THE
SCOTS LAW TIMES

REPORTS

1993

General Editor: PETER A NICHOLSON, LLB

EDINBURGH
PUBLISHED BY W GREEN, THE SCOTTISH LAW PUBLISHER
21 ALVA STREET

ISBN This Volume only: 0 414 01072 8
As a set: 0 414 01074 4

Printed and bound in Great Britain by
Hartnolls Limited, Bodmin, Cornwall

THE
SCOTS LAW TIMES

REPORTS

1993

Reported by

Sir C H AGNEW OF LOCHNAW
P A ARTHURSON, LLB
D BALLANTYNE, LLB
S J BATTEN, MA, LLB
M J BELL, LLB
D S CORKE, LLB
J P DOOHAN, BA, LLB
P W FERGUSON, LLB
M L B FORDE, MA, LLB
M C GEARY, MA, LLB
C S HADDOW, QC, LLB
A J HAMILTON, LLB
P G L HAMMOND, LLB
N W HOLROYD, LLB, BCL
R F HUNTER, LLB
B JOHNSTON, MA, LLB
G J JUNOR, LLB
D KELLY, LLB
D A KINLOCH, LLB
P McCORMACK, MA, LLB
L A McGEADY, LLB

C N MACNAIR, LLB
C A G McNEILL, LLB
C H S MACNEILL, LLB
A D MENNIE, LLB, PhD
I H L MILLER, MA, LLB
G D MITCHELL, LLB
S F MURPHY, MA, LLB
D E NICOL, LLB
S D D NICOLL, LLB
A W NOBLE, LLB
M H OATWAY, LLB
D C RAE, LLB
N C RITCHIE, LLB
D P SELLAR, MA, LLB
L M SHAND, LLB
R D SUTHERLAND, MA, LLB
R N THOMSON, BCom, LLB
M G J UPTON, BA, LLB
I C WYLIE, LLB
A R W YOUNG, LLB

Edited by

M G THOMSON, QC, LLB

EDINBURGH
PUBLISHED BY W GREEN, THE SCOTTISH LAW PUBLISHER
21 ALVA STREET

JUDGES OF THE COURT OF SESSION DURING 1993

FIRST DIVISION

Lord President — The Right Hon Lord HOPE,
The Hon Lord ALLANBRIDGE, The Hon Lord COWIE
and The Hon Lord MAYFIELD, MC

SECOND DIVISION

Lord Justice Clerk – The Right Hon Lord ROSS,
The Right Hon Lord MURRAY, The Hon Lord DAVIDSON,[1]
The Right Hon The Lord McCLUSKEY and The Hon Lord MORISON

LORDS ORDINARY

The Hon Lord SUTHERLAND
The Hon Lord WEIR
The Hon Lord CLYDE
The Hon Lord CULLEN
The Hon Lord PROSSER
The Hon Lord KIRKWOOD
The Hon Lord COULSFIELD
The Hon Lord MILLIGAN
The Right Hon The Lord MORTON of SHUNA
The Hon Lord CAPLAN
The Right Hon The Lord CAMERON of LOCHBROOM, PC
The Hon Lord MARNOCH
The Hon Lord MACLEAN
The Hon Lord PENROSE
The Hon Lord OSBORNE
The Hon Lord ABERNETHY

[1] The Hon Lord Davidson was seconded as Chairman of the Scottish Law Commission on 1 October 1988.

RETIRED JUDGES

appointed in terms of s 22 of the Law Reform (Miscellaneous Provisions) (Scotland) Act 1985 who sat in judgment in cases reported in this volume:

The Hon Lord GRIEVE, The Hon Lord BRAND, The Hon Lord KINCRAIG, The Hon Lord MAXWELL, The Hon Lord McDONALD, MC, and The Right Hon Lord WYLIE

TEMPORARY JUDGES

appointed in terms of s 35 (3) of the Law Reform (Miscellaneous Provisions) (Scotland) Act 1990 who sat in judgment in cases reported in this volume:

D B ROBERTSON, QC, T G COUTTS, QC, J M S HORSBURGH, QC, and R G McEWAN, QC

INDEX OF CASES

ACCORDING TO NAMES OF PARTIES

L signifies *House of Lords* Decision.

O signifies *Outer House* Decision.

J signifies *Justiciary Court* or *Criminal Appeal Court* Decision.

V signifies *Lands Valuation Appeal Court* and *Valuation Appeal Court* Decision.

★ signifies case reported in note form.

M v Kennedy, 431
M, Strathclyde Regional Council v, 1305
★ MRS (Distribution) Ltd, Murphy v, O 786
MT Group v James Howden & Co Ltd, O 409
MT Group v Howden Group plc, O 345
★ McAvoy v City of Glasgow District Council, O 859
McClory, Simpson v, J 861
McCluskey v HM Advocate, J 897
McColl v McColl, 617
MacColl, Strathern v, 301
McColligan v Normand, J 1026
McCormack v HM Advocate, J 1158
★ McCormick v City of Aberdeen District Council, O 1123
★ McCreadie v Clairmont Garments (Scotland) Ltd, O 823
McCrum v Ballantyne, 788
McCulloch v Scott, J 901
★ McDermid v Crown House Engineering Ltd, O 543
McDowall, McMillan v, O 311
MacFarlane, McLeod v, J 782
★ McFaulds v Reed Corrugated Cases Ltd, O 670
McGarvie, Drury v, 987
McGillivray v Davidson, O 693
MacGillivray, Johnston v, J 120
McGlennan v Beatties Bakeries Ltd, J 1109
McGlennan v Clark, J 1069
McGlennan, Hazlett v, J 74
★ McGrandles, Ferguson v, O 822
★ McGunnigal v D B Marshall (Newbridge) Ltd, O 769
★ MacInnes v MacInnes, O 1108
McInnes's Executors, Fullemann v, O 259
★ McIntosh (A H) & Co Ltd, Arbuckle v , O 857
★ McIntyre, Ferguson v, O 1269
McIntyre v Sheridan, 412
MacIver, Kamperman v, O 732
MacIver, Solicitors Estate Agency (Glasgow) Ltd v, 23
MacKenzie v Barr's Trustees, 1228
Mackie, City of Glasgow District Council v, 213
McKinnie, Council of the Law Society of Scotland v, 238
McLean, Clark v, O 492
Macleod v Clacher, O 318
McLeod v Lowe, J 471
McLeod v MacFarlane, J 782
MacLeod v Williamson, J 144
McLuckie Brothers Ltd v Newhouse Contracts Ltd, O 641
McLuskie v City of Glasgow District Council, 1102
McMahon v Lees, J 593
McMillan v McDowall, O 311
McMonagle v Secretary of State for Scotland, 807
McMurdo v Ferguson, O 193
McNair v HM Advocate, J 277
McNaughtan, Robertson v, J 1143
McNaughton, Stainton v, J 119
★ McNeil v Clelland, O 662

MacPhail, Thomson v, J 225
★ McWhinnie v British Coal Corporation, O 467
Maciocia v Alma Holdings Ltd, O 730
Mahmood v Mahmood, O 589
Mailley v HM Advocate, J 959
Maitland v HM Advocate, J 645
★ Malcolm v Fair, O 342
Marr v Heywood, J 1254
★ Marshall (D B) (Newbridge) Ltd, McGunnigal v, O 769
Martin v HM Advocate, J 197
Mason v A & R Robertson & Black, O 773
★ Massie, Exal Sampling Services Ltd v, O 1220
Matchett v Dunfermline District Council, O 537
Maxwell v Cardle, J 1017
Medicopharma (UK) BV v Cairns, O 386
Mejka v H M Advocate, J 1321
Melrose v Davidson and Robertson, 611
Mifflin Construction Ltd, Shanks & McEwan (Contractors) Ltd v, O 1124
Mikhailitchenko v Normand, J 1138
Miller v Lanarkshire Health Board, O 453
Miller and Santhouse plc, Postel Properties Ltd v, O 342
Miller Group Ltd, The v Tasker, 207
Mirestop Ltd (in administration), Scottish Exhibition Centre Ltd v, O 1034
Mirza, Fraser v, L 527
Mitchell v HAT Contracting Services Ltd (No 2), O 734
Mitchell v HAT Contracting Services Ltd (No 3), O 1199
Mitchell v Mitchell, 123
Mitchell v Mitchell, O 419
★ Moffat v Babcock Thorn Ltd, O 1130
Moir v H M Advocate, J 1191
Moore, George Thompson Services Ltd v, O 634
Moore, King v, O 1117
Moran, Wendel v, O 44
Morrison, Grieve v, O 852
Morrison v Panic Link Ltd, O 602
Morrison, Scott v, J 672
Muir v Cumbernauld and Kilsyth District Council, 287
Mullan v Anderson, 835
★ Munro v Strathclyde Regional Council, O 658
★ Murphy v MRS (Distribution) Ltd, O 786
Murray, Cardle v, J 525
★ Murray v Gent Ltd, O 482

★ Nairn Floors Ltd, Stark v, O 717
Narden Services Ltd v Secretary of State for Scotland, 871
Neizer, Hamilton v, J 992
Newhouse Contracts Ltd, McLuckie Brothers Ltd v, O 641
Nicoll v Steelpress (Supplies) Ltd, 533
Noble v City of Glasgow District Council, 800
Noble Organisation Ltd (The) v Kilmarnock and Loudoun District Council, 759
Nordic Oil Services Ltd v Berman, O 1164
Normand, Farrell v, J 793
Normand, Hughes v, J 113
Normand, Kimmins v, J 1260

REPORTS

1993 SCOTS LAW TIMES

Editor
M G THOMSON, QC, LLB

Note: **Cases in this volume may be cited 1993 SLT**

Thus: **Cordiner v HM Advocate, 1993 SLT 2.**

REPORTS

Cordiner v HM Advocate

HIGH COURT OF JUSTICIARY

THE LORD JUSTICE CLERK (ROSS),
LORDS McCLUSKEY AND MORISON

22 MARCH 1991

Justiciary — Evidence — Cross examination — Evidence of crime not charged — Accused asked whether he had suborned defence witnesses — Whether breach of statutory protection — Criminal Procedure (Scotland) Act 1975 (c 21), s 141 (1) (f).

Justiciary — Evidence — Admissibility — Statement by accused — Statement made to officer in charge of investigation after accused charged.

Justiciary — Procedure — Indictment — Form of — Single charge containing separate offences.

Justiciary — Procedure — Verdict — Single charge containing separate offences — Whether jury should be directed to return separate verdicts in respect of each offence.

Justiciary — Evidence — Credibility — Crown case presented on basis that complainer giving entirely true account — Crown suggesting for first time in address to jury that they could accept part and reject part of complainer's evidence — Whether open to jury to do so.

Justiciary — Evidence — Corroboration — Rape — Production spoken to only by complainer — Sufficiency of other corroborative evidence where further charge of attempted murder.

Justiciary — Procedure — Trial — Charge to jury — Erroneous direction that certain evidence capable of corroborating complainer — Other evidence relied on for corroboration equivocal — Whether miscarriage of justice.

An accused was charged on indictment which, after amendment, alleged that he did (a) stab to severe injury and attempt to murder, (b) assault and rape, and (c) have unnatural carnal connection with, the complainer. The accused gave evidence and was cross examined, without objection being taken, on the suggestion that he had induced defence witnesses to give false evidence. During his trial evidence was also led from the officer in charge of the investigation of a statement made to him by the accused after he had been charged. Objection was taken on the ground that the statement should have been taken by an officer unconnected with the case. The trial judge repelled the objection but left it to the jury to determine whether the statement was fairly obtained.

At the conclusion of the Crown case the trial judge refused to hear a submission of no case to answer as respects para (c) of the indictment, since the indictment contained only one charge. He subsequently directed the jury to return a single verdict, subject to any deletions they wished to make.

In addressing the jury the Crown suggested in the alternative that they could accept part of the complainer's evidence and reject her denial of having earlier had consensual intercourse as claimed by the accused,

a suggestion which contradicted the Crown's presentation of its case.

The complainer gave evidence that a pullover had been used to tie her legs prior to the accused raping her and identified a pullover found near the accused's home as the pullover concerned. There was no other evidence that the pullover was the accused's. In his charge to the jury the trial judge gave a direction that the evidence of the pullover could corroborate the complainer. The accused was convicted of paras (a) and (b) of the indictment, the jury having been directed to delete para (c), and appealed to the High Court, contending that each of the foregoing matters had resulted in a miscarriage of justice.

Held, (1) that although there had been a breach of s 141 (1) (f), (per the Lord Justice Clerk (Ross) and Lord Morison) the appellant had to be taken to have waived compliance by failing to object at the time the objectionable question had been asked, and it was too late to contend on appeal that there had been a miscarriage of justice (pp 5A-B and 10B-C); (per Lord McCluskey) the significance of the question was slight and not such as to constitute a miscarriage of justice (p 8D and F-I); (2) that the deviation from the normal practice did not itself render the statement inadmissible but was rather a circumstance bearing on the question of whether the statement was fairly obtained, and the trial judge had correctly left that matter to the jury (pp 5J-L, 8I and 10B-C); (3) that while it would have been preferable for the separate offences within the indictment to have been the subject of separate charges, no miscarriage of justice had resulted since (per the Lord Justice Clerk (Ross) and Lord Morison) the trial judge had acted within his discretion in charging the jury to return a single verdict and, having regard to deletions made by the jury, there must have been a majority in favour of the verdict returned; (per Lord McCluskey) while the judge was wrong to hold incompetent a submission of no case to answer in respect of the distinct charge of sodomy, and further should have instructed the jury to treat the charges as separate, he had made it sufficiently plain that they could delete any part of the indictment (pp 6D-F, 9B-C, 9E-G and 10B-C); (4) that having regard to the forensic evidence which suggested that intercourse might have taken place some time earlier than alleged by the complainer, the Crown were entitled to present their case on the alternative basis that the jury could accept part and disbelieve part of the complainer's evidence (pp 6J-L, 9G and 10B-C); (5) (the Crown conceding that there had been a misdirection) that the evidence concerning the pullover came from the complainer herself and so could not provide corroboration, and since the other corroborating evidence was unequivocal it was possible the jury had been influenced by the evidence of the pullover in reaching the guilty verdict, and that there had been a miscarriage of justice (pp 7J-L, 9I-10B and 10B-C); and appeal *allowed* and conviction of rape *quashed*.

Indictment

A   William Buchan Cordiner was charged at the instance of the rt hon the Lord Fraser of Carmyllie, Her Majesty's Advocate, on an indictment which libelled that he did, inter alia:

(a) on 4 July 1990 at Old Ancrum Stables assault M A O C or T, seize hold of her, stab her repeatedly on the neck and body and cut her on the face and arms and hand with a knife all to her severe injury and to the danger of her life and did attempt to murder her;

B   (b) on date and place last libelled assault said M A O C or T, present a knife at her throat, threaten her therewith, tie her legs together with a pullover, force her into the rear of the car, sit on top of her, remove her trousers and underclothes, force her legs apart, lick her breasts, punch her on the face, place his hands around her neck and compress same, kick her on the face, lie on top of her and rape her all to her severe injury; and

(c) assault said M A O C or T, insert his private member into her hinder parts and have unnatural carnal connection with her.

C   The accused pled not guilty and went to trial before Lord MacLean and a jury in the High Court at Jedburgh. The accused was found guilty of attempted murder and rape, and appealed to the High Court by note of appeal against conviction.

Statutory provisions

The Criminal Procedure (Scotland) Act 1975
D   provides:

"141.—(1) The accused shall be a competent witness for the defence at every stage of the case, whether the accused is on trial alone or along with a co-accused: Provided that—. . . (f) the accused who gives evidence on his own behalf in pursuance of this section shall not be asked, and if asked shall not be required to answer, any question tending to show that he has committed, or been convicted of, or been charged with, any offence other than that with which he is then charged, or is of
E   bad character, unless—(i) the proof that he has committed or been convicted of such other offence is admissible evidence to show that he is guilty of the offence with which he is then charged; or (ii) the accused or his counsel or solicitor has asked questions of the witnesses for the prosecution with a view to establish the accused's good character, or the accused has given evidence of his own good character, or the nature or conduct of the defence is such as to involve imputations on the character of the prosecutor or of the witnesses for the prosecution; or (iii) the accused has given evidence against
F   any other person charged in the same proceedings."

Cases referred to

Binks v HM Advocate, 1985 SLT 59; 1984 JC 108; 1984 SCCR 335.
Tonge v HM Advocate, 1982 SLT 506; 1982 JC 130; 1982 SCCR 313.

Textbook referred to

Renton and Brown, *Criminal Procedure* (5th ed), para 18-36.

Appeal

G   The accused lodged a note of appeal setting forth the following complaints, inter alia:

(1) In the course of giving evidence on his own behalf the appellant was asked questions by the advocate depute that he had committed a crime while in custody awaiting trial in respect that it was suggested to him that he had instigated the witness McGlynn to pervert the course of justice. Such questioning by the advocate depute was in contravention of s 141 (1) (f) and resulted in a miscarriage of justice.

H   (2) Evidence concerning the appellant's incriminatory statement contained in the transcription of a taped police interview on 4 July 1990 at Hawick police station, Crown production no 17 was wrongly admitted. The said statement was inadmissible in respect that: (i) the statement was taken by the officer in charge of the investigation against the appellant after the appellant had been arrested, charged and transferred to Hawick police station prior to his appearance in court the following morning, ie 5 July 1990. . . .

I   (3) The learned trial judge misdirected the jury in relation to the verdict which it could return in respect that the single charge on the indictment which was before the jury contained separate offences, namely assault, attempted murder and rape. Such misdirection resulted in a miscarriage of justice.

(4) The evidence of the complainer, M A O C or T was to the effect inter alia that she denied that she had ever had a sexual relationship with the appellant. The
J   defence to the charge of rape was that consensual intercourse had taken place between the parties some hours earlier and that the parties had a pre-existing sexual relationship. The basis of the Crown's presentation of its case was to the effect that no such relationship existed. In the course of his speech to the jury, the advocate depute submitted for the first time in the case that it would be open to the jury to accept that such a sexual relationship had indeed existed contrary to the evidence of the complainer, but nevertheless to find that the complainer had been raped on the occasion libelled in the
K   indictment. Such a suggestion was contradictory of the principal basis of the Crown's presentation of the case against the appellant. The learned trial judge failed to direct the jury that notwithstanding the right of a jury to accept a part of a witness's account and reject other parts, in the circumstances of this case it was not open to them to accept the complainer's evidence with regard to the offences libelled in the charge, but to disbelieve the complainer in respect of her evidence regarding her previous relationship with the appellant. Such failure
L   to give appropriate directions resulted in a miscarriage of justice.

(5) The Crown sought to rely for corroboration on the identification of a jersey (label no 12) as being the property of the appellant. The jersey was identified by the complainer only and accordingly could not form a separate, independent source as is required to constitute corroborative evidence. The learned trial judge failed to direct the jury that it would not be open to them to rely on such evidence for corroboration. Such

failure to give appropriate directions resulted in a miscarriage of justice.

The appeal was heard before the High Court on 22 February 1991.

On 22 March 1991 the court *allowed* the appeal and *quashed* the conviction of rape.

THE LORD JUSTICE CLERK (ROSS).—The appellant went to trial in the High Court at Jedburgh on a charge libelling abduction, attempted murder, rape and indecent assault. In the course of the trial the indictment was amended so as to delete those parts of the indictment libelling abduction. Thereafter the charge contained three paragraphs—(a) a charge of attempted murder, (b) a charge of rape, and (c) a charge of indecent assault. In the course of his charge, the trial judge directed the jury that there was no corroboration in relation to branch (c) and that the jury would require to delete (c) in the event of their returning a verdict of guilty. He also directed them that certain deletions would require to be made from branch (b) in the event of a verdict of guilty. The jury by a majority found the appellant guilty of the indictment under certain deletions. The effect of their verdict was that the appellant was found guilty of attempted murder and rape. He was sentenced to life imprisonment. He has now appealed against both conviction and sentence.

In his note of appeal five grounds of appeal have been put forward against conviction and one ground of appeal against sentence. So far as the appeal against conviction is concerned the first ground of appeal alleges that there was a contravention of the provisions of s 141 (1) (f) of the Criminal Procedure (Scotland) Act 1975 and a consequent miscarriage of justice. Section 141 (1) (f) provides that: [his Lordship quoted the terms of s 141 (1) (f) and continued:]

On behalf of the appellant it was maintained that the advocate depute in cross examining the appellant had suggested that he had committed another crime, namely that he had instigated a witness McGlynn to pervert the course of justice, that is subornation of perjury. Counsel for the appellant contended that none of the provisos was applicable.

In his report the trial judge tells us that he had arranged for the relevant passage in the shorthand notes to be extended, and in his report he sets out at length the passage from the cross examination of the appellant. In that passage the first question was in the following terms: "With regard to Mr McGlynn, did he at a stage in the end of July or possibly during the first week or two of August come and visit you in Saughton, you being there awaiting this trial, and make arrangements with you that he would say that he saw you drop M T [the complainer] off in Dalkeith and going away on your own?"

This question was not objected to but counsel on behalf of the appellant inquired whether the Crown had a basis for the question, and the advocate depute answered that he had. It was also pointed out that the question was in two parts, and there then followed further questions dealing with the first part of the original question, namely, whether the appellant and Mr McGlynn had met one another in HM Prison, Saughton. The advocate depute then proceeded to deal with the second part of the original question and asked: "To deal with the second part of the question I take it you deny any suggestion I make that on such a visit he and you agreed that he would go witness for you, if I can put it that way, and say he was in Dalkeith on the night in question, 3 July, and say you dropped M T off there and then drove away without her?"

The trial judge pointed out that that question in fact contained a number of questions and the appellant was stopped from answering. The advocate depute then proceeded as follows: "First of all you deny a suggestion that you and he agreed on a visit at the time I indicate that he would go witness for you? — I never seen him on a visit, I seen him in prison when he was untried." The advocate depute then remarked: "Well if you deny that and you say you never saw him I will leave the matter there".

From the foregoing passages it is clear that counsel for the defence did not object at the time to the line of cross examination upon the basis that it offended the provisions of s 141 (1) (f) of the Criminal Procedure (Scotland) Act 1975. In developing this ground of appeal, counsel for the appellant explained that McGlynn had been called as a witness for the defence, and he referred to certain questions addressed to McGlynn by the advocate depute, including a question to the following effect: "He discussed with you what you should say?" Counsel explained that objection was taken to this question, and he submitted that in the course of seeking to justify the question the advocate depute intimated to the court that he accepted that he was putting an offence to McGlynn. Apparently he also explained that information regarding this had only reached him recently and that accordingly it had not been possible to incorporate in the indictment an additional charge dealing with this matter.

The Solicitor General reminded us that this ground of appeal relates to the cross examination of the appellant and not to the cross examination of McGlynn. There was no ground of appeal directed to the issue of whether certain questions put to the witness McGlynn were objectionable. I agree with the Solicitor General that this ground of appeal is confined to the application of s 141 (1) (f) which is concerned with the accused as a witness. It is quite clear that when the appellant was giving his evidence no objection was taken on his behalf in terms of s 141 (1) (f).

It is plain from the terms of the subsection that the mere asking of a question tending to show that an accused has committed an offence other than that with which he has been charged may infringe the statute, but if no objection is taken the trial judge is placed in a difficult position. In the present case, if objection had been taken, the trial judge could immediately have stopped the questioning, and he would then have required to consider whether to desert the diet immediately (and, if so, whether simpliciter or pro loco et tempore) or whether the matter could be dealt with by an appropriate direction (*Binks v HM Advocate*).

In these circumstances the Solicitor General submitted that if a question which contravened the provisions of s 141 (1) (f) was put to an accused, objection had to be taken there and then so that the judge could determine whether it would be necessary to desert the diet or whether the matter could be dealt with by a direction to the jury by him. The Solicitor General maintained that since objection had not timeously been taken on behalf of the appellant, he could not now found on the provisions of s 141 (1) (f). He pointed out that in some cases the defence may wish to ask questions about a previous conviction, and that accordingly they may choose to waive compliance with the provisions of the subsection.

I have come to be of opinion that the submissions of the Solicitor General are in general well founded. Section 141 (1) (f) contains provisions which are conceived in favour of an accused person, and I agree that compliance with these provisions can be waived on behalf of that accused person. If no objection is taken at the time when the objectionable question is asked, the presumption must be that the accused is waiving compliance with the subsection, and it will thereafter be too late to raise the issue on appeal in order to suggest that there has been a miscarriage of justice.

Accordingly although the provisions of s 141 (1) (f) were in my opinion contravened, the appellant failed to take timeous objection, and, in my opinion, it is too late now to seek to raise this objection on appeal as a basis for contending that there has been a miscarriage of justice. Since the appellant had the opportunity during his trial to take this objection, I am of opinion that no miscarriage of justice resulted from the fact that the provisions of this subsection were contravened.

The second ground of appeal relates to an incriminating statement made by the appellant. In the ground of appeal it is contended that the statement was inadmissible because it was taken from the appellant by the officer in charge of the investigation. The statement was tape recorded, and at the same time a written version of the statement was made by Detective Constable Mitchell. At the trial the admissibility of the statement was challenged both on the grounds that it had been taken by the officer in charge of the investigation, and upon the ground that the written statement taken by Detective Constable Mitchell had not been produced. The trial judge rejected the objection taken to the leading of evidence relating to the statement. Before this court counsel for the appellant intimated that he was no longer insisting on the objection based upon the fact that the written statement handwritten by Detective Constable Mitchell had not been produced, but he continued to maintain that the statement was inadmissible since it had been taken by the officer in charge of the investigation.

In support of his submission counsel for the appellant referred first of all to Renton and Brown's *Criminal Procedure* (5th ed), para 18-36, where it is stated: "There have been suggestions that the police should not even receive a spontaneous statement voluntarily offered by a charged prisoner, but should instead take him before a magistrate there to make a declaration, but this is clearly not the law. The statement should, however, be taken by an officer unconnected with the case."

The authority which the learned author offers for that latter statement is *Tonge v HM Advocate.* In the course of delivering his opinion in that case Lord Cameron said (1982 SLT at p 517): "The regular and proper practice when an accused or suspect indicates or intimates he wishes to make a voluntary statement is that the statement should be taken by officers unconnected with the particular investigation, and authenticated by the signatures of the officers concerned and the maker of the statement himself."

Counsel for the appellant maintained that what Lord Cameron said in this connection amounted to a rule of law requiring that statements should be taken from accused persons or suspects by officers unconnected with the particular investigation. I do not so read Lord Cameron's opinion. In this part of his opinion he makes it clear that what he is referring to is simply "the regular and well-known practice of police officers". The language which he uses in that connection is to be contrasted with what he says regarding the giving of a caution to an accused person when he is charged, because he there refers to that as "the rule of law". In my opinion all that Lord Cameron is referring to in connection with the taking of statements is the practice of police officers. He is not to be taken as stating that if that practice is not followed a statement taken from an accused person will be inadmissible. In my opinion if a statement has not been taken by police officers unconnected with the investigation, that may be a circumstance bearing upon the question of whether the statement is to be regarded by the jury as a voluntary statement fairly obtained. The test is one of fairness, and that is for the jury to determine.

In the present case the trial judge reminded the jury that the evidence had disclosed that it was the ordinary and normal practice for officers unconnected with the investigation to take a voluntary statement, and he directed the jury that it was for them to determine whether the statement was a voluntary statement fairly obtained and voluntarily given. In his report the trial judge tells us of the circumstances giving rise to the making of this statement. It appears that after being cautioned and charged, the appellant was transferred to Hawick police station. While there he spoke to the police officer who had charge of him and said that he wanted to speak to "the DCI". This was a reference to Detective Chief Inspector Jones who was the officer in charge of the investigation and to whom the statement was ultimately made. There were other officers in the police station unconnected with the case who could have taken the statement, but it is significant that it was apparently the appellant himself who had expressly asked to be given the opportunity of speaking to the officer who in fact took the statement. I am satisfied that the trial judge dealt with this question in an entirely proper manner and that there is no reason for concluding that there was any miscarriage of justice upon this ground.

The third ground of appeal alleges misdirection on the part of the trial judge in that he directed the jury that the indictment before them contained a single charge upon which they would require to bring one

verdict. Counsel for the appellant recognised that the
A Crown had chosen to libel the offences in this way. At
the conclusion of the Crown case counsel had made a
submission of no case to answer in relation to para (c)
of the indictment. In replying to that submission the
advocate depute maintained that the indictment contained only one charge, and that it would not accordingly be competent to make a motion of no case to
answer in respect of part of a charge. The trial judge
in dealing with that submission held that the indictment
contained one charge, and that accordingly the submis-
B sion of no case to answer in relation to part of that charge
could not be entertained. When he came to charge the
jury, the trial judge directed them as follows: "Your
verdict may be unanimous or by a majority. If your
verdict is to be one of guilty then at least eight of you
have to be in favour of that verdict, and that is because
there are 15 of you in number and there are two alternative forms of the verdict of acquittal. You may find
the accused guilty as libelled, subject of course to such
deletions as I have suggested you make, or under any
other deletions that you yourselves wish to make."
C
After explaining to them what the acquittal verdicts
were he added: "Now you will be asked to return, as
I indicated to you earlier, in this charge one verdict,
although of course there are now before you two separate
offences, (a) and (b). So ladies and gentlemen, if you
are minded to convict the accused there must be at least
eight of you in favour of that verdict."

Counsel for the appellant maintained that in the circumstances of this case the jury should have been
D instructed to return a separate verdict on each of the
charges contained in (a), (b) and (c), and that in any event
they should have been expressly instructed that eight
of their number required to be in favour of a verdict
of guilty of each separate crime. The jury had returned
a single verdict with deletions. Counsel maintained that
in returning their verdict which meant that the appellant was guilty of attempted murder and rape, it was
possible that eight or more of the jury had been in favour
of guilty of one of these crimes, but less than eight of
E them in favour of guilty of the other crime. He accordingly submitted that the directions which the trial judge
gave to the jury were inadequate.

Although it would have been preferable if the trial
judge had directed the jury to return a separate verdict
in respect of each of paras (a), (b) and (c) (and that is
the course which I would have followed if I had been
the trial judge), I am satisfied that what the trial judge
did say to the jury in this connection did not amount
to a misdirection. It was within his discretion to charge
F the jury as he did. The jury were clearly directed that
if they were to bring in a verdict of guilty at least eight
of their number must be in favour of that verdict; they
were also told that they could make deletions. At the
end of the day they returned a verdict of guilty with
deletions, and in my opinion, having regard to the directions which they had been given, that verdict must mean
that at least eight of the jury were in favour of the verdict
in the terms in which they returned it. At the same time
I regard as unfortunate that the Crown chose to frame
the indictment in the form of a single charge. The indictment in fact libelled a number of separate offences, and,

in my opinion, each of these offences should have been
made the subject of a separate charge, and the jury G
should have been instructed to return a separate verdict
on each charge. It would have been preferable if the
Crown had framed the indictment differently, but I am
not persuaded that any miscarriage of justice has resulted
from their failure to do so. The verdict of guilty which
the jury did return was a clear and unambiguous verdict.

In the fourth ground of appeal the appellant seeks
to contend that it was not open to the Crown to put
their case forward upon an alternative basis. The matter
arises in this way. It was part of the Crown case that H
the appellant had raped the complainer at Old Ancrum
stables between 12 midnight and 2 am on Wednesday,
4 July 1990. Part of the evidence upon which the Crown
relied was evidence from forensic scientists to the effect
that a swab taken at about 9 am on 4 July 1990 from
the complainer was indicative of semen which had been
deposited between 6 and 12 hours before, since the spermatozoa were seen to be intact. That accordingly meant
that on the basis of that evidence intercourse had taken
place at earliest about 9 pm the previous night. There
was also evidence of semen being found in the back of I
the car, and in the opinion of the scientists this had also
recently been deposited because intact spermatozoa were
found. The appellant put forward an alternative explanation for the presence of semen in the complainer's
vagina. He maintained that he had had consensual intercourse with her in his daughter's house about 7 pm on
Tuesday, 3 July 1990. This was strongly denied by the
complainer.

The advocate depute stated to the jury that even if
they thought contrary to the complainer's evidence that J
she and the appellant had had consensual intercourse
about 7 pm, it did not follow that the appellant had not
raped her early the next morning at Old Ancrum stables.
In his report the trial judge explains that apart from
the evidence of the forensic scientists there was evidence
of the complainer's distressed, injured and shocked state
at 4.30 am when she complained that she had been
raped. That evidence was consistent with forcible intercourse at the time when she said she had been attacked,
and was not consistent with consensual intercourse at K
7 pm the previous night.

In my opinion having regard to the nature of the evidence from the forensic scientists, it was open to the
Crown to present the case to the jury upon the basis
that the complainer was entirely credible, and that they
should accept her evidence that she had been raped at
Old Ancrum stables early on 4 July 1990 and also to
accept her evidence that she had not had intercourse
with the appellant around 7 pm the earlier evening. The
Crown were also entitled to submit to the jury that even L
if they did not believe her denial in relation to the suggestion that she had had intercourse at 7 pm on 3 July
1990, they could still hold her as credible in relation
to the allegation of rape in the early hours of 4 July 1990.
Having regard to the evidence from the forensic scientists, I am satisfied that on the evidence the Crown were
entitled to present the case upon that alternative basis,
and I am also satisfied that there was no misdirection
on the part of the trial judge in this connection. In particular I am satisfied that he would not have been justified in directing the jury to disregard the Crown's

alternative case as suggested by counsel for the
A appellant.

The final ground of appeal against conviction relates
to evidence in relation to a pullover said to belong to
the appellant. It was part of the libel that the appellant
prior to committing rape had tied the complainer's legs
together with a pullover. Crown label production 12
is a pullover and the complainer identified this as the
pullover which was used in an attempt to tie her legs
in the course of the assault. This pullover was subsequently found in a blue disposal refuse bag in a con-
B cealed position under a bridge over the Burdiehouse
Burn on the Gilmerton Road near to where the appellant was living in Edinburgh. The inference which the
jury were invited to draw was that in order to get rid
of incriminating items including the pullover, the appellant had left his house, driven to the bridge, dumped
the bag containing inter alia the pullover and returned
to his house.

The complaint which is made is of misdirection. In
his charge the trial judge correctly reminded the jury
C that the pullover was not put to the appellant in his
evidence, and he then added: "So we do not know
whether he would accept or reject that jersey as his, and
in any event you must ask yourselves the question, how
far does it take you, the fact that Mrs [T] identified
this as a jersey that was in the back of the accused's
car and used to tie her legs, and the fact that it was found
in a blue bag dumped in a burn near where the accused
lives. It is a matter for you how far that single piece
of evidence takes you, but you may, or may not, doubt
D whether it could amount satisfactorily to corroboration
by itself of Mrs [T]'s account."

In the final part of that quotation, it is plain that the
trial judge is directing the jury that they may treat the
evidence in relation to the jersey as corroborating the
complainer's account. Counsel for the appellant maintained that that constituted a misdirection on the part
of the trial judge since the evidence that the jersey was
the appellant's came only from the complainer and she
could not corroborate herself.

E   The Solicitor General accepted that the pullover could
not constitute corroboration since it was not evidence
coming from a source other than the complainer herself.
Accordingly there was misdirection on the part of the
trial judge. As the trial judge tells us in his report, the
evidence regarding the pullover might be thought to
support the complainer's credibility, but it is now a
matter of admission that it could not amount to corroboration. The question for us must therefore be
whether that misdirection on the part of the trial judge
F gave rise to a miscarriage of justice. Counsel for the
appellant stressed that this had been a majority verdict,
and he maintained that this misdirection may have
influenced some of the majority. He therefore contended
that there had been a miscarriage of justice and that
accordingly it would be appropriate to quash that part
of the verdict under para (b). The Solicitor General on
the other hand maintained that we should conclude that
there had been no miscarriage of justice. He reminded
us that there had been other corroboration available.
In his report the trial judge reminds us that the Crown
relied for corroboration of the complainer's account

upon the evidence of the freshness of the semen within
her vagina, upon the fresh semen found on the rear seat   G
of the appellant's car, and the semen found liberally on
her pants and her track suit bottoms. Blood was also
found on the straw within the barn where she said she
was attacked and that was blood which could have come
from her. Her lighter was also found there. Moreover
there was a discarded paper tissue which was found
there with wetted blood on it which was the same group
as the accused's. In her evidence the complainer gave
evidence that after intercourse the accused had been
sweating freely and that he had taken a tissue to wipe   H
himself free of sweat. The Crown also relied for corroboration of the complainer's story upon her general
extremely distressed and shocked state when she arrived
at Kirklands Lodge where she complained of having
been raped.

As regards the evidence relied upon for corroboration, it must be recognised that the Crown presented
the case upon an alternative basis, and that accordingly
the jury may not have believed the complainer's denial
that she had had intercourse with the appellant at 7 pm,   I
in which event there may have been an innocent explanation for the semen being found in her vagina and on
her clothing. Earlier intercourse at 7 pm in the appellant's daughter's house, however, would not account
for the finding of fresh semen on the rear seat of the
appellant's car. That latter evidence was available as
corroboration of the complainer's account that forcible
intercourse had taken place in the back of the car.

One of the problems in the present case was that the
evidence of the complainer's distress when she arrived   J
at Kirklands Lodge was somewhat equivocal because
that distress might at least to some extent be referable
to the fact that she had been the victim of attempted
murder. The trial judge reminded the jury of this aspect
of the evidence. Accordingly although the jury were
entitled to rely on the evidence of distress as corroborating the complainer's story that she had been raped, the
jury may not have attached as much weight to this evidence as would usually be the case because there was
an alternative explanation for her distress, namely that
she had been the victim of attempted murder.   K

Having regard to the nature of the evidence relied
upon by the Crown as corroboration of the complainer's
story that she had been raped, I have reached the conclusion that some of the jury who voted in favour of
the verdict of guilty of rape may have been influenced
by the evidence relating to the pullover. One certainly
cannot exclude the possibility that in this case where
the other evidence relied upon for corroboration was
not unequivocal, one or more of the jurors who formed
the majority may have relied for corroboration upon the   L
evidence relating to the pullover. It is clear from the
trial judge's charge that the advocate depute had referred
to this evidence when addressing the jury, and the trial
judge dealt with the evidence relating to the pullover
in a little detail. In these circumstances it cannot be suggested that the evidence relating to the pullover was not
put forward as forming part of the case which the Crown
sought to make against the appellant. Since the evidence
relating to the pullover could not constitute corroboration, I am of opinion that the proper inference must

be that the misdirection in relation to the pullover gave
rise to a miscarriage of justice.

I would accordingly move your Lordships to sustain
the appellant's appeal in relation to the charge of rape.
Counsel for the appellant agreed that the submissions
which he put forward related to the conviction for rape
only. I would accordingly move your Lordships further
to set aside the verdict of the trial court, and to substitute therefor the following amended verdict of guilty,
that is, "guilty on the indictment as amended under
deletion of paragraphs (b) and (c)".

This means that the appellant still stands convicted
of attempted murder, and we shall proceed to hear his
appeal against sentence.

LORD McCLUSKEY.—Your Lordship in the chair
has explained the background to this trial and has dealt
with all five grounds of appeal. It is not necessary for
me to deal with each of them as fully as your Lordship
has done but I shall express my opinion in relation to
each.

The first ground of appeal, as developed by counsel
before us, related to questions asked by the advocate
depute at the trial; the submission was that the questioning was in contravention of s 141 (1) (f) of the Criminal Procedure (Scotland) Act 1975 and resulted in a
miscarriage of justice. Your Lordship has set out fully
what took place and it is indeed correct to say that
counsel for the defence did not object at the time to
the questioning upon the basis that it was prohibited
by s 141 (1) (f). The Solicitor General did not dispute
that the advocate depute at the trial asked questions
which tended to show that the appellant had committed an offence other than that with which he was then
charged. He did not seek to argue that the questioning
was justified by any of the exceptions (i) or (ii) or (iii).
It appears to me, therefore, that there was a contravention of s 141 (1) (f). The mere asking of the question
in circumstances where the question is not justifiable
in terms of one of the numbered exceptions is a contravention of the section.

Accordingly, in my view, there was a contravention
of the section even before counsel for the defence arose
to intervene in the way narrated by your Lordship. I
do not suggest that once the prosecutor has contravened
the section by asking a question which the section prohibits the defence counsel is entitled to refrain from
objecting. He should object. The purpose of his objection will be to ensure that there is no further contravention of the section, a contravention which would occur
if the accused person were required to answer the question that should not have been asked. A secondary
purpose of objecting would be to demonstrate that the
accused is not acquiescing in the asking of such a question. That is a not unimportant purpose because it commonly happens that one party does not take all the
objections which are competent to him to take. A third
purpose of the objection, of course, is to enable the
prosecutor to explain, if he can, why he has asked the
question. The trial judge is then able to determine
whether or not the matter is serious enough to warrant
his deserting the diet immediately or whether any
damage that might have been done can be remedied by

the giving of an appropriate direction to the jury in relation to what has happened.

Although the provisions of the section were, in my
opinion, contravened in the way I have indicated, I am
not persuaded that there is any reason to suppose that
a miscarriage of justice has resulted. In the first place,
when one looks at the questioning, although it was questioning tending to show that the appellant had committed the offence of attempted subornation of perjury by
trying to persuade a potential defence witness to tell
a false story to the criminal authorities, this is very
similar to the kind of allegation that is properly made
in many trials, namely the allegation that the accused
and his witness are telling lies and that the telling has
been orchestrated in some unspecified way beforehand.
Furthermore, I do not doubt that if objection had been
taken at the time upon the basis of a contravention of
s 141 (1) (f), the trial judge would have been able to
deal with the matter satisfactorily by appropriate directions to the jury. The very failure of defence counsel
to mention s 141 (1) (f) at the time is an indication of
how unimportant this aspect of the matter was at the
trial itself. It is essential not to exaggerate the importance of such a matter given that at the trial its significance was so slight. Looking at the whole context,
therefore, I see no basis for concluding that a miscarriage of justice resulted from the putting of these improper
questions by the advocate depute.

In relation to the second ground of appeal, relating
to the circumstances of the taking of a statement from
the appellant by the officer in charge of the investigation, I have nothing to add to what your Lordship has
said. I agree that the trial judge dealt with this issue
properly and that this ground of appeal is unsound.

The third ground of appeal relates to the alleged misdirection on the part of the trial judge in directing the
jury to treat the separate paragraphs of the indictment
as containing a single charge. In my opinion this indictment and the view of it taken by the advocate depute
and the trial judge resulted in a muddle. It began with
the words: "you are indicted at the instance of the right
hon the Lord Fraser of Carmyllie, Her Majesty's Advocate, and the charge against you is are [sic] that", etc.

Although the minute of proceedings reveals a number
of amendments to the indictment (principally in order
to remove the abduction charge originally contained in
the original para (a)) it does not appear that any amendment was made to attempt to make sense of the last
seven words which I have quoted. The minute of
proceedings, however, reveals that at the conclusion of
the Crown case counsel for the accused stated that he
wished to make a submission to the court and, the jury
having retired, he sought to make a motion of no case
to answer under s 140A of the 1975 Act, restricted to
the assault by sodomy charge, which by then was charge
(c). He was not allowed to do so because the trial judge
ruled, on the motion of the advocate depute, that the
indictment contained only one charge, and that it was
therefore incompetent to do what counsel was seeking
to do, namely to move the court to acquit the accused
in respect of what was only one part of a charge.

I regret to say that I consider that this was an entirely
mistaken view of the indictment. Referring to the three

paras which were lettered (a), (b) and (c), after the amendment of the indictment, the narrative in (a) is of an assault by repeated stabbing all to the severe injury of the victim and to the danger of her life; and it is further characterised as an attempt to murder. Despite its preceding the charge contained in (b) on the indictment, the evidence indicated that chronologically the events giving rise to (b) preceded those giving rise to (a). Nonetheless (b) libelled a "further" assault upon the same victim. The assault did not include any stabbing with a knife but gave a wholly different narrative of acts constituting assault, and concluded by narrating various indecent acts culminating in rape. The final paragraph, now lettered (c), included the entirely different and distinct assault by sodomising the victim. These three quite separate matters have in common the date, the place, the victim and the appellant but are otherwise quite separate. In my opinion there can be no room for doubt that these were three separate crimes and that, whatever the punctuation, they were and should have been treated as three distinct charges; and that the trial judge was wrong to hold it incompetent to make a s 140A motion in respect of the distinct charge of assault by sodomising the victim. In the result, the appellant was undoubtedly denied his right to be acquitted at that stage in relation to that charge: he should have been acquitted then because the evidence was insufficient in law to justify his conviction on that charge.

It is not possible for us to know the precise consequences of that denial to him of his statutory right. It is at least conceivable that the appellant might have been legally advised that it would be better not to enter the witness box to give evidence in relation to charges (a) and (b) but felt that he had no choice but to do so and give evidence in order to repudiate the distinct charge of assault coupled with sodomy, (c). In any event, because that charge remained on the indictment, he faced cross examination in relation to it which he would not have had to do if the s 140A motion anent it had been allowed, as it should have been, it being plain that the trial judge was satisfied that the evidence led by the prosecution at that stage was insufficient in law to justify the appellant being convicted of that charge; so the appellant would have been acquitted before the start of the defence case. Another unfortunate consequence of this muddle was that it was possible that the jury might have been confused in the course of their deliberations, if, having considered the evidence in relation to charges (a) and (b), there were fewer than eight in favour of a guilty verdict on one of those charges but substantially more than eight in favour of a guilty verdict on the other. The correct direction for the trial judge to give would have been to instruct the jury to treat the three charges as being entirely separate and to make it clear that the jury could not return a verdict of guilty on any one of the three distinct charges unless, in relation to that charge considered separately, there was a majority of eight or more in favour of guilty.

Your Lordship has drawn attention to the trial judge's directions to the jury. For the reasons I have set forth I do not consider that the directions were good directions. Indeed, once the trial judge made the error of treating the indictment as containing only one charge, there was no certain route out of the difficulty. However,

with some hesitation, and after considering the opinion of your Lordship in the chair, I am prepared to agree that the trial judge made it sufficiently plain to the jury that they could delete any part of the indictment which they did not consider proved and that therefore it cannot be said that any miscarriage of justice resulted from what happened.

In relation to the fourth ground of appeal I need add nothing to what your Lordship in the chair has said. I agree with it.

The final ground of appeal, as your Lordship has explained, relates to the evidence about a pullover. I need not repeat the circumstances narrated by your Lordship. It is, however, clear that evidence given by the complainer, Mrs M T, about the pullover could in no circumstances be corroborative of Mrs T's evidence about anything else. The minute of proceedings, as pointed out by counsel for the appellant in the course of his submission, confirms that at the close of the case for the appellant counsel formally submitted to the trial judge that the whole evidence about the pullover came from Mrs T and from no one else. Despite that, the trial judge told the jury: "It is a matter for you how far that single piece of evidence takes you, but you may, *or may not* [my emphasis] doubt whether it could amount satisfactorily to corroboration by itself of Mrs T's account."

That is clearly a misdirection. The pullover could not provide corroboration of Mrs T in any respect, because only she spoke about it. Remarkably, the appellant had not even been asked about it when he gave evidence. The Solicitor General did not dispute that what was said constituted a misdirection.

In these circumstances, I am not prepared to hold that this misdirection did not result in a miscarriage of justice. The Solicitor General pointed to the other material which had been relied upon for corroboration and which is fully narrated by the trial judge in his report. Some of that evidence is consistent with consensual intercourse, which the appellant maintained had taken place. The rest of it is consistent with the assault referred to in para (a) of the amended indictment. The discarded paper tissue which was found with wetted blood on it appears to have been spoken to by others in addition to Mrs T, so it might also have provided an adminicle of corroboration as explained by your Lordship in the chair, even though it was not proved to be the appellant's blood. The only other corroboration was said to come from evidence as to the complainer's state of distress some time later, though that again could just as readily be referable to the assault. In these circumstances it appears to me that although there was a little evidence which might or might not have been treated by a jury as corroborative, it was by no means overwhelming and much if not all of it could be regarded as equivocal in the sense that it could have been referable to the other assault and to earlier consensual intercourse. That being so, the misdirection about the possible corroborative weight of the evidence about the jumper appears to me to be sufficiently important to compel us to the conclusion that the misdirection led to a miscarriage of justice. The fact that elsewhere in his charge the trial judge explained cor-

A roboration in clear terms cannot cure this misdirection. Corroboration is, I believe, a difficult concept for laymen to grasp. A judge may describe it academically in what appear to be clear terms; but if he then contradicts himself by telling the jury that some piece of evidence which, in terms of his earlier exposition, cannot be regarded as corroboration may nevertheless be used as corroboration, or indeed may "*amount to corroboration*" he is likely to leave the jury in a state of confusion. In relation to the rape charge, corroboration lay at the heart of the matter. It is impossible to assess what effect this misdirection might have had upon this jury. The verdict

B was by a majority only. In these circumstances the correct course, in my opinion, is to quash the conviction for rape. As counsel for the accused accepted, success in relation to this submission alone would result in the quashing of the rape conviction only.

I would accordingly conclude that the appellant's appeal against conviction should succeed to this limited extent.

C **LORD MORISON.**—I agree with your Lordship in the chair regarding all the points raised in this appeal and have nothing to add.

Counsel for Appellant, Drummond, QC, Di Rollo; Solicitors, Drummond & Co, WS — Counsel for Respondent, Solicitor General (Rodger, QC); Solicitor, I Dean, Crown Agent.

S D D N

D

Lord Advocate v Butt

SECOND DIVISION

E THE LORD JUSTICE CLERK (ROSS), LORDS MORISON AND WYLIE

20 DECEMBER 1991

Revenue — Income tax — Prescription — Negative prescription — Unpaid tax due under assessment — Interest thereon — Interest accruing from day to day — Whether "sum of money due . . . by way of interest" — Whether due "in respect of a particular period" — Taxes Management Act 1970 (c 9), ss 68 (1), 69 and 86 (1) — Prescription and Limitation (Scotland) Act 1973 (c 52), s 6 and
F *Sched 1, para 1 (a).*

Prescription — Negative prescription — Claim for unpaid taxes assessed — Interest thereon — Interest accruing from day to day — Whether "sum of money due . . . by way of interest" — Whether due "in respect of a particular period" — Taxes Management Act 1970 (c 9), ss 68 (1), 69 and 86 (1) — Prescription and Limitation (Scotland) Act 1973 (c 52), s 6 and Sched 1, para 1 (a).

Interest — Unpaid tax due under assessment — Interest thereon — Prescription — Negative prescription — Interest

accruing from day to day — Whether obligation to pay sum of money by way of interest an obligation in respect G *of a particular period — Taxes Management Act 1970 (c 9), ss 68 (1), 69 and 86 (1) — Prescription and Limitation (Scotland) Act 1973 (c 52), s 6 and Sched 1, para 1 (a).*

The Prescription and Limitation (Scotland) Act 1973, s 6 and Sched 1, para 1 (a), provides that "any obligation to pay a sum of money due in respect of a particular period — (i) by way of interest" shall be extinguished after a period of five years where no relevant claim has been made in relation to the obligation and the subsistence of the obligation has not been relevantly H acknowledged. Section 69 of the Taxes Management Act 1970 provides that interest charged on overdue tax shall be treated for the purposes of inter alia s 68 (which provides for the recovery of tax as a debt due to the Crown) "as if it were tax charged and due and payable under the assessment to which it relates".

The Inland Revenue raised an action against taxpayers seeking payment of unpaid taxes and interest. The taxpayers defended the action on the grounds that the claim had prescribed in terms of the 1973 Act. When the I action came before the Lord Ordinary on procedure roll he upheld the taxpayers' argument in respect of the claim for interest only, holding as respects that claim that the 1973 Act was not restricted to private rights or obligations, and that where, as here, interest accrued from day to day, para 1 (a) applied to exclude a claim for interest in respect of a particular day when the obligation to pay that interest had subsisted for a continuous period of five years. The revenue reclaimed. The taxpayers did not challenge the decision that the claim for unpaid tax had not prescribed. J

Held, (1) that since in terms of s 69 of the 1970 Act the interest fell to be treated as if it were tax, it could not be treated as interest subject to the short negative prescription under the 1973 Act (pp 12J-L, 14B-D and 15G-I); (2) that the obligation to pay interest which accrued continually for an indefinite period was not an obligation to pay interest "in respect of a particular period" within Sched 1, para 1 (a) (i) (pp 13C-E, 14F-H and 15L-16A); and reclaiming motion *granted.*

K

Action of payment
(Reported 1991 SLT 248)

The Lord Advocate as representing the Commissioners of Inland Revenue raised an action of payment against Mohammed Sadiq Butt and others, the partners of a dissolved firm, for several sums allegedly due by them. Conclusions 1 and 2 of the summons related to income tax and interest due thereon; conclusion 3 L related to unpaid social security contributions. The defenders argued that the claim had prescribed in terms of s 6 of and Sched 1, para 1 (a) (i) to the Prescription and Limitation (Scotland) Act 1973. The case came before the Lord Ordinary (Prosser) on procedure roll.

Statutory provisions
The Taxes Management Act 1970, prior to amendment (as respects s 86) by the Finance Act 1989, provides:

"68.—(1) Any tax may be sued for and recovered from

the person charged therewith in the High Court as a debt due to the Crown, or by any other means whereby any debt of record or otherwise due to the Crown can, or may at any time, be sued for and recovered, as well as by the other means specially provided by this Act for levying the tax.

"(2) All matters within the jurisdiction of the High Court under this section shall be assigned in Scotland to the Court of Session sitting as the Court of Exchequer.

"69. Interest charged under Part IX of this Act shall be treated for the purposes — (a) of sections 61, 63 and 65 to 68 above . . . as if it were tax charged and due and payable under the assessment to which it relates. . . .

"PART IX
"INTEREST ON OVERDUE TAX

"86.—(1) Any tax charged by an assessment to which this section applies shall carry interest at the prescribed rate from the reckonable date until payment.

"(2) This section applies to — (a) an assessment to income tax under Schedule A, Schedule C, Schedule D or Schedule E."

The Prescription and Limitation (Scotland) Act 1973 provides:

"6.—(1) If, after the appropriate date, an obligation to which this section applies has subsisted for a continuous period of five years — (a) without any relevant claim having been made in relation to the obligation, and (b) without the subsistence of the obligation having been relevantly acknowledged, then as from the expiration of that period the obligation shall be extinguished: Provided that in its application to an obligation under a bill of exchange or a promissory note this subsection shall have effect as if paragraph (b) thereof was omitted.

"(2) Schedule 1 to this Act shall have effect for defining the obligations to which this section applies.

"(3) In subsection (1) above the reference to the appropriate date, in relation to an obligation of any kind specified in Schedule 2 to this Act is a reference to the date specified in that Schedule in relation to obligations of that kind, and in relation to an obligation of any other kind is a reference to the date when the obligation became enforceable. . . .

"SCHEDULE 1
"OBLIGATIONS AFFECTED BY PRESCRIPTIVE PERIODS OF FIVE YEARS UNDER SECTION 6

"1 Subject to paragraph 2 below, section 6 of this Act applies —

"(a) to any obligation to pay a sum of money due in respect of a particular period — (i) by way of interest; (ii) by way of an instalment of an annuity; (iii) by way of feuduty or other periodical payment under a feu grant; (iv) by way of ground annual or other periodical payment under a contract of ground annual; (v) by way of rent or other periodical payment under a lease; (vi) by way of a periodical payment in respect of the occupancy or use of land, not being an obligation falling within any other provision of this sub-paragraph; (vii) by way of a periodical payment under a land obligation, not being an obligation falling within any other provision of this sub-paragraph;

"(b) to any obligation based on redress of unjustified enrichment, including without prejudice to that generality any obligation of restitution, repetition or recompense;

"(c) to any obligation arising from negotiorum gestio;

"(d) to any obligation arising from liability (whether arising from any enactment or from any rule of law) to make reparation;

"(e) to any obligation under a bill of exchange or a promissory note;

"(f) to any obligation of accounting, other than accounting for trust funds;

"(g) to any obligation arising from, or by reason of any breach of, a contract or promise, not being an obligation falling within any other provision of this paragraph."

On 21 November 1990 the Lord Ordinary *found* the pursuer entitled to decree for the principal sums but *excluded* his claim for interest in respect of those periods caught by the short negative prescription. (Reported 1991 SLT 248.)

The pursuer reclaimed.

Reclaiming motion

The reclaiming motion was heard before the Second Division on 14 and 15 November 1991.

On 20 December 1991 the court *allowed* the reclaiming motion.

THE LORD JUSTICE CLERK (ROSS).—In this action the Lord Advocate on behalf of the Commissioners of Inland Revenue sought payment from the defenders of tax and class 4 contributions under the Social Security Act 1975. In the first conclusion payment was sought of income tax remaining payable and unpaid with interest thereon from 6 July 1989. In the second conclusion the pursuer sought payment of a sum in respect of interest from the reckonable dates to 6 July 1989, and in the third conclusion the pursuer sought payment of the class 4 contributions. In their defences the defenders included two pleas in law, nos 4 and 6, which raised the issue of prescription. The pursuer had a sixth plea in law to the effect that the defences were irrelevant and lacking in specification and should be repelled, and decree pronounced de plano. After sundry procedure the Lord Ordinary on 21 November 1990 pronounced an interlocutor sustaining the sixth plea in law for the pursuer to the extent indicated in his opinion. He proceeded to grant decree against the defenders in terms of the first conclusion, the third conclusion, and in respect of part of the second conclusion. The summons had been served on 9 October 1989, and the restricted sum for which decree was pronounced in terms of the second conclusion represented the interest due from 9 October 1984 to

A 6 July 1989, that is for a period commencing with the date five years before the action was raised. Against that interlocutor of the Lord Ordinary the pursuer has reclaimed. No reclaiming motion was made by the defenders and no cross appeal was put forward on their behalf.

Accordingly the sole issue raised in this reclaiming motion is whether on a proper construction of the Prescription and Limitation (Scotland) Act 1973 Parliament intended to apply the short negative prescription of five years to claims for interest on unpaid tax. Counsel B for the pursuer pointed out that claims for interest on unpaid tax were not subject to any short negative prescription prior to the passing of the Act of 1973. They also contended that principal sums due as tax were not subject to any short negative prescription either before or after the Act of 1973 had come into force, and that they were not liable to any limitation under the law of England. In these circumstances they contended that the Lord Ordinary had erred in holding that interest on unpaid tax was subject to the short negative C prescription.

Before this court counsel for the pursuer put forward four principal submissions. The first submission was that before 1973, a taxpayer's obligations to pay tax, penalties and interest on unpaid tax were not subject to prescription, and that there was nothing in the wording of the Act of 1973 to show that Parliament intended to innovate by making these obligations subject to the short negative prescription. The second submission was that the court will not favour a construction D of an Act which will give rise to an anomaly in the recovery of taxation between Scotland and other United Kingdom jurisdictions whereby a claim to tax would be cut off in one jurisdiction but not in the other. The third submission was that holding that interest on unpaid tax is subject to the short negative prescription rests ill with some provisions of the Taxes Management Act 1970 and is inconsistent with other provisions of that statute. The fourth submission was that in any event the reference in Sched 1, para 1 (a) (i) to the Act of 1973 to a sum of money due by way of interest does E not, on a proper construction, cover interest on tax.

Although counsel developed all these submissions before the court in detail and with considerable skill, I do not find it necessary to express an opinion upon all the issues raised. In dealing with the claim for interest, the Lord Ordinary recognised that interest on unpaid tax did not fit precisely into what is laid down in para 1 (a) (i) of Sched 1 to the Act of 1973. However, he held that claims for interest were plainly intended F to be subject to the five year prescription and he accordingly decided in favour of the defenders apparently on the view that since interest accrued from day to day, the interest in respect of a particular day fell to be treated as prescribing when the obligation to pay that interest had subsisted for a continuous period of five years.

The relevant statutory provisions appear in s 6 of and Sched 1 to the Prescription and Limitation (Scotland) Act 1973. Section 6 provides inter alia as follows: [his Lordship quoted the terms of s 6 (1)-(3) and continued:]

Schedule 1 is headed "Obligations Affected By

Prescriptive Periods of Five Years Under Section 6". Paragraph 1 is in the following terms: [his Lordship G quoted its terms and continued:]

For the sake of completeness it should be observed that para 2 of Sched 1 lists certain obligations to which s 6 of the Act does not apply.

Counsel for the defenders sought to refute each of the propositions for which the pursuer had contended, and maintained that interest on unpaid tax fell squarely within Sched 1, para 1 (a) (i). Interest on tax was a debt due to the Crown and was no different to any other debt H due to the Crown or any other creditor. The Act of 1973 binds the Crown (s 24). Interest accrued from day to day; the particular period was a single day, and there was a series of obligations each for one day. The Lord Ordinary had reached the correct conclusion.

Having considered all the submissions advanced before us I am satisfied that there are two principal reasons for concluding that the Lord Ordinary arrived at the wrong conclusion so far as interest was concerned and that the submissions on behalf of the pursuer fall I to be preferred. In my opinion when considering the question of interest on unpaid tax, the Lord Ordinary failed to attach proper weight to the provisions of the Taxes Management Act 1970. In terms of s 86 (1) of that Act, any tax charged by any assessment, including assessment under Sched D, shall carry interest at the prescribed rate from the date when the tax becomes due and payable until payment. Section 88 (1) also provides for interest on tax recovered to make good a loss due to the taxpayer's fault. Section 68 provides that any tax may be sued for and recovered from the person charged J therewith as a debt due to the Crown in the Court of Session sitting as Court of Exchequer. Section 69 is of particular importance. It provides that interest charged under Pt IX of this Act (which deals with interest on overdue tax) shall be treated for the purposes of inter alia s 68 "as if it were tax charged and due and payable under the assessment to which it relates". This means that interest charged under s 86 & s 88 of the Act of 1970 falls to be treated as tax. If it falls to be treated as tax, it cannot be interest under the Act of 1973. In K the present action the Lord Ordinary has correctly held that the obligation to pay tax is not covered by the short negative prescription. Since interest for the purposes of the present action falls to be treated as tax it must follow that the obligation to pay interest is likewise not subject to the short negative prescription. It is not really a claim for interest at all but a claim for a principal sum due as tax. Since Sched 1 does not apply to the principal sum, it likewise does not apply to interest that falls to be treated as part of it. In my opinion the Lord Ordi- L nary has erred in failing to give effect to the provisions of s 69 providing that the interest charged on unpaid tax shall be treated as if it were tax.

There is a second reason for holding that the Lord Ordinary did not arrive at the correct conclusion so far as the claim for interest is concerned. This turns upon the terms of Sched 1. It is important to observe that by virtue of para 1 (a) (i) of Sched 1, s 6 applies not to any obligation to pay a sum of money due by way of interest but to any obligation to pay a sum of money

due *in respect of a particular period* by way of interest.
A   In order to give effect to the words which I have
emphasised the Lord Ordinary held that interest accrued
from day to day, and that there was thus a series of obligations to pay interest in respect of a particular day.
Counsel for the respondent sought to support this
reasoning of the Lord Ordinary and maintained that the
proper approach in this case was to regard there as being
a series of obligations to pay interest, each obligation
being for one day. I do not regard that as a reasonable
or appropriate approach. For example when s 86 (1)
B   of the Taxes Management Act 1970 provides that any
tax charged by any assessment shall carry interest from
the date when the tax becomes due and payable until
payment, that prescribes a period commencing with the
date when the tax becomes due and terminating with
the date when payment is made. It does not impose an
obligation to pay interest for a single day followed by
a series of obligations to pay interest each for a single
day. I agree that interest does accrue continually, and
that in practice it is calculated on a daily basis, but the
method by which it is calculated does not define the
C   nature of the obligation. The obligation to pay interest
imposed by s 86 is an obligation to pay interest for an
indefinite period, and I agree with counsel for the
pursuer that an indefinite period is not a particular
period. The fallacy in the approach of the respondents
is that they seek to construe para 1 (a) (i) of Sched 1
as though the words "in respect of a particular period"
did not appear. Furthermore, on a proper construction
of para 1 (a) of Sched 1, it appears to me that the subheads (ii) to (vii) all relate to obligations to pay a sum
D   of money by way of regular periodical payments; all the
obligations are private contractual obligations, and all
are independent and stand on their own, in other words
they are not ancillary to another obligation. That is a
strong indication that the obligation being referred to
in para 1 (a) (i) is of a similar nature — noscitur a sociis.
This shows that the obligation to pay a sum of money
due by way of interest is an obligation to pay interest
by means of regular periodical payments. The obligation to pay interest on unpaid tax from the date when
E   the tax becomes due and payable until payment is not
such an obligation. The language used in para 1 (a) (i)
does not, in my opinion, cover the situation where
interest is accruing indefinitely during a period of non-
payment of the principal sum.

For the foregoing reasons I am of opinion that the
Lord Ordinary's conclusion that the obligation to pay
interest had prescribed five years later is not a sound
one. As I have already indicated, counsel for the pursuer
presented a number of other arguments in support of
F   his submission that the reclaiming motion should be
granted. Thus counsel contended that there was a
presumption that Parliament had not intended to change
the general law in the absence of clear expressions to
that effect; it was also submitted that Parliament cannot
have intended to provide for different treatment of
interest on unpaid tax in Scotland and in England; and
it was submitted that if the Lord Ordinary were correct
there would be certain anomalies when regard was had
to the terms of the Taxes Management Act 1970.
Counsel for the defender challenged these contentions.

Being satisfied for other reasons that the Lord Ordinary's decision cannot stand so far as interest is con-   G
cerned, I do not find it necessary to consider these other
submissions.

I would accordingly move your Lordships to grant
the reclaiming motion, and to recall the interlocutor of
the Lord Ordinary of 21 November 1990 in so far as
he pronounced decree for £3,188.12 under (2), and in
place of that part of the decree I would under (2) grant
decree for payment of the sum of £5,549.77; quoad ultra
I would adhere to the interlocutor of the Lord Ordinary.
                                                          H
LORD MORISON.—The sum which is in issue in
this reclaiming motion is an amount which represents
interest on certain assessments of income tax liability
made on the defenders, and which is claimed to have
arisen in respect of a period before 9 October 1984. The
Lord Ordinary pronounced decree for the balance of
the principal sums to which the defenders had been
assessed for the period 1979 to 1982, rejecting their
argument that these sums had prescribed by virtue of
provisions contained in the Prescription and Limitation
(Scotland) Act 1973 (hereinafter referred to as "the 1973   I
Act"). However, he held that the revenue's claim for
interest on these sums had prescribed so far as it related
to the period more than five years before the action was
raised, which was on 9 October 1989. His decision
rejecting the defenders' contentions regarding the principal sums is not challenged. The pursuer has however
reclaimed against the Lord Ordinary's interlocutor so
far as relating to interest for which liability is claimed
to have arisen before 9 October 1984.
                                                          J
The Lord Ordinary held that the obligation to pay
the sum which is now the subject of dispute was an obligation which fell within the classes specified in Sched
1, para 1 to the 1973 Act. By virtue of s 6 (1) of that
Act, if such an obligation has subsisted for a continuous period of five years without any relevant claim or
relevant acknowledgment of its subsistence, it is extinguished from the expiration of that period. The only
question therefore which arises for our decision is
whether the obligation to pay interest is one which falls   K
within the classes specified in the said para 1. That paragraph refers to the application of s 6 inter alia "(a) to
any obligation to pay a sum of money due in respect
of a particular period — (i) by way of interest". The
Lord Ordinary held the obligation in issue to be such
an obligation.

In any case where a dispute arises whether an obligation is one of those referred to in Sched 1, it is clearly
necessary first to define with precision the nature of the
obligation in question. The Lord Ordinary's opinion   L
does not reveal any decision on that matter, so far as
the claim for interest is concerned. In fact that claim
arises by virtue of s 86 (1) of the Taxes Management
Act 1970 which provides that "Any tax charged by an
assessment to which this section applies shall carry
interest . . . from the reckonable date until payment."

The assessments made on the defenders on which
interest is claimed are assessments to which the section
applies; and it is by virtue of this provision that the sum
in dispute is claimed.

Further provision is however made in the 1970 Act which is relevant to a determination of the nature of the obligation to pay interest. Section 69 thereof provides that: "Interest charged . . . shall be treated for the purposes — (a) of sections 61, 63 and 65 to 68 above . . . as if it were tax charged and due and payable under the assessment to which it relates."

Section 68 provides inter alia that: "(1) Any tax may be sued for and recovered from the person charged therewith . . . as a debt due to the Crown, or by any other means whereby any debt of record or otherwise due to the Crown can, or may at any time, be sued for and recovered."

The effect of these provisions is in my view clearly relevant to the defenders' contention that the obligation has been extinguished by prescription. That plea would, if successful, prevent the revenue from recovering the amount in dispute. But, for the purpose of recovery, interest has to be treated "as if it were tax charged and due and payable under the assessment to which it relates". For this purpose therefore the claims for interest and principal sums are to be treated in the same way, and not as if they were independent of each other. The obligation which is in issue cannot therefore be treated independently, as if it were a separate "obligation to pay a sum . . . by way of interest". It is not now disputed that the obligation to pay the principal sums due under the assessments is not one of those to which s 6 of the 1973 Act applies. The result must be that the obligation to pay interest has similarly not prescribed.

That conclusion appears to me to be the inevitable result of the statutory provisions to which I have referred. But it seems to me to be also in accordance with what must have been intended by the legislature. It would be most surprising if the principal sums due under the assessments were held to have been excluded from the effect of s 6, but interest on these sums was not excluded from that effect. Claims not only for the amounts due under assessments but also those for penalties and for repayment to the taxpayer are unaffected by the provisions of the 1973 Act. I can see no good reason why the revenue's claims for interest should not similarly be unaffected in Scotland, particularly since they are apparently unaffected by the statutory provisions applying to limitation in England. To construe the provisions to which I have referred in a way favourable to the defenders' contentions would in my view lead to an illogical result.

However, that illogical result is in my opinion also avoided by a proper construction of the wording used in para 1 of the Schedule. Even on the assumption that the respondents' obligation to pay interest is to be treated as arising independently of their obligation to pay under the assessments (contrary to the view which I have expressed), in my opinion it still does not fall within the category referred to in para 1 (a) (i). The Lord Ordinary recognised that the "constantly extending period" in which interest is due "does not appear . . . to fit the words of the statute at all well". In my opinion the defenders' obligation to pay interest is wholly inconsistent with the words used to describe the obligation referred to in para 1 (a) (i). The defenders' obligation to pay is one in which the amount due accrues indefinitely. It does not fall to be discharged periodically, although no doubt a calculation of the amount due on any particular date may be, as it generally is, based on the number of days during which the obligation has subsisted. The obligation to pay is not therefore one to pay a sum of money "due in respect of a particular period". The only content which can reasonably be given to the latter words in the context of interest, is that they make provision for a case in which it is stipulated that payment must be made on a particular date in respect of a particular period. This construction as applied to the obligation to pay interest fits well with the other classes of obligations defined in para 1 (a), all of which relate to periodical payments. It was suggested that the "particular period" in respect of which interest became due in the present case was a period of one day at the end of which a new obligation arose to pay in respect of the following day. This appears to be the suggestion which found favour with the Lord Ordinary, but in my opinion the concept of a series of recurring obligations is contrary to the ordinary notion of liability for accruing interest. Moreover, if in the absence of express stipulation as to the date on which payment is to be made, an obligation to pay interest does arise in respect of each day, all claims for interest would be struck at, and there would thus be no need to include the words "in respect of a particular period". Finally, the defenders' submission would lead to the illogical result that interest on claims for principal sums which are expressly excluded from prescription by virtue of para 2 of the Schedule, would not be excluded. In my opinion therefore para 1 (a) (i) is, like the other obligations to pay which are specified in the subparagraph, confined to obligations to pay interest which becomes due for payment on a particular date, which the defenders' obligation did not.

Submissions were made on behalf of the reclaimer based on what was submitted to be a presumption that the previous law, particularly relating to liability to pay tax, should not be regarded as altered by the 1973 Act in the absence of a clear indication that this was intended. I was not impressed by this argument, since the 1973 Act introduced specific provision relating to prescription of interest which appears to innovate on the general law then existing. The Crown is expressly bound by the Act, and no exception is made in favour of the revenue which would entitle them to plead that they were in a special position in this respect. I agree with the defenders' submission that the provisions of the 1973 Act must be construed only in light of the general intention to afford protection to alleged debtors against stale claims. In my opinion the reclaiming motion turns only on the construction of the legislative provisions to which I have referred, in the context of that general intention. On this approach and for the reasons which I have given I agree that the reclaiming motion should be granted, and decree pronounced as proposed by your Lordship.

LORD WYLIE.—The live issue in this case, so far as the reclaiming motion is concerned, is a narrow one, albeit one of some significance. In terms of the first conclusion of the summons the pursuer and reclaimer sought payment of the balance outstanding on certain assessments to income tax (Sched D) in respect of the three income tax years 1979-80 to 1981-82. The Lord Ordinary pronounced decree for the principal sums involved and this decision, like his decision to pronounce decree in terms of the third conclusion for the principal sum due in respect of class 4 contributions due under the Social Security Act 1975, is not now being challenged. In the second conclusion the pursuer seeks payment of the sum of £5,549.77, being the aggregated interest payable on the principal sums outstanding under the assessments. The Lord Ordinary likewise reached the conclusion that the pursuer was entitled to interest in respect of the period since 9 October 1984, being the date on which the action was raised, but held that the claim for interest prior thereto had prescribed. He accordingly pronounced decree in respect of the second conclusion in the restricted sum of £3,188.12 and it is against the Lord Ordinary's decision to exclude the pursuer's claim to interest prior to 9 October 1984 that this reclaiming motion has been taken.

The narrow issue is accordingly whether or not interest due in respect of non-payment of tax falls within the provisions of s 6 of the Prescription and Limitation (Scotland) Act 1973, and in particular whether or not it constitutes one of the defined obligations to which the section applies in terms of para 1 of Sched 1 to the Act. Section 6 provides for the extinction of certain obligations by prescription and subs (1), read short, is in these terms: "If . . . an obligation to which this section applies has subsisted for a continuous period of five years — (a) without any relevant claim having been made in relation to the obligation, and (b) without the subsistence of the obligation having been relevantly acknowledged, then as from the expiration of that period the obligation shall be extinguished."

Subsection (2) provides that Sched 1 to the Act shall have effect for defining the obligations to which the section applies, and paras 1 and 2 thereof respectively set out the obligations to which the section does and does not apply. It is to be observed that para 2 is not exhaustive. It contains no reference to tax but it is accepted that principal sums due in respect of tax are not struck at by the section, and indeed the list has been added to from time to time. The critical wording of para 1 is as follows: "Subject to paragraph 2 below, section 6 of this Act applies — (a) to any obligation to pay a sum of money due in respect of a particular period — (i) by way of interest". In the last resort it is the construction to be placed on these words that must decide the issue in this reclaiming motion.

Counsel for the pursuer submitted, in my view correctly, that in addressing this issue regard must be had to the statutory background which set out the nature of the obligations now in dispute as having been affected by these provisions. The starting point is the provisions of s 86 of the Taxes Management Act 1970, subs (1) of which provides: [his Lordship quoted the terms of s 86 (1) and continued:] This is the statutory basis on which the disputed sum is claimed. A similar provision is to be found in s 88 (1) in relation to interest on tax recovered to make good loss due to the taxpayer's fault. Moreover, a highly significant provision in relation to

interest on tax is to be found in s 69 which, read short, provides that: "Interest charged . . . shall be treated for the purposes — (a) of sections 61, 63 and 65 to 68 above . . . as if it were tax charged and due and payable under the assessment to which it relates".

Under these provisions interest has accordingly to be treated as forming part of the principal sum due as tax, a principal sum which itself is not subject to prescription under s 6 of the Act of 1973. These provisions, read together with s 68 which provides that "Any tax may be sued for and recovered from the person charged therewith . . . as a debt due to the Crown", indicate to me that at all stages up to recovery interest falls to be treated as an integral part of the principal sum due under an assessment. On that view the sum being claimed in the second conclusion in proceedings under s 68 (2) in this court as the Court of Exchequer is not strictly a distinct and separate claim for interest but rather, by virtue of s 69, it is a claim for part of the principal sum due as tax due under these assessments. To such a claim the Schedule has no application.

This was the argument primarily advanced by senior counsel for the pursuer. It is not clear whether it was advanced before the Lord Ordinary but it is certainly not canvassed in his opinion. In my view however it is a well founded argument, on the basis of which the pursuer would succeed.

An alternative argument however was also deployed in support of the reclaiming motion, based on the actual wording of para 1 (a) (i). On the assumption that interest on tax is a distinct and separate obligation from the obligation in relation to payment of the principal sums due, on a proper construction of the provisions in the Schedule, para 1 (a) (i) is not apt to cover a claim for interest accruing generally on a principal sum due and payable throughout the whole period of non-payment. It was not a catch all provision covering all claims for interest. It does not apply "to any obligation to pay a sum of money due — (i) by way of interest". On the contrary, the obligation is narrowed down by the interposition of the words "in respect of a particular period". This provision, so it was argued, would be deprived of any content if interest accruing continuously to the principal sum throughout the period of non-payment fell to be covered. Such an obligation could not be said to be referable to a particular period. On the contrary it was an obligation to pay interest for a quite indefinite period. The counter argument, which found favour with the Lord Ordinary, was that the provision could be read in such a way as to constitute a "rolling" prescription, with the obligation to pay interest in respect of a particular day prescribing, day by day, five years later. The Lord Ordinary appears to have accepted this argument on the broad view that claims for interest were intended to be subject to the five year prescription but, with respect to the Lord Ordinary, that view appears to overlook the limitation imposed by the qualification incorporated in the opening words.

I have little hesitation in reaching the conclusion that para 1 (a) (i) applies only to claims for interest which fall due for payment on a particular date, as indeed is the case of all the other categories itemised in para 1 (a), all of which in terms relate to periodical payments. The obligation to pay interest at a prescribed rate on a principal sum does not arise on a day to day basis, notwithstanding that for practical purposes the calculation of the amount due at any particular time may do so. For these reasons I am satisfied that the interest claimed in this case is not struck at by s 6 of the Act of 1973. I would only add that I agree with counsel for the pursuer that it would indeed be difficult to explain why Parliament should single out interest due on a principal sum as being subject to prescription under the Act while the principal sum itself, like penalties for delayed payment and claims for repayment of tax, remains unaffected. I would accordingly grant the reclaiming motion.

_____

Counsel for Pursuer, G N H Emslie, QC; Hodge; Solicitor, T H Scott, Solicitor of Inland Revenue (Scotland) — Counsel for Defenders, Tyre; Solicitors, John G Gray & Co, SSC.

M C G

Roxburgh Dinardo & Partners' Judicial Factor v Dinardo

SECOND DIVISION
THE LORD JUSTICE CLERK (ROSS),
LORDS MURRAY AND SUTHERLAND
17 JANUARY 1992

Partnership — Dissolution — Scheme of division — Assets in hands of one partner — Whether appropriate for judicial factor to allow interest at commercial rather than judicial rate — Whether appropriate to apply compound interest.

Interest — Partnership — Dissolution — Scheme of division — Assets in hands of one partner — Whether appropriate for judicial factor to allow interest at commercial rather than judicial rate — Whether appropriate to apply compound interest.

A judicial factor on the sequestrated estates of a firm petitioned for approval of the factory accounts and scheme of division. When the partners had separated one of them, D, had taken all the net assets and the other, R, the net liabilities. The judicial factor, with the concurrence of the accountant of court, charged compound interest at the rate of 3 per cent above base against D in respect of the partnership assets in his hands. No objection to this had been taken prior to the accountant of court's report. When the case came before the court on the petitioner's motion to approve the report, D objected to the application of compound interest at that rate and sought leave to amend to raise the issue of interest. The Lord Ordinary having refused that motion as too late and on the ground that no specific amendment was being proposed, and approved the

report, D reclaimed, arguing (1) that interest should have been charged at the judicial rate, and (2) that compound interest could only be charged in special circumstances which did not exist in this case.

Held, (1) that there was no rule to the effect that the judicial rate of interest had to apply in all circumstances and the judicial factor and accountant of court were entitled to exercise their discretion to conclude that a commercial rate was appropriate (pp 17L-18A, 21C-D and 22I-J); (2) that while it was correct to say that compound interest could only be applied in special or exceptional circumstances, (per the Lord Justice Clerk (Ross) and Lord Murray) such circumstances existed in this case since (a) the partner who took the net liabilities had to finance these by overdraft and pay compound interest thereon, and (b) the assets in the hands of D were subject to a constructive trust, giving rise to a fiduciary relationship under which it was permissible to apply compound interest; (per Lord Sutherland) it was clear that there was a possible exception where there was a fiduciary relationship and, there being no proper pleadings on the facts, D could only succeed by establishing that there were no circumstances in which he could be liable for other than simple interest (pp 20A-F, 22A-B and 23F-H) and reclaiming motion *refused.*

_____

Petition for approval of a scheme of division and exoneration and discharge

Ian Henry Ogle, CA, judicial factor on the sequestrated estates of the firm of Roxburgh Dinardo & Partners, dissolved on 9 July 1982, petitioned the court to have the accounts of the factory and the proposed scheme of division approved by the court and for his exoneration and discharge. After sundry procedure the petition was remitted to the accountant of court to report on the state of the funds and scheme of division, which he did on 7 September 1990.

The petition came before the Lord Ordinary (Prosser) for approval of the accountant's report when the respondent Carlo Dinardo objected to the application of compound interest.

Cases referred to

Ahmed Musaji Saleji v Hashim Ebrahim Saleji (1915) LR 42 Ind App 91.
Blair v Murray (1843) 5 D 1315.
Blair's Trustees v Payne (1884) 12 R 104.
Bunten v Hart (1902) 9 SLT 476.
Campbell v Cordale Investment Ltd, 1985 SLT 305.
Chapman v James Dickie & Co (Drop Forgings) Ltd, 1985 SLT 380.
Douglas v Douglas's Trustees (1867) 5 M 827.
Graham's Executors v Fletcher's Executors (1870) 9 M 298.
Lees' Trustees v Dun, 1912 SC 50; 1913 SC (HL) 12.
McNiven v Peffers (1868) 7 M 181.
Montgomerie (Lady) v Wauchope (1822) 1 S 453.
Munro's Trustees v Murray & Ferrier (1871) 9 SLR 174.
Plaine v Thomson (1836) 15 S 194.
Thomson v Glasgow Corporation, 1962 SLT 105; 1962 SC (HL) 36.
Wellwood's Trustees v Hill (1856) 19 D 187.

Textbooks referred to

A   Bell, *Commentaries,* i, 690, 693, 695-698.
Erskine, *Institute,* III iii 81.
Gloag, *Contract* (2nd ed), pp 518-519, 683.
Green's Encyclopaedia of the Law of Scotland, Vol 11, paras 149 and 166.
Maclaren, *Court of Session Practice,* pp 304-305.
Munro, *Notes for Judicial Factors,* p 175.

On 5 December 1990 the Lord Ordinary *refused* the respondent leave to amend and *approved* the state of funds and scheme of division.

B

The respondent Carlo Dinardo reclaimed.

Reclaiming motion

The reclaiming motion was heard before the Second Division on 27 and 28 November 1991.

On 17 January 1992 the court *refused* the reclaiming motion.

C   **THE LORD JUSTICE CLERK (ROSS).—**In his opinion dated 5 December 1990 the Lord Ordinary has described the circumstances giving rise to the motion in respect of which he pronounced the interlocutor of 5 December 1990. It is accordingly unnecessary in this opinion to repeat what the Lord Ordinary said in that connection. The motion before the Lord Ordinary at the instance of the petitioner was to approve the updated state of funds and scheme of division, and to authorise the petitioner to distribute in accordance with that scheme, subject to adjustment as necessary in relation to taxation and completion costs. At the hearing on the motion roll, counsel for the respondent Carlo Dinardo moved for leave to lodge a minute of amendment. Having heard parties on the motion roll the Lord Ordinary refused to grant leave for further amendment, and approved the state of funds and scheme, and authorised the petitioner to distribute in accordance with the scheme with such adjustments as might be necessary in relation to taxation and the costs of the factory, as these might be approved by the accountant of court. The Lord Ordinary granted leave to reclaim, and the respondent Carlo Dinardo has now reclaimed against that interlocutor of the Lord Ordinary.

On behalf of the respondent Carlo Dinardo two grounds of appeal were stated. The first ground of appeal was to the effect that the Lord Ordinary had erred in law in approving the state of funds and scheme of division in that interest had been charged against the respondent Carlo Dinardo at the rate of 3 per cent per F   annum above base rate compounded annually whereas it was asserted that interest should not have been compounded and should have been charged at the legal rate. The second ground of appeal was to the effect that the Lord Ordinary had erred in law and had exercised his discretion unreasonably in refusing the respondent's motion for leave to amend, the amendment being sought to challenge the treatment of interest in the state of funds and scheme of division.

In opening the appeal counsel for the respondent Carlo Dinardo made it plain that the two grounds of appeal were interlinked. The issue which he was raising in both grounds of appeal was whether the petitioner G had been correct in charging interest against the respondent at overdraft rates, and in charging compound interest.

So far as amendment was concerned, counsel submitted that the Lord Ordinary had erred. He founded upon *Chapman v James Dickie & Co (Drop Forgings) Ltd.* He pointed out that in that case Lord Justice Clerk Wheatley had indicated (at p 381) that when considering whether or not to allow a minute of amendment: "The overriding consideration is fairness and the interests of H justice: prejudice to the defenders must be a major element in such a consideration."

He also founded upon *Campbell v Cordale Investment Ltd* where the pursuer was allowed to amend since the defenders would not be prejudiced thereby. Counsel pointed out that in the present case the Lord Ordinary had not concluded that there would be prejudice to either party if the amendment were allowed. Counsel accordingly submitted that the Lord Ordinary had exercised his discretion to refuse the amendment upon a I wrong basis. He contended that the reason which the Lord Ordinary gave for exercising his discretion so as to refuse the minute of amendment was that he was satisfied that the matter of interest had been correctly treated by the judicial factor and the accountant of court. Counsel maintained that if the Lord Ordinary were in error in concluding that the matter of interest had been correctly treated by the judicial factor and the accountant of court, then it would produce a manifest injustice to the parties to adhere to the Lord Ordinary's interlocutor refusing the amendment merely because he had J exercised his discretion.

In my opinion the question of the late amendment and the question of whether the matter of interest has been treated correctly in the state of funds and scheme of division are indeed closely linked, and I agree that whether or not an amendment should be allowed, and indeed whether or not an amendment is necessary can only be determined once a decision is reached on the treatment of interest.   K

As already indicated, two matters arise regarding interest. So far as rate of interest is concerned, counsel maintained that the rate to be charged varied according to the circumstances. In the present case the rate which had been charged was overdraft interest, that is 3 per cent above base rate. That was said to be the commercial rate of interest. He maintained that there was no warrant for applying a commercial rate of interest. He submitted that it was a question of what was considered reasonable. On the other hand he accepted that L it was for the judicial factor and the accountant of court to consider what rate was reasonable in the circumstances and he recognised that it was difficult for him to advance an argument to the effect that they were not entitled to conclude that a commercial rate of interest was appropriate in the circumstances.

I am quite satisfied that it was for the judicial factor and the accountant of court to determine what rate of interest was appropriate in the circumstances. There is no rule to the effect that the legal rate of interest must be applied in all circumstances. In my opinion the judicial factor and the accountant of court were entitled to exercise their discretion to conclude that a commercial rate of interest was appropriate and there is no reason to think that they exercised that discretion on a wrong basis. Accordingly I am satisfied that this court would not be entitled to interfere with their decision upon that matter.

The major question raised however is whether the judicial factor and the accountant of court were justified in compounding the interest. Counsel maintained that compound interest was only due in special circumstances and that the circumstances of the present case were not special. He referred to Maclaren's *Court of Session Practice*, pp 304-305; Erskine's *Institute*, III iii 81; and Bell's *Commentaries*, i, 690, 695-696, 697-698.

It is unnecessary to examine all these authorities in detail because the subject of compound interest is dealt with very plainly in Maclaren's *Court of Session Practice* at p 304: "(iii) *Compound Interest.* — Compound interest is usually restricted to cases where persons are in breach of their duty, where banks lend money, and where it is allowed by usage or acquiescence or by special agreement. As Lord Justice Clerk Patton has said, 'A claim for compound interest, with annual rests, is a demand which can only be maintained, either in the case of a fixed usage in commercial dealings, or where there has been an abuse in a party trusted with funds and violating his trust. In dealing with money in a bank, interest is accumulated because the course of practice in reference to banks dealing in money is fixed. Where there is a fiduciary relation constituted between the parties, so that the party who is trustee is either bound to recover or to account for sums of money and fails in his duty, or, it may be, used the property held by him in trust for his own purposes, he shall be held to account upon the very strictest system of accounting.' Accordingly, *tutors or curators, factors, trustees, agents,* and others who have retained money for which they were bound to account or to invest are liable in compound interest from the date they ought to have done so."

The passage which Maclaren cites is from the opinion of Lord Justice Clerk Patton in *Douglas v Douglas's Trs* at p 836. (There is however an error in the quotation in *Maclaren* because whereas in the final sentence of the quotation it is stated "and fails in his duty, or, it may be", what the Lord Justice Clerk in fact said according to the report of the case is "and fails in his duty, and, it may be". An error in relation to this quotation is also made in Gloag on *Contract* (2nd ed), p 683 where this quotation from *Douglas v Douglas's Trs* is per incuriam attributed in a footnote to Lord Justice Clerk Inglis.) In *Douglas v Douglas's Trs* Lord Benholme at p 831 said: "I must observe, however, that the very ground on which he is entitled to demand interest as purely a creditor upon his brother's estate, in my opinion excludes him from claiming accumulation, or in other words compound interest, upon his debt. The ordinary rule of our law is against compound interest, and the General's character of creditor, ascertained by the judgment of the Court in 1859, does not entitle him to so unusual a benefit as that which compound interest would confer upon him."

Counsel for the respondent Dinardo also referred to *Graham's Exrs v Fletcher's Exrs*. In that case at p 304 Lord Kinloch said: "It is only in cases special and exceptional that yearly accumulation of interest with principal is permitted. One of these exceptional cases is commonly considered to be that of bankers, who are known invariably to balance once a year, and must, in the general case, be dealt with on the footing of annual accumulation. Where accounts are rendered year by year by the creditor, with the balance yearly accumulated, acquiescence in this rendering by the debtor may very reasonably raise an implied contract in favour of such accumulation. But where neither agreement nor usage sanctions the claim, I consider a charge of compound interest excluded; and so I hold it in the present case, which has no exceptional character."

Bunten v Hart was a case where compound interest was refused, but the report is very short and does not afford assistance in the present case. In *Munro's Trs v Murray and Ferrier* compound interest was again disallowed. Lord Kinloch in delivering the leading opinion repeated what he had said in *Graham's Exrs v Fletcher's Exrs* to the effect that compound interest is only allowed in special and exceptional cases. *Blair's Trs v Payne* deals with the circumstances in which interest may be charged, but does not throw any light upon the question of whether interest in any particular case should be compounded.

Counsel for the respondent Dinardo recognised that compound interest has been allowed in certain cases. He cited two examples of this, namely *Lady Montgomerie v Wauchope* and *Blair v Murray*. The former case appeared to turn upon practice, and in the latter case compound interest appears to have been conceded.

Counsel maintained that none of the cases cited was similar to the present case, and that the Lord Ordinary had erred in holding that the present case was one where compound interest was warranted. In his opinion the Lord Ordinary expressed the view that this was not a case of debt but a case "in the field of accountability and agency". He held that each of the partners was holding and operating with partnership assets, and as such was an agent for the partnership and was thus accountable for what he did with those assets while he had them. Counsel maintained that this was an incorrect statement of the position; the true situation was not that the respondent Carlo Dinardo had taken away and retained some asset of the partnership; it was simply an accounting exercise, and examination of the accounts showed that the partnership asset which was principally concerned was work in progress. Counsel thus maintained that the respondent Carlo Dinardo had not retained any asset which could have earned a return, and that accordingly he had no obligation to account.

Counsel proceeded to examine the legal consequences of dissolution of partnership, and referred to *Green's Encyclopaedia of the Law of Scotland*, Vol 11, para 149. He also referred to para 166 where it is stated inter alia: "this consists with a well-settled rule of the common law that when on the dissolution of a firm one of the partners retains in his hands assets of the firm without

A a settlement of accounts, and applies them in continuing a business for his own benefit, he may be ordered to account for these assets with interest thereon quite apart from any fraud or misconduct."

The foregoing passage is taken from an Indian case, *Ahmed Musaji Saleji v Hashim Ebrahim Saleji*, where the words are used by Lord Sumner.

Counsel for the respondent Dinardo referred finally to *Lees' Trs v Dun*. In that case where there had been negligence on the part of trustees interest was awarded without accumulations. Lord Dundas described the
B claim for compound interest as "scarcely stateable". Lord Salvesen also stated that the claim for compound interest was not stateable, and he stated that the court had not been referred to any case where compound interest had been given.

In these circumstances counsel maintained that there was no justification for awarding compound interest in the circumstances of the present case; to do so would, he maintained, be contrary to principle.

C Counsel for the petitioner, on the other hand, maintained that whether or not to allow a minute of amendment at this stage was a matter for the discretion of the Lord Ordinary. The Lord Ordinary had exercised his discretion and had refused the motion made on behalf of the respondent Carlo Dinardo for leave for further amendment. In that situation this court should not interfere unless it could be shown that the Lord Ordinary had been plainly wrong. Counsel referred to *Thomson v Glasgow Corporation*. He also pointed out under refer-
D ence to the dissolution accounting statement that it was obvious that interest was being compounded. He also maintained that it must have been obvious that a rate in excess of legal rate was being applied and yet no objection had been taken in that respect. He agreed that the Lord Ordinary had not dealt expressly with the matter of any prejudice which would occur in the event of late amendment being allowed, but he maintained that the Lord Ordinary had been justified in refusing the late amendment.

E Counsel for the petitioner, however, recognised that the issue raised in relation to interest was a matter of law, and that that issue could be determined without the necessity for any minute of amendment. Moreover, insofar as the issue was a matter of law, the court was bound to give effect to what the law was. Accordingly, at the end of the day what the court had to do was to determine the matter of law, and his submission was that the Lord Ordinary had been well founded when he expressed the conclusion that compound interest was due in the present circumstances and that there had been
F no error on the part of the judicial factor and the accountant of court in that respect. He stressed that the relationship of partners to each other was a fiduciary one, and that on dissolution of the partnership that fiduciary duty survived with the result that each partner holds partnership property taken by him subject to a duty to account, and that property is held by him on a constructive trust (*McNiven v Peffers*). He maintained that the judicial factor was entitled to take the view that equality of treatment of the partners was only possible by applying compound interest. There was clear authority

for the view that compound interest is appropriate in cases involving a fiduciary relationship. In addition to G founding upon Maclaren's *Court of Session Practice*, p 304, counsel for the petitioner relied upon *Lady Montgomerie v Wauchope* and *Wellwood's Trs v Hill*.

Under reference to the dissolution accounting statement, counsel for the petitioner pointed out that the partnership had financed itself by overdraft, and that until property was sold in 1983 the judicial factor had had to continue the overdraft. That had involved the payment of interest at the base rate plus 3 per cent, and that interest was compounded. He also pointed out H under reference to the dissolution accounting statement that there had been no ordinary division of the assets but that the partners had simply taken certain assets of the partnership in an arbitrary manner. There was an inequality of division, and each partner had a duty to account and was liable to a constructive trust. The dissolution accounting statement showed that overall the respondent Carlo Dinardo had taken net assets whereas the respondent Graham Roxburgh had taken net liabilities which he had to finance by bank borrow- I ing. In these circumstances, he maintained that in order to achieve a fair result the judicial factor had to make an interest calculation, and that in doing so he was justified in adopting a rate of interest of base rate plus 3 per cent and of compounding that interest. Without doing so, no real equality between the two respondents could be achieved. He also pointed out that the respondent Carlo Dinardo had been asked at an early stage to make a contribution to the assets held by the judicial factor. The request was ignored and no significant sum was paid until 1990. Counsel submitted that if the J respondent Carlo Dinardo had made payment earlier, the imbalance between the two former partners would have been corrected, and a large part of the sum now sought would not have been payable.

In all the circumstances he maintained that the decision of the judicial factor was appropriate and in accordance with legal principle. He therefore moved the court to refuse the reclaiming motion.

Counsel for the respondent Graham Roxburgh also K moved the court to refuse the reclaiming motion. He adopted the submissions of counsel for the petitioner. He maintained that the Lord Ordinary had been entitled in the exercise of his discretion to refuse leave to amend. He recognised that whether or not interest should be compounded raised a question of law, but he maintained that the question of the rate of interest to be applied was a matter for the discretion of the judicial factor and the accountant of court and did not raise a matter of law. Accordingly if the issue of the rate of L interest were to be raised, that would require amendment of the pleadings.

So far as the claim for compound interest was concerned, counsel for the respondent Roxburgh emphasised that there was a fiduciary relationship involved, and that the assets in the hands of the respondent Carlo Dinardo were subject to a constructive trust. Accordingly on authority compound interest was appropriate. He also submitted on the authority of *Plaine v Thomson* that compound interest was due where

the beneficiary of an estate ad interim took part of the
estate and made use of the assets. He contended that
there had been no true agreement as to the division of
the assets, and no orderly division. At the end of the
day he submitted that the approach of the judicial factor
and the accountant of court had produced a fair and
equitable result.

Having considered the submissions made, I am satisfied that those of counsel for the petitioner and counsel
for the respondent Roxburgh fall to be preferred. I
entirely accept that it is only in special or exceptional
circumstances that compound interest can be demanded
(*Douglas v Douglas's Trs; Graham's Exrs v Fletcher's
Exrs;* Maclaren's *Court of Session Practice,* p 304). The
critical question is whether the present case is such a
special and exceptional case. I have come to the conclusion that the present case is such a special or exceptional one. I am not persuaded that compound interest
would be appropriate in every case where the estates
of a partnership have been sequestrated, but the present
case clearly has unusual features. As counsel pointed
out, there had been no agreement as to the division of
the assets and liabilities of the firm, and the consequence
was that one partner took with him net assets whereas
the other partner was left with net liabilities. The partnership had financed itself to some extent by overdraft,
and the partner who took the net liabilities had to
finance these by overdraft; he thus had to pay interest
at the rate appropriate to overdrafts. Compound interest
is charged on overdrafts. In the unusual circumstances
of this case, in order to secure equality of treatment,
the judicial factor had to make interest calculations. In
the circumstances as I have already described them, I
am satisfied that the judicial factor was entitled to conclude that compound interest was due.

In any event I agree with counsel for the petitioner
and counsel for the respondent Graham Roxburgh that
there was a fiduciary relationship between the parties,
and that the assets in the hands of the respondent Carlo
Dinardo were subject to a constructive trust (*McNiven
v Peffers*). In these circumstances in the present case
I am satisfied that the judicial factor and the accountant of court were entitled to conclude that the respondent Carlo Dinardo who had retained partnership assets
for which he was bound to account was liable to pay
compound interest. The case appears to me to be
covered by the words used by Lord Justice Clerk Patton
in *Douglas v Douglas's Trs:* "Where there is a fiduciary
relation constituted between two parties, so that the
party who is trustee is bound either to recover or to
account for sums of money, and fails in his duty, and,
it may be, uses the property held by him in trust for
his own purposes, he shall be held to account upon the
very strictest system of accounting."

Support for this view is also found in the passage
already cited from Maclaren to the effect that a trustee
who has retained money for which he is bound to
account is liable in compound interest. Although some
of the cases cited appear to have turned on practice or
concession, it appears to me that the case for compound
interest in the present case also receives support from
Lady Montgomerie v Wauchope, Plaine v Thomson and
Blair v Murray. I was not impressed by counsel for the

respondent Dinardo's argument that the respondent
Carlo Dinardo had not retained any asset which could
have earned a return. As the dissolution accounting
statement shows, he had retained net assets. Moreover
he had done so at a time when the respondent Graham
Roxburgh had taken over net liabilities. In any event,
in view of the fact that the respondent Graham
Roxburgh had to finance these net liabilities by bank
borrowing which was subject to the overdraft rate of
interest which was compounded, it appears to me to
be reasonable for the judicial factor and the accountant
of court to conclude that compound interest was due
by the respondent Carlo Dinardo in the circumstances.
Unless that were done a fair and equitable division
would not be achieved.

In the foregoing circumstances I am satisfied that the
reclaimer has failed to demonstrate any error on the part
of the judicial factor and the accountant of court either
as to the rate of interest or the compounding of interest.
I am also satisfied that the Lord Ordinary was well
founded in his conclusions as to interest and in deciding not to allow late amendment. I would accordingly
move your Lordships to refuse this reclaiming motion
and to adhere to the interlocutor of the Lord Ordinary.

LORD MURRAY.—On 15 November 1978 the
petitioner was appointed judicial factor ad interim in
the Court of Session on the firm of Roxburgh Dinardo
& Partners. On 9 July 1982 the firm was dissolved and
the petitioner was confirmed as judicial factor to its
sequestrated estates. In this petition the judicial factor
applies to the court to have the accounts and the proposed scheme of division approved so that the judicial
factory may be closed. One of the partners, Carlo
Dinardo, opposes the petition; the other partner,
Graham Roxburgh, does not.

After sundry procedure the petition was remitted to
the accountant of court to report upon the state of the
funds and the scheme of division. He reported on 7 September 1990 after dealing with all the objections made
to him. He asked if there were any further objections
and there were none. No complaint is made now about
the way in which he dealt with those objections. In particular no objection was made in regard to the rate of
interest charged by the judicial factor against the respondent Carlo Dinardo in respect of partnership assets in
his hands. But when the petition came before the Lord
Ordinary on a motion to approve of the accountant of
court's report, objection to the rate of interest was mentioned for the first time. Counsel for the respondent
Dinardo sought leave to lodge a minute of amendment
raising this issue of interest. Having heard parties the
Lord Ordinary refused this motion on the ground that
it came too late, the stage for objections having long
past, and that the respondent was not in a position to
specify the amendment proposed. In dealing with that
decision in the reclaiming motion counsel for the respondent Dinardo maintained that amendment was necessary in order to focus a proper legal issue between the
parties which had not been resolved so that there was
no room for prejudice, a matter with which the Lord
Ordinary did not expressly deal. It was accepted that
the decision on this head was entirely a matter for the

discretion of the Lord Ordinary. In light of the history

A of this case I have no doubt whatever that the Lord Ordinary exercised his discretion properly in refusing to allow amendment at this late stage. It is hard to understand how the respondent, who could have availed himself of the professional advice of his accountant and his solicitor, failed to challenge the amount of interest being charged against him at the stage of objections. At the same time I have some disquiet that accounts where an exceptional rate or mode of interest is being applied can be regarded as complete in the absence of

B a note indicating why this has been done.

Counsel for both sides accepted nonetheless that the motion before the Lord Ordinary had raised a genuine issue of law as to whether the judicial factor was, in the circumstances, entitled to apply the exceptional rate of interest which he did. The Lord Ordinary had decided this matter against the respondent and this issue could be raised in the reclaiming motion independently of the question of amendment.

As regards interest counsel for the respondent Dinardo

C maintained first that the judicial factor should have charged interest against the respondent at the legal rate rather than at base rate plus 3 per cent. In the second place he submitted that there was no basis in law for the judicial factor to charge compound interest as he did in this case. The first point can be disposed of rapidly as it was accepted on behalf of the respondent that the actual rate of simple interest to be charged by a judicial factor was within his discretion and no ground for querying the exercise of his discretion was before

D the court. Accordingly the appeal on this point cannot succeed.

Turning to the second point (which was the first ground of appeal), that there was no legal basis for charging compound interest, counsel for the respondent Dinardo submitted that compound interest was not generally applicable and was not, for instance, a matter within the discretion of the judicial factor. Compound interest was allowable as a matter of law only in certain established categories of exceptional cases. There was

E an exception for banks and where compound interest was permitted by custom of trade. Compound interest was also exceptionally allowed where there was a breach of trust or where funds had wrongfully been withheld from the person entitled thereto. None of these exceptions applied to the present case. It could not be said that the respondent was wrongfully withholding assets from his former partner or the judicial factor simply because he had been in possession of the major part of the partnership assets. When the partnership broke up

F each partner had been left de facto in possession of different parts of the assets so that the situation was tantamount to allocation of the assets by agreement. None of the exceptions applied and as a matter of law the judicial factor should have applied simple interest.

Counsel for the respondent Dinardo, in support of his submission that he had exhaustively enumerated the categories of cases in which compound interest was legally permitted, referred to the following: Maclaren on *Court of Session Practice*, p 304; Bell's *Commentaries*, i, 693, 696 and 698; *Douglas v Douglas's Trs* at pp 831,

834, 836, 838 and 839; *Graham's Exrs v Fletcher's Exrs* at pp 301-304; *Bunten v Hart*; *Munro's Trs v Murray* G *& Ferrier* at p 109; *Montgomerie v Wauchope* at p 454; Munro's *Notes for Judicial Factors*, p 175; and *Blair v Murray*; *Green's Encyclopaedia*, Vol 11, paras 149 and 166; and *Lees' Trs v Dun*. At the conclusion of his submissions counsel for the respondent informed the court that he had now received a reply from the accountant of court by letter dated 27 November 1991 to the earlier inquiry on behalf of the respondent whether the accountant of court was aware of any precedent or any rule of practice in regard to the application of compound H interest on the capital accounts of partners. The letter stated that the accountant knew of no precedent and that there was no rule of practice in this matter.

In reply counsel for the petitioner submitted that it was clear on authority that the relationship between partners inter se and with the partnership was a fiduciary one: Gloag on *Contract* (2nd ed), pp 518-519; Partnership Act 1890, s 39; and *McNiven v Peffers*. It was also clear on authority that, in the case of fiduciary relationships, compound interest could competently be I applied: Maclaren on *Court of Session Practice*, p 304; *Douglas v Douglas's Trs*, per Lord Justice Clerk Patton at p 836; *Wellwood's Trs v Hill*, per Lord President McNeill at pp 193-194; and *Montgomerie v Wauchope* at p 454. Furthermore the division of partnership assets in the present case had been far from agreed but rather grab what you can. As a result the lion's share of the assets were taken by the respondent and net liabilities went to his partner. This was very far from an agreed or fair division of assets. In effect Mr Roxburgh, the J other partner, had over a period to fund the partnership deficit on a basis which could be assumed to be overdraft rate at compound interest. Bearing these circumstances in mind the judicial factor had taken the view that the imbalance between the advantages and disadvantages borne by the two partners respectively required him to redress the balance in favour of the disadvantaged partner. This could only be done realistically by charging the respondent compound interest. On 30 November 1982 the judicial factor had requested K the respondent to pay the sum of £120,000 to account on the basis of this differential between the parties. The respondent took no action on this request. The circumstances here were such that a clear fiduciary relationship between the parties existed and, in terms of his actings, the respondent had fiduciary duties to the judicial factor and to Mr Roxburgh in respect of the assets which he had retained in his possession. The present case fell evidently into one or more of the categories within which it was permissible to apply compound interest and it was plainly equitable for the judicial factor L to apply it in the present case. The reclaiming motion should be refused.

Counsel for Mr Roxburgh, who though supporting the petitioner was separately represented, adopted the argument of the petitioner. He referred the court to the case of *Plaine v Thomson* in which a legatee under a testator's settlement was allowed by the trustees to overdraw her share of the proceeds because dividends were paid at only distant intervals. On the trust being wound up the legatee was charged compound interest on the

A advances which had been made to her. She sought to challenge this before the Lord Ordinary maintaining that only simple interest should have been charged. The Lord Ordinary repelled this objection and the Second Division adhered to his interlocutor.

I am satisfied that the submissions for the petitioner and Mr Roxburgh are soundly based in this case both because partners are in a fiduciary relationship and because the respondent, by virtue of his retaining possession of all or most of the partnership assets, placed himself in a position of trust in relation to Mr Roxburgh
B and the judicial factor. Accordingly it was open as a matter of law for the judicial factor, exercising his discretion, to charge compound interest against the respondent if that was an equitable way to proceed. It is clear that no general rule can be stated as to when it is appropriate to charge compound interest in such circumstances, given that it is competent so to do. Furthermore the case of *Plaine v Thomson*, to which we were referred by counsel for Mr Roxburgh, destroys the universality of the so called general principle for
C which the respondent contended, for the case of *Plaine* does not fall under any of the categories in the exhaustive enumeration which counsel for the respondent sought to present. The reclaiming motion accordingly fails.

LORD SUTHERLAND.—The petitioner as judicial factor on the sequestrated estates of Roxburgh Dinardo & Partners brings this petition with a view to having the accounts and scheme of division approved,
D ascertaining and dividing the free balance of the partnership estate between the former partners, and exoneration and discharge. The petition is opposed by one of the former partners, the respondent Mr Dinardo. The petition was remitted to the accountant of court to report upon the statement of funds and scheme of division. The accountant of court's report of 7 September 1990 shows that he had called upon both of the former partners to lodge any objections they had to the scheme of division with him. The respondent's solicitors intimated a number of objections although they said that they
E might have further objections to follow. The accountant of court subsequently asked if there were any further objections but none was forthcoming. The objections which were lodged were dealt with by the accountant of court and no exception is now taken to his decision on these matters. The objections which were intimated did not include any objection of any kind to the matter of the interest which was charged against the respondent. The petition came again before the Lord Ordinary on a motion to approve of the report of the
F accountant of court and at that stage the respondent for the first time raised the matter of interest. Counsel for the respondent sought time in which to lodge a minute of amendment to deal with this matter and after hearing submissions the Lord Ordinary refused leave to amend. His ground for doing so was that this matter was raised far too late and even at that stage no specific amendment was being proposed.

In the present reclaiming motion it was argued that the Lord Ordinary exercised his discretion unreasonably in refusing the respondent's motion for leave to

amend. It was said that amendment would be necessary in order to raise the proper issue between the parties G and it was argued that the Lord Ordinary had failed to demonstrate that there would be any prejudice to any other party if amendment was allowed. It is true that the Lord Ordinary does not deal specifically with the matter of prejudice but it is clear that if leave to amend was granted any disputed facts (and it is clear from the hearing before this court that there would be some disputed facts) would have to be decided either by further remit to the accountant of court or by proof. This would cause yet further delay in a judicial factory which has H already lasted for 13 years. In these circumstances I am quite unable to say that the Lord Ordinary exercised his discretion wrongly. This does not mean that if the case can be decided on a pure question of law any injustice will be done to the respondent, as counsel for the petitioner was prepared to concede that a pure question of law could be argued at this stage even in the absence of any pleadings to cover the point specifically.

The questions of law which are said to be raised are two in number. In the first place it is argued that the I rate of interest charged against the respondent should have been at the legal rate rather than at the rate of 3 per cent above base rate. Counsel for the respondent accepted that the decision as to the appropriate rate was on the authorities a matter for the discretion of the judicial factor. That being so, it would be necessary, before any question of law could be decided, to ascertain the detailed grounds upon which the judicial factor exercised his discretion to find out whether or not his discretion was properly exercised. No material is properly before us which would entitle us to decide this ques- J tion and accordingly this ground of appeal must fail.

The second question raised is whether there was an error of law in charging interest against the partners on a compound basis. Counsel for the respondent argued that the general rule is that compounding of interest will only be allowed in certain special circumstances, none of which is present in this case. Apart from certain recognised exceptions such as banker's accounts or where custom of trade is established, the only other circumstances in which compound interest would be K allowed would be where there has been a wrongful withholding of funds or a breach of trust and in such cases the allowance of compound interest is to be regarded as a penalty to mark the disapprobation of the conduct of the holder of the assets. In the present case the partnership assets taken over by the respondent on dissolution which led to the differential benefit to him were not in the form of cash and were taken by agreement. There was therefore no wrongful withholding or breach L of trust. Accordingly the general rule should be applied and only simple interest allowed. Counsel for the petitioner argued that partners are in a fiduciary relationship to each other and to the firm. In *McNiven v Peffers* it was said that a partner stipulating for private advantage will be compelled to hold it as trustee for the benefit of other partners and this principle was enshrined in s 39 of the Partnership Act 1890. There is ample authority for the view that compound interest may be applicable in cases of a fiduciary relationship. In Maclaren, *Court of Session Practice*, p 304, it is said that tutors or curators, factors, trustees, agents and others who have retained money for which they were bound to account or to invest are liable in compound interest from the date they ought to have done so. The principal authority for this proposition is *Douglas v Douglas's Trs*. In that case the Lord Justice Clerk said: "Where there is a fiduciary relation constituted between two parties, so that the party who is trustee is bound either to recover or to account for sums of money, and fails in his duty, and, it may be, uses the property held by him in trust for his own purposes, he shall be held to account upon the very strictest system of accounting."

Counsel did not accept the proposition that the divided assets were taken by agreement. What happened according to him was that there was a division of assets and liabilities carried out on a de facto basis which was not a proper agreement although it was eventually acquiesced in. The result of this exercise was that 150 per cent of the net assets went to the respondent and − 50 per cent went to Mr Roxburgh, the other partner. As a result Mr Roxburgh had to finance the partnership deficit and it would therefore be only proper on an equitable basis that he should be entitled to recover interest at an overdraft rate on a compound basis as that would be the basis upon which he would have to finance the deficit. Counsel explained that the judicial factor took the view that it was necessary to redress the differential in advantage between the partners and he did so by taking the view that this could only be done by the interest calculation. Furthermore, on 30 November 1982 the judicial factor wrote to the respondent requesting £120,000 to be paid to account on the basis of the differential benefit which was already apparent. This request was ignored by the respondent who did not pay any of the sums sought under this letter. Had he made the payment requested at that time, the present claim for interest would have been largely if not entirely avoided. In the whole circumstances it was clear that there was a fiduciary relationship between the partners and that in such circumstances compounding of interest could be appropriate. It could not therefore be said as a matter of law that the judicial factor was inevitably wrong in deciding to allow compound interest in this case. Counsel for Mr Roxburgh adopted the argument advanced by counsel for the petitioner. He also referred to *Plaine v Thomson*, which is the earliest reported case in which compound interest was allowed. In that case a beneficiary was allowed to overdraw her share of the proceeds of a trust estate. On the trust being wound up she was charged at the rate of 5 per cent on all advances so made with annual accumulations. It was held that this was a proper charge. It is accordingly apparent from this case that there is no need for wrongful withholding or breach of trust to allow the compounding of interest.

I accept that as a general rule only simple interest will be allowed. It is clear however from what was said by Maclaren and by the Lord Justice Clerk in *Douglas* that where there is a fiduciary relationship it is possible for an exception to be made to this rule. Whether such an exception should be made will in my opinion depend upon the circumstances of each case. Because the facts are not properly before this court in the absence of any

proper pleadings, it would follow that for the respondent to succeed on a pure question of law he would require to establish that as a matter of law there would be no circumstances in which a partner in his position could be liable for other than simple interest. In my opinion that proposition cannot be laid down as a pure matter of law. If it had been conceded by the petitioner that there were no special circumstances in this case which would take it outwith the general rule, then of course different considerations would apply. The petitioner has, however, contended that the case could fall within the admittedly limited exceptions suggested in *Douglas* and I am unable to say as a matter of law that this contention is necessarily unsound. That being so, the respondent's argument must necessarily fail and I would refuse this reclaiming motion.

Counsel for Petitioner and Respondent, Drummond Young, QC, Andrew Smith; Solicitors, Macroberts, WS — Counsel for First Respondent and Reclaimer (Dinardo), J L Mitchell, QC; Solicitors, McGrigor Donald — Counsel for Second Respondent (Roxburgh), Howie; Solicitors, McClure Naismith Anderson & Gardiner.

D E N

Solicitors Estate Agency (Glasgow) Ltd v MacIver

SECOND DIVISION

THE LORD JUSTICE CLERK (ROSS), LORDS MURRAY AND MARNOCH

27 MARCH 1992

Contract — Agency — Estate agent — Failure by estate agent to comply with statutory obligations — Contract enforceable at discretion of court — Court to have regard to prejudice and culpability — Court having regard to relevant factors but not considering one of two breaches of statutory obligations — Whether exercise of discretion open to review — Estate Agents Act 1979 (c 38), s 18 (1), (2), (5) and (6).

Process — Appeal — Appeal to sheriff principal — Exercise of discretion by sheriff — Court to have regard to prejudice and culpability arising from breach of statutory obligations — Court having regard to relevant factors but not considering one of two breaches of statutory obligations — Whether exercise of discretion open to review — Estate Agents Act 1979 (c 38), s 18 (1), (2), (5) and (6).

The Estate Agents Act 1979, s 18 (1) and (2) imposes certain obligations on estate agents in their dealings with clients, including by subs (2) (a) an obligation to give particulars of the circumstances in which clients become liable to pay remuneration, and by subs (2) (d) an obligation to give information as to the manner in which

A   advertising costs would be calculated. Section 18 (5) provides that if such obligations are not complied with the contract is not enforceable except pursuant to an order of the court under s 18 (6), in terms of which the court must consider the questions of prejudice and culpability.

An estate agency sued a client in the sheriff court for payment of fees and outlays. After proof the sheriff held that the pursuers had failed to comply with their obligations under s 18 (2) (d) of the 1979 Act in failing to disclose a discount on advertising charges allowed them by a newspaper, and that the contract was unenforcea-
B   ble except pursuant to an order by the sheriff under s 18 (6). The sheriff decided that the failure to disclose or credit the discount to the client was significantly culpable, but that that culpability and the resulting prejudice to the defender were not sufficient to render the contract unenforceable and he accordingly determined that the contract be enforced but that a reduced amount be payable. On appeal, the sheriff principal held that the sheriff had misdirected himself in that he should have found the pursuers in breach of s 18 (2) (a) as well
C   as (d), and thus the exercise of the discretion in s 18 (6) was at large for him. He determined that the contract should not be enforced. On appeal to the Court of Session it was argued that although the sheriff had misdirected himself on the question of breach of the statutory obligations, the misdirection was not material to the decision he made in exercise of his discretion under s 18 (6).

Held, that although the sheriff had misdirected himself, the misdirection was not material and did not
D   affect the exercise by him of the discretion he had under s 18 (6): in exercising his discretion he had had regard to all the matters giving rise to the breaches of s 18 (2) (a) and (d), and the sheriff principal had not been entitled to interfere with his exercise of his discretion (pp 27G-H and 27L-28B); and appeal *allowed* and sheriff's interlocutors *affirmed*.

Appeal from the sheriff court

E   The Solicitors Estate Agency (Glasgow) Ltd raised an action of payment in the sheriff court at Dumbarton against Donald MacIver in respect of fees and outlays incurred in marketing property owned by the defender.

The case came to proof before the sheriff (J T Fitzsimons).

Statutory provisions

The Estate Agents Act 1979 provides:

F   "18.—(1) Subject to subsection (2) below, before any person (in this section referred to as 'the client') enters into a contract with another (in this section referred to as 'the agent') under which the agent will engage in estate agency work on behalf of the client, the agent shall give that client — (a) the information specified in subsection (2) below; and (b) any additional information which may be prescribed under subsection (4) below.

"(2) The following is the information to be given under subsection (1) (a) above — (a) particulars of the

circumstances in which the client will become liable to
G   pay remuneration to the agent for carrying out estate agency work; (b) particulars of the amount of the agent's remuneration for carrying out estate agency work or, if that amount is not ascertainable at the time the information is given, particulars of the manner in which the remuneration will be calculated; (c) particulars of any payments which do not form part of the agent's remuneration for carrying out estate agency work or a contract or pre-contract deposit but which, under the contract referred to in subsection (1) above, will or may in certain circumstances be payable by the client to the
H   agent or any other person and particulars of the circumstances in which any such payments will become payable; and (d) particulars of the amount of any payment falling within paragraph (c) above or, if that amount is not ascertainable at the time the information is given, an estimate of that amount together with particulars of the manner in which it will be calculated. . . .

"(5) If any person — (a) fails to comply with the obligation under subsection (1) above with respect to a contract or with any provision of regulations under
I   subsection (4) above relating to that obligation, . . . the contract or, as the case may be, the variation of it shall not be enforceable by him except pursuant to an order of the court under subsection (6) below.

"(6) If, in a case where subsection (5) above applies in relation to a contract or a variation of a contract, the agent concerned makes an application to the court for the enforcement of the contract or, as the case may be, of a contract as varied by the variation,—(a) the court shall dismiss the application if, but only if, it considers
J   it just to do so having regard to prejudice caused to the client by the agent's failure to comply with his obligation and the degree of culpability for the failure; and (b) where the court does not dismiss the application, it may nevertheless order that any sum payable by the client under the contract or, as the case may be, under the contract as varied shall be reduced or discharged so as to compensate the client for prejudice suffered as a result of the agent's failure to comply with his obligation."

K

Cases referred to

Bellenden v Satterthwaite [1948] 1 All ER 343.
Ronaldson v Drummond & Reid (1881) 8 R 956.
Thomson v Glasgow Corporation, 1962 SLT 105; 1962 SC (HL) 36.

Textbook referred to

Gloag, *Contract* (2nd ed), pp 521-522.

On 20 December 1989 the sheriff *held* the pursuers   L
to have been in breach of s 18 (2) (d) of the 1979 Act and *determined* that the contract should be enforced with the exception of a proportion of the sum due by the defender by way of advertising outlays.

The defender appealed to the sheriff principal.

On 22 March 1990 the sheriff principal (R C Hay, WS) *allowed* the appeal and *assoilzied* the defender.

The pursuers appealed to the Court of Session.

Appeal

The appeal was heard by the Second Division on 3 March 1992.

On 27 March 1992 the court *allowed* the appeal and *affirmed* the interlocutors of the sheriff dated 20 December 1989 and 18 January 1990.

The following opinion of the court was delivered by the Lord Justice Clerk (Ross):

OPINION OF THE COURT.—In this action, the pursuers, who carry on business as estate agents, seek payment of fees in the form of commission, and outlays in the form of advertising costs, due to them under a contract with the defender in terms of which the pursuers undertook to advertise and market the defender's property at 30 Forth Road, Bearsden. The defender resists payment on the ground that the contract between the parties is unenforceable due to failure on the part of the pursuers to comply with the obligation placed upon them by the terms of s 18 (1) of the Estate Agents Act 1979.

In their pleadings the pursuers put forward their case on alternative grounds. In the first place they aver that they were not in breach of the provisions of s 18 (1) and (2) of the Act of 1979, and that accordingly they are entitled to enforce the contract. Alternatively they aver that if they failed to comply with the terms and conditions laid down in s 18 (1) and (2) so that they are not entitled to enforce the contract in accordance with s 18 (5) of the said Act, they are entitled to apply to the court for enforcement of the contract in terms of s 18 (6) of the Act of 1979.

The sheriff heard evidence at a proof, and he held that the pursuers had failed to comply with their obligation under s 18 (1) of the Act of 1979 in respect that they had failed to give the defender the information required by s 18 (2) (d) of the said Act. He accordingly held in terms of s 18 (5) (a) of the Act of 1979 that the contract was not enforceable by the pursuers except pursuant to an order of court under s 18 (6) of the Act. In terms of s 18 (6) the sheriff held that it was not just, having regard to the prejudice caused to the defender and the degree of culpability on the part of the pursuers, that the said application should be dismissed in terms of s 18 (6) (a) of the Act. He therefore determined that the contract should be enforced, but he further held that the sum payable by the defender under the contract should be reduced by the sum of £317.49 as compensation to the defender in terms of s 18 (6) (d) of the Act of 1979, in respect of prejudice suffered as a result of the pursuers' failure to comply with their said obligation.

Against that decision of the sheriff the defender appealed to the sheriff principal. After hearing parties the sheriff principal varied the interlocutor of the sheriff and held in terms of s 18 (6) that it was just, having regard to the prejudice caused to the defender and to the degree of culpability on the part of the pursuers, that the application of the pursuers for enforcement of the contract should be dismissed, and that the contract should not be enforced. He accordingly assoilzied the defender from the conclusions of the action (by which we assume he meant the crave of the initial writ).

Against that decision of the sheriff principal the pursuers have appealed to this court.

This appeal turns upon the provisions of s 18 of the Act of 1979. The relevant provisions of s 18 have been set forth by both the sheriff and the sheriff principal in the notes annexed to their interlocutors, and it is unnecessary to repeat these provisions again ad longum. In his note the sheriff records that the solicitor for the pursuers had conceded that the pursuers could not succeed on their primary case since on any view of the evidence they had not complied with the requirements of s 18 (1) and (2). He accepted that the pursuers had failed to comply with the requirements of s 18 (2) (d) in that they had not given the defender information as to the manner in which the advertising costs would be calculated. On the pursuers' behalf it was accordingly accepted that the contract with the defender was not enforceable in terms of s 18 (5); it was however submitted that the court should not consider it just to dismiss the application having regard to the prejudice caused to the defender by the pursuers' failure to comply with their obligations and their degree of culpability for that failure. The pursuers accordingly submitted that the court should make an order for payment by the defender to the pursuer, reduced if need be in terms of s 18 (6) (b).

On the defender's behalf it was submitted to the sheriff that there had been a breach of obligation under s 18 (1) and (2) in respect of failures to provide the information specified in s 18 (2) (a), (c) and (d). In these circumstances the defender's solicitor stressed the high degree of culpability and high level of prejudice, and accordingly maintained that the court should dismiss the application since it should consider it just to do so in terms of s 18 (6) (a).

After considering all the evidence adduced before him, the sheriff concluded that there had been no breach by the pursuers of those parts of their obligation covered by paras (a), (b) or (c) of s 18 (2). He observed that it had not been claimed by the defender that there had been any breach of para (b). The sheriff did, however, accept that there had been a failure to comply with part of the obligation contained in s 18 (2) (d), in respect that although the pursuers through Mr Neilson had informed the defender of the approximate cost of outlays in relation to advertisements, they had not provided him with particulars of the manner in which the outlays would be calculated. The sheriff accordingly recognised that the contract between the parties was not enforceable by the pursuers and that he required to consider the application by the pursuers for enforcement in terms of s 18 (5) and (6). The sheriff then proceeded to consider, as he was required to do, the question of culpability and the question of prejudice. He decided that there had been a not insignificant degree of culpability for the failure to supply the required information under s 18 (2) (d). So far as prejudice was concerned, he took the view that in the circumstances of the case the defender had not been prejudiced to any significant extent. Having considered these elements of prejudice and culpability, the sheriff concluded that it would not be just in his view to dismiss the application and thereby to deprive the pursuers of any payment under the contract. Indeed he concluded that it would be positively

A unjust to take such a course in the circumstances of this case.

Having decided that it would not be just to dismiss the application, the sheriff then proceeded to consider the provisions of s 18 (6) (b) which allowed him to reduce or discharge any sum payable by the defender under the contract so as to compensate him for prejudice suffered as a result of the pursuers' failure to comply with their obligations. In the event, he came to the conclusion that in order to compensate the defender for the prejudice caused, the sum payable by him under the
B contract should be reduced by an amount equivalent to 50 per cent of the total sum due (including VAT) in respect of the advertisements instructed between 18 March and 24 June. The sum to be deducted amounted to £317.49, and the sheriff gave effect to that decision in his interlocutor.

Before the sheriff principal it was submitted on behalf of the defender that the sheriff should also have found that the pursuers were in breach of their obligation under s 18 (2) (a) to give particulars of the circumstances
C in which the defender would become liable to pay remuneration to the pursuers, and that he erred in law by failing so to find. This argument was based upon the proposition that by failing to disclose and to account to the defender for the discount of 18 per cent allowed to them by the newspaper, the pursuers were in fact taking undisclosed remuneration from him and that this was in breach of their obligation under s 18 (2) (a). This is the matter referred to in finding 9 and finding 12 of the sheriff's interlocutor to the effect that it was the
D practice of the pursuers to advertise in the *Glasgow Herald* newspaper by means of a block advertisement containing details of a number of properties being offered by them for sale on the instructions of their clients, and to the fact that George Outram & Co Ltd, owners of the *Glasgow Herald*, allowed the pursuers a discount of 18 per cent in respect of the total cost of the block advertisement. As is made plain in finding 24, this discount of 18 per cent allowed to the pursuers by the *Glasgow Herald* was not passed on to the pur-
E suers' clients. Finding 24 is in the following terms: "(24) The discount of 18 per cent allowed to the pursuers by the *Glasgow Herald* was not passed on to the pursuers' clients, but was recorded in the pursuers' purchase day book as commission from George Outram & Co Ltd. The defender was not given any information by Mr Donald Neilson, or any other representative of the pursuers, regarding the said discount or its effect in the calculation of charges for advertisements. It was the policy of the pursuers at the time of this transaction not to inform clients or potential clients of the dis-
F count allowed by the *Glasgow Herald*."

The sheriff principal accepted that this argument had not been addressed to the sheriff. The only argument presented to the sheriff in relation to s 18 (2) (a) appears to have been that the agent must specify an identifiable point of time for payment. That argument had been rightly rejected by the sheriff. However the sheriff principal, in the light of the argument now advanced to him, concluded that there had been breach by the pursuers of their obligation under s 18 (2) (a). He explained that he was persuaded that the discount on advertising

G charges allowed by the newspaper to the pursuers which was not disclosed and not passed on to their clients properly fell within the definition of "remuneration" for which the client was liable to pay, within the meaning of s 18 (2) (a).

The sheriff principal accordingly decided that the sheriff had misdirected himself by finding that the pursuers were not in breach of s 18 (2) (a), and that being so he concluded that the exercise of the discretion in terms of s 18 (6) was at large for him. Having regard to the terms of s 18 (6) (a) the sheriff principal proceeded to consider the matter of culpability and the matter of
H prejudice. Although he agreed with the sheriff's assessment of the degree of prejudice actually suffered by the defender, he disagreed with the sheriff on the subject of culpability. The sheriff principal held that the sheriff had misdirected himself in treating as an aspect of the pursuers' failure to provide their clients with details of how the advertising costs were charged, their deliberate policy not to pass on to clients the discount allowed by the newspaper and to conceal from their clients that they were doing so. He reached the conclusion that this
I was an entirely separate act from the pursuers' failure to disclose to their clients the rather involved system which they adopted for apportioning among their clients the costs of the block advertisement. The sheriff principal stated that having regard to the fact that the taking, at the defender's expense, of the undisclosed profit on advertising charges was a policy deliberately adopted by the pursuers, the degree of culpability was so high that it would not be just that this contract should be enforced. That being so the sheriff principal dismissed the application by the pursuers for the enforcement of
J the contract.

Counsel for the pursuers accepted that the sheriff principal was entitled to hold that there had been a breach of s 18 (2) (a) in addition to the breach of s 18 (2) (d) to which the sheriff had referred. He submitted however that although the sheriff had not held that there had been any breach of the obligation under s 18 (2) (a), he had taken account of the fact that the 18 per cent
K discount had not been passed on to the defender in consequence of a deliberate policy on the part of the pursuers to that effect. Although the sheriff principal had been entitled to hold that there had been a failure to supply the information specified in s 18 (2) (a) and s 18 (2) (d), he submitted that it was only one obligation which had been breached. The language of s 18 (5) made it clear that s 18 (1) imposed a single obligation, although a party might fail to comply with that obligation in a number of different respects specified in s 18 (2). It was clear from the note annexed to the sheriff's interlocu-
L tor that he had treated the pursuers' failure to disclose the remuneration which they received by way of discount from George Outram & Co Ltd as culpable. The truth of the matter is that the sheriff had approached the matter in the correct way. He had identified two separate failures to provide information but had treated them under one paragraph of s 18 (2). Moreover, he had considered both culpability and prejudice and had put them in the balance. Although the sheriff had not recognised that there had been any failure to comply with the obligation in respect of the matters specified

in s 18 (2) (a), in the circumstances of the present case
A the same matters fell under s 18 (2) (a) and 18 (2) (d);
whether the pursuers were regarded as having been in
breach of one or two paragraphs of s 18 (2) did not
matter. In exercising his discretion, the sheriff had had
regard to all the material facts, and in particular all the
material breaches on the part of the pursuers. He submitted that any misdirection on the part of the sheriff
in finding that the pursuers were not in breach of s 18
(2) (a) was not material to the decision which he was
making under s 18 (6) (a).

B   Counsel for the defender on the other hand submitted that it was plain that the sheriff had failed to appreciate the proper legal category into which the facts fell.
Section 28 (2) set forth four different types of particulars, and it was plain that these fell into two groups.
(a) and (b) were both concerned with remuneration
payable to the agent, whereas (c) and (d) were concerned
with items other than remuneration such as outlays. It
followed that in the present case there had been failure
on the part of the sheriff to recognise that the pursuers
C had been in breach of an obligation in relation to
remuneration as well as an obligation in relation to
outlays. He submitted that this failure to disclose
remuneration over and above what had been contracted
for was a serious matter. Under reference to Gloag on
Contract (2nd ed), pp 521-522, and *Ronaldson v Drummond & Reid*, he reminded us that at common law an
agent was bound to credit his client with any discount
which he might receive from a person whom he has
employed on behalf of a client. Counsel also pointed
out that parties had been agreed before the sheriff that
D the number and nature of the contraventions of the obligation might be of significance in relation to questions
of prejudice and culpability when the court was considering an application for enforcement of the contract
under s 18 (6). Counsel also pointed out that when the
sheriff stated in his note that the pursuers had complied
with those parts of their obligation under s 18 (2) (a),
(b) and (c) it was clear that the sheriff had not properly
applied his mind to the fact that there had been wrongful appropriation of money. He had clearly misdirected
E himself in holding that there had been no failure to
comply with the requirements of s 18 (2) (a) and that
vitiated his decision. Counsel submitted that in these
circumstances the matter was at large for the sheriff principal and that in the circumstances he was entitled to
conclude that it was just for the court to dismiss the
pursuers' application having regard to the prejudice
caused to the defender and the degree of culpability of
the pursuers. He accordingly invited us to dismiss the
appeal.

F   We have considerable sympathy with the sheriff
because although parties are now agreed that the sheriff
principal was correct in holding that the pursuers were
in breach of their obligation under s 18 (2) (a), no argument to that effect had ever been advanced before the
sheriff. Accordingly the sheriff can hardly be blamed
for not holding that there had been a breach of the obligation under s 18 (2) (a) in this respect. The important
question however is whether that misdirection on the
part of the sheriff means that his exercise of his discretion in terms of s 18 (6) fell to be set aside, and that
the matter was at large for the sheriff principal.

We are not persuaded that the misdirection by the
sheriff meant that the exercise of discretion was at large G
for the sheriff principal. In our opinion the reasoning
of the sheriff principal is flawed in that he has failed
to recognise that when the sheriff considered the question of whether it was just to dismiss the application,
he had regard to all the relevant material relating to both
prejudice and culpability. Although he approached the
case as though the only breach had been a breach of
the obligation under s 18 (2) (d), he took fully into
account all the matters which it is now agreed also gave
rise to a breach of the obligation under s 18 (2) (a). The
sheriff principal concluded that the pursuers were in H
breach of their obligation under s 18 (2) (a), "in that
the practical effect of their policy not to reveal or to
account to their clients for the discount received from
the newspaper was that the defender became liable to
pay undisclosed remuneration to the pursuers for
carrying out estate agency work".

It is, however, clear that the sheriff took these matters
into account when he was assessing the culpability of
the pursuers. In his note, the sheriff states: "it was their
policy not to inform clients of the discount received from I
the *Glasgow Herald* and a fortiori not to disclose the
manner in which that discount was taken into acount
in the calculation of advertising outlays in relation to
individual clients".

In an ensuing passage in his note the sheriff refers
to *Ronaldson v Drummond & Reid* and to the fact that
the pursuers were bound to account to the defender for
the discount. The sheriff states: "In the present case
the pursuers were acting as agents for the defender in
relation to the instruction of advertisements for inser- J
tion in the *Glasgow Herald*, and what they have done
is to charge their clients, including the defender, more
than was actually charged to them by the *Glasgow Herald*
by not crediting the discount to their clients. They have
therefore charged more than they were entitled to, and
increased the burden on their clients, which they had
no right to do while acting as agents on their behalf."

When the sheriff came to consider the subject of culpability, he expressed the view that there was a not insignificant degree of culpability from the failure to supply K
the required information under s 18 (2) (d) in that the
failure was the result of a deliberate decision not to
inform clients of the manner of calculation of outlays
in respect of advertising. The sheriff went on to say:
"In particular the question of the discount was of crucial
importance in the calculation of outlays, and failure to
credit the discount or at the very least to disclose the
effect of the discount on the calculation was in my view
significantly culpable."

When the sheriff came to consider the question of L
prejudice, he stated: "The main elements of prejudice
appear to me to be, first, the fact that the defender was
deprived of the benefit of the 18 per cent discount, and
secondly, and perhaps more importantly, that he was
deprived of information which may have led him to consider his position more carefully and perhaps seek a quotation elsewhere."

In these circumstances we are satisfied that when the
sheriff was exercising his discretion under s 18 (6), and
was determining whether it was just to dismiss the appli-

cation, he in fact had regard to all the matters which
A have been put forward in support of the conclusion that
the pursuers had been in breach not only of their obligation under s 18 (2) (d) but also their obligation under
s 18 (2) (a). In these circumstances we are satisfied that
the sheriff principal was not entitled to hold that the
failure of the sheriff to recognise that there had been
a breach of the obligation under s 18 (2) (a) meant that
the exercise of his discretion was vitiated. In our opinion
although the sheriff may have misdirected himself, the
misdirection was not material and did not affect the exer-
B cise by him of this discretion. We agree with counsel
for the pursuers that the sheriff principal was not well
founded when he criticised the sheriff for treating as
one act of default two quite separate matters arising
under s 18 (2). What is of importance is not whether
there were one or two acts of default; but the nature
and substance of the breaches which took place.

We are satisfied that in exercising his discretion the
sheriff did have regard to all material matters, and
indeed in one passage in his note the sheriff principal
C himself appears to recognise that the sheriff had had
regard to the matters which arise under s 18 (2) (a) and
s 18 (2) (d): "In my respectful opinion, the learned
sheriff seems at this stage to have treated as one act of
default two quite separate matters arising under s 18
(2), namely, (1) the failure which he has found in the
obligation under s 18 (2) (d) to disclose details of how
the advertising costs were charged, and (2) the
undisclosed profit of 18 per cent on advertising charges
which the pursuers took from the defender by not
passing on the discount."
D
If the sheriff treated these two quite separate matters
as one act of default, that can only mean that he had
regard to both these matters and took them into account.

In a later passage in his note, the sheriff principal
again makes it plain that he recognised that the sheriff
had taken account of the matters which in the sheriff
principal's view showed that there had been a breach
of the obligation under s 18 (2) (a). The sheriff principal stated: "The learned sheriff has found that the
E pursuers' failure to account for or at least to disclose
the effect of the discount was significantly culpable. In
that I agree with him."

In all the circumstances we are satisfied that the
sheriff's approach under s 18 (6) (a) was correct; he had
regard to prejudice caused to the defender by the pursuers' failure to comply with their obligation, and he
also had regard to the degree of culpability of the pursuers. The sheriff principal recognised that the sheriff
F had a discretion in this matter, and that he would not
be entitled to interfere with the exercise by the sheriff
of his discretion unless the sheriff had proceeded upon
some wrong principle. In this connection the sheriff
principal referred to *Bellenden v Satterthwaite* at p 345.
Reference might also be made to *Thomson v Glasgow
Corporation*, 1962 SLT at p 107. The sheriff principal
seeks to justify his interfering with the exercise by the
sheriff of his discretion by holding that there had been
a misdirection by the sheriff in relation to the breach
of obligation under s 18 (2) (a). We have already pointed
out that the sheriff principal was in error in this regard

because he failed to recognise that any misdirection in
that connection was not material. The sheriff principal G
expresses the view that the breach of the pursuers' obligation under s 18 (2) (d) which the sheriff found to be
established, and in relation to which he took the
undisclosed commission into account, would in itself
have justified the court in dismissing the application
for relief in terms of s 18 (6) (a). What the sheriff principal has done is to substitute his view upon this matter
for the view of the sheriff, and that was something which
he was not entitled to do since he had no good grounds
for concluding that the sheriff had exercised his discretion on any wrong basis. The matter was not at large H
for the sheriff principal and he was not entitled to substitute his view upon this matter for the view of the
sheriff.

In all the circumstances therefore we have come to
the conclusion that the sheriff principal was not entitled to alter the sheriff's interlocutor as he did. We shall
accordingly allow the appeal, recall the interlocutors of
the sheriff principal dated 24 April 1990 and 11 May
1990, and we shall affirm the interlocutors of the sheriff
dated 20 December 1989 and 18 January 1990. I

*Counsel for Pursuers and Appellants, Drummond
Young, QC; Solicitors, Cochran Sayers & Cook — Counsel
for Defender and Respondent, A P Campbell; Solicitors,
Drummond Miller, WS (for Harpers, Glasgow).*

D E N

J

Gray v Criminal Injuries Compensation Board

OUTER HOUSE

LORD WEIR   K

13 MAY 1992

*Administrative law — Criminal Injuries Compensation
Scheme — Bigamous marriage — Sexual intercourse
after pretended marriage ceremony — Whether crime of
violence under Criminal Injuries Compensation Scheme
— 1990 Scheme, para 4 (a) — Sexual Offences (Scotland)
Act 1976 (c 67), s 2 (1) (b).*

Justiciary — Crime — Crime of violence — Sexual inter- L
*course by bigamous husband after marriage ceremony —
Whether crime of violence committed.*

The Criminal Injuries Compensation Scheme provides payment of compensation to persons who have
suffered personal injury attributable to a crime of
violence.

A woman was deceived into undergoing a pretended
marriage ceremony with a man who was already
married. They lived together thereafter as man and wife
and engaged in sexual intercourse. When the man dis-

appeared the bigamy was discovered. The woman
required treatment from her doctor for stress. She
applied for compensation under the Criminal Injuries
Compensation Scheme. Her application was refused on
the ground that no crime of violence had been committed. She applied for judicial review of that decision and
argued that the crime of procuring sexual intercourse
with her was in these circumstances a crime of violence
since, on discovery of the bigamy, the woman had
suffered injury to her health.

Held, (1) that the nature of the crime and not its effect
upon the victim should be looked at in determining
whether a criminal act was a crime of violence (p 31A);
(2) that the root cause of the injury suffered by the petitioner was the commission of the crime of bigamy and
its discovery (p 31A); (3) that sexual intercourse within
a bigamous marriage did not amount to a crime (p 31B);
(4) that, even if s 2 (1) (b) of the Sexual Offences (Scotland) Act 1976 applied to the circumstances, no crime
of violence had taken place (p 31B); and application
refused.

R v Criminal Injuries Compensation Board, ex p Webb
[1987] 1 QB 74, *approved* and *followed.*

Petition for judicial review

Jane Kilpatrick Gray applied for judicial review of
a decision by the Criminal Injuries Compensation Board
refusing her claim for compensation presented following her discovery that she had been deceived into entering a bigamous marriage.

The case came for a first hearing before the Lord Ordinary (Weir).

Statutory provisions

The Sexual Offences (Scotland) Act 1976 provides:

"2.—(1) Any person who — . . . (b) by false pretences
or false representations procures any woman or girl to
have any unlawful intercourse in any part of the world,
. . . shall be liable on conviction on indictment to
imprisonment for a term not exceeding two years or on
a summary conviction to imprisonment for a term not
exceeding three months."

Terms of scheme

The Criminal Injuries Compensation Scheme 1990
provides:

"4. The Board will entertain applications for ex gratia
payments of compensation in any case where the applicant . . . sustained in Great Britain . . . personal injury
directly attributable: (a) to a crime of violence (including arson or poisoning)".

Cases referred to

Advocate (HM) v Sweenie (1853) 3 Irvine 109.
Brutus v Cozens [1973] AC 854; [1972] 3 WLR 521;
    [1972] 2 All ER 1297.
R v Criminal Injuries Compensation Board, ex p Clowes
    [1977] 1 WLR 1353; [1977] 3 All ER 854.
R v Criminal Injuries Compensation Board, ex p Webb
    [1987] QB 74; [1986] 3 WLR 251; [1986] 2 All
    ER 478.

On 13 May 1992 his Lordship *dismissed* the petition.

LORD WEIR.—Paragraph 4 (a) of the compensation scheme administered by the Criminal Injuries Compensation Board provides that the board will entertain
applications for ex gratia payments of compensation in
any case where an applicant sustained in Great Britain
personal injury directly attributable to a crime of
violence.

The petitioner applied to the board for an award of
compensation. Initially her application was considered
by a single member of the board and on refusal of an
award by him the matter was referred to a hearing of
three members of the board in terms of para 22 of the
scheme. The hearing took place in Glasgow on 19
August 1991 when evidence was given by the petitioner.
The board members (Mr T A K Drummond, QC, Mr
Donald S Mackay, QC, and Mr David Barker, QC) disallowed the application and in due course issued a
written decision setting out their reasons. The petitioner
now seeks reduction of the board's decision by way of
judicial review.

It was accepted by counsel for the board that the court
has power to review decisions of the board and it was
agreed that if the court was minded to grant reduction
the proper course would be to order the board to reconsider the petitioner's application.

The facts giving rise to the claim are recorded in the
following passages taken from the written decision of
the board.

"The applicant stated that in 1987 she became
friendly with a man named Kenneth Watson. She began
to see him on a regular basis. No sexual intercourse took
place between them, although Watson attempted to persuade her to do so. On a number of occasions during
the summer of 1988 Watson asked her to marry him
but she declined his invitation to become engaged.
During the later months of 1988 he renewed his
proposal of marriage. Eventually on 10 December 1988
the applicant became engaged to Watson. At that time
the applicant understood from what she had been told
by Watson that he was a divorced man, that he had been
so for some four to five years, and that his former wife
resided in Nottingham. After their engagement and
before their marriage the applicant and Watson had
sexual relations on one occasion. They married on 24
March 1989 at Dumfries and thereafter resided together
at the applicant's house. After the marriage they had
sexual intercourse together on approximately six occasions. On 21 August 1989 Watson disappeared. The
applicant reported this to Dumfries police station. Investigation disclosed that Watson had given up his job the
previous Friday. Later police officers advised the applicant that they had found Watson living in Carlisle. His
true name was Kenneth Murray Dolman and he was
married to a woman in Carlisle where he was living with
her and his children. The applicant stated that the discovery that her marriage was bigamous had caused her
great distress. She particularly stressed that following
upon Watson's deception of her she had sexual intercourse with him. She confirmed that she had been
divorced herself in 1972 because of her former husband's affair with her sister. Her former husband and

A her sister had two children. The applicant claimed that the realisation that she had married a bigamist had a devastating effect on her. She had required to attend her doctor for stress. She had indicated that if she had known that Watson had been married she would never have gone out with him, far less had a sexual relationship with him. No medical evidence was produced on behalf of the applicant."

It is not clear from the decision whether the board accepted the petitioner's evidence on these matters, par-
B ticularly as regards the effect of her discovery of Watson's true status on her health, but counsel for the board indicated that for the purpose of this hearing it could be assumed that these facts were accepted by the board.

The submission made by the petitioner's solicitor to the board was to the effect that Watson had committed the crime of rape which was a crime of violence within the meaning of para 4 (a) of the scheme. This argument was advanced upon the basis that on the occasions when
C Watson had sexual relations with the petitioner he did so either intending that the applicant would suffer mental and physical distress when she found out that he was still married or with reckless indifference as to whether she might suffer such distress on becoming aware that he was still married. Having considered the evidence and the submissions the board disallowed the application under reference to para 4 (a) of the scheme. The reason given for refusal is contained in a single and concise sentence: "We were not persuaded that either the crime of rape or any other crime of violence is com-
D mitted in circumstances when a female is persuaded to have sexual intercourse with a male by reason of false pretences of the nature made towards the applicant by Watson."

Counsel for the petitioner departed from the argu-
ment advanced to the board. In particular he did not contend that for the application to succeed the petitioner had to satisfy the board that injury was directly attributable to "a crime of violence". He submitted that the
E crime in this case was that of procuring sexual inter-
course with the applicant on a false pretence, namely that she was free to marry, and in circumstances in which had she been aware of the true position, she would not have agreed to sexual intercourse. This crime he said was perpetrated on each occasion when the parties had intercourse after the pretended marriage ceremony. In this connection he referred me to s 2 (1) (b) of the Sexual Offences (Scotland) Act 1976 which makes it an offence for any person to procure by false pretence or false
F representation any woman to have unlawful sexual inter-
course in any part of the world. He also submitted that the conduct of Watson was analogous to an indecent assault such as where a man has sexual relations with a sleeping woman (*HM Advocate v Sweenie*). Although no actual violence was inflicted on the petitioner, indeed she freely consented to the sexual act, it was necessary to consider the effect on her on discovering that Watson was a bigamist. Viewing the conduct of Watson in the light of the consequences to her health when the truth became known, it could be said that the sexual acts in the circumstances were crimes of violence.

G The issue in this case is a narrow one. If there was no crime of violence, the petitioner's application is clearly not within the scheme. On the other hand if it can be said that there was a crime of violence and that the petitioner's personal injury was directly attributable to such a crime, her application is within the scheme and in such circumstances the board, in refusing to entertain her application, erred in law.

The expression "crime of violence" is not defined in the scheme. It is significant, in my view, that para 4 (a) of the scheme does not give rise to a possible claim for compensation where the personal injury sustained
H was directly attributable to "a crime". The original scheme introduced in 1964 made provision for compen-
sation in such terms but these were altered at a subse-
quent stage. The addition of the words "of violence" are words of qualification and limitation. In order to ascertain in a particular case what is meant by a crime of violence, it is necessary to look at the nature of the crime in question. This problem has been the subject of study in certain English cases, notably in *R v CICB, ex p Clowes* [1977] 1 WLR at p. 1364; and in a deci-
I sion of the Court of Appeal in *R v CICB, ex p Webb*. In the latter case Lawton LJ, [1987] QB at p 77 said: "The words 'crime of violence' are not a term of art. The scheme is not a statutory one. The government has made funds available for the payment of compensation without being under a statutory duty to do so. It follows, in my judgment, that the court should not construe the scheme as if it were a statute but as a public announcement of what the government was willing to do. This entails the court deciding what would be a reasonable and literate man's understanding of the circumstances
J in which he could under the scheme be paid compen-
sation for personal injuries caused by a crime of violence."

In a later passage in his judgment, at p 79, Lawton LJ, referring to a submission of counsel for the board, said: "In my judgment, Mr Wright's submission that what matters is the nature of the crime, not its likely consequences, is well founded. It is for the board to decide whether unlawful conduct, because of its nature,
K not its consequences, amounts to a crime of violence. As Lord Widgery C.J. pointed out in *Clowes*' case, at p. 1364 following what Lord Reid had said in *Cozens v. Brutus* [1973] A.C. 854, the meaning of 'crime of violence' is 'very much a jury point'. Most crimes of violence will involve the infliction or threat of force but some may not. I do not think it prudent to attempt a definition of words of ordinary usage in English which the board, as a fact finding body, have to apply to the case before them. They will recognise a crime of vio-
L lence when they hear about it, even though as a matter of semantics it may be difficult to produce a definition which is not too narrow or so wide as to produce absurd consequences."

I am content to follow the approach to this question set out in the passages in the judgment of Lawton LJ which I have quoted. Indeed the board in their written decision make it clear that they themselves followed the same approach. The argument of counsel for the petitioner in support of the existence of a crime of violence in this case depended upon looking at the effect of the

behaviour of the wrongdoer on the petitioner rather than upon the nature of the crime he committed. But this is directly in conflict with the approach stated in *Webb*. The proper approach is to look at the nature of the crime and ask the question, were the acts of sexual intercourse crimes of violence? In my opinion, the answer to that question must be in the negative. The root cause of the injury suffered by the petitioner was the commission by Watson of the crime of bigamy and the discovery by the petitioner of that fact. It is to that act that her injury is attributable. Neither that in itself nor the deception involved towards the petitioner contained any element of violence. The ambit of s 2 (1) (b) of the Sexual Offences (Scotland) Act 1976 was not explored in argument, but assuming that it could apply to the circumstances of this case, while it may be said that an offence had been committed, the offence was not one attended with violence. Moreover I am not prepared to affirm in the absence of authority that acts of sexual intercourse in the context of a bigamous marriage constitute a crime at common law, let alone a crime of violence.

It is difficult to refrain from expressing a feeling of considerable sympathy for the petitioner who was cruelly deceived by the man that she thought she had married. She may very well have a claim for damages against him under civil law but these proceedings are concerned with the interpretation and application of the scheme as it stands. I am unable to detect any error in law in the manner in which the board dealt with the application and therefore the petition must be dismissed.

Counsel for Petitioner, Clancy; Solicitors, Brodies, WS — Counsel for Respondent, Brailsford; Solicitor, R Brodie, Solicitor to the Secretary of State for Scotland.

S F M

Wilson v Donald

HIGH COURT OF JUSTICIARY

LORDS ALLANBRIDGE, MURRAY AND CULLEN

5 JUNE 1992

Justiciary — Procedure — Summary procedure — Sentence — Adjournment to obtain DVLA printout for period in excess of three weeks — Whether order competent — Criminal Procedure (Scotland) Act 1975 (c 21), ss 380 (1) and 432.

An accused person pled guilty to two charges of contravention of the Road Traffic Act 1988, and as the accused claimed that he did not hold a driving licence, the sheriff purported to defer sentence so that the court could obtain a DVLA printout. The diet was adjourned for a period in excess of three weeks. At the next calling of the case it was argued that the proceedings were incompetent because an adjournment under s 380 of the 1975 Act could not be for a period in excess of three

weeks. The sheriff sustained the objection and dismissed the complaint. The Crown sought advocation of the sheriff's decision, arguing that the sheriff had power at common law to adjourn after conviction, but that in any event s 380 (1) did not apply to a DVLA printout and, furthermore, the adjournment could be justified by s 432 (1).

Held, (1) that the common law power to adjourn a criminal case after conviction had been restricted by s 380 (1) (p 33A-B); (2) that the wider provisions of s 432 could not be invoked to avoid the restriction in s 380 (1) (p 33D-F); (3) that the terms of s 380 (1) applied to an adjournment for the purposes of obtaining a printout from the DVLA and accordingly the adjournment was incompetent (p 33B-D); and bill *refused*.

HM Advocate v Clegg, 1991 SLT 192, *applied*.

Observed, that if ss 179 and 380 of the 1975 Act were now causing administrative problems then legislative amendment might provide at least one method of overcoming them (p 33F).

Bill of advocation

Andrew Taylor Watt Wilson, procurator fiscal, Airdrie, presented a bill of advocation to the High Court seeking recall of the decision of Sheriff J H Stewart dated 3 March 1992 dismissing a summary complaint.

Statement of facts

The bill contained the following statement of facts:

1. The respondent appeared at Airdrie sheriff court on 20 January 1992 on a summary complaint at the instance of the complainer charging him with: (1) a contravention of s 143 (1) and (2) of the Road Traffic Act 1988; and (2) a contravention of s 103 (1) (b) of the said Act. The respondent pled guilty to the said charges.

2. On conviction on both said offences any driving licence held or to be held by the respondent was liable to endorsement in terms of s 44 of the Road Traffic Offenders Act 1988. The respondent intimated to the court that he did not hold a driving licence and the court thereafter deferred sentence until 26 February 1992 to enable the complainer to obtain such a document as is specified in s 32 of that Act to ascertain particulars of any previous convictions or disqualification pertaining to the respondent and any penalty points ordered to be endorsed on any licence held by the respondent.

3. At the diet of 26 February 1992 it was submitted on behalf of the respondent that on 20 January 1992 the diet had in fact been adjourned in terms of s 380 of the Criminal Procedure (Scotland) Act 1975 and that because the diet had been adjourned for a single period exceeding three weeks further proceedings on the said complaint were incompetent. The sheriff upheld the said submission and dismissed the said complaint.

4. The decision of the said sheriff was erroneous and contrary to law. The diet was not adjourned on 20 January 1992 for any purpose in terms of s 380 of the Criminal Procedure (Scotland) Act 1975. The minute of 20 January 1992 recorded that sentence was deferred until 26 February 1992. Esto notwithstanding the terms

of the minute the continuation of the diet on 29 January
1992 was not a deferral of sentence but in fact an
adjournment, the court had power at common law to
adjourn the diet for such a period as it saw fit in order
to allow the said document specified in s 32 of the Road
Traffic Offenders Act 1988 to be produced to the court.

Statutory provisions

The Criminal Procedure (Scotland) Act 1975
provides:

"380.—(1) It is hereby declared that the power of a
court to adjourn the hearing of a case includes power,
after a person has been convicted or the court has found
that he committed the offence and before he has been
sentenced or otherwise dealt with, to adjourn the case
for the purpose of enabling inquiries to be made or of
determining the most suitable method of dealing with
his case and where the court so adjourns the case it shall
remand the accused in custody or on bail or ordain him
to appear at the adjourned diet; Provided that a court
shall not for the purpose aforesaid adjourn the hearing
of a case for a single period exceeding three weeks. . . .

"432.—(1) It shall be competent for a court to defer
sentence after conviction for a period and on such conditions as the court may determine and the fact that an
accused has been convicted shall not prevent the court
from making, in due course, a probation order under
section 384 of this Act."

Cases referred to

Advocate (HM) v Clegg, 1991 SLT 192; 1990 SCCR
293.
Bruce v Linton (1861) 23 D 85.

Textbook referred to

Renton and Brown, *Criminal Procedure* (5th ed), para
14-55.

Bill

The bill contained the following plea in law:

The decision of the sheriff on 26 February 1992
holding that further proceedings on the complaint were
incompetent and dismissing the said complaint being
erroneous and contrary to law, should be recalled and
the case remitted to the said sheriff to proceed to sentence the respondent.

The bill was argued before the High Court on 21 May
1992.

On 5 June 1992 the court *refused* to pass the bill.

The following opinion of the court was delivered by
Lord Allanbridge:

OPINION OF THE COURT.—The respondent
appeared at Airdrie sheriff court on 20 January 1992
and pled guilty on a summary complaint to two contraventions of the Road Traffic Act 1988. On conviction of both said offences, any driving licence held or
to be held by the respondent was liable to endorsement
in terms of s 44 of the Road Traffic Offenders Act 1988.
The respondent intimated to the court that he did not
hold a driving licence and the court thereafter

"deferred" sentence until 26 February 1992 to enable
the complainer to obtain such a document as is specified in s 32 of that Act as "purporting to be a note of
information contained in the records" and as more fully
described in that section, in order to ascertain particulars
of any previous convictions or disqualifications pertaining to the respondent and any penalty points endorsed
on any licence held by him.

At the diet of 26 February 1992 it was submitted on
behalf of the respondent that on 20 January 1992 the
diet had been adjourned in terms of s 380 of the Criminal Procedure (Scotland) Act 1975 and that because the
diet had been adjourned for a single period exceeding
three weeks, further proceedings on the said complaint
were incompetent. The sheriff, after hearing a debate
on the matter on 3 March 1992, upheld the said submission and dismissed the said complaint. The complainer has raised this bill of advocation against that
decision of the sheriff.

Section 380 (1) of the 1975 Act reads as follows: [his
Lordship quoted the terms of s 380 (1) and continued:]

In the present case the minutes of procedure in this
case for 20 January 1992 read as follows: "The accused
in answer to the complaint pled guilty to charge 1 and
pled guilty to charge 2. The court deferred sentence
for the purpose of obtaining a printout from DVLA
until 25 February 1992 at 10 am and ordained the
accused then to appear."

In addressing us on behalf of the complainer, the advocate depute explained that it is very often not possible
to obtain such printouts within a period of three weeks
and that sometimes they take five or six weeks to arrive.
In these circumstances for obvious administrative convenience the court will adjourn the case for a period
longer than three weeks. He submitted that it was not
incompetent for the court to do so. Under common law
the court has an inherent power to adjourn where necessary in the interests of justice. (See Renton and Brown's
Criminal Procedure, para 14-55, and *Bruce v Linton*
(1861) 23 D 85.) He argued that said s 380 did not restrict that power; in any event the section did not apply
to the situation where such a printout was being
obtained as it was not covered by the terms of the
section. The section was limited in its application to
obtaining reports which might require the interviewing of the accused such as social inquiry reports and
medical reports and where in some circumstances it
might, for example, be necessary to remand the accused
in custody and in which event a time limit of 21 days
could be considered appropriate. In a case such as the
present no prejudice which could otherwise be avoided
would be suffered by the respondent. In a subsidiary
argument he submitted that as in the present case sentence had specifically been "deferred", the terms of s
432 (1) of the 1975 Act applied and made it competent
for the court "to defer sentence after conviction for a
period and on such conditions as the court may
determine".

We do not accept these arguments put forward on
behalf of the Crown. There is no doubt that the court
has a common law power to adjourn a criminal case
before the accused has pled or been found guilty. At

p 94 of *Bruce v Linton*, Lord Justice Clerk Inglis stated;
"a power to adjourn is a power inherent in every court,
which must be exercised according to the discretion of
the judge". However, it is to be noted that that case
was concerned with adjourning a case before conviction. Paragraph 14-55 of Renton and Brown, supra,
referred to by the advocate depute, was concerned with
s 337 (b) of the 1975 Act which applies to a situation
where pleas of not guilty are tendered by an accused
and the case is thereafter adjourned from time to time.
The situation, however, may be different after conviction where by statute the common law power to adjourn
a case further has been restricted in certain circumstances. Section 380 (1) imposes such a restriction to
an adjournment limited to 21 days where the subsection applies.

We are of the opinion that the terms of s 380 (1) do
apply to an adjournment for the purposes of obtaining
a printout from the DVLA. In such a situation the case
is clearly being adjourned "for the purpose of enabling
inquiries to be made". Such "inquiries" are not further
defined in that subsection. These words are clearly apt
in our view to include the obtaining of the further information which may be contained in the printout. The
alternative words "or of determining the most suitable
method of dealing with his case" could also be said to
apply as the appropriate disposal of the case might well
depend, at least to some extent, on what is revealed in
the printout as regards his driving record. In this situation we are satisfied that the words of s 380 (1) are wide
enough to include an adjournment for the purpose of
obtaining such a printout. As the period granted in this
case exceeded 21 days it was in breach of the terms of
the subsection and therefore incompetent.

We do not consider that the fact that the minute of
procedure records that sentence was "deferred" assists
the Crown. As counsel for the respondent pointed out,
the case of *HM Advocate v Clegg* makes it clear that the
device of invoking the wider provisions of s 219 of the
1975 Act in solemn procedure, which relates to the
court's power to defer sentence, in an attempt to avoid
the terms of s 179 (the equivalent in solemn procedure
of s 380 in summary procedure) cannot succeed. That
case was concerned with a situation where the sheriff
ordered that sentence be deferred for a period of three
weeks and one day for the purpose of obtaining social
inquiry and community service reports and the court
made it clear that the practice, if it existed, of using
s 219 for reasons of administrative convenience cannot
be condoned. In our opinion and for the same reasons
as expressed in *Clegg's* case we cannot condone an
attempt, if it be such an attempt in this case, to avoid
the equivalent provisions in a summary case by relying
on the provisions of s 432 of the Act.

We therefore refuse to pass the bill and this appeal
fails. We should only add, as noted in the [SCCR] commentary to *Clegg's* case, that if ss 179 and 380 of the
1975 Act are now causing administrative problems, then
legislative amendment may provide at least one method
of overcoming them.

---

*Counsel for Complainer, G J Davidson, AD; Solicitor,
J D Lowe, Crown Agent — Counsel for Respondent, C
A G McNeill; Solicitors, Russel & Aitken, WS.*

P W F

Casey v HM Advocate

HIGH COURT OF JUSTICIARY

THE LORD JUSTICE CLERK (ROSS),
LORDS SUTHERLAND AND KINCRAIG

3 JULY 1992

*Justiciary — Evidence — Witness — Compellability —
"Spouse" — Cohabitee of accused who had lived with him
for six years — Whether compellable witness for Crown
— Criminal Procedure (Scotland) Act 1975 (c 21), s 143.*

*Justiciary — Evidence — Witness — Socius criminis —
Socius criminis incriminating accused — Crown case partly
based upon evidence of socius but Crown inviting jury to
find both accused and socius guilty so that jury asked to
accept part and reject part of socius' evidence — Failure
of judge to give cum nota warning to jury — Whether misdirection.*

Section 143 (1) of the Criminal Procedure (Scotland)
Act 1975 enables a spouse of a person charged with an
offence to be called as a witness. Section 143 (2) provides inter alia that: "Nothing in this section shall make
the spouse of an accused a compellable witness for . . .
the prosecutor in a case where such a spouse would not
be so compellable at common law".

An accused person was tried in the High Court on
a charge of, inter alia, murder. A witness for the Crown
was the accused's cohabitee with whom he had lived
for six years and who called herself his common law
wife. The trial judge did not warn her that she was not
a compellable witness in terms of s 143 (2) of the 1975
Act. A co-accused, in his own defence, spoke to an
incrimination lodged against the accused. The trial
judge, in his charge to the jury, failed to give them a
cum nota warning in respect of the co-accused's evidence
when they were considering the case against the accused.
The Crown case rested partly on the evidence of the
co-accused but the Crown invited the jury to convict
both accused and accordingly to accept part and reject
part of the co-accused's evidence. The accused was convicted and appealed, contending inter alia that (1) the
cohabitee should have been advised by the trial judge
that she was not a compellable witness; and (2) that the
trial judge should have given a cum nota warning to
the jury in respect of the evidence of the co-accused.

Held, (1) that the word "spouse" in s 143 could be
applied only to persons who were married to each other
and not to those who were cohabiting with each other
but not married, so that the cohabitee had been a compellable witness (p 35E-F); and (2) that there was no
rule that a trial judge had to direct the jury that the
evidence of a socius criminis should be scrutinised with
special care, and although there might be cases where
the trial judge would think it appropriate to give the
jury directions which would assist them in dealing with
the credibility of particular witnesses, it would have been
wrong for the judge to do so where the co-accused had
been entitled to the presumption of innocence (p
35H-J); and appeal *refused*.

McKay v HM Advocate, 1992 SLT 138, *distinguished;
McCourt v HM Advocate*, 1977 SLT (Notes) 22, and
Docherty v HM Advocate, 1987 SLT 784, *applied.*

Indictment

A   James Casey and George Douglas Cameron McNairn were charged at the instance of the rt hon the Lord Fraser of Carmyllie, Her Majesty's Advocate, on an indictment which libelled inter alia the following: "on 16 or 17 September 1990 (1) at the Social and Recreational Club, Castle Road, Invergordon, you James Casey and George Douglas Cameron McNairn did assault Ian David MacBeth, manager there, and did repeatedly strike him on the head with a hammer or a similar instrument or instruments to his severe injury, knock

B   him to the ground, rob him of a bank book, a bank wallet and £1,260 of money, drag him along the ground, place him in a motor car, remove his trousers and did convey him against his will to woodlands near to the unclassified Delny to Scotsburn road, Kindeace, place handcuffs on his wrists, take him from said car into said woodlands, strike him repeatedly on the head and body with a sign, gag him, handcuff him to a tree and abandon him there, as a result of which he died there and you did murder him . . . (2) place above libelled you James Casey and George Douglas Cameron McNairn did steal

C   a motor car registered number F291 TJS; (3) in Castle Road, Invergordon, the A9 public road between Invergordon and Delny, the unclassified Delny to Scotsburn road, the Invergordon to Tomich road, Inverbreakie industrial estate and other public roads in the District of Ross and Cromarty, you George Douglas Cameron McNairn did use a motor vehicle namely said motor car, without there being in force in relation to the use of the vehicle by you such a policy of insurance or such a security in respect of third party risks as complied

D   with the requirements of Pt VI of the Road Traffic Act 1988: contrary to the Road Traffic Act 1988, s 143 (1) and (2)".

The accused pled not guilty and the case proceeded to trial before Lord MacLean and a jury in the High Court at Inverness. Casey was convicted of charges 1 and 2; McNairn was convicted of robbery in charge 1 and of charges 2 and 3 as libelled. Casey appealed to the High Court by note of appeal against conviction.

E   ### Statutory provisions

The Criminal Procedure (Scotland) Act 1975 provides:

"143.—(1) The spouse of a person charged with an offence may be called as a witness — (a) by that person; (b) by a co-accused or by the prosecutor without the consent of that person.

"(2) Nothing in this section shall — (a) make the spouse of an accused a compellable witness for a co-

F   accused or for the prosecutor in a case where such spouse would not be so compellable at common law; (b) compel a spouse to disclose any communication made between the spouses during the marriage.

"(3) The failure of the spouse of an accused to give evidence shall not be commented on by the defence or the prosecutor."

Cases referred to

Docherty v HM Advocate, 1987 SLT 784; 1987 SCCR 418.

McCourt v HM Advocate, 1977 SLT (Notes) 22.
McKay v HM Advocate, 1992 SLT 138; 1991 SCCR   G 364.

Appeal

The note of appeal contained various grounds, the fifth of which was in the following terms:

(5) The learned trial judge erred in law in failing to advise Mrs Isobel Aitchison Begg or Casey, witness no 12 on the Crown list, that she was not a compellable witness. Although she and the appellant were not formally married the evidence regarding their relationship   H disclosed that she was entitled to the protection afforded to "spouses" by the Criminal Procedure (Scotland) Act 1975, s 143 (2). This constitutes a miscarriage of justice.

The accused subsequently lodged two further grounds of appeal, the second of which was as follows:

The decision to allow each co-accused to lodge special defences of incrimination against each other, with respect was an error in law — thus resulting in a miscarriage of justice.   I

The appeal came before the High Court on 13 June 1991 when it was continued to a date to be afterwards fixed. It called again on 5 July 1991 when it was again continued to a date to be afterwards fixed. On 21 November 1991 the appeal was continued to a date to be afterwards fixed to enable investigations to continue with respect to possible additional evidence and amended grounds of appeal. On 20 March 1992 the appeal was again continued to a date to be afterwards   J fixed, the appeal finally being heard by the High Court on 11 June 1992.

On 3 July 1992 the court *refused* the appeal.

The following opinion of the court was delivered by the Lord Justice Clerk (Ross):

OPINION OF THE COURT.—The appellant is James Casey who went to trial along with a co-accused George Douglas Cameron McNairn in the High Court   K at Inverness on an indictment containing three charges. Charges 1 and 2 were directed against both the appellant and his co-accused; charge 1 was a charge of the murder of Ian David MacBeth, and charge 2 libelled the theft of a motor car. Charge 3 libelled a contravention of s 143 (1) and (2) of the Road Traffic Act 1988, and was directed against the co-accused only. In the course of the trial the first charge was amended in a number of respects, and an amendment was also made to charge 2. At the end of the day the jury unanimously   L found the appellant guilty of charges 1 and 2, and unanimously found the co-accused guilty of robbery on charge 1 and unanimously guilty of charges 2 and 3. The appellant was sentenced to life imprisonment, and in terms of s 205A of the Criminal Procedure (Scotland) Act 1975, the trial judge recommended that a minimum period of 20 years should elapse before the Secretary of State released the appellant on licence. The appellant has now appealed against conviction, but he has not appealed against the recommendation which the trial judge made in terms of s 205A of the Act of 1975.

The note of appeal was lodged on 18 April 1991. The appellant's appeal against conviction was stated to be on the following grounds: [his Lordship quoted the grounds of appeal and continued:]

The appellant was convicted and sentenced on 7 February 1991.

[His Lordship narrated the procedural history of the appeal and continued:]

After making some preliminary observations, the appellant proceeded to deal with each of his grounds of appeal in turn. [His Lordship dealt with grounds of appeal with which this report is not concerned and continued:]

(5) In this ground of appeal it is contended that the trial judge erred in law in failing to advise Mrs Isobel Casey that she was not a compellable witness. Apparently the situation is that this witness and the appellant were not married to one another although they had cohabited for six years. In his report, the trial judge states that no objection was taken to the evidence given by this witness. He took the view that the word "spouse" in s 143 of the Criminal Procedure (Scotland) Act 1975 meant someone who had gone through a ceremony of marriage or been declared by law to be married to the person charged with the offence, and that it did not include what is often referred to as a common law wife.

In support of his submissions, the appellant sought to rely on *McKay v HM Advocate*. In that case it was held that sudden and overwhelming indignation on the discovery of infidelity, which the law recognised as constituting provocation, might be just as powerful in the case of cohabitees as it was in the case of people married to each other. In our opinion, however, that case does not assist the appellant. In *McKay v HM Advocate,* the court was considering the application of a doctrine of the common law, whereas in the present case under s 143 of the Act of 1975, the question which arises is one as to the interpretation of a statute. In s 143, the word which is used is "the spouse" and we are satisfied that it is only persons who are married to each other who are properly referred to in law as spouses. We see no justification for attaching the expression "spouse" to persons who are cohabiting with one another but are not married. In the circumstances we are quite satisfied that the witness Mrs Isobel Casey was a compellable witness, and that the trial judge would have been in error if he had advised her that she was not compellable.

In any event, as the trial judge points out in his report, none of this witness's evidence incriminated the appellant directly in the murder of the victim, and there is accordingly no basis whatsoever for the assertion that a miscarriage of justice has occurred in this respect. [His Lordship dealt with other grounds of appeal with which this report is not concerned, and continued:]

The second additional issue which the appellant raised was related to his additional ground of appeal dated 1 June 1992. His complaint appeared to be that since his co-accused sought to incriminate him, the burden of proof had in some way been altered. At the same time the appellant returned to his first ground of appeal maintaining that the jury should have been directed to treat the evidence of his co-accused with particular care.

In our opinion this ground of appeal is misconceived. It is true that part of the Crown case against the appellant was based upon the evidence given by his co-accused, but the Crown were inviting the jury to find both the appellant and his co-accused guilty of the charge, and although they relied on some of the evidence given by the co-accused in support of their case against the appellant, they also invited the jury to reject parts of the evidence given by the co-accused. It was authoritatively laid down in *Docherty v HM Advocate* that there was no rule that a trial judge must direct the jury that the evidence of a socius criminis should be scrutinised with special care. At the same time it was recognised that there might be cases where the trial judge would think it appropriate to give the jury directions which would assist them in dealing with the credibility of particular witnesses. We are quite clear however that there was no obligation upon the trial judge in this case to give the jury any warning to the effect that they required to scrutinise the evidence of the co-accused with care, and indeed that it would have been wrong for him to have done so. We agree with the Lord Advocate who appeared for the Crown in this appeal that for the trial judge to have given any such direction would have been contrary to the spirit of *McCourt v HM Advocate.* Throughout the trial the co-accused was entitled to the presumption of innocence, and accordingly the trial judge would not have been justified in directing the jury that they should treat the evidence of the co-accused with particular care.

[His Lordship then dealt with another ground of appeal with which this report is not concerned, and continued:]

Having duly considered all the grounds of appeal put forward by the appellant, and the submissions which he put forward, we have reached the clear conclusion that he has failed to demonstrate any miscarriage of justice in this case. There was sufficient evidence if the jury accepted it to entitle them to convict the appellant, and nothing which he has said would justify us in interfering with the jury's verdict. It follows that the appeal against conviction must be refused.

For Appellant, Party — Counsel for Respondent, Lord Advocate (Lord Rodger of Earlsferry, QC); Solicitor, J D Lowe, Crown Agent.

R F H

AB v Glasgow and West of Scotland Blood Transfusion Service

OUTER HOUSE

LORD MORISON

21 DECEMBER 1989

Process — Order for disclosure of information — Petitioner contracting human immune deficiency virus through transfusion of infected blood — Petitioner seeking information as to person donating blood for transfusion — Public interest — Secretary of State claiming risk to supply of blood for transfusion — Whether petitioner's right to sue donor should prevail over public interest — Administration of Justice (Scotland) Act 1972 (c 59), s 1.

Crown — Public interest immunity — National Health Service — Records of blood transfusion service — Disclosure of identity of blood donor to person contracting human immune deficiency virus from transfused blood — Whether public interest threatened — Whether information subject to public interest immunity — Whether petitioner's interest capable of overriding public interest — Considerations for court in assessing claims of Secretary of State and of blood transfusion service — Administration of Justice (Scotland) Act 1972 (c 59), s 1.

A person who averred that he had been infected with human immune deficiency virus as a result of blood transfusions administered to him, presented a petition seeking an order under s 1 of the Administration of Justice (Scotland) Act 1972 for disclosure of information as to the identity of the donor of the blood which was transfused. The petitioner's only purpose in seeking such an order was to enable him to raise an action of damages against the donor on the ground, inter alia, that the donor negligently donated blood for transfusion knowing that there was a high risk of it being infected.

The petition was opposed by the blood transfusion service and by the Secretary of State for Scotland, who lodged answers intimating that he had concluded that the documents in question ought to be protected on the ground of public policy, since any infringement of donor anonymity would put at risk the supply of donor blood to the health service nationally. The petitioner conceded that the court was not entitled to investigate the validity of the conclusion expressed by the minister unless it appeared that the conclusion was patently unreasonable or had been expressed on an erroneous basis, but argued that the petitioner's private right to sue the donor was of such magnitude as to prevail over the public interest advanced by the Secretary of State.

Held, that the petitioner's concession was correct and, while the extent of the alleged risk was a relevant consideration for the court, it was impossible to hold that his pecuniary interest should prevail over a material risk to the sufficiency of the national supply of blood for transfusion (pp 37H-I and K and 38B); and prayer of the petition *refused.*

Observed, that it was offensive to any notion of justice that persons should be deprived of the ability to claim damages from those by whose negligence they had been injured. If public policy required this, it seemed reasonable for public policy to provide also some alternative means of compensation (p 38A).

Opinion, that the court's approach to the blood transfusion service's objections to disclosure of information relating to the donor would be different from that which applied to ministerial objection based on public interest immunity: in particular, the court would be free to consider and assess the merits of the objection in the light of the nature of the work which was sought to be protected by non-disclosure (p 38D-E).

Petition under s 1 of the Administration of Justice (Scotland) Act 1972

AB presented a petition under s 1 of the Administration of Justice (Scotland) Act 1972 for disclosure to him and his legal advisers by the respondents, the Glasgow and West of Scotland Blood Transfusion Service, of the name and address of a blood donor whose blood he had received in a transfusion, to enable the petitioner to raise an action of damages against the donor. Answers to the petition were lodged by the respondents and the Secretary of State for Scotland as representing the public interest by virtue of his responsibility under the National Health Service (Scotland) Act 1978 to maintain and promote that service.

The petition came before the Lord Ordinary (Morison).

Statutory provisions

The Administration of Justice (Scotland) Act 1972 provides:

"1.— . . . (1A) Without prejudice to the existing powers of the Court of Session and of the sheriff court, those courts shall have power, subject to subsection (4) of this section, to order any person to disclose such information as he has as to the identity of any persons who appear to the court to be persons who — (a) might be witnesses in any existing civil proceedings before that court or in civil proceedings which are likely to be brought; or (b) might be defenders in any civil proceedings which appear to the court to be likely to be brought."

Cases referred to

Glasgow Corporation v Central Land Board, 1956 SLT 41; 1956 SC (HL) 1.
Rogers v Orr, 1939 SLT 403; 1939 SC 492.

On 21 December 1989 his Lordship *refused* the prayer of the petition and *dismissed* the petition.

LORD MORISON.—This is an application by a person who avers that he became infected with human immune deficiency virus as a result of blood transfusions administered to him in 1986 by the respondents, the Glasgow and West of Scotland Blood Transfusion Service. The petitioner proceeds upon provisions contained in s 1 of the Administration of Justice (Scotland) Act 1972, and in effect he seeks an order of the court for disclosure to him and his legal advisers of the name and address of the person who donated the blood which was transfused. The petitioner's only purpose in seeking such an order is to enable him to raise an action of damages against the donor, on the ground that he negligently failed to disclose to the respondents his high risk of HIV infection, negligently failed to complete accurately a health questionnaire which donors are asked to complete, and negligently donated blood for transfusion knowing that there was a high risk of it being infected. If the donor were voluntarily to disclose his identity to the petitioner, there would be no need to obtain an order from the court, but he has not done so yet, and the petitioner is accordingly unable to raise an action against him, although he is suing the respondents on the ground that their screening procedures were inadequate.

The case came before the court on 13 December 1989 when there was appearance both for the respondents and for the Lord Advocate, on whom the petition had also been served. It was continued for a week to enable the Lord Advocate to consider his position in relation to the public interest which it was submitted might be affected by the disclosure sought. At the continued hearing on 20 December, the application was opposed both by the respondents and by the Secretary of State for Scotland as representing the public interest by virtue of his responsibility under the National Health Service (Scotland) Act 1978 to maintain and promote that service.

The Secretary of State opposes the disclosure sought, on the ground that it would be injurious to the public interest. That injury is particularised in answers to the petition lodged by him as follows: "These documents [ie those which disclose the donor's identity] . . . fall within the class of documents which ought to be afforded protection on the ground of public policy in order to ensure that there is and continues to be a sufficient supply of donor blood to the health service nationally. Such supply is required for necessary and often emergency medical procedures in the treatment of illness (including injury). The Secretary of State has duly considered the matter and has concluded that any infringement of donor anonymity would put such supply at risk. Prospective donors, he has concluded, would be discouraged from providing donations by reason of apprehension that they might be subjected to legal action (whether justified or not) on the basis of some adverse effect resulting from the use of the blood for transfusion purposes."

It is to be noted that this conclusion relates to any infringement whatever of donor anonymity. The disclosure which the petitioner seeks is confined to himself and his legal advisers. It is not to be assumed, and it was not contended, that if the petitioner raised an action against the donor, the donor's name would necessarily be disclosed to the public. The attitude of prospective donors upon which the Secretary of State is relying is exclusively the apprehension that they might be sued, justifiably or not, in relation to their conduct, not that their names might thereby be publicised.

Such apprehension is one which anybody whose conduct affects other persons might experience. In the case of blood donors there seems to me to be every reason to suppose that they are actuated by the very highest motives of altruism and commitment to the public welfare. It is not immediately apparent to me why such persons would be deterred from pursuing these motives by an apprehension that they might be unjustifiably sued. If on the other hand there are any persons who give blood without due regard to their responsibilities, the public interest would plainly be served if they were discouraged from doing so. But it was conceded on behalf of the petitioner that I was not entitled to investigate the validity of the conclusion expressed by the Secretary of State unless it appeared that the conclusion was patently unreasonable or had been expressed on an erroneous basis, and this obviously cannot be said in the present case. In view of the observations contained in the speeches of Lord Normand and Lord Keith in the case of *Glasgow Corporation v Central Land Board*, I consider that this concession was rightly made. Whilst in Scotland the court has the inherent power to override the objection of a responsible minister based on the public interest, that power is not to be exercised upon the basis of an assessment of the merits of the objection. Thus in the present case there may well be matters upon which the Secretary of State has been informed of which I am not aware and which are not contained in the information before me. For present purposes I must accept that "any infringement of donor anonymity" would put at risk the sufficiency of the national supply of donor blood.

On this assumption, the scope for any reasoned argument as to whether or not the Secretary of State's objection should be overridden is limited. On behalf of the petitioner it was submitted that his private right to sue the donor was of such "magnitude" (to use the word employed by Lord Moncrieff in *Rogers v Orr*, 1939 SLT at p 406) as to prevail over the public interest advanced by the Secretary of State. But the only right which the petitioner seeks to assert in the proceedings which he proposes is the right to claim damages, and although his claim is a very large one, it seems to me to be impossible to hold that such a pecuniary interest should prevail over a material risk to the sufficiency of the national supply of blood for purposes of transfusion. It was submitted also that there were other persons apart from the petitioner whose right to claim damages would similarly be affected if disclosure were not made. I can conceive of cases in which such a consideration might be material, but I was not informed that there is a large number of persons likely to be prejudiced by non-disclosure to them of the names of donors, and I do not think that this matter substantially affects the issue. It was further submitted that it was a matter of public interest that the administration of justice should not be selective. This is undoubtedly true, but such an argument could be advanced in any case where disclosure

A of relevant information is subject to ministerial objection and counsel were unable to inform me of any case in which such an objection had been overridden by the court. However I entirely agree that it is offensive to any notion of justice that persons should be deprived of the ability to claim damages from those by whose negligence they have been injured. If public policy requires this, it seems to me that it would be reasonable for public policy to provide also some alternative means of compensation.

B Counsel for the petitioner also pointed out that the extent of the alleged risk to the public blood supply was not indicated by the objection. Contrary to submissions made on behalf of the Secretary of State, I consider that this is indeed a relevant consideration in determination of the issue which is before me. It seems to me that it would be much easier for the court to override an objection based on a slight risk to the public interest than one based on a substantial probability of damage to that interest. But it is obvious that the consequences of a national deficiency in the supply of blood for transfu-
C sion would be appalling. If there is any material risk of such an occurrence resulting from disclosure of the donor's name in the present case — and this is what I have to assume — it seems to me to be clear that the objection to that disclosure must prevail over the interests advanced on the petitioner's behalf.

For these reasons I shall refuse to pronounce the order which the petitioner seeks. It was agreed that if this were my determination, I should refuse the motion, dismiss the petition and order the return to the respondents of
D the documents recovered from them. I shall issue an interlocutor in these terms.

I should add that the respondents advanced arguments similar to those of the Secretary of State, to support their submission that the donor's identity should not be revealed to the petitioner. The respondents are providing a public service and they have an obvious duty (subject only to an order of the court) to promote that valuable service and to maintain the confidentiality of persons upon whom they rely to provide it. Neverthe-
E less I consider that the court's approach to their objection would be different from that which applies to a ministerial objection based on the public interest. In particular, it would in my opinion be legitimate for the court to consider and assess the merits of the respondents' objection in light of the nature of the work which they perform, so as to determine whether or not the petitioner's interest should prevail over that objection. This would involve consideration of the quality of the evidence upon which the respondents rely, and it might
F also involve a determination whether their own procedures are adequate to support the immunity which they say ought to be accorded to donors. However on the view which I have formed in respect of the Secretary of State's objection, it is unnecessary for me to reach any conclusion as to the respondents' contentions, and I refrain from doing so.

Counsel for Petitioner, Haddow, QC, G M Henderson; Solicitors, J & A Hastie, SSC — Counsel for Respondents,

G *J A Cameron, QC, C A L Scott (Scottish Blood Transfusion Service), A C Hamilton, QC (Secretary of State for Scotland); Solicitor, R Brodie, Solicitor to the Secretary of State for Scotland.*

M L B F

[The publication of this report has been requested.]

H

British Coal Corporation v South of Scotland Electricity Board (No 2)

OUTER HOUSE

LORD DERVAIRD

28 DECEMBER 1989

I

Contract — Construction — Waiver — Whether departure from term of contract by limited period agreement waived right to insist in reversion to original term after expiry of limited period agreement.

Contract — Construction — Tacit relocation — Whether limited period agreement departing from terms of original contract could be extended by tacit relocation.

British Coal raised an action against the SSEB seeking to enforce an agreement entered into between them in J 1962 for the supply of coal to a power station. The agreement was for a 25 year period commencing when the power station started to generate electricity and contained both upper and lower limits on the quantity of coal to be supplied and a formula for fixing the price per ton of such coal. The parties subsequently entered into two fixed term agreements, in 1977 and 1986 respectively, which departed from the original pricing arrangement but specifically retained the original agreement except so far as inconsistent with the new terms.

K The electricity board argued that as the short term agreements covered their entire coal requirements from British Coal and departed from the original price formula, they had acted in the belief that the original contract was no longer being insisted in and, accordingly, that British Coal had waived the right to insist therein. They further argued that as one of the generators had been operational for a few hours in June 1967 before a design modification was made, the agreement would terminate in June 1992 even if it could be insisted in. British Coal, on the other hand, argued that this was L a case of temporary variations in a contract with an identifiable term, and that the agreement was provided to run until the end of 1992.

Held, (1) that, as the parties had accepted in terms of the temporary arrangements that the original agreement remained in force, its terms could only be affected for so long as the temporary arrangement remained in operation, and the right to insist on performance of the original agreement at a future stage was not thereby waived (pp 40H-41A); (2) that the limited operation of

the generator before the design fault was remedied was
A not intended as a commencement of operations and was
in any event de minimis and, the agreement ran from
August 1967, when significant quantities of coal were
first consumed, and, since the agreement should
properly be interpreted as running for a maximum of
25 years, it would accordingly expire in August 1992
(pp 43B-F and 43K-44B); and declarator *pronounced* and
decree of specific implement *granted*, limited to the
expiry date of 24 August 1992.

B **Observed**, that a fixed term arrangement could not
continue in force by tacit relocation where it conflicted
with the original agreement (p 40J-K).

———————

Action of declarator and implement
    The British Coal Corporation (formerly the National
Coal Board) raised an action in the Court of Session
against the South of Scotland Electricity Board concluding inter alia for declarator that the board were bound
C to receive from them all the coal necessary for the operation of the board's Cockenzie power station and for
specific implement of those contractual obligations.

    The action was conjoined with a similar action
between the parties relative to the board's Longannet
power station (*British Coal Corporation v South of Scotland Electricity Board*, 1991 SLT 302). Both cases came
to proof before answer before the Lord Ordinary
(Dervaird).

D **Cases referred to**
Armia Ltd v Daejan Developments Ltd, 1979 SLT 147;
    1979 SC (HL) 56.
*British Coal Corporation v South of Scotland Electricity
    Board*, 1991 SLT 302.
Carron Co Ltd v Henderson's Trustees (1896) 4 SLT 91;
    (1896) 23 R 1042.
McArthur v Lawson (1877) 4 R 1134.
Moore v Paterson (1881) 9 R 337.
E *Rowtor Steamship Co v Love & Stewart Ltd*, 1916 2 SLT
    124; 1916 SC (HL) 199.

Textbook referred to
Chitty, *Contracts* (24th ed), p 784.

    On 28 December 1989 the Lord Ordinary *pronounced*
decree of declarator and *granted* decree for specific
implement limited to the expiry date of 24 August 1992.

F **LORD DERVAIRD.**—For the general background
to this case I refer to my opinion in *British Coal Corporation v SSEB*, the Longannet action. Parties were
agreed that all the evidence heard should be treated as
applicable to each case as might be appropriate. In the
Cockenzie case, however, matters were less susceptible
to evidential considerations in respect that the main issue
between the parties related to the construction of a
formal document, the heads of agreement between the
parties (hereinafter referred to as BCC and SSEB respectively) of 9 and 23 March 1962. That document, hereinafter referred to as the 1962 agreement, was executed

in anticipation of the construction of a 300 megawatt
power station at Cockenzie, and purported to lay down G
certain provisions for the supply of coal by BCC to that
power station and the terms on which SSEB was to purchase and to take it.

    Coal was first delivered by BCC to Cockenzie on 6
June 1966. For present immediate purposes the date
of commencement of generation of electricity is not relevant, but substantial quantities of coal have been taken
by SSEB at Cockenzie ever since from BCC. Production 400 in the Longannet action shows the amount of
such coal acquired from BCC in each of the fiscal years H
from 1969-70 to date (in kilotonnes). The schedule to
the 1962 agreement appears to relate to calendar years
and is in tons. This makes it difficult to be clear about
what the measure of difference precisely is between the
figures in that schedule and the actual performance in
respect of purchase and supply of coal; but it was
accepted by the Dean of Faculty for BCC that there
had been supplies both less than and in excess of the
stipulated tonnages in that period. Further, in certain
years where less than the stipulated tonnage appears to I
have been taken from BCC, coal was taken from other
sources.

    In 1977 the parties agreed upon terms for the supply
of coal to SSEB during the five year period from 1
October 1977. In terms of cl 3 of that agreement it was
provided: "The existing Longannet and Cockenzie
Agreements between BCC and SSEB shall continue to
operate except that where conflict exists between this
Agreement and the Longannet and Cockenzie Agreements, this Agreement shall prevail." In terms of the J
1977 agreement an illustrative statement of the amounts
of coal expected to be consumed by SSEB under certain
stated assumptions was set forth in one of the appen-
dices. Specific provision was made for the price of coal
so supplied. That agreement came to an end on 30
September 1982. It is averred by SSEB and admitted
by BCC that minimum and maximum quantities contained in the schedule to the 1962 agreement were
breached in 1981, 1984 and 1985. In 1984 the minimum
quantity provision was breached, that being the year
of the miners' strike. In 1981 and 1985 the maximum K
quantities were exceeded.

    In 1986 the parties entered into a further agreement
relative to the supply of coal for the three year period
from 1 April 1985. In terms of para 3.1 of that agreement SSEB undertook to take from BCC not less than
90 per cent of their total coal requirements as defined,
and cl 3.3 provided that the balance of SSEB's total coal
requirement should be purchased from private coal suppliers. Elaborate provisions were also made as to price. L
Clause 9 was in these terms:

    "*Existing Station Agreements*. The provisons of the
    Agreements between NCB and SSEB relating to Lon-
    gannet and Cockenzie Power Stations insofar as still in
    force at the commencement of this Agreement shall con-
    tinue to operate, except that where conflict exists
    between the terms of this Agreement and the Longan-
    net or Cockenzie Agreements this Agreement shall
    prevail."

    For BCC the submission was simple. The 1962 agree-

A ment was a formal binding agreement still in force and expressly saved by the 1977 and 1986 agreements. A price could be fixed in terms of art 3 of that agreement, and Mr Hustings' evidence which I do not here rehearse showed how this was appropriately to be calculated. I do not think it necessary to rehearse that evidence because the joint minute for the parties records their agreement as to the arithmetical correctness of the figures contained in the relevant conclusions on the hypothesis of fact on which they are made.

B SSEB argued on the other hand that by their actings since 1982 in particular BCC had waived their rights to enforce performance of the 1962 agreement. Between 1977 and 1982 it was recognised in terms of the 1977 agreement that the 1962 agreement was in existence. Thereafter, the situation was quite different. Paragraph 6 of the joint minute demonstrated that whereas in terms of cl 3 of the 1962 agreement the price paid by SSEB for coal was to be in accordance with coal price structure (Scottish list price) (with the modifications set out in cl 4 of the 1962 agreement where appropriate), from C 1977 until October 1982 the prices charged had been East Midlands and Yorkshire prices as set out in the coal price structure with certain modifications. Between November 1982 and October 1983 the price charged was that paid in October 1982 with a 6.65 per cent increase. However, it was invoiced to SSEB, on the basis of Scottish list prices as set out in the coal price structure with a discount of 9.03 per cent. From November 1983 a two tranche, or at times three tranche system D was in operation whereby a certain amount was charged at one level, and the remainder at lesser prices. At some stages this was specific to Cockenzie in that a fixed tonnage for Cockenzie was payable at the initial rate and the balance at a discount or discounts. At other times the pricing arrangements were related to the whole coal requirements of SSEB and expressed in percentage terms. From this I was entitled to infer that after the expiry of the 1977 agreement in 1982 there were simply several agreements as to price unrelated to the coal price structure (except for purposes of invoicing). During that E period also, and before (as production 400 of the Longannet action confirmed), as was indeed accepted by Mr Edwards in his evidence for BCC, variations from the figures specified for take had occurred without any protest on the part of BCC. Likewise coal had been purchased from other sources without any objection in principle to what was taking place. SSEB had acted in reliance on their belief that the 1962 contract was no longer being insisted in, in that they entered into agreements whereby they had bound themselves to take F certain specified tonnages (whereas in relation to Longannet there had been no obligation of a minimum take). The whole negotiations in 1986 leading up to the agreement with effect from 1 April 1985 were geared to negotiations in an overall context for all coal being supplied to SSEB at a uniform price, leaving it to SSEB to determine what quantity should go to what station. SSEB had relied on the concept of overall negotiations. *Armia Ltd v Daejan Developments Ltd* and in particular the speech of Lord Keith at 1979 SLT, p 165, demonstrated that the question whether or not there has been

G a waiver of a right was a question of fact to be determined objectively upon a consideration of all the relevant evidence. In reply on this point the Dean of Faculty observed that the only relevant period where the situation was unclear was the period 1983 to 1985 which had been the time of the miners' strike and its aftermath. This case was, he said, one where during the currency of a contract with an identifiable term there had been temporary variations. But such temporary variations did not themselves bring to an end obligations in that contract not affected by the temporary variations. The well known case of *Carron Co v Henderson's Trs* H demonstrated that consent to particular acts did not amount to a discharge of an obligation for the future.

In my opinion the facts in the present case do not demonstrate that BCC waived its right to insist on the performance of the 1962 agreement at any future stage. It is clear that it was convenient to the parties to arrive at agreements from time to time which could not be implemented commensurately with the whole terms of the 1962 agreement because these agreements cover the supply of coal to the whole of the power stations under I the control of SSEB. But it is a very different question whether by entering into such agreements BCC waived any rights it had to revert to the 1962 agreement in its entirety once these earlier agreements which were all expressed to run for specific short periods had terminated. In my opinion on the facts before me that would have been at best a doubtful proposition: but it is excluded by the clear acceptance by the parties in terms of these temporary arrangements that the 1962 agreement remained in force. Clause 3 of the 1977 agreement J was explicit that the existing Cockenzie agreement should continue to operate subject only to the 1977 agreement prevailing in case of conflict. It seems to me plain that this could only affect or limit the force and effect of the 1962 agreement for so long as the 1977 agreement itself remained in operation. It was contended on behalf of BCC that between 1982 and 1985 the 1977 agreement continued in force by tacit relocation. In the case of Cockenzie I do not see how that can be said to arise: if there is an agreement governing the relations K of the parties for a tract of time extending beyond the five year period which is expressly affected by the 1977 agreement I do not see upon what basis in law tacit relocation can arise at the end of that five year period to maintain in force a limited period agreement which is in conflict with the original agreement. That cannot in my view be done tacitly. If that view be right, then the 1962 agreement would, having been kept in force throughout the duration of the 1977 agreement expressly in terms thereof, have resumed its full force L and effect in 1982 when the 1977 agreement terminated. Plainly there were departures from the terms of the 1962 agreement both as to price and as to quantities of coal in the ensuing period up until 1 April 1985. But that period as I have already indicated covered the very special circumstances of the miners' strike and the necessity to restock with coal thereafter. Clause 9 of the 1986 agreement provides as already stated that the position of the Cockenzie agreement insofar as still in force at the commencement of this agreement should continue to operate with the same exception as had been stated in the 1977 agreement. It appears to me that in entering into an agreement in these terms BCC did not waive any rights it had relating to the 1962 agreement and its enforcement at the expiry of the three year period of the 1986 agreement on 31 March 1988. For these reasons which I have tried briefly to express, the case of waiver fails, and BCC has not waived its right to insist in due performance of the 1962 agreement.

An argument was then advanced for SSEB to the effect that there was a difficult question as to the proper construction of cl second (b) of the 1962 agreement, given that the object of coal supply to SSEB under that agreement was for consumption in the generating station, and that the obligation under cl second (b) was "Such quantities of coal as are necessary for the operation of the generating station". In partial response to some of the criticisms advanced BCC amended their conclusions to make the obligations as set forth in their conclusions subject to the exercise of cl ninth of the 1962 agreement (which permitted either party to cancel from the contract the appropriate quantity of coal in any instance where for one of the specified causes it was not practicable either for BCC to supply or SSEB to accept delivery of the same). But SSEB claimed that there was nothing in the 1962 agreement which prevented them from closing the station altogether. The response to this on behalf of BCC was that SSEB having regard to cl ninth had no discretion in relation to cl second (b) as to running the station. Their obligation under that clause was unavoidable subject only to their rights under cl ninth and provided that the station was operating. As I understood him, the Dean of Faculty contended that so long as the station was operating, SSEB was obliged to take the minimum quantity of 600,000 tonnes of coal per annum. The last part of cl second (b) would have made it possible for the parties to agree fixed quantities at an earlier stage but that had not happened. In my opinion the points raised on behalf of SSEB do not justify the claim founded on *McArthur v Lawson* that the contract was so uncertain and incapable of enforcement that there was in truth no contract at all. While it may be that under certain circumstances SSEB may be able to avoid this contract altogether by ceasing to operate the station, *so long as they continue to operate Cockenzie Power Station for the purpose of generating electricity* within the timescale covered by the agreement they are in my opinion bound to take coal supplied by BCC within the limit specified.

A further point raised by the defenders related to the question whether coal to be taken in a year related to consumption in that year, in particular how it might be affected by the acquisition of coal in any previous year. In my opinion the last amendment to the conclusions by BCC which related to the provision of coal during a calendar year removed any dubiety on that score. Just as when under cl second (a) of the 1962 agreement a fixed quantity was to be taken each year irrespective of consumption, so under cl second (b) a quantity within the fixed parameters and therefore always at least 600,000 tonnes has to be taken irrespective of consumption. Lastly, I do not consider this to be a case such

as is exemplified by *Moore v Paterson* where there is an equitable basis for refusing to order specific implement.

On what had been expected to be the last day of the case, counsel for SSEB indicated that having regard to advice now received by him he required leave to withdraw from item 4 of the joint minute which had very recently been lodged. That item stated the parties' agreement that Cockenzie power station started generating electricity for the grid in December 1967. It was indicated that an earlier date in the view of SSEB was appropriate; and that that in turn would or could have very significant effects on the duration of the Cockenzie agreement should I hold that to be enforceable. The possible commercial importance of the matter was accepted by the Dean of Faculty. Accordingly I permitted SSEB to withdraw from item 4 of the joint minute. Thereafter a further minute of amendment was lodged averring that the generating station at Cockenzie commenced operation on 13 June 1967. Answers were lodged for BCC. Further proof in the case and further submissions were heard on 1 December 1989.

Cockenzie power station consists of four generating sets. Each generating set is capable of operating independently, although all four share certain common services. In the late 60s and early 70s stations of the size of Cockenzie represented a considerable increase in size over the conventional power stations of the previous decade, and in certain respects were at the then limits of technology. One consequence was that the level of breakdowns or outage was considerably higher than that which had been experienced in the smaller 30 to 60 megawatt stations which had been previously the normal size. The no 1 generating set at Cockenzie had been intended to come into operation first, in 1966. Because of defects in the boiler construction it was greatly delayed, and it was in fact no 2 set which first came into operation. Mr Ilett, who was operations superintendent at Cockenzie between 1965 and October 1967 explained that each generating unit contains amongst other things a boiler and a turbine generator. For the purposes of supplying the national grid the generator required to supply electricity into an alternating current system and it was necessary for the generators to be running at the same speed. The basic speed was 3,000 revolutions per minute. Once turbine generators had achieved that speed they were electrically locked together (and thereafter the speed of all the generators so locked together might vary in response to load factors). It was therefore necessary for an individual generator to be synchronised with the system. Once that had been achieved and only once that had been achieved the generator could generate electricity into the grid. Until that had been done it was impossible for a generator to supply any current to the grid.

Production 298 which was produced for the last hearing was a schedule of weekly output from Cockenzie from June 1967 to the end of the year. The first column showed the electricity generated in gigawatts (GWH). The station itself was a heavy consumer of electricity which was also shown in one of the columns of production 298 and the final column showed the balance

A over each week of electricity consumed as opposed to electricity generated. That table demonstrated that in the week ending 16 June 1967 the no 2 generating set in fact generated 1.249 GWH, and in that week there was a surplus of electricity generated over electricity consumed of 0.322 GWH. It was accepted, as I understood it by Mr Ilett, that in respect of a 300 megawatt station, as Cockenzie was, 1.249 GWH represented about four hours' generation. Over June as a whole there was a deficit of 0.699 GWH. The reason was that after the week ending 16 June 1967 the no 2 set did not

B operate again until the week ending 25 August 1967. There were two problems; one related to the stator, which was a design problem which had to be attended to. There was also an incident involving a water hammer. Mr Ilett accepted that it might always have been intended that after synchronisation the generator was to be taken out of service until August in order to have the design problem relating to the stator attended to, and that the minute of the liaison committee held on 13 June 1967 (coincidentally the day on which syn-

C chronisation was in the event actually achieved) appeared to make it clear that the necessity for design modifications had already been appreciated coupled with the understanding that the station would become "operative" by August 1967. In fact generation of electricity from no 2 set next took place in the week ending 25 August 1967 and continued, with a break of one week, into the first week of October. At that point a design weakness in relation to the turbine glands was revealed, and that had to be put right before the set could recom-

D mence generation which did not take place until towards the end of December 1967.

In order to start up the generator at Cockenzie it was necessary to use oil. Coal was only introduced to the furnaces at the time that the generator was synchronised, at which stage pulverised coal fuel was injected into the boiler furnace. Oil was still retained as a constituent of the fuel until the set was on approximately two thirds load, it being necessary to maintain ignition by means of oil until the coal had become mutually supportive.

E Coal was first delivered to Cockenzie in June 1966 and a stock was built up. It had always been anticipated that stock would be built up prior to the operation of the station, and the delay resulting from the defects in the no 1 generating set did not determine the build up of coal stocks. Instead some special arrangements were made whereby BCC were able to stockpile the coal at Cockenzie in anticipation of the operation of the station. Throughout the latter part of 1967 coal continued to be delivered to the power station. By 1 September 1967

F over 250,000 tonnes of coal had been delivered to Cockenzie. By the same date 2,400 tonnes of coal had actually been consumed. The station had produced electricity in each of the three weeks ending 16 June, 25 August and 1 September 1967.

The amounts of electricity generated were 1.249 GWH, 6.075 GWH and 5.734 GWH respectively. At the output rate postulated these represented 4, 20 and 19 hours' operation respectively. Mr Ilett explained that the output of 1.249 GWH in June 1967 was not achievable by the use of oil alone and that some of the 2,400

G tonnes of coal must have been burnt on that occasion. Since the electricity generated in that period was a little less than 10 per cent of that generated up until 1 September 1967 it seems not unreasonable to assume that some 10 per cent of the 2,400 tonnes would have been consumed in June 1967, ie about 240 tonnes.

It was explained that the individual generating sets were commissioned separately. The actual process of commissioning each generator was a complex one as different items were brought into operation at different stages. The date of commissioning being taken in

H the view of the SSEB as the date of handover by the contractor to them was the date when the generator in question was synchronised for the first time. (In fact certain items could not be brought into operation and could not therefore technically be commissioned until after synchronisation had been achieved.)

For BCC Mr George McNeill was recalled. He explained that commissioning and synchronising were not expressions regularly used by BCC. What BCC were looking to was the time when a station would consume

I coal on what he called a normal burning basis. In the whole period to December 1967 the station burnt some 25,000 tonnes of coal which in no way could be described as six months' normal coal burning. He agreed that the station might be regarded as commencing operation when it first provided power to the grid, but that was subject to qualification that that was so only if it was done on a regular basis as opposed to an experimental or irregular basis.

J It is clear on the evidence that the no 2 generating set was in fact synchronised on 13 June 1967 and was therefore at that date capable of generating electricity and supplying it to the grid. It is further clear that some electricity was in fact supplied to the grid in the course of that week, and that in order to provide that electricity some coal, as well as oil, must have been burnt in the boiler furnace. However it seems likely that the total number of hours when the set was supplying electricity was about four, and that the coal consumed was about 240 tonnes. It also seems likely that it was known prior

K to synchronisation on 13 June 1967 that a design problem existed in relation to the stator which would require several weeks' further work during which the set could not generate electricity, with the result that the station was not, at the time of synchronisation, expected by either SSEB or BCC to be functioning until about August 1967 in its normal role. The importance of this matter is that in terms of cl second of the 1962 agreement BCC undertook certain supply obligations "as from the date on which the said generating station

L commences operations". Commencing operations is not otherwise defined. In cl fourth which deals with a "commercial addition" to be paid in respect of certain types of coal, it was agreed by subcl (b) "That for the first five years after the date on which the said generating station is brought into commercial use by SSEB the commercial addition will be four shillings per tonne." For SSEB it was argued that the date on which the station commenced operation was 13 June 1967. On that date the no 2 generator was synchronised and capable of supplying electricity to the grid and did actually do

so. That having occurred it did not matter what hap-
A pened thereafter. For BCC it was claimed that against
the whole background circumstances the end of 1967
was the appropriate date to take. It was not until then
that the generator could be described as operating normally. Clause ninth of the heads of agreement in 1962
enabled SSEB to cancel coal from the specified schedule of tonnages when it was not practical for SSEB to
accept delivery by means inter alia of breakdown of
machinery or plant and it was admitted on record that
no such cancellation had been sought by SSEB, which
B must be taken as an indication that SSEB had not considered that the station had yet come into operation.

In my opinion the limited operation of the station in
the week of 16 June 1967 did not constitute a commencement of operations within the meaning of cl
second. It appears to me that the period of commencement of operations being specifically related to an obligation to supply coal to SSEB for consumption in that
station, it falls to be related to a point in time from which
the station was expected by the parties to operate on
C a normal basis as a power station supplying power to
the grid and burning coal for that purpose. In other
words I do not think that any distinction was intended
to be drawn between the station commencing operations
and being brought into commercial use. It is clear on
the other hand that commissioning as used in cl first
is not the same as commencing operations in cl second.
It is clear from the minute of 13 June 1967 that SSEB
did not at that stage intend to put the station into normal
operation, because they were aware of a design fault
D which was going to require attention and prevent the
station from functioning for at least some weeks thereafter. The use of the phrase "would be operative" in
that minute is at least some indication of what the parties
had in mind as regards the commencement of operations. In the whole circumstances I consider that the
functioning of the generator in June 1967 was not
intended to be a commencement of operations.
Moreover I take the view in any event that in the whole
context that operation falls to be treated as de minimis.
E It appears to me that if the June operation is rejected
as the commencement of operations, there is no reason
for challenging the view that the station did indeed commence operations in August 1967. At that stage the
generator commenced to generate electricity and supplied the grid for a period of several weeks and it consumed quantities of coal. Neither the electricity then
generated nor the coal consumed can be regarded as
insignificant. Moreover there was no planned "outage"
of the station to take place thereafter. The fact that
F breakdown occurred does not mean that the station had
not commenced operation. Accordingly I hold that
Cockenzie power station commenced operation within
the meaning of cl second in the week commencing 25
August 1967, and since the precise date in that week
cannot now be determined, parties were agreed that in
that event the date should be taken as 25 August 1967.

The whole purpose of this extra evidence was to
support an argument by SSEB that the period during
which they came under any obligation to take coal from
BCC in terms of the 1962 agreement was limited to a

period of 25 years from the date of commencement,
which on the approach just indicated would take them G
to 24 August 1992 and not 31 December 1992 as
claimed in the conclusions of the summons. For BCC
it was argued that this whole chapter of evidence was
irrelevant having regard to the actual terms of cl second
which is in these terms: "NCB undertake that they will,
as from the date on which the said generating station
commences operation and during the life of the station
which for the purposes of this agreement shall be taken
as 25 years thereafter, supply to SSEB for consumption in said generating station and SSEB agree to pur- H
chase and take (a) in respect of each year during the
period from 1966 to 1980 both inclusive the quantities
of coal specified in the schedule hereto attached. . . .
(b) In respect of each year during the succeeding period
up until 31 December 1992 such quantities of coal as
are necessary for the operation of the generating station
with a minimum of 600,000 tonnes p.a. and a maximum
of 1,500,000 tonnes p.a. SSEB will during the year 1975
provide NCB with estimates of demand for each year
of the last mentioned period; and the sources, quanti- I
ties and type of coal to be supplied against this demand
will then be agreed between the parties in the light of
the circumstances then obtaining."

Clause second, said BCC, was internally inconsistent,
and obviously so, since while the life of the station was
to be taken as 25 years, the two subheads refer to specific
periods, a 15 year period from 1966 to 1980 with defined
quantities in each year to be taken as set out in the schedule and a further 12 year period described as "the succeeding period up to 31 December 1992". That meant, J
said BCC, that the whole matter was inconsistent. The
parties had clearly intended that the contract should
endure for a substantial period and when they had
provided explicitly for the termination date effect should
be given to their intention. I was referred to Chitty, Contracts (24th ed), p 784, and to the Scottish case of Rowtor
Steamship Co v Love & Stewart in support of that proposition. The appropriate way was to read 25 years in the
initial part of the clause as meaning "more or less" and
thus indicating it was only an overall estimate.   K

That interpretation appears to me itself to pose
difficulty. The undertaking by BCC is limited to a
period of 25 years after the date on which the generating station commences operation. If the period specified in cl second (a) and (b) were literally to govern then
a period of 25 years could never ever have been right.
It is a reasonable inference from cll first, second (a) and
the schedule that the parties anticipated in 1962 that
the station would commence operating at some stage L
in 1966, and the period specified in cl second (a) might
therefore be only just over 14 years. But if that literal
effect is to be given to cl second (a) and likewise to subcl
(b) the result will always have been that a minimum
of just over 26 years and a maximum of precisely 27
years was in contemplation. It appears to me that the
true intention of the parties may be gauged in this way;
cl first makes it plain that the parties contemplated there
was to be a successive commissioning of the generating sets comprising the whole station. The precise time
when the station would commence operation could not

be precisely known in 1962 when the agreement was made but was expected to take place sometime between the years 1966 and 1968 and over that period. Clause second (a) might therefore be taken as the period from 1966 to 1980 starting in that period whenever during that period the generating station commenced operation. Clause second (b) refers to the succeeding period up to 31 December 1992. The phrase "the succeeding period" has to be given some content. If the BCC contention was sound these words mean no more than "thereafter". If on the other hand the phrase means such part of the 25 year period that remains up to if necessary but no further than 31 December 1992 it appears to give some content to the reference to 25 years, which on this basis becomes a maximum period controlling the whole undertaking. On this basis I conclude that effect can and should be given to the wording of the clause, and the result is that the succeeding period by virtue of the operation of the 25 year rule will end at 24 August 1992. In support of that construction I would further point out that if one treats the words in cl second (a) and (b) as determinative of the length of the period of agreement the whole reference to the life of the station in the initial part of that clause appears to become devoid of meaning. There is no other point in the agreement than cl second where that phrase appears to have any role to play.

In the whole circumstances therefore I am of opinion that BCC are entitled to a declarator that the 1962 agreement is in force between the parties and that the obligations stated in the first conclusion are incumbent on SSEB. The date, however, at which that obligation will expire is in my view in light of the evidence which has been led not 31 December 1992 but 24 August of that year. I also consider that BCC are entitled not only to a declarator but also to a decree of specific implement in respect of the same matter and accordingly I shall grant decree in terms of the second conclusion similarly limited in point of time to 24 August 1992.

Counsel for Pursuers, Dean of Faculty (Johnston, QC), Reid; Solicitors, McClure Naismith Anderson & Gardiner — Counsel for Defenders, Mackay, QC, Davidson; Solicitors, Shepherd & Wedderburn, WS.

R F H

[This case has been reported by request.]

Wendel v Moran

OUTER HOUSE
LORD CULLEN
13 NOVEMBER 1991

International law — Recognition of foreign judgment — Judgment of United States court — Judgment in action resulting from tort — Jurisdiction of court issuing judgment based on locus of tort in territory of court — Whether judgment may only be recognised if defender resident or present in territory of foreign court when action brought there.

Parties brought an action seeking decree conform to a judgment obtained by them against the defender and a company in a New York court. They sought $1,745,102.99, averring that this was the sum for which judgment had been given in the United States. The defender maintained (1) that he was not domiciled in Scotland and that as a result the Court of Session had no jurisdiction over him, and (2) that, as the pursuers had not established that the New York court was a court of competent jurisdiction in terms of Scottish private international law, the pursuers' averments were irrelevant. The pursuers argued that the New York court was a court of competent jurisdiction, and its judgment should therefore be recognised, since (1) the tortious acts on which the New York action was founded had taken place in the territory of the court, and (2) the defender had agreed with the pursuers that United States laws would apply to their transactions.

Held, (1) that it was appropriate for the court to consider the recognition question prior to the jurisdiction question (p 45D); (2) that, so far as the recognition question was concerned, there was no significant difference between Scots law and English law, and at common law the residence or presence of the defender in the territory of the foreign court at the time when the action was commenced provided a basis for recognition while the mere fact that the cause of action arose in the territory of the foreign court did not (p 48A-B); (3) that the provisions of the 1968 Brussels Jurisdiction and Judgments Convention had no bearing on the common law rules applicable in disputes concerning non-contracting states (p 48G-H); and (4) that there was no relevant averment by the pursuers that the defender had submitted, expressly or by implication, to the jurisdiction of the New York court (p 48H-I); and action *dismissed.*

Action for decree conform

Jeffrey Wendel and others raised an action against Christopher Moran for a decree conform to a judgment obtained against the defender and another in a United States court.

The case came before the Lord Ordinary (Cullen) on procedure roll, where the defender argued that the pursuers' averments were irrelevant and lacking in specification.

Cases referred to

Adams v Cape Industries plc [1990] Ch 433; [1990] 2 WLR 657; [1991] 1 All ER 929.

Dallas & Co v McArdle, 1949 SLT 375; 1949 SC 481.

Kerr v R & W Ferguson, 1931 SLT 540; 1931 SC 736.

Pick v Stewart, Galbraith & Co Ltd (1907) 15 SLT 447.

Singh (Sirdar Gurdyal) v Rajah of Faridkote [1894] AC 670.

Société Cooperative Sidmetal v Titan International Ltd [1966] 1 QB 828; [1965] 3 WLR 847; [1965] 3 All ER 494.

Waygood & Co v Bennie (1885) 12 R 651.

Textbooks referred to

A Anton, *Private International Law* (2nd ed), pp 24-25, 222.

Dicey & Morris, *Conflict of Laws* (11th ed), pp 436-437.

Duncan & Dykes, *Principles of Civil Jurisdiction,* pp 291-293.

Lorimer, *Institutes of the Law of Nations,* p 328.

Story, *Conflict of Laws,* pp 752, 754.

Von Bar, *Theory and Practice of Private International Law* (Gillespie's ed), s 425.

B On 13 November 1991 the Lord Ordinary *sustained* the defender's third plea in law and *dismissed* the action.

LORD CULLEN.—In this action the pursuers seek decree against the defender conform to a judgment obtained by them against the defender and Christopher Moran & Co Ltd in the United States district court for the Southern District of New York. It is averred that the sum sued for in dollars, namely, $1,745,102.99 is the sum for which judgment was given on 19 June 1989, subject to rectification by the court on 30 April 1990 C of certain clerical errors.

When the case called before me on procedure roll the defender challenged the relevancy and specification of the pursuers' averments on the ground that even if they were true they did not establish that the New York court fell for the purposes of the present case to be regarded as a court of competent jurisdiction according to the rules of private international law in the law of Scotland. At this point I should mention that the defender has D also challenged the jurisdiction of this court on the basis that he is not domiciled in Scotland. It is well established that questions of jurisdiction should be decided in limine rather than reserved for decision along with the merits of a case *(Dallas & Co v McArdle)*. It was not in dispute in the present case, and it was in any event my view, that it was appropriate to deal with recognition as a matter of relevancy even before a question of jurisdiction. This is plainly expedient since it may avoid an unnecessary inquiry into the factual basis E for the assertion that the court has jurisdiction over the defender.

In the course of the discussion before me the pursuers founded upon two separate grounds for the argument that the jurisdiction of the New York court should be recognised.

The first was founded upon the pursuers' averments that: "the jurisdiction of the said court was founded inter alia upon the commission by the defenders of tortious acts within the territorial jurisdiction of the court. . . . F Said judgment was pronounced in respect of fraudulent misrepresentations made by the defender to the pursuers in New York City in relation to the purchase of shares in Zondervan Corporation." The pursuers go on to aver: "Service of the action was made on the defender in England on 19 December 1988 following a number of abortive attempts to arrange a meeting with the defender via his secretary. All subsequent steps of procedure of the US district court were notified to the defender. The US district court had jurisdiction over the defender by reason inter alia of the delictual acts

of the defender within New York State and the presence of the defender and his agents transacting business in G New York State. The said delictual acts were committed prior to and during March 1987 by the defender when he was physically present in New York City, New York."

The second ground for recognition was founded upon the pursuers' averments, as amended at the beginning of the debate, as follows: "Explained and averred that the defender submitted by agreement with the pursuers to all laws of the United States in respect of transactions in Zondervan shares in filings made by him to the Securities Exchange Council." H

Although the debate was concerned with the defender's attack on the relevancy and specification of the pursuers' averments it is convenient to begin by setting out the pursuers' arguments in support of recognition.

Counsel for the pursuers submitted, in support of the first ground for recognition, that the New York court should be regarded as having jurisdiction by reason of I the delict having been committed within the territory of that court, coupled with the fact that service of the action had been made on the defender as averred. Counsel accepted that according to the common law the Court of Session, prior to the enactment of the Law Reform (Jurisdiction in Delict) (Scotland) Act 1971, did not assert its jurisdiction over a defender on the basis that the cause of action had arisen in Scotland unless the defender had been personally cited within Scotland. That had been held in *Kerr v R & W Ferguson,* a deci- J sion of the First Division with four consulted judges. However, opinions delivered in that case, such as that of Lord Justice Clerk Alness at 1931 SLT, p 549, recognised that the requirement for personal citation in Scotland was anomalous. It did not follow that as a matter of private international law the same requirement would be made in considering the recognition of the judgment of a foreign court which was based on the commission of a wrong within its territory. Counsel founded on the dissenting opinions of Lord Hunter and Lord Blackburn K in *Kerr* and pointed out that at pp 552-553 Lord Hunter founded upon a passage in von Bar's *Theory and Practice of Private International Law* which supported his argument. It was in the following terms: "It needs no further exposition to show that, in the case of a claim arising on a delict, the *forum delicti commissi* must be recognised as having international jurisdiction. . . . The *forum delicti commissi* is, therefore, merely the court of the place in which the person who did the act, and against whom the claim is subsequently brought, is resi- L dent at the time the act is done; it is not the court of the place in which the effects of the act are felt, or in which the injured person is resident. We must not, however, require, as a condition of recognising the *forum delicti commissi,* personal service of the action within the jurisdiction or possession of property there" (Gillespie's ed, s 425).

Although there was no authority which was in point, counsel founded upon the decision of Lord McLaren in *Waygood & Co v Bennie,* in which it was held that

the Court of Session should recognise the jurisdiction
of the High Court in England to prevent a wrong being
done in England where the alleged wrongdoer was a
person carrying on trade in Scotland, and, on that basis,
to give a decree for the costs of the preventive procedure.
At pp 654-655 Lord McLaren, whose decision was
affirmed in the Inner House, set out a number of considerations which he regarded as relevant to his decision. He referred in the first place to the Roman law,
continuing as follows: "On this subject Savigny has a
very important observation (vol. viii. sec. 371, 6), where
he insists that the *forum delicti* is by no means to be
regarded as a particular application of the jurisdiction
founded on obligation and known as *forum contractus;*
for, he proceeds, the *forum delicti* is not founded on the
voluntary submission of the party, and is not subject
to the restriction prescribed with respect to jurisdiction
founded on obligation (*i.e.,* the restriction that the
respondent must be found within the territory). He adds
that it is a jurisdiction founded on the enforced submission of the party, consequent on his violation of the
law, and that it is a jurisdiction established, not in the
interest of the defender, but very clearly in the interest
of the demandant."

Counsel emphasised the distinction between contract
and delict as the cause of action on which jurisdiction
was founded. The proposition that in the case of delict
jurisdiction was founded upon the enforced submission
of the party and that his presence within the territory
was not required applied to all delictual cases, whether
or not they were concerned with the exercise of a preventive jurisdiction. This was in accordance with considerations of fairness and common sense, particularly so in
modern times when the opportunities for communications between different countries had been so greatly
increased. Counsel also referred to Duncan & Dykes,
Principles of Civil Jurisdiction, pp 291-293. He also
founded on Lorimer's *Institutes of the Law of Nations*
at p 328 where the author sets out "the only conditions
imposed by reason, and recognised by practice" in the
recognition of foreign judgments, none of which
included any restriction as to the citation of the defender
within the territory. As regards English law counsel submitted that the law as to recognition in that country
had grown up in a different way from Scotland. No distinction had been drawn between contract and tort as
the cause of action. It was inappropriate that the concept
of submission, which implied a voluntary act, should
be applied without discrimination to both contract and
tort cases. Counsel also submitted that his approach to
recognition was supported by the enactment of the Civil
Jurisdiction and Judgments Act 1982. Article 5 of the
1968 Convention provided: "A person domiciled in a
Contracting State may, in another Contracting State be
sued . . . (3) in matters relating to tort, delict and quasi-
delict, in the courts for the place where the harmful
event occurred." The Convention, he submitted,
reflected the general international legal principles which
the contracting states had agreed to adopt. He also
pointed out that Anton, *Private International Law* (2nd
ed), p 222 suggested that it was possible that in the light
of the 1982 Act the Scottish courts would review the

common law grounds on which they conceded international competence to the courts of other countries.

In reply counsel for the defender submitted that the
pursuers' submissions were not borne out by the
authorities upon which they founded. The decision in
Kerr had laid to rest any doubt which might have existed
that personal citation in Scotland was required in order
to give a Scottish court jurisdiction ratione loci delicti.
Although this requirement might well be imperfect as
a means of ensuring the effectiveness of the eventual
judgment, it ensured and evidenced the presence of the
defender within the territory at the time when the action
was raised (see Lord Ormidale, 1931 SLT at p 550 and
Lord Anderson at p 554). The passage from von Bar
merely set out a theory which had not been accepted
in practice. As regards the decision of Lord McLaren
in *Waygood & Co,* it was pointed out that the passage
in Savigny to which he referred formed part of a larger
discussion as to the forum of the obligation in regard
to contracts, unilateral permitted acts and delicts. After
that passage he had stated (at p 220 of the same translation): "The jurisdiction of the obligation can be made
effective only if the debtor is either present in the territory, or possesses property there." It was pointed out
that this later passage was quoted in *Kerr* by Lord
Justice Clerk Alness at p 547, following which he
referred to Story's *Conflict of Laws* (8th ed) where the
writer said at p 752: "The civil law contemplated
another place of jurisdiction; to wit, the place where
a contract was made or was to be fulfilled, or where
any other act was done, if the defendant or his property
could be found there, although it was not the place of
his domicil"; and at p 754: "Considered in an international point of view, jurisdiction, to be rightfully exercised, must be founded either upon the person being
within the territory, or upon the thing being within the
territory . . . no sovereignty can extend its process
beyond its own territorial limits to subject either persons
or property to its judicial decisions. Every exertion of
authority of this sort beyond this limit is a mere nullity,
and incapable of binding such persons or property in
any other tribunals."

There was no warrant for applying Lord McLaren's
conclusion that personal citation within the jurisdiction
was not necessary beyond cases which involved the court
exercising a preventive jurisdiction within its own territory. Lorimer should not be regarded as an authoritative source of the rules of private international law (see
Anton, pp 24-25). Counsel submitted that, leaving aside
submission, territoriality was the basic consideration
upon which recognition was founded. This was clearly
recognised in English law in which the decisions were
of highly persuasive value in the present case. In *Sirdar
Gurdyal Singh v The Rajah of Faridkote* it was held that
money decrees passed by the court in Faridkote against
the defendant who had been the treasurer of the late
Rajah in that state but had decamped to the state of
Jhind in which he was domiciled, were a nullity by international law. At pp 683-684 the Earl of Selborne, after
referring to the fundamental rule that the plaintiff must
sue in the court to which the defendant is subject at
the time of suit — actor sequitur forum rei — stated:

"Territorial jurisdiction attaches (with special exceptions) upon all persons either permanently or temporarily resident within the territory while they are within it; but it does not follow them after they have withdrawn from it, and when they are living in another independent country. It exists always as to land within the territory, and it may be exercised over moveables within the territory; and, in questions of status or succession governed by domicil, it may exist as to persons domiciled, or who when living were domiciled, within the territory. As between different provinces under one sovereignty (eg under the Roman Empire) legislation of the sovereign may distribute and regulate jurisdiction; but no territorial legislation can give jurisdiction which any foreign Court ought to recognise against foreigners, who owe no allegiance or obedience to the Power which so legislates.

"In a personal action to which none of these causes of jurisdiction apply, a decree pronounced in absentem by a foreign Court, to the jurisdiction of which the defendant has not in any way submitted himself, is by international law an absolute nullity. He is under no obligation of any kind to obey it; and it must be regarded as a mere nullity by the Courts of every nation except (when authorised by special local legislation) in the country of the forum by which it was pronounced."

He then stated that those doctrines were laid down by all the leading authorities on international law, including Story's *Conflict of Laws*. It was also pointed out that in English law the extent to which a foreign judgment in personam was recognised was determined not by comity but primarily by reference to whether the defendant had a duty to observe its terms (*Société Cooperative Sidmetal v Titan International Ltd*). My attention was drawn to rule 37 in Dicey & Morris, *Conflict of Laws* (11th ed) at pp 436-437. The first case under that rule states that, subject to certain rules which are not of significance for present purposes, a court of a foreign country outside the United Kingdom has jurisdiction to give a judgment in personam capable of enforcement or recognition "if the judgment debtor was, at the time the proceedings were instituted, resident (or, perhaps, present) in the foreign country". That statement fell to be read along with the recent decision of the Court of Appeal in *Adams v Cape Industries plc*. At [1991] 1 All ER, p 1003 Slade LJ, giving the decision of the court, stated that in the absence of any form of submission to the foreign court the competence of the foreign court to summon the defendants before it and to decide such matters as it has decided depended on the physical presence of the defendant in the country concerned at the time of suit. It appeared that the date of service of process rather than the date of issue of proceedings was to be treated as the time of suit for these purposes, but no final view was expressed on this point. Further, the temporary presence of a defendant in the foreign country would suffice provided at least that it was voluntary (ie not induced by compulsion, fraud or duress). At p 1004 Slade LJ said that the court regarded the source of the territorial jurisdiction of the court of a foreign country to summon a defendant to appear before it as being his obligation for the time being to abide by its laws and accept the jurisdiction of its courts while present in its territory: "So long as he remains physically present in that country, he has the benefit of its laws, and must take the rough with the smooth, by accepting his amenability to the process of its courts. In the absence of authority compelling a contrary conclusion, we would conclude that the voluntary presence of an individual in a foreign country, whether permanent or temporary, and whether or not accompanied by residence, is sufficient to give the courts of that country territorial jurisdiction over him under our rules of private international law."

Counsel submitted that the approach in England was wholly consistent with the approach in Scots law. In *Waygood & Co* Lord McLaren had recognised the significance of territoriality. At p 655 he said: "*Prima facie*, I should assume the jurisdiction to be as wide as the necessity of restraining infringements of public or private right within the territory may from time to time prescribe." In *Pick v Stewart, Galbraith & Co Ltd* Lord Salvesen refused to enforce the decree of a New York court against a limited company which had its registered office in Scotland. He followed English authority and pointed out that in the case of *Sirdar Gurdyal Singh* the Privy Council had expressly decided that the mere fact that the cause of action arose within the jurisdiction of the court in which the judgment was pronounced would not in a personal action give jurisdiction over a defendant who was personally resident elsewhere. He went on to state that, assuming that the accidental presence and citation of a director of the defender's company in New York was sufficient, according to the law there prevailing, to confer jurisdiction on the American judge to pronounce the judgment in question, that had no relevancy in the present action unless the ground of jurisdiction was one which the Scottish courts ought to recognise. On English authority it was obvious that the jurisdiction on the grounds claimed could not be recognised. In the present case senior counsel for the defender conceded that he would not have argued against recognition of the jurisdiction of the New York court if the defender had been present and served in the territory of that court. As regards the 1982 Act counsel submitted that this resulted from a combination of steps taken by the government in acceding to the Convention and Parliament making the consequential legislation. This had no bearing on the existing common law of Scotland.

As regards the second ground put forward for recognition of the jurisdiction of the New York court, counsel for the pursuers submitted that a submission to all laws was apt to include a submission to the jurisdiction of courts including the court in question. Counsel for the defender argued that, quite apart from the fact that the pursuers' averments lacked specification as to where, when and in what terms the agreement was expressed, it did not follow from any submission to all laws that there was a submission to the court in question.

In dealing with these arguments I require to apply the private international rules of Scots law as to the recognition of foreign judgments in actions in personam, and more specifically where the action arises out of a delict committed in the territory of the foreign court.

A In the light of the discussion before me, I am not persuaded that there is any significant difference between the approach which would be followed in Scotland and the approach which has been taken in England. Leaving aside cases of express or implied submission to the jurisdiction of the foreign court, with which the present case is not concerned, these rules require that the defender was resident or at any rate present in the territory of the foreign court when the action was commenced. The principle which appears to underlie this ground of recog-

B nition is that by his residence or presence at the relevant time he has rendered himself subject to the orders of the foreign court so that in this sense the foreign court possessed an effective jurisdiction over him. There is no authority to support the proposition that the mere fact that the cause of action arose in the territory of the foreign court is sufficient to warrant recognition of its judgment. Such a proposition was emphatically rejected in the Privy Council case of *Sirdar Gurdyal Singh,* followed by the Scottish case of *Pick.* The view advocated

C by von Bar, namely that what mattered was the place of residence of the defender at the time of the delict, has not been adopted. Such an approach would have had no relation in itself to the ability of the foreign court to exercise an effective jurisdiction over the defender by means of the proceedings in question.

While the private international rules as to the recognition of foreign judgments do not necessarily coincide with the domestic rules of jurisdiction it is, in my view, of some significance that in Scotland the domestic rules

D at common law were clearly based on considerations of effectiveness. Thus, where jurisdiction was claimed ratione contractus or ratione delicti it was essential that personal service should have been effected on the defender in Scotland (*Dallas & Co v McArdle* and *Kerr v R & W Ferguson*). The reasoning adopted by the majority of the court in the latter case shows that for the purposes of the domestic rules the principles appropriate to international recognition were applied.

E Quite apart from the considerations which I have mentioned above, I do not consider that Lord McLaren's decision in *Waygood & Co* provides a basis for holding that in the case of a foreign judgment for payment in a case based on delict it is sufficient that the delict occurred in the territory of the foreign court. It is clear that although Savigny treated jurisdiction in the case of delict as an enforced jurisdiction, he made it clear that the presence of the defender in the territory was necessary in order to provide an effective jurisdiction.

F Further, I do not consider that it is correct to extend the application of the approach which is taken in cases involving the exercise of a preventive jurisdiction. Such cases appear to me to fall into a special category. In the case of preventive jurisdiction the court acts in order to protect rights within its own territory. It is understandable that the courts of other countries should recognise its jurisdiction regardless of whether the defender is resident or present in the country at the time when the preventive proceedings are taken. On the other hand, in the case of a pecuniary claim based upon the commission of a delict, there is no reason why the court

of the territory where the delict was committed should be regarded as specially qualified to deal with such a G claim. It may also be noted that in the case of the domestic rules of jurisdiction in Scotland the jurisdiction exercised for preventive purposes was not regarded as providing a basis at common law for jurisdiction in regard to pecuniary claims arising out of the commission of the delict. As regards the 1982 Act I am wholly in agreement with the defender's submission that terms which are agreed between the contracting states and enacted in those states in consequence of that agreement have no bearing on the common law as between a Scot- H tish court and a court in non-contracting state.

For these reasons I am of opinion that the defender's attack on the first ground put forward by the pursuers for the recognition of the jurisdiction of the New York court is well founded.

As regards the second ground, which was briefly argued on either side, I am of opinion that the pursuers' averments are fundamentally lacking in any relevant averment which demonstrates that the defender sub- I mitted, either expressly or by implication, to the jurisdiction of the court which pronounced the judgment.

In these circumstances I shall sustain the defender's third plea in law and dismiss the action.

Counsel for Pursuers, Davidson; Solicitors, Shepherd & Wedderburn, WS — Counsel for Defender, Hamilton, QC, Hodge; Solicitors, Brodies, WS.

A M   J

Paterson v Lees

HIGH COURT OF JUSTICIARY   K

THE LORD JUSTICE CLERK (ROSS), LORDS MORISON AND CAPLAN

12 DECEMBER 1991

Justiciary — Statutory offence — Carrying out gas work without being competent to do it — Failing to carry out gas work in proper and workmanlike manner — Accused installing and thereafter repairing gas central heating boiler — Bad practices employed by accused exposing complainer subsequently to carbon monoxide fumes — Meaning of L *"competent" — Whether work not done "in a proper and workmanlike manner" — Gas Safety (Installation and Use) Regulations 1984 (SI 1984/1358), regs 3 (1) and 4 (3).*

Regulation 3 (1) of the Gas Safety (Installation and Use) Regulations 1984 provides that no person shall carry out any work in relation to a gas fitting unless he is competent to do so. Regulation 4 (3) provides that no person shall carry out any work in relation to a gas fitting otherwise than in a proper and workmanlike manner.

Two accused persons were charged on summary complaint with two offences, namely (1) carrying out work in relation to an open flued gas central heating boiler without being competent to do so, and (2) failing to carry out work in relation to that gas fitting in a proper and workmanlike manner whereby carbon monoxide gas spilled into the complainer's flat and endangered her life, contrary to regs 3 (1) and 4 (3) of the Gas Safety (Installation and Use) Regulations 1984. In convicting the accused on charge 1 the sheriff relied on inter alia the factors that the accused had installed an open flued boiler in a tenement ground floor flat with no proper flueing; they had failed to instal any permanent ventilation; and they had fitted the flue terminal on the surface of the wall in contravention of the British Standard Code of Practice for flues and air supply gas appliances. On charge 2 the sheriff found that in December 1988 the boiler emitted black smoke, was sooted up and was certified unsafe by the Gas Board. Shortly thereafter the accused cleaned and serviced the boiler. They installed a right angled bend on the terminal of the flue so that the flue was vertical and not horizontal, and was close to the wall, both of which were bad practice. Thereafter the boiler was put back into service and four finches in a bird cage in the complainer's flat died. No measurements were however taken of the level of concentration of carbon monoxide in the flat or in the complainer's blood. The accused appealed on the grounds that while the accused might have been negligent they were not proved to have lacked competence; that no facts had been stated from which the sheriff was entitled to conclude that they were guilty of charge 2; and in any event, there were no findings to support the aggravation that the work carried out by the accused had caused spillage of combustion products and endangered the complainer's life. In stating the case the sheriff refused to make a finding in fact as proposed by the Crown that neither accused was competent to instal the boiler because he considered that that was a matter of opinion to be drawn from the facts.

Held, (1) that a person who was competent to carry out any work was a person who had the knowledge and ability necessary to perform it properly (p 53I); (2) that having regard to the factors listed, the sheriff was entitled to infer that neither accused had the knowledge and ability to do the job properly and accordingly that neither was competent to instal the boiler (p 53I-J); (3) that the sheriff was entitled to conclude from the findings that the accused had failed to carry out the work of rectification in a proper and workmanlike manner and that it had endangered the complainer's life (pp 53L-54A and 54E-F); and appeal *refused*.

Observed, that the sheriff ought to have recorded the inference which he had drawn from the facts as part of his findings in fact (p 53A-B).

Mundie v Cardle, 1991 SCCR 118, *applied*.

Summary complaint

William Paterson and John McPherson were charged at the instance of Robert F Lees, procurator fiscal, Edin-

burgh, on a summary complaint which contained the following charges: "(1) on 31 October 1986, at the flat occupied by Jacqueline Wells, 12 Rossie Place, Edinburgh, you did carry out work in relation to a gas fitting namely did instal a Glow-worm Fuelsaver 30 Mk II open flued gas central heating boiler in the kitchen of the said flat without being competent to do so: contrary to reg 3 (1) of the Gas Safety (Installation and Use) Regulations 1984 and s 33 (1) (c) of the Health and Safety at Work, etc Act 1974 and in terms of s 34 of the Health and Safety at Work, etc Act 1974, as amended by the Gas Act 1986 (Appointed Day) Order 1986, Sched 7, para 18, evidence sufficient in the opinion of the Health and Safety Executive to justify proceedings came to the knowledge of the Health and Safety Executive on 11 December 1989; (2) on 15 December 1988 at place above libelled you did fail to carry out work in a proper and workmanlike manner in relation to a gas fitting, namely the rectification of faults to the construction of the flue of the abovementioned appliance previously installed by you as above libelled, whereby did cause spillage of combustion products including carbon monoxide into the said flat which did endanger the life of said Jacqueline Wells when she was affected by carbon monoxide poisoning on 21 November 1989 and 25 November 1989: Contrary to reg 4 (3) of the Gas Safety (Installation and Use) Regulations 1984 and s 33 (1) (c) of the Health and Safety at Work, etc Act 1974 and in terms of s 34 of the Health and Safety at Work, etc Act 1974, as amended by the Gas Act 1986 (Appointed Day) Order 1986, Sched 7, para 18, evidence sufficient in the opinion of the Health and Safety Executive to justify proceedings came to the knowledge of the Health and Safety Executive on 11 December 1989."

The accused pled not guilty and proceeded to trial. After trial the temporary sheriff (D T Crowe) found the accused guilty.

The accused appealed by way of stated case to the High Court against the decision of the sheriff.

Findings in fact

The sheriff found the following facts admitted or proved:

(1) The appellants are both full time firemen. They worked part time as plumbers trading as "McPherson and Paterson". They installed an open flue gas central heating boiler at the home of Miss Jacqueline Wells at 12 Rossie Place, Edinburgh. Said work was carried out in October 1986, the boiler being a Glowworm Fuelsaver Mk II. They were paid a total of £2,285.00 for said work. Notwithstanding their choice of part time trade, neither appellants were apparently conversant with or had a gas tightness gauge which is an essential piece of equipment used in gas fittings. (2) Said boiler was installed on an internal wall in the kitchen of said house, it being on the ground floor of a tenement. As the burner for said boiler is fuelled by gas, an adequate supply of air is required to ensure efficient combustion. There was no permanent air vent to supply air to said boiler either in the kitchen itself or in the adjoining

livingroom from which it was separated by louvred doors. This was contrary to the installation instructions (production 2), para 2.5.1. (3) When installed said boiler flue rose vertically for an adequate distance and then turned at right angles and ran horizontally before terminating slightly proud of the exterior face of the outside wall. This was contrary to para 2.3.1 of production 2 and paras 12.5 and 12.8.3 of production 3 which was the code of practice BS 5440. Said flue was inserted through a piece of board covering the aperture of a blocked off window. Adjoining said flue pipe was an extractor fan of the "xpelair" variety. Said fan was installed by the electrician who was asked by the appellants on the complainer's behalf to wire up the boiler. There was no other window in said kitchen. No apparent steps had been taken to comply with para 2.6, production 2. (4) In December 1988 the boiler emitted black smoke. The burner was found to be sooted up. The appliance was certified unsafe by the Gas Board pending modification. (5) Shortly thereafter the appellants cleaned and serviced the boiler and installed a right angled bend on the terminal of the flue so that the flue terminal was vertical and not horizontal. The terminal was close to the external wall. The boiler was put back in service.

(6) Said boiler was operated by a timer. Normally said boiler was operated automatically from 6 am to 9 am and from 5 pm to 10.30 pm. (7) On 21 November Miss Wells, who had been ill for some weeks with pelvic inflammatory disease, suffered a bad headache about 6 pm. She had been at home that day with the central heating on most of the time. She fell asleep on the settee in the livingroom and woke up about 8.50 pm feeling her head was about to explode. She went into the bathroom and thereafter fainted for about five minutes. She phoned her brother. She was semi-conscious and dizzy. She was taken to hospital. She was diagnosed as having a virus, discharged and went to her parents. She had recovered from her symptoms in a few hours. (8) She returned from her parents about 11 pm on 24 November 1989. She went to bed about midnight having spent about an hour talking to her zebra finches who lived in a cage on a chair in the livingroom. (9) She woke about 9 am on 25 November 1989 with an explosive headache. She put her head under the covers. Sometime thereafter she crawled to the bathroom. She felt weak and dizzy. She felt faint. The four zebra finches were lying dead at the bottom of their cage. (10) She phoned her brother Tony Wells between 11 and 11.30 am. He came immediately from his house close by and found her lying on the floor in the hall. She was crying, mumbling and very distressed. There was a smell of gas in the house. He switched off the gas supply and called the Gas Board.

(11) Shortly after noon on 25 November 1989 the Gas Board employees attended the flat. The heat exchanger in the boiler was sooted up. The reading of carbon monoxide in the primary flue, which was taken by inserting a probe attached to a Telegan meter through a grille in the casing of the boiler into the primary flue, exceeded 2,000 parts per million. The Telegan meter to measure same is only calibrated up to 2,000. Any reading over 1,000 requires that the appliance be sealed off as being dangerous. No readings were taken of carbon monoxide levels in the atmosphere of the flat. No tests were carried out to determine whether carbon monoxide was leaking from the boiler. (12) The boiler was subsequently replaced. (13) An open flued boiler is impractical in a ground floor flat of a tenement unless it can be vented to an existing chimney. Otherwise the flue pipe would have to extend above the height of the eaves of the building but the cooling effect of the exhaust gases would be such as to cause them to condense and preclude the efficient working of the flue, leading to a risk of flue gases spilling into the room in which the boiler was situated. Production 3 at para 12.6 deals with such problems. (14) The recommended form of boiler in such a flat is balanced flue boiler or fan assisted boiler. Both draw air from outside the building and expel combustion products to the open air. Both are sealed from the atmosphere of the room in which they operate. (15) The installation of an xpelair fan in a non-ventilated room containing an open flue boiler would possibly cause spillage of combustion products from the boiler into the atmosphere of the room, as the operation of the fan exhausts the air from the room with possible reversal of the operation of the boiler flue.

(16) Although there was no permanent ventilation in the kitchen or livingroom there was a blocked off fireplace in the livingroom. There was a brick missing from the bricked up fireplace. Behind said brick was soot and debris. As the open flued boiler flue was at a lesser height than the chimney which served the livingroom then, assuming the chimney to be unobstructed, the draw in the chimney would tend to overcome the draw in the boiler flue thus pulling combustion products into the room. (17) The insertion of right angled bends in a flue is bad practice. They restrict the natural convection effect of the hot gases. They cause turbulence. They enhance the likelihood of spillages into the room. (18) The termination of a flue close to and at right angles to an external wall is bad practice. There is a lessening of the draught which would dispel the flue gases and create a vacuum thus creating a draught in the flue. The termination of the flue parallel but close to the extension wall when coupled with a further right angled bend is bad practice. The additional bend mitigates against creating a good draught and the proximity of the terminal to the external wall reduces the effective air circulation surrounding same. (19) On the evening of 21 November and the morning of 25 November Miss Wells had symptoms commensurate with a significant level of carbon monoxide poisoning which might have been caused by a spillage of combustion products including carbon monoxide. The symptoms described by Miss Wells in evidence could be diagnosed as being commensurate with other medical conditions not related to carbon monoxide poisoning. Carbon monoxide is a colourless odourless gas. It is one of the combustion products from a gas fired boiler. It is attracted to the bloodstream and is accepted therein by the haemoglobin in preference to oxygen. It is potentially fatal to animals and birds depending on the length of exposure, the concentration of the gas, and the state of the victim. On

removal of the victim from the contaminated atmosphere recovery is spontaneous. Carbon monoxide poisoning in humans is often misdiagnosed as a virus. The complainer exhibited symptoms which were indicative of a potential life threatening concentration of carbon monoxide. (20) The level of concentration of carbon monoxide in the flat was never measured nor was the concentration in Miss Wells's blood. No tests were carried out to establish the cause of death of the birds. (21) If the combustion of the gas in the burner of a boiler is inefficient because of an inadequate oxygen supply, then the burner and heat exchanger will become sooted up and eventually blocked with carbon. Inadequate combustion will lead to the formation of abnormal quantities of carbon monoxide. Inadequate combustion may be caused by a lack of oxygen because of the lack of oxygen in the room containing the boiler or the absence of adequate oxygen at the burner because of the lack of dispersal of the products of combustion, or both.

Statutory provisions

The Gas Safety (Installation and Use) Regulations 1984 provide:

"3.—(1) No person shall carry out any work in relation to a gas fitting unless he is competent to do so. . . .

"4.— . . . (3) No person shall carry out any work in relation to a gas fitting otherwise than in a proper and workmanlike manner."

Cases referred to

Brazier v The Skipton Rock Co Ltd [1962] 1 WLR 471; [1962] 1 All ER 955.
Gibson v Skibs A/S Marina [1966] 2 All ER 476.
Mundie v Cardle, 1991 SCCR 118.

The sheriff appended a note to the findings in fact in the following terms, inter alia:

THE SHERIFF (D T CROWE).— . . . I heard evidence from two health and safety inspectors, from the complainer, her flatmate and her brother, three Gas Board employees, the senior medical adviser to the health and safety inspector and the professor of pathology. I found the witnesses both credible and reliable. No evidence was led for the defence.

With regard to charge 1 I had to have regard to the question of "competence" within the meaning of the regulations. I was referred by counsel for the appellants to *Brazier v The Skipton Rock Co Ltd*. It seemed to me that one must assess competence in a practical way using ordinary values. I accept that a competent person may act in a negligent manner but it did not seem to me that the scenario here was of that nature. The appellants committed a series of cardinal errors and indeed when recalled after the first incident, still remained blind to what was obvious to the competent fitters from the gas board who gave evidence. In making my findings I included the last sentence in finding 1 — not because it had any direct bearing on the charges but because it served to underline the appellants' woeful lack of elementary knowledge. I was told that the gas tightness gauge was a simple "U" tube with liquid therein

which would detect any leaks in the system between the meter and the several appliances and that the gauge was used as a matter of routine in all installations and servicing. . . .

The procurator fiscal depute said that their lack of competence was adequately illustrated by: (a) the installation of an open flued boiler in a tenement ground floor flat with no proper flueing; (b) the failure to instal any permanent ventilation; (c) the right angled bend and the horizontal run in the flue; (d) the insertion of the xpelair; (e) the fitting of the terminal on the surface of the wall in contravention of para 12.8.3 of production 3; (f) the uncorroborated but unchallenged evidence of the brick missing from the blocked off fireplace; (g) the installation of the boiler on an internal wall.

I would concur with what she said with the exception of para (f). Although clearly the installation on the internal wall increased the length of the flue, I would not be prepared to hold that this was bad practice, merely undesirable. In fairness I should also add that there was no evidence as to when the brick went missing from the fireplace other than that it was missing on 25 November 1989. I accordingly convicted both appellants on charge 1.

With regard to charge 2, I understood counsel to argue that I was obliged to look only at what was done to the installation by way of modification or rectification, in December 1988, namely the installation of the second 90 degree bend and the servicing and cleaning, in determining whether or not the works were proper and workmanlike. In other words, in terms of the regulations "work" could only cover acts and not omissions. I did not accept this argument. The appellants were the original installers. The Gas Board employee who inspected the installation on 1 December 1988 reported "boiler soot-up caused by no ventilation and badly fitted flue. Also xpelair fan fitted in kitchen". In my view the board merely made a diagnosis — it was left to the expertise of the installer to rectify the faults. That apart, the small amount of modification they did, did not even encompass all the points made by the board employee.

The Crown's position was that the construction of the flue was fundamentally bad and no modification could overcome the difficulties. I took the view that the appellants had a second opportunity to make good a fundamentally defective installation. They failed to grasp this chance.

The aggravation of endangering the life of Miss Wells was the final factor to consider. There was no evidence of analysis of the atmosphere in the flat. At best the primary flue showed a very high level of carbon monoxide. In contrast the heat exchanger was sooted up, the flue construction mitigated against dispersal of the flue gases, the flat lacked permanent ventilation, the central heating boiler had been on and in addition on two occasions the occupant showed symptoms identical with carbon monoxide poisoning. On the second occasion the birds were found dead. In my view there is an irresistible inference to be drawn, namely that Miss Wells was suffering on those two occasions from carbon monoxide poisoning.

A   That leaves the question of whether the level of poisoning was such as to allow me to conclude that her life was in danger. The evidence that Dr Morrison and Professor Busuttil gave, both of whose evidence was by way of opinion, suggested that Miss Wells had symptoms consistent with carbon monoxide poisoning of between 20 and 50 per cent. Above 50 per cent in the blood is likely to be fatal. I concluded that there was a danger to life because Miss Wells exhibited symptoms consistent with a significant level of contamination and except for her actings in contacting her

B   brother, there was nothing apparent to remove the contamination from the atmosphere and the mere cessation of the boiler would not remove the carbon monoxide. I was told that as the gas has a greater affinity with the blood than oxygen then the process of saturation of the blood will continue until the subject is removed from the contaminated atmosphere or dies, although it has to be conceded that with the increased takeup of carbon monoxide, respiration slows so that the takeup into the bloodstream slows. Dr Morrison stated that to cause

C   death in a canary (not a zebra finch) he would expect a concentration in excess of 1,200 parts per million. In a resting adult a similar concentration would cause death in something over two hours.

    In my opinion it is only by good fortune that a tragedy was averted. If I understand correctly, the Gas Board make a diagnosis of the apparent faults in the installation. Thereafter the occupier takes steps to rectify the faults by employing a contractor. Once the faults are rectified or even if nothing is done, the occupier can

D   then inform the Gas Board that the installation has been reconnected. There is no check by a Gas Board official that the remedial work has been properly done nor if it has been done at all. I therefore welcome the introduction of the registration scheme for gas installers which I understand is shortly to come into effect.

Appeal

E   The sheriff posed the following questions for the opinion of the High Court, inter alia:

    (1) Was I correct to repel a submission of no case to answer in respect of the first named appellant?

    (2) Was I correct to repel a submission of no case to answer in respect of the second named appellant? . . .

    (4) Do the findings in fact disclose sufficient evidence to entitle me to convict the appellants or either of them on charge 1?

F   (5) Is there sufficient evidence narrated in my findings in fact to entitle me to have convicted the appellants or either of them on charge 2?

    (6) Was I entitled to convict either or both of the appellants of all or part of the aggravation libelled in charge 2, namely "whereby did cause spillage of combustion products including carbon monoxide into the said flat which did endanger the life of said Jacqueline Wells when she was affected by carbon monoxide on 21 November 1989 and 25 November 1989"?

    (7) Was I entitled to hold that either or both of the appellants' failure to carry out certain work in a proper G and workmanlike manner could, having regard to the definition of "work" contained in reg 2 of the Gas Safety (Installation and Use) Regulations 1984, include failure to replace the flue mentioned in the libel of charge 2?

    (8) Was there sufficient evidence disclosed in my findings in fact to entitle me to hold that the Crown had proved beyond reasonable doubt that combustion products were spilled into the premises mentioned in the libel of charge 2? . . .

    (10) Was I entitled to hold that the Crown had proved H beyond reasonable doubt that the said Jacqueline Wells was affected by carbon monoxide poisoning?

    (11) Was I entitled to conclude that Dr Lightfoot and Mr Boyd were not exercising powers conferred upon them by s 20 of the Health and Safety at Work, etc Act 1974 when they interviewed the accused?

    The appeals were argued before the High Court on 20 November 1991.

                                      I

    On 12 December 1991 the court *answered* all of the questions except question 12 (which related to sentence) in the *affirmative*, *answered* question 12 in the *negative* and *refused* the appeals.

    The following opinion of the court was delivered by the Lord Justice Clerk (Ross):

OPINION OF THE COURT.—The appellants are William Paterson and John McPherson. They went to J trial in the sheriff court at Edinburgh on a complaint libelling two charges. The first charge libelled a contravention of reg 3 (1) of the Gas Safety (Installation and Use) Regulations 1984, and the second charge libelled a contravention of reg 4 (3) of the same regulations. After a fairly lengthy trial both appellants were found guilty as libelled; they were each fined £350 on the first charge and £500 on the second charge. They have both appealed against conviction and sentence by means of a stated case. K

    In opening the appeal, counsel on behalf of both appellants drew attention to the terms of the regulations which were said to have been breached. Regulation 3 (1) of the Gas Safety (Installation and Use) Regulations 1984 (SI 1984/1358) provides as follows: [his Lordship quoted the terms of reg 3 (1) and then reg 4 (3) and continued:]

    As regards the conviction of the appellants on charge 1, counsel pointed out that the essence of the charge L was that work had been carried out by the appellants when they were not competent to do the work. He drew attention to the fact that there was no finding in fact to the effect that the appellants were not competent to do the work, and he submitted that that was fatal to their conviction on this charge. He recognised under reference to a letter dated 15 April 1991 from the Crown Office with proposed adjustments for the respondent, that the respondent had invited the sheriff to make a finding to the following effect: "Neither appellant was competent to instal said boiler." The sheriff has indi-

cated in the stated case that he rejected that adjustment
as it appeared to him that this was not a matter of fact
but a matter of opinion to be drawn from the facts. The
advocate depute pointed out under reference to *Mundie
v Cardle* that the sheriff was under misapprehension
regarding this and that he ought to have made a finding
in fact in these terms.

We agree with the advocate depute that the sheriff
has not dealt with this issue properly. It is clear from
the sheriff's note that he accepted the submission of the
respondent's depute to the effect that lack of competence on the part of the appellants had been established.
He clearly drew an inference of lack of competence from
a number of factors which were placed before him. In
these circumstances what the sheriff ought to have done
was to record the inference which he had drawn from
the facts as part of his findings in fact. What the sheriff
has failed to do is to state the case in accordance with
what the court said in *Mundie v Cardle*. In that case
it was pointed out that if a sheriff has drawn an inference from the facts, then the inference which he has
drawn should be recorded as part of his findings in fact.
Accordingly provided that the sheriff was justified in
drawing the inference, he ought to have made a finding
in fact to the effect that neither appellant was competent to instal said boiler. In terms of s 452 (4) (f) of the
Criminal Procedure (Scotland) Act 1975 this court is
entitled in hearing this appeal to take account of any
matter proposed in any adjustment rejected by the trial
judge and of the reasons for such rejection. We are
accordingly entitled to proceed upon the basis that the
sheriff was satisfied by the evidence that the appellants
were not competent to instal the gas boiler. It is,
however, necessary for this court to consider whether
the sheriff was entitled to draw that inference from the
facts found proved. The question then arises as to what
is meant by the words "unless he is competent to do so".

Counsel drew attention to *Brazier v The Skipton Rock
Co Ltd*. That case concerned regulations requiring an
inspection to be carried out by a competent person.
When considering what was meant by a competent
person in that context, Winn J (as he then was) said:
"In my judgment it means a man who, on a fair assessment of the requirements of the task, of the factors
involved, the problems to be studied and the degree of
risk of danger implicit, can fairly as well as reasonably
be regarded by the manager, and in fact is regarded at
the time by the manager as competent to perform such
an inspection."

Counsel also referred to *Gibson v Skibs A/S Marina*.
In that case under different regulations examination and
testing required to be carried out by a competent person.
Cantley J said: "I think that a competent person for
this task is a person who is a practical and reasonable
man, who knows what to look for and knows how to
recognise it when he sees it."

Counsel maintained that the test was an objective one.
He also submitted that a competent person might make
a mistake and might be negligent, and he maintained
that on the findings made in the present case no inference of lack of competence could be drawn. At the
highest the appellants might be thought to have been
negligent but he maintained that there was no justification for drawing the inference that they lacked competence.

Counsel subjected the findings which the sheriff made
in relation to charge 1 to a close examination. We do
not, however, consider it necessary to consider these
findings seriatim. In his note the sheriff sets out various
factors based upon the findings in fact which the Crown
maintained demonstrated lack of competence. These are
numbered (a) to (g). Before this court the advocate
depute founded only upon the items (a) to (e). When
considering what was meant by the words "unless he
is competent to do so" in reg 3 (1) the advocate depute
accepted that there was a distinction between being
negligent and being incompetent. He submitted that
essentially it was a difference between knowing how to
do the job properly and being careless in the execution
of the work on the one hand and not knowing how to
do it properly in the first place on the other hand. A
man lacked competence if he did not know how to do
the job properly in the first place.

In our opinion that distinction drawn by the advocate depute is a valid one. A person who is competent
to carry out any work is a person who has the knowledge
and ability necessary to perform it properly. In the light
of the factors listed (a) to (e) the sheriff was entitled to
draw an inference of lack of competence. These factors
upon which he relied are as follows: [his Lordship
quoted factors (a) to (e) set out in the sheriff's note at
p 51G-H, and continued:]

Having regard to the foregoing factors, we are satisfied that the sheriff was entitled to draw the inference
that neither of the appellants had the knowledge and
ability to do the job properly and that accordingly
neither was competent to instal the boiler.

As regards charge 2, counsel pointed out that the question was whether the remedial work carried out on 15
December 1988 had been carried out in a proper and
workmanlike manner. He submitted that there was no
specification of the work which the appellants were
alleged to have carried out in an unworkmanlike
manner, and he contended that no facts had been stated
from which the sheriff was entitled to conclude that they
were guilty of this charge.

The advocate depute on the other hand maintained
that in the light of the findings there was sufficient
material before the sheriff to entitle him to hold that
the appellants had failed to carry out the work in a
proper and workmanlike manner. In this connection the
advocate depute drew attention in particular to findings 4, 5, 10, 11, 17, 18 and 19.

In our opinion in this context findings 4, 5, 17 and
18 are of particular significance. From these findings
it appears that in December 1988 the boiler emitted
black smoke, the burner was found to be sooted up and
the appliance was certified unsafe by the gas board
pending modification. Shortly thereafter the appellants
cleaned and serviced the boiler and installed a right
angled bend on the terminal of the flue so that the flue

A terminal was vertical, and not horizontal. The terminal was close to the external wall. The boiler was put back into service. It is plain from findings 17 and 18 that the insertion of right angled bends in a flue is bad practice, and that the termination of a flue close to and at right angles to an external wall is bad practice. In these circumstances we are satisfied that the sheriff was entitled to conclude that the appellants had failed to carry out the work of rectification in a proper and workmanlike manner.

B   Counsel's final submission in relation to charge 2 was that there were no findings in fact to support the aggravation libelled in the charge, namely, that the work carried out by the appellants had caused the spillage of combustion products including carbon monoxide into the flat which endangered the life of the complainer. Counsel drew particular attention to finding 19 and reminded the court that the sheriff's finding was that on the two occasions in question the complainer had symptoms commensurate with a significant level of carbon monoxide poisoning which might have been C caused by a spillage of combustion products including carbon monoxide. The advocate depute, however, pointed out that the Crown's case depended upon circumstantial evidence. It was true as stated in finding 20 that the level of concentration of carbon monoxide in the flat was never measured nor was the concentration in the complainer's blood, but the question was whether the aggravation of the charge was established by circumstantial evidence. The advocate depute maintained that the whole circumstances narrated by the D sheriff including the fact that carbon monoxide is potentially fatal to animals and birds, and that the four finches in a cage in the flat died, entitled the sheriff to conclude that the aggravation was proved and that the complainer's life was endangered by the spillage of combustion products including carbon monoxide into her flat.

In his note the sheriff states: "In my view there is an irresistible inference to be drawn, namely that Miss Wells was suffering on those two occasions from carbon E monoxide poisoning." As we have already observed under reference to *Mundie v Cardle*, since the sheriff drew such an inference he should have recorded that as part of his findings in fact. Having regard to the findings in fact and the inferences which the sheriff indicates in his note he was prepared to draw, we are satisfied in relation to charge 2 that the Crown had proved a failure on the part of the appellants to carry out the work in a proper and workmanlike manner, resultant spillage of combustion products into the flat, F and the endangering of the life of the complainer when she was affected by carbon monoxide poisoning on the two dates libelled. We are accordingly satisfied that the sheriff was entitled to convict the appellant of these two charges.

No fewer than 12 questions have been stated in this case. We would accordingly answer the questions as follows: Question 1 — Yes. Question 2 — Yes. Question 3 — Counsel indicated that he was not pursuing this matter further and accordingly of consent question 3 falls to be answered in the affirmative. Question 4

— Yes. Question 5 — Yes. Question 6 — Yes. Question 7 — Yes. Question 8 — Yes. Question 9 — Counsel G did not pursue this point and accordingly of consent this question can also be answered in the affirmative. Question 10 — Yes. Question 11 — Again counsel did not pursue this point and accordingly this question can be answered of consent in the affirmative. Question 12 — Counsel explained that he only sought to raise the issue of sentence in the event of the court holding that in relation to charge 2 the Crown had proved a failure to carry out the work in a proper and workmanlike manner, but had failed to establish the aggravations H libelled in the charge. Since, however, we are satisfied that the sheriff was entitled to find the appellants guilty of charge 2 as libelled, it follows that no challenge is now being made of the penalties imposed by the sheriff. We shall accordingly answer question 12 in the negative.

Counsel for Appellants, Hamilton, QC; Solicitors, Erskine MacAskill & Co — Counsel for Respondents, Macdonald, QC, AD; Solicitor, J D Lowe, Crown Agent. I

P W F

Fitzpatrick v Inland Revenue Commissioners   J

FIRST DIVISION
THE LORD PRESIDENT (HOPE),
LORDS McCLUSKEY AND CULLEN
14 FEBRUARY 1992

Revenue — Income tax — Necessary expenses — Journalists required to purchase newspapers for background reading — Whether condition of employment — Whether K *expenses incurred "necessarily in the performance of" their duties — Income and Corporation Taxes Act 1970 (c 10), s 189 (1).*

Five taxpayers were employed as journalists by the same employer. During the year of assessment 1985-86 they were each paid an allowance for the purchase of newspapers, which formed part of their assessable emoluments. They spent their entire allowances on newspapers, chosen by themselves, which they read largely in their own time. The Inland Revenue Commissioners refused their claims to have the expenditure deducted from their assessable emoluments on the ground that it had not been incurred "wholly, exclusively and necessarily in the performance of [the duties of the employment]" in terms of s 189 (1) of the Income and Corporation Taxes Act 1970. The taxpayers appealed to the special commissioners, who found in fact that such background reading was a common practice in the industry and that if the taxpayers had not undertaken such reading they would have discharged

their duties less effectively, would have been
A reprimanded by their employers and might not have
kept their jobs, but that it was not an implied condition of their employment that they did so. The commissioners concluded that, while the tests of "wholly
and exclusively" had been met, the expenditure had not
been incurred "necessarily in the performance of [their
duties]". The taxpayers appealed to the Inner House
by way of stated cases under s 56 of the Taxes Management Act 1970. They argued that the special commissioners should have found that the reading was an
implied condition of their employment, and, in any
B event, that it was so intimately connected with their
work that it was part of their duties. It was incurred
necessarily because without it they could not have performed their work effectively.

Held (Lord McCluskey *dissenting*), (1) that on the
evidence the commissioners had been entitled to find
that it was not a condition of the taxpayers' employment that they bought and read the newspapers (pp
60G-61C, 72G and 73C-D) (per the Lord President
C (Hope): in any event, such a condition would have established at most that the expenditure had been "necessarily" incurred, but not that it had been incurred in
the performance of their duties (p 61D-E)); (2) that "the
performance of the duties" did not include putting
oneself in a position to, or enabling oneself to, perform
the duties of the employment (pp 58A-C, 63E-F and
71F) (*Humbles v Brooks* (1962) 40 TC 500, *followed*);
(3) that the taxpayers had in general bought and read
the newspapers in order to maintain a general knowledge
of current affairs, and also to provide background
D reading before investigating specific subjects, and to
avoid duplicating stories published in other papers, all
of which activities were preliminary or preparatory to
the performance of their duties, or at best were undertaken to enable them to perform their duties, rather than
having been undertaken "in the performance of" their
duties (pp 63D-G and 73H-I); (4) that while there had
been evidence in respect of one of the taxpayers that
she had on occasion used material from other papers
as a direct foundation for commentaries on topical
E events, in the absence of evidence to identify that part
of her expenditure which had been incurred for that
purpose the only conclusion available was that, taken
as a whole, the test of "wholly and exclusively" could
not be satisfied by her expenditure (pp 62G-H and
73K-L); and that accordingly it could not be said that
on the facts found by the special commissioners they
had not been entitled to refuse the appeals; and appeals
refused.

Smith v Abbott [1992] 1 WLR 201; [1991] STC 661,
F *distinguished.*

Observed (per the Lord President (Hope)), that it
was hard to understand how the special commissioners
could have held that the test of "wholly and exclusively"
had been met when they had decided that the expenditure had not been incurred "in the performance of the
duties", for it would only have been if the expenditure
had been found to have been incurred in the performance of those duties that any question could have
arisen as to whether it had been "wholly and exclusively" so incurred (p 64B-C).

Per Lord McCluskey (*dissenting*): The special commissioners had failed to make findings in fact which G
addressed precisely what were the duties of holders of
the taxpayers' employments and what was necessarily
involved in the performance thereof; if the absence of
findings in fact on essential matters had arisen from the
failure of the taxpayers to discharge the onus that rested
upon them to demonstrate their entitlement to the
deduction, then statements to that effect by the commissioners were to be expected, but were absent; given
that the commissioners had thereby failed to address
certain essential facts, the proper conclusion was that
they had reached their decision without considering all H
of the relevant issues, which they were not entitled to
do; accordingly, the court was entitled to reach its own
conclusions on the evidence, and, standing that
evidence, it could not be said that the taxpayers would
have been performing the duties of their employment
if they had been doing them so ineffectively that they
would have been reprimanded and would have put their
jobs in peril; in the nature of their work, research was
an integral part of the duties to be performed even if
it was also a preparation for a particular aspect of that I
performance; and accordingly the appeals ought to have
been allowed (pp 67L-68E, 69B-C and E-H and
70B-C, G-H, I and K).

Per the Lord President (Hope): The approach adopted
by Lord McCluskey was at variance with the law and
practice to be applied by the court in such appeals, for
the onus was on the taxpayer to satisfy the special commissioners that the assessment against which he
appealed was wrong, and it was not the practice for the
commissioners to set out facts which had not been estab- J
lished by the evidence; nor had Lord McCluskey's criticisms formed part of the taxpayers' case (p 65A-E).

**Appeal from the special commissioners of income
tax**

Thomas Fitzpatrick, Rosemary Long, Cameron
Simpson, James Traynor and Barclay McBain appealed
by stated case against decisions by the special commissioners of income tax refusing their appeals against K
refusals by the Commissioners of Inland Revenue of
their claims for the deduction, from their emoluments
assessable to income tax under Sched E, of expenditure
incurred by them on the purchase of newspapers and
periodicals. The question of law in each of the stated
cases was whether, on the facts found by the special
commissioners, they had been entitled to conclude that
no deduction could be made under s 189 (1) of the
Income and Corporation Taxes Act 1970.

Statutory provisions   L

The Income and Corporation Taxes Act 1970
provides:

"189.—(1) If the holder of an office or employment
is necessarily obliged to incur and defray out of the
emoluments thereof the expenses of travelling in the
performance of the duties of the office or employment,
or of keeping and maintaining a horse to enable him
to perform the same, or otherwise to expend money
wholly, exclusively and necessarily in the performance

A of the said duties, there may be deducted from the emoluments to be assessed the expenses so necessarily incurred and defrayed."

Cases referred to

Brown v Bullock [1961] 1 WLR 53; [1961] 1 All ER 206; (1960) 40 TC 1.

Edwards v Bairstow and Harrison [1956] AC 14; [1955] 3 WLR 410; [1955] 3 All ER 48.

Frasers (Glasgow) Bank Ltd v Commissioners of Inland Revenue, 1962 SLT 273; 1963 SLT 117; 1962 SC
B 371; 1963 SC (HL) 18.

Humbles v Brooks (1962) 40 TC 500.

Inland Revenue Commissioners v Toll Property Co Ltd, 1952 SLT 371; 1952 SC 387.

Lomax v Newton [1953] 1 WLR 1123; [1953] 2 All ER 801; (1953) 34 TC 558.

Pook v Owen [1970] AC 244; [1969] 2 WLR 775; [1969] 2 All ER 1; (1969) 45 TC 571.

Ricketts v Colquhoun [1926] AC 1; (1926) 10 TC 118.

Simpson v Tate [1925] 2 KB 214; (1925) 9 TC 314.
C *Smith v Abbott* [1992] 1 WLR 201; [1991] STC 661.

Taylor v Provan [1975] AC 194; [1974] 2 WLR 394; [1974] 1 All ER 1201.

Appeal

The appeals were heard by the First Division on 14, 15, 16 and 17 January 1992.

On 14 February 1992 the court *answered* the questions of law in the *affirmative* and *refused* the appeals.
D
THE LORD PRESIDENT (HOPE).—The question for decision by the special commissioners in each of these appeals was whether a deduction should be made from the appellants' emoluments to be assessed to income tax under Sched E for expenditure incurred by them on the purchase of newspapers and periodicals.

The appellants were all employed as journalists by George Outram & Co Ltd during the year of assessment,
E which was 1985-86. They each received from the company during that year an allowance of £1,063 for the purchase of newspapers, which formed part of their assessable emoluments. It was agreed between the parties in each case that the whole of that allowance was spent on purchasing newspapers and periodicals during the year. The appellants' claims for the deduction of that expenditure from their assessable emoluments under s 189 (1) of the Income and Corporation Taxes Act 1970 were refused, and it was against that refusal that they appealed to the special commissioners.
F Their appeals were all heard together at a single hearing, since they had been selected as test cases for a number of other similar appeals, and it was agreed that the evidence given in each case could be treated as evidence in the other four. Each of the appellants was employed in a different capacity, so although the background to the question of law was the same in each case the facts of each case required to some extent to be considered separately. Each appellant gave evidence in support of his or her own appeal in order to explain the work which was done and the purposes for which the expenditure

was incurred. Various documents were produced in each case, but there was no other evidence. It was held by G the special commissioners that no deduction could be made for the expenditure because the evidence had not established that it fell within the terms of the subsection. The reasons for their determination were set out in a single written decision which they issued on 18 May 1989. The appellants expressed dissatisfaction with the determination as being erroneous in point of law and requested the commissioners to state a case for the opinion of this court. The question of law which we now have to decide is whether, on the facts found by H them to be admitted or proved, the special commissioners were entitled to conclude that the deduction claimed in each case could not be made.

It was necessary for the special commissioners to prepare a separate stated case for the purposes of each appeal in terms of s 56 of the Taxes Management Act 1970. But the cases which they signed on 28 August 1990 were extremely brief because they contained no findings of fact and were confined largely to matters of form and procedure. A copy of the decision of 18 I May 1989 was appended to each case. When the appeals first came before the court in the single bills the appellants claimed that the cases were defective in two respects. The first was that the commissioners had failed to include sufficient questions in each case to focus the issues of law between the parties. The second was that they had failed to set out in each case their findings of fact. There appeared to us to be no substance in the first point, but we were satisfied that the commissioners had failed to fulfil their statutory duty in terms of s 56 J (4) to set forth in the cases stated the facts upon which the cases were being stated for our determination. On 28 September 1990, for reasons given in the opinion of that date, we remitted each case to the commissioners for amendment [reported 1991 SLT 841]. The cases which are now before us have been amended in accordance with our interlocutor by the setting out in the body of each stated case in separate numbered paragraphs the facts which the commissioners found admitted or proved and the contentions of each party K to these appeals. The appellants were at first dissatisfied with the cases as so amended, and on 9 July 1991 they appeared again in the single bills on a motion which sought to have the cases remitted again to the commissioners so that findings of fact in respect of all the witnesses could be incorporated in each case and points on which the appellants had asked for findings to be made could be considered further. Their motions were refused in hoc statu on the ground that it would be more appropriate for the matter to be considered in detail at L the hearing of the appeals. The appellants were still dissatisfied, and they presented an application for judicial review of the determination of the commissioners on the ground that fundamental defects in the procedure had vitiated the proceedings. On 26 November 1991 Lord Coulsfield sustained the respondents' plea to the relevancy and dismissed the application [reported 1992 SLT 1069, sub nom *Simpson v Inland Revenue Commissioners*].

But all these difficulties had been resolved by the stage

A when the appeals came before us for the hearing of the argument. A joint minute has now been lodged in each case, in which it has been agreed between the parties that the findings of fact in each of the stated cases may be treated as including the findings of fact in the stated cases in the associated appeals. It has also been agreed that the decision of the special commissioners dated 18 May 1989 may be treated as appended to each stated case. Counsel for both parties accepted that the findings of fact and the contentions which are set out in each case had, to that extent, superseded the decision,

B but it was agreed that the decision might nevertheless be looked at for the reasons given by the special commissioners for refusing the appeals. Consequently no motion was made to us at any stage in the course of the hearing that the cases should be remitted to the special commissioners for further findings. Counsel for the appellants said that, except in regard to an argument about their conditions of employment to which I shall return later in this opinion, he did not wish to add to or detract from any of the findings, and it was

C on the facts found by the commissioners that he invited us to answer the question of law in each case in the negative and allow the appeals.

George Outram & Co Ltd own two newspapers known as the *Glasgow Herald* and the *Evening Times*. The *Glasgow Herald* circulates throughout Scotland, but the *Evening Times* circulates mainly in the area of Glasgow. As has already been indicated, the appellants were each employed in a different capacity during the year of assessment. Thomas Fitzpatrick was working

D as an assistant picture editor with the *Evening Times*. Rosemary Long was also working for the *Evening Times*, as a features writer and weekly columnist. The other three appellants all worked for the *Glasgow Herald*, on which Barclay McBain was a staff reporter. Cameron Simpson was a general sub-editor and deputy television editor and he did some feature writing. James Traynor was a sports sub-editor. We were informed that, although it was agreed that the evidence of each could be treated as evidence in the other appeals, the appel-

E lants spoke almost exclusively about their own circumstances. There is no indication in the findings of fact that any of the appellants knew what the others were doing in the course of their working day. It was left to each of them to decide for themselves which newspapers or periodicals to purchase with the newspaper allowance which they received.

Section 189 (1) of the 1970 Act is in these terms: [his Lordship quoted the terms of s 189 (1) and continued:]

F This provision was first enacted many years ago, at a time when the conditions under which people worked, and travelled to work, were very different from what they are today. Nevertheless the rule, which appeared in s 51 of the Income Tax Act 1853, has been re-enacted in almost exactly the same terms ever since. It is now to be found in s 198 (1) of the Income and Corporation Taxes Act 1988. We must take the provision as we find it and apply it as it stands to the facts. This is not a case about the expenses of travelling, nor is it one of those cases, which must now be extremely rare, about the expenses of keeping and maintaining a horse to

G perform the duties of the office or employment. So the important elements for present purposes are to be found in the third branch of the rule, in the phrase "or otherwise to expend money wholly, exclusively and necessarily in the performance of the said duties" — that is to say, the duties of the office or employment out of the emoluments of which the expenses have been necessarily incurred and defrayed.

There was no dispute in the argument before us in these appeals about the tests which must be applied. Counsel for the appellant taxpayers accepted that the

H requirements of the subsection were exceedingly strict, and that in order to succeed the appellants had to demonstrate to the commissioners that the expenditure was incurred necessarily in the performance of the duties of the employment. He recognised that, following *Ricketts v Colquhoun* and later cases, the phrase "in the performance of the duties" must be given a strict interpretation and that it does not mean "in order to enable the duties to be performed". His position was that the tests had been applied too rigidly to the facts

I by the commissioners, and that, in the words of Lord Radcliffe in *Edwards v Bairstow* [1956] AC at p 36, the true and only reasonable conclusion from their findings in each case was that the expenditure satisfied the necessary tests and should be allowed as a deduction. He drew our attention to the conclusion by the special commissioners that what they described as the "wholly and exclusively" test was satisfied. He directed his argument to the remaining part of the statutory formula, that is to the words "necessarily in the performance of the said

J duties". He said that the conclusion to be drawn from the findings was that the appellants' expenditure was so closely tied to the performance of their duties as journalists that it should be regarded as having been incurred in the performance of these duties. He accepted that an objective test was to be applied. As he put it, the duties must demand the outlays, irrespective of the appellants' own views as to what was required.

In support of these submissions he referred us to a number of authorities. In *Simpson v Tate* it was held

K that a county medical officer was not entitled to deduct from his emoluments sums expended by him as subscriptions to various professional societies to which he belonged. Rowlatt J saw this expenditure as incurred not in the performance of the duties of the office but in order to keep himself qualified to perform them, by keeping himself abreast of developments and knowledge of the day. In *Brown v Bullock* the manager of a branch of a bank in the West End of London was unsuccessful in his claim that there should be allowed as a deduc-

L tion part of the annual subscription for membership of a West End club which was paid by the bank and was agreed to form part of his emoluments. There was a finding in that case that club membership was virtually a condition or requisite of managerial appointment and that it would be unlikely that a manager would be appointed who would refuse to join the appropriate club or clubs. Nevertheless when the question was asked whether the sum paid was necessarily incurred in the performance of his duties as a bank manager, the short answer was seen to be "no". Lord Evershed MR at p 10

A said: "What his employers may think is desirable for him to do, socially, is one thing. Performance of the duties of manager of their branch is something else".

Counsel for the appellants accepted these decisions as illustrative of the point which was discussed at greater length by Ungoed-Thomas J in *Humbles v Brooks* at pp 502-504. He pointed out in that case that "in the performance of the duties" does not include qualifying initially to perform the duties of the office, or even keeping qualified to perform them, nor does the require-
B ment of the employer that the expenditure should be incurred, of itself, bring the expense within the rule. In that case, which concerned the headmaster at a primary school, the cost of attending a series of weekend lectures in history at a college for adult education for the purpose of improving his background knowledge was disallowed as a deduction. The taxpayer felt that the course was essential to keep himself up to date so as provide him with material which he reproduced in the history lessons which he was required to give. In
C his comment on this argument Ungoed-Thomas J said this at p 504: "It is, to my mind, qualifying for lecturing, or putting himself in a position to prepare a lecture. It is not the preparation of a lecture. In this sense the distinction is between preparation for lecturing on the one hand and preparation of a lecture on the other".

This, said counsel for the appellants, was the crux of the argument in the present appeals. When the findings in the cases were examined it could be seen that the expenditure on the purchase of the newspapers and
D the periodicals was related to the performance of the duties, not merely to preparation for their performance. The special commissioners had erred in law because they ought to have held that it was a condition of the employment that this expenditure should be incurred. In any event they should have held that it was so intimately connected with what the appellants did as journalists that it was incurred as part of the duties of their employment. And it was plainly necessary, because it was clear on the findings that without this expenditure,
E and the reading and cutting which went with it, the appellants simply could not do their job effectively as journalists.

Counsel for the Commissioners of Inland Revenue, in moving us to refuse the appeals, submitted that the argument should be approached in this way. The issues were (1) whether the expenditure was incurred in the performance of the duties of the employment and (2) whether, if so, it was wholly, exclusively and necessar-
F ily so incurred. The proper starting point was to ask the question whether, on the facts found by the commissioners, the appellants read the newspapers and periodicals and took cuttings from them in the performance of the duties of their employment. Only if that question was answered in the affirmative should one then ask whether any of the restrictive adverbs apply. It was submitted that there were no findings in the cases which met the narrow tests which were prescribed by s 189 (1). In particular, it could not be said that the true and only reasonable conclusion which the special commissioners could have reached on these findings was that

the appellants incurred the expenditure in the performance of the duties of their employment. This test was G strict, narrow and objective. In *Ricketts v Colquhoun* at (1926) 10 TC, p 133 Viscount Cave LC said, in regard to travelling expenses: "They must be expenses which the holder of an office is necessarily obliged to incur — that is to say, obliged by the very fact that he holds the office, and has to perform the duties — and they must be incurred in, that is, in the course of, the performance of those duties".

We were referred also to *Taylor v Provan* in which *Ricketts v Colquhoun* was distinguished and the expenses H of travelling were held to have been necessarily incurred in the performance of the duties of the taxpayer's office as a non-resident director. The significant point about that case for present purposes was that the majority of their Lordships accepted the propositions of law which were laid down in *Ricketts v Colquhoun* as correct. Lord Salmon at [1975] AC, p 226 said: "In my view, the decision in *Ricketts v Colquhoun* does no more than confirm the proposition that 'in the performance of the duties' must be given a strict interpretation and does not mean I 'in order to enable the duties to be performed' ".

It was said that on a proper analysis of the findings in these stated cases there was no sound basis for the appellants' argument that there had been any error of law by the commissioners. The issue was plainly one of fact and degree for them to decide, and at this stage it was sufficient for the respondents to say that it had not been shown that the determination was one which, on the findings, they were not entitled to reach.

The approach which we were invited by the respon- J dents to take to these appeals therefore was to look at the facts found and to see whether they justified the determination by the commissioners. The point was made that their determination must be accepted unless they were bound by those facts to decide the case the other way. Reference was made to *Frasers (Glasgow) Bank Ltd v Commissioners of Inland Revenue*, in which the onus which rests on the taxpayer in such cases was discussed. The facts which were admitted or proved in the case were said by Lord President Clyde at 1962 K SLT, p 279 to be somewhat meagre and to justify the special commissioners in concluding that the appellants had not established that the assessment was wrong. Lord Guthrie, who dissented, said at p 283 that the ground stated by the commissioners for their determination was unconvincing and that he did not think that it was correct. The appeal was refused because the majority held that the determination was justified by the facts found by the special commissioners. In the House of Lords, 1963 SLT at p 118, Lord Reid endorsed this L approach when he said: "I have no doubt that the decision of the Special Commissioners was right. The reasons given by the Special Commissioners are not very adequate and the majority of the First Division reached their decision on the facts without relying on the decision of the Special Commissioners. I would take the same course".

The point of this reference was to support the submission that it was primarily to the facts found by the commissioners and not to the reasoning stated in their

decision that we should look in order to see whether
the determination was one which they were entitled to
make on these findings.

It has long been recognised that the requirements
which must be satisfied to obtain the deduction are
much more severe than those which enable a deduction to be made when computing the amount of profits
or gains to be charged to income tax under Sched D.
In *Ricketts v Colquhoun* at p 135 Lord Blanesburgh said
this of the rule: "Undoubtedly its most striking characteristic is its jealously restricted language, some of it
repeated apparently to heighten its effect. But I am also
struck by this, that, as it seems to me, although undoubtedly less obtrusively, the language of the Rule points
to the expenses with which it is concerned as being confined to those which each and every occupant of the
particular office is necessarily obliged to incur in the
performance of its duties, to expenses imposed upon
each holder and ex necessitate of his office and to such
expenses only".

In *Lomax v Newton* [1953] 1 WLR at p 1125, Vaisey
J observed that the provisions of the rule are notoriously rigid, narrow and restricted in their operation.
In *Brown v Bullock* at p 6, Danckwerts J said that the
rule had again and again been criticised judicially for
being extremely narrow, and that it was undoubtedly
in terms much more severe and much more narrow than
the corresponding rule for Sched D. I mention these
remarks only to emphasise the importance of precision
in a case of this kind. It is necessary to adhere precisely
to the language of the subsection, because any attempt
to rephrase or paraphrase the language may easily lead
to a softening of the rule. It is also necessary for precision to be exercised in the examination of the evidence
and, at the stage of an appeal by case stated, in the
examination of the findings by the commissioners. In
my opinion the court must always be careful not to
attempt to decide these cases on any other basis than
that which the commissioners have provided in their
findings of fact, since our jurisdiction in terms of s 56
(6) of the Taxes Management Act 1970 is limited to
determining any question or questions of law arising
on the case.

I think that it is also worth quoting in this context
a passage in the speech of Lord Morris of Borth-y-Gest
in *Taylor v Provan* [1975] AC at pp 210-211, where
he was discussing the rule as it appeared in para 7 of
Sched 9 to the Income Tax Act 1952, which was in identical terms to s 189 (1) of the 1970 Act: "In considering in any particular case whether the wording of para
7 is applicable it seems to me that it is first essential
to have clear and explicit findings of fact. Thereafter
the application of the words of the paragraph should
not in most cases present much difficulty. I regard many
of the reported cases as being no more than illustrative
of the divergent sets of circumstances that may arise
and of the way in which in reference to particular facts
the words of para 7 have in particular cases been applied.
Most of the words are, as words, well understood. I refer
to the words 'necessarily' and 'wholly' and 'exclusively'.
There is little room for doubt as to the meaning of those
words. They are not ambiguous. It will, however, always

be essential to have clear findings of fact on certain
matters. In the first place, it will be necessary to know
what exactly was the office or employment that a person
held. In the second place, it will be necessary to know
what exactly were the duties of the office or
employment."

In the same case at p 215 Lord Wilberforce said: "The
relevant word for the purpose of this case is 'necessarily'.
It is a word which has a long history of interpretation
and application. It does not mean what the ordinary taxpayer might think it should mean. To do any job, it
is necessary to get there: but it is settled law that
expenses of travelling to work cannot be deducted
against the emoluments of the employment. It is only
if the job requires a man to travel that his expenses of
that travel can be deducted: i.e. if he is travelling on
his work, as distinct from travelling to his work."

The point which he was making here, as I understand
it, is that the word "necessarily" has to be understood
in the context of the phrase as a whole. It is not sufficient that the man feels obliged to incur the expenditure. He must show that it was necessary for him to
do so in the performance of his work. At p 216 Lord
Wilberforce went on to say that he regarded *Ricketts
v Colquhoun* as an authority for the proposition that the
office or employment must be objectively considered:
what is its nature: what did it call for, or involve, in
the way of duties; and as an authority against the proposition that the individual's personal circumstances can
be brought in as part of the duties of the office, or as
indicating what is necessary for its performance.
Although both *Ricketts v Colquhoun* and *Taylor v
Provan* were cases about travelling expenses, these comments apply with equal force to a case such as the
present where the deduction is sought under the third
branch of the rule.

In my opinion the starting point for an examination
of the facts in these stated cases must be to ask whether
the expenditure was incurred "in the performance of
the duties". The special commissioners held that the
expenditure fell on the wrong side of the dividing line
indicated in *Humbles v Brooks*. They did so because they
held that the appellants were, generally speaking at any
rate, providing themselves with background material
with which to approach their respective tasks. They
were not, at the time when they were reading the
newspapers or periodicals, preparing articles, photographs or reports for publication but were preparing
themselves to carry out the duties of their employment.
They hesitated in Miss Long's case only because it
appeared that on some occasions she used pieces from
other newspapers as a direct foundation for her commentary on topical events. But in the end they concluded in her case also that the statutory test was not
satisfied because it was for her to decide how the topi-
cality required by her column was achieved. So the
expenditure was not determined by the employment,
as the objective test requires. As I understand their decision, while they held in the case of the four other appellants that the expenditure was not incurred in the
performance of their duties, in her case the primary
reason for refusing her appeal was that the expenditure

A was not necessarily so incurred. But in her case also it is appropriate to ask whether, on the facts in her stated case, the expenditure which is claimed to be deductible could properly be said to have been incurred in the performance of her duties as a journalist. If the facts found proved by the commissioners require that question to be answered in the negative, then the statutory test cannot be satisfied, whatever view one might take about the necessity of the expenditure.

B There were identical findings in each case that the appellants were employed under a contract of employment which, in respect of matters such as payment, hours of work, holidays and disciplinary procedures, incorporated the terms of an agreement currently in force between the employer company and the National Union of Journalists of which the appellants were all members. The agreement, which was dated 28 July 1983 and was in force for the year 1985-86, which was the year of assessment, included a clause about expenses which was cl 12. Paragraph (a) of this clause was in these terms: "Expenses will be paid to Chapel members, who incur expenditure in the course of their duties, in accordance with appendix 'B' of this agreement".

C Paragraph 3 of appendix B under the heading "Newspaper and TV Licence Expenses" provided as follows: "In compliance with Inland Revenue regulations all expenses associated with the purchase of newspapers and television licence were grossed up and consolidated into salaries with effect from 1st October, 1982. Journalists employed by the company at that time have the option of having these expenses paid on a monthly or six-monthly basis".

D There were also findings, which although differently worded in each case were all broadly to the same effect, that the appellants would have been reprimanded if they did not purchase and read other newspapers and periodicals since this was expected of them by their superiors. Finding xii in Mr Simpson's case is a typical example of this point. The appellants' argument before the commissioners was that it was a condition of their employment in each case that the appellants should purchase and read newspapers and periodicals and counsel for the appellants renewed that argument in support of the appeals. He accepted that this was not conclusive of the question whether the expenditure was deductible but it was, he said, a good starting point.

E He sought to support this argument by reference to the terms of the agreement. His contention was that the provision in appendix B which I have quoted must be read together with para 3 of appendix B in a previous version of the agreement between the company and the National Union of Journalists which was dated 11 July 1980 and was among the documents produced to the commissioners in each case. This paragraph under the heading "Newspaper Expenses" was in these terms: "Recognising the need for supporting reading, the company will make a payment of up to £10 per week to journalists employed on the Glasgow Herald and Evening Times for the purchase of newspapers and magazines required by them in furtherance of their duties. Such payments to be claimed on the company's expenses claim form."

F

G Counsel for the appellants stressed the use of the phrases "recognising the need" and "required by them in furtherance of their duties" which appear in this version of the paragraph. He contended that the effect of these phrases was that it was a condition of the employment that the expenditure should be incurred, and he submitted that the special commissioners had erred in law in their decision to the contrary. But there are various difficulties in the way of that argument, and I reject it as unsound. In the first place the only findings which were made by the commissioners relate to the agreement which was in force in the year of assessment. There is no reference either in their findings or in their decision to the earlier version of it, which had plainly been superseded by the date which is relevant to these appeals. Indeed this point is made abundantly clear by cl 1 (b) of the later version which provides: "This agreement supersedes all other House Agreements between the Company and the Chapels". Next, there is no indication in the wording of para 3 of the relevant agreement that reference requires to be made to the earlier version. It seems to me, therefore, that the earlier version must be ignored, and that the commissioners were right not to make any mention of it in their findings. But even if it were legitimate to have regard to the earlier version on this point, I do not think that it supports the argument of counsel for the appellants. A recognition of the need for supporting reading seems to me to fall far short of a statement that the reading has to be done in the performance of the duties of the employment. The need which is referred to here is for "supporting reading", which seems to me to point to what is required to enable the journalists to do their job rather than what is necessary in the performance of it.

H

I

J

An alternative argument was advanced with reference to the findings in each case that the appellants would have been reprimanded if they had not read other newspapers and periodicals. Counsel for the appellants said that it was to be inferred from these findings that it was an implied condition of their employment that they should do so. It is not clear whether an argument was presented to the special commissioners in these terms, but in any event I do not think that the findings support it. It does not appear from the findings that the particular implied condition for which counsel for the appellants contended was necessary to give their contracts efficacy. I do not say that a duty in more general terms might not be implied. But what counsel for the appellants was asking for was an implied condition specifically directed to the reading of other newspapers and periodicals, and I am not persuaded that the special commissioners were in error in not making a finding that a condition to this effect was to be implied.

K

L

Counsel for the appellants then referred us to what appears in para VI of each stated case. The commissioners state in this paragraph that they were unable to find on the evidence, as they had been invited to do by counsel for the appellants, that reading a number of newspapers and magazines was a condition of the appellants' employment, nor did the evidence establish that such reading was the universal practice for such journalists working in the newspaper industry. But they were satisfied that wide reading of other newspapers and magazines is a common practice among journalists of all kinds, and that without that reading the appellants would have discharged the duties of their employment less effectively and might not have kept their jobs on the newspapers on which they were employed. It was under reference to these comments that counsel for the appellants submitted that the practice of reading newspapers and periodicals was so widespread among journalists of the categories involved in these appeals as to amount to a universal practice, that one would expect it to be a condition of their employment in these circumstances and that a condition to this effect was to be implied. He invited us to hold that the commissioners had erred in law in their decision that it was not a condition of their employment that they should incur this expenditure.

I see no grounds for reversing the decision of the special commissioners on this point. It was agreed that the evidence given by each appellant was available to be considered in support of the other appeals. No doubt it was on a consideration of all that evidence that the commissioners were satisfied that it was common practice for journalists of all kinds to devote time to a wide reading of other newspapers and periodicals. But they were entitled to conclude that the evidence did not establish that this was the universal practice for the particular categories of journalists involved in these appeals, since this was a question of fact for them to determine on the evidence. Even if they had been persuaded to the contrary, I think that a finding to this effect would have failed to satisfy the requirement that the expenditure must be incurred in the performance of the duties. The argument of counsel for the appellants on this whole issue therefore seemed to me to fall short of what was required to disturb the determination by the special commissioners, because at best for him the condition of employment which he was seeking to establish was an indication that the expenditure was necessarily incurred. But the crucial issue on the facts of these cases is whether the expenditure was incurred in the performance of the duties which each appellant was required to perform.

It is now necessary to look at each case separately because the findings of fact in each case which are relevant to this issue are not the same. What the special commissioners have done, after dealing with the agreement between the company and the National Union of Journalists, is to make findings of fact based on the evidence which each appellant gave in support of his own appeal. They describe what each of them did in the course of their working day, the various duties which they were required to perform, the newspapers and periodicals which they purchased, why they purchased them and the uses to which they were put. It was suggested in the course of the argument that some of these findings were not proper findings of fact. Typical of the findings which were criticised in this way is finding xviii in Mr Fitzpatrick's case which is in these terms: "He considered that he was working when he was reading and cutting newspapers and magazines at home in the evenings and on his rest days".

In my opinion this criticism was not justified. It would have been different if the words used were merely a record that this was his evidence without giving any indication that the evidence had been accepted by the special commissioners as true. As it is, statements to the effect that the appellant considered something to be the case, or that he regarded himself as doing something, imply an acceptance by the commissioners that the evidence given on this point was honest and reliable and that they believed it. The explanation why some of the findings are expressed in this form may be found in the fact that the evidence in these cases was confined to that of the journalists themselves. There was no independent evidence as to what the duties of their employment required or as to the relationship between those duties and the practice of purchasing and reading newspapers. There was no evidence from the editors nor was there any evidence from the managers of the newspapers on these points. As I see it, the special commissioners were being careful, when making findings in this form, to indicate that this part of the evidence which they accepted was necessarily subjective. They were entitled to refrain from making findings which might have suggested that there was more than this in the evidence. So I would resist any criticism of the special commissioners on the ground that the stated cases which are before us have not been properly stated by them.

I shall take the cases in the same order as they appear in the decision of the commissioners where they summarise the facts of each case. I do not require to set out again all the facts. Instead what I wish to do is to point to those findings on the issue as to whether the expenditure was incurred in the performance of the duties which have led me to the conclusion that they provide ample support for the determination which the commissioners have made.

Mr Fitzpatrick, the assistant picture editor of the *Evening Times*, was in charge of a section of seven full time photographers and part of his working day was spent in the office, organising the work of his section. But he was also free to go out on assignments of his own as a photo-journalist. He is a compulsive buyer of newspapers and magazines, and he had bought 10 daily newspapers and some magazines for 20 years or more. A list is given of those which he regularly bought in 1985-86, which comprises nine daily papers, three Sunday papers and eight magazines. There is an element of personal choice in his selection, but he found it necessary to make purchases on the scale of this list to do his job as a photo-journalist. He had to know about politics, sport, fashion and current affairs, but he also had a particular reason for purchasing the daily papers. This was not only to get ideas which the *Evening Times* might use but also to see what pictures were in them. He had to avoid printing in the *Evening Times* a picture which had already appeared in another paper. He also read the papers and took cuttings from them during the three days of the week, Friday, Saturday and Sunday when he was not required to work, and even when he was on holiday he tried to keep abreast of events. Then there is the finding which I have already quoted that

A he considered that he was working when he was reading and cutting newspapers and magazines at home in the evenings and on his rest days. But there is no finding that his purchases were made for the purposes of any particular assignment, or that there was any editorial direction or control over what he bought. The clear impression which is conveyed by these findings is of personal choice, of the building up and maintaining of a general knowledge of affairs, of his equipping himself to do his job. Some of what he read, and some of the cuttings which he took, might prove to be useful but

B some might not. There is a finding that he found about 20 per cent of the cuttings to be useful in his work. I find this to be a clear indication that it was the enabling function — that is keeping himself equipped to fulfil his duties as a journalist — which was the motive for these purchases and that the money was not being expended in the performance of those duties. The only possible exception lies in finding xxiv which is that he had to avoid printing in the *Evening Times* a picture which had appeared in another paper. But the limits

C of this duty are not clearly defined. It does not appear that he was under any precise duty of censorship, or that he was required to scrutinise any particular paper or papers while he was at work in the office as assistant picture editor. In the absence of precise findings to that effect I think that the commissioners were entitled to regard this as just part of a single activity of general background reading, the value of which might manifest itself in various ways during the working day.

D Miss Long, as a features writer and weekly columnist with the *Evening Times*, was expected to produce ideas for features and put them to the features editor. She got her ideas for features from her wide reading of other papers and from going about her ordinary life, talking to people. Her weekly column could be filled entirely with her own ideas, but that might not produce the topical column which was expected of her by the editor. She found it necessary to read other newspapers and magazines to find out what matters were of topical

E interest. She considered that the reading and cutting of magazines and newspapers was an essential part of her work without which she would not have been able to produce a satisfactory column. Details are given of the newspapers, both daily and on Sundays, and of the magazines which she took. Finding xiv states that she took some magazines regularly as useful background reading and others when it seemed from the cover that they might have something which would be useful to her work. Most of her reading of newspapers was done

F at home in the evening, and finding xi tells us that this reading provided her with background knowledge and enabled her to get a feel for the subjects which might interest her readers. Here again the emphasis is on personal choice and of enabling the journalist to do her job. Her reading and cutting was over before she went to see the features editor to put to him her ideas. I can find nothing to indicate, so far as her work as a features writer was concerned, that her reading and cutting was done in the performance of her duties in writing features. The only possible exception in her case, as the special commissioners have pointed out in their deci-

G sion, is that there seems to have been evidence that on occasions she used pieces from other papers as a direct foundation for her commentaries on topical events. Finding xii states that she read more widely on Sundays and on Mondays when she was writing her Tuesday column. Had there been more precise information on this point, and had there also been evidence to identify that part of the expenditure which was incurred for this purpose, there might have been a basis for allowing it as a deduction. But Miss Long's case was not presented in that way, since her claim was for a deduction from

H her emoluments of the whole of the newspaper allowance which she received. In her case therefore I think that the only conclusion which can reasonably be reached on the findings is that the expenditure, when looked at as a whole, was not incurred in the performance of her duties and that the statutory test was not satisfied. In any event the findings demonstrate that it was not wholly and exclusively so incurred.

I Mr McBain was a staff reporter on the *Glasgow Herald*. The findings in his case show that he covered stories for most sections of the newspaper, under the direction of the news editor who decided what subjects were to be covered and by whom, after listening to suggestions. In his case also the choice of publications which he purchased was his own. There were four newspapers every weekday and two Sunday newspapers. He regularly bought eight magazines or periodicals, and there were two others on his list which he sometimes bought. Here again the emphasis is on personal choice and background reading to enable him to do his job.

J Finding xi is of particular significance, because it is stated here that he read newspapers and magazines partly to improve his general knowledge of current affairs, partly to provide background reading against which to conduct interviews and attend press conferences on specific subjects, and partly to obtain ideas for future articles which he might write up later. This, together with finding xiii which states that it is essential for him to read the specialist publications to keep himself informed on energy and education matters, presents a clear picture of the conscientious journalist

K who keeps himself well informed to do his job. But it falls well short of what is needed to show that the expenditure was incurred in the performance of his duties within the strict requirements of the subsection. The reading and cutting in his case was all preparatory by way of background to what he had to do when he came to perform these duties.

L Mr Simpson worked as a general sub-editor on the *Glasgow Herald*. He had to know what was going on in the world, because his task was to make up the pages for which he was responsible with stories of interest to his readers, and he had to recognise which stories were new and which were stale when they came in. The choice of newspapers and periodicals was his own, and the emphasis was on background reading to enable himself to do his job. Finding xviii tells us that he read even more widely on Sundays than on weekdays to obtain an overview of current topics. And finding xix states that while he was at work he relied heavily on his recollection of what he had read at home, all of which

A helped him with his awareness of current affairs. It was part of his duties as sub-editor to be careful to avoid printing stories lifted from other papers which had been submitted by outside contributors. But the implication of this finding is that this was just one of the aspects of his job for which he relied on the background reading which he had previously done. I do not find here a basis for a finding that the newspapers and periodicals which he took were read and cut by him in the performance of his duties as sub-editor.

B Lastly, there was Mr Traynor who was a sports sub-editor on the *Glasgow Herald*. His duties at the sports desk were to receive stories from the sports writers, put headlines on them and adapt them to fit the spaces on the page. He also did some feature writing and occasional match reports. He bought eight newspapers on weekdays, five on Sundays and various magazines. Finding xii states that his purpose in all that reading was to gather information to enable him to do his job, and finding xiii is that his reading went far beyond the sports pages, partly because, as a journalist, he was C interested in general news but also because background information of direct value in his own work could be gleaned from other parts of the papers. Here again, the emphasis is on personal choice, on the enabling function, on background reading to equip himself to do his job as a journalist. But there is nothing here to show that, in the strict sense required by the statutory rule, any of this reading was done in the performance of the duties of his employment.

D It seems to me that in all these cases there is a consistent pattern which reflects the general finding in para VI in each case that wide reading of other newspapers and magazines is a common practice among journalists of all kinds. Each of the appellants when speaking of his or her own activities considered that this reading was necessary to enable them to do their job. No doubt an essential part of the equipment of a good journalist is to be well informed and up to date. Whether he works as a reporter, as a writer, as a sub-editor or as a pho-E tographer the creation, selection and rejection of ideas requires a sound measure of general knowledge and a good deal of information on what is topical. An obvious source for information in the field in which he works is that which is provided by other newspapers and periodicals. But it does not follow that money which is expended by him on the purchase of newspapers and periodicals for this purpose has been expended in the performance of the duties of his employment. Whether this can be said to be the case must be a question of fact. Moreover these duties cannot, for the purposes of F the statutory role, include a general duty on the journalist to keep himself informed or in some other way qualified or equipped to perform the duties of the employment. That is to be seen as a preliminary to the performance of those duties when they require to be performed. So one must be careful to distinguish between what is preliminary or preparatory in that general sense and what is done in the performance of the duties of the employment when they are being performed. I consider that the special commissioners were entitled on the findings to hold, as they did in all cases

except that of Miss Long, that the expenditure fell on the wrong side of this dividing line. But I think that G the findings in Miss Long's case, when read as a whole, show that in her case also this part of the statutory test was not satisfied.

There was very little argument in the appeal to which we listened as to whether the restrictive words "wholly, exclusively and necessarily" were satisfied. Counsel for the appellants submitted that the expenditure was all necessary, to which he accepted an objective test had to be applied. But the findings on which he relied were, for the reasons already discussed, directed to the prelimi-H nary or preparatory stage of enabling the journalist to do his job. He pointed to findings about the practice in the newspaper industry and submitted that, given the experience of the journalists who gave evidence in this case and the variety of occupations in the industry which they described, it was clear that the reading which was done was what was demanded by the job and that it was necessary. But I think that this argument became detached from the wording of the rest of the subsection with which the word "necessarily" must be read. I The test of what has been necessarily expended in the performance of the duties cannot be satisfied by showing that the expenditure has been necessarily incurred on something else. The decision of the special commissioners contains little by way of discussion of the question whether the expenditure was necessarily incurred, but I do not think that they needed to examine this issue to any great extent in view of their decision that, except perhaps in Miss Long's case, it had not been proved that the appellants were not, at the time when they were J reading and cutting, engaged in the performance of the duties of their employment as journalists.

For the same reason it is not necessary to dwell at any length on the issue as to whether the expenditure was incurred "wholly" or "exclusively" in the performance of these duties. Counsel for the appellants maintained that counsel for the Crown had conceded this point by stating in terms to the commissioners that, if they found that the expenditure was necessarily incurred K in the performance of the duties, he would not challenge the proposition that it was wholly and exclusively incurred. Senior counsel for the respondents insisted that no such concession had been made, and he stated that in any event if there had been such a concession he wished to withdraw it. He pointed out that the phrase "wholly and exclusively" ought not to be read separately from the remainder of the statutory test. The whole phrase was qualified by the words "in the performance of the duties", and there had been no concession by the L respondents at any stage in these appeals that the expenditure was incurred in the performance of the duties of the employment to any extent. In reply counsel for the appellants submitted that it was too late for the concession which he insisted had been made to be withdrawn, but in response to this argument senior counsel for the respondents said that anything said by counsel on this point to the commissioners was at the stage of submissions after the leading of the evidence and was simply a comment on the evidence which he was entitled to withdraw.

A The special commissioners' brief discussion of this point has caused me some difficulty, but this is not on the issue raised by counsel for the appellants as to whether or not it had been conceded by counsel for the respondents. If there had been such a concession I would have expected the commissioners to say so in terms. As it is, their statement that the proposition was not seriously in dispute suggests the contrary, namely that the point had been left to them to decide. That seems to me appropriate, because the proposition to which they refer was in broad terms which did not meet the terms of the statutory test. What I find hard to understand

B is how they could have held that the test was satisfied without having decided that the expenditure was incurred in the performance of the duties of the employment in which it was incurred. As I have said repeatedly throughout this opinion, it seems to me that the starting point for an examination of the facts in each of these appeals must be to examine the latter question, and that it would only be if the expenditure was found to have been incurred in the performance of those duties

C that any question would arise as to whether the expenditure was wholly and exclusively so incurred.

But the true position seems to me, in light of the findings by the commissioners, that except in Miss Long's case, this point is not of any real importance. There was no dispute about the amount which had been spent by each of the appellants in purchasing newspapers and periodicals during the year of assessment, and no attempt was made to distinguish between expenditure on some newspapers and periodicals and expenditure

D on others. The appellants' argument was that the whole of the expenditure was necessarily incurred in the performance of the duties of their employment, while the argument for the respondents in response to this generalised approach was to say that none of the expenditure fell within the terms of the subsection. Furthermore the submissions which were made to us under reference to these words were extremely brief. I propose to say nothing further on this point, since I do not think that, except in Miss Long's case, the appellants' argu-

E ment reached the stage at which it became relevant to a decision in these appeals. In her case the point is easily disposed of, because her case was presented on the basis that the expenditure which she incurred was to be looked at as a whole. Since the expense of buying newspapers for use in her column was not separately identified and, as the special commissioners point out, might in any case be difficult to identify, this expenditure had to be taken together with the rest and, plainly, the whole expenditure could not be said to have been

F incurred wholly and exclusively for use in the performance of her duties as a columnist.

I should mention finally that we were referred by counsel for the appellants at the commencement of his argument to the decision of Warner J in *Smith v Abbott*. That case also was concerned with the question whether expenditure incurred by journalists in the purchase of newspapers and periodicals was necessarily incurred by them in the performance of the duties of their employment. As in the present case there were five journalists whose assessments were taken to appeal, and they all

worked for the same employer in different capacities on two different newspapers. The general commis- G
sioners allowed their appeals, holding that the statutory tests had all been satisfied and that the newspaper allowance which they had received from their employers was deductible under s 189 (1) of the 1970 Act. Warner J dismissed the Crown's appeals in the case of four journalists in whose cases there was an express finding by the commissioners that reading newspapers and periodicals was a necessary part of the duties of their employment and was not merely required to qualify them or maintain their qualification to do their duties. H
There was no such finding in the other case, which was that of Mr Abbott, and the judge held that on the findings the only true and reasonable conclusion was that the expenditure had been incurred by this journalist to keep him qualified to perform the duties of his employment. It is clear from an examination of the reasoning in that case that the decisive point in favour of the four journalists who were successful in resisting the appeals was the express finding in their cases that the expenditure was necessarily incurred in the performance of their I
duties. The judge was satisfied that the general commissioners were aware of the distinction which had to be made between preparation and performance. He found that the other findings in these cases were such as to make the critical finding both intelligible and consistent with the law. It was the absence of such a finding in Abbott's case that led to his decision to allow the appeal in his case.

We were informed that both sides have now appealed against that decision. Although counsel for the appel- J
lants stressed its importance, I do not think that it can be regarded as of any material assistance in the present case. I agree that it would be unreal to ignore the fact that these are both test cases, and I have no doubt that it is desirable to avoid unnecessary differences in the result. But the facts stated by the special commissioners in these appeals are not the same as those which were before Warner J. There are important differences, including the absence of the critical finding which was decisive of the four appeals which he refused. The K
evidence was also different, because in addition to the documents and the oral evidence from the five taxpayers the general commissioners in that case heard evidence from the deputy managing editor of one of the newspapers who was responsible for all aspects of the paper including employee contracts. It is clear that the general commissioners relied upon and accepted his evidence as well as that of the taxpayers when they came to make the critical findings in the case. In all these cases, as Warner J pointed out at [1992] 1 WLR, p 216, the ques- L
tion at the stage of an appeal is whether the facts found by the commissioners are fairly capable of leading to the conclusion at which they have arrived. In my opinion all that can be said about *Smith v Abbott* for the purposes of the present case is that it must be distinguished on its facts.

For these reasons I would answer the question of law in each of these cases in the affirmative and refuse the appeals. Before parting with the case however I should say that I have had the opportunity of reading Lord

McCluskey's opinion, with which I have the misfortune to disagree. He has made numerous criticisms of the findings of fact by the special commissioners on the ground that they have not addressed the correct questions in the correct way and that the findings which they have made are inadequate. These criticisms form the basis for his opinion that the court is free to come to its own conclusions and that the appeals should be allowed. In my opinion, however, this approach is at variance with the law and practice to be applied by this court in appeals from the commissioners. The onus is on the taxpayer to satisfy the commissioners that the assessment which he has appealed against is wrong, and the question at this stage is whether on the facts found by the commissioners they were entitled to arrive at their decision that this onus had not been discharged. It is not the practice for the commissioners to set out the facts which were not established by the evidence, and I believe that it would be unreasonable to expect the commissioners to have addressed the facts as listed by Lord McCluskey since nobody, so far as I am aware, has previously analysed s 189 (1) in that way.

It is also necessary to point out that Lord McCluskey's criticisms formed no part of the argument of counsel for the taxpayers in support of these appeals. We were informed by senior counsel for the respondents that at no stage in the complicated history of this case did the appellants seek findings from the special commissioners of the kind which Lord McCluskey considers ought to have been made by them. Had there been a basis for these criticisms the proper course, in fairness to the special commissioners and also to the respondents to these appeals, would have been to remit the case to the commissioners for further findings. But I would only have been willing to follow that course if counsel for the appellants had been able to persuade us that this was necessary for the proper disposal of these appeals and if it was clear also that findings in the terms suggested had been requested of the special commissioners but they had declined to make them. As it is, since no motion to that effect was made to us by counsel for the appellants who was content to address us on the facts found by the commissioners, I think that we have no alternative but to decide these appeals on the basis of these facts only, and that on these facts they must be refused.

LORD McCLUSKEY.—Your Lordship in the chair has fully narrated the background to these appeals and the arguments presented to this court; I can, therefore, turn at once to the issues they raise.

These cases ultimately depend upon the application to their respective circumstances of s 189 (1) of the Income and Corporation Taxes Act 1970. Reading that subsection short, and with a minor change in the order of words, what is provided is, "If the holder of an office or employment is necessarily obliged . . . to expend money wholly, exclusively and necessarily in the performance of the duties of the office or employment . . . the expenses so necessarily incurred and defrayed . . . may be deducted from the emoluments [of the office or employment]."

I note that the wording is different from that contained in s 130, para (a) and I acknowledge that the tests which have to be passed before deduction may properly be claimed under s 189 (1) are more stringent than those contained in s 130. In particular s 189 (1) repeatedly introduces the concept of necessity. Furthermore, whereas s 130, para (a) speaks of expenditure "for the purposes of" the trade, profession or vocation, s 189 (1) requires the expenditure to be "in the performance of the duties". We must take the words of the section as we find them, recognising that these words have been re-enacted by Parliament in the knowledge that the courts have interpreted them and it must be assumed that the modern enactments, by repeating the wording dating from the middle of the 19th century, are intended to have the same meaning as the courts have put upon them.

Nonetheless, there is little to admire in the wording of the section as it now stands. Quite apart from the reference to the keeping and maintaining of a horse to enable the holder of the office or employment to perform the duties, there is much tautology. The word "necessarily" appears three times, and that is in addition to the element of necessity contained in the word "obliged". I have felt a temptation to try to rewrite or to paraphrase the wording of the section but I have decided against succumbing to it in case by doing so I make subtle changes in the meaning. Nonetheless it appears to me evident that, when a person seeks deduction under the section in respect of expenses, he has a responsibility to establish certain facts. These facts are: (1) the claimant holds an office or employment; (2) as the holder he expends money; (3) he does so because, as the holder, he is "necessarily obliged to" (ie, he has to, he is not free to refrain from expending the money); (4) the spending is in the performance of the duties of the office or employment; (5) the whole expenditure claimed is incurred in meeting demands flowing directly from such performance; and (6) the expenditure claimed is incurred for no purpose other than in meeting those demands.

The foregoing list contains some facts which in particular circumstances will be primary facts and others which are inferential facts, that is to say matters of fact which are inferred from primary facts established directly in evidence; this is the distinction drawn by Lord Reid in *Taylor v Provan* [1975] AC at p 206, where he says of a particular conclusion reached by the special commissioners in that case: "But that is not a finding in fact. It is an inference which they draw from the findings which precede the decision in the case stated." In the circumstances of the present cases, facts 1 and 2 are simple primary facts, but facts 3 and 4 are rather more complex facts and may depend upon the establishing or other primary or incidental facts. Thus, in relation to no 4, it is probably necessary to discover in relation to each appellant taxpayer what is the work of the office or employment which he holds, what is embraced in it, what is involved in the performance of the work, and whether or not what is so involved is in the performance of duties which are duties of the employment. It may be necessary to determine at what

times the taxpayer is performing the duties of the
employment and at what times he is not. It may be
necessary to examine carefully how the expenditure
claimed relates to the alleged performance of the alleged
duties of the employment. It may well be necessary to
discover whether the performance could have been
achieved without the expenditure. Furthermore, because
the section contains the words "necessarily in the performance of the said duties", facts 3 and 4 are interrelated to a material degree. These are matters of the
kind that Lord Morris of Borth-y-Gest was speaking
about in the context of the factual background to *Taylor
v Provan* at p 211. Where any one of the essential factual
matters is not a primary fact but a fact inferred from
other primary facts, then the taxpayer has to establish
in evidence the other facts from which the vital fact may
be properly inferred.

It follows that in a properly stated case there should
be comprehensive findings in fact relating to each of
the six matters listed above so as to enable clear, explicit
and complete findings to be made, whether simply or
by inference, as to each of them. I respectfully adopt
what Lord Morris of Borth-y-Gest said in *Taylor v
Provan* at p 210: "In considering in any particular case
whether the wording [of the statute] is applicable it
seems to me that it is first essential to have clear and
explicit findings of fact". Alternatively if, whether
because of lack of evidence or lack of persuasive and
satisfactory evidence, the commissioners are unable to
hold that any such essential fact has been established,
one would expect a clear statement that they recognised
that the establishing of such a fact was essential to the
success of the claim but were unable to hold that fact
established because of the state of the evidence: in that
type of case it would be clear, and would be made
explicit, that the party on whom the onus rested failed
because he had not discharged that onus. Accordingly,
to put it another way, in a properly stated case, each
of the essential matters listed will be clearly addressed
by the commissioners. If each of the essential facts is
addressed and in the light of that addressing the commissioners determine how the section applies to the
circumstances established, then this court has no power
to interfere except upon the basis spelled out by Lord
Radcliffe in *Edwards v Bairstow* [1956] AC at pp 35-36.
In my opinion, however, if the commissioners do not
adequately address the essential matters of fact derived
from the subsection, then the conclusion is not that the
appellant fails, but that the case has not been properly
stated. The commissioners are not entitled to reach a
conclusion which has to be inferred or deduced from
other facts unless they have all those other facts before
them. If the commissioners have reached a conclusion
upon the application of the section to the circumstances
without properly considering the issue by addressing
all the matters which the section requires them to
address, then it would follow that the commissioners
"were not entitled to reach the conclusion which they
did, that they must have misdirected themselves in law"
(the words used by Lord President Cooper in *IRC v
Toll Property Co Ltd*, 1952 SLT at p 374). Even inadequate submissions could not properly justify a failure

by commissioners to deal with, ie to address, the essential facts, whether by holding them proved, disproved
or unproved or even by pointing out that they have been
neglected by whichever party had the onus of establishing them.

In the present case there is no problem with facts 1,
2 and 5. I leave aside fact 6 for the present. It is facts
3 and 4 which go to the heart of the present cases and
the first question for me is whether or not the commissioners have properly addressed these essentials. It
appears to me that we are concerned here with how the
essentials are dealt with in the stated cases; one must
look to see whether or not the essential matters have
been addressed within the four walls of the cases themselves. Ultimately that is because the question of law
for the opinion of the court is: "Whether, on the facts
found, we were entitled to conclude that no deduction
could be made under s 189 (1) of the Taxes Act 1970
for the expenditure in question".

The reference there to "the facts found" is, of course,
a reference back to the facts found in the stated case.
Nonetheless, it would be unfair to ignore the reasoning contained in the decision which is referred to in para
IX of each case. That decision, dated 18 May 1989, was
referred to in argument by the appellants and the
revenue. Before I turn to look at the facts found,
however, I should make it clear that I accept that if it
is plain that the commissioners have addressed all but
one of the relevant matters and have reached a decision
fatally adverse to the taxpayer in relation to any one
of the essentials addressed, and that decision is one
which they were entitled to arrive at, a failure to address
properly the other one of the other essential matters
would not be fatal to their overall decision (provided
that matter was discrete and separate): obviously, if the
taxpayer falls at the third hurdle then it hardly matters
how he performs in relation to the fifth hurdle, if any
single fall is sufficient to disqualify him from further
participation in the race.

Although the material facts which I have numbered
3 and 4 above are separate, on one view they are very
closely related (indeed facts 5 and 6 are also closely
related to 4). When it comes to the commissioners' findings in fact there are several findings which relate to
both or could relate to either. I shall, therefore, look
at the findings in fact which relate to facts 3 and 4. I
start with the case of Cameron Simpson, the first case
upon which we were addressed. Findings V (ii) and (iii)
shows that this appellant's paid hours of work were
restricted to those specified in his written contract. V
(iv) refers to cl 12 of the agreement (expenses) but, given
the wording of cl 12 and appendix (B), it cannot be said
that it was a matter of contract that any expenditure
by this appellant in the course of his duties on purchasing newspapers was necessarily to be regarded as expenditure in the course of his duties: on this issue I agree
entirely with your Lordship in the chair. Mr Simpson's
job was to act as a general sub-editor on his paper and
as deputy television editor. He also had to write features and review books (V (v)). He spent four eight-and-
a-half-hour shifts in the office. He was one of 40 or so

in a pool of general sub-editors similarly employed (V (vi) and (vii)). His duties involved news and feature items but he also had to deal with sport or anything else which the editor or night editor might allocate to him; it is stated "he was thought to be knowledgeable on motoring matters" (V (vii)). He had to know what was going on because he had to make up pages that would interest the readers (V (viii)). The paper had to be fresh; and part of his job was to carry forward stories that the readers might have encountered earlier on radio or TV (V (ix)).

Finding V (x) is of particular importance. It shows that, as sub-editor, the appellant had a duty to be properly informed so that he could distinguish between new and stale stories and could recognise whether or not a story submitted by an outside contributor was in fact a secondhand story lifted from elsewhere; he had a responsibility not to print stories lifted from other papers. This, taken along with other findings, is a clear recognition that in and as a necessary condition of the performance of the duties of the employment he had to be aware of and constantly to make himself freshly aware of the changing press scene. Plainly he could not perform the duties referred to in this finding unless he was constantly keeping himself up to date by studying other newspapers. Finding V (xii) records that his superiors "expected him" to read a number of other newspapers and magazines. If he failed to do so that would become obvious to them each day and he would have expected to be reprimanded. It is unfortunate that this finding (V (xii)) refers to what the appellant's superiors "expected", without the special commissioners' having at any time addressed themselves as to the bearing of that finding upon the precise question as to whether or not it was one of the duties of a sub-editor's employment to read a number of other newspapers and magazines. If it was the duty of a sub-editor on each occasion when he was sub-editing to bring to that task knowledge obtainable only from reading other daily newspapers and recently published magazines, and if that was expected of him to the extent that a failure to do what was expected would result in his exposure and reprimand, then it is more than just unfortunate that the commissioners did not hold whether or not the reading was one of the duties of a sub-editor's employment. In my opinion, in the absence of any such finding they materially disabled themselves from determining whether or not in performing the reading this appellant was performing one of the duties of the employment of a sub-editor.

Finding V (xiii) records the "opinion" of the appellant that such reading was "an intrinsic part of his job"; but, without saying that that "opinion" evidence is accepted or that it is rejected or otherwise discussing it, the commissioners make no finding as to whether or not such reading was an intrinsic part of the job. Unlike your Lordship in the chair, who deals with this point in relation to finding V (xxvii) in Mr Fitzpatrick's case, I consider that there is no adequate finding in fact here. What each journalist honestly thought, considered, believed or held an opinion about is interesting and valuable and worth recording as a relevant primary fact; but

— leaving aside the special case where a party fails to discharge his onus — the commissioners must determine what the objective facts are, even if they have to draw inferences to do so. Was such a reading an intrinsic part of the job or was it not? The commissioners do not expressly tell us in the findings in fact; and in the reasoning they do not tell us what they made of this or similar evidence and why it was not used to infer a finding as to the relevant objective fact. Findings V (xiv) to V (xvii) merely record Mr Simpson's practice in relation to which papers he read and when and where. Finding V (xviii) records that he took a lot of cuttings and retained them for as long as necessary and that the cutting service of the office library was "not sufficient for his needs". This implies, though the implication is neither stated nor negatived, that his personal or home cuttings were related to "his needs". But this finding also makes it plain that "he had little time for reading or cutting newspapers in the office"; the necessary implication of this in its context is that he could not do what was expected of him without reading out of office hours. As finding V (xix) shows, the purpose of all this reading and cutting was to stock or calibrate his mind for the immediate responsibilities of his daily task. The findings in fact certainly reflect the submission made on behalf of the appellant that the reading of newspapers and magazines was necessary because the job required an immediacy of knowledge, a daily updating in relation to the state of the daily published news; but they do not show that the commissioners have properly and adequately addressed this point by relating it to the performance of the duties of the job. Findings V (xx) and V (xxi) again record that the appellant regarded such reading "as simply part of his job" and considered himself to be working when he was reading and cutting newspapers at home, but the commissioners do not address themselves at all as to what they considered in relation to these matters. Before I turn to para VI I wish to make the comment that, as the authorities referred to by your Lordship in the chair make clear, the section requires an examination not of the personal circumstances of the particular holder of the office or employment but of the duties of "the holder", as such. Yet all the findings in fact in para V really relate to the appellant's personal habits, understandings and activities. Thus there are no "clear and explicit" findings in para V which expressly deal with what the holder as such necessarily does in the performance of the duties of the holder of the office or employment in question; it appears as if the commissioners might have thought that what was important was the situation of each individual appellant.

In para VI the commissioners record that they were unable to find that reading a number of newspapers and magazines was a "condition" of this appellant's employment nor that such reading was "the universal practice" for sub-editors or feature writers in the newspaper industry. It appears from the way that this matter is put in the findings that what is recorded here was in response to an invitation from counsel for the appellant, an invitation which the commissioners felt they could not accept. But, whoever is responsible for it, it

A appears here that the commissioners were looking at the wrong thing, as well as not looking at the right thing. The determining issue was not one as to the conditions of the employment; it was an issue as to what was necessarily involved in the performance of the duties of the employment. These are not the same things or co-extensive things. The conditions of the employment do not necessarily correspond exactly to the duties of the employment. Equally the question of "the universal practice" is not the real point; the point is whether it was necessary in the performance of the duties of the

B holder of the office or employment of sub-editor or feature writer to engage in such out of office reading. After addressing the wrong questions in the first sentence of para VI the commissioners then made the mistake of dealing with the wrong matters in the second sentence. I need say no more about para (i). In relation to para VI (ii), what is recorded is that "without that reading Mr Simpson would have discharged the duties of his employment less effectively and might not have kept his job on the *Glasgow Herald*". This I consider

C to be an unsatisfactory and insufficient finding because it is not made clear what the commissioners mean by "less effectively", nor is it made plain how long they thought he might have retained his job if he had not engaged in the reading. How effective is "less effective"? All one can do in relation to that vital matter is to go back to finding V (xii) and the other related findings referred to where it is recorded that his superiors expected him to do the reading, that his failure to do so would have become obvious each day, that the first

D such failure would have resulted in a reprimand and that he regarded it as an indispensable part of his job. In relation to the words in s 189 (1) I do not see how it can be said that a person is "performing" the duties of the employment if he is doing them so ineffectively that he will be reprimanded daily, will manifestly disappoint the "expectations" of his superiors and so put his job in peril. Furthermore, the fact that the choice of newspapers was made by the journalist does not weigh against the appellant's contention. In this, as in

E the other cases, the journalist was expected to keep abreast of the current state of printed news etc. How he chose to do that, which papers he chose to read, would inevitably be left to his professional judgment. This observation applies to all the appellants.

It thus appears to me that the special commissioners did not address themselves properly to the interrelated questions 3 and 4 which I have listed earlier. In arriving at that view I have had regard to the written deci-

F sion of 18 May 1989 as well. I can find in that no satisfactory addressing of the question of necessity. On p 9 thereof it is recorded: "As to the element of necessity Mr Whiteman asked us to find on the evidence, first, that it was a condition of the employment in each case that the appellant should read and cut newspapers at home, since failure to do so would soon have become apparent, rendering the employee liable to disciplinary action, possibly dismissal; and secondly that the duties of each appellant could not have been performed properly without reading at home, which was accordingly essential to the performance of those duties. Mr

G McNeil concedes only that the duties would have been performed less well without home reading and he disputes the proposition that it was a condition of the employment".

This passage reflects matters dealt with in para VI but takes the matter no further. There is no other passage in which the question of necessity is satisfactorily addressed. On the passage of what was necessarily involved "in the performance of the duties of the employment", certain passages on pp 11 and 12 do purport to address this matter but principally in rela-

H tion to what the general practice is, and in particular it is said: "It does not follow necessarily that they were carrying out the duties of their employments and we can find no grounds for saying that they were. The *only possible* conclusion on the evidence is, in our opinion, that the duties of each appellant started when he or she arrived at the office . . . and finished when he or she left the office".

This is not a proper conclusion, to my mind, in the light of their failure to address precisely what was meant

I in context by the performance of the duties of the office and by their failure to discuss the reasons for not drawing the obvious inferences from the facts established. I find it startling that they say that this was "the only possible conclusion". That appears to me to be a plain indication in the written decision that they have misunderstood the evidence which they have recorded as findings in fact. It appears to me that the commissioners have been misled by supposing that these cases are like *Humbles v Brooks*, a case in which a headmaster

J and history teacher who attended weekend lectures in history at a college for adult education for the purpose of improving his background knowledge was held, in so improving his background knowledge, not to be engaged in performing his work as a headmaster or teacher. No doubt that case indicates that there is a dividing line between what might properly be called preparation for the work and the carrying out or performance of the work itself. In the present case, however, it appears to me to be perfectly plain that if

K the appellant had sat in the newspaper office at the start of his working day reading through the newspapers and magazines in question for the purpose of alerting his mind to the matters for which he had to look out during the rest of the day when he was putting pen to paper or participating in decision making, there could have been no question that in doing so he was performing the duties of his employment. I fail to see how he is not performing the duties of his employment when he does precisely the same thing before arriving at the office

L or indeed between working days. This was something he had to do in order to do his job properly. It was expected of him and any failure to do it would have shown up instantly. No doubt cases like *Humbles v Brooks* illustrates how the words of the statute have been applied in other cases and by providing analogies assist the argument as to the application of the words; but as Lord Morris of Borth-y-Gest said in *Taylor v Provan* at p 210: "I regard many of the reported cases as being no more than illustrative of the divergent sets of circumstances that may arise and of the way in which in

reference to particular facts the words . . . have in particular cases been applied".

The analogy between a journalist on a daily newspaper
and a history teacher is singularly weak. A better analogy
would be with a television interviewer who once per
week for 30 minutes, interviews live on television a
prominent politician who is closely involved with a
rapidly changing political scene. In his preparation for
the 30 minutes of the broadcast the interviewer would
have to spend many hours researching the subject, the
person to be interviewed, the opinions of others and
the very latest developments and utterances relevant to
the possible subject matter of the interview. In my view,
it would be absurd to say that the interviewer was performing his duties only when the studio lights were
turned up and the broadcast began. The correct view
would be that the preparation, reading and research
would be done in the performance of the interviewer's
work, whether it was done on the premises of the television station or at the interviewer's home or in a university library: in this kind of task the researching is an
integral part of the duties to be performed even if it
is also a preparation for a particular aspect of the performance. An analogy might also be drawn with a
member of an orchestra who on Tuesday at home prac-
tises and on Thursday in the concert hall rehearses the
part he has to play in a public concert on Friday. I
should have thought he was engaged in the performance
of his work on all occasions even although he was
preparing on Tuesday and Thursday for what the public
was to hear on Friday. Practising the piece to be performed in public would be part of his duties. Arguments
based on the fact that the appellant was paid an hourly
rate for hours spent in the office and received no pay
or overtime emolument in respect of any other hours
appear to me to miss the obvious reality, that employed
members of many professions perform their work
outwith office hours but do not expect, seek or obtain
extra remuneration. Payment by the week, the day or
the hour is just a convenient technique for calculating
pay and differentials.

The logic of my approach, therefore, is that the commissioners have not addressed the correct questions in
the correct way and that accordingly their conclusion
cannot be sustained unless it is justified upon the
primary facts themselves, properly understood, and
sound inferences from them. The commissioners' conclusion is one which purports to relate to all the material
facts but does not, in my view, rest upon a consideration of or even an addressing of all the material facts.
I contrast the findings in these cases with the clear,
explicit and comprehensive findings in *Smith v Abbott*,
the report of several cases which your Lordship in the
chair distinguishes on the facts. It is also useful,
however, to contrast the character of the findings in
those cases with the character of the findings in the
present cases; doing that assists me to the conclusion
that the present findings are not adequate to justify the
conclusion drawn by the special commissioners.

In these circumstances, if the primary facts are sufficient for the purpose, this court is, in my opinion, able
to come to its own conclusion upon the taxpayer's claim.
I think that they are sufficient and that the proper conclusion is that the expenditure of this appellant was
expenditure necessarily in the performance of the duties
of the employment. I have already noted that there
appeared to be no dispute in relation to question 5. So
far as question 6 is concerned, the commissioners themselves made no finding that the expenditure claimed was
incurred for any purpose other than to meet the
demands of the duties of the employment and I see no
proper basis on the material in this case to reach any
such conclusion. It would be unfair to hold that the taxpayer failed in relation to question 6 simply because
the commissioners decided it was unnecessary to address
this essential matter, if that is what truly happened. But
it appears just as likely that they did not address the
point because the revenue did not press them to find
against the taxpayer on this matter. Accordingly I should
allow this appeal.

I now turn to the case of Thomas Fitzpatrick. The
general background findings in fact are the same. This
appellant, however, was a photographer, and was
employed as assistant picture editor in charge of several
staff, both full time and part time; he also sometimes
acted as a "photo-journalist". He was expected to
produce ideas for the editor's consideration and he in
fact obtained many of these ideas from reading other
newspapers and taking cuttings from them (V (ix)). One
of his first duties after reaching the newspaper offices
and following upon a meeting with the editor was to
have a discussion with the picture editor to decide which
of the available photographs should be used in the
paper's first edition; similar decisions in relation to the
use of photographs had to be taken for later editions,
subject to changes in the light of events. He actually
used his cuttings in his discussions with the picture
editor (see findings V (xii) and V (xiii)). He could not
rely upon the cuttings library and had to have his own
cuttings. He found about 20 per cent of the cuttings
which he took to be useful (finding V (xiv)). I pause
to observe that, in my opinion, it is a fallacy to say, as
I understood counsel for the revenue to urge us to
accept, that even if the work involved in obtaining the
20 per cent fell within the performance of the duties
of the employment the work connected with the remaining 80 per cent did not. Plainly, if, in the performance
of his duties he took 100 cuttings any of which he might
actually use or discard as not needed, the fact that he
eventually used only 20 of them and discarded the other
80 would not somehow have the result that the taking
of these 80 would fall outwith the scope of the performance of his duties. The observation which I have just
made has the appearance of circularity, but the point
is that, if the reading etc was done in the performance
of the work, the fact that it did not directly influence
what came to be published would not change that. It
is very important to observe in this case that it is found
without qualification that the pressures of his work
within the office left Mr Fitzpatrick with no time to
take cuttings during the day (V (xviii)): thus this essential work had to be done probably outside the office and
certainly outside office hours. Finding V (xxiv) makes

it plain that he had to read the papers not only to get
ideas but also to see what pictures were printed in other
newspapers in order to avoid printing in the *Evening
Times*, in which he was employed, any picture that had
already appeared in another paper. When he was
engaged for the job he was told by the editor that he,
the editor, would not employ anyone on the paper who
was not a "reading man" (finding V (xxx)). Paragraph
VI is identical in this case, and indeed all the cases, to
that contained in Cameron Simpson's case. In my
opinion, it fails to address the issues for the reasons that
I have given in dealing with Cameron Simpson's case.
In my opinion the determination by the special commissioners in this case also is defective because of their
failure to address the correct issues. Upon a consideration of the facts as they appear from what is recorded
as findings in fact I would draw the conclusion that the
expenditure that this appellant incurred was such that
it is proper to describe it as necessarily incurred by him
as holder of the office or employment which he held
in the performance of the duties of that employment.
So far as facts 5 and 6 are concerned I have nothing
additional to say in relation to this particular appellant.
I should therefore allow this appeal.

Barclay McBain was a staff reporter with the *Glasgow
Herald*. It is plain from the findings relating to him in
para V that he was expected to cover stories over a very
wide field, as narrated in V (vi). In V (viii) it is narrated that "he was expected to have read other papers"
when he arrived at the office (my emphasis). He was also
"expected" then, ie on arrival, to have ideas on what
stories might have been followed up or what subjects
might be covered in features articles though the decisions were for the editor to take. It is evident that he
had to discuss these matters with the editor. Furthermore he had been told when he was appointed to the
job that he *had* to read other newspapers (my emphasis) and would have expected to have been reprimanded
had he not done so. He regarded his obligation so to
read as an unofficial condition of his employment; but
again we are not told if the commissioners agreed with
him, or why they disagreed, if they did. Finding V (xiii)
narrates his own view that it was necessary for him to
study the publications in question to do his job properly
and he had to take cuttings because the office cutting
service was inadequate; as elsewhere, the commissioners
are silent as to what they concluded about necessity in
this regard. There was no time to read and take cuttings in the office (V (iv)). As in the cases previously
dealt with, it is evident, in my opinion, that in this case
too the special commissioners have not approached the
correct issues in the correct way and have not addressed
themselves to the matters which are essential; thus their
conclusion is flawed. On the basis of the facts which,
in my opinion, fall to be treated as primary facts the
proper conclusion, in my opinion, is that in reading the
newspapers etc in question this appellant was engaged
in the performance of the duties of the employment and
that the holder could not have performed those duties
without such reading and, at least in that sense, the
reading was necessary. I see no reason to hold that there
was a failure to establish the fact I have numbered 5.

So far as fact 6 is concerned, finding V (xi) refers to
his reading as being "partly to improve his general
knowledge of current affairs", but the continuation of
that sentence indicates that this was an aspect of stock-
ing his mind so that he could tackle any job that he
would be given by the editor. The immediacy of this
kind of knowledge of current affairs is obviously a matter
of crucial importance and I do not consider that it would
be proper to hold that the expenditure claimed was
incurred for a purpose other than meeting the demands
arising directly from the need to perform the duties of
the office. Otherwise the observations I have made in
relation to Mr Simpson's appeal apply here also.

I can deal with the case of Rosemary Long more
shortly. It was not in dispute that this was the strongest case and it is perfectly evident that she could not
have done her job properly unless she did the reading
in question V (xviii). Furthermore that reading was
necessary because her superiors expected her to read
it, because they required her column to be topical,
because she had to produce ideas for features and put
them to the features editor and because generally she
had to keep abreast of things in view of what was
required of her. The reasoning applicable to the other
cases applies to this one mutatis mutandis. I should also
allow this appeal for the reasons already given.

Mr James Traynor was a sports sub-editor, feature
writer and match reporter who did some of his reading
in the office and some outside (finding V (x)). He could
not rely on the office cutting service and had his own
cuttings file. He could not do his job without knowing
what was happening in the world of sport and indeed
without knowing what was being written about sport
in other newspapers. He had to read beyond the sports
pages for reasons explained in finding V (xiii). There
is nothing in the special commissioners' treatment of
this case to indicate that they adequately addressed the
questions which, in my opinion, it was necessary for
them to address. On the facts as recorded and properly
understood the correct inference, in my opinion, is that
it was necessary for him in the performance of the work
of sports sub-editor and feature writer to incur the
expenditure in question. Accordingly I consider that this
appeal too should be allowed, for the same reasons
generally as are given in relation to the other appeals.
I should note that so far as the facts I have called 5 and
6 are concerned, that there is no record in the contentions on behalf of the Commissioners of Inland
Revenue, contained in para VIII of the stated cases, that
the appellants should fail because they fail to satisfy
these tests. So far as these matters are concerned I am
content with what the commissioners appear to have
accepted, albeit their decision is not clearly spelled out.

I wish to add one other observation about *Smith v
Abbott*. I have already referred to what appears to me
to be the striking contrast between the character of the
findings in fact in that group of cases and the purported
findings in these five appeals. I appreciate that one
cannot graft the facts from one set of cases with another
set of cases when the fact finding processes are distinct.
But, comparing the two sets of facts found, I am left

A with a profound sense of the unreality of the exercise which we were invited by the revenue (and effectively by the special commissioners) to undertake in the present appeals. It appears to me to be somewhat unreal to be asked to distinguish *Smith v Abbott* from the present cases on the basis that the facts are different. To my mind the more likely reason why the facts are not broadly the same for the same category of journalists is that in the present five stated cases the "facts" are not properly stated at all.

B I regret that my conclusions are different from those arrived at by your Lordships. And I am very conscious of the fact, noted by both your Lordships, that the submissions addressed to us for the appellants were narrower in some ways than the approach that has commended itself to me. But, as the history of the case shows, the appellants were never content with the way the cases were stated or the facts found but were unable to find a mechanism for having the cases stated adequately (as they judged it). In the event, they adopted the approach described by your Lordship in the chair.

C In my view, however, the essence of their argument was that the conclusions reached by the commissioners upon the inferential issues and, in consequence, upon the essential questions of fact and law were not conclusions which the commissioners were entitled to reach upon the facts as properly understood; and that this court was free to draw its own conclusions based upon those facts. That is the view of the case which I have concluded is the correct one.

D **LORD CULLEN.**—In each of these appeals the question for the opinion of this court is whether, on the facts found by the special commissioners, they were entitled to conclude that no deduction could be made under s 189 (1) of the Income and Corporation Taxes Act 1970 for the expenditure in question.

Section 189 (1) provides as follows: [his Lordship quoted the terms of s 189 (1) and continued:]

E It was not in dispute that in order to justify that deduction in the present cases each of the appellants required to establish that as the holder of an employment he or she was "necessarily obliged" to expend money in question "wholly, exclusively and necessarily in the performance of" the duties of that employment. There was no dispute as to the interpretation of these terms in the light of a number of authoritative decisions. The expression "necessarily obliged" means that the taxpayer must be obliged by the very fact that he holds the employment in question. It imposes an objective test (*Ricketts v Colquhoun*, per Viscount Cave at (1926) 10 TC, p 133

F and Lord Blanesburgh at p 135). A correct interpretation of "in the performance of" the duties involves distinguishing between what is done in performance of the duties and what is done in qualifying or preparing to perform them (*Humbles v Brooks* at pp 502-503). Further, it falls to be distinguished from what is done in order to enable the duties to be performed (*Taylor v Provan* [1975] AC, per Lord Salmon at p 226). An expenditure may be "necessary" for the holder of an employment without being necessary in the performance

of the duties of that employment. The latter is required by the last part of the expression "wholly, exclusively G and necessarily" (*Lomax v Newton*, per Vaisey J at (1953) 34 TC, p 562). This again imposes an objective test. It has long been recognised that the terms of s 189 (1) and its antecedents from the middle of the 19th century impose a strict and rigid set of requirements which may be contrasted with the less stringent provisions relating to deductions in connection with taxation under Sched D.

At this point it is useful to bring into sharp focus the H question which has been posed for our opinion. It is clear that this court can reverse a decision of the special commissioners only if they have erred in point of law. There was no argument before us in the present cases that the commissioners had misinterpreted or misapplied the law in some relevant particular. Further, there was no argument, as there had been at an earlier stage in the history of these appeals, that they had failed to make proper findings. Subject to certain exceptions relating to inferences from the primary facts, to which I will refer later in this opinion, it was not argued that I they had failed to make a finding in regard to a particular matter when they should have done so. We were not asked to remit the cases to them for further consideration of the findings. Had the court on cause shown remitted the cases to them they would have been given the opportunity to set out the evidence, if any, which was relevant to such a possible finding and their reasons for not making a finding to that effect, so that this court could ascertain whether there was evidence on the basis of which the finding could have been made; and, if so, J whether there was any reasonable ground on which the finding could have been withheld.

In these circumstances the submission by counsel for the appellants was, and required to be, that on the facts found by the commissioners the true and only reasonable conclusion contradicted their determination, and in that sense they had fallen into an error of law. This formulation follows the terms of the classic statement of Lord Radcliffe in *Edwards v Bairstow* [1956] AC at K p 36.

I would make a number of observations at this point. First, it is plainly for the appellant, upon whom the onus lies to obtain authority for the deduction, to have led evidence which is relevant, adequate and persuasive for the purpose of obtaining from the commissioners findings which are adequate to meet the challenge which is posed by this test. Secondly, it is important to keep firmly in view that the question for this court is whether on the facts found by the commissioners they were L entitled to reach the determination which they did. If those facts warranted a determination either way, and there was no misinterpretation or misapplication of the law, there is no room for this court's interference. The question would be a matter of degree and therefore of fact, giving rise to no question of error in law. Thirdly, it is clear from the nature of the submission which was made to us that we are to compare on the one hand the facts found by the commissioners and on the other the determination which they made. Even if the reasons

A given by them for their determination are unconvincing the question would still remain whether their determination was one to which they were not entitled, on the facts found by them, to come. Unless it can be shown that the true and only reasonable conclusion contradicts the determination, the court is not warranted in interfering.

It is convenient and not inappropriate to deal first with the application of the expression "in the performance of", since it is clear that in the case of all the appellants, apart from Miss Long, their appeals failed

B before the commissioners on this point. Further, as Lord Salmon observed in *Taylor v Provan* at [1975] AC, p 225, a consideration of this expression comes logically before the question whether the expenditure was "necessarily" incurred. Following this approach I will at this stage consider the appeals other than that of Miss Long, and defer my discussion of her appeal until a later stage in this opinion.

The written decision of the commissioners dated 18

C May 1989 which is appended to each of the cases shows that it was argued for each of the appellants that the duties of their employment were performed in part at home, and that these duties included the reading and cutting of newspapers and periodicals. The commissioners evidently rejected this and no findings to this effect appear in any of the cases.

In support of their submission that the appellants' duties were performed partly at home they invited the commissioners to find that, like the standby doctor in

D *Pook v Owen*, each of the appellants was while at home "on call" and received and gave advice and instructions relating to his employment. The commissioners rejected such a comparison and it was not renewed in argument before us. Accordingly I do not require to consider it further.

Counsel for the appellants renewed an argument which had been presented to the commissioners that it was a condition of employment of each of the appel-

E lants that he carry out reading and cutting of newspapers and periodicals. Counsel founded on the terms of an agreement between the employers, George Outram & Co Ltd, and the National Union of Journalists (NUJ) dated 11 July 1980. He also drew attention to findings in certain of the cases which showed that it had been made clear to the appellants from the outset that they were expected to read newspapers and periodicals. They also showed that if they had not done so this would soon have become obvious and they would have faced a repri-

F mand. He also pointed out that the appellants themselves took the view that they did not regard their work as stopping at the limits of the recognised working hours. Counsel criticised the commissioners for not finding as a fact that it was a condition of employment that each appellant carry out reading and cutting. He also maintained that a finding that a particular appellant "considered that he was engaged on the duties of his employment when he was reading and taking cuttings from those newspapers and magazines" was not a proper finding, in respect that the commissioners should have decided whether that was the case or not.

The answer to the question of condition of employment is clearly relevant to whether the appellant was G "necessarily obliged". Nevertheless it may have a bearing on whether when reading and cutting each of the appellants was performing the duties of his employment. The commissioners state in each case that on the evidence before them they were unable to make a finding that there was such a condition. I do not consider that such a finding could not reasonably have been withheld. The appellants' attempt to found on the terms of the 1980 agreement was in my view misconceived, for the reasons set out by your Lordship in the chair. There H was no basis for such a finding in the terms of the contract of employment which was current in 1985-86. The appellants were not paid for reading and cutting at home outwith the recognised working hours. There was no arrangement between them and the employers to this effect. The commissioners were entitled to treat the appellants' own views on this matter as not decisive. I am unable to agree that the type of finding which was criticised was not a proper finding. It would, of course, be wrong for the commissioners to set out a purported I finding which was merely a statement that a witness had given evidence to a certain effect, since the commissioners could not abdicate the responsibility of deciding whether they accepted the truth of what was testified. Here the point is different. The commissioners plainly rejected the proposition that each of the appellants was performing the duties of his employment while at home. The finding indicates that each appellant genuinely took the opposite view.

Counsel for the appellants also presented an alter- J native argument in favour of the implication of a term in the appellants' contract of employment that each of them was to carry out reading and cutting of newspapers. This argument was also used in support of an approach to the word "necessarily" which was independent of the contract of employment. Counsel submitted that it should be inferred from the commissioners' findings that it was a general practice among journalists, and particularly those in the same type of employment as each of the appellants, that they carried K on such reading and cutting at home. The commissioners had declined to find that it was a universal practice among journalists but accepted that it was a common one. In their written decision they stated: "In the absence of any special circumstances, however, it seems to us that the practice is to be regarded as part of a professional journalist's way of life rather than an incident in the duties of a particular employment in the newspaper industry. The terms of the journalists' contracts in this case are more consistent with that view L of the matter than with the opposing view that reading is part of the employees' duties. There is no requirement that it should be done nor is any time made available for it. The practice is recognised and approved by payment of the newspaper allowance but the activity is clearly to be carried on out of working hours in the employee's own time."

Counsel criticised the commissioners' finding "that wide reading of other newspapers and magazines is a common practice among journalists of all kinds". This was, he said, a finding which no reasonable commissioners would have made. He went on to submit that the findings made by the commissioners showed that the work of the appellants could not be performed without the activity of reading and cutting newspapers and periodicals at home, renewing a submission to that effect which had been made to the commissioners. The commissioners did not in terms state what was their view in regard to that proposition. However in each of the cases they stated that they were satisfied that without a wide reading of other newspapers and magazines the appellant "would have discharged the duties of his employment less effectively and might not have kept his job" on the newspaper in question. Counsel for the appellants founded strongly on a number of findings as supporting the view that this statement, which echoed the submission which had been made by the respondents before the commissioners, fell a long way short of what was an inevitable inference from certain of the findings as to what each of the appellants found it essential to do in equipping himself for the working day.

It was in my view open to the commissioners who heard only the evidence of the appellants and, for aught yet seen, only in regard to what was the practice which each of them followed, to decline to find that the practice of reading and cutting was universal among journalists. As regards the proposition that such reading and cutting were essential to the proper performance by each appellant of the duties of his employment, the facts found by the commissioners could readily have led to the inference that this was the case. However I am unable to say that the commissioners were bound to reach this conclusion. In any event a conclusion on this point could not be decisive in the present appeals. The critical question was whether the reading and cutting of newspapers and periodicals formed part of the performance of the duties of employment in the case of each of the appellants.

In order to meet this test counsel for the appellants argued that the reading and cutting was so closely tied to what was done by each appellant within the recognised working hours that it fell to be regarded as part and parcel of it. Not long after they had been gleaned from this activity materials and ideas were put to actual use at the office or on assignments by each of the appellants. Thereafter they would be redundant. In response counsel for the respondents pointed out by reference to the findings that the appellants received no payment for the time spent on reading and cutting which on any view was outside the recognised working hours. Each of them had a personal choice of which newspapers or periodicals to purchase. The character of the activity of buying and reading was substantially unchanged with the passing of time. It had no regard to whether the appellant was working or was on holiday. It had no regard to any particular assignment on which he was to be engaged. The reading and cutting was completed in most cases before the appellant arrived at the office where he was given the task which he was to perform during recognised working hours, such as writing an article or carrying out an assignment. At the time of reading and cutting the appellant did not know whether

what he read would be used for the purpose of performing a particular task. The reading provided background knowledge, information of general interest and information which might be useful.

The commissioners' view on this aspect of the matter, as expressed in their written decision, was that: "By reading newspapers and magazines the appellants, generally speaking at any rate, provided themselves with background material with which to approach their respective tasks as reporter, feature writer, sub-editor or photo-journalist as the case might be. They were not at any time preparing articles, photographs or reports for publication, but preparing themselves to carry out the duties of their employments."

I do not propose to go into the detail of individual cases, since in the light of the findings founded upon by the respondents which I have outlined above I am unable to take the view that the commissioners were not entitled to conclude that the appellants had failed to establish that the expenditure of money on newspapers and periodicals was "in the performance of" the duties of their respective employments. They were entitled, in my view, to regard the findings as indicating that the activity of reading and cutting newspapers and periodicals was preparatory to the performance of their duties. Even if this were regarded as an unconvincing description of this activity, they would in any event have been entitled to regard the activity as being carried on in order to enable the duties to be performed rather than as being part of the performance itself.

It remains for me to deal with the case of Miss Long. In her case the commissioners were evidently hesitant about reaching the conclusion that when she was reading newspapers and periodicals at home she was not carrying out the duties of her employment. They observed in their written decision: "There seem to have been occasions when she used pieces from other papers as the direct foundation for her commentary on topical events, adding her own twist to the subject". Instead they treated as determinative that the expenditure could not satisfy the objective test required by s 189 (1) as it was dictated in their view not by the employment but by her chosen method of work, which was personal to her. At the same time the commissioners made it clear that only part of the expense would have qualified for deduction if the objective test had been satisfied. They pointed out that identification would presumably be difficult since she also bought papers as background information. It is clear that the appellant presented her case for deduction in such a way as not to distinguish between the expenditure on different newspapers and periodicals. Accordingly the question whether expenditure was "wholly" and "exclusively" in the performance of the duties of her employment fell to be considered by the commissioners with reference to the total expenditure. In the light of the way in which this appellant's case was presented and the commissioners' observation that only part of that expenditure could have been incurred in the performance of those duties, it can be seen that the test of "wholly" and "exclusively" could not be satisfied. In those circumstances the commis-

sioners were entitled on this point also to conclude that
A no deduction could be made for the expenditure in question. I do not overlook the fact that the commissioners
recorded that the respondents did not seriously dispute
the proposition that the expenditure on newspapers
"was incurred wholly and exclusively for the purposes
of" the employment of each of the appellants. However, that broad proposition is sufficient to encompass
the expending of money in preparation for or for the
purposes of enabling the performance of the duties of
an employment. Section 189 (1) of the 1970 Act imposes
B a more stringent test by requiring that the expenditure
is "in the performance of" the duties; and the words
"wholly" and "exclusively" must be read in conjunction
with that requirement and not in isolation.

For these reasons I am in agreement with your Lordship in the chair that in each of these cases the question of law should be answered in the affirmative and
the appeals refused.

C
*Counsel for Appellants, R N M Anderson; Solicitors,
Haig Scott & Co — Counsel for Respondents, G N H
Emslie, QC, Hodge; Solicitor, T H Scott, Solicitor of
Inland Revenue, Scotland.*

M G J U

[An appeal to the House of Lords has been presented.]

D

Hazlett v McGlennan

HIGH COURT OF JUSTICIARY

THE LORD JUSTICE CLERK (ROSS),
LORDS MORISON AND GRIEVE

7 JULY 1992

E
*Justiciary — Procedure — Summary procedure — 40 day
custody rule — Whether 40 day period calculated by including first day — Whether period elapses at first moment
of 40th day — Criminal Procedure (Scotland) Act 1975
(c 21), s 331A (1).*

Section 331A (1) of the Criminal Procedure (Scotland)
Act 1975 provides inter alia that a person charged with
a summary offence shall not be detained in that respect
for a total of more than 40 days after the bringing of
F the complaint in court unless his trial is commenced
within that period, failing which he shall be liberated
forthwith and thereafter shall be forever free from all
question or process for that offence.

Two accused persons appeared in court on 5 February
1992 charged on summary complaint. They pled not
guilty, trial was fixed for 16 March 1992 and they were
remanded in custody. At the trial diet the accused moved
the sheriff to dismiss the complaints on the ground that
they had been detained in custody for 41 days. The
sheriff repelled the plea and the accused pled guilty and

were sentenced. The accused appealed by bill of suspension, contending that the whole of the first day, 5 G
February 1992, should be included in the computation
of the 40 day period and, additionally, that the period
was completed at the first moment of the 40th day, on
the basis of the maxim dies inceptus pro completo
habetur.

Held, (1) that in calculating the period of 40 days
under s 331A (1), the first day (5 February 1992) fell
to be excluded from the calculation and accordingly 16
March 1992 was the 40th day (p 76B); (2) that while
s 331A (1) might be regarded as conferring a right upon H
a person charged with a summary offence, the fact that
Parliament envisaged a trial being commenced within
the 40 day period showed that the 40th day would not
elapse until the end of the 24 hours of that day (p
76G-H); and bills *refused*.

Lees v Lovell, 1992 SLT 967, *followed*.

Bill of suspension and liberation   I
Madeleine Hazlett and Paula Elizabeth McCrory
brought bills of suspension against J G M McGlennan,
procurator fiscal, Kilmarnock, praying the High Court
of Justiciary to suspend their pretended convictions and
sentences imposed by Sheriff A W Noble on 16 March
1992 for attempting to pervert the course of justice. The
facts of the case are set forth in the opinion of the court.

Statutory provisions
The Criminal Procedure (Scotland) Act 1975
provides: J

"331A.—(1) Subject to subsections (2) and (3) below,
a person charged with a summary offence shall not be
detained in that respect for a total of more than forty
days after the bringing of the complaint in court unless
his trial is commenced within that period, failing which
he shall be liberated forthwith and thereafter he shall
be forever free from all question or process for that
offence."

Cases referred to   K
Blair v Magistrates of Edinburgh (1704) Mor 3468.
Frew v Morris (1897) 24 R (J) 50.
Grugen v Jessop, 1988 SCCR 182.
Keenan v Carmichael, 1992 SLT 814; 1991 SCCR 680.
Lees v Lovell, 1992 SLT 967.
Thomson v Kirkcudbright Magistrates (1878) 5 R 561.

Textbooks referred to
Erskine, *Institute*, III viii 96.
Green's *Encyclopaedia*, Vol 14, para 1039.   L
Stair Memorial Encyclopaedia, Vol 17, para 699, and
    Vol 22, paras 819, 822 and 823.

The bills were heard before the High Court on 7 July
1992.

Eo die the court *refused* to pass the bills.

The following opinion of the court was delivered by
the Lord Justice Clerk (Ross):

OPINION OF THE COURT.—By agreement of

A parties these two bills of suspension were heard together as they raise the same issues. On 5 February 1992 the two complainers appeared in Kilmarnock sheriff court on a summary complaint containing against each complainer charges of theft, and attempting to pervert the course of justice. In the case of the complainer Paula Elizabeth McCrory there were also charges of contravening the provisions of the Bail etc (Scotland) Act 1980. The complainers both pled not guilty to the charges and a trial diet was fixed for 16 March 1992. The com-

B plainers were both remanded in custody pending trial.

When the case called for trial against the complainers on 16 March 1992 the solicitors for the complainers moved the court to dismiss the complainers from the proceedings on the ground that they had been detained in custody for a period exceeding 40 days contrary to s 331A of the Criminal Procedure (Scotland) Act 1975. After hearing submissions from the solicitors and the procurator fiscal depute, the sheriff repelled this plea. Thereafter the complainers pled guilty to certain charges

C on the complaint and were sentenced by the sheriff to periods of imprisonment. They have now presented these bills of suspension in which they maintain that the sheriff reached the wrong decision on the motion made to him. They both contend that they had been detained for a total of more than 40 days after the bringing of the complaint in court without their trial having commenced, and that accordingly they are entitled to be liberated and to be forever free from all question or process in respect of that complaint.

D

The question which arises in these bills is as to how the 40 day period referred to in s 331A of the Act of 1975 falls to be calculated. Section 331A (1) provides as follows: [his Lordship quoted the terms of s 331A (1) and continued:]

In the present case the complaint against the complainers was brought in court on 5 February 1992. The trial diet was 16 March 1992. Counsel for the complainer Madeleine Hazlett maintained that when cal-

E culating the period of 40 days after the bringing of the complaint, the date upon which the complaint was brought had to be taken into account; accordingly 16 March 1992 was the 41st day after the complaint had been brought into court on 5 February 1992. On the other hand he recognised that if the day upon which the complaint was brought in court fell to be omitted from the calculation, 16 March 1992 was then the 40th day after the bringing of the complaint.

F

In support of his contention, counsel referred to the *Stair Memorial Encyclopaedia of the Laws of Scotland*, Vol 17, para 699, and the *Stair Memorial Encyclopaedia of the Laws of Scotland*, Vol 22, para 819. Under reference to para 819 he maintained that when calculating the extent of a period of time it was necessary to determine the method of computation to be employed which might be naturalis computatio or civilis computatio. It was also necesary to determine when the period commenced and when it terminated. He did not suggest that naturalis computatio fell to be employed as that would have meant that time fell to be calculated de

momento in momentum. Counsel recognised that where civilis computatio was adopted, the general rule was that G the whole of the first day fell to be excluded and that the last day fell to be included. However he contended that this general rule did not apply in the circumstances.

He maintained that support for this proposition was to be found in para 699 of Vol 17 of the *Stair Memorial Encyclopaedia of the Laws of Scotland*. In that paragraph it is stated: "The 40 day rule starts from the time the complaint is brought to court providing the accused is detained from that time onwards". In our opinion, however, that statement begs the question of when the H 40 day period commences.

Counsel also prayed in aid *Grugen v Jessop*. In the course of his opinion in that case the Lord Justice General at p 184 mentioned that as a matter of arithmetic the complainer had spent 34 days in custody before 1 September 1987. In the circumstances of that case that meant that the first day was included in the calculation. It is clear, however, that that observation by the Lord Justice General was obiter, and the court I does not appear to have received any argument on the question of whether or not the first day fell to be included in the calculation. The point was not critical in that case.

In our opinion counsel for the complainer Hazlett has failed to demonstrate that the general rule in civilis computatio does not apply. We see no reason why the general rule should not be followed in this case. As already observed, the general rule is that fractions of a day are ignored, and that the day from which the J period runs is excluded, the period being deemed to commence at midnight on that day (para 822 of Vol 22 of the *Stair Memorial Encyclopaedia of the Laws of Scotland*). In that paragraph reference is made to what Lord Ivory wrote in a note to Erskine's *Institute*, III viii 96, commenting on a case where a deed was reduced under the law of deathbed: "The ground of decision in the House of Lords is important, as fixing the rule of computation, 'that the *terminus a quo*, mentioned in the Act, is descriptive of a period of time, viz the date or day K of the death, which is indivisible; and *60 days after* is descriptive of another and subsequent period, which begins when the first period is completed. The day of making the deed must therefore be excluded."

In these circumstances, we are satisfied as matter of principle that in the present case the day which forms the terminus a quo (5 February 1992) falls to be omitted from the calculation of the 40 days. Confirmation for this view is to be found in *Lees v Lovell*, upon which L the Solicitor General relied in seeking to support the decision of the sheriff. That case was concerned with the six month period of time bar under s 331 of the Act of 1975. The language used in s 331 is similar to the language used in s 331A. In s 331 it is provided that proceedings must be commenced within six months "after the contravention occurred". In s 331A, reference is made to "a total of more than 40 days after the bringing of the complaint in court". In *Lees v Lovell* the Lord Justice General in delivering the opinion of the court said: "For the reasons explained in *Keenan*

A *v Carmichael*, however, which we need not repeat in detail in this opinion, the correct approach to the matter is to calculate the period of six months referred to in s 331 (1) de die in diem and accordingly to leave the date when the contravention occurred out of account. This is the normal rule which is applied in the computation of time, the relevance of which to criminal cases was explained by Lord Justice Clerk Macdonald in *Frew v Morris* at p 51: 'I think that in the ordinary sense of our criminal law the word "time" means the day on which the fact or offence occurred, and the rule of law

B applies, that in computing a period from the time or day of the occurrence of any event, the day of that occurrence is not to be counted.' "

For the foregoing reasons we are satisfied that counsel's first submission was ill founded, and that in calculating the period of 40 days under s 331A, the first day, namely, 5 February 1992, fell to be excluded from the calculation. It follows that 16 March 1992 was the 40th day.

C Counsel for the complainer Hazlett, however, had a second submission which he asked the court to uphold in the event of the court being against him on his first submission. He contended that even if the day which formed the terminus a quo fell to be omitted from the calculation, and the 40th day was 16 March 1992, the last day should be held as completed at the first moment of that day in accordance with the maxim dies inceptus pro completo habetur. In *Lees v Lovell*, the Lord Justice General appears to have accepted the Crown's conten-

D tion that the six month period expired at midnight on 29 December 1991. It appears, however, that it was not suggested to the court in that case that the maxim dies inceptus pro completo habetur applied, and accordingly the court did not express any opinion upon this matter.

Counsel referred to Vol 22 of the *Stair Memorial Encyclopaedia of the Laws of Scotland*, para 823. It is there stated: "When computation is by *civilis computatio* and the day upon which the period commenced has been excluded, it is to be expected that the final

E day will be included, and this is the general rule." It is also observed however that questions do arise as to the terminus ad quem: at what point of the day is the period to be deemed to have terminated? One possibility is that a period of time will expire at the earliest moment of the final day on the principle dies inceptus pro completo habetur. It has been held that the maxim applies only when a right is being acquired (*Thomson v Kirkcudbright Magistrates* at p 563).

F Counsel also referred to Green's *Encyclopaedia of the Laws of Scotland*, Vol 14, para 1039. The maxim is again referred to and the view expressed that it applies in the acquisition of rights: "Thus a debtor who was entitled to be liberated under the Act of Grace 1696, c 32, after ten days, was held entitled to be liberated at the commencement of the tenth day." In this context too, counsel referred to *Blair v Magistrates of Edinburgh*.

We are not persuaded that the maxim dies inceptus pro completo habetur applies to the present case. As was made plain in the *Stair Memorial Encyclopaedia*,

Vol 22, and Green's *Encyclopaedia*, Vol 14, the general rule is that the whole of the final day is included. We G recognise that s 331A (1) might be regarded in a sense as conferring a right upon a person charged with a summary offence, but we cannot believe that Parliament intended that such a right could be acquired at one minute past midnight on the 40th day when there could be no question of a trial commencing at such an hour. The fact that Parliament envisaged a trial being commenced within the 40 day period shows, in our opinion, that the 40th day will not elapse until the end of the 24 hours of that day. If the period was held to expire H at the earliest moment of the final day, the consequence would be that in effect the period was reduced from 40 days to 39 days, and we are not persuaded that that can have been the intention of Parliament. Accordingly we are satisfied that the general rule applies in this case and that since the first day was excluded from the calculation, the whole of the final day falls to be included. It follows that the sheriff was well founded in concluding that the motion made by the complainers should be refused. I

Counsel for the complainer Paula Elizabeth McCrory adopted the submissions made by counsel for the complainer Hazlett, but recognised that her client was not in as strong a position as the complainer Hazlett. During the whole of the 40 day period, this complainer was serving a sentence of imprisonment on other matters. Counsel recognised that in cases which fell under the 110 day rule (that is, s 101 of the Act of 1975), a sentence of imprisonment has been held to interrupt the running of the 110 day period. She realised that there J was much to be said for the view that a sentence would similarly interrupt the running of the 40 day period in summary procedure. In view of the decision at which we have arrived on the basis of the submissions made by counsel for the complainer Hazlett, it is not necessary to consider the special features which exist in the case of the complainer McCrory.

We have refused to pass both bills of suspension.

———————

K

Counsel for Complainer Hazlett, Allardice; Solicitors, Macbeth Currie & Co, WS — Counsel for Complainer McCrory, McNeill; Solicitors, Simpson & Marwick, WS — Counsel for Respondent, Solicitor General (Dawson, QC); Solicitor, J D Lowe, Crown Agent.

P W F

L

K v HM Advocate

A HIGH COURT OF JUSTICIARY

THE LORD JUSTICE GENERAL (HOPE),
LORDS ALLANBRIDGE AND MURRAY

21 DECEMBER 1990

Justiciary — Procedure — Trial — Accused committed to prison — Accused subsequently granted bail with condition that they reside at school containing secure unit — Whether accused continued to be detained and subject to statutory time limits — Criminal Procedure (Scotland) Act 1975 (c 21), s 101 (2).

B

Two children, K and B, appeared on petition and were committed to prison on production of certificates that they were so unruly that they could not safely be detained in a place of safety chosen by the local authority. They were later granted bail on condition inter alia that they reside at named schools which contained secure units. They remained there and, in respect of B, in custody relating to other proceedings, for longer than 110 days. After being served with indictments they intimated pleas in bar of trial that the indictments had not been served within 80 days following their committal and that they had been detained for longer than 110 days, contrary to s 101 (2) of the Criminal Procedure (Scotland) Act 1975. The sheriff repelled the pleas but granted leave to appeal. On appeal it was argued for the appellants that bail meant the release of an accused person and that the appellants could not be said to have been liberated while incarcerated in the secure unit of a school. The Crown submitted that the orders had been made under the Bail etc (Scotland) Act 1980 in petitions for bail at the appellants' instance, that a review of the conditions could have been sought and that the appellants had no longer been detained by virtue of the original committals.

C

D

Held, that although the appellants had been granted bail this had been no more than a device to ensure that they were detained in suitable and secure conditions until brought to trial, and as the factual position was that they had not been set at liberty but continued to be detained by virtue of their committal they remained entitled to the benefit of the statutory time limits and to plead them in bar of trial (pp 79G and 80B-C); and appeals *allowed* and pleas in bar of trial *sustained*.

E

HM Advocate v McCann, 1977 JC 1, *applied*.

F

_____

Indictment

On 8 May 1990, K and B appeared on petition at Arbroath sheriff court and were committed to prison until liberated in due course of law, certificates having been produced in terms of the Criminal Procedure (Scotland) Act 1975, s 24. They were subsequently granted bail with the additional condition that they reside at named schools which contained secure units.

On 30 August 1990, K and B were indicted at the instance of the rt hon the Lord Fraser of Carmyllie, Her Majesty's Advocate, for trial on 26 November 1990.

G

The accused lodged minutes of notice requesting that a preliminary diet be held to consider a plea in bar of trial.

On 19 November 1990 the sheriff (C Smith) *repelled* the pleas in bar of trial but *granted* leave to appeal.

The accused appealed to the High Court by note of appeal in terms of s 76A of the Criminal Procedure (Scotland) Act 1975.

H

Statutory provisions

The Social Work (Scotland) Act 1968 provides:

"58A.— . . . (3) Where a children's hearing decide, in accordance with section 44 of this Act, that a child is in need of compulsory measures of care, and they are satisfied that either — (a) he has a history of absconding, and — (i) he is likely to abscond unless he is kept in secure accommodation; and (ii) if he absconds, it is likely that his physical, mental or moral welfare will be at risk; or (b) he is likely to injure himself or other persons unless he is kept in secure accommodation, they may make it a condition of a supervision requirement under subsection (1) (b) of the said section 44 that the child shall be liable to be placed and kept in secure accommodation in the named residential establishment at such times as the person in charge of that establishment, with the agreement of the director of social work of the local authority required to give effect to the supervision requirement, considers it necessary that he do so."

I

J

The Criminal Procedure (Scotland) Act 1975 provides:

"24.—(1) Any court, on remanding or committing for trial a child who is not liberated on bail shall, instead of committing him to prison, commit him to the local authority in whose area the court is situated to be detained in a place of safety chosen by the local authority for the period for which he is remanded or until he is liberated in due course of law. Provided that in the case of a child over 14 years of age it shall not be obligatory on the court so to commit him if the court certifies that he is of so unruly a character that he cannot safely be so committed or that he is of so depraved a character that he is not a fit person to be so detained; but the court shall not so certify a child unless such conditions as the Secretary of State may by order made by statutory instrument prescribe are satisfied in relation to the child. . . .

K

L

"101.— . . . (2) Subject to subsections (3), (4) and (5) below, an accused who is committed for any offence until liberated in due course of law shall not be detained by virtue of that committal for a total period of more than — (a) 80 days, unless within that period the indictment is served on him, which failing he shall be liberated forthwith; or (b) 110 days, unless the trial of the case is commenced within that period, which failing he shall be liberated forthwith and thereafter he shall be for ever free from all question or process for that offence."

Cases referred to

HM Advocate v Bickerstaff, 1926 SLT 121; 1926 JC 65.

HM Advocate v McCann, 1977 SLT (Notes) 19; 1977 JC 1.

Appeal

The grounds of appeal were as follows:

(1) The learned sheriff erred in holding that the minuter had not been detained by virtue of his committal for longer than 110 days, and that the indictment had not been required to be served within 80 days of committal, all in terms of s 101 (2) (a) and 101 (2) (b) of the Criminal Procedure (Scotland) Act 1975.

(2) The learned sheriff erred in holding that being held within a secure unit did not equiparate with being held on remand.

(3) The learned sheriff erred in holding that the consent of the minuter to the additional condition of bail, obviated the necessity of the Crown to comply with the provisions of s 101 (2) (a) and 101 (2) (b) of the Criminal Procedure (Scotland) Act 1975.

The appeals were argued before the High Court on 6 December 1990.

On 21 December 1990 the court *allowed* the appeals and *sustained* the pleas in bar of trial.

The following opinion of the court was delivered by the Lord Justice General (Hope):

OPINION OF THE COURT.—The appellants are both children under the age of 16 years. On 8 May 1990 they appeared on petition in the sheriff court at Arbroath on various charges of assault, abduction, threatening violence, contravening s 41 (1) (a) of the Police (Scotland) Act 1967, breach of the peace and malicious damage. These charges all related to incidents which were said to have taken place at Lunan Unit, Rossie School, Montrose, on 30 April and 1 May 1990. A certificate was given in terms of s 24 (1) of the Criminal Procedure (Scotland) Act 1975 that the appellants were of so unruly a character that they could not safely be detained in a place of safety chosen by the local authority, and accordingly they were committed to HM Prison in Perth until liberated in due course of law. On 25 June 1990 the appellant B appeared again in the same court. He was granted bail on the usual conditions together with an additional condition which was in these terms: "That the accused now resides at Keerlaw School, Stevenston, Ayrshire". Keerlaw school is a list D school with a secure unit and the purpose of the additional condition was that he should be detained there until he was brought to trial rather than that he be committed to prison or to a remand centre. On 3 July 1990 the

appellant K appeared in the same court and he also was granted bail. In his case, in addition to the usual conditions, there was an additional condition in these terms: "That the accused reside within the secure unit of St Mary's List D School, Bishopbriggs". The purpose of this additional condition was, as in B's case, that he should be detained in the secure unit there rather than in prison or a remand centre until he was brought to trial.

The appellant K has continued to reside at Kenmure St Mary's list D school. He did so in accordance with the condition to which he had been admitted to bail, but since 25 October 1990 his residence there has been in terms of a condition of a supervision requirement made by a children's hearing under s 58A of the Social Work (Scotland) Act 1968. In the case of the appellant B the history is more complicated. On 19 July 1990 he appeared on petition in the sheriff court at Kilmarnock, having been taken there from Keerlaw school, and he was remanded in custody. On 1 August 1990 the proceedings were reduced to summary and he pled not guilty, but on 31 August 1990 he pled guilty and sentence was deferred until 14 September 1990. On that date he was remitted to the children's panel in Glenrothes and released from custody. On 29 October 1990 he appeared on petition on another matter and was refused bail, and, an appeal against the refusal having also been refused, he is at present being held in the young offenders institution at Polmont on remand.

On 30 August 1990 the appellants were served with an indictment for trial in the sheriff court at Arbroath on 26 November 1990. This related to the various matters on which they had originally appeared on petition on 8 May 1990. The indictment was served more than 80 days after their committal to prison on that date and, since the 110th day occurred on 26 August 1990, the trial date was fixed for a day more than 110 days after their committal. On 19 November 1990 a preliminary diet was held in the sheriff court in which the sheriff had before him minutes of notice by both appellants intimating pleas in bar of trial. The basis of these pleas was that the indictment had not been served on them within the period of 80 days following their committal, contrary to s 101 (2) (a) of the 1975 Act and that they had been detained for longer than 110 days contrary to s 101 (2) (b) of that Act. It was submitted on their behalf that the effect of the additional conditions on which the appellants had been granted bail was that they were still being detained and were not at liberty, with the result that the 80 and 110 day rules continued to apply. The procurator fiscal depute's argument was that since the appellants had been granted bail on conditions to which they had agreed and which they had not sought to have reviewed by the court they had ceased to be detained in custody for the purposes of s 101 (2). The sheriff repelled the pleas in bar of trial and the appellants have now appealed to this court.

Counsel for the appellant K submitted that it was of the essence of bail that the accused should be released from custody. As he pointed out, "bail" is defined in s 462 (1) of the Act as meaning "release of an accused or appellant on conditions, or conditions imposed on bail, as the context requires". The appellant could not be said to have been liberated in due course of law for the purposes of s 101 (2) while he continued to be incarcerated in a secure unit in a list D school in terms of the bail condition. This was in no sense a voluntary arrangement. Counsel agreed that it would have been competent for the appellant to have applied for a review of the bail condition under s 299 of the Act, but this would have been a pointless exercise as the Crown would no doubt have opposed the appellant's release and, if the sheriff had decided to revoke the additional condition, the consequence would have been a committal of the appellant to prison or to a remand centre in terms of the proviso to s 24 (1). The factual situation was what mattered here, and the statutory provisions should be construed benignly in favour of liberty rather than against it. We were referred to dicta to that effect in *HM Advocate v McCann* per Lord Justice Clerk Wheatley at 1977 SLT (Notes), p 21 and *HM Advocate v Bickerstaff*, per Lord Justice General Clyde at 1926 SLT, pp 122-123. The proper approach to this case was said therefore to be to regard the committal of 8 May 1990 as not having been altered by the order for bail because the appellant had been granted bail on a condition which prevented his release. Counsel for the appellant B adopted this argument. He recognised that in B's case the additional condition of bail did not say that the appellant was to reside in the secure unit at Keerlaw school, but that was in fact what happened and that was what the condition was intended to achieve. The practical effect was that he was taken away to reside in the approved school behind locked doors. This was an entirely different case from one where a person had been required by an additional condition of bail to reside in his own home and which he was free to comply with or disregard of his own free will. He accepted that there had been a genuine intention to avoid holding the appellant in prison or in a remand centre, but what was done here ought not to deprive him of the protection of s 101 (2).

In his reply the learned advocate depute did not seek to distinguish between the position of the two appellants, despite the differences in the terms of the additional conditions. He accepted that what had been done in these cases, in a very difficult situation, was not within the spirit of the statutory provisions about bail. Nevertheless the orders were made under the Bail etc (Scotland) Act 1980 in petitions for bail at the appellants' own instance, and from then on the initiative lay with them as to whether they were to remain on bail subject to the additional conditions or whether a review of these conditions should be sought. If they were no longer unruly, for example, their residence within secure units in the list D schools would no longer be necessary, and it was to be expected that they would be released if there was no other compulsitor for them to be in custody. The effect of the bail orders was that they were no longer being held by virtue of the original committals of 8 May 1990 but that they had been liberated from these committals in due course of law.

The problem which has arisen in this case is an unusual one. The circumstances are highly special because it is clear that, although the appellants were granted bail, this was in fact no more than a device which was resorted to in order to ensure that they were detained in suitable and secure conditions until they were brought to trial. It is plain that it was not the intention, when bail was granted to them, that they should be released from custody. The only question was where they were to be detained, in view of their ages and their unruly character which made it unsafe for them to be committed to the local authority to be detained in a place of safety under s 24 (1) of the Act without the assurance that they could be kept in secure accommodation. As it happens, the appellant K is now in secure accommodation as a result of a condition made by a children's hearing under s 58A of the Social Work (Scotland) Act 1968 because the conditions of subs (3) of that section are satisfied. But we must assume that it was not clear when bail was granted to the appellants that a children's hearing would make a condition in these terms, or at least that there might be some delay in the making of such a condition. The object was to achieve the same result by a different route from that which s 58A provides. Now it is clear that, if such a condition had been in force at the time when the appellants applied for bail, there would have been no point in admitting them to bail subject to the additional conditions. The same result could have been achieved by the more orthodox route of committing them to the local authority under s 24 (1) to be detained in a place of safety chosen by the local authority until they were liberated in due course of law. Had that been done, by means of a combination of s 24 (1) and the existence of a condition made under s 58A of the 1968 Act, the protection of s 101 (2) would undoubtedly have been available to the appellants. Why then should they lose this protection where the result has been achieved by a means which was not, as the advocate depute accepts, within the spirit of a grant of bail?

The argument for the Crown is that the appellants, once granted bail, were no longer being detained by virtue of their committal on 8 May 1990 until liberated in due course of law. They were being detained instead by virtue of a condition of bail to which they had agreed, and the whole matter was to be seen as a voluntary arrangement in which they had taken the initiative. If this is the correct view of the matter, s 101 (2) does not apply and the appellants are not entitled to the benefit of the statutory time limits. In our opinion, however, this approach ignores the reality of the situation and it is contrary to what s 101 (2) is designed to achieve. The purpose of the subsection, like that of the corresponding provisions in s 43 of the Criminal Procedure (Scotland) Act 1887, is to secure that, where the accused has been detained in custody, there shall be no undue delay in serving him with the indictment and bringing him to trial. In *HM*

Advocate v McCann the accused had been committed
until liberated in due course of law. He was released
from prison on the instructions of the procurator fiscal
96 days after his committal and thereafter remained at
liberty. The question then arose whether the 110 days
continued to run, since his release proceeded simply
on the procurator fiscal's authority and not on the
order of the court. Lord Justice Clerk Wheatley at
1977 SLT (Notes), p 21, said: "As I understood the
argument the respondent was still notionally detained
in prison and the 110 days kept running. . . . I cannot
accept this argument. Basically the matter is a factual
one. The respondent was set at liberty and regained
his liberty, so that the statutory safeguard against
undue detention was achieved." In the present case
the factual position is the reverse. The appellants,
although granted bail, were not set at liberty because
of the additional conditions of bail which were
imposed on them. The critical question, so far as the
application of s 101 (2) is concerned, is whether they
were still being "detained by virtue of that
committal", that is to say by virtue of their committal
on 8 May 1990 for the offences for which the Crown
now seeks to bring them to trial. In our opinion they
continued to be so detained, because the bail orders
did not result in their release from custody. In this
situation the appellants are, we think, entitled to the
benefit of the statutory time limits and to plead them
in bar of trial.

For these reasons we consider that these appeals
should be allowed and that the pleas in bar of trial
which have been stated on behalf of the appellants
should be sustained.

---

*Counsel for First Appellant (K), Bell; Solicitors, More
& Co — Counsel for Second Appellant (B), Donaldson;
Solicitors, Michael T McSherry, Glasgow — Counsel for
Respondent, Macdonald, QC, AD; Solicitor, I Dean,
Crown Agent.*

D K

Dawson International plc v Coats Paton plc

OUTER HOUSE

LORD PROSSER

22 MARCH 1991

*Company — Takeover — Agreement by board of offeree
company to recommend offer to its members — Whether
legally enforceable — Whether implied term not to solicit
or co-operate with potential competing offerors —
Whether implied term breached.*

*Contract — Company — Takeover — Agreement by
offeree company to recommend offer — Whether agree-*
*ment legally enforceable — Whether implied term not to
solicit or co-operate with potential competing offeror —
Whether breach of implied term — Whether breach
caused loss — Measure of loss.*

A listed company raised an action against another
such company and two of the second company's
directors arising out of an abortive offer by the first
company to purchase the shares of the second company. The first company concluded for a sum which
was averred to represent the costs of underwriting,
printing and professional services incurred in connection with the intended takeover and certain capital
gains tax which would be chargeable if the first
company recovered those costs.

The first company averred that the parties had
reached an agreement that the second company would
not co-operate with any competing bid, that such a bid
had been made and that the second company through
its directors had co-operated with that bid in breach of
the agreement between the parties.

It was held after proof that after negotiations
between certain directors of the two companies as to
the detailed terms of the proposed offer, the board of
the second company had agreed to recommend it. The
board of the first company had also resolved to make
an offer and the two companies had issued a joint press
announcement which referred to an agreed merger
between them, set out the terms of the offer and stated
that the board of the second company would recommend to their shareholders that they accept that offer.
After that announcement a representative of a third
company indicated to the second company that it
wished to make a higher offer. The second company
and its merchant bankers initially replied that they
would not negotiate and that it was for the third
company to make a specific offer. The second company's merchant bank later gave specific advice to the
bank acting for the third company as to the terms of
its proposed offer which would lead to the second
defenders' directors recommending it. After negotiations between the representatives of the second and
third companies the directors of the latter resolved to
make an offer and those of the second company
withdrew their recommendation of the first defenders'
offer. The first company submitted that they and the
second company had entered into a contract under
which the latter would recommend the offer by the
former and that that contract had contained, as
implied terms, (1) that the board of the second
company could withdraw its recommendation if they
bona fide considered that it no longer remained in the
interests of their shareholders, but (2) that the
directors would not solicit for, or co-operate with, a
competing offeror except to comply with the requirement of the City Code on Takeovers and Mergers
("the code") that an offeree company provide all
offerors with the same information. The first company
submitted further that the second company had acted
in breach of that second implied term. The first
company had also pleaded a case of misrepresentation
by the representatives of the second company but the

A Lord Ordinary held as a matter of fact that there had been no misrepresentations.

Held, (1) that there was nothing in the actions of the first and second companies which indicated that they were entering into a binding contract; when the actings of the companies were judged in the context of the requirement of the code that the board of an offeree company advise its shareholders of its view on any intended offer, the minutes of the meetings of their respective boards in making and recommending the first company's offer were not indicating that

B any contract had been concluded; the joint press announcement as a whole was, in that context, consistent with it containing statements of the parties' intention rather than of obligation, particularly as the alleged obligation to recommend the first defenders' offer was admittedly qualified (pp 94C-K, 95L-96D and 96I-97F); (2) that, if there had been an enforceable contract between the parties, there would have been an implied term that the second company would not solicit for, or co-operate with, potential competing

C offerors on the ground that an obligant should not be free to alter the surrounding circumstances so as to enable him to avoid his obligation (p 98H-L); (3) that, if there had been an enforceable contract, the second company would have been in breach of that implied term through the actings of their merchant bankers, who had assisted the third company to formulate their eventual offer when their proposed offer had been uncertain (p 99B-C); and defenders *assoilzied*.

Opinion, (1) that, even if the second company had

D acted in breach of any contract with the first company, that breach had caused no loss to the latter in that, but for the co-operation given, the third company would on the balance of probabilities have made a more attractive bid which would have succeeded and the first company's expenditure would have been abortive (p 100F-H); and (2) that if the first company had sustained a loss, that would have included tax losses which they had applied to reduce their gain on the sale of shares in the second company, which they had

E purchased, and would otherwise have applied to reduce other gains (p 101B).

Action of damages

Dawson International plc raised an action against Coats Paton plc and two of its former directors in which the pursuers concluded for damages for loss which they claimed to have sustained as a result of alleged misrepresentation and breach of contract by

F the defenders. After a procedure roll debate the action was dismissed so far as laid against the directors (see 1988 SLT 854 and 1989 SLT 655).

The action came to proof before the Lord Ordinary (Prosser).

Cases referred to

Dempster (R & J) Ltd v Motherwell Bridge & Engineering Co Ltd, 1964 SLT 353; 1964 SC 308.
Edwards v Skyways Ltd [1964] 1 WLR 349; [1964] 1 All ER 494.

Houldsworth v Brand's Trustees (1877) 4 R 369.
Kleinwort Benson Ltd v Malaysia Mining Corp Berhad G [1989] 1 WLR 379; [1989] 1 All ER 785.
Muirhead & Turnbull v Dickson (1905) 8 SLT 151; (1905) 7 F 680.
R v City Panel on Takeovers and Mergers, ex p Datafin plc [1987] QB 815; [1987] 2 WLR 699; [1987] 1 All ER 564.
R v City Panel on Takeovers and Mergers, ex p Guinness plc [1990] 1 QB 146; [1989] 2 WLR 863; [1989] 1 All ER 509.

H On 22 March 1991 the Lord Ordinary *assoilzied* the defenders.

LORD PROSSER.—
I. Background

The defenders are a major textile company, based in Scotland. In 1984, their turnover, in round terms, was over £1,000m, and their pre-tax profit on ordinary activities was over £100m. In 1985, they were vulner-

I able to takeover, despite their size. Their financial advisers, Morgan Grenfell & Co Ltd, prepared a document entitled "Project Dunkirk", containing various analyses of the company's position, and in particular of the risks of takeover bids and the appropriate defence strategy should such a bid emerge. By the end of 1985, this document had been through five drafts, and a sixth was due in January 1986. In addition to the risk of a "predatory" takeover bid, perhaps with a view to the breakup of the company, the defenders'

J market ratings were sufficiently poor to open up possibilities of takeover or merger proposals from other, perhaps smaller, companies in the textile field, which it would be difficult to resist. In the latter part of 1985, these possibilities had been considered by Vantona Viyella plc ("Vantona") with their financial advisers N M Rothschild & Sons Ltd, and by the pursuers in the present action, with their financial advisers Samuel Montagu & Co Ltd. The code names adopted for the defenders by Rothschilds and Samuel Montagu were "Peach" and "Dodo" respectively. Despite this

K rather trivial (and transparent) terminology, the defenders' vulnerability to takeover was in both cases identified as real.

The origins of the present action can be briefly summarised. Meetings between representatives of the pursuers and the defenders in mid-January 1986 led to a press announcement on behalf of the boards of both companies, to the effect that terms had been agreed for a merger, which would be implemented by means of

L recommended offers on behalf of the pursuers to acquire the whole issued share capital of the defenders. Over the next fortnight, the formal offer document was prepared, and it was due to go out to shareholders on 10 February 1986. However, during that fortnight, the defenders' board and the board of Vantona agreed the terms of a merger between their two companies. That merger was to be effected by means of a recommended offer by Vantona for the defenders' share capital, which put a higher value on the defenders' shares than the pursuers' proposed

offer had done. In these circumstances, the defenders'
A　board withdrew their support for the pursuers' offer,
and the offer document which had been prepared was
not sent out. In due course, the merger with Vantona
went ahead. The pursuers incurred substantial underwriting costs, and certain other fees, in connection with
their proposed offer for the defenders' share capital.
They now seek damages or reimbursement from the
defenders based upon their abortive expenditure,
claiming that their loss resulted either from breach of
contract by the defenders, or from the pursuers having
B　relied on representations made fraudulently, or negligently, by the defenders.

The pursuers are themselves a major textile company, based in Scotland. In the year to March 1985,
they had an annual turnover of over £250m, with a pre-
tax profit of about £35m. They were thus much smaller
than the defenders. While both were textile companies,
their strengths lay in different fields of operation, and
indeed in different parts of the world. They also had
very different management approaches, the defenders'
C　reflecting their size and their long history, the pursuers' reflecting the strong personal views and abilities
of their chairman and chief executive, Mr Ronald
Miller. A further and crucial difference between the
two companies was that in 1985, the pursuers' market
ratings were very much better than the defenders'. It
was only this fact which opened up the possibility of
merger or takeover proposals which might both attract
the defenders' shareholders, and appear advantageous
D　to the pursuers'.

II. Contacts between the parties
In December 1985, Mr Miller telephoned Sir
William Coats, the defenders' chairman. While remaining as chairman, Sir William had just ceased to be the
defenders' chief executive, being succeeded by Mr
James McAdam. Mr Miller wanted a meeting to
discuss merger possibilities, but understandably
approached the matter somewhat obliquely, with
E　references to a previous meeting in 1983, and generalities about both being Scottish textile companies who
should be friendly, and the speculations about possible
takeover of the defenders by others. In evidence, Mr
Miller was clear that he had sufficiently shown his
purpose, and indeed recalled Sir William saying that
they had often thought of getting together with
Dawsons but could not see how it could be done.
However, Sir William's evidence was that if Mr Miller
had intended to raise the question of merger, he had
F　failed to get this through. Given the ambiguity of
expressions such as "get together", and Sir William's
perhaps superficial view that the defenders were too
big to be taken over by a company such as the pursuers,
I am satisfied that Sir William did not in fact
understand what Mr Miller had in mind. As Mr
McAdam had taken over as chief executive, it was
arranged that the proposed meeting should be with him
rather than Sir William, and I am satisfied that Sir
William did not give Mr McAdam an account of
matters which would suggest that the pursuers wanted
to discuss merger.

Mr Miller and Mr McAdam subsequently arranged
a meeting for 15 January 1986, it being agreed that Mr　G
McAdam would be accompanied by Michael Bell, a
director of the defenders, while Mr Miller would have
with him two of his fellow directors, John Waterton
and John Embrey. Very shortly after his conversation
with Sir William Coats, Mr Miller prepared notes for
the proposed meeting, which were passed to Mr
Embrey and Mr Waterton for their consideration, and
subsequently in early January he prepared a note with
alternative bases for his conduct of the meeting. In
addition, the pursuers obtained from Samuel Montagu　H
an updated memorandum on the "Dodo" acquisition.
This illustrated the effects of an offer for the defenders'
shares upon a number of assumptions, envisaging that
an offer of 111 new shares in the pursuers for every 100
shares in the defenders, and providing for a cash
alternative by means of underwriting the new shares.
Questions of gearing, the cost of acquisition, and the
effects of dilution on the pursuers' existing shareholders' interests were all covered.

So far as the defenders' representatives are con-　I
cerned, their known vulnerability and the "Dunkirk"
studies would mean that many of the necessary considerations in relation to possible merger would be in
the front of their minds. I am however satisfied that
they had not given specific consideration to the possibility, or effects, of proposals for takeover or merger
which might be made by the pursuers. It is to be
observed that the Dunkirk document was primarily
concerned with predatory bids of a type which the
defenders would wish to resist, and that so far as　J
acceptable mergers were concerned, the defenders had
in mid-1985 appreciated the difficulty which they
would find in attempting takeover of smaller companies, and had considered (in a document entitled
"Think Piece") an alternative strategy by way of
"Mega Merger" with a company whose "financial
business and problem profile" was similar to their
own. They had identified Courtaulds as a possible
candidate for "Mega Merger", and that document is
essentially concerned with that specific possibility.　K
Merger with a company such as the pursuers might
well have significant advantages, but I see no reason to
think that any such merger with the pursuers had been
contemplated by the defenders in advance of the
meeting of 15 January. In evidence Mr McAdam
acknowledged that the defenders had in the past looked
at the possibility of some structural get together
between themselves and the pursuers, and thought
they had probably mentioned this at the meeting on 15
January or the following day. They had known quite a　L
lot about the pursuers, having had a working lunch in
1983, and having operated alongside of them in both
Britain and the United States, but they had not seen
any way in which the two companies could come
together structurally, and had not regarded it as a
serious possibility. I would accept that evidence.

III. The meeting of 15 January 1986
The meeting took place as arranged, at the pursuers'
premises at Kinross. Mr Bell, who accompanied Mr

McAdam, and who was closely involved in the events
of the succeeding month, has unfortunately since died.
Mr McAdam, Mr Miller and the other two directors of
the pursuers all gave evidence as to what passed at this
meeting, and indeed the further meeting the next day.
There are fairly substantial differences between the
evidence of Mr McAdam and the evidence of the three
pursuers' representatives, and indeed in certain
respects between those three representatives. I have
however come to the view that these differences find
their explanation in the lapse of time and differences of
memory, together with differences in perception and
the interpretation of what was going on in the minds
of the other side. It is clear that after opening
generalities, and talk of a possible threatened takeover
by others, Mr Miller quite quickly (and indeed more
quickly than he had expected or intended) moved from
talk of the pursuers intervening if a takeover was
attempted by others, to positive suggestions of a
merger between the pursuers and defenders being
advantageous for both. The speed with which this
stage was reached, coupled with Mr Miller's
understanding that Sir William Coats had been told the
pursuers' purpose in seeking a meeting, led the
pursuers' representatives to think that the defenders
were prepared for, and indeed quite keen on, actual
negotiation of possible friendly merger arrangements.
Mr McAdam appears to have shown no surprise at
what was being put forward, which no doubt
confirmed the impression gained by the pursuers'
representatives. But Mr McAdam does not strike me as
a man who could evince surprise, unless he saw some
advantage in doing so, and I would accept his evidence
that he was quite sympathetic to what was being
suggested, and wanted to hear what detailed
suggestions the pursuers might make. While the
pursuers were obviously raising the idea of a merger,
I would accept Mr McAdam's evidence that he did not
wish matters, at that meeting, to proceed beyond that
stage, into a situation where the defenders could be said
to be negotiating. While I would thus accept that in his
eyes at least, matters remained at an exploratory stage,
and that even where both sides were at one, it would
be wrong to see this as a provisional agreement of any
kind, I think it is clear that there was what could
properly be described as detailed discussion, running
over a wide range of topics, with the defenders' representatives making a quite positive contribution.

In relation to the possible mechanisms of takeover or
merger, it is clear that the possibility of creating a new
company, to acquire the shares of both pursuers and
defenders, was raised and discounted: there were
variations on the evidence on this subject, but they do
not appear to me to matter, or to throw light upon any
other material issue. Matters proceeded upon the basis
that any merger would have to take the form of an
acquisition of the defenders' share capital by the
pursuers, and the two sides thus came to discuss the
question of price. Given that the discussion was
between members of the two boards, I think it is plain
that what was being discussed was not, or was not
merely, the level at which a bid might be expected to
succeed (in terms of acceptance by shareholders), but
was rather the level at which a suggested price would
be seriously considered by, and gain the recommendation of, the defenders' board. Thus far, and whatever
precise language was used, I do not think that the two
sides really differ. But in Mr Miller's eyes, the
pursuers would not have been interested in making a
bid which had not been so recommended, and he
regarded the whole subsequent dealings between the
two companies as having proceeded on that basis, to
the knowledge of both. I would accept that that was his
view of the matter, and that quite apart from issues of
price, he saw a hostile bid as neither likely to succeed,
nor capable of producing a workable merger, given the
pursuers' need for co-operation and support, after the
merger, from the defenders' senior management team.
Nonetheless, I am not satisfied that a hostile bid from
the pursuers was so patently impossible, or so
explicitly and convincingly ruled out, as to put it out
of Mr McAdam's contemplation, and I would accept
that he, and subsequently the defenders' board, saw it
as a real possibility. (Such a bid might be at a level
which could attract shareholders, and moreover
"trigger" higher predatory bids.) I am satisfied that he
was determined neither to put the defenders "in play",
nor to divulge anything material as to their position.

Discussion of price appears to have started with talk
of the need for a substantial premium over the then
market price of the defenders' shares. Mr Miller,
producing Samuel Montagu's documentation, suggested a 40 per cent premium, which would have
represented about 200p per share, and one way or
another it is clear that this suggestion was advanced to
a figure of 225p per share. At that level, Mr Miller was
indicating that the pursuers could go no further having
regard to the effects of dilution on their shareholders'
interests. For the defenders, Mr McAdam made it clear
that such a figure was not likely to be enough,
commenting that at that figure there would be "lots of
sharks in the pool". With this indication that such a
price was likely to be outbid by a third party, Mr Miller
then sought a figure from the defenders, and was told
not less than 250p per share. The basis for that figure
was that it represented a "breakup" valuation of the
various parts of the defenders' business, and could thus
be obtained by their shareholders by accepting a bid
from a "predator" intent on such breakup. The
evidence varies somewhat as to quite what was said on
this matter, but I am not persuaded that the differences
are as important as they may have seemed. If a price is
enough to reflect breakup value, then it is likely to be
enough to deter bids from predators intent on breakup.
One is dealing with likelihoods, not certainties, but the
two issues are essentially two sides of the same coin, as
it seems to me. In the interpretation which he put upon
this part of the meeting, Mr Miller recalled language
which concentrates on the deterrent aspect: lockout,
and avoiding takeover by others. With that emphasis,
he saw the parties as having been proceeding upon a
mutual understanding that they would not merely
expect other bids to be deterred by the price in
question, but would want and try to deter such other

bids. Mr McAdam did not recall that deterrent
A language, and emphasised that the figure mentioned as
one which would merit the consideration, and perhaps
recommendation, of the board. For him, the fact that
it was likely to better other bids explained its likely
acceptability, but the exclusion or rejection of other
bids was not the essence of the matter. I am satisfied
that the expression "lockout" was probably used; but
whether one talks of common understandings, or
assumptions, or aims, or agreements, the evidence does
not appear to me to show that the defenders were at this
B stage positively joining in an attempt to make the
pursuers' proposed takeover succeed. In their pleadings, the pursuers aver that the defenders' directors
represented to the pursuers that if agreement could be
reached on certain other matters, the merger would
proceed as an agreed merger, recommended by the
defenders' board, "with the object of achieving a
'lockout' situation" in which it was understood that the
defenders' board would not encourage or co-operate
with any competing offer. I am not satisfied that at this
C meeting any such representation was made or that any
such understanding was reached, upon the basis of
these words or otherwise.

   While the discussion appears to have used the
terminology of "price", what was primarily envisaged
was the issue of new shares in the pursuers in exchange
for shares in the defenders, not a cash price as such.
The need for a cash alternative was however discussed,
the defenders' representatives seeing it as essential, and
D the pursuers resisting the idea. Certain other issues
were aired by the pursuers' representatives, both in
regard to the possible advantages of "synergy", and in
regard to the possible structures of the board. The
evidence varied as to quite how deeply matters had
been discussed and how much "progress" had been
achieved, but it again does not appear to me that
anything really turns upon these differences. One way
and another the parties had had enough for one day and
agreed to meet again the next day. I think it is true, as
E counsel for the pursuers submitted, that Mr Miller saw
matters in terms of a mutual endeavour of repelling
unwelcome competition, with an offer from the pursuers of 250p as a means to that end. If the defenders
had been genuinely afraid of a predatory takeover, and
had been looking for a "white knight", then this
concept of a mutual endeavour would make sense. But
I am not satisfied that anything had been said by Mr
McAdam or Mr Bell to suggest that that was their
position, and I would accept Mr McAdam's evidence
F that so far as the main supposed predator was concerned, he did not fear any immediate bid, and was not
at this stage positively looking for a merger such as the
pursuers proposed.

IV. The meeting of 16 Jaunary 1986

   The meeting of 15 January gives the background,
and may explain the subsequent attitudes and assumptions of the parties. The meeting on the following day,
at the Sheraton hotel in Edinburgh, lies more directly
at the heart of the pursuers' case. It is clear that early
on in the meeting, Mr Miller asked whether the

defenders had been having discussions with anyone
else. It was clear that what he meant was discussions G
about merger or takeover, and it was clear that he was
trying to establish whether he had a clear field.
According to Mr McAdam, the first question was in
general terms, and the reply had been one which
fobbed off inquiry, to the effect that they had had
discussions with lots of people. Mr Miller had then
followed up his general question with a specific one, as
to whether they had had any offers, and he had replied
in the negative. According to Mr McAdam, he would
not have been able to tell the pursuers about dealings H
with third parties, and he said that he did not see how
they could expect to know whether there was competition in this way. Nonetheless, I think that Mr
McAdam clearly appreciated that whatever was being
asked was not a mere inquiry as to the historical past,
but was being asked in order to discover whether there
was any current competition. The pursuers' representatives gave somewhat varying accounts of precisely
what words were used, but, to take Mr Miller, he was
very sure that after a more general question, he had I
asked whether there was anyone else "in the wings".
He was even more certain that the reply was that there
was no one else in the wings, and that the defenders had
talked with no one else. Mr Waterton's account,
although differing somewhat in detail, confirmed the
use of the expression "in the wings" and he was
confident that they had been told that there was no one
lurking in the wings. He claimed that on this matter his
recollection was "photographic". Judging by the
exuberance with which Mr Waterton gave his evidence J
in general, I suspect that his memory is painterly rather
than photographic, and I would not in general be
disposed to rely upon it as precise. Mr Embrey's recollection of the episode did not include the use of the
words "in the wings" and indeed bore out the
questions and answers which Mr McAdam recalled
having been asked and given. Mr Embrey however
recalled a further question, in which Mr Miller had
asked whether the defenders had had merger discussions with others, and had received a negative reply K
to that.

   Whether or not Mr Miller could reasonably expect
to be given a clear assurance that he had the field to
himself, I think it is clear that he wanted such an
assurance, and saw it as important before proceeding
further. I think it unlikely that he would have limited
his question to the specific one regarding offers, which
Mr McAdam recalled. Whether or not the precise
words "in the wings" were used I think it highly likely
that a question would have been asked as to whether L
there were competitors around, and overall I have
come to the view that a question was asked with that
as its plain purpose and meaning, and that it received
a negative reply. I am not sure that I regard the phrase
"in the wings" as particularly vivid, but on balance I
am disposed to accept Mr Miller's clear recollection of
its use, confirmed as it is by Mr Waterton. Whatever
the precise words of the question or the answer, I am
satisfied that the defenders gave the pursuers an
assurance to the effect that there was no one else in the

wings, in the sense of there being no one else with
A whom discussions as to merger could be regarded as
current or live.

Vagueness and ambiguity are no doubt inherent in
talks of this kind. I accept that Mr McAdam tried to fob
Mr Miller off, and I would also accept that he would
not have identified any rival that there may or might
have been. But Mr McAdam said that if he had given
a negative answer, on being asked whether there was
anyone else in the wings, such an answer would in fact
have been true. I am satisfied that he gave an answer
B to that effect; and the issue between the parties, as to
whether it was true or false, is one to which I shall
return in due course. I am satisfied that at the meeting
of 16 January, Mr Miller was relying upon that reply,
and would not have proceeded there and then to
discuss price or other details as he did, if he had been
told that there were current talks with others, or if that
issue had been left unresolved. The question of any
subsequent approach by a third party, and how the
defenders might treat it, was not expressly raised at this
C meeting; and while I am satisfied that Mr Miller
continued, after the meeting, to proceed upon the
assumption that there were still no current contacts of
that kind, this is not the point at which to discuss
whether the representation given on 16 January, along
with the defenders' subsequent handling of this matter,
afforded an abiding basis for Mr Miller's abiding
assumption.

In relation to the representation on 16 January, I
D would only add that some passages in the evidence
describe questions by Mr Miller, and answers by Mr
McAdam, relating to the past, rather than the current,
situation. Correspondingly, I understood Mr Miller to
say that even if there had been past discussions of
merger, he would have proceeded no further, and I
understood Mr McAdam to rely in some measure upon
the view that only the past, and not the current
situation, had been raised and dealt with. I am not
persuaded that the revelation of past talks would have
E brought proceedings to an end: any such revelation
would necessarily have raised the question of whether
the talks were still live, or were dead. If Mr Miller had
been assured that they were dead, I do not doubt that
he would have proceeded as he did. Equally, even if the
past tense was used, I did not understand Mr McAdam
really to deny that the purpose of the inquiry was plain,
and related to the current position. This aspect of the
matter does not alter my view that a representation as
to the current position was in fact made.

F The other "preliminary" issue which was raised at
this meeting related to the authority of Messrs
McAdam and Bell. I accept that they made it plain that
they were not vested with any particular ad hoc
authority to agree anything on behalf of the board. In
that context, it may well be that they were only there
to listen. I am not persuaded that the precise words
used are of much significance. I am satisfied that in fact
Messrs McAdam and Bell did much more than simply
listen, and that they took an active part in discussion.
On the other hand, I am satisfied that what was being

discussed was the way in which a merger between the
two companies might work in practice and what terms G
would be required in any offer by the pursuers, for
Messrs McAdam and Bell to conclude that it was worth
putting to the board, and for the board to be likely to
give the offer their recommendation. Mr McAdam
being the chief executive, his willingness to put it to the
board, and the likelihood, in his opinion, of the board
giving it their recommendation may not be very
different matters. But the discussions which I have
described do appear to me to be different from the two
sides attempting to reach an "agreement" to the effect H
that an offer in agreed terms would be made and
recommended, subject only to "ratification" of that
agreement by the boards of the two companies. These
concepts of "agreement" and "ratification" do not
seem to me to be appropriate or helpful in relation to
what was going on.

There was a fair amount of evidence as to the detailed
discussions which took place at this meeting. The
details do not appear to me to be of much importance.
So far as price is concerned, both sides had considered
Samuel Montagu's figures overnight, and Mr Miller
moved from his previous figure of 225p to 235p. His
position at that stage was however that the defenders'
figure of 250p, despite its logic as a breakup figure,
would not make sense from the point of view of the
pursuers' shareholders. Other issues, such as the
necessity, level and extent of a cash alternative, and
underwriting and who should pay for it, were also
discussed. The "philosophy" and possible "synergy" J
of the combined business were further discussed and
clarified, and similarly there was discussion as to board
structures, the chairmanship and the post of chief
executive. While I do not think that the terminology of
agreement and ratification is right, it seems to me that
a good deal of progress was made at this meeting
towards identifying a common "vision" and establishing what Mr Miller called a strong "chemistry"
between the representatives of the two sides. I am satisfied that by the end of the meeting, enough clarification K
of each side's views had been achieved for both sides
to feel that a potentially "recommendable" offer could
be envisaged, despite differences on particular issues,
if only the fundamental difference as to price could be
overcome.

V. The sequel to the meetings

Over the next four days, no substantive progress was
made between the two sides. Some of the main
outstanding issues were discussed over the phone
between Mr Miller and Mr McAdam on 17 January, L
and by the Tuesday the unacceptability of 235p had
evidently been made plain. On the Tuesday (21
January) however, Mr Miller had a long conversation
with his non-executive directors, and it was agreed that
they were prepared to go to a price of 250p (share for
share, at a sensible ratio). Other aspects of the pursuers'
position were settled, including their proposals as to
the size and composition of the board, the company
name and the location of the head office. Certain other
matters remained open: while they would prefer the

price to be all share, the need for a cash alternative and
A underwriting, and the possibility that underwriting
costs might be shared were noted, as was the need for
a full meeting on "philosophy" before they went
further. On the defenders' side, Mr McAdam had contacted his non-executive directors after the meeting of
16 January, and he and Mr Bell discussed matters with
Sir William Coats and Lord McFadzean in London on
17 January. That meeting led to a contact with
Courtaulds to which I shall have to return; and by the
Tuesday, Mr McAdam had alerted board members,
B had further discussion with Sir William and Lord
McFadzean, and had taken advice from Mr Peter
Cadbury of Morgan Grenfell. I am satisfied that they
felt a genuine unease that Mr Miller might make a
hostile bid, and indeed that they were concerned as to
whether their shareholders would be "loyal" in the
face of such a bid at 235p. The next day, Mr Cadbury
contacted Mr Ian McIntosh of Samuel Montagu, the
pursuers' financial advisers, and arranged to meet.
However, Mr Miller contacted Mr McAdam direct,
C and put the figure of 250p to him along with the other
details settled with his non-executive directors the
previous day. There are some discrepancies as to the
details of his conversation, but I think that it is clear
that Mr Miller (as Mr McAdam put it) was "coming
across very strong" and wanted the defenders' reaction
very soon.

By this time, also, the pursuers had begun to buy
shares in the defenders, but desisted on Mr McAdam
asking them to do so. This request by Mr McAdam has
D been interpreted as showing a lack of good faith in his
dealings with the pursuers, but at the end of the day,
counsel for the pursuers accepted that this was probably an ill founded suspicion, particularly in view of
the advice that he had evidently received as to what was
proper in the circumstances. That is certainly my view.

Whether triggered by the pursuers' relatively limited
purchases or not, the defenders' share price moved
sharply up on the following day, Thursday 23 January.
E A joint announcement by the two sides was discussed,
but the pursuers did not wish to join in this, and the
defenders unilaterally announced that they had
received an approach which might or might not lead to
an offer. At a meeting of the defenders' board that day,
Mr McAdam advised the board that the pursuers were
prepared to make a share-for-share offer, valuing the
defenders' shares at 250p, with a cash alternative of
225p. The whole issue was discussed, and it was agreed
that Mr McAdam and Lord McFadzean should meet
F Mr Miller, with a remit to secure agreement for a
structure which took due account of the international
complexity of the company's business, and the
interests of its management and employees. Lord
McFadzean and Mr McAdam in fact met Mr Miller
later that day. At a further meeting of the defenders'
board the following day, 24 January, Mr Cadbury gave
details as to how matters would be handled, including
a proposed press announcement on Monday 27
January, and the board agreed that provided details of
this and other matters were satisfactory to a committee
of the board, it would recommend to shareholders

acceptance of the proposed offer by the pursuers. It is
recorded in the minute of this meeting that the board G
agreed to give public support to the merger "in a form
that would not compromise the company's position in
the event that the Dawson bid were thwarted". At a
meeting of the pursuers' board, also on 24 January, the
offer and cash alternative were approved in principle,
and power was delegated to a small committee to do all
that was required (including, without limitation, the
underwriting agreement) in connection with the
merger and the usual documentation and the like. Over
the weekend there was considerable contact between H
the two sides in relation to the proposed press release,
leading to agreement as to its terms and a rehearsal of
the proposed press announcement.

VI. The press announcement

On Monday 27 January, a press conference was held
at which the agreed announcement was released. The
heading to the announcement referred to an "agreed
merger"; the opening paragraph states that the boards
of the two companies announced "that terms have been I
agreed for a merger" of the two companies, and that
"The merger will be implemented by means of
recommended offers" by Samuel Montagu on behalf of
the pursuers; and the next paragraph states that the
boards of the two companies together with their
financial advisers consider that the terms of the
proposed merger are fair and reasonable to their
respective shareholders, and that "the Board of Coats
Paton will recommend" Coats Paton shareholders to
accept the ordinary offer. Upon this narrative of what J
had been agreed depends the pursuers' case for breach
of contract.

VII. Defenders' contacts with third parties

It is convenient at this point to turn from a
consideration of what passed between the pursuers and
the defenders, to the history of the defenders' contacts
with other companies, concerning a possible takeover
or merger, up to the date of the issue of the press
announcement.   K

(1) Courtaulds

I have already mentioned that the defenders had
identified Courtaulds as possible partners in a "Mega
Merger" in the summer of 1985. There was indeed a
meeting in July, which at least put the possibility of a
merger into the minds of the Courtaulds board; but
they were not really interested as matters then stood,
and the meeting was inconclusive. By the autumn,
circumstances had changed significantly, with L
Courtaulds' price being stronger and the defenders'
price having weakened. A true "merger" was no longer
likely to be feasible, but the possibility of a takeover,
with Courtaulds acquiring the defenders' shares, had
become more credible. Courtaulds accordingly sought
a further meeting, and a long meeting was held on
28 November between Sir William, Mr McAdam and
Mr Bell, and Sir Christopher Hogg, chairman of
Courtaulds, and a number of others on their side. After
a long discussion as to the nature and compatibility of
their businesses, they agreed to meet again, and did so

on 5 December. This time, the primary subject for A discussion was the financial aspect of any "get together". It seems to have been rapidly apparent that acquisition of the defenders' shares by Courtaulds was the appropriate mechanism, and discussion centred on a suggestion that the "price" for the defenders' shares would have to be at a level some 40 per cent above their current market value. On behalf of Courtaulds, it was indicated that this would involve too great a dilution to be attractive to them or their shareholders. The alternative lower prices and premium suggested by Sir B Christopher Hogg were rejected by the defenders' representatives.

Neither side seems to have expected the matter to progress further, given these differences, but at Sir Christopher Hogg's request, a further meeting over dinner was arranged for 10 January 1986, Mr McAdam having become chief executive just after the previous meeting. The holding of this meeting at first sight suggests that there was still a live prospect of merger, after the previous meeting. Indeed, at one point Sir C Christopher Hogg said that acceptance of a 10 per cent dilution in earnings on their part would enable them to make an offer which gave the defenders around a 40 per cent premium on the basis of current share prices. Nonetheless, I am satisfied that at least in the mind of Sir Christopher Hogg and Courtaulds, when the meeting of 10 January ended, discussions of a possible merger had effectively ended, with no expectation of further meetings in the foreseeable future. On the basis of what had happened up to that time, one would D expect that also to have been the view of the defenders in their representatives. According to Mr McAdam it was so.

On that basis Courtaulds would not have been "in the wings" on 15 and 16 January. However, on Friday 17 January, in the evening, Mr McAdam and Mr Bell saw Sir Christopher Hogg again for an hour and a half. Sir Christopher's note of that meeting, with the perhaps significant heading "Philadelphia", can in my E view be taken as accurate. It quotes the defenders' representatives as having said that as a result of the evening they had spent together the previous week, "they had understood that we would still be interested in our two companies getting together provided that it could be done on a sensible basis". They are recorded as having gone on to say that they wanted to tell Sir Christopher about something which had arisen within the previous two days (plainly their meetings with the pursuers) and which they thought he should know F given the conversation of the previous week. As they saw it events might now move in a way which Courtaulds might subsequently regret not having had the opportunity to determine. Without revealing the pursuers' identity, they insisted that if Courtaulds were going to make a move, they should do so within days. They were clear that they would prefer to link with Courtaulds provided that Courtaulds could offer sufficient premium both to enlist their support and shut out possible competition. Their view was that the minimum price that had to be offered was 230p and they suggested strongly that it should be half cash and

half shares, the cash element being important. Sir Christopher does not appear to have given the sugges- G tion of a renewed interest by Courtaulds any encouragement, and on 21 January, he intimated that he did not wish to continue the previous discussions between the two companies.

The pursuers submit that in the light of this further meeting, after the pursuers and defenders had met on 15 and 16 January, it was clear that Courtaulds had still indeed been "in the wings" on those dates, at least in the mind of the defenders. On 17 January, the H defenders were to be found using the talks with the pursuers as a means of inducing Courtaulds into a takeover bid. One should infer that on the two previous days, when talking to the pursuers, they saw Courtaulds as a potential bidder, and were endeavouring to obtain as high a figure as possible from the pursuers, not with a view to accepting or even considering it, but in bad faith, with a view to using it as a lever on Courtaulds. Courtaulds were in the wings, and the denial that they were so was given in bad faith. Leaving aside any question of the propriety of this visit I to Courtaulds on 17 January, I am satisfied that the pursuers' interpretation of that visit, as indicating that Courtaulds were regarded as being in the wings on 16 January, is unsound. I can understand that sinister interpretation being reached, when the pursuers discovered that there had been a meeting on 17 January. But I am satisfied that this further approach to Courtaulds was probably at the suggestion of Lord McFadzean, with whom Mr McAdam and Mr Bell had been discussing matters earlier that day. Lord J McFadzean's evidence was that Courtaulds struck all of them as a much better "fit" than the pursuers, that he had known of the discussions in 1985 which had come to nothing, and that while they had decided that McAdam and Bell should go and see the chairman of Courtaulds, this was with no optimism: now that the company was "in play", they thought he might again be interested, but Lord McFadzean was not surprised when Sir Christopher said "No". I do not consider that this further approach to Sir Christopher, followed as it K was by a prompt negative, is inconsistent with the view to which all the other evidence points, that after 10 January, Courtaulds was not regarded by the defenders, any more than by Courtaulds, as in any true sense "in the wings".

It remains true that the defenders had been talking to Courtaulds about possible merger. The true answer to any question as to whether they had been talking to others would therefore have been an affirmative. The only affirmative answer which Mr McAdam appears to L have given was in his general "fob off" reply, that they had talked to lots of people. The defenders had not received an offer from Courtaulds; and it appears to me that any other specific question was related not merely to the past, but to the current position. In these circumstances, I do not think that the contacts with Courtaulds were falsely described by any of the answers which Mr McAdam gave at a the meeting on 16 January. When they met Courtaulds on 10 January, talks were live, if moribund. When they parted that day, I accept that the talks were dead.

(2) Vantona Viyella

A   Vantona had been interested in the possibility of taking over the defenders for some time. The initial review of "Peach" was dated 22 September 1985, was prepared within the company, for discussion purposes, and extends to 53 pages. In October 1985, Vantona's financial advisers, N M Rothschild & Sons, prepared a memorandum on "Peach" extending to 19 pages. The defenders were seen as a prime acquisition candidate in general terms, and from Vantona's point of view merger had major benefit by way of internationa-

B   lisation, widening the product base and in other ways. Without personal contacts on the defenders' board, it was necessary to approach the question cautiously. Contact was made by Vantona's chairman, Sir James Spooner, and their chief executive, David (now Sir David) Alliance. This appears to have been in November 1985, but the Vantona representatives were careful to keep the conversation general, without any mention of the possibility of merger. I accept Sir David's evidence that that was the last thing he would

C   have mentioned. I see him as a man well able to conceal his thoughts. In January 1986, Sir David discussed the possibility of takeover further with Rothschilds, and arrangements were made for him to lunch with representatives of the defenders' board on 17 January 1986. An arrangement was also made for the chairmen of the two companies to dine together. In his own mind, Sir David was thus preparing very definitely for a possible takeover bid, but despite the substantial work already done, he was not yet ready to move

D   openly. One problem was his wish to "hive off" the engineering side of the defenders' business, and positive advantages in delay were seen, with an expectation that in the next few months, the price-to-price ratio of Vantona's shares to the defenders' would improve in Vantona's favour. Even at the meeting on 17 January Sir David appears to have succeeded in giving no hint of his intentions. The pursuers do not now suggest that these contacts between Vantona and the defenders amounted to Vantona being "in the

E   wings" on 16 January for the purposes of their misrepresentation case, despite the fact that on that date Mr McAdam would be aware that he was meeting Vantona representatives the following day. The contacts are, however, the background to later events.

VIII. Vantona Viyella's bid

The announcement on 23 January by the defenders, that they had received an approach, surprised Sir David, and made him somewhat despondent. On 24

F   January, the matter was discussed by Sir David with Vantona's advisers, but they had no clear idea of who the approach might have come from. Various names, including the pursuers' were considered, and a document was prepared covering the ability of such companies to acquire the defenders. This included computations for the pursuers, Courtaulds and Reckitt and Coleman taking hypothetical prices of 200p, 220p and 240p. While Sir David had not wished to move yet, the announcement on 23 January plainly made it necessary for him to consider having to move more quickly.

G   When the pursuers' offer was announced on 27 January, he moved at once: he telephoned the defenders, asking to "get together" and for the first time talked not merely of a possible purchase of subsidiaries, but said that he was interested in making a bid. He said this in order to ensure that they would see him, and in fact Mr McAdam and Mr Bell went to see him that same day. The fact that they went to see Sir David, rather than him coming to see them, can be seen as an indication that they were positively soliciting or encouraging a bid from him. In context, I do not think that this is a fair inference. Mr McAdam's notes

H   of the meeting show that Sir David tried to get them to discuss merger, but record both that Lord McFadzean had agreed beforehand that they should have a drink but show themselves solidly behind the merger, and that at the meeting, the Coats Paton representatives were "very poker faced". In evidence Sir David said that he had told them that Vantona would consider a higher price, but that Mr McAdam had merely said "I hear you", and had said that they had recommended the pursuers' bid and that that was

I   where they stood. It is sometimes said that a "No" to a wooer can carry an indication of "Yes". Even if that is so, I do not see any basis for such an inference here.

Sir David resolved to try again. I accept his evidence that his mind had been made up long before, and that he intended to achieve his aim. He accordingly telephoned Mr McAdam the next day, Lord McFadzean being with Mr McAdam at the time, but Mr McAdam's note of his response is "Pity he didn't speak before but we are men of honour and stand

J   behind deal and in any event good deal for shareholders". The defenders' wholly negative response is confirmed by Sir David. He himself went further than he had previously done: he said that Vantona were prepared to make a better offer, but not if they did not get the defenders' management support. He wanted to discuss the "position re positions" and said that he wished with all his heart that they could put a deal together. At or about this time, Mr McAdam took advice from Mr Cadbury of Morgan Grenfell, and Mr

K   Cadbury's note records that this was "at first on a hypothetical basis and subsequently on a specific basis about how they should react should an approach be received from a third party". He told them that they would always have to place the interests of the shareholders and employees first, and "could not, therefore, refuse to entertain an approach". As a practical matter, however, he advised against entering into "negotiations" or taking any "initiatives". He added that "This was very different, however, from reacting to an

L   approach or from seeking clarification about the precise terms of an offer." He notes that the defenders had adopted this line very strictly with regard to the initial approach which they had received from Vantona. His advice is summarised in Mr McAdam's note in the words "No hope if hypothetical."

The same evening, Mr Cadbury telephoned Ian McIntosh of Samuel Montagu, the pursuers' advisers, and told him that "a fly had been cast" over Coats with a view to the possibility of a third party making a

counter offer. Mr Cadbury's note records that he said
A they "had not given this third party any encouragement" whereas Mr McIntosh recalls Mr Cadbury
saying that they had "rebuffed" it. Both parties to the
conversation saw a significant difference in these two
versions, and if some concrete approach had been
made, I can see that the difference might be important.
But in the context of a fly being cast, I think either
version would mean that the defenders had behaved as
in fact they had behaved — in a wholly negative
manner. Mr Miller seems to have been told of the "fly
B cast" by both Mr McAdam direct, and by Mr
McIntosh, although it is not clear which told him first.
He seems to have received the "no encouragement"
version from Mr McAdam, and the "rebuffed" version
from Mr McIntosh, but either way, was not greatly
concerned. A further issue arising out of this information was that it was seen as possibly "insider" information, which might inhibit the purchase of the
defenders' shares by the pursuers; and there was a
measure of disagreement between Messrs Cadbury and
C McIntosh as to what the defenders should or should
not tell the pursuers. Mr Cadbury's notes are written
some time after the events, and indeed after 10
February. In this and other respects I think that they
may suffer from being a later and slightly overaware
historical recollection, rather than a contemporary
note. In any event, I am not prepared to draw an inference that the defenders, or their advisers, were at this
stage attempting to damage the pursuers' position, or
that they felt any freer to embark upon negotiation with
D Vantona as the result of anything which was said by the
pursuers or their advisers. However, I think it probable
that these particular events made it less likely that the
defenders would keep the pursuers informed of any
further or more specific indications of interest from
Vantona or others.

The following day, the issue of the pursuers' offer
document was postponed from 3 February to 10
February. The reason given for this was that the
defenders' auditors could not provide the required
E details on working capital, cash balances and borrowing. In the light of subsequent events, some scepticism
has arisen on the pursuers' side as to whether this was
a genuine reason, or whether the defenders were
playing for time, knowing of the possibility of a bid
from Vantona. I am satisfied that the reason given
makes sense, and that on this matter also, an inference
of bad faith is not warranted.

Quite how much contact there was between Sir
David and the defenders over the succeeding days is
F not clear. An accurate picture is probably obtained
from the evidence of Sir James Spooner, to the effect
that they spoke daily, with Vantona trying to wear
down the other side, but that the defenders' reaction
was that they already had an agreement, and that that
was positive unless they received an offer so obviously
attractive to their shareholders that they could not but
put it to them. Sir David was "constantly at them".
There appears also to have been some contact at
merchant banker level between Rothschilds and
Morgan Grenfell. The message however seems to have

been much the same: that unless Vantona came and
said what they would offer and in what terms, there G
could be no talks. There is a specific record, in notes
made by Mr Bell, of a phone call from Sir David to Mr
McAdam on Friday 31 January. Sir David is recorded
as having suggested talking over the weekend, and
having lunch. Mr McAdam's reply is recorded as
"No". It is also recorded that Lord McFadzean considered going in Mr McAdam's place, but after discussion, both agreed that there should be no meeting
"as we were behind the deal with Kinross". It is clear
that by this stage all was not well between the pursuers H
and the defenders, reaction to the announced merger
not having been good, and in terms of Mr Bell's note
"management irritation was considerable". Nonetheless, it appears to me that up to this point, the attitude
of the defenders' board had remained consistently one
of refusal to talk unless a specific offer was put forward,
and that no indication had been given of what sort of
offer would induce them to talk. It is to be noted that
at a meeting of the defenders' board on the Thursday,
30 January, Mr McAdam reported on the terms of the I
press announcement issued on 27 January "and the
events both preceding and following that announcement", and the board confirmed its support for all
action taken thus far. A committee was appointed with
full powers to act in connection with the offer to be
made by the pursuers.

What perhaps opened up the impasse between the
defenders and Vantona was the intervention of a Mr
Richard Webb, one of Mr Cadbury's partners at
Morgan Grenfell. Mr Webb apparently knew Sir J
James Spooner well, and was seeing him on a quite
unrelated matter. The message which Sir James
Spooner received from Mr Webb was to the effect that
Vantona must come forward with something very
serious, or Coats Paton would not talk. It is not quite
clear whose idea it was to use Mr Webb as an inter-
mediary, to talk to the other side in this way. Mr Webb
had however been involved to some extent in the
defenders' preparations for the takeover by the pursuers, and there is an indication in a note by the K
defenders' company secretary that it was Mr McAdam,
rather than merely Mr Cadbury, who "passed
messages through Richard Webb (friend of James
Spooner)". This account of the messages states "made
position clear that unless got a letter with appreciably
better terms couldn't meet". I think the wooer was by
now being told at least "No, but".

Whoever instigated this contact between the
defenders' merchant bankers and the Vantona chair- L
man, it resulted in a letter from Sir James to Mr
McAdam, dated 3 February, in which he says: "We
wondered if you and your colleagues might not wish to
examine other alternatives which we are sure would be
equally as attractive to your shareholders and the
management of your Group as the offer made by
Dawson." The letter says that it is important that Mr
McAdam and Sir David should have the opportunity
to meet and discuss the possible benefits, and goes on
to say that there is some ground to cover "before we
reach the stage which might lead to a possible merger,

A
and the necessity to make an announcement". (A handwritten postscript says "I have told DA you will call him as soon as you are ready", but I think that this does not reflect any prior agreement on Mr McAdam's part to meet: it appears to me merely to be part of Vantona's efforts to draw Mr McAdam into such a meeting.) An annotated copy of this letter appears to suggest the substitution of the words "more" and "than" for the words "equally" and "as". Further up the page are the words "demonstrably" and "clearly" bracketed together, with the word "more" after them.

B
This is evidently the work of the defenders' financial advisers, regarding what had been received as inadequate to justify talks, but adumbrating a terminology which would justify talks.

On 4 February, Sir James wrote to Mr McAdam again expressing his concern "that the financial advisers do not appear to be advancing this matter as quickly as they might". He refers to the inadvisability of making a specific commitment as to merger terms before full discussion between Mr McAdam and Sir

C
David had taken place and goes on to say that he is sure that Mr McAdam would understand that "We would not have considered it worthwhile approaching you were we not fully confident that such terms would prove to be clearly more attractive than those which are at present in front of you." It seems clear that the stronger terminology of this letter did not result merely from thought or advice on the part of Vantona or Rothschilds, but was a response to indications from Morgan Grenfell that such stronger terminology

D
would be required. Furthermore, it is apparent that having received the letter with this stronger terminology, Mr Cadbury was not satisfied that it would yet justify a meeting between the two companies. There is a note by him dated 4 February 1986, referring to Vantona and the defenders as "Seychelles" and "Mauritius" respectively, which (in the fuller of two versions of the note) reads as follows: "I indicated to the advisers of 'Seychelles' that the chief executive of 'Mauritius' would be prepared to meet the chairman

E
and/or chief executive of 'Seychelles' on the understanding that the words 'more attractive' contained in the letter from the chairman of 'Seychelles' dated 4 February 1986 reflected a discussion between Morgan Grenfell & Co Ltd and N M Rothschild. In this M G made it clear that 'Mauritius' could only consider proposals which contained both a wholly cash offer at least 10 per cent above the cash alternative offered by Louis" (plainly Dawson) "and also a wholly equity offer by 'Seychelles' which all parties felt confident

F
would stand at an appreciably higher level than such cash offer by 'Seychelles' after the announcement of its proposals.

"N M R stated that although they could make no prior commitments on price, they understood our position on terms, and accepted that in order to obtain the recommendation of the 'Mauritius' board it would be necessary to demonstrate that the offer by 'Seychelles' was superior in all respects."

It is to be observed that this note records no new

G
clarification of Vantona's intention, or ability, to make an offer at any specified level, and records Rothschilds' understanding of Morgan Grenfell's position, rather than the other way around. The note moreover shows the defenders' financial advisers giving quite specific advice to Vantona's advisers as to the need for Vantona to replace the generalised expression "more attractive" with a determinate cash offer related to Dawson's cash alternative, and an equity offer appreciably higher than that cash offer at the relevant date. Morgan Grenfell thus effectively told Rothschilds what offer could lead

H
to a meeting to discuss merger more generally, and were impliedly indicating the level of price which could achieve recommendation if other merger terms could be satisfactorily resolved. Rothschilds are not recorded as accepting that the words "more attractive" in fact "reflected a discussion" between the merchant bankers, nor do they appear to agree that they can be so read from then on. Judging by Mr Cadbury's own advice to the defenders, he appears at this meeting to have gone well beyond "seeking clarification about the precise terms of an offer" and appears to me to have

I
been "entering into negotiations" and taking an initiative in being the first to put a figure into those negotiations. He is therefore as merchant banker to the defenders apparently doing something which they themselves could not in his view properly have done. In commenting on Sir James's letter of 4 February, Mr Cadbury said in evidence that having received a serious letter, he felt it necessary to find out what Vantona had in mind. The defenders' shareholders were entitled to this, in view of the very positive words used. But his

J
attempt to find out what Vantona had in mind apparently took the form of telling Vantona what he, or the defenders, had in mind. As I understood his evidence, Rothschild's representative had not agreed to the suggested 10 per cent figure, although he had accepted that there must be a demonstrable superiority in all respects. At all events, and whichever side had achieved a better understanding of the other's position, the letter of 4 February, coupled rather loosely with this meeting, was evidently seen as a sufficient basis for

K
the defenders to meet Vantona and discuss merger.

That stage having been reached, it is plain that substantial negotiations took place on the whole range of topics upon which a common understanding would be necessary before any offer could receive the recommendation of the defenders' board. The board met on Friday 7 February 1986, and Mr McAdam advised the board of the "further unsolicited approaches to the Company" from Vantona. He reported inter alia that

L
all aspects other than the financial terms had been resolved to the satisfaction of himself and Mr Bell. He described to the board a number of the matters which had been covered, and these appear to me to reflect very substantial discussion and negotiation between the two companies. The board concluded that were a satisfactory agreement reached on price, it would be in the interests of shareholders, employees and customers alike to merge with Vantona. It is recorded that in "long and exhaustive negotiations" it had become clear that the board had to make a decision as to whether a

cash alternative of 238.24p was acceptable and defensible. They authorised Mr McAdam and Mr Bell to secure the best possible terms for the merger with Vantona with a cash alternative of not less than that figure. The meeting then adjourned and following the adjournment Mr McAdam reported that agreement had been reached with Vantona on the minimum terms agreed by the board. It was noted that posting of the Dawson offer document could not occur without the written approval of the committee consisting of Mr McAdam and Mr Bell, whose approval would not be forthcoming should it become absolutely clear that the Vantona Viyella offer would proceed. Subject to that written approval not being given, a committee was appointed with full powers to take the necessary steps in connection with an offer from Vantona.

The Vantona board met on Sunday 9 February, and resolved to make the offer. At 8.30 on the morning of Monday 10 February, Mr Cadbury went to tell Samuel Montagu that the defenders' board would be issuing a joint press announcement with Vantona at 9.30 that morning, recommending a merger between the defenders and Vantona, and that accordingly it would not be possible to give a letter of recommendation from the defenders in relation to the pursuers' offer documents. He said that they had been restrained from talking earlier, and attributed this (according to one of his later notes) partly to the conversation which I have mentioned with Ian McIntosh, but more particularly to a condition placed on them by Rothschilds that they should not communicate with any third party, and in particular Dawson, prior to the release of the under-writing document which was held in escrow until 8.30 that morning. He intimated that in view of the fact that they had been aware of the proposal from the previous Friday, if they received a request for payment of the bulk printing of the offer document over the weekend, this would probably be given sympathetic considera-tion. The press announcement by the defenders and Vantona was duly made that day, and in the event, that takeover went ahead and has been put into effect.

IX. Fraudulent or negligent misrepresentation

The pursuers' case founded upon fraudulent or negligent misrepresentation is based upon a represen-tation allegedly made at the meeting between repre-sentatives of the pursuers and defenders on 16 January 1986. It is averred that at that meeting, the pursuers' representatives specifically asked whether there had been any approach by or discussion with any other possible bidder and were informed that there had not. It is then averred that the representation that there had not been any approach by or discussion with any other possible bidder was untrue and falsely represented the defenders' position. The averments of falseness are based upon averments as to discussions with Courtaulds. It is averred that the defenders did not reveal such discussions, and materially misrepresented the situation by alleging that there were no such discussions. There are further averments that the pursuers relied on these representations, and would not have proceeded with the discussions if they had been aware of other discussions between the defenders and a potential third party bidder. After further averments concerned with contacts between the defenders and Vantona Viyella the pursuers expand their case of misrepresentation. They aver that in the whole circum-stances, the representation made on 16 January was intended by the defenders, and understood by the pursuers, to be "repeated throughout their subsequent discussions" and the subsequent discussions are said in fact to have been conducted subject to that intention and understanding. Upon that basis, the pursuers' pleadings proceed to aver not merely that there had been discussions with Vantona, as well as Courtaulds, at the time of the original representation, but that the discussions with both of these companies continued thereafter. They continue with averments that the representation was at no time throughout the subse-quent discussions retracted or modified, and allege that in these circumstances the defenders fraudulently misrepresented the true position regarding other possible bidders throughout the entire period 15 to 28 January. (It is the original misrepresentation which thus continues: it is not suggested that any new representation is implied, as to new events arising after the meeting on 16 January.) In the alternative, they aver that the defenders negligently misrepre-sented the true position regarding other possible bidders. This alternative averment is based upon aver-ments that the defenders knew or ought to have known that the pursuers would rely on any representation of this kind, and owed to the pursuers a duty to take reasonable care that any such representation was accurate.

On the facts which I have found to be established, no false representation was made on 16 January. So far as Vantona are concerned, counsel for the pursuers accepted that the evidence as to the defenders' knowledge of Vantona's intentions at that time would not suffice as a basis for his case of misrepresentation, either in relation to 16 January, or in relation to the subsequent period up to 28 January. So far as Courtaulds are concerned, it was accepted that from 21 January onwards, they could not be regarded by the defenders as "possible bidders" in any current sense. Using the other terminology, which appears to under-lie, and is in my view reasonably consistent with, what is said in the pleadings, Courtaulds after 21 January could no longer be regarded as "in the wings". On the view which I have taken, Courtaulds were not potential bidders, or in the wings, between 16 and 21 January. But even if they still were so on 16 January, or indeed became so again on 17 January, any original or supervening falsity in the representation which had been given appears to me, as was submitted by counsel for the defenders, not to have any sufficient causal connection with the pursuers' decision to make an offer, and accept the underwriting liabilities which went with it. Whatever the precise terms of any repre-sentation, the reliance placed upon it by Mr Miller appears to me to have been plainly related to the exist-ence of third parties who could reasonbly be regarded as rival bidders. Whatever Courtaulds' position had

A been before 16 January, or may temporarily have been again thereafter, the understanding upon which he was proceeding, that the field was clear of known potential bidders, was in my opinion correct, by the time that he proceeded with the actions which led to abortive expenditure. A somewhat broader formulation of the misrepresentation case presents the falseness of the representation (whether intentional or negligent) as something which would, if revealed, have destroyed Mr Miller's trust in the defenders and their board, and would have led him to have terminated his approach,

B notwithstanding that the one outside bidder in relation to whom the representation was false had subsequently dropped out of the category. Even on the assumption of original falseness, I am not satisfied that it would have had this destructive effect, if the defenders had told Mr Miller of the history of their dealings with Courtaulds, or if he had asked for confirmation or otherwise discovered the position, before moving into the position of formal approach and intimation of intended offer, on 22 January and succeeding days. I

C am satisfied that the pursuers' case based upon misrepresentation fails.

X. Contract

The other basis upon which the pursuers found their case is breach of contract. Some passages in the pursuers' pleadings perhaps suggest that they claim that a contract was concluded at the meeting on 15 January 1986 (albeit with conditions or provisos which would require to be purified). This was not the

D eventual submission. While sometimes using the terminology of "agreement" and subsequent "ratification" counsel for the pursuers did not, as I understood him, submit that the required consensus between the parties, even subject to further ratification or purification of conditions, was to be found in what passed between them at the meeting on 15 January. Nor was it a matter of assurances given by the defenders; rather it was a question of a mutual understanding having been reached. This would accord with a passage in the

E pursuers' pleadings which ends with these understandings becoming terms of the alleged contract, and is worth setting out quite fully:

"The expression 'lockout' was introduced into the discussion by Mr McAdam, and Mr McAdam and Mr Bell indicated that a 'lockout' would be likely to be achieved at the price of £2.50. It was explained that this figure was based on calculations . . . prepared . . . to determine a break up of the constituent parts of the defenders' enterprise. . . . The directors of the

F defenders . . . represented to the pursuers that, if agreement could be reached on the valuation of the defenders' shares and the other terms of the offer, including the cash alternative, the merger would proceed as an agreed merger recommended by the defenders' board with the object of achieving a 'lockout' situation. It was understood that in such a situation having regard to the whole circumstances and in particular the price per share, a bid from any outside party would be deterred. It was further understood that, in accordance with normal City practice in such

a situation, neither party to such an agreed merger would solicit any competing offer by a third party or G encourage or co-operate with any potential competing offerer either by the provision of information, except to the extent required by the Takeover Code, or by discussion of post-merger arrangements or otherwise. The said understandings remained in force at all material times thereafter and were implied terms of the contract which was made between the parties as hereinafter condescended upon."

The averments as to the actual constitution of the contract are found somewhat later in the pleadings, as H follows:

"By at latest the said joint meeting of 26 January 1986, followed by the joint press announcement of 27 January 1986 the defenders and the pursuers had agreed that the pursuers would offer to buy the entire share capital of the defenders at the price stated in the press announcement. The defenders had by the same date contracted that they would recommend the said offer to their shareholders and that neither they, nor I anyone on their behalf would solicit any competing offer by a third party or encourage or co-operate with any potential competing offeror, all in accordance with the understandings hereinbefore condescended upon."

For convenience, I shall refer to this last implied term as the "no-encouragement" provision. Counsel for the pursuers submitted that the contract was in fact completed when the parties reached agreement on Friday, 24 January. The subsequent discussions as to the terms of the press release, and the rehearsal of the J press announcement, did not alter the terms of the contract. Correspondingly, the press release was to be regarded not as a document constituting the contract, but a narrative of it. It is to be noted that despite the early origin of the understandings which are said to have become implied terms of the contract, the alleged contract itself comes at a time when the chapter concerning misrepresentation and Courtaulds is at an end, and the chapter of dealings with Vantona, which K is alleged to show a breach of the no-encouragement provision, has yet to begin.

XI. The code

Before I come to consider the existence, terms and effect of any contract, it is convenient to say something about the City Code on Takeovers and Mergers. In considering the history of events, I have intentionally left over until now the interrelation between the code and these events. But much of what various parties did, and indeed took care not to do, and many of their L reactions to what others were doing, find their explanation in the requirements of the code, or at least in parties' understanding of what those requirements entailed or might entail. Whether and how the requirements of the code may affect legal obligations is a matter to which I shall come shortly. The code itself states that it is not, and does not seek to have, the force of law; but it continues by saying that "those who wish to take advantage of the facilities of the securities markets in the United Kingdom should conduct

A themselves in matters relating to takeovers according to the code. Those who do not so conduct themselves cannot expect to enjoy those facilities and may find that they are withheld".

In that way at least, I am in no doubt that the provisions of the code were regarded as applicable and binding by all those concerned in the events which I have had to consider. That being so, care was obviously required, and was obviously being taken by various parties at various stages, to hold back from those events envisaged by the code as altering parties'
B obligations under it, until those involved were fully satisfied that the time was right for that particular event. The desire not to have made an "approach" while matters could still be plausibly treated as exploratory or hypothetical, or the desire not to notify an offeree board of a firm intention to make an offer free of preconditions, seems to me to be entirely understandable, when one considers the changes in responsibility and obligation which such events produce, or can produce under the code. These con-
C siderations underlie the insistence which one finds upon the exploratory nature of talks and the want of any specific authority vested in representatives by their board, and explain a general wish to work things out as fully as possible, before allowing the next formal stage to be reached. I appreciate the principles and far reaching practical considerations which have given rise to these rules. I understand the tendency to "hold off" when in other legal contexts an offer with multiple conditions might have been a sensible mechanism. But
D there is a pervasive if explicable artificiality in many of the contacts made in the process which leads to a formal announcement, and in due course an actual offer to shareholders. Most particularly, contacts between the two sides' financial advisers, rather than between actual board representatives, seem to be regarded as somehow holding matters on a hypothetical level, even in circumstances where the financial advisers are, or are coming dangerously close to, speaking directly on behalf of their principals. And
E the terminology of utterances such as the press announcement seems to me to be (despite both ambiguity and some variation in practice) stylised in a way which says more about what professional advisers think has to be said, than it does about what the parties have actually done.

In the present case, these considerations seem to me to be worth noting as part of the context of what went on. More specifically, it is plain that the major steps taken by the parties were seen as taken in terms of the
F code. Specific obligations under the code are not founded upon by the pursuers as having been breached. Rather, the provisions of the code are brought in because it is acknowledged that they would have to be complied with, and such compliance is treated as permissible, notwithstanding what would otherwise be a general contractual obligation to the contrary. I shall come back to this effect of the code, in limiting the *scope* of a supposed contractual obligation; but it is convenient to consider whether a contractual obligation existed, before considering in detail what its scope may have been.

G In considering the more fundamental question, of whether there was any contractual relationship between the parties at any stage, the code seems to me to be important in the analysis of what parties were really doing. For example, bearing in mind that the press announcement of 27 January was essentially an announcement of the kind required by the code, it may be important to remember that what would trigger it would not on the face of it be some contract which required to be announced, but merely the notification to the board of the offeree company, from a serious source, of a firm intention to make an offer, free of
H preconditions (rule 2.2 (a)). Again, one should not forget that in such announcements, what is being announced is this "firm intention to make an offer" with details of the intended offer as required by rule 2.5. And while the offer (in itself of course an offer to shareholders) must be put forward in the first instance to the board of the offeree company or its advisers (rule 1 (a)), a firm announcement brings about certain further positive obligations under the code: upon the offeree company promptly to send a copy of the press
I notice, or a summary of the offer, to its shareholders, and upon the offeror, to proceed with the offer, except in certain rather special circumstances. Each party having these obligations under the code, it appears to me less necessary to search for a contract, as a basis and explanation for either the one party feeling obliged to do particular things, or for the other party relying upon them being done.

Again, considering the nature of any "recommen-
J dation" given by the offeree board, it is to be remembered that rule 25.1 requires that such a board must circulate "its views on the offer" as well as making known to its shareholders the substance of the advice which it is obliged to take from independent advisers under rule 3.1. It may well be that a potential offeror will not make a firm offer unless and until it has ascertained the views of the offeree board as to the merits of the proposed offer. But if those views have been ascertained, and the offeror proceeds formally to
K notify to the board of the offeree company a firm intention to make an offer, the fact that each party can reasonably rely upon the other complying with the code perhaps suggests that contractual stipulations would be superfluous, and that what is going on is indeed a statement by one party as to its intentions, and a statement by the other party as to its views and the advice it has received. Scrutiny of a particular set of dealings, or of a particular press announcement describing them, may of course reveal that a particular contractual bargain has been struck. But the various
L processes contemplated by the code do not appear to necessitate and entail any such contractual relationship, and in identifying and describing any party's "obligations" in this area, one will have to be careful to distinguish between such obligations arising from contractual stipulation, and obligations in the sense of duties imposed by the code upon those who are subject to it.

As regards the interrelation between the code and any contractual bargain, and in particular any terms alleged to be implied in terms of such a bargain, I would add that the acceptance or expectation by each party that the other will comply with the code will not merely eliminate the need for contractual provision in certain areas, but would appear to rule out, in practical if not in absolute terms, the possibility of any implied term imposing an obligation to act in a manner contrary to the requirements of the code. In the present case, if there was a contract between the parties, and if that contract included an implied term such as the no-encouragement provision averred by the pursuers, then I am satisfied that the expression "except to the extent required by the Takeover Code" which is used by the pursuers would indeed have to be built in as a qualification to what might otherwise be a more general implied term forbidding soliciting, encouraging or co-operating by the provision of information. If compliance with the code required provision of information, I cannot readily envisage an implied term which did not allow for that. But was there a contract at all? And if so, did it contain an implied no-encouragement provision, even with this qualification?

XII. Existence of a contract

If the parties saw themselves as making a contract, one would expect perhaps to find this reflected in the official record of their decisions, in their board minutes. In the minute of the defenders' board meeting on 24 January, as I have noted at head V, the board agreed that provided details of the press announcement and related matters were in a form satisfactory to a committee comprising Mr McAdam and others, "it would recommend to shareholders acceptance of the proposed offer by Dawson of shares in Dawson having a value of 250p at the close of business that day or a cash alternative at no greater discount than 10 per cent of the value of the share offer". It was agreed "to give public support to the merger in a form that would not compromise the company's position in the event that the Dawson bid were thwarted". On the face of it, that does not appear to me to be the language of contract. Rather, it expresses unilateral decisions as to what will be done in the event of the pursuers making an offer to the defenders' shareholders, in defined terms. The language also appears to me to fit the non-contractual requirements of the code, governing what the defenders' board would have to do in the circumstances.

Contractual obligations may of course relate to contingent future circumstances. But even in the context of substantial discussion and indeed "agreement" as to the structures and policies which would be adopted in the contingency of the takeover/merger going ahead, the terms of the minute do not to my mind indicate that the defenders or their board saw themselves as "agreeing", or being about to agree, "that the pursuers would offer to buy the entire share capital of the defenders at the price stated in the press announcement" as averred by the pursuers on record. I see no real basis for the pursuers being bound, or taken bound, by a contractual bargain in that respect. Nor does the language of the minute to my mind indicate

that the defenders had "contracted" that they would recommend the offer to their shareholders, or that they were about to do so, or indeed that this was any more than a decision by the board as to what they would do in fulfilment of their obligations under the code, if the offer were to be made. I do not doubt that the making of the offer was itself dependent upon the defenders having reached these decisions and being willing to give public intimation of them along with the public intimation of the proposed offer. But thus far at least, it does not seem to me that contractual concepts are either necessary, or implicit in what the defenders' board said they were doing.

Somewhat similarly, the terms of the minutes of the meeting of the pursuers' board held on 24 January show that the meeting had been called for the purpose of approving the principle of an offer to be made on behalf of the company for the share capital of the defenders, and the main resolution is indeed to that effect. Neither that resolution, nor the further resolution to set up a committee with full powers is expressed as involving any contractual bargain with the defenders or their board. Again, while I do not question that the publication of the proposed offer was seen as dependent on the defenders' board recommending acceptance, I see no necessary implication, and nothing in the terms of what was resolved, indicating that a contract was seen as necessary, or existing, to bind the parties in advance to do what, by the press announcement, they announced in due course that they were doing. If two parties propose to do something together, and either can abstain from moving unless and until the other moves with him, there seems nothing particularly surprising in the period up to joint announcement being regulated by ordinary assurance and reliance, without any contractual bond.

As counsel for the defenders conceded, some of the subjects of prior discussion can be seen as having reached the stage of being "agreements" — but agreements (whatever their status) as to what would happen afterwards, in the event of a merger occurring, with no implication of a contractual agreement to the effect that the pursuers would make an offer, or that the defenders, or their board, would recommend such an offer.

I come to the press announcement of 27 January 1986. Counsel for the defenders insisted, and counsel for the pursuers at least accepted, that the press announcement was essentially a narrative of what the two boards had already done, rather than itself constituting any juridical step in their dealings with one another. At least if one is looking for a contract, that appears to me to be the correct view. So too, the offer by the pursuers to the defenders' shareholders remained in the future, and even the recommendation of that offer is properly to be seen as something which would follow on the press announcement, rather than being constituted by what was said about recommendation in that announcement. The language of the announcement was subjected to close scrutiny, both by counsel in their submissions, and indeed by a variety of witnesses familiar with announcements of this kind. While some of the evidence emphasised the extent to which the matters set out in the announcement would be regarded as "binding" in the City and financial circles, the view that something was thus binding can be seen as a matter of honour, or as a requirement of the code, regardless of contract. Moreover, the announcement was not merely a communication to the City and such circles, but was used (and is envisaged in the code as usable) as the means for informing shareholders, in language with no cryptic significance for initiates, of what is proposed. That being so, I consider that interpretation is essentially a matter for the court, and not for expert evidence.

There are two main aspects of the announcement which might be seen as pointing to the existence of a contract. First, there is a good deal of talk of "agreement". The heading refers to an "agreed merger", and the very first sentence of the announcement is to the effect that the boards of the two companies announce "that terms have been agreed for a merger". Secondly, there is repeated use of a positive future tense. The merger "will be" implemented by means of recommended offers on behalf of Dawson. The board of Coats Paton "will recommend" Coats Paton's shareholders to accept the ordinary offer. On behalf of the pursuers, it was contended that this use of the future tense, particularly in the context of the language of agreement, was to be read as promissory or obligatory, and not merely as indicating intention. Counsel for the defenders, on the other hand, did not merely repudiate the suggestion of an obligatory content in these words, but contended that they were not even expressive of intention. They reflected the intention of the parties involved, but they were not to be interpreted as similar words might be interpreted when spoken, in the first person, by one party to another. They were essentially statements of a narrative or descriptive kind, saying to others what would happen, or what a particular party would do. The words were appropriate because the particular party had decided, and no doubt intended, to do something. There was no obligatory content either in the words themselves, or in what they described.

In contending for an obligatory or contractual interpretation of the words "will recommend", counsel for the pursuers emphasised the difference between statements of present fact on the one hand, and unqualified expressions as to future conduct on the other. Statements of present fact might constitute representations, but words as to future conduct were to be understood as promissory, and contractual. In the context of commercial arrangements, one should prefer a "binding" construction, and treat the words as prima facie obligatory. Only thus would the commercial dealings of parties become effective, and in the absence of any clear indication that the arrangement was not intended to be binding, one should proceed upon the basis that it was. Reference was made to such cases as *R & J Dempster Ltd v Motherwell Bridge*; *Muirhead & Turnbull v Dickson*; *Kleinwort Benson Ltd v Malaysia Mining*; and *Edwards v Skyways Ltd*. According to this approach, one has the pursuers (in simplified terms) saying something about their proposed offer, and adding something like "We want your recommendation — will you give it?"; and the defenders replying in the affirmative. Having regard to the importance and the commercial nature of the matter, that was said to constitute an agreement. It was that agreement which was described in the terms of the press announcement. It was proper, if not determinative, to have regard to the views of those familiar with such transactions and announcements. Both Mr McIntosh, and Mr David Hudson, a witness with substantial experience in merchant and investment banking, took the view that the defenders had promised their recommendation, and while other witnesses such as Mr Cadbury, and Antony Beevor, Director General of the Panel on Takeovers and Mergers, took a different view, that was said to turn essentially upon the problem of vires, which was solved if one built in the qualifications which would give primacy to the requirements of the code. On a correct view of matters, the code had been applied by all parties, and it itself, to all intents and purposes, had the force of law.

Reference was made to *R v The Panel, ex p Datafin plc* and *R v The Panel, ex p Guinness*. In such a situation, the parties' dealings overall were regulated by law, and in saying that they would recommend the offer, the defenders, whatever they may have thought they were doing, were making a statement as to their future conduct which should be interpreted as promissory and binding. While a particular context, like that of a social invitation, could remove the promissory effect of future statements, the context here pointed in quite the opposite direction. There was a contract on the one side to make the proposed offer, and on the other side to recommend it to shareholders.

Speaking generally, I would accept that when two parties are talking to one another about a matter which has commercial significance to both, a statement by one party that he will do some particular thing will normally be construed as obligatory, or as an offer, rather than as a mere statement of intention, if the words and deeds of the other party indicate that the statement was so understood, and the obligation confirmed or the offer accepted so that parties appeared to regard the commercial "deal" as concluded. But in considering whether there is indeed a contract between the parties, in any particular case, it will always be essential to look at the particular facts, with a view to discovering whether these facts, rather than some general rule of thumb, can be said to reveal consensus and an intention to conclude a contract.

In the present case, I am not persuaded that it was the intention of the parties to form a contract whereby they became reciprocally obliged to make and recommend the proposed offer to the defenders' shareholders. It is not merely that the use of the future tense is found in a statement to third parties, rather than in a statement made by one party to another. Indeed, it is not difficult to imagine circumstances in which a public statement to third parties, incorporating an

A indication of acceptance or agreement, might be evidence of prior agreement, or might itself constitute the contract between the parties. But in the present case, the language of the press announcement appears to me, when taken along with the language in which the two sides describe the decisions they were taking, to reflect agreement (whether contractual or not) as to various things that will be done in the event of a merger, without any prior contractual obligation on the pursuers to make the offer, and (in the absence of that obligation upon the pursuers) with no reciprocal

B obligation upon the defenders. Moreover, one must look at the subject matter. Where the subject matter is a simple commercial act, such as the delivery of goods, it seems to me to be a quite simple step to an inference of concluded contractual intent. But in the present case, with the two sides discussing changes which would be effected by contracts between the pursuers and the defenders' shareholders, the suggestion of a prior contract, with obligations to make the offer and recommend it, strikes me as much less natural. The

C unlikelihood of a preliminary contract of that kind is increased by the fact that the wish of each party, to be able to rely upon the other fulfilling his stated intentions, could be met without contractual ties, by relying on the code being followed, and by each side's commitment only being expressed in the one joint statement by both. Whether there was any contract as to what would be done after merger is another matter. I am not satisfied by the language used that there was any contract in relation to the steps of offer and

D recommendation which would precede any eventual merger.

I have concentrated thus far upon the use of the future tense, and the language of agreement, in the press announcement. But there is a second aspect of that statement which may be important in considering whether the parties had contracted to make and recommend the proposed offer. The subject matter of the alleged contract is the making and "recommend-

E ing" of an offer. I see no real problem in the concept of one party binding himself, in a contract with another party, to make an offer to third parties. But the position in relation to recommendation is perhaps more complicated. What is in issue is not a de praesenti recommendation; what is in issue is a binding obligation, undertaken at one point in time, to make a recommendation at a subsequent point in time — presumably the time when the offer is open for acceptance. Counsel for the pursuers acknowledged that the nature of

F recommendation was what gave rise to some of the problems or complexities in regard to the supposed contract. I do not think it necessary or appropriate to embark on any attempt at a definition of "recommendation", but whether as an integral part of its meaning, or as a prerequisite of any bona fide recommendation, it appears to me (and was not I think disputed) that recommendation entails or implies that the person making the recommendation believes that what he is recommending is good and appropriate. If a future recommendation is contemplated, this belief must also be in the future.

G To bind oneself to do something which is dependent on one's future beliefs, or even to bind oneself to believe something in the future, is no doubt possible in law. But where it is suggested that someone has done this, I would be inclined to be slow in putting such a construction upon their words and deeds. And more specifically, if someone has thus bound themselves, I think it is clear that any such contract, or the rules regulating its enforcement, would have to allow for the possibility that the person who has bound himself to make the recommendation quite simply cannot do so in good faith, for want of the necessary belief in it. In

H some circumstances, it might be that this "let out" might legitimately be read into the contract as an implied term. It might also be a question of construction, in relation to a particular contract, whether the person undertaking the obligation to recommend was warranting his belief at the time of that undertaking.

But apart from the specific construction of a specific contract, it appears to me that in relation to the alleged contract in the present case, the "let out" would be

I available to the defenders, if they no longer felt able bona fide to recommend the pursuers' offer, as a matter of the general law applicable to such a contract. They would not in my view be required to do that which in good faith they could not do. This matter has already been covered at some length in previous decisions in the present case [see 1988 SLT 854 and 1989 SLT 655], and I do not feel it necessary or appropriate to go into it further. Nonetheless, the fact that the obligation in question is one which is not open to simple enforcement, but is dependent for its enforceability upon the

J defenders' state of mind at a subsequent date, makes it all the more important to question whether any such undertaking was in truth given, or whether one was in the field of statements of intention. "I will do X, but you need not expect me to do so if I have honestly changed my mind" may be an unfair description of the alleged undertaking. But I do not think that it is wholly unfair, and it is perilously close to a fair description of a statement of intention, and its consequences. The introduction of the "let out" is no doubt essential to a

K contract to recommend; but the "let out" comes very close to bridging the gap back from contract to a mere statement of intent. I am not persuaded, in the light of all the considerations I have mentioned, that the defenders moved beyond a statement of intent, which for non-contractual reasons they would feel obliged to fulfil, unless they had honestly changed their mind.

There is a further consideration which I believe

L points in the same direction. Distinctions between the actions of a board and the actions of a company can of course become unreal. This is not the place to embark upon any general consideration of the circumstances in which, or the basis upon which, the actions of a board (as such or as individuals) might not be regarded as the actions of the company. But if there is to be a contract, that contract would in my view have to be the company's, rather than the board's. If there is merely a statement of intention, then even if the company might eventually be seen as answerable for that statement and its consequences, I find it easier to regard the statement, in quite simple terms, as being a joint statement by the members of the board, as a board, of their intentions. A recommendation can properly be seen in this way, in my opinion, as being the board's and reflecting the board's belief. Correspondingly, a statement that a recommendation will be made appears to me to be more naturally construed as a statement of the board's intentions, rather than a contract made by the company through them.

I would add that this non-contractual construction of what the parties said they would do as steps before merger seems to me to fit well with the proper construction of the steps that they "agreed" would be taken after the merger, if it happened. As I have indicated, I would regard that as essentially a separate matter, so that the one stage might be regulated contractually, while the other was not. But the assertion of a contract at the offer/recommendation stage finds some of its basis in the language of agreement used in the press announcement, which in turn flows, at least partly, from the various issues which had been "agreed" in relation to the post-merger stage. While it is perhaps unnecessary for me to reach any concluded view as to whether the agreements as to the post-merger stage are to be regarded as contractual or not, I very much doubt whether they are. Ex hypothesi these matters would require to be regulated at a time when the defenders' shares had passed into the ownership of the pursuers, the pursuers' shareholding would have been transformed, and all questions as to the structure and policy of the pursuers, and indeed the defenders, would be a matter for decision at that time and in these circumstances. Firm indication of what will happen if the offer is accepted may be a crucial carrot to put before the City and the shareholders. My impressions may be coloured by hindsight, but I do not find it difficult to envisage a situation in which apparently firm pre-merger "agreements" would not be carried out. If the basis for this were to be questioned, I would expect it to be in terms of breach of faith rather than breach of contract. Any actual contract as to who should be chairman, or where the head office should be or the like would in my view require "let out" provisions, or non-enforceability rules, of the type discussed above in relation to recommendation. There would also be questions as to title and interest to enforce, in the wholly altered circumstances. It appears to me that the "agreements" in relation to the post-merger stage are probably only statements of common intention, which if honestly made at the time, could be relied upon as matter of honesty and trust, but not as a matter of obligation and law. These matters may help to explain the use of the language of agreement in the press announcement. They do not support a contractual construction of that language in relation to the prior, pre-merger stage.

XIII. The implied term

I return to the alleged contract regulating the pre-merger stage. As averred by the pursuers, this appears to be a bilateral contract, with an obligation on the pursuers to buy the entire share capital of the defenders at the price stated in the press announcement (although the consensus on that price and other matters is seen as having been reached before the actual announcement). In this action, it is of course the defenders' obligations which are founded upon. As set out by the pursuers in their pleadings, these are not limited to the simple obligation to recommend the offer, but include what I have called the no-encouragement provision. That provision is seen as an implied term of the contract, flowing from an understanding which is itself said to be in accordance with normal City practice in such a situation. But for the presence of that implied term, which is averred to have been breached, there would be no breach of contract upon which the pursuers could found: the defenders' failure to recommend the pursuers' offer cannot be said, in the circumstances which had in fact emerged, to be attributable to anything other than a bona fide change of belief as to what was in the best interests of their shareholders. The switch in recommendation was in itself covered by the "let out" provided by the general law. The alleged breach of contract thus lies solely in an alleged breach of the no-encouragement provision.

In terms of what would be understood between the parties, and in terms of what may be called normal City practice, I am satisfied that after the press announcement, the defenders were in a situation where they "ought" not to have solicited any competing offer by a third party, and moreover, in relation to any potential competing offeror, ought not to have given encouragement or co-operation of certain kinds. That understanding and practice do not appear to me, on the basis of the evidence which I heard, to be dependent on any contractual basis or background. Even with no contract to make an offer, or to recommend an offer, the announcement that an offer would be made, and that it would be recommended, would mean that the parties would proceed upon the basis (again non-contractual) that it would be wrong in such circumstances for the party which had said that it would recommend the proposed offer to solicit any competing offer, or to give encouragement or co-operation in the way that I have mentioned. In that wholly non-contractual context the law of contract will not provide the appropriate criteria for identifying or defining the boundaries of the encouragement and co-operation which would thus be seen as wrong, or as something which ought not to occur, or as constituting a breach of some non-contractual, or indeed non-legal rule. But I think a rationale for this understanding and practice can be found in common sense. Some new circumstances, of which one example would be a new competing offer, might quite properly lead to a switch of recommendation. But parties who have publicly stated that they will recommend a previous offer should not seek or help to undermine the basis of their own intentions, or seek or help to change circumstances in such a way that they would be free not to do that which they have said they will do. Anything which was done in order to comply with the code would not offend against this rather broad principle. Moreover, in a changing situation, a stage might be reached where enough was actually known as to the terms and likelihood of a competing offer from a particular source, and as to the kind of benefits which might be expected from it, for those who had said that they would recommend the original offer to have lost any real belief that acceptance of that offer was in their shareholders' interests. The evidence of the witnesses experienced in these matters varied quite widely in the terminology used. I conclude however from that evidence that until one reached the state of knowledge about the competing bid which I have just described, it would be seen as "wrong", and an unacceptable form of encouragement and co-operation, to do anything which would help the competing offeror so to alter his offer, or the information regarding his offer, that that stage of knowledge would in fact thereby be reached; but that once that stage had been reached, without such encouragement and co-operation, subsequent discussion or negotiation with him, including the provision of business information, would not be seen as wrong. Application of the principle to particular facts might be difficult. But my conclusion is that the principle is as I have described it.

The opinions expressed by witnesses as to why the board of a company were entitled to withhold a recommendation which they had said they would give, and indeed as to why they were entitled at a given stage to move from a stance of non-co-operation to one of active discussion, tended to lay significant emphasis upon the fiduciary duty of directors, and the interests of the company and its shareholders. If the justification for withholding a recommendation, or for beginning to talk to another potential offeror, is seen in those terms, so be it. But issues as to directors' fiduciary duties, and the interests of the company or its shareholders, are in my view primarily of significance in relation to possible clashes between those interests and the interests of the directors personally. Even in the context of non-contractual obligations, or non-legal obligations, it does not seem to me that shareholders' interests, or company interests, afford a satisfactory reason for saying that an otherwise subsisting obligation need not be fulfilled. Once it has been said that a recommendation will be given (and whether that is seen as a matter of intention or obligation), the justification for not making the recommendation, and the justification at some stage for beginning to talk to a potential rival bidder, is in my view to be found in the broader principles which I have discussed above, which indeed I should have thought could be invoked by anyone, without recourse to the specialities of fiduciary duty. If a natural individual, free to act in his own interests, had said that he would give a recommendation, that would in my opinion naturally be understood as carrying with it both a "let out" and a no-encouragement understanding, and indeed a release from that no-encouragement understanding, of the kinds and in the circumstances which I have discussed.

I have discussed these matters in the non-contractual context first, because that is where they appear to have their origins, both in the pursuers' pleadings and in fact. It is these non-contractual understandings which are said to become implied terms in the context of the alleged contract. It is not suggested that the implied contractual terms differ in any way from the terms of the understandings which would exist before, or indeed without, the conclusion of any contract imposing obligations to make or recommend an offer. While I have come to the view that there was here no such contract, the question remains whether, if I am wrong in that respect, the contract would include an implied term, of the type which I have described as a no-encouragement provision, and if so, whether that implied term was breached as the pursuers claim. On behalf of the defenders, it was contended that the incorporation of such a provision into the supposed contract was not justified by the rules regarding implied terms in contracts. But in my opinion we are not here really concerned with the rules which allow for an additional and unexpressed term to be read into a contract as implied, perhaps on a basis such as custom of trade or necessity. It may be that such an approach could be seen as justifying the incorporation into a contract of a City practice. But I am not disposed to see the no-encouragement provision as a specific and extra term of the contract, requiring such a specific justification if it is to be implied. It appears to me to be an implication arising from the nature of contract in general, and from the purpose of the particular contract in question. Having undertaken an obligation, an obligant cannot be regarded as free to set about changing circumstances in such a way that his obligation will fly off or become unenforceable, and the contract thus ineffectual. More specifically, in the case of an obligation to recommend an offer for shares, just as it is inherent in such an obligation that it will not be enforceable if there is a bona fide change of mind, so also it seems to me to be inherent in that "let out" that the obligant cannot be free to take steps so to change circumstances that he will be enabled to change his mind. There was some dispute as to the history and content of the pursuers' pleadings in relation to the implied term of contract; but I am satisfied that there is enough on record to cover an implication of this kind. I am satisfied in these circumstances that if the parties had contracted respectively to make and recommend the pursuers' proposed offer, it was implicit in that contract that the defenders were subject to a no-encouragement provision of the kind which I have discussed in relation to the non-contractual situation.

XIV. Breach of contract

Upon the hypothesis that there was a contract, including such an implied term, were the defenders in breach of that implied term? Initially, it is clear that the defenders, and in particular Mr McAdam, were complying with the no-encouragement provision, whether one sees it as contractual or non-contractual. Equally, during the latter stages, it is clear that they regarded themselves (on professional advice) as having reached the stage where they were free to talk to the competing potential offeror, and that they in fact did so in the way in which I have described as justified once the requisite level of knowledge concerning the competing offer has been reached. In the absence of a contract, it would not be for me to judge whether particular actings amounted to a breach of, or a departure from, the understandings and practices which I have held to exist apart from contract. Moreover, having concluded that there was no contract, I have some misgivings over expressing a view upon the hypothesis that there was a contract, as to whether particular actings constituted a breach of its implied no-encouragement term. I am however satisfied that I should do so; and my view is that Vantona Viyella, at a stage when the terms and likelihood of any offer by them remained very unclear and uncertain, received information and help which led to their formulating and intimating a potential offer in more precise terms, and with more definite indications that such an offer was likely to be made. The fact that such information and help came from the defenders' financial advisers does not in the circumstances seem to me to make it extraneous. On the facts as I have found them to be, the help and information must be seen as given by and on behalf of the defenders, and I am satisfied that on the hypothesis of a contract, these actings were such, and at such a stage, as to constitute a breach of what I have called the no-encouragement provision. In the event however, I have held that there was no contract to breach. The view which I have expressed plainly indicates that these same actings failed to comply with the understandings and practice which exist quite apart from contract. Without wishing to embark upon judgment or criticism in fields which are not regulated by the courts, I should add that I think the defenders' failure flowed from the views, advice and actings of their advisers, and in particular Mr Cadbury; and that I see what he did not as deliberately furtive or devious, but as a shift from adherence to the right principle in theory, into an error in applying it, in circumstances which were increasingly unreal as the pure demands of the principles were subjected to the practical pressures applied by Vantona Viyella. Whether that pressure was proper, in the context of what was understood to be improper for the defenders' board, is a question, but not for this court. I hold that the pursuers' case based upon breach of contract fails.

XV. Damages

Upon the view which I have taken, questions of damages or reimbursement do not arise. I should however express my opinion upon these matters, on the assumption that the pursuers had established either breach of contract, or fraudulent or negligent misrepresentation. It is agreed that the pursuers incurred underwriting costs totalling £5,371,024.77 in connection with their proposed offer to purchase the defenders' share capital. It is however further agreed that the pursuers realised a gross profit of £1,946,585.50 on the sale of shares in the defenders which the pursuers purchased between January and 3

February 1986, and which they sold after the withdrawal of their offer for the defenders' share capital. The pursuers accept that in asserting their claim for abortive underwriting costs, they would have to deduct from those costs the profit which they made from the sale of shares in the defenders. If the appropriate deduction was the gross profit which I have mentioned, the claim for underwriting costs would thus be brought down to a figure of £3,424,439.27. According to the pursuers, however, that would reflect too great a deduction. The deduction in respect of profit on the sale of shares should not be the gross figure, but should be a figure net of a tax liability which they claim they would otherwise have avoided, amounting to £559,152. If one adds back that figure, after making the gross deduction, the claim comes to £3,963,571.27. It is however agreed that the pursuers paid fees to a number of bodies, amounting to £157,500, for work done in relation to the offer, after 15 January but before the offer was withdrawn. The pursuers claim that these form part of their loss, and their total claim is accordingly £4,121,071.27. In addition to this principal sum the pursuers sought interest at the rate of 15 per cent per annum from the date of citation, 17 March 1986. It was however accepted that interest should run not upon the total claim, but upon that figure minus the tax element of £559,152, since the gross profit on shares had been obtained, but the tax had not yet been paid.

The pursuers' claim is essentially for abortive or wasted expenditure. But for the alleged misrepresentation, they would never have embarked upon the underwriting expenditure, or incurred fees in question. Having embarked on the expenditure, and incurred these fees on the faith of the contract, and the whole proceedings being in reliance on the misrepresentations, the pursuers were entitled (on one basis or the other) to recover what they had spent, the expenditure having proved wholly abortive as a result of the defenders' fraudulence or negligence in their representations, or their breach of the no-encouragement provision. The context in which the expenditure was incurred was one in which the defenders were to recommend the pursuers' offer. The quid pro quo for the expenditure was to be that recommendation. It was not given, and that was why the expenditure was rendered abortive. It would be wrong to think that the quid pro quo for the expenditure was shareholders' acceptance of the offer. That could never have been guaranteed, and neither party could have ensured that outcome. The purpose of the expenditure was less uncertain: the pursuers were spending money in order to get their hat in the ring with the defenders' recommendation. That was what they had lost through the defenders' breach of contract or misrepresentation. Against this line of argument the defenders argued that the expenditure would have been abortive in any event.

In relation to breach of contract, it was accepted that the basic rule was that the pursuers be put where they would have been if the contract had been performed.

Reference was made to *Houldsworth v Brand's Trs*.
A Normally there would be a claim for loss of profit, which was not sought here. Where such a claim was made, it would be for profit net of expenditure. It was competent to claim abortive expenditure, without a claim for profit, but it would be necessary to show not merely that the expense had been incurred, but that it would have been recovered if the breach of contract had not occurred. While proof might be difficult the onus lay upon the pursuer to show that the expenditure which had in fact proved abortive, would
B have been recovered but for the breach of contract. (Counsel referred to an indication in English authority that in the case of recovery of expenditure, the onus might shift to the defender. However, I do not think that English authority is of real assistance in a matter relating to damages of this kind, and in any event, after evidence, it does not seem to me that questions of onus are still of importance.)

Counsel for the defenders submitted that upon the evidence, the balance of probabilities was that the
C underwriting costs would have been irrecoverable, even if the actions founded upon as constituting breach of contract had never been taken. The probabilities were that even without these actions, Vantona would have made a bid, without the defenders' recommendation, probably initially at the same level as the pursuers' bid. Even at that level, it was improbable that the pursuers' bid would be preferred to Vantona's, but it was plain that if need be Vantona would have raised their bid, and improbable
D that the pursuers could have improved on their existing offer. Even if they could have done so, it was improbable that they could have succeeded in a contest with Vantona. In any event, if they had had to make a further and improved offer, the cost of underwriting their original offer would have been wasted and not recovered. The possibility of their succeeding with a later bid would effectively be unrelated to the original underwriting and the cost thereof. Overall, the fact was that Vantona wanted to
E take over the defenders, and indeed were determined to do so. While they had of course wanted to do so with the recommendation of the defenders' board, and to do so as cheaply as possible, the evidence showed that they could and would have done so even without initial recommendation, and at a price significantly above anything that the pursuers would have been able to put forward. Even if the probabilities were not positively as suggested on behalf of the defenders, it was submitted that the pursuers had failed to show
F any probability that the underwriting costs would have been recovered.

While I appreciate the difficulty of assessing the probable outcome of so uncertain a matter, I am satisfied that upon the evidence, Vantona's interest in taking over the defenders, and their determination to achieve that result, was such that if the defenders' board had maintained their refusal to talk, Vantona would have made an unrecommended bid. The precise course of events which would have followed upon such a bid is no doubt even more uncertain. I am

nonetheless satisfied that faced with a hostile bid of this kind, it is highly improbable that the pursuers'
G recommended offer, or indeed the defenders' board's recommendation of it, could have stood unaltered, far less have succeeded. The underwriting costs of that offer would in these circumstances have been abortive, even if an altered and improved offer, perhaps still holding a recommendation, could have been made by the pursuers, and perhaps accepted. But I am again satisfied that such an improvement, and in any event the holding of the recommendation, must be seen as something which was improbable, and in the end of
H the day, I am satisfied that Vantona having entered the contest were always the probable winners.

I would see some force in the argument advanced by counsel for the pursuers, to the effect that the pursuers were really putting out this money in order to get their hat in the ring with the recommendation, if the obligation to give the recommendation had been a simple one, with no risk of the recommendation being withdrawn through a change of circumstances, and no risk of rival bids which might necessitate an
I improvement in the pursuers' own offer. But quite apart from the uncertainties as to eventual acceptance of any offer, these were in my view real risks. That reinforces what I think would be true in any event, that this was not one of those situations where the wronged party is to be regarded as damnified at such an early or intermediate stage, rather than when a more tangible loss has actually, on the balance of probabilities, accrued. If a loss of profit were being claimed, I do not consider that one would value the
J hat in the ring: one would be looking at the later stage of probable gains flowing from acceptance. In my opinion, the expenditure on underwriting was something which the pursuers did at their own risk, which is perhaps partly why they wished that expenditure to be shared. The expenditure has proved abortive, and on my view of the probabilities, it would have been so in any event, even without the actions which are said to constitute breach of contract. In these circumstances, even if breach of contract were
K established, it does not appear to me that the costs of underwriting would constitute a loss attributable to that breach.

The other expenditure by way of fees may in theory include elements which might have made them recoverable as loss due to breach of contract. However, they are dealt with on a broad basis as expenditure on the contract and this element of the breach of contract claim must in my opinion fail upon
L the same basis as the claim for underwriting costs. In the circumstances, questions related to the deduction of the pursuers' profit on the sale of the defenders' shares, and in particular the question of tax liability, would not arise. The probability is that no tax liability would arise directly in respect of the profit made on the sale of these shares. There were sufficient losses available to exclude such a liability, but by using these losses to eliminate liability to tax in respect of these profits, the pursuers no longer had those losses available to set off against future planned gains. A

liability to tax would therefore emerge in respect of
A those gains, and this liability, according to the
pursuers, is one which they would not have sustained,
but for the defenders' breach of contract. The matter
is perhaps somewhat speculative, and is dependent on
the continuing availability of a scheme operating by
the pursuers for planning gains which could be set off
against losses. On behalf of the defenders, it was
submitted that in buying the defenders' shares, the
pursuers were precisely allowing for the possibility
that their offer would not succeed, and in that
B eventuality were plainly intending to use their
available losses to avoid tax on a resultant profit.
Nonetheless, it appears to me that the future planned
gain, and liability to tax in respect of it, are to be taken
as probabilities as matters stand. Overall, it appears
probable that that liability would not have emerged, if
the previously available losses had not been used to set
off against the profits on the sale of the defenders'
shares. However, upon the view which I have already
expressed as to what would probably have happened
C if the defenders had never talked to Vantona, it seems
probable that the pursuers would have finished up
selling the defenders' shares which they had bought,
and using their available losses to offset profits on that
sale. While dates and prices might have differed, it
thus seems probable that a liability to tax on the future
planned gain would have emerged in any event, the
losses having been used up on the sale of the
defenders' shares. It may be that upon a different view
from mine as to whether the underwriting costs
D constituted a loss, there would be a correspondingly
different view as to whether the tax liability on these
future gains was to be taken into account in computing
the deduction of profit on the share sales, but in my
view, that was a liability which was probably going to
emerge in any event.

The case founded upon misrepresentation raises
rather different issues. The basic principle may be the
same in relation to misrepresentation or breach of
E contract, that the pursuers would be entitled to a
pecuniary award which would restore them to the
position in which they would have been but for the
wrong. Nonetheless, there is a fundamental difference
between the two cases. In the breach of contract case,
the wrong is not said to have led to the expenditure,
but to have rendered abortive expenditure which
would have occurred in any event. In the misrepresentation case the misrepresentation is said to have led to
expenditure which was indeed abortive, but which but
F for the wrong would not have been incurred at all. In
that situation, the crucial issue is not whether the
expenditure would have been recovered apart from the
wrong. It is the quite different causal question, of
whether the incurring of the expenditure resulted
from the wrong. Questions of quantification, and in
particular the specific question as to whether the
profit from sale of shares should be deducted gross, or
net of the tax liability, are still in point. In relation to
the misrepresentation case, it seems to me that if the
expenditure is seen as a result of the misrepresentation, so too is the purchase of the defenders' shares,

and on that basis the deduction of profit on the sale of
shares should be of the profit net of the tax liability G
which would not otherwise have emerged. If the
alleged misrepresentation had caused the pursuers'
loss I would have awarded the whole loss claimed by
the pursuers. But in my opinion there was no misrepresentation. And if there was a misrepresentation
then as I have already indicated, I am not satisfied that
it caused the pursuers to proceed to the stage of
contract and the incurring of the items of expenditure
in question.

In all these circumstances, I assoilzie the defenders. H

---

*Counsel for Pursuers, Nimmo Smith, QC, Brailsford;
Solicitors, Dundas & Wilson, CS — Counsel for
Defenders, D R A Emslie, QC, Keen; Solicitors, Maclay
Murray & Spens.*

D P S

I

Collins v HM Advocate

HIGH COURT OF JUSTICIARY
THE LORD JUSTICE CLERK (ROSS),
LORDS MURRAY AND WEIR
11 JULY 1991   J

*Justiciary — Procedure — Trial — Charge to jury — Self
exonerating statements made by accused to police —
Direction that part of statement which was self
exonerating could not be relied upon as evidence —
Whether statements self exonerating in fact — Whether
misdirection — Whether miscarriage of justice.*

*Justiciary — Procedure — Trial — Charge to jury —
Notices of incrimination among co-accused — Whether
required to be read out or referred to in charge — Whether* K
misdirection to refer to one notice and not another.

*Justiciary — Evidence — Admissibility — Statements by
accused — Whether statement partly self exonerating —
Whether self exonerating part admissible.*

*Justiciary — Procedure — Trial — Jury having retired
requesting sight of productions — Statements by co-
accused — Whether judge entitled to refuse jury's request.*

Justiciary — Procedure — Trial — Counsel's address to L
*jury — Propriety of commenting on questions of law —
Propriety of commenting on co-accused's failure to give
evidence.*

An accused and four others were charged on
indictment with, inter alia, murder. At trial, evidence
was led of a statement made to the police by the
accused in which he admitted collecting the gun subsequently used in the murder. Parts of the statement
suggested that the accused had been forced to
participate in the alleged offence because he was

afraid. The trial judge directed the jury that anything
in the statement which was self exculpatory could not
be relied on by the defence. After the jury retired they
asked to see transcripts of interviews with the accused,
and some of his co-accused, which had been lodged as
productions by the Crown. The trial judge refused to
allow the jury access to the transcripts because of the
risk of the jury's accepting them as evidence against
the remaining co-accused. The accused was convicted
and appealed.

Held, (1) that the judge had misdirected the jury but
that the statements were not self exculpatory, coercion
not having been raised as a defence to the charge, and
that accordingly no miscarriage of justice had occurred
(pp 103H-L and 104H-I and J); and (2) that it was a
matter for the discretion of the trial judge as to which
productions the jury should see and that there was no
basis for concluding that he had exercised his
discretion wrongly (p 104A-C, H-I and J); and appeal
refused.

Opinion, that counsel should not use their address
to the jury as a vehicle for inviting directions in law
from the trial judge (pp 103C and 104H-I and K-L).

Opinion, per the Lord Justice Clerk (Ross), that
although there was no express statutory prohibition
against an accused person commenting upon the
failure of a co-accused to give evidence, such comment
should not be made as it was inconsistent with the
principle on which rested the prohibition against the
prosecutor making such comment (p 103C-E).

Opinion reserved, per Lords Murray and Weir,
on this point (p 104I-J and J-K).

Indictment

Thomas Collins was charged together with four co-
accused at the instance of the rt hon the Lord Fraser
of Carmyllie, Her Majesty's Advocate on an indictment which contained the following charge, inter alia:
"(6) you . . . did [on 8 October 1988], in an area of
woodland in the vicinity of Kilmarnock, Galston,
Moscow, Hurlford, Fenwick, Stewarton, Kilmaurs
and other areas all in Ayrshire, assault Paul Leslie
Thorne, formerly of 29 Declifford Road, Bristol,
repeatedly discharge a shotgun or similar firearm at
him and shoot him in the head whereby he was so
seriously injured that he died there and then and you
did murder him".

The accused pled not guilty and proceeded to trial
in the High Court at Glasgow before Lord
Allanbridge and a jury.

The accused was convicted and appealed to the
High Court by way of note of appeal.

Cases referred to

Hendry v HM Advocate, 1986 SLT 186; 1985 JC 105;
    1985 SCCR 274.
McShane v HM Advocate, 1989 SCCR 687.
Morrison v HM Advocate, 1991 SLT 57; 1990 JC 299;
    1990 SCCR 235.

Textbook referred to

Renton and Brown, *Criminal Procedure* (5th ed), paras
    10-33 and 10-53.

Appeal

The accused lodged grounds of appeal in the
following terms, inter alia:

(3) The trial judge misdirected the jury regarding
the position in fact and law and of the evidential value
of the tape recorded interview between the appellant
and the police and the transcript of said interview and
also the transcript of the appellant's judicial
examination.

(4) The trial judge at no time mentioned to the jury
that the appellant had lodged a notice of incrimination of the panels John Paul McFadyen and Ricardo
Blanco.

(5) The trial judge wrongly and unreasonably
refused to allow the jury to see transcripts of the
interviews between the police and the appellant and
the panel Thomas Currie during their deliberations. . . .

Accordingly, for the foregoing reasons, there was a
miscarriage of justice.

The appeal was argued before the High Court on 14
June 1991.

On 11 July 1991 the court *refused* the appeal.

THE LORD JUSTICE CLERK (ROSS).—The
appellant is Thomas Collins who went to trial in the
High Court at Glasgow along with several co-accused
on an indictment libelling a number of charges
including a charge of murder. The appellant was
found guilty of charge 4 and charge 6. Charge 4 was
a charge of contravening s 4 (3) (b) of the Misuse of
Drugs Act 1971, and charge 6 was a charge of murder.
The appellant has appealed against his conviction on
charge 6; he has not appealed against his conviction on
charge 4. In his note of appeal, six grounds of appeal
were put forward, but counsel for the appellant
informed the court that he was not seeking to support
the first ground of appeal. He did however advance
arguments to the court in respect of the remaining
grounds of appeal.

[His Lordship dealt with grounds of appeal with
which this report is not concerned, and continued:]

Counsel for the appellant then dealt with grounds 3
and 5 together. The complaint here is that the trial
judge misdirected the jury as to the evidential value of
the tape recorded interview between the appellant and
the police, and the transcript of that interview. It is
also maintained that the trial judge wrongly refused to
allow the jury to see the transcripts of the interviews
between the police and the appellant, and the police
and the co-accused Thomas Currie during the jury's
deliberations.

Counsel's principal point was that the trial judge
had erred in law in directing the jury that anything in
the statement which was self incriminating was
competent evidence against the accused but that
anything in the statement which was self exonerating
could not be used by the defence as evidence in the
case. Although the passage in the judge's charge is not
entirely clear, it does appear that the trial judge gave
the jury directions on this matter and in accordance

with *Hendry v HM Advocate*. The problem arises because that case was overruled by *Morrison v HM Advocate*.

The problem was compounded by the fact that in his address to the jury counsel for John Paul McFadyen repeatedly commented upon the fact that the appellant had failed to give evidence in the witness box, and that all he did was to rely upon what was contained in his statement to the police. He also in the course of his speech invited the trial judge to direct the jury that anything in a statement wich was self exonerating could not be used by the defence as evidence in the case, and that the only proper place for self exonerating evidence was in the witness box. At one stage in his speech counsel stated: "I suggest to you that it would be a principle of the law of Scotland that they cannot sit back and point to those statements as evidence of those facts unless they go into the witness box and give evidence".

I am bound to say that I am very surprised at some of the things which counsel for John Paul McFadyen said in his address to the jury. I do not approve of counsel using his address to the jury as a vehicle for inviting directions on law from the trial judge. Moreover I am concerned that counsel for one of the co-accused who was seeking to incriminate another co-accused, should comment adversely upon the fact that the latter had failed to give evidence. Although such comment is not expressly prohibited by the Act of 1975, it is, in my opinion, undesirable that counsel for one co-accused should do what the prosecutor is not permitted to do in this regard. In terms of s 141 (1) (b) the prosecutor is prohibited from commenting upon the failure of an accused to give evidence. In terms of s 143 (3) the failure of the spouse of an accused to give evidence shall not be commented on by the defence or the prosecutor. However there is no express prohibition in the statute against a co-accused commenting upon the failure of a co-accused to give evidence (Renton and Brown, *Criminal Procedure* (5th ed), para 10-53). Nonetheless in my opinion, although there is no express prohibition in the statute against such comment being made on behalf of one co-accused who is seeking to incriminate a co-accused who has failed to give evidence, such comment should not be made as it is inconsistent with the principle on which s 141 (1) (b) rests. Since the matter was not fully debated before us I reserve my opinion upon the question of whether it would make any difference if two co-accused were incriminating each other and the co-accused on whose behalf the comment had been made had himself entered the witness box and given evidence, so that a contrast was being made between his position and that of the other co-accused who had not given evidence. I would also observe that in the present appeal no specific ground of appeal was directed to the fact that these comments had been made.

Under reference to *Morrison v HM Advocate* counsel for the appellant maintained strongly that there had been a misdirection in law in relation to the use that could be made of the appellant's statement to the police, and that this had accordingly resulted in a miscarriage of justice. The advocate depute pointed out that in his charge the trial judge made it plain that

he was not going to give the jury one of the particular directions which counsel for John Paul McFadyen had requested him to give. As I read the portion of the charge however, the trial judge did direct the jury in accordance with *Hendry v HM Advocate* that the self exonerating parts of a statement could not be used by the defence; the direction which he declined to give was a direction to the effect that the only place where such self exonerating evidence could be given was in the witness box. Indeed the trial judge makes this plain in his report when he says: "I should explain that the further direction which counsel for McFadyen asked me to give and I quite intentionally did not give, was when he asked me to indicate that the place for explanations by an accused was in the witness box".

One can feel sympathy for the trial judge. What he was doing was following the case of *Hendry v HM Advocate* which was subsequently overruled. In view of the decision in *Morrison v HM Advocate*, it thus appears that he did indeed misdirect the jury when he indicated to them that the defence could not rely on those parts of the statement which were self exonerating. In the present case, however, I am satisfied that any misdirection which there was did not cause a miscarriage of justice. The fact of the matter is that the statement of the appellant Collins was not to any extent a self exonerating statement. When counsel for the appellant was invited to say what parts of the statement were self exonerating, he found it difficult to draw attention to any particular part of the statement. At the end of the day all he could do was to point to the fact that the appellant Collins had stated that the gun had been obtained for use against bouncers, and that there was nothing in the statement to show that he knew that the gun was in the car. The fact of the matter is, as the advocate depute maintained, that there were no parts of the statement which could properly be described as self exonerating. Having regard to the nature of charge 6, to say that the gun had originally been obtained for use against bouncers was in no way self exonerating. The statement as a whole shows that the appellant knew about the gun at all material times, and the statement also makes it clear that he knew what the gun was to be used for before the first shots were fired. There are passages in the statement suggesting that the appellant was acting because he was afraid of John Paul McFadyen. Accordingly if there had been a legitimate defence of coercion, then certain passages in the statement might be regarded as self exonerating, but in fact coercion was not raised by counsel for the appellant and was never mentioned in the charge. For the foregoing reasons I am therefore satisfied that even though there was a misdirection in this case, it did not result in any miscarriage of justice.

So far as ground of appeal 5 is concerned, counsel for the appellant maintained that the trial judge had declined to allow the jury to see the transcripts of the interviews during their deliberations because he had formed the view that the jury were only entitled to see those parts of the statement which contained self incriminating material. The advocate depute, however, drew attention to what the trial judge said about this matter in his report. In his report the trial judge points out that it is always a matter for the discretion of the trial judge as to what productions the jury should see. The jury here had asked to see all three transcripts of the police interviews of Mitchell, Currie and the appellant. Since Mitchell had given evidence his statement was superseded by his evidence, and the trial judge felt that the jury may have wanted to remind themselves of what evidence he had given against all the accused in his statement. He also had in mind that there was a danger that the jury might have used the statements of the appellant and his co-accused Currie as evidence against the co-accused Blanco and McFadyen, although they had been repeatedly told not to do so. In these circumstances the trial judge concluded that in the interests of all four accused it was necessary for him to refuse to allow the jury to see the transcripts. In my opinion the trial judge dealt with this matter in an entirely correct fashion and there is no reason to conclude that he exercised his discretion on any wrong basis. He exercised his discretion in the interests of justice, and it follows that there is no substance in ground of appeal 5.

There remains ground of appeal 4, which complains that the trial judge at no time mentioned to the jury that the appellant had lodged a notice of incrimination of John Paul McFadyen and Ricardo Blanco. It is clear from the judge's charge that he had referred in his charge to the fact that Ricardo Blanco and John Paul McFadyen had lodged notices of incrimination. In these circumstances counsel for the appellant maintained that he ought also to have referred in his charge to the notice of incrimination lodged by the appellant. As I understood it, this ground of appeal was put forward as a makeweight; it was accepted that it was not sufficient on its own, but it was suggested that it was of importance when taken along with ground of appeal 6 [an alleged misdirection of material fact by suggesting that the appellant had prior knowledge of the presence of a firearm among the accused, a ground rejected since there was other evidence that the appellant knew that a murder was to be carried out]. Since I have already rejected ground of appeal 6, this ground of appeal would not appear to have any real weight. In any event I am quite satisfied that this ground of appeal has no validity. A notice of intention to lead evidence incriminating a co-accused is different from a special defence and does not require to be read out or to be referred to in the judge's charge (*McShane v HM Advocate*). In Renton and Brown, *Criminal Procedure* (5th ed), para 10-33, it is stated: "It remains, however, the practice to read special defences to the jury. It is also the practice to read them any notice of intention to incriminate a co-accused which has been lodged".

The experience of the members of this court is that the current practice in relation to a notice of intention to incriminate a co-accused is not as described by the learned editor of Renton and Brown. In our experience it is not the practice for such notices of intention to incriminate to be read unless counsel specifically requests that that should be done. It is in any event clear that there is no requirement for such a notice to be read to the jury or referred to by the trial judge in his charge. In addition to that the trial judge

in his report states that it was quite obvious to the jury throughout the trial that on the one side counsel for the appellant and Currie were contending that Blanco and McFadyen were guilty of the murder, whereas on the other side McFadyen's counsel was maintaining that Currie, Mitchell and the appellant had carried out the murder. I agree with the trial judge that no one on the jury can have been in any doubt that these two groups were blaming one another, and that it did not matter that the trial judge at no time in his charge made specific reference to the notice of incrimination lodged by the appellant.

For the foregoing reasons I am of opinion that no grounds exist for concluding that there has been any miscarriage of justice so far as the conviction of the appellant on charge 6 is concerned, and I would accordingly move your Lordships to refuse his appeal against conviction.

LORD MURRAY.—I agree with the opinion of your Lordship in the chair and with the observations which you make about the role of counsel in addressing the jury. I would, however, go further than your Lordship in reserving my view about the consequences of there being no express prohibition in the 1975 Act against comment being made on behalf of one accused that a co-accused did not give evidence on his own behalf. I find myself unable at present to discern any ground upon which such comment can be regarded as inconsistent with a principle underlying the provisions of s 141 (1) (b) of the Act. I would have thought that the reasoning behind the prohibition against comment by the prosecutor is that the burden of proof is, and remains, on him throughout the trial, so that an accused's failure to testify is irrelevant. In contrast there is no burden of proof upon an accused, not even — as I understand it — upon an accused who formally incriminates a co-accused.

LORD WEIR.—I also agree with your Lordship in the chair that this appeal should be dismissed, although I wish to reserve my opinion on the propriety of making comment on behalf of one accused on the failure of a co-accused to give evidence. There may be a distinction to be drawn in relation to such comments between, on the one hand, a situation where the accused has not himself given evidence and where, on the other hand, he has given evidence. However, in my opinion, such matters are better reserved for decision in a future case, particularly as no argument was presented to us on the subject.

I would associate myself with the comments made by your Lordship expressing disapproval of the practice of counsel using his address to the jury as a means of inviting directions on law from the trial judge. There has been an increasing tendency in recent times for counsel, whether for the Crown or for the accused, to address the jury with some elaboration on the law which has to be applied to the evidence in the case. While reference to the law may sometimes be inevitable in order to give some context to the submissions on the evidence, in my view, the proper practice is to confine such reference to the bare minimum necessary for the purpose.

A   *Counsel for Appellant, Bell, QC, Small; Solicitors, Allan McDougall & Co, SSC — Counsel for Respondent, Drummond, QC, AD, Sinclair; Solicitor, J D Lowe, Crown Agent.*

S D D N

(NOTE)

B # Duncan v Ross Harper & Murphy

OUTER HOUSE

LORD KIRKWOOD

19 FEBRUARY 1992

Damages — Indemnity — Motor Insurers' Bureau — Injured person passenger in stolen car — Whether injured
C *person only learned of theft at a time when unreasonable for him to alight — Onus of proof.*

Damages — Amount — Solatium and loss of earning capacity — Pelvis — Serious pelvic fracture with associated internal injuries with permanent consequences, including sterility and inability to undertake any but light work.

A 19 year old man whose only employment each year had been limited to about six months' casual farm
D work was injured when a passenger in a car. His injuries included a severe pelvic injury with fractures and internal injuries. After the accident he required a colostomy and was initially impotent and permanently sterile. His permanent disabilities limited his ability to work. It was held that the car had been stolen and that the pursuer had been involved in the theft. He was accordingly held not entitled to recover damages from the driver.

Opinion, that, in any event, the pursuer would not
E have been able to enforce a decree against the Motor Insurers' Bureau since he accepted that he had been aware, before the accident, that the car had been stolen and was unable to prove that he only became so aware at a time when it was unreasonable to expect him to have alighted, it being for him to prove that any exception to the Motor Insurers' Bureau agreement would have applied, the Bureau having discharged the onus on them of proving knowledge by the pursuer of the theft.

F   **Opinion,** further, that damages of £27,000 for solatium and £8,000 for loss of earning capacity would have been appropriate.

———

William Duncan raised an action of damages against a firm of solicitors, Messrs Ross Harper & Murphy, in respect of the alleged professional negligence of a solicitor in having failed timeously to raise an action of damages for personal injuries. An agreement between the Motor Insurers' Bureau and the Minister

of Transport provides that decrees against uninsured drivers are, with certain exceptions, recoverable from G the Bureau. The pursuer, on 21 September 1985, while a passenger, along with an acquaintance James McLean, in a car driven by John Chalmers, was injured in an accident near Marlee, Perthshire, about 10.30 pm, caused by the fault of the driver. The pursuer was then aged 19. The car had been stolen from Parnie Street, Glasgow, between 4 and 5 pm by the driver who, accordingly, had not been insured.

After a proof the Lord Ordinary (Kirkwood) held that the solicitor had been negligent in failing to raise H the action timeously. He assoilzied the defenders on the ground that the pursuer would not have recovered any damages had the action been raised. In so deciding his Lordship said:

"Counsel for the defenders submitted that, even if the defenders had been in breach of contract in failing to raise an action on the pursuer's behalf, the pursuer had not suffered any loss as, on a balance of probabilities, an action against Chalmers would not have been successful. Counsel submitted that, on the basis I of the principle *ex turpi causa non oritur actio*, a driver did not owe a duty of care to his passengers when they had all participated in a continuing joint illegal act (*Winnik v Dick*, 1984 SLT 185, per Lord Hunter at p 189; *Lindsay v Poole*, 1984 SLT 269, and *Pitts v Hunt* [1991] 1 QB 24). In this case Chalmers did not owe a duty of care to the pursuer or McLean as all three of them had participated in the theft of the Ford Escort when it was parked in Parnie Street. Counsel accepted that the onus was on the defenders J to prove, on a balance of probabilities, that the pursuer had participated in the theft of the car (*Sloan v Triplett*, 1985 SLT 294) and he submitted that the defenders had discharged the onus which lay upon them. [His Lordship narrated the defenders' submissions on the evidence in relation to the theft of the car and continued:]

"Counsel for the defenders went on to submit that, even if the pursuer had not taken part in the theft of the Ford Escort, and he had succeeded in obtaining an K award of damages for personal injuries in an action against Chalmers, it was clear that such damages as would have been awarded could not have been recovered from Chalmers, who was not insured. Accordingly, the pursuer would have had to have attempted to recover the amount awarded from the Motor Insurers' Bureau. However, the Motor Insurers' Bureau would not have been liable to satisfy the decree as the pursuer had known that the vehicle had been stolen. Clause 2 of the Motor Insurers' Bureau Agreement of 22 November 1972 provides L that if a judgment is not satisfied by the debtor then the Motor Insurers' Bureau will, subject to the provisions of cll 4, 5 and 6 of the agreement, pay to the person in whose favour the judgment was given any sum payable or remaining payable thereunder. However, cl 6 (1) of the agreement provides inter alia as follows:

" 'Exemptions

" '6. (1) M.I.B. shall not incur any liability under Clause 2 of this Agreement in a case where — . . . (c)

A at the time of the accident the person suffering death or bodily injury in respect of which the claim is made was allowing himself to be carried in a vehicle and — (i) knew or had reason to believe that the vehicle had been taken without the consent of the owner or other lawful authority except in a case where — . . . (B) he had learned of the circumstances of the taking of the vehicle since the commencement of the journey and it would be unreasonable to expect him to have alighted from the vehicle'.

B "Counsel submitted that it would have been for the Motor Insurers' Bureau to raise the issue and the onus would have been on the Motor Insurers' Bureau to satisfy the court that at the time of the accident the pursuer had known or had had reason to believe that the vehicle had been taken without the consent of the owner. Once this initial onus had been discharged, it was for the pursuer to satisfy the court that he had learned of the circumstances of the taking of the vehicle since the commencement of the journey and it would be unreasonable to expect him to have alighted C from the vehicle. While the onus of proof was normally on a defender to bring himself within the terms of an exception, in this case the Motor Insurers' Bureau would be founding on an exception to an exception. In the circumstances of this case the issue as to whether the pursuer had known that the car was stolen would have been raised by the Motor Insurers' Bureau and the evidence had established that the pursuer had known, at the time of the accident, that the car had been stolen. The pursuer had given D evidence that when the Ford Escort was being chased by the police car, and the driver had accelerated, he had been aware that the car was stolen so that he knew at the time of the accident that he was in a stolen car. Counsel accepted that if the pursuer had only learned for the first time that the car was stolen when it was being chased by the police then, having regard to (a) the fact that the car had only two doors, (b) the fact that the pursuer was in the back seat, and (c) the speed at which the car was being driven, it would have been unreasonable for him to have alighted from the E vehicle. However, in the circumstances the court should not believe the evidence of the pursuer that he had not learned that the car was stolen until it was being chased by the police. Counsel accepted that there was no evidence that the pursuer had known Chalmers before he got into the car in Glasgow but he submitted that, as the pursuer and Chalmers had been together for about five hours prior to the accident, during which time they had visited a public house, the caravan and a caravan site, there must have been some F discussion of the circumstances in which Chalmers came to be driving the car. The pursuer had said that he had been sitting in the back seat of the car looking at the scenery but part of the journey had taken place in darkness. Counsel invited me to reject the evidence of the pursuer to the effect that he had only learned that the car was stolen when they were being chased by the police car and to hold that he had not discharged the onus placed on him by virtue of cl 6 (1) (c) (i) (B) of the agreement. In the circumstances the defenders had established that, even if an action had been raised against Chalmers and an award of damages

G had been made in the sheriff court, the pursuer could not have enforced the decree against the Motor Insurers' Bureau and accordingly he had not suffered any loss as a result of the defenders' breach of contract.

[His Lordship then narrated the submissions by counsel for the pursuer in relation to the participation of the pursuer in the theft and continued:]

"Counsel for the pursuer further submitted that if the defenders had raised an action of damages on behalf of the pursuer against Chalmers, the action H would have been successful and the pursuer would have been entitled to have the decree satisfied by the Motor Insurers' Bureau. Counsel referred to the Motor Insurers' Bureau Agreement and submitted that the burden of proof was on the defenders to establish that the exemption from liability set out in cl 6 (1) (c) (i) applied. Counsel referred to *Coul v Ayr County Council*, 1909 1 SLT 144, per Lord Dundas at p 145 (1909 SC 422); *Railway Executive v Brydon*, 1957 SLT 106, per Lord Patrick at p 110 (1957 SC 282); and *Nimmo v Alexander Cowan & Sons Ltd*, I 1967 SLT 277, per Lord Wilberforce at pp 283-284 (1967 SC (HL) 79). The onus of proving that the exception applied was upon the defenders as they were, in effect, seeking to adopt the position of the Motor Insurers' Bureau on the assumption that an action against Chalmers had been successful. The pursuer had given evidence that he had not known that the car was stolen until the police car chased them and the driver accelerated away and his evidence on this matter had been supported by both McLean and J Chalmers. The only averment made by the defenders, in seeking to attribute to the pursuer knowledge that the car was stolen, was to the effect that the car was of a type and age which Chalmers was unlikely to have owned. [His Lordship narrated further submissions and continued:]

"The first question for consideration is whether the defenders have proved that the pursuer was one of the men who took part in the theft of the Ford Escort from Parnie Street. Having considered the evidence and the K submissions made by counsel, I have reached the conclusion that the submissions made by counsel for the defenders are well founded. The car was stolen from Parnie Street by three young men, although the witnesses who saw the car being driven away could not identify any of the men involved, and I was satisfied that the theft took place between 4 pm and 5 pm. Chalmers admitted that he was one of the three men who took the car and the pursuer admitted that he and McLean were passengers in the car when it left L Glasgow, driven by Chalmers, shortly after 5.30 pm. He was still in the car when the accident took place near Meikleour at about 10.30 pm. Having regard to their demeanour in the witness box, their admitted criminal records and the content of their evidence, I did not regard the pursuer, Chalmers or McLean as being credible or reliable witnesses and I thought that the criticisms of their evidence which were made by counsel for the defenders were fully justified. . . . On the basis of the evidence which was led, including the replies made to the police by Chalmers and McLean,

A and the fact that the car was stolen by three young men and the pursuer was admittedly one of three young men in the car not long after it had been stolen, I am satisfied, on a balance of probabilities, that the pursuer took part in the theft of the Ford Escort. That being so, it was a matter of admission that, even if the defenders had raised an action on his behalf against Chalmers, the principle ex turpi causa non oritur actio would have applied and the action would have been bound to fail. If the action was bound to fail, then the pursuer has failed to establish that he has suffered any

B loss in consequence of the defenders' breach of contract. For these reasons I consider that the defenders are entitled to decree of absolvitor.

"If I had reached the conclusion that the defenders had failed to establish that the pursuer had taken part in the theft of the car from Parnie Street and I had accepted that he had got into the car when Chalmers was driving it some time after it had been stolen, and that an action at his instance against Chalmers would

C have been successful, the next question for consideration is whether the Motor Insurers' Bureau would have been bound to satisfy the decree. Clause 6 of the Motor Insurers' Bureau Agreement provides that the Board shall not incur any liability under cl 2 in a case where 'at the time of the accident the person suffering . . . bodily injury in respect of which the claim is made was allowing himself to be carried in a vehicle and . . . knew or had reason to believe that the vehicle had been taken without the consent of the owner'.

D However, this provision is subject to the exception set out in subpara (B), namely, where 'he had learned of the circumstances of the taking of the vehicle since the commencement of the journey and it would be unreasonable to expect him to have alighted from the vehicle'. In my opinion, counsel for the defenders was well founded when he submitted that the onus was on the defenders to establish that at the time of the accident the pursuer knew, or had reason to believe, that the vehicle had been stolen and that, once that

E had been established, it was for the pursuer to bring himself within the terms of the exception set out in subpara (B). In this case the pursuer admitted that at the time of the accident he knew that the car had been stolen and, having regard to the fact that the car was being chased by the police and the speed at which the car was being driven by Chalmers shortly before the accident, I have no difficulty in accepting that he knew at the time of the accident that the car was stolen. However, the pursuer said that he had not learned

F from Chalmers that it was a stolen car until they were being chased by the police. If that was the case, it would, at that stage, clearly have been unreasonable for him to have alighted from the vehicle. However, as I have already said, I did not regard the pursuer as a credible or reliable witness, nor did I accept the account of events given by Chalmers and McLean. For some five hours prior to the accident the pursuer had been in the company of Chalmers, a habitual car thief, who admitted that he had stolen the car, and the pursuer said that he had got into the car at the same time as McLean, who admitted to the police that he

had been involved in the theft and that he had allowed himself to be carried in a stolen car. In the circum- G stances I was not prepared to accept the pursuer's evidence that he did not learn that the car had been stolen until it was too late for him to get out. That being so, I would have reached the conclusion that the pursuer had failed to bring himself within the terms of the exception set out in subpara (B). In these circumstances the Motor Insurers' Bureau would not have been required to satisfy any decree which he had obtained and accordingly the pursuer has failed to establish that he has suffered any loss as a result of the H defenders' breach of contract."

In relation to damages his Lordship continued:

"Turning to the issue of damages, parties were agreed that, if the pursuer was entitled to damages for breach of contract, the measure of his loss was the amount of damages which he would have been awarded if an action had been raised in the sheriff court and the decree had been satisfied by the Motor Insurers' Bureau. Counsel for the pursuer accepted I that it would have been necessary for the pursuer to go to proof on his claim for damages and that, particularly in light of the evidence given by Mr Townsend, there would have been no prospect of an offer being made in settlement. In relation to the injuries sustained by the pursuer, and his residual disabilities, counsel for the pursuer referred to three medical reports, namely (1) report by Mr Peter J Paterson, consultant urologist, dated 20 April 1990, (2) report by Dr William F Durward, consultant J neurologist, dated 14 November 1990, and (3) report by Mr A W Kinninmonth, consultant orthopaedic surgeon, dated 14 May 1991. These reports are agreed reports and constitute the medical evidence for the pursuer. According to Mr Kinninmonth's report, the pursuer sustained a severe pelvic injury with diastasis of the pubic symphysis and a transverse ileal fracture in the immediate left supra-acetabular region with a probable intra-articular component. In addition, there was a longitudinal displaced fracture through the right K wing of the sacrum which damaged the sacral nerve roots on the right side. The pursuer also had internal abdominal injuries which necessitated a defunctioning colostomy and a suprapubic catheterisation. He had about two weeks of assisted ventilation. He underwent surgery to the pelvic fracture which amounted to a wire loop applied across the pubic rami to hold the diastasis together. He was then placed on skeletal traction for eight to nine weeks to allow the pelvic fracture to heal. In 1986 the defunctioning colostomy L was closed, although he had urological dysfunction for about a year, and he was then able to gain an erection. He still has discomfort over the pubic region and in the left groin and anterior aspect of the left ilium. His walking distance is limited to less than 200 yds and if he tries to walk any further than that his pain increases with distance. He still gets occasional dysuria and dribbling of urine from his urethra. There are areas of anaesthesia over the buttocks. He walks with a limp and there is restriction of movement of the left hip. The pursuer was initially impotent and although his

A impotence has been resolved he has been rendered sterile by reason of retrograde ejaculation. The altered sensation in his buttocks is likely to be permanent. There is a small but significant risk that he may get degenerative change in his left hip as time progresses. He remains tender across the area of the pubic symphysis diastasis and it is possible that the broken wire loop which is still present may be causing some irritation of the local tissues. Mr Paterson confirmed the diagnosis of retrograde ejaculation and he expressed the opinion that the pursuer's sexual

B dysfunction is related to the accident and it is unlikely that he will be able to offer the pursuer any effective treatment. Dr Durward performed a lumbar radiculography and he stated that the cause of the pursuer's sexual difficulties was not to be found in the lower lumbar spine but was related to structural damage affecting the pelvic nerves. He does not know of any further therapeutic steps which can be offered to improve sexual function and he considers it likely that retrograde ejaculation will be a permanent problem.

C Abnormal sensation in the left leg and groin is perhaps more of an irritant than a handicap but it is also likely to be permanent.

"The pursuer gave evidence that he cannot walk very far and that he has pain if he sits or stands for any length of time. He cannot do any heavy lifting and he has difficulty bending. He cannot now play football. When walking, he does not now require the aid of a stick. Although he is capable of sexual intercourse he has been advised that he is now sterile.

D
"Counsel for the pursuer submitted that the injuries which the pursuer sustained were of considerable severity. No question of contributory negligence arose in this case, so that the pursuer would be entitled to recover from the defenders a sum representing the full amount of the loss and damage which he has sustained as a result of the accident. In relation to solatium, counsel referred to *Keith v Fraser*, 1973 SLT (Notes)

E 42, *Davies v Scottish Stamping and Engineering Co Ltd* (Case Note 16/09 in McEwan and Paton on *Damages in Scotland*, p 506) and *Deery v Johnson* and *Hodgson v Harrison* (Cases F5/017 and 019 in Kemp & Kemp on *Quantum of Damages*, Vol 2), and he submitted that an appropriate award of solatium would be £30,000. So far as loss of earning capacity was concerned, the pursuer had given evidence relating to his continuing disabilities and it is clear that he will never be able to return to the casual farming work on which he had been engaged before the accident. The pursuer said

F that he had left school at the age of 16 with no formal qualifications and that he had been engaged on casual farming work for about six months each year and was unemployed for the other six months. He had not worked since the accident. He had looked for light work, such as driving, but had not been successful. He is now 25 years of age and has most of his working life ahead of him. As there was no evidence as to how much he was earning before the accident, the court should adopt a broad approach. In the circumstances an award of £10,000 should be made in respect of the pursuer's loss of earning capacity.

G "Counsel for the defenders referred to the terms of the agreed medical reports and he pointed out that Dr Durward had observed that as a consequence of retrograde ejaculation the pursuer may be infertile so that infertility was not certain. In relation to the pursuer's claim for solatium, counsel referred to *Hunter v Glasgow Corporation*, 1971 SC 220, *Kelly v Smith*, 1974 SLT (Notes) 70 and *Wilson v National Coal Board*, 1978 SLT (Notes) 36, and he submitted that an award in name of solatium should not exceed £25,000. So far as the pursuer's claim in respect of loss of earning capacity was concerned, counsel were

H agreed that, as there was no evidence as to how much the pursuer had been earning from casual farm work, the court should adopt a broad approach. However, the pursuer had stated that he had only worked about six months a year as a farm labourer. Further, Dr Durward had expressed the opinion that the pursuer may well be fit for light work if he can find it in the current economic climate in the area where he lives. He is able to drive and it is possible that he could obtain employment as a driver. In the circumstances,

I and having regard to the fact that the pursuer has never been in full time employment, an appropriate award in the name of loss of earning capacity would be £7,000.

"There is no doubt that as a result of the accident the pursuer sustained serious injuries. Details of these injuries and their sequelae are set out in the agreed medical reports. Had I been awarding damages I would, having regard to the evidence given by the

J pursuer and the terms of the medical reports, have assessed solatium at the sum of £27,000. So far as the pursuer's claim for loss of earning capacity is concerned, it appears that prior to the accident he had been doing casual farming work for about six months each year but there was no evidence as to how much he had earned. He has apparently tried to obtain light work but so far he has not been successful. In the circumstances, and having regard to his age, I would have awarded £8,000 in respect of loss of earning

K capacity so that the total award of damages would have been £35,000 plus interest. However, as I have found in favour of the defenders on the merits, I shall pronounce decree of absolvitor."

Counsel for Pursuer, Ivey; Solicitors, Lindsays, WS (for Peacock Johnston, Glasgow) — Counsel for Defenders, I W F Ferguson; Solicitors, Dundas & Wilson, CS.

C H L

[A note on quantum in the related case, *McLean v Ross Harper & Murphy*, is published at 1992 SLT 1007.]

Perfect Swivel Ltd v City of Dundee District Licensing Board (No 1)

EXTRA DIVISION

LORDS ALLANBRIDGE, MURRAY AND BRAND

4 MARCH 1992

Licensing — Licence — Suspension of licence — Appeal — Procedure — Failure to serve writ on chief constable timeously — Whether writ required to be served — Whether sheriff entitled to exercise dispensing power — Sheriff Courts (Scotland) Act 1907 (7 Edw VII, c 51), s 50 and Sched, rule 1, as amended — Act of Sederunt (Appeals under the Licensing (Scotland) Act 1976) 1977 (SI 1977/1622), para 3, as amended — Act of Sederunt (Ordinary Cause Rules, Sheriff Court) 1983 (SI 1983/747), para 5.

Paragraph 3 (b) of the Act of Sederunt (Appeals under the Licensing (Scotland) Act 1976) 1977 (as amended) provides that where an applicant under the 1976 Act appeals to the sheriff against a decision of a licensing board, he must serve a copy of the initial writ on all parties who appeared at the hearing of the board "at the same time as" the lodging of the writ "or as soon as may be thereafter". Paragraph 2 provides that appeals under s 39 of the 1976 Act are to be disposed of as summary applications as defined by the Sheriff Courts (Scotland) Act 1907. Paragraph 5 of the Act of Sederunt (Ordinary Cause Rules, Sheriff Court) 1983 provides that rule 1 (dispensing power of sheriff) applies to summary applications insofar as not inconsistent with s 50 of the 1907 Act. Section 50 provides inter alia that nothing in the Act shall affect any right of appeal provided by any Act of Parliament under which a summary application is brought.

A licence was suspended as a result of a complaint to the licensing board by a chief constable. The licence holders appealed, but failed to effect service on the chief constable timeously. The sheriff held that para 3 was mandatory and dismissed the appeal. The licence holders appealed to the Court of Session, arguing that the sheriff's dispensing power in terms of rule 1 applied to appeals under s 39 of the 1976 Act such as the present one by virtue of s 39 of the 1976 Act and para 5 of the 1983 Act of Sederunt. The licence holders also argued that, in any event, they were not obliged to effect service on the chief constable, because the requirement of service on "all other parties who appeared at the hearing" in para 3 (b) applied only to "the applicant at the hearing", and they had not been the applicants at the hearing.

Held, (1) that the effect of s 50 of the 1907 Act was that the dispensing power in rule 1 did not affect the statutory right of appeal provided by the 1976 Act nor the statutory rules relative thereto, of which para 3 was mandatory (*Binnie v City of Glasgow District Licensing Board*, 1979 SLT 286 and *Russell v Ross*, 1980 SLT 10, *followed*) (pp 110L-111A); (2) that in an appeal against suspension, the chief constable could properly be described as "the applicant" and a licence holder who objected to suspension as "the objector", in which case when the latter appealed he was bound by para 3 (c) to serve the writ on "the applicant", ie, the chief constable (p 111G-I); and (3) that even if that interpretation was wrong, if the expression "the applicant" comprehended a licence holder who was applying not to have his licence suspended but to retain it, then the appellants were bound to effect service on the chief constable as "an objector" in terms of para 3 (b) (p 111I-J); and appeal *refused*.

Appeal from the sheriff court

Perfect Swivel Ltd appealed against an interlocutor of the sheriff dismissing as incompetent an appeal by them under s 39 of the Licensing (Scotland) Act 1976 against a decision by the City of Dundee District Licensing Board that they were no longer "a fit and proper person" to hold a licence in terms of s 31 (2) (a) of the 1976 Act and suspending their licence for a period of one year.

Statutory provisions

The Act of Sederunt (Appeals under the Licensing (Scotland) Act 1976) 1977, as amended, provides:

"2. Any appeal to the sheriff under section 39 of the 1976 Act against a decision of a licensing board shall be made by way of initial writ under the Sheriff Courts (Scotland) Acts 1907 and 1913 and such appeals shall be disposed of as a summary application as defined in the said Acts.

"3. At the same time as the initial writ is lodged with the sheriff clerk or as soon as may be thereafter, the appellant shall serve a copy of the initial writ—(a) on the clerk of the licensing board; and (b) if he was the applicant at the hearing before the licensing board, on all other parties who appeared (whether personally or by means of a representative) at the hearing; and (c) if he was an objector at that hearing, on the applicant."

The Act of Sederunt (Ordinary Cause Rules, Sheriff Court) 1983 provides:

"5. Rules 1, 3, 4, 5 (2), 10 to 12 and 14 to 19 of the Ordinary Cause Rules shall apply to a summary application in so far as they are not inconsistent with section 50 of the Act of 1907."

The Sheriff Courts (Scotland) Act 1907 provides:

"50. In summary applications (where a hearing is necessary) the sheriff shall appoint the application to be heard at a diet to be fixed by him, and at that or any subsequent diet (without record of evidence unless the sheriff shall order a record) shall summarily dispose of the matter and give his judgment in writing: Provided that wherever in any Act of Parliament an application is directed to be heard, tried and determined summarily or in the manner provided by section 52 of the Sheriff Courts (Scotland) Act 1876,

A such direction shall be read and construed as if it referred to this section of this Act: Provided also that nothing contained in this Act shall affect any right of appeal provided by any Act of Parliament under which a summary application is brought."

"[Sched] 1. The sheriff may in his discretion relieve any party from the consequences of any failure to comply with the provisions of these Rules which is shown to be due to mistake, oversight or other cause, not being wilful non-observance of the same, on such terms and conditions as shall seem just."

B

Cases referred to

Binnie v City of Glasgow District Licensing Board, 1979 SLT 286.
Padda v Strathkelvin District Licensing Board, 1988 SCLR 349.
Russell v Ross, 1980 SLT 10.
Sangha v Bute and Cowal Divisional Licensing Board, 1990 SCLR 409.

C **Textbook referred to**

Macphail, *Sheriff Court Practice*, p 877n.

Appeal

The appeal was heard before an Extra Division on 6 February 1992.

On 4 March 1992 the court *refused* the appeal.

The following opinion of the court was delivered by
D Lord Allanbridge:

OPINION OF THE COURT.—On 19 April 1990 the respondents held a hearing of the licensing board to consider whether or not to suspend the appellants' licence following on a complaint to them by the chief constable. Following on that hearing the respondents ordered, in terms of s 31 of the Licensing (Scotland) Act 1976, that the appellants were no longer "a fit and proper person" to hold such a licence in view of certain criminal convictions relating to two of their directors and suspended the appellants' licence for a period of one year. In terms of s 31 (8) of the 1976 Act the appellants took an appeal to the sheriff against that order.

The appeals procedure for such an appeal is laid down in the Act of Sederunt (Appeals under the Licensing (Scotland) Act 1976) 1977 (SI 1977/1622), as amended by the Act of Sederunt (Appeals under the Licensing (Scotland) Act 1976) (Amendment) 1979 (SI
F 1979/1520). Paragraphs 2 and 3 of the now amended Act of Sederunt provide as follows: [his Lordship quoted the terms of paras 2 and 3 and continued:]

In this case the initial writ was lodged with the sheriff clerk on 1 May 1990 but a copy was not served upon the chief constable until 20 June 1990. In this situation counsel for the appellants accepted that the terms of para 3 of the Act of Sederunt had not been complied with by the appellants as a copy of the initial writ had not been served on the chief constable "at the same time as the initial writ is lodged with the sheriff

clerk or as soon as may be thereafter", as required in said para 3. The sheriff held that the terms of para 3 G were mandatory and as they had not been complied with, he upheld the respondents' plea to the competency and dismissed the appeal.

It was argued before the sheriff, and also before this court, that when the Act of Sederunt (Ordinary Cause Rules, Sheriff Court) 1983 (SI 1983/747) came into operation on 1 September 1983 it had the effect of extending the dispensing power of the sheriff in terms of rule 1 of the new and substituted sheriff court rules, to inter alia para 3 of the said Act of Sederunt of 1977, H as now amended. According to counsel for the appellants, the foundation for this submission was to be found in para 5 of the 1983 Act of Sederunt which reads as follows: [his Lordship quoted the terms of para 5 and continued:]

Counsel argued that as the present appeal fell to be disposed of as a summary application then said para 5 applied to all summary applications including the present appeal, in accordance with the maxim I expressio unius est exclusio alterius (see Trayner's *Latin Maxims and Phrases* (4th ed), p 210), which is to the effect that the special mention of one thing operates as the exclusion of things differing from it. The effect of para 5 therefore was, according to the appellants' counsel, that whereas prior to the 1983 Act of Sederunt, the provisions of said s 3 of the 1977 Act of Sederunt may have been mandatory, that was no longer the case because the sheriff's dispensing power in rule 1 of the sheriff court rules applied to the whole J of the procedure regarding summary applications. In this situation the provisions of para 3 were no longer mandatory and he invited us to allow the appeal and remit back to the sheriff to allow him to exercise his discretion in terms of rule 1 in relation to the failure of the appellants to serve a copy of the initial writ "timeously" and to reach a decision on that matter.

This was a bold and somewhat startling submission on the part of the appellants' counsel, faced as he was by the decisions in the two cases of *Binnie v City of* K *Glasgow District Licensing Board* and *Russell v Ross*, where both the First and Second Divisions respectively had held that the terms of para 3 were mandatory. He also referred to two other cases, namely, *Padda v Strathkelvin District Licensing Board and Sangha v Bute and Cowal Divisional Licensing Board*, but neither of these cases afforded any clear support to his main argument. We found it difficult to understand the relevance of counsel's quotation of Latin maxims when a close examination is made of L para 5. Paragraph 5 refers to s 50 of the 1907 Act which applies to summary applications in the sheriff court and is in the following terms: [his Lordship quoted the terms of s 50 and continued:]

The final proviso at the end of s 50 indicates that nothing contained in the Act shall affect any right of appeal provided by any Act of Parliament under which a summary application is brought. The appeal in the present case was brought in terms of s 31 (8) of the 1976 Act. Section 39 (9) of that Act authorised the

Court of Session to make rules for the conduct of appeals to the sheriff by Act of Sederunt and the 1977 Act of Sederunt, as amended, made such rules. In this situation we consider that the sheriff's dispensing power contained in rule 1 of the First Schedule to the 1907 Act does not and cannot "affect" the statutory right of appeal, and the statutory rules relating to it, which are provided in terms of the 1976 Act.

In these circumstances we agree with the sheriff in this case where he concludes that his discretion in terms of rule 1 only applied to breaches of the sheriff court rules and not to statutory rules directly controlling particular appeals. Rule 1 commences by stating: "The sheriff may in his discretion relieve any party from the consequences of any failure to comply with the provisions of *these rules*". "These rules" are the sheriff court rules which follow and cannot include statutory rules made in an Act of Sederunt relating to procedures for appeals under another Act of Parliament. It would indeed be surprising if Parliament, having given power to the Court of Session to make statutory rules, also intended to give the sheriff a power of discretion to determine whether non-compliance with such statutory rules should be excused unless such a power of discretion was expressly given in the legislation. In these circumstances we reject the main argument of counsel for the appellants in this case.

There was also a subsidiary argument put forward by counsel for the appellants. This arose because counsel for the respondents very properly drew our attention to footnote 58, at p 877 of Macphail's *Sheriff Court Practice*, where the author suggests there is a lacuna in para 3 of the 1977 Act of Sederunt as amended, because no provision is made therein for intimation to the parties who appeared before a licensing board when the appeal relates to the suspension of a licence. Counsel for the appellants argued that as regards an appeal against a suspension there was such a lacuna because the appellant was not "the applicant at the hearing" referred to in para 3 (b), and he could not be the objector in terms of para 3 (c). In these circumstances the only person on whom the appellant required to serve a copy of the initial writ was the clerk of the licensing board in terms of para 3 (a).

It would be surprising if this substituted and new para 3 did not apply to appeals against suspension of a licence where normally the appellant would be the licence holder. There is no dispute that the original para 3 did apply to such appeals but counsel for the appellant suggested that the new section was drafted so as to exclude its application to appeals relating to the suspension of a licence. We consider that at least one of the reasons why para 3 was re-drafted in the 1979 Act of Sederunt was probably to avoid the problem created by *Russell's* case which held that an objector required to effect service on all other objectors however many these might be. The new para 3 only required such an objector to serve on the applicant for the licence as well as the clerk of the

licensing board. We are quite satisfied that the new para 3 can still be read as applying to appeals against suspension. In such an appeal where suspension has been in issue the appellant will be the licence holder. In terms of s 31 (2) (a) of the 1976 Act a licence holder may have his licence suspended if he is no longer a fit and proper person to be the holder of a licence. He has then ceased to be an applicant for a licence but is no longer a fit and proper person to be a licence holder. Suspension is initiated by a complaint in terms of s 31 (1). In this case the chief constable made such a complaint and the licensing board decided to hold a hearing on the issue in terms of s 31 (4). "The applicant" for that hearing to consider a suspension can properly be described as the chief constable. He is applying for a suspension of the licence. The licence holder objected to such a suspension being granted and can properly be described as "the objector" at that hearing. In that event when the appellant appealed as the objector he was bound in terms of subpara (c) of para 3 to serve a copy of the initial writ on "the applicant" who was the chief constable. The same person must be "the applicant" throughout the reading of para 3, whomsoever that person may be. If that interpretation were to be wrong and "the applicant" within the meaning of the section was to be read as meaning the appellant in this case, namely, the licence holder, because he was applying not to have the licence suspended but to retain it, and the chief constable was "the objector", then he was bound in terms of subpara (b) to serve a copy of the initial writ on the chief constable as one of the persons who appeared at the hearing. The paragraph makes it clear that there must be an "applicant at the hearing" and that can be interpreted as either the chief constable, which is our preferred interpretation in the circumstances of this case, or the licence holder. On either interpretation, because "the applicant" must remain the same person throughout the reading of the paragraph, the paragraph does provide for service on the chief constable in the circumstances of this appeal. There is thus no lacuna in the paragraph.

On the whole matter we have no doubt that the provisions regarding service contained in para 3 of the 1977 Act of Sederunt, as now amended, are mandatory. In *Binnie's* case, supra, the First Division clearly held in 1978 that the terms of the original para 3 were mandatory and furthermore that at that time no statutory power had been given to the sheriff to waive compliance with statutory and mandatory requirements. For the reasons given earlier in this opinion we are satisfied that the 1983 Act of Sederunt, which substituted new sheriff court rules, did not alter the law on this matter or give the sheriff the necessary statutory power of discretion. In these circumstances as such mandatory provisions were breached in the present appeal we consider the sheriff was correct when he dismissed the appeal as incompetent.

We therefore refuse the appeal and uphold the sheriff's interlocutor of 14 August 1990.

A *Counsel for Pursuers and Appellants, Bovey; Solicitors, Bennett & Robertson, WS — Counsel for Defenders and Respondents, Agnew of Lochnaw; Solicitors, Haig-Scott & Co, WS.*

M G J U

B (NOTE)

Perfect Swivel Ltd v City of Dundee District Licensing Board (No 2)

OUTER HOUSE

LORD ABERNETHY

26 MARCH 1992

C

Administrative law — Judicial review — Competency — Whether barred by mora, taciturnity and acquiescence — Refusal of licensing application — Immediate steps to challenge decision not taken but further applications made before judicial review of original decision sought.

Holders of an hotel licence applied for regular extension of permitted hours. The application was heard and refused on 20 June 1991. That refusal was
D made the subject of a petition for judicial review, lodged on 8 January 1992. The applicants had previously applied and been refused a regular extension of hours in October 1990. The earlier refusal had been subjected to judicial review and reduced of consent; the application had been remitted to the licensing board and was again refused in July 1991. A further petition for judicial review against the July decision had been presented but had not proceeded with since any grant on the original application would have expired in October 1991. A further application for regular
E extension was made in October 1991 and again refused. The licensing board argued that the petition for judicial review of the 20 June 1991 refusal was barred by mora, taciturnity and acquiescence.

Opinion, that there was no mora established.

R v Dairy Produce Quota Tribunal for England and Wales, ex p Caswell [1990] 2 AC 738, *considered.*

Opinion reserved, on whether acquiescence by
F applicants without any resultant alteration of the licensing board's position was sufficient to bar judicial review.

Hanlon v Traffic Commissioner, 1988 SLT 802, *distinguished.*

Perfect Swivel Ltd petitioned, along with the person responsible for the day to day running of an hotel operated by the company, for judicial review of a decision of the City of Dundee District Licensing Board. The decision, given on 20 June 1991, was a
G refusal of an application for regular extension of permitted hours. The petitioners, both before and after that application, had made similar applications the history of which was detailed by the Lord Ordinary (Abernethy) thus:

"The factual position is somewhat complicated and it is appropriate that I set it out in a little detail. The petitioners made a similar application for the regular extension of permitted hours in October 1990. That application was refused. After the petitioners had
H petitioned by way of judicial review for reduction of that decision it was agreed that the decision of refusal be reduced and the application remitted to the licensing board for reconsideration. The reconsideration took place at a hearing in July 1991. The licensing board again refused the application. A petition for judicial review of that decision was presented but a date for the first hearing could not be arranged until shortly before any grant of the application would have expired, in October 1991. Accordingly the petition
I was not proceeded with. Another application in similar terms was made in October 1991. However, by reason of the provisions of s 64 (9) of the 1976 Act, it was dropped. This subsection was introduced by s 74 of and Sched 8, para 12 to the Law Reform (Miscellaneous Provisions) (Scotland) Act 1990. It was thought to be in force and it prohibited an application within one year of the refusal of a previous application. In fact there is doubt as to whether the provision came into force on 1 January 1991 or 1 January 1992
J and I was informed that a decision on the point is expected shortly from the Inner House. From the answers it appears that there has been yet a further application in similar terms, which was heard by the respondents on 16 January 1992 and again refused and I understood from the petitioners' counsel that this was in fact the case. I assume this application was entertained on the basis that s 64 (9) did not come into force until 1 January 1992."

The petition for judicial review was based on the
K failure by the board to explain their decision that there was no need for a regular extension in the locality. His Lordship held that the application for judicial review failed on the ground that, although it had been for the applicants to demonstrate the need for a regular extension, they had not attempted to do so. His Lordship accordingly dismissed the petition. In relation to a submission by the board that the petition should be dismissed for mora, taciturnity and acquiescence his Lordship said:
L

"That is sufficient for the disposal of this petition but I should mention that a further argument was advanced by counsel for the respondents, which was directed at the competency of the petition. It was explained that the particular incompetency was that the petitioners were barred by mora, taciturnity and acquiescence from presenting the petition. The respondents' first and second pleas in law were therefore to be taken together. Counsel for the respondents drew attention to the history of the various applications between October 1990 and January 1992 and the way in which they had been dealt with. He contended that by making a new application for regular extension of permitted hours in October 1991 the respondents had given a clear indication that they were abandoning any attack on the June 1991 decision and were acquiescing in it. Furthermore, when the October 1991 application was withdrawn, there was no indication at all that the June 1991 decision was to be disputed. Then a further application was lodged for the January 1992 board meeting. This application was lodged in December 1991 and although the present judicial review was lodged in the Court of Session on 8 January 1992, the application lodged in December 1991 was heard by the respondents on 16 January 1992. Although it could not be said that the board had acted in such a way as to alter their position as a result of the petitioners' actings, mere acquiescence was enough. Counsel referred me to Bell's *Principles* (10th ed), para 946 and *Trades House of Glasgow v Heritors of Govan Parish* (1887) 14 R 910, in support of this proposition. Furthermore, although there was no time limit in the Rules of Court regarding judicial review, the nature of judicial review required that in principle promptness in presenting petitions was desirable and that judicial review should not be used in such a way as would be detrimental to good administration. Reference was made to the two rules on these matters which are part of the judicial review rules in England and to the comments of Lord Goff of Chieveley in *R v Dairy Produce Quota Tribunal for England and Wales, ex p Caswell* [1990] 2 AC 738 at pp 748-750. It was accepted that what was prompt and what was detrimental to good administration was a question of fact and degree but in the present case both matters should be decided in the respondents' favour.

"In my opinion it is clear that acquiescence is a concept which can be properly considered in the present context. That was accepted in the case of *Hanlon v Traffic Commissioner*, 1988 SLT 802. However, in that case the petitioners' acquiescence in the decision which had been made had led to a material change in circumstances and for that reason they were barred from seeking judicial review. The circumstances of the present case are in my opinion quite different and I would wish to reserve my opinion as to whether mere acquiescence without any alteration on the part of the respondents of their position would be sufficient. As for the principles behind the rules governing judicial review in England, they are in my opinion relevant considerations for a court in Scotland. The remedy is an equitable one and the court has a discretion in the matter (*Hanlon*, at p 805L). However, in the present case I am not satisfied that the present petition comes so late that that in itself would justify dismissal. Nor am I satisfied in the present circumstances that reconsideration now of the June 1991 decision would be so detrimental to good administration as in itself to justify dismissal of the petition. The reconsideration of the October 1990 hearing took place without apparent difficulty some nine months later and after the June 1991 decision had been given on a subsequent application."

Counsel for Petitioners, R W J Anderson; Solicitors, Drummond Miller, WS — Counsel for Respondents, Agnew of Lochnaw; Solicitors, Haig-Scott & Co, WS.

C H

Hughes v Normand

HIGH COURT OF JUSTICIARY
THE LORD JUSTICE CLERK (ROSS),
LORDS SUTHERLAND AND WYLIE
22 SEPTEMBER 1992

Justiciary — Procedure — Warrant to take blood sample — Accused charged with assaulting two persons causing each to bleed — Accused's shirt apparently bloodstained — Crown seeking warrant to take blood sample from accused for simultaneous analysis of accused's blood and shirt stains — Not known whether stains on shirt could be victims' blood — Whether special circumstances — Whether warrant premature.

An accused person was charged on petition, along with another person, with assaulting two men to their severe injury. Both victims suffered lacerations which bled. When the accused was arrested the police recovered an apparently bloodstained shirt from him. Thereafter the Crown applied to the sheriff for a warrant to take a sample of blood from the accused so that it could be analysed along with the victims' blood samples and the stains on the accused's shirt. The victims' blood had not by then been analysed and it was not known whether the stains on the accused's shirt were in fact blood. The sheriff granted the warrant and the accused appealed by bill of suspension.

Held, that where the Crown were unable to say that the shirt did contain bloodstaining or that such bloodstaining on the shirt could have come from either of the injured individuals, the Crown's application was premature as no special circumstances had been made out (p 114G-J); and bill *passed* and warrant *suspended.*

Morris v MacNeill, 1991 SLT 607, *applied.*

Bill of suspension

David Hughes brought a bill of suspension against A C Normand, procurator fiscal, Glasgow, praying the High Court to suspend a warrant granted by Sheriff A B Wilkinson at Glasgow to take a sample of blood from the complainer. The facts of the case are set forth in the opinion of the court.

Case referred to

Morris v MacNeill, 1991 SLT 607; 1991 SCCR 722.

The bill was argued before the High Court on 22 September 1992.

A Eo die the court *passed* the bill and *suspended* the warrant.

The following opinion of the court was delivered by the Lord Justice Clerk (Ross):

OPINION OF THE COURT.—This is a bill of suspension at the instance of David Hughes against the procurator fiscal, Glasgow.

B In the bill it is explained that the complainer is applying for suspension of a warrant granted by the sheriff at Glasgow on 3 August 1992. That warrant ordered the complainer to give a blood sample and in the statement of facts for the complainer it is maintained that the warrant which was granted lacked specification and was premature.

The warrant has not been set out, but the terms of the petition seeking the warrant have been set out and it appears that on 28 July 1992 the complainer appeared on petition charging him, while acting along with another named individual, with assaulting two persons, Desmond Friel and Mark Whitelaw, to their severe injury. It is also stated in that petition that as a consequence of the incident giving rise to the charges, Desmond Friel suffered three stab wounds which bled and that Mark Whitelaw suffered six lacerations which bled. It is also averred that on 27 July 1992 when the complainer was arrested, the arresting police officers recovered an apparently blood stained shirt. It is maintained that in these circumstances a blood sample from the complainer should be D ordered. As we say the sheriff granted the warrant but we have no report from him explaining the circumstances under which he did so.

In inviting us to pass the bill counsel for the complainer has maintained that the petition which sought the warrant lacked specification because it did not set out that anything was to be gained by taking a blood sample from the complainer, and he also maintained that the petition was premature in that it was not said that the shirt did bear bloodstains, nor E was it said that any bloodstains on the shirt were of blood which could have come from either Desmond Friel or Mark Whitelaw. Counsel for the complainer drew attention to the case of *Morris v MacNeill*, and stressed that it was only where the circumstances were special and the balance between the public interest and the interests of the complainer favoured granting such a warrant that a warrant of this kind could be granted.

F In opposing the passing of the bill the Solicitor General accepted the test laid down in *Morris v MacNeill*. He maintained that there were special circumstances present in this case. The inquiry related to an alleged assault to severe injury in which two persons were said to have been injured and to have lost blood. The petition also disclosed that a shirt had been discovered in the possession of the complainer and in these circumstances the learned Solicitor General maintained that it was legitimate, first, that the blood on the shirt should be analysed and grouped, secondly that samples from the two injured individuals should

likewise be analysed and grouped, and thirdly that a sample from the complainer should likewise be G analysed and grouped. He explained that it was in accordance with the practice of the Crown to arrange for all these analyses to be carried out together.

We can readily understand why the Crown should wish the analyses to be carried out together and it, no doubt, is a matter of convenience that that should be so. However, it appears to us in the light of the information which is presently available that the application to take a blood sample from the complainer may well be premature. In the first place, it is H not yet known whether the stains on the shirt are indeed stains of blood at all. The situation might have been different if, in the petition seeking a warrant, the Crown had been able to say that the shirt contained bloodstains, but that is not what the Crown said; the most they have said is that the police have recovered "an apparently bloodstained shirt". Not only that, but it appears that any blood samples taken from the two individuals who are alleged to have been injured have not, so far, been analysed or grouped. If the shirt does I contain bloodstains it may be that an analysis of the blood obtained from the two injured individuals will reveal that any blood on the shirt could not have come from either of them, and if that is so then there would be no ground for requiring a sample of blood for comparison purposes to be provided by the complainer. It accordingly appears to us that the present application is indeed premature and that where the Crown are unable to say that the shirt did contain bloodstaining or that such bloodstaining on the shirt J could have come from either of the two injured individuals, the Crown are not justified in presenting this petition seeking warrant to take a blood sample from the complainer. It appears to us that no special circumstances have been made out by the Crown such as were said to be necessary in the case of *Morris v MacNeill*, and for these reasons we shall accordingly pass the bill and suspend the warrant granted by the sheriff.

K

Counsel for Complainer, McVicar; Solicitors, Drummond Miller, WS (for J Stuart Cobb, Glasgow) — Counsel for Respondent, Solicitor General (Dawson, QC); Solicitor, J D Lowe, Crown Agent.

P W F

L

Singh v Secretary of State for the Home Department

HOUSE OF LORDS

LORD TEMPLEMAN, LORD ACKNER,
LORD JAUNCEY OF TULLICHETTLE,
LORD BROWNE-WILKINSON AND
LORD MUSTILL

15 OCTOBER 1992

Administrative law — Judicial review — Subordinate legislation — Whether ultra vires — Regulations requiring immigration officers to give written notice of deportation order unless whereabouts or place of abode of recipient unknown — Whether included power to make written notice unnecessary — Whether included power to provide that notice might be sent to recipient's last known address — Immigration Act 1971 (c 77), s 18 (1) — Immigration Appeals (Notices) Regulations 1984 (SI 1984/2040), regs 3 (1) and (4) and 6.

Immigration — Deportation order — Competency — Decision to make deportation order not intimated since address of person to be deported not known — Decision to make deportation order only appealable within 14 days — Subordinate legislation made under statutory power to make regulations about notice of decisions providing for no notice where address unknown — Regulation providing notice might be sent to subject's last known address — Whether regulations ultra vires — Immigration Act 1971 (c 77), s 18 (1) — Immigration Appeals (Notices) Regulations 1984 (SI 1984/2040), regs 3 (1) and (4) and 6.

Section 18 (1) (a) of the Immigration Act 1971 empowers the Secretary of State to make regulations providing for written notice to be given to a person in respect of any decision or action taken in respect of him which is appealable under Pt II of the Act. In terms of s 18 (1) (d), the Secretary of State is empowered to provide for the form of any such notice and the way in which it may be given. Regulation 3 (4) of the Immigration Appeals (Notices) Regulations 1984 provides that written notice under reg 3 (1) of the decision to make a deportation order is not necessary if the immigration officer or authority has no knowledge of the whereabouts or place of abode of the person to whom it is to be given. Regulation 6 provides that written notice may be sent to the person's last known address.

A man subject to a deportation order petitioned for judicial review seeking to challenge the validity of the order. The petitioner had remained clandestinely in the United Kingdom after the expiry of the period for which he had been given leave to enter, without taking any steps to extend this period. On 20 December 1985 the Secretary of State decided to make a deportation order. Notice of the decision was sent to the petitioner at his last known address but it was returned undelivered. Notice was also sent to the home of his sister. The deportation order was made on 13 June 1986. The petitioner was apprehended in Glasgow in 1989. He was disabled from appealing against the decision to

make a deportation order as the prescribed time within which notice to appeal had to be given had expired. The petitioner argued (1) that reg 3 (4) was ultra vires s 18 inasmuch as that section did not empower the Secretary of State to make regulations which dispensed altogether with the service of a notice of a decision, and (2) that no notice had been given by the Secretary of State, because to send a notice to an address at which the petitioner was known not to be abiding was unreasonable in the *Wednesbury* sense and did not therefore constitute compliance with reg 6. The Lord Ordinary having dismissed the petition and a reclaiming motion having been refused, the petitioner appealed to the House of Lords.

Held, (1) that the Secretary of State was required by s 18 to make regulations to enable persons with rights of appeal to exercise them effectively (p 117I-K); (2) that s 18 (1) did not require the Secretary of State to provide for the giving of notice in circumstances where there was no reasonable prospect of that notice being effective, nor did it imply that a deportation order could not be made until notice had been given, and accordingly that reg 3 (4) was intra vires s 18 (1) (p 118D-E); and (3) that there was no warrant for construing "last known place of abode" in reg 6 as "last known place of abode at which there is any reason to believe he might still be abiding", and that in the present case the Secretary of State had acted entirely reasonably in complying with the requirements of reg 6 and had gone further than the regulations required him to go by sending notice of his decision both to the appellant's last known place of abode and to the address of his sister (p 118H and J); and appeal *dismissed.*

R v Secretary of State for the Home Department, ex p Makhan Singh [1977] Imm AR 66n, *approved.*

Observed, that in considering the question of reasonableness it had to be remembered that persons having rights of appeal under Pt II of the 1971 Act were non-patrials who were only present in the United Kingdom by virtue of leave granted to them, and that it was therefore quite reasonable that they should provide the authorities with addresses to which notices might be given and if they failed so to provide they could hardly complain if notices did not reach them (p 118I-J).

Petition for judicial review
(Reported 1990 SLT 300 and 1992 SLT 200)
Pargan Singh applied for judicial review of a decision of the Secretary of State for the Home Department to make a deportation order against him.

The petition came for a first hearing before the Lord Ordinary (Weir).

Statutory provisions
The Immigration Act 1971 provides:

"18.—(1) The Secretary of State may by regulations provide: (a) for written notice to be given to a person of any such decision or action taken in respect of him as is appealable under this Part of this Act (whether or not he is in the facts of his case entitled to appeal) or would be so appealable but for the ground on which it is taken; (b) for any such notice to include a statement of the reasons for the decision or action and, where the action is the giving of directions for the removal of any person from the United Kingdom, of the country or territory to which he is to be removed; (c) for any such notice to be accompanied by a statement containing particulars of the rights of appeal available under this Part of this Act and of the procedure by which those rights may be exercised; (d) for the form of any such notice or statement and the way in which a notice is to be or may be given."

The Immigration Appeals (Notices) Regulations 1984 provide:

"3.—(1) Subject to the following provisions of this Regulation, written notice of any decision or action which is appealable (or would be appealable but for the grounds of the decision or action) shall as soon as practicable be given in accordance with the provisions of the Regulations to the person in respect of whom the decision or action was taken. . . .

"(4) It shall not be necessary for notice to be given in compliance with the provisions of paragraph (1) if the officer or authority required by paragraph (2) to give it has no knowledge of the whereabouts or place of abode of the person to whom it is to be given. . . .

"(6) Any notice required by regulation 3 to be given to any person may be delivered, or sent by post in a registered letter or by recorded delivery service to — (a) that person's last known or usual place of abode; or (b) an address provided by him for receipt of the notice."

Cases referred to

Associated Provincial Picture Houses Ltd v Wednesbury Corporation [1948] 1 KB 223.
R v Immigration Appeal Tribunal, ex p Ekrem Mehmet [1977] 1 WLR 795; [1977] 2 All ER 602; [1977] Imm AR 56.
R v Secretary of State for the Home Department, ex p Makhan Singh [1977] Imm AR 66n.
R v Secretary of State for the Home Department, ex p Oladehinde [1991] 1 AC 254; [1990] 3 WLR 797; [1990] 3 All ER 393.
R v Secretary of State for the Home Department, ex p Yeboah [1987] 1 WLR 1586; [1987] 3 All ER 999.
Rhemtulla v Immigration Appeal Tribunal [1980] Imm AR 168.

On 10 May 1989 the Lord Ordinary *dismissed* the petition. (Reported 1990 SLT 300.)

The petitioner reclaimed.

Reclaiming motion

The reclaiming motion was heard before the Second Division on 12 December 1990.

On 18 January 1991 the court *refused* the reclaiming motion. (Reported 1992 SLT 200.)

The petitioner appealed to the House of Lords.

Appeal

The appeal was heard before Lord Templeman, Lord Ackner, Lord Jauncey of Tullichettle, Lord Browne-Wilkinson and Lord Mustill on 1 and 2 July 1992.

On 15 October 1992 the House *dismissed* the appeal.

LORD TEMPLEMAN.—For the reasons contained in the speech to be delivered by my noble and learned friend Lord Jauncey of Tullichettle, I would dismiss this appeal.

LORD ACKNER.—I too would dismiss this appeal for the reasons given in the speech of my noble and learned friend, Lord Jauncey of Tullichettle.

LORD JAUNCEY OF TULLICHETTLE.— There are two issues in this appeal from the Court of Session, namely: (1) whether reg 3 (4) of the Immigration Appeals (Notices) Regulations 1984 (SI 1984/ 2040) (the "Notices Regulations") is ultra vires s 18 of the Immigration Act 1971, and (2) whether in the particular circumstances of the case the Secretary of State acted unreasonably in serving on the appellant at his last known place of abode in accordance with reg 6 of the Notices Regulations a notice of his decision to deport him.

The appellant entered the United Kingdom from India in February 1983 having been granted leave to remain for a period of three months in order to marry. He remained in the United Kingdom after the expiry of the three month period without having applied for an extension and, on the advice of members of the Indian community in Birmingham, he "went underground". On 20 December 1985 the Secretary of State decided to make a deportation order under s 3 (5) of the Immigration Act 1971 and notice thereof was sent both to his last known address and to the home of his sister. The first notice was returned undelivered. On 13 June 1986 a deportation order was made. In early 1989 the appellant was traced to Glasgow and arrested. Thereafter he sought to challenge the validity of the deportation order by way of judicial review procedure. The Lord Ordinary refused to grant him the relief which he sought and the Second Division adhered to the interlocutor of the Lord Ordinary.

Section 1 of the Act of 1971 divides persons into those having a right of abode in the United Kingdom, who are later referred to in the Act as patrials, and those who require permission to live, work and settle in the United Kingdom. Section 3 (1) provides that a person who is not patrial shall not enter the United Kingdom unless given leave with or without conditions to do so, and s 3 (5) provides that such a person shall be liable to deportation in certain specified circumstances, including his remaining beyond the time limited by his leave. Part II of the Act, which extends to some 12 sections, makes provision for appeals. Section 13 applies to persons who are refused leave to enter the United Kingdom. Section 14 allows persons who have a limited leave to enter or remain in the United Kingdom to appeal against a variation of that leave or a refusal to vary it. Section 15 provides for appeals against a decision of the Secretary of State to make a deportation order by virtue of s 3 (5) or a refusal, by him, to revoke a deportation order. Section 15 (2) provides that a deportation order shall not be made under s 3 (5) during the period allowed for appeal against the decision to make it nor during the period of any pending appeal. Regulation 4 (7) of the Immigrations Appeals (Procedure) Rules 1984 (SI 1984/2041), which were made under powers contained in s 22 of the Act, provides that notice of an appeal against a decision to make a deportation order may be given not later than 14 days after the decision. Thus the procedure involved in making a deportation order involves two stages, namely: (1) the decision to make the order, which decision is appealable, and (2) the making of the order if the decision is not appealed or any appeal is unsuccessful. Section 18 (1) of the Act is in the following terms: [his Lordship quoted the terms of s 18 (1) and continued:]

The Secretary of State first exercised his powers under the foregoing subsection in 1972 in regulations which were revoked by the Notices Regulations. The latter regulations provide inter alia: [his Lordship quoted the terms of regs 3 (1) and (4) and 6 and continued:]

Regulation 3 (4) of the 1972 Notices Regulations was in terms identical to those of reg 3 (4) of the 1984 Notices Regulations.

Counsel for the appellant advanced two arguments in support of his motion that the appeal be allowed and the deportation order quashed. He submitted (first) that reg 3 (4) was ultra vires s 18 inasmuch as that section did not empower the Secretary of State to make regulations which dispensed altogether with the service of a notice of a decision, and (second) that no notice had been given by the Secretary of State, because to send a notice to an address at which the appellant was known not to be abiding was unreasonable in the *Wednesbury* sense and did not therefore constitute compliance with reg 6. It followed therefore that no valid notice of the decision to deport having been given and there being no power in the Secretary of State to dispense by regulation with the giving of notice the deportation order was invalid and should be quashed. In advancing the first argument counsel accepted that if it were correct it would be necessary for this House to overrule three English cases in which it had been held that reg 3 (4) was intra vires s 18.

In my view the first question to be addressed is the scope of s 18. Differing views have been expressed in England as to whether the Secretary of State is required by the section to make regulations or whether he has a discretion as to the making or not making thereof. In *R v Immigration Appeal Tribunal, ex p Ekrem Mehmet* Slynn J (as he then was), in delivering the judgment of a divisional court consisting of Lord Widgery CJ, Forbes J and himself, said at [1977] Imm AR, p 66 that s 18 (1) gave the Secretary of State "a discretion as to whether and how he should make regulations". A few weeks later in *Makhan Singh v*

Her Majesty's Secretary of State for Home Affairs (reported only partially as a footnote at p 66 in *Ekrem Mehmet*) Bridge LJ (as he then was) in the Court of Appeal said: "When I look at section 18 (1), with all respect to the Divisional Court, I gravely doubt whether that is right and whether it can be said that Parliament intended to leave it to the Secretary of State to decide whether any regulations at all should be made under this section. I attach particular significance to paragraphs (b) and (c) of subsection (1). Paragraph (b) says that the regulations may provide for a notice to include a statement of the reasons for the decision, and by subsection (2) such a statement is made conclusive of the ground on which the decision was made. Under paragraph (c) provision may be made for the notice to be accompanied by a statement containing particulars which are designed to provide important safeguards for potential appellants of the rights of appeal available. Looking at these provisions, it seems to me that one should construe subsection (1) not as leaving it open to the Secretary of State's discretion whether he makes any regulations at all, but as requiring him to make regulations under the subsection."

My Lords, I entirely agree with the views of Bridge LJ on this matter and indeed would go further. Sections 13-16 of the Act confer rights of appeal upon persons in relation to various actions and decisions affecting them, such as refusal of leave to enter the United Kingdom, variations of limited leave to enter the United Kingdom, deportation orders and directions for removal. If those rights are to be effective the persons concerned must, where possible, be given such notice as will enable them to exercise the rights. In my view Parliament intended that the Secretary of State should be required to make regulations which would ensure, so far as practicable, that persons upon whom the rights of appeal had been conferred should be enabled effectively to exercise those rights. It follows that the Secretary of State does not have a discretion as to whether or not he shall make regulations.

The next question is what must be contained in those regulations. I turn to consider the three English cases which counsel asked your Lordships to overrule. In *Ekrem Mehmet* Slynn J at p 66 said: "Accordingly in our judgment regulation 3 (4) was made by the Secretary of State within the powers conferred upon him by section 18 of the Immigration Act 1971." In *Makhan Singh,* in which the Court of Appeal held reg 3 (4) to be intra vires, Lord Denning MR said: "If a decision to deport is made, the structure of the Act contemplates that notice is to be given whenever the circumstances are such that notice can reasonably be given. Otherwise his right of appeal would be useless. But, if no notice can be given because it is impracticable (as a man's address or place of abode is not known) in these circumstances the regulations can provide that no notice is necessary. It cannot be supposed that the Act is to be rendered nugatory simply because a man has gone to ground and cannot be found. So sub-paragraph (4) is valid. It is not necessary for notice to be given if the Home Office has

A   no knowledge of the present whereabouts or place of abode of the man.''

Bridge LJ said: "I am perfectly satisfied that the provision in regulation 3 (4) of the 1972 Regulations is *intra vires* because it is an absurdity to suppose that Parliament intended to compel the Secretary of State to make a regulation requiring written notice to be served in a situation where in practical terms it is not possible to serve it; and it is perfectly legitimate and proper in my judgment for the regulations to spell out, as they do, an exception to the obligation to serve notice in a case where, as here, notice cannot be served because the Secretary of State does not know the whereabouts of the person upon whom notice would otherwise be required to be served.''

B

Finally, in *Rhemtulla v Immigration Tribunal Appeal* the Court of Appeal once again held that reg 3 (4) was intra vires. Bridge LJ at p 174 said: "As I have said that decision [*Makhan Singh*] (the reasoning of which I need not examine) is clearly and unmistakably to the effect that regulation 3 (4) of the Immigration Appeals (Notices) Regulations, which dispenses with the necessity for the notice on a person of whose whereabouts the Secretary of State has no knowledge is valid and intra vires. So that disposes once and for all of that point.''

C

Counsel for the appellant submitted that these cases were wrongly decided. Section 18, although not requiring regulations made thereunder to provide for receipt as well as giving of notice, nevertheless required that some form of substituted service be provided for, such as edictal service or advertisement.

D

My Lords, I reject this submission and agree entirely with the reasoning of Lord Denning MR and Bridge LJ in *Makhan Singh*. Section 18 (1) requires the Secretary of State to make regulations for the purpose to which I have already referred but it does not require him to provide for the giving of notice in circumstances where there is no reasonable prospect of that notice being effective, nor does the subsection provide by implication that in no circumstances can a deportation order be made until notice has been given. So to provide would indeed place a premium on disappearance. When the Notices Regulations are looked at as a whole it appears that they have catered for all eventualities which can reasonably be anticipated. Regulation 3 (1) provides for written notice of a decision being given as soon as practicable. Regulation 6 provides that any such notice shall be sent to a person's "last known or usual place of abode" or to an address provided by him for receipt of the notice. Regulation 3 (4) dispenses with the notice if the "whereabouts or place of abode" of a person are unknown. Thus if a person's usual abode is known or if he has provided an address for service notice must be sent to that address. If his present abode is unknown but his last abode is known the notice will be sent there. If his present abode is unknown and he had no last known abode service is not required. In my view reg 3 (4) is only intended to apply where a person's present and last place of abode is unknown and it does not overlap with reg 6. Indeed, reg 3 (4) is likely to operate only in rare cases, for example, where a person has given a false address or where his last known abode has ceased to exist for some

E

F

reason such as demolition. My Lords, in my view reg 3 (4) is a sensible provision which is undoubtedly intra vires s 18 (1).   G

I would add that in a situation where reg 3 (4) is applied so that a deportation order has been made without notice of the decision to deport having been given, all is not necessarily lost for a non-patrial. He may apply for a revocation of the order and if his application is refused he may appeal against the refusal after he has left the United Kingdom (s 15 (1) (b) and (5)).

Counsel for the appellant's argument that service on a person at his last known abode when he is known not   H to be there is *Wednesbury* unreasonable also fails. It is to be noted that the attack is not on the vires of reg 6 but upon its exercise in the particular circumstances of this case. This argument necessarily involves construing "last known place of abode" as meaning "last known place of abode at which there is reason to believe he might still be abiding". There is no warrant for such a construction. "Last known place of abode" means exactly what it says, no more and no less. If it is known where a person was living but it is not known where he is now living, the former is his last known   I place of abode at which the regulation directs notice to be given. The formula is well known. For example, RSC order 10, rule 1 (2) (a) provides for service of an originating process by posting to the defendant "at his usual or last known address". Furthermore in considering the question of reasonableness it must be remembered that persons having rights of appeal under Pt II of the Act of 1971 are non-patrials who are only present in the United Kingdom by virtue of leave granted to them. It is therefore quite reasonable that   J they should provide the authorities with addresses to which notices may be given and if they fail so to provide they can hardly complain if notices do not reach them. In the present case the Secretary of State acted entirely reasonably in complying with the requirements of reg 6 and indeed he went further than the regulations required him to go by sending notice of his decision both to the appellant's last known place of abode and to the address of his sister.

My Lords for all the foregoing reasons I would dismiss the appeal and affirm the interlocutor of the   K Second Division.

LORD BROWNE-WILKINSON.—I too would dismiss this appeal for the reasons given in the speech of my noble and learned friend, Lord Jauncey of Tullichettle.

LORD MUSTILL.—I have had the advantage of reading in draft the speech prepared by my noble and learned friend Lord Jauncey of Tullichettle. I agree with it, and for the reasons given, I too would dismiss   L this appeal.

Counsel for Petitioner and Appellant, J L Mitchell, QC, P M Macdonald; Solicitors, Drummond Miller, WS (for Philip Rooney & Co, Paisley), Oswald Hickson Collier & Co, London — Counsel for Respondent, R D Mackay, QC, Reith; Solicitor, R Brodie, Solicitor in Scotland to the Secretary of State for the Home Department, Treasury Solicitor, London.

M G T

Stainton v McNaughton

A HIGH COURT OF JUSTICIARY

THE LORD JUSTICE CLERK (ROSS),
LORDS MURRAY AND BRAND

19 DECEMBER 1990

Justiciary — Statutory offence — Licensing — Sale of alcohol for consumption other than as ancillary to a meal — Whether both licence holder and employee could be charged and convicted — Licensing (Scotland) Act 1976
B *(c 66), s 99.*

By s 99 (a) of the Licensing (Scotland) Act 1976, "The holder of a restaurant licence or his employee or agent" shall be guilty of an offence if he sells or supplies alcoholic liquor for consumption on the premises, except for consumption as ancillary to a meal.

The holder of a restaurant licence and an employee working for him were charged on summary complaint which libelled two charges of supplying alcohol for
C consumption other than by persons taking meals in the premises. On being convicted they appealed, arguing inter alia that in view of the terms of s 99 it was not competent to convict both the licence holder and his employee.

Held, that since the provisions of s 67 of and Sched 5 to the Act (penalties) envisaged vicarious liability on the part of the licence holder inter alia where the offence was committed under s 99 (a), proceedings
D might be instituted against both a licence holder and an employee who was alleged to have committed the offence (p 120B-D).

Docherty v Stakis Hotels Ltd, 1992 SLT 381, *distinguished.*

Summary complaint

Leonard Charles Stainton and Kaey Anderson or Seiler were charged at the instance of I S McNaughton,
E procurator fiscal, Peterhead, on a summary complaint which libelled two contraventions of s 99 (a) of the Licensing (Scotland) Act 1976. Both accused pled not guilty and proceeded to trial in the district court at Peterhead. After trial the justices convicted the accused.

The accused appealed by way of stated case to the High Court against the decision of the justices.

F   The facts of the case are set forth in the opinion of the court.

Statutory provisions

The Licensing (Scotland) Act 1976 provides:

"99. The holder of a restaurant licence or his employee or agent shall be guilty of an offence if — (a) he sells or supplies any alcoholic liquor for consumption on the premises, except to persons taking meals in the premises, for consumption by such a person as an ancillary to his meal."

Cases referred to

Davies v Smith, 1983 SLT 644; 1983 SCCR 232.   G
Docherty v Stakis Hotels Ltd, 1992 SLT 381; 1991 SCCR 6.

Appeal

The appeal was argued before the High Court on 19 December 1990.

Eo die the court *quashed* the conviction in respect of charge 1 but quoad ultra *refused* the appeal.   H

The following opinion of the court was delivered by the Lord Justice Clerk (Ross):

OPINION OF THE COURT.—This is an appeal by way of stated case at the instance of Leonard Charles Stainton and Kaey Anderson or Seiler. They were found guilty in the district court of Banff and Buchan at Peterhead of two charges on a complaint. Each libelled a contravention of s 99 (a) of the Licensing I (Scotland) Act 1976, the charges being that the appellant being the holder of a restaurant licence in respect of premises at Queen Street, Peterhead, did by the hands of his agent or employee, the appellant Seiler, sell and supply alcoholic liquor for consumption on the premises other than to persons taking meals in the premises for consumption by such persons as an ancillary to their meal. The first charge related to events on 12 February 1989 and the second to events on 18 and 19 February 1989.   J

There are three questions in the case but counsel for the appellants explained that he was not presenting any argument on question 2. The first question asks whether the justices had been correct in rejecting a submission of no case to answer made under s 345A of the Criminal Procedure (Scotland) Act 1975. Before addressing us on the sufficiency of evidence, counsel for the appellants sought to take a point on competency and when he had raised this issue on an earlier occasion the appeal had been continued for the purpose of allow- K ing the Crown to consider this matter. Put shortly the submission of counsel for the appellants was that it was not competent to convict both appellants on this complaint. He founded upon the provisions of s 99 of the Act of 1976 which provides: "The holder of a restaurant licence or his employee or agent shall be guilty of an offence if"; there then follow the circumstances which will give rise to the offence. Counsel's submission was that the word "or" was disjunctive and that L both the holder of the licence and his employee could not be guilty of the offence charged.

In this connection he founded upon a decision of this court in *Docherty v Stakis Hotels Ltd*. That case was one where under reference to the Food Hygiene (Scotland) Regulations 1959 the view was expressed by the court that in reg 32 (2) of the regulations the word "or" was disjunctive and not conjunctive. These were however very different regulations from the statute with which the present appeal is concerned, and the result

A in the case of *Docherty v Stakis Hotels Ltd* depended upon the nature of the language used in reg 32 (2) of the regulations founded upon. We are not satisfied that any assistance in this case is to be derived from that decision.

Reference was made in *Docherty v Stakis Hotels Ltd* to *Davies v Smith*. That was a case arising out of the provisions of the Prevention of Oil Pollution Act 1971 which provided that liability could arise on behalf of "the owner or master of the vessel". It was held in that case that the word "or" had to be given a conjunctive

B meaning and that it was competent in that case to charge both the owners and the master of the vessel. Quite apart from that the learned advocate depute in the present case drew attention to provisions of s 67 (1) (a) and 67 (2) of the Licensing (Scotland) Act 1976. The effect of these provisions is that in certain circumstances the licence holder has vicarious liability and that proceedings may be instituted against the licence holder whether or not proceedings had been instituted against the person who committed the offence.

C Schedule 5 to the Act is referred to in these subsections and when the terms of Sched 5 are considered it is to be seen that s 99 (a) is one of those sections where vicarious liability on the part of the licence holder does exist. It follows therefore that the point of competency which counsel for the appellants sought to raise is not a sound one because this is one of those situations where proceedings may be instituted both against the licence holder and someone such as his agent or employee who is alleged to have committed the offence.

D [The court then considered submissions on sufficiency of evidence with which this report is not concerned.]

Counsel for Appellants, P W Ferguson; Solicitors, Simpson & Marwick, WS (for Masson & Glennie, Peterhead) — Counsel for Respondent, Macdonald, QC, AD; Solicitor, I Dean, Crown Agent.

E SDDN

Johnston v MacGillivray

HIGH COURT OF JUSTICIARY
THE LORD JUSTICE GENERAL (HOPE),
F LORDS COWIE AND GRIEVE
19 DECEMBER 1991

Justiciary — Procedure — Summary procedure — Accused challenging validity of statutory instrument under which prosecuted — Sheriff ordering accused to lead evidence at hearing on competency — No plea being taken but accused appealing to High Court — Criminal Procedure (Scotland) Act 1975 (c 21), s 334 (2A) — Act of Adjournal (Consolidation) 1988 (SI 1988/110), rule 128 (1).

Section 334 (2A) of the Criminal Procedure (Scot-
G land) Act 1975 provides, inter alia, that a party may, with leave of the court and in accordance with such procedure as may be prescribed by Act of Adjournal, appeal to the High Court against a decision of the court of first instance (other than a decision not to grant leave) which relates to an objection to the competency or relevancy of the complaint or the proceedings. Rule 128 (1) of the Act of Adjournal (Consolidation) 1988 provides that an accused may only apply for leave to appeal against a decision on an objection after stating how he pleads to the charge.

H An accused person who was the skipper and owner of a British fishing boat, was charged on a summary complaint with a contravention of art 3 of the Inshore Fishing (Prohibition of Carriage of Monofilament Gill Nets) (Scotland) Order 1986 and ss 2 and 4 of the Inshore Fishing (Scotland) Act 1984. He stated a plea to the competency of the charge on the ground that the 1986 Order was invalid and ultra vires because the Secretary of State had failed to carry out consultations in terms of s 2 of the 1984 Act before making the order.
I The sheriff held that the onus of proving the invalidity of the order should rest on the accused who challenged its invalidity, and ordained the accused to lead at the hearing of evidence on the preliminary plea. Without stating how he intended to plead, the accused appealed contending that the sheriff erred in placing the onus on the accused. In the High Court the accused and the Crown were agreed that the appropriate course was for the issue to be dealt with by the sheriff at the trial diet. The High Court accordingly, but without expressing
J their view on the matter, allowed the appeal only to the extent of directing the sheriff to call upon the accused to state how he pleaded and thereafter, if he pleaded not guilty, to adjourn the case to a trial diet.

Observed, that in practice the preferable course would always be for the Crown to lead such evidence as it could on the point which was at issue, so that the court might be properly informed before it came to resolve the issue about the validity of the 1986 Order
K (p 122J-K).

Opinion reserved, as to (1) whether the onus was on the Crown or the accused (p 122I); (2) whether the note of appeal was competent in terms of rule 128 (1) of the Act of Adjournal since no plea had been taken from the accused (p 122D-E); (3) since the sheriff's decision was not to repel the plea to competency, whether it was a decision which was capable of being appealed under s 334 (2A) of the 1975 Act (p 122E); and (4) whether it was appropriate for the sheriff to
L hear evidence while hearing a debate on competency (p 122H-I).

Summary complaint

Nigel Maurice Johnston was charged at the instance of James I M MacGillivray, procurator fiscal, Fort William on a summary complaint which libelled a contravention of art 3 of the Inshore Fishing (Prohibition of Carriage of Monofilament Gill Nets) (Scotland)

Order 1986 and ss 2 and 4 of the Inshore Fishing (Scotland) Act 1984 in respect that he carried on a British fishing boat, of which he was skipper and owner, while the boat was on waters within a specified sea area at Mallaig harbour, a quantity of monofilament gill nets. The accused stated a plea to the competency of the charge on the ground that the order, which was made by the Secretary of State for Scotland on 14 January 1986, was invalid and ultra vires in that the Secretary of State had failed to carry out consultations in terms of s 2 of the 1984 Act before making the order. The sheriff held that the plea should be dealt with before the accused was called on to plead and that the onus lay on the accused to prove the invalidity of the 1986 Order, and ordained the accused to lead evidence first at a hearing of evidence on the preliminary plea.

The accused appealed, with leave of the sheriff, to the High Court against the decision of the sheriff.

Statutory provisions

The Criminal Procedure (Scotland) Act 1975 provides:

"334.—. . . (2A) Without prejudice to any right of appeal under section 442 or 453A of this Act, a party may, with the leave of the court (granted either on the motion of that party or *ex proprio motu*) and in accordance with such procedure as may be prescribed by Act of Adjournal under this Act, appeal to the High Court against a decision of the court of first instance (other than a decision not to grant leave under this subsection) which relates to such objection or denial as is mentioned in subsection (1) above; but such appeal must be taken not later than two days after such decision. . . ."

"353.—. . . (2) Any order by any of the departments of state or government or any local authority or public body made under powers conferred by any statute, or a print or copy of such order, shall when produced in a summary prosecution be received in evidence of the due making, confirmation, and existence of such order without being sworn to by any witness and without any further or other proof, but without prejudice to any right competent to the accused to challenge any such order as being *ultra vires* of the authority making it or on any other competent ground, and where any such order is referred to in the complaint it shall not be necessary to enter it in the record of the proceedings as a documentary production."

The Act of Adjournal (Consolidation) 1988 provides inter alia:

"128.—(1) If — (a) an accused states an objection to the competency or relevancy of the complaint or the proceedings; and (b) that objection is repelled, he may only apply for leave to appeal against that decision under section 334 (2A) after stating how he pleads to the charge or charges set out in the complaint."

Cases referred to

Francis v Cardle, 1988 SLT 578; 1987 SCCR 1.
McCartney v Tudhope, 1986 SLT 159; 1986 JC 7; 1985 SCCR 373.
Walkingshaw v Marshall, 1992 SLT 1167; 1991 SCCR 397.

Appeal

The appeal was argued before the High Court on 3 December 1991.

On 19 December 1991 the court *allowed* the appeal (of consent of the Crown) only to the extent of *directing* the sheriff to call upon the accused to plead and, if necessary, to *adjourn* the case to a trial diet.

The following opinion of the court was delivered by the Lord Justice General (Hope):

OPINION OF THE COURT.—The appellant was charged with carrying on a British fishing boat, of which he is skipper and owner, while the vessel was on waters within a specified sea area at Mallaig harbour, a quantity of monofilament gill nets, contrary to art 3 of the Inshore Fishing (Prohibition of Carriage of Monofilament Gill Nets) (Scotland) Order 1986 and ss 2 and 4 of the Inshore Fishing (Scotland) Act 1984. He has taken a plea to the competency of the charge on the grounds that the order which was made by the Secretary of State for Scotland on 14 January 1986 is invalid and ultra vires in that the Secretary of State failed to carry out consultations in terms of s 2 of the Act before making the order.

On 6 June 1991, at the diet at which this plea was intimated, the appellant's motion that the prosecutor should be ordained to lead evidence at the diet of debate was deferred by the sheriff until the diet of debate which he fixed for 5 September 1991. On that date the motion was renewed and the sheriff heard argument for both parties on the question whether the onus was on the Crown to prove that the order had been validly made by the Secretary of State in terms of s 2 of the Act. He then adjourned the diet until 4 October 1991 when he issued his decision on the points which had been raised in argument with reference to the plea to the competency. He held that when an accused challenges an order as being ultra vires of the authority which has made it the onus of proving the invalidity of the order should rest on the party challenging its validity. He also held that the plea to the competency in this case should be dealt with before the appellant was called upon to plead, by a hearing on 24 January 1992 at which the defence and the Crown were to be entitled to lead evidence. In view of his decision that the onus was on the party who challenged the validity of the order he held that it was appropriate that the appellant should lead his evidence first, adding that the Crown were to be entitled but not bound to lead evidence.

The appellant has now appealed to this court. The point which he sought to bring under review is the sheriff's decision that at any hearing of evidence relating to the plea to the competency the appellant should lead evidence to prove the invalidity of the order. It is contended in the note of appeal that the sheriff erred in law by placing the onus on the accused, since he failed to follow the fundamental rule in a Scots criminal prosecution that the onus rests on the Crown. His decision is also said to be inconsistent with the opinion

of Sheriff Kelbie in *Francis v Cardle* at 1987 SCCR,
p 6, which was followed by Sheriff J R Smith in
Walkingshaw v Marshall [1992 SLT at p 1179D-H],
that the onus was on the Crown.

It is clear that this case has raised an issue of general
importance, but at the hearing before us in this appeal
counsel for the appellant and the advocate depute were
both agreed that it was not appropriate for the sheriff
to hear evidence at a preliminary hearing on competency and that the issue should be dealt with by him
at the trial. Counsel for the appellant said that what the
sheriff should have done was to call upon the appellant
to state how he pled to the charge and, assuming that
his plea was one of not guilty, to fix a diet for the trial.
He also submitted that the sheriff went too far in his
comments about onus because, if they were to be
applied according to their terms, the effect would be
that if the Crown were to lead no evidence at all about
the circumstances in which the order came to be made
and the appellant was unable to adduce any such
evidence the challenge to the competency of the order
would inevitably fail. The advocate depute informed us
that the Crown's position was that it was normally
inappropriate for a sheriff to hear evidence on preliminary matters, and that the sheriff would normally be
expected to deal with all issues which required the
hearing of evidence at the trial. He submitted that it
was not appropriate for us to attempt to resolve the
issue about onus at this stage, although he indicated
that the sheriff had reached the right decision on this
point. He invited us to remit the matter to the sheriff
to take the appellant's plea and to fix a diet for the trial.

The brief discussion to which we listened did not
provide us with a satisfactory basis for resolving the
various issues which have arisen in this case. One is the
procedural point to which the sheriff has drawn our
attention in his report. This is that according to rule
128 (1) of the Act of Adjournal (Consolidation) 1988 an
accused may only apply for leave to appeal against a
decision on an objection to competency after stating
how he pleads to the charge. No plea has been taken in
this case, and it is open to question whether the note
of appeal is competent. Another is whether the
sheriff's decision of 4 October 1991, which was not to
repel the plea to competency but to order that it should
be dealt with before the appellant was called upon to
plead and that a diet should be fixed for the hearing of
evidence at which the appellant should lead his
evidence first, is a decision which is capable of being
appealed under s 334 (2A) of the 1975 Act. The advocate depute drew our attention to these points, but he
did not find it necessary to challenge the appeal on
these grounds since the parties were agreed that the
case should be remitted to the sheriff to take a plea and
to hear any evidence at the trial.

The third issue is whether the sheriff was right, as he
appears to have been invited to do by the appellant's
solicitor, to allow evidence to be led at the preliminary
diet at which the issue of competency was to be discussed. It is no doubt true that in *Francis v Cardle*, 1987
SCCR at p 10 the Lord Justice Clerk said that the
sheriff in that case was well entitled to conclude that he
should not hear evidence at the stage of hearing pleas

to competency. But at p 8 in the same case the Lord
Justice Clerk recognised that there may be cases where
it would be appropriate for a sheriff to hear evidence
while hearing a debate on competency. In *McCartney
v Tudhope*, 1986 SLT at p 161, where the question
raised was one of time bar, the Lord Justice Clerk
observed that unless the relevant facts could be agreed
between the parties the preferable course would be for
evidence to be heard on the preliminary plea. So far as
the issue in this case is concerned, it is not obvious that
any evidence on the question as to the validity of the
order would be relevant to the issues on the merits as
to whether the appellant was in breach of art 3 of the
1986 order. In *Walkingshaw v Marshall* the parties
were agreed that the questions as to validity which
remained in that case should be dealt with at the trial.
In the event, as the sheriff observed in his decision on
22 April 1991, all the facts relevant to the contravention of the order were admitted, and the only matters
on which evidence was led related to the issues as to the
validity of the order. In these circumstances we are not
to be taken as having reached any view of our own as
to whether the sheriff was wrong to decide to allow
evidence to be led. In remitting the matter to him to
proceed to take a plea and fix a diet for the trial we are
doing no more than giving effect to what the parties are
agreed should be done.

The question as to whether the onus is on the Crown
or on the accused in regard to the question of validity
was not argued and we must reserve our opinion on this
matter also. It is sufficient to say at this stage that in
view of the provisions of s 353 (2) of the 1975 Act, an
order made by the Secretary of State will be presumed
to be validly made unless a challenge to its validity is
made by the accused. And any challenge to its validity
must be made in terms which are sufficiently specific
to give notice to the Crown of the basis upon which the
challenge is to be made. Difficult questions then may
arise, especially where all the facts relevant to the issue
of validity may be expected to be known by or available
to the Crown, as to how much, if any, evidence needs
to be led by the accused. For this reason it would be
unwise for the Crown to assume that it is unnecessary
for it to lead any evidence on the matter. In practice the
preferable course will always be for the Crown to lead
such evidence as it can on the point which is at issue,
so that the court may be properly informed about the
facts before it comes to resolve the issue which has been
raised by the accused about the validity of the order.

For these reasons we shall allow the appeal only to
the extent of directing the sheriff to call upon the appellant at the commencement of the hearing on 24 January
1992 to state how he pleads to the charge and thereafter, if he pleads not guilty, to adjourn the case to a
diet for the trial.

---

*Counsel for Appellant, Geary; Solicitors, Pearsons, WS
(for Primrose & Gordon, Dumfries) — Counsel for
Respondent, Bonomy, AD; Solicitor, J D Lowe, Crown
Agent.*

P W F

Mitchell v Mitchell

A   EXTRA DIVISION

LORDS ALLANBRIDGE, COWIE AND GRIEVE

23 APRIL 1992

Husband and wife — Divorce — Proceedings also taking place in another jurisdiction — Sisting of action — Whether appropriate for other proceedings to be disposed of first — Relevant factors — Domicile and Matrimonial Proceedings Act 1973 (c 45), Sched 3, para 9 (1).

B

Jurisdiction — Consistorial action — Proceedings also taking place in another jurisdiction — Sisting of action — Whether appropriate for other proceedings to be disposed of first — Relevant factors — Domicile and Matrimonial Proceedings Act 1973 (c 45), Sched 3, para 9 (1).

Process — Sist — Action of divorce — Proceedings also taking place in another jurisdiction — Whether action should be sisted so that foreign proceedings might be disposed of first — Relevant factors — Domicile and
C *Matrimonial Proceedings Act 1973 (c 45), Sched 3, para 9 (1).*

Paragraph 9 (1) of Sched 3 to the Domicile and Matrimonial Proceedings Act 1973 provides that a Scottish court may sist a consistorial action before the beginning of the proof if it appears that proceedings are continuing in another jurisdiction in respect of the marriage or capable of affecting its validity and that the balance of fairness between the parties is such that it is appropriate for those other proceedings to be disposed
D of before further steps are taken in the Scottish action.

A husband and wife were married on 10 June 1977. They lived together in Edinburgh until April 1989 when they moved to France, where they lived together until they separated in July 1990. The wife raised an action of divorce in Scotland in January 1991 while still residing in France. The husband raised an action of divorce in France in March 1991. The wife returned to Scotland in September 1991. There was a dispute
E between the parties as to where their various assets were located although the husband maintained that they were substantially based in France where he continued to reside. In September 1991 the husband enrolled a motion to sist the Scottish action. He averred that he was domiciled in France, that he had raised an action of divorce in France on the grounds of his wife's adultery in France in March 1991, and that both parties resided in France and were habitually resident there throughout the year prior to their separation. He
F argued that in those circumstances the French court was the appropriate forum. The Lord Ordinary adopted the reasoning of the House of Lords in *de Dampierre v de Dampierre* [1988] AC 92 and refused the motion.

The husband reclaimed. He argued that the Lord Ordinary had erred in law (1) in concluding that he should approach the question of the balance of fairness, primarily from the angle of the "overall connection of the marriage" with Scotland and the entitlement of the Scottish spouse to obtain a remedy in Scotland, the

proper approach being the principle of forum non conveniens; (2) in failing properly to take into account G the other circumstances by reason of which justice required that a sist should be granted, namely (a) the parties' residence in France; (b) the location of their assets in France; and (c) the facts connected with the merits of the case having occurred in France and the requirement that primarily French witnesses would speak to them; (3) in taking into account the order in which the actions commenced et separatim the wife's application to the French court that jurisdiction should be declined; and (4) in taking into account a dispute H concerning a property in Edinburgh, and an allegation that the husband resided there.

Held, (1) that the proper approach was first to consider the overall connection of the marriage with the jurisdictions in question: if the overall connection was prima facie with one forum, that should ordinarily be the appropriate forum unless there were circumstances by reason of which justice required otherwise (pp 125L and 126B and E); (2) that the Lord Ordinary had correctly decided that the overall connection of the marri- I age was with Scotland (p 126C-E); (3) that on the state of the pleadings before the Lord Ordinary and the information available to him there were no circumstances regarding the parties' respective income and capital which made it more appropriate in the interests of justice that the action should be sisted (p 126J-L); (4) that, in the circumstances of this case, the convenience of witnesses was not a factor making it more appropriate that the action be heard in France (pp 126L-127B); (5) that the question of which proceedings were raised J first was of no real significance, both actions being in their initial stages (p 127D-E); (6) that the French court having reached a decision on the matter of its own jurisdiction, this was no longer a relevant factor for consideration (p 127H-I); and (7) that the Lord Ordinary was entitled to conclude that the property in Edinburgh remained an important subject of dispute between the parties and one which might more conveniently be resolved in a Scottish court (p 127K-L); and reclaiming motion *refused.* K

De Dampierre v De Dampierre [1988] AC 92, *followed.*

Action of divorce

(Reported 1992 SLT 410)

Mrs Aileen Catherine Finlayson Robinson or Mitchell raised an action of divorce in the Court of Session against James Frederick Mitchell. The defender raised an action of divorce against the pursuer L in France. The defender enrolled a motion to have the action sisted pending the disposal of the French action in terms of para 9 (1) of Sched 3 to the Domicile and Matrimonial Proceedings Act 1973.

The case came before the Lord Ordinary (Marnoch) on the motion roll.

Statutory provisions

The Domicile and Matrimonial Proceedings Act 1973 provides in Sched 3:

"9.—(1) Where before the beginning of the proof in any consistorial action which is continuing in the Court of Session or in a sheriff court, it appears to the court concerned — (a) that any other proceedings in respect of the marriage in question or capable of affecting its validity are continuing in another jurisdiction, and (b) that the balance of fairness (including convenience) as between the parties to the marriage is such that it is appropriate for those other proceedings to be disposed of before further steps are taken in the action in the said court, the court may then if it thinks fit sist the action.

"(2) In considering the balance of fairness and convenience for the purposes of sub-paragraph (1) (b) above, the court shall have regard to all factors appearing to be relevant, including the convenience of witnesses and any delay or expense which may result from the proceedings being sisted, or not being sisted."

Cases referred to

Abidin Daver (The) [1984] AC 398.
Argyllshire Weavers Ltd v A Macaulay (Tweeds) Ltd, 1962 SLT 310; 1962 SC 388.
de Dampierre v de Dampierre [1988] AC 92; [1987] 2 WLR 1006; [1987] 2 All ER 1.
Sim v Robinow (1892) 14 R 665.
Société du Gaz de Paris v Société Anonyme de Navigation "Les Armateurs Français", 1926 SLT 33; 1926 SC (HL) 13.
Spiliada Maritime Corporation v Cansulex Ltd [1987] AC 460; [1986] 3 WLR 972; [1986] 3 All ER 843.

On 27 September 1991 the Lord Ordinary *refused* the motion. (Reported 1992 SLT 410.)

The defender reclaimed.

Reclaiming motion

The reclaiming motion was heard before an Extra Division on 27 March 1992.

On 23 April 1992 the Extra Division *refused* the reclaiming motion.

The following opinion of the court was delivered by Lord Allanbridge:

OPINION OF THE COURT.—This is an action of divorce by a wife, who is the pursuer and respondent, against her husband, the defender and reclaimer. Her action was raised on 31 January 1991 in the Court of Session and on 18 March 1991 her husband petitioned for divorce in the district court of Draguignan in France. On 27 September 1991 the Lord Ordinary refused a motion to sist the cause in terms of para 9 (1) of Sched 3 to the Domicile and Matrimonial Proceedings Act 1973. The husband has now reclaimed against the Lord Ordinary's interlocutor of 27 September 1991 which refused to sist the present action to allow the French proceedings to be disposed of before further steps are taken in the present action.

The relevant parts of said para 9 are as follows: [his Lordship quoted the terms of para 9 (1) set out supra and continued:]

At the time the Lord Ordinary heard the motion to sist in September 1991, the facts, as contained in the summons and defences which were then unadjusted, were that the wife averred that the Court of Session had jurisdiction as she was domiciled in Edinburgh on the date when the action was begun. (See s 7 (2) (a) of the Domicile and Matrimonial Proceedings Act 1973.) On the other hand the husband avers that he is domiciled in France, that he had raised an action of divorce in France on the ground of the wife's adultery in France in March 1991, and that both parties resided in France and were habitually resident in France throughout the year prior to their separation. In these circumstances the husband averred that the French court was the appropriate forum to dispose of the present dispute between the parties.

The parties were married at Edinburgh on 10 June 1977. At the time the present action was raised there was one child of the parties under 16 years of age, namely, Euan Fraser Mitchell born on 15 September 1975, but that child is now over 16 years of age. After the marriage the parties lived together in Edinburgh until about April 1989 when, as stated in the Lord Ordinary's opinion, it seems that the parties moved to France where they lived together until finally separating in July 1990. At the time the present proceedings were raised by the wife in January 1991 the instance shows she was then residing in France, although in September 1991 the Lord Ordinary was told that she had recently returned to live in this country. There was a dispute between the parties as to where their various assets were situated and in particular it was maintained by senior counsel for the husband, that as the husband's assets were now substantially based in France where he presently resides, the French court was the appropriate forum. On the whole matter senior counsel for the reclaimer had submitted that having regard to the present or recent whereabouts of both parties, the fact that they had lived together in France, the fact that the most part of their assets was, at least, arguably located in France and the fact that the witnesses to the merits were presumably resident in France, the balance of fairness (including that of convenience) as between the parties made it appropriate that the present proceedings should be sisted in Scotland.

The leading case on the interpretation of the English equivalent of said para 9 is *de Dampierre v de Dampierre*. Paragraph 9, which relates to the sisting of consistorial actions in Scotland, is contained in Sched 3 to the 1973 Act whereas the English equivalent in similar terms is contained in Sched 1 to the same Act. In this case the House of Lords allowed an appeal by a French husband who had raised an action for divorce against his French wife in France and had been refused a sist to stay the wife's action for divorce in England. The Lord Ordinary in the present case adopted the reasoning of the House of Lords in that case and in

particular founded on what Lord Templeman said, at
A [1988] AC, p 102F-H, regarding the situation of the
French wife which the Lord Ordinary considered was
very similar to the situation of the Scottish wife in the
present case. The Lord Ordinary said that he construed
the decision in *de Dampierre*'s case as leaving open, as
a very relevant consideration in deciding whether or
not to sist the proceedings, the "overall connection of
the marriage" with the jurisdiction or jurisdictions in
question. With that approach in mind he said he had
little doubt that the motion in the present case should
B be refused but that, even without the benefit of that
approach, he would still, he thought, on balance, have
refused the motion.

In the appeal before us senior counsel for the
reclaimer submitted that the Lord Ordinary had erred
in law in concluding that he should approach the question of the balance of fairness, primarily from the angle
of the "overall connection of the marriage" and the
entitlement of the "Scottish" spouse in terms of the
dicta of Lord Templeman. This is the first and most
C important of the husband's grounds of appeal which
are very clearly and helpfully set out in his written
grounds of appeal in this case.

Lords Templeman and Goff each delivered speeches
in *de Dampierre*'s case. For the purposes of this appeal
it is necessary to refer to a passage from each of their
separate speeches. At p 102F-H Lord Templeman said:
"In my opinion it is not unfair to the wife in the present
circumstances to deprive her of the advantages of
D seeking from an English court maintenance which she
might not obtain from a French court. The wife's connections with England were tenuous and she voluntarily severed all connection with England before
instituting her English divorce proceedings. The wife
is French; she was married in France, she can litigate
in France as easily as in England and she can obtain
from the French court all the redress to which she is
entitled under French law. The wife cannot sever her
direct French connections derived from ancestry,
E birth, nationality, education, culture and marriage
laws, or her indirect French connections through her
husband and child. On the one hand it is logical and not
unfair to the wife to treat her as a French wife entitled
to the rights conferred by French law on divorced
wives. On the other hand it would be unfair to the
husband to treat the wife as if she were an English wife
entitled to the rights conferred by English law on
divorced wives when, in truth, the wife is a French
wife, resides at present in the United States and has no
F connection with England."

At pp 107H to 108C Lord Goff said: "Under the
principle of forum non conveniens now applicable in
England as well as in Scotland, the court may exercise
its discretion under its inherent jurisdiction to grant a
stay where 'it is satisfied that there is some other
tribunal, having competent jurisdiction, in which the
case may be tried more suitably for the interests of the
parties and for the ends of justice': see *Sim v Robinow*
(1892) 19 R (Ct of Sess) 665 at p 668, per Lord
Kinnear. The effect is that the court in this country

looks first to see what factors there are which connect
the case with another forum. If, on the basis of that G
inquiry, the court concludes that there is another available forum which, prima facie, is clearly more appropriate for the trial of the action, it will ordinarily grant
a stay, unless there are circumstances by reason of
which justice requires that a stay should nevertheless
not be granted: see the *Spiliada* case [1987] AC 460,
475-478. The same principle is applicable whether or
not there are other relevant proceedings already
pending in the alternative forum: see *The Abidin Daver*
[1984] AC 398, 411, per Lord Diplock. However, the H
existence of such proceedings may, depending on the
circumstances, be relevant to the inquiry. Sometimes
they may be of no relevance at all, for example, if one
party has commenced the proceedings for the purpose
of demonstrating the existence of a competing jurisdiction, or the proceedings have not passed beyond the
stage of the initiating process. But if, for example,
genuine proceedings have been started and have not
merely been started but have developed to the stage
where they have had some impact upon the dispute I
between the parties, especially if such impact is likely
to have a continuing effect, then this may be a relevant
factor to be taken into account when considering
whether the foreign jurisdiction provides the appropriate forum for the resolution of the dispute between
the parties."

In presenting his main argument, senior counsel for
the reclaimer drew our attention to the fact that Lord
Goff at p 107H of the English case, had explained that
the principle of forum non conveniens which had J
become established in Scotland was now available in
England in choosing the appropriate forum. This,
according to senior counsel for the reclaimer, was the
proper approach and he referred to what was said by
Lord Dunedin, at 1926 SLT, p 34 in *Société du Gaz de
Paris v Armateurs Français* to the effect that the test
was whether there was another court of competent
jursidiction in which the case may be tried "more suitably for the interests of all the parties and for the ends
of justice". Senior counsel for the reclaimer submitted K
that Lord Templeman had gone too far and departed
from the accepted test laid down in the forum non conveniens cases and that his observations regarding the
French wife, quoted and founded on by the Lord
Ordinary in his opinion in this case, were obiter and
did not form part of the ratio of the decision of the
House of Lords in that case and that being so Lord
Templeman's approach was not one which required to
be followed in the courts in Scotland.

This was a bold approach by senior counsel for the L
reclaimer and it is not one with which we agree. We
consider it is quite clear from what was said by Lord
Goff in the passage quoted supra, that the court should
look first to see what factors there are which connect
the case with another forum. Once that has been done
and prima facie there is a more appropriate forum on
the basis of that connection, then unless there are
circumstances by reason of which justice requires that
that should not be the forum, that should ordinarily be
the appropriate forum.

The speeches of both Lords Templeman and Goff of Chieveley were read in draft by Lord Keith of Kinkel, Lord Brandon of Oakbrook and Lord Ackner who each agreed with them (see pp 98C-D and 103E), and Lords Templeman and Goff each agreed with each other's speech (see pp 102B-C and 110F-G), so that all their Lordships agreed with Lord Goff's explanation of the initial approach in such cases and the result of taking that approach is explained in some detail in Lord Templeman's speech in the passage from it we have quoted.

In these circumstances we are quite satisfied that the Lord Ordinary was correct to adopt the approach that he did in the present case. The initial approach should be to consider the overall connection of the marriage with the jurisdictions in question. In this case the parties were married in Scotland in June 1977 and lived there together for about 12 years when they apparently went to France in April 1989 and lived together for about 15 months before they separated in July 1990. They are British nationals and their respective backgrounds are Scottish and by far the greater part of their married life was spent living together in Scotland. In the English case, Lord Templeman referred to the fact that the wife was French and she was married in France and she had a direct French connection derived from "ancestry, birth, nationality, education, culture and marriage laws" and an indirect connection through her husband and child. We agree with the Lord Ordinary that the wife in this case is in a similar situation to the French wife in that case. It is true, as pointed out by senior counsel for the reclaimer, that the French wife had voluntarily severed all connection with England before instituting her English divorce proceedings, whereas the wife in this case was still resident in France when she instituted her present divorce proceedings in Scotland. However, we do not consider that is a sufficiently important distinction to counter the overall connection of the marriage with Scotland, especially as in this case the wife was relying on her Scottish domicile as founding jurisdiction on the Scottish courts.

Having correctly decided that the overall connection of this marriage was prima facie with Scotland, the Lord Ordinary would only have been entitled to grant the sist if he took the view that there were, nevertheless, other circumstances by reason of which justice required that a sist should be granted. These circumstances were put to the Lord Ordinary and repeated to us by senior counsel for the reclaimer. They are detailed in his written grounds of appeal. The first circumstance is based on the parties' residence in France. We accept that this is a circumstance to be taken into account but there is a considerable dispute between the parties as to the nature of their respective residences. The wife, according to the counsel who appeared for her before the Lord Ordinary, had recently returned to live in this country but it was suggested that the husband, at least from time to time, resided in Edinburgh at the former matrimonial home named "The Whitehouse". It was said on behalf of the husband that both he and the wife still resided in France. Because of this dispute the Lord Ordinary was unable to reach a concluded view on this particular matter which will no doubt require to be the subject of evidence.

The second circumstance is based on the parties' admitted last residence being in France, under reference to a comparison between said para 9 with para 8 of Sched 3 to the 1973 Act. A sist would have been mandatory in terms of para 8 had the other proceedings been continuing in another "related" jurisdiction such as England (see para 3 (2) of Sched 3). However, that comparison may raise other questions regarding "related" jurisdictions as contrasted with foreign jurisdictions and it is not disputed that para 9 applies in the circumstances of this case. We get no assistance on the basis of this comparison.

The third circumstance was the "admitted" absence of any assets of the wife in Scotland, her assets being said to be in France and the business interests and assets of the husband being also in France. Whilst it is averred by the wife that she has a share in the parties' joint property in France, she also avers she has the proceeds of sale of her business in Scotland and the husband himself avers she is a director along with her mother of two companies, namely Edoborg Ltd and Addside Ltd, which are clearly not in France. As regards the husband's assets we can well understand why the Lord Ordinary said he was far from satisfied that the location of the husband's many and varied assets could at that stage be ascertained with any certainty. He also said particular doubts surrounded the beneficial interest in "The Whitehouse" which he was informed had recently been sold for £750,000 to a company registered in the Isle of Man, although it was eventually acknowledged that the defender himself had an interest in that company, albeit the extent of that interest was unknown to his legal advisers. Suffice it to say that nothing was said to us which further clarified the husband's position regarding his various assets. His wife avers that not only is he the proprietor of "The Whitehouse" but that he also owns or owned adjacent property, has substantial banking arrangements in the Isle of Man and owns a number of valuable motor cars. Finally the only source of income disclosed by the husband in his present pleadings is £17,000 superannuation from the National Health Service. In this state of the pleadings before the Lord Ordinary and the information available to him, we do not consider there are any circumstances regarding the parties' respective income and capital which would make it more appropriate in the interests of justice that a motion to sist this action should have been granted.

The fourth and fifth circumstances founded on by senior counsel for the reclaimer related to his submission that the facts connected with the merits of the case had occurred in France and the consequent requirement for "primarily" French witnesses to speak to the facts. Also the financial aspects of the case would require witnesses from France. The "convenience of witnesses" is one of the factors to which the court must have regard in terms of para 9 (2). With regard to the merits of the action, senior counsel who appeared before us on behalf of the wife, pointed out that the grounds of the wife's divorce depended on her husband's behaviour throughout the marriage and the wife, her mother and her sister would be the main witnesses whereas only one French witness would be required to speak to the final matter of the alleged assault in France at the end of 1990. In these circumstances we do not consider that the convenience of such witnesses could be said to be a factor making it more appropriate that the action be heard in France. There may well be other witnesses speaking to the parties' respective assets but, as already indicated, in the present state of uncertainty regarding these assets, the court could not be expected to know at this stage which other witnesses are likely to be required to give evidence.

Two other grounds of appeal were argued before us. The first was that the Lord Ordinary had erred by taking into account the order in which the actions were commenced et separatim the existence of an application by the wife to the French court that jurisdiction should be declined in terms of art 21 of the Convention of Brussels. Senior counsel for the reclaimer also referred to what Lord President Clyde said at 1962 SLT, p 312 of *Argyllshire Weavers Ltd v A Macaulay (Tweeds) Ltd* which demonstrated that in Scotland litiscontestation takes place when defences are lodged. In the present case defences were not lodged by the husband until August 1991, as correctly noted by the Lord Ordinary in his opinion at 1992 SLT, p 411. In fairness to the Lord Ordinary it is to be noted that he only took the date of the commencement of the respective proceedings into account when considering whether there were any factors that would require him to change his mind, having decided correctly in our view, that the marriage was so closely connected with Scotland that the action regarding it should proceed there. He said he bore in mind that in terms of procedural fairness the present action was raised in advance of the husband's petition. We do not consider that the question of which proceedings were raised first is of any real significance in this case at the time the motion to sist was made. Lord Goff deals with this matter in the second part of the extract from his speech that we have already quoted supra, where he indicates that sometimes the matter of whether other proceedings are already pending may be of no relevance at all. In this case both the proceedings in the Scottish and French courts could be said to be still in their initial stages. Neither counsel suggested that any substantial weight should be attached to the fact that the Scottish action was commenced first. We agree with that approach by counsel in the circumstances of this case. We do not consider that the Lord Ordinary attached any significant weight to this factor although he correctly said he had to bear it in mind.

As regards the Lord Ordinary's view that there was much to be said for awaiting the outcome of the French court's decision on the matter of its own jurisdiction, we were told by senior counsel for the reclaimer that this matter had now been resolved by the French court which had decided it had jurisdiction, although the date when it did so was not entirely clear. However, on 18 March 1992 the French court had decided, as reconciliation of the couple did not seem possible, to give the husband leave to sue his wife for divorce within three months. According to senior counsel for the reclaimer the objection to the jurisdiction of the French court had been based on art 21 of the Convention of Brussels of 27 September 1968 which stated that the second jurisdiction chosen must be relinquished in favour of the court in which jurisdiction was first chosen. However, this Convention did not apply to matrimonial actions in the United Kingdom (see Civil Jurisdiction and Judgments Act 1982, Sched 1, which gives the text of the Convention as amended and, in Title 1, explains that the scope of the Convention does not apply to matrimonial disputes), or in France. In these circumstances there was no longer any dispute as to whether the French courts had jurisdiction and no longer any suggestion that this matter still required to be determined. Senior counsel for the respondent did not offer any contrary submissions on this matter and did not submit that this question of jurisdiction in the French courts was still outstanding. That being so this factor, which formed the basis of the third ground of appeal, has now gone as a reason for refusing to grant the sist but it was relevant at the time the Lord Ordinary was reaching his decision on the motion roll.

The fourth and last ground of appeal related to the former matrimonial home known as "The Whitehouse". It was to the effect that the Lord Ordinary was wrong to take the property, or the alleged fact that the husband resided there, into account in reaching his decision. We consider that the Lord Ordinary was fully entitled to conclude that "The Whitehouse" remains, on any view, an important subject of dispute between the parties. We have already referred to his earlier remarks in his opinion regarding it. A copy of a minute, dated 17 July 1990, signed by the husband and wife, both therein described as then residing at "The Whitehouse" was shown to us, in terms of which the wife purports to acknowledge that that property is not matrimonial property in terms of the Family Law (Scotland) Act 1985. A copy of the disposition, dated 8 February 1991, was also shown to us. It is a disposition by the husband in favour of Pageant Investments Ltd, whose registered office is in the Isle of Man and in terms of which the husband purports to sell "The Whitehouse" to the company for a sum of £750,000. We are further informed that the wife has now adjusted her pleadings to seek orders from the court setting aside both these documents. This further information merely serves to confirm that this property still remains a subject of dispute between the parties and one which might more conveniently be resolved in a Scottish rather than a French court.

For all these reasons we can find nothing in the husband's four main grounds of appeal, argued before us in such careful detail by senior counsel for the reclaimer, which persuades us that this appeal should be allowed. We consider the Lord Ordinary's approach in this case was the proper one. He did not err in law and correctly followed the approach laid down by the

A House of Lords in the *de Dampierre* case. We have decided this reclaiming motion on the information that was made available to the Lord Ordinary and the arguments presented to him when he heard and refused the motion for sist in September 1991. We need only add that had we decided that he had erred in exercising his discretion and that we required to consider the matter anew in the light of up to date information, we ourselves would have refused to sist the wife's action in Scotland. We need not rehearse the further information provided to us, although some of it has already been referred to in this opinion. We were informed by

B senior counsel for the respondent that the wife has not lived in France for about six months but has lived in England and Scotland at various addresses and has as yet no fixed abode. We were told by senior counsel for the respondent that a draft, unsigned and undated affidavit shown to us by senior counsel for the reclaimer regarding his wife's recent residence, was inaccurate. We were further informed that the most recent electoral roll and community charge roll indicated that the husband resided at "The Whitehouse".

C In addition senior counsel for the respondent submitted that whilst the wife could speak some French it would be difficult for her to understand the language in French court proceedings and that as the natural language of both parties was English, it was more appropriate that the divorce proceedings should take place in a Scottish court. That was a further factor we would have taken into account had we required to consider the motion de novo but we accept the contention of senior counsel for the reclaimer that it was not a

D factor argued before the Lord Ordinary.

On the whole matter we therefore refuse the reclaiming motion and adhere to the Lord Ordinary's interlocutor of 27 September 1991.

Counsel for Pursuer and Respondent, McGhie, QC, J J Mitchell; Solicitors, Morton Fraser Milligan, WS — Counsel for Defender and Reclaimer, Sutherland, QC, Dorrian; Solicitors, Drummond Miller, WS.

E

[The defender sought and was refused leave to appeal to the House of Lords.]

M C G

EFT Commercial Ltd v
F # Security Change Ltd (No 1)

FIRST DIVISION
THE LORD PRESIDENT (HOPE),
LORDS WEIR AND CAPLAN

8 MAY 1992

Contract — Construction — Lease of moveables — Term enabling lessor to terminate lease in event of receiver being appointed to lessee — Term providing that on any such termination certain sums would become payable by lessee — Whether penalty clause — Whether enforceable.

G Lessors leased an item of printing equipment to a limited company. A guarantee was granted in respect of the performance of the lessee's obligations under the lease. The lease agreement was subject to certain standard terms and conditions. Amongst these terms was a provision which enabled the lessors to terminate the agreement by notice in writing to the lessee in the event of, inter alia, a receiver being appointed to it. A receiver was appointed to the lessee and the lessors gave written notice terminating the lease agreement in reliance upon that provision. The consequences of ter-

H mination were the subject of further provisions by which the lessee became due to pay certain sums to the lessors as agreed compensation for loss of profit. The lessee failed to pay the sums sought and the lessors sued the guarantors for the sums in terms of their guarantee. The guarantors refused to pay, arguing that the provision for payment of these sums amounted to a penalty and was unenforceable. The lessors argued that the sums due to them by the lessee were due as the result of the occurrence of a particular specified event which entitled them to terminate the lease, and not as a result

I of breach of that agreement. The sums sued for were accordingly not damages for breach of contract, but payments agreed to be due in terms of the lease in respect of the events which had occurred, and therefore not a penalty. The Lord Ordinary held that as the event which gave rise to liability to pay was not a breach of contract by the lessee, the law concerning penalty clauses did not apply. The guarantors reclaimed.

Held, (1) that it was well settled in both Scotland and England that the rules about the unenforceability of J penalty clauses applied only to cases of breach of contract (pp 133B, 134F and I-J and 135A-B); (2) that there was a distinction to be drawn between payments which a party undertook to make on a specified event, which were enforceable, and payments which he undertook to make on a breach of contract, which could be looked at to see if they constituted a penalty and were therefore unenforceable (pp 133D-F, 134K-L and 135F-K); and reclaiming motion *refused*.

Granor Finance Ltd v Liquidator of Eastore Ltd, 1974 K SLT 296, *followed*.

Action of payment

EFT Commercial Ltd raised an action of payment against (first) Security Change Ltd and (second) Gresham House plc as guarantors for a limited company, Financial and General Print Ltd, which was L lessee under a lease of printing machinery from the pursuers, following the appointment of a receiver to the lessee. The case came before the Lord Ordinary (Coulsfield) on procedure roll when the pursuers challenged the relevancy of the defences and the defenders argued that the provision in question was unenforceable.

Terms of lease

The following narrative is taken from the opinion of the Lord Ordinary:

The lease is contained in a standard printed form. It
A specifies the equipment which was the subject of the
lease and states the cash price of that equipment as
£610,000. Clause 2 of the lease provides, inter alia:

"The lessee agrees: (a) to pay to the lessor on or
before the date of agreement the first rental (if any) and
to pay all the primary rentals on the due dates during
the primary period as specified in the schedule . . . (b)
to pay to the lessor interest by way of additional rentals
on all rentals and insurance premiums (if any) and on
all other sums payable under this agreement which are
B not paid on the due date at the per annum rate of 5%
over Clydesdale Bank base rate calculated on a day to
day basis . . . (g) that if at the end of the primary period
the whole terms and conditions of this agreement have
been complied with and all payments whether of
rentals, insurance premiums (if any) or otherwise have
been paid and if secondary rentals have been specified
in the schedule, then the lessee at its option may continue the hire for the secondary period and will be
deemed to have done so unless at least 3 months prior
C to the end of the primary period the lessee shall have
served written notice on the lessor stating that the lease
will terminate at the end of the primary period".

The primary period, in this case, was 120 months
and the first rental was £29,029.90 payable on the date
of agreement; this was to be followed by 39 quarterly
rentals of £29,029.90 payable on the appropriate day of
each quarter, commencing on 1 July 1990. It was
further provided that there should be a secondary
D period of five years, commencing on 1 April 2000, and
that the secondary rental should be £3,050.00 per
annum.

Clause 8 of the lease is headed "Termination" and
provides, inter alia, by subcl (e), that if the lessee, being
a company, shall have a receiver appointed the lessor
may, without prejudice to any other rights under the
lease or claims for breach of it, immediately and absolutely terminate the agreement and/or the hiring under
it by notice in writing to the lessee. Clause 8 also
E permits the lessor to terminate the lease by notice on
the occurrence of a number of other events including
failure to pay any rent on the due date, any breach by
the lessee of the terms and conditions of the agreement,
any diligence permitted to be done against the assets of
the lessee, the death of the lessee, the cancellation of
insurance or any risk which in the opinion of the lessor
may result in the equipment passing from the control
of the lessee.

F Clause 9 is headed "Consequences of Termination"
and provides, inter alia that if the lessor terminates the
agreement under cl 8 the lessee's right to retain the
goods shall cease and the lessee shall pay to the lessor
a sum equal to the total of arrears of rental and other
payments due, costs and expenses incurred by the
lessor in recovering possession of the goods, an amount
certified by the lessor as compensation for breaking
fixed deposits or re-employing funds, certain other
sums calculated by reference to the effect of capital
allowances and other matters relating to taxation upon
the payments due under the lease; and an amount

defined in subcl (b) (iv) as follows: "as agreed compensation for the lessor's loss of profit, the total of all G
rentals (including VAT) and insurance premiums (if
any) which would have been payable during the
unexpired primary period of this agreement together
with the first secondary rental (if any) discounted at
5% per annum on a day to day basis compounded
quarterly".

Clause 9 (b) further provides that in determining the
sum payable by the lessee there shall be deducted from
the total of the sums above summarised, "if the goods
are recovered by the lessor, the net proceeds of sale of H
the goods (if any) provided that where no such sale is
effected within a period of 3 months from the date of
termination there shall be substituted the value which
would be placed on the goods after any repairs required
under paragraph (b) (ii) of this Clause had been carried
out as determined by a dealer appointed for the
purpose of such valuation by the lessor".

Clause 9 (c) provides: "that the amount payable
under Clause 9 (b) above shall in the case of termination by the lessor be recoverable as liquidate damages I
and the whole provisions of this Clause 9 shall remain
in full force and effect notwithstanding termination of
this agreement".

Cases referred to
Apex Supply Co Ltd, Re [1942] Ch 108.
Bell Brothers (HP) Ltd v Aitken, 1939 SLT 453; 1939
SC 577.
*Bernstein (Philip) (Successors) Ltd v Lydiate Textiles
Ltd*, CA, 26 June 1982, unreported. J
Bridge v Campbell Discount Co Ltd [1962] AC 600;
[1962] 2 WLR 439; [1962] 1 All ER 385.
Chester & Cole v Wright, unreported, referred to in *Re
Apex Supply Co Ltd*, supra, at p 119.
*Clydebank Engineering and Shipbuilding Co Ltd v Don
Jose Ramos Yzquierdo y Castaneda* (1904) 12 SLT
498; (sub nom *Castaneda v Clydebank Engineering
and Shipbuilding Co Ltd*) 1904 7F (HL) 77.
Craig v McBeath (1863) 1M 1020.
Dunlop Pneumatic Tyre Co Ltd v New Garage and K
Motor Co Ltd [1915] AC 79.
Elsey & Co Ltd v Hyde, unreported, referred to in *Re
Apex Supply Co Ltd*, supra, at pp 116-117.
*Export Credits Guarantee Dept v Universal Oil Products
Co* [1983] 1 WLR 399; [1983] 2 All ER 205.
Gatty v Maclaine, 1921 1 SLT 51; 1921 SC (HL) 1.
Granor Finance Ltd v Liquidator of Eastore Ltd, 1974
SLT 296.
Home v Hepburn (1549) Mor 10033.
Robertson v Driver's Trs (1881) 8R 555. L

Textbooks referred to
Bell, *Commentaries*, i, 699-700.
Stair, *Institutions*, I x 14 and IV xviii 3.

On 2 October 1991 the Lord Ordinary *issued* an
opinion concluding that the pursuers' plea fell to be
sustained and *put out* the case by order to permit adjustment of the amount of the decree to follow thereon.

The defenders reclaimed.

Reclaiming motion

A   The reclaiming motion was heard by the First Division on 26 and 27 March 1992.

On 8 May 1992 the court *refused* the reclaiming motion.

THE LORD PRESIDENT (HOPE).—This is a reclaiming motion by the defenders against an interlocutor in which the Lord Ordinary pronounced decree for payment by the defenders to the pursuers of a sum

B   due under a guarantee. The pursuers had leased an item of printing equipment to Financial and General Print Ltd under a lease agreement in which the pursuers were referred to as the lessor and that company was referred to as the lessee. The lease agreement was subject to certain terms and conditions which were set out on a standard printed form. Amongst these terms and conditions was a provision in cl 8 which enabled the pursuers to terminate the agreement by notice in writing to the lessee in the event inter alia of the lessee

C   becoming apparently insolvent or, in addition to various other such events, having a receiver appointed to the company. On 17 December 1990, following the appointment of an administrative receiver to the lessee, the pursuers terminated the lease agreement by serving a notice of termination in reliance upon that clause. The consequences of termination under cl 8 were the subject of further provisions set out in cl 9. This clause provided that, upon the agreement being terminated by the lessor, the lessee was to pay to the lessor upon

D   demand a sum which was to include, in addition to arrears of rentals and insurance premiums and the expenses of recovering possession of the goods and certain other items, an amount which was described in subcl (b) (iv) in these terms: [his Lordship quoted the terms of cl 9 (b) (iv) set out supra and continued:] In terms of cl 9 (c) it was agreed that the amount payable under cl 9 (b) was, in the case of termination by the lessor, to be recoverable as liquidate damages.

E   The defenders bound themselves jointly and severally to guarantee to the pursuers on demand payment, performance and satisfaction of all sums and obligations due and prestable by the lessee. The pursuers sought payment from the administrative receiver of the sum which they calculated to be due to them under cl 9 in consequence of the termination, but the sum demanded was not paid. It was in these circumstances that they then sought payment from the defenders under the guarantee and, following the defenders'

F   refusal to make payment, raised the present action. They were met by the argument that cl 9 (b), and in particular cl 9 (b) (iv), when properly construed, amounted to a penalty and was unenforceable. It was averred in the defences that cl 9 (b) stipulated for a sum which could not have been regarded as a genuine preestimate of the approximate loss which the termination of the agreement was likely to have caused to the pursuers. The pursuers' response to this argument was that the sums due to them by the lessee were due as the result of the occurrence of a particular specified event which entitled them to terminate the lease agreement,

and not as a result of breach of that agreement. The

G   sum sued for was accordingly sought not as damages for breach of contract but as a payment agreed to be due in terms of the lease agreement in the events which had occurred. After hearing parties on the procedure roll on the question of relevancy raised in the defences the Lord Ordinary held that the defenders' argument that the clause was unenforceable was unsound, since the event which gave rise to the liability to pay was not a breach of contract by the lessee and the law concerning penalty clauses did not apply in this case. He sustained

H   the pursuers' plea in law to the effect that the defences were irrelevant, and at a later date he granted decree de plano for a sum agreed by the parties to be due in that event.

The question raised in this case is of some general interest, but like the Lord Ordinary I think that it can be reduced to a quite narrow compass and that in the end there is no doubt about the principles which must be applied. On the one hand there is the principle that it is the function of the court to enforce contracts according to the bargain which the parties have made   I

for themselves. It is not for the court to interfere in order to modify a bargain which one of the parties later considers to be unfair. As Lord Birkenhead LC said in *Gatty v Maclaine*, 1921 SLT at p 54: "It would be both undesirable and dangerous that courts of law should set up an elastic, and, from the nature of the case, an undefinable judicial discretion in substitution for the expressed agreement of the parties to the instrument".

On the other there is the principle which distin-   J

guishes a penalty from liquidated damages — the question being whether the sum which the party seeks to recover is an agreed sum of damages or, in the words of Lord Halsbury LC in *Clydebank Engineering & Shipbuilding Co Ltd v Don Jose Ramos Yzquierdo y Castaneda* (1904) 12 SLT at p 498: "is simply a penalty to be held over the other party in terrorem — whether it is what I think gave the jurisdiction to the courts in both countries to interfere at all in an agreement between the parties — unconscionable and extravagant   K

— and one which no court ought to allow to be enforced?"

The defenders' contention is that the principle that a sum in the nature of a penalty is not recoverable is not confined to cases of breach of contract. A penalty, they say, is a punishment, and on their averments the sum payable under cl 9 (b) (iv) amounts to a punishment and ought not to be enforced. This argument was rejected by the Lord Ordinary after a consideration of both Scottish and English authority.   L

The first case to mention is *Granor Finance Ltd v Liquidator of Eastore Ltd* since, as the Lord Ordinary pointed out, it is indistinguishable from the present case on its facts. The agreement was one for the hire of certain machinery. It provided that in the event of the hirers going into voluntary liquidation the owners were to be entitled to take repossession of the machinery and that, should they do so, the hirers were then to pay to the owners a sum of money calculated as set forth in the agreement. The liquidator resisted the owners' claim for payment on the ground that on a proper construction of this provision it amounted to an agreement for payment of a penalty and was unenforceable. The owners' argument was, as it has been in the present case, that the chapter of law dealing with the distinction between penalty and liquidated damages had no application since their claim did not arise out of any breach of contract but rested simply on an agreement by the hirers, forming part of the contractual terms, to pay the owners a sum of money, calculated in the stipulated manner, upon the occurrence of a particular event. Lord Keith held that the owners had stated a relevant case for enforceability of the clause. He pointed out that the provision was expressed as intended to take effect in any of three different sets of circumstances, one of which was the occurrence of an event amounting to a breach of contract, in which event the provision could be construed as a penalty and would be unenforceable. But the sum was also expressed to be payable should the hirers exercise their option to terminate the agreement and in the event of its being terminated by the owners in circumstances which did not involve a breach of agreement at all, such as the hirers going into voluntary liquidation. The basis for his decision appears from this passage at p 298: "I am unable to accept that the law about penalty and liquidated damages has any application in a case which is not a case of breach of contract, and I consider that *Bell Brothers (HP) Ltd v Aitken* is authority binding upon me for the view that it has no such application. I can see no distinction, for this purpose, between the situation where the provision in question is sought to be applied following the exercise by the hirer of an option to terminate the contract, and that where it is sought to be applied in other circumstances not involving breach of contract".

It is clear that, if that case was correctly decided, the same approach must be taken to this case and that the Lord Ordinary was right to hold that the defenders' contention that the clause in question here amounts to a penalty is irrelevant.

Counsel for the defenders sought to persuade us that the decision in *Bell Brothers (HP) Ltd v Aitken* had not been correctly analysed by Lord Keith in *Granor Finance Ltd,* and that on its true ratio it was not to be taken as authority for the proposition that the law about penalty clauses had no application to cases other than breach of contract. It was pointed out that this was the only Scottish case which was referred to by Lord Keith in his opinion. Absent from his discussion were a number of earlier Scottish authorities which, it was said, showed that the only question for inquiry was whether the sum which had been stipulated for could be regarded as a penalty. If it could be so regarded, then it was not recoverable.

The point at issue in *Bell Brothers (HP) Ltd* was not precisely the same as that which arose in *Granor Finance Ltd,* but it does not seem to me that Lord Keith misunderstood its effect. That was a case where the event which gave rise to the owners' claim for payment was the exercise by the hirer of his option to terminate

the hiring of a motor car before the end of the period of hiring. It was held that the clause was to be regarded, in that event, as laying down expressly the financial conditions upon which the hirer could return the car to its owner before the due date, and accordingly that no question of penalty or liquidated damages arose. Counsel submitted that the ratio of this decision was that the hirer in that case was exercising a personal privilege, the consideration for which was payment of the sum which had been stipulated to be payable if that option was exercised. The present case on the other hand was one where the termination had taken place at the option of the owner, over whose actions the hirer had no choice or control and from which he had derived no advantage. It was accepted that the decision in *Bell* was correct on its own facts. But it was emphasised that the crucial point in the case was that the hirer could exercise control over the event which gave rise to the liability to payment, and that accordingly the whole matter was at his option. The point of this distinction was that, while a payment which was at the hirer's option could not be described as a penalty, that description could properly be applied to a sum payable in an event over which the hirer had no control. We were referred to the last paragraph of the opinion of Lord President Normand at 1939 SLT, p 462 and to the following passage in Lord Moncrieff's opinion at p 464: "Where a hirer contracts in favour of himself for a personal privilege which, as such a privilege, is the only subject of regulation as to its terms, it is idle to say that these terms are penal because similar or even identical terms are conditioned as applying to the wholly different question of what award of damages shall follow on a breach of contract".

It is true that none of the judges in *Bell Brothers (HP) Ltd* said anything about the situation which has arisen in this case, which is a termination not by the hirer but by the owner in circumstances where no breach of contract has taken place. But the only circumstances in which the liquidated damages were agreed to be payable in that case were the event of the hirer returning the vehicle to the owners in the exercise of his option to do so, and the event of the owner retaking possession of the vehicle on default in payment of the rent or the hirer's failure to observe any of the stipulations of the agreement — that is, in the event of the hirer's breach of contract. The dicta to which we were referred must be read according to the facts of that case. The view which Lord Keith took of the decision is that no distinction could be drawn between cases where the provision for payment was sought to be applied following the exercise by the hirer of an option to terminate and where it was sought to be applied in any other circumstances not involving breach of contract. It seems to me, with respect, that he was right to see that case as authority for the view that the rule about penalty and liquidated damages does not apply in a case which is not a case of breach of contract. In any event it is significant that nowhere in *Bell Brothers (HP) Ltd* is it stated that the rule is not confined in its application to cases of breach of contract but applies generally to all cases where the sum payable is said to amount to a penalty.

Nor am I persuaded that the more general principle
A for which the defenders contended has ever been
accepted as part of Scots law. Reference was made to
Stair, I x 14 and IV xviii 3 and to Bell's *Commentaries*,
i, 699-700 where there is some discussion about the
power vested in the court for mitigating penalties and,
as Bell puts it, "reducing them to the actual or probable
amount of such damage". These passages did not seem
to me to provide any support for the defenders' argument, and Bell's comments in regard to penalties in the
context of money obligations are at least consistent
B with the view that the court can intervene only in cases
where there is an obligation to pay damages upon a
breach of contract such as a failure to pay on the due
date. But the defenders relied for their argument principally upon the opinions of Lord Justice Clerk Inglis
in *Craig v McBeath* at p 1022 and of Lord Young in
Robertson v Driver's Trs at p 562.

In *Craig v McBeath*, the passage at p 1022 to which
our attention was drawn was one in which Lord Justice
Clerk Inglis said this: "Perhaps it is somewhat
C inaccurate to call such sums by the name of penalty,
because, properly speaking, a penalty is a punishment,
and nothing can be clearer than this, that parties are
not entitled to make punishment the subject of agreement. Parties cannot lawfully enter into an agreement
that the one party shall be punished at the suit of the
other."

This was said to be authority for the broad proposition that no sum which can be regarded as a penalty can
D be recovered, whatever the circumstances in which it
has been agreed that the sum is to be paid. But the significance of the passage is to be found in its context,
which was a claim for breach of contract. This can be
seen from a passage which immediately precedes the
words which I have just quoted, which is in these
terms: "And the first question is, whether this penalty
is in truth, not a penalty in the proper sense of the term,
but liquidate damage agreed to be taken to be the
amount of loss in the event of breach of contract, and
E therefore not subject to modification by the court. I
think this sum is not liquidate damage, but that it is a
penalty of that kind which we are bound to modify to
the actual loss if duly required by the defender to do
so."

As I understand his opinion, Lord Justice Clerk
Inglis then went on, in the words on which the
defenders now rely, to explain the principle which he
had just expressed. I do not think that it was his inten-
F tion to affirm a principle of more general application
which could be invoked in circumstances other than a
breach of contract. This can be seen from a comment
later on the same page where he said that the question
in such cases resolves itself into this: "whether the sum
stipulated to be paid in the event of breach of contract
is liquidate damage, or merely represents the general
agreement that a money payment shall be made to the
extent of the damage caused by breach of contract". A
similar comment is to be found in the opinion of Lord
Benholme at p 1024. In *Robertson v Driver's Trs* the
argument was about a deduction from the contract

price of an agreed sum for each day the work remained
unfinished after the date stipulated for completion of G
the contract for repairs and alterations. Lord Young
said at p 562: "Where there is a distinct time bargain
and a stipulation by the parties that if the contractor
fail to complete the contract within the time distinctly
limited, he shall be liable for a certain sum of money
for every day or week during which it remains incomplete, the court will generally give effect to that bargain
if it be reasonable that damages be paid. But if, again,
the penalty be truly a penalty — that is, a punishment
— the court will not allow that, because the law will not H
let people punish each other."

Here again the passage relied on seems to me to be
directed to the question whether the sum stipulated to
be payable for a breach of contract was to be regarded
as a penalty. The broad proposition that the law will
not let people punish each other is made only by way
of explanation of the rule about penalty and liquidated
damages, and is not to be read as laying down a
principle that the court will always intervene in any
case where a stipulation in a contract appears to it to I
be in the nature of a penalty.

Accordingly I do not find anything in these passages
to support the proposition which was contended for by
the defenders that the rule applies to a case which is not
one of breach of contract. On the contrary, the reference by Lord Justice Clerk Inglis to the function of the
court as being to modify the sum to the actual loss
seems to me to confine the application of the rule to
those cases where there is an underlying obligation to J
pay damages. If the defenders' argument were to be
accepted in the present case the only course open to us
would be to hold the provision in question to be void
and unenforceable. We would have no basis for substituting any other figure as the amount to be paid by
the defenders, since the event which gave rise to the
claim for payment was not one which could be said to
have created an obligation to pay any other sum except
that stipulated for in the contract. I do not think that
Lord Justice Clerk Inglis had in contemplation a case K
where the provision in question was agreed to be
payable in the event of a rescission of the contract in
circumstances not inferring a breach of contract to
which the ordinary rules for the quantification of
damages could not apply.

Senior counsel for the defenders said that we should
not allow the pursuers to attempt by their contract to
circumvent what he described as the court's undoubted
equitable control over the terms of a contract. His point
was that the principle was in danger of being narrowed L
down to a point where contracts could be drawn so as
to avoid the court's equitable control over penalty
clauses in cases of breach of contract. He invited us to
look to the substance of the contract and not its form.
In my opinion, however, that argument must be
rejected both on the narrow ground that it has no basis
on the facts of this case and on the wider ground that
it is inconsistent with the principles which have confined the rule to cases of breach of contract.

On the narrow point it is sufficient to say that there

is no hint in the defenders' pleadings that the event which gave rise to termination in this case was properly to be described as a breach of contract. Some of the events referred to in cl 9, such as failure to pay in full any rental and the lessee's breach of any of the terms and conditions of the agreement, could no doubt be so described. But we are dealing in this case with an event which, quite independently of any question of breach of contract, has entitled the lessor to terminate the agreement, and there is no question here of any attempt having been made to treat a breach of contract as being something else. On the broader point, I consider that it is now well settled that the rule about penalty and liquidated damages applies only to cases of breach of contract. The argument of senior counsel for the defenders, if accepted, would open up contracts to modification at the hand of the court in a manner which cannot be reconciled with the other principle to which I referred earlier in this opinion, that contracts are to be enforced according to the agreement which the parties have made for themselves. I agree with the Lord Ordinary that to accept the defenders' argument would involve a very considerable inroad upon the principle of freedom of contract. Difficulties to which the defenders provided no satisfactory answer would arise if the court were to attempt to compare the sum payable under the contract on the occurrence of a specified event not amounting to a breach of contract with any loss or harm that has actually been sustained. These problems seem to me to confirm the desirability of confining the rule to the limited case of breach of contract to which it has always been applied.

An examination of the English cases, some of which were mentioned by Lord Keith in *Granor Finance Ltd,* confirms this approach. In *Dunlop Pneumatic Tyre Co Ltd v New Garage and Motor Co Ltd* at pp 86-87, Lord Dunedin set out the various propositions on this branch of the law which were deducible from the authorities. Among these was the dictum of Lord Halsbury LC in the *Clydebank* case, supra. I do not need to quote these propositions, because the only point about them which is significant for the purposes of this discussion is that it is clear from the way in which they were framed by Lord Dunedin that the only situation which he had in mind as being one in which the court must find out whether the payment stipulated is in truth a penalty or liquidated damages was that of breach of contract. In *Re Apex Supply Co Ltd* Simonds J held that the question whether the sum claimed was a penalty or liquidated damages did not arise because it was agreed to be payable in the event of the termination of the agreement on the liquidation of the hiring company. That case is of importance for present purposes, because it cannot be distinguished on its facts from *Granor Finance Ltd* or from the present case. If we were to sustain the defenders' argument it would have to be in recognition of there being a difference on this matter from the approach which has been taken in England. But I see no justification for recognising any such difference.

In reaching his decision Simonds J followed dicta in several unreported cases, the material parts of which

are set out in his opinion. The passages which he quoted at pp 116-117 from Salter J in *Elsey & Co Ltd v Hyde* and at p 119 from Greer LJ's opinion in *Chester & Cole v Wright* seem to me to contain nothing which is inconsistent with the Scottish approach. It is sufficient to quote from the opinion of Greer LJ where he said: "There is no reason in law why, for a sufficient consideration, there should not be on the same document, two contracts, one a contract to hire the motor car on the terms of the agreement, and another, a contract that if that contract comes to an end, then a certain sum will be payable by the hirer; and it may very well be that the view which is, I think, the view of Salter J, in *Elsey & Co Ltd v Hyde,* which was cited before us, is the right way to look at this clause, namely, that it is not either liquidated damages or a penalty, but it is a sum payable in respect of one event, namely, the determination and end of the hiring agreement, whether that end of the hiring agreement arises from the hirer delivering the car back again, or whether it arises from the owner taking it out of the possession of the hirer in the events in which he is entitled to take it out."

The distinction between payments which by the terms of the contract a party undertakes to make on a specified event and payments which he undertakes to make on a breach of a contract were the subject of comment in *Bridge v Campbell Discount Co* [1962] AC, by Lord Denning at p 631 and Lord Devlin at p 634 on the ground, as Lord Denning put it, that it is a paradox that equity will grant relief to a man who breaks his contract but will penalise the man who keeps it. But, as Lord Keith in *Granor Finance* pointed out, their views were not shared by the other peers who contributed to the decision and it seemed to him that their reasoning was based on English principles of equity which are not familiar in Scotland.

Furthermore, the position in England was put beyond doubt in *Export Credits Guarantee Department v Universal Oil Products Co* [1983] 1 WLR, where at p 403H Lord Roskill, with whom all their Lordships agreed, said: "My Lords, one purpose, perhaps the main purpose, of the law relating to penalty clauses is to prevent a plantiff recovering a sum of money in respect of a breach of contract committed by a defendant which bears little or no relationship to the loss actually suffered by the plaintiff as a result of the breach by the defendant. But it is not and never has been for the courts to relieve a party from the consequences of what may in the event prove to be an onerous or possibly even a commercially imprudent bargain."

He concluded his opinion at p 404C with this quotation from the opinion of Diplock LJ, as he then was, in an unreported decision of the Court of Appeal in *Philip Bernstein (Successors) Ltd v Lydiate Textiles Ltd:* "I, for my part, am not prepared to extend the law by relieving against an obligation in a contract entered into between two parties which does not fall within the well defined limits in which the court has in the past shown itself willing to interfere."

A In my opinion these observations are consistent with principles which are well settled in Scotland, and I am satisfied that these principles ought not to be disturbed.

For these reasons I would refuse this reclaiming motion and adhere to the interlocutor of the Lord Ordinary.

LORD WEIR.—This case is concerned with the right of the pursuers to terminate their contract and the consequences of the termination to the hirers and, in B this instance, their guarantors who are the defenders and reclaimers. It raises the question whether the agreement must be enforced in accordance with its terms or whether, as the defenders contend, the court has an equitable power to override the financial consequences.

Your Lordship in the chair has set out the relevant provisions of the agreement with which we are concerned. It is claimed by the defenders that cl 9 (b) is a C penalty clause and their argument before us proceeded upon the assumption that this is how it fell to be regarded. On that basis it was contended that there was a general power residing in the court to strike down such a clause or at least modify its rigour.

There is no doubt that the court may exercise its equitable power in relation to a penalty clause where a contract has come to an end as the result of a breach of its terms. The theory behind a penalty clause is that of punishment, and "it is not legal to stipulate for punish-D ment" (*Craig v McBeath*, per Lord Justice Clerk Inglis at p 1022). "The essence of a penalty of money stipulated is in terrorem of the offending party" (*Dunlop Pneumatic Tyre Co Ltd v New Garage and Motor Co Ltd*, per Lord Dunedin at p 86). For there to be punishment there must be a wrongdoer and in this context, the wrongdoer is the person who breaks his contract. Breach of contract gives rise at common law to a claim for damages and there is no difficulty in finding a practicable remedy in substitution for the enforcement E of a penalty clause. Accordingly the principle that a penalty clause may not be enforced because it is illegal to punish someone who is in breach of his contract is very well understood and the operation of the alternative remedy in such circumstances is in principle straightforward.

In the agreement under consideration, termination may come about in a number of stipulated circumstances, only one of which is breach of contract by the hirers. There are other events not involving breach of F contract which may have come about due to circumstances beyond the hirers' control. The event here was the appointment of a receiver to the hirers. It is not averred by the defenders that this event amounted to a breach of contract and the question is whether in the absence of a breach of contract the court has any power to strike down the penalty clause which the pursuers seek to enforce.

In my opinion, the equitable power of the court to intervene is not available if a contract is terminated as the result of an event other than a breach of contract.

It is possible to discern the shadowy outline of a prin- G ciple of wider application in the 16th and 17th centuries (*Home v Hepburn*; Stair, I x 14), but this failed to acquire substance as our mercantile law developed. The dicta of Lord Justice Clerk Inglis and Lord Dunedin, which I have already quoted, were stated only in the context of a breach of contract. There is nothing said in *Bell Brothers (HP) Ltd v Aitken,* on which the defenders strongly founded, to show that the rule on penalty clauses had any application beyond cases of breach of contract. In *Granor Finance Ltd v Liquidator of Eastore Ltd* at p 298, Lord Keith con- H sidered the question in light of both Scottish and English authorities and concluded that the law about penalty and liquidated damages had no application in a case which was not a case of breach of contract. Your Lordship in the chair has analysed the line of authority in some detail and I agree with your Lordship's conclusions. In my opinion there is no Scottish authority to support the wider application of the rule.

In England, where the law is the same (*Dunlop* I *Pneumatic Tyre Co Ltd*) the position is put decisively by Diplock LJ in a passage in the unreported case of *Philip Bernstein (Successors) Ltd v Lydiate Textiles Ltd* which was approved in the House of Lords in *Export Credits Guarantee Department v Universal Oil Products Co* [1983] 1 WLR at p 404: "I, for my part, am not prepared to extend the law by relieving against an obligation in a contract entered into between two parties which does not fall within the well defined limits in which the court has in the past shown itself willing to J interfere."

Counsel for the defenders submitted that the court should not be bound by authority but should approach the matter on a broad basis of principle. It was submitted that if it was wrong to stipulate for punishment against someone who was a wrongdoer by breaching his contract, it was even more unjust to punish the innocent such as a party who had fallen into financial difficulties or was otherwise not in control of the events referred to in the clauses of a contract. While recog- K nising that there may be an anomaly in these circumstances, I do not consider that the court in the absence of clear authority can or should innovate on the law. The fundamental principle is that where a bargain is freely entered into, the parties will be held to its terms. This applies, in my view, when parties have agreed that in the event of termination certain payments will have to be made by one to the other. It may appear that the consequences, should they arise, are unfair to one party but for the court to intervene to strike out or L modify these consequences would amount to it passing judgment on what is a fair bargain. The only exception to the fundamental principle is where there has been a breach of contract and where the common law remedy of damages is available as a substitute for the effects of a penalty clause. If the court was to intervene on the application of a wider principle, it is not clear under what circumstances it should do so, under what rule of law it was doing so, and in what manner and to what extent its powers should be used.

In my opinion the Lord Ordinary reached the right decision for the right reasons and I agree that the reclaiming motion should be refused.

LORD CAPLAN.—I agree entirely with the views expressed by your Lordship in the chair. Under our common law it is well established that generally the court will not intervene to reform parties' bargains on the ground that they may be unduly disadvantageous to one of the parties. In a limited category of cases the court may exercise a degree of equitable control. For example such control will in certain circumstances be exercised in relation to an agreed provision for payment of a penalty or liquidate damages upon a breach of contract, to the operation of irritancies, and to the forfeiture of vested rights in property. The older authorities we were referred to clearly relate to such restricted category of situations. The reclaimers did not contest the appellants' right to terminate the contract under cl 8 of the leasing agreement which on one view may be regarded as providing for an irritancy. Rather they challenged the validity of cl 9 (b) of the leasing agreement which provides for payment by the lessee of certain sums in the event of the lessor terminating the agreement under cl 8. No question of loss of vested property rights arises in this case. At one point the reclaimers appeared to argue that cl 8 in effect provides that each of the events which would give rise to a right on the part of the lessor to terminate the leasing agreement was to be regarded as being essentially a breach of contract. However this will not do. Thus for example cl 8 (b) differentiates quite clearly between a breach of any term and condition of the leasing agreement and a breach of any other such agreement (which latter event would also give rise to a right to terminate). There is a clear difference between the effect of an event merely giving a right to terminate the contract and a breach of the contract. Thus for example in the latter situation alone the party relying upon a breach may be able to continue with the contract and also claim damages.

The reclaimers therefore are thrown back on the contention that the principles governing the court's regulation of stipulations for the payment of a penalty or liquidated damages upon a breach of contract must extend to any case where there is an agreed provision for payment of an amount of compensation which can be regarded as penal. It was suggested that a contract would not be open to judicial scrutiny if it provided for a payment upon the exercise of a privilege. However it was said that a payment due as a result of a right to terminate at the lessor's hand fell to be regarded differently from a payment due as the consideration payable upon the exercise of a privilege. It was contended that any payment due to the lessor as compensation for the termination of the agreement must be regarded as equivalent to pactional damages in every respect.

In my view the cases concerning the regulation of conventional penalties or liquidate damages upon a breach of contract relate to a situation which is essentially different to that raised by this case. In a case where there has been a material breach of contract the aggrieved party has a right to terminate the contract and has an established right under the law to recover damages. The authorities show that the courts regard it as unacceptable that, a breach of contract having occurred, the parties should substitute for the established common law remedy of damages a remedy requiring payment of a sum totally disproportionate in measure to the appropriate legal compensation. In such a situation the party who imposes a provision for recovery of a payment is not seeking to facilitate the recovery of true compensation but rather is attempting to ensure performance of the contract by the introduction of exorbitantly penal provisions which would take effect upon breach. The only question for the court is to assess the true objective of the provision for liquidate damages and in performing this task the court can pay regard to the proper measure of damages. This measure can be assessed on the basis of well established principles. If the court regards the agreed arrangements for damages as unacceptable the effect of the court's intervention is to restrict recovery to the proper amount of damages. A question has regularly been discussed by the courts (particularly in England) as to whether the exercise of a conventional provision for termination of a contract in circumstances which amount to a breach of contract may take the case out of the general rule regarding liquidate damages, but that is not the issue which concerns us.

Where the contract provides the obligor with an option to terminate it on the happening of an event which is not breach of contract and to recover a sum of money in consequence the provision cannot be equated with a provision for liquidate damages upon a breach of contract. This applies in whatever terms the conventional payment is described in the contract. The parties are not seeking to provide remedies alternative to, and more onerous than, those provided by the processes of law, because upon termination of a contract on the occurrence of an event not amounting to breach no provision for compensation exists other than that agreed by the parties themselves. Since compensation arises only by agreement the court has no measure to apply to test what should be the proper level of compensation. It cannot be assumed that agreed compensation is intended to reflect or should reflect the damages which would be recoverable upon breach of contract. For example the obligor may when fixing the rate of rent due under a leasing agreement take into account the level of compensation which would be payable under the agreement should the agreement require to be terminated prematurely. Moreover the judicial intervention required by the reclaimers is not that the court should confine parties to the proper measure of compensation (because there is no such measure in non-breach of contract cases) but effectively that the court should hold that the compensation stipulation is null and void. In this case condition 8 of the leasing agreement (the lessor's right to terminate) and condition 9 (the consequences of termination) are set out in separate contractual clauses but I am not sure that it is realistic to regard them as being totally independent of

A one another. When deciding whether or not to terminate the contract the lessor will look at the whole package and take account of the agreement on the compensation he is to receive. If that agreement were not effective he would receive no compensation at all and the consequences of the specified event occurring would be quite different to what was agreed. When the lessor terminates the contract he may not know if his right to receive compensation is to be challenged. The termination and compensation provisions will in some contracts appear in the one clause. Thus if the

B reclaimers are in effect contending that the court will not enforce contractual terms which have an unduly penal effect it is not inconceivable that in another case a lessee could challenge the validity of the lessor's right to terminate the contract on the basis that this would impose upon the lessee an obligation to pay an exorbitant amount of compensation.

This highlights the difference between the present case and the liquidate damages cases where no question of a right to terminate would arise and the only issue

C relates to the amount of damages to be recovered. What the reclaimers are here seeking is not the application of established principles of law but a material extension of these principles which has no warrant in authority. Indeed essentially what the reclaimers are saying here is that the agreed reservation by the lessors of the right to terminate the contract in certain events not in themselves breaches of contract and on certain compensation terms is an unreasonable stipulation because it is unduly harsh on the lessee. As I have already said it is

D quite clear that under our common law the court will not interfere with contractual terms merely because they may be unfair or disadvantageous to one or other of the parties. I think it has to be acknowledged that in practice the difference between the rights available on a breach of contract and the rights which may be available by agreement in other circumstances can give rise to anomalies. However the court must apply the law as it stands.

In my view the approach taken by the Lord Ordinary

E was quite correct and for that reason the reclaiming motion falls to be dismissed.

Counsel for Pursuers and Respondents, M G Clarke, QC, Peoples; Solicitors, Morton Fraser Milligan, WS — Counsel for Defenders and Reclaimers, Haddow QC, Boyd; Solicitors, Biggart Baillie & Gifford.

D A K

F [An appeal to the House of Lords has been presented.]

Boots the Chemist Ltd v G A Estates Ltd

G

SECOND DIVISION

THE LORD JUSTICE CLERK (ROSS),
LORDS MURRAY AND GRIEVE

12 JUNE 1992

Damages — Interest on damages — Reparation — Date from which interest to run on loss from non-personal injuries — Principles applicable — Interest on Damages (Scotland) Act 1958 (6 & 7 Eliz II, c 61), s 1 (1).

H

Section 1 (1) of the Interest on Damages (Scotland) Act 1958, as amended, empowers a court, when awarding damages, to award interest on the whole or part of the principal sum for the whole or part of any period between the date when the right of action arose and the date of the award.

An action of damages based on negligence and nuisance and arising out of flood damage suffered in 1984 was signeted in 1987 and settled in about March 1991. Under a joint minute agreement was reached on various heads of loss sustained on particular dates. The parties submitted to the determination of the court the matter of interest on the various sums.

I

It was argued for the pursuers that s 1 (1) of the 1958 Act permitted the court to award interest from the date when the right of action arose, being when damnum and injuria occurred and that the amendment made by the Interest on Damages (Scotland) Act 1971 had altered the emphasis of the section which now required the court to ascertain if there was a reason not to award interest from the date when the action arose. They further argued that the expenditure of money in the present case by the pursuers was analogous to their having lost an interest bearing chattel or something which otherwise would have secured a profit for them. The defenders contended that the rate of interest and the period for which it was awarded should be restricted. No judicial demand had been made of the defenders until the summons called early in 1988. Despite requests, the defenders had not been provided with the full detailed claim until five years after the event. The defenders argued that any award should be at a rate less than the judicial rate. They also argued that interest should not run until, at earliest, the date of citation and in fact not until the amount of loss had been established by the joint minute.

J

K

The Lord Ordinary awarded interest on loss of stock from the date of citation to the date of decree, and on the remaining items from the dates on which the expenditure had been incurred, at the judicial rate prevailing at the time. The defenders reclaimed.

L

Held, (1) that a pursuer might recover interest by way of damages where he was deprived of an interest bearing security or a profit producing chattel or where money had been wrongfully withheld (p 143B-D); (2) that even if damages had not been quantified, interest might reasonably be held to run from a date when the

A damages might reasonably be regarded as quantifiable or capable of ascertainment, and that from that date the wrongdoer could reasonably be regarded as wrongfully withholding the damages (p 143H); and (3) that in the absence of special circumstances, inordinate delay in prosecuting an action should not result in a pursuer being deprived of interest on items of damages which were capable of being ascertained and in respect of which expenditure had been incurred by the injured party (p 144E-G); and reclaiming motion *refused*.

B
Action of damages
Boots the Chemist Ltd raised an action against G A Estates Ltd. Messrs Thorburn Associates were called as third party.

Prior to proof the Lord Ordinary (Lord Cameron of Lochbroom) was advised that settlement had taken place as respects the principal sums claimed on the basis of a joint minute of admissions. The Lord Ordinary was addressed on the question of interest on damages.

C

Statutory provisions
The Interest on Damages (Scotland) Act 1958, as originally enacted, provided:

"1.—(1) Where the court having jurisdiction in any action for damages pronounces an interlocutor decerning for payment by any person of a sum of money as damages, the interlocutor may, if the circumstances D warrant such a course, include decree for payment by that person of interest on the sum or any part thereof at such rate as may be specified in the interlocutor, from such date as may be so specified (being a date not earlier than the date on which the action was commenced against that person) until the date of the interlocutor."

The 1958 Act, as amended by the Interest on Damages (Scotland) Act 1971, provides:

E "1.—(1) Where a court pronounces an interlocutor decerning for payment by any person of a sum of money as damages, the interlocutor may include decree for payment by that person of interest, at such rate or rates as may be specified in the interlocutor, on the whole or any part of that sum for the whole or any part of the period between the date when the right of action arose and the date of the interlocutor.

"(1A) Where a court pronounces an interlocutor F decerning for payment of a sum which consists of or includes damages or solatium in respect of personal injuries sustained by the pursuer or any other person, then (without prejudice to the exercise of the power conferred by subsection (1) of this section in relation to any part of that sum which does not represent such damages or solatium) the court shall exercise that power so as to include in that sum interest on those damages and on that solatium or on such part of each as the court considers appropriate, unless the court is satisfied that there are reasons special to the case why no interest should be given in respect thereof."

Cases referred to
Associated Provincial Picture Houses Ltd v Wednesbury G *Corporation* [1948] 1 KB 223.
Bell's Sports Centre (Perth) Ltd v William Briggs & Sons Ltd, 1971 SLT (Notes) 48.
Buchan v J Marr (Aberdeen) Ltd, 1987 SLT 521.
Buchanan (James) & Co Ltd v Stewart Cameron (Drymen) Ltd, 1973 SLT (Notes) 78; 1973 SC 285.
Carmichael v Caledonian Railway Co (1870) 8 M (HL) 119.
Finnegan v British Gas Corporation, OH, 1 February H 1991, unreported (1991 GWD 9-540).
Fraser v Morton Wilson Ltd, 1966 SLT 22.
Green (F W) & Co Ltd v Brown & Gracie Ltd, 1960 SLT (Notes) 43.
Kolbin & Sons v Kinnear & Co, 1931 SLT 464; 1931 SC (HL) 128.
M & I Instrument Engineers Ltd v Varsada, 1991 SLT 106.
MacRae v Reed & Mallik Ltd, 1961 SLT 96; 1961 SC 68.   I
Nacap Ltd v Moffat Plant Ltd, 1986 SLT 326 (revd on another point 1987 SLT 221).
Osenton (Charles) & Co v Johnston [1942] AC 130.
Twomax Ltd v Dickson, McFarlane & Robinson, 1983 SLT 98; 1984 SLT 424; 1982 SC 113.
Wordie Property Co Ltd v Secretary of State for Scotland, 1984 SLT 345.

Terms of joint minute
The joint minute between the parties was in the fol- J lowing terms, inter alia:

"the parties have agreed and hereby agree that the pursuers suffered the following loss and damage upon the dates hereinafter specified as a result of the flooding of their premises on 3 November 1984 condescended upon upon record:

Head of loss	Sum £	Date incurred
Loss of stock	1,030.28	3 November 1984
Supply and fitting of skirting	310.72	1 January 1985
Honda generator	38.14	15 November 1984
Repair to electrical services	501.00	27 November 1984
Container hoists	165.00	1 January 1985
Additional staff costs	440.16	23 November 1984
Additional shopfitting costs	8,100.28	14 December 1984
Loss of sales	1,874.76	5 November 1984"

K

L

A On 21 June 1991 the Lord Ordinary *pronounced* decree with interest at the judicial rate from the date of citation in respect of the agreed loss of stock claim and from the various agreed dates on which the other heads of loss had been incurred.

LORD CAMERON OF LOCHBROOM.—When this proof was called, I was advised by counsel that settlement had taken place on the basis of a joint minute of admissions. The joint minute sets out that the parties were agreed that [his Lordship summarised

B the terms of the joint minute set out supra and continued:]

The action concerns an incident of flooding from a blocked culvert which occurred at the Cameron Toll shopping centre, Edinburgh, on 3 November 1984. Floodwater entered the premises within the centre, including those let to the pursuers, and caused loss and damage. The present action is one of some 28 claims arising from the flooding. The summons in the present

C action was apparently signeted in November 1987 though it did not call until February 1988. At that time it was directed against the present defenders as the developer of the centre and a second defender, as the owner of the land on which the blocked culvert was situated. The basis of the action was in negligence and in nuisance. The record was initially closed in May 1988 but subsequently restored to the adjustment roll on the pursuers' motion in June 1988. In July 1988 the defenders convened the present third party to the action on the basis of averments of negligence. In

D August 1988 the pursuers abandoned the action so far as laid against the second defenders on condition of no expenses being found due to or by either party. Thereafter the first defenders were blamed in both capacities, as developer and as owner of the land on which the culvert was situated. After sundry procedure in the course of which the pursuers adopted and amplified the defenders' case of fault against the third party, the record was closed in July 1989. It was then sent to the

E procedure roll on the defenders' motion. Thereafter both the pursuers and the defenders amended their pleadings. There was delay until June 1990 in the lodging of the prints of the closed record as amended. A diet of procedure roll debate was fixed for 20 September 1990 but the parties agreed upon a proof before answer. Subsequently the pleadings were further the subject of proposed amendment in February 1991. However, by letters dated 26 and 27 March 1991 the defenders' agents, following discussions with the third party's agents, proposed to the pur-

F suers terms for settlement on the basis of an agreed principal sum and, failing agreement as to the matter of interest, then interest to be subject to the determination of the court. The conclusion of those negotiations give rise to the joint minute of admissions and the present submission of the matter of interest on the various sums comprising the agreed principal sum to the court's determination. Before leaving the history of the case, I note that in the closed record as further amended and printed in June 1990, the sum concluded for is stated to be £50,000 with interest at the rate of

15 per cent from 3 November 1984 until payment. Furthermore, in their averments in art 13 of the con- G descendence the pursuers make general averments of their three principal heads of loss, namely damage to stock, fabric, fixtures and fittings, expenditure incurred for wages and overtime paid to staff and outside contractors to clear the damage and loss of profit suffered from the closure of the premises between 3 and 5 November 1984.

In addition the parties have produced correspondence passing between them relative to the issue of quantum. It appears that in February 1988 the H defenders' agents wrote to the pursuers' agents indicating that the defenders were anxious "if at all possible, to agree the quantification of the pursuers' claim in the action leaving only the matter of liability to be argued before the court". Thereafter the letter suggested that an attempt be made to reach agreement on quantum through the parties' respective loss adjusters. A response to this approach was given in April 1989, advising that various vouchers in support of the pursuers' claim had been sent to the loss adjusters, but that I there were still "a good more to come" and that it was hoped to have these as soon as possible. In November 1989 the pursuers' agents wrote direct to the defenders' loss adjusters enclosing a schedule of losses. This schedule contained eight items, of which the first five had already been vouched. The sixth head was for additional staff costs amounting to £440.16. No vouchers were then provided in support of the claim. The seventh head of claim was for additional shopfitting costs amounting to £8,100.28. A breakdown was J provided in the letter without supporting vouchers. Finally a loss of profit figure of £1,874.76 was intimated as being calculated by reference to the previous week's trading. The last three heads of claim accord with the sixth, seventh and eighth heads of loss in the joint minute of admissions. It was agreed by counsel that the remaining items represented the remaining heads of loss in the joint minute. In October 1990 the pursuers' agents wrote to the defenders' loss adjusters as well as the agents for the third parties, inquiring K whether they were prepared on behalf of their respective clients to agree quantum. That letter made reference to the vouchers in support of the claim having been produced and the position being fully set out in the letter of 3 November 1989.

Counsel for the pursuers submitted that the discretion given to the court by s 1 (1) of the Interest on Damages (Scotland) Act 1958 as substituted by the Interest on Damages (Scotland) Act 1971, permitted L the court to order interest to be paid from the date when the right of action arose, ie when damnum and injuria occurred. He said that the effect of the amendment introduced by the 1971 Act was to effect a change of emphasis such that the court should now look for a reason not to award interest from the date when the right of action arose. He referred to *James Buchanan & Co Ltd v Stewart Cameron (Drymen) Ltd.* The expenditure of money in the present case by the pursuers was, he said, analogous to the loss of an interest bearing chattel or of something which otherwise would have secured a profit. He referred to *Twomax Ltd v Dickson* and *Nacap Ltd v Moffat Plant Ltd* as examples of cases where, in analogous circumstances, awards of interest had been made to run from the date when the loss occurred or the money was expended. He further referred to *M & I Instrument Engineers Ltd v Varsada.* There the pursuer had been defrauded of moneys on a certain date and the Lord Ordinary had been persuaded, only by reason of delay in prosecuting the claim, to award interest from a date later than the date when the fraud took place.

Counsel for the defenders on the other hand contended that the principle of doing justice between the parties inherent in making any such discretionary award required that both the period for which interest be allowed and the rate awarded should be restricted. Under reference to the background circumstances in this case, he submitted that the defenders had faced no judicial demand until the summons called in early 1988, that it had not been until five years after the event that the defenders or their loss adjusters had been provided with full and detailed claims and that for some two years prior to that the pursuers had, despite requests and reminders, failed to produce any adequate documentation. He submitted that any award should be at a rate less than the judicial rate. As regards the commencement of interest, it could not be said that the defenders had wrongfully withheld any sums properly due until, at the earliest, the date of citation. Even at that time on averment the sum sued for remained uncertain in extent and accordingly there was nothing like a debt due and resting owing. It was therefore appropriate that the pursuers should bear responsibility for any delay until the resolution of their claims, having in mind that the settlement sum was substantially less than the sum sued for. Counsel made reference to the common law principle as stated by Lord Atkin in *Kolbin & Sons v Kinnear & Co,* 1931 SLT at p 468 which is cited by Lord Maxwell in *Buchanan v Cameron.* The 1958 Act, he argued, had permitted interest to be awarded prior to the date of final decree but no earlier than the date of citation, where a proper demand for payment had been made and the sum sued for was then put forward. Under reference to *MacRae v Reed & Mallik Ltd, Fraser v J Morton Wilson Ltd* and *Bell's Sports Centre (Perth) Ltd v William Briggs & Sons Ltd* he said that the practice of the court had been to look at the question from the point of view of whether there had been wrongful withholding of some reasonably ascertained sum which the defender had been given an opportunity to pay and had failed to do so. He further submitted that notwithstanding the changes made by the 1971 Act, there was nevertheless a distinction between personal injury and non-personal injury cases such that, in the latter case, guidance could be obtained from earlier authority. While accepting in general the approach adopted by Lord Maxwell in *Buchanan v Cameron,* with the qualification that his gloss upon the *Bell's Sports Centre* case might not be correct, he argued that the ascertainment of loss and the wrongful withholding of moneys were the proper principles to be adopted in determining the court's approach. As regards the cases cited by the pursuers in favour of awards of interest earlier than date of citation, he pointed out that in none of *Twomax, Nacap* or *M & I Instrument Engineers Ltd* had any argument been presented on the matter of the starting point for interest or the appropriate rate. In the present case he argued that the claims made were not claims in respect of income bearing securities or profit making chattels. In particular, there was no basis for seeking any award of interest in relation to loss of sales, where loss of stock had already been claimed. Furthermore, it was impossible to know when any profit would have been obtained on the stock lost. It could not be said that it would have earned a profit ratio of as much as 15 per cent, nor could it be said how it could have been used. Furthermore, standing the failure to vouch fully the claims until at least 1989, there had been no wrongful withholding of a reasonably ascertainable sum prior to that date. Indeed it was not until the letter of 3 November 1989 that the items forming heads 6, 7 and 8 were formally identified. Accordingly at best any interest on those items should run from 1989. Finally, under reference to *Nacap Ltd v Moffat Plant Ltd,* and *Buchan v J Marr (Aberdeen) Ltd* he argued that some allowance should be made for the delay in prosecuting the action where settlement was not achieved until six and a half years after the flooding giving rise to the action. Counsel also submitted that it was unreasonable that interest at the rate of 15 per cent be awarded in a case where it was not self evident that the pursuers would have secured interest of 15 per cent on the money laid out if otherwise employed by them. If the courts were to award such high interest, this would be an incentive, he said, to pursuers to spin out the proceedings. Finally he observed that in any event, the judicial rate prior to August 1985 had been 12 per cent, and if the court were to award interest prior to that date at the judicial rate it could be no greater than that rate.

In my opinion, the approach adopted by Lord Maxwell in *Buchanan v Cameron* as to the effect of the amendment introduced by the 1971 Act, reached after consideration of the 1958 Act and the 1971 Act, and an analysis of them, is correct. At 1973 SLT (Notes), p 79 he said: "Whatever the position may have been under the 1958 Act, I consider that the court now can and should award interest on damages (in non-personal injury cases) back to such date (not earlier than the date when the right of action arises) as in all the circumstances seems just. I am of the opinion that the court, in exercising this power is not inhibited by the prior practice which precluded awards of interest on awards of damages, as such, in respect of periods earlier than the date of citation." I would also point out that in s 1 (1A), which is concerned with personal injury actions, it is provided that in such actions the power conferred by subs (1) is to be exercised in relation to any part of the sum of damages which does not represent damages or solatium in respect of personal injuries. While the case of *MacRae v Reed & Mallik Ltd* was concerned with the provisions of the 1958 Act, there are in that case two expressions of general principle which remain, in my opinion, relevant. At 1961

SLT, pp 97 and 98 Lord Justice Clerk Thomson was concerned to consider assessment of damages in a typical action of damages for personal injuries. The first of the three familiar heads to which he referred was "out of pocket expenses". He then said: "It would be reasonable for the Lord Ordinary to award interest at what he regarded as the correct rate on the out of pockets. That would be a figure which he would have assessed at the date of the trial and he would be well justified in thinking that it was within the general intendment of the statute that interest should run on that sum from the commencement of the action as some compensation for the fact that the pursuer has been standing out of his wages. But when one passes to what is awarded in respect of loss of future earnings, the circumstances are different. Up to the date of the trial the pursuer had lost nothing under this head. It could not be said that he had been deprived of the use of the money so awarded. If he were awarded interest from the date of the commencement of the action, this would be tantamount to giving him some kind of bonus for which it is difficult to see any warrant in the circumstances of the ordinary straightforward sort of case which I am envisaging." Later on he said this: "The ruling principle must be that, as interest assumes the existence of a principal sum, interest falls to be awarded only where there is a principal sum, which but for the law's normal delays the pursuer would have enjoyed. This is consonant with the accepted principle that ordinarily interest is payable only where there is a principal debt payment of which has been improperly or unjustifiably withheld." At the end of his opinion, the Lord Justice Clerk in reference to the award made by the Lord Ordinary in that case said this: "The Lord Ordinary seems to think that as the pursuer was standing out of his money from the date of the accident, this could be made up to him by an award under the statute. But if Parliament had intended the pre-action period to be taken into account, it would have said so. It deliberately selected the date of citation in preference to the date of the accident." By the amendment introduced in the 1971 Act, Parliament has now remedied the situation to which the Lord Justice Clerk alluded. In doing so, while it has given an emphasis to damages in personal injury actions, it has not, I consider, entrenched upon the ruling principle set out by the Lord Justice Clerk and this, in my opinion, remains relevant in dealing with the latter form of action.

In the same case Lord Patrick said this: "The next point which arises is whether the section authorises a Lord Ordinary to punish a defender for the heinous nature of his negligence, or because of the grave nature of the results of his negligence, or for the fact that the conduct of the defence has delayed the date on which the pursuer receives his award. The cardinal rule in awards of damages has hitherto been that the tribunal which tries the case should seek to put the injured party, so far as money can do so, into the same position as he would have been if he had not been injured, and I can see nothing in the statute to lead me to believe that that cardinal rule has been departed from. On the contrary, I think the purpose of the statute was to give the court power to give fuller effect to that cardinal rule, a power which it did not previously have." In my opinion that cardinal rule has been given yet fuller effect to by the amendment effected by the 1971 Act. The decision in *Twomax* is consistent with that cardinal principle, the pursuers in that case having been standing out of money by reason of the defenders' negligence from the date when they paid for the shareholding. I agree with counsel for the defenders that it is difficult to look at *Nacap Ltd v Moffat Plant Ltd* as a decision which is helpful in determining the appropriate date from which interest should be awarded in the ordinary case where no deduction falls to be made for delay. I observe that in that case the contractors were seeking to recover costs incurred by them in making good damage suffered by them on 18 February 1976. No argument appears to have been presented to the Lord Ordinary to the effect that the award should not, at worst for the defenders, take effect until the date when the costs were incurred. In the case of *M & I Instrument Engineers Ltd* the Lord Ordinary does appear to have accepted that, but for delay, the interest would fall to be awarded from the date when the sum of which the pursuers were defrauded was lost to them and this is consistent again with the cardinal principle. In personal injury actions where there is a related claim for damages, as for instance a damaged motor car in a road accident involving personal injury, depending upon whether the car is a total loss or has been repaired, it has, as I understand, been in general the practice to award interest from the date of the accident or the date when the repair outlays were incurred.

In the present case the heads of loss which are immediately analogous to what might be termed "out of pocket expenses", are those forming items 2 to 7 of the heads of loss set out in the joint minute of admissions. Subject to the consideration of what effect, if any, delay in prosecuting the case or some such similar consideration special to the case should have, in the ordinary case I would accept that reference to the cardinal principle would normally entitle the pursuers to an award of interest from the date when the expenditure was incurred and the pursuers were standing out of their money. These cases can be equiparated to the type of case where a pursuer has been deprived of an interest bearing security. In the case of item 8, loss of sales, this again represents money which the pursuers could have expected to receive if the premises had been open, and is akin to loss of wages in a personal injury action. Again, subject to the consideration of what effect any delay may have in prosecuting the claim or some similar consideration special to the case, in the ordinary case it would seem appropriate to award interest from the date when that loss occurred. The last item, namely item 1, loss of stock, is in my opinion in a different category. This gives rise to the same problem which confronted Lord Maxwell in *Buchanan v Cameron*, namely where the award is for the principal value of an asset lost or destroyed. In *Buchanan v Cameron* Lord Maxwell observed at pp

79-80 that he had "no grounds for assuming that the whisky and the advertising material would, if not destroyed, have earned profit for the pursuers from any particular date. It may be that in cases such as *Bell's Sports Centre (Perth) Ltd v William Briggs & Sons Ltd*, where the pursuers have had to expend money to repair their loss, the case can be equiparated to the type of case where the pursuers have been 'deprived of an interest bearing security', since money not otherwise expended can always earn interest, but there is no such suggestion in this case". Likewise, the pursuers in this case have not provided any information to me to suggest when or to what extent they would have expected to make a profit on the stock which was lost, nor do they suggest that they expended money to repair the loss of stock suffered. Furthermore, it may be reasonably said that the head of loss of sales may encompass a return on stock which was in fact destroyed. I agree with Lord Maxwell that the mere fact that a right of action has arisen on a particular date in respect of an asset lost or destroyed through negligence or breach of contract does not per se justify an award of interest from that date. Accordingly there is nothing which invests the date 3 November 1984, when the loss of stock was suffered, with any significance in the determination of the date from which an award of interest should be made on that head. In this case I consider that by analogy with *Buchanan v Cameron* the date of citation and no earlier date to be the appropriate date from which an award of interest on this head should run.

I have now to consider whether having regard to the particular circumstances of this case there is ground for restricting the period from which any award of interest on each item should run. In my opinion, there is no justification for doing so. From the outset the defenders made clear that they intended to contest liability. While it may be said that the items of loss were not identified with precision even at the date when the action was raised, that was not the reason for which settlement of the action was delayed. They could fairly be regarded as quantifiable from an early stage and indeed well before the action was raised. The fact that no agreement on quantum was reached before February 1991 was not a matter which gave rise to the action being unduly lengthened. The defenders pleaded from the first that the pursuers' averments were lacking in relevancy and specification and maintained that the case should go to procedure roll until September 1990. By that time the pursuers had made available to the defenders' loss adjusters the full details of the pursuers' claim and indeed, as appears from the joint minute, it was on that basis that quantum was eventually agreed. It could not be said that the apparent inflation of the pursuers' claim at the date when the action was raised had any material effect upon the subsequent course of the action. If the defenders had been anxious to discover the details of the pursuers' claim they could have done so by way of enrolling for commission and diligence for recovery of documents. They did not do so. I would also observe that in this case a claim was put forward some two years or so

prior to the date when the action was raised so that the defenders had ample time within which to consider their position in relation to this claim.

I propose therefore to award interest on each of the items 2 to 8 in the joint minute of admissions from the dates set out as the dates when such loss was incurred. In regard to item 1 I shall award interest from the date of citation. As regards the rate of interest, I see no reason to depart from the usual practice of awarding interest at the appropriate judicial rate until the date of decree. This is the normal practice of the court in such circumstances and nothing that was said by the defenders indicated any element special to this case to lead me to consider that a lower rate would be appropriate. I shall therefore grant decree in the sum of £12,460.34; of that sum £1,030.28 will bear interest at the rate of 15 per cent per annum from the date of citation until decree; the remaining items will bear interest at the appropriate judicial rate from the date on which the various sums are agreed to have been incurred, that is to say at the rate of 12 per cent per annum for each period up to 15 August 1985 and thereafter at the rate of 15 per cent per annum until decree.

The defenders reclaimed.

Reclaiming motion

The reclaiming motion was heard before the Second Division on 7 May 1992.

On 12 June 1992 the court *refused* the reclaiming motion.

THE LORD JUSTICE CLERK (ROSS).—This is an action of damages arising out of flooding which occurred at the Cameron Toll shopping centre, Edinburgh, on 3 November 1984. In the action the pursuers who were the tenants of store premises at the shopping centre sought damages from the defenders and the third parties in respect of damage caused by the ingress of water to their premises. After sundry procedure, the case was called for proof before the Lord Ordinary. He was then advised by counsel that settlement had been reached, and that it was agreed that decree should be pronounced for payment to the pursuers of the sum of £12,460.34. Agreement had not, however, been reached on the matter of interest, and that issue was left for determination by the Lord Ordinary.

In connection with the claim for interest, a joint minute of admissions was lodged. The joint minute contained the following agreement of parties: [his Lordship quoted the terms of the joint minute set out supra and continued:]

After hearing parties' submissions on the matter of interest, the Lord Ordinary on 21 June 1991 pronounced an interlocutor decerning for payment to the pursuers of the principal sum, and awarding interest as follows. On the sum of £1,030.28, he awarded interest at the rate of 15 per cent per annum from the

A date of citation to the date of decree. On the remaining items mentioned in the joint minute, namely 2 to 8, he awarded interest from the dates on which the expenditure had been incurred; interest was awarded at the judicial rate prevailing at the time. The Lord Ordinary was informed that the judicial rate of interest had been increased from 12 per cent to 15 per cent on 15 August 1985, and accordingly where appropriate he ordered interest to run at the rate of 12 per cent until 15 August 1985 and thereafter at the rate of 15 per cent per annum. Against that interlocutor of the Lord Ordinary the defenders have reclaimed.

B

In support of the reclaiming motion, senior counsel for the defenders explained that his submissions were being made both for the defenders and the third parties, although the latter were not separately represented. He submitted that although the Lord Ordinary had a discretion as to whether to award interest, the exercise by him of that discretion was fatally flawed. He contended that in a number of respects the Lord Ordinary had misdirected himself in law; he had applied wrong principles to the award of interest, he had failed to give any effective weight to certain factors which, as he put it graphically, "cried out for some restriction" in the interest awarded. He accordingly maintained that the result at which the Lord Ordinary had arrived was one which no reasonable Lord Ordinary could have reached. In support of this part of his submissions he cited *Charles Osenton & Co v Johnston*; *Associated Provincial Picture Houses Ltd v Wednesbury Corporation*; and *Wordie Property Co Ltd v Secretary of State for Scotland*. Under reference to these authorities senior counsel for the defenders submitted that this court would be entitled to reverse the Lord Ordinary if he had misdirected himself, and in particular if he had failed to attach appropriate weight to any relevant factor considered by him. He further submitted that, if the Lord Ordinary's decision was so unreasonable that no reasonable Lord Ordinary could have arrived at it, his decision was open to review, and the question of whether interest should be awarded and from what date would be at large for this court.

C

D

E

On behalf of the pursuers the learned Dean of Faculty did not quarrel with what senior counsel for the defenders said in regard to the circumstances which would entitle the Inner House to interfere. He accepted that if the Lord Ordinary had misdirected himself, the question would then be at large for this court. He did however emphasise that the onus was upon the defenders to show that the Lord Ordinary had exercised his discretion upon wrong principles or reached a wholly unreasonable result. I readily accept that the law regarding the right of an appellate court to interfere with the exercise of discretion by a court of first instance is as counsel agreed it to be.

F

Senior counsel for the defenders explained that apart from interest on the loss of stock, the Lord Ordinary had awarded interest at the full judicial rate for the whole period that had elapsed from the date when the loss had been incurred, and he submitted that it was wholly unreasonable for the Lord Ordinary to have

done so. He submitted that there had been a series of misdirections on the part of the Lord Ordinary. As I understood it, the principal submissions of senior counsel for the defenders were as follows: (1) there was no presumption that the pursuers were entitled to an award of interest in respect of the full period from the date when the loss was incurred, and the Lord Ordinary was in error in holding that there was a presumption to that effect; (2) the present case was not one where there had been any wrongful withholding of money on the part of the defenders, nor could it be suggested that the pursuers were in the position of having been deprived of an interest bearing security or a profit producing chattel; (3) the Lord Ordinary also erred in holding that the cardinal rule to be followed was restitutio in integrum; (4) the Lord Ordinary had also erred in treating the different items of loss 2 to 8 as being reasonably quantifiable from an early stage and indeed well before the action was raised.

G

H

Senior counsel for the defenders maintained that this reclaiming motion raised a question of general importance as to the proper approach to the awarding of interest on damages under the relevant statute in non-personal injury cases. The common law relating to interest had been altered by the enactment of the Interest on Damages (Scotland) Act 1958. The statute had been considered by the court in *MacRae v Reed & Mallik Ltd*. That case had been decided in the Inner House, and thereafter there had been a number of Outer House cases dealing with the matter. These included *Fraser v Morton Wilson Ltd* and *Bell's Sports Centre (Perth) Ltd v William Briggs & Sons Ltd*. The Interest on Damages (Scotland) Act 1958 had been amended by the Interest on Damages (Scotland) Act 1971, and the provisions of the amended statute had been considered in the Outer House in *James Buchanan & Co Ltd v Stewart Cameron (Drymen) Ltd*. Senior counsel for the defenders submitted that since the Lord Ordinary had gone wrong in law, this court should consider the matter afresh. He drew attention to the terms of the correspondence which had been exchanged between parties' solicitors and stressed that the pursuers' solicitors had failed to produce vouchers when asked to. That being so he submitted that interest on items 6, 7 and 8 should be restricted to 3 November 1989 being the date of the letter from the pursuers' solicitors to the defenders' loss adjusters; as regards items 1 to 5 he accepted that vouchers had been sent previously and he accordingly suggested that in these instances interest should run from 3 November 1988. Alternatively he submitted that on no view should any interest be awarded prior to the date of citation, and he maintained that even that date was a difficult one to justify in the present case. His ultimate long stop position was that interest should not be awarded any earlier than the date when the claim was put forward, which was two years or so prior to the date when the action was raised, ie 3 November 1985.

I

J

K

L

The Dean of Faculty on behalf of the pursuers maintained that there had been no misdirection on the part of the Lord Ordinary; he submitted that the Lord

Ordinary had reached the right result. He stressed that the Lord Ordinary had not awarded interest from the date when the loss was incurred but from the date when the expenditure had been incurred. He accepted that the Act of 1958 (as amended) had granted wide power to the court, but he agreed with senior counsel for the defender that it was still necessary to consider what the common law rules regarding interest were. In this connection he referred to *MacRae v Reed & Mallik Ltd* and *Kolbin & Sons v Kinnear & Co*. He argued in support of the common law rule that a pursuer might recover interest by way of damages where he is deprived of an interest bearing security or a profit producing chattel or where a principal sum has been wrongfully withheld. He submitted that anyone who committed a delict was wrongfully withholding damages from the moment when the delict occurred, but he accepted that interest was not due unless the injured party could show that he had sustained loss of interest; he would not get interest until it had been demanded or incurred. He maintained that the fallacy of the approach of senior counsel for the defenders was that it ignored the fact that there was a continuing obligation to pay damages from the moment when the delict was committed; it did not matter that the damages were not quantified at that time; what was important was that they should be capable of quantification.

I have come to the conclusion that the general approach of the learned Dean of Faculty is to be preferred. I agree with counsel for both parties that the Act of 1958 did not sweep away the previous law relating to damages. As Lord Mackintosh observed in *MacRae v Reed & Mallik Ltd* at 1961 SLT, p 100, the Act did not profess to abrogate the general rule relating to damages nor to do away with the former practice. Accordingly the general principle laid down in *Carmichael v Caledonian Railway Co* and *Kolbin & Sons v Kinnear & Co* still applies, that is to say, that a pursuer may recover interest by way of damages where he is deprived of an interest bearing security or a profit producing chattel or where money has been wrongfully withheld. Where a delict has been committed, the delinquent is liable to pay damages. In the normal case, however, the amount of damages cannot be quantified there and then, and damages cannot be regarded as being wrongfully withheld at a date when they are incapable of quantification. On the other hand, even though damages have not been quantified, if they become capable of ascertainment then the injured party can properly be regarded as standing out of his money, and the damages can be regarded as being wrongfully withheld (*Fraser v Morton Wilson Ltd* and *Bell's Sports Centre v Briggs & Sons Ltd*).

The Act of 1958 empowered the court to award interest from a date not earlier than the date on which the action was commenced against the defender, ie the date of citation. The Act of 1971 extended that power to an earlier date by enabling the court to award interest for the whole or part of the period between the date when the right of action arose and the interlocutor awarding damages. The right of action may

well have arisen long before the pursuer has cited the defender in the action of damages. I agree with Lord Maxwell in *Buchanan v Cameron* that the mere fact that a right of action arose on a particular date does not per se justify an award of interest from that date, but in my opinion interest may properly be awarded from a date when the damage suffered was capable of ascertainment (*Bell's Sports Centre (Perth) Ltd v William Briggs & Sons Ltd*). This appears to me to be consistent with the principle adverted to by Lord Keith of Avonholm in *F W Green & Co Ltd v Brown & Gracie Ltd* where he observed of damages for breach of contract that quantification would generally fix the earliest date from which interest could reasonably be taken to run. In my opinion, however, even if damages have not been quantified, interest may be reasonably be held to run from a date when the damages may reasonably be regarded as quantifiable or capable of ascertainment. From that date the wrongdoer can reasonably be regarded as wrongfully withholding the damages. It is, in my opinion, a fair implication that in both *Fraser v Morton Wilson Ltd* and *Bell's Sports Centre (Perth) Ltd v William Briggs & Sons Ltd* damages would have been awarded from a date before the date of citation if the law at that date had permitted such a course.

In the present case the stock was lost on 3 November 1984, but there was no material before the Lord Ordinary to enable him to conclude whether that stock, if not destroyed, would have earned profit for the pursuers from any particular date. As the Lord Ordinary observed: "There is nothing which invests the date 3 November 1984, when the loss of stock was suffered, with any significance in the determination of the date from which an award of interest should be made on that head." He accordingly awarded interest on item 1 from the date of citation. The learned Dean of Faculty for the pursuers accepted that the date of citation was the appropriate date in respect of this item. I do not accept the submission of senior counsel for the defenders that interest should not be awarded from any date earlier than 3 November 1988 in respect of this item, and I agree with the result at which the Lord Ordinary arrived so far as item 1 is concerned.

So far as the remaining items are concerned, the Lord Ordinary awarded interest on each of them from the dates shown in the joint minute as the dates when the loss was incurred. It is plain from the terms of the joint minute that the dates shown in the joint minute are the dates when these items were reasonably quantifiable. As the Lord Ordinary correctly observes, items 2 to 7 are analogous to what might be termed "out of pocket expenses". The dates shown in the joint minute are the dates when the expenditure on these items was incurred. At that date the pursuers were standing out of their money, and it follows, in my opinion, that the wrongdoer was wrongfully withholding money. Liability to pay damages attaches to a delinquent, and once the injured party has incurred expenditure to repair the loss, it appears to me to be entirely reasonable to regard the wrongdoer as wrongfully withholding money and not paying that money

A on the date when it ought to be paid (*Carmichael v Caledonian Railway Co*). From the date when the pursuer has incurred the expenditure the amount of his loss is clearly ascertainable, and it is in accordance with principle that interest should run from that date.

Senior counsel for the defenders failed to persuade me that the Lord Ordinary had exercised his discretion upon any wrong basis. In one passage of his opinion, the Lord Ordinary appears to be suggesting that in the ordinary case there is a presumption in favour of awarding interest on damages to a pursuer.
B There is no such presumption, but earlier in his opinion under reference to *MacRae v Reed & Mallik Ltd*, the Lord Ordinary correctly identifies the cardinal or ruling principle. In these circumstances, I am satisfied that the Lord Ordinary was entitled to exercise his discretion to award interest as he did.

Before the Lord Ordinary it was submitted on behalf of the defenders that there was a ground for restricting the period from which any award of interest should
C run having regard to the particular circumstances of this case, and reference was made to certain correspondence. Senior counsel for the defenders also referred to this correspondence, and as I understood it the suggestion was that because of the failure of the pursuers to provide adequate information regarding their claim when asked to do so, they should not be held entitled to interest from the dates specified in the joint minute. This appeared to be the basis for the alternative submissions which senior counsel for the defenders made.
D I am not persuaded that this is a correct approach. Senior counsel for the defenders referred to a number of cases where Outer House judges in awarding interest on damages had had regard to the question of who had been responsible for procedural delays throughout the course of the action. In some cases interest was not allowed at the beginning of the period, and in others interest was not allowed at the end of the period. In this connection we were referred to *Nacap Ltd v Moffat Plant Ltd*; *Buchan v J Marr
E (Aberdeen) Ltd* and *M & I Instrument Engineers Ltd v Varsada*. We were also referred to the unreported case of *Finnegan v British Gas*. I am not persuaded that inordinate delay on the part of the pursuer in prosecuting his action should justify any modification of interest. If there has been such inordinate delay, the result must be that the defenders have had use of money for a longer period than they should have had it. Accordingly even where there has been inordinate delay on the part of the pursuer, I see no reason why
F interest should not be awarded from the date when the loss was capable of ascertainment. It appears to me to be wrong in principle to deprive a pursuer of interest from the date when the loss was capable of ascertainment merely because he has delayed in prosecuting his claim. From the date when the loss was capable of ascertainment, the defender should have made payment in respect of that loss, and it appears wrong that the wrongdoer should be permitted to enjoy the use of that money during a period when the money ought to have been paid to the injured party. Accordingly in the absence of any

G special circumstances, I am not satisfied that inordinate delay in prosecuting the action should result in a pursuer being deprived of interest on items of damages which have been capable of ascertainment and in respect of which expenditure has been incurred by the injured party. In the present case, I have no complaint to find in the manner in which the Lord Ordinary has dealt with the allegations of delay.

For the foregoing reasons I am satisfied that the Lord Ordinary was fully entitled to exercise his discretion as he did, and that the award of interest which he made was in accordance with principle and authority. H I would accordingly move your Lordships to refuse the reclaiming motion and to adhere to the interlocutor of the Lord Ordinary.

LORD MURRAY.—I concur and have nothing to add.

LORD GRIEVE.—I agree, for the reasons given by your Lordship, that this reclaiming motion should be refused.
I

Counsel for Pursuers and Respondents, Dean of Faculty (Johnston, QC), McVicar; Solicitors, Dundas & Wilson, CS — Counsel for Defenders and Reclaimers, G N H Emslie, QC, J R Campbell; Solicitors, J & F Anderson, WS.

P A

J

MacLeod v Williamson

HIGH COURT OF JUSTICIARY
THE LORD JUSTICE CLERK (ROSS),
LORDS SUTHERLAND AND WYLIE
9 OCTOBER 1992
K

Justiciary — Procedure — Summary procedure — Desertion — Trial — Desertion simpliciter by court ex proprio motu after sheriff overhearing Crown witness, outside court, describing his evidence to prosecutor — Whether competent — Whether sheriff entitled to continue with trial — Appropriate course where sheriff felt unable to continue.

An accused person was tried on a summary complaint libelling assault to injury with a machete and possessing a machete in a public place, contrary to s 1 L (1) of the Prevention of Crime Act 1953. The Crown adduced evidence from three witnesses to the effect that the accused had struck the complainer with a machete or similar instrument. The trial was then adjourned for luncheon. After other parties in the trial and the public had left the court building, the procurator fiscal depute met police witnesses outside the courtroom to discuss whether any of them could be excused attendance in the afternoon. While this discussion was taking place, the sheriff walked past. After

A luncheon the sheriff in court intimated that as he had been walking past he had overheard one of the police witnesses state that his evidence concerned only "recovering the machete in his possession". The sheriff invited submissions on what he should do. Thereafter he stated that he felt unable to cast completely from his mind what he had overheard and, after further submissions, he ex proprio motu deserted the diet simpliciter. The Crown sought advocation of the sheriff's decision, contending that either he should have put out of his mind what he had overheard and

B continued with the trial or, alternatively, he should have discharged the diet and fixed a fresh diet to proceed before another sheriff.

Held, (1) that the sheriff was entitled to decide that the trial could not proceed, although he might well have concluded that the trial could proceed despite his having heard the remark (p 146H-I); but (2) that the sheriff was not entitled, either under statute or at common law, ex proprio motu to desert the diet simpliciter (p 146J); and (3) that the appropriate course

C for the sheriff to have followed was to discharge the diet of trial and fix a fresh diet to proceed before another sheriff (pp 146K and 147A); and bill *passed*, decision *recalled*, diet *discharged* and case *remitted* to sheriff to fix a fresh diet of trial to proceed before another sheriff.

Platt v Lockhart, 1988 SLT 845, *applied*; observations of Lord Pitmilly in *HM Advocate v Mary Elder or Smith* (1827) 1 Syme 71, *approved*.

D ————————

Bill of advocation

Ian Angus MacLeod, procurator fiscal, Perth, presented a bill of advocation praying the High Court of Justiciary to recall the decision of Temporary Sheriff D J May, QC, on 22 June 1992 whereby, in the course of a summary trial, the sheriff ex proprio motu deserted the diet simpliciter.

E **Statement of facts**

The bill contained the following statement of facts:

Stat 1. The respondent was charged at the instance of the complainer on a summary complaint, a copy of which is annexed hereto, libelling a charge of assault and a charge of contravening the Prevention of Crime Act 1953, s 1 (1).

Stat 2. The trial of the respondent proceeded on 22 June 1992 and evidence was adduced by the com-

F plainer from three witnesses that the respondent had struck the alleged victim of the assault with a machete or similar instrument.

Stat 3. At 1 pm the trial was adjourned until 2 pm, and after other parties in the trial had left the court building the complainer's depute met police witnesses in the trial of the respondent outside the courtroom to discuss whether any of the said witnesses might be excused attendance that afternoon. In the course of the said discussion the sheriff happened to walk past the complainer's depute and the witnesses.

G Stat 4. When the case against the respondent called again at 2 pm the sheriff intimated that during the adjournment he had overheard one of the police witnesses state to the complainer's depute that his evidence concerned only "recovering the machete in his possession". The sheriff expressed the view that this might have an effect on his ability to hear further evidence in the case. The sheriff invited the respondent's solicitor to consider whether she should submit that his hearing of the remark by the police witness would have a prejudicial effect upon the respondent

H and the respondent's solicitor made a submission to that effect.

Stat 5. The sheriff then invited the complainer's depute to address him. The complainer's depute stated that the sheriff had overheard the witness incorrectly and invited the sheriff to put out of his mind what he considered he had overheard and to proceed with the trial of the respondent.

Stat 6. The sheriff thereafter stated that he felt unable to cast completely from his mind what he had

I overheard, and following further submissions by the complainer's depute and the respondent's solicitor the sheriff ex proprio motu deserted the diet simpliciter.

Stat 7. The decision of the sheriff to desert the diet simpliciter was unjust, erroneous and contrary to law. The sheriff had a duty in discharging his judicial function to put from his mind any extraneous considerations, to proceed with the trial of the respondent and to reach a verdict based solely on the evidence heard by him in court. Esto the sheriff was correct not to

J proceed further with the trial of the respondent, it was his duty to discharge the diet of trial and to fix a fresh diet of trial to proceed before another sheriff.

Cases referred to

Advocate (HM) v Mary Elder or Smith (1827) 1 Syme 71.
Carmichael v Monaghan, 1986 SLT 338; 1986 SCCR 598.
Platt v Lockhart, 1988 SLT 845; 1988 SCCR 308.

K The bill contained the following pleas in law:

(1) The decision of the sheriff not to proceed further with the trial of the respondent and to desert the diet simpliciter being unjust, erroneous and contrary to law should be recalled and the case remitted to the sheriff to proceed with the trial of the respondent.

(2) Esto the decision of the sheriff not to proceed further with the trial of the respondent was correct, his decision to desert the diet simpliciter being unjust,

L erroneous and contrary to law should be recalled and the case remitted to the sheriff court at Perth for trial before another sheriff.

The bill was argued before the High Court on 22 September 1992.

On 9 October 1992 the court *passed* the bill, *recalled* the decision, *discharged* the diet of trial and *remitted* to the sheriff to fix a fresh diet to proceed before another sheriff.

The following opinion of the court was delivered by the Lord Justice Clerk (Ross):

OPINION OF THE COURT.—This is a bill of advocation at the instance of the procurator fiscal, Perth. The bill arises from events which took place at a trial of the respondent in Perth sheriff court. [His Lordship rehearsed the facts as set out in the statement of facts and continued:]

On behalf of the complainer it is contended that the sheriff's decision to desert the diet simpliciter was erroneous, and that he ought to have proceeded with the trial putting out of his mind any extraneous considerations. Alternatively, it is contended that if the sheriff was correct not to proceed further with the trial, he ought to have discharged the diet of trial and fixed a fresh diet of trial to proceed before another sheriff.

The sheriff has provided a report in this case in which he explains what he overheard. The sheriff also explains that the complainer's depute submitted that there was no statutory provision to enable him to desert pro loco et tempore and that he should deal with the matter by simply putting what he had heard out of his mind. The solicitor for the respondent, on the other hand, submitted that the trial should be deserted, and that the desertion should be simpliciter. The sheriff goes on to explain that subsequently the complainer's depute submitted that the proper course for the sheriff to follow would be to desert simpliciter in which event the Crown could appeal by way of bill of advocation. He explained to the sheriff that in the event of the appeal being successful, a new trial could then be held before a different sheriff. The sheriff further observes that he understood the position of both the Crown and the defence ultimately to be that if the trial was not to proceed in front of him, the only course open to him was to desert simpliciter.

In inviting the court to pass the bill and to advocate the proceedings, the Solicitor General submitted that the sheriff had no power to desert simpliciter. He submitted that what the sheriff ought to have done was to proceed to hear the evidence and to put out of his mind what he had overheard. Alternatively if the sheriff was justified in not proceeding further with the trial, the Solicitor General submitted that what he ought to have done was to discharge the diet of trial and to fix a fresh diet of trial to proceed before another sheriff.

Counsel for the respondent contended that it was not incompetent for a sheriff to desert the diet simpliciter. She also submitted that at common law he could have deserted the diet pro loco et tempore. However since he had deserted the diet simpliciter, she submitted that his decision should stand, and that this court should refuse to pass the bill. She contended that the sheriff could not discharge the diet of trial once the trial had proceeded and witnesses had been called.

We have some sympathy with the sheriff in the position in which he found himself. It is clear from his report that he was anxious to do justice between the parties and to ensure that the trial was fairly conducted and that justice was not only done but was seen to be done. However, we are not persuaded that the sheriff's disposal of this case was appropriate.

In the events which occurred, we are of opinion that the sheriff might well have concluded that the trial should be allowed to proceed with him disregarding what he had overheard. The situation is similar to that which obtains where a sheriff has heard evidence which ought not to have been placed before him. In such a case under summary procedure it ought to be possible for a sheriff to allow the trial to proceed since the sheriff ought to be able to put out of his mind the material which is improperly before him. As was observed in *Carmichael v Monaghan*, it ought to be possible for a sheriff to apply his good sense in this connection.

In the present case, however, we are not prepared to hold that the sheriff was not entitled to decide that the trial could not proceed. Although we consider that the sheriff might well have concluded that the trial could proceed despite his having overheard this remark, we are not prepared to fault the sheriff for reaching a different conclusion upon this matter, particularly since it is obvious that he was concerned to ensure that the trial was conducted fairly. However, when the sheriff determined that the trial could not proceed further, we are of opinion that he was not justified ex proprio motu in deserting the diet simpliciter. Counsel referred to the terms of s 338A of the Criminal Procedure (Scotland) Act 1975. Counsel were agreed that the present case did not fall within the terms of that section. Counsel also remarked that it was conceded in *Carmichael v Monaghan* that it was not competent for the sheriff in that case to have deserted the diet simpliciter. We are not persuaded that the sheriff either under statute or at common law was entitled to desert the diet simpliciter in this case.

There was, however, another course which the sheriff could and should have taken once he decided that the trial could not proceed further. We agree with the Solicitor General, that the appropriate course for the sheriff to have followed was to discharge the diet of trial and fix a fresh diet of trial to proceed before another sheriff. That was the course followed in *Platt v Lockhart*. Although the circumstances were different in that case, we are satisfied that that case is authority for the proposition that once the sheriff had determined that the case could not proceed further, he could appropriately have discharged the diet and adjourned the case for a fresh diet of trial. As in *Platt v Lockhart*, a question of time bar would have arisen if there had been any question of deserting the diet pro loco et tempore. However, as the sheriff himself recognises in his report, it is in the public interest that the accused having been charged on this summary complaint should be brought to trial and a verdict reached in respect of the charges. Once the sheriff concluded that the trial before him could not proceed, we are satisfied that there must be some method by which the trial of the respondent can proceed. In *Platt v Lockhart* the court referred to the observations of Lord Pitmilly in *HM Advocate v Mary Elder or Smith*. These observations appear equally apt in the present case.

In all the circumstances therefore we agree with the learned Solicitor General that once the sheriff decided not to proceed further with the trial, what he ought to have done was to discharge the diet of trial and to fix a fresh diet of trial to proceed before another sheriff. It was not appropriate for him to desert the diet simpliciter.

For the foregoing reasons we shall pass the bill, advocate the proceedings, recall the decision of the sheriff, discharge the diet of trial which proceeded on 22 June 1992, and remit to the sheriff to fix a fresh diet of trial to take place before a different sheriff.

Counsel for Complainer, Solicitor General (Dawson, QC); Solicitor, J D Lowe, Crown Agent — Counsel for Respondent, Powrie; Solicitors, Simpson & Marwick, WS (for Drew-Paul & Murray, Perth).

P W F

Venter v Scottish Legal Aid Board

FIRST DIVISION
THE LORD PRESIDENT (HOPE),
LORDS COWIE AND SUTHERLAND
5 NOVEMBER 1992

Administrative law — Judicial review — Legal aid — Work likely to involve unusually large expenditure — Court granting open commission to take evidence in South Africa — Refusal by Scottish Legal Aid Board of prior approval — Whether unreasonable — Relevant considerations — Civil Legal Aid (Scotland) Regulations 1987 (SI 1987/381), reg 21, as amended.

Expenses — Legal aid — Work likely to involve unusually large expenditure — Court granting open commission to take evidence in South Africa — Refusal by Scottish Legal Aid Board of prior approval — Whether unreasonable — Relevant considerations — Proper time to seek approval — Civil Legal Aid (Scotland) Regulations 1987 (SI 1987/381), reg 21, as amended.

Regulation 21 of the Civil Legal Aid (Scotland) Regulations 1987, as amended, provides that the prior approval of the Scottish Legal Aid Board must be obtained for legally aided work of an unusual nature or likely to involve unusually large expenditure.

In proceedings by way of minute and answers for variation of an award of custody made in 1989, the petitioner, who was legally aided, applied to the court for interrogatories to be dispensed with and for an open

commission to take the evidence of two witnesses in South Africa. This motion was granted. Thereafter a further motion was enrolled to allow the evidence of additional witnesses also to be taken on open commission. The Lord Ordinary who granted this motion was also to conduct the proof and he appointed himself judge commissioner. An application was made to the board for authority for the commission as this would involve an unusually large expenditure. The board refused the application, noting that there had been a costly commission in the original custody proceedings and also noting that evidence could be taken by way of interrogatories. The board also referred to what private litigants might be expected to do in such circumstances. The petitioner's solicitors asked the board to reconsider the matter. The Lord Ordinary who was to conduct the commission had his view made known to the board that the commission was essential for the conduct of the litigation. The board adhered to their decision. The petitioner sought judicial review of the board's decision as unreasonable and failing to take into account the proper considerations. The Lord Ordinary found in favour of the petitioner and reduced the decisions. The board reclaimed, arguing that there was no duty on them to give reasons for their decisions, and any reasons given need not be the complete reasons. The question was whether a case had been made for unusually large expenditure to be incurred from public funds. The petitioner submitted that it was for the court and not the board to determine what was appropriate procedure and it was not for the board to substitute its view for that of the court.

Held, (1) that where prior approval of the board was required prior to unusually large expenditure being incurred the question was whether that could be justified as a charge on the legal aid fund (p 153C); (2) that the board had to consider, first, whether there was any other reasonable alternative but to incur the expenditure and, secondly, if there was, whether the step proposed should be approved in preference to the available alternatives (p 153D); (3) that there was a duty on the applicant to explain the basis of the request, and the board could call for such information as it might require (p 153E); (4) that in all legally aided cases where the court was to be asked to authorise a course of action for which the prior approval of the board was required, the proper procedure was for the approval of the board to be sought before an application was made to the court: a refusal would not necessarily be conclusive although the court had no jurisdiction to order the board to grant prior approval (p 154D-F); (5) that the cost of the previous commission, and what private litigants could reasonably be expected to do in similar circumstances, were both factors to which the board was entitled to have regard (pp 155D and 156A-B); (6) that the taking of evidence on interrogatories was an available alternative and, the petitioner's solicitors having failed to provide any reasoned explanation of why this would not be satisfactory, the board was entitled to take the view that it had not been shown that it was essential for the evidence to be taken on open commission: its silence on the effects of the board's

A decision did not indicate a failure to consider the requirements and achievements of justice (p 155F-H and K-L); (7) that in the whole circumstances the decision of the board could not be said to have been unreasonable or perverse (p 156B-E); and reclaiming motion *allowed*, interlocutor of the Lord Ordinary *recalled* and petition *dismissed*.

Observed, that the court should be careful not to be drawn into direct argument with the board on matters relating to legal aid, and that any guidance or advice from the court to the board should be said only from
B the bench (p 155A-C).

Petition for judicial review
Herman Lodewyk Venter applied for judicial review of a decision of the Scottish Legal Aid Board refusing to grant authorisation for expenditure for an open commission to take evidence in South Africa.

The petition called for a first hearing before the Lord
C Ordinary (Prosser).

Statutory provisions
The Civil Legal Aid (Scotland) Regulations 1987, as amended, provide:

"21.—(1) Subject to paragraph (2) below, the prior approval of the Board shall be required — (a) for the employment in the House of Lords of counsel other than Scottish counsel; (b) for the employment in the Court of Session of senior counsel or of more than one
D junior counsel; (c) for the employment of counsel in the sheriff court, the Scottish Land Court, the Lands Tribunal for Scotland or the Employment Appeal Tribunal; (d) for the employment of any expert witness; and (e) for work of an unusual nature or likely to involve unusually large expenditure.

"(2) Paragraph (1) above shall not apply where the Board, on an application made to it for retrospective approval for the employment of counsel or, as the case may be, of an expert witness, considers that that
E employment would have been approved by them and that there was special reason why prior approval was not applied for."

Cases referred to
AB v Scottish Legal Aid Board, 1991 SCLR 702.
Associated Provincial Picture Houses Ltd v Wednesbury Corporation [1948] 1 KB 223.
Council of Civil Service Unions v Minister for the Civil Service [1985] 1 AC 374; [1984] 1 WLR 1174;
F [1984] 3 All ER 935.
K v Scottish Legal Aid Board, 1989 SLT 617; 1989 SCLR 144.

On 2 October 1992 his Lordship *granted* decree of reduction.

The respondents reclaimed.

Reclaiming motion
The reclaiming motion was heard before the First Division on 23 October 1992.

On 5 November 1992 the court *allowed* the reclaiming motion, *recalled* the interlocutor of the Lord
G Ordinary and *dismissed* the petition.

The following opinion of the court was delivered by the Lord President (Hope):

OPINION OF THE COURT.—This is a petition for judicial review of a decision of the Scottish Legal Aid Board refusing to grant prior approval for work likely to involve unusually large expenditure. The reasons for the refusal were set out in two letters from the board to the petitioners' solicitors dated 10 August
H 1992 and, following further consideration of the matter by the board's legal aid committee, 26 August 1992. The application came before the Lord Ordinary for the first hearing on 23 September 1992. There was no material dispute as to fact and the Lord Ordinary was invited to dispose of the issue on the petitioner's pleadings and the documents lodged by him. On 2 October 1992, having come to the view that each of the decision letters, or both taken together, must be seen as expressing a decision which was unreasonable and perverse in
I the required sense, he reduced the decision. The board has now reclaimed against that interlocutor. Answers have been lodged but, subject only to one point of detail which does not affect the main issue in the case, the factual background remains the same as that which was before the Lord Odinary.

The petitioner, who is resident in Johannesburg in the Republic of South Africa, has raised proceedings in the Court of Session by way of minute for variation of an interlocutor dated 16 March 1990 in regard to the
J custody of his child Beverley. The respondent in that application is his former wife, Lorna Margaret Wallace or Venter, to whom he was married on 2 October 1982 and from whom he was divorced in about March 1990. Beverley, who was the only child of the marriage and was born on 12 September 1985, lived with her parents in Scotland for the first years of her life. After the parties had separated, but while they and the child were still in Scotland, the petitioner applied by petition to the Court of Session for an order for her custody. A
K proof was heard on various dates in March, May and June 1989, in the course of which the evidence of several witnesses was taken on open commission in South Africa. These included the petitioner's mother and stepfather, Mr and Mrs Reid. Their evidence, like that of the other witnesses whose evidence was taken on commission, was concerned with the circumstances in South Africa, since the petitioner was about to return to that country. After the proof the Lord Ordinary, Lord Weir, indicated that he would award custody of
L the child to Mrs Venter, provided that she returned with Beverley to make their home in South Africa. Mrs Venter gave an undertaking to that effect, and the Lord Ordinary then pronounced the interlocutor of 16 March 1990 by which he awarded custody of the child to her. The petitioner was awarded residential access to the child each alternative weekend. Mrs Venter returned to South Africa with Beverley, as did the petitioner, and she made her home there for a time. But in about June 1991, contrary to the petitioner's wishes, she returned with the child to live in Scotland. The

petitioner then applied to the board for legal aid to raise proceedings for variation of the interlocutor of 16 March 1990 and to seek an award of custody in his own favour. On 5 October 1991 the board granted him a legal aid certificate. Mrs Venter lodged answers to the minute which was then served on her, and she also now has the benefit of legal aid — as did both parties for purposes of the original proceedings which resulted in the interlocutor which the petitioner now seeks to have varied.

On 26 March 1992 a proof before answer was allowed on the minute and answers, which contained detailed averments as to whether it is in Beverley's best interests to remain in Scotland or to return to South Africa. The petitioner avers that for the majority of her life she has lived in South Africa, and that this is the country with which she is most familiar and in which she was well settled. There are averments about the accommodation which is available there in which he would care for the child, about schooling arrangements and the assistance and support which the petitioner would have from his fiancée Mrs Jansen. It is said that Beverley has many friends and relatives in South Africa, separation from whom would be detrimental to her wellbeing. There are also averments about the love and affection which the petitioner showed to the child at all times while she was in his care. The petitioner's case at the proof is to consist largely of the evidence of witnesses who are resident in South Africa. These include his mother and stepfather, Mr and Mrs Reid, who are said to be unfit to travel to Scotland to give evidence.

A motion was enrolled at the petitioner's instance for the evidence of Mr and Mrs Reid to be taken on open commission in South Africa. This motion, which was not opposed, was heard and granted by Lord Weir on 10 July 1992. The name of the commissioner was left blank at that stage, on the basis that this should be decided by the Lord Ordinary who was to hear the proof. It appears that, when issuing that interlocutor, Lord Weir suggested that the Lord Ordinary should consider whether he ought to go to South Africa himself to hear the evidence of the witnesses there. The petitioner's solicitor then wrote to the board by letter dated 15 July 1992 informing them that counsel had recommended that they call Mr and Mrs Reid as witnesses, that, owing to ill health on their part, they were unable to travel to Scotland and that they had now obtained permission from the Court of Session to obtain their evidence on commission. They also said that, in the light of Lord Weir's comment, they had enrolled a motion for the evidence of their remaining witnesses, except for that of the petitioner, to be taken on commission and that the judge who was to deal with the case would then decide whether that motion should be granted and whether he should appoint himself as commissioner. In support of their request for authority from the board for the commission to take place in South Africa, they mentioned that Mrs Venter's solicitors had advised them that they wished the evidence of a further eight witnesses to be taken on commission there. They also informed the board that the petitioner's counsel considered it inappropriate for the

evidence of the petitioner's witnesses to be taken on interrogatories.

In the meantime, arrangements had been made for the proof on the minute and answers to be taken by Lord Abernethy. Lord Weir had indicated that, in his view, it was not appropriate that he should hear it, in view of his previous involvement in the case. On 17 July 1992 Lord Abernethy granted the motion by the petitioner to allow the evidence of his five other main witnesses to be taken on open commission in South Africa. He also allowed a motion on behalf of Mrs Venter that the evidence of a further seven witnesses whom she wished to call should also be taken there on open commission. He granted commission to himself to take the evidence of all these witnesses as judge commissioner, and his name was inserted as commissioner in the interlocutor of 10 July 1992 which had been granted by Lord Weir. The two motions which were granted on 17 July 1992 were marked of consent. Neither Lord Weir nor Lord Abernethy issued an opinion to explain the reasons for the decision recorded in these interlocutors. On one view this is not at all surprising, because there was no dispute between Mr and Mrs Venter that the evidence of all these witnesses was necessary and that an open commission in South Africa was appropriate. Lord Weir was also well aware of the background to the case, having already heard the lengthy proof on the issue of Beverley's custody which included the previous open commission in South Africa. We are in no doubt that he gave careful consideration to the matter, and the view, which is implicit in his decision, that it was in the best interests of the child that the evidence of Mr and Mrs Reid should be taken on open commission was one which he was entitled to reach on the information before him and in all the circumstances. Nevertheless there was another important issue which appears not to have been raised with either judge on the motion roll, and on which the board had had no opportunity to make representations, which relates to the provision of legal aid.

The petitioner has, as we have said, the benefit of civil legal aid in the proceedings which he has now raised for variation of the order about custody. Section 13 (2) of the Legal Aid (Scotland) Act 1986 provides that "civil legal aid" means representation by a solicitor and, where appropriate, by counsel in any proceedings mentioned in Pt I of Sched 2 to the Act, which includes civil proceedings in the Court of Session, on the terms provided for in the Act. Where civil legal aid is made available to a person who has applied for it the burden of his expenses fall on a fund established and maintained by the board under s 4 (1) of the Act, known as the Scottish Legal Aid Fund. Subsection (2) (a) of that section provides that there are to be paid out of the fund such sums as are, by virtue of the Act or any regulations made thereunder, due out of the fund to any solicitor or counsel in respect of fees and outlays properly incurred by him in connection with the provision, in accordance with the Act, of legal aid. Much of the detail about the provision of legal aid and the exercise by the board of its functions has been left by the Act to regulations made under s 36 by the Secretary of State. The principal regulations which affect the provision of civil legal aid are the Civil Legal Aid (Scotland) Regulations 1987. Part V of these Regulations deals with the conduct of proceedings, and it comprises two regulations which require the prior approval of the board for certain items of expenditure. Similar, but not identical, provisions as to the obtaining of prior approval from the board are to be found in reg 14 of the Criminal Legal Aid (Scotland) Regulations 1987.

Regulation 21 (1) of the Civil Legal Aid (Scotland) Regulations 1987, as amended by the Civil Legal Aid (Scotland) Amendment Regulations 1992, is in these terms: [his Lordship quoted the terms of reg 21 (1), as amended, and continued:]

We were informed that subpara (e), which was added by the 1992 Regulations with effect from 3 April 1992, was inserted in the light of the expenditure incurred on the previous commission to South Africa in this case, the cost of which was in excess of £30,000.

The petitioner's solicitors did not seek the prior approval of the board under reg 21 (1) (e) before enrolling the motions which resulted in the interlocutors of 10 and 17 July 1992. We shall return later in this opinion to the question whether it is appropriate that motions relating to expenditure of this nature should be enrolled before the prior approval of the board has been obtained. The solicitor's letter of 15 July 1992, however, was in effect, although not in terms, a request for prior approval under reg 21 (1) (e), and it was treated as such by the board. On 17 July 1992 the board wrote to the petitioner's solicitors pointing out, under reference to the previous commission in South Africa, that they had not dealt in any detail with the evidence which was to be given on this occasion by the witnesses, or as to why they required to be led and how that evidence was to be obtained. An explanation was sought as to why it was thought that it was not appropriate for their evidence to be taken on interrogatories. The letter concluded with a sentence in these terms: "The Board would expect detailed consideration of the relative merits, or otherwise, of leading such witnesses as are absolutely necessary, obtaining evidence taken on interrogatories or on commission."

The petitioner's solicitors replied by letter dated 23 July 1992. They said in this letter that the only witnesses on their present list who had previously given evidence were Mr and Mrs Reid. They maintained that their evidence was different from what it had been previously because the petitioner had thereafter returned to South Africa, had set up home there and had looked after Beverley an equal share of the time. They then went on to say this: "Mr and Mrs Reid will be able to speak to all these circumstances and again to the position in South Africa with regard to schooling, accommodation, etc, should Beverley return there if Mr Venter's case is successful. They would also speak to the political situation in South Africa. For these reasons the evidence of Mr and Mrs Reid is essential for our client. Mr and Mrs Reid are both unable to travel to Scotland through ill health." Reference was made to the medical reports which had been placed before Lord Weir on 10 July 1992 and to the fact that Lord Weir had dispensed with interrogatories and stressed that the Lord Ordinary who was to hear the

case should consider himself going to South Africa to hear the evidence of these two witnesses, the remaining five witnesses for the pursuer and any witnesses which the respondent wished to call. They added: "The situation therefore is that the evidence of Mr and Mrs Reid must be taken in South Africa since they are not available to attend court here and since Lord Weir has dispensed with interrogatories." After a brief summary of the evidence to be given by the other five witnesses, they concluded their letter by saying this: "In the circumstances of the court having ordered this procedure we are not aware of any basis on which you can now refuse this request."

The board was not satisfied by this information, and it declined to give its prior approval to the expenditure. This decision was intimated by letter dated 10 August 1992 in these terms:

"It was noted that there had been a prior Commission to South Africa involving the same parties in 1989. The cost of this to the Fund had been around £33,000.

"The Board decided that it would be an unreasonable use of public funds to grant the application, which is accordingly refused. The Board noted that evidence from South Africa could be obtained by way of interrogatories."

The petitioner's solicitors replied by letter dated 18 August 1992 asking the board to reconsider the matter. They also asked the board to consider a letter which Lord Abernethy was said to have instructed the Keeper of the Rolls to write to the board, a copy of which had been made available to them. This letter, which was dated 14 August 1992, contained a paragraph in these terms: "I have spoken to Lord Abernethy, who granted the commission, about this matter and he has asked me to inform you that he considered this matter carefully before granting the commission and that in his view it is essential for the conduct of the litigation that the commission take place. I would be grateful, therefore, if you would place this letter before the Legal Aid Board for their consideration when disposing of this application." The petitioner's solicitors went on to say that, the court having been satisfied that it was appropriate that a commission should take place, it was an unreasonable and ultra vires exercise of the board's power to refuse to grant approval for the cost of the commission.

The matter was reconsidered by the board's legal aid committee, but the request for prior approval of the expenditure was again refused. This decision was intimated by the board's solicitor in a letter dated 26 August 1992 which is in these terms:

"I refer to previous correspondence in the above, and in particular to my letter of 10 August. The request contained in your recent letter regarding the above has received further consideration, but I have to advise you that it is not considered reasonable that the proposed Commission to South Africa be undertaken at public expense. This view has been arrived at, both in consideration of the Board's stewardship of public funds and having regard to what private litigants could reasonably be expected to do in similar circumstances, particularly bearing in mind that there has already

A been a Commission to take evidence in South Africa involving these parties in quite recent times, at a cost in excess of £30,000.

"I would also draw to your attention that (as a result of that very matter) the Legal Aid legislation was amended earlier this year to require prior approval of the Board for all work likely to involve unusually large expenditure and notification of this change was made to all firms of solicitors by the Board on 26 March last, particularly calling attention to cases involving travel to and from foreign countries, and you should, there-

B fore, have sought approval of the Board before embarking on this exercise. In all the circumstances, it is considered to be an unreasonable expenditure of public funds and the request is accordingly refused."

It is the two decisions recorded in the board's letters dated 10 and 26 August 1992 which the petitioner seeks to have reduced.

The petitioner does not dispute the fact that the proposed open commission in South Africa will involve unusually large expenditure and that the prior

C approval of the board is required. Nor does he suggest that in reaching its decision the board departed from any particular requirement, since the regulation provides only that the "prior approval" of the board is required. Its power to grant approval is at its discretion, and its discretion is not fettered by any requirement that particular criteria are to be applied or particular factors are or are not to be taken into account. The basis of his challenge, according to the averments and the pleas in law in the petition, rests on

D the broad propositions that the board left out of account relevant and material considerations, that it took into account irrelevant considerations and that the decision is unreasonable. But it became clear in the course of the debate before the Lord Ordinary that the essential ground upon which reduction was being sought was that the decision was, in the familiar sense, unreasonable as being one which no reasonable authority acting with due appreciation of its responsibilities could have made.

E In his careful analysis of the argument, which has been of considerable assistance to us in this case, the Lord Ordinary says that he was not persuaded that in relation to the witnesses other than Mr and Mrs Reid the petitioner's pleadings revealed any unreasonableness on the part of the board. He accepted that the issue as to how the evidence of the other witnesses was to be taken was a matter which had no determinative weight in their decision, which was essentially one in relation to the primary question whether there should

F be an open commission to take the evidence of Mr and Mrs Reid. He then dealt with some points which he considered to be minor — the suggestion that the board might have had doubts about the ability of either of the Reids to travel, and the argument that the material before the board did not show that their evidence was essential. He said that it did not appear to him that, on the material before it, any reasonable board could have taken that view of these matters. But he was satisfied that these considerations did not have a decisive role in the board's considerations, and he concentrated his attention on the grounds stated in the letters by which

the decisions were intimated. He then dealt with the

G question whether the cost of the prior dispute about custody was a factor to which the board could have had regard. His conclusion was that, while this could not, standing on its own, be a reasonable basis for refusal, it could not be said to be a wholly illegitimate consideration for the board although this could not constitute more than makeweight consideration, to confirm that approval should be refused for expenditure which was regarded as unreasonable on its own terms. As to whether the stated reasons revealed that the board was proceeding upon some consideration other than the

H cost of the previous commission, he conceded that, on a fair reading of the letter of 10 August 1992, the board was saying that interrogatories were a reasonable alternative in the circumstances. And he was prepared, with hesitation, to concede that, if that was itself a reasonable view, the decision could not be attacked as unreasonable. As for the letter of 26 August 1992, he said that the decision appeared no longer to proceed on the basis that interrogatories constituted a reasonable alternative, the only matter then being founded upon being what private litigants could reasonably be

I expected to do in similar circumstances. Here again, if there were a reasonable basis for the refusal, he did not think that the reference to the prior commission would lead one to see the decision as unreasonable.

Having reached this position, the Lord Ordinary then dealt with the principal argument which the Dean of Faculty had advanced for the petitioner. His submission had been that the board had left out of account the fact that in the view of the Lord Ordinary the Reids'

J evidence was essential and that interrogatories were inappropriate. It was for the court, not the board, to decide how litigation should be conducted. And since the practical result of its refusal to approve the expenditure was that their evidence could not be obtained in the only way which the court had expressly held to be reasonable, its decision to that effect was perverse. The Lord Ordinary saw much force in this argument, and in his discussion of it he made remarks which, by implication at least, were highly critical of the board. This

K was on the ground that its decision showed a lack of courtesy to the court and that it was effectively saying that high quality justice could not be afforded and only very inadequate alternatives could be provided. He said that he would be shocked and saddened by any decision of the board to that effect. But he did not feel able to uphold the Dean's submissions that the board could not take a view of its own on this matter or to say that any such decision could be described as inherently irrational or perverse. Nor in his view was it inherently

L irrational or perverse to conclude that private litigants would not do something which the court, on being asked, had seen as essential.

Thus far the Lord Ordinary's observations were against, rather than in favour of, the petitioner. But in the concluding paragraph of his opinion he said that he had come to the view that each of the decision letters, or both taken together, must be seen as expressing a decision which was unreasonable and perverse in the required sense. He appears to have reached that view on two grounds. The first is that the letters, separately or together, demonstrated that the primary ground for the board's decision was the cost of the previous commission in the same process. He described the other points about the alternative method of interrogatories and about what private litigants would do as representing merely a technical possibility and a dubious speculation. He referred also to the board's silence as to the effects of the decision, particularly in the face of the views of the court. He saw in this not only an astonishing discourtesy but also a failure to consider the requirements and achievement of justice. The essence of his view is described in this sentence: "That silence and failure, coupled with the primacy which they give to the secondary background, leave me in no material doubt that it is not merely the expression of their reasons but their reasoning itself, which ignored the crucial issues, and was diverted on to other matters, the significance and consequences of which were not sufficiently considered to provide a rational basis for refusal."

Counsel for the board submitted that if either of the two parts of the ratio for the Lord Ordinary's decision were erroneous there was no proper basis for his view that the board's decisions were unreasonable. He dealt first with the Lord Ordinary's point that the board had failed to take account of the effect of a decision not to approve the expenditure. He pointed out that this was not a point which had been raised by the petitioner's averments. This was therefore not an issue on which the Lord Ordinary had been addressed and his opinion, although expressed with a high degree of confidence, was based on errors. The suggestion was that the Lord Ordinary's view was influenced more by his evident dislike of the decisions, which he had criticised as astonishingly discourteous, than by a clear understanding of the issues which were of concern to the board. The board was not required by reg 21 (1) (e) to give reasons for a decision to grant or withhold prior approval. It followed that, if reasons were to be given, they did not need to be complete. It was not to be inferred merely from the board's silence on the point that it had not been considered. In any event the board's concern was with the facts and circumstances of this case, and their function was to decide, not how the litigation was to be conducted, but whether the petitioner had made out a case for this unusually large expenditure to be incurred out of public funds. Furthermore, it had not been demonstrated that, if the board had taken account of the effects of this decision, this would have made any difference, given the extent and nature of the information which had been given to it in support of the request. Lastly the other point made by the Lord Ordinary, that the cost of the prior commission was the prime point on which the decisions were based, this was a misunderstanding of the meaning and effect of the decision letters. It was a relevant factor, since the board was necessarily concerned with the question of cost in the performance of its functions. But it was not to be taken in isolation as the only active reason for the decisions. The other reasons, which had been dismissed by the Lord Ordinary as merely speculation, were important and legitimate factors to which the board was entitled to have regard.

We were invited by the Dean of Faculty to reject these submissions and to adhere to the view taken by the Lord Ordinary. His principal argument was that it was for the court to determine the course of action which is appropriate and that it was not reasonable for the board to substitute its own view on this matter for the view taken by the court. The Dean did not go so far as to assert that this was a matter of absolute obligation. Nevertheless the court's decision in this case that interrogatories were to be dispensed with, being an order on a matter of procedure, was binding on the board. And it was self evident that the evidence of Mr and Mrs Reid was essential to the case being made by the petitioner. The board did not seem to have challenged this point or to have questioned their inability to travel to this country to give evidence. So the only point left was the matter of procedure for taking the evidence, which was a matter not for the board but for the court. He was willing to accept that the board was, even on 26 August, looking for a further explanation from the petitioner's solicitors as to why the Reids' evidence could not be taken on interrogatories. But this was a matter which had already been excluded by the court, as was clear not only from Lord Weir's interlocutor but also from Lord Abernethy's views as recorded in the letter written by the Keeper of the Rolls to the board. That disposed of the reason based on the possibility of the evidence being taken on interrogatories. The reference to what private litigants would do was just an assumption on the board's part, and it was not to be treated as a reason for the decision to which it was attached. This left as the only substantial point made by the board the fact that the previous commission had cost so much. But the present dispute about Beverley's custody was a new dispute which was being conducted in different circumstances. A decision based on this point, the effect of which would be to upset the court's view of what was appropriate, was unreasonable and perverse, and the Lord Ordinary was right to reduce the decision as intimated in the two letters of 10 and 26 August.

It is unfortunate that this case has been seen as a confrontation between the board and the court. In our opinion that is a misrepresentation of the important issues which have been raised by the amendment to reg 21 (1), and in particular of what has occurred in this case. The description of the board's decisions — the letters of 10 and 26 August 1992 are, strictly speaking, two decisions although both to the same effect — as astonishingly discourteous attributes to the board, and especially to its legal aid committee, an attitude to the court which has no basis at all in the words used in the decision letters. It is an attitude which should not be inferred lightly under any circumstances, and we are entirely satisfied that it is not to be attributed to the board in this case. It should also be mentioned that on 26 August 1992 the board wrote to the Keeper of the Rolls, saying that the terms of his letter that it was Lord Abernethy's view that it was essential that the commission take place were carefully considered, but that for the reasons outlined in the letters of 10 and 26 August it had been decided to refuse the request to sanction the

A
B
expenditure. The Lord Ordinary was not aware of this letter, which was mentioned for the first time in the board's answers. But it does at least put on record the fact that the board gave careful consideration to Lord Abernethy's view and it shows that trouble was taken to provide the Keeper, and through him Lord Abernethy, with an assurance to this effect. We mention these points not only in fairness to the board in the face of the Lord Ordinary's criticisms. It is fundamental to a proper and just decision in this case that it should be stripped of any suggestion of discourtesy to the court, since this tends to deflect attention from the true issues which, as was pointed out by the Dean of Faculty, are of considerable practical importance to the profession and to the board.

C
D
It is necessary first to examine the issue which the board had to decide. There is no doubt that the holding of an open commission abroad is likely to involve unusually large expenditure. This means that, in terms of reg 21 (1) (e), the prior approval of the board is required. The question, as in all those cases where the prior approval of the board is required in terms of the regulations about both criminal and civil legal aid, is the same. In each of these cases the question is whether the step to be taken, or the expenditure to be incurred, can be said to be justified as a charge on the legal aid fund. If the board is satisfied that there is no other reasonable alternative but to incur the expenditure, the proper course will be for it to grant its approval. This is because the expenditure will then fall into the category of necessary expenditure in the proceedings for which legal aid has already been made available under the Act. But the regulations assume that there may be a choice in this matter, as for example on the question as to whether senior counsel is to be employed: see *AB v Scottish Legal Aid Board*. This then is the first question which the board has a duty to consider in each case. If the answer to it is that there is a choice, the next question is whether the step which is proposed should be approved in preference to the alternative or alternatives which are available. There is a duty on the applicant to explain the basis of the request, and the board is entitled to call for such information as it may require to reach its decision. All this is implied by the regulations and the statutory duty which they impose on the board.

E
F
The court also has a function where the taking of evidence on commission is thought to be appropriate. Section 10 of the Court of Session Act 1988 confers power on the Lord Ordinary to grant a commission for the taking of evidence in the case of any witness who is resident beyond the jurisdiction of the court or who, by reason of age, infirmity or sickness, is unable to attend the diet of proof or trial. The matter is dealt with also in rule 100 of the Rules of Court. The granting or refusal of a commission and diligence lies in the discretion of the Lord Ordinary, as also is the decision as to whether the evidence is to be taken on open commission or by interrogatories. The party who seeks the commission must show cause as to why it should be granted, and if he seeks an open commission he must also show cause as to why this alternative is to be

G
H
I
preferred to the taking of the evidence on interrogatories. Expense is a relevant factor, since the expenses of the commission will ultimately form part of the expenses in the cause and are likely thus to have to be borne by the unsuccessful party in the end of the day. In terms of Rule of Court 97 (a), as applied to a commission for the examination of witnesses by Rule of Court 100 (d), the report of the commission must have endorsed thereon a note of all fees and outlays incurred to or by the commissioner and his clerk. Where the parties are agreed that an open commission is necessary or appropriate, there is unlikely to be an issue on the question of expense. But a motion for an open commission may be opposed on the ground that the course proposed is unnecessarily expensive. In that event the party who seeks the commission will be required to justify his application to the satisfaction of the Lord Ordinary, and questions of detail may be raised in regard to the alternatives which may be available. In such cases the court's decision as to what is desirable in the interests of justice will take account of the expense which is likely to be incurred as well as the relevance and importance of the evidence which the party seeks to have taken in this way.

J
K
In cases, such as the present, where both parties are on legal aid there is not the same pressure on them to subject the cost of the commission to close analysis. The private litigant, aware that he must pay for the commission out of his own funds in the first instance and that he is likely to be held liable in expenses if he loses the action at the end of the day, may be expected to have examined this matter carefully before the motion for a commission is enrolled. And his opponent, if he also is paying for the litigation out of his own money, is likely to do the same in deciding whether or not to oppose it. In legal aid cases the court is, of course, especially vigilant in the knowledge that the expenditure will have to be met from the legal aid fund. But the question is unlikely to be the subject of the same detailed submission and analysis as in cases which are contested on this issue, and the party with the primary interest in the matter, namely the Scottish Legal Aid Board, is normally absent. That indeed is the origin of the principal difficulty which has arisen in this case.

L
On the broad issue, therefore, as to what is required to achieve justice in the case, both the board and the court have functions to perform. But these functions are not the same, and the decisions which they must take are not necessarily to be reached by reference to the same criteria. The court is best placed to assess the relevance and importance of the evidence to the issues in the case, and to express a view as to whether the nature of the evidence is such that it may, or that it should not, be taken on interrogatories. The board is best placed to assess the financial implications of the competing alternatives, and to express a view as to whether, taking its own view of that factor into account, the more expensive alternative should be adopted. The judge is entitled to decide the issue on the basis of such information as may be in process and has been placed before him on the motion roll. The board

is entitled to decide the issue, in the exercise of its statu-
A tory duty, on the basis of such information as may be
placed before it by the applicant, including any
answers which it may receive to requests for further
information if this is required.

The Dean of Faculty informed us that Lord Weir,
who granted the motion on 10 July 1992 for the Reids'
evidence to be taken on open commission in South
Africa, was not told that this would involve unusually
large expenditure for which the prior approval of the
board was required. There is no indication that this
B point was drawn to Lord Abernethy's attention on 17
July 1992 when he granted the motions in regard to the
other witnesses and appointed himself to be the commissioner. The point was of course of lesser importance at that stage, because the critical decision had
already been taken by Lord Weir. On the Dean's argument it was immaterial whether Lord Weir was or was
not aware of this point, because the question was essentially one for the court to decide as a matter of procedure and it was not for the board to substitute its own
C view for the view taken by the court. This argument
raises two further questions of importance with which
we must now deal. The first is whether it was appropriate for the petitioner to apply to the court to grant
the commissions to take the evidence before he had
obtained the prior approval of the board to this expenditure. The second is whether the issue was one of procedure which it was for the court only to decide and not
the board.

D Now reg 21 (1)(e) does not in terms require the prior
approval of the board before a motion for an open commission may be enrolled. Nor is there any provision to
that effect in the Rules of Court. Nevertheless we are
in no doubt that the proper procedure, in all legally
aided cases where the court is to be asked to authorise
a course of action which is of an unusual nature or is
likely to involve unusually large expenditure, is for the
party who is in receipt of legal aid to seek the prior
approval of the board before that course of action is
E proposed to the court. There is a close analogy in this
regard to the way in which the matter would be
handled if the case was to be paid for out of, or was
being supported by, private funds. Good sense requires
that the alternative courses of action be assessed and
the appropriate calculations carried out before the
party commits himself to the expenditure. There
would be no point in the privately funded case for the
litigant asking for an open commission unless this is
something which he is satisfied he ought to and can pay
for. In view of the board's interest in the matter, there-
F fore, this is something which ought to be taken up with
the board first before the application is made to the
court. If prior approval is refused, that is not necessarily an end of the matter. The view which may be
taken by the court, as to the importance from its point
of view of the evidence, may be a factor which the
board would find decisive in reaching its decision, on
further consideration, as to whether the expenditure
should be approved. But the court should be aware in
expressing this view that it has no jurisdiction to order
the board to grant prior approval for the expenditure.

This matter has been committed by the regulation to
the decision of the board, which has the responsibility G
in the public interest for administering the legal aid
fund. Thus, the court's decision on what the Dean
described as a matter of procedure is not binding on the
board. We agree on this point with the Lord Ordinary,
who felt unable to uphold the argument that the board
could not take a view of its own as to what should be
paid for out of public funds.

If the court is to express a view on this matter it
should, of course, be based only on the pleadings and
other documents in process and on such other informa- H
tion as may be provided to it by the parties on
the motion roll. It should be recorded in a note or
opinion in the process which is issued to the parties in
the normal manner, a copy of which can then be provided to the board. No such note or opinion is available
in this case to record the factors which Lord Weir took
into account in reaching his decision on 10 July 1992.
This is, as we have already said, unsurprising because
the motion which he heard was unopposed and he was
not told of the requirement for the prior approval of the I
board to be obtained. The only record which we have
seen of what Lord Abernethy had in mind on 17 July
1992 is the letter which the Keeper of the Rolls sent to
the board at his request. In this letter he expressed the
view that it was essential to the conduct of the litigation
that the commission should take place. The Dean of
Faculty told us that this letter was prompted by a joint
approach by the parties to Lord Abernethy's clerk for
Lord Abernethy's views to be sought. No doubt they
were influenced in this matter by the urgency which
was then being expressed to the board for a decision to J
be taken if Lord Abernethy was to be able to conduct
the commission in South Africa on the intended date.

Whatever the circumstances, however, and however
well intentioned Lord Abernethy was to respond to it
as he did, this procedure should not have been adopted
and the letter was, in effect, worthless as an expression
of his view. The matter should have been raised with
the judge by motion in open court. His view should
then have been expressed in a note or opinion in the K
process which set out the reasons for it, so as to make
it plain that his view was based solely on the information which was in process or had been put before him
by the parties. As it is, the basis for his view is unclear.
The motions which he heard were marked of consent.
He was not required to decide whether the evidence of
Mr and Mrs Reid should be taken on open commission, since that matter had already been decided by
Lord Weir. And it is not clear that his view was
expressed only in regard to the question whether the L
Reids' evidence should be taken in this way, or whether
it was a view expressed generally in regard to the taking
of the evidence of all the witnesses whose names had
been entered into the three interlocutors. The result of
this was that the board was presented with no more
than the fact that decisions had been taken by the court
in its absence, without any reasoned explanation of the
view, if any, which had been formed on the issue about
the necessity of taking the Reids' evidence on open
commission, which was the point of critical importance
to the board.

The provisions of reg 21 (1) (e) may raise difficult issues for all concerned where strong views are held by the parties that an item of work of an unusual nature, or which is likely to involve unusually large expenditure, is necessary and appropriate to the case and the board disagrees with this view. But a judge, or sheriff where the matter is raised in the sheriff court, should be careful not to be drawn into direct argument with the board on matters relating to legal aid. The board's decisions are in the last resort subject to the remedy of judicial review, and the impartiality of the court in this aspect of the matter must be preserved. It is essential that anything which is to be communicated by way of guidance or advice from the court to the board should be said only from the bench. The judge or sheriff should be careful also not to commit himself to the position that an item of expenditure is essential unless he is satisfied, by careful and detailed argument in open court, that no other reasonable alternative is available. By doing so in circumstances where it is open to the board to take a different view, he may put himself in difficulty in taking any further part in the case if a step which he has said is essential cannot be carried out. It is preferable that he should confine himself to saying whether or not in his view the course proposed by the parties is desirable, together with a statement of the factors which have led him to this view. There is no reason to think that the board will not give close attention, in forming its own view on the matter, to what he has said.

We can now turn to the reasons for the decisions which were held by the Lord Ordinary not to provide a rational basis for the refusal. In our opinion the costs of the previous commission in South Africa was a factor to which the board was entitled to have regard. It was relevant as a guide to the likely cost of the expenditure which would be incurred on this occasion. The cost of a further commission in South Africa was of direct concern to the board, as this was expenditure which would require to be met out of the legal aid fund. It cannot be doubted that the scale of the unusually large expenditure was a relevant factor, although we agree with the Lord Ordinary that a decision which was based solely on cost without regard to other factors would be unreasonable in the *Wednesbury* sense: see *Associated Provincial Picture Houses Ltd v Wednesbury Corporation* [1948] 1 KB, per Lord Greene MR at p 229. We cannot accept, however, the view taken by the Lord Ordinary that the cost was, as he put it, the prime point on which the decisions were based and that the other points mentioned in the decision letters are to be dismissed as mere speculation, indicating a line of reasoning which was diverted from the critical issues.

In its letter dated 10 August 1992 the board, having set out its decision that it would be an unreasonable use of public funds to grant the application, added that it had noted that evidence from South Africa could be obtained by way of interrogatories. In the context this must be taken to be an indication of a further factor to which the board had had regard as well as the issue of cost. As a statement of fact the point was entirely accurate. The evidence of Mr and Mrs Reid could be,

and can still be, obtained by interrogatories. Implicit in this statement was the point raised in the board's letter to the petitioner's solicitors dated 17 July 1992, that it would expect detailed consideration to be given to the relative merits of obtaining evidence taken on interrogatories or on open commission. In their reply dated 23 July 1992 the petitioner's solicitors did not deal with this matter. They said that the evidence of Mr and Mrs Reid was essential for their client and that they could not travel to Scotland. But they did not explain why it would not be satisfactory for their evidence not to be taken on interrogatories. They based the argument solely on the fact that Lord Weir had dispensed with interrogatories, without providing the board with any reasoned explanation of why this had been done. In our opinion the board was entitled to take the view that it had not been shown that it was essential for this evidence to be taken on open commission, and that the taking of the Reids' evidence on interrogatories was an alternative method of taking their evidence which was available.

Indeed we ourselves are far from being satisfied that the expensive step of an open commission to take the Reids' evidence is really necessary in this case. The Lord Ordinary will have the benefit of seeing both the petitioner and Mrs Venter at the proof in Edinburgh, since it is not intended that their evidence should be taken on commission. They are the principal parties in the dispute about Beverley's custody. The petitioner's fiancée, Mrs Jansen, is fit to travel to this country as are all the other witnesses whom the parties may wish to call. There are averments in the minute and answers about the accommodation which would be available for Beverley in South Africa and other matters affecting her care and wellbeing should her custody be awarded to the petitioner. But there is no suggestion in the averments that any of these matters are exclusively within the knowledge of Mr and Mrs Reid, nor has it been suggested that on the points about which they can speak there are particular issues of difficulty or of credibility which might arise. Their state of health, the fact that they reside at a different address from that where the petitioner now resides with Mrs Jansen, and the lack of any reference to them by name in the averments all suggest that they are likely to play a relatively minor part in Beverley's care and upbringing and that their evidence is unlikely to be critical to the decision about her custody. These were, of course, all matters for the board to consider in taking the decision as to whether to approve the expenditure. It is sufficient for us to say that we reject the Lord Ordinary's view that the board's silence on the effects of the decision, which is that the Reids' evidence will have to be taken on interrogatories, indicates a failure to consider the requirements and achievement of justice in this case. These broad concepts resolve themselves into the very questions on which the board had sought answers from the petitioner's solicitors and to which, the board was entitled to think, no satisfactory answer had been provided in reply.

There remains the point about what private litigants could reasonably be expected to do in similar circum-

A stances, which was stated in the letter dated 26 August 1992 as a factor to which the board had had regard. The Lord Ordinary dismissed this point as something which, while not inherently irrational, had been only touched on by the board as a possibility. It was in his view not the prime point of the decision. We do not agree with this construction of the board's letter. The point about what a private litigant would do is stated as one of the factors which the board had in view. It is entitled to at least equal weight along with the other factors about the board's stewardship for public funds

B and the cost of the prior commission in this case. And it raises the same basic issue about the need for a careful and detailed consideration of the relative merits of obtaining the Reids' evidence on interrogatories and on commission, which was the subject of the comment in the previous decision letter and to which, the board were again entitled to think, no satisfactory answer had yet been given.

On the whole matter we consider that the board's decision to refuse approval for the expenditure as inti-

C mated in the letters of 10 and 26 August 1992 cannot be said to have been unreasonable. As Lord Cullen pointed out in *K v Scottish Legal Aid Board*, 1989 SLT at p 620, and again in *AB v Scottish Legal Aid Board*, 1991 SCLR at p 704, the test which requires to be satisfied to demonstrate unreasonableness in this context is an exacting one. We can find nothing in the decisions to justify applying to them Lord Diplock's description of an unreasonable decision as being one which is "so outrageous in its defiance of logic or of accepted moral

D standards that no sensible person who had applied his mind to the question to be decided could have arrived at it": *Council of Civil Service Unions v Minister for the Civil Service* [1985] 1 AC at p 410. It appears to us to be a decision which fell clearly within the limits of the discretion which has been committed to the board by reg 21 (1) (e). We are not persuaded that the board left out of account relevant or material considerations or that it took into account considerations which were irrelevant. Nor can the decisions, when properly

E understood in their context and in the light of the statutory duty which the board must perform, be said to be perverse.

Accordingly, we shall allow this reclaiming motion and recall the interlocutor of the Lord Ordinary. We shall sustain the first plea in law for the board and dismiss the petition on the ground that the petitioner's averments are irrelevant.

———

F   *Counsel for Petitioner, Dean of Faculty (Johnston, QC), Sutherland; Solicitors, Robson McLean, WS — Counsel for Respondents, Stewart, QC, Thomson; Solicitors, Shepherd & Wedderburn, WS.*

R D S

John Walker & Sons Ltd v Douglas Laing & Co Ltd

OUTER HOUSE
LORD MAXWELL
19 OCTOBER 1976

Trade marks and names — Passing off — Interdict — Breach — Interdict against supplying Scotch whisky for purpose of enabling spirits containing spirits other than Scotch to be passed off as Scotch whisky — Respondents exporting Scotch whisky to Panama under brand name of "King of Scots" which consisted of 20 per cent of Scotch malt and 80 per cent of Panamanian cane spirit — Respondents instructing Panamanian agents to ensure that all labels and materials clearly indicated that product was blend of Scotch whisky and Panamanian spirit — Cartons sold in Panama for use with Scotch whisky and for use with blend to some extent the same — Bottles used to sell Scotch whisky and blend almost identical — Whether calculated to enable passing off to be achieved.

Interdict — Breach — Passing off — Proof — Interdict against supplying Scotch whisky for purpose of enabling spirits containing spirits other than Scotch to be passed off as Scotch whisky — Respondents exporting Scotch whisky to Panama under brand name of "King of Scots" which consisted of 20 per cent of Scotch malt and 80 per cent of Panamanian cane spirit — Respondents instructing Panamanian agents to ensure that all labels and materials clearly indicated that product was blend of Scotch whisky and Panamanian spirit — Cartons sold in Panama for use with Scotch whisky and for use with blend to some extent the same — Bottles used to sell Scotch whisky and blend almost identical — Whether calculated to enable passing off to be achieved.

In 1973 the respondents were interdicted from inter alia supplying Scotch whisky, bottles or labels or permitting the use of any trade mark or label or doing any other acts for the purpose of enabling or which were calculated to enable spirits containing spirits other than Scotch to be passed off as Scotch whisky, under exception of the supply by them of Scotch whisky for admixture purposes (being the production of a mixture consisting of Scotch whisky and a spirit or spirits other than Scotch whisky) if the respondents had reasonable grounds for believing and did in fact believe that such admixture would not be passed off as and for Scotch whisky. The respondents exported Scotch whisky under the brand name of "King of Scots" to Panama which consisted of 20 per cent of Scotch malt and 80 per cent of Panamanian cane spirit. They instructed their Panamanian agents to ensure that all labels and materials used for presentation of "King of Scots" had clearly to indicate that although the product could be termed whisky, it could not be termed Scotch whisky, and that it had to be clearly indicated on the labels that the product was a blend of Scotch malt whisky and local Panamanian spirit. The cartons for use with Scotch whisky and for

use with the admix sold in Panama were to some
A extent the same, each having the name "King of
Scots" prominently displayed and identical colouring
and pictorial design. The bottles used to sell Scotch
whisky and the Panama bottles were almost identical
and the bottles and cartons were sent in cardboard
boxes bearing the words "King of Scots" and
"whisky" although the wording was usually obscured
by government despatch labels. In these circumstances, the petitioners presented a complaint to the
Inner House in which they claimed that the respondents had breached the terms of the interdict as the
B malt, bottles, cartons and boxes which had been
supplied were "calculated" in the objective sense to
enable passing off to be achieved. The Second
Division remitted the cause to the Outer House for a
hearing on the petition and complaint. The respondents contended that their actings fell within the
exception to the prohibition. The petitioners contended inter alia that the onus of proof in that regard
fell on the respondents.

C   **Held,** by the Lord Ordinary, (1) that the onus of
proof rested with the petitioners throughout as the
interdict should be construed in the sense most
favourable to the liberty of the respondents
(p 162D); (2) that to establish what was meant by
"passing off" in the context of this case it was
necessary for the petitioners to prove first that
Scotch whisky had a reputation in Panama,
secondly that that reputation was attached to
Scotch whisky properly so called, and thirdly that
D things supplied by the respondents were calculated
to enable "King of Scots" to be sold in such a way
that purchasers were likely to be misled into thinking that it was of the same nature and had the same
characteristic as regards geographical origin as
Scotch whisky, whether or not those customers
knew the precise facts of that nature and characteristic (pp 162L-163B); (3) that although proof of
the remote possibility of an occasional deception
would not establish likelihood of being misled, the
petitioners need not go as far as proving the proba-
E bility of frequent passing off (p 163F-G); (4) that
although it was essential to rely on evidence from
Panama in this case, it was for the Court of Session
to decide on the facts rather than on the opinion
of witnesses whether passing off was likely
(p 163G-H); (5) that on the evidence the petitioners
had proved the three matters they required to establish passing off (pp 163H-164B); and (6) that it was
clear beyond reasonable doubt that the respondents
did not have reasonable grounds for believing that
F the admix would not be passed off either intentionally or inadvertently, for throughout they had a full
and detailed knowledge on how "King of Scots"
was made, marketed and advertised (pp 166L-
167C); and order that interdict had been breached
pronounced accordingly.

Observed, that where actual passing off was not
alleged, but merely the enabling of passing off to be
achieved, proof of actual instance was not essential
(p 164C).

Petition and complaint

John Walker & Sons Ltd and John Dewar & Sons G
Ltd, blenders and exporters of Scotch whisky,
obtained an interdict pronounced by the First
Division on 6 July 1973 against Douglas Laing & Co
Ltd, Frederick Douglas Laing and Morag Ross Laing
prohibiting them from supplying Scotch whisky,
bottles or labels or permitting the use of any trade
mark or label or doing any other acts for the purpose
of enabling or which were calculated to enable spirits
containing spirits other than Scotch to be passed off as
Scotch whisky. A petition and complaint was subse- H
quently initiated by the petitioners against the respondents for breach of that interdict.

Pleadings

The parties averred, inter alia:

Stat 2. On 4 August 1970 the petitioners raised an
action of interdict and reparation against the first
named respondents in the Court of Session. The
summons in the said action concluded for interdict
against the first named respondents either under their   I
own name or the name of Langside Distillers or under
any other name, and any person or persons acting on
their behalf, using or supplying to any other person or
persons any Scotch whisky, bottles, labels, or other
things or documents, or causing licensing or permitting the use of any trade mark or label, or doing
any other acts, for the purpose of enabling, or which
were calculated to enable, spirits that consist of or
include spirits that were not obtained by distillation in
Scotland from a mash of cereal grain saccharified by   J
the diastase of malt, to be passed off in any country as
and for Scotch whisky. On 9 March 1972 the Lord
Ordinary (Avonside), having heard counsel for the
parties in the procedure roll, pronounced an interlocutor granting interdict de plano as concluded for.
The first named respondents reclaimed against the
said interlocutor, but prior to the hearing of the
reclaiming motion the action was settled extra-
judicially. On 6 July 1973 your Lordships pronounced
the following interlocutor therein: K

"Edinburgh, 6 July 1973.

"The Lords interpone authority to the joint minute
for the parties no 94 of process and in respect and in
terms thereof recall the interdict pronounced by the
Lord Ordinary on 9 March 1972 and of new interdict
prohibit and discharge the defenders either under
their own name or the name of Langside Distillers or
under any other name, and any person or persons   L
acting on their behalf, using or supplying to any other
person or persons any Scotch whisky, bottles, labels or
other things or documents, or causing licensing or permitting the use of any trade mark or label or doing any
other acts, for the purpose of enabling, or which are
calculated to enable, spirits that consist of or include
spirits that were not obtained by distillation in Scotland from a mash of cereal grain saccharified by the
diastase of malt, to be passed off as and for Scotch
whisky, excepting, however, the supply by the
defenders or their foresaids, as the case may be, of

A Scotch whisky or any of the abovementioned articles, (i) if the defenders or their foresaids, as the case may be, have reasonable grounds for believing, and do in fact believe, that such Scotch whisky or articles will not be used for admixture purposes (meaning thereby the production of a mixture consisting of Scotch whisky and a spirit or spirits other than Scotch whisky) or (ii) for such admixture purposes if the defenders or their foresaids, as the case may be, have reasonable grounds for believing, and do in fact believe, that such admixture will not be passed off as

B and for Scotch whisky; quoad ultra assoilzie the defenders from the whole conclusions of the summons and decern; find no expenses due to or by either party."

Ans 2. Admitted.

On 13 November 1975 the Second Division *allowed* a proof before answer to be heard by the Lord Ordinary; and *remitted* the case to him to hear the evidence of parties and report back to the Inner House.

C

The proof before answer was heard before the Lord Ordinary (Maxwell) on 1 June 1976 and following days.

Cases referred to

Argyllshire Weavers Ltd v A Macaulay (Tweeds) Ltd,
    1965 SLT 21.
Bollinger v Costa Brava Wine Co [1960] 1 Ch 262;
    [1961] 1 WLR 277.
Cellular Clothing Co v White (1953) 70 RPC 9.
D *Coleman & Co v Smith,* 29 RPC 81.
Eutectic Welding Alloys Co Ltd v Whitting, 1969 SLT
    (Notes) 79.
Gribben v Gribben, 1976 SLT 266.
Haig (John) & Co Ltd v Forth Blending Co Ltd, 1954
    SLT 2; 1954 SC 35.
Henderson & Turnbull Ltd v Adair, 1939 SLT 478.
Johnston v Orr Ewing (1882) 7 App Cas 219.
King v Gilloch (1905) 22 RPC 327.
Nimmo v Alexander Cowan & Sons Ltd, 1967 SLT
    277; 1967 SC (HL) 79.
E
*Office Cleaning Services v Westminster Window &
    General Cleaners Ltd* (1946) 63 RPC 69.
Park Court Hotel Ltd v Transworld Hotels Ltd [1970]
    PLR 89; [1972] RPC 27.
Schweppes v Gibbens (1905) 22 RPC 601.
Vine Products Ltd v Mackenzie & Co Ltd [1969]
    RPC 1.
*Walker (John) & Sons Ltd v Douglas McGibbon & Co
    Ltd,* 1972 SLT 128.
F *Walker (John) & Sons Ltd v Henry Ost & Co Ltd*
    [1970] 1 WLR 917.
Weingarten v Bayer & Co (1905) 22 RPC 341.
Wertheimer v Stewart Cooper & Co (1906) 23 RPC
    481.

Textbook referred to

Kerley, *Trade Marks* (10th ed), p 428.

On 19 October 1976 the Lord Ordinary *found* that the interdict had been breached and *reported* to the Inner House accordingly.

LORD MAXWELL.—In pursuance of your Lordships' interlocutor of 13 November 1975 I took a G proof of the parties' respective averments in this petition and complaint and answers on 1 June 1976 and following days and now report as follows:

The petitioners led the evidence of Mr Bryce, a legal adviser in the trade marks department of the Distillers Co Ltd; Mr Boyter, a director of MacDonald Greenlees Ltd, a subsidiary of the Distillers Co Ltd; Senor Mendez, a director of a company based in Panama City carrying on business as importers and distributors of liquor in Panama. He has also held H various appointments in the business and commercial sphere in Panama such as President of the Chamber of Commerce; Senor de Obaldia, a Panamanian businessman, who was at one time a customs official in Panama, rising to the position of customs director and who was also president of and is still a member of the Panamanian Tariff Commission, and Senor Brostella, president of a company based in Panama City carrying on business as distributors of liquor in Panama. The respondents led the evidence of Mr I Laing, the second named respondent, who is managing director of and who owns all but one share in the first named respondents (the one remaining share being owned by his wife, the third named respondent); Senor Arias, a Cuban who has lived in Panama since about 1960. He has been engaged in the liquor business since he arrived in Panama. In 1970 he joined the firm of Diers & Ullrich, aftermentioned, as sales director. Since 1973 he has been vice president of that firm and for practical purposes the manager thereof; J and Mr Nam Sing Lao, a Panamanian of Chinese extraction, who is manager of a company based in Panama City and carrying on business as liquor distributors in Panama.

[His Lordship commented on the credibility of the various witnesses and continued:]

The following facts are admitted on record or are spoken to in evidence, which I considered was reliable and which was not I think challenged by counsel on K either side. I do not suggest that all of these matters are relevant to the present issue, but this being a report, I think it right to set out fairly fully the matters which were subject of evidence and in my view clearly established.

The Republic of Panama has a population of about 1½ million, of whom one third or rather more live in Panama City. The language of the country is Spanish. English is a compulsory language in schools and a substantial proportion of the population, particularly in L Panama City, speak English to some degree, though I consider that Mr Laing was clearly exaggerating when he said that everyone there speaks English. In Spanish there is only one word, "Escoces", for "Scotch", "Scottish" and "Scots".

For many years Scotch whisky (by which expression in this report I mean whisky the whole alcoholic content of which has been distilled in Scotland) has been imported into and sold in Panama in large quantities and in many brands. It is a very popular drink particularly with the more affluent inhabitants. The principal outlets are supermarkets and "bodegas" (which are smaller shops selling liquors), where it is sold in bottles sometimes in and sometimes without cartons, and bars, restaurants, nightclubs and the like, where it is sold mainly by the measure but sometimes by the bottle. Many of the bars, nightclubs etc are dimly lit. Scotch whisky as imported into Panama usually, if not invariably, bears the words "Scotch Whisky" on the bottles and cartons.

For some years, though for how long I do not know, there have been on the market in Panama a number of brands of liquor of a whisky type, which I refer to in this report as "admixes". These admixes consist of malt distilled in Scotland and imported in bulk and mixed with a spirit distilled in Panama. They may also contain water added in Panama. Some of these admixes have brand names which to a Scotsman, but not necessarily to a Panamanian, would suggest an association with Scotland, such as "Old Mackay". One of them, "Old Scotty", suggests even more strongly an association with Scotland. An admix at least at one time made and marketed in Panama by Diers & Ullrich under the brand name Royal Club specifically and clearly purports on the main label of the bottle to be a "produce of", "distilled in", and "blended in" Scotland and to be Scotch whisky. I am not satisfied on the evidence of Senor Arias as to whether and if so when the marketing of this product with this label has ceased. Another admix produced by Diers & Ullrich and marketed in Panama is called "Windsor Castle". The main label on the bottle of this product at least at one time, described the product as "Tipo de Scotch Whisky". It is not clear to me whether this would be understood in Panama to mean a variety of Scotch whisky or merely a liquor of the Scotch whisky type. Admixes are sold through the same outlets as Scotch whisky. Admixes in general sell at a substantially lower price than Scotch whisky. Certain Canadian and American whiskies are also sold in Panama and through the same outlets, though they are not as popular as Scotch whisky.

The first respondents have for many years exported Scotch whisky under the brand name "King of Scots" to various parts of the world. In about 1963, with a view to entering the Panama market, they approached Diers & Ullrich, of Colon, Panama. Following discussions, it was agreed that Diers & Ullrich would place on the Panama market under the brand name "King of Scots", an admix mixed in Panama and consisting of Scotch malt to be supplied in bulk by the first respondents and a neutral spirit distilled from cane in Panama by or for Diers & Ullrich. It was further agreed that the first respondents should provide from Scotland all the packaging materials, that is to say bottles, labels, bottle cartons and larger cases when used. This arrangement was carried into effect and is still in operation. The admix sold in Panama under this arrangement is comprised, as to 20 per cent, of Scotch malt and, as to 80 per cent, of Panamanian cane spirit. I am not clear whether there is also an addition of water in Panama.

Selling of the "King of Scots" admix in Panama started in 1965 or 1966. Originally it was sold without individual bottle cartons, but at some stage a carton was introduced. This carton bears on all four sides the words "King of Scots" in large red gothic letters underneath which are printed in smaller black letters the words "Blended Scotch Whisky", and below that again in smaller black letters the words "with finest local neutral spirit". There is also written in fairly small letters the words "shipped by the owners Douglas Laing & Co Ltd, Glasgow, Scotland". This carton bears pictures of a Scottish piper and female Highland dancers in appropriate dress. At a date of which I am not informed this carton was replaced by a slightly different carton, the only significant difference being the deletion of the word "Scotch" so that the words below "King of Scots" read simply "blended whisky". No cartons of either of these two types have been supplied by the respondents since the aftermentioned interdict of 6 July 1973 was pronounced. I do not have an example of the bottle in use in Panama before July 1973.

In August 1970 the present petitioners raised an action against the first respondents concluding for interdict in certain terms against passing off as "Scotch whisky". In March 1972, having heard argument in procedure roll, Lord Avonside granted interdict de plano as concluded for. The first named respondents reclaimed, but before the reclaiming motion was heard the parties reached an agreement as a result of which, on 6 July 1973, an interdict was pronounced in pursuance of a joint minute the wording of which is more restricted than that originally concluded for.

At about the time the terms of the interdict were agreed the respondents determined to adopt a new and more dignified style of carton, not only for the admix sold in Panama but also for the "King of Scots" brand of Scotch whisky exported to other countries. They commissioned the design of a carton for use in the marketing of Scotch whisky. An example of this is no 16 of process, which was purchased in Portugal. At the same time they commissioned a modified design of the carton for use with the admix sold in Panama, having regard to the terms of the interdict. The carton for use with Scotch whisky and the carton for the Panama admix are the same to this extent. First, the most prominent feature of both is, on the front, the name "King of Scots" in large white gothic characters against a black background. Secondly, they have identical colouring and pictorial design. They both show on the front a picture of the bottle contained in the carton with the front and shoulder labels of the bottles visible, two half full glasses, the bottle cap with the name "King of Scots" visible thereon, a sprig of white heather and a Cairngorm brooch. On one side they both show more heather, some old books and a picture of a man in Highland dress. On the other side they show more old books and an antique flask. Apart from writing, the back in each case is plain. The main differences are as follows. Whereas the Scotch whisky carton has under the words "King of Scots" on the front in fairly large yellow letters the words "Blended Scotch Whisky", the Panama carton bears, in the same place and in similar letters, the words "A blend of Scotch Malt Whisky and Panamanian Spirit". While nothing like so prominent as the words "King of Scots", this lettering, to anyone of reasonable eyesight is clearly legible from a considerable distance. The Scotch whisky carton bears, on both sides, the words "Douglas Laing & Co Ltd, Glasgow, Scotland". No wording appears on the sides of the Panama carton. On the back of the Scotch whisky carton are the words "Product of Scotland" "100% Scotch Whisky" and "Distilled Blended and Bottled by Douglas Laing & Co Ltd, Glasgow, Scotland". None of these words appear on the back of the Panama carton, but instead there is written in Spanish, "La malta Escocesa que contiene este producto es destilado y anejado en Escocia y combinado conselectos espiritus destilados en Panama", which means "the Scottish Malt which is contained in this product is distilled and matured in Scotland and combined with select spirit distilled in Panama". At the bottom of the back of the carton is written "Producto Nacional de Panama". All of this writing on the back of the Panama carton is in fairly large white letters which stand out clearly against a black background and are legible from a considerable distance. The pictures of the bottle on the fronts of the two cartons respectively also differ to the extent that the labels on the bottles themselves differ.

As regards the bottles themselves, it is not clear to me whether their style or labelling underwent a change at the time of the introduction of the new cartons. In any event the bottle sent to Panama since the date of the interdict has a cap bearing the words "King of Scots" and also the words "Douglas Laing & Co Ltd, Glasgow, Scotland". This wording on the cap is likely to be wholly or partly obscured, at the time of sale, by the government stamp aftermentioned. To the front there is a shoulder label bearing very prominently the words "King of Scots" in gothic letters. The front label which was in use initially following the interdict (referred to on record as "type A") has a device which, I think, has no significance. It again bears prominently the words "King of Scots" in gothic letters. Beneath this in fairly large letters are the words "Blended Whisky". Beneath this again in very small letters, only legible on close inspection, are the words in Spanish "Mezclas de maltas escocesas y espiritu de granos panamenos bajo la supervigilancia de Douglas Laing & Co Ltd, Glasgow, Scotland" and "Fabricado por (which I understood can mean either 'made by' or 'made for') Diers & Ullrich SA Colon Rep de Panama". There are also in extremely small letters the words "printed in Scotland". On the back is a label bearing a lion rampant device and, again in small letters, the words "Producto Nacional", "Diers & Ullrich SA Colon" and in extremely small letters "permitido su consumo y aprobado por el quimico oficial". The bottle used for the sale of Scotch whisky is almost identical to the Panama bottle first described except that, first, the front label under the words "King of Scots" describes the product as "Blended

Scotch Whisky" and bears the words "Product of Scotland", "100% Scotch Whiskies" and "Blended by Douglas Laing & Co Ltd, Glasgow, Scotland" and "Printed in Scotland" and does not of course bear any of the wording in Spanish. Similarly the back label does not bear the Spanish wording to which I have referred, but simply bears the words "Distilled in Scotland".

At some date after the interdict but before the proof the respondents made changes to the front labels of the bottles sent to Panama. The new label (called on record "type B") differs from the type A in respect that the word "blended" is deleted, so that, after the words "King of Scots", there follows simply the word "whisky". Further, in type B, the words "Bajo la Supervigilancia de Douglas Laing & Co Ltd, Glasgow, Scotland" do not appear and nor do the words "printed in Scotland".

The Spanish wording on the backs of the cartons was a translation made by a teacher of English in Panama of words initially provided in English by Mr Laing. There was some disagreement between Senor Arias and Mr Laing as to how the Spanish wording on the labels on the bottles was obtained.

Following the interdict there elapsed a few months, during which no material was sent by the respondents to Panama, but since then they have regularly despatched to Diers & Ullrich large quantities of Scotch malt with the appropriate number of bottles and cartons as above described. The bottles and cartons are sent in large cardboard boxes which bear the words "King of Scots" and "whisky" but this wording on the large boxes is usually obscured by despatch labels.

Diers & Ullrich prepare the admix as already described and market it in large quantities throughout Panama in the bottles and cartons provided by the respondents. Mr Nam Sing Lao's company (which is one of the four largest liquor wholesalers in Panama) alone sells about 50 cases a month, as compared with 200 cases of Scotch whisky.

As required by Panamanian law all bottles of "King of Scots", when leaving Diers & Ullrich, must bear across the top a government adhesive stamp appropriate to national products. This stamp, at any rate as at the time of the proof, is pale blue and white in colour and bears the words in rather small writing "Botellas", "Republica de Panama", "Timbre Para Licores Nacionales" and a reference to the relevant article of the fiscal code. This contrasts with a white and pink adhesive stamp applied to imported products such as Scotch whisky, which bears the words in not very legible writing "Republica de Panama", "Timbre para licores extranjeros". Imported bottles of Scotch whisky or some of them at least also have a small blue and yellow official adhesive stamp on the shoulder at the back.

By far the largest outlet for "King of Scots" in Panama is through supermarkets. The photographs produced show clearly the general manner in which it is displayed in the supermarkets and also in the smaller bodegas. It will be seen that it is displayed in large quantities. It is often, probably more often than not, displayed on shelves close to Scotch whiskies, but it is not necessarily adjacent thereto being frequently separated from Scotch whiskies, by other liquors. Mr Boyter gave evidence of having seen, in more than one supermarket, Scotch whisky displayed on the shelves in descending order of price with "King of Scots" immediately adjacent to the cheapest Scotch whisky. While I have no doubt that this sometimes occurs, the photographs demonstrate that it is by no means the regular arrangement for display. In the supermarkets cartons of "King of Scots" are sometimes displayed in the large cardboard case to which I have referred, the cases being cut so as partially to reveal the contents. Mr Bryce expressed the opinion that the large cases are cut deliberately in such a way that the words "King of Scots" on the front of the cartons are visible, but not the words "A blend of Scotch Malt Whisky and Panamanian Spirit". I do not think it proved and the photographs do not suggest that this is a regular and deliberate practice. On the other hand it is obvious that from time to time the cartons and bottles may be displayed, whether intentionally or inadvertently, in such a way that the only reasonably legible and visible words are "King of Scots".

"King of Scots" is also sold in some quantities by the measure or in bottles in bars, restaurants, night clubs etc. When it is sold by the measure and where, which is by no means always the case, the bottle from which the measure is poured is visible to the customer I take it as self evident that, depending on lighting and distance from the bar or counter, the customer will frequently be able to read the words on the bottle "King of Scots" and perhaps the words "Whisky" or "Blended Whisky", but not the small writing "mezclas de maltas escocesas y espiritu de granos panamenos". In such cases the cap will have been removed and the government stamp will not be visible.

"King of Scots" is widely advertised in the Panama press. A number of advertisements have been lodged in process. Sometimes it is advertised by itself. In no 78 of process the advertisement includes a picture showing the front of the carton with the words "A blend of Scotch Malt Whisky and Panamanian spirit" visible but nowhere is there visible and reasonably legible a statement in Spanish as to the nature of the product. While the layout of such advertisements no doubt varies it is reasonable to assume that no 78 of process is not untypical. Sometimes, particularly by supermarkets, a number of liquors including "King of Scots" are dealt with in one advertisement. In some instances all the advertised products including "King of Scots" are described as "Whisky" and all but "King of Scots" are in fact "Scotch Whiskies". In other examples of these group advertisements "King of Scots" is advertised along with other liquors, some of which are Scotch whiskies and some of which are not, being for example, beer, wine etc. So far as can be judged from the advertisements produced it is not

the custom in advertisements to describe Scotch whisky as "Scotch Whisky", though the words "Scotch Whisky" are sometimes legible on the pictures of the bottles portrayed. Newspaper advertisements of liquor usually and perhaps invariably state clearly the retail price of the product.

"King of Scots" is frequently advertised on television in Panama but I do not have sufficiently precise evidence to describe the nature of such advertising.

There was, at the time of the proof, a sign advertising "King of Scots", hanging in a busy thoroughfare in Panama City describing "King of Scots" as "Scotch Whisky". This is shown in photograph 34 of no 26 of process.

At one time there were at least two large roadside hoardings advertising "King of Scots" as "Realment Escoces". According to Senor Arias he ordered them to be removed in 1973 and there is no evidence that they are still in position.

The normal retail price of "King of Scots" sold in supermarkets and bodegas in Panama is about $4.25-$4.50 per bottle. The normal price for Scotch whisky varies from about $7.50 per bottle for the standard brands to up to $14 or more for de luxe brands. There may be some Scotch whiskies that normally retail at less than $7.50, but certainly none retail normally at anything like as low a price as $4.50 and they could not be sold economically at that price having regard to Panamanian import duty. There was a great deal of detailed evidence on this matter, the general effect of which was as follows: For imported liquors there is generally a high import duty. In certain cases an importer can enter into a special arrangement with the Panamanian government by which he can import liquor paying little or no import duty, mix it with a locally produced liquor and sell the product as a national product paying the duty levied on national liquors. The latter duty plus the little, if any, import duty he requires to pay, is far less than the import duty on a corresponding quantity of imported liquor. Diers & Ullrich have an arrangement of this kind with the government in relation to "King of Scots". The retail price of at least some of the other admixes on the market is substantially lower than "King of Scots", probably because they contain a smaller proportion of Scotch malt. Although the normal prices of whisky are as above stated, it is common in Panama for liquor such as whisky to be sold temporarily at substantially reduced prices as sales promotions, though there is no evidence that Scotch whisky is ever sold by the bottle in supermarkets or bodegas at as low a price as the normal price of "King of Scots". The price at which "King of Scots" and Scotch whiskies are sold by the measure in bars, restaurants, nightclubs etc varies greatly according to the class and nature of the establishment and in some such establishments there is no differentiation in the price charged for "King of Scots" and for Scotch whiskies.

At the time when the interdict was pronounced Mr Laing sent a letter to Diers & Ullrich instructing them inter alia that all labels and materials used for the presentation of "King of Scots" must clearly indicate that the product can be termed whisky but not Scotch whisky and that it must be clearly indicated on the labels that the product is a blend of Scotch malt whisky and local Panamanian spirit "so that there is no doubt in the mind of the purchaser what is being purchased", and that all advertising "must clearly indicate the correct description of the product".

The Scotch Whisky Association from time to time issues advices to its members. One such advice was a circular of 2 July 1973. The respondents are not members of the association but Mr Laing had seen the circular of 2 July 1973, which dealt with admixes. This document afforded ammunition for cross examination but I do not think it otherwise relevant.

[His Lordship quoted the terms of the interdict and continued:]

Counsel for the petitioners disclaimed any suggestion that the respondents supplied anything "for the purpose of enabling" passing off to be achieved (see also opinion of the Second Division of 13 November 1975). Accordingly I am concerned only with whether the malt, bottles, cartons and boxes, admittedly supplied, are "calculated", in the objective sense, to enable passing off to be achieved.

Counsel for the respondents did not and obviously could not seek to rely on exception (i) of the two exceptions, but he did rely on exception (ii). Counsel for the petitioners contended that the onus of proof in regard to this exception rested on the respondents, referring to *Nimmo v Alexander Cowan & Sons Ltd.* I do not agree. This is not a statute but an interdict, the terms of which were devised or agreed to by the petitioners. It is designed for their protection and I think that it should be construed in the sense most favourable to the liberty of the respondents and that the onus of proof of breach should be on the petitioners throughout.

Counsel for the parties were agreed that the onus of proof so far as resting on the petitioners required to be discharged beyond reasonable doubt (*Eutectic Welding Alloys Co Ltd v Whitting; Gribben v Gribben*).

There is no dispute as to the things supplied by the respondents and, leaving aside the exception, the question is whether it is proved beyond reasonable doubt that these things used in combination are calculated to enable an admix to be passed off in Panama as and for Scotch whisky. I have considered first what is involved in the conception of "passing off as and for Scotch whisky" in a foreign country. The normal run of passing off cases concerns the misleading of the purchaser into thinking that the article he purchases is of a particular brand or the product of a particular manufacturer but it is not quite so clear what it is a purchaser has to be misled into thinking to achieve "passing off" as and for Scotch whisky. The interdict refers to a definition of Scotch whisky which has no statutory authority, but quite clearly no ordinary Panamanian would be misled into thinking that "King

of Scots" was obtained by "distillation in Scotland from a mash of cereal grain saccharified by the diastase of malt". Even if translated into Spanish he would not have the faintest idea what those words meant. In order to understand the issue I have thought it necessary to consider certain authorities which were briefly mentioned in argument but not considered by either side in any detail.

Passing off actions in relation to geographical origin appear to be a relatively new development in Scots and English law. In *Bollinger v Costa Brava Wine Co* the defendants were restrained from using the name "Spanish Champagne" in relation to a Spanish wine. In *Vine Products Ltd v Mackenzie & Co Ltd* it was held unlawful to describe as "sherry" wine which had no connection with the Jerez district of Spain, though it was further held that the use of the description "British Sherry" could not now be restrained by the Spanish producers as the description had been used for a very long period without objection. In *John Walker & Sons Ltd v Henry Ost & Co Ltd*, a case similar to the present (though perhaps stronger) relating to the supply of malt and bottles and labels for admixture purposes, it was held that a wrong had been committed in enabling passing off as Scotch whisky to be achieved in Ecuador. As regards Scottish cases, in *Argyllshire Weavers Ltd v A Macaulay (Tweeds) Ltd* Lord Hunter stated obiter that, if necessary, he would have followed *Bollinger v Costa Brava Wine Co.* In *John Walker & Sons Ltd v Douglas McGibbon & Co Ltd*, a case similar to the present relating to Honduras, Lord Avonside, in allowing a proof before answer followed and applied the *Ost* case, though this to some extent proceeded on a concession. In his opinion of 24 February 1972 in the action for the present interdict Lord Avonside, as it were, incorporated by reference his opinion in the *McGibbon* case.

As I read them the *Bollinger* and *Vine Products* cases, though they are called "passing off" cases, involve somewhat different principles from those usually associated with passing off. In these cases it was not, I think, suggested that anyone would be misled as to the true nature of the product. No purchaser would think that "Spanish champagne" came from France or "British Sherry" from Spain. The wrong in these cases was not deception as to the origin of the product but debasement or dilution of the names "champagne" and "sherry". It is in my view unnecessary to consider the possibility of "passing off" of that kind in the present case, since I do not understand it to be suggested by the petitioners either in their pleadings or in argument and I do not think that either party read the interdict as meaning that there might be "passing off" even if a purchaser was aware at the time of purchase that "King of Scots" was an admix.

The *Ost* case on the other hand does, I think, exemplify the kind of "passing off" contemplated by this interdict. Following that case I consider that it is first necessary for the petitioners to prove that Scotch whisky has a reputation in Panama. Obviously a person cannot be misled into thinking that "A" is "B"

unless he is aware of "B", and reputation is a necessary element of passing off cases generally (see, eg
Haig v Forth Blending Co). Secondly, again following
the *Ost* case, I think that the petitioners must show
that the reputation attached to Scotch whisky in
Panama is attached to Scotch whisky properly so
called, that is to say that the expression or its Spanish
equivalent "Whisky Escoces" has not lost its geographical meaning and become debased into a merely
generic description (*Henderson & Turnbull Ltd v
Adair*), covering a broad class of liquor wherever
made. Thirdly, I think that the petitioners require to
prove that things supplied by the respondents are
calculated to enable "King of Scots" to be sold in such
a way that purchasers are likely to be misled into
thinking that it is of the same nature and has the same
characteristic as regards geographical origin as Scotch
whisky, whether or not those customers know the
precise facts of that nature and characteristic. In
putting the matter in this way I am setting perhaps a
lower standard than that applied in *Ost*. In that case
it was found as a fact that "an Ecuadorian of whatever
repute knows today that 'Whisky Escoces' means a
blend of whiskies distilled in Scotland". I could not
make a corresponding finding in this case. I was surprised at how little the Panamanian witnesses, who
were dealers in liquor, appeared to know about how
whisky, or other liquors, are made. I doubt whether
many Panamanians even know of the existence of the
distillation process and there is no evidence that any
Panamanians know that it is the Scottish locality of the
distillation process, as opposed to any other part of the
process from the growing of the cereal to the bottling
of the blended product, which distinguishes Scotch
whisky from other whiskies. I do not however see why
a Panamanian should not be considered a victim of
passing off if he is misled into thinking that "King of
Scots" is whisky having the same connection with
Scotland as Scotch whisky even though he has no clear
idea as to what that connection is, subject however to
this, that it can be assumed without evidence, since, as
I say, this is the basis on which the case is approached
by both parties, that no Panamanian would be so
misled if he was aware that "King of Scots" was an
admix. In stating this third matter that has to be
proved I use the expression "likely to be misled".
Counsel for the respondents, by reference particularly
to *Park Court Hotel Ltd v Transworld Hotels Ltd* and
*Office Cleaning Services v Westminster Window &
General Cleaners Ltd*, argued that the petitioners must
prove more than merely some risk of confusion, and
small differences in "get up" will be enough to
exonerate the respondents. I can understand why in
those cases a particularly heavy onus was held to lie on
those claiming passing off, since they were in effect
seeking to acquire for their own property or business
a monopoly of general descriptive words to which they
had no natural right. I do not think that these cases
apply here where the petitioners are seeking to protect
a name which is in fact peculiarly appropriate to the
product to which it is generally applied. However, I
accept that there is a matter of degree involved. Proof
of the remote possibility of an occasional deception

would not, I consider, be enough, but on the other
hand I do not think that the petitioners need go as far
as proving the probability of frequent "passing off".

I accept a general submission by counsel for the
respondents that in this case it is essential to rely on
evidence from Panama in respect of matters, which, if
one were concerned with passing off in the United
Kingdom, would be too well known to require proof,
and opinion evidence from Panama as to likely
reactions of the public in particular circumstances is
more useful than it would be in a United Kingdom
case. On the other hand in my opinion, at the end of
the day it is for the court to decide on the facts rather
than on the opinion of witnesses whether "passing
off" is likely (*Coleman & Co v Smith*, Farwell LJ at
p 98; *Park Court Hotel Ltd v Transworld Hotels Ltd*).

Turning to the first matter to be proved I consider
the reputation of Scotch whisky in Panama is established beyond doubt. The quantity in which it has
been sold for so long and the fact that the words
"Scotch Whisky" appear on the bottles are significant.
All of the Panamanian witnesses speak expressly or by
implication to the popularity of Scotch whisky and
there is no contrary evidence. Diers & Ullrich saw fit,
at least at one time, to advertise "King of Scots" as
"realmente escoces". Although Senor Mendez said
that Scotch whisky is sometimes ordered as "Scotch",
the other evidence, particularly that of Senor
Brostella, and of the advertisements, suggests that this
is not usually so. It is usually either simply asked for
by the word "whisky" or by reference to the particular
brand name. However the reason for this is a fact
which, in my opinion, is of considerable importance in
this case. The word "whisky" in Panama has no technically defined meaning, but in practice, used by
itself, it is taken to mean Scotch whisky. If a Panamanian orders "whisky" he expects to get Scotch whisky.
If he wants, for example, Canadian whisky, he
requires to say so expressly. The evidence to this effect
is very clear. It is spoken to by Senor Mendez, Senor
de Obaldia and Senor Brostella and there is no evidence to a contrary effect.

As regards the second matter to be proved, I think
it clearly established that the expression "Scotch
whisky" has not become debased so as to be merely
descriptive of a type of liquor. The fact that "whisky"
normally means Scotch whisky does not involve the
opposite proposition that "Scotch whisky" means any
whisky. Senor Mendez said that persons expect
"Scotch whisky" to come from Scotland, and again,
"We know that 'Scotch' comes from Scotland". Senor
de Obaldia said that Scotch whisky means to the
ordinary Panamanian "whisky made in Scotland" and
that Panamanians "prefer the Scotch whisky to
others". Mr Nam Sing Lao said: "My clients" (I think
he was speaking of retailers) "they make orders by
phone — they order these foreign Scotch whiskies and
imported in bottles in Panama — they right away
know the difference", and, asked if a high proportion
of those who did drink alcohol in Panama do in fact
like Scotch whisky, he said: "Yes, they know the

difference; the whisky drinkers know what they are drinking." On this matter again there was no contrary evidence.

Turning to the third question, which is the real matter in dispute, I am satisfied beyond reasonable doubt that there is a likelihood of purchasers in Panama being misled into believing that "King of Scots", marketed as it is in the bottles and with the labels and cartons provided by the respondents, has the same nature and the same characteristics as regards geographical origin as Scotch whisky. I am satisfied beyond reasonable doubt that the likelihood is far more than minimal. I am accordingly satisfied beyond reasonable doubt that the things supplied by the respondents to Diers & Ullrich are calculated to enable "passing off", within the meaning of the interdict, to be achieved.

Counsel for the respondents argued forcefully that proof beyond reasonable doubt being required, the petitioners could scarcely hope to succeed, since, as is correct, they had not led evidence of a single instance in which passing off had in fact occurred. It is I think clear on authority that, at any rate where actual passing off is not alleged, but merely the enabling of passing off to be achieved, proof of actual instance is not essential (*Haig v Forth Blending Co; John Walker & Sons Ltd v Henry Ost & Co Ltd; Coleman & Co v Smith; Weingarten v Bayer & Co; King v Gilloch*). Nevertheless the absence of evidence of actual instances has caused me some surprise and anxiety in this case. However the fact that the evidence is not there does not exonerate me from reaching a conclusion on such evidence as I have and I do not think that a petition and complaint must fail because the petitioner has not proved something which would have made his case even stronger.

The nearest approach to evidence of actual passing off was the evidence of Mr Bryce and Mr Boyter regarding certain instances of what might be called "test orders". These gentlemen, separately, visited certain supermarkets in Panama with a view to securing evidence on this matter. Evidence of these visits was objected to on the grounds inter alia that the names of the supermarket assistants were not given and that, at the time of the orders, the assistants in question were not informed of their purpose. Reference was made to *Cellular Clothing Co v White* and Kerley, *Trade Marks* (10th ed), p 428. In the present case, where neither the assistants in question nor their employers were themselves accused of passing off I did not consider that these authorities justified me in refusing to hear this evidence. An attempt was made to lead evidence of a large number of other "test orders" made in about March of this year which differed from those I have first referred to in respect that no reference was made to them on record. I sustained the objections to evidence of these further orders, taking the view that fairness in accordance with our practice required specific notice of such matters on record, as had been given in the case of the orders by Mr Bryce and Mr Boyter above referred to.

I also refused leave to amend to incorporate a reference on record to these further orders, having been informed by counsel for the respondents that he would require time to answer involving adjournment of the proof. I would have allowed the amendment and adjournment had this been an ordinary civil action, but I took the view that a respondent in a petition and complaint ought in general to be entitled to have the matter disposed of on the basis of pleadings prepared no later than the date on which the proof is heard. As regards the test orders of which I allowed evidence, in two instances in the case of Mr Bryce and a further two in the case of Mr Boyter, the shop assistant said, in response to inquiry, that "King of Scots" on display was "Scotch whisky". The evidence of these instances was criticised on the ground of language difficulties and the absence of a precise written note of the conversation, but I have no doubt as to the effect of the conversations in each case. These of course are not instances of passing off since neither Mr Bryce nor Mr Boyter was in fact misled, but they demonstrate that, at least in these instances, either the shop assistant was prepared to attempt to mislead or that he was himself misled.

Senor de Obaldia said that he had supposed until a few months before the proof that "King of Scots" was a Scotch whisky bottled in Panama. He also gave evidence, which I accepted, of a recent occasion when he was served with "King of Scots" at a bar and was told by the bartender that it was "pure Scotch". He himself was not deceived. Again I do not know whether the bartender was himself misled or was trying to mislead.

These instances concerning Mr Bryce, Mr Boyter and Senor de Obaldia are far from conclusive but they go some distance in confirming my opinion as to the likelihood of passing off. I should refer at this point to certain evidence of Senor Brostella, to the effect that he also thought, until recently, that "King of Scots" was Scotch whisky imported in bulk and mixed with water and bottled in Panama. This matter took up much time at the proof. Counsel for the respondents contended that he was not telling the truth on this matter, first because he as a liquor dealer must have known that it is illegal to import Scotch whisky in bulk and mix it with water in Panama, secondly, because with his experience, he must have known that, having regard to the import regulations and tariffs, it would not be possible to sell Scotch whisky imported in bulk at such a low price, and thirdly, because of a price list of Senor Brostella's firm which clearly shows "King of Scots" as an admix. I am not satisfied on the evidence that it is in fact illegal to import Scotch whisky in bulk into Panama and mix it there with water. As regards import duties, my impression was that the witnesses who were liquor dealers had little precise knowledge of the complex local laws and tariffs except as they specifically affected their own particular operations. As regards the price list, this unfortunately was lodged after Senor Brostella had given evidence and accordingly was not put to him. I am not prepared to hold that Senor Brostella was lying. I did

A not think that he was. On the other hand I think it safer in the circumstances to ignore his evidence as to what he himself had thought was the composition of "King of Scots".

Turning from evidence of actual instances, I consider first the situation of "King of Scots" sold in cartons in supermarkets and bodegas and advertised by pictures of the cartons. The evidence shows that the pictorial design of Highland dress, white heather, etc would have no geographical significance to the average Panamanian and I think that no more can be
B made of it than that it certainly does not suggest a Panamanian connection and it has some foreign flavour about it. The most important matter by far, indeed the matter on which I consider the case turns, is the name "King of Scots" itself, which is so prominent on both bottle and carton. It is clear that the product is sold and described in Panama as "whisky" and it is so described on the carton and the picture of the bottle on the carton. In my opinion that, in a market where "whisky" prima facie means "Scotch"
C whisky and where the language makes no difference between "Scots" and "Scotch", it is inevitable that from time to time purchasers of a liquor of the whisky type called "King of Scots" will think that the article is Scotch whisky unless they are sufficiently clearly and quickly disabused of that notion. Mr Laing conceded that if it were marketed as "King of Scots Scotch Whisky" it would be misleading, but it appears to me that, in practical effect, there is not a very great difference between calling it "King of Scots" and
D "Whisky" and calling it "King of Scots Scotch Whisky". The respondents contended that as the product contained an element of Scotch whisky it was reasonable for them to show a Scottish connection in the brand name and that the whisky was sold as and would always be understood as being not Scotch whisky but a cheap substitute for Scotch whisky. It may well be that he thought he was acting "reasonably", but I think that the difficulty in this argument is that the distinction between a "cheap substitute
E for" and a "cheap variety of" a product is a narrow one and one which the less discerning, prudent and knowledgeable customer could not be relied upon to make.

It is clear that the advertisements and the manner of display on the shelves do not always, by reason of juxtaposition with Scotch whiskies, tend to suggest that "King of Scots" is Scotch whisky, but I think it also clear that juxtaposition will frequently occur in such
F a way as to suggest at first glance that it probably is.

Turning to the indiciae on the carton as to the true nature of the product, in my opinion the writing in Spanish on the back is not sufficient to remove the risk of confusion. I think that if in fact a Spanish speaking purchaser read that writing he would know the true nature of the product. There was evidence, disputed by Senor Arias, that the word "espiritu" is not, in Panama, an appropriate word to use in relation to alcohol. Be that so, I do not believe that a Panamanian who took the trouble to read the wording on the back

would be misled. But the evidence of some of the witnesses that purchasers would not normally and cer- G
tainly not always trouble to read the wording on the back, confirms what I should have thought obvious and shows that, in this respect at least, Panamanian purchasers are no different from British. Mr Laing gave evidence of having examined, with some interest, and with what might be called a "professional eye" a bottle of "Royal Club" which he had taken down from a shelf in a supermarket, but he conceded that he did not look at the back of the bottle and therefore did not observe the small explanatory label that appears H
thereon.

The wording on the front of the carton is in my opinion more significant. While nothing like as prominent as "King of Scots" it is certainly large and legible. It is written in English, the effect of which in my opinion, is that a non-English-speaking Panamanian either would not try to read it at all, or, if he did try to read it would not entirely understand it. The mere fact that it is written in English suggests that the product is foreign. Moreover, while I do not think the I
non-English speaking Panamanians would understand the whole of the English wording on the front of the carton, it contains two words which on the evidence are very well known to Panamanians, namely "Scotch" and "Whisky". If a non-English-speaking Panamanian sees a product called "King of Scots" and underneath a passage in English including the words "Scotch" and "Whisky", I find it impossible to believe that there is not a serious risk of confusion. It is true that he will presumably also recognise the word J
"Panamanian", but I do not think it follows that he will understand the significance of that word in its context. In my opinion, again confirmed by the views of the Panamanian witnesses called for the petitioners, the wording on the front of the carton is insufficient protection against the likelihood of passing off.

Counsel for the respondents relied strongly on certain authorities which emphasised that in relation to passing off by "get up" one must look at the get up K
fairly and as a whole, and further that the test is the purchaser of reasonable apprehension and eyesight and who takes the trouble to read (*Schweppes v Gibbens; King v Gilloch; Coleman & Co v Smith; Wertheimer v Stewart Cooper & Co*). While I do not of course dissent from the dicta in these cases in their context and I agree that any person who in fact read and understood either the English or the Spanish writing on the carton would not be misled, I think it is dangerous to try to apply, as generalisations, dicta L
made in particular cases especially when they do not concern the type of geographical passing off here in issue. In my opinion one can do no more than try to decide whether passing off is likely having regard to the manner of sale and conditions of the market. *Johnston v Orr Ewing* was a case in which it was thought appropriate to take into account the incautious or illiterate purchaser and *Haig & Co v Forth Blending Co* was a case where, having regard to the conditions in which the product was sold, interdict was granted although a purchaser who could and did

read the labels on the bottles plainly would not be deceived. I do not think that there is anything on the carton in this case which is sufficient to eliminate the serious risk of confusion.

Turning to the case where the bottle is displayed out of its carton, in my opinion the risk of confusion is even greater. The only words which are legible on the front of the bottle, other than on very close inspection, are "King of Scots" and "Whisky" or "Blended Whisky". As I have already said I consider these words are likely to lead to passing off unless their prima facie inference is adequately corrected. The words of explanation on the front label "mezclas de maltas escocesas y espiritu de granos panamenos" would in my opinion, if read by a Panamanian, dispel the illusion, but having regard to their small size, I consider it inevitable that they frequently would not be read. I am by no means satisfied that the words on the back label, even if read, would be sufficient, but they are again in very small writing and being on the back in many cases would certainly not be noticed. I should add here that the evidence shows that the lion rampant device is of no significance to the Panamanian. I do not take it into account. There is one feature on the bottles which is not visible on the cartons, namely the blue revenue stamp. I consider it most unlikely that a purchaser would read the small writing on this stamp and it seems to me hopeless to suggest that he would recognise and appreciate the significance of the blue colour of the stamp, even assuming, which is by no means clear on the evidence, that that colour is always used for national as opposed to imported liquors. As I have already said the Panamanians, who might be expected to be experts on the subject of import duties and the like, were hazy on the details and I do not believe that the average Panamanian has the colour code of the tariff stamps at his fingertips.

The third principal mode of sale of "King of Scots" is by measure at bars and nightclubs etc. It is possible that in such circumstances, and where the customer does not see the bottle, the mere use of the words "King of Scots" could involve a passing off but I doubt if the petitioners' pleadings or the terms of the interdict would justify a finding of breach of interdict on that ground. However in the cases where the order is made at a bar and the bottle, face foremost, is visible to the customer, I consider that passing off is even more likely than in the case of sale of an uncartoned bottle in a supermarket or bodega. In such circumstances the words "King of Scots" and "Whisky" would very likely be legible but the Spanish writing beneath almost certainly would not.

Counsel for the respondents submitted that there was one further major protection against the risk of passing off, namely the price at which the product is sold. On the evidence, in my opinion, this protection would in any event not operate in the case of sales by measure at bars and the like, but in sales in shops and supermarkets and in advertising the price difference is very marked, though the habit of selling at cut prices

for sales promotion may go some way to blur the difference in the public mind. In any event in my opinion the price difference would have only a limited effect on the likelihood of passing off. Leaving aside Senor Brostella's evidence, Senor de Obaldia, a man whose experience should have given him a better than average understanding of these things, thought "King of Scots" was Scotch whisky bottled in Panama. It is evident that the cause of the price difference is, at least to a large extent, the special tariff concessions which Senor Arias has obtained by using local spirit, but the relative ignorance of the more or less expert Panamanian witnesses convince me that the average Panamanian would be most unlikely to know, merely because the product is relatively cheap, that its alcoholic content is not wholly imported. He would certainly think that it was a very cheap brand of whisky, but I do not see why that means that he would know that it was not a very cheap brand of Scotch whisky.

The three Panamanian witnesses called by the petitioners were clearly of the opinion that "King of Scots", particularly by reason of its name, was likely to mislead as to its origin. While the view of Mr Nam Sing Lao on this was not clear, one part of his evidence, as to the purport of which I had no doubt, I thought also favoured the petitioners. He said that he would not try to sell "King of Scots" as Scotch whisky because a purchaser might subsequently discover he had been misled and return with a complaint, implying, not that passing off could not be achieved, but rather that it might well be achieved, but with the risk of subsequent recrimination. Senor Arias professed to see no danger of passing off, but I preferred the evidence of the other Panamanians.

It is further, I consider, significant that at least at one time "King of Scots" was sold and advertised in Panama as Scotch whisky. I refer to the first type of carton used before the interdict and particularly to the roadside hoardings. While the view I have formed does not turn on this matter, I think it all the more likely that Panamanians will now think that "King of Scots" is Scotch whisky, when at least for a time not so long ago they were expressly told that it was.

Counsel for the petitioners made considerable play with the similarity between the get up used to sell "King of Scots" Scotch whisky in other countries and the "King of Scots" admix in Panama. Intention, however, not being in issue, I do not attach importance to this point. But for the other reasons I have set out I am satisfied beyond reasonable doubt as to the likelihood of passing off by reason of the things supplied by the petitioners.

Counsel for the respondents argued that, even if the things supplied were calculated to enable passing off to be achieved, the respondents were still not shown to be in breach because of the second exception in the interdict. I do not agree. In view of the concession as regards intention, I am not concerned with what Mr Laing in fact believed, but I am satisfied beyond reasonable doubt that he did not have reasonable

grounds for believing that the admix would not be
passed off either intentionally or inadvertently. As I
understand it, the exception is designed to cover the
situation where the likelihood of passing off arises
from some method of marketing or some other circumstance in Panama of which the respondents were not
aware and had no reason to contemplate. No such
matter arises in this case. Mr Laing makes frequent
visits to Panama in connection with the business. He
has all along had a full and detailed knowledge on how
"King of Scots" is made, marketed and advertised. It
is possible that he did not wholly appreciate the extent
to which, as revealed at the proof, for the Pana-
nians, whisky is prima facie Scotch whisky. He may
not have appreciated the full extent of the ignorance
as to the details of tariff regulations, or the size of the
non-English-speaking part of the population. But
matters of this kind are matters of degree which, in my
opinion, if not precisely within his knowledge, ought
to have been within his contemplation. There is in my
opinion on the evidence no significant matter of fact
which he neither knew nor could reasonably be
expected to have contemplated.

In the whole circumstances I have to report to your
Lordships that in my opinion the interdict has been
breached. If this is correct it is clear that the first and
second respondents are in breach. Counsel for the
petitioners did not in the end press for a finding of
breach against the third respondent and in my
opinion, despite certain admissions on record, such a
finding would not be justified, as there was no
evidence as to the extent, if any, of her knowledge or
involvement.

---

*Counsel for Petitioners and Complainers, Mackay,
QC, MacKenzie; Solicitors, Dundas & Wilson, CS,
Davidson & Syme, WS — Counsel for Respondents,
Robertson, QC, Horsburgh; Solicitors, Connell &
Connell, WS.*

R F H

[On 2 December 1976 the Second Division (Lord Justice
Clerk Wheatley, Lord Kissen and Lord Leechman)
pronounced the following interlocutor: The Lords having
called the cause by order and having resumed consideration
of the petition and complaint and answers together with the
report by Lord Maxwell, no 88 of process and heard counsel
thereon, counsel for the respondents stating that the respondents accepted the conclusion reached by Lord Maxwell in
the said report; find that the first and second respondents by
their actings and proceedings complained of and set forth in
the petition and complaint have acted illegally and have been
guilty of breach and violation of the interdict granted by the
interlocutor of the First Division dated 6 July 1973 therefore
fine and amerciate the first named respondents Douglas
Laing & Co Ltd in the sum of two hundred and fifty pounds
(£250) and the second named respondent Frederick Douglas
Laing in the sum of five hundred pounds (£500) said sums
to be paid to The Director, Scottish Courts Administration,
28 North Bridge, Edinburgh within 14 days from this date;
find the first and second respondents jointly and severally
liable to the petitioners in expenses and remit the account
thereof, when lodged, to the auditor of court to tax and to
report.]

[This case has been reported by request.]

Young v Carmichael

HIGH COURT OF JUSTICIARY

THE LORD JUSTICE CLERK (ROSS),
LORDS MURRAY AND BRAND

18 DECEMBER 1990

*Justiciary — Statutory offence — Driving while unfit
through drink — Failure to provide breath specimen —
Car park within grounds of private property — Whether
"road or other public place" — Road Traffic Act 1972
(c 20), ss 7 (4) and 8 (7).*

An accused person was discovered by police officers
in the driving seat of his car attempting to extricate
the vehicle from a garden next to a car park located within
the grounds of a building comprising a number of
privately owned apartments. He was smelling of
alcohol and was required to provide specimens of
breath for analysis but refused to do so. He was
charged with contraventions of ss 7 (4) and 8 (7) of the
1972 Act. At trial the accused argued that neither the
garden nor the car park was a "road or other public
place" within the Road Traffic Acts. The accused was
convicted on both charges and appealed.

Held, (1) by concession of the Crown, that there
was an absence of evidence of the public in fact using
the car park and the sheriff had erred in holding that
the car park was a public place (p 169J-K); (2) that it
followed that no offence under the Act could have
been committed at the locus and accordingly an investigation in relation to such an offence was not being
carried out (p 170A); and appeal *allowed* and convictions *quashed*.

Summary complaint

John Young was charged on summary complaint at
the instance of William George Carmichael, procurator fiscal, Hamilton, with contraventions of ss 7 (4)
and 8 (7) of the Road Traffic Act 1972. The accused
pled not guilty and proceeded to trial. After evidence
led for the Crown the sheriff allowed an amendment
to charge 1 by adding after the word "road" the words
"or other public place". The accused led no evidence
and after submissions the sheriff convicted on both
charges. The accused appealed by way of stated case.
The facts giving rise to the appeal are set forth in the
opinion of the court.

Cases referred to

Cheyne v Macneill, 1973 SLT 27.
Dunn v Keane, 1976 JC 39.
Harrison v Hill, 1931 SLT 598; 1932 JC 13.
Hogg v Nicholson, 1968 SLT 265.
Pugh v Knipe [1972] RTR 286.
R v Waters (1963) 47 Cr App R 149.

Appeal

The sheriff posed the following questions for the
opinion of the court:

A   (1) Did I err in holding that the lawn of the garden ground was not a road or other public place within the meaning of the Act?

(2) Did I err in holding that the car park was a road or other public place within the meaning of the Act?

(3) Was I entitled on the evidence to infer that the appellant had been driving in the car park?

(4) On the facts stated was I entitled to convict the appellant on charge 1?

B   (5) Was the sentence imposed excessive in the circumstances?

The appeal was argued before the High Court on 18 December 1990.

Eo die the court *allowed* the appeal and *quashed* the convictions.

The following opinion of the court was delivered by the Lord Justice Clerk (Ross):

C   **OPINION OF THE COURT.**—The appellant is John Young who went to trial in the sheriff court at Hamilton on a complaint libelling two charges. The first charge was a charge of contravening s 7 (4) of the Road Traffic Act 1972, and the second charge was a charge of contravening s 8 (7) of the Road Traffic Act 1972. After evidence had been led for the Crown the respondent sought and obtained leave to amend the first charge by adding after the word "road" the words "or other public place". The first charge accordingly

D   libelled that the appellant had failed without reasonable excuse to provide a specimen of breath for a breath test, he "being a person who was on 14 March 1989 driving a motor vehicle, namely motor car registration mark LGE 761Y on a road or other public place, namely, within the grounds of Dalzell House, Dalzell Drive, Motherwell".

No evidence was led for the appellant, and after hearing submissions, the sheriff found the appellant guilty as libelled on both charges. He has now

E   appealed against conviction by means of a stated case.

The case contained five questions: [his Lordship quoted the terms of the questions and continued:]

The case first called before this court on 24 October 1990. Having considered the appeal, on the motion of counsel for the appellant, we allowed a sixth question to be added to the case, namely: "On the facts stated was I entitled to convict the appellant on charge 2?" At this hearing the advocate depute conceded that the

F   car park was not a road within the meaning of the statutory legislation, and the court accordingly remitted to the sheriff at Hamilton to state whether he was satisfied that the car park was a public place and to provide any additional findings in fact together with his reasons for so finding.

On 18 December 1990 the appeal again called before this court. The sheriff had prepared a report in answer to the foregoing remit and in the course of that report he indicated that he was satisfied that the car park was a public place. Counsel for the appellant maintained

that the sheriff was not entitled so to hold. He drew attention to the findings in fact. These reveal that G Dalzell House is a building comprising a number of privately owned apartments. It is situated within Dalzell public park, access being afforded via Dalzell Drive which is a public carriageway which leads eventually to Dalzell House. There are road signs on it indicating "Private Property" and a two strand wire fence surrounds the grounds of Dalzell House with a gap in the fence to allow the roadway to pass through. There are two parking places within the grounds of Dalzell House and signs saying "No Entry" or H "Private Property" or "Residents Only". One of these car parks is at the western side of Dalzell House. From this car park a shallow flight of steps leads down to a garden area which is set aside for the use of the residents. It is further found in fact that this car park at the western side normally has several cars parked in it, and that the car park is also used by the police when they call and by the usual tradesmen as well as by the residents and their guests.

Two police officers arrived at Dalzell House at I about 4 am on the date libelled. They found the appellant seated in the driving seat of a motor car which was in the garden. The engine was running and the wheels were spinning on the lawn. They formed the impression that the car had been driven from the car park, down the steps, and onto the lawn. The appellant was apparently trying to extricate the vehicle, but it was merely becoming more deeply embedded in the grass. There was a strong smell of alcohol from the appellant's breath and the police officers reasonably sus- J pected him of having alcohol in his body. He was taken to the police car which was parked in the car park at the western side of Dalzell House, and he was there requested to provide a specimen of breath for analysis, which request he refused without reasonable excuse. He was subsequently arrested and taken to Motherwell police station where he was informed of his rights and requested to provide two specimens of breath for analysis, but he unreasonably refused to do so in respect that he persistently blew down the side K of the mouthpiece. He was then cautioned and charged with the offences libelled, but made no reply. The sheriff then proceeded to make the following three findings in fact: "(9) The place where the appellant was driving the vehicle at the time the police officers arrived, namely on the lawn of the garden of Dalzell House, was not a 'road or other public place'. (10) The car ended up on the lawn as a result of being driven there by the appellant from the car park at the western side of Dalzell House and down the steps L referred to. (11) The car park was a 'road or other public place'."

In the course of adjustment the appellant had proposed the deletion of findings 10 and 11 in their entirety, and before this court it was accepted that the appellant was entitled to challenge the making of these findings.

As we have already observed, at the hearing on 24 October 1990, the advocate depute conceded that the car park was not a road within the meaning of the statutory legislation. As the sheriff points out in his report, no such concession was made at the trial diet. The advocate depute, however, explained how it came about that the Crown had made this concession. Under reference to s 192 (1) of the Road Traffic Act 1988, he pointed out that "road", in relation to England and Wales, means any highway and any other road to which the public has access, and includes bridges over which a road passes. Accordingly in England and Wales the test was whether the particular road was a road to which the public had access. In terms of s 192 (2) of the Act of 1988, in relation to Scotland, "road" has the same meaning as in the Roads (Scotland) Act 1984. By virtue of s 151 (1) of the last mentioned Act "road" means, subject to an exception which does not apply in the present case, "any way (other than a waterway) over which there is a public right of passage (by whatever means) and includes the road's verge, and any bridge (whether permanent or temporary) over which, or tunnel through which, the road passes; and any reference to a road includes a part thereof".

The advocate depute emphasised the difference between the definition of "road" in the two jurisdictions, and pointed out that, so far as Scotland is concerned, the car park in the present appeal was not a road since it could not be suggested on the findings that there was any public right of passage over the car park. In this connection also he pointed out that the case of *Harrison v Hill* had been decided at a time when the definition of "road" in Scotland was the same as in England, ie "any highway and any other road to which the public has access" (s 121 (1) of the Road Traffic Act 1930).

Counsel for the appellant recognised that in his report the sheriff had stated that he was satisfied that the car park was a public place, but counsel pointed out that the sheriff had made no additional findings in fact. Under reference to *Harrison v Hill*, he reminded us that the Lord Justice General at 1931 SLT, p 600 had stated: "I think that, when the statute speaks of 'the public' in this connection, what is meant is the public generally, and not the special class of members of the public who have occasion for business or social purposes to go to the farmhouse or to any part of the farm itself; were it otherwise, the definition might just as well have included all private roads as well as all public highways. I think also that, when the statute speaks of the public having 'access' to the road, what is meant is neither (at one extreme) that the public has a positive right of its own to access, nor (at the other extreme) that there exists no physical obstruction, of greater or less impenetrability, against physical access by the public; but that the public actually and legally enjoys access to it. It is, I think, a certain state of use or possession that is pointed to. There must be, as matter of fact, walking or driving by the public on the road, and such walking or driving must be lawfully performed — that is to say, must be permitted or allowed, either expressly or implicitly, by the person or persons to whom the road belongs."

In his report the sheriff gives his reasons for concluding that the car park was a public place. He observed that the car park was situated within the curtilage of Dalzell House which comprised a number of apartments individually occupied. He stated: "The car park was therefore a place to which a number of people must have access — all the occupants, their families and their guests, the tradesmen who supplied them or attended to their properties, and a great variety of persons who might have some occasion or other to resort to it."

Counsel for the appellant pointed out that what is stated in that portion of the sheriff's report had not been made the subject of any finding in fact. Moreover, what the sheriff said in relation to this car park might equally be said of what was undoubtedly a private road leading to a private property. In the note annexed to the stated case the sheriff gave reasons for concluding that the garden ground or lawn was not a road or other public place. His reasons for so concluding could equally apply to the car park. As in the case of the lawn, there was no evidence to show that members of the public in general had access to it in the sense that they normally resorted to it and so might be expected to be there. So far as the residents were concerned they were a restricted class of the public. In addition to that it was plain from findings 1 and 2 that there were road signs making it clear that the public were in fact being denied access to inter alia the car park in question. The advocate depute did not seek to dispute that the car park was not a public place. He referred to a number of cases including *Hogg v Nicholson, Cheyne v Macneill, Dunn v Keane, R v Waters* and *Pugh v Knipe*. The advocate depute accepted that in the present case there was an absence of evidence of the public in fact using the car park, and having regard to the findings which had been made and in particular findings 1 and 2, he accepted that the learned sheriff had erred in holding that the car park was a public place. In these circumstances the advocate depute accepted that the sheriff had not been entitled to find the appellant guilty of charge 1.

In his note the sheriff explained that the respondent had submitted that even if charge 1 was not proved, the appellant must nonetheless be convicted of charge 2. The sheriff expressed the view that that submission was irresistible. He pointed out that it was an offence to fail without reasonable excuse to provide a breath specimen in a response to a requirement made by a constable "in the course of an investigation whether a person has committed an offence under section 5 or section 6". He also observed that such a requirement might now be made whether or not the person had been arrested, let alone lawfully arrested. He further expressed the view that even if it should eventually transpire that the person was not even driving the car at the time, the requirement would still be a valid one, provided there was no question of misconduct on the part of the police. He proceeded then to refer to two English authorities and to two Scottish authorities. We do not find it necessary to examine these authorities because they appear to have been dealing with a

different factual situation. As the advocate depute
recognised in the present case, the result of holding
that the car park was not a road or public place was
that the appellant could not possibly have committed
a traffic offence while driving a motor car in that
place. The police officers could not have been investigating whether the appellant had committed an
offence under s 5 or s 6 since he could not possibly
have committed such an offence in the place libelled.
Charge 2 libelled: "you, being a person who in the
course of an investigation as to whether you had committed an offence under s 5 or s 6 of the Act first hereafter mentioned in respect of the alleged driving by
you of a motor vehicle, namely, said motor car registration mark LGE 761Y within the grounds of Dalzell
House, Dalzell Drive, Motherwell on 14 March
1989". It has, however, been held that the place
libelled was not a road or other public place, and the
result of that must be that no offence under s 5 or s
6 could have been committed at the locus. The Crown
accordingly could not show that an investigation as to
whether such an offence had been committed was
being carried out. The advocate depute accordingly
accepted that the sheriff was not entitled to convict the
appellant of charge 2.

For the foregoing reasons we have of consent
answered the questions in the case as follows:

(1) No.
(2) Yes.
(3) We have not found it necessary to answer this
question.
(4) No.
(5) This question does not arise.
(6) No.

---

*Counsel for Appellant, McBride; Solicitors, Pairman
Miller & Murray, WS (for Barrowman & Partners,
Cumbernauld) — Counsel for Respondent, Macdonald,
QC, AD; Solicitor, I Dean, Crown Agent.*

S D D N

Forth Wines Ltd, Petitioners

FIRST DIVISION

THE LORD PRESIDENT (HOPE),
LORDS COWIE AND MORISON

14 JUNE 1991

*Company — Capital — Reduction — Variation of share
capital — Special resolution passed for conversion of
ordinary shares to redeemable deferred shares — Whether
competent — Companies Act 1985 (c 6), s 135 (1).*

Section 135 (1) of the Companies Act 1985 provides
that, subject to confirmation by the court, a company
may by special resolution reduce its share capital in
any way.

A company presented a petition for confirmation of
reduction of capital and cancellation of share premium
account. On 11 December 1989 it had passed special
resolutions adopting new articles of association and for
the effecting of the reconstruction of the company's
share capital. The company had authorised share
capital of £3,000,000 divided into 3,000,000 ordinary
shares of £1 each, of which 342,000 ordinary shares of
£1 each were issued and fully paid. The special resolutions provided, inter alia, for the 342,000 shares to be
converted into deferred shares of £1 each, and that,
subject to confirmation by the court, all the deferred
shares should be redeemable as at 31 October 1991.
On 27 November 1990 special resolutions were passed
for cancellation of the company's share premium
account and for reduction of its share capital by cancelling paid up capital which was unrepresented by
available assets. The Inner House confirmed the
reduction of capital resolved on by the November
1990 special resolutions but refused cancellation of the
share premium account.

The petition thereafter came again before the Inner
House for a consideration of the resolution for the
reconstruction of the company's share capital passed
in December 1989. The petitioners averred that the
conversion of the 342,000 ordinary shares to redeemable deferred shares constituted one of the reductions
of capital in respect of which confirmation was sought.
The reporter was of the view that the resolution of
December 1989 was objectionable on the ground that
issued shares could not competently be converted into
redeemable shares. The petitioners argued that the
conversion should be seen simply as a mechanism by
which the shares were to be paid off and that in a way
which would protect the creditors of the company, by
deferring the reduction of the capital to an appropriate
date.

Held, (1) that the proposed conversion of the issued
ordinary shares into redeemable deferred shares was
within the powers of the company under s 135 (1) of
the 1985 Act: in essence this was a proposal for the
reduction of the company's share capital in a particular but unusual way (p 172D-E); and (2) that the
company having sought and obtained the approval of
its members in terms of resolutions which were
appropriate to a reduction of its share capital, all that
the court was concerned with was whether, having
regard to the interests of creditors, the proposal was
one which it should confirm (p 172E-F); and case
remitted to reporter for a supplementary report.

Re St James' Court Ltd [1944] Ch 6, *distinguished*.

Petition for reduction of capital

Forth Wines Ltd presented a petition to the Court
of Session praying for confirmation of reduction of
capital and cancellation of share premium account.

Facts

The following narrative is taken from the opinion of
the court:

This is a petition for confirmation of reduction of
A capital and cancellation of share premium account.
The company is said to have suffered a serious loss of
capital as a result of the bankruptcy of one of its
customers. In order to continue trading it required to
raise capital from institutional investors, from one of
its trade suppliers and from a new managing director.
As part of these arrangements resolutions were passed
for the reconstruction of the company's share capital
and for the reduction of capital and cancellation of
share premium account with which this application is
B concerned.

On 11 December 1989 special resolutions were
passed by the company adopting new articles of association and for the effecting of the reconstruction of the
company's share capital. On 27 November 1990
special resolutions were passed for cancellation of the
company's share premium account and for the reduction of its share capital by cancelling paid up capital
which was unrepresented by available assets. We have
C already dealt with that part of this application which
is concerned with the resolutions passed on 27
November 1990. On 22 March 1991, having considered the reporter's report, we pronounced an interlocutor confirming the reduction of capital resolved on
by the special resolutions of 27 November 1990 but
refusing cancellation of the share premium account. A
minute in terms appropriate to that stage in the application was approved and directed to be registered by
the registrar of companies. We have to deal now only
D with the resolution for the reconstruction of the
company's share capital which was passed on 11
December 1989.

Immediately prior to 11 December 1989 the authorised share capital of the company was £3,000,000
divided into 3,000,000 ordinary shares of £1 each, of
which 342,000 ordinary shares of £1 each were issued
and fully paid. By the special resolution passed on that
date the authorised share capital was diminished by
the cancellation of 1,158,000 ordinary shares of £1
E each, none of which had been taken or agreed to be
taken by any person. The remaining 1,500,000
unissued shares of £1 were converted and reclassified
into 1,000,000 12% "A" cumulative redeemable
preference shares, 225,000 "A" ordinary shares and
275,000 "new" ordinary shares, all of £1 each. The
342,000 ordinary shares of £1 each then in issue were
to be converted into deferred shares of £1 each, in
terms of the following provision in the special resolution: "(e) Each of the shares in the Company presently
F in issue be converted into a Deferred Share of £1
having the rights and being subject to the restrictions
set out in the said new Articles of Association and that,
subject to confirmation by the Court of Session, all the
Deferred Shares shall be redeemable as at 31 October
1991, all in terms of Article 3 (B) (v) of the said new
Articles of Association." It is stated in the petition that
the conversion of the 342,000 ordinary shares to
redeemable deferred shares constitutes one of the
reductions of capital in respect of which confirmation
is sought by the company.

The petition again called before the First Division
on the matter of the resolution passed on 11 December G
1989 for the reconstruction of the company's share
capital.

The reporter's report called into question the competency of the proposed course.

Statutory provisions
The Companies Act 1985 provides:

"135.—(1) Subject to confirmation by the court, a
company limited by shares or a company limited by
guarantee and having a share capital may, if so H
authorised by its articles, by special resolution reduce
its share capital in any way."

Case referred to
St James' Court Estate Ltd, Re [1944] Ch 6.

On 14 June 1991 the court *repelled* the objection of
the reporter to the issued shares being converted into
redeemable shares, and *remitted* the case to him for a
supplementary report.   I

The following opinion of the court was delivered by
the Lord President (Hope):

OPINION OF THE COURT.—[After the narrative set out supra his Lordship continued:] The
reporter has brought a point to our attention on which
we heard counsel in the single bills. He considers the
special resolution which we have quoted to be objectionable on the following grounds: "Your reporter
considers that issued shares cannot competently be J
converted into redeemable shares (*Re St James' Court
Estate Ltd* [1944] Ch 6; Gower (4th ed), para 13.8.1).
The shares require to be regarded as deferred shares
only as they are so described in the articles of association. Redeemable shares normally require to be
redeemed out of distributable profits. The company
does not have such profits. In any event there are no
facts and circumstances set forth in the petition to
enable the reporter to consider such a reduction of
capital."
                                                         K
No objection has been raised by him to the conversion of the ordinary shares of £1 each into deferred
shares, since this in itself does not constitute a reduction of capital. It is the provision that all the deferred
shares are to be redeemable as at 31 October 1991
which gives rise to the objection. It is the reduction of
capital which will result from their redemption which
makes it necessary for the reduction to be confirmed
by the court.

Counsel submitted that this was in substance a L
straightforward reduction of capital. The conversion
of the ordinary shares into deferred shares which were
to be redeemable on 31 October 1991 should be seen
simply as a mechanism by which these shares were to
be paid off. The sole purpose of the relevant provisions of the Companies Act 1985 was to avoid
prejudice to creditors. Section 135 (1) provides that,
subject to confirmation by the court, a company may
by special resolution reduce its share capital in any
way. The resolution sought only to achieve this in a
way which would protect the creditors of the

company, by deferring the reduction of capital to an appropriate date. We were invited to distinguish the decision in *Re St James' Court*. In that case the question was whether a scheme of arrangement should be sanctioned on the ground that the conversion of issued preference shares into redeemable preference shares was authorised by s 46 (1) of the Companies Act 1929, now re-enacted as s 159 (1) of the 1985 Act. Simonds J declined to sanction the scheme as it stood, because he considered that the conversion of issued preference shares into redeemable preference shares was not within s 46 (1). He held that a conversion of that kind could take place only if the steps appropriate to a reduction and simultaneous increase of capital had been taken. The petition was adjourned so that the company might have an opportunity to submit resolutions of that kind to its members. But, as counsel for the petitioners pointed out, the scheme which was before the court in that case did not provide that the redeemable preference shares into which the issued preference shares were to be converted, were to be redeemed on a particular date. The scheme was presented as one for the surrender and exchange of shares only, and as one which did not require resolutions of the company appropriate to a reduction and simultaneous increase of its share capital. What was proposed to be done in this case was presented as a reduction of the company's share capital and not just a scheme for the surrender and exchange of shares, and it was supported by the appropriate resolutions.

We are satisfied that the proposed conversion of the issued ordinary shares into redeemable deferred shares is within the powers of the company under s 135 (1). The conversion of the ordinary shares into deferred shares does not of itself constitute a reduction of share capital. But the only purpose of this conversion is to provide a mechanism, in terms of the new articles of association, whereby the share capital can be paid off at a given date. The date for redemption is to be deferred in the interests of creditors, but in essence this is a proposal for the reduction of the company's share capital in a particular but unusual way. Furthermore, the objection to the scheme which the court was asked to sanction in *Re St James' Court Ltd* was that the company was seeking to convert issued preference shares into redeemable preference shares without having first obtained the appropriate resolutions for a reduction and increase in capital in terms of the Act. In the present case there can be no such objection because the company has sought and obtained the approval of its members in terms of resolutions which are appropriate to a reduction of its share capital. All we are concerned with now is whether, having regard to the interests of creditors, the proposal is one which we should confirm by making the appropriate order in terms of ss 135 to 137 of the Act.

That is sufficient to dispose of the point which the reporter has very properly drawn to our attention, and we must now remit this case to him for a supplementary report. We require to be advised as to the regularity of the proceedings on 11 December 1989 when the special resolution was passed by the company, and

as to whether the proposed reduction of capital can be achieved by the redemption of the deferred shares on 31 October 1991 without prejudice to its creditors, having regard to the averments in art 11 of the petition.

Counsel for Petitioners, Drummond Young, QC; Solicitors, Morton Fraser & Milligan, WS.

R F H

Khan v HM Advocate

HIGH COURT OF JUSTICIARY

THE LORD JUSTICE GENERAL (HOPE), LORDS ALLANBRIDGE AND KINCRAIG

1 NOVEMBER 1991

Justiciary — Evidence — Admissibility — Statement by accused — Whether statement both exculpatory and incriminatory in character — Other evidence pointing to truth of statement — Trial judge directing jury to treat statement as wholly exculpatory — Whether misdirection.

Justiciary — Procedure — Trial — Charge to jury — Statement by accused — Statement led in evidence by accused both exculpatory and incriminatory in character — Trial judge directing jury to treat statement as wholly exculpatory — Whether misdirection — Whether miscarriage of justice.

Justiciary — Procedure — Trial — Charge to jury — Judge directing jury on the evidence that if they acquitted first accused, necessary also to acquit second accused — Whether prejudicial to first accused.

Two accused persons (A and M) were convicted of inter alia being knowingly concerned in the fraudulent evasion of the prohibition in s 3 (1) of the Misuse of Drugs Act 1971 against the importation of controlled drugs. Whilst in detention, they both made statements. A's statement was made to customs officers under caution and in the presence of his solicitor; M's statement consisted of replies by him to a police officer under caution when he was being searched. Neither accused gave evidence at their trial but their counsel referred to the respective statements in their speeches to the jury on the basis that the statements had been both incriminatory and exculpatory in character and that they should be considered by the jury as a whole. In A's case, evidence of his statement had been led by the Crown but the trial judge was of the view that the Crown case did not depend to any extent upon admissions which that statement contained; in M's case the statement had been elicited as evidence by his own counsel and had never been founded upon by the Crown. The trial judge directed the jury that, while the statements could be founded on as indicating that the accused had been consistent in their denial of guilt, they could not be regarded as a substitute for

evidence in the witness box because the statements
A were, in the judge's opinion, wholly exculpatory. He
also directed the jury that if M were to be acquitted,
A had to be acquitted as well. Both accused appealed
to the High Court.

Held, (1) that there was no unfairness to M in the
direction that A had to be acquitted if M was, since
that reflected the Crown's approach and the point had
to be made in fairness to A (p 175H-I); (2) that a statement did not lose its incriminatory character simply
because there was other evidence in the case pointing
B to the truth of the admission, and as there had been
an admission in A's statement which had not been the
subject of any evidence elsewhere in the case and it
was clear that that statement had been treated by the
Crown as being in part incriminatory, that whole
statement had been admissible; and, accordingly (the
Crown conceding), that there had been a misdirection
in relation to A's statement leading to a miscarriage of
justice (pp 176L-177B); (3) that although M's state-
C ment could not be regarded as other than a mixed
statement, capable of being both incriminatory and
exculpatory, the use made of it at the trial had to be
looked at since the point underlying the rule in respect
of mixed statements was that of fairness to the accused
(pp 177K-178B); (4) that since the defence had led
evidence of the statement for the sole purpose of exculpating the accused, the fact that the trial judge had
chosen to direct the jury on the basis that M's statement had been wholly exculpatory could not be said
to have resulted in a miscarriage of justice (p 178E-F);
D and A's appeal *allowed* with authority to the Crown to
bring a new prosecution and M's appeal *refused*.

Morrison v HM Advocate, 1991 SLT 57, *explained*
and *applied*.

Indictment
Mumraiz Khan and Aman Khan were charged at
E the instance of the rt hon the Lord Fraser of
Carmyllie, Her Majesty's Advocate, on an indictment
which libelled inter alia the following charge: "(1)
between 6th and 8th December 1990, both dates inclusive, at Heathrow airport and at the Heathrow Penta
hotel, both Hounslow, Middlesex, at Aberdeen airport
and in Market Street, Aberdeen, and elsewhere in the
United Kingdom, you were, in relation to a controlled
drug, namely diamorphine, knowingly concerned in
the fraudulent evasion of the prohibition in force with
F respect to the importation of said drug under the
Misuse of Drugs Act 1971, s 3: contrary to the
Customs and Excise Management Act 1979, s 170 (2)
(b); (2) between the dates above libelled, both dates
inclusive, places above libelled, you were concerned in
the supplying to another or others of a controlled
drug, namely diamorphine, a class A drug specified in
Pt I of Sched 2 to the aftermentioned Act, in con-
travention of s 4 (1) (b) of said Act: contrary to the
Misuse of Drugs Act 1971, s 4 (3) (b); and (3) on 8
December 1990, at Aberdeen airport, in Market
Street, Aberdeen, and elsewhere in Aberdeen, you did

have in your possession a controlled drug, namely
diamorphine, a class A drug specified in Pt I of Sched G
2 to the aftermentioned Act, with intent to supply it
to another or others in contravention of s 4 (1) of said
Act: contrary to the Misuse of Drugs Act 1971, s 5
(3)". The accused pled not guilty and proceeded to
trial before Lord Morison and a jury in the High
Court at Aberdeen. After trial the accused Mumraiz
Khan was convicted of charges 1 and 3 and the
accused Aman Khan was convicted of charges 1 and 2.

The accused appealed to the High Court by note of
appeal against conviction. The facts of the case are set H
forth in the opinion of the court.

Cases referred to
Morrison v HM Advocate, 1991 SLT 57; 1990 JC 299;
    1990 SCCR 235.
Owens v HM Advocate, 1946 SLT 227; 1946 JC 119.

Appeal
The grounds of appeal for the first appellant
(Mumraiz Khan) included the following: I

(1) The learned trial judge misdirected the jury by
failing to direct them that evidence of statements
implicating the appellant, made by the co-accused
outwith the presence of the appellant, was not admissible as evidence against the appellant. Said misdirection amounts to a miscarriage of justice.

(2) The learned trial judge misdirected the jury by
directing them that the statements, which were
capable of being both incriminatory and exculpatory, J
made by the appellant prior to trial, were admissible
only for the limited purpose of showing that he had
been consistent, and were not a substitute for evidence. Said misdirection amounts to a miscarriage of
justice. (Said statements were contained in the appellant's replies to the police under caution.)

The grounds of appeal for the second appellant
(Aman Khan) included the following:

The learned trial judge misdirected the jury as to the K
status of a pre-trial statement made by the appellant. . . . The pre-trial statement given by this appellant was led by the Crown and relied upon as
incriminating. Every point covered by the judge . . .
was admitted in that statement by this appellant but
was accompanied by an explanation. The Crown
relied upon the admissions and invited the jury to
convict on that basis. By his direction the judge
removed the explanations from the jury's consideration. The said statement was a "mixed statement" L
capable of being both incriminating and exculpatory.
As such it was admissible as evidence of the facts in
it. The trial judge told the jury wrongly that it was not
evidence and that it could be "used only to show that
he had been consistent".

As this appellant did not give evidence there was
nothing for the said statement to be consistent with.
It follows that a misdirection led to a miscarriage of
justice as the defence case was not allowed to be considered by the jury.

The appeal was argued in the High Court on 15 October 1991.

On 1 November 1991, the court *allowed* Aman Khan's appeal but *granted* authority to Her Majesty's Advocate to bring a new prosecution, if so advised; and *refused* Mumraiz Khan's appeal.

The following opinion of the court was delivered by the Lord Justice General (Hope):

OPINION OF THE COURT.—The appellants were found guilty at the High Court in Aberdeen of being knowingly concerned in the fraudulent evasion of the prohibition in s 3 (1) of the Misuse of Drugs Act 1971 against the importation of controlled drugs. The drug involved in this case was diamorphine. The first appellant Mumraiz Khan was also convicted of possessing that drug with intent to supply it to others. The second appellant was acquitted on that charge by direction of the trial judge, but he was convicted of being concerned in the supplying of the drug. Mumraiz Khan was sentenced to seven years on each of the charges of which he was convicted. The sentence on Aman Khan was 10 years' imprisonment.

Much of the background of fact in this case was agreed by joint minute, and the other facts were not seriously in dispute. Mumraiz Khan entered the United Kingdom at Heathrow airport on 6 December 1990 on a flight from Islamabad, Pakistan. He had with him a suitcase within the top and bottom compartments of which were concealed 24 polythene bags containing almost 2 kg of diamorphine of exceptional purity. These compartments were formed between the inside lining of the suitcase and its outside. The drugs were discovered when an alert customs officer noticed that the suitcase had a lip which was slightly larger than usual. He pierced the case with a dart and extracted some powder which gave a positive reaction when tested for the presence of diamorphine. The suitcase was collected by the unsuspecting Mumraiz, who was allowed to go through customs and leave the terminal. After waiting for a short time outside he went back, apparently to collect a bag which he had left behind. This required him to go once more through the customs hall with the suitcase, and once again he was allowed to pass through the hall by the customs officer. He then went by taxi to the Penta hotel at Heathrow where he booked himself into a room. He remained there until 8 December when he checked out of the hotel and travelled by a British Airways flight to Aberdeen. His hotel bill was paid by Aman Khan who authorised payment of it from his Clydesdale Bank Access account by telephone from Aberdeen. Aman also made the arrangements for Mumraiz's flight to Aberdeen and for the cost of the ticket to be charged to his account. A telephone booking was made by or on his instructions during the afternoon of 7 December on a Dan Air flight to Aberdeen later that day, and the price of the ticket was charged to Aman's Bank of Scotland Visa account. A few minutes later that booking was cancelled by or on

his instructions, and another booking was made instead for an evening flight by British Airways the next day, the cost of which was charged to the same account. When he reached Aberdeen on that flight on a single ticket Mumraiz was met at the airport by Aman who drove him in his car to Market Street. They both alighted there from the car and Aman removed the suitcase from the boot, whereupon both men were detained by the police.

The Crown's case against Mumraiz was that he knew that the suitcase contained diamorphine and that he was engaged in importing this controlled drug into the United Kingdom for the purpose of supplying it to others. His knowledge of the contents was to be inferred from his possession of the suitcase which contained the drugs and from various deceptions by him regarding his visit to this country which were described in the evidence. The address which he gave in his application for a visa in Islamabad as that of his host or sponsor in the United Kingdom turned out to be false. He also stated in his application that he was a business agriculturalist with a substantial annual income, but the bill for his stay at the hotel was paid for by means of Aman's credit card and on his instructions. It was Aman who arranged and paid for the flight to Aberdeen. The landing card which Mumraiz produced to immigration control at Heathrow stated that his address in the United Kingdom would be in Cardiff, and he said to the immigration officer that his visit would be for about six weeks and that its purpose was to see his sister who was his only relative in this country. Yet during his stay at the Penta hotel he made only three telephone calls from the hotel, two of which were to Pakistan. The third was to Aman's number in Aberdeen on 7 December, and it was made about half an hour before the booking by telephone by or on Aman's instructions for the Dan Air flight to Aberdeen.

The case against Aman depended upon evidence of his association with Mumraiz, from which the necessary inferences of knowledge and participation were sought to be drawn. The argument was that there were sufficient facts to justify the inference that he was knowingly concerned in the importation of drugs, in that he made the necessary financial and other arrangements for Mumraiz to travel with them to Aberdeen where he was to receive them. These facts were that Aman's passport showed that he had visited Pakistan for about four weeks, returning to the United Kingdom about 11 days prior to Mumraiz's arrival at Heathrow. When Mumraiz was searched by the police he was found to be in possession of an address book which contained Aman's name, address and telephone number. The only telephone call within the United Kingdom which was made by Mumraiz from the Penta hotel was to Aman's telephone number in Aberdeen. As already mentioned, the cost of Mumraiz's stay at the hotel and of his transportation by air to Aberdeen was met entirely by Aman. It was Aman also who made all the arrangements for the driving of Mumraiz from the Penta hotel to the terminal at Heathrow and who met him on arrival at Aberdeen

airport. Mumraiz had stated to the immigration officer
that he had 550 US dollars with him, but he had no
other money and he appeared to be financially dependent on Aman. There was no indication that Mumraiz
had the money to pay the cost of his journey back to
London from Aberdeen. A search of Aman's house in
Aberdeen revealed that he was in possession of 38,675
rupees, which was worth approximately £1,000.
Rupees are a restricted currency in the United
Kingdom, since their exchange involves application to
an international division of a bank, but they are usable
as currency in Pakistan. In addition evidence was led
by the Crown of a statement which Aman made in the
early hours of 9 December to officers of the Customs
and Excise at Aberdeen. In the course of this statement he said that he had met Mumraiz during his visit
to Pakistan shortly before Mumraiz's arrival in the
United Kingdom and that he had given him his Aberdeen address and telephone number. He maintained
that he had no knowledge of the contents of the suitcase and that he had only helped Mumraiz because
they came from the same village in Pakistan.

There was no challenge at the trial to the sufficiency
of the evidence against Mumraiz, but it was submitted
on behalf of Aman that there was no case for him to
answer and his first ground of appeal is that this submission was wrongly repelled by the trial judge.
Counsel for Aman pointed out that Aman had very
little contact with the suitcase which contained the
diamorphine. There was, he said, no evidence from
which it could be inferred that he had any particular
interest in this suitcase. The arrangements which he
made for Mumraiz's accommodation and travel to
Aberdeen indicated that he had an interest in
Mumraiz, but that was because they came from the
same village and had previously met in Pakistan. The
various facts relied on by the Crown were not capable
either singly or in combination of supporting the
inference that he was aware that Mumraiz had drugs
with him when he arrived at Heathrow. We are in no
doubt however that there was ample evidence to
entitle the jury to draw that inference. As the Solicitor
General pointed out, all the various facts to which we
have referred should be seen against the background
of the admitted fact that Mumraiz had with him a suitcase within which a substantial quantity of diamorphine had been concealed. There was no direct
evidence that Aman was aware of that fact, but there
was ample circumstantial evidence to support the
inference that everything that he did following
Mumraiz's arrival at Heathrow was done in the knowledge that Mumraiz had the drugs with him and to
ensure that he travelled with them to Aberdeen.

It is convenient to turn next to the third ground of
appeal for Mumraiz which raises a short point about
a passage in the judge's charge. This passage follows
a direction that the case against each accused had to be
considered separately on each of the charges against
them. Having said that the trial judge then pointed out
that the case against Aman depended largely on his
association with Mumraiz. He directed the jury that if
they were to acquit Mumraiz there would be insuf-

ficient evidence as a matter of law to establish the guilt
of Aman. He told them that this was because unless
Mumraiz knew that he had drugs in his suitcase there
would be insufficient evidence based on the association between the two men to justify a verdict of guilty
against Aman. Counsel for Mumraiz contended that
these directions, while no doubt favourable to Aman,
were prejudicial to Mumraiz and that they should not
have been given. They amounted, he said, to a direction that if they wanted to convict Aman they first had
to convict Mumraiz, which was unfair to Mumraiz
because the jury might otherwise have felt able to
acquit him even although they had decided to convict
Aman. In our opinion the words used by the trial
judge, which were an accurate statement of the
approach taken by the Crown, do not bear this construction. The point had to be made, in view of the
Crown's approach and in fairness to Aman, that if
Mumraiz were to be acquitted then Aman would have
to be acquitted as well. The direction which was given
on this point was both clear and accurate, and we can
find no basis in it for the criticism that it was prejudicial to Mumraiz.

We turn now to Mumraiz's first ground of appeal,
which is that the trial judge misdirected the jury by
failing to direct them that evidence of statements
implicating the appellant made by Aman outwith
Mumraiz's presence was not admissible as evidence
against Mumraiz. The statement in question is that
given by Aman to officers of the Customs and Excise
in Aberdeen to which we have already referred. It was
a long statement given over a period of 38 minutes in
the early hours of 9 December. The only part of it
which is founded on in the ground of appeal is a brief
passage near the beginning in which Aman described
his telephone conversations with Mumraiz while he
was staying in the hotel at Heathrow. The relevant
parts of this passage are these: "Mumreze [sic] came
up in ah Heathrow airports and he has been ah staying
in some hotel, I don't know what's its name. He phone
on a Friday when I was busy, somebody told me,
somebody's on the line who canna speak English.

"I came up and he told me his name then I knew
who he is.

"The I told hims, well all right where you staying,
he give me the hotel number plus his room numbers.

"Then I told him alright, I'll get arranged the
things and then you come to see me and he says no he
cant come up because some person going to take his
ah stuff.

"While what is brough it for him ands thats it, after
that I phone him and I, I said alright I book the seat
for you."

The trial judge did not give the direction which is
said to have been necessary, nor was he asked to do so
at any stage in the trial. He tells us in his report that
the Crown did not at any time found on any part of
Aman's statement as having a bearing on the case
against Mumraiz. Counsel for Mumraiz accepts this
account, and he informed us also that the contents of

the statement formed no part of the address to the jury
A which he made on Mumraiz's behalf. He told us that
he addressed them only on the basis of what Mumraiz
himself said and what he did. Nevertheless, said
counsel, the direction should have been given because
there was no other evidence of prior association in
Pakistan than the references in Aman's statement to
his visit there shortly before Mumraiz came to this
country. In a case which was so dependent on inferences the jury ought not to have been left in ignorance
of the fact that Aman's statement to this effect was not
B evidence against Mumraiz. Now the only passage in
the statement referred to in the written grounds of
appeal is that quoted above, and this makes no reference to a prior association in Pakistan. The trial judge
says that if it had been suggested to him that a direction should be given he would probably have been
averse to mentioning this passage to the jury. It might
then have appeared to them that it had some significance to the charges against Mumraiz which up until
that point no one had attached to it. There is consider-
C able force in this observation, and we are not persuaded that the trial judge was in error in not giving
the direction. The passage in question seems to us to
have no material bearing on the case against Mumraiz,
and it cannot be said that there was a miscarriage of
justice simply because the jury were not directed on
this point. It is accepted that the admissible evidence
against Mumraiz, which was virtually undisputed,
was sufficient in law for the jury to be entitled to
convict.

D   We are left now with the third ground of appeal for
Mumraiz and the second ground of appeal for Aman.
These grounds are concerned also with alleged misdirections by the trial judge. The directions which are
under challenge here relate to two separate statements
made by the appellants after they had been detained.
In Mumraiz's case this consisted of replies by him to
a police officer under caution when he was being
searched. In Aman's case the statement was that made
to the officers of the Customs and Excise to which we
E have already referred. It was made under caution and
in the presence of a solicitor. Neither of the appellants
gave evidence, but their counsel made reference to the
statements when addressing the jury on the basis that
they were both incriminatory and exculpatory in
character and that they were to be considered as a
whole. The trial judge disagreed with this approach,
and he directed the jury that, while the statements
could be founded on as indicating that the accused had
been consistent in their denial of guilt, they could not
F be regarded as a substitute for evidence from the
witness box. He gave this direction because in his
opinion the statements were wholly exculpatory. In
Mumraiz's case the statement was elicited as evidence
by his own counsel and it was not at any time founded
on by the Crown. In Aman's case evidence of the statement was led by the Crown, but in the view of the trial
judge the Crown case did not depend to any extent
upon admissions which the statement contained.

   There is no doubt that, if the statements in question
were wholly exculpatory, the directions by the trial

judge were both appropriate and correct. They would
then fall under the third rule described by the Lord G
Justice Clerk in *Morrison v HM Advocate*, 1991 SLT
at p 62 which is in these terms: "(3) A prior statement
of an accused which is not to any extent incriminatory
is admissible for the limited purpose of proving that
the statement was made, and of the attitude or reaction
of the accused at the time when it was made, which is
part of the general picture which the jury have to consider, but is not evidence of the facts contained in the
statement."

   But the appellants maintain that the statements H
which they made were capable of being both incriminatory and exculpatory and that they fell under the
second rule, which is as follows: "(2) Where the
Crown lead evidence, or where evidence is led by the
defence without objection from the Crown of a statement made by an accused person prior to the trial
which is capable of being both incriminatory and
exculpatory, the whole statement is admissible as
evidence of the facts contained in the statement."

   In Aman's case there is little which we need say on I
this issue. The statement was, as we have said, a long
one and we shall not repeat all that was said. It contained his answers to questions which were put to him
on a variety of matters relating to his association with
Mumraiz. Many of his answers were exculpatory, but
they included references to his visit to Pakistan where
he met Mumraiz. There were two passages dealing
with this matter, including that which we quoted
earlier in regard to Mumraiz's first ground of appeal. J
Now the only evidence that Aman had met Mumraiz
prior to his arrival at Heathrow and that it was he who
had given Mumraiz his address and telephone number
came from Aman's own statements to that effect.
There was other evidence from Aman's passport to
show that he had indeed visited Pakistan and his
name, address and telephone number were found to be
in Mumraiz's possession. But the evidence of direct
contact between the two men at this stage came only
from Aman's statement. The minutes of proceedings K
state that in her response to the motion of no case to
answer the advocate depute referred to pp 3 and 9 of
the transcript of the statement where the relevant
passages appear. She founded on the fact that Aman
had had a conversation with Mumraiz in Pakistan
shortly before Mumraiz travelled to the United
Kingdom. The Solicitor General has confirmed that
the advocate depute relied on this evidence as the
starting point of the Crown case. In these circumstances we are in no doubt that the trial judge was mis- L
taken when he regarded this statement as wholly
exculpatory in relation to the crimes charged. The
explanation for the view which he took on this point
lies in a comment in his report that the fact that
certain evidence founded on by the Crown was the
subject of admission in the statement did not alter its
exculpatory character so far as the substance of the
charges was concerned. This suggests that in considering whether the statement was wholly exculpatory he
applied the wrong test. The question to be decided is
whether the statement itself is capable of being both

incriminatory and exculpatory. A statement does not lose its incriminatory character simply because there is other evidence in the case pointing to the truth of the admission and in this case one of the admissions, about the contact between the two men in Pakistan, was not the subject of any evidence elsewhere in the case. Furthermore the Crown led the statement in evidence and relied upon the admissions as part of the case against Aman. That is sufficient to dispose of the matter, because it is clear that the statement was being treated by the Crown as being in part incriminatory. In these circumstances the whole statement was admissible, and the jury should have been directed to consider the whole of it because, as the Lord Justice Clerk pointed out in *Morrison*, 1991 SLT at p 62, it would be unfair to admit the admission without also admitting the explanation. In our opinion the misdirection in regard to this long statement led to a miscarriage of justice in Aman's case, and this point was not disputed by the Crown.

The point which has been raised by Mumraiz is more difficult, for two reasons. The first is that it is less obvious that it contains anything which was incriminatory of the appellant. The second is that his statement was led in evidence not by the Crown but by Mumraiz's own counsel in cross examination of the police officer. It did not at any stage form part of the Crown case against Mumraiz. Nevertheless it was led by the defence without objection from the Crown, and if it was capable of being both incriminatory and exculpatory it was one to which, on a strict reading of the opening words of the second rule in *Morrison*, that rule should have been applied. Both points were disputed by the Solicitor General, and we must turn to examine these arguments in more detail.

The statement which Mumraiz gave consisted of his replies to three questions by the police. These were put to him when he was confronted with the suitcase and its contents, and the replies were in these terms:

"I was given it by Hadi Sarwas in Islamabad, but the contents are mine."

"I didn't know it contained drugs. If I did, I would not have brought it. I will tell you if you ask any questions."

"Someone has deceived me, I don't know what it is."

The trial judge regarded these replies as being wholly exculpatory in regard to the crimes charged.

Counsel for Mumraiz's submission was that the first sentence was not wholly of that character. He founded in particular on the phrase "the contents are mine", on the ground that that had a material bearing on the crucial issue in the case which was whether Mumraiz was aware that the suitcase contained drugs. He did not suggest that the words "the contents" could be taken to include the drugs themselves because in the very next answer Mumraiz said that he did not know it contained drugs and that he would not have brought it if he had known. But the admissions to owning the contents within the suitcase and that he had been

given the suitcase by someone else in Islamabad were capable of supporting the inference, when taken with other facts in the case, that he knew that the suitcase contained drugs. He pointed out that the Crown case as described in the judge's charge was that Mumraiz's possession of the suitcase was itself sufficient to entitle the jury to hold that he must have known that he was carrying a quantity of drugs, especially having regard to the weight and volume of the drugs concerned. The fact that he admitted that the contents were his was relevant to the question whether he was aware, because of their weight, that the drugs were also there concealed in the suitcase.

The Solicitor General at first resisted this approach because, as he put it, the statements did not go to the heart of the case against Mumraiz, which was not whether he had the suitcase with him but whether he knew what it contained. The admissions were open to the construction that he had obtained the case and packed the contents himself, but that was all. However he then went on to accept that one might just find something in the statement which was incriminating of Mumraiz, since it did put him into a relationship with the suitcase. He agreed that it was capable on close analysis of being used as an adminicle of evidence against him. He then directed the main part of his argument to the use which was made of the statement at the trial. In *Morrison* the statement in question was essential to the Crown case and it was relied upon by the Crown. In the case of Aman Khan the statement was used in part by the Crown as the starting point of its case against him, and it was led by the Crown in evidence. But this statement did not form any part of the Crown case against Mumraiz at all. It had been introduced entirely for self serving purposes by the defence. While there might be an issue in retrospect as to whether it was capable of being both incriminatory and exculpatory, the use made of it at the trial was simply to exculpate the appellant.

We have reached the conclusion, having examined the statement as we are able to do with the assistance of counsel in this appeal, that it cannot be regarded as other than a mixed statement, capable of being both incriminatory and exculpatory within the meaning of the second rule in *Morrison*. It contained two admissions, one that Mumraiz was given the suitcase by someone in Islamabad, and the other that the contents of the suitcase were his. The suitcase had concealed within it about 2 kg of diamorphine, which is a substantial quantity. The suitcase was a production in the trial, and the jury would be entitled to consider whether a person who packed the suitcase, which from his admissions Mumraiz could be assumed to have done, would have been aware of the presence of the drugs because of their weight. There was no admission of knowledge, but the case against Mumraiz depended on inferences from various facts from which that state of knowledge could be inferred, and the facts revealed by these admissions cannot be dismissed as entirely irrelevant to that exercise. Nor is there room here for questions of degree. A statement is either capable of

A being incriminatory and exculpatory or it is not. That question is ultimately one for the jury, but it is enough to satisfy this test for the purposes of the rule that the statement is in part incriminatory in the sense that a reasonable jury would be entitled so to regard it, in knowledge of all the facts of the case.

But this case illustrates a problem about so called mixed statements which cannot be resolved satisfactorily by looking only to what the statement contains. The use made of it at the trial may also be relevant, since the point which underlies the rule is that of fairness to the accused. The discussion in *Morrison*
B proceeded upon an acceptance of a passage in the opinion of Lord Justice General Normand in *Owens v HM Advocate* in which he said, of an admission which contained an explanation, "The Crown cannot, we think, take advantage of the admission without displacing the explanation." In that case the admission was made by the panel when he came to give evidence, but that principle applies to all cases where the Crown seeks to take advantage of an admission. The essential
C point which was decided in *Morrison* was that a jury must consider the whole statement, both the incriminatory parts and the exculpatory parts. And the reason given for the second rule is that it would be unfair to admit the admission without admitting the explanation. The purpose of the preamble to that rule is to define the circumstances in which the rule is to be applied in order to prevent unfairness. But it would be an abuse of the rule to apply it in circumstances where there could be no unfairness to the accused,
D especially where, as is suggested in this case, the defence led the evidence of the statement for the sole purpose of exculpating the accused. The Crown could not object to this evidence, because a statement which is exculpatory is admissible for the limited purpose of showing that the accused has been consistent in his denial of guilt. It was not known at the time whether Mumraiz himself was to give evidence. If he did, the statement would be admissible for the limited purpose of rebutting a challenge to his credibility which the
E Crown would be bound to make if he continued to deny his guilt. But in the event there was no such challenge, because Mumraiz did not give evidence.

While it can no doubt be said that the preamble to the second rule was satisfied because the Crown did not object to the evidence and that, since we have held that this must be regarded as a mixed statement, the rule has to be applied, we regard that result as wholly unsatisfactory in this case. The use made of the state-
F ment at the trial was all one way, and that was to exculpate the appellant without putting him into the witness box. There was no question of any part of the statement being used against him in any way which was unfair, since no mention of it was made at any stage by the Crown. For these reasons we are satisfied that the fact that the trial judge chose to direct the jury in terms of the third rule in *Morrison* on the basis that the statement was wholly exculpatory cannot be said to have resulted in a miscarriage of justice in Mumraiz's case. His decision was in accordance with the way the statement was approached both by the

G Crown and the defence and it reflected the reality of the situation as it emerged at the trial. It was not possible for him to conduct the exercise which we have been able to undertake in this appeal of examining the statement with the benefit of counsel to see whether some significance could be attached to it as being incriminatory which was not obvious and which had not been suggested by anybody in the course of the trial.

Accordingly we reject this ground of appeal in the case of Mumraiz Khan and, since we have decided that there is no substance in his other grounds of H appeal, it follows that his appeal against conviction must be refused. The situation is different in the case of Aman Khan for the reasons already given, and on this ground only we must allow his appeal against conviction and set aside the verdict of the trial court. But since we have held that there was sufficient evidence in his case and because the appeal is being allowed solely on the ground of the misdirection by the trial judge we shall give effect to the motion made by the Solicitor General, which counsel for Aman Khan very I properly felt unable to resist, that authority should be given to the Crown to bring a new prosecution against Aman Khan in accordance with s 255 of the Act.

———————

Counsel for First Appellant (Mumraiz Khan), Drummond, QC; Solicitors, Balfour & Manson, Nightingale & Bell (for Mackie & Dewar, Aberdeen) — Counsel for Second Appellant (Aman Khan), Mitchell, QC; Solicitors, Macbeth, Currie & Co, WS (for Beltrami & Co, J
Glasgow) — Counsel for Respondent, Solicitor General (Rodger, QC); Solicitor, J D Lowe, Crown Agent.

R F H

(NOTE)   K

Gribb v Gribb

OUTER HOUSE
LORD WEIR
7 MAY 1992

Process — Remit to sheriff court — Action of divorce defended on financial conclusions only — Action raised in Court of Session to avoid local publicity — Extra expense L
to defender in defending in Court of Session — Whether remit appropriate — Law Reform (Miscellaneous Provisions) (Scotland) Act 1985 (c 73), s 14.

A wife raised a divorce action in the Court of Session, having selected the Court of Session instead of the sheriff court to avoid publicity in the local press. The husband sought a remit to the sheriff court to avoid expense which he would have difficulty in meeting.

Held, that the wife's desire to avoid publicity was

A outweighed by the difficulty involved in the extra expense of defending an action in the Court of Session; and action *remitted* to the sheriff court.

———————

Section 14 of the Law Reform (Miscellaneous Provisions) (Scotland) Act 1985 empowers the Court of Session to remit an action to the appropriate sheriff court where "in the opinion of the Court, the nature of the action makes it appropriate to do so". Margaret Gribb raised an action in the Court of Session against B her husband, William Gribb. She concluded for divorce, for payments to her and for an order transferring the matrimonial home to her. The action was not defended on the merits but was contested on the financial aspects, including the claim by the wife for payment of a substantial capital sum. The parties were both retired. The husband moved the court to remit the action to the local sheriff court. In granting the husband's motion the Lord Ordinary (Weir) said:

C "It was explained to me that while the pursuer was on legal aid the defender was not. His means were such that he fell just above the legal aid limit and if proceedings were to continue in the Court of Session he would be unable to afford to defend the action. An action in this court would involve both counsel and two firms of solicitors and to afford such advisers was beyond his means. On the other hand by proceeding in the sheriff court the defender would be better able to defend the case. The only ground advanced on behalf of the pursuer in opposition to this motion was D that she chose to raise proceedings in the Court of Session in order to avoid publicity in the local press. . . .

"I am satisfied that the nature of this action, being perfectly straightforward, is such as to be appropriate for a remit to the sheriff court. While fear of publicity is no doubt a genuine apprehension, I do not consider that a dispute over finance in a consistorial case will be likely to be regarded locally as newsworthy. In any E event this factor is outweighed in my opinion by the difficulties which the defender at present faces in affording to defend the action in the Court of Session. If he is able to afford to defend in the sheriff court in contrast to his position in the Court of Session, this is a powerful reason for remitting the action."

———————

Counsel for Pursuer, Mackie; Solicitors, Ketchen & Stevens, WS — Counsel for Defender, Davie; Solicitors, F *Drummond Miller, WS.*

C H

Lockhart v Kevin Oliphant Ltd

G

HIGH COURT OF JUSTICIARY
THE LORD JUSTICE CLERK (ROSS),
LORDS SUTHERLAND AND MORISON
25 JUNE 1992

Justiciary — Statutory offence — Health and safety at work — Failure to ensure health and safety so far as reasonably practicable — Employee electrocuted when erecting lamp post under power cable not marked on plans — Plans prepared by consulting engineers for employers' H *main contractors — Main contractors' engineer wrongly locating lamp post under cable — Deceased's employers relying on plans and engineer's location marking — Whether sufficient case of breach of duty — Whether onus shifting to accused — Whether onus of proving not reasonably practicable discharged by accused — Health and Safety at Work etc Act 1974 (c 37), ss 2 (1) and (2), 33 (1) (a) and 40.*

Section 40 of the Health and Safety at Work etc Act I 1974 provides that in any proceedings for an offence under inter alia any statutory provision requiring that something be done so far as is reasonably practicable, it is for the accused to prove that it was not reasonably practicable to do more than was in fact done to satisfy the duty.

A limited company was charged on a summary complaint with a contravention of ss 2 (1) and (2) and 33 (1) (a) of the Health and Safety at Work etc Act 1974 J by failing to ensure, so far as was reasonably practicable, the health, safety and welfare of an employee in respect that they failed to provide a system of work that was, so far as was reasonably practicable, safe and without risk to health, and to ensure the provision of such information and supervision as was necessary to ensure, so far as was reasonably practicable, the employee's health and safety at work. One of the company's employees was electrocuted when a street lamp post which he was assisting in erecting touched an overhead power line. The deceased had been provided K with an incorrect plan which did not show a particular high voltage power line which was in existence when the plan was prepared. The plan had subsequently been updated by consulting engineers working for the company's main contractors. The main contractors' site engineer had also wrongly measured and marked the location of the lamp post underneath the power line. After trial the sheriff acquitted the company on the view that the Crown had not established a sufficient case against it because it was entitled to rely on L the plans and on the location marking of the lamp post. The Crown appealed, contending that the company had failed to discharge the onus which fell on them in terms of s 40 of the 1974 Act.

Held, (1) that the sheriff erred in his approach to the case because (a) the company prima facie clearly failed to ensure the deceased's safety as he died as a result of being electrocuted in the course of his employment while erecting lamp posts at the site, (b) prima facie the company's systems of work were not

A safe and without risk to health for the same reason, and (c) prima facie the information and supervision provided by the company did not ensure the deceased's health and safety at work (p 183B-D); (2) that once a prima facie breach of the 1974 Act arose, the onus in terms of s 40 was on the company to prove that it was not reasonably practicable to do more than the company did to satisfy the statutory duty (p 183F); (3) that the company had not discharged the onus since merely to hold that the company was entitled to rely on the engineers was quite insufficient to prove

B that it was not reasonably practicable to ensure what the company was under a duty to ensure (pp 183L and 184B-C); and appeal *allowed* and case *remitted* to sheriff with a direction to convict.

Dictum in *Marshall v Gotham Co Ltd* [1954] AC 360 at p 373, *applied*.

Summary complaint

C Kevin Oliphant Ltd was charged at the instance of S W Lockhart, procurator fiscal, Aberdeen, on a summary complaint which contained the following charge: "you, being the employer of Mark Webster Robbie, 75 The Corse, Crimmond, Aberdeenshire, in terms of the Health and Safety at Work etc Act 1974, did on 28 September 1990, at the new perimeter road, Kingswells, Aberdeen, fail to ensure, so far as was reasonably practicable, the health, safety and welfare at work of all your employees and in particular said

D Mark Webster Robbie, in that you did fail to ensure (a) a system of work that was, so far as was reasonably practicable, safe and without risk to health, and (b) the provision of such information and supervision as was necessary to ensure, so far as was reasonably practicable, the health and safety at work of your employees and did fail to ensure that a street lighting column erected by your employees was located and erected at a safe distance from overhead power lines, and an 11.5 m street lighting column was lifted by means of a JCB

E digger in such close proximity to an overhead 11,000 KV [sic] electricity power line, that said column came near to, or made contact with, said power line and said employee, Mark Webster Robbie, then holding the bottom end of said column in order to guide it into its locating position, was electrocuted and died shortly thereafter: contrary to the Health and Safety at Work etc Act 1974, s 2 (1) (2) and s 33 (1) (a)''. The accused pled not guilty and proceeded to trial. After trial the temporary sheriff (K C Marshall) acquitted the accused.

F The procurator fiscal appealed by way of stated case to the High Court against the decision of the sheriff.

Findings in fact

The sheriff found the following facts to be admitted or proved:

(1) In connection with the then new perimeter road at Kingswells, Aberdeen, a company known as MTM Construction Ltd were the main contractors (referred to hereafter as "MTM"). (2) The accused company

were asked to tender for subcontract work, in particular the installation of street lighting and the G associated cabling. To enable the accused to tender for the work a very detailed plan of the site prepared by Messrs Fairhursts, consulting civil engineers, was sent by MTM to the accused. The plan was more detailed than was usual for tender purposes. The plan showed existing power cables and other services and the proposed location of lamp standards with one important omission referred to in finding in fact 4. Because of the amount of information on the plan and the detailed nature of the plan the accused were entitled to rely on H that plan and the information contained on it as being comprehensive and correct. Using the plan for reference and without any site visit, the accused tendered for the subcontract work and obtained a contract from MTM for the installation of the lamp posts and associated cabling. (3) It is usual for contractors to discuss proposed works with the local electricity board and MTM had discussion with the North of Scotland Hydro Electric Board to clear with them any construction difficulties due to power lines. The accused were I not present nor were expected to be present at these discussions. The Health and Safety Executive produces a Guidance Note GS6 entitled "Avoidance of Danger from Overhead Electric Lines", a copy of which is produced. Paragraph 17 of said note reads: "The first essential step in complying with the Construction (General Provisions) Regulations is to ascertain whether danger exists in the working area. Consequently an inspection must be made to ascertain whether or not there is any overhead electric line J within or immediately adjoining the work area, or across any route to it. If there are any electric lines over the site, near the site boundaries, or over access road to the site, it is essential that the contractor or employer undertaking the work should consult the owners of the lines (usually the Electricity Board) without delay in order that the proposed work can be discussed and full time given for the line to be diverted or made dead or for other precautions to be taken as described below." Neither MTM nor the accused K carried out such an inspection. (4) The plan referred to was incorrect in that it did not show one particular high voltage power line which was in existence at the time the plan was prepared and the plan updated. Because of this omission there was no discussion between MTM and the Hydro Board about that power line. The accused, relying on the plan and its detail, were not aware of the existence and location of that same particular power line. Apart from consulting the plan the accused took no steps to check whether employees would be in danger from overhead cables L when carrying out their work. The scheme of work for erecting the lamp standards was that the site engineer from MTM would go on site and measure out and mark the position for each lamp post on the roadway. The accused's employees would then come and dig out and prepare an appropriate lined hole for each lamp post to slot into beside the markers prepared by MTM's site engineer. The holes were dug by employees of the accused other than the deceased, Mr Graham Robbie, Mr Brown and Mr Mowatt. (5) The lighting scheme was to be taken over by the Grampian Regional Council on completion and because of that MTM exhibited plans, without correction of the omitted power line, to their lighting engineer for approval. The plans were approved without the local authority going on site to verify the position of the lamp standards or the location of any high voltage electricity wires.

(6) MTM's site engineer wrongly measured and marked the location of two lamp posts. One of the lamp posts was marked to be erected within two metres from overhead power lines carrying 11,000 volts. (7) The power line which was omitted from the plan was the same power line below which MTM's site engineer had wrongly fixed the location of one of the lamp standards. The said power line crossed the new perimeter road at almost right angles. MTM had erected coloured bunting lines across the roadway near to the overhead cabling so that site construction traffic would be aware of the dangers of those power lines. (8) The erection of the lamp posts was behind the scheduled time because of a change in specification for the cabling. The roadway was thus in use before the lamp standards were erected and the bunting was no longer strung across the roadway giving warning of the danger. (9) The accused had no influence with the main contractors over the location of the lamp standards. MTM decided on the location of the lamp standards and they were responsible for marking the roadway. (10) It is not normal practice for a subcontractor erecting lamp posts to go to the consulting engineers to check the plans of their location and other services.

(11) On 28 September 1990 Mark Webster Robbie (hereinafter referred to as the "deceased"), then of 75 The Corse, Crimmond, Aberdeenshire, was an employee of the accused. The deceased had been employed by the accused for approximately two years prior to his death and was very experienced in erecting lamp posts. (12) On 28 September 1990 the deceased was working in a gang of three erecting lamp posts. The gang consisted of himself, his father Graham Webster Robbie and Mr Alexander Brown. A fourth man, a Mr Mowatt, had been in the gang earlier that week but was not on site on 28 September as he was attending a wedding. Mr Mowatt was normally in charge of this squad and in his absence no other person was designated as being in charge. On 27 September Mr Mowatt had shown Mr Graham Webster Robbie a plan of where the lamp posts were to be erected the following day and discussed with him how they were to be erected. The plan did not show any high voltage electricity wires at the location of the poles. (13) On 28 September 1990 a lorry carried the lamp posts on site and left one lamp post beside each of the pre-prepared holes and slots where they were to be erected. Graham Webster Robbie drove a JCB tractor unit with a hydraulic arm which had a lifting eye at the front of its bucket. On to the lifting eye was attached a sample sling which would be tied round the lamp post being erected above the point of balance of the post. When the lifting arm was raised the lamp

post was swung upwards and the foot of the lamp post would be held down by one of the other two men in the gang and eased into the pre-prepared slot. The sling would then be slipped and the JCB driven along to the next location where the next pole would be erected using the same system. This system had been in use for a considerable period. Mr Graham Webster Robbie had been employed by the accused for 14 years and was experienced in this system. The deceased was the accused's most experienced lamp standard erector and had recently helped erect over 450 lamp posts at another location. When in the course of erecting the fourth or fifth lamp post on the morning of 28 September the lamp post came very close to or touched an 11,000 volt power line whilst the deceased was holding the foot of the lamp post, about to guide it into its pre-prepared slot. As a result of this the electricity from the cables discharged through the now deceased and he was electrocuted and died as a result. (14) The JCB driver had not seen the overhead wires until he descended from the cab of the tractor after his son had been electrocuted. The JCB tractor had a solid non-transparent roof. Neither the deceased nor the third man in the gang had indicated that they were aware of any overhead wires in the vicinity before the erection of that particular lamp post. (15) Each lamp post is approximately 12.5 m in length. The high voltage electricity wires were approximately 9 m above ground level. The JCB driver had worked near high voltage wires on average once per week. Both he and the deceased had been at training courses arranged by the accused covering inter alia the dangers of working near high voltage lines.

(16) The gang of three men had 10 lamp posts to erect on 28 September. The poles were approximately 100 yds apart and it would take only a matter of minutes to erect each pole. There is a warning notice stating "Danger of Death" on a plaque approximately 8 in × 4 in affixed to the electricity pylon carrying the high voltage wires. What remained of the bunting referred to in finding 8 was attached to a pole close by the pylon and both this and the plaque were clearly visible from the road and verge where the deceased was working. (17) Mark Webster Robbie died on 28 September 1990 as a result of electrocution in the course of his employment whilst erecting lamp posts at Kingswells perimeter road, Aberdeen.

Statutory provisions

The Health and Safety at Work etc Act 1974 provides:

"2.—(1) It shall be the duty of every employer to ensure, so far as is reasonably practicable, the health, safety and welfare at work of all his employees.

"(2) Without prejudice to the generality of an employer's duty under the preceding subsection, the matters to which that duty extends include in particular — (a) the provision and maintenance of plant and systems of work that are, so far as is reasonably practicable, safe and without risks to health; . . . (c) the provision of such information, instruction, training and supervision as is necessary to ensure, so far as is

A reasonably practicable, the health and safety at work of his employees. . . .

"40. In any proceedings for an offence under any of the relevant statutory provisions consisting of a failure to comply with a duty or requirement to do something so far as is practicable or so far as is reasonably practicable, or to use the best practicable means to do something, it shall be for the accused to prove (as the case may be) that it was not practicable or not reasonably practicable to do more than was in fact done to satisfy the duty or requirement, or that there was no better

B practicable means than was in fact used to satisfy the duty or requirement."

Cases referred to

Edwards v National Coal Board [1949] 1 KB 704.
Marshall v Gotham Co Ltd [1954] AC 360; [1954] 2 WLR 812; [1954] 1 All ER 437.
Nimmo v Alexander Cowan & Sons Ltd, 1967 SLT 277; 1967 SC (HL) 79.

C **Appeal**

The sheriff posed the following questions for the opinion of the High Court:

(1) Did I err in law on the facts as stated above in finding the case against the accused not proven?

(2) Did I err in law in holding that the respondent was entitled to rely exclusively on the plan prepared by consulting civil engineers?

D (3) Did I err in law in holding that the respondent had satisfied the evidential burden laid upon it by s 40 of the Health and Safety at Work Act 1974?

The appeal was argued before the High Court on 9 June 1992.

On 25 June 1992 the court *answered* questions 1 and 3 in the *affirmative, declined* to answer question 2, *allowed* the appeal and *remitted* to the sheriff with a direction to proceed to conviction.

E The following opinion of the court was delivered by the Lord Justice Clerk (Ross):

OPINION OF THE COURT.—This is an appeal at the instance of the procurator fiscal, Aberdeen. The respondent is Kevin Oliphant Ltd. The respondent was charged in the sheriff court at Aberdeen on a complaint libelling a contravention of s 2 (1) and (2) and s 33 (1) (a) of the Health and Safety at Work etc Act

F 1974. The charge was in the following terms: [his Lordship quoted the terms of the charge and continued:]

Section 2 of the Act of 1974 provides inter alia as follows: [his Lordship quoted the terms of s 2 set out supra and continued:] Section 33 (1) (a) of the Act of 1974 provides inter alia that it is an offence for a person to fail to discharge a duty to which he is subject by virtue of s 2.

Section 40 of the Act of 1974 deals with the onus of proving limits of what is practicable. It provides as

follows: [his Lordship quoted the terms of s 40 and continued:]   G

At the trial of the respondent three joint minutes of admission were lodged and a number of productions were also lodged in evidence by the appellant and the respondent. After the evidence had been concluded the sheriff found the charge against the respondent not proven. Against that decision of the sheriff the appellant has appealed by way of stated case. The case contains three questions for the opinion of the court: [his Lordship quoted the terms of the questions and   H continued:]

The advocate depute drew attention to the terms of various findings in fact, and submitted that they gave rise to a prima facie case against the respondent, and that the onus had therefore been transferred to the respondent in terms of s 40. He further contended that it was also clear from the findings that the respondent had failed to discharge that onus.

Senior counsel for the respondent on the other hand   I maintained that the sheriff had been well founded in concluding that the onus of proof had never shifted. He contended that the presence of the words "so far as is reasonably practicable" in s 2 (1) and s 2 (2) (a) and (c) showed that the duty imposed by that section was not an absolute duty. He maintained that the sheriff had been well founded in holding that when regard was had to the whole evidence in the case the proper conclusion was that the Crown had not established a sufficient case against the respondent. He   J stressed, as the sheriff had stressed, that the findings showed that the respondent had been provided with an incorrect plan which had been prepared by consulting civil engineers, and sent to the respondent who was a subcontractor by the main contractors. The respondent had relied upon this plan and had not carried out any inspection of the site. The plan in fact was incorrect in that it did not show one particular high voltage power line which was in existence at the time when the plan was prepared and when the plan was updated.   K Because the respondent relied on this plan it was not aware of the existence and location of that particular power line. Moreover the scheme of working for erecting lamp standards was that the site engineer from the main contractors would go to the site and measure out and mark the position for each lamp post on the roadway. The site engineer wrongly measured and marked the location of two lamp posts, one of which was marked to be erected within two metres from overhead power lines carrying 11,000 volts. The   L power line which was omitted from the plan was the same power line below which the main contractors' site engineer had wrongly fixed the location of one of the lamp standards. The accident had occurred when this particular lamp standard was being erected. Senior counsel for the respondent drew attention to the fact that in his note, on more than one occasion, the sheriff expressed the view that the respondent was entitled to rely on the very detailed plans prepared by the consulting engineers and on the location marking of each lamp post prepared and marked by the main

contractors. The sheriff held that the respondent had
employed a system of work that was safe in the erection of the lamp posts.

In our opinion the sheriff erred in his approach to
this case. The respondent has been charged with contravening s 2 (1) and 2 (2) of the Act of 1974. In terms
of s 2 (1) the duty is to ensure so far as is reasonably
practicable the health, safety and welfare at work of all
its employees. In terms of s 40 the onus of proving
that it was not reasonably practicable to have done
more than was in fact done to ensure the health, safety
and welfare of its employees including the deceased
rested upon the respondent. Accordingly the first
question must be whether the evidence led discloses a
prima facie case that the respondent failed to ensure
the health, safety and welfare at work of its employees.
In our opinion having regard to the findings in fact,
it is quite clear that prima facie the respondent failed
to ensure the safety at work of its employee Mark
Webster Robbie. The respondent was his employer,
and at the time of his death he was engaged at work
in his employment with the respondent. It clearly
failed to ensure his safety because as is clear from findings 13 and 17 he died as a result of being electrocuted
in the course of his employment while erecting lamp
posts at the site. Likewise, having regard to the findings, prima facie the respondent's systems of work
were not safe and without risks to health, since Mark
Webster Robbie died in the course of his employment
while erecting lamp posts. Similarly on the findings
prima facie the information and supervision provided
by the respondent did not ensure the health and safety
at work of Mark Webster Robbie. We are accordingly
satisfied that the findings in fact disclosed a prima
facie case against the respondent of breach of s 2 (1)
and s 2 (2) (a) and (c) of the Act of 1974.

In our opinion the sheriff erred in his conclusion
that the Crown had not established a sufficient case
against the respondent. The fallacy in the sheriff's
approach is that he has approached the case as if the
words "so far as is reasonably practicable" were an
integral part of the offence, so that accordingly there
could be no prima facie case against the respondent
unless it appeared prima facie that it was reasonably
practicable to secure the result which the statute
provided that the employer had to ensure. There is,
however, high authority for the view that the words
"so far as is reasonably practicable" are not an integral
part of an offence such as that alleged in the present
case (*Nimmo v Alexander Cowan & Sons Ltd*). Section
2 (1) of the Act of 1974 is clearly intended to secure
that a stated result is achieved, namely, the health,
safety and welfare at work of all the respondent's
employees. Once it is established that that stated result
was not achieved, a prima facie case of breach of
statute arises, and in terms of s 40 the onus is on the
respondent to prove that it was not reasonably practicable to do more than the respondent did to satisfy
the statutory duty.

The question then arises as to whether that onus was
discharged. In that connection regard must be had to
all the evidence which was adduced before the sheriff.
Because the sheriff held that the Crown had not established a sufficient case against the respondent it was
unnecessary for him to consider whether that onus had
been discharged. However, in the further note which
he supplied dealing with proposed adjustments, the
sheriff said this: "Had I held that the Crown had
established such a case and the burden then fell upon
the accused to discharge, I would have held that they
had discharged it for the reasons given in the findings
and [sic] fact and this note."

The advocate depute contended that insofar as the
sheriff did comment on discharging the onus in this
case he had not considered the proper question which
fell to be determined when s 40 was relied upon. As
we have already observed, it is clear from the findings
in the sheriff's note that he attached great importance
to the fact that the respondent had been supplied with
a more than usually detailed plan of the site. He went
on to express the following conclusion: "My view was
that an experienced engineering company such as the
accused was entitled to rely on the main contractor's
site engineer and consulting civil engineers and had
not breached the terms of the Act by acting in the way
that the company did. The company had employed a
system of work that was safe in the erection of the
lamp post. The company had provided information by
way of lectures and courses to ensure that their
employees were well aware of the dangers of working
at or near high voltage wires. The particular
employees of the company were very experienced in
that one had been working with the company for 14
years doing similar work and the deceased had erected
over 450 lamp standards using the same system and it
was not in my view necessary that they should be
supervised in their work."

Senior counsel for the respondent accepted that the
respondent had carried out no inspection, but he
maintained that there was no reason to conclude that
any inspection which might have taken place before
the location of the lamp posts had been marked by the
main contractors would have disclosed the presence of
danger; he accordingly concluded that there was no
reason to link inspection with the later fatality.

In our opinion in concentrating upon the question
of whether the respondent was entitled to rely on the
plans prepared by the consulting engineers and on the
location marking of the lamp posts submitted by the
main contractor, the sheriff was directing himself to
the wrong issue. Where as here the result which
Parliament has stated has to be ensured has not been
achieved, it is for the respondent to prove that it was
not reasonably practicable to do so. In our opinion the
material placed before the sheriff was quite inadequate
to demonstrate any such thing. Such evidence as was
led did not demonstrate that it would not have been
practicable to ensure that the lamp post which the
deceased was holding did not come very close to or
touched the overhead power line. As Lord Reid
observed in *Marshall v Gotham Co Ltd* [1954] AC at
p 373: "I think it enough to say that if a precaution

A　is practicable it must be taken unless in the whole circumstances that would be unreasonable."

It has been observed that the fact that a precaution is physically possible does not mean that it is reasonably practicable, but when considering whether a precaution is reasonably practicable a computation must be made in which the degree of risk is weighed against the cost in money, time or trouble of the measures necessary to avert risk (*Edwards v National Coal Board*).

B　In the present case the sheriff did not undertake any such exercise. He did not address himself to these matters at all (no doubt because no evidence to enable him to do so was adduced by the respondent), and it follows that the onus of proving that it was not reasonably practicable to do more than was in fact done was not discharged. Merely to hold that the respondent was entitled to rely on the main contractor's engineer and the consulting civil engineers is quite insufficient to prove that it was not reasonably practicable to achieve the result which Parliament has said the C　respondent was under a duty to ensure.

For the foregoing reasons we answer the first question in the case in the affirmative and the third question likewise in the affirmative. The second question does not require to be answered since it is defective in form; the sheriff did not hold that the respondent was entitled to rely exclusively on the plan prepared by the consulting civil engineers. Having answered questions 1 and 3, we shall remit to the sheriff with a direction that he should proceed as accords, and should find the D　respondent guilty of the charge.

Counsel for Appellant, Bonomy, AD; Solicitor, J D Lowe, Crown Agent — Counsel for Respondent, Nimmo Smith, QC, Baird; Solicitors, Shepherd & Wedderburn, WS.

P W F

E

Brooks v Brooks

OUTER HOUSE

LORD MARNOCH

25 JUNE 1992

F　*Husband and wife — Divorce — Financial provision — Capital sum — Pension rights — Method of valuation — Whether pension should be valued according to actuarial evidence or by reference to multiplier — Whether income rights or capital value — Family Law (Scotland) Act 1985 (c 37), s 10.*

A wife raised an action of divorce in which she concluded for payment of a capital sum. The parties agreed that there should be equal division of the total net value of the items of matrimonial property as at the date of separation. The main matter of dispute between the parties was the valuation of the husband's

rights in a pension. The pursuer led evidence from an actuary who, after certain adjustments, put a capital G value on the pension rights. The defender argued that the valuation should be obtained by applying a multiplier as had been done in personal injuries cases. The defender further contended that the actuarial figure was an assessment of income rights rather than an immediately realisable capital sum and thus it should be treated as a maximum rather than an actual amount; and that extract should be superseded by six months and interest postponed for a similar period.

Held, (1) that the value of the pension rights was H properly obtained from the actuarial evidence rather than by use of a multiplier (p 186A-C); (2) that as there were other assets capable of realisation it was fair and reasonable to treat the actuarial figure as a capital asset (p 185I-J); and decree for capital sum with interest from the date of decree *granted* accordingly but with extract superseded for four months.

I

Action of divorce

Virginia Mary Tunstall or Brooks raised an action of divorce against William Brooks. She concluded inter alia for payment of a capital sum.

The case proceeded to proof before the Lord Ordinary (Marnoch).

Statutory provisions

The Family Law (Scotland) Act 1985 provides:

"10.—(1) In applying the principle set out in section J 9 (1) (a) of this Act, the net value of the matrimonial property shall be taken to be shared fairly bweween the parties to the marriage when it is shared equally or in such other proportions as are justified by special circumstances. . . .

"(5) The proportion of any rights or interests of either party under a life policy or occupational pension scheme or similar arrangement referable to the period to which subsection (4) (b) above refers K shall be taken to form part of the matrimonial property.

"(6) In subsection (1) above 'special circumstances', without prejudice to the generality of the words, may include—. . . (c) any destruction, dissipation or alienation of property by either party; (d) the nature of the matrimonial property, the use made of it (including use for business purposes or as a matrimonial home) and the extent to which it is reasonable to expect it to L be realised or divided or used as security."

Cases referred to

Little v Little, 1990 SLT 785.
Mitchell v Glenrothes Development Corporation, 1991 SLT 284.
O'Brien's Curator Bonis v British Steel plc, 1991 SLT 477.

On 25 June 1992 the Lord Ordinary *pronounced* decree of divorce, *awarded* the pursuer a capital sum

of £23,884 with interest from the date of decree and
A *superseded* extract for four months.

LORD MARNOCH.—In this action, having heard
the evidence of both parties, I am satisfied that decree
of divorce should be pronounced and I accordingly
uphold the pursuer's first plea in law to that effect.

The only other conclusion insisted in by the pursuer
is her fourth conclusion to the extent of seeking
payment of a capital sum. On that matter the parties
are to be commended on having reached agreement as
B to all items of matrimonial property and as to the
values of most of them, all as set out in the joint
minute. They are also agreed that the total net value
of that property assessed as at the date of separation,
namely 15 November 1988, should be equally divided
between them in accordance with the presumption
normally applicable under and in terms of s 10 (1) of
the Family Law (Scotland) Act 1985. Several of the
items, including three heritable properties, are already
held in their joint names and nothing further need be
C said about these items. Indeed, it follows from the
foregoing that the capital sum, as agreed in principle,
can be derived quite simply from a comparison
between the values of matrimonial property held
exclusively in the respective names of each party. [His
Lordship considered a matter with which this report
is not concerned and continued:] I accordingly assess
the total value of the matrimonial property [at the
relevant date] in the name of the pursuer as being
£48,626.
D

Turning now to the value of such property in the
name of the defender it is common ground that he
holds items having a total value, as at the relevant
date, of £14,000. In addition, however, the defender is
in right of a pension from Grindlay's Bank and it was
the valuation of this item which was the main subject
of dispute as between the parties.

The pursuer led evidence from an actuary, Mr
E Hurcombe, who unfortunately had been misinformed
as to the age of the defender and who in consequence
accepted that his valuation should be reduced by
between 6 per cent and 8 per cent. In these circumstances I consider that the appropriate reduction to
make is one of 7 per cent. As can be seen from his
report, Mr Hurcombe prepared valuations on two distinct bases, the first assuming 4 per cent annual
increases in the pension and the second assuming
increases restricted to the guaranteed minimum rate of
3 per cent per annum. In support of the former Mr
F Hurcombe referred to a change of policy subsequent
to November 1988 but readily agreed in cross examination that this could not have been a factor in valuation as at the relevant date. He was, however, aware
that in the single year preceding the relevant date a
discretionary addition of 1 per cent had been awarded
and this, he thought, went some way, although not the
whole way, towards supporting the higher of the two
valuations. In the whole circumstances I consider that
the proper course is to take as a starting point the
figure midway between these two valuations as

reduced by 7 per cent for the reason referred to above.
This produces a figure of £101,974 and on the basis G
of the actuarial evidence I did not understand counsel
for the defender seriously to dispute that starting
point. Of that figure, however, a sum of, in round
terms, £15,000 was attributable to widow's rights and
Mr Hurcombe accepted that a divorced wife would
not be eligible to claim these. Moreover the defender
was 51 years of age as at the date of separation and at
that age Mr Hurcombe thought that the statistical
probability of remarriage was "considerably less than
100 per cent". In truth, however, he had not really H
applied his mind to that matter. In the foregoing circumstances counsel for the defender submitted that
for purposes of valuation as at the relevant date (being
the date of separation), the figure of £15,000 should be
deducted. In my opinion he was well founded in that
submission and I am not sure that counsel for the
pursuer had any real argument to the contrary. In any
event, however, if for some reason this were not a
matter to be taken into account at the stage of valuation I should have thought there might be a case for I
making special allowance for it under s 10 (6) (c) or (d)
of the 1985 Act.

In the result, I assess the value of the pension as
being £86,974. Counsel for the defender submitted
that this was a "ceiling" figure, in the sense that it was
a valuation of the income rights rather than an assessment of an immediately realisable capital sum.
However, where, as here, there are other assets which
are capable of realisation I consider that the figure in
question is a fair and reasonable one: cf *Little v Little*, J
per Lord President Hope at pp 788-789.

It follows from the above that I assess the total value
of the matrimonial property held by the defender as
being £100,974, namely £52,348 in excess of that held
by the pursuer. Half of the difference is £26,174, but
there is a debt due by the defender to the pursuer's
mother in the sum of £4,580. In terms of s 10 (2) of
the Act that debt must be borne equally by the parties
and I accordingly award the pursuer a capital sum of K
£23,884. I shall sustain the pursuer's third plea in law
to that effect. In view of the fact that heritable
property may have to be realised in order to finance
this sum both parties accepted that it was appropriate
to supersede extract for a limited period. Counsel for
the defender suggested that a period of six months was
appropriate. Counsel for the pursuer suggested that
three months would be sufficient. In the result, I have
decided to supersede extract for a period of four
months but, despite the submission to the contrary by L
counsel for the defender, I am satisfied that in the
present case interest at the legal rate should run from
the present date.

Before parting with this case I have to record that,
in the course of his submissions, counsel for the
defender sought to persuade me that in valuing the
defender's pension I should disregard the actuarial
evidence entirely and proceed instead on what he
maintained was the "conventional" approach of
applying a multiplier to the amount of the pension. In

A this connection he referred me to the decision of Lord Clyde in *Mitchell v Glenrothes Development Corporation*, as referred to with approval by the Inner House in *O'Brien's Curator Bonis v British Steel plc*. These however were both actions for damages which, in my opinion, raise considerations very different from those which arise when valuing matrimonial property. In particular, I note that at p 289 of the *Mitchell* report Lord Clyde gave two specific reasons for rejecting the actuarial approach as being immediately relevant in assessing damages. In the first place, it expressly took

B account of supposed future inflation and, secondly, it was too imprecise insofar as it reflected only the expectations of the average man. Neither criticism, it seems to me, is in the same way applicable to the valuation of pension rights as an item of matrimonial property. Moreover, so far as authority is concerned, counsel for the defender fully accepted that he could cite no case which threw light on what would be an appropriate multiplier to cover the full life expectancy of a man aged 51 years. Instead he invited me simply to accept

C his own assertion that a multiplier of 10 would, in the circumstances, be a reasonable one to take. As already indicated, however, I am not prepared to give effect to his submissions on this matter. On the contrary, I am quite satisfied as to the propriety and usefulness of the actuarial evidence which was led in the present case and on which I have based my assessment of the value of the pension rights in question. I may say that I am fortified in that view by the knowledge that, as matter of practice, such evidence has frequently been relied

D upon in the past; cf, eg, *Little v Little*.

Counsel for Pursuer, J G Thomson; Solicitors, Aitken Nairn, WS — Counsel for Defender, J J Mitchell; Solicitors, Allan McDougall & Co, SSC.

C A G M

E

Breingan v Jamieson

OUTER HOUSE

LORD MACLEAN

26 JUNE 1992

Parent and child — Custody — Best interests of child —
F *Death of mother of young child — Whether child ought to be returned to natural father who maintained contact with her or remain with aunt where she was happy and well settled.*

The father of a young female child petitioned for her custody following the death of the mother when the child was nearly seven years old. The child's parents had separated and were divorced when the child was still only three. Both parents had remarried. The child had remained with her mother although her father had maintained contact with her. He had initially been

granted access for two days a week but, on divorce,
G access was reduced to once per month. The father and his new wife had no family. The mother's second husband, the first respondent, also sought custody but worked abroad for long periods. After the death of the child's mother and in accordance with the child's wishes the child had gone to live with the child's aunt and her husband. They had one very young child. The child's mother had made provisions in an unexecuted will that the child be looked after by the child's aunt in the event of the mother's death. The child was happy and well settled there and had a secure and
H stable environment. She also enjoyed her access visits to the petitioner and his second wife.

Held, (1) that the paramount consideration was the child's welfare and what the court had to decide was what would be in her best interests (p 187F); (2) that since the child was happy and well settled where she was, she had endured numerous upheavals in her life already and to remove her now to a new environment would be disruptive of her settled, happy life, her best
I interests were to remain in the care of the aunt and her husband (p 190E-F); and custody and parental rights *granted* accordingly with access to the petitioner.

Petition for custody

Scott Dalrymple Breingan petitioned for custody of his daughter Nicola Breingan following the death of Nicola's mother. Nicola's stepfather Thomas Brinley Jamieson was called as first respondent and her aunt
J and the aunt's husband, Christine and Ninian Jamieson, were called as second respondents. The second respondents concluded for parental rights of Nicola and for her custody.

The petition came before the Lord Ordinary (MacLean).

On 26 June 1992 his Lordship *granted* custody and parental rights to the second respondents and access to
K the petitioner.

LORD MACLEAN.—Nicola Breingan was born on 4 September 1984. She is the child of the petitioner and his first wife Linda Dickson, who were married on 19 December 1978 and divorced on 31 May 1988. On 18 December 1989 Linda Dickson married Thomas Brinley Jamieson, the first respondent, whom she had known since about May 1989. Nicola's mother died on 23 July 1991, aged 38. On 5 March 1992 the peti-
L tioner married Clare Breingan whom he had known since about 1986, the year after he and Nicola's mother separated. Upon separation the petitioner continued to live in the family home but his first wife went to live with her parents, taking Nicola with her. Nicola then lived in family with her mother, her grandparents and her mother's younger sister, Christine Dickson who is 11 years younger than her sister, until about the time when her parents were divorced, when she and her mother went to live in a flat in Eaglesham. After her mother remarried, Nicola

A
lived with her mother and the first respondent.
Christine Dickson, Nicola's aunt, married her
husband Ninian in August 1988 and then became Mrs
Jamieson. They have one child, William, who is about
18 months old. She and her husband are the second
respondents. Mr Tom Jamieson and Mr Ninian
Jamieson are not related. It will be seen from these
bare statements of fact that Nicola has not lived with
her father since December 1985, and that thereafter
she has been cared for by her mother, her mother's
family, and her stepfather.

B
Her father, the petitioner, however continued to
maintain contact with Nicola after he and Nicola's
mother separated. On 14 August 1986 he was granted
access by the sheriff court at Paisley on two days a
week. Upon divorce the amount of access the petitioner enjoyed was reduced to once per month from 10
am to 6 pm or such other times as might be agreed
between the parties. The petitioner maintained that he
exercised access more frequently than that, which was
disputed by the respondents, although the petitioner
C
accepted that when Nicola went to school first in
August 1989 he saw less of her because she was being
teased about having two "Daddies". Then, he said, he
voluntarily reduced access so as not to disturb the
child. I have to say that I was not influenced or
affected by the evidence led by both sides about the
reasons for the breakdown of the marriage — whether
it was the petitioner's alleged violence or Linda
Dickson's alleged alcoholism or an interaction
between the two. This evidence seemed to me to have
D
only a very remote bearing upon what *now* was in the
best interests of Nicola, especially as it was not said
that the petitioner was ever violent towards Nicola or
in her presence. The regularity of the access which the
petitioner exercised seemed to me to have a little more
relevance, but only if it was being maintained that the
petitioner was interested in Nicola only after her
mother died. That I do not think was the case
although, as I shall recount later, her mother's death
did stimulate him immediately into seeking her
E
custody. It may be the case that on occasions the petitioner missed access periods, but the important fact
seems to me to be that he was never able to exercise
residential access to her until March 1992 on the eve
of his wedding and that as a result of the order of the
court.

If I may, I would like to repeat at this point what I
said at the close of the proof, and I do so in explanation of my decision not to rehearse all or even most of
F
the evidence which was led before me, which in
another type of case I would normally do in a written
judgment. The paramount consideration in this case is
Nicola's welfare and what I have to decide upon is
what, in my judgment, will be her best interests. The
parties to the action — the petitioner on the one hand
and all the respondents on the other — are obviously
very sincere in the views they hold about what is in
Nicola's best interests. Unless it can be seen to have
some relevance to that question I do not think it is
helpful to express my opinion with regard to the past
conduct of those involved in caring for Nicola,

especially as all those who are concerned in her
upbringing will have to co-operate with each other and G
try to get on reasonably well together, no matter who
is awarded her custody. So, for example, I do not
intend to condescend in any detail about the positions
parties took at the obviously hard fought motions
before this court in September 1991 and February
1992 when I think there was to a certain extent some
misunderstanding between the parties about their
respective motives and objectives. What I want to
make clear, in short, is that a strained and difficult
relationship between those involved in Nicola's care
and upbringing will not be in her best interests. What H
I wish to do is to avoid making unnecessary judgments
about past conduct that might cause friction or otherwise have an adverse effect upon that future relationship.

The event which has focused attention upon
Nicola's custody was the tragic early death of her
mother in July 1991. Until then arrangements for her
upbringing had worked tolerably well, with her
mother having her custody and her father exercising I
access to her fairly regularly. What I have to consider
is whether that event has brought about such a change
of circumstances as would justify removing Nicola
from the care of the second respondents and placing
her in the custody of the petitioner.

Shortly after he learnt of Nicola's mother's death the
petitioner tried to find out where Nicola was, being as
he said, concerned about her and being desirous of her
custody. He spoke to the first respondent on the inter-
com at his flat, asking if he could take his daughter J
home, a request which the first respondent refused
without telling him where Nicola was. In fact when
her mother fell ill Nicola went to stay with her grandparents, and two weeks after her mother died she went
to live with the second respondents in the village of
Loans, just outside Troon, where she has lived ever
since. Being concerned, as I think without justification, that the first respondent intended to take Nicola
out of the jurisdiction, the petitioner raised the
present action and obtained interim interdict against K
the first respondent from removing Nicola from the
jurisdiction in the vacation court on 31 July 1991. I
should add that on the day of Mrs Linda Jamieson's
cremation a writ was served on the petitioner at the
instance of the second respondents seeking custody of
the child. These proceedings, which were raised in the
sheriff court, have been sisted, pending the outcome
of this action.

The petitioner, who is aged 37, said that he wished L
to have custody of Nicola because he did not want her
to be ignored or pushed aside. He had a very good relationship with Nicola, as did his wife, Clare, who had
known Nicola since about 1986. As her father he could
offer her love and affection. She would be brought up
close to his brother's children, and she was especially
close to her cousin Laura who is about the same age.
She was like a sister to Nicola. He thought that if she
remained with the second respondents it was as if she
was being brought up by adults. "She would" he said,
"be an old maid." He did not want her to be passed

round the family between stepfather, grandparents
A and uncle and aunt "dressed to the nines". He added:
"She's not treated as a wee girl. She is treated as a
show piece." In East Kilbride she would go to school
with her cousins. He was anxious that the second
respondents, as they had more children of their own,
would tend to ignore Nicola. According to the petitioner Nicola was quite happy to come to live with
him and Clare. She had chosen the bunkbeds and the
wallpaper for her bedroom. He considered that Nicola
was not in the right environment. She was not with
her father and mother, and her mother was no longer
B alive. He concluded his position with regard to
custody thus: "Her aunt and uncle will have more
children who will know that Nicola is not their sister.
I am the natural father and want to resume her
custody. There is no reason for me to differentiate
between Nicola and any other children I may have."

Mrs Clare Breingan who is aged 27 and is a trained
general nurse undergoing midwifery training, confirmed that the petitioner and Nicola were very close,
C especially since residential access had been exercised.
She was perfectly happy for the petitioner to have
custody of Nicola whom she would treat as her own
daughter. When her course was completed in August
she and the petitioner planned to begin a family. She
got on very well with Nicola. She was "like a wee
pal". Not only did the petitioner's family live near
them in East Kilbride, but so also did her own family.
It was obvious that Nicola was being looked after well
enough at present, but it would be "great" if she could
D come back to live with her father. That, she thought,
would be better for Nicola. After all, the petitioner
was "her only blood relative". I formed the clear
impression that if Mrs Clare Breingan has any children they will have a very nice caring mother and it
did not surprise me to learn later in the evidence that
Nicola spoke very positively about Clare and said that
she liked her a lot.

Mrs Anne Breingan, the petitioner's mother, confirmed that Nicola and her cousin Laura were very
E friendly. She also said of her daughter in law Clare:
"She gets on very well with Nicola. It is very brave of
her. She's young. She's newly married. She's got very
close to her." But Clare was very happy to include
Nicola in her family. The petitioner's position was
well summed up by his mother: "She's his wee girl,
isn't she? Why should she live with almost strangers?
It's his daughter. It's his blood. She doesn't belong to
grandparents." Of the second respondents she said
that they would have other family and cousins always
F came second. Her son's home was "her proper home".
Clare was a very capable girl. The petitioner could
provide a settled and stable home life for Nicola. If the
petitioner were to be awarded Nicola's custody I
thought Mrs Anne Breingan would be a warm and
attentive grandmother.

The first respondent, Nicola's stepfather, explained
the reasons why he, the second respondents and
Nicola's grandparents thought that they should take
steps immediately after Linda's death to obtain
Nicola's custody. His position in relation to custody

was, he had been advised, pretty weak. Linda, his
wife, had always thought that it would be better for G
Nicola to live with her aunt and uncle if anything were
to happen to her. Indeed she had put this in her will.
The draft will which had not been executed and was
thought to predate Linda's divorce, was produced
which included a provision to this effect. Besides, the
petitioner had called, stating that he was going to take
Nicola away since he was the child's father. He told
the petitioner that the petitioner was not Nicola's real
dad in the sense that she did not regard him as her
father. Nicola, in his view, could be quite shy, but she H
could quickly open up. She was "very intelligent and
articulate and extremely inquisitive". She had got over
her mother's death and was now much more open and
confident. She enjoyed the stables attached to the
second respondents' home. She loved her cousin
William very much. She treated him as a brother, but
knew him as a cousin. Nicola regarded him as dad and
called him such. As for the second respondents, Nicola
had known them almost all her life. They were the
people who had always provided her with security and I
stability. After his wife died he asked Nicola what she
wanted and she said that she wanted to live with the
second respondents. He and the second respondents
had been worried that in view of his claims as Nicola's
father, if the petitioner then had access to Nicola he
might not return her. For that reason initially they did
not tell him where she was. He himself worked as a
geologist with an oilfield services group in drilling off
the West African coast. His job involved him being
abroad a lot, perhaps as much as six to eight weeks at J
a time. He intended making financial provision for
Nicola in the form of an endowment fund for her continuing education which he would contribute to
whatever decision was made regarding her custody.
He was still accumulating money to provide a lump
sum. Dr Brenda Robson, child psychologist, had been
instructed to provide a report on Nicola simply in an
attempt to obtain an independent view of whether he
and the second respondents were doing the right
thing. Whether that report was truly independent K
depended on the integrity of the compiler of the
report. While Nicola sometimes stayed with her
grandparents, she never stayed with him.

Mrs Christine Jamieson, who is aged 28 and is
Nicola's aunt, recounted how her sister had asked her
and Ninian before she married him to look after
Nicola if anything were to happen to her, and said that
she had made provision for this in her will. "We grew
extremely fond of Nicola when she lived with us in
Newton Mearns," she said. "So we agreed to look L
after her." After she married Ninian Jamieson in
August 1988 she continued to see Nicola most weekends. Nicola used to come to see her horse. When she
lived with her sister and Nicola in her parents' house
there were occasions especially on Saturdays when she
looked after Nicola. Nicola had, after all, lived in
family with her for about two and a half years. It was,
she said, impossible not to be involved with "such a
charming wee girl". After her mother's sudden death
Nicola did not want to see her father and "We [that

A is the respondents and Nicola's grandparents] thought it best that he should not see her until it was all sorted out by the court." Everyone at that time thought it would have been a disaster if Nicola had been removed from her own environment. They were apprehensive that the petitioner might not return Nicola if he exercised access to her since, following Linda Jamieson's death, he had come to take her back. They had given Nicola a pony in August believing that that would help her get over her mother's death and in the hope that she would enjoy it as much as her

B aunt had done. Nicola was now involved in Troon Riding Club. She had been at Wellington school in Ayr since September 1991. There she was happy, apart from a passing difficulty with one other pupil, and she was doing very well. Her reports were complimentary. This was confirmed by her teacher Miss Godfrey, who said in evidence that Nicola was shy when she came to school and not so confident as she now was. According to Miss Godfrey she seemed to be very well adjusted and very happy. She occasionally

C talked about her father to her teacher. As for her school work, it had progressed very satisfactorily.

Mrs Jamieson said that she and her husband were extending the accommodation they had by converting a byre. Their new accommodation was expected to be completed by the autumn. Nicola was quite taken with the second respondents' child William. Right from the start she called him her brother. He was as good as a brother to her although she appreciated that he was her cousin. Mrs Jamieson said that she had no

D problem dealing with Nicola as her own child, adding, "You just get on with your life." Nicola was only 15 months old when her parents separated. Mrs Jamieson said: "She has formed relationships with us and that's where the problem lies. I can't help it if she enjoys living with us." Because they were all worried about Nicola's future and thought it would be catastrophic if she were to be removed from the family group they sought advice from a child psychologist. That was how Dr Robson came to be instructed. Mrs Jamieson

E frankly admitted that she would be very upset if Nicola were to be taken away from herself and her family. "I'd hate to see her going anywhere else," she said in conclusion.

Ninian Jamieson, her husband who is aged 30, is a building inspector with the National House Building Council, his area being south west Scotland. This work does not take him away from home overnight. He had known Nicola practically all her life since he had been going out with her aunt when she was born.

F After Linda Jamieson died he believed that it was right that Nicola should come to live with him and his wife. He said: "She had a very close relationship with Christine and her grandmother and we thought that that should be maintained." They thought that the acquisition of the pony was a good idea, partly to take her mind off the loss of her mother. She settled down very quickly in Troon, and her stepfather on occasions came down to stay. She was very good with his son William. With them she had as stable and normal a life as possible. She did, however, enjoy her visits to her

father, although she was always a bit quieter when she returned. While Nicola's views were an important G factor, they were not the only important factor. Besides, she might not know what was in her best interests.

I have not the slightest doubt that the second respondents love Nicola and have been strongly attached to her for most of her life. I do not see them differentiating between William (or any other children they may have) and Nicola. Their wish to bring Nicola up is positive and genuine and not based on any preconceived views that Nicola will be materially H better off with them. They both impressed me as sensible and caring and not motivated, as they might have been, by a negative desire to prevent the pursuer resuming custody of his own child.

Dr Brenda Robson made a visit to the second respondents' home in Troon about four weeks before giving evidence. There she saw Nicola and talked to her alone in the course of a walk. Following her visit she compiled her report which is dated 19 May 1992. I Dr Robson's qualifications are set out in her report. In addition, however, to being a chartered psychologist she is a certificated primary school teacher. She is married and the 36 year old mother of four children. She was engaged as a reporter by a number of sheriff courts and was experienced as an expert witness in such matters. She made it very clear that in this case she could not make a conclusive recommendation since she had not seen all the parties. (With every justification, in my view, the petitioner did not partici- J pate in Dr Robson's investigation.) She was impressed that there was a lot of care and love going on in the house. Nicola was enthusiastic about Wellington school and positive towards it. Even if the Jamiesons moved away from where they lived Nicola would continue to attend that school. She was totally attached to her pony. For her part Dr Robson did not criticise this gift. It was designed to cheer her up and provide her with a pony in a riding environment when everyone else had either a horse or a pony. She talked of K William as her brother and treated him as such. For her, "Daddy" was the first respondent, but when she was with her father she called him "Daddy". Otherwise she called him "Scott". Dr Robson reported that Nicola expressed a wish not to go to live with her father. It was not true what he said to the contrary. She frequently told him that, but he would not listen to her, she said. In Dr Robson's opinion there was no evidence that Nicola had been coached to say things or to say that she wanted to live with the second respon- L dents. Nicola spoke very positively about Mrs Clare Breingan and liked her a lot, although she did not want to call her "Mum". She had a very strong bond with her stepfather who had regular contact with her when he was back in this country. She had a similar bond with her father of whom she was very fond. "Coming to me," said Dr Robson, "is the message that Nicola wants to see him but does not want to live with him." Her long term interest dictated that she should maintain contact with her father. There was no problem about access. Nicola came back saying that

A she had enjoyed it. Dr Robson agreed that material considerations did have an effect upon a child. For that reason one should not take a child's desires or views wholly into account. No doubt the pony did influence Nicola against more frequent access because she wanted to be with it. However, all her security and strongest attachments were with the family who had looked after her. She seemed to have a stronger than usual attachment to her maternal grandmother. These relationships were strong and intense. She herself did not wish to move, and Dr Robson would have been

B very surprised if she had, in all these circumstances, wanted to move.

There is a limit, plainly to the extent to which I can be influenced by evidence given by someone like Dr Robson and by the contents of her report. Mine is the decision as to what is in Nicola's best interests. On the other hand, since I was not allowed the opportunity myself to listen to what Nicola had to say and to ask her questions myself, I do not see why I should not give weight to a skilled child psychologist's evidence

C which reflects, filters and passes expert judgment upon the child's own views. There was no doubt in my mind that Dr Robson's evidence was objective and balanced and it is probable that her interview of Nicola is more structured and penetrating than any interview I might have conducted myself.

Nicola will be eight years old in September. Her life has not been an easy one so far. There was, I assume, never a time that she can remember when she lived

D with her parents. Effectively, she was brought up by her mother, her aunt and her grandparents. Then before she was even seven years old her mother died suddenly. That must have been very tragic for her. The fact that she seems to have overcome this is a tribute to the love and care she has enjoyed with her aunt and uncle. It is entirely understandable that, once her mother had died, her father should wish to resume her custody, especially as he has now remarried someone who knows Nicola and with whom Nicola

E gets on. His claim, however, is based effectively upon his role as the child's natural or biological parent. No criticism can be made of the second respondents except that they are Nicola's aunt and uncle and not her mother and father. What impresses me is that Nicola is happy and settled where she is. There she has a stable and secure environment, which is hardly surprising because she has been brought up, if I may put it this way, in the bosom of the Dickson family. Nor do I anticipate that she will become unhappy

F where she is. Her life in my opinion has been disturbed enough so far. To remove her now to a totally different environment would be disruptive of her settled, happy life and detrimental to her best interests which are in my view to remain in the care of the second respondents. In reaching this conclusion it will, I hope, be appreciated from all that I have said so far, that I have not been affected by any material advantages Nicola is likely to have from one family rather than another. I shall therefore make an order for parental rights in terms of the first conclusion for the second respondents. I shall also find the second

G respondents entitled to Nicola's custody in terms of their third conclusion. Her contact with her father and Clare Breingan must be maintained and fostered. To that end I shall find the petitioner entitled to residential access to Nicola one weekend per month from Friday evening to Sunday evening; for one week during the Easter holidays; for two weeks during the summer holidays; and for alternative Christmas days with the petitioner having access at Christmas 1993, the exact dates and times to be mutually agreed between the parties. I have restricted access to once

H per month because of all the activities Nicola currently has at weekends and because she is bound up with the family in which she lives. But as time passes and the memories of the present action fade I would like to think that such weekend access could be increased by agreement between the parties. If the petitioner and Clare Breingan have family which I, for one, hope that they do, Nicola no doubt will want to feel as close to that family as she can, given the fact that she has been brought up by others.

I

Counsel for Petitioner, Illius; Solicitors, Macbeth Currie & Co, WS (for James K Cameron, Glasgow) — Counsel for First and Second Respondents, Cowan; Solicitors, Wright, Johnston & MacKenzie.

J P D

J

Centri-Force Engineering Ltd v Bank of Scotland

OUTER HOUSE

LORD ABERNETHY

28 OCTOBER 1992

K

Bank — Letter of credit — Document in order on its face presented to issuing bank fraudulently certified by party other than beneficiary — Whether terms and conditions of credit complied with — Whether prima facie case to seek interdict against issuing bank making payment under the credit — Uniform Customs and Practice for Documentary Credits (1983 Revision), International Chamber of Commerce publication no 400, art 3.

A company entered into a contract with suppliers L for the supply and installation of pasteurising equipment at the premises of customers of the company. In terms of the contract 50 per cent of the purchase price was payable under irrevocable letter of credit issued by the company's bank through the suppliers' bank, which latter bank confirmed the credit, on production inter alia of a copy certificate by engineers, employed by the suppliers to carry out the commissioning of the equipment, evidencing that the equipment had been properly commissioned and was in working condition satisfactory to the company.

A A certificate was subsequently issued by the engineers which on its face complied with the relevant terms and conditions of the credit. The company sought interdict against its bank from making payment under the letter of credit, averring that the certificate had been fraudulently issued in that at the time of its issue the equipment was not in satisfactory working condition and that the signatory knew that the certificate was false or was reckless as to whether it was true or false. The company moved for interim interdict.

B The bank argued that, except in circumstances of fraud on the part of a beneficiary in relation to the documents presented by him to the bank, the obligation to make payment under a credit whose terms and conditions had been complied with had to be strictly enforced notwithstanding any contractual dispute arising from the contract of supply.

Held, that the obligation under a letter of credit being distinct from the contract on which the letter of credit might be based, where documents in order on C their face and complying with the terms and conditions of the letter of credit were presented, there was an absolute obligation on the relevant bank to make payment under the credit, and the only exception to this rule was that payment could not be enforced where the beneficiary himself presented the documents required by the letter of credit and they were forged or fraudulent, and the petitioners had accordingly failed to aver a prima facie case (pp 192K-193F); and interim interdict *refused.*

D Dicta in *Edward Owen Engineering Ltd v Barclays Bank* [1978] 1 QB 159 and *United City Merchants (Investments) v Royal Bank of Canada* [1983] AC 168, *followed.*

———————

Petition for interdict

Centri-Force Engineering Ltd presented a petition seeking interdict and interim interdict to prevent the E Bank of Scotland from debiting the petitioners' account or making payment to Software Systems of any moneys representing payment under a letter of credit issued by the bank on application of the petitioners in respect of payments due under a contract of supply between the petitioners and Software Systems.

The case came before Lord Ordinary (Abernethy) on the petitioners' motion for interim interdict.

F

Conditions of letter of credit

The letter of credit was subject to the Uniform Customs and Practice for Documentary Credits (1983 Revision), International Chamber of Commerce publication no 400, which provides, inter alia:

"3. Credits, by their nature, are separate transactions from sales or other contract(s) on which they may be based and banks are in no way concerned with or bound by such contract(s), even if any reference to such contract(s) is included in credit."

Cases referred to

Bolivinter Oil SA v Chase Manhattan Bank NA [1984] G 1 WLR 392.
Malas (Hamzeh) & Sons v British Imex Industries Ltd [1958] 2 QB 127; [1958] 2 WLR 100; [1958] 1 All ER 262.
Owen (Edward) Engineering Ltd v Barclays Bank International [1978] 1 QB 159; [1978] 1 All ER 976; [1977] 3 WLR 764.
Toynar Ltd v Whitbread & Co plc, 1988 SLT 433.
United City Merchants (Investments) v Royal Bank of Canada [1983] AC 168; [1982] 2 WLR 1039; H [1982] 2 All ER 270.

Textbook referred to

Goode, *Commercial Law,* pp 675-678.

On 28 October 1991 the Lord Ordinary *refused* the motion for interim interdict.

LORD ABERNETHY.—In a continued hearing on the motion roll counsel for the petitioners sought I interim interdict to prevent the Bank of Scotland ("the Bank") from debiting the petitioners' account or making payment to Software Systems ("Software") of any moneys representing payment under a letter of credit issued on 21 August 1992.

As I understood it from the averments in the petition and the documents which have been lodged as productions in the process, the letter of credit was issued in the following circumstances. The petitioners and Software entered into a contract for the supply J and installation of pasteurising equipment by Software at the premises of the petitioners' customers, G R Tanner & Co Ltd, Halstead, Essex. The purchase price was £83,000 payable 50 per cent in advance and 50 per cent by irrevocable letter of credit payable on production, inter alia, of a copy commissioning certificate issued by Poul Hansen Engineers ("Poul Hansen") evidencing that the equipment had been properly commissioned and was in satisfactory working condition to the petitioners' satisfaction. Poul K Hansen had been employed by Software to carry out the commissioning of the equipment.

A letter of credit containing this condition was issued by the Bank on 21 August 1992. On 1 September 1992 a commissioning certificate was issued by Poul Hansen Nyborg A/S. It was signed by Mr Poul Hansen who I understand is the principal of Poul Hansen. It confirmed that the equipment "has been properly commissioned by Poul Hansen engineers, L and it is in a satisfactory working condition to Centri-Force Engineering Co Limited satisfaction".

No point was taken that the issue of the certificate was by Poul Hansen Nyborg A/S rather than Poul Hansen Engineers and I assume for present purposes that they are one and the same organisation. The petitioners aver, however, that the commissioning certificate is false and, indeed, was issued fraudulently. The information available at the time of the hearing differed in detail from what is averred in the petition but the gravamen of it is that as at 1 September 1992 the plant had not been commissioned and, indeed, an employee of Poul Hansen, one Jens Erik Ankjaer, was working on the equipment and trying to deal with problems in it for some days afterwards. It is averred that his efforts were unsuccessful and that the equipment is still not in satisfactory working condition. The point for present purposes, however, was that the commissioning certificate issued on 1 September 1992 was false and, indeed, fraudulent. Mr Poul Hansen either knew that it was false or was reckless as to whether it was true or false.

Counsel for the Bank submitted that the averments and supporting documentation did not come up to the standard required for fraud. In my opinion, however, no 7/4 of process, which is a copy of a day to day report by Jens Erik Ankjaer and which was sent by Poul Hansen to the petitioners, makes it sufficiently clear prima facie that the plant was not properly commissioned and was not in a satisfactory working condition by 1 September 1992. Accordingly, in my view the prima facie position is that either the commissioning certificate was issued knowing it to be false or else it was issued without prior inquiry of Jens Erik Ankjaer and therefore recklessly as to whether it was true or false. I have therefore come to the prima facie conclusion that the commissioning certificate was issued fraudulently by Mr Poul Hansen.

Counsel for the Bank, however, submitted that there was a further reason why interim interdict should not be pronounced. International commerce and trade relied on letters of credit being honoured. That consideration should not be overcome by a dispute between the petitioners and Software as to the performance of their contract. Although there was no authority on the point in Scotland, there was recent English authority in which it had been held that in English law there was a well established, strict general rule which required payment under a letter of credit when the documents were in order on their face. The only exception to this rule was that the Bank ought not to pay under the letter of credit if the documents were presented by the beneficiary (Software) and the Bank knows that they are forged or that the request for payment is made fraudulently in circumstances when there is no right to payment (*Edward Owen Ltd v Barclays Bank; UCM v Royal Bank of Canada*). The principle underlying these authorities, counsel submitted, applied equally in Scots law. Since there were no averments to support a case of fraud on the part of the beneficiary, the strict general rule should apply. The motion for interim interdict preventing payment under the letter of credit should therefore be refused.

In reply to his argument counsel for the petitioners accepted that his averments were not at present enough to bring home a case of fraud involving Software and he was not in a position to make such averments. The nearest he could get was to say that there was a nexus between Software and Poul Hansen in that the principal of Software was Mr Gregors Hansen, who is the son of Mr Poul Hansen. He also said that the equipment in question here had previously been the subject of a contract contemplated but never furthered between Poul Hansen and the petitioners.

In order to deal with this point, which was not raised at the first hearing of this motion, it is appropriate first to set out in a little detail the contractual relationships of the various parties involved. The petitioners and Software had entered into a contract, one of the terms of which was that the purchase price was payable as to 50 per cent by irrevocable letter of credit. It is to be noted that in terms of Software's quotation the first part of the equipment was to be released after receipt of prepayment and a confirmed letter of credit by Den Danske Bank, which was Software's bank in Denmark. Application for the letter of credit was made by the petitioners to the Bank on 19 August 1992. It was an application for an irrevocable letter of credit. The beneficiary is stated to be Software; the beneficiary's bank Den Danske Bank. The letter is also stated to be subject to Uniform Customs and Practice for Documentary Credits (1983 Revision), International Chamber of Commerce publication no 400. The relevance of this is that art 3 of this document provides that: [his Lordship quoted the terms of art 3 and continued:] The application was signed with the petitioners' authorised signature and in response to it the letter of credit was issued in favour of Software on 21 August 1992.

Accordingly, there are now at least two contracts: one between the petitioners and Software and the other between the petitioners and the Bank. And it is provided in the latter that the two are separate and the Bank is in no way concerned with the former. There are, of course, other contractual relationships as well. In terms of the letter of credit the receiving bank is Den Danske Bank, which, as already noted, is the beneficiary's (Software's) bank. There are therefore contractual relationships between that bank and Software and between that bank and the Bank. I was informed that Den Danske Bank had already credited Software with the sum in the letter of credit. It had done so on the basis that the Bank had indicated the documents were in order and that in accordance with the well known practice in international trade and commerce the Bank would honour the letter of credit.

In my opinion the further submission advanced by counsel for the Bank is well founded. As I have tried to show, it is in my view fully supported by the terms of the petitioners' contract with the Bank. But it also receives powerful support from what was said about the law concerning letters of credit in the unanimous decision of the Court of Appeal in *Edward Owen Engineering v Barclays Bank* and of the House of Lords in *UCM v Royal Bank of Canada*. In stating the basic position in the *Edward Owen* case Lord Denning MR, with whom the other members of the Court of Appeal agreed, said this (at [1978] QB, p 169A-D): "It has been long established that when a letter of credit is issued and confirmed by a bank, the bank must pay it if the documents are in order and the terms of the

credit are satisfied. Any dispute between buyer and
A seller must be settled between themselves. The bank
must honour the credit. That was clearly stated in
Hamzeh Malas & Sons v British Imex Industries Ltd
[1958] 2 QB 127. Jenkins LJ giving the judgment of
this court, said at p 129: '. . . it seems to be plain
enough that the opening of a confirmed letter of credit
constitutes a bargain between the banker and the
vendor of the goods, which imposes upon the banker
an absolute obligation to pay, irrespective of any
dispute there may be between the parties as to whether
the goods are up to contract or not. An elaborate com-
B mercial system has been built up on the footing that
bankers' confirmed credits are of that character, and,
in my judgment, it would be wrong for this court in
the present case to interfere with the established
practice.'"

As Lord Diplock put it in *UCM v Royal Bank of
Canada* (at [1983] AC, p 183F): "The whole
commercial purpose for which the system of confirmed irrevocable documentary credits has been
C developed in international trade is to give to the seller
an assured right to be paid before he parts with control
of the goods that does not permit of any dispute with
the buyer as to the performance of the contract of sale
being used as a ground for non-payment or reduction
or deferment of payment." Of course there are differences in fact between those two cases and this case but
there is in my opinion no basis for distinguishing them
in principle. The considerations which give rise to the
basic rule in England apply equally in Scotland in my
opinion.
D
The only exception to the basic rule recognised by
English law, drawing on authority from the United
States of America, is where the beneficiary himself
presents the documents required by the letter of credit
and they are forged or fraudulent. That exception was
explained by Lord Diplock in *UCM v Royal Bank of
Canada* ([1983] AC at p 184A-B) as follows: "The
exception for fraud on the part of the beneficiary
seeking to avail himself of the credit is a clear applica-
E tion of the maxim *ex turpi causa non oritur actio* or, if
plain English is to be preferred, 'fraud unravels all'.
The courts will not allow their process to be used by
a dishonest person to carry out a fraud." I have no
reason to doubt that for the same reason that exception
would apply in Scots law. But it does not assist on the
facts of this case. Although prima facie the commissioning certificate was in my view presented fraudulently, it was not presented by or on behalf of the
beneficiary. It was presented by a third party, Poul
F Hansen.

For these reasons I am of opinion that there are no
averments in the petition which would justify interfering with the honouring of the credit. To put it in the
context of the Scots approach to interim interdict the
petitioners have not in my opinion established a prima
facie case. It follows, therefore, that consideration of
the balance of convenience does not arise (see *Toynar
Ltd v Whitbread & Co plc*).

I shall accordingly refuse the motion for interim
interdict. I should record that I was also referred to

Bolivinter Oil SA v Chase Manhattan Bank NA and
Goode on *Commercial Law*, pp 675-678.   G

*Counsel for Petitioners, S D D Nicoll; Solicitors, Haig-
Scott & Co, WS — Counsel for Respondents, Davidson;
Solicitors, Anderson Strathern, WS.*

M L B F

H

McMurdo v Ferguson

OUTER HOUSE

LORD MURRAY

29 MAY 1992

*Reparation — Defamation — Anticipated publication of
newspaper article — Petitioner alleging article to be* I
*defamatory — Newspaper denying content defamatory
and arguing also that public interest favoured refusal of
interim interdict — Balance between damage to
individual and public interest.*

*Interdict — Interim interdict — Balance of convenience
— Defamatory matter in newspaper article about to be
published — Article dealing with alleged dispute between
parties in the public eye — Public interest.*

A sporting personalities' agent and consultant J
brought a petition for suspension and interdict against
a journalist and the managers and proprietors of a
newspaper in respect of an article due to be published
within hours of the hearing of the motion for interim
interdict. The article concerned a prominent former
football personality and stated that the petitioner had
held himself out as being the footballer's agent and
that the petitioner had improperly deprived the footballer and his family of assets rightly belonging to
them. Counsel for the petitioner submitted that the
article was prima facie defamatory and threatened the K
petitioner's reputation and means of livelihood. In
those circumstances the balance of convenience
favoured interim interdict. For the respondents it was
argued that, even if the article was prima facie defamatory, the public interest favoured publication of a
newsworthy row between these two personalities with
protection of the petitioner's interests being given by
his right to sue for damages.

Held, that the article was prima facie defamatory
and that while there was public interest in rows L
between public figures, the matter was likely to
remain newsworthy in the time required to remove
any potentially damaging material from the article,
whereas loss of the petitioner's professional reputation
and its consequences could be immediate and irreparable even if he had a remedy under the law of defamation, and the balance of convenience favoured the
petitioner (p 194G-I); and interim interdict *pronounced.*

Petition for suspension and interdict

A   William McMurdo, a sporting personalities' agent and consultant, presented a petition seeking interdict against Ian Ferguson, a journalist, and the managers and proprietors of the *Daily Record*, from publishing an article which was allegedly defamatory of the petitioner.

The case came before the Lord Ordinary (Murray) on the petitioner's motion for interim interdict.

On 29 May 1992 his Lordship *granted* interim
B interdict.

   LORD MURRAY.—The petitioner, who is a sporting personalities' agent and consultant, has brought the present petition for suspension and interdict against a journalist who writes for the *Daily Record* and the managers and proprietors of the newspaper in respect of an article to be published on Saturday, 30 May 1992, within hours of the motion being heard on Friday night, about a prominent football personality in which the petitioner figures. By the time
C when the motion began (about 9.15 pm) a second edition of the proposed article was available in "fax" form. This is no 7/2 of process and was taken as the relevant text for the purposes of the motion.

   The petitioner claims that there are material statements in the article about him which are false and calumnious. In particular the article falsely represents that he has falsely held himself out as still being the said footballer's agent and falsely represents that the petition improperly deprived the said footballer and
D members of his family of assets rightly belonging to them.

   Counsel for the petitioner submitted that there were two elements of innuendo in the article, first, that the petitioner was dishonest personally and untrustworthy professionally, and secondly that he had used his position for personal gain at the expense of his client. The article was prima facie defamatory. The balance of convenience favoured interim interdict being pronounced. The loss of the petitioner's reputation and
E means of livelihood which was potentially involved outweighed the public interest in a public row between prominent figures in the sporting world.

   Counsel for the respondents submitted that, subject to correction of certain inaccurate detail in regard to a company connected with the former footballer, the article could not be said to be prima facie defamatory. All that was really involved was a public row between the petitioner and the former footballer in which the former asserted that he was the latter's agent while the
F latter vigorously denied that he was. But even if the article were defamatory (which was denied) the balance of convenience favoured refusal of interim interdict. There was public interest in a newsworthy row between these two sporting individuals. The petitioner would be adequately protected against possible defamation by his right to sue for damages.

   In reply counsel for the petitioner pointed out that the row which existed was not about whether the petitioner was the former footballer's agent. It was accepted by both sides that he no longer is his agent.

That was why the allegation of holding out was falsely attributed to him. Counsel for the respondents then G quoted an alleged verbatim assertion by the petitioner to the contrary.

   Having retired briefly to consider the position I reached the conclusion that, even with the proposed alterations as to detail, the article no 7/2 of process is prima facie defamatory.

   The balance of convenience, however, gave me much more difficulty. I recognise that there is public interest in rows between public figures. However, this particular article appears to present the row in relation H to the personal and professional integrity of the petitioner rather than in terms of disagreement as to fact or opinion. Nor am I persuaded that the row will not remain newsworthy in the time which could be taken to remove any damaging material, or potentially damaging material, from the contents of the article. On the other hand the petitioner's loss of professional reputation and means of earning a livelihood could be immediate and irreparable, even if the law of defamation could ultimately provide a remedy. I

   In my opinion the balance of convenience is very even but it does come down in favour of the petitioner. Accordingly interim interdict falls to be pronounced in terms of the prayer of the petition in regard to the article which is no 7/2 of process.

Counsel for Petitioner, Doherty; Solicitors, Gray Muirhead, WS — Counsel for Respondents, Brailsford; J *Solicitors, McGrigor Donald.*

                            I C W

Tahir v Tahir

OUTER HOUSE
LORD SUTHERLAND   K
3 JUNE 1992

Husband and wife — Divorce — Foreign decree obtained during currency of Scottish action — Recognition by Scottish court — Whether contrary to public policy — Availability of right to financial provision even although party divorced — Matrimonial and Family Proceedings Act 1984 (c 42), s 28 (1) — Family Law Act 1986 (c 55), s 51 (3) (c). L

International law — Recognition of foreign decree — Divorce — Whether foreign decree of divorce depriving party of right to claim financial provision — Whether recognition of decree manifestly contrary to public policy where right still available — Family Law Act 1986 (c 55), s 51 (3) (c).

   The Family Law Act 1986 provides in s 51 (3) (c) that a foreign decree of divorce may be refused recognition if recognition would be "manifestly contrary to public policy".

A The Matrimonial and Family Proceedings Act 1984 provides in s 28 (1) for application to the Scottish courts by a divorced person for financial provision where a divorce has taken place abroad, where that divorce is one that is recognised by the Scottish courts and where there would have been jurisdiction for the divorce to have proceeded in Scotland.

An action of divorce with conclusions for financial provision was raised by a wife in 1986. When the matter came to proof in 1992 one defence to the action was that the defender had already divorced the B pursuer in Pakistan in 1989. The pursuer argued that the motive of the husband defender in obtaining the divorce in Pakistan had to be looked at, and there was nothing in his evidence to override the inference that he had obtained the divorce to avoid his wife's claim for financial provision. Recognition would thus be "manifestly contrary to public policy" in terms of s 51 (3) (c) of the 1986 Act.

Held, that the pursuer's rights to claim financial provision having been preserved under the 1984 Act, C there could be no public policy objection to recognition of the foreign decree on grounds of deprivation of those rights (p 196I-K); and action, so far as relating to divorce, *dismissed* as incompetent.

Chaudhary v Chaudhary [1985] Fam 19, *distinguished.*

Action of divorce

Shagufta Tahir raised an action of divorce against her husband Irshad Tahir on the ground of irretriev-
D able breakdown of the marriage by reason of the defender's behaviour, concluding for divorce and ancillary financial payments.

The case came before the Lord Ordinary (Sutherland) for a preliminary proof on the defender's averments that he had, since the raising of the present action, divorced the pursuer in Pakistan, and the question of recognition of that decree.

Statutory provisions
E The Family Law Act 1986 provides:

"51.—. . . (3) Subject to section 52 of this Act, recognition by virtue of section 45 of this Act of the validity of an overseas divorce, annulment or legal separation may be refused if . . . (c) in either case [whether or not obtained 'by means of proceedings'], recognition of the divorce, annulment or legal separation would be manifestly contrary to public policy."

The Matrimonial and Family Proceedings Act 1984
F provides:

"28.—(1) Where parties to a marriage have been divorced in an overseas country, then, subject to subsection (4) below, if the jurisdictional requirements and the conditions set out in subsections (2) and (3) below respectively are satisfied, the court may entertain an application by one of the parties for an order for financial provision."

Case referred to
Chaudhary v Chaudhary [1985] Fam 19; [1985] 2 WLR 350; [1984] 3 All ER 1017.

On 3 June 1992 his Lordship *sustained* the defender's third plea in law and *dismissed* the action so G far as relating to divorce.

LORD SUTHERLAND.—This is an action of divorce with ancillary conclusions and one defence to the action is that the defender divorced the pursuer in Pakistan in 1989. Although there was no plea that this matter should be dealt with by way of preliminary proof, it was agreed by the parties that it would be appropriate to deal with this as a preliminary issue. At the beginning of the proof the pursuer's counsel con-
H ceded that in the first place the Pakistan divorce was validly obtained by means of proceedings, and in the second place that the only ground for opposing recognition was that it was "manifestly contrary to public policy", to quote the words from s 51 (3) (c) of the Family Law Act 1986.

The defender gave evidence to the effect that the parties were married in 1979 in Glasgow and at that time he had dual nationality, British and Pakistani, which he still has. The pursuer at the time was only I a national of Pakistan. The marriage was an arranged one, the defender never having met the pursuer before, and she came to Scotland as his fiancée. After about a year the parties separated for a period when in Pakistan. They resumed cohabitation after about a year and finally separated in 1985 again in Pakistan. Since then they have not lived together. In 1986 the pursuer raised the present action. In December 1988 the defender went to Pakistan because his mother was ill and while there he instituted formal divorce J proceedings. His evidence was that in February 1988 he had spoken to the mufti of the central mosque in Glasgow and discussed the state of his marriage. At that time he obtained divorce from his wife in accordance with Islamic law and a formal document to this effect, which is in process, was produced and countersigned by the mufti. This document would of course have no validity for the purpose of ending a marriage under the law of Scotland. The defender's evidence was that when he went to Pakistan at the end of 1988 he discussed the matter with elders there and was K advised that he should go to the formal proceedings before the arbitration council which is the proper method of obtaining divorce in Pakistan. This he did and a notice of divorce was sent to the pursuer as at 11 January 1989. She was given the opportunity to appear before the council which she did not take and eventually the divorce was, to use our words, finalised in April 1989. It should be said at this stage that even if the pursuer had appeared before the council there could be no question of her preventing the defender L from divorcing her. The only purpose of any appearance would be to make representations relating to certain limited financial matters. This is made clear from the evidence of the mufti which was given on commission.

In the light of this evidence counsel for the pursuer argued that it was clear that apart from certain visits to Pakistan the parties spent all their married life in Scotland and essentially their home was there. The defender by defending the present action had sub-

mitted himself to the jurisdiction of this court. It was
clear from the mufti's evidence that once the divorce
was pronounced nothing the wife could do would
change the position or make it ineffective. There was
no adequate explanation by the defender for his
actions which would override the inference that he
deliberately sought divorce in order to avoid having to
face his wife's claim for financial provision in this
present litigation. Counsel referred to the case of
Chaudhary v Chaudhary. In that case recognition of a
Pakistani divorce was refused but the main ground for
refusal was that it had not been obtained by means of
proceedings. As a subsidiary matter however, it was
also held that even if it had been properly obtained, it
would be contrary to public policy to recognise it
because it would be against the policy of the law in
England where both parties to a marriage are
domiciled in England to permit one of them to avoid
the incidents of the law of England and to deprive the
other party to the marriage of her rights under that law
by the simple process of travelling to a country whose
laws appear to be more favourable. It is important to
notice that *Chaudhary* was decided before the coming
into effect of the Matrimonial and Family Proceedings
Act 1984. Counsel for the pursuer argued that what
had to be looked at was the motive of the husband in
obtaining a divorce in Pakistan and if the only reasonable explanation for obtaining that divorce was that he
wished to put an end to his wife's claim, then it would
be contrary to public policy to recognise the decree so
obtained. Furthermore, having submitted to the jurisdiction of the Scottish courts he should not be permitted to go off and take proceedings elsewhere, which
was effectively acting in contempt of the Scottish
court.

Counsel for the defender argued that the evidence
was clear that the defender had dual nationality, that
the marriage was an arranged one, that there was only
a period of six years before the final separation and
during that period there were two substantial visits to
Pakistan. He accepted that the matrimonial home
would have to be regarded as being in Scotland but
there was still a substantial connection with Pakistan.
He then argued that it was not open to the defender
to avoid submitting to jurisdiction in this case. The
case was defended not only on financial provision but
was also defended on the merits and it was only yesterday that an alternative ground for divorce on the basis
of non-cohabitation for a period of five years was
added and that only as an alternative to the existing
ground of divorce for unreasonable behaviour. The
defender's evidence should be accepted that if his wife
wanted a divorce he would be satisfied to give her one
and that is why he went through the proceedings
which he did. Finally, counsel argued that the 1984
Act takes the whole substance out of the decision in
Chaudhary. If the pursuer had recognised the
Pakistani divorce when she should have done, she
would have been able to preserve her rights of a
financial nature by taking proceedings under the 1984
Act. There is therefore no ground for saying that it is
contrary to public policy for a Pakistani national to

exercise the rights which he undoubtedly has to obtain
a divorce in his own country when this will have no
effect on the financial rights of the pursuer in this
country. Finally, counsel argued that if the decree was
not recognised it would mean that the whole merits
would have to be investigated at length in this proof
at public expense. This is an argument which in the
present case might have very little substance because
it would be open simply to agree that the appropriate
form of divorce would be on the basis of non-
cohabitation for five years and therefore proof on the
merits would take a matter of minutes rather than
days. On the other hand it can certainly be said that
there might be cases where, for example, the ground
of divorce was unreasonable behaviour but only a com-
paratively short period had elapsed since the separation when it might well be contrary to public policy
to insist on carrying through a lengthy divorce proof
when parties had already effectively been divorced
elsewhere.

In my opinion the defender's evidence that he
divorced his wife because she was wanting a divorce
may have had some substance, particularly to avoid a
proof on what was then the only ground of unreasonable behaviour. On the other hand I cannot avoid the
suspicion that the timing of the original declaration of
divorce in February 1988 just before a proof date was
fixed in March 1988 may also bear upon his motives.
However in my view motive is not a conclusive factor
in this case. What I have to look at is the decree which
was pronounced in Pakistan. It would be contrary to
public policy to recognise it, according to *Chaudhary,*
if both the motive and the effect were to deprive the
pursuer of her rights in Scotland. That however is not
the position because her rights are preserved under s
28 of the 1984 Act. There can therefore, in my view,
be no public policy objection to recognition of this
divorce based on deprivation of the pursuer's financial
rights. As I understood the submission made to me, it
was only on the basis that she would be deprived of
such rights that it was argued that there was a public
policy objection to recognition. As I hold that that
submission is not well founded I cannot find that the
recognition of the Pakistani decree would be
manifestly contrary to public policy which is the test
which I require to apply. In these circumstances it
follows that under the terms of s 51 of the 1986 Act
I must recognise the Pakistani divorce and it follows,
therefore, that the present divorce proceedings would
not be competent in that the parties are not at the
present moment married. In the whole circumstances
I shall sustain the defender's third plea in law and
dismiss the action so far as based on the first conclusion of the summons.

---

*Counsel for Pursuer, Bennett; Solicitors, Allan
McDougall & Co, SSC — Counsel for Defender, J R
Campbell; Solicitors, Drummond Miller, WS.*

I C W

Martin v HM Advocate

A HIGH COURT OF JUSTICIARY

THE LORD JUSTICE CLERK (ROSS),
LORDS COWIE AND BRAND

25 OCTOBER 1990

*Justiciary — Procedure — Trial — Charge to jury —
Judge charging jury that there were three verdicts open to
them — Whether necessary that judge direct jury as to distinctions between each verdict — Whether misdirection.*

B
An accused person went to trial before the sheriff
and a jury. At the conclusion of the evidence the
sheriff in his charge to the jury stated: "There are
three verdicts open to you. These verdicts are guilty,
not guilty and not proven." He did not explain the
meaning of these verdicts or explain that both not
guilty and not proven were acquittal verdicts. The
accused was convicted and appealed to the High
Court.

C
Held, that the sheriff had informed the jury of the
alternative verdicts which it was open to them to
return and that was all that was required (p 198C-D);
and appeal *refused*.

MacDermid v HM Advocate, 1948 SLT 202, *considered*.

Indictment

D
Eric Marshall Martin was indicted at the instance of
the rt hon the Lord Fraser of Carmyllie, Her
Majesty's Advocate, on 13 charges libelling contravention of the Misuse of Drugs Act 1971. The accused
pled not guilty and proceeded to trial before Sheriff A
V Sheehan and a jury at Falkirk. Nine charges having
been withdrawn from the jury, the accused was convicted on the remaining four charges, charges 7 and
11, which libelled contravention of s 5 (2) of the 1971
Act, and charges 8 and 12, which libelled contravention of s 5 (3).

E
The accused appealed to the High Court by way of
note of appeal against conviction.

Cases referred to

MacDermid v HM Advocate, 1948 SLT 202; 1948 JC
12.
Smith (Madeleine), Notable Scottish Trials series.

The sheriff directed the jury inter alia as follows:

F
THE SHERIFF (A V SHEEHAN).— . . . So
really when the accused said, "I didn't have it with
intent to supply," if you believe him, that's the end of
the matter. If you don't believe him completely but
you have a reasonable doubt about him, then again
that's an end of the matter, you must acquit. If you
don't believe him and he has not raised a doubt and
you look at the Crown case and you are satisfied on the
Crown case beyond a reasonable doubt that the Crown
have proved the case, then of course you must bring
in a verdict of guilty.

So really ladies and gentlemen really what it boils
down to is this, while it's a matter entirely for you, I G
think you will have little difficulty with the charges
relating to simple possession, namely 7 and 11, but
you will have to look very carefully at charges 8 and
12 because that is where the real dispute is between
the parties. You have really got to be satisfied. . . . Are
you satisfied beyond reasonable doubt that so far as
the cannabis resin is concerned he had it with intent
to supply and with regard to the other charge are you
satisfied beyond reasonable doubt that he had the
amphetamines with intent to supply, and these are the H
issues, or the main issues for you to decide, ladies and
gentlemen.

Now there are three verdicts open to you. These verdicts are guilty, not guilty and not proven. You must
return a separate verdict in respect of each charge.
When you come back the clerk of court will ask you
first of all what is your verdict with regard to charge
7, and you will return a verdict on that guilty, not
guilty, not proven. Then he will ask you what is your I
verdict in regard to charge 8 and you will give your
verdict on that, then you will be asked your verdict on
charge 11 and you will give your verdict on that, and
then your verdict on charge 12 and you will give your
verdict on that.

The verdicts need not be unanimous and that means
if you are not unanimous I can accept a verdict by a
majority, but if you are for guilty, there must be at
least eight of you — at least eight of you in favour of
a guilty verdict. J

Appeal

The note of appeal contained the following ground,
inter alia:

The presiding sheriff misdirected the jury by failing
to direct them as to the distinctions between the three
verdicts open to them and the meaning of each.

The appeal was argued before the High Court on 25 K
October 1990.

Eo die the court *refused* the appeal.

The following opinion of the court was delivered by
the Lord Justice Clerk (Ross):

OPINION OF THE COURT.—The appellant is
Eric Marshall Martin who went to trial in Falkirk
sheriff court on an indictment containing a number of
charges. He was found guilty of four charges on the L
indictment. Two of these charges libelled contraventions of s 5 (2) of the Misuse of Drugs Act 1971. The
other two charges were of contraventions of s 5 (3) of
the same Act. He has appealed against conviction and
three grounds of appeal were put forward in his note
of appeal. Today on his behalf counsel has intimated
that he is not proposing to argue the third ground of
appeal. [His Lordship dealt with the first ground of
appeal with which this report is not concerned, and
then continued:]

The second ground of appeal is in the following

A terms: [his Lordship quoted the terms of ground 2 and continued:] In his charge the sheriff stated to the jury: "Now, there are three verdicts open to you. These verdicts are guilty, not guilty and not proven." He went on to explain that they must return a separate verdict in respect of each charge and he went on also to tell them that if there was to be a finding of guilty there must be at least eight of them in favour of such a verdict. Counsel for the appellant maintained, as we understood it, that what the sheriff ought to have done

B was to go on and explain the meaning of these verdicts or at least to explain to the jury that either not guilty or not proven would lead to acquittal. We recognise that many judges do explain to the jury that not guilty or not proven would lead to acquittal but we are not persuaded that that is something which must be done in every case. In *MacDermid v HM Advocate* the Lord Justice General expressed the view that he was unwilling to believe that any Scottish jury did not know that there were three possible verdicts, namely, guilty, not guilty and not proven. He went on to observe that in

C the case of *Madeleine Smith* it appears from the published report that Lord Justice Clerk Hope never even alluded to the possibility of a not proven verdict which was of course the verdict which the jury returned in that case. What the Lord Justice General said in *MacDermid* was this: "Nevertheless I repeat that it is always proper and desirable that the jury should be specifically informed by the presiding judge of the alternative verdicts which they can return." We are satisfied that the sheriff in this case did just that. He

D did inform the jury of the alternative verdicts which it was open for them to return. For these reasons we are satisfied that the second ground of appeal also is not made out. The appellant has failed to show that there has been any miscarriage of justice on either of these grounds and the appeal against conviction is accordingly refused.

Counsel for Appellant, Turnbull; Solicitors, Russel &

E *Aitken, WS, Falkirk — Counsel for Respondent, Macdonald, QC, AD; Solicitor, I Dean, Crown Agent.*

S D D N

F # City of Glasgow District Council v Secretary of State for Scotland (No 1)

EXTRA DIVISION

LORDS McCLUSKEY, CAPLAN AND WYLIE

18 JANUARY 1991

Administrative law — Natural justice — Town and country planning — Planning permission — Appeal — Secretary of State directing that he would himself deter-

mine an appeal which would, by regulations, normally be determined by reporter — Secretary of State involved in G *promoting subject of planning application — Whether contrary to natural justice for Secretary of State to hear appeal.*

Town and country planning — Planning permission — Appeal — Secretary of State directing that he would himself determine an appeal which would, by regulations, normally be determined by reporter — Secretary of State involved in promoting subject of planning application — Whether contrary to natural justice for Secretary of State H *to hear appeal.*

Town and country planning — Planning permission — Appeal — Determination by Secretary of State — Departure from recommendations of reporter — Whether sufficient reasons given for decision.

Process — Appeal — Grounds of appeal — Sufficiency — Alleged breach of natural justice — Rules of Court 1965, rule 290 (c).

A district planning authority applied to the Court of I Session to exercise their power under s 233 (4) (b) of the Town and Country Planning (Scotland) Act 1972 to quash a decision of the Secretary of State allowing an appeal against the authority's refusal of planning permission for the construction of part of a road. An inquiry had been held to determine the appeal and consider objections. In terms of the Town and Country Planning (Determination of Appeals by Appointed Persons) (Prescribed Classes) (Scotland) Regulations 1987, the appeal came into a class to be J determined by a person appointed by the Secretary of State rather than by the Secretary of State himself. However, in the exercise of his powers under Sched 7, para 3 (1) to the 1972 Act the Secretary of State directed that he would consider the appeal himself. The reporter recommended acceptance of the proposed route, subject to conditions and minor modifications, and the Secretary of State allowed the appeal.

The planning authority contended that: (1) the Secretary of State had acted contrary to natural justice K in that, being the promoter through the Scottish Development Department of the road outwith the appellants' area, he was closely identified with the promoters within it so that a reasonable man might be suspicious as regards his motives in choosing to determine the appeal himself; (2) he had failed to take all of the reporter's recommendations and considerations into account and had given insufficient reasons for his decision; and (3) he had erred in considering that the reporter had gone beyond his remit in looking at flood L control measures as the reporter had not in fact stated that any particular measures ought to be adopted.

Held, (1) that it was entirely proper for the Secretary of State to appoint a reporter but to reserve to himself the responsibility for the final decisions in what he was entitled to regard as a matter of strategic importance (pp 201J, 205C-D and 206L); (2) that it could not be said that because he differed on some matters from the reporter a reasonable person would conclude that he was biased (pp 201K, 205F-G and

A 206L); (3) that although the reasons for the decision could have been more detailed, they were sufficiently intelligible and passed the test formulated in *Wordie Property Co v Secretary of State for Scotland*, 1984 SLT 345 (pp 202L-203C, 203E, 205I-J and 206L); and (4) that the Secretary of State had correctly understood that the reporter, in making recommendations concerning flood control, had improperly interfered with the regional council's statutory responsibility to promote appropriate flood control measures (pp 204A-B, 206H-J and 206L); and appeal *refused*.

B   **Observed**, that a challenge on the ground of natural justice should be the subject of a specific ground of appeal under Rules of Court 1965, rule 290 (c) and it was accordingly insufficient to rely on a statement in one of the grounds relating to the conditions that the decision was contrary to the principles of natural justice (pp 200J-K, 204E-F and 206L).

C   **Appeal from the Secretary of State for Scotland**
The City of Glasgow District Council, as a local planning authority, appealed to the Court of Session against a decision of the Secretary of State for Scotland in respect of the Secretary of State's allowance of an appeal concerning the council's refusal of planning permission for the construction of part of a road in Strathclyde Region. The council asked the court to exercise its power under s 233 (4) (b) of the Town and Country Planning (Scotland) Act 1972 to quash the Secretary of State's decision. The applicants, Strathclyde Regional Council, appeared as second respondents.

D

Statutory provisions
The Town and Country Planning (Scotland) Act 1972 provides:

"233.—. . . (4) On any application under this section the Court of Session — . . . (b) if satisfied that the order or action in question is not within the powers of E this Act, or that the interests of the applicant have been substantially prejudiced by a failure to comply with any of the relevant requirements in relation thereto, may quash that order or action. . . .

"[Sched 7] 3.—(1) The Secretary of State may, if he thinks fit, direct that an appeal, which by virtue of paragraph 1 of this Schedule and apart from this subparagraph, falls to be determined by a person appointed by the Secretary of State shall instead be determined by the Secretary of State."

F

The Roads (Scotland) Act 1984 provides:

"7.—. . . (6) A scheme under this section authorising the provision of a special road shall — . . . (b) in the case of a road to be provided by a local roads authority, be made by that authority and confirmed by the Secretary of State, in accordance with the provisions of Parts II and III of Schedule 1 to this Act.

"(7) Before making or confirming a scheme under this section, the Secretary of State shall give due con-

sideration to the requirements of local and national planning, and to the requirements of agriculture and G industry."

Cases referred to
Albyn Properties v Knox, 1977 SLT 41; 1977 SC 108.
Barrs v British Wool Marketing Board, 1957 SLT 153; 1957 SC 72.
Bradford v McLeod, 1986 SLT 244; 1985 SCCR 379.
Iveagh (Earl of) v Minister of Housing and Local Government [1964] 1 QB 395; [1963] 3 WLR 974. H
Lavender (H) & Son Ltd v Minister of Housing and Local Government [1970] 1 WLR 1231; [1970] 3 All ER 871.
Law v Chartered Institute of Patent Agents [1919] 2 Ch 276.
Lithgow v Secretary of State for Scotland, 1973 SLT 81; 1973 SC 1.
London and Clydeside Estates Ltd v Secretary of State for Scotland, 1987 SLT 459.
Poyser and Mills' Arbitration, Re [1964] 2 QB 467; I [1963] 2 WLR 1309; [1963] 1 All ER 612.
Wordie Property Co Ltd v Secretary of State for Scotland, 1984 SLT 345.

The appeal was heard by an Extra Division on 4 and 5 December 1990.

On 18 January 1991 the court *refused* the appeal.

LORD McCLUSKEY.—This is an application by J City of Glasgow District Council, the appellants, in which the appellants ask this court to exercise its power under s 233 (4) (b) of the Town and Country Planning (Scotland) Act 1972, and to quash a decision of the Secretary of State for Scotland (the first respondent) contained in a letter dated 8 September and signed by Mrs M B Gunn on Scottish Development Department notepaper on behalf of the first respondent. The letter contains the first respondent's decisions on a total of 10 schemes and orders listed in K the letter and also on an appeal by the second respondents against the refusal (in 1987) of planning permission by the appellants for the construction of the A77 Ayr Road route in Glasgow. The decision letter intimated that the first respondent had decided to sustain the appeal against the refusal of planning permission and to grant planning permission subject to conditions and also to make or confirm the various schemes and orders, in some cases with modifications, being the schemes and orders specified in the letter. L

Before turning to consider the submissions of parties at the hearing of the appeal I should describe the general background to the various decisions. The Ayr Road, which forms the subject matter of the proposed schemes, is to extend for 11 km from the south end of the M77 to a junction with the A77 at Malletsheugh. It would be constructed with dual two-lane carriageways and grade separated junctions. Within the city of Glasgow the road would be constructed by the second respondents as a special road (6.7 km) and

A outside it to the same standards by the Scottish Development Department as a trunk road (4.3 km). The road would be capable of extension to dual three-lane. The total cost of the scheme as proposed would be approximately £50m, at 1987 prices. The appellants, as planning authority, refused planning permission for the section of the road within the City of Glasgow District. The reasons for the refusal are set forth in appendix 1. An inquiry was duly held to determine the appeal lodged by the second respondents and to consider objections to the road schemes and orders.

B That inquiry, a public local inquiry, was held between 23 March and 20 May 1988 by Mr Brian K Parnell, BSc, ACGI, DipTP, FRTPI. Under the Town and Country Planning (Determination of Appeals by Appointed Persons) (Prescribed Classes) (Scotland) Regulations 1987, the planning appeal came into a class of appeal to be determined by a person appointed by the Secretary of State rather than by the Secretary of State himself. However, in exercise of his powers under para 3 (1) of Sched 7 to the Town and Country

C Planning (Scotland) Act 1972, the first respondent directed on 26 November 1987 that he would determine the appeal himself because it was expedient to consider it jointly with the schemes and orders promoted in connection with the proposed Ayr Road route. The promoters of the road within the City of Glasgow District were the second named respondents. The promoters of the road outwith the city boundary were the Scottish Development Department.

D In due course the reporter issued parts 1 and 2 of his report containing his summary of the evidence led, of the arguments advanced, his findings in fact and his reasoning, conclusions and recommendations. On the evidence, he accepted that the need for, and the value of, the Ayr Road route had been established, and went on to consider whether the Ayr Road route would have harmful effects on the local environment such as to outweigh the likely benefits, and whether any of the harmful effects could be mitigated. He concluded that the proposed road would be generally beneficial for

E traffic movement and in the reduction of pollution and accidents and that it was desirable in principle. However, he also concluded that it would harm the environment of certain communities along the proposed route. Putting the matter briefly, the reporter recommended acceptance of the route of the proposed road and the associated connecting roads, that the appeal by the second respondents against the refusal of planning permission by the first respondent should be sustained, subject to the conditions, and that the

F various schemes and orders for the road should be approved, subject to minor modifications.

The letter of 8 September 1989 deals with all these matters in more detail and contains a section entitled, "Consideration by the Secretary of State". Paragraph 9 thereof says as follows:

"9. The Secretary of State has carefully considered all the evidence presented at the Inquiry, the representations and written submissions made on the proposals and the Reporter's Findings of Fact, conclusions and

recommendations thereon. He accepts the Reporter's Findings of Fact and agrees generally with the G Reporter's conclusions and reasons therefor. However, the Secretary of State does not accept two of the Reporter's recommended conditions to be attached to the Strathclyde Regional Council's planning permission, namely those referred to by the Reporter as numbers R.1.1(iii) and R.1.1(iv) on pages 127 and 128 of his Report."

Recommended condition R 1.1(iii) is a condition relating to the replacement of the Pollok playing fields. Recommendation R 1.1(iv) is a condition relat- H ing to the construction of the road between Kennishead Road and Deaconsbank. The submissions of parties largely related to these two matters. The terms of the proposed conditions are set out below.

In opening the appeal, however, counsel for the appellants presented a submission which, in my opinion, is not foreshadowed, or at the very least is not made explicit, in the grounds of appeal. That submission was that, in determining the planning appeal, the I first respondent acted in a way contrary to natural justice, in respect that an opportunity was afforded for injustice to be done and there were circumstances calculated to induce in the mind of a reasonable man a suspicion as to the first respondent's impartiality. It was pointed out on behalf of the respondents that the appellants had not stated any proposition to this effect in the grounds of appeal, as required by Rule of Court 290 (c). In reply the appellants argued that as the grounds of appeal stated that the first respondent's J decision was "contrary to the principles of natural justice" they were entitled to advance this argument. In my view there is no warrant whatsoever in the grounds of appeal for this submission. The principles of natural justice are indeed referred to but only in a rubber stamp way, incidentally to the grounds of appeal relating to the two matters covered by R 1.1(iii) and R 1.1(iv). I deplore the attempt to advance a substantial submission of this character without clear notice having been given. I would not, however, wish K to reject the argument solely upon technical grounds, particularly as the respondents were able to offer us a full submission in response to it. I shall accordingly deal with it, albeit briefly. It was argued that the first respondent, in considering matters of the kind which were before him in the present instance, though not acting fully judicially, had an obligation to conform to certain standards of fair play (*Barrs v British Wool Marketing Board*). In that case the Lord President (Clyde), speaking of the relevant principle of natural L justice, said (1957 SC at p 82): "It is important to observe the width of this principle. It is not a question of whether the Tribunal has arrived at the fair result; for in most cases that would involve an examination into the merits of the case, upon which the tribunal is final. The question is whether the tribunal has dealt fairly and equally with the parties before it in arriving at that result. The test is not, 'Has an unjust result been reached?' but, 'Was there an opportunity afforded for injustice to be done?' If there was such an opportunity, the decision cannot stand."

A Counsel for the appellant also referred to what the Lord Justice Clerk said in *Bradford v McLeod*, 1986 SLT at p 247, quoting with approval Eve J in *Law v Chartered Institute of Patent Agents* [1919] 2 Ch at p 289: "If he has a bias which renders him otherwise than an impartial judge he is disqualified from performing his duty. Nay, more (so jealous is the policy of our law of the purity of the administration of justice), if there are circumstances so affecting a person acting in a judicial capacity as to be calculated to create in the mind of a reasonable man a suspicion

B of that person's impartiality, those circumstances are themselves sufficient to disqualify although in fact no bias exists."

Reference was also made to *H Lavender & Son Ltd v Minister of Housing and Local Government* [1970] 1 WLR at pp 1240-1241. Counsel accepted that, in considering the report of the public local inquiry, the first respondent was bound to act in a way that avoided any appearance of being the judge in his own cause. These dicta were directly relevant; the first

C respondent was acting in a dual capacity. He was not only considering a planning appeal but was also the confirming authority in terms of s 7 (6) (b) of the Roads (Scotland) Act 1984. In that capacity he had a duty, under subs (7), to give due consideration to the requirements of local and national planning. But in this instance, although he was not the promoter of the road within the Glasgow City District boundary, he was the promoter, through the Scottish Development Department, of the rest of the road, so he was closely

D identified with the promoters of the road and their aims. That was evidenced by the fact that both respondents were represented at the public local inquiry by the same counsel. The planning appeal came into a class of appeal to be determined by a person appointed by the Secretary of State rather than by the Secretary of State himself: it was accepted that the first respondent had powers to direct that he would in fact determine the appeal himself and it was not suggested that it was itself improper for him to do so. Nonetheless

E that factor, taken along with others, was likely to induce in the mind of a reasonable man a suspicion as to his impartiality in determining this particular planning appeal. The other factors included the circumstances that the decision on the appeal was announced on the notepaper of the Scottish Development Department and that the decision of the Secretary of State was contrary to the recommendations of the reporter in the two important respects mentioned.

F In reply, counsel for both respondents accepted that the principles of natural justice applied generally to the exercise by the first respondent of his planning functions under the 1972 Act, notably in relation to determining planning appeals. However it was obvious that that Act, like the Roads Act itself, contemplated that the Secretary of State might frequently have to determine matters in which he had an interest. Accordingly, the principle that no man should be the judge in his own case had to yield to necessity derived from the provisions of the legislation (*London and Clydeside Estates Ltd v Secretary of State for Scotland*).

The Secretary of State, in determining a planning appeal such as the present, was acting in an executive G or administrative capacity (*Lithgow v Secretary of State for Scotland*). Any planning authority, including the appellants themselves when the issue was before them as a planning authority, might have a responsibility to determine a planning appeal in which they had an interest. A planning authority might have an interest, for example as the partners of a developer making a planning application to them. The appellants were not suggesting, and it could not be suggested, that the first respondent had acted incompetently or improperly in H exercising his powers under para 3 (1) of Sched 7 to the Town and Country Planning (Scotland) Act 1972 and deciding to determine the appeal himself. It was not disputed that there was a proximity of interest between the first and second respondents in relation to the Ayr Road route. The Ayr route was part of government policy, as had been explained at the public local inquiry. It was perfectly appropriate that the same counsel should appear for both respondents at the public local inquiry; indeed the appellants were not I suggesting otherwise. It was very usual for decisions of the Secretary of State to be issued by the Scottish Development Department in such a case. It was entirely appropriate that in considering no fewer than 10 schemes and orders the Secretary of State should decide to determine these himself. The fact that he differed from the reporter in two relatively minor respects could not be prayed in aid as a factor which would lead a reasonable man to suppose that he had not acted impartially in determining the planning J appeal.

In my opinion, there is no merit whatsoever in this submission advanced by the appellants. It was entirely proper, and it was not suggested otherwise, for the first respondent to appoint a reporter but to reserve to himself the responsibility for the final decisions in what he was entitled to regard as a matter of such strategic importance. It would have been absurd for the first respondent to ask a Secretary of State from another United Kingdom department to take the final K decision on the 10 schemes and orders or on the associated planning appeal, as was at one point suggested by the appellants. It appears to us to be equally unstatable to suggest that because the first respondent differed from the reporter on some matters therefore a reasonable person would conclude that the first respondent was biased. The other points made were trivial. Nothing in the circumstances individually or collectively was calculated to induce in the mind of a reasonable man any suspicion as to the first L respondent in particular in relation to his non-acceptance of the said conditions proposed by the reporter. I have no hesitation in rejecting this opening submission.

Counsel for the appellants next advanced an argument of which notice was given in the first of the grounds of appeal. I need not rehearse here what is stated in that ground. It was pointed out that the reporter had heard and had accepted evidence showing that the proposed road would have adverse effects

A   upon the communities of Darnley and Arden, communities between which the road was to pass; the effects on Darnley were said to be "unacceptable". The reporter, in the light of that evidence and his findings in fact, had recommended that the particular section of the road between Kennishead Road and Deaconsbank should not be constructed as proposed by the promoters but that new plans should be submitted for the approval of the appellants providing for the road to pass under Nitshill Road, all as detailed in recommendation R 1.1(iv). Section 12 (1) of the Tribunals

B   and Inquiries Act 1971 laid upon the first respondent a duty "to furnish a statement . . . of the reasons for the decision". Reference was made to *Re Poyser and Mills' Arbitration, Earl of Iveagh v Minister of Housing and Local Government* and *Albyn Properties v Knox*. The requirements for the formulation of such reasons were summarised in the words of the Lord President (Emslie) in *Wordie Property Co Ltd v Secretary of State for Scotland*, at p 348: "all that requires to be said is that in order to comply with the statutory duty

C   imposed upon him the Secretary of State must give proper and adequate reasons for his decision which deal with the substantial questions in issue in an intelligible way. The decision must, in short, leave the informed reader and the court in no real and substantial doubt as to what the reasons for it were and what were the material considerations which were taken into account in reaching it".

In the present case, it was plain that the reporter had

D   concluded that the cumulative effects of the Ayr Road built as proposed would be unacceptable for Darnley and damaging for Arden. The harmful effects he identified were noise, air pollution, obstruction to movement between the two communities, visual intrusion and obstruction, and danger for pedestrians obliged to walk along Nitshill Road, all matters referred to in the appellants' original reasons for refusing the planning application in 1987. The condition he had recommended would avoid or minimise these effects, other

E   than the air pollution effect. The Secretary of State's reasons, however, seemed to relate only to noise and, indeed, to the effects of noise upon only some of the houses, namely those which would qualify for help under the Noise Insulation (Scotland) Regulations 1975. Thus he had given no reasons for differing from the reporter in relation to the effects of noise upon houses which would not qualify under those regulations, or in relation to the incidental exacerbation of the problems of dampness in houses affected by noise,

F   the obstruction to movement between the two communities resulting from the separation effect of the road, the visual intrusion of the high road upon the communities, particularly the occupants of houses in Darnley, and the dangers to pedestrians. Furthermore, the reporter had indicated that the solution enshrined in the condition which was recommended would cost between £4m and £5m and the Secretary of State had given no justification whatsoever for his bald statement that that additional cost would outweigh the benefits which would accrue from spending it. It was not clear from the letter that the first respondent had

G   given consideration to these matters which were relevant to the reporter's recommendation. The need to make the reasons clear was, it was submitted, all the greater in the light of the consideration advanced as supporting the preliminary submission.

In reply, counsel for the respondents made it clear that he had no quarrel with the requirements indicated in the dictum of the Lord President quoted from *Wordie*, above. The decision letter met those requirements. It referred explicitly, in para 7, to all those parts of the report in which the reporter set out all the

H   detailed considerations pertaining to the local communities. Furthermore, in para 11 the first respondent had expressly accepted that the imposition of the recommended condition would materially alleviate the effects of the proposed road on both Darnley and Arden. But he went on to make it plain that in his judgment the additional cost to the second respondents outweighed the benefits that would accrue. That was a judgment which he was perfectly entitled to make. It was clear that his approach to the whole

I   matter of the road was that value should be obtained for money. There was really no other way to express this decision. The benefits that would result from that expenditure were not capable of being measured and expressed in arithmetical and monetary terms so that the value of the benefits could be added up and set against the expenditure required to produce them. The benefits that would accrue were all dealt with in paras 11 and 12 of the decision letter. It was perfectly proper to confine his observations to "the occupants

J   of the limited number of houses who would be *substantially* affected by the impact of the new road". Obviously, others might be affected less than substantially, and it was not necessary to deal particularly with the occupants of other houses upon whom the impact would be less than substantial. Paragraph 11 also dealt with visual intrusion, as did conditions 12.3 and 12.5 contained in para 12. Paragraph 11 and para 12.4 dealt in terms with the arrangements for pedestrians crossing the new road and showed clearly that the Secretary of State was not satisfied with the

K   promoters' plans in this regard. For that reason he had imposed condition 12.4 which would ameliorate the position for pedestrians passing between the two communities. The question of dampness associated with measures taken to exclude noise was part of a much larger and already existing problem of dampness as the evidence before the reporter and his findings in fact demonstrated. It was appropriate for the Secretary of State to deal with the matter of noise as he had done and not to enter separately upon the much larger pre-

L   existing problem of dampness. What should be borne in mind was that it was unnecessary for the first respondent to reiterate all the findings and observations of the reporter. He had effectively incorporated them in the decision letter by the references he made to them. Nobody could fail to understand that the first respondent rejected the reporter's recommendation because he considered that the cost of achieving the specified benefits was too high.

In my opinion, the argument of the respondents is

to be preferred. In saying that, I express the view that
I should have been happier had the first respondent
chosen to put more of the detail into para 11 than he
chose to do. I am satisfied, nonetheless, that, as the
respondent submitted, the reasoning is sufficiently
plain. I do not consider that the considerations
advanced in support of the preliminary submission
affect the test propounded by the Lord President in
Wordie, which I accept is the test we must apply. The
first respondent is clearly saying that, having considered the detailed findings in fact and recommendations put before him by the reporter, he has made
a judgment that although there would indeed be
material alleviation of the adverse impact of the proposed road on Darnley and Arden housing estates by
adopting the design proposals preferred by the
reporter, the cost does not justify making that change
to the design. The first respondent has gone on to
make it clear that some at least of the effects could be
mitigated in the ways detailed in paras 11 and 12 of
the letter and already referred to. In my opinion, the
reasons given are sufficiently intelligible and pass the
test formulated by the Lord President in *Wordie*.

Counsel for the appellants went on to argue that the
first respondent had acted ultra vires by failing to take
account of relevant considerations. This argument was
closely related to the previous argument but, as I
understood it, the appellants were suggesting that, if
the reasons given were intelligible, they showed the
first respondent's failure to take into account matters
that had to be taken into account. It was suggested in
particular that the first respondent had failed to take
account of the fact noted by the reporter that dampness in the houses would be exacerbated by physical
noise insulation measures taken on the houses themselves, that he had not dealt with the whole matter of
the isolation and separation of the two communities
and that he had omitted to deal with the adverse
effects both on noise and visual amenity upon persons
occupying houses not immediately adjacent to or over-
looking the road. In my opinion, the respondents'
answer to the immediately preceding submission
covers these matters as well and it is sufficiently clear
from the decision letter that the first respondent has
taken account of these matters. He has not ignored
these matters. He has referred to them expressly or by
reference. He had decided that the cost necessary to
achieve what the reporter believes can be achieved by
the imposition of the condition is too high.

In support of the second ground of appeal, it was
suggested that the first respondent had simply misunderstood the reporter's reasoning and his recommendation. The background to this matter was that
the new road would pass through the recreational area
of Pollok Park containing some 15 football pitches.
The reporter had found that "these pitches are an
essential part of Glasgow District Council's recreation
provision". The reporter had considered the circumstance that the area of the pitches provided a flood
water storage for the Brock burn and that a number of
options were being considered for better flood control
measures. He had also accepted that there were

various difficulties attending the proposals advanced
by the second respondents for the replacement of the
pitches. The reporter had come to a perfectly proper
conclusion in para II.8.4: "The decision about which
flood control plan should be adopted is clearly outside
the scope of the Inquiry, but I believe that a scheme
which protects at least 5 pitches on the west side of the
Ayr Road should be adopted and that these pitches
should accord with the specification submitted to the
Inquiry by G.D.C. (three artificial pitches, one all-
weather grass and one Cresta pitch) or with such other
specifications and numbers as the two Authorities may
agree."

The Secretary of State, in para 10, had erred in
supposing that this meant that the reporter believed
that a particular flood control plan had to be adopted.
His recommendation did not exclude a variety of flood
control plans. It was also quite wrong to suggest that
the question of the reinstatement of the playing fields
was, as the first respondent had put it, "a matter of
accommodation works which will fall to be settled
between Glasgow District Council and Strathclyde
Regional Council".

In reply the respondent submitted that there was no
warrant whatsoever in the evidence or the findings in
fact for suggesting that it would be proper to protect
new playing pitches by bunding on the west side of the
Brock burn. In any event it was plain that if a measure
of that kind were taken it might place significant
restrictions upon the design of other flood control
measures which were likely to prove to be necessary in
the future, as the reporter had recognised. To that
extent the recommendation by the reporter as to what
was to be done and as to how it was to be achieved
improperly interfered with the statutory responsibility
of the regional council to promote appropriate flood
control measures, under the Flood Prevention (Scotland) Act 1961, s 1 (1): the provision of bunding would
circumscribe their options. While it was accepted that
the concept of "accommodation works" was not to be
found in the planning legislation, the true context of
the reference in para 11 to accommodation works was
that the reporter at the inquiry and the first respondent were both dealing with compulsory purchase of
the ground upon which the road itself was to be built.
Order no (ix) was the Strathclyde Regional Council
(Ayr Road Route Drumbreck to Glasgow City Boundary) Compulsory Purchase Order 1986. That order
related to the line of the road itself and the ground
upon which it was to be built. It was perfectly proper
and usual in that context to refer to accommodation
works. It was usual for the acquiring authority to seek
to carry out accommodation works on land not
acquired with the consent of the landowner thereof
from whom land was to be compulsorily purchased in
order to mitigate the effects of the acquisition of the
land so acquired and, at the same time, to diminish the
amount of compensation that required to be paid. It
was perfectly proper for the Secretary of State to contemplate that the appellants and the second respondents would continue to negotiate to see if the matter
could be settled by agreement involving such accom-

A modation works. Although settlement had not been achieved prior to the public local inquiry the decision itself created a new context in which the parties could again seek agreement. In the event of their failing to do so the remedy available to the appellants was to seek compensation under the Land Compensation (Scotland) Act 1963.

In my opinion the first respondent has correctly understood the basis upon which the reporter recommended condition R 1.1(iii). There is in fact no basis in the findings in fact for his recommendation about

B bunding. It is abundantly clear that by adopting the solution proposed by the reporter, including bunding, the design of any future flood control plan might be inhibited. Indeed it is plain from the evidence that the measures proposed at this point of the Brock burn might cause problems downstream. Plainly it is at least conceivable that bunding on the west side of the Brock burn at this location could have that effect. I have no difficulty in holding that the respondents are correct in their submissions as to the reference in the

C letter to accommodation works. I have equally no doubt that the first respondent was correct to conclude that the door was open for further negotiation between the appellants and the second respondents on this matter and that, failing agreement, the appellants would be entitled to compensation and could use the proceeds to assist in providing alternative playing field accommodation to replace that lost. In my opinion this ground of appeal also fails.

D   The appellants did not seek to argue the third ground of appeal, relating to expenses.

In the whole circumstances I recommend to your Lordships that the appeal be refused.

LORD CAPLAN.—The first case argued by the appellants was that the decision of the Secretary of State for Scotland as embodied in the letter from the Scottish Development Department dated 8 September 1989 was invalid as being contrary to natural justice.

E   In the first place it is my view that the appellants have not competently placed before the court the points on this matter which we were urged to consider. Rule 290 (c) of the Rules of Court provides that in relation to statutory appeals (such as the present appeal) the appeal shall state in brief numbered propositions the grounds of appeal. The appellant has lodged grounds of appeal and ground 1 and ground 2 deal respectively with the Secretary of State's decision

F to reject the reporter's recommendations in respect of the Darnley-Arden undercut proposal and the South Pollok playing fields. In each of these grounds of appeal there is a bare averment that the Secretary of State's decision is contrary to the principles of natural justice. The requirements of rule 290 (c) are modest enough but I think the rule is designed to achieve more than a mere rubber stamp indication of a ground of appeal. The purpose of the rule is obviously to ensure that a respondent will receive fair advance notice of any points to be taken in the appeal. A decision making authority may theoretically violate

natural justice in manifold ways. In the present case the appellants have failed completely to focus the G nature of their complaint against the Secretary of State in respect of the alleged departure from rules of natural justice. Moreover this arises in the context of a case where the second respondents in their answers have specific calls for greater specification in relation to the appellants' natural justice case. The first named respondent — the Secretary of State for Scotland — has a plea in law to the relevancy and lack of specification of the grounds of appeal.

However in a matter involving considerable public H interest such as the relevant road proposals it would be unfortunate that any attack on the Secretary of State's decision should fail on a technical ground. In fact pending our decision on the technical question we permitted the appellants to develop their case on the natural justice issue and this has permitted me to conclude that there is in any event no merit in this ground of attack on the Secretary of State's determination. As I understood the appellants' argument it was underpinned by the general consideration that in relation to I a planning application justice must not only be done but must be seen to be done. We were asked to take into account a number of circumstances surrounding the Secretary of State's determination of the relevant matters. In the first place the Secretary of State was himself the promoter of the part of the road scheme which lies outside Glasgow. Therefore he had an indirect but very real interest in seeing the part of the scheme promoted by the regional council proceed. The Secretary of State could have left the planning J appeal to be determined by the reporter in terms of the Town and Country Planning (Determination of Appeals by Appointed Persons) (Prescribed Classes) (Scotland) Regulations 1987. Instead he exercised his powers under para 3 (1) of Sched 7 to the Town and Country Planning (Scotland) Act 1972 to call in the appeal for his own decision. This it was suggested would give the interested persons an impression that he was personally adjudicating upon a matter in which he had an interest. At the public inquiry both the K Secretary of State and the regional council were represented by the same senior counsel. The decision letter was issued through the Scottish Development Department. Finally the terms of the Secretary of State's determination in respect of the Darnley-Arden undercut were vague and would suggest that the Secretary of State had not given proper consideration to points made by the reporter in support of his recommendation. At the last resort it was not contended that these considerations, if viewed individually, were L sufficient departures from natural justice to negate the determination, but it was said that if the points were viewed cumulatively they could strongly suggest that the Secretary of State had not acted fairly or impartially.

In my view it has not been demonstrated that the Secretary of State in any respects departed from such obligations to observe rules of natural justice as may have rested upon him. I would accept that there are certain rules of natural justice that are so fundamental that they would apply to a minister carrying out an executive responsibility as much as to a tribunal with a more exclusively judicial role. The obligation to act bona fide is an example of one. However, in regarding the authorities quoted I think it could be misleading to equate a government minister making an administrative decision with a body which has a neutral adjudicative role. A minister cannot be expected to abdicate from his statutory responsibilities and eventually the appellants' senior counsel required to concede that the statutory requirements of office and statutory procedures could circumscribe how a minister might go about making a decision falling to him. It must be remembered that the determination letter of 8 September 1989 (and the public inquiry which preceded it) were not only concerned with the appeal against Strathclyde Regional Council's planning application but with the determination by the Secretary of State of questions arising for his decision under 10 separate schemes and orders. These included the relevant special road schemes under the Roads (Scotland) Act 1984 and related compulsory orders, and they require direct decision by the Secretary of State himself. The road schemes under consideration were part of a major project estimated to cost about £50m. In his decision letter it is stated that the Secretary of State exercised his powers to determine the planning appeal himself because it was expedient to consider it jointly with the other schemes and orders promoted in connection with the proposed Ayr Road route. Given the interrelationship between the various matters to be decided and the Secretary of State's overall responsibility, it is difficult to regard his decision to deal with these matters together as other than sensible and practical. If a minister or authority has to make a decision in respect of a statutory function the fact that such decision may bear upon the exercise of another statutory function is not in my view a disqualifying factor. This applies equally to planning applications. Moreover it is well illustrated in the present case, for when the appellants decided the second respondents' original planning application by refusing it, it could be said that they had a competing interest in that in another of their capacities as local authority they were the owners of the very football fields which are affected by the road proposals. They certainly did not suggest that they were disqualified from exercising their planning function in an impartial manner. The employment of the same senior counsel by the Secretary of State and regional council at the planning inquiry no doubt reflected the fact that each of these promoters was concerned with a different section of the proposed route and therefore there was no obvious conflict of interest. On the contrary it is obvious that there would be many points concerning the proposals which would be common to each promoter. Given that it was road proposals which generated the various matters arising for decision, the fact that the decisions emerged in a letter from the Scottish Development Department is scarcely irregular or surprising. Complaints were made that the reasons given by the Secretary of State for rejecting the relevant recommendation of the reporter relating

to the Darnley undercut showed that he had not taken into account all matters which should have been considered. If the Secretary of State did not give fair and full consideration to the report this may well vitiate his decision. However this question arises in relation to the appellants' other case that this part of the Secretary of State's decision is ultra vires. The question remains whether or not the Secretary of State has set out sufficient reasons for his decision and this will have to be decided irrespective of any considerations particular to principles of natural justice.

In relation to the matters dealt with in para 11 of the Secretary of State's decision letter (that is to say the rejection of the reporter's recommendation that it should be a condition of planning that the proposed road through Darnley and Arden should be sited in an undercut), the appellants argued that the reasons given by the Secretary of State for rejecting the reporter were inadequate in that they did not indicate that any consideration was given to other than the noise question. Certainly all parties seemed to accept the tests laid down by Lord President Emslie in *Wordie Property Co Ltd v Secretary of State for Scotland*, 1984 SLT at pp 347 and 348. On the basis of the Lord President's dicta the question is whether the reasons stated by the Secretary of State for his determination of the planning appeal on the relevant point would leave the informed reader in real and substantial doubt as to what the reasons were.

I would accept that the reasons set out in para 11 of the decision letter may well be worthy of rather more precise and comprehensive articulation than they received. Nevertheless the question to be answered is whether the reasonably informed reader could have been left in any serious doubt as to the Secretary of State's reasons for refusing the undercut proposal. In my view the Secretary of State's reasons for refusing the proposal in question are perfectly plain. He did not consider that the necessary expenditure of £4m to £5m would be justified by the benefits which would accrue from the expenditure. Whether or not particular benefits to members of a community are worth a specific amount of expenditure is essentially a value judgment over which views may differ. It is a question which the Secretary of State is especially well placed to answer being aware as he will of the competing claims on scarce road resources. However it is not a matter which lends itself to much elaboration or scrutiny. The Secretary of State having taken the decision it is difficult to contend that his view is so totally and obviously unreasonable as to amount to an improper exercise of his determinative function. However the appellants have argued that not only are the Secretary of State's reasons not adequately set out but further, insofar as reasons are set out, it is clear that the Secretary of State has failed to take significant elements in the report into account. I cannot accept this. The reporter lists five problems which the construction of the new road could create for the Darnley-Arden area, namely noise, air pollution, visual intrusion, obstruction to movement, and obstruction and danger to pedestrians obliged to walk along Nitshill

Road (II.9.8). The reporter only specifically lists reduction in noise and visual impact as being benefits which would flow from adopting the uncovered cut proposal (II.9.11 and II.9.13). It may be that the proposal would also alleviate problems of pedestrian movement by permitting a "green bridge" (II.9.14). Certainly in para 9 of the decision letter it is indicated that the Secretary of State has carefully considered all the evidence presented at the inquiry and the reporter's findings of fact and general conclusions and reasons. Again in para 11 the Secretary of State is said to accept that the imposition of condition R I.I(iv) would materially alleviate the effects of the proposed road on the Darnley and Arden housing estates. It is difficult to suppose that this concession would be made if the problems arising for these estates and the extent of the alleviation which would flow from the reporter's recommendations had not been looked at and examined. The Secretary of State then proceeds to refer specifically to the benefit to the occupants of houses which would be "substantially affected" by the impact of the new road. It is to be noted that the Secretary of State refers to the benefits to "occupants" and not to "houses", so that it may well be supposed that these benefits would include the issues of visual impact and also increased difficulty of pedestrian movement for such occupants. There is a subsequent reference to the Noise Insulation (Scotland) Regulations but this may flow from the fact that the reporter had suggested that if the cut proposal was adopted it might not be necessary to apply these regulations. In any event it is quite obvious from the balance of the paragraph that the Secretary of State has not been oblivious to questions of pedestrian movement and visual impact because he proceeds to make specific provision for a further pedestrian survey and for the submission by Strathclyde Regional Council of landscaping proposals. In the whole circumstances when the Secretary of State has indicated the view that the cost of the cut proposal would outweigh the benefits, there is nothing to suggest that this is a flagrantly unreasonable decision nor that it proceeds on an incomplete appreciation of the exact benefits to be taken into account.

With regard to the reporter's recommendation that the planning approval should be fenced with a condition that five football pitches be provided on the west side of the South Pollok playing fields and protected by bunding against frequent flooding from the Brock burn, the Secretary of State gave three reasons for rejecting this suggestion. One of these was that this suggestion was a matter of accommodation works which should be settled between Glasgow District Council and Strathclyde Regional Council. Certainly on one view the restoration of the appellants' football ground can properly be described as apt for accommodation works. The problem can be viewed as arising out of the injurious affection of the appellants' football ground as a result of the proposed road dissecting that ground. The works are not to be effected on the land compulsorily acquired but on land remaining in the appellants' ownership. Moreover the proposed new football pitches will give rise to flood control problems, and since these measures may involve other affected parties there may be grounds for preferring the rearrangement of the football fields to be effected by way of negotiated accommodation works rather than by way of imposed condition. The effect of the road works on the football grounds will certainly jeopardise an important recreational facility so that I do not doubt that this would have significant planning implications. However the question is not whether the restoration of the football pitches can only be regarded as a matter for accommodation works, but rather whether the Secretary of State is entitled to prefer proceeding by way of negotiated works rather than by way of an imposed planning condition. Given that there seems to be little doubt about the appellants' own desire to recreate the necessary football pitches and the increased flexibility that could arise from negotiated arrangements particularly on the flooding questions, I cannot hold that it · was intrinsically unreasonable for the Secretary of State to reject the reporter's proposal for the particular reason I have been discussing. In any event the Secretary of State has two additional linked reasons for rejecting the reporter's proposal. These are that the requirement that the pitches should be protected against flooding by bunding is not supported by any finding in fact and in any event is a matter outwith the reporter's remit. The reporter himself acknowledges that protection against flooding was beyond the scope of the inquiry. Certainly there is nothing we were referred to in the findings in fact to suggest that protection by bunding is the only or best method of flood control. Nor is it clear that such protection could be afforded without affecting other land or downstream proprietors and without additional statutory procedures. Moreover given the absence of flood control from the reporter's remit it cannot be assumed that the implications of flood protection were properly and fully ventilated before him. In short I can see nothing wrong with the Secretary of State's reasons for rejecting this recommendation.

In the whole circumstances the appellants have failed to establish their grounds of appeal.

LORD WYLIE.—I have had the opportunity to read the opinions both of your Lordship in the chair and of Lord Caplan. I agree with them and there is nothing which I feel I can usefully add.

Counsel for Appellants, Haddow, QC, Menzies; Solicitors, Campbell Smith & Co, WS — Counsel for First Respondent, Reed; Solicitor, R Brodie, Solicitor to the Secretary of State for Scotland — Counsel for Second Respondents, Macfadyen, QC; Solicitors, Simpson & Marwick, WS.

R F H

The Miller Group Ltd v Tasker

A EXTRA DIVISION

LORDS MURRAY, WEIR AND BRAND

11 JUNE 1991

*Heritable property — Common property — Division and
sale — Sale by public roup or private bargain — Whether
presumption in favour of sale by private bargain —
Applicable considerations in exercise by court of equitable
jurisdiction.*

B *Property — Heritable property — Common property —
Division and sale — Sale by public roup or private
bargain — Whether presumption in favour of sale by
private bargain — Applicable considerations in exercise
by court of equitable jurisdiction.*

An action of division or sale was raised in the sheriff
court by heritable proprietors of common property
against their co-proprietors. The parties were agreed
that the property should be sold but disagreed upon
whether the sale should proceed by way of public roup
C or private bargain. The heritable proprietors sought
declarator that the subjects should be sold by public
roup. They argued that they were entitled in law to
such a declarator. The co-proprietors contended that
there was a presumption that such a sale should be by
private bargain and that there were no relevant averments to rebut that presumption or support a sale by
public roup. The sheriff did not reach a conclusion on
the parties' arguments but ordered a proof before
answer. Parties were agreed that such a course was
D inappropriate and an appeal was marked to the Court
of Session where the arguments were restated.

Held, (1) that in the case of a judicial sale of this
kind, the court was exercising an equitable jurisdiction
(p 208H); (2) that in exercising this jurisdiction, the
court had to have regard to the interests of all the co-
proprietors and the aim had to be to effect a sale which
was fair to all parties (p 208I); (3) that reference to
presumptions was unhelpful in the court's approach to
what was essentially a practical question and flexibility
E of approach was to be preferred (p 208H and K); and
(4) that the pursuers having declined to amend the
crave to leave open the mode of sale, there was no
alternative but to dismiss the action (p 209A-C); and
appeal *allowed* and action *dismissed*.

Appeal from the sheriff court

The Miller Group Ltd raised an action of division
F or sale in the sheriff court at Edinburgh against Colin
Moray Tasker and others, their co-proprietors of an
area of land known as Gogar Park. While the parties
were in agreement that the land should be sold they
were in disagreement as to the mode of sale. The pursuers in their second crave sought declarator that the
subjects should be sold by public roup and the
defenders contended that there was a presumption in
law in favour of sale by private bargain.

The case came before the sheriff (I A Poole) for
debate.

Cases referred to

Anderson v Anderson (1857) 19 D 700.   G
Brock v Hamilton (1852) 19 D 701n.
Campbell v Murray, 1972 SLT 249; 1972 SC 310.
Upper Crathes Fishings Ltd v Bailey's Executors, 1991
SLT 747.

Textbooks referred to

Dobie, *Sheriff Court Practice*, p 505.
Maclaren, *Court of Session Practice*, p 778.

On 16 August 1990, without reaching a conclusion H
on the arguments presented by the parties, the sheriff
allowed a proof before answer.

The defenders appealed to the Court of Session.

Appeal

The appeal was heard before an Extra Division on
11 June 1991.

Eo die the court *allowed* the appeal and *dismissed* the I
action.

The following opinion of the court was delivered by
Lord Weir:

OPINION OF THE COURT.—At the western
edge of the City of Edinburgh there is land known as
Gogar Park. The subjects were owned by certain
individuals as trustees for and partners of the firm of
D M Hall & Son, chartered surveyors. In 1986 the J
partners became pro indiviso owners as individuals,
and by 1989 one of the partners, James Firth Hall, had
become vested in a share to the extent of approximately 52 per cent. In that year he conveyed his share
to the respondents. The remaining shares are held by
the other partners of the firm and they are the appellants. The land is of considerable value on account of
its potential for development. An attempt was made
by the respondents to purchase the interests of the
appellants but this failed and they have proceeded to K
raise an action in the sheriff court for division or sale
of the subjects.

There is no dispute that division of the property
would not be easy or satisfactory and that its sale is the
proper solution. The appellants do not challenge the
right of the respondents to insist upon the sale. What
is at the heart of the controversy is the manner in
which the sale should be carried out. The respondents
sought declarator from the sheriff that the subjects L
should be sold by public roup and they maintained
before the sheriff and before this court that they are
entitled as a matter of law to such a declarator. On the
other hand, the appellants contended before the sheriff
that the sale should be by way of private bargain and
it was submitted on their behalf to the sheriff and also
to us that there is a presumption that such a sale
should be by private bargain, that the respondents had
failed to make relevant averments to rebut that
presumption or to support a sale by public roup, and
accordingly that the action should be dismissed.

A The sheriff did not reach a concluded view on these arguments and decided that before doing so the appropriate course was to allow a proof before answer. Neither of the parties had asked the sheriff to take such a course and before us they agreed that such a course was inappropriate.

In submitting that there was a presumption in favour of sale by private bargain, counsel for the appellants relied upon the case of *Campbell v Murray*. This case was concerned with the division or sale of a small hotel. The action was not contested and it is

B to be observed that a report had been obtained by the pursuers from a valuer who recommended against the sale by public roup. The matter was considered by the Lord Ordinary (Lord Fraser) and he refused the pursuers' motion seeking authority to sell by private bargain. In his opinion the Lord Ordinary said (at 1972 SC, p 311): "The difficulty, however, is that sales for division of common property are always made by public roup. I have been referred to the case of *Brock v Hamilton*, reported as a foot-note to *Anderson*

C *v Anderson* (1857) 19 D 700, where Lord Rutherfurd held that a sale of common heritable property was proper and added (at p 703) that 'public sale, under authority of the Court, became plainly the only course'. Lord Rutherfurd was, of course, not considering the alternative of a private sale, but all the textbooks to which I have referred state that sale by public roup is the regular practice. See Maclaren on *Court of Session Practice*, p 778, and Dobie on *Sheriff Court Practice*, p 505. I have made inquiries from the Court

D offices, and I am informed that one officer of the Court, whose recollection extends over the last 35 years, has never known of a sale for the purpose of division to be in any other way than by public roup.

"Having regard to this long, well-established and regular practice, I do not think it would be proper for me to make any departure from it, particularly as the circumstances of the present case do not impress me as outstandingly strong. If any change of practice is required now, in order to conform with modern condi-

E tions, I think it would have to be authorised by the Inner House."

In the Inner House, the practice was re-examined and Lord President Emslie, in delivering the opinion of the court, observed that they had been unable to discover any statement of principle which would justify slavish adherence to the practice of sale by public roup in all circumstances. His Lordship said (at p 313; 1972 SLT at p 250): "In these circumstances, examining

F the practice for ourselves, we have little doubt that the practice of sale by public roup was adopted since it was, at the time of its adoption, and subsequently, then the most likely way of securing sale at the best price in circumstances in which the market had been tested.

"The question for us now is whether, in the conditions of 1972, sale by public roup can still be regarded as invariably the best method of testing the market and securing the best price. In our opinion it cannot."

The conclusion of the court was expressed as

follows: "All these indications go to confirm that, whatever the merits of sale by public roup once were, G sale by this method is now seen to be less likely than sale by private bargain, after an adequate test of the relevant market, to lead to sale at the best price which can reasonably be obtained."

The effect of the case of *Campbell* was to displace what might have been regarded as a presumption based on practice in favour of sale by public roup but it did not, in our view, substitute for it a presumption in favour of sale by private bargain. It is apparent that the court, while sanctioning sale by private bargain, H did not exclude the possibility of there being sales by public roup in suitable cases. In any event, we do not consider that it is helpful to approach what is essentially a practical question by reference to presumptions. It has to be remembered that in the case of a judicial sale of this kind, the court is exercising an equitable jurisdiction. That is made clear in the opinion of the Lord President in *Upper Crathes Fishings Ltd v Bailey's Exrs*. This equitable jurisdiction may be concerned not only with whether there I should be a division or a sale but also, in our opinion, with the manner in which the sale is conducted. When exercising this jurisdiction, the court must have regard to the interests of all the co-owners and the aim must be to effect a sale which is fair to all parties. The common goal of all parties obviously is to achieve the best bargain which can be obtained in all the circumstances. It is to be assumed that in conducting a judicial sale, the court will have available to it all the expert advice which is necessary and it is a well recog- J nised practice to remit to a valuer to examine and report on all questions which may arise in connection with that sale. It may well be the case that in modern times a sale by private bargain will in most cases prove to be the best way, as was recognised in *Campbell v Murray*. On the other hand, for all the court knows, there may be situations in which a sale by public roup is to be preferred. These are questions upon which the court may wish to inform itself, not least when the co-owners have, as in this case, expressed different views K on the proper way in which to proceed. We wish to emphasise that the matter is basically a practical one and accordingly there is everything to be said for flexibility of approach rather than the court creating presumptions to which adherence may be required.

While we are not inclined to accept the submission by counsel for the appellants in the manner in which it was advanced, the views which we have expressed are, on the other hand, fatal to the submission of L counsel for the respondents in insisting, as he did, upon a sale in this case by public roup. Counsel for the respondents advanced a list of reasons why a sale by public roup in this instance should be ordered by the court without further ado. He explained that such a sale would be speedier and would avoid the complicated business of considering competing offers each containing, as may well be the case, different conflicting conditions. Counsel went so far as to say that when parties were not in agreement as to the mode of sale, the court should accede to a motion for sale by public

A roup, but he produced no authority for that proposition. It is clear to us that these submissions were not based on law but were of the nature of ex parte statements concerned with the practical mechanics of a sale of property. In our opinion such problems are properly for the court, acting upon the advice of a reporter, to resolve. In short, the respondents have failed to demonstrate any basis in law for the declarator sought by them.

It was suggested by us that the respondents might amend the second crave by deleting the words "by B public roup", thereby leaving open the mode of sale, but counsel declined to avail himself of that opportunity. In these circumstances we consider that the appellants were fully entitled to contest not only the allowance of proof by the sheriff but also the insistence of the respondents on their crave for a sale by public roup.

Had the respondents been prepared to delete reference in the crave to sale by public roup, we would have been disposed to remit the case to the sheriff to C order a sale and leave it to her to determine on a valuer's report covering all relevant matters what was the proper mode of sale. However, standing the pursuers' failure to amend we have no alternative but to allow the appeal and to dismiss the action.

Counsel for Pursuers and Respondents, McNeill, QC; Solicitors, Bird Semple Fyfe Ireland, WS — Counsel for Defenders and Appellants, Nimmo Smith, QC; Solicitors, McGrigor Donald.

D

M C G

A Links & Co Ltd v Rose

FIRST DIVISION
E THE LORD PRESIDENT (HOPE),
LORDS McCLUSKEY AND WEIR
12 JUNE 1991

Employment — Unfair dismissal — Employee dismissed after being certified as medically unfit for work — Duty of employer to consult with employee prior to dismissal on grounds of ill health — Whether sufficient consultation — Employment Protection (Consolidation) Act 1978 (c 44),
F *s 57 (1) (a), (2) (a), (3) and (4).*

Process — Appeal — Appeal to employment appeal tribunal — Failure of industrial tribunal to determine all material facts.

An employee suffered two heart attacks after six years' service in an onerous position which required long hours, and was certified as medically unfit for work. After several months the employers' directors became concerned about the employee's future with the company and required him to undergo medical examination. The employee failed to present himself for the examination arranged, and thereafter provided a report from his own doctor. Three months later, G after one meeting with one of the employers' directors, the employee was dismissed. He applied to an industrial tribunal who concluded that he had been unfairly dismissed as he had not been given fair warning and an opportunity to show that he could do the job. The employers appealed to the employment appeal tribunal, who upheld the tribunal's decision on the grounds that there had not been sufficient consultation between employers and employee. The employers appealed to the Court of Session, contending that it H was plain from the tribunal's findings that consultation had taken place and there had been insufficient findings to show whether dismissal was fair in all the circumstances.

Held, (1) that an industrial tribunal, in approaching the question as to whether an employer acted fairly or unfairly, had to determine as a matter of fact and judgment (a) what consultation, if any, was necessary or desirable in the known circumstances of the particular case, (b) what consultation, if any, took place, I and (c) whether that consultation process was adequate in all the circumstances (p 213C); (2) that there was insufficient material in the tribunal's findings in fact to enable the adequacy of the consultation process to be assessed (p 213F); and (3) that the tribunal had failed to take account of all relevant material and in the absence of circumstances which made it abundantly plain that a properly directed tribunal could only have reached one conclusion, it was not possible for the court to make a finding to that effect (p 213H-I); and J appeal *allowed* and case *remitted* to a fresh industrial tribunal.

Appeal from the employment appeal tribunal
George Rose made application to an industrial tribunal for a finding that he had been unfairly dismissed by his former employers, A Links & Co Ltd.

Findings in fact   K
The tribunal made the following findings in fact:

(1) that the applicant had completed at the date of his dismissal six years' service at the Reardon Snooker Centre in Glasgow, a business operated by the respondent company; (2) that the duties of his position were onerous and required the attendance of the applicant at the centre for long hours every week; (3) that in August 1987 the applicant suffered two heart attacks, was then certified unfit for work and remained so L certified until now; (4) that by December 1987 the future of the applicant within the respondent company's business was causing concern to the directors; (5) that the directors by letter (R1) required the applicant to undergo medical examination; (6) that the applicant did not present himself for the examination arranged; (7) that through his solicitor the applicant provided, in January 1988, a medical report (R5) on his condition from his own doctor; (8) that no medical report was provided to the respondents by or on behalf of the applicant after January 1988; (9) that the

respondents' directors perceived suspicion and hos-
A tility towards them by the applicant from about
November 1987; (10) that the applicant was suspicious
of the respondents' directors' motives and behaviour
and believed he was being unfairly treated by them;
(11) that between their receipt of the medical report
and 22 April, the date of the dismissal of the applicant,
one meeting was held between the applicant and Mr
David Links; (12) that on 22 April 1988 by letter the
respondents gave notice of dismissal to the applicant
with effect from 3 June 1988.

B **Statutory provisions**

The Employment Protection (Consolidation) Act
1978, as amended, provides:

"57.—(1) In determining for the purposes of this
Part whether the dismissal of an employee was fair or
unfair, it shall be for the employer to show — (a) what
was the reason (or, if there was more than one, the
principal reason) for the dismissal, and (b) that it was
a reason falling within subsection (2) or some other
substantial reason of a kind such as to justify the dis-
C missal of an employee holding the position which that
employee held.

"(2) In subsection (1) (b) the reference to a reason
falling within this subsection is a reference to a reason
which — (a) related to the capability or qualifications
of the employee for performing work of the kind
which he was employed by the employer to do . . .

"(3) Where the employer has fulfilled the requirements of subsection (1), then, subject to sections 58 to
D 62, the determination of the question whether the dismissal was fair or unfair, having regard to the reason
shown by the employer, shall depend on whether in
the circumstances (including the size and administrative resources of the employer's undertaking) the
employer acted reasonably or unreasonably in treating
it as a sufficient reason for dismissing the employee;
and that question shall be determined in accordance
with equity and the substantial merits of the case.

"(4) In this section, in relation to an employee, — (a)
E 'capability' means capability assessed by reference to
skill, aptitude, health or any other physical or mental
quality".

Cases referred to

East Lindsey District Council v G E Daubney [1977]
ICR 566; [1977] IRLR 181.
Polkey v A E Dayton Services Ltd [1988] AC 344;
[1987] 3 WLR 1153; [1987] 3 All ER 974.
Sherratt (David) Ltd v Williams, EAT, 8 March 1977,
unreported.
F *Spencer v Paragon Wallpapers Ltd* [1977] ICR 301.
Taylorplan Catering (Scotland) Ltd v McInally [1980]
IRLR 53.

On 28 December 1988 the industrial tribunal *found*
that the applicant had been unfairly dismissed.

The employers appealed to the employment appeal
tribunal.

On 26 April 1989 the employment appeal tribunal
dismissed the appeal.

The employers, with leave of the employment
appeal tribunal, appealed to the Court of Session.   G

Appeal

The appeal was heard before the First Division on
23 May 1991.

On 12 June 1991 the court *allowed* the appeal and
remitted the cause to a fresh industrial tribunal.

The following opinion of the court was delivered by
Lord McCluskey:

OPINION OF THE COURT.—This is an appeal H
on a question of law from a decision of the employment appeal tribunal, with the leave of the tribunal,
under s 136 (4) of the Employment Protection (Consolidation) Act 1978 (as amended). The decision of the
employment appeal tribunal, dated 26 April 1989, was
to dismiss an appeal taken against a decision of an
industrial tribunal dated 28 December 1988. The
issue before the industrial tribunal was whether or not
the present respondent (who will hereinafter be
referred to as "the applicant") had been unfairly dis- I
missed by the present appellants (hereinafter referred
to as "the employers").

The applicant had been employed by the employers
for some six years at a snooker centre in Glasgow
which the employers owned. In August 1987 he fell ill
with heart trouble and was certified unfit for work. He
remained so certified until, and indeed beyond, the
date when the employers dismissed him from his
employment, 22 April 1988. The industrial tribunal
concluded, and it has not been an issue since then, that J
the reason that the employers had for dismissing him
was that his state of health was such that he was no
longer capable of performing the work which he had
been employed to do, and that that was a reason which
fell within s 57 (2) (a) of the Employment Protection
(Consolidation) Act 1978 (as amended). It was also
accepted by both parties that the employer had shown
that that was the reason for the dismissal, as required
by s 57 (1) (a). The question which the industrial
tribunal was required to resolve upon the evidence K
presented to them was the question referred to in s 57
(3) of the 1978 Act, namely whether the dismissal was
fair or unfair. That section, as amended, provides: [his
Lordship quoted the terms of subs (3) and continued:]
It should be noted that s 57 (4) contains the following
provision: [his Lordship quoted the terms of s 57 (4)
set out supra and continued:]

It follows, therefore, that this question had to be
approached upon the basis that the employers dismissed the applicant from his employment because L
they concluded that he was incapable of performing
his work because of his ill health. When the industrial
tribunal issued its decision, that the dismissal had
been unfair, the full reasons which accompanied that
decision contained findings in fact derived from the
evidence which the tribunal had heard and reasoning
in support of the conclusion based upon those findings
in fact. As the findings in fact are fairly short it is convenient to set them out. They are in the following
terms: [his Lordship quoted the findings and continued:] The full reasons also contained the state-

ment: "The above findings in fact are those which in the opinion of the tribunal suffice to support the conclusion it reached. They are extracted from lengthy evidence regarding the relationship between the applicant and his employers."

The tribunal's reasons go on to make it plain that the tribunal had difficulty in reaching conclusions upon the basis of that evidence upon certain matters of fact but considered that it was not necessary to determine all the facts in dispute, because the facts 1 to 12 were sufficient to enable the case to be determined. The reasoning contained in the full reasons demonstrates why they reached this conclusion. The tribunal had been referred to a speech by Lord Bridge of Harwich in *Polkey v A E Dayton Services* containing an obiter passage which the tribunal considered afforded a clear indication as to the approach to be taken. As that dictum was also referred to by the employment appeal tribunal and was the subject of some analysis in the submissions before us it should be quoted in full. It is as follows: "Employers contesting a claim of unfair dismissal will commonly advance as their reason for dismissal one of the reasons specifically recognised as valid by s 57 (2) (a), (b) and (c) of the Employment Protection (Consolidation) Act 1978. These, put shortly, are: (a) that the employee could not do his job properly; (b) that he had been guilty of misconduct; (c) that he was redundant. But an employer having prima facie grounds to dismiss for one of these reasons will in the great majority of cases not act reasonably in treating the reason as a sufficient reason for dismissal unless and until he has taken the steps, conveniently classified in most of the authorities as 'procedural', which are necessary in the circumstances of the case to justify that course of action. Thus, in the case of incapacity, the employer will normally not act reasonably unless he gives the employee fair warning and an opportunity to mend his ways and show that he can do the job."

The first two sentences of that passage, which were not quoted by the tribunal, indicate that his Lordship was intending to indicate what the duty of employers was in relation to dismissal for a reason recognised as valid by para (a) or (b) or (c) of s 57 (2). The tribunal, having quoted the latter part of that passage, stated: "In accordance with our findings in fact which show (nos 11 and 12) that there was no warning or opportunity as envisaged by Lord Bridge, the respondents [scil the employers] must therefore be held to have dismissed the applicant unfairly in that they did not act reasonably in treating the reason as a sufficient reason for the dismissal in that they disregarded the steps described by Lord Bridge above."

The employers appealed to the employment appeal tribunal on grounds of appeal which need not be quoted in full. In summary, the employers submitted that it was incorrect in fact to conclude that whatever procedural steps were necessary had not been taken, that Lord Bridge's observations did not apply to a case of medical incapacity and that the notion of "fair warning and an opportunity to mend his ways" had no application to a case of incapacity resulting from long

term, serious illness. The employment appeal tribunal concluded that the industrial tribunal had "incorrectly applied the dicta of Lord Bridge to the instant situation in that what he said did not strictly apply to the situation where the employee was off work because of sickness". The judgment of the employment appeal tribunal explained: "In that particular passage, it seemed to us that Lord Bridge was dealing with capability in the sense that the employee was not carrying out his work adequately. In that situation, of course, a warning and an opportunity to mend his ways would be appropriate. In the present case of illness, warnings are not appropriate (*Taylorplan Catering (Scotland) Ltd v McInally*)."

However, the employment appeal tribunal recognised that the case of *Polkey* did point to the need for consultation. The employment appeal tribunal construed the industrial tribunal's findings in fact to the following effect: "There was no consultation in fact between the appellants and the respondent." They went on to apply the rule, derived from various cases, that "unless there are wholly exceptional circumstances, before an employee is dismissed on the grounds of ill health it is necessary that he should be consulted and the matter discussed with him, and that in one way or another steps should be taken by the employer to discover the true medical position and the employee's future".

The judgment then contains the following conclusion: "It is, in this tribunal's view, sufficiently clear from the industrial tribunal decision that there was in fact no consultation between the appellants and the respondent before the decision was taken to dismiss, and the industrial tribunal were entitled to hold that the dismissal was unfair." On this basis the appeal was dismissed. Both the industrial tribunal and the employment appeal tribunal dealt with the assessment of the award, but no submissions were made to us in relation to that matter and we need say nothing about it.

In support of the appeal from the judgment of the employment appeal tribunal, counsel for the employers argued that the industrial tribunal had misdirected themselves by supposing that the observations by Lord Bridge applied to a situation in which the evidence demonstrated that the reason for the dismissal was that the employee suffered from a serious illness such that he was permanently incapacitated from carrying out the duties of his position. The idea that an employer would be acting unfairly if he dismissed such an employee without first giving him "fair warning and an opportunity to mend his ways" was absurd in such a situation. Warnings and such opportunities had no place in a case of this character. The result, he maintained, was that the industrial tribunal approached the whole question of unfair dismissal in the wrong way, and, as a result, had made insufficient findings in fact. No doubt the findings they had made might be sufficient to enable them to answer the question which they posed. But they had not posed the correct question. It was plain that there

had been some substantial communication between
A the employers and their solicitors on the one hand and
the applicant and his solicitors on the other, that there
had been a number of attempts by the employers to
obtain satisfactory medical evidence as to the applicant's state of health and that at least one meeting was
held between the applicant and a representative of the
employers. Unfortunately, because the findings in fact
were so exiguous none of these matters were canvassed
in the findings in fact, and it was not possible to find
out what the attitude of the tribunal would have been
B to the real question, namely whether or not the dismissal was unfair in all the circumstances, and principally by having regard to the neglected issue as to
whether or not the consultation which undoubtedly
did take place was adequate. Discussion and consultation there had been but the findings in fact did not
enable a conclusion to be reached as to the sufficiency
and adequacy of the consultation process. The matter
should go back to the industrial tribunal in order that
the necessary findings in fact be made and to allow the
C tribunal to address its mind to the correct question.
The weakness of the employment appeal tribunal's
judgment was that, although it recognised that the
industrial tribunal had erred by applying Lord
Bridge's observations to the present case, it failed to
recognise that as a consequence of that the industrial
tribunal had not made the necessary findings in fact.
These matters of fact, principally relating to the
character of the consultation that did take place
between the applicant and the employer's represen-
D tative, were the very ones that had to be resolved in
order to enable a sound decision to be taken upon all
the facts. In short, the industrial tribunal had, as a
result of misdirecting itself, failed to make the necessary findings in fact, and had thus failed to take into
account relevant facts; the employment appeal
tribunal had failed to see that the industrial tribunal's
decision was flawed as a result.

In reply counsel for the applicant agreed with the
submission that the employment appeal tribunal were
E correct in saying that consultation was necessary
before an employee was dismissed on the grounds of
ill health. In his submission, however, the Court of
Session should recognise that the industrial tribunal
had reached a unanimous decision on an issue of fact
and had produced findings in fact and full reasons
which were adequate to support the conclusion they
had reached. They had indeed addressed the correct
issue, namely whether or not the applicant was
unfairly dismissed. They alone had heard the evidence
F and had reached a view upon the basis of that evidence
in relation to the correct question. The decision on
unfair dismissal was essentially a question of fact,
although it was an inference from the findings of
primary fact. However, the findings of primary fact
adequately justified the inference made. He accepted
that it was not entirely accurate to say, as the industrial tribunal had said, that "there was no warning or
opportunity as envisaged by Lord Bridge", and that it
was not entirely accurate to say, as the employment
appeal tribunal had stated: "It is . . . sufficiently clear

from the industrial tribunal decision that there was in
fact no consultation between the appellants and the G
respondent before the decision was taken to dismiss."
Nonetheless, properly read, what these passages indicated was that there had been no adequate consultation, no proper consultation, and that for that reason
it was correct to characterise the dismissal as "unfair".
The appeal should be refused. If the matter had to go
back to the industrial tribunal it would be better if it
went back to the same tribunal, not to a fresh tribunal
as happened in the case of Polkey.

The law in relation to the duty of an employer who   H
is considering dismissing an employee on the grounds
of ill health, being ill health which appears to be such
as to incapacitate the employee from performing the
duties attached to his position, is not in dispute
between the parties. We were referred to two cases
where the employer's duty is described. It is sufficient
to quote them. In the first, East Lindsey District
Council v G E Daubney, Phillips J said, at [1977]
IRLR, p 184, para 18: "There have been several
decisions of the Appeal Tribunal in which considera-   I
tion has been given to what are the appropriate steps
to be taken by an employer who is considering the dismissal of an employee on the ground of ill health.
Spencer v Paragon Wallpapers Ltd [1976] IRLR 373
and David Sherratt Ltd v Williams are examples. It
comes to this. Unless there are wholly exceptional circumstances, before an employee is dismissed on the
ground of ill health it is necessary that he should be
consulted and the matter discussed with him, and that
in one way or another steps should be taken by the   J
employer to discover the true medical position. We do
not propose to lay down detailed principles to be
applied in such cases, for what will be necessary in one
case may not be appropriate in another. But if in every
case employers take such steps as are sensible according to the circumstances to consult the employee and
to discuss the matter with him, and to inform themselves upon the true medical position, it will be found
in practice that all that is necessary has been done.
Discussions and consultation will often bring to light   K
facts and circumstances of which the employers were
unaware, and which will throw new light on the
problem."

In the second case, Taylorplan Catering (Scotland)
Ltd, Lord McDonald said, at p 55, paras 9 and 10:
"There is no doubt that in the normal case a measure
of consultation is expected of an employer before he
decides to dismiss an employee for ill health. Apart
from considerations of general courtesy the reason for   L
this is to secure that the situation can be weighed up,
balancing the employer's need for the work to be done
on the one hand, against the employee's need for time
to recover his health on the other."

It does not appear to us that the passage in the
speech of Lord Bridge in Polkey is in any way inconsistent with these earlier cases. Lord Bridge was
plainly addressing himself generally to cases of incapacity; that is clear from his reference to s 57 (2) (a).
It is true that the concept of "fair warning and an

opportunity to mend his ways" is not one which can
be applied readily to a situation where the ill health
which has rendered the employee unfit for the work he
has been doing is of such a character that it is likely
to be permanent. But it is easy enough to envisage
cases in which an employee's incapacity might result
from ill health which in turn flowed directly from
some circumstance within the control of the employee
himself. It might be, for example, that his ill health
took the form of obesity and that with reasonable
dieting he could cure his condition and restore his
capacity to do the job. Another example would be one
where the physical incapacity to perform the work
could be remedied by a simple operation which the
employee was, for no apparent reason, neglecting to
take. It would be easy to multiply examples but it is
not necessary to do so. Lord Bridge, in any event,
qualified his remarks in this passage by the adverb,
"normally". Accordingly the relevant law appears to
us to be that stated by Phillips J and Lord McDonald
in the passages quoted. It follows, in our opinion, that
an industrial tribunal, in approaching the question as
to whether the employer acted fairly or unfairly must
determine, as a matter of fact and judgment, what consultation, if any, was necessary or desirable in the
known circumstances of the particular case, what consultation, if any, in fact took place, and whether or not
that consultation process was adequate in all the circumstances. If it was not adequate the dismissal will
be unfair, as explained by Lord Bridge.

When we turn to the findings in fact of the industrial tribunal and the full reasons, what we see is that
the industrial tribunal, despite the terms of finding in
fact 11 and despite their narrative of the evidence as
to what transpired at the meeting there referred to,
concluded that there was "no warning or opportunity". Furthermore, in arriving at that conclusion, they
ignore the substantial correspondence starting with
the letter of 7 December 1987, referred to in finding
4, which appears to demonstrate that various warnings
were given, and they also ignore the evidence that the
attempts of the employers to communicate with the
applicant in order to ascertain his medical position
were unsuccessful because the applicant's solicitors
wrote, on 18 December 1987, saying, "In the meantime Mr Rose has asked us to request that you do not
attempt to contact him regarding the matter of his continuing ill health as often as you have been recently."
Furthermore one of the letters, dated 23 December
1987, refers in the postscript to a further meeting
between the applicant and the employers, but that
matter is not dealt with at all either in the findings in
fact or in the full reasons. It is not for us to determine
matters of fact but we are unable to find in the findings in fact which we have quoted from the decision
of the industrial tribunal sufficient material to enable
the adequacy of the consultation process to be
assessed. What we should have expected to see would
have been findings in fact which dealt with all the
exchanges between the parties and their respective
solicitors bearing upon warnings, attempts to ascertain
the applicant's medical position, and consultations

about the possible alternatives to a full return to full
duties. We should also have expected the tribunal to
make findings in fact as to what took place between
the date when the applicant went off work and the date
when he was dismissed. It is the responsibility of a
judicial tribunal to determine, on a balance of probabilities, what the material facts are. If the evidence
does not enable findings of fact to be made upon
matters that are material, the rules as to onus of proof
will come into operation.

In the whole circumstances, we are persuaded that
the industrial tribunal failed to take into account all
the material that was relevant to the matter that they
had to decide, namely whether or not the so called
"procedural" steps (inquiry, warning, consultation
and consideration of alternatives) appropriate to the
circumstances of this case were taken by the
employers. It is regrettable that after such a long
period this matter has to go back to a tribunal, but this
court hears appeals in these cases on questions of law
only and the ultimate question here, as counsel for the
applicant persuaded us, is a question of fact. If the circumstances had been that it was abundantly plain that
a tribunal properly directed could have reached but
one conclusion it would no doubt have been possible
for this court to make a finding to that effect. That,
however, is not the position here. In the whole circumstances we will allow the appeal and remit the matter
to a fresh industrial tribunal as was done in the case
of *Polkey*.

---

*Counsel for Appellants, May, QC; Solicitors,
Drummond Miller, WS (for Cannon, Orpin & Co,
Glasgow) — Counsel for Respondent, Peoples; Solicitors,
Balfour & Manson, Nightingale & Bell.*

R F H

City of Glasgow District Council v Mackie

FIRST DIVISION

THE LORD PRESIDENT (HOPE),
LORDS MAYFIELD AND KINCRAIG

25 JULY 1991

*Compulsory powers — Purchase — Compensation —
Compensation for disturbance — Discretionary payment
for displacement from land — Assessment — Competency
— Whether Lands Tribunal had jurisdiction to determine
amount of payment — Land Compensation (Scotland)
Act 1973 (c 56), ss 34 (4) and 35 (4).*

Section 34 (4) of the Land Compensation (Scotland)
Act 1973 provides that where a person is displaced
from any land but is not entitled to a disturbance
payment or to compensation for disturbance under

any other enactment, the authority may, if it thinks fit,
A make a payment determined in accordance with s 35
(1) to (3). Section 35 (4) provides: "Any dispute as to
the amount of disturbance payment shall be referred
to and determined by the Lands Tribunal."

A tenant of a shop applied to the Lands Tribunal
under s 35 (4) of the 1973 Act in respect of his claim
for compensation for disturbance on having to vacate
the shop. At the hearing the tenant accepted that he
could not seek a disturbance payment under s 34 (1)
(d) of the Act but confined his claim to that of a discre-
B tionary payment under s 34 (4). The housing association responsible for the development affecting the
subjects argued that the application was incompetent,
that a discretionary payment under s 34 (4) was not a
"disturbance payment" within the meaning of s 35 (4)
and that the tribunal therefore had no jurisdiction.
The tribunal repelled the competency pleas and the
association appealed to the Inner House.

Held, (1) that s 35 (4) was concerned only with dis-
C putes about the amount of a disturbance payment
which, applying the language used in s 34, the
payment in dispute in this case was not and there was
no indication in s 34 (4) that the amount of discretionary payment, if in dispute, was to be referred to and
determined by the Lands Tribunal under s 35 (4)
(p 215G-H); (2) that there was no basis in the Act for
treating a payment under s 34 (4) as a "discretionary
disturbance payment" for the purposes of s 35 (4) (p
216A); (3) that a discretionary payment was not some-
D thing which could be sued for and it was not
unreasonable to leave it to the authority to resolve all
questions of fact and degree so long as the particular
exercises which were described in s 35 (1) to (3) were
carried out (p 216F-G); and appeal *allowed.*

Gozra v Hackney Borough Council (1988) 46 EG 87,
not followed.

Observed, (1) that sidenotes were at best a poor
guide to construction of an enactment (p 215K); and
E (2) that a decision of a local authority on an application
for a discretionary payment would be amenable to
judicial review (pp 216I-J and 217F-G).

Appeal from the Lands Tribunal for Scotland

Duncan G Mackie applied to the Lands Tribunal
for Scotland for a determination in respect of an
assessment of a discretionary payment under s 35 (4)
F of the Land Compensation (Scotland) Act 1973 for his
displacement from shop premises in Glasgow which
had been the subject of a comprehensive improvement
scheme carried out by Yoker Housing Association as
agents for the City of Glasgow District Council. The
council and association were called in the application
as first and second respondents respectively and pled
that the application was incompetent.

Statutory provisions

The Land Compensation (Scotland) Act 1973
provides:

"34.— . . . (4) Where a person is displaced from any
land as mentioned in subsection (1) above but is not G
entitled, as against the authority there mentioned, to
a disturbance payment or to compensation for disturbance under any other enactment, the authority may,
if they think fit, make a payment to him determined
in accordance with section 35 (1) to (3) below."

"35.— . . . (4) Any dispute as to the amount of disturbance payment shall be referred to and determined
by the Lands Tribunal."

Cases referred to   H

Glasgow Corporation v Anderson, 1976 SLT 225.
Gozra v Hackney Borough Council (1988) 46 EG 87;
    (1989) 57 P & CR 211.
Lanarkshire and Dunbartonshire Railway Co v Main
    (1895) 22 R 912.
McMonagle v Westminster City Council [1990] 2 AC
    716; [1990] 2 WLR 823; [1990] 1 All ER 993.
R v Federal Steam Navigation Co Ltd [1974] 1 WLR
    505; [1974] 2 All ER 97.
                                                                            I

The Lands Tribunal *repelled* the respondents' competency pleas and *assessed* compensation.

The respondents appealed to the Inner House by
way of stated case.

Appeal

The appeal was heard before the First Division on
11 July 1991.

On 25 July 1991 the court *allowed* the appeal and J
upheld the pleas to competency.

The following opinion of the court was delivered by
the Lord President (Hope):

OPINION OF THE COURT.—This is an appeal
by case stated by the Lands Tribunal for Scotland
under the Tribunals and Inquiries Act 1971 and Rule
of Court 291. The respondent was the lessee of a shop
in Glasgow. His lease was due to terminate in 1992, K
but the tenement in which the shop was located was
the subject of a comprehensive improvement scheme
as a result of which he was obliged to move out of the
property in 1987. It was originally envisaged that his
loss of occupation of the premises would be only temporary, but the contractor went into liquidation and
the work was delayed. The respondent alleges that he
was not able to return to the premises and that he was
permanently displaced. He negotiated a renunciation
of his lease with his landlords, as a result of which it L
was determined in 1989. The improvement scheme
was being carried out by the housing association who
allege that they were acting as agents for the district
council.

This case is concerned only with the appellants'
pleas to the competency of the respondent's application to the Lands Tribunal for determination of his
claim for compensation for legal costs and loss of
profits resulting from these events.

The respondent's application to the tribunal was in

A terms of s 35 (4) of the Land Compensation (Scotland) Act 1973 which provides that: "Any dispute as to the amount of disturbance payment shall be referred to and determined by the Lands Tribunal."

His claim was originally presented as being one for a disturbance payment in terms of s 34 (1) (d) of the Act, by which it was provided for the first time that a payment could be recovered as of right by a person displaced from any land, and also for a discretionary payment in terms of s 34 (4) which replaced the power to make an allowance to persons displaced in s 38 of
B the Land Compensation Act 1963. But his solicitor accepted in the hearing before the tribunal on the preliminary pleas that, as the housing association were not the owners of the land, s 34 (1) (d) did not apply. He confined himself to the respondent's claim for the determination of the amount of a discretionary payment under s 34 (4), which is in thse terms: [his Lordship quoted the terms of s 34 (4) and continued:] The appellants' submission was that this was not a
C question which was open for determination by the tribunal, since a discretionary payment under that subsection was not a "disturbance payment" within the meaning of s 35 (4). The tribunal rejected that argument and repelled the pleas to competency on the ground that it had jurisdiction under the subsection to determine the amount which is in dispute.

The tribunal noted that the respondent had no statutory entitlement to any payment under s 34 (4). But they pointed out that the housing association had
D already exercised their discretion by agreeing to make a payment under that subsection to the respondent at the rate of £240 per week for the period of 20 weeks originally envisaged for the completion of the works. The subsection requires that the amount of any payment under s 34 (4) is to be determined by the authority in accordance with s 35 (1) to (3). They considered these provisions to be mandatory and not directory, and said that it would be surprising if Parliament had given no statutory remedy to a dis-
E placed person if an authority did not determine the payment in accordance with what s 35 (1) to (3) requires. They held that a payment, once it had been assessed under s 35, became a discretionary displacement payment and thus that it was a disturbance payment within the meaning of s 35 (4) which could be referred to and determined by the Lands Tribunal if there was a dispute as to its amount.

In our opinion this approach is not in accordance with the words used by the legislature. The jurisdic-
F tion of the Lands Tribunal is defined by s 35 (4) which refers to "any dispute as to the amount of a disturbance payment". But the only dispute which remains in this case relates to a payment under s 34 (4) which is to be made at the discretion of the authority. The phrase "disturbance payment" is used in s 34 (1) to define the payment which a person who is displaced from land is entitled to receive as of right in the circumstances to which that subsection refers. Section 34 (4) applies in terms only where the person who is displaced is *not* entitled to receive a disturbance payment.

The phrase which is used to describe the discretionary payment which may be made under that subsection is G "a payment . . . determined in accordance with section 35 (1) to (3) below". Thus, whether one starts with s 35 (4) or with s 34 (4) the result is the same. Section 35 (4) is concerned only with disputes about the amount of a disturbance payment which, applying the language used in s 34, the payment in dispute in this case is not. And s 34 (4) says that the amount payable under that subsection is to be determined in accordance with s 35 (1) to (3), not in accordance with s 35 (1) to (4). There is no indication in s 34 (4) that the H amount of the discretionary payment, if in dispute, is to be referred to and determined by the Lands Tribunal under s 35 (4).

Counsel for the respondent submitted that there was an ambiguity as to the scope of the phrase "discretionary payment" as used in s 35 (4). He pointed out that s 34 (1), when describing the payment with which that subsection is concerned, says that it is "hereafter referred to as 'a disturbance payment'". It was open to question whether the word "hereafter" meant I simply "hereafter within this section" or whether the definition was intended to apply also to s 35. Moreover, s 35 (1), which is among the group of subsections referred to in s 35 (4) and which sets out the formula to be applied, describes the amount which is to be arrived at as the "amount of a disturbance payment". This showed that a payment under s 34 (4) could reasonably be described as a "discretionary disturbance payment", and that s 35 (4) applied because it referred to any dispute about the amount of a distur- J bance payment. He invited us to examine the sidenotes and the heading to these two sections in support of this approach. His point was that the phrase "disturbance payment" was used in the plural both in the heading and in the sidenote to s 34 in order to describe the subject matter. So it was appropriate to regard s 34 as being concerned with two different types of disturbance payment, namely a "discretionary disturbance payment", which is what a payment under s 34 (4) amounted to, as well as the "disturbance payment" K which is defined in s 34 (1).

We are not persuaded that there is any such ambiguity, and in our opinion the use of the plural in the heading and in the sidenote to s 34 is of no significance in view of the clarity which which s 34 is expressed. A sidenote is at best a poor guide to the construction of an enactment, and such guidance as we may derive from the heading is outweighed by the definition in s 34 (1). This confines the expression L "disturbance payment" to a payment to which there is an entitlement in terms of the Act. This approach is confirmed when one comes to s 34 (5) which provides that a disturbance payment shall carry interest from the date of displacement until payment. That provision would be inappropriate to the discretionary payment to which subs (4) refers. And the word "hereafter" in s 34 (1) is not qualified in such a way as to restrict the meaning which it gives to the words "disturbance payment" to their use in that section only. So the same meaning should be given to these words in any following sections in which they appear, as being a reference back to what 34 (1) provides. In short, there is no statutory basis for the use of the expression "discretionary disturbance payment" as a guide to the proper construction of s 35 (4).

We were invited nevertheless by counsel for the respondent to construe s 35 (4) in what he described as a purposive manner with regard to the consequences of the competing arguments. It should be noted, as background to this part of his submissions, that counsel for the appellants accepted that the provision in s 34 (4) that a payment under that subsection was to be determined in accordance with s 35 (1) to (3) was mandatory. There was a discretion as to whether or not to make the payment, but once it had been decided to make it the amount of it had to be determined in accordance with those subsections. Thus there was no discretion as to how its amount was to be calculated, in contrast for example to the wide terms of s 83 (1) of the Local Government (Scotland) Act 1973 which gives power to local authorities to incur expenditure which in their opinion is in the interests of their area or any part of it or all or some of its inhabitants. That being so, said counsel for the respondent, there would be an anomaly if a dispute as to the amount of a disturbance payment within the meaning of s 34 (1) could be referred to the Lands Tribunal and a dispute as to the amount of a discretionary payment under s 34 (4) could not. The provisions of s 35 (1) to (3) applied to them both and in both cases they were mandatory. It was not to be thought that Parliament intended that a different result should be arrived at in each case. Yet that could well happen if, in the case of a discretionary payment, the only method open to resolve any dispute was that of judicial review.

This argument reflects the comment by the Lands Tribunal in its opinion in this case that it would be surprising if Parliament gave no statutory remedy to a displaced person if an authority did not determine the payment in accordance with the provisions to which s 34 (1) refers. But it is not obvious that the intention of Parliament was that the remedy in each case should be the same. It makes good sense, in the case of a disturbance payment, to make express provision for the determination of a dispute as to its amount. There is an entitlement to this payment under the statute in those cases to which s 34 (1) applies. It is an amount which can be sued for, if necessary, if it is not paid. The effect of s 35 (4) is to exclude all questions as to the amount of a disturbance payment from the courts, because these questions are to be referred to and determined by the Lands Tribunal. This is in accordance with a long tradition in cases where compensation is due as of right in cases of compulsory acquisition by bodies with statutory powers, that determination of the amount to be paid is to be by arbitration and is not a matter for the court: see Lord McLaren's comments in *Lanarkshire and Dunbartonshire Railway Co v Main* at p 920. But a discretionary payment is in a quite different category. It is not something which can be sued for because it is

in the discretion of the authority as to whether or not it is to be paid. The amount of the payment is prescribed by s 34 (4) under reference to s 35 (1) to (3). But it seems not unreasonable to leave it to the authority to resolve all questions of fact and degree — or of circumstance and degree, as they were described in *Glasgow Corporation v Anderson* — so long as the particular exercises which are described in s 35 (1) to (3) are carried out. Questions as to what was or was not reasonable for the express purpose of these subsections would thus be left to them to decide. Their decision as to what was or was not reasonable might well be relevant to a decision as to whether or not the payment should be made. It might well be thought to be anomalous for an authority, having decided to exercise their discretion to make a payment under s 34 (4) and having proceeded to do so upon their own view of what was reasonable entirely in accordance with s 35 (1) to (3), to be at risk of the amount of the payment being reviewed in every detail by the Lands Tribunal. They might then find that the amount to be paid was greater than had been assumed when the discretion was exercised simply because the Lands Tribunal took a different view of the facts. Assuming that a petition for judicial review would be competent in those cases where the payment is at the discretion of the authority — and counsel for the appellants conceded this point, at least in those cases where the authority had already agreed to make the payment — this would still leave all questions which were pure questions of fact and degree to the authority. That seems to us to be consistent with the nature of a discretionary payment under s 34 (4), as to which the displaced person has no right of action under the statute. It is also consistent with the wording of s 34 (4) which says that the amount of the payment is to be "determined" in accordance with s 35 (1) to (3) — determined, that is to say, by the authority, since the absence of a reference here to s 35 (4) seems to us to exclude its determination under that subsection by the Lands Tribunal.

In our opinion this is not one of those cases where it can be said that to apply the words used by the legislature according to their ordinary meaning would produce a result which cannot have been intended by Parliament. It has been recognised that it may be permissible for a word to be struck out and another substituted for it where without such a substitution the provision is unintelligible or absurd or totally unworkable, or where by giving effect to the words used in it the operation of the statute would be rendered insensible, absurd or ineffective to achieve its evident purpose: see *R v Federal Steam Navigation Co Ltd* [1974] 1 WLR per Lord Reid at p 509B, and *McMonagle v Westminster City Council* [1990] 2 AC at p 726E. But that is not the situation in the present case, and we do not think that we would be justified in departing from the clear language of the statute which we would require to do if we were to give effect to counsel's argument.

We were referred to a decision of the Court of Appeal in *Gozra v Hackney Borough Council* in which, contrary to the opinion which we have formed in this

case, it was held that the Lands Tribunal had jurisdic-
A tion to determine a dispute as to the amount of a discretionary payment. That was a case where the
claimant was a weekly tenant of a dwellinghouse who,
on being rehoused, claimed a disturbance payment. It
was agreed that the payment could only be made
under s 37 (5) of the Land Compensation Act 1973,
which is in the same terms as s 34 (4) of the Scottish
Act of 1973 except for the section numbers. It provides that the amount of the payment under that subsection is to be determined in accordance with s 38 (1)
B to (3) of the English Act. A preliminary question was
raised as to the jurisdiction of the Lands Tribunal to
determine the amount of a payment made or decided
upon under s 37 (5) which was in dispute. All three
members of the Court of Appeal were of the opinion
that the disputed question was referable to the
tribunal. That decision, which is not binding on us, is
entitled to respect and we would be disposed to follow
it if we could since the legislation is, for all practical
purposes, identical. But we regret that we are unable
C to do so because we disagree with the opinions which
were expressed. Under reference to the construction of
the statute which we favour Nourse LJ said: "As a
matter of cool statutory interpretation, that submission has some sterile appeal to it. But I do not think
that it can be the function of the court to put such a
construction on the Act unless the material provisions
absolutely require it. As the Lands Tribunal pointed
out, it would produce an incongruous difference of
remedy for settling disputes as to the amount of
D section 37 (1) payments on the one hand and section
37 (5) payments on the other, even though they have
to be determined according to precisely the same
criteria. Not only would the remedy be different. In
the case of a section 37 (5) payment the remedy would
be that of judicial review, a remedy far inferior to an
absolute right to have the amount of the payment
determined by the Lands Tribunal under section 38
(4)."

E   Having identified the problem in this way he found
the solution to it, with which Mann LJ and Lord
Donaldson of Lymington MR both agreed, in holding
that since s 37 (5) required there to be determined the
equivalent of an amount equal to a disturbance
payment, a dispute as to that amount was referable to
the Lands Tribunal as being a dispute about the
amount of a disturbance payment. We find ourselves
unable to agree with this approach. It seems to us that
the decision overlooks the significance of the point
that the question whether to make the payment is
F entirely at the discretion of the authority and that, in
contrast to a disturbance payment, there is no entitlement to sue for this amount. The reference to the
remedy of judicial review as a far inferior remedy
seems to recognise, in our view correctly, that the
amount of a discretionary payment could not be the
subject of a dispute in the courts since no action could
be raised to recover it. But it does not seem to us to be
incongruous in these circumstances that the only
remedy in the event of a dispute should be that of judicial review, leaving all matters of fact and degree to the

determination of the authority. Nor does it seem to be
unreasonable that disputes about a disturbance G
payment, for which there is a right of action, are to be
referred to the Lands Tribunal for determination there
rather than in the exercise of its ordinary jurisdiction
by the court.

For these reasons we consider that the decision
reached by the Lands Tribunal in this case was
unsound and we shall allow this appeal. We answer
the single question of law for the City of Glasgow District Council and the first question of law for Yoker
Housing Association both in the affirmative. We find H
it unnecessary to answer questions 2 to 5 for Yoker
Housing Association since these questions were not
argued and are in any event superseded by our
decision.

---

*Counsel for Appellants and Respondents, McNeill,
QC; Solicitors, Campbell Smith & Co, WS (District
Council), MacRoberts (Housing Association) — Counsel* I
*for Respondent and Claimant, Moynihan; Solicitors,
McClure Naismith Anderson & Gardiner.*

R F H

Spence v Davie   J

OUTER HOUSE
LORD CAMERON OF LOCHBROOM
19 NOVEMBER 1991

*Jurisdiction — Sheriff court — Whether sheriff sitting in
one court within sheriffdom has jurisdiction throughout
sheriffdom.*

*Process — Review — Reduction as mode of review —
Whether decree may be reduced even though other means* K
*of review were available but not used — Whether reduc-
tion competent where failure to seek review by other
means was result of advice from solicitors — Whether
decree may be reduced where statutory remedy still available to pursuer with no consequent miscarriage of justice.*

A pursuer sought production and reduction of (i) a
decree pronounced by the sheriff at Duns sheriff court
for payment of £846.45 together with interest and
expenses; (ii) an extract decree thereof; (iii) a charge
for payment served on her pursuant to the extract; (iv) L
the execution of the charge; and (v) an interlocutor
awarding the sequestration of her estates and appointing an interim trustee. The sheriff court action had
concerned a tenancy of immovable property in North
Berwick.

The pursuer argued (1) that Duns sheriff court had
lacked jurisdiction as the court for the place where the
property was situated had exclusive jurisdiction in
terms of rule 4 (1) (a) of Sched 8 to the Civil Jurisdiction and Judgments Act 1982, and that it was open to

the Court of Session to reduce a decree granted in an
action in which the court concerned did not have jurisdiction; and (2) that in the extract decree the sum
decerned for was erroneously stated to be £1,000
together with interest and expenses, and that as a
result the extract decree and the subsequent writs
should be reduced.

Held, (1) that the jurisdiction of a sheriff sitting in
any court within a sheriffdom extended throughout
the whole sheriffdom, and that the sheriff at Duns
therefore had jurisdiction to entertain the dispute concerning immovable property at North Berwick (p
219D); (2) that in exceptional circumstances reduction
might be granted even if the party seeking reduction
had failed to take advantage of other available means
of review (p 220B-C); but (3) that the pursuer was still
entitled, after making payment of the sum due, to
make use of the procedure for recall of a sequestration
set out in ss 16 and 17 of the Bankruptcy (Scotland)
Act 1985, and that as that statutory remedy was still
available to the pursuer, and its use would result in no
miscarriage of justice, there was no basis upon which
the court could exercise its discretion in favour of
reduction (p 220J-L); and action *dismissed.*

Opinion, that, since the error in the extract decree
was one for which neither the pursuer nor her legal
advisers bore any responsibility, even assuming that
failure to advise her of any rights and remedies she
might have had at various stages amounted to professional negligence on the part of those advisers, the
averments relating to such matters did not necessarily
exclude her from the "exceptional circumstances"
which might otherwise justify reduction (p 220F-H).

Action of production and reduction

Mrs Urzula Borowskah or Spence brought an action
for production and reduction of an extract decree and
related writs. She called as defenders Ian Davie and
another, the pursuers in the first action, and William
Cleghorn, the interim trustee appointed on her
sequestrated estates.

The case came before the Lord Ordinary (Lord
Cameron of Lochbroom) on procedure roll, when the
defenders sought to have the action dismissed on the
basis that the pursuer's averments disclosed no relevant case.

Statutory provisions

The Civil Jurisdiction and Judgments Act 1982 provides in Sched 8:

"4.—(1) Notwithstanding anything contained in any
of the Rules 1 to 3 above or 5 to 8 below, the following
courts shall have exclusive jurisdiction — (a) in
proceedings which have as their object rights *in rem*
in, or tenancies of, immoveable property, the courts
for the place where the property is situated".

Cases referred to

Adair v Colville & Sons Ltd, 1926 SLT 590; 1926 SC
(HL) 51.

Bain v Hugh L S McConnell Ltd, 1991 SLT 691.
Bruce v British Motor Trading Corporation Ltd, 1924
SLT 723; 1924 SC 908.
Central Motor Engineering Co v Gibbs, 1918 2 SLT
177; 1918 SC 755.
Hall v Riverlodge Ltd, 1980 SLT 141.
Halliday v Pattison, 1988 SLT 235.
Kirkwood v City of Glasgow District Council, 1988
SLT 430.
McCormick v Campbell (1926) 42 Sh Ct Rep 124.
Simpson v Bruce, 1984 SLT (Sh Ct) 38.
Tait v Johnston (1891) 18 R 606.
Yeaman v Mathewson (1900) 8 SLT 23; (1900) 2 F
873.

Textbook referred to
Stewart, *Diligence,* p 281.

On 19 November 1991 the Lord Ordinary *sustained*
the defenders' pleas in law to the relevancy and *dismissed* the action.

LORD CAMERON OF LOCHBROOM.—The
pursuer has raised the present action, first, for production and reduction of an interlocutor pronounced
by the sheriff at the sheriff court at Duns on 28
September 1988 finding the pursuer liable to the
defenders in the sum of £846.45 with interest thereon
at the rate of 15 per cent per annum from the date of
citation in said action and further finding the pursuer
liable to the defenders in the expenses of said action;
secondly, for production and reduction of an extract
decree issued in respect of said action on 13 October
1988; thirdly, for production and reduction of a
charge for payment served on the pursuer on 16
February 1989 pursuant to said extract; fourthly, for
production and reduction of the execution of said
charge dated 16 February 1989 and, fifthly, for production and reduction of the interlocutor of the sheriff
at the sheriff court at Duns dated 26 April 1989
awarding the sequestration of the estate of the pursuer
and appointing William Thomson Mercer Cleghorn,
now the third defender, to be interim trustee of said
estate, and of the act and warrant to follow thereon.
The present action bears to be signeted on 16 October
1990.

The interlocutor was pronounced after proof in an
action which, it is averred, had as its object a tenancy
of immovable property situated in North Berwick. In
the writ initiating the action the pursuer is cited as a
defender resident in Duns. However, it was common
ground between parties that jurisdiction in the sheriff
court action fell to be determined by reference to rule
4 (1) (a) of Sched 8 to the Civil Jurisdiction and Judgments Act 1982.

The pursuer avers that the sheriff court at Duns
lacked jurisdiction in the action and by virtue of that
the decree of the sheriff court at Duns was null and
void.

Rule 4 (1) (a) is in the following terms: [his Lordship
quoted the terms of rule 4 set out *supra* and con-

tinued:] I note at this point that the counsel for the
defenders concede for the purposes of the action that
the quoted rule applies although it appears from the
terms of the summary cause action that it was concerned with breach of conditions in missives of let in
respect that damage had arisen from the pursuer's
keeping of pets within the property, contrary to the
terms of two clauses within the missives of let.

The question thus arises as to which are the courts
for the place where the property was situated, namely
North Berwick. There was no dispute that North
Berwick was a place situated within the Sheriffdom of
Lothian and Borders. A sheriff sitting in any court
within the sheriffdom to which he is appointed has a
jurisdiction which extends over the whole county.
This is clearly stipulated in terms of s 7 of the Sheriff
Courts (Scotland) Act 1971. That section merely
confirms what was understood to be the law obtaining until that date (*Tait v Johnston*; *McCormick v
Campbell*; *Simpson v Bruce*). Nothing in the rule
quoted, in my opinion, expressly or by necessary
implication entrenches upon a sheriff's jurisdiction
under statute.

Counsel for the pursuer referred to *Bruce v British
Motor Trading Corporation Ltd* and *Yeaman v
Mathewson* for the proposition that reduction of a
decree whether in absence or in foro is competent
where there is lack of jurisdiction or the court has
exercised a jurisdiction it did not possess. That may
well be so, but neither case bears upon the issue as to
whether a sheriff exercises his jurisdiction over the
whole sheriffdom when he is sitting in one court
within the sheriffdom or whether his jurisdiction is
then limited to the district within which that court
lies. In my opinion, the former and not the latter is the
case.

In these circumstances I am satisfied that the
defenders are well founded in their submissions that
there is no relevant case stated to entitle the pursuer
to decree of reduction in terms of the first conclusion.

The pursuer's case in relation to the remaining
conclusions is based upon the fact, which all parties
admit, that the sheriff at Duns, after proof, pronounced an interlocutor under which the present
pursuer was found liable to the present first and
second defenders in the sum of £846.45 with interest
thereon at the rate of 15 per cent per annum from the
date of citation of the cause. That interlocutor was
dated 28 September 1988. It was not appealed. On 13
October 1988 the sheriff clerk issued an extract decree
in which the sum decerned for was stated to be £1,000
with interest at the rate of 15 per cent annually from
the date of citation until payment and £656.03 of
expenses. Warrant was also granted for all lawful execution thereon. It is admitted that the extract decree
is not in conformity with the principal sum for which
the sheriff pronounced decree in the interlocutor on
28 September 1988. On 16 February 1989 a charge for
payment of money was served on the pursuer bearing
to proceed on the basis of the extract decree. The
pursuer admits that until service of the charge she had

no knowledge of the terms of the extract decree.
Following the execution of the charge, which the first
and second defenders admit to be excessive to the
extent of £200, a petition at the instance of the first
and second defenders was on 12 April 1989 presented
to the sheriff court at Duns. The petition proceeded
on averments that the first and second defenders as
petitioners were creditors of the pursuer as debtor to
the extent of £1,656.03 approximately in terms of
decree granted against the pursuer as debtor by the
sheriff of Lothian and Borders at Duns on 28
September 1988: that no sums had been received by
the first and second defenders as petitioners since the
date of decree: that apparent insolvency of the pursuer
as debtor was constituted within four months preceding the presentation of the petition by virtue of the
charge served on the pursuer as debtor: that the
pursuer as debtor had failed to obtemper the terms of
the charge and was accordingly insolvent in terms of
s 7 of the Bankruptcy (Scotland) Act 1985.

On 26 April 1989 the sheriff at Duns pronounced an
interlocutor setting out that he was satisfied that the
petition had been presented in accordance with the
Bankruptcy (Scotland) Act 1985, that proper citation
had been made of the pursuer as debtor, that the
requirements of the Bankruptcy (Scotland) Act 1985
relating to apparent insolvency had been fulfilled, and
that he therefore sequestrated the pursuer's estate and
declared the same to belong to the pursuer's creditors
for the purposes of the Act. By the same interlocutor
the third defender was appointed to be interim trustee.

The present action was raised on 16 October 1990.
The pursuer makes no averment that she has paid any
sum towards meeting the sum awarded by the sheriff's
interlocutor dated 28 September 1988. Her case is that
after service of the charge she sought advice from her
solicitors who at that time advised her that it was too
late for her to lodge an appeal against the sheriff's
interlocutor of 28 September 1988. The pursuer does
not make any averment that she entered the sequestration process. Her explanation on record is that she
was advised by the sheriff clerk at Jedburgh in May
1989 that she was no longer able to appeal against the
sheriff's decision in the action against her by the first
and second defenders, that further advice was received
from solicitors in May 1989 and in early 1990 to the
effect that she had no grounds for challenging the
charge as a basis for the sequestration, that there was
nothing which could be done to recall the sequestration and that there was no avenue of appeal open to
her. The pursuer goes on to aver that none of the solicitors consulted by her gave her any advice on the
matter of suspension or reduction of the decree or the
charge, or of recall or reduction of the sequestration on
the basis of suspension or recall of the decree, extract
decree or charge. She further avers that she has
brought the present proceedings within a reasonable
time of being advised that there were rights and
remedies available to her in respect of the subject
matter of the present proceedings.

At this stage it is appropriate to notice that in the
first and second defenders' answers they aver that they

have limited their claim in the sequestration to the
restricted sum for which decree was granted on 28
September 1988, namely £846.45 plus interest of
£167.31 and expenses of £662.70. It only falls to be
noted that the pursuer does not admit this averment
and that the answers for the third defender would
appear to deny it.

Counsel for the pursuer conceded in the course of
his submissions that before ordering reduction, the
court would have regard to the equities, reduction
being an equitable remedy. For that reason his averments relative to the pursuer's dealing with solicitors
as averred in art 7 of the condescendence were relevant. I consider that counsel was well founded in
making this concession having regard to the general
principle set out in the case of *Bain v Hugh L S
McConnell Ltd,* namely that in exceptional circumstances a court may grant reduction even where other
means of review of the decrees or steps in process
which it is sought to review have been prescribed and
the party seeking reduction has failed to take advantage of them. At p 695 the Lord Justice Clerk (Ross)
said: "It is, in our opinion, well established that a
decree may be reduced in exceptional circumstances if
reduction is necessary to produce substantial justice."
That sentence is to be read in the context of earlier
references to the speeches of Viscount Dunedin and of
Lord Carson in *Adair v Colville & Sons Ltd* which
stressed the importance of there being a miscarriage of
justice if reduction was to be justified.

In the present action all parties accept that the
extract decree is incorrect in referring to the principal
sum as being £1,000. That error is not one for which
either of the parties to the sheriff court action are
responsible. All the procedure since the decree was
extracted, took place by reference to the extract
decree. I have no doubt that if the pursuer had sought
to do so she could have reduced the extract decree by
virtue of the mistake in the extract decree issued by
the sheriff clerk (*Hall v Riverlodge Ltd*). I am also satisfied that following service of the charge, the charge
could have been suspended and the extract set aside
(Graham Stewart on *The Law of Diligence,* p 281). I am
also satisfied that upon service of the petition for
sequestration it was open to the pursuer to enter the
process to show cause why sequestration could not
competently be awarded (s 12 of the Bankruptcy (Scotland) Act 1985). It would further have been open to
the pursuer to petition the court in terms of s 16 of the
1985 Act for recall of the award of sequestration at any
time within 10 weeks after the date of sequestration.
Thereafter she can do so upon payment of the full sum
due under the terms of the decree granted by the
sheriff on 28 September 1988. I refer to the terms of
s 17 (1) (a) of the 1985 Act.

Counsel for the third defenders submitted that
where the only ground for excusing the pursuer lay in
blaming her solicitors for wrongly advising her, there
was no proper basis for seeking reduction (*Halliday v
Pattison; Kirkwood v City of Glasgow District Council*).
As at present advised, particularly since the error in

the extract decree is one for which neither herself nor
her legal advisers bear any responsibility, I would be
of the view that even assuming that failure to advise
the pursuer of any rights and remedies she might have
at various stages amounted to professional negligence
on the part of her then advisers, the averments relating
to such matters do not necessarily operate to bar the
pursuer from seeking to bring herself within the
generality of the exceptional case to which the court
made reference in *Bain v Hugh L S McConnell Ltd.* I
would therefore, if otherwise disposed to grant a proof
on the second branch of the case, have held these averments sufficiently relevant for the purposes of justifying the relative conclusions.

Counsel for the first and second defenders referred
to *Central Motor Engineering Co v Gibbs* in support of
a proposition that the pursuer must fail unless she
could excuse her failure to follow the statutory procedure in the sequestration process. That case was
concerned with reduction of a sequestration sought on
the ground that citation of two partners in a company
had been inept. The decision of the court proceeded
upon the basis that there was nothing exceptional in
the circumstances to justify reduction, more particularly since statute had provided a remedy in
recall.

The contention for the pursuer was that since all the
steps that had followed the extract decree were tainted
by the mistake in the extract decree, they should be set
aside. In my opinion, this argument is fatally flawed.
There is outstanding and effective a decree which
cannot be challenged by the pursuer and under which
she is obliged to make payment of sums certain to the
first and second defenders. In order to justify reduction, she has to establish that there is no other step
available to her and that but for reduction a miscarriage of justice will occur. That miscarriage of
justice can only occur if as a consequence of the
sequestration proceedings, she is now being called
upon to pay more than that which she could otherwise
properly be called upon to pay if the sequestration
proceedings had followed upon an extract decree in
the proper terms, with a charge for the proper sum. It
is at this point that it seems to me the pursuer's submissions break down. It is plain on the face of her
averments that she has made no payment whatsoever
in satisfaction of the decree pronounced against her.
She makes no offer to satisfy the decree. Yet she can
seek to have the sequestration recalled having made
full payment in terms of that decree, on the ground
that she is not obliged to make payment over and
above that which appears on the face of the decree in
terms of the sheriff's interlocutor. It is plain therefore
on the face of the pursuer's averments that she is still
entitled to make use of the statutory procedure for
recall of the sequestration in terms of ss 16 and 17 of
the 1985 Act.

I should add that if, as the first and second defenders
aver, it were to be established by proof that they had
submitted a claim in the sequestration which did no
more than seek a payment conform to the decree
which was pronounced by the sheriff on 28 September

1988, any suggestion of miscarriage of justice disappears and the pursuer's action must inevitably fail.

However being satisfied as I am that a remedy under the statutory procedure is still available to the pursuer of which she has not availed herself and which would result in no miscarriage of justice, then in the absence of any averments of miscarriage of justice, I must conclude that there is no basis upon which the court could exercise its equitable jurisdiction by pronouncing any of the orders for production and reduction that are sought in terms of the second to fifth conclusions of the action.

In the whole circumstances I am of opinion that the pursuer's averments disclose no relevant case for the action in any of its branches. I shall therefore sustain the second plea in law for the first and second defenders and the fourth plea in law for the third defenders and dismiss the action.

Counsel for Pursuer, Fitzpatrick; Solicitors, Maclachlan & Mackenzie, SSC — Counsel for First and Second Defenders, Gale; Solicitors, Bird Semple Fyfe Ireland, WS — Counsel for Third Defender, Bovey; Solicitors, Morton Fraser Milligan, WS.

A M

Rutherford v Radio Rentals Ltd

FIRST DIVISION
THE LORD PRESIDENT (HOPE),
LORDS ALLANBRIDGE AND MAYFIELD
21 NOVEMBER 1991

Employment — Contract of employment — Conditions of employment indemnifying employee against accident at work — Whether employers under any contractual obligation to pay sum claimed to employee.

Process — Form of action — Alleged failure to pay benefit due under contract of employment — Action of damages for breach of contract rather than of payment under contract — Whether relevant.

A contract of employment provided the employee with personal accident cover in the event of an accident at work, which in the event of permanent total disablement provided a benefit of five times the employee's average annual earnings. There was no express provision in the contract for payment of any sum by the employer to the employee. The employee suffered an accident at work which resulted in the termination of his employment on medical grounds. His employers did not pay him any sum in terms of his contract. Following the failure of an action of damages against his employers based on their alleged

fault and negligence, the employee raised an action of damages against them based on their alleged breach of contract. The employers argued that the action was irrelevant as they were under no contractual obligation to make any payment to the employee. The employee had chosen the wrong form of action. The employee accepted that an action for payment might have been more apposite but contended that he had relevantly averred that he was entitled to a benefit which he had not received. The Lord Ordinary allowed a proof before answer on the whole case and reserved all pleas to the relevancy. The employers reclaimed.

Held, (1) that if the employee could prove his averments of fact, it could not be affirmed at this stage that he would not be entitled to the sum sued for in terms of the contract (pp 222L-223A); (2) that, although an action for payment would have been more appropriate, the basis of the employee's action was sufficiently averred and the employers could not be said to have suffered any prejudice by the way in which the remedy was sought (p 223B); and reclaiming motion *refused*.

Action of damages

Robert Rutherford raised an action of damages against Radio Rentals Ltd based on their alleged breach of a term of his contract of employment whereby he became entitled to an insurance payment in the event of permanent total disablement from work. The company sought dismissal of the action on the grounds (a) that they were under no contractual obligation to make payment to the pursuer, and (b) that in any event the wrong type of action had been raised and it was therefore irrelevant.

The action came before the Lord Ordinary (Coulsfield) on procedure roll.

On 12 July 1990 the Lord Ordinary *allowed* a proof before answer and *reserved* all pleas to the relevancy.

The defenders reclaimed.

Reclaiming motion

The reclaiming motion was heard before the First Division on 21 November 1991.

Eo die the court *refused* the reclaiming motion.

The following opinion of the court was delivered by Lord Allanbridge:

OPINION OF THE COURT.—This is an action for payment raised by the pursuer against the defenders who were his employers in May 1985. On 30 May 1985 he avers he suffered an accident when he injured his back carrying a television set in the course of his employment. On 28 February 1986 the defenders terminated his employment on medical grounds. The pursuer then raised an action for damages against the defenders arising out of this accident but failed to establish any fault against them. In the present action he seeks payment of £25,000

which he alleges is due to him in terms of para 4.2.2
A of the staff handbook which describes the defenders'
standard terms and conditions of employment.

The foreword to the said handbook was in the
following terms: "This handbook is designed to give
members of staff a brief indication of our principal
activities, objectives and philosophies. It also describes the company's standard Terms and Conditions
of employment, its training and development policies,
and the concessions and facilities which are available
to its staff. These Terms and Conditions, together
B with those contained in the employee's letter of
appointment, constitute the main provisions of his or
her contract of employment with this Company.
Members of staff should, therefore, read this booklet
and keep it in a safe place for future reference."

Paragraph 4.2.2 of the said handbook, so far as relevant to the present action, provided as follows:

"*Personal accident cover*
"This takes the form of an earnings related insur-
C ance covering all employees in respect of any accident
that might occur to any employee whilst engaged on
the business of the company. Subject to the terms and
conditions of the policy, details of cover provided and
the time in which it operates are as follows:

"Benefits
"Death: permanent loss of use of limb(s); eye(s);
permanent total disablement from carrying out usual
occupation — five times average annual earnings."

D   After hearing argument by both parties on the procedure roll the Lord Ordinary allowed a proof before
answer on the whole case and reserved all pleas to the
relevancy. It had been argued before him by counsel
for the defenders that the action should be dismissed
on the ground that they were not under any contractual obligation to pay the sum claimed to the pursuer.
In allowing a proof before answer the Lord Ordinary
said he accepted that the contract of employment did
not contain any express term obliging the defenders to
E make any payment to the pursuer but that he considered there were a number of terms which must be
implied in order to give the contract business efficacy.
He outlines these implied terms in his opinion and
then added that an alternative and much simpler way
of giving the contract business efficacy would be to
read para 4.2.2 as imposing an obligation upon the
defenders to make payment to the pursuer in the event
of his becoming disabled in circumstances which fall
within the terms of the policy referred to in the
F contract.

Counsel for the defenders argued that whilst he
might be prepared to accept the applicability of some
of these implied terms, they were not averred by the
pursuer and formed no part of his present case on
record. Counsel for the pursuer accepted this situation
and explained that it was the Lord Ordinary who had
introduced the question of implied terms into the
debate and that as far as the pursuer was concerned it
was accepted, whatever may be the position in future
if amendments are made, that on his present pleadings

the question of implied terms could not be raised or
founded on by the pursuer. What the pursuer did rely G
on in his present pleadings was the simple case that
the pursuer was entitled to a benefit in terms of para
4.2.2 and he had not received that benefit.

In these circumstances we can now concentrate on
the defenders' counsel's attack on what was described
by the Lord Ordinary as the simple and alternative
way of giving the contract business efficacy. Counsel
for the defenders accepted that the proper interpretation of para 4.2.2 lay at the heart of the dispute H
between the parties. The action was one based on
breach of contract as indicated in cond 3 and the first
plea in law for the pursuer. It was not disputed that
there might be an action available to the pursuer but
it was submitted that it was not the action as presently
averred. He submitted that in cond 3 the pursuer
averred that by failing to pay the sum sued for the
defenders were in breach of their contract with him.
He stressed that in terms of para 4.2.2 the defenders
were under no obligation to pay any sum to the
pursuer. Furthermore, the pursuer had not taken, for I
example, any steps to recover the insurance policy by
diligence or otherwise and therefore had not as yet
made any attempt to rely on its terms. The pursuer
had not averred that the defenders had failed to take
out the appropriate policy or failed to submit a claim
when asked by the pursuer to do so, or otherwise made
a relevant case that the defenders were in breach of the
pursuer's contract of employment.

In reply counsel for the pursuer explained that his J
case was a simple and straightforward one. The
pursuer was in the circumstances averred entitled to
the benefit described in para 4.2.2. In his pleadings he
averred that he had sustained an accident whilst
engaged on the business of the company which had
resulted in permanent total disablement from carrying
out his normal occupation. In that event the benefit to
which he was entitled was five times his average
annual earnings. His annual earnings were £5,000 per
annum at the time and the benefit claimed was there- K
fore £25,000. He accepted that he would require to
prove these particular facts in order to meet the terms
of para 4.2.2 but if he did so then he was entitled to
receive the sum sued for as the appropriate benefit.
Pursuer's counsel accepted that to describe the
defenders' failure to pay him this sum as a breach of
contract was not entirely apt because what the
defenders had done was to fail to pay him a sum to
which he was entitled. He accepted that his action
could more properly be regarded as an action for L
payment for a sum due rather than payment of
damages for a breach of contract.

Having considered the matter we are satisfied that
the pursuer has made sufficient and relevant averments to entitle him to a proof before answer in this
case. We find it impossible to affirm at this stage,
assuming that the pursuer can establish the essential
facts as presently averred by him, that he would not
be entitled to receive the sum sued for on the basis that
it was a benefit to which he would be entitled in terms

of para 4.2.2. We agree with the Lord Ordinary that,
on the present pleadings, if there is any dispute
between the defenders and the insurance company
upon the contract between them then that would be a
matter for them to resolve without involving the
pursuer. We also consider that if there is any dispute
arising between the pursuer and the defenders regarding the full terms of the pursuer's contract of employment and/or the policy referred to in the said
paragraph, then that cannot be resolved in the absence
of both documents. We accept that the pursuer's averments in cond 3 and in his first plea in law are not very
happily or accurately phrased and that a straightforward action for payment of a benefit due would be
more appropriate. Nevertheless in the context of this
action the remedy of payment which the pursuer seeks
and his reasons for seeking it are sufficiently set out in
his pleadings and the defenders cannot be said to have
suffered any prejudice by the way in which the remedy
is sought. As we are refusing the reclaiming motion
and the case is to proceed to proof with all pleas standing, we do not consider it necessary or even advisable
to express any further views at this stage on the
matters in dispute between the parties.

On the whole matter we therefore refuse this
reclaiming motion and adhere to the Lord Ordinary's
interlocutor.

---

*Counsel for Pursuer and Respondent, Peoples; Solici-
tors, Lawford Kidd & Co, WS — Counsel for Defenders
and Reclaimers, Brailsford; Solicitors, Gray Muirhead,
WS.*

M C G

Archer Car Sales (Airdrie) Ltd v Gregory's Trustee

OUTER HOUSE

TEMPORARY JUDGE J M S HORSBURGH, QC

26 NOVEMBER 1991

*Bankruptcy — Sequestration — Recall — Sequestration
on petition of trustee under debtor's trust deed for
creditors — Whether trustee acting for debtor or creditors
— Bankruptcy (Scotland) Act 1985 (c 66), s 5 (2) (c).*

*Statute — Construction — Reference to report of Scottish
Law Commission — Purpose for which reference may be
made — Statute not ambiguous.*

The Bankruptcy (Scotland) Act 1985 provides in s 5
(2) that those who may petition for sequestration are
(a) the debtor, with the concurrence of a qualified
creditor, (b) a qualified creditor, and (c) a trustee
under a voluntary trust deed for creditors granted by
the debtor. Section 17 gives to the court a general discretionary power of recall of an award.

A debtor granted a trust deed and the trustee then
sought and obtained an award of sequestration. At the
date of the trust deed a creditor had raised an action
of payment against the debtor and had recorded an
inhibition on the dependence of the action. On procedure roll the creditors sought recall of the sequestration and of the trustee's appointment as permanent
trustee on the basis that the trustee had not been
acting independently for behoof of the creditors of the
debtor but had been acting for the debtor. In advancing his contention, counsel for the creditors argued
that reference to the Scottish Law Commission's
Report on Bankruptcy was competent in construing the
provisions of the 1985 Act.

Held, (1) that the trustee's investigations and advice
to the debtor before she granted the trust deed did not
bar the trustee under the trust deed from petitioning
for sequestration or being appointed as permanent
trustee on the sequestrated estates (p 225A-B); (2) that
in petitioning for sequestration the trustee had not
been acting as the debtor's agent (p 225E-F); and petition for recall *dismissed*.

Opinion, that it was not legitimate to look at the
Scottish Law Commission's report to provide a gloss
on a statutory provision which was, in any event,
unambiguous (p 225H).

Petition for recall of sequestration

Archer Car Sales (Airdrie) Ltd petitioned for the
recall of the sequestration of Mrs Lillian Stark or
Gregory, the first respondent. George Stewart Paton,
the permanent trustee on the sequestrated estate of the
first respondent, was called as second respondent. He
opposed the petition.

The case came before Temporary Judge J M S
Horsburgh, QC, on procedure roll.

Statutory provisions

The Bankruptcy (Scotland) Act 1985 provides:

"5.—. . . (2) The sequestration of the estate of a
living debtor shall be on the petition of — (a) the
debtor, with the concurrence of a qualified creditor or
qualified creditors; (b) a qualified creditor or qualified
creditors, if the debtor is apparently insolvent; or (c)
the trustee acting under a voluntary trust deed granted
by or on behalf of the debtor whereby his estate is conveyed to the trustee for the benefit of his creditors
generally (in this Act referred to as a 'trust deed'). . . .

"17.—(1) The Court of Session may recall an award
of sequestration if it is satisfied that in all the circumstances of the case (including those arising after the
date of the award of sequestration) it is appropriate to
do so and, without prejudice to the foregoing generality, may recall the award if it is satisfied that — (a)
the debtor has paid his debts in full or has given sufficient security for their payment; (b) a majority in value
of the creditors reside in a country other than Scotland
and that it is more appropriate for the debtor's estate
to be administered in that other country; or (c) one or

A more other awards of sequestration of the estate or analogous remedies (as defined in section 10 (5) of this Act) have been granted."

Cases referred to

Aswan Engineering Establishment Co v Lupdine Ltd
    [1987] 1 WLR 1; [1987] 1 All ER 135.
Keith v Texaco Ltd, 1977 SLT (Lands Tr) 16.
R v Shivpuri [1987] AC 1; [1986] 2 WLR 988; [1986]
    2 All ER 334.

B **Textbook referred to**

McBryde, *Bankruptcy*, pp 39-41, 243.

On 26 November 1991 the temporary judge *dismissed* the petition.

J M S HORSBURGH, QC.—In this petition, which called before me on procedure roll, recall of the sequestration of the first respondent awarded by the sheriff at Airdrie on 29 November 1990 is sought.
C That is opposed by the second respondent, the permanent trustee on the estates of the first respondent.

From the averments of the petitioners and the second respondent and the productions referred to and incorporated brevitatis causa, it appears that on 17 December 1989 the petitioners raised an action for payment of £68,283 against the first respondent, and on 20 December 1989 they recorded an inhibition on the dependence of the action against her. On 26 October 1990 the first respondent signed a trust deed
D for behoof of her whole creditors, conveying her whole assets to the second respondent as trustee. The second respondent with her concurrence then petitioned for the first respondent's sequestration under s 5 (2) (c) of the Bankruptcy (Scotland) Act 1985. On 9 November 1990 he was appointed interim trustee.

Certain correspondence with the petitioners' solicitors is relevant to the history of the matter. On 27 November 1990 the second respondent wrote to them, informing them that the first respondent was not his
E client, that she had signed a trust deed in his favour in order that a sequestration petition could be lodged, that the sequestration would follow the "small assets" procedure, and requesting assistance in tracing assets in the first respondent's name. On 29 November the second respondent wrote further that the first respondent had been referred to him by her solicitors, owing to the state of her finances and for advice thereon. Her assets appeared to be £1.00, her liabilities approximately £9,700.00, her income invalidity benefit of
F £59.21 weekly. He concluded that she could not pay her creditors, advised her of the options available and of the effect of sequestration. He stated that in the week following his giving advice the first respondent signed the trust deed in his favour, and he then arranged presentation of the sequestration petition.

Sequestration was awarded on 29 November 1990, the sheriff having rejected an argument based on the letter of 27 November that such an award would be incompetent. On 31 December the second respondent was appointed permanent trustee.

In terms of s 17 (1) the present petitioners seek recall of the award as appropriate in all the circumstances of G the case on the basis that the sole purpose of the trust deed was to enable sequestration to be applied for, the second respondent having taken no further steps under the trust deed. In terms of his first plea in law the second respondent seeks dismissal of the petition.

In support of his argument counsel for the petitioners contended that s 5 (2) demonstrates that in insolvency debtors are not free to do with their assets as they please. For a sequestration petition, qualified creditors or a trustee under a trust deed must be H involved. This is to protect creditors' interests. The second respondent however had acted in the debtor's interest, and as her agent, without considering the interests of the creditors. His letters indicated that she had consulted him for advice on her financial position, and that about a week later she had signed the trust deed in order that a petition could be lodged. It could be inferred that the second respondent had decided a petition for sequestration was appropriate prior to the first respondent signing the trust deed. In presenting I it he had not acted for the creditors, but for the debtor, and had not considered if sequestration was in the creditors' interests.

Under reference to *Keith v Texaco Ltd, Aswan Engineering Establishment Co v Lupdine Ltd* and *R v Shivpuri*, counsel for the petitioners contended that reference could be made to the Scottish Law Commission's *Report on Bankruptcy* of 1982 for the limited purpose of discovering the mischief sought to be remedied by the statutory provision. Section 5 (2) of J the Act and cl 5 (2) of the commission's draft Bill were identical. Paragraph 5.23 of the report favoured involvement of creditors in sequestration to make available a creditor's view on the appropriateness of the proceedings and as a safeguard against debtors applying for their own sequestrations for ulterior purposes. Paragraph 24.18 emphasised the independent function of a trustee under a trust deed for creditors.

In reply senior counsel for the second respondent K sought dismissal. His argument was that by signing the trust deed the first respondent admitted her financial position was hopeless. The trustee appointed, an insolvency practitioner, had to act independently of her and required to investigate her affairs. With small assets cases that investigation normally preceded the signing of the trust deed as a matter of convenience. In this case the correspondence showed the second respondent had carried out his duties. The procedure outlined in McBryde on *Bankruptcy*, pp 39-41 and L p 243 had been followed, and what had happened complied with the Act. There was no relevant attack on the trust deed, nor was it claimed that the sequestration was a device to defeat the creditors' rights.

It was accepted that Law Commission material might be looked at to identify the mischief corrected by an Act of Parliament, but that was not a general aid to construction where, as here, the meaning of the statute was clear.

I have reached the view that the argument for the

A second respondent is correct, and that the petition falls to be dismissed as irrelevant. It is not claimed that the trust deed entered by the first respondent was not for the benefit of her whole creditors, or that its purposes were invalid or that it was defectively executed. It is not claimed that the sequestration petition which followed was designed to defeat illegitimately the rights of creditors. What is claimed is that the independence of the second respondent's actions as trustee for the whole creditors had been undermined by his having given the first respondent advice on her finances before the trust deed was signed, and by B acting as her agent then and thereafter. I do not consider either attack on the second respondent's actings to be soundly based.

I reject the argument that per se the second respondent's status as trustee for the creditors was tainted by his having previously advised the debtor. In many cases investigations by trustees for creditors into debtors' finances take place after the execution of trust deeds, but with small assets cases I consider it is both C convenient and reasonable that such investigations may take place before the deeds are signed. I also consider it reasonable that in such cases debtors may have received advice on their financial circumstances from persons appointed their trustees under trust deeds subsequently entered. There is nothing in the Act which strikes at the appointment of a debtor's adviser as trustee for his creditors.

Once the trust deed is signed, the trustee must take D up a position independent of the debtor, and he has a responsibility for investigating the debtor's financial affairs. I consider that responsibility may be properly discharged by taking into account investigations made prior to the signing of the trust deed. The decision to petition for sequestration is of course the trustee's and not the creditor's. One reason why the Act authorises a trustee under a trust deed to petition is to avoid the need to obtain the concurrence of creditors, which in the state of the first respondent's finances might not E have been easily got. Indeed, as Professor McBryde observes at p 40 (foot), there may be a variety of reasons for a trustee under a trust deed petitioning for a debtor's sequestration, among them securing his fees and outlays out of public funds in a small assets case.

I also reject the petitioners' argument that in petitioning for her sequestration the second respondent was acting as the first respondent's agent and not on behalf of her creditors. There are no relevant averments to support this. The petitioners admit that by F the trust deed the first respondent conveyed her whole assets to the second respondent as trustee for her whole creditors. In terms of s 5 (2) (c) he was thus qualified to petition. The procedure which followed was strictly in accordance with the Act. The petitioners' argument sits uncomfortably with the admission. Further, perusal of the two letters founded on by the petitioners shows the situation to have been that the second respondent was acting on behalf of the whole creditors and not as agent for the first respondent. In these letters, written after the trust deed had

been signed, the second respondent stated that the debtor was not his client, disclosed the results of his G earlier financial investigations, and requested assistance from the petitioners' solicitors in tracing assets in the name of the first respondent. That is not consistent with agency, but entirely consistent with acting on behalf of the creditors in general. The letter of 27 November 1990 also shows that, contrary to the petitioners' submission, the second respondent did take steps to ascertain the debtor's financial position after she had signed the trust deed. For these reasons I reject the petitioners' arguments. H

In my opinion there is no need in the circumstances of this case to refer to the report of the Law Commission. As I understood the reference it was made not so much to ascertain the mischief the following legislation was designed to cure, but to provide a gloss on the meaning of s 5 of the Act. I do not regard that as legitimate. In any event, the statutory provision itself is quite clear and I do not consider that reference to such pre-enactment sources is required.

In conclusion, I do not regard the practice which I was adopted by the second respondent as trustee to be objectionable in any way. The course followed was a convenient method of achieving sequestration where a plainly insolvent debtor, pressed by creditors, was seeking a solution to her financial problems. The course adopted was one clearly sanctioned by the Act and in the absence of relevant averments attacking its competency or the actings of the second respondent as trustee, I consider the petition falls to be dismissed. J

Counsel for Petitioner, Maher; Solicitors, Brodies, WS — No appearance for First Respondent (Debtor) — Counsel for Second Respondent (Permanent Trustee), Drummond Young, QC; Solicitors, Bishop & Robertson Chalmers.

J P D

K

Thomson v MacPhail

HIGH COURT OF JUSTICIARY

THE LORD JUSTICE CLERK (ROSS), LORDS McCLUSKEY AND KIRKWOOD

18 MARCH 1992   L

Justiciary — Statutory offence — Driving while unfit through drink — Failure to provide breath specimen — Notice describing road as a private road with entry by appointment only — Road used by members of public including members of a private fishing club and hill-walkers — Whether road or other public place — Road Traffic Act 1988 (c 52), ss 5 (1) (a) and 7 (6).

Section 5 (1) (a) of the Road Traffic Act 1988 makes it an offence for a person to drive or attempt to drive

A a motor vehicle on a road or other public place when the proportion of alcohol in that person's breath, blood or urine exceeds a prescribed limit. Section 7 empowers a constable to require a breath specimen from a person he has reasonable cause to suspect of driving on a road or other public place with alcohol in his body. Section 7 (6) makes it an offence to fail to provide such a specimen.

An accused person was convicted of failing to provide two specimens of breath for analysis which were required to ascertain the proportion of alcohol in
B his breath while he was driving a vehicle on a certain road. A notice described the road as a private road and made it clear that entry was by appointment. The road was, however, used by members of the public including members of a private fishing club and hillwalkers. The defence submitted that the road did not fall within the statutory prohibition. The sheriff rejected this view and held that the road was one over which there was a public right of access. The accused appealed by stated case.

C **Held,** that the test was whether the place in question was a place on which members of the public might be expected to be found and over which they might be expected to be passing or over which they were in use to have access, and, applying that test, the road was a public place within the meaning of the Act (p 228G-H); and appeal refused.

Brown v Braid, 1985 SLT 37, *applied*; *Young v Carmichael*, 1993 SLT 167, *distinguished*.

D **Observed,** that the sheriff might have gone too far in affirming a right of access in the public (p 228F).

———————

Summary complaint
Frederick Thomson was charged at the instance of Malcolm MacPhail, procurator fiscal, Perth, on a summary complaint which libelled the following charge: "On 19 May 1991 at Divisional Police Headquarters, Barrack Street, Perth, Perth and Kinross
E District you did without reasonable excuse, fail to provide two specimens of breath for analysis by means of a device of a type approved by the Secretary of State in pursuance of a requirement imposed under the Road Traffic Act 1988, s 7; contrary to said Act, s 7 (6), and it will be shown that the said specimens of breath were required to ascertain your ability to drive or the proportion of alcohol in your breath at the time you were driving motor vehicle namely a motor tractor on 19 May 1991 on the road to Glenquey Reservoir
F at its junction with the road to Glenquey Farm, Glendevon, Perth and Kinross District".

The accused pled not guilty and proceeded to trial before the temporary sheriff (K R W Hogg), after which he was found guilty as libelled.

The accused appealed by way of stated case to the High Court against conviction.

Findings in fact
The sheriff found inter alia the following facts admitted or proved:

(1) On the 19 May 1991 in the early hours of the morning two police officers in uniform, being Con- G stables Pover and Miller, were on mobile patrol on Glendevon Road, Perth and Kinross District. The officers received a radio message to go to Glenquey House, Glendevon at approximately 2 am. (2) Glenquey House and Glenquey farm were in a rural setting and known to the officers. They were reached by turning off the main Glendevon Road which in itself was a two lane tarmacadamed road running through countryside, such turnoff being at an unobstructed junction. The road then became a single track tarma- H cadamed road which ran for a distance of approximately a mile passing at least one house before dividing again with the single track tarmacadamed road continuing on to Glenquey House and reservoir and an unmetalled road commencing at a gate and cattle grid running downhill for a distance of approximately 500 yds before arriving at the farm steading known as Glenquey farm. The single track tarmacadamed road was surrounded by open countryside and hillside and was of an undulating nature and had I telegraph poles running its length. (3) At the commencement of the single track tarmacadamed road, on the left hand side set back from the road, stood a signboard bearing the legend "Fife Regional Council, Glenquey Reservoir, private road, entry by appointment only". Approximately 100 yds further on up an incline there was a cattle grid and a gate which was open. The tarmacadamed single track road gave access to Glenquey reservoir, a warden's house there, Glenquey House, Glenquey farm and one or possibly two J dwellinghouses. (4) Both police constables were aware that the road was used for access to these properties and was also used by members of the public in particular members of a private fishing club and also hillwalkers. Both constables at times had seen examples of members of the public walking and driving on the tarmacadamed single track road and had also taken access themselves in the past in a police vehicle. Neither officer had ever challenged any member of the public on the said road if they had made an appoint- K ment. The tarmacadamed single track road was a road to which the public had access and to which the terms of the Road Traffic Act 1988 applied. . . . (8) . . . From their position the officers could not see the junction of the farm road and the single track tarmacadamed road and could not see Glenquey farm and steading all of which were down in an undulation in the valley. The officers having seen the vehicle and formed the conclusion that it was on the single track tarmacadamed road some distance down that road from the junction L with Glenquey farm road noticed that the tractor appeared to turn and head back. The officers were suspicious that the appellant who had been previously warned might be driving the tractor and turned their motor vehicle and gave chase to the tractor. They noticed that the tractor was not displaying red tail lights. . . . (10) When the police officers finally caught up with the tractor it was being driven round in circles in a field and was eventually stopped when one of the police officers climbed on board the tractor and terminated the ignition. At the time that the tractor was

A boarded it was still displaying white lights to the front but no red tail light.

(11) The tractor stopped was the same tractor which had driven on to the single track tarmacadamed road and was driven by the appellant being the same person who had been warned earlier on not to drive a vehicle. There was no other person in the immediate vicinity who could have been the driver of the vehicle except for the appellant.

Statutory provisions

B The Road Traffic Act 1988 provides:

"5.—(1) If a person — (a) drives or attempts to drive a motor vehicle on a road or other public place . . . after consuming so much alcohol that the proportion of it in his breath, blood or urine exceeds the prescribed limit he is guilty of an offence. . . .

"7.—. . . (6) A person who, without reasonable excuse, fails to provide a specimen when required to do so in pursuance of this section is guilty of an offence."

C

Cases referred to

Brown v Braid, 1985 SLT 37; 1984 SCCR 286.
Harrison v Hill, 1931 SLT 598; 1932 JC 13.
Paterson v Ogilvy, 1957 SLT 354; 1957 JC 42.
Young v Carmichael, 1993 SLT 167; 1991 SCCR 332.

Appeal

The sheriff posed the following questions for the opinion of the High Court:

D (1) Was I entitled to hold on the evidence that the appellant had been driving on a road within the meaning of the Act?

(2) Was I entitled to hold that the road was a road within the meaning of the Act?

(3) On the facts stated was I entitled to convict the appellant?

The appeal was heard by the High Court on 18 E February 1992.

On 18 March 1992 the court answered question 2 of consent in the *negative* and question 3 in the *affirmative* and *refused* the appeal.

The following opinion of the court was delivered by the Lord Justice Clerk (Ross):

OPINION OF THE COURT.—The appellant is F Frederick Thomson who went to trial in the sheriff court at Perth on a complaint libelling a contravention of s 7 (6) of the Road Traffic Act 1988. In the charge it was alleged that he had failed to provide two specimens of breath for analysis, and it was further libelled as follows: "and it will be shown that the said specimens of breath were required to ascertain your ability to drive or the proportion of alcohol in your breath at the time you were driving motor vehicle namely a motor tractor on 19 May 1991 on the road to Glenquey Reservoir at its junction with the road to Glenquey Farm, Glendevon, Perth and Kinross District".

After evidence had been led by the Crown, and after the appellant had given evidence, the sheriff found the G appellant guilty of the charge. Against his conviction he has appealed by way of stated case. Three questions are stated in the case, but counsel for the appellant intimated that he was dropping the first question. He explained that the contention for the appellant was that the sheriff was not entitled to hold that the road where the appellant had been was a road within the meaning of the Road Traffic Act 1988. He accordingly invited the court to answer the second and third questions in the case in the negative. H

Counsel for the appellant drew attention to the relevant findings in the case. These findings are in the following terms: [his Lordship quoted the terms of findings 2, 3 and 4 and continued:]

Counsel for the appellant maintained that the final sentence of finding 4 was incorrect. He maintained that the road was not a road to which the public had access and to which the terms of the Road Traffic Act 1988 applied. He referred to *Young v Carmichael* and I pointed out that in that case it had been recognised that for the purposes of the Road Traffic Act 1972 "road" was defined as "any way . . . over which there is a public right of passage". He submitted that in the present case there could be no question of the public having any right of passage over the road because there was a notice describing the road as a private road and making it clear that entry was by appointment only.

Counsel for the appellant also founded on *Harrison* J *v Hill*. At 1931 SLT, p 600 the Lord Justice General said: "I think that, when the statute speaks of 'the public' in this connection, what is meant is the public generally, and not the special class of members of the public who have occasion for business or social purposes to go to the farmhouse or to any part of the farm itself; were it otherwise, the definition might just as well have included all private roads as well as all public highways."

In that case Lord Sands at p 601 stated: "In my K view, access means, not right of access, but ingress in fact without any physical hindrance and without any wilful intrusion." Subsequently he stated: "In my view, any road may be regarded as a road to which the public have access upon which members of the public are to be found who have not obtained access either by overcoming a physical obstruction or in defiance of prohibition express or implied."

Counsel maintained that having regard to what was L stated in finding 3 regarding the legend on the signboard, any member of the public who was on the road could only have got there in defiance of the implied prohibition on the signboard.

The advocate depute under reference to *Young v Carmichael* conceded that the sheriff had not been entitled to hold that the road in question was a road within the meaning of the Act of 1988 as it then stood. He reminded us that the definition of "road" has been altered by the Road Traffic Act 1991, but the amend-

ment will not be effective until 1 July 1992 whereas
A the offence was alleged to have been committed on 19
May 1991. Accordingly at the time when the offence
was alleged to have been committed the definition of
road was the same as the definition which was in force
in *Young v Carmichael*. On the basis of the findings in
the present case it was clear that the road was a private
road and not a way over which there was a public right
of passage.

However, the advocate depute maintained that there
was in the case ample material to hold that the road
B in question was a public place within the meaning of
the Act. The charge had libelled that the specimens of
breath were required to ascertain the appellant's
ability to drive or the proportion of alcohol in his
breath at the time he was driving a motor vehicle on
the road in question. Section 5 (1) (a) of the Road
Traffic Act 1988 makes it an offence for a person to
drive or attempt to drive a motor vehicle on a road or
other public place. The advocate depute submitted
that having regard to the findings and in particular
C finding 4 it was clear that the road in question was a
public place. The road was used for access to a
number of properties, and it was also used by
members of the public including members of a private
fishing club and hillwalkers. He submitted that the
case was different to *Young v Carmichael* where it was
plain that access was limited to the residents and their
guests. In that case there was no evidence that
members of the public in general had access to the car
park.

D
We are satisfied that the submissions of the advocate
depute in this connection are to be preferred to those
of counsel for the appellant. It is clear upon the findings that the road was in fact used by the public. The
matter is also made clear by the sheriff in his note
where he explains why he thought that the present
case was different to *Young v Carmichael*. In his note
he states inter alia: "I had the benefit of the photographs which showed a roadway going for some dis-
E tance into undulating hillside and a roadway which
appeared to serve various places, and also went to a
reservoir which I would understand would be an
allurement for the public and that reservoir had a
fishing club which operated. The police had also given
evidence that in the past they had seen hillwalkers and
vehicles parked and therefore it was my judgment that
the road was a road to which the public had on an
implied basis a right of access since no one appeared
to have prevented them."

F   The sheriff may have gone too far in affirming a
right of access in the public, but the facts certainly
showed that the road was used for access by the
public. Subsequently the sheriff stated: "I therefore
formed a conclusion that there was both walking and
driving by members of the public on the single track
tarmacadamed road and that it was lawfully performed
being allowed both expressly and implicitly by the
person or persons to whom the road belonged."

That account of the evidence which the sheriff gives
appeared to us to justify the conclusion that this road

was used by the public and thus was a public place
within the meaning of the statute.   G

The advocate depute also referred to *Paterson v
Ogilvy* where it had been observed that a place did not
cease to be a public place merely because it was fre-
quented by a special section of the public only. He also
founded upon *Brown v Braid* where it was observed
that the test which ought to be applied was whether
the place in question was a place on which members
of the public might be expected to be found and over
which they might be expected to be passing or over
which they were in use to have access.   H

Accepting that test, we are of opinion that despite
the existence of the signboard referred to in finding 3,
the fact of the matter is that having regard to the terms
of finding 4 members of the public might be expected
to be found upon this road. It was accordingly a public
place within the meaning of the Act.

For the foregoing reasons we shall of consent answer
question 2 in the negative, and we shall answer question 3 in the affirmative. It follows that the appeal is I
refused.

---

*Counsel for Appellant, P W Ferguson; Solicitors,
Drummond Miller, WS (for Peddie Smith & Maloco,
Dunfermline) — Counsel for Respondent, Macdonald,
QC, AD; Solicitor, J D Lowe, Crown Agent.*

                                              R F H

                                                          J

Cumming v Secretary of State for Scotland

EXTRA DIVISION

LORDS MURRAY, CULLEN AND WYLIE   K
5 JUNE 1992

*Town and country planning — Planning permission —
Application for outline permission — Full details of
application not given in application itself or in advertisement in local newspaper — Whether application and
advertisement required to give full details of application
— Whether grant of application ultra vires — Town and
Country Planning (General Development) (Scotland)
Order 1981 (SI 1981/830), arts 7 (5) (c) and 8, as L
amended.*

*Town and country planning — Planning permission —
Appeal — "Person aggrieved" — Local resident not
objecting to application — Application inadequately
described — Resident becoming aware of nature of
application prior to appeal by applicants but not appearing in appeal — Whether "person aggrieved" — Whether
entitled to appeal against grant of planning permission —
Town and Country Planning (Scotland) Act 1972 (c 52),
s 233 (1).*

An application for outline planning permission was
A lodged in which the development was described as the
"building of a roadside petrol station and service
area". The application was also advertised in the
Stirling Observer as "proposed development of a roadside petrol station and service area". The application
also had appended to it a location plan and a drawing
purporting to be the proposed layout for the development. The drawing showed that the application was in
fact for a separate petrol station for each of two roadside sites, together with a 40 bed lodge, a restaurant
B and two car parks with parking for 120 cars on the
north side of the road, and a further restaurant and car
park for 49 cars on the south side. A reporter was
appointed by the Secretary of State to consider the
applicants' appeal against the failure of the district
council to deal with the application. The reporter
granted outline planning permission for the
development.

A local resident and owner of an inn in the locality
then appealed the reporter's decision under s 233 of
C the Town and Country Planning (Scotland) Act 1972.
He had not objected to the original application or
made any representations to the reporter. The appellant argued that as the advertisement had made no
mention of roadside lodges or residential accommodation which the applicants proposed to build, the
regulations relating to advertisement had not been
complied with. He also argued that as the application
itself made no mention of these matters the reporter
had acted ultra vires in that he had granted planning
D permission for a development in respect of which no
application had been made. He argued that as a result
of the defects in the application and the advertisement
he had had no opportunity to make representations to
the reporter. He argued that he was a "person
aggrieved" within the meaning of s 233 (1) of the 1972
Act as he was one of the persons at whom the
advertisement had been directed, and the phrase had
been given a wide interpretation in decisions in
England and Scotland since 1961. The Secretary of
E State and the applicants argued that the application
had referred to a "service area" and that this was wide
enough to extend to overnight accommodation and the
provision of restaurants. Even if the reporter's
decision was ultra vires the appellant could not
challenge it unless he was a "person aggrieved". The
appellant was not a "person aggrieved" as he had been
notified in correspondence of the nature of the
application, had had the opportunity to object to the
application and had failed to do so.

F **Held,** (1) that any description in an application, and
advertisement of the application, for planning permission should be accurate, convey the substance of
what was applied for, and of itself give full and fair
notice to the planning authority, to interested parties
upon whom the application might be served, and to
the general public, of the grant which the applicant
hoped to obtain (p 234G-H); (2) that the description in
the application failed to comply with each of these
requirements and that therefore the reporter in granting the application was acting ultra vires (p 234F and

H-I); (3) that in determining whether the appellant
was a "person aggrieved" the central issue was G
whether he was genuinely deprived by the procedure
of an opportunity to make representations which
might (at least in his view) have affected the result
(p 235C-D); and (4) that as the application and advertisement failed to comply with the requirements the
appellant had been deprived of the full opportunity to
make representations and therefore was a "person
aggrieved" (p 235F-H); and appeal *allowed* and grant
of planning permission *quashed*.

———————————   H

Appeal from the Secretary of State for Scotland

Frederick L Cumming appealed to the Court of
Session under s 233 of the Town and Country Planning (Scotland) Act 1972 against the determination of
a reporter appointed by the Secretary of State for Scotland allowing an appeal by the trustees of Mrs P A
Stirling-Aird's 1988 accumulation and maintenance
trust against the failure of Stirling District Council to
give a decision on an application by them for outline I
planning permission.

Statutory provisions

The Town and Country Planning (Scotland) Act
1972 provides:

"233.—(1) If any person — . . . (b) is aggrieved by
any action on the part of the Secretary of State to
which this section applies and desires to question the
validity of that action, on the grounds that the action
is not within the powers of this Act, or that any of the J
relevant requirements have not been complied with in
relation to that action, he may, within six weeks from
the date on which the order is confirmed or the action
is taken, as the case may be, make an application to the
Court of Session under this section. . . .

"(3) This section applies to any such order as is
mentioned in subsection (2) of section 231 of this Act
(other than an order under section 203 (1) (a) of this
Act) and to any such action on the part of the Secretary
of State as is mentioned in subsection (3) of the said K
section 231."

The Town and Country Planning (General
Development) (Scotland) Order 1981, as amended,
provides:

"7.—(1) Subject to paragraph (4) of this Article an
applicant for planning permission or for approval of
reserved matters under Articles 8 and 9 shall serve on
any party who holds a notifiable interest in neighbouring land and who has not been served in terms of L
section 24 of the Act with a notice in the form set out
in Part IV of Schedule 3 (or in a form substantially to
the like effect) stating — (a) that the plans or drawings
relating to the application may be inspected in the
register kept by the planning authority in terms of
Article 17 (1); and (b) the address at which the plans
may be so inspected if different from the address of
the planning authority shown on the application;
and (c) the period within which the plans may be
inspected. . . .

"(5) . . . (c) where the application relates to development of one or more of the classes specified in Schedule 2 which classes are hereby prescribed in terms of section 23 (1) (b) of the Act for the purpose of publication as hereinafter mentioned; the planning authority shall publish a notice (containing similar information to that required to be included in a notice served in accordance with paragraph (1) of this Article) in a newspaper circulating in the locality in which the neighbouring land is situated. . . .

"8.—(1) An application to a planning authority for planning permission shall be made on a form issued by the planning authority and obtainable from that authority and shall include the particulars required by such form to be supplied and be accompanied by a plan sufficient to identify the land to which it relates and such other plans and drawings as are necessary to describe the development which is the subject of the application, together with such additional number of copies, not exceeding three, of the form and plans and drawings as may be required by the planning authority; and a planning authority may by a direction in writing addressed to the applicant require such further information as may be specified in the direction to be given to them in respect of an application for permission made to them under this paragraph, to enable them to determine that application.

"(2) Where an applicant so desires, an application may be made for outline planning permission and, where such permission is granted, the subsequent approval of the planning authority shall be required to such reserved matters as may be specified by the authority in granting such permission. The application shall be made on a form, as required by the preceding paragraph, shall describe the development to which it relates, shall be accompanied by a plan sufficient to identify the land to which it relates (together with such additional copies, not exceeding three, of the form and plan as may be required by the planning authority) and may contain such further information (if any) as to the proposal as the applicant desires: Provided that, where the authority are of the opinion that in the circumstances of the case the application ought not to be considered separately from the siting or the design or external appearance of the building, or the means of access thereto or the landscaping of the site, they shall within the period of one month from receipt of the application notify the applicant that they are unable to entertain it unless further details are submitted, specifying the matters as to which they require further information for the purpose of arriving at a decision in respect of the proposed development; and the applicant may either furnish the information so required or appeal to the Secretary of State within six months of receiving such notice, or such longer period as the Secretary of State may at any time allow, as if his application had been refused by the authority."

Cases referred to

Arsenal Football Club v Ende [1979] AC 1; [1977] 2 WLR 974; [1977] 2 All ER 267.

Att Gen of the Gambia v N'Jie [1961] AC 617; [1961] 2 WLR 845; [1961] 2 All ER 504.

Falkirk District Council v Secretary of State for Scotland, 1991 SLT 553.

Simpson v Edinburgh Corporation, 1960 SLT (Notes) 65; 1960 SC 313.

Strathclyde Regional Council v Secretary of State for Scotland (No 2), 1990 SLT 149.

Turner v Secretary of State for the Environment (1974) 28 P & CR 123.

The appellant tabled the following grounds of appeal:

Ground I. The application for planning permission to which the foregoing determination applies describes the proposed development as the building of a roadside petrol station and service area. In particular it does not mention or specify roadside lodges or other form of residential accommodation. No reference is made to a roadside lodge or other form of accommodation in the statutory advertisement relating to the planning application which appeared in the *Stirling Observer*. . . . Had the appellant known that a roadside lodge or other form of residential accommodation would be considered by the planning authority as part of the application he would have objected to the said application. . . .

Ground II. The appeal which resulted in the foregoing determination was conducted by way of written submissions. It was not advertised by the respondent. The respondent knew or ought to have known of the advertisement by the local authority. The appellant, as an interested party, had no opportunity to be represented or to make representations in connection with said appeal to which the foregoing determination relates.

Ground III. Notwithstanding the absence of notice in both of the said planning application and relative advertisement, the respondent's reporter purported to consider a plan which was submitted to him and which showed inter alia a roadside lodge providing 40 bedrooms. He thereupon granted outline planning permission for a petrol filling station and service area on two parcels of ground on either side and at the north end of the bypass at Dunblane . . . subject to certain conditions.

Ground IV. In the foregoing circumstances the appellant is aggrieved by the said decision. The requirements of the Town and Country Planning (Scotland) Act 1972, and the regulations made thereunder relating to advertisement, were not complied with. The appellant has been substantially prejudiced by said failure. Separatim the respondent has acted ultra vires. He has purported to grant planning permission for a development in respect of which no application was made. Accordingly the said decision should be quashed.

The pleas in law for the first respondent (the Secretary of State) were as follows:

(1) The appeal being incompetent in respect that the

appellant is not an aggrieved person within the meaning of the Town and Country Planning (Scotland) Act 1972, s 233 (1) (b), should be dismissed.

(2) The grounds of appeal being irrelevant et separatim lacking in specification the appeal should be dismissed.

(3) The said decision having been validly made within the powers of the Act and there having been no failure to comply with a relevant requirement to the prejudice of the appellant the appeal should be refused.

The pleas in law for the second respondents (the applicants) were as follows:

(1) The appellant not being a person aggrieved and lacking title and interest in the appeal the appeal should be dismissed.

(2) The appellant's averments being irrelevant et separatim lacking in specification the appeal should be refused.

Appeal

The appeal was heard by an Extra Division on 19 and 20 March 1992.

On 5 June 1992 the court *allowed* the appeal and *quashed* the decision of the reporter.

The following opinion of the court was delivered by Lord Murray:

OPINION OF THE COURT.—The present case is an appeal under the provisions of s 233 of the Town and Country Planning (Scotland) Act 1972 against a determination of a reporter appointed by the Secretary of State for Scotland dated 26 July 1990 whereby he sustained an appeal by the trustees of Mrs P A Stirling-Aird's 1988 accumulation and maintenance trust against the failure of Stirling District Council to give a decision on an application by them for outline planning permission for development of land at the north end of the road bypass at Dunblane. The appellant is a local resident and the owner of the Red Comyn inn in the centre of Dunblane. The Secretary of State and the said trustees are respectively the first and second respondents. The appellant was not a party to proceedings in respect of the planning application. He did not object to the application while it was before the district council for decision nor did he make representations to the Secretary of State after the second respondents had appealed to him.

The second respondents' planning application was dated 28 June 1989 and related, as the statutory form in process shows, to 3.14 ha of agricultural land for development described as "building of a roadside petrol station and service area". It is common ground between the parties, for reasons set out later in this opinion, that this application required to be advertised in a local newspaper. An advertisement in the following terms was published on 19 July 1989 in the *Stirling Observer* at the instance of the district council: "North end, Dunblane bypass, by Duthieston House,

Dunblane — proposed development of a roadside petrol station and service area."

The present application was the first of a number of applications for planning permission on which comments were invited within 21 days along with information that details of the application could be seen at an address in Stirling between certain hours on weekdays. The heading of the whole advertisement was: "Will YOU be affected when these decisions are made?" The reporter dealt with the appeal by way of written submissions and an accompanied inspection of the appeal site and surroundings on 20 March 1990. In paras 1 and 2 of his decision letter the reporter describes the appeal site as being two parcels of ground on either side of the bypass on the northern outskirts of Dunblane. He identified three determining issues: (1) whether policy ENP07 of the Stirling-Alloa structure plan should be applied; (2) whether policy 10.2 of the Dunblane area local plan, and SDD circular 24 of 1985, would be contravened to a material extent; and (3) whether the effect of the appeal proposal upon the appearance and character of its surroundings was sufficiently adverse to justify a refusal of planning permission. In paras 4 and 5 respectively he reaches conclusions favourable to the application on the first and second issues which he had identified. In para 6 he deals with the third issue in the following terms: "Turning now to the third issue, I agree that the wooded knoll upon which Duthieston House is situated is an attractive natural feature at the northern entrance to Dunblane. I appreciate also that petrol filling station complexes often appear garish and alien to the appearance and character of their surroundings. Nevertheless taking into account that they are necessary features of the national road network, that they are often to be found in the countryside remote from towns and villages, and that the appeal sites are not within an area designated as, for example, green belt or an area of great landscape value within which there may have been a presumption against most forms of development, I think that this is insufficient reason of itself to justify a refusal of planning permission. Furthermore, much of the site on the south side of the bypass is some 1-2 metres lower than the carriageway of that road. For this reason, provided the proposed development avoids the higher ground near the south-west and north-west boundaries of the site, and incorporates the planting of trees, it should not be unacceptably conspicuous. Similarly, the site to the north-west side of the bypass is large enough to include earth mounding and substantial areas of tree planting. It is also well screened from the south-west and south by high ground on the north-west side of the cutting through which the road passes."

After dealing with certain specific qualifications the reporter continues in para 10: "For the above reasons, and in the exercise of the powers delegated to me, I hereby sustain this appeal and grant outline planning permission for a petrol filling station and service area on two parcels of ground on either side, and at the north end, of the bypass at Dunblane in accordance

A with application no N/89/272 of 28 June 1989 subject" to seven conditions which the reporter set forth at the end of para 10. The fourth of these conditions was in the following terms: "The proposed lodge shall not exceed two storeys in height and all other buildings shall be of a single storey."

It was agreed by the parties that the original application form had appended to it a location plan (as envisaged by the relevant regulations) and a drawing purporting to be the proposed layout for "petrol stations". The latter, however, in addition to showing

B a separate petrol station for each of the two roadside sites also shows a lodge (40 bed), a restaurant, and two separate car parks, one for 72 spaces and the other for 48 spaces, all on the north side; and on the south side, a restaurant and car park with 49 spaces. It is also common ground that the reporter's decision letter makes no mention of the lodge, restaurants or designated car parks except in condition 4.

The appellant tabled four grounds of appeal which

C are set out below: [his Lordship then quoted the terms of the grounds of appeal set out supra and continued:]

In their answers the respondents respectively made various admissions of fact demonstrating that there are few contentious issues of fact in the appeal.

The pleas in law for the first respondent were as follows: [his Lordship quoted the terms of the pleas in law for the first respondent, followed by those of the

D second respondents, and continued:]

For the appellant it was submitted that on the face of it the decision letter had granted planning permission going beyond the scope of the application by including a motel or other residential accommodation not mentioned in the application. The press advertisement issued by the district council repeated the words of the application and made no reference to residential accommodation. If more had been granted than was sought the Secretary of State must have acted ultra

E vires. Two questions arose: (1) what was applied for by the developers?; (2) what planning permission did the Secretary of State give?

The first question took one to the application itself which was by statutory form in terms of the Town and Country (General Development) (Scotland) Order 1981 (SI 1981/830, as amended by SI 1984/237), art 8. The completed entries on the form determined the subject matter of the application. It was also necessary

F that there should be a location plan to determine the place and further documents and drawings could be lodged with the application to describe the development. But it was plain that neither the location plan nor any other document could extend the scope of the application beyond what the form stated the development to be. For the present grant of planning permission to have been competent the application in the form should have been for petrol filling stations, service areas, motel, restaurants and designated parking areas. This was supported by reference to art 3 (5) (c) of and to the Schedule to the Town and

Country Planning (Use Classes) (Scotland) Order 1989 (SI 1989/147). Applications for the sale of G vehicle fuel were sui generis but the planning permission granted here included use classes 1, 3 and 12 in addition. The latter were not mentioned in the application form submitted by the second respondents.

By art 2 of the Town and Country Planning (General Development) (Scotland) Amendment Order 1984 a new art 7 was inserted in the 1981 Order which, by subpara (5) (c), required publication in a local newspaper of "similar information to that H required" for service on a party with a notifiable interest under art 7 (1) which refers inter alia to service of a copy of the planning application. This requirement applied because the application related to development falling within Sched 2 ("bad neighbourhood" development). Publication by advertisement was also required by reason of art 12 (1) of the 1981 General Development Order and para 2 (a) of the direction of 1981 (contrary to the development plan).

For the foregoing reasons it was contended that the I Secretary of State had exceeded his powers in the grant of planning permission made. Indeed it was difficult to see how this contention could be resisted.

However the appellant had to demonstrate that he was entitled to challenge the vires of the decision in an appeal under s 233 of the 1972 Act. It was plain that the appellant as a local resident and owner of an hotel in the centre of Dunblane had an interest in the development of residential/restaurant accommodation J in the locality. His interest might not seem adversely affected by the application as advertised in the *Stirling Observer*. The development could be cast as a bad neighbourhood development for the locality in terms of s 23 (1) of the 1972 Act and para 15 of Sched 2 to the 1984 Order. This was not disputed by the first respondent nor did the second respondents dispute that the newspaper advertisement made no reference to proposed residential accommodation.

The foregoing issue depended on whether the appel- K lant was a "person aggrieved" within the meaning of s 233 (1) of the Act, which was the second main issue in the appeal. It was submitted that he was so qualified by being one of the persons at whom the public advertisement had been directed and who was opposed to the development. If the development were nonetheless granted planning permission he would be "aggrieved" by that decision. Since the introduction of planning legislation the courts had moved from a strict and legalistic interpretation of the words "person L aggrieved" to a meaning more in accord with ordinary language.

The turning point in the courts' interpretation of "person aggrieved" was the Privy Council case of *Att Gen of the Gambia v N'Jie*. At [1961] AC, p 634, in delivering the advice of the Privy Council, Lord Denning said: "The words 'person aggrieved' are of wide import and should not be subjected to a restrictive interpretation. They do not include, of course, a mere busybody who is interfering in things which do not concern him: but they do include a person who has a genuine grievance because an order has been made which prejudicially affects his interests."

This opinion contrasted sharply with that of Lord Guest in the Outer House case of *Simpson v Edinburgh Corporation.* The Scottish courts did not follow that restrictive approach in the case of *Strathclyde Regional Council v Secretary of State for Scotland (No 2)* where the Inner House held that a regional council which was not party to a district council planning issue but had made representations at the inquiry held was a "person aggrieved" within the meaning of s 233 (1). The same trend was illustrated in the case of *Turner v Secretary of State for the Environment* where Ackner J (as he then was) said, at pp 138-139: "I see no merit in the proposition that a person who has merely been given notice of the existence of the inquiry at the request of and not by the requirement of the Secretary of State and whose right to attend and make his representations has resulted from the exercise of the inspector's discretion should be obliged to sit by and accept the decision, which, *ex hypothesi*, is bad in law. I can see no compelling matter of policy which requires this form of silence to be imposed on a person who has, again *ex hypothesi*, a clear grievance in law. On the other hand I see good reason, so long as the grounds of appeal are so restricted, for ensuring that any person who, in the ordinary sense of the word, is aggrieved by the decision, and certainly any person who has attended and made representations at the inquiry, should have the right to establish in the courts that the decision is bad in law because it is *ultra vires* or for some other good reason."

It would be wrong to give "person aggrieved" a restrictive interpretation when it was an objective of the planning legislation that the public should be made aware of planning proposals and that they should be given an opportunity of making representations about them: see *Falkirk District Council v Secretary of State for Scotland* at p 555D. There were no set limits to the persons who could be heard at a public planning inquiry. It followed that a person who could have made such representations but was not alerted by an inadequate description in the application and newspaper advertisement should not be rejected as a "person aggrieved". The wrong description of the proposed development had misled the appellant and deprived him of an opportunity of making representations against it. The action of the Secretary of State in granting planning permission should be quashed by the court under s 233 (4) (b).

Counsel for the first respondent indicated that he would deal first with the competency point and then turn to vires. He accepted the effect of the decisions illustrated by *Turner*. Nor did he, under reference to *Arsenal Football Club v Ende*, maintain that a "person aggrieved" had to be hit in the pocket. What could be drawn from the cases was that a person aggrieved had to have a genuine grievance and be prejudicially affected. The appellant here did not qualify on either score. His grievance was not genuine. By letter dated 19 February 1990 he had been informed that the application in question was under appeal and that it involved residential and restaurant accommodation as well as petrol filling facilities. He had full notice then of what was involved and an opportunity to make representations of his own to the reporter who made no decision on the appeal for some months thereafter. The appellant was not deprived of an opportunity to make representations on the merits of the application. The opportunity was there and he did not take it. If he had made representations to the first respondent he would have been a "person aggrieved" within the meaning of *Turner*.

In the print of his grounds of appeal the appellant did not present himself as a local resident concerned to uphold the district plan in the general interest. What he said was that his economic interest would be adversely affected. Recognising that this was not a sound planning argument, he was now claiming to have been deprived of an opportunity to present an argument on amenity. It was difficult to see what threat there was to amenity in the provision of petrol filling stations and associated service area facilities on a major road. The *Stirling Observer* advertisement had given the appellant fair notice of a proposal with consequences for amenity which was contrary to the district plan. Yet he did nothing about it. Even now the appellant made no point on the merits of the district plan. The appellant had failed to demonstrate prejudice and he had failed to demonstrate that he had a genuine grievance. Accordingly he should not be held to be a "person aggrieved" within the sense of *Att Gen for the Gambia* and *Turner*.

As regards the complaint of ultra vires the appellant gave this an isolated mention (preceded by the word "separatim") as follows: "Separatim the respondent has acted ultra vires. He has purported to grant planning permission for a development in respect of which no application was made. Accordingly the said decision should be quashed."

Yet by the time when he received the letter from Stirling District Council dated 19 February 1990 it had been confirmed to the appellant that a motel and restaurant were under consideration and that the application was being appealed. Means of full knowledge of the application and the proposal were then available to the appellant. The fact that a decision was ultra vires (if it was) did not confer aggrieved person status on anybody who cared to assert that. The appellant had to be aggrieved in the sense of having been aggrieved by the decision itself, whatever its vires. He had to have a genuine complaint that the decision was wrong. The appellant's actual complaints on vires in the printed record were minimal. They were not supported by relevant averments. The application was for roadside petrol filling and associated service area facilities. The only point in the grant of planning permission on which the appellant could put his finger was the reference in condition 4 of para 10 relating to the proposed lodge. If the appellant was right, then this condition was inept, but that was all.

It was accepted that under art 8 (1) and (2) of the 1981 Regulations a plan accompanying an application for planning permission could not expand its scope. But it could explain or illustrate words used in the description. For road users today the facilities to be expected in a roadside service area were widespread and diverse. The Roads (Scotland) Act 1984 defined "service area" in a manner which covered the present application in ss 119 (2) and 164 (3) (c). Provision of overnight accommodation and restaurants was within the scope of roadside service area facilities for the travelling public. The appeal should be refused.

Counsel for the second respondents pressed similar arguments to those of the first respondent against the appellant. Particular emphasis was laid on behalf of the second respondents on the state of the appellant's knowledge of the planning application and its progress. A professional adviser for the appellant had sent a fax letter to Stirling District Council dated 16 February 1990 which sought "confirmation on the status of the application for a new motel on the outskirts of Dunblane". In response the letter dated 19 February 1990 which had been referred to was sent to the appellant. The appellant was accordingly aware in a general sense that the proposal involved residential accommodation, yet he took no steps to make representations even when that was confirmed. Counsel for the second respondents also urged strongly that the concept of roadside service area facilities reflected in the Roads (Scotland) Act 1984 was one which was well known to road users and to the public generally. It was well known and accepted that service area facilities extended to overnight accommodation and provision of restaurants. The planning application made by these respondents disclosed all these elements to anyone who cared to inspect the form and its accompanying documents. The attack on vires was without foundation and the appeal should be refused.

We take up first the question of whether the reporter's decision was ultra vires as, in our opinion, this is the easier of the two main issues to resolve. There was no real dispute in the end of the day that the information entered in the form under the heading "description" determined, as a matter of law, the content of a planning application. Its scope could not be extended by the location plan or any ancillary document but these could serve to illustrate or to explain the terminology of the description. The argument for both respondents was that the description, illustrated and explained by the accompanying ancillary documents, covered what was granted by the reporter. We do not doubt that the reporter was able by perusal of all these documents to understand the grant which the applicants intended or hoped to obtain from the application. However the critical point is whether what was contained in the accompanying ancillary documents went beyond the scope of the "description" of the planning application. We have no doubt that it did. In our opinion the reporter wrongly allowed the application to extend beyond the proper scope of the description. It is thus our conclusion that the reporter's decision was ultra vires.

The description in the application is plainly material to the question of vires. Its importance, so far as the public is concerned, lies in the fact that the planning authority will use the description, as they did in the present case, in the required advertisement and in council business. We consider that the description, whether it is long or short, should be accurate, convey the substance of what is applied for and of itself give full and fair notice to the planning authority, to interested parties upon whom the application may be served and to the general public, of the grant which the applicant hopes to obtain.

In our opinion the description in the present application falls at the first hurdle. It is not accurate in that the application was intended to be for two petrol filling stations, not one, and that it related not to a single site, but to adjacent sites on opposite sides of the Dunblane bypass. More fundamentally it does not convey the substance of what was sought, which was the provision of comprehensive roadside service facilities, including provision of fuel, for travellers in both southbound and northbound directions. We do not think that the description was apt to give fair notice to those concerned with the application or to the public generally that something of the nature of comprehensive roadside service areas were in contemplation. Indeed when the first entry in the *Stirling Observer* advertisement which related to the present application is compared with the fourth entry relating to a proposed interpretation centre, petrol filling station, business/technology park, 100 bedroom hotel, etc, the meagre description of the present development could well mislead the reader or at least put him off his guard. In short in our opinion the description given does not convey in any accurate or realistic sense the extent of the grant which the applicants had in mind.

The issue of locus standi is more difficult than vires and not simply because of the transition which the courts have made from a restrictive interpretation of the words "person aggrieved" to a more liberal one following the case of *Att Gen for the Gambia v N'Jie.* It was argued strongly before us on behalf of the first respondent that, to be a person aggrieved, there were two requirements, namely, that the person must have a genuine grievance and be prejudiced by the decision. It was said against the appellant that it could certainly be said that he was prejudiced economically by the decision, on which the emphasis was laid in his grounds of appeal, but that this was not a proper planning consideration. His remaining grounds of opposition on the merits related to amenity on which the appellant's averments were thin and lacking in specification. The appellant had not succeeded in making out that he was prejudiced in the sense of being adversely affected in any material way. We consider that while there is force in this criticism it goes too far. It is generally accepted that it is a cornerstone of planning legislation that planning proposals and decisions should be in the public domain and this requires the public to be properly informed and given an opportunity, if they consider that they are adversely affected, to make appropriate representations about it. Such representations, we conceive, may extend over an extremely wide spectrum, from precisely articulated planning objections at one end to simple abhorrence of the proposal at the other. In that context it hardly seems appropriate to introduce from formal pleading concepts such as relevancy so as to exclude objections in limine. The practice of reporters in exercising their discretion at planning inquiries widely so as to give an opportunity to all or most who wish to make representations to be heard or to have their letter considered, appears to be appropriate. In short it must be for the objector himself to decide whether he is adversely affected by a planning proposal and to take appropriate action as a result. His response need not be confined to making formal or informal representations at a planning inquiry. He may seek to marshal public opinion against the proposal. He may organise a petition against it or take other similar steps. A member of the public may be deprived of this opportunity as well as that of making representations in the planning process if accurate information about planning proposals is not made public. In this sense we consider that counsel for the first respondent went too far asserting that the present appellant had failed to show that he was prejudiced by the decision.

The question of the genuineness of his grievance is, however, much more delicately balanced. The attack on this aspect was stressed strongly on behalf of both respondents. The central issue, it appears to us, was whether the appellant was genuinely deprived by the procedure in the present planning application of an opportunity to make representations which might (at least in his view) have affected the result. On the fact of it it is difficult to resist the contentions for the respondents that by February 1990 the appellant had available to him all the means of knowledge to enable him to assess the true nature of the application and to make representations to the Secretary of State, who still had the matter before him, on the merits of the applications and indeed on the issue of vires. He did not avail himself of this opportunity. Is this necessarily fatal to his status as a person aggrieved? Senior counsel for the appellant urged that it was not. On any view he had been informed belatedly and indirectly by the planning authority what the application was and that it was under appeal before the Secretary of State. He was not told expressly of his right to make representations in the matter to the Secretary of State. He might well have taken the view, with or without legal advice, that the disparity between the advertised description in the application and the development for which planning permission was said to be under consideration was so great that the grant was unlikely to be made. But we doubt whether it would be sufficient for the appellant to rely on the foregoing alone. However, looking at the matter in a somewhat broader context, we consider that, in the peculiar circumstances of the present case, there is the feature that the description of the development in the planning application form was so inadequate as to mislead or put a member of the public off his guard about what

its real purpose was. The appellant puts himself plainly in that position. If so, it follows that, because of the faulty description, he was given less than a full opportunity at the time of the advertisement in the *Stirling Observer* to comment or make representations to the planning authority about the proposed development within the 21 days mentioned in the notice. There seems no good reason to us why the appellant should not be accepted as genuine about that.

If then we are right about the inadequacy of the description, in the application and advertisement, then the appellant has been deprived of the full opportunity which should have been open to him under the planning procedures to make representations about the proposal. The issue is a narrow one but we are satisfied, in the special circumstances of the present case, that the appellant does have the status of a "person aggrieved". In our opinion the planning permission sought and granted went far beyond the description which was in law determinative of the scope of the application. As an aggrieved person the appellant is entitled to found upon this fundamental defect in purported grant of planning permission in this case.

In the foregoing circumstances the appeal succeeds and the action of the Secretary of State in granting planning permission falls to be quashed.

―――――――

Counsel for Appellant, Hardie, QC, Boyd; Solicitors, Drummond Miller, WS — Counsel for First Respondent, Moynihan; Solicitor, R Brodie, Solicitor to the Secretary of State for Scotland — Counsel for Second Respondents, Steele, P W Ferguson; Solicitors, Dundas & Wilson, CS.

D A K

(NOTE)

Wilson v Imrie Engineering Services Ltd

OUTER HOUSE

TEMPORARY JUDGE T G COUTTS, QC

24 JULY 1992

Process — Proof — Reopening of proof — Action of damages for personal injuries — Second defenders' proof proceeding and closing before first defenders' proof — Pursuer abandoning against first defenders before first defenders' proof opened — Whether second defenders to be allowed to reopen proof to lead evidence of medical witness who was to have been witness for first defenders.

At a proof against two defenders, the second defenders led their evidence ahead of the first

A defenders because the first defenders' only witness was not available. After the second defenders closed their case, the pursuer abandoned against the first defenders. The second defenders sought to reopen their proof to adduce the evidence of the first defenders' witness, a consultant orthopaedic surgeon.

Held, that justice demanded that the second defenders be allowed to reopen their proof; and motion *granted.*

B Archibald Wilson raised an action of damages against, first, his employers Imrie Engineering Services Ltd and, second, a firm of contractors who had carried out work as subcontractors to his employers. The case proceeded to a proof and, on the third day of the proof, the pursuer abandoned his case against the first defenders. The second defenders' proof had been led and closed by that time but, because the first defenders' witness had not been avail-

C able, the first defenders' proof had not been commenced. The second defenders then sought to reopen their proof to enable them to lead the evidence of the consultant orthopaedic surgeon who was to have been the first defenders' sole witness. The pursuer opposed the reopening of the proof. In allowing the second defenders to reopen their proof the temporary judge (T G Coutts, QC) said:

"A procedural difficulty occurred on the morning of

D the third day of the proof in this action of reparation in which the pursuer sued both his employers and the firm of contractors in respect of injuries he had received on 10 October 1985. At that time the pursuer, whose case against his employers, the first defenders, had been restricted at procedure roll to an allegation of breach of statutory duty in respect of the alleged failure to make and keep safe the pursuer's place of work, abandoned his action against the first defenders. On the previous day the pursuer had closed

E his case and, because the first defenders' only witness, an orthopaedic consultant, was not to be available until the next day, by agreement, the second defenders led their only witness, their managing director. At the end of his evidence counsel for the second defenders closed his case. When the pursuer abandoned against the first defenders, counsel for the second defenders sought to have his proof reopened in order that he might lead the said medical witness who was then present and able to give evidence. He stated that he had anticipated that the first defenders would lead the

F medical evidence and that he had arranged with the counsel for the first defenders to adopt it so that it would be both defenders' medical evidence. He frankly stated that he had had no idea that the pursuer might abandon against the first defenders and that if he had thought of such an eventuality, the second defenders' case would not have been closed. Counsel for the pursuer objected to a reopening of the proof, saying that he was no party to any arrangement about medical evidence and that if the defenders had closed their case that should be the end of the matter. He

cited Maclaren, *Court of Session Practice,* p 562.

G Counsel for the second defenders, citing the same page in Maclaren and *Roy v Carron Co,* 1967 SLT (Notes) 84, submitted that it was competent for the proof to be reopened. In that case Lord Cameron said: 'I do not doubt that it is competent to apply for leave to tender an additional witness after a proof has been led and that the court, if satisfied that the ends of justice require it, may, on sufficiently weighty grounds, grant such a motion but the occasions must be rare when such a motion can properly be made and the grounds in its support weighty'. The cases cited in Maclaren

H were all special cases of a single defender in actions of affiliation and aliment and added nothing to the dictum above quoted.

"I regarded the matter as one of discretion which I exercised in favour of allowing the second defenders to reopen their proof and lead the medical consultant as a witness. It appeared to me, primarily, that the interests of justice demanded that this be done since it was plain throughout the proof that there was a con-flict of medical evidence upon which it was anticipated

I the court would adjudicate; and, secondly, having regard to the particular circumstances in which the counsel for the second defenders had closed his case, I could accept that he was under a genuine misappre-hension of the course the proof would take. At worst he made a mistake. Further, counsel for the second defenders would have been perfectly entitled to insist upon an adjournment of the proof and to decline to interpose his evidence before that of the first defenders, but all parties had agreed that this could be

J done. In the circumstances of this case it seemed to me that the counsel for the second defenders had merely intended to indicate that his evidence was at an end and not that the whole of the defenders' case, in a two defender case, was closed. I considered it unfortunate that the pursuer, by the timing of his abandonment, sought to gain an incidental advantage by precluding the defenders' medical evidence being available to the court and I did not think that that was in the interests of justice. I would add, however, that the abandon-

K ment of the case against the first defenders by the pursuer was wholly justified on the evidence which had been led and that counsel's action in abandoning was entirely proper. He was correct in adopting the view that he could not succeed against the first defenders."

Counsel for Pursuer, Ogg; Solicitors, J & A Hastie, SSC — Counsel for Second Defenders, Macfadyen, QC; L *Solicitors, Simpson & Marwick, WS.*

[After the proof was concluded the temporary judge held that the pursuer had failed to prove his case and granted decree of absolvitor.]

C H

K v HM Advocate

A HIGH COURT OF JUSTICIARY

THE LORD JUSTICE CLERK (ROSS),
LORDS CAMERON OF LOCHBROOM AND
GRIEVE

22 MARCH 1991

*Justiciary — Sentence — Competency — Child sentenced
to be detained without limit of time — Whether sentence
available other than in case of murder conviction —*
B *Whether requirement to "specify" period satisfied —
Criminal Procedure (Scotland) Act 1975 (c 21), s 206.*

Section 206 of the Criminal Procedure (Scotland)
Act 1975 provides that subject to s 205 [conviction for
murder], in relation to a child the court "may sentence
him to be detained for a period which it shall specify
in the sentence".

A boy aged 12 was convicted of culpable homicide.
The trial judge sentenced him to be detained without
C limit of time. An appeal against sentence was taken in
which the competency of such a disposal under s 206
was challenged.

Held, (1) that it did not follow from the provisions
of s 205 that the court was fettered in the sentences
which could be imposed under s 206 in cases other
than murder (p 237K-L); (2) that the sentence was
competent because it was one specifying a period for
the detention (pp 237L-238A); and appeal *refused*.

D ————————————

Indictment

R J K was indicted at the instance of the rt hon the
Lord Fraser of Carmyllie, Her Majesty's Advocate, on
a charge of murder of a child aged three. He pled not
guilty and proceeded to trial before Lord Sutherland
and a jury in the High Court at Glasgow. The accused
was convicted of culpable homicide and sentenced to
be detained without limit of time.

E   The accused appealed to the High Court by note of
appeal against sentence.

Statutory provisions

The Criminal Procedure (Scotland) Act 1975, as
amended, provides:

"205.— . . . (2) Where a person convicted of murder
is under the age of 18 years he shall not be sentenced
to imprisonment for life but to be detained without
F limit of time and shall be liable to be detained in such
place, and under such conditions, as the Secretary of
State may direct.

"206. Subject to section 205 of this Act, where a
child is convicted and the court is of the opinion that
no other method of dealing with him is appropriate, it
may sentence him to be detained for a period which it
shall specify in the sentence; and the child shall
during that period be liable to be detained in such
place and on such conditions as the Secretary of State
may direct."

The appeal was heard before the High Court on 22
March 1991.   G

Eo die the court *refused* the appeal.

The following opinion of the court was delivered by
the Lord Justice Clerk (Ross):

OPINION OF THE COURT.—The appellant is
R J K who was convicted after trial in the High Court
at Glasgow of culpable homicide. He is 12 years of age
and having heard counsel and considered the various   H
reports placed before him, the trial judge sentenced
him to be detained without limit of time. The minute
in the book of adjournal records the sentence as
follows: "Sentence the accused [R J K] to be detained
without limit of time in terms of ss 205/206 of the
Criminal Procedure (Scotland) Act 1975". He has
appealed against sentence and today on his behalf
counsel has raised as a preliminary matter the question
of whether that sentence was competent.

The first ground of appeal is to the effect that the   I
sentence was incompetent. It draws attention to
the fact that s 205 of the Act of 1975 applies only
to the crime of murder and it is submitted on behalf
of the appellant that the words "without limit of time"
are not a period specified in the sentence. Today
counsel has repeated that submission and has contended that a sentence imposed in terms of s 206 must
be for a definite period and he maintains that the sentence imposed in the present case does not meet that
requirement. Section 206 (1) provides as follows: [his   J
Lordship quoted the terms of s 206 (1) and continued:]

The advocate depute in reply to counsel's submissions drew attention to the opening words of that subsection with their reference to s 205. Section 205 is
dealing with the punishment for murder and s 205 (2)
provides as follows: [his Lordship quoted its terms
and continued:] The advocate depute has pointed out
that with reference to a person under the age of 18   K
years where he has been convicted of murder there is
a mandatory sentence, namely detention without limit
of time. That is the equivalent of life imprisonment in
the case of a person over that age. The words
"detained without limit of time" in s 205 (2) do not
appear in s 206, but we agree with the advocate depute
that the purpose of s 205 (2) was to impose a mandatory sentence in the case of murder and that it does not
follow that the absence of these words in s 206 was
intended to impose some fetter or limit upon the sent-   L
ence which could be imposed in other cases.

Having regard to the language used in s 206, the
question must be whether the sentence which was
imposed in this case met the requirements of that subsection. That in turn raises the question of whether
what the court did was to sentence the appellant to be
detained for a period which it specified. We have come
to the conclusion that the order which the trial judge
made in this case was a competent order because in
ordering that the appellant should be detained without

limit of time, he was specifying a period for the deten-
A tion. The order was that the appellant was to be
detained for an unlimited period but it was still a
period which was being specified for his detention.
That being so we are satisfied that the sentence was a
proper one. The only other comment which may be
made in this connection is this, that in his report to us,
the trial judge in giving us the benefit of his opinion
upon the matter of competency has drawn attention to
provisions of s 206 (2) of the Act of 1975. It appears
however, that that provision was repealed by para 12
of Sched 2 to the Prisons (Scotland) Act 1989 and
B accordingly the opinion at which we have arrived does
not depend to any extent upon the provisions of any
of the other subsections of s 206 which have been
repealed. For the foregoing reasons the first ground of
appeal put forward by counsel for the accused is held
to be unsound.

[The court then considered and rejected the ground
of appeal that sentence was excessive.]

C

*Counsel for Appellant, Findlay, QC; Solicitors,
Pairman Miller & Murray, WS — Counsel for Respon-
dent, Macdonald, QC, AD; Solicitor, I Dean, Crown
Agent.*

S D D N

D

Council of the Law Society of Scotland v McKinnie

FIRST DIVISION
THE LORD PRESIDENT (HOPE),
LORDS ALLANBRIDGE AND McDONALD
8 MAY 1991

E *Bankruptcy — Sequestration — Solicitor — Judicial
factor appointed to solicitor's estates — Factor authorised
to divide sum at credit of client account among clients —
Solicitor's estates then sequestrated and permanent
trustee appointed — Whether funds at credit of client
account vested in trustee — Whether accountant of court
entitled to order judicial factor to hand over funds to
trustee — Solicitors (Scotland) Act 1980 (c 46), s 42 —
Bankruptcy (Scotland) Act 1985 (c 66), s 33 (1).*

*Judicial factor — Factor appointed to solicitor's estates —
F Factor authorised to divide sum at credit of client account
among clients — Solicitor's estates then sequestrated and
permanent trustee appointed — Whether funds at credit
of client account vested in trustee — Whether accountant
of court entitled to order judicial factor to hand over
funds to trustee — Solicitors (Scotland) Act 1980 (c 46),
s 42 — Bankruptcy (Scotland) Act 1985 (c 66), s 33 (1).*

*Solicitor — Judicial factor appointed to solicitor's estates
— Factor authorised to divide sum at credit of client
account among clients — Solicitor's estates then sequestrated and permanent trustee appointed — Whether funds*

*at credit of client account vested in trustee — Whether
accountant of court entitled to order judicial factor to* G
*hand over funds to trustee — Solicitors (Scotland) Act
1980 (c 46), s 42 — Bankruptcy (Scotland) Act 1985
(c 66), s 33 (1).*

Section 42 of the Solicitors (Scotland) Act 1980 provides, in the event of the sequestration of a solicitor,
the granting by him of a trust deed for behoof of
creditors or the appointment of a judicial factor on his
estate, for clients' funds being divided proportionately
among the solicitor's clients according to the respective sums received by him in the course of his practice H
on their behalf and remaining due by him to them.

Section 31 (1) of the Bankruptcy (Scotland) Act 1985
vests the sequestrated estates of a debtor in the permanent trustee, and s 33 (1) excludes from vesting
property held on trust by the debtor for any other
person.

Following a petition at the instance of the Council
of the Law Society of Scotland, a judicial factor was
appointed to the estates of a solicitor whereby the I
factor was authorised, inter alia: "to make payments
from or out of any bank account or sum or sums
lodged on deposit receipt in the name of [the solicitor
or his firm], subject always to the provisions of s 42
of the Solicitors (Scotland) Act 1980 and to divide the
sum at credit of the client account of the said [solicitor
or his firm] among his clients in terms of said s 42". The
solicitor's estate was subsequently sequestrated and a
permanent trustee was appointed. As at the date of
sequestration those estates vested in the permanent J
trustee for the benefit of the solicitor's creditors in
terms of s 31 (1) of the Bankruptcy (Scotland) Act
1985.

In the audit report to the judicial factor on the first
account of his interim intromissions, the accountant of
court noted that the factor had handed over to the permanent trustee only £206.37 and that he had retained
in his own hands all sums at credit of the solicitor's
client account. The accountant ordered that the factor
make over to the trustee all the clients' funds in K
accordance with the usual practice. The factor
objected to this instruction. The accountant of court
reported the matter to the Inner House with a view to
obtaining a judicial decision as to who was the proper
party to administer the funds held on the client
account.

Held, (1) that sums held at credit of the client
account were fiduciary in nature and accordingly s 33
(1) (b) of the 1985 Act operated to exclude them from L
the property which vested in the permanent trustee (p
240I); and (2) that the appropriate officer to attend to
the task of dividing those sums was the judicial factor,
and even if the solicitor were then sequestrated or
granted a trust deed for creditors, any clients' money
should remain with the judicial factor for division in
terms of s 42 (1) of the 1980 Act (p 241B-D); and
accountant's instruction *reversed* and audit and report
remitted to accountant of court to consider additional
matters.

Report by accountant of court

A   Following upon an application by the Council of the Law Society of Scotland, a judicial factor was appointed to the estates of a solicitor, Iain James Walker McKinnie, trading as McKinnie & Co, under and in terms of s 41 of the Solicitors (Scotland) Act 1980. The solicitor subsequently became sequestrated and a permanent trustee was appointed. In his audit report to the judicial factor on the first account of his interim intromissions the accountant of court instructed him, in conformity to the usual practice, to
B   hand over to the trustee all the solicitor's client funds. The judicial factor objected to the instruction.

The accountant of court reported the matter to the Inner House.

Statutory provisions

The Solicitors (Scotland) Act 1980 provides:

"42.—(1) Subject to the provisions of this section, where, in any of the events mentioned in subsection
C   (2) or (2A), the sum at the credit of any client account kept by a solicitor or an incorporated practice (or where several such accounts are kept by him or, as the case may be, by it the total of the sums at the credit of those accounts) is less than the total of the sums received by him in the course of his practice on behalf of his clients or, as the case may be, by it on behalf of its clients and remaining due by him or, as the case may be, by it to them, then, notwithstanding any rule of law to the contrary, the sum at the credit of the
D   client account (or where several such accounts are kept, the total of the sums at the credit of those accounts) shall be divisible proportionately among the clients of the solicitor or, as the case may be, the incorporated practice according to the respective sums received by him in the course of his practice on their behalf or, as the case may be, by it on their behalf and remaining due by him or, as the case may be, by it to them."

E   ### Cases referred to

Devaynes v Noble (Clayton's Case) (1816) 1 Mer 529.
Jopp v Johnston's Trustee (1904) 12 SLT 279; (1904) 6 F 1028.

The report came before the First Division.

On 8 May 1991 the court *reversed* the accountant's report insofar as it related to the instruction objected to and *remitted* the accountant's audit and report to the accountant in regard to other matters raised.

F   The following opinion of the court was delivered by the Lord President (Hope):

OPINION OF THE COURT.—This is a report by the accountant of court in terms of s 15 of the Judicial Factors Act 1849 arising from his report on the intromissions and management of the judicial factor on the estates of Iain James Walker McKinnie, trading as McKinnie & Co, against which written objections have been lodged. The judicial factor was appointed in

terms of s 41 of the Solicitors (Scotland) Act 1980 at the instance of the Council of the Law Society of Scot-   G land. The appointment was sought on the ground that the solicitor had failed to a material extent to comply with the provisions of the Solicitors (Scotland) Accounts Rules 1986, and that his liabilities exceeded his assets and there were reasonable grounds for apprehending that a claim on the guarantee fund might arise. An appointment ad interim was made on 24 May 1988 and this was followed on 23 June 1988 by a full appointment in terms of which the judicial factor was authorised inter alia: "to make payments   H from or out of any bank account or sum or sums lodged on deposit receipt in the name of the said Iain James Walker McKinnie, or McKinnie & Co, subject always to the provisions of s 42 of the Solicitors (Scotland) Act 1980 and to divide the sum at credit of the client account of the said Iain James Walker McKinnie, or McKinnie & Co, among his clients in terms of said s 42".

On 28 October 1988 the solicitor's estates were   I sequestrated, and on 6 February 1989 C I Rankin, CA, was appointed to be his permanent trustee. As at the date of his sequestration the whole estate of the solicitor vested in the permanent trustee for the benefit of his creditors in terms of s 31 (1) of the Bankruptcy (Scotland) Act 1985.

The point raised in the report relates to note 8 in the audit report to the judicial factor on the first account of his interim intromissions from 24 May 1988 to 30 September 1989. The accountant noted that the judi-   J cial factor had handed over to the permanent trustee a sum amounting only to £206.37, and that he had retained in his own hands all sums at the credit of the client account. His comment on this item in note 8 is in the following terms: "Section 42 of the Solicitors (Scotland) Act 1980 makes provision for clients' funds being dealt with by a trustee in sequestration. In all other such cases where a Solicitors Act appointment has been superseded by sequestration the client funds have been handed over to the trustee and accordingly   K the accountant must require the factor to do so in this case."

The judicial factor has objected to this instruction in the following terms: "The judicial factor agrees that s 42 (1) of the Solicitors (Scotland) Act 1980 makes provision, on the appointment of (a) a trustee in sequestration; (b) a trustee in a trust deed; (c) a judicial factor, for clients' funds being divided proportionately among the clients of the solicitor according to the   L respective sums seized by him in the course of his practice on their behalf and remaining due by him to them. It is not clear, however, whether s 42 does in fact give the appointee power to sign cheques out of the clients' bank account. If such power is implied by the provisions of s 42 (1) and (2) of the Solicitors (Scotland) Act 1980 why does the Court of Session consider it necessary, in the interlocutor appointing the judicial factor, to give specific powers 'to make payment from or out of any bank account or sum or sums lodged on deposit receipt in the name of the said Iain James

A Walker McKinnie or McKinnie & Co'? Furthermore, s 33 (1) of the Bankruptcy (Scotland) Act 1985 states that: 'property held in trust by the debtor for any other person shall not vest in the trustee'. In view of the foregoing the judicial factor is not in a position to hand over the clients' fund to the trustee."

In these circumstances the accountant has reported this matter with a view to obtaining a judicial decision as to who is the proper party to administer the funds held on the client account and as to whether the judicial factor was correct in objecting to the terms of note 8 to the audit report on the account of his intromissions to 30 September 1989.

B

Section 42 (1) of the 1980 Act is a re-enactment of a provision which was first introduced by s 16 (1) of the Solicitors (Scotland) Act 1958. As amended by the Law Reform (Miscellaneous Provisions) (Scotland) Act 1985, Sched 1, para 20 in regard to incorporated practices, the subsection is in the following terms: [his Lordship quoted the terms of s 42 (1) and continued:] In subs (2) of that section it is provided that the events to which subs (1) applies are, in relation to any solicitor, (a) the sequestration of his estate, (b) the granting by him of a trust deed for behoof of creditors and (c) the appointment of a judicial factor on his estate. The effect of this provision is to eliminate the risk of the application to sums held at credit of these accounts of the rule in *Clayton's Case (Devaynes v Noble)* at p 572, by which payments on the credit side of the account are held to extinguish the items on the debit side in the order of their date. In place of the first in, first out rule which would operate unfairly against those clients whose sums had most recently been paid in, sums at credit of the client account or, where several such accounts are kept, the total of the sums at the credit of those accounts, are to be divisible proportionately among the clients of the solicitor. But, contrary to what was suggested by the accountant in the first sentence of note 8, the subsection does not say by whom the sums at credit of these accounts are to be divided and paid out. The practice which has been adopted by the court is to provide expressly in its interlocutor, as it did in this case, that the judicial factor is authorised to divide the sum at credit of the client account among the clients of the solicitor in terms of s 42. On the other hand we were informed that hitherto, where a sequestration has followed upon the appointment of a judicial factor, the practice has been for the accountant of court to instruct the factor to make over clients' funds to the trustee in the sequestration so that the permanent trustee may perform the function of distributing the funds in terms of s 42 (1) to the clients of the solicitor.

C

D

E

F

In our opinion this practice, despite its obvious convenience, has no sound basis in law and the judicial factor is well founded in the objection which he has taken to the instruction that he should follow it in this case. The key to the matter lies, as counsel for the accountant very properly pointed out, in the nature of the client account kept by a solicitor and whether, having regard to its nature, funds at credit of that

account as at the date of the sequestration can properly be said to have vested in the permanent trustee. For G it is only property which has vested in the permanent trustee that may be ingathered by him for the purpose of ensuring that the estate of the debtor is realised and distributed among his creditors in settlement of their claims on his estate. The order of priority in distribution which is prescribed by s 51 of the 1985 Act leaves no room for doubt that if sums at credit of the clients' account were to be regarded as having vested in the permanent trustee, these funds would be exposed to the claims of all those entitled to a ranking on the H debtor's estate. But property held on trust by the debtor for any other person lies outside this scheme of distribution altogether.

Section 33 (1) (b) of the Act provides that such property shall not vest in the permanent trustee. So if sums at credit of the clients' account are to be regarded as having been held by the solicitor on trust on his clients' behalf, it must follow that these sums do not vest in the permanent trustee on the sequestration of the solicitor, and accordingly that the judicial factor I was right to resist the instruction by the accountant that the sums held on clients' account in this case were to be made over to the permanent trustee.

We are in no doubt that sums held to the credit of the clients' account are fiduciary in character and that for this reason they are sums to which s 33 (1) (b) of the 1985 Act applies. It is well settled that a solicitor stands in a fiduciary relation to his client in regard to all sums of money which he has received on the J client's behalf. For example, in *Jopp v Johnston's Tr,* a law agent sold certain shares belonging to his client and paid the price which he obtained for them into his bank account. He later died insolvent and his estates were thereafter sequestrated. It was held that, since he was in the position of a trustee in regard to the sum realised for the sale of his client's shares, the amount in the account at his death which represented the trust moneys still belonged to his client and did not form part of his sequestrated estate. The case was concerned K principally with the problem which had been created by the fact that the client's money had been inmixed by the law agent with his own funds. But on the issue which is relevant to the present case Lord Justice Clerk Macdonald said this at (1904) 12 SLT, p 282: "Now, there can be no doubt whatever that throughout the whole time during which the price of these shares was dealt with, Mr Johnston stood in a fiduciary relation to Mrs Jopp. When he received the price of the shares he held it with responsibility to L hold it for her and for no one else."

Another passage in his opinion at p 283 expresses the same point: "Now, here, whatever Mr Johnston did, the fiduciary relation of agent undoubtedly subsisted, and to have uplifted the whole of these deposit-receipts and used the contents for his own purposes would undoubtedly have been an absolute breach of his duty and the fiduciary position in which he stood."

As the Lord Ordinary had pointed out at p 280, to allow the deposit receipts to be treated as property in

A which the agent alone was concerned would enable his general creditors to benefit by his breach of the trust relation in which he stood in regard to his client.

The whole matter is, of course, now regulated by the Solicitors (Scotland) Accounts Rules 1989, by which, subject to the detailed provisions of these rules, a solicitor is required to pay clients' money into a client account in the name of the solicitor in the title of which the word "client", "trustee", "trust" or other fiduciary term appears. The fiduciary nature of the client account is recognised in the definitions of this
B expression in rule 2 (1) of the Accounts Rules and also in s 65 (1) of the Solicitors (Scotland) Act 1980. The concluding words of s 42 (1) of the 1980 Act are consistent with these definitions, since they refer to sums received by the solicitor in the course of his practice on his clients' behalf and remaining due by him to them. There can be no question therefore of sums at credit of any client account kept by the solicitor vesting in his permanent trustee in the event of his sequestration. So the appropriate officer to attend to
C the task of dividing sums at credit of the client account, or the total of the sums at the credit of the client accounts if more than one, is the judicial factor appointed on the estate of the solicitor in terms of s 41 of the Act. Even if the solicitor is thereafter sequestrated or grants a trust deed for behoof of his creditors, any clients' money remaining in the hands of the judicial factor should remain with him for division in terms of s 42 (1) and it should not be paid over to the permanent trustee or to the trustee appointed under the trust deed.

D For these reasons, since we are satisfied that the instruction in note 8 to the accountant's report was erroneous, we shall reverse his report in that respect. It should be noted that the accountant felt it appropriate to report this matter to the court for guidance in the absence of any previous decision on the point and also in view of the practice which has grown up and which, prior to this case, had not been called into question.

E We appreciate that questions may now arise as to the remuneration, if any, which is to be paid to the judicial factor for his work in dividing among the clients of the solicitor any such funds which may remain in his hands, and as to the source from which any such remuneration is to be paid. Some of these questions are raised in note 9 to the accountant's report and the factor's replies to it, but we cannot resolve these questions at this stage, especially in the absence of the permanent trustee. Accordingly we shall, as we were invited to do, remit the accountant's
F audit and report back to him in regard to the issues raised in note 9 so that he may reconsider them in the light of any further representations that may be made to him by the judicial factor and, if so advised, submit a further report to the court in due course.

Counsel for Petitioners, Dunlop, QC; Solicitors, Balfour & Manson, Nightingale & Bell — Counsel for Accountant of Court, Reed; Solicitor, R Brodie.

R F H

Hollywood Bowl (Scotland) Ltd v Horsburgh

G

OUTER HOUSE
LORD OSBORNE
13 JUNE 1991

Administrative law — Judicial review — Title to sue — Licensing — Petitioner objecting to liquor licence failing to object to grant of occasional licence while appeal against grant of liquor licence pending — Whether sufficient interest to challenge grant of occasional licence.

H

Licensing — Occasional licence — Grant for period of more than one day — Whether ultra vires — "Event" taking place over period of 14 days — Licensing (Scotland) Act 1976 (c 66), s 33 (1) and (7).

The Licensing (Scotland) Act 1976 provides in s 33 for the grant of an occasional licence to the holder of a licence authorising the sale of alcoholic liquor, during such hours and on such day as the board may determine, in the course of catering for an event taking place outwith the licensed premises.

I

A company applied for an entertainment licence in respect of premises owned by the company. This application was objected to. The licensing board granted the application. The objectors appealed to the sheriff court. Prior to the hearing set down in respect of that appeal, the applicant company applied for an occasional licence, in terms of s 33 (1) of the Act, for permission to sell alcoholic liquor at the same premises to which the application for the entertainment licence applied, for catering for "an event" at
J the premises, namely a "high score" bowling competition (the application being made in the applicant company's capacity as licence holders in respect of other licensed premises). The objectors to the original application did not lodge an objection to the application for an occasional licence. The latter application was granted by the clerk to the licensing board, subject to conditions, for the period 4 to 17 June 1991.

The objectors then presented a petition for judicial
K review seeking suspension ad interim and reduction of the decision to grant the occasional licence. They argued that the clerk had acted ultra vires and had erred in law inter alia because s 33 (1) provided for the grant of a licence on a single day only; that the application had been granted in respect of the supply of alcoholic liquor in the normal course of business relating to the premises (a bowling centre) and not in relation to "an event" within the meaning of s 33 (1); and that the grant effectively enabled the applicants to operate the premises as if an entertainment licence was in full
L force and effect. The clerk and the applicants argued that the objectors had no title to sue.

Held, that the failure to object to the occasional licence application precluded the objectors from having the necessary locus standi, which would otherwise have been conferred upon them by reason of their objection to the grant of the entertainment licence, and accordingly the objectors had no title to sue (pp 244I-J and 245A); and motion for interim suspension *refused.*

Opinion, (1) that upon a proper interpretation of the statutory provisions, an occasional licence might be granted in terms of s 33 (1) for a period of more than one day (p 245C-D); and (2) that in the particular circumstances of the case, "an event" was taking place in the premises within the meaning of s 33 (1) (p 245G-H).

Petition for judicial review

Hollywood Bowl (Scotland) Ltd presented a petition for judicial review seeking suspension ad interim and reduction of a decision of Charles Horsburgh, clerk to the City of Glasgow Licensing Board, on 31 May 1991 to grant to County Properties and Developments Ltd an occasional licence, in terms of s 33 (1) of the Licensing (Scotland) Act 1976, for the provision of alcoholic liquor during a "high score" bowling competition at their premises at 30/52 Finnieston Street, Glasgow, for the period 4 to 17 June 1991.

The petition came before the Lord Ordinary (Osborne) for a first hearing on 7 June 1991. After argument a first order was granted and the petitioners' interim motion was continued until 11 June 1991. The case was further continued on that date to 12 June 1991, in order that the petitioners and second named respondents could produce to the court affidavits in support of their respective positions.

Statutory provisions

The Licensing (Scotland) Act 1976 provides:

"33.—(1) A licensing board may grant an occasional licence to the holder of a licence authorising him to sell alcoholic liquor, during such hours and on such day as the board may determine, in the course of catering for an event taking place outwith the licensed premises in respect of which he is the holder of a licence. . . .

"(7) An application for an occasional licence under this section shall be made in writing to the clerk of the licensing board and shall specify . . . the hours and period for which the licence is requested."

The Interpretation Act 1978 provides:

"6. In any Act, unless the contrary intention appears, . . . (c) words in the singular include the plural and words in the plural include the singular."

Cases referred to

Black v Tennent (1899) 6 SLT 298; (1899) 1 F 423.
McDonald v Finlay, 1957 SLT 81; (sub nom *McDonald v Chambers*) 1956 SC 542.
Nicol (D & J) v Dundee Harbour Trustees, 1914 2 SLT 418; 1915 SC (HL) 7.
Patmor Ltd v City of Edinburgh District Licensing Board, 1987 SLT 492.
Scottish Old People's Welfare Council, Petitioners, 1987 SLT 179.

On 13 June 1991 the Lord Ordinary *refused* the petitioners' motion for suspension ad interim and reduction of the first named respondent's decision.

LORD OSBORNE.—In this petition for judicial review, the petitioners, who have a place of business at Port Street, Glasgow, where they carry on the business of a bowling centre, seek suspension ad interim and reduction of a decision by the first named respondent, taken on 31 May 1991, to grant an application under s 33 (1) of the Licensing (Scotland) Act 1976 by the second named respondents for an occasional licence authorising the sale of alcoholic liquor at their premises at 30/52 Finnieston Street, Glasgow, during the period of 4 June to 17 June 1981, between the hours of 11 am and 12 midnight each day. In the form in which the petition stood when originally presented to the court, it bore to relate to two alleged decisions said to have been taken by the first named respondent; however during the course of argument before me on the petitioners' motion for suspension ad interim, to which this opinion relates, it was amended by the petitioners to take the form which I have described.

The undisputed background to this matter is that the first named respondent, who is clerk to the City of Glasgow Licensing Board, has power delegated to him by that board to determine any application for an occasional licence under s 33 (1) of the Act of 1976 made in respect of an event taking place within the City of Glasgow District. The second named respondents, who are holders of a public house licence under the Act of 1976 in respect of subjects known as Moll Flanders, South Road, Cumbernauld, made an application for the occasional licence, to which I have already referred, in that capacity. The application, dated 10 May 1991, describes the event for which the occasional licence was required as "Playing of bowls in connection with high score competition. Final to be held Saturday of each week". The date of the event is specified therein as 4 to 17 June 1991. This application was not the first to be made by the second named respondents. They had previously made and had granted similar applications in respect of the periods 7 to 20 May and 21 May to 3 June 1991, for the same premises upon a similar basis as regards the event concerned. Those premises at 30/52 Finnieston Street, Glasgow, a location in the same neighbourhood as those of the petitioners to which I have already referred, are fitted out for use as a tenpin bowling centre with 44 bowling lanes and other facilities. Earlier in 1991 the second named respondents had applied for an entertainment licence, as defined in Sched 1 to the Act of 1976, to supply alcoholic liquor as ancillary to the entertainment provided in the premises concerned, the application having been made to the licensing board of which the first named respondent is clerk. That application, to which the petitioners objected in terms of s 16 (1) (a) of the Act of 1976, as "any person owning or occupying property situated in the neighbourhood of the premises to which the application relates", was granted on 11 March 1991. Subsequently, the petitioners appealed to the sheriff against the decision of the licensing board granting the application for the entertainment licence, as they were entitled to do under s 17 (5) of the Act of 1976. That appeal is due to be heard on 29

July 1991. It is a feature of the Act of 1976 that, by
A virtue of s 30 (1) (b) thereof, a new licence does not
come into effect until, where an appeal has been
lodged against the grant, that appeal has been abandoned or determined in favour of the applicant for the
licence. Thus the entertainment licence to which I
have referred above is not at present in force.

Following the making by the second named respondents of their application for an occasional licence
dated 10 May 1991, no objection thereto was lodged
by the petitioners, although it would have been open
B to them to do so in terms of s 16 (1) (a) of the Act of
1976. It appears that the first named respondent had
certain concerns about the operation of the earlier
occasional licences referred to above based upon information passed to him by the police, who have been
closely involved in the supervision of that operation.
As a result there took place telephone conversations
and a meeting between the respondents, and two
letters dated 30 and 31 May 1991 were written by the
solicitors of the second named respondents, Messrs
C McVey and Quar, to the first named respondent. The
former contained an undertaking by the second named
respondents to the licensing board "that all bowling
will, forthwith, be competition bowling and that this
condition will be made plain to all patrons by advertisement and announcement and when they book-in to
bowl". The letter set forth a number of steps taken by
the second named respondents with a view to ensuring
that the competition referred to in the application of
10 May 1992 was the only context in which bowling
D would be permitted in the premises concerned during
the currency of the contemplated occasional licence.
Rules for the competition had been drafted and were
sent, along with the letter of 31 May 1991, to the first
named respondent. Those rules are set out on a card
in process. The result of those various communications was that the first named respondent's concerns
were allayed and he issued the occasional licence dated
31 May 1991, which is the subject of the petition.
That licence purports to authorise the second named
E respondents to sell alcoholic liquor "during the hours
of 11.00 am to 12 midnight on 4 to 17 June 1991, in
connection with an event to take place at Fastlane
Superbowl, 30/52 Finnieston Street, Glasgow, subject
to the undernoted conditions. . . . Conditions referred
to: Playing of Bowls in connection with High Score
Competition. Final to be held Saturday of each week.
. . . That the premises at all times are operated in
accordance with the undertaking given by Messrs
McVey and Quar, Solicitors, in a letter dated 30 May
F 1991 and that no public bowling will take place".

In the foregoing circumstances, in their petition the
petitioners claim that the first named respondent acted
ultra vires and erred in law in granting the second
named respondents' application for an occasional
licence dated 10 May 1991. It is there contended that
that state of matters is evident from the fact that the
application was granted for a period of 14 days and not
for a day as provided for in s 33 (1) of the Act of 1976;
that the application was granted in respect of the
ordinary business of the said bowling centre and not

for the supply of alcoholic liquor in the course of
catering for an event taking place at the said premises; G
that alcoholic liquor is provided, not in the course of
catering for an event, but in the ordinary course of the
business of the premises. It is further contended that
the first named respondent has effectively made a
decision which enables the said bowling centre to be
operated as if the application for an entertainment
licence had resulted in a licence being granted which
was now of full force and effect, thus circumventing
the provisions of s 30 of the said Act of 1976. Finally,
the petitioners aver that the granting of the said appli- H
cation for an occasional licence dated 10 May 1991 has
resulted in the business of the petitioners being
adversely affected.

The petition came before me on Friday, 7 June
1991, for a first order and on the petitioners' motion
for interim suspension in terms of their plea in law no
1. At that time the first named respondent was
represented in consequence of there existing a relevant
caveat. The second named respondents were not
represented. After hearing some argument, I granted I
the first order and continued the motion for interim
suspension until Tuesday, 11 June 1991. On that date
all parties were represented. The petitioners and
second named respondents moved me to continue the
motion further until Wednesday, 12 June 1991, to
enable affidavits to be produced in support of their
positions. This I did. On that day I heard full arguments from all parties.

It was a matter of common ground between the J
parties that before interim suspension could be
granted, it was incumbent upon the petitioners to
show that they had a prima facie case. If they could do
that, the matter was then one for the discretion of the
court having regard to the balance of convenience. In
this situation, the first issue which I have to address
is the question of whether the petitioners can show a
prima facie case. As the arguments were developed,
this issue was refined into two separate questions: (1)
whether the petitioners had demonstrated a title to K
sue, and (2) whether the averred basis of the petition
was relevant in law to justify the remedies sought.

On the matter of title to sue, a number of authorities
were cited to me and I did not understand parties to
be at odds as regards their effect. Reference was made
to the dictum of Lord Dunedin in *D & J Nicol v
Dundee Harbour Trs*, 1914 2 SLT at pp 420-421:
"when a complainer can only say that he is a rival
trader and nothing more, he qualifies an interest but
not a title. L

"By the law of Scotland a litigant, and in particular
a pursuer, must always qualify title and interest.
Though the phrase 'title to sue' has been a heading
under which cases have been collected from at least
the time of Morison's Dictionary and Brown's Synop-
sis I am not aware that anyone of authority has risked
a definition of what constitutes title to sue. I am not
disposed to do so, but I think it may fairly be said that
for a person to have such title he must be a party
(using the word in its widest sense) to some legal rela-

A tion which gives him some right which the person against whom he raises the action either infringes or denies."

This classic explanation of the concept of title to sue has recently been reaffirmed in *Scottish Old People's Welfare Council, Petrs* by Lord Clyde at p 184K-L. In relation to licensing matters, it is evident from *McDonald v Finlay* that a member of the public having no qualification other than that had no title to sue. Again in relation to the licensing context guidance can, in my opinion, be got from *Patmor Ltd v City of*

B *Edinburgh District Licensing Board.* Dealing with title to sue at pp 494-495, Lord Jauncey made it clear that, in his opinion, petitioners had no title to sue, by reason alone of their holding a gaming licence, to take action to protect the value of the benefits flowing from that licence, for example by limiting competition. However, as objectors to a competitor's application, he considered that they did have the right to see that their objection, and hence the competitor's applica-

C tion, were dealt with in accordance with the relevant statutory provisions. As objectors they would be entitled to pursue a matter involving the allegation of ultra vires action on the part of a licensing board. In this connection, Lord Jauncey made reference to the dictum of Lord Adam in *Black v Tennent*: "They have a statutory right to object to the certificate being granted, and to appear and be heard before the Justices, and it appears to me, as it does to the Lord Ordinary, that they have a right and title to see that their objections are disposed of in accordance with the

D provisions of statute". It is in the light of the guidance which these dicta afford that I approach the question of title to sue in this case.

The argument of the respondents was, quite simply, that the circumstances disclosed here did not afford the petitioners a title to sue, according to the recognised legal approach to the matter. Section 33 (9) of the Act of 1976 contemplated the making of objections to an application for an occasional licence. Objections

E could be made by the various persons listed in s 16 (1) of the Act. Having regard to the terms of ss 16 (1) (a) and 139, the petitioners could have lodged objections to the application in question, but did not do so. Section 20 of the Act made provision for the keeping by the clerk of each licensing board of a register of applications for licences and the decisions taken on them, which is available to members of the public for inspection. Thus the petitioners could have informed themselves of the existence of the application con-

F cerned had they exercised diligence. They not having done so, had failed to put themselves into any legal relation which gave them a right which could be said to have been infringed by the first named respondent.

For the petitioners it was argued that their title derived from the circumstance of their involvement, as objectors and appellants in the matter of the application of the second named respondents for the entertainment licence. Section 30 (1) (b) enacted that, standing the appeal, the licence granted should not come into effect. The effect of that statutory provision

G was being circumvented by the grant of the application for the occasional licence. The practical result of that grant was the same result as would follow if the petitioners' appeal to the sheriff had failed, yet that had not happened. The petitioners had been informed by a member of the first named respondent's department, at least as at 24 May 1991, that occasional licences had been granted in the second named respondents' favour enduring until 6 July 1991. To that extent the petitioners had been misled. The petitioners' advisers had not been aware that a remedy by

H way of objection had been available to them. In a matter where an allegation of ultra vires action was involved, the petitioners' failure to avail themselves of the opportunity to object should not be held against them.

In my opinion, in reaching a conclusion in regard to the matter of title to sue, it is important to keep in mind the distinction between the second named respondents' application for an entertainment licence and the application made by them for an occasional

I licence in question here. The petitioners have plainly put themselves in a legal relation with those involved in the handling of the entertainment licence application made by the second named respondents and the appeal to the sheriff from its grant, by virtue of their objecting to that application and their initiating that appeal, which would, in my opinion, confer upon them a title to ensure the proper conduct of their objections and the appeal. However, there is no parallel in relation to the application for the occasional

J licence in question. In that matter the petitioners were not objectors, although they could have made themselves so by first informing themselves of the existence of the application by examination of the register kept under s 20 of the Act of 1976 and thereafter taking the appropriate steps. I am not persuaded by the petitioners' argument that the title or locus standi which the petitioners have in relation to the entertainment licence application and appeal confers upon them a title to sue the present petition. In a superficial

K sense the grant of the application for the occasional licence in question may perhaps be thought to involve the circumventing of the terms of s 30 (1) (b) of the Act, but if one considers the whole circumstances of the two applications made by the first named respondents, I do not consider that the realities bear out that impression. The fact of the matter is that the entertainment licence, if effective, would confer the right to sell by retail or supply alcoholic liquor to persons frequenting the premises for consumption on the

L premises as an ancillary to the entertainment provided, subject to the particular conditions attaching to that grant. The occasional licence, on the other hand, permits the holder to sell alcoholic liquor only during the hours and period permitted by it, in the course of catering for an event, in this case the high score bowling competition, taking place outwith the licensed premises in respect of which he is the holder of a licence authorising him to sell alcoholic liquor, and that on the particular conditions attaching to that grant, which are plainly different from those which would apply to the operative entertainment licence. In my opinion, these two rights or privileges are of a markedly different character and the availability of one cannot properly be seen as, in any real sense, a substitute for the other. Thus the conclusion which I have reached is that the petitioners have failed in this petition to qualify a title to sue. The result is that they cannot be regarded as having demonstrated any prima facie case. In these circumstances I shall refuse the petitioners' motion for interim suspension.

Having reached the foregoing conclusion in relation to the matter of title to sue, that is sufficient for the disposal of the motion before me. However in deference to the full arguments which were presented to me, I intend to state briefly my opinion in relation to the other main issue focused in those arguments, namely the relevance of the averred basis of the petition. Two criticisms in particular of the first named respondent's decision were relied upon as a basis for the remedies claimed. The first of these was that the terms of s 33 (1) of the Act of 1976, as it was enacted, do not permit the granting of an occasional licence which would endure for more than one day as a maximum. This contention I understand to be based on the words "on such day" appearing in the subsection. I was not impressed by this argument. Section 6 (c) of the Interpretation Act 1978 provides that words in the singular include the plural unless a contrary intention appears, in the same way as did its statutory predecessor s 1 (1) (b) of the Interpretation Act 1889, in force when the Act of 1976 was passed. I can discern no contrary intention in the provisions of the Act of 1976. Further, I observe that s 33 (7), which makes provision for the form of an application for an occasional licence, refers to the necessity for specifying "the hours and period for which the licence is requested". I emphasise the use of the word "period", rather than day. I was also referred to the language used in s 60 of the Licensing (Scotland) Act 1959, the statutory predecessor of s 33 of the Act of 1976. In relation to the "special permission" there provided for, the section made reference to the "period for which the permission is to be in force". It is not obvious to me from the terms of the Act of 1976 that Parliament intended to narrow the scope of this type of permission or licence. Finally, on this aspect of the matter, I was informed that in practice occasional licences are frequently granted to cover a period of more than one day. To require the issue of a separate licence for each day or part of a day over which any event extended would cause serious practical difficulties, which Parliament cannot have intended. For all these reasons, had it been necessary for me to do so, I would have rejected this particular ground of criticism of the first respondent's decision. In these circumstances, it is not necessary for me to comment on a further contention advanced by the first named respondent to the effect that, in any event, the terms of s 33 of the Act had already been amended by recent legislation authorising the grant of an occasional licence for a period of up to 14 days.

The second ground of criticism of that decision was based upon the necessity for there to be "an event" taking place outwith the licensed premises in respect of which the applicant for the occasional licence is the holder of a licence. In the present case, it was argued that it was not open to the first named respondent to hold that there was "an event" within the meaning of s 33 (1). With that argument I also disagree. Looking, as I consider one must, at the circumstances as they were presented to the first named respondent, prior to his taking the decision concerned, in my opinion, he was fully entitled to proceed upon the basis that "an event" within the meaning of s 33 (1) of the Act, namely the high score bowling competition, was to take place. Much attention was paid during the course of the debate before me to allegations that the conditions attached to the occasional licence concerned had been breached and, in particular, that public bowling unrelated to the competition was taking place. In my opinion, such considerations have no relevance to the question of whether the first named respondent's prior decision was or was not ultra vires and I express no view about them.

Counsel for Petitioners, Reith; Solicitors, McGrigor Donald — Counsel for First Respondent (Clerk), Reed; Solicitors, Simpson & Marwick, WS — Counsel for Second Respondents, MacLeod; Solicitors, Allan McDougall & Co (for Hughes Dowdall, Glasgow).

L A McG

Campbell v HM Advocate

HIGH COURT OF JUSTICIARY

THE LORD JUSTICE CLERK (ROSS), LORDS MURRAY AND WEIR

27 SEPTEMBER 1991

Justiciary — Evidence — Admissibility — Police having grounds for suspicion that two persons using hired car in possession of drugs — Police stopping car and discovering third occupant — Third occupant being searched — Whether reasonable grounds for suspecting third occupant in possession of controlled drugs — Misuse of Drugs Act 1971 (c 38), s 23 (2).

Justiciary — Procedure — Search — Police having grounds for suspicion that two persons using hired car in possession of drugs — Police stopping car and discovering third occupant — Third occupant being searched — Whether reasonable grounds for suspecting third occupant in possession of controlled drugs — Misuse of Drugs Act 1971 (c 38), s 23 (2).

The Misuse of Drugs Act 1971, s 23 (2), provides inter alia that if a constable has reasonable grounds to suspect that any person is unlawfully in possession of a controlled drug, he may search that person, and detain him for the purpose of searching him.

Police acting on information about two persons using a hired car, whom they suspected to be in possession of controlled drugs, stopped the vehicle and discovered a third occupant of whom they had no knowledge. He was detained and a search of the car was then carried out, during which a bag of cannabis resin was discovered under the seat behind which he had been sitting. The third occupant was searched without his consent and a knife with traces of cannabis resin was recovered from his holdall. At his trial on a charge of possession of cannabis resin with intent to supply, the sheriff repelled an objection that the search was illegal and the evidence recovered inadmissible, in that the police officers had no reasonable grounds for suspicion in terms of s 23 (2) of the 1971 Act. On conviction the accused appealed to the High Court.

Held, (1) that the question was whether the circumstances gave the police reasonable grounds to entertain the suspicion that the accused was in possession of drugs (pp 247I-248A); (2) that where the police information was not related simply to the two other occupants but also to the car as being used for conveying drugs they were entitled to a reasonable suspicion and therefore had authority to detain and search the accused (p 248B-C); and appeal *refused*.

Indictment

Duncan McNeil Campbell was charged together with two co-accused at the instance of the rt hon the Lord Fraser of Carmyllie, Her Majesty's Advocate, on an indictment which libelled inter alia contravention of s 5 (3) of the Misuse of Drugs Act 1971. The accused pled not guilty and proceeded to trial before Sheriff D Noble and a jury in the sheriff court at Oban. In the course of the trial the sheriff repelled an objection on behalf of the accused to the admissibility of evidence of a police search. The accused was convicted and appealed to the High Court by note of appeal.

Statutory provisions

The Misuse of Drugs Act 1971 provides:

"23.—. . . (2) If a constable has reasonable grounds to suspect that any person is in possession of a controlled drug in contravention of this Act or of any regulations made thereunder, the constable may—(a) search that person, and detain him for the purpose of searching him; (b) search any vehicle or vessel in which the constable suspects that the drug may be found, and for that purpose require the person in control of the vehicle or vessel to stop it; (c) seize and detain, for the purposes of proceedings under this Act, anything found in the course of the search which appears to the constable to be evidence of an offence under this Act . . .; and nothing in this subsection shall prejudice any power of search or any power to seize or detain property which is exercisable by a constable apart from this subsection."

Cases referred to

Guthrie v Hamilton, 1988 SLT 823; 1988 SCCR 330.
Lucas v Lockhart, 1980 SCCR (Supp) 256.
Wither v Reid, 1979 SLT 192; 1980 JC 7.

Appeal

The note of appeal contained the following grounds of appeal, inter alia:

The police officers in Oban received reliable information on Friday, 12 January 1990, that two local men (the appellant's co-accused) were due to travel to Glasgow in a hired motor vehicle F267 KHS. On the basis of information received the police officers were suspicious and their suspicions centred on the Misuse of Drugs Act. The police set up a roadblock in order to stop this vehicle on its return to Oban and when it arrived in Oban the two suspected persons were in the driver's seat and the passenger seat respectively. The appellant was in the back seat. The officers did not expect to find anyone else in the car other than the two suspected persons. They did not know the appellant nor did they have any independent suspicions of the appellant other than the fact that he was in the motor vehicle. Despite having no suspicions of him, they detained him and searched him in terms of their statutory warrant to search granted by s 23 (2) of the Misuse of Drugs Act. The appellant did not agree to the search and was not invited to submit to a search.

It was argued that the search was illegal and that further, the detention was illegal. Timeous objection was taken to the evidence of the search. Authority for the proposition that the search was irregular was offered to the court (*Lucas v Lockhart*). Sheriff Noble repelled the objection and allowed evidence of the search to go on to the jury. In this respect it is averred that the learned sheriff erred in law in holding that the suspicion which centred on the co-accused was transferable to the appellant in the circumstances of his presence within the motor vehicle.

The appeal was heard on 27 September 1991.

Eo die the court *refused* the appeal.

The following opinion of the court was delivered by the Lord Justice Clerk (Ross):

OPINION OF THE COURT.—The appellant is Duncan McNeil Campbell who was found guilty in the sheriff court at Oban of charge 1 on an indictment which was a charge of contravening s 5 (3) of the Misuse of Drugs Act 1971. That was a charge that along with two co-accused in a motor vehicle he unlawfully had in his possession a controlled drug, namely cannabis resin, with intent to supply it to another. He has appealed against conviction and the note of appeal contains three grounds of appeal. Today on his behalf counsel has intimated that he is no longer insisting on grounds 2 and 3 and he has concentrated upon ground 1. Ground 1 is to the effect that it is alleged that the search of the appellant by the police was illegal and that his detention was illegal.

The sheriff in his report describes the circumstances
A which gave rise to this prosecution. It appears that on
Friday evening, 12 January, police officers at Oban
received a telephone call giving them reliable information that the appellant's two co-accused had hired a
motor vehicle registered number F267 KHS for the
purpose of making a return journey to Glasgow that
night. The police officers had reasonable grounds to
suspect that the purpose of the journey was to obtain
controlled drugs in the Glasgow area and to bring
them to Oban. The sheriff further informs us that
B acting on this information the police set up a roadblock on the outskirts of Oban and that at about 2 am
on Saturday, 13 January, the car was stopped at the
roadblock and was found to contain three persons.
These three persons were the appellant and his two co-
accused. The two co-accused were apparently in the
front driving and passenger seats and the appellant
was in the rear seat behind the front passenger seat.
The sheriff tells us that lying on the floor under the
front passenger seat was a plastic bin bag containing
C a slab of a substance about 4 in × 3 in × 1 in which was
subsequently identified as cannabis resin. On the rear
seat next to the appellant was a holdall bag containing
personal clothing and a knife which was found to have
minute particles adhering to its blade which were subsequently identified as cannabis resin. The appellant
admitted ownership of the bag and the personal clothing but denied any knowledge of the knife.

In presenting the appeal counsel has maintained that
when the two co-accused and the appellant were
D detained the police had not yet searched the car and
were not aware of the presence of the slab or the
holdall bag. He informed us that the history of the
matter was that the three individuals were detained
and removed to the police station in a police vehicle
and that their vehicle, that is the vehicle in which they
had been found, was then driven to the police station
where it was searched and these items were discovered. Counsel's submission was that so far as the
appellant was concerned the police had not been
E entitled to detain him in terms of s 23 (2) (a) of the
Misuse of Drugs Act 1971. Under reference to the
case of *Wither v Reid*, counsel stressed that the section
in question has been referred to in that case to the
effect that the statute was a penal statute which had to
be construed strictly. He recognised that having
regard to what the sheriff says in his report the police
no doubt had reasonable grounds to suspect that the
two co-accused were in possession of a controlled drug
and thus to search them and detain them for the
F purpose of a search but he maintained that in the circumstances that right did not extend to the appellant
who was merely found to be a third individual in the
car when it was stopped.

Counsel founded on the case of *Lucas v Lockhart*.
That was a case where the police had stopped a car in
order to inquire about the ownership of the car and
having done so recognised the driver as being a person
with whom they had had dealings previously in connection with drug offences. They then proceeded to
search the driver and also two passengers, one of

whom was the appellant in that case who was found
to have in his possession a quantity of cannabis. It was   G
conceded upon appeal in that case that in the circumstances the police were not entitled to exercise their
power of search under s 23 (2) to search the appellant
in that case. It must be recognised however that that
case differs materially from the present case on its
facts because the vehicle in the case of *Lucas* had not
been stopped because there was any suspicion that
drugs were being conveyed in the vehicle but it had
been stopped for an entirely different purpose namely
to inquire about the ownership of the vehicle.   H
Moreover in the case of *Lucas* the sole suspicion which
the police entertained when they stopped the vehicle
was in connection with the driver of that vehicle and
its ownership. There was no question in the case of
Lucas of the police ever having had suspicion that the
vehicle was in some way involved in drug dealing.
Nonetheless counsel maintained that in the circumstances of this case the mere fact that the appellant was
present in the car in the company of two other men
who were suspected of being involved with drugs was   I
no justification for detaining and searching him under
the powers contained in s 23 (2).

The advocate depute on the other hand maintained
that in the circumstances the police were entitled to
detain and search all the individuals whom they found
in the car. They had received information not merely
that the two co-accused were likely to be involved in
obtaining controlled drugs, but information that this
particular car had been hired for the purpose of conveying these two men to and from Glasgow in order   J
to obtain controlled drugs in the Glasgow area and to
bring them to Oban. When they accordingly set up a
roadblock and stopped the car the situation was not
merely that the co-accused were suspected of being
involved but this particular car was suspected of being
used for the conveying of drugs. In these circumstances the advocate depute maintained that when the
police discovered not two men but three men in the
car they had reasonable grounds to suspect that all the   K
individuals in the car were in possession of controlled
drugs and accordingly to search and detain all three.
In this connection the advocate depute founded on the
case of *Guthrie v Hamilton*. That case was of course
different on its facts but in our opinion the principle
which was approved of in that case is also applicable
to the circumstances of the present case. In that case
the police had obtained a warrant under s 23 (3) in
respect of premises and they were engaged in searching the premises when the appellant called at the
house. He was detained on the doorstep and found to   L
be in possession of drugs. At his trial it was suggested
that the evidence of the drugs found in his possession
had been illegally obtained but it was held that the
search of him had been properly carried out under
s 23 (2). In the course of the opinion delivered in that
case it was pointed out that the real question was
whether the facts and circumstances gave the police
reasonable grounds to entertain the particular suspicion and the following was stated in the opinion: "In
the present case the situation was that because the

A police had reasonable grounds to suspect that controlled drugs were in the possession of a person in the premises at 45 Church Street they applied for and obtained a search warrant. When a caller came to the door during the search and that caller had no obvious innocent reason for being there, we are of opinion that the police officers were justified in suspecting that the caller was a person in possession of controlled drugs. We agree that the situation might well have been different if there had been some obvious innocent explanation for the caller's presence" (1988 SLT at p

B 825A-B).

In the present case when the vehicle was stopped by the police with the prior knowledge which they had and the vehicle was found to contain not merely the two men whose names the police officers already had but a third party, namely the appellant, we are satisfied that in the circumstances the police officers were entitled to conclude reasonably that that person, namely the third party, was in possession of drugs and that therefore they had authority to search him and to

C detain him for the purpose of searching him. Accordingly we are satisfied that the detention and search of the appellant were in the circumstances legal.

In the course of presenting his submissions counsel stressed that the appellant had been detained before the articles were found in the car and before he admitted ownership of the holdall bag and the personal clothing in it and denied knowledge of the knife. The advocate depute however pointed out that there would have been sufficient evidence to warrant con-

D viction of the appellant even without the admission because the fact of the matter was that he was found in the car with the slab of cannabis under the front seat behind which he was sitting, that is at his feet, and with this holdall at his side. We agree with the advocate depute that that is indeed the situation and for all these reasons we are satisfied that there was no miscarriage of justice in this case and the appeal against conviction must accordingly be refused.

E ─────────

F

Inland Revenue Commissioners v Stenhouse's Trustees

OUTER HOUSE

LORD COULSFIELD

26 NOVEMBER 1991

Evidence — Admissibility — Valuation of shares in private company for capital transfer tax — Hypothetical open market valuation — Relevance of evidence of transactions not in open market and of previous agreements as to value with Inland Revenue — Whether special commissioner entitled to reject such evidence as irrelevant — Finance Act 1975 (c 7), s 38.

Revenue — Capital transfer tax — Valuations of shares in private company — Whether previous agreements as to value of sums paid in transfers between relatives relevant to valuation — Finance Act 1975 (c 7), s 38.

Trustees under an inter vivos trust owned shares in a private limited company. The trustees made a distribution of these shares and as a result capital transfer tax was payable on the value of the shares transferred. The trustees were unable to agree a value for the shares with the Inland Revenue and a hearing took place before the special commissioners to have a value fixed. At the hearing the trustees led a witness who gave evidence as to his valuation of the shares, which was based on the latest available accounts of the companies. It was the intention of the Inland Revenue to lead evidence of a number of previous transactions in the shares and the price then paid for them. On questions being asked by counsel for the Inland Revenue on the subject of actual transactions in the shares and of agreements as to their value, counsel for the trustees objected. The special commissioner ruled that the cross examination was irrelevant, on the basis that the only evidence which was relevant was evidence of "sales of shares between actual parties for cash at arms length which are similar as regards both amount and time". The effect of the commissioner's ruling was to rule out evidence of any transactions more than a few months before or after the transaction with which the hearing was concerned, which excluded the evidence which the Inland Revenue had proposed to lead. The Inland Revenue appealed the commissioner's ruling to the Court of Session under s 17 of the Court of Exchequer (Scotland) Act 1856.

Held, (1) that the general rule was that evidence was relevant if it was logically connected with the matters in dispute (unless it was excluded by some peremptory rule of law) (p 251E); (2) that although the objective in this case was to determine a hypothetical value of shares in a hypothetical sale between a hypothetical vendor and purchaser, the evidence of actual transactions or agreements as to value was not necessarily irrelevant and the whole circumstances should be open to consideration, although the weight to be given to such evidence was a matter for the commissioner (pp 251K-252F); and appeal *allowed*.

Appeal from the special commissioners

A   The Commissioners of Inland Revenue brought an appeal under s 17 of the Court of Exchequer (Scotland) Act 1856. The appeal was against a decision of a special commissioner not to allow certain evidence proposed to be given during a hearing for the determination of the value of certain shares for capital transfer tax purposes.

Statutory provisions

The Finance Act 1975 provided:

B   "38.—(1) Except as otherwise provided by this part of this Act, the value at any time of any property shall for the purposes of capital transfer tax be the price which the property might reasonably be expected to fetch if sold in the open market at that time; but that price shall not be assumed to be reduced on the ground that the whole property is to be placed on the market at one and the same time.

"(2) Schedule 10 to this Act shall have effect with
C   respect to the valuation of property for the purposes of capital transfer tax and the determination of the value transferred by a transfer of value. . . .

"[Sched 10] 13.—(1) In determining the price which unquoted shares or securities might reasonably be expected to fetch if sold in the open market it shall be assumed that in that market there is available to any prospective purchaser of the shares or securities all the information which a prudent prospective purchaser might reasonably require if he were proposing to pur-
D   chase them from a willing vendor by private treaty and at arm's length.

"(2) In this paragraph 'unquoted shares or securities' means shares or securities which are not quoted on a recognised stock exchange."

Cases referred to

Holt, Re [1953] 1 WLR 1488.
Lynall, Re [1972] AC 680; (1971) 47 TC 375.
E   *McNamee v IRC* [1954] IR 214.
Portland (Duke of) v Woods' Trustees, 1926 SLT 321, 417; 1926 SC 640.

Textbook referred to

Walker and Walker, *Evidence*, pp 1, 5 and 6.

On 26 November 1991 his Lordship *sustained* the appeal, *quashed* the special commissioner's ruling and *remitted* the case to the special commissioners to
F   proceed as accords.

LORD COULSFIELD.—This is an appeal under s 17 of the Court of Exchequer (Scotland) Act 1856 by the Commissioners of Inland Revenue against a decision of the special commissioners dated 27 March 1990. The decision was made in the course of proceedings to determine the value for capital transfer tax purposes of certain shares included in a capital distribution made by the respondents on 17 March 1978. The respondents are the trustees of the inter vivos trust of the late H C Stenhouse. The distribution

consisted of shares in three companies, namely, Haddockston Holdings Ltd ("Haddockston"), Scot- G tish Western Trust Holdings Ltd ("SWTH") and Second Haddockston Holdings Ltd, but, by the time of the hearing, the values attributable to the shares in SWTH and Second Haddockston Holdings Ltd for the purposes of assessment of tax on the transfer had been agreed. Haddockston was an investment company and on 17 March 1978 its investments consisted principally of shares in SWTH. SWTH itself was an investment company whose assets included shares in a quoted company, Stenhouse Holdings Ltd. H Haddockston and SWTH were both unquoted companies and, as I understand the position, the articles of each company contained restrictions on the transfer of shares in the companies. The respondents were not, as trustees, involved in the management of either Haddockston or SWTH.

The value of any property for the purposes of capital transfer tax was at the relevant date defined by s 38 of the Finance Act 1975, which provides: [his Lordship quoted the terms of s 38 of and then Sched 10, para I 13 (1) and (2) to the Act and continued:] Paragraph 13 was, it appears, designed to alter the law laid down in *Re Lynall*.

At the hearing on 27 March 1990, before a single commissioner, the respondents led evidence first. One of their principal witnesses, Professor J S Macleod, gave evidence as to the value of the shares and explained that in arriving at his estimate of the value he had relied on the accounts of the companies to 31 J March 1977, the latest available date, and on information in the public domain, such as information available through Stock Exchange sources, showing the general approach of stock market investors to investment trust companies and the level of yield which such investors might expect. Professor Macleod did not take account of any actual transactions in shares of Haddockston or SWTH. In cross examination, counsel for the appellants asked him whether he had taken into account actual transactions in, or agree- K ments on value in respect of, shares of the two companies. Counsel for the respondents objected to that question. After hearing a short argument and retiring briefly to consider it, the special commissioner made the determination which is the subject of this appeal. One of the issues in the appeal is what the precise effect of the determination was but, on any view, it indicates some limitation on the extent to which cross examination would be permitted, or evidence allowed to be led as to actual transactions in, or agreements L relating to the value of, shares in the two companies. It was, it appears, the intention of the appellants to lead evidence of, inter alia, a number of transactions in the shares both of Haddockston and SWTH, at known values, involving members of the family of the late Mr Stenhouse or trusts or companies in which they had an interest. Further, there had been earlier capital distributions from the inter vivos trust and agreements had been reached between the appellants and the respondents as to the appropriate formula to be adopted in valuing the shares of Haddockston and

SWTH for tax purposes. The formula involved discounting the net asset value of each company and represented a materially different approach to valuation from that adopted by Professor Macleod in his evidence. After the determination of the special commissioner was announced, the appellants took the view that their ability to lead appropriate evidence would be unduly restricted. Nothing further was done at the hearing and this appeal was then taken. As a result, the special commissioner was never asked to rule on the admissibility or relevance of any question or any item of evidence relating to any particular transaction or agreement and never had before him any detailed information about any such transaction or agreement.

In his determination, the special commissioner explained the question which had arisen and referred to s 38 of the 1975 Act and also to s 52 of the Taxes Management Act 1970 which imposes a duty on appeal commissioners to hear lawful evidence. Strictly speaking, that reference was in error because s 52 of the 1970 Act applies to proceedings in relation to income tax assessments and the relevant provision for the purposes of the present proceedings is contained in para 9 of Sched 4 to the Finance Act 1975, which is in slightly different terms, but nothing turns on the difference. After some other introductory remarks, the determination continued: "It seems to me that the question I have to deal with is of fundamental importance in the valuation of shares in a private company for which there is no actual market. The function of the commissioners, or, if the matter comes before the Court at first instance, of the Court, is, to adopt so much as I can remember of a phrase of Danckwerts J. in *Holt v IRC* [1953] 1 WLR 1488, 'a dim world peopled by the indeterminate spirits of fictitious or unborn sales'.

"Fundamentally it seems to me that the question which I have to determine is wholly hypothetical. Where there is a market one looks at values in the market. When there is no market, one has to indulge in the sort of calculations that are fundamental to the present appeal.

"With that background I approach this present case. The relevance of other actual transactions is limited first by the consideration that they must be transactions which both as regards time and quantity resemble this particular asset, namely a holding on this particular date. The relevance to my mind of any actual transaction which may have taken place is as a sounding board for the hypothetical calculations.

"Now the hypothetical calculation is, as we know, of a sale in a notional open market between a notionally willing vendor and a notionally willing purchaser. I would add a rider that the articles of association of two of the companies with which I am concerned contain embargoes on transfers of shares. I make the assumption that there is no embargo on the hypothetical purchaser in the hypothetical sale but that the purchaser will thereafter take subject to the embargoes. I therefore have to consider what is admissible as a test of the calculations which the experts make.

For my part I rule out entirely what other experts in other cases even of similar holdings of shares on the same day have said. I also rule out agreements arrived at between taxpayers and the Inland Revenue. To accept such evidence would be — to some extent — to substitute for my jurisdiction the 'horse trading' negotiations of other taxpayers with the Inland Revenue. However, I do not rule out as necessarily irrelevant such real open market transactions (if any) as may be shown to have existed at this time or shortly before or shortly afterwards of similar amounts of holdings of shares in these companies. In order to be admissible such evidence must be of sales for cash between vendors and purchasers at arms length and, as I have said, of similar quantities of the same shares. If pressed as to the time I would be inclined (although I make no ruling on this particular point) having regard to the fact that 1978 was a year of great inflation and great economic turbulence, to rule out evidence of transactions separated by more than a few months from March 1978.

"I am conscious that my jurisdiction is limited in a number of ways. In particular there is no interlocutory appeal. A rider to that is that there could be an application to the Court of Session by way of judicial review. I am also conscious of the fact that the appeal allowed by statute is by way of case stated. With these facts in mind I must err on the side of admitting evidence which is in doubt. Even bearing that in mind, I rule out as irrelevant everything except sales between actual parties for cash at arms length which are similar both as regards amount and time, as I have mentioned, and I so decide."

An appeal under s 17 of the 1856 Act is competent where at the date of passing of the Act a writ of habeas or of certiorari might competently have been issued from the Court of Exchequer. There was some discussion of the circumstances in which certiorari is competent but there was, in the end, no real dispute on this issue. As I understand the position, it is accepted that certiorari is competent where an error in law is patent on the record of the proceedings of an inferior tribunal or authority and it is not necessary that the error should be one going to the jurisdiction of the tribunal or, in other words, one which renders its proceedings ultra vires. There must, however, be an error of law, not merely one relating to matters of fact or in the exercise of discretion, within the limits of reasonableness.

The first question which has to be considered is, I think, what the effect of the special commissioner's determination is. As I have explained, the determination was made on an objection to a very broad question. At one stage of the argument, I was inclined to think that all that the commissioner had done was to assist the parties, as would be appropriate in proceedings of the character in question, by indicating in broad terms the attitude which he would be disposed to take to particular issues as they arose. The commissioner did not, as I read his determination, give an express ruling on the objection to the question which

A had actually been asked. Further, since the commissioner did not have the opportunity to apply the views which he had formed to particular instances, and could not be expected, in a extempore ruling of this kind, to consider instances or examples in detail, there is some difficulty in appreciating the precise effect of his determination. I am still inclined to think that it might have been more satisfactory if the appellants had gone a stage further with the hearing and endeavoured to put some questions about specific instances, before taking the matter to appeal. I have,
B however, come to the view that, at least in certain respects, the determination is sufficiently precise to allow me to consider whether it is correct in law. In the first place, the special commissioner has, I think, positively ruled out evidence of agreements reached between the taxpayers and the Inland Revenue arising out of previous distributions of, or including, shares in the same companies. Secondly, he has indicated that evidence of transactions will be admissible only if the transactions were "sales for cash between vendors and
C purchasers at arms length . . . of similar quantities of the same shares". Although it would have been particularly helpful to have had the benefit of the special commissioner's views on individual transactions in order to appreciate how he intended to apply these requirements, I think that, in view of the emphasis put on "sales for cash at arms length", it is fair to take the ruling as intended to exclude at least the bulk of the transactions on which the appellants intended to rely. All these transactions involved relatives of the late Mr
D Stenhouse or trusts or companies in which they were involved, and, in that respect, could be said not to be at arms length. These were the transactions with which the parties were concerned in the debate before the commissioner and it is reasonable to conclude that the ruling was intended to deal with them. Certainly, the appellants seem to have understood that their ability to lead evidence of these transactions was at least severely limited.

E   I heard a full argument and was referred to a number of authorities, but in the end of the day the issue, for the present purposes, seems to me to become quite narrow. The general rule of law, which is not in doubt, is that evidence which is relevant to the issue in the case is admissible unless it is excluded by some peremptory rule of law (see Walkers, *Evidence*, p 1). Evidence is relevant if it is in some way logically connected with the matters in dispute or if it is consistent or inconsistent with, or gives rise to a logical inference regarding, the facts in issue (Walkers, pp 5 and 6). No
F peremptory rule of law of evidence was referred to in the present case and the question was argued as one of relevance of evidence. Put shortly, the appellants' contention was that evidence of agreements as to the open market value of shares in the companies and evidence of actual transactions in those shares must be relevant to the issue in the present dispute, even if such evidence might not be determinative or even of very great weight. The respondents argued that the issue between the parties was a hypothetical one, namely the price which would be paid in the open market for

the shares under valuation, and that it followed from the nature of that issue that it was correct to take the G approach of their witnesses as the primary approach; that regard could only be had to any transactions in the shares to the limited extent allowed by the special commissioner; and that evidence of agreements was not relevant at all. Reference was made to *Re Holt, McNamee v IRC* and *Re Lynall* as showing the nature of the issue, the approach to valuation and the information which might be taken into account.

Re Lynall was concerned with an open market valuation under s 7 (5) of the Finance Act 1894 and Lord H Reid remarked (47 TC at p 406) that s 7 (5) was merely machinery for estimating value. He also pointed out that sale in the open market may take many forms. It is true, as the respondents argued, that the objective is to ascertain the hypothetical value of the property in a hypothetical sale between hypothetical vendor and purchaser. It is also true that it is necessary to define, as a matter of law, the assumptions which the valuer must make. For example, in the case of *Re Lynall* itself, it was necessary to define the type of I information which the purchaser is to be assumed to have. Beyond that, however, valuation seems to me to be a matter of fact and expert opinion. The appellants referred to *Duke of Portland v Woods' Trs* where Lord President Clyde said, at 1926 SLT, p 327: "The measures employed to estimate the money value of anything (including the damage flowing from a breach of contract) are not to be confounded with the value which it is sought to estimate; and the true value may only be found after employing more measures than J one — in themselves all legitimate, but none of them necessarily conclusive by itself — and checking one result with another. As Lord Stair puts it in the section quoted above [I xvii 16]: 'It is rather in the arbitrament of the judge to ponder all circumstances.'"

That was a case of damages for breach of contract, but the observations seem to me to be applicable more generally. I do not see why, in the present case, the type of evidence admissible should be restricted by the K nature of the issue in the way suggested by the respondents. No doubt the best evidence of open market value is evidence of sales of the same or similar property on the open market. It is not, however, necessarily the case that where evidence of open market sales is available, other evidence is excluded. If it is suggested that conditions have changed, in some material respect, the evidence of market sales may have to be qualified by taking account of other evidence. The evidence of market sales is only evidence L of value, and is not necessarily conclusive by itself. Similarly, in the case of a hypothetical sale, the calculation made by the respondents' witnesses are, in my view, only evidence of value, and cannot be regarded as, in themselves, conclusive. I therefore do not understand why it is said to follow from the fact that value has to be ascertained on a hypothesis, that any evidence of actual transactions should be ruled out as so irrelevant as to be inadmissible. Whether it is correct to start, as the respondents' witnesses did, with the accounts of the companies and information available

in the public domain, is in my opinion a question of
fact and opinion, not one of law. Similarly, the question whether any weight, and if so how much, is to be
attached to evidence of transactions seems to me to be
a question of fact and opinion. Some of the transactions on which the appellants rely may be of no use:
but there may be others which took place between
parties who were genuinely trying to strike an open
market value, and I do not see why such cases should
simply be ignored. As I understand the position, the
special commissioner accepted, as the respondents also
did in argument, that it is relevant to lead evidence of
some transactions, albeit in a secondary role, as a
check or sounding board for a conclusion reached
upon the basis of their preferred approach. Once that
concession is made, it seems to me to be difficult to
rule out ab ante the evidence which the appellants seek
to lead as necessarily inadmissible. Whether any particular part of that evidence is of assistance must, in my
view, be a question of fact and circumstance.

The same line of argument is, in my view, applicable with regard to the agreements. The basis on
which it is sought to lead the evidence is that it concerns cases in which the taxpayers did agree values as
open market values. That evidence may not be of
much strength as against other types of evidence, but
I am unable to see that it is so valueless as not to be
admissible at all. In other fields, such as valuation for
rating, evidence of agreements reached is regularly
admitted as evidence of the value which would be
arrived at in hypothetical transactions and I do not see
that there is any reason to regard such evidence as
inadmissible in the field with which this case is concerned. The commissioner's particular reason for
rejecting evidence of agreements is that to accept it
would be to substitute for his jurisdiction the "horse
trading" negotiations of other taxpayers with the
Inland Revenue. With all respect to his views, it seems
to me that the conclusion that a particular value, or a
particular method of valuation, was appropriate in
those particular cases, as a measure of or a means of
reaching the market value, is a consideration which
cannot be regarded as necessarily irrelevant. There
may be every reason for treating such evidence with
care but the reasons are not sufficient, in my view, to
form a legal barrier to admitting the evidence at all.
Again, I am assisted by the fact that the respondents
conceded that it would be open to the appellants to
cross examine expert witnesses who had adopted a
different approach in a previous valuation with regard
to the reasons why they had done so. If that is correct,
it seems to me that it follows that the whole circumstances of the previous occasion must be open for consideration in order to assess the significance of any
answers that may be given in cross examination. I can
see difficulties in dealing with evidence concerning
previous agreements if the appellants are not prepared
to reveal the approach which they themselves took in
arriving at the value in question, but that is a problem
which requires to be dealt with as the evidence is
heard.

The special commissioners are a specialist tribunal,

following a relatively informal procedure, and it is a
valuable feature of that procedure that the commissioners should employ their expertise and experience
to regulate the proceedings by, inter alia, indicating
what evidence may or may not, in their view, assist
them in determining the question at issue before them.
In the present case, however, I feel obliged to conclude that the commissioner went too far and gave a
ruling which would have the effect of preventing the
appellants from leading evidence which, as a matter of
law, is admissible. In all the circumstances, therefore,
I shall sustain the appeal, quash the ruling and remit
to the special commissioners to proceed as accords.

*Counsel for Appellants, G N H Emslie, QC, McNeill,
QC; Solicitor, T H Scott, Solicitor of Inland Revenue,
Scotland — Counsel for Respondents, Nimmo Smith,
QC, Hodge; Solicitors, Simpson & Marwick, WS (for
Boyds, Glasgow).*

D A K

[Section 38 (1) of the Finance Act 1975 has been re-enacted
as s 160 of the Inheritance Tax Act 1984.]

Bank of Scotland v Graham's Trustee

FIRST DIVISION
THE LORD PRESIDENT (HOPE),
LORDS MAYFIELD AND McCLUSKEY
11 DECEMBER 1991

*Writ — Rectification — Standard security — Proforma
personal bond and standard security only completed
quoad personal bond — Whether competent to rectify
quoad standard security — Law Reform (Miscellaneous
Provisions) (Scotland) Act 1985 (c 73), s 8 (1) (b).*

*Heritable property — Standard security — Defective
form — Standard form signed by debtors qua debtors but
not qua proprietors — Whether nature of defect such that
court empowered to order rectification — Law Reform
(Miscellaneous Provisions) (Scotland) Act 1985 (c 73),
s 8 (1).*

The Law Reform (Miscellaneous Provisions) (Scotland) Act 1985, s 8 provides that where the court is
satisfied that a document fails to express accurately the
common intention of the parties it may order the document to be rectified in order to give effect to that
intention.

The joint heritable proprietors of subjects at
Broxburn, West Lothian, executed a standard security
in favour of a bank which was recorded on 4 June
1985. After one of the heritable proprietors had been
sequestrated, it was discovered that the security was
defective. The heritable proprietors had signed the

A security as debtors but had failed to do so as proprietors. They had also signed the schedule as relative to the dispositive clause. The bank petitioned the court to rectify the deed in terms of the Law Reform (Miscellaneous Provisions) (Scotland) Act 1985, s 8 (1). The trustee in sequestration opposed the petition on the grounds (a) that the proprietors had granted a personal bond only and accordingly the court had no power to rectify a part of a document which had not been granted by the grantor; and (b) that the provisions of s 8 (1) were limited to errors of expression

B within the terminology of the document and did not extend to a defect in its execution. The Lord Ordinary allowed a proof before answer on the bank's averments. The trustee in sequestration reclaimed.

Held, (1) that the signature of the proprietors on the schedule was sufficient to show from what appeared on the face of the document itself that the signatories were holding themselves out as proprietors of the subjects and that their purpose in signing the schedule was to create a standard security (p 254K-L); (2) that

C the phrase "express accurately" could cover a range of inaccuracies from errors of expression to errors of omission (p 255C); (3) that a case of defective form filling fell within the range of these inaccuracies so long as the court was not being asked to supply signatures which were not there at all or to cure other defects of such a fundamental kind that the deed could not be said to have been executed at all (p 255D); and (4) that the present case fell within the range of inaccuracies described (p 255E); and reclaiming

D motion *refused*.

Petition under s 8 (1) of the Law Reform (Miscellaneous Provisions) (Scotland) Act 1985

(Reported 1991 SLT 879)

The Governor and Company of the Bank of Scotland presented a petition under the Law Reform (Miscellaneous Provisions) (Scotland) Act 1985 seeking

E rectification by the court of a standard security contained in a document constituting a personal bond and standard security in favour of the bank by Gordon Alexander Graham and Mrs Brenda Noble Graham. The second respondent, R B M Graham, CA, the trustee in sequestration of Gordon Alexander Graham, opposed the application on the grounds that the signatories had granted a personal bond only and the Act only empowered the court to alter errors of expression within the terminology of the document. The first

F respondents, Mr and Mrs Graham, did not lodge answers to the petition.

The case came before the Lord Ordinary (Milligan) on procedure roll.

Statutory provisions

The Law Reform (Miscellaneous Provisions) (Scotland) Act 1985 provides:

"8.—(1) Subject to section 9 of this Act, where the court is satisfied, on an application made to it, that —
(a) a document intended to express or to give effect to

an agreement fails to express accurately the common intention of the parties to the agreement at the date G when it was made; or (b) a document intended to create, transfer, vary or renounce a right, not being a document falling within paragraph (a) above, fails to express accurately the intention of the grantor of the document at the date when it was executed, it may order the document to be rectified in any manner that it may specify in order to give effect to that intention."

Case referred to

Hudson v Hudson's Trustees, 1978 SLT 88; (sub nom H *Hudson v St John*) 1977 SC 255.

On 13 February 1991 the Lord Ordinary *allowed* a proof before answer. (Reported 1991 SLT 879.)

The trustee in sequestration reclaimed.

Reclaiming motion

The reclaiming motion was heard by the First Division on 28 November 1991. I

On 11 December 1991 the court *refused* the reclaiming motion.

The following opinion of the court was delivered by the Lord President (Hope):

OPINION OF THE COURT.—This is a reclaiming motion by the second respondent against an interlocutor of the Lord Ordinary by which he allowed a proof before answer in this petition for rectification of J a document and the answers thereto as adjusted. The second respondent is the trustee on the sequestrated estate of Gordon Alexander Graham who was at one time resident with his wife at 32 New Holygate, Broxburn, West Lothian. Mr and Mrs Graham were and still are the heritable proprietors of these subjects, and they are the first respondents to this petition. Their present whereabouts are unknown and they have not lodged answers. The petitioners aver that the first respondents wished to grant a standard security K in their favour over the subjects and for this purpose had instructed a firm of solicitors to act on their behalf. The petitioners sent to the solicitors their standard form security document form no 613, and in due course this document was sent by the solicitors for recording in the division of the General Register of Sasines for the County of West Lothian. It was recorded on 4 June 1985, but upon examination the document was found to be defective. This application L has been brought to have these defects rectified.

The petition has been presented under s 8 (1) of the Law Reform (Miscellaneous Provisions) (Scotland) Act 1985. That subsection is in these terms: [his Lordship narrated the terms of s 8 (1) set out supra and continued:]

The document with which we are concerned is a unilateral deed, not an agreement, so the relevant provision for present purposes is para (b). The question is whether the nature of the defect is such that the court has power to order the document to be rectified in order that it may receive the effect contended for by the petitioners. The Lord Ordinary was satisfied that there was within the terms of the document itself material which, taken together with proof of the intentions of the first respondents offered by the petitioners in their averments, would entitle the court to grant this remedy. The second respondent submits that the petition ought to be dismissed on the ground that the section does not enable the court to rectify defects of the nature which have arisen in this case which, on his approach, are to be seen as related essentially to the execution of the document, as a result of which there is no standard security at all.

The petitioners' standard form is a printed document which extends to four pages and is provided with a backing on which the words "Standard Security" appear. The first page contains a definition clause in these terms: "In this deed the expression [sic] set out below shall have the meanings and effect respectively set opposite to them:—". There are then set out four separate boxes or panels, three of which are left blank for completion in order to identify the debtor, the proprietor and the subjects. There is also a panel which defines the bank as meaning the petitioners. Then there is set out an undertaking by the debtor to pay to the bank all sums due to the bank in terms which are sufficient to constitute a personal bond by the debtor. The next part of the form is designed to create the heritable security. It begins with a clause in these terms: "For all which sums the Proprietor Grants a Standard Security in favour of the Bank and its assignees over All and Whole the subjects and others described in the Schedule annexed and signed as relative hereto: Declaring that the said Schedule forms part of the dispositive clause of these presents".

Reference is then made to the standard conditions specified in Sched 3 to the Conveyancing and Feudal Reform (Scotland) Acts 1970 and 1971 and to several variations to these standard conditions which it is agreed are to have effect. The body of the deed concludes with a warrandice clause by the proprietor and a clause of consent to registration for execution by both the debtor and the proprietor. The testing clause which then follows is set out on the second page of the printed form in such a way as to require execution separately before witnesses by both the debtor and the proprietor. Beneath the relevant spaces for these signatures there appear the words "Signature of Debtor(s)" and "Signature of Proprietor(s)" respectively. The third page of the document begins with a space for completion which is headed "Schedule referred to in the foregoing Standard Security". Beneath a suitable space for the insertion of the relevant details places are provided for two signatures. In this instance there are no words to indicate the identity of the signatories, but it is to be assumed under reference to the passage from the dispositive clause which we have quoted that they are the proprietors of the subjects described in the schedule and that their purpose in subscribing their names here is to sign the schedule as relative to the dispositive clause.

The defects which have arisen in this case are confined to the way in which the blanks in the form have been completed. There are no material misprints in the text of the standard form, nor are there any errors in the expression of those parts that have been filled in. But the panel to identify the proprietor has been left blank and no signatures have been included in that part of the testing clause for signature by the proprietors. The deed has been completed in such a way as to identify the debtor only and the first respondents' signatures appear only in that part of the testing clause which is designed for signature by the debtors. It should be noted that their signatures also appear in the spaces provided beneath the schedule. The defects have attracted the argument by the second respondent that the standard security is invalid and of no effect on the ground that it does not conform as closely as may be to form A of Sched 2 to the Conveyancing and Feudal Reform (Scotland) Act 1970. It is admitted that the first respondents were heritable proprietors of the subjects, but the second respondent's contention is that since they did not sign the form in that capacity the only effect of their signatures is to constitute a personal bond between them and the bank and that it cannot receive effect as a heritable security.

The first submission in support of the reclaiming motion was that on a proper interpretation of s 8 (1) (b) the court had no power to rectify any part of a document which had not been granted by the grantor at the date when it was executed. The basis for this submission was the contention that what the first respondents had done in this case was to grant a personal bond only, and that there had been a total failure on their part to execute the standard security. This was not just a failure to express accurately the intention to grant a standard security in favour of the petitioners. It was a failure to create the right at all, and it was not the purpose of the subsection to enable an entirely new, or an entirely different, right to be created than that which had been granted. It is not, we think, necessary to examine this argument in any detail because, taking the petitioners' averments pro veritate, the basis for it is unsound. This is not a case where there can be said to be a clear separation between one part of the document which has been executed and another part of it which has not. The fact that the first respondents' signatures appear beneath the schedule on p 3 of the document, which is declared on p 2 to form part of the dispositive clause and to have been signed as relative thereto, is sufficient to show, from what appears on the face of the document itself, that the first respondents were holding themselves out as the proprietors of the subjects and that their purpose in signing the schedule was to create a standard security over the subjects in favour of the petitioners. They did not do everything that the standard form required to express that intention accurately, but it cannot be said that there was a complete failure on their part to demonstrate that their intention was to be the grantors of the standard security.

The second submission was substantially the same

as the first, namely that the provisions of s 8 (1) (b) did not entitle the court to create a standard security where none existed before — in other words that the court could not transform the only part of the deed which had been executed into something entirely new which the grantor had not executed at all. But the third raised a somewhat different point. It was said that the power of rectification which this provision conferred was limited to errors of expression within the terminology of the document. What the Lord Ordinary had done was to allow a proof before answer on averments which were designed to rectify a defect of a quite different nature, namely a defect in its execution, which the court had no power to do.

We think that it would be unwise to attempt to define all the circumstances to which the power of rectification under s 8 (1) (b) can apply. The only express limitations which the provision contains are that it must be related to the intention of the grantor of the document at the time when it was executed and that it is in order to express accurately that intention that the power is available to be exercised. The phrase "express accurately" can cover a range of inaccuracies from errors of expression on the one hand to errors of omission on the other. Ambiguities may be corrected, and so also may more substantial defects such as errors in the expression of the grantor's intention in the dispositive clause of the deed which, if uncorrected, might leave intended grantees without the rights which the grantor intended to confer. *Hudson v Hudson's Trs* provides a good example of the error of the latter kind for which the subsection was intended to provide a more convenient remedy. A case of defective form filling falls naturally within the range of these inaccuracies, so long as the court is not being asked to supply signatures which are not there at all or to cure other defects of such a fundamental kind that the deed cannot be said to have been executed at all. The intention of the grantor at the date when the deed was executed is a matter for evidence, and it is to all relevant evidence whether written or oral that the court may have regard.

The present case seems to us, on the petitioners' averments, to fall within the range of inaccuracies which we have described. We have here a document which has been executed, albeit imperfectly. The grantors have signed it in one place before witnesses and they have signed it in another place in such a way as to show an intention to create a standard security as well as to subject themselves to a personal bond. Their form filling has been incomplete because they have failed to enter their names in the panel marked "Proprietor", and because they have failed to execute the document a second time in that capacity before witnesses. But both inaccuracies are capable of being rectified in the manner set out in the prayer to the petition without it being necessary for any further signatures to be obtained. In these circumstances the power under s 8 (1) (b) is available to be exercised by the court. We shall refuse the reclaiming motion and adhere to the interlocutor of the Lord Ordinary.

_____

Counsel for Petitioners and Respondents, Stewart, QC; Solicitors, Bonar Mackenzie, WS — No appearance for First Named Respondents — Counsel for Second Named Respondent and Reclaimer, Fleming, QC; Solicitors, Clark & Co.

M C G

Edmund Nuttall Ltd v Amec Projects Ltd

FIRST DIVISION

THE LORD PRESIDENT (HOPE),
LORDS COWIE AND SUTHERLAND

20 DECEMBER 1991

Arbitration — Stated case — Arbiter postponing stating a case — Nobile officium — Petition to ordain arbiter to state case — Competency — Whether provided for by Rules of Court — Whether matter within regulatory powers of court — Whether rule of court ultra vires — Rules of Court 1965, rule 277 (c) — Administration of Justice (Scotland) Act 1972 (c 59), s 3 (1) — Court of Session Act 1988 (c 36), s 5.

Nobile officium — Competency — Petition to ordain arbiter to state case — Arbiter postponing stating case — Whether provided for by Rules of Court — Whether matter within regulatory powers of court — Whether rule of court ultra vires — Rules of Court 1965, rule 277 (c) — Administration of Justice (Scotland) Act 1972 (c 59), s 3 (1) — Court of Session Act 1988 (c 36), s 5.

The respondents in an arbitration lodged a counterclaim. The claimants took a plea to the relevancy of the counterclaim, but the arbiter issued a proposed interlocutor allowing proof before answer of both the original claim and the counterclaim. The claimants applied to the arbiter under s 3 of the Administration of Justice (Scotland) Act 1972 and Rule of Court 277 for him to state a case for the court, but he declined to do so on the ground that it was expedient that the facts should be ascertained before their application was determined, in terms of Rule of Court 277 (c). It was not open to the petitioners to apply to the court for a remedy under Rule of Court 278, on the ground that the arbiter had refused to state a case, because he had merely postponed their application. The petitioners therefore presented a petition to the nobile officium for an order ordaining the arbiter to state a case.

The petitioners accepted that the nobile officium was excluded in the case of tribunals to which the court's rule making power applied, but contended that no rules had in fact been made for the obtaining of a stated case from an arbiter who refused to do so, for on a proper construction of Rules of Court 276-280, only rules 279 and 280 applied to a stated case from an arbiter. In any event the court had no power under s 3 of the Administration of Justice (Scotland) Act

A 1972 to regulate the obtaining of a stated case from an arbiter; moreover, even if such a power was to be implied, it could not be exercised so as to extinguish the substantive right of a party to an arbitration to apply for a stated case at any time. Rule of Court 277 (c) was accordingly ultra vires.

Held, (1) that Rule of Court 277 applied to the obtaining of a stated case from an arbiter, for on a proper reading of rule 276, all references to "the tribunal" in rules 277-280 were to be taken to include an arbiter (p 259C-D); (2) that s 5 of the Court of
B Session Act 1988, taken together with s 3 (1) of the 1972 Act, entitled the court to regulate the manner in which, the time within which, and the conditions upon which the right of an arbiter to state a case or the power of the court to order him to do so, could be exercised (pp 257L-258D); (3) that while s 3 (1) conferred a right to obtain a stated case from an arbiter if the court so directed it was inappropriate for the court to be required to entertain questions of law which the arbiter had decided he was not going to decide for the
C time being, and it was consistent with existing law and practice for rule 277 (c), which related only to timing and procedure, to give the arbiter a discretion on the receipt of an application to state a case to postpone further consideration of the application until the facts had been ascertained (p 258E-I); and petition *dismissed* as incompetent.

John L Haley Ltd v Dumfries and Galloway Regional Council, 1985 SLT 109, *followed.*

D

_____

Petition to the nobile officium

Edmund Nuttall Ltd presented a petition to the nobile officium of the Court of Session seeking an order ordaining the arbiter in an arbitration between the petitioners and Amec Projects Ltd to state a case for the opinion of the court.

Statutory provisions

The Administration of Justice (Scotland) Act 1972
E provides:

"3.—(1) Subject to express provision to the contrary in an agreement to refer to arbitration, the arbiter or oversman may, on the application of a party to the arbitration, and shall, if the Court of Session on such an application so directs, at any stage in the arbitration state a case for the opinion of that Court on any question of law arising in the arbitration."

The Court of Session Act 1988 provides:
F

"5. The Court shall have power by act of sederunt — (a) to regulate and prescribe the procedure and practice to be followed in various categories of causes in the Court or in execution or diligence following on such causes, whether originating in the said Court or brought there by way of appeal, removal, remit, stated case, or other like process, and any matters incidental or relating to any such procedure or practice including (but without prejudice to the foregoing generality) the manner in which, the time within which, and the conditions on which any interlocutor of a Lord Ordinary

may be submitted to the review of the Inner House, or any application to the Court, or any thing required G or authorised to be done in relation to any such causes as aforesaid shall or may be made or done; . . . (l) to make such regulations as may be necessary to carry out the provisions of this Act or of any Act conferring powers or imposing duties on the Court or relating to proceedings therein".

The Rules of Court 1965 provide:

"276. All appeals by way of stated case, special case, H case, reference or submission (hereinafter referred to as 'the case') against the decision of any court, the Secretary of State, a Minister, a Department statutory tribunal, referee or authority (hereinafter referred to as 'the tribunal') and all stated cases by an arbiter and all statutory proceedings for obtaining the opinion of the court on a question either prior to the issue of a decision by the tribunal or by way of appeal against a decision by the tribunal, shall subject to the provisions of the statute allowing such appeal or proceedings (hereinafter referred to as 'the statute') and these Rules I be regulated by Rules 277 to 280, provided that 'the question' shall in the said Rules be construed as 'the question of law' unless the statute allows an appeal on a question other than a question of law.

"277. Where the court is authorised to make regulations by Act of Sederunt for obtaining, settling, stating and authenticating the case for presentation to the court, the following provisions shall have effect: . . . (c) If the application is presented before the facts have J been ascertained by the tribunal, and if the tribunal is of opinion that it is necessary or expedient that the facts should be ascertained before the application is disposed of, it may postpone further consideration of the application until the facts have been ascertained by it. . . .

"278. When the tribunal has refused to state and sign a case the party whose application has been refused may, within fourteen days from date of such refusal, apply by a written note to one of the divisions K of the Inner House lodged in the General Department for an order upon the other party to shew cause why a case should not be stated."

Cases referred to

Bennets v Bennet (1903) 10 SLT 609; (1903) 5 F 376.
Clydebank District Council v Clink, 1977 SLT 190; 1977 SC 147.
Gunac Ltd v Inverclyde District Council, 1982 SLT 388; 1983 SLT 130. L
Haley (John L) Ltd v Dumfries and Galloway Regional Council, 1985 SLT 109.
McGregor (John G) (Contractors) Ltd v Grampian Regional Council, 1989 SLT 299.

The petition came before the First Division on 11 December 1991.

On 20 December 1991 the court *dismissed* the petition as incompetent.

The following opinion of the court was delivered by
the Lord President (Hope):

OPINION OF THE COURT.—In this petition
the petitioners seek an order under the nobile officium
ordaining an arbiter to state a case for the opinion of
the Court of Session on a question of law which they
desire to raise in an arbitration.

The arbiter has been appointed to determine a
number of disputes which have arisen between the
petitioners and the respondents, with whom the petitioners entered into a building subcontract for work in
the construction of a semiconductor construction
facility at South Queensferry. The petitioners have
lodged a statement of claim in the arbitration to which
the respondents have lodged answers and a counterclaim. A diet of debate took place on 13 May 1991 at
which the petitioners submitted argument in support
of their plea to the relevancy of certain aspects of the
counterclaim. The arbiter issued a proposed interlocutor in June 1991 by which he intimated his intention to allow a proof before answer of the claim and
counterclaim with all pleas left standing. The petitioners' agents made representations against his proposed interlocutor, and on 11 September 1991, on
being told that he did not propose to alter its terms,
they requested him in terms of s 3 of the Administration of Justice (Scotland) Act 1972 and Rule of
Court 277 to state a case for the opinion of the court.
On 9 October 1991 the clerk to the arbiter intimated
to the parties that the arbiter had decided to postpone
the application for a stated case in terms of rule 277
(c), being of the opinion that it was expedient that the
facts should be ascertained before the application was
disposed of. The petitioners are dissatisfied with this
decision, because they maintain that it is not expedient
that any facts should be ascertained before their application for a stated case is disposed of. But, standing
that decision which has been made by the arbiter
under reference to Rule of Court 277 (c), it is not open
to them to apply to the court under Rule of Court 278
on the ground that the arbiter has refused to state a
case. An application under that rule requires to be
accompanied by a certificate of refusal, and the arbiter
in this case has decided not to refuse the application
but only to postpone it. It is in these circumstances
that the petitioners seek a remedy from the court in
the exercise of the nobile officium.

Counsel for the petitioners accepted that, standing
the provisions of Rule of Court 277 (c), it was necessary for him first to satisfy us as to the competency of
the application. He also accepted that, in the case of
those tribunals to which the court's rule making power
applies, the nobile officium of the court was excluded
by the power delegated to the court and the court's
exercise of its powers in terms of rules 276 to 280. But
he submitted that no such power had been delegated
to the court under s 3 of the Administration of Justice
(Scotland) Act 1972, his argument being that that provision gave no authority to the court to regulate the
obtaining of a stated case from an arbiter. Even if such
a power was to be implied, it could not be exercised

so as to cut down the substantive right of a party to
apply for a stated case at any time. For this reason
Rule of Court 277 (c) was outwith the powers of the
court. He also submitted that, on a proper construction of rules 276–280, the only rules which could
be said to apply to a stated case by an arbiter were
rules 279 and 280 and that no procedure had been laid
down by these rules for the obtaining of a stated case
from an arbiter who refused to state a case.

In support of his first argument counsel for the petitioners pointed out that s 3 (1) of the 1972 Act makes
no express provision for the making of any rules with
regard to cases stated by arbiters for the opinion of the
court. He accepted that the power given by s 16 (a) of
the Administration of Justice (Scotland) Act 1933,
now to be found in s 5 (a) of the Court of Session Act
1988, to regulate and prescribe by Act of Sederunt the
procedure and practice to be followed in this court was
sufficient to enable the Court of Session, without any
express authority in s 3 (1) of the 1972 Act, to make
rules about the procedure and practice to be followed,
about the form of stated cases and what was to be done
with them when they were received. But he submitted
that the Court of Session had no power without
express authority to make provision as to the obtaining
of a stated case from an arbiter. We were referred to
s 13 of the Tribunals and Inquiries Act 1971, which
sets out in considerable detail the various matters
which may be provided for by rules of court in regard
to appeals from the various tribunals to which that
section applies. Subsection (2) of that section, read
with subs (6) (a), confers express power on the Court
of Session to make rules of court authorising or requiring a tribunal to state a case for the opinion of the
Court of Session. Reference was also made to s 234 of
the Town and Country Planning (Scotland) Act 1972,
which makes express provision for various matters in
connection with appeals to the Court of Session
against decisions by the Secretary of State to be dealt
with by the exercise of the power to make rules of
court. No doubt various other examples of the conferring of express powers in addition to those already
available to the court under its general power might be
cited. One need look no further than the 1972 Act
itself, since s 1 (3) makes express provision that the
general power conferred on the court by s 16 of the
1933 Act to regulate its own procedure and by s 32 of
the Sheriff Courts (Scotland) Act 1971 to regulate the
procedure of the sheriff court may be exercised for the
purposes of that subsection, while s 3 of the same Act
with which we are concerned in this case makes no
such provision.

But the fact that Parliament has chosen to make
express provision for the making of rules in other
enactments does not have the effect of restricting the
general rule making powers which have been given to
the court. The question in each case, when no express
provision has been made, is whether the general
powers are wide enough to authorise the making of the
rules. The power which is given to the court to regulate its own procedures is expressed in wide terms.
Section 5 (a) of the Court of Session Act 1988 — it is

A convenient to refer to the provisions which are now in force rather than to s 16 of the 1933 Act which has been repealed — enables the power to be exercised to prescribe the procedure and practice to be followed in regard to causes brought to the Court of Session by way of stated case. This power is not confined to regulating the form of the stated case or what is to be done with it when it is received. It extends to "any matters incidental or relating to any such procedure or practice including (but without prejudice to the fore-going generality) the manner in which, the time

B within which, and the conditions on which . . . any application to the Court . . . shall or may be made". Section 5 (a) enables the court to make such regulations as may be necessary to carry out the provisions of any Act conferring powers or imposing duties on the court or relating to proceedings therein. When these powers are compared with what s 3 (1) of the 1972 Act provides, it can be seen clearly that the rule making power extends to regulating and prescribing the procedure to be followed in an application to the

C arbiter to state a case for the opinion of the court. The power given to the arbiter to state a case must obviously be subject to some regulation, in the interests of the court, as to the manner in which, the time within which and the conditions on which it is to be exercised. So also the power given to the court by s 3 (1) of the 1972 Act to direct an arbiter to state a case implies that a procedure must be laid down as to the manner and time within which, and the conditions on which, an order under that subsection may be sought.

D In these circumstances there was no need for any further express rule making power to be given.

This bring us to counsel for the petitioner's next point, which was that even if the court had the necessary rule making power, it could not be exercised in such a way as to cut down the substantive right of a party to apply for a stated case from an arbiter at any stage in the arbitration. He submitted that rule 277 (c) was in conflict with this principle and that since, in terms of rule 276, rules 276 to 280 all had to be read

E "subject to the provisions of the statute allowing such appeal or proceedings", para (c) had no application to stated cases by an arbiter. Rule 277 (c) is in these terms: [his Lordship quoted its terms and continued:]

But there does not seem to us to be any conflict between that power and what s 3 (1) of the 1972 Act provides. The only substantial right relevant to this issue which is conferred by s 3 (1) is to obtain a stated

F case from an arbiter if the Court of Session on such application so directs. A stated case can be obtained at any stage in the arbitration, but this does not mean that it will be appropriate for an arbiter to be directed to state a case at every stage. What rule 277 (c) does is to confer a measure of discretion on the arbiter, who may feel that it is premature for a case to be stated on a question of law which he does not propose to entertain until the facts have been ascertained. If that is his opinion, he is enabled by the rule to postpone further consideration of the application until this stage has been reached. As counsel for the respondents pointed

out, it is inappropriate for the court to be required to entertain questions of law which the arbiter has G decided he is not going to decide for the time being. Furthermore, as can be seen from what was said by Lord Kinnear in *Bennets v Bennet* (1903) 10 SLT at p 612, it is well established that determinations on the procedure to be followed by an arbiter are matters for him to decide. The question whether the facts should be ascertained before an arbiter decides disputed questions on the merits is one for the arbiter as one of procedure, which the court does not have jurisdiction to review. So it is entirely consistent with the existing H law and practice of arbitration in Scotland that an arbiter should be given the discretion which rule 277 (c) extends to all tribunals on the receipt of an application to state a case. The substantive right to have the application considered by the court is not to be seen as having been cut down by this rule. It is a provision relating only to timing and procedure, and it does not remove the right to obtain a stated case if the arbiter decides to state a case, or apply to the court for an order on him to state a case, if he refuses to do so. I

The last point on the question of the rules is whether, on a proper construction of rules 276 to 280, the provisions of rule 277 can have any application to the obtaining of a stated case from an arbiter. The argument was that the expression "the tribunal" in rule 276 did not extend to an arbiter, having regard to the very limited amendment which was made to this rule by the Act of Sederunt (Rules of Court Amendment No 7) 1972. The only amendment which was made was to insert the words "and all stated cases by J an arbiter" between the words "hereinafter referred to as 'the tribunal'" and the words "and all statutory proceedings". This, it was argued, made it impossible to read the word "tribunal" in that rule and in rule 277 as including an arbiter. In the result the only rules which could be applied to arbiters were those in which the expression "tribunal" did not appear. At first sight there was something to be said for this argument, since the amendment which was made to the relevant rules by the Act of Sederunt may be thought to be lacking K in clarity. And this is not the first time the point has been raised. In *Clydebank District Council v Clink* Lord President Emslie observed, 1977 SC at p 152, that there was at least some doubt whether rule 278 of the Rules of Court read together with rule 276 is applicable when an arbiter has refused to state a case. On the other hand, it does not appear to have been thought necessary at that stage to remove the doubt by an amendment to the rules. In practice rules 277 and 278 have been applied to the obtaining of stated cases L from an arbiter from time to time without it being suggested that this was incompetent. It was no doubt in recognition of that practice that the petitioners themselves invoked rule 277 when they made their application to the arbiter in these proceedings to state a case. And there are other examples. In *Gunac Ltd v Inverclyde District Council* the court declined to ordain an arbiter to state a case until a certificate of refusal had been lodged in terms of rule 278. A certificate of refusal which conformed to the requirements of rule

A 277 (d) was then lodged in process, and the prayer of the note was then granted on the ground that the claimants had failed to show cause under rule 278 why a case should not be stated: 1983 SLT 130.

Counsel for the petitioners submitted that no importance should be attached to that case, since there was no dispute between the parties in *Gunac Ltd v Inverclyde District Council* as to whether Rules of Court 277 and 278 applied to arbitrations. That is so, but when the point was raised again in *John L Haley Ltd v Dumfries and Galloway Regional Council* it was argued,

B and after considering the arguments the court held, that on a proper reading of rule 276 these rules apply to all stated cases by an arbiter. This was because rule 276 states expressly that "all stated cases by an arbiter . . . shall . . . be regulated by Rules 277 to 280". Reference was made to the fact that this had already been recognised by the court in *Gunac Ltd v Inverclyde District Council*. It is also worth noting that in *John G McGregor (Contractors) Ltd v Grampian Regional Council* the court granted an application under rule

C 278 for an order requiring an arbiter to state a case in respect of questions on which he had refused to state a case. The main point in dispute was whether it was competent for the court to make such an order in a case where the arbiter had agreed to state a case on some questions but not on others. But there was no dispute on the general question as to whether Rule of Court 278 applied at all. That point is no longer open to argument, following the decision in *John L Haley Ltd v Dumfries & Galloway Regional Council*. In the

D result, all references to "the tribunal" in rules 277 to 280 must be taken to include an arbiter since rule 276 provides that all stated cases by an arbiter are to be regulated by these rules.

For these reasons the petitioners' application to the nobile officium for an order ordaining the arbiter to state a case is incompetent. It is unnecessary, therefore, for us to deal with the arguments which were presented to us on the merits of the application. The question whether or not to state a case before the facts

E were ascertained was a matter for the arbiter, and since he has expressed the opinion that the facts should be ascertained first, the petitioners' application to the court for an order seeking him to be ordained to state a case is excluded for the time being by rule 277 (c). We shall therefore dismiss this application.

F *Counsel for Petitioners, Keen; Solicitors, McGrigor Donald — Counsel for Respondents, A C Hamilton, QC; Solicitors, Shepherd & Wedderburn, WS.*

M G J U

Fullemann v McInnes's Executors

OUTER HOUSE

LORD CULLEN

27 DECEMBER 1991

Damages — Amount — Solatium and patrimonial loss — Head and back — Minor compression fracture of lumbar vertebra with continuing discomfort — Brain damage leading to neurological deficits, difficulties in speech, short term amnesia, difficulties in concentration, reduced intellectual skills and personality change.

Process — Decree — Decree in foreign currency — Patrimonial loss suffered and to be suffered by Swiss resident — Competency of awarding such loss in foreign currency.

The 39 year old owner of a company with a garage business in Switzerland was seriously injured in a road accident on 1 October 1983. He had been the front seat passenger in a car which had collided with another car. The executors of the driver of the other car admitted liability to make reparation to the pursuer. In the accident the pursuer received face injuries, including a bone fracture, undisplaced fractures of bones in his right foot and a minor compression fracture of a lumbar vertebra. From these physical injuries the pursuer made a good recovery, although he continued to have symptoms relating to the back injury. The most serious consequence to the pursuer was injury to his brain. After an initial period of amnesia the pursuer suffered from a number of neurological deficits, severe neuro-psychological deficits and a change of personality. At the time of the accident the pursuer had been successfully operating a garage business of which he held 99 per cent of the share capital. After the accident he was advised to, and did, sell the business. His injuries also prevented him expanding his business by the acquisition of another garage concern. The pursuer sought decree for his patrimonial loss in Swiss francs.

Held, (1) that solatium was properly valued at £42,500 (p 262C); (2) that the loss sustained by the pursuer's company and the loss in value of the company were not the pursuer's loss and were not recoverable by him and that the pursuer's loss was the loss of his income from the company (p 265F-K); (3) that the appropriate multiplier for future loss was 11 years from the date of the proof, a figure derived from Scottish practice and checked against the tables produced by the Ogden committee (p 267B-D); and (4) that decree for the patrimonial loss should be expressed in Swiss francs with the alternative of the equivalent in sterling at the date of payment or at the date of extract, whichever was the earlier (p 268C-F).

Vaughan v Greater Glasgow Passenger Transport Executive, 1984 SLT 44, *considered; The "Despina R"* [1979] AC 685, *followed*.

Action of damages

A   Alex Peter Herman Fullemann, a Swiss national, raised an action of damages against the executors of the late James Vasey McInnes in respect of personal injuries sustained by the pursuer in a road accident on 1 October 1983. At that date the pursuer was aged 39.

The case came to a proof on quantum before the Lord Ordinary (Cullen), liability having been admitted.

Cases referred to

B   *Solatium*
Barrett v Strathclyde Fire Brigade, 1984 SLT 325.
Bohling v George, 21 July 1986, unreported (*Butterworths Personal Injury Litigation Service*).
Caygill v Hughes, 16 April 1986, unreported (*Butterworths Personal Injury Litigation Service*).
Convery v Kirkwood, 1985 SLT 483.
Docherty's Curator Bonis v UIE Shipbuilding (Scotland) Ltd, 1989 SLT 197.
Gerrard v Swanson's Executor, 1980 SLT (Notes) 43.
C   *Jeffries v McNeill*, 8 December 1987, unreported (*Butterworths Personal Injury Litigation Service*).
Macdonald's Curator v Westminster Corporation, 1981 SLT (Notes) 92.
McKinlay v British Steel Corporation, 1987 SLT 522 (affd on another point, 1988 SLT 810).
Wilson v Norman J Stewart & Co (1970) Ltd, 1986 SLT 469.
Winter v News Scotland Ltd, 1991 SLT 828.

D   *Patrimonial loss*
Allan v Barclay (1864) 2 M 873.
Ashcroft v Curtin [1971] 1 WLR 1731; [1971] 3 All ER 1208.
Bellingham v Dhillon [1973] 1 QB 304; [1972] 3 WLR 730; [1973] 1 All ER 20.
Breslin v Britoil plc, 1992 SLT 414.
Esso Petroleum Co v Mardon [1976] QB 801; [1976] 2 WLR 583; [1976] 2 All ER 5.
Fox v P Caulfield & Co Ltd, 1975 SLT (Notes) 71.
Lee v Sheard [1956] 1 QB 192; [1955] 3 WLR 951;
E   [1955] 3 All ER 777.
Mitchell v Glenrothes Development Corporation, 1991 SLT 284.
O'Brien's Curator Bonis v British Steel plc, 1991 SLT 477.
Smith v Heeps, 1990 SLT 871.
Vaughan v Greater Glasgow Passenger Transport Executive, 1984 SLT 44; 1984 SC 32.

F   *Currency of decree*
Commerzbank Aktiengesellschaft v Large, 1977 SLT 219; 1977 SC 375.
"Despina R" (The) [1979] AC 685; [1978] 3 WLR 804; [1979] 1 All ER 421.
Hoffman v Sofaer [1982] 1 WLR 1350.
Miliangos v George Frank (Textiles) [1976] AC 443; [1975] 3 WLR 758; [1975] 3 All ER 801.
North Scottish Helicopters Ltd v United Technologies Corporation Inc (No 2), 1988 SLT 778.

On 27 December 1991 the Lord Ordinary, having assessed damages, had the case *put out* by order to con-sider how to take account of an interim award made at the conclusion of the proof.

G

LORD CULLEN.—In this action, in which liability is admitted, the pursuer seeks damages in respect of the personal injuries sustained by him in an accident on 1 October 1983 when a motor car in which he was a front seat passenger was in collision with a motor car driven by the late James Vasey McInnes, of whom the defenders are the executors. The proof was directed to the pursuer's claims for solatium, financial loss and various matters connected with these claims.

H

The assessment of solatium

At the time of the accident the pursuer was spending a shooting holiday in Scotland. His home was in Weesen, Switzerland, where he ran a garage business. After the collision the pursuer was taken to Ayr County hospital where it was found that he had sustained (i) a displaced and comminuted fracture of the right malar bone, along with various injuries to his nose and the right side of his face; (ii) undisplaced fractures of a number of bones in his right foot and an injury to the great toenail of that foot; (iii) a minor compression fracture of the body of the fifth lumbar vertebra. On 5 October 1983 the pursuer was transferred by air ambulance to Zurich where he received treatment as an inpatient for the repositioning and fixing of the malar bone. Thereafter he was discharged home.

I

The pursuer made a remarkably good recovery from the physical injuries to his body. However, as a result of the fractured vertebra he requires to wear a special shoe, and frequently suffers back pain if, for example, he stands for more than an hour. This can be alleviated by walking or frequent changes in body position. Further, the severity of back pain can be limited by physiotherapy or regular physical exercises such as swimming.

J

The major disabilities which the pursuer has suffered since the accident arise out of the injury to his head which was found to have involved severe trauma to the basal and frontal structures on both sides of the brain. Immediately following the accident he suffered a short period of unconsciousness, followed by a period of post-traumatic disorientation and disordered behaviour. He had amnesia in respect of a period of at least two weeks. He has since then suffered from (i) a number of neurological deficits such as a slight motor hemisyndrome on the right side and hypoaesthesia in the maxillary branch of the trigeminal nerve on the right side of the face; (ii) severe neuro-psychological deficits, which initially included some difficulty in speech production, but throughout have comprised amnesia in regard to short term memory, difficulty in concentration and reduced motor and intellectual skills; and (iii) a change of personality. In regard to these matters I had the benefit of the agreed medical reports of Professor V Henn, of the Chair of Neurology at Zurich University Hospital, Dr M Regard, senior neuro-psychologist at that hospital, and Professor D N Brooks of Balerno, Midlothian.

K

L

The neuro-psychological deficits from which the pursuer suffers may be illustrated in a number of ways. He finds it difficult to follow a conversation involving more than one other participant. Faced with a task involving the organisation of information his span of concentration is not more than one hour. During such a period he suffers from increasingly severe difficulty in auditory and visual concentration, diminished speed and flexibility of cognition and decreased ability to suppress intrusions. This is associated with an increasing complaint of headache which results from stress or the "overflow" of information with which the pursuer is unable to cope. Such headaches are felt as a dull pain and a feeling of pressure around the head. They are not amenable to treatment by ordinary medication. The pursuer requires to retreat to a darkened room for a period until he recovers. This was clearly illustrated during the course of the pursuer's evidence, which required to be taken in several parts on this account. The pursuer attended a rehabilitation centre in Bellikon, Switzerland, for two months in 1984 and again in 1985, where he was given exercises in cognition, psychotherapy, occupational therapy and fitness training. These do not appear to have been of much benefit to him. In addition he received training in Zurich in ways of dealing with his concentration and other deficits. Professor Henn expressed the view that the pursuer's brain dysfunction should be classified as medium to severe. While there was some room for a degree of recovery up to two years after the accident the disability remaining thereafter was likely to be permanent with no likelihood of further improvement.

The pursuer's change in personality arose through reaction to his disabilities and their effect on his life. Professor Henn described him as tending to be irritable, easily frustrated and less stable in emotion. This was very likely to affect family life and his relationship with friends. Professor Brooks, who also noted the pursuer's irritability, mentioned the pursuer's difficulty in tolerating noise as well as information overload and his suffering episodes of what he interpreted as panic attacks. There had been a deterioration in the pursuer's emotional state over a period of two or three years after the accident which was a very common result of an accident victim realising his disabilities. On occasions the pursuer's feelings of worthlessness and failure had been so great that he contemplated suicide. There had been an improvement in the pursuer's emotional state since 1987. He expected further improvement but he pointed out that the pursuer would always have problems relating to his memory and concentration.

When the pursuer attempted to return to work in 1984 he found that he could not concentrate for more than one or one and a half hours at a time. In this way he could achieve two periods of work during the day, and then only when he was free to work at his own pace. He had difficulty even in writing out cheques. Before the accident he had been a very good businessman and an excellent mechanic, working hours well beyond the average. Oskar Hauser, who knew the pursuer through the motor trade, described the difference in the pursuer before and after the accident as

"like day and night". The pursuer was not able to concentrate on decision making or evaluate consequences. He forgot dates and failed to keep to arrangements. Mrs Margaret Biggar, who was the secretary in the garage business, described the pursuer's very limited capacity for work and said that when he succumbed to a headache it was impossible to talk to him. Stephan Boni, who was a lifelong friend of the pursuer and a fellow engineer, found that after the accident the pursuer was "completely different". He thought he could do things but he got them wrong. He gave as an example the pursuer's bad judgment in buying second hand motor cars in the United States. His mind was "uncontrolled": one minute he said this; the next something completely different; and yet the pursuer did not accept that he was no longer able to be a businessman. His friend, Derek Mackie, said that the pursuer's headaches were liable to occur more rapidly in overcast weather. When carrying out small repair jobs he would hurt himself, do more damage than repair and become quickly frustrated. I am in no doubt that Professor Henn was right in concluding that while some form of occupation is within the pursuer's capability, provided that he undertakes it in his own time and at his own pace, he is and has been since the accident incapable of carrying out his pre-accident work and indeed any form of employment since this would involve working under pressure in one way or another. Professor Henn observed in his report that the pursuer "would utterly fail in a free contest in a competitive market if he were measured against similar aged men of comparable training".

At the time of the accident the pursuer was married and had two sons. A daughter was born in 1983 after the accident. His wife left him in November 1984 and a divorce followed in 1987. The pursuer did not dispute that there had been difficulties between himself and his wife prior to the accident. This was due to the fact that he spent long hours in the business, and in particular on the sales side in the evenings. He said that he had intended to rebuild the marriage. He and his wife had discussed living in the south of Switzerland from which she came. In this connection the purchase of a garage company in Lugano, to which I shall refer later, would have assisted. He thought that if there had been no accident he would still be married to her. The pursuer's wife, whose evidence was taken on interrogatories before the area court in the Swiss Canton of Sargans, confirmed that immediately prior to the accident her relationship with the pursuer was no longer harmonious. She said that she had been thinking of leaving the pursuer when she was expecting her daughter. Mr Boni and Mr Mackie expressed the opinion that had there been no accident the pursuer would still be with his wife, or at any rate he would have been able to pull the marriage together. Having considered the whole evidence which is available to me on this matter, and in particular the evidence of the pursuer's wife and the pursuer's concession as to the state of relations with his wife prior to the accident, I am not satisfied on the balance of probabilities that in the absence of the accident the pursuer would have succeeded in preserving his marriage. Accordingly I do not consider that the breakup of his marriage was caused by his accident.

Counsel for the pursuer invited me to assess solatium at the figure of £60,000, under reference to the decisions in the English cases of *Caygill v Hughes, Bohling v George* and *Jeffries v McNeill*, dated 16 April, 21 July 1986 and 8 December 1987, all unreported (noted in Butterworth's *Personal Injury Litigation Service*, IX/207-208); and the Scottish case of *Winter v News Scotland Ltd*. For the defenders the Dean of Faculty invited me to assess solatium at the figure of £40,000 under reference to the Scottish decisions in *McKinlay v British Steel Corporation; Convery v Kirkwood; Wilson v Norman J Stewart & Co (1970) Ltd; Barrett v Strathclyde Fire Brigade; Gerrard v Swanson's Exr; Docherty's CB v UIE Shipbuilding (Scotland) Ltd;* and *Macdonald's Curator v Westminster Corporation*.

Having regard to the evidence and the submissions of counsel I have reached the view that a figure of £42,500 is an appropriate figure in respect of solatium.

The garage business operated by the pursuer

After serving an apprenticeship in his native village the pursuer obtained an engineering qualification and started a garage business on his own account. Thereafter in 1979 he incorporated Fullemann Garage AG as a limited company. Since that time he has held 99 per cent of its share capital. In the same year this company acquired premises in which its business was thereafter carried on. These premises included not only a garage but also a number of flats, one of which was occupied by the pursuer and his family. The company's business was initially concerned with the repairing and servicing of motor vehicles. It expanded in due course to include the sale of motor fuel and spare parts, and the sale of motor vehicles and motor boats. The business acquired agencies, initially from Fiat and latterly from Volvo Switzerland. The agency with Volvo was classed as a "B" agency, that description applying to a business which sold at least 15 motor vehicles a year. The premises did not include a showroom. A few motor vehicles were kept in the street and catalogues were provided for prospective purchasers. The business achieved a place in the top third of the "B" agencies in the east of Switzerland and won awards from Volvo for exceeding sales targets. At the time of the accident the pursuer had built up a team of employees consisting of two mechanics, two or three apprentices and a secretary. The pursuer worked some 13-14 hours per day in the business and was the only person who was involved in its management. At the beginning of the day he would divide work among mechanics, deal with office work in conjunction with the secretary and then take part in the repair work. Most of his time was spent on repairs, where he took on the more complicated work and instructed apprentices. He also checked cars which were submitted for certificates of roadworthiness. He dealt with sales only in the evenings or to some extent after lunch as he did not have time to do so otherwise.

Each year the pursuer's remuneration was fixed by him after discussion with OBT Treuhand AG, a firm of accountants whose branch at St Gallen provided the business with bookkeeping services, management advice and auditing. The amount which was treated as remuneration depended naturally on the profits of the business. The pursuer said in evidence that he paid himself less than the profits as he kept investing in the company. The amount of the remuneration which had been fixed in this way was credited to his loan account with the company. The pursuer drew on that account from time to time to meet his personal requirements. The profits remaining after allowance for his remuneration were subject to taxation as the net profits of the company, and, in accordance with Swiss law, the tax formed a deduction from the gross profits of the company in the following year. The pursuer's remuneration, whether or not it was drawn upon by him, was treated as his income for his own tax liability in the year in question.

Some months after the pursuer attempted to return to his former work it became clear that he was unable to manage the business or to do other work on it. On the advice of OBT the business employed a manager from June 1984 to deal with the repair and servicing side of the business. He was Martin Muller, who was a qualified motor engineer. Following his accident the pursuer continued to draw on his loan account with the company although he was no longer credited with a true remuneration.

In due course the pursuer was advised that the motor business, which comprised the garage business with the exception of business relating to the heritable property and investments of the company, should be sold, since the pursuer was unable to manage the business himself and in these circumstances it was no longer viable. This advice was given by OBT and the pursuer's friends. The pursuer himself was initially reluctant to agree to this. The motor business was advertised for sale by OBT on several occasions in 1987. Following various attempts to achieve a sale an agreement was made whereby the assets of the motor business were sold to Garage Martin Muller AG, a company incorporated by Mr Muller. The takeover date was 1 November 1987, at which date Mr Muller ceased to be employed by Fullemann Garage AG. The total consideration for the takeover included payment of a capital sum by one company to the other amounting to SF 340,000 (Swiss francs). It was also agreed that Garage Martin Muller AG should pay an initial rent of SF 45,600 per annum, which was made up of a true rent of SF 32,000 and a goodwill premium of SF 13,600. The lease was to subsist for a period of 10 years, subject to an option to renew for a further five years. Mr Daniel Stoop of OBT said that there was a substantial reason for not allowing the existing operation of the business to continue indefinitely. It could not be expected that Mr Muller would be willing to continue indefinitely as an employee. He would want to be "his own businessman". I am entirely satisfied that the sale of the motor business was in all the circumstances a reasonable step to take.

Following upon the sale of the motor business the pursuer drew very substantially upon his loan account with Fullemann Garage AG not merely in order to meet his living expenses but also to meet his liabilities to his wife arising out of their divorce in 1987; and in order to invest money in the purchase of a flat and a restaurant business in Spain in 1987. The latter business proved to be a total financial failure in 1988 and 1989. The pursuer said: "I tried but everything seemed to go wrong." The pursuer's borrowing from the company rose from SF 577,799.60 at the end of 1988 to SF 1,193,928.96 at the end of 1989. The pursuer accepted in evidence that he required to repay this borrowing and said that he would do so when he could. In a letter to the pursuer in regard to the affairs of Fullemann Garage AG for the year 1989 dated 22 April 1991 OBT pointed out as auditors of the company that: "The ability to repay this debt (SF 1,193,928.96) cannot be conclusively judged at this time." They went on to state: "In the event of the debt claim against Alex Fullemann being wholly or partially non recoverable, adjustments would be necessary, which could lead to risk of excessive debt. For this eventuality we refer the Board to the provisions of Article 725 OR. In addition we would point out that Mr Alex Fullemann's credit balance current account represents a violation of the prohibition against refunding of deposits under Article 680 para 2 OR." The articles referred to in this quotation form part of the Swiss Company Code.

It may be noted that in 1989 or 1990 the pursuer visited the United States of America along with a friend and there bought a number of secondhand motor cars at auctions which he imported to Switzerland. These were not a source of significant income to the pursuer. Few of them were sold and in general they were of poor quality. This activity represented no more than a hobby or interest for the pursuer, and, as I have indicated earlier in this opinion, it appears that the pursuer's power of judgment in this matter was poor.

In August and September 1983 the pursuer had discussed the acquisition by Fullemann Garage AG of the whole shares of a company which carried on a garage business at 10 Via Maggio, Lugano, Southern Switzerland. The owner of the company was Giuseppe Guscio who had operated a garage business for many years in Lugano. Currently it held a Volvo "A" dealership, being appropriate for a business selling more than 50 motor vehicles per annum. This business had 23 employees. Mr Guscio, who was then 63 years of age, had had a heart attack and was in a weak financial position, wished to sell his company and retire from business. Two of the personnel of Volvo Switzerland, Mr Oskar Hauser and Mr Charles Blochliger, recommended the pursuer as a suitable person to be the purchaser. The pursuer for his part considered that the existing business of Fullemann

Garage AG was too small and that there were no prospects of expansion at Weesen. Lugano was some 200 km from Weesen. However, the pursuer knew the area. His holiday home was 40 km north of Lugano. Further, as the pursuer explained, his wife preferred the warmer climate of the south. He said that he expected that the operation of the business at Lugano would provide higher profits since it had a larger business and had access to a larger catchment of population. Mr Hauser said in evidence that he had advised the pursuer about the potential of the Lugano business. He could see a good business for Volvo, with a big increase in sales and greater customer satisfaction. Volvo would have been likely to approve the takeover of the dealership. Negotiations between the pursuer and Mr Guscio before the pursuer's accident had reached a point at which they had "shaken hands" on the deal after discussing a price of, in Mr Guscio's words, "around SF 400,000 more or less". This appeared to be subject to the pursuer's inspection of the books of the company. At that stage the pursuer had apparently not made up his mind as to whether or not the existing business in Weesen would be retained by Fullemann Garage AG. It was possible that it would be sold as his friends advised him. However, he was reluctant to sell as he had "founded it and was attached to it". If it was to be retained, perhaps for the pursuer's sons, it would have required the employment of a manager. No date for the takeover had been agreed before the pursuer sustained his accident. Mr Guscio was anxious that it should be as soon as possible. The pursuer had not reached the stage of examining the books of the company. There was no evidence as to how the purchase of the shares would have been financed and with what results on the net profits of Fullemann Garage AG. The pursuer's accident had dashed Mr Guscio's expectations of a sale. However, he was able to find an alternative purchaser to whom the shares were sold in August 1984, and at a price in excess of SF 400,000. In the light of the evidence summarised above I am satisfied that it is likely that had it not been for the pursuer's accident, Fullemann Garage AG would have acquired the Lugano company. I consider the financial implications of this later in this opinion.

The parties' submissions in regard to the assessment of financial loss

The pursuer led the evidence of Mr M M Kapoor, FCIS, who is a very experienced loss assessor and accountant. I will require to deal with certain aspects of his evidence in more detail later in this opinion but for the present it is sufficient to set out the main outline of his approach. He set out to quantify (i) the loss of or diminution in the profits of the motor business (before allowance for the pursuer's remuneration) which resulted from the pursuer's incapacity; (ii) the loss of benefits sustained by the pursuer as a result of that incapacity; and (iii) the loss of goodwill of the motor business.

As regards the first, he took as his basis for projection the net operating profits of the company for the years 1979-83 which on average were SF 99,800 per annum before, and SF 109,494 after, certain adjustments made by him. For the projection from 1984 onwards he made annual allowances for trends in favourable business and in price inflation; and took a reparation period until the year 2009 when the pursuer would be 65 years of age. Against this he set the adjusted net profits for 1984-87 and the anticipated income from the investment of the proceeds of sale of the motor business to Garage Martin Muller AG. This brought out a loss to 1987 of SF 401,873; and to the year 2009 of SF 3,290,087. He then converted the past and future loss to a present value by applying compound interest at 5 per cent per annum. As regards the second, he took the difference between the past and anticipated benefits to the year 2009, subject to an annual allowance for price inflation, and the actual benefits enjoyed in the years 1984-87. This brought out a figure of SF 991,244, which was similarly converted to a present value. As regards the third he used the same formula for the valuation of goodwill which had been used by OBT in regard to the sale of the motor business in 1987 but applied it to the information which was available at the end of 1983. On this basis he determined that the goodwill of the business would have commanded a higher value at that time. He accordingly quantified a corresponding shortfall in the premium rent for the 10 years of the initial lease of the premises. The total amounted to SF 126,650 which was again converted to a present value.

In his closing submissions counsel for the pursuer put before me certain further computations which incorporated certain parts of the work of Mr Kapoor but were also based on other evidence.

The first two of these computations were designed to quantify loss under the three headings to which Mr Kapoor had directed his attention. The loss was divided into what had been sustained to the end of 1991 on the one hand, and future loss on the other. Counsel founded on evidence given by Mr Hauser and by Mr Stoop, to which I will refer later, in support of the view that the net profits of the Lugano business would have been at least double those of the Weesen business. Accordingly counsel for the pursuer used as the annual loss of profit SF 219,000 (on the basis of Mr Kapoor's adjusted figure of SF 109,494 for Weesen), which failing SF 198,000 (on the basis of the unadjusted figure of SF 99,800). This produced a figure to the end of 1991 of SF 1,779,276 (or SF 1,551,144). On the assumption that the pursuer would have worked to the age of 70, a multiplier of 13.5 was applied to a continuing loss, as at the end of 1991, of SF 240,000 (or SF 219,000) per annum, giving a further loss of SF 3,240,000 (or SF 2,956,500). The third and last computation was based on the assumption that the pursuer was entitled to claim loss of remuneration (as opposed to the loss of profits on the business). In reliance on evidence given by Mr Stoop this computation showed an annual remuneration of SF 75,000 in 1984 rising in stages to SF 180,000 in 1991. The computation to the end of 1991 (which also included a claim for loss of benefits and the loss of

goodwill of the motor business) amounted to SF 1,137,831. Further loss of remuneration and benefits was computed at 13.5 years' purchase (as before), giving a future loss of SF 2,814,736.

It is clear from the above that the pursuer's primary approach to the claim in respect of financial loss was based on the treatment of the company's loss of profit and of goodwill as suffered by the pursuer himself. I should add that no case was put forward that the pursuer was entitled to claim any diminution in the value in his shares in Fullemann Garage AG, whatever may have been the extent of any diminution.

At this point in my opinion it is therefore necessary for me to consider whether the pursuer is entitled to claim the company's loss of profit and loss of goodwill as his own. In support of that claim counsel for the pursuer referred to *Vaughan v Greater Glasgow Passenger Transport Executive*. In that case the pursuer who was a partner in a firm of electrical engineers was rewarded for his labours by entitlement of 55 per cent of the profits of the partnership. The loss of this was treated as a foreseeable claim in respect of loss of earnings (see, for example, Lord President Emslie, 1984 SLT at p 46). Counsel also relied upon a number of English cases. In *Lee v Sheard* the Court of Appeal took the view that the loss of £1,500 which the plaintiff shareholder would have received from his company if he had not sustained an accident was neither too remote nor fell to be regarded as the company's loss rather than his own. In *Ashcroft v Curtin* the plaintiff who was injured was the major shareholder in a private company in which he worked as an engineer. At the trial a claim was made for the extent to which the company's profits had decreased after his accident. It was clear that such a claim had the approval in principle of the trial judge and apparently the Court of Appeal. The trial judge is quoted by Edmund Davies LJ at [1971] 1 WLR pp 1734-1735 as saying that it was of little practical significance that the plaintiff held 40 per cent of the shareholding where his wife held 20 per cent and his two children 15 per cent each. He said: "this company, like so many private companies, distributes its profits entirely in accordance with the wishes of the founder, and entirely with a view to producing the minimum of taxation. . . . Any fluctuations in profit will be taken up by [the plaintiff] for his own benefit". He also said: "On any break-up of the company, matters would have been so organised that [the plaintiff] got the money, and his was the loss (and the only loss) which flows from any lack of profitability consequent upon this accident." However the claim failed in that case owing to the unreliability of the accounts. The plaintiff was awarded damages in respect of the risk of his being thrown on to the labour market and being unable to find a livelihood. Counsel also pointed out that in *Bellingham v Dhillon*, which was concerned with a claim of loss of profits in regard to a business venture, it was agreed that the loss of the plaintiff's company fell to be treated as his loss; and in *Esso Petroleum Co v Mardon* the Court of Appeal did not distinguish between the money which the defendant's

company had lost as a result of the plaintiff's negligent
A misstatement and what the defendant had lost. In the
present case the pursuer's remuneration was artificial.
It had been put in "merely to keep the tax straight".
It was of no significance whether taxation fell on the
part of the profits which were designated as his
remuneration or on the part which was retained by the
company.

In reply the Dean of Faculty submitted that it was
essential to keep in view the distinct and separate
persona of the limited company. In *Allan v Barclay*
B Lord Kinloch at p 874 set out the well known grand
rule on the subject of damages as being that: "none
can be claimed except as naturally and directly arise
out of the wrong done; and such, therefore, as may
reasonably be supposed to have been in the view of the
wrongdoer. . . . The personal injuries of the individual
himself will be properly held to have been in the contemplation of the wrongdoer. But he cannot be held
bound to have surmised the secondary injuries done to
all holding relations with the individual, whether that
C of master, or any other". It followed that the court
should be concerned only with the loss of earnings
suffered by the pursuer himself and not with the company's loss of profits or any loss in the value of its
assets such as the goodwill of the business. The
creation of a limited company entailed not merely
benefits but also disadvantages to the incorporator.
The pursuer could not claim that he fell to be identified with the company in regard to the alleged losses,
and yet deny that identification when it came to claims
D against the company. He would not in fact be required
to pay the debts of the company. By the same token
he could not claim the company's losses as if they were
his own. This did not involve any injustice: incor-
porators could not claim the protection of a limited
company and yet "lift the veil" whenever it suited
them to do so. The Dean of Faculty pointed out that
in *Vaughan* the pursuer was held entitled to recover
for loss of profits only insofar as they represented the
agreed remuneration to him for his labours in the
E work of the partnership, and that no doubt was cast on
the correctness of the decision of Lord McDonald in
Fox v P Caulfield & Co Ltd. In that case he withheld
from probation a claim in respect of the loss of the
share of company profits which the pursuer would
have received in the event of the company being
wound up or taken over. In *Vaughan* it was observed
that this was not a claim for loss of earnings. As
regards the English cases the Dean of Faculty submitted that the sum awarded in *Lee* was at least consis-
F tent with having been a loss of earnings. In *Ashcroft*
the point at issue in the present case was not taken but
was apparently conceded by the defendant. The passages quoted from the opinion of the trial judge
involved a failure to address a difficulty of a fundamental character. In *Bellingham* there was an
express concession that the loss of the company should
be treated as the loss of the plaintiff.

In my opinion the pursuer's claim in respect of the
loss of profit of the motor business and the loss of
goodwill is not well founded in law and upon the facts

of the present case. It is not based on any authoritative
decision in the law of Scotland; and the opinions G
delivered by the members of the court in *Vaughan* do
not support it but tend to exclude it. A clear distinction was drawn in that case between a claim in
respect of loss of earnings, however quantification fell
to be carried out, and a claim in respect of loss of value
to the corporator. In the present case any loss of profit
or loss on the value of goodwill was sustained by the
company. The first could not be regarded as the pursuer's loss of earnings unless the difference between
the company and the pursuer is ignored. The second H
was an asset which could never be regarded as belonging to the pursuer unless what belonged to the
company was treated as belonging to him. Even then,
on no view could it be regarded as a loss of earnings,
even though it might be valued by reference to loss of
profits. An examination of the facts in the present
case, far from supporting the pursuer's claim, demonstrates that it is unsound. It may well be that the
pursuer had a considerable amount of discretion each
year as to the amount which should be determined as
his remuneration. But the fact that he had such a dis- I
cretion does not go to show that the determination can
simply be ignored as if it had never taken place. As I
have quoted above, it determined what was left in the
company's hands as an investment for future trading
— no doubt for good business reasons. What was fixed
as the pursuer's remuneration was credited to his loan
account with the company. The existence of this
account and the crediting or debiting of sums to this
account demonstrate the separation, both legal and
factual, between the company on the one hand and the J
pursuer on the other. This is also illustrated by the
letter from OBT dated 22 April 1991 to which I
referred earlier; and by the different tax treatment
accorded on the one hand to the remuneration fixed
for the pursuer and on the other the profits of the
company remaining after allowance had been made for
that remuneration.

In these circumstances I am of opinion that the
pursuer's claim in respect of financial loss is limited to
a claim relating to loss of past and prospective earn- K
ings and benefits. I turn now to the assessment of such
a claim.

The assessment of financial loss

I am satisfied that it is appropriate to proceed to
assess this loss by dividing it into the loss to date
(taken as being the end of 1991) and future loss. I leave
over for the time being questions in regard to taxation
and in regard to the currency in which decree should
be pronounced.   L

The pursuer's remuneration in the years 1980-83
inclusive amounted on average to just under SF
75,000. [His Lordship considered the evidence including evidence about the possible profitability of the
Lugano concern, in relation to which his Lordship
concluded that the profits of the Lugano business were
likely to be greater than those of the concern founded
by the pursuer but that he had no information about
the actual effect on the pursuer's income. His Lordship concluded:]

In the light of these considerations I consider that it
A is right that I should allow for a progressive increase
in the pursuer's remuneration not merely in the light
of the passage of time but also in the light of the likely
acquisition of the Lugano company. However, I can
only do so by proceeding on a broad basis which takes
into account the quality of the evidence with which I
have to deal and the uncertainties which were inherent
in it. In the light of these considerations I assess the
pursuer's loss on the basis that his salary would have
been SF 75,000 in 1984 and 1985; SF 100,000 in
B 1986, 1987 and 1988; SF 120,000 in 1989 and 1990;
and SF 140,000 in 1991. It was not in dispute that the
average annual value of benefits enjoyed by the
pursuer over the period 1979-83 amounted to SF
28,499. I accept counsel for the pursuer's submission
that this sum should be added to the loss of remuneration for each of the years 1984 to 1991. Against this
total fall to be set (i) certain payments actually received
by the pursuer from Fullemann Garage AG in the
years 1984-87 amounting to SF 1,900, 1,206, 15,300
C and 4,140; and (ii) the value of benefits received in
those years being SF 22,417 per annum. The resulting
figure amounts to SF 945,778.

I turn now to consider future loss. In the light of my
conclusions as to the level of remuneration which the
pursuer would have been likely to earn in 1991 the
continuing loss falls to be assessed on the basis of
SF 140,000 per annum to which SF 28,499 in respect
of loss of benefits falls to be added, giving a total
SF 168,499 per annum. It is appropriate to treat this
D as the multiplicand. The question then is as to the
appropriate multiplier, having regard to what would
have been the prospective working life of the pursuer,
subject to the various contingencies which were liable
to have affected it.

The pursuer's argument in favour of a multiplier of
13.5 was based on the following approach. He
founded on the evidence of the pursuer that he would
have worked as long as he could, without setting a
E particular limit in advance. He would work at least
until the age of 70. Counsel sought to support this by
table 43 from a work entitled "Barwerttafeln" which
was published in Zurich in 1989. Dr Josef Zurkirchen,
a Swiss lawyer who was employed by SUVA, a mutual
company which deals with accident insurance,
explained that such a table was used in Swiss courts
and by his company. The table gave the average
period of "activity" for men and women of various
ages. This was based, he said, on the activity period
for all who worked for money. It showed that a man
F who was 47 years of age, which is the current age of
the pursuer, would have a prospective period of
activity of 22.49 years. This type of information
would be used in order to arrive at a capitalisation of
annual sums. Counsel for the pursuer also referred me
to the recent decision of the First Division in
O'Brien's CB v British Steel plc. He founded on table
3 of the tables produced by the Ogden committee in
1984. This showed that for men aged 47 at the date
of trial the multiplier for loss of earnings to the age of
65, after allowance for population mortality and a rate

of interest of 4½ per cent, was 11.5. The Ogden committee did not provide a table for loss of earnings to G
the age of 70 but he pointed out that, according to the
same table, for a man aged 42 at the date of trial the
corresponding multiplier was 13.5. According to table
42 of "Barwerttafeln", the expectation of life of a man
of 47 years of age was 31.69 years; whereas according
to appendix II to Munkman on *Damages for Personal
Injuries and Death*, which was based on the Registrar
General's tables constructed from mortality experience in 1974-76, the expectation of life of men aged 45
and 50 years was 27.8 and 23.4 years respectively. He H
also submitted that the contingencies other than death
were less significant for the pursuer than for ordinary
employees. The contingencies of redundancy, dismissal and company failure did not apply in the
present case. Accordingly there should be no reduction for contingencies other than death. In any event
the multiplier should not be below 13.

In reply the Dean of Faculty submitted that I was
not bound to follow the tables produced by the Ogden
committee. In *O'Brien's CB* it had been observed that I
they were no more than a useful guide. He renewed an
objection to the use of the tables in "Barwerttafeln"
on a number of grounds. In particular their use was
not foreshadowed on record; the tables without the
rest of the work were incomprehensible; and in any
event the basis and accuracy of the tables had not been
proved. He had declined in these circumstances to
cross examine Dr Zurkirchen. He invited me to follow
the general line indicated for the appropriate multiplier in a number of recent Scottish decisions. In J
Smith v Heeps and *Mitchell v Glenrothes Development
Corporation* the court took the view that a multiplier
of 8 was appropriate for arriving at loss of earnings or
pension value in the case of a man approaching 50
years of age. In *Breslin v Britoil plc* a multiplier of 6
had been adopted in the case of an offshore worker
aged 49, who had the prospect of working offshore
"for a number of years, perhaps until his early to
mid-50s. Thereafter he might have continued as a
rigger onshore". K

The pursuer's approach to quantification appears to
me to face a number of significant difficulties. In
O'Brien's CB the court made it clear that where
possible the court should follow the traditional
approach of basing an award on a conventional figure
derived from experience and from awards in comparable cases; and that while there was no reason why
judicial notice should not be taken of the tables
produced by the Ogden committee they should not be L
used as a starting point but could be used to check
multipliers arrived at by other means (see Lord President Hope at pp 486-487). In the present case counsel
for the pursuer made no attempt to relate his figure of
13.5 to any Scottish award. Further, his use of table
3 as a means of arriving at the multiplier for loss of
earnings to the age of 70 appears to me to be unsound.
Common sense would suggest that the risk of mortality increases with advancing age, and accordingly
that it does not follow that the prospective loss of a
man aged 42 until a retiring age of 65 is the same as

the prospective loss of a man aged 47 with a retiring
age of 70. The exercise is further complicated, if not
made more obscure, by counsel's resort to the tables
in "Barwerttafeln". The expectation of life which is
shown in table 42, however that is arrived at, appears
significantly longer than that shown in the life expectancy tables which are referred to in connection with
the tables produced by the Ogden committee. I do
not understand why only excerpts from "Barwerttafeln"
were produced; or at any rate why the pursuer's
advisers did not take steps to obtain evidence as to the
basis on which they were arrived at or reach agreement
with the defenders as to the facts of the matter. I do
not know on what data, relating to what period and by
what method these tables were arrived at. I am wholly
sympathetic to the defenders' objection on this point
and I sustain their objection to the use of the tables
taken from this work. I propose to base my choice of
the Scottish multiplier upon what I consider to be the
current practice in Scotland and to check this so far as
I can do so against table 3 produced by the Ogden
committee. The Scottish decisions to which I was
referred by the Dean of Faculty support the use of a
multiplier of 8 in the case of employees who were aged
between 47 and 48 and had a prospective working life
until the age of 65. A multiplier of 8 would represent
in those cases a discount of just over 3 in the light of
what is shown in table 3, given a return of 4½ per
cent. I accept that in the case of the pursuer there was
no predetermined limit to his working life and it was
likely that, given that he was fit to do so, he would
have taken whatever opportunity he had to go on
working after the age of 65. I also accept that as the
major shareholder in a garage company he was less
vulnerable to loss of employment for reasons to do
with business conditions. These considerations
indicate to me that it is appropriate in the case of the
pursuer to raise the undiscounted multiplier to 13 and
to discount it by 2. I accordingly adopt a multiplier of
11. On that basis the resulting figure for loss of earnings and benefit is SF 1,853,489. [His Lordship then
dealt with a question with which this report is not concerned and continued:]

The effect of taxation

It was agreed between the parties by joint minute,
that: "Esto the pursuer is to be regarded as a Swiss
resident for Swiss tax law purposes he would require
to pay Swiss federal tax on any award of solatium and
that any award of solatium requires to be uprated for
such tax." It was not in dispute that the relevant rate
for this purpose, if it arose, was 11.5 per cent in
accordance with the tax table set out in no 82 of
process. It was, however, in dispute whether the
assumption in terms of the joint minute had been
proved. On record the pursuer also avers that an
award in respect of loss of earnings should be based
upon his gross earnings in respect that under the law
of Switzerland awards of damages in respect of loss of
earnings and other taxable receipts are subject to
income tax. Mr Stoop in the course of his evidence
spoke to this being the situation under Swiss law.
However, the significance of this for the present case

depended once more upon whether the pursuer was to
be regarded as a Swiss resident for Swiss tax law purposes. [His Lordship considered this point and concluded:]

I have come to the conclusion that the evidence to
which I have referred is adequate to enable me to infer
that the assumption set out in the joint minute is
proved and that my assessment of solatium falls to be
increased by a figure which will enable that sum to
remain after tax at 11.5 per cent has been deducted in
accordance with Swiss law. The additional figure for
this purpose is £5,522, giving a gross figure of
£48,022. It also follows that my assessment of loss of
remuneration should remain, as above, on the basis of
gross earnings.

Costs incurred by the pursuer

The remaining items of patrimonial loss for which
the pursuer claims are concerned with the medical
costs incurred and to be incurred by him including the
air transfer costs arising out of the accident. It is
agreed that these amount to SF 54,642.35.

The currency in which decree should be given in respect of patrimonial loss

For the pursuer it was argued by junior counsel that
the principle of restitutio in integrum could be fulfilled only if the award in regard to patrimonial loss
was expressed in Swiss francs or the sterling equivalent at the date of payment or enforcement, whichever
was the earlier. Otherwise the pursuer would be at the
risk of currency fluctuations. There was no reason
why that just result could not be achieved. It was
pointed out that in *Miliangos v Frank* the House of
Lords had reserved its opinion as to the currency in
which judgment should be given in cases of tort.
However, in *The "Despina R"* it was recognised that
it was competent in a case of tort to make an award
expressed in a foreign currency so long as it was one
in which the foreign plaintiff had suffered his loss.
Reference was made to the speeches of Lord Wilberforce [1979] AC at pp 696-697 and Lord Russell of
Killowen at pp 703-704. In the former of these
passages Lord Wilberforce observed that to give
judgment in the currency in which the plaintiff's loss
was sustained gave him exactly what he had lost and
committed him only to the risk of changes in the value
of that currency, or those currencies which are either
his currency or those which he had chosen to use. This
was followed in the case of a claim for personal injury
in *Hoffman v Sofaer*. There was no authority in Scots
law to the effect that decree required to be given in
sterling in a case of delict. It was pointed out in *North
Scottish Helicopters Ltd v United Technologies Corporation Inc (No 2)* that decree would not have been given
in a foreign currency since it was not proved that the
trading accounts had been maintained in that
currency.

Junior counsel for the defenders maintained that the
question was not one of competency but whether it
was appropriate to grant decree which allowed for conversion at a date later than the date of judgment. The

A only authority which was relevant was the decision in *The "Despina R"*. However, it was not binding; and in any event should be distinguished since it was concerned with dealing with the argument that conversion from the foreign currency to sterling should be as at the date of breach. In the present case the defenders maintained that the conversion should be as at the date of decree. Parties were agreed that at that date the appropriate exchange rate was SF 2.55 to the pound sterling. Sterling was the appropriate currency in which to express the judgment. Any other approach could be prejudicial to the defenders. The true

B measure of their liability fell to be established at the date of the judgment on the proof. It was not equitable to increase this having regard to external factors. The pursuer was protected against currency fluctuations by means of the interest which would run on the decree. The relatively high rate of interest reflected the position of the pound sterling on the money market. A higher return would be obtained than the pursuer would receive in Switzerland. Junior counsel for the defenders also suggested that it was illogical for

C the pursuer to accept a decree in sterling in respect of solatium but to seek a decree by reference to Swiss currency in regard to patrimonial loss.

There is no doubt in the present case that the patrimonial loss which was and will continue to be suffered by the pursuer is one suffered in Swiss currency. I see no reason either in principle or on the facts of this case to reject or distinguish the approach adopted in *The "Despina R"*. That approach implies

D that judgment is given in the particular foreign currency with a view to its conversion at the latest practicable date, in accordance with the general considerations set out in the earlier case of *Miliangos*. I note that in the Scottish case of *Commerzbank Aktiengesellschaft v Large*, in which the case of *Miliangos* was considered, Lord President Emslie observed, 1977 SLT at p 224 that "ideally the conversion date should be the date when the debt is actually paid. If, of course, the debt is not paid voluntarily when decree is taken, the search must be for the latest

E practicable date for conversion in order to reduce to a minimum the risk that the foreign creditor who has to enforce his decree will suffer by reason of an adverse fluctuation of the value of sterling as against the currency of account". I do not consider that this approach is any less appropriate in days when interest rates in this country are even higher than they were in 1977. While the relative strength or weakness of the pound sterling on the money market may be a factor which affects the rate of interest which is applied to decrees

F for payment of damages, it does not in my view follow that fluctuations in the value of the pound sterling for conversion purposes can be ignored. Accordingly it is in my view appropriate that as regards patrimonial loss decree should be expressed in Swiss currency with the alternative of the equivalent in sterling at the date of payment or at the date of extract, whichever is the earlier.

Interest on damages

The pursuer sought interest on past solatium which was estimated as being 40 per cent of the total figure of £48,022, namely £19,209. Having regard to the

G change in the rate of interest on decrees in August 1985 from 12 per cent to 15 per cent I consider that it is appropriate to award interest at the rate of 7.125 per cent on the sum of £19,209. The pursuer also sought interest on past financial loss. This was resisted by the Dean of Faculty who submitted that interest should be withheld or reduced in respect that the case had taken an inordinate length of time to reach the stage of a proof, having been sisted for over three years at the instance of the pursuer. I am not convinced that

H in the somewhat special circumstances of the present case which involved a foreign pursuer and foreign advisers, along with the outcome of business carried on in Switzerland, that it would be right to deny the pursuer the appropriate rate of interest on his financial loss. I accordingly award him interest at the rate of 7.125 per cent on the figure of SF 945,778, which is my assessment of his past financial loss.

Further procedure

On 16 October 1991 before making avizandum I

I granted a motion for the pursuer, which was consented to by the defenders, for interim decree for payment of the sum of £150,000. In these circumstances it is appropriate that parties should be heard as to the appropriate form of decree in the light of the terms of this opinion and any payment made in terms of the interim decree. This case will accordingly be put out by order for this purpose.

_____

J *Counsel for Pursuer, McEachran, QC, Reed; Solicitors, Gray Muirhead, WS (for Holmes Mackillop, Glasgow) — Counsel for Defenders, Dean of Faculty (Johnston, QC), Sturrock; Solicitors, Balfour & Manson, Nightingale & Bell.*

C H

[Both parties have marked reclaiming motions against the Lord Ordinary's interlocutor.]

K

City of Glasgow District Council v Secretary of State for Scotland (No 2)

FIRST DIVISION

THE LORD PRESIDENT (HOPE),
LORDS ALLANBRIDGE AND MAYFIELD

L 11 JUNE 1992

Town and country planning — Planning permission — Enterprise zone — Scheme originally authorising residential development without permission amended to require permission — Building warrant in respect of proposed residential development applied for prior to amendment of scheme but issued after amendment — Development commenced prior to amendment of scheme and prior to

A
issue of warrant — Enforcement notice — Whether development lawfully commenced — Whether developers entitled to found on works prior to issue of building warrant as "specified operations" determining date of commencement of development — Extent of development commenced by works undertaken — Town and Country Planning (Scotland) Act 1972 (c 52), s 40 (1) and (2) — Local Government, Planning and Land Act 1980 (c 65), Sched 32, para 21.

B
Paragraph 21 of Sched 32 to the Local Government, Planning and Land Act 1980 provides that modifications to an enterprise zone scheme do not affect planning permission under the scheme in any case where the development authorised by it was begun before the modifications took effect. Section 40 of the Town and Country Planning (Scotland) Act 1972 provides that development shall be taken to be begun on the earliest date on which any of certain specified operations comprised in the development begins to be carried out.

C
Developers acquired a site within an enterprise zone in early 1990. In late 1989 the developers had discussed a proposal for residential development on the site with the planning authority and asked for written confirmation that such a development would not require planning approval. By letter of 13 December 1989 the director of planning replied that planning permission for residential development was granted subject to the standard conditions specified in para 5 of the zone description document. In March 1990 the developers applied for a building warrant in respect of

D
detailed plans lodged with the application. By the beginning of July the developers and the planning authority were aware that the issue of a warrant was imminent. Construction work started by 9 July 1990 at the site. On 10 July 1990 the planning authority made a direction the effect of which was to exclude houses and all residential development from the planning permission granted by the enterprise zone designation order. The direction came into effect on 11 July 1990, providing that it "shall not affect planning per-

E
mission under the said Scheme in any case where development authorised by it has been begun before that date". Thereafter work proceeded on the site. ·The planning authority served an enforcement notice on the developers on the basis that the construction was proceeding without the necessary planning permission. An appeal was lodged. The reporter determined the appeal in favour of the developers and directed that the enforcement notice be quashed. The planning authority appealed to the Inner House,

F
arguing (1) that development without a building warrant was not authorised by the scheme and being unlawful could not be relied on by the developers, and (2) that in any event it was only those buildings on which work had actually begun that were not affected by the direction.

Held, (1) that as the development of the site for housing was not excluded by the 1981 Order and the standard conditions were complied with, it had to be deemed to have been authorised by planning permission in terms of the scheme attached to the order,

G
within the meaning of para 21 of Sched 32 to the 1980 Act, prior to 11 July 1990 and it was immaterial for that purpose that the building warrant was not obtained until after that date (pp 263K-L and 274B-C); (2) that as certain of the specified operations begun on the site before 11 July 1990 did not require a building warrant the reporter was entitled to find that the housing development had begun by that date (p 274D-G); (3) that since the developers had applied for a building warrant in March 1990 and knew at the beginning of July that there was no impediment to its being granted, the reporter was entitled in the circum-

H
stances and where there was no turpitude on the part of the developers, to have regard to the operations for which building warrant was required (pp 274L-275B); (4) that the reporter was entitled to consider the question of the extent of the development as one of fact and, since planning permission was deemed to have been granted, to consider the plans lodged with the building warrant application as "proxy" for the absent planning application and to regard them as reliable evidence of the proposals for development (p 275C-E); and appeal *refused.*

I
Glamorgan County Council v Carter [1963] 1 WLR 1, *distinguished.*

Doubted, whether there was a universal, inflexible rule in Scots law, especially in matters of planning, that once a statutory offence had been committed the court could not have regard to all the facts and circumstances in reaching a decision as to whether some other statutory requirement had been satisfied (p 274J-K).

J
_____

Appeal from the Secretary of State for Scotland
The City of Glasgow District Council appealed against a decision of the chief reporter sustaining an appeal by Laing Homes Ltd against an enforcement notice dated 15 October 1990, concerning a residential development begun by Laing Homes Ltd within an enterprise zone in the City of Glasgow District.

K
Statutory provisions
The Town and Country Planning (Scotland) Act 1972 provides:

"**40.**—(1) For the purposes of sections 38 and 39 of this Act [duration of planning permission], development shall be taken to be begun on the earliest date on which any specified operation comprised in the development begins to be carried out.

L
"(2) In subsection (1) of this section 'specified operation' means any of the following, that is to say — (a) any work of construction in the course of the erection of a building; (b) the digging of a trench which is to contain the foundations, or part of the foundations, of a building; (c) the laying of any underground main or pipe to the foundations, or part of the foundations, of a building or to any such trench as is mentioned in the last preceding paragraph; (d) any operation in the course of laying out or constructing a road or part of a road; (e) any change in the use of any land, where that change constitutes material development. . . .

"85.—(1) A person on whom an enforcement notice
A is served, or any other person having an interest in the
land may, at any time before the date specified in the
notice as the date on which it is to take effect, appeal
to the Secretary of State against the notice on any of
the following grounds — . . . (b) that the matters
alleged in the notice do not constitute a breach of planning control; (bb) that the breach of planning control
alleged in the notice has not taken place."

The Local Government, Planning and Land Act
B 1980, as amended, provides in Sched 32:

"21. Modifications to [an enterprise zone] scheme
do not affect planning permission under the scheme in
any case where the development authorised by it has
been begun before the modifications take effect."

Cases referred to

*Dunfermline District Council v Secretary of State for
Scotland*, 1990 SLT 469.
Etheridge v Secretary of State for the Environment
(1984) 48 P & CR 35.
C *Glamorgan County Council v Carter* [1963] 1 WLR 1;
[1962] 3 All ER 866.
Paul v Ayrshire County Council, 1964 SLT 207; 1964
SC 116.
*R v Secretary of State for the Environment, ex p Percy
Bilton Industrial Properties Ltd* (1975) 31 P & CR
154.
Spackman v Secretary of State for the Environment
[1977] 1 All ER 257; (1976) 33 P & CR 430.

D **Textbooks referred to**

Bennion, *Statutory Interpretation* (1984), codes 127,
345 and 354, at pp 295, 298-299, 759-760 and
779.
Maxwell, *Interpretation of Statutes* (12th ed), pp
274-275.

Terms of enterprise zone scheme
"City of Glasgow District Council
"Proposals for an Enterprise Zone Scheme
E "1. *Introduction*

"These proposals have been prepared by the City of
Glasgow District Council with a view to the designation of those areas of Yoker defined in the annexed
plan as the Glasgow Enterprise Zone.

"Following adoption of the scheme by the Council
and designation of the Enterprise Zone by the Secretary of State, planning permission subject only to the
exclusions and conditions set out below will be
granted for development within the Enterprise Zone.
F
"2. *Boundaries*
"The boundaries of the Enterprise Zone are shown
delineated in black on the annexed map. . . .

"3. *Permitted Development*
"Planning permission will be granted within the
Enterprise Zone subject to the exclusions as described
in Paragraph 4 and the standard conditions as
described in Paragraph 5, below, for all development
normally requiring permission under the Town and
Country Planning (Scotland) Act, 1972.

"4. *Exclusions*
[List does not include 'houses' or residential G
development.]

"5. *Standard Conditions*
"Nothing in this scheme relieves the applicant from
the responsibility of ensuring that the following
Highway conditions are complied with:— [There
follows a list of highway matters.]

"6. *Building Control, Health and Safety Requirements,
etc.*
"The planning permission given by this scheme H
does not relieve applicants from obtaining the necessary statutory permissions under Building, Health,
Safety, Fire, Pollution or Licensing Controls from
statutory notification requirements or from ensuring
that Strathclyde Regional Council is consulted regarding the provision of Sewerage and Water facilities.
(Refer to Annex E for guidelines and list of contacts,
names and addresses for sewerage and water facilities.)

"Within Glasgow District Council authority is
delegated to the Director of Building Control to grant I
applications for Warrant under the Building (Scotland) Acts, 1959/1970 where the application meets the
Building Regulations and is unopposed.

"7. *Procedures for other Planning Matters*
"Arrangements have been made to ensure that
applications for development which are not granted
automatic planning consent under this scheme will be
expeditiously handled by the planning authority.

"For development applications in the Glasgow area
of the Enterprise Zone, contact:—   J

The Director of Planning,
City of Glasgow District Council,
84 Queen Street,
Glasgow G1 3DP."

The appeal was heard before the First Division on
14 May 1992.

On 11 June 1992 the court *refused* the appeal.   K

The following opinion of the court was delivered by
Lord Allanbridge:

OPINION OF THE COURT.—In 1981 the
Secretary of State for Scotland, the first respondent in
this appeal, made an order in exercise of his powers in
terms of s 179 of and para 5 of Sched 32 to the Local
Government, Planning and Land Act 1980. This was
the City of Glasgow Enterprise Zone Designation
Order 1981 which came into operation on 18 August L
1981. The appeal site lies within the enterprise zone
and was acquired by Laing Homes Ltd, the second
respondents in this appeal, in early 1990.

The facts found by the reporter were not disputed
by the parties in the appeal before us and we narrate
them in historical sequence. In late 1989 the second
respondents discussed a proposal for residential
development on the appeal site with the appellants'
planning department. They then asked for written
confirmation that such a development would not

require planning approval. By letter dated 13
A December 1989 the director of planning replied that
planning permission for residential development was
granted subject to the standard conditions specified in
para 5 of the zone description document.

The parts of that descriptive document which are
relevant to this appeal read as follows: [his Lordship
quoted the provisions set out supra and continued:]

On 15 March 1990 the second respondents wrote to
the director of building control applying for a building
warrant for phase 1 (59 houses). The full fee for the
B whole development of £4,010 was paid with this initial
application which was also accompanied by site
layouts and detailed plans. These plans showed that
the site was to be developed in three phases, with
phase 1 being for 89 houses, phase 2 for 84 houses and
phase 3 for 73 houses, giving a total of 216 houses.

Following various surveys it was decided that the
houses should be built on trench filled or piled foundations. On 1 June 1990 the second respondents
C accepted the tender of Hercules Piling to carry out the
works. On 15 June 1990 the requisite construction
consent was issued by the Strathclyde Regional
Council for the roadworks.

By 9 July 1990 certain construction work had been
started and at a site meeting Mr Murie of the appellants' building control department warned the second
respondents' representatives that an offence had been
committed by starting work on phase 1 before the
building warrant in respect of it had been issued, and
D a similar warning was given at a meeting within the
building department. However, Mr Murie agreed in
evidence that by the beginning of July 1990 his staff
would have been aware that the issuing of the warrant
was imminent. It was not in fact issued until 17 July
1990.

On 10 July 1990 direction no 4 was made to the
enterprise zone in exercise of the appellants' powers
conferred on them by para 17 (4) and (5) of Sched 32
to the 1980 Act, as amended, and with the approval of
E the first respondent. The effect of this direction was
to exclude houses and all residential development
from the planning permission granted by the 1981
Order. The direction came into effect on 11 July 1990
but it specifically provided that it "shall not affect
planning permission under the said Scheme in any
case where development authorised by it has been
begun before that date".

Thereafter work proceeded with the construction of
the houses in phase 1. An enforcement notice was then
F served by the appellants on the second respondents on
10 October 1990 on the basis that this construction
was proceeding without the necessary planning permission and the appellants required that steps should
be taken within 28 days to cease such work. The
notice was said to take effect on 14 November 1990
unless an appeal was taken before that date. An appeal
was timeously lodged under s 85 (1) and (2) of the
1972 Act, as amended, on grounds (b) and (bb) of s 85
(1). These grounds were: [his Lordship quoted the
terms of s 85 (1) (b) and (bb) and continued:]

The appeal was also intimated on ground (a) of s 85
(1) but that ground of appeal was withdrawn on 25 G
January 1991. The chief reporter was appointed to
determine the appeal and conducted a public local
inquiry into the appeal on 18 March 1991. By letter
dated 22 May 1991 he determined the appeal in favour
of the first respondents and directed that the enforcement notice be quashed. It is against that determination that the appeal to this court is taken by the
appellants under s 233 of the 1972 Act.

The decision in this appeal turns on the interpretation of the words at the end of para 2 of direction no H
4 already quoted supra. This was a modification to the
enterprise zone scheme and it is provided in para 21
of Sched 32 to the 1980 Act, as amended, as follows:
[his Lordship quoted para 21 and continued:]

The words used in the said direction are to the same
effect and in this case it is therefore essential to determine whether the housing development on the appeal
site and authorised by the scheme had begun by 11
July 1990 which was the date when the direction came I
into effect. Paragraph 26 (1A) (b) of said Sched 32, as
amended, states that in Scotland subss (1) to (3) of s 40
of the 1972 Act shall apply for the purposes of that
Schedule when development shall be taken to be
begun. Section 40 (1) and (2) of the 1972 Act, which
therefore apply to the interpretation of said para 21,
is in the following terms: [his Lordship quoted its
terms and continued:]

The reporter therefore required to decide what
"specified operations", if any, had taken place on site J
by 11 July 1990. Photographs had been taken on that
date both by the appellants and the second respondents and were available to him. He also heard
evidence. The facts found by him in relation to this
aspect of the appeal are to be found at paras 9 and 10
of his letter of determination. They include inter alia
(first) the corner block at the northwest section of the
site (block A on the plan — see minute of admissions
now signed and lodged by the parties) "had its structural strip foundations cast on the trench filled con- K
crete with all the underbuilding walls up to the soffit
of the precast ground floor slab"; (second) "The
ground works contractor had completed the construction of a manhole in the roadway just inside the site
entrance," and (third) "A piling rig was operating on
site and 14 piles had been driven to set for another
corner block with the two 761 house types which is on
land requiring piled foundations" (block F in the
plan).

The reporter concluded that the development had L
begun on the site because "specified operations" had
begun on site in respect of heads (a) and (b) of said s 40
(2) and that such development was a residential
development of the whole site. (See paras 30 and 27
respectively of his said determination letter.) He therefore sustained the appeal.

The appellants' grounds of appeal as argued before
us by their counsel were to the effect that the reporter
had erred in law in a number of respects. In the first
place he argued that development without a building

A warrant was (a) not authorised by the scheme and (b) was unlawful and therefore could not be relied upon. The building warrant was not issued until 17 July 1990, the second respondents had been warned not to proceed with their work and such work was not "authorised" by the enterprise zone scheme because the terms of para 6 of the scheme relating to building control had not been met. The development was also "unlawful" because an offence had been committed in terms of the Building (Scotland) Act 1959. Section 6

B (1) of that Act stated that no person should conduct any operations for the construction of a building unless a warrant has been obtained from the local authority for such construction and any contravention thereof was an offence. Fines were payable for such an offence and for every day the offence was continued in terms of s 19 (2). In these circumstances counsel for the appellants argued that it was contrary to principle to allow a developer to found on his own illegal acts to escape from the consequences of direction no 4 (see Bennion on *Statutory Interpretation* (1984), codes 127, 345 and 354 at pp 295, 759-760 and 779, and Maxwell

C on *Interpretation of Statutes* (12th ed), at pp 274-275).

Counsel then founded on the case of *Glamorgan County Council v Carter* (referred to by Bennion at pp 298-299 and Maxwell at p 275). This case was concerned with s 12 (5) of the Town and Country Planning Act 1947 which provided that: "permission shall not be required under this part . . . (c) in the case of land which on the appointed day is unoccupied, in respect of the use of the land for the purpose for which

D it was last used". The use in question involved the commission of an offence under the Cardiff Rural Town Planning Scheme. Salmon J said (at [1963] 1 WLR, p 5): "It seems to me plain on principle that Mrs James could not acquire any legal right by the illegal use to which she was putting the land. In my view it is plain that the use referred to in section 12 (5) (c) of the Town and Country Planning Act, 1947, must mean lawful use, at any rate in this sense, that it cannot include use which constitutes the commis-

E sion of a criminal or quasi-criminal offence"; and at p 6: "The construction which I favour . . . only involves applying the well-known principle that it is impossible to acquire a right by committing a quasi-criminal offence."

Counsel argued that if this principle was applied to the circumstances of the present case then the second respondents could not found on any construction works at their site which had begun by 11 July 1990 as these works were illegal as no building warrant for

F them was issued until 17 July 1990.

In the second place counsel submitted that if his first argument that the developers' actings were illegal was wrong, then it was only those buildings on which work had actually begun by 11 July 1990 that were not affected by direction no 4. These were block A, where foundation works had commenced and block F, where piling work had also been commenced. He explained that a concession had been made at the hearing before the reporter that if the construction works were not illegal then it was only blocks A and F which were

saved by the wording of s 42 (2) of the 1972 Act. The "development" could only be the actual buildings on G which work had begun in terms of that subsection, and the reporter was not entitled to rely on the plans which were submitted along with the application for the building warrant made on 15 March 1990 and which he said served as a "proxy" for the absent planning application (see para 27 of the direction letter).

At this stage we should deal with what all parties accept was a factual error by the reporter. At para 24 of his direction letter he indicates that he had understood that the appellants' concession applied to "the H two blocks (now erected)". By the date of the hearing construction work on the site had progressed to the extent that blocks A and C had been completed but that block B had been partially constructed, but block F remained as it had been on 11 July 1990 with some 14 piles driven on site. This is made clear in the minute of admissions which was lodged prior to the appeal being heard by this court. The reporter stated that because he thought the concession applied to blocks A and C he "found it inconsistent that the I development of the block with piled foundations (block F) should not also be saved".

In fact there was no inconsistency as the concession applied to blocks A and F and not blocks A and C. This inconsistency was said to be an error of law in the appellants' third written ground of appeal. We consider it was clearly a factual error, and that it was only incidental to the reporter's reasons for sustaining the second respondents' appeal and does not vitiate his J determination in any way. We should also add that counsel for the appellants suggested that because the minute of admissions did not include any reference to the construction of the manhole in the roadway that was no longer a fact admitted by the parties which the court could take into account. We were informed by counsel for the first respondent that the minute of admissions was prepared solely to correct the reporter's misunderstanding about the concession regarding the appropriate two blocks. We accept that K that clearly was the intention of the minute of admissions, that it was not intended to be exhaustive of all the facts regarding construction work as at 11 July 1990, and that therefore the construction of the manhole is a fact which we can consider in the context of this appeal to this court.

In arguing that the reporter was not entitled to rely on the plans in this case, counsel referred to the case of *Dunfermline District Council v Secretary of State for Scotland*. He also stated that if this argument was not L accepted then there would be uncertainty as to what would be the actual development in the future as plans and intentions could change as the development proceeded. In conclusion counsel stated that he founded most strongly on his "unlawful" argument, but he submitted that both his main arguments were sound and invited us to allow the appeal and overturn the chief reporter's direction that the enforcement notice be quashed.

In reply counsel for the first respondent submitted

that the housing development was development "authorised" by the enterprise zone scheme as a matter of planning law and that para 6 of the scheme served merely as a reminder that separate and collateral statutory requirements would also require to be fulfilled. He then submitted that the fact that the second respondents anticipated the granting of a building warrant and proceeded with the construction work was of no consequence when considering land use development. There was a clear distinction between planning and building statutory requirements which relate to safety, health and other purposes. Furthermore, this was a case where there was no flagrant abuse of the building regulations but an anticipation of a formal grant. He did not dispute that an offence had been committed but said one should look at the nature and extent of the wrongdoing. It was nowhere suggested that this was a deliberate act to get past the effect of direction no 4. What the appellants were trying to do in this case was to use a building law objection to achieve a planning law result. It was analogous to an attempt to create a public right of way by means of an enforcement notice and refusal of planning permission which was disapproved in the case of *Paul v Ayrshire County Council*, per Lord Justice Clerk Grant at 1964 SLT, p 211. The true question was the planning one of whether work was carried out in compliance with the plans and this was a question of fact and degree. (See *Spackman v Secretary of State for the Environment* [1977] 1 All ER at p 260D.) The principle that it was impossible to acquire a right by committing a quasi-criminal offence was too broadly stated at least in its application to Scots law. In the *Glamorgan* case such a broad principle was not necessary for the decision and all that required to be said was that the previous land use was not to be taken into account and furthermore the decision in the case depended upon planning law requirements.

Counsel then said that the appellants' argument required inserting the word "lawful" before the word "development" in considering what was the development which had begun by 11 July 1990 and this was not justified. There was no question of turpitude in the present case on the part of the developers as the parties knew the warrant was in the pipeline. In any event he submitted on the facts that the second respondents had full consents for roadworks and the "specified operations" in (a), (b) and (d) of said s 40 (2) had all been begun on the relevant date. Thus the construction of the manhole and the digging of a trench which did not require a building warrant could not be said to be tainted with any illegality.

As regards the appellants' second ground of appeal counsel submitted that the development was properly treated as a unum quid on the evidence available to the reporter. The documentary evidence was to be found in the developers' building application plans. One required to look at the development as a whole as if it had been an outline planning permission for the whole site albeit that separate detailed plans might be submitted later (see *R v Secretary of State for the Environment, ex p Percy Bilton Industrial Properties Ltd* at

p 158 and *Etheridge v Secretary of State for the Environment* at pp 40-41). He added that the case of *Dunfermline District Council*, cited by counsel for the appellants, was not of assistance as it related to plans actually submitted for planning permission and not deemed planning permission as in the present case.

Counsel for the second respondents adopted counsel for the first respondent's submissions. He added that the defenders had applied for building warrants in March 1990 and knew by the beginning of July 1990 that the issuing of the necessary warrants was imminent as found in fact by the reporter. He emphasised that there were certain works commenced by 11 July 1990 that did not require building warrants, such as the construction of the manhole in the roadway and the digging of the trench to take the foundations for block A.

Counsel for the appellants in a short final speech submitted that the case of *Spackman* was not of assistance as it related to deviations made in error and not unlawfully. He said that the general principle that persons should not be allowed to benefit from their own illegal acts was applicable in Scotland as in England.

We will deal with the two main arguments of the appellants in the order in which they were presented to us by counsel. They are summarised in the first and second written grounds of appeal in the case. The first concerns the question of whether the reporter had erred in law in holding that by 11 July 1990 an authorised development had begun in respect that no works on the site were legally authorised and no building warrant had been issued by that date.

The first question raised in this ground of appeal is whether the works had been "authorised" by the scheme in such a situation. We are satisfied that the effect of the City of Glasgow District Zone Designation Order 1981, which came into operation on 11 August 1981, to which were attached proposals for an enterprise zone scheme which were adopted by the council, had the effect of granting planning permission for, and therefore authorising, developments which were not excluded by the exclusions listed in para 4 of the scheme. Houses and residential development were not excluded by para 4. The adopted scheme in para 3 stated that planning permission would be granted within the enterprise zone: "subject to the exclusions as described in paragraph 4 and the standard conditions in paragraph 5, below, for all development normally requiring permission under the Town and Country Planning (Scotland) Act 1972". The standard conditions related only to highway conditions being complied with. There is no suggestion in the present case that these highway conditions were not met and it is found as a fact by the reporter that on 15 June 1990 the requisite construction consent was issued by Strathclyde Regional Council for the roadworks in accordance with the submitted plans (see determination letter, para 8). Thus, since the development of the appellants' site for housing was not excluded development and the standard conditions were complied with, the development must be deemed to have been authorised by planning permission in terms of the scheme. Paragraph 6 of the scheme relating to "Building Control, Health and Safety Requirements, etc" was not made a condition of the planning permission. What it did was to state that the planning permission given by the scheme did "not relieve the applicants from obtaining the necessary statutory permissions under Building, Health, Safety, Fire, Pollution or Licensing Controls". This was a reference to the statutory permissions which are always required where appropriate after planning permissions are granted in the normal case but whose presence or absence do not, as such, affect the validity of the planning permission. This paragraph merely serves as a reminder to that effect and makes it clear that such statutory permission must be obtained where appropriate. In our opinion therefore the development of the site for housing was authorised by the scheme within the meaning of para 21 of Sched 32 to the 1980 Act prior to 11 July 1990, and it is immaterial for this purpose that the building warrant was not obtained until after that date.

The second question raised in the appellants' first ground of appeal was whether the fact that the building warrant was not obtained until after 11 July 1990 means that the developers cannot rely on "specified operations" said to have begun on that date in terms of s 40 (2) of the 1980 Act, as amended. These operations were said to be illegal, but it became clear during the hearing of this appeal that on any view such criticisms could not be levelled against all the "specified operations" which the reporter found established in this case and also the facts he found relating to the manhole in the roadway. A close examination of the definition of "specified operations" in s 40 (2) demonstrates that operation (a) relates to "any work of construction". Section 6 (1) of the Building (Scotland) Act 1959 refers to the requirement of obtaining a warrant for any operations for "the construction" of a building. Section 40 (2) (b) on the other hand refers to "the digging of a trench which is to contain the foundations, or part of the foundations, of a building", and thus makes it a separate specified operation clearly distinguished from the construction of a building. There is nothing in the 1959 Act to suggest that a building warrant was required before a trench was dug to contain the foundations because at that stage no act of construction of a building had begun. The trench could have been left empty or backfilled, and it was not until the actual construction of the building was started within the trench that a building warrant, as its name implies, was required. It is therefore apparent that in the present case at some stage before 11 July 1990 the trenches were dug which were thereafter used to contain the foundations of the building. The second respondents have therefore established that such a specified operation in terms of s 40 (2) (b) must have begun on the site before 11 July 1990, and such an operation did not require a building warrant. The same is true of the manhole constructed within the meaning of s 40 (2) (d) as it was an operation in the course of laying out or constructing a road.

Thus there were two operations which were established by the second respondents in evidence as being specified operations which were begun before 11 July 1990. They did not require a building warrant and therefore were unaffected by the fact that no such warrant had been issued by that date. That being so, the reporter was entitled to find that the housing development had begun by that date as regards s 40 (2) (b) and did not err in law in so finding. He would also have been entitled to find that the housing development had begun by that date as regards s 40 (2) (d) as we have already indicated. The argument based on the illegality of the actual construction work therefore only affects the specified operation of construction of a building in terms of s 40 (2) (a). However, as this approach was said to be one of the strongest arguments for the appellants we will now express our views upon it although it is not necessary for our decision on this first ground of appeal.

In support of his argument that the building operations were illegal, counsel for the appellants did not distinguish between the specified operations in s 40 (2) but submitted, at least by implication, that the absence of a building warrant affected all of them. For the reasons we have already explained we think that that was too general an approach in view of the particular facts in this case, but we now consider his general argument on this matter. It was based on a general principle, said to be formulated by Bennion and Maxwell in their respective textbooks and expressed by Salmon J at p 6 of *Glamorgan County Council v Carter*. That principle, according to Salmon J, was "that it is *impossible* to acquire a right by committing a quasi-criminal offence". We stress the use of the word "impossible" as that indicates that this is a universal rule applicable in all circumstances. We doubt whether such an inflexible rule is applicable universally in Scots law, especially in matters of planning, or is such that once a statutory offence has been committed, as was conceded to have occurred in this case, the court cannot have regard to all the facts and circumstances disclosed in the evidence in reaching a decision as to whether some other statutory requirement has been satisfied. We know of no authority in Scots law that would support such a wide and inflexible approach and none was cited to us. Furthermore, the case of *Glamorgan County Council* was concerned with an offence under a planning scheme in the context of the construction of a planning Act. It can therefore be distinguished from the present case where the statutory offence was committed under the building legislation which is an entirely separate matter from the commission of an offence under the planning legislation.

That being so, we consider that the reporter was entitled in the circumstances of this particular case to have regard to the history of events and to take the view that the fact that the developers were not granted a building warrant until 17 July 1990 did not prevent them from establishing that they had begun the necessary "specified operations" on the appeal site under planning legislation. They had applied for a building warrant in March 1990. The reporter has found as a fact that it was generally known at the beginning of July that there was no impediment to the granting of the building warrant (see para 25 of determination letter). The reporter considered that the developer took "what might be regarded as a calculated risk starting in advance of the warrant, which constitutes a criminal offence under the Building Act". However, the reporter goes on to opine that there was no doubt that the development carried out by 11 July was subsequently ratified by the issue of the warrant. In the whole circumstances, and where there was clearly no turpitude on the part of the developers and no suggestion that they intentionally breached the Building Act requirements so as to establish a case under s 40 (2), we are satisfied that the reporter did not err in law as far as this part of the first ground of appeal is concerned.

We now turn to the second written ground of appeal which was presented on an alternative or esto basis, to the effect that any development authorised by the scheme only extended to the two blocks A and F on which construction had actually started by 11 July 1990 and that the reporter was not entitled to look at the plans lodged with the application for a building warrant in March 1990 as showing the extent of the development. We are of the opinion that in deciding what was the extent of the development for housing the reporter was fully entitled to treat this question as one of fact to be determined on the evidence. In a normal planning application the extent of the development would be determined by the granting of an application for outline planning permission in accordance with the plans submitted to the planning authority. In this enterprise zone case no such planning permission was required as it was granted or at least deemed to be granted by the scheme itself. The whole site owned by the second respondents could therefore be developed for housing without application to the appellants' planning department.

In para 27 of his determination letter, the reporter indicates he took into account the plans which were lodged with the application for a building warrant in March 1990 and said he considered they must serve as "proxy" for the absent planning application. In such a situation we think that this was a sensible and legitimate approach since he was dealing with a situation where there was a deemed planning consent under the unusual conditions of an enterprise zone scheme. We note the reporter's finding in para 6 that the full fee for the whole development was paid with the initial application, which was also accompanied by site layouts and detailed house type plans. The reporter was entitled to regard this as reliable evidence of the proposals for development. We do not find the cases to which we were referred by counsel for the parties on this ground of appeal of assistance, as these cases were concerned with actual applications for planning consent. The reporter says in terms in said para 27 that: "From the facts I can find no room for doubt that the development which your client began prior to 11 July 1990 was a residential development of the whole site." We are quite satisfied that the reporter did not make an error in law in taking into account the build-

ing warrant application plans. We therefore reject the appellants' second ground of appeal.

In the whole circumstances we are therefore satisfied that the chief reporter did not err in law in reaching his determination of 22 May 1991. This appeal under s 233 of the Town and Country Planning (Scotland) Act 1972 is therefore refused.

Counsel for Appellants, Menzies, QC; Solicitors, Gray Muirhead, WS — Counsel for First Respondent, Hodge; Solicitor, R Brodie, Solicitor to the Secretary of State for Scotland — Counsel for Second Respondents, Steele; Solicitors, Wright, Johnston & McKenzie.

P A

(NOTE)

Gow v Lord Advocate

OUTER HOUSE
LORD CAPLAN
17 JULY 1992

Husband and wife — Marriage — Constitution — Irregular marriage — Cohabitation with habit and repute — Divided repute — Whether sufficient repute to infer consent to marriage.

A widower commenced a relationship with a woman. The woman moved to live with the man and lived with him until her death 10 years later. For the last seven years prior to her death she had been free to marry him. He sought declarator that they had been married by cohabitation with habit and repute. There was divided repute on the issue as to whether the man and woman were married.

Held, that the man had failed to prove a general repute that they were married; and decree of absolvitor *pronounced.*

Robert Gow sought declarator that he had been married by cohabitation with habit and repute to a woman, May Thompson, with whom he had cohabited for about 10 years prior to her death. The relationship had not always been harmonious. The pursuer was about 61 years of age when his cohabitee died. He had been a widower when the relationship started. The woman had been married when she first commenced the relationship and was divorced by her husband about seven years before her death. The pursuer had two children by his first marriage. The woman had four children by her first marriage. In refusing decree of declarator the Lord Ordinary (Caplan) said:

"In my view the law applicable to this case is quite clear. As Lord Moncrieff indicated as early as 1845 in *Lapsley v Grierson* (1845) 8 D 34 at p 61, cohabitation with the assumption of the character of husband and wife and repute to that effect, does not constitute marriage. However these circumstances may prove marriage. Moreover Lord Stott stated in *Shaw v Henderson*, 1982 SLT 211 at p 212: 'all that requires to be inferred under Scots law is that the parties tacitly consented to the status of a married couple'. However any presumption of marriage which may be available can be rebutted if it is cogently shown by the evidence that there was no actual mutual consent to the assumption of the status of marriage (*Mackenzie v Scott*, 1980 SLT (Notes) 9; *Shaw v Henderson*, supra). Moreover before the presumption of marriage arises at all the repute of marriage must be general. As Lord Robertson observed in *Low v Gorman*, 1970 SLT 357 at p 359: 'Although the repute need not be universal, it must be general, substantially unvarying and consistent, and not divided'.

"In the present case any question of marriage could only arise after the deceased became free to marry following upon her divorce in 1979. It has in the past been suggested that if a relationship involving cohabitation is flagrantly illicit to begin with because the parties are not free to marry, then proof that they tacitly consented to marriage when they became free to contract marriage becomes more onerous. However I think the modern and correct view is that the issue always remains one of fact, the question being whether it has been shown that the parties contracted marriage by habit and repute after they became free to marry during the cohabitation. Indeed, in my view, if the parties clearly showed an inclination to adopt the married state even before they became free to marry, this could reflect on their attitude to the relationship if cohabitation continues when freedom to marry arises. In the present case, as far as the evidence showed, the parties' presentation of their relationship to the world does not seem to have altered significantly after the date of the deceased's divorce. The pursuer and the deceased undoubtedly were prepared to represent themselves as married to a few neighbours and strangers. However this is not conclusive in itself because no doubt they wanted to spare themselves the needless embarrassment of explaining their true situation to persons who were not close to them. Perhaps this is illustrated by the fact that the deceased did not refute the suggestion coming from [the pursuer's son's] friends that she was his mother, although that she certainly was not. However any repute that the pursuer and the deceased were married was in no sense general and undivided. Mr Johnston, the friend of the deceased, did not consider the deceased to have been married. Not only did the deceased continue to call herself May Thompson at work but there was no convincing evidence that any of her workmates considered her to be a married person after her divorce. Certainly Mrs Knight, a colleague at work, appears to have addressed a wedding invitation to 'Mr and Mrs Gow', but only after she had inquired as to how to address the envelope in order to save embarrassment. None of the Thompson family appeared to have thought of the deceased as being married to the pursuer. Even the pursuer's own son, Ian, gave evidence that he did not consider his father to be married to the deceased. If he meant by this that he merely did not consider that his father and the deceased had gone through a formal wedding ceremony, he did not make that clear. After the deceased had died, Mrs Nisbet's mother told Mrs Nisbet [the pursuer's immediate neighbour, who had believed the pursuer and Mrs Thompson to have been married] that the deceased and the pursuer were not married. She had known the deceased all her life. In any event, even if the repute of marriage were sufficiently wide to give rise to the presumption of marriage, the evidence, in my view, made it absolutely plain that the deceased at no time considered herself to be married to the pursuer.

"I can accept that the pursuer wanted to marry the deceased and may have often invited her to become his wife. However she persistently refused to marry him. The case must be viewed against the background of modern social conditions where it is not at all uncommon for a man and woman to live together openly in an intimate relationship while retaining a distinct disinclination to enter the married state. The fact that the deceased throughout signed herself 'May Thompson' may be a pointer to her state of mind, although this would not in itself be conclusive. However there was more direct evidence of her view that she had never been married to the pursuer. Mr Bowman, the insurance collector who called from time to time at the pursuer's home, had first thought that the deceased was married to the pursuer but eventually was told by her that she and the pursuer were not in fact married. In my view the evidence that the deceased did not consider herself to be married goes beyond a response to the fact that there had been no formal ceremony. Mrs McManus, a sister of the deceased, testified that the deceased had told her that she would never get married. Mrs Cassidy, her daughter, gave evidence to the same effect. Likewise Mrs Campbell [a niece of the deceased] indicated that the deceased had told her that she would never marry the pursuer. Mrs Jarvis, the elder daughter of the deceased, stated in evidence that her Aunt Minnie (a sister of the deceased who is herself now deceased) had suggested to the deceased that since she was cohabiting with the pursuer she would be better to marry him. The deceased had replied that she would never marry him. I find this evidence of the attitude of the deceased consistent and acceptable. The pursuer himself accepted that he and the deceased often discussed the question of marriage and he was unable to explain in satisfactory terms why in such circumstances no wedding had ever taken place. I think the fact that marriage was a regular topic of conversation between the pursuer and the deceased confirms the view that the pursuer was not happy about the formal status of the relationship. Moreover, the actings of the deceased in relation to her few assets rather confirm the view that she did not consider the pursuer to be her husband. Indeed she was at pains to secure that her own children got such money as she had at her death."

Counsel for Pursuer, Mackinnon; Solicitors, Allan McDougall & Co, SSC (for Johnston & Herron, Lochgelly) — No appearance for First Defender (Lord Advocate) — Counsel for Second to Fifth Defenders (Relatives of Deceased), Dunlop; Solicitors, Balfour & Manson, Nightingale & Bell (for Ian Smith & Co, Aberdeen).

C H

McNair v HM Advocate

A HIGH COURT OF JUSTICIARY

THE LORD JUSTICE CLERK (ROSS),
LORDS CAPLAN AND BRAND

25 JANUARY 1991

*Justiciary — Evidence — Admissibility — Hearsay —
Best evidence — Boy witness not available to give
evidence — Whether evidence of police officer regarding
questions put to boy and his ability to identify anyone at
B identity parade admissible — Whether miscarriage of
justice.*

An accused person was charged with, inter alia,
attempted murder. During the police investigation of
the alleged offence a boy who had been at the locus
and who had witnessed certain events attended an
identity parade. He was not on the Crown list of witnesses but was cited on behalf of the defence. In the
course of the trial it was discovered that the boy had
not answered his citation and that he had been excused
C by the Crown. A medical certificate was produced
giving reasons why the boy was considered to be an
unreliable witness. In cross examination of a police
witness counsel for the accused sought to elicit
evidence of the type of questions which had been put
to the boy at the identity parade and of whether or not
he had been able to identify anyone on the parade.
The trial judge sustained the Crown's objection to the
leading of such evidence on the ground that it was
seeking to elicit hearsay and was thus incompetent.
D The accused was convicted and appealed on the
ground, inter alia, that the trial judge had erred in
excluding the evidence sought to be led.

Held, (1) that while the boy may not have been a
reliable witness it could not be said that he had been
unable to give evidence (p 278A); (2) that the best
evidence would have been that of the boy and what
was sought to be elicited was second best evidence and
the trial judge had been correct to exclude it (p 278G
and I-J), and appeal *refused*.

E **Opinion**, that even if the evidence had been
wrongly excluded, no miscarriage of justice would
have resulted as there was more than sufficient identification of the accused by other witnesses (p 278L).

Indictment

Stephen George Patrick McNair was indicted at the
instance of the rt hon the Lord Fraser of Carmyllie,
F Her Majesty's Advocate, on charges of, inter alia,
attempted murder.

The accused pled not guilty and proceeded to trial
in the High Court at Edinburgh before Lord Marnoch
and a jury.

The accused was convicted and appealed by way of
note of appeal to the High Court.

Appeal

The note of appeal contained the following grounds
of appeal:

(1) That the learned trial judge erred in holding
that evidence of a statement read out by Detective G
Inspector Irving to the boy [W N] at an identification
parade held at St Leonard's police station on 6 June
1989 was inadmissible hearsay.

(2) That the learned trial judge erred in holding that
the evidence of the said Detective Inspector Irving as
to whether the said boy [W N] had been able to identify anyone at said identification parade was inadmissible as being irrelevant.

(3) That in the circumstances of the case in which H
the evidence incriminating the appellant was eyewitness identification, the wrongful exclusion of said
evidence amounted to a miscarriage of justice.

The appeal was argued before the High Court on 25
January 1991.

Eo die the court *refused* the appeal.

The following opinion of the court was delivered by
the Lord Justice Clerk (Ross):   I

OPINION OF THE COURT.—The appellant is
Stephen George McNair who was found guilty in the
High Court at Edinburgh of charge 5 on an indictment which was a charge of assault to severe injury,
permanent disfigurement and to the danger of life and
attempted murder. He has appealed against conviction. Today counsel has addressed us on the first two
grounds of appeal. What is raised in this appeal is that
the trial judge is said to have erred in holding that
evidence of a statement read out by a police inspector J
to a boy N at an identification parade was inadmissible
hearsay. The second ground of appeal narrows the
matter down and suggests that the trial judge erred in
another respect, namely in holding that evidence from
that police officer as to whether the boy had been able
to identify anyone at an identification parade was inadmissible.

The circumstances which have given rise to these
grounds of appeal are these. In the course of investigating the case identification parades had been held K
and a number of persons had attended the identification parade, including a boy W N. He was not on the
Crown list of witnesses but had been cited for the
defence. Counsel for the appellant informed us that
while he was conducting the defence he discovered
that the boy had not answered his citation and he
understood that the boy had been excused by the
Crown. He understood there was a soul and conscience medical certificate and he also was given to L
understand that the boy attended a special school. He
informs us that in these circumstances he accepted
that it was not possible for him to lead the evidence
of the boy. The Solicitor General has however
informed us of the terms of the medical certificate.
The medical certificate apparently indicated that the
boy was someone who was attending a special school
because of educational difficulties which were aggravated by disturbed behaviour and temporal lobe
epilepsy. It was apparently certified that because of
these difficulties it was considered that he would be an

A unreliable witness and it was also considered that if he was placed under pressure that might lead to his behaviour worsening. These were the terms of the medical certificate. It appears to us that the boy might still have been called as a witness by the defence. The medical certificate did not say that he was unable to give evidence. It is one thing to say that someone would be an unreliable witness, quite another to say that he could not give evidence. Accordingly although counsel for the appellant appears to have accepted that it was not possible to lead the boy as a witness, it B appears to us that in the light of the information contained in the medical certificate, the boy indeed was capable of being a witness.

The trial judge in his report explains that when Detective Inspector Irving was giving evidence he was asked by the defence the following question: "Was he [that is W N] asked the following question at the identification parade: 'Do you see here a man who on 25 May 1990 you saw in The Quilts, Edinburgh running from the scene of a fight in the company of others?'" C Objection was taken to that question and the trial judge heard submissions in the absence of the jury. The trial judge points out that it became clear that for the evidence sought to be elicited to be at all meaningful and therefore relevant one had to know what the person was being asked to do in the way of identification. He points out in his report that there was no evidence as to what the boy was being asked to do at the parade other than the evidence sought to be elicited in answer to the question to which objection D was taken and that that question referred to something allegedly said by the boy on an earlier occasion. In these circumstances he upheld the Crown's objection to that particular question upon the ground that it was seeking to elicit hearsay and was thus incompetent.

As we understand it counsel for the appellant now accepts that that ruling was correct but he maintains that there was a subsequent question put by him to the witness which was objected to, which objection the trial judge upheld. He explains that subsequently in E questioning this police officer he put the following question to the officer under reference to W N: "Could he identify anyone?" He tells us that that question was objected to in the presence of the jury and the trial judge explained that he was sustaining the objection on the same grounds. Counsel for the appellant maintained that the trial judge had erred in sustaining the objection to that question and he went on to explain that the exclusion of this evidence amounted to a miscarriage of justice. He maintained F that it was not necessary for W N to have been a witness for him to be entitled to take evidence of this nature from the police inspector. He submitted that it was not necessary to call witnesses to say that they had either identified or had not identified someone at an identification parade. He realised that the situation would obviously be different if the witness had died or had left the country and was not available because in such circumstances an exception to the hearsay rule is recognised, but he maintained that in the circumstances here all he was asking was whether the witness could identify anyone; it was not necessary for him to

have called the witness or to be in a position to do so. We do not agree. When the question is raised as to G whether an individual has identified anyone at an identification parade the best evidence of that must be the witness himself and what counsel for the appellant was seeking to do by addressing this question to the police inspector was to take second best evidence, namely evidence of the police inspector as to whether the boy had been able to identify anyone.

Counsel for the appellant explained to us that what he, of course, had been hoping to do was to get a negative answer to that question. That he maintains would H have been relevant because evidence had been given by another witness, Mrs Finlayson, who spoke to seeing the person responsible for this offence arriving at the locus with another man at the end of the fight and she said that he had slapped W N on the face and that a knife had been seen. The individual had then gone into the garden where the stabbing took place. The witness apparently indicated in her evidence that W N would have had a good view of the events. Counsel for the appellant explained that this witness's I evidence was inconsistent with other evidence in the case but he maintained that having regard to what she said and particularly her statement that the boy had had a good view of events, it would have been helpful to the defence if evidence from the police inspector had been given to the effect that the boy had not been able to identify anyone. As we say, we are satisfied that the trial judge was correct to sustain the objection taken to the second question upon the view that the best evidence would have been W N. Even if that were J not the case, we are not persuaded that eliciting the answer "no" to that second question would have been of any great assistance to the defence. Counsel for the appellant stressed that the case depended upon identification evidence and that some of the identification evidence was confused and he reminded us again that Mrs Finlayson had said that the boy had a good view. Nonetheless we are not persuaded that if the witness had replied in the negative to that question, this would really have assisted the defence. The trial judge would K have been bound to point out to the jury that they did not have the evidence from the boy himself and that there may well have been explanations for his not having been in a position to identify anyone. Even if it be correct, as Mrs Finlayson maintained, that W N had a good view, he might have some perfectly good explanation for not being able to identify anyone, perhaps because he was not looking in the particular direction at that time. Accordingly we are not persuaded that even if this evidence was wrongly L excluded that fact could have caused a miscarriage of justice in this case. In reaching that conclusion we are mindful of the fact that the trial judge tells us in his report that there were no less than 10 witnesses who spoke to seeing the accused at the scene of the crime. In all the circumstances counsel for the appellant has failed to persuade us that there was any miscarriage of justice in this case and it follows that the appeal against conviction must be refused.

A *Counsel for Appellant, Batchelor; Solicitors, Drummond & Co, WS — Counsel for Respondent, Solicitor General (Rodger, QC); Solicitor, I Dean, Crown Agent.*

S D D N

Baron Meats Ltd v Lockhart

B HIGH COURT OF JUSTICIARY

THE LORD JUSTICE CLERK (ROSS),
LORDS CAPLAN AND BRAND

14 FEBRUARY 1991

Justiciary — Statutory offence — Failing to use tachograph recording equipment — Exemption for door to door selling — Accused driving refrigerated van with meat for sale — Van stopped after first visit when travelling 43 miles to second visit before travelling 18 miles to third
C *visit — Evidence that van might make average of 30-40 visits per day — Justice concluding that exemption from regulations not established by evidence of three visits — Whether exemption established — Council Regulation (EEC) Nos 3820/85 and 3821/85 — Transport Act 1968 (c 73), s 97 (1) (c) — Community Drivers' Hours and Recording Equipment (Exemptions and Supplementary Provisions) Regulations 1986 (SI 1986/1456), reg 4 (1) and Sched, Pt I, para 6.*

Section 97 of the Transport Act 1968 provides that
D no person shall use, or cause or permit to be used, a vehicle unless inter alia there is in the vehicle tachograph recording equipment which is being used as provided by arts 13 to 15 of EEC Council Regulation No 3821/85, as read with the Community Drivers' Hours and Recording Equipment (Exemptions and Supplementary Provisions) Regulations 1986. Article 14 of the 1985 Regulations provides for the issue by an employer of a sufficient number of record sheets to drivers and art 15 provides that drivers shall use the
E record sheets every day on which they are driving, starting from the moment they take over the vehicle. Regulation 4 (1) of, and Pt I of the Schedule to, the 1986 Regulations provide that any vehicle which is being used for door to door selling and is specially fitted for such use is exempted from the provisions of the 1985 Council Regulation.

A van salesman and his employers were charged on summary complaint with inter alia two offences under
F s 97 of the Transport Act 1968 in respect of failing to issue to the driver tachograph recording sheets and failing to use the sheets in the vehicle. The vehicle was a van specially fitted for door to door selling of refrigerated meat. The vehicle was stopped after it had made its first visit to a shop and while it was en route to the next visit 43 miles away, after which it was to travel 18 miles to a third visit. There was evidence that the vehicle could make approximately 30-40 visits on an average day. The justice held that since there was no evidence in detail of more than three visits having been made, the accused had failed to establish

that the vehicle was exempted, and accordingly convicted the accused who appealed by stated case.   G

Held, (1) that whether the activity of selling involved frequent stops in any particular case was a question of fact and degree (p 283K); (2) that since the salesman must have made something of the order of five visits per hour, the activity of selling did involve frequent stops and the proper conclusion to be drawn from the findings in the evidence was that at the material time the vehicle was being used for door to door selling, and was exempted (pp 283L-284A); and
H appeals *allowed*.

R v Scott [1984] ECR 2863, *applied*; *Struthers (Lochwinnoch) Ltd v Tudhope*, 1982 SLT 393, *distinguished*.

Summary complaint

Baron Meats Ltd and Brian Edward McMenemy were charged at the instance of Staniforth Wilson Lockhart, procurator fiscal, Aberdeen on a summary complaint which contained the following charges, I inter alia: "(1) Between 23 December 1988 and 4 January 1989, both dates inclusive, at Weasenham Lane, Wisbech, Cambridgeshire, or elsewhere, you Baron Meats Ltd being the employer of Brian Edward McMenemy, the driver of goods vehicle C381 DYB, being a vehicle to which s 97 of the aftermentioned Act applies and which was fitted with tachograph recording equipment, did fail to issue to said Brian Edward McMenemy, a sufficient number of record sheets as provided by art 14 (1) of the European J Economic Community Council Regulation (EEC) No 3821/85, in respect that no record sheets had been issued to said Brian Edward McMenemy: contrary to the Transport Act 1968, s 97 (1) (c).

"(2) On 4 January 1989, in Jesmond Drive, Bridge of Don, Aberdeen, you Brian Edward McMenemy, being the driver of goods vehicle C381 DYB, a vehicle to which s 97 of the aftermentioned Act applies and which was fitted with tachograph recording equipment, did use said vehicle and tachograph recording K equipment other than as provided by art 15 (2) of the European Community Council Regulation (EEC) No 3821/85, in respect that no record sheet was inserted in the tachograph recording equipment for that day: contrary to the Transport Act 1968, s 97 (1) (c)."

The accused pled not guilty and proceeded to trial in the district court. After the trial the justice (J Quarterman) convicted both accused.

The accused appealed by way of stated case to the L High Court against the decision of the justice.

Findings in fact

The justice found the following facts to be admitted or proved:

(1) The appellants Baron Meats are a limited company with a place of business at Weasenham Lane, Wisbech, Cambridgeshire and they carry on business as manufacturers and wholesalers of meat and bakery products. (2) The appellants Baron Meats employ a

number of men as salesmen/drivers of lorries leased by
the appellants and two salesmen/drivers operate from
a base at Aberdeen. One driver is employed to do the
local run within the city of Aberdeen. The other
driver, who was Brian McMenemy, was employed to
travel to the outlying districts outside Aberdeen. This
could involve travelling as far north as Fraserburgh.
(3) On 4 January 1989 at approximately 8.00 am one
of the salesmen/drivers from the Aberdeen base,
namely the appellant Brian McMenemy of 51 Fair-
view Crescent, Danestone, Aberdeen, was driving one
of Baron Meats' lorries, goods vehicle registration
number C381 DYB in Jesmond Avenue, Bridge of
Don, Aberdeen, when he was stopped by two police
officers who had recorded the vehicle travelling in
excess of the speed limit. (4) Vehicle C381 DYB is a
vehicle to which s 97 of the Transport Act 1968
applies. The appellant Brian McMenemy produced a
log book detailing his hours of working but did not
have a chart inserted in the tachograph recording
equipment. (5) The appellants Baron Meats Ltd had
never provided McMenemy with any record sheets.
(6) Mercedes van C381 DYB comprised of a standard
cabin chassis bought from the manufacturers and the
bodywork was provided by Wincanton Vehicle
Rentals to suit the purposes of the appellants Baron
Meats. (7) The body of the van was a refrigerated unit.
Racks and shelving were fitted along three sides of the
van designed to carry trays which would slide out and
give easy access to a maximum amount of product.
There was a clear walkway up the centre of the van
and a strip light was fitted. The doorway was not of
the width usual to allow palette loading but was a
normal sized door and steps were fitted to allow access
for the driver/salesman and customers. (8) The appellant McMenemy like other driver/salesmen employed
by Baron Meats was paid a basic wage plus commission on sales. McMenemy was expected not only to
call on regular customers but also to canvass for new
business. (9) McMenemy was the van salesman for the
Aberdeen area who made the outlying calls and on a
normal day would call on an average of 30 retail
outlets. Each call was speculative and no orders were
placed in advance. McMenemy would take payment
in cash or make out an invoice. He would then order
sufficient supplies to make up his stock from the
Baron Meats depot in East Kilbride. (10) The 4
January 1989 was a Thursday and McMenemy had
been on holiday. He could not recall whether he had
worked between Christmas and New Year. On 4
January 1989 his first call was at Gateway in the
Bridge of Don area of Aberdeen and he was stopped
by the police en route to his second call, Gateway in
Fraserburgh, some 43 miles away. From there he was
travelling to Gateway in Peterhead some 18 miles
from Fraserburgh. (11) The motor van registration
number C381 DYB was not being used for door to
door selling as required in reg 4 of (and para 6 (b) of
the Schedule to) the Community Drivers' Hours and
Recording Equipment (Exemptions and Supplementary Provisions) Regulations 1986.

Statutory provisions

The Transport Act 1968, as amended, provides:

"(1) No person shall use, or cause or permit to be
used, a vehicle to which this section applies unless
there is in the vehicle recording equipment which —
(a) has been installed in accordance with the Community Recording Equipment Regulation; (b) complies
with Annexes I and II to that Regulation; and (c) is
being used as provided by Articles 13 to 15 of that
Regulation, and any person who contravenes this subsection shall be liable on summary conviction to a fine
not exceeding level 4 on the standard scale. . . .

"(6) This section applies at any time to any vehicle
to which this Part of this Act applies if, at that time,
Article 3 of the Community Recording Equipment
Regulation requires recording equipment to be
installed and used in that vehicle; and in this section
and sections 97A and 97B of this Act any expression
which is also used in that Regulation has the same
meaning as in that Regulation.

"(7) In this Part of this Act — 'the Community
Recording Equipment Regulation' means Council
Regulation (EEC) No. 3821/85 of 20th December
1985 on recording equipment in road transport as read
with the Community Drivers' Hours and Recording
Equipment (Exemptions and Supplementary Provisions) Regulations 1986; 'recording equipment' means
equipment for recording information as to the use of
a vehicle'."

Council Regulation (EEC) No 3820/85 provides:

"13.1. Each Member State may grant exceptions on
its own territories or, with the agreement of the States
concerned, on the territory of another Member State
from any provision of this Regulation applicable to
carriage by means of a vehicle belonging to one or
more of the following categories: . . . (f) vehicles used
as shops at local markets or for door-to-door selling, or
used for mobile banking, exchange or saving transactions, for worship, for the lending of books, records
or cassettes, for cultural events or exhibitions, and
specially fitted for such uses."

Council Regulation (EEC) No 3821/85 provides:

"14.1. The employer shall issue a sufficient number
of record sheets to drivers, bearing in mind the fact
that these sheets are personal in character, the length
of the period of service and the possible obligation to
replace sheets which are damaged, or have been taken
by an authorized inspecting officer. The employer
shall issue to drivers only sheets of an approved model
suitable for use in the equipment installed in the
vehicle. . . .

"15. . . . 2. Drivers shall use the record sheets every
day on which they are driving, starting from the
moment they take over the vehicle. The record sheet
shall not be withdrawn before the end of the daily
working period unless its withdrawal is otherwise
authorized. No record sheet may be used to cover a
period longer than that for which it is intended."

The Community Drivers' Hours and Recording Equipment (Exemptions and Supplementary Provisions) Regulations 1986 provide:

"4.—(1) Pursuant to Article 3 (2) of the Community Recording Equipment Regulation, exemption is granted from the provisions of that Regulation in respect of any vehicle falling within a description specified in Part I of the Schedule to these Regulations. . . .

"[Sched, Pt I] 6. Any vehicle which is being used — (a) as a shop at a local market; (b) for door-to-door selling; (c) for mobile banking, exchange or saving transactions; (d) for worship; (e) for the lending of books, records or cassettes; or (f) for cultural events or exhibitions, and is specially fitted for that use."

Cases referred to

R v Thomas Scott & Sons (Bakers) Ltd (133/83) [1984] ECR 2863; [1984] RTR 337.
Struthers (Lochwinnoch) Ltd v Tudhope, 1982 SLT 393.

Appeal

The justice posed the following questions for the opinion of the High Court:

(a) Was I entitled to hold that the goods vehicle C381 DYB was not a vehicle being used at the material time for door to door selling in terms of reg 4 of (and para 6 (b) of the Schedule to) the Community Drivers' Hours and Recording Equipment (Exemptions and Supplementary Provisions) Regulations 1986?

(b) Was I correct in holding that there was insufficient evidence to establish the exception referred to in the said reg 4?

(c) Was I entitled to consider that the evidence of Mr Bill Walker, sales manager for Scotland of the first appellants was irrelevant anent the expected calls which would be made on 4 January 1989?

(d) Was I entitled to make finding in fact 11?

The appeal was argued in the High Court on 23 January 1991.

On 14 February 1991 the court *answered* the four questions in the *negative, allowed* the appeals and *quashed* the convictions.

The following opinion of the court was delivered by the Lord Justice Clerk (Ross):

OPINION OF THE COURT.—The appellants went to trial in the district court of the city of Aberdeen on a complaint libelling a number of charges. The charges which are the subject of this appeal were as follows: [his Lordship quoted the terms of charges 1 and 2 and continued:]

The justice found both appellants guilty of the charges as libelled, and against their convictions on these charges the appellants have both appealed. In presenting their appeals counsel referred to the findings in fact made by the justice. The appellants Baron Meats Ltd carry on business as manufacturers and wholesalers of meat and bakery products. They employ a number of men as salesmen/drivers, and in particular they employ two salesmen/drivers who operate from a base at Aberdeen. One of these drivers is employed to do the local run within the city of Aberdeen, and the other driver, who was the appellant Brian Edward McMenemy, was employed to travel to the outlying districts outside Aberdeen. This could involve travelling as far north as Fraserburgh. On 4 January 1989 the appellant Brian Edward McMenemy was stopped by police officers who had recorded that his vehicle was travelling in excess of the speed limit.

Finding 4 is in the following terms: [his Lordship quoted its terms and continued:]

Counsel maintained that that finding really begged the question. He submitted that s 97 (6) of the Transport Act 1968 only applied in respect of a vehicle which at the relevant time required recording equipment in terms of art 3 of Regulation (EEC) No 3821/85. If the vehicle was an exempted vehicle under the relevant Regulations, it would not be a vehicle to which s 97 of the Act of 1968 applied.

The findings go on to describe the vehicle C381 DYB. It comprised a standard cabin chassis and the bodywork was provided by Wincanton Vehicle Rentals to suit the purposes of the appellants, Baron Meats Ltd.

Finding 7 is in the following terms: [his Lordship quoted its terms and continued:]

The findings go on to explain that the appellant McMenemy like other driver/salesmen employed by Baron Meats Ltd was paid a basic wage plus commission on sales. He was expected not only to call on regular customers but also to canvass for new business. The appellant McMenemy on a normal day would call on an average of 30 retail outlets. Each call was speculative and no orders were placed in advance. The appellant McMenemy would take payment in cash or make out an invoice, and he would then order sufficient supplies to make up his stock from the depot of Baron Meats Ltd in East Kilbride.

On 4 January 1989 the appellant McMenemy's first call was at Gateway in the Bridge of Don area of Aberdeen and he was stopped by the police en route to his second call, Gateway in Fraserburgh some 43 miles away. From there he was to travel to Gateway in Peterhead some 18 miles from Fraserburgh.

Finding 11 is in the following terms: [his Lordship quoted its terms and continued:]

That finding is challenged by the appellants, and question (d) in the case asks whether the justice was entitled to make that finding in fact. Counsel explained that the issue which he sought to raise in the appeal was whether the vehicle was exempt. This issue was dealt with in questions (a), (b) and (d). He explained that question (c) dealt with the relevancy of certain evidence given by the appellants Baron Meats Ltd's Scottish sales manager.

Counsel next drew attention to the relevant statutory provisions. Section 97 of the Transport Act 1968, as amended, provides inter alia as follows: [his Lordship quoted the terms of s 97 (1), (6) and (7) and continued:]

Regulation (EEC) 3821/85 of 20 December 1985 provides in art 14 for the issue by an employer of a sufficient number of record sheets to drivers. Article 15 provides that drivers shall use the record sheets every day on which they are driving starting from the moment they take over the vehicle.

In para 2 of art 3, provision is made for member states to exempt vehicles mentioned in art 13 (1) of Regulation (EEC) No 3820/85 from application of this regulation.

Article 13 (1) of Regulation (EEC) 3820/85 of 20 December 1985 provides inter alia as follows: [his Lordship quoted the terms of art 13 (1) and continued:]

By virtue of the powers contained in the foregoing enabling legislation, the following regulations have been made — the Community Drivers' Hours and Recording Equipment (Exemptions and Supplementary Provisions) Regulations 1986 (SI 1986/1456). Regulation 4 (1) provides: [his Lordship quoted the terms of reg 4 (1), followed by para 6 of Pt I of the Schedule, and continued:]

Under reference to these provisions, counsel accordingly pointed out that in the present case the vehicle would be exempt from the provisions of the Community Recording Equipment Regulation provided that it was being used for door to door selling and had been specially fitted for that use. He also reminded us that under earlier regulations namely the Drivers' Hours (Keeping of Records) Regulations 1976 (SI 1976/1447) and the Community Road Transport Rules (Exemptions) Regulations 1978 (SI 1978/1158) exemption was afforded in respect of operations carried on by the employer of a British goods vehicle, whereas under the current regulations exemption was given in respect of a vehicle which was being used for a specific purpose and was specially fitted for that use.

Counsel pointed out that in the present case the justice had accepted that the vehicle concerned had been specially fitted for door to door selling (finding 7). The question then arose as to whether at the material time the vehicle was being used for door to door selling. The meaning of "door to door" selling had been considered in *Struthers (Lochwinnoch) Ltd v Tudhope*. In that case the Lord Justice Clerk had said: "The expression 'door-to-door selling' appeared to me to indicate a salesman making a series of calls, travelling from the premises of one potential customer to those of another. 'Door-to-door' is defined in *Chambers Twentieth Century Dictionary* (1972 ed) as 'calling at each house in an area for purposes of selling, canvassing, etc'."

Counsel maintained that that was too narrow a definition having regard to what had been stated by the European Court of Justice in a later case. It should however be observed that in *Struthers (Lochwinnoch) Ltd v Tudhope*, although the vehicle in question had been specially designed to facilitate door to door selling of the company's soft drinks, at the time when the vehicle was stopped the vehicle was in fact carrying a load of cases of empty bottles, and the driver was on his way back from delivering to one customer a load of full bottles. The findings show that the vehicle was used for door to door selling on three days of the week only, and that on the other two days the vehicle was used to transport a full load of soft drinks to one customer and to return with a full load of empties. The court accordingly held that the operations carried on by the accused company on the date libelled on the complaint could not be described as door to door selling.

The expression "door-to-door selling" was considered by the European Court of Justice in *R v Thomas Scott & Sons Bakers Ltd*. The House of Lords had referred the case to the European Court of Justice for a preliminary ruling on inter alia what was meant by door to door selling. In the decision it is stated:

"22. The purpose of the second question put to the Court by the House of Lords is to ascertain whether the activity of door-to-door selling is meant to apply only to a methodical calling at one house after another for the purpose of selling to the ultimate consumer or whether it also includes a selling activity characterized by frequent stops, whether at the homes of individuals or at the premises of wholesale customers such as canteens, old-peoples homes or supermarkets.

"23. The defendants in the main proceedings and the United Kingdom, in the observations which they have submitted to the Court, express the view that the term 'door-to-door selling' should be given a wide interpretation. They contend, in effect, that the exemption in question can, without compromising the objectives of Regulation No 543/69, cover drivers who drive for only quite short periods where the time spent driving is secondary to their selling activity.

"24. The French Government and the Commission propose that in order to ensure the efficacy of checks, only itinerant retail sales to individuals at their homes should be exempted and add that the wording of the contested provision is not sufficiently clear and precise to justify a wider interpretation.

"25. Whilst it is true that such a conclusion seems to be supported by the wording of some language versions of Article 14a (3) (a) of Regulation [EEC] No 543/69, other language versions point more to a wider interpretation.

"26. It is not necessary to give the concept of door-to-door selling a strict interpretation in order to ensure the effective checking of compliance with the Community rules. It follows from the foregoing considerations that the basic guarantee of compliance with the provisions of Regulation No 543/69 is the fact that the vehicle has permanent characteristics ensuring that it will not be used other than for door-to-door selling. In such circumstances it does not matter whether such

A door-to-door selling is to individuals, to wholesalers or to other customers provided that the activity of selling is characterized by frequent stops.

"27. The answer to the second question should therefore be that the activity of 'door-to-door selling' within the meaning of Article 14a (3) (a) of Regulation No 543/69 may consist of calls on potential wholesale customers, such as shops, works canteens, old-people's homes or supermarkets provided that the activity of selling is characterized by frequent stops by the specialized vehicle."

B Although that case was decided under earlier regulations, the case is important as explaining what is meant by "door-to-door selling".

In the light of the foregoing authorities, counsel submitted that the justice had taken too narrow a view of what was meant by door to door selling. He stressed that in his evidence the appellant McMenemy had stated that his calls averaged 30 to 40 on a day such as this when he was going to Fraserburgh and Peter-
C head. The evidence of Mr Walker had been that their salesmen would average about 40 calls in one day and never less than about 28. In these circumstances counsel submitted that the proper conclusion from the evidence was that this vehicle was being used for door to door selling on the date in question. He maintained that having regard to the evidence and the findings it was plain that the primary function on which the appellant McMenemy was engaged was selling and not driving. This had been recognised by the justice
D who recorded that the divisional general manager of Baron Meats Ltd had stated that the appellant McMenemy was employed not as a driver but as a van salesman. Counsel accordingly submitted that questions (a), (b) and (d) should all be answered in the negative.

For the Crown the Solicitor General welcomed the fact that this case had been brought before the court. He stated frankly that he shared counsel's doubts
E regarding the approach adopted by the justice. The justice had failed to attach sufficient weight to the fact that the appellant McMenemy was engaged on a normal day's work at the time when the vehicle was stopped. The Solicitor General pointed out that the purpose of Regulation (EEC) 3821/85 was to lay down provisions dealing with drivers' hours and rest periods. Regulation (EEC) 3821/85 dealt with recording equipment, the purpose of which was to ensure that the provisions regarding driving hours and rest
F periods were complied with. He accepted that in the present case the critical question was whether the driving involved frequent stops. What was important was how the vehicle was being used and there was no question of having to determine what constituted the driver's main activity, as might be the case where an exemption was claimed under para 7 (2) of Pt I of the Schedule to the Community Drivers' Hours and Recording Equipment (Exemptions and Supplementary Provisions) Regulations 1986 (SI 1986/1456). Although he did not expressly concede the point, we understood the Solicitor General to accept that the

proper conclusion from the evidence and findings in this case was that on the day in question the selling in G which the appellant McMenemy had been engaged did involve frequent stops by his specially fitted vehicle.

In our opinion the justice in this case has adopted too narrow an approach. It is clear from the note in the case that he was influenced by the fact that when the vehicle had been stopped the driver had only made one call, and was in the process of undertaking a journey of 43 miles before he made his second call. He also commented that there was very little evidence H relating to the calls being made on 4 January 1989, and indeed he states that he considers that some detailed evidence regarding the existence of more than three stops should have been presented.

We are satisfied that sufficient material was placed before the justice to enable him to decide this matter. The vehicle was stopped after making its first call that day. What it is important to know is what use was being made of the vehicle that day. It is clear from the I findings that the present case is not one like Struthers (Lochwinnoch) Ltd v Tudhope where, although the vehicle was specially fitted for door to door selling, it was not in fact being used for such a purpose on the day in question. In the present case it is clear that the appellant McMenemy was engaged upon his normal work with the vehicle. According to Mr Walker, a van salesman in this area would average about 40 calls in one day and never less than about 28. This was accepted by the justice, and in finding 9 he states that on a normal day the appellant McMenemy would call J on an average of 30 retail outlets. It is true that on this day he was intending to travel to Fraserburgh and then to Peterhead, but the findings make it clear that even on such days the average is approximately 30 calls. The evidence of McMenemy himself was that on that specific day he had made 30 to 40 calls. The justice appears to have concluded that the exemption had not been established because of the evidence that the appellant had to travel 43 miles to Fraserburgh and 18 miles from Fraserburgh to Peterhead. As the justice K himself recognised, however, in rural localities the distance between stops will necessarily be greater. In our opinion, whether the activity of selling involves frequent stops in any particular case is a question of fact and degree. Within an urban area a vehicle engaged on selling will no doubt stop more frequently than will a vehicle which is engaged on selling in a rural area. It appears to be accepted in the findings that the appellant McMenemy averaged 30 retail outlets per day. He must accordingly have made something of the order of L five calls per hour, and if that be so we are satisfied that in his case the activity of selling did involve frequent stops. The vehicle which he was using was a specialised vehicle and he was using it not as a driver but as a van salesman. Accordingly, we are satisfied that the proper conclusion to be drawn from the findings in the evidence is that at the material time the vehicle in question was being used for door to door selling. The stops made by the vehicle were sufficiently frequent having regard to the nature of the locality within which the vehicle was being used.

In the course of his note the justice makes it clear
A that he regarded the evidence of Mr Walker regarding
the expected calls which would be made on 4 January
1989 as irrelevant. We do not agree that evidence of
this kind is irrelevant. If, as in the present case, a
vehicle is stopped by the police shortly after it has set
off on its day's work, the question of whether or not
it is being used for door to door selling must depend
upon how it was intended to be used that day. If that
were not so, a vehicle which set off on a journey with
the intention of being engaged genuinely in door to
B door selling might fail to qualify for exemption if the
vehicle suffered a puncture or a breakdown. We are
not persuaded that that would be a sensible result. Of
course, if as in *Struthers (Lochwinnoch) Ltd v Tudhope*
a specialised vehicle was in fact being used for another
purpose, it would not be entitled to the exemption. In
our opinion the evidence of Mr Walker regarding the
calls which the appellant McMenemy might be
expected to make that day was relevant to the issue of
whether the vehicle was being used for door to door
C selling on the date in question.

For the foregoing reasons we shall answer all four
questions in the negative.

*Counsel for Appellants, Keen; Solicitors, Dundas &
Wilson, CS (for Raeburn, Christie & Co, Aberdeen) —
Counsel for Respondent, Solicitor General (Rodger, QC);
Solicitor, I Dean, Crown Agent.*

D
P W F

United Wholesale Grocers Ltd
E **v Sher**

OUTER HOUSE
LORD CULLEN
25 JULY 1991

*Reparation — Negligence — Vicarious liability — Inde-
pendent contractor — Test to be applied in determining
whether person an independent contractor or a casual
employee.*

F
The proprietors of warehouse premises raised an
action of damages against an individual who had contracted with them to carry out joinery and flooring
work to the premises. The individual entrusted the
work to three workmen. These men were to be paid
on a daily basis but without deductions. The
individual provided the initial materials necessary for
their work. During the period when the work was in
progress the premises were damaged by fire. The pursuers contended that one of the workmen had negligently discarded a cigarette and that each of the

workmen had been employed by the defender who was
accordingly vicariously liable for their negligence. G
The defender admitted that one of the workmen was
his employee but contended that the other two had
been independent subcontractors.

Opinion, (1) that in the absence of any determining
principle which fell to be applied, the status of the two
workmen depended upon an assessment of all the
factors which appeared to be relevant to the particular
case (p 287B); (2) that the control exercised by the
alleged employer over the way in which the work was
done was a very important consideration but was not H
conclusive (p 287B-C); (3) that an important consideration was whether the work carried out by the
workmen fell to be regarded as part and parcel of a
business carried out by the alleged employer or as
forming part of what they were doing on their own
account (p 287D); and (4) that in the circumstances
all three workmen had been employees of the
defender when carrying out the work on the premises
which the defender had contracted to undertake
(p 287D-G). I

Action of damages

United Wholesale Grocers Ltd raised an action concluding for damages against Falak Sher in respect of
losses sustained by the pursuers as a result of a fire at
their premises.

The case came to proof before the Lord Ordinary J
(Cullen).

Cases referred to

Kilboy v South Eastern Fire Area Joint Committee,
1952 SLT 332; 1952 SC 280.
Marshall v William Sharp & Sons Ltd, 1991 SLT 114.
Rose v Plenty [1976] 1 WLR 141; [1976] 1 All ER 97.
Stephen v Thurso Police Commissioners (1876) 3 R 535.

On 25 July 1991 the Lord Ordinary *assoilzied* the K
defender.

LORD CULLEN.—In this action the pursuers,
who were the proprietors of premises at 164-166
Maxwell Road, Pollokshields, Glasgow, sue the
defender for damages in respect of losses sustained by
them as a result of a fire at the premises on the night
of 30 June 1984. It is agreed between the parties that
for the purpose of any award of damages these losses
amount to £250,000 inclusive of all interest to the date L
of decree.

The premises were used by the pursuers as a wholesale cash and carry warehouse. They consisted of a flat
roofed brick building adjoined on three sides by open
ground used for the parking of vehicles. Within the
premises there was a brick walled store on the east
wall. A small suite of offices was on the north wall.
The rest of the interior was set out with shelved steel
racks in parallel rows to hold the goods which were
displayed for sale. Adjoining the offices was the main

entrance for customers. On the west side of the premises there was a secondary entrance. On the south side there was a vehicle entrance.

On 30 June 1984 the premises were not open for normal business as this was the day of a Muslim festival. However, certain work was being carried on within the premises. Thomas Clark was performing joinery work within the offices; and John McLeish and James Lickrish were engaged in filling cracks in the concrete floor of the premises, and in particular between the vehicle entrance and the southern ends of the rows of steel racks.

In the light of the evidence and the submission of parties the issues in this case can be expressed in the following questions: (i) Was the fire caused by the smouldering of a discarded light? (ii) If so, was it a cigarette discarded by one or other of Mr Clark, Mr McLeish and Mr Lickrish? (iii) Was each of them employed by the defender who was accordingly vicariously responsible for their negligence?

I take each of these issues in turn.

The causation of the fire

Mohammed Sarwar, a director of the pursuers, gave evidence that he had been outside the vehicle entrance until the three workmen had finished and left the premises, which was between 4 pm and 5 pm. A few minutes later he closed the premises, in the company of two friends, Nobahar Ullah and Safraz Ahmed, who had joined him earlier in the afternoon. Having locked the vehicle entrance from inside and having put on the intruder alarm he left the premises, locking the secondary entrance behind him. His two friends gave evidence which was broadly to the same effect. Only Mr Sarwar and his brother, Mohammed Ramzan, held keys to the premises. They gave evidence that they retained the keys and did not return to the premises in the evening. I accept that as from the time when the premises were closed they were in a secure state until after the outbreak of fire at the premises was discovered about 1 am on 1 July. [His Lordship considered the evidence, including evidence from a fire brigade officer and individuals experienced in investigating the causation of fires and concluded:] In all these circumstances I have come to the conclusion that the fire was caused by the dropping of a light, and in particular a cigarette prior to the closing of the premises.

The discarding of a cigarette by one of the workmen

In approaching this part of the case, it is necessary to bear in mind that the pursuers' case is based upon inference. In art 6 of the condescendence they aver: "During 30 June 1984 the defender's said employees were all smoking in the warehouse premises. They were the only persons smoking in the warehouse premises on 30 June 1984. They were the only persons in the warehouse premises after 2 pm on said date."

It was not in dispute that if one of the workmen dis-

carded a lit cigarette by throwing it into goods stored on a shelf at "S" [the seat of the fire, as denoted in the plan forming part of the fire investigator's report] he was at fault in doing so. [His Lordship then considered the evidence as to who all had been present in the warehouse premises on 30 June 1984 and which of these persons had been smoking, and concluded that there had been at least one other present during the course of the afternoon who had been smoking cigarettes. His Lordship continued:] In these circumstances I am not satisfied on the balance of probabilities that in the later part of the afternoon the three workmen were the only persons, and the only persons smoking, inside the premises. . . . The evidence of Dr Gibb [who gave expert evidence as a fire investigator] as to periods of time over which smouldering could take place, which I accept, was that the fire was consistent with a cigarette having been discarded at any time between mid-afternoon and the closing of the premises between 4 pm and 5 pm. Accordingly the fire could have been due to a cigarette dropped by some other person than one of the workmen prior to McLeish and Lickrish leaving the premises. In these circumstances I am not satisfied on the balance of probabilities that the pursuers have established the inference upon which their case against the defender depends.

The status of the workmen

In view of the evidence and submissions devoted to this matter, I propose to indicate my views upon it although by reason of my conclusion in the last paragraph, it has become academic.

In ans 3 the defender admits that he entered into a contract to carry out certain joinery work at the premises, including the creation of a hatchway through a partition wall. He also admits that Mr Clark was employed by him to carry out that work and that he was paid by him for it. He also admits that he paid both Mr McLeish and Mr Lickrish, but without any explanation as to how he came to do so. In the light of the evidence I have reached a number of findings which are as follows:

(i) The defender entered into a contract with the pursuers to carry out both the joinery and the flooring work. This resulted from Mr Sarwar getting in touch with the defender who, he believed, carried on business as the West End Building Co. Having seen at the premises what was involved, the defender agreed a price for the work with Mr Sarwar which was in the region of £500-£600. I accept the evidence of Mr Sarwar to this effect. It is supported by Mr Ramzan's understanding that his brother had arranged for the whole work to be done by the defender who had a building business. It is also supported by the evidence of Mr Clark, Mr McLeish and Mr Lickrish that they were looking to the defender for payment and did not understand anyone else was the contracting party. I reject the evidence of the defender that he had not gone to the premises to see what was involved in the work but that someone else, Bruce Galley, had done so; that he had had no discussions with Mr Sarwar but that Mr Galley had done so; and that Mr Galley had asked him to see to the carrying out of the joinery work for which he would be paid £100; but that he had had no concern with the flooring work. The defender's evidence on these points is so completely at odds with the rest of the evidence that I have no hesitation in rejecting it and preferring the evidence of Mr Sarwar. Mr Galley was not led as a witness by either party.

(ii) In order to carry out the joinery work, the defender got in touch with Mr Clark three or four days before 30 June 1984. Mr Clark had worked for him in 1983 in his building business but not continuously. He had not worked for him recently.

(iii) In order to carry out the flooring work, the defender got in touch with Mr McLeish two to three days before 30 June 1984. No specific price or rate was mentioned between them but Mr McLeish expected to be paid by the defender at the rate of £15 per day without any deductions. In 1984 he had done work for the defender at his shop which required extensive repairs, including plaster and roughcast work. This involved him working there several times a week. He had also worked for the defender alongside Mr Clark on two jobs, one in a shop, probably the defender's, and the other in a house. It is unclear how long Mr McLeish expected the work on the flooring to take, but it appears that at the outset he expected it to take a day, but when he saw what was involved he knew that it would take several occasions of weekend working in addition to the work on 30 June 1984. These findings are made in reliance on the evidence of Mr Clark and Mr McLeish, which I prefer to the evidence given by the defender.

(iv) Mr McLeish was expected by the defender to arrange for a second man to assist him with the flooring work. For this purpose he got in touch with Mr Lickrish who was a friend and neighbour with whom he had worked once before. He asked Mr Lickrish if he wanted the work, mentioning the rate of £15 per day. Mr Lickrish agreed. He understood the payment would be made by the defender. He had not previously worked for him.

(v) On 30 June 1984 the defender drove Mr McLeish and Mr Lickrish to the premises in his van, which was marked with the name of the West End Building Co, after they had met at the defender's house. Mr Clark followed in his own car. They arrived between 8 am and 9 am. On their arrival the defender showed all of them what work had to be done. Before that they had not personally seen what was involved. The second last sentence of these findings is based on the evidence given by Mr Ramzan, Mr Clark and Mr McLeish. I reject the evidence of the defender who said that Mr Galley showed Mr McLeish and Mr Lickrish what flooring work was to be done.

(vi) In the van the defender brought tools belonging to Mr Lickrish and some materials for flooring repairs. He also brought some materials for Mr Clark to use. Mr Clark had his own tools in his car.

(vii) After 15-20 minutes at the premises the defender left. He did not instruct the three workmen how to do their work. This was unnecessary. He did not supervise their work. He made at least one further visit to the premises, that being in mid-afternoon. The last sentence is based on the evidence of Mr Sarwar and the defender. Mr Ramzan also said that the defender returned in the morning with another Asian and inspected the work, but I am doubtful whether this evidence is reliable as it is unsupported by any other evidence.

(viii) Mr Galley visited the premises in the early part of the morning. He inspected the joinery and flooring work and materials in accordance with an arrangement which Mr Sarwar had made with him after making his contract with the defender. At Mr McLeish's request he went to a builder's merchant to collect further materials. His visit to the premises was after the defender had left. These findings are based on the evidence of Mr Sarwar as to the arrangement which he had made; Mr Ramzan as to what Mr Galley did and said; and Mr McLeish and Mr Lickrish as to the former's request for Mr Galley's assistance. There was, however, a conflict in the evidence between Mr McLeish who said that he had no materials and Mr Lickrish who said that the materials with which they had come to the premises were too coarse.

(ix) The defender gave evidence that Mr Galley had left a note in his shop asking him to pay the three workmen and saying that he would settle up with him. The defender said that he did not himself pay them but that someone in his shop did so.

Counsel for the pursuers laid particular stress on the admission made by the defender on record that he had employed Mr Clark. He submitted that the way in which Mr McLeish and Mr Lickrish had been engaged, performed their work and been paid for it showed no material distinction between them and Mr Clark. Counsel for the defender submitted that Mr McLeish and Mr Lickrish were independent contractors. He pointed to what he submitted was the absence of a permanent and continuing business, the absence of any exercise of control by the defender as to the way in which these workmen performed their work; and the differences between those workmen and Mr Clark in regard to any previous connection with the defender as a builder.

In connection with their submissions counsel referred me to *Stephen v Thurso Police Commissioners*, in which the importance of control was emphasised in regard to the question whether a person was vicariously liable for the negligence of a third party. This falls to be read along with the view expressed by Lord President Cooper in *Kilboy v South Eastern Fire Area Joint Committee*, 1952 SLT at p 335, where he said that "Being unable now to find any sure foothold in legal principle, I must take the matter on a broad overhead view". Reference was also made to *Marshall v William Sharp & Sons Ltd*. At p 125 Lord Dunpark, after referring to the cases of *Stephen* and *Kilboy* said: "One must have regard to all the relevant factors, which include the intention of the parties, power of selection, the method of payment and the reasons for that, the nature of the work and the power of dismissal." Counsel for the pursuers also relied upon a dictum of Scarman LJ in *Rose v Plenty* [1976] 1 WLR at p 147 that the reason for the vicarious liability of an employer is that, having put matters into motion, he should be liable if the motion which he has originated leads to damage to another.

In approaching the parties' submissions, the basic question which I have to consider is whether Mr McLeish and Mr Lickrish should be regarded as having undertaken to serve the defender and for that purpose provide him with their labour and skill in return for remuneration or as having undertaken to provide him with the end result of a job of work. In the absence of any determining principle which falls to be applied, the answer to the question depends upon an assessment of all the factors which appear to be relevant to the particular case. The control exercised by the alleged employer over the way in which the work is done is obviously a very important consideration. However, there must be many cases in which such control is not exercised either because it was unnecessary or because the employer lacks the skill to exercise such control. In the present case there was no instruction given by the defender as to the way in which the flooring work was to be done, let alone supervision of the way in which it was being done. However, the work was clearly not such as to require this. It was enough that the defender indicated to the two workmen what had to be done. It seems to me that an important consideration is whether the work carried out by these workmen fell to be regarded as part and parcel of a business carried out by the defender; or, on the other hand, as forming part of what they were doing on their own account. On any view the defender operated a building business in 1983. He claimed in evidence that he had discontinued this business after undergoing an operation. However, his admission in regard to Mr Clark would tend to imply the existence of some form of business, even if the engagement was of a relatively casual nature. On the basis of the evidence of Mr Sarwar and Mr Ramzan which I accept on these points, the defender undertook to carry out personally and through any necessary labour both the joinery and the flooring work for a total price. Accordingly in regard to both, the defender undertook contractual obligations and, since there was a fixed price (although the precise figure is not known) it was he who ran any financial risk associated with the execution of that work. The two workers were to be paid by the defender, as I accept, either directly or indirectly. The type of payment which they were to receive was not related to the end product but to their work on a daily basis. On the other hand, it appears they were to be paid without any deductions and that Mr Lickrish, like Mr Clark, brought his own tools with him. The initial materials were on any view provided by the defender. The evidence does not indicate who paid for any additional materials which were provided by Mr

Galley in accordance with the request made by Mr McLeish.

In the light of the factors which I have set out in the previous paragraph, I conclude that in addition to Mr Clark both Mr McLeish and Mr Lickrish were employed by the defender, although on any view that employent was on an extremely casual basis.

In the circumstances I shall sustain the defender's third plea in law and assoilzie him from the first conclusion of the summons.

Counsel for Pursuers, Keen; Solicitors, Dundas & Wilson, CS (for Brechin Robb, Glasgow) — Counsel for Defender, M G Clarke, QC, Howie; Solicitors, Cochran, Sayers & Cook.

I H L M

Muir v Cumbernauld and Kilsyth District Council

EXTRA DIVISION

LORDS MURRAY, McCLUSKEY
AND SUTHERLAND

20 DECEMBER 1991

Reparation — Negligence — Duty of care — Foreseeability — Causation — Type of injury — Pursuer injured in finger either by glancing blow from sharp object in refuse sack or by piercing of sack and glove worn by pursuer — Defenders supplying PVC gloves — Probability that use of latex gloves would have prevented injury caused by glancing blow but not if caused by piercing — Whether defenders under duty of care to supply latex gloves — Whether defenders negligent.

A refuse collector injured his finger in the course of his employment while picking up a refuse sack and raised an action of damages against his employers. The injury was caused either by a glancing blow from a sharp object in the sack or by the piercing of the sack and PVC glove worn by the pursuer and supplied to him by the defenders. The evidence showed that if the injury was caused by a glancing blow the use of latex gloves would probably have prevented the injury, but not if the injury was caused by piercing. The sheriff found that the injury was sustained through the negligence of the defenders in failing to provide gloves which gave adequate protection and granted decree in the pursuer's favour. The defenders appealed to the Court of Session on the ground that the sheriff had made no express finding of fact that had the defenders supplied to the pursuer the superior type of gloves this would have prevented the accident or materially reduced the risk of the accident occurring.

Held, (1) that the accepted test was that a pursuer had to prove on a balance of probabilities that the

A defender's breach of duty caused or materially contributed to his injury (p 289L); (2) that although the evidence as to precisely how the pursuer's finger came to be cut was scanty, it was more probable that the cut was of a glancing nature, which it was conceded the provision of latex gloves would on a balance of probabilities have prevented (p 290C-E); and appeal *refused.*

Porter v Strathclyde Regional Council, 1991 SLT 446, *explained.*

B   **Opinion,** that even if the matter of a glancing or a piercing blow had been left in the balance, the pursuer would be entitled to succeed on the basis that these two types of blow were not entirely different types of injury but were merely manifestations of the same type of injury, namely a cutting injury (p 290F-G).

Appeal from the sheriff court

William Muir raised an action of damages against C Cumbernauld and Kilsyth District Council in the sheriff court in respect of an injury caused to the fourth finger of his right hand in the course of his employment with them.

Case referred to

Porter v Strathclyde Regional Council, 1991 SLT 446.

After proof, the sheriff *granted* decree in favour of the pursuer in the agreed sum of damages.

D   The defenders appealed to the Court of Session.

Appeal

The appeal was heard before an Extra Division on 21 and 22 November 1991.

On 20 December 1991 the court *refused* the appeal.

The following opinion of the court was delivered by Lord Sutherland:

E   **OPINION OF THE COURT.**—The pursuer is employed by the defenders as a refuse collector. On 3 May 1988 the pursuer sustained injury to the fourth finger of his right hand when collecting refuse sacks from a block of flats in Cumbernauld. The accident occurred when the pursuer was removing three or four filled or partly filled plastic sacks. Grasping each sack at its top he swung them over his shoulders. At the time he was wearing cotton lined PVC gloves. A sharp object carelessly deposited in one of the plastic sacks F by a resident pierced the sack and the glove which the pursuer was wearing and lacerated his finger. At the time the pursuer did not know that he had been injured and was not aware of his injury until a fellow employee drew his attention to blood running down his right arm. The pursuer then observed a cut in the relevant finger of his glove and also a cut to his finger.

After proof the sheriff found that the regular careless disposal by householders of sharp objects including broken glass, cans, needles and the like is a widespread and well known hazard. In relation to the gloves provided by the defenders for the pursuer's use the sheriff made the following finding: "The type of G gloves which the pursuer was using has been supplied for a number of years. It affords inadequate protection against accidental penetration by sharp objects protruding from refuse bags. The defenders were aware of that inefficacy and, from time to time, supplied their refuse collectors with sample alternative gloves for short periods of time. Pliable working gloves suitable for the work of refuse collection and offering the wearer a materially greater degree of protection than those supplied to the pursuer were and are available to H the defenders on the market. . . . The use of such gloves has been considered and rejected by the defenders because they are rather more expensive than those which they have regularly supplied and which the pursuer was wearing."

The sheriff found that the injury was sustained through the negligence of the defenders in failing to provide gloves which gave adequate protection and accordingly granted decree for the agreed damages. The defenders have appealed against the sheriff's I interlocutor on the ground that the sheriff made no express finding of fact that had the defenders supplied to the pursuer the superior type of gloves this would have prevented the accident or materially reduced the risk of the accident occurring. Accordingly the sheriff was not entitled to hold that the accident was caused by the fault and negligence of the defenders. In presenting this ground of appeal counsel for the defenders argued that the failure to make such an express finding of fact vitiated the whole of the J sheriff's reasoning and that it was accordingly for this court to consider the evidence on causation. If that evidence was properly considered on a fair reading it would not support the view that the accident was caused by the failure of the defenders to provide the superior type of gloves.

The problem about causation arises in this way. It is clear on the evidence as accepted by counsel for the defenders that if the injury was caused by a glancing K blow from a sharp object the use of latex gloves as opposed to PVC gloves would probably have prevented the injury. If however the injury was caused by piercing, even a latex glove might not have been able to prevent the injury. Counsel for the defenders argued that the evidence did not establish which type of blow caused the injury. If therefore there was an equal chance that it was caused by a piercing blow, and as the evidence indicated that at best latex gloves might have prevented rather than probably would L have prevented such injury, the pursuer must fail on causation. In order to consider this argument it is necessary to look at the evidence. The only evidence relevant to this matter came from the pursuer and an expert witness, Mr Stuart. The pursuer described the manner in which he normally lifted bags and accepted that he was unaware of his injury until it was pointed out to him by a fellow employee. When asked what he thought it was that cut him he replied, "I don't know. It was either the glass or the tins." He described the damage to his glove at different points in his evidence

as being ripped, torn or cut. In cross examination he
was not asked about the way in which he sustained
injury but in answer to the sheriff at the end of his
evidence when asked how he thought he came in
contact with something sharp, he said that he thought
it must have happened when he swung the bags on to
his shoulder.

Mr Stuart's evidence was in general terms that the
PVC gloves supplied by the defenders provided quite
inadequate protection against a cutting injury. Latex
gloves, which were available, were far superior as far
as the resistance to cutting was concerned. He
described tests that he had carried out drawing the
blade of a Stanley knife across latex gloves and said
that the texture of the rubber would resist cutting.
The matter of piercing first arose from a question by
the sheriff who asked Mr Stuart whether the latex
glove would prevent a cut with a sharp pointed needle
such as that of a hypodermic syringe. Mr Stuart's
answer was that it possibly would. He went on to say:
"If it was a light, glancing blow on to the syringe I
don't think it would go through it, but having said
that, I am sure I could get it to go through it if I really
wanted to force it to go through it. I don't think there
is any glove on the market which will protect under
every situation a glove from being pierced, but that is
quite different from getting a glancing cut. So piercing
is a problem with all types of glove". He went on to
say that from the tests he carried out his opinion
would be that a latex glove would protect against a
glancing blow from glass or a tin can lid or some
similar sharp item. As far as a direct pierce was concerned, whether or not a thing would pierce depends
very much on the speed at which it contacts the glove.
Having said that, he considered that on a straight comparison between piercing a PVC glove and piercing a
latex glove, the latex glove would stand up better
under the same test conditions. In cross examination
the only question which might be thought to have a
bearing on the question of causation was in the following terms: "I think your evidence also was that you
were unable to say with any great confidence whether
or not a glove of the rubber sort could actually have
prevented the accident in any event." Mr Stuart's
answer was: "If that is the impression you got, I don't
think that is quite true." He went on to say that in the
case of rubber gloves they offer better resistance to
cuts. He then added: "I think my Lord also brought
up the point about piercing, and ignoring that, these
two gloves have better resistance to cuts than the PVC
glove — without a doubt — because of the material."
Neither the cross examiner nor the sheriff took up the
question of piercing any further with this witness. The
only medical evidence in the case came from two
agreed medical reports. In the report by Mr Simpson,
he says that there was a cut over the back of the ring
finger caused presumably by a sharp object which had
penetrated the bin bag. The cut was curved enclosing
a flap of skin. Mr Simpson considered that the injury
involved skin and subcutaneous tissue. The treatment
was the insertion of three stitches. It does not appear
from the sheriff's findings in fact or from his note that

the distinction between a glancing cut and a piercing
cut was ever raised as an issue before him nor that any
point was taken at the hearing about causation. From
the evidence it is clear that this was not a matter which
was considered in any detail. In these circumstances it
is perhaps not surprising that the sheriff did not make
any specific finding relating to causation.

On this evidence counsel for the defenders submitted that the pursuer did not differentiate between
a cut caused by a glancing blow or by a piercing blow
and nothing in his evidence would justify the inference that this was a glancing blow which could have
been warded off by the provision of latex gloves. If it
was a blow of a piercing type, Mr Stuart's evidence
did not come up to saying that a latex glove would
probably have prevented penetration. Therefore the
pursuer had to prove on a balance of probabilities that
it was a glancing blow, and as he has failed to do so
he must also fail on causation. Counsel for the pursuer
argued in the first place under reference to *Porter v
Strathclyde Regional Council* that the sheriff's finding
that latex would provide "a materially greater degree
of protection" was equivalent to saying that there was
a material reduction in the risk, and that this led to the
inevitable conclusion that provision of latex gloves
would probably have prevented the accident. In our
view this submission involves a misreading of what
was said in *Porter*. The particular passage founded on
reads (at p 448K): "As the Lord Ordinary found, the
risk of someone slipping on food on the floor was 'a
reasonably foreseeable danger'. If the defenders
operated a system designed to preclude or reduce this
danger, then, in our opinion, the inevitable inference
is that such a system would probably have prevented
this accident." The system referred to was a system
whereby there should be continuous supervision with
the cleaning up of any spillage of food as soon as it
occurred. Quite clearly on the facts of that case the
operation of that stringent system would have
prevented any spilled food lying on the floor for any
material length of time, and accordingly the probability that an accident occasioned by slipping on
spilled food would be prevented was indeed an inevitable inference. We cannot however read into this
passage any general proposition to the effect that
where a pursuer establishes a failure to take a precaution which was designed to reduce a danger, this
inevitably implies that had the precaution been taken
the accident would probably have been prevented. It
would in our view be a question of fact in each particular case whether or not the failure to take a desiderated precaution was a cause of the accident. In *Porter*
the "inevitable inference" was specifically related to
"*this* accident" and on the facts of that particular case
we can well understand how the court came to that
conclusion. We are accordingly satisfied that *Porter* in
no way derogates from the accepted test which is that
a pursuer must prove on a balance of probabilities that
the breach of duty caused or materially contributed to
his injury.

Counsel for the pursuer then argued that Mr
Stuart's evidence properly read as a whole is not to the

effect that the category of injury caused by piercing as defined by him is an exception to his general evidence that latex gloves would have materially lessened the risk of injury caused by sharp objects. It was clear from his evidence as a whole that latex gloves were far more resistant to cutting of any kind than PVC gloves. Properly read, the passage in his evidence relating to a piercing type of injury merely indicates that no glove can give an absolute protection against piercing, and that if contact is fast and forceful an instrument such as a needle could penetrate even a latex glove. The difference between a glancing blow and a piercing blow is merely one of degree and they should not be regarded as two entirely distinct and different types of blow. There is no doubt on Mr Stuart's evidence that latex gloves provide substantially more resistance to any type of cutting injury and accordingly it is by no means unreasonable to say that the provision of latex gloves would have materially reduced the risk of injury to the pursuer in this case. Counsel further argued that in any event the evidence, while admittedly far from clear, indicated a glancing type of blow rather than a piercing type of blow. The injury was not of the nature of a hole which might be expected from a piercing injury but was a cut of reasonably substantial dimensions which required three stitches. It appeared from the medical evidence to be a fairly superficial cut over its length rather than a deep cut. The pursuer's evidence that he considered the likely cause of such a cut to be broken glass or a sharp piece of tin can was not challenged, nor was his evidence about the nature of the cut or tear to the finger of the glove. His evidence about the way in which he lifted the bag would tend to preclude the inference that either forceful contact or fast contact with a piercing type object was involved. In the whole circumstances therefore on a balance of probabilities the pursuer has established that it was a glancing blow which he sustained and therefore, as the defenders now accept, injury to his finger would probably have been prevented by the provision of latex gloves.

In our opinion the argument by counsel for the pursuer should be preferred. It is true that the evidence as to precisely how the pursuer's finger came to be cut is scanty but we consider that for the reasons advanced by counsel for the pursuer it is more probable that the cut was of a glancing nature. Certainly a needle would not produce the type of injury which he sustained, and if it was a piercing type of blow caused for example by the point of a broken piece of glass we would have expected an injury deeper in the centre than at the edges and almost certainly one which would have been felt by the pursuer at the time it was sustained. We would accordingly be prepared to hold that on the evidence the pursuer has established on a balance of probabilities that he sustained a glancing blow and if this be so, as the defenders would concede, he has established that the provision of latex gloves would on a balance of probabilities have prevented the accident. Even if the matter of glancing or piercing blow had been left in the balance, we would still have considered that the pursuer would be entitled to succeed on the basis that these two types of blow are not entirely different types of injury but are merely manifestations of the same type of injury, namely a cutting injury. On the evidence of Mr Stuart read as a whole, it is clear that the provision of latex gloves would have provided much better resistance to a cutting injury. It may very well be that certain types of blow administered with sufficient force could penetrate even latex gloves, but all that the pursuer requires to establish is that on a balance of probabilities his injury would have been prevented by the provision of such gloves. On the whole matter therefore we shall refuse this appeal.

As the matter of causation has now been raised it is appropriate that there should be a finding in fact to deal with it. We shall therefore add a further finding in fact in the following terms: "10. The wearing of gloves of a type referred to in finding 9 would have materially lessened the risk of the pursuer sustaining an injury of the type he in fact sustained and would probably have prevented said accident." The existing finding 10 should be renumbered accordingly.

Counsel for Pursuer (Respondent), Peebles; Solicitors, Digby, Brown & Co — Counsel for Defenders (Appellants), Currie; Solicitors, Bishop & Robertson Chalmers.

R F H

Gall v HM Advocate

HIGH COURT OF JUSTICIARY
THE LORD JUSTICE GENERAL (HOPE),
LORDS COWIE AND WYLIE
5 MARCH 1992

Justiciary — Procedure — Trial — Charge to jury — Crown witness prevaricating, being detained on advocate depute's instructions, charged by police with perjury and detained overnight — Witness recalled, incriminating accused and cross examined about these events — Trial judge not directing jury to disregard witness's evidence — Whether misdirection.

Justiciary — Procedure — Witness — Recall — Crown witness prevaricating, being detained on advocate depute's instructions, charged by police with perjury and detained overnight — Witness recalled, incriminating accused and cross examined about these events — Whether trial judge erred in allowing recall of witness — Criminal Procedure (Scotland) Act 1975 (c 21), s 148A.

Section 148A of the Criminal Procedure (Scotland) Act 1975 provides: "In any trial, on the motion of either party, the presiding judge may permit a witness who has been examined to be recalled."

An accused person was charged on indictment with inter alia a contravention of s 4 (3) (b) of the Misuse

of Drugs Act 1971. One of the essential Crown wit-
A nesses, C, gave evidence on the first day of the trial
but prevaricated and was not cross examined. At the
conclusion of his evidence C was detained by the
police on the instructions of the advocate depute and
charged by them with perjury. He was held in custody
overnight and the next morning he returned to court
where outwith the presence of the jury the trial judge
warned him that he was considering holding him in
contempt. The Crown then sought permission to
recall C to give evidence in terms of s 148A of the
B 1975 Act, which motion was opposed on behalf of the
accused but was granted by the trial judge. At the conclusion of his evidence in chief C was cross examined
as to why he had changed his evidence. The effect of
the cross examination was to reveal to the jury matters
of which they had hitherto been unaware, namely that
C had been detained, charged by the police with
perjury and that he had been warned by the trial judge
that he was considering holding him in contempt. In
charging the jury the trial judge directed them as to
C how they should approach the evidence of witnesses
who are "trying to say as little as they can get away
with and have to be put under pressure of various
kinds in order to get them to say anything at all". He
did not direct the jury to disregard C's evidence. The
accused was convicted and appealed, contending that
the trial judge erred in allowing C to be recalled
because of what had happened to him after he had
completed his evidence on the first day and that he
misdirected the jury in not telling them to disregard
D C's evidence.

Held, (1) that the decision to permit a witness to be
recalled was a matter entirely at the discretion of the
trial judge (p 294F); (2) that the trial judge did not err
in the exercise of his discretion (a) since the jury at
that stage knew nothing of the various steps which had
been taken in the light of C's behaviour the previous
day, nor were they present when he was warned by the
trial judge that he was considering holding him in con-
E tempt, (b) since it was difficult to imagine a case where
the recall of a witness was likely to be less disruptive
to the fair and orderly progress of the trial, and (c)
since it was a sound practice to allow a witness to
purge his contempt (p 294F-I); (3) that a trial judge
would only be justified in directing a jury to disregard
the whole of a witness's evidence if he were satisfied
that no reasonable jury properly directed could assess
the evidence impartially in fairness to the accused and
nothing that was said or done in the course of C's evidence would have justified the trial judge in taking that
F extreme step (p 295D-G); and appeal *refused*.

Williamson v HM Advocate, 1978 SLT (Notes) 58,
applied.

Indictment
Daniel Campbell Gall was charged along with
Arthur Thomas Swankie at the instance of the rt hon
the Lord Fraser of Carmyllie, Her Majesty's Advocate, on an indictment which included the following

charge, inter alia: "(1) between 1 January and 10
August 1990, both dates inclusive, in the house G
occupied by you Arthur Thomas Swankie at 15 Jamieson Street, Arbroath, and elsewhere in Arbroath and
Tayside to the Prosecutor unknown, you Arthur
Thomas Swankie and Daniel Campbell Gall were concerned in the supplying of a controlled drug, namely
Lysergide, a class A drug specified in Pt I of Sched 2
to the aftermentioned Act, to another in contravention
of s 4 (1) of said Act: Contrary to the Misuse of Drugs
Act 1971, s 4 (3) (b)". The accused pled not guilty and
proceeded to trial before Lord Coulsfield and a jury in H
the High Court at Dundee. After trial the accused was
found   guilty   and   sentenced   to   five   years'
imprisonment.

The accused appealed by note of appeal against conviction and sentence.

Statutory provisions
The Criminal Procedure (Scotland) Act 1975, as
amended, provides: I

"148A. In any trial, on the motion of either party,
the presiding judge may permit a witness who has
been examined to be recalled."

Cases referred to
Hutchison v HM Advocate, 1984 SLT 233; 1983
SCCR 504.
Thomson v HM Advocate, 1989 SLT 22; 1988 SCCR
354.
Williamson v HM Advocate, 1978 SLT (Notes) 58; J
1979 JC 36.

The trial judge gave the following directions to the
jury, inter alia:

LORD COULSFIELD.—. . . Now I have said
several times that the evidence must be credible and
reliable and there are a number of aspects of that again
which it may be helpful if I mention in this case. One
point is that you can never draw an inference that K
because somebody has said something which you
think is false, therefore the opposite, something contrary to that, must be true. If a witness gives evidence
which is false, then you have to put it aside and you
have to proceed only upon the evidence which you can
accept as reliable. The assessment of that is entirely a
matter for you, but you will appreciate that in a
criminal trial the Crown — and indeed in many cases
the defence — have to proceed upon the evidence
which is there. It would be very helpful if matters L
could be arranged so that there was always a witness
of unimpeachable credit available to speak about the
circumstances in which crimes are committed, but
that is not usually the situation. And in many cases we
have to proceed upon the evidence which is the best
that can be got, and that means there may be witnesses
who are reluctant to say anything, perhaps because
they have been threatened, perhaps because they have
got some previous involvement, they have got some
involvement of their own, some interest which they
are trying to protect, sometimes because they are

A simply hostile to the law and to the police, and to any interference with what they look on as their own affairs. So you may very well have witnesses who are trying to say as little as they can get away with and have to be put under pressure of various kinds in order to get then to say anything at all.

When you get such a situation it is a matter for you to judge on the particular case what you think of the evidence that results. Sometimes it can even be a point in favour of believing something that a witness said that it is something that is dragged out of him like B drawing teeth, when it is obvious he would much rather not say it. On the other hand, it may be in such a situation that you think that the evidence is so tainted, so corrupted, by the obvious self interest of the witness that you can't rely upon it. That is why it is important in a case like this that you have to sift the evidence according to your recollection of it and your judgment of it, and do so carefully, and you do pick and choose among it.

C In this case I don't think I am trespassing upon your province by saying that I doubt if anyone in court has the least doubt that all the witnesses, apart from the police witnesses at least, did not tell the whole truth, and in some instances probably certainly told lies. But that doesn't mean that there may not be parts of the evidence which you can identify as credible and that those parts may not be enough for the Crown. On the other hand, as I have said, it may mean that the evidence is so unsatisfactory and so tainted that you can't D reach any safe conclusion.

I don't think anyone can give you any help about this. The reason why juries are employed in serious criminal cases like this is precisely that it is thought that the collective judgment and experience of 15 people like yourselves is a much more reliable way of determining whether a case can be proved upon the evidence, the application of that wisdom and judgment is a much more reliable way of deciding it than to entrust such decisions to those of us who spend all E our lives in these courts. But what I do have to stress to you is that you have to look at the evidence and analyse it carefully in a case like this to see what conclusion you can draw.

Counsel for the accused Gall drew your attention to discrepancies between the evidence of the various witnesses about the amount of LSD that was seen, Mr Cuthill saying there was 100 tablets, Mr Cooper 500, Mr Swankie 15 to 20 at the most; and he drew your attention to, most importantly perhaps, the sorry F history of the way the evidence has come before you and the various statements which have been made to the police, and the various differences in the way the witnesses changed their statements from time to time. All that is a matter which you must consider.

Ladies and gentlemen, as I say, there is evidence put before you by the Crown which meets the legal test, the minimum legal test, there is evidence which is sufficient in law, but the vital question for you is whether that evidence or enough of it to establish the Crown case is credible and reliable, and that is the issue to which you must now address yourselves. If you are not satisfied on that evidence that the Crown G have proved their case beyond reasonable doubt, then you must of course in accordance with your oath acquit. Equally, of course, if you think the case is proved beyond reasonable doubt, it is your duty to convict.

Appeal

The note of appeal contained the following grounds of appeal: H

That the learned trial judge erred in allowing against opposition the advocate depute's motion to recall to the witness stand the Crown witness no 5 Craig Brian Cooper against the background of

(1) Cooper's having been called as a prosecution witness on the prior afternoon and having concluded his evidence then and been stood down as a witness;

(2) Cooper's thereafter being detained by police on I the instructions of the trial advocate depute outwith the courtroom after his initially being called as a witness and having been charged by them on the latter's instructions with perjury arising out of the manner of his giving and the content of his evidence;

(3) Cooper's having been detained overnight by the police on that latter matter and returned to the court building to appear on petition before the sheriff therefor; and

(4) Cooper's having been brought into court at the J request of the learned trial judge outwith the presence of the jury and being upbraided by the latter for insulting the court's intelligence both by the manner and content of his earlier evidence, being questioned by the latter as to his telling lies in court earlier and by the latter advising him that he was minded to hold him in contempt but that he would be given an opportunity to give further evidence whereafter the learned trial judge would see what his penalty was to be.

K In a case where the evidence was to that point marginal in relation to the indictment charges both in content and quality, where issues of credibility and reliability were narrow and crucial and in a situation where, if Cooper were to change his evidence by incriminating the accused on being recalled, it was obvious that the defence would either be oppressively confined in cross examination of the witness or constrained to cross examine as to why he had changed his evidence, which would inevitably bring to the know- L ledge of the jury that the witness was in the eyes of the prosecution a perjurer and had been so charged and/or that he had been recalled after rebuke by the learned trial judge, in any of which instances the accused's position would be or would be seen to be prejudiced as a result of which, and in the absence of adequate direction to the jury by the learned trial judge on these aspects, there was a miscarriage of justice.

The appeal was argued before the High Court on 7 February 1992.

On 5 March 1992 the court *refused* the appeal.

The following opinion of the court was delivered by the Lord Justice General (Hope):

OPINION OF THE COURT.—The appellants, who are Arthur Thomas Swankie and Daniel Campbell Gall, appeared for trial in the High Court at Dundee on an indictment which contained numerous charges under the Misuse of Drugs Act 1971. The first of these charges was that between 1 January and 10 August 1990 in the house occupied by Swankie and elsewhere in Arbroath and Tayside, the appellants were concerned in the supplying of a class A controlled drug, namely Lysergide, to another contrary to s 4 (3) (b) of the Act. At the commencement of the trial Swankie pled guilty to this charge under substitution of the date 1 May for 1 January, and quoad ultra not guilty. These pleas were accepted by the Crown. Gall pled not guilty to all charges, and after trial he was convicted of charge 1 as libelled and acquitted of the remaining charges. The appellants were both sentenced to five years' imprisonment. Swankie has appealed against this sentence on the ground that it is excessive. Gall has appealed against both conviction and sentence, and it is appropriate that we should deal first with his appeal against conviction.

The evidence against Gall came in the first place from Swankie, who was called as a witness by the Crown. There were only two other civilian witnesses, named Stephen Cuthill and Craig Cooper. The remainder of the evidence against Gall came from police officers. The trial judge tells us that neither Cuthill nor Cooper were satisfactory witnesses. Cuthill's evidence was at times vague and contradictory. Cooper's evidence was at first of no assistance at all to the Crown, as he was obviously prevaricating. It was so devoid of content that, when he completed his evidence in chief at the end of the first day of the trial, no questions were asked of him in cross examination. But he was recalled to give evidence the next day, and on this occasion he gave some evidence which tended to incriminate Gall. It is not suggested that the evidence of these witnesses was insufficient to justify Gall's conviction on the first charge. His ground of appeal is that the trial judge erred in allowing Cooper to be recalled to give evidence, and that in any event, in the absence of an adequate direction to the jury as to the consequences of this, there was a miscarriage of justice.

The background to this argument is set out in Gall's note of appeal, and it has also been described by the trial judge for our benefit in his report. Cooper's manner of answering the questions which were put to him was unsatisfactory, alternating between indifference and impertinence, and he was warned by the advocate depute and by the trial judge of the consequences of perjury. At the conclusion of his evidence that day he was detained by the police on the instructions of the advocate depute. He was then charged by them with perjury and held overnight in custody. The following morning he was brought back to court,

having had the benefit of legal advice. He was warned by the trial judge, outwith the presence of the jury, that the judge was considering holding him in contempt. The advocate depute then made a motion in terms of s 148A of the Criminal Procedure (Scotland) Act 1975 that Cooper be allowed to be recalled to give evidence. This motion was opposed by Gall's counsel but it was granted, and the trial judge then informed Cooper that he was being given an opportunity to give further evidence. At the conclusion of his evidence in chief he was cross examined as to why he had changed his story. He was asked whether he felt under pressure when he was recalled, and he was reminded by defence counsel of the consequences of perjury. He said that he had given different evidence because he did not want to go to jail for lying and that he had thought about the position overnight. He was then asked where he had been overnight, and he said that he had been kept in a cell for lying in court. Initially he said that he had not been charged, but when the question was repeated he said that he had been charged with perjury. He was also asked whether he had been warned about the risk of contempt that morning and he said that he had, and he also said that he had obtained legal advice. He was finally asked whether he was telling a different story to save himself from prison and he said that he was. The effect of this cross examination was to reveal to the jury things of which they had hitherto been unaware, because nothing had been said in their presence about the advocate depute's instructions that Cooper was to be detained, or of the fact that he had been charged with perjury by the police, or that he had been warned by the trial judge that he was considering holding him in contempt.

The trial judge felt it appropriate in these circumstances to give directions to the jury as to how they should approach the evidence of witnesses who were, as he put it, trying to say as little as they could get away with and had to be put under pressure of various kinds in order to get them to say anything at all. He told them that it was a matter for them to judge what they thought of the evidence that had resulted and that it was open to them, having sifted the evidence, to pick and choose among it as they thought fit. He went on to say this at [p 292C-D, supra]: "In this case I don't think I am trespassing upon your province by saying that I doubt if anyone in court has the least doubt that all the witnesses, apart from the police witnesses at least, did not tell the whole truth, and in some instances probably certainly told lies. But that doesn't mean that there may not be parts of the evidence which you can identify as credible and that those parts may not be enough for the Crown. On the other hand, as I have said, it may mean that the evidence is so unsatisfactory and so tainted that you can't reach any safe conclusion." In a later passage, after having summarised the evidence, he reminded the jury that the vital question for them was whether that evidence or enough of it to establish the Crown case was credible and reliable.

Counsel, in presenting the argument in support of Gall's appeal against conviction, made no criticism of these directions as far as they went. His submission was that the trial judge erred in allowing Cooper to be recalled because of what had happened to him after he had completed his evidence on the first day. It was said that there was nothing to prevent the prosecution from waiting until the end of the trial before taking proceedings against him, but the advocate depute had elected to have Cooper charged with perjury there and then and had then moved to have him recalled. As a consequence, said counsel, he had, as counsel for the defence, been driven into the position of having to ask questions in cross examination of Cooper in order to reveal to the jury the fact that this had been done. He submitted that if this had all been brought to the attention of the jury by the Crown, that would have been fatal to the conviction in a case such as this, where the evidence as a whole was far from satisfactory. The fact that he had been left with no alternative but to do this himself should have the same result. The trial judge should, in any event, having heard the effect of this cross examination, have directed the jury to totally disregard Cooper's evidence. Only in that way could the prejudice to the appellant which had been created by the advocate depute's actions be removed. Any direction short of that would have been inadequate, so the directions which the trial judge gave, while not in themselves open to criticism, had resulted in a miscarriage of justice.

There were two things about Cooper which the trial judge had to decide in the course of this trial. The first was whether to permit him to be recalled, in view of the fact that the Crown's motion to this effect was opposed. The second was what directions to give to the jury in regard to this man's evidence in the course of his charge. Both of these decisions are under attack in this appeal, but the point which is crucial to the argument on both points is the same, namely that Cooper had been detained and charged with perjury at the conclusion of his evidence on the first day. It was not suggested that the trial judge or the Crown said or did anything at that stage which was prejudicial to the appellant. But it was contended that the trial judge ought to have appreciated that, if Cooper was recalled, the defence would be bound to reveal what happened if he were then to give any evidence which was favourable to the Crown, and that once he had done this the risk of prejudice was so grave that no direction by him could remove it.

On the first point we cannot accept that the trial judge erred in granting the motion for Cooper's recall. Section 148A of the 1975 Act, as inserted by s 73 of the Criminal Justice Act 1982, provides: [his Lordship quoted the terms of s 148A and continued:] The matter is entirely at the discretion of the trial judge. In *Thomson v HM Advocate* it was held that there was no justification for reading into this section qualifications and restrictions which are not there. Counsel did not suggest otherwise, but nothing in his argument has persuaded us that the trial judge erred in the exercise of his discretion to permit Cooper to be recalled. At that stage the jury knew nothing of the various steps which had been taken in the light of his

behaviour the previous day. Nothing had been said in their presence to the effect that he was to be detained and charged with perjury. Nor were they present when Cooper was warned by the trial judge that he was considering holding him to be in contempt. What had been done was done privately and outwith the hearing and sight of the jury, in accordance with the procedure referred to with approval by Lord Cameron in *Hutchison v HM Advocate*, at 1984 SLT, pp 239-240, and with para 3 of the memorandum by the Lord Justice General on contempt of court. Furthermore, Cooper was the last witness to give evidence the previous day. He had not been cross examined at all on that evidence, and the Crown case was still in progress with many more witnesses on the Crown list who might yet be called. It is difficult to imagine a case where the recall of a witness was likely to be less disruptive to the fair and orderly progress of the trial. And by allowing Cooper to purge his contempt by returning to the witness box to give the evidence which he had earlier refused or failed to give, the trial judge was following the practice which was approved in *Thomson v HM Advocate* as a sound practice. As for counsel's point that it was inevitable that, if Cooper was recalled, he would have to be cross examined as to what had led to the change in his evidence, this was not a good reason for refusing the motion for his recall. If it were, this would mean that a witness who has been detained for prevarication could never be recalled to allow him to purge his contempt, since any attempt to do this would always be open to cross examination of this kind. Counsel's particular objection seemed to be related to the fact that Cooper had been charged with perjury, but we do not agree that it would have been obvious to the trial judge that he had no alternative but to reveal this fact in his cross examination of the witness.

The trial judge then had to decide, having listened to the whole of Cooper's evidence, what directions he should give to the jury about this in his charge. He tells us in his report that it did not occur to him that, in the circumstances, any special direction should be given in relation to Cooper's evidence. There were arguments addressed to the jury on both sides about Cooper's credibility, and he referred to these in the course of his charge when dealing with the evidence. He also gave the general directions about witnesses who were unwilling to give evidence to which we have referred earlier in this opinion. But, said counsel, that did not meet the circumstances of this case because once the jury were made aware of the fact that Cooper had been charged with perjury, this made it impossible for them to make an impartial assessment of his credibility. It made no difference, he said, that the questions which revealed this fact to the jury came from the defence and not from the Crown. It was the Crown who had placed him in the position of having to ask these questions by insisting on the recall of the witness, and it would be a sham to disregard the fact that the Crown was ultimately responsible for what had occurred.

This argument was put very forcibly, but we con-

sider it to be unsound. A trial judge will only be justi-
A fied in directing a jury to disregard the whole of a witness's evidence in such circumstances if he is satisfied
that no reasonable jury, properly directed, could assess
that evidence impartially in fairness to the accused. It
is hard to conceive of circumstances where questions
put by the defence could ever lead to that result. This
is because questions put by the defence must be
assumed to have been put in the interests of the
accused. An attack on the credibility of a Crown
witness may include the putting of questions which, in
B fairness, could not properly be put to him by the
Crown. But if the defence choose to put questions of
that kind, it must be assumed that this is because they
wish them to be answered and accordingly that the
evidence is evidence which they wish the jury to hear.
The situation in this case is entirely different from
that which occurs where either the trial judge or the
prosecutor says or does something in the presence of
the jury which is likely to cause prejudice to a fair
trial. That is what happened in *Hutchison v HM*
C *Advocate*, where the course of action followed by the
trial judge at the invitation of the advocate depute was
said to have been likely to convey to the jury that the
judge had formed an adverse opinion of the credibility
or reliability of the witness. Nothing like that happened in this case. The position in which the trial
judge found himself was no different in principle from
that discussed in *Williamson v HM Advocate*, to which
counsel referred, where a witness had been
approached by a police officer during the overnight
D adjournment of a trial at which he was giving evidence. The submission in that case was that the sheriff
should have directed the jury that the evidence given
by the witness after his meetings with the police
officer should not be taken into their consideration.
Lord Justice General Emslie said of this argument at
1978 SLT (Notes), pp 59-60: "Only in an exceptional
case will it be possible for a judge to say upon the evidence to which he has listened that an approach was so
improper as to require him to exclude from a jury's
E consideration the subsequent evidence given by the
witness approached. The problem for the judge is not
very different from that which a judge faces regularly
when objection is taken to the admissibility of statements alleged to have been made by an accused person
and guidance to judges on that problem is of considerable assistance in resolving the slightly different
problem which this case has focused. . . . [W]hen
objection is made to the admissibility of the evidence
of a witness on the ground that he has been
F approached by a police officer or anyone else before
his evidence has been concluded, the judge will only
be justified in excluding the subsequent evidence
given by that witness from consideration by a jury if
he is able to say, having heard the evidence of the surrounding circumstances, that no reasonable jury,
properly directed, could possibly regard the evidence
given by the witness after the intervention as sufficiently reliable to accept."

In this case nothing that was said or done in the
course of Cooper's evidence would have justified the

trial judge in taking the extreme step contended for by
counsel, and we reject this criticism of the directions G
in the charge as misconceived. We shall accordingly
refuse Gall's appeal against his conviction.

[His Lordship then dealt with and refused the
appeals against sentence, with which this report is not
concerned.]

Counsel for Appellant, Murray; Solicitors, More & Co
— Counsel for Respondent, Solicitor General (Rodger,
QC); Solicitor, J D Lowe, Crown Agent. H

P W F

[The witness Cooper, at the conclusion of the trial, was
found to be in contempt of court and sentenced to a period
of detention.]

I

Kennedy v R's Curator ad Litem

FIRST DIVISION
THE LORD PRESIDENT (HOPE),
LORDS COWIE AND CULLEN
6 MARCH 1992

Children and young persons — Children's hearing — J
Application to sheriff for findings whether or not grounds
of referral established — Grounds admitted at outset of
children's hearing by mother of child — Whether com-
petent for admission to be withdrawn at hearing before
sheriff — Social Work (Scotland) Act 1968 (c 49), s 42
(1) and (4).

Children and young persons — Children's hearing —
Application to sheriff for findings whether or not grounds
of referral established — Child living with mother at K
separate address from father but with access allowed by
mother twice per week — Whether child living in same
household as father — Whether sheriff entitled to dis-
charge referral without hearing mother's evidence —
Social Work (Scotland) Act 1968 (c 49), s 32 (2) (d).

Process — Appeal — Stated case — Form of — Proper
form of findings — Whether sheriff entitled to make
findings where no prima facie case held to be made out —
Rules of Court 1965, rules 277-280.

At a children's hearing in August 1990 it was estab- L
lished that a 13 year old child had been subjected to
lewd and indecent practices by her father. In January
1991 the child's half sister was also referred to a
children's hearing. The grounds of referral were that
in terms of s 32 (2) (d) of the Social Work (Scotland)
Act 1968, the child was a member of the same household as a person who had committed an offence
mentioned in Sched 1 (e) to the Criminal Procedure
(Scotland) Act 1975. Her mother and father accepted
the grounds, but the children's hearing were satisfied

that the child was too young to understand the
A explanation of these grounds given by the chairman at
the commencement of the hearing and made a direction under s 42 (7) by which the reporter had to apply
to the sheriff for a finding as to whether the grounds
had been established. Shortly thereafter the child's
mother removed herself and the child from the family
home to her mother's house. She was still there when
the case called before the sheriff in February 1991. In
view of this change of circumstances she moved the
sheriff for leave to withdraw her acceptance of the
B grounds of referral. The sheriff refused this request as
incompetent, adjourned the case and ordered that a
curator ad litem be appointed to the child. At the
adjourned diet the case called before a different sheriff
who allowed the mother to contest the referral. After
hearing evidence from the reporter the sheriff
accepted submissions on behalf of the mother that no
prima facie case had been made out that the child was
a member of the same household as her father and discharged the referral. He found that the mother
retained affection for the father and allowed him to see
C the child, but had no intention of resuming cohabitation in case she lost custody of the child. The reporter
appealed arguing, first, that there was no statutory
scheme which enabled a party who had accepted the
grounds of referral to withdraw that acceptance, and
secondly, that in the circumstances the child was still
a member of the same household as the father.

Held, (1) that where application to the sheriff was
necessary the fact that a party had accepted the
grounds of referral before the children's hearing did
D not restrict in any way the right of that party to dispute the grounds before the sheriff at the hearing of
the application, and the acceptance required to be
restated in the course of the proceedings before the
sheriff if it was to be taken as establishing the ground
of referral (p 298E and H); (2) that the important question in deciding whether a person was a member of a
household was whether the ties of affection and
regular contact which held the parties together as a
group still continued, and the fact that persons were
E separated temporarily or only due to the intervention
of the authorities would not generally mean that they
were not members of the same household (pp 299L-
300B); (3) that in the circumstances the sheriff could
not properly decide whether there was a prima facie
case without hearing the mother's evidence (p 300F);
and appeal *allowed* and case *remitted* to the sheriff for
the hearing of further evidence.

McGregor v H, 1983 SLT 626, and *R v Birmingham
Juvenile Court, ex p S (a Minor)* [1984] Fam 93,
F *followed.*

Observed, (1) that the procedure in an appeal by
way of stated case against the decision of a court was
regulated by Rules of Court 277 to 280 and required
that the stated case should state in articulate numbered
paragraphs the facts and circumstances out of which
the case arose (pp 298L-299A); and (2) that the sheriff
could not properly decide what facts were established
until he had heard all the evidence and was in a
position to decide what evidence he should believe
(p 300D-E).

Kennedy v A, 1986 SLT 358, and *Sloan v B*, 1991
SLT 530, *applied.*
G

Appeal from the sheriff court
Frederick J Kennedy, reporter for Strathclyde
Region, referred a child ER to a children's hearing on
the following grounds:

"(A) That she is, or is likely to become, a member
of the same household as a person who has committed
an offence mentioned in Sched 1 (e) to the Criminal
Procedure (Scotland) Act 1975, namely an offence H
involving the use of lewd, indecent or libidinous
practice or behaviour towards a child under the age of
17 years, this being grounds for referral in terms of
s 32 (2) (dd) of the Social Work (Scotland) Act 1968.

"(B) That any of the offences mentioned in Sched 1
(e) to the Criminal Procedure (Scotland) Act 1975 has
been committed in respect of a child who is a member
of the same household, this being grounds for referral
in terms of s 32 (2) (d) of the Social Work (Scotland)
Act 1968."
I

On 22 January 1991 the case came before a children's hearing when the child's mother and father
both accepted the grounds of referral but the children's hearing, being satisfied that the child was too
young to understand the grounds of referral, made an
application to the sheriff in terms of s 42 (7) of the
1968 Act. Before the sheriff the child's mother sought
to withdraw her acceptance of the grounds of referral
given to the children's hearing.

Statutory provisions
J
The Social Work (Scotland) Act 1968 provides:

"32.—(1) A child may be in need of compulsory
measures of care within the meaning of this Part of
this Act if any of the conditions mentioned in the next
following subsection is satisfied with respect to him.

"(2) The conditions referred to in subsection (1) of
this section are that — . . . (d) any of the offences mentioned in Schedule 1 to the Criminal Procedure (Scotland) Act 1975 has been committed in respect of him K
or in respect of a child who is a member of the same
household; (dd) the child is, or is likely to become, a
member of the same household as a person who has
committed any of the offences mentioned in Schedule
1 to the Criminal Procedure (Scotland) Act 1975. . . .

"42.—(1) Subject to the provisions of subsections (7)
and (8) of this section, at the commencement of a
children's hearing and before proceeding to the consideration of the case, it shall be the duty of the chairman to explain to the child and his parent the grounds L
stated by the reporter for the referral of the case for the
purpose of ascertaining whether these grounds are
accepted in whole or in part by the child and his
parent. . . .

"(6A) . . . where, in the course of the proceedings
before the sheriff, the child and his parent accept any
of the grounds in respect of which the application has
been made, the sheriff may dispense with the hearing
of evidence relating to that ground unless he is satisfied that in all the circumstances such evidence should

be heard, and deem that ground to have been established for the purposes of this section.

"(7) Where a children's hearing are satisfied that the child for any reason is not capable of understanding the explanation of the grounds of referral required by subsection (1) of this section, or in the course of, or at the conclusion of that explanation, it appears not to be understood by the child, the hearing shall, unless they decide to discharge the referral, direct the reporter to make application to the sheriff for a finding as to whether any of the grounds for the referral have been established, and the provisions of this section relating to an application to the sheriff under subsection (2) (c) thereof shall apply as they apply to an application under that subsection except that where any of the grounds for the referral are accepted by the child's parent, whether or not accepted by the child, then, notwithstanding subsection (6A) of this section, the sheriff may dispense with the hearing of evidence relating to that ground if he is satisfied that in all the circumstances it would be reasonable to do so."

Cases referred to
Kennedy v A, 1986 SLT 358.
Kennedy v B, 1973 SLT 38.
McGregor v H, 1983 SLT 626.
R v Birmingham Juvenile Court, ex p S (A Minor) [1984] Fam 93; [1984] 3 WLR 387; [1984] 2 All ER 688.
Sloan v B, 1991 SLT 530.

On 20 February 1991 the sheriff *refused* the mother's motion, *adjourned* the case and *ordered* that a curator ad litem be appointed to the child.

On 13 March 1991 the case called before another sheriff who *allowed* the mother to be represented and, after hearing the evidence for the reporter, *upheld* a submission for the mother that no prima facie case had been made out, *dismissed* the application and *discharged* the referral.

The reporter appealed.

Appeal
The appeal was heard before the First Division on 21 February 1992.

On 6 March 1992 the court *recalled* the sheriff's interlocutor and *remitted* the case to him to hear further evidence.

The following opinion of the court was delivered by the Lord President (Hope):

OPINION OF THE COURT.—This is an appeal by way of stated case under s 50 of the Social Work (Scotland) Act 1968. It has been brought against the decision of the sheriff under s 42 (5) of the Act to discharge the referral of the case of ER to a children's hearing on the following grounds: [his Lordship quoted the grounds of referral and continued:]

In his statement of the grounds for the referral the appellant provided a brief narrative of the circum-stances of the case. It appears from this narrative that ER was born on 30 June 1989 and is half sister to RR who was born on 11 August 1977. She normally resided with her father and mother at an address in Glasgow which was described as the family home. On 20 August 1990 at Glasgow sheriff court grounds for the referral of the case of RR to a children's hearing under s 32 (2) (d) were established. These were that on various occasions in 1988, the exact dates unknown, within the family home her father had forced the child to have oral sex with him and to masturbate him. The case of ER came before a children's hearing on 22 January 1991. Her mother and father accepted the grounds for referral, but the children's hearing were satisfied that ER was too young to understand the explanation of these grounds which the chairman had given at the commencement of the hearing under s 42 (1). Accordingly they made a direction under s 42 (7) by which the reporter was required to make application to the sheriff for a finding as to whether the grounds for the referral had been established.

Shortly thereafter, on 6 February 1991, the child's mother removed herself from the family home. She took ER with her and went to stay with her mother at a different address in Glasgow. She was still there when the case came before the sheriff on 20 February 1991. In the light of this change in the circumstances she moved the sheriff for leave to withdraw her acceptance of the grounds for the referral. This request was refused by the sheriff as incompetent, and he adjourned the case to a later date and ordered that a curator ad litem be appointed to the child ER. On 25 February 1991 Miss C Kelly, solicitor, Drumchapel, was appointed to be curator ad litem. When the case came before a different sheriff on 13 March 1991 the appellant, ER's mother and the curator ad litem were all present and evidence was led. The appellant submitted at the outset that ER's mother had no right to be heard because she had accepted the grounds for the referral and because the sheriff on 20 February 1991 had refused her motion to be allowed to withdraw her acceptance. But the sheriff was of the opinion that he had to hear the evidence as at the date when the case came before him and accordingly that he had no alternative but to allow the mother to be heard.

It is convenient to deal at this stage with the first question in this stated case which relates to this point of procedure. The question is whether ER's mother, having accepted the grounds of referral at the commencement of the children's hearing and having been refused permission by the sheriff to withdraw her acceptance of them, was nevertheless entitled to be represented at the proof on 13 March 1991 and to contest the grounds for the referral at that stage. Counsel for the appellant invited us to answer this question in the negative. He did so on the ground that there was no provision in the statutory scheme which enabled a party who had accepted the grounds for the referral under s 42 (2) to withdraw that acceptance. He submitted that ER's mother was thus disabled from taking any active role in the proceedings before the sheriff, and that she ought not to have been allowed to take advantage of the fact that the case had been remitted to the sheriff under s 42 (7) to change her mind as to her acceptance of the grounds. In our opinion, however, the sheriff's decision on this matter was correct and he was right to allow ER's mother to be heard. We consider that the submissions to the contrary were based on a misconception of the effect of the statutory scheme.

It is clear that the acceptance by the child and his parent of the grounds for the referral is an important step in the procedure at the commencement of a children's hearing. The reasons for this were discussed in *Sloan v B* at p 548A-F, where it was explained that the right of the child and the parent to dispute the grounds provides the context for s 42 (1), which sets out the duty of the claimant to explain to the child and his parent the grounds stated by the reporter for the referral of the case. This is an essential part of the system which the Act has laid down, since it gives the protection which is needed to ensure that a children's hearing do not proceed to a consideration of the case with a view to the compulsory measures of care which may be required until any dispute about the facts has been resolved. If, following the chairman's explanation, the grounds for the referral are accepted, that is an end of the matter, and the children's hearing are then free to proceed to the disposal of the case. There is no provision in the Act for an acceptance of the grounds for the referral to be withdrawn. But what if one of these parties does not accept the grounds, or the child is not capable of understanding the explanation required by s 42 (1), or it appears not to have understood it? In this situation the children's hearing must direct the reporter to make application to the sheriff for a finding as to whether the grounds for the referral are established. The acceptance of the grounds by one of the parties at the commencement of the children's hearing then ceases to be of significance. The hearing is unable in these circumstances to act on that acceptance, since the whole matter as to whether the grounds for the referral are established must be referred to the sheriff for a decision.

When the matter comes before the sheriff therefore the fact that at the commencement of the children's hearing a party accepted the grounds for the referral in whole or in part does not restrict in any way the right of that party to dispute the grounds before the sheriff at the hearing of the application. The various statutory rules are without qualification as to the rights which he has at that stage. He has a right to attend the hearing of the application and to be represented at any diet thereof in terms of s 42 (4). Rule 6 of the Social Work (Sheriff Court Procedure) Rules 1971 provides for the citation of the child and for intimation of the hearing to be made to any parent whose whereabouts are known to the reporter. Rule 8 (2) provides that at the close of the case for the reporter the sheriff shall, unless he considers that a prima facie case has not been made out, tell the child and his parent or representative and any safeguarder appointed that they may give evidence or make a statement and call witnesses.

It is, of course, open to a party to state in the course of the proceedings before the sheriff that he accepts any of the grounds in respect of which the application has been made by the reporter. Section 42 (6A) provides that where the child and his parent accept the grounds in the course of the proceedings before him the sheriff may dispense with the hearing of evidence relating to that ground and deem it to be established. But the acceptance of the grounds in the course of the proceedings before the sheriff in terms of s 42 (6A) is an entirely separate matter from the acceptance of the grounds at the commencement of the children's hearing in terms of s 42 (2). A party is not to be taken to have accepted the grounds in the course of the proceedings before the sheriff simply because he accepted them at the commencement of the children's hearing. His acceptance of the grounds at that stage has been superseded by the application to the sheriff, and it must be restated in the course of the proceedings before the sheriff if it is to have any effect at that stage for the purposes of s 42 (6A).

For these reasons ER's mother was entitled to appear and be represented at the hearing of the application before the sheriff on 11 March 1991 and to give such evidence and make such submissions to the sheriff as she saw fit, even if these contradicted her earlier acceptance of the grounds for the referral at the commencement of the children's hearing.

In the event there was no dispute that, if the facts had been the same as those which had been accepted by the parties before the children's hearing on 22 January 1991, the grounds for the referral would have been established. It was clear that on these facts ER was residing in the same house as both her stepsister and her father who had committed an offence against her stepsister of the kind mentioned in Sched 1 (e) to the Criminal Procedure (Scotland) Act 1975. The issue which the sheriff had to decide was whether the change of circumstances which occurred when ER and her mother went to live elsewhere made all the difference because the child could no longer be regarded as being, or as likely to become, a member of the same household. At the conclusion of the evidence led by the appellant the mother's solicitor submitted in terms of rule 8 (2) of the 1971 Rules that a prima facie case had not been made out, having regard to the change of circumstances which had occurred. The sheriff upheld this submission, and accordingly no further evidence was led and the sheriff dismissed the application and discharged the referral.

The principal question to be decided in this appeal, therefore, is whether the sheriff was entitled to hold that a prima facie case had not been made out by the appellant's evidence. Unfortunately, the stated case which the sheriff has prepared on this matter leaves a great deal to be desired. This may be due in part to the form of the questions, as to which we shall have something to say later in this opinion. But the fact is that the sheriff has made no attempt to state a case in the statutory form. As was pointed out in *Kennedy v A* at p 361A, this being an appeal by way of stated case against the decision of a court, the procedure to be

followed is regulated by Rules of Court 277 to 280: see
A also *Sloan v B* at p 544J-K. Rule 279 (a) requires that
the case shall state in articulate numbered paragraphs
the facts and circumstances out of which the case
arises. The sheriff has completely ignored this requirement. He has provided us with a narrative of the background to the case and of the procedure, together with
some reasons for the decision which he took. But he
has failed to address himself to the essential task of
setting out in articulate numbered paragraphs the
evidence relied upon in support of the grounds for the
B referral which in his opinion was insufficient to make
out a prima facie case.

Counsel for the appellant accepted that he was
unable in the circumstances to advance any argument
with regard to the second ground for the referral,
which is that under s 32 (2) (d). This is because the
sheriff has omitted to say in the stated case what happened to RR when ER and her mother left the family
home and went to live elsewhere. He has failed to tell
us what evidence was led about her circumstances by
C the appellant. In this situation we cannot begin to
address the question whether there was a prima facie
case that at the date of the hearing before the sheriff
ER was still a member of the same household as her
stepsister. In this situation counsel was content not to
make any submissions in regard to this ground of
referral. He directed his argument to the second
ground of referral under reference to s 32 (2) (dd). He
submitted that sufficient facts and circumstances were
disclosed by the stated case to show that the sheriff
D was not entitled to hold that ER was not a member of
the same household as her father. His contention was
that the only conclusion which was open to the sheriff
on these facts was that ER remained a member of the
same household as her father despite the fact that her
mother had taken her to live elsewhere, and that he
ought not to have discharged the referral. Counsel for
the respondent invited us to hold that the effect of
this move was to demonstrate an intention on the
mother's part to remain in separate homes indefinitely
E and that the family unit had broken down. She submitted that this was sufficient to deprive the appellant
of a prima facie case, and that the sheriff was entitled
to discharge the referral without hearing any further
evidence.

The facts on which counsel for the appellant relied
are to be found in the following observations by the
sheriff in the stated case: "I was satisfied that all the
relevant statements of facts accepted by the parties
F before the children's hearing upon 22 January 1991
were established at that date . . . I was further satisfied
that despite the fact that the mother still had affection
for the father and still allowed the father to visit the
said child at least twice a week at her mother's house
in her or her mother's presence, nevertheless she had
no intention of resuming cohabitation with the said
father in case she thereby lost custody of the said
child."

Now there is no doubt that the sheriff required to
take account of the change of circumstances which had

occurred. In *Kennedy v B* it was held that the sheriff,
in deciding whether or not the ground for referral was G
established, had to take into account the change of circumstances which had occurred since the appearance
before the children's hearing. As Lord Justice Clerk
Grant pointed out at p 40, it would be an unfortunate
situation if the sheriff had to hold as established
grounds of referral which were based on a situation
which, at the date of the hearing, had fundamentally
altered and indeed had ceased to exist. Accordingly
everything depended in the present case on what was
to be made of the change of circumstances which had H
occurred when ER moved from the family home to
another address.

The question which the sheriff had to consider in
regard to the ground of referral under s 32 (2) (dd) was
whether there was a prima facie case that despite this
move ER was still, or was likely to become, a member
of the same household as her father, who had committed the offence. He was referred to *McGregor v H*
where the ground of referral was under s 32 (2) (d),
namely that the child, who had been taken into com- I
pulsory care, was nevertheless still a member of the
same household as the victim of the relevant offence.
The sheriff discharged the referral on the ground that
the child was no longer living in the same house as the
victim. But it was pointed out that this was a misdirection, because all that was required by s 32 (2) (d) was
that the child shall be "a member of the same household" as the victim. Lord President Emslie explained
the expression in these words (at p 628): "The word
'household' in s 32 is plainly intended to connote a J
family unit or something akin to a family unit — a
group of persons, held together by a particular kind of
tie who normally live together, even if individual
members of the group may be temporarily separated
from it."

Similar dicta are to be found in *R v Birmingham
Juvenile Court, ex p S (a Minor)*. In that case it was
held that the question whether people were members
of the same household was a question of fact and K
degree and that the concept of household was of a
group of persons and not the location in which those
persons lived. Sir John Arnold P said at p 91 that the
context of the care and welfare of the child was relevant to the question of what is a household to which
one child and the other must belong. He went on to
say this: "It is of course quite true that, if there is a
complete severance of locality between the household
one has to consider at one stage and that which has to
be considered at a later stage, it is more obvious L
perhaps, in a case in which there has been a real
change of household, that that is the fact if the house-
holds are differently located. But at the heart of the
concept it is the persons who comprise the household
which have to be considered I think and not the place
where the household is located as a matter of
residence."

In our opinion the same approach is appropriate
where the question arises under reference to s 32 (2)
(dd). Accordingly the fact that persons are living for

the time being in separate houses is not decisive of the question whether they are members of the same household. The important question, since the issue is whether the child is in need of compulsory measures of care in terms of s 32 of the Act, is whether the ties of affection and regular contact which hold the parties together as a group of persons still continue. Since the criterion is that of relationship rather than locality, it is necessary to examine closely the reasons given for the suggestion that the relationship has broken down. A temporary separation will not do, especially as s 32 (2) (dd) looks to the future as well as the present state of affairs. Nor will a separation which is due only to the intervention of the authorities or to a fear that steps may be taken by them which may result in compulsory measures of care. To accept that the parties were no longer members of the same household in these circumstances would be likely to defeat the object of the provision, which is to protect the child against the risk of abuse or corruption due to the informality and frequency of contact which occurs within that relationship.

The sheriff said that he was satisfied that ER's mother had no intention of resuming cohabitation with the father in case she thereby lost custody of the child. But it is far from clear how he could have been satisfied that this was her intention, since the only evidence which he heard was the evidence led by the appellant and the mother did not give evidence. Indeed there appears to have been a confusion in the sheriff's mind as to the point which he had to examine in order to decide, for the purposes of rule 8 (2), whether or not a prima facie case had been made out. The only question which he had to examine at that stage was whether the evidence relied on by the appellant was sufficient, if accepted, to make out such a case. It was both unnecessary and inappropriate for him to decide what facts were established by that evidence. He could not properly do this until he had heard all the evidence and was in a position to decide what evidence he should believe. Moreover the reason which was given as to why the mother had no intention of resuming cohabitation with the father raises a question as to whether her separation from him was merely temporary and due only to the risk which she perceived that she might otherwise lose the child's custody. It is not at all clear what her attitude would have been if the referral were to be discharged and she were to be left with the impression that the risk of compulsory measures of care being taken against the child had been removed. The sheriff states that he was satisfied that the mother still had affection for the father and that she still allowed him to visit the child at least twice a week at her mother's house in her or her mother's presence. There is here a sufficient indication of a continuing relationship which makes it very difficult to accept that there was no prima facie case that the child was or was likely to become a member of the same household as her father.

In our opinion the sheriff could not in these circumstances properly decide this issue without hearing the mother's evidence. It was necessary to hear her own explanation of the decision which she had taken for her removal of the child to another address, and to examine precisely the reasons why she appeared to have no intention of returning to live with the father. He ought not to have sustained the submission that there was no prima facie case, and accordingly he was in error in dismissing the application and discharging the referral.

For these reasons we are unable to provide satisfactory answers to the questions which are before us in this stated case except for question 1 which deals with the procedural issue and which we shall answer in the affirmative. None of the remaining questions is directed to the issue whether the sheriff was entitled to discharge the referral on the ground that a prima facie case had not been made out. Had there been a question in these terms we would have answered it in the negative. As it is, the remaining questions all seem to assume, incorrectly, that the evidence which was before the sheriff was complete and that he was in a position to decide what facts had been proved. In these circumstances the only course which we can properly take in this confused and unsatisfactory situation is to decline to answer the remaining questions. What we shall do is recall the sheriff's interlocutor by which he dismissed the application and discharged the referral. We shall direct him to fix a further diet in this case at which the parent and the curator ad litem may give evidence or make a statement and call witnesses all in terms of rule 8 (2) of the 1971 Rules. It will then be for the sheriff to decide in the light of all the evidence what facts have been proved and whether on the facts proved or admitted the child ER is or is likely to become a member of the same household as her father or a member of the same household as her stepsister, all as more fully specified in the grounds of referral. If the parties are content with his decision on these points there need be no further reference of the case to this court. But any appeal against his decision will require to be the subject of a fresh stated case, and we trust that in that event the requirements of rule 279 (a) as to the form of the stated case will be observed by setting out in appropriately numbered paragraphs a full and accurate statement of all the facts established by the evidence.

Counsel for Appellant, McGhie, QC; Solicitors, Biggart Baillie & Gifford, WS — Counsel for Respondent, Raeburn, QC; Solicitors, Drummond Miller, WS.

D A K L

Strathern v MacColl

A SECOND DIVISION

LORDS McCLUSKEY, MORISON AND
PROSSER

3 APRIL 1992

*Landlord and tenant — Croft — Common grazings —
Extraction of minerals by landlord — Permanent reduction in extent of grazing available for pasturage —
Crofter entitled to compensation for damage to grazing —*
B *Whether crofter's security of tenure at risk from landlord's operations — Whether interdict justified where
encroachment by landlord not such as to determine crofting tenure — Crofters (Scotland) Act 1955 (3 & 4 Eliz
II, c 21), s 3 and Sched 2, para 10.*

*Process — Sheriff court — Competency — Application
for interdict of landlord's actings on croft land —
Whether action should have been raised in Land Court —
Crofters (Scotland) Act 1961 (9 & 10 Eliz II, c 58), s 4.*

C   Section 3 of the Crofters (Scotland) Act 1955 provides that a crofter shall not be subject to be removed
from the croft of which he is tenant except in consequence of the breach of one or more of the conditions
set out in the Second Schedule to the Act, other than
the condition as to payment of rent. Paragraph 3 of the
Second Schedule provides that the crofter shall cultivate his croft and para 10 provides that the crofter
shall permit the landlord to exercise the right of taking
minerals, subject to payment by the landlord of such
D compensation as the Land Court may find reasonable
in respect of any damage occasioned thereby. Section
12 of the Act provides for the resumption of the croft
by the landlord in circumstances where there is a
reasonable purpose to do so which is related to the
good of the croft, the estate or the public interest,
subject to the Land Court's authorisation. Section 4 of
the Crofters (Scotland) Act 1961 provides that the
Land Court shall have power to determine any question of fact or law arising under the Act of 1955.

E   A crofting tenant owned shares in common grazings
extending to about 24 acres. His landlords extracted
sand and gravel from the common grazings resulting
in a diminution of the area available for grazing. The
Land Court awarded compensation to the crofters for
the loss of five acres caused by the landlords' operations. The landlords proposed to continue to extract
minerals. The crofting tenant raised an action in the
sheriff court seeking to interdict the landlords from
F extending the area of extraction in such a way as
materially and permanently to reduce the extent of
grazing available for pasturage. The landlords
accepted that such a reduction would necessarily
result from his operations. Following a proof, the
sheriff granted interdict against the landlords. The
landlords appealed to the Court of Session. They
argued that there was no evidence that the statutory
relationship between the crofting tenant and themselves would effectively be ended by any additional
operations. The crofting tenant contended that any
substantial interference with his activities would con-

stitute a legal wrong as the stage had now been reached
when any further extraction of the subsoil would con- G
stitute such interference. The landlords further submitted that the appropriate and competent forum for
the crofter's application was the Land Court.

Held, (1) that the contractual relationship between
a crofting tenant and his landlord could not effectively
be terminated by the exercise of rights whose exercise
was expressed as a condition of the contract between
them: if the purported exercise of any of the rights
mentioned in para 10 rendered a croft incapable of
crofting tenure, that would be unlawful (p 303G-H); H
(2) that the right in para 10 was unlimited except to
the extent that it had to be exercised in such a way as
to allow the crofting tenure to be maintained, and,
there being no finding in fact that the additional operations proposed by the landlords would necessarily
result in the termination of the crofting tenure, the
sheriff had erred in holding that the extraction of sand
and gravel by the landlords exceeded the limit of a
landlord's right under para 10 (pp 303J and 304I-J);
(3) that accordingly the landlords would be com- I
mitting no wrong by further encroachment on the
grazings and could not be interdicted from undertaking operations involving such further encroachment (p 304J); and (4) that, while the Land Court
would have been entitled to dispose of the application,
there was no particular convenience in having it
disposed of by the Land Court rather than the sheriff
court (pp 304L-305A); and appeal *allowed* and crave of
initial writ *refused*.

Dictum of Lord Clyde in *Trs of the Tenth Duke of* J
Argyll v MacCormick, 1991 SLT 900, *not followed*.

Observed, that it was clear that the rights conferred
by para 10 (a) and (b) of the Second Schedule were not
limited to operations undertaken only for estate purposes (p 304C).

MacAskill v Basil Baird & Sons Ltd, 1987 SLT
(Land Ct) 34, *doubted*.

―――――――――   K

Appeal from the sheriff court
Michael Strathern, tenant of a croft and shareholder
in common grazings at Keil, Benderloch, Argyll,
raised an action of interdict against Hugh Solamh
James MacColl and others in the sheriff court at
Oban. The crave of the initial writ sought interdict of
the defenders and all others acting under their authority from extending the present areas of extraction of
gravel or sand in the grazings so as to reduce the present L
extent of common grazings available for pasturage.

The case came before the sheriff for proof.

Statutory provisions
The Crofters (Scotland) Act 1955 provides:

"3.— . . . (3) A crofter shall not be subject to be
removed from the croft of which he is tenant except
— (a) where one year's rent of the croft is unpaid; (b)
in consequence of the breach of one or more of the
conditions set out in the Second Schedule to this Act

(in this Act referred to as 'the statutory conditions'), other than the condition as to payment of rent; or (c) in pursuance of any enactment, including any enactment contained in this Act. . . .

"12.—(1) The Land Court may, on the application of the landlord and on being satisfied that he desires to resume the croft, or part thereof, for some reasonable purpose having relation to the good of the croft or of the estate or to the public interest, authorise the resumption thereof by the landlord upon such terms and conditions as they may think fit."

"[Sched 2] 3. The crofter shall, by himself or his family, with or without hired labour, cultivate his croft. . . .

"10. The crofter shall permit the landlord or any person authorised by the landlord in that behalf to enter upon the croft for the purpose of exercising (subject always to the payment of such compensation as in case of dispute the Land Court may find to be reasonable in respect of any damage done or occasioned thereby) any of the following rights, and shall not obstruct the landlord or any person authorised as aforesaid in the exercise of any of such rights, that is to say — (a) mining or taking minerals, or digging or searching for minerals; (b) quarrying or taking stone, marble, gravel, sand, clay, slate or other workable mineral; (c) using for any estate purpose any springs of water rising on the croft and not required for the use thereof; (d) cutting or taking timber or peats, excepting timber and other trees planted by the crofter or any of his predecessors in the tenancy, or which may be necessary for ornament or shelter, and excepting also such peats as may be required for the use of the croft; (e) opening or making roads, fences, drains and water-courses; (f) passing and re-passing to and from the shore of the sea or any loch with or without vehicles for the purpose of exercising any right of property or other right belonging to the landlord; (g) viewing or examining at reasonable times the state of the croft and all buildings or improvements thereon; (h) hunting, shooting, fishing or taking game or fish, wild birds or vermin."

The Crofters (Scotland) Act 1961 provides:

"4.—(1) Without prejudice to any jurisdiction exercisable by them under any enactment, the Land Court shall have power to determine, either on the application of any person having an interest or on a reference made to them by the Commission, any question of fact or law arising under the Act of 1955."

Cases referred to

Argyll (Trustees of the Tenth Duke of) v MacCormick, 1991 SLT 900.

MacAskill v Basil Baird & Sons Ltd, 1987 SLT (Land Ct) 34.

On 12 August 1991 the sheriff *pronounced* decree of perpetual interdict against the defenders.

The defenders appealed to the Court of Session.

Appeal

The appeal was heard before the Second Division on 10 March 1992.

On 3 April 1992 the court *allowed* the appeal, *recalled* the interlocutor of the sheriff dated 12 April 1991, and *refused* the crave of the initial writ.

The following opinion of the court was delivered by Lord Morison:

OPINION OF THE COURT.—The defenders and appellants are landlords of ground at Keil Township, Benderloch, Argyll, which comprises a number of crofts. The pursuer and respondent is the registered crofter of one of these crofts. Along with the other Keil crofters he has a share in the common grazings which occupy an area of ground between the crofts and the foreshore of Ardmucknish Bay. There are 23 shares in these grazings of which 20 have been allocated amongst the crofters. Two of these shares have been allocated to the pursuer, and these entitle him to graze two cows and followers in the grazings between May and September.

The subsoil of the common grazings consists of sand and shingle and for many years crofters and others have occasionally removed sand and gravel for their own use. In 1949 the defenders' predecessor in title was granted planning consent for the extraction of sand and gravel. Particularly since 1976, extraction by the landlords of sand and gravel from the area in accordance with this planning consent has resulted in a diminution of the area of common grazings. This has occurred as a result of soil erosion, excavation without restoration, and the presence of heaps of excavated gravel which have not been removed. In 1986 the Land Court assessed compensation due by the landlords to the crofters for the loss of five acres caused by these operations. The position at the date of the proof in these proceedings (which was closed in October 1990) was that the grassland of the grazings extended to about 24 acres, 12 of these being of poor quality. That grazing was then insufficient to support the existing souming of 20 cows with followers. The pursuer therefore has to purchase additional feed for his cows and followers.

The defenders propose to continue to undertake extraction of sand and gravel from the grazings. The rate and method of extraction would depend on market demand from time to time. The pursuer's action sought to interdict the defenders or persons acting for them from extending the area of extraction in such a way as materially and permanently to reduce the extent of grazing available for pasturage. It was not disputed that any continuation of the defenders' operations would necessarily result in such a reduction. By interlocutor dated 12 August 1991 the sheriff pronounced decree of interdict ad perpetuam in the pursuer's favour against the defenders and all others acting under their authority from extending the present areas of extraction of gravel or sand in the grazings so as to reduce the present extent of common grazings available for pasturage. The defenders have appealed against this interlocutor.

The relationship of the pursuer and defenders as crofter and landlords is primarily governed by the statutory provisions contained in the Crofters (Scotland) Act 1955. This Act makes provision for a crofter's security of tenure in s 3 (3). The subsection provides: [his Lordship quoted the terms of s 3 (3) and continued:]

It is a notable feature of the Act that subs (3) (b) constitutes the only reference to the statutory conditions set out in the Second Schedule, and that these conditions are nowhere expressly stated to be binding on the crofter except to the extent that he is subject to removal if he is in breach of one or more of them. However, parties were agreed that the statutory conditions did, at least by implication, constitute conditions which were generally binding on the crofter, and we proceed on this basis.

The statutory conditions inter alia make provision obliging the crofter to pay his rent and to cultivate his croft. Paragraph 10 thereof recognises the existence of certain rights which the landlord has in respect of the land which forms the holding. It provides that the crofter shall permit the landlord or persons authorised by him to enter on the land for the purpose of exercising these rights, and shall not obstruct him in the exercise of them. This provision is, however, expressed to be subject to payment of such compensation for damage done or occasioned in exercise of the rights as in case of dispute is found to be reasonable by the Land Court. It was by virtue of this provision that an award was made for loss of five acres of the common grazing in 1986 for the damage done or occasioned to the grazing by the defenders' operations.

The landlord's rights specified in para 10 are as follows: [his Lordship quoted the terms of para 10 (a)-(h) and continued:]

The sheriff held that "the stated intentions of the defenders grossly exceed the right to extract sand or gravel provided by (a) and (b) of paragraph 10". But the interdict which he pronounced was one which prohibited the defenders from reducing by any extent the pasturage presently available to the pursuer. That interdict accordingly must have proceeded not on a consideration of the defenders' ultimate intentions, but on the view that the stage has now been reached at which the defenders are no longer entitled, even to a slight extent, to exercise the right of quarrying in the area of common grazing. This was the position adopted by pursuer's counsel in the hearing before us, and it is reflected also by the terms in which interdict was sought.

The basis upon which this submission primarily proceeded was that the rights specified in para 10 which the landlord was entitled to exercise were not to be regarded as unqualified. The obligation imposed on the crofter to allow the exercise of these rights was, it was submitted, one which assumed the continuation of the relationship between the landlord and the crofting tenant. If the purported exercise by the landlord of one or more of these rights effectively involved the destruction of that relationship, the crofter's security

of tenure, which the Act sought to protect, would disappear. The exercise of the landlord's rights was circumscribed by the general purpose of the legislation which was to afford security to the crofter, subject to certain conditions, in maintaining occupation and cultivation of his croft.

We agree with this general view of the legislation. As a matter of general principle applicable to any contractual relationship we do not consider that the relationship between a crofting tenant and his landlord may effectively be terminated by the exercise of rights whose exercise is expressed as a condition of the contract between them. It would not make sense to construe legislation which affords security of tenure to the crofter as being subject to a condition which allows the landlord to nullify that security. If the purported exercise of any of the rights mentioned in para 10 would render the crofts or any of them incapable of crofting tenure, we would regard that exercise as illegal. This view is supported by the fact that s 12 of the 1955 Act makes provision for resumption of the croft by the landlord in circumstances where there is a reasonable purpose to do so which is related to the good of the croft, the estate or the public interest. Resumption under this section is conditional on the Land Court's authorisation. It appears to us to be clear that the legislature envisaged termination of a crofting tenure as being allowable only if the crofter might be removed by virtue of the provisions of s 3 (3) on account of failure to comply with his obligations; or by authorisation of the Land Court in pursuance of the provisions contained in s 12.

But there is no finding in the present case which remotely supports the view that the statutory relationship between the pursuer and the defenders would effectively be ended by any additional operations, however slight, undertaken by the defenders which have the effect of reducing the pasturage now available to the pursuer. The sheriff describes the grazings as an "essential" part of the pursuer's holding. But it is plain that this does not mean that if there were any further curtailment of the grazings the crofting tenure could no longer continue, because he adds that further substantial curtailment would merely involve that the holding "would likely cease to be viable". Whatever is meant by the word "viable", the finding clearly does not infer that cultivation of the pursuer's croft, which is a principal obligation imposed on the tenant in the special conditions, would become impracticable. It is on the contrary clear from the sheriff's other findings that some further reduction of the grazings would merely result in the pursuer having to purchase more feed for his cattle than he has to purchase at present, or, at most, some curtailment of his activities. The additional expense or loss involved would be expense or loss for which the defenders would be liable to compensate him. There is no finding to suggest that a further curtailment of the grazings would render the whole subjects which the pursuer now occupies incapable of crofting tenure.

However, it is not altogether clear that the sheriff decided the case upon the basis that the statutory rela-

tionship between the pursuer and the defenders would
be effectively terminated if further reduction of the
grazings occurred. Both in his note relative to
allowance of proof after debate, and in the note accompanying the interlocutor appealed against, he appears
to have attached considerable weight to observations
made by the Land Court in the case of *MacAskill v
Basil Baird & Sons Ltd*. In that case application was
made by a crofter for an order authorising her to
acquire the croft. The landlords objected on the
ground that they proposed to commence commercial
peat extraction over a large part of the croft by virtue
of the right referred to in para 10 (d). It was held that
this right did not extend to the commercial extraction
of peat but only extraction for estate use, apparently
because the wording of para 10 (d) "has its origin in
s 1 (7) of the Crofters (Scotland) Act 1886 when it
could hardly have been contemplated that large scale
commercial peat extraction would be undertaken by
landlords".

We doubt the reasoning of this decision, but it is
unnecessary for us to determine whether the case was
correctly decided, since in our view it is abundantly
clear that the rights referred to in para 10 (a) and (b)
are not limited to operations undertaken only for
estate purposes. These rights plainly envisage the
commercial extraction of minerals and of gravel and
sand. Insofar as the sheriff's decision proceeded in
reliance on the case we considered that he misdirected
himself.

The sheriff also relied on an observation of Lord
Clyde in the case of *Trs of the Tenth Duke of Argyll v
MacCormick*. That was a case in which the question
was whether a crofter's right to share in the value of
land resumed by a landlord included the mineral value
of the land resumed. In the course of his opinion (at
p 907) Lord Clyde observed that: "If the excavation
process reasonably requires the destruction of the relevant area for crofting purposes then the landlord will
require to resume all rights over that area."

Except insofar as it accords with the general view of
the legislation which we have expressed above, we do
not agree with this observation, which was plainly
obiter. In our opinion a landlord who wishes to exercise the right of excavation is entitled to do so without
resumption of the area concerned, even if that excavation involves destruction of that area to the detriment
of the crofter's holding. Paragraph 10 (b) expressly
recognises his right to do so without resumption,
subject to payment of compensation for the damage
caused. Similarly, roads may be constructed without
resumption of the land which they would occupy, by
virtue of the right recognised in para 10 (e). In our
opinion the sheriff erred in proceeding on the
authority of this dictum.

If further curtailment of the grazing does not
involve the effective termination of the pursuer's
crofting tenure, if it is not prohibited by the consideration that the operation would be commercial, and if it
is not prohibited on account of the defenders' failure
to apply for resumption, we find it difficult to understand on what other basis the sheriff may have proceeded. Counsel for the pursuer experienced similar
difficulty in formulating any legal proposition to
justify his submission that something less than the
effective determination of the crofting tenure justified
the grant of the interdict which he sought. Ultimately
he submitted that any substantial interference with the
crofter's activities would constitute a legal wrong, and
that the stage had now been reached, although it had
not been reached previously, when any further extraction of the subsoil would constitute such interference.

There would be great difficulty in determining in
any case at what stage interference with the crofter's
tenure became "substantial", if this were the test to be
applied. In the present case it is impossible to extract
from the relevant findings any consequence to the
pursuer of further curtailment of the grazings other
than the need to purchase more feed for his cattle, or
some undefined curtailment of his activities, for
which, as we have observed, he would be compensated. But in our opinion such questions do not arise,
because the right expressed in para 10 (b) is clearly
unlimited except to the extent that it must be exercised in such a way as to allow the crofting tenure to
be maintained. If some other limitation on the exercise
of the right had been intended, it would have been
expressed. In our opinion the sheriff was in error in
holding that the "extraction of sand and gravel by the
defenders . . . has exceeded the limit of a landlord's
right under para 10 (a) and (b)". He was also in error
in holding that because the pursuer "was unable to
exercise fully his grazing rights" a wrong had been
committed and that the defenders should be interdicted from further encroachment.

Accordingly we consider that the defenders would
be committing no wrong by further encroachment on
the grazings, and that they cannot be interdicted from
undertaking operations involving any such further
encroachment. The question whether the defenders
would be permitted to undertake operations which
effectively involved the total abstraction of the
common grazing from the township does not arise,
since the only remedy sought by the pursuer is interdict against any reduction whatever of the existing
pasturage.

We should mention finally that on behalf of the
defenders it was submitted that the pursuer's action
should have been brought in the Land Court by virtue
of the provisions contained in s 4 (1) of the Crofters
(Scotland) Act 1961. That subsection provides inter
alia that "the Land Court shall have power to determine . . . any question of fact or law arising under the
Act of 1955". No doubt the Land Court would be
entitled by virtue of this provision to entertain the
questions of fact and law which have arisen in the
present case. But the provision is not particularly
directed to determination of an application by a crofter
for interdict on the ground that operations by a landlord would constitute unwarrantable interference with
his crofting tenure, and we see no particular convenience in the present case in having that question

determined by the Land Court rather than by the
A sheriff court. The subsection is clearly expressed in a
way in which the jurisdiction of the ordinary courts is
not excluded. In our opinion the sheriff court was an
appropriate and competent forum for the determination of the pursuer's action.

Because reduction of the existing extent of the
common grazing caused by the defenders' proposed
operations would not constitute a wrong, the
defenders cannot be interdicted from extracting
minerals, gravel or sand on the ground that such a
B reduction would occur. We therefore sustain the
appeal, recall the interlocutor of the sheriff dated 12
August 1991, repel the pursuer's first plea in law, and
refuse the crave of the initial writ.

---

*Counsel for Pursuer and Respondent, A P Campbell;
Solicitors, Russel & Aitken, WS (for Anderson, Banks
& Co, Oban) — Counsel for Defenders and Appellants,*
C *Philip, QC; Solicitors, McClure Naismith Anderson &
Gardiner.*

M C G

Carmichael, Complainer

D HIGH COURT OF JUSTICIARY

THE LORD JUSTICE GENERAL (HOPE),
LORDS ALLANBRIDGE AND COWIE

29 APRIL 1992

*Justiciary — Procedure — Warrant — Precognition on
oath — Complainer's statement to police materially
different from precognition to procurator fiscal — Crown
seeking warrant to precognosce complainer on oath —*
E *Sheriff refusing warrant as unnecessary — Whether
sheriff's refusal justified.*

A procurator fiscal presented a petition to the sheriff
for a warrant to cite the complainer in an assault case
for precognition on oath in order to investigate the
crime. The complainer had been precognosced by the
procurator fiscal but her precognition was materially
different from the terms of the statement which she
had given to the police officers on an earlier occasion.
F The sheriff refused the application as he considered it
to be unnecessary in order to investigate the crime
because the crime had already been investigated by the
police and the procurator fiscal, and the precognition
which would be obtained on oath would only be what
she had said to the police, or the procurator fiscal, or
a third version but it would not assure the prosecutor
as to what the complainer was likely to say at the trial.
The sheriff also considered that the complainer was
not a reluctant witness but only an inconsistent
witness. The procurator fiscal sought advocation of
the sheriff's decision.

Held, (1) that the sheriff was wrong to think that a
precognition of the complainer on oath would not give G
some assurance to the prosecutor as to what she was
likely to say when she gave evidence at the trial
(p 307H); (2) that the difference between a reluctant
and an inconsistent witness was a distinction without
a difference since witnesses commonly gave inconsistent statements when they were reluctant to tell the
truth (p 307H-I); (3) that the prosecutor had good
reasons for wishing to precognosce the complainer on
oath and his explanation ought to have been accepted
by the sheriff (p 307I); and bill *passed* and cause H
remitted to the sheriff to proceed as accords.

Bill of advocation

William G Carmichael, procurator fiscal, Hamilton,
presented a bill of advocation to the High Court of
Justiciary praying the court to recall the decision of
Sheriff W E Gibson dated 18 February 1992 whereby
he refused to grant the procurator fiscal's petition for I
warrant to cite Tracy Hamill, the complainer in an
assault charge, for precognition on oath. The factors
giving rise to the bill appear from the sheriff's report.

Case referred to

Coll, Petitioner, 1977 SLT 58; 1977 JC 29.

Textbooks referred to

Alison, *Criminal Law*, ii, pp 137-139.
Hume, *Crimes* (3rd ed), ii, 82.   J

The sheriff submitted the following report to the
High Court:

THE SHERIFF (W E GIBSON).—On 18
February 1992 the complainer presented to me a petition in the following terms:

"(1) That on 17 June 1991, Allan James Cairns and
Gaynor Copland appeared at Hamilton sheriff court
on petition at the instance of the procurator fiscal on K
charges of assault and con Bail etc (Scotland) Act
1980, s 3 (1) (b) and were committed for further examination until liberated in due course of law.

"(2) That it is necessary for the investigation of said
crime that Tracy Hamill, 5 Spruce Avenue, Blantyre,
be precognosced on oath before the sheriff.

"(3) That the statement provided by said Tracy
Hamill at precognition was materially different to the
original statement provided to the police.   L

"The petitioner accordingly craves your Lordship
to grant warrent to cite said Tracy Hamill to attend for
precognition before your Lordship on 26 February
1992 at 10.00 am in the sheriff court, Beckford Street,
Hamilton, or to do so otherwise as to your Lordship
may seem proper."

Having considered its terms, I decided not to grant
it unless the complainer satisfied me by oral submissions that I should. I advised him of this and invited
him to address me but he declined.

In my view it was not necessary as averred in art 2
A of the petition to precognosce the witness on oath to
investigate the crime. The alleged crime had already
been investigated, first, by the police who had taken
a statement from the witness, and then, by a member
of the complainer's staff who, having interviewed the
witness, had prepared a precognition.

As the terms of the statement and of the precognition were materially different it followed that the
terms of at least one, if not both, of them were inaccurate. A precognition on oath, at best, could do no
B more than reiterate the terms of either one or the other
and might provide yet another statement. It would
neither establish which, if either, was true nor assure
the complainer what would be the evidence of the
witness in the course of the ensuing trial.

Certainly, if I had granted the warrant and the evidence of the witness at the ensuing trial were materially
different from the terms of the precognition on oath,
the precognition would be available as evidence if the
complainer were to prosecute the witness for perjury.
C But that, as I understand it, is not the purpose of
citing a witness for precognition on oath. The purpose
is to elicit information from a reluctant witness who
may be apprehended and brought before the sheriff
and thereafter, if he refuses to take the oath or
obstinately refuses to answer the questions put to him,
may "be coerced with imprisonment" until he complies (Hume, ii, 82). The witness whom the complainer
craved warrant to cite for precognition on oath was not,
so far as the petition disclosed, a reluctant witness,
D only an inconsistent one.

In any event, were the evidence of the witness
during the trial to be materially different from the
statement to the police, that statement would be evidence to allow the complainer to charge the witness
with perjury, regardless of whether her evidence were
consistent with either the terms of the precognition on
oath or the terms of the earlier precognition.

E **Bill**
The plea in law in the bill was as follows:

The decision of the sheriff in refusing to grant the
said warrant being unjust, erroneous and contrary to
law should be recalled and he should be ordained to
grant warrant to cite the said witness for precognition
on oath on such date as may be determined.

The bill was argued before the High Court on 29
April 1992.
F
Eo die the court *passed* the bill, *advocated* the cause
and *remitted* to the sheriff to proceed as accords.

The following opinion of the court was delivered by
the Lord Justice General (Hope):

OPINION OF THE COURT.—This is a bill of
advocation by the procurator fiscal at Hamilton which
arises out of an application by him for a warrant to
precognosce a witness on oath before the sheriff. The
sheriff refused to grant the crave of the petition

because in his view it was unnecessary to do so, and
an appeal has now been taken by the prosecutor G
against that decision. The application was made
against the background of the following set of circumstances. On 17 June 1991 two persons named Allan
James Cairns and Gaynor Copland appeared at
Hamilton sheriff court on petition at the instance of
the complainer. They were charged with assault and
contraventions of the Bail etc (Scotland) Act 1980, s 3
(1) (b), and they were committed for further examination until liberated in due course of law. In the course
of investigating the assault the complainer precog- H
nosced the alleged victim who was a witness named
Tracy Hamill. The precognition which he then
obtained was materially different from the terms of the
statement which she had provided to the police
officers at an earlier date. It was because of this inconsistency between the precognition and her statement
to the police that the complainer wished to precognosce this witness on oath before the sheriff, and in
due course he presented a petition to the sheriff for a
warrant to enable this to be done. I

The sheriff decided to refuse the application for
reasons which have been explained in his report. He
tells us that in his view it was not necessary for this
witness to be precognosced on oath in order to investigate the crime. This was because the crime had
already been investigated, first by the police who had
taken a statement from the witness, and then by the
obtaining of a precognition by a member of the prosecutor's staff who had interviewed the witness. It
seemed to him that, although there was an incon- J
sistency between the two statements so far obtained, a
precognition on oath could at best do no more than
reiterate the terms of one or the other, or might indeed
provide yet a third version of the facts. Neither of
them would establish which, if either, of the previous
versions was true, nor assure the complainer what
would be the evidence of the witness in the course of
the trial. He accepted that if he were to grant the
warrant and the evidence of the witness at the trial was
to turn out to be materially different from the terms K
of the precognition on oath, that precognition would
be available as evidence if the complainer were to
prosecute the witness for perjury. But that in his view
was not the purpose of citing a witness for precognition on oath. As he saw it, the purpose was to elicit
information from a reluctant witness who may be
apprehended and brought before the sheriff and thereafter, if he refused to take the oath or absolutely
refused to answer the questions put to him, might be
coerced with imprisonment until he complied. The L
view which he took was that, since the witness in the
present case had already provided a statement and a
precognition, she could not be described as a reluctant
witness, only an inconsistent one.

In presenting his argument in support of the bill,
the learned advocate depute assured us that the
purpose of the prosecutor in seeking to precognosce
the witness was not to obtain a basis for the prosecution of this witness for perjury. His only purpose was
to investigate the crime in the public interest. It was

A in the interests of the prosecutor to explore in advance of the trial what this witness was likely to say at the trial when she was put on oath. It was necessary for him to do this in order to assess the strength of her evidence. There was therefore a perfectly reasonable ground for asking the sheriff to grant the warrant, and the sheriff was wrong in refusing to grant it.

The sheriff found support for his approach in a passage in Hume, ii, 82 where it is stated that witnesses who have refused to attend for precognition may be brought before a judge to be examined and if B they obstinately refuse to answer they may be coerced with imprisonment. In a further passage on the same page Hume states: "Nay more, though it is not the ordinary course of proceeding, yet still, in those cases, where, owing to popular favour toward the prisoner, or toward the offence, the truth cannot otherwise be obtained, it is lawful, and has often been practised, to put the witnesses on their oath; which if they refuse, they are, for this contempt also, liable to be imprisoned."

C These passages provide a convenient summary of the previous practice and of the consequences for the witness if he refused to comply. But there is no clear guidance as to the circumstances in which it was thought to be appropriate for a warrant to precognosce on oath to be granted and those in which it would not. The advocate depute referred us to Alison's *Practice* at pp 137-139 where there is a more complete discussion of the matter. Alison begins with the following proposition at p 137: "The Judge-examinator may grant D warrant for citing witnesses for their precognition, and, if necessary, put them on oath, in order to elicit the truth, provided this last is not done to the party accused, or any other intended to be brought to trial, or to any one to whose testimony there would be a legal objection."

Then at p 139 he expands upon the concluding words of the opening paragraph by saying this: "No steps of coercion, therefore, should be adopted against E witnesses in a precognition, except such persons, and in relation to such questions, as are competent to be examined or put at the trial."

The references to the inquisitorial function of the judge or magistrate are, of course, obsolete. But the practice of examining witnesses on oath where appropriate has survived, and the limits to it which Alison has described, remain relevant.

A warrant for a witness to be precognosced on oath F should not be granted unless the sheriff is satisfied that the person who is to be examined would be a competent witness at the trial. The sheriff must also be satisfied, on a consideration of the information with which he has been presented, that it is in the public interest that this measure of compulsion should be exercised. Weight will normally be given to an assurance by the prosecutor that it is necessary for the investigation of crime that the witness should be examined on oath before the sheriff. Various reasons for this may exist, and it is not unreasonable for the prosecutor to wish to test the evidence of an inconsistent

witness, or one who has a tendency to prevaricate, by this means. As Lord Justice Clerk Wheatley men- G tioned in *Coll, Petr*, 1977 SLT at p 59, the obtaining of a precognition on oath may be a valuable safeguard against the witness going back on his or her statement at the trial.

The sheriff's comment that a precognition on oath of the witness in the present case could at best do no more than reiterate the terms of one or other of her previous statements and might provide yet another was an underestimate of its importance and effect. It would not of course establish the truth, since that H matter had to be reserved until evidence was given at the trial. But the sheriff was wrong to think that a precognition of the witness on oath could not give some assurance to the prosecutor as to what she was likely to say when she gave evidence at the trial. We also disagree with the sheriff's comment that the witness was not a reluctant witness but only an inconsistent one. In our opinion that was a distinction without a difference for present purposes, since witnesses commonly gave inconsistent statements when I they are reluctant to tell the truth. It seems to us that the prosecutor has good reasons in the circumstances for wishing to precognosce this witness on oath, and that his explanation for the view which he had taken ought to have been accepted by the sheriff.

In all these circumstances we consider that there was no sound reason for the sheriff to refuse to grant the warrant which was requested by the prosecutor. We shall accordingly pass the bill, advocate the cause and remit to the sheriff to proceed as accords.   J

Counsel for Complainer, Matthews, QC, AD; Solicitor, J D Lowe, Crown Agent — No appearance for Respondent.

P W F

K

Byrne v Ross

FIRST DIVISION
THE LORD PRESIDENT (HOPE),
LORDS COWIE AND McCLUSKEY
9 JULY 1992

L

Interdict — Breach of interdict — Finding of breach of interdict in respect of an incident not averred in proceedings for breach and not intimated to Lord Advocate for his concurrence — Whether competent to find there had been a breach.

Interdict — Breach of interdict — Proof — Whether corroboration required — Civil Evidence (Scotland) Act 1988 (c 32), s 1 (1).

Interdict — Breach of interdict — Penalty — Breach of interdict preventing molestation.

In 1988 a woman obtained an interdict against a
A man interdicting him from molesting her. The woman
later brought proceedings for breach of interdict, averring that the respondent had breached the interdict in
five separate respects between July 1990 and October
1991. After hearing evidence the Lord Ordinary found
it established that the respondent had breached the
interdict in three respects, one of which related to an
incident which had not been averred as a breach. He
imposed a period of imprisonment of four months in
respect of the breaches. The respondent appealed and
B argued that with regard to the incident which had not
been averred the Lord Ordinary had erred in finding
a breach established for the following reasons: (1) the
incident had not been brought to the attention of the
Lord Advocate, not having been averred in the petition which was intimated to him for his concurrence
in the proceedings; (2) there was no corroboration of
the incident; and (3) as there were no averments
regarding the incident the Lord Ordinary had been
wrong to allow the evidence of it to be received and
C was wrong to regard it as a breach of interdict.

Held, (1) that a breach of interdict constituted a
contempt of court which might lead to punishment,
and it was necessary in the interests of fairness that the
alleged contempt should be clearly and distinctly
averred and that the proceedings for contempt should
be confined to the averments (p 310C-D); (2) that
although the Lord Ordinary was entitled to attach to
evidence of the incident, which had been led without
objection, such significance as was appropriate in
D reaching his decision as to whether the respondent had
breached the interdict in the respects averred by the
petitioner, he was not entitled to treat the incident as
amounting in itself to a breach of interdict which
should attract punishment (p 310D-E); (3) that the
Lord Ordinary was entitled to find the remaining two
breaches established (p 309F-H); and sentence of four
months' imprisonment *recalled* and three months
substituted.

E *Eutectic Welding Alloys Co v Whitting*, 1969 SLT
(Notes) 79, and *Gribben v Gribben*, 1976 SLT 266,
followed.

Opinion, (1) that although the general practice was
that it was necessary to intimate all proceedings for
breach of interdict to the Lord Advocate and to obtain
his concurrence for the institution of proceedings, it
was not necessary to intimate to him all adjustments
to the pleadings, and therefore the lack of notice to the
Lord Advocate of a particular incident said to consti-
F tute a breach did not bar a finding of breach of interdict in respect of that incident (p 310F-H); (2) that
proceedings for breach of interdict were civil proceedings to which s 1 (1) of the Civil Evidence (Scotland)
Act applied and corroboration was not necessary
(p 310I-J).

Petition for interdict

Anne Byrne petitioned for interdict against Ian
Gordon Ross from telephoning her, from molesting

her by abusing her verbally, threatening her, putting
her in a state of fear and alarm or distress or using G
violence towards her or by accosting her in public or
by calling at her house or place of work. Interim interdict was granted on 15 March 1988 and made perpetual on 3 May 1988.

The petitioner subsequently brought proceedings
averring five separate breaches of interdict.

The case came to proof before the temporary judge
(J M S Horsburgh, QC).   H

Statutory provisions

The Civil Evidence (Scotland) Act 1988 provides:

"1.—(1) In any civil proceedings the court or, as the
case may be, the jury, if satisfied that any fact has been
established by evidence in those proceedings, shall be
entitled to find that fact proved by that evidence notwithstanding that the evidence is not corroborated."

Cases referred to
Eutectic Welding Alloys Co v Whitting, 1969 SLT   I
(Notes) 79.
Gribben v Gribben, 1976 SLT 266.

On 8 May 1992 the temporary judge *found* the
respondent to have been in breach of interdict in three
separate respects and *sentenced* him to four months'
imprisonment.

The respondent reclaimed.   J

Reclaiming motion

The reclaiming motion was heard before the First
Division on 9 July 1992.

Eo die the court *recalled* the interlocutor of the
temporary judge only to the extent of substituting a
sentence of three months' imprisonment.

The following opinion of the court was delivered by
the Lord President (Hope):   K

OPINION OF THE COURT.—The respondent
seeks review in this reclaiming motion of an interlocutor in which he was found to be in breach of interdict and sentenced to four months' imprisonment.

The petitioner, at whose instance the interdict was
pronounced ad interim on 15 March 1988 and made
perpetual on 3 May 1988, had previously lived with
the respondent and shared a flat with him. Following   L
their separation in about September 1987, the respondent began telephoning her at her home and at work
and molesting her in various ways. She became distressed by his harassment of her, and sought and
obtained interdict against him from telephoning her,
from molesting her by abusing her verbally, threatening her, putting her in a state of fear and alarm or distress or using violence towards her or by accosting her
in public or by calling at her house or her place of
work within the administration offices at Waverley
Station, Edinburgh. The respondent continued never-

theless to molest her, and on 8 July 1988 he was found
to have breached the interdict and fined £100. He was
warned that any further breach of the interdict was
likely to result in his imprisonment. Further proceedings for breach were brought against him as a result
of which he was found on 3 May 1990 to have been
guilty of repeatedly and wilfully breaching the interdict. The diet was adjourned to allow him to attend for
psychiatric examination and undertake such treatment
as was thought to be appropriate. On 13 July 1990 the
proceedings were again adjourned upon the respondent's undertaking that he would attend for a further
psychiatric examination and for treatment. Despite
these attempts to deal leniently with him, the respondent continued to cause alarm and distress to the petitioner, who brought this third petition and complaint
for breach of interdict upon averments that the
respondent had repeatedly and wilfully breached the
interdict on various occasions since 13 July 1990.

When the matter came to proof before the Temporary Lord Ordinary the petition contained averments that the respondent had breached the interdict
in five separate respects between 16 July 1990 and late
October 1991. The Lord Ordinary heard evidence
from the petitioner and her witnesses, but the respondent did not give evidence. He was satisfied that it had
been proved beyond reasonable doubt that the respondent was in breach of the interdict in three respects
including two of those averred. The first was on 16
July 1990, when between 9 and 10 pm he was seen
standing in the roadway looking up at the third floor
flat where the petitioner and her flatmate were then
living. The flatmate saw him when she went to close
the curtains, whereupon he called up to her and then
moved off. He had no reason to be there as his house
was about 15 miles away, and the Lord Ordinary
found that the petitioner was greatly alarmed by the
incident. The second occasion, which was mentioned
in the averments, was in October 1990. The petitioner's flatmate observed the respondent peering
through the inner glass doors of their flat. She told the
petitioner, who did not see the respondent but was
alarmed by what she had been told. The third occasion
was in late October 1991. The respondent telephoned
the petitioner's mother's house and, when the petitioner answered the telephone, asked to speak to a
friend who was visiting her at the time. The friend had
not told the respondent that she was going to visit the
petitioner, and the fact that he was aware that she was
in the house indicated that he must have been watch-
ing it from a position nearby.

Counsel for the respondent submitted that the Lord
Ordinary was wrong to hold it established that the
respondent had acted in breach of interdict on these
three occasions. He did not challenge any of the facts
as narrated in the Lord Ordinary's opinion. His argument as regards the first and third occasions was that
the respondent's conduct was not such as to warrant
a finding that he was in breach of the interdict. But we
are not persuaded that there is any substance in the
points which he raised by way of criticism of the Lord
Ordinary's conclusions about these incidents. The

respondent's conduct on 16 July 1990 could reasonably be described as calling at the house, and the Lord
Ordinary was entitled to draw the inference that this
was a deliberate act on his part which caused alarm to
the petitioner. He was also entitled to reach the conclusion which he did about the occasion in late
October 1991. Although the respondent asked to
speak to the petitioner's friend, his act in telephoning
the house where he knew the petitioner was then
living was a deliberate act on his part to warn her that
she was being watched and that the respondent was
aware of what she was doing. We need say no more
about these incidents, because we are entirely satisfied
that the Lord Ordinary was entitled to find that the
respondent was in breach of the interdict on these two
occasions.

There remains however the second incident in
October 1990. The Lord Ordinary's conclusion about
this incident was criticised in several respects. Counsel's first point was that he was wrong to repel an
objection which was taken in the course of the evidence about this incident on the ground that it was not
averred on record. He submitted that the Lord
Ordinary was in any event wrong to take account of it
since, having not been the subject of averment, it had
not been drawn to the attention of the Lord Advocate
when his concurrence in the petition and complaint
was obtained. And he also argued that, since the only
witness who spoke to the incident was the petitioner's
friend, as the petitioner herself was not asked about it
at any stage in the course of her evidence, the friend's
evidence was not corroborated and on this further
ground the occasion ought not to have been taken into
account.

The Lord Ordinary repelled the objection based on
the absence of record on the ground that it was made
too late. It was not until after the witness had given all
the details about the incident, except the fact that it
took place in October 1990, that the objection was
taken. Counsel for the petitioner informed us that the
witness had prefaced her remarks by saying that she
had seen the respondent a few months after the first
incident in July 1990. She then embarked on a
description of the incident as narrated by the Lord
Ordinary. Now the only incidents mentioned in the
averments as having taken place after the first occasion
on 16 July 1990 consisted of the making of various
telephone calls to friends of the petitioner, to her place
of work and her mother's house. The incident which
the witness began to describe was quite unlike any of
the incidents described in the averments. It ought to
have been obvious prior to the point at which the
objection was taken that the evidence was objectionable on this ground. Had the only issue been whether
the Lord Ordinary was right to repel the objection at
that stage, we would have had little difficulty in
holding that he was entitled to do so, having regard to
the amount of evidence about the incident which had
already been given without objection.

But there is a more fundamental point which arises
from the absence of averment which the Lord

Ordinary did not take into account. The petitioner's
A complaint was that the respondent had wilfully and
repeatedly breached the interdict in the respects specified in her averments. In the prayer of her petition she
sought a finding from the court that the respondent
"by his actings and behaviour above set forth as complained of has been guilty of wilfully and repeatedly
breaching the said interdict and interdict ad interim
and of the contempt of the authority of your Lordships; and in respect thereof to inflict such punishment by way of imprisonment, fine or otherwise on
B the respondent as may be deemed by your Lordships
to be appropriate". This wording, which is in the
usual style appropriate to proceedings of this kind,
demonstrates the importance of the averments, since it
was only in the respects set forth in the averments that
the respondent was said to have breached the interdict
and that punishment was being sought for his breach.
In *Eutectic Welding Alloys Co v Whitting*, Lord Avonside said that where accusations of this nature are
made they must be demonstrated with clarity and that
he inclined to the view that the standard of proof in
C these proceedings was proof beyond reasonable doubt.
His view as to the standard of proof in proceedings for
breach of interdict was approved in *Gribben v Gribben*,
at p 269. In our opinion the same principle must be
applied to the averments in the petition and complaint. A breach of interdict constitutes a contempt of
court which may lead to punishment, and it is necessary in the interests of fairness that the alleged contempt should be clearly and distinctly averred and that
the proceedings for contempt be confined to the
D averments.

The Lord Ordinary was, of course, entitled to treat
such evidence as had been led without objection as
evidence in the case and to attach such significance to
it as was appropriate in reaching his decision as to
whether the respondent had breached the interdict in
the respects averred by the petitioner. But what he was
not entitled to do, in the absence of averment, was to
treat the incident mentioned by the witness as a
E separate and distinct incident amounting in itself to a
breach of the interdict which should attract punishment. In the circumstances of this case, since the incident which the witness described seems to have had no
bearing on any of the other incidents mentioned in the
averments, the proper course, following the objection,
was for him to disregard the incident completely. He
ought therefore to have taken account of the objection
at the stage when he came to assess the relevance and
competency of this evidence, since the incident was
not one of the breaches set forth in the averments in
F respect of which he was invited in the prayer to inflict
punishment.

The point that this incident was not drawn to the
attention of the Lord Advocate was not taken before
the Lord Ordinary. But in any event we would not
have regarded this as a sound objection independent of
that based on the lack of averment. The general rule
as approved in *Gribben v Gribben* is that all proceedings for breach of interdict must be intimated to the
Lord Advocate at the outset. His concurrence in the
proceedings is a necessary prerequisite of the pro-

cedure. But it is not, and never has been, the practice
for all adjustments or amendments to the petition to G
be intimated to the Lord Advocate once he has indicated that he does not intend to intervene. The Lord
Advocate's concurrence to these proceedings was
obtained on 16 August 1990. Several of the incidents
which were before the Lord Ordinary at the proof
were the subject of averments which were made after
that date. This was inevitable since they related to
alleged breaches all of which occurred in or about
October 1991. But they were all part of the same
course of conduct as that mentioned in the original
averments, and there was no need to refer these H
further allegations to the Lord Advocate since he had
already indicated that he did not intend to intervene.
We note also that the respondent did not ask for the
additional averments to be intimated to the Lord
Advocate, as he might have been expected to do if he
thought that he was truly being exposed to the double
jeopardy of being prosecuted for a criminal offence as
well as being punished for contempt. There is no
reason to think that his position would have been any
different if this further incident had also been the I
subject of averment.

As for the final point that the witness's evidence was
not corroborated, it is sufficient to say that there is no
longer any rule to that effect in proceedings for breach
of interdict. These are civil proceedings to which s 1
(1) of the Civil Evidence (Scotland) Act 1988 applies,
and the Lord Ordinary was entitled to find the facts
spoken to by the witness as proved by her evidence, if
he was satisfied that her evidence established these
facts. It is questionable whether he should have J
accepted the evidence of the witness that the petitioner
was alarmed by the incident when the petitioner
herself was not asked about it when she gave her evidence. But we need not examine this point any further,
since we are of the opinion that the incident ought not
to have been taken into account because it was not the
subject of averment.

The remaining question is whether the sentence of
four months' imprisonment was excessive, given that
the Lord Ordinary ought not to have taken this addi- K
tional incident into account in deciding upon the
appropriate penalty. We concur in everything that he
says in his opinion about the need for a more severe
punishment than the respondent had received previously, and counsel for the respondent did not suggest
that in all the circumstances a custodial sentence was
not justified. But in our opinion the appropriate
punishment for the two breaches which were established by the evidence, one on 16 July 1990 and the
other in late October 1991, is three months' imprison- L
ment. To that extent only we shall recall the interlocutor pronounced by the Temporary Lord Ordinary and
order that the respondent be imprisoned for a period
of three months from the date of his interlocutor.
Quoad ultra his interlocutor will be affirmed.

*Counsel for Petitioner, Dorrian; Solicitors, Robson
McLean, WS — Counsel for Respondent, Bennett; Solicitors, Allan McDougall & Co, SSC.*

D A K

McMillan v McDowall

OUTER HOUSE

TEMPORARY JUDGE T G COUTTS, QC

30 JULY 1992

Damages — Amount — Solatium, loss of earnings, necessary services rendered to injured person and expense occasioned by injury — Loss of accommodation provided with employment — Whether account to be taken of accommodation provided by parents — Cost of future care — Paraplegia in young man.

An 18 year old shepherd was rendered paraplegic in a road accident. The case came to proof almost six years after the accident. Liability was admitted subject to an agreed contribution of 20 per cent for the pursuer's own negligence. The assessment of damages was contested.

Held, (1) that solatium was properly valued at £70,000 (p 312I); (2) that his future free accommodation that he would have been entitled to in his employment was a benefit the loss of which was recoverable in damages as part of his earnings, and the gratuitous provision of accommodation by his parents fell to be disregarded under s 10 (f) of the Administration of Justice Act 1982 (*Edgar v Lord Advocate*, 1965 SLT 158, *distinguished*) (p 313D-F); (3) that the appropriate multiplier for future loss of earnings was 15 years discounted by two years for the possibility of future employment (p 313K-L); (4) that the cost of a buggy capable of use over rough ground was a necessary expenditure (p 314F-G); (5) that the pursuer required a lightweight wheelchair with a capital cost of £1,850 (p 315C-D); (6) that maintenance costs and additional clothing costs of £750 a year were appropriate with a multiplier of 18 years (p 315E-F); (7) that in assessing past services rendered by a relative, the starting point was the rate provided by outside agencies, and that the appropriate total for services to date was £9,200 (pp 315K-316A and 316F-H); (8) that future care should be calculated using an overall multiplier of 17½ years (pp 316L and 317F); (9) that the cost of provision of a specially built house should be 2 per cent per annum of the cost with a 15 year multiplier applied (p 317K-L); and (10) that an award should be made for the extra cost of holidays using a multiplier of 13 years (p 318B-C); and decree for £285,432 *pronounced*.

Action of damages

John Logan McMillan raised an action of damages against Kenneth McDowall seeking damages for injuries sustained in a car accident on 26 September 1986. The pursuer had been the passenger in and the defender the driver of the car.

The case came to proof before the temporary judge (T G Coutts, QC).

Statutory provisions

The Administration of Justice Act 1982 provides:

"10. Subject to any agreement to the contrary, in assessing the amount of damages payable to the injured person in respect of personal injuries there shall not be taken into account so as to reduce that amount — . . . (f) subject to paragraph (iv) below, any payment of a benevolent character made to the injured person or to any relative of his by any person following upon the injuries in question; but there shall be taken into account — . . . (iv) any payment of a benevolent character made to the injured person or to any relative of his by the responsible person following on the injuries in question, where such a payment is made directly and not through a trust or other fund from which the injured person or his relatives have benefited or may benefit."

Cases referred to

Donnelly v Joyce [1974] 2 QB 454; [1973] 3 WLR 514; [1973] 3 All ER 475.
Edgar v Lord Advocate, 1965 SLT 158; 1965 SC 67.
Forsyth's Curator Bonis v Govan Shipbuilders Ltd, 1989 SLT 91.
Geddes v Lothian Health Board, 1992 SLT 986.
Gordon v Wilson, 1992 SLT 849.
Liffen v Watson [1940] 1 KB 556.
McLoone v British Railways Board, 1981 SLT (Notes) 65.
O'Brien's Curator Bonis v British Steel plc, 1991 SLT 477.
Parry v Cleaver [1970] AC 1; [1969] 2 WLR 821; [1969] 1 All ER 555.
Roberts v Johnstone [1989] 1 QB 878.
Tuttle v Edinburgh University, 1984 SLT 173.
Will v Charles Will Ltd, 1980 SLT (Notes) 37.

Textbook referred to

Walker, *Damages*, pp 594, 605.

On 30 July 1992 the temporary judge *pronounced* decree in favour of the pursuer for £285,432.

T G COUTTS, QC.—The pursuer was injured in the early hours of the morning of 26 September 1986 while a passenger in a motor car being driven by the defender. They had spent an evening in a public house. At the proof liability for the accident was admitted by the defender and a contribution of 20 per cent to the cause of injury was admitted by the pursuer.

As a result of the accident the pursuer, then an 18 year old shepherd, suffered a dislocation fracture of the sixth dorsal vertebra and as a result was rendered paraplegic. He was treated at Ayr County and Philipshill hospitals, where he was regularly visited by his parents. His parents were first able to have him at home for weekends around Christmas 1986 and did so until his final release from hospital into their care in April 1987. He has remained in his parents' house since that date. That house has required to be adapted to a minor extent to help to meet his needs, but he intends to build a house for himself on a patch of ground close to his parents' house so that he can achieve a further measure of independence.

The pursuer was a remarkable young man. He obviously has had and benefited from devoted care and attention from both his parents. He was a person who was not academic in his interests or outlook on life but was a truly outdoor person. As a result of the accident, therefore, his entire chosen way of life has been destroyed and he has no other compensating mental interest. Instead of becoming depressed, self neglectful or careless he has made commendable efforts to cope with his disabilities. His attitude as expressed in evidence and to those persons who had the responsibility of his care has been one of fortitude and cheerfulness. Shortly after his return home he was provided by his father, in my view as a necessary part of his treatment, with a small all terrain vehicle, known as a "Yamaha buggy". This has enabled him to move about the farm and to provide a useful service to his father which, although not essential to his father, has plainly proved therapeutic. As a result of being able to move about he is able to take an interest in the farm stock and to inspect and report upon the condition of farm equipment such as fences. He also has some capability with his hands and has been attempting to make shepherds' crooks and do homecraft in a very modest way. He is fiercely determined to become even more independent, a feature which his mother views with some concern, and there can be no doubt from his evidence and from what he has achieved so far that he can be independent for a considerable period of time into the future, subject only to having emergency help available to him if required and also subject to his having necessary aids and equipment, about which detailed submissions were made and with which I deal later.

The pursuer is incontinent of urine and his bowel function has been seriously disrupted, although he has retained a minor degree of sensation which enables him to avoid the disability of total lack of control of bowel function. He has developed extremely strong musculature in his upper body and that enables him to move about using his arms. He can, for example, with the use of his normal NHS wheelchair manoeuvre himself into the ordinary motor car which he has, take his wheelchair into the car with him and go and visit friends. Inevitably with the passage of time that ability may become significantly lessened. His expectation of life has been only slightly affected. It may be restricted by about five years, according to his surgeon Mr Freeman. He has lost, on the balance of probabilities, any real prospect of a wife and family and he has possible problems of urinary infection and skin sores. Such however has been his attention to his own welfare that the only time he had a urinary infection was in hospital. He has never suffered from skin breakdown. He requires to perform exercises to keep tendon tone and will require to do these for the rest of his life either with or without assistance. His mother has in fact also been supplying some form of massage to the lower limbs but the medical evidence was that this was not necessary and I accept that medical evidence.

The figure which without benefit of submission or authority came to mind as appropriate for solatium in this case was £70,000. That was the figure which was suggested by counsel for the pursuer. Counsel for the defender suggested £65,000. Counsel founded upon the case of *Tuttle v Edinburgh University* which was suggested as a case highly similar to the present. There on 1 November 1983 the Lord Ordinary awarded £40,000 to a student of 21 years of age who was rendered paraplegic. There is not any material distinction other than on detail, so far as appears from the report, between that case and the present and I was informed that if the inflation factor given in Kemp and Kemp on *Quantum of Damages* was applied to Lord McDonald's award, a figure of just under £65,000 would be produced. While the assessment of solatium is not a precise science and has frequently been called a jury question, the view of Lord McDonald in a similar case must be treated with respect. It is, however, to be borne in mind in awards of the size the court requires to deal with in a case of this kind, that large round numbers tend to be used. It is unlikely, for example, that Lord McDonald would have awarded other than an apportionate round sum and that is exemplified by his later approach to special needs. I do not think that applying an inflation factor to his award thus producing a sum of less than £70,000 does justice to the pursuer and my assessment of the appropriate sum for solatium for this pursuer is £70,000. Parties were agreed that interest at the rate of 7½ per cent per annum should be given on 40 per cent of the sum for solatium, agreed at £14,857.

While there was no marked disagreement between counsel on that part of the case, there was on almost every other aspect. I was provided with two helpful documents scheduling the damages claimed by each party and their different contentions and insofar as was possible, matters had been agreed in a joint minute of some length and complexity. Parties were agreed that there was a net wage loss of £19,900 to which interest of £8,468 should be added. It was accepted by the pursuer's counsel, rightly, that a sum required to be deducted from that for the costs saved while in hospital and that sum was agreed at £1,410. Counsel for the pursuer went on to claim that there had been a loss of accommodation and other benefits. The pursuer, although he had not yet done so, would have been entitled shortly after the date of the accident to a house with his employment. The fact of such provision of accommodation was agreed by para 10 of the joint minute and the benefits which he would have received exclusive of accommodation were agreed at para 11 of the joint minute at £10 per week. Counsel for the pursuer sought £30 a week in respect of the accommodation and the £10 a week in respect of the loss of other benefits plus interest from 7 September 1987, a date agreed in the joint minute.

The pursuer's contentions were that these sums were part of the pursuer's remuneration and were simply payments in kind rather than in cash. This meant that a board and lodging element of earnings could be recovered despite free accommodation being provided subsequent to the accident. He cited the English authority of *Liffen v Watson* and *Donnelly v Joyce*. *Liffen* was cited by Professor Walker in his

work on *Damages*, pp 594, 605. I note, however, that
that work was published in 1955. Counsel for the
defender's contention was that Scots law was different
in this respect, that to date the pursuer had not
incurred any expense for replacement of those items of
benefit and as a result had not suffered any loss and
thus could not recover compensation. *Liffen* and
Donnelly were not part of Scots law and on the
authority of *Edgar v Lord Advocate*, especially per
Lord President Clyde at 1965 SLT, p 160, it could not
be said that the pursuer had lost anything. The principle in *Edgar* was reaffirmed in *Forsyth's CB v Govan
Shipbuilders Ltd*, 1989 SLT at p 95. In reply counsel
for the pursuer contended that *Edgar* was not in point,
that his claim was not that the pursuer had suffered
dislocation of benefit; and that this was not a provision
of care claim but a direct loss. There was evidence that
the pursuer had indeed paid his mother for his keep,
but even if the provision of accommodation and
keep by the pursuer's parents were a gratuitous
benefit, it would require to be disregarded by virtue of
s 10 (f) of the Administration of Justice Act 1982
which provides that "any benefit of a benevolent
character made to the injured person . . . by any
person following upon the injuries" has to be disregarded. He further cited Lord Reid in *Parry v
Cleaver* [1970] AC at p 14: "It would be revolting to
the ordinary man's sense of justice, and therefore contrary to public policy, that the sufferer should have his
damages reduced so that he would gain nothing from
the benevolence of his friends or relations or of the
public at large, and that the only gainer would be the
wrongdoer."

It is correct that the Scots approach is not to look at
whether the wrongdoer gains or is penalised but only
at whether the sufferer requires to be compensated or
recompensed for loss. I have, however, come to the
view that the claims in this instance are part of a loss
of remuneration claim and are not to be regarded in
the same way as the disallowed claim for loss of earnings by the pursuer's wife in *Edgar*. In my view it is
incorrect to look at the provision of accommodation
and particularly at the loss of the other benefits or perquisites which the pursuer would have had from his
employment as being distinct from the financial loss
he suffered when his package of remuneration for his
employment ceased as a result of the accident. The
benefits in question can truly be regarded as part of his
earnings. It follows therefore that the provision of
accommodation to him by his parents in their house
thereafter was a gratuitous benefit which can be disregarded in terms of the Act. I accordingly find the
pursuer's total loss of earnings to date is £29,499, to
which interest requires to be added (a) on the net wage
loss in the sum of £8,468 as agreed in the joint minute
and (b) at 7½ per cent from 7 September 1987 to date
in relation to the other sums being £3,310. The arithmetical calculation was not disputed by the defender's
counsel if accommodation and benefits truly fell to be
added in to the amount due for past loss.

The element for loss of future remuneration was in
dispute only as to the multiplier. Parties were agreed

that the multiplicand was £7,250. The pursuer contended for a multiplier of 15 and the defender for a
multiplier of 12. Because of the long lapse of time
since the accident of 26 September 1986 the pursuer
is now 24 years of age. Counsel for the defender did
not dispute a multiplier of 15 as being appropriate if
it had been established that the pursuer would never
earn again. He contended that there was evidence to
the contrary. The pursuer's counsel under reference to
the recent case of *O'Brien's CB v British Steel plc* and
under reference to the actuarial evidence led from Mr
Kershaw and the "Ogden tables" suggested that 15
was an appropriate multiplier taking into account on
the one hand the possibility that the pursuer might
have become a farm manager and, on the other hand,
the prospect that he might have some form of
remunerative employment in the future. He referred
to *Will v Charles Will Ltd* where a multiplier of 15 was
agreed between counsel for a 21 year old farmworker
and *McLoone v British Railways Board* where for a 20
year old with a double amputation of legs a multiplier
of 13 was adopted.

In the present case there was also evidence led for
the defender from Dr Cornes that the pursuer was
capable of retraining. Thereafter he would be able to
earn and he is mobile. He had excellent handicraft O
grades. He was enterprising. He was in fact keeping
and making some profit from specially imported
Belgian sheep that he had a plan to breed and develop.
There was also evidence from Mr Freeman, the
surgeon, that there were some prospects of remunerative employment, but the pursuer had not been
appraised of any of the opportunities open to him.
The defender contended with reference to the pursuer's prospects of advancement to the hoped for position as farm manager that the pursuer's absence of any
qualification by way of theoretical training was a
pointer against his obtaining such a post. On the other
hand his friends and those who knew him well and in
particular Mr David Seton (a farm manager with no
paper qualifications) indicated that in a farming
locality where the expertise of a particular employee
was known locally, the absence of qualifications might
even be an advantage if set against practical knowledge, achievement and a recognised competence in
the job.

Weighing these opposing contentions I am of
opinion that to discount two years from the multiplier
of 15 which I would have considered appropriate, had
the pursuer been totally disabled from any prospect of
remunerative work, does justice to the position. I
accordingly assess future loss using a multiplier of 13
at £97,760.

The next head of damages claimed by the pursuer
was described as "special needs", divided into past
and future outlays. The pursuer claimed that his
parents regularly visited him while he was in hospital
and incurred expense in doing so and produced a
schedule of expenses. That schedule brought out
travelling expenses of £2,480. Counsel for the
defender pointed out that the schedule disclosed

A expenses met not only by the parents going to hospital but also by "other family members". Pursuer's counsel contended that this was simply part of the costs met by the parents in relation to visiting which was a necessary service whether they went themselves or otherwise provided visiting for the pursuer. Both parties agreed that this would be a claim which fell under s 8 of the Administration of Justice Act 1982 but the defender stated that this went beyond the pleadings and the appropriate amount would require to be a sum suffering some deduction from that in the schedule. The defender proposed the sum of £2,184 to

B which interest was required to be added, making a total of £3,684. The pursuer claimed the whole sums in the schedule plus interest which would give a total of £4,212. The defender's proposed reduction could appear to be somewhat arbitrary but nonetheless I cannot hold that the pursuer has fully established the claim made on record about the parents' expenses in visiting. Since the defender is prepared to concede a sum of £2,184 as expenses with interest of £1,500 I

C feel able to award that sum.

The other two items of past outlays claimed by the pursuer were in relation to alterations to the farmhouse net of local authority grants and the cost of a buggy and a replacement buggy. The pursuer pled that he had incurred these costs. The evidence was that the costs had been incurred, but that they had been met by the pursuer's father in relation to the alterations and in relation to the purchase of the first buggy. In the course of his response to the defender's

D submissions, counsel for the pursuer sought to amend his pleadings to make it clear that these were expenses necessarily incurred by the father on behalf of the pursuer. Amendment was opposed on the ground that there was prejudice in that the amendment came after all the evidence had been led and that no investigation, given the state of the pleadings, had been made as to the enhancement, if any, which the alterations to the farmhouse might have brought to the value of the property. Despite the fact that the amendment came

E so late, I allowed it. I did not consider having heard the whole evidence that the defender had in fact been prejudiced in any material way by any flaw in the pleadings. It was clear and plain that the expenditure had been incurred, that it was both necessary and reasonable, nor would it enhance the value of the parents' house to any material extent, being the addition of a bathroom on the ground floor attached to what would be a guest bedroom if not occupied by the pursuer. The defender's position must have been one

F in which he was in no doubt that these were appropriate expenses. The costs of the alterations to the farm house net of grant were agreed, if relevant, in the joint minute at the modest sum of £2,241; and it was agreed that interest would fall to be added to that sum which at 15 per cent from July 1987 would be £1,613, a total of £3,854.

The first buggy was purchased by the pursuer's father. It was contended by the defender that this was not a necessary service. I consider that contention to be wholly unfounded. I cannot think of a more suit-

G able beneficial piece of therapeutic equipment for this pursuer than the provision of that buggy. In his case I consider it was not only necessary to his recovery but vital. I have no hesitation in allowing that expense. The costs which were claimed by pursuer's counsel amounted to £1,390 (having taken into account a sum as trade in or discount) on which interest at 15 per cent amounts to £938, a total of £2,328. So far as the second buggy is concerned, a replacement, the evidence was that the pursuer had traded in the old buggy and paid a balance of £1,000. I allow that £1,000.

H It was in relation to future outlays (and also future care) that the main dispute appeared between the parties. I was provided with a report by and evidence from a Mr Bartle Hellyer, a solicitor who is a paraplegic and who makes a specialty of formulating and advising litigants upon claims such as the present. There was also a considerable body of useful evidence from the principal medical witnesses in the case, Mr Freeman and Mr Edmond in particular. I regret to say that I did not find Mr Hellyer's report or his approach

I to be of much assistance. It proceeded upon the basis of a single visit to the pursuer on 7 July 1988 and it was constructed after that visit. No attempt had been made by Mr Hellyer to ascertain whether any of the items referred to in his report had proved to be necessary or whether any of his suggestions had been followed up; he never spoke to the pursuer again. Despite that he produced a report for the court which bore the date 21 February 1992 and on the face of it bore to be an assessment at that date. It turned out that

J this was no more than the original report he had compiled with the costings therein revised. So, for example, there appeared in that report the following: "III Manual wheelchair. Mr McMillan has been supplied with a standard National Health issue chair *but like most other paraplegics*, finds it heavy and unwieldy to use. He proposes to purchase a light-weight chair." Any inquiry of the pursuer would have ascertained that he had not by 1992 purchased such a chair; that he did not, according to the evidence before

K me, find the National Health issue chair heavy or unwieldy to use and indeed when in court so demonstrated. It is unsatisfactory to say the least when documents are provided as some form of assessment of the needs of the pursuer but which bear little if any relation to the facts of the situation at the time of the proof. Again, under the heading, "Items which Mr McMillan will require in his own home in future" there appears "13.14 Home computer system" with a costing attached to it. Mr McMillan has not and has

L never had any interest in a home computer and any inquiry of him would have ascertained that. There were other examples of wholly exaggerated alleged requirements and costs and I disregard that document. I note further, in particular, that despite the judicial strictures in *Tuttle* and the cases cited therein of a claim based on a projection of replacement costs on an annual basis, that appears still to be the procedure adopted in this report. No doubt the advice of such as Mr Hellyer can be helpful at the preliminary stages of the formulation of a claim and useful in assisting

parties to recognise the implications of a disability
such as that suffered by the pursuer and by helping
them to consider what amelioration could be achieved
by suitable appliances, but that should be the sole
purpose of such a report.

Because of the obvious evidential difficulties with
Mr Hellyer's report, the defender's counsel suggested
that a contingency fund was the appropriate way to
deal with the future needs of the pursuer and
suggested £5,000. While that approach has some
superficial attraction, I do not think that it does justice
to the pursuer's needs. In the end of the day counsel
for the pursuer restricted his capital cost claim to
£1,863.50. This comprised: physiotherapy weights
£30, lightweight wheelchair £1,215, exercise mat £60,
protective pad £129, easy reacher helping hand £8.50,
portable ramp £246, cordless telephone £100, natural
sheepskin £30, sheepskin for wheelchair £15, and
adjustable table £30. As can be seen the principal item
was the lightweight wheelchair for which the pursuer
has not seen any particular need at this stage. If,
however, he were to be travelling on any regular basis,
he could well find it useful and on full consideration
I am prepared to allow the capital cost only of such an
item because I do not consider that the pursuer will
use it so extensively as to require the type of replacement or maintenance contended for it at £393
annually. The evidence of capital costs was somewhat
vague and a variety of costs were illustrated in the
productions. I allow £1,850 under this head. The
pursuer will also have replacement and maintenance
costs for his buggy but again these are overstated in
Mr Hellyer's report. In the pursuer's revised claim at
proof various sums were produced by counsel for the
pursuer which gave a total annual outlay of £1,560.80.
Discounting substantially the substantial items in that
calculation expressed as "annual replacement cost"
which relate to the wheelchair and buggy, I accept that
the pursuer will have additional expenses and will
have replacement costs for various items. He will have
additional washing and clothing requirements. He will
need his sheepskin and he will need a measure of
maintenance for his equipment including the buggy.
I consider an annual outlay of £750 is adequate to deal
with such annual expense over normal that the
pursuer will have. I propose to take a multiplier of 18
as suggested by pursuer's counsel for that head of
damages, which amounts to £13,500. I recognise that
in so doing I have departed somewhat from the
approach adopted by Lord McDonald in *Tuttle* but
only to the extent that he did not include under that
head the items that have been included in the
present by way of running costs, special clothing and
dressing.

A further area of major dispute between the parties
was the past and future cost of care and the appropriate sums to be taken as both multiplier and multiplicand in that regard. Up until the date of the proof
and for a short time thereafter, until the pursuer's own
house is built, the pursuer has been and will be cared
for by his parents and in particular by his mother. She
has done so devotedly. She has spent a great deal of

time and effort on this task. I do not doubt that she has
done so and that she has devoted the hours that she
indicated but I am not persuaded that strictly all this
was necessary. In particular, when it was suggested to
Dr Freeman that the pursuer's mother required to
spend three hours a day on his care he indicated that
he felt that a maximum of one and a half hours per day
was all that was necessary. Both parties chose to
present their argument on the basis of the cost which
would be incurred were these services to be provided
by an outside agency.

In this case they both started from the "Crossroads"
care rate which was set out in the productions. These
rates were payable to a non-profit-making organisation
not setting out to provide skilled nursing care. Both
counsel proposed that the past care should be divided
into distinct parts. The first was the weekend care
necessary when the pursuer was released from hospital
at weekends between Christmas 1986 and April 1987.
The pursuer claimed that thereafter six hours per day
were needed for the first year at home and after that
three hours daily to the present time. The defender
suggested that a higher involvement for the first six
months only should be taken and that thereafter 10½
hours per week was all that was necessary. Although
the rates suggested were such as require to be paid to
an outside agency, the defender contended these rates
were not appropriate when evaluating the care
provided by a relative since they were what the
recipient of the care would have paid and not what the
provider would have received. They did not represent
reasonable remuneration for a relative and deductions
should be made for the administrative costs included
in the "Crossroads" care rate, tax and a further
deduction said "To reflect nature of payments to
mother". Applying their different calculations the
defender produced a figure for past care inclusive of
interest of £7,451 and the pursuer's counsel a sum of
£23,370.

Both parties, no doubt conscious of the views
expressed by Lord Clyde in *Forsyth's CB v Govan
Shipbuilders Ltd* and adopted and expanded by Lord
Penrose in *Gordon v Wilson*, provided various rates for
the court to consider in order to ascertain the cost or
equivalent cost of services. Lord Penrose indicated
that a deduction of some element for commission, tax
and insurance was appropriate but declined to make
any further deduction to reflect the fact that the
services were provided in the home. In my opinion it
is important to refer to equivalent hourly rates for
similar services by outside agencies, here the "Crossroads" rates, to assist in determining the sum to be
awarded to represent appropriate remuneration for the
relative providing the services. I do not consider that
the use of the word remuneration means that the
provider has to be paid as if she were an independent
employee; indeed there is something repugnant about
the idea of a caring relative being awarded an hourly
wage rate. What, in my view, the comparative rates do
provide is material against which the court can check
its impression of the sum to be given as appropriate
remuneration. It appears to me that except in cases

involving 24 hour care, there must always be some
A variation in the amount of time spent, the time at
which it is spent and the amount of effort required
from the relative providing care which means that no
accurate calculation of a precise sum of money can
ever be made in this regard.

In the present case I find that necessary services
would amount in all to about one and a half hours a
day. I accept that further services were and are being
provided, but these were and are not necessary.
Further, I recognise that the one and a half hours per
B day are provided at odd times and not necessarily at
one extended period which no doubt makes the provision easier for the provider, so long as she is a
relative in the same house, but impossible to quantify
on a calculation of what a person such as a home help
person would require to be paid. This pursuer
requires an emergency stand-by service which is virtually unquantifiable. The relevant "Crossroads" rate
for a home help can be found in 38/1 of process. I do
not consider that, at least in this case, it is possible to
C achieve the kind of accuracy attempted by Lord
Penrose in *Gordon* and I assess this element using
rather less precise calculations than he seemed to be
able to make. The level of care was high in the initial
stages. It began at Christmas 1986 and involved 12
weekends, virtually full time. Then the pursuer came
home. He was by then reasonably well able to look
after himself, but plainly required a great deal of
assistance until the appropriate alterations were done
to his parents' house to enable him to achieve a satis-
D factory degree of independence. Thereafter the
requirement for services diminished until by, say a
year after the accident, they were of the order of the
one and a half hours spoken to by Mr Freeman as
being appropriate. Counsel for the pursuer claimed
that £835 would be an appropriate sum for the period
prior to the pursuer's final return home and that
£6,351 would be appropriate for the year thereafter.
The effect of counsel for the defender's calculations
brought out a sum for £700 for the period from
E Christmas 1986 to 30 June 1987 and £809 for the
period 1 July 1987 to 30 June 1988. Counsel for the
defender's figures included a deduction of 20 per cent
as the administration element in the "Crossroads"
daily care rate as well as a deduction for tax and a
further deduction of 10 per cent for the fact of services
being provided in the home. There was no precise
evidence about the administrative content of the
"Crossroads" care rate. There was evidence from the
area superintendent of an organisation known as
F "Allied Medicare" which would indicate that there
were some administrative costs in the charges that her
organisation levied. Mr Hellyer's report and evidence
was again of no assistance, since it did not take account
of any of these matters, merely assuming that the full
rate would always require to be paid.

I assess reasonable remuneration for the pursuer's
relatives as follows: (1) for the period between
Christmas 1986 and April 1987 when the pursuer was
being assisted virtually 24 hours a day at £700 for such
time as he spent at home, (2) for the period from 1

April 1987 to 1 April 1988 when the level of care had
fully stabilised at £2,500 reflecting a progressive G
diminution from six to one and a half hours and
bearing in mind an undiscounted "Crossroads" care
rate of £2.90 an hour, (3) thereafter and to date at
£6,000 which in my view adequately reflects necessary
care of one and a half hours, has regard to an average
home help rate of about £3.40 an hour undiscounted,
and makes allowance for the incidence of taxation and
a counter allowance for the irregular hours of work
and responsibility. This gives the total sum for past
care for the pursuer for the purposes of his s 8 claim H
of £9,200. To these sums interest requires to be added
at 15 per cent from April 1987 on the sum of £750
which I calculate in round figures at £565, again at 15
per cent on £2,500 for four years, ie £1,500 and at 7½
per cent for three years on £6,000, ie £1,350.

Turning to the need for future care, the evidence
which I accept was that the pursuer would initially
require nothing beyond what he presently needs other
than the presence of an emergency backup service
when he acquires his own home and independence. I
Thereafter he will require progressively more care
which his mother will be less able to provide, until
ultimately he will require a resident housekeeper. The
doctors assessed that 20-25 years would elapse before
he would be in the position of so requiring, given no
major upsets in his health between now and then. The
question thus becomes one of how appropriately to
reflect that sequence of events (which I find on the
balance of probabilities will occur) by way of a sum
payable now. Actuarial evidence was led by the J
pursuer from Mr Kershaw, who spoke to his own calculations and to the "Ogden tables". His calculations
which were based on a real rate of interest of 4.38 per
cent and on a no risk policy, would indicate a
multiplier of between 18 and 20. In his report he
assumes a real rate of interest using that week's stock
exchange prices for index linked gilt-edged securities
of 4.38 per cent, giving a net rate of interest at 3.25
per cent after tax at current rates. Both these rates
can, obviously, fluctuate. He reckoned that a multi- K
plier of 14.5 would be required from age 25 to 45 and
thereafter one of 8.79. Counsel for the pursuer
approached this problem on the basis that for short
term care I should simply multiply, as indicated by the
actuary's report, the sum which he said was appropriate on the basis of three hours a day. As I have
stated I do not accept three hours a day but instead
accept one and a half hours at £3 hourly instead of
£3.50 per hour at the "Crossroads" rate. In addition
increasing help may have to be paid for as a supple- L
ment to his mother's care increasing over the later
years. Overall it seems reasonable to take £1,642.50
per year as the multiplicand. Using the multiplier in
the actuary's reports of 14.5 would bring out a total of
£23,816 for that element. The pursuer had before the
proof entered into a formal agreement with his mother
to pay her for more hours of care and at a sum greater
than I have allowed. He has thus surmounted the
difficulty with s 8 before it was amended which was
noted in *Forsyth's CB v Govan Shipbuilders*. The

pursuer went on to calculate basic long term residential care at an employed housekeeper's cost of £50 a week but with a certain amount of relief residential care at £46.50 a week in addition, together with extra maintenance costs of £3,261, giving a total of £8,279. Applying the multiplier as given in the actuary's report of 8.7, he brought out a total of £72,027.30.

The defender's approach was different. He divided future care into the first 10 years at 14 hours a week and the second 10 years at a sum involving the provision of care for 20 hours per week, part of which would require to be bought in. He proposed 20 hours at an average rate of £4 for the weekly rate and eight hours at a weekend rate of £5.84, giving £126.72 and proposed a multiplier of 3 for each of these two years. This in fact would give an overall multiplier of 15 for the first 20 years. Thereafter in later life he accepted multiplicand of £50 per week for a housekeeper with carer's living expenses of £3,261 would be met by the pursuer and with relief help of some 10 hours at the "Crossroads" care rate of £3.89 per hour, ie £39.80 per week, or annually, £2,022. This gave a total later life multiplicand of £7,883. He then proposed a multiplier of 2 and a deduction for attendance allowance for those two years. He used an overall multiplier of 17.

I prefer the pursuer's simpler approach in relation to the first period of 20 years and adopt, modified as above noted, the pursuer's figures. With regard to later life, while I have little doubt that some form of allowance will be available from the state in respect of the necessity for full time care, there can be no projection as to when that would be granted or when the pursuer would be judged in need of a full or part time attendance allowance. I consider that all I can do is to bear that in mind as a factor when considering the appropriateness of a multiplier in later life. Mr Kershaw in cross examination indicated that any discounting made by the court for loss of expectation of life and or any of the other vicissitudes of fortune should be loaded towards the later end of the calculation. He suggested that 10 per cent of his figures might be appropriate. This would give a total multiplier looking at the Ogden tables of 16½ to 20 which would indicate that the remaining part of the multiplier would be of the order of 3, rather than the 8.7 contended for by the pursuer. I regard the appropriate multiplicand for later life as being, in the first instance, of £50 a week plus living expenses plus some relief help. The relief help in the pursuer's calculation costs about as much as the residential carer and I do not think that this is reasonable. The defender suggested a sum of £2,022 extrapolating from the "Crossroads" care rate. I accept that calculation but I am unable to quantify any deduction for attendance allowance. That being so, accepting the defender's multiplicand of £7,883 and adopting a multiplier of 3 which I consider to be reasonable, that element of future care costs amounts to £23,649. The total under this head is thus £47,465. I have utilised an overall multiplier of 17½.

The pursuer sought damages for the costs incurred by him with regard to his accommodation. The pursuer's counsel contended that of the alternatives put forward, it was plainly economical for the pursuer to have a bungalow built to his specification having the special features he required. He accepted that there should be no capital windfall in this respect. In *Roberts v Johnstone*, in similar circumstances the English court adopted the principle of an annualised cost of acquisition over a set number of years. That approach was accepted in *Geddes v Lothian Health Board*, but at 1992 SLT, p 988 the Lord Ordinary indicated various problems in finding what sum it was appropriate to adopt as an annualised cost. He desiderated evidence, for example, of finance costs and the actual outlay to be incurred. He envisaged a correctly based claim as potentially quite complex. In the present case, parties were agreed that 2 per cent per annum of the cost was the appropriate base on which to proceed, but defender's counsel disputed the pursuer's calculation on the basis that it was inappropriate to take the entire building cost as indicated in 33/9 of process of the purpose built house. Mr Rutherford, the architectural assistant who gave evidence, said that he had included in his estimate "every conceivable item which may be required and costed it". He had not discussed the pursuer's needs with the pursuer. I was not satisfied that the figure produced of £140,500 was the appropriate figure to take, particularly in the light of that evidence from Mr Rutherford. Counsel for the defender suggested that about £14,000 would require to be deducted from that estimate, since the only truly additional items to an ordinary house would be the hand and guard rails, a matter of a few hundred pounds. I agree with counsel for the defender that the figure of £140,502 in 33/10 of process is overstated and accept his suggestion that £14,000 should be deducted from those figures. This gives the cost of the house and building plot at £143,500 of which 2 per cent is £2,870. In *Roberts v Johnstone* a multiplier of 16 was taken as appropriate in such a case. In the present case the pursuer contended for 18 and the defender for 11. In support of his contention defender's counsel urged that the amount would be given now, whereas the house had not yet been built and the costs not yet incurred and further, that if he had been a shepherd with his tied cottage, the pursuer's employment and tenancy would have ceased at age 65, in which case he would have required to fund rent or make alternative arrangements. Bearing in mind that the outlay has not yet been incurred and may not be for at least a year, I consider that the appropriate multiplier is 15 and under this head award £41,700. It was claimed that there was left out of the calculation a sum of £10,000 which would represent the sum by which a prospective purchaser would discount his price because of the unwanted things in a house built to accommodate a paraplegic and the necessity to alter levels and the like. I think it would be wrong as contended for by the pursuer to award such a sum now on the basis of some prospective loss of that amount described by the pursuer's counsel as "cost representing non-enhancement". I think I have

A fully allowed for that possibility by applying a multiplier of 15 to the annualised cost as I have done.

The final item claimed by the pursuer was additional cost of holidays. This was a matter which was spoken to by Mr Hellyer. The pursuer himself has never yet taken a holiday, although he said he would like to and it is reasonably clear that in order to have a satisfactory holiday away from the farm, the pursuer would require to be accompanied. He might well be accompanied by a relative and he might well require special arrangements to be made. The pursuer suggested £400 a year for this with a multiplier of 18. The defender contended that that additional cost was a contingency to be met under the general fund he had already proposed. Since I have not accepted in principle the contention for a general fund, I do consider that there is an element of additional cost for holidays. I do not think that £400 a year would be exceptional, but must bear in mind that the pursuer's ability to go away on holiday will become restricted as he requires full time residential care. Accordingly in this respect C I propose to apply the multiplier of 13 which I have applied to the element of wage loss; this gives a further sum of £5,200. On the whole matter therefore, the pursuer is entitled to decree in the sum of £285,432 being £356,790 less £71,358 being 20 per cent thereof, made up as follows:

(i)	Solatium		£70,000
	(a) Interest thereon		14,857
(ii)	Past loss of earnings		29,499
	(a) Interest thereon		11,778
(iii)	Future loss of earnings		97,760
(iv)	Past special needs and care (s 8)		
	(a) Past care		9,200
	Interest thereon		3,415
	(b) Travel by parents		2,184
	Interest thereon		1,500
	(c) Outlays by father		
	Alteration to farmhouse (with interest)		3,854
	Buggy (with interest)		2,328
	Replacement buggy (paid by pursuer)		1,000
(v)	Future special needs		
	Capital outlays		1,850
	Replacement and other special costs		13,500
(vi)	Future care		
	(a) while largely independent	£23,816	
	(b) while largely dependent	£23,649	
			47,465
(vii)	Accommodation costs		41,700
(viii)	Holidays in future		5,200
			£356,790
	less 20 per cent (contributory negligence)		71,358
			£285,432

Counsel for Pursuer, Brodie, QC, Maguire; Solicitors, Simpson & Marwick, WS (for A B & A Matthews, Newton Stewart) — Counsel for Defender, Jones, QC, Reith; Solicitors, Cochran, Sayers & Cook.

C H

Macleod v Clacher

OUTER HOUSE

LORD COULSFIELD

15 MARCH 1991

Church — Church property — Recovery of possession — Title to sue — Title to property in name of trustees for congregation — No trustees in office — Title to sue of finance committee empowered to undertake duties in relation to church property.

Process — Title to sue — Church property — Recovery of possession — Title to property in name of trustees for congregation — No trustees in office — Title to sue of finance committee empowered to undertake duties in relation to church property.

From 1982 the manse of a congregation of the Free Church of Scotland was occupied by an individual in good faith and with the consent of the majority of the congregation. Title to the manse was in the name of the former trustees for the congregation. The finance committee of the congregation raised an action for recovery of possession of the manse. At the time of raising the action there were no trustees in office. On procedure roll the defender moved that the action should be dismissed. He argued that the finance committee had no title to sue, contending that in terms of the trust deed the trustees alone had the power to raise an action relating to heritable property while the deacons' court had the exclusive power to manage the property. Esto the deacons' court had power to raise such an action the defender further argued that the 1976 Act Anent Finance Committees, which made provision for the undertaking by finance committees of the duties normally discharged by a deacons' court, did not delegate such a power to the finance committee. It was further argued that there was insufficient specification that the finance committee had been properly appointed in terms of the 1976 Act.

Held, (1) that the deacons had authority to manage church property in terms of the trust deed and that that included the power to take legal proceedings for the safeguarding or recovery of possession of property of the congregation (p 321E-F); (2) that the purpose of the 1976 Act was to confer on finance committees the power to perform the functions normally carried out by deacons' courts, and the delegation to the deacons in the trust deed was incomplete without reference to the powers of the church to authorise others to perform the functions normally entrusted to the deacons (pp 321J and 322A-D); and (3) that, in the absence of any likelihood of significant prejudice to the defender from the want of specification, the action should go to proof (p 322E-F); and proof before answer *allowed.*

Action of declarator and ejection

The Reverend Murdo Macleod and others, as the finance committee of the congregation of the Free

A Church of Scotland of Raasay, raised an action against Robert Clacher seeking declarator that the defender had no right, title or interest to continue to occupy the Free Church manse on Raasay, warrant for his ejection and payment of a sum of money as violent profits.

The case came before the Lord Ordinary (Coulsfield) on procedure roll on the defender's plea of no title to sue and on his plea to the relevancy of the action.

B On 15 March 1991 the Lord Ordinary *allowed* a proof before answer, leaving all pleas standing.

LORD COULSFIELD.—The pursuers in this action describe themselves as the persons presently constituting the finance committee of the congregation of the Free Church of Scotland of Raasay. The defender is, and has been since about 1982, in occupation of the Free Church manse in Raasay. The pursuers seek declarator that the defender has no right, title or interest to continue to occupy the subjects,
C warrant for his ejection and payment of a sum of money as violent profits. The defender does not aver that he has any right or title to occupy the subjects, apart from stating that he has possessed and continues to possess them in good faith with the consent of the majority of the communicant members of the Free Church of Scotland at Raasay. The defender does not aver that he is a member of the church. He pleads, however, that the pursuers have no title to sue and that the action is irrelevant.
D
The case came before me in the procedure roll on 1 March 1991, when counsel for the defender submitted that his plea of no title to sue, and, so far as bearing on questions of title to sue, his plea to the relevancy, should be sustained, and the action dismissed. Counsel for the pursuer submitted that a proof before answer should be allowed. The facts and circumstances bearing on the question of title to sue are substantially agreed between the parties, apart from one
E matter which will be mentioned later. These facts are, perhaps, not fully set out in the pleadings, but they appear from the averments when taken with the documents referred to on record and the circumstances agreed between the parties.

The heritable title to the subjects in question was constituted by a disposition dated 3 December 1862 granted by George Rainy in favour of the trustees then acting for the congregation of the Free Church of Scotland in Raasay. The disposition bears to be granted in
F favour of a number of named individuals described as "Trustees for the congregation of the body of Christians called the Free Church of Scotland at present worshipping in Raasay", and continues: "and to the successors in office of the Minister and elders of the said Free Church in Raasay to be from time to time appointed by the said congregation in the way and manner provided for the appointment of new or additional trustees in the disposition after referred to". Subsequently, it is provided that the disposition is granted "always with the powers and under the con-

ditions, provisions, and declarations contained and specially enumerated from *primo* to *duodecimo* both G
inclusive in the disposition before referred to . . . all which powers, conditions, provisions and declarations are here held as repeated *brevitatis causa*". The disposition referred to was one granted in 1844 to certain individuals named therein and described as trustees for the congregation of St George's Free Church of Edinburgh. In applying the powers and provisions of the 1844 disposition to the subjects relevant in the present action, the disposition of 1862 conformed to the practice of the Free Church of Scotland, dating H
back to an Act of the church of 1844. The 1844 disposition itself is conveniently referred to, in the practice of the church, as the model trust deed.

For the purposes of the present action, the material provisions of the model trust deed are cll thirdly, fifthly and eighthly. Clause thirdly, so far as material, provides: "That the said building or place of worship, erected, or to be erected, as said is, and whole pertinents thereof, and generally the whole subjects hereby disponed, shall be under the immediate charge and I
management . . . of the elders and deacons, or elders acting as deacons, for the time being, of the congregation in the use, occupation, and enjoyment for the time, of such building or place of worship — such elders and deacons, or elders acting as deacons, being always subject to such control as shall, or may, be provided from time to time, by the said body, or united body, of Christians, through the medium of its kirk sessions, presbyteries, provincial synods and general assemblies or in the way and manner generally J
in use in the said body, or united body, for the time: declaring always, as it is hereby expressly provided and declared, that it shall not be in the power of the said deacons, or elders, or any of them, or of any, or all, of the individual members of the congregation . . . either to maintain themselves in any use, possession, occupation, or enjoyment of the same, as against the said trustees or trustee, acting for the time, or to institute against the said trustees or trustee, acting for the time, any action, suit, or proceeding, before any K
court of law or justice, for the purpose either of obtaining or maintaining such possession, use, occupation, or enjoyment or of controlling in any way the said trustees or trustee in reference to the use, possession, occupation or enjoyment, or management and disposal of such building, or place of worship, unless with the express consent and concurrence of the general assembly of the said body or united body of Christians".

Clause fifthly provides: "It is hereby expressly L
provided and declared that the said trustees, or trustee, acting for the time, shall always have full power and liberty to raise, prosecute, and follow forth, whatever action, suit or proceeding they may think proper in whatever court, or courts, of law or justice, for the purpose or with the intent and object of excluding any party or parties whatsoever, from all or any use, possession, occupation, or enjoyment of the building or place of worship . . . and that no party, or parties, whatsoever, shall have any right or title what-

soever to defend such action, suit or proceeding either in virtue of these presents or otherwise, unless with the express consent and concurrence, as aforesaid, of the general assembly of the said body".

Clause eighthly provides: "It is hereby further expressly provided and declared that it shall be, at all times, in the power of the congregation . . . to appoint . . . additional trustees to act under these presents along with the trustees who at the date of such appointment are surviving and acting; . . . and the said trustees or trustee acting for the time shall on every occasion of such appointment of additional trustee be bound and obliged to execute a formal deed of assumption of such additional trustees containing a formal and in all respects complete conveyance of the subjects hereby disponed in favour of such additional trustees and of themselves and otherwise in terms of these presents".

Two points are immediately apparent. First, the trustees appointed by the disposition of 1862 are not trustees ex officio, so that their successors require to be appointed from time to time in the appropriate manner defined by the trust deed. Secondly, the members of the kirk session or the deacons' court of a congregation are not necessarily the trustees of the subjects. On occasion, an individual may be both an elder or deacon and a trustee, but that is a coincidence and the offices are distinct. Indeed, I was informed that in practice, for various reasons, in certain parts of Scotland trustees may not be appointed for substantial periods of time, the management of the property of the church being carried on by the deacons until some event, such as a sale of property, occurs which requires trustees to deal with conveyance of a title. I should note also at this stage, that, although s 26 of the Titles to Land (Consolidation) (Scotland) Act 1868 made it unnecessary for deeds to be executed conveying trust property upon the appointment of new trustees, for a religious body, counsel for the defender reserved his position on the question whether it might still be necessary that new trustees should, in the case of a trust incorporating the model trust deed, be formally assumed to act in the trust.

The model trust deed does not itself specify who are to be the deacons to whom the management of church property is entrusted or how deacons are to be appointed. Both parties accepted that, for the purposes of this debate, the position of deacons in the church was authoritatively described in a book entitled *The Practice of the Free Church of Scotland* published in 1964, a copy of which was produced. With regard to the constitution of the deacons' court, it is stated inter alia: "1. The pastor or pastors of each congregation, along with the ruling elders and the deacons, constitute the deacons' court.

"2. The deacon's function is the administering of the temporal affairs of a congregation. The higher office scripturally includes the lower. The pastor and ruling elders are, therefore, not excluded from the exercise of the deacon's function. . . . Deacons are elected for life, or until they cease to be members of the congregation, ...

"3. The election of deacons belongs to the members of the congregation in full communion."

With regard to the powers and functions of the deacons' court, it is stated:

"The deacons' court have charge of the whole property belonging to the congregation, or held for the congregation's use by trustees appointed in terms of deeds which the general assembly has sanctioned; also of all the congregation's secular affairs. . . .

"The powers and functions thus generally described are exemplified in detail as follows:

"1. The deacons' court has no power of discipline even over its own members. It can neither admit to the office of deaconship, nor depose from it. . . .

"3. The members of the deacons' court are not necessarily themselves the local trustees in whom the congregational property is vested, but the general assembly approve only of such title deeds as require the trustees to leave the management in the hands of the deacons' court. It is competent and not unusual for members of the deacons' court to be named as the trustees".

In 1976 it was found necessary to make further provision for the administration of congregational affairs by an Act of the general assembly entitled An Act Anent Finance Committees. So far as material, the Act provides:

"The general assembly noting that finance committees exist in many congregations without the benefit of formal legislative recognition enact that the following regulations shall apply to the appointment and duties of finance committees:

"(1) In ordinary circumstances a congregational finance committee shall be appointed only in the absence of a sufficient number of suitably qualified male members whose names are on the congregational roll and who are willing to accept office as deacons after being duly elected by the congregation.

"(2) The necessity for appointing a finance committee and the number of its members should be determined by the kirk session in the same manner as they decide upon the appointment of office bearers.

"(3) Election should be by the congregation, preferably annually, on the recommendation of the kirk session.

"(4) The finance committee shall undertake to discharge all the duties normally discharged by a deacons' court, in whose place they shall be called upon to express formally their opinion on all matters affecting the financial obligations of the congregation, or the oversight of congregational property, requiring decisions by the general assembly, its commission or court of the church".

The Act proceeds to make provision for a finance committee to come to an end when circumstances permit the election of a deacons' court. In 1977, the general assembly approved an expansion of the Act, in the following terms:

A "The general assembly expressly state that no section of the foregoing legislation confers the status of office bearer on members of finance committees. These committees are recognised only as temporary expedients which should be replaced in terms of the preceding paragraph: as temporary expedients they do not rank as church courts".

In the present case, it appears that at the date when the action was raised there were no trustees of the Raasay property in office. New trustees were appointed on 9 May 1989, some time after the service B of the summons. The pursuers do not claim title to sue in any capacity other than as the finance committee of the congregation and concede that if the position is that only the trustees have a title to sue for recovery of possession of the subjects, the action is irrelevant.

The first submission for the defender was that cl fifthly of the model trust deed declared that the trustees had the right to pursue actions, including actions such as the present. In terms of cl thirdly, the C power to manage the property was conferred upon the deacons but that management power could well be interpreted, consistently with cl fifthly, as falling short of any power to bring an action in court for recovery of possession of heritable property. The fact that cl thirdly contained an express prohibition upon the deacons instituting any legal proceedings against the trustees did not imply that the deacons had any power to raise proceedings other than proceedings against the trustees. The provisions in question were only a form D of internal procedure for the resolution of disputes. The clear intent was to give the final say to the infeft proprietors. For the pursuers, it was submitted that the power of management conferred upon the deacons would include taking steps, including legal proceedings, for recovery of possession of the property which it was their duty to manage. It was further submitted that the declaration in cl thirdly made it clear that the deacons did have such a power, apart from the case of legal proceedings against the trustees.

E   Clause thirdly clearly provides that the property shall be under the immediate charge and management of the deacons. This power of management is not conferred on the deacons as agents or factors acting on behalf of the trustees. Indeed, as the description of the practice of the church, quoted above, shows, the trustees are expected to leave the management of the property to the deacons. The deacons, therefore, have authority to manage in virtue of a provision of the trust deed itself, not derived from any power or F authority granted by the trustees. In that context, the words of cl thirdly, in my opinion, confer a wide general power upon the deacons and that power is wide enough to include authority to take legal proceedings to safeguard the property of the congregation or recover it from a person who does not claim to be a member of the church. The provisions of cl fifthly are, in my view, designed to deal with the situation where a dispute arises between members of the church, and there is nothing in that provision to limit the authority of the deacon to raise proceedings in a

case such as this. In my opinion, accordingly, the first argument for the defender falls to be rejected.   G

The second argument for the defender was that, on the assumption that deacons would have had a title to sue the present action, no title or authority belonged to a finance committee appointed in terms of the Act of 1976. This argument was presented under two heads. First, it was submitted that the Act of 1976 required the finance committee to discharge the *duties* normally discharged by a deacons' court, but did not confer upon them any power to bring an action to H vindicate possession of church property. It was submitted that there was a difference in law between duties and powers, and that while the Act might, for example, place on the finance committee the obligation to see to repairs of the property, it did not give them power to reclaim possession of it by legal proceedings. This was further shown by the provisions of s 4 of the Act, which required the finance committee to perform the duties of the deacons' court in regard to expressing an opinion on matters requiring decisions by the general assembly. That was an I indication of the sort of matters which the finance committee were entitled to deal with. If it had been intended that they should have power to take proceedings, that would have been said expressly. For the pursuers it was submitted that the word "duty" should not be construed so narrowly and that what was intended was that the finance committee should perform the functions of the deacons' court. The finance committee would, indeed, be failing in a duty if they did not take the steps necessary to recover J possession of church property. In my opinion, the pursuers' submission on this point is correct. Looking at the 1976 Act as a whole, it is plain, in my view, that its purpose was to provide for the carrying out of all those functions which are normally performed by a deacons' court by the appointment of a finance committee and that the Act is intended to confer on the committee the power necessary to perform these functions.

K The second head of this argument for the defender was that the model trust deed specifically delegated the power of management to the deacons ex officio. The deacons' court was a court of the church and deacons were office bearers of the church. The finance committee, on the other hand, was specifically said not to be a court of the church and its members were not office bearers. Clause thirdly was a provision of the trust deed which could not be varied by an Act of the general assembly. That was emphasised if the L defender's first submission was rejected, because the deacons would be exercising the trustees' power in managing the property. If the powers of deacons were to be transferred to some other persons or body it would be necessary to vary the trust purposes by some means. The Act of the general assembly might be binding upon members of the church, but the assembly had no authority either to vary a trust purpose or to legislate in a way binding upon outsiders. Counsel for the pursuers accepted that the model trust deed contained no express power to place the management of the church property in the hands of persons other than deacons, so that if the deed were strictly construed a variation might be necessary. He submitted, however, that such a narrow construction was inappropriate.

I have come to the conclusion that this argument should also be rejected. It is true that the model trust deed confers the power of management on the deacons. However, there is no provision in the model trust deed which defines or identifies the persons who are the deacons for the purposes of its provisions. It must follow that the trust deed left to the church the power to provide, according to its own rules and practices, for the election or appointment of the persons who are to have the power of management as deacons. Clause thirdly itself provides for control to be exercised by other courts of the church over the deacons. That being so, it is not, in my view, unreasonable to construe the power left to the church under the trust deed as extending to the authorisation of arrangements for the election of persons who, in exceptional circumstances, may perform the functions normally entrusted to the deacons. If the model trust deed itself contained provision for the appointment of deacons, there would be greater force in the defender's argument that a variation of the deed would be necessary in order to confer any powers upon a finance committee rather than upon the deacons' court. As matters stand, however, the trust deed cannot be regarded as complete in itself and there must be reliance upon the church to provide for the method by which the persons who are to perform the functions of deacons under the trust deed are to be appointed. In my opinion, therefore, the defender's second argument against the pursuers' title to sue also fails.

The third submission for the defender was that, on the assumption that a properly appointed finance committee would have a title to sue, the pursuers in the present action do not specifically aver either that the kirk session has decided that it is necessary to appoint a finance committee, in terms of s 2 of the Act of 1976, or that the pursuers have been elected in terms of s 3 of that Act. Counsel for the pursuers accepted that these matters were not specified but submitted that he had sufficiently averred the pursuers' title by averring that they presently constitute the finance committee of the church. This is a point of specification only and, while I think that it would have been better for the pursuers to make averments upon the points raised by counsel for the defender, it does not seem to me that the defender is likely to sustain any significant prejudice if the action proceeds to a proof. If the pursuers fail to prove that the necessary resolution of the kirk session and the necessary election were held, the action will of course fail.

In the whole circumstances, in my opinion, the proper course is to allow a proof before answer upon the whole case, leaving all pleas standing.

Counsel for Pursuers, Brailsford; Solicitors, Simpson & Marwick, WS — Counsel for Defender, I G Mitchell; Solicitors, Drummond & Co, WS.

N C R

R Peter & Co Ltd v The Pancake Place Ltd

OUTER HOUSE
LORD MARNOCH
22 MARCH 1991

Prescription — Negative prescription — Commencement date of prescriptive period — Action raised in respect of latest of three distinct invoices — Subsequent adjustments adding claims in respect of earlier invoices — Whether transactions charged on continuing account — Prescription and Limitation (Scotland) Act 1973 (c 52), Sched 2, para 1.

Prescription — Negative prescription — Interruption of prescriptive period — "Relevant claim" — Preliminary notice of arbitration — No prior agreement to arbitrate or subsequent arbitration proceedings undertaken — Prescription and Limitation (Scotland) Act 1973 (c 52), ss 4 (4), 6 (1) and 9.

Prescription — Negative prescription — Interruption of prescriptive period — "Relevant acknowledgment" — Whether short negative prescriptive period capable of running after making of relevant acknowledgment — Prescription and Limitation (Scotland) Act 1973 (c 52), ss 6 (1) and 7 (1).

A building company in liquidation sought recovery of certain unpaid balances contained in three invoices which related to building work allegedly carried out for a restaurant company at three separate locations. It was accepted that the action had been raised timeously in respect of the last in date of the three invoices, and that the first two invoices in date had been added by adjustment outwith the prescriptive period. The defenders argued that any obligations to make payment in respect of the first two invoices had prescribed. The builders contended (1) under reference to para 1 of Sched 2 to the Prescription and Limitation (Scotland) Act 1973, that all three transactions had been charged "to the defenders' continuing account", thus "saving" the two earlier invoices; (2) that averments on record concerning letters passing between the builders and the defenders wherein the parties "gave each other preliminary notice stating the nature of their respective claims with a view to arbitration" were averments of a claim made in arbitration proceedings and thus a "relevant claim" within the meaning of s 9 of the Act, and that the date of the "preliminary notice" for the purposes of s 9 (3) was the date of the making of that claim; and (3) that as regards payments made by the defenders to account which might or might not have been made more than five years prior to the raising of the action, these constituted "relevant acknowledgments" of the claims within the meaning of s 10 (1) (a) of the Act, and the obligation having been acknowledged within five years of the obligation first becoming enforceable it could thereafter only prescribe by reason of the 20 year prescriptive period provided in s 7.

Held, (1) that there were no averments of a consolidated demand for payment or other facts sufficient to establish that there was a continuing account, but rather the builders' averments were of three separate transactions and thus the earlier claims were not saved by the terms of para 1 of Sched 2 to the 1973 Act (p 324D-G); (2) that averments on record relating to a "relevant claim" in an arbitration were irrelevant since there had been no concluded agreement to arbitrate and no arbitration had taken place (p 324I-K); (3) that a relevant acknowledgment required to have been made within five years before the raising of the action to prevent the claim from having prescribed (p 325D-H); and averments in respect of the first two invoices in date *excluded* from probation, and proof before answer *allowed* in respect of the final invoice.

Dicta in *H G Robertson v Murray International Metals Ltd*, 1988 SLT 747, *approved*.

Action of payment

R Peter & Co Ltd and its liquidator raised an action against The Pancake Place Ltd for payment of certain unpaid balances contained in each of three invoices.

The case came before the Lord Ordinary (Marnoch) on procedure roll on the defenders' plea that the claims under the first two invoices had prescribed.

Statutory provisions

The Prescription and Limitation (Scotland) Act 1973, as amended, provides:

"4.— . . . (4) In the foregoing subsection 'preliminary notice' in relation to an arbitration means a notice served by one party to the arbitration on the other party or parties requiring him or them to appoint an arbiter or to agree to the appointment of an arbiter, or, where the arbitration agreement or any relevant enactment provides that the reference shall be to a person therein named or designated, a notice requiring him or them to submit the dispute to the person so named or designated. . . .

"6.—(1) If, after the appropriate date, an obligation to which this section applies has subsisted for a continuous period of five years — (a) without any relevant claim having been made in relation to the obligation, and (b) without the subsistence of the obligation having been relevantly acknowledged, then as from the expiration of that period the obligation shall be extinguished: Provided that in its application to an obligation under a bill of exchange or a promissory note this subsection shall have effect as if paragraph (b) thereof were omitted.

"(2) Schedule 1 to this Act shall have effect for defining the obligations to which this section applies.

"(3) In subsection (1) above the reference to the appropriate date, in relation to an obligation of any kind specified in Schedule 2 to this Act is a reference to the date specified in that Schedule in relation to obligations of that kind, and in relation to an obligation of any other kind is a reference to the date when the obligation became enforceable. . . .

"7.—(1) If, after the date when any obligation to which this section applies has become enforceable, the obligation has subsisted for a continuous period of twenty years — (a) without any relevant claim having been made in relation to the obligation, and (b) without the subsistence of the obligation having been relevantly acknowledged, then as from the expiration of that period the obligation shall be extinguished: Provided that in its application to an obligation under a bill of exchange or a promissory note this subsection shall have effect as if paragraph (b) thereof were omitted. . . .

"9.—(1) In sections 6, 7 and 8A of this Act the expression 'relevant claim', in relation to an obligation, means a claim made by or on behalf of the creditor for implement or part-implement of the obligation, being a claim made — (a) in appropriate proceedings, . . .

"(3) Where a claim which, in accordance with the foregoing provisions of this section, is a relevant claim for the purposes of sections 6, 7, 8 or 8A of this Act is made in an arbitration, and the nature of the claim has been stated in a preliminary notice relating to that arbitration, the date when the notice was served shall be taken for those purposes to be the date of the making of the claim. . . .

"10.—(1) The subsistence of an obligation shall be regarded for the purposes of sections 6, 7 and 8A of this Act as having been relevantly acknowledged if, and only if, either of the following conditions is satisfied, namely — (a) that there has been such performance by or on behalf of the debtor towards implement of the obligation as clearly indicates that the obligation still subsists. . . .

"[Sched 2] 1.—(1) This paragraph applies to any obligation, not being part of a banking transaction, to pay money in respect of — (a) goods supplied on sale or hire, or (b) services rendered, in a series of transactions between the same parties (whether under a single contract or under several contracts) and charged on continuing account. . . .

(4) The appropriate date in relation to an obligation to which this paragraph applies is the date on which payment for the goods last supplied, or, as the case may be, the services last rendered, became due."

Cases referred to

Garden v Rigg (1734) Mor 11274.
Robertson (H G) v Murray International Metals Ltd, 1988 SLT 747.

Textbook referred to

Walker, *The Law of Prescription and Limitation of Actions in Scotland* (4th ed), p 65.

On 22 March 1991 the Lord Ordinary *sustained* the defenders' second plea in law excluding from probation the claims related to the earlier invoices and quoad ultra *allowed* a proof before answer.

LORD MARNOCH.—In this action the pursuers seek to recover certain unpaid balances contained in

A each of three invoices which relate to building work carried out or allegedly carried out for the defenders at three separate locations.

The case came before me on procedure roll in respect of the defenders' second plea in law which, as amended at the bar, seeks to exclude from probation the averments in respect of two of the locations on the basis that any obligations to make payment in respect of the relevant invoices have prescribed. The invoices in question were due to be paid in February and July 1983 respectively and it is not disputed that claims in

B respect of these invoices were first added by adjustment on 5 December 1988 which is, of course, well in excess of the quinquennial prescriptive period. In that situation it was further not disputed that the onus was on the pursuers to aver facts and circumstances to overcome the presumption of prescription. However counsel for the pursuers maintained that this had been done in the present case and in support of that submission advanced three distinct propositions to which I now turn.

C

First, it was pointed out that the last in date of the three invoices had been due for payment on or before 27 September 1983 and that it was accepted that in respect of that invoice the action had been raised timeously. In that connection, however, it was now averred by the pursuers that all three transactions had been charged "to the defenders' continuing account" and, under reference to the provisions of para 1 of Sched 2 to the Prescription and Limitation (Scotland) Act

D 1973, it was submitted that the effect of that averment was to "save" the earlier two invoices. In my opinion this submission was ill founded. In the first place, the raising of the action in a form which concluded only for payment of the third invoice and made no reference whatever to either of the earlier invoices seems to me almost certainly incompatible with the notion of a single obligation arising out of a "continuing account" within the meaning of the statutory provisions. In the second place, I respectfully agree with Lord

E McCluskey's interpretation of these provisions in the case of *H G Robertson v Murray International Metals Ltd*, 1988 SLT at p 749 where, in agreement with Professor Walker, he conceives of them as covering the situation where "parties are repeatedly transacting and one of them, usually the creditor, keeps a record of what is due but does not bother to render a specific account on the occasion of each transaction". In that case there was a specific averment that "the defenders . . . were not invoiced for every item separately". No

F such averment appears in the present case and, on the contrary, the pursuers themselves have lodged in process three invoices (whose terms are incorporated in the pleadings) which bear different dates and which appear, on the face of them, to be entirely separate and distinct. In the words of senior counsel for the defenders, there are here no averments of a "consolidated demand for payment", which I accept is of the essence of the statutory requirement that the transactions to which it applies be "charged on continuing account". In all the foregoing circumstances the mere assertion in the pleadings that the various transactions

in the present case were charged by the pursuers "*to the defenders' continuing account*", whatever that G may mean, is not, in my opinion, sufficient.

The second submission by counsel for the pursuers was based on averments at the end of cond 3 to the effect that, by various specified letters in 1984 and 1985, "the first named pursuers and the defenders gave each other preliminary notice stating the nature of their respective claims with a view to arbitration". It was submitted that, as regards the invoices in question, these averments were averments of a claim made in arbitration proceedings and thus "a relevant claim" H within the meaning of s 9 of the 1973 Act. In particular, it was submitted that in terms of s 9 (3) of the Act the date of the "preliminary notice" given by the pursuers should be taken to be the date of the making of that claim. Before I examine that submission I should record that counsel for the pursuers quite specifically did not maintain that I could, or should, read into these averments any prior agreement between the parties to proceed to arbitration. I should also record that it is a matter of averment by the pur- I suers that, following the exchange of the aforesaid correspondence, the parties did not, as matter of fact, proceed to arbitration. In these circumstances I am of opinion that counsel for the defenders were well founded in their argument that the averments in question were irrelevant and that, before there can be made any "relevant claim" in an arbitration within the meaning of s 9, there must be in existence an actual arbitration process which presupposes, at the least, a concluded agreement to arbitrate. Accordingly, I do J not accept the submission on behalf of the pursuers that the references to arbitration should be construed as including references to "putative arbitration" and it is, I think, instructive that "preliminary notice" is defined in s 4 (4) of the Act as meaning, "a notice served by one party to the arbitration on the other party or parties". In my opinion these words go a long way to supporting the construction contended for by counsel for the defenders.

I turn now to the third and last submission advanced K on behalf of the pursuers which was based on averments that, in respect of each of the two invoices in question, the defenders had made certain payments "to account". It was argued that these payments could be seen as performance by the defenders towards implement of the obligations such as clearly indicated that the obligations still subsisted within the meaning and effect of s 10 (1) (a) of the 1973 Act. In short, such payments constituted "relevant acknowledgments" of the claims in question. In this connection, the L defenders' position was that there were no averments that any of these payments had been made within five years of the raising of the action and that, on the contrary, the strong inference from the terms of the two invoices was that they had been made very much earlier. It was also pointed out that the averments in question were denied by the defenders who in turn averred that the pursuers were "not entitled to any further payments". At worst, therefore, a preliminary proof on prescription would be required.

In the event, senior counsel for the pursuers
A accepted that there were no averments of any payment
to account or "relevant acknowledgment" of either of
the disputed claims within the five year period preceding
the raising of the action. He argued, however, that,
on a proper construction of the 1973 Act, no such
averments were necessary. According to this argument
the provisions of s 6 of the 1973 Act regarding the
quinquennial prescription had to be seen in the
context or framework of the provisions of s 7 of the
Act which was concerned with the 20 year negative
B prescriptive period. In this connection, it was particularly
instructive that, in terms of s 7 (2) of the Act, the
20 year prescriptive period applied to an obligation of
any kind "including an obligation to which s 6 of this
Act applies". The provisions of s 6 were accordingly
"circumscribed" by the provisions of s 7 and, against
that background, it was submitted that, where, as in
the present case, the existence of an obligation had
been acknowledged within five years, that was conclusive
against the continued operation of the quinquennial
C prescription. To put the matter another way, so
the argument went, the provisions of s 6 of the Act
only operated for five years after the "appropriate
date" which, in terms of s 6 (3) and apart from the
special situations dealt with in Sched 2 to the Act, was
the date when the obligation in question first became
enforceable. If the existence of the obligation was
acknowledged within that period, then it mattered not
that no "relevant claim" was made for more than five
years thereafter. Finally, according to this argument,
D an obligation, having once been acknowledged, could
still be "caught" by the 20 year prescriptive period
provided for in s 7 and this, it was said, was the only
construction which gave content to the reference in s
7 (2) to obligations "to which s 6 of this Act applies".

In my opinion, this last submission on behalf of the
pursuers, while both interesting and original, is
unsound. In the first place, I have to observe that the
only difference in wording between s 6 (1) and s 7 (1)
E of the Act is that in the former reference is made to
"the appropriate date" whereas in the latter the reference
is to "the date when any obligation to which this
section applies has become enforceable". Apart from
the special situations dealt with in Sched 2 to the Act
the respective provisions are accordingly identical in
their effect. If, therefore, the argument were correct
that any "relevant acknowledgment" is conclusive
against the continued operation of the provisions of s
6, I have great difficulty in seeing why such an
acknowledgment should not also be conclusive against
F the continued operation of the provisions of s 7 of the
Act. In the second place, it respectfully seems to me
that other content can readily be found for the reference
to what might be termed s 6 obligations in s 7 (2)
of the Act in that, for purposes of calculating the 20
year prescriptive period, the provisions of s 6 (4) anent
the disregard of periods during which the debtor
labours under fraud or error and while the creditor is
under legal disability have apparently no application.
Thirdly, I am of opinion that the construction for
which the pursuers contend involves reading into the

opening provisions of s 6 (1) words such as "from
and" so that these provisions would read "If, from and G
after the appropriate date, an obligation . . . has subsisted
for a continuous period of five years". In the circumstances
I see no reason whatever for doing that
and, on the contrary, I consider that counsel for the
defenders were correct in reading these provisions in
an unrestricted way and as thus covering the situation
where at any time after the "appropriate date" an
obligation has subsisted for a period of five years
without either its subsistence having been
acknowledged or a claim having been made. I may say H
that I am fortified in this view by noting that it is
shared by Professor David M Walker in his book
entitled *The Law of Prescription and Limitation of
Actions in Scotland* (4th ed), at p 65.

Having found against the pursuers so far, it is
unnecessary for me to examine in any detail the
further proposition that the obligation to pay money
in respect of each of the invoices in question was, on
any view, an indivisible one, with the result that any
payment made under either invoice — even on the I
express basis that no further sum was due — was conclusive
of the existence of that obligation, and thus
against the operation of prescription. In principle, I
find it difficult to fault that proposition, although it
does mean that, where monetary obligations are
involved, the more refined provisions of s 10 (1) of the
Act are difficult, if not impossible, to operate. In the
particular circumstances of the present case, however,
I agree with senior counsel for the defenders that it
would be going "too far too fast", as the saying goes, J
to assume that for purposes of the Act each invoice
reflected a single monetary obligation. Accordingly,
had I been in favour of the pursuers in their first submission,
I would still have thought it necessary to
allow a preliminary proof before disposing finally of
the defenders' second plea in law. As it is, I shall
sustain that plea and quoad ultra — that is as regards
the latest in date of the three invoices — allow a proof
before answer, which was the course accepted by both
parties as being appropriate in these circumstances. K

In conclusion, I should perhaps record that there
was cited to me during the debate the old case of
Garden v Rigg. On close analysis I do not find it
altogether easy to extract the true ratio of that decision
and I think, indeed, that the report of the case rather
suggests that at common law a debtor could, perhaps
inadvertently, defeat his own plea of prescription by
himself ascribing a general or indefinite payment as
having been made towards one of several obligations.
In that respect the provisions of s 10 (1) of the 1973 L
Act are not perhaps wholly synonymous with those of
the common law.

---

*Counsel for Pursuers, Dean of Faculty (Johnston,
QC), D I Mackay; Solicitors, Simpson & Marwick, WS
— Counsel for Defenders, Drummond Young, QC,
Dunlop; Solicitors, Brodies, WS.*

G D M

Shanks v British Broadcasting Corporation

OUTER HOUSE

LORD OSBORNE

31 MAY 1991

Process — Mode of inquiry — Proof or jury trial — Defamation — Complex issues of fact — Difficult and complex issues of mixed fact and law — Television broadcast in which conduct in business of pursuer and another stated to be fraudulent or inept — Pursuer having involvement in various different capacities in a multiplicity of limited companies — Companies entering into a series of complex inter-company transactions and schemes — Separate defences of veritas and fair comment — Nine separate innuendos set out — Whether "special cause" for withholding case from jury trial — Court of Session Act 1988 (c 36), s 9.

In an action of damages for defamation the pursuer, a practising accountant, claimed that he had been defamed in a television broadcast which, he averred, falsely and calumniously represented, directly and by innuendo, inter alia, that his conduct in business was fraudulent or inept, that he had been guilty of disgraceful conduct and breach of trust, and that he had been guilty of conduct unbecoming of a chartered accountant. In his pleadings the pursuer set out nine separate innuendos. He further averred that certain statements had been made in the broadcast for the purposes inter alia of discrediting and defaming him. The defenders averred that the statements of fact broadcast were true, and that the expressions of opinion were fair comment honestly made on matters of public interest, and based on facts which were essentially true and which afforded a reasonable basis for the comments. The pleadings disclosed that over a substantial period of time the pursuer was said to have been involved in a series of inter-company transactions including "hive down" operations and other dealings. The pursuer had acted in the different capacities of accountant, financial director, director and shareholder in the course of these dealings. Twenty seven different companies, nine changes of company name and eight inter-company dealings were referred to on record. The pursuer had stated no plea to the relevancy of the defenders' averments. The defenders had stated a plea to the relevancy of certain of the pursuer's averments.

On procedure roll the defenders sought to exclude from probation, as being irrelevant, the pursuer's averments relating to material not published in the broadcast. The defenders argued that if these averments were not excluded from probation they nonetheless amounted to matters of doubtful relevancy, rendering the case unsuitable for trial by jury. They further argued that in any event special cause existed which rendered the case unsuitable for trial by jury. The defenders submitted that there were other averments of doubtful relevance in the pursuer's pleadings including averments as to the defenders' said alleged intentions in broadcasting certain state-

ments. They further submitted that the case raised difficult and complex issues of mixed fact and law. The defenders argued that even if the intention of a defamer was relevant in a question of possible aggravation of damages, the law on enhancement of damages was unsettled and it would be difficult to charge a jury properly. They contended that the complexity of the factual background to the action gave rise to the risk of confusion and misapprehension if the case were to be determined by a jury. They further submitted that in order to exercise a critical judgment of the pursuer's conduct it would be necessary to have an understanding of the fiduciary duties owed by a director of a limited company to the company, the matter of professional duties owed by an accountant to his client, and the concepts of conflicts of interest in different circumstances. The defenders also argued that the two separate defences of veritas and fair comment would involve consideration of the two different roles which the element of truth played in each of those defences. The pursuer argued inter alia that defamation actions were particularly appropriate for trial by jury and contended that there was no case in which a defamation action had been withheld from trial by jury on account of "special cause".

Held, (1) that the pursuer's averments relating to the unpublished material might be relevant to the defence of fair comment and that the defenders' motion to exclude them from probation should be refused (p 336G-H); (2) that in determining whether "special cause" had been shown defamation cases should be treated no differently from other cases, although what might amount to "special cause" might be different, and the many cases of reparation actions in which "special cause" was argued were of only limited assistance to the extent that they set out the criteria to be taken account of by the court in exercising its sound discretion (p 337E-F and J-K); and (3) that "special cause" had been shown for withholding the case from jury trial since (i) a jury was likely to be confused by the complexity of the averments relating to the pursuer's professional activities over a substantial period of time and to miss the point of the various dealings referred to (p 338D-E); (ii) a jury would likewise be confused by the matters requiring to be considered in determining the professional duties incumbent on the pursuer and the standards of conduct by which he ought to be judged (p 338F); (iii) a substantial volume of educational evidence would require to be led to enable the jury to understand the point of the various dealings referred to and to judge the pursuer's conduct (p 338G); (iv) the range and variety of different issues and defences gave rise to a serious risk that a jury would become very confused if faced with the necessity of making a series of separate decisions on these matters (p 338J-L); (v) passages relating to the unpublished material were of doubtful relevancy and the uncertainty in law about the effect on damages of the defenders' intentions would make it difficult to charge a jury (pp 338L-339C); (vi) the pursuer's averments of loss were confused and unclear (p 339C); and (vii) the difficult and delicate issues of mixed fact and law concerning the fiduciary duties of directors of companies, the duties of accountants and the possible conflicts of interest in the pursuer's conduct rendered the case unsuitable for jury trial (p 339D-F); and issues *refused* and proof before answer *allowed* on the whole averments in the closed record as amended.

Observed, (1) that in considering the issue of "special cause" in terms of s 9 of the Court of Session Act 1988, it was appropriate to look at the authorities decided under s 4 of the Evidence (Scotland) Act 1866 (p 336J-K); and (2) that in determining whether "special cause" existed for witholding a case from jury trial the citation of English authority and practice was of no assistance to the court (p 337I-J).

Action of damages

James Shanks raised an action of damages against the British Broadcasting Corporation, claiming that he had been defamed by them.

The case called on procedure roll before the Lord Ordinary (Osborne) when, on the unopposed motion of the defenders, the Lord Ordinary allowed amendment of the record by the addition of a plea in law to the effect that the case was unsuitable for jury trial. Thereafter debate proceeded on the defenders' pleas to the relevancy and the new plea in law.

Statutory provisions

The Court of Session Act 1988 provides:

"9. The Lord Ordinary may allow a proof—. . . (b) in any action enumerated [in section 11 of this Act], if the parties to the action consent thereto or if special cause is shown. . . .

"11. Subject to section 9 (b) of this Act, the following actions if remitted to probation shall be tried by jury—(a) an action of damages for personal injuries; (b) an action for libel or defamation".

The Evidence (Scotland) Act 1866 provides:

"4. If both parties consent thereto, or if special cause be shown, it shall be competent to the Lord Ordinary to take proof in the manner above provided in section first hereof in any cause which may be in dependence before him, notwithstanding of the provisions contained in the Court of Sessions Act, 1825, section twenty-eight, and the provisions contained in the Court of Session Act, 1850, section forty-nine; and the judgment to be pronounced by him upon such proof shall be subject to review in the like manner as other judgments pronounced by him."

Cases referred to

Anderson v Grieve, 1970 SLT (Notes) 39.
Bygate v Edinburgh Corporation, 1967 SLT (Notes) 65.
Cowie v London, Midland and Scottish Railway Co, 1934 SLT 409; 1934 SC 433.
Cunningham v Duncan & Jamieson (1889) 16 R 383.
Dornan v Forrest, 1932 SLT 365; 1932 SC 562.

Gardner v A B Fleming & Co Ltd, 1969 SLT (Notes) 93.
Graham v John Paterson & Son Ltd, 1938 SLT 174; 1938 SC 119.
Higgins v Burton, 1968 SLT (Notes) 14.
Hines v Davidson, 1935 SLT 137; 1935 SC 30.
Hunter v Hanley, 1955 SLT 213; 1955 SC 200.
Lamond v The Daily Record (Glasgow) Ltd, 1923 SLT 512.
Lever Brothers Ltd v Daily Record and Mail Ltd, 1909 1 SLT 553; (sub nom *Lever Brothers Ltd v The Daily Record (Glasgow) Ltd*) 1909 SC 1004.
Macdonald v Martin, 1935 SLT 379; 1935 SC 621.
McFaull v Compania Navigacion Sota y Anzar, 1937 SLT 118.
McGinnigle v McLuskie, 1974 SLT (Notes) 34.
McGinty v Smith & McLean Ltd, 1964 SLT (Notes) 9.
McKenzie v Donachie, 1969 SLT (Notes) 3.
Moffat v London Express Newspapers Ltd, 1951 SLT (Notes) 8.
Ogston & Tennant Ltd v The Daily Record, Glasgow, Ltd, 1909 1 SLT 551; 1910 2 SLT 230; 1909 SC 1000.
Rhind v Kemp & Co (1893) 1 SLT 367.
Rigley v Remington Rand Ltd, 1964 SLT (Notes) 100.
Robertson v Bannigan, 1965 SLT (Notes) 90; 1965 SC 20.
Robertson v T & H Smith Ltd, 1962 SLT (Notes) 64; 1962 SC 628.
Rogers v Orr, 1939 SLT 43 and 403; 1939 SC 121.
Taylor v Dumbarton Tramways Co, 1918 1 SLT 391; 1918 SC (HL) 96.
Taylor v National Coal Board, 1953 SLT 246; 1953 SC 349.
Walker v Pitlochry Motor Co, 1930 SLT 367; 1930 SC 565.
White v Dixon (1875) 2 R 904.

Textbooks referred to

Cooper, *Defamation and Verbal Injury* (2nd ed), pp 238, 265 and 269.
Gatley, *Libel and Slander* (8th ed), para 1265.
Gloag and Henderson, *An Introduction to the Law of Scotland* (9th ed), p 607.
Maclaren, *Court of Session Practice*, pp 546, 585 and 586.
Maxwell, *Practice of the Court of Session*, p 297.

On 31 May 1991 the Lord Ordinary *upheld* the defenders' new plea in law and *allowed* a proof before answer on the whole averments in the closed record as amended.

LORD OSBORNE.—In this action the pursuer seeks damages of £900,000 from the defenders on the ground that he has been defamed by them. The pursuer avers that on 14 November 1985, between the hours of 8 and 8.25 pm, the defenders broadcast on BBC1 Scotland a programme entitled "Keeping Bad Companies", a programme in the series known as the "Reid Report". The said programme was produced by David Scott and presented by James Reid, both of whom were at the relevant time employees of the

defenders. The pursuer avers that the programme was
intended to and did defame both the pursuer and
David Cunningham, who was at the relevant time a
practising advocate and an accountant, by stating that
their conduct in business was fraudulent or grossly
inept. The pursuer produces a written transcript of
the broadcast, the whole terms of which are adopted
and held as repeated as part of his pleadings. There is
no dispute between the parties as regards the basic fact
of the production and broadcast of the programme
concerned.

The pursuer specifies his case in this way. He avers
that the presenter, James Reid, made the following
statements in the course of the broadcast: "Together
they have lost millions of pounds of other people's
money. In tonight's 'Reid Report' I am saying their
conduct in business has either been fraudulent or
grossly inept. Posing as saviours, they have taken over
businesses but instead of saving them, the businesses
have collapsed with hundreds of thousands of pounds
of debts. They have betrayed the loyalty that we
normally place in their respective professions. Individuals, large and small businesses, have all been ruth-
lessly exploited as the two men enjoyed expensive
cars, top quality restaurants, and a remarkable fast
spending existence."

[His Lordship described particular allegations made
in the programme and continued:]

In cond 5 of his summons the pursuer sets out his
grounds of action. He avers that the representations
made in the said broadcast were false and calumnious.
The said broadcast falsely and calumniously represented that the pursuer had abused his position of
trust in respect of the Fraser Construction, Alex
Ferguson, Gentil Soap and Forthprint businesses in
order to defraud shareholders and creditors for the
benefit of himself. In describing the pursuer as posing
as a saviour, the broadcast implied that the pursuer's
efforts to rescue the businesses in which he was
involved were not genuine. Since the pursuer commenced in business on his own account, the cars
driven by him were his own personal property and
were not charged to any of the businesses with which
the pursuer was associated. In its reference to the
company George Martin & Sons of Paisley, with
which the pursuer was also involved, the broadcast
implied that the pursuer was dealing dishonestly with
the assets of the business and that the pursuer had
endeavoured to conceal information from the receiver
of the company. The development of the chocolate
business of Alex Ferguson (Confectioners) Ltd was a
serious business undertaking. The chocolates produced were generally considered to be excellent and
had a shelf life of about three months. The observations in the programme of David Harris and Alex
Clark on the company's chocolate production gave the
television viewer to understand that the pursuer was
not capable of manufacturing chocolates and that his
only purpose in so doing was to obtain money from
third parties dishonestly. This innuendo was enforced
by the playing of an excerpt from the music of "Big
Spender". The presenter deliberately portrayed the

pursuer as a ruthless exploiter of third parties and one
who abused their trust in order to finance high living
with money which should have been paid to creditors
of the companies with which he was associated and the
exploitation of which caused their collapse. There was
no connection between the chocolate business and the
soap business and, in any event, the pursuer had no
interest at all in the soap company. The purpose of
James Reid's and David Harris's suggestions anent the
use of the same moulds for the production of chocolate
and soap was to ridicule, discredit and defame the
pursuer. Likewise, with reference to the creditors'
meeting in the Edinburgh hotel in July in relation to
Ferguson's debts, the explicit suggestion is that the
pursuer had personally incurred the debts and then
concealed them from the liquidator.

There then follow in the pursuer's case certain averments which were the subject of a particular argument
to which I shall make reference in due course. These
are as follows: "When asked, in the course of a lengthy
interview with James Reid prior to the said broadcast
about the extent of the debts of companies with which
he had been associated, the pursuer took care to
explain that the vast proportion of the debts related to
the Fraser Construction Co whose deficit was well in
excess of £2½ million and in any event existed before
any association between the pursuer and the company.
He also made it clear to James Reid that the moneys
owed were owed not by the pursuer but by the companies and they were only owed by him to the extent that
he was the guarantor in respect of a small number of
debts. None of the pursuer's reasonable explanations
on these matters was incorporated into the broadcast
and the broadcast deliberately left the television
viewer with the impression that it was only by virtue
of the pursuer's association with the companies that
debts of such a magnitude had been created."

The pursuer's averments continue as follows:
"Likewise, the statement that the payment of £75,000
to creditors favoured those in whom he had a personal
interest or was a friend or associate, was designed to
suggest to the television viewer that there were
improper motives behind the payment of the debts.
The pursuer has had no contact with the said Robert
Beattie since 1974 when the pursuer required to terminate their business relationship. Again the suggestion
to the television viewer is that it was the association
of the pursuer with the joint business venture with
Robert Beattie which led to their collapse."

In response to these averments, the defenders, in ans
5, set forth their defences to the pursuer's claim. After
making a number of admissions concerning certain of
the pursuer's averments, to which it is not necessary
for me to refer in any detail, the defenders continue as
follows. The statements of fact made in the said broadcast were all true or at least substantially true. The
expressions of opinion set forth in said broadcast were
fair comment, fairly and honestly made on matters of
public interest and were based on facts which were
substantially true and which afforded a reasonable
foundation for the comments made therein.

[His Lordship narrated further averments in explanation by the defenders and the pursuer's answers thereto and continued:]

In cond 6 of his summons, the pursuer further elaborates the ground of action. In particular there are there set forth a number of innuendos. I consider it necessary to narrate these averments in detail. They are as follows. The said broadcast falsely and calumniously represented, and was understood by members of the public and in particular friends, professional and business colleagues, clients and bankers of the pursuer, to represent directly and by innuendo that the pursuer was dishonest, and that he had been guilty of fraudulent and disgraceful conduct and breach of trust. The pursuer was in practice as a chartered accountant at the time of the broadcast and the programme gave prominence to that fact. It falsely and calumniously represented and was intended to and understood to represent directly and by innuendo that the pursuer was guilty of conduct which was unbecoming of a chartered accountant and that he was not fit to continue in that profession. Likewise, it falsely and calumniously represented and was intended to and understood to represent directly and by innuendo that the pursuer was a ruthless exploiter of innocent third parties' business interests whose sole interest was to line his own pocket in order to finance an extravagant lifestyle at the expense of others and that he should not be permitted to control a business. The said broadcast also made inter alia the various allegations more particularly hereinbefore referred to in art 4 of condescendence. Each and all of the said representations made concerning the pursuer are untrue and grossly defamatory of the pursuer. The defenders have slandered the pursuer by broadcasting the said programme containing the said representations condescended on. Prior to the broadcasting of the programme there was an extensive advertising campaign on television, in the *Radio Times*, and in the *Glasgow Herald* newspaper, drawing attention to the forthcoming programme. As a consequence the programme was watched by a very large audience including many members of the business and financial community. In consequence of the said broadcast the pursuer has suffered the serious loss and damage hereinafter condescended on. The defenders' response to this condescendence is to make a number of admissions, to which I need not refer, but otherwise to deny the pursuer's averments.

In cond and ans 7 there are to be found the averments of the pursuer and the answers of the defenders concerning the damage which the pursuer claims to have sustained as a consequence of the defenders' alleged defamation. Since arguments were addressed to me concerning these matters, it is necessary for me to narrate these averments, in order to make sense of what I have to say subsequently. The pursuer claims that he has suffered serious injury to his feelings, standing and professional reputation as a result of the broadcast by the defenders of the said false and calumnious allegations. The defamatory representations made in the said programme have obtained wide currency by reason of their broadcast on the defenders' BBC1 Scotland network at peak viewing time. The pursuer's social position and professional standing have been injured by the defamatory representations made in the said programme. Friends, professional and business colleagues, clients and bankers, have contacted the pursuer to ask for an explanation of the various matters canvassed in the said programme. Prior to the broadcast of the programme, the pursuer's services as a chartered accountant had been in great demand and he had built up a thriving and expanding practice, being able in particular to expand into newly refurbished offices on four floors at 22 Alva Street, Edinburgh. After the said broadcast, clients ceased to engage the pursuer and demand for his services fell off dramatically. The pursuer's creditworthiness and in particular his creditworthiness with his banking connections has been seriously affected. His integrity, and in particular, his integrity with finance houses, has been seriously impaired. His practice as a chartered accountant and his business dealings have been seriously affected by the said programme. The success of the pursuer's practice and business interests were substantially dependent upon his reputation. At the time of the broadcast of the said programme, the pursuer's said practice and business interests were thriving and he was looking forward to a period of steady expansion and growth. To that end, he had engaged additional staff, expended moneys on additional office equipment, and moved into the said larger premises. Due to the adverse publicity occasioned by the programme and the slur on his character, the anticipated expansion and growth did not materialise.

The earning capacity of the pursuer's practice was severely prejudiced as was his whole future in the professional and business world. He qualified as a chartered accountant in February 1957 and has the qualifications MA, LLB, CA. In the course of a long and successful career, prior to the said broadcast, he was employed inter alia by Pilkingtons as their tax adviser and by Plessey and GEC. From 1971 he was a self employed consultant with various companies with a strong Scottish emphasis. He commenced practice on his own account in 1981. In the first four years of practice his net income, before tax, increased from £8,021 to £111,292. It was forecast that his net income would grow to £121,500 in the year to 30 April 1986 and to £142,000 in the year to 30 April 1987. Thereafter, it was forecast that his net income would level out at approximately £150,000 per annum before tax, having been in practice for some seven years. In consequence of the said programme, his income dropped and his business made a loss of £34,155 in the year to 30 April 1986. In the three years prior to the broadcast of the programme, in November 1985, the turnover of the pursuer's business was £329,071.59. Over the three year period the annual turnover increased from £74,329 to £190,680.

The pursuer reasonably believes that the same level of growth would have been maintained over the following three years. Accordingly the pursuer would have enjoyed a turnover of £900,000, whereas, as a consequence of the said defamation, his turnover in the said period since the broadcast, to 31 October 1988, has totalled £129,741. After deductions for tax of £100,000, the pursuer's loss of income over the three year period is £670,000. Allowing for a small continuing increase in turnover thereafter the pursuer reasonably anticipates that over a six year period his gross income would be approximately £1,400,000. After deduction of overheads of 40 per cent his net loss of income over the period is £840,000. As a consequence of the said defamation all of the pursuer's 13 employees left his employment, and most of his clients removed their files. The pursuer required to vacate the four floor office building in Alva Street and effectively commence his practice anew from home. Because of the substantial fall in the pursuer's income, he was unable to meet the borrowings of the business which had been incurred in connection with the expansion into larger premises and the equipping of them. The creditors were not prepared to give the pursuer time to pay and he was the recipient of numerous writs which have caused him much distress and hardships as he endeavoured to find the means to settle with creditors without at the same time becoming bankrupt. Of the 48 clients listed in the years to 30 November 1985, who produced the income of £190,680, only 10 remained as a source of income in the year to 30 November 1986. Of the total of 14 clients who were the source of the pursuer's practice income in the year to 30 November 1986, six were new clients who were prepared to use the pursuer's services. Of the eight clients in 1986 who had been clients in 1985, two terminated the pursuer's agency but were persuaded by him to continue it.

Further, the said defamation had a traumatic effect on the pursuer's domestic life. All of his family were greatly affected emotionally by the said broadcast and by the unwanted attention that followed upon it. The pursuer was heartbroken at the sight of his family suffering. It was because of the extreme financial circumstances to which the pursuer was reduced as a consequence of the defamation that he was having to work every day of the week. The pursuer reasonably anticipates that it will take him a period of at least six years from the date of the defamation to restore his practice to the income level which he previously enjoyed. His reputation and earning capacity have been seriously damaged as a result of the broadcast by the defenders of the said defamatory representations. The pursuer has suffered a serious loss of income. He has lost and will continue to lose earnings of a substantial nature. In these circumstances the sum sued for is a reasonable estimate of the loss, injury and damage suffered by the pursuer.

In answer to this statement of the pursuer's claim of damages, the defenders aver that by about the summer of 1985 the pursuer's accountancy business had begun to decline. He fell out with several of his staff upon whom he relied heavily for the efficient operation of his accountancy business, as he spent much of his time in connection with the Fraser Construction and Alex Ferguson businesses. In about the autumn of 1985 two individuals whose services he had engaged on a self employed basis left him. They had to raise actions against him before he would pay them the remuneration to which they were entitled. They set up business with another accountant and many of the pursuer's clients left the pursuer preferring the accountancy services of those said individuals. In the course of his public examination in relation to the winding up of Sales, the pursuer stated that he lost all his staff on the date that company went into liquidation, i e 8 November 1985. The defenders believe and aver that that statement of the pursuer was true. However, they aver that more recently the pursuer has commenced business as a chartered accountant in the Aberdeen area and his business is believed to be prospering. By letter dated 5 January 1987 to the said liquidator of Owald Nine Ltd, the pursuer informed him that his financial position had steadily improved in the course of 1986. In the closing passages of cond 7, the pursuer sets out his responses to the defenders' averments in ans 7, but I do not require to refer to these.

When this case came before me in procedure roll, at the outset the defenders had three preliminary pleas, nos 1, 2 and 3 of their pleas in law. No preliminary pleas were stated for the pursuer. At the commencement of the debate, counsel for the defenders sought leave to amend the defenders' pleadings by the addition of a new plea in law, of a preliminary character. The plea which he sought to add by amendment was in the following terms: "The cause giving rise to difficult questions of fact and law, any inquiry should be by means of proof." There being no objection to this proposed amendment, I allowed it, the new plea in law becoming no 4 for the defenders; the defenders' existing pleas nos 4 to 8 were, as a consequence, renumbered as pleas nos 5 to 9. I should also mention that at the outset of the debate counsel for the defenders indicated to me that he did not wish to argue plea in law no 2 for the defenders, a preliminary plea which related to averments which had in fact been removed from the pursuer's pleadings. Accordingly, on his invitation, I repelled plea in law no 2 for the defenders. In this situation the debate took place upon pleas nos 1, 3 and 4 for the defenders. It is appropriate at this stage to note that among the defenders' pleas in law on the merits of the case are to be found plea in law no 7 which reflects a defence of veritas, and plea in law no 8 in which the defence of fair comment is stated.

Outlining the defenders' general position, counsel indicated to me that the main issue in the debate was the question of whether investigation of the pursuer's case should be by way of jury trial, or alternatively by way of proof before answer. In addition, it was indicated that the defenders were seeking the exclusion from inquiry of certain averments in the closed record on the basis of the plea in law no 3. These averments, to which I have already drawn attention, are concerned with what is said to have been a lengthy interview which took place betwen the pursuer and James Reid prior to the broadcast which is the subject of the action.

The pursuer's initial position in the debate was that the whole case, as it stood at the outset of the debate,

A   was appropriate and relevant for inquiry by way of jury trial. However, during the course of the speech by senior counsel for the pursuer towards the end of the debate, the pursuer sought leave to make certain amendments to his pleadings. There was no objection to the making of these amendments by the defenders. Accordingly, I allowed them to be made. [His Lordship described the amendments and continued:]

B   Counsel for the defenders began by addressing me on his motion to exclude the averments which I have mentioned relating to the pre-broadcast interview between James Reid and the pursuer. The defenders' simple position was that that passage dealt exclusively with matters which were not broadcast. The answer to the question of whether the programme was defamatory had to be decided by reference to what the programme did contain. What was said in unpublished material was not relevant. The pursuer had sought to justify the relevance of this passage by saying that it was pertinent to the defence of fair comment. Any such connection, if indeed there was

C   one, was not made clear in the pursuer's averments themselves. If the pursuer's position was that the defenders knew to be true certain exculpatory circumstances, which they had suppressed in the programme, the defenders accepted that that would be a matter relevant to the fairness of any comment which the defenders had made. However, there were no averments to that effect. It was not sufficient for the pursuer to say in his averments simply that he had made certain statements to James Reid. To render

D   such material relevant to the issue of fair comment, it would be necessary for him to go further and to relate what had been said prior to the broadcast specifically to the defence of fair comment. If the court was not prepared to exclude the passage concerned from any factual investigation, it should at least determine that that passage was of doubtful relevancy, rendering the case unsuitable for trial by jury.

E   Turning to the principal submission for the defenders, it was argued that in the circumstances of this case, "special cause" existed, which justified the action being withheld from trial by jury. The defenders of course recognised that, in terms of s 11 of the Court of Session Act 1988, it was provided that an action, such as the present one, for defamation "if remitted to probation shall be tried by jury", subject to s 9 (b) of that Act, which provides that the Lord Ordinary may allow a proof in any action enumerated in s 11 of the Act, "if the parties to the action consent

F   thereto or if special cause is shown". The defenders accepted that the cause for withholding a case from trial by jury must be "special" to the case in question. Decisions made by the court under s 4 of the Evidence (Scotland) Act 1866, the statutory predecessor of s 9 of the said Act of 1988, could be of assistance in indicating the approach which the court ought to take in the exercise of its discretion. One such case was *Walker v Pitlochry Motor Co.* At 1930 SLT, pp 372 and 373 guidance was given as to the approach which should be taken. Whether "special cause" existed was a question to be determined, not by reference to any

G   legal principle or category, but as a matter of sound discretion. "Special cause" was a flexible concept. The pursuer's ordinary right was to have his case heard by a jury. It was only where the circumstances were not ordinary, but special, that the court had a discretion to withhold the case from that mode of investigation (*Graham v Paterson & Son Ltd*, 1938 SLT at p 176). In Maclaren, *Court of Session Practice*, at p 546, it was indicated that "special cause" had been shown where actions were of doubtful relevance, were partly relevant and partly irrelevant, where there was difficulty in adjusting issues, and where there were

H   questions of great delicacy, both of fact and law. Maxwell in his work on *The Practice of the Court of Session* at p 297 recognised that complexity of fact could amount to "special cause". Further, there could be a jury trial only upon the basis of a properly drawn record. In considering the question of "special cause", the court ought to look at the context of the case as a whole, not simply at the pleadings of one party (*McKenzie v Donachie*). Pursuers could protect them-

I   selves against dubiously relevant defences, the purpose of which was to prevent trial by jury, by stating and insisting upon a plea to the relevancy of such defences or averments by defenders. The pursuer in the present case had stated no relevancy plea to the defenders' averments and accordingly it was proper for the court to take into account all of those averments in judging whether "special cause" existed. The question of whether "special cause" existed had to be judged according to the standards of the time.

J   Decisions showed that the tendency was towards to a less rigorous standard of "special cause" than was once thought necessary before an action appropriated to trial by jury could be sent to proof before a judge without a jury (*Dornan v Forrest*).

K   Counsel for the defenders went on to submit that there were a variety of considerations which, in the past, the court had regarded as constituting "special cause". Among these considerations was the presence in a case of difficult and delicate questions of mixed fact and law. *Bygate v Edinburgh Corporation* was an example of such a case. The court considered that it would have been difficult to charge a jury adequately in the circumstances of that case. That was a test which the court ought to apply in the present case. Further, the presence in a case of factual complexities could, in appropriate circumstances, justify the withholding of that case from trial by jury. That was evident from *Robertson v T & H Smith Ltd*. There

L   Lord Strachan considered that the technical and complex nature of the factual questions raised in the case, which was concerned with an accident which had occurred during a complicated chemical process, constituted "special cause". *Robertson*'s case was mentioned with approval in *Rigley v Remington Rand Ltd*. In the later case of *McGinnigle v McLuskie*, there were involved two different species of contributory negligence. The court withheld the case from trial by jury upon the view that it would be difficult to make the distinction between them clear to the jury and that there was doubt as to whether the jury would fully grasp it and apply it properly. Finally, argued counsel for the defenders, the presence in a case of averments of doubtful relevancy constituted special cause for withholding it from trial by jury. There were numerous examples of that situation, including *Robertson v T & H Smith Ltd*. It was not feasible to hold a jury trial if a plea to the relevancy of averments in the case was left standing. There could be no admission of evidence in a jury trial under reservation of questions of relevancy. In considering questions of "special cause", there was no justification for a difference in treatment of defamation cases and other cases, contrary to the argument of the pursuer. The position was that in ss 9 and 11 of the Court of Session Act 1988 no such distinction was recognised. The proposition to be found in Cooper on *Defamation and Verbal Injury* (2nd ed), at p 265 to the effect that "it is extremely doubtful whether the Court would order proof before a judge instead of jury trial if either party — and particularly if the pursuer — objected to its being so dealt with", in a defamation action was wrong and unsupported by the authority cited, *Rhind v Kemp & Co*.

Focusing attention on the particular circumstances of the present case, counsel for the defenders indicated that there were three branches to the defenders' submission that "special cause" existed. First, the pursuer's pleadings contained numerous examples of averments of doubtful relevancy; secondly the case involved difficult and delicate questions of mixed fact and law; and thirdly the technical and complicated nature of the issues raised amounted to a justification for withholding the case from trial by jury.

Dealing first with matters of doubtful relevancy, attention was drawn principally to three areas of the pursuer's pleadings. In the first place, in cond 5 the passage to the effect that the purpose of James Reid and David Harris's suggestions anent the use of the same moulds for the production of chocolate and soap was to ridicule, discredit and defame the pursuer, was of doubtful relevance. The reference to ridicule was of no significance in the context of an allegation of defamation. Furthermore, this passage of the pursuer's averments related to the alleged purpose of the suggestions concerned. The purpose or intention with which a statement was made was not relevant to the question of whether or not it was defamatory. In any event, if it were accepted that there was some authority to justify the view that such considerations were relevant, the legal standing of that authority was open to doubt. In this connection reference is made to *Cunningham v Duncan & Jamieson*, in which the issue of aggravation of damages in an action of defamation was considered. In that case it was alleged that the defamatory material was part of a systematic plan on the part of the defenders to destroy the pursuer's character. The Lord President at pp 386 and 387 expressed the view that such an allegation would be relevant to possible aggravation of damages. Lord Mure agreed with that view. Lord Shand at pp 388 and 389 appeared to adopt a different position. He stated that the amount of injury done would not be affected by proof of what was the state of mind of the

writer when the defamatory material was written. Lord Adam at p 390 agreed with the majority. The defenders argued that one was left not knowing exactly what was the view of the court in relation to the question of enhancement of damages. It was contrary to the normal principles upon which damages were awarded that they should be in any sense punitive. If the view was taken that the intention of the defamer was relevant, in accordance with the views of the majority in *Cunningham*'s case, it was by no means clear that the principles set out by the majority were applicable in the circumstances of the present case. The pursuer's averments here did not sufficiently clearly demonstrate the allegation of a campaign on the defenders' part against him. In relation to this aspect of the case, there would be very serious difficulties in charging a jury satisfactorily, in the light of the uncertainty in the law and the difficulty of its application to the pursuer's case.

In the second place, assuming that the court was not to accede to the defenders' motion that the averments in cond 5 relating to the contents of the interview between James Reid and the pursuer should be excluded from probation, on any view, those averments were of doubtful relevance. There were no adequate averments to show how the passage concerned was to be related to the defence of fair comment, to which it was argued that it was relevant.

In the third place, the pursuer's averments in cond 7 relating to his pecuniary loss were confused and unclear. At different points in the condescendence the pursuer referred to the earning capacity of his practice, his net income before tax, the turnover of his business, his loss of income after tax, and his gross income. It was not clear upon what basis the pursuer sought to claim damages for pecuniary loss. In the passage in cond 7 in which the pursuer made averments about the level of his business turnover, there was a conflict between the figures and the verbal content of the averments. All of these factors gave rise to doubt as to the pursuer's approach to the quantification of damages for pecuniary loss.

The defenders' arguments relating to the existence of difficult and delicate questions of mixed fact and law and the technical and complicated nature of the issues arising were presented together. Counsel for the defenders argued that the backcloth of fact against which the issues for decision in the present case arose, was extremely complicated. Looking at the matter in a practical way, it was to be observed that no fewer than 27 separate companies were referred to in the pleadings of the parties and documents which were incorporated therein. Nine changes of company name were the subject of averment. There were eight separate inter-company dealings referred to in the pleadings. In the course of these transactions the pursuer was said to have acted in different capacities. He had acted as Martins' accountant and financial adviser, he had acted as chairman and director of New Fraser and Holdings, he had acted as a shareholder and director of Alex Ferguson (Confectioners) Ltd and as director and shareholder of Alex Ferguson (Sales)

Ltd. The complexity of the factual background involved a substantial risk that a jury would be likely to be puzzled and confused and accordingly apt to miss the point of the various dealings. These considerations had influenced the court to decide against juries in the cases of *McKenzie v Donachie* and *McGinty v Smith & McLean Ltd.* It would certainly be very difficult for any judge to present the issues which arose in this case lucidly to a jury without the risk that they would become confused. Looking at the particular issues which arose in the case, there were a number of transactions which it would be difficult for a jury to follow. In particular, the Martins "hive down" scheme was one such. In connection with that matter, any jury would require to consider whether any reasonably competent accountant or financial adviser would have advised that such a scheme or transaction should take place in the particular circumstances. That of itself was a difficult issue. It was quite obvious that, if a jury were to hear this case, there would have to be a considerable volume of evidence to educate the jury in the intricacies of various company procedures and transactions. In the field of actions of reparation for professional negligence, issues of a less complicated kind than those which arose in the present case were regarded as involving "special cause" (*Robertson v Bannigan*). The present case was far removed in complexity from any ordinary type of reparation action. It was concerned with the whole conduct of the pursuer's professional and business life over a period of time. This involved the examination of a whole series of complex commercial transactions which had ramifications which affected one another. Justice would be much more likely to be done by the avoidance of risks of confusion and misapprehension if the case were to be determined by the judge after proof, rather than by a jury. Furthermore, an understanding of and the undertaking of a critical judgment in relation to the pursuer's conduct required that there should be an understanding of several matters of mixed fact and law. These were unsuitable for a jury. The matters concerned were (1) the fiduciary duties owed by a director of a limited company to the company and how those duties would apply to the complicated facts of this case; (2) the matter of the professional duties owed by an accountant to his clients; and (3) the concept of conflicts of interest and the exercise of a judgment as to whether particular circumstances involved a conflict of interest, including the making of a judgment as to whether the pursuer's behaviour in a conflict of interest situation was proper. These were all matters of very great delicacy and intricacy rendering them quite unsuitable for consideration by a jury. The present case was very much more complicated than the average professional negligence claim. Many of such claims were not now dealt with by juries.

The law of defamation itself in its application to the circumstances of the present was a matter of difficulty and delicacy. Even with the clearest of directions, it would be extremely difficult to present the case comprehensibly to a jury. While it was not necessary at this stage to consider the form of any issue and counter

issue which might be involved if a jury trial were permitted, it was instructive to consider those matters in order to see what complexities the case involved. So far as the issue was concerned, it would require to have appended to it the transcript of the broadcast concerned, or at least substantial excerpts from it. While that in itself did not present any particular difficulty, that was not the end of the matter. The issue would require to set out the innuendos relied upon by the pursuer. Accordingly, it was necessary to consider what these were. Examination of the pleadings revealed that the pursuer relied upon no less than nine separate innuendos. All of these would require to be spelled out individually in the issue. The jury would be faced with such a multiplicity of questions for determination that there would be serious risk of confusion. Turning to the matter of the counter issue, it was plain that there would require to be a counter issue of veritas (Cooper on *Defamation and Verbal Injury*, p 238; Maclaren's *Court of Session Practice*, p 586). While at an earlier time, the other defence of fair comment would not have been reflected in a separate counter issue (Cooper, p 238; Maclaren, p 585), the position appeared to have changed following changes in the Rules of Court. This was apparent from the decision of *Moffat v London Express Newspapers Ltd.* The relevant Rule of Court was now 114 (5) which referred to "any question of fact". In this connection reference was also made to *Taylor v The National Coal Board*, a case in which general guidance was given as to the circumstances in which it was appropriate for there to be tabled a counter issue. Having regard to all of these considerations, the defenders submitted that, if the case went to trial by jury, there would be a necessity for two counter issues. A further difficulty which would arise in the case, having regard to the existence of the two separate defences of veritas and fair comment, would be that the element of truth played two different roles in these defences. In the case of the defence of veritas the issue was simply that of truth or falsehood. In the case of the defence of fair comment, the question arose as to whether the facts upon which the comment was based were substantially true or not. In summary, it was quite plain from the various considerations to which reference had been made that a jury would lose its way in the present case with the result that injustice would be done.

Counsel for the pursuer in his argument dealt first of all with the defenders' contention that the passage of the pursuer's averments dealing with the interview between James Reid and the pursuer prior to the broadcast concerned should be excluded from probation. It was contended for the pursuer that these averments, while they related to material which had not been broadcast, were nevertheless relevant to the validity or otherwise of the defence of fair comment relied upon by the defenders. It was very pertinent to that matter for the court to hear about material which the pursuer had conveyed to the defenders before the broadcast, which constituted the context of the broadcast concerned.

Turning to the matter of the mode of investigation,

A counsel for the pursuer argued that, apart from the consent of the pursuer, which was not available here, there was only one ground for the avoidance of a jury trial, namely, the existence of "special cause". In the absence of "special cause" there was a right on the part of the pursuer to trial by jury in this kind of action. Counsel for the pursuer then went on to refer to a number of general considerations which supported the submission which he was making to the effect that "special cause" did not exist in this case. First, he argued that defamation was a matter which

B was particularly appropriate for trial by jury. It was the view of Cooper in his *Defamation and Verbal Injury* (2nd ed), p 265, that it was extremely doubtful whether the court would order proof before a judge instead of a jury trial in a defamation action if either party, and particularly if the pursuer, objected to its being so dealt with. That was a correct statement of the approach of the court. Here the alleged defamation was one which was published in the most public way possible by means of a television broadcast. That cir-

C cumstance made trial by jury very appropriate. Secondly, the court should not accept the defenders' argument that a jury, which was composed of members of the public, would not properly understand the issues arising in the present action. The position was that the defenders had thought fit to broadcast the material which was the subject of the pursuer's complaint to the public in general. It had to be assumed that the defenders thought that the public would understand the allegedly complex matters

D which were the subject matter of the broadcast.

Thirdly, counsel for the pursuer referred to a number of authorities which it was contended showed that quite complicated issues were sent for trial by jury and that there had to be very substantial reasons in existence for not taking that course. In *Graham v John Paterson & Son Ltd* the issue of "special cause" arose. The Lord Justice Clerk at p 176 emphasised that, in the absence of either consent or "special cause", the

E pursuer had a statutory right to have his or her claim adjudicated upon by a jury. At p 178 he said: "Special cause means some real ground of substance making the case unsuitable for jury trial. It must not be a mere hypothetical difficulty conjured up by the ingenuity of counsel. It ought to be something that is capable of articulate formulation, and not a mere generality". At p 178 of the report the Lord Justice Clerk drew attention to the importance of the quality of finality which attached to a jury's verdict. That was an asset of which

F the pursuer should not be lightly deprived. In *Rigley v Remington Rand Ltd* the court made clear that the existence of a probable disagreement between expert witnesses would not constitute "special cause". The course which was taken in *Higgins v Burton* showed the importance which the court attached to the pursuer's right to trial by jury. Although *Cowie v London, Midland and Scottish Railway Co* involved issues relating to the operation of a piece of complicated machinery, namely a railway locomotive, that was not considered to give rise to "special cause". In *Gardner v A B Fleming & Co Ltd*, the court took the view that

G the existence of difficult questions of medical causation in an action of reparation did not justify the case being sent to a proof. Such complicated questions of fact were considered to be quite suitable for trial by jury. Further, it was noteworthy that in *Hunter v Hanley*, a leading case in the law of professional negligence, there had been a jury trial. *Anderson v Grieve* showed that a jury trial could be held where the legal background to the case involved questions of breach of statutory duty and a fairly involved issue of causation.

H Counsel for the pursuer went on to refer me to a number of cases involving defamation. All of these, which demonstrated varying degrees of complexity, had been sent to trial by jury. In *Lamond v The Daily Record (Glasgow) Ltd*, an action of damages for verbal injury, a fairly complicated issue was adjusted and adjudicated upon by a jury. The allegedly objectionable material was contained in a newspaper article, the terms of which were set forth in a schedule to the issue. That showed that there was no particular difficulty in dealing with the kind of material which was in issue in the present case. The transcript of the

I broadcast could be appended to the issue to be submitted to the jury. *Macdonald v Martin* was an example of a very complex case being sent for adjudication by a jury. Veritas and fair comment were both raised and there were no less than 21 issues put forward. Those finally adjusted for submission to the jury appeared at pp 386-387 of the report. It was evident from them that the questions which the jury had to answer were numerous and complex. Again, the

J case of *Rogers v Orr* involved an action of defamation being sent for trial by jury in which the issues were elaborate and complicated. In that case, in addition to other matters, the jury had to consider the issue of privilege. The case of *Hines v Davidson* was an action of defamation which arose out of a very complicated series of events. It showed that it was acceptable for complicated issues to be determined by a jury. Further examples of complicated actions of defamation being dealt with before juries were to be found in the cases of *Ogston & Tennant Ltd v The Daily Record, Glasgow,*

K *Ltd* and *Lever Brothers Ltd v Daily Record and Mail Ltd*. In these cases issues had been approved which extended to 150 and 163 pages of print respectively. In each case loss of profit claims were advanced. The questions of fact and law arising in these cases were numerous and difficult. In the former of the two cases, as appeared from a report in 1910 2 SLT 230, the pursuers moved the court to send the action to trial by special jury, urging as grounds the magnitude of the case, the complexity of the evidence to be led, and the

L large amount of the damages involved. The pursuers' motion was granted. In modern practice the ordinary jury had come in place of the special jury. It was to be taken that the modern jury was capable of undertaking all tasks previously undertaken by a special jury. All of the foregoing cases, argued counsel for the pursuer, demonstrated that there was no justification for holding that "special cause" existed in the present case upon the ground of factual complexity.

The pursuer's counsel informed me that the court

was dealing with a unique situation. Their researches
A had revealed no case in which a defamation action had
been withheld from trial by jury on account of the
existence of "special cause". It was remarkable that
over 125 years had passed since the concept of
"special cause" had been introduced by the Evidence
(Scotland) Act 1866, yet there existed not one reported
case of such "special cause" having been sustained in
relation to an action of defamation. In supplement to
that, it could be said that juries in Scotland have
frequently been called upon to determine cases at least
B as intricate as that with which the court was now concerned. The existence of the defences of fair comment
and veritas did not bring the case into the category in
which there was "special cause". Such defences
frequently were tabled in actions where the media
were involved. There was nothing special about them.
The assessment of such pleas was a classic task for a
jury. The present case was no different from many
others in which a businessman claimed to have been
defamed by the media. The recent libel action directed
C against Count Tolstoy, heard in England, was an indication of just how complicated an action might be
heard by a jury, although it had to be accepted that the
grounds upon which a jury trial could be avoided in
England, in actions for libel or slander, were different
from the concept of "special cause" utilised in Scotland (Gatley on *Libel and Slander* (8th ed), para 1265).
One of the most striking cases in which questions of
great complexity had been sent for determination by
a jury in an action of defamation was *Cunningham v*
D *Duncan & Jamieson*. In that case there were 16 articles
of condescendence, a plea of fair comment, and other
difficulties. It was stated to be a very important case
of some novelty. There was in substance no difference
between that kind of case and the present one. Both
involved complicated facts.

Counsel for the pursuer went on to respond to the
defenders' arguments in favour of the existence of
"special cause" based upon doubtful relevancy and
the existence of difficult and delicate questions of
E mixed fact and law. At the outset it was contended that
it was not sufficient for the defenders to point to a
single averment of doubtful relevance in order to
achieve the withdrawal of the case from trial by jury.
What had to be shown was that the case was of doubtful relevancy. Only then could it be withheld from
jury trial. No particular problem would arise if an
essentially relevant case, which nevertheless contained
certain dubiously relevant averments, was sent to trial
by jury. The presiding judge could simply direct the
F jury to ignore evidence which related to the questionable averments, if it turned out that they were not relevant to the issues arising in the case. All that was
necessary was for the pursuer to have pled relevantly
the essentials of the case. These were set forth in
Cooper, p 269. The defenders' submissions in the
present case were insufficient to warrant the court
holding that special cause existed on this particular
ground, since it had not been submitted that the pursuer's case in its essentials was of doubtful relevancy.
It had to be re-emphasised that "special cause"

required to be some real ground of substance (*Graham
v Paterson*).   G

Turning to the particular points made by the
defenders, it was argued that the reference to
"ridicule" in cond 5 was not an attempt on the part
of the pursuer to go outwith the proper scope of an
action of defamation and into the field of verbal
injury. This was simply a further aspect of the pursuer's claim that the defenders had intended deliberately to defame the pursuer and was thus relevant to
the matter of the quantum of damages (*Cunningham v
Duncan & Jamieson*; Gloag and Henderson, *Introduc-*   H
tion to the Law of Scotland (9th ed), p 607). As regards
the passage in the pursuer's averments related to the
interview between the pursuer and James Reid prior
to the broadcast, that material was relevant to the
defenders' intention in emitting the broadcast in question and also to the defence of fair comment. On the
topic of the defenders' criticisms of the pursuer's averments of loss, the terminology used in the averments
had to be looked at in context. The pursuer's position
had been made sufficiently clear to enable the matter   I
to be put before a jury. The averment concerning the
earning capacity of the pursuer's practice formed no
part of the computation of his claim of damages.
Further, the arithmetical points made by the
defenders would create no serious confusion in the
mind of a jury.

The defenders had argued that in the averments in
the present case there were references to the pursuer
acting in several different capacities in relation to the   J
companies which featured in the case; it had been said
that this aspect of the case would cause the likelihood
of difficulty and confusion for a jury. However, in the
case of *McFaull v Compania Navigacion Sota y Anzar*
it was held that no "special cause" existed despite the
fact that the case was one involving the different
capacities of invitee, licensee and trespasser. Further,
there was no substance in the defenders' argument
that difficult and delicate questions would be likely to
arise on account of the different parts played by truth   K
in relation to the defence of veritas and the defence of
fair comment.

Counsel for the pursuer submitted that very little
assistance could be got from a consideration of the
proof or jury trial issue in the context of other types
of reparation case, in particular cases arising from
accidents. Dealing with the authorities relied upon by
the defenders, counsel for the pursuer contended first
that *McGinty v Smith & McLean Ltd* had been   L
wrongly decided. The circumstances relied upon as
constituting special cause in that case were in fact
insufficient for that purpose. In *McKenzie v Donachie*
there had been several defenders, varying averments
of fault, and questions of contribution between wrong-
doers. It was understandable that, in these circumstances, the case was considered unsuitable for trial
by jury. *McGinnigle v McLuskie* was a case in which
there were several claimants and difficult questions
relating to contributory negligence on the part of a
husband and wife who had been passengers in the

same motor car. In these circumstances the court's
A decision to withhold the case from jury trial was
understandable. In *Bygate v Edinburgh Corporation*
difficult and delicate questions arose in relation to the
risks associated with the behaviour of animals. That
again was an understandable basis for withholding the
case from trial by jury. The case of *Robertson v T &*
H Smith Ltd could be distinguished from the circumstances of the present case. It did not involve simply
complexities of fact, but rather technical complexities
of scientific process. There were no such factors
B present in this case. Where the issues were simply
questions of fact, albeit of a complex nature, "special
cause" did not exist, as appeared from the cases of
Cowie v London, Midland and Scottish Railway Co,
Rigley v Remington Rand Ltd and *Gardner v A B*
Fleming & Co Ltd.

Summarising the pursuer's position, it was contended that almost all cases of a public defamation of
a businessman would involve areas of fact which
might not be capable of being presented in a clear and
C simple way. Every case of defamation of that type
would inevitably involve legal issues of the same kind
as those in the present case. The question before the
court here was whether there was anything in the
circumstances of the present case which took it out of
the class of relatively straightforward actions of defamation arising from the publication of objectionable
material by the media. The answer to that question
was that there was nothing out of the ordinary here.
If the court were to hold that "special cause" existed
D here, then no businessman who averred that he had
suffered loss of profit in consequence of being
defamed in a television programme could ever have his
case heard by a jury. That was a startling situation. In
the present case one started from the position that
there was no difficulty whatever in the proof of the
statements which had been made; further there was no
difficulty in deciding that those statements related to
the pursuer. On the merits of the case there were only
very few questions to be decided. These were: (1) were
E the statements made true? (2) were they substantially
true? and (3) were the comments made by the
defenders fair? Those were the simple issues for
decision. There was no reason why a jury should not
be able to deal with these matters under proper direction from the court. Such directions would not need
to be unduly complex. For all these reasons issues
should be allowed.

The arguments presented by the parties in this case
F related to two matters. First, the issue was raised of
the relevance for inquiry of the averments of the
pursuer in cond 5 relating to the interview between
James Reid and the pursuer prior to the broadcast,
upon the contents of which this action is founded. It
was contended that I should exclude those averments
from probation. Secondly, elaborate arguments were
developed by both parties in relation to the question
of the mode of inquiry, which featured as the principal
subject of the lengthy debate before me. I deal first
with the matter of the relevance of the averments
referred to above. Prima facie, it appears to me that

there is much to be said for the view advanced by the
defenders that, since these averments relate to matters G
which formed no part of the broadcast which is the
subject of complaint, they have no bearing on the
issues raised in the action. However, in my opinion,
it is conceivable that these averments which amount to
what are described as reasonable explanations in
relation to the circumstances in which the pursuer was
acting in the various transactions which are the subject
of the action, may be relevant to the defence of fair
comment which has been tabled by the defenders,
although it cannot with confidence be said that they H
are so. It would have been very much easier to relate
those averments to that defence if they had been
accompanied by averments which defined the connection between them and that defence. In the
circumstances, I feel unable, at this stage, to exclude
the averments in question from probation. In view of
their uncertain connection with the defence referred
to above, however, in my opinion they assume a
significance in relation to the matter to which I next
turn, that is to say, the appropriate mode of inquiry in I
this case.

In terms of the Court of Session Act 1988, s 11, it
is provided that: [his Lordship then quoted the terms
of s 11 and then those of s 9 (b) set out supra and continued:] These provisions are the statutory successor
of s 4 of the Evidence (Scotland) Act 1866. Having
regard to the tems of ss 9 and 11 of the Act of 1988,
there is a statutory requirement that an enumerated
action shall be tried by jury unless the parties to the
action consent to the allowance of a proof, or unless J
the Lord Ordinary is satisfied that "special cause" for
the allowance of a proof has been shown. In the debate
before me both parties were agreed that the meaning
of the expression "special cause" in s 9 (b) of the Act
of 1988 was the same as that of the same expression
in s 4 of the Act of 1866. It therefore follows that in
considering the issue of "special cause" under the Act
of 1988 in relation to the circumstances of the present
case, it is appropriate to look at the authorities decided
under s 4 of the Act of 1866. The nature of "special K
cause" has been considered in numerous reported
cases. In some of these the general approach which the
court should take in relation to the issue has been
explained. It is appropriate that I should mention
them. In *Walker v Pitlochry Motor Co*, the Lord President said at 1930 SLT, p 372: "A special cause
implies some specialty or other about the case or its
circumstances, but the Court has always refrained
from any attempt to lay down rules on the subject; nor
is anything gained by pointing out that this or that L
general consideration will not be enough in itself to
constitute special cause. Whether this or that special
feature — or some combination of special features —
amounts to 'special cause' is a question to be determined, not by reference to any legal principle or
category, but as a matter of sound discretion, and the
discretion rests mainly and in the first instance with
the Lord Ordinary whose duty it is to try the case."

In the same case at p 373 Lord Blackburn [quoting
from *White v Dixon* (1875) 2 R 904 per Lord Gifford]

went on to say: "'the rule as to the nature of the
A special cause which requires to be shown is rather flexible,' and I myself doubt whether it is possible to formulate any precise rule as to what does or does not
constitute a 'special cause'. Of course it must be a
cause special to the particular case."

Further, it is apparent from *Dornan v Forrest* that
views as to what might constitute "special cause" have
varied with time. At 1932 SLT, p 367 of that case the
Lord President said: "I think, at the present day, the
tendency is towards a less rigorous standard of special
B cause than was once thought necessary before an
'appropriated' action could be sent to proof before a
judge without a jury", although, as no doubt a
warning against the adoption of too lax a criterion, in
Graham v Paterson & Son Ltd the Lord Justice Clerk
at p 176 said: "I have recited these provisions in order
to emphasise that the right of the subject, who has
suffered injury to his or her person, to have his or her
claim adjudicated upon by a jury, except of consent,
or where special cause is shown, is a statutory right.
C It is a right conferred by the express direction of
Parliament; in substance, as Lord Shaw expressed it in
Taylor v Dumbarton Tramways Co (1918 SC (HL) 96
at p 108), 'a constitutional right', no encroachment
upon which can be sanctioned except by the Legislature itself." At p 178 he continued: "Special cause
means some real ground of substance making the case
unsuitable for jury trial. It must not be a mere
hypothetical difficulty conjured up by the ingenuity of
counsel. It ought to be something that is capable of
D articulate formulation, and not a mere generality."

In dealing with the circumstances of the present
case, I seek to follow the approach which is described
in these dicta.

Counsel for the pursuer sought to persuade me that,
in assessing whether "special cause" existed, it was
appropriate to adopt a different standard in relation to
"an action for libel or defamation" as compared with
the other actions enumerated in s 11 of the Act of
E 1988. He contended that in a case such as the present
there was "an almost irresistible presumption in
favour of allowing issues". In this connection he
referred to the passage, already mentioned, to be
found at p 265 of Cooper on *Defamation and Verbal
Injury* (2nd ed). I have come to the conclusion that this
contention is unsound, although, of course, I recognise that it is likely that in actions for defamation the
factors which may be thought to amount to special
cause will be different from those which may be simi-
F larly viewed in, for example, an action for damages for
personal injuries, since "special cause" must relate to
the circumstances of the particular case under consideration. In the provisions of the Act of 1988, which
I have already quoted, I note that no distinction is
drawn between "an action for libel or defamation"
and any of the other enumerated actions. In the work
mentioned, Cooper at p 265 says: "it is extremely
doubtful whether the Court would order proof before
a judge instead of a jury trial if either party — and particularly if the pursuer — objected to its being so dealt

with", in an action for defamation. In support of this
proposition the learned author cited the case of *Rhind* G
v Kemp & Co. That case was, so far as appears from
the very brief report, an action of damages based upon
the taking of decree in absence for a debt previously
paid. In a reclaiming motion it was held that the Lord
Ordinary had erred in holding that "special cause"
existed in the circumstances of that case. As it was
presented in the reclaiming motion, the case was not
an action of defamation. In my opinion, this authority
does not support the proposition contained in the
passage from the work which I have already quoted, H
which in my view is incorrect.

During the debate before me, some consideration
was given to the method of handling of actions for
defamation in the courts in England. So far as I was
concerned, that proved to be more of an educational
experience than of any practical assistance in relation
to the circumstances of the present case. The legislation which deals with the mode of inquiry in cases
such as this is exclusively Scottish and has no parallel
in England, so far as I am aware. Accordingly I think I
that it would be misleading to consider the criteria
which are applied by a master in making a decision in
an English action of defamation as to the mode of
inquiry. The criteria which are applied in England, as
I understand it, are set out in s 6 (1) of the Administration of Justice (Miscellaneous Provisions) Act 1933,
and bear no similarity to the provisions which are in
force in Scotland. In all these circumstances, I propose
to approach the issue of "special cause" in this case
without reference to English practice.
J

In the course of the debate before me, very many
authorities were quoted relating to "special cause" in
what were described as ordinary reparation actions. In
my opinion, these can be of only limited assistance in
relation to the present action, since what I have to do
is to endeavour to exercise a "sound discretion" in
relation to the particular facts of this case. However,
these cases can provide some guidance as to the kind
of criteria or standards which may properly be applied
in assessing the matter of "special cause". Indeed such K
cases are, in a sense, the only source of such guidance,
it being accepted by both counsel for the pursuer and
for the defenders that they were unaware of any
reported case in which the issue of "special cause" had
been raised in relation to a defamation action. It
appears to me from my consideration of the cases
which were put before me that the court has taken the
view that there exists, for example, a certain degree of
complexity in the circumstances of a case beyond
which a jury has been thought likely to "miss the L
point", or become confused, with consequent injustice
occurring. Furthermore, it appears that the court has
in the past been influenced in relation to the question
of "special cause" by the degree of difficulty which
might be experienced by the trial judge in providing
lucid directions to the jury in the circumstances of the
case in question. The cases which have caused me to
reach these conclusions are *Robertson v T & H Smith
Ltd*; *McGinnigle v McLuskie*; *Bygate v Edinburgh Corporation*; *McKenzie v Donachie*; and *McGinty v Smith
& McLean Ltd*.

Counsel for the pursuer referred me to many
A reported cases in which actions of damages for defamation involving greater or lesser degrees of complexity had been, or were to be, tried by juries. These cases frequently involved defences of veritas, fair comment, and privilege, alone or in combination. Among the more complex of these cases are *Cunningham v Duncan & Jamieson*; *Ogston & Tennant Ltd v The Daily Record, Glasgow, Ltd*; *Lever Brothers Ltd v Daily Record and Mail Ltd*; *Lamond v The Daily Record (Glasgow) Ltd*; *Macdonald v Martin*; and *Rogers v Orr*.
B While I would readily acknowledge that, in many of these cases, issues of considerable complexity were put before juries for inquiry, sometimes with very elaborate issues and counter issues, in my opinion, that situation does not avail the pursuer in the present case. The fact of the matter is that, in none of these cases, was the issue of "special cause" ever argued, so far as I am aware. For reasons which no doubt seemed good to both the pursuers and the defenders in those cases, they were content that they should be dealt with
C before juries. Thus they do not appear to me to afford any criteria in relation to the issue of "special cause" in defamation actions, which might be useful to me in the circumstances of the present case. I am therefore left to proceed to endeavour to exercise a "sound discretion" according to the considerations to which I have already referred above, derived from decisions in actions other than defamation actions.

Approaching the issue of mode of inquiry raised here in the way which I have outlined, the conclusion
D which I have reached is that "special cause" has been shown by the defenders why a proof rather than a jury trial should be allowed. Prominent among my reasons for having reached this conclusion is the very substantial complexity of the averments which I have thought fit to quote, the relevance of which is not challenged, made by the defenders relating to the pursuer's professional activities over a substantial period of time. These averments make reference to a considerable
E number of different companies, several of which, during the period of time in question, underwent changes of name. Against this complicated background the averments deal with a series of inter-company transactions, including "hive down" operations and other inter-company dealings, with the pursuer acting in a number of different capacities. In my opinion, any ordinary jury would be likely to be puzzled and confused when faced with issues relating to these matters. I consider that there would be a very serious risk of such a jury losing its way and missing
F the point, to put the matter as it was put in the cases of *McKenzie v Donachie* and *McGinty v Smith & McLean Ltd*. In addition to the difficulties to which I have just made reference, there are also raised issues concerning the actions of the pursuer, which are criticised by reference to the standards which might have been attained by a reasonably competent accountant. That aspect of the matter renders the present case one akin to an action of professional negligence. This feature adds a further degree of complexity to the litigation. Having regard to the difficult and complicated

background to the transactions which are the subject of averment, in my opinion, if a jury trial were to be G allowed, there would have to be a substantial volume of what I might call "educational evidence", the purpose of which would be to inform a jury as to the nature and purposes of the various transactions involved. That, in my opinion, itself constitutes a further reason why trial by jury is inappropriate. In a proof before a judge, such evidence would be unlikely to be required.

In the argument before me much was made on behalf of the pursuer of the circumstances that the H defenders had included the complicated material to which I have made reference in their broadcast and that therefore, so ran the argument, it could be assumed that the defenders at that stage considered that the general public would be able to follow this material without difficulty. Thus it was said that any jury, which consisted of ordinary members of the public, would be likely to be able to follow the issues raised in the action without difficulty. It appears to me that this argument involves a non sequitur. In my I opinion, it cannot be assumed that the defenders necessarily directed their broadcast to members of the public in general. It may well be that it was assumed simply that the broadcast would be comprehensible to those who were professionally interested in the matters with which it was concerned.

In addition to the difficulties to which I have already referred, it appears to me that the pursuer's claim for damages would be likely to involve complicated J material relating to the profitability of the pursuer's business, including accountancy evidence, which a jury would be likely to find difficulty in following. I consider that the evidence relating to damages in the present case would be far removed from the sort of evidence which is presented to a jury in what might be described as an ordinary reparation action.

I was also impressed by the argument of the defenders that the number and variety of the different issues arising in the case would create an additional K likelihood of confusion and consequent injustice. It is the case that, upon the pleadings as they stand, no less than nine different innuendos are involved. In addition, the defences of fair comment and veritas have been tabled, involving in different ways and to different extents the element of truth. There are also involved allegations of dishonesty, fraudulent conduct, conduct unbecoming of a chartered accountant, and ineptitude. In my opinion, the range and variety of the different issues arising constitute, in L themselves, a good reason for withholding the case from trial by jury, since I consider that there would be a serious risk that a jury would become very confused if faced with the necessity of making a series of separate decisions concerning these matters.

In addition to the foregoing considerations, I have reached the conclusion that there are a number of passages in the averments of the pursuer which are of doubtful relevance and accordingly, in my opinion, constitute "special cause" for withholding the case from trial by jury, since I cannot agree with the pursuer's contention that it would be acceptable for a case to go before a jury, although the pleadings contained averments of doubtful relevance, provided that there were relevantly averred "the essentials" of the case. In a different context I have already made reference to the averments in cond 5 which relate to the interview between James Reid and the pursuer prior to the emission of the broadcast. For reasons which I have already explained, I consider these averments are of doubtful relevance. In addition, at various points in the pursuer's case there are references to the alleged purpose with which the defenders, or those for whom they are responsible, made certain statements in the course of the broadcast. In my opinion, having regard to the dicta in the case of *Cunningham v Duncan & Jamieson*, to which I have already referred, in any jury trial, the court would be faced with the very considerable difficulty of charging a jury against a background in which, prima facie, there appears to be an uncertainty in the law. Such an uncertainty would necessarily be likely to encourage the advancing of arguments of an essentially legal nature on either side at any inquiry. Those considerations, in my opinion, render the case unsuitable for trial by jury. Finally, in connection with the arguments relating to doubtful relevance, I am persuaded that the pursuer's averments of loss are confused and unclear. I consider that those averments would create very serious difficulties in the way of a clear presentation of the case on damages to a jury.

In addition to the aspects of the case which I have already mentioned as reasons making the case unsuitable for trial by jury, I consider that there are raised in the averments of the parties as they stand a number of issues which involve what might be described as difficult and delicate issues of mixed fact and law. These, in my opinion, constitute further reasons why the case is, in my opinion, unsuitable for trial by jury. In particular, in this connection, I refer to the issues concerning the fiduciary duties of directors of companies. Such considerations involve sophisticated concepts of company law and would be difficult for a jury to apply to the facts of the case. Further, in my opinion, the averments concerning the duties of accountants to their clients involve considerations which would be difficult to apply against the background of the facts in the present case. Finally, the proper decision of the case would involve the resolution of issues concerned with conflicts of interest and duties in relation to the pursuer's conduct. Such matters, in my opinion, would be inappropriate for consideration by a jury.

For all of these reasons, I am persuaded that it would be unsafe to allow a jury to adjudicate on the facts in the present case. Accordingly I shall sustain plea in law no 4 for the defenders and allow a proof before answer on the whole averments in the closed record as amended.

Counsel for Pursuer, Sutherland, QC, Geary; Solicitors, Drummond & Co, WS (for Friel & Co, Uddingston) — Counsel for Defenders, Macfadyen, QC, J G Reid; Solicitors, McGrigor Donald.

L M S

Lambert v HM Advocate

HIGH COURT OF JUSTICIARY

THE LORD JUSTICE GENERAL (HOPE), LORDS ALLANBRIDGE AND BRAND

27 JUNE 1991

Justiciary — Procedure — Plea in bar of trial — Prejudice — Pre-trial publicity — Detailed criticism of accused in treatment of elderly patients in residential home — Sheriff holding that effect of such publicity might be short lived — Whether accused could be ensured fair trial.

An accused person was charged on an indictment containing 31 charges of cruel and unnatural treatment of elderly residents in a residential home, nearly all of whom were now deceased. There had been detailed criticism in the media surrounding the operation and management of the residential home featured in all the charges, and of the accused herself, which extended largely over the period May 1989 to May 1990, after which time the police investigations commenced. In these circumstances the accused tendered a plea in bar of trial on the basis that the prejudicial pre-trial publicity would render a fair trial impossible. The sheriff repelled the plea in bar of trial, holding that there was not such potential prejudice as could not be removed by proper direction to the jury.

Held, that the sheriff had applied the correct tests and was entitled to reach the conclusion that he did (p 341I-J); and appeal *refused*.

Stuurman v HM Advocate, 1980 SLT (Notes) 95, *applied*.

Indictment

Mrs Gladys Muirden or Lambert was charged at the instance of the rt hon the Lord Fraser of Carmyllie, Her Majesty's Advocate, on an indictment which libelled 31 charges of cruel and unnatural treatment of elderly residents in a residential home called "Moorheads", covering a substantial period of time.

The accused tendered a plea in bar of trial in respect of certain prejudicial pre-trial publicity in the press covering largely the period May 1989 to May 1990, after which time the police had started their investigations into the matters raised in the indictment. A preliminary diet was held in the sheriff court at Dumfries before Sheriff K G Barr on 6 June 1991, trial being due on 18 June.

A The sheriff repelled the accused's plea in bar of trial and the accused appealed by way of note of appeal to the High Court.

Cases referred to

H v Sweeney, 1983 SLT 498; (sub nom *X v Sweeney*) 1982 JC 70; 1982 SCCR 161.

Kilbane v HM Advocate, 1990 SLT 108; 1989 SCCR 313.

Spink v HM Advocate, 1989 SCCR 413.

Stuurman v HM Advocate, 1980 SLT (Notes) 95; 1980 B JC 111.

In his report to the High Court the sheriff made the following observations, inter alia:

THE SHERIFF (K G BARR).—[After dealing with submissions to the effect that there had been undue delay in proceeding to trial in respect of the charges in the indictment, with which this report is not concerned, the sheriff continued:]

C The second plea in bar of trial advanced was a plea of prejudicial publicity making it impossible for the appellant to receive a fair and impartial trial. The publicity complained of was mainly in the period between May 1989 and May 1990.

The appellant's complaint covered local television and radio, but the principal complaint centred around a series of articles in the *Dumfries and Galloway Standard* newspaper during that period. Complaint was particularly made of articles appearing in that D newspaper on 21 February, 23 and 28 March 1990. I was informed on the appellant's behalf that the newspaper is published twice weekly with a circulation in excess of 20,000 copies per issue. The list of assize, I was told, only covers 4,000 persons a year and it would be impossible for anyone on the jury list not to have read the articles or to be unaware of the publicity resulting from the discussion of these matters in the local press. That discussion was, it was submitted, totally adverse to the appellant's interests. It would E make it impossible for her to receive a fair trial. Reference was made to *Stuurman v HM Advocate*; *H v Sweeney*; *Kilbane v HM Advocate*; and *Spink v HM Advocate*.

For the Crown in reply it was submitted that even if there had been publicity which was prejudicial to the appellant, that could be removed by an appropriate direction to the jury. The period involved in the present case between the publicity and the trial was a much longer one than in any of the cases referred to.

F Your Lordships will no doubt be invited to read the detail of the newspaper reports of which the appellant makes complaint. The wording and layout of the articles is really impossible to summarise but the subject matter concerns the two separate reports which were made to the social work committee of Dumfries and Galloway Regional Council after the two inquiries already referred to in this report had been carried out into the allegations relating to the running of Moorheads. The newspaper articles gave more and more details of the allegations which had

been made, and these allegations covered many matters which are now detailed in charges in the G present indictment. Reference was also made in the articles to the fact that staff at Moorheads felt intimidated by the officer in charge. Then for the first time in an article in the issue dated 21 February 1990 the *Dumfries and Galloway Standard* named the appellant as the officer in charge and reported her resignation as from 16 January 1990, and her absence from work since the preceding November when the second inquiry was instituted. The issue of 23 March 1990 reported an interview with a former member of staff at Moorheads, Mrs Margaret Glasson (who is on the H list of witnesses appended to the indictment) as to her concern about her experiences while there. Later in that issue the opinion of the depute director of social services and of the reporter was quoted to the effect that the standard of care being displayed by staff towards residents was currently satisfactory and gave no continued cause for concern.

What caused particular complaint, however, from counsel for the appellant was that the *Dumfries and Galloway Standard* in its issues of 23 and 28 March I 1990 then in effect quoted the terms of the second report which had just been submitted to the social work committee of the local authority. Considerable detail was given of the allegations which had been made about the running of Moorheads. Allegations of intimidation of staff by the appellant during the course of the first inquiry were quoted in the article of 28 March 1990 and the very trenchant criticisms which the second report made of the appellant personally were also quoted in full in this article. J

The later newspaper reports did not mention the appellant personally but kept the whole matter of Moorheads before the public until the final article dated 2 May 1990 intimated that a police investigation into the allegations was under way.

I considered that although the publicity complained of had been sustained over a considerable period in the local press, and although it was potentially prejudicial to the appellant, this potential prejudice could be K removed by a clear direction to the jury to disregard any information which they had already obtained through the press, radio or television and to judge the case solely upon the evidence led before them in the course of the trial. The publicity complained of in the present case was now of some considerable age — far longer than the periods involved in the cases cited on behalf of the appellant which had in any event all proceeded to trial. I had particular regard to what was said by Lord Justice General Emslie in *Stuurman v HM Advocate* at p 123 to effect that that court is "well L entitled to bear in mind that the public memory of newspaper articles and news broadcasts and of their detailed contents is notoriously short and, . . . the residual risk of prejudice to the prospects of a fair trial . . . could reasonably be expected to be removed by careful directions".

I accordingly repelled both these pleas in bar of trial, taking the view that the matter was in each case one for careful direction of the jury in the light of the evidence led at the trial.

Appeal

A   The appeal was argued before the High Court on 27 June 1991.

Eo die the court *refused* the appeal.

The following opinion of the court was delivered by Lord Allanbridge:

OPINION OF THE COURT.—The appellant is Mrs Gladys Muirden or Lambert. The appeal arises out of the second preliminary diet in respect of the 31
B   charges in the indictment. Two grounds of appeal were argued in this court by counsel for the appellant. In the first place he submitted that there had been such undue delay between the dates of the various offences charged and bringing the matter to trial that the indictment should now be dismissed as incompetent and oppressive. In the second place he argued that there had been such widespread publicity extending over such a long period of time surrounding the operation and management of the residential home for
C   the elderly featuring in all the charges that the effect of such publicity should operate as a bar to any trial. [His Lordship summarised the arguments in support of the first ground of appeal, with which this report is not concerned, and continued:]

The second argument submitted by counsel for the appellant was to the effect that the publicity had been such in this particular case that it was impossible to cure the adverse effect of it even by a suitable direction by the trial judge. He carefully went through various
D   cases which are reported on this matter. In the first place he referred to the case of *Stuurman v HM Advocate*. As regards that case he said it could be distinguished from the present because although allegations there were made of previous convictions the allegations did not extend in the press over the period of about a year as applied in the present case. He then turned to the case of *Sweeney*, which was the Glasgow rape case, and there again he said that although there was great publicity attached to that case, it was not as
E   prolonged as in the present case. He lastly referred to two other cases, *Kilbane v HM Advocate* and *Spink v HM Advocate*, and in both of these he said that in each only one article was written in the press and that in contrast to the present case there was a minimal exposure in the press.

We have considered these two grounds of appeal and the arguments submitted in support of each of them. [His Lordship considered and refused the first ground of appeal and continued:]

F   The second ground of appeal was based on a plea of prejudicial publicity making it impossible for the appellant to receive a fair and impartial trial. The publicity complained of was mainly in the period between May 1989 and May 1990 after which the police investigations commenced. Counsel for the appellant has taken us carefully through the various articles published in the newspaper concerned and we have studied them with care. There is no doubt that there is a good deal of detailed criticism of the appellant herself in them. Nonetheless, as the sheriff pointed out, such publicity may well be short lived as the memory of people reading it is usually not long. In
G   this respect the sheriff referred in his report to what was said by Lord Justice General Emslie in *Stuurman*, 1980 JC at p 123 where he said: "the court was well entitled to bear in mind that the public memory of newspaper articles and news broadcasts and of their detailed contents is notoriously short . . . the residual risk of prejudice to the prospects of fair trial . . . could reasonably be expected to be removed by careful directions".

We have considered the four cases to which counsel
H   for the appellant referred us in this respect and we accept that this particular case can be distinguished from all of them. Nonetheless in this particular case the sheriff was not satisfied that there was such publicity as could not be removed by proper direction. The sheriff hearing this case was the local sheriff who must have been conversant with the public knowledge of the particular residential home in question and the publicity which the running of that home has received in the past. We are therefore of the opinion that no
I   grounds have been put before us which demonstrate the sheriff was wrong in reaching the conclusion that he did as regards the second ground.

In conclusion we would add that this preliminary diet was heard by the sheriff and both grounds of appeal were matters of fact to be decided by him. It is always difficult to decide in advance what prejudice an appellant may suffer at a trial. In this particular case we are satisfied that the sheriff applied the right tests and that he was entitled in our view to reach the con-
J   clusions that he did. Counsel for the appellant was invited to explain to us where the sheriff had gone wrong in applying the appropriate tests and he very frankly conceded as regards both his arguments that really what he submitted was that the sheriff had failed to apply sufficient weight to the particular factors which he, counsel, stressed. We are quite satisfied that in the whole circumstances the sheriff was entitled to reach the view that he did and the appeal is refused. Further, we order that there be no publication of the facts set out in this appeal until after the trial has taken
K   place and any further procedure in the case has finally been disposed of.

Counsel for Appellant, Baird; Solicitors, Braidwoods, Dumfries — Counsel for Respondent, Macdonald, QC, AD; Solicitor, J D Lowe, Crown Agent.

R F H   L

A

(NOTE)

Malcolm v Fair

OUTER HOUSE

LORD CAMERON OF LOCHBROOM

3 JULY 1991

Reparation — Negligence — Road accident — Divided blame — Pedestrian crossing road without keeping proper lookout — Driver also not keeping proper lookout.

B

A pedestrian who was under the influence of alcohol started to cross a road without having observed an approaching car. The car driver was driving at a reasonable speed but failed to see the pedestrian crossing from nearside to offside until too late to avoid striking the pedestrian.

Held, that pedestrian and driver were equally to blame; and decree *pronounced* in favour of the pedestrian subject to a reduction of 50 per cent for contributory negligence.

C

––––––––––––

William Alexander Malcolm raised an action against Ian William Fair for injuries sustained in a road accident about 6.45 pm on 26 December 1986. The pursuer was a pedestrian crossing a wide road in Edinburgh from east to west. The defender's evidence was that he was driving his car northwards on the road in the outer of the two southbound lanes at a speed of

D

about 25 mph. After a proof before the Lord Ordinary (Lord Cameron of Lochbroom) his Lordship held it established that the pursuer had been under the influence of drink, and that the defender had only seen the pursuer when the defender was almost upon him and had swerved but caught the pursuer on the offside of the car towards the rear. In apportioning blame for the accident equally the Lord Ordinary said: "While I am satisfied on the evidence that the pursuer was under the influence of drink at the time of the

E

accident, I do not consider that there is any evidence to substantiate the defender's case that the pursuer 'dashed out from beside parked cars'. There was nothing to suggest that the pursuer was in a hurry and indeed his own evidence was to the effect that he considered it safe to proceed across Leith Walk. There was no evidence to suggest that the conditions of lighting might disguise the pursuer's movement across the carriageway from being observed by a motorist travelling southwards up Leith Walk. Furthermore, having

F

regard to the width of Leith Walk at that point and the fact that according to [a police constable who gave evidence] only one half of the inside southbound lane would have been taken up by parked cars, the pursuer must have moved a considerable distance across the total width of the southbound carriageway of Leith Walk prior to the accident. This would accord with the pursuer's evidence that he was looking southwards up Leith Walk. The defender accepted that at such time of night and on Boxing Day it would be reasonable to anticipate that pedestrians would be crossing the carriageway. There was nothing to prevent his

observing the movement of the pursuer out from the pavement between parked cars and from there into the G carriageway itself if he had been paying attention. In the circumstances I must conclude that he was not paying sufficient attention to the roadway ahead of him as he was approaching and passing the junction of Dalmeny Street and Leith Walk and accordingly that the accident was caused by his fault despite his attempts to avoid the pursuer when he was eventually seen by him.

"On the other hand, I am in no doubt that the pursuer must accept blame also. There was nothing in H the evidence to suggest that the defender was proceeding at an excessive speed, and indeed the fact that the car must have come to a halt very quickly after the impact is not suggestive of excessive speed. I believe the defender's evidence as to his speed. From the fact that the defender passed through the pedestrian lights while they were in his favour and that when the pursuer looked down Leith Walk they were then at red, I conclude that the defender's car was already south of the lights by the time that the pursuer moved I out onto the carriageway of Leith Walk. It is of some note that according to the pursuer, he only looked northwards for southbound traffic at the edge of the kerb and thus before he moved out between the parked cars and that immediately before the accident he was looking southwards for northgoing traffic, although at that time he must still have been crossing the east [southbound] carriageway of Leith Walk. I conclude from the evidence that he had not taken proper care for his own safety as he moved out onto the carriage- J way, that he failed to observe the approach of the defender's car although this must have been obvious to him if he had been keeping a proper lookout. This failure is consistent with his being under the influence of drink at the time. Furthermore, and in particular, I hold that the pursuer failed to carry out the appropriate drill for ascertaining whether traffic was approaching towards him from the north, namely by looking again for such traffic once he got to the offside of the cars parked on the kerb. If he had done so I hold that K there was nothing to prevent his observing the approach of the defender's car and for himself to have taken steps to avoid moving into its path. On a broad view of the matter I have reached the conclusion that each party was equally to blame for the accident. In the circumstances I shall sustain the first plea in law for the pursuer and the fourth plea in law for the defender and assess the degree of contributory negligence on the part of the pursuer at one half."

In terms of the joint minute I shall accordingly L pronounce decree in the sum of £6,000, of which £4,000 will bear interest at the rate of 7½ per cent from the date of the accident, 26 December 1986, to date.

––––––––––––

Counsel for Pursuer, Tyre; Solicitors, Boyd Jameson, WS — Counsel for Defender, Allardice; Solicitors, Balfour & Manson, Nightingale & Bell.

C H

Skarpaas v Skarpaas

A FIRST DIVISION

THE LORD PRESIDENT (HOPE),
LORDS COWIE AND MAYFIELD

11 DECEMBER 1991

Husband and wife — Divorce — Financial provision — Valuation of matrimonial property — Award of damages made after relevant date in respect of accident occurring between date of marriage and relevant date — Method of valuing right to damages at relevant date — Whether sheriff entitled to take the sum awarded as value of the asset at relevant date — Family Law (Scotland) Act 1985 (c 37), s 10 (4).

In an action of divorce the wife pursuer claimed a capital sum representing a proportion of an award of damages made after the relevant date in respect of an accident occurring during the course of the marriage and prior to the relevant date. The sheriff rejected the defender's argument that the award was not matrimonial property. The defender's averments set out details of the sums awarded to him, but he made no averments that as the action had not been concluded by the relevant date the value of the claim was different or less than the sums ultimately awarded. The sheriff based his award on the sum awarded in damages, having deducted certain elements of that award including the sums awarded for solatium and interest, and for future wage loss, giving the wife pursuer a sum which was more than half the sum arrived at after deductions. The defender appealed to the sheriff principal, arguing inter alia that the claim had no value at the relevant date. The sheriff principal affirmed the sheriff on this point. The defender appealed to the Court of Session. The defender accepted in argument that the claim for damages was matrimonial property and had a value, but argued that the sheriff should have approached his valuation not on the sums actually awarded, but on the basis of the sum for which the claim could have been assigned at the relevant date.

Held, that as the defender had put no material before the sheriff other than details of the sums awarded, the sheriff was entitled to value the award on that basis (p 345F-G); and appeal *refused*.

Cooper v Cooper, 1971 SLT (Notes) 31, *commented on*.

Observed, that in principle there was much to be said for the view that a claim for damages which was yet to be quantified and admitted would attract less if offered for sale in the market place than the amount awarded by decree which was obtained at the end of the day. Common experience suggested that a discount would be insisted upon for the uncertainties inherent in litigation (p 345C).

Appeal from the sheriff court
(Reported 1991 SLT (Sh Ct) 15)

Mrs Dorothy Margaret Hand or Macdonald or Skarpaas raised an action of divorce against her husband Torstein Edgar Skarpaas, concluding inter alia for a capital sum representing a proportion of an award of damages made to the defender after the relevant date in respect of an accident occurring during the course of the marriage and prior to the relevant date.

The case came to proof before the sheriff (A L Stewart).

Statutory provisions

The Family Law (Scotland) Act 1985, as originally enacted, provided:

"8.—(1) In an action for divorce, either party to the marriage may apply to the court for one or more of the following orders — (a) an order for the payment of a capital sum or the transfer of property to him by the other party to the marriage; . . .

"10.— . . . (4) Subject to subsection (5) below, in this section and in section 11 of this Act 'the matrimonial property' means all the property belonging to the parties or either of them at the relevant date which was acquired by them or him (otherwise than by way of gift or succession from a third party) — (a) before the marriage for use by them as a family home or as furniture or plenishings for such home; or (b) during the marriage but before the relevant date."

Cases referred to

Cooper v Cooper, 1971 SLT (Notes) 31.
Mackenzie v Middleton, Ross and Arnot, 1983 SLT 286.
Traill & Sons v Actieselskabat Dalbeattie Ltd (1904) 12 SLT 129; (1904) 6 F 798.

On 29 May 1990 the sheriff *awarded* the pursuer a capital sum of £25,000 with interest thereon from the date of citation. (Reported 1991 SLT (Sh Ct) 15.)

The defender appealed to the sheriff principal.

On 21 November 1990 the sheriff principal *allowed* the appeal to the extent only of substituting interest from the date of decree. (Reported 1991 SLT (Sh Ct) 15.)

The defender appealed to the Court of Session.

Appeal

The appeal was heard before the First Division on 29 November 1991.

On 11 December 1991 the court *refused* the appeal.

The following opinion of the court was delivered by the Lord President (Hope):

OPINION OF THE COURT.—This is an action of divorce in which the appellant, who was the respondent's husband, is the defender. The only outstanding issue relates to the pursuer's claim for the payment of a capital sum in terms of s 8 (1) (a) of the Family Law (Scotland) Act 1985. The sheriff awarded the pursuer a capital sum of £25,000 with interest at the rate of 15

per cent per annum from the date of citation until
payment. The defender appealed against this award to
the sheriff principal, who refused the appeal as regards
the amount of the capital sum but varied the sheriff's
interlocutor in regard to interest to the effect that
interest was to be payable from the date of the decree
of divorce. The sheriff principal's decision as regards
interest has not been challenged in the appeal to this
court. But the defender contends that he erred in law
in his decision as to the amount of the award.

The only property which belonged to the parties at
the relevant date was a claim by the defender for
damages as a result of an injury which he had sustained in the course of his employment with North Sea
Engineering Ltd. The accident occurred on 1
December 1984 and the effect of the injury was that
he did not work again during the course of the
marriage. He subsequently raised an action of
damages against his employers in Aberdeen sheriff
court. That action had not yet come to proof by the
date when the parties ceased to cohabit, which was 28
July 1988. That is the relevant date in terms of s 10
(3) of the 1985 Act. On 12 June 1989 the sheriff
granted decree in that action for the sum of £98,000
with interest. Payment of the sum due under this
decree amounting to £105,528·89 was made to the
defender on 8 August 1989. The only capital asset
which he had at the time of the divorce on 29 March
1990 was what was left of this sum.

The sheriff held that the claim for damages was
matrimonial property within the meaning of s 10 (4)
of the 1985 Act since it was an asset which could be
assigned: *Traill & Sons v Actieselskabat Dalbeattie Ltd*.
Although the claim was not quantified until after the
relevant date and payment was not made to the
defender until later still, the sheriff was satisfied that
the value of the claim should be assessed in conformity
with the sums awarded by the sheriff who assessed
damages. He made no deduction or other adjustment
to the principal sum to allow for the fact that it was
not received until after the relevant date, but he made
a small adjustment on this account to the interest
which was awarded on the amounts for solatium and
past loss of wages. He then made various deductions
for the defender's liability for extrajudicial expenses
and for debts incurred during the marriage in order to
arrive at a figure for the net value of the matrimonial
property. He then had regard to the nature of the
matrimonial property, this being one of the special
circumstances referred to in s 10 (6) (d), and discounted the whole of the sums included in the award
of damages for solatium with interest and for loss of
future earning capacity. The effect of all this was to
reduce the amount to be shared between the parties to
£46,255. The final step in his calculations was to take
account of the economic disadvantage which he considered the pursuer to have suffered in the interests of
the defender following his accident and in respect of
his consumption of alcohol, in accordance with the
principle described in s 9 (1) (b). Taking a broad view
of the matter he awarded the pursuer the sum of
£25,000 which was rather more than half of the sum

which was to be shared between the parties. The foundation for all his calculations was the sum awarded by
the sheriff as damages approximately one year after
the relevant date.

The argument for the defender in the appeal to the
sheriff principal was that the claim for damages had no
value at all at the relevant date. It was agreed that the
claim was assignable but the contention was that it had
no value until it was either settled or decree was
granted. It was said that the claim was only a potential
asset at the relevant date, which might turn out to be
a liability in the event of the defender losing his action
and becoming liable in expenses. For these reasons it
was argued that the claim was not at that date capable
of valuation. This argument appears to have been
advanced as one of principle, because there is no indication in the sheriff's findings of fact or in his note
that any evidence was led to this effect. Not surprisingly the argument was rejected by the sheriff principal. He agreed with the sheriff that the claim itself
was matrimonial property even although it had not
been quantified at the relevant date. And he rejected
the argument that it necessarily had no value, on the
view that it was reasonable to think that a potential
assignee after considering the available evidence
would have been prepared to offer something to
acquire the claim. There was no criticism in the
appeal of any of the detail of the calculations by which
the sheriff had arrived at the sum of £25,000 which he
awarded to the pursuer.

Counsel for the defender accepted that the sheriff
principal was well founded in holding that the
defender's claim of damages was an asset which had a
value at the relevant date. She did not seek to support
the only argument which appears to have been
advanced in the appeal to the sheriff principal by way
of challenge to the award. She assured us, however,
that the question how this asset ought to be valued was
raised in that appeal, and on the basis that it was open
to her to renew the argument in the appeal to this
court, she submitted that the sheriff principal was in
error in holding that the sheriff was well founded in
basing his award on the sum paid to the defender as
damages. Her contention was that the claim for
damages, which was the only asset which was assignable at the relevant date, was fundamentally different
in character from the award of damages which the
defender ultimately received. We were referred to
Cooper v Cooper in which Lord Robertson refused a
claim by the wife for award of a capital sum on
divorce. This was because he declined to take account
of the husband's claim for damages for personal injury
which had not yet been quantified or admitted. He
held that it would be impossible to make a fair or
realistic assessment of the amount to be paid as a
capital payment without knowing the sum of damages
awarded and at least the approximate value of the
various elements included therein. Reference was also
made to *Mackenzie v Middleton, Ross and Arnot*, in
order to illustrate the point that the hypothetical assignee would be likely to have offered less for the claim
for damages than the sum ultimately awarded because

of the material risks inherent in a litigation. In that case the figure which was arrived at as being the value of the claim which had been lost due to the solicitor's failure to raise the action timeously was regarded as the amount which it would have been sound business for the insurers to tender to the family and which would have been regarded by the family as a tender which it would have been folly to ignore: per Lord President Emslie at p 290. Counsel for the defenders accepted that no facts had been put before the sheriff in evidence — and certainly none are set out in his findings in fact — which would have enabled this approach to valuation to be adopted in the present case. Her solution to this difficulty is to invite us to remit the case to the sheriff so that he might hear additional evidence on this point and make the necessary findings on that evidence.

There would have been force in this argument if the necessary basis for it had been laid in the defender's pleadings and in the evidence which was led at the proof. In principle there is much to be said for the view that a claim of damages which is yet to be quantified and admitted will attract less if offered for sale in the market place than the amount awarded by the decree which is obtained at the end of the day. Common experience suggests that a discount will be insisted upon for the uncertainties inherent in the litigation, and the greater the uncertainty the larger the discount is likely to be. But an exercise of valuation on this basis cannot be carried out without some evidence to support it. At the very least some evidence is needed to identify those parts of the claim which are in dispute and the extent to which they are likely to be disputed. An examination of the pleadings for the defender in this case shows that no attempt was made by his agent to join issue with the pursuer on this point at the proof. The pursuer made it perfectly clear in her pleadings that her claim for a capital sum was based on the amount of the award, and she contended that that award was matrimonial property within the meaning of s 10 of the Act. The defender in his averments in reply described the various payments made by him out of the sum which he received in settlement of his claim and he analysed the principal sum which was awarded to him into its various component parts. His averments concluded with a denial that the whole of that award amounted to matrimonial property in terms of s 10, the implication being that it was conceded that part of that award was comprised in the matrimonial property. Nowhere in these averments was it suggested by the defender that it was the claim only as at the relevant date and not the award itself which ought to be taken as being matrimonial property. Nor were there any averments to the effect that the claim had no value as at the relevant date or, if it had a value, how that value ought to be quantified. These omissions are significant, because all the facts relevant to an assessment of the amount or value of the claim as at the relevant date were within the knowledge of the defender. The obvious inference to be drawn from the pleadings is that the defender was content to accept the amount of the award as the basis

for the calculations to be made in respect of the pursuer's claim for a capital sum. It is not surprising that when he came to make his calculations the sheriff followed this approach. The only facts before him which were relevant to the question of value were those relating to the amount of the award and its various component parts. In the absence of any evidence to the contrary he was entitled to assess the value of the claim as being the amount which was awarded in respect of it. It was this additional evidence which was lacking in *Cooper v Cooper* and was the principal reason why Lord Robertson felt unable to make any award in that case.

We have no hesitation, therefore, in rejecting this part of counsel for the defender's argument. The motion that we should remit the case to the sheriff to hear further evidence as to the value to be attached to the claim must also be rejected. There is no indication that a motion to this effect was made to the sheriff principal. In any event, as counsel for the pursuer pointed out, it cannot possibly be suggested that the defender has only now come into possession of the relevant facts. A remit to hear further evidence can be justified only in very exceptional circumstances and will not be granted where, as is plainly the case here, the evidence which is sought to be led could have been made available at the proof.

[The court then dealt with and rejected an argument that the sheriff erred in allowing the pursuer more than an equal share, with which this report is not concerned.]

Counsel for Pursuer and Respondent, Macnair; Solicitors, Shepherd & Wedderburn, WS (for Cooper & Hay, Aberdeen) — Counsel for Defender and Appellant, Stacey; Solicitors, Drummond Miller, WS (for The Frank Lefevre Practice, Aberdeen).

C H A of L

M T Group v Howden Group plc

OUTER HOUSE

LORD CULLEN

14 JANUARY 1992

Diligence — Inhibition and arrestment on dependence — Recall — Whether nimious and oppressive — Action raised against guarantor — Dispute as to whether liability under guarantee limited to same extent as principal obligation — Defenders intending to plead forum non conveniens.

Jurisdiction — Forum non conveniens — Claim by Danish company against Scottish company — Claim under guarantee executed in English but subject to Danish

law in respect of contract to be performed in Denmark —
A *Dispute as to effect of Danish law.*

A Danish company raised an action, as a commercial cause, seeking declarator that, in terms of an agreement previously entered into, a Scottish company was obliged to take steps necessary to secure performance of the obligations of its subsidiary company and to indemnify the pursuers against losses arising from the non-performance of those obligations. The declarator was sought because the defenders had argued that their guarantee was restricted to the same extent as the
B principal obligant's liability. The pursuers also sought decree for payment of a sum which they maintained was a reasonable estimate of their unrestricted losses resulting from the non-performance of the obligations. (In a separate action brought against the subsidiary of the Scottish company the pursuers had sought decree for damages for breach of contract.) Inhibition and arrestment were effected on the basis of the warrant contained in the summons. Prior to the calling of the summons the defenders moved for recall of the inhibi-
C tion and arrestment, maintaining that they were nimious and oppressive. When moving for recall, the defenders argued that the action should more properly be decided in the Danish courts. Although the defenders were domiciled in Scotland, the contract related to a construction project in Denmark, the guarantee was executed in Denmark and fell to be executed in accordance with Danish law.

Held, (1) that the pursuers had a proper basis for
D seeking to maintain inhibition and arrestment for the full amount of their claim against the defenders, the defenders' obligation to indemnify them arguably not being affected by the clauses restricting liability in the contract between the company and the pursuers (p 347H-J); and (2) that so far as the defenders' plea of forum non conveniens was concerned, the various considerations as to the appropriateness of the Scottish court rather than a Danish court did not indicate that the inhibition and arrestment were nimious and oppressive (p 348G-H); and motion for recall *refused.*
E

Crédit Chimique v James Scott Engineering Group Ltd, 1982 SLT 131, *considered.*

Action of declarator and payment

The M T Group brought an action against the Howden Group plc for declarator that the defenders were bound to indemnify the pursuers in terms of an
F agreement previously entered into and for payment in terms of the agreement.

Prior to the calling of the summons the defenders moved for the recall of the inhibition and arrestment which had proceeded on the warrant contained in the summons. The motion for recall came before the Lord Ordinary (Cullen).

Case referred to

Crédit Chimique v James Scott Engineering Group Ltd, 1982 SLT 131; 1979 SC 406.

On 14 January 1992 the Lord Ordinary *refused* the defenders' motion.
G

LORD CULLEN.—This commercial cause is concerned with a guarantee executed by the defenders in favour of the pursuer on 29 November 1988 in connection with a contract between the pursuer and James Howden & Co Ltd, which I will refer to as "James Howden", for the design, manufacture and supply by James Howden for the pursuer of four tunnel boring machines for use in the construction of a railway tunnel under the Storebaelt in Denmark. The
H defenders own the share capital of James Howden. The contract was dated 25 November 1988, subject to amendments on 15 December 1989 and 16 November 1990.

The summons passed the signet on 20 December and was served on 23 December 1991. On the latter date inhibition and arrestment were effected on the basis of the warrant contained in the summons.

The pursuer seeks decree of declarator as follows:
"(a) That in terms of a guarantee executed by the I defenders on 29 November 1988, in respect that James Howden & Co Ltd have failed to perform and are in breach of the obligations incumbent upon them in terms of a contract with the pursuer dated 25 November 1988, the defenders themselves are bound to take whatever steps may be necessary to achieve performance of the obligations of James Howden & Co Ltd and are bound to indemnify and keep indemnified the pursuer against any loss, damage, costs or expense arising from said failure or breach.
J

"(b) That the said obligation on the part of the defenders to indemnify is not subject to the purported limitations on damages contained in arts XVI and XXV of said contract dated 25 November 1988 between the pursuer and James Howden & Co Ltd."

The pursuer also seeks decree for payment to it by the defenders of the sum of DKK 747,821,100 (Danish Kroner), the sterling equivalent of which is about £70,000,000, as being a reasonable estimate of
K the loss, damage, costs and expense sustained by it. In a separate action against James Howden the pursuer seeks decree for payment of the same sum as being loss and damage sustained by it as a result of breach of contract on the part of James Howden. In that connection the pursuer avers in art 11 of the condescendence annexed to the present summons that: "There is, however, no likelihood of any duplication in recovery of damages. James Howden & Co Ltd are unlikely to be able to pay more than a small proportion of any
L damages awarded against them. For this reason the defenders submitted themselves to said guarantee. In any event the pursuer is desirous of having as soon as possible a decision from the court on the question whether the defenders' obligation to indemnify is subject to the purported limitation on damages recoverable by the pursuer under arts XVI and XXV of the contract with James Howden & Co Ltd and thereafter to sist this action pending conclusion of the arbitration between them and James Howden & Co Ltd in Denmark."

Articles XVI and XXV of the contract provide, respectively, that James Howden are only to be responsible for indirect or consequential losses up to a maximum of £4,000,000; and that the contract is to be subject to certain liquidated damages and penalties which overall are not to exceed 20 per cent of the price of each of the tunnel boring machines. I was informed that the overall liability of James Howden under these contractual provisions could not exceed £12,000,000.

In terms of the guarantee executed on 29 November 1988 the defenders as James Howden's ultimate holding company entered into a number of "unconditional irrevocable undertakings" with the pursuer. The particular undertaking which is of most relevance for present purposes was in the following terms: "2. That if James Howden & Co Ltd shall in any respect fail to perform all its obligations contained in the said contract or commits any breach thereof we shall ourselves perform or take whatever steps may be necessary to achieve performance of the obligations of James Howden & Co Ltd and we shall indemnify and keep indemnified the purchaser [the pursuer] against any loss, damage, costs or expense howsoever arising from the said failure or breach."

On 10 January 1992, before the calling of the summons, I heard a motion by the defenders for the recall of the inhibition and arrestment, which was opposed by the pursuer. At the same time I heard a similar motion by James Howden in the separate action against them to which I have referred above. On 14 January I refused both motions.

In support of their submission that the inhibition and arrestment fell to be recalled unconditionally as being nimious and oppressive, counsel for the defenders presented a number of arguments, the first and second of which challenged the pursuer's action in whole or in part.

In the first place counsel for the defenders submitted that the pursuer had failed to address the fact that both the contract and the guarantee were, according to their terms, to be construed and take effect in accordance with Danish law. Where there was an explicit provision that a foreign law was to apply, there was no room for the presumption that foreign law was to the same effect as Scots law. As regards Danish law the defenders had been advised by experts in Danish law, including Professor Norgard, that the obligations of the defenders under the guarantee were no wider than the underlying contractual obligations on the part of James Howden. In other words the defenders were bound in no more than an accessory way. It followed that the defenders' liability to indemnify was no wider than any liability on the part of James Howden in respect of breach of contract. It was to be noted that in the present action the pursuer did not rely, as they did in the action against James Howden, on the proposition that James Howden were grossly negligent in maintaining that the defenders' obligation to indemnify was not subject to the restrictions imposed by arts XVI and XXV of the contract.

In response counsel for the pursuer submitted that

its position was that the guarantee, which was referred to in Danish law as a contract of "kaution", imposed on the guarantor an obligation to perform the contractual obligations of the contractor and to procure such performance. The extent of the obligation to indemnify was the same as that of this primary obligation. It followed that the obligation on the part of the defenders to indemnify was not subject to the restrictive provisions contained in arts XVI and XXV of the contract which, unless they were rendered inapplicable in the circumstances which occurred, applied to regulate the extent of any liability on the part of James Howden. The pursuer's position was based upon advice which had been tendered to it by Mr Jacob Norager-Neilsen, a practising Danish lawyer and the author of a commentary on the Danish Sale of Goods Act.

I was satisfied that on the interpretation of the scope of the guarantee the pursuer has the basis for an argument that it is not affected by the restrictions contained in arts XVI and XXV of the contract, being a ground which is entirely independent of whether the pursuer is successful in establishing that, in the circumstances which have occurred, the liability of James Howden is not affected by the restrictions contained in those articles. It followed that there could be a situation in which the liability of James Howden did not exceed £12,000,000, but the balance of the pursuer's loss and damage would be recoverable from the defenders alone. These considerations indicated that, so far as concerned the extent of its claim, the pursuer had a proper basis for seeking to maintain inhibition and arrestment for the full amount of their pecuniary claim against the defenders.

In the second place counsel for the defenders indicated that it was their intention to plead that the Court of Session was forum non conveniens and outlined the argument in support of that plea. It was pointed out that the guarantee was executed in Denmark and fell to be construed in accordance with Danish law. It was not an argument in favour of a forum that diligence could be effected or had been effected there. Reference was made to the decision of Lord Jauncey in *Crédit Chimique v James Scott Engineering Group Ltd* in which, despite the fact that the defenders had their domicile in Scotland and that there was a warrant to arrest on the dependence, he held that the plea of forum non conveniens should be sustained and the action sisted to enable the pursuers to pursue their claim in the French courts. In that case a group of French banks had sued a Scottish company as guarantors for credit which had been extended to a French company. Lord Jauncey held that because of the accessory nature of the alleged guarantee and the many and complex questions of French law which were likely to be involved the ends of justice were more likely to be secured if the subject matter was pursued in a French court. Counsel for the defenders also submitted that his clients had been advised that in a Danish court the construction of a document could be ascertained by reference to collateral material in a way which went far beyond what would be permitted in a Scottish court.

This raised a problem in the present case. Was a Scottish court to admit such material on the basis that it was in accordance with Danish law? Further, was it reasonable for a Scottish court to determine the construction of the guarantee, which had been sought only as a secondary security and would be relevant only if breach of contract on the part of James Howden had been established? It was submitted that the only reason why the Court of Session had been asked to determine the construction of the guarantee was to put pressure on the defenders by means of inhibition and arrestment.

In reply counsel for the pursuer pointed out that there was only one reported case in which a plea of forum non conveniens had been upheld where the defenders had their domicile in Scotland, namely the decision in *Crédit Chimique*. In that case Lord Jauncey had no difficulty in accepting that the Scottish domicile of the defenders was a matter to be taken into account in the exercise of the court's discretion. However he concluded that if there were other and more weighty considerations militating against the court exercising its discretion in a particular case, those considerations would not require to give way solely to the fact that the defenders' domicile was Scottish. The present case did not resemble the circumstances of *Crédit Chimique*, in which there were numerous and complex questions of French law both in regard to the alleged guarantee and in regard to the credit facilities extended to the French company and the liquidation of that company (see 1982 SLT, p 134). In the present case all that the Court of Session was being asked to do was to determine whether the defenders' liability under the guarantee was or was not limited. The pursuer intended to establish that by Danish law it was not, and to do this at an early stage. The flexible procedure which was available in a commercial cause could be used in order to obtain an early proof on this restricted point. The guarantee itself did not give rise to any difficulty of language since it was in English. It should also be borne in mind that under art II of the Convention on Jurisdiction and the Enforcement of Judgments in Civil and Commercial Matters the primary rule of jurisdiction was that persons domiciled in a contracting state should be sued in the courts of that state. There was nothing artificial about proceedings being taken against a person in a court of the contracting state in which he was domiciled. The defenders' assets were likely to be in Scotland; and it was only through the Scottish courts that liability on the part of the defenders could be enforced. There was no reason why the pursuer should not have the advantage of diligence which Scottish litigants enjoyed.

The arguments in regard to the question of forum non conveniens were set out for me by the parties in outline only. No doubt if the defenders are to press for a hearing of that plea the arguments will be developed in more detail. The question for me was whether I found the defenders' attack on the forum persuasive in regard to the question whether the inhibition and arrestment were nimious and oppressive. I found that the pursuer's argument in reliance on the defenders' domicile and the presence of their assets in Scotland to be of considerable weight. The present case does not appear to me to present anything like the degree and extent of complexity of foreign legal questions which were presented in the case of *Crédit Chimique*. In that case Lord Jauncey pointed out that the mere fact that a case raised matters of foreign law was of itself not necessarily determinative of whether the Scottish court should sustain the plea. Having considered the submissions made on either side I did not find myself persuaded that considerations as to the appropriateness of the forum indicated that the inhibition and arrestment were nimious and oppressive.

The defenders also relied upon a number of further considerations. It was pointed out that, according to its averments in art 11 of the condescendence, the pursuer had sought the defenders' guarantee in view of the fact that James Howden were unlikely to be able to pay more than a small proportion of any damages awarded against them. The pursuer had not insisted on the defenders providing any further security at the time. However, they were now seeking to obtain a fresh layer of security without any averments as to a change of circumstances which justified their departure from relying solely on the guarantee. Any obligation on the part of the defenders to indemnify was dependent on the outcome of the arbitration between the pursuer and James Howden and the failure on the part of James Howden to meet any liability which had been established against them in that arbitration; and it was dependent on the existing security which was provided by bank guarantees and sums retained amounting in total to about £15,784,000 proving to be inadequate. In order to reach that point the pursuer required to surmount a number of hurdles, including disputes in regard to foreign law, which would not be achieved until a considerable time had elapsed. In the meantime the inhibition had caused considerable inconvenience and the arrestment had caused embarrassment. This was not in the interests of the defenders. They were a substantial trading concern. Counsel informed me, without further elaboration, that they had net assets of £90,000,000.

In response counsel for the pursuer emphasised that the defenders had been required to give a guarantee as James Howden had relatively small resources. The breaches of contract which had taken place were very significant in the sense that they had given rise to extremely large claims. The existing security covered only a small part of the pursuer's claim if the pursuer was entitled to damages against James Howden or the defenders on a basis which was unrestricted by arts XVI and XXV of the contract.

I appreciated that the liability of the defenders was dependent upon a number of matters and that it is likely to be a substantial time before the arbitration is concluded and the extent of any liability on the part of the defenders is established. However, it is commonplace that the outcome of any proceedings is dependent upon the resolution of matters of fact and law and may take a considerable time to achieve com-

A pletion; and yet in the meantime it may be appropriate that inhibition and arrestment remain in force. In the present case, while on one view the position of the defenders was that of providing a secondary security with respect to any liability on the part of James Howden, there could be a situation in which their liability was more extensive than that of James Howden. This arises from the point which I have noted above, namely that the ground upon which it is maintained that the restrictive provisions of arts XVI and XXV do not apply to any liability on the part of

B the defenders is entirely independent of the ground on which it is maintained that those provisions do not restrict any liability on the part of James Howden. This point appears to me, if anything, to strengthen the pursuer's hand in relying on the inhibition and arrestment. Throughout the discussion before me the defenders' position was that both should be recalled unconditionally. I was not persuaded by the various considerations which I have discussed in the last section of this opinion, either taken by themselves or along with the other matters to which I have referred

C earlier in this opinion, that the inhibition and arrestment should be recalled. I considered on balancing the matters which were drawn to my attention that the defenders had failed to persuade me that they were nimious and oppressive.

Counsel for Pursuers, Drummond Young, QC, Currie; Solicitors, W & J Burness, WS — Counsel for Defenders, Dean of Faculty (Johnston, QC), Keen; Soli-

D _citors, Maclay Murray & Spens._

A M

Young v Webster

HIGH COURT OF JUSTICIARY

E THE LORD JUSTICE GENERAL (HOPE), LORDS ALLANBRIDGE AND MAYFIELD

9 JULY 1992

Justiciary — Evidence — Sufficiency — Theft — Accused passengers in car with dinghy and trailer 30 minutes after dinghy and trailer stolen — Accused stopped at 11.45 pm on country road in car used to steal dinghy and trailer — Whether sufficient evidence that accused possessing dinghy and trailer — Whether sufficient evidence of theft.

F
Three accused persons went to trial along with a fourth man on a summary complaint which libelled theft of a dinghy and trailer. The evidence disclosed that at 11.15 pm a car drove rather quickly into the grounds of a sailing club, an unidentified male person got out of the passenger door and the dinghy and trailer were hitched to the back of the car. The car then left suddenly. At 11.45 pm police officers stopped the car on a twisting country road leading to Glasgow, about 12 miles from the sailing club. There were five men in the car, including the three accused

and the fourth man who was the driver. At the close of the Crown case it was submitted that there was no G case for the three accused to answer as it could not be said that they had been in possession of the dinghy and trailer when the car was stopped by the police. The sheriff repelled the submission. The accused did not give evidence and were convicted of theft. The accused appealed.

Held, that it was a reasonable inference that the accused knew of the presence of the dinghy and trailer and that there were sufficient circumstances to entitle the sheriff to infer that the accused were involved in H the same enterprise as the driver and to enable possession of the stolen property to be attributed to them (p 352G-J); and appeals _refused_.

Opinion, that in the absence of a sufficient explanation by the accused for their presence in the car, there was ample evidence for a conviction at least of reset (p 352J).

Summary complaint   I
Ronald Alexander Laing Young, William Douglas and David Maloney, along with another person, were charged at the instance of D L Webster, procurator fiscal, Dunoon, on a summary complaint which contained the following charge: "on 14 August 1991, from the Holy Loch Sailing Club, Shore Road, Sandbank, Argyll, you did steal a dinghy and trailer". The accused pled not guilty and proceeded to trial. After trial the sheriff (C W Palmer) convicted the accused.

The accused appealed by way of stated case to the J High Court against the decision of the sheriff.

Cases referred to
Fox v Patterson, 1948 SLT 547; 1948 JC 104.
Hipson v Tudhope, 1983 SCCR 247.

The sheriff in the stated case provided a note in the following terms:

THE SHERIFF (C W PALMER).—The Crown K evidence was as follows:

Alexander Collier is a retired gentleman aged 67 and is the sailing secretary of the Holy Loch Sailing Club, Shore Road, Sandbank, Argyll. The premises of the sailing club are located 100 yds from the witness's house. Mr Collier said that he knew a boat and trailer belonging to a member of the club, a Mr McChlery. He described the boat as a 13 ft boat containing a small cabin or, as it is called, a cuddy. At 11.15 pm exactly on 14 August 1991 he saw a light coloured L hatchback drive into the grounds of the sailing club rather fast. The boat and trailer belonging to Mr McChlery was in fact the only boat left on the premises at the time, the others having been moved out for the coming weekend. The trailer and boat were hitched up to the back of the car. He saw a male person get out of the car beforehand and he said that that person emerged from the passenger door of the car. Once the boat and trailer were hooked onto the rear of the car the car very suddenly took off and left the sailing club premises through the opposite gate.

A The car, boat and trailer then went up what is known locally as Rankin's Brae in order to join the main Dunoon to Cairndow road. The witness said that the Why Not public house is located on the main road at the top of Rankin's Brae.

Constables David Ferguson and David Stone were, on Wednesday, 14 August 1991, at 11.45 pm occupied in an anti-crime patrol driving north in a marked police car on the A815 Dunoon to Cairndow road at the north end of Loch Eck and about one mile south of Glen Branter. They estimated that the driving time B from the Why Not public house to the place where they came across this Ford Fiesta would be between 18 and 20 minutes. The distance involved is 12 miles along a twisty country road. The trailer was showing no lights to the rear and the police signalled it to stop by putting on the blue light. It did so. The police had no information that any crime had been committed but intended to stop and check out any vehicles moving that night. They then approached the car. He identified the co-accused McGarrigle as the driver. C There were five males in the car. They identified the three appellants and the co-accused. They asked the driver, the co-accused McGarrigle, to explain where he had obtained the boat. McGarrigle said that he had bought the boat from an American in a public house for £300. The officers accepted that the question and answer may not have been heard by the other occupants of the car. One of the police officers looked inside the cabin and saw a tool box with the name McChlery on it. He knew of the name McChlery and D contacted the police to check it out. All five men were asked to accompany the police officers to Dunoon police office on a voluntary basis. They agreed to do so. The police officers then summoned assistance and while they were waiting for assistance to arrive the fifth member of the party disappeared from the locus and was not seen again. On arrival at the police office the witness McChlery was shown the boat and trailer and identified them. At 1.20 am all four were arrested and cautioned and charged. The appellants Maloney E and Young made no reply. The appellant Douglas replied: "You're talking a load of shite". The police officers said that there was no number plate showing to the rear of the trailer. The police also confirmed that at that time of night there was no ferry connection between the Cowal Peninsula and the mainland and the only way out of Dunoon was via the A815 Dunoon to Cairndow road meeting up with the A83 Campbeltown to Glasgow road.

Robert McChlery, a member of the sailing club at F Holy Loch, recalled being summoned to Dunoon police office about 12.30 am one morning. He went to the police office via the sailing club where he noticed that the boat and trailer were missing. He had last seen them at 5.15 pm that evening, that is on 14 August. When he arrived at the police station the boat and trailer had not yet arrived. In due course they did. He then identified them as his. The cabin or cuddy on the boat was locked and he opened it with a key which he had in his possession. Inside was located his tool box with his name on it. He placed a value of £650 on the boat and £50 damage had been incurred.

The solicitor for the appellant Young made a sub-G mission in terms of s 345A of the Criminal Procedure (Scotland) Act 1975 that there was no case to answer. In his submission the Crown were relying on the doctrine of recent possession and the appellant Young was not in possession. He relied heavily on the case of *Hipson v Tudhope*. The appellant Young was a passenger in the car which was towing stolen property. For there to be possession the court would have to be satisfied that he had knowledge and control and there was no evidence that he had control over the property in question. The solicitor for the appellant Douglas adopted the solicitor for the appellant H Young's submission. The solicitor for the appellant Maloney did the same and added that the Crown would have to establish art and part and there was no evidence whatsoever of concert.

In response the procurator fiscal invited me to distinguish the facts in this case from those in *Hipson v Tudhope*. Here one was not dealing with an allegedly stolen car but a car towing stolen items. These items were clearly visible and thus all four occupants of the car had knowledge of them. The important point in I his view was that the possession was very recent indeed and that at the very least there was sufficient to infer that they were privy to the retention of stolen property and therefore there was a sufficiency to establish the crime of reset.

It seemed implicit from the submissions made on behalf of the appellants that what they were effectively saying was that only the driver could be in possession of the boat and trailer because only the driver had control over the boat and trailer. I have no difficulty J in distinguishing the facts in this case from the facts in *Hipson*. That case involved a stolen car and it is accepted that the accused had accepted a lift in it. As I read the case of *Hipson*, it does not directly address the question whether a passenger in a car can be said to be in possession of it. In my respectful view it all depends on the circumstances of each individual case whether or not possession can be inferred. In my view it would be simplistic and artificial to suggest that only a driver and owner of a car could have had possession K of it and by extension as I understood to be submitted here, have possession of items attached thereto. If, for example, one had a situation where a boat and trailer were being towed by a vehicle, the vehicle was driven by a chauffeur and his employer was present in the car, in my submission the chauffeur would have possession and control of the car and trailer subject, of course, to the instructions of his employer. That must also mean in my view that the employer, the owner of the boat and trailer, also has possession and control. In L the same way if in fact a number of people owned the boat and trailer jointly and these people were all present in the car with the chauffeur then the situation would be that all occupants of the car would be in possession of the boat and trailer. They would all have knowledge of them and they would have, to a degree, control of them. At this stage in proceedings I had no explanation as to how these three appellants came to be in the car. The Crown case is in short compass, the boat and trailer were stolen at 11.15 pm exactly from the premises of the Holy Loch Sailing Club, Sandbank. The vehicle used was a light coloured hatchback. Only one person was seen by the witness Collier and that person emerged from the passenger's side of the car. That clearly infers that there were at least two people in that car at that time. Exactly half an hour later, some 12 miles and, according to police evidence at least 18-20 minutes' drive north on what is accepted is a slow and twisty road, late at night, the entire combination was stopped by the police. The trailer was showing no lights and no number plate. In my view, the short passage of time is crucial and not simply to the application of the doctrine of recent possession. The shortage of time, namely 30 minutes, in the circumstances of this case is tantamount to being caught red handed. The shortage of time is such that in my view, standing that we know that at least two people were in that car when the boat and trailer were taken at 11.15, that concert can clearly be inferred by the presence of the three appellants in that car, as can the joint possession of the boat and trailer. This is not a situation such as in *Hipson* where one was only concerned with the car itself and where it was accepted that the passenger had accepted a lift in the car. Here the boat and trailer were there for all to see, including the three appellants and, picking up the procurator fiscal's point, the circumstances were such that it was reasonable to infer that anyone in that car would be aware that the boat and trailer were stolen and that made all three appellants at the very least privy to the retention of the stolen property. I had no hesitation, therefore, in repelling the submissions.

Appeal

The sheriff posed the following questions for the opinion of the High Court:

(1) Was I correct in repelling the submissions made in terms of s 345A of the Criminal Procedure (Scotland) Act 1975?

(2) Was I entitled to infer that the appellants were in possession of the stolen boat and trailer? Or, alternatively, was I entitled to infer that they were privy to their retention?

(3) On the facts stated was I entitled to convict?

The appeal was argued before the High Court on 23 June 1992.

On 9 July 1992 the court *answered* question 1 in the *affirmative*, *declined* to answer question 2 as unnecessary, *answered* question 3, of consent of the accused, in the *affirmative*, and *refused* the appeals.

The following opinion of the court was delivered by the Lord Justice General (Hope):

OPINION OF THE COURT.—The appellants went to trial in the sheriff court at Dunoon with a co-accused named Robert Michael McGarrigle on a charge of stealing a dinghy and trailer from the Holy Loch Sailing Club, Sandbank. A motion was made by the appellants' solicitors at the end of the Crown case under s 345A of the Criminal Procedure (Scotland) Act 1975 that there was no case to answer, but the

sheriff repelled this submission in each case. McGarrigle then gave evidence on his own behalf and his solicitor led one other witness in his defence. None of the appellants gave evidence. In the event the sheriff found all the appellants and their co-accused guilty of the charge. The appellants have now appealed against their conviction on the ground that the sheriff erred in law in repelling the motion of no case to answer. They submit that he was not entitled to infer from the Crown evidence that they were involved in the commission of the crime libelled in the complaint, or that they were at any time in possession of the stolen goods or privy to their retention. We were informed at the outset of the hearing of these appeals that the appeal by William Douglas against the sentence of imprisonment which he received was not being insisted upon.

The Crown case comprised the evidence of four witnesses. The first was Alexander Collier, who was the sailing secretary of the sailing club. His house was 100 yds from the club premises, and he was an eyewitness to the theft. The dinghy, which was 13 ft long and was on its trailer at the time, was the only boat left on the premises. All the others had been moved out for the coming weekend. At 11.15 pm on the night in question he saw a light coloured hatchback car drive into the grounds of the club rather fast. A male person got out of the passenger door, and the trailer and boat were hitched up to the back of the car. The car then took off suddenly and left the premises up a brae in the direction of the A815 Dunoon to Cairndow road. The next two witnesses were two police officers who were on an anti-crime patrol on the A815 road that evening. They were about 12 miles and between 18 and 20 minutes' driving time from the point where the brae joins the main road. At 11.45 pm they observed a Ford Fiesta car pulling a boat and trailer which was showing no lights to the rear. There were five men in the car, including the appellants and the co-accused McGarrigle who was the driver. They stopped the car and a conversation then took place between the police and McGarrigle which may not have been heard by the other occupants of the car. One of the police officers looked inside the cabin of the boat and saw a tool box with the name McChlery on it. They asked the five men to accompany them to Dunoon police office, which they agreed to do. One of the party then disappeared and was not seen again. The other four went to the police office where Robert McChlery, who was the fourth witness for the Crown, was shown the boat and trailer and identified them as his property. At 1.20 am the four remaining occupants of the car were arrested, cautioned and charged with the theft.

It was submitted to the sheriff that the appellants could not be said to have been in possession of the boat and trailer when the car was stopped by the police since they were merely passengers in the car. There was no evidence that any of them had participated in the theft because Collier saw only one person emerge from the passenger door of the car whom he did not identify. Only the driver could be said to have had control over the boat and trailer. There was no evidence from which an inference to that effect could be drawn in the case of the passengers. Reference was made to *Hipson v Tudhope*, in which it was held that there was nothing to indicate that a passenger in a stolen car, who was not implicated in the theft of it, was aware of the fact that it was stolen and was privy to its retention. But the sheriff noted that that case did not address directly the question whether a passenger in a car can be said to be in possession of it, and in his view it all depended on the circumstances whether or not possession could be inferred. So far as the present case was concerned he found sufficient in the facts and circumstances to enable him to draw the inference. It seemed to him that, in view of the short passage of time between the theft and the stopping of the car by the police, the appellants had really been caught red handed, and in any event the boat and trailer were there for all to see and the appellants were at least privy to the retention of the stolen property.

Counsel for the appellants did not challenge the sheriff's inference that the car which was stopped by the police was the same car as that which was involved in the theft. He accepted that the sheriff was entitled to infer that it was the same car, and that those who were in the car would be aware that it was towing a boat and trailer when it was stopped. The important question however was whether they were in the car when the theft took place. On this point the evidence in the Crown case was insufficient, because Collier had observed only one person leaving the car by the passenger door whom he could not identify. There was no evidence that any of the appellants were in the car at that time. The only evidence about them was that they were passengers in the car later in the evening when it was stopped, and there was nothing to suggest that they had anything to do with the theft or were aware that the boat and trailer had been stolen.

This argument is, as the advocate depute pointed out, open to the criticism that the Crown did not need to lead evidence to show that the appellants had participated in the theft. It was sufficient for the Crown that there was a case to answer on a charge of reset, so it was not necessary for there to have been evidence that the appellants were present in the car when the boat and trailer were taken from the sailing club. But the point remains that, unless there was evidence to enable the inference to be drawn that they were in possession of the stolen property when the car was stopped by the police, the appellants were entitled to be acquitted both of theft and of reset. There was evidence that the property had very recently been stolen, and there were other criminative circumstances in that the boat and trailer were being towed late at night along a twisty country road with no lights showing to the rear. The critical question therefore, according to the rule described by Lord Justice General Cooper in *Fox v Patterson*, 1948 SLT at p 548, is whether the stolen goods were in the possession of the passengers in the car as well as its driver when it was stopped by the police about half an hour after the theft.

Counsel for the appellants accepted that the driver of the car was in possession of the boat and trailer since they were attached to the car while he was driving it along the road. He knew that they were attached to the car and they were under his control. But knowledge that there was a boat and trailer attached to the car can also be attributed to the passengers. It is a reasonable inference that they would have seen them when they got into the car — assuming in their favour that they were not already in the car at the time of the theft. The only remaining question therefore is whether there were other facts and circumstances to enable possession of the stolen property to be attributed to them also although they were not actually driving the car.

Now the fact that they were travelling in the same car as the driver does not of itself justify the inference that they were also in possession of the stolen property. But the significance of their presence in the car cannot be judged without taking into account also the circumstances. And in our opinion the circumstances were sufficient to entitle the sheriff to infer that they were all involved in the same enterprise as the driver of the car. Here were five men travelling together in the same car as that used to carry out the theft only a short time after it was committed. They were travelling together late at night on a country road leading to Glasgow from the scene of the crime. It was, to say the least, unlikely that the driver of the car, with the stolen dinghy and trailer still attached to it, would have stopped to pick up passengers after the theft unless they were implicated in it in some way. There was sufficient evidence in these circumstances to warrant the inference that the passengers were as much in possession of the stolen property as the driver, and that they were stopped while they were in the act of taking it away from the place from which it had been stolen. In our opinion there was ample evidence here for a conviction at least of reset in the absence of a sufficient explanation by the appellants for their presence in the car.

For these reasons we considered that the sheriff was right to repel the submissions which were made to him in terms of s 345A of the 1975 Act, and we shall answer the first question in each case in the affirmative. It is not necessary for us to answer the second question since the point raised by it is implicit in our answer to the first. Counsel for the appellants did not argue the third question as he accepted that, when all the evidence in the case was considered, there was sufficient to entitle the sheriff to convict. We shall answer this question in the affirmative and refuse the appeals.

Counsel for Appellants, McBride; Solicitors, (Young) Drummond Miller, WS (for T M Cairns & Co, Glasgow), (Douglas) Gray Muirhead, WS (for Lavery Smith & Co, Glasgow), (Maloney) Aitken Nairn, WS (for Dunlop, Allen, McConnachie & Co, Glasgow) — Counsel for Respondent, Bonomy, AD; Solicitor, J D Lowe, Crown Agent.

P W F

Postel Properties Ltd v Miller and Santhouse plc

OUTER HOUSE

LORD SUTHERLAND

9 JULY 1992

Landlord and tenant — Lease — Construction — Lease of shop unit in shopping centre — Obligation on tenant to keep and use leased premises as retail premises — Whether positive obligation capable of being enforced by decree ad factum praestandum.

Process — Decree — Decree ad factum praestandum — Whether competent against limited company — Law Reform (Miscellaneous Provisions) (Scotland) Act 1940 (3 & 4 Geo VI, c 42), s 1.

The lease of a shop unit in a shopping centre provided that it should endure for 25 years and that the tenants should keep and use the leased premises solely as retail premises throughout the duration of the lease. The tenants were taken bound to indemnify the landlords against all loss or damage suffered by the landlords in consequence of the tenants' failure to occupy the leased premises. The lease also contained other clauses explicitly prohibiting acts which might cause a nuisance or endanger the insurance of the shopping centre. The tenants were a limited company. They used the premises for retail purposes for a period but then closed the shop because it was trading at a loss. The landlords raised an action seeking a decree ordaining the tenants to occupy the premises and trade therefrom. The tenants challenged the competency and relevancy of the action.

Held, (1) that the phrase "to keep and use the leased premises solely as retail premises" should, in the context of the lease as a whole, be construed as a positive obligation and hence there was a prima facie duty on the tenants to occupy the premises and use them for retail purposes (p 356C-D); (2) that not all terms of a lease or other contract were capable of being made the subject of an order for specific implement and, where what was required to be done by one party was not a clear and specific act to be performed at a clear and specific time, but was simply a general duty to be performed over a long period during which circumstances might change, an order ad factum praestandum would not be granted and accordingly, since the order sought by the landlords lacked the necessary precision it was incompetent (p 356E-I); and action *dismissed*.

Grosvenor Developments (Scotland) plc v Argyll Stores Ltd, 1987 SLT 738, *followed*.

Opinion, (1) that an order ad factum praestandum could be competently granted against a company since the penalty for failure was not, given the control provided to the court by the Law Reform (Miscellaneous Provisions) (Scotland) Act 1940, s 1, necessarily imprisonment (pp 356J-357A and 357D-E); (2) that when an obligation in a lease was fortified by a penalty, it was nonetheless open to the creditor to enforce the obligation and the debtor could not escape simply by paying the penalty: thus the mere fact that the tenants were obliged under the contract to indemnify the landlords did not of itself preclude the landlords from seeking a decree ad factum praestandum (p 357J-K).

Gloag, Contract (2nd ed), p 720, *approved*.

Action of specific implement

Postel Properties Ltd, the owners of a shopping centre, raised an action of specific implement against Miller and Santhouse plc, tenants of a unit in the centre, in respect of the failure of the tenants to implement a term of the lease relating to the occupation of the unit. The tenants challenged the competency and relevancy of the landlords' pleadings.

The case came before the Lord Ordinary (Sutherland) on procedure roll on the defenders' pleas to the competency and relevancy of the action and on the pursuers' plea to the relevancy of the defences.

Statutory provisions

The Law Reform (Miscellaneous Provisions) (Scotland) Act 1940, s 1 provides:

"1.—(1) No person shall be apprehended or imprisoned on account of his failure to comply with a decree ad factum praestandum except in accordance with the following provisions—(i) On an application by the person in right of such a decree (hereinafter referred to as the applicant) to the court by which the decree was granted, the court may, if it is satisfied that the person against whom such decree was granted (hereinafter referred to as the respondent) is wilfully refusing to comply with the decree, grant warrant for his imprisonment for any period not exceeding six months; . . .

"(2) On any application in pursuance of the foregoing subsection, the court may, in lieu of granting warrant for imprisonment, recall the decree on which the application proceeds and make an order for the payment by the respondent to the applicant of a specified sum or make such other order as appears to the court to be just and equitable in the circumstances, including, in the case where the decree on which the application proceeds is a decree for delivery of corporeal moveables, a warrant to officers of court to search any premises in the occupation of the respondent or of such other person as may be named in the warrant, and to take possession of, and deliver to the applicant, any such moveables which may be found in such premises."

Cases referred to

Fleming & Ferguson v Burgh of Paisley, 1948 SLT 457; 1948 SC 547.

Grahame v Magistrates of Kirkcaldy (1882) 9 R (HL) 91.

Grosvenor Developments (Scotland) plc v Argyll Stores Ltd, 1987 SLT 738.

Hendry v Marshall (1878) 5 R 687.

Lochgelly Iron & Coal Co v North British Railway Co, 1913 1 SLT 405.

McArthur v Lawson (1877) 4 R 1134.

A
MacLeod v Alexander Sutherland Ltd, 1977 SLT
(Notes) 44.
Middleton v Leslie (1892) 19 R 801.
*Salaried Staff London Loan Co Ltd v Swears and Wells
Ltd*, 1985 SLT 326.
White & Carter (Councils) Ltd v McGregor, 1962 SLT
9; 1962 SC (HL) 1.

Textbooks referred to
Burn-Murdoch, *Interdict*, p 158.
Gloag, *Contract* (2nd ed), pp 657, 659 and 720.
B
Walker, *Civil Remedies*, p 269.

On 9 July 1992 his Lordship *sustained* the
defenders' competency plea and *dismissed* the action.

LORD SUTHERLAND.—In this action the pursuers as landlords under a lease of shop premises seek
decree ordaining the defenders as tenants under the
lease to occupy the premises and trade therefrom, with
a further conclusion for damages. The leased premises
are a shop unit in the Sauchiehall Centre, Glasgow.
C The lease was for a period from 17 April 1987 to 16
April 2012.

Clause 5 of pt IV of the lease provides: "Within ten
weeks of the date of entry under this lease to install in
the leased premises suitable and necessary fixtures, fit-
ments and fittings of good quality required to make
the leased premises suitable in all respects for the permitted use thereof, any necessary planning consent
and/or building warrant being obtained by the tenants
at their expense and the drawings and specifications in
D relation to any fitting out works by the tenants as
aforesaid shall be submitted for the landlords'
approval, such approval not to be unreasonably withheld or delayed and the tenant shall occupy the leased
premises and shall not without the written consent of
the landlords leave the leased premises unoccupied for
a period exceeding 21 days, the tenants indemnifying
the landlords against all loss or damage suffered by the
landlords in consequence of the failure by the tenants
to occupy the leased premises including without
E prejudice to the foregoing generality any loss or
damage to or depreciation in the capital or rental value
of the leased premises attributable to the tenant's
failure to occupy or in consequence of any other
breach by the tenants of the tenant's obligations."

Clause 13 of pt IV provides: "To keep and use the
leased premises solely as retail premises within Class
1 of the Town and Country Planning (Use Classes)
(Scotland) Order 1973", followed by certain other restrictions on use. Clauses 14 and 15, which deal with
F prohibition of acts causing a nuisance or endangering
the insurance of the centre, commence respectively
with the words "not to do or permit to be done upon
or in connection with the leased premises or any part
thereof any act or thing", and "not to do or permit to
be done or omit to do within or upon the leased
premises or any part of the centre any act or thing".

The pursuers aver that the defenders used the
premises for a period but then closed the shop and
ceased trading there. The defenders admit that they
closed the shop and explained that the reason that they

did so was because their activities were producing a
loss. They aver that they endeavoured to find another G
tenant for the premises to whom their rights and obligations under the lease could be assigned in terms of
cl 30 (b) but they have been unable to do so.

The case came on procedure roll on the first and
second pleas of the defenders which are pleas to competency and relevancy and the fourth plea for the pursuers which seeks decree de plano. Under their first
plea the defenders argued that the pursuers' conclusion for implement was incompetent on three
grounds, namely, lack of precision, lack of enforce- H
ability and exclusion of that remedy in terms of the
lease. On the first ground it was argued that an order
ad factum praestandum must be precise, a proposition
vouched in general by Walker on *Civil Remedies*,
p 269, Burn-Murdoch on *Interdict*, p 158, *Middleton v
Leslie, Fleming & Ferguson v Burgh of Paisley* and
Hendry v Marshall. In connection with leases the
defenders referred to *Grosvenor Developments (Scotland) plc v Argyll Stores Ltd*. In *Grosvenor Developments* the defenders were the tenants of a supermarket I
within a development owned by the pursuers and the
lease ran from 1974 to 2016. The lease provided that
the subjects were let for the retail sale of all foodstuffs
and all hardware, electrical goods and non-foods "as
commonly sold in supermarkets and discount stores",
and the use of part of the premises as an off licence.
It was provided that "the tenants shall take possession
of and use and occupy the premises for the foregoing
purpose(s) within three calendar months from the date
of entry hereunder and shall thereafter continue to use J
and occupy the same for said purpose(s) and during all
normal business hours shall keep the premises open
for business throughout the whole period of this
lease". The defenders intimated their intention to discontinue trading and the pursuers sought interdict
against the defenders from ceasing to continue to
occupy and use the supermarket premises. It was held
that it was not competent to obtain an interdict which
in terms compelled the performance of an act and
accordingly the action was dismissed. In addition,
however, it was held that the obligation sought to be K
implemented was too general to be enforced by
specific implement. The obligation to occupy and use
premises and carry on a business therein involved continuous acts of management in which multifarious
actions are required and it also required decisions over
a period of 42 years as to what at any one time is commonly sold in supermarkets. Accordingly the obligation was one where the defenders would have
difficulty in deciding at any given time whether they
were acting in breach of it or not. An order from the L
court must be precise and specific so that the
defenders know throughout the period when the order
is enforced exactly what they are required to do and
what they are prohibited from doing. A further
problem raised in the opinion of Lord Jauncey was
that the order sought was that the defenders continue
to occupy and use the premises without any limitation,
whereas certain provisions in the lease contemplated
an interruption of occupancy and use in the event, for
example, of the premises being damaged or destroyed
or the lease being irritated. The terms of the interdict

A sought therefore required the defenders to do more than they were required to do in terms of the lease.

Counsel for the defenders in the present case founded strongly on *Grosvenor Developments* as showing that an obligation to carry on commercial activity will not be enforced by specific implement because the order would inevitably lack the necessary precision. Furthermore the terms of cl 13 in the present lease do not even make it clear that there is a positive obligation to trade from the premises. All that is said is that the premises must be kept and used

B solely for the purpose of retail trade within class 1 of the relevant regulations. This should be construed as meaning that cl 13 was purely a restrictive clause and did not provide any positive obligation. In any event even if there was an obligation to use the premises, does that necessarily mean that the defenders require to continue trading in a particular fashion? Would it be sufficient to open the shop for half an hour per week with one employee selling matches stationed at a counter just inside the door? If that would not be

C enough, what would be sufficient to comply and how can the defenders know what it is that they must do? In these circumstances there is a total lack of precision in the pursuers' first conclusion and accordingly that conclusion is incompetent.

In reply counsel for the pursuers argued that specific implement is a normal remedy which should be granted unless there is some special hardship or exceptional circumstances or implement is impossible.

D It is for the defenders to aver and prove what such exceptional circumstances would be and if they are unable to do so they have no answer to a claim for implement. In *McArthur v Lawson* it was said by Lord President Inglis that a contract which cannot be enforced by specific implement insofar as regards its form and substance is no contract at all and cannot form the ground of an action of damages. It was not argued by the defenders in this case that there was anything wrong with the contract of lease or that it

E was unenforceable and if that be so then its terms must be enforceable by specific implement. Where a contract has been repudiated the innocent party has an option. He may either accept the repudiation and sue for damages for breach of contract or if he chooses he may refuse to accept the repudiation and then the contract remains in full effect: *White & Carter (Councils) Ltd v McGregor*; *Salaried Staff London Loan Co Ltd v Swears and Wells Ltd*. All that the pursuers are seeking to do here is to enforce the terms of a contract which

F the defenders do not attack as being in any way defective in form or substance. *Grosvenor Developments* is not in point as the issue there was whether interdict was an appropriate remedy and the other observations in the case were obiter. In any event the decision only amounted to saying that the terms of the clause in that particular lease were too vague to be enforceable. There is no difficulty in understanding the concept of occupying premises nor is there any difficulty in understanding the concept of using the premises for the purposes of retail trade. The obligation in cl 13 is to keep and use the premises and if this was intended

G only to be a negative obligation it could easily have been phrased in precisely the same way as cll 14 and 15. The difference in wording shows that it was intended to be a positive obligation. This is perfectly comprehensible in the context of a commercial lease of a unit in a shopping development because lack of use detracts from the viability of a shopping centre. The point taken by Lord Jauncey in *Grosvenor Developments* about other clauses in the lease giving rise to circumstances where occupancy and use could not be enforced is not a valid one, as if decree is granted in the present case this would not abolish all the other

H clauses in the lease but would merely be tantamount to saying that the whole terms of the lease should remain in full force and effect.

Counsel for the pursuers went on to argue that the defenders' averments relating to the loss which they were making in their trading and their difficulties in finding an alternative tenant were irrelevant. The circumstances required to deprive the pursuers of their right to a decree ad factum praestandum would

I have to be exceptional: *Grahame v Magistrates of Kirkcaldy*, *White & Carter (Councils) Ltd* and *Salaried Staff London Loan Co Ltd*. It is no answer for a party in breach to say that it appears that the contract into which he entered has become unduly onerous. There is nothing exceptional in a company trading at a loss in times of recession and equally there is nothing unusual in a company finding difficulty in obtaining alternative tenants for a development which is, in any event, substantially unlet. It is nowhere suggested by the defenders that the pursuers do not have an interest

J to enforce the contract rather than merely claim the alternative remedy of damages. That being so the defenders' averments which purport to show that there are some exceptional circumstances which would justify the court in exercising its equitable jurisdiction to refuse a decree for specific implement are irrelevant and therefore decree should be granted de plano.

In reply to this latter point, counsel for the defenders pointed out that in the case of *Salaried Staff*

K *London Loan Co* where what was sought was payment of rent for the period up to the date when the action was raised, the Lord President said that if the pursuers continued to maintain the contract and continued to sue for payment of unpaid rent in subsequent actions, it may well be that different considerations would arise. Lord Ross observed that it was significant that the defenders made no averments which might justify the view that it would be manifestly unjust and unreasonable to allow the pursuers the remedy which

L they sought in that action, namely payment of the rent. The defenders offered no explanation for purporting to renounce the lease. They did not say that it had become uneconomic for them to continue as tenants, nor that it would be uneconomic for any other tenant and they did not aver that any attempt had been made by them to find a substitute tenant or that it had been impossible to find such a substitute tenant. Lord Ross went on to observe that the lack of any such averments appeared to be fatal to the defenders' contention, as there was no material in that case which would

A justify the court in concluding that it would be manifestly unjust and unreasonable to allow the pursuers the remedy which they were seeking. In the present case the defenders had made appropriate averments. They gave an explanation for ceasing to trade, namely that it had become uneconomic for them to do so. They averred that the centre was not a popular development and they aver that they have made substantial efforts to find a substitute tenant, even to the extent of offering a substantial premium to any incoming tenant, but that they have been unable to find

B anyone to take on the obligations. It was argued that it was a reasonable inference from Lord Ross's opinion that had the averments made in the present case been made in that case, he would have been prepared to accept that there was sufficient at least to go to proof on the question of whether or not it was unjust and unreasonable to allow the pursuers even the limited remedy which they were seeking in that case. A fortiori these averments are very relevant when what is sought is a decree ordaining the defenders to continue uneconomic trading for the next 20 years, or until

C such time as they can find a substitute tenant which, at present, appears to be a virtual impossibility.

The first matter to be considered is what is meant by the words "to keep and use the leased premises solely as retail premises" within the meaning of cl 13. In my opinion as a matter of construction this is intended to be a positive obligation. It is expressed as a positive obligation even though all the rest of the clause produces further restrictions upon what use can be made of the premises. Had it been intended to be

D a negative restriction, it would have been perfectly possible to phrase it in exactly the same way as cll 14 and 15, in other words "not to keep and use the leased premises other than as retail premises" etc. Prima facie therefore there is a duty on the defenders to occupy the premises and to use the premises as retail premises wthin the terms of cll 5 and 13. I have no doubt that a perfectly valid contract can be framed in terms such as this and such a contract could not be said to be void from uncertainty. It does not however,

E in my opinion, necessarily follow that every term in a valid contract can necessarily be made the subject of an order for specific implement. The obvious example is a term providing for the payment of money. Another example would be where a contract provides that one party should use their best endeavours to do certain things. This is not an uncommon form of words in a perfectly valid contract, but plainly could not be made the subject of an order for specific implement. Finally, there is the position as appears in

F *Grosvenor Developments* where what was said to be a perfectly valid lease was nevertheless regarded as being unsuitable for pronouncing an order for specific implement. Where what is required to be done by one party is not a clear and specific act to be performed at a clear and specific time, but is simply a general duty to be performed over a long period during which circumstances might change, I consider that the inevitable aura of vagueness which must surround any such proposition is fatal to a party seeking an order ad factum praestandum. It will not, in my opinion, do for the pursuers simply to say that everybody knows what

is meant by occupying a shop and everybody knows what is meant by using a shop as retail premises. If G that argument was valid, all that would be necessary in the pursuers' first conclusion would be an order ordaining the defenders to carry out their obligations under the lease without giving any further specification and it is, in my opinion, clear that the court would never pronounce such an order. While *Salaried Staff London Loan Co* was a case involving only payment of rent, the observations made by the court in that case would fortify the view that the court would be slow to grant a decree of specific implement which would

H involve active participation by the defenders in trading from premises for the next 20 years. No case was put before me where such an onerous obligation was imposed by the court. The only case which comes anything near it is *Grosvenor Developments* and in that case the proposition was firmly rejected. I see no material ground for distinguishing this case from *Grosvenor Developments* and accordingly I take the view that what is sought by the pursuers in this case lacks the necessary precision for a decree ad factum

I praestandum.

The second ground upon which it was said that the action was incompetent was that the defenders being a limited company cannot have a decree ad factum praestandum pronounced against them. The historic sanction for breach of such an order was imprisonment and a corporate body cannot be imprisoned. In *Lochgelly Iron & Coal Co v North British Railway Co*, Lord Kinnear expressed doubts as to whether a company could be subject to a decree ad factum

J praestandum because it could not be imprisoned. In *Gloag on Contract*, p 659 it is said that such a conclusion cannot be brought against a company without an alternative conclusion for damages. There have been some cases in which an order ad factum praestandum appears to have been pronounced against a corporate body, but it also appears that in those cases no point was taken that such an order was incompetent. Whatever may be the historic basis for the idea that the only sanction for breach of an order ad factum praestandum is imprisonment, it does not appear to

K me that such a proposition in modern times could any longer be sustainable. The Law Reform (Miscellaneous Provisions) (Scotland) Act 1940, s 1 provides that no person shall be apprehended or imprisoned on account of his failure to comply with a decree ad factum praestandum except in accordance with certain conditions. These conditions include a provision that the person in right of such a decree has to make an application to the court which will not grant warrant for imprisonment unless satisfied that the defender has

L wilfully refused to comply with the decree. Under subs (2) it is provided that on any application in pursuance of subs (1), the court may in lieu of granting warrant for imprisonment, recall the decree on which the application proceeds and make an order for payment by the respondent to the applicant of a specified sum or make such other order as appears to the court to be just and equitable in the circumstances. It may well be that this Act was not intended to cover the situation where a company or corporate body was the defender as it proceeds on the basis that an application

A can be made for imprisonment of the defender. It is however, clear that the court is empowered on any view to substitute for the decree ad factum praestandum an order for payment or such other order as appears appropriate.

The pursuers contended that the idea that the only sanction was imprisonment was based historically on the proposition that a person in right of a decree was entitled at his own hand to enforce the decree by imprisonment and that the 1940 Act had removed that absolute right. The position was however different

B where the matter was in the control of the court. If a party is in breach of a court order then that party can be brought before the court and will be treated as being in contempt of court. The penalty for contempt of court may be imprisonment but may, of course, also be any such other order as the court may think appropriate. Accordingly if a decree ad factum praestandum is passed against a corporate body and that body wilfully refuses to comply with the order, it can be brought before the court as being in contempt and the court can pronounce such remedy as appears

C to be appropriate in the circumstances. Counsel for the defenders argued that it is clear from what was said by Lord Kinnear that the historical basis undoubtedly was that imprisonment was the only proper remedy for failure to obtemper a decree ad factum praestandum and that there was no good reason for having any change in that position. Counsel accepted that it was perhaps somewhat illogical that interdicts can be and are daily pronounced against corporate bodies whereas a decree ordaining a corporate body to perform a parti-

D cular act should for technical and historical reasons be regarded as incompetent.

In my view it is indeed illogical that the court cannot pronounce a decree to which an innocent party would prima facie be entitled, just because there was thought to be historically only one penalty for breach of that order. I see no reason whatsoever why a party in breach of an order ordaining performance of a specific act should not be treated in exactly the same way as a party who is in breach of interdict and if that be so

E there is no reason why a decree ad factum praestandum should not pass against a corporate body. As was said in Gloag on *Contract*, p 657, the object of a decree is to enable the pursuer to secure his right, not to punish the defender. If that is correct, it would appear strange that difficulties in punishing the defender should prevent an innocent pursuer securing his right. In *MacLeod v Alexander Sutherland Ltd*, the pursuers sought implement of a clause in missives providing that the defenders should perform certain specified building works. The defenders were a company which

F was in receivership. Lord Stott refused decree of implement on the ground that as a receiver had been appointed, the company was not in a position to obtemper any decree and might find itself in the position of being in breach of an order if the receiver chose not to act. He added some observations on the subject of enforcement in the following terms: "The only sanction suggested by counsel for the pursuer for failure to obtemper such a decree against a limited company would be the imposition of a monetary penalty, and counsel was unable to refer to any report of such having been done. That, I think, is why the

learned author of Gloag on *Contract* at p 659 suggests that an action against a corporate body concluding for G the performance of some act which can be performed vicariously is incompetent without an alternative conclusion for damages, and may afford the explanation also for Lord Kinnear's observations in *Lochgelly Iron & Coal Co Ltd v North British Railway Co* where he had expressed doubts as to whether a contract with the railway company would support a decree ad factum praestandum. For the purposes of the present case, it is unnecessary to affirm so wide a proposition, and counsel for the defenders did not invite me to do so. . . . It would, I think, be inequitable to grant a H decree ad factum praestandum against a company which can act only through the agency of a receiver and which, if the receiver should decline to act, would inevitably be in contempt of court in respect of an omission which they would be powerless to remedy. To pronounce such an order in a case in which the sanction of a monetary penalty would have to be imposed on defenders for a contempt which they have no means of purging except through the intervention of an agent whose actings they have no power to I control, would not only be ineffective, but would as it seems to me, be unfair to the defenders and no doubt also to their creditors."

It would appear from these observations that his Lordship would have accepted that if decree ad factum praestandum could have been pronounced against the defenders, he would have been prepared to do so and that the sanction of a monetary penalty appeared to him to be an appropriate sanction in the event of there being a breach of the order. For these reasons in my opinion, the defenders' attack on the competency on J this ground must fail.

The defenders' third ground of attack was that the remedy of specific implement was excluded by the terms of the lease. Clause 5 provides for the situation where the tenants failed to occupy the premises for a period exceeding 21 days and in that situation it is provided that the tenants should indemnify the landlords against all loss and damage suffered by them. The lease has accordingly provided the appropriate sanction for a failure to occupy the premises and it K would not be appropriate for the court to order specific implement. In my opinion the complete answer to this proposition can be found in Gloag on *Contract*, p 720 where the learned author says that when an obligation is fortified by a penalty it is still open to enforce the obligation and the debtor cannot escape simply by paying the penalty.

[His Lordship dealt with two points with which this report is not concerned and concluded:]

On the whole matter I shall sustain the defenders' L first plea in law and dismiss the action.

Counsel for Pursuers, Sutherland, QC, Skinner; Solicitors, Tods Murray, WS — Counsel for Defenders, Hamilton, QC, Ivey; Solicitors, Archibald Campbell & Harley, WS.

N W H

Russell v HM Advocate

A   HIGH COURT OF JUSTICIARY

THE LORD JUSTICE GENERAL (HOPE),
LORDS ALLANBRIDGE AND COWIE

31 MAY 1991

Justiciary — Procedure — Trial — Previous convictions — Procurator fiscal's speech referring to previous conviction in respect of which accused disqualified from driving for life — Whether breach of statutory prohibition —
B *Criminal Procedure (Scotland) Act 1975 (c 21), ss 160 (1) and (2) and 161 (5).*

Section 160 (1) of the Criminal Procedure (Scotland) Act 1975 provides inter alia that no reference shall be made to previous convictions of the accused in presence of the jury before the verdict is returned. Section 161 (1) prevents such convictions being laid before the presiding judge until the prosecution moves for sentence. Sections 160 (2) and 161 (5) provide exceptions where it is competent to lead evidence of
C   such convictions in support of a substantive charge.

An accused person was charged on an indictment which libelled, inter alia, a charge of driving while disqualified. An extract of the accused's conviction in respect of which disqualification from driving had been imposed was lodged as a production. The procurator fiscal's speech to the jury made reference to the extract conviction, its date and the fact that the disqualification had been imposed for life. The accused
D   was convicted and appealed to the High Court on the ground that this disclosure had prejudiced the jury against him.

Held, (1) that the evidence as to the accused's previous conviction was competent as it was within the limits of the exception to the prohibition set forth in ss 160 (2) and 161 (5) of the Criminal Procedure (Scotland) Act 1975 (p 360E and F); and (2) that the disclosure did not go beyond what it was appropriate for the jury to be told in order to satisfy them that the
E   evidence was sufficient to establish the necessary facts in the indictment (p 360E-F); and appeal *refused*.

Observed, that it was open to an accused to agree the fact of his disqualification by joint minute if he wished such details to be withheld from the jury (p 360A).

F   **Indictment**

Douglas Johnston Brown Russell was indicted at the instance of the rt hon the Lord Fraser of Carmyllie, Her Majesty's Advocate, on charges which read, inter alia, as follows: "(1) you being a person disqualified for holding or obtaining a licence to drive a motor vehicle did on 18 January 1990 in Shawmoss Road, Glasgow near Morton Gardens (while so disqualified) drive motor vehicle registered number F746 LDS; contrary to s 103 (1) (b) of the Road Traffic Act 1988".

The accused pled not guilty and proceeded to trial

in the sheriff court at Glasgow before Sheriff A A Bell, QC, and a jury.   G

The accused was convicted and appealed by way of note of appeal to the High Court.

Statutory provisions

The Criminal Procedure (Scotland) Act 1975 provides:

"68.—(1) No mention shall be made in the indictment of previous convictions, nor shall extracts of previous convictions be included in the list of productions annexed to the indictment.   H

"(2) If the prosecutor desires to place before the court any previous conviction, he shall cause to be served on the accused along with the indictment a notice in the form of Form No 1 of Schedule 7 to the Criminal Justice (Scotland) Act 1949 or in the form set out in an Act of Adjournal under this Act or as nearly as may be in such form, and any conviction set forth in that notice shall be held to apply to the accused   I unless he gives, in accordance with subsection (3) of this section, written intimation objecting to such conviction on the ground that it does not apply to him or is otherwise inadmissible. . . .

"160.—(1) Previous convictions against the accused shall not be laid before the jury, nor shall reference be made thereto in presence of the jury before the verdict is returned.

"(2) Nothing in this section shall prevent the prose-   J cutor from laying before the jury evidence of previous convictions where, by the existing law, it is competent to lead evidence of such previous convictions as evidence in causa in support of the substantive charge, or where the accused shall lead evidence to prove previous good character."

"161.—. . . (5) Nothing in this section or in section 68 of this Act shall prevent evidence of previous convictions being led in any case where such evidence is competent in support of a substantive charge."   K

Case referred to

Boustead v McLeod, 1979 SLT (Notes) 48; 1979 JC 70.

In addressing the jury the procurator fiscal depute made the following remarks, inter alia:

"Now, I think you all got copies of the indictment with the charges on it. The offences, really, in this   L case are quite straightforward. The first charge is driving while disqualified. Now, that's straightforward. You may have heard me put up productions nos 2 and 3 to his Lordship. Now, what those are — production no 2 is what's called an extract of disqualification. Now, that's a document which sets out the fact that Mr Russell here was disqualified from driving on the 28 November 1988 and he was disqualified for life. So, he was in fact disqualified on the 18 January 1990. Production no 3 was a document which is signed by the person who has served an extract dis qualification on Mr Russell — that's a requirement. It has to be served on Mr Russell and once that's done — done on time before the trial and there is no exception taken to it — he is not saying that I am not Mr Russell — once that's done then those documents prove that he was disqualified for life in November '88. So, we don't have to worry about that."

Appeal

The accused lodged a note of appeal which contained the following ground of appeal:

"I feel that the procurator fiscal misdirected the jury as well as the sheriff as facts were made known to the jury and the sheriff with [sic] I feel made both parties [biased]. And a vital piece of evidence for the Crown was not produced in court, which would have proved my innocence (the HORT I form which was signed by the driver)."

The appeal was argued before the High Court on 7 February 1991.

Eo die the court *continued* the appeal and *ordered* the extension of the notes of the procurator fiscal's speech to the jury.

On 31 May 1991 the appeal was argued further before the High Court.

Eo die the court *refused* the appeal.

The following opinion of the court was delivered by the Lord Justice General (Hope):

OPINION OF THE COURT.—The appellant is Douglas Johnston Brown Russell who appeared before us originally on 7 February 1991. The background to this appeal and the issues which are raised by it are summarised in our opinion of that date and we do not need to repeat the various points which were made at that stage. We have before us today a transcript of the speech to the jury by the procurator fiscal depute on the occasion of the appellant's trial which it was necessary for us to see in order to consider one of the arguments. We have now had a chance of reading that speech and we have also been addressed by the appellant on various passages from it which he considered to be of relevance to his argument. Against that background we can now dispose of this appeal.

It will be recalled that there are three charges in the indictment and that the appellant was found guilty on all three of them. The first of these charges was one to the effect that he was driving a motor vehicle in a street in Glasgow on 18 January 1990 while he was disqualified from holding or obtaining a licence. There was also a charge of driving without insurance, and there was a charge which alleged that he had attempted to pervert the course of justice by concealing his true identity and deceiving police officers. The various issues which were presented by the appellant, who has argued this appeal on his own behalf, were focused in our previous opinion, and what we shall do is go through these issues in the same order in which they appear in that previous opinion.

The first issue is one which relates to the point which formed the basis of the first charge on the indictment. As we have said the charge was one of driving while disqualified and it was therefore necessary for the Crown, in order to prove the various elements in the charge and obtain a conviction, to establish that the appellant was in fact disqualified from holding or obtaining a licence to drive a motor vehicle on the day in question. The matter is referred to by the sheriff in his charge where he says this: "you may have little difficulty with one part of [the charge], and that is the disqualification. As the fiscal pointed out there is an extract of the accused having been disqualified from driving and that has been served on him. There is production of that. There is no exception taken, so you may take it that the accused on the day in question in this indictment was disqualified from driving."

The appellant did not take any exception to the way in which the matter had been dealt with by the sheriff. His complaint was that the procurator fiscal depute in addressing the jury on this matter had referred to the fact that he was disqualified from driving for life. There is no dispute that that was in fact the position of the appellant on the day in question. But the appellant said that by revealing the terms of the disqualification to the jury the procurator fiscal depute had prejudiced the jury against him, and he told us that that appeared to be the jury's reaction when they heard reference to this matter from the procurator fiscal depute herself. The relevant passage in her speech which we have now before us begins by referring by number to the productions which had been lodged in order to deal with this matter. These were productions nos 2 and 3. She then explained to the jury what these productions contained: "Now, what those are — production no 2 is what's called an extract of disqualification. Now, that's a document which sets out the fact that Mr Russell here was disqualified from driving on the 28 November 1988 and he was disqualified for life. So, he was in fact disqualified on the 18 January 1990."

She then explained to the jury that production no 3 was a document which had been signed by the person who served the extract disqualification on Mr Russell and that no exception had been taken to it. She repeated that what these documents did was to prove that he was disqualified for life in November 1988.

The procedure which the procurator fiscal depute was following is one which is set out in s 68 in the Criminal Procedure (Scotland) Act 1975. Subsection (1) of that section provides that no mention shall be made in the indictment of previous convictions nor shall extracts of previous convictions be included in the list of productions annexed to the indictment. Subsection (2) then sets out the formal procedure which may be followed if the prosecutor desires to place before the court any previous conviction. It was that procedure which had been followed in this case, and no objection was taken by the solicitor who represented the appellant at his trial to what was done. If the fact that the appellant's disqualification was for life was thought to be prejudicial to the appellant, there was of course a means available to the defence by which that detail could have been withheld from the jury. What could have been done is for the fact that the appellant was disqualified for driving on the relevant date to be agreed between the defence and the prosecution in the form of a joint minute. That was not done for reasons which we have not been told about, but it can be assumed that this was not due to any lack of notice that it was the intention of the prosecutor to put this matter before the jury as she had to do in order to establish the charge and as she was permitted to do by s 161 (5) of the Act.

The situation therefore seems to us to be this: in the absence of a joint minute it was necessary for the prosecutor to place before the court the extract conviction together with the relevant notice, and then to explain to the jury enough about these documents to enable them to appreciate the point that these productions established that the appellant had been disqualified from driving and was still disqualified on the day in question. In our opinion the procurator fiscal depute confined herself in her address to the facts which were relevant to the charge. This case is different from those cases where it can be said that the details which were revealed to the sheriff or to the jury went beyond those which were necessary to establish the facts libelled in the complaint or indictment. For example, in *Boustead v McLeod* an appeal against conviction on a summary complaint was allowed on the ground that an extract conviction had been wrongly admitted in evidence. That extract conviction contained reference to two previous convictions, one of which had no relevance to the matter at issue and its admission was held to have introduced a fatal flaw into the proceedings. We do not need to refer in detail to what Lord Cameron said at 1979 SLT (Notes), p 50, but it was the admission of what he described as "this incompetent and highly prejudicial evidence" which introduced the fatal flaw into the proceedings, with the result that the conviction of the appellant could not stand. It was evidence which was outwith the limits of the exception to the general rule about previous convictions which is to be found in s 357 (5) and, in solemn cases, s 161 (5). We consider that that approach is not one which can be taken in the present case, for the simple reason that the details which were revealed to the jury were details which were relevant to the charge. They did not go beyond what was appropriate for the jury to be told in order to satisfy them that the productions were sufficient to establish the necessary facts. The evidence was competent, and it was within the limits of the exception in s 161 (5). Since the appellant was in fact disqualified from driving for life and was accused of driving in breach of that disqualification, it cannot be said to be unjust for that fact to be revealed to the jury in order to make it plain to them that he was in fact disqualified on the day in question when he was seen to be driving the vehicle.

[His Lordship then dealt with other grounds of appeal with which this report is not concerned and concluded:]

For these various reasons we are not persuaded that there is any substance in any of the grounds of appeal with which we have been dealing and we have no alternative but to refuse this appeal.

_____

For Appellant, Party — Counsel for Respondent, Macdonald, QC, AD; Solicitor, J D Lowe, Crown Agent.

S D D N

_____

(NOTE)

BOC Ltd v Groves

OUTER HOUSE
LORD PENROSE
11 JULY 1991

Reparation — Negligence — Road accident — Allocation of blame — Car driver negligently losing control of car on motorway slip road — Lorry driver negligently failing to observe crashed car and driving into collision with it — Liability to be apportioned to each driver.

A car driver lost control of his car, causing it to overturn. It came to rest upside down. A lorry driver who was approaching at speed failed to take reasonable steps to avoid colliding with the upturned car.

Held, that liability for the consequent damage to the lorry should be apportioned as to 75 per cent to the car driver and as to 25 per cent to the lorry driver.

_____

BOC Ltd raised an action against Anthony Groves for payment of damages following the destruction of their gas road tanker in a collision with a Mini that had been driven by the defender.

The accident, which occurred at 11.50 pm on 20 July 1983, happened near to the junction of the slip road from the westbound carriageway of the M8 motorway to the northbound carriageway of the M898, A898 road leading to the Erskine Bridge. At the date of the accident the M8 had been for some time and still was undergoing extensive repair. The eastbound carriageway was closed to the west of the slip road from the bridge, and a contraflow was in operation on the westbound carriageway. There was no dispute between the parties as to how the car driven by the defender came to be in its position immediately before the accident with the pursuers' tanker. The defender and three others had spent the evening in a hotel in Dumbarton. All four had been drinking. They were on their way home. The car was driven south over the Erskine Bridge. As it approached the eastbound carriageway of the M8 it failed to take the bend, mounted the grass verge bordering the slip road some

85 m from the motorway, continued along the verge into the closed section of the eastbound carriageway and struck the kerb of the central reservation. It struck and mounted the crash barrier on the eastbound carriageway, became airborne, and arrived on, and to some extent crossed, the westbound carriageway. As the car lay after these events, it was struck by the pursuers' tanker driven by Mr William Hendry.

After a proof before the Lord Ordinary (Penrose) his Lordship held that the defender had lost control of the car through a combination of the effects of alcohol and excessive speed, that the car had come to rest obstructing the westbound carriageway to a material extent and in a position of danger, that the defenders' driver, Hendry, had been driving at about 60 mph until, according to the evidence of the lorry's tachograph, the speed was dropped, starting at a distance of 282 m from the point of impact, to 51 mph at a point only about 20 m from the point of impact, followed by rapid deceleration and the tanker going out of control. In relation to the braking his Lordship concluded:

"I considered that Mr Hendry must have started to brake lightly over a short distance before he entered the contraflow section of the road. Emergency braking was concentrated in the final phase prior to impact. There was no evidence of any serious attempt to brake the vehicle between these stages. . . . It seemed to me to be clear from Mr Manderson's evidence that the vehicle was out of control over the final 40 m over which the tachograph operated and, further, that emergency braking was taking place. Neither Mr Jamieson nor Mr Tracey observed this. But it must have occurred. However, it was clear from their evidence that the tanker went out of control at or near that point of impact, swerved across the carriageway, struck the crash barrier, ricocheted off it and went over on its side after which it went towards its final resting place on the grass verge. Taking the matter generally, it appeared to me that on balance the evidence demonstrated that Mr Hendry . . . did not brake progressively, that at a late stage he began emergency braking which neither Mr Jamieson nor Mr Tracey observed, that he went totally out of control, and that the orientation and movement of the tanker from the point at which he lost control became a matter of conjecture."

In relation to the fault of the tanker driver and to the apportionment of blame his Lordship continued:

"I considered it to have been proved that Mr Hendry was driving too fast in the circumstances and that he lost control of the vehicle when confronted with the emergency presented by the obstacle of the Mini in his path. When he saw that obstacle it was still a considerable distance ahead and there was ample opportunity to bring his vehicle to a halt or alternatively to slow it to such an extent that he would have been able to negotiate a passage between the two vehicles in his sight [the second vehicle being a car stopped 20 m east of the Mini on the other lane of the contraflow system, facing east with its hazard lights on]. Even ignoring his own estimate of stopping distances the total distance available was considerable. If one accepted that he intended to leave by the slip way it nonetheless seemed necessary that he should brake given the configuration of the road, which he knew. There was no natural gradient to slow him or indeed to prevent him from coming into very considerable danger as he crested the slip way and approached the bend under the motorway. Even had he intended to leave the motorway by the slip way, serious braking of the vehicle would have been required. Had he begun to do so, his ability to stop before the collision would have been increased. Quite apart from objective factors, on his evidence he was not driving the vehicle within the limits of his own capacity to control it properly in an emergency. Even if his choice of escape route were beyond criticism, the risk of there being pedestrians in the vicinity of a crashed vehicle should have indicated a need to slow the vehicle considerably. He braked little, with the result that when he was deprived of the escape route he had selected [by the presence of a pedestrian], he had inadequate time to brake under control before impact. I am of opinion that it has been proved that Mr Hendry was negligent in that, having regard to the speed of his vehicle, he failed to use his brakes as part of his response to the emergency he faced until it was too late to do so effectively. . . .

"I am of opinion that the accident was caused by two factors, in the first place by the negligent driving of the defender which caused the Mini motor car to come to a halt in a position of danger on the westbound lane of the contraflow section of the motorway in a position in which it presented a serious obstacle to traffic moving westwards on the motorway, and in the second place by the speed of driving and loss of control by Mr Hendry of the tanker as it approached the locus. Without the coincidence of the negligence of both drivers, this accident would not have happened. In apportioning blame I have had regard to the situation in which Mr Hendry found himself. He drove into an emergency and failed to react to it and to respond in a proper way. However, the emergency was created by the driving of the defender. Having regard to the blameworthiness which is inherent in the situation I am of opinion that the defender was 75 per cent to blame for this accident and Mr Hendry 25 per cent to blame."

Counsel for Pursuers, D S Mackay, QC, Hofford; Solicitors, Allan McDougall & Co (for Bell Russell & Co, Airdrie) — Counsel for Defenders, Jones, QC, I M Scott; Solicitors, Simpson & Marwick, WS.

C H

Carson v Orr

A HIGH COURT OF JUSTICIARY

THE LORD JUSTICE GENERAL (HOPE),
LORDS COWIE AND GRIEVE

3 DECEMBER 1991

Justiciary — Statutory offence — Being in charge of vehicle while unfit through drink — Breath analyser readings 29 microgrammes apart after one minute interval — Machine calibrating properly and not unsatis-
B *factory on previous occasions when used — Whether police entitled to regard machine as reliable — Road Traffic Act 1988 (c 52), ss 5 (1) (b) and 7 (1) (a) and (3) (b).*

An accused person was charged with inter alia being in charge of a moped with an excess of alcohol in his breath, contrary to s 5 (1) (b) of the Road Traffic Act 1988. The evidence was to the effect that the accused's breath smelled of alcohol when he was first observed by police officers. He was asked to provide a breath
C specimen for a roadside breath test and when he refused to do so he was arrested. At police headquarters the Camic breath analyser calibrated correctly when switched on and again between and after the specimens provided by the accused, but gave readings of 87 and 58 microgrammes of alcohol in 100 millilitres of breath for the two specimens which were provided one minute apart. The police concluded on these readings that the machine was working satisfactorily. There was also evidence that the machine had
D been used on previous occasions when calibration tests had been carried out and on none of these occasions was there anything to indicate that the machine was not working within acceptable limits. The accused did not give evidence. The sheriff convicted the accused on the basis that he was satisfied that there were no circumstances which showed that the breath analyser was unreliable or cast reasonable doubt on its reliability. The accused appealed by stated case.

E **Held,** (1) that it was for the police officers to form their own judgment in the light of all the facts and circumstances known to them as to whether the device was reliable and that judgment was open to examination if their decision was one which no police officer acting reasonably and applying the subjective test could have reached (p 364K-L); (2) that since there had been no indication that there was anything wrong with the machine, and since the results were not so absurdly apart as to indicate that no police officer acting reasonably could regard them as having been
F produced by a reliable machine, the decision was one which the police were entitled to reach (pp 364L-365A); and appeal *refused.*

Burnett v Smith, 1990 SLT 537, *applied.*

Summary complaint

David Frederick Carson was charged at the instance of W W Orr, procurator fiscal, Inverness, on a summary complaint which libelled inter alia: "(2) [on 3 February 1991] you were in charge of a motor vehicle, namely said moped which was on a road or G other public place, namely [Academy Street, opposite the Market Police Office, Inverness] after consuming so much alcohol that the proportion of it in your breath was 58 microgrammes of alcohol in 100 millilitres of breath which exceeded the prescribed limit, namely 35 microgrammes of alcohol in 100 millilitres of breath: contrary to s 5 (1) (b) of the Road Traffic Act 1988". The accused pled not guilty and proceeded to trial. After trial the sheriff (D Booker-Milburn) found the accused guilty. H

The accused appealed to the High Court by way of stated case, against the decision of the sheriff.

Findings in fact

The sheriff found the following facts to be admitted or proved, inter alia:

(2) The officers saw the appellant astride a moped on Academy Street. He was wearing no crash helmet. The engine of the moped was running and the appel- I lant was preparing to drive off. (3) Sergeant McCloy spoke to the appellant about his lack of helmet. The appellant said it had been stolen earlier that evening and that he was about to drive home. (4) Sergeant McCloy smelt alcohol on the appellant's breath and required him to provide a specimen of breath. The appellant was warned of the consequences of refusal. He refused. He was crying and sobbing and appeared to be verging on becoming hysterical. (5) Sergeant Elder told the appellant that he was arresting him for J refusing the requirement to provide a specimen of breath for a breath test. (6) The appellant was arrested and taken to police headquarters. (7) At police headquarters Sergeant McCloy explained to the appellant that he was going to require him to provide two specimens of breath for analysis by the Camic machine. He explained the procedures to the appellant and then made the requirement and gave the warning contained in Pt 1 of Form R361 under the heading "Statement to the Accused". The accused agreed to provide two K specimens. (8) The machine was switched on and calibration check no 1 produced a reading of 33 microgrammes in 100 millilitres. There followed a zero check which produced a reading of zero microgrammes in 100 millilitres. Breath test no 1 was carried out at 0151 hours and produced a reading of 87 microgrammes of alcohol in 100 millilitres of breath. There followed a zero check which produced a reading of zero microgrammes in 100 millilitres. Breath test no 2 was carried out at 0152 hours and produced a L reading of 58 microgrammes of alcohol in 100 millilitres of breath, a difference of 29 microgrammes after the elapse of one minute. There then followed calibration check no 2 which produced a reading of 34 microgrammes of alcohol in 100 millilitres. (9) The appellant was handed a certified copy of the statement produced by the approved device showing the lower proportion of alcohol in a specimen of breath provided by him to be 58 microgrammes of alcohol in 100 millilitres of breath. He accepted the said copy statement and signed the form acknowledging receipt of the copy

statement. (10) The machine used to analyse the said two specimens of breath had been tested on 26 January 1991 at 0810 hours when the two calibration checks had produced readings of 33 and 34 microgrammes respectively and the machine was pronounced by police officers to be in order. The machine was used at 0051 hours on 27 January 1991 when the two calibration checks produced readings of 34 microgrammes and tests 1 and 2 produced readings of 118 and 117 microgrammes in 100 millilitres of breath respectively.

(11) The said machine was tested on the following dates at the following times with the following results:

27 January 1991	1015 hrs	32	35
28 January 1991	0814 hrs	34	34
29 January 1991	0745 hrs	33	33
30 January 1991	0735 hrs	33	34
31 January 1991	0729 hrs	32	32
1 February 1991	0915 hrs	33	33

On each of the above occasions the said machine was pronounced by police officers to be in order. (12) At 0725 hours on 2 February 1991 the simulator solution was changed and the machine was tested at 0833 hours and produced readings of 34 microgrammes on both calibration checks. A customer was tested on the machine on 3 February 1991 at 0115 hours when calibration check no 1 showed a reading of 33, test no 1 a reading of 78, test no 2 a reading of 75 and calibration check no 2 a reading of 33. Then came the appellant with the results as found in finding 8. (13) The said machine was tested on the following dates at the following times with the following results:

3 February 1991	0710 hrs	34	35
4 February 1991	0726 hrs	35	33
5 February 1991	0730 hrs	33	32
6 February 1991	0720 hrs	33	34

On each of the above occasions the said machine was pronounced by police officers to be in order. (14) A customer was tested on 7 February 1991 at 0308 hours and the following readings were obtained: 34 : 79 : 75 : 33. On the same date the said machine was tested at 0735 hours and produced readings of 35 and 34. The machine was pronounced by police officers to be in order. (15) Two customers were tested on 8 February 1991 with the following results:

0145 hours	33 : 42 : 39 : 33
0239 hours	34 : 52 : 50 : 34

The machine was tested on the same date at 0818 hours and produced readings of 34 and 34. The machine was pronounced by police officers to be in order. A further customer was tested on the same date at 2359 hours with the following results: 33 : 131 : 129 : 35. (16) From the foregoing tests on customers, none, apart from the appellant's, showed a difference of more than four on the second test. In every case the machine had calibrated correctly. If the machine had a fault, it would not have calibrated correctly. The machine calibrated correctly at the time of the appellant's tests. (17) It is known that if a person produces wind from his stomach which is then blown into the machine whilst the first specimen is being given and the second specimen contains breath only from the lungs, there may be a large difference between the first reading and the second reading. This may have happened in the case of the appellant although neither police officer was aware of it happening.

Cases referred to

Burnett v Smith, 1990 SLT 537; 1989 SCCR 628.
Lunney v Cardle, 1988 SLT 440; 1988 SCCR 104.
Ross v Allan, 1986 SLT 349; 1986 SCCR 100.
Tudhope v Craig, 1985 SCCR 214.

Appeal

The sheriff posed the following questions for the opinion of the High Court:

(1) Was I entitled to rely on the lower proportion of alcohol in a specimen of breath provided by the appellant?

(2) On the facts stated was I entitled to find the appellant guilty of charge 2?

The appeal was argued before the High Court on 3 December 1991.

Eo die the court *answered* both questions in the *affirmative* and *refused* the appeal.

The following opinion of the court was delivered by the Lord Justice General (Hope):

OPINION OF THE COURT.—The appellant is David Frederick Carson who was found guilty in the sheriff court at Inverness on two charges brought against him under the Road Traffic Act 1988. The first was a charge of failing without reasonable excuse to provide a specimen of breath for a breath test and the second was one of being in charge of a moped with an excess of alcohol in his breath. He has appealed against his conviction, but the grounds of appeal and the argument to which we listened were directed only to the second charge, that is the charge of being in charge of the moped with an excess of alcohol in his breath. The issue which has been raised relates to the reliability of the Camic machine which was used to obtain the specimens for analysis. Shortly put, the submission is that the results obtained when the specimens were taken were so far apart as to raise a reasonable doubt about the reliability of the machine, with the consequence that the officers should have departed from this method and instead requested a sample of blood for analysis.

The findings of fact which set out the background do not need to be elaborated upon in any detail. It is enough to say that police officers saw the appellant sitting astride a moped in Academy Street, Inverness. He appeared to be preparing to drive off and, since alcohol was smelt on his breath, he was asked to provide a specimen of breath. When he refused to do so he was arrested and taken to the police head-

A quarters. It was there that the specimens of breath for analysis by means of the Camic machine were obtained. The machine was duly switched on, and a calibration check, check no 1, produced a reading of 33 microgrammes in 100 millilitres, which is within the acceptable range. There then followed a zero check, which produced a reading of zero microgrammes in 100 millilitres, which also showed that the machine was operating satisfactorily. Then breath test no 1 was carried out. It produced a reading of 87 microgrammes of alcohol in 100 millilitres of breath,

B which can at least be said to be consistent with the fact that the appellant was found to be smelling of alcohol when he was seen in Academy Street. There then followed a further zero check, which produced a reading of zero microgrammes in 100 millilitres. This was followed by breath test no 2, carried out one minute after the first, which produced a reading of 58 microgrammes of alcohol, in 100 millilitres of breath. This was a difference of 29 microgrammes after the elapse of one minute from the first test. The proce-

C dures were completed by a final calibration check which produced a reading of 34 microgrammes of alcohol in 100 millilitres and once again was within the permitted range.

In the light of those various readings obtained in these various ways the police officers concluded that the machine was working satisfactorily. They decided to proceed upon the basis that the samples of breath had been provided by means of a reliable device, and as required by the statute they proceeded upon the

D lower of the two readings for the purposes of further procedures. It should be noted that the machine had been used to analyse breath on previous occasions when calibration tests had also been carried out. These are fully set out in the stated case, and it is not necessary to recite them for the purposes of this opinion. The important point is that there was nothing on any of these previous occasions to indicate that the machine was not working within acceptable limits. Indeed every finding or test that was obtained or carried out tended to confirm that the machine was

E working satisfactorily and could be relied upon to provide acceptable results. Accordingly the only indication to the contrary is the fact that on the occasion when the specimens of breath were obtained from the appellant there was a difference of 29 microgrammes between the first test and the second, with the result that the reading obtained on the first occasion was 50 per cent higher than the reading on the second. Finding 17 is in these terms: [his Lordship quoted the terms of finding 17 and continued:]

F Against the background of these findings counsel submitted that there was an aura of unreliability in this case because of the difference between the first and second tests. He submitted that this raised a presumption of unreliability, and that it was for the police officers applying the test subjectively to overcome that presumption by reference to the facts and circumstances in which the tests were obtained. We were referred to a number of cases to illustrate that argument and the way in which the approach has developed to the obtaining of specimens of breath for

analysis by means of an approved device. In *Tudhope*
G *v Craig* there was a minute difference between the two readings obtained on the zero test, and it was held that that could not reasonably be taken as an indication of malfunction. In *Ross v Allan* the readings obtained when the specimens were taken were very far apart. The first reading showed a figure of 75 microgrammes whereas the second showed zero, although the appellant had been found to be smelling of alcohol. The police officers were held to be entitled in these circumstances to regard the machine as unreliable and to

H require a sample of blood to be provided, the reason being that the zero reading was contradicted by the smell of alcohol from the person who was providing the specimen. In *Lunney v Cardle* there was again a wide discrepancy between the results obtained for the specimens of breath provided by the appellant. The lower reading was 14 microgrammes and the upper reading was 92, and the extent of this discrepancy was held to be enough to justify the police officers in their conclusion that the machine was unreliable. Lord McDonald said that the test of reliability was a subjec-

I tive one, for the judgment of the police officer who seeks to make use of the device. The other members of the court reserved their opinions on this point, but this was held to be the proper test in *Burnett v Smith*, where again the difference between the readings for the two specimens of breath was substantial. The first specimen gave a reading of 39 microgrammes, while the second gave a reading of 55 microgrammes. There was also a brief flashing of a green light at an unex-

J pected stage of the procedure. So the police decided that the machine was unreliable and required a blood specimen. The court held that the police were entitled to do that, the test being a subjective one and that so long as they concluded on reasonable grounds that the device was unreliable their decision was one which could not be held to be one they were not entitled to take.

The present case, as counsel pointed out, is the reverse of what occurred in *Burnett v Smith*. In this

K case, despite the substantial difference between the two readings for the specimens of breath, the police decided that the device was reliable. But this case illustrates the effect of applying the subjective test. In the end of the day it is a matter for the police officers at the time to form their own judgment in the light of all the facts and circumstances known to them as to whether the device is reliable. That judgment is, of course, open to examination if the decision is one which no police officer acting reasonably and applying the subjective test could have reached. But in the

L present case, in support of the view taken by the police, there is the fact that a considerable number of tests of various kinds over a substantial period all indicated that the machine was reliable. Neither on the occasion when these specimens were taken nor on all previous occasions referred to in the findings was there any indication that there was anything wrong with the machine. Nor can it be said that the results themselves were so absurdly far apart as to indicate that no police officer acting reasonably could have

A regarded them as having been produced by a reliable machine. We are not dealing here with a machine which has produced a zero reading from a man who is smelling of alcohol, and finding 17 provides a reasonable explanation for the results, even although no "burp" was actually observed.

For all these reasons we are satisfied that the decision which was reached in this case was one which the police officers were entitled to reach. That means that the sheriff in his turn was entitled to rely on the lower proportion of alcohol in the specimens of breath
B provided by the appellant. We shall accordingly answer both questions in the affirmative and refuse the appeal.

Counsel for Appellant, Baird; Solicitors, Drummond Miller, WS (for Sutherland & Co, Inverness) — Counsel for Respondent, Bonomy, AD; Solicitor, J D Lowe, Crown Agent.

P W F

C

Leech v Secretary of State for Scotland

EXTRA DIVISION

D LORDS McCLUSKEY, SUTHERLAND AND GRIEVE

13 DECEMBER 1991

Administrative law — Judicial review — Prisons — Prison rules and standing orders — Extent of prisoner's right to confidentiality in correspondence between his legal advisers and himself concerning potential legal proceedings — Whether prison rules and standing orders of
E *Secretary of State purporting to accord him a right to read and censor such correspondence ultra vires — Prisons (Scotland) Act 1989 (c 45), ss 39 (1) and 42 (1) — Prison (Scotland) Rules 1952 (SI 1952/565), rule 74 (4).*

Constitutional law — Civil liberties — Prisons — Judicial review — Prison rules and standing orders — Communications with legal advisers — Confidentiality — Whether prisoner entitled to unimpeded and uncensored correspondence with legal advisers concerning potential legal proceedings — Whether prison rules and
F *standing orders of Secretary of State purporting to accord to him a right to read and censor letters passing between prisoner and his legal adviser concerning potential legal proceedings ultra vires — Prisons (Scotland) Act 1989 (c 45), ss 39 (1) and 42 (1) — Prison (Scotland) Rules 1952 (SI 1952/565), rule 74 (4).*

Section 39 (1) of the Prisons (Scotland) Act 1989 empowers the Secretary of State to make rules for the regulation and inspection of prisons and for the classification, treatment, employment, discipline and control of persons required to be detained therein.

Rule 74 (4) of the Prison (Scotland) Rules 1952 pro-
G vides, inter alia, that: "every letter to or from a prisoner shall be read by the governor . . . and it shall be within the discretion of the governor to stop any letter if he considers that the contents are objectionable". Rule 76 provides that: "The legal adviser of a prisoner shall be given reasonable facilities to consult him on any legal business. The interview shall take place in the sight but not in the hearing of an officer." The Secretary of State also issues standing orders which represent the detailed management procedure to be applied within prisons in Scotland. In terms of
H Section M thereof, the prison authorities are accorded a right to read and censor letters concerning potential legal proceedings passing between a prisoner and his legal advisers.

A prisoner, who was engaged in or contemplating a number of litigations, presented a petition for judicial review in which he sought declarator that he was entitled to unrestricted correspondence with his legal adviser, and that such correspondence was privileged; that rule 74 (4) was ultra vires; and that the Prison
I (Scotland) Standing Orders were ultra vires insofar as they purported to provide for the discipline and control of prisoners and in particular to censor correspondence with their legal advisers. The petition was dismissed by the Lord Ordinary. The prisoner reclaimed.

Held, (1) that rule 74 covered all communications, including correspondence between a prisoner and his legal adviser (p 368L); (2) that the particular standing
J orders objected to merely regulated and in some respects enlarged the prisoner's rights under rule 74 (4) and therefore the real question for the court was whether rule 74 (4) was ultra vires (p 371H-J); (3) that the right of access to the courts was a basic civil right which could not be extinguished except by clear and express enactment, and comprehended within that right was a right of access to a solicitor for confidential advice and assistance (pp 370I-J and 371J-K); (4) that rule 74 could not be looked at in isolation but fell
K to be considered in its whole context (pp 370I and 371G-H); (5) that the 1952 Rules, read as a whole, did enable a prisoner to seek and receive confidential advice from his solicitor, the prisoner being able to obtain such advice at an interview under rule 76, and there being nothing in rule 74 (4) entitling the governor to stop a letter in which a prisoner merely invited his legal adviser to come for interview regarding a confidential matter (p 371K-L); (6) that rule 74 (4) was therefore not ultra vires (p 372A); and (7) that
L the rule of confidentiality applied to the recovery of documents incidental to a litigation; it was not a basic civil right and had no bearing on the issues raised in the petition (p 372E); and reclaiming motion *refused*.

Opinion reserved, as to the vires of the standing orders and as to whether a prisoner had title or interest to complain that the standing orders were ultra vires where they merely enlarged the rights conferred upon him by rule 74 (4) (p 372B-D).

Petition for judicial review

(Reported 1991 SLT 910)

Mark Francis Leech, a prisoner at HM Prison, Blundeston, presented a petition for judicial review in the Court of Session in which the Secretary of State for Scotland was called as respondent. The object of the petition was to determine the contention of the respondent that the prison authority in Scotland was entitled to peruse, and if thought fit, stop, written correspondence between a prisoner in Scotland and his legal adviser concerning current and prospective litigation.

The case called for a first hearing before the Lord Ordinary (Caplan).

Statutory provisions

The Prisons (Scotland) Act 1989 provides:

"39.—(1) The Secretary of State may make rules for the regulation and management of prisons, remand centres and young offenders institutions respectively, and for the classification, treatment, employment, discipline and control of persons required to be detained therein.

"(2) Rules made under this section shall make provision for ensuring that a person who is charged with any offence under the rules shall be given a proper opportunity of presenting his case. . . .

"42.—(1) Any power of the Secretary of State to make rules or regulations under this Act, and the power of the Secretary of State to make an order under section 22 (2), 30 (6) or (7), 32 (5) or 37 (1) of this Act, shall be exercisable by statutory instrument.

"(2) Any statutory instrument containing regulations made under section 12 or an order made under section 37 (1) of this Act and the draft of any statutory instrument containing rules made under section 39 of this Act shall be laid before Parliament."

The Prison (Scotland) Rules 1952 provide:

"74.—(1) Communications between prisoners and their relatives and friends shall be allowed in accordance with the following provisions, subject to such restrictions as may be laid down by the Secretary of State with a view to the maintenance of discipline and order and the prevention of crime, and no other person shall be allowed to communicate with a prisoner without the authority of the Secretary of State.

"(2) Every prisoner shall be allowed to write and to receive a letter on his admission, and shall thereafter be allowed to write and receive letters and to receive visits at intervals laid down by the Secretary of State. The intervals so described may be extended as a punishment for misconduct, but shall not be extended so as to preclude a prisoner from writing and receiving a letter, and receiving a visit, every eight weeks.

"(3) When a prisoner who becomes entitled to write a letter or receive a visit is at the time subject to confinement to cell the writing of the letter or the receipt

of the visit may, in the Governor's discretion, be deferred until the period of such confinement has expired but not so as to extend the interval between letters or visits beyond eight weeks.

"(4) Subject to the provisions of Rule 50 (4) every letter to or from a prisoner shall be read by the Governor or by an officer deputed by him for that purpose and it shall be within the discretion of the Governor to stop any letter if he considers that the contents are objectionable.

"(5) The Governor may allow any prisoner entitled to receive a visit to write a letter and receive a reply in lieu of such visit, and if he considers that the circumstances justify such a concession may allow any prisoner to write a special letter and receive a reply, or to receive a special visit, or may prolong the period of a visit. . . .

"76. The legal adviser of a prisoner shall be given reasonable facilities to consult him on any legal business. The interview shall take place in the sight but not in the hearing of an officer."

Standing orders

The Prison Standing Orders provide:

"*Censorship*

"Ma6 . . . (e) General Correspondence: that is to say correspondence with family, friends and other individuals, with organisations or public bodies and most correspondence with legal advisers about matters other than legal proceedings and forthcoming adjudications. . . .

"*General Correspondence*

"Ma7 [Prohibited material] . . . (j) Complaints about prison treatment which the inmate has not yet raised through the prescribed procedures, unless the complaints are about a matter already decided at Headquarters or the complaints are about a matter which does not require investigation or in which no corrective or remedial action is possible (such as complaints of a general nature about conditions — eg about overcrowding or poor facilities — which are basically descriptive of the conditions the inmate is experiencing and his feelings about them). As soon as a complaint about prison treatment has been made through the prescribed procedures it may be mentioned in correspondence. The prescribed procedures are: (i) with respect to a disciplinary hearing, by petition to the Secretary of State; (ii) with respect to an allegation of misconduct or impropriety by a member of staff, in writing to the Governor or by petition to the Secretary of State; (iii) in relation to any other matter by petition to the Secretary of State or by application to the Visiting Committee or a Visiting Officer of the Secretary of State or a Sheriff or Justice of the Peace visiting an establishment under section 15 of the Prisons (Scotland) Act 1952. . . .

"*Correspondence with a Legal Adviser about Legal Proceedings*

"Ma8. Correspondence with a legal adviser about

legal proceedings to which an inmate is already a party or about a forthcoming adjudication, may not be read or stopped unless the Governor has reason to suppose it contains other material. Such a letter may be examined for illicit enclosures, but should only be opened for that purpose in the presence of the inmate by whom it is sent or to whom it is addressed.

"Other correspondence with a legal adviser may be read and may not contain anything specified in Standing Order Ma7 (a)-(i) and (k)-(n). Such correspondence may not be stopped on the ground that it contains material prohibited by Standing Order Ma7 (j) unless it is clear that the inmate is not seeking legal advice but is writing for some other purpose.

"See Standing Order Mf7 for Correspondence with a Legal Adviser about a Petition to the European Commission of Human Rights. . . .

"*Visits by Legal Advisers*
"Mb20.—(1) Inmates may be visited by legal advisers acting in their professional capacity. Visiting Orders need not be surrendered.

"(2) All visits between inmates and legal advisers should be in the sight of a prison officer. An inmate who is party to legal proceedings is entitled to a visit with his legal adviser out of the hearing of a prison officer to discuss those proceedings. Other visits with a legal adviser acting in his professional capacity should also be allowed out of hearing, provided the subject to be discussed is disclosed to the Governor in advance. Visits by members of the legal profession as a friend or relative of an inmate are subject to the general rules on domestic visits.

"(3) An inmate's legal adviser may be allowed to use a cassette recorder when interviewing the inmate, provided he gives a written undertaking that the tape will be kept in his office and will be used solely in connection with the proceedings or the legal business which the visit was to discuss."

Cases referred to
McGowan v Wright (1852) 15 D 229.
Munro v Fraser (1858) 21 D 103.
R v Deputy Governor of Parkhurst Prison, ex p Hague [1990] 3 WLR 1210; [1990] 3 All ER 687 (affd [1992] 1 AC 58; [1991] 3 WLR 340; [1991] 3 All ER 733).
R v Secretary of State for the Home Department, ex p Anderson [1984] QB 778; [1984] 2 WLR 725; [1984] 1 All ER 920.
R v Secretary of State for the Home Department, ex p Leech, QBD, 22 October 1991, unreported ([1992] COD 168).
Raymond v Honey [1983] AC 1; [1982] 2 WLR 465; [1982] 1 All ER 756.

On 26 October 1990 the Lord Ordinary *dismissed* the petition. (Reported 1991 SLT 910.)

The petitioner reclaimed.

Reclaiming motion
The grounds of appeal for the petitioner were in the following terms:

(1) The Lord Ordinary has failed to address the fundamental point of the judicial review, namely, that all rules relating to a prisoner's "classification, treatment, employment, discipline and control" as referred to in section 39 of the Prisons (Scotland) Act 1989, must be issued, not by way of standing orders, but by statutory instrument.

(2) The Lord Ordinary has misdirected himself in holding that the requirement in terms of rule 76 of the said Prison (Scotland) Rules 1952 that a prisoner must be given reasonable facilities to consult a legal adviser outwith the hearing of a prison officer, is sufficient fulfilment of the requirement, which the Lord Ordinary found established, that a prisoner should be permitted an effective and unconditional opportunity of seeking confidential legal advice by some practical means.

(3) The Lord Ordinary has failed to recognise the right of privilege which attaches to communications for the purpose of obtaining legal advice and which was not removed by the Prisons (Scotland) Act 1989.

The reclaiming motion was heard by an Extra Division on 7 November 1991.

On 13 December 1991 the court *refused* the reclaiming motion.

The following opinion of the court was delivered by Lord McCluskey:

OPINION OF THE COURT.—This is a petition for judicial review brought by a person who was a prisoner in HM Prison, Blundeston, at the time when the petition was raised but had been transferrred to HM Prison, Saughton, by the time the appeal was heard. In August 1987 he was sentenced at Inverness High Court to six years' imprisonment and we were informed that his earliest release date was now 27 November 1991. In the instance of the petition the appellant seeks judicial review of rule 74 (4) of the Prison (Scotland) Rules and of certain specified sections of the Prison (Scotland) Standing Orders. It is important at the outset to identify precisely what it is that the petitioner and appellant is seeking in these proceedings. In order to ascertain that we turn to his pleadings.

In art 8 of the petition the following averments appear:

"The petitioner seeks declarator that

"1. He is entitled to unrestricted correspondence with his legal adviser, and that such correspondence is privileged.

"2. The Prison (Scotland) Standing Orders so far as purporting to provide for the discipline and control of prisoners and in particular to censor correspondence with his legal adviser are ultra vires.

"3. The said rule 74 (4) is ultra vires. The petitioner craves the court to pronounce such further or other decree or orders as may seem to the court to be just and reasonable in all the circumstances of the case."

The pleas in law for the petitioner are in the following terms:

"1. Rule 74 (4) of the Prison (Scotland) Rules 1952 being ultra vires and contrary to law, *insofar as it purports to restrict correspondence between the petitioner and his legal advisers*, declarator should be pronounced accordingly. [Emphasis added.]

"2. The Section [sic] Ma6 (e), Ma7 (j), Ma8 and Mb20 (2) of the Prison (Scotland) Standing Orders, being ultra vires and contrary to law insofar as they seek to restrict communication between the petitioner and his legal advisers, declarator should be pronounced accordingly.

"3. The petitioner's correspondence with his legal adviser being privileged and not subject to third party scrutiny, declarator should be pronounced accordingly.

"4. The petitioner being entitled to unimpeded and uncensored correspondence with his legal adviser, declarator should be pronounced accordingly."

From the averments in the petition and the supporting documents, it appears that the appellant, whilst imprisoned in Scotland, did not enjoy the right to correspond with his legal adviser in the way he would like. In particular, he complains not only that letters passing between him and his legal adviser were unwarrantably examined by the prison authorities but also that, equally unwarrantably, they claimed to exercise a right to prevent any such letter reaching the addressee. He was thus denied an unimpeded right of access to his legal adviser for confidential consultation and advice and, as a direct consequence, was denied unimpeded access to the courts. The restrictions upon his freedom to correspond freely and confidentially with his legal adviser are said to be contained in the rule and the standing orders in respect of which he now seeks judicial review. The rule and standing orders which were applied and invoked by the respondent and the prison authorities to warrant interception and examination of such correspondence are said to have been and to be ultra vires.

The Lord Ordinary examined the rules and the standing orders referred to (and which are quoted below) in the light of the submissions made to him and concluded that rule 74 (4) was not ultra vires. This was seen to be the critical issue, because, as the Lord Ordinary records, it was recognised before him that if rule 74 (4) was valid then the petitioner could not obtain the practical relief that he sought by attacking the standing orders: for the effect of the standing orders, properly construed, was to enlarge the rights of prisoners rather than to diminish them; and a prisoner had no interest to challenge orders which served only to enlarge his rights. The Lord Ordinary refused the petition. The grounds of appeal are in the following terms: [his Lordship quoted the grounds of appeal and continued:]

Counsel for the petitioner intimated that he proposed to present all three grounds of appeal but would treat the third ground as a subhead of the first ground.

The rule which was attacked as ultra vires, rule 74, was contained in the Prison (Scotland) Rules 1952. These rules were made in the exercise of powers conferred on the Secretary of State by the Criminal Justice (Scotland) Act 1949. They had since been amended and now derived their validity from the Prisons (Scotland) Act 1989. Section 39 (1) of the 1989 Act provided: [his Lordship quoted the terms of s 39 (1) and continued:]

Reference was also made to s 39 (2): [his Lordship quoted the terms of s 39 (2) and continued:]

The exercise of the power to make such rules was governed by s 42 (1) and (2): [his Lordship quoted the terms of s 42 (1) and (2) and continued:]

The relevant parliamentary procedure was governed by the Statutory Instruments Act 1946. Parts of rule 74 appeared to govern correspondence between prisoners and other persons, including legal advisers; and other parts regulated inter alia visits to prisoners. It is convenient to set out the parts of rule 74 which were discussed in the submissions before this court [his Lordship quoted the terms of rule 74 (1)-(5) and continued:]

Rule 76, which was also referred to, is in the following terms: [his Lordship quoted its terms and continued:] "Legal adviser" is defined in rule 1 of the 1952 Rules as "an advocate or a solicitor within the meaning of the Solicitors (Scotland) Act 1933, or the authorised clerk of an advocate or solicitor". That Act has now been superseded by the Solicitors (Scotland) Act 1980.

Counsel for the petitioner pointed out that the Lord Ordinary had addressed the question as to whether or not the provisions in rule 74 relating to correspondence governed not all communications between prisoners and others but only those between prisoners on the one hand and "their relatives and friends" on the other. However, having regard to the terms of rule 74 (4) and of the provisions of rule 50 (4) it was accepted, and it was the appellant's submission, that rule 74 did relate to correspondence between prisoners and their legal advisers. Apart from this rule, the rules were silent on the matter of letters between convicted prisoners and their legal advisers. On this point, it is appropriate for us to record here that counsel for the respondent submitted that, on a proper construction of rule 74 (1), it covered all communications between a prisoner on the one hand and any other party; the final words "no other person shall be allowed to communicate with a prisoner without the authority of the Secretary of State", governed all persons other than relatives and friends and accordingly governed legal advisers. In our opinion, the Lord Ordinary, in treating rule 74 (4) as being applicable to inter alia correspondence which the prisoner had with his legal adviser, adopted the correct approach on this matter. His approach was not seriously challenged by either party and we proceed upon the basis that rule 74 purports to cover all communications, including correspondence between a prisoner and his legal adviser.

Counsel conceded that rule 76 gave the prisoner and his legal adviser a right to communicate face to face outwith the hearing of any prison officer; but he pointed to what he described as the illogicality of permitting unrestricted communication between a prisoner and his legal adviser when they met face to face but prohibiting unsupervised communication by letter. The provisions of rules 121 to 124 of the 1952 Rules, governing corresponding rights of untried prisoners, were referred to. They, it was said, appeared to confer larger privileges upon untried prisoners than upon convicted persons but they too contained contradictory and anomalous provisions which could not be said to be logical. The standing orders, Section M of which (dealing with communications) is printed in the appendix to the reclaiming print, contained a number of provisions relating to or bearing upon correspondence between a convicted prisoner and his legal adviser; these were the orders which the appellant particularly sought to bring under review. They were Ma6 (e) and (f), Ma7 (j), Ma8 and Mb20. Ma6 (e) and (f) and Ma7 (j) were referred to, but were incidental to Ma8. Mb20 related to visits by legal advisers. Ma8 was in the following terms: [his Lordship quoted its terms and continued:]

It was submitted that this regulation was satisfactory so far as it went but it dealt only with legal proceedings to which the inmate was already a party, and not to possible future proceedings to which the inmate might wish to become a party. In particular this standing order conferred no right upon the inmate in respect of proceedings which he was thinking of taking against the prison authorities themselves. The effect of the relevant provisions in the standing orders was that, even in circumstances where a convicted prisoner wanted to receive legal advice about the possibility of taking legal proceedings against the prison authorities, or against any particular member of the prison staff, or against the Secretary of State, the prison authorities were exercising the right to examine the correspondence and the prisoner was denied confidential communication via correspondence with his legal adviser.

Counsel for the petitioner submitted that the so called standing orders were effectively "rules for the regulation in management of prisons . . . and for the . . . treatment . . . discipline and control of persons required to be detained therein" (words quoted from s 39 (1)). But, as rules under s 39 require to be incorporated in a statutory instrument laid before Parliament (for negative resolution procedure) and as that procedure had not been followed in relation to the Prison (Scotland) Standing Orders, these orders were not legally made within the Secretary of State's statutory powers. Neither s 39 of the 1989 Act nor the 1952 Rules reserved to the respondent any power to make subsidiary rules which were not to be laid before Parliament. Nonetheless, counsel accepted that the Secretary of State could supervise the prisons and could send out circulars or other such instructions which could properly govern the matters addressed by them, provided such circulars or instructions were not inconsistent with the rules. In this case, however, it was clear that the so called standing orders were an undated, unpublished and virtually secret code, which was not available from the Stationery Office, regulating matters that fell properly to be regulated under rules laid before Parliament in terms of ss 39 and 42 of the 1989 Act. The Secretary of State could not make rules by such a back door procedure, that is to say, by describing them as "standing orders".

Additionally, rule 74 (4) was itself ultra vires. It was not now to be argued that rule 74 (4) was ultra vires on the ground of irrationality. The Lord Ordinary's decison on this matter was not challenged. What was still submitted was that the rule was void for illegality, because it effectively violated the right of a prisoner to have unimpeded access to a solicitor; that led inevitably or at least effectively to a violation of his right to have unimpeded access to the courts. It was clear on the basis of English authority, which it was submitted applied principles equally applicable in Scotland, that a convicted person retained all his civil rights which were not taken away expressly or by necessary implication; prisoners retained the right of access to the courts and that right carried with it the right of access to a solicitor: Lord Wilberforce in *Raymond v Honey* [1983] AC at p 10; and *R v Secretary of State for the Home Department, ex p Anderson* [1984] QB at p 793. Access to a solicitor for the purpose of receiving advice and assistance in connection with the possible instituting of civil proceedings in the courts formed an inseparable part of the right of access to the courts themselves. As the court had stated in *Anderson*'s case: "It must, we consider, be inherent in the logic of the decision of the House of Lords in *Raymond v Honey* that an inmate's right of access to a solicitor for the purpose of obtaining advice and assistance with a view to instituting proceedings should be unimpeded, in the same way as his right to initiate proceedings by despatching the necessary documents for that purpose by post is unimpeded" (p 794).

The latter reference there was the right that an inmate had to despatch the necessary documents direct by post to the court itself. Any rule which impeded the right of access to the court, and therefore any rule which impeded the right of access to the solicitor, invaded a fundamental right. That fundamental right embraced as an integral part of it the right to send a letter to the inmate's solicitor without that letter being opened. The right conferred by rule 76 to have a confidential interview with the legal adviser was not sufficient to preserve the prisoner's fundamental right because a prisoner and his solicitor could be faced with many difficulties of a practical character which would render face to face interview impracticable at times; the prisoner might be far away from his legal adviser; the legal adviser might be heavily committed in some proceedings so that he could not travel to the prison; in any event the cost of travelling to the prison for an interview might be prohibitive. In the United States, it was submitted, the prison authorities were forbidden to open incoming or outgoing mail between a prisoner and his attorney once the status of the outside correspondent had been

A satisfactorily established. The Lord Ordinary had not properly addressed this issue by confining his attention to the alternative methods whereby the prisoner might communicate with his solicitor in confidence. It was, furthermore, a matter of trite law that all communications between a person, including a prison inmate, and his solicitor were protected by confidentiality. Among other cases illustrating this trite law were *McGowan v Wright* at p 237 and *Munro v Fraser* at p 107.

B In reply, counsel for the Secretary of State submitted that, on a correct reading, the present petition was not an all embracing attack on all the standing orders. The appellant's counsel in addressing this court had not dealt with any alleged illegality of all the orders; he had drawn attention to and had criticised only a few specified orders. The Lord Ordinary's manner of dealing with the vires of the orders was not now expressly challenged by counsel in presenting the appeal. So far as the first ground of appeal was con-

C cerned, it itself did not address the correct question. In framing and publishing standing orders, the respondent was not making rules within the meaning of s 39. His obligations in relation to prisons derived from s 1 of the 1989 Act, which preserved all the traditional powers and jurisdictions exercisable by the political authority in relation to prisons and prisoners, and s 2, which empowered the Secretary of State to employ persons for the purposes of the Prisons (Scotland) Act 1989. Section 3 vested the general superin-

D tendence of the prisons in the Secretary of State and s 4 imposed general duties upon the Secretary of State in relation to prisons and prisoners. Section 39 was a permissive section. But quite apart from s 39 the Secretary of State, in performance of the functions conferred upon him by ss 1 to 4, could plainly issue circulars or individual orders or standing orders. He was entitled to give orders to the persons engaged by him and to clarify how they might perform their duties under the Act or under rules made in terms of

E s 39. That was what the present standing orders did. They were of equivalent status to circular letters or particular orders which the Secretary of State might properly make or instructions he might give. The court recognised the competence of the Secretary of State to issue circulars containing instructions: see *R v Deputy Governor of Parkhurst Prison, ex p Hague* [1990] 3 WLR at p 1218B (Ralph Gibson LJ). Rule 74 (1) itself recognised that in regulating communications between prisoners and their relatives and friends

F the Secretary of State had the right to lay down restrictions; he could do so in writing, for example by promulgating standing orders. Similarly the Secretary of State under the same rule had the right to grant or withhold authority in relation to communications between prisoners and other persons. Rule 74 (2) envisaged that the Secretary of State would lay down intervals for the receipt and sending of letters; this could be effected by some form of circular or standing order. The 1952 Rules were made with the authority of Parliament, but in these and other respects could not receive effect unless the Secretary of State made

G some form of standing orders which governed these and many other such matters. There could be no doubt that rule 74 (4), the principal rule under attack, was made by a statutory instrument approved by Parliament in accordance with the statutory procedure. To hold that it was ultra vires would be to take a remarkable step. It would be less remarkable to hold that the standing orders themselves were ultra vires; but properly understood they simply relaxed the general rule contained in 74 (4) to the effect that every letter has to be read, and the appellant as a prisoner

H had no title to complain of a relaxation of that rule in his favour.

So far as the vires of rule 74 (4) were concerned, it was important to note that the Lord Ordinary's decision on irrationality was no longer attacked. The Lord Ordinary, however, had properly analysed the law in relation to illegality as well and it should be adopted. That correct approach was that the rules fell to be read as a whole. Rule 76 imposed no restriction upon confidential communication between the legal

I adviser and the prisoner; indeed it expressly authorised such communication. The question as to whether or not rule 74 was ultra vires could not be determined by looking at that rule alone; it fell to be considered in its whole context, of which rule 76 was a part. Without adopting the notion of a "fundamental" right, it was accepted that the right of access to the courts was a basic civil right which the court would not hold to be extinguished except by clear and express enactment intra vires. For present purposes it

J could also be accepted that that basic civil right included the right of access to a solicitor for confidential advice and assistance. However, the right to send and receive confidential letters to and from a solicitor was not a necessary part of the basic civil right and it was not itself the right. The cases founded upon by the appellant, the principles of which were not challenged, did not vouch the proposition that the right of access to a solicitor should be unregulated, nor even that the right of access to the courts could be

K wholly unregulated. The rule which reflected the basic civil right was that access to the courts should be unimpeded. The Lord Ordinary had properly analysed the principles discussed in *Raymond v Honey*. The House of Lords had also upheld the reasoning of the divisional court in that case and had thus affirmed the rule that the mere stopping of a letter from the prisoner to his solicitor did not itself impede the prisoner's access to the courts; there was no contempt of court involved in stopping a letter: cf

L p 14. In *R v Secretary of State for the Home Department, ex p Anderson* it was not suggested that the regulation of correspondence with other parties was ultra vires. All that was held was that the so called "simultaneous ventilation rule" was an impediment to the prisoner's right of access to a legal adviser unless the prisoner first lodged a complaint with the prison authorities. Reference was made to the opinion of the court delivered by Goff LJ, as he then was, in the *Anderson* case where it was said (p 792): "we have to consider Mr Brown's submission that the simultaneous ventilation rule does no more than regulate the circumstances in which inmates of prisons may have access to solicitors. We, for our part, accept that it is proper, and indeed inevitable, that some regulations must exist for that purpose. We can see a good example of such a regulation in Order 5A34 itself, which provides that 'Other visits with a legal adviser . . . should be allowed out of hearing provided the subject to be discussed *is disclosed to the Governor in advance*' ".

If correspondence is regulated but visits are permitted during which confidential instructions may be given and confidential advice received then the difficulties founded upon by the appellant could, it was submitted, be seen to be overstated: a solicitor who agreed to act had an obligation to act for a client; if the solicitor himself could not readily visit the prisoner in the prison then local correspondents could be instructed; unqualified staff could be sent; in special circumstances the prisoner had the right to apply for a transfer to another prison. The Lord Ordinary's consideration of this matter was correct. If the true position is that it is permitted to regulate the right of access to the solicitor, without impeding it, then regulation of the kind that is condescended upon in the present case cannot be said to block the prisoner's access to the court. It might have been more difficult to defend rule 74 (4) had it stood alone, but it did not stand alone: rule 76 was also there, and it ensured that there were no unacceptable difficulties in the way of a prisoner's obtaining access to his solicitor. The correct approach could also be found in the opinion of Webster J in *R v Secretary of State for the Home Department, ex p Mark Francis Leech* (22 October 1991) in which there was being considered a similar submission on behalf of a prisoner, who was in fact the present appellant. At pp 5 to 6 of the unreported judgment Webster J said, "For the purpose of deciding whether the rules in question are ultra vires, I would, in the absence of authority, simply ask myself the following question. First, do they have the effect of removing, frustrating or denying the exercise of any relevant right, and, if so, is that effect within the rule-making power conferred by section 47? Secondly, do they restrict the exercise of any relevant right and, if so, to what extent? If and to the extent they restrict the exercise of such a right, does section 47 give power to restrict to that extent?" (Section 47 is in similer terms to s 39 (1) of the Prisons (Scotland) Act 1989.)

Where the right of access to the court survived but serious impediments were placed in the way, then it was conceded that, in certain circumstances, those impediments could amount to a denial of access to confidential legal advice or to the court. In such circumstances, the vires question would be determined by considering whether or not the practical effect of the restrictions was materially to impede access to the court; it could become a matter of degree. But, as Webster J had said (at p 9): "the Rules may in principle properly restrict or regulate the right of a prisoner to correspond with his solicitor". The rules about confidentiality had no bearing upon the present issue. All kinds of correspondence, for example, correspondence with a spouse or with a doctor, were regarded in legal procedure as confidential when one party to a litigation sought to recover documents that might have a bearing upon the facts in dispute. That rule of confidentiality was not relevant to the vires of the rules and standing orders made by the Secretary of State in the present case.

In our opinion, the respondent's submissions are to be preferred, subject to one reservation noted in the next paragraph. The real issue, as the learned Solicitor General submitted, is whether or not rule 74 (4) falls to be regarded as ultra vires. Accepting as we do that rule 74 (4) does relate to correspondence between a prisoner and his legal adviser, it can be seen that the rule requires the governor or an officer deputed by him for the purpose to read every such letter and empowers the governor to stop any letter if he considers that the contents are objectionable. If that rule is ultra vires then the related standing orders could not be defended because they plainly regulate various matters which are incidental to the overriding power to interfere with correspondence which is conferred by rule 74 (4). If, on the other hand, rule 74 (4) is found to be intra vires, then it is plain that the directions contained in the standing orders do not purport to restrict the prisoner's rights as contained in rule 74 (4) but simply to regulate them and in some respects to enlarge them, and the appellant's criticism of them as additionally and unwarrantably restrictive would fail. Accordingly, what we have to decide is whether rule 74 (4) is ultra vires because it unwarrantably removes a basic civil right in a way not intended by Parliament when it enacted the primary legislation. We have no hesitation in approving the proposition, about which the parties were not in dispute, that all persons have a basic civil right of access to the courts. The so called "right" of access to a solicitor, is incidental to that right. There is no automatic right of access to a solicitor, for example to make a will or to receive advice from him in his capacity as an estate agent or a financial adviser. However, any rule which prevented altogether a right of confidential communication with a prisoner's solicitor might well fall to be regarded as creating such an impediment to access to the courts that it could readily be described as ultra vires. But any rule criticised as having such an effect must be looked at in its whole context. In our view, it is clear that the 1952 Rules, read as a whole, do permit and enable the prisoner to seek and receive confidential advice from his legal adviser. He can obtain such advice at an interview conducted under rule 76. That rule creates absolute rights in the prisoner which enable him to receive confidential advice. It does not appear to us that anything in rule 74 (4) would entitle the governor or his officers to stop any letter in which the prisoner simply invited his legal adviser to come for interview in order that a confidential matter, unspecified in the letter, could be discussed. We accept also that, in any particular case, it could well be necessary to look at the particular regulations embodying restrictions upon communications with the legal

A adviser to see whether or not they might have the practical effect that access to confidential legal advice with a view to taking part in court proceedings was denied; in many cases it would become a question of degree. In the circumstances here, there is no absolute impediment at all, because rule 76 is there. In our view, the appellant's attack upon the vires of rule 74 on the ground of illegality in that that rule denies the prisoner a basic civil right fails. The prisoner has access to the courts and has the means to obtain unsupervised confidential advice from his legal

B adviser. The rules, which include rule 74 (4), do not remove the prisoner's basic civil right or fence it round with such restrictions as to render it nugatory.

In our view, it is not necessary, in order to decide the issues raised in the pleadings, to determine whether or not all, or any other parts of, the standing orders fall outwith the expression "rules for the regulation and management of prisons . . . and for the classification, treatment, employment, discipline and control of persons required to be detained therein",

C contained in s 39 (1). The petition does not invite us to consider any rules other than those which purport to regulate correspondence between the prisoner and others, notably the legal adviser. In our view, it is clear that the rules mentioned by the appellant do no more than to regulate matters which rule 74 envisages fall to be regulated in an incidental way by the Secretary of State and the prison governor. It is not, therefore, necessary to express any opinion on the soundness of the respondent's submission that, if rule 74 (4) itself

D is intra vires, then the prisoner who finds that his rights or privileges in relation to correspondence are in fact enlarged and that the regime is relaxed in relation to correspondence by such standing orders has no interest or title to complain that they are ultra vires. As the petition itself makes plain, the only complaint against the particular orders founded upon is that they diminish his rights. We do not see them as doing anything of the kind.

E We have no difficulty in accepting counsel for the petitioner's submission that, in certain circumstances, correspondence between a person and his legal adviser is confidential. However, this rule or privilege applies essentially to the procedure for the recovery of documents incidental to the conduct of some litigation; it is in no sense a "basic" civil right for all purposes. The right of confidentiality, properly understood, does not appear to us to have any bearing upon the issues raised in this petition.

F In the whole circumstances, agreeing with the Lord Ordinary and his reasoning, we shall refuse the reclaiming motion.

Counsel for Petitioner and Reclaimer, Henderson, QC; Solicitors, Shepherd & Wedderburn, WS — Counsel for Respondent, Solicitor General (Rodger, QC), Keen; Solicitor, R Brodie, Solicitor to the Secretary of State for Scotland.

A N

Kenny v Lord Advocate

G

OUTER HOUSE
LORD KIRKWOOD
24 JANUARY 1992

Expenses — Tender and acceptance — Imminent proof — Reasonable time for consideration of tender — Whether pursuer entitled to expenses of proof — Auditor's discretion.

An employee raised an action of damages for personal injuries. Proof was fixed for Thursday 6 December. On Friday 30 November the defender tendered £22,000. This was reported to the pursuer and a consultation to consider the matter was fixed for Monday 2 December. After the consultation the pursuer wanted to consider the matter overnight with his wife. The following day, 3 December, the tender was accepted and on 6 December the pursuer was found entitled to expenses "to the date of tender". By 3 December counsel for the pursuer had been instructed for the proof. At taxation the auditor disallowed counsel's fee for the first day of the proof. He did so on the assumption that possible settlement figures had been discussed previously by the pursuer and his advisers, so that the pursuer would have been in a position to consider the tender more speedily. The pursuer lodged a note of objections to the auditor's report which came before the Lord Ordinary. In seeking to uphold the auditor's decision the defender argued that the pursuer should have made his decision at the end of the consultation rather than considering it overnight.

Held, (1) that although the matter was initially within the auditor's discretion, by relying on an assumption which was not established the auditor had misdirected himself and the question was open to be considered by the court (pp 374H and 375G-H); (2) that the pursuer was entitled to a reasonable time to consider the tender and in the circumstances the minute of acceptance the day after the consultation was timeous (p 375F-G and I); and pursuer's objection *sustained*.

Observed, that the true reason for the late acceptance of the tender was the late lodging of the tender (p 375H-I).

Action of damages

Stephen Kenny raised an action of damages for personal injuries against the Lord Advocate as representing his employers, the Ministry of Defence. The action was settled by decree upon a minute of tender and minute of acceptance. The pursuer's account of expenses was lodged with the Auditor of the Court of Session to tax and report. The pursuer was not satisfied with the auditor's report and lodged a note of objections thereto.

The case came before the Lord Ordinary (Kirkwood) on the note of objections.

Cases referred to

A   *Gysin v Pochin (Joinery) Ltd*, 1970 SLT (Notes) 9.
Morton v O'Donnell, 1979 SLT (Notes) 26.
Wood v Miller, 1960 SLT (Notes) 7; 1960 SC 86.

On 24 January 1992 the Lord Ordinary *sustained* the pursuer's objection to the auditor's report and *ordained* the auditor to amend his report by *allowing* counsel for the pursuer's fee for the first day of the proof as a good charge against the defender.

B   **LORD KIRKWOOD.**—On or about 25 March 1987 the pursuer was working in the course of his employment as a general labourer with the Ministry of Defence at RNAD Crombie when he tripped over a power cable and sustained certain injuries. On 6 March 1990 he raised the present action of damages against the Lord Advocate as representing the Ministry of Defence. After sundry procedure the proof was due to commence on Thursday 6 December 1990. On Friday 30 November 1990 the defender lodged a

C   minute of tender for £22,000 and the taxed expenses of process to date and the minute was intimated to the pursuer's agents by fax at about 3 pm that day. The pursuer's agents at once reported the terms of the tender to the pursuer and a consultation with counsel to consider the tender was arranged for 4 pm on Monday 3 December. The consultation duly took place and when it ended the pursuer stated that he wished to consider overnight the advice which he had received and discuss it with his wife. On the Tuesday

D   morning, 4 December, the pursuer informed his agents that he had decided to accept the tender and later that morning a minute of acceptance of tender was lodged. By interlocutor dated 6 December 1990 the pursuer was found entitled to expenses against the defender to the date of the tender. Counsel for the pursuer had been instructed for the proof on Friday 30 November but parties were agreed that, in the case of a proof commencing on a Thursday, it was appropriate for counsel to be instructed on the preceding

E   Monday.

The pursuer's agents subsequently lodged their account of expenses for taxation and at the diet of taxation the auditor disallowed the fee paid to counsel in respect of the first day of the proof. On 5 November 1991 the pursuer lodged a note of objections to the auditor's report and on 28 November 1991 the auditor lodged a minute setting out the reason for his decision. In his minute the auditor stated that, after consideration of the information given to him, he "was of

F   opinion that the pursuer had had a reasonable and sufficient amount of time within which to consider the tender no 27 of process to make unnecessary the instruction of his counsel for the first day of the diet of proof". In the note appended to the minute, the auditor stated that he was informed that a pre-proof consultation was held with the pursuer on 5 November 1990 at which the auditor would have expected the pursuer to be fully advised about the prospect of success in his action and the likely level of award he could expect. The auditor went on to state

that he was informed that on Friday morning, 30 November, the defender's agents contacted the pur- G suer's agents by telephone and suggested settlement of the action in the sum of £22,000 with expenses of process. They were immediately informed that that amount would not be acceptable but that the pursuer might settle for £23,000 or possibly £22,500 and from this reply the auditor understood that the pursuer would have been given such advice at the pre-proof consultation. The defender refused to increase the offer to any extent and that same day tendered the sum of £22,000 with expenses. The auditor went on to H state that the pursuer's agents forthwith reported the terms of the tender to the pursuer and in so doing "the Auditor would expect them to have commented thereon, thereby affording their client the opportunity of considering the tender over the weekend". The auditor then referred to the case of *Wood v Miller* and the last two paragraphs of his note are in the following terms:

"If, in the circumstances of the present case, it was considered necessary to have a consultation with I counsel the pursuer's agents had a duty to arrange for one to be held at the earliest opportunity. The consultation having taken place, the auditor was of opinion that the pursuer had had a reasonable amount of time to consider the tender, with his solicitors' views thereon when reporting it to him, and the advice of his counsel at the recent previous consultation, so enabling him to give instructions on the tender late on Monday afternoon. If he had done so it would have avoided the instructing of counsel by the Monday J evening for the proof due to commence on the Thursday, as to the timing of which reference is made to the case of *Morton v O'Donnell* at p 28.

"The auditor having regard to the pursuer's solicitors' immediate response to the verbal offer by the defender and the apparent relatively small difference between the offered and mentioned sum, and setting that against the expenses which would be incurred in a proof, formed the opinion that the pursuer could reasonably have been expected to make a decision on K the tender at the conclusion of the consultation thereon. The auditor, therefore, felt obliged to disallow the pursuer's counsel's fee for the first day of the proof, which did not take place, so far as being a charge against the defender."

Counsel for the pursuer submitted that it was reasonable for the pursuer to have a consultation with counsel in order to receive advice as to whether or not the tender should be accepted and that as the minute L of tender had not been intimated to the pursuer's agents until 3 pm on Friday 30 November the consultation with counsel had been held at the earliest possible opportunity, the Monday being the next sederunt day. At the consultation the pursuer had been advised to accept the tender although he was also told that there were prospects that an award would exceed the sum tendered. The pursuer's request to consider the matter overnight, and discuss it with his wife, could not be regarded as unreasonable, and his decision to accept the tender had been made, and the

A minute of acceptance of tender lodged, on the morning of the second sederunt day after the tender was intimated. A period of two or three sederunt days was usually regarded as a reasonable time for considering a tender (*Wood v Miller; Gysin v Pochin (Joinery) Ltd,* and *Morton v O'Donnell,* per Lord Ross at p 28). In reaching his decision to disallow counsel's fee for the first day of the proof the auditor had relied on the fact that a pre-proof consultation had taken place on 5 November 1990 and the terms of the telephone conversation between the parties' agents on the morning

B of Friday 30 November. At the pre-proof consultation, the purpose of which was to decide on preparations for the proof, there had been some discussion as to whether or not the defender's plea of contributory negligence was likely to succeed and the pursuer had been given a range of possible awards but there had been no discussion at to what figure the pursuer would be prepared to accept as no offer had been made at that stage. When the defender's agents had contacted the pursuer's agents by telephone on the morning of

C Friday 30 November and suggested settlement of the action in the sum of £22,000 the assistant who took the call had merely said that the pursuer might settle for £23,000 or possibly £22,500. While there had been informal discussions between the parties' agents relating to the value of the pursuer's claim, it was not until 30 November that a firm offer had been made and the pursuer had to be allowed a reasonable time in which to decide whether or not to accept it in light of the advice which he received from counsel. The pursuer

D should not be rushed into making a hasty decision because the defender had delayed lodging a tender until a few days before the proof. In this case the auditor had erred in placing weight on advice which he thought that the pursuer had received at the pre-proof consultation and the conversation which had taken place between the parties' agents on the Friday morning, and his decision not to allow counsel's fee for the first day of the proof had been unreasonable.

E Counsel for the defender submitted that the decision whether or not to allow the first day's fee was a matter for the exercise of the auditor's discretion and was peculiarly within his province (*Wood v Miller,* per Lord Justice Clerk Thomson at pp 97-98) and the auditor had had information which is not available to the court. There had been informal discussions between the parties' agents concerning possible settlement of the case early in November 1990. In particular, the pursuer's agents had intimated that they considered that the value of the pursuer's claim, on

F the basis of contributory negligence of 25 per cent, and taking account of the risks inherent in litigation, was £23,670. The auditor was entitled to assume that when these informal discussions had been taking place the pursuer was being kept fully informed. When the formal tender for £22,000 was lodged it had not been necessary for the pursuer to have a consultation with counsel as the offer had been based on the assessment of the value of the claim which had been made by the pursuer's agents. If a consultation was necessary, counsel conceded that it had been held timeously and

she also conceded that at the diet of taxation the defender had not suggested that the expense of the G consultation was not a proper charge against the defender. In the circumstances, however, it was unreasonable for the pursuer to say that he wanted to consider overnight the advice which he had received at the consultation and he should have made his decision at the consultation. If he had done so, the instructions which had been given to pursuer's counsel for the first day of the proof could have been cancelled forthwith and that expense could have been saved.
H

The issue as to whether or not counsel's fee for the first day of the proof is a proper charge against the defender is initially a matter for the exercise of the auditor's discretion and, as Lord Justice Clerk Thomson observed in *Wood v Miller,* 1960 SC at p 98: "It is not the function of a Judge reviewing an exercise of a discretion to substitute his own view of the material under consideration. The decision of the Auditor stands in a not dissimilar position to the verdict of a jury. If the Auditor had no material to go I on, his exercise will fall, but if he had material, then, so long as the decision he reached on it was not unreasonable, it cannot readily be upset."

In considering whether or not counsel's fee for the first day of the proof should be allowed as a charge against the defender, the principles to be applied were not in dispute. If a tender is lodged when a trial is imminent, consideration of the tender should be treated as a matter of urgency. However, the pursuer J must be allowed a reasonable time to consider whether he should accept the tender and what is a reasonable time must depend on the circumstances of each individual case. As Lord Justice Clerk Thomson observed in *Wood v Miller* at p 98: "Defenders who delay making tenders until a late date do not deserve much sympathy, and are not to be allowed to hustle pursuers into what may be hurried and hasty decisions."

In this case the proof had been fixed for Thursday K 6 December and the minute of tender was intimated to the pursuer's agents at about 3 pm on Friday 30 November. A consultation was arranged in order that the pursuer could receive the advice of counsel in relation to the tender and the consultation was held at 4 pm on Monday 3 December, which was the next sederunt day after the minute of tender was lodged. The tender was a substantial one and it is, I think, clear that it was reasonable for the pursuer to seek the advice of counsel before he took his decision whether L or not to accept the tender, and the expense incurred in holding the consultation was not challenged by the defender and was allowed by the auditor as a proper charge against the defender. On the basis that a consultation was justified it was accepted by counsel for the defender that it had been held timeously. It took place at 4 pm on the Monday afternoon and at the conclusion of the consultation the pursuer stated that he wished to consider overnight the advice which he had received and discuss the matter with his wife. On the

A face of it, that request was not unreasonable as the tender had only been lodged on the Friday and involved a substantial sum. However, the auditor decided that the pursuer had had a reasonable amount of time to consider the tender and that he could reasonably have been expected to make a decision on the tender at the conclusion of the consultation. In these circumstances he felt obliged to disallow counsel's fee for the first day of the proof. In reaching that decision the auditor founded on (a) the advice which he expected that the pursuer would have received at

B the pre-proof consultation; (b) the conversation between the parties' agents on the Friday morning; and (c) the views which he expected that the pursuer's agents would have expressed when they reported the terms of the tender to the pursuer. However, if the auditor had information to the effect that the pursuer had actually been advised at the pre-proof consultation as to what sum he should accept I would have expected this information to have been contained in the auditor's note and counsel for the pursuer indicated that at the pre-proof consultation he had not

C advised the pursuer that he should accept any particular figure as no offer had then been made. In any event, when the tender was eventually lodged it would have had to have been considered in light of all the information then available, including such additional information as had come to light in the course of the preparations for the proof. With regard to the conversation between the parties' agents on the Friday morning, it appears that all that was said by the pursuer's agent was that the pursuer might accept

D £23,000 or possibly £22,500. Further, if the auditor had information to the effect that, when the pursuer's agents had informed him that the tender had been lodged, they had actually given advice as to whether or not it should be accepted, I would have expected that information to have been contained in the note. In any event, the consultation on the Monday was held so that the pursuer could obtain the advice of counsel and it also gave him the opportunity of discussing with counsel all the factors involved, including the possible consequences, so far as expenses were

E concerned, of not accepting the tender.

In the circumstances there is no information before me to show that, prior to the consultation on Monday 3 December, the pursuer had, in fact, received advice from his counsel or his agents as to whether or not he should accept the sum of £22,000 in settlement of his claim. While I was informed that during November informal discussions had taken place between the parties' solicitors regarding the value of the pursuer's

F claim, these discussions were not referred to by the auditor and there is no indication in the papers before me that the pursuer was privy to them and, of course, no formal offer had been made which required his consideration. In the particular circumstances of this case it does not seem to me that the auditor was entitled to take the view that, by the end of the consultation held on Monday 3 December, the pursuer had had a reasonable amount of time to consider the tender which had been lodged on the Friday afternoon and that he should have given his decision in the course of the consultation. The sum tendered was substantial

and the decision which the pursuer had to make was an important one. He was entitled to a reasonable time G to consider the advice which he had received from his counsel at the consultation. In the circumstances, and having regard to the fact that the consultation was held late on the Monday afternoon, I do not consider that the pursuer's request to be allowed to consider the matter overnight, and discuss it with his wife, was unreasonable. In my opinion the auditor, in relying on advice which he expected that the pursuer would have received at an earlier stage, but which the pursuer has not been shown actually to have received, misdirected H himself and on the basis of the information before me I consider that it was unreasonable for him to have decided that the pursuer should have instructed acceptance of the tender in the course of the Monday afternoon consultation. It seems to me that the difficulty which arose in this case was occasioned by the fact that, although the accident took place in 1987 and the action was raised in March 1990, the defender delayed lodging the minute of tender until the Friday afternoon before the proof. As I have said, the pursuer was entitled to a reasonable time to consider the tender and I the advice which he had received from counsel and in the circumstances I consider that the lodging of the minute of acceptance of tender on the Tuesday morning was timeous. I will therefore sustain the objection in the pursuer's note and ordain the auditor to amend his report to give effect to the decision which I have reached by allowing counsel for the pursuer's fee for the first day of the proof as a proper charge against the defender. As parties were agreed that expenses should follow success I shall find the J defender liable to the pursuer in the expenses of the procedure on the note.

Counsel for Pursuer, Bell, QC; Solicitors, Allan McDougall & Co, SSC — Counsel for Defender, Paterson; Solicitors, Robson, McLean, WS.

C A G M

K

Taylor, Noter

SECOND DIVISION

THE LORD JUSTICE CLERK (ROSS),
LORDS McCLUSKEY AND MORISON

3 APRIL 1992 L

Bankruptcy — Sequestration — Powers of trustee — Whether competent for trustee to agree that administration of sequestrated estate proceed jointly with company winding up — Bankruptcy (Scotland) Act 1913 (3 & 4 Geo V, c 20), s 172.

Company — Winding up — Powers of liquidator — Note — Competency of order that winding up of two companies proceed jointly with sequestration of estate of director — Companies Act 1948 (11 & 12 Geo VI, c 38), s 245 (1) (f).

Two companies were wound up by order of the court, and the estate of a director of the companies was subsequently sequestrated. The official liquidator of the companies presented a note in which he averred that no formal or statutory accounts had ever been prepared for the companies, that the books and records of the companies were incomplete, and that the director had operated only one bank account through which all transactions had been effected. He averred that the liabilities of the companies and of the director personally were so intermingled that it was impossible to determine which creditors had claims against one or other of the companies and which had claims against the director's sequestrated estate. He sought (1) an order that the winding up of the companies should proceed jointly with the sequestration of the director's estate, and (2) an order ordaining himself and the trustee on the sequestrated estate to prepare a single scheme of ranking and division of the joint assets of the companies and of the sequestrated estate. The director argued that the proposed note was incompetent and also disputed certain facts.

The Lord Ordinary held that the note was a competent proceeding, but that inquiry was necessary into the matters of fact in dispute between the parties before the court could ascertain whether the orders should be granted. Without hearing parties, he remitted the note and the director's answers to a member of the bar to inquire and to report. The director reclaimed. He contended, inter alia, that if there was to be inquiry it should be by way of proof before answer, failing which the remit should be to a practising chartered accountant, as proposed by the noter.

Held, (1) that it was unnecessary and undesirable to decide now whether the orders sought were competent or incompetent, since inquiry might show that the factual basis of the note was unsound, or agreement might be reached between the creditors, but if it were established that the assets of the companies and of the sequestrated estate were so confused that it was impossible separately to identify the assets of each, and if it was practically impossible to determine who were the creditors' true debtors, then it would be open to the liquidator to enter into a compromise arrangement in conjunction with the trustee so as to enable an overall settlement to be reached with all the creditors, having regard to the terms of s 245 (1) (f) of the Companies Act 1948 and s 172 of the Bankruptcy (Scotland) Act 1913 (pp 381L-382C); (2) that a remit to a reporter was a sensible course which was more likely to lead to an early and less expensive resolution of the problems than a proof before answer (p 382C); (3) that it would be more suitable for a practising chartered accountant to act as reporter than a member of the bar (p 382H); and reclaiming motion *allowed* to the extent of recalling the remit to a member of the bar, and case *put out* by order for parties to intimate whether they had reached agreement on who might act as reporter.

Observed, that if a Lord Ordinary, after making avizandum, came to be of the view that a particular course of action might be followed which had not been canvassed before him, the correct course to follow was to put the case out by order, with or without issuing an opinion, to enable parties to make representations about the competency and propriety of the course proposed (p 382F-G).

Note in petition for liquidation

Peter Cranbourne Taylor, the official liquidator of George Morris (Hotels) Ltd and of Argyll Hotels (Ullapool) Co Ltd, presented a note seeking orders that the winding up of the two companies should proceed jointly with the sequestration of the estate of George Morris, a director of the companies, and that he and the trustee on the sequestrated estate should prepare a single scheme of ranking and division of the joint assets of the companies and of the sequestrated estate.

George Morris lodged answers to the note.

The case came before the Lord Ordinary (Osborne).

Statutory provisions

The Bankruptcy (Scotland) Act 1913 povided:

"172. The trustee may, with consent of the commissioners, compound and transact or refer to arbitration any questions which may arise in the course of the sequestration regarding the estate, or any demand or claim made thereon, and the compromise, transaction, or decree arbitral shall be binding on the creditors and the bankrupt."

The Companies Act 1948 provided:

"245.—(1) The liquidator in a winding up by the court shall have power, with the sanction either of the court or of the committee of inspection . . . (f) to compromise all calls and liabilities to calls, debts and liabilities capable of resulting in debts, and all claims, present or future, certain or contingent, ascertained or sounding only in damages, subsisting or supposed to subsist between the company and a contributory or alleged contributory or other debtor or person apprehending liability to the company, and all questions in any way relating to or affecting the assets or the winding up of the company, on such terms as may be agreed."

Cases referred to

Albert Life Assurance Co (Re) (1871) 6 Ch App 381.
Juba Property Co Ltd, OH, Lord Kincraig, 17 January 1978, unreported.
Sharpe (Isaac) Ltd, 1966, unreported.
Trix Ltd (Re); *Re Ewart Holdings Ltd* [1970] 1 WLR 1421; [1970] 3 All ER 397.

Textbooks referred to

Goudy, *Bankruptcy* (4th ed), pp 336-337.
Palmer's Company Law (25th ed), Vol 2, para 15.123.
Wilton, *Company Liquidation Law and Practice*, p 146.

On 5 June 1991 the Lord Ordinary *held* the note to

be competent, and *remitted* the note and answers to a member of the bar to inquire and to report.

LORD OSBORNE.—The noter avers that on 23 January 1981 Peter Hamish Armour, chartered accountant, was appointed by the court to be provisional liquidator of George Morris (Hotels) Ltd, Argyll Hotels (Ullapool) Co Ltd, and George Morris (Greengairs) Ltd. Subsequently by an interlocutor dated 19 February 1981 the court ordered George Morris (Hotels) Ltd and Argyll Hotels (Ullapool) Co Ltd to be wound up. On 24 April 1981, George Morris (Greengairs) Ltd was ordered to be wound up. Peter Hamish Armour was appointed to be official liquidator of all three of the said companies. On 21 October 1988 the noter was appointed official liquidator to George Morris (Hotels) Ltd and Argyll Hotels (Ullapool) Co Ltd in room and place of the said Peter Hamish Armour.

George Morris, who has lodged answers in the note and is hereinafter referred to as the respondent, signed a trust deed dated 2 February 1981 in favour of Robin Wight Wilson, chartered accountant. On 28 January 1986 the estate of the respondent was sequestrated by the Sheriff of Tayside, Central and Fife at Stirling. Robin Wight Wilson was appointed trustee on the said estate. Mrs Morris, the wife of the respondent, also signed a trust deed in favour of the said Robin Wight Wilson on 4 February 1981. Her estate has not been sequestrated.

The noter goes on to aver that prior to 1981 George Morris (Hotels) Ltd and Argyll Hotels (Ullapool) Co Ltd, hereinafter referred to as the companies, operated farms and estates in Perthshire. In addition, George Morris (Hotels) Ltd owned and operated the Tighnabruich hotel. The sole directors of the companies were the respondent and his wife. Prior to the liquidation of the said companies and the signing of the trust deed by the respondent, he operated only one bank account through which all the transactions for the hotel and the farms and estates were conducted. The noter avers that no formal or statutory accounts were ever prepared on behalf of the companies. The books and records of the companies were incomplete.

The noter avers that upon taking up his duty in 1981, the official liquidator sent out a questionnaire to the creditors of the said companies. In said questionnaire, the creditors were asked to specify against whom they had a claim. None of the creditors, in their responses to the questionnaire, named one of the companies as their debtor. Instead their claims were directed either against various properties belonging to the companies, such as Tighnabruich hotel, Killin, and the Kinnell estate, Killin, or against the respondent himself. It appeared to the official liquidator that the liabilities of George Morris (Hotels) Ltd, Argyll Hotels (Ullapool) Co Ltd and of the respondent as an individual were intermingled. Accordingly he and Robin Wight Wilson, in their respective capacities as liquidator and trustee, arranged for a joint meeting of creditors to be held in Edinburgh on 26 March 1981.

The liquidator determined that the creditors of George Morris (Greengairs) Ltd were ascertainable. The assets of said company were principally heritable property situated in Lanarkshire, consisting of a quarry and a farmhouse, which were fully secured to the bank. An account of charge and discharge in respect of that company for the period from 23 January 1981 until 29 May 1984 was prepared. Said account had disclosed that there were no moveable assets to provide funds for the liquidation. The administration outlays for the said period were met by the secured creditor over the company's heritable property. On 8 May 1985, the court dissolved that company and authorised the accountant of court to deliver up the liquidator's bond of caution. As the dissolution was effected by means of summary procedure the liquidator was not formally discharged from office.

Neither the original official liquidator of the companies nor the noter has been able to determine which creditors have claims against George Morris (Hotels) Ltd, which against Argyll Hotels (Ullapool) Co Ltd and which against the sequestrated estate of the respondent. Accordingly, avers the noter, it has not been possible to adjudicate on the creditors' claims. The liquidation of the companies has proceeded upon the basis that it is not possible to differentiate between the assets and liabilities of the companies and of the respondent personally. A statement of assets for each company dated 3 October 1988 shows assets of £199,243.77. The noter and Robin Wight Wilson, as trustee on the sequestrated estate of the respondent, have both reached the stage where, subject to possible claims against the estates handled by each other, they are in a position to wind up the respective estates for which they are responsible. The assets were realised by the liquidator on an understanding between himself and the said trustee that the estates would be eventually divided amongst all the creditors. The said trustee has informally intimated a claim of £350,000 against the liquidated estates of the said companies. If the liquidations and the said sequestration are not permitted to proceed jointly, the noter claims that the said trustee will require to submit a formal claim.

In these circumstances the noter submits that it is in the best interests of the creditors of the companies and the sequestrated estate of the respondent that the two liquidations should now proceed jointly with the sequestration of the estate of the respondent to the effect that a single scheme of division should be prepared. He states that to do so would avoid unnecessary expense and delay which would be involved if a decision required to be taken as to whether claims were properly directed against the noter or the said trustee. The trustee has agreed to this proposal, as also have the committees of inspection of the creditors of the companies. In these circumstances the noter submits that the court may properly grant the prayer of the note, which seeks an order to ordain that the winding up of George Morris (Hotels) Ltd and of Argyll Hotels (Ullapool) Co Ltd should proceed jointly with the sequestration of the estate of the respondent, and to ordain the noter and Robin Wight

Wilson to prepare a single scheme of ranking and
division of the joint assets of the companies and of the
sequestrated estate. Reference is made to s 245 (1) (f)
of the Companies Act 1948.

The respondent, in his answers to the foregoing
note, admits much of what is averred by the noter.
However, a number of matters appear to be in dispute.
In particular, the respondent avers that his wife has
raised an action against the said Robin Wight Wilson,
as trustee under the trust deed signed by her, seeking
an accounting and requiring him to denude in her
favour. Furthermore, the respondent avers that the
Tighnabruich hotel was owned and operated by a
company called Satron Ltd, and not by George Morris
(Hotels) Ltd. Further he claims that he had bank
accounts with a number of different banks, among
others the Royal Bank of Scotland, the Bank of Scotland and the Allied Irish Bank. In addition he claims
that the business books relating to George Morris
(Hotels) Ltd were complete and were audited by
Messrs Spicer Watson of Edinburgh. He claims that
these auditors continued to assist in auditing the books
of that company subsequent to the appointment of the
provisional liquidator referred to above and at his
request.

In relation to the form of the claims which the noter
says were received by his predecessor as official liquidator, the respondent avers that the claims took that
form as a consequence of the official liquidator's
failure to carry out his duties properly and effectively.
He calls upon the noter to produce copies of all the
correspondence with purported creditors, lists of
creditors, and documents showing the efforts which
have been made in correspondence with the said
Robin Wight Wilson as trustee in bankruptcy of the
respondent to establish which debts alleged are of the
company and which are relevant to the respondent as
an individual. The respondent goes on to claim that he
has currently pending legal actions which, if successful, will substantially increase his assets. He says that
he also intends to take proceedings against the said
Robin Wight Wilson personally in respect of his
conduct of the sequestration as trustee. The respondent also claims that the noter and his trustee in
bankruptcy have previously acknowledged that the
estates of the respondent and of his wife were inextricably linked.

At the outset of the hearing before me, counsel for
the respondent indicated that he wished to argue that
the note was incompetent, although no such argument
was foreshadowed in the respondent's pleadings.
Counsel for the noter recognised that it was open to
the court to consider matters of competency, albeit
that there was no plea or averment relating to the
matter. Accordingly, I permitted counsel for the
respondent to make a submission on the matter of
competency. He argued that the remedy which the
noter sought was one which the court could not grant.
He claimed that he knew of no cases in Scotland or
England which would constitute a precedent for the
granting of this remedy. Power to grant the remedy

sought could only be found in the relevant legislation,
which, having regard to the dates of the relevant liquidations and sequestration, was the Companies Act
1948 and the Bankruptcy (Scotland) Act 1913. Examination of that legislation revealed that it contained
nothing which would justify the granting of the
remedy which the noter sought in this case. The note
could not be treated as an application to the nobile
officium. While s 245 (1) (f) of the Companies Act
1948 was referred to in the note, that section gave no
power to the court to grant the prayer of this note.

Looking at the matter more widely, the remedy
which the noter sought was inimical to the whole
concept of corporate identity. The noter was seeking
a remedy which involved the lumping together of the
estates of the companies in liquidation along with the
estate controlled by the trustee in bankruptcy of the
respondent. Such an approach was contrary to the provisions of liquidation and bankruptcy law, which
required the noter, as official liquidator, and the
trustee in bankruptcy to make decisions or adjudications on claims by creditors and to identify the ownership of assets. It was not open to the court to make an
order which would have the effect of requiring that the
estates of the two companies in liquidation and that of
the respondent should be dealt with together. Counsel
for the respondent referred me to a passage in Goudy
on *The Law of Bankruptcy* (4th ed), at pp 336-337, in
which it was stated that the office of trustee in
bankruptcy, with its accompanying rights and duties,
was strictly personal and could not be shared with
another person, so as to confer on them any of its
privileges or make them responsible for any of its obligations. Thus the trustee in bankruptcy was not
empowered to engage in the kind of co-operative procedure with the noter which was contemplated.

Counsel for the noter contended that the note was
competent and that the remedy sought had previously
been granted in other unreported cases. In this connection he made reference to the liquidation of *Isaac
Sharpe Ltd* in 1966 and the case of *Juba Property Co
Ltd* in 1976. During the course of the debate attempts
were made to retrieve the processes in these cases from
the Scottish Record Office. These efforts were
successful in the case of the liquidation of *Juba
Property Co Ltd*. It appeared from the process in that
case that a note had been presented to the court
seeking an order in similar terms to that sought in the
present note. By an interlocutor of 17 January 1978,
on the unopposed motion of the noter, the order
sought had been granted by the hon Lord Kincraig.
Counsel for the noter went on to elaborate the statutory basis for the note. In particular he referred to
s 245 (1) (f) of the Companies Act 1948, which applied
to these liquidations. [His Lordship narrated the
terms of s 245 (1) set out supra and continued:]

In the light of this wording, argued counsel for the
noter, it was perfectly proper for the noter to adopt the
course which was proposed. Section 172 of the
Bankruptcy (Scotland) Act 1913 provided that: [his
Lordship narrated the terms of s 172 and continued:]

It was thus clear that it was open also to the trustee in bankruptcy of the respondent to adopt the same approach. There was no question of any fundamental attack being made upon the integrity of a corporate persona. What was sought to be done was to divide the estates in the control of the noter and the trustee in sequestration of the respondent in the same manner as that in which the estates had been administered previously, namely as one estate. The granting of the prayer of the note was the only practicable way in which the noter and the trustee in bankruptcy could obtain their discharge by the settlement of claims. They had an overriding duty to ingather and distribute the estate yet, unless the note were granted, distribution could not take place, since there was no rational basis upon which claims could be allocated to particular estates. The creditors in the liquidations and in the sequestration were the same persons. There would be no prejudice involved in proceeding as the noter proposed.

The conclusion which I have reached on the issue of the competency of the present note is that it is a competent proceeding. It appears to me that the wording of s 245 (1) (f) of the Companies Act 1948 is quite wide enough to authorise the liquidator, provided he has the sanction either of the court or of the committee of inspection, to take the course proposed. I refer in particular to the words appearing in subpara (f): "to compromise . . . all questions in any way relating to or affecting the assets or the winding up of the company, on such terms as may be agreed". Further, I am reinforced in my view by the terms of the interlocutor pronounced by the hon Lord Kincraig on 17 January 1978 in the note by the official liquidator of *Juba Property Co Ltd*, already referred to. Further, it appears to me that there need be no anxiety relating to the propriety of the trustee in sequestration of the respondent taking the course proposed, in the light of the terms of s 172 of the Act of 1913, already quoted.

Counsel for the noter went on to address me on the merits of the note, upon the assumption that it was a competent proceeding. Prominent among the considerations to which he made reference in seeking to persuade me at this stage to grant the prayer of the note was the situation in which the noter found himself. That situation was one in which the noter was unable to allocate the creditors between the companies and the respondent as an individual. This difficulty simply reflected the laxity with which the affairs of the companies and of the respondent had been conducted prior to the liquidations and the sequestration. The noter was not in a position to determine which creditors had claims against any particular company or against the sequestrated estate of the respondent. Accordingly it had been impossible to adjudicate on the creditors' claims. This confused situation had become apparent in response to the questionnaire issued to the creditors of the companies by the official liquidator in 1981. All interests would be protected by the requirement that the noter would have to bring his final scheme of distribution before the court for approval. Counsel for the noter argued that the prayer of the petition should be granted at this stage. The respondent had demonstrated no interest to resist the grant of the prayer. There were no averments showing how he personally would be prejudiced if the prayer were granted. Those who would be affected directly by the proposal, namely the creditors, agreed to the course proposed. That course was the only practicable way in which the liquidations and incidentally the sequestration of the respondent could be expeditiously brought to a close. If the prayer of the note was not granted, the only course which the noter could take would be to make a completely arbitrary adjudication, which was unacceptable, or present a petition to the nobile officium of the court. The respondent's answers contained no relevant material which would constitute a reason why the prayer of the note should not be granted.

Counsel for the respondent submitted that the court should not grant the prayer of the note at this stage. There was an important area of disputed fact in existence. The position of the respondent was that the difficulties faced by the official liquidator in allocating creditors' claims as between the companies and the respondent himself were difficulties of his own creation. It was quite insufficient for the noter to rely on the confused replies given by creditors to the questionnaire issued by the official liquidator in 1981. The official liquidator should have taken further steps by way of inquiry with the creditors to clarify the correct debtors. Further the position regarding the ownership of the Tighnabruich hotel was a matter in dispute. In addition, it was disputed that the respondent had operated only one bank account. The court should not grant the prayer of the note unless and until it was clearly established that no other practicable course could be followed by the noter to bring the liquidations to a conclusion.

Having considered the terms of the parties' averments in this note and answers and having heard the arguments based upon them, I have reached the conclusion that it would not be proper for me to grant the prayer of the note at this stage. It is evident from the averments made by the noter that the essential basis of the note is the contention that the noter has been unable to determine which creditors have claims against George Morris (Hotels) Ltd, which against Argyll Hotels (Ullapool) Co Ltd and which against the sequestrated estate of the respondent. However, it is, in my opinion, plain from the answers that the respondent contends that insufficient efforts have been made to inquire into the correct debtors in the creditors' claims. Furthermore there is a factual dispute between the parties about the extent to which the said companies and the affairs of the respondent were conducted without regard to the different legal personae involved. In these circumstances it appears to me necessary for inquiry to be undertaken into the matters of dispute between the parties before the court can properly reach a conclusion as to whether the prayer of the note should be granted. In this situation I have decided to remit the note and answers to a reporter for inquiry into the facts, a course which I consider open to me both at common law and in terms of s 25 (2) of the Court of Session Act 1988. In my opinion it would be appropriate for a member of the Faculty of Advocates to undertake this task and accordingly I shall pronounce the requisite interlocutor.

The respondent reclaimed.

Reclaiming motion

The reclaiming motion was heard before the Second Division on 28 February 1992.

On 3 April 1992 the court *allowed* the reclaiming motion to the extent of *recalling* the remit to the member of the bar, and *put out* the case by order for parties to intimate whether they had agreed on a suitable practising chartered accountant to act as reporter.

The following opinion of the court was delivered by Lord McCluskey:

OPINION OF THE COURT.—The noter was appointed official liquidator to George Morris (Hotels) Ltd and Argyll Hotels (Ullapool) Co Ltd on 21 October 1988 in room and place of Peter Hamish Armour who had been appointed by the court to be official liquidator of those companies when they were ordered to be wound up in 1981. The reclaimer (who was the respondent in the note) is George Morris who lodged answers to the note. He signed a trust deed in 1981 in favour of Robin Wight Wilson, chartered accountant; his estate was sequestrated in 1986 and Mr Wilson was appointed trustee on the estate. The background to this matter is narrated very fully in the opinion of the Lord Ordinary dated 5 June 1991, which in turn summarises the position as set forth in the pleadings of the parties.

It is unnecessary to rehearse the averments in any detail here. In essence, what the noter avers is that, prior to the appointment of Mr Armour as liquidator of the companies, the businesses carried on by the companies and at various farms and estates, including the Tighnabruich hotel, were carried on in a way that did not enable the business transactions of the different entities to be distinguished and separated from each other. The sole directors of the companies were the reclaimer and his wife; all the transactions for the hotel, the farms and estates were conducted through one bank account; no formal or statutory accounts were prepared on behalf of the companies and the books and records of the companies were incomplete. It is said that the official liquidator discovered that the liabilities of the companies and of the reclaimer as an individual were so intermingled that he was unable to ascertain which creditors had claims against which of the companies and which creditors had claims against the sequestrated estate of the respondent. Thus it was not possible to adjudicate upon the creditors' claims. The liquidation of the companies had proceeded upon the basis that it was not possible to differentiate between the assets and liabilities of the companies and

of the reclaimer. Upon that narrative the noter invites the court to grant the prayer of the note, which includes the following: "to ordain that the winding up of George Morris (Hotels) Ltd and of Argyll Hotels (Ullapool) Co Ltd should proceed jointly with the sequestration of the estates of George Morris; and to ordain the noter and Robin Wight Wilson to prepare a single scheme of ranking and division of the joint assets of the companies and of the sequestrated estates".

The reclaimer in his answers disputes some of the material facts averred by the noter. In particular he claims that there were several bank accounts and that there were business books relating to George Morris (Hotels) Ltd which were complete and audited. There are other matters of fact about which the parties are in dispute.

When the case came before the Lord Ordinary counsel for the respondent indicated that he wished to argue that the note was incompetent. Although there was no plea to the competency the Lord Ordinary permitted counsel for the reclaimer to make a submission on the matter of competency. The submissions for both parties on that question are fully narrated in the opinion of the Lord Ordinary. It is unnecessary to repeat them. The same submissions were made to this court by both parties. At the conclusion of the debate the Lord Ordinary pronounced an interlocutor in the following terms: "The Lord Ordinary having further considered the note and answers, nos 61 and 70 of process, remits same to Mr R Anderson, advocate, to inquire into the facts and to report, said report to be transmitted to the Deputy Principal Clerk of Session, 2 Parliament Square, Edinburgh; appoints the solicitor for the noter to instruct said reporter within 14 days from this date, to provide him with copies of all relevant documents, including a copy of this interlocutor, and the opinion herein dated of even date and to be responsible in the first instance for payment of his fee; having heard counsel on the respondent's oral motion made at the bar for leave to reclaim this interlocutor, grants same."

In this court it was argued that the order pronounced by the Lord Ordinary was not one that it was competent for him to grant. The submission was that the remedy which the noter was seeking in the prayer of the note was inimical to the whole concept of corporate identity. It was submitted that there was no common law power to do what was sought in the prayer and that the relevant statutory provision conferred no power upon the court either. The statutory provision upon which the noter relied before the Lord Ordinary, and upon which the Lord Ordinary relied, was contained in s 245 (1) (f) of the Companies Act 1948, the statute which applied to these liquidations. The relevant part provided that: [his Lordship quoted the terms of s 245 (1) set out supra and continued:]

It was submitted that this provision was designed to enable the liquidator to deal with particular claims in regard to the company. It was concerned only with what was permitted within what counsel described as the "four corners" of the liquidation proceedings. It

A simply could not have been the intention of Parliament to permit confusion between corporate assets and the assets of individuals when there was a liquidation of a company proceeding at the same time as the sequestration of an individual person, however close his connections with the company in liquidation. In order to achieve the dramatic result which the Lord Ordinary had held was permitted by the statute the language would have had to be much clearer than in fact it was. Counsel had been unable to find any case

B in which this provision, or its predecessors or successors, had been construed by a court in such a way as to shed light on the competency question. Reference was, however, made to *Re Trix Ltd*; *Re Ewart Holdings Ltd* in which the court had declined to sanction a conditional agreement of compromise under s 245 of the Companies Act 1948 made between the liquidator and a company in circumstances where not all the creditors were agreeable to the compromise. All that could really be said about that case in relation

C to the matter of competency was that no issue of competency was argued there. Counsel submitted that the liquidator's duty was to adjudicate upon the claims as best he could. The liquidator was properly described as an agent of the company: *Palmer's Company Law*, Vol 2, para 15.123. He was responsible for the assets of the company. There were limits upon the power of a liquidator just as there were limits upon the power of a trustee in a sequestration. He was not entitled to say, as the noter was saying, that an adjudication was

D impossible. Furthermore, under reference to the passage in Goudy on *The Law of Bankruptcy* (4th ed), at pp 336-337, referred to by the Lord Ordinary, it was submitted that the office of trustee in bankruptcy was strictly personal and could not be shared with another person. In short, neither the liquidator nor the trustee had any statutory power to have the winding up and the sequestration conjoined with a consequent inmixing and confusion of the assets of the two companies and of the estate of the reclaimer. It was incor-

E rect to speak of "the joint assets of the companies and of the sequestrated estates", as the prayer of the note did.

In reply to the arguments on competency, counsel for the noter submitted that the language of s 245 (1) (f) was sufficiently clear and unambiguous to show that the liquidator had power to engage in any compromise or arrangement that the company could have engaged in. The power of the trustee in bankruptcy contained in s 172 of the Bankruptcy (Scotland) Act

F 1913 was similarly wide. In his submission, if it could be said that a company and an individual closely connected with the company could have entered into an arrangement whereby they jointly made a compromise with a number of creditors who had potential claims against both or either, then a similar arrangement could properly and competently be made between the company and a trustee on the sequestrated estate of that individual, or between the individual and the liquidator of the company, or, as in this case, between the liquidator of the company and the trustee on the

sequestrated estate of the individual. Support for this view could be found in the opinion of James LJ in *Re* G *Albert Life Assurance Co*, at p 386. In that case, under reference to sections of the Companies Act 1862, which contained wording indistinguishable for this purpose from that in s 245 (1) (f), James LJ had said: "The 159th and 160th sections seem to me to provide that a company by its official liquidators, with the sanction of the Court, is to have exactly the same power of compromising both with its creditors and its debtors as an individual would have."

That dictum was quoted by Wilton in *Company* H *Liquidation Law and Practice*, p 146, as applicable to Scotland. The legislature must be taken to have had knowledge of that statement of the law when enacting the 1948 Act. It was quite incorrect to describe what was proposed here as a flagrant attack on the whole notion of corporate identity. The noter was seeking merely to do what the companies and the sequestrated individual could have done by agreement. Counsel confirmed that inquiries into the cases of *Isaac Sharpe Ltd* in 1966 and *Juba Property Co Ltd* in 1976, I referred to in the opinion of the Lord Ordinary, showed that orders in similar terms to that sought in the present note had been granted, but it was accepted that in each case the order was made on an unopposed motion of the respective noter and no question of competency had been raised or decided.

Upon the assumption that it was competent to do what the Lord Ordinary had done, counsel for the reclaimer submitted that the Lord Ordinary should J not have taken the step of remitting to a reporter under s 25 (2) of the Court of Session Act 1988. It was not suggested that it was not competent for the Lord Ordinary to remit to a reporter for the purpose specified in the interlocutor; it was simply that the better course would have been to allow a proof before answer, as had been suggested to the Lord Ordinary by the reclaimer. Finally, it was submitted that if there was to be a remit, it would be better to remit to a practising accountant who would be more suitable to K investigate the background to this matter. Counsel pointed out that the idea of making a remit under s 25 (2) of the Court of Session Act 1988 had come from the Lord Ordinary himself. It had not been discussed in the course of the debate and neither party had made any submission about it or about the kind of person to whom such a remit might be made. In reply, counsel for the noter argued that the Lord Ordinary had a discretion to remit in the way he had done under s 25 (2). Following that course in the present case might well L be swifter and cheaper than the alternative of a proof before answer and the noter supported the Lord Ordinary in the course that he had followed. However, counsel also acknowledged that this matter had not been discussed before the Lord Ordinary and neither party had been invited to make suggestions as to what kind of person or indeed who might be suitable to make the necessary investigation and to report.

In our opinion, it is unnecessary and undesirable at this stage to attempt to pronounce upon the com-

A petency of granting the several distinct remedies contained in the prayer of the note. The court is not being invited at this stage to grant the prayer. We are not at this stage prepared to rule that any part of the prayer is incompetent. In our view, however, it is plain that s 245 (1) (f) permits the liquidator of a company to enter into any compromise arrangement with creditors that might have been entered into by the company itself. Similarly a trustee in bankruptcy is empowered by s 172 of the Bankruptcy (Scotland) Act 1913 to compromise with creditors in exactly the same way as

B the bankrupt himself might have compromised had the estate not been sequestrated. We see no reason to refrain from giving the wording of these two sections their ordinary meaning. In our view, if it is established that the assets of the companies and of the sequestrated estate are so confused that it is impossible separately to identify the assets of each, and if also it appears that it is practically impossible to determine who are the true debtors for those creditors who have claims arising out of some business with the com-

C panies and/or the sequestrated estate, then it would be open to the noter to enter into a compromise arrangement in conjunction with Robin Wight Wilson so as to enable an overall settlement to be reached with all the creditors. On that view, it appears to us that the course adopted by the Lord Ordinary, namely a remit, is a sensible one and, as far as can be judged, is more likely to lead to an early and less expensive resolution of the problems than the alternative proposed by the reclaimer. We reserve our opinion as to whether or not it would be competent for the court to ordain that the

D winding up of the companies should proceed "jointly" with the sequestration of the estates of the reclaimer. That is an order that might be entirely unnecessary particularly if the position is as averred by the noter in stat 10, viz: "The noter and the trustee have both reached the stage where, subject to possible claims against the estates handled by each other, they are in a position to wind up their respective estates. The assets were realised by the liquidator on an under-

E standing between himself and the trustee that the estates would be eventually divided amongst all the creditors."

It is also averred (stat 11) that the trustee and the committees of inspection of the creditors of the companies are agreed to what is proposed. Thus it may be unnecessary to consider ordaining that the winding up of the companies should proceed jointly with the sequestration. It may also be unnecessary to ordain the noter and Robin Wight Wilson to prepare a single

F scheme of ranking and division of the joint assets of the companies and of the sequestrated estates. We refrain from deciding on the competency of either course simply because it is not necessary to do so at this stage.

Parties are agreed that the Lord Ordinary decided to use his power under s 25 (2) of the Court of Session Act 1988 without having the benefit of submissions from the parties in relation to that course. If a Lord Ordinary makes avizandum after a debate and thereafter comes to be of the view that a particular course

of action might be followed, but that is not a course of action which has been canvassed before him, the G correct course for him to follow is to put the case out by order; whether or not he should, at the same time, issue an opinion will depend upon the circumstances of each particular case. Putting the case out by order will enable parties to make representations to him about the competency and propriety of the course which he has in mind. It will also, as in this type of case, enable them to make representations as to who might be appointed to report to the court. In the course of the debate before us it was indicated to H parties that if there was to be a remit, the court would be in favour of appointing as a reporter a practising chartered accountant or other suitably qualified person rather than a member of the bar; in that event it would be helpful if the parties were able to agree upon who should be appointed. If they could agree, and the court judged that he was a suitable person, the person could then be appointed. This case will, therefore, be put out by order to enable parties to intimate to the court if any such agreement has been reached. I In the absence of any such agreement the court will proceed to make its own appointment. At that stage the court will require to grant the reclaiming motion, to recall the interlocutor of 5 June 1991 insofar as it remitted the note and answers to Mr R Anderson, advocate, to remit the note and answers to another suitable person and quoad ultra to affirm the interlocutor of 5 June 1991.

J
Counsel for Noter and Respondent, J R Campbell; Solicitors, Ketchen & Stevens, WS — Counsel for Respondent and Reclaimer, Andrew Smith; Solicitors, Drummond Miller, WS (for Friels, Uddingston).

A N

The statutory provisions currently applicable are the Bankruptcy (Scotland) Act 1985, s 65, and the Insolvency Act 1986, ss 165 and 167 and Sched 4.

K

Dempsey v Celtic Football and Athletic Co Ltd

OUTER HOUSE
LORD PROSSER
15 MAY 1992

L

Company — Register of members — Transfer of shares — Failure to comply with form provided in articles of association — Petition for rectification of register — Voting rights — Whether transferee should be prevented from exercising voting rights — Transferee having right by contract to control vote of transferor should transferor remain as member — Whether interim interdict appropriate.

Company — Register of members — Transfer of shares

— *Failure to comply with form provided in articles of*
A *association — Whether proper instrument of transfer —*
Whether registration of transfer unlawful — Companies
Act 1985 (c 6), s 183 (1).

A member of a company petitioned under s 359 (1)
of the Companies Act 1985 for rectification of the
company's register of members by deletion of the
entries of 31 individuals who were registered as the
holders of partly paid shares. The petitioning member
relied upon the terms of s 183 (1) of the Companies
Act 1985 which provides that it is not lawful for a
B company to register a transfer of shares unless a
"proper instrument of transfer" has been delivered.
The Stock Transfer Act 1963 provides a statutory
form of transfer of registered securities, but the form
is only appropriate for the transfer of fully paid shares.
The articles of association of the company provided
that shares in the company were to be transferred in
the form provided in the articles. That form differed
from the statutory one in that it provided for the transferee to complete and sign the form of transfer con-
C firming the transferee's acceptance of the conditions
under which the shares were held by the transferor.
The forms purporting to transfer the shares registered
in the names of the 31 individuals had not been signed
in that manner. In the petition the member also
sought interdict and obtained interim interdict against
certain of the transferees exercising any voting rights.
Twelve of the parties so interdicted and named as
respondents subsequently sought recall of the interim
interdict. In resisting recall the petitioning member
D argued first, that the company had unlawfully
registered the transfer of the shares relating to those
parties who were affected by the interim interdict,
under and in terms of the Companies Act 1985, s 183
(1), an argument subsequently departed from, and,
secondly, that the company had been in breach of its
own articles of association by registering those shares
in name of the interdicted parties without the required
signatures. The petitioner further argued that,
pending rectification of the register of members under
E s 359 (1) of the Companies Act 1985, the alleged defective entry of the names of the interdicted parties
should not be given effect to and the interim interdict
should not be recalled.

Held, (1) that the absence of the transferee's signature on the form of transfer was a substantive matter,
and not merely a matter of form, and gave a prima
facie case for rectification (p 385G-H); but (2) that
although such an omission was a breach of the company's articles of association, the fundamental issue in
F relation to interim interdict was that of beneficial
ownership; and as beneficial ownership had passed to
the interdicted parties as a matter of contract, they
were entitled to use and control the rights, including
voting rights, otherwise ostensibly held by the relevant transferor of the shares despite the defect in the
form of transfer (p 385H-K); and interim interdict
recalled.

Opinion, that for the purposes of s 183 (1) of the
Companies Act 1985, an "instrument of transfer" was
"proper" so long as it attracted the imposition of

stamp duty, the section not being concerned with
regularity as between transferor and transferee or G
between them and the company or other members
(p 384K-L).

Re Paradise Motor Co [1968] 1 WLR 1125, *followed.*

────────

**Petition for rectification of register of members
and for interdict**
Brian John Dempsey presented a petition seeking
rectification of the register of members of the Celtic
Football and Athletic Co Ltd and for interdict and H
interim interdict. The rectification sought was the
deletion from the register of the names of 31 people
registered as holders of shares. The company and also
the 31 individuals were called as respondents. Interim
interdict against those who had not lodged caveats
against the disputed members exercising their voting
rights was granted ex parte. Thereafter certain of the
respondents enrolled for recall of the grant of interim
interdict.   I

The motion came before the Lord Ordinary
(Prosser).

Statutory provisions
The Companies Act 1985 provides:

"183.—(1) It is not lawful for a company to register
a transfer of shares in or debentures of the company
unless a proper instrument of transfer has been
delivered to it. . . . This applies notwithstanding anything in the company's articles. . . .   J

"359.—(1) If — (a) the name of any person is,
without sufficient cause, entered in or omitted from a
company's register of members . . . the person
aggrieved, or any member of the company, or the
company, may apply to the court for rectification of
the register."

Cases referred to
Paradise Motor Co, Re [1968] 1 WLR 1125; [1968] 2 K
      All ER 625.
Piccadilly Radio plc, Re [1989] BCL 683.

On 15 May 1992 his Lordship *recalled* the interim
interdict.

LORD PROSSER.—The petitioner is the holder
of a number of fully paid shares of the Celtic Football
and Athletic Co Ltd ("the company"). In this petition,
he seeks an order that the register of members of the   L
company be rectified by deletion of the entries indicating that 31 persons called as respondents are the
holders of the shares entered against their names. He
also seeks interdict against certain of these respondents in relation to the exercise of the votes attaching
to the shares at present registered in their names. On
29 March 1992, interim interdict was granted against
such of these respondents as had lodged no caveat.
They were thereby interdicted from "exercising the
votes attaching to the shares of the . . . company . . .
which are at present registered in their names unlaw-

A fully and without sufficient cause, and in respect of which the petitioner seeks rectification of the register of members . . ., and in particular from exercising those votes at the extraordinary general meeting of the said company to be held on 30 March 1992 or at any adjournment thereof or from granting a proxy to any other person to exercise on their behalf any such votes". Insofar as it relates to the particular meeting of 30 March 1992, or any adjournment thereof, the interlocutor granting interim interdict is spent. However, the more general interdict against exercising

B the votes unlawfully and without sufficient cause, or from granting a proxy to exercise such votes, remains in force. Since the interlocutor was pronounced, answers have been lodged both on behalf of the company, and on behalf of 12 of the individuals affected by the interim interdict. These individuals now seek recall of that interim interdict.

The immediate background to the petition is to be found in a notice issued on 27 February 1992, giving notice of the holding of an extraordinary general

C meeting on 30 March 1992, for the purpose of considering certain resolutions relating to the appointment and removal of directors. Put more generally, it appears that there was a potential battle for control of the board. The problem in relation to the register of members is that the Stock Transfer Act 1963 provides for the transfer of registered securities by means of an instrument in a simple form set out in a Schedule to the Act. That form is, however, only appropriate in the case of fully paid shares. Article 14 of the com-

D pany's articles provides that shares in the company shall be transferred in the form therein provided. That form, unlike the statutory one, provides for acceptance by the transferee of the conditions under which the shares were held by the transferor, and a signature by the transferee to that effect. The entries in the register which the petitioner seeks to have deleted are averred to have followed from transfers of partly paid shares, but it is said that none of the forms used in respect of these transfers contained any acceptance or signature

E by the transferee. The 12 individual respondents on whose behalf answers have been lodged admit that the form of transfer employed in respect of their acquisition of shares was not conform to the company's articles, and a similar admission is made on behalf of the company in respect of the transfers more generally. The petitioner avers, and the company admit, that since February 1992, transfers of partly paid shares have been effected in accordance with the provisions of the articles.

F In seeking deletion of the relevant entries, the petitioner in his pleadings founds not merely upon the fact that the statutory form was inappropriate, and that the form provided in the articles should have been used. He founds also upon s 183 (1) of the Companies Act 1985, which provides that "it is not lawful for a company to register a transfer of shares . . . unless a proper instrument of transfer has been delivered to it, or the transfer is an exempt transfer. . . . This applies notwithstanding anything in the company's articles". The transfers in question were not exempt, and the

petitioner avers that it was not lawful for the company to have registered the transfers.   G

In moving me to recall the interim interdict, counsel for the respondents referred to a number of matters which were apparently seen as reflecting ill upon the petitioner. The interdict had only been obtained and intimated very shortly before the crucial meeting. The petitioner had selected those against whom interdict was sought, not merely because they had lodged no caveat, but because these persons were thought to be on one side of the dispute, while the petitioner, and those against whom he did not seek interdict, were on H the other. The petitioner was thus said to be using "illegitimate" means in pursuit of his aims, and his "motive" in seeking rectification and interdict was said to be improper. His grievance was not that the register was wrong, but that some of those whose names appeared on it would vote in a way that he did not like, unless they were disenfranchised. In the context of what is now an admitted and quite widespread breach of the company's articles, I see nothing surprising in one party to a dispute of this I kind questioning the consequences of that breach, and while other votes might also have been invalidated, it does not strike me as odd that such a party should restrict his practical recourse to the law to those situations where he has an interest in doing so. I have not found this line of argument useful.

As I have indicated, the petitioner's criticism of these entries in the register is based not only upon the breach of the articles, but also upon an alleged breach J of s 183 (1) of the Companies Act 1985. On the basis of the petitioner's pleadings, the contention appears to be that since the wrong form of instrument had been used for these transfers, there was no "proper instrument of transfer" within the meaning of s 183 (1), and the registration of the transfers was thereby rendered unlawful. However, counsel for the respondents, under reference to *Re Paradise Motor Co*, submitted that this section did not render registration of these transfers unlawful, even if the wrong form had been K used. A "proper" instrument, for the purposes of this section, meant merely an instrument which would attract stamp duty. The section was not designed to ensure regularity between transferor and transferee, nor between them and the company or other members. Having regard to what was said by the court in that case, counsel for the petitioner did not seek to rely further upon this aspect of his case, and I am satisfied that it was indeed ill founded.

There is nonetheless an evident breach of the L requirement of the articles in regard to the form of transfer which was used. Moreover, in relation to partly paid shares, I am not prepared to see the absence of the transferee's signature as a mere irregularity, as it might be in relation to fully paid shares. One way of ensuring that this provision in the articles is obeyed would be to refuse to register the name of any transferee, unless the correct form, with his signature, had been used. That being so, there is in my view a prima facie case for rectification if registration has in fact been granted on the basis of a transfer form which is defective in terms of the articles. It was accepted by counsel for the petitioner that if rectification were to be ordered in such circumstances, restoration of the transferor's name to the register would be a necessary concomitant of deletion of the transferee's name. I would observe that in my opinion it would always be a question of circumstances whether the court should indeed order the clock to be put back in this way. But I am not concerned at this stage with any eventual decision as to rectification, in terms of s 359 of the Companies Act 1985. I am concerned only with the interim regulation of matters, pending resolution of that issue.

Counsel for the respondents pointed out that the transferors of their shares had been disenfranchised by the alteration of the register, and that they as transferees had been disenfranchised, for all purposes, by the interim interdict. The respondents aver that the transfer to them was made pursuant to a binding agreement between them and the transferor, and that the transferor had at no time notified any challenge in respect of the transfer or the binding nature of the agreement to transfer. The real question of principle did not relate to the form which had been used, but to the issue of beneficial ownership. That had indeed been transferred, and that being so, those who had acquired the beneficial right ought not to be deprived of the title which they had obtained by registration, even if they had obtained it in a defective manner. Counsel referred to *Re Piccadilly Radio plc*. Rectification would serve no purpose in situations where the beneficial transfer was valid and unquestioned. Moreover, where that was the situation, there was no prima facie case for disenfranchising the transferees ad interim, and more particularly, the balance of convenience was against disenfranchising a beneficial owner ad interim, when no one else could exercise the voting rights attaching to these shares.

Counsel for the petitioner emphasised that a breach of the articles was a wrong. The absence of the transferee's signature was not a technicality. The transfer of partly paid shares had been recognised as unsuitable for the simplified statutory form, and it was left to individual companies to decide what was necessary when such a transfer occurred. This company had made specific requirements as to what the transferee must do. These positive requirements had been ignored, and the transferee's names had been entered in the register "without sufficient cause" for the purposes of s 359. A defective transfer had produced a defective register, and at least prima facie, that register should be rectified, and pending rectification the defective entry should not be given effect. This was the more true when those with this defect in their title to membership might by their votes have a determinative effect on important issues. As a member of the company, the petitioner was entitled to demand compliance with the articles, and upon the consequences of non-compliance being deprived of effect. In the circumstances, he also had an interest in ensuring that non-compliance should be ineffective. While he acknowledged that there were similarities with the case of *Re Piccadilly Radio plc*, it remained true that there was a prima facie case for eventual rectification, and pending such rectification, those who had arrived upon the register in breach of the articles, and who might in due course be removed from it, should not be allowed to exercise power in the affairs of the company.

I see genuine force in these submissions. Even if registration is not unlawful in terms of s 183 of the Companies Act 1985, I see the breach of the articles, and the absence of the transferee's signature, as a substantive matter, and not merely one of "form". It is perhaps the company itself, rather than other individual members, which is primarily affected by the breach. Nonetheless, other individual members are at least prima facie entitled to complain of the breach, if their interests are, even indirectly, affected. I have, however, come to the view that as counsel for the respondents contended, the fundamental issue is that of beneficial ownership. Beneficial ownership having passed to the transferees as matter of contract, it was accepted that they would be entitled to control and direct the use of the relevant votes by the transferor, pending alteration of the register. Being less direct, that position might be less effectual than having the actual right of voting as a member on the register. But once it is accepted, as it is, that the transferees are entitled, in a question with the transferors, to insist that the vote be used as the transferees wish, the possibility of a rectification, bringing the transferors back on to the register, becomes much less significant. The transferees would then still have control of these votes, despite the removal of their names from the register, by virtue of their beneficial right in the shares. That being so, the "wrongness" of their names being on the register might be seen as one of form rather than substance. Upon such a view, it is questionable whether there is even a prima facie case for interim interdict against their using their votes. Be that as it may, if one turns to the question of balance of convenience, I am satisfied that it is more appropriate to allow acquired beneficial rights to be exercised through voting, rather than exclude the holders of these shares (i e, both the willing transferors and the willing transferees) from the voting process, pending resolution of an issue which relates primarily to methods of transfer rather than its intended effects.

In these circumstances I recall the interim interdict granted on 29 March 1992.

Counsel for Petitioner, J L Mitchell, QC, Baird; Solicitors, Drummond Miller, WS — Counsel for Respondents, Davidson; Solicitors, McGrigor Donald.

L A McG

Medicopharma (UK) BV v Cairns

OUTER HOUSE

TEMPORARY JUDGE T G COUTTS, QC

20 MAY 1992

Expenses — Caution for expenses — Foreign company ceasing to trade in United Kingdom — Whether sufficient reason for pursuers to be ordained to find caution.

In an action of payment for goods supplied by a foreign company registered in the European Community, the only defence stated was a breach of contract by reason of default of notice of termination of the agreement to supply. The defender sought to have the pursuers ordained to find caution for expenses at common law, founding on a letter indicating that the pursuers were to cease trading in the United Kingdom.

Held, (1) that there would require to be some compelling factor before a litigant was ordained to find caution (p 386G-H); (2) that the mere fact that the pursuer was a foreign company registered in the European Community was not of itself such a ground (p 386H-I); and motion *refused* in hoc statu.

Action of payment

Medicopharma (UK) BV, a company registered in the European Community but outwith the United Kingdom, raised an action of payment for goods supplied against Edward Louise Cairns, MPS, trading as Cairns Chemists. The defender lodged a minute seeking to have the pursuers ordained to find caution at common law.

The motion to have the pursuers ordained to find caution came before the temporary judge (T G Coutts, QC).

On 20 May 1992 the temporary judge *refused* the motion and *refused* leave to reclaim.

T G COUTTS, QC—In this action of payment it is admitted that goods were supplied by the pursuers to the defender. The pursuers seek payment. The only defence alleged is that there was a breach of contract by reason of default of notice of termination of the agreement to supply. The defender lodged a minute which was answered and the minute and answers came before me at a hearing to determine whether the pursuers should be ordained to find caution for expenses.

In support of the contention that the pursuers should be ordained to find caution the defender pointed to a letter indicating that they were ceasing to trade in respect of their United Kingdom operation. The caution was not sought in terms of the Companies Act but at common law. It was conceded by counsel for the defender that the common law test was higher than the test under the Companies Act whereby by s 726 it is provided that caution for expenses may be

ordered if there is credible testimony before the court that the pursuers might be unable to meet an award of expenses against them. Both parties were agreed that the matter was one of discretion for the Lord Ordinary in the whole circumstances of the case.

A litigant is not normally ordained to find caution. In order that that should happen there require to be compelling factors such as the unlikelihood of success in the action or that the litigant was an undischarged bankrupt or that some award or decree having been granted in another matter there had been a failure to pay. In the case of a company for example, a charge on a decree which had not been paid would provide grounds for a presumption that there might be an inability to pay expenses. Looking at the averments in the present case it cannot be said that the pursuers are unlikely to succeed as the averments presently stand, nor is there any evidence that the pursuer company has failed to pay its debts in another matter. The mere fact that it is a foreign company registered in the European Community would not, in my view, afford any ground for a requirement that caution be found. Indeed it would appear by way of the adjusted open record in the principal action that in fact the defender dishonoured a cheque made payable to the pursuers in part payment for goods supplied by them. In all these circumstances the request by the defender for an order upon the pursuers to find caution for expenses must be refused in hoc statu, there being, in my view, insufficient averment of fact to warrant such a course. I was moved for leave to reclaim against that refusal but since the matter is one of discretion, since the matter for appeal would further delay progress in the action and since I have otherwise continued the minute and answers for adjustment it did not seem to me to be appropriate that leave should be granted.

Counsel for Pursuers, Hanretty; Solicitors, Russel & Aitken, WS — Counsel for Defender, Andrew Smith; Solicitors, Clark & Co.

R D S

Canon (Scotland) Business Machines Ltd v GA Business Systems Ltd (in liquidation)

OUTER HOUSE

LORD CAPLAN

12 JUNE 1992

Company — Liquidator — Misfeasance — Procedure — Alleged breach of interdict by liquidator — Leave to raise proceedings against company in liquidation and liquidator — Whether disputed breach of interdict best dealt with in winding up process or interdict process — Insolvency Act 1986 (c 45), s 212 (2) and (3).

Interdict — Breach of interdict — Company in liquidation — Leave to raise proceedings — Whether disputed breach of interdict best dealt with in winding up process or interdict process.

Section 212 of the Insolvency Act 1986 gives powers to the court to restore to a company money or property or to order compensation in respect of any misfeasance or breach of statutory duty by a liquidator which has arisen in the course of the winding up of the company.

A company was supplied on credit with a photocopying machine in terms of a dealership agreement. The standard terms and conditions of sale provided that title in the machine remained with the suppliers until full payment had been made. Payment not having been made, the suppliers obtained interim interdict against the company, its agents or anyone acting on its behalf, from selling or removing or in any way interfering with certain specified equipment, including the copier. Shortly thereafter an order was made for the winding up of the company and a liquidator was appointed. Prior to the grant of interim interdict the company had delivered the copier to another business. After the grant of interim interdict the liquidator came to an agreement with the other business involving a sale of the copier. The suppliers presented a note seeking leave to raise proceedings against the company for breach of interdict, averring that the liquidator's action had affected their title to the copier. For the company and the liquidator it was argued that any question between the parties could be resolved within the context of the liquidation, that special cause was required before leave to litigate the matter could be granted, that a statutory alternative was available if the liquidator had acted improperly and that the suppliers were personally barred, because of delay, from complaining of any breach of interdict.

Held, (1) that the winding up process was designed to provide a fair procedure for settlement of the claims of creditors and contributories and that a party applying for leave to litigate against a company had to show special cause, but that the court should seek to do what was right and fair according to the circumstances of each case (p 389G-H and J-K); (2) that the winding up process was not an appropriate place to have a breach of interdict determined, particularly where the liquidator was said to have been instrumental in causing the breach, since under the insolvency provisions the court would have less pertinent powers to deal with a breach of interdict than it would in the interdict process (pp 389L-390B); and (3) that the suppliers had a prima facie case and prima facie it was appropriate that questions which had been raised be dealt with in the interdict proceedings, which also included the question of personal bar (p 390B-H); and leave to raise proceedings *granted*.

Re Grosvenor Metal Co Ltd [1950] Ch 63 and *Re Aro Co Ltd* [1980] Ch 196, *approved* and *followed*.

Petition for winding up

Canon (Scotland) Business Machines Ltd, creditors of GA Business Systems Ltd, a company which had been wound up by order of the court, presented a note seeking to raise proceedings against the company in liquidation. Answers were lodged on behalf of GA Business Systems Ltd and Stuart Fraser, the liquidator thereof.

The note and answers came before the Lord Ordinary (Caplan).

Statutory provisions

The Insolvency Act 1986 provides:

"130.— . . . (2) When a winding-up order has been made or a provisional liquidator has been appointed, no action or proceeding shall be proceeded with or commenced against the company or its property, except by leave of the court and subject to such terms as the court may impose. . . .

"212.—(1) This section applies if in the course of the winding up of a company it appears that a person who — (a) is or has been an officer of the company, (b) has acted as liquidator, administrator or administrative receiver of the company, or (c) not being a person falling within paragraph (a) or (b), is or has been concerned, or has taken part, in the promotion, formation or management of the company, has misapplied or retained, or become accountable for, any money or other property of the company, or been guilty of any misfeasance or breach of any fiduciary or other duty in relation to the company.

"(2) The reference in subsection (1) to any misfeasance or breach of any fiduciary or other duty in relation to the company includes, in the case of a person who has acted as liquidator or administrator of the company, any misfeasance or breach of any fiduciary or other duty in connection with the carrying out of his functions as liquidator or administrator of the company.

"(3) The court may, on the application of the official receiver or the liquidator, or of any creditor or contributory, examine into the conduct of the person falling within subsection (1) and compel him — (a) to repay, restore or account for the money or property or any part of it, with interest at such rate as the court thinks just, or (b) to contribute such sum to the company's assets by way of compensation in respect of the misfeasance or breach of fiduciary or other duty as the court thinks just."

Cases referred to

Advocate (Lord) v The Scotsman Publications Ltd, 1988 SLT 490 (affd 1989 SLT 705).

Armour v Thyssen Edelstahlwerke AG, 1990 SLT 891.

Aro Co Ltd, Re [1980] Ch 196; [1980] 2 WLR 453; [1980] 1 All ER 1067.

Coclas v Bruce Peebles & Co Ltd (in liquidation) (1908) 16 SLT 7.

Grosvenor Metal Co Ltd, Re [1950] Ch 63.

Main v Azotine Ltd, 1916 2 SLT 252.

Reynolds & Warren v Metropolitan Police [1982] Crim LR 831.

Smith v Lord Advocate, 1979 SLT 233; 1978 SC 259.

Smith of Maddiston Ltd v Macnab, 1975 SLT 86; 1975 JC 48.

Widenmeyer v Burn Stewart & Co Ltd, 1967 SLT 129; 1976 SC 85.

Textbooks referred to

Benjamin, *Sale of Goods* (3rd ed), para 381.

Palmer's Company Law (25th ed), Vol 2, paras 15.443, 15.697 and 15.698.

On 12 June 1992 the Lord Ordinary *granted* the prayer of the note.

LORD CAPLAN.—This is a note presented by Canon (Scotland) Business Machines Ltd in the winding up proceedings concerning GA Business Systems Ltd (the company). The note is presented under s 130 (2) of the Insolvency Act 1986 for leave to raise proceedings against the company and it is opposed both by the company and by Mr Stuart Fraser, the liquidator.

The background facts giving rise to the note are as follows. The noters are suppliers of business equipment and on 11 January 1991 they supplied the company with a Canon Colour Laser Copier 200 machine. The machine was supplied on credit and in terms of a dealership agreement dated 5 February 1990 between the noters and the company. It is common ground that the company has not paid the noters for this machine. In terms of condition 5 of the standard terms and conditions of sale incorporated into the dealership agreement the title in the copier machine remains with the noters until they have received payment of the full purchase price of the machine together with any VAT and interest which is also payable. Moreover until such payment in full the noters may require the company to deliver the equipment to the noters on demand.

Although this note is concerned only with the said CLC 200 copier machine it would appear that the noters had also sold other equipment to the company which at the beginning of 1991 remained unpaid for. In any event on 22 January 1991 the noters, upon presenting a summons to the Court of Session, obtained interim interdict against the company interdicting the company or their agents or anyone acting on their behalf from selling or removing or in any way interfering with certain specified equipment including the said Canon copier. The said summons narrated that the company had refused to honour a demand that the equipment specified in the summons be redelivered to the noters and that the noters were apprehensive that the company would seek to sell the equipment in question.

On 24 January 1991 the court made an order for the winding up of the company and Mr Stuart Fraser was on the same date appointed liquidator.

It would appear that on about 14 January 1991 the company delivered the said Canon copier to a firm known as Sloppy Joe's, Falkirk. The noters claim that this delivery was made in pursuance of an agreement recorded in a letter dated 7 January 1991 from Mr John O'Donnell representing the company to Mr James Fraser (who apparently controls Sloppy Joe's). The letter was in the following terms:

"Further to our recent discussion regarding the problems you have encountered with your CLC Mark 1. In order to keep customer relations at the optimum, I can confirm that we will swap you Mark 1 CLC for a CLC 200.

"I trust this will meet with your approval and I look forward to hearing from you."

When the noters attempted to recover the CLC 200 machine from Sloppy Joe's on 13 February 1991 the firm refused to hand over the machine and by letter to the noters of the same date their solicitors, Messrs Peacock Johnson, indicated that Sloppy Joe's claimed to be the owners of the copier having acquired it from the company. In a further letter dated 21 February 1991 the said solicitors wrote to the noters' solicitors and said: "You will see because of business relations GA Business Systems decided to do a swap of one machine for another." The noters have all along contended that an exchange of their Canon CLC copier for a Mark 1 CLC machine was not an effective transfer of title to Sloppy Joe's (in particular because the transaction was not one for valuable consideration). It was contended that, whereas a CLC 200 machine at the time of the purported transfer had a value of £14,000, the Mark 1 machine was only worth about £2,500.

The present note was presented in November 1991. The noters aver that the liquidator of the company had sought and obtained from Sloppy Joe's valuable consideration for the said machine. In their answers the respondents aver that in January 1991 the CLC Mark 1 copier was traded in for an allowance of £9,000 against a new CLC 200 copier at a price of £12,500 excluding VAT. The respondents further aver that after extensive correspondence the debt owed by Sloppy Joe's to the company has been collected. The noters claim that the liquidator's action in transacting with Sloppy Joe's may have affected the legal title to the said Canon copier and that to their disadvantage. They say therefore that the company is in breach of interdict.

In addressing me counsel for the noters argued that in transacting with Sloppy Joe's the liquidator had essentially been acting as an agent for the company and that his actings must be regarded as a breach of interdict on the part of the company. I was referred to *Smith v Lord Advocate*. Furthermore I was referred to *Armour v Thyssen Edelstahlwerke AG*, an authority for the submission that the noters could properly preserve their ownership of the relevant machine until it was paid for. It would appear from the earlier correspondence that the original transaction between the company and Sloppy Joe's was not a sale transaction but a barter transaction. In terms of s 2 (1) of the Sale of Goods Act 1979 a sale requires a money consideration. The passing of the title under a barter transaction is regulated under common law. In this respect I was referred to *Widenmeyer v Burn Stewart & Co*. Moreover in terms of s 25 (1) of the Sale of Goods Act 1979 a buyer receiving goods belonging to another only receives an effective title if he receives the goods in good faith. Moreover s 2 (1) and s 5 of the Factors Act 1889 would apply and the sale or disposition of goods would only transfer title if there were a valuable consideration. It is doubtful whether Sloppy Joe's have acted in good faith if there was a barter arrangement in the terms described in the earlier correspondence. In any event they did not pay a valuable consideration. By negotiating with Sloppy Joe's for the payment of a monetary price the liquidator has interfered with the legal standing of the goods. Sloppy Joe's may now be in a position to claim that they have paid a valuable consideration for the goods. Moreover it would seem that in effect the liquidator had negotiated sale terms where none previously existed. The company have therefore been in breach of interdict and the noters should be allowed to bring the matter to the attention of the court.

Counsel for the respondents contended that the note should be refused. The interdict had been pronounced before the liquidator was appointed. The dealership agreement only gave the noters a limited right. There was, for example, no provision that the proceeds of any sale of the equipment by the company should be kept in a special fund. I was referred to Benjamin on *Sale of Goods* (3rd ed), para 381. Thus the liquidator had no duty to account to the noters for the proceeds of any sale. The interdict could not be made binding on the liquidator. Reference was made to *Lord Advocate v The Scotsman Publications Ltd* and to *Smith of Maddiston Ltd v Macnab*. In relation to the circumstances under which a court should allow proceedings to continue against a liquidator I was referred to Palmer on *Company Law*, Vol 2, paras 15.443, 15.697 and 15.698. The test was whether litigation was expedient having regard to the interests of the creditors generally. I was further referred to *Re Aro Co Ltd*. The judgment in that case approves of a dictum of Vaisey J in *Re Grosvenor Metal Co Ltd* where he said: "The section seems to give the court a free hand to do what is right and fair according to the circumstances of each case."

It was argued that leave should be refused where, as here, any question between the parties could be resolved within the context of the liquidation. Before leave to litigate should be granted there ought to be special cause as defined in *Coclas v Bruce Peebles* and *Main v Azotine Ltd*. The noters could resort to the court under s 212 (2) and (3) of the Insolvency Act if they considered that the liquidator had acted improperly in any way. Moreover, because of delay in pursuing the note the noters were personally barred from complaining of any breach of interdict. The noters had all along been well aware of what the liquidator had been attempting to do in relation to the transaction with Sloppy Joe's. In any event the liquidator's actings could not be described as "interference" with the copier machine. Reference was made to *Reynolds & Warren v Metropolitan Police*.

I was not referred to any recent Scottish authority having a bearing on the circumstances under which the court would entertain an application made by virtue of s 130 (2) of the Insolvency Act. The cases of *Coclas* and *Main Ltd* are not particularly helpful in relation to the question I have to decide. The reason why litigation against a company in the course of winding up is controlled is clearly to prevent a spate of actions against the company by competing creditors. The winding up process is designed to provide a fair procedure for settlement of the claims of creditors and contributories. In that situation litigation against the company would generally be somewhat otiose and in any event contrary to the interests of the body of creditors regarded as a whole. Thus I have no difficulty in agreeing with Lord Guthrie in *Coclas* that a party applying for leave to litigate against a company must show special cause — that is as I understand it an exceptional factor justifying the request to litigate. However, in *Coclas* the court was dealing with an action to constitute a debt against the company. In *Main* the applicant was refused leave to litigate to secure for himself an allotment of shares. However, although the Lord Ordinary gave no opinion he seemingly accepted the argument that settlement of the list of contributories was properly a matter to be determined in the first instance by the liquidator. It was suggested to me that the test was whether litigation was expedient having regard to the interests of the creditors generally. Whatever merit there may be in regarding that as a general test it is plainly not exhaustive. For example, in a breach of interdict situation the court has an interest not to allow the authority of its decrees to be ignored and that is an interest which should override the concern of the general body of creditors. In fact in the present case it would clearly be to the advantage of the creditors if they were allowed to enjoy undisturbed the realisation proceeds of a machine belonging to the noters, but that factor cannot be conclusive. I think myself that there is much to be said for following the flexible test set out by Vaisey J in *Re Grosvenor Metal Co Ltd* and approved by the Court of Appeal in *Re Aro Co Ltd*. That is to say the court should seek to do what is right and fair according to the circumstances of each case.

When a party enjoys the protection of an interdict pronounced by this court it is a serious matter if it can be demonstrated that the interdict has been breached. The party who has suffered from the breach is entitled to have an opportunity to complain to the court which pronounced the interdict. I do not see the winding up process as being an appropriate place to have such a complaint determined. That must particularly be so where the liquidator himself is said to have been instrumental in causing the breach. Nor do I think, as was suggested to me by the respondents, that an application to the court under s 212 (2) and (3) would be the appropriate way to raise a question of breach of interdict. In the first place it is difficult to see how even at the practical level an attempt to invoke s 212 would be a simpler or less expensive procedure than a minute in the interdict process. In any event even if a breach of interdict were established in a s 212 application the court would have less pertinent powers to take appropriate action than a judge dealing with a breach of interdict. Section 212 (3) gives the court power to restore the position of the company following upon a breach of duty by the liquidator, but that power would be of no avail to the noters. In any event if the liquidator is at all concerned in any breach of interdict committed by the company it is not in his particular capacity as liquidator but rather as a person responsible for the acts of the company itself.

Thus in general I would favour granting leave to a party seeking to pursue breach of interdict proceedings against a company which is in the course of winding up. But of course I am entitled to be satisfied that the noters have a prima facie case to make. It is clear in my view that some of the questions which breach of interdict proceedings could raise are not without difficulty, but my only concern is that there should be legitimate issues to try. The present application is not the place to decide all the questions which were presented to me. There may or may not be questions as to the effect of winding up on the interdict and the liquidator's responsibility to observe it. It was not disputed that its terms had been brought to the liquidator's notice before the acts complained of took place. If there is a question about his duties it is eminently one to be decided in the interdict process. In respect of the liquidator's actings there is certainly room for a contention that the original transaction between the company and Sloppy Joe's was a straightforward "swap". Indeed both the company and Sloppy Joe's solicitors described the transaction thus in the earlier correspondence. The respondents now claim that the original transaction was not simple barter but a sale in terms of which Sloppy Joe's were due to pay a balance of an agreed price. However, counsel for the respondents was unable to refer me to any voucher authenticating that the transaction was originally a sale in the terms now claimed. Indeed he supposed that details of the terms of the purported sale had come solely from the directors of the company. There must therefore be some question mark as to the circumstances under which Sloppy Joe's originally obtained possession of the copier. If the machine was originally acquired either by barter or by sale for less than a valuable consideration, I am not clear as to how any subsequent intervention on the part of the company through the liquidator will have affected the noters' rights. However, if there has been a breach of interdict they are entitled to complain to the court even if it were the case that the breach has not been effective in disturbing their rights. There is a question as to whether the interdict only prohibits physical interference with the goods or whether in context it must be taken to include the wider concept of intermeddling with them. In any event although not presently part of the noters' proposals for presenting the breach of interdict, a question could arise as to whether or not the company has since the interdict converted what was originally a barter contract into a sale contract. As I have said, questions such as these should appropriately be raised and determined in the interdict proceedings but they certainly seem to me to be serious issues.

In response to the case of personal bar the noters' counsel explained to me why it has taken from November 1991 until May 1992 to have his note brought before a judge for decision. He claimed that it was only in the autumn of 1991 that the noters first became aware that the liquidator had collected part of a purported price from Sloppy Joe's. Certainly on the face of it it seems most unfortunate that an application such as this should take seven months from first coming to court before it is presented to a judge for decision. However, a part of the delay may have been outwith the control of the parties themselves. In any event any question of personal bar should again be dealt with in the interdict proceedings.

In the whole circumstances I shall grant the note and give the noters leave to raise the breach of interdict proceedings which they propose.

Counsel for Noters, MacIver; Solicitors, Bird Semple Fyfe Ireland, WS — Counsel for Respondents (Company and Liquidator), Mackinnon; Solicitors, Dorman Jeffrey & Co.

R D S

Ahmed's Trustee v Ahmed (No 1)

OUTER HOUSE

LORD PENROSE

24 JUNE 1992

Expenses — Taxation — Counsel's fees — Defender's agents withdrawing — Proof set down for Tuesday discharged on previous Friday — First day's fee (including proof preparation) disallowed — Note of objections — Approach of auditor — Test to be applied — Rules of Court 1965, rule 347 (a).

Rule of Court 347 (a) provides: "Only such expenses shall be allowed as are reasonable for conducting the case in a proper manner."

In an action against five defenders, only the second and third defenders lodged defences, and shared solicitors and counsel. The action was due to go to proof on 5 November 1991. On 11 October 1991 the defenders' solicitors advised the pursuer's agents that they no longer acted for the second defender. The pursuer's agents continued to prepare for the proof, a consultation being held on 24 October. At an undisclosed date prior to 1 pm on 1 November 1991, counsel for the pursuer was instructed for the proof. On 30 October new solicitors for the second defenders intimated the enrolment of a motion for discharge of the proof. On

Friday 1 November the proof diet was discharged, and the defenders were found liable jointly and severally for the pursuer's expenses as taxed.

In the account of expenses, counsel's fee in respect of the instructions for the first day of the proof included preparation for the proof. The auditor taxed off the whole of the fee for the first day of the proof. He took the view that it was not reasonable in the circumstances for the pursuer to instruct counsel prior to 1 pm on the Friday prior to a proof due to commence the following Tuesday. Authorities on the subject indicated conventional periods which the auditor hesitated to increase.

In a note of objections for the pursuer to the report of the auditor, the case was said to be complex, requiring counsel to be instructed well before the proof. Considerable preparation had been necessary before the proof was discharged. The element of the fee claimed for the first day of the proof was for the preparation. The auditor had erred in that he had failed to consider what might be proper remuneration of counsel in the circumstances in preparing for the proof, and the rule adopted on timing of instructions lacked any legal basis, being merely conventional. The defenders argued that after 11 October it ought to have been known that the proof diet was likely to be lost, and that by 30 October it was clear that the diet would be discharged.

Held, (1) that in its current form the only relevant test under rule 347 (a) was that of reasonableness in the context of the conduct of the case in a proper manner (p 393H-I); (2) that in general the application of any test predicated on a fixed interval before a hearing was incompatible with a rule stipulating a single criterion of reasonableness related to the proper conduct of a case (p 393K-L); (3) that the auditor had misdirected himself (a) in considering significant the withdrawal of the second defender's representation when judging the reasonableness of the continuation by the pursuer's solicitors of preparations for the proof, and (b) in expecting the pre-proof consultation to complete relevant proof preparation, which in any event should be remunerated, and consequently in failing to consider whether counsel was entitled to remuneration for preparation work which was properly instructed (pp 393L-394A, 394E-H and 395C); and case *remitted* to auditor for reconsideration.

Wood v Miller, 1960 SC 86 and *Kenny v Lord Advocate*, 1992 SLT 372, *distinguished*.

Observed, that postponement of instructions to counsel to attend at a hearing to a point as close to it as envisaged by the auditor must have as one consequence the postponement of decision on the conduct of the case to a stage at which disruption of the business of the court would appear inevitable (p 395B).

Action of reduction

Colin Anthony Hastings Fisher, trustee in sequestration of Maqsood Ahmed, brought an action against Maqsood Ahmed and four other defenders, seeking inter alia reduction of an assignation of a lease by the third to the second defender and seeking an assignation instead in favour of the first defender. The second and third defenders lodged defences. Proof was set down for 5 November 1991 and subsequent days. On 11 October 1991 the solicitors previously acting for the second and third defenders intimated to the pursuer's solicitors that they no longer acted for the second defender. The second defender consulted new solicitors who on 30 October intimated their intention to seek discharge of the diet of proof. Discharge was granted on 1 November with the defenders being found liable jointly and severally for the expenses incurred by the pursuer. Following taxation of the pursuer's account of expenses, the pursuer presented an application by note of objections to the report of the auditor of court, who had taxed off the whole of the fee payable to counsel in respect of the first day of the proof.

The note was heard before the Lord Ordinary (Penrose).

Statutory provisions

Rule of Court 347 (a) provides:

"Only such expenses shall be allowed as are reasonable for conducting the case in a proper manner."

Cases referred to

Davidson v Scott, 1915 2 SLT 113.
Kenny v Lord Advocate, 1993 SLT 372.
Morton v O'Donnell, 1979 SLT (Notes) 26.
Wood v Miller, 1960 SLT (Notes) 7; 1960 SC 86.

On 24 June 1992 the Lord Ordinary *remitted* the matter to the auditor for reconsideration.

LORD PENROSE.—This is an application by note of objections to a report by the auditor of court on the taxation of the account of expenses incurred by the pursuer for which the second and third defenders were found liable, jointly and severally, by interlocutor dated 19 November 1991. That finding followed the discharge of a diet of proof set down for 5 November 1991 and the three subsequent days, on the motion of the second defender. The summons in the action was signeted on 19 December 1989. Initially the action was sisted to enable the first, fourth and fifth defenders to apply for legal aid. None of these defenders has lodged defences. The sist was recalled on 3 July 1990. The third defender sought to have the cause sisted of new on 10 July 1990. That motion was refused. The second defender was allowed to lodge defences late on 21 August 1990, and a similar motion by the third defender was allowed on 28 August of that year. The record was closed on 5 December 1990 and proof was thereafter allowed.

Throughout the preparation and adjustment of the pleadings the second and third defenders had common solicitors and counsel. Early in October 1991 a view

A was formed that there was a conflict of interest between the compearing defenders. The solicitors previously acting for those defenders wrote to the pursuer's agents on 11 October to inform them that they no longer acted for the second defender. The pursuer's representatives continued with their preparation for the proof on the view that it was a peremptory diet. A consultation was held on 24 October as part of those preparations. Counsel was instructed for the proof. The date of instruction was not disclosed, but it was prior to 1 pm on Friday, 1 November 1991.

B The second defender consulted new solicitors and, on 30 October, they intimated to the other parties their intention to enrol a motion for discharge of the diet of proof. In the ordinary course that motion would have come before the court on Tuesday, 5 November, the first day of the proof. Of consent of the pursuer the motion was brought before the court on Friday, 1 November. After hearing counsel the Lord Ordinary discharged the diet.

C In preparing the party and party account of expenses, the pursuer's liability to counsel in respect of the instructions for the first day of the proof was included. Apart from an allowance for the accelerated motion roll hearing, for which counsel made no separate charge, the auditor taxed off the whole of the fee payable. It is against this decision that the present objection is taken.

In his minute the auditor narrated his determination in the following terms: "After consideration of the D information given to him, the auditor was of opinion that it was not reasonable in the circumstances for the pursuer to instruct counsel prior to 1 pm on the Friday prior to a proof due to commence on the following Tuesday."

The minute contains much of the factual narrative already contained in this opinion. The reasons for the auditor's views appear from the following paragraphs:

"(2) The auditor was informed that the second E defender's now former solicitors expected the pursuer's solicitors to enrol a motion requesting the court to ordain the second defender to intimate to the court, if he still insisted in his defence to the action, the identity of his new solicitors, if any. However, that procedure was not adopted by the pursuer's solicitors who regarded the proof diet as being peremptory and therefore the responsibility of the second defender to arrange for appropriate representation at it. . . .

"(5) The auditor would expect that prior to and at F the pre-proof consultation counsel would have reviewed all the evidence to be led at proof in support of the pursuer's case and to discuss it with the pursuer and his solicitors. The possibility of the diet of proof being discharged could not reasonably have been ignored, more especially as the second defender through no fault of his own was without the services of the solicitors who had acted for him throughout the case until less than one month beforehand."

The auditor proceeds to state: "The auditor appreciates that the court is unable to lay down guidelines as to how far in advance it may be reasonable to instruct counsel for a proof or procedure roll hearing as cir- G cumstances vary in each case. Such comments bearing on the matter, as are known to the auditor, are contained in cases of some years' standing and, although it may be considered that they are no longer in tune with the times, the auditor is however hesitant to increase unilaterally what are probably regarded as conventional periods." He then proceeds to refer to a number of authorities from which he drew the inference that it was not reasonable for counsel in the present case to be instructed prior to 1 pm on the Friday prior to the proof. H

In the note of objections certain matters of history were set out by the pursuer, and, in addition, it was stated that the case was a complex case involving 15 witnesses who had been cited to give evidence in addition to the pursuer. It had been necessary to instruct counsel well in advance of the proof and counsel had required to carry out considerable preparation by the time the proof was discharged. There was a further reference to passing the papers to I other counsel, but this was not insisted in as a point before me.

In presenting the argument for the pursuer, the Dean of Faculty emphasised that his concern related only to the element within the first day's fee which was attributable to counsel's preparation for the proof. No criticism was made of the decision so far as it related to remuneration for counsel's appearance on the first day of the proof. The Dean invited me to apply the test set out in comments of Lord Justice J Clerk Thomson in *Wood v Miller*, 1960 SC at p 98 as a correct statement of the approach to be taken in considering objections to a report by the auditor. There the Lord Justice Clerk said: "It is not the function of a judge reviewing an exercise of a discretion to substitute his own view of the material under consideration. The decision of the Auditor stands in a not dissimilar position to the verdict of a jury. If the Auditor had no material to go on, his exercise will fall, but if he had material, then, so long as the decision he reached on K it was not unreasonable, it cannot readily be upset. There is, however, this difference between a Judge exercising a discretion and a jury that a Judge is usually expected to give and does give reasons. If, on a scrutiny of these reasons, it clearly appears that he has misstated or mistaken or misunderstood the material put before him there may well be grounds for interfering. But if as appears to be the case here, the Lord Ordinary's criticism on analysis comes only to a disapproval of the relative weight attached by the Auditor to the various elements involved, the Lord L Ordinary is simply substituting his own view of the relevant factors."

In addition to the background circumstances particular to the present case, the Dean reminded me that preparation was now commonly remunerated separately from appearance in court, and that the legal aid scheme as presently administered provided for payment of such fees. This was a material factor not only as between counsel and agent for the party giving instructions, but as between parties in considering what was reasonable to expect a party to pay when found liable in expenses of a late discharge of a proof. In every case it would be a question of circumstances what would be a reasonable charge. However the approach of the auditor in the present case was objectionable on three grounds: (1) he had failed to consider at all what might be proper remuneration for counsel for preparation for the proof in the circumstances of the case, preparation being included in this case in the instruction fee for the first day of the proof; (2) he had applied his mind to authorities which related to liability for expenses where that was affected by a judicial tender, and that was a different situation; and (3) he had followed a conventional rule relating to the timing of instructions which had no legal basis at all. Had the auditor applied his mind to the question of the level of remuneration for preparation properly chargeable against the party whose late motion had rendered that preparation nugatory, his decision must have been otherwise.

For the defenders, counsel contended that as between party and party preparation should not be provided for, as a civil fine as it were, since the taxation of accounts as between party and party properly took account of the test of due economy. The withdrawal of the solicitors for the second defender should have sounded a klaxon horn of warning on 11 October, when the second defender was left without representation, that the diet was likely to be lost. By 30 October it should have been obvious that the diet would be discharged. The auditor had looked at the proceedings and concluded that it would not have been proper to consider preparation for the proof beyond what would in any event have been carried out prior to and at the pre-proof consultation. Following on the abandonment of the second defender, very little inquiry had been made. The auditor's decision could not be faulted. The only rule was that of reasonableness as between parties.

In its present form rule 347 (a) provides that: "Only such expenses shall be allowed as are reasonable for conducting the case in a proper manner." That formulation represents a material change from earlier provisions regulating the basis of taxation as between party and party. In Maclaren on *Expenses* the then current provisions were contained in the General Regulations as to the Preparation and Taxation of Accounts for Judicial Proceedings of 1876. Regulation 4 was in the following terms: "In order that the expense of litigation may be kept within proper and reasonable limits, only such expenses shall be allowed, in taxing accounts between party and party, as are absolutely necessary for conducting it in a proper manner, with due regard to economy; ex gratia the party shall think proper to employ an unnecessary number of counsel, or to pay higher fees than are warranted by ordinary practice, the extra expense occasioned thereby shall not be allowed against the opposite party." In the consolidating Acts of Sederunt of 1948 and 1965 the test of necessity remained, albeit in a modified form. In each case the provision was: "Only such expenses shall be allowed against the opposite party as are

necessary for conducting the case in a proper manner with due regard to economy".

Rule 347 was substantially amended by the Act of Sederunt (Rules of Court Amendment No 1) of 1966 (SI 1966/335). No criterion was specified. The present formulation was introduced with effect from 1 November 1974 by Act of Sederunt (Rules of Court Amendment No 6) 1974 (SI 1974/1686) and applies without discrimination as between party and party and agent and client. The repeal of s 5 (g) of the Court of Session Act 1988, by the Law Reform (Miscellaneous Provisions) (Scotland) Act 1990, Sched 9, which will affect the rule, has not yet been brought into effect.

The development of the rules from 1966 onwards appears deliberately to have departed from the tests of necessity, whether absolute or otherwise, and excludes specific reference to economy. These changes were clearly significant. They support the approach adopted by both counsel in this case that the only relevant test presently applicable is the test of reasonableness in the context of the conduct of the case in a proper manner. The change is important in considering the relevance in current practice of any authority relating to circumstances obtaining prior to 1 November 1974. In addition to the authorities mentioned by the auditor, counsel referred to *Davidson v Scott*. The circumstances in that case were far removed from the present, and given the terms of the Act of Sederunt then regulating the taxation of accounts, I have found the case of no assistance for present purposes. The authorities referred to by the auditor all relate to situations in which taxation took place against the background of a judicial tender. In *Morton v O'Donnell* the Lord Ordinary, Lord Ross, referred at p 27 to the special considerations which apply in the taxation of accounts in such a context. Whether the circumstance that taxation was affected by a tender is sufficient to distinguish a case such as the present I consider it unnecessary to say. It is clear from *Wood v Miller* and from *Kenny v Lord Advocate* that what was involved in each case was the instruction for appearance at the hearing, without the separate question of instructions for preparation and the carrying out of preparation having been separately considered. It is that factor which appears to me to require particular consideration in the present case and I have found no assistance in the authorities in resolving the problem that it raises. In general, however, it would appear to be incompatible with a rule stipulating a single criterion of reasonableness related to the proper conduct of a case to apply any test defined by reference to a fixed period prior to a hearing.

Within the limits of his jurisdiction, the auditor is the proper officer to determine the question whether expenditure is reasonably incurred for the proper conduct of litigation. In this case, however, there are substantial reasons to question his decision. In the first place, in my opinion, the auditor has misdirected himself in attaching significance to the intimation of withdrawal of representation from the second defender in forming his judgment on the reasonableness of the actions of the pursuer's solicitors in continuing with preparations for the proof. While his reasoning is far from clear, he did pass a fee for counsel for the pre-proof consultation held on 24 October but was otherwise critical of the continuing preparations, and it must be assumed that he has identified this factor because it was material in his approach to the contentious issue raised in the present objections. There are two problems associated with this point. It is unclear what timetable the auditor had in mind. The intimation of withdrawal was made by letter written on 11 October, a Friday. The earliest day on which a motion might have been enrolled to bring the matter to the attention of the court would have been Monday, 14 October, ignoring any question of obtaining the pursuer's instructions or of intimation to the third defender's solicitors. If the motion were heard before the end of the then current week, and granted, the usual induciae would have been 14 days for intimation by the second defender whether the defence was to be insisted in. It is almost inconceivable that all necessary steps would have been completed before the time for instructing counsel for the proof in accordance with the rule which the auditor had purported to apply in taxing the account. Secondly, it would have been irresponsible for those advising the pursuer to have suspended their preparations until the matter had been disposed of. It would not have been appropriate for them to anticipate the court's disposal of a discretionary issue to the possible prejudice of the pursuer's interests in the litigation. The auditor has not expressed a view as to the point at which the pursuer's solicitors should have acted on the view that they could not reasonably ignore the possibility of discharge of the diet of proof and suspended preparation. If the auditor were correct in his determination, then prima facie at 11 October, there was ample time for the second defender to obtain and instruct fresh representation. It is difficult to identify any stage at which the responsibility of the pursuer's solicitors to concern themselves with the risk of discharge of the proof would have emerged. The auditor's implied criticism of the pursuer's solicitors for acknowledging their responsibility to the pursuer and to the court in continuing with preparation for the proof is without foundation in any fact set out in his minute.

In the second place I consider that the auditor has misdirected himself in his approach to the general question of counsel's remuneration for preparation. The auditor has stated that he would expect that prior to and at the pre-proof consultation counsel would have reviewed all the evidence to be led at the proof in support of the pursuer's case and discussed it with the pursuer and his solicitors. The basis of that assumption is not set out in the minute. Even if it were correct, it would relate to one aspect only of the question whether the whole of counsel's fee for the first day of the proof should have been taxed off. In this case counsel included the charge for preparation for the proof in the fee for the first day. It is not suggested that that preparation was remunerated by any other item in the account. If the auditor were correct that the whole relevant preparation for the proof had been completed, in accordance with his expectations, and therefore one must assume properly in his view, prior to and at the pre-proof consultation, the corollary would appear to be that counsel should have been remunerated at that stage for the work. Even if counsel has chosen to postpone the demand for payment he cannot be assumed to have elected to forego the payment to which he was entitled unless properly instructed for the first day's attendance at the proof. Put another way, it would appear to follow from the auditor's assumption that the proper time for solicitors to instruct counsel for preparation for the proof is prior to the pre-proof consultation, so that that consultation may satisfy the requirements of full discussion of all aspects of the pursuer's case. If that is correct, there can be no reason why counsel should fail to recover proper remuneration for work so instructed and carried out. If the charge has been included in a fee for the first day of preparation, some part of that fee would appear to be due, whatever the position between parties in respect of the appearance fee. It must be said, however, that the auditor's experience, which no doubt explains his assumption, appears to have been singular in this matter. The reality in many cases is that preparation is a continuing process, requiring reappraisal of a changing body of information as proof approaches. Late lodging of documentary and other productions is not uncommon. Indeed it is a frequent cause of dispute before the court. Response to documents allowed late is necessary, and decisions taken without sight of them must be reviewed. Experience would suggest that other forms of information also change and require review of evidence to be led and strategies and tactics to be adopted at proof or trial. Such work, properly instructed and carried out, will usually be of a kind which is reasonable for the proper conduct of the case, in the absence of contrary indications in the particular case, and will, equally properly, qualify for appropriate remuneration whatever rule applies in taxing accounts of expenses relating to the first day of proof. It could hardly be appropriate for instructions for preparation for a proof due to commence on a Tuesday to be postponed until 1 pm on the previous Friday. In my opinion the Dean of Faculty was well founded in challenging the basis on which the auditor approached this matter, so far as it concerned the determination of a proper level of remuneration for counsel for preparation. In the light of the disposal of this matter, it is clearly unfortunate that counsel did not charge separately for the preparation work which was carried out. Had he done so the auditor's mind might have focused more directly upon the proper level of remuneration for that work. But in the whole circumstances it appears to me to be clear that the auditor's reasons confused the two elements of the question, namely, whether the work was done, and whether the work was remunerated otherwise than by the first day's fee; and, further, that he has given inappropriate consideration to the implications of withdrawal of the second defender's solicitors.

The final section of the auditor's minute is concerned with the question of general rules or guidelines. It is clearly correct, as he observed, that the court cannot lay down guidelines as to how far in advance it may be reasonable to instruct counsel for an appearance before the court, or for preparation. That must depend upon the circumstances of the particular case and a general rule amplifying the Rule of Court is much more likely to be misleading than helpful. Solicitors and counsel have responsibilities to clients and to the court and to all those whose interests are affected by litigation. The postponement of instructions to counsel to attend at a hearing to a point as close to it as envisaged by the auditor must have as one consequence the postponement of decision on the conduct of the case to a stage at which disruption of the business of the court would appear to be inevitable. There is at least a question whether, in present circumstances, late instruction should be encouraged in the wider public interest. Similarly the postponement of instruction to a point at which no effective decision can be taken on the response to late lodged documents and to the lodging of documents is unlikely to be in the interests of the client and a similar factor may arise in connection with the citation of witnesses. However, the resolution of such matters of general interest would appear to be irrelevant to the issue properly raised on the argument before me. On the limited question argued, I consider that the auditor did misdirect himself in failing to consider the question of counsel's entitlement to remuneration for work of preparation properly instructed. I shall remit the matter to him for reconsideration in the light of these observations. It will be for him to decide whether in the whole circumstances an additional sum should be allowed, and, if so, what that sum should be.

Counsel for Pursuer, Dean of Faculty (Johnston, QC); Solicitors, Brodies, WS — Counsel for Defenders, G M Henderson; Solicitors, Drummond Miller, WS (Second Defender); Macbeth, Currie & Co, WS (Third Defender).

D B

HM Advocate v Birkett

HIGH COURT OF JUSTICIARY

THE LORD JUSTICE CLERK (ROSS)

17 JULY 1992

Justiciary — Procedure — Competency — Petition for order authorising giving of evidence by live television link — Court not satisfied prior to trial that cause shown for making order — Whether competent to refuse motion in hoc statu for consideration by trial judge — Law Reform (Miscellaneous Provisions) (Scotland) Act 1990 (c 40), s 56 — Act of Adjournal (Consolidation Amendment No 2) (Evidence of Children) 1991 (SI 1991/1916), rule 61A.

Section 56 of the Law Reform (Miscellaneous Provisions) (Scotland) Act 1990 provides that on cause shown the court may make an order authorising the giving of evidence by means of a live television link. Rule 61A of the Act of Adjournal (Consolidation Amendment No 2) (Evidence of Children) 1991 provides that an application for this purpose must be made not later than 14 clear days before the trial diet except on cause shown.

An accused person was charged with attempted murder of a three year old boy, assault to injury and permanent disfigurement and malicious damage. Among the Crown witnesses were the six year old sister and eight year old brother of the complainer on the attempted murder charge and two other children aged four and six years. The Crown petitioned the court for an order in terms of s 56 of the 1990 Act authorising the giving of the children's evidence by means of a live television link. In the course of the hearing, because the court was not satisfied that cause had been shown at that stage for granting the application, a question arose as to the competency of continuing the application for consideration by the trial judge.

Held, that if the trial was taking place in a building where the facilities existed, there was no reason why the trial judge should not be able to order that the evidence of a child should be taken by a live television link (p 397G-I); and application *refused* in hoc statu.

Petition for an order under s 56 of the Law Reform (Miscellaneous Provisions) (Scotland) Act 1990

Gary Alistair Birkett was charged at the instance of the rt hon the Lord Rodger of Earlsferry, Her Majesty's Advocate, on an indictment which libelled the following charges: "(1) on various occasions between 24 December 1991 and 3 April 1992, both dates inclusive, the precise dates being to the prosecutor unknown, at [address], you did assault A G B, date of birth 27 January 1989, son of and residing with A S P there and did seize hold of his face, repeatedly slap him on the face and head, punch and kick him repeatedly on the head and body, throw him down a flight of stairs, throw him on a chair, throw a knife at him, push him onto a fire, force his head under water and attempt to drown him all to his injury and you did attempt to murder him; (2) on various occasions between 24 December 1991 and 3 April 1992, both dates inclusive, the precise dates being to the prosecutor unknown, at [address], you did assault said A S P of said address, threaten her with violence, seize her by the throat, punch and kick her repeatedly on the head and body, repeatedly butt her on the face, throw a chair at her, cause a piece of plate to strike her on the face, push her down a flight of stairs, present and brandish a knife at her, throw a knife at her, strike her on the head and stab her on the hand with a knife all to her injury and permanent disfigurement; and (3) on various occasions between 24 December 1991 and 3 April 1992, both dates inclusive, the precise dates being to the prosecutor unknown, at [address], you did

maliciously damage a stereo unit and break a
window."

The Crown presented an application to the High
Court for an order in terms of s 56 of the Law Reform
(Miscellaneous Provisions) (Scotland) Act 1990 authorising the giving of the evidence of five children aged
between three years and eight years by means of a live
television link. The application was not opposed in
respect of the three year old complainer on the charge
of attempted murder. The facts of the case appear
from the opinion of the Lord Justice Clerk (Ross).

Statutory provisions

The Law Reform (Miscellaneous Provisions) (Scotland) Act 1990 provides:

"56.—(1) Subject to subsections (2) and (3) below,
where a child has been cited to give evidence in a trial,
the court may, on an application being made to it,
authorise the giving of evidence by the child by means
of a live television link.

"(2) The court may grant an application under subsection (1) above only on cause shown having regard
in particular to — (a) the possible effect on the child
if required to give evidence, no such application
having been granted; and (b) whether it is likely that
the child would be better able to give evidence if such
application were granted.

"(3) In considering whether to grant an application
under subsection (1) above, the court may take into
account, where appropriate, any of the following — (a)
the age and maturity of the child; (b) the nature of the
alleged offence; (c) the nature of the evidence which
the child is likely to be called on to give; and (d) the
relationship, if any, between the child and the
accused."

The Act of Adjournal (Consolidation Amendment
No 2) (Evidence of Children) 1991 provides inter alia:

"61A.—(1) An application to the court under section
56 (1) of the Law Reform (Miscellaneous Provisions)
(Scotland) Act 1990 for authorisation of the giving of
evidence by a child by means of a live television link
shall be made by petition in Form 28D (1) or Form
28D (2) of Schedule 1.

"(2) An application referred to in paragraph (1) shall
— (a) where it relates to proceedings in the High
Court, be lodged with the Clerk of Justiciary; and (b)
where it relates to proceedings in the sheriff court, be
lodged with the sheriff clerk, not later than 14 clear
days before the trial diet (except on special cause
shown).

"(3) The court shall, on the application being placed
before it — (a) order intimation of the application to
be made to the other party or parties to the proceedings; and (b) fix a diet for hearing the application on
the earliest practicable date.

"(4) After hearing the parties and allowing such
further procedure as the court thinks fit — (a) the
court may make an order granting or refusing the
application."

The application was heard in the High Court on 10
July 1992.

On 17 July 1992 the court (of consent of the
accused) *authorised* the giving of evidence by one
Crown witness by means of a live television link but
refused the application in hoc statu in respect of four
other child witnesses.

THE LORD JUSTICE CLERK (ROSS).—This
is a petition at the instance of the Lord Advocate
seeking an order under s 56 of the Law Reform (Miscellaneous Provisions) (Scotland) Act 1990 authorising
the giving of evidence by five children by means of a
live television link. The children are A G B, L J B,
C J B, W S G and A D G.

A G B is the complainer in charge 1, and I was
informed that he is aged three. He has been precognosced by the procurator fiscal himself and I was
informed that he is frightened of the accused, and that
the view of the procurator fiscal is that he would be
better able to give evidence outwith the presence of
the accused. Counsel for the accused did not oppose
the application in respect of A G B, and accordingly
I agreed to grant the application so far as he was concerned.

As regards the children L J B (aged six) and C J B
(aged eight), who are the sister and brother respectively of A G B, it was said that they are both quiet
and hesitant witnesses and that they will be required
to give evidence of a traumatic nature. It was said that
L J B might be inhibited in the presence of the
accused. It was also said that A S P who is the complainer in charge 2 might be ready to protect the
accused. As regards C J B, I was informed that he felt
loyalty both to his mother A S P and the accused with
whom he had had a close relationship. It was felt that
there was divided loyalty in his case. It was suggested
that they would be better able to give evidence outwith
the accused's presence.

As regards W S G (aged four) and A D G (aged six)
it was said that they were to give evidence regarding
charge 1 and in particular evidence regarding the use
of a knife. It was said that the evidence they could give
was of a frightening nature, and again that they would
be better able to give evidence outwith the accused's
presence.

In terms of s 56 (2) of the Act of 1990, cause has to
be shown before the court may grant an application
such as this. In determining whether cause had been
shown regard must be had in particular to the possible
effect on the child if required to give evidence, no such
application having been granted, and whether it is
likely that the child would be better able to give
evidence if the application were granted.

Section 56 (3) specifies the criteria to be taken into
account when considering whether to grant an application such as this. Counsel for the accused maintained
that the application should be refused in relation to
the four children other than A G B. She stressed that
it was not suggested in their case that they were frightened, and she emphasised that age was not in itself a
sufficient ground for granting the application. She
stated that L J B and C J B had had a close relationship with the accused, and that C J B had had a par-

ticularly good relationship with him. They only spoke
A to part of the matters libelled. As regards the other two
children, they were not related to the accused or the
complainers and they had not lived in the same household as them. She recognised that the children would
be speaking to a somewhat frightening event, but she
emphasised that that would be so whether they gave
evidence in open court or by means of a live television
link. This was not a case involving sexual abuse.

On the information placed before me I was not satisfied that cause had been shown at this stage for the
B granting of the application. On the other hand I was
conscious that difficulties might be encountered when
the evidence of the children was sought to be taken in
open court, and I was anxious that at that stage, the
trial judge, if he thought fit, could order that the
evidence of these children should be taken by means
of a television link. A question then arose in my mind
as to whether it would be competent to continue the
matter for consideration by the trial judge.

C   The Act of Adjournal (Consolidation Amendment
No 2) (Evidence of Children) 1991 sets out the form
of applications under s 56 of the Act of 1990, and
prescribes the procedure to be followed. Rule 61A
provides for an application for this purpose being
made by petition not later than 14 clear days before
the trial diet (except on special cause shown). In my
opinion, the purpose of providing that applications
should be made 14 days before the trial diet is to
ensure that the trial takes place within a building
D where facilities exist for taking evidence by means of
a live television link. If an application is granted then
arrangements will be made for the trial to take place
in such a building. On the other hand if an application
is refused, there will be no need for any such arrangements to be made. The advocate depute agreed that it
would not be incompetent to continue an application
of this kind for consideration by the trial judge, but he
stressed that it would be undesirable to do so. He
explained that where child witnesses are concerned,
E steps have to be taken before a trial to put them at
their ease. They are given guidance by procurators
fiscal, and other agencies may also be involved in this
respect. They are visited before the trial and it is
explained to them what is going to happen. In order
to reduce any uncertainties that the children may have
it will be explained to them where they will have to
stand when giving their evidence, and they may be
taken and shown a court room for that purpose. He
accordingly submitted that if the application were to
F be continued and it was uncertain whether a particular
child's evidence was to be given in open court or by
means of a live television link, the result would be
most unsatisfactory.

I fully appreciate the force of these observations
which the advocate depute made. On the other hand
I was concerned that if I refused the application out
of hand, and it subsequently transpired that any of the
witnesses was having difficulty in giving evidence in
court, it might be desirable if the trial judge could
arrange to have the evidence of the child taken by

means of a live television link. Since the application
was being granted in relation to the complainer in G
charge 1, the trial would be taking place within a
building where that facility existed. I appreciate that
the Act of Adjournal does not envisage successive
applications being made in relation to the evidence of
particular children, nor does it envisage the application being dealt with by a trial judge at the trial.
Nonetheless, if a trial is taking place in a building
where facilities for taking evidence by a live television
link exist, I see no reason why the trial judge should
not be able to order that the evidence of a child should H
be taken in that way. I recognise however that if in
relation to that child an application had previously
been refused, the trial judge might be reluctant to
order the child's evidence to be taken by means of a
live television link in the event of that facility being
available.

Since I was not satisfied in relation to the four
children to whom I have referred that cause had been
shown at this stage for the granting of the application,
I was not prepared to grant the application. I have I
however refused to grant the application in hoc statu
in order to emphasise that if circumstances have
changed by the time of the trial, and if it appears
appropriate to the trial judge to order that the evidence of all or any of these children should be taken by
means of a live television link, he will be able to do so
by making an order in terms of the petition which is
presently before me.

For the sake of completeness, it should be noted that
the advocate depute contended that even if an applica- J
tion had been refused by one judge before the trial had
commenced, it would be open to the Crown or the
accused to lodge a further petition before the trial
judge seeking an order for the taking of the evidence
of the child by means of a live television link. Special
cause might be shown as to why that petition had not
been lodged 14 clear days before the trial diet, and the
advocate depute contended that in the event of a
change of circumstances there was no reason why a
subsequent petition should not be granted. It is K
unnecessary for me to determine whether successive
petitions under this procedure would be competent,
since by refusing the present application in hoc statu
I have kept the existing petition in existence, and left
it open to the trial judge, if so advised, to grant the
application which has at present been refused in hoc
statu. However, since the application has at present
been refused, the Crown should proceed upon the
basis that the evidence of these children is to be taken
in open court, and the guidance which is given to the L
children pre-trial should proceed upon that basis.

---

*Counsel for Petitioner, Bonomy, AD; Solicitor, J D
Lowe, Crown Agent — Counsel for Respondent, M E
Scott; Solicitors, Sinclairs, SSC.*

P W F

Williams v Cleveland and Highland Holdings Ltd

OUTER HOUSE

LORD PENROSE

9 JULY 1991

Process — Division or sale — Remit to person of skill — Objections to report — Relevancy of objections — Whether competent to object that reporter had not dealt with certain issues when not required by terms of remit to do so — Whether party entitled to require remit to reporter for reconsideration in light of objections to report — Whether reporter entitled to entertain arguments for division based on sentimental interests of one party where pecuniary interests of other party would be prejudiced — Whether appropriate on remit for reconsideration to expand on terms of original remit.

An individual, one of two pro indiviso heritable proprietors of the island of Eigg, raised an action against the other, a company, seeking division or sale. A remit was made to a person of skill to report as to whether the subjects were capable of division, having regard to the interests of the parties; whether sale was proper and necessary; whether any sale should be of the whole subjects, or of lots; and to advise on upset prices. The report rejected division on the ground that the aggregate value of the subjects would be diminished.

The company sought to have the cause remitted back to the reporter for him to reconsider his report in the light of objections lodged by them. The objections, so far as not agreed between the parties were: (1) that in considering the practicability of division, although the reporter had recognised that a road across the island divided it into two equal hefts of sheep, he had failed to acknowledge that, in view of the numbers of sheep, certain EEC regulations effectively required that division; (2) that while the reporter had reported that the two areas were very different, he had not explained why that should render division impracticable; (3) that the reporter had not considered whether any shortfall in value between divided parts could be made up to the parties' satisfaction; (4) that the reporter had failed to address the company's desire and interest to retain at least part of the island in order to fulfil existing responsibilities to the islanders, as employees, tenants or inhabitants, and to a charitable wildlife trust, and consequently had not taken into consideration that any reduction in the market value of the company's own share caused by the division would be offset by the gain to the company of being able to fulfil these responsibilities, and would therefore be of no consequence; (5) that the reporter did not explain why any lots would consist of individual dwellinghouses rather than larger units such as the island's two farms; (6) that the reporter did not explain why, despite acknowledging the island's ability to cope with a large number of visitors, he considered that the greater number of viewers which a sale by lots

would entail would raise transport and accommodation problems; and (7) that the reporter had not considered offering the island for sale as a whole or in lots, leaving the choice to be determined by the market.

Held, (1) that the remit had proceeded upon an interlocutor which both defined the issues to be decided by the reporter, and prescribed the procedure to be followed by him, and, no objection to the terms of the interlocutor having been taken, the parties were to be held to them (p 401B); (2) that it was not open to a party to include in a note of objections, contentions on the approach which the reporter might have adopted in carrying out the remit, where such contentions sought to innovate on the terms of the interlocutor, or otherwise to present argument which could properly have been made at the time of the remit (p 401D-E); (3) that the right to a remit for reconsideration arose only where there were cogent and articulate objections relating to the performance by the reporter of his duty under the remit, or to some issue of principle identifiable ex facie of the report (p 401J-K); (4) that where division would prejudice the pecuniary interests of one party, a reporter was not entitled to entertain opposing arguments based on sentimental or other non-economic interests of another party (p 402H-I and K-L); (5) that there was substance in the company's second, fifth and seventh objections (p 403D and H-J); (6) that in the circumstances it would not be appropriate to enlarge the original remit, the terms of which would remain binding on the reporter (p 403K-L); and second, fifth and seventh objections *upheld* and in respect thereof cause *remitted* to the reporter for reconsideration.

Dixon v Monkland Canal Co (1821) 1 S 145; 1 W & S 636, and *Thom v Macbeth* (1875) 3 R 161, *followed; Morrison v Kirk*, 1911 2 SLT 355; 1912 SC 44, *distinguished.*

Action of division or sale

The hon Mrs Margaret De Hauteville Udny-Hamilton or Schellenberg or Williams raised an action against (first) Cleveland and Highland Holdings Ltd, (second) Clifford Keith Wayne Schellenberg, and (third) Highland and Islands Development Board, seeking an order for division, or, if that were impracticable, sale of heritable subjects, in particular the island of Eigg. The case was remitted to Mr C J Campbell, FRICS, as a person of skill to report. The first defenders lodged a note of objections to the report.

The first defenders enrolled a motion seeking, in the first place, an order that the report should not be approved or at least, primo loco, that the matter should be remitted to the reporter to reconsider his report in the light of the note of objections. Failing this the first defenders sought authority to purchase the pursuer's half share of the subjects at valuation. The pursuer enrolled a motion seeking an order repelling the note of objections, approving of the report,

A and granting a warrant for sale, and certain further orders.

The case came before the Lord Ordinary (Penrose) on the motion roll on a discussion restricted to the issue of a further remit.

Statutory provisions

The Codifying Act of Sederunt 1913 provided in Book C, chap II:

B "13. When, in any cause, a report has been obtained from an accountant or other professional person, and the parties, or either of them, shall be dissatisfied with the report, the cause shall be enrolled before the Lord Ordinary, for debate on the report, and a note of the objections shall be furnished to the opposite party forty-eight hours before the enrolment; and at the time of enrolling the cause, a copy of the note of objections shall be furnished to the Lord Ordinary's clerk, for his Lordship's use; and, upon hearing parties, the Lord Ordinary may order answers or otherwise dispose of C the note of objections as he sees cause."

Cases referred to

Blantyre (Lord) v Glasgow Railway Co (1851) 13 D 570.

Bruce v Bain (1883) 11 R 192.

Dixon v Monkland Canal Co (1821) 1 S 145; 1 W & S 636.

Edinburgh Northern Tramways Co v Mann (1896) 4 SLT 90; (1896) 23 R 1056.

D *Hunter v Duke of Queensberry's Executors* (1827) 6 S 89.

Meason v Duke of Queensberry's Executors (1827) 6 S 326.

Morrison v Kirk, 1911 2 SLT 355; 1912 SC 44.

Muir v Anderson (1833) 12 S 129.

Quin's Executrix v James Gardner & Sons Ltd (1888) 15 R 776.

Rowat v Whitehead (1826) 5 S 19.

Thom v Macbeth (1875) 3 R 161.

E **Textbook referred to**

Maxwell, *Practice of the Court of Session*, p 314.

On 9 July 1991 the Lord Ordinary *remitted* the case to the reporter for reconsideration.

LORD PENROSE.—In this action the pursuer seeks an order for division, or, if that be impracticable, for sale of the heritable subjects described in a disposi-
F tion in favour of the pursuer and the second defender dated 2 and 8 July 1976, and comprising in particular the island of Eigg. After extensive procedure the vacation judge, on 7 August 1990, remitted to Mr C J Campbell, FRICS, to examine the subjects and to report whether, with due regard to the interests of the parties, the subjects were incapable of division among the pro indiviso proprietors, and whether it was proper and necessary that they should be sold; further to report whether they should be sold as a whole or in lots, to suggest the lots and to suggest the upset price or prices.

G Mr Campbell submitted his report on 11 March 1991. On 8 May, the pursuer enrolled a motion for an order for sale. This was opposed. On 10 May the matter came before Lord Morton of Shuna. It was intimated that the defenders were to lodge a note of objections to the report. The pursuer's motion was dropped. In due course a note of objections was presented on behalf of the first defenders, Cleveland and Highland Holdings Ltd, to whom I shall refer as "the company".

H The pursuer and the company have each enrolled motions. The company seeks, in the first place, an order that the report should not be approved, or at least, primo loco, that the matter be remitted to the reporter to reconsider his report in the light of the objections contained in the note lodged on behalf of the company, failing which, authority to purchase the pursuer's half share at valuation on one or other of two specified bases. The pursuer's motion seeks an order repelling the note of objections, approving of the report, and a warrant for sale and for certain further
I orders. At the hearing before me on 6 June 1991, it was agreed between counsel that the discussion should be restricted to the questions raised by that part of the company's motion which sought a remit for reconsideration of the report in the light of the note of objections. Counsel for the pursuer accepted certain of the points of criticism made of the report and did not contend that the report could be approved without qualification at this stage.

The objections set out in the note are as follows:
J "1. The first defenders contend that the question addressed by the reporter at para 3.1 (namely 'whether with due regard to the interest of the party said subjects are incapable of division among the pro indiviso proprietors thereof') has not been adequately addressed and in particular (a) that although the reporter in consideration of the practicability of division recognises the 'obvious physical division' (believed to be division by the council road which divides the island by a south east to north west
K physical line almost exactly) and that (para 5.3) 'the present farming system is based on a total of 2,000 ewes carried in two equal hefts divided by the council road', he does not acknowledge (all as discussed with him by the farm manager) that sheep farming of the land (the only practicable farming activity) was required by new EEC regulations (in particular Council regulation EEC No 3013/89 which effectively limits sheep farming subsidy to 1,000 ewes under any one ownership) to be carried out in two different hold-
L ings on either side of the road (to which end division has in part already been made by fencing and livestock road grids); (b) and even if the reporter is right — which is disputed — to report that each area of potential division is very different from the other (there being in fact the same number of houses and cottages on each and there being negligible geophysical and environmental differences) the reporter does not explain why that would make division impracticable having regard to the interest of the parties; (c) the reporter does not explain adequately — nor is it

believed could he — why the parties would require to agree to share mutual costs such as transport; (d) the reporter did not raise and does not report having raised with parties the question of whether any short-fall in value between divided parts could be made up to their satisfaction; (e) the reporter does not address or attempt to balance the real desire and interest of the first defenders, a family company, to retain possession of at least part of the island — not only for themselves but also to fulfil existing extensive responsibilities to employees, inhabitants, tenants and others such as the Scottish Wildlife Trust or that relative to that consideration, for the first defenders at least, a reduction in market value of their share would be of no consequence. The reporter does not further indicate to what degree in his view a division would reduce the market value of each party's share.

"2. The first defenders further contend that the question addressed by the reporter at para 3.3 (namely 'Whether it is proper and necessary that they should be sold as a whole or in lots, to suggest lots') has not been adequately addressed, in particular (a) that he does not explain why in his view if there were to be lotting it would be of individual dwellinghouses as opposed for example to the two halves of the estate represented on the one hand by Kildonan and Howlin farms and on the other by Galmisdale and Sandavore farms with the lodge and its policies and a cottage as a further lot and perhaps the disputed forestry area as a fourth lot; (b) does not adequately explain how despite his acknowledgment of the number of visitors and the island's ability to cope therewith (see, eg paras 5.1 and 5.8) the fact of 'considerably more viewers wishing to visit the island' would raise transport and accommodation problems; (c) that the reporter does not consider (which is believed to be the norm) the option of offering for sale the estate as a whole or in lots (such as those described in para (a) above) leaving it to the market to determine, the market potentially including those who may not wish to carry the burden of responsibility both social and financial which ownership of the whole does demand".

For the pursuer counsel accepted that there was force in the criticism that the report gave inadequate information on the diminution in value which would result from division of the subjects. Further he accepted that the passage in para 3.1 of the report referring to mutual costs such as transport was unintelligible, as the report stood, and would require explanation. In the circumstances a remit to the reporter to reconsider his report was unavoidable. But with the exception of these topics the parties were in dispute.

Counsel for the company contended that there was a broad general right available to any party who was dissatisfied with the report of a man of skill to require that he reconsider his report in the light of objections. This was reflected in the terms of the consolidating Act of Sederunt of 1913, C ii, 13, quoted in Maxwell on *The Practice of the Court of Session*, p 314. It was consistent with parties' general rights. With the exception of cases of certain identifiable kinds in which the

court might make a remit without consent, a party was entitled to insist in proof of averments made by or against him: *Quin's Exrx v James Gardner & Sons Ltd*, per Lord President Inglis and Lord Shand. By agreeing to a remit, or not opposing a remit, a party waived important rights. It followed that unless there were authorities clearly restricting the grounds on which a party could seek reconsideration of a report, the court should be slow to prevent him from requesting as a matter of right such a further step in procedure. Counsel recognised that it might not be sufficient for a party simply to express dissatisfaction with the report, but argued that it would be sufficient to indicate an area of disagreement with the reporter's views, and to invite a remit for reconsideration on the basis of the points of disagreement. The authorities, he said, supported the view that matters were at large as to the nature of objections which might be taken, and that this was reflected in the terms of the Act of Sederunt. Counsel for the pursuer responded that the proper view was that there was a right to object to a report, but that it was narrow, and arose only where the reporter failed to obtemper the court's order, by failing to exhaust the remit, or by exceeding the scope of the remit, or by failing to give reasons, or by reporting in terms which disclosed fundamental error on some material particular in issue between the parties. He sought support from the realities of the situation. Where reports were sought of consent and without opposition the parties were to be held to have elected the particular mode of proof provided in the remit, and must be held to the result as conclusive of the issues so dealt with, unless there were clear grounds for disputing the reporter's findings. The remit was a mode of inquiry intended to exhaust the particular issue remitted as between the parties. The Act of Sederunt was concerned with procedure only and was not determinative of the substantive issues of law involved.

In developing their submissions counsel drew on substantially the same body of authority. Reference was made to *Dixon v Monkland Canal Co, Rowat v Whitehead, Hunter v Duke of Queensberry's Exrs, Meason v Duke of Queensberry's Exrs, Muir v Anderson, Lord Blantyre v Glasgow Railway Co, Thom v Macbeth, Edinburgh Northern Tramways Co v Mann, Morrison v Kirk,* and *Quin's Exrx.* In addition counsel for the pursuer referred to *Bruce v Bain.* I did not find *Muir v Anderson* or *Bruce v Bain* to be helpful. There was no dispute between counsel that where parties elect to proceed by remit to a man of skill, that becomes the exclusive mode of proof of the issues comprised in the remit. There was similarly no dispute that there was a right to object to a report, and that the procedure following on a relevant note of objection would require a remit to the same reporter, if available, for reconsideration of his report. It was, further, a matter of agreement that after a fresh report it would be only where there was gross error on the part of the reporter that the court might resort to a different mode of proof.

In my opinion it is clear that in cases where remit

to a man of skill depends upon agreement or the initia-
A tive of one party without opposition from the other or
others, there is considerable freedom in defining the
scope of the remit, and in providing for procedure
before the reporter. In the present case the matter was
left largely to the court to prescribe in a common form
interlocutor. Since comment was made on the matter,
I note that the terms of the motion which resulted in
the remit were: "to remit to Mr C J Fraser . . . and
to report to the Court whether or not the property is
capable of division and if not to recommend an upset
B price".

The motion in these terms was intimated and was
not opposed. It was not granted in its terms. The
interlocutor which was pronounced both defined the
issues for the reporter and prescribed the procedure to
be followed by him. No one took issue with that interlocutor, and the whole parties must be held to its
terms. That was the approach adopted by the House
of Lords in *Dixon v Monkland Canal Co*, notwithstanding that the remit to the reporter, Mr Telford,
C was regarded as altogether a singular step for the court
to have taken, having regard to the scope of the
dispute on the pleadings. It was held that Mr Dixon
had acquiesced in the remit. In that context it was
further held that he was bound by consent to the judgment of the reporter.

That the parties might have sought further or other
provision had they wished is clearly illustrated by the
case of *Hunter v Duke of Queensberry's Exrs*, where the
D interlocutor provided for probation and for a hearing
of parties and their agents. In particular had any party
so wished in this case, it would have been competent
to have sought an order requiring the reporter to have
regard to oral or written representations of the parties
on matters falling within the scope of the remit. That
was not done. In my opinion it is not legitimate for a
party to include by way of note of objections contentions on the approach which the reporter might have
adopted in carrying out the remit which are in sub-
E stance innovations on the procedure provided for in
the remit, nor to use the procedure by way of objection
to present argument which might have preceded
decision, as distinct from criticisms of the decision
arrived at by the reporter.

In *Rowat v Whitehead*, the opinion of Lord Pitmilly,
with which Lord Alloway and Lord Justice Clerk
Boyle concurred, was that for a remit to a reporter to
reconsider his report there had to be specific objections, or allegations of omission of duty. Counsel for
F the pursuer relied on *Hunter v Duke of Queensberry's
Exrs* for support for this approach. However the
reasoning in that case appears to me to have been
peculiar to the situation in which there was provision
for a hearing. In *Meason v Duke of Queensberry's Exrs*,
the issue before the court was whether, following a
report by men of skill, there should be a trial of
damages. In rejecting such a mode of proof, the court
had before it allegations that the reporters had not
taken proper steps to ascertain the loss, and had
neglected to investigate a particular matter altogether.

The interlocutor pronounced inter alia remitted the
case to the Lord Ordinary "to receive articulate objec- G
tions to the report already made, and to do therein as
he shall see cause". The Lord Justice Clerk referred
to the further procedure and said: "Here, if sufficient
objections are condescended on, there may be grounds
for remitting to the same persons". The reference to
articulate objections in the interlocutor is reflected in
Lord Pitmilly's opinion. In *Lord Blantyre v Glasgow
Railway Co*, the report did not exhaust the remit. Lord
Blantyre sought to avoid its results so far as it went by
seeking an order for proof prout de jure. One of the H
reporters had died. The Lord Ordinary reported the
case, and, in his report, at p 572 said: "when parties
have adopted or agreed to one mode of proof in a court
of justice, one of them shall not — because he is dissatisfied with it — be at liberty to depart from it and
require another to be taken. That being the rule, the
practical result is, that the report obtained from the
parties remitted to, shall either be binding and conclusive, where it properly exhausts the matter of
inquiry, and affords sufficient materials for judgment; I
or if not, that a re-remit shall be made to supply the
farther information that may be deemed needful".

The case was remitted to the Lord Ordinary to
proceed further as should be just. In *Edinburgh
Northern Tramways Co v Mann*, Lord McLaren at
(1896) 4 SLT, pp 90-91 lends support to the view that
objections must relate to the nature of the duty
entrusted to the reporter or to wrong conclusions on
some matter of principle.

In my opinion there is no support in any of these J
authorities for the position adopted by the company.
On the contrary the emphasis is on the finality of the
reporter's findings subject only to a remit for reconsideration on the basis of articulate objections made to
the report provided, and on restricted grounds.
Whether a further remit is made must, in my opinion,
depend upon the cogency of the objections, considered
in the light of the original remit, and on those objections relating to the performance by the reporter of his K
duty under the remit, or to some issue of principle
identifiable on the face of the report.

The remit in the present case identified three issues:
the scope for physical division of the subjects, having
due regard to the interests of the parties; whether it
was proper and necessary that the subject should be
sold; and whether a sale should be of the whole subjects, or of lots to be defined by the reporter, with
advice on upset prices.

In approaching the question of a remit to a reporter L
in the context of division or sale, the parties have both
an opportunity, and in my opinion, an obligation to
define the issues with clarity, since it is they who have
to determine the scope of the reporter's power to bind
them by his decision. Where the subjects consist of a
number of more or less homogeneous units, division
will present a range of problems reflecting that fact.
Where there is a single holding of land with varying
physical and other characteristics the range of
problems which will arise will reflect that fact. It is

obvious that valuation of the whole, and of the component or possible component parts, is among those issues. However it seems to me to be a matter for the parties also to consider what use might be made of the information provided. Before one can have a division into two parts of differing characteristics of a single unit of land, there must be a mechanism which binds the parties to the value of the whole, and of the parts, and which provides for compensating payments as appropriate. It is not relevant to object to a report that the reporter has not dealt with issues of this kind unless particular provision has been made requiring him to do so. If it be the case that a physical division can only be achieved at the cost of a reduction in value which is material, sale of the whole would appear to be unavoidable unless the reporter's powers extend to defining the parts, fixing the values, identifying the party to receive particular subjects, and specifying balancing payments to be made and by whom. These are not issues which can arise after the report has been made on a remit in common form and that remit has been exhausted. In the present case the reporter was not required to determine values for the subjects at all, nor was any basis of valuation specified, and the parties were not bound by the remit to accept a valuation for any purpose of determining their financial interests inter se. Relative values were a factor relevant to deciding whether the subjects could be divided, having due regard to the interests of the parties, but there was no requirement for the reporter to determine a value which might be realised in an open, or any other, market. In *Morrison v Kirk* the reporter (whose findings are quoted at 1912 SC, p 45) did provide a value, and reported that division was possible using the competent parts of the value with a balancing payment. The circumstances appear to have favoured division particularly, and it appears not to have been argued that the valuation was other than a proper measure of the parties' rights inter se. That could not be said in this case where it is a reasonable inference from the terms of the respective motions that the company considers the suggested prices are sufficiently favourable to use as a basis for acquisition without testing the market, and the pursuer reserves her position on the value as a whole.

Turning to the terms of the interlocutor, the first issue of construction which falls to be determined is whether the interests of the parties properly to be taken into account were confined to economic interests or included wider interests such as social and charitable interests and interests in the welfare of wildlife. This issue arose out of the terms of para 1 (e) of the note of objections. Having regard to the discussion before me it can perhaps best be considered with reference to the example of the Scottish Wildlife Trust. I was informed that that is a charitable trust concerned with the protection and the interests of wild species. In the report, para 5.6 (iv), it is said that the trust have been involved with Eigg for about 16 years, which would appear to include a period prior to the disposition in favour of the pursuer and second defender. There is no lease or other form of right which would bind the successor of the present proprietors. The specific sites of interest are not located on any one area, but are spread between the two parts of the island identified by the public road. The "responsibility" towards the trust referred to in the objections is a moral responsibility related to the second defender's interest in wildlife welfare, and attributed in this case to the company. It was not made clear to me how a company might formulate its attitude towards such a responsibility. But it is perhaps best treated as an illustration of an attachment to the land which the company maintains should have been weighed in the balance when the reporter was considering the issue of physical division of the subjects. As already observed, no provision was made for a hearing or for representations in this case. I have very considerable difficulty in understanding how the reporter could have investigated questions such as the emotional attachment of parties to the land, or how he could have been expected to evaluate such factors, as an expert, in assessing the feasibility of the physical division of the land. However, apart from such considerations, I am of the opinion that factors such as the emotional attachment of parties to the subject are not relevant considerations. In *Thom v Macbeth*, the defender objected to a sale on the ground that "looking to the nature of the estate, if it was not to be retained as a whole, it was much more for his interest, as an individual, and for the interest of the trust-estate which he represented, that it should be divided". As matters progressed in that case, it appeared that the defender considered that the land had development potential in part as in whole. The opposing view was based wholly on the economics of division at the time. Lord Justice Clerk Inglis said: "The only question is whether the estate can be reasonably divided in such a manner as to protect the just interests of all concerned. . . . Now . . . when division is not reasonably practicable without sacrificing to an appreciable extent the interests of some or all of the parties the only resort is a sale and division of the price. . . . [The] proprietors who wish to realise are not bound to run the risk of the market. They are entitled to have their present interest realised. They want money, and a division of the estate would be clearly a pecuniary loss to them at present, to which the defender has no right to subject them".

In view of the emphasis on pecuniary interests in that case, and the mechanism sanctioned to ensure that any individual who had speculative or sentimental objectives might bid, I consider it to be clear that the reporter would not have been entitled on the terms of the remit in the present case to have entertained argument based on the interests of the company in continuing physical occupation of part of the subjects, even had that part been defined.

Further, the basis on which division and sale is entertained is that a party cannot be held bound in a communion of interests against his will, in the absence of contract. It is no doubt a frequent occurrence that co-proprietors of heritable property have interests in common which extend beyond, and perhaps even conflict with, their economic interests in the subjects. So long as the common interest subsists they may indulge such non-economic interests to the extent they agree inter se. However when the common interest dissolves, the continuing emotional, or sentimental, or other non-economic interests of those wishing to retain the subjects or part of the subjects can be sustained only at the expense of the others. That, in substance, would maintain an element of the community against the will of those wishing to obtain the proceeds of sale. In circumstances such as arise in the present case, I am of the opinion that the company is not entitled to require weight to be given to non-economic interests or objectives to the detriment of the pursuer's interests in realising the full value of her present interest in the subjects. With the exception of the last sentence, para 1 (e) of the objections is, in my view, irrelevant.

Paragraph 1 (a) refers to certain EEC regulations which may have as their effect the subdivision of farming units. It is not maintained that the effect of these regulations would be to require any significant change in beneficial ownership in or occupation of the subjects. Paragraph 5.3 of the report illustrates, though the discussion is incomplete, one method of dividing occupation by the use of limited partnerships which may avoid disturbing underlying ownership or the substantial economic interests of proprietors in agricultural subjects. In my opinion nothing in this subparagraph bears upon the performance by the reporter of his duties such as to require him to report further on the topic.

Paragraph 1 (b) of the note of objections attacks the lack of reasons in the report for the view that division is impracticable having regard to the interests of the parties. Insofar as this relates to the economic interests of the parties, I consider that the objection is valid. The report does not provide the materials required for judgment on the issue and will require to be supplemented. Paragraph 1 (c) refers to a single sentence in para 3.1 of the report. It was agreed in argument that the sentence was incomprehensible.

Paragraph 1 (d) of the note of objections may be no more than a comment on the consequences of lack of information of comparative values on subdivision. But it appeared to me to raise an issue of some importance. I have already referred to *Morrison v Kirk* where a balancing payment was proposed. It is relatively easy to imagine a case involving co-proprietorship of a number of units of more or less equal value, but of such number that the division must be unequal. Two co-proprietors could not divide an odd number of identical houses equally. If the unit value could be agreed or determined by a man of skill, a balancing payment would be a simple means of resolving the problems of disposing of the final unit. *Morrison* may have been such a case. However where there is a single unit incapable of subdivision into two homogeneous parts, the problems of identification and of valuation of the parts of the whole must interact. If the aggregate value of the parts is less than the value of the whole,

a compensating payment would require to reflect the reporter's views of the values of the individual units of subdivision, and of the difference between the sum of those values and the value of the whole. The remit in the present case does not require such an exercise to be carried out. More significantly the scope of the remit does not bind the parties to accept the reporter's adjudication on such a matter. It seems to me that the exercise is altogether different in concept from an issue which takes differences in value simply as an indicator of the practicability or impracticability of subdivision (as *Thom* demonstrates). I am of the opinion that this objection is irrelevant. It does not arise on the terms of the remit.

The second chapter of objections relates to the reporter's opinions on sale. Paragraph 2 (a) is closely related to the other objections that inadequate information has been provided as to the reporter's reasons for his opinions. There may be obvious reasons for the reporter's approach. He has rejected division on the ground that the aggregate value will be diminished. He recognises the possibility of separate disposals of individual dwellings which, from his report, can be seen clearly to include empty properties. But to go further would involve speculation. Further reasons must be provided by the reporter. Paragraph (c) appears to be related. Again one might expect particulars of sale, which the reporter was not instructed to draft, to provide conventional options, and it may be that it would not be inconsistent with the recommendation that the whole should be offered as a unit that particulars of sale would provide for alternatives. It is for the reporter to comment on this matter.

Paragraph 2 (b) relates to a passage in s 3 of the report. In my opinion the import of the comment is clear. The reporter is dealing with the implications of offering individual houses for sale, including the attraction of an increased number of potential bidders. It was a matter for his judgment whether inconvenience and expense associated with any particular system of lotting were justified by the prospects of increased competition. I do not consider that there is substance in the attack on his judgment on this matter by pointing to alleged inconsistencies with comments made in other contexts.

It is necessary for the court to be advised of the reasons for the reporter's views, and, to ascertain those views, I shall remit to him to reconsider and to re-report on certain issues. However I do not consider it appropriate to enlarge the original remit in any way, and the order must not be construed by the reporter or by the parties as an invitation to him to deal with issues which were not properly comprehended in the initial remit.

In relation to value, the report should indicate the degree or extent of reduction on division, so that its materiality can be considered. In relation to the identities of potential units, the report should explain the reasons for the reporter's views, having regard to the factors identified in the objections and to any other factors considered by the reporter to be relevant. The

A reference to sharing of mutual costs will require to be clarified in the context of the reporter's views on the practical management of the units he has in mind. Since the result will be that parts only of the note of objections will be considered by the reporter I have thought it necessary to repeat in the interlocutor in this case those matters which fall properly to be reconsidered by him, in my opinion, rather than simply to remit the note of objections to him to consider in its terms.

B

Counsel for Pursuer, Keen; Solicitors, Dundas & Wilson, CS — Counsel for First Defenders, D R A Emslie, QC; Solicitors, A C Bennett & Robertsons, WS (for Ledingham & Chalmers, Aberdeen) — No appearance for Second or Third Defenders.

P G L H

C

HM Advocate v Sutherland

HIGH COURT OF JUSTICIARY

THE LORD JUSTICE CLERK (ROSS),
LORDS MORISON AND MILLIGAN

25 OCTOBER 1991

D *Justiciary — Procedure — Plea in bar of trial — Postponement — Accused charged in capacity of debtor whose estates had been sequestrated — Proceedings raised in Court of Session to reduce award of sequestration — Whether contrary to interests of justice to proceed to trial until resolution of civil action — Whether competent to challenge award of sequestration in criminal trial.*

An accused person was indicted, along with her co-accused, on various charges of breaches of the provisions of the Bankruptcy (Scotland) Act 1985. The
E libel against her charged her in the capacity of a "debtor whose estates had been sequestrated" on a particular date. At a preliminary diet the accused argued that she was not, in fact, such a debtor; that she had raised an action for suspension and reduction of the award of sequestration in the Court of Session; and that it would not be in the interests of justice that the trial should proceed until those civil proceedings had been resolved. Ex proprio motu, the sheriff deserted the charges against the accused and granted leave to
F the Crown to re-raise proceedings at a later date. The Crown presented a bill of advocation against the sheriff's decision.

Held, (1) that while the sheriff's decision was a discretionary one, the court could interfere since (a) he had not appreciated that it would be competent in the criminal proceedings for the defence to challenge the validity of the award of sequestration, and (b) he had not attached sufficient weight to the fact that an inevitable consequence of his actions would be a considerable delay before the accused could be brought to

trial in respect of the charges which had been deserted (p 405G-J); and (2) that since the respondent would G not be prejudiced by allowing the trial to proceed, it was in the interests of justice that it should do so (p 405J); and bill *passed.*

David Lawson Ltd v Torrance, 1929 SLT 519, *followed.*

Bill of advocation

The rt hon the Lord Fraser of Carmyllie, Her Majesty's Advocate, presented a bill of advocation to H the High Court against the decision of Sheriff A Pollock at Aberdeen sheriff court in which he deserted certain charges on an indictment which alleged that Charlotte Liston Sutherland, "being a debtor whose estates had been sequestrated in the Court of Session, Edinburgh, on 31 January 1989", and Douglas Andrew Arthur had, inter alia, breached certain provisions of the Bankruptcy (Scotland) Act 1985. The first named accused had requested a preliminary diet I by way of minute of notice under s 76 of the Criminal Procedure (Scotland) Act 1975 and argued that, as she had raised an action in the Court of Session for suspension and reduction of the award of sequestration and was thus contesting her capacity as a sequestrated debtor at the material time, it was not in the interests of justice that the trial should proceed pending resolution of that action.

Case referred to

Lawson (David) Ltd v Torrance, 1929 SLT 519; 1929 J JC 119.

The sheriff, ex proprio motu, deserted the relevant charges, being charges 7, 8, 10, 11, 12, 15 and 16 on the indictment; granted leave to the Crown to re-raise these matters at a later date; et separatim dismissed charge 14 as irrelevant.

The bill was argued before the High Court on 25 October 1991. K

Eo die their Lordships *passed* the bill and *recalled* the decision of the sheriff under exception of the decision to dismiss charge 14.

The following opinion of the court was delivered by the Lord Justice Clerk (Ross):

OPINION OF THE COURT.—This is a bill of advocation at the instance of the Lord Advocate as L complainer against Charlotte Liston Sutherland, first respondent, and Douglas Andrew Arthur, second respondent. As the Solicitor General explained, an unusual situation has arisen in this case. The respondents have been charged on indictment with a number of charges. By minute of notice the first respondent sought a preliminary diet to raise certain matters at that diet. What she seeks to raise is that despite what appears on the indictment, she is not a debtor whose estates have been sequestrated at the Court of Session on 31 January 1989, and she also raises the point that she has raised in the Court of Session an action of suspension and an action of reduction of a purported decree of sequestration dated 9 March 1989. In these circumstances the submission on her behalf is that it is not in the interests of justice that the present proceedings should proceed until these civil actions have been disposed of.

The preliminary diet was heard before the sheriff at Aberdeen and in the event the sheriff deserted quoad charges 7, 8, 10, 11, 12, 15 and 16 against the first respondent. The sheriff also dealt with charge 14 but no point is now taken on his decision on that matter by the complainer. What is challenged by this bill of advocation is the sheriff's decision ex proprio motu to desert the charges which we have listed. Putting the matter shortly, the Solicitor General recognised that these charges on the indictment proceeded upon the basis that the first respondent was a debtor whose estates had been sequestrated at the Court of Session on 31 January 1989. That being so, as the sheriff recognised, before there could be any question of any conviction it would be for the Crown to prove that. The first respondent has, however, raised proceedings in the Court of Session for reduction and, putting the matter shortly, the sheriff's reason for deserting quoad these charges was that it would be appropriate to wait until the outcome of the Court of Session proceedings before making it necessary for the first respondent to face these charges. It is unnecessary to examine in detail the basis upon which the action of reduction has been presented. It is plain, however, that the first respondent's contention is that certain requirements of the Bankruptcy (Scotland) Act 1985 were not complied with. The principal matter which the Solicitor General raised was this. He recognised that the issue of the validity of the award of sequestration had been raised in these civil proceedings but he maintained, under reference to the case of *David Lawson Ltd v Torrance,* that it would be competent for the first respondent at a trial to challenge the validity of the sequestration. That being so, he submitted that the sheriff had been wrong to reach the view that it was not in the interests of justice for her trial on these specific charges to be allowed to proceed until the outcome of the civil proceedings.

Counsel on behalf of the first respondent, on the other hand, maintained that the sheriff had been entitled to arrive at the decision which he had reached. He stressed that the appropriate forum in which to determine the validity of the award of sequestration was the Court of Session, and he maintained that there were substantial grounds for thinking that the action of reduction would succeed. He accepted that as a result of the sheriff's decision there would be delay in the respondent being tried upon these specified charges but, none the less, he maintained that we should not interfere with the decision of the sheriff, which had been arrived at by him at the preliminary diet. He stressed that the sheriff had a discretion when he had to determine whether or not to accede to the submission made on behalf of the first respondent.

Counsel for the second respondent intimated initially that he was adopting a neutral position, although as time went on he appeared to identify himself with the first respondent and to seek to support the submissions on behalf of the first respondent.

Having considered the submissions made, we have come to the conclusion that the submissions of the Solicitor General are well founded. We recognise that the sheriff was exercising a discretion, but we feel justified in interfering in this case because, so far as we can see from the very careful report which the sheriff has written, his attention was not drawn to *David Lawson Ltd v Torrance* and he does not appear to have appreciated that it would be competent in the criminal proceedings for the defence to challenge the validity of the award of sequestration. The case of *David Lawson Ltd v Torrance* arose under summary procedure, but we agree with the Solicitor General that the same principle would be equally applicable under solemn procedure and that under solemn procedure it would be competent for the defence to challenge the award of sequestration. Not only that but, as we read the sheriff's report, he does not appear to us to have attached sufficient weight to the fact that a consequence of acting as he did must inevitably be that there would be considerable delay before there could be any question of the first respondent being brought to trial in respect of these specified charges. It is obvious that it might be many months before a decision was arrived at in the action of reduction. The decision might be the subject of a reclaiming motion and in these circumstances it is obvious that a considerable period might elapse before the way was open, if it is open, for the first respondent to be brought to trial in respect of these charges. When regard is had to the fact that her position in relation to the award of sequestration would not be prejudiced by allowing the trial to proceed because it would be competent for her to challenge the award of sequestration during these proceedings, we are satisfied that it would be in the interests of justice that the trial should proceed on, among others, these specified charges. That being so, we shall pass the bill and we shall recall the decision of the sheriff except to the extent that it related to charge 14 and we shall remit to the sheriff to proceed as accords.

Counsel for Complainer, Solicitor General (Rodger, QC); Solicitor, J D Lowe, Crown Agent — Counsel for First Respondent, Conway; Solicitors, Liam Robertson & Co, Glasgow — Counsel for Second Respondent, McBride; Solicitors, Liam Robertson & Co, Glasgow.

R F H

[Both accused subsequently went to trial and were convicted of certain charges. The sheriff rejected arguments directed to the validity of the sequestration and his decision was upheld on appeal to the High Court on 19 November 1992. A report is in preparation.]

Orr v Urquhart

A HIGH COURT OF JUSTICIARY

THE LORD JUSTICE CLERK (ROSS),
LORDS MORISON AND CAPLAN

12 DECEMBER 1991

Justiciary — Statutory offence — Being in charge of vehicle while having excess of alcohol — Accused required to provide roadside breath test — No evidence that police officers in uniform — Accused arrested and required to B *provide specimens for analysis on Camic machine on which prosecution based — Whether necessary for officers to be in uniform — Whether prima facie case — Road Traffic Act 1988 (c 52), s 5 (1) (b).*

Section 6 (1) (b) of the Road Traffic Act 1988 provides that where a constable in uniform has reasonable cause to suspect that a person has been driving or attempting to drive or been in charge of a motor vehicle with alcohol in his body and that that person C still has alcohol in his body, he may require him to provide a specimen of breath for a breath test. Section 7 (1) (a) provides that in the course of an investigation into whether a person has committed an offence under s 4 or s 5 a constable may require him to provide two specimens of breath for analysis by means of a device of a type approved by the Secretary of State.

An accused person was charged with being in charge of a motor car while having excess alcohol in his body contrary to s 5 (1) (b) of the Road Traffic Act 1988. D The evidence at his trial established that the accused's car was parked partly on the road and partly on the verge with the accused asleep in the driver's seat. In his hands was an empty vodka bottle. The keys were in the ignition, the engine off but the radio was playing. The accused on being awakened had slurred speech and glazed eyes. He was required to provide a roadside breath test which proved positive and he was arrested. At the police station in response to a requirement the accused provided two breath specimens for E analysis on the Camic breath analyser. At the accused's trial it was submitted that there was no case for him to answer because it had not been established in evidence that the police officers were in uniform when they administered the roadside breath test or during the subsequent Camic procedure. The sheriff, considering that the question for him was whether he was entitled to infer that the officers were in uniform, upheld the submission and acquitted the accused. The procurator fiscal appealed contending that the Crown F were entitled to rely on the results of the Camic breath analyser so long as they were obtained in the course of an investigation into an offence under s 4 or s 5 and that the Crown did not require to rely on the evidence of the roadside breath test. Accordingly it was unnecessary to establish that the officers were in uniform when they required the provision of a breath specimen for a roadside breath test.

Held, (1) that it was not necessary for the procedure in s 6 to have been followed at all provided that the procedure laid down in s 7 had been observed (p 408G); (2) that accordingly, even though there was no evidence that the police officers were in uniform, G the evidence led without objection regarding the specimens of breath provided for analysis on the Camic breath analyser was clearly sufficient to constitute a case to answer (p 408I-J); and appeal *allowed* and case *remitted* to sheriff to proceed as accords.

Richards v West [1980] RTR 215, *distinguished.*

Observed, (1) that even if the arrest of a person under s 6 should appear to be invalid, that would not render invalid any procedure properly carried out H under s 7 (p 408G-H); and (2) that having regard to the facts relating to the accused when he was found by the police, the police would have been entitled to arrest the accused without warrant under s 4 (6) (which permits "a constable" to arrest a person without warrant if he has reasonable cause to suspect that he has been or is committing an offence under that section) (p 408K-L).

I

Summary complaint

Colin Murdoch Urquhart was charged at the instance of William W Orr, procurator fiscal, Inverness on a summary complaint which was in the following terms: "on 27 October 1990 you were in charge of a motor vehicle, namely motor car registered number MSE 933V which was on a road or other public place, namely on the Inverness to Essich road, at a part 400 yds or thereby west of the Essich roundabout, District of Inverness, after consuming so much alcohol that the J proportion of it in your breath was 131 microgrammes of alcohol in 100 millilitres of breath which exceeded the prescribed limit, namely 35 microgrammes of alcohol in 100 millilitres of breath: contrary to the Road Traffic Act 1988, s 5 (1) (b)". The accused pled not guilty and proceeded to trial. After trial the sheriff (I D Smith) upheld a submission of no case to answer and acquitted the accused.

The procurator fiscal appealed by way of stated case to the High Court against the decision of the sheriff. K The facts of the case appear from the opinion of the court.

Statutory provisions

The Road Traffic Act 1988 provides:

"4.—. . . (2) Without prejudice to subsection (1) above, a person who, when in charge of a motor vehicle which is on a road or other public place, is unfit to drive through drink or drugs is guilty of an L offence. . . .

"(6) A constable may arrest a person without warrant if he has reasonable cause to suspect that that person is or has been committing an offence under this section. . . .

"6.—(1) Where a constable in uniform has reasonable cause to suspect — . . . (b) that a person has been driving or attempting to drive or been in charge of a motor vehicle on a road or other public place with alcohol in his body and that that person still has

A alcohol in his body . . . he may, subject to section 9 of this Act, require him to provide a specimen of breath for a breath test. . . .

"(4) A person who, without reasonable excuse, fails to provide a specimen of breath when required to do so in pursuance of this section is guilty of an offence.

"(5) A constable may arrest a person without warrant if — (a) as a result of a breath test he has reasonable cause to suspect that the proportion of alcohol in that person's breath or blood exceeds the prescribed limit, or (b) that person has failed to B provide a specimen of breath for a breath test when required to do so in pursuance of this section and the constable has reasonable cause to suspect that he has alcohol in his body, but a person shall not be arrested by virtue of this subsection when he is at a hospital as a patient. . . .

"7.—(1) In the course of an investigation into whether a person has committed an offence under section 4 or 5 of this Act a constable may, subject to the following provisions of this section and section 9 C of this Act, require him — (a) to provide two specimens of breath for analysis by means of a device of a type approved by the Secretary of State, or (b) to provide a specimen of blood or urine for a laboratory test."

Cases referred to

Cooper v Rowlands [1971] RTR 291.
R v Fox [1985] RTR 337; [1985] 1 WLR 1126; [1985] 3 All ER 992.
D *Richards v West* [1980] RTR 215.

Appeal

The sheriff posed the following questions for the opinion of the High Court:

(1) Did I err in holding that the prosecution was fatally flawed in the absence of evidence that Constables Allan and Patience had been in uniform at the time the accused was required to provide a specimen E of breath on the Essich Road?

(2) Did I, therefore, err in law in upholding the submission made by the defence agent made in terms of s 345A of the Criminal Procedure (Scotland) Act 1975 that the evidence of the analysis of the specimens of breath provided by the respondent was inadmissible?

The appeal was argued before the High Court on 20 November 1991.

F On 12 December 1991 the court *answered* both questions in the *affirmative, allowed* the appeal and *remitted* the case to the sheriff to proceed as accords.

The following opinion of the court was delivered by the Lord Justice Clerk (Ross):

OPINION OF THE COURT.—This is a Crown appeal. The appellant is the procurator fiscal, Inverness, and the respondent is Colin Murdoch Urquhart. The respondent went to trial in the sheriff court at Inverness on a complaint libelling a contravention of

s 5 (1) (b) of the Road Traffic Act 1988. At the end of the Crown case, the solicitor for the respondent made G a submission of no case to answer in terms of s 345A of the Criminal Procedure (Scotland) Act 1975. Having heard parties the sheriff sustained the submission and acquitted the respondent. Against that decision of the sheriff the appellant has appealed by means of a stated case.

In the case the sheriff narrates the evidence which was led on behalf of the Crown. Two constables gave evidence that on the date libelled they had been on mobile patrol when they received a radio message to H attend upon a car which was stationary near a roundabout. On arriving at the locus they discovered a car partly on the verge and partly on the road. The respondent was in the driver's seat asleep. In his hands which were between his legs was an empty half bottle of vodka. The keys were in the ignition, the engine was off although the radio was playing. One of the officers woke the accused and spoke to him. Both officers observed that his speech was slurred and his eyes glazed. He was required to provide a roadside I breath test on a breathalyser device. The specimen proved positive. The respondent was then arrested and taken to Inverness police station where in response to a requirement made by one of the constables he provided two specimens of breath for analysis on a Camic breath analyser. The lower of the readings produced was 131 microgrammes of alcohol in 100 millilitres of breath.

The submission of no case to answer was based J upon the fact that no evidence had been led that the two policemen involved in the case were in uniform at the time they administered the roadside breath test nor during the subsequent Camic procedure. The sheriff states that there was agreement between the respondent's solicitor, the procurator fiscal depute and himself that no evidence had been led that the two policemen were in uniform at the relevant time. Section 6 (1) (b) of the Road Traffic Act 1988 provides as follows: [his Lordship quoted the terms of s 6 (1) K set out supra and continued:]

The submission made by the respondent's solicitor was that since there was no evidence that the two constables were in uniform, the whole breathalyser and Camic procedure was fatally flawed. The sheriff narrates that he was referred to *Richards v West*, which concerned a breath test which an accused was required to provide by a special constable, and *Cooper v Rowlands*. The sheriff expressed the view that the question for him was whether he was entitled to infer L that the two officers were in uniform. At the end of the day the sheriff concluded that there were insufficient facts and circumstances to allow him to make the necessary inference that the two police constables were in uniform.

The advocate depute pointed out that although there were two questions in the case there was no question relating to the procedure carried out with the Camic breath analyser. The advocate depute also maintained that the sheriff and the procurator fiscal had concentrated on the wrong provisions of the Act. He stated that lack of evidence that the constable requiring the roadside breath test had been in uniform might have been a good point if the charge against the respondent had been under s 6 (4). That subsection provides: [his Lordship quoted its terms and continued:]

The advocate depute drew attention to the fact that s 7 of the Act of 1988 which deals with the provision of specimens for analysis in the police station, does not refer to s 6 and the provision of a specimen of breath in pursuance of s 6. Section 7 (1) opens with the words: [his Lordship quoted the terms of s 7 (1) set out supra and continued:] It will be observed that in the opening words of s 7, when reference is made to a constable, there is no stipulation that that constable has to be in uniform.

Put shortly the advocate depute's argument was that the sheriff had erred because he had been influenced by the former law which was to be found in the Road Traffic Act 1972, and that he had not appreciated that different provisions were now operative. The advocate depute maintained that in the present case it did not matter whether or not the constable who had required the respondent to provide a specimen of breath at the roadside was in uniform because there was a case to answer in respect that evidence had been led of his providing two specimens of breath in the police station which produced a result in excess of the permitted limit. In other words the Crown did not require to rely on the evidence of the roadside breath test in order to make out a prima facie case; they were entitled to rely on the results obtained from the Camic breath analyser in the police station so long as these results were obtained in the course of an investigation into whether an offence under s 4 or 5 had been committed.

Counsel for the respondent maintained that since there had been no direct evidence that the police constables had been in uniform, it followed that the Crown had not led evidence that the roadside breath test had been carried out in a legal manner. He maintained that that vitiated all subsequent procedures, and that the sheriff had been well founded in concluding that the later procedure had been fatally flawed because there was no evidence that the two police constables had been in uniform when the roadside breath test was obtained.

We are satisfied that the argument of the advocate depute is to be preferred. We agree with the advocate depute that the sheriff may have been misled because of the terms of the earlier legislation. Under the provisions of the Road Traffic Act 1972 as originally enacted, the requirement of a specimen of blood or urine could only be made of the person if he had been arrested under the provisions of s 5 or s 8. These provisions were however amended by the Transport Act 1981, and in the substituted s 8 (the provisions of which are now to be found in s 7 of the Act of 1988) there is no requirement that the person should have been arrested. Under the provisions of what is now

s 7 of the Act of 1988, the requirement to provide two specimens of breath for analysis can be given in the course of an investigation into whether a person has committed an offence under s 4 or 5 of the Act of 1988. Accordingly it is not necessary for the procedure in s 6 to have been followed at all provided that the procedure laid down in s 7 has been observed. We are also satisfied that there is no reason why any failure to follow the procedural requirements of s 6 should render any subsequent procedure invalid. Indeed, even if the arrest of a person under s 6 (5) should appear to be invalid, that would not, in our opinion, render invalid any procedure properly carried out under s 7. In *R v Fox* which was a case under s 6 (1) of the Road Traffic Act 1972 as substituted by s 25 (3) of and Sched 8 to the Transport Act 1981, the House of Lords held that on a true construction of s 8 (1) of the Act of 1972, a lawful arrest was not an essential prerequisite of a breath test. In his speech, Lord Fraser of Tullybelton observed that following upon the amendments made to the Act of 1972 by the Act of 1981, the divisional court had been right "in treating the fact that the appellant was in the police station because he had been unlawfully arrested merely as a historical fact, with which the court was not concerned".

For the foregoing reasons we are satisfied that the sheriff erred in concluding that the prosecution was fatally flawed in the absence of evidence that the two police constables had been in uniform at the time when the respondent was required to undergo the roadside breath test. Even though there was no evidence that the police officers were in uniform, the evidence led without objection regarding the specimens of breath provided for analysis on the Camic breath analyser, was clearly sufficient to constitute a case to answer. As we understand it, the evidence which was adduced regarding the provision of specimens of breath for analysis on the Camic breath analyser was not objected to, and having regard to the provisions of s 15 (2) of the Road Traffic Offenders Act 1988 there clearly was a case to answer.

We would only make one other point. From the sheriff's narration of the evidence it would appear that the respondent was arrested following upon his having provided a specimen which proved positive on the breathalyser. It should be noted however that in terms of s 4 (6) of the Road Traffic Act 1988 a constable may arrest a person without warrant if he has reasonable cause to suspect that that person is or has been committing an offence under that section. A constable does not require to be in uniform to exercise his right to arrest in terms of s 4 (6). In the present case having regard to the fact that the respondent was found asleep in the driver's seat of the car which was partially on the verge and partially on the road, and having regard to the fact that there was an empty half bottle of vodka in his hands, and that his speech was slurred and his eyes glazed, we are clearly of opinion that the constables would have been entitled to arrest him in terms of s 4 (6).

A For all the foregoing reasons we are satisfied that the sheriff reached the wrong conclusion in this case. We shall accordingly answer both questions in the case in the affirmative and we shall remit the case to the sheriff to proceed as accords.

Counsel for Appellant, Macdonald, QC, A-D; Solicitor, J D Lowe, Crown Agent — Counsel for Respondent, Hofford; Solicitors, Wheatley & Co (for Fleetwood & Robb, Inverness).

B

P W F

MT Group v James Howden & Co Ltd

C OUTER HOUSE

LORD CAMERON OF LOCHBROOM

26 FEBRUARY 1992

Jurisdiction — Plea of no jurisdiction — Defences on jurisdiction and on merits — Motion by defenders for order for inspection of property — Whether departure from plea of no jurisdiction — Civil Jurisdiction and Judgments Act 1982 (c 27), Sched 8, rule 6 — Rules of Court 1965, rule 83 (e).

D

Process — Commission and diligence — Examination of property — Motion by defenders for pursuers to be ordained to allow named individuals to examine property — Defence of no jurisdiction — Court not likely to be asked to determine merits of dispute — Whether competent or appropriate for motion to be granted — Administration of Justice (Scotland) Act 1972 (c 59), s 1.

Process — Sist of process — Sist sought by pursuers — Merits of dispute likely to be determined elsewhere —
E _Record not yet closed and plea of no jurisdiction to be determined — Whether appropriate for motion to be granted._

In an action of damages for breach of contract, the defenders lodged defences relating both to the jurisdiction of the court and to the merits of the action. With regard to jurisdiction, the defenders maintained that the parties had agreed that the Danish Court of Arbitration would have jurisdiction in disputes between them. The pursuers had initiated proceedings
F in the Court of Arbitration (by requiring the appointment of experts by their court), and it was agreed by the parties that the merits of the Scottish action should be decided in the Danish proceedings. The pursuers stated that the reason for raising the Scottish proceedings had been to seek arrestment and inhibition on the dependence and to facilitate the execution of any Danish decree arbitral. The defenders moved for an order in terms of s 1 of the Administration of Justice (Scotland) Act 1972 for the inspection of specified machinery, and the pursuers moved for the action to

be sisted on account of its real nature. Both motions
G were opposed. The pursuers argued, inter alia, that by lodging defences on the merits and seeking to invoke the power of the court in terms of s 1 of the 1972 Act, the defenders must be held to have departed from their plea that the Scottish court had no jurisdiction. The defenders argued that it was not appropriate for the action to be sisted prior to the closing of the record.

Held, (1) that as the defenders were intending to argue, and had not departed from, their plea of no jurisdiction and the question of jurisdiction was separate from the merits of the action, and as there
H were proceedings elsewhere concerned with the merits of the dispute and no question concerning the merits was likely to require to be resolved by the court, it was not appropriate for, and perhaps not competent for, the court to make an order in terms of s 1 of the 1972 Act, the Danish Court of Arbitration in any event being the tribunal which should be requested to make orders concerning the discovery or preservation of material (pp 411L-412D); and (2) that as the pleadings were still being adjusted, the plea of no jurisdiction
I had still to be determined and there were no special circumstances to warrant sisting the action, it would not be appropriate for the action to be sisted (p 412F-G); and defenders' motion _refused_ and pursuers' motion _refused_ in hoc statu.

Opinion, that it was competent for the courts in Scotland to make ancillary orders such as relating to diligence on the dependence even where the Scottish courts had no jurisdiction (p 411G-H).

J

Action of damages

The MT Group brought an action of damages for breach of contract against James Howden & Co Ltd. The defenders pled, inter alia, no jurisdiction. The action came before the Lord Ordinary (Lord Cameron of Lochbroom) on the motion roll on the defenders' motion for an order in terms of s 1 of the Administration of Justice (Scotland) Act 1972 and on the
K pursuers' motion for the action to be sisted pending contractually agreed arbitration proceedings in Denmark.

Statutory provisions

The Civil Jurisdiction and Judgments Act 1982 provides in Sched 8 (Rules as to Jurisdiction in Scotland):

"5.—(1) If the parties have agreed that a court is to have jurisdiction to settle any disputes which have arisen or which may arise in connection with a par-
L ticular legal relationship, that court shall have exclusive jurisdiction.

"(2) Such an agreement conferring jurisdiction shall be either in writing or evidenced in writing or, in trade or commerce, in a form which accords with practices in that trade or commerce of which the parties are or ought to have been aware. . . .

"6.—(1) Apart from jurisdiction derived from other provisions of this Schedule, a court before whom a defender enters an appearance shall have jurisdiction.

A "(2) This rule shall not apply where appearance was entered solely to contest jurisdiction, or where another court has exclusive jurisdiction by virtue of rule 4 or where rule 4 (3) applies."

The Rules of Court provide:

"83.—. . . (e) Where a defender intends to contest the jurisdiction of the court, he must—(i) lodge defences relating only to the question of jurisdiction in the first instance; and if unsuccessful, be allowed to amend his defences to defend on the substantive issues
B of the action within such time as the court may allow; or (ii) lodge defences relating to both jurisdiction and the substantive issues of the action without submitting to the jurisdiction of the court."

Cases referred to

Albyn Housing Society Ltd v Taylor Woodrow Homes Ltd, 1985 SLT 309; 1985 SC 104.
East Kilbride Development Corporation v Whatlings (Building) Ltd, 1990 SLT 492.
C *Hamlyn & Co v The Talisker Distillery* (1894) 2 SLT 12; (1894) 21 R (HL) 21.
McDougall (D & J) Ltd v Argyll & Bute District Council, 1987 SLT 7.
Redpath Dorman Long Ltd v Tarmac Construction Ltd, 1982 SLT 442; 1982 SC 14.
Sanderson (A) & Son v Armour & Co Ltd, 1922 SLT 285; 1922 SC (HL) 117.

On 26 February 1992 the Lord Ordinary *refused* the
D defenders' motion for an order under the 1972 Act and *refused* in hoc statu the pursuers' motion for a sist.

LORD CAMERON OF LOCHBROOM.—In this action the defenders sought an order in terms of s 1 (1) of the Administration of Justice (Scotland) Act 1972. The motion sought to have the pursuers ordained to give certain individuals or such other persons as the court may sanction, free access to and all necessary facilities for inspecting, surveying, pho-
E tographing and examining the "Fionia" (tunnel boring machine no 3) and the "Jutlandia" (tunnel boring machine no 4) at Sprogo, Denmark, under the possession and control of the pursuers, including those parts thereof which had been removed by the pursuers to RKS at Avallon, France, ABB, Denmark and Rexroth, Germany. At the same time I heard a similar motion by the Howden Group plc in a commercial cause which was raised by the pursuers against them at the same time as they raised the present
F action.

The nature of this action and its history to date were set out in the opinion of Lord Cullen dated 14 January 1992 when he refused a motion by the defenders for the recall of inhibition and arrestment [reported 1993 SLT 345]. Thereafter a reclaiming motion was marked against the interlocutor of Lord Cullen at the instance of the defenders. The reclaiming motion was not proceeded with. On 20 February 1992 the First Division refused the motion for review and remitted back to the Outer House to proceed as accords. There-

after defences were lodged to the action. They are directed both to the issue of jurisdiction and to the G merits of the action. A plea of no jurisdiction is stated.

The plea of no jurisdiction proceeds upon a denial of the pursuers' averment that there are no proceedings continuing in any other court between the parties concerning the subject matter of this action and that no agreement exists to prorogate the jurisdiction of any other court and further that this court has jurisdiction. In ans 10 of the defences the defenders admit the terms of art XXIX of the contract between the parties which provides for the settlement of disputes between H the parties in connection with or arising out of the contract. They further admit that the pursuers lodged an application with the Danish Court of Arbitration on 9 December 1991. However they contend that the Danish Court of Arbitration is a tribunal and therefore a court within the meaning of s 50 of the Civil Jurisdiction and Judgments Act 1982. Under reference to rule 5 of Sched 8 to that Act, the defenders contend that the Danish Court of Arbitration has exclusive I jurisdiction to settle the dispute between the parties to this action and that the Court of Session has no jurisdiction in the present action. At the hearing before me I was advised by counsel for the defenders that in fact the pursuers made the first approach to the Danish Court of Arbitration on 8 February 1991 when they requested the appointment of experts by that court for a technical appraisal of the screw conveyors on the tunnel boring machines. I did not understand counsel for the pursuers to demur to this statement. Thereafter by statement of claims dated 21 February 1991 J and 16 August 1991 two cases were instigated before the Danish Court of Arbitration by the defenders in the present action. It is a matter of agreement between parties that the issues on the merits which arise in the present action are the subject matter of the claims which are now before the Danish Court of Arbitration.

For the defenders it was submitted that the two machines named in the motion are property to which questions may arise in the Scottish proceedings. The K size of the machines and the method of their operation were such that they could only be inspected in situ. They are at present undergoing repair following a flooding incident. The defences in this action indicate the complexity of the issues which arise in the disputes between the parties. Reference was made to the averments in the summons with respect to defects and to contamination within the hydraulic systems as also to the fact that some repairs have already been carried out but others remain to be carried out upon the L machines. The matters complained of extended beyond the issue of the operation of the screw conveyors which was the subject of the pursuers' request in February 1991. It was important, counsel contended, in order that the defenders should not be prejudiced in their defences to this action that they should be entitled to inspect the two machines, more particularly to observe what repairs are still being carried out, whether they involve alterations to the machines, whether in the course of continuing repair the existence and nature of any of the alleged defects can be discovered and also what is the nature of any modifications to the machines that may have been made since their manufacture and assembly on site. Counsel explained that for a period of time until about October 1991 representatives of the defenders had been able to remain on site and observe the machines in operation and the nature of any problems which had arisen during that operation. By then experts had been appointed to the Danish Court of Arbitration for the purpose of the limited appraisal of the screw conveyors. From early in October 1991 it appeared however that representatives of the defenders had been forbidden access to the control cabinet of the machines during excavation and ring fill. I was advised that correspondence had passed between the legal representatives of the parties thereafter in an attempt to resolve the matters of access. In late November it appeared that access was being wholly refused. The matter of access was then raised by the defenders' legal representative with the Danish Court of Arbitration by letter dated 6 December 1991. On 24 January 1992 the Danish Court of Arbitration sat to consider the request by the defenders' legal representative inter alia that the pursuers give the defenders' site personnel access to the tunnel boring machines "Jutlandia" and "Fionia" situated on Sprogo under the condition that the safety rules were complied with. It appeared that before the court the request is being resisted by the pursuers' representative. That hearing is not completed. It was originally set down for further hearing on 5 February 1992 but owing to illness, the court was unable to sit on that date. A further hearing has now been set down for 4 March 1992. It is anticipated that the hearing may be completed on that date.

Counsel further maintained that since the defenders had been permitted to monitor the operation of the machines at least until about August 1991 without any opposition by the pursuers, and since the stripping and repairing of the machines which is continuing at the moment may result in the destruction of material evidence, it should be done at the sight of the defenders' representatives. It was therefore appropriate to grant the motion. There was no objection to persons carrying out such examination on behalf of the defenders being accompanied by representatives of the pursuers. It was important that the persons named in the motion were individuals who were familiar with the machines when they were originally assembled and thus were in a position, unlike third party experts, to determine what, if any, defects there were and what, if any, modifications had been made since manufacture and assembly. In particular counsel considered that the greatest priority attached to Dr Davies, and Messrs Brander, Hamilton, Hughes and Brown by reason of their positions and expertise, although in addition the first four individuals named in the motion had been present when facilities for access were available, being respectively site manager, quality engineer and two mechanical engineers. All would thus have first hand knowledge of the assembly and the operation of the machines.

In my opinion this motion falls to be determined

having regard to the fact that the defenders' position, as averred in the defences, is that in terms of rule 5 of Sched 8 to the Civil Jurisdiction and Judgments Act 1982 the Danish Court of Arbitration has exclusive jurisdiction to settle the dispute between the parties to the action. A plea of no jurisdiction is stated. Counsel for the defenders contended that if the plea was well taken, then the action should not be before this court and accordingly the pursuers should not have the benefit of the diligence effected under the warrant contained in the summons. I am doubtful if this is so. As Lord Cullen pointed out, the jurisdiction of this court can be invoked in order to give effect to an arbitration award at the conclusion of the arbitration proceedings and meantime prevent the disposal of assets to the prejudice of the claim pending in the arbitration proceedings. It does not appear to me, as at present advised, that such ancillary orders in any way detract from the exclusive nature of a court's jurisdiction to settle the dispute which has arisen between parties and which is the nature of the exclusive jurisdiction given by rule 5 of Sched 8 to the 1982 Act. However, I do not decide this matter at this juncture. Nevertheless the logic of the defenders' submissions must be that any order of this court pertaining to the merits of the action would likewise be invalidated by a finding that it had no jurisdiction to entertain the action in the first place.

Counsel for the pursuers drew attention to the terms of rule 6, and in particular para (2), of Sched 8 which provides that a defender merely by entering appearance shall not be held to have prorogated the jurisdiction of a court where appearance was entered solely to contest jurisdiction. He argued that in the present case not only have the defenders lodged defences addressed to the issue of jurisdiction but they have also done so in relation to the merits of the action. Furthermore they have sought to invoke the power of the court in terms of s 1 (1) of the Administration of Justice (Scotland) Act 1972 for the purpose of the defence on the merits. The defenders must therefore be held to have departed from their plea of no jurisdiction.

Under rule of court 83 (e) it is provided that: [his Lordship narrated the terms of the rule and continued:] Thus it is permissible to lodge defences which include averments relating both to jurisdiction and to the substantive issues of the action without submitting to the jurisdiction of the court. Thus by stating and insisting on a plea of no jurisdiction, the defender is not deprived of the right to contest the jurisdiction of this court. As counsel for the defenders here clearly stated the defenders' intention to argue their plea of no jurisdiction in limine and there are proceedings current elsewhere to which the parties to this action are party and which will determine the substantive issues averred in this action, it is not appropriate, in my opinion, for this court to pronounce an order relating to the substantive issues of the action. Indeed it may be said that such an order is not open to this court to pronounce since such issues are not before the court at present, at least until the plea is repelled. Thus it is made clear by the terms of rule of court 83 (e) (i) that

A it is open to a defender to limit his initial defence to that of jurisdiction and that he need not be required to state his defence on the substantive issues until after the court has determined the issue of jurisdiction, though by para (e) (ii) the defender is not precluded from stating his defence on the substantive issues at the initial stage, as indeed a defender was required to do under the former law. I have therefore refused the defenders' motion.

B While that is sufficient for the determination of the motion, I would add that if, as parties agree, the substantive issues fall to be decided in the Danish proceedings, then that tribunal, having jurisdiction to settle the issues in dispute, is the proper tribunal to which application should be made for the purpose of discovery or preservation of material for evidential purposes in the proceedings before it. Its rules of evidence and of procedure must regulate its proceedings and its determination, not those of this court, which can at best act only in its auxiliary capacity.

C The plea of no jurisdiction, being a preliminary defence, has the effect that the court has no power to pronounce an enforceable decree against the defenders. The questions of jurisdiction and of the merits are not bound up together in the present case. Whether or not the court has such power to pronounce a decree must be decided in limine and before any proof as to the merits of the case. Looking to the terms of s 1 (1) of the Administration of Justice (Scotland) Act 1972 it cannot be said at present that in the proceedings before this court any question is likely to

D arise in relation to the merits. Indeed both parties appear to be content that the Danish Court of Arbitration should settle the issue of the merits of the disputes between them, for not only do the defenders argue for the exclusive jurisdiction of that court, but the pursuers seek a sist of the present action for that purpose.

Counsel for the pursuers moved me to sist the present action. He did so on the basis that the present proceedings in this court were merely to facilitate

E execution of any decree arbitral that might be pronounced in the Danish proceedings and in order to do diligence. This was perfectly competent. Counsel for the defenders did not dispute that a sist might be competent in due course. He argued under reference to a well known line of cases beginning with *Hamlyn & Co v Talisker Distillery, Sanderson & Son v Armour & Co, Redpath Dorman Long Ltd v Tarmac Construction Ltd, Albyn Housing Society Ltd v Taylor Woodrow Homes Ltd, D & J McDougall Ltd v Argyll and Bute District*

F *Council* and *East Kilbride Development Corporation v Whatlings (Building) Ltd*, that in normal circumstances such a motion should not be entertained by the court until after the record was closed.

The motion is made after the point at which s 1 (1) of the Arbitration Act 1975 would be applicable has passed. Defences have been lodged. As I have already indicated, I did not agree with counsel for the pursuers that by moving their motion at this stage the defenders have effectively invoked the jurisdiction of this court under rule 6 (1) of Sched 8 to the 1982 Act on the

G ground that they have not entered appearance *solely* to contest jurisdiction. The pleadings are still at the stage of adjustment. The plea of no jurisdiction has yet to be determined. There are no special circumstances which persuade me that it will be appropriate at this stage to sist the action. A live issue presently remains to be decided in the action, leaving aside the substantive issues of the action which parties agree fall to be determined in the Danish proceedings. I have therefore refused the pursuers' motion for sist in hoc statu.

H *Counsel for Pursuers, Drummond Young, QC, Currie; Solicitors, W & J Burness, WS — Counsel for Defenders, Nimmo Smith, QC, Keen; Solicitors, Maclay Murray & Spens.*

A M

[In another action at the instance of the same pursuers against Howden Group plc in which the jurisdiction point did not arise the Lord Ordinary, on the same day, pronounced an order ordaining the pursuers to give facilities

I for examining and photographing the two named machines, subject to certain conditions. All three interlocutors were reclaimed. The reclaiming motion against the interlocutor in the other action was refused. The cross reclaiming motions in the action against James Howden & Co Ltd were both abandoned.]

J

McIntyre v Sheridan

SECOND DIVISION

THE LORD JUSTICE CLERK (ROSS), LORDS MURRAY AND MARNOCH

6 MARCH 1992

Interdict — Precision — Interdict from "disrupting,
K *impeding or otherwise interfering with" execution of warrant sale — Whether "impeding" or "interfering" required to be a physical act — Whether interdict expressed too widely to be enforceable.*

Interdict — Breach of interdict — Interdict from "disrupting, impeding or otherwise interfering with" execution of warrant sale — Respondent taking charge of crowd disrupting sale and making inflammatory speech — Whether "impeding" or "interfering" required to be a physical act — Whether breach.

L
Interdict — Breach of interdict — Penalty — Interdict against disrupting execution of warrant sale — Public defiance of court orders.

On 27 September 1991 sheriff officers obtained interim interdict preventing two individuals, Sheridan and Landells, or anyone on their behalf, (1) from attending a warrant sale at Strathclyde Regional Council premises on 1 October 1991; and (2) from disrupting, impeding or otherwise interfering with their day to day business or that of their agents or employees and the carrying out of their lawful duties, in particular the execution of the said warrant sale; and from encouraging or instructing the Inverclyde Anti-Poll Tax Union or anyone else to do so.

On 1 October 1991 when two of the sheriff officers' employees attended at the council premises in order to carry out the warrant sale, their van was attacked by a crowd which had gathered there. The police eventually restored order but the sale had to be abandoned. The sheriff officers presented a minute alleging breach of interdict by Sheridan in that, by virtue of his attendance at, and actions prior to, the proposed warrant sale, he had been in breach of the interim order. After a proof the Lord Ordinary found it established that Sheridan had attended at the premises on 1 October, had climbed onto a platform and had addressed the crowd appealing to the police not to allow the warrant sale to take place. Further, he had torn up a copy of the interdict in front of the crowd and said that as far as they were concerned there would be no sale; it was cancelled and so was every other one. The Lord Ordinary held that there had been a flagrant and calculated breach of the interdict and sentenced the respondent to six months' imprisonment.

The respondent reclaimed and argued (1) that for there to be a breach of interdict there had to be physical interference and as there had been no such physical interference on his part there had been no breach of interdict; (2) that the making of speeches at the warrant sale could not in any event amount to a breach of interdict because the interdict was expressed in very wide terms and, read strictly, might have prevented him from making a speech in another part of Scotland; and (3) that the sentence of six months' imprisonment was excessive.

Held, (1) that the words "interfere" and "impede" had to be given their ordinary and natural meaning and that there was no justification for placing a narrow interpretation on them which would require a physical element to any interference or impedance (p 418C); (2) that, in any event, in associating with and taking charge of the crowd the first respondent had added his weight to the crowd, and that this in itself was a physical act of interference (p 418D-F); (3) that the respondent's actions in tearing up the interdict could only be taken as a representation to the crowd that their purposes merited ignoring the rule of law and amounted to a breach of the order (p 418J-L); and (4) that the period of six months' imprisonment was not excessive (p 419F-G); and reclaiming motion *refused*.

Opinion reserved, on the question of whether the respondent might have breached the interdict by making a speech in another part of Scotland (p 419A).

Petition for interdict

Robert McIntyre and others, sheriff officers, petitioned for interdict against (first) Thomas Sheridan and (second) David Landells. The petitioners sought and obtained ex parte interim interdict in the following terms:

"Interdicts the respondents ad interim or anyone on their behalf (1) from attending the warrant sale at Strathclyde Regional Council premises at Turnbull Street, Glasgow on 1 October 1991; (2) from disrupting, impeding or otherwise interfering with the day to day business of the petitioners or their agents or employees and the carrying out of their lawful duties, in particular the execution of the said warrant sale; and from encouraging or instructing the Inverclyde Anti-Poll Tax Union or anyone else to do so".

The petitioners subsequently presented a minute averring breach of the interim interdict.

A proof took place on the minute and answers thereto before the Lord Ordinary (Caplan). The minuters did not insist in their case against the respondent Landells.

Cases referred to

Hunter v Wilson (1848) 10 D 893.
Murdoch v Murdoch, 1973 SLT (Notes) 13.

Textbook referred to

Burn-Murdoch, *Interdict,* paras 109, 110, 114 and 448.

On 28 January 1992 the Lord Ordinary *found* the respondent Sheridan to have been in breach of the interim interdict.

LORD CAPLAN.—The first respondent (who is now the only respondent) is Thomas Sheridan who resides at 265 Linthaugh Road, Pollok, Glasgow. By interlocutor of this court dated 27 September 1991 in a petition brought by the present minuters against Thomas Sheridan and a certain David Landells I pronounced interdict ad interim against the respondents in the petition. No caveat having been lodged the interdict was pronounced on the basis of an ex parte application. The minuters had been instructed by Strathclyde Regional Council to collect certain arrears of community charge due by a Mrs Ann Brennan of Port Glasgow and following upon a summary warrant and a poinding they were proposing to conduct a warrant sale at 11 am on 1 October 1991 within premises owned by the regional council at Turnbull Street, Glasgow. The terms of the interim interdict were essentially to interdict the respondent from attending the said warrant sale or from disrupting, impeding, or otherwise interfering with the day to day business of the petitioners and the carrying out of their lawful duties, including the execution of the said warrant sale or from encouraging or instructing others to do so.

The interdict was served personally on the respondent during the afternoon of 30 September 1991. Thus there was a measure of delay in serving the interdict but there is a perfectly understandable reason for this. When the minuters' Edinburgh solicitors were first instructed to present the interdict, they were informed that the warrant sale would take place within the regional council's premises and they erroneously

A assumed that this meant Glasgow City Chambers. Therefore when the interlocutor was granted on Friday 27 September, the interlocutor I pronounced gave the location of the warrant sale as being the City Chambers. The error was discovered when the minuters were preparing to have the interim interdict served and on the morning of Monday 30 September I amended the interim interdict to show the correct location of the warrant sale. When counsel for the parties were addressing me, I was informed that there was no dispute that the interim interdict had been B pronounced, that it applied to the first respondent, that at the time of the events complained of it was in force, and that the respondent was at that time aware of its terms.

The events which the minuters complain of occurred in the morning of 1 October 1991 prior to the proposed warrant sale. The minuters led four witnesses in support of their version of events, namely Mr Robert McIntyre and Mrs Freda Reilly, both partners of Abernethy McIntyre & Co, Hugh Doherty C who is the senior press officer of Strathclyde Regional Council and Inspector John Cattell who is second in command of the policemen present at the incident. These witnesses gave a fairly consistent account of events and I had no difficulty in accepting the significant features of their evidence.

Two video recordings were played to me. One was a short excerpt from a BBC programme. The other was a longer recording taken by the police at the time D of the incident. The BBC programme was very short and the police recording neither gave a total overview of what was happening nor did it cover more than about half of the time occupied by the incident. However these videos gave important confirmation to certain points made by the four witnesses I have mentioned.

The effects of Mrs Brennan to be sold at the sale were five items of furniture with an appraised value of £360. At Turnbull Street there is an enclosed yard E where the sale was to take place and the effects to be sold were in a van which had been left overnight in the yard. Robert McIntyre who was proposing to conduct the auction sale and Freda Reilly who was to assist him arrived at the yard early in the morning of 1 October. After checking the sale items they sat in the cabin of the van. About 9.50 am 30 or 40 people came into the yard. They battered the side of the van. They let down the tyres of the van. They began to shake the van to and fro from side to side and someone asked the F crowd to stand clear of one side of the van, giving the occupants of the van the impression that the intention was to overturn the van. Mr McIntyre managed to avert that possibility by edging the van forward a short distance so that it stood between two pillars. £1,400 worth of damage was done to the van by these actions. During this phase of the incident Mr McIntyre and Mrs Reilly were terrified. Mr McIntyre pumped his horn frantically, hoping to attract police assistance. Meanwhile the crowd in the yard were increasing.

Inspector Cattell was in Turnbull Street outside the yard and he had a sizeable police contingent of about G 60 officers at his disposal. When he saw the size of the crowd pouring into the yard, he instructed some of his policemen to follow them in. After a struggle the policemen who entered the yard were able to interpose themselves between the van and the assembled crowd. They were also able to restore order. The respondent, according to his own evidence, entered the yard towards the rear of the crowd. He stated that at the time there was some shouting, there was a clatter of metal against metal, the van was moving to and fro H and its horn was sounding. Eventually there was a crowd of about 200-250 people in the yard.

After the police had surrounded the van the crowd became more pacific particularly as the sale was not due to take place for about an hour and no other action was imminent. Many of the assembled crowd carried placards protesting against the sale, some chanted "No no warrant sale" and shouts of "Scum" were directed at the two sheriff officers. There was some waving of fists and some isolated scuffling. During this stage of I the incident the respondent stood on some kind of platform on a number of occasions and addressed the crowd. He was the only person present who thus addressed the crowd. On one occasion he said: "We would appeal to the polis not to protect these people. These people are nothing but scum and they shouldnae allow the warrant sale to take place". At another point of time in addressing the crowd the respondent held up a piece of paper and said: "This interdict is to stop me and every single one of youse J from being here today. As far as I'm concerned this is what they can do with their bloody interdict". The respondent then tore the paper he was holding and threw the bits into the crowd. There was some division of view as to the precise expletive that Mr Sheridan used when he referred to the interdict but I hardly think this is important. At another point of time Mr Sheridan said to the crowd: "The sale that they're going to try and carry out is due to take place at 11 o'clock. That's one hour and five minutes. As far K as we're concerned there will be no sale". The witnesses got the impression that the respondent was a person the crowd looked to for leadership. When he addressed the crowd he spoke with an obvious degree of aggression. The crowd listened attentively and responded to him enthusiastically. Moreover members of the crowd who appeared to be active in the demonstration conferred with him from time to time.

As the time for the sale approached some members L of the crowd began again to concentrate their attention in the direction of the van and the mood of a section of the crowd became distinctly more menacing. Mr McIntyre heard a voice shout: "If they try to take the furniture out of the van", although because of the noise from the crowd he could not hear the end of the sentence. Mr McIntyre consulted with Inspector Cattell, Inspector Cattell also adjudged the mood of the crowd to be menacing and he informed the sheriff officers that although he could ensure that they would not be murdered he could not guarantee that they might not suffer some injury if the sale were to proceed. It was therefore decided to cancel the sale and Mr Doherty announced this through a megaphone about 10.50 am. The crowd responded to the news with jubilation. Given the numbers of persons gathered at the yard and the threatening behaviour that some elements had shown themselves to be capable of, there was no practical possibility that the sale could have taken place.

Even after the sale was cancelled the crowd remained in the yard. The respondent again addressed the crowd and said: "When this van goes out of the yard we're prepared to go out of the yard. What we are saying loud and clear is that this warrant sale is cancelled and so is every other one. Let's go back to all the housing estates and all the colleges and let's build the campaign. If any of these people turn up in the Polloks, Drumchapels, the Castlemilks we'll chase them to hell". Thereafter Mr Sheridan approached Inspector Cattell and said that he could arrange to allow the van to leave the yard but the crowd would not leave before the van. Mr McIntyre signified he was prepared to drive the van away. Thereafter the respondent once more addressed the crowd and said: "We've got a guarantee now folks. They're going to take the van away. If we let them get out of here the van's away. The warrant sale's off so we can get everybody this end." After Mr Sheridan spoke the crowd cleared a path for the van and Mr McIntyre drove it away.

Only Mr Sheridan gave evidence on his own behalf. He is 27 years of age. He accepted that he was the chairman of the Scottish Anti-Poll Tax Federation and that this organisation had arranged the assembly of the crowd at Turnbull Street, although it was said that this had been done before the interdict had been received. The interdict had been received by Mr Sheridan about 3.15 pm on 30 September and this had angered him because it did not leave him enough time to get it recalled. The respondent said that he personally had never interfered with the van, although he did not deny that he had made speeches at least equivalent to those attributed to him. In essence his position was that his attendance and activities at Turnbull Street were simply a legitimate, political protest. He claimed that he had not called on the crowd to stop the warrant sale. As he put it: "I said nothing as specific as that." After the incident he approached the police because everyone was saying that they were not going to leave the yard until the van had left. People were telling him that they were frightened that the warrant sale might be held after they had left. Mr Sheridan accepted that people do tend to listen to what he says. The respondent accepted that the crowd had been directing chants of "Scum" at the sheriff officers and he said that such a chant is what one would expect from "an angry individual". Mr Sheridan claimed that if the warrant sale had proceeded his federation would have ensured that any bids would have been of a ludicrous nature. The respondent said he viewed "his attendance at the sale" as being in a personal capacity. He was not going

to play "a key role" in any interference which took place. The respondent claimed that he had torn up the interdict to demonstrate his contempt for the manner in which it had been served. He ended his evidence by declaring that it was obvious from his statements and acts that he had no intention of being bound by the interdict.

Counsel for the minuter argued that it was plain from the evidence that the respondent had breached all aspects of interim interdict. He had attended at the sale. He had interfered with and impeded the business of the petitioners. He had also encouraged others to do so. The terms of an interim interdict should be read in a practical way and not like a deed of entail (Burn-Murdoch, p 456).

Counsel for the respondent argued that the terms of the interdict must be strictly construed contra proferentem. I was referred to *Murdoch v Murdoch*. Interdict is a personal remedy. The respondent had not been interdicted as chairman of the Scottish Anti-Poll Tax Federation or as part of a crowd. An intention to violate an interdict or a mere attempt to contravene its terms does not constitute a breach of interdict. I was referred to *Hunter v Wilson*. Mr Sheridan had not attended the warrant sale since under the relevant legislation this was not due to commence until 11 am. I was referred to the relevant legislation and to Burn-Murdoch on *Interdict*, paras 109, 110 and 114. In relation to the remainder of the interdict the respondent had not impeded the sheriff officers. He had not physically impeded or interfered with them. The minuters required to prove that he had personally intervened in a physical fashion and they had failed to do so. It was not a breach of interdict to make a speech or participate in a political protest. The crowd had already assembled and would have interrupted the sale whatever the respondent had done. It was not shown that he personally had contributed to any impeding of the activities of the petitioners.

In my view the actions of the respondent amounted to a flagrant and calculated breach of interim interdict. Counsel for the respondent argued that it cannot be contended that the respondent attended the warrant sale because the sale was not due to begin until 11 am. This is certainly an arguable submission because it is at least possible that the respondent could have left the yard at 10.55 am. However, I need form no concluded view on the matter since I have no difficulty in deciding that the respondent impeded and interfered with the petitioners' representatives as they carried out their lawful duties. He also encouraged others thus to interfere and impede. It can scarcely be contested that the crowd gathered in the courtyard at Turnbull Street impeded and interfered with the sheriff officers in the conduct of their business. Indeed the effect of such interference was that the warrant sale had to be cancelled. Nor can it be disputed that the crowd had gathered with the object of stopping the sale. Handbills had been distributed prior to 1 October by the Anti-Poll Tax Federation urging members of the public to stop the warrant sale. As Mr Sheridan

A himself volunteered, after the sale had been cancelled the crowd would not disperse because people were saying that if the crowd went away the sale might take place. What clearer indication could there be that the object of the crowd was to stop the sale? The respondent is quite mistaken if he considered that before it could be said that he had impeded or interfered with the sheriff officers it had to be shown that he had personally interfered with them in a physical manner. One impedes or interferes with sheriff officers if one does anything calculated and likely to obstruct the

B conduct of their lawful activities. To a large extent a crowd or mob gathers its intimidatory character by force of numbers. Thus if a person deliberately attaches himself to a crowd bent upon impeding sheriff officers then at the simplest level, adding weight to the mob can itself be an act of interference when this is done with a view to associating oneself with the activities of those assembled.

However, in this case the activities of the respon-
C dent go beyond mere attachment to the crowd. He knew that the crowd contained elements who were unruly and aggressive. He accepts that he had entered the yard while there were violent activities taking place around the van. Nevertheless, aware of the potential of a section of the crowd for aggression, the respondent addressed the crowd in a manner which could only be described as inflammatory both in content and manner of delivery. He asked the police to withdraw protection from sheriff officers who had
D recently been the subject of vicious attack. He declared that no warrant sale would take place. By declaring that "The sale they're going to try to carry out is due to take place at 11 o'clock", the respondent was manifestly inferring that difficulties would be placed in the way of the intention to carry out the sale. The respondent contemptuously tore up what appeared to be the interim interdict which could only be taken as a representation to the crowd that the crowd's purposes merited ignoring the rule of law. Mr Sheridan obviously had influence over the crowd. The
E response of the crowd in the videoed scenes makes that quite clear. He was able at the end of the incident to get the crowd to clear a path for the van and he even volunteered to do this. Put at its lowest Mr Sheridan's words were predictably likely to cause the sheriff officers serious apprehension as to their safety and this in itself would interfere with their work. However, I have no doubt that what he said and what he did encouraged the crowd to continue in its efforts to hinder and impede the sheriff officers. He plainly rein-
F forced the determination of the crowd to maintain its attempts to stop the sale. As the only person who addressed the crowd, he chose deliberately to give them a lead. Mr Sheridan claims that he was angry because he did not have a sufficient opportunity to have the interim interdict recalled. That is absolutely no excuse for ignoring an order of the court. Indeed he is extremely sanguine if he imagines that any court in Scotland would ever tolerate activities which result in physical interference with the lawful business of persons specifically appointed to act as officers of the

court itself. I should state quite clearly that to interfere aggressively with officers of court going about their G lawful business is in itself a crime under the law of Scotland and that fact should be carefully considered by the respondent and those who may be tempted to repeat what happened at Turnbull Street. In a democracy such as ours there are many forms of political protest which are available, but ignoring court orders and obstructing sheriff officers are not among their number.

I therefore find the breach of interdict set out in the minute proved and sustain the minuters' plea in law. H I shall grant decree declaring that there has been a breach of the interim interdict by the respondent.

Eo die, after affording counsel for the respondent Sheridan an opportunity to state any matters in mitigation, the Lord Ordinary *adjudged* him to be imprisoned for six months.

LORD CAPLAN.—In the opinion which I deli-
vered at the conclusion of the proof I stated my I reasons for finding the respondent Thomas Sheridan guilty of breach of interdict. After I had announced that finding, counsel for Mr Sheridan was given an opportunity to state any matters which he wanted me to consider in mitigation of penalty but he declared that he had been specifically instructed to say nothing. I considered that Mr Sheridan's offence had very serious implications. His actions had been deliberate and calculated. His was not the case of an individual acting impulsively in pursuance of some private J matter but rather he had chosen publicly to challenge the authority of the courts. He flagrantly flouted the interdict of the court in front of a crowd which he knew contained violent and disorderly elements. He must have known that his challenge to the authority of the law would be likely to receive widespread publicity. He actively participated in a crowd and in activities which prevented sheriff officers from going about their lawful business as officers of the court. Given the whole circumstances I considered that Mr K Sheridan's conduct merited a sentence of six months' imprisonment. When I imposed that sentence I indicated to Mr Sheridan that had it been shown that he had been directly involved in the serious violence directed against the sheriff officers at the beginning of the incident I should have imposed a heavier sentence.

The respondent reclaimed. L

Reclaiming motion
The respondent submitted the following grounds of appeal:

(1) That upon a true construction of its terms, the first respondent did not breach the interim interdict granted on 27 September 1991 as averred by the minuters in that (a) he did not physically impede or interfere in the execution of any warrant sale to be carried out in Turnbull Street, Glasgow on 1 October

1991 or in the day to day business of the minuters or
A the carrying out of their lawful duties on said date; (b)
in the speeches made by him against warrant sales on
said date, he did not instruct or encourage any other
persons to impede or interfere in the day to day business of the minuters or the carrying out of their lawful
duties.

(2) That esto the first respondent was in breach of
the interim interdict, the sentence of six months'
imprisonment was excessive having regard to (a) his
non-physical involvement other than by his presence
B in Turnbull Street, aforesaid on said date; (b) the non-
interference by the crowd or any part of the crowd
whilst the first respondent was present and, in particular, whilst and after he addressed them; and (c) his
right, subject to the terms of interim interdict to
express lawfully his opposition to the use of warrant
sales to enforce payment of arrears of the community
charge.

The reclaiming motion was heard before the Second
C Division on 6 March 1992.

Eo die the court *refused* the reclaiming motion.

The following opinion of the court was delivered by
the Lord Justice Clerk (Ross):

OPINION OF THE COURT.—This is a reclaiming motion against an interlocutor of the Lord Ordinary dated 28 January 1992 in which the Lord
Ordinary found that the first respondent had breached
D the interim interdict granted on 27 September 1991
and adjudged the first respondent to be imprisoned for
a period of six months. This interlocutor was pronounced following upon a proof which took place on
a minute and answers. In the minute the minuters
refer to a petition presented by them, and to the fact
that on 27 September 1991 the Lord Ordinary
pronounced interim interdict in the following terms:
[his Lordship quoted the terms of the interlocutor set
out supra and continued:]
E
The minute contains further averments to the effect
that in defiance of the interlocutor the respondents
(and this includes the first respondent) attended said
sale and impeded the petitioners from carrying out the
sale. Answers were lodged to the minute and subsequently a proof was heard on the minute and answers.
In the course of the proof the minuters intimated that
they no longer insisted in the minute in respect of the
second respondent who was assoilzied from the first
F crave of the minute. After having heard the proof
adduced and having been addressed by counsel for the
parties, the Lord Ordinary held that the first respondent had breached the interim interdict, and he
adjudged him to be imprisoned as already mentioned.

In challenging that decision of the Lord Ordinary
the first respondent put forward two grounds of
appeal. These were in the following terms: [his Lordship narrated the terms of the grounds of appeal set
out supra and continued:]

In presenting the appeal counsel for the first respon-

dent explained that there was no real dispute on the
facts and that he accepted the narration of the facts G
contained in the Lord Ordinary's opinion dated 28
January 1992. His principal submission was that there
had been no breach of interdict because there had been
no physical interference on the part of the first respondent. He submitted that there was no evidence of
direct interference with the petitioners on the part of
the first respondent, and no proof that the crowd had
been encouraged by him to interfere with the minuters
or their employees in carrying out their lawful duties.
He stressed that on the description of the facts given H
by the Lord Ordinary, it was clear that any violence
had taken place before the arrival of the first respondent, and that any intimidation of the sheriff officers
had occurred before the first respondent's arrival at
the scene. Counsel explained that the first respondent
did not dispute that he had made speeches to the
crowd, and that the crowd had listened to him, but he
submitted that there was insufficient material to
justify the Lord Ordinary in concluding that there had
been any breach of interdict. He submitted that before I
there could be interference there required to be on the
part of the first respondent some physical activity, and
he maintained that there had been no physical intervention on the part of the first respondent. He stressed
that making speeches could not in itself constitute a
breach of the interim interdict, because the interim
interdict was expressed in very wide terms, and read
strictly might have prevented the first respondent
from making a speech in another part of Scotland in
which he attacked the holding of warrant sales.   J

Counsel for the first respondent recognised that the
fact that the interim interdict also struck at the
encouragement of others to interfere with the day to
day business of the sheriff officers and the carrying out
of their lawful duties made it more difficult for him,
but he maintained that the evidence was insufficient to
justify the conclusion that the first respondent had
encouraged others to act in that way.

Counsel for the minuters, on the other hand, main- K
tained that the Lord Ordinary had been fully entitled
to hold breach of interdict established. She maintained
that it was erroneous to contend that for interference
there required to have been some physical act; so far
as encouragement was concerned she maintained that
one had to consider the terms of the speeches made by
the first respondent and also the effect which they had
upon the crowd. She then proceeded to rehearse the
evidence referred to by the Lord Ordinary and at the
end of the day submitted that there had been no error L
on his part.

On the basis of the facts which the Lord Ordinary
found proved, we are satisfied that he was fully
entitled to conclude that there had been breach of
interdict. We are not persuaded that before the first
respondent could be held to have interfered with the
day to day business of the sheriff officers or their
employees in the carrying out of their lawful duties, it
was necessary to show that he had carried out some
physical act. We agree with counsel for the minuters

that the word "interfere" should be given its ordinary
A and natural meaning. There is no justification for
limiting that to physical interference. In the *Oxford
English Dictionary* one of the meanings of the verb
"interfere" is stated to be: "Of persons and things: To
come into non-physical collision or contact, to clash in
opinions, tendencies, etc". Other meanings in the
Oxford English Dictionary include: "Of persons: to
meddle with; to interpose and take part in something,
especially without having the right to do so; to
intermeddle", and: "To interpose, take part, so as to
B affect some action; to intervene".

Counsel for the minuters also drew attention to the
definition in the *Oxford English Dictionary* of
"impede". The definition includes: "To retard in
progress or action by putting obstacles in the way; to
obstruct; to hinder; to stand in the way of". She also
pointed out that in that dictionary the verb "obstruct"
has inter alia the following definition: "To interrupt,
render difficult, or retard the passage or progress of;
to impede, hinder, or retard (a person or thing in its
C motion)".

We agree with counsel for the minuters that the
words "impede" and "interfere" should be given their
ordinary and natural meaning, and that there is no
justification for placing some narrow interpretation
upon them as counsel for the first respondent
suggested. In particular we are satisfied that interference need not have a physical element. However,
although that is so, we are inclined to the view that in
D the present case there was in any event a physical
element to the interference by the first respondent.
The Lord Ordinary makes it plain in his opinion that
the first respondent himself accepted that he entered
the yard towards the rear of the crowd at a time when
there was shouting, a clatter of metal against metal,
and the van was being moved to and fro with its horn
sounding. This accordingly must have been towards
the end of the stage when the crowd was behaving in
a violent manner towards the sheriff officers in the
E van. Having arrived there it is plain from the Lord
Ordinary's findings that the first respondent proceeded to associate himself with the crowd and indeed
to take charge of the crowd. He addressed the crowd,
and he was the only person to address the crowd.
Witnesses got the impression that the first respondent
was a person to whom the crowd looked for leadership. When he addressed the crowd before the
decision to cancel the sale was made he spoke with an
obvious degree of aggression and the crowd listened
F attentively to him and responded enthusiastically. In
these circumstances we are of opinion that the Lord
Ordinary would have been entitled to conclude that
there had been a physical element in the first respondent's interference with the day to day business of the
minuters and the carrying out of their lawful duties.

As it was in his opinion the Lord Ordinary
expressed the view that an individual impeded or
interfered with sheriff officers if he did anything
calculated and likely to obstruct the conduct of their
lawful activities. He pointed out that to a large extent

a crowd or mob gathers its intimidatory character by
force of numbers and that if a person deliberately G
attaches himself to a crowd bent upon impeding
sheriff officers, then at the simplest level, adding
weight to the mob or crowd can itself be an act of
interference when this is done with a view to associating oneself with the activities of those assembled. We
agree with that expression of opinion by the Lord
Ordinary. Moreover, as the Lord Ordinary himself
recognised, the activities of the first respondent went
beyond mere attachment to the crowd. As we have
already observed, the first respondent appears to have H
assumed leadership of the crowd, and to have been
treated by the crowd as their leader. Indeed, when one
has regard to the speeches made by the first respondent to the crowd, we are satisfied that there was
ample material to justify the conclusion that the first
respondent not only impeded or interfered with the
sheriff officers in their day to day business and the
carrying out of their lawful duties, but also
encouraged others to do the same.

When he addressed the crowd he at one stage stated: I
"We would appeal to the polis not to protect these
people. These people are nothing but scum and they
shouldnae allow the warrant sale to take place".

At another point when addressing the crowd the
first respondent held up a piece of paper and said:
"This interdict is to stop me and every single one of
youse from being here today. As far as I'm concerned
this is what they can do with their bloody interdict".
The first respondent then tore the paper he was J
holding and threw the bits into the crowd. At another
point of time the first respondent addressed the crowd
as follows: "The sale that they're going to try and
carry out is due to take place at 11 o'clock. That's one
hour and five minutes. As far as we're concerned there
will be no sale".

We agree with the Lord Ordinary that the manner
in which the first respondent addressed the crowd
could properly be described as inflammatory both in
content and in manner of delivery. By declaring: "The K
sale they're going to try to carry out is due to take
place at 11 o'clock", and: "As far as we're concerned
there will be no sale", the first respondent was plainly
inferring that difficulties would and should be placed
in the way of the intention to carry out the sale. We
also agree with the Lord Ordinary that the first
respondent's action in tearing up what appeared to be
the interim interdict could only be taken as a representation to the crowd that their purposes merited ignoring the rule of law. The Lord Ordinary mentions that L
at the end of his evidence, the first respondent
declared that it was obvious from his statements and
acts that he had no intention of being bound by the
interdict.

In these circumstances we are quite satisfied that the
Lord Ordinary was well founded in concluding that
there had been what he described as "a flagrant and
calculated breach of interim interdict". The findings
made by the Lord Ordinary fully support the conclusion at which he arrived, and counsel for the first

respondent failed to persuade us that any error could
A be detected in the Lord Ordinary's reasoning. As
regards counsel's criticisms of the width of the interim
interdict, it is unnecessary for us to express any view
upon the question of whether the first respondent
might have breached the interdict by making a speech
against warrant sales in another part of Scotland. The
speeches upon which the minuter founds were
speeches which were made at the place where the
warrant sale was to take place.

B Counsel's second ground of appeal was that the
period of imprisonment of six months was excessive.
Under reference to the second ground of appeal, he
contended that it was excessive having regard to the
non-physical involvement of the first respondent, the
non-interference by the crowd whilst he was present,
and his right to express lawfully his opposition to the
use of warrant sales. We are quite satisfied that there
is no merit in this ground of appeal. As we have
already observed there was a real physical element in
the first respondent's involvement. In any event even
C if his involvement could properly be categorised as
non-physical, what he did was to commit a flagrant
and calculated breach of interim interdict. Although
the main violence appears to have taken place just
before the first respondent arrived, there can be no
doubt that the crowd continued to behave in an
intimidatory manner whilst he was present, and the
speeches which he made would certainly have
encouraged them to do so. We entirely accept that the
first respondent, if so advised, is entitled to express
D lawfully his opposition to the use of warrant sales to
enforce payments of arrears of the community charge,
but that is, as the ground of appeal recognises, subject
to the terms of the interim interdict.

In his supplementary opinion the Lord Ordinary
explains that the first respondent's actions on the day
in question had been deliberate and calculated, and
that he had chosen publicly to challenge the authority
of the courts. He flagrantly flouted the interim inter-
E dict pronounced by the court in front of a crowd
which he knew contained violent and disorderly
elements. Not only that but he actively participated in
the crowd, and assumed leadership of the crowd.

Counsel for the first respondent himself recognised
that if the Lord Ordinary was well founded in concluding that there had been a flagrant and calculated
breach of interim interdict, then civil imprisonment
was well nigh inevitable. He urged us however to substitute a lesser period for the period of six months
F selected by the Lord Ordinary.

We are satisfied that the Lord Ordinary was fully
entitled to select a period of six months as the period
of imprisonment in this case. We fully agree with the
Lord Ordinary that if the evidence had shown that the
first respondent had been directly involved in the
serious violence directed against the sheriff officers at
the beginning of the incident a heavier sentence would
have been called for. Nothing which counsel for the
first respondent said persuaded us that a period of six
months in the circumstances could be regarded as

excessive. For these reasons we refuse the reclaiming
motion at the instance of the first respondent and G
adhere to the interlocutor of the Lord Ordinary of 28
January 1992.

*Counsel for Minuters and Respondents, Dorrian; Soli-
citors, Drummond Miller, WS — Counsel for First
Respondent and Reclaimer, Batchelor; Solicitors, David
Clark & Co.*

D A K
H

Mitchell v Mitchell

OUTER HOUSE
LORD CAMERON OF LOCHBROOM
5 NOVEMBER 1992
I

*Husband and wife — Divorce — Financial provision —
Periodical allowance — Variation of award made prior
to coming into force of Family Law (Scotland) Act 1985
— Competency of varying both level and duration of
periodical allowance — Payer alleged to have voluntarily
altered his financial position — Divorce (Scotland) Act
1976 (c 39), s 5 (4) — Family Law (Scotland) Act 1985
(c 37), s 28 (3).*

A woman was divorced from her husband in 1976 J
and awarded a periodical allowance. The periodical
allowance was subsequently increased to £23 per
week. The former husband enrolled a motion to have
the periodical allowance reduced for a set period of
time followed by a further reduction to nil. He had
taken early retirement and had also undertaken certain
financial obligations on behalf of his mother. The
woman questioned the competency of the order
sought. She also argued that her former husband had
voluntarily altered his financial position.
K

Held, (1) that it was competent for the court to
make a variation in the level of a periodical allowance
granted under the 1976 Act at the same time as fixing
a limited duration of payment of the periodical
allowance (p 421A-B); (2) that no sinister interpretation could be placed upon the former husband's
actings (p 421C-E); but (3) that while it was reasonable
that some final limit should be put upon the liability
to pay periodical allowance, the woman was entitled to
a lengthy period in which to adjust to the changed L
financial arrangements (p 421G); and decree *pronounced* reducing periodical allowance to £10 per week
until 30 April 1994, when the award to cease.

Action of divorce

Helen Mitchell raised an action of divorce against
her husband Robert Mitchell in which decree of
divorce was pronounced on 29 October 1976. She was

A also awarded custody, aliment and a periodical allowance. The periodical allowance was subsequently increased to £23 per week, the last increase having been made on 29 April 1986. The defender enrolled a motion for a variation of the award on account of a material change in his financial circumstances. He sought a reduction to nil after a period of reduced payments.

The case came before the Lord Ordinary (Lord Cameron of Lochbroom) on the motion roll.

B **Case referred to**
Smith v Smith, 1988 SLT 840.

Statutory provisions

The Divorce (Scotland) Act 1976 provides:

"5.—. . . (4) Any order made under this section relating to the payment of a periodical allowance may, on an application by or on behalf of either party to the marriage (or his executor) on a change of circumstances, be varied or recalled by a subsequent order."

C

The Family Law (Scotland) Act 1985 provides:

"28.—. . . (3) Nothing in subsection (2) above [repeals] shall affect the operation of section 5 (orders for financial provision) of the Divorce (Scotland) Act 1976 in relation to an action for divorce brought before the commencement of this Act; but in the continued operation of that section the powers of the court — (a) to make an order for payment of periodical allowance D under subsection (2) thereof; and (b) to vary such an order under subsection (4) thereof, shall include power to make such an order for a definite or an indefinite period or until the happening of a specified event."

On 5 November 1992, his Lordship *varied* the periodical allowance by reducing it to £10 per week and *ordered* that it be paid until 30 April 1994.

LORD CAMERON OF LOCHBROOM.—The defender was divorced from the pursuer on 29 October E 1976. There were then four children of the marriage. Two of these were under 16 years of age. The pursuer was found entitled to custody of the children with aliment for each child until 16 years of age. In addition, she was awarded a periodical allowance of £6 per week payable until remarriage or death. The youngest child was 16 on 16 July 1981. Since decree of divorce the periodical allowance has been varied on several occasions. The last variation was on 29 April 1986. Payment of £23 per week was then ordered. The F parties were married in 1955. Accordingly the marriage which lasted for some 21 years, has now been terminated for some 16 years.

The defender was employed by British Telecommunications as a telephone engineer until 5 June 1992 when he took voluntary retirement. Prior to doing so, he had been earning about £1,375 net per month. I was advised that in April 1986 he had been earning between £650 and £700 net per month. At that time he was living with his mother and was paying about £130 per week for bed and board. More

recently he has moved out to live with another woman. He continues to give his mother a monthly allowance G of £162 which is dedicated to paying the mortgage on his mother's house. She is a widow and elderly. Upon retirement the defender became entitled to a capital payment of some £23,800 and a continuing pension, presently in the sum of £605 net per month. Some £20,000 of the capital sum has been invested. It presently yields an income of £75 net per month. Some £3,500 was distributed by him by way of a gift to his mother and the surviving children of the marriage. The balance was used to reduce his lia- H bilities to the bank and otherwise.

The defender presently lives in, and shares the expenses of, the house owned by his cohabitee. These include payments of £150 per month, being one half of the monthly payment on the mortgage on the house, and £118 per month, being one half of the premium on the related endowment policy. In addition monthly payments totalling some £80 are made for various outstanding loan accounts for house improvements and household goods. He also pays £70 per I month to reduce the outstanding debit balance upon a Giro bank account presently overdrawn to the extent of just under £1,300. These payments, together with his further necessary household payments, amount to and account for the whole of his present income.

Counsel invited me to grant the motion in its terms. It had been framed in such a manner as to give time for the pursuer to adjust to a reduction of the periodical allowance to nil by incorporating a reduced J payment for a sufficiently long period to enable this to happen in a reasonable manner. This could competently be done within the provisions of s 5 of the Divorce (Scotland) Act 1976 and s 28 (3) of the Family Law (Scotland) Act 1985. Counsel also referred to *Smith v Smith* where, at 1988 SLT, p 841L, the Lord Justice Clerk said: "Since the present action was an action for divorce brought before the commencement of the Act of 1985, s 5 of the Act of 1976 continues to apply to the making of an order for periodical K allowance or the variation of such an order, the only difference being that the court is now empowered to make an order for a definite or indefinite period or until the happening of a specified event. . . . Having regard to the terms of s 5 of the Act of 1976, it is clear that what the court has to have regard to are the respective means of the parties and all the circumstances of the case."

Counsel for the pursuer in opposing the motion, criticised what he called the "restructured financial L arrangements" whereby the defender had taken voluntary retirement when it was not necessary for him to do so. He had also voluntarily undertaken to meet his mother's mortgage payments, though under no legal obligation to do so since a child was no longer bound to aliment a needy parent. In addition he voluntarily undertook to pay towards his cohabitee's mortgage. The cohabitee herself earned £488 per month net as documents in process showed. The pursuer was in employment and earned between £500 to £580 net per month. She had regular outgoings of some £300 per month, including mortgage payments of £155 per month. There was no justification, counsel said, for a variation and in any event none for a variation to nil. Counsel also questioned, in the light of the limited power given to the court in s 28 (3) of the Act of 1985, the competency of the motion which sought to vary an award of periodical allowance in predetermined stages to nil.

In my opinion, the court is now able, on a motion to vary an award of periodical allowance, to determine that the award should continue only for a fixed period and further determine that within that period the award should be at a level different from the award subsisting at the date when the motion is heard. I note that the terms of s 28 (3) of the Act of 1985 provide that the power to vary a periodical allowance "shall *include*" (my emphasis) "power . . . to make such an order for a definite period".

In the present case it was not in dispute that both parties had been in employment during the marriage, the pursuer as an auxiliary nurse, and that both had continued employment after the divorce. It was a relatively lengthy marriage. The surviving children are now adult. The award of periodical allowance when made was pronounced until the pursuer's remarriage or death. The court may intervene however in particular circumstances in any case to impose a limit to the period during which the award would be payable short of remarriage or death (*Smith v Smith*). In the present case the defender has undertaken certain financial obligations voluntarily, by way of mortgage payments, at a level which extends his outgoings materially. I accept that his circumstances changed markedly in June 1992 and that it would be appropriate to consider a variation of the periodical allowance in these circumstances. The fact that retirement was voluntary may, in certain circumstances, have a sinister reflection upon a party's motives. In the present case no suggestion was made that the defender had a long working life potentially ahead of him. He offers to pay £10 per week, that is about £40 per month, for a limited period. I am persuaded that having regard to the respective means of the parties which approximate much more closely than they did before June 1992, such a figure is not unreasonable. But I have in mind that the defender, unlike the pursuer, has now some free capital assets from which he derives an income, and to which he could apply. The question is whether that level of award should continue for a definite or indefinite period. In the latter case, it would then be left open to the parties to return to the court at some later stage if there was a further material change of circumstance. But the defender's working life is now over. It may well be that shortly the pursuer's will also be. There is no suggestion that the parties' respective lifestyles were or are materially different one from the other. However, put in broad terms, the defender's contribution by way of periodical allowance since 1986 has amounted to what is a very substantial proportion of the pursuer's present monthly outgoings for her mortgage payments. I consider that while it can reasonably be said that some final limit should be now put upon the defender's contribution to the pursuer's support, there must be a reasonably long period for the adjustment in the pursuer's finances occasioned by a change in the present arrangements to be absorbed. In my opinion, looking to all the circumstances, a period of 18 months from the granting of motion would be appropriate. I shall therefore make an order varying the award of periodical allowance by reducing the amount to £10 per week, but will make that award continue until 30 April 1994.

Counsel for Pursuer, H K Small; Solicitors, Balfour & Manson, Nightingale & Bell — Counsel for Defender, Kinroy; Solicitors, Tods Murray, WS.

A R W Y

Bell v Lothiansure Ltd

SECOND DIVISION
THE LORD JUSTICE CLERK (ROSS),
LORDS MURRAY AND CULLEN
1 FEBRUARY 1991

Insurance — Professional indemnity insurance — Construction of contract — Liability to indemnify insurance brokers against negligence excluded where claim arose from insolvency of insurance company — Whether proper exclusion clause — Fraudulently operated insurance company going into liquidation — Whether insurance company within meaning of exclusion clause — Members of public having purchased policies through brokers' negligence — Whether their claims arising from insolvency of insurance company.

A company trading as insurance brokers took out professional indemnity insurance with underwriters whereby the underwriters agreed to indemnify the brokers, inter alia, in respect of claims made against them for any negligent act, error or omission committed by them. Under the heading "Exclusions", the relevant contracts provided: "The Underwriters shall not indemnify The Assured against any claim or loss arising from . . . 2. The insolvency of any insurance company." The brokers publicised and recommended a "Gilt Bond" which was issued by a company registered in Gibraltar known as Signal Life Assurance Co Ltd, and as a result a number of members of the public purchased Gilt Bonds through the agency of the brokers. The Gilt Bond prospectus described the bond as a guaranteed and secured bond, whereas the only securities held by Signal Life were worthless

A Weimar Republic bonds. Signal Life subsequently went into liquidation, having been absolutely insolvent since before the bond was issued. The purchasers of the bonds raised actions against the brokers, which also went into liquidation, and the underwriters. On the basis that they would otherwise have invested their money in secure investments yielding interest of at least 11 per cent, the amounts they sued for represented the sums used to purchase the bonds with interest at 11 per cent from the date of purchase. When the conjoined actions came before the Lord Ordinary the underwriters accepted that the brokers

B had been negligent, but claimed they were entitled to avoid liability under exclusion 2. The Lord Ordinary having rejected their contention, the underwriters reclaimed. It was agreed between the parties that "arising from" meant "proximately caused by". The purchasers argued that exclusion 2 was not properly an exclusion, since it excluded what no one would think was included in the insuring clause, and therefore did not affect the construction to be placed on the words in the insuring clause. They also argued that

C Signal Life, as a fraud from beginning to end, was not an insurance company within the meaning of exclusion 2. The underwriters argued that there were two proximate causes of the purchasers' claims, the negligence of the brokers, and the insolvency of Signal Life, and they therefore were not obliged to indemnify the brokers.

Held, (1) that it had not been demonstrated that exclusion 2 had merely been added ob majorem cautelam and effect required to be given to its terms

D (pp 426A-C, 430A and 431B); (2) that Signal Life may have been the tool whereby a fraudulent scheme was perpetrated, but it was not in itself a fraudulent scheme, being properly incorporated and registered, with objects enabling it to carry on business as an insurance company; moreover, it had carried on business, and operated bank accounts, and the Gilt Bonds were single premium life assurance bonds (pp 426G-J, 430A and 431B); (3) (per the Lord Justice Clerk (Ross) and Lord Murray) that the Lord Ordinary's conclu-

E sion that Signal Life's insolvency was not the proximate cause was a finding in fact, and therefore could only be disturbed if the Lord Ordinary had misdirected himself, or the court could be satisfied that his conclusion could not be justified by any advantage enjoyed by him by reason of having seen and heard the witnesses, and while there was sometimes a confusion between claims and losses in the Lord Ordinary's opinion, it was not sufficient to overturn the Lord Ordinary's conclusion (pp 429A-C and 430A); and

F reclaiming motion *refused.*

Opinion, that considering the matter de novo, Signal Life's insolvency was not the proximate cause; the actions were concerned with the purchasers' claims, not losses; there was a concurrence of damnum and injuria when the worthless policies had been purchased; the purchasers were not seeking payment of what they could have obtained under the policies had Signal Life not been unable to meet the sums due, but the purchase price of the policies together with what they would have received as interest had the purchase

price been securely invested (pp 429D-J, 430A and 431F-I); and, per the Lord Justice Clerk (Ross) (Lord G Murray concurring): that it was not possible to have two proximate causes; if there were two causes which were approximately equal in effectiveness, there was no proximate cause (pp 428E-F and 430A).

Action of damages and declarator

Ian Forrest Bell and 57 others raised actions in Dundee sheriff court against (first) Lothiansure Ltd and (second) Nicholas Charles Haydon, as represent- H ing the underwriters of the first defenders' professional indemnity insurance, seeking damages from the first defenders for alleged negligence and declarator that the first defenders had a right of indemnity against the underwriters, that that right had been transferred to and vested in the pursuers, and that the underwriters were bound to make payment to the pursuers of the sums sued for. The actions were all remitted to the Court of Session.

The conjoined actions came to proof before the I Lord Ordinary (Lord Cameron of Lochbroom).

Terms of policy

The first defenders' professional indemnity insurance policy provided in the insuring clauses inter alia:

"The Underwriters shall indemnify The Assured in respect of:

"1.A. Claims first made against The Assured during the Period of Insurance for any negligent act, error, J omission, libel, slander or defamation committed by or on behalf of The Assured or any firm with which The Assured is acting jointly.

"B. (i) Claims first made against The Assured during The Period of Insurance—

"(ii) Losses sustained by The Assured which they first discover during The Period of Insurance—

"in consequence of any dishonest or fraudulent act K or omission of The Assured or any former or present employee of The Assured."

Under "Exclusions", the policy provided inter alia:

"The Underwriters shall not indemnify The Assured against any claim or loss arising from:

"1. The Assured's activities as manager of any insurance company.

"2. The insolvency of any insurance company.

"3. The failure to account for money, except as L provided for in Insuring Clause 1.B."

Cases referred to

Burger v Indemnity Mutual Marine Assurance Co [1900] 2 QB 348.

Curtis & Sons v Mathews [1919] 1 KB 425.

Dunlop v McGowans, 1980 SLT 129; 1980 SC (HL) 73.

Leyland Shipping Co Ltd v Norwich Union Fire Insurance Society Ltd [1918] AC 350.

Lloyd (J J) Instruments Ltd v Northern Star Insurance Co Ltd (The "Miss Jay Jay") [1987] 1 Lloyd's Rep 32.
Thomas v Thomas, 1948 SLT 2; 1947 SC (HL) 45.
Wayne Tank and Pump Co Ltd v Employers Liability Assurance Corporation Ltd [1974] 1 QB 57.

Textbooks referred to
Halsbury's Laws of England (4th ed), Vol 25, para 181.
MacGillivray and Parkington, *Insurance Law* (8th ed), paras 1077-1079.

On 19 January 1990 the Lord Ordinary *pronounced* decree as craved, subject to the insertion of references to the excess on the insurance policy in relation to the declaratory craves.

The second defender reclaimed.

Reclaiming motion

The reclaiming motion was heard before the Second Division.

On 1 February 1991 the court *refused* the reclaiming motion and *adhered* to the interlocutor of the Lord Ordinary.

THE LORD JUSTICE CLERK (ROSS).—In these conjoined actions, the crave is divided into three parts. Under branch (a) the pursuers seek payment from the first defenders of sums of money calculated by reference to the amount which he (or she) paid to the first defenders in respect of a premium for the purchase of a "Gilt Bond", issued by Signal Life Assurance Co Ltd (hereinafter referred to as "Signal Life"), a company which was registered in Gibraltar. In each instance the pursuers purchased the bond through the agency of the first defenders who traded as Lothian Insurance Brokers and acted as insurance brokers, insurance consultants and insurance agents. In each case the pursuers did so as a result of publicity for the bond issued by the first defenders. This publicity took the form of advertisement in newspapers or elsewhere, personal calls from employees of the first defenders or the sending of a letter from the first defenders dated 19 May 1982. In each of these ways the first defenders represented that the Gilt Bond was a good investment, and it was described as a guaranteed bond. Investment in the bond was recommended by the first defenders. In each instance the pursuers completed a proposal form and paid the sum to the first defenders to be invested on their behalf in the purchase of a bond. In some cases a policy document was issued to the pursuers, but none of the pursuers have ever received any payment in terms of their investment.

The conjoined actions were all raised in 1986 or 1987. The first defenders were wound up upon orders pronounced by the sheriff at Dundee on 20 May 1987. They originally lodged defences to the actions, but since their liquidation they have taken no further part in the present proceedings, and they were not represented at the proof before the Lord Ordinary.

The second defender represents the underwriters who subscribed to professional indemnity policies whereby they bound themselves to indemnify the first defenders in respect of certain claims and losses, which policies were effective from 23 April 1982 until 22 April 1985.

Initially the actions were raised in the sheriff court at Dundee, but on 9 October 1987 the sheriff remitted the causes to the Court of Session in terms of s 37 (1) (b) of the Sheriff Courts (Scotland) Act 1971. After sundry procedure a proof took place before the Lord Ordinary in October 1989. On 19 January 1990 the Lord Ordinary pronounced an interlocutor sustaining the first plea in law for the pursuers and decerning against the first defenders for payment to the pursuers of the respective sums craved in terms of crave (a), sustaining the fifth plea in law for the pursuers and finding and declaring as craved in terms of crave (b) of the initial writ subject always to the proviso that the contract of insurance contained an excess of £2,000, the proportion whereof attributable to the claims made by the pursuers is £417, and finding and declaring as craved in terms of crave (c) of the initial writ subject to the proviso that the second defender was bound to make payment to the pursuers of the sums decerned in terms of crave (a) together with expenses under deduction of the proportion of the excess attributable to the claims. Against that interlocutor of the Lord Ordinary the second defender has now reclaimed.

In his grounds of appeal, the second defender put forward one ground of appeal in the following terms: "The Lord Ordinary erred in finding that the insolvency of Signal Life, in either the absolute or the practical sense, was not a proximate cause of the pursuers' claims or losses. Accordingly the Lord Ordinary should have found that the pursuers' claims or losses were caused by an excepted peril under the policy."

Since the pursuers were not wishing to bring the interlocutor of the Lord Ordinary under review, they were not required under Rule of Court 294B to lodge grounds of appeal. However, since the pursuers wished to challenge certain views expressed by the Lord Ordinary in his opinion, they sought and obtained leave to lodge a note of submissions giving notice of the matters which they wished to raise.

As the Lord Ordinary observes in his opinion, the proof was substantially shortened because the pursuers and the second defender entered into joint minutes whereby the salient matters of fact were agreed. For convenience I refer to the Lord Ordinary's summary of what had been agreed:

"It is agreed that at all material times there was current a contract of professional indemnity insurance between the first defenders and the second defender constituted by proposal form, no 532 of process, and policies and others, nos 524, 525 and 526 of process, that the claims made by the pursuers against the first defenders in this action were first made during the period of insurance specified in that contract, that all

conditions of that contract including conditions pre-
A cedent to the right to indemnity so far as relevant have
been met and complied with by the first defenders,
and that the pursuers' claims and others' claims
arising out of the same circumstances but not forming
part of the present proceedings, are deemed to be one
claim for the purposes of determining the second
defender's liability under that contract including the
provisions of insuring clauses 3 and 4 of policy no
H2D141, no 524 of process. It is also agreed that the
deemed claim bears an excess of £2,000 and that the
B proportion thereof attributable to the claims is £417.

"The parties are further agreed that in respect of the
claims made by the pursuers against the first
defenders, the first defenders are liable to make reparation to the pursuers in the amounts of principal and
interest at the judicial rate in force from time to time
commencing from the dates as craved in part (a) of the
crave with such expenses as the court may award.
They are also agreed that the grounds of liability to
make reparation are those specified in the articles of
C condescendence in this action, that they constitute
negligent acts, errors and omissions committed by or
on behalf of the first defenders as the assured within
the meaning of clause A of the insuring clauses of
policy no H2D141 and that such negligent acts, errors
and omissions occurred in the course of activities
undertaken by the first defenders falling within the
scope of cover provided by the contract. However no
admission is made by the second defender that the
claims made are claims in respect of which a right of
D indemnity arises in terms of the contract and the
second defender makes the admission relative to the
first defenders' negligence without prejudice to his
contention that the claims arose from the insolvency of
an insurance company.

"The parties are also agreed that the purported facts
set out in the documents nos 620 to 644 of process,
nos 648 to 651 of process and no 655 of process are
correct in all respects and that the affidavit and supplementary affidavit by Mr G A Weiss, the liquidator
E of Signal Life, are to be treated as his evidence."

The Lord Ordinary also explains in his opinion that
in addition to the joint minutes and the agreed documents and affidavit evidence, he also heard evidence
from Mr Gordon Shaw, an insurance consultant, who
gave evidence for the pursuers, and from Mr Peter
Taylor, an insolvency practitioner, who gave evidence
for the second defender.

In his opinion the Lord Ordinary proceeds to set out
F the facts which he holds to have been established. As
I understand it there is no dispute between the parties
regarding the facts which the Lord Ordinary has held
to be proved, although parties are in dispute regarding
certain conclusions which the Lord Ordinary drew
from the proved facts.

As already observed, it is not disputed that the pursuers are entitled to decree for payment against the
first defenders. The basis of the pursuers' claim
against the second defender is that he is bound to
indemnify the first defenders, and that the first

defenders' right to be indemnified in the amount of
the sums sued for has been transferred to and is now G
vested in the pursuers by virtue of the Third Parties
(Rights against Insurers) Act 1930, with the result that
the pursuers are entitled to decree against the second
defender in terms of crave (b) and (c). This alleged
obligation on the part of the second defender to
indemnify the first defenders is said to arise from the
terms of the professional indemnity policies of insurance nos 524, 525 and 526. In terms of these policies,
the second defender as underwriter agreed to insure
against loss, damage or liability to the extent and in H
the manner provided in the policy. For the purposes
of this reclaiming motion, it is necessary to consider
the terms of both the "Insuring Clauses" and the
"Exclusions" in the policies. The relevant portion of
the insuring clauses is in the following terms: [his
Lordship quoted the terms of the insuring clause set
out supra, followed by those of the exclusions, and
continued:]

On behalf of the second defender it was submitted
that the second defender was not bound to indemnify I
the first defenders against the pursuers' claims because
these claims arose from the insolvency of an insurance
company, namely, Signal Life. In his opinion the Lord
Ordinary expressed the view that in the exclusions the
words "arising from" should be given a narrow
meaning, and before this court it was not disputed that
in this context "arising from" meant "proximately
caused by". In the action, it is clear that the claim
forming the subject matter of the conjoined actions is
a claim for negligent acts, errors and omissions by the J
first defenders. Accordingly the critical question is
whether it has been established that the insolvency of
Signal Life was the proximate cause of the pursuers'
claim. Before considering that issue, however, it
would be desirable to deal with various subsidiary
matters raised by the pursuers in the course of this
reclaiming motion.

Before the Lord Ordinary there was some discussion
regarding the evidence as to the insolvency of Signal K
Life. It was not disputed that Signal Life was absolutely insolvent prior to the promotion and issue of the
Gilt Bonds, in the sense that its liabilities, including
the contingent claims of holders of bonds, exceeded its
assets available to satisfy those claims. The Lord
Ordinary however accepted that Signal Life was not
practically insolvent prior to 9 August 1982 in the
sense that it had control of sufficient funds to meet its
then current liabilities. Before this court counsel for
the pursuers maintained that the Lord Ordinary had L
not been well founded in holding that Signal Life was
not practically insolvent until 9 August 1982. I am not
persuaded that the date upon which Signal Life
became practically insolvent has any relevance to the
issues which require to be determined in this cause. I
understood counsel on behalf of the second defender
to accept that the date of practical insolvency was not
relevant for the purposes of the present reclaiming
motion. That also appeared to be the attitude of
counsel for the pursuer. In seeking to challenge the
Lord Ordinary's finding upon this matter, counsel for

A the pursuer referred to part of the evidence given by Mr Taylor and submitted that the evidence as a whole was insufficient to allow the Lord Ordinary to reach this conclusion. It appears to me, however, that there was material before the Lord Ordinary sufficient to entitle him to reach this conclusion, and I am not persuaded that his conclusion was incorrect. In any event, since parties appear to be agreed that practical insolvency is irrelevant for the purposes of the present reclaiming motion, it is unnecessary to say any more upon this topic.

B Counsel for the pursuers next presented a submission to the effect that exclusion 2, on a correct construction of the exclusions, was not an exclusion in the proper sense of the word. Counsel maintained that the provision had been included under the exclusions for what is sometimes described as "superabundant caution". In other words counsel contended that exclusion 2 should be regarded as excluding a risk which no one would sensibly imagine was included in the insuring clause, and that accordingly it did not C alter the construction to be placed upon the words in the insuring clause.

Counsel for the pursuers referred to various basic principles which fall to be applied in the construction of policies of insurance.

"It is an accepted canon of construction that a commercial document, such as an insurance policy, should be construed in accordance with sound commercial principles and good business sense, so that its provi-D sions receive a fair and sensible application. Several consequences flow from this principle. The literal meaning of words must not be permitted to prevail where it would produce an unrealistic and generally unanticipated result, as, for example, where it would absolve the insurer from liability on the chief risks sought to be covered by the policy" (MacGillivray and Parkington, *Insurance Law* (8th ed), para 1077).

"It follows that in interpreting any clause of a policy, it is correct to bear in mind the commercial E object or function of the clause and its apparent relation to the contract as a whole. It may then become apparent that the literal meaning of the clause must yield to business sense or that an ambiguity in the wording can be resolved, or that the ordinary meaning of the words used may need to be modified (para 1078).

"If the wording of a clause is ambiguous, and one reading produces a fairer result than the alternative, the reasonable interpretation should be adopted" (para F 1079).

I agree that certain exceptions may fall to be regarded not as true exceptions in the sense that they exclude a risk, but that they should be regarded as merely ensuring that the insured risk does not cover a particular situation.

In *Burger v Indemnity Mutual Marine Assurance Co*, the court held that a proviso which had been added by way of superabundant caution did not alter the meaning of the clear words which preceded it. A L

Smith LJ said (at p 351): "It appears to me that the proviso was inserted ex majori cautela and was not G really necessary."

Vaughan Williams LJ said (at p 352): "If the words defining the subject-matters of insurance under the collision clause are clear, I do not think that we can extend or alter their effect by reason of the introduction of a proviso, which, when we look at it, appears to be one which a prudent underwriter might well think it desirable as a matter of caution to introduce into every policy containing a collision clause whatever its terms might be." H

Romer LJ said (at p 352): "I agree that the proviso with regard to loss of life and personal injury is really useless, and was merely added by way of superabundant caution. I do not think that the addition of such a proviso can alter the meaning of fairly plain words preceding it."

In *Curtis & Sons v Mathews* at p 430, Bankes LJ adopted the following words of the judge of first instance: "I cannot regard the insertion of words ex I abundanti cautela in this later connection as altering or affecting the plain and natural construction of the words in the earlier part of the clause."

Counsel for the pursuers maintained that the position of exclusion 2 in the list of exclusions was significant. Counsel contended that exclusion 1 and exclusion 3 were plainly not proper exclusions. Having regard to the definition of "The Assured" in the schedule to the policy, it was clear that there was J no question of the definition covering the assured acting as the manager of an insurance company. Accordingly exclusion 1 must be regarded not as excluding something from the insuring clauses, but as ensuring that no one advanced the argument that the manager of an insurance company was within the definition of "The Assured". Admittedly provision could be made in the schedule for scheduling other activities on which the assured might be engaged, but it would hardly make sense to schedule being manager of an K insurance company as one of the activities on which the assured might become engaged, and at the same time to exclude such activities under the exclusions. Likewise, counsel contended that exclusion 3 was not a proper exclusion since it did not seek to exclude anything from insuring clause 1B but merely to confirm what was provided for in insuring clause 1B.

As counsel put it, if an insurance company was insolvent, but there had been no negligence, a claim could hardly be put forward merely on the ground of L insolvency, as insolvency per se was not an insured risk. Accordingly counsel submitted that it was clear that exclusion 2 had merely been put forward for the avoidance of doubt.

Counsel for the second defender, on the other hand, maintained that exclusion 2 had not been included merely ob majorem cautelam. An insurance company might become insolvent for a number of reasons; there might have been negligence on the part of the managers or there might simply have been bad luck.

I am not persuaded that exclusion 2 was merely added ob majorem cautelam and so has no real effect. The explanation for the presence of exclusion 2 may well be that special provision is made for the provision of indemnity insurance by practising insurance brokers in terms of the Insurance Brokers (Registration) Act 1977 and the Insurance Brokers Registration Council (Indemnity Insurance and Grants Scheme) Rules Approval Order 1979 (SI 1979/408). Different provisions have been enacted for the protection of policyholders in the event of an insurance company becoming insolvent (Policyholders Protection Act 1975). That being so, exclusion 2 may well have been included among the exclusions because the insurers of an insurance broker were not prepared to indemnify their assured where the claim or loss was properly attributable to the insolvency of an insurance company since persons prejudiced by such insolvency could look elsewhere for satisfaction of their loss. (I appreciate that Signal Life was a foreign company and that it was not a company to which the provisions of the Policyholders Protection Act 1975 applied, but that does not affect the construction to be placed upon this policy.) In these circumstances, I see no reason why effect should not be given to exclusion 2 in any case where it can be shown that the claim or loss in question arose from the insolvency of any insurance company.

Counsel for the pursuers also presented an argument to the effect that on the basis of his findings the Lord Ordinary was not entitled to conclude that Signal Life was an insurance company within the meaning of exclusion 2. Counsel submitted that exclusion 2 could only apply where there is a company which is in form an insurance company and which carries on genuine and not fraudulent insurance business. Counsel contended that in the present case the Lord Ordinary had held that Signal Life was a fraud from beginning to end, and counsel submitted that exclusion 2 could not apply where there was a purported insurance company which in a practical sense was a fraud or a sham. Counsel for the second defender, on the other hand, pointed out that Signal Life had operated bank accounts, had issued two series of bonds, and had together with Hong Kong and Shanghai Bank Trustee (Jersey) Ltd executed a trust deed dated 22 October 1981 whereby the latter company was to act as trustee of one or more funds each consisting of assets derived from premiums to be paid to Signal Life in respect of insurance policies to be issued by Signal Life. Signal Life had taken in money in exchange for bonds which ex facie gave valuable contractual rights against Signal Life. In these circumstances counsel for the second defender contended that it could not be maintained that Signal Life had been a sham from the start. In art 8 of the condescendence the pursuers aver: "The pursuers now believe and aver that Signal Life was not a bona fide insurance company but was rather a fraudulent scheme carried out by its promoters and managers for their own benefit and for the benefit of their associates. In any event the Gilt Bond issued was a fraudulent scheme."

In my opinion, for the reasons advanced by counsel for the second defender, it cannot properly be maintained that Signal Life was itself a fraudulent scheme. It may have been a tool by which a fraudulent scheme was perpetrated, but that does not mean that Signal Life itself was a fraudulent scheme. This argument was considered by the Lord Ordinary who expressed the view that the pursuers' contention was misconceived. In his opinion the Lord Ordinary disposed of the matter as follows: "Signal Life was properly incorporated as a limited company and registered as required by the laws of Gibraltar. It had a memorandum and articles of association, the objects of which were designed to enable it to carry on business as an insurance company. It was given a certificate to do so under the laws of Gibraltar. It was recognised as a legal person both in the actions against it in the High Court of Justice in England and the Royal Court of Jersey in August 1982 and again as a petitioner for winding up, following a properly constituted company meeting, in the High Court in England in November 1982. It has been the subject of liquidation proceedings in the course of which it has never been suggested that it was anything other than a properly constituted company. Furthermore I am satisfied on the evidence of Mr Shaw that on any view the bonds promoted by Signal Life could properly be regarded as single premium life assurance bonds from the insurance point of view, so that its business was conducted as that of an insurance company."

I entirely agree with what the Lord Ordinary says in this respect, and when regard is also had to the fact that Signal Life operated bank accounts, issued bonds, and entered into arrangements with Hong Kong and Shanghai Bank Trustee (Jersey) Ltd, I am entirely satisfied that the Lord Ordinary was right to reject this submission made on behalf of the pursuers.

In my opinion the real issue to be decided in this case is whether the second defender has established the defence which is formulated in his sixth plea in law. That plea in law is in the following terms: "Separatim, in respect that the claims condescended on arise from the insolvency of an insurance company, the defenders are not entitled to indemnity in terms of the said policies of insurance, and the second named defender should be assoilzied."

As already observed, in terms of the joint minute it is matter of admission that the first defenders are liable to make reparation to the pursuers, and that the grounds of that liability constitute negligent acts, errors and omissions on behalf of the first defenders within the meaning of cl 1.A of the insuring clauses of the policy, and that the acts, errors and omissions occurred in the course of the activities undertaken by the first defenders falling within the scope of the cover provided by the policy. In the circumstances it was not disputed that the second defender could only succeed in his defence to this action if the Lord Ordinary ought to have found that the pursuers' claims arose from the insolvency of Signal Life and so were an excepted peril under the policy.

It is, in my opinion, important to emphasise that the subject matter of the present conjoined actions is the pursuers' claim against the first defenders who are the assured under the policy. This is made plain in art 10 of the condescendence. It is there stated inter alia: "The claim forming the subject matter to the present conjoined actions was first made during the period of insurance. It is a claim for negligent acts, errors and omissions by the first defenders trading as Lothian Insurance Brokers and acting as insurance brokers and consultants. In terms of said policies the second defender and those whom he represents are bound to indemnify the first defenders in respect of said claim."

That the claim is the subject matter of the conjoined actions is recognised by the second defender in the averments made on his behalf in ans 10. It is also recognised in the language used in the pleas in law for the parties and in particular in plea in law 8 for the pursuers and pleas in law 5 and 6 for the second defender. Moreover this is consistent with the terms of the policy itself. In the policy a distinction is drawn between claims and losses. Thus under the insuring clauses, cl 1.A deals with claims first made against the assured for inter alia any negligent act, error or omission. Clause 1.B is divided into two parts: (i) deals with claims first made against the assured during the period of insurance, and (ii) deals with losses sustained by the assured which they first discover during the period of insurance. The opening words of the exclusions are: "The Underwriters shall not indemnify The Assured against any claim or loss arising from—".

In my opinion, the words "any claim or loss" in the exclusions must refer to the claims or losses defined in the insuring clauses. In other words, the words "claim" and "loss" in the exclusions must have the same meaning as they have in the insuring clauses. I am accordingly satisfied that, as averred by the pursuers, the subject matter of the present conjoined actions is the claim made against the first defenders by the pursuers in respect of the first defenders' negligent act, error or omission; that is a claim under cl 1.A of the insuring clauses. Accordingly if the second defender is to exclude the right to indemnity under the insuring clauses, he can only do so if he shows that the pursuers' claim against the first defenders arose from the insolvency of Signal Life.

This is important because, with all respect to the Lord Ordinary, there is some confusion in his opinion between claims on the one hand and losses on the other. Thus on p 17 of his opinion, he correctly identifies the issue which falls to be decided. What he said was this: "In my opinion, and I did not understand either counsel to demur from this, the exclusion upon which the second defender founds, namely a claim arising from the insolvency of an insurance company, can only operate as an exclusion from the right to indemnity if the insolvency is a proximate cause of the claim." (As already observed, before this court it was accepted by both sides that the phrase "arising from" meant "proximately caused by".)

Having correctly identified the question which had to be decided, the Lord Ordinary unfortunately went on to confuse claim with loss. Thus on p 18 of his opinion, he stated: "The real question at the end of the day comes to be whether the negligent act of the first defenders was a proximate cause of the pursuers' loss, and, if so, whether a proximate cause was also the insolvency of Signal Life."

Thereafter in his opinion on numerous occasions the Lord Ordinary proceeded to consider what was the proximate cause of the pursuers' loss. This confusion has been carried into the second defender's grounds of appeal, where reference is made to "a proximate cause of the pursuers' claims or losses", and a further reference to the allegation that "the pursuers' claims or losses were caused by an excepted peril under the policy".

Despite the references in the Lord Ordinary's opinion to the proximate cause of the pursuers' loss, counsel on both sides of the bar were agreed before this court that the real issue was that originally identified by the Lord Ordinary, namely, whether the insolvency of Signal Life was a proximate cause of the pursuers' claim.

We were referred to a number of authorities dealing with causation in the context of policies of insurance. Although these cases are helpful, it must be observed that they were all cases dealing with the proximate cause of loss or damage, and none of them was addressing the question of what was the proximate cause of a claim of the type which is being put forward by the pursuers in the present case.

Leyland Shipping Co Ltd v Norwich Union Fire Insurance Society Ltd was a case concerning a ship which was torpedoed by a German submarine and subsequently foundered in the harbour of Havre where she had been taken with the aid of tugs. The shipowners contended that the ship was lost by a peril of the sea, whereas the insurers contended that the loss was caused by the torpedoing, and that they were protected by the warranty against the consequences of hostilities. Lord Dunedin said in his speech at p 362: "My lords, we have had a large citation of authority in this case, and much discussion on what is the true meaning of causa proxima. Yet I think the case turns on a pure question of fact to be determined by common-sense principles. What was the cause of the loss of the ship? I do not think the ordinary man would have any difficulty in answering she was lost because she was torpedoed".

Subsequently he stated at p 363: "The solution will always lie in settling as a question of fact which of the two causes was what I will venture to call (though I shrink from the multiplication of epithets) the dominant cause of the two. In other words, you seek for the causa proxima, if it is well understood that the question of which is proxima is not solved by the mere point of order in time".

In the same case Lord Shaw of Dunfermline stated at pp 368-369: "The doctrine of cause has been, since the time of Aristotle and the famous category of

material, formal, efficient, and final causes, one
A involving the subtlest of distinctions. The doctrine
applied in these to existences rather than to occurrences. But the idea of the cause of an occurrence or
the production of an event or the bringing about of a
result is an idea perfectly familiar to the mind and to
the law, and it is in connection with that that the
notion of proxima causa is introduced.''

He subsequently observed that it was out of the
question to treat proxima causa as the cause which was
nearest in time. Thereafter he stated at p 369: "What
B does 'proximate' here mean? To treat proximate cause
as if it was the cause which is proximate in time is, as
I have said, out of the question. The cause which is
truly proximate is that which is proximate in efficiency. That efficiency may have been preserved
although other causes may meantime have sprung up
which have yet not destroyed it, or truly impaired it,
and it may culminate in a result of which it still
remains the real efficient cause to which the event can
be ascribed.''
C
At p 370 he added: "In my opinion, accordingly,
proximate cause is an expression referring to the
efficiency as an operating factor upon the result.
Where various factors or causes are concurrent, and
one has to be selected, the matter is determined as one
of fact, and the choice falls upon the one to which may
be variously ascribed the qualities of reality, pre-
dominance, efficiency. Fortunately, this much would
appear to be in accordance with the principles of a
D plain business transaction, and it is not at all foreign
to the law.''

In *Wayne Tank and Pump Co Ltd v Employers
Liability Assurance Corporation Ltd* a question arose as
to the proximate cause of damage. In that case the
court considered what the position would be where
there were two causes which were equal or nearly
equal in their efficiency in bringing about the damage,
that is, where there was more than one proximate
cause. The court appears to have accepted that in
E some cases there might be two causes which were
approximately equal in effectiveness, that is to say two
proximate causes. With all respect to the distinguished
judges who delivered opinions in that case, I find it
difficult to conceive of a situation where there are two
proximate causes. Indeed this appears to me, with all
respect, to involve a contradiction in terms. If there
are two causes which are approximately equal in effectiveness, then, in my opinion there is no proximate
cause of the loss or damage. Counsel for the second
F defender founded upon this case for the proposition
that there might be two proximate causes, and submitted that where there are two proximate causes of
damage one of which is within the general words of
the policy and one within an exception to it, the
insurers can then rely upon the exception. Since I find
it difficult to accept that there could be two proximate
causes of loss or damage, I have not found this case of
assistance.

The pursuers also relied upon *J J Lloyd Instruments
Ltd v Northern Star Insurance Co Ltd (the "Miss Jay*

Jay"). In that case, a question arose as to what had
been the sole cause of the loss. The court referred with G
approval to *Wayne Tank and Pump Co Ltd v
Employers Liability Assurance Corporation Ltd* and
held that where there were two concurrent and effective causes of a marine loss and one came within the
terms of the policy and the other did not, the insurers
must pay.

The distinction between the two cases appears to be
this: in *Wayne Tank Co v Employers Liability Ltd* it
was recognised that where there were two causes of
damage, one within the general words of the policy H
and one within an exception to it, the insurers could
rely upon the exception. On the other hand in *The
"Miss Jay Jay"* the court approved the legal position
stated in *Halsbury's Laws of England* (4th ed), Vol 25,
para 181 relating to marine insurance policies: "It
seems that there may be more than one proximate (in
the sense of effective or direct) cause of a loss. If one
of these causes is insured against under the policy, and
none of the others is expressly excluded from the
policy, the assured will be entitled to recover.'' I

Counsel for the second defender maintained that in
the present case there were three causes each of which
could be described as a causa sine qua non: there was
the insolvency of Signal Life, there was the negligence
of the first defenders, and there was the fraud.
Counsel maintained that there was possibly a fourth
cause sine qua non in respect of the absence of security. As I understood it, however, counsel's principal
submission was that in the present case there were two J
proximate causes of the pursuers' loss, namely, the
insolvency of Signal Life and the negligence of the
first defenders. That being so, counsel contended that
since one of these proximate causes was within the
words of an exclusion, the second defender was
entitled to rely upon that exclusion and so to avoid
making indemnity.

When junior counsel for the second defender made
his submissions, they were upon the basis that the
insolvency of Signal Life was a proximate cause of the K
pursuers' loss. As already observed, the important
question is not as to the proximate cause of the pursuers' loss but as to the proximate cause of the pursuers' claim. This was recognised by senior counsel
for the second defender, who submitted that the insolvency of Signal Life was a proximate cause of the pursuers' claim. As I understood it, senior counsel
accepted that the negligence of the first defenders was
also a proximate cause of the pursuers' claim, but he
maintained that there were two proximate causes of L
the claim. Since one of these proximate causes fell
within the terms of exclusion 2, he maintained that the
first defenders were entitled to rely upon exclusion 2.

Although the Lord Ordinary confused the pursuers'
loss with the pursuers' claim, he expressed the conclusion that the insolvency of Signal Life did not cause
the pursuers' loss. In his opinion, under reference to
the insolvency of Signal Life, he stated: "It was merely
the means whereby the extent of the pursuers' loss
came to be quantified. It was rather the fraudulent

A actings of those controlling Signal Life in issuing the brochure for the Series Two Bond and the negligence of the first defenders which together caused the loss of the pursuers' investment and are to be regarded as proximate causes of their loss."

Although the Lord Ordinary has confused the claim with the loss, I am of opinion that that passage in his opinion ought to be read as meaning that he was satisfied that the pursuers' claim had been caused by the negligence of the first defenders and not by the insolvency of Signal Life. As was observed in *Leyland Ship-*
B *ping Co v Norwich Union Fire Insurance Society*, the question of what has caused a loss is a question of fact. Since the Lord Ordinary appears to me to have decided as matter of fact that the cause of the loss was not the insolvency of Signal Life but the negligence of the first defenders, this court would not be entitled to come to a different conclusion from the Lord Ordinary unless he had misdirected himself or this court could be satisfied that the trial judge's conclusion could not be justified by any advantage enjoyed by him by
C reason of having seen and heard the witnesses (*Thomas v Thomas*).

I am not disposed to think that this is a case where this court would be justified in overturning the Lord Ordinary's conclusion on this essential matter of fact. However, counsel for the second defender maintained that the approach of the Lord Ordinary was clearly vitiated because he had wrongly addressed himself to the question of what had caused the pursuers' loss
D instead of directing his attention to the question of what had caused the pursuers' claim. Since there was this confusion in the Lord Ordinary's opinion, it may be that his conclusion on this crucial matter of fact is open to review by this court. However, even if the question of what was the proximate cause of the pursuers' claim is at large for this court, I am clearly of opinion that the proper conclusion to draw from the Lord Ordinary's findings is that the proximate cause of the pursuers' claim was the negligence of the first
E defenders. Indeed, even if the question had been what caused the pursuers' loss, I am of opinion that it would not be correct to say that the loss was caused by the insolvency of Signal Life. I agree with counsel for the pursuers that the loss which resulted from the insolvency of Signal Life was that company's inability to pay its debts, that is, its inability to return to the pursuers their premiums and the interest thereupon. But that is not the loss which is claimed for in this action. What the pursuers are claiming for in this action is the loss of a secure investment. In art 8 of the condescen-
F dence it is stated: "Each of the pursuers was looking for a secure investment giving a reasonable income. If they had not taken out said Gilt Bond policies they would have been [sic] invested said sums in British government securities or an investment of similar security from which they would have received a return to capital of at least 11 per cent per annum during the period of investment. They would also have got their capital back. The principal sum sued for represents the capital plus interest at 11 per cent per annum for the period of investment in each case."

G On behalf of the second defender, it was maintained that the pursuers would not have had any claim unless Signal Life had been insolvent. If Signal Life had been solvent the pursuers would have recovered from them the amount of their investment with interest thereon. The submission was that the pursuers only lost their capital when Signal Life became insolvent on 13 December 1982. In my opinion, however, this is not the correct view. What each of the pursuers purchased was a Gilt Bond described as a guaranteed bond having security underwritten by first class banking
H institutions. The truth was that the Gilt Bond prospectus was nonsense and that the company neither held nor had rights in any government securities other than in worthless Weimar bonds. Accordingly as soon as each of the pursuers handed over money and purchased a bond, the bond which each of the pursuers obtained was worth considerably less than its face value. In fact the bond was probably worthless, but in any event it was clearly worth less than the purchase price. That being so, as soon as a
I bond was purchased by investment of the relevant premium, each of the pursuers had a claim against the first defenders on the basis of the negligence of the first defenders as insurance brokers. At that stage there was a concurrence of injuria and damnum (*Dunlop v McGowans*).

The claim of the pursuers was thus a claim which was proximately caused by the negligence of the first defenders as insurance brokers. In my opinion, that was the sole proximate cause of the claim. Even if
J Signal Life had been solvent, the pursuers would have had a claim against the first defenders once it became clear that the bond was not guaranteed and that there was no security. That would have made the bond less valuable. The bonds issued by Signal Life were assignable, and had a bond been assigned after it had been purchased, it clearly would have realised less than the purchase price paid in the form of a single premium once it was appreciated that the bond was not a guaranteed bond and that there was no security. Once
K it was recognised that Signal Life was insolvent, that no doubt fixed the amount of the pursuers' loss, but the pursuers' claim was not caused by the insolvency of Signal Life but by the negligence of the first defenders as insurance brokers. If, as has been suggested in the reported cases, the man in the street were to be asked what was the proximate cause of the pursuers' claim, I am in no doubt that the answer given would be the negligence of the first defenders as insurance brokers. I do not understand how the pursuers'
L claim as opposed to their loss could ever be described as having been caused by the insolvency of Signal Life. Since the pursuers' claim was caused by the negligence of the first defenders, it was caused by a cause which fell within the insuring clauses. There is, in my opinion, no basis for holding that the pursuers' claim was caused by the excepted peril. The second defender has failed to discharge the onus of establishing that the pursuers' claim was caused by the insolvency of Signal Life, and accordingly there is no question of exclusion 2 having been established.

In these circumstances I am of opinion that the Lord
A Ordinary arrived at the correct conclusion in this case.
I would accordingly move your Lordships to refuse
the reclaiming motion and to adhere to the interlocutor of the Lord Ordinary.

LORD MURRAY.—I agree entirely with the
opinion of your Lordship in the chair and I have
nothing to add.

LORD CULLEN.—It is common ground between
the pursuers and respondents on the one hand and the
B second defender and reclaimer on the other that the
first defenders are liable to the pursuers in this action
and that the claims for which the first defenders are so
liable are "Claims first made against The Assured
during The Period of Insurance for any negligent act,
error, omission . . . committed by or on behalf of The
Assured", within the meaning of those words as they
appear in insuring clause 1.A of the professional
indemnity policy which the first defenders had with
the underwriters whom the second defender
C represents. It follows that the second defender is
bound to indemnify the first defenders against, and in
view of the winding up of the first defenders to meet,
those claims unless the terms of the policy are such as
to exclude the liability which otherwise would rest
upon him. The second defender's contention, which
was rejected by the Lord Ordinary, was that such
exclusion of liability was effected by exclusion clause
2, which states that: "The Underwriters shall not
indemnify The Assured against any claim or loss
D arising from: . . . 2. The insolvency of any insurance
company".

During the course of the discussion on the reclaiming motion counsel for the second defender accepted,
and in my view correctly in view of the terms of the
policy, that in the present action the relevant word was
"claim" rather than "loss", so that the issue between
him and the pursuers is whether their claims arose out
of the insolvency of an insurance company, namely
Signal Life.

E The reclaimer cited a number of decisions on the
law of insurance. These vouched the proposition that
an insurer is not liable in respect of a loss which is
otherwise covered where the proximate (or effective)
cause of the loss is a risk or peril which is excepted.
In the case of *Wayne Tank and Pump Co Ltd v
Employers Liability Ltd* the Court of Appeal considered the situation in which there were two proximate
(or effective) causes. In that case defective apparatus
had been installed by the insured engineers in a
F factory. An employee of the insured had put the
apparatus into operation before it had been tested.
Lord Denning MR and Roskill LJ held that the proximate cause of the destruction of the factory was the
defective nature of the apparatus, which fell within an
exception clause in the policy of liability insurance.
However, on the basis that a second proximate cause
was the negligent conduct of the employee which,
taken alone, would fall within an insuring clause, they
expressed the opinion that the insurers would not be
liable. On that basis Lord Denning said at p 67: "The

result is that, although this accident comes within the
general words at the opening of the policy, neverthe- G
less seeing that there is a particular exception, the
exception takes priority over the general words.
General words always have to give way to particular
provisions. In the present case one of the causes which
was efficient to produce the damage was the nature of
the goods supplied by the insured. The insurers are
exempt from liability for it. Their exemption is not
taken away by the fact that there was another cause
equally efficient also operating to cause the loss".

Cairns LJ on the other hand was not disposed to   H
differentiate between the two causes. At pp 68-69 he
said: "But for my part I do not consider that the court
should strain to find a dominant cause if, as here, there
are two causes both of which can properly be
described as effective causes of the loss. Mr Le Quesne
recognised that if there are two causes which are
approximately equal in effectiveness, then it is impossible to call one rather than the other the dominant
cause. I should prefer to say that unless one cause is
clearly more decisive than the other, it should be   I
accepted that there are two causes of the loss and no
attempt should be made to give one of them the
quality of dominance. On this approach if one cause
is within the words of the policy and the other comes
within an exception in the policy, it must be taken that
the loss cannot be recovered under the policy. The
effect of an exception is to save the insurer from
liability for a loss which but for the exception would
be covered. The effect of the cover is not to impose on
the insurer liability for something which is within the   J
exception".

The second defender argued that there were at least
three causes of the pursuers' losses and of their claims
which were at least causae sine qua non. These were
the insolvency of Signal Life, the negligence of the
first defenders and the fraudulent actings of those in
control of Signal Life. On the other hand the first and
second of these causes should be regarded as proximate (or effective) causes of the pursuers' losses and   K
their claims. These arose out of the inability of Signal
Life to pay. The reason why the pursuers had made
their claims was because they had put their money
into a company which did not have the assets to meet
its obligations either as to the payment of interest or
as to the repayment of capital on the date of maturity.
It was accepted, as the Lord Ordinary had found, that
Signal Life was all along absolutely insolvent; and that
the pursuers had paid their premiums for worthless
investments. However it was pointed out by junior   L
counsel that for some months after they had paid their
premiums the pursuers could not have known that
they had sustained loss. The Lord Ordinary had held
that Signal Life were not practically insolvent prior to
9 August 1982. If the court accepted the second
defender's arguments, it should not be astute to find
that, as between two causes which were efficient in the
case of the respondents' claims, one of them was a
dominant cause.

The pursuers defended the decision of the Lord

Ordinary and also submitted a number of further argu-
A ments. They submitted that the clause founded upon
by the reclaimer was not a true exception to the cover
provided by insuring clause 1.A but was merely
inserted ex abundanti cautela; and maintained that
this construction was consistent with the declaration
in the policy that it was taken out pursuant to the
Insurance Brokers Registration Council (Indemnity
Insurance and Grants Scheme) Rules 1979. They also
submitted that even if the clause was a true exclusion
clause it could not apply where the "insurance
B company" had been conceived and operated as a
means of perpetrating a fraud on investors, as it was
in the present case. As regards these arguments I agree
that they fall to be rejected for the reasons given by
your Lordship in the chair. This leaves for decision
the question whether the second defender has established that his liability is excluded by exclusion clause
2.

Although the pursuers defended the decision of the
Lord Ordinary they pointed out that in his opinion
C there had been a blurring of the distinction between a
"claim" and a "loss". In approaching the second
defender's contention that his liability was excluded
the Lord Ordinary had correctly observed that the
exclusion upon which he founded could only operate
as an exclusion from the right to indemnity if the
insolvency was a proximate cause of the *claim*.
However thereafter he had concentrated on the *loss*
sustained by the pursuers. He concluded: "Thus
insolvency as a legal state of indebtedness did not, in
D my opinion, cause the pursuers' loss. It was merely the
means whereby the extent of the pursuers' loss came
to be quantified. It was rather the fraudulent actings
of those controlling Signal Life in issuing the brochure
for the Series Two Bond and the negligence of the first
defenders which together caused the loss of the pursuers' investment and are to be regarded as proximate
causes of their loss".

These statements do not appear to address squarely
E the question of the proximate cause or causes of the
pursuers' claims. However they appear to imply that
the insolvency of Signal Life was not a proximate
cause of the pursuers' claims. Accordingly the second
defender is faced in this reclaiming motion with the
task of attacking the Lord Ordinary's findings on
matters of fact. I will however assume that it is open
to this court to review the matter of proximate cause.

At the outset it is important to consider the nature
of the pursuers' claims. In summary, the pursuers'
F complaint is that they were induced by the first
defenders' negligence to make a worthless investment.
The first defenders should have advised them not to
invest in the Series Two Bonds, or at any rate not
advised them to invest in them. The pursuers seek to
be placed in the position in which they would have
been if they had not made this investment. Accordingly they seek reparation equivalent to the premiums
which they expended together with the interest which
they would otherwise have received from investing in
British government securities. The bonds were assign-

able but worthless. It follows that from the time when
each of the pursuers made their investment there was   G
a concurrence of injuria and damnum, so entitling
each pursuer to sue the first defenders.

As regards the insolvency of Signal Life, it is
obvious that this did not play any part in bringing
about the pursuers' investment in the bonds. It was an
existing state of affairs to which the pursuers were
exposed as a result of that investment. It may also be
noted that the damnum suffered by the pursuers as a
result of that investment was twofold. In the first place
the pretended security which was advertised in the   H
brochure for the Series Two Bonds and which the pursuers aver that the first defenders should have investigated was non-existent. In the second place the
insolvency of Signal Life entailed that no payment
would be made to unsecured creditors such as the pursuers. In these circumstances the fact that the pursuers
were affected by the insolvency of Signal Life can be
seen to be only part of the disadvantageous consequences of the pursuers' actions in making these
investments. In these circumstances I do not consider I
that the insolvency of Signal Life was a proximate (or
effective) cause of the pursuers' claims.

For these reasons I agree with your Lordship in the
chair that the reclaiming motion should be refused.

───────────

*Counsel for Pursuers and Respondents, Stewart, QC,
Sellar; Solicitors, McClure Naismith Anderson &
Gardiner (for D M Ogilvie, Dundee) — No appearance* J
*for First Defenders — Counsel for Second Defender and
Reclaimer, Nimmo Smith, QC, R Smith; Solicitors,
Maclay Murray & Spens.*

A N

M v Kennedy   K

SECOND DIVISION
THE LORD JUSTICE CLERK (ROSS),
LORDS MURRAY AND KIRKWOOD
11 JULY 1991

*Children and young persons — Children's hearing —
Application to sheriff for findings whether or not grounds
of referral established — Finding that grounds of referral
established under deletion of words specifying locus —*   L
*Whether children's hearing entitled to proceed upon belief
of social work department that offence had taken place at
the particular locus — Social Work (Scotland) Act 1968
(c 49), ss 39 (4) and 43 (1).*

A mentally handicapped child was referred to a children's hearing on the ground that an offence had been
committed in respect of her. One of the statements of
fact provided inter alia that "within the family home
or elsewhere in Glasgow the child was the subject of
unlawful sexual intercourse". At the hearing the

appellants accepted the statement under deletion of the words "within the family home". The reporter applied to the sheriff for a finding as to whether such grounds of referral as were not accepted by the appellants were established. The sheriff found "the grounds for referral" established under deletion of the words "within the family home or elsewhere in Glasgow" and remitted the matter back to the children's hearing. The children's hearing made a supervision requirement requiring the child to live with foster parents. Their decision proceeded, notwithstanding the decision of the sheriff, upon the basis that the family home "may have been the setting of any abuse". Upon appeal, a different sheriff held that the children's panel were entitled to approach the issue on that basis because the sheriff's finding was not negative (i e abuse did not take place at the home), but indicated that he was not satisfied that it had been proved that abuse had taken place at home. The parents appealed to the Court of Session by stated case. The court remitted the case to the first sheriff to clarify his findings. He reported that he had found that abuse had not taken place in the family home.

Held, that the children's hearing were not entitled to ignore the sheriff's finding that no abuse had taken place in the family home and proceed upon the "belief" of the social work department, notwithstanding the deletion, that abuse had taken place in the home (p 434H-J); and appeal *allowed* and case *remitted* to the sheriff to remit to the children's hearing to reconsider the case upon the basis that sexual intercourse did not take place within the family home.

Appeal from the sheriff court

Mr and Mrs M, the parents of S M, appealed to the Court of Session by stated case against a decision of the sheriff upholding a decision of a children's hearing imposing a residential supervision requirement on S M requiring her to live with foster parents.

Statutory provisions

The Social Work (Scotland) Act 1968 provides:

"39.— . . . (4) Where the reporter has arranged a children's hearing in pursuance of the last foregoing subsection, he shall request from the local authority a report on the child and his social background and it shall be the duty of the authority to supply the report which may contain information from any such person as the reporter or the local authority may think fit. . . .

"43.—(1) When a children's hearing have considered the grounds for the referral of a case, accepted or established under the last foregoing section, the report obtained under section 39 (4) of this Act and such other relevant information as may be available to them, they shall proceed in accordance with the subsequent provisions of this section to consider on what course they should decide in the best interests of the child."

The appeal was heard before the Second Division on 21 June 1991.

On 11 July 1991 the court *allowed* the appeal and *remitted* the case to the sheriff to remit to the children's hearing.

The following opinion of the court was delivered by the Lord Justice Clerk (Ross):

OPINION OF THE COURT.—The appellants are the parents of a child S M, who was born on 9 March 1976. The child is mentally handicapped, and for some years resided normally with the appellants in the family home. During 1990 the said child was referred to a children's hearing on the grounds that an offence had been committed in respect of her. One of the statements of fact in support of this was in the following terms: "That between 9 March 1989 and 6 April 1990 within the family home or elsewhere in Glasgow, the child was the subject of unlawful sexual intercourse being a girl of or above the age of 13 years and under the age of 16 years. This being a contravention of s 4 of the Sexual Offences (Scotland) Act 1976."

At a children's hearing the appellants indicated that they accepted the statement of facts under deletion of the words "within the family home". Since the whole grounds for referral were not accepted by the appellants, the children's hearing directed the reporter to make application to the sheriff for a finding as to whether such grounds for referral as were not accepted by the appellants were established. It is thus clear that in this case the sole issue to be determined by the sheriff was whether it had been established that the unlawful sexual intercourse had taken place within the family home.

Proof was heard before the sheriff on 8 and 15 June 1990. It is stated in the stated case that he pronounced an interlocutor in the following terms: "Evidence further led and closed. Having heard parties on the evidence led, finds the grounds for referral established under deletion of the words 'within the family home or elsewhere in Glasgow' and remits the case to the reporter to make arrangements for a children's hearing for consideration and determination of the case."

Thereafter the children's hearing on 28 June 1990 considered the case and decided that the child should reside at a children's home, and the area manager of the social work department undertook to have the case reviewed under s 48 (2) of the Social Work (Scotland) Act 1968. After some further incidental procedure a further children's hearing was held on 2 August 1990, and the supervision requirement was varied so that the child was to live with named foster parents. In their statement of reasons for their decision, the children's hearing stated inter alia:

"The social work department is of the view that while the sheriff did not find it happened at home it cannot discount S's disclosure to the nursery staff and to return her to a setting that may have been the setting of any abuse would not be in her best interests.

"She is a handicapped child who must be protected
and we accept that the parents consider we are being
over zealous in this and we also acknowledge the
difficulties for the SWD in making a recommendation
that appears to fly in the face of judicial finding but
like the SWD we consider S should not return home
at this time."

Against that decision of the children's hearing the
appellants appealed to the sheriff. The appeal came
before a different sheriff on 6 September 1990. In the
course of his submissions to the sheriff the agent for
the appellants stated that he was sure that the original
sheriff by deleting the words "within the family home
or elsewhere in Glasgow" meant to indicate that in his
view the abuse had not taken place at the family home.
He accordingly submitted that the children's hearing
had improperly taken into account matters which had
been excluded from the statement of facts by the
sheriff. The reporter, on the other hand, maintained
that while the children's hearing were bound by the
facts as found by the sheriff, what the sheriff had
found did not preclude the decision which they had
taken. The reporter reminded the sheriff that it was
not necessary when referring a child to a children's
hearing under s 32 (2) (d) of the Social Work (Scotland) Act 1968 to name the perpetrator.

The sheriff states that he found this a difficult case,
but at the end of the day he took the view that the
appeal had failed and that the decision of the children's hearing should be confirmed. In his note the
sheriff made inter alia the following comment: "It was
not disputed that abuse had occurred. The sheriff's
findings were not negative findings, i e they did not
say 'I found that abuse did not take place at home'.
The sheriff deleted the averred locus. This appeared
to me to be an indication that he was not satisfied that
it had been established that the abuse had taken place
at home."

Subsequently the sheriff indicated that it appeared
to him from reading the statement of reasons of the
children's hearing that they based their decision on
two elements — (1) they took the view that they were
entitled to approach the matter on the basis that the
abuse might have occurred at home, and (2) they also
took the view that in the circumstances the girl being
mentally handicapped with limited social contact she
would be better placed with a foster family having
experience in dealing with children in such a condition. The sheriff went on to say that with some hesitation he reached the conclusion that the children's
hearing were entitled to approach the matter in that
way and to come to the decision which they did.

When the appeal was first before this court on 23
April 1991 counsel for the appellants accepted that
when the original sheriff had deleted the words
"within the family home or elsewhere in Glasgow"
that might have been because the locus had not been
established to his satisfaction or because he was satisfied that it had not happened at that locus. He accordingly moved the court to invite the original sheriff to
provide a report for the court. Counsel for the appel-

lants accepted that it was not necessary for the locus
to be established nor was it necessary for the perpetrator to be named. However in this case the locus had
been specified by the reporter in the statement of facts
and the only matter referred to the sheriff for proof
had been whether the specified locus fell to be deleted
from the statement of facts. He submitted that if the
children's hearing were entitled to disregard what the
sheriff had decided in relation to the locus, the procedure of referring the matter to the sheriff for proof had
been a waste of time.

Counsel for the reporter on the other hand,
reminded us that where the sheriff was satisfied on the
evidence before him that the ground of referral had
been established, he was required to remit the case to
the reporter to make arrangements for a children's
hearing for consideration and determination of the
case (s 42 (6A) of the Act of 1968). He also submitted
that since the original sheriff had deleted the words
"within the family home or elsewhere in Glasgow"
this showed that he was not satisfied what the locus
was. He maintained however that it could not be
assumed that the sheriff was excluding the family
home as a possible locus. Accordingly the children's
hearing had been entitled to proceed upon the basis
that the family home may have been the place where
the offence took place.

The court concluded that the appropriate course to
follow in the unusual circumstances of this case was to
remit to the original sheriff so that he could give full
reasons for deleting from the grounds of referral the
words "within the family home" and "elsewhere in
Glasgow".

The case called again before this court on 21 June
1991 when the court had before it a full report by the
original sheriff. In that report he deals very fully with
the evidence which was led before him, and in his conclusion he states that he was not satisfied that it had
been established that sexual intercourse had taken
place within the family home. Subsequently in his
report he stated: "I am able to add to my formal conclusion that, on the evidence submitted to me, it is my
view that the abuse had not taken place within the
family home."

Having regard to the terms of the sheriff's report,
counsel for the appellants maintained that once the
sheriff had determined that the abuse had not taken
place within the family home, it was not open to the
children's hearing to continue to approach the case
upon the basis that the abuse might have taken place
within the family home.

Counsel for the reporter on the other hand maintained first that the sheriff had not been entitled to
make a negative finding, and that the material before
the sheriff had not justified him in reaching that conclusion. Alternatively she submitted that whereas her
grounds of referral had been held to have been established, the children's hearing were still obliged to have
regard to the whole circumstances of the case. She
relied particularly upon the provisions of s 43 (1) of

the Act of 1968 which provides as follows: [his Lordship quoted the terms of s 43 (1) and continued:]

Counsel reminded the court of the terms of s 39 (4) of the Act of 1968. That subsection provides: [his Lordship quoted the terms of s 39 (4) and continued:]

Counsel then drew attention to the terms of a report which is no 55 of process and which is dated 22 June 1990. This is a report to the children's hearing from the social work department and is the report referred to by the children's hearing in their statement of reasons annexed to the decision of 2 August 1990. The final two paragraphs of that report under the heading "Conclusion" are in the following terms:

"The question now arises about S's future needs and protection. While the proof hearing failed to establish where the abuse occurred, the Social Work Department still hold the belief that it has occurred within the family home.

"Given this latter opinion, it is believed that compulsory measures of care are necessary to ensure S's protection and that her developmental needs are met. Hence, it is believed that S's best interests would be served through a Residential Supervision Requirement. At the time of writing, however, an appropriate residential placement has not been identified."

In some cases where there is a ground of referral under s 32 (2) (d) the locus of the offence may not be material. However, in the present case the question of where the offence had taken place was highly material. There was no dispute that abuse had occurred, and the only issue which the sheriff had to determine was whether the words "within the family home" fell to be deleted from the statement of facts. As the original sheriff puts it in his report: "A proof had then been fixed for 8 June 1990 to find whether the words 'within the family home' were established." As already observed in his report the original sheriff now makes it plain that this was not merely a case where it had not been established that sexual intercourse had taken place within the family home, but that it was a case where he was satisfied that the sexual intercourse had not taken place within the family home.

Accordingly, having regard to the circumstances which gave rise to the case being referred to the sheriff, we are of opinion that the children's hearing are bound to proceed upon the basis that the sexual intercourse did not take place within the family home. That was the issue which was referred to the sheriff, and he heard evidence and made conclusions based upon that evidence. The sheriff makes it plain that he held the ground of referral to be established upon the basis that the abuse did not take place within the family home, and that is the basis upon which the children's hearing must now proceed. We are not persuaded that, in the light of the sheriff's findings, it is open to the children's hearing to disregard the sheriff's conclusion and to proceed upon the basis that the sexual intercourse may have taken place within the family home. For the children's hearing to proceed upon that basis would be inconsistent with and contradictory of the sheriff's conclusions.

We recognise that in terms of s 43 of the Act of 1968 the children's hearing have to consider a number of matters including the grounds for referral, but in the circumstances of the present case we are satisfied that it is not open to the children's hearing to proceed upon the basis that the abuse may have taken place within the family home when the sheriff has negatived any such possibility.

At one stage of her argument counsel for the respondent maintained that the sheriff had not been entitled to make a negative finding to the effect that the abuse had not taken place within the family home. Having regard to what the original sheriff says in his report regarding the evidence led before him and the conclusions at which he arrived on the evidence, we are satisfied that there was material before the sheriff upon which he could find that unlawful sexual intercourse had not taken place within the family home.

We entirely agree that the children's hearing were entitled to take into account that a serious offence had been committed in relation to this child, that she was mentally handicapped and required to be protected, but we are also satisfied that they were not entitled to proceed upon the basis that the offence against her may have been committed within the family home.

In the report dated 22 June 1990, what the social work department appear to be saying is that even though the sheriff has excluded the possibility that the sexual intercourse took place within the family home, the children's hearing are still entitled to proceed upon the belief of the social work department that it has occurred there. In our opinion so to hold is to ignore the findings which the sheriff made upon the issue which was referred to him for determination.

Accordingly in the circumstances of this case we are clearly of opinion that the two questions in the case should be answered in the negative. Having so answered these questions we shall remit the case to the sheriff to proceed as accords, and to remit to the children's hearing to reconsider the case upon the basis that sexual intercourse did not take place within the family home.

Counsel for Appellants (Parents), Raeburn; Solicitors, Macbeth, Currie & Co, WS — Counsel for Respondent (Reporter), Patrick; Solicitors, Biggart, Baillie & Gifford, WS.

C H A of L

HM Advocate v Lewis

HIGH COURT OF JUSTICIARY

THE LORD JUSTICE CLERK (ROSS),
LORDS MORISON AND MILLIGAN

13 NOVEMBER 1991

Justiciary — Procedure — Prevention of delay — 110 day rule — Transfer of serving prisoner within United Kingdom — Accused sentenced in Scotland and transferred to England on Home Secretary's order — Accused absconding in England, committing offences in Scotland and being arrested there — Accused fully committed in custody for offences in Scotland — No formal order retransferring accused to Scotland — Whether order necessary to prevent running of 110 day period — Criminal Justice Act 1961 (9 & 10 Eliz II, c 39), ss 26 (1) and (4), 28 (1), 29 (1) and 30 (1) and (3) — Criminal Procedure (Scotland) Act 1975 (c 21), s 101 (2) (b).

Administrative law — Prisons — Transfer of prisoner — Transfer to another part of United Kingdom — Prisoner absconding and arrested in part where originally sentenced — Power of Secretary of State to make further transfer order — Criminal Justice Act 1961 (9 & 10 Eliz II, c 34), ss 26 (1) and (4), 28 (1), 29 (1) and 30 (1) and (3).

Section 26 (1) of the Criminal Justice Act 1961, as amended, provides that the responsible minister may on the application of a serving prisoner, make an order for his transfer to another part of, inter alia, the United Kingdom, there to serve the remainder of his sentence. Section 28 (4) provides that such a prisoner "shall be treated for the purposes of detention, release, recall and otherwise as if that sentence (and any other sentence to which he may be subject) had been passed by a court there". Section 28 (1) provides that where it appears to the responsible minister that a serving prisoner should be transferred to another part of the United Kingdom to attend criminal proceedings against him there, the minister may make an order for the prisoner's transfer.

An accused person was charged on indictment with various charges of theft, reset and fraud allegedly committed between 17 July and 26 October 1990. He had been sentenced in March 1988 to consecutive terms of imprisonment totalling over five years, in respect of other offences. He commenced his sentence in Scotland but in February 1989 he was transferred to prison in England in terms of s 26 (1) of the 1961 Act. He failed to return to prison following a short home leave. On 26 October 1990 he was apprehended in Aberdeen and was fully committed in custody on 5 November 1990. He was served with an indictment calling him for trial at Aberdeen sheriff court on 30 September 1991. When the indictment called for trial the accused submitted in bar of trial that he had been detained in custody for longer than 110 days because his detention was referable not to the warrants of March 1988 but to the warrant of 5 November 1990 since no formal order had been made by the Home Secretary transferring him to Aberdeen prison. The sheriff sustained the

plea on that ground and dismissed the indictment. The Crown appealed by bill of advocation, contending that there was no need for an order transferring the accused to Scotland since the sentences of imprisonment imposed in 1988 had never flown off and had revived as soon as the accused had left England.

Held, that since in terms of s 26 (4) of the 1961 Act the sentences passed in March 1988 fell to be treated as if they had been passed by an English court, and since the order transferring the accused to England in February 1990 had never been superseded by any subsequent order, when the accused was taken into custody on 26 October 1990 the only warrants for his detention in Scotland were the petition and committal warrants, and accordingly the sheriff had reached the correct decision (p 438B-D); and bill *refused*.

Observed, (1) that when the accused had been apprehended in Scotland it would not have been open to the Home Secretary to make an order under s 28 (1) since the accused was already in prison in Scotland (p 438D-E); but (2) that when he was apprehended the accused could and should have been returned to England and then it would have been open to the Home Secretary, if so advised, to transfer the accused to Scotland for the purpose of attending criminal proceedings against him under s 28 (1) (p 438G-H).

Bill of advocation

The rt hon the Lord Fraser of Carmyllie, Her Majesty's Advocate presented a bill of advocation to the High Court of Justiciary against Kevin John Lewis craving the court to recall the decision of Sheriff David Kelbie at Aberdeen dated 2 October 1991 to dismiss the indictment against Lewis on the ground that there had been a failure to comply with the terms of s 101 (2) (b) of the Criminal Procedure (Scotland) Act 1975. The facts of the case are set forth in the opinion of the court.

Statutory provisions

The Criminal Procedure (Scotland) Act 1975 provides:

"101.—. . . (2) Subject to subsections (3), (4) and (5) below, an accused who is committed for any offence until liberated in due course of law shall not be detained by virtue of that committal for a total period of more than — . . . (b) 110 days, unless the trial of the case is commenced within that period, which failing he shall be liberated forthwith and thereafter he shall be for ever free from all question or process for that offence."

The Criminal Justice Act 1961, as amended, provides:

"26.—(1) The responsible Minister may, on the application of a person serving a sentence of imprisonment or detention in any part of the United Kingdom, make an order for his transfer to another part of the United Kingdom or to any of the Channel Islands or the Isle of Man, there to serve the remainder of his

sentence, and for his removal to an appropriate institu-
A tion there. . . .

"(4) Subject to the following provisions of this
section, a person transferred under this section to any
part of the United Kingdom or to any of the Channel
Islands or the Isle of Man there to serve his sentence
or the remainder of his sentence shall be treated for
purposes of detention, release, recall and otherwise as
if that sentence (and any other sentence to which he
may be subject) had been passed by a court there and,
where it is not a sentence which could be so passed,
B as if it could be so passed. . . .

"28.—(1) If it appears to the responsible Minister
that a person serving a sentence of imprisonment or
detention in any part of the United Kingdom or to any
of the Channel Islands or the Isle of Man should be
transferred to another part of the United Kingdom for
the purpose of attending criminal proceedings against
him there, that Minister may make an order for his
transfer to that other part or that island, and for his
C removal to a prison or other institution there. . . .

"29.—(1) If the responsible Minister is satisfied, in
the case of a person detailed in any part of the United
Kingdom in a prison, borstal institution, remand
centre, detention centre or place of safety that the
attendance of that person at any place in that or any
other part of the United Kingdom or in any of the
Channel Islands or the Isle of Man is desirable in the
interests of justice or for the purposes of any public
inquiry, the responsible Minister may direct that
D person to be taken to that place. . . .

"30.—(1) The following enactments (relating to the
arrest and return of prisoners and other persons
unlawfully at large) that is to say — (a) subsection (1)
of section forty-nine of the Prison Act 1952; (b) subsection (1) of section thirty-seven of the Prisons (Scotland) Act 1952; and (c) subsection (1) of section
thirty-eight of the Prison Act (Northern Ireland) 1953,
shall extend throughout the United Kingdom, the
Channel Islands and the Isle of Man; and any refer-
E ence in those enactments to a constable shall include
a reference to a person being a constable under the law
of any part of the United Kingdom or of the Isle of
Man, to a member of the police in Jersey, and to an
officer of police within the meaning of section forty-
three of the Larceny (Guernsey) Law 1958 or any
corresponding law for the time being in force. . . .

"(3) Where a person who, having been sentenced to
imprisonment or detention, is unlawfully at large
during any period during which he is liable to be
F detained in a prison, borstal institution or detention
centre in any part of the United Kingdom is sentenced
to imprisonment or detention by a court in another
part of the United Kingdom, the provisions of section
twenty-six of this Act relating to the treatment of
persons transferred under that section shall apply to
him, while he remains in that other part of the United
Kingdom, as if he had been transferred there under
that section immediately before he was so sentenced,
and the responsible Minister may, if he thinks fit,
make an order under that section (but without applica-

tion in that behalf) transferring him back to the part
of the United Kingdom from which he was unlawfully G
at large."

Bill

The bill contained the following plea in law:

The decision of the sheriff to dismiss said indictment being unjust, erroneous and contrary to law,
should be recalled, and he should be ordained to
proceed as accords. H

The bill was heard in the High Court on 22 October
1991.

On 13 November 1991 the court *refused* to pass the
bill.

The following opinion of the court was delivered by
the Lord Justice Clerk (Ross):
I

OPINION OF THE COURT.—This is a bill of
advocation at the instance of the Lord Advocate
challenging a decision of the sheriff of Grampian,
Highland and Islands at Aberdeen whereby he sustained a plea to the competency of an indictment on
the ground that the complainer had failed to comply
with the terms of s 101 (2) (b) of the Criminal Procedure (Scotland) Act 1975 in that the respondent had
been detained in custody for longer than 110 days
from the date of his committal. J

The facts giving rise to this bill are set forth in the
statement of facts for the complainer. On 3 March
1988 at Aberdeen sheriff court the respondent was
sentenced to periods of imprisonment totalling two
years three months. On 8 March 1988 at the High
Court in Edinburgh the respondent was sentenced to
a period of three years' imprisonment to commence
upon the expiry of said sentences totalling two years
three months. The respondent commenced serving his K
sentences at Shotts prison, Scotland, but on 14 February 1989 he was transferred in terms of s 26 (1) of the
Criminal Justice Act 1961 to England for the
remainder of his sentences to be served in an English
prison. He was first transferred to Durham prison and
subsequently to Verne prison, Gloucester.

The respondent was released from Verne prison on
short home leave for the period 25 to 28 September
1990 but failed to return to Verne prison at the expiry
of said short home leave. Subsequently he was appre- L
hended by officers of Grampian Police on Friday 26
October 1990 in Aberdeen and taken into custody in
connection with the charges which now appear on the
present indictment. He appeared on petition before
the sheriff in Aberdeen on 29 October 1990 and was
committed for further examination in custody. He
appeared again on the said petition containing these
charges on 5 November 1990 when he was committed
until liberated in due course of law. Following upon
his appearance on petition on 5 November 1990 the

A respondent was committed to Aberdeen prison, and it is averred by the complainer that the respondent then recommended serving his prison sentences there. It is also averred that no formal order was made by the Home Secretary transferring him from Verne prison, Gloucester to Aberdeen prison.

The respondent was lawfully served with the said indictment for a sitting at Aberdeen sheriff court commencing 30 September 1991. The indictment called for trial on 2 October 1991. At the calling of the indictment on 2 October 1991 counsel for the respon-

B dent sought and was granted leave to take a preliminary plea to the effect that since no formal order had been made transferring the respondent from Verne prison, Gloucester, England, to Aberdeen prison, Scotland, his detention in Aberdeen prison was not referable to the warrants for his imprisonment granted on 3 March 1988 and 8 March 1988 but was referable to the warrant granted for his committal until liberated in due course of law at Aberdeen sheriff court on 5 November 1990, and that accordingly he had been

C detained in custody for longer than 110 days and should therefore be liberated forthwith, and thereafter be forever free from all question or process in respect of the offences libelled in the charges on said petition. The sheriff, after hearing submissions by counsel for the respondent and the procurator fiscal depute, sustained the plea.

In moving the court to pass the bill, the Solicitor General drew attention to the relevant provisions of

D the Criminal Justice Act 1961 (as amended). Part III deals with the transfer, supervision and recall of prisoners within the British Islands. Section 26 (1) provides as follows: [his Lordship quoted the terms of s 26 (1), followed by s 26 (4) and s 28 (1) and continued:]

For the sake of completeness it should be observed that s 29 (1) contains provisions authorising the removal of a person to another part of the United Kingdom where that is desirable in the interests of

E justice or for the purposes of any public inquiry. Section 30 (1) provides as follows: [his Lordship quoted the terms of s 30 (1) and continued:]

Section 30 (3) contains provisions relating to a person who has been sentenced to imprisonment or detention, and is unlawfully at large during any period when he is liable to be so detained, and is then sentenced to imprisonment or detention by a court in another part of the United Kingdom. The effect of

F these provisions is that if a person who has been sentenced to imprisonment or detention is unlawfully at large and is then sentenced to a further period of imprisonment in another part of the United Kingdom, the provisions of s 26 of the Act of 1961 shall apply to him while he remains in that other part of the United Kingdom as if he had been transferred there under s 26 immediately before he was so sentenced. This provision does not, however, apply to the respondent, as he has not been sentenced to any further period of imprisonment since being apprehended in Aberdeen on 26 October 1990.

At the hearing on 2 October 1991 the sheriff held that having regard to the provisions of s 26 (4) of the G Act of 1961, the sentences and warrants pronounced on 3 March 1988 and 8 March 1988 no longer justified the detention of the respondent in a Scottish prison. At one stage in his note the sheriff appears to express the view that in the present case after the respondent had been apprehended, the Home Secretary could have made an order under s 28 (1) of the Act of 1961 for his transfer to Scotland and for his removal to a prison there. The Solicitor General maintained that this was not so since the respondent was already H in Scotland; he maintained that an order for transfer of a prisoner to Scotland and for his removal to a prison there could only be made by the Home Secretary if that prisoner was in England.

The Solicitor General contended that the original sentences imposed in Scotland had never flown off; there was no need for an order to be made by the Home Secretary re-transferring the respondent to Scotland; in the circumstances here s 26 (4) of the Act I of 1961 did not apply. His submission was that it would be a misuse of language to invoke s 26 (4) in the present case. The words "as if that sentence . . . had been passed by a court there" created a fiction, whereas in this case there was no need for any fiction that the sentence had been passed by a court in Scotland since the original sentence had in fact been passed by a Scottish court. He submitted that the fiction under s 26 (4) ceased to have effect as soon as the respondent left England; when that occurred the original sentences and warrants revived. J

Counsel on behalf of the respondent moved us to refuse to pass the bill. He disputed the averment in the bill to the effect that on 5 November 1990 the respondent recommenced serving his prison sentences in Aberdeen. He maintained that on 5 November 1990 the only warrant which was in force in Scotland was the committal warrant. The warrants relative to the sentences of imprisonment imposed on 3 March 1988 and 8 March 1988 fell to be treated as English K warrants in terms of s 26 (4) of the Act of 1961. He drew attention to a passage in the sheriff's note in the following terms: "As I understand it, the fact that an English court has sentenced someone to a period of imprisonment is no authority for his detention in a prison in Scotland to serve the sentence of what is, in effect, a foreign court. In the present case, the warrants of the Scottish courts, photocopies of which were produced, have to be read subject to s 26 of the Criminal Justice Act 1961. For the purposes of deten- L tion the sentences referred to must now be regarded as sentences passed by an English court. The warrants do not, therefore, any longer give authority for detention in a Scottish prison".

Counsel maintained that the sheriff was well founded in these views. He submitted that when the respondent was apprehended on 26 October 1990 he could have been returned to England where he had been imprisoned at the time when he failed to return on the expiry of his short home leave. Thereafter if

necessary he could have been returned to Scotland by
A virtue of the provisions of s 28 (1). If he were not
returned to England on being apprehended, then
counsel maintained that the only warrant for his
detention was the committal warrant in which case he
was subject to the 110 day rule by virtue of s 101 (2)
(b) of the Act of 1975. He accordingly submitted that
the sheriff had arrived at the correct decision in this
case and he therefore contended that this court should
refuse to pass the bill.

B   We have reached the conclusion that the submissions of counsel for the respondent are to be preferred
to those of the learned Solicitor General, and that the
sheriff reached the correct decision in this case. The
order made on 14 February 1989 for the transfer and
removal of the respondent to England to serve the
remainder of his sentence is still in existence; it has
never been superseded by any subsequent order. That
being so, effect must continue to be given to the order
of 14 February 1989. In terms of s 26 (4) the respondent falls to be treated for the purposes of detention,
C release, recall and otherwise as if the sentences passed
on 3 March 1988 and 8 March 1988 had been passed
by an English court. Accordingly when the respondent was apprehended in Scotland on 26 October 1990
and was taken into custody in connection with the
charges which now appear on the present indictment,
the only warrants for his detention in Scotland were
first the petition and then the committal warrants. In
our opinion the warrants granted by the Scottish
courts on 3 March 1988 and 8 March 1988 no longer
D justified the respondent's detention in Scotland
because, by virtue of s 26 (4), the respondent fell to be
treated as if these sentences had been passed not by a
Scottish court but by a court in England.

We agree with the Solicitor General that when the
respondent had been apprehended in Scotland, it
would not have been open to the Home Secretary to
make an order under s 28 (1) of the Act of 1961 for the
transfer and removal of the respondent to Scotland
E since he was already in Scotland. However we disagree
with the learned Solicitor General's submission that it
would be a misuse of language to invoke s 26 (4) in the
present case. No doubt the language used in that subsection creates a fiction, but once the fact that the sentences had originally been passed by a court in
Scotland has been replaced by the fiction that the sentences had been passed by an English court, that
fiction must continue to operate until the responsible
minister makes another order superseding the first
F order. In our opinion the fallacy of the Solicitor
General's argument is that he is seeking to persuade
the court to read s 26 (4) as if it included words which
are not there; he is really contending that s 26 (4)
should be read as if there were inserted after the words
"shall be treated" the words "during the period of his
detention in that other part of the United Kingdom".
These words do not appear in s 26 (4) and we are not
prepared to read s 26 (4) as if these words were there.
Having regard to the language used in s 26 (4), we see
no reason for construing that subsection as operating
for only a limited duration. Nor are we persuaded that

the original sentence will automatically be revived in
the event of the person sentenced leaving without G
authority the other part of the United Kingdom
named in the s 26 (1) order as the place where he is
to serve the remainder of his sentence.

We also agree with counsel for the respondent that
when the respondent was apprehended on 26 October
1990, he could and should have been returned to
England where he had been ordered to serve the
remainder of his sentence and where he had been
imprisoned at the time when he absconded. It would
then have been open to the Home Secretary, if so H
advised, to transfer the respondent to Scotland for the
purpose of attending criminal proceedings against him
which had been made the subject of the present
indictment.

In all the circumstances we are satisfied that the
sheriff arrived at a correct conclusion in this case, and
accordingly we refuse to pass the bill.

———————

I

*Counsel for Complainer, Solicitor General (Rodger,
QC); Solicitor, J D Lowe, Crown Agent — Counsel for
Respondent, McBride; Solicitors, Stronachs, Aberdeen.*

                                                    P W F

J

Stuart v Crowe

HIGH COURT OF JUSTICIARY
THE LORD JUSTICE CLERK (ROSS),
LORDS MORISON AND WYLIE
13 NOVEMBER 1991

*Justiciary — Procedure — Warrant to search — Police
searching house of suspected drugs dealer when accused* K
*arriving — Accused searched but nothing drug related
found — Police then obtaining warrant to search
accused's house, and discovering incriminating drug
related documents — Police thereafter obtaining warrant
to search accused's garage premises, and discovering drug
related material — Accused subsequently indicted on
charges based on evidence discovered in searches —
Whether reasonable grounds for suspecting accused in possession of controlled drugs — Misuse of Drugs Act 1971
(c 38), s 23 (2).*
                                                        L

During a search by the police of a house of a suspected drugs dealer under a warrant granted in terms
of the Misuse of Drugs Act 1971, the accused arrived
and was searched by the police but nothing of a drug
related nature was found on his person. His motor car
was then searched and a number of shirts were found
but nothing of a drug related nature was found. The
accused was detained under s 2 of the Criminal Justice
(Scotland) Act 1980. The police thereafter applied for
and were granted a warrant under s 23 (2) of the

Misuse of Drugs Act 1971 to search the accused's
A house where certain documents of a potentially drug
related nature were found. Thereafter the police
obtained another warrant under the 1971 Act to search
the accused's garage premises where drug related
material was found. The accused was subsequently
indicted along with inter alios the person whose house
had first been searched, on a charge under s 1 of the
Trade Descriptions Act 1968 in relation to the shirts
and various contraventions of the Misuse of Drugs Act
1971. The accused before his trial sought suspension
B of the two warrants on the ground that the police had
no reasonable grounds for applying for them under the
1971 Act.

Held, that if at the time when the accused arrived
at the premises the police had reasonable grounds to
entertain a suspicion that he was involved with drugs,
which was the reason for the police's searching these
premises, then that suspicion also gave the police
reasonable grounds for taking the matter further and
obtaining a warrant to search the accused's premises
C (p 440H); and bill *refused*.

Guthrie v Hamilton, 1988 SLT 823, *applied*.

Bill of suspension

Raymond Malcolm Stuart presented a bill of suspension to the High Court of Justiciary against F R
Crowe, procurator fiscal, Kirkcaldy, praying the court
to suspend two search warrants dated 1 August 1991
D granted by a justice of the peace under s 23 (2) of the
Misuse of Drugs Act 1971. The facts of the case are
set forth in the opinion of the court.

Statutory provisions

The Misuse of Drugs Act 1971 provides:

"23.— . . . (2) If a constable has reasonable grounds
to suspect that any person is in possession of a controlled drug in contravention of this Act or of any
regulations made thereunder, the constable may — (a)
E search that person, and detain him for the purpose of
searching him; (b) search any vehicle or vessel in
which the constable suspects that the drug may be
found, and for that purpose require the person in
control of the vehicle or vessel to stop it; (c) seize and
detain, for the purposes of proceedings under this Act,
anything found in the course of the search which
appears to the constable to be evidence of an offence
under this Act."

F **Cases referred to**

Allan v Tant, 1986 SCCR 175.
Bell v Black and Morrison (1865) 5 Irv 57.
Guthrie v Hamilton, 1988 SLT 823; 1988 SCCR 330.

The bill was argued before the High Court on 13
November 1991.

Eo die the court *refused* to pass the bill.

The following opinion of the court was delivered by
the Lord Justice Clerk (Ross):

OPINION OF THE COURT.—This is a bill of
suspension at the instance of Raymond Malcolm G
Stuart. The respondent is the procurator fiscal,
Kirkcaldy. In the bill the complainer seeks to reduce
two warrants granted by a justice at Kirkcaldy for the
search of the complainer's house and garage premises.
The statement of facts sets forth the background to
this application. It is narrated that the two warrants
which it is sought to reduce are ex facie valid and give
apparent authority under the Misuse of Drugs Act
1971 for police officers to search the complainer's
house and garage premises used by him. We note that H
in presenting the bill today counsel for the complainer
submitted that it was appropriate to raise this matter
at this stage rather than at the stage of the trial and he
referred to *Bell v Black and Morrison* and *Allan v Tant*.
The advocate depute agreed that it was appropriate for
this issue to be raised by means of a bill of suspension
at this stage. Counsel for the complainer also
explained that although there were two warrants, they
stood or fell together.

What led to these warrants being applied for and I
granted was that on 1 August 1991 police officers were
engaged in a search under the authority of a different
search warrant at the dwellinghouse of the complainer's first co-accused, a man Thomas Forrest
Fairfull at 36 Chapel Place, Kirkcaldy. While the
police were so engaged, the complainer arrived at that
address. He was taken into the house by the police
who there searched his person under colour of the
warrant to search the premises. Nothing of a drug
related nature was found on his person. His car was J
then searched again under colour of the warrant and
there was found in it a number of shirts which formed
the basis of charge 13 on the indictment which the
complainer is presently facing. Nothing of a drug
related nature was there found. The complainer was
detained under s 2 of the Criminal Justice (Scotland)
Act 1980 in relation to the finding of the shirts. It
appeared that thereafter police officers applied for and
were granted the first warrant which is now complained of, that was a warrant which related to a search K
of the complainer's dwellinghouse in Kirkcaldy. It is
narrated in the statement of facts that the warrant was
executed and that certain documents of a potentially
drug related nature were found in the dwellinghouse.
Thereafter the second warrant complained of was
applied for. It related to garage premises used by the
complainer in Kirkcaldy. It is said that the obtaining
of that warrant was wholly dependent upon the execution of the first warrant. The execution of the second
warrant resulted in the recovery of material which L
relates to charges 1, 3, 14 and 15 on the indictment.
The complainer maintains that the application for the
first warrant was in the circumstances unfounded in
the reasonableness of belief as to his involvement with
drug related matters. The warrants are before us and
it is plain that the warrants proceeded upon the basis
that the police had reasonable grounds for suspecting
that controlled drugs were in possession of the complainer on the premises named in the warrant. The
short point which counsel made was that in the cir-

A cumstances the police could not have had any such reasonable belief.

The advocate depute stated that the sole reason for the police suspicion of the complainer was his arrival at a house which they thought was the home of a drug dealer and which they were at the time searching on the authority of another warrant which authorised search of that other individual's premises. The advocate depute also maintained that the complainer had not put forward any good reason for his being there,

B and accordingly since he had arrived at the premises of Fairfull which were being searched by a warrant granted under the Misuse of Drugs Act 1971, the police were entitled to search the appellant's person when he arrived there and that although they found nothing of a drug related nature they were then on the basis of that suspicion entitled to go to a justice and obtain successively the two warrants referred to in the bill.

The point is a very short one because counsel simply

C maintained that in these circumstances the police had no reasonable grounds for suspicion of the complainer in relation to drugs and that therefore there was no proper basis upon which the justice could have granted these two warrants. We were referred to the case of *Guthrie v Hamilton*. That case is certainly authority for the view that when the police were searching the premises of a third party and the complainer arrived there, they were entitled to search him. Counsel for the complainer pointed out that they

D would have been entitled to search that complainer because he was a person found on the premises and the warrant would be in its terms wide enough to authorise the search of any persons found on the premises. However the case of *Guthrie v Hamilton* is of assistance because it goes further than that and deals with the right of police officers to search and detain someone when they had reasonable grounds to suspect that he is in possession of a controlled drug. It seems plain from what was said in that case that if police are

E searching premises by virtue of a warrant under the Misuse of Drugs Act 1971, and a caller arrives there who has no obvious innocent reason for being there, the police are then justified in suspecting that he is involved with controlled drugs. The point was made in that case that the situation might be different if there was an obvious innocent explanation for the caller's presence. If he had been a postman or a milkman or a visiting clergyman then no doubt the police would not be justified in entertaining a sus-

F picion about them in relation to controlled drugs, but that was not the position in the present case and all we were told was that there was certainly no obvious explanation for the complainer's presence on these premises.

It appears to us to be a matter of common sense that if, as here, police officers are searching premises because they suspect that there are controlled drugs on these premises and someone arrives at the premises the police are entitled to suspect that that person is also involved with controlled drugs and therefore to

search his person. *Guthrie v Hamilton* is authority for that. The police did search the complainer's person G but found nothing. In our opinion, however, since he had called at these premises which they believed to be the house of a drug dealer, the police were entitled on the basis of the suspicion which they entertained about the complainer, then to go to the justice and obtain a warrant to search the dwellinghouse and other premises of the complainer. That, as we say, appears to us to be a matter of common sense and it is also, we think, justified by what was said in *Guthrie v Hamilton* as to the reasonableness of the suspicion which the H police had in relation to a caller for whom there is no innocent explanation for his presence. If at the time when the caller arrives at the premises the police have reasonable grounds to entertain a suspicion that he is involved with drugs, which is the reason for the police searching these premises, then in our opinion that suspicion also gives the police reasonable grounds for taking the matter further and obtaining a warrant to search the premises of the complainer. They were entitled to search his person by virtue of the warrant I which they had for searching the premises of Fairfull and, in our opinion, they were justified in the circumstances in thereafter seeking a warrant to search his own premises. It follows that the challenge which is sought to be made in this bill is not in our view a sound one and we shall accordingly refuse to pass the bill.

Counsel for Complainer, Skinner; Solicitors, More & Co — Counsel for Respondent, Burns, QC, AD; Solicitor, J D Lowe, Crown Agent. J

P W F

Stewart's Executors v Stewart

OUTER HOUSE K

LORD KIRKWOOD

3 APRIL 1992

Heritable property — Sale — Informal agreement followed by homologation — Proof of existence of agreement — Whether writ of defenders referable to agreement.

Property — Heritable property — Sale — Informal agreement followed by homologation — Proof of existence of agreement — Whether writ of defenders referable to L agreement.

Contract — Sale of heritage — Formation of contract — Informal agreement followed by homologation — Proof of existence of agreement — Whether writ of defenders referable to agreement.

Agent and principal — Solicitor — Solicitor averred to have granted receipts as defenders' agents — No averment as to instructions — Relevancy.

Prescription — Negative prescription — Contract for sale

of heritage — Obligation to grant disposition — Whether imprescriptible obligation — Prescription and Limitation (Scotland) Act 1973 (c 52), Sched 3, para (h).

Prescription — Negative prescription — Contract for sale of heritage — When obligation enforceable — Relevant acknowledgment — Acceptance by seller of interest on agreed price — Minute of agreement giving right of preemption — Whether performance towards implement — Prescription and Limitation (Scotland) Act 1973 (c 52), s 10 (1).

The father of four children (three sons and a daughter) left a farm to his daughter and one of his sons but expressed a wish that the farm would be sold at a price of £8,000 to another son, who had been tenant of the farm.

When the father died the two to whom the farm had been left agreed in January 1953 with the tenant that the farm would be sold in terms of the will. Subsequently payments of interest and capital were made and receipts granted by solicitors on behalf of the son and daughter. The daughter had been paid £4,000 of capital by 1972 and the other son had continued to receive payments of interest. In March 1973 a minute of agreement was entered into by which the son who had agreed to purchase the farm granted to his brother a right of pre-emption over the farm at a fixed price. After the death in 1988 of the son who had agreed to purchase, an action for declarator and implement of the obligation to grant a disposition was raised by his executors.

The defenders contended (1) that there were no relevant averments of a contract to sell the farm, nor of any informal agreement capable of being homologated; (2) that there were insufficient averments that the solicitors had granted the receipts as the defenders' agents; (3) that the acceptance of interest did not relate unequivocally to the alleged agreement and could not amount to homologation; and (4) that any obligation had prescribed by January 1973.

Held, (1) that an agreement to sell heritage being an obligatio literis, it could not be created by homologation, homologation only validating an informal agreement proved by writ or oath (p 449C-D); (2) that averments that the receipts were issued by solicitors who acted for the defenders would be sufficient for proof although the terms of their instructions were not averred (pp 449G-H and 450C-D); (3) that the receipts were not writs unambiguously referable to an antecedent agreement to sell heritage to which the brother and sister were parties (pp 449H-I and 450D); (4) that the minute of agreement was a sufficient writ to seek to establish that the brother had agreed to the sale (pp 449I-450A); but (5) that since the sale averred was a sale of the whole property and not of a pro indiviso share the executors were not entitled to succeed against one defender and not the other (pp 449E-F and 450F) and action *dismissed.*

Opinion, (1) that the obligation to grant a disposition was not an imprescriptible obligation in terms of para (h) of Sched 3 to the Prescription and Limitation (Scotland) Act 1973 (p 450H-I); (2) that the obligation

was enforceable in 1953 in that the purchaser could then, on tendering the price, have demanded delivery of a disposition (p 450J-K); and (3) that proof before answer would have been allowed on whether or not the receipt of interest and capital amounted to such performance towards implement of the obligation as clearly to indicate that the obligation still subsisted in terms of s 10 (1) (a) of the 1973 Act (pp 450L-451A).

———————

Action of declarator and implement

Mrs Maggie Bella Halkett or Stewart and Keith Douglas Falconer Stewart Jr, the executors nominate of the late Charles Stewart, raised an action against (first) William Stewart and (second) Mrs Catherine Stewart or McCall-Smith. The pursuers sought inter alia declarator that the defender had failed to implement an agreement entered into with the deceased to dispone a farm to him, and implement of the obligation to do so.

The action was raised in the sheriff court and then remitted to the Court of Session.

The case came before the Lord Ordinary (Kirkwood) on procedure roll on the defenders' pleas to the relevancy and that the right founded on had prescribed.

Statutory provisions

The Prescription and Limitation (Scotland) Act 1973 provides:

"7.—(1) If, after the date when any obligation to which this section applies has become enforceable, the obligation has subsisted for a continuous period of twenty years — (a) without any relevant claim having been made in relation to the obligation, and (b) without the subsistence of the obligation having been relevantly acknowledged, then as from the expiration of that period the obligation shall be extinguished. . . .

"10.—(1) The subsistence of an obligation shall be regarded for the purposes of sections 6, 7 and 8A of this Act as having been relevantly acknowledged if, and only if, either of the following conditions is satisfied, namely — (a) that there has been such performance by or on behalf of the debtor towards implement of the obligation as clearly indicates that the obligation still subsists; (b) that there has been made by or on behalf of the debtor to the creditor or his agent an unequivocal written admission clearly acknowledging that the obligation still subsists. . . .

"[Sched 3] The following are imprescriptible rights and obligations for the purposes of sections 7 (2) and 8 (2) of, and paragraph 2 (h) of Schedule 1 to, this Act, namely — . . . (h) any right to be served as heir to an ancestor or to take any steps necessary for making up or completing title to any interest in land."

Cases referred to

Danish Dairy Co Ltd v Gillespie, 1922 SLT 487; 1922 SC 656.
Dryburgh v Macpherson, 1944 SLT 116.

Errol v Walker, 1966 SLT 159; 1966 SC 93.

A *Fisher v Fisher*, 1952 SLT 350; 1952 SC 347.

Gibson v Carson, 1980 SC 356.

Greater Glasgow Health Board v Baxter Clark & Paul, 1992 SLT 35.

Kermack v Kermack (1874) 2 R 156.

McAdam v McAdam (1879) 6 R 1256.

Macdonald v North of Scotland Bank, 1942 SLT 196; 1942 SC 369.

Macdonald v Scott's Executors, 1981 SLT 128; 1981 SC 75.

B *McGregor v McGregor* (1860) 22 D 1264.

Morrison-Low v Paterson, 1985 SLT 255; 1985 SC (HL) 49.

Robb and Co v Stornoway Pier & Harbour Commissioners, 1932 SLT 214; 1932 SC 290.

Shaw v Shaw (1851) 13 D 877.

Textbooks referred to

Bell, *Principles*, p 16.

Gloag and Henderson, *Introduction to the Law of Scotland* (6th ed), p 149.

C Halliday, *Conveyancing Law and Practice*, Vol IV, para 48-24.

Walker and Walker, *Evidence*, p 315.

On 3 April 1992 the Lord Ordinary *dismissed* the action.

LORD KIRKWOOD.—In this action the pursuers are the executors nominate of the late Charles Stewart, D farmer, who resided at Cocklarachy, Huntly, Aberdeenshire, and who died on 10 June 1988. The defenders are the brother and sister of the said Charles Stewart.

The pursuers seek inter alia decree of declarator that the defenders "have failed to implement an agreement entered into between them and the said late Charles Stewart, Farmer of Cocklarachy, Huntly, Aberdeenshire, on or about 18 January 1953, and in particular E have failed to make, execute and deliver to the said Charles Stewart, a valid Disposition of All and Whole the Farm of Cocklarachy in the Parish of Drumblade and County of Aberdeen, together with Eighty acres or thereby of the Ba'hill Wood adjoining the said farm". The second crave seeks decree ordaining the defenders "to implement and fulfil said agreement in all respects within one month from the date of decree to follow hereon, and in particular to make, execute and deliver to the pursuers, in return for the balance of the purchase price, a valid disposition of the said F subjects in favour of the pursuers, the executors nominate of the said Charles Stewart, and to make and execute such other deeds as may be necessary in order to give the pursuers a valid title to the said subjects". The pursuers also crave the court, failing the execution of said deed or deeds, to dispense with the granting of them by the defenders and to direct the Depute Principal Clerk of Session to execute the same. Alternatively, the pursuers seek payment (a) by the first named defender (Dr Stewart) of the sum of £196,000 and (b) by the second named defender (Mrs McCall-

Smith, formerly Miss Catherine M Stewart) of the sum of £200,000, with interest.   G

The late William Stewart, who was the father of Charles Stewart and the defenders, died on 18 January 1953 leaving a trust disposition and settlement dated 31 March 1952 and registered in the Books of Council and Session on 10 February 1953. Clause (second) of the said trust disposition and settlement provided as follows: "I leave and bequeath free of government duties and all expenses the Farm of Cocklarachy belonging to me, and of which my son Charles Stewart is tenant, equally between my son William James   H Morrison Stewart and my daughter Catherine Margaret Stewart: declaring that it is my desire that the said Charles Stewart, will acquire the farm from his brother and sister at the price of Eight Thousand Pounds and that he will pay to his said brother and sister interest at the rate of four *per centum per annum* on the value of the farm or on such portion thereof as shall remain unpaid."

I was informed that at the time of his father's death   I Charles Stewart was the tenant of the farm and that he paid his father a rent of £307 a year.

The pursuers aver that upon the death of William Stewart the defenders "agreed with their brother, the said Charles Stewart, to sell to him the farm and lands of Cocklarachy as directed by and on the terms and conditions stipulated in their father's said trust disposition and settlement". The pursuers aver that interest at the rate of 4 per cent per annum on the said sum of £8,000 was paid by Charles Stewart to the   J defenders as from the date of their father's death, and refer to a receipted "Statement of Sums due by Mr Charles Stewart" dated 9 June 1954 and issued by Messrs Murdoch McMath & Mitchell, solicitors, Huntly, who then acted for the defenders. That document (which is no 39 of process) gives details of inter alia sums paid as "interest due to Dr William J M Stewart and Miss Catherine M Stewart jointly in terms of will". The statement acknowledges payment   K of interest to the terms of Martinmas 1953 and Whitsunday 1954 as well as a proportion of interest from the date of death of the said William Stewart to 15 May 1953. The pursuers go on to aver that after the issue of that statement, payments of interest on the outstanding balances due to the defenders were acknowledged by further half yearly receipts issued by said solicitors on behalf of each of the defenders and the receipts narrated that the sums acknowledged were collected "on behalf of Dr W J M Stewart" and "on   L behalf of Mrs M McCall-Smith" respectively. In any event, by accepting these sums from said solicitors the second defender ratified the solicitors' actings on her behalf. In or about 1954 Charles Stewart paid £1,000 to his sister towards settlement of her share of the purchase price and he thereafter paid interest at the rate of 4 per cent per annum to his brother on £4,000 and to his sister on £3,000. The pursuers produce and found on two receipts dated 27 April 1972 (nos 40 and 41 of process) in terms of which it is averred that the solicitors acknowledged having received from Charles

Stewart interest in respect of the farm of Cocklarachy
A amounting to £80 and £60 on behalf of the first and
second defenders respectively. These amounts of £80
and £60 represented one half year's interest on the
sums of £4,000 and £3,000 at the rate of 4 per cent per
annum. The pursuers then aver that the defenders'
"agreement to sell said farm to their said brother is
accordingly evidenced and acknowledged by the writ
and actings" of the defenders and their agents.

The pursuers further aver that in or about 1972
Charles Stewart paid the balance of £3,000 to his
B sister, so that she had then received the whole of her
share of the purchase price, and that the contract and
payments of interest and capital are referred to and
further evidenced by a minute of agreement between
Charles Stewart and Dr Stewart dated 9 March 1973
and registered in the Books of Council and Session on
23 March 1973. The minute of agreement narrates
inter alia as follows: "And Whereas the said William
Stewart, by Purpose (Second) of his Trust Disposition
and Settlement dated the Thirty-first day of March
C Nineteen hundred and fifty-two and registered in the
Books of the Lords of Council and Session on Tenth
February Nineteen hundred and fifty-three left and
bequeathed, free of Government duties and all
expenses, the farm of Cocklarachy which belonged to
him and of which his son the said Charles Stewart (the
Second Party) was tenant, equally between his son the
said William James Morrison Stewart and his daughter Catherine Margaret Stewart (now Mrs Catherine
Margaret Stewart or McCall Smith residing at Adam-
D ston, Drumblade in the said County of Aberdeen); and
the said deceased declared in said Purpose (Second)
that it was his desire that the said Charles Stewart
would acquire the said farm of Cocklarachy from the
said William James Morrison Stewart and Catherine
Margaret Stewart (now Mrs Catherine Margaret
Stewart or McCall Smith as aforesaid) at the price of
Eight Thousand Pounds (that is Four Thousand
Pounds would be paid to each of them) and that the
said Charles Stewart would pay to his said brother and
E sister, Interest at the rate of Four *per centum per
annum* on the said sum of Eight thousand pounds or
on such proportion thereof as should remain unpaid
(the total sum and accrued Interest due to the said Mrs
Catherine Margaret Stewart or McCall Smith having
been paid to her prior to the date of these presents);
And Whereas the said Charles Stewart pays Interest
twice annually to the said William James Morrison
Stewart in respect of the sum of Four thousand
pounds due by the said Charles Stewart to the said
F William James Morrison Stewart; And Whereas no
Disposition by the Trustees and Executors of the
deceased William Stewart has ever been granted with
the consent of the said William James Morrison
Stewart and the said Catherine Margaret Stewart (now
Mrs Catherine Margaret Stewart or McCall Smith as
aforesaid) since the said William James Morrison
Stewart has never consented to the granting of such a
Disposition, having declared that the said farm and
lands of Cocklarachy aforesaid must be retained in the
'Stewart' family for as long as possible and practicable;

And Whereas the said William James Morrison
Stewart has advanced on loan the sum of approxi- G
mately Thirty Thousand Pounds or such other greater
or lesser sum as may be brought out in a final statement following the completion of erection of the steading aftermentioned, to the said Charles Stewart for the
erection of a new Steading on the said farm of Cocklarachy, Therefore the said Charles Stewart has
irrevocably Agreed and Hereby Agrees and Binds
himself and his heirs, executors, representatives, assignees, creditors and any other party or parties who may
have an interest in his estate whether during his life- H
time or on his death that the said farm of Cocklarachy
which is and shall be held to include the whole buildings and erections on said Farm, the whole fittings and
fixtures, fencing, gates, all standing and fallen timber
and generally everything in, on or about said subjects
(except the Stock and Implements of Husbandry) shall
never be sold by him or by his foresaids under any
circumstances whatsoever without his or their giving
the first option to purchase the said farm of Cocklarachy including the buildings and others detailed as I
aforesaid to the said William James Morrison Stewart
or his nominees at a price of Thirty Thousand Pounds
which price has been agreed and is hereby confirmed
between them as the price of said whole subjects and
that in addition to any sum outstanding at the time
being of said loan of Thirty Thousand Pounds".

The pursuers aver that by his acceptance of the right
of pre-emption, Dr Stewart acknowledged his
brother's ownership of the farm. After the date of the
minute of agreement Charles Stewart ceased payments J
of interest on the part of the purchase price still due
to Dr Stewart and in respect of the sum due to Dr
Stewart, Charles Stewart thereafter wintered cattle
belonging to Dr Stewart on the farm without charge
and he did so in lieu of further payments of interest.
This service continued until the death of Charles
Stewart and was accepted by Dr Stewart in place of
interest on the purchase price of his share of the farm.
The pursuers aver that all of the payments of capital
and interest were made by Charles Stewart in reliance K
upon the contract to purchase the farm from the
defenders upon the terms and conditions stipulated in
his father's trust disposition and settlement and that
these payments were accepted by the defenders on the
basis of that contract.

The pursuers go on to aver that at the time of his
death in 1988 Charles Stewart had still not paid the
balance of £4,000 to his brother and had not obtained
a disposition of the farm. The pursuers state that they
are willing to pay the balance of the purchase price L
and any outstanding interest thereon. They further
aver that, if they do not receive a valid disposition of
the subjects, they will sustain considerable loss and
damage. The value of the subjects has risen considerably since the date of the agreement between Charles
Stewart and the defenders and they are now reasonably valued at £400,000. In these circumstances the
pursuers seek decree for payment to them (a) by Dr
Stewart of the sum of £196,000 and (b) by Mrs
McCall-Smith of the sum of £200,000. The present
action was raised in 1988.

Each of the defenders has inter alia a general plea to
A the relevancy of the pursuers' averments and a plea
that any obligation has been extinguished by
prescription.

Counsel for Dr Stewart submitted that the pursuers'
averments were irrelevant and that the action should
be dismissed. Counsel began by attacking the pursuers' averments relating to the formation of the
alleged contract for the sale of the farm and submitted
that the averments were totally lacking in specifica-
B tion. The pursuers did not specify what form the contract had taken. In particular, it was not stated
whether the contract had been entered into verbally or
in writing, or in what circumstances it had been
entered into. It was significant that the pursuers did
not seek decree of declarator that a contract of sale had
been entered into. While the first crave referred to "an
agreement", the craves in the initial writ did not
specify the terms of the alleged agreement. Further,
the pursuers' pleadings referred to one agreement but
as each of the defenders had succeeded to a one half
C pro indiviso share of the farm, it would have been
necessary for both of them to agree to sell the subjects
to Charles Stewart.

Further, while the pursuers averred that the
defenders' agreement to sell the farm to their brother
was "evidenced and acknowledged by the writ and
actings" of the defenders and their agents, the pleadings did not make clear what writ was being referred
to. The alleged agreement related to a sale of heritage
D but it was not suggested that the agreement had been
constituted by a holograph or tested writing. In these
circumstances the pursuers' case was that there was an
informal agreement followed by homologation. However, the pursuers first had to make relevant averments of an agreement on the part of the defenders to
sell the farm to Charles Stewart. As the alleged contract related to the sale of heritage it was an obligatio
literis and an informal agreement to sell the farm
could only be proved by the writ or oath of the
E defenders. In relation to an alleged contract for the
sale of heritage, it was necessary for the pursuers to
aver the form which the agreement had taken, particularly as the defenders denied that any such agreement
had been concluded. It was not suggested that there
had been an informal writing by either of the
defenders in January 1953 agreeing to sell the farm to
Charles Stewart and the pursuers were not seeking to
refer the matter to the oath of either of the defenders.
It followed that there were no relevant averments of an
F agreement on the part of both of the defenders to sell
the farm to Charles Stewart and on that short ground
the action fell to be dismissed.

In any event, the pursuers aver that the alleged
agreement to sell the farm to Charles Stewart was evidenced by the writ of the defenders and their agents
and, so far as Dr Stewart was concerned, they sought
to found on the receipts nos 39 and 40 of process and
the 1973 minute of agreement. However, in this connection any writ founded on by the pursuers must be
capable of demonstrating unequivocally that the

parties had entered into a binding agreement to sell
the farm (*Robb & Co v Stornoway Pier and Harbour* G
Commissioners per Lord President Clyde at 1932 SLT,
p 217). None of the writs which the pursuers sought
to found on made any reference to a contract for the
sale of the farm. The solicitors' "Statement of Sums
due by Mr Charles Stewart, Cocklarachy" (no 39 of
process) simply referred to interest due to the
defenders jointly "in terms of Will". The receipt (no
40 of process) referred to "Half Year's Interest on
Bond". The pursuers cannot found on the terms of the
trust disposition and settlement of the late William H
Stewart as it was not a writ of the defenders or of
Charles Stewart. The minute of agreement did not
contain any reference to a contract for the sale of the
farm. On the contrary, it stated that Dr Stewart had
never consented to the granting of a disposition of the
farm. In the circumstances, the documents founded on
by the pursuers, either individually or taken together,
do not allow the inference to be drawn that an agreement to sell the farm had been concluded.

Further, there were no relevant averments that the I
documents nos 39 and 40 of process fell to be regarded
as writs of Dr Stewart. While there may be circumstances in which a writ by a solicitor can be regarded
as the constructive writ of his client, the alleged debtor
in the obligation, the party seeking to attribute the
writ to the client must aver that the agent was
instructed to commit the client to the agreement being
founded on (*McGregor v McGregor; Danish Dairy Co
v Gillespie* and *Dryburgh v Macpherson*). As Lord President Clyde observed in *Danish Dairy Co v Gillespie* J
(1922 SLT at p 491): "Authority to make a complete
and binding agreement on behalf of a client is not to
be lightly inferred in the case of a law agent." In a case
such as the present, the pursuers must aver that the
agents were expressly instructed to commit Dr Stewart
to the agreement in question and there was no such
averment. In the absence of such an averment the two
receipts founded on by the pursuers cannot be
regarded as writs of Dr Stewart. Even if the pursuers
had made relevant averments to the effect that there K
was an informal agreement to sell the farm to Charles
Stewart, they would have had to go on to aver that
there had been homologation on the part of Dr
Stewart, but there were no averments that there had
been homologation. The actings from which homologation is to be inferred must be "such acts of the
obligor as imply distinct and unequivocal consent"
(Bell's *Principles*, p 16). Any such actings must relate
unequivocally to the alleged agreement. In this case
the pursuers sought to found on Dr Stewart's accep- L
tance of interest from Charles Stewart as inferring
homologation. However, the acceptance of interest
cannot be regarded as demonstrating Dr Stewart's
express approval of the fact that there was in existence
an agreement to sell the farm. While acceptance of
interest may be sufficient evidence of homologation in
a case where the existence of a debt is in dispute, it is
not sufficient in the case of an alleged agreement to
sell heritage. In the circumstances, the pursuers had
not relevantly averred (a) the existence of an informal

agreement on the part of Dr Stewart to sell the farm, or (b) the fact that the alleged agreement had been validated by homologation.

Turning to the issue of prescription, counsel pointed out that the pursuers were founding on an agreement to sell the farm which was alleged to have been concluded on or about 18 January 1953. By virtue of the old negative prescription the obligation would have prescribed in January 1973, whereas the present action was not raised until 1988 (Gloag and Henderson, *Introduction to the Law of Scotland* (6th ed), p 149; s 17 (1) of the Conveyancing (Scotland) Act 1924). Counsel accepted that the defenders' pleadings made no reference to the long negative prescription. However, the Prescription and Limitation (Scotland) Act 1973 came into force in July 1976. Counsel referred to the provisions of s 7 (1) of the Act. Subsection (2) provides that the section applies to an obligation of any kind, not being an obligation specified in Sched 3 as an imprescriptible obligation. Section 10 (1) defines a relevant acknowledgment and provides inter alia that there must have been "an unequivocal written admission clearly acknowledging that the obligation still subsists". The pursuers aver that the contract of sale was entered into on or about 18 January 1953 and, if that was the case, it was clear that Charles Stewart could at once have enforced the contract by tendering the price and demanding a disposition of the subjects (*Macdonald v North of Scotland Bank*). It could not be contended that the prescriptive period did not begin to run simply because Charles Stewart was not in a position to tender payment of the price, and that the obligation only became enforceable when he had acquired the funds to enable him to tender the full price. He could have borrowed the money and the creditor in an obligation cannot delay the start of the prescriptive period if it is within his power to purify the obligation (*Gibson v Carson*). In the circumstances the prescriptive period had commenced in January 1953 and the obligation had been extinguished by prescription in January 1973. Receipts for the payment of interest did not constitute an unequivocal written admission "clearly acknowledging" that the obligation to grant a disposition of the heritage still subsisted, nor did they constitute a relevant acknowledgment within the meaning of s 10 (1) (a). The receipt of interest could amount to an acknowledgment of the existence of a debt (*Kermack v Kermack* (1874) 2 R, per Lord President Inglis at p 159) but not to an acknowledgment of the existence of a contract to sell land or an obligation to grant a disposition. If the payments and receipt of interest did not operate to interrupt the prescriptive period, the obligation had prescribed in January 1973 and the pursuers could not seek, in relation to the issue of prescription, to found on the minute of agreement which was executed in March 1973. In any event, the minute of agreement did not constitute a new obligation to convey the farm, nor did it amount to an "unequivocal written admission clearly acknowledging" that the obligation still subsisted, particularly as it referred to the fact that Dr Stewart had never con-

sented to the granting of a disposition. It is important to recognise that a "relevant acknowledgment" within the meaning of ss 7 and 10 of the Act must be a clear and unequivocal acknowledgment of the obligation in question (in this case, an obligation to grant a disposition of the farm) (cf *Greater Glasgow Health Board v Baxter Clark & Paul*), but none of the documents founded on by the pursuers was capable of being construed as such an acknowledgment.

Further, the obligation in question was not an imprescriptible obligation within the meaning of para (h) of Sched 3 to the Act. Paragraph (h) referred to "any right . . . to take any steps necessary for making up or completing title to any interest in land". A person who has a contractual right to heritage cannot properly be described as a person who has a right to make up or complete title to any interest in land, as it would be necessary for him to enforce his contractual obligation, and obtain a disposition of the subjects, before he reached the stage of being able to take steps to make up or complete title (Halliday, *Conveyancing Law and Practice*, Vol IV, para 48-24; s 24 of the Conveyancing (Scotland) Act 1924). A party must have a title to complete before he could be in a position to found on the terms of para (h) of Sched 3. In the circumstances, even if the pursuers had relevantly averred the existence of an obligation to convey the farm to Charles Stewart, that obligation had been extinguished by the operation of prescription.

With regard to the pursuers' averments relating to the loss and damage which they have sustained, the 1973 minute of agreement had conferred on Dr Stewart a right of pre-emption of the farm at a price of £30,000 and that right of pre-emption would have been binding on the pursuers. The pursuers were only entitled to be placed in the position they would have been in had the disposition been granted. Even if the pursuers had succeeded in obtaining a disposition of the subjects, Dr Stewart would have had the right to purchase the farm from them at the price of £30,000 and it followed that the pursuers' total loss would be limited to that figure. However, on the whole matter, counsel invited me to dismiss the action.

Counsel for Mrs McCall-Smith adopted the submissions which had been made by counsel for Dr Stewart. In the first place, counsel submitted that the pursuers had not relevantly averred the existence of an agreement on the part of Mrs McCall-Smith to convey to them the one half pro indiviso share of the farm which had been bequeathed to her by her father. The alleged agreement for the sale of the farm was an obligatio literis and as such there were restrictions on the mode of constitution of such an obligation. The pursuers appeared to be contending that the actings of the parties after January 1953 demonstrated that an agreement to sell the farm must have been concluded as the actings were only consistent with there having been a contract of sale. However, an agreement to sell heritage cannot be proved by evidence of the subsequent actings of the parties (cf *Morrison-Low v Paterson*). The pursuers had to aver that an agreement to

sell the farm had been established by communings
A passing between the parties within a short time after
William Stewart's death, but the issue was confused
by the pursuers' fifth plea in law which stated that the
agreement had been evidenced by the writ, actual or
constructive, of the defenders. The pursuers have no
relevant averments that there were communings
between Charles Stewart and Mrs McCall-Smith
leading to an agreement in January 1953. It was necessary for the pursuers to specify the exact nature of the
alleged communings as the existence of a contract to
B sell heritage could only be established by (a) a judicial
admission by Mrs McCall-Smith, (b) a reference to her
oath, or (c) her writing. The existence of an agreement
could not be proved by parole evidence. There was no
judicial admission of any agreement and the pursuers
do not propose to refer the issue to Mrs McCall-
Smith's oath. If the issue as to whether or not there
was an agreement had been going to be referred to her
oath, it would have been particularly important for the
pursuers to specify exactly what form the alleged
C agreement had taken. The documents founded on by
the pursuers are not capable of providing evidence
that Mrs McCall-Smith was party to an agreement to
sell the farm to Charles Stewart. The pursuers would
have to be able to produce a writing or writings of Mrs
McCall-Smith referring unequivocally to an agreement to sell the farm in January 1953, but the documents founded on by the pursuers do not justify such
an inference being drawn. The "Statement of Sums
due by Charles Stewart" (no 39 of process) refers to
D interest due "in terms of Will" but there is no reference to an agreement to sell the farm. The trust disposition and settlement of the late William Stewart was
not a writing of any of the parties to the alleged agreement and, in any event, it only contained an expression of the testator's desire that the farm should be
acquired by Charles Stewart at the price specified. It
did not give rise to any legal obligation. It was necessary for there to have been a subsequent agreement on
the part of both defenders to sell the farm to Charles
E Stewart. The "Statement of Sums due by Charles
Stewart" simply shows that the solicitors who prepared it had been under a mistaken apprehension as to
the effect of the will but it does not support the existence of an agreement between Charles Stewart and
Mrs McCall-Smith to sell the farm to him. Indeed, it
appears to assume that a separate agreement was not
necessary and this militates against an agreement
having been concluded. The receipt for interest is
even more remote from an obligation to convey
F heritage as it bears to relate to a half year's interest on
a bond. In the circumstances the pursuers had not
relevantly averred that an agreement to sell the farm
had been concluded in January 1953.

Even if the pursuers had made relevant averments
that there had been an informal agreement in January
1953 to sell the heritage, they would then have had to
aver that there had been homologation. There were no
averments of homologation and, in any event, the
documents, and the actings, founded on by the pursuers are not unequivocally referable to, and approba-

tory of, an agreement to sell heritage. Further, the
writs founded on by the pursuers cannot be regarded G
constructively as being writs of Mrs McCall-Smith.
She disputes that the relationship of agent and client
existed and she is faced with a bald assertion by the
pursuers that the firm of solicitors acted for her. In
this connection the calls made by Mrs McCall-Smith
have not been answered. She is entitled to specification as to how the pursuers will be seeking to prove
that the relationship of agent and client existed, particularly as, apart from the question of acceptance by her
of interest, proof of such a relationship is critical to the H
pursuers' case against her (a) in relation to proof of the
alleged agreement, (b) in relation to proof of homologation, and (c) in relation to the issue of prescription,
particularly the application of s 10 (1) of the 1973 Act.
She was entitled to know how the solicitors are said to
have had authority to bind her in the way it is alleged
that she was bound (*Danish Dairy Co v Gillespie*).

So far as homologation is concerned, the pursuers
must establish (a) that the relationship of agent and
client existed, and (b) that the agents were given the I
necessary authority (*Fisher v Fisher*). Further, it must
be shown that she knew of the defect in her legal right
and that she had the right to resile (*Shaw v Shaw*
(1851) 13 D per Lord Cockburn at pp 879-880;
Walker and Walker on *Evidence*, p 315). To establish
homologation there must be a state of knowledge far
beyond what is alleged in this case. While the pursuers
rely on the actings of the firm of solicitors, they do not
aver why these actings should be regarded as the
actings of Mrs McCall-Smith. Proof of payment of the J
price and interest would not constitute homologation
unless the pursuers averred that Mrs McCall-Smith
had knowledge of the alleged informal agreement and
the fact that the acceptance of the money amounted to
homologation. So far as the pursuers' averment relating to alleged ratification was concerned, this was not
a relevant averment as the fact that she accepted
money from a firm of solicitors does not infer ratification of actings by them which bound her in a legal
relationship. There was no averment that she was K
aware of what the solicitors were purportedly doing on
her behalf.

Turning to the issue of prescription, counsel
founded on the terms of s 7 of the 1973 Act. The
present action had been commenced in September
1988 but, if a contract for the sale of the farm had been
concluded in January 1953, as the pursuers aver, there
had been an enforceable obligation in existence since
that date. The personal financial circumstances of L
Charles Stewart had no bearing on the existence of
such an enforceable obligation. Charles Stewart could
have tendered the full price in January 1953 and
demanded a disposition of the subjects but he had not
done so. It was not for the defenders to prove that he
was in a position to pay the price. The pursuers could
not rely on s 10 (1) of the Act as there had been no relevant acknowledgment of the subsistence of the obligation to grant a disposition of the farm. An obligation
to pay money, even if it arises out of the same contractual relationship, does not affect the obligation to

grant a conveyance. The fact that Charles Stewart had paid Mrs McCall-Smith interest on the price, and then the price itself, had nothing to do with the obligation to grant a disposition of the subjects (*Gibson v Carson*, per Lord Allanbridge at pp 360-361). Section 10 (1) (b) requires the debtor to have given an unequivocal written admission that the obligation to convey the farm still subsisted (cf *Greater Glasgow Health Board v Baxter Clark & Paul*). The documents founded on by the pursuers did not meet the requirements of s 10 (1) (b) nor were there averments of a relevant acknowledgment in terms of s 10 (1) (a) of the Act. For example, no 39 of process simply referred to interest due to Mrs McCall-Smith in terms of the will and there were no relevant averments of agency. Further, the obligation founded on by the pursuers could not be regarded as being imprescriptible. The right to a conveyance following on a contract for the sale of heritage is quite different from a right to make up or complete title to the subject matter of the contract. Paragraph (h) of Sched 3 had nothing to do with the earlier procedure of obtaining a disposition of the property (*McAdam v McAdam*). Paragraph (h) refers to the process of converting a personal right to land to a real or feudalised right (*Macdonald v Scott's Exrs*). On the whole matter counsel submitted that the action should be dismissed as irrelevant. If a proof was to be allowed, it should be a proof habili modo.

Counsel for the pursuers submitted that it was important to bear in mind the circumstances in which the present dispute had arisen. Charles Stewart had been the tenant of the farm since 1940 and he had paid his father a rent of £307 a year until his death in January 1953 and his tenant's rights in the farm continued after his father's death. In his trust disposition and settlement the late William Stewart had left the farm to the defenders but had expressed the desire that they should sell it to Charles Stewart at the price of £8,000. He had not bequeathed any property to his fourth child, Keith Stewart, as he had already provided for him by setting him up in another farm. It was plain that the whole family had accepted that the father's wishes should be implemented. In 1953 the sum of £8,000 was a substantial one and it was not unreasonable to suppose that the family should have agreed to act in accordance with his expressed desire. After the father's death there had been actings over a period of years on the part of Charles Stewart and the defenders which followed the terms of the father's expressed wish, and the trust disposition and settlement made it clear what the father intended should happen. These actings were clearly and solely referable to the agreement to carry into effect the wishes of the late William Stewart. The "Statement of Sums due by Charles Stewart" (no 39 of process) referred to interest due in terms of the will and this obviously referred to the proposed terms of sale contained in the trust disposition and settlement of the late William Stewart. Accordingly, the document was clearly referable to an agreement to sell the farm to Charles Stewart, interest being payable on the purchase price at 4 per cent per annum. In or about 1954 Charles

Stewart paid the sum of £1,000 to Mrs McCall-Smith. This was payment of part of her share of the price, and she admitted that she had received that sum from her solicitors. Thereafter Charles Stewart paid interest on £7,000, being the outstanding balance of the purchase price. Counsel referred to the two receipts dated 27 April 1972 (nos 40 and 41 of process), which related to payments of interest on £4,000 to Dr Stewart and on £3,000 to Mrs McCall-Smith, both at the rate of 4 per cent per annum. These payments of interest were clearly referable to the agreement to sell the farm to Charles Stewart and his obligation to pay interest on the unpaid balance of the price. The defenders admit receipt of the interest payments. In 1972 Mrs McCall-Smith received the sum of £3,000, being the balance of her one half share of the purchase price. The sum of £3,000 was paid to her by Dr Stewart and Charles Stewart undertook to repay that sum to Dr Stewart.

In March 1973 Dr Stewart and Charles Stewart entered into a minute of agreement which narrated the terms of the late William Stewart's trust disposition and settlement and stated that Charles Stewart had paid interest on the sum of £4,000 due by him to Dr Stewart. This reference to £4,000 was clearly a reference to Dr Stewart's share of the purchase price of the farm. The minute of agreement stated that Dr Stewart had never consented to the granting of a disposition of the farm "having declared that the said farm and lands of Cocklarachy aforesaid must be retained in the 'Stewart' family for as long as possible and practicable". However, the minute of agreement did not state that Dr Stewart was not obliged to grant a disposition of the farm. Further, in terms of the minute of agreement Charles Stewart granted to Dr Stewart an option to purchase the farm if he decided to sell it. This showed that Charles Stewart was entitled to a disposition of the farm once he was in a position to tender the price. It was also significant that neither of the defenders had ever sought a title to their one half pro indiviso shares of the farm. All these facts and circumstances averred by the pursuers demonstrated that on or about the date of the late William Stewart's death an informal agreement had been reached between the parties in terms of which the defenders sold the farm to Charles Stewart in accordance with their father's expressed wish. The pursuers had relevantly averred the existence of an agreement to sell the farm. The agreement could have been reached at a meeting or by the parties knowing of their father's expressed desire and acting on it. However, senior counsel stated quite frankly that he was not in a position to aver what form the alleged agreement had taken. An agreement to sell heritage can be established by (a) an informal written agreement validated by homologation, (b) a verbal agreement validated by homologation, or (c) proved actings which show that an agreement had been reached, i e that the only proper inference from the parties' actings was that there had been an agreement to sell the farm (*Errol v Walker*). Counsel founded on the trust disposition and settlement of the late William Stewart as the foundation document and submitted that the rights of all the parties to this action depended

on it. The writ founded on did not need to be the writ
A of any of the parties to the alleged agreement. While
an informal agreement to sell heritage could only be
proved by writ or oath, the trust disposition and settlement and the other documents produced and founded
on by the pursuers went a long way towards establishing the existence of the agreement to sell the farm. In
this case the actings of the parties averred by the pursuers and evidenced by the documents founded on by
them clearly demonstrate that an agreement to sell the
farm was reached (*Morrison-Low v Paterson*, per Lord
B Fraser, 1985 SLT at p 266).

Even if the writings produced do not establish the
existence of an informal agreement to sell the farm,
the facts and circumstances averred by the pursuers
show that such an agreement was reached. It was suggested that the pursuers had to aver that the solicitors
were authorised to act for the defenders. However, the
solicitors were the family firm of solicitors. They had
collected the interest on behalf of the defenders and
both defenders had admitted that they had received
C the money. The solicitors' acceptance of interest on
behalf of the defenders was plainly within the scope of
their ostensible authority. It was not necessary for the
pursuers to aver the precise nature of the instructions
given by the defenders to their solicitors and, indeed,
they were not in a position to do so. In any event, Mrs
McCall-Smith, by accepting the payments of interest
from her solicitors, had ratified their actings on her
behalf. It was inconceivable that Mrs McCall-Smith
could have believed that all the sums which she
D received from her solicitors over a period of 20 years
were payments in respect of a legacy under her father's
will. In the circumstances it was for the defenders to
show that their solicitors had not been given the necessary authority or that they were acting beyond the
scope of their ostensible authority. Further, Mrs
McCall-Smith had received payment of the whole of
her share of the purchase price.

Turning to the issue of prescription, counsel sub-
E mitted that the obligation to grant a disposition of the
farm was imprescriptible in terms of para (h) of Sched
3 to the 1973 Act. If, however, the obligation to grant
a disposition was capable of being extinguished by
prescription, it had not been extinguished in 1973 but
had been kept alive by the payments of interest which
were accepted by the defenders (*Macdonald v North of
Scotland Bank*). Charles Stewart was under an obligation to pay the purchase price and, until he did so, to
pay interest at the agreed rate on the unpaid balance
F of the price. The defenders were under an obligation,
once the price was tendered, to grant a disposition of
the farm. These obligations were bound up together
and prescription did not begin to run until Charles
Stewart stopped paying interest. Prior to 1973 he had
paid part of the purchase price and he had made
regular payments of interest. In the circumstances, the
obligation to deliver the disposition was held in sus-
pense and prescription did not begin to run until
1973. As the present action was raised in 1988, the
obligation had not been extinguished by prescription.
Mrs McCall-Smith had received regular payments of

interest until 1972 and she had then received the
balance of her share of the purchase price. Accord- G
ingly, in 1972 she had been under an obligation to
grant a disposition to Charles Stewart of her one half
pro indiviso share of the farm. The acceptance of
interest amounted to such performance by her towards
implement of the obligation as clearly to indicate that
it still subsisted (s 10 (1) (a) of the 1973 Act). So far
as s 10 (1) (b) was concerned, the only written
acknowledgment by her that the obligation still subsisted was the receipt for the payment of interest. So
far as Dr Stewart was concerned, he had also accepted H
the payments of interest until 1973. Further, the
probative minute of agreement entered into in 1973
amounted to a relevant acknowledgment by him that
the obligation still subsisted within the meaning of s
10 (1) (b) of the 1973 Act. Alternatively, the obligation
to convey his share of the farm was reconstituted by
the minute of agreement but on a different footing as
the minute of agreement effectively acknowledged that
Charles Stewart had an interest in the land and that
the only obstacle to the granting of a disposition was I
Dr Stewart's refusal to do so for family reasons. In the
circumstances a proof before answer should be
allowed, leaving all the parties' pleas in law, including
those relating to prescription, standing. Alternatively,
a proof habili modo should be allowed.

The pursuers aver that on or about 18 January 1953
the defenders agreed to sell the farm of Cocklarachy to
Charles Stewart. The price was to be £8,000 and
Charles Stewart was to pay to the defenders interest at
the rate of 4 per cent per annum on the value of the J
farm or on such portion thereof as remained unpaid.
It is averred that this agreement carried into effect the
desire which the late William Stewart, who died on 18
January 1953, had expressed in his trust disposition
and settlement. Senior counsel for the pursuers quite
frankly stated that they were not in a position to aver
the circumstances in which the alleged agreement had
been reached or the form which the agreement had
taken. Thus, they could not say if it had been an infor- K
mal written agreement or a verbal agreement nor
could they say where and when the agreement had
been reached. They have not produced any writing in
January 1953 which refers to an agreement to purchase the farm. In particular, there was no evidence
that Charles Stewart had made a written offer, either
probative or improbative, to purchase the farm.
Indeed, it is clear that the pursuers' case is that the
existence of an agreement to sell the farm should be
implied from the actings of the parties after January L
1953. The pursuers' case on record is that the
defenders' agreement to sell the farm to Charles
Stewart is "evidenced and acknowledged by the writ
and actings" of the defenders and their agents.
Counsel for the pursuers submitted that the actings of
the parties, and the documents produced, demonstrated that there had been an informal agreement, at
about the time of their father's death, to give effect to
the desire which he had expressed in his trust disposition and settlement. It was contended that the only
inference which could be drawn from the actings of

the parties, and the documents produced, was that the defenders had agreed to sell the farm to Charles Stewart on the terms proposed by their father. In seeking to prove the existence of an agreement on the part of the defenders to sell the farm, the pursuers found on (a) the expression of desire by the late William Stewart in his trust disposition and settlement, (b) the "Statement of Sums due by Charles Stewart" (no 39 of process), (c) the two receipts for interest dated 27 April 1972 (nos 40 and 41 of process) and (d) the minute of agreement between Charles Stewart and Dr Stewart dated 9 March 1973. Further, since January 1953 Charles Stewart had paid the interest due on such part of the total price as had not been paid, and he had also paid Mrs McCall-Smith her one half share of the purchase price, and these payments had been accepted by the defenders. As I understood the pursuers' arguments, it was not suggested that there was a binding contract in January 1953 — what was said was that there was at that time consensus in idem upon the essentials of a contract of sale and that there was therefore an agreement which could be validated by homologation.

The agreement which the pursuers seek to establish is an agreement to sell heritage and, as such, it is an obligatio literis. It is settled that such an obligation may be constituted only in one of two ways, namely (1) by a writing which is tested or holograph or (2) by an informal agreement which is proved by writ or oath and validated by homologation or rei interventus. In this case the pursuers seek to establish that there was an informal agreement between the parties and that it was validated by homologation. However, homologation can never operate to create an agreement — it can only operate to formalise a pre-existing agreement. Accordingly, before the pursuers can reach the stage of proving that there has been homologation, they must aver and prove the existence of the informal agreement and this can only be done by the writ or oath of the defenders. The issue as to whether or not there was such an agreement is not proposed to be referred to the oath of either of the defenders and accordingly the pursuers must be in a position to found on a writ or writs which demonstrate that both defenders had agreed to sell the farm to Charles Stewart in January 1953. It is not suggested that the agreement was evidenced by any writing in January 1953 and the pursuers' averments are consistent with the alleged agreement having been entered into verbally. Further, the pursuers aver that there was a contract for the sale of the whole property, not of a pro indiviso share, and in these circumstances I do not consider that they would be entitled to succeed against one of the defenders and not against the other. Accordingly, unless the pursuers have relevantly averred that both defenders were parties to the alleged agreement in January 1953, I consider that the action would fall to be dismissed.

So far as Dr Stewart is concerned, the pursuers aver that Charles Stewart paid him interest at the rate of 4 per cent per annum on his one half share of the purchase price until 1973 and that thereafter, until

Charles Stewart's death in 1988, he kept and grazed Dr Stewart's cattle on Cocklarachy in lieu of interest. The pursuers found on the receipted "Statement of Sums due by Mr Charles Stewart, Cocklarachy" dated 9 June 1954 issued by Messrs Murdoch McMath & Mitchell, solicitors, Huntly, and that firm's receipt for interest "collected on behalf of Dr W J M Stewart" dated 27 April 1972 and they aver that Messrs Murdoch McMath & Mitchell issued the receipts on behalf of Dr Stewart. While it was argued on behalf of Dr Stewart that the pursuers could not found on these receipts as being constructively his writs unless they had averred the basis upon which it was alleged that the firm had acted as his agents, and the instructions which the firm of solicitors had received, I consider that the pursuers' averments would be sufficient to entitle them to seek to prove that the solicitors, in granting receipts for the sums in question, were acting on behalf of Dr Stewart. However, even if these two receipts could properly be regarded as being writs of Dr Stewart, I do not consider that they would, by themselves, be sufficient to demonstrate that Dr Stewart had entered into an agreement to sell the farm. In particular, the 1954 receipt related to payments of interest due "in terms of Will" and the 1972 receipt bears to relate to the payment of interest due under a bond. Neither of the receipts makes any reference to an agreement to sell the farm. However, the pursuers also found on the 1973 minute of agreement between Charles Stewart and Dr Stewart which was a probative document. The minute of agreement narrates the relevant section of the late William Stewart's trust disposition and settlement, wherein he expressed the desire that Charles Stewart should acquire the farm from the defenders at the price of £8,000, and it also states that Charles Stewart paid interest twice annually to Dr Stewart in respect of the sum of £4,000 "due by the said Charles Stewart to the said William James Morrison Stewart". The pursuers' case is that the sum of £4,000 could not have been due to Dr Stewart in 1973, and the payments of interest on that sum would not have been made, unless Dr Stewart had been a party to an agreement to sell the farm to Charles Stewart. The minute of agreement goes on to state that the late William Stewart's trustees had never granted a disposition of the farm "since the said William James Morrison Stewart has never consented to the granting of such a Disposition, having declared that the said farm and lands of Cocklarachy aforesaid must be retained in the 'Stewart' family for as long as possible and practicable". Further, in terms of the minute of agreement Charles Stewart granted to Dr Stewart a right of pre-emption of the farm at a price of £30,000. On behalf of the pursuers it was submitted that the terms of the minute of agreement, particularly the reference to the testator's expressed desire in his trust disposition and settlement, the admission that the sum of £4,000 was due by Charles Stewart to Dr Stewart and the granting by Charles Stewart of the right of pre-emption in favour of Dr Stewart, were consistent only with Dr Stewart having agreed to sell the farm to Charles Stewart on the terms and conditions stipulated in his father's trust disposition and

A settlement and that the minute of agreement amounted to an acknowledgment by Dr Stewart that such an agreement had been entered into. Further, the receipt by him of the payments of interest over a period of almost 20 years showed that he had homologated the informal agreement to sell the farm. In the circumstances I would have taken the view that the pursuers' averments are sufficient to entitle them to seek to prove that Dr Stewart was a party to an agreement to sell the farm to Charles Stewart in 1953.

B The next question is whether the pursuers have relevantly averred that Mrs McCall-Smith was a party to the alleged agreement to sell the farm to Charles Stewart. She was not a party to the minute of agreement but the pursuers found on the two receipts granted by Messrs Murdoch McMath & Mitchell as being constructively the writs of Mrs McCall-Smith. The pursuers contend that Messrs Murdoch McMath & Mitchell issued the receipts on behalf of Mrs McCall-Smith and that they can properly be regarded C as her writs. They also aver that, in any event, by accepting the payments of interest from the firm of solicitors Mrs McCall-Smith ratified their actings on her behalf. On behalf of Mrs McCall-Smith it was submitted that the receipts could not be treated as her writs unless the pursuers had averred the basis on which they allege that the solicitors had acted as her agents and what instructions they had been given by her. In the circumstances I would have been inclined to regard the pursuers' averments on this particular D issue as sufficient to entitle them to go to proof before answer. However, even if the two receipts were to be treated constructively as writs of Mrs McCall-Smith, I do not consider that they are capable of establishing that she was a party to an agreement to sell the farm. As I have said, one refers to interest due "in terms of Will" and the other bears to relate to interest due on a bond. While the amounts of interest involved are consistent with being payments of interest on such part of her share of the purchase price as remained E unpaid, the receipts do not contain any reference to an agreement to sell the farm. While they may well be relevant to the issue of homologation, I have reached the conclusion that they are not capable of being regarded as writs which are unambiguously referable to an antecedent agreement to sell the heritage. That being so, the pursuers have not, in my opinion, relevantly averred that there is a writ of Mrs McCall-Smith which demonstrates that she was a party to the alleged agreement to sell the farm in January 1953. As F they do not seek to refer the matter to her oath, it follows, in my view, that they have not relevantly averred that she was a party to the alleged agreement, and on that short ground I consider that the action must be dismissed. As I have already observed, I consider that, in the circumstances of this case, it is necessary for the pursuers relevantly to aver that both of the defenders agreed to sell the farm to Charles Stewart. If there had been relevant averments that Mrs McCall-Smith had agreed to sell the farm, then the averments to the effect that she accepted interest and received her one half share of the price would, in my view, have

been sufficient to entitle the pursuers to seek to prove that she had homologated the agreement. However, I G consider that, in the absence of relevant averments that she was a party to the alleged agreement to sell the farm, the pursuers do not reach the stage of being able to prove homologation.

If I had reached the conclusion that the pursuers had relevantly averred that both of the defenders had been parties to an informal agreement to sell the farm, and that the agreement had been validated by homologation, I would have had to consider the submissions which were made to me on the issue of prescription. H

In the first place, I do not consider that the obligation to grant a disposition of the farm can be regarded as an imprescriptible obligation within the meaning of para (h) of Sched 3 to the 1973 Act. Paragraph (h) refers, not to an obligation, but to "any right . . . to take any steps necessary for making up or completing title to any interest in land". In my opinion, a party is not in a position to take steps to make up or complete title until he is in possession of a disposition of the subjects. I do not consider that para (h) can be construed as applying to an obligation to grant a disposition.

Section 7 (1) of the Act provides as follows: [his Lordship quoted the terms of s 7 (1) and continued:]

Section 10 (1) provides inter alia that the subsistence of an obligation shall be regarded for the purposes of s 7 as having been relevantly acknowledged: [his Lordship quoted the terms of s 10 (1) after "acknowledged" to the end and continued:] J

The obligation which is founded on in this case is an obligation by the defenders to grant a disposition of the subjects in favour of Charles Stewart. If an agreement to sell the farm was concluded in January 1953, as the pursuers aver, I am of the opinion that that obligation was enforceable by Charles Stewart in January 1953 in that he could then have enforced it by tendering payment of the full price and requesting a disposition of the subjects. There is no suggestion in the K pleadings that he was not at that time in a financial position to make payment of the price but, even if such an averment had been made, I do not consider that any impecuniosity on his part would have prevented the running of the prescriptive period. The pursuers do not aver that at any time during the following 20 years Charles Stewart tendered the full price of the farm and demanded a conveyance of the subjects. The next question is whether the defenders had, prior to 18 January 1973, made a relevant acknowledgment that the obligation still subsisted L within the meaning of s 10 (1) of the Act. So far as s 10 (1) (b) is concerned, even if the 1973 minute of agreement could be regarded as constituting an unequivocal written admission by Dr Stewart that the obligation to grant a disposition of the farm still subsisted, this would not avail the pursuers if the obligation had already prescribed in January 1973. However, if I had taken the view that the pursuers had relevantly averred the existence of an agreement on the part of the defenders to sell the farm, I would not

have sustained the defenders' pleas of prescription but
I would have allowed a proof before answer so that the
court could decide, after evidence had been led,
whether, in terms of s 10 (1) (a) of the Act, the acceptance of interest and, in the case of Mrs McCall-
Smith, the receipt of her share of the price, amounted
to such performance towards implement of the obligation as to clearly indicate that the obligation still subsisted.

Counsel for Dr Stewart sought to argue that the pursuers' averments of loss were irrelevant because Dr
Stewart had been granted a right of pre-emption in
1973, giving him the right to purchase the farm at a
price of £30,000 and, accordingly, that the pursuers'
loss would be limited to that figure. In my opinion,
however, this argument is unsound. If the pursuers
did not receive a valid disposition of the subjects, they
would be entitled to be placed as far as possible in the
position they would have been in if they had acquired
a title to the property. If they had obtained a disposition, they would then have been the owners of a farm
which they state is now valued at £400,000, but they
would not have been under any obligation to sell the
subjects.

However, as I have taken the view that the pursuers
have not relevantly averred that both defenders
entered into an agreement to sell the farm to Charles
Stewart, I shall sustain the first plea in law for Dr
Stewart and the second plea in law for Mrs McCall-
Smith and dismiss the action.

_Counsel for Pursuers, Coutts, QC, J R Campbell;
Solicitors, Drummond Miller, WS (for Burnett & Reid,
Aberdeen) — Counsel for First Defender, C J Macaulay,
QC, MacIver; Solicitors, Lindsays, WS — Counsel for
Second Defender, Hamilton, QC, Davidson; Solicitors,
W & J Burness, WS._

S D D N

[A reclaiming motion has been enrolled by the pursuers.]

Landcatch Ltd v Sea Catch plc

OUTER HOUSE
LORD SUTHERLAND
2 JUNE 1992

_Diligence — Arrestment — Recall — Pursuers arresting
funds in hands of bank — Funds held in name of pursuers
in trust on behalf of defenders — Whether arrestments
competent — Whether arrestments to be recalled._

In relation to two actions raised by a limited
company against the same defenders, one action

seeking damages for breach of contract and the other
payment of interest arising out of contract, the pursuers served arrestments on the dependence on a bank.
The pursuers sold salmon on behalf of the defenders
on terms whereby the receipts were placed by the pursuers in an account in their name marked as being in
trust for the defenders. Each month the money so collected was transferred to the defenders' order and the
defenders were then to pay back a commission of 5 per
cent. The arrestments were intended to be effective
against money held in the account in the pursuers'
name but marked as being in trust for the defenders.
The defenders enrolled motions for recall of the arrestments on the ground that they were incompetent. The
pursuers argued that the arrestments were competent
since, although the funds arrested were held in the
pursuers' hands, they were so held as trustees for the
defenders.

Held, (1) that as any control over the account by the
pursuers was exercised only as trustees on behalf of
the defenders, the account was held in a character
different from that in which they were the pursuers in
the actions (p 452I-J); and (2) that if the funds had
been transferred to the beneficial ownership of the
defenders upon having been paid into the account the
arrestments would also be valid (p 452J-K); and recall
refused.

Action of damages
Action of payment

Landcatch Ltd raised two actions against Sea Catch
plc, seeking, in one action, damages for alleged breach
of a contract under which the defenders were obliged
to supply a quantity of fish for rearing under the
management of the pursuers, and, in the second
action, interest, on a contractual basis, arising from
the performance of the pursuers' contractual obligations. The pursuers served arrestments on the Bank of
Scotland on the dependence of the actions. The
defenders enrolled motions in each action seeking
recall of the arrestments.

The motions came before the Lord Ordinary
(Sutherland).

Textbook referred to
Stewart, _Diligence,_ p 105.

Terms of contract
The agreement between the parties provided inter
alia:

"20. Commission on Sales: All monies received by
the manager from sales of the owner's salmon shall
belong to the owner and shall be separately banked by
the manager in a bank account or bank accounts
specifically marked that they are in trust for the owner
or in name of the owner; at the end of each calendar
month after sales of salmon shall have commenced and
throughout the period of this contract, the manager
shall cause all sums in such bank accounts to be trans-

A ferred immediately to any bank account notified by the owner for the purposes hereof and shall, at the same time, supply to the owner a detailed schedule showing all receipts including names of customers, dates of payment and the like and reconciling the same with each transfer of monies; within three days after the receipt by the owner of such documentation, then, in the absence of manifest error, the owner shall transfer back into the manager's bank account as sales commission, a sum being 5% of all receipts from sales during the relevant period covered by the remittance and

B documentation received from the manager."

On 2 June 1992 the Lord Ordinary *refused* the defenders' motions.

LORD SUTHERLAND.—In these two actions the pursuers seek damages for alleged breach of contract and interest on a contractual basis from the defenders, the total sum involved being in the region of £216,000. The pursuers have arrested the sum of

C £240,000 in the hands of the Bank of Scotland and the motion before me today was for the recall of these arrestments. It is not necessary for me to go into detail of the actions as it is a matter of agreement that the essential feature which has bearing on the present motion is that the relationship between the parties is governed inter alia by a management contract of which cl 20 is in the following terms: [his Lordship quoted its terms and continued:]

D In this contract the pursuers are the manager and the defenders are the owner. Under the terms of this clause the pursuers opened a bank account with the Bank of Scotland in the name of the defenders and there is currently at credit of that account some £242,000. It is this account which the pursuers have arrested and which is the subject of the present motion.

Both parties accepted and indeed founded upon what is said by Graham Stewart on *Diligence*, p 105,

E which is in the following terms: "Arrestment is competent in the hands of him who is debtor to the arrester's debtor. It is an incompetent diligence to attach moveables in the hands of the debtor himself or in the hands of the arrester. To this there are but three exceptions . . . (3) an arrester may arrest in his own hands funds which he holds in a different character to that in which he is pursuer."

The argument for the defenders was that the arrest

F ment offends against the principle that moveables in the hands of the arrester cannot be arrested. Under the terms of cl 20, although the account with the Bank of Scotland is in the name of the defenders, it is in fact the pursuers' account and under their control. They may have an obligation at the end of each calendar month to cause the balance to be transferred to any bank account notified by the owner, but in the meantime it is their account and they alone can control it. That being so the present diligence is incompetent and should be recalled. In particular because of the arrangement of cl 20, the bank do not have any duty

G to account for the balance in this account to the defenders but would only have a duty to account to the pursuers. That being so the diligence cannot be effective as an arrestment can only be effective if the bank had a duty to account to the defenders.

In reply counsel for the pursuers founded upon the exception which is referred to by Graham Stewart. It is clear that until the end of the calendar month, the funds are under the control of the pursuers, but during that period the pursuers are not holding the funds as beneficial owners, but only in trust for the defenders. The account may nominally be in the name

H of the defenders, but in truth it is an account being maintained by the pursuers for funds being held in trust for the defenders until the end of the calendar month when they will finally be paid away. Accordingly, as the pursuers are holding these funds as trustees for the defenders, they are entitled to arrest the funds albeit in their own hands when they are suing not as trustees but as individuals. The only other possibility would be that the funds as soon as

I placed in the account would automatically be transferred to the ownership of the defenders although the defenders would not have a right to have them transferred to any other bank account until the end of a calendar month. Either way the arrestment is valid and should not be recalled.

In my opinion the pursuers' analysis is the correct one and their argument should prevail. Whatever might be the position in the absence of cl 20, it is clear from the terms of that clause that insofar as the pur

J suers retain control over the money in the bank account, this control is being exercised only as trustees on behalf of the defenders. That being so, in my opinion, the funds are being held in a different character to that in which they are pursuers in the present actions and accordingly the case falls within the third exception narrated by Graham Stewart. If the position be that the funds have been transferred to the beneficial ownership of the defenders as soon as they were paid into the account, then the bank would have an obligation to account to the defenders and again the

K arrestment would be valid. The only other possibility that could be advanced would be that the funds in the bank account were in the beneficial ownership of the pursuers and that in my view, having regard to the terms of cl 20, cannot be a tenable proposition. For these reasons I shall refuse the defenders' motion to recall the arrestments.

Counsel for Pursuers, McNeill, QC, Grotrian; Solicitors, Snell & Co, WS — Counsel for Defenders, Martin, QC; Solicitors, Brodies, WS.

B J

Miller v Lanarkshire Health Board

OUTER HOUSE

LORD COULSFIELD

16 JUNE 1992

Process — Mode of inquiry — Proof or jury trial — Medical negligence — Whether complexity of likely proof outweighed simplicity of parties' pleadings.

A patient sued in respect of allegedly negligent performance of a laparoscopy whereby, it was claimed, a trocar punctured the left common iliac artery. At procedure roll the pursuer moved for issues, that motion being opposed. The pursuer's averments were simple, her proposition being that if a practitioner of ordinary competence displayed due skill in performance of the procedure, the artery would not be pierced. The defenders averred that because the technique was blind, and because of variables between patients, the occurrence of such a wound was not per se suggestive of substandard skill and care.

Held, that while the pleadings set out relatively simple positions, and there would be no difficulty in framing an appropriate issue, in applying the rule governing the standard of care to the facts it would probably be necessary to draw inferences from the primary facts, which would involve precise consideration of detailed anatomical evidence, and accordingly the case was not suitable for jury trial (p 454E-F and I-L); and proof before answer *allowed.*

Action of damages

Maureen Martha Murdoch Waterson or Miller raised an action of reparation against Lanarkshire Health Board in respect of injuries allegedly sustained in the course of a laparoscopy operation performed on 16 August 1988.

The case came on procedure roll before the Lord Ordinary (Coulsfield) when the pursuer sought issues and the defenders a proof before answer.

Cases referred to

Beswick v North Manchester Health Board Authority, HH Judge Humphreys, QBD, 14 March 1989, unreported.

Bolam v Friern Hospital Management Committee [1957] 1 WLR 582.

Hunter v Hanley, 1955 SLT 213; 1955 SC 200.

Whitehouse v Jordan [1981] 1 WLR 246.

On 16 June 1992 his Lordship *refused* issues and *allowed* a proof before answer.

LORD COULSFIELD.—The pursuer in this action was admitted to Monklands General hospital on 16 August 1988 for laparoscopy, an operation in which portholes are created in the abdominal wall to permit the insertion of a telescope by which the internal organs may be inspected. The operation was carried out by Dr M Deeny, for whom the defenders accept responsibility. The character of the operation and the method by which it was carried out in the pursuer's case are substantially agreed in the averments of parties. It involves the insertion of a hollow tube into the abdomen through an incision in the supra-pubic area, the inflation of the abdomen by the introduction of carbon dioxide gas through the tube, and the insertion of a trocar inside an outer sleeve cannula. The trocar is a sharp instrument which must be directed at the pelvic brim, in order to avoid contact with the great blood vessels within the abdomen. Thereafter, the trocar is withdrawn, the necessary inspection procedures are carried out through the cannula and, in due course, the instruments are withdrawn and the gas released. In the pursuer's case, the procedures were carried out without apparent incident, but some time afterwards her condition deteriorated and emergency action, including a laparotomy, had to be carried out. It was discovered that she had sustained a puncture wound to the left common iliac artery, about 1 cm below the bifurcation of the aorta. The wound was treated but the pursuer suffered various ill effects, for which she seeks damages.

The action came before me in the procedure roll on 7 May 1992. The pursuer moved for issues but the defenders submitted that the action was unsuitable for jury trial. The pursuer's case of fault and the defenders' answer to it are stated quite simply and briefly on record. The pursuer avers that the injury to the iliac artery must have been caused by Dr Deeny during the laparoscopy and, while the defenders do not in terms admit that it was so caused, they do not suggest any other possible cause. The pursuer avers that if a gynaecologist of ordinary competence displays the standard of skill and care reasonably to be expected while carrying out a laparoscopy, a wound of the left common iliac artery will not be caused. The defenders aver that the technique is blind, that because of variables between patients, such as the position of the bifurcation and the angle of the right common iliac artery, damage can occur and that the occurrence of a wound in the position above described is not per se suggestive of substandard skill and care. They further aver that Dr Deeny carried out the operation with her usual standard of technique.

The contentions of the parties can also be set out quite briefly. The defenders submitted that the case involved difficult and delicate questions in the application of the proper standard of care in an action against a professional person, in a field in which there was considerable conflict of medical opinion. The pursuer submitted that the standard of care was well established by cases such as *Hunter v Hanley* and *Bolam v Friern Hospital Management Committee* and that there would be no difficulty in framing an issue for the trial of the cause or in explaining to a jury the question which they had to decide. Counsel for the pursuer stressed that special cause had to be shown to render an action unsuitable for jury trial if it fell within the enumerated causes.

A The defenders referred me to *Beswick v North Manchester Health Board Authority,* an unreported decision of Judge Humphreys, sitting as a judge of the High Court, dated 14 March 1989. The circumstances of that case were very similar to those of the present case. In that case, a laparoscopy was carried out through an incision at a different point from that in the present case and the plaintiff sustained a wound of the right, rather than the left, common iliac artery but these differences are not, so far as can be judged at this stage, material. Judge Humphreys heard evidence on B behalf of the plaintiff from two consultant surgeons who stated that their opinion was that if proper care had been taken the artery would not have been penetrated. He heard evidence that none of the witnesses had any personal experience of right common iliac artery damage in laparoscopy, although their experience ran to thousands of occasions of the procedure, and he was also referred to a number of textbooks which appear, at least prima facie, to support the view that damage will not occur if proper care is taken. On the other hand he also heard evidence from C three consultants called as witnesses by the defendants who took a different view and said that, as the defenders maintain in the present case, the mere occurrence of damage does not indicate that proper care has not been taken. The evidence is not analysed in depth in the judgment. In summary, Judge Humphreys indicated that he was less impressed by the experts led on behalf of the plaintiff than by those led on behalf of the defendants, and that he took the view that the literature, although at first sight favourable to the plaintiff's case, might be setting out a standard greater than that required by the law. The judge D gave considerable weight to the evidence of the doctors who had actually carried out the operation and accepted that they had done so by an acceptable technique within acceptable limits and that there had not been any failure in care and skill. He therefore held that the defendants were not liable to the plaintiff. There was also, in that case, an issue as to the after care of the plaintiff which does not arise in the present case; on that issue also the judge held in favour of the defendants.

E Since this action falls into the class of enumerated causes, it is for the defenders to show special cause rendering it unsuitable for jury trial. The circumstances most often founded on as special cause have been difficulty in framing an appropriate issue and difficulty in explaining to a jury the legal questions and considerations involved in a proper decision of an action. In the present case, I do not think that there would be any difficulty in framing an appropriate issue. The question is one of fault and the normal F form of issue appropriate to any action of personal injuries is equally appropriate here. Again, I do not think that there is particular difficulty in stating in general terms the legal rule governing the standard of care to be expected of a professional person in a manner which a reasonable juryman might be expected to understand. As was submitted on behalf of the pursuer, it is well established that what is required of a doctor is that he should exercise the skill and care of an ordinary competent practitioner of the particular branch of the profession on which he is engaged and that in judging the application of that standard it must

be borne in mind that the obligation is not to guarantee a successful result but to exercise proper G care in carrying out the procedure. I do not think that these general statements are necessarily beyond the comprehension of an average person called to serve on a jury. However, when the general rule has to be applied to particular facts, much greater difficulties are, in my opinion, likely to arise. With all due respect to the decision in *Beswick* it seems to me that the broad approach adopted in that case of preferring one body of evidence to another in general terms may not be wholly satisfactory. If the procedure of laparoscopy is normally carried out without any ill effects, one might H expect that it would be possible to suggest some reasons why it went wrong in a particular case. There is some indication in the judgment in *Beswick* of some of the factors relied on by the defendants. It was suggested that the technique is blind, because the operator cannot see inside the abdomen, while the trocar is a very sharp instrument and the vessels are very close to the target area, so that a variation in position of 1 or 2 cm, which is within the natural variation to be expected, can cause a vessel to be hit. These statements do not, however, in my view, advance the I position very far because if they are accepted as correct, without further explanation, it is not easy to see why incidents of striking a major vessel are as rare as, apparently, they are.

These considerations indicate, in my view, that it is likely to be necessary to determine, so far as possible, what gave rise to the injury in the present case. In order to do so, it seems to me that it is likely to be necessary, as it was in *Whitehouse v Jordan,* to draw J inferences from the primary facts and that in order to do so it may be necessary to consider with some precision detailed evidence as to anatomical matters. It further seems to me that it will only be possible to consider the question whether the proper standard of care was exercised in the light of some assessment of the reason or possible reasons for the unfortunate consequences of the operation in this case. It is, I think, an oversimplification to express the issue as a straightforward choice between a body of opinion to the effect that proper skill and care will avoid any damage of the K kind which occurred, on the one hand, and, on the other, a body of opinion to the effect that even if all proper care is exercised, injury may occur. In any event, even if in the end of the day the question does resolve into a choice of that kind, it seems to me that it is a choice which can only properly be made in the light of a much fuller assessment of the facts and circumstances than is possible looking at the pleadings as they stand. It follows, in my opinion, that this is a case in which the application of the proper legal standard can only be carried out after the particular facts have L been established with some precision and that accordingly the case is not suitable for jury trial. I shall therefore refuse the pursuer's motion for issues and allow a proof before answer.

Counsel for Pursuer, Woolman; Solicitors, Balfour & Manson, Nightingale & Bell — Counsel for Defenders, R W J Anderson; Solicitor, R F MacDonald.

R N T

B, Petitioner

A HIGH COURT OF JUSTICIARY

THE LORD JUSTICE CLERK (ROSS),
LORDS CULLEN AND WYLIE

14 MAY 1992

Justiciary — Procedure — Place of safety order — Sheriff granting warrant to detain accused youth in custody of local authority — Extract warrant for committal stating that sheriff granted warrant to detain accused in named

B *assessment centre — Accused subsequently moved to another centre — Accused petitioning nobile officium against transfer — Whether court had power to specify particular place of safety — Criminal Procedure (Scotland) Act 1975 (c 21), s 24 (1).*

Section 24 (1) of the Criminal Procedure (Scotland) Act 1975 provides: "Any court, on remanding or committing for trial a child who is not liberated on bail shall, instead of committing him to prison, commit him to the local authority in whose area the court is

C situated to be detained in a place of safety chosen by the local authority for the period for which he is remanded or until he is liberated in due course of law".

A 15 year old youth appeared on petition charged with murder and attempted murder. The sheriff pronounced a place of safety order under s 24 (1) of the 1975 Act that the youth be kept at Newfield Assessment Centre, Johnstone. He was thereafter fully com-

D mitted. Subsequently, he was transferred from that centre to Kerelaw, Stevenston, Ayrshire. The extract warrant of committal showed that the sheriff granted warrant to detain the youth in the custody of Strathclyde Region authority at Newfield Assessment Centre but the record of proceedings showed that the sheriff in fact granted warrant to detain the youth in a place of safety in the custody of Strathclyde Region therein to be detained until liberated in due course of law, without specification of the place at which the youth was to be detained. The youth presented a peti-

E tion to the nobile officium of the High Court and maintained that his transfer from the one centre to the other was contrary to the terms of the place of safety order which the sheriff had made.

Held, (1) that s 24 (1) required the court to commit the child in question to the appropriate local authority for him to be detained in a place of safety chosen by that authority, so that the place of safety should not have been specified in the extract warrant and the

F actual warrant had been correct in not specifying that place (p 456C-D); and (2) that, accordingly, it would not be competent to grant the remedy sought (p 456E); and petition *dismissed*.

Petition to the nobile officium

E P C B, born 4 August 1976, charged with murder and attempted murder and subsequently detained, presented a petition to the nobile officium of the High Court of Justiciary against his transfer from Newfield

Assessment Centre, Johnstone, to Kerelaw, Stevenston, Ayrshire. The petitioner maintained that G that transfer was contrary to the place of safety order pronounced by the sheriff (G Evans) at Glasgow sheriff court on 24 March 1992 which had indicated that the place of safety was to be Newfield Assessment Centre. The facts appear from the opinion of the court.

Statutory provisions

The Criminal Procedure (Scotland) Act 1975 provides: H

"24.—(1) Any court, on remanding or committing for trial a child who is not liberated on bail shall, instead of committing him to prison, commit him to the local authority in whose area the court is situated to be detained in a place of safety chosen by the local authority for the period for which he is remanded or until he is liberated in due course of law."

The petition was heard before the High Court on 14 May 1992.   I

Eo die their Lordships *refused* the prayer of the petition.

The following opinion of the court was delivered by the Lord Justice Clerk (Ross):

OPINION OF THE COURT.—This is a petition addressed to the nobile officium of the court at the instance of E B. The petitioner is 15 years of age J and the petition narrates that on 16 March 1992 he appeared at Glasgow sheriff court on petition. He was charged along with others with murder and attempted murder. It is averred that on that date the sheriff made a place of safety order that the petitioner should be kept at Newfield Assessment Centre, Johnstone. It is further narrated that on 23 March 1992 the petitioner appeared before the sheriff when he was fully committed. The petitioner goes on to explain that although he was originally taken to Newfield Assess- K ment Centre, Johnstone, subsequently he had been moved to Kerelaw, Stevenston, Ayrshire, and he maintains that that was contrary to the terms of the place of safety order which the sheriff had made.

In the petition the petitioner goes on to seek to be admitted to bail, but today counsel on his behalf has explained that he is no longer pursuing the issue of bail. He does, however, invite the court to review the detention of the petitioner upon the view that since the sheriff stipulated that the petitioner should be kept L at Newfield Assessment Centre, Johnstone, he should not have been moved to Kerelaw, Stevenston.

It appears that the sheriff was acting under the powers conferred upon him by s 24 (1) of the Criminal Procedure (Scotland) Act 1975. Section 24 (1) provides inter alia as follows: [his Lordship quoted the terms of s 24 (1) set out supra and continued:] That appears to have been the statutory power under which the sheriff acted when he made this place of safety order. There has been produced to us an extract warrant of committal which bears that on 24 March the sheriff granted warrant to detain the petitioner in the custody of Strathclyde Region authority at Newfield Assessment Centre. On the other hand when we examine the record of proceedings it appears that on 24 March 1992 what the sheriff in fact did was to grant warrant to detain the petitioner in a place of safety in the custody of Strathclyde Region, therein to be detained until liberated in due course of law. On that document there is no specification of the place at which the petitioner was to be detained.

It appears to us that that order which the sheriff made on 24 March 1992 was one which he was empowered to make under s 24 (1). The mistake appears to be that in the extract warrant the place at which the petitioner is to be detained has been entered, although that place does not appear in the actual warrant granted by the sheriff. We can readily understand that before a sheriff decides to make a place of safety order he will wish to be satisfied that the local authority concerned has a place available for detaining the individual in question and we are given to understand that what happened on this occasion was that before the order was made Strathclyde Regional Council were approached and were asked whether a place could be made available for detaining this youth and that the court was informed that Newfield Assessment Centre would be the appropriate place. No doubt that is why the reference to Newfield Assessment Centre appears in the extract warrant. We are quite clear however that that place should not have been specified in the extract warrant, and that it was correct that it was not specified in the actual warrant. We say that because it is plain from the terms of s 24 (1) that what the court ought to do is to commit the child to the appropriate local authority for the child to be detained in a place of safety chosen by the local authority. The statute makes it quite plain that it is the authority and not the court which requires to select the particular place of safety where the child is to be detained. That being so we are satisfied that the reference to Newfield Assessment Centre should not have appeared in the extract warrant, but that the extract warrant should merely have recorded that the sheriff had granted warrant to detain the petitioner in the custody of Strathclyde Region authority. It would then be for Strathclyde Region authority to determine the appropriate place for this child to be detained. It is for the local authority and not the court to determine that matter.

It follows that neither the sheriff nor this court has any power to specify the particular place of safety where the petitioner should be detained, and that accordingly it would not be competent for this court to grant counsel for the petitioner the remedy which he seeks. Counsel for the petitioner did explain that there were difficulties for the petitioner's parents in visiting him at Kerelaw and that there were other problems there because of the presence at Kerelaw of a nephew of the victim referred to in the petition. We can well understand that these matters do give rise to problems, but the Solicitor General explained that his information was that the local authority had moved the petitioner to Kerelaw because there had been a lack of security at the assessment centre where he was originally detained. The question of where he should be detained, as we say, is, however, a matter for the local authority and it is not open to this court to direct the local authority as to where the individual should be detained in a place of safety. For the foregoing reasons we therefore refuse the prayer of this petition.

Counsel for Petitioner, Armstrong; Solicitors, Macbeth Currie & Co, WS — Counsel for Respondent, Solicitor General (Dawson, QC); Solicitor, J D Lowe, Crown Agent.

R F H

(NOTE)

Buchanan v Lanarkshire Health Board

OUTER HOUSE

LORD KIRKWOOD

29 JULY 1992

Damages — Amount — Solatium and loss of earnings — Back — Mechanical low back pain resulting in significant disability — Future wage loss calculated using a 5 year multiplier for lady aged 53 at date of proof.

A 50 year old auxiliary nurse slipped and fell, apparently causing a muscular strain in her groin. She returned to work after about two weeks but thereafter found her back to be giving her trouble, finally leading to her having to give up work about 16 months later. She suffered continuing disability symptoms.

Held, that solatium was properly assessed at £10,000 and that future loss should be calculated using a multiplier of 5 years; and decree *pronounced* accordingly.

Sophia Buchanan raised an action against her employers, Lanarkshire Health Board, for damages following an accident in the course of her work as an auxiliary nurse on 2 April 1989. She was then aged 50. She had slipped and fallen awkwardly. After a proof the Lord Ordinary (Kirkwood) held that she had slipped on oil left on the floor from maintenance work being carried out on laundry trolleys. His Lordship held the defenders liable. In relation to damages his Lordship said:

"I now turn to the issue of damages. Parties were agreed that the pursuer's loss of pension is £10,000, that the value of her claim for services rendered to her in terms of s 8 of the Administration of Justice Act 1982 is £1,000 and that the expenses which she incurred, inclusive of interest, amounted to £300.

However, there was a dispute as to the value of her claim for solatium and the amount of her total wage loss.

"So far as solatium is concerned, the pursuer gave evidence that immediately after her fall she had pain in her left groin and she went to the duty room. When she left the duty room her back and groin were very painful and she was seen in the hospital's casualty department. She was advised that she had sustained a muscular strain in her groin and that she should go home and rest. She went home and she was off work for two to three weeks. After she returned to work she found it difficult to cope at times and she was assisted by her fellow employees who had seen that she was in discomfort. She took painkillers most nights. She said that she had returned to work because of the shortage of staff and because she had been losing wages. Her husband was not well paid and her income was important to them. Further, she had been told that her injury was only muscular and she expected it to improve but it did not do so. She usually rested at home prior to working at weekends but she became able to do less and less at work and at home and her progress was gradually downhill and her back pain became steadily worse. She had difficulty walking and eventually, in August 1990, the nursing officer told her that she was not fit to be at work and she was sent to the casualty department and then taken home by ambulance. Between April 1989 and August 1990 she had visited her general practitioner but she had not told him about her back pain as she wished to continue working if at all possible. In November 1990 she was admitted to hospital for about two and a half weeks and she was on traction for 10 days and was then in bed awaiting a myleogram. The traction appeared to have improved the condition of her back but after being put on a bed pan one day the pain got worse again. In June 1991 she received acupuncture treatment after she had been referred to the pain clinic, and she also received steroid injections. In addition, she had yoga treatment and stress relief therapy which helped her to cope mentally with her disability. There had, however, been little change in her condition. She is unable to lift heavy objects or do any gardening and she has difficulty pushing a hoover and putting on her tights. She had regularly looked after her grandchildren two nights a week when her daughter was working, a task which she had enjoyed, but she had had to stop looking after them. Prior to the accident she had been a very active person and she had had no trouble with her back or her legs. Her disability had resulted in a total change in her lifestyle and has left her feeling frustrated and, at times, depressed. She cannot now sit or stand for any length of time and she does not like going out socially and prefers to stay at home. She has had to give up her former hobbies of sewing, knitting and crocheting as she cannot sit comfortably. She has pain in her back which radiates into her foot and on occasions she lies on the floor in an effort to relieve the pain. She finds it difficult to get in and out of a bath. Her ability to perform the straight leg raising test depended upon the degree of pain from which she was suffering and what she had been doing before the test. Since the accident she had never walked really freely and at times she dragged her foot, and she has had reduced skin sensation in her left leg. On occasions she has had sharp pains in her left knee and also hot and cold sensations. She denied that she had been exaggerating her symptoms.

"The pursuer's husband, David Buchanan, gave evidence that prior to the accident the pursuer had enjoyed her work at the hospital. After the accident she had complained of pain in her lower back but she did not want to stop working. During the 16 months after the accident her back had become progressively worse and there were many things in the house which she found that she was unable to do, particularly the heavier housework and gardening. She used to look after her grandchildren two nights a week but she eventually had to give up looking after them. She could not cope physically and she became frustrated. Until she stopped work in August 1990 there was a progressive deterioration in her condition and the pain was too much for her. Since she stopped work she had been unable to do any heavy work in the house and she had obvious pain in her back and legs. She cannot now pursue her hobby of knitting as she cannot sit for long. He has seen her lying on the floor in an effort to ease the pain. The degree of pain appears to vary and if she rests the pain seems to be less severe. She has difficulty bending and lifting and her walking is restricted. Prior to the accident she had been a very active person.

"Mrs Hazel Whyte, the pursuer's daughter, said that she went to see the pursuer the day after the accident and found her lying on a couch looking very strained and in pain from her back and hip. She was off work for about two weeks and during that time she could not do anything and Mrs Whyte had to do the housework and the cooking and help her to dress. Before the accident the pursuer had been very active and she had enjoyed her work at the hospital. Between April 1989 and August 1990 the pursuer had gradually got worse and she had to give up looking after Mrs Whyte's two children two nights a week. The pursuer had stopped working in August 1990 and by then she could not walk without difficulty. She has had to give up knitting and she cannot sit or stand for any length of time. On occasions she lies down on the couch or on the floor. Her condition now is much the same as it was in August 1990. She is probably coping better mentally although she still becomes frustrated at her inability to do things which she could have done prior to the accident. She was certain that her mother was not exaggerating her symptoms. There was no cross examination of Mrs Whyte's evidence. [His Lordship then narrated the similar evidence given by other friends and neighbours. His Lordship thereafter narrated the import of the evidence of the pursuer's general practitioner and of the orthopaedic surgeons who gave evidence and continued:]

"Counsel for the pursuer invited me to accept the evidence of the pursuer and the witnesses led on her

A behalf. The fact that the pursuer had actively sought a variety of different treatments, and had sought a second opinion from Professor Waddell, a specialist in back pain, showed that her complaints of pain were genuine and that she was trying to bring about an improvement in her condition. The fact that she had had to stop looking after her grandchildren for two nights a week, a task which she had enjoyed, was another indication that her complaints were genuine. She had worked on for some 16 months after the accident in spite of suffering pain and discomfort but

B this was because of a shortage of staff and because she had enjoyed her work and did not want to stop working. She only stopped working because she was told to stop as it had become clear that she was not fit to carry on. Dr Logan, her general practitioner, had known her for 17 years and he had always regarded her as a genuine person. Mr Graham [the consultant orthopaedic surgeon led on behalf of the prusuer] also took the view that her pain was genuine and that there was an organic basis for it. The pursuer has been

C showing the classical symptoms of low back pain which is a recognised condition. Mr Scott [a consultant orthopaedic surgeon led by the defenders] had examined the pursuer on only one occasion and he had agreed that his findings were only one part of the overall picture. He had accepted that she was suffering from back pain although he had also expressed the view that she had been exaggerating her symptoms. On the evidence it had been established that the pursuer has been suffering from mechanical low back

D pain which was due to the accident in April 1989 and that the pain is constant although it varies in severity. Mr Graham had said that the pursuer's back pain will be likely to persist until she is in her late 60s or early 70s and it would then probably ease off so that the pursuer will have a significant disability for most of the rest of her life. The pursuer is not now able to do things which she could do before the accident and this has led to frustration, particularly as it is clear that prior to the accident she was a very

E active person. With regard to the issue of functional overlay, there was admittedly evidence that the pursuer had exaggerated her condition to a certain extent when she was being examined by the two orthopaedic surgeons. Although Mr Graham had found certain inappropriate responses he still concluded that her pain was genuine. While Mr Scott had taken the view that the pursuer was exaggerating her symptoms, he had accepted that she was suffering pain. He did not go so far as to say that she was malingering or was

F being deliberately untruthful. He had agreed that it would have been helpful if he had seen her more than once and that it was necessary to take into account all the other information which was now available to the court and which had a bearing on her condition. He had also stated (a) that most people try to impress him with the extent to which their lifestyles had been disrupted, (b) that the more a person's life had been disrupted the greater was the likelihood that there would be inappropriate responses, and (c) that a sizeable proportion of patients demonstrated inappropriate responses on examination. It was clear that the pur-

G suer's lifestyle had been seriously disrupted and she was also under stress when she was being examined by the defenders' specialist. The presence of a degree of functional overlay did not mean that the pursuer was malingering. Functional overlay can be deliberate or unconscious. In this case it was clear that the pursuer had not intentionally exaggerated her symptoms. Taken as a whole, the evidence had established that her complaints of pain and disability were genuine. Counsel referred to *Martin v Grootcon (UK) Ltd*, 1990 SLT 566; *Campbell v Dumfries and Galloway Health Board*, 1991 SLT 624; *Harrison v R B Tennent Ltd*, H 1992 SLT 1060, and *Duncan v Scottish Marine Biological Association*, 1992 SLT 554, and submitted that an appropriate award of solatium would be in the region of £12,000 of which one third should be attributed to the past.

"Counsel for the defenders submitted that while the pursuer had some back pain she was clearly exaggerating her symptoms to a significant extent, and to the extent that she was exaggerating them she was not I entitled to damages. The court had to try to ascertain the extent of her pain and suffering which was truly attributable to the accident. After the accident the pursuer had worked on for about 16 months and during that time she had never consulted her general practitioner about her back pain although she had consulted him on other matters. The fact that she had not sought the advice of her general practitioner during that period showed that the pain from which she was suffering was not as great as she had tried to make out and was not severe enough to justify seeking medical J advice. Counsel founded heavily on the evidence of Mr Scott which, he said, showed that the pursuer had been deliberately exaggerating her symptoms and Mr Scott had said that her exaggeration bordered on malingering. The evidence had shown that there was no organic basis for her alleged pain and that there is now very little physically wrong with her. The evidence of her relatives, colleagues and Mrs Soutar [a friend and neighbour] had been of little assistance as they had simply accepted her complaints at face value. K The evidence of the orthopaedic consultants had been more objective and they had both expressed the opinion that she had been exaggerating her symptoms. Counsel accepted that inappropriate responses on medical examination do not necessarily indicate that the patient is malingering but the extent of the inappropriate responses found by Mr Scott showed that the pursuer was intentionally exaggerating. There was evidence that there was an element of functional overlay and if the pursuer had wished to establish that L that was due to an underlying psychiatric condition, and that her exaggeration was not deliberate, then she should have led the evidence of a psychiatrist but she had not done so. In the absence of such evidence, the existence of a functional overlay could not sound in damages. Counsel referred to *Easton v National Coal Board*, 1981 SLT (Notes) 73, *Zabiega v Borders Health Board*, 1984 SLT 394, and *Murray v British Railways Board*, 1990 SLT 853, and submitted that even if the pursuer's evidence was accepted at face value and there had been no significant exaggeration on her part an award of solatium should not exceed £6,000. However, in the circumstances of this case that figure would fall to be reduced to give effect to the extent to which she had been exaggerating her symptoms and two thirds of the award should be attributed to the past.

"I listened very carefully to the pursuer when she gave evidence and I had regard to her demeanour and the manner in which she gave her evidence and I formed the view that, when she was speaking of her disabilities since the accident, she was a credible and reliable witness. The evidence of the pursuer was supported by that of her husband, Mrs Soutar and her daughter, Mrs Whyte and I believed the evidence of these witnesses. The pursuer was off work for two to three weeks after the accident and she then worked on until August 1990 and during that time she admittedly did not consult Dr Logan about the condition of her back. However, I accepted her evidence that she enjoyed her work, that her income was important to her and her husband and that she did not wish to give up work. I think that she carried on working for as long as she was able to do so in spite of the fact that she was suffering increasing pain and discomfort. In this connection I accepted the evidence of Mrs Smith and Mrs Mellors and I considered that Mrs Smith was right when she said that she thought that the pursuer was simply gritting her teeth and getting on with it. However, by August 1990 it had become clear that the pursuer was no longer fit to do her job properly and the nursing officer was called and she was sent home.

"I was also very impressed by Dr Logan, who had been the pursuer's general practitioner for many years. He had always considered her to be a genuine character and he did not consider that she had been exaggerating her symptoms to him. Mr Graham, the consultant orthopaedic surgeon who was called as a witness by the pursuer, gave evidence that in his opinion she was suffering from mechanical low back pain which was due to the accident, that her back pain had an organic basis, that her complaints of pain were genuine and that she will continue to have mechanical low back pain although it will probably ease off when she is in her 60s and 70s as the back naturally stiffens. He took the view that there will be very little change in the pursuer's condition over the next 15 years. He also stated that although, on examination, she had exaggerated her symptoms to a certain extent, this exaggeration had not been deliberate and he was satisfied that she had not been malingering. I found Mr Graham to be a most impressive witness and I accepted his evidence.

"Mr Scott, the consultant orthopaedic surgeon called by the defenders, spoke to a number of inappropriate responses and he expressed the opinion that the pursuer had been grossly exaggerating her symptoms. He said that she was attempting to impress him to a degree which was bordering on malingering. However, Mr Scott examined the pursuer on only one occasion, in July 1991, and he agreed that his findings were only one factor for the court to take into account in determining the true extent of the pursuer's disabilities. He also said that the more a person's lifestyle had been disrupted, the greater the likelihood of inappropriate responses due to unintentional functional overlay. He said that a majority of patients showed inappropriate responses. He also referred to the fact that the pursuer had not consulted her general practitioner about her back during the 16 month period she worked on after the accident and he assumed that she was not in sufficient pain to warrant seeking medical advice, but I did not accept his evidence on this matter. There was certainly evidence that the pursuer exaggerated her symptoms to a greater or lesser extent when she was being examined by the two orthopaedic consultants and that this was due to functional overlay. In this connection it seemed to me that the two consultants were perfectly familiar with the concept of functional overlay in relation to back pain and I took the view that they were both sufficiently well qualified to express these opinions on that aspect of the case.

"It is clear that if there is an element of functional overlay the patient's exaggeration can be either deliberate or unintentional. Mr Graham expressed the opinion that her exaggeration was unintentional while Mr Scott took the view that she was exaggerating to such an extent as to be bordering on malingering. Having seen and heard the pursuer giving evidence, I was satisfied that she did not, in the witness box, seek to exaggerate the disabilities from which she has been suffering and I accepted Mr Graham's evidence that her exaggeration in the course of clinical examination was not intentional. In the circumstances I had no hesitation in reaching the conclusion that the pursuer is not a malingerer. On the whole matter I accepted the evidence of the pursuer, and her supporting witnesses, as to the extent of the disabilities from which she has been suffering since the accident. She used to be a very active person but as a result of the accident she has suffered from mechanical low back pain which has left her with significant disabilities. Further, there is unlikely to be any significant improvement in her condition over the next 15 years. Having considered all the evidence, and making due allowance for the extent to which she exaggerated her symptoms when she was being examined by the two orthopaedic consultants, I have reached the conclusion that the value of her claim for solatium is £10,000.

"With regard to loss of wages, the pursuer was off work for two to three weeks after the accident and thereafter she returned to work and she worked on until August 1990. She has not worked since and it is agreed that her employment with the defenders was terminated on 16 September 1991 on the grounds of incapacity and that her net wage loss to date is £7,844.62 inclusive of interest. Parties are also agreed that her present annual net wage, if she had remained in the defenders' employment, would be £6,824.48.

"The pursuer gave evidence that since August 1990 she has been unfit to return to her work as an auxiliary nurse due to her restricted movement and her difficulty in walking, bending and lifting. In June 1991 she attended a hearing before the unit general manager, the director of nursing services and the unit personnel manager which considered a recommendation for termination of her employment on the grounds of incapacity. As a result of that hearing her employment was terminated with effect from 16 September 1991 and she was not required to work the period of notice. She said that but for the accident she would have continued to work as an auxiliary nurse until she reached the age of 65 and that she would have had the option of doing so. Before the accident she had begun to pay superannuation contributions. Her husband is six years older than her and is not very well paid and she would have worked on until she was eligible for her pension. If her condition does not improve she did not consider that she would be fit for any kind of employment, particularly as she cannot sit or stand for any length of time.

"The pursuer's husband expressed the opinion that she was not fit to return to work as an auxiliary nurse. Her daughter, Mrs Whyte, stated that, but for the accident, her mother would have worked on for as long as she was able to do so, probably until the age of 65. Dr Logan gave evidence that the pursuer was not fit to return to work and, unless there is a material improvement in her condition, he could not suggest any job which she would be capable of undertaking. Mr Graham said that he would expect the pursuer to continue to suffer from mechanical low back pain and that it would not be likely to ease off until she was in her late 60s or early 70s. He thought that there would be very little change in her condition over the next 15 years. In his opinion she will not be able to return to work as an auxiliary nurse. As she cannot stay in one position for long, it is difficult to envisage any form of employment which she would be likely to be able to undertake. He did not see her getting back to work at all as a result of the accident. Mr Scott stated that he was not convinced that the pursuer is as restricted as she is claiming and felt that she probably could get back to work as an auxiliary nurse in theatre. If she was not fit to return to work as an auxiliary nurse then she would still be fit for some other forms of employment. However, he accepted that if the condition of the pursuer's back was as bad as she said it was, then she could not return to her pre-accident employment and it was unlikely that she could carry out any full time work.

"Counsel for the pursuer submitted that the evidence had established that the pursuer has been unfit for work as an auxiliary nurse since August 1990 and that it is unlikely that she will ever be able to take gainful employment in the future. She is now 53 years of age and but for the accident she would have worked on until she reached 65. In these circumstances she was entitled to the agreed figure for loss of wages to date and she was also entitled to an award in respect of future loss of wages, the appropriate multiplier being 6. Counsel for the defenders submitted that the pursuer is fit to return to work as an auxiliary nurse. If she is not able to return to her pre-accident employ-

ment she is still fit for some forms of light work. She was not entitled to any award for future wage loss. If, however, such an award was to be made then, having regard to her age, the appropriate multiplier should not be greater than 4.

"I had no hesitation in accepting the evidence of the pursuer, and her supporting witnesses, that she is not fit to return to her pre-accident employment as a nursing auxiliary. In this connection it is, I think, significant that her employment with the defenders was terminated on 16 September 1991 on the grounds of incapacity and that the defenders stated that they were unable to offer her any suitable alternative employment. Further, having regard to the nature of her disabilities, I do not consider that she is likely to be able to take any other form of gainful employment in the foreseeable future. She is now 53 years of age and she stated that it had been her intention to work on until the age of 65 if she was fit to do so. Whether she would have been able to do so must be, to some extent, a matter of conjecture but Dr Logan stated that there was nothing in her medical records which would be likely to have prevented her from working on until that age. In the circumstances I consider that an appropriate multiplier, for the purpose of calculating her future loss of wages, will be 5.

"On the whole matter I find the pursuer entitled to (a) the agreed sum of £10,000 in respect of her loss of pension, (b) the agreed sum of £1,000 in respect of the services rendered to her, (c) her expenses of £300, inclusive of interest to date, (d) the sum of £10,000 in name of solatium, (e) the sum of £7,844.62 being her net wage loss to date inclusive of interest, and (f) the sum of £34,122.40 in name of future loss of wages, making a total of £63,267.02. So far as solatium is concerned, I consider that one third should be attributed to the past and that the pursuer is entitled to interest thereon from 2 April 1989 to date at the rate of 7½ per cent per annum."

Counsel for Pursuer, H H Campbell, QC, Caldwell; Solicitors, Robin Thompson & Partners — Counsel for Defenders, Ardrey; Solicitor, R F MacDonald.

C H

Lord Advocate's Reference No 2 of 1992

HIGH COURT OF JUSTICIARY
THE LORD JUSTICE CLERK (ROSS), LORDS COWIE AND SUTHERLAND
23 OCTOBER 1992

Justiciary — Crime — Assault — Accused admitting actions constituting actus reus of assault but explaining that they were done as a joke — Whether motive — Whether defence to charge of assault.

An accused person was tried on indictment for a
A contravention of s 17 (2) and (5) of the Firearms Act
1968 and attempted robbery by assaulting two shopkeepers, presenting an imitation handgun at them,
placing them in a state of fear and alarm for their
safety, demanding money and demanding that they lie
on the ground. The Crown led evidence that the
accused in the late afternoon entered the premises and,
holding the gun in both hands with his arms outstretched in front of him, said words to the effect:
"Get the money out of the till and lay on the floor".
B Another member of staff then stood up from behind
the counter and the accused, seeing her, ran out of the
door. The accused admitted entering the shop,
presenting an imitation firearm, stating "this is a hold
up", ordering them to get down on the floor and
demanding money from them. He accepted that the
shopkeepers were alarmed by his actings but his
defence was that his actions were a joke and that he
had no evil intent to assault or rob. The trial judge
directed the jury that if they believed the accused that
he had no evil intent they would acquit him, but on
C the other hand, they might wish to judge the accused's
actings objectively of how other people appreciated his
actings if they were not satisfied with his explanation
of his intent.

The accused was acquitted and the Lord Advocate
presented a petition to the High Court in terms of
s 263A (1) of the Criminal Procedure (Scotland) Act
1975 to obtain the court's opinion on whether the
evidence of the accused that his admitted actions were
carried out as a joke constituted in all the circum-
D stances a relevant defence to the charges libelled
against him. The Crown, however, restricted the question to the charge of assault.

Held, that the accused's assertion that it was a joke
meant no more than that it was his motive or ulterior
intention in acting as he did, and as it was plain that
when the accused entered the shop, presented the
handgun and uttered the words which he did, he was
acting deliberately, the accused had the necessary
E intent for his actions to amount to assault and his
motive was irrelevant (pp 464F-H, 466D-E and 467D-E).

Dictum of Lord Justice Clerk Inglis in *HM Advocate
v Elizabeth Edmiston* (1866) 5 Irv 219, *applied*.

Opinion reserved, on whether the claim that it
was a joke would be a relevant defence to the crime of
attempted robbery and whether the jury were entitled
to hold that the charge of attempted robbery was not
proven (pp 464L-465A, 466E and 467F-G).

F ——————————

**Reference by the Lord Advocate to the High
Court**
The rt hon the Lord Rodger of Earlsferry, Her
Majesty's Advocate, presented a petition to the High
Court of Justiciary in terms of s 263A (1) of the
Criminal Procedure (Scotland) Act 1975. The petition
was in the following terms:

(1) That the material facts which give rise to this
reference are as follows:

(a) A person (hereinafter referred to as "X") was
indicted for trial in the High Court of Justiciary on G
charges of (1) assault with intent to rob and attempted
robbery; and (2) contravention of the Firearms Act
1968, s 17 (2) and (5);

(b) The case proceeded to trial before Lord
MacLean at the sitting of the High Court of Justiciary
at Glasgow which began on 17 February 1992. The
jury found each charge not proven by a majority;

(c) The complainers in Charge 1 were Marie
Carberry or Daly and Tiffany Sali Rubin. In the H
course of the trial Mrs Daly gave evidence that in the
late afternoon of 4 November 1991 she was standing
behind part of the counter in the shop premises mentioned in charge (1) when the door was thrown open
and X entered the shop and presented a handgun at
her. He was holding the gun in both hands with his
arms outstretched in front of him. He said words to
the effect "get the money out of the till and lay on the
floor". At this time Tiffany Sali Rubin was crouched
down behind a different part of the counter putting a I
jacket onto a small boy who was there with his mother.
Miss Rubin stood up to see what was happening and
X, seeing her, ran out of the door. Mrs Daly stated
that she did not take what the accused did as being a
joke and that if she had been in the shop herself she
would probably have handed over the money to him.
Miss Rubin gave evidence that at approximately
quarter to five or 20 minutes to five on the afternoon
of 4 November 1991 she was working in the shop and
was trying to get a jacket onto a little boy who was in J
the shop with his mother. At that time she was
crouched down behind the counter, her head being
below the counter. She heard a buzzer which operated
when the door was opened and looked up to see X
pointing a gun at Mrs Daly. X was standing with his
arms extended in front of him and the gun between his
hands. X said words to the effect: "Get the money out
of the till and lie down on the floor." She said that he
sounded serious and she took him seriously. She stood
up and X, upon seeing her, ran out of the shop. She K
said that she did not find the incident funny and she
took it as a serious incident;

(d) In the course of the trial, X admitted entering the
premises mentioned in charge 1, presenting an imitation firearm at the complainers in charge 1, stating
"This is a hold up", ordering them to get down on the
floor, and demanding money from them. He accepted
that they were alarmed by his actings;

(e) X's defence was that his actions were a joke, that L
he had no evil intent to assault or rob the complainers
and that accordingly his actions lacked the criminal
intent necessary for the commission of the crimes
libelled;

(f) The advocate depute in her address to the jury
submitted that it was not a relevant defence to an
assault charge that the actions constituting the assault
were carried out as a joke;

(g) Counsel for X in his address to the jury submitted that if the jury accepted X's evidence that the

A actions were carried out as a joke the necessary evil intent for the commission of the crime of assault would be lacking and X would require to be acquitted;

(h) The trial judge directed the jury that assault is any attack on the person of another with evil intent, that whether or not there was evil intent was at the heart of the instant case, that the accused's evidence was that his actions were a joke and there was no evil intent, and that if the jury believed X's evidence that he had no evil intent they would acquit him.

B (2) It is submitted that the trial judge ought to have directed the jury in relation to charge 1 that the accused's admitted actions constituted the crime of assault; that the necessary evil intent was inevitably to be inferred from the deliberate commission of the acts themselves; that it was not a relevant defence that the said acts were committed as a joke; and that if the jury accepted that the said acts were committed as a joke, the jury, if otherwise satisfied as to the accused's guilt, were bound to convict.

C The petitioner accordingly refers the following point of law to your Lordships for an opinion:

Did the evidence of the accused that his admitted actions were carried out as a joke constitute, in all the circumstances, a relevant defence to the charges libelled against him?

Cases referred to

Advocate (HM) v Edmiston (Elizabeth) (1866) 5 Irv 219.
D *Atkinson v HM Advocate*, 1987 SLT 534.
Butcher v Jessop, 1989 SLT 593; 1989 SCCR 119.
Ralston v HM Advocate, 1989 SLT 474; 1988 SCCR 590.
Young v McGlennan, 1991 SCCR 739.

Textbooks referred to

Gordon, *Criminal Law* (2nd ed), para 29-30.
Macdonald, *Criminal Law* (5th ed), pp 1, 115.

E The petition was heard before the High Court on 24 September 1992.

On 23 October 1992 the court *answered* the question in the *negative*.

THE LORD JUSTICE CLERK (ROSS).—The circumstances which have given rise to this reference in terms of s 263A of the Criminal Procedure (Scotland) Act 1975 are that a person, X, was indicted for
F trial in the High Court of Justiciary at Glasgow on charges of (1) assault with intent to rob and attempted robbery; and (2) contravention of the Firearms Act 1968, s 17 (2) and (5). The case proceeded to trial at the sitting which began on 17 February 1992. The jury found each of the charges on the indictment not proven by a majority.

The first charge on the indictment was in the following terms: "(1) On 4 November 1991 in the premises known as Pablo's Clothing Babywear, 1116 Maryhill Road, Glasgow, you did assault Marie Carberry or Daly, proprietrix there and Tiffany Sali Rubin, employee there, present an imitation handgun at G them, place them in a state of fear and alarm for their safety, demand money, demand that they lie on the ground all with intent to rob and you did attempt to rob them."

In the course of the trial Mrs Daly gave evidence that in the late afternoon of 4 November 1991 she was standing behind part of the counter in the shop premises referred to in charge 1 when the door was thrown open and X entered the shop and presented a handgun at her. He was holding the gun in both hands H with his arms outstretched in front of him. He said words to the effect: "Get the money out of the till and lay on the floor." At this time Tiffany Sali Rubin was crouched down behind a different part of the counter putting a jacket onto a small boy who was there with his mother. Miss Rubin stood up to see what was happening, and X, seeing her, ran out of the door.

In the course of the trial X admitted entering the premises mentioned in charge 1, presenting an imita- I tion firearm at the complainers in charge 1, stating "This is a hold up", ordering them to get down on the floor, and demanding money from them. He accepted that they were alarmed by his actings. His defence was that his actions were a joke, that he had no evil intent to assault or rob the complainers, and that accordingly his actions lacked the criminal intent necessary for the commission of the crimes libelled.

Mrs Daly in her evidence stated that she did not take what the accused did as being a joke, and that if she J had been in the shop herself she would probably have handed over the money to him. She said that she just froze and felt terrible. Miss Rubin spoke to having stood up from behind the counter and having seen X pointing a gun at Mrs Daly. She said he was standing with his arms extended in front of him and the gun between his hands. She confirmed that he had said the words attributed to him by Mrs Daly. Miss Rubin stated that X sounded serious and she took him seriously. She said that she did not find the incident funny K and she took it as a serious incident: she added, "I got a hell of a fright."

The advocate depute in her address to the jury submitted that it was not a relevant defence to an assault charge that the actions constituting the assault were carried out as a joke. Counsel for X in his address to the jury submitted that if the jury accepted X's evidence that the actions were carried out as a joke, the necessary evil intent for the commission of the crime of assault would be lacking and X would require to be L acquitted.

The trial judge directed the jury that assault is an attack on the person of another with evil intent, that whether or not there was evil intent was at the heart of the case, that X's evidence was that his actions were a joke and there was no evil intent, and that if the jury believed X's evidence that he had no evil intent, they would acquit him.

In this reference it is submitted on behalf of the

Lord Advocate that the trial judge ought to have directed the jury in relation to charge 1 that the accused admitted actions which constituted the crime of assault; that the necessary evil intent was inevitably to be inferred from the deliberate commission of the acts themselves; that it was not a relevant defence that the said acts were committed as a joke; and that if the jury accepted that the said acts were committed as a joke, the jury, if otherwise satisfied as to the accused's guilt, were bound to convict.

The Lord Advocate has accordingly referred to this court for its opinion the following question: [his Lordship quoted the question set out supra and continued:]

At the hearing the advocate depute submitted that the foregoing question should be answered in the negative. Counsel who represented X, submitted that the question should be answered in the affirmative.

In presenting his submissions, the advocate depute referred in detail to the evidence given by Mrs Daly, Miss Rubin and the accused. However I am satisfied that what I have already said regarding their evidence is an accurate summary of it. The advocate depute also referred to the transcript of the speech for the advocate depute and the speech for defence counsel. Again what I have already said constitutes a sufficient summary of these speeches.

So far as the judge's charge is concerned the following is the relevant passage: "The crimes set out in this first charge are those of assault and attempted robbery. What is an assault? Any attack on the person of another with evil intent is an assault, the attack has to be deliberately aimed or directed at the other and intended to harm. Harm, of course, may not be physical on the body. The attack with that intent has to be proved beyond reasonable doubt by corroborated evidence and as I have indicated to you a moment or two ago it is not necessary for every detail of the assault to be subject to corroborated evidence. With assault you may consider the question of acting in self defence or an action in support and in this case, of course, you may consider if there was a threat which is not intended to cause harm — a joke, a prank — and that of course, as you will appreciate, is at the heart of this case because, let me repeat again the direction I gave you about what is an assault — an attack on the person of another with evil intent and whether or not there was evil intent is at the heart of this case. The Crown maintain that there was such evil intent on the part of the accused and the accused has told you that he had no such evil intent. It was a joke — as his counsel said to him 'a gey sick joke' and he agreed with that, that it was a sick joke, there was no evil intent and therefore assault would not be established. How do you determine that? Of course it will depend upon your appreciation of the evidence and the evidence which the accused has given, the evidence that was given by the two ladies in the shop, the evidence they gave of their reaction to what happened. It is true you can't look into a man's mind. A man may express, of course, what he thinks was in his own mind and if you believe

the accused in this case that he had no such evil intent you would acquit him. You may, however on the other hand, wish to judge the actings objectively of how the other people appreciated it if you are not satisfied of his own explanation of his intent — that is to say, how other people looked at what he did, what he intended to do."

The trial judge went on in his charge to deal with intent to rob, and advised the jury that the two crimes in the charge were interacted with each other, and that they stood together or fell together.

In his report the trial judge states that X admitted to the police when he attended voluntarily at the police station on the evening of the date libelled, that he had gone into the shop, that he had said: "Right. Get down on the floor and that". He had clicked the gun twice. "I just kidded on it was a hold-up. It was a laugh. I wouldn't have taken the money". He told the police it was only a child's gun, that it was in a house in Ruchill and he would take the police to it. The police went to that house and recovered the gun, which became label production 1.

The advocate depute supported the submission which is contained in the petition to this court. He maintained that the trial judge had confused intent with motive, and that motive was irrelevant to criminal responsibility. He contended that if a person carries out an actus reus with mens rea, he is guilty of the crime, and that his motive is irrelevant to the question of guilt. The advocate depute drew attention to *HM Advocate v Elizabeth Edmiston* where it was held that the writing and sending of threatening letters was a crime, whatever may have been the motive. He contended that the same principle should be applied here. In charging the jury in that case the Lord Justice Clerk said: "The writing or sending of letters expressed in these terms is in itself in the eye of the law a crime, no matter what the motive. Supposing it to be perfectly true that all that was designed was frolic, the writing and sending of such letters as these would still be a crime, and the counsel for the prisoner seriously misunderstood the true and proper meaning of those words which expressed the quality of the act charged against the panel, that she did wickedly and feloniously write and send these letters. Every crime is wicked and felonious, and the moment you arrive at the conclusion that the act charged against the prisoner is a crime, that of itself is sufficient proof of wicked and felonious intent. The words mean no more than that the act is criminal. If the act is shown to be criminal, from the nature of the act itself there is no necessity for any proof of malice as regards any of the ordinary crimes."

The advocate depute submitted that the same principles should be applied to the present case, and that the trial judge ought to have directed the jury that it was no defence to say that it had all been a joke. He also referred to *Ralston v HM Advocate.* In that case the appellant maintained that the sheriff had erred in giving directions to the jury to the effect that even if they thought that the appellant's motives were blame-

A less, nonetheless they must convict him. In the course of my opinion I stated at 1989 SLT, p 476: "Whether or not any particular acts amount to a breach of the peace is a question of fact depending upon the particular circumstances of the case. Since it is a question of fact, it was for the jury to determine that matter. Whatever the appellant's motives may have been, it was for the jury to decide on the evidence whether his actings amounted to a breach of the peace."

B The advocate depute maintained that in the present case the actions of X had been deliberate, and that accordingly they constituted the crime of assault. The advocate depute recognised that in some areas of human activity difficult situations might arise. He submitted that to bring another person down by means of a rugby tackle would not constitute assault in the course of a game of rugby, but that it would be criminal if the person tackled was a stranger in a public street. He also maintained that between friends no crime would be committed if one friend perpetrated a joke upon another. The situation he submitted was different where strangers were involved. At the end of the day his submission was that the crime of assault was committed once it was plain that the appellant was acting deliberately. He contended that there was a risk that the direction given by the trial judge could become a "Robbers' Charter".

C Counsel for X on the other hand contended that the directions given by the trial judge were sound and proper. He submitted that it was necessary for the jury to consider all the circumstances before they could determine whether there had been evil intent or dole. He maintained that the accused's assertion that it was a joke was one factor which had to be taken into account in the overall evaluation of the existence of dole; if the jury accepted that that factor negatived evil intent, they were entitled to acquit. He submitted that the assertion that it was a joke was not relevant to the issue of motive; it was a factor which required to be considered when the jury determined whether or not there had been evil intent. All that was decided in *HM Advocate v Elizabeth Edmiston* was that the prosecutor was not required to establish a motive for the crime (Macdonald's *Criminal Law* (5th ed), p 1. He also referred to *Atkinson v HM Advocate* and *Young v McGlennan*. Senior counsel further submitted that it was not the correct approach to hold that the accused's assertion that it was a joke came too late, that is, after the assault had been committed. He maintained that there was no justification for any cut off point in evaluating the overall circumstances of the incident. It was necessary to look at the whole circumstances when determining whether or not the necessary evil intent was present.

In my opinion the accused's assertion that it was a joke means no more than that it was his motive or ulterior intention in acting as he did. It has often been said that evil intention is of the essence of assault (Macdonald's *Criminal Law*, p 115). But what that means is that assault cannot be committed accidentally or recklessly or negligently (Gordon's *Criminal Law*

D

E

F

(2nd ed), para 29-30). In the present case, it is plain that when the accused entered the shop, presented the G handgun at Mrs Daly and uttered the words which he did, he was acting deliberately. That being so, in my opinion, he had the necessary intent for his actions to amount to assault, and his motive for acting as he did was irrelevant. I agree with the advocate depute that the principle laid down by the Lord Justice Clerk in *HM Advocate v Elizabeth Edmiston* would apply to the present case, and that even if the accused was believed when he stated it was a joke, his acting as he did would still constitute the crime of assault. H

The advocate depute raised the question of there being possible difficult situations. I agree with him that it would be a crime to rugby tackle a stranger on the public street, although a rugby tackle in the course of a game of rugby would not amount to an assault. The reason for that is that for conduct in a sporting game to be criminal, it would require to be shown to be outwith the normal scope of the sport (*Butcher v Jessop* at 1989 SLT, p 598). As regards a joke between friends, if a friend, for example, deliberately tripped I up his companion as a joke, the crime of assault would still have been committed although if it took place in the context of joking between friends, any prosecution would be unlikely.

I am not persuaded that the approach of counsel for X is a sound one. It is clear that even where conduct has taken place against the background of good natured joking, an assault may be committed if an accused has acted deliberately when he has carried out J an attack upon another (*Young v McGlennan*). It is well established that an assault may be constituted by threatening gestures sufficient to produce alarm (*Atkinson v HM Advocate*). The actings of the accused in the present case included threatening gestures and produced fear and alarm in the two complainers.

When he gave his evidence at the trial, X stated that after he had told the complainer Mrs Daly that it was a hold up, that she should get the money and get down on the floor, he started laughing and stated "I'm only K kidding" as he left the shop. Neither of the complainers spoke to this; they did not say that he started laughing or that he said "I'm only kidding". On the other hand, the jury may have accepted X's evidence in this regard, but even if they did, I am satisfied that by the time he claims to have started laughing, the crime of assault had been committed; his laughing and statement to the effect that it was a joke came too late to alter the quality of his conduct.

The submissions on behalf of the Lord Advocate L contained in the petition relate to the crime of assault only. The court was not invited to determine whether the assertion that the acts were committed as a joke would be a relevant defence to the charge that the assault had been with intent to rob and that X had attempted to rob the complainers. The trial judge had directed the jury that the two crimes of assault and attempted robbery stood or fell together. I reserve my opinion upon the question of whether the claim that it was a joke would be a relevant defence to the crime

A of attempted robbery and whether in the circumstances the jury were entitled to hold that the charge of attempted robbery was not proven. I am, however, satisfied that insofar as the question in the petition relates to the crime of assault, the question falls to be answered in the negative.

LORD COWIE.—This is a petition by the Lord Advocate to the High Court of Justiciary under the provisions of s 263A of the Criminal Procedure (Scotland) Act 1975 for the opinion of the court on a point
B of law which arose in the course of a trial at the High Court in Glasgow.

In that trial the panel was indicted on charges of (1) assault with intent to rob and attempted robbery, and (2) a contravention of the Firearms Act 1968, s 17 (2) and (5). In the end of the day the jury found both charges not proven.

During the course of the evidence two Crown witnesses stated that in the late afternoon of 4 November 1991 the panel entered the shop premises where
C they were working, presented a hand gun at one of them and said words to the effect: "Get the money out of the till and lay on the floor." The other witness who had been crouched below the level of the counter putting a jacket on a small boy who had come into the shop with his mother, stood up at this point and on seeing her the panel turned and ran out of the shop.

The panel gave evidence on his own behalf and admitted entering the shop premises, presenting an
D imitation firearm at the first witness and stating "This is a hold up." He also admitted ordering the witness to get down on the floor and demanding money from her. He then said that he started laughing and that he said "I am only kidding." He went on to say that he then turned and ran away.

Later in his evidence he said that he accepted that the Crown witnesses would have been alarmed by his actings but that "It was just a joke" and that he had had no intention of going into the shop to assault and
E rob the occupants.

When the advocate depute came to address the jury, she submitted that it was not a relevant defence to a crime of assault to say that the actions constituting the assault were carried out as a joke.

On the other hand counsel for the panel submitted to the jury that if they accepted the panel's evidence that what he had done was a joke then there was none of the evil intent present which was necessary to
F establish the crime of assault and that they would require to acquit the panel of the charges libelled.

The trial judge directed the jury that assault is any attack on the person of another with evil intent; that whether or not there was evil intent was at the heart of the instant case; that the panel's evidence was that his actions were a joke and that there was no evil intent; and that if the jury believed the panel's evidence that he had no evil intent they should acquit him. As stated above the jury proceeded to find the charges not proven.

G The Lord Advocate has taken issue with the terms of the directions which the trial judge gave in this case.

In this petition he submits that the trial judge ought to have directed the jury, in relation to the first charge, that the panel's admitted actions constituted the crime of assault; that the necessary evil intent was inevitably to be inferred from the deliberate commission of the acts themselves; that it was not a relevant defence that the said acts were committed as a joke; and that if the
H jury accepted that the said acts were committed as a joke, the jury if otherwise satisfied as to the appellant's guilt were bound to convict.

In these circumstances the Lord Advocate poses the following question of law for the opinion of the court: [his Lordship quoted the question set out supra and continued:]

Notwithstanding the wide terms of the question, I understood it to be directed only to the part of the first charge libelling assault. That was the basis on which both the advocate depute and counsel who represented
I the panel presented their arguments, and I shall approach the matter in the same way. In elaboration of the submissions outlined above the advocate depute maintained that once a crime has been committed the motive is irrelevant. In the present case the crime of assault had been committed before any question of it being a joke had arisen, and since that was the motive for the offence it could not be a defence to the charge.

In that connection he referred to the case of *HM
J Advocate v Edmiston* in which a woman had been charged with writing and sending threatening letters, having "wickedly and feloniously" written or caused to be written and sent or caused to be sent a threatening letter to two separate individuals.

The defence was that although she had written and sent the letters, the prosecution had not proved that they were sent and delivered "wickedly and feloniously" and that, on the contrary, the panel had made it clear that the letters were written as a frolic. Accord-
K ingly it was submitted that what was done was done without that intention and without that disposition of mind necessary to produce guilt.

The Lord Justice Clerk in charging the jury said this: "The writing or sending of letters expressed in these terms is in itself in the eye of the law a crime, no matter what the motive. Supposing it to be perfectly true that all that was designed was frolic, the writing and sending of such letters as these would still
L be a crime, and the counsel for the prisoner seriously misunderstood the true and proper meaning of those words which expressed the quality of the act charged against the panel, that she did wickedly and feloniously write and send these letters."

It was on that basis that the advocate depute in the present case argued that once the crime of assault was established it was no defence for the panel to say that what he did was a joke. The advocate depute maintained that even if the panel's evidence that he laughed and said he was only kidding before he ran away, was

A accepted by the jury, that was too late to be a defence to the charge because the crime had already been committed by that time, and the motive was irrelevant.

Counsel for the panel on the other hand argued that that was too narrow an approach. He submitted that since evil intent was of the essence of the crime of assault, a jury was entitled to consider all the circumstances surrounding the incident in deciding whether evil intent had been established. In particular he submitted that the trial judge was justified in leaving to the jury the question whether the panel's actings had
B indeed been a joke.

In my opinion however, the submission of counsel for the panel is not correct in the present case. The point is a short one and it depends upon what is meant by the words "evil intent" insofar as they form an essential element in the crime of assault. In my opinion the meaning of the words in the context of this offence is not to be obtained from a wide review of the circumstances surrounding the incident but is to be
C derived directly from the quality of the act in the first place, and in the second place, whether that act was committed deliberately as opposed to carelessly, recklessly or negligently. It is the quality of the act itself, assuming that there was no justification for it, which must be considered in deciding whether it was evil. That was the position in the case of *Edmiston* where the Lord Justice Clerk indicated that it was the quality of the act which justified the description of the writing and sending of the threatening letters as "wicked and
D felonious". Having established that the act is an evil one all that is then required to constitute the crime of assault is that that act was done deliberately and not carelessly, recklessly or negligently.

Accordingly, in my opinion, the approach of counsel for the panel was too wide and in relation to the facts is not appropriate in deciding whether evil intent had been established in the present case.

The evil intent was established when the panel
E deliberately and without justification pointed the hand gun at the person in the shop premises and said: "Get the money out of the till and lay on the floor." At that point the crime of assault was established and the subsequent actions suggesting that it was all a joke were wholly irrelevant as a defence to that crime. For these reasons I have no hesitation in saying that in the present case, the trial judge misdirected the jury and that he ought to have directed them along the lines set out in para 2 of the petition.

F Accordingly I would answer the question posed for our opinion in the negative.

LORD SUTHERLAND.—In this petition the Lord Advocate seeks the opinion of the court on a matter of law arising from a charge given to the jury in a trial in the High Court in Glasgow. The charges faced by the panel were charges of assault with intent to rob and attempted robbery and a contravention of s 17 (2) and (5) of the Firearms Act 1968.

The material facts which were not seriously in

dispute were that the panel entered a shop in Glasgow and pointed a hand gun at the shop assistant behind G the counter. He said words to the effect: "Lie on the floor and get your money out of the till." At this point another person in the shop showed herself to the panel who then left the shop. The panel's defence was that his actions were a joke and that he had no evil intent to assault or rob the complainers. The advocate depute at the trial, in addressing the jury, submitted that it was not a relevant defence to an assault charge that the actions constituting the assault were carried out as a joke. Counsel for the panel in addressing the jury sub- H mitted that if the jury accepted the panel's evidence that his actions were carried out as a joke, the necessary evil intent for the commission of the crime of assault would be lacking. The trial judge directed the jury that any attack on the person of another with evil intent is an assault, and that the attack has to be deliberately aimed or directed at the other and intended to harm. He went on to say: "With assault you may consider the question of acting in self defence or an action in support and in this case, of course, you I may consider if there was a threat which is not intended to cause harm — a joke, a prank".

In the petition it is submitted that the trial judge ought to have directed the jury in relation to charge 1 that the accused's admitted actions constituted the crime of assault; that the necessary evil intent was inevitably to be inferred from the deliberate commission of the acts themselves; that it was not a relevant defence that the said acts were committed as a joke; and that if the jury accepted that the said acts were J committed as a joke the jury, if otherwise satisfied as to the accused's guilt, were bound to convict. It will be noted that that submission relates to the crime of assault and does not specifically deal with the aggravation of assault, namely, with intent to rob or the additional crime of attempted robbery. The point of law, however, which is referred to the court is: [his Lordship quoted the question set out supra and continued:]

In seeking to have the question of law answered in K the negative the advocate depute submitted that the judge should have directed that the necessary intent inevitably had to be inferred from deliberate acts. There was no doubt about the actings of the panel in that he pointed a gun at the complainer and uttered threatening words. It was submitted that intent involving mens rea was confused with motive by the trial judge and this led him to a misdirection. If the actus reus is accompanied by the requisite mens rea then L motive is irrelevant. The advocate depute referred to the cases of *HM Advocate v Edmiston* and *HM Advocate v Ralston*. These cases make it clear that where a criminal act has been carried out it is quite immaterial what was the motive of the perpetrator. Where, as here, the actings of the panel were quite deliberate and constituted a criminal act there is no room for a defence based on the proposition that his motive was merely to perform some practical joke. Counsel for the panel contended that the direction given by the trial judge was the usual direction in cases of assault and was entirely appropriate and proper. What had to be looked at were both the actus reas and the mens rea and in deciding whether the Crown had established the necessary mens rea the whole circumstances of the alleged crime had to be looked at. The jury would have to be satisfied that there was evil intent on the part of the panel and if the Crown failed to prove that evil intent the panel was entitled to be acquitted. If therefore the jury accepted that what the panel did was by way of a joke and was without evil intent the appropriate verdict would be one of acquittal and the trial judge's direction on the matter was correct. The Crown's approach was wrong in equiparating a joke with motive as the proper test is whether or not the panel's intention was an evil one or was merely in jest.

The words "evil intent" have an eminently respectable pedigree, being used by Hume when he describes dole or mens rea as "that corrupt and evil intention which is essential to the guilt of any crime". It is however perfectly possible to have an intention to perform particular acts without necessarily intending evil consequences from those acts. The use of the word "intention" may therefore be confusing in itself. If intention means motive then plainly it is irrelevant. If on the other hand intention means nothing more than wilful, intentional or deliberate as opposed to accidental, careless or even reckless, then plainly it is relevant in that a criminal act cannot be performed other than deliberately. This latter view appears to commend itself to Macdonald, *Criminal Law,* p 115 and Gordon, *Criminal Law,* para 29-30. If, therefore, a person deliberately performs an act which would in itself be criminal then both the actus reus and the mens rea co-exist and a crime has been committed. The pointing of a gun at a shop assistant accompanied by words such as those used by the panel would undoubtedly constitute the actus reus of the crime of assault, and if these things are done deliberately and intentionally as they were done here the mens rea is also, in my opinion, established. The panel undoubtedly knew what he was doing and knew that what he did would be likely to cause alarm and distress. That is sufficient to constitute the crime of assault and his motive for doing it was quite irrelevant. I am therefore satisfied that at least as far as the crime of assault is concerned the trial judge misdirected the jury in leaving open to them consideration of the alleged defence that it was all a joke.

In his submissions the advocate depute did not seek to distinguish between assault, assault with intent to rob and attempted robbery insofar as he maintained that the alleged defence was irrelevant. Counsel for the panel also made no distinction between these three separate aspects of the case and consequently we did not hear any argument presented as to any possible distinction to be made between the three. While I am satisfied that the necessary mens rea was established for the crime of assault I would wish to hear further argument, particularly in relation to the specific aggravation of assault with intent to rob, before deciding that the sort of defence put forward in the present case was irrelevant. The submissions in para 2 of the petition relate only to the crime of assault. I would prefer therefore to reserve my opinion on the question of whether or not a defence such as put forward in the present case would be relevant to any other crime charged. I would therefore answer the question posed in the petition in the negative, subject to deletion of the word "charges" and the substitution of the words "charge of assault".

Counsel for Petitioner, Macdonald, QC, AD; Solicitor, J D Lowe, Crown Agent. — Counsel for Accused, Kerrigan, QC, Armstrong; Solicitors, Ian McCarry, Glasgow.

P W F

(NOTE)

McWhinnie v British Coal Corporation

OUTER HOUSE

TEMPORARY JUDGE D B ROBERTSON, QC

23 OCTOBER 1992

Damages — Amount — Solatium and loss of earnings — Injury leading to painful and permanent disability with a psychological component — Multiplier of 9 used where pursuer 44 at proof and likely to have retired at 62.

A 41 year old miner struck his back. This resulted in a permanent condition of muscle spasm which was both painful and permanently disabling. He would normally have retired at the age of 62.

Held, that solatium was properly assessed at £20,000 and that future loss should be calculated using a multiplier of 9 years; and decree *pronounced* accordingly.

James McWhinnie raised an action against his former employers the British Coal Corporation. He had been employed as a power loader by the defenders at Castlebridge colliery until 19 June 1989. He claimed damages for injuries allegedly sustained in two accidents in the course of his employment at the said colliery on 21 December 1987 and 19 June 1989. Each of the said accidents was averred to have been caused by the fault of the defenders. The action came to proof before Temporary Judge D B Robertson, QC.

In relation to the first accident, in which the pursuer had hurt his back, liability was in dispute but total damages on a full liability basis were agreed at £2,500 inclusive of interest. As regards the second accident of 19 June 1989, when the pursuer was aged 41, the defenders accepted full liability therefor but disputed damages which were concluded for in the sum of

£200,000. The temporary judge held liability estab-
A lished in relation to the first accident. In relation to the
second accident he continued:

"The sole issue arising from the averments with
regard to the second accident on 19 June 1989 when
the pursuer was struck in the lower back by an oil
drum of five gallon capacity which was allowed to
slide down a belt in the said colliery, is damages.
Liability is accepted by the defenders. The defenders
however maintain that the pursuer did not sustain any
significant injury as a result of this accident, no
B serious abnormality being found when he was
examined at Stirling Royal infirmary shortly thereafter. It is their position that apart from a short period
the pursuer was not disabled from working due to this
accident and that he has over the years exaggerated,
and is presently grossly exaggerating, his symptoms
consciously and deliberately. It is averred that he
exhibited inappropriate responses to objective testing
and that he dramatised and magnified his purported
symptoms consciously and deliberately with a view to
C enhancing his prospects of obtaining compensation.
They maintain that the bruising injury, which is all
the pursuer sustained, should have resolved completely within a period of no more than about three
months and that he should have made a complete
recovery from the effects thereof by about September
1989. It is further averred that even if the pursuer is
not now deliberately and consciously exaggerating but
has a genuine inability to work by reason of psychological reaction, which is denied, that reaction and
D inability are caused not by the accident of June 1989
but by a conversion hysteria or the conversion of his
previous initial conscious and deliberate exaggeration
of symptoms into a state of chronic invalidism.

"It is not disputed that following the accident the
pursuer had severe pain in his back and he was taken
to Stirling Royal infirmary where x-ray disclosed that
there were no fractures and it is noted in the records
that there was bruising and tenderness over the lower
E thoracic and lumbar spine. He was discharged the
same day and advised to rest and was given pain
killers. Dr Walters, the pursuer's general practitioner,
indicated that the pursuer had been seen initially by
one of his partners, Dr Webster, but thereafter Dr
Walters himself saw the pursuer frequently from 28
June 1989. The pursuer was complaining of pain on
the right side of his back going down his right leg and
into his foot and this pain has persisted to the present
day. He has been using a stick to assist his walking
F since about August 1989 and Dr Walters has been
signing him off as unfit for work up to the present day.

"The pursuer has been known to Dr Walters for at
least 15 years, although he did not often see the
pursuer as a patient before the first accident in 1987.
After the pursuer had been attending him following
the second accident and matters did not appear to be
improving by about August 1989, Dr Walters referred
the pursuer for physiotherapy. The physiotherapist
found the pursuer to have a tremendous amount of
painful spasm in his back which appeared to be

intractable and did not respond to physiotherapy. In
December 1989 Dr Walters referred the pursuer to G
Mr Isbister, a consultant orthopaedic surgeon, to see
if surgery or some other drastic procedure might assist
the pursuer and alleviate his pain. Mr Isbister
reported back to Dr Walters in April 1990 to the effect
that while it was possible that the pursuer did have
some genuine pain he had formed the impression that
Mr McWhinnie was deliberately and consciously
exaggerating any symptoms which he had. Mr Isbister
gave it as his opinion that the back received no significant injury at all; that it was simply bruised and that H
Mr McWhinnie was probably trying to maximise any
compensation which he might receive. He further
stated that the pursuer would probably never admit to
any improvement until his case was settled and might
well be on the way to developing a chronic pattern of
illness behaviour which could last indefinitely.

"Dr Walters said frankly that this report caused him
to reconsider the pursuer's case very carefully. He
went through all his notes and turned over in his mind
his assessment and knowledge of the pursuer over I
many years and during the period following the
accident when he was seeing the pursuer about once
a month. Having done this he rejected the opinion of
Mr Isbister and stated in evidence that in his view the
pursuer was suffering genuine pain and was not consciously exaggerating his symptoms. He had himself
observed the very extreme reactions of the pursuer
commented upon by Mr Isbister in his report, but he
did not regard these as indicating a malingering or pretence. In cross examination Dr Walters agreed that he J
referred patients to Mr Isbister or one of his colleagues
fairly frequently but said that he did so to see if
surgery or some other treatment a consultant can order
might help. When asked if it followed that Mr
Isbister's opinion was one which he valued in that connection, Dr Walters replied 'not always' and he added
that he had been in practice for 22 years and had seen
consultants make mistakes, sometimes very big ones.
Dr Walters was quite satisfied that the pursuer was
suffering pain and was not consciously and deliber- K
ately inventing or exaggerating his symptoms. Dr
Walters regarded the pursuer as being unfit for any
work in the future.

"Professor Michael Richard Bond, whose experience included work as a general surgeon and a neurosurgeon, but who also specialises in psychological
medicine, being a fellow of the Royal College of
Psychologists as well as the Royal College of Surgeons
and Physicians of Glasgow and the Royal College of
Surgeons at Edinburgh, has had as his special interest L
for about 20 years the study of chronic pain and back
injury. He is regarded as the foremost expert in his
field in Scotland. He examined the pursuer on 21
September 1990 and again on 13 January 1992 when
he also interviewed the pursuer's brother in law Mr
Cole. Number 25/12 of process is his report dated 14
January 1992. He was fully conversant with the pursuer's history and had access to the pursuer's medical
records. Professor Bond's impression of the pursuer
was that he was a shy and anxious man who showed

A a marked degree of disability in excess of what would have been expected from the injury sustained in the accident. Professor Bond indeed found the same apparently grossly excessive reactions during examination as were found by Dr Walters and as were remarked upon by Mr Isbister. Professor Bond's view was that the pursuer was fully recovered from the effects of the first accident in 1987 but that the second accident in June 1989 left him with low back pain which extended into his right leg. This pain was due mainly to attacks of muscle spasm. He was not fit for

B any work due to the painful spasm associated with gross anxiety and psychological reaction. Professor Bond's view was that the greater part of the pursuer's disability is psychologically determined at an unconscious level and his lack of activity has compounded the problem as disuse increased the likelihood of pain. The pursuer's condition is, in Professor Bond's opinion, so firmly fixed that even specialist rehabilitation, were it available, would not produce more than a marginal improvement. His opinion was that no

C marked degree of recovery was likely nor was it likely that the pursuer would return to any form of employment. He was adamant that no part of Mr McWhinnie's condition was ever consciously motivated or related to any claim for compensation."

The temporary judge then narrated the evidence of Professor Gordon Waddell, a consultant orthopaedic surgeon who ran the specialist spine referral clinic for the west of Scotland, concluding:

D "Professor Waddell gave it as his opinion that 90 per cent of injuries of the nature of Mr McWhinnie's, would be expected to settle sufficiently to permit a return to work within approximately six weeks, although recovery could be slower and could possibly take several months in view of the previous history of an earlier back injury and the heavy physical nature of Mr McWhinnie's job. The protracted time off work appears in Professor Waddell's opinion to be due to the secondary development of muscle spasm, anxiety,

E fear avoidance, psychological distress and abnormal illness behaviour. Mr McWhinnie is now almost totally adapted to an invalid lifestyle affecting all aspects of his life and including severe restriction of all physical activities and the use of a stick. Professor Waddell considered that this entire pattern of clinical presentation and the change in all aspects of his life is entirely unconscious and psychological in nature and is not due to any conscious magnification or exaggeration related to his claim for compensation. . . .

F "Professor Waddell was of opinion that Mr McWhinnie would continue to have entirely genuine low back pain related to continued muscle spasm, deranged movements and a severe disuse syndrome. He considered that because of this the pursuer was not physically capable of undertaking his previous physical work. The degree of total disability and invalidity is however out of proportion to the objective clinical findings and in his view this extreme disability is due mainly to the psychological overlay and abnormal illness behaviour. There is no physical basis to

G expect any significant physical complications such as osteo-arthritis or serious deterioration and while he agreed with Professor Bond in theory and from a purely physical perspective that Mr McWhinnie might be rehabilitated sufficiently to return to light work, he considered that it was very unlikely that he could ever return to his previous job or to comparable heavy physical work. The disuse syndrome, psychological overlay, abnormal illness behaviour and invalidity were however now firmly established and were now likely to be very resistant to any form of

H medical, psychological or psychiatric treatment or rehabilitation. For these reasons he considered that the possibility of actually getting Mr McWhinnie back to any form of gainful employment within a foreseeable number of years is less than 10 per cent. This was not likely to be influenced by the settlement of his legal proceedings."

The temporary judge next narrated the evidence of Mr Isbister and three other medically qualified witnesses led by the defenders, Dr Alan Melville, a general practitioner, Mr Brian Dean, an orthopaedic

I surgeon and Dr Ian Kennedy, a consultant psychiatrist. He then continued:

"I was most impressed with the evidence of both Professor Bond and Mr Waddell and while I consider that Mr Isbister plainly had grave doubts as to the genuineness of Mr McWhinnie's complaints and disability and as to whether these were conscious and deliberate, I do feel that he did not consider the psychological aspects of the case in the same way or

J indeed with the same expertise that both Bond and Waddell did. The pursuer's own general practitioner, Dr Walters, who had applied his mind specifically to the matter of conscious and deliberate exaggeration when it was raised by Mr Isbister in his report to him, gave it as his carefully considered opinion that the pursuer was not consciously or deliberately exaggerating or inventing symptoms. This view was adhered to despite having observed the same dramatic unusual and apparently excessive reaction by the pursuer to

K physical examination as was observed by Mr Isbister and indeed all the other medical witnesses who examined Mr McWhinnie. I give great weight to Dr Walters' evidence not only as an experienced and commonsense general practitioner in a mining community but also as a man who has seen the pursuer more often and over a longer period of time than the other medical witnesses and was a doctor searching for some treatment or procedure as a solution to the problems the pursuer claimed to have. Waddell and

L Bond, both acknowledged experts in their fields, also saw the pursuer's behaviour when examining him but both were convinced that while part of the disability was psychological, the pursuer was not a malingerer and was not consciously or deliberately faking or exaggerating pain or disability. Even Mr Dean, the orthopaedic surgeon who was led for the defenders, agreed on this point, although he stood alone in his opinion that there was an actual disc problem. He spoke of functional overlay and exaggeration but agrees that the pursuer is gravely disabled as a result of the accident in 1989 and that while he may initially have exaggerated his symptoms this was not for gain. He thought there may have been a degree of voluntary behaviour at an early stage but there is a strong involuntary element which has nothing to do with compensation. He agreed in effect with Dr Walters, and Professors Waddell and Bond, that the pursuer is not and never has been a malingerer, acting dishonestly for some ulterior motive connected with compensation.

"I cannot attach any great weight to Dr Kennedy's evidence. He never saw the pursuer and spoke in wholly general terms. Isbister, as I have already observed, gave no consideration to the psychological aspects and my impression was that in the end he would give way to the opinions of Bond and Waddell in such matters. If I am mistaken in that impression then I must say that I prefer the evidence of Dr Walters, and Bond and Waddell. So far as Dr Melville's evidence is concerned he certainly took the view that the pursuer was unfit for work in the coal industry and indeed that was really his remit when examining the pursuer — fitness or unfitness for work in the industry. He found some responses surprising and thought that McWhinnie was overreacting. He admitted that the question of whether these reactions were conscious or unconscious was an extremely difficult question. He accepted the physical disabilities and recommended retiral. At one point in his evidence Dr Melville indicated he thought there was a deliberate ploy on the pursuer's part but then said that if he had been prescribing treatment he felt 'counselling would be a number one priority'.

"I found it very difficult to understand why if a man is thought to be deliberately and dishonestly exaggerating symptoms to inflate his claim, counselling should be considered as a priority. The prescribing of counselling would seem to me consistent with a diagnosis of some psychological problem. If a man is a malingerer and engaged in some ploy to exaggerate his symptoms I cannot see that counselling is an appropriate procedure. That evidence indicated to me that Dr Melville, as he did say in other parts of his evidence, thought there were strong psychological aspects to Mr McWhinnie's behaviour and condition. Dr Melville indeed agreed there was abnormal illness behaviour and that it was difficult for him to say how much was conscious or unconscious.

"The overwhelming weight of the evidence from the medical men which I have accepted is to the effect that the pursuer has suffered and is suffering genuine pain and disability from a condition (of muscular spasm) resulting from the injury sustained on 19 June 1989 and that he is not and never has been malingering, nor dishonestly exaggerating the physical symptoms of back pain and pain radiating into his right leg which disable him from working. My own assessment of the pursuer, for what it is worth, is that he is not a dishonest man but he is certainly of very limited intelligence. There was evidence that he went to a special school and it appeared in the course of his evidence that he had considerable difficulty in reading. The manner in which he spoke of his working career in the mines persuaded me that he did genuinely enjoy his job and this impression assisted me in assessing him as a man who would not wish to give up his job on some pretext or simply to inflate his claim for damages. He gave the impression of being a somewhat inadequate and solitary man who, however, felt part of a team in the mines and got satisfaction from being in the mining industry. Indeed, I got the distinct impression that he felt pride in being a miner and doing a job which was both difficult and dangerous and involved working conditions which most outsiders would regard as uncongenial.

"Since the accident the pursuer has suffered pain in his back with radiation into his right leg. Physiotherapy has relieved the pain to some extent but the pain and discomfort, while varying in intensity, is always present to some extent. His sleep is disturbed and most nights he gets only three to four hours' rest. He is unable to bend or stoop without increased pain and while he is able to walk only 50 yds at a time and that with the assistance of a stick, discomfort manifests itself after an hour or so even in a sitting position. He requires the assistance of his mother, with whom he lives, for the performance of many everyday tasks. He is no longer able to attend football matches unless he is taken by car and is able to have a seat. The accident was in 1989 when the pursuer was aged 41 and the pain and suffering will continue at about the same level of intensity from now into the future. I was referred to the case of *Duncan v Scottish Marine Biological Association*, OH, 20 December 1991 (1992 GWD 6-319). The pursuer there suffered a back injury and thereafter continued to suffer disabling and depressing pain in his back and right leg with recurrent exacerbations. Solatium of £15,000 was awarded. It is difficult from the very brief report [see now 1992 SLT 554] to compare the pain suffered by Mr Duncan with that of the pursuer in this case but having regard to the pursuer's age, he being some seven years younger and from his description of his pain and discomfort in the witness box, I think a somewhat higher figure is justified here. Taking into account the pain and suffering and also the loss of a job which the pursuer plainly enjoyed and was proud of I consider that solatium could reasonably be assessed at the sum of £20,000. Having regard to his age and the fact that, as noted, the pain and suffering will continue in the future, I allocate one third of the solatium to the past and award interest at 7½ per cent on that third.

"The pursuer is plainly disabled from any job requiring more than the slightest physical agility and so far as sedentary occupation is concerned, apart from his inability to sustain the sitting position for any length of time without acute discomfort, he obviously lacks any real skills or intellectual capacity for most non-manual occupations. In my opinion the likelihood of the pursuer being able for light work is low and from the medical evidence for all practical purposes he must be regarded as being unlikely ever to work again.

"Past loss of wages to 31 January 1992 is agreed at

£22,400 and it was agreed that that loss will be
A increased at the rate of £180.33 per week to the date
of decree. It was agreed that interest on the total past
loss should run at 7½ per cent per annum.

"On the evidence the pursuer could have taken
retirement at the age of 53. On the evidence of the pursuer's attitude to his work, which I accepted, and my
own impression of him as above indicated and bearing
in mind that he is a single man now with few outside
interests, I think it is unlikely that he would have
taken early retirement at the earlier age of 53. I accept
B the submission made on his behalf that the likely
retiral age would be 62. Since he is now 44 years of
age that would have given 18 working years till retirement. Under reference to *McGeechan v George Russell
(Steel) Ltd*, 1970 SLT (Notes) 76, a multiplier of 9 was
proposed. I do not think this is unreasonable. On the
agreed multiplicand of £9,377 this gives a sum of
£84,393 for future loss. So far as the loss of pension
rights is concerned, parties were agreed that the lump
sum of £20,000 should be awarded under this head of
C damage. The remaining heads of damage are those
claimed under ss 8 and 9 of the Administration of
Justice (Scotland) Act 1982 and these again have been
agreed in the sum of £500."

---

*Counsel for Pursuer, Miller, QC, Allardice; Solicitors,
Robin Thompson & Partners — Counsel for Defenders,
Howie; Solicitors, McClure Naismith Anderson &
Gardiner.*

D

C H

McLeod v Lowe

HIGH COURT OF JUSTICIARY
E THE LORD JUSTICE CLERK (ROSS),
LORDS MURRAY AND GRIEVE

15 MAY 1991

*Justiciary — Evidence — Admissibility — Hearsay —
Police officers acting on reasonable suspicion — Whether
officers entitled to speak to what was said to them by
third party.*

*Justiciary — Evidence — Sufficiency — Reasonable
grounds for suspicion by police — Accused detained under
F Misuse of Drugs Act 1971 to be searched — Police acting
on information from hotel staff but no evidence of what
police told by staff — Whether sheriff entitled to hold
police had reasonable grounds to detain — Misuse of
Drugs Act 1971 (c 38), s 23 (4) (a).*

*Justiciary — Procedure — Summary procedure —
Appeal — Additional evidence relevant to alleged miscar-
riage of justice — Sheriff wrongly sustaining objection to
Crown evidence but convicting on what was held to be
insufficient evidence — Criminal Procedure (Scotland)
Act 1975 (c 21), s 452 (4) (b).*

Section 23 (2) of the Misuse of Drugs Act 1971 provides inter alia that if a constable has reasonable   G
grounds to suspect that any person is in possession of
a controlled drug in contravention of the Act, the constable may search that person, and detain him for the
purpose of searching him. Section 452 (4) (b) of the
Criminal Procedure (Scotland) Act 1975 provides that
the High Court on hearing a stated case may, inter
alia, hear any additional evidence relevant to any
alleged miscarriage of justice.

An accused person was charged with inter alia
obstructing police officers in the exercise of their   H
powers under the Misuse of Drugs Act 1971 by refusing to permit them to search him and struggling with
them, contrary to s 23 (4) (b) of the Misuse of Drugs
Act 1971. The evidence disclosed that a report was
received by the police of an alleged contravention of
the 1971 Act at an hotel. On arrival at the hotel the
police were given certain information by the hotel staff
and were taken to one of the bars where the officers'
attention was directed to the accused. The police told
the accused that he was being detained under the 1971   I
Act as they had information which led them to believe
that he was in possession of a controlled substance.
Outside the hotel, when the accused was told that he
was to be searched, he became aggressive, abusive and
unco-operative; he lashed out and broke free from the
grasp of the police and ran away but was eventually
captured. A search did not reveal the possession of any
controlled drug. In the course of the trial the defence
had objected to the Crown's attempt to lead evidence
from the police officers as to what was said to them by
the hotel staff and the sheriff sustained the objection   J
on the ground that only the hotel staff, who were not
led in evidence, could testify as to whether they had
pointed out the accused.

A submission of no case to answer was made on the
ground that there was no evidence to show that the
police had reasonable cause to suspect that the accused
was in possession of drugs and accordingly the police
had no right to detain him. The sheriff repelled the
submission and convicted the accused, who appealed.
                                                              K
Held, (1) that the sheriff had erred in upholding the
objection since what was at issue was the information
on which the police acted and evidence as to that could
competently have been given either by the hotel staff
or by the police themselves (pp 475D-E, 475L and
476C-D); (2) (Lord Murray *dissenting*) that the evidence before the sheriff was insufficient to show that the
police officers had reasonable grounds to suspect
that the accused was in possession of drugs since it was
impossible to determine whether the police officers
had such reasonable grounds without knowing what it   L
was the officers were told by the hotel staff (pp 475G,
475J-K and 476F); and (3) that having regard to how
it came about that no evidence was led regarding what
the police officers were told by the hotel staff, the
appeal court ought to hear additional evidence upon
this matter in terms of s 452 (4) (b) of the 1975 Act (pp
475I, 475L and 476G-H); and appeal *continued* and
hearing of additional evidence *ordered*.

Per Lord Murray (*dissenting*): Whether or not there
was a case to answer turned entirely on whether the

findings were sufficient to justify the inference that
A the police had reasonable grounds to suspect that the
accused was in possession of controlled drugs and not
whether any suspicion was in fact justified, and
accordingly the sheriff was entitled to repel the submission (p 475J-L).

_____

Summary complaint

Raymond Donald McLeod was charged at the
instance of John D Lowe, procurator fiscal, Edin-
B burgh, on a summary complaint which was in the
following terms: "(1) On 17 June 1990 at the rear of
the Willowbrae hotel, 224 Willowbrae Road, Edinburgh, you did intentionally obstruct Sergeant
Thomas Martin and Constable Brian Cooper in the
exercise of their powers under s 23 of the Misuse of
Drugs Act 1971 and did refuse to permit them to
search you and struggle violently with them: Contrary
to the Misuse of Drugs Act 1971, s 23 (4) (a). (2) Date
and place above libelled you did conduct yourself in
C a disorderly manner, shout and swear and commit a
breach of the peace. (3) You being an accused person
and having been granted bail on 29 March 1990 at
Edinburgh sheriff court in terms of the Criminal
Procedure (Scotland) Act 1975 and the Bail etc (Scotland) Act 1980 and being subject to the condition inter
alia that you would not commit an offence while on
bail, did on date and place libelled in charges 1 and 2
above, fail without reasonable excuse to comply with
said condition, in respect that you committed the
D offences libelled in charges 1 and 2 above: Contrary to
the Bail etc (Scotland) Act 1980, s 3 (1) (b)."

The accused pled not guilty and proceeded to trial.
The temporary sheriff (K A McLernan) convicted the
accused.

The accused appealed by way of stated case to the
High Court against the decision of the sheriff.

Statutory provisions

E The Misuse of Drugs Act 1971 provides:

"23.—. . . (2) If a constable has reasonable grounds
to suspect that any person is in possession of a controlled drug in contravention of this Act or of any
regulations made thereunder, the constable may — (a)
search that person, and detain him for the purpose of
searching him . . .

"(4) A person commits an offence if he — (a) intentionally obstructs a person in the exercise of his
F powers under this section".

The Criminal Procedure (Scotland) Act 1975
provides:

"452.—. . . (4) Without prejudice to any existing
power of the High Court, that court may in hearing
a stated case — . . . (b) hear any additional evidence
relevant to any alleged miscarriage of justice or order
such evidence to be heard by a judge of the High
Court or by such other person as it may appoint for
that purpose."

Cases referred to

Dryburgh v Galt, 1981 SLT 151; 1981 JC 69; 1981 G
    SCCR 26.
Guthrie v Hamilton, 1988 SLT 823; 1988 SCCR 330.
McNicol v Peters, 1969 SLT 261.
Twycross v Farrell, 1973 SLT (Notes) 85.
Weir v Jessop, 1992 SLT 533; 1991 SCCR 242.

Textbook referred to

Walker and Walker, *Evidence*, pp 394, 396.

Findings in fact H

The sheriff found the following facts to be admitted
or proved:

(1) On 17 June 1990 a report was received at Portobello police station of an alleged contravention of the
Misuse of Drugs Act 1971 on the premises of Willowbrae hotel, 224 Willowbrae Road, Edinburgh.
Sergeant Martin and Constable Cooper were
instructed to investigate. No evidence was led as to
where said report came from. (2) Said two police I
officers proceeded to said hotel and on arrival there
they were given certain information by the hotel staff,
and conducted by the hotel staff to one of the bars.
Their attention was directed by the hotel staff to a
man seated at one of the tables in a bar. That man was
Raymond Donald McLeod the present accused. (3)
The police officers had reasonable grounds to suspect
that said Raymond Donald McLeod was in possession
of a controlled drug. (4) The two police officers
approached the man, informed him that he was being
detained under the Misuse of Drugs Act as they had J
information which led them to believe he was in possession of a controlled substance, and they asked him
to accompany them outside the premises. The man
made no comment, he co-operated with the police and
was escorted by them through a door which led out
from the bar into a rear garden area. (5) Once out in
the garden area the accused was again informed by
Sergeant Martin that he was being detained under the
Misuse of Drugs Act with a view to their carrying out K
a search of his person as it had been alleged that he
was in possession of a controlled substance. (6) He
then became aggressive and abusive and unco-
operative. He lashed out with his arms and legs and
broke free from the grasp of the police and ran away.
A chase took place round the garden; he evaded
capture for some time but was eventually caught. (7)
He continued to struggle and resist a search and
shouted and swore at the police. He stated that if any
drugs were found on him the police would have L
planted them on him. He also referred to the police as
"fucking scrote bags". (8) The chase, capture and
struggle were witnessed by patrons who had come out
of the bar into the garden area. (9) No search took
place at the garden. (10) The accused was taken from
Willowbrae hotel to Portobello police station and a
search was carried out there. The search did not reveal
the possession of any drugs. (11) A check at the police
station revealed that there was a bail order in force
relating to the accused. He was cautioned and charged
with a breach of the peace, breach of the Misuse

of Drugs Act and breach of the Bail Act. He made no
A reply.

The sheriff appended a note to the findings in fact
in the following terms:

THE SHERIFF (K A McLERNAN).—At the conclusion of the Crown case the accused's agent made a
submission of "no case to answer" in terms of s 345A
of the Criminal Procedure (Scotland) Act 1975. The
basis of the submission was that there was no competent evidence led to show that the police had reason-
B able cause to suspect that the accused was in
possession of drugs. Accordingly they had no right to
arrest the accused. In these circumstances he was
entitled to resist arrest. Reference was made to the
case of *Twycross v Farrell.* In reply the procurator
fiscal accepted that if the accused's argument was
correct then charge 2 must fall, and so must also
charge 3. The issue was entirely centred on whether
the police were entitled to detain. The depute procu-
C rator fiscal argued that the police had received anonymous information that an offence was being
committed, that their attention was directed to the
accused and that they had immediately approached
him and told him they were acting under their powers
under s 23 of the Misuse of Drugs Act and that accordingly there was a clear sufficiency. No specific point
was made of the accused's silence when being asked to
accompany the policemen. I repelled the submission.
The accused did not lead evidence. I was then
addressed again by the procurator fiscal depute and
D the agent for the accused. The latter adopted his previous argument expanding it to say that it was necessary
for the Crown to prove beyond reasonable doubt that
an offence had been committed before the police were
entitled to detain under s 23, and as there was no
direct evidence, far less proof beyond reasonable
doubt, that an offence had been committed prior to the
detention then the detention was improper and the
accused was entitled to resist a search.

E   I found the accused guilty as libelled. . . .

The issue here was essentially a short one. The
police were directed to a hotel on the basis of a report
that a contravention of the Misuse of Drugs Act was
taking place in the hotel. When the police arrived at
the hotel, staff indicated a particular individual as
being the person they wished to draw to the attention
of the police. The precise terms of how the staff indicated to the police was a matter of persistent dispute.
F The defence agent objected timeously to any narrative
by both police witnesses of what was said to them by
members of the hotel staff. I upheld that objection.
Both policemen gave evidence however that they did
receive information from staff at the hotel and that
their attention was directed to a particular individual.
They approached that individual, informed him of
why they were approaching him and asked him to
accompany them outside. The argument presented to
me was that the direct evidence of the hotel staff as to
why they had indicated this man to the police was not
laid before the court, accordingly there was no evid-

ence of an offence under the Misuse of Drugs Act
1971 having taken place. In the absence of such evid- G
ence the police were not entitled to use their powers
under s 23 (1) of that Act. Their selection of the
accused from the bar customers was not based on anything they saw for themselves and thus there was no
evidence to justify their detention of the accused. I
rejected that argument. It seemed to me that the true
issue was whether the police had reasonable grounds
for acting as they did. The Act provides in s 23 (2): "If
a constable has reasonable grounds to suspect that any
person is in possession of a controlled drug in con- H
travention of this Act or of any regulations made thereunder, the constable may (a) search that person, and
detain him for the purpose of searching him".

It seemed to me that police in general are constantly
acting on information received. Some sources are
anonymous, some sources are known and respected as
reliable, some are known and suspected as being
unreliable. It is always a matter of judgment as to
whether and to what extent the police take action. The
police in this case clearly believed that the information I
they received was information on which they felt
entitled to act. While it may be material to note that
the accused made no comment when first approached,
and co-operated with the police until he got outside
and was informed that he was going to be searched,
that does not form any part of my decision. I took the
view that the police having received information from
a source which they believed to be reliable, acted
within their powers in making a detention under s 23.

_____
J

Appeal

The sheriff posed the following questions for the
opinion of the High Court:

(1) Was I entitled in the circumstances to repel the
submission made at the conclusion of the Crown case?

(2) Was I entitled on the evidence to make finding
in fact 3?

(3) On the basis of the facts found was I entitled to K
convict the accused as libelled?

The appeal was argued before the High Court on 19
March 1991.

On 15 May 1991 the court *continued* the appeal and
ordered the hearing of additional evidence by the High
Court as to what was said to the police officers by
members of the hotel staff.
L

THE LORD JUSTICE CLERK (ROSS).—The
appellant went to trial in the sheriff court at Edinburgh on a summary complaint containing three
charges. The first charge libelled a contravention of s
23 (4) (a) of the Misuse of Drugs Act 1971; the second
charge was a charge of breach of the peace, and the
third charge libelled a contravention of s 3 (1) (b) of
the Bail etc (Scotland) Act 1980. At the conclusion of
the Crown case the solicitor for the appellant made a
submission of no case to answer in terms of s 345A of

the Criminal Procedure (Scotland) Act 1975. The
A basis of the submission was that there was no competent evidence led to show that the police had reasonable cause to suspect that the appellant was in
possession of drugs, and that accordingly they had no
right to arrest him. In these circumstances, it was
claimed that he was entitled to resist arrest (*Twycross
v Farrell*). It was accepted by the respondent that if the
appellant's argument was sound, then charge 2 must
fall as would charge 3. The respondent maintained
that there was sufficient evidence to establish that the
B police had reasonable cause to suspect that the accused
was in possession of drugs. The sheriff repelled the
submission. No evidence was led on behalf of the
appellant and after hearing the respondent and the
solicitor for the appellant the sheriff found the appellant guilty as libelled. The appellant has now appealed
against conviction by means of a stated case.

In presenting his appeal counsel on behalf of the
appellant drew attention to the findings in fact. Put
shortly the facts stated are that on 17 June 1990 a
C report was received at Portobello police station of an
alleged contravention of the Misuse of Drugs Act 1971
on the premises of an hotel. Two police officers were
instructed to investigate. Finding 2 is in the following
terms: [his Lordship quoted its terms and then those
of finding 3 and continued:]

The appellant challenged [finding 3], and there is a
question in the case asking whether the sheriff was
entitled on the evidence to make finding in fact 3. Sub-
D sequent findings reveal that the two police officers
approached the appellant and informed him that he
was being detained under the Misuse of Drugs Act as
they had information which led them to believe he was
in possession of a controlled substance. They asked
him to accompany them outside the premises, and he
did so and co-operated with the police at that stage.
Once outside the premises and in the garden area the
appellant was again informed as to why he was being
detained and he was told that this was with a view to
E the police carrying out a search of his person since it
had been alleged that he was in possession of a controlled substance. At that stage the appellant became
aggressive, abusive and unco-operative. He lashed out
with his arms and legs and broke free from the grasp
of the police and ran away. He was pursued and eventually captured. He continued to struggle and resist a
search and shouted and swore at the police, maintaining that if any drugs were found on him the police
would have planted them. No search took place in the
F garden. The appellant was eventually taken from the
hotel to Portobello police station where a search was
carried out. The search did not reveal the possession
of any drugs. When cautioned and charged with the
three offences which ultimately appeared on the complaint, the appellant made no reply.

Counsel for the appellant maintained that it was
clear from these findings and from what the sheriff
stated in his note that the police had acted not on
anonymous information but on information from the
hotel staff. It was also evident that when the police

officers arrived at the hotel they had no reason to
suspect the appellant until the hotel staff pointed him G
out. Counsel emphasised that the sheriff did not know
what information the hotel staff had or conveyed to
the police, and he accordingly contended that it was
impossible to know whether the police officers had
any reasonable grounds to suspect that the appellant
was in possession of controlled drugs. None of the
hotel staff had been called as witnesses, and accordingly there was no evidence as to why they pointed the
appellant out to the police officers. In these circumstances he maintained that there was no evidence to
entitle the court to hold that the police officers had H
reasonable grounds to suspect that the appellant was
in possession of drugs and thus to search and detain
him in terms of s 23 (2) of the Misuse of Drugs Act
1971.

In support of his submissions, counsel for the appellant referred to a number of cases. *Guthrie v Hamilton*
was a case where the police had obtained a warrant in
respect of certain premises, and while they were
searching the premises the accused called at the door. I
He was detained on the doorstep and found to be in
possession of drugs. In the circumstances the court
held that the sheriff was fully justified in accepting
that at the material time the constables had reasonable
grounds to suspect that the accused was in possession
of drugs and that they were accordingly entitled to
detain and search him. That case turned upon its own
facts, and I have not found it of assistance in deciding
the present appeal.

The next case referred to was *Weir v Jessop*. In that J
case the police received anonymous information to the
effect that an individual on the fourth landing of a
block of flats was involved in the misuse of drugs. The
police proceeded to the locus and discovered only one
person there namely the accused. He was asked if he
was involved in using drugs and replied "No", but
added that he had been involved with drugs in the
past. He was then searched and was found to be in
possession of controlled drugs. In these circumstances
the court held that the police officer had reasonable K
grounds to suspect that the appellant was in possession of drugs and accordingly was entitled to search
and detain him under s 23 (2) of the Act of 1971.
Counsel pointed out that in that case the information
given to the police by the informant was detailed, and
accordingly the court knew upon what information the
police were relying when they maintained that they
had reasonable grounds to suspect that the appellant
was in possession of controlled drugs. He submitted
that the present case was different since the court did L
not know what the information was which was said to
give rise to the suspicion. Moreover in the present case
there was no question of the appellant being the only
person who was in the hotel bar when the police
arrived.

Counsel finally referred to *Dryburgh v Galt*. That
was a road traffic case where an anonymous caller had
telephoned a police station with information that a
particular car had almost collided with him and that
he considered that the driver was drunk. The informa-

tion was passed to police constables on traffic patrol
A who ascertained the address of the registered owner
and proceeded to that address. On their way they saw
the car being driven normally and it entered a car park
at the owner's address. The owner who was driving
left the car and was intercepted by the police who
noticed a smell of drink on his breath. He was
required to take a breath test which proved positive.
Under reference to s 8 (1) of the Road Traffic Act
1972, the court held that the police officers in the circumstances had reasonable cause to suspect that the
B accused who was driving the vehicle had alcohol in his
body. In this case again the nature of the information
conveyed by the anonymous caller to the police was
before the court.

The advocate depute maintained that on the findings in the case, the sheriff was entitled to hold that
the police officers had reasonable grounds to suspect
that the appellant was in possession of controlled
drugs. Following on the report received at Portobello
police station the police officers had proceeded to the
C premises, and while there their attention was directed
by the hotel staff to the appellant. The advocate
depute maintained that these circumstances justified
the police officers in suspecting that the appellant was
in possession of drugs. The advocate depute recognised that *Dryburgh v Galt* differed from the present
case in that the court was aware of the nature of the
information conveyed by the anonymous caller to the
police. In the present case the respondent had
endeavoured to lead evidence as to what was said to
D the police officers by members of the hotel staff, but
the appellant had objected to that evidence and the
sheriff had upheld the objection. He apparently did so
upon the view that only the members of the hotel staff
could have testified as to why they had pointed the
appellant out to the police officers.

I agree with the advocate depute that the sheriff's
decision in which he upheld the objection to this evidence was misconceived. What was at issue was the
E information upon which the police acted. Evidence
about that could competently have been given by
either the hotel staff or the police officers themselves.
The evidence of the police officers to this effect would
not have proved the truth of what they were told by
the hotel staff but it could have proved that the statements were made. In other words what the Crown
were endeavouring to lead from the police witnesses
was primary hearsay which was admissible as direct
evidence that the statement was made irrespective of
its truth or falsehood (Walker and Walker, *Law of*
F *Evidence in Scotland*, p 394). Subsequently at p 396 it
is observed that it is frequently necessary to prove that
a statement has been made, and it is stated: "The
party leading the evidence does so merely to establish
that the statement was made. He is probably not concerned with its truth, and indeed his case may be that
it was untrue." I accordingly agree with the advocate
depute that the sheriff was wrong to have upheld the
objection to the evidence which it was sought to take
from the police officers as to what was said to them by
members of the hotel staff.

In my opinion the evidence before the sheriff was
not sufficient to show that the police officers had   G
reasonable grounds to suspect that the appellant was
in possession of drugs. It is not possible to determine
whether the police officers had such reasonable
grounds without knowing what it was that the police
officers were told by members of the hotel staff. The
sheriff did not have this information, and in the
absence of that information he was not entitled to conclude that the police officers were acting within their
powers in making a detention and search under s 23
(2) of the Act of 1971. On the other hand it is no fault   H
of the respondent that the sheriff did not have this
information. The sheriff would have had that information if he had repelled the objection to the evidence as
he should have done. In these circumstances without
knowing what the police officers were told by the hotel
staff, it is impossible to determine whether the sheriff
was entitled to make finding in fact 3. In terms of
s 452 (4) (b) this court in hearing a stated case has
power to hear any additional evidence relevant to any
alleged miscarriage of justice. Having regard to how it   I
came about that no evidence was led regarding what
the police officers were told by the hotel staff, I am of
opinion that the present case is one where the court
ought to exercise this statutory power and ought to
hear additional evidence upon this matter. It is only
when this court has been apprised of what the police
officers were told by the hotel staff that this court will
be able to determine whether there has been any miscarriage of justice as suggested by the appellant. I
would accordingly move your Lordships to continue   J
the appeal, and to order the hearing by this court of
additional evidence as to what was said to the police
officers by members of the hotel staff.

LORD MURRAY.—I read the findings in this
stated case to the effect that communication of suspicion that a drugs offence was being committed at a
named hotel was made by telephone to the police. In
consequence they attended at the hotel where they
were received by hotel staff and taken to a particular   K
bar where a particular person, the appellant, was
pointed out to them. The appellant was then detained
for search. Accordingly I am unable to agree with the
expression of opinion by your Lordship in the chair
that the findings are insufficient to justify the inference which the sheriff drew that the police had reasonable grounds to suspect that the appellant was in
possession of controlled drugs. The central issue in
the appeal, whether or not there is a case to answer,
turns entirely upon that point, not on whether any   L
suspicion is in fact justified. However, in light of the
sheriff's mistaken exclusion of material and relevant
evidence through ill founded objection on the part of
the appellant's agent, I entirely agree that it is
appropriate in this case for the court to exercise its
powers under s 452 (4) (b) of the 1975 Act to hear
additional evidence upon the matter.

LORD GRIEVE.—Section 23 (2) of the Misuse of
Drugs Act 1971 entitles a constable, who has reasonable grounds to suspect that a person is in possession

of a controlled drug, to search that person and to detain him for the purpose of searching him.

The complaint against the appellant on charge 1 was that he "did intentionally obstruct Sergeant Thomas Martin and Constable Brian Cooper in the exercise of their powers under s 23 of the Misuse of Drugs Act 1971 and did refuse to permit them to search [him] and did struggle violently with them: contrary to the Misuse of Drugs Act 1971, s 23 (4) (a)".

In this appeal by stated case the appellant challenges the right of the constables to detain him for the purpose of searching him. This he does on the ground that, on the facts found proved in the stated case, they had no reasonable grounds to suspect that he was in possession of controlled drugs.

The circumstances which gave rise to the constables' actings are set out in findings 1 to 4 of the stated case and are as follows: [his Lordship quoted the terms of findings 1 to 4 and continued:]

It is to be noted that in finding 1 the alleged contravention of the Act is not specified. That of itself is perhaps not important, but, in the light of what happened as a result of it, it is not insignificant. In finding 2 there is nothing to indicate what information the hotel staff gave to the police officers, but from the sheriff's note, we know that this was because the agent for the appellant took objection to any narrative by the police officers of what was said to them by the hotel staff, and because the sheriff, wrongly in my opinion, sustained that objection.

Before us counsel for the appellant was put in the anomalous position of submitting that the evidence to which objection had been taken at the trial by the appellant's agent was crucial to a decision as to the appellant's guilt or innocence. In the absence of any information in finding in fact 2 as to why the appellant had been pointed out by the hotel staff, when there were other people in the bar at the time, the court was in ignorance as to the grounds on which the police officers had proceeded to detain the appellant; there was no case to answer and question 1 should be answered in the negative as indeed should question 3.

It was submitted on behalf of the Crown that, albeit there was no evidence as to the precise information on which the police officers had proceeded to detain the appellant, there was sufficient in the findings, read as a whole, to justify the sheriff in deciding that there was a case to answer, and thereafter that the police officers had had reasonable grounds to suspect that the appellant was in possession of a controlled drug.

This case raises important issues. As was pointed out in *Dryburgh v Galt*, 1981 SLT at pp 155-156, the legitimacy of police officers proceeding on information received depends on the source and content of that information. In my opinion it is not possible for a court to decide whether a police officer had reasonable grounds to suspect that a person was in possession of a controlled drug, until it knows on what information the police officer had proceeded. The facts will vary from case to case, but the kind of information on

which a police officer can legitimately proceed to detain and search a suspect is to be found in the cases of *Dryburgh* and *Weir v Jessop*.

The course which your Lordship proposes we should take would enable the court to decide, bearing in mind the general considerations set out in *McNicol v Peters*, whether or not the police officers in this case had reasonable grounds to suspect that the appellant was in possession of controlled drugs at the material time. In my opinion without the information which the additional evidence will provide it is not possible to answer any of the questions in the stated case. I agree that the case should be dealt with in the way in which your Lordship in the chair proposes, and for these reasons which your Lordship gives.

Counsel for Appellant, Bell, QC; Solicitors, More & Co — Counsel for Respondent, Macdonald, QC, AD; Solicitor, J D Lowe, Crown Agent.

P W F

[On 20 November 1991 the appeal was continued until 17 December 1991 when the appellant was ordained to appear. It is understood that on that date the appeal was dismissed.]

Drummond v HM Advocate

HIGH COURT OF JUSTICIARY
THE LORD JUSTICE GENERAL (HOPE),
LORDS MURRAY AND MORISON
6 DECEMBER 1991

Justiciary — Evidence — Admissibility — Improperly obtained evidence — Warrant to search house referring to property stolen from furniture store — Items found in wardrobe relating to separate theft of clothing — Sheriff sustaining objection to evidence of one officer who had been searching for items outwith terms of warrant but repelling objection to evidence from second officer who stated that he was searching for furniture — Whether that officer's evidence admissible in light of successful earlier objection.

An accused person was convicted of a charge of theft by housebreaking of certain clothing from a particular location. Police officers had come to his house with a search warrant which referred to property stolen from a furniture store. Officers opened a wardrobe in the accused's bedroom where four sweaters and a cardigan which were similar to garments stolen in the clothing theft incident were found. The first officer stated in evidence that he had opened the wardrobe because he was looking for items from that incident. An objection to his evidence was then upheld. The accused objected to the evidence of a second officer involved in the search as to the items recovered from the wardrobe on the basis that that evidence had already been held to

A be inadmissible by reason of the sheriff's decision in upholding the objection to the first officer's evidence. That objection was repelled. The second officer stated in evidence that he was searching for items allegedly stolen in respect of the furniture theft, that the furniture he was looking for included smaller items as well as large pieces and that that was what he was looking for in the wardrobe, but that certain items of clothing attracted his attention because he felt that they were proceeds from another break in. The accused appealed against conviction and argued that the sheriff had been B wrong to hold competent the second officer's evidence regarding the search standing that the evidence of the first officer had been held by him to be inadmissible.

Held, (1) that, although a deliberate attempt to search for property stolen from other premises than those covered by the search warrant was excluded by its terms, the police officers were not prevented from taking possession of other articles of a plainly incriminatory character which they happened to come across in the course of their search for the furniture C (pp 478L-479A); (2) that each officer could speak only to what he was doing when the wardrobe was opened and, although the first officer's evidence was rendered inadmissible as soon as he said that he was initially looking for stuff from the clothing theft, nothing had been said which excluded the possibility that the second officer might have been acting within the terms of the warrant, and thus the second officer's evidence that the opening of the wardrobe had been done within the terms of the warrant would result in his D evidence of what he found inside the wardrobe, if believed by the jury, being admissible (p 479A-C); and appeal *refused*.

Indictment

Thomas Drummond, Kevin Munro Steele, David Landells Forbes and two others were charged at the instance of the rt hon the Lord Fraser of Carmyllie, Her Majesty's Advocate on an indictment which con-E tained several charges of theft by housebreaking. The accused pled not guilty and proceeded to trial before the sheriff and a jury. Drummond was convicted of charge 8 on the indictment being a charge of theft by housebreaking from premises at Eastfield industrial estate, Penicuik, occupied by Edinburgh Crystal and Peter Anderson Woollens.

Drummond appealed against conviction by way of note of appeal to the High Court. The facts giving rise to the appeal appear from the opinion of the court.

F

Case referred to

Advocate (HM) v Hepper, 1958 SLT 160; 1958 JC 39.

Appeal

The appeal was heard by the High Court on 26 September 1991.

On 6 December 1991 the court *allowed* the appeal only to the extent of substituting a verdict of guilty of reset for that of guilty of theft.

The following opinion of the court was delivered by the Lord Justice General (Hope): G

OPINION OF THE COURT.—The appellant is Thomas Drummond, who went to trial with Kevin Munro Steele and David Landells Forbes and two others on an indictment which contained several charges of theft by housebreaking. Steele and Forbes were each found guilty as libelled on three of the housebreaking charges. They appealed against these convictions, and for the reasons given in the opinion of the court dated 26 September 1991 [1992 SLT 847] the convictions were set aside and amended verdicts of H guilty of reset were substituted on all the charges of which they were convicted. The appellant was found guilty as libelled on one charge only, this being charge 8 which was a single charge of theft by housebreaking from premises at Eastfield industrial estate, Penicuik, occupied by Edinburgh Crystal and Peter Anderson Woollens. He also has appealed against his conviction, but he has done so on grounds which in some respects are different from those advanced by his co-accused and this opinion is concerned with his appeal. I

The first point which was argued by counsel on the appellant's behalf appears as the second ground on the sheet attached to his note of appeal. This is that the sheriff erred in holding that the evidence of DC Morrison regarding the search of the appellant's house at 4/5 Redbraes Place, Edinburgh, was competent standing that the evidence of DC Patterson was held by him to be inadmissible. The significance of this point lies in the fact that an important part of the evidence against the appellant in charge 8 was the finding J of labels 104 and 105 in a wardrobe in the front bedroom of his house. Label 104 comprised four Lyle and Scott sweaters, and label 105 was a cardigan manufactured by Peter Anderson Woollens who operated a franchise within the premises occupied by Edinburgh Crystal at Penicuik. These garments were identified as being similar to garments stolen in the housebreaking referred to in this charge. The other evidence which linked the appellant with the housebreaking referred to in charge 8 consisted of his K presence at a lockup in South Queensferry on 11 and 16 January 1990, outside which was found a bag which must have come from within the lockup containing security tag pins labels 106 and 107 which were similar in all respects to security tag pins stolen from Peter Anderson.

The search at the appellant's house was spoken to first by DC Patterson and then by DC Morrison. DC Patterson explained at the outset of his evidence that they were in possession of a search warrant for that L house, to look for property stolen at Landmark, Westfield Avenue, Edinburgh. The housebreaking at those premises was the subject of another charge on the indictment in which the appellant was not involved. This was charge 4, which related to the theft by housebreaking of various pieces of furniture and other household items from a warehouse at Westfield Avenue which was occupied by Landmark House Furnishings. Counsel took objection to this evidence on the ground that any items taken from the house

A were unlawfully obtained. Her point was that the warrant was to search for furniture, which confined the police officers to searching for items which were clearly visible in the house and did not entitle them to look into wardrobes or open drawers in a search for smaller items. The sheriff repelled the objection in the first instance, and DC Patterson then continued with his evidence. He confirmed that the warrant was to search for furniture, and that the items which he found were in a wardrobe unit in a bedroom of the house. There then followed this passage in his evid-
B ence: "Q. Now, tell me why were you in this wardrobe initially, why were you looking in there? — Initially when I was looking in the wardrobe I was looking for stuff from the break in at the Crystal Works."

At this point counsel renewed her objection on the ground that on this evidence the police officer was searching for items which clearly were not covered by the warrant to search for furniture from Landmark. The sheriff sustained the objection, and he directed the jury in due course to disregard the evidence which
C they had heard prior to the objection about the finding of certain other items in the house not relevant to charge 8.

At a later stage in the trial DC Morrison gave his evidence. He described the terms of the search warrant, which he said was for articles of furniture stolen or unlawfully carried off from Landmark, and he also described his arrival at the house with other police officers to carry out the search. Counsel then took objection on the ground that in view of the
D finding by the sheriff that the search by DC Patterson was illegal, evidence of the search by this police officer on the same search warrant should also be held to be inadmissible on the same ground. The sheriff was not satisfied that it was right for him to sustain the objection without having heard the evidence of this police officer about what he was doing in the course of the search. DC Morrison then returned to the witness box. He stated that he was working with DC Patterson and that there were two other police officers in
E another part of the house. He explained that he was searching for furniture, but that he had a list of the property stolen from Landmark which included table lamps and pictures and that the furniture he was looking for included smaller items as well as large pieces. His position was explained in this part of his evidence:

"Q. Why was the wardrobe opened, do you know? — We were searching for stolen property.

F "Q. Look again at your search warrant would you? What stolen property does that search warrant allow you to search for? — Furniture.

"Q. What furniture were you looking for in this wardrobe? — I had a property list of stolen property in my possession from Landmark which was some pages long. As well as the furniture it also included table lamps and pictures.

"Q. I see, so you were aware that the furniture you were looking for wasn't just three piece suites but included smaller items as well? — That is correct.

"Q. When you opened this wardrobe did you see anything there that attracted your attention? — I saw G certain items of clothing which attracted my attention, yes.

"Q. So they attracted your attention? — Yes, because I felt they were proceeds from another break in."

According to him therefore the wardrobe was opened because they were searching for property of the description in the warrant when certain items of clothing attracted his attention. He explained that he H felt that these items were proceeds from another break in at Dalmahoy Golf Club. This break in was the subject of charge 1 in the indictment. He explained that a number of the items had the Dalmahoy motif on the clothing and that he thought that everything which he took from the wardrobe might relate to Dalmahoy. The items which he took included labels 104 and 105, and he took them because at the time he felt that they were part of the proceeds of the Dalmahoy break in. The sweaters comprised in label I 104 were, he said, the kind of sweaters which a golfer might wear.

Counsel submitted that the sheriff was wrong to allow evidence of the search in the wardrobe to be taken from DC Morrison. This was, she said, a single search carried out by the two police officers as a team. What they did could not be valid for one and not for the other, because they both had the same search warrant and they were acting together in what they did. The learned advocate depute in reply accepted J that if evidence of labels 104 and 105 was inadmissible there would be insufficient evidence to convict the appellant. But he submitted that the question as to the admissibility of the search was one which should be answered by reference to the evidence of each police officer as to what he thought he was doing at the time. DC Patterson said that initially when he was looking in the wardrobe he was looking for stuff from the break in at Edinburgh Crystal. This was something for which he had no warrant to search at all, and quite K clearly in the light of that answer anything which he found in the wardrobe was inadmissible against the appellant. On the other hand when DC Morrison was asked what the stolen property was which he was searching for when the wardrobe was opened he replied that he had a list of stolen property in his possession from Landmark which included smaller items. He justified the opening of the wardrobe by the fact that some of the items on his list were small pieces of furniture such as table lamps and pictures. It was sub- L mitted that his evidence about what was found in the wardrobe was not rendered inadmissible merely because the other police officer who was working with him said that he was looking for something else.

The authority which was conferred on the police officers by their search warrant was to search only for furniture stolen or unlawfully carried off from Landmark. A deliberate attempt to search for property stolen from other premises was excluded by its terms. But the police officers were not prevented from taking possession of other articles of a plainly incriminatory character which they happened to come across in the course of their search for the furniture: see *HM Advocate v Hepper*, 1958 SLT per Lord Guthrie at p 160. So if the opening of the wardrobe could be justified on the ground that the police officers were looking for small items of furniture, evidence about the finding of other articles of an incriminatory character was, without doubt, admissible. On this matter, at least on the evidence which was led in this case, each police officer could speak only for himself as to what he was doing when the wardrobe was opened. As soon as he said that initially when he was looking in the wardrobe he was looking for stuff from the break in at the Crystal Works, DC Patterson rendered any further evidence about what he found in the wardrobe inadmissible. But he was not asked whether he had discussed with DC Morrison whether the wardrobe should be opened, nor was anything said by him which excluded the possibility that DC Morrison might have been acting within the terms of the warrant at the time. As it happened, on the evidence of DC Morrison the opening of the wardrobe was done within the terms of the warrant, so, having regard to what he said about this in his evidence, if it was believed by the jury, what he found inside the wardrobe was admissible. In these circumstances the sheriff was not precluded by the fact that he had sustained the objection to DC Patterson's evidence from repelling the same objection to DC Morrison's evidence and allowing this evidence to go to the jury. We reject this ground of appeal.

[His Lordship dealt with a ground with which this report is not concerned and concluded:]

The third ground raises the same issue as that which was the subject of the appeal against conviction by the appellant's co-accused Kevin Munro Steele and David Landells Forbes. The reasons which we gave in our opinion dated 26 September 1991 for allowing their appeals against their convictions for theft and for substituting convictions for reset apply also to the appellant's conviction for theft on charge 8. Accordingly we shall allow this appeal to the extent only of setting aside the verdict of guilty of theft on charge 8 and substituting a verdict of guilty of reset on that charge.

Counsel for Appellants, Powrie; Solicitors, Gordon McBain — Counsel for Respondent, Macdonald, QC, AD; Solicitor, J D Lowe, Crown Agent.

R F H

Davidson v City of Glasgow District Council

OUTER HOUSE

TEMPORARY JUDGE D B ROBERTSON, QC

23 JANUARY 1992

Reparation — Negligence — Averments — Relevancy — Novus actus interveniens — Causation — Whether determinable without proof.

Process — Pleadings — Relevancy — Novus actus interveniens — Causation — Whether determinable without proof.

A scaffolder sought reparation for injuries sustained in a fall from scaffolding. He averred that the board which gave way, causing the accident, did so because it was of inadequate length. He raised an action against his employers and against the scaffolding suppliers who had hired the equipment, including boards, to his employers. It was averred that before the accident the employers had required to return all the boards supplied as they were of insufficient length; that substitute boards had been supplied, and that the board which gave way was an original board which had not been returned or alternatively a substitute board of insufficient length. He tabled a number of cases at common law and under the Construction (Working Places) Regulations 1966 against his employers, including a case based on alleged failure to inspect all scaffolding boards before use. The pursuer also averred a case at common law against the scaffolding suppliers for supplying boards which they knew or ought to have known were too short, and in particular for failing to inspect the boards prior to supplying them. The employers adopted this case against the suppliers and also alleged breach of contract of hire by them. The suppliers sought dismissal of the pursuer's case of fault against them, arguing that the weaker of the two alternative factual situations pled by the pursuer was that the employers, having discovered the defects, had omitted to withdraw from use and return all short boards with the result that one such short board had been used. That failure had broken the causal link between any initial negligent supply by the suppliers and the accident and amounted to novus actus interveniens. In reply it was argued that there could be several contributing causes to the accident, and, even where an intermediate examination had taken place, that there was not necessarily an interruption of the chain of causation.

Held, that without the whole evidence of the surrounding facts and circumstances which would emerge at proof, it was impossible to hold that the employers' failure to discover that one of the planks had remained and been inadvertently used was negligent, or that it broke the chain of causation of the negligence by the suppliers and was the sole cause of the accident (p 482C-D); and proof before answer *allowed*.

Miller v South of Scotland Electricity Board, 1958

A SLT 229, *followed*; *Knightley v Johns* [1982] 1 WLR 349; and *Taylor v Rover Co Ltd* [1966] 1 WLR 1491, *commented on*.

Action of damages

Leslie Davidson raised an action of damages against (first) City of Glasgow District Council, his employers, and (second) Stephens & Carter Ltd, suppliers of scaffolding to his employers, following an accident in the course of his employment when he fell B from scaffolding.

The case called on procedure roll before the temporary judge (D B Robertson, QC) when the second defenders' plea to the relevancy of the pursuer's case of fault against them was argued.

Cases referred to

Clay v A J Crump & Sons Ltd [1964] 1 QB 533; [1963] 3 WLR 866; [1963] 3 All ER 687.
Grant v Sun Shipping Co Ltd, 1949 SLT 25; 1948 SC C (HL) 73.
Knightley v Johns [1982] 1 WLR 349; [1982] 1 All ER 851.
Miller v South of Scotland Electricity Board, 1958 SLT 229; 1958 SC (HL) 20.
Taylor v Rover Co Ltd [1966] 1 WLR 1491; [1966] 2 All ER 181.

On 23 January 1992 the temporary judge *allowed* a proof before answer, leaving all preliminary pleas D standing.

D B ROBERTSON, QC.—The pursuer seeks

reparation for injuries sustained on 13 September 1987 when he was engaged in the course of his employment as a scaffolder with City of Glasgow District Council at a building in Burghead Drive, Glasgow, where scaffolding was being erected. The scaffolding was being erected on the front of the said property and at a gable end thereof. The front E scaffolding had four bays, three of which were 8 ft bays and the fourth was a 4 ft bay, and on the said date this scaffolding was incomplete, being erected only to a one level height. It is averred that the pursuer stepped on the 4 ft bay and a board thereon gave way causing the pursuer to fall to the ground and sustain his injuries. It is alleged that the scaffolding board which moved was not resting securely because it was of inadequate length for use in a 4 ft bay. The scaffolding equipment including boards was supplied to the F pursuer's employers by Stephens & Carter Ltd under a contract of hire. The pursuer has convened both his employers and Messrs Stephens & Carter as defenders. While it is not clear when the scaffolding was first delivered to the first defenders, nor when they commenced the erection of the scaffolding, it is averred that in April 1987, five months before the accident, the first defenders required to gather up and return all the boards supplied for use in the 4 ft bay because said boards were only 4 ft 1 in or less in length and of insufficient length to be used safely in the said scaffolding. New boards were supplied by the second

defenders in substitution. The first defenders, it is alleged, instituted no system for the checking of the G length of said substitute boards, or any scaffolding boards remaining on site. It is explained and averred that the board which gave way was one of the original boards which had not been returned to the second defenders or alternatively a board provided in substitution by the second defenders but of insufficient length for its purpose.

The pursuer tables a number of cases of fault against his employers both at common law and under the Construction Regulations 1966, but since the debate H before me did not concern the relevancy of the cases against the first defenders it is sufficient to notice that the common law case against the first defenders involves inter alia an alleged failure to inspect all scaffolding boards for length before use, it being averred that they knew or ought to have known that "some of the original [short] boards might remain on site". The case of fault at common law made by the pursuer against the second defenders is that they supplied boards which they knew or ought to have I known were too short for use in 4 ft bays and this case is particularised by an averment that they failed in a duty to inspect the boards to ensure that they were of the correct size prior to supplying them for use of the first defenders. The first defenders adopt this case of fault against the second defenders and further allege breach of contract of hire by the second defenders.

Both defenders have relevancy pleas to the pursuer's averments, and the second defenders have also pleas directed at the first defenders' cases of fault and breach J of contract against them, but I was addressed only on the second defenders' plea to the relevancy of the pursuer's case of fault against them.

Counsel for the second defenders' submission was, accepting that on the pursuer's case, if proved, the second defenders were liable in law for the initial supply of defective or dangerous boards, and taking the weaker of the two alternative possible factual situations pled by the pursuer, namely that the first K defenders having discovered the defects and having omitted to withdraw and return all the short boards so that at least one short board had been used on the scaffolding, that broke the causal link between the initial negligent supply by the second defenders and the accident. That omission and the subsequent damage was not a natural and probable consequence of the original negligence which ought reasonably to have been foreseen. There was here in that situation, it was submitted, a novus actus interveniens so that L the original negligence on the part of the second defenders as suppliers ceases to be relevant. There had, in effect, been an intermediate examination which disclosed the dangerous feature of the boards supplied.

In his compelling address counsel for the second defenders referred to a number of authorities and he founded strongly in particular on two English cases — *Knightley v Johns* and *Taylor v Rover Co Ltd*. Before dealing with these cases and the applicability of the

A reasoning there to the present case, it is important to remember that these decisions were made after proof of all the facts and circumstances because in England, since the abolition of demurrer in 1883, the English courts usually have an inquiry into the whole facts and circumstances in negligence cases. In both these cases it was found that there had been acts and omissions breaking the chain of causation between one negligent act and ultimate damage.

B In *Knightley* the first defendant was involved in a road accident near the exit of a tunnel carrying one way traffic which had a sharp bend in the middle obscuring the exit and the site of the first defendant's accident to drivers entering the tunnel. The police inspector in charge at the scene of the accident, realising he had forgotten to close the tunnel to oncoming traffic, ordered two police officers on motorcycles, one of whom was the plaintiff, to go back against the oncoming traffic and close the tunnel. One of the police officers — the plaintiff — collided with an C oncoming motor car and was injured. That motorist was found on the facts not to have been negligent. The plaintiff claimed damages from inter alios the first defendant, the police inspector and the chief constable. The first defendant admitted negligence but claimed that the negligence of the other defenders and/or of the plaintiff had caused or contributed to the accident. The trial judge found that neither the plaintiff nor the police inspector had been negligent and that their actions had not broken the chain of causa-D tion between the first defendant's accident and the plaintiff's accident. He found the first defendant wholly liable for the plaintiff's injuries. On appeal, after a detailed consideration of evidence, the Court of Appeal found that the inspector's negligence in not closing the tunnel and in ordering the plaintiff to remedy that negligence by a dangerous manoeuvre had been the real cause of the plaintiff's injuries and was a new cause which disturbed and interrupted the sequence of events between the first defendant's negli-E gence and the plaintiff's accident. The inspector's negligence therefore made the plaintiff's injuries too remote from the first defendant's wrongdoing to be a consequence of it. While this is an interesting example of a court finding a novus actus interveniens established on evidence and indeed taking a different view on the evidence from the trial judge, in my opinion it merely emphasises the difficulty and unwisdom of making judgment on questions of causation and foreseeability without proof of the whole facts and circum-F stances. In the course of the Court of Appeal's very detailed consideration of the evidence it was said that in deciding whether the whole sequence of events which emanated from a negligent act was a natural and probable consequence and a reasonably foreseeable result or whether an event or events in the sequence was or were a novus actus interveniens it is helpful but not decisive to consider which events were deliberate choices to do positive acts, which events were omissions or failures to act, which acts were innocent mistakes or miscalculations and which acts or omissions were negligent. Since negligent conduct is more likely to break the chain of causation than conduct which is G not, positive acts will more easily constitute new causes than inaction and mistakes and mischances are to be expected of human beings in a crisis ([1982] 1 WLR at pp 366-367). In other words, in deciding matters of causation and foreseeability many and varied factors must be considered.

The next case referred to, *Taylor v Rover Co Ltd*, while superficially more similar in its facts to the present case since it involved the liability of a supplier of dangerous chisels where the employers of a man injured by a piece flying from the chisel had kept it in H circulation despite there having been previous incidents when a piece had flown from the chisel, involved other considerations including the responsibility of the manufacturer and a third party who carried out the hardening of the chisel. Here again of course all the facts and circumstances were before the court. These cases were of course decisions on their particular facts and do not lay down any principles of universal application. What can be adduced from them however is that whether a particular event or piece of conduct I does or does not have the effect of a novus actus interveniens is a question of evaluation of fact for the court having considered the evidence and weighed up the relative importance of the different factors which have combined to bring about the damage.

In reply it was submitted that the pursuer had averred more than one operating cause of the accident and one being the negligence of the second defenders as suppliers. There could be several contributing causes and even if the dangerous plank was one which J was inadvertently left on site and even if that was proved to be the sole responsibility of the first defenders and was negligent (which would itself depend on the surrounding facts and circumstances) it did not follow that the actings or omissions of the first defenders was the sole cause. Reference was made to *Grant v Sun Shipping Co*. As Lord du Parcq said in his speech in that case (1949 SLT at p 36): "If the negligence or breach of duty of one person is the cause of injury to another, the wrongdoer cannot in all circum-K stances escape liability by proving that, though he was to blame, yet but for the negligence of a third person the injured man would not have suffered the damage of which he complains. There is abundant authority for the proposition that the mere fact that a subsequent act of negligence has been the immediate cause of disaster does not (necessarily) exonerate the original offender." Reference was also made to *Clay v Crump & Son*. Here a wall was left standing in a dangerous condition by demolition contractors and there were L then successive failures by an architect and building contractors to inspect properly and discover the dangerous condition of the wall, which eventually fell and injured an employee. The court rejected the proposition that the building contractors, as having the last opportunity of examining and having actually made an examination (which was held to be careless), should bear the whole liability to the workman. Applying *Grant v Sun Shipping Co Ltd* the Court of Appeal held that the demolition contractors and the architect and the building contractors were all liable in

A negligence and responsibility was apportioned among them. This case is quite specific authority for the submission on behalf of the pursuer that even where an intermediate examination has taken place, that does not per se in all circumstances interrupt the chain of causation between earlier negligence and subsequent damage.

The submission for the pursuer that the case against the second defenders should go to a proof before answer was reinforced by reference to *Miller v South of Scotland Electricity Board* and well known dicta
B therein on foreseeability and the difficulty of disposing of cases of negligence on a preliminary plea without inquiry into the facts. As Lord Keith of Avonholm says (1958 SLT at p 236): "In claims of damages for alleged negligence it can only be in rare and exceptional cases that an action can be disposed of on relevancy . . . the law of negligence in Scotland proceeds on principles of *culpa*, breach of the duty to take that care which the circumstances demand from a reasonable man. These circumstances in any parti-
C cular case will normally have to be ascertained by evidence. They vary infinitely. The facets and detail of a case on which an assessment of the law must depend cannot be conveyed to the mind by mere averments of the bare bones of the case, and the weighing of the facts for or against negligence may often present a delicate task to the tribunal charged with applying the law."

Even although there was in effect an intermediate inspection, and assuming on the alternative that the
D first defenders failed to discover that one of the planks remained and was inadvertently used, it does not follow that that was negligence or that it broke the chain of causation and was the sole cause of the accident. That may be the position depending on the evidence of the surrounding facts and circumstances which emerges at a proof, but without the whole evidence of such facts and circumstances it is impossible to hold at this stage that it is. The argument presented for the second defenders may well succeed after all the
E facts are out. I am not saying that the judge after a proof must find negligence on the part of the second defenders or must find that such negligence was a cause of the damage or must hold that there is not a novus actus interveniens, but he may do. The second defenders' argument cannot be sustained without an inquiry into the facts. The pursuer has stated a relevant case against the second defenders. Parties were agreed that any inquiry must be by way of proof before answer, leaving all preliminary pleas standing. There will be a proof before answer. I should like to add that
F I was much assisted in this debate by excellent addresses from both sides of the bar.

Counsel for Pursuer, Gibson; Solicitors, Aitken Nairn, WS (for McVey & Murricane, Glasgow) — Counsel for First Defenders, R A Smith; Solicitors, Campbell Smith & Co, WS — Counsel for Second Defenders, Sturrock; Solicitors, Gray Muirhead, WS (for Holmes Mackillop, Glasgow).

D S C

(NOTE)

Murray v Gent Ltd

OUTER HOUSE

TEMPORARY JUDGE R G McEWAN, QC

26 FEBRUARY 1992

Damages — Amount — Solatium and loss of earning capacity — Fingers — Cut tendon in right ring finger leading to permanent disability.

A 56 year old foreman electrician cut his fingers, severing a tendon of his right ring finger. The finger was left permanently bent and was painful in damp weather.

Opinion, that solatium was properly assessed at £3,000 and that disadvantage in the labour market was properly valued at £200.

John Jackson Murray raised an action against his employers, Gent Ltd, for damages for injuries sustained in an accident at work on 12 April 1988. He was then aged 56 and was employed as a foreman electrician. He was removing from a wall a metal plate which came away in his hand causing a severe cut to each of the long and ring fingers of his right hand. He was right handed. After a proof before the temporary judge (R G McEwan, QC) it was held that liability had not been established. The employers were assoilzied. In relation to damages the temporary judge said:

"The metal plate cut two fingers on the right hand. The long finger was cut but not seriously. It was cleaned and sutured. The cut to the ring finger severed a tendon at the terminal point. Surgical procedure has made it permanently bent at 30 degrees on that joint. The injury and treatment were both painful and unpleasant. There is cosmetic deformity and some continuing disability. The pursuer suffers pain from it in damp weather. He remains in his present job. There was no wage loss. There is a very slight risk that if he lost his job, he would be at a disadvantage in the labour market. Had I been awarding damages I would have awarded the pursuer £3,000 for what was a nasty injury. I would have awarded £200 for loss of prospects. I allocate one half of solatium to the past. I would have awarded interest on past solatium of £1,500 at 7½ per cent to date."

Counsel for Pursuer, Ardrey; Solicitors, Lawford Kidd & Co, WS — Counsel for Defenders, Keen; Solicitors, Digby, Brown & Co.

C H

Craig v HM Advocate

A HIGH COURT OF JUSTICIARY

THE LORD JUSTICE CLERK (ROSS),
LORDS MORISON AND PENROSE

20 MARCH 1992

Justiciary — Evidence — Admissibility — Character of possible associates of accused — Accused charged with being concerned in supplying drugs — Evidence of police officer as to his knowledge of names and nicknames in
B *notebook found in accused's house and that known drug dealers were persons of those names — Whether evidence speculative — Whether prior notice ought to have been given to defence — Whether evidence properly left to jury.*

Two accused persons were convicted in the sheriff court of contraventions of ss 4 (3) (b) and 5 (2) of the Misuse of Drugs Act 1971. One Crown witness was a police officer who had been involved in the detection of a large number of drug offences. During the course of his evidence he was shown a notebook on which
C there was a list of names and nicknames and was asked by the prosecutor if he recognised any names on the list. The defence objected to this question on the ground that as the names were commonly used names the officer would not be able to say that any of the names referred to the same persons as the officer had known in previous illegal drug dealing and that, accordingly, when he was being asked to give evidence the officer would only be speculating. The sheriff repelled the objection on the ground that it was rele-
D vant for the officer to give evidence that he knew persons who were involved with drugs, some of whose names or nicknames were the same as the names and nicknames on the list, and that, although the officer could not say that the names or nicknames referred to the same persons, it would be a matter for the jury to decide what inference, if any, they could draw from such evidence. The sheriff directed the jury accordingly. The accused appealed to the High Court and contended that the sheriff had erred in (a) allowing the
E officer's evidence (i) as to his knowledge of the names on the list; and (ii) as to his speculation that the names were of known drug dealers; and (b) failing to direct the jury that that evidence was speculative and not evidence of fact and that it should be disregarded.

Held, (1) that, having regard to the fact that the officer could not say that the names or nicknames on the list referred to persons whom he knew but could merely say that he knew persons who had similar
F names or nicknames, the sheriff had properly repelled the defence objection (p 485A); and (2) that the sheriff had been correct to direct the jury that it was for them to determine what, if anything, they made of that evidence (p 485B); and appeals *refused.*

Opinion, that no notice required to be given to the defence of the intention to lead the officer's evidence because in this case the evidence was not being led to suggest that the names on the lists definitely referred to persons whom the police officers knew, but only that they were similar (p 484J-K).

Forsyth v HM Advocate, 1992 SLT 189, *distinguished.* G

Indictment

Jacqueline Craig and John Thomson were charged at the instance of the rt hon the Lord Fraser of Carmyllie, Her Majesty's Advocate, on an indictment which libelled inter alia: "(1) you Jacqueline Craig and John Thomson were on 17 January 1990 in the house occupied by you at 8 Kenmar Terrace, Hamilton, and elsewhere in Scotland, concerned in the supply to H other persons of a controlled drug namely cannabis resin, a class B drug specified in Pt II of Sched 2 to the aftermentioned Act in contravention of s 4 (1) of said Act: contrary to the Misuse of Drugs Act 1971, s 4 (3) (b); (2) you Jacqueline Craig and John Thomson did date libelled in charge 1 hereof at said house at 8 Kenmar Terrace aforesaid, unlawfully have in your possession a controlled drug namely cannabis resin, a class B drug specified in Pt II of Sched 2 to the aftermentioned Act in contravention of s 5 (1) of said Act: I contrary to the Misuse of Drugs Act 1971, s 5 (2)".

The accused pled not guilty and proceeded to trial in the sheriff court at Hamilton before Sheriff W E Gibson and a jury.

The defence objected to evidence led by the Crown which sought to elicit from a police officer his knowledge of the names found on, inter alia, a notebook and his speculation that the names were those of known drug dealers. The sheriff repelled the objection. The jury convicted the accused of charges 1 and J 2. The accused appealed by way of note of appeal to the High Court.

Case referred to

Forsyth v HM Advocate, 1992 SLT 189; 1991 SCCR 861.

Appeal

The grounds of appeal for the accused Craig were in the following terms, inter alia: K

(1) That the trial judge erred in holding that he was entitled to allow the evidence of Crown witness no 1, John Kelly, as to his knowledge of the names on the Crown productions nos 8 and 4.

(2) That the trial judge erred in holding that he was entitled to allow the evidence of Crown witness no 1, John Kelly, in relation to his speculation that the said names were of known drug dealers. The trial judge erred in law in repelling the objections to the said L evidence.

(3) That the trial judge failed to direct the jury that the said evidence was speculative and not evidence of fact and should be disregarded.

The grounds of appeal for the accused Thomson were substantially similar.

The appeals were argued before the High Court on 20 March 1992.

Eo die the court *refused* the appeals.

The following opinion of the court was delivered by the Lord Justice Clerk (Ross):

OPINION OF THE COURT.—These are appeals at the instance of Jacqueline Craig and John Thomson. They were both found guilty of charges 1 and 2 on an indictment and each was sentenced to 18 months' imprisonment. Charge 1 was a charge of contravening s 4 (3) (b) of the Misuse of Drugs Act 1971 and charge 2 was a charge of contravening s 5 (2) of the same Act. They have both appealed against conviction. Originally both appealed against sentence also but the appeal against sentence at the instance of John Thomson was abandoned. The appellant Jacqueline Craig still maintains an appeal against sentence. So far as the appeal against conviction is concerned, although the grounds of appeal are expressed differently in the two appeals, they both relate to the same issue and raise what is essentially the same point. The grounds of appeal in the case of the appellant Jacqueline Craig which were founded on before us, were grounds 1, 2 and 3. These are in the following terms: [his Lordship quoted the grounds of appeal set out supra and continued:]

As we say the ground of appeal against conviction in the case of the appellant John Thomson is expressed in different terms, but again it is suggested on his behalf that the sheriff erred in allowing evidence from this police officer about names on a list found in the house, which evidence was of a purely speculative nature. In seeking to advance this ground of appeal counsel for the appellant Jacqueline Craig reminded us of what the sheriff said in his report. It appears that one of the productions was a list in the form of what is usually referred to as a "tick list". One of the officers who found this list, Detective Constable John Kelly, spoke to the list of names which appeared in a notebook. He gave evidence that he had been involved in the past in the detection of a large number of contraventions of the Misuse of Drugs Act and at that stage the procurator fiscal depute sought to ask him if he recognised any names on the list. The agent for the appellant objected and the objection appears to have been on the ground that as the names were commonly used names the officer was unable to say that any of the names referred to one and the same person as the officer had known in previous illegal drug dealing and that accordingly when he was being asked to give evidence he was only speculating. The Crown maintained that the question was a proper one to ask because the officer, in the course of his work as a policeman, had come to know who were drug addicts and it would be a matter for the jury to decide if the names on the list had any significance. The sheriff took the view that it was relevant for the officer to give evidence that he knew persons who were involved with drugs, some of whose names or nicknames were the same as the names and nicknames on the list. He recognised that the officer could not say that they referred to the same person but it would be a matter for the jury to decide what inference, if any, they could draw from such

evidence. He accordingly allowed the evidence to be led. When he came to charge the jury, in the course of his charge the sheriff referred to the evidence which Detective Constable Kelly gave about recognising names and then said this: "Clearly, PC Kelly was unable to say that the names in the book definitely referred to the people involved in his drug cases and cases which he said related to the drug cannabis resin. I don't know what you will make of that evidence. For example you may think there is some significance in that or you may regard it as coincidental."

Both counsel for the appellant Craig and counsel who appeared for the appellant John Thomson referred to the recent case of *Forsyth v HM Advocate*. That case related to evidence which had been led regarding surveillance operations carried out by the police in the course of which the police had observed the two accused in the company of two individuals whom the police knew had had convictions for drug offences. As we understand the ratio of that case, it was held that there had been a risk of unfairness by the leading of such evidence because no notice had been given to the accused of the intention to lead evidence of the association of the accused with these two men who had convictions for drug offences. It will thus be seen that the situation which arose in *Forsyth* was different to the situation which arose here. In the case of *Forsyth* evidence had been led of association between the two accused and two named and identified individuals whom the police witnesses indicated had had drug convictions. On the other hand, as the sheriff reminded the jury in the present case, Detective Constable Kelly was not able to say that the names in the book definitely referred to people whom he knew to have been involved in drug cases. All that could be said was that the names or nicknames on the list were similar to the names or nicknames of individuals whom the police officer knew. The situation as we say appears to us to be different from a case where evidence has been given of a surveillance operation where the accused are seen in the company of definite identifiable persons. That was not the situation here. Whilst it may be in a case such as *Forsyth* that notice has to be given, whether notice has to be given must depend upon the circumstances and we are not persuaded that notice had to be given in a case like the present where evidence was not being led to suggest that the names on the lists definitely referred to persons whom the police officers knew. In any event it is difficult to see how notice could be given where only a nickname is known. Quite apart from that, as the sheriff makes plain in his report, when objection was taken before him the objection was not upon the ground that there had been a failure to give notice but merely upon the ground that the evidence which the officer would be giving would be speculation. Likewise when the grounds of appeal in the two appeals were stated in the notes of appeal the ground is stated on the same basis as the objections were taken before the sheriff, namely, that the evidence involved speculation and the ground of appeal does not proceed upon the basis that there had been any failure to give notice.

That being so, the appellants are not in a position to found upon anything said in the case of *Forsyth*.

In our judgment, having regard to the evidence which the police officers gave and to the fact that Detective Constable Kelly could not say that the names or nicknames on the list referred to persons whom he knew, but could merely say that he knew persons who had similar names or nicknames, the objection which was taken to the leading of this evidence was correctly repelled by the sheriff. We are satisfied that the evidence of Detective Constable Kelly in this case was properly before the jury and, as the sheriff directed the jury, it was for them to determine what, if anything, they made of that evidence and it was for them to determine whether they thought that evidence was of significance or whether they thought the fact that the names or nicknames were the same was mere coincidence. That is the sole ground of appeal against conviction and we have come to the conclusion that the ground is not a good one and that the appellants have failed to establish any miscarriage of justice on that ground. It follows that the appeal against conviction of both appellants must be refused.

[His Lordship then dealt with, and refused, the appeal against sentence by Jacqueline Craig, with which this report is not concerned.]

Counsel for Appellant Craig, Armstrong; Solicitors, Strathern & Blair, WS (for N J Scullion & Co, Hamilton) — Counsel for Appellant Thomson, Duguid; Solicitors, Wheatley & Co, SSC (for J A Bryan & Co, Hamilton) —Counsel for Respondent, McFarlane, QC, AD; Solicitor, J D Lowe, Crown Agent.

R F H

Palmer v Beck

OUTER HOUSE
LORD KIRKWOOD
7 APRIL 1992

Heritable property — Sale — Warrandice — Whether actual or threatened eviction necessary to found claim for breach of warrandice.

Property — Heritable property — Sale — Warrandice — Whether actual or threatened eviction necessary to found claim for breach of warrandice.

Damages — Amount — Solatium — Breach of contract for sale of heritage — Resultant distress suffered by purchaser.

Damages — Breach of warrandice — Whether claim for solatium relevant.

The purchaser of a house and garden received a title containing less than she had contracted to purchase but more than the sellers had title to convey to her.

The sellers had intended to acquire the extra area, having negotiated with the owners of it. The purchaser moved out of the house because of the defect in the title and eventually sold on. She required to purchase the extra area to enable her to sell the house and garden. She sought damages on the grounds of fraudulent misrepresentation, negligent misrepresentation and breach of warrandice. The misrepresentation cases were not established at proof. The purchaser contended that the breach of warrandice case was relevant, arguing that the undoubted lack of title rendering the subjects virtually unsaleable was a sufficient basis for the operation of the remedy. The purchaser sought an award of damages including solatium both on the cases based on misrepresentation and on the case based on breach of warrandice.

Held, (1) that an undeniable absence of title did not amount to eviction (pp 488L-489A); and (2) that there had been no actual eviction or threat of eviction (p 489A-D); and decree of absolvitor *pronounced.*

Opinion, that, had the claim for fraudulent misrepresentation succeeded, damages would have been awarded for the financial loss directly attributable to the defect and solatium assessed at £5,000 (p 491E-H).

Opinion, that, had the claim for breach of warrandice succeeded, damages would have been awarded for indemnification only, with no award for solatium (pp 491I-J and 492C-E).

Dictum of Lord Morison in *Watson v Swift & Co's Judicial Factor,* 1986 SLT 217 at p 220I-J, *not followed.*

Action of damages

Mrs Sheila Doris Cole or Palmer raised an action against Harold William Bryan Beck and Mrs Pamela Lucy Beck for damages arising from the sale by the defenders to the pursuer of a house and garden ground. The case was variously laid on fraudulent misrepresentation, negligent misrepresentation and breach of contract.

The case came to proof before the Lord Ordinary (Kirkwood).

Cases referred to

Allan v Barclay (1864) 2 M 873.
Hadley v Baxendale (1854) 9 Ex 341.
Hutchison v Davidson, 1946 SLT 11; 1945 SC 395.
Leith Heritages Co v Edinburgh and Leith Glass Co (1876) 3 R 789.
Melville v Wemyss (1842) 4 D 385.
Smith v Ross (1672) Mor 16596.
Smith v Sim, 1954 SC 357.
Watson v Swift & Co's Judicial Factor, 1986 SLT 217.
Welsh v Russell (1894) 2 SLT 27; (1894) 21 R 769.

Textbooks referred to

Bell, *Lectures on Conveyancing* (3rd ed), Vol I, pp 214, 217 and 643.
Bell, *Principles* (10th ed), paras 121, 895.

Erskine, *Institute,* II iii 30.

Gordon, *Scottish Land Law,* para 12-68.

Halliday, *Conveyancing Law and Practice,* Vol I, paras 4-44, 4-47.

Macdonald, *Conveyancing Manual* (4th ed), para 12.10.

Stair, *Institutions,* II iii 46.

Walker, *Civil Remedies,* pp 753, 754-755.

On 7 April 1992 the Lord Ordinary *pronounced* decree of absolvitor.

LORD KIRKWOOD.—In 1973 the defenders purchased the subjects known as "Summerside", Mosstowie, Elgin which comprised a dwellinghouse and an area of garden ground. To the east and south of the garden ground was a raised area of rough ground which was bounded on the east by a fence and which did not form part of the subjects purchased by the defenders. This area of rough ground was owned by Mr and Mrs Allan Smith, the proprietors of the adjoining farm of Lower Whitefield. One day in 1974 the first defender spoke to Mr Smith and asked him if he would be willing to sell the raised area of ground. Mr Smith indicated that he was prepared to sell that area of ground to the defenders provided that he could retain an access to his field to the south and a price of £40 was agreed. The first defender consulted his solicitor, Mr Kean, of Messrs R & R Urquhart, solicitors, Forres, and on 26 April 1974 Mr Kean submitted to the solicitors acting for Mr and Mrs Smith a formal offer to purchase the additional area of ground at the price of £40. On 26 April 1974 the offer was accepted. On 7 May 1974 the defenders' solicitor sent to Mr and Mrs Smith's solicitors a cheque for £40 in settlement of the purchase price and on 8 May 1974 Mr and Mrs Smith's solicitors gave a formal undertaking to deliver a validly executed disposition within 14 days of the receipt by them of the engrossment of the draft disposition. No such disposition was ever delivered. The defenders cleared the raised area of its existing gorse and the building materials and rubbish which were lying on it, removed a number of tree stumps and spread on it about 100 tons of topsoil which was seeded with grass. They later planted a hedge close to the existing fence and the whole garden was landscaped. Once this work had been carried out, the raised area of ground had effectively been incorporated into, and formed part of, the garden ground of "Summerside".

In 1975 the defenders decided to sell the subjects and on their instructions particulars of sale were prepared by Geoffrey Smith & Partners, chartered surveyors. The particulars of sale referred to the garden of the subjects as being mostly grassed out with numerous rowans and other small trees/hedging around the perimeter and stated that the gently undulating nature of the garden added to its attractiveness. In March 1975 the pursuer and her husband came to view the subjects and they were shown round by the first defender. The pursuer was told by him that the garden ground included the raised area and that the garden extended as far as the line of the hedge adjoining the fence lying to the east. She was told that to the south the garden included the raised area and extended as far as certain yellow gorse bushes some little distance short of the hedge line. The whole of the garden area pointed out to the pursuer was covered with grass and the first defender told her that he had increased the size of the garden by acquiring additional land from the neighbouring farmer. The pursuer was impressed by the house and the garden and she decided to submit an offer to purchase the subjects. On 26 March 1975 the pursuer's solicitors, Messrs Macpherson & Black, solicitors, Edinburgh submitted a formal offer to purchase the subjects at a price of £23,000 and the offer was accepted on 27 March 1975. The missives are nos 8 and 9 of process. The purchase was financed inter alia by a mortgage of £11,000 from the Halifax Building Society and a £5,500 loan from the Norwich Union Insurance Company.

In May 1975 the pursuer, her husband and their five children moved into the house. A few days after they had moved in Mr Allan Smith came to the door and informed the pursuer that he owned the raised area forming part of the garden to the east and south. The pursuer paid £11,000 to account of the purchase price but she decided to withhold payment of the balance of the price until the issue of the disputed area of garden ground was resolved. However, in July 1975 the defenders raised an action against the pursuer in Elgin sheriff court seeking (1) decree ordaining the pursuer to implement and fulfil her part of the missives of sale by making payment of the balance of the price, namely, £12,000 with interest in exchange for a valid disposition of the subjects and (2) failing implement, for payment of the sum of £2,600 and decree ordaining the present pursuer to remove from the subjects. Skeleton defences were lodged on behalf of the pursuer and on 24 September 1975 the case called in the debate roll. The solicitor who appeared for Mrs Palmer stated that he was not prepared to argue that the pursuers' case was irrelevant and that he only wished time to make the necessary arrangements for payment of the balance of the price. He said that there had been some suggestion that the boundaries of the property as taken over by Mrs Palmer were not exactly what she had been led to believe they were but he agreed that he could not elaborate the skeleton defences. He consented to an interlocutor being pronounced granting the crave for implement and payment of the balance of the purchase price but asked that the time for payment of the balance of the price should be one month from the date of the interlocutor. The sheriff pronounced an interlocutor ordaining Mrs Palmer to implement and fulfil her part of the missives of sale within 14 days by making payment of the balance of the purchase price of £12,000 in exchange for a valid disposition of the subjects. The present pursuer appealed to the sheriff principal and the appeal was heard on 23 October 1975. Counsel for the appellant asked for time to prepare and lodge a minute of amendment expanding the defences and stated that he wished to aver circumstances which would justify retention of a limited part of the purchase price of the subjects, but the sheriff principal refused the motion for time to prepare and lodge a minute of amendment and ordained the appellant to implement the sheriff's interlocutor within seven days. The present pursuer did not make payment of the balance of the purchase price within the stipulated period and on 5 November 1975 decree of removing was pronounced. The pursuer was then faced with the choice of paying the balance of the price or removing from the subjects and she made payment of the sum of £12,000 being the balance of the price. On 2 July 1976 the defenders executed a disposition of the subjects in favour of the pursuer and it was delivered to her. That disposition is no 10 of process and it contained a grant of warrandice. However, the subjects conveyed by the disposition did not include the whole of the garden ground which had been pointed out to the pursuer by the first defender in March 1975.

On 7 December 1976 the defenders' solicitors wrote to the solicitors acting for Mr Smith. The letter pointed out that Mr Smith had never granted a title to the additional area of garden ground referred to in the 1974 missives, and that the price of £40 had been paid to Mr Smith in May 1974 and requested that the money should now be repaid. The letter observed that it may very well be that the purchaser of "Summerside" would be interested in coming to a further agreement with Mr Smith. On 9 December 1976 the solicitors acting for Mr Smith returned the purchase price of £40.

Early in 1976 the pursuer, her husband and family had moved out of "Summerside" and gone to live in a council house at 5 Dean of Guild Way, Elgin and they are still living there. The pursuer stated that she felt that she should move out and get the title deeds put right and they could then move back to "Summerside". However, she said that her nerves had been badly affected by the legal difficulties with which she had been faced in relation to the purchase of the property and by 1977 she felt that she did not want to return to live there and she decided to sell the subjects. They were advertised for sale and by missives dated 18 and 21 October 1977 the pursuer agreed to sell them to a Mr and Mrs McGregor at a price of £24,500. However, the purchasers wished a title to the whole of the garden ground, including the additional area of ground which still belonged to Mr and Mrs Smith. It was therefore agreed that Mr and Mrs McGregor would make payment of the sum of £9,500 on the date of entry (1 April 1978) and that the balance of £15,000 plus interest would be paid when they obtained a title to the additional area of garden ground. In the event, it took many years before the title position was able to be regularised with the assistance of the Halifax Building Society. In January 1984 the pursuer granted a disposition in favour of Mr and Mrs McGregor of the house and garden ground which she owned and Mr and Mrs Smith granted a disposition in their favour of the additional area of garden ground, having received £600 as the purchase price thereof. On 22 May 1984

the pursuer received the sum of £26,296.28 being the balance of the purchase price (namely, £15,000) and interest thereon amounting to £11,296.58.

The present action was raised in October 1980 and the pursuer seeks damages for fraudulent misrepresentation et separatim negligent misrepresentation and breach of contract.

[His Lordship rehearsed the evidence, considered the pursuer's cases of fraudulent misrepresentation, which he held she had failed to prove, and negligent misrepresentation, which he held was not open to her since the events took place prior to the coming into force of s 10 of the Law Reform (Miscellaneous Provisions) (Scotland) Act 1985, and continued:]

Breach of warrandice

The pursuer has made averments of breach of contract and breach of warrandice, but her counsel stated that the pursuer's case of breach of contract was based only on the allegation that there had been a breach of the warrandice clause contained in the disposition granted by the defenders in July 1976. The disposition granted by the defenders in favour of the pursuer contained a clause of absolute warrandice in the usual terms and counsel for the pursuer submitted that a warrandice clause was an express contractual term, the breach of which sounds in damages. The averments relating to breach of warrandice are contained in art 7 of the condescendence, and counsel conceded that the disposition did not purport to convey area no 4 specified in art 3 of the condescendence (the green area shown in the plan no 81 of process). However, the disposition by the defenders bore to convey to the pursuer inter alia the orange area and part of the blue area (both parts of the raised area of ground) and it was conceded that the defenders did not have a title to these areas of ground. In the circumstances, there was no defence to the claim based on breach of warrandice. Such defence as was advanced appeared to be based on the old fashioned notion that actual eviction, or the threat of eviction, was necessary before a claim under a warrandice clause could be made. However, in *Watson v Swift & Co's JF* it was held that a claim for breach of warrandice was competent where there had been no eviction if an unquestionable burden on the subjects arose (see also Gordon, *Scottish Land Law*, para 12-68). Accordingly, a claim for breach of warrandice arose even though the pursuer had not been evicted from that part of the subjects specified in the disposition to which she had not obtained a good title. However, in the present case, the circumstances amounted to full eviction from the whole subjects as the fact that the pursuer had not received a valid title to part of the garden ground which the disposition had purported to convey to her had rendered the subjects virtually unsaleable. In any event, the defenders had threatened to evict the pursuer from the subjects as they had obtained decree of removing in the sheriff court and the pursuer had moved out because of the defect in her title. The later disposition by Mr and Mrs Smith had conveyed to Mr and Mrs McGregor the orange, blue and green areas shown in the plan no 81 of process.

A   Counsel for the defenders submitted that the pursuer's averments relating to breach of warrandice were irrelevant. Warrandice imports an obligation to indemnify the purchaser if there is a breach of the warrandice clause but this obligation does not arise until there has been eviction, or at least the threat of eviction, of the purchaser from the subjects or part of them. The reason for the necessity for eviction, or threatened eviction, is that if the purchaser takes entry and occupies the disputed subjects peaceably for the whole of the prescriptive period, then the purchaser's

B   title will be safe from challenge. Where it is alleged that the seller did not have a title to part of the subjects conveyed by the disposition, there could not be a claim for breach of warrandice unless and until the purchaser had been evicted, or there had been a threat of eviction, by the true owner. The fact that the true owner could readily establish his right to part of the subjects conveyed by the disposition was not relevant and could not give rise to a claim based on breach of warrandice. The claim could not arise until the true

C   owner actually evicted the purchaser from the area of ground in question or there was a real threat of eviction by him in relation to which there was no statable defence. Counsel referred to Bell's *Principles* (10th ed), para 121; Bell's *Lectures on Conveyancing*, Vol I, pp 217 and 643; Stair, II iii 46; Erskine, *Institute*, II iii 30; Halliday, *Conveyancing Law and Practice*, Vol I, para 4-44; Walker, *Civil Remedies*, p 753; *Smith v Ross*; *Melville v Wemyss* and *Leith Heritages Co v Edinburgh and Leith Glass Co*. In the present case the

D   owners of the area of ground in question, Mr and Mrs Smith, had not sought to evict the pursuer from any part of the raised area to which they still had a title. They had not raised proceedings against her and they had not even requested her not to use the area of ground which they owned. Mr Smith gave evidence that he did not sue the pursuer and that he had no intention of suing her, and the pursuer and her husband gave evidence that there had never been any threat of proceedings being taken. The pursuer

E   averred that she eventually had to pay the sum of £600 to Mr and Mrs Smith "in order to avoid the possibility of eviction", but a possibility of eviction was not sufficient. In any event, Mr and Mrs Smith had later agreed to sell the raised area to enable a title to that area to be given to Mr and Mrs McGregor. Although the pursuer and her family moved out of the subjects, they did not do so because of any action taken, or threatened, by Mr and Mrs Smith. Further, in the case of breach of warrandice, the obligation of the

F   seller is one of indemnification only and counsel for the pursuer was wrong to suggest that a claim for breach of warrandice was no different from any other breach of contract. In the case of *Watson v Swift & Co's JF*, an action had been raised against the pursuers by a party with a prior title and the raising of the action had constituted a threat of eviction. Further, in expressing the views which he did in that case, Lord Morison had stated that he was not satisfied that a full citation of the relevant authorities had been furnished to him. As there had been no eviction, or threatened eviction, of the pursuer by the true owners in this case,

the claim for breach of warrandice had not been established.   G

In Bell's *Lectures on Conveyancing* (3rd ed), Vol I, p 214, warrandice is defined as "the obligation of the granter of any conveyance, or other deed, that the deed and the right thereby granted shall be good and effectual to the grantee; implying, or expressing, that, — in case of reduction of the deed, or of eviction of the subject contained in it, in whole or in part, on account of any fact or deed of the granter, or of his predecessors, or any defect in the granter's title, or it may be on any ground not attributable to the grantee, —   H   the granter shall make good the loss or damage thence arising to the grantee." In Bell's *Principles* (at para 895) it is stated: "Warrandice is not an obligation to protect, but only to indemnify in case of eviction . . . Thus, there is no action of warrandice till judicial eviction, unless the ground of demand be unquestionable, and proceeding from the fault of the seller". As Lord McLaren observed in *Welsh v Russell* (1894) 21 R at p 773, warrandice "remains latent until the conditions come into existence that give it force and effect, and   I   it continues to affect the granter and his heirs until the possibility of adverse claims has been extinguished by the long prescription". It has been held that an action for breach of warrandice can lie even where the pursuer has not been physically evicted from the subjects (*Leith Heritages Co v Edinburgh and Leith Glass Co*, per Lord Ormidale at p 796; *Watson v Swift & Co's JF*).

In the present case the pursuer founds on the   J   warrandice clause contained in the 1976 disposition. She did not seek to found on any obligation of warrandice implied in the missives which were superseded by the disposition. In terms of the missives the sellers undertook to give a good marketable title to the subjects of sale. If, once the titles were examined, it was ascertained that the sellers did not have a title to certain of the ground to which the missives related, then the existence of the defect in the sellers' title would entitle the purchaser to refuse to proceed with   K   the transaction. In this case, however, the purchase price was paid, the disposition was delivered and the pursuer seeks to found on the clause of absolute warrandice contained in the disposition. The pursuer avers that the defenders did not have a title to part of the garden ground which the disposition purported to convey to her. It is clear that, in a case of absence of title, a claim for breach of warrandice will arise if the purchaser is judicially evicted by the true owner from the subjects of sale or part of them. Further, a claim   L   for breach of warrandice can arise if there is a real threat of eviction as, for example, when the true owner raises proceedings seeking to evict the purchaser and there is no statable defence to the action. As Lord Morison observed in *Watson v Swift & Co's JF* (at p 220): "the warrandice clause came into effect at least as soon as the action against the pursuers was raised, if . . . they had no defence to such an action". What constitutes a threat of eviction giving rise to a claim for breach of warrandice must depend on the circumstances of each individual case. In my opinion,

however, the mere absence of title does not at once
A give rise to a claim for breach of warrandice. In the
present case counsel for the pursuer submitted that
there had, in effect, been eviction of the pursuer from
the whole subjects as, without the area of ground in
question, the subjects were virtually unsaleable. In my
opinion, however, it cannot be said, in the circumstances of this case, that the pursuer was ever evicted
from that part of the property to which she acquired
a good title by virtue of the disposition. She was
certainly not evicted from any part of the garden
B ground by the true owners. On the question as to
whether or not there had been a threat of eviction
counsel submitted that the defenders had threatened
to evict her from the subjects by obtaining a decree of
removing in the sheriff court action. However, this
action related to the whole subjects and it was raised
by the defenders because the pursuer had not paid the
balance of the price. Further, the decree of removing
was pronounced some eight months before the disposition was delivered. It is clear that there was no
C attempt by the true owners to evict the pursuer from
the area of garden ground to which the disposition
related but which was still in their ownership. The
evidence demonstrated that Mr and Mrs Smith at no
stage raised proceedings against the pursuer with a
view to evicting her from the area of ground in
question, nor did they ever threaten to do so. Indeed,
at no stage did they even request her to vacate the
ground. In the circumstances I do not consider that
the pursuer has established that she was ever evicted
D from the area of garden ground or that there was at
any stage a threat of eviction which gave rise to a
claim for breach of warrandice. I have therefore
reached the conclusion that the pursuer has not made
out her case that she is entitled to damages for breach
of warrandice. For the foregoing reasons I am satisfied that the defenders are entitled to decree of
absolvitor.

E **Damages**

Counsel for the pursuer dealt first with the measure
of damages on the basis of delict, namely, if the
pursuer had established that she had been induced to
purchase the subjects by fraudulent or negligent misrepresentation on the part of the defenders. So far as
the pursuer's financial loss was concerned, counsel
submitted that the amount of damages to be awarded
was essentially a jury question, taking into account all
the circumstances of the case (*Hutchison v Davidson*,
F 1946 SLT per Lord Russell at pp 15-16 and 17). The
object of an award of damages was to endeavour, as far
as possible, to put the pursuer back into the position
she would have been in if she had never entered into
the contract to purchase the property. Counsel
submitted that the measure of the pursuer's financial
loss was the difference between (a) her expenditure
resulting from entering into the contract and (b) the
moneys received by her on the later sale of the subjects. He summarised the pursuer's financial claim as
follows:

I *Expenditure*

(a) Purchase price of house	23,000	G
(b) Interest on loan from Halifax Building Society	11,881	
(c) Interest on loan from Norwich Union	7,090	
(d) Expenses incurred —		
1. Solicitors' fees (Norwich Union)	1,380	
2. Solicitors' fees (Halifax Building Society)	2,594	
3. Other legal fees	690	H
4. Recording dues	33	
5. Insurance	325	
6. Price paid for additional ground	600	
	5,622	
	£47,593	

II *Receipts*

(a) Sale price of subjects	24,500	I
(b) Interest paid by purchasers	11,296	
(c) Sum received from Mr and Mrs Robertson	150	
	£35,946	

The difference between the pursuer's expenditure
and the total amount which she received following the
sale of the property was £11,647 and this represented
her financial loss. She was also entitled to an award in
name of solatium and she had clearly suffered con- J
siderable anxiety and distress over a long period as a
result of the defenders' misrepresentation. She moved
out of the property because of the title difficulties and
she and her husband and five children moved into a
small council house where they still reside. Counsel
accepted that it had not been proved that it was necessary for the pursuer and her family to move out of the
property but he submitted that she had moved out
because of the defect in her title and that, in the
circumstances, it could not be suggested that she had K
acted unreasonably. Since the title difficulties arose
she has been suffering from anxiety and nervous
tension and has required medical treatment although
there may be some improvement once the present
action is resolved. While it had been suggested in cross
examination that the pursuer had failed to mitigate her
loss, objection had been taken to the line of questioning as the defenders have no record for a case based on
her alleged failure to mitigate her loss. In the circumstances solatium could reasonably be assessed at L
£10,000 so that the total value of the pursuer's claim
for damages was £21,647 plus interest.

So far as the pursuer's claim for damages for breach
of warrandice was concerned, counsel submitted that
the measure of her financial loss was the diminution
in the value of the subjects as at the date of resale, the
purchasers having taken entry on 1 April 1978. There
was unchallenged evidence from Mr Geoffrey Smith,
the surveyor, that the property could, at that date,
have been sold for £30,000 if the whole of the garden

ground, including the raised area, had been able to be conveyed to a purchaser. From this figure there fell to be deducted the loans of £16,500 and the expenses of sale which could reasonably be estimated at £1,000, bringing out a figure of £12,500. To this sum should be added the additional expenses incurred by the pursuer, which counsel estimated at £4,000, so that her financial loss could reasonably be estimated at £16,500. She was also entitled to solatium of £10,000 as a breach of warrandice was, so far as an award of damages was concerned, in no different position from any other breach of contract which sounds in damages. In the circumstances the value of the pursuer's claim for damages for breach of warrandice was £26,500.

In relation to the pursuer's claim for damages based on fraudulent or negligent misrepresentation, counsel for the defenders referred to *Allan v Barclay* and *Hadley v Baxendale*. He submitted that it was for the pursuer to show that her loss flowed from the alleged misrepresentation and was such as in the ordinary course of events would flow from such a misrepresentation. However, there were two extraordinary factors involved in this case which affected the pursuer's right to claim damages. In the first place, the sheriff court action had had a major influence on later events. The present pursuer's solicitor had consented to decree being granted, although the pursuer was by then well aware of the defect in her title, and that had been the proximate cause of a number of the losses being claimed by the pursuer. The pursuer should have defended the sheriff court action on the ground that the title she was being offered was not the title contracted for in the missives. Alternatively, she could have resiled from the missives. However, instead of adopting either of these courses, her solicitor consented to decree and the pursuer later paid the balance of the purchase price. In the circumstances the pursuer's alleged losses incurred after decree was pronounced in the sheriff court action were not directly attributable to the alleged misrepresentation. Secondly, in October 1977 the pursuer had entered into missives to sell the subjects to Mr and Mrs McGregor, but she had done so in the knowledge that she was not at that time in a position to give Mr and Mrs McGregor a valid title to the whole of the subjects of sale. Further, the pursuer said that she had, in consequence of the defect in her title, accepted a price which was below the true value of the subjects. She had stated in evidence that her priority was to have the title put right and then decide what to do, but her decision to enter into missives before she had a title to the rest of the garden ground had created further problems. The fact that she had entered into missives in October 1977, when she did not have a title to the whole of the subjects of sale, had been the proximate cause of her claims in respect of building society loan interest repayments and certain of the legal fees involved. If the title position had been put right before the pursuer entered into missives to sell the subjects, the purchaser would have paid the full market value and the loans from the Halifax Building Society and the Norwich Union could have been paid

off at once. Counsel accepted that a claim for solatium would be competent and he submitted that, if an award under this head was appropriate, the sum of £5,000 would be reasonable.

He went on to attack certain of the items contained in the calculation of the pursuer's claim for financial loss. In particular, in relation to the legal fees of £690 paid to Messrs Grigor & Young, the pursuer could not recover both the legal fees involved in selling the property and the mortgage payments. In any event, the bulk of these legal fees would have been incurred in any event, and only fees of £200 plus VAT could be described as additional fees. The recording dues of £33 would have been incurred whenever the loan was repaid. In relation to the Halifax Building Society loan, the pursuer's statement of claim did not take account of credits amounting to £1,358.52. The legal fees due to the Norwich Union are not recoverable as these fees were attributable to the fact that the pursuer had failed to keep up the payments due on the loan and the Norwich Union had successfully taken action against her in the Court of Session. With regard to the interest payments set out in no 102 of process, the pursuer had made only one payment and the collateral life policy had then lapsed due to non-payment of the premium. The pursuer's failure to make payments of interest was not related to any misrepresentation on the part of the defenders. In any event, the pursuer was not entitled to recover the payments of interest due before 1 April 1978 as these payments would have had to be made whether the pursuer had decided to sell or to stay in the property. The pursuer had failed to take reasonable steps to mitigate her loss.

Counsel for the defenders went on to submit that the measure of damages in a case based on breach of warrandice is more limited than in the case of a claim arising from delict. The pursuer was entitled to be indemnified for the loss which she had sustained as a result of the breach of warrandice and in the circumstances of this case the sole measure of her loss was the diminution in the value of the subjects in consequence of the breach of the obligation to maintain her in possession of the area of ground referred to in the disposition to which the defenders had not had a title (*Welsh v Russell* (1894) 21 R per Lord McLaren at p 774 and Lord Kinnear at p 775; Macdonald's *Conveyancing Manual* (4th ed), para 12.10; Walker, *Civil Remedies*, pp 754-755; Halliday, *Conveyancing Law and Practice*, Vol I, para 4-47). Further, the diminution in the value of the subjects fell to be measured at the date of eviction or threatened eviction. However, the pursuer could not offer a date when that loss should be calculated. Mr Geoffrey Smith had given evidence that as at 1 April 1978, when Mr and Mrs McGregor took entry, the value of the subjects, if the whole of the enclosed garden ground had been included, would have been £30,000 whereas the sale price had only been £24,500, apparently bringing out a loss of £5,500. Mr Smith's evidence of the diminution in the value of the subjects only related to 1 April 1978. However, the pursuer had not been evicted from the area of ground in question and there was no suggestion

that any threat of eviction had taken place on 1 April
1978, when Mr and Mrs McGregor took entry. In
these circumstances the evidence of Mr Geoffrey
Smith was of no assistance to the pursuer's case so far
as it related to a diminution in the value of the
subjects. The extent of the diminution in the value of
the subjects at any other date could not be taken as
being within judicial knowledge. Further, a breach of
warrandice did not give rise to a claim for solatium in
respect of any anxiety or distress suffered by the
pursuer. In the circumstances, the pursuer had failed
to prove that she had suffered any loss as a result of
the alleged breach of warrandice.

In relation to quantum of damages for fraudulent or
negligent misrepresentation, counsel for the defenders
submitted that the pursuer should have defended the
sheriff court action on the ground that the defenders
could not offer her a disposition of the whole subjects
which they had agreed to sell to her. It would clearly
have been better if the action had been defended, but
the pursuer explained that she did not instruct her
solicitor to consent to decree and I accepted her evidence on that matter. At the same time it should be
borne in mind that the defenders raised the action
although they were not in a position to grant a title to
the whole area of ground which had been pointed out
by Mr Beck as being included in the sale. In the
circumstances I do not feel that it is right to be too
critical of the pursuer because of the actual outcome
of the sheriff court action. It is true that the pursuer
entered into missives with Mr and Mrs McGregor at
a time when she was not in a position to grant a valid
title to the whole subjects of sale and it might have
been better if she had delayed the sale until she had
acquired the balance of the garden ground from Mr
and Mrs Smith. However, she sold in the expectation
of being able to acquire the additional ground, she
eventually succeeded in acquiring that ground and Mr
and Mrs McGregor were aware of the position. While
it was unfortunate that it took so long to regularise the
position, the pursuer received interest on the balance
of the purchase price from 1 April 1978 until a full
title was able to be given. In the particular circumstances of this case I do not consider that the pursuer's
action in proceeding with the sale in 1977, once she
had found a willing purchaser, could be categorised as
unreasonable. In my opinion, the general approach of
counsel for the pursuer to the assessment of the
measure of damages was the correct one, but I would
deduct from the items of expenditure (a) the payments
of interest due to the Norwich Union prior to 1 April
1978 (£1,920.42), (b) the legal fees incurred by the
Norwich Union (£1,380) as they were incurred
because the pursuer failed to meet the interest payments, and (c) the Halifax Building Society credits of
£1,358.52 which were not taken into account in the
pursuer's calculation of her loss. These sums total
£4,658.94 and they would fall to be deducted from the
pursuer's estimated financial loss of £11,647 so that
her total loss amounted to £6,988. She is also entitled
to an award in name of solatium. In this connection,
there is no doubt that, as a result of the title difficulties

which emerged, she understandably suffered anxiety
and distress and she required medical treatment. She
has not, however, demonstrated that there was any
need for her to move out of "Summerside" when she
did and her husband gave evidence that the property
had been vacated on the advice tendered by their
solicitor. I am not satisfied that, viewed objectively, it
was reasonable for her to have moved out in January
1976. Further, it is not easy to assess how much of her
anxiety and distress could be said to be attributable to
the defenders' alleged fraudulent or negligent misrepresentation and how much was attributable to the
other things which went wrong with the transaction.
In the circumstances I would have been disposed, so
far as solatium was concerned, to make an award of
£5,000, which was the figure suggested by counsel for
the defenders. On the whole matter, if I had been
awarding the pursuer damages for fraudulent or negligent misrepresentation, I would have awarded her
£6,988 in respect of financial loss and £5,000 in name
of solatium, making a total of £11,988.

Turning to the pursuer's claim for damages for
breach of warrandice, a breach of warrandice gives rise
to a claim for indemnification and the amount of the
loss will normally be calculated as at the date of eviction (Bell's *Principles*, para 895; Bell's *Lectures on Conveyancing*, Vol I, p 217). In this case it seems to me
that the measure of the pursuer's loss would be the
diminution in the value of the subjects arising from
the breach of warrandice, namely, the difference
between the value of the subjects validly conveyed to
her and the value of the subjects if they had included
the area of ground specified in the disposition to
which the defenders did not have a title. Further, I
consider that the diminution in value would fall to be
calculated at the date when the eviction or threat of
eviction occurred. In my opinion, the pursuer is not
entitled to recover, under this head, any damages
resulting from the fact that she vacated the subjects
because she had moved out some six months before
the disposition was granted. The pursuer led evidence
from Mr Geoffrey Smith which was apparently
designed to demonstrate the diminution in the value
of the property as at 1 April 1978 when Mr and Mrs
McGregor took entry. Mr Smith said that the value of
the subjects, including the whole area of garden
ground, would have been £30,000, but the pursuer
could only obtain a price of £24,500. However,
counsel for the pursuer, as I understood him, did not
seek to argue that the pursuer's claim should be based
on the difference between these two values and I must
confess that I had some difficulty in understanding the
basis of the claim which he did make. However, if the
proper measure of damages is the diminution in the
value of the property resulting from the alleged breach
of warrandice, the question would arise as to the date
on which that diminution in value fell to be calculated.
If, contrary to the view which I have taken, there was
a threat of eviction then it would appear that it must
have existed as soon as the disposition was delivered
to the pursuer on the basis that she did not thereby
acquire a title to the area of garden ground in question

A and was therefore liable at any time to be evicted from it by the true owners. On the evidence, there was no threat of eviction on 1 April 1978, but that was the only date to which Mr Geoffrey Smith's evidence of value was directed. There was no evidence relating to the diminution in the value of the subjects as at July 1976 or to any loss sustained by the pursuer at that time. In any event, Mr Geoffrey Smith's evidence did not relate to the difference between (a) the value of the subjects validly conveyed to the pursuer and (b) the value of the subjects if they had also included the additional area of garden ground specified in the disposi-
B tion and to which the defenders did not have a title. It is important to bear in mind that although the missives apparently related to the whole of the enclosed garden ground, the disposition did not purport to convey to the pursuer the green area shown in plan no 81 of process which was part of the garden pointed out to the pursuer and was also part of the subjects in respect of which Mr and Mrs McGregor paid the price of £24,500. Even if the disposition had conferred on the pursuer a valid title to the subjects therein
C specified, she would not have received a title to the green area. However, Mr Geoffrey Smith's valuation of £30,000 was based on the assumption that the purchaser had obtained a conveyance of the whole of the garden ground. In these circumstances it seems to me that the evidence of Mr Smith was not properly directed to the true measure of the pursuer's loss, even if it had related to the date when a threat of eviction arose. For these reasons I do not consider that the pursuer has proved what financial loss she sustained as a result of any breach of warrandice on the part of the
D defenders. I am also of the opinion that, as the pursuer's claim would be for indemnification, she is not entitled to an award of damages for solatium for the anxiety and distress which she allegedly suffered as a result of the breach of warrandice. While Lord Morison appeared to express the view in *Watson* that a claim for damages for breach of warrandice could include a claim for solatium, I was not referred to any case in which an award of solatium had been made to a pursuer in an action for breach of warrandice. In my
E opinion, a breach of warrandice only entitles the pursuer to be indemnified in respect of the financial loss which has been sustained in consequence of the breach. In any event, having regard to the number of things which went wrong with this unfortunate transaction, it would be difficult to assess how much of the anxiety and distress suffered by the pursuer was actually attributable to the alleged breach of warrandice. For the reasons which I have endeavoured to give, I would have reached the conclusion that the pursuer has failed to prove what loss she sustained in conse-
F quence of the defenders' breach of warrandice.

On the whole matter, as I have found in favour of the defenders on the merits, I shall pronounce decree of absolvitor.

Counsel for Pursuer, Sutherland, QC, Clancy; Solicitors, Drummond Miller, WS (for Grigor & Young, Elgin) — Counsel for Defenders, I W F Ferguson; Solicitors, Strathern & Blair, WS.

C H

Clark v McLean

G

OUTER HOUSE

TEMPORARY JUDGE R G McEWAN, QC

2 JULY 1992

Limitation of actions — Reparation — Negligence — Time bar — Action raised outwith triennium — Discretion to allow action to proceed — Action raised eight months after expiry of triennium — Pursuer girlfriend of defender — Effect on triennium of parties' relationship —
Prescription and Limitation (Scotland) Act 1973 (c 52), H *s 19A.*

Section 19A of the Prescription and Limitation (Scotland) Act 1973 empowers the court to allow a person to bring an action which would otherwise be time barred under s 17, if it seems to the court equitable to do so.

A passenger was injured in a motorcycle accident on 12 January 1983. She became of full age on 18 June 1984. She did not raise an action of reparation against I the driver of the motorcycle, who had then been her boyfriend, until 17 February 1988, about eight months beyond the extended triennium. Nine days before the expiry of the extended triennium, the pursuer had consulted a solicitor who had referred her to another solicitor who had advised her that her claim had already become time barred on the third anniversary of the accident. He nevertheless investigated the case further, intimated a claim in December 1987 and applied for legal aid. A summons was instructed on 15 January 1988. The pursuer moved the court to exer- J cise its discretion in terms of s 19A of the 1973 Act to allow the action to proceed. The pursuer's averred reason for not having taken advice earlier was sympathy for the defender. The defender argued that the action should be dismissed since the pursuer had an alternative remedy against her solicitor.

Held, that it would be premature to dismiss the action as time barred, particularly because of the doubt about the quantification of any alternative claim against the solicitor and the delay which would be K involved in seeking to recover from the solicitor (p 494F-H); and proof before answer *allowed*.

Action of damages

Janette Shiona Clark raised an action of damages against Derek Paul McLean and the Motor Insurers Bureau in respect of injuries sustained by her in a motorcycle accident on 12 January 1983. The first L defender had been the pursuer's boyfriend at the time of the accident. The action was raised outwith the triennium.

The case came before the temporary judge (R G McEwan, QC) on procedure roll when the first defender moved that the action be dismissed and the pursuer moved that the action be allowed to proceed.

Statutory provisions

The Prescription and Limitation (Scotland) Act 1973 provides:

"17.— . . . (2) Subject to subsection (3) below and
section 19A of this Act, no action to which this section
applies shall be brought unless it is commenced within
a period of 3 years after — (a) the date on which the
injuries were sustained or, where the act or omission
to which the injuries were attributable was a continuing one, that date or the date on which the act or
omission ceased, whichever is the later; or (b) the date
(if later than any date mentioned in paragraph (a)
above) on which the pursuer in the action became, or
on which, in the opinion of the court, it would have
been reasonably practicable for him in all the circumstances to become, aware of all the following facts —
(i) that the injuries in question were sufficiently
serious to justify his bringing an action of damages on
the assumption that the person against whom the
action was brought did not dispute liability and was
able to satisfy a decree; (ii) that the injuries were
attributable in whole or in part to an act or omission;
and (iii) that the defender was a person to whose act
or omission the injuries were attributable in whole or
in part or the employer or principal of such a person.

"(3) In the computation of the period specified in
subsection (2) above there shall be disregarded any
time during which the person who sustained the
injuries was under legal disability by reason of nonage
or unsoundness of mind. . . .

"19A.—(1) Where a person would be entitled, but
for any of the provisions of section 17 or section 18
and 18A of this Act, to bring an action, the court may,
if it seems to it equitable to do so, allow him to bring
the action notwithstanding that provision."

Cases referred to

Anderson v City of Glasgow District Council, 1987 SLT
   279.
Bain v Philip, OH, 11 March 1992, unreported.
Comber v Greater Glasgow Health Board, 1989 SLT
   639.
Craw v Gallagher, 1988 SLT 204.
Donald v Rutherford, 1984 SLT 70.
Forsyth v A F Stoddard & Co Ltd, 1985 SLT 51.
Mackenzie v Middleton, Ross and Arnot, 1983 SLT
   286.

Textbook referred to

Jackson and Powell, *Professional Negligence* (1987),
   para 4/140.

On 2 July 1992 the temporary judge *allowed* a proof
before answer leaving all pleas standing.

R G MCEWAN, QC—In this case the pursuer
sues the defender in reparation for injuries she sustained in a motorcycle accident in Edinburgh on 12
January 1983. At the material time the parties were
boyfriend and girlfriend. The pursuer at the time was
aged 16 years and six months.

The action was served on the first defender on 17
February 1988. It was a matter of agreement that
because of nonage time did not begin to run against
the pursuer until her 18th birthday on 18 June 1984.
The triennium would therefore expire on 18 June

1987. The action was thus eight months late and
prima facie time barred.

In seeking to have the court allow her to continue
with the action the pursuer avers that following the
accident she was hospitalised but told she would make
a full recovery. Because of sympathy for the defender
she took no legal advice until 9 June 1987 (i e nine
days before the time ran out). Her first solicitor
referred her to another solicitor who was of the view
that her claim had already become barred on 12
January 1986. He investigated the case, intimated a
claim to the first defender on 2 December 1987 and
applied for legal aid in January 1988. A summons was
instructed on 15 January 1988.

Counsel who appeared for the first defender moved
me to sustain his first and second pleas in law and
dismiss the action. The action was eight months late
although the pursuer had taken legal advice in time.
The balance of equity did not favour the pursuer and
the agent should have sued at once or at least sooner
into the expiry. He had erred in his initial view, then
delayed longer: *Forsyth v A F Stoddard & Co Ltd* and
Bain v Philip.

The facts were nearly 10 years old and to allow the
action to proceed would deny the defender his statutory defence. Although the pursuer would lose a
chance to sue a defender who had been convicted of
reckless driving she had a very good claim against her
own solicitor. Interest would protect her against the
delay in another action and solatium would increase.

The pursuer moved me first to amend at the bar the
word "proposals" to "prospects" and the date "7
February" to "2 December". Of consent I allowed
this.

Thereafter, before answer, I should allow proof on
the whole cause was the argument. The proper tests
were set out in *Craw v Gallagher*, 1988 SLT at
pp 205K and 206A. The present case raised a number
of special factors.

It was accepted that the defender would lose the
benefit of the statutory defence: *Forsyth* at p 54.
However the delay in raising the action did not of
itself cause prejudice to him. The real issue was how
significant was any supposed prejudice (*Comber v
Greater Glasgow Health Board* at p 641F-G; *Donald v
Rutherford* at p 79).

The prospects of suing the solicitor were uncertain.
The pursuer would have to show negligence which
caused loss, a hypothetical date for proof and what
possible early settlement might have been effected.
(Counsel referred me to Jackson and Powell, *Professional Negligence* (1987), para 4/140.) Where the case
was difficult you had to speculate and this was such a
case.

Even the quantification against the solicitor would
be difficult. The court would have to speculate about
the opinions of doctors, solicitors and counsel had the
case proceeded timeously. The claim itself might
suffer a reduction to take account of any tender offered
and accepted (*Mackenzie v Middleton, Ross and Arnot*
at p 289). Suing the solicitor would mean that receipt

of any damages would be delayed some years
A (*Anderson v Glasgow District Council* at p 289; *Donald v Rutherford* at p 77).

The material facts were, in any case, within the defender's knowledge and he had been put on notice in December 1987. Also he had the benefit of legal aid and it was unlikely he would have to pay any expenses. This was an important factor in *Forsyth* but absent here. The case against this defender was not strong. The pursuer knew he had been drinking yet put herself in a position where she could not get off the
B motorcycle. She could be wholly to blame for her misfortune.

The pursuer was within her rights to delay during nonage and the triennium. That could not be inherently culpable. It was a matter of proof when she lost sympathy for the defender. There would be greater prejudice in dismissing the action than in allowing it to proceed.

In my opinion it would be premature to dismiss this
C action as time barred. The matter is entirely one for the exercise of my discretion provided I exercise that within the circumstances of this particular case and fairly balance all the competing considerations. These I apprehend to be the proper tests set out by the Inner House first in *Donald v Rutherford* by Lord Cameron at p 75, and in *Forsyth v A F Stoddard & Co Ltd* per the Lord Justice Clerk at p 53 and Lord Hunter at p 55.

Here the defender can only point to a few factors
D some of which are neutral. These are, first, that the case is now 10 years old and, secondly, that the defender has lost the statutory protection afforded him if the action is allowed to proceed through no fault of his own. It is also complained that the action could have been raised sooner and that there is a good case against the solicitor. In my view it is nothing to the point that the case is now old. It is not said that evidence has been lost or witnesses have forgotten the facts. Indeed the defender himself must have knowledge of all the material facts. It is not said that
E the investigation of the case has been prejudiced. The defender has been on notice since December 1987. For the same reasons I do not accept that the eight month delay into the triennium has any special significance here. It is not claimed that that per se has caused prejudice. In this context I refer to and rely on *Comber v Greater Glasgow Health Board* and *Forsyth* at p 54.

It is true that the defender is prejudiced by the loss of the time bar defence, but in this case this has to be
F balanced against the supposed remedy against the second solicitor.

Notwithstanding the defender's conviction, the case against the solicitor raises problems. Liability against the defender is not certain. The case raises issues of the consumption of alcohol by the defender to the pursuer's knowledge. It also sharply raises the issue of contributory negligence. Proof on these matters is bound to affect the claim upon the solicitor. In that state of affairs I am of the view that the quantification of the claim against the solicitor may be problematical

as was seen and explained by Lord President Emslie in *Mackenzie v Middleton, Ross and Arnot* at p 289. I
G also attach importance to the inevitability of the pursuer's damages being delayed by years if the action has to proceed elsewhere. That was not seriously disputed and is well vouched by Inner House dicta: see *Anderson v Glasgow District Council* at p 289 per Lord Ross and *Donald v Rutherford* at p 77 per Lord Cameron.

In my opinion to force the pursuer to bring a second action against this background would be inequitable.
H

There remain some minor matters in the scales. Loss of his statutory protection is not likely to cause the defender any expense as he is legally aided (this was considered an important point in *Forsyth* and is absent here). To force the pursuer to apply again for legal aid would be an excessive use of public funds in my view.

Finally I have some reservations as to whether the pursuer herself was to blame. The issue will turn on the continuing nature of her relationship with the
I defender after the accident. That is in my view a suitable subject for proof in the same way as it was in *Comber*.

Since the pursuer did not move me to repel the defender's first plea and as I am satisfied that the equities clearly lie in her favour, I will, before answer, allow a proof leaving all pleas standing.

J

Counsel for Pursuer, Kinroy; Solicitors, Robson McLean, WS — Counsel for First Defender, P W Ferguson; Solicitors, Menzies Dougal & Milligan, WS — No appearance for Second Defenders.

J P D

K

Geddes v Geddes

FIRST DIVISION
THE LORD PRESIDENT (HOPE),
LORDS ALLANBRIDGE AND MAYFIELD
15 JANUARY 1993

Husband and wife — Divorce — Financial provision —
L *Capital sum — Fair sharing of matrimonial property — Interest claimed for period prior to decree — Competency — Circumstances where appropriate — Family Law (Scotland) Act 1985 (c 37), s 14 (1) and (2) (j).*

Section 14 (1) of the Family Law (Scotland) Act 1985 provides that before, on or after granting or refusal of decree of divorce, a court may under s 8 (2) make an "incidental order", which by s 14 (2) (j) includes "an order as to the date from which interest on any amount awarded shall run".

A husband raised an action of divorce against his
A wife. They had been married in 1966 and separated in
1982. The only issue between the parties related to the
wife's counterclaim for payment of a capital sum.
After proof, the property upon which the sheriff based
his calculation of net value of the matrimonial
property consisted entirely of property belonging to
the husband, principally a farm. The husband had
purchased the farm, where he continued to live and
work, shortly before the marriage, for use as the family
home. The sheriff decided to depart from the general
B principle of s 10 (1) of the Family Law (Scotland) Act
1985, that matrimonial property should be shared
equally, and awarded the wife a one fifth share of the
net value, to be paid in six equal instalments commencing six months from the date of decree. The
sheriff also considered that s 14 (2) (j) of the Act
allowed the court a discretion as to the date from
which interest on any sum awarded should run and he
awarded interest from the date of citation, on the view
that ex hypothesi the sum was due when the action
was raised.

C   The wife appealed to the sheriff principal who
refused the appeal but modified the sheriff's award of
interest, ordering that it should run from the date of
decree on the view that an award from an earlier date
was incompetent.

In an appeal to the Court of Session the wife argued
that s 14 (2) (j) of the Act extended the common law
position that interest was awarded on a capital sum
only from the date of decree and conferred on the
D court a complete discretion in the matter.

Held, (1) that the purpose of including interest
among the list of incidental orders in s 14 (2) of the
1985 Act was to give the court a power beyond that
which already existed at common law and that s 14 (2)
(j) conferred a discretion on the court to award interest
from a date prior to the date of decree (pp 499F-I,
501D-E and 501F); (2) that the basis of an award of
interest from a date prior to decree was not compensa-
E tion for wrongful withholding of the principal sum,
but was to facilitate the fair sharing of the matrimonial
property between the parties, and such an order for
interest had to be seen as an integral part of the order
for financial provision, justified by the principles set
out in s 9 of the Act (pp 499I-J, 500C-E, 500K-L,
501D-E and 501G); and (3) that while the sheriff's
reasoning in selecting the date of citation as the
appropriate date from which interest should run was
based on a misconception, the result he reached was
not so obviously unreasonable that it would be wrong
F to give effect to it (pp 499L and 501B-D, D-E and
H-I); and appeal *allowed* and sheriff's interlocutor
affirmed.

Carpenter v Carpenter, 1990 SLT (Sh Ct) 68 and
Skarpaas v Skarpaas, 1991 SLT (Sh Ct) 15, *overruled*
in part.

Observed (per the Lord President (Hope)), that
circumstances in which it might be appropriate to
award interest from a date prior to decree might
include those where one party had had sole use or

possession of the property since the relevant date,
interest being awarded in consideration of the use G
enjoyed; where the use or possession had resulted in
a benefit not otherwise included in the calculation of
the financial provision; or where payment of the
principal sum was postponed to a later date (pp
500K-501A).

*Stirling & Dunfermline Railway Co v Edinburgh &
Glasgow Railway Co* (1857) 19 D 598, *applied.*

Action of divorce   H
William Geddes raised an action of divorce in the
sheriff court at Banff, against Marilyn Louise
McDonald or Geddes. The merits of the action were
not contested. The defender lodged a counterclaim,
craving payment of a capital sum. The case came to
proof before the sheriff (Cameron) for proof on the
question of financial provision.

Statutory provisions
The Family Law (Scotland) Act 1985, as originally I
enacted, provided:

"8.—. . . (2) Where an application has been made
. . . the court shall make such an order [for financial
provision], if any, as is (a) justified by the principles
set out in section 9 of the Act; and (b) reasonable
having regard to the resources of the parties. . . .

"14.—(1) Subject to subsection (3) below, an
incidental order may be made under section 8 (2) of
this Act before, on or after the granting or refusal of J
decree of divorce.

"(2) In this Act, 'an incidental order' means one or
more of the following orders—. . . (j) an order as to the
date from which any interest on any amount awarded
shall run".

Cases referred to
Birrell Ltd v City of Edinburgh District Council, 1982
    SLT 363; 1982 SC (HL) 75.
Blair's Trustees v Payne (1884) 12 R 104.   K
*Buchanan (James) & Co Ltd v Stewart Cameron
    (Drymen) Ltd,* 1973 SLT (Notes) 78.
Carmichael v Caledonian Railway Co (1870) 8 M (HL)
    119.
Carpenter v Carpenter, 1990 SLT (Sh Ct) 68.
Carroll v Carroll, 1988 SCLR 104.
*Greenock Harbour Trustees v Glasgow and South
    Western Railway Co,* 1909 2 SLT 53; 1909 SC
    1438; 1909 SC (HL) 49.
Gulline v Gulline, 1992 SLT (Sh Ct) 71.
Kolbin & Sons v Kinnear & Co, 1931 SLT 464; 1931 L
    SC (HL) 128.
Little v Little, 1990 SLT 785.
Macrae v Reed & Malik Ltd, 1961 SLT 96; 1961 SC
    68.
Muir v Muir, 1989 SCLR 445.
Skarpaas v Skarpaas, 1991 SLT (Sh Ct) 15 (affd on
    another point, 1993 SLT 343).
*Stirling & Dunfermline Railway Co v Edinburgh &
    Glasgow Railway Co* (1857) 19 D 598.
Wallis v Wallis, 1992 SLT 676.

Textbook referred to

A Gloag, *Contract* (2nd ed), pp 681-682.

On 15 June 1990, the sheriff *granted* decree of divorce and *awarded* the defender a capital sum of £8,400, payable in six instalments commencing six months from date of decree, with interest thereon from the date of citation in the pursuer's action.

The defender appealed to the sheriff principal (R A Bennett, QC) who *refused* the appeal but *modified* the
B sheriff's award of interest and *ordered* that interest should run from the date of decree.

The defender appealed to the Court of Session.

Appeal

The appeal was heard by the First Division on 18 December 1992.

On 15 January 1993 the court *allowed* the appeal and
C *affirmed* the sheriff's interlocutor.

THE LORD PRESIDENT (HOPE).—This is an appeal from an interlocutor of the sheriff principal by which, with one modification, he refused an appeal against the amount of the capital sum which the sheriff awarded to the defender in an action of divorce. There is no longer any dispute about the principal sum, nor is it disputed that the sheriff was entitled to order it to be paid to the defender in instalments. The
D only remaining issue relates to the date as from which interest should run on that award. The sheriff decided that interest should run from the date of citation, but the sheriff principal held that the appropriate date for the running of interest was the date of decree. It was to this extent only that he modified the sheriff's interlocutor. The defender submits in her appeal to this court that the sheriff principal erred in failing to appreciate that, in terms of s 14 (2) (j) of the Family Law (Scotland) Act 1985, the sheriff was entitled to
E award interest on any amount awarded as a financial provision under that Act to run from any date whether before or after the date of the decree.

The parties were married on 14 October 1966 and lived together until 21 September 1982 when they separated. The pursuer's action, in which he sought divorce from the defender on the ground that the marriage had broken down irretrievably as established by the parties' non-cohabitation for a continuous period of five years or more, was raised on 8
F November 1988. On 10 January 1989 the defender lodged a counterclaim in which she concluded for payment of a capital sum of £30,000 with interest at the rate of 15 per cent per annum from the date of decree or such other date as to the court seemed appropriate until payment. The pursuer is a farmer, having purchased the farm where he resides in 1966 for use by him and the defender as their family home. The sheriff held that the net value of all the property belonging to the pursuer which was acquired during the marriage, and also before the marriage for use as

the family home, after deduction of debts incurred during the marriage, was approximately £48,000. G None of that property was acquired by way of gift or succession from a third party, and the defender did not own any property of significant value. The property which the sheriff decided to value in order to arrive at the net value of the matrimonial property at the relevant date consisted therefore entirely of property belonging to the pursuer. Apart from the farm and the equipment and stock on it, the only other asset was an insurance policy in name of and on the life of the pursuer, whose surrender value as at the date of the H separation was £722. After a careful examination of all the circumstances, the sheriff decided that it was appropriate in this case to depart from the principle in s 10 (1) of the 1985 Act that the net value of the matrimonial property shall be taken to be shared fairly between the parties when it is shared equally. He decided to award the defender a one fifth share of the net value, after deduction of a sum of £1,200 which had been wrongly paid to her as interim aliment on her representation that she was indigent when she was I in fact being supported by a third party. His calculations resulted in the figure of £8,400, which he ordered to be paid to the defender by six equal instalments commencing six months from the date of decree.

When he came to pronounce his decree on 15 June 1990, the sheriff had regard to the provisions of s 14 (2) (j) of the 1985 Act which, in his view, allowed the court a discretion as to the date from which interest on any amount awarded is to run. He noted that the J defender herself would have been absolutely entitled to divorce the pursuer at any time after 21 September 1987, if so minded, but that she had chosen not to do so. He did not think it appropriate for the running of interest to commence prior to the date of citation in the action. On the view that ex hypothesi the sum which he awarded was due when the action was raised he considered that interest should run from that date. These were the only reasons which he gave for deciding to award interest on the capital sum from 8 K November 1988 which, it should be noted, was the date of citation in the pursuer's action, not the date of the lodging of the defender's counterclaim. The only reason which the sheriff principal gives for modifying the sheriff's award of interest and ordering that interest should run from the date of decree was that he felt bound to follow his own decision in *Skarpaas v Skarpaas,* in which he held that the earliest date from which interest on a capital sum could run was the date of decree.   L

Prior to the Family Law (Scotland) Act 1985 none of the statutory provisions for the making of orders for the financial provision of spouses on divorce made any mention of interest. The practice was for interest on any capital sum to be awarded from the date of decree. This was consistent with the principle that, apart from contract, a party will only be entitled to interest by virtue of the principal sum having been wrongfully withheld, and not paid on the day when it ought to have been paid: *Caledonian Railway Co v Carmichael,*

per Lord Westbury at p 131; *Kolbin & Sons v Kinnear*
A *& Co,* 1931 SLT per Lord Atkin at p 468. Under the
Interest on Damages (Scotland) Acts 1958 and 1971
the court now has a discretion to award interest on
damages for the whole or any part of the period
between the date when the right of action arose and
the date of decree. But this was an innovation on the
previous practice as regards damages, which was
explained in *Macrae v Reed & Malik Ltd* by Lord
Justice Clerk Thomson at 1961 SLT, p 97 as follows:
"It has long been our practice that where in actions of
B damages damages are awarded interest runs only from
the date of the final decree. The reason is that it is
then and only then that the illiquid claim for damages
is quantified and made liquid. Once there is a final
decree for a specified sum that sum is payable at the
date of the final decree and if it is not then paid, it
carries interest as payment is wrongfully withheld.
That is in consonance with the accepted principle as
laid down in *Carmichael* by Lord Westbury where he
said: 'Interest can be demanded only in virtue of a
C contract, express or implied, or by virtue of the
principal sum of money having been wrongfully withheld, and not paid on the day when it ought to have
been paid'."

The same approach was taken to an order for the
payment of a capital sum on divorce, because the right
to payment of the capital sum arose only on divorce
and it was only on the date of the order that the
amount of the capital sum to be paid on divorce was
quantified.
D
One of the many changes introduced by the 1985
Act was to confer on the court a power to award
interest, as one of the incidental orders which it might
make in an action of divorce. Section 8 (2) of the Act
provides that the court shall make such order for
financial provision, if any, as is justified by the principles set out in s 9 and reasonable having regard to
the resources of the parties. Section 14 (1) provides
that an incidental order may be made under s 8 (2)
E before, on or after the granting or refusal of decree of
divorce. There then follows in s 14 (2) a list of the
various incidental orders which may be made, including in s 14 (2) (j) one about interest which is in these
terms: "an order as to the date from which any interest
on any amount awarded shall run".

Counsel's submission for the defender in this case
was that there was no need for this provision if it was
intended merely to re-state the position at common
law which, hitherto, had been that interest was
F awarded on a capital sum only from the date of decree.
Its purpose must have been to alter the common law,
and he submitted that its effect was to confer a complete discretion in this matter on the court. Counsel
for the pursuer submitted that the court was not
entitled under this provision to award interest from
any date prior to the date of decree, and that in any
event any award of interest could only be made if it
was justified by the principles set out in s 9 and was
reasonable having regard to the resources of the
parties.

A difference of practice in this matter has emerged
in the sheriff court. In *Carroll v Carroll* the sheriff G
refused the pursuer's claim for interest on the capital
sum from the date of separation. He said that, while
he could see some superficial attraction that interest
should be awarded from that date, the 1985 Act did
not, so far as he could see, contain any provision for
the inclusion of interest in this way and over such a
period. He noted that s 12 of the Act, which contains
various provisions about the structure of an order for
payment of a capital sum and provides among other
things for payment of that sum by instalments, con- H
tains no mention of interest. But he made no reference
to s 14 (1) which, read together with s 14 (2) (j) enables
an order for interest to be made as an incidental order
under s 8 (2). He decided to award interest from the
date of citation, following the practice that if a debt is
constituted by the raising of the action interest should
be craved and awarded from the date of citation. He
did this on the view that, once an order for payment
of a capital sum is pronounced, its effect is that the
capital sum is then constituted as an enforceable debt. I
It is difficult to follow the sheriff's reasoning, because
if the debt is not constituted until the order for it is
pronounced it cannot be right to follow the rule which
applies where the debt is constituted by the raising of
the action. In any event, in the absence of any reference to s 14 (2) (j), counsel for the defender did not
place any reliance on this decision as a guide to how
that provision should be applied.

In *Muir v Muir* the defender craved interest on the
capital sum from the date of the lodging of her J
counterclaim. The sheriff observed that he had power
to make an order as to the date from which interest
should run under s 14 (2) (j). It was not contended by
the pursuer that there was no power to award interest
from any date prior to decree. The only point which
was argued related to the amount on which interest
should be awarded from the date of the lodging of the
claim for the capital sum. The defender's agent was
prepared to accept interest at a lower rate than the K
legal rate of 15 per cent on part of the value attributed
to the dwellinghouse, while the pursuer's agent
accepted that any interest allowed from the date prior
to the date of decree should be based on the difference
between the sum awarded and the offer which the
pursuer had made in his answer to the counterclaim.
The sheriff preferred the pursuer's approach on the
ground that it was more logical. He observed that
interest is not to be regarded as a mechanism whereby
values already determined may be readjusted in favour
of one or other of the parties and that its purpose was L
to compensate a creditor for late payment of a sum
due. He awarded interest at the full legal rate on the
difference between these two sums from the date of
the counterclaim and on the whole amount from the
date of the decree. Counsel for the defender submitted
that the sheriff's approach was correct, insofar as he
regarded it as within his discretion to award interest
from a date prior to the date of decree. But he recognised that this point was not the subject of argument
in that case.

As against these two cases in which interest was
A awarded from a date prior to decree, there are a
number of other cases in which it has been held that
a claim for interest on a capital sum prior to the date
of decree is incompetent. The first of these is
Carpenter v Carpenter. The sheriff pointed out that
while s 14 (2) (j) entitled the court to make an order
as to the date from which any interest on any award
should run, there was no provision to guide as to when
interest should run. He went on to say this at p 73: "In
particular there is no provision whatsoever that
B interest shall run from 'the relevant date' which is the
date on which the net value of the matrimonial
property has to be calculated in terms of s 10 (2). I
considered that had it been the intention of Parliament to entitle a party to seek interest from that
date there would have been specific mention of it in
the Act".

His attention does not seem to have been drawn to
either *Carroll* or *Muir,* and he noted that despite
careful research counsel for the pursuer had been
C unable to refer him to any case in which interest had
been awarded from the relevant date as opposed to the
date of divorce. In his view there was no ground for
seeking interest before the date of divorce, since until
a divorce is granted a party has no right to a capital
sum and accordingly has no right to claim interest for
a period prior to the date on which that right arises.
This case can be seen as an application of the ordinary
common law principle that interest is not due on an
illiquid claim until decree. In effect what the sheriff
D was doing was declining to make any incidental order
about interest under the Act. In *Skarpaas v Skarpaas*
the sheriff was invited to follow *Carroll* and to award
interest from the date of citation. Since the defender's
solicitor made no submissions on the matter the sheriff
agreed to do so, but he added this comment at
p 20: "I wish to reserve my opinion on whether the
date of citation is truly the appropriate date in an
action of divorce. The reason for my reservation is
that a party in a divorce action has no right at all to
E payment of a capital sum until decree of divorce is
granted. It is therefore arguable — I put it no more
highly — that interest should run only from the date
of decree".

The defender appealed to the sheriff principal, who
was referred to *Carpenter* and also to *Muir.* He agreed
with the sheriff's reasoning in *Carpenter,* and he
declined to follow *Muir* since there was no argument
in that case that the award of interest prior to decree
F was incompetent. This was the decision which he felt
obliged to follow in the present case.

The only other decision on the matter of interest to
which we were referred is *Gulline v Gulline,* in which
it was accepted by the defender's solicitor, following
Skarpaas, that she could not claim interest from a date
prior to the date of decree. The argument in that case
was whether an award of interest from the date of
decree was appropriate, when the date of payment of
the capital sum was postponed under s 12 (2) of the
1985 Act to a later date. The award of the capital sum

was based on the value of the pursuer's rights under
a police pension scheme, under which he was entitled G
to a tax free lump sum on his retirement. The sheriff
ordered the capital sum to be paid on his retirement
date, which was approximately eight years after the
date of the decree. He awarded interest at 7½ per cent,
this being one half of the legal rate, from the date of
decree to compensate the defender for the fact that
payment of the capital sum had to be postponed. I
think that this decision is a good example of an appropriate exercise of the power under s 14 (2) (j). But it
offers no guidance on the question whether the power H
can be exercised so as to award interest from a date
prior to the date of the decree which fixes the amount
of the capital sum.

It can be seen from this brief narrative of the
reported decisions in the sheriff court that the words
used in s 14 (2) (j) have given rise to some difficulty.
On the one hand there is the series of cases starting
with *Carpenter* in which it has been held that there is
no authority in the language of the statute for awarding interest on the amount of a capital sum from any I
date prior to the date when the award is made. This
approach follows the common law principle that
interest is not awarded from any date prior to that
when the amount due has been ascertained, and it is
based on the view that there is no right to payment of
a capital sum until decree of divorce. As I have already
mentioned, it seems to me to imply a refusal to make
an incidental order about it under the statute because
it is the common law power to order payment of
interest which is being exercised. On the other hand J
there are the cases where the view has been taken that
what s 14 (2) (j) does is to confer a discretion on the
court to award interest from a date prior to the date of
decree. That was also the view taken by the sheriff in
the present case. But there is no recognition in these
cases of the fact that an order under s 14 (2) (j) is an
incidental order which requires to be made in accordance with s 8 (2) of the Act.

In developing his argument in support of the latter K
alternative, counsel for the defender said that the
purpose of s 14 (2) (j) was to alter the previous law in
order to allow interest to be awarded from a date prior
to decree, and that there was no need of this provision
if it was intended merely to state that the common law
rule was to apply. The words of the provision were
entirely general, and they conferred a wide discretion
on the court as to the date from which interest should
be awarded. He drew our attention to a passage in the
report of the Scottish Law Commission on *Aliment
and Financial Provision* (Scot Law Com no 67), in L
which the question of interest is discussed. It was
noted in para 3.139 of this report that under their
proposals the court might award a capital sum in
instalments or a capital sum payable at a future date.
The report then went on to say this: "Depending on
the circumstances it may be appropriate to award
interest from the date of citation or decree or from
some future date. It may even be appropriate to award
interest as from a date prior to citation. . . . This could
not be done under the present common law, under

which the general rule in relation to illiquid claims is that interest can be awarded only from the date of the final decree. We conclude therefore that the Court should be given power to award interest from any date on any sum awarded as financial provision on divorce."

Clause 14 (2) (j) of the draft Bill attached to that report was in the same terms as s 14 (2) (j) of the Act, and counsel for the defender submitted that in the event of ambiguity it was legitimate to have regard to the comments of the Scottish Law Commission as a guide to its construction. In any event it was consistent with the scheme of the Act that the court should be able to award interest from a date prior to the date of decree, as the matrimonial property was to be valued at the relevant date: *Little v Little,* 1990 SLT at p 787J-K; see also *Wallis v Wallis,* 1992 SLT at p 679E-F. He pointed out that there would inevitably be some lapse of time between the relevant date which, as defined in s 9 (3), would normally be the date of separation, and the date of the raising of the action. This could, he said, result in injustice because of the delay between the relevant date and the obtaining of decree, and the court ought to be able to take this into account. The purpose of the provision was to enable the court to award interest as compensation for being kept out of the money since the relevant date.

Counsel for the pursuer resisted this approach, on the ground that a capital sum did not become due until the decree was pronounced by which the amount of the capital sum was established. This was a financial provision to be made on divorce, not before it, and it was illogical to require interest to be paid from a date earlier than that on which it was decided what the amount was that had to be paid. It was not appropriate for interest to be awarded in order to make up the difference in value between the relevant date and the date of making the award. With reference to a point made by counsel for the defender that interest should be used to encourage early settlement, she submitted that it ought not to be awarded in order to penalise a party for delay. She was also critical of the sheriff's award in the present case on the ground that, if he had power to award interest from a date prior to decree, he had not done this by reference to the principles of the Act. But, as counsel for the defender pointed out, the pursuer does not have a ground of appeal directed to this point, and I consider that a review of the sheriff's decision is beyond the scope of the arguments which we can properly entertain in this case.

I think that it can be assumed that the purpose of including an order for interest among the list of incidental orders in s 14 (2) was to give the court a power which it would not otherwise be able to exercise. There was no need to legislate on this matter if all that was intended was to allow the court to award interest from the date when payment was due in terms of the decree. The power to award interest from that date exists already at common law. It is inherent in the principle that interest may be recovered by virtue of the principal sum having been wrongfully withheld

and not paid on the date when it ought to have been paid. The amount of the principal sum is fixed by the court's decree, and the date of the decree is, unless it states otherwise, the date when that sum ought to be paid. The award of interest follows naturally from the pronouncing of decree for payment of the principal sum. Furthermore, the fact that an order for interest is an incidental order, which, if made, must be made under s 8 (2) of the Act, suggests that the provisions of that subsection will have some relevance to the question as to the date as from which any interest on any amount awarded should run. It is difficult to see what relevance that subsection could have to a decision to award interest, if the court was not to be entitled to award interest from a date other than the date of payment in terms of the decree.

For these reasons I think that it can be inferred that the purpose of s 14 (2) (j) is to enable the court to award interest on the whole, or any part, of any amount awarded as a financial provision as from such date as it thinks appropriate, even although this may be a date earlier than the date of payment in terms of the decree. I should add that I have reached this view without finding it necessary to rely on what was said on this point in the report of the Scottish Law Commission. But if an order for interest is to be made as an incidental order under s 14 (2) (j) it must, as s 8 (2) provides, be justified by the principles set out in s 9 of the Act and be reasonable having regard to the resources of the parties. It should therefore be seen as an integral part of the order for financial provision, and not as something which is to be added on afterwards once all the exercises to arrive at this provision are complete. The order must also be made having regard to the purpose for which interest is awarded by the court.

In reaching a contrary view on this point in *Carpenter* the sheriff was clearly, and in my view rightly, concerned that he was being invited under reference to s 14 (2) (j) to depart from principle. Concern on the same point was expressed by the sheriff in *Skarpaas,* and it was no doubt for the same reason that the sheriff principal in that case decided to follow the decision in *Carpenter.* But I think that the decisions in these cases cannot be supported on a proper construction of ss 8 and 14 of the Act. I consider that they were wrongly decided insofar as they held that it was incompetent for interest to be awarded by way of an incidental order under s 14 (2) (j) from a date earlier than the date of the decree for payment. It follows that we ought, in my opinion, to allow this appeal and, since the sheriff's decision has not been challenged on any ground other than that it was incompetent, we should affirm the sheriff's interlocutor.

But it is clear from the various decisions in the sheriff court, and from the discussion to which we listened in this case, that merely to assert that the court may award interest from a date earlier than the date when payment is due in terms of the decree will leave the proper approach to interest under s 14 (2) (j)

in a state of uncertainty. No detailed examination has
A been given to this question in any of the cases, and
neither counsel addressed us on the issues of principle
which underlie the whole question. As I said earlier in
this opinion, a review of the sheriff's decision is
beyond the scope of the arguments which we can
properly entertain in this case, as no ground of appeal
has been lodged to challenge his interlocutor. On the
other hand I should not like it to be thought that, in
saying that his interlocutor should be affirmed, I am
in agreement with the reason which he gave for
B deciding to award interest from the date of citation.
He said that this was because the sum which he
awarded as a capital sum was ex hypothesi due when
the action was raised. It seems to me, however, that he
based his decision on a misconception because, as was
pointed out in *Carpenter* and also by the sheriff in
Skarpaas, there is no right to payment of a capital
sum until decree of divorce has been pronounced.
Since a capital sum cannot be assumed to have been
due for payment on any earlier date, some other basis
C must be found for awarding interest from a date before
payment is due. In these circumstances it may be
helpful for me to say something about the way in
which I think s 14 (2) (j) ought to be applied.

The first thing to be said is that a claim for financial
provision on divorce is unlike the more familiar
categories of claim which attract interest from a date
earlier than the date of decree. No part of any amount
awarded under s 8 (2) can be said to have been wrongfully withheld and not paid on the date when it ought
D to have been paid until, at the earliest, decree of
divorce has been pronounced. It is not a claim in the
nature of a debt, on which interest is due from the date
of the judicial demand, which is the date of citation:
Blair's Trs v Payne, per Lord Fraser at p 112. It is not
a claim in the nature of damages, on which under s 1
(1) of the Interest on Damages (Scotland) Act 1958 as
amended, the court may, in non-personal-injury cases,
award interest from such date not earlier than the date
when the right of action arises as in all the circum-
E stances seems just: *James Buchanan & Co Ltd v
Stewart Cameron (Drymen) Ltd*, per Lord Maxwell at
p 79. There is no right of action for a financial provision, in the sense of a right which may attract
interest on it, until decree of divorce has been granted
since a reconciliation is possible at any time until
decree.

On the other hand some guidance as to the cases in
which an incidental order for interest under s 14 (2) (j)
F may be appropriate may be found in the rule that,
where possession is given on a sale of land, interest is
due on the price from the date when possession is
taken, although the price may not then be settled, or
although the seller may not then be able to give a good
title: see Gloag on *Contract* (2nd ed), pp 681-682. In
*Greenock Harbour Trs v Glasgow and South Western
Railway Co* where an award of interest was made on
this basis, some doubt was expressed in the Inner
House as to whether this rule of law was really based
on principle. Lord McLaren said at 1909 SC,
p 1441: "It is perhaps, as the law is so fixed, of no

great importance to say upon what principle such a
payment of interest falls to be awarded, but the way G
in which I can most easily represent the principle to
my mind is that the interest is given in place of rent,
because before the transaction has been completed by
the payment of the price, the purchaser has been put
in possession, and therefore he must pay interest as
a substitute for rent, or as consideration for the
possession he has had during this intermediate
period".

But Lord Shaw of Dunfermline, in the House of
Lords, at 1909 SC (HL), pp 51-52, seems to have been H
satisfied that the rule could be justified on a broad
equitable basis, since he saw no difference in principle
between the accepted general principle, as stated by
Lord Westbury's statement in *Carmichael v Caledonian Railway Co*, that interest can be demanded only
in virtue of a contract, express or implied, or by virtue
of a principal sum of money having been wrongfully
withheld and not paid on the date when it ought to
have been paid, and the rule with regard to the
acquisition of lands of which possession is taken I
without payment of the price, as stated by Lord
Cowan in *Stirling & Dunfermline Railway Co v Edinburgh & Glasgow Railway Co* at p 621 in these terms:
"It would be contrary to all equity, to allow the purchaser to possess the subjects with their fruits, without
accounting for interest on the price which he has
continued to hold in his hands. The interest is equivalent for the fruits, and drawing the one he must pay
the other".
J
This rule of the common law, which is confined to
the possession of land before the price is paid for it,
has been applied to the acquisition of land by the purchasing authority by virtue of a compulsory purchase
order made under a public act: *Birrell Ltd v City of
Edinburgh District Council*, per Lord Fraser of
Tullybelton at pp 367-368.

It would seem therefore to be not unreasonable to
follow the guidance afforded by this rule, in suitable
cases, in the exercise of the statutory power under s 14 K
(2) (j), which enables interest to be awarded as part of
the financial provision under s 8 (2) of the Act from
a date prior to the date of payment in terms of the
decree. When it makes a financial provision on divorce
the court is not, as I have said, dealing with claims in
the nature of debt or damages. It is concerned essentially, so far as an order for the payment of a capital
sum is concerned, with the division of property
between the parties. What it is required to do, when
the capital sum is awarded with reference to the net L
value of the matrimonial property, is to share fairly the
net value of all the matrimonial property as at the relevant date. In most cases this will be the date of the
final separation: see s 10 (3) (a). There may be circumstances where a party who has had the sole use or
possession of an asset since the relevant date, the
whole or part of the value of which is to be shared with
the other party on divorce, should be required to pay
interest as consideration for the use or possession
which he has had between the relevant date and the

date of decree. An order for interest may, for example, be appropriate where the use or possession has resulted in a benefit which has not been taken into account in some other way in making the order for financial provision. It may also be appropriate where, as in *Gulline,* the amount of the principal sum is fixed by the decree but payment of it, in whole or in part, is postponed to a later date. Whether interest should be awarded on this basis, and if so on what part of the award, from what date and what the rate of interest should be is in the discretion of the court, bearing in mind that an incidental order for interest under s 14 (2) (j) is an integral part of the order for financial provision under s 8 (2) of the Act.

In the present case the principal asset which was taken into account by the sheriff was the value of the farm, of which the pursuer has had the sole possession since the date of the separation. It does not seem to be wholly inappropriate that he should be required to pay something by way of interest on the defender's share of that value, since the value was fixed at the date of separation and the pursuer has had the benefit of that share, represented by his possession of the farm. The sheriff took the date of citation in the action of divorce, and not the date of the defender's counterclaim, as the appropriate date from which interest should run. The justification for this was not the subject of argument in this appeal. I have already said that I do not agree with his reasoning. But it can at least be said that the result which he reached was not, in the particular circumstances of this case, so obviously unreasonable that it would be wrong to give effect to it.

For these reasons I would allow this appeal by recalling the interlocutor of the sheriff principal and affirming the sheriff's interlocutor.

LORD ALLANBRIDGE.—I agree that this appeal should be allowed for the reasons given by your Lordship in the chair. In particular I agree that s 14 (2) (j) of the 1985 Act is very wide in its terms and gives power to the court to award interest on any capital amount from any date considered appropriate either before, on or after the date of decree. I also agree that where, for example, one party has had the sole use of any part of the matrimonial property after the relevant date, then in appropriate cases compensation therefor by way of interest awarded to the other party could be considered justified and reasonable in terms of s 8 (2) of the Act.

LORD MAYFIELD.—I also agree that this appeal be allowed. I am persuaded that the reason for including an order for interest in a list of the incidental orders in s 14 (2) was to give the court a power which hitherto had not been available to it. There was no need to include an order for interest if all that was intended was to grant a power which already existed at common law, that is, to award interest from the date of decree.

I agree with your Lordship in the chair that an order

under s 14 (2) (j) is an incidental order which, if made, must be made under s 8 (2) of the Act and that points to the conclusion that s 8 (2) must have some relevance as to the selection of the date from which interest is to run having regard to the particular facts and circumstances in the case. I also agree that in the making of an order it is also necessary, as s 8 (2) provides, that regard be paid to the principles set out in s 9 of the Act and that the order must be reasonable having regard to the resources of the parties.

From the facts and circumstances in the present case the sheriff took the view that the principal asset was the value of the farm. The pursuer had had sole possession of the farm since the date of separation at which date the value of the farm was fixed. The sheriff accordingly considered that the pursuer should be required to pay something by way of interest on the defender's share of that value as the pursuer has had the benefit of that share because of his possession of the farm. In pursuance of that conclusion he accordingly decided to select the date of citation in the action of divorce as the date from which interest should run. It was not argued that the date of the defender's counterclaim might have been a more appropriate date. I agree however with your Lordship in the chair that the choice of date by the sheriff was not so unreasonable as to warrant interference by this court.

Accordingly as a matter of construction I agree with the conclusion that the Act extends the common law rule that interest only runs from the date of decree and that interest may run from an earlier date depending on the facts and circumstances of the particular case and having regard to the provisions of s 8 (2) of the Act.

Counsel for Pursuer and Respondent, S A O Raeburn, QC; Solicitors, Gray Muirhead, WS (for Walter Gerrard & Co, Macduff) — Counsel for Defender and Appellant, Agnew of Lochnaw; Solicitors, Balfour & Manson, Nightingale & Bell (for Stronachs, Aberdeen).

C A G M

Abbas v Secretary of State for the Home Department

A

OUTER HOUSE

LORD MARNOCH

7 FEBRUARY 1991

Administrative law — Judicial review — Competency — Decision open to review — Secretary of State setting up advisory panel to hear representations from persons aggrieved by decision to deport them on grounds of
B *national security — Secretary of State refusing to allow legal representation before panel — Whether refusal subject to review.*

Immigration — Deportation — Grounds of national security — Secretary of State setting up advisory panel to hear representations from persons aggrieved by decision to deport them — Secretary of State refusing to allow legal representation before panel — Whether exercise of discretion — Whether unreasonable exercise — Whether exer-
C *cise of discretion improperly fettered.*

Two persons subject to proposed deportation orders in the interests of national security petitioned for judicial review of alleged decisions by the Home Secretary, who had previously set up an extra-statutory advisory panel to hear representations from persons aggrieved by such decisions, intimating that each petitioner could make representations to the panel but that he could not be legally represented before it. The petitioners argued that while the panel had no
D legal personality distinct from the Home Secretary, the Home Secretary would be bound himself to consider representations which emanated from legal advisers.

Held, (1) that while the Home Secretary had to exercise a discretionary power on the matter of deportation, and might have a duty to give rational grounds for his decision and an opportunity to comment on those grounds, that did not involve the exercise of any
E particular discretion in regard to the matter of legal representation, and he was entitled to decide in advance that in no circumstances would he allow legal representation before the panel any more than he would have permitted such representation before himself (pp 503L-504B); (2) that in any event it was impossible to state ab ante that no reasonable Home Secretary would have done other than allow the petitioners legal representation, and that accordingly the petitions were incompetent and premature (p 504C-
F D); and petitions *dismissed*.

Doubted, whether the petitioners' rights and expectations had yet been affected in such a way that the alleged decisions were properly the subject of judicial review (p 503A).

Council of Civil Service Unions v Minister for the Civil Service [1985] 1 AC 374, *followed.*

Opinion, that had the respondent had an obligation to exercise a discretion as to legal representation his inflexible policy of denying legal representation would have improperly fettered the exercise of such discretion (p 504J-K).

G

Petition for judicial review

Fakhir Fakhil Abbas and Ibrahim Ramadhan Agool respectively petitioned the court for judicial review of an alleged decision by the Secretary of State for the Home Department denying them an opportunity to be legally represented before an advisory panel to whom they wished to make representations against decisions of the Secretary of State to deport them in the interests
H of national security.

A first hearing took place before the Lord Ordinary (Marnoch).

Cases referred to

Airey v Ireland [1979] 2 EHRR 305.
Council of Civil Service Unions v Minister for the Civil Service [1985] 1 AC 374; [1984] 3 WLR 1174; [1984] 3 All ER 935.
R v Secretary of State for Home Affairs, ex p Hosenball I [1977] 1 WLR 766.
R v Board of Visitors of the Maze Prison, ex p Hone [1988] 1 AC 379; [1988] 2 WLR 177; [1988] 1 All ER 321.
R v Secretary of State for the Home Department, ex p Tarrant [1985] QB 251; [1984] 2 WLR 613; [1984] 1 All ER 799.

On 7 February 1991 the Lord Ordinary *dismissed* the petitions.
J

LORD MARNOCH.—These are petitions for judicial review relative to the proposed deporation of the petitioners under s 3 (5) (b) of the Immigration Act 1971. [His Lordship dealt with matters with which this report is not concerned and continued:]

In the result, only one issue now remains for my consideration, namely the question of whether the petitioners are entitled to legal representation before the advisory panel which has been set up by the
K respondent on an extra-statutory basis in order to hear representations from persons aggrieved by his decision to deport them in the interests of national security under ss 3 (5) (b) and 15 (3) of the Immigration Act 1971 and on whose advice the respondent may or may not reaffirm such decisions.

So far as the petitioners are concerned, what was said to be, for present purposes, a quite distinct "decision" that they would not be entitled to legal representation is to be found in letters written on
L behalf of the respondent to each petitioner dated 3 January 1991, and, in the case of Mr Abbas, the letter itself is produced. It was accepted on behalf of the respondent that a letter had been written in identical terms to Mr Agool, and it can be taken, therefore, that, in terms of written communications on or about 3 January 1991, both petitioners were advised inter alia that they could make representations to the panel but that they could not be represented before it. Counsel for the petitioners sought review of these "decisions"

and judicial declarators that his clients were, on the contrary, entitled to legal representation at the hearings in question.

At the outset I confess to having some considerable doubt whether the alleged "decisions" in these cases are properly the subject of judicial review. In this connection I can do no better than respectfully adopt the words of Lord Diplock in *Council of Civil Service Unions v Minister for Civil Service* at p 408: "The subject matter of every judicial review is a decision made by some person (or body of persons) whom I will call the 'decision-maker' or else a refusal by him to make a decision.

"To qualify as a subject for judicial review the decision must have consequences which affect some person (or body of persons) other than the decision-maker, although it may affect him too. It must affect such other person either: (a) by altering rights or obligations of that person which are enforceable by or against him in private law; or (b) by depriving him of some benefit or advantage which . . . he had in the past been permitted by the decision-maker to enjoy and which he can legitimately expect to be permitted to continue to do until there has been communicated to him some rational grounds for withdrawing it on which he has been given an opportunity to comment."

In the present case, I can see that the petitioners might legitimately expect to complete their allotted periods of residence in this country, and that they are accordingly entitled to have communicated to them rational grounds for withdrawing that privilege and to have the opportunity to comment on these grounds. However, it is only when the Secretary of State makes a deportation order that these particular rights or expectations are affected, and it respectfully seems to me that it is at that stage that any review should be sought of the minister's decision, either on the grounds of its unreasonableness or on the ground of flawed procedure leading up to, and thus invalidating, the decision. This, indeed, was the course followed in two English cases where, in differing respects, the circumstances were closely similar to those of the petitioners, namely *R v Secretary of State for Home Affairs, ex p Hosenball* and *R v Maze Visitors, ex p Hone*; and, despite counsel's researches, no authority could be cited to me to the contrary effect. There was some faint suggestion that in this general area the Scottish procedure of judicial review might differ from that of England, but the only reference made in that connection was to Rule of Court 260B (10) which refers, in passing, to "the decision, act or omission in question". For myself, I do not see how that provision is in any way inconsistent with English authority in this area of the law. In any event, it cannot be assumed that the Secretary of State will in due course reaffirm his decisions in respect of these petitioners, and, to that extent, the present applications can also be seen as being both hypothetical and premature.

Having said all that, I have to record that counsel for the respondent was not disposed to argue for either incompetency or prematurity along the lines above indicated, and, in view of the importance attached by both parties to a judicial decision on the remaining point argued, I think it appropriate to give my opinion on that matter.

The principal, if not, in the end, the only authority founded on by counsel for the petitioners for the proposition that his clients should have the right of legal representation before the advisory panel was the case of *R v Home Secretary, ex p Tarrant*, subsequently approved, as it happens, by the House of Lords in *R v Maze Visitors*. In that case certain decisions of two boards of prison visitors were quashed on the ground that the boards had been unaware of, and had thus failed to exercise, a discretion to permit legal representation in the proceedings before them. In two instances the decisions were quashed on the further ground that, having regard to the gravity and complexity of the charges, any reasonable tribunal, properly exercising their discretion, would have been bound to allow such representation. In the final formulation of his argument it was submitted by counsel for the petitioners that, in the same way, the respondent, in exercising his functions under s 3 (5) (b) of the Immigration Act 1971, was bound to exercise a discretion on the matter of whether he should allow legal representations to be made to him in connection with any decision made by him under that section. In this connection, counsel for the petitioners recognised — quite rightly in my opinion — that the extra-statutory advisory panel had no separate legal personality and, indeed, that it had no separate existence from the Secretary of State for Home Affairs. It had simply been devised by him as an aid to the discharge of his functions under ss 3 (5) (b) and 15 (3) of the 1971 Act, and counsel for the petitioners was accordingly content to test his proposition against what the Secretary of State would himself have required to do if no panel had been set up in the first place. It seems to me that another way of expressing the same concept is that, having been set up, the panel could properly be instructed to do, or not to do, whatever might have been done, or not done, by the Secretary of State himself. In this connection, counsel for the petitioners instanced the example of the Secretary of State deciding himself to ask for written representations and receiving, by way of such a representation, a letter from a firm of solicitors. He could not dismiss the representation because it emanated from a firm of solicitors and this demonstrated that, likewise, legal representation before the advisory panel was a matter which had to be considered.

In my opinion the submissions of counsel for the petitioners on this matter are unsound. As regards the particular example given by counsel, I find that in *R v Maze Visitors* Lord Goff, with whose reasoning all the other members of the committee agreed, drew a clear distinction between the right of legal representation before a tribunal and the right of a man to employ an agent to communicate with a body performing an administrative act. For the rest, it respectfully seems to me that there is a world of difference between domestic tribunals regulating their own procedure,

including the allowance or otherwise of legal represen-
A tation, which was the context of the case founded
upon on the one hand, and a minister exercising a discretionary power within the privacy of his office or
ministry on the other hand. In the latter case he may,
in the words of Lord Diplock, have a duty to give
"rational grounds" for his decision and an opportunity to comment on these grounds, but that does not
involve, at least as I see it, the exercise of any particular discretion in regard to the matter of legal
representation. It follows, in my opinion, that, in
B setting up his extra-statutory panel of advisers, the
Secretary of State was fully entitled to do what counsel
for the petitioners submits he in fact did, namely to
determine in advance that in no circumstances would
he allow legal representation before the panel, any
more than he would have permitted such representation before himself. I say this without regard to what
might loosely be termed the "merits" of that decision
since, as to those, I heard little argument on behalf of
the respondent and since, as I see it, they are in any
C event irrelevant to the only legal issue involved. It
almost goes without saying that it is with that issue
alone that I am concerned.

Even supposing that I am wrong so far and that the
minister and, through him, the panel are in each case
under an obligation to exercise a discretion on the
matter of legal representation, the further question
arises whether, in respect of the petitioners, it can be
said that no reasonable Home Secretary or panel of
advisers would have done other than allow the peti-
D tioners the legal representation which they seek. In my
opinion, it is quite impossible to answer that question
ab ante in the affirmative, and this, indeed, is another
reason why I regard the applications as being, on any
view, premature. Counsel for the petitioners
emphasised the gravity of the subject matter of the
hearings and instanced ways in which a lawyer might
be able to assist persons in the position of the petitioners. However, bearing in mind that the only issue
is one of national security and that counsel for the peti-
E tioners accepts the restraints thereby imposed, it is far
from self evident that in every case, or indeed any case,
the questions would be sufficiently complex, or the
circumstances of the inquiry such, that legal representation would be justified or appropriate. On the contrary, as was made clear in the authorities referred to
above, everything must turn on the particular facts of
the particular case. Lest it be thought that I have overlooked it, I find nothing in the decision in *Airey v
Ireland* which suggests that the European Court of
F Human Rights would take any different view. It
follows that on this aspect of the case, also, I am
against the petitioners.

I have only to add that counsel for the respondent
was prepared to argue that, were it necessary for the
respondent to do so, the respondent was still able
validly to exercise a discretion in the matter of legal
representation for the petitioners. According to this
submission the statement made by the respondent's
predecessor in the House of Commons in 1971, of
which a copy was sent to each petitioner as embodying

the procedure for the hearings, fell properly to be construed as indicating that there would be no entitle- G
ment, as matter of right, to legal representation, but
that such representation might still be allowed. I
confess that I have had the greatest difficulty with this
submission. It seems to me that, on any fair construction, the statement in question indicates quite clearly
that an aggrieved person will not be permitted legal
representation but may be assisted by a friend to such
extent as the advisers sanction. I am fortified in this
view having regard to the terms of the letters written
to both petitioners on 3 January 1991, the further H
letter written to Mr Agool's London agents dated 30
January 1991 and the contents of the attendance note
produced in the petition at the instance of Mr Abbas.
According to counsel for the respondent all these
letters and communications — despite the terms of the
letter dated 30 January — were simply reformulations
of the 1971 statement according to the liberal construction for which he contended. He went on to
submit that there was accordingly, as yet, no decision
by the respondent on the matter of legal representa- I
tion for the petitioners and that for this reason the
applications were premature. This was particularly so
in the case of Mr Agool where a further request had
been made for legal representation in a letter from his
solicitors to the Home Office dated 31 January 1991.
In this connection, however, counsel for the respondent was unable to say whether any reply would be
sent to that letter and was certainly not prepared to
give any reply himself.

I am against counsel for the respondent in these J
latter submissions. I am satisfied that since 1971 the
Secretary of State for Home Affairs has had a clear and
inflexible policy of denying legal representation before
the advisory panel and that this policy was reflected,
so far as the petitioners are concerned, in the letters of
3 January 1991 and, again, in the later communications to which I have referred. As it happens, and for
the reasons given above, I am of opinion that the
respondent was entitled to adopt that policy, but I am
left in little doubt that it would improperly have K
fettered the exercise of a discretion in regard to the
matter in issue had such an exercise been required.

In the result, my decision is that these petitions were
incompetent and premature, but that, even if I am
wrong about this, they fail on their merits so far as the
only remaining issue is concerned. I accordingly
dismiss both of them.

Counsel for Petitioners, Bovey; Solicitors, Lawford L
Kidd & Co, WS — Counsel for Respondent, Davidson;
Solicitor, R Brodie, Solicitor in Scotland to the Secretary
of State for the Home Department.

R N T

Kilmarnock and Loudoun
A # District Council v Young

FIRST DIVISION

THE LORD PRESIDENT (HOPE),
LORDS ALLANBRIDGE AND McCLUSKEY

15 NOVEMBER 1991

B
Local government — Burial grounds — Provision of — Procedure — Statutory requirement for special meeting of local authority requisitioned by two members or 10 ratepayers — Whether mandatory — Committee of local authority approving proposed extension of burial ground and resolving to petition sheriff for designation of ground — Whether sufficient compliance with statute — Burial Grounds (Scotland) Act 1855 (18 & 19 Vict, c 68), ss 9 and 10 — Local Government (Scotland) Act 1973 (c 65), s 56.

Process — Sheriff court — Petition for designation of burial ground — Whether sheriff exercising adminis-
C *trative or judicial function — Competency of person other than owner of affected land appearing or leading evidence — Burial Grounds (Scotland) Act 1855 (18 & 19 Vict, c 68), s 10.*

Process — Appeal — Appeal from sheriff court — Competency — Appeal without leave — Appeal to Inner House — Statutes providing for appeal to Lord Ordinary — Burial Grounds (Scotland) Act 1855 (18 & 19 Vict, c 68), s 10 — Sheriff Courts (Scotland) Act 1907 (7 Edw
D *VII, c 51), s 28.*

Sections 9 and 10 of the Burial Grounds (Scotland) Act 1855, as amended, provide for the convening of a special meeting of the district council on the requisition of 10 or more ratepayers or two or more members of the council for the purpose of determining whether a burial ground shall be provided under the Act for the district. If no suitable ground is provided within six months after such requisition, it shall be lawful to petition the sheriff to have a suitable portion of land
E designated, intimation being made to the owner. The sheriff "shall examine such witnesses and make such inquiry as he shall think proper", with an appeal lying "to any of the Lords Ordinary of the Court of Session".

A district council resolved to investigate the possible purchase of suitable land for a cemetery extension. A committee of the council agreed to pursue the acquisition of a site identified as suitable and, failing agreement with the tenant, to petition the sheriff under the
F 1855 Act. No agreement was reached and the council petitioned the sheriff accordingly. The tenant lodged answers and challenged the competency of the petition as no special meeting of the council had been requisitioned. The council argued that the statutory procedure was not mandatory and that what had in fact taken place was consistent with the purpose of the 1855 Act. They further argued that s 9 of that Act fell to be read with s 56 of the Local Government (Scotland) Act 1973, which permitted them to arrange for the discharge of their functions by committee, sub-

committee or officer. The sheriff repelled the plea to competency and sustained the council's plea that the G tenant had no title or interest to challenge the council's decision except on competency. The tenant appealed without leave to the Inner House under s 28 of the Sheriff Courts (Scotland) Act 1907.

Held, (1) that the statutory procedure having been left unamended despite other amendments to the 1855 Act, it was not open to the court to read the provisions as to requisition pro non scripto or to excuse observance on the view that they prescribed useless formalities (pp 507E-G, 508H-I and 510L-511B); (2) that H the requisitioning process was not a "function" of the council within s 56 of the 1973 Act and the council could not invoke that section to satisfy the requirements of the 1855 Act (pp 508H-I and 511H-I); (3) that since there had been no requisition and no special meeting was convened (the meeting of the committee not being a special meeting of the council for the purpose of the 1855 Act), the council had no power to present the petition under s 10 of the Act (pp 508H-I and 511F-G and I); and appeal *allowed* and petition I *dismissed.*

Observed, (1) (per the Lord President (Hope)) that in view of the terms of Rule of Court 290, appeals under the 1855 Act were properly taken to the Inner House and not to a particular Lord Ordinary (pp 507L-508A); and (2) that the present appeal, brought under s 28 of the 1907 Act, was of doubtful competence (pp 508C-D, 508H-I and 510D).

Opinion, that since the role of the sheriff under J s 10 was administrative rather than judicial, it was for him to determine how proceedings were to be conducted and the essential requirement of fairness observed; but that natural justice required that a person wishing to object should be allowed to be heard (pp 508F-G, 508H-I and 511L-512H).

Appeal from the sheriff court

Kilmarnock and Loudoun District Council applied K by summary petition to the sheriff at Kilmarnock to have certain ground designated and set apart for the purposes of a burial ground in terms of the Burial Grounds (Scotland) Act 1855. Following advertisement of the petition, John Young, the tenant of the land in question, lodged answers inter alia challenging the competency of the petition.

On 15 January 1991 the sheriff heard parties in debate. L

Statutory provisions

The Burial Grounds (Scotland) Act 1855, as originally enacted, provided:

"IX. Although no Burial Ground in the Parish has been closed by Order in Council, the Inspector of the Poor of any Parish not within Burgh, and the Town Clerk in the Case of any Parish within Burgh, shall be bound, upon the Requisition in Writing of Ten or more Persons assessed for Relief of the Poor of the

Parish, or upon the Requisition in Writing of any
A Two or more Members of the Parochial Board of the
Parish, to convene a Special Meeting of the Parochial
Board of such Parish, for the Purpose of determining
whether a Burial Ground shall be provided under this
Act for the Parish; and if a majority of such meeting
of the Parochial Board shall resolve that a Burial
Ground shall be provided under this Act for the
Parish, such new Burial Ground shall be provided in
the same Manner as if an old Burial Ground had been
closed by order in Council.

B "X. Whenever any Burial Ground shall have been
closed by Order in Council, the Parochial Board shall
forthwith proceed to provide a suitable and convenient
Burial Ground for the Parish, and to make Arrangements for facilitating Interments therein; and in the
event of a suitable Burial Ground not being provided
by the Parochial Board within Six Months after such
Order or Requisition as aforesaid, it shall be lawful for
such Board, or for any Ten or more Persons assessed
for Relief of the Poor in the Parish, or any Two or
C more members of the Parochial Board, to apply by
summary Petition to the Sheriff to have a suitable
Portion of Land designated for the Purpose of a Burial
Ground; and the Sheriff shall examine such Witnesses
and made such Inquiry as he shall think proper, and
shall keep a Note of such Evidence as may be adduced,
and, if he thinks fit, shall thereupon proceed to designate and set apart such Portion as he may deem necessary of any Lands in such Parish suitable for the
Purpose, not being Part of any Policy, Pleasure
D Ground, or Garden attached to any Dwelling House;
Provided always, that due Intimation shall have been
given of not less than Ten Days to the Owner of such
Lands, that he may be heard for his Interest before
such Designation is actually made, subject always to
an appeal to any of the Lords Ordinary of the Court
of Session, whose Decision shall be final, such Appeal
always being presented within Fourteen Days of the
Date of the Sheriff's Judgment; and provided also,
that no Land shall be so designated nearer than One
E hundred yards to any Dwelling House without the
Consent in Writing of the owner of such Dwelling
House; and on such Land being so designated the
Parochial Board shall proceed to acquire the same in
manner herein-after provided."

The Act, as amended, now provides:

"9. Although no burial ground in the (District) has
been closed by Order in Council the proper officer of
the islands or district council shall be bound, upon the
F requisition of ten or more ratepayers or upon the
requisition in writing of any two or more members of
the District Council, to convene a special meeting of
the District Council for the purpose of determining
whether a burial ground shall be provided under this
Act for the (District); and if a majority of such meeting
of the District Council shall resolve that a burial
ground shall be provided under this Act for the (District), such new burial ground shall be provided in the
same manner as if an old burial ground had been
closed by Order in Council.

"10. Whenever any burial ground shall have been
closed by Order in Council, the District Council shall G
forthwith proceed to provide a suitable and convenient
burial ground for the (District) and to make arrangements for facilitating interments therein; and in the
event of a suitable burial ground not being provided
by the District Council within six months after such
Order or requisition as aforesaid, it shall be lawful for
such Council, or for any ten or more ratepayers residing in the (District) or any two or more members of
the District Council, to apply by summary petition to
the sheriff to have a suitable portion of land designated H
for the purpose of a burial ground; and the sheriff
shall examine such witnesses and make such inquiry
as he shall think proper, and shall keep a note of such
evidence as may be adduced, and, if he thinks fit, shall
thereupon proceed to designate and set apart such
portion as he may deem necessary of any lands in such
parish suitable for the purpose, not being part of any
policy, pleasure ground, or garden attached to any
dwelling house: Provided always, that due intimation
shall have been given of not less than ten days to the I
owner of such lands, that he may be heard for his
interest before such designation is actually made,
subject always to an appeal to any of the Lords
Ordinary of the Court of Session, whose decision shall
be final, such appeal always being presented within
fourteen days of the date of the sheriff's judgment:
And provided also, that no land shall be so designated
nearer than one hundred yards to any dwelling house
without the consent in writing of the owner of such
dwelling house; and on such land being so designated J
the District Council shall proceed to acquire the same
in manner herein-after provided."

The Sheriff Courts (Scotland) Act 1907 provides:

"28.—(1) Subject to the provisions of this Act, it
shall be competent to appeal to the Court of Session
against a judgment either of a sheriff or of a sheriff-
substitute if the interlocutor appealed against is a final
judgment. . . .

"(2) Nothing in this section nor in section 27 of this K
Act contained shall affect any right of appeal or exclusion of such right provided by any Act of Parliament
in force for the time being."

Cases referred to
Bailey, Hay & Co Ltd, Re [1971] 1 WLR 1357.
Covington v Wright [1963] 2 QB 469; [1963] 2 WLR
  1232; [1963] 2 All ER 212.
Express Engineering Works Ltd, Re [1920] 1 Ch 466. L
Liddall v Ballingry Parish Council (1908) 16 SLT 258;
  1908 SC 1082.
Ostreicher v Secretary of State for the Environment
  [1978] 1 WLR 810; [1978] 1 All ER 591.
Strichen Parish Council v Goodwillie (1908) 16 SLT 70;
  1908 SC 835.
University of London Charitable Trusts, Re [1964] Ch
  282; [1963] 3 WLR 1081; [1963] 3 All ER 859.

Textbook referred to
Maxwell, *Practice of the Court of Session*, p 645.

On 29 January 1991 the sheriff *repelled* the respondent's plea to the competency, *sustained* the petitioners' plea challenging the respondent's title and interest to challenge their decision to proceed except as relating to competency, and *appointed* a further hearing.

The respondent appealed to the Court of Session.

Appeal

The appeal was heard before the First Division on 18 October 1991.

On 15 November 1991 the court *allowed* the appeal and *dismissed* the petition.

THE LORD PRESIDENT (HOPE).—I have had the advantage of reading the opinion which has been prepared by Lord McCluskey. He has set out very fully the background to this case, and I do not wish to add anything to what he has said about this or to his description of the various amendments which have been made to ss 9 and 10 of the Burial Grounds (Scotland) Act 1855 as originally enacted. For the reasons which he gives, I agree that there is no escape from the conclusion that the petition to the sheriff was incompetent and that it must be dismissed.

This is not a result which I regard as satisfactory, since it seems to me that the procedural problems which have arisen in this case show very clearly that the 1855 Act is in need of reform. It lays down a procedure for the obtaining of a resolution by the district council that a burial ground shall be provided which is out of touch with the way in which local authorities in modern practice conduct their affairs. And it lays down a procedure for appeal to this court against a decision of the sheriff under s 10 which, at first sight, does not fit easily with our current practice by which statutory appeals are heard in the Inner House and not by a particular Lord Ordinary.

Fortunately the latter point is one, as I shall mention later, which is capable of being dealt with by the Rules of Court. But, as Lord McCluskey has explained, it is not open to this court to disregard the requirements of the statute about the formalities which must be observed before a resolution can competently be made under s 9. Counsel for the district council submitted that on a proper construction of that section these formalities were not essential, and that the district council was entitled to proceed to a decision in any way it thought fit so long as it acted within its powers under the Local Government (Scotland) Act 1973. He pointed to the fact that the functions of councils under the 1855 Act were transferred to and vested in the district council by s 169 (1) of the 1973 Act, and contended that it was not appropriate to insist that there must be a special meeting convened by requisition in the cases where the council had resolved, after considering the issue, that a burial ground must be provided. But in my opinion the words "such meeting" in the second part of s 9 and the timetable provided for by s 10 under reference to "such order or

requisition as aforesaid", make it impossible to construe s 9 in this way. Furthermore, we are dealing here with the requirements of a statute and not with rules, such as those of a club or the articles of association of a company, which are capable of being altered by agreement. A local authority does not have the same power in regard to the requirements of a statute as that which may be exercised by a company in general meeting to authorise steps which have been taken in breach of its articles. Since it is a creature entirely of statute, it can act only in accordance with what the statutes provide. It is a matter for regret that Parliament has not yet thought fit to amend the procedural provisions of s 9 of the 1855 Act, despite the various amendments which have been made to reflect changes in the authorities entrusted with responsibility for local government. The provision that requisition must be by 10 or more ratepayers or by two or more members of the district council seems now to have little to commend it, since the effect of the Abolition of Domestic Rates Etc (Scotland) Act 1987 is to restrict the power of requisition which was given to ratepayers to those who pay non-domestic rates. No provision was made by that Act to enable those who now pay the community charges to requisition a meeting under this section. This may have been an oversight, and the opportunity may yet be taken when that Act is itself repealed to correct the anomalies which now exist. Nevertheless we must apply the statute as we find it, and since there was no requisition and no special meeting was convened in terms of s 9, the district council had no power to present this petition under s 10 of the Act.

There was some discussion as to whether this appeal is itself competent having regard on the one hand to the provisions of s 10, which provide only for an appeal from the sheriff to any Lord Ordinary, and to the requirements of s 28 (1) of the Sheriff Courts (Scotland) Act 1907 about leave to appeal. Now it is clear that if this had been a competent petition under s 10 and the decision appealed against was a decision of the sheriff taken under that section also, the only method by which it could be appealed would have been by appeal under that statute. In *Strichen Parish Council v Goodwillie* at p 837, Lord President Dunedin said: "It is impossible to read the provisions of the Burial Grounds (Scotland) Act 1855 without seeing that the only appeal allowed is an appeal to the Lord Ordinary under certain limited conditions, and that there is no appeal from the Sheriff-substitute to the Sheriff."

That is still the case, subject to the fact that the appeal lies now to the Inner House as a statutory appeal under Rule of Court 290 and not to the Lord Ordinary, since that rule provides that it is to have effect notwithstanding anything in any Act of Parliament to the contrary: see also s 5 (m) of the Court of Session Act 1988. It might avoid confusion if s 10 were now to be amended to conform with the Rule of Court, but the Rule of Court is clear on this matter and the procedure which it prescribes is separate and distinct from that by which appeals are made from the sheriff court to the Court of Session under s 28 of the 1907 Act.

This appeal however has been brought before us, without leave, as an appeal under the 1907 Act. I do not think that leave was necessary, because the sheriff's decision, which was to repel the appellant's pleas to the competency and to sustain the district council's plea that the appellant had no title to challenge their claim except on competency, was a final judgment so far as the appellant was concerned. But was it competent for him to appeal that decision under s 28 of the 1907 Act, given that the district council's petition was presented to the sheriff as a summary application under the 1855 Act, and having regard also to s 28 (2) of the 1907 Act which provides that nothing in that section is to affect any exclusion of any right of appeal provided by any Act of Parliament in force for the time being? No assistance is to be gained from *Liddall v Ballingry Parish Council,* where the powers of the sheriff under the 1855 Act were reviewed by the Inner House, because in that case the sheriff's decision on expenses was the subject of a suspension which was brought in the Court of Session. The reference to that case in Maxwell's *Court of Session Practice* at p 645 as an example of an appeal under s 10 of the 1855 Act is incorrect. I am not aware of any previous example of a petition under s 10 being appealed under the provisions of the 1907 Act at the preliminary stage following a debate on preliminary pleas. With some hesitation, however, I am content to treat this as a competent appeal, since the point which is raised here is a pure question of law and is directed solely to the competency of the proceedings. But this case must not be taken as an indication that the court will sanction a departure from the method of appeal which s 10 of the 1855 Act requires where the sheriff has proceeded to fulfil the administrative function which is given to him by that section.

The only other point on which I wish to comment is the role of the sheriff in the administrative proceedings under that section if a person, in response to an interlocutor calling upon all parties having an interest and who desire to be heard, appears before him on the date which he appoints for the inquiry. As Lord Denning MR pointed out in *Ostreicher v Secretary of State for the Environment* [1978] 1 WLR at p 815: "It is one of the elementary principles of natural justice, no matter whether it is in a judicial proceeding or an administrative inquiry, that everything should be done fairly: and that any party or objector should be given a fair opportunity of being heard."

It was submitted for the appellant not only that he had a right to be heard but that this right extended also to his becoming a party to the proceedings with the same rights as to the leading of evidence as the district council would enjoy as petitioners. I agree with Lord McCluskey, however, that since this is an administrative proceeding it is a matter for the discretion of the sheriff as to how it is to be conducted and thus how the essential requirement of fairness is to be observed. It is sufficient to say that it would not be consistent with this requirement if a person who wished to object to the designation of the land as a burial ground and who appeared at the inquiry was not allowed to be heard at all; and that it would be open to the sheriff in these circumstances, if he thought fit, to allow the objector to become a party to the proceedings in the full sense of these words. No doubt he would be guided in this matter by the nature of the objection which was to be advanced and the extent to which it might involve the leading of witnesses and challenge to evidence led for the petitioners.

For these reasons and for those given by Lord McCluskey I agree that this appeal should be allowed, and I concur with his proposal as to the terms of the interlocutor which we should pronounce.

LORD ALLANBRIDGE.—I have had the advantage of reading the opinions of both your Lordship in the chair and Lord McCluskey. For the reasons set forth in these opinions I agree that this appeal should be allowed.

LORD McCLUSKEY.—The petitioners in these proceedings, which were brought in Kilmarnock sheriff court, are Kilmarnock and Loudoun District Council, a local authority incorporated under the Local Government (Scotland) Act 1973; they are also the respondents in this appeal. For convenience I shall refer to them as "the district council". The appellant in the present appeal was the respondent in the petition brought by the district council in the sheriff court and he will usually be referred to in this opinion as "the appellant".

On 16 December 1987, at a meeting of the district council there was submitted a report, dated 3 December 1987, by the parks manager, stating that a recent survey had found that there would be a need for new cemetery extensions at Riccarton and Galston. The council agreed that certain steps be taken by officials with a view to investigating the possible purchase of suitable land and preparing a programme of phased development for cemetery extensions of land at Riccarton and Galston. On 20 February 1990 a committee of the district council, known as the general purposes committee, received a progress report, dated 2 February 1990, prepared by the director of administration and legal services, in relation to the extension of Riccarton cemetery. The report had previously been circulated presumably to members of that committee. The minute of the meeting included an item in the following terms:

"Riccarton Cemetery — Extension
"There was submitted progress report dated 2 February 1990 (circulated) by Director of Administration and Legal Services.

"The Committee agreed that authority be remitted to the Director of Administration and Legal Services, viz:— (1) to arrange a meeting with the tenant and owners of the site to discuss the acquisition of the site with vacant possession; (2) failing an early agreement, to acquire the cemetery extension site with early entry,

by a petition in terms of the Burial Grounds (Scotland)
A Act 1855; and (3) to conclude an appropriate agreement, in consultation with the directors of leisure and technical services, with the developer of the adjacent site regarding access, wayleaves and compensation in money or land."

The present appellant is the person referred to in that minute as "the tenant" and the site there referred to is that identified in para 1 of the crave in the petition, being an area of land extending to 6.3 acres presently in the ownership of the Trustees of the
B Buchanan Bequest, lying on the southern side of Riccarton Road, Kilmarnock, and to the north of the existing Riccarton cemetery. The appellant is the agricultural tenant of the holding of Kaimshill of which the subjects form part.

In the autumn of 1990 the district council, as the burial grounds authority for the Kilmarnock and Loudoun District for the purposes of the Burial Grounds (Scotland) Act 1855 (hereinafter referred to
C as the 1855 Act) in terms of s 169 (1) of the Local Government (Scotland) Act 1973, applied by summary petition to the sheriff to have the ground specified in the petition designated and set apart for the purposes of a burial ground for the parish of Riccarton in terms of the 1855 Act, and, in particular, s 9 thereof. The petition containing the application also contained craves for certain incidental authority and powers exercisable under the 1855 Act. On 26 October 1990 the sheriff signed an interlocutor in the following terms:
D

"Kilmarnock: 26 October 1990. The sheriff, having considered the foregoing petition together with the productions lodged, appoints intimation of the import thereof and of this deliverance to be made by advertisement once in each of the *Glasgow Herald* and *Kilmarnock Standard* newspapers calling upon all parties having an interest, who desire to be heard, to appear before the sheriff within the Sheriff Court House, St Marnock Street, Kilmarnock, on Wednes-
E day, 5 December 1990 at 10.00 am; requires said intimation to be made at least 21 days before the said diet; meantime appoints a copy of the petition and relative productions to lie in the hands of the Sheriff Clerk, Sheriff Court House, Kilmarnock, to be available for inspection by anyone having an interest."

The appellant lodged answers to the petition and on 5 December 1990 the sheriff, on the joint motion of the district council and the appellant, appointed parties to be heard on the application on 15 January
F 1991 "as a hearing". On 15 January 1991, the sheriff heard the parties' procurators on the debate roll and made avizandum. On 29 January 1991, he repelled the first plea in law for the appellant (the respondent in the petition); that plea is in the following terms: "(1) The petition being incompetent should be refused."

He also sustained the district council's plea no 4, which was in the following terms: "(4) The respondent having neither title nor interest to challenge the said decision except on competency his averments anent the merits of the said decision should not be

admitted to probation." The "said decision" referred
to in the district council's fourth plea is the decision G
of the general purposes committee of 20 February
1990 narrated above.

The interlocutor pronounced by the sheriff was in the following terms:

"Kilmarnock: 29 January 1991. The sheriff having resumed consideration of the cause repels the first plea in law for the respondent; sustains plea in law no 4 for the petitioners; appoints the cause to the roll of 6 February 1991 reserving any question of expenses." H
Appended to the interlocutor of 29 January 1991 was a note by the sheriff explaining the background, narrating submissions made to him by the parties' procurators or counsel and explaining why he had dealt with the pleas in the way recorded in that interlocutor.

It will be seen from this brief narrative that the appellant sought to persuade the sheriff that the petition was incompetent. The district council resisted that submission and in turn argued that the appellant had no title or interest to appear as a party in the I petition process or, as a party, to challenge the merits of the petition. It was not disputed, however, that the appellant had the right to appear in the petition process to challenge the competency of the petition itself. Not all the matters which were argued before the sheriff were argued before this court and the appellant's counsel respectfully criticised the sheriff's note as not having fully recorded and canvassed all the submissions made to him at the hearing on 15 January 1991. In all the circumstances, it is sufficient for the J purposes of this court to narrate the submissions of parties as they were made to this court. These submissions addressed three matters: (a) the competency of the petition; (b) the right of the appellant to appear, as a party, in the proceedings on the merits of the petition; and (c) whether or not certain matters relating to the necessity of designating the ground in question for burial purposes and the effect of such a designation upon the viability of the appellant's tenanted farm were matters which were properly the K subject of whatever inquiry was intended by the Act.

Before turning to deal with these issues it is necessary to narrate the terms of the sections, as now amended, of the 1855 Act in terms of which this petition was brought. Counsel for the district council accepted that the relevant sections were ss 9 and 10; this was not an application purporting to be under s 11 of the Act. Section 9, as originally enacted, was in the following terms: [his Lordship quoted the L original terms of s 9, followed by those of s 10, and continued:] In terms of the Local Government (Scotland) Act 1894, Pt III, the parochial boards ceased to function and were replaced by parish councils (later replaced by town or county councils). The functions of councils under the Burial Grounds (Scotland) Act 1855 were transferred to and vested in islands or district councils by s 169 (1) of the Local Government (Scotland) Act 1973. Certain words from s 9 as originally enacted, namely "the Inspector of the Poor of any Parish not within Burgh, and the Town Clerk, in the

A case of any Parish within Burgh, shall be bound, upon the requisition in writing of ten or more persons assessed for relief of the Poor of the Parish", were replaced in 1930 by the words "the County Clerk or the Town Clerk as the case may be shall be bound upon the requisition in writing, of ten or more ratepayers", by virtue of the Local Government (Scotland) (Adaptation of Enactments) Order 1930 (SR & O 1930/1026). The National Assistance (Adaptation of Enactments) Regulations 1952 (SI 1952/1334) substituted the word "ratepayers" for the words "persons

B assessed for relief of the poor" in s 10. As a result of the Local Government (Scotland) Act 1973, Sched 27, Pt I, para 2 (1) the function of convening a special meeting in terms of s 9 is now conferred upon the proper officer of the islands or district council. Accordingly, although I suspect that the amendments have not been made as carefully as they might have been, the effect is that the sections now read as if they were in the following terms: [his Lordship quoted the terms of ss 9 and 10 as amended and continued:]

C Our attention was also drawn to s 27 (1) of the Abolition of Domestic Rates Etc (Scotland) Act 1987 which provided inter alia: "In this Act and in any other enactment, whether passed or made before or after the passing of this Act, and unless the context otherwise requires — (a) the word 'rate' shall mean (i) the non-domestic rate (ii) the non-domestic water rate and (iii) the non-domestic sewerage rate . . . and cognate expressions shall be construed accordingly".

D It was suggested that this provision fell to be applied to the word "ratepayers" in ss 9 and 10 of the 1855 Act. For completeness, both parties were agreed that the present appeal to the Inner House of the Court of Session was competent under Rule of Court 290, despite the wording of s 10 aforesaid. I share the concern of your Lordship in the chair on this matter, but it was not argued before us.

E Against this statutory background, the appellant presented the argument that the petition was incompetent because no petition could be presented under ss 9 and 10 unless there had first been a special meeting of the district council convened by the proper officer of the council following upon the requisition of 10 or more "ratepayers" or upon the requisition in writing of any two or more members of the district council. In the present instance, it was plain, and indeed it was conceded, that there had been no requisition by any ratepayers or by members of the district council, that there had been no special meeting and that accord-

F ingly the statutory procedure laid down by s 9 had not been complied with. That procedure was both statutory and mandatory. Accordingly it was incompetent for the district council to apply by summary petition to the sheriff in terms of s 10. The link between the two sections was clear when one observed that the petition could not be presented until six months after the "requisition as aforesaid". It was the requisition, whether by ratepayers or by members of the council, which started the six month period running, not the convening of the special meeting, or the majority

G decision at any such meeting. It was submitted that the district council had no common law power to provide burial grounds or to apply by summary petition to the sheriff to have land designated for the purpose of a burial ground. The powers of the district council fell to be ascertained from the sections as amended and there was no power to act without there being a requisition. Whether or not the term "ratepayers" in the amended s 9 or the amended s 10 fell to be read as restricted to non-domestic ratepayers because of the effect of the 1987 Act had no bearing upon the issue because it was a matter of concession H that there had been no requisition whether by ratepayers or by members of the district council.

In reply, counsel for the district council argued that the court should have regard to the evident purpose of the 1855 Act, as amended; it was appropriate to give it a beneficent or benign construction and to read s 9 as including a power in the district council itself to determine to provide a burial ground even although there was no formal requisition. In any event, it was I argued, the formalities of requisition envisaged by s 9 were unnecessary formalities. It was clear that a special meeting could have been convened following upon a requisition in writing by any two members of the district council. Although that had not been done, it was obvious that at the meeting of the general purposes committee on 20 February 1990 more than two members of the district council had favoured the provision of the burial ground at the site which was the subject of the petition to the sheriff, and indeed the whole committee had resolved to petition the sheriff. J Accordingly, for the court to insist upon a strict compliance with the precise procedures contained in s 9, would be to insist upon the observance of useless formalities. The court could dispense with the observance of useless formalities where it was plain that the failure to comply with them had made and could make no difference; the court should apply common sense: *Covington v Wright* and *Re University of London Charitable Trusts*. The court had waived unnecessary formalities in *Re Bailey, Hay & Co Ltd* and *Re Express* K *Engineering Works Ltd*.

It was also argued that on a sound construction of s 9, the first part — down to the semicolon — was concerned with the requisition process, but the second part could properly be read independently of the first part so as to allow a meeting of the district council to resolve that a burial ground should be provided under the Act even although there had been no preceding requisition. The provisions about requisition were not L mandatory. It was further argued that the provisions in s 9 fell to be read in the light of s 56 of the Local Government (Scotland) Act 1973 which permitted the local authority to arrange for the discharge of any of their functions by a committee of the authority, a subcommittee or an officer of the authority. The provision in s 56 (1) fell to be read along with the provision in s 56 (14).

In my opinion, it is not open to this court to read the provisions as to "requisition" pro non scripto or

A to excuse observance of them on the view that they prescribe what are, in circumstances such as are disclosed here, useless formalities. The Act of 1855 has been repeatedly amended both by primary and by secondary legislation since its enactment and is specifically referred to in the Local Government (Scotland) Act 1973, but the provisions in question have been left substantially intact, even although their form has changed. There can be no room for doubt that in 1855 the taking of action by summary petition to the sheriff was intended, in any case where no burial ground has

B been closed by order in council, to be initiated by a requisition. Despite the various amendments of ss 9 and 10, the requirement for a requisition has survived.

Requisition appears to me to have a twofold function. In s 9, the requisition, by whomsoever made, causes the proper officer of the council to convene a "special meeting" of the district council for the express purpose of determining whether a burial ground should be provided under the 1855 Act. In s 10, the date of the requisition "as aforesaid" is part

C of the mechanism that precedes the application by summary petition to the sheriff and determines when such an application may be made. Where there is ambiguity, it is sometimes possible to give a benign construction to the provisions of a statute whose evident purpose is clear, if that evident purpose would not be achieved without benign construction. However, it is important to remember that the procedures envisaged by ss 9 and 10 may lead to adverse effects upon the interests of some persons residing or having

D business within the area of the district council and, more particularly, within the area close to the proposed burial ground; the court should not lightly adopt a construction which might serve to frustrate these interests. Equally, it is not easy to assume that the detailed procedures which are required before a special meeting of the district council is convened are to be characterised as useless formalities. It may be possible in the case of a club regulated by its own rules or a company regulated by articles of association to

E conclude that certain formalities of procedure might be dispensed with where it is plain that what has been done informally could readily have been done formally, because everything was done with the full agreement of all interested persons; and examples were put to us in argument to illustrate how that may happen. But it is an entirely different matter for the court simply to write out of a statute words which have been deliberately inserted and deliberately left in place.

F Furthermore I do not find it possible to read s 9 as if it were in two distinct parts, the first concerned with formalities leading to a meeting and the second dealing independently with what might happen at a meeting not commenced in the prescribed way. The words following the semicolon are: "and if a majority of *such meeting* of the District Council shall resolve"; and the meeting there referred to is "a special meeting of the District Council". In the present case, it is a matter of concession that there was no "special meeting" of the district council, although it was recognised that the

current legislation (Local Government (Scotland) Act 1973, Sched 7, para 1 (4)) regulates the conditions G under which a "special meeting" may be called. In any event, the meeting founded upon in the petition and for the purposes of this appeal was a meeting of the general purposes committee. In no sense could that be said to be a special meeting of the district council convened for the purpose of determining whether a burial ground should be provided under the Act. Finally, s 56 (1) of the 1973 Act empowers a local authority to arrange for the discharge of any of their functions by a committee, by a subcommittee or by an H officer of the authority. What s 9 is concerned with, however, is a requisitioning process which empowers either 10 or more ratepayers or two or more district council members to require the proper officer to convene a special meeting. The requisitioning process carried out by ratepayers or by individual members of the council is not a "function" of the council. It does not appear to me that s 56 (1) enables the district council in the present instance to say that the requisites of s 9 and s 10 had been met. In the whole I circumstances, I conclude that the petition to the sheriff is incompetent. It follows that the decision of the sheriff to repel the first plea in law for the appellant (then the respondent) as recorded in the interlocutor of 29 January 1991 was unsound. In my opinion, therefore, that interlocutor must be recalled.

The effect of that decision, about which we are agreed, is that the petition falls to be dismissed. It follows from that that it is not necessary for this court to express any opinion as to the other matters, namely J the right of the appellant to participate as a party in any proceedings before the sheriff or the matters which it might be relevant for the sheriff to take into account. However it would be unrealistic not to acknowledge that it is open to the district council to start the whole process again and, after due observance of the requisition and special meeting procedure, to present, in due time, a fresh application by summary petition to the sheriff; and, unless the circumstances have changed, it is possible that the present appellant K would wish to lay his concerns before the sheriff. For this reason and also because we were addressed on this matter it appears to me to be appropriate for the court to offer some guidance in case a fresh petition should be presented.

In my opinion, the role of the sheriff in s 10 is administrative rather than judicial. The important words relating to his function are: "and the sheriff shall examine such witnesses and make such inquiry L as he shall think proper, and shall keep a note of such evidence as may be adduced, and, if he thinks fit, shall thereupon proceed to designate and set apart such portion as he may deem necessary of any lands in such parish suitable for the purpose".

The section specifically envisages that interests other than those of the applicants may be considered by the sheriff. In particular the proviso says: "Provided always, that due intimation shall have been given of not less than ten days to the owner of such lands, that he may be heard for his interest before such designation is actually made".

Accordingly it is plain that the owner would be entitled to present submissions and evidence in support of any contention that he advanced if the sheriff thought it proper to hear such submissions and to examine such witnesses. Where there was opposition by the owner of the lands then, if the sheriff decided to permit the applicants (ie the petitioners) to present evidence and to make submissions, the rules of natural justice would almost certainly require him to afford the same facilities to the owner who was seeking to have his interests laid before the sheriff and taken into account. Accordingly, for the section to work, the sheriff should give careful consideration to the possibility of allowing both the petitioners and the owner to present to him material which is relevant to the decision he has to make. Next, it appears to me to be clear that the sheriff is not limited to hearing only those witnesses suggested by the petitioners or by the owner of the lands. One can envisage many circumstances in which interests other than those of the owner of the lands might be affected. Again the rules of natural justice would appear to require that if a person, in response to an interlocutor such as that pronounced by the sheriff on 26 October 1990, quoted above, wished to lay evidence before or make representations to the sheriff in relation to his interest, the sheriff should give careful consideration to allowing such a person to be represented before the sheriff in the same manner as he allows the petitioner or the owner to be represented before him. Of course, as counsel for the district council pointed out, there could be circumstances in which a great many objectors might seek separate rights of representation. That might be so in some cases, though there is no reason to suppose that that would happen here; but if in a particular case there were many objectors it would be for the sheriff, in the exercise of his discretion, to determine how the separate interests might be identified and represented before him. I do not think that it is appropriate in the present proceedings for this court to try to prescribe a procedure for the sheriff in carrying out this administrative function. It is enough to indicate that he must bear in mind that his discretion is not absolute and unfettered despite the words "as he shall think proper" in s 10. If he omitted to take into account considerations which he should have taken into account, or took into account matters which he should have left out of account, or conducted the proceedings in such a way as to constitute a breach of the elementary rules of natural justice, then whatever decision he made could be attacked. It is for the sheriff, with the assistance of parties' representatives, and in the light of these broad principles to determine how each should be represented before him and what facilities might be afforded to each in order to allow each party fairly to make his case to the sheriff for or against the designation. Again, though this must in the circumstances be an obiter view, the question as to whether or not it is *necessary* to designate the lands in question as burial grounds appears to be one that is relevant for inquiry, when it is explicitly disputed, and is a question upon which the sheriff might obtain assistance from others than the petitioners, who have an obvious interest to argue in favour of necessity. Equally, the effects of designating this ground upon the legitimate patrimonial interests of an affected person such as the present appellant should not be ignored. In my opinion, it is going too far too fast to say that the present appellant cannot appear as a party or through a procurator at any future hearing before the sheriff, that at best he may appear as a witness and that, even if he appears as a witness, he will not be allowed to speak about what is to him the important matter of the continuing viability of his farm.

For the reasons which have been given, this court should recall the interlocutor of 29 January 1991, sustain the first plea in law for the appellant and dismiss the petition.

Counsel for Petitioners and Respondents, McNeill, QC, Bovey; Solicitors, Bonar Mackenzie, WS — Counsel for Respondent and Appellant, Philip, QC, Abercrombie; Solicitors, Connell & Connell, WS.

D E N

King v Gebbie

OUTER HOUSE

LORD CAPLAN

27 MAY 1992

Heritable property — Sale — Missives — Obligation to build house in accordance with drawings and specification — Whether collateral obligation — Whether obligation limited to works completed after conclusion of missives — Patent defects — Effect of subsequent disposition.

Contract — Sale of heritage — Missives of sale — Collateral obligation to build house in accordance with drawings and specification — Whether obligation limited to works completed after conclusion of missives — Patent defects — Effect of subsequent disposition.

Property — Heritable property — Missives of sale — Obligation to build house in accordance with drawings and specification — Whether collateral obligation — Whether obligation limited to works completed after conclusion of missives — Patent defects — Effect of subsequent disposition.

Missives were concluded for the purchase of a house which was in the process of completion. The seller averred that, at the date of conclusion of missives, the external part of the house had been 90 per cent completed and the whole house was approximately 75 per cent completed. It was a term of the contract that the seller would complete the house in accordance with

the architect's drawings and specification and, in
A particular, that kitchen and bathroom fittings to a
certain value would be installed. Shortly after taking
entry to the house, the purchaser discovered certain
deficiencies in the construction of the house. The purchaser brought an action against the seller for breach
of contract and averred that the seller was in breach of
the warranty to build the house in accordance with the
drawings and specification. The seller's primary contention was that the acceptance of the disposition
superseded any contractual obligations contained in
B the missives. The purchaser attacked the relevancy of
this defence and averred that the obligation to build
the house was a collateral one which continued beyond
delivery of the disposition. The seller argued (i) that
the obligation to build the house was not collateral
since the house was virtually complete and therefore
the obligations to build and to convey could not be
separated; (ii) that if there was a collateral obligation,
it related solely to the fitting out work in the kitchen
and bathroom; and (iii) that even if the obligation to
C build the house in accordance with the drawings and
specification was collateral, it was clear from the
missives and, in particular, the inspection of the house
by the purchaser's surveyor, that the parties had
accepted that any obligation in relation to patent
defects would cease at settlement.

Held, (1) that the obligation imposed under the
missives was to give entry to a house which was built
in accordance with the drawings and specification and
that this obligation extended to works carried out both
D before and after conclusion of missives (pp
516G-517C); (2) that an obligation to build or complete a house was collateral to the contract of sale as
it was separate and independent from the normal incidents of conveyancing (p 517F-I); (3) that the conditions in the missives could not be interpreted to
prevent the purchaser claiming damages for defects
which were reasonably discoverable prior to settlement (p 518I-K); and defender's fifth plea in law,
seeking absolvitor on the ground that acceptance of
E the disposition discharged the seller of his obligations
under the missives, *repelled.*

Observed, that a condition in missives to produce
planning permission, building warrants and completion certificates and which warranted that no statutory notices were in existence was not a collateral
obligation and would be superseded by delivery of the
disposition (p 518L).

McKillop v Mutual Securities Ltd, 1945 SLT 198,
F *followed; Winston v Patrick,* 1981 SLT 41, and
Hardwick v Gebbie, 1991 SLT 255, *commented on.*

Action of damages

Dr A G King raised an action of damages against
Mrs Shirley Gebbie in respect of a house which the
pursuer alleged the defender had failed to build
conform to drawings and a specification referred to in
the missives of sale. The first defender averred that
her solicitors, Messrs Peter Anderson & Co, had had

no authority to conclude missives on her behalf and
they were convened into the action as second G
defenders. The pursuer sought the cost of repairing
the alleged defects.

The first defender pleaded inter alia:

(5) Separatim — A disposition of the subjects having
been delivered to and accepted by the pursuer and said
missives having been thereby superseded and discharged, the first defender should be assoilzied.

(6) Separatim — Esto the first defender was in
breach of contract, the pursuer having acquiesced in H
the said breach and having waived any rights arising
therefrom, the defender should be assoilzied.

The case came on procedure roll before the Lord
Ordinary (Caplan) in respect of the relevancy of the
first defender's fifth plea in law.

Cases referred to
Hardwick v Gebbie, 1991 SLT 258.
Hoey v Butler, 1975 SC 87.
Lee v Alexander (1883) 10 R (HL) 91.   I
McKillop v Mutual Securities Ltd, 1945 SLT 198;
   1945 SC 166.
Pena v Ray, 1987 SLT 609.
Taylor v McLeod, 1990 SLT 194.
Winston v Patrick, 1981 SLT 41; 1980 SC 246.

Terms of missives

The formal offer to sell the subjects contained, inter
alia, the following conditions:

"6. It is understood that prior to settlement our J
clients will exhibit the planning permission, building
warrant and completion certificate required in respect
of the erection and completion of the dwellinghouse
hereinafter referred to. It is understood that there are
no notices, orders or the like of the local authority
either current or pending which could affect the continued use of said subjects as a private dwellinghouse.

"7. Prior to settlement our clients will cause to have
completed upon the plot of ground hereinbefore K
referred to a dwellinghouse all in accordance with the
architect's drawings and specification annexed and
signed as relative hereto. Notwithstanding the terms
of said specification it is understood that included in
the purchase price are prime cost sums to the supply
and fitting of sanitary ware and kitchen fixtures and
fittings, namely: (a) £250 for sanitary ware in each
bathroom, (b) £1,250 for kitchen fixtures and fittings,
and, (c) £75 for sanitary ware in the cloakroom. In the
event of your client requesting our client to supply L
sanitary ware or kitchen fixtures or fittings beyond the
value of the foregoing respective sums the additional
cost shall be charged as an extra at settlement together
with such other extra items or workmanship as may be
specified for by your client beyond that set out in the
specification hereinbefore referred to."

On 27 May 1992 the Lord Ordinary *sustained* the
pursuer's first and second pleas in law, *repelled* the
first defender's fifth plea in law, *excluded* from probation the first defender's averments in support of her

A fifth plea in law and quoad ultra *allowed* a proof before answer.

LORD CAPLAN.—By missives entered into on 19 April 1985 between solicitors acting for the pursuer and solicitors purportedly acting for the first defender, the pursuer contracted to purchase from the first defender a dwellinghouse at 5 Wilson Terrace, Troon. At the time the missives were concluded the construction of the said dwellinghouse had not been completed and it was a term of the contract that the first defender
B should complete the house before settlement. In terms of the missives the purchase price to be paid by the pursuer was £67,900. The date of entry was to be 31 May 1985 or such earlier date as may be mutually agreed. At the procedure roll hearing before me I was referred to the terms of the formal offer to sell which was purportedly issued by solicitors on behalf of the first defender. This was in the form of a letter dated 4 April 1985 from Peter Anderson & Co, purportedly acting on behalf of the first defender, to the pursuer's
C solicitors, J M & J H Robertson, and the offer described the subjects to be sold as a plot of ground extending to 29.86 poles or thereby together with "the dwellinghouse erected or to be erected thereon". In the exchange of missives which followed the conditions attached to this offer were qualified but it is accepted that the final missives contained conditions as set out in conditions 6 and 7 of the said letter. These conditions are in the terms following: [his Lordship quoted the terms of the conditions set out supra and
D continued:]

The pursuer's pleadings are not entirely specific as to the date when entry and settlement occurred, but the first defender avers that the transaction was settled on 20 June 1985 when the pursuer paid the purchase price and received a disposition in exchange therefor. I did not understand that fact to be disputed by the pursuer.

The foundation of the pursuer's action is the claim
E that shortly after entry to the subjects the pursuer became aware of fundamental faults in the construction of the dwellinghouse. These alleged faults are specified in art 4 of the condescendence and are eight in number. It is alleged that in respect of these faults the first defender departed from the specification provided for in the missives. Moreover it is said that the quality of workmanship was substantially lower than that which would have been expected from a reasonably competent contractor. It is further averred
F that certain items had been completed to a standard which was below the standard required by the architect's drawings and specification. These items are specified in the said article of condescendence and are seven in number. It should perhaps be noted at this point that the pursuer nowhere avers that the alleged departures from specification and the additional seven deficiencies were latent at the date of settlement.

The pursuer avers that the first defender was in breach of contract in respect of the said 15 matters which he complains of. It is averred that it was an

express term of the missives between the parties that
G the said house should be completed in accordance with the architect's drawings and specifications. It was an implied term of the missives that works necessary to complete said house would be executed with a reasonable degree of care and skill, that the materials would be sound and adequate and that in the result they would be reasonably fit for the purpose for which they were intended. The pursuer further avers that the foregoing terms whether express or implied were intended by the parties to the missives to impose obligations which continued beyond delivery of the
H disposition. The said defects in the building represent a breach of these terms. The pursuer accordingly sues the first defender for damages amounting to £41,605. This is the alleged cost of the remedial work said to be needed to make the house conform to contract.

The first defender claims that the said solicitors Peter Anderson & Co had no authority to complete the alleged missives on her behalf. As a result these solicitors have been brought into the action as second
I defenders. However they were not represented at the procedure roll hearing before me and the disputed question of authority has no bearing on the matters which were argued.

The first defender avers in answer that when missives were concluded the external construction of the house was 90 per cent completed and the whole works required on the house were about 75 per cent completed. It is further averred that the house was inspected by a surveyor on the pursuer's behalf before
J entry and settlement. It is averred that the surveyor "passed it as constructed in accordance with the missives". The first defender has set out in her averments specific answers to each of the 15 complaints of the pursuer and in a number of these answers she avers that the work complained of by the pursuer had been effected prior to the completion of missives. She avers that if she was bound by the missives they had been superseded and discharged by the subsequent delivery of a disposition concerning the subjects. The first
K defender has a general plea to the relevancy of the pursuer's case. Her fifth and sixth pleas in law are in the following terms: [his Lordship quoted the terms of the pleas in law set out supra and continued:]

The pursuer's first and second pleas in law attack the relevancy of the defences.

The first defender is content that her preliminary pleas be reserved for proof before answer and the matter came before me on the procedure roll on the
L pursuer's said preliminary pleas. Senior counsel for the pursuer attacked the first defender's fifth plea in law as irrelevant. He requested that it be repelled at this stage. He also attacked as irrelevant the first defender's averments to the effect that certain of the work complained about had been carried out prior to the conclusion of missives. He wanted these averments excluded from probation. Otherwise he was content that the other issues in the case (including the question of waiver raised by the first defender's sixth plea in law) should proceed to proof before answer.

In supporting his said pleas in law senior counsel for
A the pursuer accepted that the general rule as stated in
Lee v Alexander was that the delivery and acceptance
of a disposition totally superseded earlier communings
between the parties including, in particular, the
missives. However in *Winston v Patrick* the Lord
Justice Clerk had formulated recognised exceptions to
this rule. One of these exceptions was where missives
contained a collateral obligation which was separate
from the obligation to convey heritage. Condition 7 of
the present missives was said to be such a collateral
B obligation involving as it does an obligation to complete a building. Thus it was contended that the
missives in the present case incorporated not only a
contract for the sale of heritage but in addition a
collateral building contract. In this regard the case was
indistinguishable from *McKillop v Mutual Securities
Ltd*, where an agreement in missives to complete a
shop in the course of erection was held to be an obligation collateral to the sale contract which was not discharged by the taking of a formal disposition. The
C contract in the present case is to the effect that the first
defender will complete the dwellinghouse prior to
settlement. Accordingly the first defender has up to
settlement before it can be said that she is in default.
Senior counsel contended that it would be absurd if
the first defender's obligations under the building contract ceased to be enforceable at the very moment of
default. I was referred to *Pena v Ray* and *Taylor v
McLeod*, but senior counsel recognised that these cases
were concerned with special considerations not parti-
D cularly relevant to this case. *Hoey v Butler* was
however a significant case because it decided that
where a pursuer claims implement and damages in
respect of building work to be done before settlement
of a sale transaction and in terms of missives for sale,
the pursuer's remedy was not restricted to rescission
and damages. The basis of the decision in *Hoey* was
that the pursuer's action was not in the nature of an
actio quanti minoris.

E   Senior counsel for the pursuer then referred me to
Hardwick v Gebbie. This was a highly relevant
decision not only because it was very recent but particularly because it involved the same defender as in
the present action and for practical purposes the
missives in *Hardwick* contained contractual terms
identical to those founded on in the present case. In
Hardwick, after the pursuer, who was the purchaser,
had taken entry and paid the purchase price he discovered certain discrepancies between the work
carried out by the defender and the prior specification
F of that work. The pursuer sued for breach of contract
and claimed damages based on the cost of rectifying
the defender's errors and omissions in carrying out the
building work. The seller argued that the fact that the
obligations under the missives were collateral to the
sale did not form an exception to the general rule that
the disposition supersedes the missives where the
claim under the collateral agreement was based on a
building contract which had been breached by building deficiencies which were patent and discoverable at
the time of settlement. The Lord Ordinary (Lord

McCluskey) appeared to hold that on the construction
of the particular contract before him the parties had G
intended that the disposition would supersede the
missives in respect of claims based on defects reasonably discoverable prior to settlement. His Lordship
then proceeds to hold that even if the pursuer had discovered defects prior to settlement, on the basis of
Hoey v Butler, the pursuer could have settled the
transaction and then sued for damages. Therefore his
Lordship concluded that the pursuer was entitled to a
proof before answer despite the fact that he had not
averred that the defects he was founding upon were H
latent as at the time of settlement. Senior counsel for
the pursuer was content enough to found on the
decision in *Hardwick* (which was essentially in support
of his own case). However he found considerable difficulty with the Lord Ordinary's reasoning. He was
unable to reconcile the Lord Ordinary's apparent
finding that the parties intended the disposition to
supersede claims based on discoverable defects with
his decision to apply *Hoey v Butler.* Senior counsel
argued that the Lord Ordinary was in error in holding I
that the disposition was intended to supersede the
missives on the relevant matters, although he accepted
that the Lord Ordinary had otherwise correctly
decided the case. As a second issue senior counsel for
the pursuer asked me to exclude from probation the
references in the answers of the first defender to the
fact that certain of the work claimed by the pursuer to
have been defective had been completed prior to the
conclusion of missives. It was contended that on a
proper construction of condition 7 of the missives the J
first defender had to bring the entire dwellinghouse up
to the proper standard prior to settlement and that the
fact that some defective work may have been
completed before the missives would not affect that
obligation.

   Counsel for the first defender contended that condition 7 of the missives did not constitute obligations
collateral to the contract of sale otherwise contained in
the missives. In any event condition 7 related only to
the carrying out of such work as had not been effected K
as at the date of the missives. In effect the seller had
only undertaken to complete the fitting of the kitchen
and the bathroom. The distinction between an obligation to complete the building and a warranty that the
building sold would be in a particular condition was
artificial. It was not critical to the decision in *Winston
v Patrick* that the clause under consideration did not
require future action on the part of the seller. An obligation to deliver a valid title represents an obligation
to take future action if it is viewed at the time when L
the missives are concluded. The cases of *Hoey v Butler*
and *McKillop v Mutual Securities Ltd* are distinguishable from the present case. In *Hoey* and in *McKillop*
it was envisaged that a substantial period of time
would occur between the missives and settlement.
Major building work had to be completed over that
period. It is clear from the first defender's averments
in the present case that condition 7 was a mere adjunct
to a contract of sale of heritage. Ninety per cent of the
external work on the building had been completed

prior to the missives and 75 per cent of the remaining

A work. Only five weeks were to elapse between the conclusion of the missives and the date for settlement, which shows that the work to be done by the first defender was relatively minor. The house being purchased was substantially completed and the seller's obligation was merely to put it into a particular state before the sale was settled. There was no apportionment of the consideration which was essentially a price for the house. In any event the parties envisaged that all obligations accepted by the seller were to be ful-

B filled prior to settlement. Since any work which had to be performed by the seller related only to the kitchen and bathroom, any collateral obligation undertaken must be restricted to that work only. Under the terms of the missives it was clearly contemplated that any obligations arising under condition 7 would lapse at settlement of the sale. In *Pena v Ray* the Lord Ordinary had indicated that parties could agree in respect of an obligation in missives that it should not endure after the settlement. It was clear from consider-

C ing condition 7 along with condition 6 that this was the parties' understanding in the present case. Before settlement the local authority were expected to have considered the drawings and specifications. They were to certify the building as being complete. The building was in fact to be complete prior to settlement. In any event if any obligations under condition 7 remained after settlement, this could only be in respect of defects which were latent at the time of settlement. Just as counsel for the pursuer had

D experienced difficulty with the Lord Ordinary's reasoning in *Hardwick v Gebbie*, so counsel for the first defender indicated that he could not reconcile Lord McCluskey's view that the disposition superseded cl 7 in respect of discoverable defects with his decision that the pursuer's case should go to proof before answer. Counsel contended that the Lord Ordinary was correct in finding that cl 7 had been superseded but he had erred in holding that nevertheless the pursuer's case may have been relevant. It emerged from the

E terms of cl 6 that the pursuer was expected to discover and complain about any discoverable defects before settlement. The pursuer's case was irrelevant because he had failed to aver that any of the matters complained about were not readily discoverable prior to settlement. The pursuer accepts that his surveyor had been given an opportunity to inspect the property before settlement. Although the first defender had originally been content to offer a proof before answer in fact the pursuer's case ought to be dismissed as

F irrelevant. Otherwise a proof before answer should be allowed, reserving in particular all pleas directed against the relevancy of the first defender's defences.

The pursuer founds his case on such obligations on the seller as can be taken from the terms of condition 7 of the missives. Logically therefore the first question to consider is the extent of the obligation which that condition imposes on the seller. It was maintained on behalf of the first defender that the obligation on the seller is restricted to carrying out the work specified in the architect's drawings and specifications which had

not been effected prior to the missives. Thus it was contended that the seller had no responsibility except G in relation to the limited work which he required to have done on the house. This was essentially work to the bathroom and kitchen (a matter which the first defender was prepared to prove). It was also suggested that if I was not prepared to accept the first defender's construction of the contract at this stage, proof of the facts would assist such construction. I cannot accept any of the contentions for the first defender on these matters. It is beyond question that the pursuer was buying a house which at the time he took it over would H be newly constructed. In the missives the offer made on behalf of the seller describes the property as "erected or to be erected", thus implying that even the seller was not entirely certain of how to describe the state of the works at that point of time. Only five weeks were expected to elapse between the missives and the prescribed time of settlement. It is obvious that the house would first be in a complete state at a point of time very close to settlement. It is, I think, notorious that newly completed building works are I likely to have some defects and most building contracts in fact make provision for this contingency. It is therefore eminently likely that a purchaser acquiring a newly built building would expect to have some recourse if it proved to be the case that the building had not been properly erected. The first defender certainly avers that the pursuer inspected the property before the missives but is not offering to prove that the pursuer sought or had an opportunity to carry out the particular kind of inspection that would be necessary J to decide if works which had been carried out at that date conformed to the drawings and specification. If what the parties intended in their contract was that before transfer of the property to the purchaser, the seller had the responsibility for bringing the house in its entirety up to the standards set out in the drawings and specification then that would be a contract leading to practicable and enforceable obligations. On the other hand if the seller was only taking responsibility for work still to be completed and not for the whole K works, one would have expected in the contract some definition of the incomplete work (or alternatively of the work which had already been completed). Otherwise the purchaser would have difficulty in knowing the precise state of the works at the time when missives were concluded. He might well have practical difficulty in knowing whether a particular defect was due to work which postdated the missives. The missives themselves took some weeks to complete and presumably even during that period work may well L have been proceeding. An obligation to do only some of the work up to the standard specified in the drawings and specification could be impossible to fulfil if the earlier work did not conform to these. For example, it could be difficult to fit a bathroom suite in accordance with drawings if the plumbing had earlier been put in the wrong place. In my view it is obvious that what the purchaser required was that at settlement he should be given entry to a new house that had been built conform to the drawings and specification. That is indeed the plain meaning of con-

dition 7. If the seller was only undertaking to do any
A work not already effected and to carry out such
remaining work in accordance with the drawings and
specification, it would have been easy enough to
express such limited obligation clearly. However what
I find in condition 7 is not that certain work is to be
carried out in accordance with the drawings and
specification, but rather that the dwellinghouse is to
be completed in accordance with these documents.
The fact that the house may have been substantially
completed at the date of the missives may have
B reduced the practical burden of the condition but does
not affect its meaning. Thus, in my view, the seller
undertook in the missives that prior to settlement the
house would be put in the state provided for by the
drawings and specification. This means an express
obligation to ensure that all the work set out in the
relevant documents had been effected and that the
standard of work was in accordance with the specification. As to the implied obligations founded on by the
pursuer, the first defender's counsel did not dispute
C that these would attach to such area of building works
as a seller was held to have assumed responsibility for
so that I need not pronounce particularly on these
matters.

The next question is whether the obligations arising
from condition 7 are discharged by the pursuer having
settled the purchase of the house and if so to what
extent. It is agreed that in fact the pursuer had entered
into the subjects, taken delivery of a disposition and
paid the full price. It is well established law that, in
D general, acceptance by a purchaser of a disposition will
have the effect of preventing recourse to any obligations owed to him under the missives. It should
however be noted that the said general rule was enunciated in cases concerned with attempts to invoke conditions in missives which were naturally incidental to
a contract concerned exclusively with the acquisition
of heritage. This is not surprising since traditionally
missives tended to be limited in scope and the conditions therein confined to matters which were clearly
E elements of the sale transaction, including title and the
definition of the land and rights to be conveyed. The
modern tendency to elaborate the conditions attached
to missives perhaps explains why the application of
the said general rule has recently been the subject of
close scrutiny in a number of cases. Perhaps the most
significant of these cases is *Winston v Patrick* because
the Lord Justice Clerk there clearly articulated the
recognised exceptions to the general rule and these
exceptions included situations where the obligation in
F the missives is collateral rather than intrinsic to the
sale transaction. That conditions in missives of sale
which are collateral to the main contract can survive
the delivery of a disposition is vouched by other
authorities and I think is now well established.

In my view it is now also well vouched that conditions in missives which amount to an obligation to
perform building work are to be regarded as collateral
to the contract of sale itself. This is perhaps again not
surprising. Certain obligations under missives such as
an obligation to exhibit the title, or to exhibit a clear

search, may put the seller under an obligation to do
something in the future but performance is related to G
the normal incidents of conveyancing. An acceptance
of obligations to perform building work takes the
seller beyond the range of obligations normally
associated with a sale transaction itself. Thus the obligations which expressly or impliedly attach to a contract to carry out building work can be regarded as
exclusive to that contract alone. They are separate and
independent obligations. That is not to say that there
will not be an interrelationship between the collateral
building contract and the main provisions of the mis- H
sives. The acceptance of a disposition may be readily
taken to imply that the purchaser is satisfied that all
he has to receive upon the acquisition of the property
is regulated by the disposition. However, the disposition can scarcely be said to bear on whether or not he
is satisfied with building work which may in certain
cases give rise to problems some considerable time
after the conveyancing matters have been settled. I am
unable to find any reason for distinguishing this case
from *McKillop v Mutual Securities Ltd* in respect of the I
point that an obligation to build in missives is
collateral to the contract of sale. As Lord Moncrieff
said at 1945 SC, p 172: "But if in the missives there
be not only an agreement for purchase and sale but be
also, as I have suggested there is here, a second
independent though collateral agreement for the doing
of supplementary work and the doing of that work
skilfully, such an independent agreement will not be
discharged by the taking of a formal disposition,
seeing that the formal disposition does not enter into J
the area of that particular separate agreement."

The first defender argues that even if the disposition
has not superseded the obligations arising under condition 7, the only obligations which survive settlement
are those which raise matters not discoverable before
settlement. It is contended that the pursuer cannot
recover in respect of defects which were patent at the
point of settlement. Certainly were the distinction
made by the first defender a correct one, the pursuer's K
case would be irrelevant because he does not clearly
aver that the defects complained of were not discoverable before settlement was effected. The first defender
founds on observations made by Lord Moncrieff in
McKillop v Mutual Securities Ltd and also by the Lord
Ordinary in *Hardwick v Gebbie*. In *McKillop* Lord
Moncrieff said at pp 173-174: "Now, had the defect
of which the pursuer complains as attaching to the
subjects when they were transferred to her been patent
and open to reasonable discovery upon reasonable
inspection, I should have hesitated to allow the claim L
to go further." As Lord Kincraig observed in *Hoey v
Butler* (at p 91): "It is not easy to determine just
exactly what Lord Moncrieff had in mind when he
contrasted the position in law where the defect was
patent and discoverable on reasonable examination
with that where the defect was latent." In *McKillop*
the pursuer had pleaded her case as being one of latent
defect and specifically expressed her right under the
contract as including "a right to receive the property
free from latent defect of any kind". Thus Lord

A Moncrieff was dealing with a case where the pursuer was basing the case exclusively on latent defect. Moreover the case was one where prima facie the defenders may have had a strong defence based on waiver of the defects had they been patent at settlement. The defenders had indeed pleaded such a defence founding on the fact that the pursuer had occupied the subjects for six years without complaint. Moreover the pursuer had undertaken certain obligations to maintain and repair the subjects which may have led to a ready inference that upon entry the

B pursuer accepted the subjects as being in a certain state of repair. Once it is accepted that a building contract is collateral and independent in respect of the sale provisions of the missives, then as I have indicated the acceptance by the pursuer of a disposition cannot be taken as meaning that the terms of the disposition have superseded those of the missives in respect of building matters. Certainly the purchaser has paid the price. Although in the present missives the price is unallocated, it must be assumed that it contains an

C element as consideration for the building work to be carried out. However in respect of a building contract mere payment of the price would not preclude the employer from suing for damages in respect of a breach of conditions of the contract unless there was either waiver of right or express agreement that payment of the price would discharge the builder from further obligation. I see no reason why the situation should be different when the building contract is incorporated as a collateral agreement in missives of

D sale. Even if defects are discoverable at the time for settlement of the sale the buyer may have sound reason for wanting to settle the transaction and obtain entry to the subjects. He may have sold his previous residence and require to occupy as a residence the property to be purchased. He may not at the point of settlement be able to define exactly the extent of the defects or to quantify his loss. Of course payment of the price without complaint may in certain circumstances amount to a waiver of further claim. The first

E defender has such a case and the pursuer is content to let that go to proof before answer. Even if the first defender should prove to have a sound case based on waiver, the difference between such a case and the position which the first defender maintains in respect of requiring to show latent defect could involve a significant difference in onus.

The first defender sought to make a case that the terms of the missives themselves indicated that the

F seller was to be discharged from any responsibility for patent defects upon settlement of the transaction. He also founded on the reasoning of the Lord Ordinary in *Hardwick v Gebbie* although he resisted his conclusion. I must confess to having a certain difficulty in reconciling all that was said by Lord McCluskey in *Hardwick* although I have no difficulty in agreeing with his conclusions. It may be that his Lordship was saying that prima facie the parties intended in the missives that all claims in respect of patent defects should be made before settlement, but that such could not have been their effective intention because a party is

G entitled to settle the conveyancing transaction and then pursue a claim for damages. It seems to me that there are essentially two separate questions. The first is whether or not the disposition supersedes the purchaser's rights and in the case of collateral building contract conditions such as in this case, the settlement had no effect unless there is waiver or express agreement that the settlement should supersede such obligations. The second question concerns the remedies available to a purchaser should the purchaser have rights that will not be superseded by accepting a disposition and settling the transaction. In my view

H *Hoey v Butler* is a case dealing with the second question, that is to say, the question of remedies open to a purchaser who has continuing rights. Leaving aside the issue of waiver the pursuer in this case could only have his right to found on the building contract superseded by the fact that he has settled the transaction of sale, if there is a clear agreement in the missives that this should be the case. On the other hand if it were the case that the parties had agreed that any claims in respect of discoverable defects would be

I superseded by the settlement of the sale, then the remedies said to be available by the case of *Hoey* would be of no assistance since there would be no effective rights to pursue.

Looking at conditions 6 and 7 of the missives I cannot conclude that the terms of these deprive the purchaser of the right he would otherwise have to settle the sale and then claim for damages for breach of condition 7. In condition 7 there is a stipulation that

J the building is to be completed prior to settlement. However that, in my view, simply gives the purchaser a right to have his building completed before the prescribed settlement date. Thus if the building is not completed by the said date the purchaser could choose to delay settlement of the sale or could settle the sale and claim damages for the consequences of the failure to complete the building. However, the condition does not bear to affect the purchaser's right at any stage to complain about defects. There is no obvious reason

K why it should since it could be very difficult for the purchaser to be completely satisfied about the work until he had unrestricted occupation of the building. Condition 6 refers to the seller's obligation to provide certain statutory certificates including a completion certificate. However, I consider that condition 6 is quite separate from condition 7. It refers to the production of statutory documents and it warrants the absence of statutory impediments to use. Without this condition the purchaser might have his continued

L enjoyment of the property at serious risk. Unlike condition 7 which is collateral to the contract of sale, I consider that condition 6 is an intrinsic and normal element of a sale contract and that it would be superseded by the settlement of the sale. The completion certificate would signify that the local authority was satisfied that the building met all statutory building requirements. It would not signify that the completed building corresponded exactly with the drawings and specification. The employer who contracts for building work is entitled to have the work

A performed to his own satisfaction as well as to the satisfaction of the building authority. The fact that he requires delivery prior to settlement of statutory documents which could be critical to his continued interest in the building, does not imply that he foregoes any right he may have to complain about defects thereafter.

Thus, in my view, the first defender's fifth plea in law is not relevant and falls to be repelled at this stage. Moreover in the light of the view I have taken of the meaning of condition 7 the fact that certain work has

B been carried out prior to the missives is likewise not relevant. Therefore I shall at this stage sustain the pursuer's first and second pleas in law to the effect of repelling the first defender's fifth plea in law and I shall exclude from probation all references in ans 4 to certain work having been carried out prior to completion of the missives. Otherwise I shall meantime reserve the parties' preliminary pleas and allow a proof before answer.

C ———————————

Counsel for Pursuer, Dunlop, QC; Solicitors, Bennett & Robertson — Counsel for First Defender, Abercrombie; Solicitors, Shepherd & Wedderburn, WS (for Graeme McKinstry & Co, Ayr) — No appearance for Second Defenders.

A R W Y

D

House of Fraser plc v Prudential Assurance Co Ltd

OUTER HOUSE

LORD CULLEN

18 JUNE 1992

E *Landlord and tenant — Lease — Full repairing and insuring lease — Liability for repairs — Retaining wall — Whether obligations imposed by terms of lease were wide enough to cover both ordinary and extraordinary repairs — Whether tenants under obligation to reimburse landlords for cost of repairs.*

The pursuers were tenants and the defenders were landlords of office premises forming three floors of a building in Glasgow. The lease bound the landlords

F inter alia to keep in good and substantial repair the foundations, roof, main walls and main structural members, and bound the tenants to reimburse the landlords a proportionate part of "all amounts, costs, sums and expenses of each and every kind whatsoever" reasonably expended by the landlords. A retaining wall pertaining to the premises became in urgent need of repair. The landlords proposed to take down the wall and rebuild it. The tenants sought declarator that in terms of the lease they were not obliged to reimburse the landlords for the cost of that

work. Two questions arose: first, whether the work on the retaining wall fell within the scope of the repairing G obligations imposed on the landlords by the terms of the lease, and secondly, if so, whether the tenants were under any obligation to reimburse the landlords for the cost of the work.

The tenants argued (1) that the work was an extraordinary repair for which there was no provision in the lease, and, further, that the work was work of "renewal" and not "repair" and thus fell outwith its terms; and (2) that since it had been held in previous cases that tenants were not obliged to execute extra- H ordinary repairs to urban property unless this was expressly stipulated in the lease or was a necessary inference from it, it followed that the same should apply to the tenants' obligation as to reimbursement.

The landlords argued (1) that the wording of the provisions which required the landlords to carry out repairs was general and unlimited except with respect to the parts of the building to which they related, and there was no warrant for interpreting them so as to exclude extraordinary repairs; and (2) that the struc- I ture of the lease was such as to show that the landlords' obligation as to the carrying out of repairs was distinct from the tenants' obligation as to the reimbursement of the cost of repairs, and it followed that if the landlords' obligations covered extraordinary repairs the tenants were bound to reimburse the cost of carrying them out.

Held, (1) that the language of the relevant provisions of the lease was wide enough to include both ordinary and extraordinary repairs and reflected the J position at common law, and there was no basis for a necessary inference that the provision extended only to ordinary repairs (p 522C-D); and (2) that the language of the provisions did not warrant the imposition of a restriction on the scope of the tenants' obligations to reimburse the landlords, and accordingly the tenants were obliged to reimburse the cost of the work on the retaining wall (p 522G-I); and action *dismissed*.

Observed, that the Scottish courts had avoided K becoming involved in fine distinctions of language in working out the scope of a stipulation that the tenant of urban property was obliged to keep it in repair. The broad distinction between ordinary and extraordinary repairs had provided a practical and reasonable way of expressing the distinction between the responsibilities of the parties (p 522F-G).

———————————

Action of declarator   L

House of Fraser plc raised a commercial action seeking declarator that, in terms of a lease between themselves as tenants and Prudential Assurance Co Ltd as landlords, they were not obliged to pay the landlords for repairs to a retaining wall which, it was averred, had to be taken down and rebuilt. The defenders pled that the action was irrelevant. The pursuers sought a proof before answer.

The case came before the Lord Ordinary (Cullen) on procedure roll.

Cases referred to

A *Cantors Properties (Scotland) Ltd v Swears & Wells Ltd*, 1980 SLT 165; 1978 SC 310.
Napier v Ferrier (1847) 9 D 1354.
Sharp v Thomson, 1930 SLT 785; 1930 SC 1092.
Turner's Trustees v Steel (1900) 2 F 363.

On 18 June 1992 the Lord Ordinary *sustained* the defenders' plea to the relevancy and *dismissed* the action.

B **LORD CULLEN.**—This commercial cause is concerned with a dispute as to the application of the terms of a lease between the pursuers as tenants and the defenders as landlords of subjects known as Caledonian House, being the office premises on the second, third and fourth floors of 10 Buchanan Street, Glasgow.

The original lease, which was between the defenders and the pursuers' predecessors, House of Fraser Ltd, was dated 25 August and 4 September 1952 and C recorded on 15 July 1976. That lease related to larger subjects. It was varied on a number of occasions in connection with the conversion of part of the original subjects into shop units which were assigned to third parties. For present purposes it is sufficient to refer to the terms of the minute of variation between the defenders and House of Fraser Ltd dated 2 December 1976 and 11 January 1977 and recorded on 10 August 1978 which contains the terms of lease which have applied to the office premises occupied by the pur-D suers at all times relevant to the dispute with which the present action is concerned.

According to the pursuers' averments, "the said premises have a retaining wall on the east facing Morrison's Court. By about 1989 it was in urgent need of rebuilding. Various cracks had appeared. Said wall was heavily perforated with windows, such that for structural purposes it was considered an assemblage of narrow stone piers and lintels rather than a E wall as such. By design, it was a slender, fragile structure with minimal lateral restraint provided by timber floor diaphragms. Since being built, a further storey has been added to said wall. Steel plates, rods and bands have had to be fitted in the past to strengthen it. It was an inherently weak structure." The pursuers also aver that in these circumstances the defenders proposed to take down the wall and rebuild it. The proposed work for this purpose was set up in a bill of approximate quantities prepared principally by Miller F & Co, chartered quantity surveyors, in April 1989. In view of the dangerous state of the wall the pursuers granted vacant possession of certain areas adjacent to the wall but without admission of liability and under reservation of their whole rights and pleas. The pursuers also explain that "the east facing elevation of the wall was dismantled to be totally rebuilt above ground level. Sandstone is being replaced with engineering brick. The said works also involve the application of concrete at basement level of the wall. Ancillary work to north and south facing elevations involves partial rebuilding thereof together with concrete being

pumped into chimney flues and the replacement of a wall plate."   G

The pursuers aver that "the said work as condescended upon amounts to an extraordinary repair, for which there is no provision in the said lease, and accordingly the defenders as landlords rather than the pursuers are liable therefor". In this action the pursuers seek declarator that in terms of the lease they are not obliged to pay the defenders for that work.

The distinction between "ordinary repairs" and "extraordinary repairs" is well established in the law H of Scotland in the context of the interpretation of a stipulation in an urban lease that the tenant should be responsible for carrying out repairs. The decisions in *Napier v Ferrier* and *Turner's Trs v Steel* provide authority for the proposition that, in the absence of express stipulation, or a necessary inference, to the contrary, the tenant is responsible only for "ordinary repairs", whereas the responsibility for carrying out "extraordinary repairs" falls upon the landlord. In *Turner's Trs* Lord Kinnear at p 368 gave the following I examples of cases in which the landlord might be liable: "where the cause of disrepair is an extraordinary accident or a latent defect, or the inevitable deterioration of the structure owing to the long lapse of time".

In the present case the landlords bound themselves by cl fifth to perform certain actions. In terms of the first three subclauses these were: "(1) With all due diligence to keep the foundations, the roof, the main walls, main structural members and the supporting J columns of the building, the Service Yard and the pipes, wires, water, gas, drainage and electricity services in the Common Parts and the Service Yard in good and substantial repair and condition so far as such services are not maintainable by a statutory undertaker but so that this undertaking shall not extend to the repair and maintenance of fascias and shop fronts in the subjects let and the Building;

"(2) To paint with good quality paint or otherwise preserve and clean the outside wood, metal work, K paint work, brick work and stone work of the subjects let and the Building and the Common Parts and all additions thereto and to repair the same as may be necessary but so that the Landlords shall not be liable hereunder for any repairs undertaken to be carried out by the Tenants under the provisions of this Lease nor for the repair and maintenance of the fascias and shop fronts in the subjects let and the Building;

"(3) That the Landlords will use their best L endeavours (subject to the receipt by the Landlords of the Service Charge from the Tenants) throughout the duration of this Lease to provide and carry out or procure the provision and carrying out of the works and services particulars of which are set out in the Second Schedule hereto provided that (without affecting the generality of this subclause) the Landlords shall not be liable for any failure or omission at any time or from time to time during the period of the Lease to provide, supply or procure any or all of the said works and services if it shall be prevented,

A hampered or restricted in any way from so doing by virtue of strikes, lock-outs, non-availability of materials or labour or other services, weather conditions, inevitable accidents, emergency, Act of God or by any cause whatsoever or howsoever arising and not within the control of the Landlords."

It is common ground that the retaining wall is a "main wall" within the meaning of subcl (1), and that it is not one of the "Common Parts" of the building. In para 2 of the second schedule referred to, the particulars of works and services are given as "the repair
B and decoration which the Landlords undertake to effect in the foregoing Lease".

The fourth and final subclause of cl fifth makes provision for insurance by the landlords at full reinstatement costs against certain insured risks and obliges the landlords in the event of destruction or damage rendering the building unfit for occupation or use to rebuild and reinstate so as to restore it to a state equivalent to that at the date of such destruction or
C damage.

Under cl third the tenants bound and obliged themselves inter alia: "(iv) To accept the subjects let in their present condition and throughout the duration of this Lease well and substantially to repair, maintain and clean the subjects let and all additions thereto with all due diligence (but so that the Tenants shall not be liable hereunder for any repairs undertaken to be carried out by the Landlords under the provisions of this Lease) and to keep the same well and substantially
D repaired, maintained and cleaned (damage by any of the insured risks excepted so long as such insurance shall not have been vitiated or payment of the policy monies refused or withheld in whole or in part through any act or default of the Tenants)".

The obligation on the part of the tenants to pay "the Service Charge" is contained in cl second (in the second place) which provides that: "In addition to the rent hereinbefore made payable as a further rent charge (hereinafter called 'the Service Charge') com-
E prising (a) a proportionate part calculated according to the ratio which the floor area of the subjects let bears to the total or combined floor areas from time to time of all the premises in the Building for the time being let or available for letting (but for the purposes of such calculation as aforesaid excluding the Common Parts) of all amounts, costs, sums and expense of each and every kind whatsoever which are from time to time or are at any time hereafter throughout the duration of this Lease reasonably and properly expended,
F incurred or payable by the Landlords computed upon the basis of providing an indemnity to the Landlords in respect of the works and services particulars of which are set out in the Second Schedule hereto but excluding works and services relating to the Shop Facilities and Office Facilities and the windows and window frames of those parts of the Building let or available for letting separately".

The defenders claim that the pursuers are obliged to make payment in respect of the work done to the retaining wall and base that claim upon this provision.

When the case came before me on procedure roll counsel for the defenders sought dismissal of the G action on the basis that, assuming that the work amounted to an extraordinary repair, the pursuers had set forth no relevant answer to their claim for reimbursement. Counsel for the pursuers resisted that submission and submitted that, given that the defenders did not admit that the work amounted to an extraordinary repair, inquiry should be allowed by way of proof before answer.

The discussion before me was concerned essentially with two main questions. The first was whether the H work on the retaining wall fell within the scope of the obligations imposed on the landlords by the terms of cl fifth and the second schedule. It is clear that if it did not do so there could be no question of the tenants being under obligation to reimburse the cost of that work. The second question was whether, in any event, the tenants were under any obligation to reimburse the cost of the work on the retaining wall.

In regard to the first question, the defenders sub- I mitted that the wording of the provisions which obliged the landlords to carry out repairs was general and unlimited except with respect to the parts of the building to which they related. These provisions were what one would expect, being in accordance with the position at common law. There was no warrant for interpreting them so as to exclude "extraordinary repairs". This interpretation was supported (i) by the fact that the repairing obligation was related to parts of the building such as foundations. It was difficult to J see what scope there was for ordinary repairs in the case of such parts; and (ii) by the wide language in which a repairing obligation was initially imposed on the tenants in subcl (iv) of cl third. This included the repair of damage which was substantial enough to have been caused by an insured risk.

In response the pursuers submitted that the provisions of cl fifth and the second schedule did not include extraordinary repairs. This was not required by any express language or necessary implication. The K provisions were consistent with the landlords' obligation in regard to extraordinary repairs resting solely upon the common law. It was suggested that it was possible to conceive of a number of examples of ordinary repairs to parts of the building such as foundations. The terms of cl third were also consistent with this approach. It was further argued that the work on the boundary wall should be regarded as work of "renewal" as opposed to "repair" and on that ground it fell outside the scope of the provisions of cl L fifth and the second schedule. In this connection I was referred to *Sharp v Thomson* and *Cantors Properties (Scotland) Ltd v Swears and Wells Ltd*.

Before turning to the second question I should note that the defenders submitted a subsidiary argument, which was only briefly presented, that assuming that the express language of cl fifth was not such as to impose on the landlords an obligation to effect extraordinary repairs, this was in any event to be implied; and that the terms of the second schedule were such as to be capable of including reference to such an implied obligation.

In regard to the second question the defenders submitted that the structure of the lease was such as to show that the landlords' obligation as to the carrying out of repairs was distinct from the tenants' obligation as to the reimbursement of the cost of repairs. On any view the landlords would require to carry out and in the first instance to defray the cost of carrying out the repairs. The breach of those respective obligations would be distinct and have separate consequences. It followed that if the landlords' obligations covered extraordinary repairs the tenants were bound to reimburse the cost of carrying them out.

In response the tenants submitted that, in view of the fact that it had been held in cases such as *Napier* and *Turner's Trs* that tenants were not obliged to execute extraordinary repairs to urban property unless this was expressly stipulated in the lease or was the necessary inference from it, it followed that the same should apply to the tenants' obligation as to reimbursement. To take the opposite view would involve the tenants in undertaking to indemnify the landlord against latent defects. The liability to reimburse the cost of repair should be looked at from the tenants' point of view. On that approach the tenants were not liable to reimburse the landlords in respect of these extraordinary repairs.

I am satisfied that the language of cl fifth and the second schedule is wide enough to include both ordinary and extraordinary repairs and that there is no basis for a necessary inference that extends only to ordinary repairs. Such a construction of the provisions is in line with the position at common law. Further, it is difficult to see what would be the point of the provisions covering only ordinary repairs, leaving extraordinary repairs to be covered by the common law. This approach to the interpretation of these provisions is supported by the various considerations upon which the defenders relied. I should, however, say that if I had disagreed with the defenders' interpretation of cl fifth and found that the defenders' obligation to carry out extraordinary repairs rested solely upon implication from the lease, I would have found it difficult to reach the conclusion that they were repairs which, in the language of the second schedule, "the Landlords undertake to effect in the foregoing Lease". In the event that point does not arise. I reject the pursuers' argument that the work on the retaining wall fell to be regarded as "renewal" rather than "repair". This argument appeared to me to conflict with their averment, which I have quoted earlier in this opinion, that "the said work as condescended upon amounts to an extraordinary repair". In any event the argument seems to me to run into conflict with the Scottish decisions upon which they relied for the main thrust of their submission. These demonstrate that the Scottish courts have avoided becoming involved in fine distinctions of language in working out the scope of a stipulation that the tenant of urban property is obliged to keep it in repair. Instead the broad distinction between ordinary and extraordinary repairs has

provided a practical and reasonable way of expressing the distinction between the responsibilities of the parties. In these circumstances I am of the opinion that the work on the retaining wall, as averred by the pursuers, fell within the scope of the obligations imposed on the landlords by the terms of the lease.

Turning now to the remaining question and to the pursuers' argument that the distinction drawn in these decisions should be applied to the tenants' obligation to reimburse the cost of repair, I would not deny that at first sight this approach has some attraction. However, I consider that it is unsound. The defenders were, in my view, entirely correct in pointing out the legal and practical distinctions between landlords' obligations to repair and the tenants' obligation to reimburse. The language of the provisions does not warrant the imposition of a restriction on the scope of the obligation to reimburse. In these circumstances I am of opinion that the pursuers are obliged to reimburse the cost of the work on the retaining wall which they themselves aver "amounts to an extraordinary repair".

Accordingly I will sustain the defenders' first plea in law and dismiss the action.

Counsel for Pursuers, Martin, QC, R A Smith; Solicitors, Maclay Murray & Spens — Counsel for Defenders, D R A Emslie, QC, J G Reid; Solicitors, Balfour & Manson, Nightingale & Bell (for Borland Johnston & Orr, Glasgow).

G D M

[A reclaiming motion by the pursuers was due to be heard on 27 and 28 April 1993.]

Deigan v Wilson

HIGH COURT OF JUSTICIARY

LORDS ALLANBRIDGE, CULLEN AND WYLIE

10 JULY 1992

Justiciary — Procedure — Summary procedure — Accused charged with another person, and both appearing at call over at trial diet — Accused subsequently detained on suspicion of interfering with trial witness — Crown moving outwith presence of accused for adjournment of diet to other date — Co-accused present and adhering to not guilty plea — Trial diet adjourned in respect of both accused — Whether adjournment competent — Whether breach of natural justice.

An accused person was charged along with another person on a summary complaint. Both pled not guilty and a trial diet was fixed for 11 June 1992. On that date the case was called over and the accused who was present was represented by a solicitor who intimated a plea of not guilty. The case was then adjourned until later in the day. The accused was thereafter detained under s 2 of the Criminal Justice (Scotland) Act 1980

A on suspicion of an attempt to pervert the course of justice or subornation of perjury. The accused was not granted access to his solicitor. The case later called before the sheriff. The Crown refused to have the accused brought back to court but moved to adjourn the diet to another date because of the allegation in respect of which the accused had been detained. The accused's solicitor objected to the case being heard outwith the presence of the accused. The sheriff adjourned the diet to 2 July 1992 in respect of both accused, the second accused being present and adher-

B ing to his plea previously tendered. The accused sought advocation on the grounds that the adjournment was incompetent since the later calling of the case was the commencement of the trial and therefore required to take place in the presence of the accused and, in any event, was contrary to natural justice.

Held, (1) that the question whether the trial of the accused was commenced could not be affected by what was done in regard to the other accused (p 524I-J); (2) that having regard to the fact that no plea was ten-

C dered or renewed on behalf of the accused who was not present, his trial did not commence on 11 June 1992 and the adjournment was therefore competent (p 524H); (3) that since no material prejudice was or was likely to have been sustained by the accused as a result of the diet being adjourned, the adjournment did not involve any breach of natural justice for which a remedy should be given (p 524K); and bill *refused*.

D **Bill of advocation**

William Deigan presented a bill of advocation praying the High Court of Justiciary to recall an order of Sheriff I C Simpson at Airdrie sheriff court dated 11 June 1992 adjourning the trial diet of the complainer and his co-accused to another date. The facts of the case appear from the opinion of the court.

Cases referred to

E *Aitken v Wood*, 1921 2 SLT 124; 1921 JC 84.
Gardiner v HM Advocate (1976) SCCR Supp 159.

Textbooks referred to

Hume, *Crimes* (3rd ed), ii, 269, 270.
Renton and Brown, *Criminal Procedure* (5th ed), para 14-44.

The bill was argued before the High Court on 1 July 1992.

F On 10 July 1992 the court *refused* to pass the bill.

The following opinion of the court was delivered by Lord Cullen:

OPINION OF THE COURT.—In this bill of advocation the complainer challenges the decision of the sheriff on 11 June 1992 to adjourn the trial of the complainer.

The complainer was charged along with a co-accused on a summary complaint that on 14 December

G 1991 he broke into school premises and there stole certain property. On 27 April 1992 both accused pled not guilty at a pleading diet. An intermediate diet was fixed for 28 May 1992, and a trial diet was fixed for 11 June 1992.

On 11 June 1992 the case was "called over" before the sheriff. The complainer appeared in court and, being represented by a solicitor, intimated a plea of not guilty. The case was continued by the sheriff until later in the day. At that stage the respondent's depute informed the sheriff that he wished to carry out certain

H investigations in the light of information which had come to his attention.

Following the "calling over" of the case the complainer was detained by police officers under s 2 of the Criminal Justice (Scotland) Act 1980. It appears that this was on the basis that there was a suspicion of an attempt to pervert the course of justice or subornation of perjury. The respondent's depute informed the complainer's solicitor that the complainer would not be granted access to his solicitor during his detention,

I with the result that the solicitor was unable to communicate with him. The complainer's detention was instructed by the respondent's depute in the light of information given by a witness who had been cited to the complainer's trial.

While the complainer was still under detention the case was called before the sheriff. The respondent's depute refused to have the complainer brought back to court for this purpose. He moved the sheriff to adjourn the diet to another date because of the allega-

J tion in respect of which the complainer had been detained. The respondent avers that he advised the sheriff that the information which was then in his possession made it impracticable to proceed with the trial of the complainer that day. The complainer's solicitor objected to the matter being dealt with outwith the presence of the complainer, and submitted that the proposed proceedings were incompetent, oppressive and contrary to natural justice. However, the sheriff

K adjourned the diet to 2 July 1992.

The minutes relating to the summary complaint on 11 June 1992 record that the complainer was absent but represented by his solicitor. They then state: "The Court on the motion of the Prosecutor Adjourned the diet to a notional diet of trial in respect that the accused is not available for today's diet until 02nd July 1992 at 10.00 a.m. and Ordained the Accused then to appear."

L The minutes thereunder record that the other accused was present and represented by his solicitor. They then state: "The Accused being asked to confirm the plea previously tendered pled Not Guilty."

Thereafter it is stated in the minutes that: "The Court on the motion of the Prosecutor Adjourned the diet to a notional diet of trial in respect that the first accused is not available for today's diet until 02nd July 1992 at 10.00 a.m. and Ordained the Accused then to appear."

A Counsel who appeared on behalf of the complainer invited this court to pass the bill. He submitted that it was not competent for the sheriff to adjourn the diet. In any event it was contrary to natural justice. He contended that the later calling of the case before the sheriff constituted the commencement of the trial. It was a rule that all proceedings at the trial diet required to take place in the presence of the accused. He referred to the case of *Aitken v Wood*, which related to the taking of evidence in summary proceedings. Counsel contended that the diet fell to be treated as a

B whole, and accordingly that it was not proper for the two accused to be treated separately in regard to that diet. In these circumstances the sheriff should not have entertained the motion of the prosecutor to adjourn the diet. Here the prosecutor had required the case to be called when he knew that he had prevented the complainer from having access to his solicitor, with the result that the solicitor had no means of knowing what was the position of the complainer in regard to an adjournment. If the prosecutor was

C seeking an adjournment he should have had the complainer brought to court; or at any rate enabled him to give instructions to his solicitor. The prosecutor could in any event have deserted the case pro loco et tempore, which did not require the presence of the complainer.

It may be noted at this stage that the basis for the complainer's submissions which we have outlined above differs from that set out in the bill and put before the sheriff by the complainer's solicitor. This

D was that the complainer had "already answered said complaint and intimated a plea of not guilty". This is plainly a reference to the "calling over" of the case earlier in the same day. However, counsel accepted that this "calling over" was not part of the trial of the accused. In accordance with normal practice it was not minuted (cf Renton and Brown's *Criminal Procedure*, para 14-44). Accordingly the complainer's submissions were based exclusively on the events which took place later in the day and to which the minutes relate.

E We should also add that counsel accepted that, even if he was correct in his submissions, it did not follow that, as was sought in the bill, this court should desert the complaint simpliciter. He accepted that, while the instance in the complaint would fall if the adjournment was invalid, it was open as matters stood for the prosecutor to raise a fresh complaint. Accordingly the limited result of his submissions would be that the court would recall the sheriff's order for adjournment of the trial diet.

F For the respondent the advocate depute submitted that while the case had been called later in the day it was clear that no plea had been required to be taken of the complainer. In these circumstances the trial did not commence. It was academic that a plea was taken from the co-accused. In any event the trial against both accused was adjourned to 2 July. Even if what happened constituted the commencement of the trial it was competent to adjourn the trial. Reference was made to a statement in Hume's *Commentaries*, ii, 269 and 270 which was quoted by the court in *Gardiner v*

HM Advocate. In that passage the learned author, after

G discussing the rule that no proceedings can take place in the absence of the accused, states: "On these grounds, the peremptory rule has long been settled, of requiring the personal presence of the pannel in every step, from first to last, of the trial, with the exception only of continuations of the diet." As regards the complaint of breach of natural justice no prejudice to the complainer had been shown.

For the purposes of the present case it is not necessary for us to set out a comprehensive definition of what may constitute the commencement of the trial in

H summary proceedings. It is sufficient for us to state that, having regard to the fact that in this case no plea was tendered or renewed on behalf of the complainer who was not present, his trial did not commence on 11 June 1992. Instead the sheriff on the motion of the prosecutor adjourned the diet to 2 July. From the way in which the minutes are expressed it is clear that what was adjourned was the diet of the trial so far as concerned proceedings against the complainer. The separate treatment of each accused for this purpose

I was competent. On that basis the trial of the complainer did not commence. It may be noted in passing that s 338 of the Criminal Procedure (Scotland) Act 1975 makes express provision in subs (1) (a) for the court adjourning the trial to another diet where the accused in a summary prosecution fails to appear at any diet of which he has received intimation, or to which he has been cited. The question whether the trial of the complainer was commenced could not in

J our view be affected by what was done in regard to the other accused. Accordingly even if it be the case that the trial of the second accused was commenced by his renewing of his plea of not guilty, as to which we express no opinion, this could not and did not effect the commencement of the trial of the complainer. The distinction between the two accused is in any event somewhat academic as the trial was adjourned in respect of both of them until the same date. In these circumstances we are of opinion that the order made by the sheriff was competent. We are not satisfied that

K it involved any breach of natural justice for which a remedy should be given, in respect that we are not satisfied that any material prejudice was, or was likely to have been, sustained by the complainer as a result of the diet being adjourned in the circumstances of the present case.

For these reasons we will refuse to pass the bill.

L
Counsel for Complainer, Baird; Solicitors, Simpson & Marwick, WS — Counsel for Respondent, McFarlane, QC, AD; Solicitor, J D Lowe, Crown Agent.

P W F

Cardle v Murray

A HIGH COURT OF JUSTICIARY

THE LORD JUSTICE GENERAL (HOPE),
LORDS ALLANBRIDGE AND COWIE

11 DECEMBER 1992

Justiciary — Statutory offence — Resisting police in execution of duty — Police restraining accused by placing hand on accused's arm to stop him moving away, in order to warn accused about conduct — Accused "break-
B *dancing" in busy street — Accused struggling, shouting and swearing when police restraining him — Whether restraint lawful — Whether accused entitled to resist — Police (Scotland) Act 1967 (c 77), s 41 (1) (a).*

An accused person was charged with breach of the peace and resisting the police in the execution of their duty, contrary to s 41 (1) (a) of the Police (Scotland) Act 1967. The evidence disclosed that the accused was engaged in "breakdancing" in a busy shopping
C precinct, and accidentally bumped into an elderly lady, nearly knocking her down. A police officer walked towards the accused in order to warn him about his conduct. The accused continued to break-dance and backed away from the officer as he approached. At that point the officer took hold of the accused's arm and said "Excuse me". The accused swore at the officer and continued to dance away so that the officer could not speak to him. The officer kept hold of the accused's arm and tried to calm him
D down but the accused shouted and tried to draw away, whereupon he was arrested for committing a breach of the peace. The accused continued to resist the police as he was handcuffed and walked to the police car, in the police car and at the police station. The sheriff sustained a submission that the accused had no case to answer and acquitted the accused on the ground that at the initial stage the accused was restrained unlawfully and he was accordingly entitled to use reasonable force to resist. The Crown appealed.

E **Held,** that as there was no justification for the officer to take hold of the accused which was an attempt to restrain or detain him unlawfully against his will, the accused was not committing an offence when he continued to protest and struggle (p 527F-G and H-I); and Crown appeal *refused.*

Summary complaint

F Brendan Francis Murray was charged at the instance of James Cardle, procurator fiscal, Dumbarton on a summary complaint which contained the following charges: "(1) on 30 September 1991, in Main Street, Milngavie, you did conduct yourself in a disorderly manner, shout, swear and commit a breach of the peace; (2) on date and place above libelled you did resist Frank Anderson and Neil Stewart, Constables, Strathclyde Police, in the execution of their duty and did struggle violently: contrary to the Police (Scotland) Act 1967, s 41 (1) (a); and (3) on date above libelled in Milngavie police office, Main Street,

Milngavie, you did conduct yourself in a disorderly manner and commit a breach of the peace".   G

The accused pled not guilty and proceeded to trial in the sheriff court at Dumbarton before Temporary Sheriff R M Webster.

At the close of the Crown case the sheriff sustained a submission that the accused had no case to answer and acquitted the accused. The Crown appealed by way of stated case to the High Court against the decision of the sheriff. The facts of the case are set forth in the opinion of the court.   H

Cases referred to
Ingram v Cuthbertson, High Court of Justiciary, 2 July 1991, unreported (1992 GWD 26-1488).
McFarlane v Valentine, High Court of Justiciary, 20 November 1990, unreported (1991 GWD 7-379).
Swankie v Milne, 1973 SLT (Notes) 28; 1973 JC 1.
Twycross v Farrell, 1973 SLT (Notes) 85.

Appeal   I
The sheriff posed the following questions for the opinion of the High Court:

(1) On the evidence, was I entitled to hold that the respondent had been unlawfully restrained, arrested or detained?

(2) On the evidence, was I entitled to hold that the respondent's conduct did not constitute any of the offences libelled in charges 1, 2 or 3?

(3) Was I correct in holding that the respondent had J no case to answer on charge 1?

(4) Was I correct in holding that the respondent had no case to answer on charge 2?

(5) Was I correct in holding that the respondent had no case to answer on charge 3?

The appeal was argued on 2 December 1992.

On 11 December 1992 the court *answered* all the K questions in the *affirmative* and *refused* the appeal.

The following opinion of the court was delivered by the Lord Justice General (Hope):

OPINION OF THE COURT.—The respondent was charged on summary complaint in the sheriff court at Dumbarton with committing a breach of the peace in Main Street, Milngavie; with resisting two police officers in the execution of their duty there, L contrary to s 41 (1) (a) of the Police (Scotland) Act 1967, and with committing a further breach of the peace in Milngavie police station. He pled not guilty and went to trial. Evidence was led from four police officers in support of the Crown case. A motion was then made on the respondent's behalf under s 345A of the Criminal Procedure (Scotland) Act 1975 that there was no case to answer on any of the charges in the complaint. The sheriff upheld this submission, and he acquitted the respondent on all charges. It is against that decision that the appellant has now appealed, on the ground that the sheriff erred in law in holding that the respondent's conduct did not constitute the offences libelled in the complaint.

The whole matter turns on the evidence about what occurred at the outset of this incident. The respondent first came to the notice of two police officers who were on uniformed patrol in a police car in Milngavie. They were passing the shopping precinct in Main Street at about 2.45 pm. It was the afternoon of a public holiday and there were many people shopping in the street. The police officers saw the respondent break-dancing in among the shoppers and dancing into a shop. They returned about five minutes later to see him come out of the shop, still breakdancing. They saw him accidentally knock into an elderly lady, nearly knocking her down. At this point they decided to stop, and one of the police officers got out of the police car and went over to speak to the respondent about his conduct. Breakdancing is a particularly energetic and individualistic type of street dancing. In the course of it the dancer constantly moves his arms around and dances backwards and forwards and from side to side. The movement is such that he cannot always see where he is going. No doubt the police officer was concerned that he might knock into someone else if he continued to breakdance among the shoppers in the street. But he had not received any complaints from anybody about the respondent's conduct when he went over to speak to him. The respondent had not been shouting or swearing up to that point, and he had not been committing a criminal offence.

The police officer walked towards the respondent, intending to warn him about his conduct. The respondent continued to breakdance, backing away from the police officer as he approached. It was at this point that the police officer took hold of the respondent's right arm and said "Excuse me". The respondent's reaction to being touched in this manner was to say "Fuck off, get your hands off me you prick". He kept going backwards all the time so that the police officer could not speak to him. The police officer kept hold of his arm and told him to calm down. The respondent shouted and tried to draw away again with the police officer still holding onto him. He was then arrested for committing a breach of the peace. The police officer explained in his evidence that the only reason why he arrested the respondent was because of his conduct in shouting and swearing at him, and not because he had been breakdancing. The respondent continued despite this arrest to try to breakdance, and he struggled, shouted and swore at the police officers as he was handcuffed and walked to the police car. He resisted being put into the police car and struggled when he was in the car. He continued to shout and struggle, although still in handcuffs, when he was in the police station.

There was ample evidence that the respondent behaved in a disorderly manner and shouted and swore both in Main Street and in the police station, and that he resisted the police officers by struggling with them when he was being arrested. But the ques-

tion is whether, before any of the alleged offences had been committed, he was unlawfully detained by the police officer who first went over to speak to him. There is no dispute that if this was the position the respondent was entitled to resist him as he did. As Lord Cameron pointed out in *Swankie v Milne*, 1973 SLT (Notes) at p 29, an arrest is something which in law differs from a detention by the police at their invitation or suggestion: "In the latter case a person detained or invited to accompany police officers is, at that stage, under no legal compulsion to accept the detention or invitation. It may well be that in a particular case refusal to comply could lead to formal arrest, but until that stage is reached there is theoretical freedom to exercise a right to refuse to accept detention at the hands of police officers who are not armed with a warrant. I think it is important always to keep clear the distinction between arrest, which is a legal act taken by officers of the law duly authorised to do so and while acting in the course of their duty, carrying with it certain important legal consequences, and the mere detention of a person by a police officer".

These comments must of course now be read subject to the point that, under s 2 (1) of the Criminal Justice (Scotland) Act 1980, a constable who has reasonable grounds for suspecting that a person has committed or is committing an offence punishable by imprisonment may detain that person for the purposes which that subsection describes. But the principle remains that a person has the right to refuse to accept detention at the hands of a police officer unless the officer is armed with a warrant or is exercising a statutory right to detain him upon suspicion that he has committed or is committing an offence.

In *Twycross v Farrell* the appellant was asked by a police constable what he was doing and asked for his name and address. When he made no answer, swore at the constable and started to run away the constable seized hold of him, whereupon the appellant struggled and shouted and was only with difficulty detained until further police constables arrived. His conviction of resisting, obstructing, molesting and hindering the constable in the execution of his duty and of attempting to resist arrest was quashed on appeal. The report of the case does not set out the terms of the opinion which was delivered, but it is stated in it that in allowing the appeal and quashing the conviction the court indicated that, since there were no findings in the case to support the existence of a reasonable belief by the constable that the appellant had committed an offence, the constable had no right to attempt to stop the appellant from moving smartly away from the spot and that the appellant, having been so stopped, was entitled to struggle as he did.

The sheriff took the view, on a consideration of these and other authorities, that at the initial stage of the incident the respondent was restrained or detained or arrested unlawfully by the police officer. In his view it did not matter what label was given to the restraint because no form of restraint was justified. It

followed that the police officers, when restraining the
A respondent, were not in the execution of their lawful
duty, and their actions continued to be unlawful until
he was released. And the respondent was entitled to
use reasonable force to resist his detention. Any action
by him within these limits which was directly referable to his unlawful detention was not an offence.

The advocate depute submitted that the police constable had seen circumstances which would have justified the making of a complaint, since the respondent
was behaving irresponsibly by breakdancing among
B the shoppers in the street. She accepted that no formal
complaint had yet been made, and that the police constable was not attempting to arrest the respondent or
to detain him in terms of the statute. Nevertheless the
sheriff ought to have held in all the circumstances,
looked at objectively, that the constable's actions in
laying his hand on the respondent to restrain him were
lawful. He was justified in taking the action which he
did, so that he could talk to the respondent about his
conduct. He was simply trying to settle him down so
C that he could speak to him, which was reasonable since
the respondent was continuing to breakdance all the
time and to move away. In support of her argument
she referred to *McFarlane v Valentine*, in which the
appellant appealed unsuccessfully against his conviction for breach of the peace. He was convicted of
shouting and swearing in a public place when he was
spoken to by police officers who asked for his name,
and he continued to do so when he was warned by
them that he might be taken to the police station. But
D there was no suggestion in that case that the police
officers laid their hands on him or attempted to restrain him by any other means before he had committed
the breach of the peace. She referred also to *Ingram v
Cuthbertson* where, on being asked to move on by the
police, the respondent shouted and swore at them and
was then arrested for committing a breach of the
peace. He was acquitted by the sheriff of that charge
and of resisting arrest, but on the latter point the
sheriff's decision was reversed on appeal. That case
E also is of no assistance here, because there was no
attempt by the police to restrain the appellant until
after he had begun to shout and swear at them in a
manner which, in their opinion, amounted to a breach
of the peace.

In the present case, as counsel for the respondent
emphasised in the course of his argument, the police
constable's action in laying his hand on the respondent
was not preceded by any complaint by anybody or by
any conduct which, in the view of the police officer,
F gave reasonable grounds for his suspecting that the
respondent was committing or had committed an
offence. There is no doubt either that his purpose in
laying his hand on the respondent was to restrain or
to detain him, even although this was, initially at least,
for the purpose only of speaking to him to warn him
about his conduct. We agree with the sheriff that the
respondent was entitled to protest at this action and to
back away from the police constable, who had no right
to stop him from continuing to move away. The police
constable's action in holding on to him at this point

was clearly unlawful, and the respondent cannot be
said to have been committing an offence when he con-   G
tinued to protest and struggle as he did. It follows that
his actions thereafter, as he was being taken under
arrest to the police car and from the car into the police
station, must be seen also as lawful conduct on his part
in his attempts to resist the unlawful actions by the
police.

We have some sympathy with the police constable,
who was sufficiently concerned at what he saw to
think it right to go over to the respondent to warn him
about his conduct in breakdancing in this busy street.   H
There was no doubt a risk that as he moved among the
shoppers in this way he would knock into other
people, as he had just done when he knocked accidentally into the elderly lady as he was being watched
by the police. A caution about the risk to others and
the need to take care would not have been unreasonable. There was however no justification at that stage
for the police constable to take hold of the respondent
which, in the circumstances, could not have been seen
as anything other than an attempt to restrain or detain   I
him unlawfully against his will. It is on this short
point that the case depends, and we consider that the
sheriff was right to conclude that the respondent had
no case to answer on any of the charges in the complaint, which were the result of his attempts to resist
the actions of the police constable.

Accordingly we shall answer all five questions in the
case in the affirmative and refuse the appeal.

——————————   J

*Counsel for Appellant, Jarvie, AD; Solicitor, J D
Lowe, Crown Agent — Counsel for Respondent,
McBride; Solicitors, Drummond Miller, WS (for
Fitzpatrick & Co, Glasgow).*

P W F

K

Fraser v Mirza

HOUSE OF LORDS

LORD KEITH OF KINKEL, LORD GOFF OF
CHIEVELEY, LORD JAUNCEY OF
TULLICHETTLE, LORD SLYNN OF HADLEY   L
AND LORD WOOLF

25 FEBRUARY 1993

*Reparation — Defamation — Qualified privilege —
Malice — False complaints against police officer —
Whether malice demonstrated by known falsity of allega-
tions made.*

A police officer claimed damages for defamation in
respect of allegations contained in a letter written to
his chief constable, the author of which had been

A charged by the officer with the reset of two television sets. The defamatory allegations were that threats had been made by the officer and his colleague in the course of their investigation of the charges against the complainant. The charges had later been found not proven in a sheriff court prosecution. There was a further allegation that the two policemen "were not after the case (justice) but they were after my name, Job, My Colour and Justice of the Peace", the complainant having been a justice of the peace and in employment. At proof the pursuer accepted that the

B occasion was covered by qualified privilege and that he required to prove malice. The defender stated in evidence that he had intended in the sentence quoted to convey that the police officers had had no evidence to justify the charges against him. The Lord Ordinary accepted that the words used could fairly be construed in that way and that malice was established by the fact that the defender must have known this to be untrue, and awarded damages assessed at £5,000. The defender reclaimed, contending that the words used in

C the letter were not capable of being construed as having the defamatory meaning ascribed to them by the pursuer. The Second Division allowed the reclaiming motion on the basis (1) that the quoted sentence in the complainant's letter implied that the charges against him would not have been made if he had not been of Asian origin and a justice of the peace, but did not carry the further implication that the police officer had no evidence justifying the charges, that the Lord Ordinary had therefore been wrong in

D holding that the letter carried such an implication, that although the letter was defamatory in alleging that the officer had been actuated by racial and other prejudice, that was not his real complaint, which was that the complainant had alleged that he had had no reasonable grounds for charging him, and that since the terms of the letter did not support that innuendo, that was the end of the case; and (2) that although the Lord Ordinary's finding that a factual statement in the letter was knowingly untrue entitled him to hold that

E the statement was made maliciously, the statement did not have a defamatory meaning, because it did not support the innuendo that the police officer had no reasonable grounds for charging the complainant, and that although the quoted sentence contained a defamatory allegation of prejudice it had not been established in the evidence that the complainant knew that allegation to be untrue, so that in relation to that particular allegation there was no evidence of malice. The police officer appealed to the House of Lords.

F **Held,** that absence of belief in the truth of a defamatory allegation actually conveyed was usually conclusive evidence of improper motive amounting to express malice, and that there was no valid reason for not holding that the same inference was necessarily to be drawn where the maker of the communication was proved to have intended by it to convey a defamatory allegation in the truth of which he did not believe, but which on a proper construction of the communication it was found not to bear: in each case a similar light was shed on the state of mind of the maker of the com-

G munication, and if then the communication was found to bear some untrue defamatory allegation, albeit not as serious as the maker of it intended, the qualified privilege was lost, because the occasion giving rise to it had been misused (pp 531L-532B); and appeal *allowed* and interlocutor of the Lord Ordinary *restored*.

Observed, that the Lord Ordinary, having had the considerable advantage of having seen and heard the complainant in the witness box, was well entitled to make the finding that the complainant had no honest belief even in the allegation that the police officer was actuated by prejudice (p 532B-D).

H

Action of damages
(Reported 1991 SLT 784 and 1992 SLT 740)

Leslie Fraser, a detective constable with Strathclyde Police, raised an action of damages for defamation against Mohammed Mirza, who had submitted a written complaint about Fraser and a colleague to the chief constable.

I

The case came to proof before answer before the Lord Ordinary (Marnoch).

Case referred to
Horrocks v Lowe [1975] AC 135; [1974] 2 WLR 282; [1974] 1 All ER 662.

Terms of letter
The letter dated 20 January 1986 from the defender J to the Chief Constable of Strathclyde Police Force was in the following terms:

"Dear Sir,

"I want to draw your kind attention regarding my case which I was charged on 5th Jan 1984 for reset of Televisions by D.C. FRASER and other D.C.

"I appreciate that they did their duty and try to bring the case for justice.

"But in my case D.C. Fraser and other D.C. accompanied by him did exceed their power. Authority and exaggerated my case.

K

"(1) When I was charged and taken to Pollok Police Station, I requested to both Detectives that I want to give my statement in writting but refused.

"(2) Televisions in my possession were given with out hesitation. After handing over the Televisions I was kept in police cell about 4 Hours.

"(3) They phoned to my employer same day that I was charged for reset.

L

"(4) They went to my Assistant Miss Ellen O'Connors, 535 Eglinton Street at present address 9 MYRTL PL Glasgow GS12, house and told her and mother that Mr Mirza is not coming back. She should find another job.

"(5) They went to Shaukat Hussian House and threaten him and told him you are telling lies. Even his wife was threatened while he was away to Pakistan.

A "(6) D.C. Fraser also told me that Daily Record Reporter is asking this case.

"D.C. FRASER & other D.C. were not after the case (justice) but they were after my name, Job, My Colour and Justice of the Peace.

"May please be investigated this case as I am providing names and Addresses of those person who can give you all information in detail.

(1) MR SHAUKAT HUSSIAN 664 Eglinton Street G5

B (2) MR MASOOD AKHTAR, 6 Roukenburn Street g46

(3) MISS FLORA BALLANTYNE 6 Roukenburn Street G/L

(4) Mr Masood may provide the Samee's Address.

"Above mentioned name were threatened by D.C. FRASER

"Thanking you

Yours sincerely

C   M.H. Mirza"

On 21 August 1990 the Lord Ordinary *found* that the defamatory statements had been made maliciously by the defender and *awarded* the pursuer £5,000 in damages. (Reported 1991 SLT 784.)

The defender reclaimed.

Reclaiming motion

D The reclaiming motion was heard before the Second Division on 5, 6, 7, 8, 12 and 13 November 1991.

On 27 December 1991 the court *allowed* the reclaiming motion, *recalled* the interlocutor of the Lord Ordinary and *granted* decree of absolvitor in favour of the defender. (Reported 1992 SLT 740.)

The pursuer appealed to the House of Lords.

E **Appeal**

The appeal was heard before Lord Keith of Kinkel, Lord Goff of Chieveley, Lord Jauncey of Tullichettle, Lord Slynn of Hadley and Lord Woolf on 25 and 26 January 1993.

On 25 February 1993 the House *allowed* the appeal and *restored* the interlocutor of the Lord Ordinary.

LORD KEITH OF KINKEL.—This is an action of

F damages for defamation at the instance of a police officer in the Strathclyde police force against an individual who had written a letter to the chief constable complaining of his conduct.

The facts are that on 5 January 1984 the pursuer, the appellant in this House, arrested the defender and charged him with the reset of two television sets. The defender was later prosecuted by the procurator fiscal in Glasgow sheriff court. On 20 June 1985 the sheriff found the charges not proven. On 20 January 1986 the defender, who is a prominent member of the Pakistani community in Glasgow and a justice of the peace, sent

G to the chief constable of Strathclyde a letter in these terms: [his Lordship quoted the terms of the letter and continued:]

The sentence which follows the numbered para (6) may conveniently be referred to as the "justice" sentence. On 1 May 1986 the appellant's solicitor wrote to the respondent intimating a claim for defamation, in particular in respect of the "complaint that Mr Fraser acted in this manner because of racial prejudice and because of your position as Justice of the Peace". On

H 9 May 1986 the respondent's solicitor replied that he had no intention of withdrawing the complaint. On 23 May 1986 the chief constable intimated that no action would be taken on the complaint.

The appellant raised the present action on 19 January 1989, claiming damages of £5,000 as reparation for defamation. In cond 4 of the summons the appellant averred inter alia that in the letter complained of the defender alleged that the pursuer "only charged the defender with said criminal offences

I because the defender was of Asian origin and a justice of the peace". The respondent did not plead veritas but he claimed qualified privilege. However, the appellant averred in cond 5 that the defender made the allegations maliciously. A proof took place before Lord Marnoch. Counsel for the appellant at first argued that the occasion was not privileged but eventually conceded that it was. Since the respondent did not dispute that the letter was defamatory the only issue came to be whether the plea of qualified privilege

J was defeated by express malice. The Lord Ordinary held that it was, and he awarded damages of £5,000, the sum sued for. On all important disputed issues of fact (and many unimportant ones) the Lord Ordinary preferred the evidence for the appellant to that of the respondent. Indeed he gave the respondent a broad certificate of no credibility. He found the following significant facts to be proved: (i) that the statement in para (2) of the respondent's letter, that he had given up the television sets without hesitation, was untrue;

K (ii) that the allegation in para (5) of the letter, that the appellant had threatened Shaukat Hussain, was untrue; (iii) that the respondent's intention in making the statement that "D.C. Fraser and other D.C. were not after the case (justice) but they were after my name, Job, My Colour and Justice of the Peace" was to convey the meaning that the appellant and the other police officers had had no evidence of any kind justifying the charges laid against him; and (iv) that the

L respondent knew at the time when he wrote the letter that it was not true that the appellant and other police officer had no such evidence.

The finding (iii) arose out of certain passages in the evidence of the respondent. In the course of examination in chief he was asked, "Are you suggesting in any way that the police officers did not have any kind of evidence to bring any kind of prosecution against you?" It is clear that counsel was expecting a negative answer to this question and indeed counsel for the appellant objected to the question as leading. How-

ever, the Lord Ordinary allowed the question, and no
A   doubt to everyone's surprise, the respondent answered
it "yes". Then in the cross examination of the respondent there is this passage:

Q. So for the rest of my cross examination can I
proceed upon the basis that having sat through the
criminal trial and having sat throughout the evidence
in this proof, you still have the belief that there was
no evidence against you recovered by the police
officers in the course of their investigation? — Yes,
still I feel that.

B
Q. Does that not mean that in making these allegations against Constable Fraser and his colleague, you
were alleging that in the absence of any evidence they
were after your case merely because you were called
'Mr Mirza' and you were a Post Office employee, you
were of a certain colour and you were a justice of the
peace? — Yes.

Q. That is what you claim to believe? — That's
right.

C
The Lord Ordinary did not accept that the respondent had an honest belief in the truth of what he
intended to convey. This was largely based on his
finding about the untruth of the statement that the
respondent had given up the two television sets
without hesitation. The Lord Ordinary's examination
of the evidence showed that this was very far from
being the case, so that the statement must have been
deliberately untrue. Clearly the circumstances under
which the television sets were eventually recovered
D   were extremely significant from the point of view of
whether there was evidence upon which the respondent might properly be charged with reset, and the
Lord Ordinary regarded this false statement as in itself
intended to convey that the appellant had no reasonable grounds for charging the respondent. Its deliberate falsity indicated that the respondent had no honest
belief in the truth of that allegation. So the Lord
Ordinary held that the plea of qualified privilege was
rebutted by proof of express malice, established by
E   evidence that the respondent had intended to tell
deliberate untruths. Counsel for the respondent
argued that his intention was irrelevant; what
mattered was the meaning of the defamatory statements objectively construed according to the natural
and ordinary meaning of words, that being so construed the "justice" sentence of the letter meant not
that the appellant had no evidence upon which he
might properly charge the respondent with reset but
merely that in doing so he was actuated to some extent
F   by racial prejudice and the fact of the respondent
being a justice of the peace, and further that the
respondent honestly believed that to be so. The Lord
Ordinary, however, held that even reading the sentence in that limited sense the respondent had no
honest belief in its truth.

The respondent reclaimed, and the reclaiming
motion was heard by the Second Division of the Inner
House (Lord Justice Clerk (Ross), Lord Murray
and Lord Milligan), who on 27 December 1991
allowed it and recalled the interlocutors of the Lord

Ordinary. The appellant now appeals to your Lordships' House.   G

The opinion of the Lord Justice Clerk stated two
separate grounds for finding in the respondent's
favour. His reasoning on the first ground proceeded
on these lines: the "justice" sentence in the respondent's letter implied that the charges against him
would not have been made if the respondent had not
been of Asian origin and a justice of the peace, but did
not carry the further implication that the appellant
had no evidence justifying the charges; the Lord
Ordinary was therefore wrong in holding that the   H
letter carried such an implication, and in any event it
had not been pleaded by the appellant; that although
the letter was defamatory in alleging that the appellant
had been actuated by racial and other prejudice, that
was not the appellant's real complaint, which was that
the respondent had alleged that he had had no reasonable grounds for charging the respondent; and that
since the terms of the letter did not support any such
innuendo, that was the end of the case. In my opinion
that ground for the decision is quite unsupportable.   I
The appellant was complaining about the allegation
of prejudice, whether or not he was also complaining about an allegation that he had charged the respondent without any evidence to warrant it. He was
also complaining about the allegation of threats to
witnesses.

The second ground for the Lord Justice Clerk's
decision was that although the Lord Ordinary's
finding that the respondent's statement in the letter   J
about giving up the television sets was knowingly
untrue entitled him to hold that that statement was
made maliciously, the statement did not have a
defamatory meaning, because it did not support the
innuendo that the appellant had no reasonable
grounds for charging the respondent; and that
although the "justice" sentence contained a defamatory allegation of prejudice it was not established in
the evidence that the respondent knew that allegation
to be untrue; so in relation to that particular allegation K
there was no evidence of malice. Both Lord Murray
and Lord Milligan agreed with the Lord Justice Clerk
that the restricted meaning of the "justice" sentence
in the letter was the correct one, and that in relation
to the conveying of that meaning malice had not been
proved.

In his submission to the Appellate Committee
counsel for the appellant accepted that the "justice"
sentence in the letter bore the restricted meaning
found by the Inner House. He argued, however, that   L
while an allegedly defamatory statement falls to be
construed objectively by reference to the ordinary and
natural meaning of words, the question whether it was
made maliciously depends upon the ascertainment of
the subjective state of mind of the maker of the statement at the time it was made. The question was
whether the respondent wrote what he did to the chief
constable in pursuance of a duty or to protect a legitimate interest, or from a desire to injure the appellant.
The circumstance that the respondent told at least one

A untruth in the letter (about giving up the television sets without hesitation) and that he intended to tell another which he knew to be untrue (namely that the appellant had no evidence to warrant charging him), indicated that he was not acting in pursuance of a duty or to protect an interest but out of desire to injure the appellant. Malice on his part had thus been established, and it was not relevant that the defamatory allegation which he actually conveyed was less serious than that which he had intended to convey. The judges of the Second Division had fallen into error in

B holding it necessary for the appellant to prove malice specifically related to the defamatory meaning actually conveyed. It was further argued that in any event the Lord Ordinary had found that the respondent had no honest belief even in the truth of the defamatory allegation borne by the "justice" sentence on the restricted interpretation of it, a point apparently overlooked in the Inner House. Finally, it was argued that the Lord Ordinary's finding that the allegation that the appellant had threatened witnesses was "simply

C untrue" amounted to a finding that the respondent had acted maliciously in making that allegation. This point also was not addressed by the Second Division.

In *Horrocks v Lowe* [1975] AC at pp 149-150, Lord Diplock said:

"My Lords, as a general rule English law gives effect to the ninth commandment that a man shall not speak evil falsely of his neighbour. It supplies a temporal sanction: if he cannot prove that defamatory matter which he published was true, he is liable in

D damages to whomever he has defamed, except where the publication is oral only, causes no damage and falls outside the categories of slander actionable per se. The public interest that the law should provide an effective means whereby a man can vindicate his reputation against calumny has nevertheless to be accommodated to the competing public interest in permitting men to communicate frankly and freely with one another about matters in respect of which the law recognises that they have a duty to perform or an interest to

E protect in doing so. What is published in good faith on matters of these kinds is published on a privileged occasion. It is not actionable even though it be defamatory and turns out to be untrue. With some exceptions which are irrelevant to the instant appeal, the privilege is not absolute but qualified. It is lost if the occasion which gives rise to it is misused. For in all cases of qualified privilege there is some special reason of public policy why the law accords immunity from suit — the existence of some public or private duty,

F whether legal or moral, on the part of the maker of the defamatory statement which justifies his communicating it or of some interest of his own which he is entitled to protect by doing so. If he uses the occasion for some other reason he loses the protection of the privilege.

"So, the motive with which the defendant on a privileged occasion made a statement defamatory of the plaintiff becomes crucial. The protection might, however, be illusory if the onus lay on him to prove that he was actuated solely by a sense of the relevant

duty or a desire to protect the relevant interest. So he is entitled to be protected by the privilege unless some

G other dominant and improper motive on his part is proved. 'Express malice' is the term of art descriptive of such a motive. Broadly speaking, it means malice in the popular sense of a desire to injure the person who is defamed and this is generally the motive which the plaintiff sets out to prove. But to destroy the privilege the desire to injure must be the dominant motive for the defamatory publication; knowledge that it will have that effect is not enough if the defendant is nevertheless acting in accordance with a sense of duty or in

H bona fide protection of his own legitimate interests.

"The motive with which a person published defamatory matter can only be inferred from what he did or said or knew. If it be proved that he did not believe that what he published was true this is generally conclusive evidence of express malice, for no sense of duty or desire to protect his own legitimate interests can justify a man in telling deliberate and injurious falsehoods about another, save in the exceptional case

I where a person may be under a duty to pass on, without endorsing, defamatory reports made by some other person."

The occasion upon which the respondent wrote his letter to the chief constable was that of a citizen making a complaint about the conduct of a police officer. If the citizen has grounds for making such a complaint he has a duty, which can properly be described as a public duty, to make these grounds known to the appropriate authority. So the occasion

J here was a privileged one, and the appellant accepts that. The question is whether the respondent, to use Lord Diplock's words, "misused" the occasion. It was for the appellant to prove that he did so. Such proof involved that it should be established that the respondent was actuated by some improper motive which was dominant in his mind. That is what is meant by express malice. The motive with which a person made a defamatory communication can only be ascertained from an examination of his state of mind at the time

K he made it, which as Lord Diplock said, can only be inferred from what he did or said or knew. In this case the respondent knew that he did not give up the television sets without hesitation, but he wrote that he did. It is an unusual feature of the case that according to his own evidence the respondent intended by his letter to convey that the appellant had charged him with reset without having any evidence to warrant that course. It is now accepted by the appellant that upon its true construction the letter did not bear that

L meaning, but that meaning is nevertheless capable of being regarded as a possible one. In the circumstances I am of opinion that the respondent's intentions in respect of what he was trying to convey by the letter are properly to be taken into account for the purpose of ascertaining what was the dominant motive operating on his mind at the time he wrote it. The Lord Ordinary found that the respondent had no belief in the truth of that aspect of the defamatory allegations he was seeking to convey. Absence of belief in the truth of a defamatory allegation actually conveyed is, as Lord Diplock said, usually conclusive evidence of improper motive amounting to express malice. There is no valid reason for not holding that the same inference is necessarily to be drawn where the maker of the communication is proved to have intended by it to convey a defamatory allegation in the truth of which he did not believe, but which on a proper construction of the communication it is found not to bear. In each case a similar light is shed on the state of mind of the maker of the communication. If then the communication is found to bear some untrue defamatory allegation, albeit not as serious as the maker of it intended, then the qualified privilege is lost, because the occasion giving rise to it has been misused. The allegation here of prejudice against the respondent, for racial and other reasons, was without doubt seriously defamatory.

That is sufficient for the conclusion that the appellant must succeed in this appeal. But it is to be observed that the Lord Ordinary made a clear finding, having considered the relevant parts of the evidence with care, that "the respondent had no honest belief even in the allegation that the appellant was actuated by prejudice". The Lord Justice Clerk said in the course of his opinion (1992 SLT at p 745D) that it was not established in the evidence that the respondent knew that it was false to state that the appellant was actuated by prejudice. He did not make any examination of the grounds upon which the Lord Ordinary came to a contrary conclusion. In this case it must have been a considerable advantage for the Lord Ordinary to have seen and heard the respondent in the witness box, an experience which led him to reject the respondent as a credible witness upon all matters of importance. In the circumstances the Lord Ordinary was well entitled to make the finding he did.

As regards the allegations of threats against the witnesses there was evidence that the respondent was informed that the appellant had warned witnesses that if they did not tell the truth they might get into serious trouble and even go to jail. Whether or not the respondent was correct to describe this as the making of threats is not of great significance. The respondent's motive in sending the letter was to injure the appellant, and he thereby abused the privileged occasion. The letter contained quite sufficient defamatory matter to entitle the appellant to substantial damages quite apart from the allegation of threats.

My Lords, for these reasons I would allow the appeal and restore the interlocutor of the Lord Ordinary.

Counsel for the respondent sought to maintain that the arguments advanced by counsel for the appellant were such as could and should have been but were not relied on before the Inner House, and that this ought to be reflected in any award of expenses and costs. The position is that the respondent reclaimed against the Lord Ordinary's decision and succeeded in obtaining before the Inner House a contrary decision which he should not have obtained, thus necessitating the present appeal. It is not apparent that the appellant's

counsel could have succeeded by any means in averting the errors into which the Second Division fell. In addition, a large part of the argument there was concerned with whether want of probable cause in making the publication required to be proved by the appellant. The respondent failed on that issue and did not take it up again before your Lordships' House. In all the circumstances the respondent must pay the whole of the appellant's expenses before the Inner House and his costs in this House.

LORD GOFF OF CHIEVELEY.—I have had the advantage of reading in draft the speech prepared by my noble and learned friend Lord Keith of Kinkel. For the reasons he gives I too would allow the appeal.

LORD JAUNCEY OF TULLICHETTLE.—I have had the advantage of reading in draft the speech prepared by my noble and learned friend Lord Keith of Kinkel. For the reasons he gives I too would allow the appeal.

LORD SLYNN OF HADLEY.—I have had the opportunity of considering in draft the speech prepared by my noble and learned friend Lord Keith of Kinkel. I agree that for the reasons he gives this appeal should be allowed and an order for costs be made in the terms he indicates.

LORD WOOLF.—I have had the advantage of reading in draft the speech prepared by my noble and learned friend Lord Keith of Kinkel. For the reasons he gives I too would allow the appeal.

Counsel for Pursuer and Appellant, M S Jones, QC, Hodge; Solicitors, Allan McDougall & Co, SSC (for Hughes Dowdall, Glasgow), Bayer Rosin, London — Counsel for Defender and Respondent, J L Mitchell, QC, J J Mitchell, QC; Solicitors, Macbeth Currie & Co, WS, Radcliffe & Co, London.

M G T

Nicoll v Steelpress (Supplies) Ltd

EXTRA DIVISION

LORDS MURRAY, SUTHERLAND AND MILLIGAN

20 DECEMBER 1991

Company — Insolvency — Unfair preference — Reciprocal obligations — Endorsement of cheque from debtor of company in favour of creditor of company in exchange for delivery of supplies — Whether unfair preference — Whether reciprocal obligation involved broad equivalence or strict equivalence — Insolvency Act 1986 (c 45), s 243 (2) (c).

The Insolvency Act 1986, s 243 (2) (c) provides that "a transaction whereby parties to it undertake reciprocal obligations (whether the performance by the parties of their respective obligations occurs at the same time or at different times)" is not an unfair preference in terms of s 243 (1).

A company ("RDM") were debtors of the defenders, who indicated that they were not prepared to supply RDM with further goods. An arrangement was made whereby RDM endorsed cheques in favour of the defenders in exchange for the delivery of goods. A cheque for £5,071.89 was endorsed by RDM in favour of the defenders in exchange for the supply of goods to the value of £584.96. In respect that that transaction took place less than six months before RDM's liquidation on 1 July 1987, the liquidator sought repayment of the sum so endorsed as an unfair preference in terms of s 243 (1). The defenders argued that the transaction was protected by s 243 (2) (c) as a reciprocal obligation. At debate the sheriff sustained the liquidator's pleas in law and granted decree for £5,071.89 under deduction of £584.96. The defenders appealed to the sheriff principal and the liquidator cross appealed, arguing that there should have been no deduction. The sheriff principal refused the appeal and allowed the cross appeal. The defenders appealed to the Court of Session, arguing that "reciprocal obligation" in s 243 (2) (c) implied a broad equivalence rather than a strict equivalence. It was not the invoiced value of the goods supplied but their value in RDM's hands which was the real consideration; the supply had enabled them to continue trading.

Held, (1) that prior to the 1986 Act the consideration given to the debtor in the transaction could not be less than full value to qualify for the exception for *nova debita* (pp 536L-537B); (2) that reciprocity in s 243 (2) (c) did not modify that requirement and implied nothing less than strict equivalence (p 537B-C); and appeal *refused*.

Doubted, whether reduction of prior indebtedness could ever qualify as a valid consideration in a novum debitum.

Goudy, *Bankruptcy* (4th ed), pp 90-91, *commented on.*

Appeal from the sheriff court

Peter W Nicoll, liquidator of RDM (Contracts) Ltd ("RDM"), raised an action in the sheriff court at Glasgow against Steelpress (Supplies) Ltd for repayment of £5,071.89 endorsed to them by RDM in exchange for the supply of goods to the value of £584.96.

A debate took place before the sheriff.

Pleadings

The following narrative is taken from the opinion of the court:

There is no dispute between the parties on the pleadings that on or about 27 June 1987 Mr McCormack, a director of RDM, endorsed two cheques in favour of RDM totalling £5,071.89 (which is the sum sued for) and handed them over for delivery to Steelpress on 29 June 1987. These cheques, which were dated 19 June 1987 and 25 June 1987, were presented for payment by Steelpress who have received and have retained the proceeds. It is averred for the liquidator as follows: "The transaction in terms of which the cheques were endorsed and delivered to the defenders by the company had the effect of creating a preference in favour of the defenders, who were then creditors of the company, to the prejudice of the general body of creditors. The transaction took place within the period of six months before the commencement of the winding up; the said transaction accordingly constituted an unfair preference in terms of s 243 (1) of the Insolvency Act 1986."

To this averment it is answered for the defenders: "Admitted that the transaction referred to took place within six months before the commencement of the winding up of the company, but denied that the transaction is one to which s 243 (4) of the Insolvency Act 1986 applies. . . . Said transaction was a transaction in the ordinary course of trading or business. It was a transaction under which the company and the defenders undertook reciprocal obligations and was not collusive with the purpose of prejudicing the general body of creditors."

Thereafter it is averred for the defenders that the parties dealt extensively with each other before liquidation began. Towards the beginning of May Steelpress became reluctant to continue to supply materials to RDM, but they were willing to assist if possible. A cash flow projection showing inter alia when funds were expected to be received by RDM from third parties was submitted to Steelpress with the proposal that RDM would make payments to Steelpress from these funds as they were received. In return Steelpress would agree to release certain supplies to RDM on each successive payment. The defenders aver that this method of trading became the ordinary course of trading and business between the parties during the months of May and June 1987. Four such payments were received by the defenders in accordance with this arrangement and on each occasion goods were released

in exchange. The first payment amounted to
£10,445.44 for which goods invoiced at £339.65 were
released. The second payment was for the sum of
£9,166.95 for which goods invoiced at £466.47 were
released. The third payment was for £7,009.27 for
which goods invoiced at £589 were released. The
fourth payment, which is challenged in the present
action, was £5,071.89 for which it is not in dispute
that goods valued at £584.96 were released.

After narrating the foregoing matters the defenders
aver as follows in ans 2: "The defenders were aware
that if goods were not delivered (as they were delivered
on said further occasion) to enable the company to
fulfil contractual obligations to a main contractor the
company was at risk of incurring substantial claims or
penalties under its contracts. While the precise
amount of such potential penalties and claims was not
known and could not have been known or computed
by the defenders, there was a reasonable balance of
reciprocity between the advantage to the defenders in
having said indebtedness reduced and the advantage to
the company in not incurring such claims and penalties by reason of non-delivery of goods required to
enable the company to fulfil contractual obligations.
To the extent that the assistance of the defenders
enabled the pursuers to continue to trade and fulfil
their obligations, the arrangements were to the benefit
rather than to the prejudice of any other creditors or
potential creditors."

These averments are denied by the pursuer. The
issues of relevancy on which the parties are in dispute
centre on this passage of the defenders' pleadings.

The pleas in law for the pursuer were as follows:

"(1) The pursuer as liquidator of the said RDM
(Contracts) Ltd is entitled to challenge the transaction
complained of.

"(2) The transaction complained of having created
a preference in favour of the defenders to the prejudice
of the general body of creditors and the said preference
having become effectual within the six months prior
to the liquidation of the said company, the pursuer is
entitled to decree for payment as craved.

"(3) The defenders' averments in answer being
irrelevant et separatim lacking in specification, the
defences should be repelled and decree granted de
plano as craved."

The pleas in law for the defenders were as follows:

"(1) The pursuer's averments being irrelevant et
separatim lacking in specification, the action should be
dismissed with expenses in favour of the defenders.

"(2) The transaction being a transaction excepted
from the provisions of s 243 of the Insolvency Act
1986 by virtue of the provisions of s 243 (2) of the said
Act, absolvitor should be granted with expenses in
favour of the defenders."

Statutory provisions
The Insolvency Act 1986 provides:

"243.—(1) Subject to subsection (2) below, subsection (4) below applies to a transaction entered into by
a company, whether before or after 1st April 1986,
which has the effect of creating a preference in favour
of a creditor to the prejudice of the general body of
creditors, being a preference created not earlier than
six months before the commencement of the winding
up of the company or the making of an administration
order in relation to the company.

"(2) Subsection (4) below does not apply to . . . (c)
a transaction whereby the parties to it undertake
reciprocal obligations (whether the performance by
the parties of their respective obligations occurs at the
same time or at different times) unless the transaction
was collusive as aforesaid. . . .

"(4) A transaction to which this subsection applies
is challengeable by — (a) in the case of a winding up
— (i) any creditor who is a creditor by virtue of a debt
incurred on or before the date of commencement of
the winding up, or (ii) the liquidator; and (b) in the
case of an administration order, the administrator."

Textbooks referred to
Bell, *Commentaries,* ii, 205-206.
Goudy, *Bankruptcy* (4th ed), pp 90-91.

On 3 August 1990 the sheriff *granted* decree for
payment under deduction of the value of the goods
supplied in the transaction.

The defenders appealed to the sheriff principal and
the pursuer cross appealed.

On 30 November 1990 the sheriff principal *refused*
the appeal, *allowed* the cross appeal and *granted* decree
for the full sum sued for.

The defenders appealed to the Court of Session.

Appeal
The grounds of appeal for the defenders were as
follows:

(1) The sheriff principal erred in holding that the
defenders' defence would necessarily fail even if the
defenders proved all of their averments.

(2) The sheriff principal erred in holding that, for
the obligations undertaken by the company and by the
defenders to be properly regarded as reciprocal, they
would have to arise unico contextu.

(3) Separatim the sheriff principal erred in holding
that the obligations undertaken by the company and
by the defenders did not arise unico contextu. The
company undertook to make payment of £5,071.89 in
respect of its existing indebtedness in return for the
defenders agreeing to release to the company goods
required by the company.

(4) The sheriff principal erred in holding that the
obligations of the company and the defenders, as
agreed by them, whereby the company undertook to
make payment of the sum of £5,071.89 in respect of

its existing indebtedness in return for the defenders
A agreeing to release to the company goods required by
the company, were not reciprocal.

The appeal was heard before an Extra Division on
20 November 1991.

On 20 December 1991 the court *refused* the appeal.

The following opinion of the court was delivered by
Lord Murray:

B   **OPINION OF THE COURT.**—The pursuer is
liquidator of a company known as RDM (Contracts)
Ltd ("RDM") which went into liquidation on 1 July
1987. The defenders are a trading company providing
inter alia builders' supplies. In light of ans 1 for the
defenders we refer to them as "Steelpress". It is
averred by the pursuer, but not admitted by the
defenders, that RDM passed a resolution on 26 June
1987 to present a petition to the court for its winding
up. It is however admitted by the defenders that liqui-
C dation commenced on 1 July 1987.

[His Lordship described the pleadings as narrated
supra and continued:]

The foregoing pleas in law were debated before the
sheriff in Glasgow who, by interlocutor dated 3
August 1990, apart from one matter, repelled the
defenders' pleas in law and sustained those of the
pursuer, granting decree for payment by the defenders
to the pursuer of a sum restricted to £4,486.93, being
D the sum sued for under deduction of £584.96 in
respect of goods supplied to RDM by Steelpress. The
sheriff sustained the defenders' argument to the extent
of this restriction.

The defenders appealed to the sheriff principal. The
pursuer cross appealed against the sheriff's restriction
of the sum sued for. After hearing parties and making
avizandum on 30 November 1990 the sheriff principal
sustained the third plea in law for the pursuer and
E recalled the interlocutor of the sheriff insofar as decree
had been granted for a restricted sum, pronouncing
instead decree for the full sum sued for. The defenders
have taken the present appeal against that interlocutor. Before this court neither side sought to support
the interlocutor of the sheriff insofar as it differed
from that of the sheriff principal.

The only ground upon which the defenders
appealed to the sheriff principal was that the transaction in question was excepted from challenge as falling
F under s 243 (2) (c) of the 1986 Act as one whereby the
parties undertook reciprocal obligations.

The grounds of appeal before this court were in the
following terms: [his Lordship quoted their terms and
continued:]

Counsel for the defenders stated at the outset that
ground of appeal 2 would not be argued and that the
remaining grounds of appeal turned entirely upon the
construction of s 243 (2) (c).

After summarising the submissions of parties, the

sheriff principal in his note identifies the question
before him as whether the defenders' averments G
indicate the undertaking of reciprocal obligations
within the meaning of para (c) of the section in the
transaction in issue. He then proceeds: "I have little
doubt but that difficulties in the interpretation of the
provisions of s 243 of the Insolvency Act 1986 and of
the corresponding provisions in the Bankruptcy (Scotland) Act 1985 may be resolved with the assistance of
principles developed before the passing of these Acts.
In the circumstances presented by this case however,
it has seemed to me necessary merely to interpret the H
phrase 'reciprocal obligations' and then to apply that
interpretation to the circumstances of this case.

"The *Shorter Oxford English Dictionary* (3rd ed)
offers, as one of the meanings of 'reciprocal' the word
'correlative' and the phrase 'answering to each other'.
The obligation on the company to reduce its indebtedness and the defenders' obligation to go on releasing
materials seem to me to be obligations that have
nothing of the character of being 'correlative'; nor do
they seem to me to be 'answering to each other'. These I
components of the meaning of the word 'reciprocal'
appear to me to be entirely lacking from the transaction in question. The company's obligation was none
other than its pre-existing obligation to eliminate its
pre-existing indebtedness. It was thus not correlative
to the defenders' obligation to go on supplying
materials. It had an entirely separate origin and was in
existence before the obligation undertaken by the
defenders. For these very reasons it cannot be
regarded as answering to the defenders' obligation. In J
other words, it seems to me that the obligations undertaken by the company and by the defenders cannot
properly be regarded as reciprocal because they did
not arise unico contextu.

"I am therefore of the view that even if the
defenders were to prove their averments they would
not succeed in demonstrating that the transaction was
one whereby they and the company undertook
'reciprocal obligations' within the meaning of para (c). K
They would thus not succeed in demonstrating that
the transaction in question was, prima facie, excepted
from challenge. While my approach to answering this
question is different to that adopted by the sheriff I
respectfully agree with his conclusion."

In the appeal before this court counsel for the
defenders explained that the sole issue to be brought
under review was the proper interpretation and application of s 243 (2) (c) of the 1986 Act relating to reciprocal obligations. Grounds of appeals 1, 3 and 4, but L
not ground of appeal 2, would be argued on the basis
that the transaction in question came under that
exception.

It was submitted that the sheriff principal had erred
in holding that reciprocity had not been relevantly
averred in the obligation by RDM to reduce their
indebtedness in consideration of the release of goods
by Steelpress. The sheriff principal had ignored the
averment that what was involved was payment of a
specific sum on a specific date in return for the release

of goods to which RDM were entitled in the course of
A trade under existing arrangements. He had ignored
the fact that the transaction in question was a collateral or additional agreement.

It was further submitted that the fact that a pre-
existing liability came into the transaction did not
prevent the parties from entering into a new collateral
or additional agreement that, for the reduction of
indebtedness by specified dates, Steelpress would
supply RDM with goods invoiced. This transaction
involved new and reciprocal obligations between the
B parties. It did not involve collusion and was comparable with the settlement of an action for a sum less
than the sum sued for. Like the latter it involved
equivalence in a broad sense, so that it could not be
said that the transaction was, in the circumstances, not
for real and fair value in terms of the previous
common law test. The concept of reciprocal obligations was introduced into the 1985 Act on the proposal
of the Scottish Law Commission in their report no 68
published in 1982. The Acts of 1985 and 1986 had not
C altered the law on novum debitum on which the
defenders founded. (See s 34 of the 1985 Act.)

The defenders submitted that the sheriff principal
had gone too far in holding that reciprocity implied
equality in the respective obligations of parties. He
had ignored the context including the matters averred
about previous transactions. He had not taken into
account the defenders' averments of broad equivalence, which could be quantified at a proof before
D answer. Here equivalence could not be taken at the
face value of the sums involved because of RDM's
financial predicament and liability to contractual
penalties and claims for breach of contract which they
would otherwise incur. On the averments this transaction was a novum debitum and there was a reasonable
balance of reciprocity on averment between the
parties' respective obligations. The defenders' submissions could be supported by Goudy on *Bankruptcy*
(4th ed), pp 90-91, and Bell's *Commentaries*, ii, 205.
E There were two vital factors in the present case. The
first was novum debitum and the second was broad
correspondence. The former was explicitly dealt with
in the passages from Bell and Goudy. It was not the
invoice price of goods supplied but their value in the
hands of RDM as enabling them to continue trading
which was the real consideration. The defenders could
not be blamed for want of specification of these
elements which were incapable of exact quantification
at the date of the transaction. In any event such detail
F was not within the knowledge of Steelpress.

Counsel for the pursuer submitted that the sheriff
principal's approach to s 243 of the 1986 Act rightly
proceeded upon the same premise as the common law
and the 1696 Act, namely, that a person close to insolvency should be prevented from transacting with a
particular creditor in such a way that this creditor
would receive preference over the general body of
creditors, subject only to limited exceptions now set
out in s 243. Only para (c) of subs (2) was relied upon
by the defenders. This introduced a new concept of

reciprocal obligations, but not, it was submitted, in
derogation of the foregoing basic principles. Under G
the law before the 1985 Act a novum debitum was
excepted from the operation of statutory prohibition if
the estate of the insolvent received full value in a new
or fresh transaction (Bell's *Commentaries*, ii, 205).
Nothing less than full value to the insolvent would do,
though the creditor might charge less than a full price
if the insolvent got full value, thus not diminishing the
estate available to meet the claims of creditors as a
body. The two vital ingredients were that the mutual
considerations involved were equivalent and new. H
Introduction of the concept of reciprocity did not
weaken these requirements. Full value in the strict
sense of real and fair value (Goudy) was still required
if the insolvent's estate was not to be reduced in value
by the transaction. Indeed it might be thought that the
word "reciprocity" spelt out strict bilateral equivalence of correlativity, subject to the express qualification that two reciprocal obligations did not necessarily
require to be discharged simultaneously. Reference to
para 17.38 of the Scottish Law Commission report no I
68 did not suggest that they had introduced the words
"reciprocal obligations" into their draft Bill (from
which s 243 of the 1986 Act was ultimately derived)
in any other sense. The sheriff principal's approach
was well founded in requiring nothing less than correlativity or equivalence in the respective obligations
of the parties. Far from equivalence (even in a broad
sense) the defenders' averments disclosed extreme disparity — a tenfold quantitative difference between the
parties' respective considerations. Unspecific aver- J
ments of possible penalties and breach of contract
claims could not make good this disparity. Further it
was not even averred that the transaction was a sale of
goods, for no mention of payment of the invoice price
was made. In any event it could not be said that it was
a genuinely new transaction. One side of the transaction was partial discharge of pre-existing indebtedness.
This debt was not new. It was still the old debt. The
other side of the transaction, release of the goods
invoiced, was not averred to be a new sale. Reference K
to the full passages of Bell at pp 205-206 and Goudy
at pp 90-91 made it clear that broad equivalence was
not enough — strict equivalence was required. Use of
the term "reciprocal obligations" in s 243 (2) (c) did
not affect the requirement of strict equivalence. The
sheriff principal's judgment was sound. It should be
upheld and the appeal refused.

Having considered the foregoing contentions of the
parties we are not persuaded by the argument for the
defenders that the passages cited from Bell and Goudy L
proceed on the basis of broad equivalence between the
contributions of debtor and creditor in transactions to
be excepted from the general rule against unfair
preferences. It appears to us that para 3 of Goudy,
read short from p 90 to the top of p 91, gives its overall
sense quite clearly as follows: "A *novum debitum*
strictly signifies an obligation undertaken by the
bankrupt in respect of some present consideration
received. . . . The implement of such obligations
within the days of bankruptcy is protected from the

A operation of the statute, on the ground that the bankrupt does not thereby give a preference by way of satisfaction or further security, but simply gives the specific subject which he bargained to give, and in respect of which an equivalent has accrued to his estate. . . . Moreover . . . the parties do not *quoad hoc* stand in any prior relation of debtor and creditor. The consideration given to the bankrupt must be a real one and fair value."

B We consider that the passage from Bell is to be read in a similar sense. The principle behind both passages, as we see it, is that the consideration given to the debtor in the transaction cannot be less than full value to qualify for the exception. Strict equivalence is essential in that the debtor's estate must not be diminished as a result of the transaction. This conclusion is fatal to the defenders' submission for it cannot colourably be said that the release of goods worth some £500-£600 is full and fair value for a payment of some £5,000 even allowing that the debtor may be liable for unquantified penalties and claims (which are C not liquid debts) if he does not receive the goods.

In any event we are not persuaded that the effect of using the word "reciprocal" in s 243 (2) (c) in its ordinary and natural meaning, in the context of existing insolvency law, is, as counsel for the defenders contended, to modify the requirement that full value must be given to the debtor in the transaction, so as to open the door to the concept of broad rather than a strict equivalence. Reciprocity, it is true, provides D some relaxation in that the two sides of the transaction may be successive as well as simultaneous. But where succession is not in issue, as it was not here, we see no reason to suppose that reciprocity implies anything less than strict equivalence.

Further, we doubt whether reduction of prior indebtedness could ever qualify as a valid consideration in a novum debitum. That appears to be the effect of the second last sentence of the passage from Goudy quoted above. Such consideration clearly arises from E indebtedness previously incurred which is precisely the area struck at by the law against preferential repayment of creditors. In reality it is an old debt disguised as a new consideration.

As regards specification of the full value to RDM of the contribution by Steelpress in releasing goods invoiced at a value of some £584, it seems to us that the lack of specification provided is incurable in principle. If RDM could not quantify it with some precision at the time of the transaction, then they could not F in good faith suppose that they were receiving reciprocal advantage for the reduction of some £5,000 in their indebtedness to Steelpress which was their contribution to the transaction. The manifest disparity is altogether too great.

For the foregoing reasons we consider that the sheriff principal reached the correct conclusion. Accordingly we shall refuse the appeal and affirm his interlocutor of 30 November 1990.

Counsel for Pursuer and Respondent, Drummond Young, QC; Solicitors, Bennett & Robertson (for Anderson Fyfe, Glasgow) — Counsel for Defenders and Appellants, Hodge; Solicitors, Shepherd & Wedderburn, WS (for Turnbull & Ward, Barrhead).

C H A of L

Matchett v Dunfermline District Council

OUTER HOUSE
LORD KIRKWOOD
24 JANUARY 1992

Licensing — Gaming machines — Objection to grant of permit — Objector allowed to address local authority committee — Whether objector having title and interest to seek judicial review — Gaming Act 1968 (c 65), s 34 and Sched 9, paras 6, 8, 15 and 17.

Administrative law — Judicial review — Title and interest to sue — Objector to application for gaming machine permit seeking judicial review of grant of application — Objector having no statutory right to object — Objector given hearing by local authority committee — Whether sufficient to confer title and interest.

Two individuals applied to a district council for the grant of a permit under the Gaming Act 1968 in respect of gaming machines. A business competitor of the applicants submitted a letter of objection. The licensing subcommittee of the council held a meeting at which they allowed the objector to make verbal submissions. They then refused the application. The applicants appealed to the sheriff. Before the appeal was heard, the appeal process was sisted by agreement between the district council and the applicants. The subcommittee held a hearing to consider the application afresh, having suspended their standing orders. At that hearing, the application was granted. The appeal to the sheriff was later dismissed. The objector sought judicial review on the ground that the decision by the district council to reconsider the application and then reverse their previous decision had been ultra vires. The objector contended that he had title and interest to present the application for judicial review, based on the fact that the subcommittee had permitted him to address them in support of his letter of objection. The district council and the original applicants contended (a) that the objector had no title or interest to sue; and (b) that, in any event, the district council had been entitled to grant the application.

Held, that the fact that the district council had allowed the objector to be heard in support of an objection which he had no statutory right to make was not sufficient to give him a title to present the petition for judicial review (pp 540K-541A); and petition *dismissed.*

Opinion, that, once intimation of the original decision to refuse the application had been made and the decision had been appealed to the sheriff, the district council had, quoad that application, been functus and therefore not empowered to reconsider the application and reverse their earlier decision (p 541B-C).

Petition for judicial review

Alfred Matchett presented a petition seeking judicial review of the decision by the miscellaneous licences subcommittee of Dunfermline District Council to grant an application by L Visocchi and Alan Ward, for a permit for the installation of gaming machines at certain premises. The district council and the applicants appeared as respondents and challenged inter alia the petitioner's title and interest to present the petition.

The petition came for a first hearing before the Lord Ordinary (Kirkwood).

Statutory provisions

The Gaming Act 1968 provides in Sched 9:

"6. The appropriate authority shall not refuse to grant or renew a permit without affording to the applicant or a person acting for him an opportunity of appearing before, and being heard by, the appropriate authority or (where that authority is a local authority) a committee of the local authority. . . .

"15. Where on an application under this Schedule in Scotland the appropriate authority refuse to grant or renew a permit, or grant or renew it subject to a condition, the authority shall forthwith give to the applicant notice of their decision and of the grounds on which it is made; and the applicant may, within such time, and in accordance with such rules, as may be prescribed by the Court of Session by Act of Sederunt, appeal against the decision to the sheriff having jurisdiction in the authority's area. . . .

"17.—(1) Subject to paragraph 16 of this Schedule, on any appeal under paragraph 15 of this Schedule the sheriff may allow or dismiss the appeal, or reverse or vary any part of the decision of the appropriate authority, and may deal with the application as if it had been made to the sheriff in the first instance.

"(2) The decision of the sheriff on the appeal shall be final and may include such order as to the expenses of the appeal as he thinks proper."

Cases referred to

Black v Tennent (1899) 6 SLT 298; (1899) 1 F 423.
Denton Road (No 56), Twickenham, Re [1953] 1 Ch 51.
Inland Revenue Commissioners v National Federation of Self Employed and Small Businesses [1982] AC 617.
Lindsay v Summerlee Iron Co (1907) 15 SLT 306.
McDonald v Finlay, 1957 SLT 81; (sub nom *McDonald v Chambers*) 1956 SC 542.
Patmor Ltd v City of Edinburgh District Licensing Board, 1987 SLT 492.

Scottish Old People's Welfare Council, Petitioners, 1987 SLT 179.
Swanson v Manson (1907) 14 SLT 737; 1907 SC 426.
Wilson v Independent Broadcasting Authority, 1979 SLT 279; 1979 SC 351.

On 24 January 1992 the Lord Ordinary *dismissed* the petition.

LORD KIRKWOOD.—In this application for judicial review the facts are not in dispute. The first respondents are the local authority empowered in terms of the Gaming Act 1968 to decide applications for permits in respect of gaming machines in Dunfermline District. Early in 1991 the second respondents applied for a permit under s 34 of the Act for the installation of gaming machines in the premises at 29-31 Carnegie Drive, Dunfermline. The petitioner, who is a business competitor of the second respondents, submitted to the first respondents a letter dated 26 March 1991 objecting to the application. The miscellaneous licences subcommittee of the first respondents met on 25 April 1991 to consider the application and the subcommittee allowed the petitioner to make verbal submissions in support of his objection. The subcommittee decided to refuse the application and on 29 April 1991 the first respondents gave formal intimation of the decision to refuse the application.

The second respondents then appealed to the sheriff against the decision in terms of para 15 of Sched 9 to the Gaming Act 1968. Before the appeal was heard by the sheriff the first and second respondents agreed that the appeal process should be sisted and on 26 September 1991 the first respondents' subcommittee held a hearing in order to consider the application by the second respondents afresh and the subcommittee's standing orders were suspended. At the meeting on 26 September 1991 the subcommittee decided to grant the application. The second respondents' appeal to the sheriff was later dismissed. The petitioner now seeks judicial review of the first respondents' decision to grant the application on the ground that the decision was ultra vires. The first and second respondents contend (a) that the petitioner has no title to sue and, in any event, (b) that the first respondents were entitled to grant the application on 26 September 1991.

Paragraph 8 of Sched 9 provides that the grant of a permit shall be at the discretion of the appropriate authority. Paragraph 6 provides as follows: [his Lordship quoted the terms of para 6 and continued:] Paragraph 15 provides inter alia that if the appropriate authority refuse to grant a permit the applicant may appeal against the decision to the sheriff. Paragraph 17 provides that the sheriff may allow or dismiss the appeal, or reverse or vary any part of the decision of the appropriate authority, and may deal with the application as if it had been made to the sheriff in the first instance.

Counsel for the petitioner submitted that once the

first respondents had decided to refuse the application
A and had given formal intimation of their decision to
refuse it, and the decision had been appealed to the
sheriff, the first respondents had no power to consider
the original application afresh, and then grant it, even
if they did so with the consent of the applicants. They
had refused the application, their decision had been
appealed and the appeal was still pending before the
sheriff. In these circumstances the first respondents
were not entitled to reconsider the application and
reverse their original decision, and the decision of 26
B September 1991 to grant the application was unlawful
and ultra vires. Counsel further submitted that the
petitioner had a title and interest to present the
present application for judicial review. He accepted
that the statute did not confer on any third party a
right to object to an application for a permit and that
the first respondents were not under any statutory
obligation to consider any written objection which had
been lodged or to give a hearing to anyone who had
submitted a letter of objection. He also accepted that
C the fact that the petitioner is a member of the public
and a business competitor of the second respondents
would not per se entitle him to present an application
for judicial review of the first respondents' decision to
grant the application. He did not suggest that the fact
that the petitioner had actually lodged a letter of objection was sufficient to give him title or interest to seek
judicial review of the first respondents' decision.
However, he submitted that once the first respondents' subcommittee had permitted the petitioner to
D address them in support of his letter of objection, the
subcommittee had recognised that the petitioner
would be affected by the application and he had
become part of the decision making process. That
being so, he had thereby acquired a title and interest
to sue to prevent the local authority from dealing with
the application in a way which was not authorised by
the statute. In this case, the petitioner's title and
interest were bound up together in view of the way in
which they were acquired. It could not be said that the
E application for the grant of a permit concerned only
the first and second respondents. There was a wider
public interest involved and the first respondents were
under a duty not to act unlawfully. In the circumstances the petitioner had demonstrated that he has a
title and interest to petition for judicial review of the
first respondents' decision. In support of his submissions counsel referred to *Lindsay v Summerlee Iron Co*;
*Inland Revenue Commissioners v National Federation of
Self Employed and Small Businesses* [1982] AC, per
F Lord Fraser at pp 645-646, and *Scottish Old People's
Welfare Council, Petrs.*

Counsel for the first respondents submitted that the
petitioner had no title or interest to present the present
application. It was clear that the Act did not confer on
the petitioner a right to object to the second respondents' application for a permit and, while he had
lodged a letter of objection and the first respondents
had permitted him to be heard in support of his objection, this did not confer on the petitioner a title or an
interest to challenge the actings of the first respon-

dents in dealing with the application. An analogy
could be drawn with cases under the Licensing Acts G
and there was no case in Scotland in which it had been
held that a person who appeared at a public hearing,
but was not a statutory objector, was entitled to
challenge the decision reached by the licensing board.
In *Black v Tennent* the pursuer had averred that he
had a title to sue based on his statutory entitlement to
lodge objections, but it was clear from the opinion of
the Lord Ordinary, Lord Kincairney, that the title of
a person who was not a statutory objector but had
simply turned up at the public hearing would not have H
been sustained. In *Patmor Ltd v City of Edinburgh District Licensing Board* it was held that the petitioners,
as statutory objectors to the original application for a
gaming licence, had title and interest to seek review of
the board's decision. However, the courts have been
astute to restrict the right to challenge a local
authority's decision to those who had a statutory right
to object to the original application. Counsel referred
to *Scottish Old People's Welfare Council, Petrs*, and I
submitted that Lord Clyde's decision was consistent
with the approach adopted by Lord Ardwall in
Swanson v Manson. In *Wilson v Independent Broadcasting Authority* it had been held that there was a breach
by a public body of a statutory duty owed to the public
and accordingly a member of the public had a right to
challenge the actings of the authority. However, in
this case the petitioner did not aver that the first
respondents owed any duty to the public. Turning to
the merits of the present application, counsel submitted that after the decision to refuse the application J
had been taken and appealed to the sheriff, the first
respondents had taken the view that the appeal would
be likely to be successful and in these circumstances
they had agreed with the applicants, the second
respondents, that the appeal should be sisted and the
application referred back to the subcommittee for
reconsideration. At that meeting the subcommittee's
standing orders were suspended, the application was
reconsidered and it was decided to grant it. However,
the only parties interested in the appeal to the sheriff K
were the applicants and the first respondents. The
petitioner had no interest in the appeal, and no right
to take part in the appeal process, and in the circumstances it was competent for the first and second
respondents to agree that the appeal should be sisted
and the application reconsidered by the subcommittee.
However, counsel agreed that it would have been
better if the appeal had been allowed to proceed and
the parties to the appeal had agreed that it should be
allowed or that the matter should be remitted back to L
the subcommittee. Alternatively, the applicants could
have submitted a fresh application which could then
have been granted by the first respondents. However,
it had been convenient to adopt the procedure which
was actually followed and the decision to grant the
application had been intra vires of the first respondents. Counsel referred to *McDonald v Finlay*, and *Re
56 Denton Road, Twickenham* [1953] 1 Ch, per Vaisey
J at pp 56-57.

Counsel for the second respondents adopted the

A submissions which had been made by counsel for the first respondents.

Both respondents have pleas of no title to sue. It is for the petitioner to demonstrate that he has both title and interest to pursue the present application for judicial review and in my opinion that issue falls to be considered first. I respectfully agree with the observations of Lord Clyde in *Scottish Old People's Welfare Council*, where he stated (at p 184): "In my view, the matter of locus standi is logically prior to and conceptually distinct from the merits of the case. It is properly of a

B preliminary character even although there may be cases where it cannot be resolved without inquiry into the merits."

I also agree with Lord Clyde that as a general rule in Scotland a favourable or adverse decision on the merits should not determine the existence or absence of a locus standi. The question as to whether or not a petitioner has a title and interest to present an application for judicial review must depend on the particular

C cular circumstances of each individual case and in the circumstances of this case I am satisfied that the issue of locus standi can be determined without consideration of the merits of the application. It is agreed that the provisions of the Act did not give the petitioner a right to object to the second respondents' application for a permit so that the petitioner was not able to found on the fact that he was a statutory objector. Further, para 15 of Sched 9 to the Act provides that notice of the authority's decision is only to be given to

D the applicant and it also provides that only the applicant can appeal against the decision. Accordingly, in relation to an application for a permit for gaming machines the Act appears to envisage that the only parties involved will be the applicant and the appropriate authority. On behalf of the petitioner it was not submitted that this was a case where there was a duty owed by the first respondents to the public and that as a member of the public the petitioner had a title to sue to prevent the first respondents from acting in

E breach of their statutory duty (cf *Wilson v Independent Broadcasting Authority*), nor was it suggested that the fact that he was a trade competitor of the second respondents and had written a letter of objection was sufficient to give him a title to present this application. Further, it was not contended that the petitioner was a ratepayer and that, as such, he had a title to sue to prevent the first respondents from acting in breach of their statutory duty under the Act. The basic submission made on behalf of the petitioner was that the first

F respondents, by permitting him to be heard in support of his written objection, had allowed him to become part of the decision making process and had thereby conferred on him a title and interest to see to it that the second respondents' application was properly disposed of in accordance with the provisions of the statute.

In *Black v Tennent* (1899) 1 F 423, Lord Adam observed (at p 436) as follows: "They have a statutory right to object to the certificate being granted, and to appear and be heard before the Justices, and it appears

to me, as it does to the Lord Ordinary, that they have a right and title to see that their objections are G disposed of in accordance with the provisions of the statute".

In *Patmor Ltd v City of Edinburgh District Licensing Board* it was held that the petitioners had title and interest to seek judicial review of the licensing board's decision to grant a gaming licence as they had a statutory right to lodge an objection to the application for a licence.

In *McDonald v Finlay*, the position was that s 19 of H the Licensing (Scotland) Act 1903 conferred a right to object to the granting or renewal of a certificate to keep licensed premises on "any person . . . owning or occupying property" in the neighbourhood of the premises. Section 22 gave a right of appeal against the decision of the licensing court to "any proprietor or occupier of property" in the neighbourhood. A woman, who lived with and acted as housekeeper to her father in a house which he owned and of which he was entered in the valuation roll as the owner and I occupier, lodged an objection to an application for a certificate to keep a public house. The certificate having been granted, she appealed to the licensing appeal court but without success. She then raised an action of reduction of the decisions of the licensing court and the licensing appeal court. Lord Strachan observed that the pursuer's title to sue admittedly depended upon whether she had a title to object to the application for a certificate and to appeal against the decision of the licensing court. He held that she was J not an occupier of the property in question and that she had no title under the statute either to object to the application for a certificate or to appeal to the licensing appeal court and, although she had lodged an objection and taken an appeal against the decision, he sustained the plea of no title to sue.

In this case it is agreed that the petitioner had no statutory right to object to the second respondents' application and the question which arises is whether K or not the fact that the first respondents allowed him to be heard in support of the written objection which he had, in fact, lodged is sufficient to confer on him a title to present the present application for judicial review. On behalf of the petitioner it was conceded that the lodging of the written objection did not give him a title to petition for judicial review of the decision to grant the second respondents' application and it does not seem to me that the position was materially altered by the fact that the first respondents L went a stage further and allowed him to make verbal submissions in support of his written objection. The petitioner's case was presented on a very narrow basis and, while there may be circumstances in which a decision of an appropriate authority in relation to an application for a permit will be open to challenge by means of judicial review, I have reached the conclusion, in the particular circumstances of this case and in light of the submissions which were made to me, that the fact that the first respondents allowed the petitioner to be heard in support of an objection which he had admittedly no statutory right to make was not sufficient to give him a title to present this petition for judicial review.

While I have decided that the petitioner has no locus standi to present this petition, it is right that I should briefly express my opinion on the merits of the case. Had I been dealing with the merits, I would have been satisfied that the first respondents were not entitled to grant the second respondents' application on 26 September 1991. The application was refused by the first respondents' subcommittee on 25 April 1991, and formal intimation of the decision was given in terms of para 15 of Sched 9 to the Gaming Act 1968. The second respondents then appealed against the decision to the sheriff. Before the appeal was heard the first and second respondents agreed that the appeal should be sisted and the original application remitted back to the subcommittee for reconsideration. In my opinion, however, once intimation of the decision had been made and the decision had been appealed to the sheriff, the first respondents were, in relation to that particular application, functus and they were not empowered to reconsider the application and reverse their earlier decision. I do not consider that the fact that the second respondents agreed to the course of action adopted by the first respondents could confer on the first respondents a power which they did not have under the statute. In the circumstances I would have taken the view that the first respondents acted outwith their powers in proceeding to grant the application on 26 September 1991. However, as I have decided that the petitioner has no title to sue, I shall sustain the first plea in law for both respondents and dismiss the petition.

Counsel for Petitioner, Davidson; Solicitors, J & A Hastie, SSC — Counsel for First Respondents (District Council), Currie; Solicitors, McGrigor Donald — Counsel for Second Respondents (Applicants), Henderson, QC; Solicitors, Tods Murray, WS.

D S C

Heywood v Ross

HIGH COURT OF JUSTICIARY

THE LORD JUSTICE GENERAL (HOPE), LORDS ALLANBRIDGE AND COWIE

27 MAY 1992

Justiciary — Procedure — Summary procedure — Sheriff fixing trial diet for date later than earliest available diet — Whether trial diet should be fixed for earliest practicable date.

Justiciary — Procedure — Appeal — Bill of advocation — Sheriff fixing trial diet for date later than earliest available diet — Crown seeking recall of order — Power of court to accelerate trial diet on joint application — Whether bill premature or unnecessary — Criminal Procedure (Scotland) Act 1975 (c 21), s 314 (3) and (5).

Section 314 (3) of the Criminal Procedure (Scotland) Act 1975 provides that where a diet has been fixed in a summary prosecution it shall be competent for the court, on a joint application in writing by the parties or their solicitors, to discharge the diet so fixed and fix in lieu thereof an earlier diet. Section 314 (5) confers a similar power on application by the Crown alone.

Two accused persons were charged on separate summary complaints. One accused, Gray, pled not guilty on 23 March 1992 and although there were trial diets available for the week commencing 25 May 1992, the sheriff fixed a diet for 7 December 1992. The other accused, Ross, pled not guilty on 5 November 1991 and after sundry procedure appeared again on 25 March 1992 when he adhered to his plea previously tendered. The sheriff then had a report indicating that the accused had had HIV infection for a number of years. The sheriff fixed a trial diet for 7 December 1992. The Crown sought advocation of the sheriff's decisions on the ground that by fixing such a late diet in each case he had interfered with the interests of justice and had no good reason for doing so. The sheriff reported to the High Court that he had had other complaints against Gray before him for sentence and as he had considered that the accused might be appropriate for an intensive short period of probation of six to nine months he had called for reports. The sheriff therefore did not consider an early trial diet to be either desirable or necessary. He had fixed a later trial diet in Ross's case because of his medical condition. The sheriff also suggested to the High Court that in light of the power in s 314 (3) and (5) the bills were either unnecessary or premature.

Held, (1) that since s 314 (3) and (5) assumed that the original diet had been properly fixed for good reason and that for some other reason not before the court at the time of fixing the diet a different date should be fixed, which the Crown was not suggesting, the bills were neither premature nor unnecessary (p 543B-E); (2) that in the absence of good reason to the contrary the trial diet should be fixed for the earliest practicable date in the public interest and the accused's interests (p 543G-I), and bills *passed*.

Bill of advocation

Barry K Heywood, procurator fiscal, Dundee, brought a bill of advocation against Thomas Ross craving the High Court of Justiciary to recall the decision of Sheriff G L Cox at Dundee sheriff court dated 25 March 1992 whereby the sheriff fixed a trial diet for 7 December 1992. In a separate bill of advocation against Morrison Gray the complainer sought recall of a decision of Sheriff G L Cox dated 23 March 1992 whereby he fixed a trial diet for 7 December 1992. The facts of the cases appear from the opinion of the court.

Statutory provisions

The Criminal Procedure (Scotland) Act 1975 provides:

"314.— . . . (3) Where a diet has been fixed in a summary prosecution, it shall be competent for the court, on a joint application in writing by the parties or their solicitors, to discharge the diet so fixed and fix in lieu thereof an earlier diet. . . .

"(5) Where the prosecutor has intimated to the accused that he desires to postpone or accelerate a diet which has been fixed, and the accused refuses . . . to make a joint application to the court for that purpose, the prosecutor may make an incidental application for that purpose".

The bills were argued before the High Court on 27 May 1992.

Eo die the court *passed* the bills, *recalled* the orders and *remitted* to the sheriff to fix a trial diet in each case for the earliest date available.

The following opinion of the court was delivered by the Lord Justice General (Hope):

OPINION OF THE COURT.—We have before us today two bills of advocation at the instance of the procurator fiscal, Dundee, in which, in the one case, Morrison Gray is the respondent, and in the other, Thomas Ross is the respondent. In both cases the point taken is essentially the same. The sheriff, when he came to fix a diet for trial in these two cases, selected a date very much later in the year than the dates for which trials were currently being fixed in the sheriff court at Dundee. The prosecutor takes exception to the fixing of these dates so long after the dates for which diets were available, on the ground that this is in conflict with the general and well understood principle that it is in the public interest that proceedings in matters relating to crime should be dealt with as soon as possible.

In order to understand the particular points which were advanced in argument today by the Lord Advocate we should say something about the facts in each case. Morrison Gray appeared on 23 March 1992 on summary complaint charged with two charges of assault and with a contravention of s 3 (1) (b) of the Bail etc (Scotland) Act 1980. He pled not guilty to each of the charges on this complaint. He was also before the sheriff on that date for sentence on seven other complaints, in respect of which he had previously been convicted. The prosecutor declined to accept his pleas of not guilty in the present case, and the sheriff was invited to fix a diet for trial. Although diets were then available for the week commencing 25 May 1992, the sheriff fixed a diet in this case for 7 December 1992. This clearly was very far beyond the time at which this case could reasonably have been brought to trial. Turning to the various complaints which were before him for sentence, the sheriff proceeded to deal with four of them by sentencing the respondent to a period of three months' imprisonment in each case. So far as the three remaining complaints were concerned, the respondent had pled guilty to offences committed in January and February 1992, more recently than the date of the offences libelled in the present case [22 November 1991]. The sheriff decided to defer his consideration of sentence on these three complaints, and to obtain reports from the National Children's Home Alternatives to Custody Project. It appears that he had in mind, in the case of these three complaints, ordering the respondent to undergo an intensive period of probation for a period of six to nine months. The sheriff has explained, in answer to the challenge that he acted unreasonably in not fixing an earlier date for the trial, that he did not think that an early trial diet would have been desirable or necessary in this case. That observation is made solely against the background of the disposals of the other complaints to which we have referred. No other explanation is given in his report as to why the sheriff selected a date so much later in the year than dates which were then available. He has not suggested that either the prosecutor or the respondent requested that the trial diet should be delayed. It is plain on the timetable to which we have referred that the date which he fixed for trial in this case was unlikely to secure the interests of justice in bringing the one outstanding complaint to a conclusion as soon as reasonably practicable.

Turning to the facts in the other case, Thomas Ross appeared on 5 November 1991 charged on summary complaint with a breach of the peace [on that date]. He pled not guilty at that stage, and after various intermediate diets and certain delays he appeared again on 25 March 1992 when he adhered to his plea of not guilty. There was then produced to the sheriff a medical report dated 11 March 1992 which had been signed by a consultant physician. It stated that Ross has had an HIV infection for a number of years as a consequence of injection drug misuse but that the only medical complication directly caused by this had been treated and should not recur. The report concluded with the information that Ross's current disability was related entirely to physical trauma. It was anticipated that the injuries which he had received would not interfere with his ability to attend court. The general tenor of the report is that there was no compelling medical reason why the respondent should not be regarded as fit to appear for trial. The sheriff tells us however in his report in this case that on 25 March the respondent appeared to him to be in a piteous condition and that he was plainly very unwell. This was his sole reason for the decision that a later than normal trial diet should be fixed in this case. We accept, of course, that the sheriff's description of the respondent's state of health was a reasonable assessment of his position on that date. On the other hand, as the Lord Advocate pointed out, the condition of a person may vary from day to day. So far as the long term position was concerned, relevant to the respondent's ability to stand trial at a late date, the only reliable information before the sheriff was that provided by the medical report. The date which the sheriff fixed as the diet for trial in this case was once again 7 December 1992, although diets were available for May 1992. In this case also it is clear that, measured by reference to the principle that it is in the interests of justice that criminal cases should be brought to trial as soon as reasonably practicable, the sheriff's decision falls well short of that standard.

The principal point taken by the sheriff, in the reports which he has produced in these cases, is that these bills of advocation are either unnecessary or

premature. He has referred to the provisions of s 314
(5) of the Criminal Procedure (Scotland) Act 1975
which enable the prosecutor to apply to the court for
the postponement or acceleration of a diet which has
been fixed. Section 314 (3) makes provision for a joint
application by both the prosecutor and the accused if
so desired. His suggestion is that, if the diets fixed are
thought to be oppressive or unsatisfactory, the remedy
lies in the use of these provisions and that, since the
prosecutor has not availed himself of either of them,
he ought not to be allowed to secure the same result
by means of these bills.

In our opinion, however, that is not a proper
response to the applications which have been made to
this court, for reasons which were submitted to us by
the Lord Advocate. Where an application is made to
the sheriff under s 314 (5) for the acceleration or postponement of a diet, some reason must be given to
justify the discharge of the diet which has been fixed
and the fixing of a later or earlier diet as the case may
be. That will normally involve satisfying the court
that there has been some change of circumstances. In
the present case, if the sheriff was to be invited to
depart from the decision which he originally took, he
would require to be provided with some sufficient
reason, such as a change of circumstances, to justify
the acceleration of the diet which had been fixed. But,
as the Lord Advocate pointed out, the complainer here
is not suggesting that there has been any change of circumstances. His only argument is that the diet fixed
was very much later in the year than it should have
been, that the sheriff had no good reason for postponing it for so many months and that the decision to
fix such a late date as the diet for trial ought to be
reconsidered and recalled. That is not in accordance
with what is envisaged by the section, which assumes
that the original diet has been properly fixed for good
reason, and that for some other reason not before the
court at the time of fixing it a different date should
now be fixed. Accordingly we are not persuaded by
the sheriff's comments that these bills should be dismissed on the ground that they are either premature
or unnecessary.

Turning to the merits of these applications, the
Lord Advocate submitted that the decisions under
challenge were properly to be seen as oppressive on
the ground that, by fixing such a late date as the diet
for trial in each case, the sheriff had interfered with
the interests of justice and had no good reason for
doing so. He pointed out that the sheriff court at
Dundee has a commendable record for dealing within
a reasonable time with cases brought before it on
summary complaint. The information from the sheriff
clerk depute that on 27 March this year diets were
being fixed for the week commencing on 25 May
demonstrates that this is indeed the case. Counsel who
appeared on behalf of the respondent in each case
adopted an entirely neutral position. He confirmed
that no representations had been made to the sheriff
that the trial diets in these cases should be postponed,
and he intimated that for this reason he felt unable to
take issue with the submissions of the Lord Advocate.

Very properly he accepted that the interests of justice
in both of these cases demanded that the earliest practicable trial diet should be fixed.

In our opinion no sufficient reason has been demonstrated for the fixing of diets for trial in these cases for
dates so much later than was reasonably practicable.
In Gray's case there was no need to postpone the diet
of trial on the one remaining complaint simply
because there was a prospect that a probation order
might be made following the obtaining of reports on
the other three complaints on which he had been convicted. The medical report in Ross's case indicated
that there was no compelling medical reason for delay-
ing the diet of trial. If there had been, one would have
expected a submission to that effect to have been made
on his behalf by his solicitor, yet no such submission
was advanced. The sheriff appears in both of these
cases to have lost sight of the fact that, in the absence
of a good reason to the contrary, the trial diet should
be fixed for the earliest practicable date, in the public
interest and in the interest also of the accused. For
these reasons we have decided that the only course we
can properly take is to pass these bills, and to return
the matter to the sheriff for reconsideration. We shall
recall the orders complained of in each of these two
cases, and remit them to the sheriff to fix a trial diet
in each case for the earliest date available at which it
is reasonably practicable for the trial to proceed.

---

*Counsel for Complainer, Lord Advocate (Lord Rodger
of Earlsferry, QC); Solicitor, J D Lowe, Crown Agent —
Counsel for Respondents, Duguid; Solicitors, Drummond
Miller, WS (for Bruce, Short & Co, Dundee).*

P W F

(NOTE)

McDermid v Crown House Engineering Ltd

OUTER HOUSE
LORD MORTON OF SHUNA
28 JULY 1992

*Damages — Amount — Solatium and loss of earnings —
Eye — Loss of sight of one eye with continuing pain —
Multiplier of 5 years for future loss for 28 year old where
permanent employment, but for the accident, uncertain
and where alternative employment possible.*

A 28 year old electrician's labourer fell from a ladder
causing detachment of a retina and consequent loss of
sight in the eye. He also received bruising injuries to
his back and arm. He did not return to his pre-accident
work.

Held, (1) that solatium was properly valued at
£19,000; and (2) that loss of wages to date should be

A awarded together with future loss calculated using a multiplier of 5 years; and decree *pronounced* accordingly.

Edward McDermid raised an action of damages against his former employers, Crown House Engineering Ltd, in respect of personal injuries sustained in an accident on 4 February 1987. He was then aged 28. He had been employed as an electrician's labourer. In the accident the pursuer had fallen about 20-25 ft from

B a ladder, striking some scaffolding as he fell. Liability was not in dispute, nor was the appropriate award for the bruising injuries (several hundred pounds only), but the case came to proof before the Lord Ordinary (Lord Morton of Shuna) on the issue of whether or not the detached retina which the pursuer subsequently sustained, some weeks after the accident, had been caused by his fall. The Lord Ordinary held that the fall had been the cause of the detached retina and continued:

C "The pursuer has lost the sight of his right eye and the eye has shrunk in size. He suffers pain on two or three occasions a week and takes painkillers to relieve the pain. Dr Barrie [the consultant ophthalmologist who had treated the pursuer] considered that this account of pain was what would be expected, and he also considered that there was a slight chance of further deterioration when other treatment might have to be undertaken. The pursuer was 28 years old at the date of the accident. I was referred to a variety of cases

D to assist in the assessment of solatium. Counsel for the pursuer suggested a figure of £21,000, while counsel for the defenders suggested £17,000. In my opinion, taking into account the continuing pain and the bruising to the back and arm, an appropriate figure for solatium would be £19,000. Counsel appeared to agree that interest should run on one third of that sum at 7½ per cent per annum from the date of the accident.

"The pursuer remained at work after the initial few

E days off work until he was paid off in June 1987 towards the completion of the building contract. During most of that time he was working as a storeman. He was offered re-employment with the defenders as an electrician's labourer on another contract, but did not take it up as he felt he was unfit to work from scaffolding. Since then he has not worked although he has made various attempts to obtain work. He has not received any medical or other advice as to what type of work he should or should not do. He has

F sought no advice on retraining. He impressed me as an intelligent individual and I was not impressed by his failure to obtain any advice as to what he should try to do to obtain work. He lives in an area of Glasgow with high unemployment and has, prior to the accident, worked on building contracts which is an area of work which has recently had particular difficulty. In the minute of admissions it is agreed that if the pursuer had been continuously employed by the defenders since the accident his net continuing loss of earnings, including interest and after deduction of the relevant benefits, would, as at 29 May 1992, amount

to £29,000. It was also agreed that his net wage loss in May 1992 would have been at the rate of £10,000 G per annum.

"The pursuer's counsel submitted that the pursuer should receive compensation of his net loss to date plus 13 years' purchase of his continuing loss. The defenders' counsel contended that the pursuer would not have worked continuously in the building contracting industry for the five years since the accident and that the pursuer had no justification for having turned down the offer of work that he had received on another contract. There was, he contended, no justifi- H cation for his refusal of work as an electrician's labourer. The defenders' counsel's contention was that the future loss should not be more than five years' loss bearing in mind all the various uncertainties.

"In the absence of any evidence from any witness other than the pursuer as to what an electrician's labourer with only one eye could reasonably be expected to do, or as to whether a person with one eye would ever be employed as an electrician's labourer, I or as to what the pursuer in particular could be retrained to do, I can only take a broad guess as to what is appropriate compensation. On that basis I consider that a fair award would be to allow the loss to date plus five years' loss. This would amount to £79,000 with interest on £29,000 at 7½ per cent per annum from the date of the accident."

Counsel for Pursuer, P H Brodie, QC, Maria A J *Clark; Solicitors, Allan McDougall & Co, SSC (for Gordon & Smyth, Glasgow) — Counsel for Defenders, Woolman; Solicitors, Brown Mair Mackintosh & Co, WS (for Wilson Chalmers & Hendry, Glasgow).*

C H

K

(NOTE)

Lenaghan v Ayrshire and Arran Health Board

OUTER HOUSE

LORD WEIR

30 SEPTEMBER 1992

L

Damages — Amount — Solatium, loss of earnings and earning capacity, loss of services of and necessary services rendered to injured person — Back — Injury giving rise to persistent pain but with exaggerated symptoms and personality change — Improvement likely — Multiplier of 12 from proof appropriate for permanent incapacity for lady then 45 years old.

Damages — Loss of congenial employment — Whether appropriate as a separate head of damages or included in solatium.

A 43 year old catering assistant hurt her back in a
A fall on a wet floor. This produced disabling symptoms
and depression but with a possibility of improvement
and a return to light work. She sought a separate
award for the loss of her congenial employment.

Held, (1) that it was inappropriate to make a
separate award for loss of congenial employment; (2)
that solatium should be assessed at £6,500; (3) that an
appropriate multiplier for permanent incapacity
would be 12 years but that here the award for future
loss should be limited to £15,000 where her annual
B loss was £6,400 net; (4) that an appropriate figure for
loss of personal services and necessary services, future
as well as past, was £10,000; and decree *pronounced*
accordingly restricted by 25 per cent for contributory
negligence.

———————

June Lenaghan raised an action against her former
employers, Ayrshire and Arran Health Board, for
damages for injuries sustained in an accident at work
C on 5 August 1990. She was then aged 43. She slipped
on a floor that had just been washed. She fell heavily
onto her back, striking her head as she did so. Liability
was established for a failure to erect warning signs
while the floor was being washed, but subject to a
finding of contributory negligence of one quarter. In
assessing damages, before reducing the award for contributory negligence, the Lord Ordinary (Weir) said:

"The pursuer has not worked since her accident.
D She received a blow to the back of the head from
which she quickly recovered. She also jarred her back
and neck which has given rise to the symptoms.
According to Mr I G Kelly, a consultant orthopaedic
surgeon who gave evidence on her behalf, the pursuer
suffered a significant forward flexion injury to an
already degenerative cervical spine. This has led to
persistent pain in her neck and there are complaints
also of constant pain in both her arms and in her lower
back. There is a conflict of evidence between Mr
E Kelly and the defenders' orthopaedic surgeon, Mr
Christie, and this relates to the extent to which the
symptoms which the pursuer displayed were genuine.
In his report Mr Christie puts it this way:

"'It is extremely difficult to assess the extent and
severity of her symptoms in view of the nature of her
present symptomatology and the spurious signs on
clinical examination. It is impossible for me to say
with any certainty that these symptoms actually
resulted from the incident that she has described and
F I am inclined to believe that many of the symptoms
that she describes are consciously or subconsciously
exaggerated. I do not believe that it is possible to have
an accurate picture of her symptomatology, nor is it
reasonable to attribute the symptoms that she
describes because of the plethora of spurious signs.

"'I believe that she may have shaken her back and
neck around and it is possible that she has had symptomatology afterwards and for a period of time. I would
personally find it very difficult to assess the extent and
nature of these and the importance of the injury

preventing her returning to work in the face of her
current presentation. I think that one is forced to con-   G
clude that there is so much in the way of inappropriate
presentation that an accurate assessment cannot be
made of her situation.'

"On the other hand Mr Kelly was not inclined to
share the suspicions of Mr Christie. He accepted that
upon examination she presented 'inappropriate signs'
upon examination, but he did not consider that she
was a malingerer which Mr Christie in evidence considered highly possible.
                                                             H
"What is not in dispute among the medical men is
that since the accident the pursuer has become anxious
and depressed. The evidence of her husband made it
quite clear that before her accident she was of a
straightforward and cheerful disposition. There seems
to be no doubt that her personality has changed since
the time of the accident and the interaction of her
mental state with the physical consequences of her
injuries has rendered her unable to work up till now.
It is difficult to express with conviction any opinion   I
on whether the pursuer is a malingerer or whether the
inappropriate signs which she displayed upon examination were merely a consequence of her general
mental attitude resulting from the accident. Both
specialists are experienced in this sphere of medicine
and both examined her on one occasion. Both gave
their evidence in an impressive manner. Doing the
best I can, I have come to the conclusion that there is
some force in the view of Mr Christie which I have
quoted. In my opinion, although she may have   J
exaggerated her symptoms consciously or unconsciously when seen by Mr Christie, I do not believe
that these symptoms did not exist and I accept Mr
Kelly's view that the pursuer's current disability is
related both to the effects of the physical injury and to
the psychological distress that these have caused.

"Mr Kelly expressed the view that there was a
major element of psychological distress and in these
circumstances since neither he nor Mr Christie
claimed to be experts in this field, I would have   K
expected there to be evidence from a consultant
psychiatrist led on behalf of the pursuer in proof of
her claim for damages. Such evidence would have
been highly relevant to the question of the prospects
of the pursuer returning to work since the total size of
the claim is much dependent on that factor. In fact,
somewhat to my surprise, a report by Professor Bond
of the department of psychological medicine at the
University of Glasgow dated 2 June 1992 was lodged
in process on her behalf. He was not called as a   L
witness and I was told that he was unavailable. No
attempt was made to have his evidence taken on commission. Nevertheless, the report, which is referred to
in a joint minute by the parties, is in process and I was
not asked to ignore it. Both Mr Kelly and Mr Christie
expressed the view that the pursuer was unlikely,
given her current attitude of mind, to return to work.
However, the concluding part of Professor Bond's
report is pertinent:

"'I conclude that Mrs Lenaghan experienced con-

A siderable pain as a result of her fall and reacted rapidly to the symptoms with anxiety. This was associated with a poor response to analgesics, poor mobilization and an increase in weight. All these factors would tend to increase and prolong her symptoms. She remains anxious and is well established in the invalid role. As a consequence she is unfit for work. In my view treatment will be difficult because Mrs Lenaghan requires a programme that includes psychological treatment designed to reduce her anxiety and increase her mobility. This should be coupled with a programme

B of steadily increasing exercise designed to increase her confidence in her ability to work. She will require reassurance that she has not suffered major physical injuries of any kind. I do not believe that Mrs Lenaghan has been fit to return to work as a hospital kitchen assistant since the time of her accident and given the chronicity of her present condition I find it difficult to say when she will be fit for work again, but with a suitable programme light work might be possible within six to nine months.'

C   "It is thoroughly unsatisfactory to have to proceed upon a consideration of material, only some of which was vouched by oral evidence. But it is for the pursuer to satisfy me on a balance of probabilities that her present condition is permanent and entirely attributable to the accident. The written observations of Professor Bond make it questionable whether the pursuer's condition will necessarily remain static. It is my impression that the pursuer, who was a fit and active person before the accident, suffers from some rela-

D tively minor physical disability and also painful symptoms which were brought into being by the accident, that her distress and anxiety are caused at least in part by the psychological overlay consequent upon her injury but that she is prepared to exaggerate these symptoms for the purpose of making good her claim. To that extent I accept elements of the evidence of both consultant orthopaedic surgeons. Having regard to the report of Professor Bond, I am not prepared to accept that her condition is not capable of

E improvement to some extent and to the extent in particular that she might be able to resume her housework and obtain light outside employment within the next year or so. On that basis I would assess solatium at £6,500 with interest on 50 per cent thereof at 7.5 per cent.

"Counsel for the pursuer next invited me to award the sum of £5,000 as representing 'loss of congenial employment'. So far as I am aware, this is the first

F time that the court has been asked to make an award under this special head and in support of such a claim I was invited to consider the unreported decisions of two deputy High Court judges sitting in the Queen's Bench Division of the High Court of Justice in England. I am not prepared to respond to the invitation to make a special award under this head. I recognise that to be unable due to injury to continue in a former employment which someone had found congenial is certainly an element in that person's suffering to be taken into account. As such in my opinion it is properly to be reflected in the general amount of the

G award for solatium and the amount may vary according to circumstances. There is no doubt that the pursuer in this case enjoyed working at this hospital and her fellow workers were her friends and contributed to her social life. However I consider that her sense of deprivation is adequately reflected in the overall assessment which I have made and it would be difficult to place a precise figure for that factor alone.

"For the purpose of assessing damages for future loss of earnings the multiplier is agreed at £6,400 per annum. Bearing in mind the pursuer's age (45 years)

H and assuming that she remains permanently unfit I agree with counsel for the pursuer that a multiplier of 12 would have been appropriate. This was not challenged by counsel for the defenders. Nevertheless such a multiplier is inappropriate in view of the possibility of the pursuer being fit for and obtaining light work. I consider that in these circumstances a broad approach is required and doing the best I can, and taking into account all the circumstances and the imponderables, the sum of £15,000 will be a reason-

I able figure for future loss of earnings.

"It is agreed that in any award of damages the loss of wages since the accident to the date of the proof is £6,438.75, which I round up to £6,440.

"There is a claim for services provided by the pursuer's family and also loss for services which the pursuer is unable to render in terms of ss 8 and 9 of the Administration of Justice (Scotland) Act 1982. The computation of this claim is based on a report by

J Mr Hugh Young, a senior official in the social work department of Strathclyde Regional Council. Counsel for the pursuer submitted that the court should have regard to the figure set out in Mr Young's report being based on the local authority hourly home care rate. The claim was restricted to care and to domestic tasks performed by the family and on the basis of the computations in the report to the date of proof amounted to approximately £6,000. I accept that Mr Young's figures provide a useful guide, but the rather vague

K evidence of the pursuer and her husband makes reliance difficult. Their evidence was to the effect that the pursuer needed much domestic help from her husband and from their two sons for about six months following the accident but that since then the pursuer has managed to resume many of her former household tasks. She is able to prepare meals and can do the shopping with some assistance. Some of the physical tasks in the house are still beyond her. Accordingly I am of opinion that the claim for past services is

L pitched rather too high and I would prefer to make an estimate at £4,000. It may very well be that if the pursuer receives psychological help as suggested by Professor Bond she will be able to take over most if not all of the domestic tasks within the next year or two. The pursuer has certainly not satisfied me that she is entitled to the large sum of money put forward by her counsel based on a multiplier of 12 to 13 years. In my judgment the best course is to take a round figure to cover the claims under ss 8 and 9 (as I was invited to do) and I would assess the total, both past and future,

A at £10,000. These are all the items in the claim with the exception of a minor agreed item, namely £30 for certain prescription charges.''

Counsel for Pursuer, McEachran, QC, Caldwell; Solicitors, Robin Thompson & Partners — Counsel for Defenders, R W J Anderson; Solicitor, R F Macdonald.

C H

B

Brechin Golf and Squash Club v Angus District Licensing Board

OUTER HOUSE

LORD CAPLAN

C 28 OCTOBER 1992

Administrative law — Judicial review — Reasons for decision — Sufficiency of reasons given — Failure to specify matters taken into account.

Licensing — Licence — Regular extension of permitted hours — Reasons for refusal — Sufficiency of specification of reasons — Board restricting statement to lack of satisfaction on matters without specifying basis for lack of satisfaction — Licensing (Scotland) Act 1976 (c 66), s 18.

D

Section 18 of the Licensing (Scotland) Act 1976 provides that in certain circumstances, upon being required to do so, a licensing board shall give written reasons for its decision.

A golf and squash club which operated club premises presented an application to the licensing board for the grant of a regular extension of permitted hours on Sundays from 11 am until 12.30 pm and E from 2.30 pm to 6 pm. Similar extensions to permitted hours had been granted for the 13 preceding years and operated without problems arising. There was no opposition from objectors or the police. The licensing board refused that part of the application relating to the period 11 am until 12 noon. The club required the licensing board to give a statement of the reasons for their decision under s 18 of the 1976 Act.

In a letter setting out the purported reasons for their F decision the board maintained that they were not satisfied on these matters: (a) that there was a need for golfers and squash players to be able to have a drink on Sundays between 11 am and 12 noon; (b) that, having regard to the social circumstances of the locality and to the activities taking place therein, the number of persons participating in the club's activities justified a need for an extended hour of drinking time; and (c) that the extension from 11 am to 12 noon on Sundays would be of such benefit to the community as a whole as to outweigh any detriment which the permitted extension would have.

The club petitioned for judicial review of the board's decision on the ground inter alia that the pur- G ported statement of reasons for the decision was insufficient to fulfil their statutory responsibility under s 18.

Held, that the reasons stated by the board failed to specify the circumstances they took into account in giving the foregoing reasons and the court could not be satisfied that the board had acted properly and within their statutory powers when they refused that part of the application which they did; that the reasons given by the board were accordingly not sufficiently H informative to comply with s 18 (pp 550E-551G); and decision quoad the period 11 am until 12 noon *reduced*, decree of declarator *pronounced* to the effect that the respondents had failed to give a proper statement of reasons; and board *ordained* to reconvene to reconsider the application.

Observed, that although the reasons given for a decision need not be immaculately precise and exhaustive, the interested party who looked at the reasons I should be left in no doubt as to why the licensing board had arrived at the relevant decision and a statement of reasons which was confused and ambiguous would afford the party who called for it no help whatsoever (p 550D-E).

Petition for judicial review

Brechin Golf and Squash Club presented a petition for judicial review of a decision of Angus District J Licensing Board partially refusing an application for a regular extension of permitted hours.

The petition came before the Lord Ordinary (Caplan) for a first hearing at which the petitioners sought inter alia reduction of the decision and declarator that the board had failed to give a proper statement of their reasons for the decision.

Statutory provisions

The Licensing (Scotland) Act 1976 provides: K

"18.—(1) A licensing board shall give reasons for arriving at any decisions mentioned in section 5 (2) of this Act when required to do so under subsection (2) below.

"(2) Reasons for decisions referred to in subsection (1) above may be required to be given by the board in writing on a request being made to the clerk of the board, not more than 48 hours after the decision is made, by the applicant or, as the case may be, by the L holder of the licence, or by an objector, or by any complainer who appeared at the hearing. . . .

"64.—(1) Any person holding a public house licence, a hotel licence, a restricted hotel licence, a restaurant licence, an entertainment licence or a licence under Part III of this Act, in respect of any premises, may apply to the licensing board within whose area the premises are situated for the grant of an occasional or regular extension of permitted hours, and at the same time as he makes the application he shall send a copy of the application to the chief constable. . . .

"(3) After considering the application and any objections made thereto, a licensing board may grant an application for the regular extension of permitted hours if, having regard to the social circumstances of the locality in which the premises in respect of which the application is made are situated or to activities taking place in that locality, the board considers it is desirable to do so, and such a grant shall authorise the person to whom it was granted to sell or supply alcoholic liquor in the premises to which the application relates during such period in the year succeeding the date of the grant and between such hours and on such days as may be specified in the grant."

The Law Reform (Miscellaneous Provisions) (Scotland) Act 1990 provides:

"47.—(1) A licensing board shall not grant an application under section 64 of the principal Act for an extension of permitted hours unless it is satisfied by the applicant, taking account of the factors mentioned in subsection (3) of that section — (a) that there is a need in the locality in which the premises in respect of which the application is made are situated for a regular extension of the permitted hours; and (b) that such an extension is likely to be of such benefit to the community as a whole as to outweigh any detriment to that locality.

"(2) In determining whether to grant an application for a regular extension to permitted hours in respect of any premises it shall not be a relevant consideration for the licensing board to have regard to whether any application relating to any other premises in its area has, at any time, been granted or refused or the grounds on which any such application has been granted or refused."

Cases referred to

Associated Provincial Picture Houses Ltd v Wednesbury Corporation [1948] 1 KB 223.
Elder v Ross and Cromarty District Licensing Board, 1990 SLT 307.
Martin v Ellis, 1978 SLT (Sh Ct) 38.
Speedlift Auto Salvage v Kyle and Carrick District Council, 1992 SLT (Sh Ct) 57.
Troc Sales v Kirkcaldy District Licensing Board, 1982 SLT (Sh Ct) 77.
Wordie Property Co Ltd v Secretary of State for Scotland, 1984 SLT 345.

On 28 October 1992 the Lord Ordinary *granted* decree of reduction and declarator and *ordained* the respondents to reconvene to reconsider the petitioners' application.

LORD CAPLAN.—This is a petition by Brechin Golf and Squash Club for judicial review of a decision by Angus District Licensing Board dated 23 June 1992 when they partially refused an application for a regular extension of the hours during which the applicants were permitted to sell or supply alcoholic liquor

at their clubhouse. The said clubhouse is licensed premises and the petitioners had applied under s 64 of the Licensing (Scotland) Act 1976 to have a regular extension of permitted hours on Sundays from 11 am until 12.30 pm and from 2.30 pm to 6 pm. The application insofar as relating to the afternoon hours was granted and no issue arises in respect of this, but the regular extension granted for the morning hours was restricted to the period from 12 noon until 12.30 pm rather than the period applied for. The petitioners are dissatisfied with the respondents' decision and seek to have it reviewed. No question arises as to the competency of the proceedings for review.

At the first hearing it emerged that there are no material factual differences between the parties and it was agreed by their counsel that I could determine the petition at this stage on the basis of submissions.

The background facts are that for 13 consecutive years prior to the present application the petitioners have enjoyed a regular extension of the permitted hours on Sundays between the hours of 11 am and 12.30 pm. This regular extension has never given rise to any trouble and there were no objections to the present application for a further regular extension either from the police or from other parties. When the petitioners' solicitor appeared before the respondents on 23 June 1992 he was not anticipating any difficulty about securing a further continuation of the regular extension previously enjoyed and it is agreed that the representations he made to the board are as set out in the petition. It is set out there that he said: "The said regular extension was required because many of the members of the said Golf Club who were unable to pay golf during the week due to business and other commitments, came to play on said course at 7.30 or 8 am on a Sunday morning and that such an early start was in that part (sic), necessitated by the fact that organised parties of golfers were allowed to tee-off from 10 am, thus making it impossible for others to play then. Said early golfers had completed their game, cleaned up and were in the habit of returning to said Clubhouse in order to enjoy social drinks and conversation during the period from 11 am onwards."

The situation appears to be that few if any members of the club attend the club premises on a Sunday morning merely in order to drink and those requiring drinks between 11 am and 12 noon were bona fide golfers who have completed their game. The club premises are a considerable distance from the nearest habitation. The facts relating to the position of the club premises and the category of persons who enjoy the licensed facilities on Sunday mornings do not appear to have been specifically mentioned to the board. However, these facts could have readily been ascertained by the respondents if considered significant and not already within their knowledge. During the submissions made by the petitioners' solicitor to the respondents the only intervention by a member of the board was an observation by Mr Meldrum that there would be the possibility of unfair competition between the petitioners and the public houses in

Brechin if the extension applied for were granted in
full. In any event when the petitioners' solicitor had
concluded his submissions no opposition of any kind
was advanced to the grant of the application in full.
Without retiring the respondents considered two
motions namely that the regular extension applied for
be granted or alternatively that it be restricted to the
period from 12 noon until 12.30 pm in the mornings.
On a vote the restricted period was preferred by six
votes to two.

Given the history of the matter, and the lack of any
prior indication that there would be opposition to
their proposed regular extension on the part of the
respondents, the petitioners were understandably surprised and disappointed by the decision. Accordingly
on 23 June 1992 their solicitors wrote to the respondents requesting, in terms of s 18 of the 1976 Act, a
statement of the respondents' reasons for arriving at
the partial refusal of the application. By letter dated 7
July the respondents wrote to the petitioners' solicitors setting out purported reasons for what they
described as "the decision of the licensing board to
partially grant your clients' application". In the said
letter the respondents quote the provisions of s 47 of
the Law Reform (Miscellaneous Provisions) (Scotland)
Act 1990 and also of s 64 (3) of the 1976 Act. Thereafter they set out the grounds of their decision in the
following terms:

"In the case of the above premises, the Board was
not satisfied by the applicant, ie your clients, that
there was a need for persons participating in club
activities, ie playing golf or squash to be able to have
a drink on Sundays between 11 am and 12 noon. The
Board was also not satisfied that having regard to the
social circumstances of the locality and to the activities
taking place therein that the number of persons participating in the club activities justified a need for an
extended hour of drinking time.

"The Board was also not satisfied that such an
extension in Sunday mornings would be of such
benefit to the community as a whole as to outweigh
any detriment which the extension to the permitted
hours would have."

It would appear that after the respondents had dealt
with the petitioners' application at the same sitting
they dealt with applications for a regular extension of
permitted hours on a Sunday by Kirriemuir Golf Club
and Carnoustie Golf Club. These were partially
refused in respect of the hour from 11 am until 12
noon. I was provided with a newspaper report detailing what is therein described as "a lively exchange"
between the solicitor of the Kirriemuir Club and a
councillor on the board. Views expressed by other
councillors on the board were also reported. I did not
understand counsel for the respondents to challenge
the accuracy of this report, but this is of no moment
for I do not consider that any proceedings connected
with the later applications really affect the issue before
me.

The petitioners in their petition set out four grounds
of objection to the respondents' decision on their
application: (1) they say that the purported statement

of reasons for the respondents' decision is insufficient
to fulfil their statutory responsibility in respect of
these; (2) they contend that if sufficient reasons had
been stated such reasons are in law unsustainable
because the respondents have failed to exercise their
discretion in a reasonable manner; (3) they contend
that the remarks at the hearing on the application
which were attributed to Mr Meldrum were taken into
account by the respondents and constituted an
improper consideration which influenced their
decision. Counsel for the respondents conceded that
the opinions attributed to Mr Meldrum would have
represented improper material for consideration by
the board but the petitioner's counsel did not, in fact,
persist with this ground of appeal since there was
nothing before me from which it could be inferred that
Mr Meldrum's views were taken into account by the
board; (4) the refusal of the applications relating to the
Kirriemuir and Carnoustie clubs were said to indicate
that the respondents had erred in law in applying an
inflexible policy decision to the petitioners' application. However, again at the end of the day I did not
understand that this ground of complaint was persisted in with any enthusiasm. Accordingly, the submissions of counsel for the petitioners were essentially
that the grounds given for restriction of the extension
were inadequately stated and in any event would
indicate a totally unreasonable exercise of discretion.
In relation to the sufficiency of the reasons for the
decision I was referred to *Wordie Property Co Ltd v
Secretary of State for Scotland, Martin v Ellis, Troc
Sales v Kirkcaldy District Licensing Board* and *Speedlift
Auto Salvage v Kyle and Carrick District Council*. On
the question of the exercise of discretion I was referred
to *Associated Provincial Picture Houses v Wednesbury
Corporation*.

Counsel for the respondents argued that the reasons
given by his clients for their decision were adequate in
law. *Wordie Property Co Ltd* was a complicated case
decided after considerable evidence had been led. The
respondents had simply not been satisfied in respect of
the statutory requirements which the petitioners had
to establish. They were entitled to consider each
annual application on its own merits. I was referred to
Elder v Ross and Cromarty District Licensing Board.

It has to be observed that it is not part of the petitioners' case that the proceedings themselves were
irregular or contrary to natural justice. I would
respectfully agree with Lord Weir in *Elder* that each
extension of permitted hours is only a temporary
privilege and that the board are entitled (indeed
required) to consider each annual application afresh.
The 1990 Act, of course, imposed quite new statutory
requirements on the board (although I was informed
that this year's application was not the first of the petitioners' applications which had been subject to that
Act). Thus there is no question about the respondents'
entitlement to depart from the practice of previous
years. Nevertheless, given the history of this matter it
may well have been courteous and fair for those
members of the board who were considering opposing
the application to have given the petitioners' represen-

tative some warning of a possible change in the respondents' attitude so that he could have addressed the respondents more fully and also responded to any matter particularly troubling them. As it was the petitioners seem to have been completely taken aback when their application was not granted. No doubt that explains why they were particularly anxious to examine the respondents' statement of reasons for their decision since no indication of these reasons had at any time been given to them.

In *Wordie Property Co Ltd* at p 356 Lord Cameron, who agreed with the Lord President, states: "In giving his decision the Secretary of State is required by the relevant rules to give his reasons for that decision; if he fails to do so or if his reasons are not intelligible to the mind of an informed reader then his decision will be quashed. If the letter is so obscure and would leave in the mind of an informed reader such real and substantial doubt as to the reasons for his decision and as to the matters which he did or did not take into account, it does not comply with the requirements of r 11 (1) and therefore on that ground the minister's order must be quashed."

It is quite true that *Wordie Property Co Ltd* was a complicated case where, no doubt, adequate reasons for the decision would have required a full statement. However, in my view Lord Cameron's observations are equally applicable to any statement of reasons given in response to a s 18 request. The point is that giving an interested party a right to examine the reasons of a licensing board is so that the party can satisfy himself that the relevant decision has been arrived at within the parameters set out by statute and, in particular, that it is not based on factors improperly taken into account. This does not necessarily imply that reasons given for a decision must be immaculately precise and exhaustive. However, it is critical that the interested party who looks at the reasons should at least be left in no doubt as to why the licensing board arrived at the relevant decision. A statement of reasons which is confused and ambiguous would afford the party who called for it no help whatsoever.

In the respondents' letter of 7 July they, in effect, give three reasons for their decision and I shall deal with them in reverse order. The third reason is that the board were not satisfied that the sought for extension of hours to cover from 11 am to 12 noon on a Sunday morning would be of such a benefit to the community as a whole as to outweigh any detriment which the extension to the permitted hours would have. This reason is a mere echo of the terms of s 47 (1) (b) of the 1990 Act. It is of course the case that the onus of satisfying the respondents rests squarely on the shoulders of the petitioners. However, the respondents may not have been satisfied for a number of reasons. They may have considered that the petitioners had not placed sufficient information before them to enable them to form a considered view. On the other hand, they may have decided that, even on the facts presented, the balance did not favour the petitioners' application. If so, no guidance is given as to whether the respondents considered that there was

some benefit to the community but that this was outweighed by detrimental factors or whether their position was that they considered that no advantage to the community whatsoever could have accrued from the proposed extension of hours. If it was thought that the extended hours would give rise to detrimental factors no clue is given as to what these might have been. In my view the third reason leaves the petitioners no wiser as to why their proposed extension of hours was partially refused.

The second reason is probably more closely connected with the remaining reason which I have still to refer to in that both reasons appear to be related to the criterion of need set out by s 47 (1) (a) of the 1990 Act. The reason is set out in the respondents' letter as being that: "The Board was also not satisfied that having regard to the social circumstances of the locality and to the activities taking place therein that the number of persons participating in the club activities justified a need for an extended hour of drinking time."

The introduction of the word "also" shows that what I have quoted is to be regarded as a separate reason and not a mere amplification of the first reason which refers to golf and squash players. The reference to having regard to the social circumstances of the locality and the activities taking place therein clearly refers to what has to be taken into account in terms of s 64 (3) of the 1976 Act as applied by s 47 of the 1990 Act. In any event the core of the reason would appear to be that the number of persons participating in club activities does not justify a need for an extended hour of drinking time. However, it is plainly stated that this view was arrived at having regard to the social circumstances of the locality and the activities taking place therein. Once again no guidance is given as to the particular social circumstances and activities which were taken into account. Beyond this the petitioners were granted an extension for the period of 30 minutes between midday and 12.30 pm and yet the respondents failed to signify why on the question of numbers of club members taking part in club activities they decided to differentiate between midday to 12.30 pm and 11 am to midday. If, as seems likely, considerations other than mere numbers caused the respondents to reject the earlier hour of the proposed extension, these are not particularised. In my view, the second reason is as ambiguous as the third and for that reason is equally inadequate.

The reason first stated in the letter of 7 July is in the following terms: "In the case of the above premises the Board was not satisfied by the applicant, ie your clients, that there was a need for persons participating in club activities, ie playing golf or squash, to be able to have a drink on Sundays between 11 am and 12 noon."

This is perhaps the reason which comes closest to being a sufficient reason but nevertheless it falls considerably short of being free from ambiguity. The respondents require to take account of the activities in the locality before deciding if there is a need for a regular extension of permitted hours. Such activities could be negative to the grant of an extension (such as, for example, churchgoing or activities involving young persons) or positive to the grant (such as existence of any important recreational activity where participants may reasonably require to be provided with a facility for alcohol). Apart from the separate considerations raised by s 47 (1) (b) there are two questions which arise in a case such as this. The first is whether or not the petitioners have demonstrated a local need for the proposed extension of hours. Unless this question can be answered affirmatively the application must fail. The second question is, assuming that there is such a need, is it desirable in any event to cater for it? In considering both these questions the board must take into account any relevant local activities. In the present case the first question is essentially what local need is there for licence facilities during the hours of 11 am to 12 noon on Sundays in an area where there are golfers enjoying recreational golf in the early morning. Thus to state that the board are not satisfied that there is a need for golfers and squash players to have a drink between 11 am and 12 noon on a Sunday leaves some doubt as to what considerations are motivating the board. Local need for a facility cannot be equated with the personal needs of individual club members and if the board were concerned with the issue of the need in the locality it would have been perfectly straightforward to have stated this in clear terms. The situation is complicated by the fact that on the same information about use by club members the board were apparently satisfied that there was a local need in respect of the period from 12 noon to 12.30 pm. It is difficult to escape the conclusion that in differentiating between the earlier and later part of the extension they were considering, the respondents were not exclusively moved by the question of a need in the locality for extended hours but rather by broader questions such as perhaps that drinking would be taking place relatively early on a Sunday morning. Their stated reasons might themselves lead to such an interpretation. The respondents have a certain discretion as to what they consider is desirable, but if the desirability of granting the extension was in fact taken into account then this should have been said and an indication given of the particular reasons why the respondents considered it undesirable to grant the whole extension.

In my view the reasons given by the respondents in terms of the s 18 requisition are not sufficiently informative to comply with their statutory responsibility. Given that I am not clear as to the respondents' reasons for their decision it is not necessary nor practicable to decide if they exercised their discretion reasonably. The respondents have not chosen to amplify their reasons in any way in their answers and their counsel frankly conceded that he had no reason to suppose that the respondents were in a position to add to their reasons for refusing the part of the regular extension which they rejected. In the circumstances I doubt if anything could be gained by remitting to the respondents for further amplification of their reasons.

The court cannot be satisfied that the respondents acted properly within their statutory powers when they refused the part of the proposed regular extension which they did. The decision on the application which deals with the period between 12 noon and 12.30 pm and the afternoon hours is not challenged but insofar as the decision refused an extension between the hours of 11 am and 12 noon it falls to be reduced. I shall also grant the declarator sought to the effect of declaring that the respondents have failed to give a proper statement of their reasons for their refusal of the petitioners' application quoad the said period. The decision falls to be reconsidered and I shall accordingly ordain the respondents to be reconvened as soon as convenient and to consider afresh the petitioners' application so far as relating to the said earlier period.

Counsel for Petitioners, Hajducki; Solicitors, Allan McDougall & Co, SSC (for Ferguson & Will, Brechin) — Counsel for Respondents, Ellis; Solicitors, Balfour & Manson, Nightingale & Bell.

P G L H

EFT Commercial Ltd v Security Change Ltd (No 2)

FIRST DIVISION
THE LORD PRESIDENT (HOPE),
LORDS SUTHERLAND AND CULLEN
11 NOVEMBER 1992

Process — Appeal — Appeal to House of Lords — Interim execution of decree for payment pending appeal — Whether interim execution should be granted — Whether caution for repetition sufficient protection — Court of Session Act 1988 (c 36), s 41 (1).

Section 41 (1) of the Court of Session Act 1988 provides that on an appeal from the Inner House to the House of Lords the Inner House "may regulate all matters relating to interim possession, execution and expenses already incurred as it thinks fit, having regard to the interests of the parties to the cause".

The lessors of an item of printing equipment obtained a decree against two limited companies for the sum of £650,259.65, that sum being held to be due under a guarantee granted by the companies to the lessors. The Inner House refused a reclaiming motion by the guarantors, which presented a petition of appeal to the House of Lords. Prior to the appeal being considered, the lessors applied to the court, under s 41 of the 1988 Act, for an order allowing the interlocutors to be extracted and for interim execution to proceed upon the decree. The lessors argued that there was a settled rule of practice that, pending an appeal to the House of Lords, the court would invariably allow interim execution of any sum found to be due for payment, if sufficient caution were offered for its repetition, unless cause were shown to the contrary. The guarantors argued that the terms of s 41 gave the court a wide discretion, and that they would be caused prejudice if the interim order were made. An interim order could put in jeopardy refinancing operations which one of the guarantors was carrying out. They argued further that the lessors would, in effect, receive a windfall benefit as they had been able, by other means, to avoid any significant loss from the transaction, and any sum due to them would normally have fallen due by instalments over a period of several years.

Held, (1) that there was a settled rule of practice, which was a general but not an absolute rule, that where a decree had been granted for an ascertained sum of money, the person holding the decree was entitled to have interim execution of the judgment pending an appeal to the House of Lords and upon caution being found, unless cause were shown why the rule should not be followed (pp 552J-L and 554A); (2) that a distinction was drawn between decrees for payment of money and other decrees, in that where the decree was not for payment of money the court had a wider discretion as to whether or not to grant interim execution, and in those cases it should have in mind the preservation of the status quo (p 553I-J); and (3) that the guarantors had not succeeded in showing cause why the general rule should not be followed (p 554B-E); and order for interim execution *granted.*

McGowan v Barr & Co, 1929 SLT 341, *followed; Lord Advocate v Glasgow Corporation,* 1973 SLT 153, *distinguished.*

Petition under s 41 of the Court of Session Act 1988

EFT Commercial Ltd presented a petition under s 41 of the Court of Session Act 1988 for interim execution of a joint and several decree against Security Change Ltd and Gresham House plc for the sum of £650,259.65 together with interest and expenses, pending an appeal by the respondents to the House of Lords.

Statutory provisions

The Court of Session Act 1988 provides:

"41.—(1) On an appeal to the House of Lords under section 40 of this Act, a copy of the petition of appeal shall be laid by the respondent before the Inner House which may regulate all matters relating to interim possession, execution and expenses already incurred as it thinks fit, having regard to the interests of the parties to the cause as they may be affected by the upholding or reversal of the judgment against which the appeal has been taken."

Cases referred to

Advocate (Lord) v Glasgow Corporation, 1973 SLT 153; 1972 SC 287.
McBeath v Forsythe (1887) 15 R 8.

McGowan v Barr & Co, 1929 SLT 412; 1929 SC 785.
Ross v Matheson & Son (1847) 10 D 222.

The petition came before the First Division in the single bills on 11 November 1992 on the petitioners' motion to grant the prayer of the petition.

Eo die the court *granted* the motion.

The following opinion of the court was delivered by the Lord President (Hope):

OPINION OF THE COURT.—This is an application under s 41 of the Court of Session Act 1988 for interim execution of a decree for payment pending an appeal to the House of Lords. The action was for payment by the respondents to the petitioners of a sum due under a guarantee. On 22 October 1991 the Lord Ordinary pronounced decree against the respondents for payment to the petitioners of the sum of £650,259.65 with interest at the rate of 5 per cent above the base rate of the Clydesdale Bank plc as applied from time to time from 4 January 1991 until payment. He also found the respondents liable to the petitioners in the expenses of the action except in so far as already dealt with. The respondents reclaimed against this interlocutor, but on 8 May 1992 the reclaiming motion was refused. By its interlocutor of that date the court adhered to the Lord Ordinary's interlocutor and found the respondents liable to the petitioners in the expenses of the reclaiming motion [1993 SLT 128]. On 31 July 1992 the respondents presented a petition of appeal to the House of Lords against these interlocutors. The petitioners now seek an order allowing the interlocutors to be extracted and execution to proceed upon the decrees in terms thereof notwithstanding the appeal. They are willing to find caution for the full amount of the decrees which they seek to have enforced.

Counsel for the petitioners invited us to follow the settled rule of practice that, pending an appeal to the House of Lords, the court will allow interim execution of a sum found to be due for payment, if sufficient caution is offered for its repetition, unless cause is shown to the contrary. Section 41 of the 1988 Act provides that the Inner House may regulate all matters relating to interim possession, execution and expenses already incurred as it thinks fit "having regard to the interests of the parties to the cause as they may be affected by the upholding or reversal of the judgment against which the appeal has been taken". It might seem from this wording that the court has a wide discretion in the matter, but in *McGowan v Barr & Co* it was held, on a consideration of a long line of authority to this effect, that there had emerged a general rule of practice by which petitions for interim execution of decrees for payment were invariably granted unless cause be shown to the contrary. The present case falls within that category, and the question is, as counsel for the petitioners put it, whether the respondents are able to show cause why we should not grant the order which the petitioners seek on their offer of caution for the full amount.

For the respondents it was submitted that an order for interim execution would result in prejudice to them which would be incapable of remedy in the event that they were successful in their appeal. Counsel for the respondents contended that, despite what was said in *McGowan v Barr & Co,* s 41 of the 1988 Act conferred a wide discretion on the court and that our principal concern should be to preserve the status quo. Caution would no doubt be sufficient in most cases to achieve that result, but in the present case it would not be a satisfactory remedy. Although he accepted that it was not open to him to re-argue the substance of the case, he maintained that the sum which had been found due for payment to the petitioners did not represent the amount of any actual loss to them. It was in effect a windfall, since they had been able by other means to avoid any significant loss from the transaction which was covered by the guarantee. Furthermore, by awarding them the sum sued for, the court had found the petitioners entitled to immediate payment of an amount which would otherwise have fallen due by instalments over a period of several years. Their application should be seen, therefore, as prompted by nothing more than the desire of a judgment creditor to get his money now rather than later. He contrasted the position of the petitioners with that of the respondents, Gresham House plc, on the ground that for them to be required to make payment now would put at risk a series of negotiations which were in progress for the refinancing of their business operations. No such submission was made in regard to the respondents Security Change Ltd, since that company is now in receivership. But we were shown various documents in order to demonstrate the present financial position of Gresham House plc and the attempts which they had been making to obtain additional financing from various banks and other financial institutions.

These documents demonstrate that on 8 May 1992 the company's shareholders were invited to vote in favour of a resolution to create and issue secured loan stock for issue to the financial institutions in order to reschedule group borrowing and stabilise its affairs. We were also shown an interim statement by the chairman of the company dated 30 October 1992 in which it was reported that losses would continue until the company was able to complete the negotiations, that slow progress was being made and that there was no certainty that the negotiations would be successfully concluded. The current litigation has been declared in the notes to the accounts as a contingent liability of the company pending a decision on the matter by the House of Lords. Counsel for the respondents accepted that, in comparison with the total assets of the company as disclosed by its balance sheet, the sum at issue in the present case appeared not to be significant.

But he pointed out that what was being sought from the banks and other financial institutions was refinancing, not an injection of share capital. He maintained that there was a serious risk that the banks and other financial institutions would not be willing to provide finance to Gresham House plc simply in order to enable the money to be paid over at once to the petitioners, as would be the inevitable consequence if an order for interim execution were to be pronounced. On the other hand, failure in the negotiations with these banks and financial institutions would be likely to prove fatal to the company. The result would be that repayment of the sums due in terms of the interlocutors, financed if necessary by the bond of caution, would come too late to prevent its affairs from being put into the hands of a liquidator.

We are not persuaded that an order for interim execution should not be granted in this case. Counsel for the respondents based his submission that we should exercise our discretion in favour of preserving the status quo on a passage in the opinion of Lord President Emslie in *Lord Advocate v Glasgow Corporation,* 1973 SLT at p 155, where he said: "There is force in both submissions as I have stated them but it is for us to decide, in the exercise of what is called our sound discretion, where the balance of advantage lies, having regard, as s 17 says, to the interests of the parties, and that means both parties, as they may be affected by affirmance or reversal of our interlocutor".

But in that case, which was decided under s 17 of the Court of Session Act 1808 from which s 41 of the 1988 Act is derived, the interlocutor under appeal was one ordaining the performance by the local authority of their statutory duty. It was not therefore one of those cases which fall under the settled rule of practice by which interim execution of a decree for payment will be allowed on caution being found for that amount. The distinction between cases of that type and cases where the court is asked to allow interim execution of a decree other than one for payment was noted by Lord Ormidale in *McGowan v Barr & Co,* 1929 SLT at p 413. He pointed out that the court had recognised that, when the decree was one which affected the possession of an estate, it should have in view the interests of both parties and the preservation of the status quo. But he held that the rule of practice as regards the execution of a decree for expenses was too finally settled for the court to do otherwise than grant the prayer of the petition. A decree for payment of a sum found to be due under a contract is in the same position as a decree for expenses: see *Ross v Matheson & Son.* In *McBeath v Forsythe,* interim execution was allowed of a decree for payment of a sum found to be due in an action of count, reckoning and payment. Lord President Inglis said at p 9: "When a decree has been granted for an ascertained sum of money, the person holding the judgment is entitled to have interim execution of the judgment pending an appeal to the House of Lords".

Lord Shand noted that the statute contemplated that the court should have a much larger discretion than it had been in the habit of exercising, but he said that it could not go back on what had become a settled rule. It should be noted also that in *McGowan v Barr & Co,* at p 413, Lord Ormidale said that it was not really a relevant consideration that the respondent would be prejudiced simply because she were to be called upon

A there and then to make payment of a considerable sum. He saw an order for caution as making it impossible for her to claim that she would suffer prejudice by having to pay the expenses already incurred, should she in the end be successful in her appeal.

The general rule, although a settled rule of practice, is nevertheless not to be regarded as an absolute rule, as Lord Justice Clerk Alness pointed out in *McGowan v Barr & Co* at p 413. The question then is whether the respondents have succeeded in showing cause why the rule should not be followed in this case. We were

B not impressed by the argument of counsel for the respondents that the sum found due for payment by the respondents was to be seen merely as a windfall to the petitioners. The whole point of the decision which was the basis for our interlocutor is that the petitioners are entitled to payment of that sum as a sum agreed to be due to them in the events which have occurred. Consideration of the question whether or not the petitioners are truly out of pocket by that amount would be inconsistent with the view taken by this court in

C pronouncing its interlocutor. As for the argument that to allow interim execution would prove fatal to the negotiations for the refinancing of Gresham House plc, we are not satisfied that this point has been made out. No documents were put before us to show that it was crucial to the success or otherwise of the negotiations with the banks and other financial institutions that interim execution should not be allowed. The petition was served on the respondents more than two months ago, and we would have expected this point to be capable of being demonstrated by some documen-

D tary evidence to this effect, if this was the case. As against that we have the clear impression that the difficulty and delay which the respondents have encountered in concluding their negotiations is due to a variety of other factors. The respondents' contingent liability to the petitioners has already been disclosed in their accounts, and it is not obvious why a conversion of that contingent liability into a contingent asset, supported by an appropriate bond of caution, would be regarded by the banks as unacceptable in taking their

E decision whether or not to provide the company with the financial support which it requires. On the whole the continuing decline in the company's financial position over many months persuades us that it is appropriate that the settled rule should be applied in this case and that the respondents' legitimate interests will be sufficiently protected by an appropriate bond of caution.

For these reasons we shall allow the interlocutors to be extracted and execution to proceed thereon, upon

F caution being found in common form for payment of the equivalent amount in the event of the interlocutors appealed against being reversed or altered in the House of Lords.

Counsel for Petitioners, Sturrock; Solicitors, Morton Fraser Milligan, WS — Counsel for Respondents, Glennie, Cheyne; Solicitors, Biggart Baillie & Gifford, WS.

D A K

(NOTE)

Bradnock v Liston   G

OUTER HOUSE
LORD OSBORNE
18 NOVEMBER 1992

Damages — Amount — Solatium — Spinal injury caused during childbirth — Nerve damage leading to pain and bowel problems.

A young mother suffered severe pain and episodes H of faecal urgency and incontinence over a period of about six years following the birth of her first child. She claimed that these conditions and also a fracture of the fourth sacral segment had been caused by negligence during a forceps delivery.

Opinion, that solatium for a fracture as claimed by the pursuer would have been properly valued at £1,500 and that solatium for the whole consequences would have been properly valued at £12,000.

I

Susan Bradnock raised an action against Dr William Alexander Liston and his employers the Lothian Health Board for damages said to have resulted from Dr Liston's negligence in connection with the pursuer's pregnancy and delivery of her first child by forceps on 14 March 1986. The pursuer was then aged 30.

The pursuer's case was that Dr Liston used exces- J sive force during the forceps delivery and that, as a result, she had sustained a fracture through the fourth sacral segment leading to nerve damage. Branches from the segment which innervated the pubo-rectalis muscle had been damaged, causing the whole of the pursuer's pelvic floor gradually to descend as the normal resting tone of that muscle was lost. It was said that, over time, the continuation of the pubo-rectalis muscle in a more relaxed position had led to secondary stretching of the pudendal nerve causing a secondary K pudendal neuropathy and deficient muscle tissue in the external anal sphincter. She had suffered severe pain and became demoralised. She had had severe pain opening her bowels, difficulty controlling the bowels and episodes of faecal incontinence. The pursuer claimed to continue to suffer said complaints and regularly to experience faecal urgency, which was getting worse. The defenders alleged that the pursuer had had pre-existing problems of urgency of defecation and incontinence of urine resulting from congenital condi- L tions of spina bifida occulta and talipes and, insofar as there were any problems following the birth, they were the consequences of or recognised complications of childbirth, not inferring fault.

Immediately after the birth, when the effects of anaesthesia wore off, the pursuer felt severe pain in her lower spine and could hardly walk. When the pursuer got home, she found that it was a little easier to walk, although she was still in considerable pain in the region of her back and her bottom. Attempts to open her bowels she said were excruciating. She found sitting down painful, a situation which continued for more than a month. Thereafter she continued to have intermittent but serious bowel problems leading to various courses of hospital investigations and physiotherapy and, eventually, an operation for pelvic floor repair undertaken in April 1992 after she had given birth, by Caesarean section, to two further children. That operation was likely, but not certain, to prove successful. After a proof the Lord Ordinary (Osborne) held that there had been no sacral fracture and, accordingly, no proof of negligence. The defenders were assoilzied. In relation to damages his Lordship said:

"Having already set out the details of the sequelae of the pursuer's delivery of Deborah, what I propose to do in relation to the question of damages is to summarise the positions of the parties and subsequently show how I would have resolved the questions between them had I held that the pursuer was entitled to damages. Both counsel for the pursuer and counsel for the defenders recognised that it was necessary for them to present alternative bases for an award of solatium. Dealing with the first alternative, that is to say that all of the pursuer's problems arising from her faecal incontinence and urgency were the result of the assumed fault, it was submitted on the pursuer's behalf that solatium of £15,000 would be appropriate. It was recognised by counsel for the pursuer in making this submission that he was not able to put before the court any reported cases of an award in similar circumstances to those existing in the present case. However, he made reference to *Bovenzi v Kettering Health Authority* (Kemp & Kemp, Vol 2, F4-017). The circumstances in that case were somewhat different from those of the present and the injuries involved apparently less severe. On the view that the whole of the solatium involved in this case related to the past, counsel for the pursuer submitted that interest should be awarded at the rate of 7½ per cent per annum on the sum of £15,000 from 14 March 1986 until the date of decree.

"On the alternative assumption that no causal connection had been proved between a fracture and the pursuer's problems of faecal incontinence and urgency, the submission was to the effect that £2,000 would be an appropriate sum to represent solatium. Interest on that at 15 per cent per annum should be awarded from one month after the date of the birth of Deborah, the time by which the pain experienced by the pursuer had largely subsided." His Lordship then narrated the submissions on loss of earnings made on the pursuer's behalf and on behalf of the defenders. In relation to the defenders' submissions on solatium his Lordship continued: "Turning to the question of quantum of damages, it was recognised that there were two necessary bases of approach. The first basis was that a fracture had occurred but that it had made no material contribution to the pursuer's faecal incontinence or urgency. The second basis was that it had. Dealing with the question of solatium on the first basis, it was submitted that the pursuer's claim for £2,000 was excessive. Reference was made to the case

of *Murphy v National Coal Board*, 1988 SLT 630. On the basis of that case it was suggested that an appropriate award here on this assumption would be £1,200. Interest on that sum at 15 per cent per annum from 14 April 1986 would be appropriate.

"Approaching the matter of solatium on the second basis, while there was no guarantee that the operation undertaken in April 1992 would be successful, the chances of success were high. Mr Bartolo [the surgeon who had carried out the operation] had been pleased with the results which he had seen so far. While at some stages in the period between the birth of Deborah and the present time the pursuer's faecal incontinence problem had created embarrassment and distress, it was apparent in recent times that it had made a relatively minor impact upon the pursuer's lifestyle. Her social life was now reasonably full. She had been reasonably successful in managing her problem. In the 12 months to May 1992 she had had no accidents.

"On the basis of this outline of the situation, it was submitted that solatium of £15,000 was excessive. The case of *Bovenzie v Kettering Health Authority*, cit sup, was not helpful in the circumstances of this case. No case involving a close parallel with the present circumstances could be found. The example of spinal injuries to be found in *O'Shea v Monklands District Council*, 1988 SLT 344 might be of assistance. The injuries in that case were much worse than those of the pursuer. As at 19 February 1988 an assessment of solatium of £12,500 had been made. On behalf of the defenders a figure of £8,000 for solatium upon this basis was made. . . .

"In view of the position which I have taken up in relation to the questions of causation to which I have already referred in connection with the merits of the action, it is necessary for me to express an opinion on damages on two alternative bases. Upon the first basis, that is to say upon the view that the pursuer's problems of faecal incontinence and urgency were attributable to a culpable fracture, my opinion is that solatium could properly be assessed at £12,000. I consider that that sum would be necessary to compensate the pursuer for the very considerable embarrassment and distress which were caused to her by those problems. In my view interest could properly have been awarded at 7½ per cent per annum on that sum from the date of Deborah's birth until the date of decree.

"Upon the alternative basis that I am dealing only with an assumed culpable sacral fracture, in my opinion an appropriate sum for solatium would be £1,500. Interest on that sum from 14 April 1986 could properly have been awarded at 15 per cent per annum until the date of decree."

Counsel for Pursuer, Miller, QC, Peoples; Solicitors, Alex Morison & Co, WS — Counsel for Defenders, Stewart, QC, Ellis; Solicitor, J I McCubbin.

C H

Wright's Trustees v Callender

A HOUSE OF LORDS

LORD KEITH OF KINKEL,
LORD JAUNCEY OF TULLICHETTLE,
LORD LOWRY, LORD MUSTILL AND
LORD SLYNN OF HADLEY

28 JANUARY 1993

Trust — Trust disposition and settlement — Construc-
B *tion — "Issue" — "Great-grandchildren" — Scottish*
deeds executed in 1917 and 1925 — Succession to residue
liferented by granddaughter domiciled in England and
dying in 1989 — Children of granddaughter legitimated
by operation of Legitimacy Act 1959 — Whether children
entitled to take share of residue — Legitimacy Act 1959
(7 & 8 Eliz II, c 73), s 1 (1).

Succession — Testate — Trust disposition and settlement
— Construction — "Issue" — "Great-grandchildren" —
Scottish deeds executed in 1917 and 1925 — Succession to
residue liferented by granddaughter domiciled in England
C *and dying in 1989 — Children of granddaughter legiti-*
mated by operation of Legitimacy Act 1959 — Whether
children entitled to take share of residue — Legitimacy
Act 1959 (7 & 8 Eliz II, c 73), s 1 (1).

A testator died in 1917 leaving a trust disposition
and settlement in which he granted power to his
widow to alter the "directions, purposes and powers"
of that deed. She exercised that power and executed
her own trust disposition and settlement in 1925. The
D widow died in 1932 leaving one daughter who died in
1953. That daughter had four children, one of whom,
a daughter, was domiciled in England. She had three
children, but at the date of their births she was not
married to their father, although she subsequently
married him. Those three children were not legitimated under English law until the coming into force
of the Legitimacy Act 1959. They could not be legitimated under Scots law until the coming into force of
s 4 of the Legitimation (Scotland) Act 1968. The last
E surviving grandchild of the testator and testatrix and
the mother of those three children died in 1989. At
that time she had a life interest in both of her grandparents' trust estates. In terms of her grandfather's
trust disposition and settlement succession to the
share of residue liferented by her passed to her
"issue", and in terms of her grandmother's settlement
succession to the share of residue liferented by her
passed to the grandmother's "great-grandchildren".
Vesting in these shares was suspended until the grand-
F daughter's death. A dispute arose as to the entitlement
of the children of the last granddaughter to their
mother's share of the residue of the grandfather's and
grandmother's estates and a special case was presented
to the Inner House. An Extra Division held that if a
testator was to be presumed to know the law of Scotland he also had to be presumed to know that a
person's heirs in mobilibus were determined by the
law of his domicile and that a destination to the children of a liferentrix on her death had to be construed
as to her lawful children according to the law of her
domicile at the time of her death. By that time the

granddaughter's three children had been legitimated
under the law of England and were accordingly G
entitled to benefit in both estates. Another great-
grandchild appealed to the House of Lords.

Held (per Lord Keith of Kinkel, Lord Jauncey of
Tullichettle, Lord Lowry and Lord Mustill), that a
testator was not to be regarded as having contemplated
that there might be a change in the law between his
death and the opening of the succession, and that the
more natural intention to attribute to him was that the
succession should be regulated by the law as it stood
at the time of his death and accordingly that the testa- H
tor and the testatrix had not intended that when the
succession opened the class of beneficiaries should
include "issue" and "great-grandchildren" who
answered the description of "lawful" by reason only
of changes in the law occurring after their testamentary dispositions had come into operation (pp
559I-J, 562J-563A and 563G and H); and appeal
allowed.

Observed, that it was clear from the terms of the I
Legitimacy Acts of 1926 and 1959 and the Legitimation (Scotland) Act 1968 that Parliament was concerned that deeds throughout Scotland and England
which were already in operation should not be affected
by the emergence of newly legitimated persons, and
that it would have been anomalous if Scots law, while
not recognising legitimation by the Act of 1968 as
qualifying a person to inherit under a Scottish instrument coming into operation before the commencement of that Act, were forced to recognise as so J
qualifying a person legitimated by the Act of 1959,
notwithstanding the limitation by that Act of the right
to inherit under an English instrument (pp 560A-B
and 563D-E, G and H).

Held, per Lord Slynn of Hadley, that the relevant
law was that in force at the time when the bequest fell
to vest even if there was a change in the law between
the deeds and the vesting, but that for the reasons
given by the majority of their Lordships, the
Legitimacy Acts did not operate to confer on the K
granddaughter's three children rights under the two
deeds (p 563H-K).

Special case
(Reported 1992 SLT 498)

A special case was presented to the Inner House
by (1) John Morton Miller and others, the trustees
acting under the trust disposition and settlement of
the late John Patrick Wright, WS, (2) Rupert David L
Dundonald Callender, a great-grandchild of the
testator, and (3) Anna Charlotte Holmes or Raines and
two others, great-grandchildren of the testator by a
different grandchild, concerning questions whether
the third parties fell to be regarded as "issue" in terms
of that trust disposition and settlement and "great-
grandchildren" in terms of the trust disposition and
settlement of Mrs Anna Jessie Walker Morison or
Wright, the widow of John Patrick Wright. The questions posed by the special case were:

A (1) On a proper construction of the trust disposition and settlement of each of Mr Wright and Mrs Wright and in the circumstances which have occurred, do the parties of the third part fall within the class of "issue" for the purposes thereof?

(2) On a proper construction of the trust disposition and settlement of Mrs Wright and in the circumstances which have occurred, do the parties of the third part fall within the class of "great-grandchildren" for the purposes thereof?

B The case was heard before an Extra Division on 3 and 4 October 1991.

Cases referred to

Allan, Petitioner, 1991 SLT 203.
Bell v Cheape (1845) 7 D 614.
Cockburn's Trustees v Dundas (1864) 2 M 1185.
G's Trustees v G, 1936 SLT 631; 1936 SC 837.
Maxwell v Maxwell (1864) 3 M 318.
Nimmo v Murray's Trustees (1864) 2 M 1144.
C *Smith's Trustees v Macpherson,* 1926 SLT 669; 1926 SC 983.
Spencer's Trustees v Ruggles, 1982 SLT 165; 1981 SC 289.

On 25 October 1991 the court *answered* both questions in the special case in the *affirmative* and *held* that the third parties were entitled to succeed under both trust dispositions and settlements. (Reported 1992 SLT 498.)

D The second party appealed to the House of Lords.

Appeal

The appeal was heard before Lord Keith of Kinkel, Lord Jauncey of Tullichettle, Lord Lowry, Lord Mustill and Lord Slynn of Hadley on 16 and 17 November 1992.

On 28 January 1993 the House *allowed* the appeal, E *recalled* the interlocutor of 25 October 1991 and *answered* both questions in the special case in the *negative.*

LORD KEITH OF KINKEL.—The late John Patrick Wright, Writer to the Signet ("Mr Wright") died on 19 September 1917 leaving a trust disposition and settlement dated 16 September 1912. He was survived by his widow ("Mrs Wright"), by one daughter Mrs Violet Moncreiff Lockhart Wright or Callender ("Mrs Callender") and by four children F born to Mrs Callender, Hyacinth, Winifred, Richard and David. The provisions of the trust disposition and settlement were complicated, and it is sufficient to say that the fee of the residue of the estate, after liferents in favour of Mrs Wright and after her death in favour of Mrs Callender, was destined to such of his grandchildren as should survive the period of distribution, together with the issue of any grandchild who might have predeceased the period of vesting, equally among them per stirpes. However, Mr Wright by the trust disposition and settlement conferred upon Mrs

Wright absolute power at any time during her life to G alter its purposes and provisions. Mrs Wright exercised this power by three deeds of variation of different dates, the principal effect of which as regards the residue of the estate was that certain funds were to be held for each of her grandchildren in liferent and their issue in fee with provision for accretion to the others and their issue in the event of any grandchild dying without leaving issue.

Mrs Wright died on 21 December 1932 leaving a trust disposition and settlement dated 20 June 1925, the effect of which so far as material was that (a) H certain specific funds and (b) the residue of the estate were to be held in liferent for the last survivor of her grandchildren, and upon the death of such last survivor to be paid (a) to the surviving great-grandchildren of Mrs Wright "being children of" her granddaughters and younger grandson, and (b) to surviving issue of such last surviving grandchild.

Mrs Callender died in July 1953. Her son David died on 15 September 1977 survived by one son, Rupert David Dundonald Callender. Her daughter I Winifred died without issue on 11 November 1982 and her son Richard, also without issue, on 24 January 1987. Hyacinth, the last surviving grandchild of Mr and Mrs Wright, died on 2 April 1989. She was survived by three children, Anna, Hugo and Winifred, born respectively on 15 September 1942, 29 February 1944, and 6 September 1946. At the time they were born Hyacinth was not married to their father, Alfred Holmes. He was then married to someone else and thus not free to marry Hyacinth. However, he later J became free to marry her and did so on 6 August 1954, and she then became Mrs Holmes. At all material times the family were domiciled in England. The children were not legitimated on the date of the marriage because, by virtue of s 1 (2) of the Legitimacy Act 1926, the legitimation provisions of s 1 (1) did not apply to an illegitimate person whose father or mother was married to a third person when the illegitimate person was born. However, this exception was removed by s 1 (1) of the Legitimacy Act 1959, and the K three children therefore became legitimate, so far as the law of England was concerned, three months after 29 July 1959, the date of the passing of the Act. The common law of Scotland has for centuries admitted the doctrine of legitimation per subsequens matrimonium but subject to the qualification that the parents of the child should have been free to marry each other at the date of its conception. That qualification was removed, with effect from 8 June 1968, by s 4 of the Legitimation (Scotland) Act 1968. L

At the time of her death Mrs Holmes was liferented in certain funds under the two trust dispositions and settlements, vesting of the fee being postponed till her death. So far as Mr Wright's trust disposition and settlement is concerned the persons entitled to the fee are the surviving "issue" of Mrs Holmes, whom failing the surviving "issue" of her brother David. Under Mrs Wright's trust disposition and settlement the persons entitled to the fee are Mrs Wright's surviving "great-grandchildren".

A Doubts having arisen as to whether the three children of Mrs Holmes qualified as members of the classes which Mr and Mrs Wright, on a true construction of their testamentary dispositions, intended to benefit, a special case was presented for the opinion and judgment of the Court of Session by the respective trustees as parties of the first part, Rupert David Dundonald Callender as party of the second part and the three children of Mrs Holmes as parties of the third part.

B The questions posed by the special case are these: [his Lordship quoted the terms of the questions and continued:] On 25 October 1991 an Extra Division of the Inner House of the Court of Session (Lords Allanbridge, Cullen and Brand) pronounced an interlocutor answering both questions in the affirmative. The second party now appeals to your Lordships' House.

It is common ground between the appellant and the respondent third parties that the references in the two C trust dispositions and settlements to "issue" and to "great-grandchildren" are properly to be construed as limited to issue and to great-grandchildren who are legitimate children of their parents recognised as such by the law of Scotland. There is no doubt that at the period of vesting in 1989 the third parties were so recognised, though perhaps not without qualification. I will consider that point later. The dispute turns on whether or not, on a true construction of the two deeds, the makers of them intended that possession of D the status of legitimacy at the period of vesting should be determinative of the qualification to take as a beneficiary, or whether the intention was that only those persons who would have been recognised as legitimate by the law of Scotland at the time when each deed came into operation should be so qualified. In 1917 and in 1932 children of parents who were not free to marry at the time of conception, but who had later become free to marry and had married, were not recognised as legitimate by the law of Scotland in the E case both of the father having been domiciled in Scotland at the date of the marriage and of his having been domiciled in England at that date. There is certainly no reason to suppose that the testator or the testatrix might have contemplated the possibility of the law of Scotland being changed before the period of vesting so as to result in the legitimation of persons previously incapable of it or of the law of England or any other foreign country being changed to similar effect with consequent recognition in Scotland of the legitimacy F of persons benefiting from the change.

There is no reported case, so far as the industry of counsel has revealed, in which consideration has been given to the effect of a change in the law concerning legitimacy in the period between the coming into operation of an instrument and the opening of the succession. However, a somewhat similar situation arose, in connection with changes in the Scots law of intestate succession, in *Cockburn's Trs v Dundas*. Baron Cockburn died in 1820 leaving a trust disposition and settlement dated in 1814 by which he directed that the

residue of his estate, after the expiry of certain liferents, should be paid over "to and in favour of my G own nearest heirs and executors whatsoever alive at the time of distribution, and residing in Scotland, equally among them, share and share alike". The last of the liferents expired in 1862, by which time all the testator's children but one, who resided in India, had died. There were numerous grandchildren of the testator then living, and also a number of great-grandchildren born to grandchildren who had predeceased the expiry of the liferents. Under the law of moveable intestate succession in Scotland as it stood H at the time of the testator's death the heirs in mobilibus of a person deceased were those who stood in the same relationship to him with no representation by the issue of anyone who had predeceased. Thus for example the surviving children of the deceased would take to the exclusion of issue of a child who had predeceased him. By the Intestate Moveable Succession (Scotland) Act 1855 the law was changed so as to admit of such representation. The primary argument before the Second Division revolved round the ques- I tion whether the succession was a testate or intestate one, and indeed no contentions were put forward by great-grandchildren of the testator whose parents had predeceased the expiry of the liferents. It was decided that the succession was a testate one, and that the estate should be divided among the grandchildren, share and share alike. Lord Justice Clerk Inglis said at pp 1189-1190:

"The next question is, whether the nearest heirs *in mobilibus* in 1862 are the parties who would succeed J under the old law of succession, or those who would succeed *ab intestato* under the Act of 1855. That is no doubt an important question, but I think it is to be solved by giving effect to the principle, that we must follow as nearly as possible the mind and will of the testator, for this is a case of testate and not of intestate succession. Has the testator so bequeathed the residue of his estate as to express his mind and will that it should go to those who would succeed according to the K distribution of the law? It would have been easy for him so to bequeath the residue of his estate expressly, as if he had said, After the death of the liferenters then let the law interfere and distribute the residue of my estate. In that case the law at the death of the last liferenter would be the rule for the distribution of the estate. But the question here is, has the testator by what he has said so resigned and given up his own purpose as to his succession as to commit to the law to make his will for him? I cannot so read this clause. I think that what the testator had in his mind was, that L there were various classes of his heirs *in mobilibus*, the one of whom might succeed as the other failed. If his heirs *in mobilibus* of the first class survived, and were resident in Scotland, they were to take in the first instance; then those who, according to the then existing law, would be the next class of his heirs *in mobilibus* should take next, and so on. He certainly did not contemplate that the law of succession would be altered before the lapse of the period of endurance of the liferents. When the testator directs the distribution

A of his estate without saying expressly that the law at the period of distribution, whatever that law may be, shall regulate the distribution of the fee of the residue of my estate, was it not more natural that he should have in his mind the law as it then stood, and that he should intend and contemplate that in the event of his children not taking the fee the class pointed out by the then existing law should come in and take the residue, excluding those who were not resident in Scotland? I think that by adopting that view more than by any other we shall give effect to the intention of the

B testator."

Lord Cowan said at p 1192: "I cannot hold that the Intestacy Act can be viewed as having any legitimate operation on the rights of the claimants to take equally, and share and share alike. The question is, who are the parties to whom the truster destined his moveable succession, when he directed it to be conveyed to his nearest heirs and executors? The answer seems to be — those parties who, under that character, as he understood the meaning and effect of the words,

C are within the description. And accordingly no claim has been made for great-grandchildren whose parents predeceased the time of distribution."

And Lord Benholme at p 1193 said: "But I confess I think there may be doubt on the point whether great-grandchildren are not entitled to share, on the construction that the testator left it to the law as it might stand at the opening of his succession to determine who were his nearest heirs and executors. Had

D the Intestate Succession Act passed before Baron Cockburn's death I would have inclined to the opinion that the settlement would have brought in great-grandchildren, as by direction of law equally near with grandchildren; but, on the whole, when I see that Baron Cockburn never could have foreseen the change, I think we must estimate his intention by the law he knew of, rather than by the law he knew nothing of."

Lord Neaves dissented on this point, expressing the

E view, at p 1193, that the testator meant to bequeath the succession to those who should at law be his heirs in mobilibus at the time of distribution.

The cases of *Nimmo v Murray's Trs* and *Maxwell v Maxwell*, which were referred to in argument, did not raise the same point. Both cases concerned a testator who died after the Act of 1855 leaving testamentary dispositions dated before it and containing reference in one case to "nearest heirs and successors" and in the other to "heirs, executors, and assignees". It was

F held in each case that heirs ascertained by reference to the Act of 1855 were entitled to take. I regard this as no more than a reflection of the established doctrine that a will is ambulatory and speaks from death. As Lord Justice Clerk Inglis said in *Nimmo v Murray's Trs* at p 1149, a testator so long as he is of sound disposing mind must be held to know of changes that have taken place in the law of succession, and if he does not make any alteration in his will before his death so as to show that he intended the old law to have effect then the new law must have effect.

Counsel for the third parties relied on certain passages in the judgments in *Smith's Trs v Macpherson* G and in *Spencer's Trs v Ruggles* as indicating that in all cases the question whether a person is entitled to take as answering the description of an "heir" or a "child" is to be determined by the law of the domicile of the ancestor or the parent at the time when the succession opens. Again, neither of these cases was concerned with the situation where there has been a relevant change in the applicable law between the coming into operation of the instrument and the opening of the succession. The actual decision in *Spencer's Trs v Ruggles* was that on a proper construction of the trust H deed, taking into account the whole context, the expression "lawful children" did not include a child adopted under the law of Illinois and recognised by that law as a lawful child for all purposes of inheritance.

The only guidance relevant to a solution of the problem posed in the special case is thus to be found in the opinions expressed by the majority of the judges in *Cockburn's Trs v Dundas*. These opinions indicate I that a testator is not to be regarded as having contemplated that there might be a change in the law between his death and the opening of the succession, and that the more natural intention to attribute to him is that the succession should be regulated by the law as it stood at the time of his death. Applying that approach to the circumstances of the present case the conclusion must be that the testator and the testatrix did not intend that when the succession opened, the class of beneficiaries should include "issue" and "great-grandchildren" who answered the description of J "lawful" by reason only of changes in the law occurring after their testamentary dispositions had come into operation.

While that is sufficient for the determination of the appeal, it is appropriate to deal with another aspect of the case. The English Legitimacy Act 1959, which introduced the legitimation of children whose parents had not been free to marry at the time of their births but had later legally done so, by s 1 (2) incorporated K s 10 (2) of the Legitimacy Act 1926 subject to the substitution for references to the commencement of that Act of references to the commencement of the Act of 1959. Section 10 (2) provided that nothing in the Act of 1926 should affect the operation or construction of any disposition coming into operation before the commencement of the Act. There may be room for argument as to whether "any disposition" describes only dispositions governed by English law or whether it includes also dispositions governed by some foreign L law, but whether or not that be so it remains true that the class of persons legitimated by the Act of 1959 were not legitimated for all purposes of English law. The legitimation did not extend to capacity to inherit under an English instrument that came into operation before the commencement of the Act. While it is for the law of Scotland to recognise the status of legitimacy conferred by the Act on the children of fathers domiciled in England at the time of the relevant marriage, it must also be appropriate for that law to recognise that the legitimacy so conferred was subject to limitation. So in my opinion the correct view is that Scots law must for its own purposes of conflict of laws treat the same limitation as applicable as regards instruments governed by Scots law which came into operation before the commencement of the English Act. I see no reason why Scots law should treat a legitimation which is not complete for purposes of English law as complete for its own purposes. This consideration has the more force when it is kept in mind that the Scottish Legitimation Act of 1968, which had similar effect to the English Act of 1959, contains in s 7 (2) a provision to the same effect as s 10 (2) of the Act of 1926. It would be a strange result indeed if Scots law, while not recognising legitimation by the Act of 1968 as qualifying a person to inherit under a Scottish instrument coming into operation before the commencement of that Act, were forced to recognise as so qualifying a person legitimated by the Act of 1959, notwithstanding the limitation by that Act of the right to inherit under an English instrument.

Again, if the matter is looked at from the point of view of the intention to be attributed to the maker of a Scottish instrument coming into operation before the commencement of both the Act of 1959 and that of 1968, it is absurd to suppose that the intention might have been to treat as qualified to inherit a person legitimated by the English Act but not a person legitimated by the Scottish Act.

My Lords, for these reasons I would allow the appeal and answer the two questions in the special case in the negative. The costs of both parties, by agreement, will be paid on an agent and client basis out of the trust estate.

LORD JAUNCEY OF TULLICHETTLE.—I gratefully adopt the account of events given in the speech of my noble and learned friend, Lord Keith of Kinkel, with which speech I concur.

It is matter of agreement between the parties that when the testator and the testatrix used the terms "issue" of grandchildren and "great-grandchildren (being children of my said younger grandson and granddaughters)" in their respective trust dispositions and settlements to describe the fiars, they intended to refer only to those who were legitimate. The dispute between them is as to whether the legitimacy and hence identification of these fiars is to be determined by reference to the law of the domicile of the testator and testatrix at the time of their respective deaths or to the law of the domicile of the parents of the fiars when the succession opened to them many years later. The dispute arises because during the period between the death of the testatrix, who survived the testator, and the opening of the succession to the fiars the law not only of Scotland but of England was altered by statute to treat as legitimate certain persons who at the taking effect of the trust dispositions and settlements would have been treated as illegitimate at common law.

In any question of construction of a testamentary document the court is seeking, as best it can, to ascertain the intention of the testator. In the present case the question must be whether the testator and testatrix intended that the fiars should be only those persons who had been born in wedlock or had been legitimated per subsequens matrimonium or whether they intended that any descendant who had been legitimated by supervening legislation in circumstances in which he or she could not previously have been treated as legitimate should be eligible to take as a fiar. The second party who was born legitimate contends for the first alternative; the third parties who were legitimated by operation of the Legitimacy Act 1959 contend for the second. Before turning to consider a number of authorities which were said to be relevant to this question I should point out that there is nothing in either of the trust dispositions and settlements which suggests that the testator or testatrix intended that any special meaning should be given to the terms "issue" and "great-grandchildren", except to the extent of the words in parenthesis annexed to the latter terms.

In *Nimmo v Murray's Trs* a testator, one month before the passing of the Intestate Moveable Succession (Scotland) Act 1855, executed a testamentary settlement whereby the residue of his estate was destined to his "nearest heirs and successors". The testator died three months later and a question arose as to whether his nearest heirs fell to be determined by the law at the date of the settlement or at the date of his death, by which time the Act of 1855 had come into effect. It was held that the appropriate law was that at the date of death, Lord Justice Clerk Inglis at p 1149 saying: "Now I think the principle is, that so long as he was of sound disposing mind, and had the power of altering his settlement, he must be held to know of every change that took place in the law of succession, and the effect that that change would have on the destination of the residue of his estate; and if he did not make any alteration to shew that he intended the old law of succession to have effect as regarded his residue, in place of the new law which had been introduced by Act of Parliament, the new law must take effect."

A week later the Second Division gave judgment in the case of *Cockburn's Trs v Dundas*, in which a testator who died in 1820 directed that the residue of his estate should on the expiry of certain liferents be paid over to "my own nearest heirs and executors whatsoever alive at the time of distribution, and residing in Scotland". The last liferentrix died in 1862 and the question again was whether the "nearest heirs" were those determined by the law as at the date of the testator's death or as at the date of death of the last liferentrix. Lord Justice Clerk Inglis said at pp 1189-1190: "If his heirs *in mobilibus* of the first class survived, and were resident in Scotland, they were to take in the first instance; then those who, according to the then existing law, would be the next class of his heirs *in mobilibus* should take next, and so on. He certainly did not contemplate that the law of succession would be altered before the lapse of the period of endurance of the liferents. When the testator directs the distribution of his estate without saying expressly that the law at the period of distribution, whatever that law may be, shall regulate the distribution of the fee of the residue of my estate, was it not more natural that he should have in his mind the law as it then stood, and that he should intend and contemplate that in the event of his children not taking the fee the class pointed out by the then existing law should come in and take the residue, excluding those who were not resident in Scotland? I think that by adopting that view more than by any other we shall give effect to the intention of the testator."

Lord Benholme, agreeing with the Lord Justice Clerk, concluded his judgment at p 1193 with these words: "Had the Intestate Succession Act passed before Baron Cockburn's death I would have inclined to the opinion that the settlement would have brought in great-grandchildren, as by direction of law equally near with grandchildren; but, on the whole, when I see that Baron Cockburn never could have foreseen the change, I think we must estimate his intention by the law he knew of, rather than by the law he knew nothing of."

These two cases neatly illustrate the different results which may flow from a change in the law affecting the character of a beneficiary between the date of execution of the testamentary document and the date of death of the testator, and a similar change after the death of the testator but before the succession has opened to the beneficiary.

In *Maxwell v Maxwell*, a testatrix executed a will in 1836 containing a bequest of her moveable estate to AB, "his heirs, executors, and assignees". AB died in 1852 and the testatrix survived till 1858. The issue was once again whether AB's heirs fell to be ascertained by reference to the law as it stood in 1836 or in 1858. It was held that the law in 1858 applied. In delivering the judgment of the First Division Lord Curriehill, after pointing out that the testatrix could not at the date of her settlement know who might eventually fall within the description of AB's heirs, continued at p 322: "but her intention plainly was, that the same persons, whosoever these might eventually be, who might by law have right to his succession, should also by her settlement have right to her succession. If in all cases destinations to heirs and executors, in settlements or deeds executed prior to the date of the Act in 1855, were to have a different meaning from destinations in precisely the same words in settlements or deeds executed after that date, great confusion would be introduced into successions for a long time to come. But I think that the meaning of all such destinations is just that the succession is to devolve upon the persons who may be pointed out by the law itself, whosoever these may happen to be, at

the time of the death of the person to whom they may then stand in that relation by the law itself."

The last sentence of the above citation was relied upon by the third parties in support of the proposition that the law to be applied to the description of a class of beneficiaries was, in the absence of specific indications contra, the law applicable at the date when the succession opened to that class. In my view that is to take far too much out of this sentence. The whole passage which I have just quoted is not easy to follow. The persons who would have succeeded to the moveable estate on the death of AB intestate in 1852 would have been his heirs according to the pre-1855 law. The last sentence of the passage does not therefore appear to fit the facts to which Lord Curriehill was seeking to apply the law. In the penultimate paragraph of his judgment Lord Curriehill said: "In the case of Nimmo, 3d June 1864, 2 Macph., p. 1146, the Second Division of the Court construed the Succession Act in the same way as I have done. It is said that in the case of Cockburn's Trustees, 10th June 1864, ib. p. 1185, a different decision was pronounced. But I do not think their Lordships in that case put upon the statute a construction different from that which they had adopted in the preceding week in the case of Nimmo. That case was attended with specialities. In particular, the only parties who had an interest to plead the statute, — namely, the great-grandchildren of Baron Cockburn, were not parties claimants in the Inner-House. And the opinions of some of the Judges, as I understand them, were founded upon the circumstance of the testator having been dead before the Act was passed."

In that passage Lord Curriehill appears to have been concentrating on the construction of the Act of 1855 rather than upon the construction of the settlement as evidencing the intention of the testatrix. I have no doubt that the decision in *Maxwell v Maxwell* was correct, but it was so for the simple reason that the testatrix survived the passing of the Act of 1855 for some three years without altering her settlement, and therefore in the words of Lord Justice Clerk Inglis in *Nimmo v Murray's Trs,* "the new law must take effect". I consider that *Maxwell v Maxwell* provides no support for the contentions of the third parties in a case where the law has changed between the operative date of the settlement and the opening of the succession.

In *Smith's Trs v Macpherson* a testator who died domiciled in Scotland in 1901 left a legacy on the expiry of a liferent to JM with a destination-over failing issue "to his nearest heirs". JM, who was domiciled in England at the date of death of the testator, died domiciled there in 1917 survived by the liferentrix. On her death in 1924 a question arose as to whether JM's nearest heirs fell to be ascertained according to the law of Scotland or England. The First Division held that the relevant law was that of England being the law of JM's domicile at the date of his death. Lord President Clyde, after giving the

A example of a bequest to "my brother's heirs", continued at 1926 SLT, p 673: "Further, it seems evident — in the absence of controlling context — that the question: Who are the persons who would succeed to the testator's brother on the said brother's fictional intestacy? must depend for answer on the law of the brother's domicile. For the brother's 'heirs' are incapable of ascertainment in any other way; and, if any other method were adopted, the persons called to succeed would not be *his* heirs'."

B Lord Sands at p 674, after pointing out that the word "heir" connoted not a natural but a legal relationship, went on to say: "It is a rule of international law, adopted by Scottish law, and therefore part of the law of Scotland, that the persons entitled to the moveable succession of an intestate, in other words the heirs, are the persons who are so entitled by the law of the deceased's domicile."

Lord Ashmore at p 676 said: "Moreover, it is not doubtful that the nearest heirs of the legatee must be C those who are entitled to succeed as the legal representatives of the legatee according to the law of his domicile (*Bell v. Cheape*, 7 D. 614, *per* Lord Mackenzie, p. 633, and Lord Jeffrey, p. 637). Further, it may be laid down as a general rule of law that, when a right of succession is conferred by a testator on parties called not as individuals but because of their relation to the third parties, those entitled to succeed are persons answering the description or holding the character when the succession opens or takes effect D (*Maxwell v. Maxwell* (1864) 3 Macph. 318)."

The last sentence of the above passage, which substantially echoes what Lord Curriehill said in the earlier case, was much relied upon by the third parties. However, I do not consider that it can properly be construed as stating that the description of the persons in question is to be determined by reference to the law prevailing at the time of the opening of the succession rather than at some earlier time. That was not an issue E in *Smith's Trs v Macpherson*, there being no suggestion that the law of England had changed between 1901 and 1924. The only issue was whether "heirs" fell to be determined by reference to the law of the testator's domicile or the law of the domicile of the person whose heirs were to benefit. Furthermore, it must be borne in mind, as Lord Sands pointed out, that heirship is a legal relationship whereas in this appeal the concern is with the natural relations of the propositus, a distinction which was emphasised in the F recent case of *Allan, Petr*, opinion of the court at 1991 SLT, p 205. I am therefore satisfied that *Smith's Trs v Macpherson* affords no support for the third parties' contention.

Your Lordships were also referred to *Spencer's Trs v Ruggles* in which it was held by the First Division that as a matter of construction a provision in a trust deed in favour of the son of the truster in liferent and his surviving lawful children in fee did not embrace a child adopted by the liferenter and recognised for all practical purposes as his lawful child by the law of his American domicile at the date of his death. The truster died in the early years of this century and the G decree of adoption was pronounced in 1970. Lord President Emslie at 1982 SLT, p 169 said: "There is no doubt that the 'lawful children' of Henry Arthur Spencer are those persons who are so regarded by the law of his domicile at the date of his death." Lord Cameron expressed views to a similar effect at p 167. If these statements were intended to equiparate the position of "children" to that of "heirs" I do not think that they were correct. The heir of X can only be ascertained at or after the moment of X's death and H according to the law of X's then domicile, because the relationship between X and his heirs is a creation of the law. The relationship of parent and child is a natural one and prima facie depends upon fact. A child of a liferenter can be ascertained during the life of the former and in the case of a liferentrix the class of her children can be treated as closed on her 53rd birthday (*G's Trs v G*). However, Lord Cameron at p 168 said: "The decision in any given case of the width of the ambit of the words 'lawful children' must depend on I the proper construction of the deed in which the words appear, their context and the intention of the maker of the deed as that may be ascertained from an examination of the deed itself." The Lord President at p 169 stated the question to be whether the adopted daughter "qualifies as one of the 'surviving lawful children' of Henry within the meaning of, and for the *purposes of succession* under" the relevant provisions of the trust deed (emphasis added).

J When there is a gift to a class of descendants with postponed vesting it is obvious that the members of the class who will benefit cannot be ascertained until the date of vesting. There is however nothing in the authorities to which I have referred which requires that the law which determines who is eligible to be a member of the class must always be the law of the domicile of the parent of the class member at the date of death of the parent or when the succession opens to the members. This must be purely a matter of K testamentary intention. The use of the word "issue" and "great-grandchildren" in 1917 and 1932 respectively without any other qualification or explanation would have embraced only persons born in wedlock or legitimated per subsequens matrimonium. Testators in those years would have had in mind the law as it then stood and would have been most unlikely to have contemplated that it would change to treat as legitimate persons who could not then have been legitimated at common law. The words of Lord Justice L Clerk Inglis and Lord Benholme in *Cockburn's Trs v Dundas* to which I have already referred are most apposite to the present case and I reject the contention of the third parties that the testators must be presumed to have used language wide enough to cover potential changes in the law. To introduce into the succession persons who could not have succeeded when the settlements came into operation would be to innovate upon the terms of those deeds — something which should in my view be done only by specific

legislation. That is sufficient for disposal of this
A appeal in favour of the second party but there is a
further matter which also has relevance, inter alia, to
the intentions of the testator and testatrix.

The Legitimacy Act 1926 introduced into England
for the first time the Scots law doctrine of legitimation
per subsequens matrimonium. The Legitimacy Act
1959, which applied only to England and Wales,
amended the Act of 1926 to the effect of legitimating
a child of parents who subsequently married even
although they had not been free to marry at the date
B of the child's birth. This had the effect of rendering
legitimate the third parties as from the date thereof.
However, s 10 (1) of the 1926 Act, when read together
with the 1959 Act, provided that the construction of
any disposition coming into operation after the commencement of the 1959 Act should not be affected.
Thus the third parties, although legitimated by the
Act of 1959, could not have taken a bequest to issue
or great-grandchildren under an English deed coming
C into operation before 1959. Is it to be supposed that
even if the testators had contemplated the possibility
of some change in the law of legitimation, they would
have intended to benefit persons who although treated
as legitimate in the country of their domicile for
certain purposes were, nevertheless, disabled in that
country from taking benefit from deeds such as those
about to be executed by them? The answer must, I
think, be "no".

Scots law was amended by the Legitimation (Scot-
D land) Act of 1968 to the same effect as English law had
been by the 1959 Act. Section 7 (2) of the 1968 Act
provided that the legitimation of any person under the
Act should not confer any right on that person under
a deed which came into operation before the commencement of the Act. It is clear from the terms of the
Acts of 1926, 1959 and 1968 that Parliament was concerned that deeds throughout Scotland and England
which were already in operation should not be affected
by the emergence of newly legitimated persons. If the
E arguments for the third parties were correct it would
mean that domiciled English persons legitimated
under the 1959 Act could not benefit under an English
deed in operation prior to their legitimation but could
benefit under such a Scottish one et e contra, a result
which would certainly not appear to accord with the
general intention of Parliament as expressed in the
English and Scottish Acts. An example will suffice to
show how bizarre could have been the effect of the
third parties' argument in the present case. Of the
F testator's two granddaughters only the mother of the
third parties had children. Suppose that the other
granddaughter had, by a domiciled Scotsman, children
who were subsequently legitimated by the Act of
1968. Those children would have been disabled from
taking benefit under the settlements by reason of s 7
(2) of the 1968 Act but their first cousins, being
domiciled in England, would not. While these matters
are not conclusive as to testamentary intention, they
do fortify the conclusion that the contentions of the
third parties must be rejected.

My Lords for all these reasons I would allow the
appeal, recall the interlocutor of the Court of Session G
of 25 October 1991 and answer both questions in the
special case in the negative.

LORD LOWRY.—I have had the advantage of
reading in draft the speeches of my noble and learned
friends, Lord Keith of Kinkel and Lord Jauncey of
Tullichettle. I agree with them and for the reasons
given by my noble and learned friends I, too, would
allow the appeal.

LORD MUSTILL.—I have had the advantage of H
reading in draft the speeches of my noble and learned
friends, Lord Keith of Kinkel and Lord Jauncey of
Tullichettle. I agree with them and for the reasons
given by my noble and learned friends I, too, would
allow the appeal.

LORD SLYNN OF HADLEY.—I accept counsel's
submission on behalf of the parties of the third part
that "issue" and "great-grandchildren" in the respec- I
tive trust dispositions and settlements are to be read as
meaning issue and great-grandchildren who were
legitimate according to the relevant law in force at the
time when the bequest fell to vest even if there was a
change in the law between the deeds and the vesting.
I recognise that this is not in accordance with the
decision of the Second Division of the Inner House in
Cockburn's Trs v Dundas but it is in my view consistent with all the other cases cited to the Appellate
Committee.   J

That, however, does not enable the third parties to
succeed. For the reasons given by my noble and
learned friends, Lord Keith of Kinkel and Lord
Jauncey of Tullichettle, whose speeches in draft I have
had the opportunity of reading, it is impossible when
recognising that the third parties were legitimated by
the Legitimacy Act 1959, the law of their domicile, to
ignore the limitation that the legitimation did not
extend to capacity to inherit under an English instrument which came into operation before the com- K
mencement of that Act.

For that reason I too would allow the appeal.

———————

*Counsel for Second Party and Appellants, Nimmo
Smith, QC, Howie; Solicitors, Tods Murray, WS,
Radcliffe & Co, London — Counsel for Third Parties,
D R A Emslie, QC, Cullen; Solicitors, Shepherd &
Wedderburn, WS, Dyson Bell Martin, London.*   L

M G T

Wimpey Homes Holdings Ltd
A **v Lees**

HIGH COURT OF JUSTICIARY

THE LORD JUSTICE GENERAL (HOPE),
LORDS COWIE AND CAPLAN

5 FEBRUARY 1991

*Justiciary — Statutory offence — Construction regula-
tions — Duty on employer to comply with such requirements of regulations "as affect him or any workman*
B *employed by him" — Whether supervisor was workman
— Whether necessary to prove that workmen actually on
scaffold on day libelled — Whether sufficient that scaffold
available for use of other workmen — Construction
(Lifting Operations) Regulations 1961 (SI 1961/1581),
regs 3 (1) (a) and 42 (1) — Construction (Working Places)
Regulations 1966 (SI 1966/94), regs 3 (1) (a) and 11.*

*Justiciary — Procedure — Summary procedure — Com-
plaint — Latitude of time — Complaint alleging contra-*
C *ventions of regulations on particular date — Evidence led
as to that date — Whether sheriff entitled to infer that
contraventions had taken place over preceding days.*

*Justiciary — Procedure — Summary procedure — Com-
plaint — Special capacity of accused — Accused charged
as employer of workmen who were affected by regulations
— Whether special capacity — Whether open to Crown
to take point for first time on appeal — Criminal Procedure (Scotland) Act 1975 (c 21), s 312 (x).*

D   Regulations 3 (1) (a) of the Construction (Lifting
Operations) Regulations 1961 and the Construction
(Working Places) Regulations 1966 respectively
provide that it "shall be the duty of every . . .
employer of workmen . . . to comply with such of the
requirements of the following Regulations as affect
him or any workman employed by him".

A company was charged on summary complaint
with contraventions of each set of regulations in
E respect of a scaffold and hoist on a construction site on
a particular day. The only employees of the company
on site on that day were the site agent, whose duty it
was to inspect the scaffold, and a plumber. At trial the
company argued that the Crown had failed to establish
that any of the company's workmen was affected by
the regulations on that date, since there was no evidence that the plumber required to use the scaffold or
hoist and the site agent, being a supervisor, was not a
workman within the regulations. The sheriff con-
F victed the company, rejecting these arguments and
further holding that on the basis of the latitude
allowed to the Crown, the breaches of the regulations
had persisted over the preceding 15 days. The
company appealed. On appeal the Crown argued
further that the company had been charged in a special
capacity within s 312 (x) of the Criminal Procedure
(Scotland) Act 1975, as being employers of workmen
who were affected by the regulations, and not having
challenged this by preliminary objection were to be
taken to have admitted that they possessed this qualification.

Held, (1) (of concession of the Crown) that where
the charge was framed with reference only to one   G
particular date, and evidence was led as to the state of
affairs on that date, it was not open to the sheriff, in
the absence of an amendment, to treat the charge as if
directed to a continuing breach from an earlier date
(p 568B-C); (2) that it was not open to the Crown to
contend that the company had answered the complaint
charged in a special capacity such that they could be
taken to be admitting that they were employers of
workmen affected by the requirements of the regulations, where the Crown had conducted the case   H
throughout on the basis that they had to prove that the
company's workmen were so affected (p 568E-F); (3)
that in any event the special capacity did not extend
to the proposition that the company's workmen were
affected by the regulations (p 568G-H); but (4) that the
duty of compliance was one imposed on the company
so long as the scaffolding and hoist were in position
and available for use by their employees even though
none of the workmen was actually on the scaffolding
on the day libelled (p 569B and H-I); and (5) that the
fact that an employee was designated a supervisor did   I
not remove him from the category of workman for the
purposes of the regulations (p 569G); and appeal
refused.

Summary complaint

Wimpey Homes Holdings Ltd and CFM (Roofing)
Ltd were charged on summary complaint at the
instance of Robert F Lees, procurator fiscal, Paisley,
libelling inter alia the following charges, as amended: J
"on 16 February 1989 at Crathes Court then under
construction in Braidholm Road, Giffnock, you both
undertook building operations, namely the construction of a three storey block of dwellinghouses including the tiling of a sloping roof to which the Factories
Act 1961, Construction (Working Places) Regulations
1966 and the Construction (Lifting Operations) Regulations 1961 all applied and (1) date and place above
libelled you Wimpey Homes Holdings Ltd being an
employer of workmen, regional safety officers, site   K
agent and scaffolders who are affected by the requirements of the regulations aftermentioned in this charge,
and you CFM (Roofing) Ltd being a contractor and an
employer of workmen who were undertaking a building operation and works to which the Construction
(Lifting Operations) Regulations 1961 applied at the
top scaffolding platform fail to erect a substantial
enclosure to efficiently protect persons who are liable
to be struck by any moving part of the hoist there and
did fail to fit gates where access to the hoist was   L
needed; contrary to the Factories Act 1961, s 155 (2)
and the Construction (Lifting Operations) Regulations
1961, regs 3 (1) (a) and 42 (1); (2) date and place above
libelled you Wimpey Homes Holdings Ltd being an
employer of workmen, regional safety officers, site
agent and scaffolders who are affected by the requirements of the regulations aftermentioned in this charge,
and you CFM (Roofing) Ltd being a contractor and
employer of workmen who were undertaking a building operation and works to which the Construction
(Lifting Operations) Regulations 1961 applied at the

ground level loading place of the hoist there, fail to
keep closed the gates fitted there while the platform or
cage was at rest at the top scaffolding platform; contrary to the Factories Act 1961, s 155 (2) and the Construction (Lifting Operations) Regulations 1961, regs
3 (1) (a) and 42 (1); (3) date and place above libelled
you Wimpey Homes Holdings Ltd being an employer
of workmen, regional safety officers, site agent and
scaffolders who are affected by the requirements of the
regulations aftermentioned in this charge, and you
CFM (Roofing) Ltd being a contractor and employer
of workmen who were undertaking a building operation and works to which the Construction (Working
Places) Regulations 1966 applied did fail to properly
maintain the scaffold in respect that there were no tie
bars between the hop up brackets on the first, second
and top scaffolding platforms with the result that
every part of the scaffolding was not kept so fixed,
secured or placed in position as to prevent so far as is
practicable accidental displacement; contrary to the
Factories Act 1961, s 155 (2) and the Construction
(Working Places) Regulations 1966, regs 3 (1) (a) and
11".

After trial the sheriff (C G McKay) found the
accused Wimpey Homes Holdings Ltd guilty of
charges 1, 2 and 3 and the accused CFM (Roofing)
Ltd not guilty of all charges. The accused Wimpey
Homes Holdings Ltd appealed to the High Court by
way of stated case against the decision of the sheriff.

Findings in fact

The sheriff found the following facts admitted or
proved, inter alia:

(1) On or about 16 February 1989 the appellants
were the principal contractors on a building site
known as Crathes Court in Braidholm Road,
Giffnock. They were constructing a three storey block
of dwellinghouses on this site involving the use of a
scaffold. The appellants were carrying on building
operations within the meaning of regs 2 (a) and 2 (1)
(a) of the Construction (Lifting Operations) Regulations 1961 and the Construction (Working Places)
Regulations 1966 respectively (hereinafter referred to
as "the 1961 Regulations" and "the 1966 Regulations" respectively). (2) The appellants had subcontracted the tiling of the roof of the three storey
block of dwellinghouses to the second accused. The
second accused had, to the knowledge of Mr Patrick
O'Brien, the site agent of the appellants, subcontracted the work further to Mr David M McGill,
a self employed roof tiler. Mr David McGill had
employed a gang of men including a Mr John Cullen
to carry out the roof tiling work for him. On 16
February 1989 Mr John Cullen had, whilst working
on the scaffold surrounding the three storey block of
dwellinghouses, fallen to his death. (3) Crathes Court
was a development of private dwellinghouses being
erected by the appellants. It was a three storey block
of dwellinghouses. On 16 February 1989 the external
brickwork had been completed and the roof was being
tiled. The building was surrounded by "quick stage"
scaffold. The scaffold was there to be used by all

tradesmen working on the building. The scaffold had
been erected by Mr James Kenna, an employee of the
appellants. The erection had commenced on or about
16 December 1988 and was completed at the top
storey not later than 1 February 1989. The scaffold
erected by the appellants was one to which the 1961
and 1966 Regulations applied. There was an external
materials hoist built onto the scaffold which operated
from ground level to the third storey or top level. The
hoist was there to be used by all tradesmen of the
appellants working on the building site and such
others as the appellants permitted to use the hoist.
The hoist was one to which the 1961 and 1966 Regulations applied. The hoist and scaffold had been
erected by the appellants. . . .

(5) . . . The appellants had failed to enclose the
access platform at the top storey substantially and had
failed to install a gate where access thereto was
required. The lack of substantial enclosure and lack of
a gate at the top storey had existed at least since completion of the scaffold at the top storey on or about 1
February 1989 up to and including 16 February 1989.
The scaffold and hoist had been used by bricklayers
and joiners in the employ of the appellants within the
period from 1 February to 13 February 1989. . . .

(8) On 16 February 1989 Mr John Matheson, a
plumber in the employment of the appellants, was
working on the building using the scaffold. He was
carrying out lead work at windows. He was working
within 20 ft of the roof tilers to whom the second
accused had subcontracted the roofing work. The said
John Matheson and Patrick O'Brien were workmen in
the employ of the appellants and the only workmen of
the appellants affected by both the 1961 and 1966
Regulations in terms of reg 3 (1) (a) in each case on 16
February 1989. Mr Patrick O'Brien, the appellants'
site agent, had inspected the scaffold by a complete
walking round of the scaffold for the purposes of carrying out the statutory inspection required by reg 22
of the 1966 Regulations. This inspection had preceded
the accident. The said Patrick O'Brien was on the
scaffold immediately following the accident in which
Mr John Cullen was killed. On 16 February 1989 the
said tilers were the only persons using said hoist or the
scaffolding extension which surrounds it.

Statutory provisions

The Construction (Lifting Operations) Regulations
1961 provide:

"3.—(1) It shall be the duty of every contractor, and
every employer of workmen, who is undertaking any
of the operations or works to which these Regulations
apply — (a) to comply with such of the requirements
of the following Regulations as affect him or any
workman employed by him, that is to say, Regulation
42 (1) in so far as it relates to the protection of the
hoistway, and Regulation 47; Provided that the
requirements of the said Regulations shall be deemed
not to affect any workman if and so long as his
presence in any place is not in the course of performing any work on behalf of his employer and is not

expressly or impliedly authorised or permitted by his employer".

The Construction (Working Places) Regulations 1966 provide:

"3.—(1) It shall be the duty of every contractor, and every employer of workmen, who is undertaking any of the operations or works to which these Regulations apply — (a) to comply with such of the requirements of the following Regulations as affect him or any workman employed by him, that is to say, Regulations 6 to 23, 25, 30, 31, 32, 36 and 38 and, in so far as they relate to the falling or slipping of persons, Regulations 24, 26, 27, 28, 29, 33, 34 and 35: Provided that the requirements of the said Regulations shall be deemed not to affect any workman if and so long as his presence in any place is not in the course of performing any work on behalf of his employer and is not expressly or impliedly authorised or permitted by his employer".

Cases referred to

Archibald v Plean Colliery Co, 1924 SLT 581; 1924 JC 77.

Field v Perrys (Ealing) Ltd [1950] 2 All ER 521.

Smith v George Wimpey & Co Ltd [1972] 2 QB 329; [1972] 2 WLR 1166; [1972] 2 All ER 723.

Appeal

The sheriff posed the following questions for the opinion of the High Court:

(1) Did the appellants have any obligation in terms of reg 3 (1) of both sets of regulations, on the basis of the facts found proved, to comply with the requirements of said regulation 42 (1) or of the said regulation 11 of the 1961 Regulations and 1966 Regulations respectively?

(2) On the dates libelled were any workmen employed by the appellants affected by the requirements of reg 42 (1) of the 1961 Regulations insofar as they were not complied with by the appellants as found in fact in respect of charges 1 and 2?

(3) On the date libelled were any workmen employed by the appellants affected by the requirements of reg 11 of the 1966 Regulations insofar as they were not complied with by the appellants as found in fact in respect of charge 3?

(4) On the facts found proved was I entitled to convict the appellants of an offence under s 155 (2) of the Factories Act 1961 in respect of their failures to comply with the requirements of said reg 42 (1) and the said reg 11?

(5) In the absence of any motion to amend the date libelled was I entitled to afford the Crown latitude in relation thereto, and to convict the appellants of the offences specified in charges 1, 2 and 3?

The appeal was heard before the High Court on 8 January 1991.

On 5 February 1991 the court *answered* questions 1

to 4 in the *affirmative* and question 5 in the *negative* and *refused* the appeal.

THE LORD JUSTICE GENERAL (HOPE).— The appellants were found guilty in the sheriff court at Paisley on three charges which were brought against them under regulations made under the Factories Act 1961. The first two charges were brought under the Construction (Lifting Operations) Regulations 1961, regs 3 (1) (a) and 42 (1). The third charge was brought under the Construction (Working Places) Regulations 1966, regs 3 (1) (a) and 11. These offences were said to have been committed on 16 February 1989 in Crathes Court then under construction in Braidholm Road, Giffnock, where building operations consisting of the construction of a three storey block of dwellinghouses had been undertaken by the appellants. The appellants were the principal contractors on this building site. They had subcontracted the tiling of the roof of the three storey block of dwellinghouses to CFM Roofing Ltd, who were also charged with offences under the same complaint but were acquitted on all charges. That company had subcontracted the work further to a self employed roof tiler named Mr David M McGill. Mr McGill had employed a gang of men, including a Mr John Cullen, to carry out the work for him. The construction of the three storey block of dwellinghouses on this site involved the use of a scaffold. On 16 February 1989 Mr John Cullen had, whilst working on the scaffold, fallen to his death.

The scaffold had been erected by an employee of the appellants and it was there to be used by all tradesmen working on the building. It was provided with an external materials hoist built onto the scaffold which operated from ground level to the top level of the building. The hoist was there to be used by all tradesmen of the appellants working on the building site and such others as the appellants permitted to use it. There were landings at each of the three storeys, and at the point where access from the scaffold landing to the hoist was required a scaffold platform had been constructed extending from the main scaffold surrounding the building. These platforms consisted of five scaffold boards supported on the scaffold together with a further two such boards supported on "hop up brackets". At the front or leading edge of each "hop up bracket" a bar, known as a tie bar, required to be fitted into pre-drilled holes to prevent lateral movement of the platform and the forward movement or accidental displacement of the platform boards.

There was evidence, which has not been challenged in this appeal, that the scaffolding was defective in the respects libelled in each of the three charges of which the appellants were found guilty. The first charge alleged a failure to erect a substantial enclosure to efficiently protect persons who were liable to be struck by any moving part of the hoist and a failure to fit gates where access to the hoist was needed. It was established in evidence that the appellants had failed to enclose the access platform at the top storey substantially and had failed to install a gate where access thereto was required. The lack of substantial enclosure and lack of a gate at the top storey had existed at least since completion of the scaffold at the top storey on or about 1 February 1989 up to and including 16 February 1989. The second charge alleged a failure at the ground level loading place of the hoist to keep closed the gates fitted there while the platform or cage was at rest at the top scaffolding platform. It was established in evidence that on 16 February 1989 at the ground level loading place of the hoist there was an accumulation of rubbish such as to prevent the closing of the gate fitted at that point while the platform or cage in the hoistway was at rest at the top scaffolding platform or elsewhere within the hoistway. This gate could not be and was not closed when the hoist was in use on that date. The third charge alleged a failure to properly maintain the scaffold in respect that there were no tie bars between the hop up brackets on the first, second and top scaffolding platforms, with the result that every part of the scaffolding was not kept so fixed, secured or placed in position as to prevent so far as was practicable accidental displacement. It was established in evidence that on 16 February 1989 there were no tie bars between the hop up brackets on the first, second and top access platforms from the main scaffold to the hoist. The tie bars were essential to the stability of the scaffold access platforms and they had not been kept so fixed, secured or placed in position as to prevent so far as practicable their accidental displacement. I should mention that the complaint contained two further charges which were libelled against the appellants but it is not necessary to describe these charges or the evidence which was led in support of them because the appellants were found not guilty on these charges.

The question which has been raised in this appeal is whether the appellants had any obligation in terms of reg 3 (1) of both sets of the regulations to comply with the requirements of the regulations in question. Regulation 3 (1) of the Construction (Lifting Operations) Regulations 1961 provides: [his Lordship quoted the terms of reg 3 (1) of the 1961 Regulations set out supra and continued:]

Regulation 3 (1) (a) of the Construction (Working Places) Regulations 1966 is in almost identical terms since it provides as follows: [his Lordship quoted the terms of reg 3 (1) of the 1966 Regulations set out supra and continued:]

The critical phrase for the purposes of this appeal is to be found in the opening words of para (a) of these two sets of regulations, namely "such of the requirements of the following Regulations as affect him or any workman employed by him". The appellants seek review of their conviction on charges 1, 2 and 3 on the basis that on the date libelled no workmen employed by them were likely to be affected by any of the relevant regulations and accordingly that, in terms of reg 3 (1) of each of these regulations, they had no duty to comply with the requirements of the regulations as specified in each of these charges.

Counsel for the appellants submitted that the Crown had failed to establish that any workmen employed by the appellants on the date in question were affected by the requirements of the 1961 and 1966 Regulations. He pointed out that the duty of the contractor was to comply only with such of the requirements of the regulations "as affect him or any workman employed by him". The contractor did not owe any duty under these regulations to workmen employed by others, so it was essential to the case against the appellants that workmen employed by them were affected by these requirements. He referred to *Smith v George Wimpey & Co Ltd* in which it was held that the words "him or" had been inserted in reg 3 (1) (a) of the Construction (General Provisions) Regulations 1961 in order to bring the self employed person or independent contractor within their scope so as to make him responsible for his own safety, and that they did not have the effect of extending the main contractor's duty to workmen employed by a subcontractor. There was, he said, no evidence that any of the appellants' workmen were liable to be struck by any moving part of the hoist as libelled in charge 1, or that any of them were working in such a position as to be affected by a failure to keep closed the gates fitted at the ground level loading place of the hoist referred to in charge 2. He accepted that it would be sufficient that there was evidence that it was reasonably foreseeable that the appellants' workmen would be in that position, but there were no findings to that effect. As for charge 3, he submitted that it was concerned with a failure to maintain the first, second and top platforms which provided access to the hoist. So, unless the appellants' workmen were liable to come into contact with one or other of these platforms, they could not be said to be affected by the requirements of the 1966 Regulations, of which the appellants were said to be in breach. There was, he said, no such evidence. The only employees of the appellants who were mentioned in the findings as having been on the scaffold on 16 February were the appellants' site agent Mr Patrick O'Brien and a plumber, Mr John Matheson. But there was nothing in the findings to indicate that either of these men were in the region of the hoist or on any of the platforms on that date. There was no finding that Mr Matheson ever required to use the hoist or was likely to do so, and Mr O'Brien's position was that he was not a workman within the meaning of the regulations at all. He was a supervisor, whose purpose in going on to the scaffold was to inspect it and to report on the results of his inspection as required by reg 22 of the 1966 Regulations. In *Field v Perrys (Ealing) Ltd* [1950] 2 All ER at p 523, Devlin J, as he then was, had declined to cut down the wide phrase "any workman engaged by him" in the Building Regulations 1926 to mean only any building operative or any workmen actually engaged in any part of the building operations, and had held that the regulations applied to a nightwatchman. But Mr O'Brien was in a different position because of the statutory duty which he had to perform, and it was not to be supposed that the appellants owed a duty to him to comply with the regulations which he was required to inspect. Finally, counsel for the appellants criticised a passage in the sheriff's note where the sheriff referred to Mr O'Brien's evidence that bricklayers and joiners had been on the scaffold but had

finished their work no later than 13 February 1989
A and had said that, on the basis of the latitude allowed
to the Crown in specification of the date of an alleged
offence, he was satisfied that the failure to comply
with reg 42 (1) as libelled in charge 1 had persisted
since at least 1 February 1989. He submitted that it
was unfair for the sheriff to have allowed the Crown
this latitude since the charge was directed to the situation on one particular date only, namely 16 February
1989, and no motion had been made to amend the
charge.

B　　　The learned Solicitor General accepted that the
sheriff was in error in approaching charge 1 as if it had
libelled a breach of the regulation over a period. The
charge was framed with reference only to one particular date, namely 16 February 1989, and evidence
was led as to the state of affairs on the site on that
particular date. In this situation it was not open to the
sheriff, in the absence of an amendment to the charge,
to treat it as if it was directed to a continuing breach
of the regulation from 1 February 1989, and any evid-
C ence which there might have been about the state of
the structure on days previous to 16 February 1989
was of no relevance to the case as libelled against the
appellants. I think that the Solicitor General was
plainly right on this point, and no more need be said
about it except that the sheriff did not rely exclusively
on this approach. He convicted the appellants on
charge 1 for the reason also that he found that Mr
Matheson and Mr O'Brien, both employees of the
appellants, had been on the scaffold on 16 February
D 1989. He said that he was satisfied that they were
employees of the appellants who were directly affected
on that date by the regulations.

　　　Before coming to make submissions in support of
the sheriff's decision in regard to 16 February 1989,
the Solicitor General contended that the appellants
should be held to have admitted that they were
employers of workmen who were affected by the regulations and that on that simple ground the appeal
E should be refused. They had, he said, been charged in
a special capacity as being employers of workmen who
were so affected, and since they had not challenged
this point by preliminary objection before their plea of
not guilty was recorded they were, in terms of s 312
(x) of the Criminal Procedure (Scotland) Act 1975, to
be held to have admitted that they possessed the
qualification necessary to the commission of the
offences which were libelled against them. But in my
opinion there is a short answer to this point. There is
F no indication in the stated case that this argument was
presented to the sheriff at any stage in the course of
the trial. On the contrary the case appears to have been
conducted throughout by the Crown on the basis that
it was necessary to prove that the appellants' workmen
were affected by the requirements of the regulations.
The sheriff has made findings of fact with regard to
this matter. In these circumstances it is now too late
for the Crown to seek to rely on s 312 (x). If authority
is needed for this, it is to be found in *Archibald v Plean
Colliery Co* and in particular in the opinions of Lord
Justice Clerk Alness at 1924 SLT, p 586 and Lord

Anderson at p 592. As Lord Anderson put it, the case
must be taken on the footing that parties agreed to G
determine the question by proof, there having been
nothing to prevent the Crown from waiving the statutory presumption.

　　　In any event I am not satisfied that, even if the
appellants are to be regarded as having been charged
with the offences libelled in a special capacity within
the meaning of s 312 (x), that special capacity
extended to the proposition that the workmen
employed by them were affected by the requirements
of the regulations. The way in which the charges were H
framed may seem at first sight to lend some support
to the Solicitor General's argument, but in my opinion
the special capacity, if any, is to be found in the terms
of the regulations themselves and not in the way in
which the charges have been framed. Regulation 3 (1)
of both sets of regulations begins by stating that "It
shall be the duty of every contractor, and every
employer of workmen, who is undertaking any of the
operations or works to which these Regulations
apply". Having said that, the regulations then proceed I
to set out what the duty involves. It is only when one
comes, in head (a) of each regulation, to the description of the duty that the phrase "as affect him or any
workman employed by him" appears. The phrase is
designed not to set out the qualification which the contractor or employer must possess but to identify the
requirements of the regulations with which in the
particular circumstances he must comply. For these
reasons also, although the point is obscured somewhat
by the fact that the charges do not follow precisely the
same order of language as the regulations, I must J
reject this part of the Solicitor General's argument.

　　　The only remaining question of importance therefore is whether it was established that the appellants
were under a duty on 16 February 1989 to comply
with the requirements of the regulations because
workmen employed by them were affected by these
requirements. The charges, as amended following a
preliminary debate in respect of a plea to the relevancy, all use the present tense "are affected" before K
turning to the past tense to describe the breaches of
the regulations which were said to have been present
on 16 February. But the argument on both sides
proceeded on the basis that it was necessary to find
evidence that the appellants' workmen "were
affected" by the requirements on that date. In order to
resolve this issue it is necessary to decide whether the
regulations must be applied with precision to the facts,
so that it would only be if at least one of the appellants' workmen was proved to have been in the
immediate vicinity of the hoist or on the scaffolding L
platforms themselves that day that the appellants
would be under a duty to comply with their requirements, or whether a broader approach is appropriate.
If the narrower approach is correct the appellants
must succeed in this appeal because there are no findings which place any of their workmen in precisely
that position at any time on the relevant date. But I
think that the broader approach is to be preferred,
having regard to the nature and purpose of the regulations.

It is worth noting that both sets of regulations were made by virtue of the powers conferred on the minister by ss 76 and 180 (7) of the Factories Act 1961. Section 76 confers power on the minister, if he is satisfied that any manufacture, machinery, plant, equipment, appliance, process or description of manual labour is of such a nature as to cause risk of bodily injury to the persons employed, or any class of those persons, to make such special regulations as appear to him to be reasonably practicable and to meet the necessity of the case. It is plain therefore that the purpose of the regulations is to secure, so far as reasonably practicable, the health and safety of those of the employer's workmen who are affected by the requirements, in the sense that if these requirements were not complied with they would be at risk of bodily injury. It seems to me to be appropriate therefore to include among those who are affected by the requirements any of the employer's workmen who might reasonably be expected to be exposed to that risk in the course of the work which they have to do. The proviso to reg 3 (1) (a) in each of the two sets of regulations provides further guidance as to the test which should be applied. According to that proviso the requirements shall be deemed not to affect any workman if and so long as his presence in any place is not in the course of performing any work on behalf of his employer and is not expressly or impliedly authorised or permitted by his employer. So if the workman is present in a place, in the course of such work and with the authority or permission of his employer, where he is at risk of bodily injury if the requirements are not met, he can be taken to be affected by them and his employer must comply with the requirements. Devlin J's approach in *Field v Perrys (Ealing) Ltd* to the question whether the nightwatchman was within the phrase "any workman engaged by him" is consistent with the view that, since these requirements are concerned with health and safety, a narrow or restricted interpretation is inappropriate.

The sheriff has found not only that Mr O'Brien and Mr Matheson were on the scaffold on the day in question, but also that the scaffold was there to be used by all tradesmen working on the building and that the hoist was there to be used by all tradesmen of the appellants working on the building site: see finding 3 of his findings in fact. By 16 February 1989 the external brickwork had been completed and the roof of the building was being tiled. But plainly construction work was still in progress and the scaffold together with the hoist was still in position on that date for use by tradesmen employed by the appellants as required. I think that these facts are sufficient to show that the appellants were under a duty to comply with the requirements of the regulations on the date libelled in each of the three charges. Mr O'Brien, the site agent, was on the scaffold to inspect it by a complete walking round for the purposes of the statutory inspection. The hoist was built on to the scaffold and the platform which provided access to the hoist had been constructed as an extension from the main scaffolding surrounding the building. Counsel for the appellants

argued that Mr O'Brien was not a workman for the purposes of the regulations because he was a supervisor, but I do not see why that expression, which is not defined in the regulations, should be given such a restricted meaning. In any event it is not disputed that the plumber, Mr Matheson, was a workman employed by the appellants. He was working on the building using the scaffold and the hoist was available for his use that day. Furthermore, all the other tradesmen of the appellants for whose use the scaffold and hoist were available were also affected by the requirements. I do not think that it matters that none of the other tradesmen was proved to have been on the scaffold on 16 February. The duty of compliance was a continuing one, which the appellants were bound to perform so long as the scaffold and hoist were still in position and available for use by their own workmen, even although none of the workmen affected by the requirements was actually on the scaffold at the time. The charges libelled breaches of the requirements on a particular date, but the question whether the appellants were under a duty to comply with these requirements must be answered by looking at all the facts and circumstances including the purpose of the scaffold and hoist and the fact that workmen were likely to continue to make use of these facilities at any time in the course of their work on the building while employed by the appellants.

In my opinion the sheriff was entitled, on the facts which he found proved, to convict the appellants on these three charges and I would refuse the appeal. I think that we should answer question 5 in the negative because the sheriff was in error in affording the Crown latitude in relation to the date libelled. But I would answer the first four questions in the affirmative.

LORD COWIE.—I concur in the opinion of your Lordship in the chair and have nothing to add.

LORD CAPLAN.—I agree entirely with the views expressed by your Lordship in the chair. The two sets of regulations with which this appeal is concerned have very significant safety implications for those who work on scaffolds and with or near hoists. Thus when a contractor engaged in building operations requires to consider whether any of his workmen are affected by the requirements of the regulations he must not assess his responsibility on too narrow a basis. In the present case the learned sheriff has found that the appellants provided a scaffold and hoist which were available for use by employees working on the building site. The evidence showed that from time to time workmen had been using the scaffold for a variety of purposes connected with the building operations. That use continued until 16 February 1989 when Mr O'Brien and Mr Matheson were both working on the scaffold. In my view Mr O'Brien in relation to the employer was a "workman employed by him" within the meaning of reg 3 (1) (a) in each set of regulations. An employed supervisor who uses a scaffold to carry out an inspection uses it for his "work" and I see no reason to construe "workman" in other than its general meaning of

A a person employed to do work. Since the regulations must be observed by the employer if they affect him personally, it would be difficult to construe them as applying to an employer who carries out his own inspections but not to an employed supervisor carrying out the same task. If workmen have free access to a scaffold with a hoist attached then in my view it is eminently foreseeable that their safety will be compromised if the equipment lacks the statutory safety features. There may be special cases where an employer could properly assume that there was no risk

B of his employees using or approaching particular parts of the equipment, but the learned sheriff's findings in relation to use are in general terms and do not bring the situation into such a category. Thus I have no difficulty in agreeing that it was not necessary for the Crown to prove that on 16 February 1989 a particular workman worked at or approached the hoist.

Counsel for Appellants, Dewar; Solicitors, Cochran,
C *Sayers & Cook, Glasgow — Counsel for Respondent, Solicitor General (Rodger, QC); Solicitor, I Dean, Crown Agent.*

S D D N

D # O v Rae

FIRST DIVISION

THE LORD PRESIDENT (HOPE),
LORDS MAYFIELD AND SUTHERLAND

11 DECEMBER 1991

Children and young persons — Children's hearing — Decision — Relevant considerations — Allegation in reports prepared for hearing — Allegation deleted from
E *grounds of referral accepted by parent — Whether hearing entitled to have regard to allegation — Social Work (Scotland) Act 1968 (c 49), s 43 (1).*

Section 43 (1) of the Social Work (Scotland) Act 1968 provides that when a children's hearing have considered the grounds for the referral of a case, accepted or established, the local authority report on the child and "such other relevant information as may be available to them", they shall proceed to consider on what course they should decide in the best interests

F of the child.

Four out of a father's five children were referred to a children's hearing, the eldest child, K, already being subject to compulsory measures of care. When the father did not accept the grounds of referral the reporter was directed to apply to the sheriff for a finding as to whether the grounds were established. Before the sheriff the reporter deleted from the grounds reference to an alleged sexual offence by the father on K and the remaining grounds were accepted by the father. The children were thereafter placed

G under supervision in residential care by a children's hearing. The father appealed to the sheriff who appointed a safeguarder to the four children. Reference in the safeguarder's report to K's allegation was not given any prominence and the appeal was refused. Subsequently the father requested a review of the supervision requirement relating to the four children. The children's hearing decided that all four should remain in care but that if the father could demonstrate his ability to look after the children a hearing would consider returning the children to his care. A social worker requested a further hearing, for which reports

H prepared by the social worker and the safeguarder referred to K's allegation of sexual abuse and pointed out that she had already had sexual intercourse when taken into care at 13, whatever the identity of the abuser. The father protested his innocence at the children's hearing while the mother agreed to long term fostering. The hearing determined that none of the children should be returned to live with the father, who was to be given supervised access to them. The father appealed to the sheriff, who refused the appeal,

I and thereafter to the Court of Session on the ground that the children's hearing should not have had regard to the allegation of sexual abuse since it had neither been accepted by the father nor established by the sheriff.

Held, (1) that once at least one ground of referral had been accepted or established the function of the children's hearing was to investigate the child's case so far as necessary to consider what was in the child's best interests (p 574E and G-H); (2) that their entitle-

J ment in terms of s 43 (1) of the 1968 Act to have regard to "such other relevant information as may be available to them" was not confined to information which was relevant to the grounds for the referral: the test of relevancy was whether the information was relevant to a consideration of what course should be taken in the child's best interests, which included any information relevant to making a supervision requirement once a decision had been taken that compulsory measures of care were necessary (p 574I-K); (3) that

K the information about the allegation was relevant in considering whether the father was a suitable person to look after the children and was information which the hearing were entitled to consider (p 575A-B); and (4) that there was no unfairness to the father, who had been given a fair opportunity of correcting or contradicting what had been said about or against him in the reports (p 575C-D); and appeal *refused.*

K v Finlayson, 1974 SLT (Sh Ct) 51, *overruled.*

L

Appeal from the sheriff court

William Rae, reporter to the children's panel for Wigtown District, referred four children of O to a children's hearing. The children had been taken into care following a complaint by O that their mother was neglecting them. The grounds of referral contained various facts and circumstances said to constitute lack of parental care likely to cause unnecessary suffering

or seriously impair health and development in terms
of s 32 (2) (c) of the Social Work (Scotland) Act 1968.

O did not accept the grounds of referral to the children's hearing and application was made to the sheriff in terms of s 42 (2) (c) of the Act. After an allegation of sexual abuse by O on the fifth and eldest child (K), who was already in compulsory care, was deleted, O accepted the remaining grounds and the cases were remitted to the reporter for referral to a children's hearing.

On 30 January 1990 a children's hearing decided that the four children were in need of compulsory measures of care and placed them under supervision in residential care. O appealed to the sheriff, who appointed a safeguarder to the four children. The appeal was refused.

On 27 September 1990 a children's hearing was convened at O's request to review the supervision requirement. It decided that all four children should remain in care but that if O could demonstrate his ability to look after the children a hearing would consider returning the children to his care.

On 16 December 1990 a further hearing determined that none of the children should be returned to live with O, who was to be given supervised access to them. The reasons for the decision were that: "The safeguarder has strongly recommended long term fostering after consultation with the children. The children's lives have been disrupted long enough by the matrimonial discord. Mum is in agreement with long term fostering. As long as the allegation of sexual abuse against father by his daughter K [sic], we cannot consider the children living with father."

O appealed to the sheriff.

Statutory provisions
The Social Work (Scotland) Act 1968 provides:

"43.—(1) When a children's hearing have considered the grounds for the referral of a case, accepted or established under the last foregoing section, the report obtained under section 39 (4) of this Act and such other relevant information as may be available to them, they shall proceed in accordance with the subsequent provisions of this section to consider on what course they should decide in the best interests of the child."

The Children's Hearings (Scotland) Rules 1986 provide:

"19.—(1) Unless a children's hearing consider the case of a child in the absence of the child, his parent, and any representative, the chairman shall, before the children's hearing proceed to consider the case, explain the purpose of the hearing to such of the said persons as are present.

"(2) Thereafter the children's hearing shall consider the case of the child and during such consideration shall — (a) consider a report of a local authority on the child and his social background, and any judicial remit or other relevant document and any relevant informa-

tion available to them; (b) consider any report the submission of which has been requested by the manager of the residential establishment in which the child is required to reside; (c) discuss the case with the child, parent, any safeguarder appointed under the Act and representative if attending the hearing; (d) endeavour to obtain the views of the said child, his parent, and any safeguarder appointed under the Act, if attending the hearing, on what arrangements with respect to the child would be in the best interests of the child.

"(3) The chairman shall inform the child and his parent of the substance of any reports, documents and information mentioned in paragraph (2) (a) if it appears to him that this is material to the manner in which the case of the child should be disposed of and that its disclosure would not be detrimental to the interests of the child."

Cases referred to
K v Finlayson, 1974 SLT (Sh Ct) 51.
Kennedy v A, 1986 SLT 358.

On 4 March 1991 the sheriff *refused* the appeal.

The father appealed to the Court of Session.

Appeal
The application for a stated case posed the following question for the court, inter alia:

(2) The original grounds of referral and accompanying statement of facts upon which the children were taken into care having contained no reference to any allegation of sexual abuse (such allegation having been deleted by concession of the reporter after an appeal to the sheriff by the appellant), was the panel, and subsequently the sheriff, by confirmation of the decision, entitled to take into account allegations about such sexual abuse, at the later stage of review on 17 December 1990 and in the interlocutor dated 4 March 1991?

In the stated case the sheriff stated the following questions for the court:

(1) Were the children's hearing of 17 December 1990 entitled to take the view that the child should remain under supervision?

(2) Was I entitled to hold that there was justification for said decision?

By adjustment the appellant wished the following questions to be added:

(3) Did the learned sheriff err in law in holding that the panel were entitled at the hearing to become involved in deciding upon a ground of referral, namely said allegation of sexual abuse, when said ground of referral was disputed by the appellant and had been deleted before the sheriff on 10 January 1990 and consequently had not been found to be established by him?

(4) Was the learned sheriff entitled to hold that the hearing had justification for reaching said decision on the basis of the findings in fact?

The appeal was heard before the First Division on A 26 and 27 November 1991.

On 11 December 1991 the court *refused* the appeal.

The following opinion of the court was delivered by the Lord President (Hope):

OPINION OF THE COURT.—The appellant is the father of each of the children involved in these appeals by case stated under s 50 of the Social Work (Scotland) Act 1968. The first respondent, who is now B deceased, was the reporter to the children's panel for Wigtown District. His interest was represented by counsel on the instructions of Alan Miller, the regional reporter. The second respondent is the safeguarder appointed to each of the children under s 34A of the Act, for whom there was no appearance.

The appellant is the father of five children. The eldest child, K, who is now over the age of 16 years, was referred to a children's hearing in 1986 on the C ground that she had committed an offence. She is still subject to compulsory measures of care and her case is not before us in these appeals. The remaining four children are A, now aged 13, C, now aged 11, M, now aged eight, and N, now aged seven. Prior to 2 December 1989 they had all been resident with their mother, from whom the appellant is separated. On that date the appellant complained to the police that the mother of these children was neglecting them. The matter was investigated by the police and by a social D worker, and the condition of the mother and all four children was found to be such that immediate steps were taken to obtain a place of safety order under the Act. The children were then taken into care and the reporter prepared grounds for the referral of their cases to a children's hearing. These grounds described various facts and circumstances which were said to disclose a lack of parental care in respect of each child such as was likely to cause them unnecessary suffering or seriously to impair their health and development: E see s 32 (2) (c) of the 1968 Act. At the commencement of the children's hearing the appellant did not accept these grounds of referral and the reporter was directed to make application to the sheriff in terms of s 42 (2) (c). When the application was called before the sheriff on 10 January 1990 the reporter was moved to amend the grounds of referral by deleting a passage which stated that in applying for the place of safety order the duty social worker had it in mind that the appellant was under investigation by the procurator fiscal's F department for an alleged sexual offence on one of his children. This amendment was allowed, whereupon the appellant accepted the remaining grounds of referral, and the cases were remitted to the reporter in terms of s 42 (6) to make arrangements for a children's hearing for their consideration and determination.

On 30 January 1990 a children's hearing reached the conclusion that the four children were in need of compulsory measures of care and they were placed under supervision in residential care. The appellant then appealed against this decision to the sheriff under s 49.

The second respondent was appointed by the sheriff to act as safeguarder to all four children for the pur- G poses of the appeal, and he submitted a report. In the course of the report he observed that K had made an allegation that she had been sexually abused by her uncle and that after questioning she had directed her allegation against her father, the appellant. The safeguarder went on to say that, whether or not the allegation was well founded, the fact remained that at 13 years of age when the child was taken into care she was not a virgin, and that there was clearly an absence of the requisite standard of parental care which led to H that result. It does not appear that this allegation was given any prominence in the appeal, no doubt because of the amendment of the grounds of referral which had been proposed by the reporter. Nor did it come to the notice of the children's hearing at that stage, since the appeal was refused and the decision of the children's hearing was confirmed by the sheriff under s 49 (4). The appellant's wish, however, was that the children should be returned to him and on 27 September 1990 a children's hearing was convened at his I request to review the supervision requirement of 30 January 1990. The children's hearing decided that all four children should remain in care for the time being but that if the appellant could demonstrate to the satisfaction of the social work department his ability to look after the children a further hearing could be called to consider returning the children to his care. The appellant took steps to clean up his house and improve the standard of comfort, but the social worker was sufficiently concerned about these developments J to request that the cases should be reviewed again by a children's hearing on 16 October 1990.

The purpose of this review was to reconsider the suggestion that the children might be returned to the appellant. This was seen by the social worker as being inconsistent with the social work department's plan that the children should be the subject of long term fostering. In her report the social worker who was responsible for the children stated that she found the K decision of the hearing on 27 September to be unworkable and recommended that the hearing give a decision which would allow the social work department to place for fostering all four children in new families. Among the factors of importance to which she drew attention in this report was the allegation that K had been the subject of sexual abuse. She said that she fully appreciated that there was no legal proof of this alleged offence and she noted that the procurator fiscal, to whom the police had referred the matter, had L not proceeded with the case nor dropped it. But she pointed out that when K came into care at the age of 13 she had already had sexual intercourse and added that this was a serious matter, whatever the identity of the abuser. The children's hearing decided to appoint the second respondent to act again as safeguarder to all four children and requested him to submit a further report. He was specifically asked to make contact with K in view of the allegation that she had been subjected to sexual abuse by her father. In the report which he submitted, the safeguarder said that K was persisting

in the allegation, and he also made reference to the fact
that when she was first taken into care at the age of 13
she was no longer a virgin. His advice to the children's
hearing was that he could see no reason why she
should not be believed and a great deal of reason why
she should be. His recommendation was that the children should in no circumstances be returned to their
father and that the treatment plan in the long term
should focus on preparation for long term fostering.

These reports were available when the children's
hearing met again to consider these cases on 16
December 1990. The appellant was present on this
occasion with a solicitor, as also was the safeguarder.
The safeguarder addressed the hearing and was questioned on his report. The appellant was then heard on
the report and he protested his innocence of the allegation of sexual abuse. A solicitor for the mother who
was also present intimated that she was unable to care
for any of the children and that she agreed to long
term fostering. The social worker then addressed the
hearing under reference to a series of reports which
she had prepared, and she adhered to her view that
long term fostering would be in the children's best
interests. Lastly the hearing were addressed by the
appellant's solicitor who stressed the efforts which the
appellant had made to improve the conditions of his
own home. The hearing then made their determination, which was that none of the children should be
returned to live with the appellant, and that urgent
action should be taken by the social work department
to arrange long term fostering for them on the basis
outlined by the social worker. The children were to
remain in care and the appellant was to be given one
hour's supervised access to each of them each fortnight. The reasons for the decision, as recorded in
writing by the chairman, were in these terms: [his
Lordship quoted the reasons set out at p 571C-D
supra and continued:]

The appellant then appealed to the sheriff under s
49 of the 1968 Act. On 4 March 1991 the sheriff
refused the appeal and was then requested by the
appellant to state a case for the opinion of this court.
Three questions were stated in this application, but
the only point which has been argued in the appeal to
which we listened was that mentioned in question 2,
which was in these terms: [his Lordship quoted the
terms of question 2 of the application (p 571I-J supra)
and continued:] The sheriff was of opinion that this
was a matter which was at large for the hearing and
was one which the hearing was bound to consider. In
his view it was for the hearing to decide what weight
should be attached to it, but he remarked that a continued allegation of sexual abuse against the father
would give cause for concern whatever the truth might
be, and that the fact that K was no longer a virgin at
the age of 13 would point to a lack of parental care
however the circumstances came about.

The question of law which we have to consider in
this case is whether the children's hearing were
entitled to have regard to the allegation of sexual abuse
of K. This question arises in view of the fact that this
was not one of the grounds of referral accepted by the
appellant or established to the satisfaction of the
sheriff in an application made to him under s 42.
Counsel for the appellant submitted that the sheriff
had erred in law, especially having regard to the fact
that the reference to the allegation of sexual abuse had
been deleted from the grounds for the referral before
they were accepted by the appellant. She contended
that the appellant had not been given an opportunity
to accept or deny the allegation in a way which would
require it to be tested by evidence. In fairness to him
the allegation should have been made the subject of a
fresh ground of referral so that he could state his position with regard to it in terms of s 42. As it was, since
the allegation had been deleted by the reporter at the
stage of the original appeal, the children's hearing
were entitled to proceed only with regard to the
grounds which he had accepted. Reference was made
to s 42 (2) (b) in support of this argument. It followed
that the children's hearing were not entitled to take
into account in their consideration of the case under
s 44 any information which was not directly related to
these grounds. The same applied at the stage of a
review under s 48. The effect of s 43 (1) was to confine
the children's hearing to only such information as was
relevant — relevant, that is, to the grounds of referral
which had been accepted by the appellant. As it was,
he had been severely prejudiced because his wish to
have the children returned to him had been denied on
a ground which he had not been able to have judicially
tested. In support of this argument counsel for the
appellant referred to *K v Finlayson*, in which the
sheriff held that a decision of a children's hearing
which was based on any grounds other than those
accepted by the parents, or established to the satisfaction of a sheriff, was ultra vires of their powers. In
the course of her opinion the sheriff said this (at p 53):

"I find it unthinkable that a person who has denied
the original grounds of referral against her — and
denied them successfully in two out of three cases —
should then be judged as unfit to carry out any part
of her parental role (for that is really what the condition of the child's residence in an institution amounts
to) on grounds which have not been stated as grounds
of referral and which she has no opportunity of
denying or having examined in court."

We were invited to answer question 3 in the case in
the affirmative and to remit these cases to the sheriff
with a direction that he should remit them to the children's hearing for reconsideration of their decision.

The essential points on which this argument relied
were those of openness and of fairness to the appellant. It was the absence of an opportunity to have the
allegation judicially tested which was said to constitute
the unfairness, and this was said to be all the more
unfair in view of the reporter's decision to delete the
allegation from the original grounds. The result was a
stalemate as far as the appellant was concerned,
because the last sentence of the reasons given by the
children's hearing showed that they would not consider returning the children to live with him as long
as the allegation was persisted in by K.

But it is important not to lose sight of the intention
of Parliament as expressed in Pt III of the Act. The
tests of openness and unfairness to which counsel for
the appellant drew our attention must be seen in the
context of these provisions and what it is they were
designed to achieve. Counsel for the reporter devoted
much of his argument to a careful analysis of the provisions of Pt III and of the Children's Hearings (Scotland) Rules 1986 in support of his submission that the
children's hearing were not only entitled but were also
bound to consider the allegation of sexual abuse in
their disposal of these cases. Under reference both to
the scheme of the Act and what was to be found in a
number of authorities which it is unnecessary to consider, except *K v Finlayson* which he submitted had
been wrongly decided, he invited us to answer questions 2 and 4 in the affirmative and refuse the appeal.
We are in no doubt that his was the correct approach,
and that when the decision of the children's hearing is
seen in this context it was one which the sheriff was
entitled to hold to have been justified by the reasons
which they gave.

The purpose of Pt III of the Act is to enable compulsory measures of care to be provided for children who
are in need of them. Section 32 (3) provides that
"care" in this context includes protection, control,
guidance and treatment. The first step is to establish
that the child is in need of these measures of care. This
must be done under reference to the conditions mentioned in s 32 (2), and it is with reference to these conditions that the grounds for the referral must be
prepared: see rule 17 of the 1986 Rules. Section 42 (1)
provides that the first task of the chairman at the commencement of a children's hearing is to explain the
grounds of the referral to the child and his parent so
that it may be ascertained whether they are accepted
by them in whole or in part. Provision is made for
grounds which are not accepted by both the child and
his parent to be referred to the sheriff for determination in the light of the evidence. If at the end of the
day none of the grounds is accepted and none of them
is found to have been established, that is an end of the
case. The referral on these grounds must be discharged. But so long as at least one of the grounds is
accepted or established the case is one which the
children's hearing must consider. This is because s 32
(1) provides that a child may be in need of compulsory
measures of care if any of the conditions mentioned in
subs (2) is satisfied with respect to him. It is not disputed that each of the children involved in these cases
satisfied this requirement once the appellant decided
to accept the amended grounds, and there has been no
suggestion in the submissions which were made to us
that the referral of their cases to the children's hearing
should be discharged.

The duty of the children's hearing in this situation
is set out in s 43 (1) which is in these terms: [his Lordship quoted its terms and continued:] That section
must be read together with s 44, which makes provision for how a case is to be disposed of other than
by discharge of the referral, and with s 48, which
makes provision for the review of a supervision

requirement made under s 44. These sections must
also be read together with the relevant provisions of
the 1986 Rules, especially rule 19 which provides for
the conduct of a children's hearing when they are considering a case on referral or at the stage of a review
of a supervision requirement. It is clear from a study
of these provisions that the function of the children's
hearing at this stage, once the grounds for the referral
have been accepted or established, is to consider the
case of the child. The function of the hearing is to
investigate the case so far as necessary to complete
their consideration of what is in the child's best
interests. The information to which they must have
regard in terms of s 43 (1) includes the grounds of
referral accepted or established. But it may extend
well beyond what may have been stated in these
grounds. This is because the hearing must have regard
also to a report obtained from the local authority
under s 39 (4) on the child and his social background.
As that subsection points out, this report may contain
information from any such person as the reporter or
the local authority may think fit. Furthermore they are
entitled in terms of s 43 (1) to have regard to "such
other relevant information as may be available to
them". Counsel for the appellant said that this information must be confined to information which was
relevant to the grounds for the referral, but in our
opinion that interpretation is not consistent with the
express purpose of the subsection. Its purpose is to
enable the children's hearing to consider what is in the
best interests of the child. The test of relevancy in this
context, therefore, is whether the information is relevant to a consideration of what course should be taken
in the child's best interests. Once the decision has
been taken that he is in need of compulsory measures
of care, any information which is relevant to the
making of a supervision requirement in terms of s 44
will be relevant information to which the children's
hearing may have regard. In particular, the views of
any safeguarder appointed under the Act will be relevant, especially as rule 19 (2) (d) provides that the children's hearing shall endeavour to obtain the views of
the safeguarder on what arrangements with respect to
the child would be in the best interests of the child.

It can be seen therefore that the children's hearing
have wide powers of investigation. As counsel for the
reporter pointed out, they are not just a disposing
body, and their powers are not to be seen as confined
within narrow limits determined by the grounds for
the referral. They are entitled to ask for and to consider information across a wide range and to obtain the
views of various people, including social workers and
any safeguarder, as to what would be in the best
interests of the child. To restrict their consideration of
the child's best interests by requiring them to have
regard only to what had been stated in the grounds of
referral would be inconsistent with the scheme of the
Act, to which the rules are designed to give effect. It
would be illogical to require the children's hearing to
ignore information which they were required by s 43
(1) and by rule 19 (2) to obtain.

For these reasons we consider that the decision of

the children's hearing to have regard to K's allegation of sexual abuse was one which they were clearly entitled to take. It could hardly be disputed that, applying the broad test of what would be in the best interests of the children, the information about this allegation which had been provided to the children's hearing both by the social workers and by the safeguarder, was relevant information available to the hearing which they were entitled to consider. One of the issues before the children's hearing on 16 December 1990 was whether the accommodation which the appellant was able to provide for the children was suitable. He maintained that he had made efforts to improve the material conditions of his own home to this end. In these circumstances the children's hearing were clearly entitled to consider whether the appellant himself was a suitable person to look after the children, and the relevance of the allegation to this point is inescapable.

Counsel for the appellant's objection was, as we have said, based essentially on the unfairness which she said was inherent in the fact that the appellant had no opportunity to have the allegation judicially tested. But, seen in its proper context, there was no unfairness to him in what was done in this case. The question whether the children were in need of compulsory measures of care had already been resolved. What was in issue now was the arrangements which should be made in their best interests. The children's hearing had a duty to act fairly in relation to the appellant, but that duty was fulfilled so long as they gave him a fair opportunity of correcting or contradicting what was said about him or against him in the reports. He was present at the hearing on 16 December 1990 with his solicitor, and he was given an opportunity of denying that he had sexually abused his child. It is not suggested that the provisions of rule 19 (3), by which the chairman is required to inform the child and his parent of the substance of any reports and other information available at the hearing, were not complied with in this case. The sheriff's finding is that the appellant's protestation of his innocence of the allegation of sexual abuse was considered by the hearing: see finding 7. As the Lord Justice Clerk pointed out in *Kennedy v A*, at p 362A-B, the principles of natural justice must yield to the best interests of the child, and in any event cannot be invoked to produce a result which is contrary to the clear provisions of a statutory instrument — in this case of rule 19 (2) (d) by which the children's hearing were required to obtain the views of the safeguarder. In our opinion what the rules of natural justice required here was that the proceedings of the children's hearing should be fair to the appellant. That requirement was satisfied by his being allowed to be present as the statute requires and, on being told of the allegation, being given an opportunity to contradict it.

It follows from what we have said that *K v Finlayson* was wrongly decided. The sheriff in that case was concerned to set limits to the powers of the children's hearing by reference to the principle of fair notice, which she saw as inherent in s 42 (1) which provides

for the grounds for the referral to be explained to the child and the parent. She saw this as an important safeguard against the hearing acting upon information which was other than true, unbiased and reliable, so that if the grounds were denied by the parent or the child they should be subjected to the ordinary evidential tests before being acted upon. But the sheriff's examination of the statutory provisions was incomplete. She did not consider the provisions of s 43 (1) or the rules, and she failed to appreciate the significance of the wide powers of investigation given to the children's hearing at the stage of the disposal of the case once it has been established that the child is in need of compulsory measures of care. The safeguard which the Act provides at that stage is to be found in s 49 which provides for any decision of a children's hearing to be appealed to the sheriff. The powers given to the sheriff by s 49 (3) are sufficient to enable him to review the decision in the light of the reasons which have been given for it. If the decision is one which no reasonable hearing would have taken on the information which was properly before them, then the sheriff has power under s 49 (5) to intervene on the ground that it is not justified in all the circumstances of the case. What the sheriff cannot do is to require the children's hearing to ignore information relevant to the best interests of the child on the ground that, because it might have formed the subject of a separate ground of referral, it must, if disputed, be tested by evidence.

For these reasons we shall answer questions 2 and 4 in the affirmative and refuse the appeal. We decline to answer question 1 since it was not argued, and we also decline to answer question 3 since, unlike question 2 in the application for the stated case, it does not focus accurately the question at issue in this case. It is not correct to say that the children's hearing had become involved in deciding upon the allegation of sexual abuse as a ground of referral. What they were doing was to have regard to this allegation as part of the information which was made available to them in accordance with the provisions of s 43 (1) and rule 19 (2) (d) as being relevant to what arrangements would be in the best interests of the children.

Counsel for Appellant, Raeburn, QC; Solicitors, Thomson & Baxter, WS — Counsel for First Respondent (Reporter), G N H Emslie, QC; Solicitors, Balfour & Manson, Nightingale and Bell — No appearance for Second Respondent (Safeguarder).

D K

(NOTE)

Dunn v Johnston Castings Engineering Ltd

OUTER HOUSE

LORD WEIR

24 JUNE 1992

Damages — Amount — Solatium and loss of earning capacity — Back — Injury rendering pursuer permanently unfit for pre-accident employment but fit for light work within about three years of accident.

A 38 year old employee injured his back, rendering him permanently unfit for active work but probably capable of obtaining light work within a further year or so. He continued to suffer pain from his back and had become depressed.

Held, that solatium was properly assessed at £6,000, and that in addition to loss of wages to the date of the proof an award for loss of earning capacity of £12,500 was appropriate; and decree *pronounced* accordingly.

———

Ronald Dunn raised an action against his former employers Johnston Castings Engineering Ltd for damages in respect of injuries sustained in an accident on 22 February 1990. He was then aged 38. He had been employed by the defenders for only a month when he had hurt his back lifting a heavy vice. The defenders admitted liability to make reparation for the consequences of the pursuer's injury. Their position was that he had recovered from the effects of the accident by 21 May 1990 at the very latest. On that hypothesis total damages, inclusive of interest, were agreed at £4,182. The contention for the pursuer was that he had not recovered from his injury and that he had a continuing loss. A proof on quantum was heard by the Lord Ordinary (Weir). In assessing damages his Lordship said:

"The pursuer stated in evidence that he was lifting the vice along with another employee while working on nightshift. As he started to lift he felt a sharp pain in the base of the spine and had to let go his side of the vice. The pain continued and became worse. After a few hours he felt that he could not continue so he left for home. He went to bed but the pain remained. He contacted his medical practice but for some reason which was never satisfactorily explained, he was unable to get an appointment until 5 March. By 1 March the pursuer was finding the pain unbearable and he went directly to Crosshouse hospital, near Kilmarnock. It would appear that he was seen by a junior doctor there but no x-rays were taken and he was advised to take a painkiller and to rest. The pursuer then saw Dr Gray, his general practitioner on 5 March, but no treatment appears to have been given or was contemplated. The pursuer continued to rest at home and as time went by the pain began to subside. The defenders meantime paid him off. He decided to

seek employment again. He was interviewed for a job with a company in Prestwick but this led to nothing. The pursuer during this period started to walk and he resumed playing golf. It was while playing this game in May that his back condition deteriorated and it is contended that he has been incapacitated for work ever since. In evidence the pursuer stated that at this time his back was not actually painful. He was playing a stroke from an awkward position when he felt a pain in his neck. This was so severe that he could not continue with the game. He was given a cervical collar and the pain in the neck subsided after a few days. However, shortly after this game, not more than two or three days, if that, the pursuer noticed that the pain in his back had returned. He was he said in constant pain for about a month thereafter and in fact has never been free of pain since then.

"His general practitioner suggested that he might obtain treatment from a chiropracter and in September 1990 he attended Dr Cox, a local practitioner of this skill. She made a careful examination of the pursuer, and was an impressive witness. Her x-rays revealed a right lumbar scoliosis, a lumbar lordosis and fibrositis in the sacroiliac joints. Her report contains the earliest record of radiological examination. Dr Cox also recorded the history given to her by the pursuer in which he mentioned both the episode at work and that on the golf course.

"The pursuer was also x-rayed at Crosshouse hospital in September 1990 and in March 1991, and also, in connection with this case, at Glasgow Nuffield hospital in March 1992. There is a reference in the reports from Crosshouse hospital to scoliosis. The most recent radiological report makes no reference to scoliosis but I shall return to that report in due course.

"Before dealing with the evidence of the specialists it will be convenient if I indicated my view of the pursuer. It was plain that giving evidence was something of an ordeal for him and indeed that the litigation itself was a source of unease. Mr Thomas Mann, the orthopaedic surgeon who gave evidence on behalf of the pursuer, indicated in his report that the pursuer was now depressed about life in general and this was also the impression which I received. Nevertheless the pursuer gave his evidence very clearly and with moderation. I formed a favourable view of him as a witness and as a person. I considered that he was giving his evidence truthfully and without exaggeration. His evidence on the history of his back trouble is to be regarded, in my judgment, as accurate.

"The case for the defenders as developed in the evidence of the orthopaedic surgeon, Mr Hamilton, was that the effect of the lifting episode had completely died away a few weeks after the incident and that any subsequent disability, insofar as there was any, is to be attributed to the golfing episode which was triggered off independently of and unconnected with the earlier episode. On this matter Mr Mann and Mr Hamilton disagreed."

His Lordship then considered the evidence of Mr Mann and Mr Hamilton and preferred that of Mr Mann. His Lordship continued:

"In these circumstances the pursuer has satisfied me that his loss, injury and damage is not confined to the short period between February and May 1990. Since the latter date the pursuer has suffered constantly from low back discomfort associated with damage to a lower lumbar disc. There is evidence of lumbar deformity including scoliosis and limitation of right tilting movements of the lumbar spine. Mr Mann concludes that the problems are not gross but are not likely to improve. Mr Hamilton expressed the opinion that the pursuer has long since been fit for his previous employment, but this assertion evidently came as a surprise to the defenders' counsel as she did not put this point to the pursuer. Having had the benefit of seeing the pursuer and listened to his evidence, I consider that the implication behind Mr Hamilton's assertion, namely that the pursuer was exaggerating his symptoms and might even be regarded as a malingerer, cannot be justified and I prefer Mr Mann's evidence that the pursuer is unfit permanently for active work, including bending and lifting operations. It is not suggested he was unfit for other forms of employment but bearing in mind his age and that his work experience has been in engineering, the range of work which is practically open to him is considerably restricted. The pursuer has suffered continuing pain which has reduced his quality of life and I believe that this may explain his present mood of depression. I would not be surprised however, if this mood changed after the anxiety and feelings of uncertainty caused by the present litigation have come to an end.

"In assessing damages for solatium I have had regard to the fact that due to the accident the pursuer has suffered pain and has been off work for over two years. He appears to do nothing all day and the pain is evident upon any significant degree of exertion. I also take into account the prospect of pain continuing to trouble him indefinitely. In my opinion the sum of £6,000 would be a reasonable measure of damages under this head of his claim. It was agreed that for the purposes of an award of interest the apportionment of the award should be attributed 50 per cent to the past and 50 per cent to the future.

"So far as patrimonial loss to date is concerned, it was agreed by joint minute between the parties that in the event of the court holding that the pursuer had suffered loss, injury and damage to the date of the proof attributable to the accident and that an award in respect thereof should include an award for the loss of wages for the period 22 February 1990 to the date of the proof, that sum should amount to £19,496 inclusive of interest at the rate of 7.5 per cent per annum from 22 February 1990. I am prepared to make an award on that basis. In addition the pursuer is entitled to recovery of the sum of £749 which he paid in fees to Dr Cox in respect of his various attendances upon her, which I consider were reasonably incurred.

"The assessment of damages for future loss is more problematic. The pursuer's qualifications are related to work which involves a degree of exertion for which

he is incapacitated. On the other hand he impressed me as a man of considerable intelligence and his varied work experience in the past suggests a degree of versatility and adaptability towards other forms of employment. Although sitting for any length of time is uncomfortable, the pursuer is not unfit for sedentary work and Mr Mann's view was that he should now be seeking light work. It is very difficult to assess what are the prospects of his obtaining work of a suitable kind and I estimate in a broad way that he should be capable of obtaining work within the next year or so. It cannot be readily assumed that he will earn as much as previously. This is a case where, in my opinion, it would be appropriate to award a lump sum to reflect the diminution of the pursuer's employment prospects for the future and bearing in mind that he was earning about £165 per week prior to the accident in 1990, I consider that a sum of £12,500 would be a reasonable lump sum to award under this head."

Counsel for Pursuer, Baird; Solicitors, Macbeth, Currie & Co, WS — Counsel for Defenders, Davie; Solicitors, Wright, Johnston & Mackenzie, WS.

C H

Boyle v HM Advocate

HIGH COURT OF JUSTICIARY
THE LORD JUSTICE CLERK (ROSS),
LORDS MORISON AND GRIEVE
10 JULY 1992

Justiciary — Crime — Murder — Self defence — Whether accused starting fight or going into fight armed with lethal weapon could plead self defence — Judge directing jury that accused could not so plead — Whether misdirection.

Justiciary — Procedure — Retrial — Accused charged with murder but convicted of culpable homicide — Conviction set aside and retrial authorised — Whether court could restrict retrial to culpable homicide charge — Criminal Procedure (Scotland) Act 1975 (c 21), ss 254 (1) (c) and 255 (1).

Section 254 (1) (c) of the Criminal Procedure (Scotland) Act 1975 provides that the High Court may dispose of an appeal against conviction by setting aside the verdict of the trial court and granting authority to bring a new prosecution in accordance with s 255. Section 255 (1) provides that where such authority has been granted, a new prosecution may be brought charging the accused with the same or any similar offence arising out of the same facts.

An accused person was charged with murder and breach of the peace by, inter alia, forming part of a disorderly crowd and brandishing weapons, threatening

violence to and throwing bottles at the lieges. The
A evidence disclosed that an armed group had moved
towards a public house where one of the group,
Logan, had earlier had an altercation. Another group
of persons formed an associated group some of whom
were spectators. The mob was seen before it arrived
and approximately 10 or 12 people, armed with
various weapons, left the public house and formed a
line across the road to face the approaching mob.
Eventually members of the two groups engaged in
hand to hand combat. In the course of the fighting
B Logan, who was carrying a metal bar with which he
had threatened two persons, fell to the ground. There
was evidence that both those persons had knives and
that Logan then came under threat from them. The
accused, who was armed with a knife, was one of two
or more persons who went to protect Logan. The
accused stabbed one of the persons threatening Logan.
The accused stated at his trial that he had not joined
the mob but had tagged along as a spectator and was
unarmed on arrival at the public house. He stated that
C he was given a knife to look after as he stood spectating
and that as he ran over to pick up Logan, the deceased
and his companion said that they were going to kill the
accused. He then panicked and stabbed the deceased.

The Crown's case was that the accused had been a
full member of the mob which was led by Logan and
had stabbed the deceased. The defence conceded that
the accused was guilty of breach of the peace but
suggested that he should be acquitted of the killing on
the ground of self defence. In charging the jury, the
D trial judge directed inter alia that if the accused went
into the fight armed with a lethal weapon self defence
could not be pled if the weapon were used in the
course of the fight; and that "if there is a collection of
people acting together using arms and they deliberately choose to do battle with another group also
wholly or partly armed", self defence would not be
available. The trial judge further said that someone
who engaged in the fight but broke off to rescue
someone and used violence to assist that person could
E plead self defence but that it was of critical importance
to decide how the fighting started: if the accused,
being armed, willingly entered the fight, then he lost
the right to plead self defence in respect of any
incidental episode in the fighting that resulted. The
accused was convicted of culpable homicide and
breach of the peace and appealed on the ground of
misdirection.

Held, (1) that the trial judge misdirected the jury in
F stating (a) that an accused person could not successfully plead self defence if he started the fight and was
the first to use violence (p 587E); (b) that a person
could not plead self defence if he went into the fight
armed with a lethal weapon since it might have caused
the jury to conclude that even if the accused had been
standing by as a spectator, as soon as he went forward
into the fight with the knife, he could not plead self
defence (pp 587G-H and 588A); and (c) that the critical issue was whether the accused was a spectator or
participant since whether or not self defence could be
pled depended on the circumstances and even though

the jury had concluded that the accused had participated in the breach of the peace, that did not G
necessarily mean that he could not plead self defence
(p 587I-J); (2) that as the jury may well have concluded
that it was not open to them to consider self defence
at all, the misdirections amounted to a miscarriage of
justice (p 588C); but (3) that a retrial should be
authorised (p 588D-E); and (4) that it was for the
Crown and not the court to determine what charges
should be levelled against the accused in the new
prosecution (p 588H-I); and appeal *allowed*, conviction
set aside and retrial *authorised*.
H

HM Advocate v Robertson and Donoghue, 17 October
1945, unreported, *applied.*

Indictment
Daniel Boyle was charged at the instance of the rt
hon the Lord Fraser of Carmyllie, Her Majesty's
Advocate, on an indictment which contained the
following charges, inter alia: "(1) on 27 July 1991 in
Craigton Road, Glasgow, near to the premises known I
as the Parkgate public house, you did, while acting
along with other persons, conduct yourself in a disorderly manner, form part of a disorderly crowd,
brandish sticks, baseball bats, metal bars, bottles,
knives or similar instruments or objects, shout, swear,
threaten violence to the lieges, throw bottles and other
similar objects at the lieges, place them in a state of
fear and alarm for their safety and commit a breach of
the peace; (2) date and place last above libelled, you
did assault William Murray Bennett, formerly resid- J
ing at 133 Elderpark Street, Glasgow, repeatedly stab
him on the body with a knife and did murder him".

The accused pled not guilty and proceeded to trial
before Lord McCluskey and a jury in the High Court
at Glasgow. After trial the accused was found guilty of
breach of the peace and culpable homicide. The
accused appealed against conviction by way of note of
appeal to the High Court.

K
Statutory provisions
The Criminal Procedure (Scotland) Act 1975
provides:

"254.—(1) The High Court may, subject to subsection (4) below, dispose of an appeal against conviction by — (a) affirming the verdict of the trial court;
(b) setting aside the verdict of the trial court and either
quashing the conviction or substituting therefor an
amended verdict of guilty: Provided that an amended
verdict of guilty must be one which could have been L
returned on the indictment before the trial court; or (c)
setting aside the verdict of the trial court and granting
authority to bring a new prosecution in accordance
with section 255 of this Act.

"255.—(1) Where authority is granted under section
254 (1) (c) of this Act, a new prosecution may be
brought charging the accused with the same or any
similar offence arising out of the same facts; and the
proceedings out of which the appeal arose shall not be
a bar to such new prosecution: Provided that no sent-

A
ence may be passed on conviction under the new prosecution which could not have been passed on conviction under the earlier proceedings.

Cases referred to

Advocate (HM) v Kizileviczius, 1938 SLT 245; 1938 JC 60.

Advocate (HM) v Robertson and Donoghue, 17 October 1945, unreported.

Mackenzie v HM Advocate, 1983 SLT 220; 1982 SCCR 499.

B
Textbook referred to

Gordon, *Criminal Law* (2nd ed), para 24-06.

In his charge to the jury the trial judge gave the following directions, inter alia:

LORD McCLUSKEY.— . . . Now, let's go back to the indictment. I am going to deal with charge 1. Members of the jury, both sides here, the Crown and
C
senior counsel for the defence, are agreed that you should in respect of charge 1 say guilty. In one view I could just say very well, let's pass to something else but ladies and gentlemen, why you find the accused guilty on charge 1 is important. Senior counsel for the defence put to you it is obvious that really everybody there was committing a breach of the peace and therefore convict my client, let's get on to something more important, let's look at the murder charge. Now, the advocate depute says the reason why David (sic) Boyle
D
is guilty is that he, David (sic) Boyle, was armed while a participant and for that reason convict him of forming part of a disorderly crowd brandishing weapons including knives. So, ladies and gentlemen, this charge does provide you with a focus and a necessary focus in determining what Daniel Boyle's real role in the matter was because the nature of his participation goes to the very heart of the next charge, charge 2 and particularly to the matter of self defence.

So, ladies and gentlemen, let's just take the compet-
E
ing account in relation to charge no 1 although both sides are agreed the accused should be convicted. The Crown say he formed part of a disorderly crowd right from the beginning. He was in there. He emerged down from Teucherhill into Craigton Road and along to the pub and he was armed. And he said, No, I didn't. He said, I saw the group. There is not much to do and see in Teucherhill on a Saturday afternoon. I followed down to do my nosey — I think was his expression — just to watch what was going on. Far
F
from being part of the group brandishing sticks and knives he says, I started off with a bamboo stick but as soon as I reached Craigton Road I threw it away. When I got to the scene I didn't join the fighting. I stood among the women and children and I was unarmed and remained unarmed until for some reason Frearson handed me a knife and I immediately tucked it up my sleeve out of sight.

Ladies and gentlemen, you have to resolve this question and decide where the truth lies between these two startlingly different accounts. It is not just a question

of whether the man is guilty of breach of the peace. It is really a question of what was the nature of his par-
G
ticipation of the events that took place when the real confrontation, the real conflict, began close to the pub because you see Mr Daniel Boyle says, not only was I unarmed but I didn't shout and I didn't swear and I didn't threaten violence to the lieges and I didn't throw bottles and I stood amongst the women and children and I didn't put anyone into a state of fear and alarm for their safety etc. Logically, if you accept his account it would be pretty difficult to find him guilty of this breach of the peace because he said, I
H
didn't do any of these things and I was not part of that group. Well, ladies and gentlemen, it may not matter very much whether he is guilty of breach of the peace in the whole circumstances here, but looking at the breach of the peace charge in dealing with it as carefully as you can will help you I am sure towards resolving the real question that you have got to resolve.

I do make this comment upon what senior counsel said. Really he said everybody was guilty of the breach of the peace. Ladies and gentlemen, that may or may
I
not be so. If in fact there were genuine spectators, let's say the women and the children, and they all went along to see what was happening, they didn't shout, they didn't have any weapons and they didn't join together, you wold not really find them guilty of breach of the peace because they were not part of the disorderly group. They were just hangers on who went along to see what the disorderly group was doing but it is not necessarily true that everyone in the street was guilty of breach of the peace. . . .
J

Ladies and gentlemen, I've dealt with charge no 1 and I have dealt with the bail charges and I now want to come on to the heart of the matter which is charge no 2. Again, I find myself in some disagreement with senior counsel for the defence. He said to you the law was really quite simple here. Well, it is not. In particular in relation to the matter of self defence it is not simple. I will therefore turn to the law as it applies specifically to charge no 2 and the important aspects
K
that will have to be decided by you. Let's first of all start with the easy bit. What is assault? Now, ladies and gentlemen, that is not a problem. Assault in Scotland in cases of this kind means any deliberate attack by one person, one human being upon another human being and the essence of the crime of assault is that the attacker, the assailant, carried out his account with evil intention. The prosecution does not have to demonstrate that the accused intended the precise result that was achieved. Take for example the classic case of a
L
terrorist who puts a bomb in a shop door intending to blow up a passing policeman or a passing soldier but the bomb goes off prematurely and kills a tourist. The terrorist cannot say I didn't intend to kill the tourist, I intended to kill the policeman. There is no defence there. It is still murder so the actual result may not be important. What is important is the evil intention and again you could think of a case, ladies and gentlemen, where people deliberately attack other people and there is no crime committed. The most obvious one is a boxing match. For some reason we in this country

permit two boxers to go into a boxing ring and they shake hands and for three minutes they batter one another and at the end of the three minutes they stop and sit down and at the end throw their arms round one another and this is all conducted under the Queensberry rules. It is not an assault despite the fact that one person is deliberately attacking another. For reasons in a sense of legal policy as well as other reasons the law says we will permit that, not regard that a case of evil intention. Similarly, a mother who sees her child just about to reach up and grasp the handle of the pot on the stove and his mother will seize the child and perhaps smack it and the mother is saying, don't do that again and that is everyday experience. Again, that is not regarded in law as an assault because there is an absence of evil intention but because of the special defence which I will deal with more fully it is in a sense a classic one we know in the courts. If a person's intent in using violence against another human being is not because he wishes to harm that other human being but because he wishes to protect himself or protect somebody else our law says you have a human being deliberately attacking another human being but it is not an assault because you have absence of evil intention. So, ladies and gentlemen, it is important to notice that evil intention is part of the essence of the crime of assault.

Now, let me just turn to self defence. I want to do something that I don't think was done by counsel and that is this: to make it clear to you that self defence is a defence to a charge of assault. If on this occasion Daniel Boyle was justified in using violence to defend himself against an attack by another then Daniel Boyle is not guilty of assault and because murder is just an aggravated assault he is not guilty of murder either. So the first question you ask yourself, ladies and gentlemen, is, is he guilty of assault, before we ever get to notions of murder or culpable homicide or provocation or anything of that kind. Is he guilty of assault or let me put it more formally, more accurately. A person is entitled to use force to defend himself against an attack or an intended attack by another and similarly a person is entitled to use force to defend another human being whether his brother or his son or his friend or even a stranger if he thinks that the other person is being attacked or is about to be attacked. It is important to understand why the law allows a person to use violent force in self defence without his being held to be guilty of assault and the answer is this: as I have just said the essence of the crime of assault is that the person who commits the assault is a person who uses violence with evil intent and a person who is using violence to ward off an assault or protect another is not using violence with evil intention. He has been driven to resort to violence, not with evil intention but with the trustworthy intention of preventing an assault upon another human being, whether it is himself or this other person. So, ladies and gentlemen, in this case if Daniel Boyle used violence on William Bennett to prevent Bennett from assaulting Boyle or Logan or both then he does not himself possess the evil intention which is essential before he can be found guilty of assault.

Let met put it slightly differently. It follows that self defence is a complete answer to a charge of assault. If the accused acted in self defence he must be acquitted of assault and as I have said in this type of case murder is really just an aggravated assault, an assault which results in death; if an accused acted in self defence not only is he not guilty of assault but he is not guilty of culpable homicide and he is not guilty of murder. So in other words self defence is not a plea which takes the crime of murder and turns it into culpable homicide, a lesser crime. It takes the crime of assault and turns it into an acquittal.

That is why it is logical I believe to look at self defence before we look at murder. This is the first issue to be resolved and this is it. Did the accused assault William Bennett or did the accused act in self defence? When I talk about self defence I am always talking about defending himself or another person who is being attacked. If he acted in self defence, acquit him of the whole charge. If however you reject self defence and you find he was guilty of assault then the question is, did the assault cause death, and no one disputes that the knife wounds had caused death; if he was guilty of assault and if that attack caused death then the only question becomes, do you call it murder or do you call it culpable homicide?

Ladies and gentlemen, let me repeat something I said at the beginning. It is important. The burden of proof is on the Crown throughout. The defence does not have to establish the self defence. There is no burden upon them to prove the self defence. If in a case of this kind the defence gives notice of a plea of self defence, and that was done, then the Crown must displace the self defence upon the evidence. The prosecution must satisfy you beyond reasonable doubt that despite such evidence as is pointing towards self defence the accused is nonetheless guilty of assault, assault plus death therefore of some homicide charge.

Ladies and gentlemen, I've been talking about self defence as meaning defending yourself, defending someone who needs defence against an attack. Now, not all violence used to defend oneself or to defend another can be properly described as true self defence. Let me explain what I mean by true self defence. An accused person in our courts cannot successfully plead that he acted in self defence if he started a fight, if he was first to use violence. You see, it is pretty obvious. If you think of two persons and we will call them A and B, and A uses violence on B, punches him and B in self defence uses violence on A, it would be daft for A at that point to say now, I'm going to use violence on B but from now on it is going to be in self defence. That would simply mean the law would sanction a duel or deliberately fighting, a square go, which it does not. That is the first point, if the accused started the fight. Now, there is an exception to that and that is why I say the law is rather more complicated than senior counsel for the defence suggested. If a person starts a fight with a shove, a push, mild violence and the person upon whom he has used the mild violence produces a great knife or a sword or a gun or something of the kind and the person who originally started

it with the push or even a slap or a punch, he then
A grabs an iron bar or a chair or something of the kind
to defend himself from the person that is attacking
him with the knife he could plead self defence then.
So the law is not daft about these things. If you use
mild violence and someone responds with lethal
violence of course you are entitled to defend yourself
against a lethal attack. The use of lethal violence in
response to your mild violence changes the whole
situation and you have, as it were, to go back to square
one.

B
Ladies and gentlemen, if you go into a fight,
whether it is a one upon one fight or a gang fight on
either side, if you go into the fight armed with a lethal
weapon prepared to use it then you cannot successfully plead self defence if you do use it in the course
of the fight. Ladies and gentlemen, that is true where
you alone go into a fight with one other person, you
go in armed to fight that other person and he is armed
and there is no room for self defence there for you. It
applies not just to that situation. It applies when you
C go in as part of a team or a gang or a group. It does
not matter what you call them. If there is a collection
of people acting together using arms and they deliberately choose to do battle with another group also
wholly or partly armed then, ladies and gentlemen,
self defence is not available to those who use the violence that follows in the course of the fight in which
they willingly participate.

Ladies and gentlemen, I've used the word duel and
D it is a bit old fashioned. We don't normally have
people in Glasgow Green at dawn with pistols
engaged in a duel, but the concept of the duel is well
understood so I am going to use it. The classic and
simple case is this: if two men agree to fight a duel
with guns or swords or knives and in the duel that
follows one kills the other, that is murder. There is no
room for self defence; and similarly if two men agree
to go outside a pub and fight with fists, a square go,
in that situation in law each one assaults the other.
E There is no room for self defence. That applies not
just to two men. It applies to two teams, two groups,
gangs or crowds. It is not important. If they face up
to each other willing to engage in armed conflict then
each as a willing participant is guilty of an armed
assault against those on the other side and self defence
does not come into it. Self defence, ladies and gentlemen, cannot properly arise just because in the middle
of a fight or at the end you are losing or one of your
team is losing and is down. You can't suddenly
F convert what was willing participation in an armed
conflict to a kind of rescue version in which you are
entitled to use your weapon and say, self defence.

So, ladies and gentlemen, it can be different. That
is why it is quite complicated. I don't know precisely
what view you will take of the facts but let me give you
another example. Supposing a team of five armed
youths take on another team of five armed youths to
do battle. As I have said, team A, they go in, they can't
plead self defence just because they are losing the
battle or because they notice one of their number has

gone down and needs rescued. They cannot plead self
defence. Supposing one of team B breaks off and starts G
to attack one of the spectators, one of the women or
children or any spectator, and one of team A goes to
rescue the spectator, that could be justifiable self
defence. There is nothing complicated about that. It
is just that that is not part of the attack he entered into
and he goes off to rescue someone and uses violence
to help the spectator. That could be a case of self
defence so that is why I come back in a sense to the
breach of the peace charge. It is of critical importance
for you to decide how this fighting started. It is of H
critical importance to decide what in your view, upon
the evidence, was the role of the accused. Again, was
he, putting it broadly, a spectator or was he a participant?

It is a matter for you to resolve upon the evidence
when it was that he acquired the knife because that
may be of great importance in deciding precisely what
his role was because if the evidence persuaded you
beyond reasonable doubt that the accused entered the
fight as a willing participant in which he could foresee I
or actually saw that there was going to be used or there
was actually being used weapons in an armed fight, if
you conclude that he went in armed with a big knife
then there is no room for self defence.

So in summary, ladies and gentlemen, if the
accused, being armed with a knife, willingly entered
the fight between two mobs, one of which he was a
member of, then he loses the right under our law to
plead self defence in respect of any incidental episode J
in the fighting that occurs. It may be in a particular
case and it may be in this case it is partly a question
of timing. When did he deliberately join the fray?

Ladies and gentlemen, the special defence of self
defence in this case reads as follows — this is the document lodged in court — Beltrami for the panel, Daniel
Boyle, states that in respect of charge 2 of the indictment said panel, that is Daniel Boyle, pleads not guilty
and specially and without prejudice to said plea that
on the occasion libelled he was acting in self defence K
and defence of a friend, witness no 4, J Logan, both
of whom having already been assaulted by the said
William M Bennett.

Ladies and gentlemen, the question here at the heart
of it is at what point in time this person loses the right
to plead self defence in our law. If the truth is that
Daniel Boyle was, as he said in evidence in the witness
box, merely a spectator and he moved forward from
the ranks of the spectators to assist Joe Logan to get L
up and until then he had played no part in the battle
at all, he came forward purely as a kind of stranger
determined on rescuing Joe Logan and found himself
in the middle of an attempted attack by Bennett and
companions, well, ladies and gentlemen, if that is the
truth, the spectator version, then he does not lose the
right to plead self defence, to use violence in self
defence, but if he is a willing participant, he joined in
a gang fight between two teams in which he knows
lethal weapons are likely to be used and he himself
goes in at some stage with such a weapon then he

A cannot plead self defence to excuse its use against another human being. I emphasise that because I thought that what senior counsel for the defence said to you was not a full and accurate statement of the law. I remind you that he talked about the situation and he said, and I try to summarise it because I don't pretend to have a completely accurate note, he said a situation may change and what I submit to you is this, is something you will have to listen to Lord McCluskey on on Monday morning, but that even if Logan and the others from Teucherhill were 50 per cent to blame for these boys coming down, even if they were 100 per

B cent to blame for these boys coming down, even if they went down armed, every single one of them, with a knife, even if Logan somehow having become into trouble could have got away, even if he could have got away when the point in time was reached when Logan is on the ground on his own account at the mercy of Bennett and another man, at that point in time the accused goes to try and help Logan and finds himself confronted by Bennett and another man bearing down upon him and clearly there is serious violence towards

C Logan or Boyle or both, so that is the picture senior counsel has submitted to you as one you would be entitled to arrive at on the basis of the evidence. He goes on to say, in that situation I am saying to you that in that situation the fact of the matter is that Logan, whether on his own fault or not, now finds himself vulnerable and defenceless and it is at that point, and only at that point in time, and that is the critical thing, that Daniel Boyle enters on the scene because, ladies and gentlemen, what prior to that really is very

D scrappy evidence that Daniel Boyle did not intend to enter the fray or to harm anyone. In that situation on the submission of senior counsel it is self defence.

Ladies and gentlemen, my direction to you is that that is too narrow a view. I've said this several times but because it is important I will have to say it again. If it be true as Mr Boyle said in evidence, that he went down purely as a spectator to do his nosey, as was his expression, if he was unarmed by throwing away the only thing that might look like a weapon, a 15 inch

E bamboo stick, if he had just gone and stood on the sidelines among the women and children as a spectator and saw nothing done by Bennett or by Bennett's companion, whoever he was, if Frearson came up to him and handed him a knife which he didn't really want and didn't know what to do with and did not intend to use it, just stuck it up his sleeve out of sight and folded his arms and if he went in solely for the purpose of discovering what had happened to the fallen Logan and then was driven to using a knife in order to defend

F himself and Logan against an attack by Bennett and another who were obviously armed, yes, indeed, that is self defence. Ladies and gentlemen, it is far too narrow just to say, take this slice of time at this moment he was defending himself, therefore that is self defence or he was defending Logan.

Ladies and gentlemen, I want to put it this way because again this has perhaps not been looked at with sufficient detail. There is evidence that Logan himself was armed. Now, you will decide what to make of the evidence. I am selecting bits of evidence and you will

G recollect it I hope between you and you will recollect it all. Let me remind you of some of that evidence. Thomas Boyle early on said Joe Logan had a metal pole, he slipped and he fell. Bennett came towards him and I, Thomas Boyle, backed away. I didn't see David (sic) Boyle at that time but he certainly had seen Boyle earlier and at that stage he didn't see Boyle with a knife. But that is it, he has got Logan armed with a metal pole, slipping and falling. Charles McGowan says Joe Logan had a swipe with a pole at William Bennett and then Logan fell. Bennett had a few swipes

H at Logan with a steakie. He says, I distracted Bennett by going in and throwing a brick. I ran round in front and Logan got up and away. I didn't see what Boyle did at all. Joe Logan himself said he had an iron bar. He called it an iron bar though I don't know whether he meant iron. He meant metal I think but that is for you to judge. He said he had an iron bar. It was solid and it could cause lethal injuries if used in a particular way. It was 3 feet long. He said, I didn't hit Bennett with it and Bennett didn't hit me, but he goes on to say that he fell and he demonstrated how he fell.

I Ladies and gentlemen, apart from that there is the evidence from the Stantons but you have got to wonder whether that is reliable or not but there is evidence from the Stantons that the man who was initially engaged with Bennett, battling with Bennett, if it was Bennett, was armed with a knife so there is even evidence that it was not a metal or an iron bar Logan had but it was a knife so you have to make what you can of that evidence. However, let's forget about the knife or the metal bar. Let's proceed upon the

J basis, if it is the basis of view, that Logan was armed with a substantial weapon. Now, if it is right that Logan started the trouble in a sense by going into the scheme and saying, get the troops, get the lads, get the boys, let's get tooled, and if he led his friends and others down in this fashion the whole length of Craigton Road and if at some stage in the course of that encounter he himself used his weapon to hit someone or brandish it at someone, threaten someone and wave it backwards and forwards as you have heard

K described, then, ladies and gentlemen, it is perfectly plain that he could not plead self defence in our law. It does not make any sense. There is no plea of self defence available to Logan. So if the accused stepped in and the accused uses his knife which undoubtedly he has at that stage to protect Logan, to assist Logan, to enable him to get up, could the accused ever say, my actions were justified in self defence for myself and/or Logan? The answer, ladies and gentlemen, is no if his participation was part of the whole sequence,

L the incidents in a fight, an episode in a fight in which he willingly joined while armed.

So, ladies and gentlemen, very broadly speaking that is the issue. Spectator or participant? Perhaps that is an over simplification but at least that is the kind of words I would use to summarise the matter. Was he a spectator, in which event acquit him. Was he a participant, in which event you would find him guilty of assault and you would go on to consider what the character of the assault was.

However, before I finally leave self defence there are
A a couple of matters I have to mention. One is this; that
a person is never entitled in our law to plead self
defence if he has got the option of retreating from the
scene. So your first duty in law is to run. If you choose
to stand your ground and take on your assailant when
you have the choice of leaving then you cannot plead
self defence. So a person is not entitled to plead self
defence if he had a means of escape and chose not to
use it. That is complicated of course in this case by the
circumstances that the defence is not just defending
B myself. He says, I am defending a man who is on the
ground, so the option of running is perhaps not as real
a one if that be the situation. The other point is this
and it was mentioned to you by both counsel. They
referred to what was called cruel excess. Ladies and
gentlemen, in order for a jury to acquit on the basis
of self defence there must be some degree of similarity
between the violence used or threatened by the
assaulting person and the violence used by the defending person. So if someone punches me or comes up
C threatening to punch me I can't take out a gun and
shoot him. There is a terrible disproportion between
the violence threatened and the response and if I did
behave in such a way then that is cruel excess. That
is an assault in itself. So if I am attacked with a punch
I can punch back, I can kick back, but I can't shoot
back. If I am attacked with a knife of course I can
defend myself with a knife or an axe or even possibly
a gun. So, ladies and gentlemen, it is a question of
seeing, not in too fine a scale, whether the violence
D used in response was out of all proportion to the
violence threatened and that is why it becomes important to see how many injuries were inflicted, what part
of the body did they land upon? Does that tell you anything about what was going on? Of course, it is also
cruel excess to continue to use violence after you have
overpowered your assailant. So if you do manage to
get one good blow in in self defence, even with a knife,
and that takes your opponent out of the fight it is no
longer self defence if you then move in for the kill.
E Ladies and gentlemen, you have to decide whether in
all these circumstances self defence makes sense in this
case. Bear in mind it is for the Crown to displace it,
not for the defence to prove it.

Appeal

The note of appeal contained the following grounds
of appeal:

F (1) The learned trial judge misdirected the jury as to
the doctrine of self defence as it applied to the evidence in this case. His directions could be construed as
having wrongly withdrawn the special defence from
their consideration.

(2) The learned trial judge wrongly emphasised the
importance of the jury's verdict on charge 1 on the
indictment as it related to the appellant's possible participation in assisting the witness Logan in his defence
against potentially lethal blows from the deceased and
others.

(3) The learned judge misdirected the jury on the
question of at what point in time a person can lose the G
right to plead self defence.

(4) The learned trial judge misdirected the jury as to
the level of proved participation by the appellant in
any fight or violent incident at the locus in charge 2.

(5) The learned trial judge misdirected the jury by
effectively requiring them to choose between the
appellant being a spectator in any incident or a participant. His directions on the outcome of making
such a choice as it affected the plea of self defence or H
the defence of a friend were too restrictive and
amounted to a misdirection.

The appeal was argued before the High Court on 10
July 1992.

Eo die the court *allowed* the appeal, *set aside* the conviction and *authorised* a retrial.

The following opinion of the court was delivered by I
the Lord Justice Clerk (Ross):

OPINION OF THE COURT.—The appellant is
Daniel Boyle who went to trial in the High Court at
Glasgow on an indictment containing a number of
charges. Charge 1 was a charge of breach of the peace,
charge 2 was a charge of murder, and charges 3, 4 and
5 were charges of contravening the provisions of s 3
(1) (b) of the Bail etc (Scotland) Act 1980. The jury by
a majority found the appellant guilty in respect of
charge 1 as libelled, by a majority found him guilty of J
culpable homicide in respect of charge 2 on the basis
that he acted "without murderous intent", and unanimously found the appellant guilty in respect of each
of charges 3, 4 and 5 as libelled. He was sentenced to
10 years' detention in a young offenders institution in
respect of charges 1 and 2 and to three months in
respect of each of charges 3, 4 and 5; these sentences
were ordered to run consecutively but from 30 July
1991. The appellant has now appealed against conviction and sentence.   K

A note of appeal containing grounds of appeal was
lodged on 13 January 1992. At a previous hearing of
this appeal on 21 February 1992, the court, on the
motion of counsel for the appellant, allowed fresh
grounds of appeal to be lodged and substituted for the
original grounds of appeal. At the same time they
remitted these fresh grounds of appeal to the trial
judge in order that he might prepare a supplementary
report. The substitute grounds of appeal were lodged L
on 24 February 1992. At the hearing of the appeal on
10 July 1992, counsel intimated that he sought to
support all the grounds of appeal contained in the substitute grounds of appeal. There were five grounds of
appeal against conviction, and one ground of appeal
against sentence, that ground being that the sentence
of 10 years' detention was excessive. As regards the
five grounds of appeal against conviction, counsel intimated that these were all interrelated, and that the live
issue in the appeal related to the special defence of self
defence which the appellant had put forward. It was

maintained on his behalf that the trial judge had misdirected the jury regarding self defence.

The first five grounds of appeal in the substitute grounds of appeal are in the following terms: [his Lordship narrated the grounds of appeal set out supra and continued:]

In accordance with the provisions of s 82 of the Criminal Procedure (Scotland) Act 1975, the appellant had duly given notice of a special defence of self defence. That special defence was in the following terms: "Beltrami for the panel, Daniel Boyle, states that in respect of charge 2 of the indictment said panel, that is Daniel Boyle, pleads not guilty and specially and without prejudice to said plea that on the occasion libelled he was acting in self defence and defence of a friend, witness no 4, J Logan, both of whom having already been assaulted by the said William M Bennett."

In his supplementary report the trial judge observes that the first and second charges were closely associated. He adds that the appellant was found guilty as libelled of charge 1, that is, guilty of committing a breach of the peace by forming part of a disorderly crowd which brandished weapons and threw things at and threatened the lieges. That charge, however, did not include any element of hand to hand fighting. He comments that some of those who were involved in the breach of the peace did not get involved in the subsequent fighting. The trial judge also tells us that the victim in charge 2 was William Murray Bennett who was a man aged about 50 years with a fearsome reputation for criminal activities in Glasgow.

The background to these charges is fully described by the trial judge in his supplementary report. The deceased was one of a number of persons in the Parkgate public house on the evening of 27 July 1991. A younger man, Joseph Logan, aged 22, from the Teucherhill scheme, visited the public house and had an altercation with one of the customers. The upshot was that Logan was chased out of the public house by two other persons; he fled up the road pursued by two others one of whom was known as "Uggi" Smith. The pursuit was short lived and the pursuers returned to the public house. When Logan arrived at the Teucherhill scheme, some 200 yds or so from the public house he shouted to various locals, including close friends, who were standing about there to "Get the troops and get tooled up". He wanted to lead a group down to the public house. There were perhaps 20 or 30 people who responded in one way or another to his invitation. The trial judge tells us that approximately five of them were of the same age as Logan and were closely associated with him. Another group of persons, all aged about 18, including the appellant, formed an associated group, and there were other persons including women and children, some of whom were mere spectators. Many of the Teucherhill persons armed themselves before leaving or on the way towards the public house with assorted weapons including sticks, metal bars, bricks, bottles and knives. The Teucherhill mob then proceeded towards the public house, but before they arrived they were seen by Uggi Smith who told those inside of the imminent arrival of the Teucherhill mob, and asked a barmaid to telephone the police. A large number of persons, probably about 10 or 12, then emerged from the public house armed with various weapons, principally billiard cues, but probably some had knives. The mob from the public house formed a line across the road and faced the advancing Teucherhill mob. Insults were exchanged while the two groups were just a few yards apart and objects were thrown; eventually members of the two groups engaged in close hand to hand combat.

There was evidence that several people went down on to the ground, and that one of those who fell was Logan. He had been carrying a solid metal bar with which at one point he had threatened the deceased and the deceased's companion by waving it at them. There was some dispute in the evidence as to what the deceased and his companion were armed with, but the jury could have accepted evidence which suggested that these two men were armed with knives. In the course of waving his metal bar, Logan fell awkwardly to the ground, and was temporarily unable to get up or to defend himself. There was evidence that he then came under the threat of attack from Bennett and Bennett's companion, and that the appellant was one of two or more persons who went to protect or rescue Logan. The appellant was in possession of a substantial kitchen knife which he had obtained from a friend, George Frearson. There was some dispute as to where he had received this knife; Frearson said he gave the knife to the appellant at Teucherhill, whereas the appellant said that Frearson gave it to him only after they arrived outside the public house. The appellant used the knife to stab the deceased Bennett twice, once on the left hand side, and once in the back. The stab wound in the back penetrated vital organs including a principal artery and an important vein, and the deceased died shortly afterwards from loss of blood. The appellant emerged unhurt and ran back to Teucherhill where he disposed of the bloodstained knife by dropping it down a road drain. Some time later a friend of his retrieved the knife and it was wrapped in plastic and thrown into Pollok park.

The police investigations led quickly to the appellant. At first he denied being on the scene, although he admitted witnessing others going in that direction. On a second occasion on which he was interviewed he gave a statement in which he admitted that he had been part of the Teucherhill crowd, but maintained that his only activity was to carry and throw a small bottle. Subsequently while still in the police station, the appellant became agitated and was interviewed a third time. On this occasion he conceded that he had joined the mob, had received one of the two knives that George Frearson had, and had stabbed the deceased, claiming that he did so in order to protect Logan. That account was repeated with modifications at judicial examination. The appellant gave evidence at the trial, and in the course of his evidence he stated that he had not joined the crowd led by Logan from

Teucherhill to the public house. He had simply tagged
A along as a spectator and was part of a group of
"women, weans and boys". He stated that he only followed the crowd, and that not only was he unarmed
on arrival at the public house but that on the way he
had thrown away a bottle which he had had in his
hand when the crowd set out on the way to the public
house. He had not shouted, he had brandished
nothing, he had thrown nothing and he had threatened
no one. He had not joined the line of persons confronting the line of persons who had emerged from the
B public house, he was a pure spectator. He stated that
whilst he was spectating, George Frearson had come
up and handed him the knife saying "watch it". He
maintained that he continued thereafter to stand and
watch. As he stood he noticed Logan on the ground.
He was not aware that Logan was armed. He ran over
to pick Logan up but before he reached Logan he
heard Bennett and his companion say that they were
going to kill him (the appellant). Bennett was armed
with a billiard cue and a knife; Bennett swung the
C billiard cue. The appellant stated that what had
happened next was "I panicked and stabbed him . . .
I just froze". He could not clearly recall stabbing more
than once. He denied that he had gone in with any
aggressive intention at all. He ran away and did not
know what happened to Logan.

   The Crown's case before the jury was that the appellant was a full member of the disorderly mob that was
led by Logan from Teucherhill towards the public
D house. There was other evidence that showed the
appellant to have been one of the armed mob. The
appellant admitted the stabbing with the knife, and in
the circumstances he should be found guilty of both
charges 1 and 2.

   The appellant admitted that he had stabbed Bennett
but he maintained that he had been acting in self
defence. The trial judge remarks that there was no
evidence at all, even from the appellant, that the
deceased Bennett or anyone else had attacked the
E appellant before the appellant went to help Logan.
There was however evidence that Logan, the armed
leader of the Teucherhill mob, had been fighting with
Bennett, also armed, and that eventually Logan was
temporarily on the ground and in danger; and the
appellant asserted that when he went to help Logan he
(the appellant) was then threatened by Bennett and his
companion.

   Counsel for the appellant at the trial invited the jury
F to convict the appellant of breach of the peace but to
acquit him of the second charge on the basis that he
had been acting in self defence. In doing so he invited
the jury to consider the particular time when the
stabbing took place, and he contended that the breach
of the peace was of no real moment. The trial judge
reminded the jury that both the Crown and the
defence were agreed that they should find the appellant guilty of charge 1. It is somewhat surprising that
counsel for the appellant did agree that he was guilty
of charge 1 in view of the evidence which the appellant
himself had given; convicting him of breach of the

peace was indeed inconsistent with his evidence. It
may be, of course, that counsel for the appellant G
wished to concentrate upon the main charge which
was charge 2, but conceding that he was guilty of
charge 1 might be regarded as accepting that the
appellant was not a wholly credible witness. However
that may be it was conceded that he was guilty of
breach of the peace. It is clear from the judge's charge
and from his report that he considered it of importance that this concession was made. In his supplementary report the trial judge states that the breach of
the peace charge was important because if the appellant was guilty of acting along with others, conducting H
himself in the way averred and forming part of the
armed hostile mob doing the various things libelled in
charge 1, then the consequences both for his credibility and for his role in the Logan/Bennett encounter
were bound to be significant. In a lengthy charge, the
trial judge referred to this matter on a number of
occasions. Counsel for the appellant maintained that
the trial judge was justified in stating that the concession regarding breach of the peace might affect the
credibility of the appellant, but that he had erred in I
telling the jury that the fact that the appellant was
guilty of breach of the peace assisted them in resolving
the issue of self defence.

   In his charge at [p 580C, supra] the trial judge
began giving directions regarding self defence. The
following passage appears in his charge: "Now, let me
just turn to self defence. I want to do something that
I don't think was done by counsel and that is this; to
make it clear to you that self defence is a defence to
a charge of assault. If on this occasion Daniel Boyle J
was justified in using violence to defend himself
against an attack by another then Daniel Boyle is not
guilty of assault and because murder is just an
aggravated assault he is not guilty of murder either. So
the first question you ask yourself, ladies and gentlemen, is, is he guilty of assault, before we ever get to
notions of murder or culpable homicide or provocation or anything of that kind. Is he guilty of assault or
let me put it more formally, more accurately. A person
is entitled to use force to defend himself against an K
attack or an intended attack by another and similarly
a person is entitled to use force to defend another
human being whether his brother or his son or his
friend or even a stranger if he thinks that the other
person is being attacked or is about to be attacked."

   Subsequently in his charge, the trial judge repeated
these directions, and he also stressed that the defence
did not have to establish self defence, and it was for
the Crown to displace self defence upon the evidence. L
The trial judge stated: "The prosecution must satisfy
you beyond reasonable doubt that despite such evidence as is pointing towards self defence the accused is
nonetheless guilty of assault, assault plus death therefore of some homicide charge".

   Counsel for the appellant did not complain of these
passages in the trial judge's charge, and indeed he submitted that if the trial judge had left it at that, he
would have had no cause to complain. However, the
trial judge did not leave it at that. At [p 580K, supra]

A he stated: "Now, not all violence used to defend oneself or to defend another can be properly described as true self defence. Let me explain what I mean by true self defence. An accused person in our courts cannot successfully plead that he acted in self defence if he started a fight, if he was first to use violence."

Subsequently the trial judge explained that that general statement was subject to an exception. He said: "Now, there is an exception to that and that is why I say the law is rather more complicated than senior counsel for the defence suggested. If a person B starts a fight with a shove, a push, mild violence and the person upon whom he has used the mild violence produces a great knife or a sword or a gun or something of the kind and the person who originally started it with the push or even a slap or a punch, he then grabs an iron bar or a chair or something of the kind to defend himself from the person that is attacking him with the knife he could plead self defence then. So the law is not daft about these things. If you use mild violence and someone responds with lethal C violence of course you are entitled to defend yourself against a lethal attack. The use of lethal violence in response to your mild violence changes the whole situation and you have, as it were, to go back to square one."

The trial judge then proceeded to expand on this. He said: "Ladies and gentlemen, if you go into a fight, whether it is a one upon one fight or a gang fight on either side, if you go into the fight armed with a lethal D weapon prepared to use it then you cannot successfully plead self defence if you do use it in the course of the fight. Ladies and gentlemen, that is true where you alone go into a fight with one other person, you go in armed to fight that other person and he is armed and there is no room for self defence there for you. It applies not just to that situation. It applies when you go in as part of a team or a gang or a group. It does not matter what you call them. If there is a collection of people acting together using arms and they deliberately choose to do battle with another group also E wholly or partly armed then, ladies and gentlemen, self defence is not available to those who use the violence that follows in the course of the fight in which they willingly participate."

The trial judge then went on to speak about duels, and he then added the following passage: "Self defence, ladies and gentlemen, cannot properly arise just because in the middle of a fight or at the end you are losing or one of your team is losing and is down. F You can't suddenly convert what was willing participation in an armed conflict to a kind of rescue version in which you are entitled to use your weapon and say, self defence."

The trial judge then explained to the jury that if someone who was engaged in a fight broke off and went to the rescue of someone else and used violence to assist that other person, that could amount to self defence. He then stated: "It is of critical importance for you to decide how this fighting started. It is of critical importance to decide what in your view, upon

the evidence, was the role of the accused. Again, was he, putting it broadly, a spectator or was he a par- G ticipant?"

The trial judge subsequently added: "So in summary, ladies and gentlemen, if the accused, being armed with a knife, willingly entered the fight between two mobs, one of which he was a member of, then he loses the right under our law to plead self defence in respect of any incidental episode in the fighting that occurs."

In a number of subsequent passages the trial judge H emphasised that the important question was whether the appellant was a participant in the fight or whether he was a mere spectator. At [p 582L, supra] the trial judge summarised the matter as follows: "So, ladies and gentlemen, very broadly speaking that is the issue. Spectator or participant? Perhaps that is an over simplification but at least that is the kind of words I would use to summarise the matter. Was he a spectator, in which event acquit him. Was he a participant, in which event you would find him guilty of assault and I you would go on to consider what the character of the assault was."

Counsel [who did not appear in the court below] for the appellant submitted that in describing the situation thus, the trial judge had misdirected the jury. He submitted that even if the appellant had been a participant in the fight, he might still be able to claim to have been acting in self defence. He was wrong to tell the jury that self defence cannot be pleaded by the person who was the first to use violence; he was wrong J to direct the jury that if the appellant had gone into the fight armed with a lethal weapon which he was prepared to use, then he could not plead self defence; he was wrong to direct the jury that it was of critical importance for them to decide how the fighting had started; and he was wrong to direct them that the issue was whether the appellant was a spectator or a participant. Counsel submitted that these misdirections amounted to miscarriage of justice because as a consequence of them the jury may never have considered K the issue of self defence at all. He accordingly invited the court to set aside the verdict of the jury, and if it was thought appropriate authorise the Crown to bring a fresh prosecution against the appellant.

The advocate depute accepted that it was incorrect to say that a person who started a fight could never plead self defence. He took as his starting point Gordon's *Criminal Law* (2nd ed), para 24-06, where Sheriff Gordon comments on Hume's treatment of self defence in a quarrel. He states: "This means that a L plea of self-defence cannot succeed where the accused started the quarrel, and also makes it impossible to justify the application of different rules to quarrels from those applied to self-defence against a felon."

Subsequently Sheriff Gordon proceeds to consider the present law on the matter. He does so under reference to two authorities. The first of these is *HM Advocate v Kizileviczius*. Counsel pointed out that it was clear from that case that self defence was pleaded although the quarrel between the accused and the

deceased had been initiated by the accused; the trial
A judge directed the jury that if they thought the
accused had acted in necessary self defence they could
acquit him. As Sheriff Gordon points out, there was
no suggestion that the accused was not entitled to
plead self defence at all because of his part in the
events leading up to the death. That case certainly
suggests that the trial judge was in error when he
directed the jury that an accused could not successfully plead self defence if he had started the fight and
had been the first to use violence.

B   The second authority referred to by Sheriff Gordon
is *HM Advocate v Robertson and Donoghue*. The case
is unreported and Sheriff Gordon quotes a passage
from the opinion of the Lord Justice General. The
advocate depute had obtained copies of the full
opinions of the judges in that case. As in the present
case the accused was convicted of a charge of breach
of the peace and a charge of culpable homicide. The
Lord Justice General considered that the first charge
of breach of the peace was important, and he con-
C cluded that the jury would have been influenced by it.
It is unnecessary to go into all the facts of that case
although it should be observed that the facts were very
different from the facts in the present case. However,
in the course of his opinion, the Lord Justice General
said: "It is necessary to observe that although an
accused person may commit the first assault and may
be, in general, the assailant, he is not thereby necessarily excluded from a plea of self-defence. If the
victim, in protecting himself or his property, uses
D violence altogether disproportionate to the need, and
employs savage excess, then the assailant is in his turn
entitled to defend himself against the assault by his
victim."

Subsequently he added: "Accordingly, in a case in
which there is a struggle, the right of self-defence may
be invoked by the original assailant as well as by a man
who was at the outset his victim."

In the light of these dicta, we are satisfied that the
E trial judge did misdirect the jury when he stated that
an accused person could not successfully plead that he
acted in self defence if he started the fight and was the
first to use violence. It is true that the trial judge went
on to state that there was an exception to that rule, but
the exception which he gave was of a person starting
a fight with mild violence, and the victim then producing a weapon in response to such mild violence; in
such circumstances if the original assailant himself
took hold of a weapon and struck the person attacking
F him with a knife, he could plead self defence. That
however was not the situation in the present case, and
the jury here may well have concluded that no issue
of self defence could arise because the appellant had
been the first to use violence.

The advocate depute founded upon the evidence to
the effect that the appellant had been a full member
of a disorderly mob that was led by Logan towards the
public house, and the evidence that he had been one
of the armed mob. In these circumstances since he
admitted the stabbing with the knife, the advocate

depute submitted that he was also guilty of charge 2.
He contended that even if there had been misdirection G
on the part of the trial judge that had not produced
any miscarriage of justice.

In our opinion, however, apart from the misdirection to which we have already referred, the trial judge
misdirected the jury in other respects. In our opinion,
it was an over simplification for the trial judge to
direct the jury: "If you go into the fight armed with
a lethal weapon prepared to use it then you cannot
successfully plead self defence if you do use it in the
course of the fight."   H

No doubt in giving that direction to the jury, the
trial judge was contemplating a situation where something in the nature of a duel takes place between two
persons or two gangs. His direction, however, may
well have caused the jury to conclude that even if the
appellant had been standing by as a spectator, as soon
as he went forward into the fight with the knife in his
hand, it was not open to him to plead self defence. We
are also of opinion that it was a misdirection to   I
instruct the jury that the critical issue was whether the
appellant was a spectator or was a participant.
Whether or not self defence can be pleaded must
depend upon the circumstances. As in *HM Advocate
v Robertson and Donoghue,* the fact that the appellant
was convicted of breach of the peace may well have
been important, but even though the jury had concluded that the appellant had participated in the
breach of the peace, that did not necessarily mean that
he could not plead self defence. It would have been   J
open to the jury to accept part of the appellant's evidence and to reject other parts of it. Thus, for example,
the jury might have rejected his evidence that he had
"tagged along as a spectator" from Teucherhill, and
have accepted other evidence which suggested that he
had been part of the Teucherhill mob who made their
way to the public house. On the other hand the jury
might still have accepted his evidence that on arrival
at the public house he had not joined the line of
persons confronting the line of persons who had   K
emerged from the public house and that at that stage
he was purely a spectator. They might then have
accepted his evidence that after receiving the knife
from George Frearson he had continued to stand and
watch until he noticed Logan on the ground. The jury
might then have accepted his evidence that he ran over
to pick up Logan but that before he reached him he
heard Bennett and his companion saying that they
were going to kill him (the appellant). The jury might
also have accepted that at that stage seeing that   L
Bennett was armed the appellant, as he stated,
panicked and stabbed Bennett. If so the jury would
have been entitled to hold that the appellant was
acting in self defence. Reading the charge as a
whole, we are left with the clear impression that the
jury may well have concluded that it was not open to
them to consider self defence in this case if they
accepted that the appellant had been part of the mob
moving from Teucherhill towards the public house,
and if they accepted that he had stepped forward
armed with a knife after he saw Logan lying on the

A ground apparently being attacked. We are satisfied that it was a misdirection for the trial judge to tell the jury that the appellant could not plead self defence if he was a willing participant in the sense that he joined in the fight willingly. Even if he was a participant in the sense that he stepped forward into the fight, it would all depend upon the circumstances whether self defence could be pleaded. If the jury accepted that part of his evidence in which he described how he came to step forward to go to the assistance of Logan, and how he heard the threat against himself, then in

B our opinion it would be open to the jury to accept that he was acting in self defence. If the jury believed that part of the appellant's evidence, they could hold that he was acting in self defence even though they also held that he had been, as the trial judge put it, a participant in the gang fight which was going on between the two teams. Of course, as the trial judge directed the jury, they would also require to consider whether the appellant had a means of escape and whether he used cruel excess.

C However, in view of the foregoing misdirections, we are of opinion that the jury may well have concluded that it was not open to them to consider self defence at all, whereas if they accepted the appellant's evidence as to the circumstances in which he came to stab the deceased, the issue of self defence could arise. We are accordingly satisfied that these misdirections clearly amounted to a miscarriage of justice in this case. The verdict of the jury must therefore be set aside. Although the misdirection related to charge 2

D on the indictment only, it was accepted that charges 1 and 2 were intimately connected and it is clear that charges 3, 4 and 5 were consequential charges. It therefore appears to us to be appropriate to set aside the whole verdict of the jury.

Since the miscarriage of justice arose from misdirection on the part of the trial judge, and in view of the serious nature of charge 2, we are satisfied that it is in the public interest that the Crown should be granted

E authority to bring a new prosecution in terms of ss 254 and 255 of the Criminal Procedure (Scotland) Act 1975. We are mindful too that some of the difficulty in the case appears to have arisen from the fact that counsel for the appellant conceded that he was guilty of breach of the peace, and the appellant must therefore accept some responsibility for what has occurred. The fact that there is to be a new prosecution emphasises the desirability of setting aside the jury's verdict on all charges, so that the jury at the new

F prosecution can hear all the evidence which is relevant and material to the issues which were the subject of the first indictment.

Counsel for the appellant suggested that if authority was to be granted for a new prosecution, the court as regards charge 2 should only authorise a fresh prosecution on a charge of culpable homicide, that being the offence of which he was convicted by the jury. Counsel referred to *Mackenzie v HM Advocate*. That was a case where an accused was charged with murder, and was found guilty of culpable homicide. The

verdict was set aside on the grounds of a misdirection on the part of the trial judge and authority was granted G to bring a new prosecution. As the report shows [1982 SCCR at p 508], the accused was retried on an indictment containing only a charge of culpable homicide. The advocate depute, on the other hand, contended that it was not for the court to consider what charge might be brought in the new prosecution; it was for the Crown to decide what charge should be brought.

We agree with the advocate depute. Section 254 (1) (c) enables the court to dispose of an appeal by setting aside the verdict of the trial court and granting H authority to bring a new prosecution in accordance with s 255 of the Act of 1975. Section 255 (1) makes it plain that where such authority has been granted, a new prosecution may be brought charging the accused with the same or any similar offence arising out of the same facts. In our opinion, however, it is for the Crown and not the court to determine what charges should be levelled against the accused in the new prosecution. What the court does is to grant authority for the bringing of a new prosecution leaving it to the I Crown to decide whether to exercise that right, and if so what charges to bring. In *Mackenzie v HM Advocate* it was the Crown which decided that the new indictment should contain only a charge of culpable homicide.

In all the circumstances we shall set aside the verdict of the jury and grant authority to the Crown to bring a new prosecution in terms of s 255 of the Act of 1975.

————————— J

Counsel for Appellant, McBride; Solicitors, Macbeth Currie & Co, WS (for Beltrami & Co, Glasgow) — Counsel for Respondent, Macdonald, QC, AD; Solicitor, J D Lowe, Crown Agent.

P W F

K

(NOTE)

Wilson v Grampian Regional Council

OUTER HOUSE
LORD MARNOCH
18 SEPTEMBER 1992

Administrative law — Judicial review — Title and L interest to sue — Extent of title and interest of community charge payer to object to actings of local authority.

Process — Title to sue — Local government — Extent of title and interest of community charge payer to object to actings of local authority.

Community charge payers sought to interdict a local authority from acquiring property by statutory conveyance, arguing that their interest as such entitled them to object to the local authority's purchase.

Doubted, whether an interest as a community charge payer gave title and interest to make such an application.

Ronald Wilson and others sought judicial review of a decision by Grampian Regional Council to purchase a house to provide accommodation for adults with learning difficulties. The petitioners sought interim interdict against the council purchasing the house by agreement by way of a statutory conveyance under s 70 (3) of the Local Government (Scotland) Act 1973. Such a conveyance would result in the superior and any co-feuar with a jus quaesitum tertio losing their right to enforce restrictions in the titles. The use of the house proposed by the council was in breach of the deed of feuing conditions to which the house was subject. The motion for interim interdict came before the Lord Ordinary (Marnoch). His Lordship refused the petitioners' motion, holding that there was no prima facie case that a jus quaesitum tertio had been created and that, as community charge payers, the petitioners had no interest to pursue the application so far as it was based on amenity concerns. In relation to that point, his Lordship said:

"Lastly, so far as the merits are concerned, it was argued on behalf of the petitioners that, even if they could not succeed as holders of a jus quaesitum, as community charge payers they could still complain of what was submitted to be a wholly unreasonable exercise of discretion on the part of the respondents in deciding to purchase the property in question. In this connection, it was submitted that the property was too expensive, that there were alternative sites available and that the respondents should have had regard to the petitioners' concerns regarding amenity. I confess I had some difficulty in following parts of this argument and, in particular, I take leave to doubt whether the petitioners' 'amenity concerns' could ever be relevant to a complaint by them in their capacity as payers of the community charge. I also have some doubt whether in that capacity the petitioners could in any circumstances instruct a title to sue; cf *Simpson v Edinburgh Corporation*, 1961 SLT 17; 1960 SC 313, particularly at 1961 SLT, p 19. In any event, however, I am clearly of opinion that nothing contained in the petition or affidavits or said at the bar justifies the inference that in the present case there was any such wholly unreasonable exercise of discretion on the part of the respondents as would entitle this court to interfere by way of judicial review."

Counsel for Petitioners, Menzies, QC; Solicitors, Simpson & Marwick, WS — Counsel for Defenders, Philip, QC; Solicitors, Shepherd & Wedderburn, WS.

C H

Mahmood v Mahmood

OUTER HOUSE
LORD SUTHERLAND
4 NOVEMBER 1992

Husband and wife — Marriage — Nullity — Force and fear — Woman entering into arranged marriage allegedly under duress — Woman's parents threatening to disown her and to withdraw financial support — Whether this constituting sufficient duress to vitiate woman's consent to marriage.

A woman raised an action of declarator of nullity of marriage. She averred that her marriage had been arranged between her parents and the defender's parents in 1983, without her prior knowledge or consent, and that five years later when the pursuer was aged 21, her parents had informed her that she was to marry the defender as previously arranged. The pursuer averred that she had protested against this arranged marriage but that her parents had threatened to disown her, to stop supporting her financially and to send her to live in Pakistan. She also averred that she had been told that if she refused to marry the defender she would bring disgrace to herself, to her family and to the Pakistani community in Edinburgh. In support of the seriousness of these allegations on her ability to consent the pursuer averred that her parents had already disowned her elder sister and brother for refusing to enter into arranged marriages and that she was totally reliant upon her parents for financial support. The pursuer had entered into the marriage and lived with the defender for three months before the parties separated.

At a procedure roll hearing the defender argued that, while lack of true consent as a result of duress could be a ground for nullifying a marriage, the evidence in support of such a claim had to be of a serious nature and that the averments in the present case did not constitute threats of such gravity as would sway the mind of an ordinary person.

Held, (1) that duress to a sufficient degree could vitiate consent and therefore form a ground for nullifying a marriage but that in every case it would be a question of degree as to whether or not the threats offered were such as to overcome the will of the particular pursuer (p 592A-B); (2) that in this case the averments of specific threats made to the pursuer were such as could be argued to go beyond the limits of proper parental influence, and that, in particular, the threat to cut off all financial support and to send her back to Pakistan could be regarded as matters which could overwhelm the will of a woman of her age and cultural background (p 592C-D); and (3) that it would also be necessary to explore the circumstances leading up to the threats being made and what had happened after the marriage ceremony in order to determine whether or not the pursuer's consent had been genuine (p 592D); and proof before answer *allowed.*

Observed, that the consent which had to be given

A to a marriage need not be enthusiastic consent; reluctant consent would suffice provided that the consent was genuine (p 592B-C).

Action for declarator of nullity of marriage

Shamshad Bibi or Mahmood raised an action for declarator of nullity of marriage against Zahid Mahmood, on the ground that she had not fully consented to their marriage, having entered it under duress. The pursuer's version of events was denied by

B the defender who also pled that the action was irrelevant.

The case came on procedure roll before the Lord Ordinary (Sutherland).

Cases referred to

Buckland v Buckland [1968] P 296; [1967] 2 WLR 1506; [1967] 2 All ER 300.
H v H [1954] P 258; [1953] 3 WLR 849; [1953] 2 All

C ER 1229.
Hirani v Hirani [1983] 4 FLR 232.
Pao On v Lau Yiu Long [1980] AC 614; [1979] 3 WLR 435; [1979] 3 All ER 65.
Singh v Singh [1971] P 226; [1971] 2 WLR 963; [1971] 2 All ER 828.
Szechter v Szechter [1971] P 286; [1971] 2 WLR 170; [1970] 3 All ER 905.

Textbook referred to

D Fraser, *Husband and Wife*, Vol I, p 226.

On 4 November 1992 the Lord Ordinary *allowed* a proof before answer.

LORD SUTHERLAND.—In this action the pursuer seeks to have a pretended marriage between the pursuer and the defender on 11 April 1988 declared null on the ground that the pursuer did not fully consent to the pretended marriage having

E entered into it under duress. The pursuer avers that the marriage was arranged between her parents and the defender's parents in about 1983 without the prior knowledge or consent of the pursuer. At that time the pursuer had never met the defender. In about March 1988 the pursuer's parents informed her that she was to marry the defender as previously arranged. The pursuer by this time had a boyfriend in this country of whom the pursuer's parents disapproved and she protested about the arranged marriage. It is averred

F that her parents threatened to disown her and to stop supporting her financially and threatened to send her off to live in Pakistan. They informed her that if she refused to marry the defender she would bring disgrace to herself, her family and to the Pakistani community in Edinburgh. By this time the pursuer's elder sister and her elder brother had both refused to enter into arranged marriages and had been disowned by the parents and accordingly the pursuer took the parents' threat seriously. The pursuer, who was about 21 at the time, was working in her parents' shop and was totally reliant upon her parents for financial support. The

pursuer avers that because of the gravity of these threats she entered into the marriage under duress G despite telling the defender that she did not wish to marry him. Finally she avers that they lived together between 30 April and 1 July 1988 during which time they spoke very little to each other and had sexual intercourse twice. In July 1988 they separated. The version of events narrated by the pursuer is not accepted by the defender but for the purposes of relevancy I must take the pursuer's averments pro veritate.

At procedure roll counsel for the defender sought H dismissal of the action on the ground that no sufficient averments were made which would warrant a decree of declarator of nullity on the ground of duress. There appears to be no Scottish case within the last two centuries of a decree being pronounced on this ground. The basis of the law of Scotland is to be found in Fraser on *Husband and Wife*, Vol I, p 226 where the author deals with the effect of force and fear on the consent given to marriage: "If either party is compelled by force to marry, or by some rational fear is I terrified into compliance, the law holds that there has not been given that free consent necessary to shew an agreeing mind." The examples he gives appear to be cases where physical violence of a fairly extreme nature has been used. He goes on to say that the degree of violence which is necessary to entitle a party to found upon it as a ground of nullity is a matter which cannot be brought within the precision of a rule but must vary according to circumstances such as the time, the place, the condition of the party wronged, J the sex and the age. He then deals with threats in the following terms: "Violence of a slighter kind would, unquestionably, be held sufficient in the case of a young person of delicate health, than would be required in regard to one of more mature years. Threats must not, however, resolve themselves merely into 'frownings'. It is necessary that they be threats of personal violence, or death to oneself or relations or friends, or that they be threats of loss of property, or of acts which would produce infamy, or ruin and dis- K grace." Finally he said that there is a peculiarity with reference to the case where violence is said to have been used by a parent. The reverential fear which children have towards their parents may be increased by violence used and in such a case if menaces or force more than arises ex reverentiali metu be employed, the consent is held to be extorted. It is necessary that the evidence for the violence be clear and strong and that the facts proved be weighty and atrocious or the construction of violence would not be put upon the L exercise of that influence which it is the duty of a parent to employ in order to sway his child's inclinations to a course which his wisdom approves.

Counsel argued that it was clear from Fraser's treatment of the matter that while duress could be a ground for nullifying a marriage, the evidence in support of such a claim had to be of a serious nature and that the averments in the present case did not constitute threats of such gravity as would sway the mind of an ordinary person. Counsel then turned to consider the

A English authorities on the matter which she maintained showed the same principles as those quoted from Fraser. In *Buckland v Buckland* the facts were that a 21 year old serviceman had an innocent relationship with a 15 year old girl when based in Malta. He was charged with corruption of the girl and was advised that despite the fact that he had not corrupted her he was likely to be convicted and sentenced to two years' imprisonment. The only choice open to him therefore was either to go to prison for no justified reason or to marry the girl. In the circumstances he

B married her and then left Malta eight days later without her. It was held that a fear reasonably entertained arising from external circumstances for which the plaintiff was in no way responsible would be sufficient to constitute duress. The circumstances of the case made it clear that if in fact he had defiled the girl and therefore a prosecution would have been justified, this would have been a matter which he would have brought about by his own fault and then the choice which he made would not be one made under duress.

C This case would therefore be authority for the proposition that a person faced with two unpalatable choices cannot be said to be acting under duress if he chooses one of them unless it can be said that the fact that he had to make such a choice was brought about by circumstances entirely beyond his control. *H v H* was referred to but that was a case of a pure sham marriage and is therefore of little assistance in the present case.

In *Szechter v Szechter* the purpose of the marriage was to release the wife from prison. The case,

D however, is of importance because of a dictum of Sir Jocelyn Simon P in the following terms: "It is . . . insufficient to invalidate an otherwise good marriage that a party has entered into it in order to escape from a disagreeable situation, such as penury or social degradation . . . it must be proved that the will of one of the parties thereto had been overborne by genuine and reasonably held fear caused by threat of immediate danger (for which the party is not himself responsible), to life, limb or liberty, so that the constraint

E destroys the reality of consent to ordinary wedlock."

Counsel founded strongly on this passage as showing that the President of the Probate, Admiralty and Divorce Division, as he then was was, taking the same view as that taken by Fraser. In *Singh v Singh* the Court of Appeal followed and accepted the dictum of Sir Jocelyn Simon. In *Hirani v Hirani* the Court of Appeal appears to have taken a different view. In that case the petitioner who was aged 19 had formed an association with another man which her parents

F regarded with abhorrence. To prevent the association continuing the parents arranged for her to marry a man whom neither she nor her parents had previously met. The parents put pressure on the girl to go through with the marriage, the threat being that she "wanted to marry somebody who is against our religion and if you don't marry the man we want you to, you will pack up your belongings and go". In these circumstances she agreed to go through the ceremony of marriage but the marriage was not consummated and after six weeks the petitioner left. A judge of the

Family Division had before him an undefended petition by the wife for a decree of nullity on the ground G of duress, but the judge dismissed the petition. The Court of Appeal took the view that the judge at first instance was greatly influenced by Sir Jocelyn Simon's dictum in *Szechter* but Ormrod LJ in dealing with this case said that he did not consider that the President intended the result that threat to life, limb or liberty had to be established. "He was merely contrasting a disagreeable situation with one which constituted a real threat." It is perhaps doubtful if this is a correct gloss to put upon what was said in *Szechter* and it is H particularly unfortunate that in *Hirani* the case of *Singh*, where a previous decision of the Court of Appeal had supported the dictum in *Szechter*, does not appear to have been put before the court. Ormrod LJ went on to deal with the case by saying that the opinion of Lord Scarman in *Pao On v Lau Yiu Long* should be followed when he said: "Duress, whatever form it takes, is a coercion of the will so as to vitiate consent." The crucial question was therefore said by Ormrod LJ to be whether the threats, pressure or I whatever it is, is such as to destroy the reality of consent and overbears the will of the individual. It seemed to him that the case on its facts was a classic case of a young girl wholly dependent on her parents being forced into a marriage with a man she has never seen and whom her parents have never seen in order to prevent her continuing in an association with a Muslim which the parents would regard with abhorrence. "It is as clear a case as one could want of the overbearing of the will of the petitioner and thus J invalidating or vitiating her consent."

Counsel for the defender in the present case accepted that the facts of *Hirani* were getting very much closer to the facts of the present case but sought to distinguish *Hirani* on the grounds that the timescale was very much shorter, the marriage had never been consummated and the man concerned was one whom not only the petitioner had never met but the petitioner's parents had never met. Counsel therefore submitted that the facts of the present case were such that K even if fully proved could not come up to the standard required either by Fraser or by English law as represented by *Szechter* and *Singh*. The action should accordingly be dismissed as irrelevant.

Counsel for the pursuer argued that the averments were sufficient to entitle the pursuer to proof. The pursuer knew from 1983 that the marriage had been arranged but the threats only occurred from March 1988 onwards. As the marriage took place in April 1988 the timescale was in fact similar to that in *Hirani* L and also the nature of the threats was similar to those in *Hirani* and indeed went further than the threats in *Hirani* if the report contains full details of the threats in that case. Counsel accepted that parental influence was perfectly legitimate but the threats made of disowning the pursuer, sending her back to Pakistan and cutting off all financial support went far beyond the limits of legitimate parental influence. The ultimate question must be whether there was such coercion of the pursuer's will as to vitiate consent. What con-

A stitutes duress must in every case be a matter of degree. Until the strength of the threats and the effect which they had upon the pursuer's will have been explored at proof, it is impossible ab ante to say as a matter of relevancy that the pursuer's consent was genuine and truly given. There should therefore be a proof before answer.

In my opinion the pursuer has averred sufficient in this case to justify a proof before answer. There is no doubt in my opinion that both in the law of England and Scotland duress to a sufficient degree can vitiate B consent and therefore form grounds for nullifying a marriage. It will in every case be a question of degree as to whether or not the threats offered were such as to overcome the will of a particular pursuer. I accept entirely that parental influence is perfectly legitimate and proper when the parents consider that what they are advising is in the best interests of their child. I also accept that the consent which has to be given to marriage need not be enthusiastic consent, but even reluctant consent will suffice provided that the C consent is genuine. It would not be enough for a pursuer to aver that she feared the disapproval of her parents or feared the disapproval of the community in which she lived if she withheld consent. What is averred here however is that specific threats were made to her which, if proved, could be argued to go beyond the limits of proper parental influence, and in particular the threat to cut off all financial support and to send her back to Pakistan could be regarded as matters which could overwhelm the will of a girl of D her age and cultural background. Furthermore it will be necessary to explore the circumstances leading up to the threats being made, if they were made, and also it will be necessary to explore what happened after the marriage ceremony in order to see whether or not the pursuer's consent was genuine or otherwise. Because of the specific nature of the threats I do not consider that I can say with safety at this stage that it would be impossible for the pursuer to prove a case of duress. Taking the pursuer's averments pro veritate I consider E that the appropriate course is to send the case for proof before answer.

Counsel for Pursuer, Clancy; Solicitors, Allan McDougall & Co, SSC — Counsel for Defender, Davie; Solicitors, Drummond Miller, WS.

G D M

(NOTE)

C R Smith Glaziers (Dunfermline) Ltd v Anderson

OUTER HOUSE

LORD MORTON OF SHUNA

27 NOVEMBER 1992

Interdict — Breach of interdict — Penalty — Interdict against individual being in particular employment — Interdict recalled a few weeks later but not meantime obtempered — Flagrant and deliberate defiance of court order.

A company obtained interim interdict against a former employee being in the employment of a competitor. The interdict was recalled on the application of the former employee after a month. During that period he had continued in the employment of the competitor.

Held, that an appropriate fine for the defender's flagrant and deliberate refusal to obey the interim interdict was £1,000; and fine *imposed* accordingly.

C R Smith Glaziers (Dunfermline) Ltd raised an action of interdict against a former employee, Clifford Anderson, who had entered the employment of a competitor of the company. An order for interim interdict was pronounced, preventing the defender from making use of confidential information and against his being in the employment of the competitor. About four weeks later the pursuers lodged and served a minute alleging breach of interdict. The defender then sought recall of the interdict only insofar as it related to his remaining in the employment of the competitor. He had remained in the employment of the competitor after the interdict had been served upon him and remained so employed at the time he sought recall of that part of the interdict. In recalling that part of the interdict relating to the defender's employment with the competitor (a decision thereafter reclaimed against by the pursuers), but fining him in respect of his failure to comply with the interim interdict, the Lord Ordinary (Lord Morton of Shuna) said:

"I recalled the interim interdict so far as it prohibited employment with a competitor, as it appeared to me that the prohibition was too wide in scope, and was designed to prevent competition rather than to protect trade secrets. It also appeared to me that the L balance of convenience favoured the defender, in that the pursuers had retained money due to him and the defender would lose his job if interim interdict were not recalled.

"After dealing with the motion for a recall, I was addressed on the minute averring breach of the interim interdict. Counsel for the defender admitted breach and admitted that the defender was aware of other employees of the pursuers who had been to court to seek recall of interim interdicts obtained against

A them. She explained that the defender had himself consulted a solicitor immediately the interim interdict was served on him, but that that solicitor was dilatory and the defender had thereafter changed his solicitor about 10 days prior to the court appearance. He had continued to work for Living Design and I was informed that the motion for recall was only enrolled after service of the minute alleging breach. I considered that the defender's actions were a flagrant and deliberate refusal to obey a court order and imposed a fine of £1,000. I was informed that the defender had B an income of about £3,000 per month and fixed outgoings amounting to about £2,200 per month."

Counsel for Pursuers, Macfadyen, QC, Illius; Solicitors, Macbeth Currie & Co, WS — Counsel for Defender, Dorrian; Solicitors, Drummond Miller, WS.

C H

C

McMahon v Lees

HIGH COURT OF JUSTICIARY

THE LORD JUSTICE GENERAL (HOPE),
LORDS ALLANBRIDGE AND COWIE

3 FEBRUARY 1993

D

Justiciary — Sentence — Competency — Accused pleading guilty to breach of the peace by threatening violence — Sheriff sentencing accused to six months' imprisonment — Whether an offence inferring personal violence — Criminal Procedure (Scotland) Act 1975 (c 21), s 290 (b).

Section 290 (b) of the Criminal Procedure (Scotland) Act 1975 provides that where a person is convicted by the sheriff of a second or subsequent offence inferring personal violence he may, without prejudice to any E wider powers conferred by statute, be sentenced to any period of imprisonment not exceeding six months.

An accused person who had, inter alia, seven previous convictions for assault, pled guilty to a charge of breach of the peace in respect that he had conducted himself in a disorderly manner, shouted and sworn, chanted gang slogans, challenged police officers to fight and threatened them with violence. The sheriff, considering that the offence was one which inferred personal violence, sentenced the F accused to six months' imprisonment. The accused appealed against the sentence.

Held, that since the circumstances which give rise to a breach of the peace could vary so widely from case to case, it was a clear rule that an offence of breach of the peace, if libelled as such, was not one which in its nature inferred personal violence, and accordingly that the sentence was incompetent (p 594I-K); and appeal *allowed* and sentence *quashed.*

Sharp v Tudhope, 1986 SCCR 64, *applied.*

Summary complaint

Anthony James McMahon was charged at the G instance of Robert F Lees, procurator fiscal, Edinburgh, on a summary complaint which libelled inter alia that the accused had committed a breach of the peace in respect that he had conducted himself in a disorderly manner, shouted and sworn, chanted gang slogans, challenged police officers to fight and threatened them with violence. The accused pled guilty. The sheriff sentenced the accused to six months' imprisonment.

The accused appealed by note of appeal against H sentence.

Statutory provisions

The Criminal Procedure (Scotland) Act 1975 provides:

"290. Where a person is convicted by the sheriff of — . . . (b) a second or subsequent offence inferring personal violence, he may, without prejudice to any wider powers conferred by statute, be sentenced to I imprisonment for any period not exceeding six months."

Cases referred to

Adair v Morton, 1972 SLT (Notes) 70.
Sharp v Tudhope, 1986 SCCR 64.

Appeal

The appeal was argued before the High Court on 3 February 1993.

J

Eo die the court *allowed* the appeal, *quashed* the sentence and *substituted* therefor a sentence of three months' imprisonment.

The following opinion of the court was delivered by the Lord Justice General (Hope):

OPINION OF THE COURT.—The appellant is Anthony James McMahon who appeared in the sheriff court at Edinburgh on summary complaint in answer K to charges of breach of the peace and a contravention of s 3 (1) (b) of the Bail etc (Scotland) Act 1980. The charge of breach of the peace alleged that in the Edinburgh sheriff court, and in a police vehicle travelling between there and St Leonards police station, he had conducted himself in a disorderly manner, shouted and sworn, chanted gang slogans, challenged police officers to fight, threatened them with violence and committed a breach of the peace. He had pled guilty to these charges as libelled, and consideration was then L given to sentence.

The sheriff had before her a substantial record of previous convictions. There were eight convictions of breach of the peace, seven of assault, three of offences under the Bail Act and one under the Police (Scotland) Act. All of these had been dealt with at summary level but they indicated a long course of criminal conduct, including crimes of disorder and a number of crimes inferring personal violence. When she came to consider the appropriate length of sentence, the sheriff

A had regard to the circumstances in which the breach of the peace took place. She had particular regard to the fact that it took place in the main foyer area of the sheriff court at Edinburgh before the appellant was detained, and that he had been warned on at least two occasions to desist from his conduct but had persisted in it. In mitigation it was said that he was under the influence of drink and that he had later made things up with one of the police officers who was involved. But the sheriff was not impressed by that plea, and she decided to impose the maximum sentence available to her. She took the view that the maximum sentence

B available was one of six months' imprisonment in terms of s 290 (b) of the Criminal Procedure (Scotland) Act 1975. This was on the view that the breach of the peace as libelled in this case, accompanied by the description of the facts which she was given by the prosecutor, was an offence inferring personal violence. She imposed a sentence of 60 days' imprisonment in respect of the bail offence, to be served consecutively to the sentence of six months' imprisonment.

C An appeal has been taken against these sentences, but counsel for the appellant confined his argument to the sentence of six months' imprisonment in respect of the charge of breach of the peace. He invited us to regard this as an incident which was really of a minor character. He submitted that it was over very quickly indeed, and that the sheriff had placed too much importance on the place where it occurred. The previous convictions did not reveal that the appellant had been sentenced to lengthy periods of imprisonment in the past. His various offences had been dealt with

D either by means of small fines or relatively short periods of imprisonment, and in all the circumstances a sentence of six months' imprisonment was excessive for what had occurred in this case.

The learned Solicitor General then drew our attention to the terms of s 290 (b) of the 1975 Act. He submitted that there was a question as to whether the sentence of six months' imprisonment was a competent sentence, having regard to the nature of the offence to which the appellant had pled guilty. Section 290 (b) enables a sheriff, where a person is convicted

E of a second or subsequence offence inferring personal violence, to sentence him to a period of imprisonment not exceeding six months. That is to be contrasted with the normal rule set out in s 289 (d) that the maximum sentence available to the sheriff in the exercise of his summary powers is one of three months. In *Adair v Morton* the court, without delivering opinions, held that, in respect that personal violence was not involved in the charge of breach of the peace as libelled, the equivalent provision in the Summary Jurisdiction (Scotland) Act 1954 did not apply and

F that a sentence of six months' imprisonment for a breach of the peace, which involved bawling, shouting, cursing and swearing, was therefore incompetent. The Solicitor General submitted that the same view could be taken of the present case, although he recognised that the libel here included words to the effect that the appellant had threatened the police officers with violence, which were not part of the charge as libelled in *Adair v Morton*.

Our attention was then drawn by him to another case which, in our opinion, puts this matter beyond

doubt. This was *Sharp v Tudhope* where the sheriff took the view, following a conviction for assault, that G a sentence of six months' imprisonment was open to him in view of the fact that the appellant in that case had a previous conviction for a contravention of the Prevention of Crime Act 1953, that is having an offensive weapon in his possession, and for reckless discharge of an air pistol. He regarded these as offences inferring personal violence in terms of s 290 (b). In his opinion at p 65, the Lord Justice Clerk, after referring to the terms of the section, said: "In our opinion when a sheriff is considering whether or not section 290 applies, all that he can properly look to is the list of H previous convictions, and that indeed is what the sheriff did on this occasion". Then he went on to describe the contents of the list of previous convictions and said this: "In our opinion, before the sheriff can conclude that a previous conviction does infer personal violence, it must be a necessary inference from the fact of the conviction that personal violence was involved". So far as the previous convictions libelled in that case were concerned that could not be said of them, and accordingly it was held that a sentence of six months' imprisonment was incompetent. I

In the present case there is no doubt that the appellant does have previous convictions for offences inferring personal violence. The previous convictions for assault undoubtedly fall within the ordinary meaning of that expression. So far as the conviction in the present case is concerned, however, it is for an offence which has been libelled as one of breach of the peace. It will take its place, no doubt, in due course in his list of previous convictions as a breach of the peace, and it will not be apparent from the fact of the conviction J that any personal violence was involved in the offence. It can be taken to be a clear rule that an offence of breach of the peace, if libelled as such an offence, is not one which in its nature infers personal violence. This is because the circumstances which give rise to a breach of the peace can vary so widely from case to case. The appellant pled guilty to threatening the police officers with violence, but he was charged with a breach of the peace, not assault. Accordingly the same view can be taken in the present case as in *Sharp* K *v Tudhope*, namely that the sentence of six months' imprisonment which the sheriff imposed in this case was not a sentence which was open to her in the circumstances, and accordingly that she should have restricted herself to the sentence of three months, which was the maximum available in terms of s 289 (d) of the Act.

For these reasons, since the sentence of six months' imprisonment in respect of the charge of breach of the peace was incompetent, we propose to quash that sentence and to substitute a sentence of three months' L imprisonment. We consider the imposition of the maximum sentence to be amply justified in the circumstances. The remaining sentence, not having been challenged in this appeal, will still stand.

Counsel for Appellant, McBride; Solicitors, Sinclairs — Counsel for Respondent, Solicitor General (Dawson, QC); Solicitor, J D Lowe, Crown Agent.

P W F

Jongejan v Jongejan

A FIRST DIVISION

THE LORD PRESIDENT (HOPE),
LORDS COWIE AND MAYFIELD

23 OCTOBER 1992

Administration of justice — Counsel — Effect of counsel's mandate — Joint minute settling action signed by counsel acting within terms of mandate — Competency of party reclaiming against decree in terms of joint minute on basis
B *that the terms had not been agreed.*

Husband and wife — Divorce — Financial provision — Joint minute containing agreement on financial provision — Decree in terms thereof pronounced on pursuer's motion — Competency of reclaiming motion by defender — Competency of defender seeking to set aside agreement as not fair and reasonable at time it was entered into — Family Law (Scotland) Act 1985 (c 37), s 16 (1) (b).

Process — Divorce — Joint minute containing agreement
C *on financial provision — Decree in terms thereof pronounced on pursuer's motion — Competency of reclaiming motion by defender — Competency of defender seeking to set aside agreement as not fair and reasonable at time it was entered into — Family Law (Scotland) Act 1985 (c 37), s 16 (1) (b).*

Process — Reclaiming motion — Competency — Defender reclaiming against interlocutor pronounced on pursuer's motion but in terms of joint minute.

D A wife brought an action of divorce. Her husband defended the action in relation to her claim for financial provision under s 18 of the Family Law (Scotland) Act 1985. The case came before the Lord Ordinary for proof on 30 June 1992. Affidavit evidence establishing the merits was lodged in process. Following negotiations, the Lord Ordinary was advised by counsel for both parties that agreement had been reached on the pursuer's financial claim, although one matter concerning the husband's pension scheme required to be investigated. The Lord Ordinary granted a continua-
E tion to enable a joint minute to be prepared and lodged. The case came before the Lord Ordinary again on 10 July 1992. A joint minute apparently setting out the terms of an agreement between the parties, and craving the court to interpone authority thereto and to grant decree in terms thereof, had been lodged in process. It had been signed by counsel for both parties. On 10 July 1992 another counsel appeared for the defender, counsel who had represented the defender at the proof and who had signed the joint
F minute being unable to appear. Counsel for the defender advised the court that the defender's solicitors were unaware that a joint minute had been lodged; that the joint minute did not deal with some items of matrimonial property; and that there had been insufficient time to achieve a final agreement. He sought a continuation of the case to enable the defender to be consulted about the terms of the joint minute. The Lord Ordinary refused to continue the case and granted decree of divorce and in terms of the joint minute. The defender reclaimed. The pursuer

opposed the reclaiming motion as incompetent. Counsel for the defender accepted that in normal G circumstances a decree following from a joint minute could not be reclaimed against, but on the authority of *Paterson v Magistrates of St Andrews* (1880) 7 R 712, submitted that in exceptional circumstances such a course was competent. She further relied upon the provisions of s 16 (1) (b) of the Family Law (Scotland) Act 1985 whereby agreements as to financial provision on divorce might be set aside or varied if unfair and unreasonable.

Held, (1) that when parties settled an action by joint H minute the settlement was binding and effective and there was no locus poenitentiae until the court had interponed authority to the joint minute; the circumstances of *Paterson v Magistrates of St Andrews* were very special and the case had not been decided on any clear basis of principle (pp 597G-H and 598A-D); (2) that it was well settled that a party could not reclaim against an interlocutor pronounced on his own motion, or of consent (p 597C-E); (3) that an inter- locutor pronounced on the motion of either party in I terms of a joint minute fell to be treated as an inter- locutor pronounced of consent (p 597I-J); (4) that it was not open to a party to say that a joint minute signed by counsel acting within the scope of her unrecalled mandate did not have his agreement (p 598E-F); (5) that while an agreement recorded in a joint minute fell within s 16 (1) (b), it was too late for the defender to invoke s 16 (1) (b) for the first time after decree had been pronounced since a reclaiming motion for review of the Lord Ordinary's interlocutor J had been precluded by the actings of the parties (p 599C-E); and (6) that the Lord Ordinary had not erred in refusing a continuation where the only reason advanced was to enable the defender to reconsider the terms of the joint minute (p 599F-G); and reclaiming motion *refused* as incompetent.

Dicta in *Batchelor v Pattison & Mackersy* (1876) 3 R 914, *followed*; *Young v Young (No 1)*, 1991 SLT 853, *distinguished.*   K

Action of divorce

Agnes Graham or Jongejan brought an action of divorce against her husband, Pieter Jongejan. She also sought an order for financial provision. The defender defended the action on the question of financial provision.

The case came before the Lord Ordinary for proof L on 30 June 1992.

Statutory provisions

The Family Law (Scotland) Act 1985 provides:

"16.—(1) Where the parties to a marriage have entered into an agreement as to financial provision to be made on divorce, the court may make an order setting aside or varying— . . . (b) the agreement or any term of it where the agreement was not fair and reasonable at the time it was entered into."

Cases referred to

A   *Barton v Caledon Shipbuilding and Engineering Co Ltd*, 1947 SLT (Notes) 12.

Batchelor v Pattison & Mackersy (1876) 3 R 914.

Dalzell v Dalzell, 1985 SLT 286.

Duncan v Salmond (1874) 1 R 329.

Gow v Henry (1899) 2 F 48; (sub nom *Henry v Gow*) (1899) 7 SLT 203.

Hamilton & Baird v Lewis (1893) 1 SLT 319; (1893) 21 R 120.

Lothian v Lothian, 1965 SLT 368.

B   *McAthey v Patriotic Investment Society Ltd*, 1910 1 SLT 121; 1910 SC 584.

Paterson v Kidd's Trustees (1896) 4 SLT 145; (1896) 23 R 737.

Paterson v Magistrates of St Andrews (1880) 7 R 712.

Watson v Russell (1894) 21 R 433.

Young v Young (No 1), 1991 SLT 853.

Young v Young (No 2), 1991 SLT 869.

Textbook referred to

Maclaren, *Court of Session Practice*, p 247.

C

Eo die, affidavit evidence on the merits having been lodged, and agreement having apparently been reached between the parties on the question of financial provision, the Lord Ordinary *continued* the case for a joint minute to be lodged.

On 10 July 1992 the Lord Ordinary *granted* decree of divorce and in terms of a joint minute which had been signed by counsel for both parties and lodged in

D   process.

The defender marked a reclaiming motion which the pursuer opposed as being incompetent.

Reclaiming motion

The case came before the First Division in single bills on 25 September and 23 October 1992.

On 23 October 1992 the court *refused* the reclaiming

E   motion as incompetent.

The following opinion of the court was delivered by the Lord President (Hope):

OPINION OF THE COURT.—This is an action of divorce which was defended only in regard to the pursuer's claim for financial provision under s 18 of the Family Law (Scotland) Act 1985. The case came to proof before the Lord Ordinary on 30 June 1992, when the Lord Ordinary indicated that he was satis-

F   fied on the merits in light of the affidavit evidence which had been lodged in process. He continued the case to a later date to enable a joint minute to be lodged. It came before him again on 10 July 1992 when he granted decree of divorce and made an order against the defender requiring him to transfer to the pursuer his one half pro indiviso share in a house in Middlesex which was in joint names together with his interest in the furnishings and plenishings therein within six weeks of that date. This order was made in respect and in terms of a joint minute which had been signed by counsel for both parties and lodged in

process. It was stated in the joint minute that the parties were agreed that the defender was to transfer G his interest in these subjects within the period of six weeks from the date of decree to follow thereon. It contained a number of other provisions including an agreement that the defender was to be found liable to the pursuer in the expenses of the action. The joint minute concluded by craving the court to interpone authority thereto and in the event of decree of divorce being pronounced to grant decree in terms of the paragraphs dealing with the property in Middlesex and with expenses. H

The defender has now enrolled for review of the Lord Ordinary's interlocutor dated 10 July 1992. His motion has been marked on the pursuer's behalf as incompetent. When the case came before us in the single bills on 25 September 1992 counsel for the pursuer submitted that it was incompetent for the defender to reclaim against that part of the interlocutor which had been pronounced in terms of the joint minute. Having heard argument on this point we decided to continue the matter to enable grounds of I appeal to be lodged. This was to focus more clearly the respects in which the defender sought to bring the Lord Ordinary's interlocutor under review. The defender's grounds of appeal have now been lodged and, in respect of his motion for the cause to be appointed to the summar roll for hearing, we have now heard further argument in the single bills on the issue of competency.

We were informed that, when the case called for proof before the Lord Ordinary on 30 June 1992, the J hearing was adjourned for a time to enable a settlement of the financial provision to be discussed. At about 3.40 pm that day the Lord Ordinary was advised by counsel that agreement had been reached. There was, however, one outstanding matter, relating to the pursuer's rights under the defender's pension scheme with the Royal Netherlands Navy, which required to be investigated. It was unclear whether the pursuer had to take some action to preserve her right to a widow's pension in the event of the defender's death K in light of the divorce. For this reason the parties were not able to announce the terms of the settlement and move for decree in terms thereof on that date. A continuation was granted to enable a joint minute to be prepared and thereafter lodged in process at a later date. At some stage during the period of the continuation a draft joint minute was prepared setting out the terms of an agreement between the parties in 11 numbered paragraphs. Paragraph 1 dealt with the transfer of the defender's interest in the property in L Middlesex and para 11 dealt with expenses. As we have already mentioned, the draft joint minute concluded in the normal terms by craving the court to interpone authority to it and to grant decree in terms of these paragraphs. The draft was then extended and signed by counsel for both parties, who also initialled a handwritten amendment to para 1 to the effect that the transfer was to be made within six weeks of the date of decree. Arrangements were made by the pursuer's agents for the joint minute to be lodged in process.

A When the case was put out by order on 10 July 1992, counsel who had represented the defender at the proof, and had signed and initialled the joint minute on his behalf, was unable to appear. The papers were passed to another counsel, who informed the court that those instructing him had apparently been taken by surprise by the lodging of the joint minute. Their written instructions were for a further continuation to be sought on the ground that there had been insufficient time to achieve a final agreement, and it had not been appreciated that the joint minute had already B been drafted and lodged. Counsel said that some items of matrimonial property had not been dealt with in the joint minute which was then in process, and he sought a continuation for the defender to be consulted about its terms. The Lord Ordinary refused to grant a continuation, and he pronounced the decree in terms of the joint minute against which the defender now seeks to reclaim.

The submission of counsel for the respondent that the reclaiming motion was incompetent was based on C principles which are well established and were not seriously in dispute. There is no doubt that it is incompetent for a party to reclaim against an interlocutor which has been pronounced on his own motion. In *Watson v Russell* it was held to be incompetent for a party to reclaim against an interlocutor pronounced of consent with a view to submitting a prior interlocutor to review. The reclaimer founded on s 52 of the Court of Session Act 1868, the provisions of which are now to be found in rule 262 (c) D of the Rules of Court. Lord President Robertson noted that no other argument was advanced in support of the proposition than that a party is entitled to reclaim against an interlocutor pronounced on his own motion, and added that "good sense forbids the idea". Decisions to the same effect, in regard to interlocutors pronounced of consent, are to be found in *Paterson v Kidd's Trs* and *Barton v Caledon Shipbuilding and Engineering Co Ltd*. The principle is that a party cannot seek the recall of an interlocutor which has E been granted on his own motion or with his consent, because his own actings exclude the appeal.

The interlocutor in this case was not pronounced on the defender's motion nor was it granted with his consent. It was the pursuer's motion that decree in terms of the joint minute should be pronounced, and this was opposed by the defender's counsel on the ground that a further continuation was required. But, as Lord Fraser held in *Lothian v Lothian*, a party to a joint minute is bound by the terms of the joint F minute and is not entitled to invite the court to disregard it. He explained the basis for this view in a passage at 1965 SLT, p 369 in these terms: "The general rule is, in my opinion, that when parties have settled an action by a joint minute the settlement is binding and effective although the court has not interponed authority thereto, and there is no locus poenitentiae until authority is interponed. I was not referred to any authority to that effect but in my opinion such authority is to be found in the case of *McAthey v The Patriotic Investment Society Ltd*, 1910

1 SLT 121; 1910 SC 584, which is consistent with the earlier cases of *Hamilton and Baird v Lewis* (1893) 1 G SLT 319; (1893) 21 R 120, and *Gow v Henry* (1899) 7 SLT 203; (1899) 2 F 48. All these cases were concerned with joint minutes or receipts settling a whole action, but the same principle appears to me to apply to the present joint minute which settles the only disputed question in the action."

In our opinion his conclusion on this point was amply supported by the authorities to which he referred, and in particular by the following passage in the opinion of Lord President Robertson in *McAthey* H at 1910 SC, p 586: "I think if parties by themselves or their procurators choose to make a settlement of the case, and that is authenticated in the ordinary way by joint minute, it is out of the question to hold that there is locus poenitentiae for the parties so bound until the authority of the court is interponed. The settlement is a good settlement although the court has not interponed authority thereto."

In *Dalzell v Dalzell* Lord Ross, sitting in the Outer I House, agreed with what Lord Fraser said in *Lothian*. This rule is in accordance with the ordinary principles of contract by which a party is not permitted to withdraw from a binding agreement once it has been entered into.

The pursuer's argument is that, once a joint minute has been entered into craving the court to grant decree in the agreed terms, an interlocutor in terms of that joint minute pronounced at the instance of either party is in the same position as an interlocutor which J has been pronounced of consent. Accordingly it is not competent for it to be reclaimed against by either party. This proposition seems to us to be a logical consequence of the principles which we have just mentioned, and counsel for the reclaimer did not seek to dispute it as a general rule. She accepted that a party could not normally withdraw from a joint minute which recorded the terms of a settlement and sought decree in terms thereof from the court. She also accepted that in normal circumstances a decree in K these terms could not be reclaimed against. Her argument was that there were unusual circumstances in this case which ought to be taken into account. Questions had been raised as to whether the joint minute truly represented what had been agreed. She laid particular stress on the fact that decree in terms of the joint minute was granted despite opposition on these grounds from the defender's counsel, and that it was not, and did not bear to be, pronounced of consent.

We were referred to *Paterson v Magistrates of St* L *Andrews* in which a joint minute was entered into with the pursuers by the town council, while the case was in the Inner House on a reclaiming motion, withdrawing their defence to the action. But before decree had been granted interponing authority to that joint minute a new minute was tendered by them seeking leave to withdraw the former joint minute and insist in their defence. They were allowed to do so, although the pursuers had argued that the joint minute constituted a concluded agreement from which the town council could not resile and that the fact of counsel signing the minute bound the party for whom he acted as thoroughly as if the party had signed it himself. The basis of this decision is not easy to discover from the opinions. It seems to have been accepted that the minute of withdrawal was not binding or effective until the court had interponed authority to it, and questions were also raised as to whether the resolution of the town council that their defences should be withdrawn had been fairly and regularly taken with proper notice of what was to be discussed. The circumstances of the case were described as very special by Maclaren, *Court of Session Practice*, p 247, and by Lord Fraser in *Lothian* at p 369. Certainly it does not seem to have been decided on any very clear basis of principle. Nevertheless counsel for the reclaimer sought, under reference to that case, to persuade us that the position in the present case also was unusual, under reference to what is stated in the first ground of appeal. We were informed that the defender's solicitors had expected to receive a draft joint minute from counsel so that they could take their client's instructions on it before it was signed by her. This had not been done, and the joint minute did not embody any agreement which they understood to have been reached. Counsel had explained to the Lord Ordinary on 10 July 1992, when asking for a continuation, that the joint minute had been seen only that day by his instructing solicitors and that they were not content with its terms. But we are not persuaded that the defender can be relieved on these grounds from the consequences of the general rule. Where, as in this case, a joint minute has been signed by counsel the rule is that it is as binding on the party on whose behalf it has been entered into as if the party himself had signed it. In *Duncan v Salmond* (1874) 1 R at p 334, Lord President Inglis said: "whatever is done by a counsel within his proper province in this court must be held to have been done by the client himself". He returned to this point in *Batchelor v Pattison & Mackersy* (1876) 3 R at p 918, where, in the familiar passage, he said that the legal right of counsel is to conduct the case without any regard to the wishes of his client, so long as his mandate is unrecalled, and that what he does bona fide according to his own judgment will bind his client. No doubt this legal right places a heavy responsibility upon counsel, but it is clear that it is not open to a party to say that a joint minute which has been signed by his counsel does not have his agreement. There is no suggestion in this case that the mandate to the defender's counsel to act on his behalf had been withdrawn at the time when the joint minute was signed by her or that she did not act within her mandate at the time when she signed it. In this situation the rule must be applied, and it is no answer to the point on competency to say that the defender now wishes to challenge the terms of the joint minute on the ground that an agreement had not yet been entered into or that it did not reflect what had been agreed.

Counsel for the reclaimer presented an alternative argument, which is that summarised in the second ground of appeal. This was with reference to s 16 (1)

(b) of the Family Law (Scotland) Act 1985 which provides that, where the parties to a marriage have entered into an agreement as to financial provision on divorce, the court may make an order setting aside or varying the agreement or any term of it where the agreement was not fair and reasonable at the time it was entered into. Subsection (2) provides that the court may make an order under subs (1) (b) on granting decree of divorce or within such time thereafter as the court may specify on granting decree of divorce. Subsection (4) provides that any term of an agreement purporting to exclude the right to apply for an order under subs (1) (b) shall be void. It is common ground that the Lord Ordinary's attention was not drawn to this section when counsel moved for a further continuation on 10 July 1992. It was not suggested to him at that time that there was any possibility of an application being made under s 16 (1) (b), no doubt because the point which was being taken at that stage was that the joint minute did not set out what had been agreed. Nevertheless counsel for the reclaimer submitted that this was an argument which could have been taken at any time up to the granting of decree of divorce, notwithstanding the fact that the agreement had been embodied in a joint minute. She recognised that a minute of amendment would be necessary to enable the defender to argue that the agreement contained in the joint minute should be set aside. But she submitted that it was a sufficient answer to the point on competency that this was an argument which was available to the defender which he proposed to take if his reclaiming motion were to be held to be competent.

She referred, in support of this argument, to *Young v Young (No 2)* where the defender, having been granted leave to reclaim against a decree of divorce, was allowed to lodge a minute of amendment to challenge an agreement about the financial provision to be made to the pursuer on the ground that it was not fair and reasonable and to have it set aside under s 16 (1) (b) of the Act. But the circumstances of that case were different, and it does not provide authority for what the defender in the present case seeks to do. What happened in the Outer House, in *Young v Young (No 1)*, was that the wife lodged defences to the husband's action concluding for a periodical allowance with a capital sum. The husband lodged a tender in settlement of this claim, which the wife then accepted by lodging a minute of acceptance of tender. Some months later her minute of acceptance was withdrawn and, she having failed to intimate her intention to defend the action, it proceeded as undefended. The Lord Ordinary declined to make an order in respect of financial provision on the ground that the wife's defences which contained the conclusions for the financial provision were no longer before the court and that there was no joint minute to this effect. The purpose of the reclaiming motion which then followed at the defender's instance was to set aside the agreement which had been constituted by the lodging of the minute of acceptance of tender and which would remain binding on her unless it was set aside.

There is common ground between *Young* and the present case in that here also there is an agreement which the defender wishes to have set aside under s 16 (1) (b). But there is this important difference, that the agreement in this case was recorded in a joint minute which craved the court to grant decree in terms thereof, and it was in respect and in terms of that joint minute that the Lord Ordinary pronounced the interlocutor against which the defender seeks to reclaim. It was accepted in the Inner House in *Young* that it was competent for an agreement constituted by a minute of acceptance of tender to be set aside under s 16 (1) (b). That subsection refers simply to "an agreement", and thus to any agreement, between the parties as to financial provision. It does not matter when or how the agreement was entered into so long as it is in existence when the court is asked to set it aside. An agreement recorded in a joint minute is in the same position as one which has been arrived at by the lodging of a minute of acceptance. The purpose of the subsection is to override the common law principle which applies to both forms of agreement that an agreement is binding once it has been entered into. The opportunity is there under the statute for the agreement, or any term of it, as to financial provision to be set aside on the ground that it was not fair and reasonable at the time when it was entered into. Thus an agreement as to financial provision contained in a joint minute, or any term of that agreement, may be set aside if the statutory basis for doing this can be made out.

But, there remains the question whether this can be done once the joint minute has been acted upon by the court by granting decree in respect and in terms of it, as has been done in this case. For it is one thing to invoke s 16 (1) (b) at the stage when the court has yet to be, or is being, asked to interpone authority to the joint minute. In that situation, since the provisions of subs (4) can also be invoked, the right to apply for an order under s 16 (1) (b) cannot be said to have been excluded by the terms of the joint minute. But it is quite another to invoke the subsection for the first time after decree has been pronounced. At this stage the actings of the parties preclude a reclaiming motion for review of the Lord Ordinary's interlocutor on this ground. The effect of the joint minute in the present case was that the Lord Ordinary was entitled to pronounce decree in terms of it on the motion of either party, since it was not suggested to him that an order under s 16 (1) (b) was being sought. The interlocutor is in no different position, as regards review by means of a reclaiming motion, from an interlocutor pronounced of consent.

The remaining ground of appeal is that the Lord Ordinary erred in refusing to allow a continuation to allow the defender's solicitor to seek his instructions on the terms of the joint minute. On one view of the matter a reclaiming motion on this ground might perhaps be said to be competent. But counsel for the reclaimer did not make any separate point in regard to it from those which we have already discussed. According to her argument the only reason which was advanced to the Lord Ordinary for a continuation was to enable the defender to reconsider the terms of the joint minute. But he was already bound to its terms by the signature of his counsel, and a continuation to seek his instructions — when it was admittedly not being suggested to the Lord Ordinary that s 16 (1) (b) was to be invoked — would have served no purpose since the matter had already been agreed.

In our opinion no good reasons have been advanced to excuse this case from the application of the ordinary rules, and we shall refuse this reclaiming motion as incompetent.

Counsel for Pursuer and Respondent, Macnair; Solicitors, Brodies, WS — Counsel for Defender and Reclaimer, Stacey; Solicitors, Shepherd & Wedderburn, WS.

A N

Whitelaw v Dickinson

HIGH COURT OF JUSTICIARY

THE LORD JUSTICE CLERK (ROSS),
LORDS MORISON AND PROSSER

10 DECEMBER 1992

Justiciary — Procedure — Trial — Tholed assize — Accused served with indictment fixing trial diet outwith 12 month period — Crown, being alerted to difficulty by accused, deserting diet pro loco et tempore at preliminary diet but serving summary complaint for same charges — Whether acquittal on ground of plea in course of trial tholed assize — Whether oppressive to allow summary prosecution to proceed — Criminal Procedure (Scotland) Act 1975 (c 21), s 101 (1).

Three accused persons were charged on petition with two charges of aggravated theft but the indictment was served on them for a trial diet outwith the 12 month period prescribed in s 101 (1) of the Criminal Procedure (Scotland) Act 1975. The accused lodged minutes under s 75 of the 1975 Act seeking a preliminary diet at which the Crown deserted the diet pro loco et tempore. The Crown subsequently served a summary complaint on the accused for the same offences. The accused objected to the proceedings and the sheriff dismissed the complaint on the ground that it was contrary to the public interest for the Crown to prosecute the proceedings since if the accused had not alerted the Crown to the difficulty and had taken the plea in the course of the trial, the accused would have been bound to have been acquitted and would thereby have tholed their assize. The Crown appealed on the ground of error in law.

Held, (1) that since s 101 (1) only ruled out the possibility of trial after the expiry of the 12 month period an accused in such circumstances could not be said to have tholed his assize, and fresh proceedings were competent in general terms regardless of whether there was desertion pro loco et tempore before the trial

A diet or a plea in bar sustained after the commencement of the purported trial (p 602A-B); (2) that the sheriff accordingly erred in law in holding that it would amount to oppression to allow the prosecution to proceed (p 602B-C); and Crown appeal *allowed*.

MacDougall v Russell, 1986 SLT 403, *applied*.

Opinion, that there would have been no oppression even if the accused had only become liable to fresh proceedings through the responsible actings of their solicitors (p 602C-E).

B

_____

Summary complaint

Clifford Dickinson, Richard McMahon and Vincent John Bass were charged at the instance of John Crawford Whitelaw, procurator fiscal, Jedburgh, on a summary complaint containing the following charges:

"(1) on 1 or 2 July 1991, you Clifford Dickinson, Richard McMahon and you Vincent John Bass did break into the premises occupied by John Adams and
C Son in Main Street, Yetholm, District of Roxburgh, and there steal 12,560 cigarettes, a cheque book, a number of cheques, a quantity of tobacco and a safe containing £2,900 of money.

"(2) on 8 July 1991, you Clifford Dickinson and you Richard McMahon did break into the Hirsel Golf Clubhouse, Coldstream, District of Berwickshire, with intent to steal, and there attempt to force open a lockfast gaming machine with intent to steal therefrom."

D
The accused stated a preliminary objection to the proceedings on the ground that to allow the prosecution to proceed would be oppressive. The sheriff (J V Paterson) sustained the plea and dismissed the charges.

The procurator fiscal appealed with leave of the sheriff to the High Court. The facts of the case appear from the opinion of the court.

E Statutory provisions

The Criminal Procedure (Scotland) Act 1975 provides:

"101.—(1) An accused shall not be tried on indictment for any offence unless such trial is commenced within a period of 12 months of the first appearance of that accused on petition in respect of that offence; and, failing such commencement within that period, the accused shall be discharged forthwith and thereafter he shall be for ever free from all question or
F process for that offence: Provided that — (i) nothing in this subsection shall bar the trial of an accused for whose arrest a warrant has been granted for failure to appear at a diet in the case; (ii) on application made for the purpose, the sheriff or, where an indictment has been served on the accused in respect of the High Court, a single judge of that court, may on cause shown extend the said period of 12 months."

Case referred to

MacDougall v Russell, 1986 SLT 403; 1985 SCCR 441.

Appeal

The appeals were heard in the High Court on 18 G November 1992.

On 10 December 1992 the court *allowed* the appeals, *reversed* the sheriff's decision and *directed* him to fix a new trial diet.

The following opinion of the court was delivered by Lord Prosser:

OPINION OF THE COURT.—The three respondents were charged together on a summary complaint. H Preliminary pleas to the competency of the complaint were taken on their behalf. At the hearing on these pleas, before the sheriff of Lothian and Borders at Jedburgh, three grounds of objection were advanced. The sheriff repelled the submissions made in respect of the first two grounds of objection, but he upheld the submission upon the third ground. He dismissed the complaint, granting the appellant leave to appeal. Put shortly, the submission which he upheld was to the effect that the prosecution was barred from pursuing I the proceedings, because to do so would be contrary to the public interest. The appellant appeals against that decision, on the ground that the sheriff erred in law.

On 9 July 1991, the respondents had appeared in the same court on petition. The terms of the charges contained in that petition were the same as the terms of the charges contained in the complaint with which the present appeal is concerned. On behalf of the respondents, it is said that the Crown had concluded its J investigations into these matters in August 1991. At all events, an indictment was served upon each of them in or about May 1992, and a trial diet was fixed for 15 July 1992. That diet was thus outwith the one year period prescribed by s 101 (1) of the Criminal Procedure (Scotland) Act 1975.

By minutes under s 76 of the Criminal Procedure (Scotland) Act 1975, lodged on behalf of the respondents on 2 July 1992, the point was raised that the diet K fixed for the trial would constitute a contravention of s 101 (1) of the Act. A preliminary diet was sought, and this was fixed for 6 July 1992. At that diet, the appellant intimated that he did not intend to oppose the plea in bar of trial which was set out in the respondents' minutes. He moved to desert the diet pro loco et tempore, and that motion was granted unopposed. Approximately one month after that preliminary diet, the appellant served upon the respondents the summary complaint which the sheriff has dismissed. L

It is unnecessary to discuss the first two submissions advanced on behalf of the respondents, which were repelled by the sheriff and are no longer founded upon. The third submission, which he upheld, was to the following effect. The fact that the original proceedings were time barred had been brought to the appellant's notice by the minutes lodged on behalf of the respondents. Thus alerted, he had been able to desert the diet pro loco et tempore before the trial diet. It was submitted that if the respondents' solicitors had instead chosen to do nothing until the trial diet, and had taken the time bar objection only after a jury had been empanelled and the first witness called, the respondents would have been acquitted, and having tholed their assize could not have been subjected to the present proceedings. The respondents' solicitors would not have considered that the adoption of this alternative course would have been in conformity with their professional duties and their obligations to the court. But the Crown by raising the subsequent summary complaint were "abusing the respondents' solicitors' professional integrity", and seeking to take advantage of the responsible way in which they had conducted themselves. Reference was also made to the inconvenience to potential jurors and witnesses, and the expense to the public purse, if nothing had been done until the trial diet.

The sheriff dealt with this submission very briefly, observing that it was, in his opinion, unanswerable. He considered that to allow the prosecution to proceed would amount to oppression, observing that "the fact that it can proceed at all arises out of the quite proper conduct of the solicitors acting for the respondents". After referring to the number of productions and witnesses who would have been required for the trial, the existence of a number of special defences and the number of potential jurors who would have been required for the trial, the sheriff goes on to say: "That the respondents should be penalised, and that is the only way I can describe the situation, because their solicitors acted responsibly and did not allow such a trial, which could only have ended in a not guilty direction, to take place, amounts, in my opinion, to oppression."

In summary, therefore, the sheriff's view appears to have been this. If the respondents' solicitors had not alerted the appellant as they did, the respondents would have gone to trial, and would inevitably have been acquitted. The possibility of bringing a fresh complaint against them, and thus exposing them to the risk of conviction, was thus wholly attributable to the proper decision of the respondents' solicitors not to remain silent until the trial diet. The appellant was thus taking advantage of what had been done, and exposing the respondents to a corresponding disadvantage, or penalty. The taking of that advantage, and imposing of that disadvantage, as consequences of the responsible and proper conduct of the respondents' solicitors, must be seen as oppressive.

In presenting the appeal on behalf of the appellant, the advocate depute submitted that the contrast between inevitable acquittal on the one hand, and the risk of conviction on the other hand was unsound. Even upon the hypothesis that the time bar point would not have been noticed or raised until the first witness had been called at the trial diet, it was not true that the respondents would have tholed their assize so as to be free from further prosecution by summary complaint. The effect of s 101 of the Act was that the purported trial would have been invalid. While that purported trial could not itself have resulted in any conviction, it was quite simply not an assize, and the Crown would have been just as free to initiate fresh proceedings by summary complaint as they were in any event, having deserted pro loco et tempore. There was thus no question of advantage to the appellant, or disadvantage to the respondents, flowing from the fact that matters had been disposed of at the preliminary diet. The suggestion of oppression was wholly dependent upon the appellant having gained some advantage from the respondents' solicitors having adopted the one course rather than the other. Since there was no such advantage, there could be no oppression. In any event, however, the advocate depute submitted that there would be no oppression, even if the competency of fresh proceedings was a result of the appellant having been able to desert pro loco et tempore before the purported trial had commenced. If the initiation of such fresh proceedings was competent in general after prior proceedings had been rendered ineffectual by s 101 (*MacDougall v Russell*), and if there was no oppression in the sense of oppressive delay, it was difficult to understand in what sense the initiation of fresh summary proceedings could be described as "oppressive". If the procurator fiscal had been alerted to the position by others, or had himself come to appreciate it, in advance of the fixed diet, it could not be said that there was anything oppressive in his deserting those proceedings and initiating a fresh summary complaint. That being so, the course he had adopted could not become oppressive, merely because it was the respondents' solicitors who alerted him. That was particularly true if all that they were doing was conforming to their professional obligations. The sheriff had erred, and the appeal should be upheld.

Counsel for the respondents acknowledged that in the light of *MacDougall*, she could not dispute that it was competent to proceed by summary complaint, in situations where s 101 had prevented trial under solemn procedure. She submitted however that *MacDougall*, upon its own facts, did not involve a decision that new summary proceedings could be commenced after the 12 month period had actually expired, and suggested that the decision should not be read as going so far. If it did go so far, she submitted that the court might wish to review *MacDougall*. We are however satisfied that the ratio in *MacDougall* extends to situations where the new summary proceedings are commenced after expiry of the 12 month period, and neither that matter, nor any other aspect of the present case, appears to us to call for any review of the decision in *MacDougall*.

It was accepted on behalf of the respondents that the fresh summary proceedings could only be regarded as oppressive on the basis suggested to the sheriff, and apparently accepted by him: that but for the responsible course adopted by their solicitors, they would inevitably have gone free. But upon that fundamental question, counsel added no substantive argument to the submissions which had been made to the sheriff; and upon the question of whether it would indeed be oppressive for the Crown to bring fresh proceedings, having been "saved" from a situation in which

A   acquittal would be inevitable, the submission for the respondents was simply that the sheriff was entitled to decide that this was oppressive, for the reasons given by him.

Upon the primary issue, we are satisfied that the advocate depute is well founded in submitting that fresh proceedings would have been competent, even if the solemn procedure had been held time barred only after the purported trial had been commenced. Section 101 of the Act rules out the possibility of trial after the expiry of the 12 month period, and we are satisfied

B   that an accused in such circumstances could not be said to have tholed his assize. That being so, fresh proceedings would be competent in general terms, regardless of whether there was a desertion pro loco et tempore before the trial diet, or a plea of time bar sustained after the commencement of the purported trial. That being so, no question of advantage or disadvantage, dependent upon the course adopted by the solicitors, would arise, and the only suggested basis for holding the subsequent proceedings oppressive dis-

C   appears. Furthermore, we are not satisfied that there would be any oppression, even if the actions of the respondents' solicitors made the difference between the respondents being liable to fresh prosecution (as has occurred) and their being assured of an acquittal in the solemn proceedings. We do not go into the question of whether there was a positive professional duty incumbent on the respondents' solicitors to take the course which they did, or whether, on the assumption that it could bring acquittal for their clients, they

D   could properly do nothing until the trial had commenced. But upon any view of these matters, we are not persuaded that the raising of new proceedings could be rendered oppressive, merely because what alerted the appellant to the position was a proper and responsible decision on the part of the respondents' solicitors. The assumed contrast in consequences may be seen as "hard luck" from the respondents' point of view. Nonetheless, we do not think that the course adopted by the Crown can be described as in any way

E   unfair or improper, given that it was otherwise entirely competent, and was not otherwise, in any sense, oppressively late.

Upon the whole matter, we are satisfied that the sheriff erred in holding that it would amount to oppression to allow the prosecution to proceed. We allow the appeal, reverse the sheriff's decision and direct him to fix a new trial diet.

F   *Counsel for Appellant, Macdonald, QC, A D; Solicitor, J D Lowe, Crown Agent — Counsel for Respondents Dickson and McMahon, Powrie; Solicitors, More & Co — Counsel for Respondent Bass, Carroll; Solicitors, J & A Hastie, SSC (for Baird & Co, Kirkcaldy).*

P W F

Morrison v Panic Link Ltd   G

OUTER HOUSE
LORD SUTHERLAND
18 DECEMBER 1992

Jurisdiction — Prorogation of jurisdiction — Contract providing that any action "may be brought" in England — Further provision entitling one party to raise action elsewhere — Whether jurisdiction of Scottish courts excluded where action raised by other party.

H

Jurisdiction — Forum non conveniens — Contract — Performance of contractual obligations due in Scotland — Pursuer domiciled in Scotland — Defenders domiciled in England — Whether choice of English law as proper law of contract material.

A franchisee raised an action seeking enforcement of and damages for non-performance of contractual obligations due by the franchisors under the franchise agreement. The performance of the duties was due in Scotland. The franchise agreement provided inter alia   I that the proper law of the contract was English law; that any proceedings in connection with the agreement "may be brought in any Court of competent jurisdiction in England"; and that submission to that jurisdiction did not limit the right of the franchisors to commence proceedings in any other jurisdiction. The franchisors pled that the Court of Session had no jurisdiction, arguing that the terms of the agreement conferred exclusive jurisdiction on the English courts except insofar as the franchisors would be entitled to   J proceed in another jurisdiction if they so chose. The franchisors also argued that the Scottish court was forum non conveniens because all other matters being evenly balanced, English law had been chosen as the proper law of the contract. The franchisee argued that the provisions of the agreement neither expressly conferred exclusive jurisdiction on the English courts nor did so by implication, should it be sufficient that such exclusive jurisdiction could be provided for by implication. The franchisee argued that the action had its   K most real and substantial connection with Scotland and that the choice of English law as the proper law was not material.

Held, (1) that the exclusion of jurisdiction had to be done expressly and not left to ambiguous implication, and that there was no express ousting of the jurisdiction of the Scottish courts (p 603J-L); (2) that the franchisors had not established that the English courts were a more appropriate forum (p 604F-H); and pleas to jurisdiction and of forum non conveniens *repelled*   L and proof before answer *allowed*.

Action of damages

Robert Morrison raised an action against Panic Link Ltd seeking enforcement of and damages for non-performance of contractual obligations under a franchise agreement performance of which was due in Scotland. The defenders sought dismissal, pleading no jurisdiction and forum non conveniens.

The case came before the Lord Ordinary (Suther-
A land) on procedure roll on the defenders' two preliminary pleas.

Terms of agreement

The franchise agreement provided inter alia as
follows:

"9.25 *Proper law and jurisdiction*

"9.25.1 This agreement shall be governed by
English law in every particular including formation
B and interpretation and shall be decreed to have been
made in England.

"9.25.2 Any proceedings arising out of or in connection with this agreement may be brought in any Court
of competent jurisdiction in England.

"9.25.3 The submission by the parties to such jurisdiction shall not limit the right of the franchisor to
commence any proceedings arising out of this agreement in any other jurisdiction it may consider
C appropriate."

Cases referred to

Argyllshire Weavers Ltd v A Macauley (Tweeds) Ltd,
    1962 SLT 25; 1962 SC 388.
Elderslie Steamship Co Ltd v Burrell & Son (1895) 22
    R 389.
Scotmotors (Plant Hire) Ltd v Dundee Petrosea Ltd,
    1982 SLT 181; 1980 SC 351.
Sim v Robinow (1892) 19 R 665.
Spiliada Maritime Corporation v Cansulex Ltd [1987]
D   AC 460; [1986] 3 WLR 972; [1986] 3 All ER
    843.

On 18 December 1992 the Lord Ordinary *repelled*
the defenders' preliminary pleas and *allowed* a proof
before answer.

LORD SUTHERLAND.—The pursuer in this
action seeks enforcement of and damages for non-
performance of contractual obligations, performance
E of which was due in Scotland. In July 1990 the parties
entered into a franchise agreement under which it was
stated inter alia as follows: [his Lordship quoted the
terms of the agreement set out supra and continued:]

The case came on procedure roll on two pleas in law
for the defenders, namely that the court having no
jurisdiction the action shall be dismissed, and forum
non conveniens. In support of the first plea, counsel
for the defenders argued that the terms of the agree-
F ment conferred exclusive jurisdiction on the English
courts except insofar as the defenders would be
entitled to proceed in another jurisdiction if they so
chose. Clause 9.25.1 showed that the agreement was
governed by English law. Clause 9.25.2 showed that
any proceedings may be brought in any court in
England. Counsel accepted that in cl 9.25.2 the word
"may" was used which was normally to be regarded
as permissive, but he contended that having regard to
the terms of cl 9.25.3 it was clear that what was
intended by 9.25.2 was to confer exclusive jurisdiction. Clause 9.25.3 showed that it was only the fran-

chisor who was entitled to commence any proceedings
in any other jurisdiction than England.   G

Counsel for the pursuer argued that the provisions
of this agreement did not confer exclusive jurisdiction.
If it was sought to confer exclusive jurisdiction then
it was necessary that such conferment should be
expressed and not left as a matter of implication. Even
if it could be a matter of implication it would need to
be necessary implication rather than a possible implication. He referred to *Scotmotors (Plant Hire) Ltd v
Dundee Petrosea Ltd* where the agreement provided   H
that it should be "governed and construed in accordance with the Laws of England and the parties hereto
submit to the jurisdiction of the English Courts". The
court agreed with the proposition that the jurisdiction
of the courts cannot be ousted unless the provision
therefor has been expressly specified or distinctly
expressed. It was held that the proper meaning and
effect of the agreement was that the parties agreed to
submit to the jurisdiction of the English courts if an
action was raised there, but not that the parties agreed   I
that all disputes must be submitted to the jurisdiction
of the English courts. Counsel submitted that cl
9.25.2 showed that the bringing of proceedings in a
court in England was only permissive rather than
mandatory. While cl 9.25.3 confers a specific right on
the franchisor to commence any proceedings in
another jurisdiction, it did not exclude the possibility
of the franchisee commencing any proceedings in
another jurisdiction. The only effect of cl 9.25.3
would be to prevent the franchisee objecting to
proceedings being brought in another jurisdiction on   J
the ground of forum non conveniens, on the basis that
parties to an agreement can agree that one party
should have the choice of jurisdiction: see *Elderslie
Steamship Co v Burrell & Son.*

In my opinion the argument for the pursuer is to be
preferred. I accept that it is open to parties in any contract to provide for the exclusive jurisdiction of some
particular court. If that is to be done however, it must
be done, in my view, expressly and not be left to   K
ambiguous implication. Clause 9.25.2 is merely permissive and does not confer exclusive jurisdiction in
England. Clause 9.25.3 can be given content without
necessarily implying that the franchisee is restricted to
the jurisdiction of courts in England. There is nothing
in this agreement which expressly ousts the jurisdiction of the Scottish courts, and in that situation I am
of the opinion that if jurisdiction can be founded in
Scotland on valid grounds then it has not been
excluded. It was not disputed in this case that the   L
action concerns the enforcement of and damages for
non-performance of contractual obligations, performance of which was due in Scotland and accordingly
the Scottish courts would have jurisdiction. I therefore
repel the defenders' first plea in law.

Counsel for the defenders then argued that the
appropriate jurisdiction was that of England and that
accordingly his plea of forum non conveniens should
be upheld. For a useful summary of the principles to
be applied in considering such a plea he referred to the

A speech of Lord Goff of Chieveley in *Spiliada Maritime Corporation v Cansulex Ltd* [1987] AC at p 474. The basic principle is to be found in the opinion of Lord Kinnear in *Sim v Robinow* where he said: The plea can never be sustained unless the Court is satisfied that there is some other tribunal, having competent jurisdiction, in which the case may be tried more suitably for the interests of all the parties and for the ends of justice". The word "conveniens" should not be translated as "convenient" but as "appropriate". It is for the defender to satisfy the court that there is another

B available forum which is prima facie the appropriate forum for the trial of the action. It is a factor which may be taken into account that jurisdiction is founded as of right rather than on some fragile ground. While convenience is not a factor to be taken into account by itself, the natural forum should be that with which the action has the most real and substantial connection, and in that regard convenience may be taken into account as may be expense and other factors such as the law governing the relevant transaction and the

C places where the parties respectively reside or carry on business. Counsel for the defenders argued that in the present case all other factors were equal except for the fact that parties had agreed in the agreement that the proper law was to be English law and that the proper forum was to be the English courts. In the whole circumstances the obvious and natural forum was the English court and accordingly the plea of forum non conveniens should be upheld.

D Counsel for the pursuer accepted the tests set out in Lord Goff's speech. He contended however, that the defenders had not made out a valid case for ousting the jurisdiction of the Scottish court which jurisdiction was founded not on some technicality but on the fact that the contractual obligations were due to be performed in Scotland. There was accordingly a very real connection between the contract which was the subject of the litigation and the Scottish court. The fact that parties had agreed that English law was to be applied was of no materiality. If it was to be suggested

E that there was any difference between English law and Scots law in relation to the construction of this contract, it would be necessary for the defenders to aver what that difference was in the present action. They have made no such averments, and accordingly it must be assumed that the English law is the same as Scots law as far as the construction of the contract is concerned. The pursuer is domiciled in Scotland and although the defenders are domiciled in England, the agreement related to a franchise to be operated in

F Aberdeen. It is perfectly clear therefore that Scotland is the country with which the action has the most real and substantial connection. The onus is on the defenders to show that another court was "clearly or distinctly" more appropriate, to borrow the words used in *Argyllshire Weavers Ltd v Macauley*.

In my opinion, again, the contentions of the pursuer are to be preferred. It is true that the defenders are a company domiciled in England, that English law is to be applied in the construction of the contract, and that the parties appeared to have agreed that jurisdiction in

England might be appropriate. As against that however, the pursuer is domiciled in Scotland, the G agreement relates to the operation of a franchise in Scotland, the majority of the contractual obligations which are the subject of this action were due to be performed in Scotland, and the country which has the clearest connection with the subject matter of the action is Scotland. Looking at all the factors which have been put before me, I am not satisfied that it has been shown that the English court is clearly or distinctly more appropriate as the forum in which this action should be tried than this court. It follows that H I am not satisfied that the defenders have made out suitable grounds for upholding their second plea in law and I shall repel that plea.

Parties were agreed that if the defenders' first two preliminary pleas were repelled, the case should go to proof before answer with all remaining pleas standing.

Counsel for Pursuer, Ellis; Solicitors, MacRoberts — I *Counsel for Defenders, Tyre; Solicitors, Drummond Miller, WS.*

J P D

[The defenders subsequently marked a reclaiming motion which is due to be heard on 8 July 1993.]

J

City of Glasgow District Council v Doyle

EXTRA DIVISION

LORDS McCLUSKEY, KIRKWOOD AND KINCRAIG

8 JANUARY 1993   K

Contract — Sale of heritage — Missives of sale — Construction — Public sector housing — Sale of subjects "as the same shall be determined by the Council" — Whether council entitled to determine area less than that let under existing tenancy — Whether clause a "condition" challengeable before Lands Tribunal — Tenants' Rights, Etc (Scotland) Act 1980 (c 52), ss 2, 4 (1) and 82.

Heritable property — Sale — Missives — Public sector L *housing — Purchase of dwellinghouse — Secure tenancy — Sale of subjects "as the same shall be determined by the Council" — Whether council entitled to determine area less than that let under existing tenancy — Whether clause a "condition" challengeable before Lands Tribunal — Tenants' Rights, Etc (Scotland) Act 1980 (c 52), ss 2, 4 (1) and 82.*

Property — Heritable property — Sale — Missives — Public sector housing — Purchase of dwellinghouse — Secure tenancy — Sale of subjects "as the same shall be

determined by the Council" — Whether council entitled to determine area less than that let under existing tenancy — Whether clause a "condition" challengeable before Lands Tribunal — Tenants' Rights, Etc (Scotland) Act 1980 (c 52), ss 2, 4 (1) and 82.

Landlord and tenant — Public sector housing — Tenants' rights — Purchase of dwellinghouse — Missives — Sale of subjects "as the same shall be determined by the Council" — Whether council entitled to determine area less than that let under existing tenancy — Whether clause a "condition" challengeable before Lands Tribunal — Tenants' Rights, Etc (Scotland) Act 1980 (c 52), ss 2, 4 (1) and 82.

The Tenants' Rights, Etc (Scotland) Act 1980 made provision for the sale of local authority owned dwellinghouses to their tenants. The Act allowed the local authority to set out conditions in the offer to sell, which by s 4 (1) were to be "such conditions as are reasonable [to ensure] that the tenant has as full enjoyment and use of the dwelling-house as owner as he has had as tenant". Any tenant who objected to a condition under s 2 (3) of the Act and who could not reach agreement on the matter with the local authority could refer the matter to the Lands Tribunal for Scotland under s 2 (4).

Local authority tenants exercised their right in terms of the legislation, to apply to purchase the house which they let. The offer to sell contained a brief description of the subjects to be sold "as the same shall be determined by the Council". The tenants considered that the draft disposition subsequently prepared by the local authority did not describe the whole tenancy subjects, as a substantial part of garden ground had been conveyed by a disposition of a neighbouring property, and refused to pay the price specified. The local authority raised an action seeking declarator that they were entitled to hold the contract null and payment of rent arrears. The sheriff allowed proof on the question whether the subjects described in the draft disposition were those referred to in the missives. On appeal by the local authority the sheriff principal granted decree de plano. The tenants appealed to the Court of Session. The local authority argued inter alia that the tenants' remedy had been to challenge the reasonableness of the condition before the Lands Tribunal.

Held, (1) that the central notion of the legislation was that the tenants were to become proprietors of the same subjects as those whose let they had enjoyed as tenants (p 609G-H); (2) that giving the words contained in the offer to sell their ordinary meaning they were not intended as a condition within s 2 or s 4 (1) of the 1980 Act (p 610A); (3) that the true meaning of the phrase in the offer was that it was for the local authority to delineate the boundaries of each tenant's subjects in terms of the pre-existing let and set these down in conveyancing terms (p 610C-F); and appeal *allowed* and sheriff's interlocutor *restored*, modified to allowing proof before answer.

Opinion, that where a local authority found it was incapable in law of offering to sell the whole subjects

which had been let, it might be possible to invoke the jurisdiction of the Lands Tribunal to determine the reasonableness of a condition that the subjects to be conveyed would be less than the subjects let (p 610I-K).

Appeal from the sheriff court

The City of Glasgow District Council raised an action against Hugh M Doyle and Margaret Doyle in Glasgow sheriff court seeking (1) declarator that a purported contract between the parties for the sale of subjects at 14 County Avenue, Cambuslang, Glasgow, of which the defenders were tenants, was null and void; and (2) payment of rent in respect of the defenders' continued occupation of the subjects. The defenders maintained that the subjects described in the draft disposition offered by the pursuers were not the subjects referred to in the contract of sale.

A debate took place before the sheriff.

Statutory provisions

The Tenants' Rights, Etc (Scotland) Act 1980, as amended, provided:

"2.— . . . (3) Where an offer to sell is served on a tenant and he wishes to exercise his right to purchase, but — (a) he considers that a condition contained in the offer to sell is unreasonable . . . he may request the landlord to strike out or vary the condition . . . and if the landlord agrees, it shall accordingly serve an amended offer to sell on the tenant within one month of service of the said notice setting out the request.

"(4) A tenant who is aggrieved by the refusal of the landlord to agree to strike out or vary a condition . . . may, within one month or, with the consent of the landlord given in writing before the expiry of the said period of one month, within two months of the refusal or failure, refer the matter to the Lands Tribunal for Scotland for determination.

"(5) . . . the Lands Tribunal for Scotland may, as it thinks fit, uphold the condition or strike it out or vary it, . . . and where its determination results in a variation of the terms of the offer to sell, it shall order the landlord to serve on the tenant an amended offer to sell accordingly within 2 months thereafter. . . .

"(7) Where an offer to sell (or an amended offer to sell) has been served on the tenant and a relative notice of acceptance has been duly served on the landlord, a contract of sale of the dwellinghouse shall be constituted between the landlord and the tenant on the terms contained in the offer (or amended offer) to sell. . . .

"4.—(1) Subject to section 1 (1A) of this Act an offer to sell under section 2 (2) of this Act shall contain such conditions as are reasonable, provided that — (a) the conditions shall have the effect of ensuring that the tenant has as full enjoyment and use of the dwellinghouse as owner as he has had as tenant; . . . (c) the conditions shall include such terms as are necessary to entitle the tenant to receive a good and marketable title to the dwellinghouse. . . .

"82. In Parts I to III of this Act, except where provision is made to the contrary, 'dwellinghouse' means a house or part of a house used for human habitation, and includes land let in conjunction with a dwellinghouse and outhouses and pertinents belonging to the dwellinghouse or usually enjoyed therewith".

Cases referred to

Cooper's Executors v City of Edinburgh District Council, 1990 SLT 621; 1991 SLT 518.
Houldsworth v Gordon Cumming, 1910 2 SLT 136; 1910 SC (HL) 49.

On 3 May 1991 the sheriff *allowed* a diet of proof.

The pursuers appealed to the sheriff principal.

On 22 October 1991 the sheriff principal *allowed* the appeal and *granted* decree de plano.

The defenders appealed to the Court of Session.

Appeal

The appeal was heard by an Extra Division on 1 December 1992.

On 8 January 1993 the court *allowed* the appeal and *allowed* a proof before answer on the issue whether the pursuers had offered to convey to the defenders the subjects occupied by them as tenants.

The following opinion of the court was delivered by Lord McCluskey:

OPINION OF THE COURT.—In this appeal the defenders and appellants invited the court to recall the interlocutor of the sheriff principal dated 22 October 1991 granting decree de plano, and to restore — with minor alterations — the interlocutor of the sheriff dated 3 May 1991 allowing a proof. The countermotion for the pursuers and respondents was to uphold the interlocutor of the sheriff principal. Despite the fact that in the course of the appeal questions were raised as to whether or not the position which was taken up by the pursuers and respondents at the appeal hearing was truly and fully reflected in the pleadings, no motion was made to amend the pleadings; and we must approach the case on the basis of the pleadings as they stand, although during the debate some additional explanations on incidental matters of fact were given and were not contradicted.

In 1982 the respondents as the district council were the heritable proprietors of subjects at County Avenue, Cambuslang, Glasgow. The subjects, a council estate, included no 14, occupied by the appellants as tenants and no 16, occupied by other tenants. The houses at nos 14 and 16 were adjacent terraced houses; the respondents were the landlords in each case. Each of the houses had garden ground. On 18 January 1982 the respondents as the proprietors and landlords of no 14 County Avenue offered to sell the appellants the subjects they tenanted. This offer to sell was made under s 2 (2) of the Tenants' Rights, Etc (Scotland) Act 1980 ("the Act"). On 16 March 1982 the appellants served an unqualified notice of acceptance of that offer. The result, under s 2 (7) of the Act, was that there then existed between the parties a contract of sale relating to those subjects. Section 82 of the Act contains the following definition: " 'dwellinghouse' means a house or part of a house used for human habitation, and includes lands let in conjunction with a dwelling-house and outhouses and pertinents belonging to the dwelling-house or usually enjoyed therewith". The date of entry was agreed in the missives as being six months after the date of acceptance. Before that date of entry arrived, the respondents prepared a draft disposition relating to the subjects sold. The appellants, however, considered that the garden ground described in the draft disposition was not the garden ground let to and enjoyed by them as tenants; what they aver and seek to prove is that part of the garden of no 14 let to and enjoyed by them as at the date of the contract had, since that date, been conveyed by the respondents to the former tenants (now the owners) of no 16 County Avenue. Accordingly, they say, the respondents were not in a position to give the appellants a clear title to the whole property tenanted by them as at the date of the contract; or, to put it another way, the subjects described in the draft disposition did not correspond to the subjects in the missives in respect that they did not include a substantial part of the garden effeiring to no 14, that part being a strip some 8 ft in width which, it is said, was conveyed by disposition to the new owners of no 16 in April 1982. For this reason, the appellants had refused to pay the price specified in the missives and the draft disposition was never agreed, completed or engrossed.

The respondents maintain that they were at all material times prepared to convey what the contract enshrined in the missives obliged them to convey. They maintain that, as the purchase price was not paid on the date of entry, they were entitled under para 3 of the offer to sell of 18 January 1982 (which offer contains all the terms of the contract) to hold the contract of sale null and void and to claim rent in respect of the appellants' continued occupation of the subjects. The first crave of the initial writ is accordingly in the following terms: "The pursuers crave the court: (1) To find and declare that the contract for the sale by the pursuers to the first and second defenders of the subjects known as 14 County Avenue, Cambuslang, Glasgow, and constituted by missive letters dated 18 January, 22 February and 16 March, all nineteen hundred and eighty two is null and void and that the pursuers are freed and relieved of all obligations incumbent upon them in terms thereof." The second crave seeks payment of the rent claimed, £6,176.99 with interest. There is now no dispute between the parties that if the pursuers and respondents are entitled to decree in terms of the first crave then decree should also pass for that sum, with interest, in respect of unpaid rent; for the purposes of this litigation there is now no dispute as to the quantification of the claim for rent.

The right of a local authority tenant in the spring of 1982 to purchase the dwellinghouse (as defined) of which he was tenant was conferred by s 1 (1) of the Act. Under s 2 (1) the tenant who sought to exercise his right to purchase the dwellinghouse had to serve on the landlord a notice known as the "application to purchase". Under s 2 (2) the landlord was obliged, in the ordinary case such as the present and within a specific limited period, to serve on the tenant a notice, referred to in the Act as an "offer to sell". That offer to sell had to contain certain material showing how the offer price was calculated and also "(d) any conditions which the landlord intends to impose under section 4 of this Act". The relevant part of s 4 was in the following terms: [his Lordship quoted the terms of s 4 (1) set out supra and continued:] Section 2 (3) provided inter alia: [his Lordship quoted the terms of s 2 (3), and then s 2 (4), (5) and (7), set out supra and continued:]

Counsel for the appellants submitted that the sheriff had been right to allow a proof on what was the basic and essential but disputed matter of fact, namely, whether or not the subjects described in the draft disposition were the subjects referred to in the contract of sale. The relevant part of the contract containing the description of the subjects at 14 County Avenue referred to "the terraced dwellinghouse known as and forming number 14 County Avenue, Cambuslang, Glasgow, together with the garden ground effeiring thereto (hereinafter referred to as 'the feu'), as the same shall be determined by the council, and together with the whole heritable fixtures and fittings in and upon the said subjects, the parts, privileges and pertinents and the whole rights in common after described, and that on the following terms and conditions:—".

Having regard to this wording and the context of the offer to sell, namely, the newly created statutory right of the tenant to purchase the dwellinghouse as defined in s 82, the offer to sell was an offer to sell the house and the relevant garden ground as occupied and enjoyed by the appellants as tenants as at the date of the offer and acceptance. As the appellants were maintaining in the pleadings that the subjects described in the draft disposition were different from the subjects let to the appellants as tenants it was necessary to have a proof on that issue. If, after proof, it emerged that the draft disposition contained a description of the subjects to be disponed which differed materially from the subjects let and, in particular, if the material difference was that a substantial part of the garden of no 14 enjoyed by the appellants as tenants was excluded from the description in the draft disposition, then it followed that the respondents, in offering to convey only the restricted subjects, had not been offering to perform their part of the contract. If that were the position, then they plainly had no right to seek to enforce the third condition of the contract which gave them a new and dependent contractual right to claim payment of rent from the contract date of entry. Accordingly, if the appellants were right in their factual contention, the pursuers and respondents would not be entitled to what was sought in either crave; they would fail entirely in the action. On the other hand, if, as a matter of fact, the subjects described in the draft disposition corresponded with the subjects occupied by the appellants as tenants then there would be no answer to the claim by the pursuers and respondents that they were entitled to have the contract declared null and void and to recover the sum sought as rent. Thus the only real issue in the case was this one issue of fact and it had to go to proof, though she was content that a proof before answer be allowed. She pointed to the sheriff's note where it was recorded that the agent for the pursuers and respondents had stated at the bar that "The extent of the land which the pursuers proposed to convey to the defenders was exactly the extent of the land which the pursuers considered had been let to the defenders. She [the pursuers' agent] made it clear that the pursuers were not in any way seeking to convey to the defenders an area of land *less* than had been occupied by the defenders as tenants. In these circumstances, no issue [turned] upon the proper construction of the words 'as the same shall be determined by the Council' appearing in the description of the subjects contained in the offer to sell dated 18 January 1982."

Before the sheriff principal, the pursuers and respondents had departed from that position and for the first time had argued an entirely different point, namely, that the words "as the same shall be determined by the Council" effectively gave the pursuers and respondents carte blanche to put into the disposition what they "determined" to be the garden ground effeiring to no 14. It was for that reason that the amended grounds of appeal included ground 1 (g), although counsel for the appellants conceded that in referring to personal bar it was not perhaps putting the point accurately. It was not in dispute that there were no missives of let which defined the subjects let, and it was common ground, as the sheriff had narrated, that in 1982 the pursuers and respondents did not have a specific heritable title which related exclusively to 14 County Avenue so its exact boundaries were nowhere recorded in a heritable title. The pursuers and respondents were at that date heritable proprietors of a very much larger area of ground which included the subjects at no 14. In the absence of any specific title relating exclusively to the subjects tenanted by the appellants from the respondents, the exact extent of those subjects constituting the dwellinghouse as defined in the Act had to be determined at a proof. (She did not now seek to advance the argument rejected by the sheriff and the sheriff principal to the effect that there was "delay" falling within condition no 3 of the missives.) She further submitted that it was plain from ss 2 and 4 that, whatever conditions might properly be contained in an offer to sell under the Act, there could be no condition which denied the tenant the right to purchase everything of which he had the full enjoyment and use in the dwellinghouse (as defined) as at the date of the contract. Accordingly, the words "as the same shall be determined by the Council" did not purport to confer and should not be construed as conferring upon the pursuers and respon-

A dents an unfettered right to determine what was to be included in the disposition. It was not disputed that a condition which purported to confer upon the proprietors and landlords the unfettered right to determine what the disposition should contain would be an unreasonable condition. But the phrase under consideration did not fall to be construed as creating such a condition. All that was envisaged, given that there were no specific titles for this or other neighbouring specific dwellinghouses, was that it was the responsibility of the proprietors and landlords to delineate the

B boundaries so as to ensure that each tenant was enabled to buy the dwellinghouse, including the garden ground effeiring thereto which the tenant had enjoyed and was enjoying at the material date. Understood in this sense, the alleged condition contained in these words did not detract from the rights of the defenders and respondents and could not be regarded as unreasonable. There had been no justification, therefore, for using the procedure provided under s 2 to take the steps which might have resulted in a resolu-

C tion of a dispute by the Lands Tribunal. As at the date when the offer to sell was accepted there was no dispute apparent and no reason whatsoever to suppose that any such dispute would emerge. The dispute which did emerge came to light only when the draft disposition was observed to provide a different description of the subjects from that to be understood from the description of the subjects contained in the missives. Where there was a dispute of this kind it was appropriate to have a proof: *Houldsworth v Gordon*

D *Cumming.* The sheriff principal was therefore wrong. The sheriff arrived at the correct conclusion although it was not now suggested that the first plea in law for the defenders should be repelled. The third plea in law for the pursuers should also be reserved. A proof before answer should be allowed; otherwise the interlocutor of 3 May 1991 should be restored.

In reply, counsel for the respondents submitted that the parties had entered into a contract which was valid and enforceable. It was properly entered into under

E the provisions of s 2 of the Act. The contract had not been implemented by the appellants and the reason preferred, namely, that the subjects described in the draft disposition were not those occupied by the appellants as tenants, had nothing to do with the contract contained in the missives. The reality was that the respondents had offered the appellants precisely what they were entitled to. Once the parties had entered into a s 2 contract then the terms and conditions of

F that contract were binding upon both parties even although, in terms of s 2 and s 4, the purchasing tenant might have been able at an earlier stage to challenge conditions proposed by the landlord in the offer to sell. If that was the correct view then it did not matter whether or not the purchasing tenant might have had a legitimate ground of challenge at some earlier stage against a condition imposed; once he failed to exercise his right to challenge a condition and allowed the contract of sale to be constituted on the terms and conditions proposed in the offer to sell then he simply lost forever his right to challenge the poten-

tially objectionable condition. The scheme of s 2 was plain: the offer to sell, including proposed conditions, G was to be served on the tenant and if he sought to challenge any condition on the ground of unreasonableness he could do so, if necessary by having the matter determined by the Lands Tribunal for Scotland. Under s 2 (5) that tribunal had the right to uphold the condition or to strike it out or vary it and where their determination resulted in a variation of such a condition the landlord was required to serve an amended offer to sell within two months. Thus the Act had provided a swift and final mechanism for H resolving disputes as to conditions thought by a proposed purchaser to be unreasonable. In the contract constituted by the missives in the present case, the words "as the same shall be determined by the Council" amounted to a condition that the council was to have the sole responsibility for determining what part of the garden ground effeired to the named house, 14 County Avenue. In so submitting, counsel for the respondents acknowledged that the pursuers and respondents had not explicitly averred that the I council had in fact determined the matter; but, on a correct view, the issuing of the disposition — and it was not disputed that that had been done — amounted to a determination by the council and should be treated as such. The sheriff principal had accurately stated the true effect of there being a concluded contract which contained the words, "as the same shall be determined by the Council" when he said: "The contention that the pursuers, the council, are unable to implement that offer because they cannot give title to J part of the garden ground, is unsustainable: in terms of the missive the pursuers are free to determine how much garden ground is included in the offer."

That being the correct view of the effect of these words, it followed that even if the council had consciously and deliberately offered to sell the house plus a part only — that is to say a specified fraction — of the garden then enjoyed by the tenants (eg four fifths) they could validly have done so. If that part of the K offer went unchallenged by the statutory procedure then, when the tenant served a notice of acceptance under s 2 (6), the contract of sale constituted under s 2 (7) in relation to that house and the attenuated garden was valid and enforceable; once that stage had been reached it would be too late to challenge the contract agreed. The words, "as the same shall be determined by the Council" gave the landlord council carte blanche to determine the ground to be included in the disposition. The rights of parties were to be determined by reference to the constituted contract of sale L only and all rights or potential rights that might have existed prior to the constitution of that contract under the legislation were superseded. Reference was made to *Cooper's Exrs v City of Edinburgh District Council,* where in a case concerned with similar statutory provisions, the Lord President, delivering the opinion of the Court of Session, said at 1990 SLT, p 624K: "Once the contract has been concluded the statutory object has been achieved, and it is not necessary for the purposes of the statute to insist that the rights and

A obligations under that contract must remain personal to the tenant and thus cannot transmit".

This approach was in effect the same as that taken by the respondents in the present case, namely that the only issue was the true construction of the contract constituted by the missives. Counsel for the respondents said that the words, "as the same shall be determined by the Council" should be given their ordinary meaning, namely that the council had to determine what the garden ground was. He acknowledged that if he was wrong on this matter then there would have to
B be a proof and the fifth plea in law for the pursuers and respondents would fall to be repelled; the corresponding plea for the defenders and appellants, no 2, would have to be sustained.

In our opinion, the question which arises for decision on this appeal is a narrow one. If the respondents' submissions are correct, then a proof would serve no purpose; because the council, by offering a draft disposition, would, for all practical purposes
C have "determined" which ground was to be included in the conveyance. They would in effect, therefore, have determined the question which the offer to sell, according to this submission, left open for determination by the council. If, however, the respondents' submissions are unsound and the offer to sell, properly understood, was an offer to sell all that was included in the let then subsisting, nothing more and nothing less, then the only issue in the present process (though there may be others to be resolved elsewhere) is the
D purely factual question as to whether or not the subjects described in the draft disposition corresponded with those let, notably in relation to the extent of the garden ground effeiring to the house. Accordingly we must decide which party is right about the basic issue, as to the correct construction and effect of the words "as the same shall be determined by the Council" in the contract.

We begin by considering the Act. Its principal
E purpose was to enable local authority tenants to purchase the houses (and their appurtenances) which the local authority, as landlords, had let to them as tenants: ss 1 and 82. To put it another way, its object was to enable tenants to become proprietors. Plainly, if a tenant decided that he wished to own the interests in land that he had previously enjoyed only as a tenant, there would have to be machinery for effecting the necessary legal changes and some system for establishing the terms upon which the tenancy was to be converted into ownership. The method chosen by the
F Act was to create a special statutory system whereby the landlord and tenant would enter into a concluded contract of sale relating to the subjects; and it was to have the same end result as if the two parties had been an ordinary landlord and his tenant entering into an arms length contract by missives in respect of the subjects let. The statutory system, largely contained in ss 2 and 4, gave the tenant a number of advantages that would not be enjoyed by a would be purchaser in the private sector. But once the steps envisaged in s 2, subss (1) to (6) were taken — or, in some cases, were

deliberately not taken — the parties (the local authority landlord and the local authority tenant) were G then to be in precisely the same position as if the concluded contract of sale had been constituted in the ordinary traditional way between two ordinary persons. This was, we consider, the principle which the court recognised and applied in *Cooper's Exrs v City of Edinburgh District Council.* But running through the Act, notably in ss 1, 2 and 82 (interpretation), was the central notion that the tenant was to end up as proprietor of the same subjects whose let he enjoyed at the moment when the notice of acceptance H was duly served on the landlord. Thus s 2 (7) itself provided that at that moment, "a contract of sale *of the dwellinghouse* shall be constituted" (emphasis added). So far as the tenant was concerned, nothing fundamental was to alter, except his legal relationship with the subjects and the landlord; he was to cease to be a tenant and was to become a proprietor; his legal relationship with the landlord was to cease, but his occupation and enjoyment of the subjects was to continue as before. To achieve this, the local authority landlord I had correspondingly to cease to be landlords of the whole subjects let and to convey those subjects to the tenant. Nothing in the Act envisaged their retaining ownership of any part of the subjects enjoyed by a tenant who wished to purchase; nor did anything in the Act envisage their selling any part of such subjects to anyone other than the sitting tenant. Thus, for example, a local authority was not empowered by the Act to redistribute the garden ground among several adjacent houses so that the new owners would end up J with a more equal distribution of gardens. It follows that the statutory duty of the local authority was to offer to sell precisely what had been let. It is that, and that alone, which the tenant had the right to purchase. Section 4 (1), which deals with conditions of sale, enjoined that "(a) the conditions shall have the effect of ensuring that the tenant has as full enjoyment and use of the dwellinghouse as owner as he has had as tenant".

In these circumstances, and recognising that the K offer to sell of 18 January 1982 was made under the Act (s 2 (2)), what is the court to hold is the correct meaning in the contract between the present parties of the phrase (read short) "the dwellinghouse . . . together with the garden ground effeiring thereto . . . as the same shall be determined by the Council"? Were the appellants, when they received the statutory offer to sell of 18 January 1982, to treat the last nine words quoted as constituting a "condition" which they had a right to challenge under s 2 (3), para (a) as L unreasonable? Were these words to be construed as giving effect to a common intention of the parties, namely that, despite the scheme of the Act just outlined, the council were to have a discretion to decide whether they should dispone all the subjects let or only part of them? These words, like any other words in a commercial contract, have to be given their ordinary meaning, if the court discovers that they have an ordinary meaning. We approach their construction in that way.

A In the first place, it is not at all clear that these words were an attempt to create a "condition" of the kind referred to in s 2 (2) para (d), s 2 (3) para (a) or s 4 (1). In the offer to sell of 18 January 1982 these words do not appear as one of the conditions: they appear as an appendage to the description of the subjects to be sold. Only thereafter does the letter containing the offer to sell go on to say "and that on the following terms and conditions:—", and to set forth 19 terms and conditions. To put the matter another way, if the local authority landlords had been intending to B add a statutorily challengeable condition to the effect that the offer to sell was to be read as an offer to sell something which might — at the landlord's discretion — be other than the subjects let to and enjoyed by the tenant, then one would have expected that to be listed as an explicit and clear condition and indeed as one of the terms and conditions following the words "the following terms and conditions:—".

In the second place, no ordinary reader of the offer to sell would be bound or even likely to suppose from C the words actually used that a public authority, making an offer which itself was a creature of s 2 (2) of the Act, was deliberately intending to defy the clear words and intent of the Act by offering to sell something other than that which the tenant had enjoyed as tenant. Accordingly, he would look to see if the words, "as the same shall be determined by the Council" had a meaning which was consistent with an intention to implement what the Act authorised, namely, a sale of D the whole subjects of the subsisting let. It is, in our opinion, clear that these words could, and indeed did, bear such a meaning. Against the admitted background that there were no individual titles registered for the many distinct local authority houses, it was plainly going to be necessary for someone to define in traditional conveyancing terms the boundaries of the properties, some of which at least were to be conveyed to new owners and some of which would remain, at least for the time being, the property of the local E authority landlords. The delineation and description of such boundaries would most fittingly, and indeed perhaps necessarily, be done by the local authority which, when the Act came into force, was not only the owner of all the land, and the possessor of the only heritable title thereto, but was also the landlord of each and every tenant and was uniquely in the best position to know what enjoyment and use each tenant then had in relation to each dwellinghouse and ground effeiring thereto. Thus a reasonable tenant would, in F our opinion, readily have concluded that these words were simply a recognition that the council was to have the responsibility for delineating the boundaries to achieve the same division of properties as had been achieved by the separate lets, and the concomitant responsibility to render that delineation into conveyancing terms by words, or by reference to plans, or both. It would have been entirely reasonable for the tenant reading the offer to sell to conclude that the council was simply undertaking these technical responsibilities. The alternative, namely, that the council was avowedly reserving to itself the right to act

in contravention of the statute, seems to us to be absurd. The idea that a responsible local authority G such as the respondents would, by the use of such a phrase and in the way it was used, claim the right to make a division of the let properties different from that authorised by the Act is not one which commends itself to us as a view which the reasonable man would form on reading the offer to sell of 18 January 1982. At one point in his submissions, counsel for the respondents, asserting that this phrase did indeed give the council carte blanche, was forced to concede that if it did it would be challengeable as an unreasonable H condition. We find it strange that the respondents should in effect be submitting that in this contract (and we understand many others were drafted in the same terms) the respondents sought to insert in this way, and in advance of and separate from the numbered conditions, a condition which they concede on their interpretation would be instantly challengeable as unreasonable — on the ground that it would allow the council to do what the Act envisages is not to be done, i e to convey to a tenant something other than I the subjects let to him.

We have given some consideration to a possible situation that could arise, but which the respondents maintain has not arisen here. It could happen that when the local authority landlord came to make a statutory offer to sell to a particular tenant it found that it was, in law, incapable of offering to sell the whole subjects which had been let. Part of them might have been destroyed in some way or indeed part might have been conveyed in error to an adjacent tenant who J declined to reconvey the part that perhaps should not have been conveyed to him. In such circumstances, we envisage that the local authority landlord might offer to sell the house with its garden, etc, but append in clear, explicit and unambiguous terms a condition that the subjects to be conveyed were the subjects let *less such part as it was not in their power to convey*, specifying the part. On a strict view, this would not be an offer to convey the dwellinghouse as defined in s 82; but such a situation appears to be casus improvi- K sus. In that situation, recognising that lex non cogit ad impossibilia, we consider that the machinery contained in s 2 of the Act might well be apt to enable the "reasonableness" of such a condition to be assessed by the Lands Tribunal for Scotland. But that is an entirely different kind of case from the one we have here where the respondents are claiming that this non-explicit phrase somehow gave them the right at their whim to do something other than what they were empowered to do by the Act, indeed something which L was contrary to the Act. At the very best for the respondents the phrase under consideration is capable of more than one meaning and, had it been necessary, we should have applied the contra proferentes rule. It is unnecessary, however, to invoke that rule because, in our opinion, the meaning of the phrase in the contract is sufficiently clear.

It follows that under the contract constituted by the offer and acceptance it was the duty of the council to produce a draft disposition which contained a descrip-

A tion of the subjects which corresponded to those enjoyed by the tenant as tenant. It may be that in judging whether or not the description in the disposition corresponded with an accurate description of the subjects let it would be necessary to apply a de minimis rule, because the drawing up of new boundaries in a large, occupied council estate would have to be approached in a practical manner; but we do not have to decide that in this case, because it is not suggested by the respondents that it was necessary to resort to judgmental, practical compromises; the posi-

B tion taken up by the appellants, that the respondents were unable to convey that which they undertook to convey, is simply denied by the respondents.

In our view, once the argument as to the meaning of the phrase "as the same shall be determined by the Council" has been settled it is plain that the only issue which falls to be determined in this litigation is whether or not the respondents in fact offered the subjects described in the offer to sell dated 18 January 1982. That is to say, did the respondents offer to sell

C the appellants the dwellinghouse, as defined in s 82, being the whole subjects including the whole garden enjoyed and used by the tenants as at the date of the contract? In our opinion, the learned sheriff principal reached the wrong conclusion when he held that, in terms of the missives, properly construed, the pursuers and respondents were "free to determine how much garden ground [was] included in the offer". In our opinion, the sheriff was correct to allow a proof; and that proof should be restricted to the one matter of fact which this opinion has identified.

D There is no occasion in this process to investigate the quantum of damages, or the averments in relation to the supposed delay, or any of the events which are averred to have happened in subsequent years and related to an abortive attempt to use s 19 of the Land Registration (Scotland) Act 1979 in order to produce a solution which all parties would accept. In the circumstances, we shall recall the interlocutor of the sheriff principal dated 22 October 1991 and we shall

E restore the interlocutor of the sheriff, except that, as invited by the parties, we shall reserve the first plea in law for the defenders and the third plea in law for the pursuers. The result will be that we shall allow a proof before answer of the averments of parties in relation to the one factual issue which matters in this litigation, namely whether or not the respondents were, in September 1982, in a position to offer to convey to the appellants the subjects which the appellants had occupied as tenants and did so offer by including them within the draft disposition.

F

Counsel for Pursuers and Respondents, Gibb; Solicitor, Solicitor to City of Glasgow District Council — Counsel for Defenders and Appellants, Dorrian; Solicitors, Drummond Miller, WS (for Ross Harper & Murphy, Glasgow).

R D S

[The relevant statutory provisions are now ss 64 (1), 65 and 338 of the Housing (Scotland) Act 1987.]

Melrose v Davidson and Robertson

G

FIRST DIVISION
THE LORD PRESIDENT (HOPE),
LORDS MAYFIELD AND CULLEN
5 FEBRUARY 1993

Reparation — Negligence — Duty of care — Disclaimer — Survey report to building society at request of prospective house purchaser — Disclaimer in loan application H *form signed by prospective purchaser — Whether disclaimer effective — Whether "a term of a contract" — Whether contract "relates to services of whatever kind" — Unfair Contract Terms Act 1977 (c 50), ss 15 (2) (c) and 16 (1).*

Contract — Unfair contract terms — Disclaimer — Survey report to building society at request of prospective house purchaser — Disclaimer in loan application form signed by prospective purchaser — Whether dis- I *claimer effective — Whether "a term of a contract" — Whether contract "relates to services of whatever kind" — Unfair Contract Terms Act 1977 (c 50), ss 15 (2) (c) and 16 (1).*

The Unfair Contract Terms Act 1977 provides in s 16 (1) that a term of a contract purporting to exclude or restrict liability for breach of a duty arising in the course of any business shall have no effect if it was not fair and reasonable to incorporate the term in the contract. By s 15 (2), s 16 applies to the contract "only to the extent that the contract — . . . (c) relates to services J of whatever kind, including . . . loan and services relating to the use of land".

Prospective purchasers of a house applied to a building society for a loan to enable them to purchase the house. They completed an application form which included a declaration designed to exclude liability to the purchasers on the part of the valuers who would survey the house on behalf of the building society. There was a further declaration by which the pur- K chasers accepted that the building society would provide them with a copy of the valuation report and undertook to pay for the report. The building society obtained a mortgage valuation survey from a firm of surveyors valuing the property at £38,000 and making a "nil" estimate of essential repairs then requiring to be carried out. The purchasers proceeded with the purchase of the house. Thereafter defects were discovered. The purchasers raised an action against the surveyors, averring that there were many defects in L the house which should have been apparent to surveyors of ordinary competence exercising reasonable care. The surveyors argued that, due to the express terms of the declaration in the application form, they owed no duty of care to the purchasers. The Lord Ordinary held that the exclusion clause set out in the declaration in the application form was a term of contract between the purchasers and the building society and thus that s 16 of the Unfair Contract Terms Act 1977 applied to exclude the effect of the exclusion clause, and allowed a proof before answer. The

defenders reclaimed, contending that the Lord
Ordinary had erred in law in holding that the disclaimer was part of a contract between the purchasers
and the building society, and in any event in holding
that this was a contract to which s 16 of the 1977 Act
applied. The purchasers argued inter alia that they
had a contractual right that the society consider their
application.

Held, (1) (per Lords Mayfield and Cullen, the Lord
President (Hope) expressing no concluded opinion),
that by signing and returning the application form the
purchasers did not acquire any contractual right to
have the building society process and consider their
application (pp 614I-J, 616A-B and 616J-K); (2) that
the terms of the further declaration contained in the
application form had the effect that a contract was
completed when the purchasers signed the application
form and returned it to the building society contingent
on the building society obtaining a valuation report
(pp 614K-615B, 616B-D and 616K-617A); and (3)
that the contract to provide a copy of the report related
to the services to be provided by the valuer and was
a contract of the kind to which s 16 of the 1977 Act
applied by virtue of s 15 (2) (c) of the Act (pp 615E-F,
616D and 617A-B); and reclaiming motion *refused*.

Observed, that it was not necessary for s 16 to
apply to the disclaimer, to show that there was a contract between the valuer and the prospective purchaser
(pp 614F-G, 615L and 616G).

_____

Action of damages
(Reported 1992 SLT 395)

Derek Brunton Melrose and Mrs Ann Margaret
Anderson or Melrose raised an action against the firm
of Davidson and Robertson seeking damages for
alleged professional negligence in relation to a survey
of property carried out by the defenders.

The case came on the procedure roll before the Lord
Ordinary (Lord Morton of Shuna).

Statutory provisions

The Building Societies Act 1962 provides:

"25.—(1) It shall be the duty of every director of a
building society to satisfy himself that the arrangements made for assessing the adequacy of the security
to be taken in respect of advances to be made by the
society are such as may reasonably be expected to
ensure that — . . . (b) there will be made available to
every person who has to assess the adequacy of any
security to be so taken an appropriate report as to the
value of any freehold or leasehold estate comprised in
the security and as to any matter likely to affect the
value thereof."

The Unfair Contract Terms Act 1977, as originally
enacted, provided:

"15.— . . . (2) Subject to subsection (3) below,
sections 16 to 18 of this Act apply to any contract only

to the extent that the contract — (a) relates to the
transfer of the ownership or possession of goods from
one person to another (with or without work having
been done on them); (b) constitutes a contract of
service or apprenticeship; (c) relates to services of
whatever kind, including (without prejudice to the
foregoing generality) carriage, deposit and pledge, care
and custody, mandate, agency, loan and services relating to the use of land; (d) relates to the liability of an
occupier of land to persons entering upon or using
that land; (e) relates to a grant of any right or permission to enter upon or use land not amounting to an
estate or interest in the land. . . .

"16.—(1) Where a term of a contract purports to
exclude or restrict liability for breach of duty arising
in the course of any business or from the occupation
of any premises used for business purposes of the
occupier, that term — (a) shall be void in any case
where such exclusion or restriction is in respect of
death or personal injury; (b) shall, in any other case,
have no effect if it was not fair and reasonable to incorporate the term in the contract."

Cases referred to

Hunter v General Accident Fire and Life Assurance Cor-
poration Ltd, 1909 2 SLT 99; 1909 SC (HL) 30.
Martin v Bell-Ingram, 1986 SLT 575; 1986 SC 208.
Duncan v Gumleys, 1987 SLT 729.
Robbie v Graham & Sibbald, 1989 SLT 870.
Smith v Eric S Bush; *Harris v Wyre Forest District*
Council [1990] 1 AC 831; [1989] 2 WLR 790;
[1989] 2 All ER 514.

On 17 January 1992 the Lord Ordinary *sustained* the
fourth plea in law for the pursuers challenging the
relevancy of the defenders' averments concerning an
exclusion clause and *allowed* a proof before answer on
the parties' remaining pleas. (Reported 1992 SLT
395.)

The defenders reclaimed.

Reclaiming motion

The reclaiming motion was heard before the First
Division on 15 January 1993.

On 5 February 1993 the court *refused* the reclaiming
motion.

THE LORD PRESIDENT (HOPE).—The question raised by this reclaiming motion relates to the
application of s 16 of the Unfair Contract Terms Act
1977 to a disclaimer of liability by a firm of valuers
who were instructed to provide a report and mortgage
valuation to a building society. The purpose of the disclaimer was to exclude the valuers' liability for negligence to the prospective purchasers, to whom the
disclaimer was communicated by being set out in the
society's mortgage application form.

It is accepted that the valuers owed a duty of care to
the prospective purchasers. This point is not capable
of being disputed in the circumstances of the present

case: see *Martin v Bell-Ingram*; *Duncan v Gumleys*. In
A *Smith v Bush*, it was held that a valuer instructed by
a building society to carry out a valuation of a
dwellinghouse for the purpose of enabling the society
to decide whether or not to grant a mortgage over it
owed a duty of care to the prospective purchaser to
exercise reasonable skill and care in carrying out the
valuation, if he was aware that the purchaser would
probably purchase the house in reliance on the valuation without an independent survey. A building
society requires to obtain a report from a valuer in
B order to fulfil its statutory duty under s 25 (1) of the
Building Societies Act 1962, which provides: [his
Lordship quoted the terms of s 25 (1) set out supra and
continued:]

   The society is not obliged to send a copy of any such
report and valuation to the prospective purchaser. But
it is well known that it is the practice for this to be
done, and that purchasers especially of property of
modest value do frequently rely on the care and skill
of the valuers when making their own decision as to
C whether or not to purchase the property.

   This practice has resulted in attempts by valuers to
exclude their liability to prospective purchasers by
requiring the building society to communicate a disclaimer to them on their behalf. In *Martin v Bell-
Ingram* the disclaimer was held to be of no effect
because it was not communicated to the prospective
purchasers until after the pursuers had purchased the
property in reliance on the report. That difficulty has
D been avoided in the present case by including the disclaimer in the application form. But it is agreed that,
if s 16 of the 1977 Act applies to it, the disclaimer can
have no effect. This is because the defenders are not
in a position to show that it was fair and reasonable to
incorporate it into their relationship with the purchasers. Section 16 (1) of that Act has now been
amended by s 68 (3) of the Law Reform (Miscellaneous Provisions) (Scotland) Act 1990, but this
amendment took effect on 1 April 1991, which was
E after the relevant events in this case. In its unamended
form s 16 (1) was in these terms: [his Lordship quoted
the terms of s 16 (1) and continued:]

   The question is whether the pursuers are able to
show, on the undisputed facts of this case, that s 16
applies and thus that the defenders are unable to rely
on the disclaimer.

   The pursuers wished to purchase a dwellinghouse in
Rumbling Bridge with the assistance of a loan from
F the Alliance Building Society. They completed a mortgage application form in which they were required to
provide details of the property on which the loan was
required and of their personal circumstances. They
were required also to sign a declaration form, which
contained a declaration that the particulars set out in
the form were true and correct and that they were to
form the basis of any contract between themselves and
the society at that stage. Thus far there was, in my
opinion, nothing in the application form to show that,
by signing it and submitting it to the society, the pursuers were entering into a contract with the society at

that stage. This is not a case such as *Hunter v General
Accident Fire and Life Assurance Corporation Ltd*, G
where it was held that a coupon policy of insurance in
a Letts' diary was an offer of insurance by the
defenders which could be accepted, and a contract
made, by complying with the conditions which were
set out in it. The society could not be said to be
making any offer of a loan to the pursuers by providing them with the application form which was open to
acceptance by their signing the form and returning it
to the society. Any contract of loan lay in the future,
and it was dependent upon the view which the society H
took of the information on the application form and
the condition of the property. It was only when they
decided to communicate their decision to the pursuers
to grant a loan over the property that a contract to this
effect was made between them.

   There was however a further declaration on the
same page of the application form, which was in these
terms: "I/We accept that the Society will provide
me/us with a copy of the report and mortgage valuation which the Society will obtain in relation to this   I
application. I/We understand that the Society is not
the agent of the valuer or firm of valuers and that I am
making no agreement with the valuer or firm of
valuers. I/We understand that neither the Society nor
the valuer or the firm of valuers will warrant,
represent or give any assurance to me/us that the statements, conclusions and opinions expressed or implied
in the report and mortgage valuation will be accurate
or valid and the valuer's report will be supplied
without any acceptance of responsibility on his part to J
me/us. If I/we require advice regarding the price or
condition of the property the Society will, on request,
notify me/us of the name and address of its valuer if
he is normally available to accept instructions to carry
out private surveys."

   The pursuers did not instruct a private survey or a
structural survey of the house. They relied instead on
the report and mortgage valuation, a copy of which
was sent to them by the society after they had received K
the application form. They then concluded a contract
for the purchase of the house, which they now aver
was affected by a number of defects which were
present at the time of the report and which would have
been apparent to surveyors of ordinary experience
exercising reasonable skill and care when they were
carrying out their survey.

   The pursuers' action is one of damages, on the
ground that they have sustained loss and damage due
to the defenders' fault and negligence. The defenders L
have invoked the disclaimer, on the ground that its
effect is to exclude their liability for this claim. The
pursuers' argument is that the defenders' averments
on this matter are irrelevant, on the ground that it was
not fair and reasonable to incorporate terms excluding
or restricting such liabilities into a contract between
the pursuers and the building society. The Lord
Ordinary was satisfied that s 16 of the 1977 Act
applied, on the ground that the disclaimer was a term
of the contract between the pursuers and the building

society. Since the defenders conceded that it was not
A fair and reasonable that this clause should be incorporated in the contract, he sustained the pursuers' fourth
plea in law to this effect and allowed a proof before
answer on the remaining pleas.

Counsel for the defenders submitted that the Lord
Ordinary had erred in law in holding that the disclaimer was part of a contract between the pursuers
and the building society, and in any event that he was
in error in holding that this was a contract to which
s 16 of the 1977 Act applied. He pointed out that, in
B contrast to the position in England to which Pt I of the
1977 Act applies, it was necessary to show for the purposes of s 16 of that Act that the disclaimer was "a
term of a contract". It had not been necessary to
satisfy this requirement in *Smith v Bush*, on which
some reliance appeared to have been placed by the
Lord Ordinary, since that case was concerned only
with ss 2 (2), 11 (3) and 13 (1) in the English part of
the Act. Section 2 (2) provides that a person cannot by
reference to any contract term or to a notice exclude
C or restrict his liability for negligence except insofar as
the term or notice satisfies the requirement of reasonableness. It was accepted in that case that there was a
notice to which that subsection applied, and the discussion about the effect of the 1977 Act was concerned
only with the question whether it was fair and reasonable for the valuer to rely on the disclaimer to exclude
his liability to the purchaser. As to the question
whether there was a contract in this case, it was
difficult to see how that could be spelled out of what
D was contained in the application form. There was
nothing more here than an application, which in itself
could create no legal relationship. In any event, s 16
of the 1977 Act required to be read subject to s 15,
which specifies certain types of contract to which ss 16
to 18 of the Act do and do not apply. Neither subs (3)
nor subs (4) of that section was relevant to this case
while subs (2) provides that ss 16 to 18 apply to any
contract to the extent only that the contract is of the
types specified there, none of which was relevant to
E this case either. This was not a point which had been
drawn to the attention of the Lord Ordinary, but it
was appropriate for us to consider it because, if s 16
did not apply to any contract which was created by the
pursuers' signature to and delivery of the application
form, they could not escape from the consequences of
the disclaimer. But the principal point which he made
by way of criticism of the Lord Ordinary was that he
had not analysed the terms of the declarations on the
application form. Had he done so he would have seen
F that it had no legal consequences to either party and
thus could not create any obligation on either side, so
there was no contract.

I should add that counsel for the defenders accepted
that it was not necessary for s 16 to apply to the disclaimer, to show that there was a contract between the
valuer and the prospective purchaser. There can be no
doubt that the disclaimer was included in the application form for the benefit of the valuer. Accordingly the
defenders are entitled, on the principle of the jus
quaesitum tertio, to invoke it in a question with the

pursuers, and the pursuers for their part are entitled
to seek the protection of s 16 although their contract, G
if there was one, was with the society. In *Robbie v
Graham & Sibbald*, it was conceded that a disclaimer
on the application form for a loan from a building
society was not a notice having contractual effect, and
accordingly that the pursuers, who had no contract
with the valuers, were not entitled to the protection of
the 1977 Act. But that is not the position in the
present case, since the pursuers' argument, which has
not been disputed by counsel for the defenders, is that
s 16, prior to its amendment by s 68 (3) of the Law H
Reform (Miscellaneous Provisions) (Scotland) Act
1990, was not restricted in its application to cases
where the exclusion clause was in favour of one of the
parties to the contract. This is in contrast to the provisions of s 17 of the 1977 Act, which applies only to the
case where a party to a contract which is a consumer
contract or a standard form contract seeks to exclude
or restrict his own liability to the consumer or customer for breach of an obligation in that contract.

I have difficulty with what I understood to be I
counsel for the pursuers' primary argument that by
signing and delivering the application form the pursuers had a contractual right to have the society
process and consider their application. According to
this argument, the society, by issuing the application
form, made an offer to consider any application which
was made in terms of it, and this offer was accepted
when the pursuers signed and returned the application
form. This was said to create a contract between them
for the purposes of s 16 of the Act. It seems to me, J
however, that at best there was here an expression of
willingness by the society to consider the application,
with a view to the provision of a loan to the pursuers
over the property. But this was not intended to have
any legal effect, and the society were under no obligation to consider the application when the form was
returned to them. It is unnecessary to examine this
point further, however, because I am satisfied that
there was a contract in regard to the provision of, and
payment for, a copy of the report and valuation of the K
property.

In my opinion the effect of that part of the declaration which relates to the report and valuation to be
obtained by the society was to create a contract
between the pursuers and the society, and this was a
contract of the kind to which s 16 of the 1977 Act
applies by virtue of s 15 (2) (c) of that Act. The
opening of this part of the declaration states that the
applicants "accept that the Society will provide me/us
with a copy of the report and mortgage valuation L
which the Society will obtain in relation to this application". At the end of the declaration there is a statement that the applicants enclose the inspection fee,
according to the appropriate entry in the scale of
charges for inspection of the property including VAT
which, it is stated, the society has to pay to the valuer.
It seems to me that there is here an offer by the building society to provide a copy of the report and mortgage valuation to the applicants, which the pursuers in
this case accepted by signing the declaration and

returning the application form to the society. I recognise that, since the society were under no obligation to consider the application, they were under no obligation to obtain a report and mortgage valuation from a valuer. But that does not, in my opinion, mean that there was no contract. The contract was contingent upon their obtaining this report, which they were required to do by s 25 (1) of the 1962 Act in the event of their deciding to consider granting a loan over the property. The society's obligation came into existence as soon as this implied suspensive condition was purified. The effect was, as counsel for the pursuers put it in the course of his argument, to oblige the pursuers to pay for the report, and it also had the effect of obliging the society to send a copy of the report to the pursuers. Counsel for the defenders said that the test of specific implement could not be applied to what was set out in the application form. But in my opinion it is clear that, if the pursuers were to receive the report and mortgage valuation from the society and then to refuse to pay for it — as might happen, because the purchase price which determines the amount of the inspection charge may not be known at the date of the application — their liability for the fee could be enforced by an action for payment based on the terms of the declaration in the application form.

The only remaining question is whether this was a contract of the kind to which s 16 of the 1977 Act applies. This point turns on whether the contract can be said to be one which, in terms of s 15 (2) (c), "relates to services of whatever kind, including (without prejudice to the foregoing generality) carriage, deposit and pledge, care and custody, mandate, agency, loan and services relating to the use of the land".

I do not accept counsel for the pursuers' argument that this was a contract which relates to loan. This is because I am not persuaded that the effect of submitting the application form to the society was to create a contract to the effect that their application for a loan was to be considered. In any event, it is clear that at that stage no contract of loan had yet been entered into. But loan is only one of several examples which are given in this paragraph of contracts relating to services, and all these examples are without prejudice to the generality. In my opinion a contract by the society to provide the applicants with a copy of the report and mortgage valuation was a contract relating to the services to be provided by the valuer in the preparation of that report. There is a simple and obvious relationship between the provision of these services and the valuer's wish to have the benefit of the disclaimer in order to exclude or restrict his liability for negligence in the provision of them. The effect of s 15 (2) is that, to this extent, s 16 applies to the contract which was created when the pursuers signed and returned the application form to the society. That is sufficient to enable them to obtain the benefit of s 16 (1) to defeat the application of the disclaimer since, for the reasons given by Lord Griffiths in *Smith v Bush* at [1990] 1 AC, pp 858-860, it cannot be disputed that it would not be fair and reasonable for

the defenders as professional valuers to exclude their liability to the purchasers of this dwellinghouse.

For these reasons I consider that the defenders are not entitled to the benefit of the disclaimer and that we should adhere to the interlocutor of the Lord Ordinary. I would refuse this reclaiming motion.

LORD MAYFIELD.—The pursuers sought to buy a house with the assistance of a mortgage from the Alliance Building Society. They completed a standard application form which included a declaration signed by the pursuers. The building society obtained a mortgage valuation survey from the defenders and reclaimers valuing the property at £38,000 and making a "nil" estimate of essential repairs to be carried out. In an action raised at the instance of the pursuers and respondents against the defenders and reclaimers based on negligence they averred that there were many patent defects in the house which should have been apparent to surveyors of ordinary competence exercising reasonable care. The question in the case is whether the liability of the defenders and reclaimers is excluded by the terms of the clause in the application form having regard to the provisions of the Unfair Contract Terms Act 1977. At procedure roll the Lord Ordinary allowed a proof before answer.

Counsel for the defenders and reclaimers submitted essentially that the Lord Ordinary erred in law in concluding that the declaration in the application form was part of a contract between the pursuers and the Alliance Building Society to which the provisions of s 16 of the Unfair Contract Terms Act 1977 applied and in not concluding that the declaration in the form was non-contractual in character and accordingly not caught by the provisions of the 1977 Act so far as applicable to Scotland.

Section 16 (1) (in the unamended form applicable at the time) states: [his Lordship quoted the terms of s 16 (1) and continued:]

It is accordingly necessary for the pursuers to establish that s 16 applies on the facts of this case and that the disclaimer purporting to exclude liability does not apply. It is agreed that if s 16 applies the disclaimer has no effect because the defenders are not able to show that it was fair and reasonable to incorporate the term in the contract. Section 16 applies if a contractual relationship exists between the parties and the disclaimer was a term of the contract between the pursuers and the building society. It was accepted by the defenders that it was not necessary to show that there was a contract between the valuer and the pursuers. It is also necessary to establish that the contract was of the category to which s 16 of the 1977 Act applies. That in turn depends on whether the contract falls within the provisions of s 15 (2) (c) of the Act.

Counsel for the pursuers made two main submissions. As I understood the first submission it was to the effect that when the completed application form was sent to the building society the pursuers had accepted an offer made by the building society to consider the application, and the building society were then under a contractual obligation to consider it. He referred to *Hunter v General Accident Fire and Life Assurance Corporation Ltd* where it was held that the sending of a form to the insurance company was the acceptance of an offer by the insurance company and the contract was complete on the delivery to the insurance company. In the present case however the building society did not give any undertaking to consider the application. They were under no obligation to do so. I do not accept that a contract was formed at that stage.

However, I consider that counsel for the pursuers was well founded in his second submission that a contract had been created as to the provision of and payment for the report. In the declaration it is stated that the applicants "accept that the Society will provide me/us with a copy of the report and mortgage valuation which the Society will obtain in relation to this application". It is also stated in the declaration that the appellants enclose an inspection fee based on a scale of charges which the society has to pay to the valuer. In my view the essential ingredients of a contractual relationship are present, namely an offer by the building society to provide a copy of the report and mortgage valuation to the applicants and an acceptance by, in this case, the pursuers who signed the declaration and returned the application form to the society. The contract became effective when the society obtained the report from the valuer because the society were then obliged to send it to the pursuers and at that stage the pursuers were obliged to pay the fee.

It is also clear in my view that the contract fell within the terms of a contract relating to "services of whatever kind" referred to in s 15 (2) (c) of the Act.

For the above reasons I agree with your Lordship in the chair that the reclaiming motion should be refused.

LORD CULLEN.—In this reclaiming motion the question at issue is whether the liability of the defenders for their alleged negligence in carrying out the inspection of a house is excluded by the terms of a clause in a standard application form which was completed by the pursuers and submitted by them to the Alliance Building Society in connection with the proposed purchase of that house. A report by the defenders on that house was released to the pursuers by the building society after the submission of that application; and the pursuers aver that they relied on it in deciding whether or not to purchase the house and in deciding how much to pay for it.

Whether this clause is effective in excluding the liability of the defenders depends on whether it was "a term of a contract" which "purports to exclude or restrict liability for breach of duty arising in the course of any business" within the meaning of those words as they appear in the unamended form of s 16 (1) of the Unfair Contract Terms Act 1977; and, if it was the term of such a contract, whether that contract was one to which s 16 (1) applies by virtue of falling within the scope of s 15 (2) of the Act. It was not in dispute that the terms of s 16 (1) were apt to cover the exclusion or restriction of the liability of a person who was not one of the contracting parties; and that in Scotland it was possible for a contract between two parties to be so worded as to confer the benefit of exclusion or restriction of liability on such a third party. If the clause fell within the terms of s 16 (1) there was no further issue as to whether it was fair and reasonable to incorporate it in the contract.

In approaching the question whether the clause was "a term of a contract" counsel for the pursuers recognised that at the time when the report of the defenders was released to his clients the building society had not agreed to make a loan to them. He therefore sought to demonstrate that the clause formed part of a preliminary contract at that early stage of the communings between the building society and his clients.

The primary approach which he adopted was to argue that in submitting the completed application form to the building society the pursuers accepted an offer which had been made by the building society, namely to consider the application. This was on condition that if the building society chose to procure a valuer's report as part of its consideration of the application the pursuers would be bound to pay a fee for it. He emphasised that the completion of the application form involved trouble and possible expense to applicants. He sought to draw an analogy between the present case and that of *Hunter v General Accident Fire and Life Assurance Corporation Ltd* in which it was held that a coupon insurance policy in a diary, in which the insurance company announced that they would pay a certain sum in the event of a fatal railway accident provided that the would-be insured complied with certain conditions, fell to be regarded as an offer which could be accepted and a contract so made by anyone who complied with the conditions. I am unable to accept this analogy or that a contract was made in the present case in the way suggested. The building society did not give any antecedent undertaking to consider the pursuers' application — whatever that might have entailed — and they were under no antecedent duty to do so. No doubt the respondents had reason to expect that the society would consider their application but that is a different matter. However, in the light of the terms of the declaration contained in the application, and in particular the statement that the applicants "accept that the Society will provide me/us with a copy of the report and mortgage valuation which the Society will obtain in relation to this application", I am persuaded that the building society should be taken as having offered to provide a copy of the report and mortgage valuation if they obtained it. When the pursuers submitted the application to the building society they accepted that offer, having undertaken to pay the appropriate inspection fee in return for a copy of the report and mortgage valuation, if the building society obtained it. The pleadings are silent as to whether the pursuers did in fact make payment of an inspection fee. It is enough that they undertook to pay the fee. In these circum-

A stances I am satisfied that prior to the stage of deciding whether or not to make a loan to the respondents there was a contract between the building society and the pursuers which included the disclaimer of responsibility on the part of the valuer.

The remaining question is whether that contract fell within the scope of s 15 (2) of the 1977 Act. I accept the submission that the contract fell within the terms of a contract relating "to services of whatever kind" as these words appear in subpara (c) of that subsection.

B For these reasons I am in agreement with your Lordship in the chair that this reclaiming motion should be refused.

Counsel for Pursuers and Respondents, Bovey; Solicitors, Bennett & Robertson — Counsel for Defenders and Reclaimers, Peoples; Solicitors, Simpson & Marwick, WS.

P A

C

McColl v McColl

FIRST DIVISION

THE LORD PRESIDENT (HOPE),
LORDS ALLANBRIDGE AND COWIE

5 FEBRUARY 1993

D

Husband and wife — Divorce — Financial provision — Interim aliment — Variation of award of interim aliment — Backdating of variation — Competency — Family Law (Scotland) Act 1985 (c 37), ss 2, 3 (1) (c), 5 and 6.

Husband and wife — Divorce — Financial provision — Claim for periodical allowance in action raised prior to coming into force of Family Law (Scotland) Act 1985 — Minute of amendment lodged after Act came into force
E *converting claim for periodical allowance into claim for aliment — Whether minute of amendment converted claim into claim under Act — Family Law (Scotland) Act 1985 (c 37), ss 1 (1) (a) and 2 (2) (a).*

The Family Law (Scotland) Act 1985, which came into force on 1 September 1986, provides by s 3 (1) (c) that on granting decree in an action for aliment the court may backdate the award. An action for aliment is defined in s 2 (3) as meaning inter alia a claim for aliment in an action for divorce, separation, declarator
F of marriage or declarator of nullity of marriage. Aliment is defined in s 27 (1) as not including aliment pendente lite or interim aliment.

A wife raised an action of divorce in the sheriff court against her husband in August 1986, seeking inter alia a periodical allowance and aliment for each of the two children of the marriage. On 13 August 1986 the sheriff granted the wife interim aliment for herself and for the two children at the rate of £50 per week. In March 1988, after the coming into force of the Act, the wife amended the basis of her action so that it

became an action of separation, and amended her claim for periodical allowance to one of aliment. After G proof the sheriff awarded the wife aliment for herself and the children at the rate of £30 per week, and backdated all the awards to 1 February 1989 on the basis that the husband had been unable to pay more than that by way of aliment from that date. The sheriff intended that his awards of aliment would supersede the awards of interim aliment, so that the effect of backdating would be to reduce the awards of interim aliment from £50 per week to £30 per week from 1 February 1989. The wife appealed to the sheriff principal against the backdating of the awards, arguing H that backdating a variation of interim aliment was not competent. The sheriff principal sustained the wife's appeal and deleted the reference in the sheriff's interlocutor to backdating of the award of aliment. The husband appealed to the Court of Session.

Held, (1) that although the claim for aliment by the wife for herself had not been a claim for aliment under the 1985 Act when the sheriff court action had been raised, it became a claim for aliment under the 1985 I Act as from the date of the minute of amendment altering the basis of the action, and s 3 (1) (c) of the 1985 Act gave power to backdate such a claim for aliment (p 621B-C); (2) that the children's claim for aliment was a separate claim from that of their parent since the obligations of aliment were defined separately in s 1 (1) of the 1985 Act (p 621F); (3) that although the children's claim for aliment had not been a claim under the 1985 Act when the sheriff court action had been raised, and although the minute of amendment had no effect on the claim, it became a claim for aliment J under the 1985 Act from the date of the commencement of that Act, and the awards of aliment for the children could therefore be backdated under s 3 (1) (c) of the 1985 Act (p 621I-L); (4) that claims for interim aliment and aliment were treated as separate claims in the 1985 Act so that backdating of an award of aliment did not automatically affect an award of interim aliment (pp 622K-623A); (5) that the powers given to the court to order repayment of aliment where a variation or recall of an award of aliment was made did not K apply to the variation or recall of an award of interim aliment (p 623D-E); (6) that s 6 (4) of the 1985 Act, which gave the court power to vary or recall an award of interim aliment, did not give any power to vary or recall retrospectively (p 623I-J); (7) that the 1985 Act accordingly contained no provisions which allowed a variation or recall of an award of interim aliment to be backdated, and as there was no such power at common law the awards of interim aliment could not be reduced retrospectively (p 623H and J-K); and appeal L *refused*.

Observed, that the 1985 Act might accordingly contain a defect which should be corrected (pp 623L-624A).

Appeal from the sheriff court

Mrs Anne Dearden Murray or McColl raised an action against Ian McColl in Falkirk sheriff court seeking divorce; a periodical allowance together with interim aliment; a capital sum; interdict; and custody of the two children of the marriage together with aliment and interim aliment for them. The sheriff made awards of interim aliment of £50 per week. The pursuer was subsequently allowed to substitute craves for separation and aliment for the craves for divorce and periodical allowance.

The case came to proof before the sheriff.

Statutory provisions

The Family Law (Scotland) Act 1985 provides:

"1.—(1) From the commencement of this Act, an obligation of aliment shall be owed by, and only by — (a) a husband to his wife; (b) a wife to her husband; (c) a father or mother to his or her child; (d) a person to a child (other than a child who has been boarded out with him by a local or other public authority or a voluntary organisation) who has been accepted by him as a child of his family. . . .

"2.—(1) A claim for aliment only (whether or not expenses are also sought) may be made, against any person owing an obligation of aliment, in the Court of Session or the sheriff court.

"(2) Unless the court considers it inappropriate in any particular case, a claim for aliment may also be made, against any person owing an obligation of aliment, in proceedings — (a) for divorce, separation, declarator of marriage or declarator of nullity of marriage; (b) relating to orders for financial provision; (c) concerning rights and obligations in relation to children; (d) concerning parentage or legitimacy; (e) of any other kind, where the court considers it appropriate to include a claim for aliment.

"(3) In this Act 'action for aliment' means a claim for aliment in proceedings referred to in subsection (1) or (2) above. . . .

"3.—(1) The court may, if it thinks fit, grant decree in an action for aliment, and in granting such decree shall have power — . . . (c) to backdate an award of aliment under this Act — (i) to the date of the bringing of the action or to such later date as the court thinks fit. . . .

"5.—(1) A decree granted in an action for aliment brought before or after the commencement of this Act may, on an application by or on behalf of either party to the action, be varied or recalled by an order of the court if since the date of the decree there has been a material change of circumstances.

"(2) The provisions of this Act shall apply to applications and orders under subsection (1) above as they apply to actions for aliment and decrees in such actions, subject to any necessary modifications.

"(3) On an application under subsection (1) above, the court may, pending determination of the application, make such interim order as it thinks fit.

"(4) Where the court backdates an order under subsection (1) above, the court may order any sums paid under the decree to be repaid.

"6.—(1) A claim for interim aliment shall be com-

petent — (a) in an action for aliment, by the party who claims aliment against the other party; (b) in an action for divorce, separation, declarator of marriage or declarator of nullity of marriage, by either party against the other party, on behalf of the claimant and any person on whose behalf he is entitled to act under section 2 (4) of this Act.

"(2) Where a claim under subsection (1) above has been made, then, whether or not the claim is disputed, the court may award by way of interim aliment the sum claimed or any lesser sum or may refuse to make such an award.

"(3) An award under subsection (2) above shall consist of an award of periodical payments payable only until the date of the disposal of the action in which the award was made or such earlier date as the court may specify.

"(4) An award under subsection (2) above may be varied or recalled by an order of the court; and the provisions of this section shall apply to an award so varied and the claim therefor as they applied to the original award and the claim therefor. . . .

"27.—(1) In this Act, unless the context otherwise requires — 'action' means an action brought after the commencement of this Act; 'action for aliment' has the meaning assigned to it by section 2 (3) of this Act; 'aliment' does not include aliment pendente lite or interim aliment under section 6 of this Act."

Cases referred to

Barbour v Barbour, 1965 SLT (Notes) 67; 1965 SC 158.

Beveridge v Beveridge, 1963 SLT 248; 1963 SC 572.

Donaldson v Donaldson, 1988 SLT 243.

Donnelly v Donnelly, 1959 SLT 327; 1959 SC 97.

Matheson v Matheson, 1988 SLT 238.

On 18 March 1991 the sheriff *granted* decree of separation and *awarded* aliment of £30 per week to the pursuer and each of the two children backdated to 1 February 1989.

The pursuer appealed to the sheriff principal.

On 15 August 1991 the sheriff principal *allowed* the appeal and *varied* the sheriff's interlocutor by deleting the provisions for backdating.

The defender appealed to the Court of Session.

Appeal

The appeal was heard before the First Division on 21 and 22 January 1993.

On 5 February 1993 the court *refused* the appeal.

THE LORD PRESIDENT (HOPE).—This is an appeal from an interlocutor of the sheriff principal in an action of separation and aliment. The sheriff granted decree of separation of the defender from the pursuer, found the pursuer entitled to the custody of the two children of the marriage and made an award of aliment for the pursuer and the two children at the rate of £30 per week for each of them. The only questions which were before the sheriff principal related to the sheriff's decision to backdate his award of aliment for the pursuer and the two children. These also are the only questions which are before us in this appeal, since there is no issue about the amount of the aliment or the date to which the sheriff sought to backdate his awards.

The action was brought before the commencement of the Family Law (Scotland) Act 1985 as an action for divorce. The cause tabled on 13 August 1986, and by an interlocutor of that date the sheriff granted to the pursuer interim custody of the two children, Sharon, born on 27 March 1975, and Stuart, born on 14 May 1977. He also made an order for payment by the defender to the pursuer of interim aliment at the rate of £50 per week and found the children entitled to interim aliment from the defender at the rate of £50 per week for each child. There were before the court at that stage craves for divorce on the ground that the marriage had broken down irretrievably; for payment of a periodical allowance to the pursuer, and in the meantime interim aliment; for payment to her of a capital sum; for interdict against the defender from disposing of his assets, and for interim interdict; for custody of the two children; for aliment for the two children, and in the meantime for interim aliment; for interdict and interim interdict in terms of two further conclusions; for a power of arrest to be attached to the interdicts; and for expenses.

The Family Law (Scotland) Act 1985 came into force, with certain exceptions which are not relevant to this case, on 1 September 1986 in terms of the Family Law (Scotland) Act 1985 (Commencement No 1) Order 1986. On 3 March 1988, the pursuer lodged a minute of amendment in which she sought to delete the crave for divorce, to substitute a crave for separation and to replace her claim for a periodical allowance and a capital sum on divorce with a claim for the payment of aliment. On 8 June 1988, the record was allowed to be opened up and amended to this effect, and the action thereafter proceeded as one for separation and aliment. The defender then made an unsuccessful attempt to obtain a reduction in the amount of the interim aliment. On 12 January 1989, the sheriff reduced the interim aliment to £20 per week for the pursuer and each of the two children, but on 7 February 1989 his decision was reversed by the sheriff principal. The defender made a further attempt to the same effect on 16 June 1989, when he lodged a notice of motion seeking to vary the awards of interim aliment to nil in each case. But the proof was by then imminent, and consideration of this motion was continued to the date for which the proof had been fixed. That diet was later discharged and a new date fixed, but no further consideration was given to the defender's motion at that stage.

A proof was heard on various dates between 6 December 1989 and 28 February 1990, but it was not until 18 March 1991 that the sheriff pronounced his final interlocutor for separation of the defender from the pursuer and made his awards of aliment. The part of his interlocutor which dealt with the question of aliment was in these terms: "Finds the defender liable to the pursuer in payment of aliment for herself and for each of the children, said Sharon Ann McColl and Stuart Iain McColl, at rate of thirty pounds (£30) sterling per week, said aliment in respect of the said Sharon Ann McColl and Stuart Iain McColl to be paid to the pursuer qua tutrix and curatrix of the said children and to continue as long as they are in custody and unable to earn a livelihood, all said sums of aliment being payable weekly and in advance, with interest thereon at the rate of fifteen per centum per annum on each weekly payment from the time the same falls due until payment; ordains that a concurrent receipt by the pursuer and either of the said children while in minority, shall be regarded as sufficient evidence of receipt of alimentary payments in respect of that child; backdates the awards of aliment made herein to 1 February 1989."

On 15 August 1991, the sheriff principal sustained the pursuer's appeal against the sheriff's order backdating his awards. He varied the sheriff's interlocutor by deleting from it the words "backdates the awards of aliment made herein to 1 February 1989", to the effect that aliment at the reduced rate of £30 per week for the pursuer and each of the two children was to be payable from 18 March 1991 when the sheriff pronounced decree.

What the sheriff sought to do in this case may seem to have had much to commend it in the light of the view which he formed on the evidence. Section 3 (1) (c) of the Family Law (Scotland) Act 1985 gives power to the court to backdate an award of aliment made under the Act. The sheriff was satisfied, after an examination of the defender's financial position, that his ability to pay aliment had been substantially reduced since August 1986 when he was first ordered to pay interim aliment. The defender carried on business as a fishmonger, and his only capital consisted of the matrimonial home and his business assets which were largely burdened by debt. His sole income was from his business, and there had been a downturn in its profitability while the action was in progress. There was evidence that his poorer financial position went back to at least 1987, but since he had maintained his accustomed standard of living during 1987 and 1988, and had not applied for a variation until December 1988, the sheriff saw no reason why the pursuer and the children should be made to suffer because of the way he had arranged his affairs during that time. But he was satisfied that by December 1988 the defender had been forced to adapt himself to his reduced circumstances, and that from then on he had not been able to pay aliment at a rate beyond that which the sheriff had decided to be a reasonable award. His conclusion was that it would be reasonable in the circumstances to take the end of the financial year of the defender's business on 31 January 1989 as the appropriate date for backdating.

There is no doubt that what the sheriff thought he
A should do was to reduce the amount of aliment
payable from that date from £50 to £30 for the pursuer
and each of the two children, resulting in an overall
reduction in the defender's liability from £150 to £90
per week. This was still more than the defender said
he could afford. It should be noted that he had not
been obtempering the interim order since about May
1987 when there was an unsuccessful attempt at
reconciliation which came to an end in July of that
year. Since then, when he had been paying aliment, he
B had done so at the rate of a total amount of £25 per
week. We were informed that the defender is also substantially in arrears in payment of the amount of
aliment ordered by the sheriff in terms of his final
decree. There are accordingly substantial claims for
payment of arrears of aliment in this case which the
pursuer has been taking steps to enforce. Nevertheless
there was no challenge by either party to the sheriff's
view of the evidence, nor has it been suggested that it
was unreasonable for him to consider reducing the
C defender's liability to the pursuer and the two children
to an amount of £30 per week by way of aliment for
each of them.

In this situation I would have had little hesitation in
deciding to support what the sheriff did and to affirm
his interlocutor, had it not been for the questions
which have been raised as to the competency of the
backdating of the awards of aliment and the effect of
this on the awards of interim aliment. It requires to be
stressed at the outset that the jurisdiction which the
D sheriff was invited to exercise in this case was one conferred on him not by the common law but by statute.
And it became clear in the course of the argument that
it was very difficult to find a satisfactory answer to the
questions raised under the Family Law (Scotland) Act
1985 by what the sheriff wished to do.

The first question is whether the 1985 Act applies
at all in this case, since the action was raised before the
date when that Act came into force. There can be no
E doubt that the claims made in the action at the outset
were not made under the 1985 Act. The pursuer's
claim at that stage was for a periodical allowance as a
financial provision on divorce under s 5 of the Divorce
(Scotland) Act 1976. Her claim for interim aliment
pendente lite was based on the common law principle
that a husband is bound to support his wife during the
subsistence of the marriage: see *Donnelly v Donnelly*.
The obligation to aliment and the obligation to adhere
were, as Lord Justice Clerk Grant said in *Beveridge v
F Beveridge*, 1963 SLT at p 251, co-relative to each
other, but it was settled by the authorities that a wife
was not disentitled to interim aliment where her
refusal to adhere was due to her husband's cruelty or
adultery: *Barbour v Barbour*. As for the children, their
claims for aliment and for interim aliment arose under
s 9 of the Conjugal Rights (Scotland) Amendment Act
1861, which provided that in any action for separation
or for divorce the court might from time to time make
such interim orders, and might in the final decree
make such provision as to it should seem just and
proper, with respect to the custody, maintenance and

education of any pupil children of the marriage to
which the action related. That provision was extended G
to children of under 16 years of age by s 1 of the
Custody of Children (Scotland) Act 1939. The provisions of s 9 of the 1861 Act and of s 1 of the 1939 Act
in regard to maintenance were repealed by Sched 2 to
the Family Law (Scotland) Act 1985. But they were
still in force on 13 August 1986 when the cause was
tabled and the orders were made for interim aliment.

One of the difficulties created by the 1985 Act is a
lack of clarity as to the extent to which its provisions
about aliment and interim aliment were to affect H
actions already current at the date of its commencement. Section 27 (1) of the Act defines the word
"action" as meaning an action brought after the com-
mencment of the Act. At first sight it might seem that
the effect of this definition was that the provisions of
the Act were to apply only to actions raised after that
date. There is no difficulty about this so far as actions
for divorce are concerned. The provisions of s 8, about
the orders for financial provision for which either
party to the marriage may apply in an action of I
divorce, when read subject to the definition of
"action" in s 27 (1), can apply only to actions of
divorce brought after the date of commencement.
Section 28 (3) of the Act preserves the operation of s 5
of the Divorce (Scotland) Act 1976 in regard to orders
for financial provision in actions of divorce brought
before the commencement of the 1985 Act, despite the
repeal of that section by Sched 2 to the 1985 Act as
from its commencement. Accordingly the power to
make an order for financial provision under the 1985 J
Act was to be available only in the case of actions
raised after its commencement.

On the other hand, no such transitional provision is
made in the case of the repeal of the word "maintenance" in s 9 of the 1861 Act, as amended by s 1 of
the 1939 Act, and the expression "action for aliment"
is the subject of a separate definition in s 27 (1) from
the expression "action", which makes no reference to
the date when the action was brought. Section 27 (1) K
provides that the words "action for aliment" have the
meaning assigned to them by s 2 (3) of the Act, by
which the expression is defined as meaning a claim for
aliment in proceedings referred to in subss (1) or (2)
of that section, neither of which uses the word
"action". It was on a consideration of these provisions
that Lord Clyde reached the view in *Matheson v
Matheson* at p 240J-K that the scheme of the Act was
to introduce a new regime in relation to aliment
applicable to all actions, current and future, but to L
make the new measures for financial provision on
divorce applicable in their entirety only to actions
raised after the commencement of the 1985 Act: see
also his observations in *Donaldson v Donaldson* at p
245F. It seems to me that this approach is consistent
with the provisions of s 1 (3) of the Act, which provides that any obligation of aliment arising under a
decree or by operation of law and subsisting immediately after the commencement of the Act shall, except
insofar as consistent with that section, cease to have
effect from the commencement of the Act. As Lord

Clyde said in *Matheson* at p 240I, s 1 (3) preserves
A existing obligations of aliment but only so far as consistent with the new regime. I respectfully agree with
his conclusion that the new regime in relation to
aliment applies to all actions current and future as
from the date of commencement of the 1985 Act. Like
him I have not found it easy to apply this view to the
provisions of s 6 about interim aliment, but I agree
with him that it would be unreasonable to construe the
Act in a way which would mean that ss 1 to 5 were
available for current actions and s 6 was not.

B   The question whether the sheriff had power to backdate aliment in this case is, however, a relatively
simple matter to answer from this starting point. I do
not have any difficulty at all about this as regards the
claim for aliment for the pursuer which was substituted by amendment in June 1988 for her previous
claim for a periodical allowance. This amendment was
made when her action was altered from one for divorce
to one for separation and aliment. It is clear that what
the pursuer was seeking to do at that stage was to
C enforce the defender's obligation of aliment, owed to
her as a husband to his wife, in terms of s 1 (1) (a) of
the 1985 Act. This was a claim for aliment under s 2
(2) (a), and so far as this claim was concerned there can
be no doubt that the sheriff had power, since this was
an action for aliment as defined by s 2 (3), to backdate
the award of aliment in terms of s 3 (1) (c) of the Act.
The question whether that power was available to him
also in regard to the claim for aliment for the children
is more difficult. The sheriff's reasoning on this point
D is that, although this claim was originally a claim in
proceedings for divorce, it was, by the date of his
decree, a claim in proceedings for separation and this
was good enough to enable him to say that their claim
was an action for aliment brought after the commencement of the Act. The sheriff principal thought that
there was a good deal of force in the contrary argument that both the pursuer's claim and the children's
claim, having been made in an action raised before the
commencement of the 1985 Act, were outwith its
E powers and that there was no power to backdate in the
case of either claim.

    As I have already indicated, I disagree with the
sheriff principal about the pursuer's claim for aliment,
since this claim was not made until the action became
one of separation well after the date when the Act
came into force. I was at first inclined to agree with his
view about the children's claim because, like him, I do
not find the sheriff's reasoning on this point convincing. The fact that the pursuer's action was changed
F from one of divorce to one of separation had no effect
on the children's claim for aliment, either in terms of
the 1985 Act or on the face of the pleadings. The children's claim for aliment is a separate claim from that
of their parent, since the obligations of aliment are
defined by s 1 (1) of the Act separately. For the purposes of s 2 (3) therefore, which defines the expression
"action for aliment", the claims for aliment by the
pursuer on her own behalf and, under s 2 (4) (c), on
behalf of her children, were to be seen as separate
actions. As for the pleadings, it is one of the puzzling

features of this case that the crave for aliment for the
children remained unamended from the date when the   G
action was raised until the date of final decree. When
he came to pronounce his final decree, the sheriff
granted an order which was in terms of that crave, restricting the award of aliment to the period while the
children were in the pursuer's custody and unable to
earn a livelihood. In the absence of any provision to
the contrary it would seem that the effect of this order
was to confine the award of aliment to the period when
the children were under the age of 16 years, although
s 1 (5) of the 1985 Act defines "child" for the purposes   H
of the obligation of aliment as a child under the age of
18 years. In *Matheson v Matheson* Lord Clyde held
that it was open to the pursuer in an action raised
before the commencement of the 1985 Act to amend
the conclusion so as to extend the right to apply to the
court anent aliment until the children's 18th birthday,
but no amendment to that effect was sought in this
case. The wording of the crave and of the sheriff's
interlocutor both seem to provide support for the
sheriff principal's view that this was a claim made   I
before the commencement of the Act to which the
statutory power of backdating was not available.

    On further reflection, however, I have reached the
opinion that this view cannot be reconciled with Lord
Clyde's conclusion in *Matheson* that the new regime
about aliment applies to all actions current and future
at the date of commencement of the Act. The repeal,
from the date of commencement, of the reference to
"maintenance" in s 9 of the 1861 Act as amended by
s 1 of the 1939 Act, must be held to apply to all such   J
actions, as Lord Clyde noted in *Donaldson* at p 244L.
As from the date of commencement any obligation of
aliment owed by a father or mother to his or her child,
subsisting before that date by operation of law, was
replaced by an obligation of aliment under s 1 of that
Act. Accordingly the claim which the pursuer was
making on behalf of her two children became, as from
the date of its commencement, a claim made under
that Act and not under the pre-existing law. It was
thus a claim for aliment in proceedings referred to in   K
s 2 (2) (a), and accordingly was an action of aliment for
the purposes of s 2 (3) and also for the purposes of s
3 (1) (c), which gives the power to backdate. There was
no power to backdate any award of aliment under the
repealed provisions of s 9 of the 1861 Act as amended,
but when the sheriff came to pronounce decree he was
exercising the power conferred on him by the 1985
Act by which these provisions were repealed. I am
satisfied therefore that, in the case of the children's
claims also, the sheriff had power under s 3 (1) (c) to   L
backdate the award.

    This brings me to the next question, which really
lies at the heart of this case. This relates to the effect
of the backdating of the awards of aliment on the
awards of interim aliment which were made when the
case was tabled, before the 1985 Act came into force,
and which remained in force right up to the date when
the sheriff pronounced decree. The defender had not
been implementing these awards for a long time, and
it was no doubt in order to reduce his liability for

unpaid amounts of interim aliment that he invited the
A sheriff to backdate his awards of aliment. Having
rejected the pursuer's argument that this was
incompetent, the sheriff proceeded to order backdating on the view that this would be its effect. But he
said nothing in his interlocutor about the award of
interim aliment. I find myself in agreement with the
sheriff principal that the effect of it was that the
pursuer and each of the two children were entitled to
interim aliment at the rate of £50 per week until the
date of the final decree, and in addition to a backdated
B award of aliment at the rate of £30 each per week from
1 February 1989. As the sheriff principal said, this is
an unusual result, and reference to the sheriff's note
shows that it is at variance with what he intended.

Counsel for the defender invited us to hold that,
since the sheriff makes it clear in his note that he
intended to reduce the defender's liability over the
relevant period, we should construe his interlocutor to
that effect. At one point in his argument counsel for
the pursuer seemed to be content that we should adopt
C this approach. But I do not see how we can modify the
effect of the previous interlocutor of 13 August 1986
by reference to the sheriff's note of 18 March 1991, in
the absence of any provision in the sheriff's interlocutor of that date to show that he was varying that prior
interlocutor. I agree with the sheriff principal that
what the sheriff was really seeking to do was to vary
the awards of interim aliment and to backdate his variation of these awards. Counsel for the defender then
invited us to cure what on this view was an omission
D from the sheriff's interlocutor by inserting appropriate
words in it to this effect. But this gives rise to still
further difficulties which I have, with regret, found to
be insuperable.

According to counsel for the defender's argument,
what the sheriff sought to do, but failed to do
expressly, was competent in the light of his decision
to backdate the award of aliment at the rate of £30 per
week. It was, he said, unheard of for a party to be
E entitled at the same time to both aliment and interim
aliment. The two concepts were so inconsistent with
each other that the awards of aliment must be taken to
have terminated the awards of interim aliment. This
was, by necessary implication, the result of the exercise of the power to backdate under s 3 (1) (c), and we
should recognise the practical consequences of the
sheriff's decision by inserting appropriate words in his
interlocutor. As an alternative to this approach he submitted that the sheriff had power under s 6 (3) of the
F Act to vary or recall the awards of interim aliment, and
that he had power to do this retrospectively by setting
a terminating date for these awards. He pointed out
that the awarding of interim aliment pendente lite was
inevitably an imprecise exercise. Sheriff Principal R R
Taylor had made this point in his note dated 7 February 1989 when he recalled the sheriff's interlocutor of
12 January 1989 reducing the rate of interim aliment
from £50 to £20 per week. His comment was that, in
a case where the facts were so differently stated by the
parties, the court could only proceed on a broad axe
basis and that an investigation of the correctness or

otherwise of the defender's accounts had to be left over
for proof. Counsel's information was that the sheriff G
who heard the defender's motion for variation on 16
June 1989, who was a different sheriff from that who
heard the proof, expressed his unwillingness to consider variation of the amount of interim aliment when
the proof in the action was imminent, and that he had
also made reference to the backdating provisions in s
3 (1) (c) as a means by which the court could avoid any
prejudice. Whether or not his information on this
point was accurate, there was nevertheless a widely
held view that the court was reluctant to vary awards H
of interim aliment on contradictory ex parte statements when it was about to hear evidence. It was
therefore entirely appropriate for the sheriff to review
the whole matter once he was in possession of all the
evidence and, having done so, to give effect to his conclusion that the defender was, after all, not able to pay
the full amount for which he was liable under the
interim awards.

It seems to me that there is much good sense in this
argument, but I do not think that it answers the I
problem whether what the sheriff was seeking to do
was within the powers of the Act. I take first the question whether it can be said that an order for backdating
has, by necessary implication, the effect of terminating
an award of interim aliment as from the date to which
the award of aliment is backdated. There was an initial
attraction in this argument on the view that both
awards were designed to quantify the amount of the
obligation of aliment which was sought to be enforced.
At first sight the awards of aliment and of interim J
aliment pendente lite are mutually inconsistent with
each other and they ought not to be allowed to coexist.
Interim aliment pendente lite is designed to cover the
period prior to the date of final decree when, by necessary implication, it comes to an end, while aliment
properly so called is an amount fixed as at the date of
the decree after a review of all the evidence at the
proof. But it seems to me that this approach conflicts
with the rule that an award of interim aliment pendente lite remains enforceable during the dependence K
of the action unless varied or recalled by a further
order of the court. Irrespective of whether the awards
have been fully implemented, the sums payable under
the awards remain exigible against the defender and
the pursuer is entitled to enforce them according to
their terms. This rule has been given statutory recognition in regard to interim aliment under s 6 of the
Act, which provides that an award under subs (2) of
that section may be varied or recalled by an order of
the court. There is no indication either in that sub- L
section or in s 3 (1) (c) that an order for the backdating
of aliment is to have the effect of varying or recalling
a previous award of interim aliment under s 6.
Furthermore, s 27 (1) of the Act provides that the
expression "aliment" does not include aliment pendente lite or interim aliment under s 6 of the Act. So
it cannot be suggested that these are treated by the Act
as being embraced in a single claim for the enforcement of the same obligation, with the result that an
order backdating one necessarily affects the currency

of the other. As I read the Act they are treated as separate claims, and even though an order may be made backdating aliment, an award of interim aliment under s 6 remains payable until the date of the disposal of the action or such earlier date as the court may have specified when making that award, unless it has itself been varied or recalled by an order of the court.

I do not think that there could be an objection on the grounds of competency, therefore, to the making of an order for the backdating of aliment which was intended to supplement a previous order for aliment pendente lite or for interim aliment under s 6 of the Act. The sheriff expressed a contrary view, when he said that where there is in force an award of interim aliment there cannot be a backdating of the final decree. I find myself unable to agree with him on this point, on a proper construction of the provisions of the Act. Furthermore it is not difficult to imagine circumstances where this might be appropriate, given the imprecise nature of the information on which the courts must proceed in disputed cases at the interim stage. It may be that the evidence at the proof will reveal that the amount of interim aliment which was ordered was quite inadequate having regard to the defender's resources and that, even although he has fully implemented that award, he should be ordered to pay more to the pursuer or to the children by way of aliment for a period prior to decree.

But a backdating order which was intended to reduce the liability will create difficulty if sums have already been paid under the decree for the interim award. The 1985 Act has recognised this point in s 5, which provides for the variation or recall of a decree granted in an action for aliment brought before or after the commencement of the Act. Subsection (4) of that section provides that, where the court backdates an order under that section, as it has power to do because the effect of subs (2) is that the power under s 3 (1) (c) applies to orders made under s 5, it may order any sums made under that decree to be repaid. But in view of the definition of "aliment" in s 27 (1), it is clear that that section does not apply to awards of aliment pendente lite or of interim aliment made under s 6 of the Act. The absence of any provision in the Act to enable sums paid under an award of interim aliment pendente lite or interim aliment under s 6 to be repaid as a consequence of the backdating order under s 3 (1) (c) is a further indication that a backdating order does not, by necessary implication, have the effect of reducing or terminating the liability for payment under such awards. It may seem illogical that the power to backdate can be used to increase, but not to reduce, the total amount of aliment. But, since the provisions of s 3 (1) (c) give an unqualified discretion to the court to backdate the award in an action for aliment, and since Parliament must have been well aware that awards of interim aliment are very commonly made in such cases, I do not think that it is open to us to say that this power cannot be exercised in respect of a period where there is in force an award of interim aliment. The existence of such an award is, however, a circumstance to which the court must have regard in considering whether or not a backdating order is appropriate.

The remaining question is whether, as counsel for the defender submitted, there is power in s 6 of the Act to backdate a variation or recall of an award of interim aliment. There is an initial difficulty here in that the awards of interim aliment in this case, having been made on 13 August 1986 prior to the commencement of the 1985 Act, were not awards of interim aliment made under s 6 (2) of that Act. Since the power to vary or recall under s 6 (4) applies only to awards made under s 6 (2), it seems to be clear that this is not a power which could be exercised in this case. Any variation would have to be made in the exercise of a power to vary which the court could exercise according to the law and practice in force prior to the commencement of the 1985 Act. According to that law and practice orders for variation or recall of awards of interim aliment were effective from the date of the order but not retrospectively. The power to backdate is an entirely new concept, which depends upon the powers given to the court by the 1985 Act. But even if the power to vary under s 6 (4) of the 1985 Act was available, it could not in my opinion be used to backdate the variation or recall. The absence of an express power to backdate, in contrast to that given in s 3 (1) (c), and of an express power to order the repayment of any sums made under the award, in contrast to that given in s 5 (4), both point inevitably to the conclusion that any variation or recall takes effect only from the date when the court makes its order, and that it cannot make an order retrospectively from any earlier date. The assumption must be that awards of interim aliment under s 6 will be implemented according to their terms, and that if there is to be a power to backdate an order for variation or recall, there must also be a power to order the repayment of sums paid under the award. Consequently, the absence of any power to order the repayment of sums paid under the award is a clear indication that the power in s 6 (4) cannot be exercised retrospectively, and accordingly that this alternative argument, even if it was relevant to the circumstances of this case, cannot succeed.

For these reasons I do not think that it is open to us to give effect to the sheriff's intention by re-writing his interlocutor so as to backdate a variation or recall of the awards of interim aliment. The only course which we can take is that which has already been taken by the sheriff principal, which was to delete from the sheriff's interlocutor the order for backdating which, if it was allowed to stand, would result in an increase in the defender's overall liability for a period during which the sheriff wished him to pay a reduced amount. I have reached this conclusion with regret, because it seems to me that, on the undisputed view which the sheriff took of the evidence, it was appropriate that the defender's overall liability should be reduced. The court's reluctance to alter the interim awards when the proof was imminent, and the long time when the case was at avizandum, both point to the good sense of backdating the reduced liability if this could be done. The absence of a power to backdate an order for varia-

A tion or recall of interim aliment seems to be inconsistent with the power given to the court by s 3 (1) (c) to backdate an award of aliment, and it may be that there is a defect here in the statute which should be corrected. Counsel for the defender asked us to recognise that Parliament could not foresee every circumstance and he invited us to approach the legislation on a common sense basis and, as he put it, in an adventurous manner so as to cure the difficulty which had emerged in this case. Had the problem been one of ambiguity there would have been much to be said for

B this approach to give effect to the presumed intention of Parliament. The problem in this case, however, is that there is a gap in the legislation which cannot be filled on any reasonable approach to the wording of the Act. It must therefore be left to Parliament to consider whether the legislation should now be amended to enable the court, when backdating an award of aliment, to order a corresponding variation or recall of any interim order in respect of the same obligation of aliment, and to order the repayment of any sums paid under that award.

C
For these reasons, which differ in some respects from those given by the sheriff principal, I would refuse this appeal and affirm his interlocutor.

LORD ALLANBRIDGE.—I am in complete agreement with the opinion of your Lordship in the chair and have nothing to add.

LORD COWIE.—I concur in the opinion of your
D Lordship in the chair and have nothing to add.

———————

Counsel for Pursuer and Respondent, Mackie; Solicitors, Balfour & Manson, Nightingale & Bell — Counsel for Defender and Appellant, Dewar; Solicitors, Russel & Aitken, WS.

D A K

E

Hamilton v Fife Health Board

EXTRA DIVISION
LORDS McCLUSKEY, CAPLAN AND WYLIE
24 MARCH 1993

Damages — Loss of society — Negligent act occurring prior to child being born — Child dying three days after birth as a result of negligent act — Whether injuries sus-
F *tained before birth were sustained by a "person" — Competency of loss of society claim by parents — Damages (Scotland) Act 1976 (c 13), ss 1 (1) and (4) and 10 (1).*

Reparation — Negligence — Loss of society — Negligent act occurring prior to child being born — Child dying three days after birth as a result of negligent act — Whether injuries sustained before birth were sustained by a "person" — Competency of loss of society claim by parents — Damages (Scotland) Act 1976 (c 13), ss 1 (1) and (4) and 10 (1).

The Damages (Scotland) Act 1976, s 1 (1), provides

that where "a person dies in consequence of personal injuries sustained by him", and the injuries gave rise G to liability to pay damages to "the injured person", then there also arises a liability to pay damages according to that section to any relative of the deceased. Section 10 (1) defines "personal injuries" as including "any disease or impairment of a person's physical or mental condition".

In 1976 a mother gave birth to a baby boy who died three days after he was born. The child's parents raised an action against the health board for loss of society in respect of the death of their child. According H to the parents' averments, the child died as a result of negligent acts carried out by doctors before the child was born. The defenders argued that the claim for loss of society was irrelevant as a person only came into existence on birth and therefore there was no person alive at the time the injuries were sustained. The Lord Ordinary held that the words "personal injuries" did not cover injury sustained by a child not yet born as there was no person at that stage and dismissed the action so far as relating to the conclusions for loss of
I society. The pursuers reclaimed.

Held, (1) that the only issue raised by the case was as to the meaning of s 1 (1) of the 1976 Act (pp 629A, 630F and 633K-L); (2) that there could be no liability under the section until both damnum and injuria concurred (pp 629B, 630I and 633K-L); (3) that once the unborn person was born there was a concurrence of injuria and damnum giving the newly born person a right to sue the person whose breach of duty caused the child's loss, and giving rise to a consequential
J liability under s 1 (1) to the eligible relatives (pp 629D and J-K, 630H-I, 630K-631A, 632L-633B, 633D-E and K-L); (4) that injuries sustained before the child was born were therefore properly described as personal injuries even though they were inflicted before the child acquired legal personality (pp 629E-F, 631E-F and H-K and 633K-L); and reclaiming motion *allowed.*

B v Islington Health Authority [1991] 1 QB 638, and *de Martell v Merton and Sutton Health Authority* K [1992] 3 WLR 637, *followed.*

Opinion, that the law before the passing of the 1976 Act was that certain relatives of a child who was injured whilst in the womb could have sued for damages without recourse to the common law fiction that in matters affecting its interests the unborn child in utero should be deemed to be born, and there was no reason to think that the legislature had intended to remove the right of relatives to sue for damages in L respect of injuries sustained by a child whilst still in the womb (pp 630B-C, 633I-J and K-L).

Opinion reserved (per Lord McCluskey), as to whether or not injuries sustained by a foetus early in pregnancy would be "personal injuries" (p 629H).

———————

Action of damages
(Reported 1992 SLT 1026)

Mrs Audrey Jean Hamilton raised an action against Fife Health Board seeking a loss of society award in

respect of the death, three days after his birth in
August 1976, of her baby son. The father of the child,
John David Watson, was the second pursuer. The
death was averred to be due to the negligence of
doctors at Craigtoun maternity hospital, St Andrews,
for whose actions the defenders were responsible.

The case came before the Lord Ordinary (Prosser)
on procedure roll on the defenders' preliminary pleas.

Statutory provisions

The Damages (Scotland) Act 1976 provides:

"1.—(1) Where a person dies in consequence of personal injuries sustained by him as a result of an act or omission of another person, being an act or omission giving rise to liability to pay damages to the injured person or his executor, then, subject to the following provisions of this Act, the person liable to pay those damages (in this section referred to as "the responsible person") shall also be liable to pay damages in accordance with this section to any relative of the deceased, being a relative within the meaning of Schedule 1 to this Act. . . .

"(3) The damages which the responsible person shall be liable to pay to a relative of a deceased under this section shall (subject to the provisions of this Act) be such as will compensate the relative for any loss of support suffered by him since the date of the deceased's death or likely to be suffered by him as a result of the act or omission in question, together with any reasonable expense incurred by him in connection with the deceased's funeral.

"(4) If the relative is a member of the deceased's immediate family (within the meaning of section 10 (2) of this Act) there shall be awarded, without prejudice to any claim under subsection (3) above, such sum of damages, if any, as the court thinks just by way of compensation for the loss of such non-patrimonial benefit as the relative might have been expected to derive from the deceased's society and guidance if he had not died; and a sum of damages such as is mentioned in this subsection shall be known as a 'loss of society award'. . . .

"3. There shall not be transmitted to the executor of a deceased person any right which has accrued to the deceased before his death, being a right to— (a) damages by way of solatium in respect of the death of any other person, under the law in force before the commencement of this Act; (b) a loss of society award, and accordingly the executor shall not be entitled to bring an action, or to be sisted as pursuer in any action brought by the deceased before his death, for the purpose of enforcing any such right. . . .

"10.—(1) In this Act, unless the context otherwise requires— . . . 'personal injuries' includes any disease or any impairment of a person's physical or mental condition".

Cases referred to

B v Islington Health Authority [1991] 1 QB 638;
[1991] 2 WLR 501; [1991] 1 All ER 825; affd
sub nom *Burton v Islington Health Authority*,
infra.

Bourhill v Young's Executor, 1941 SLT 364; 1941 SC
395; affd 1943 SLT 105; 1942 SC (HL) 78.
*Burton v Islington Health Authority; de Martell v
Merton and Sutton Health Authority 1992 3 WLR
637; 1992 3 All ER 833.*
Clarke v Carfin Coal Co (1891) 18 R (HL) 63.
Cohen v Shaw, 1992 SLT 1022.
Connachan v Scottish Motor Traction Co Ltd, 1946
SLT 346; 1946 SC 428.
Davidson v Sprengel, 1909 1 SLT 220; 1909 SC 566.
Dietrich v Northampton (1884) 138 Mass 14.
Donoghue v Stevenson, 1932 SLT 317; 1932 SC (HL)
31.
Duval v Seguin (1972) 26 DLR (3d) 418.
Eisten v North British Railway Co (1870) 8 M 980.
Elliot v Joicey, 1935 SC (HL) 57.
Grant v Australian Knitting Mills Ltd 1936 AC 85.
Leadbetter v National Coal Board, 1952 SLT 179.
McCluskey v HM Advocate, 1989 SLT 175; 1988
SCCR 629.
McKay v Scottish Airways Ltd, 1948 SLT 402; 1948
SC 254.
McNamara v Laird Line and Clan Line Steamers Ltd,
OH, 26 June 1924, reported in an appendix to
McKay v Scottish Airways Ltd at 1948 SLT,
p 407, and 1948 SC, p 265.
McWilliams v Lord Advocate, 1992 SLT 1045.
Pepper v Hart [1992] 3 WLR 1032.
Riddell v James Longmuir & Sons Ltd, 1971 SLT
(Notes) 33.
Roe v Wade, 410 US 113 (1973).
*Watson v Fram Reinforced Concrete Co (Scotland) Ltd
and Winget Ltd*, 1960 SLT 321; 1960 SC (HL)
92.
Watt v Rama 1972 VR 353.

Textbooks referred to

Maxwell, *Interpretation of Statutes* (12th ed), p 116.
Walker, *Delict* (2nd ed), pp 720-722.

On 21 November 1991 the Lord Ordinary *sustained*
the defenders' second plea in law and *dismissed* the
action in relation to the first and third conclusions.
(Reported 1992 SLT 1026.)

The second pursuer reclaimed.

Reclaiming motion

The reclaiming motion was heard before an Extra
Division on 24 February 1993.

On 24 March 1993 the court *allowed* the reclaiming
motion.

LORD McCLUSKEY.—The pursuers were the
parents of a baby boy who was born in August 1976
at Craigtoun maternity hospital, St Andrews. The
child died three days later. It is a matter of admission
that when the child was born he was in a poor condition of health and we must approach this case, at this
stage, upon the basis that it was the actions of doctors
at that hospital, shortly before the birth and when
attempting to deliver the child, that resulted in his
poor condition of health at the time of his birth, and

also that the child died in consequence of the same traumas sustained immediately before birth. The defenders and respondents are responsible in law for those actions. This reclaiming motion, by the second named pursuer, was concerned only with the relevancy of the claims by both parents for damages in respect of the loss they suffered as a result of the death of their child.

The defenders and respondents submitted to the Lord Ordinary that the averments of the pursuers in support of the first and third conclusions of the summons, which relate to their claims in respect of the loss of the child, were irrelevant and that the action so far as laid on these conclusions should be dismissed. The Lord Ordinary sustained the second plea in law for the defenders and respondents and dismissed the action in relation to these conclusions. The reclaiming motion before us is against the interlocutor of the Lord Ordinary sustaining that plea in law.

The parents' rights to damages in respect of the death of their child are said to derive from the Damages (Scotland) Act 1976. The applicable provisions of that Act to which we were referred are as follows: [his Lordship quoted the terms of s 1 (1) and (3) and continued:] Subsection (4) provides for an award of a "loss of society award". Subsection (7) abolishes the right to claim damages by way of solatium in respect of the death of another person. It is not in dispute that the parents qualify as relatives within the meaning of Sched 1 to the Act. Section 3 provides: [his Lordship quoted its terms and continued:] The interpretation section, s 10 (1), includes the following: "'personal injuries' includes any disease or any impairment of a person's physical or mental condition".

The issue before the Lord Ordinary and before this court was as to the meaning of s 1 (1) of the Act, quoted above. The Lord Ordinary's opinion is now reported at 1992 SLT 1026. Some seven months after the Lord Ordinary dismissed the parents' claim based upon s 1 (1) Lord Morton of Shuna reached the opposite conclusion as to the meaning of the section and upheld the claim by the parents of a baby boy whose death resulted from negligent failures in treatment of the mother in the hours preceding the birth. The opinion of Lord Morton of Shuna in relation to the relevancy of the claim by those parents is now reported as *McWilliams v Lord Advocate*. The decision by Lord Morton of Shuna was arrived at after a proof before answer but the evidence adduced at the proof was concerned with questions of negligence and damages, not with the question of relevancy. Each Lord Ordinary has fully explained his reasons for the decision that he made on the question of relevancy and it is not necessary, at this stage, to do more than refer to those reasons as reported in the *Scots Law Times*.

In the present appeal the reclaimer has lodged five grounds of appeal. It is not necessary to narrate them in full length here though they do conveniently summarise the argument which was submitted to us by counsel for the reclaimer. It is to that argument that I now turn.

Counsel for the reclaimer submitted that the issue before this court was one purely as to the meaning of s 1 (1) of the Damages (Scotland) Act 1976. Before looking at the words of the section, however, it was instructive to consider the state of the law prior to the coming into force of the 1976 Act. At that time if a person was killed negligently then certain relatives had a right to claim damages against the wrongdoer. The question as to whether or not a particular claimant had a right fell to be determined by reference to the moment of time immediately before the death of the person who had been killed. Two questions had to be asked: (1) Was the deceased a person related so closely as to give the claimant a right to damages? (2) Would the deceased have had a right of action in respect of the sustaining of his injuries? Reference was made to the opinions of the judges in *Eisten v North British Railway Co*, where it was made plain that a derivative claim, one deriving from the death of a relative, could be sustained in limited circumstances only, but they included those obtaining when the relationship between the claimant and the deceased was that of parent and child or vice versa. A claim by a posthumous child, in respect of the death of a parent who had predeceased the birth of the child, had been upheld in *Connachan v Scottish Motor Traction Co*, in *Leadbetter v National Coal Board* and in *Riddell v James Longmuir & Sons Ltd*. These cases illustrated that at common law there was no difficulty in holding that the posthumous child could claim damages in respect of the death of a parent occurring before the child's birth. In none of these cases did the child's claim appear to rest upon the civil law doctrine contained in the brocard "nasciturus pro iam nato habetur quotiens de eius commodo agitur". In *Cohen v Shaw* Lord Cullen considered that there was no sound reason in principle why the nasciturus doctrine should not apply to a reparation claim by a posthumous child arising out of the death of his parent; the doctrine was not restricted to rights of succession. There was, however, no case at common law in which the material facts were the same as those in the present case. Reference was also made to *McNamara v Laird Line and Clan Line Steamers Ltd*, reported as an appendix to *McKay v Scottish Airways*. At 1948 SLT, p 408 Lord Constable affirmed the settled rule allowing actions for damages at the instance of a parent in respect of the death of a child while noting that the claim was of an exceptional kind and, as Lord Watson had observed [in *Clarke v Carfin Coal Co* at p 65], did not rest upon "any definite principle, capable of extension to other cases which may seem to be analogous, but constitutes an arbitrary exception from the general law which excludes all such actions, found in inveterate custom, and having no other *ratio* to support it".

In *McKay v Scottish Airways* itself Lord President Cooper, at p 407, acknowledged the peculiar right of certain relatives to recover solatium for the death of a person but described the search for a basis in principle as "a forlorn hope". Although the Lord President there stated that the right of the relatives was an independent, and not a derivative or representative, right, it was difficult to express philosophically the middle view between a derivative and a non-derivative

A claim. This type of claim was in fact a hybrid type of claim. What was important, however, was that the claim of the posthumous child did not rest upon any principle embodied in the nasciturus doctrine. When it came to the construction of a statute there was a clear principle of statutory interpretation to the effect that it was to be presumed that the legislature did not intend to make any change in the existing law unless it expressed its intention with irresistible clearness: see Maxwell, *Interpretation of Statutes* (12th ed), p 116.

B No explicit and relevant change in the applicable law could be detected in s 1 of the 1976 Act: see Walker on *Delict*, p 720. The only significant change was in the characterisation of the damages claim itself; the class of claimants remained the same: Walker, op cit, pp 721-722. There was no hint that parents who would have had a common law claim previously lost it as a result of the 1976 Act. Applying common sense, it would be absurd if a woman whose child was injured immediately before birth, and died after birth as a consequence of the injuries, could make no claim,

C while a woman whose child was injured immediately after birth and died immediately thereafter could claim; no policy reason for making such a distinction could be discovered. Yet that would be the result if the Lord Ordinary's view were correct and it was a result which one should not readily accept had been legislated by inference when the 1976 Act was passed.

One could approach a claim under the section by asking four questions: (1) Has a person died? (2) Did

D that person when he died have a right of action in respect of personal injuries? (3) Did those personal injuries cause his death? (4) Is the claimant a Sched 1 relative? Question 4 did not need further consideration in this case. It was submitted that it was clear that the pursuers' child who died died as a "person". It was plain, without relying on the nasciturus doctrine, that that child had had a right of action in respect of the impairment of his physical health. There was ample authority for the view that if a duty was owed in negli-

E gence then the breach of duty must be taken to have occurred when a person to whom the duty was owed was actually injured. This was plain from *Donoghue v Stevenson*, *Bourhill v Young*, 1941 SC at p 415 (affirmed 1942 SC (HL) 78), and *Watson v Fram Reinforced Concrete Co (Scotland) Ltd and Winget Ltd*, especially in the speech of Lord Reid. The latter case was concerned with the interpretation of a different statute but the observations founded upon were of general application.

F In August 1973, shortly after the Scottish Law Commission prepared a draft of a Bill which included the clause which ultimately became s 1 (1) of the 1976 Act (and which was laid before Parliament in 1973 in Scot Law Com no 31), there was also presented to Parliament a command paper, Cmnd 5371, entitled *Liability for Ante-natal Injury*, being Scot Law Com no 30. That paper discussed various matters relating to claims in respect of ante-natal injury and included the statement: "The loss of a child before, at, or after birth represents an injury to a parent; for example, a mother

might claim in respect of a miscarriage or still-birth wrongfully caused by another, while both parents may G sue in respect of the death of a child who has been born alive but has subsequently died from harm in the ante-natal stage" (para 7).

Reference was also made to various paragraphs discussing different aspects of problems relating to ante-natal injury. The conclusion, in para 19, was "that, although there is no express Scottish decision on the point, a right to reparation would, on existing principles, be accorded by Scots law to a child for harm H wrongfully occasioned to it while in its mother's womb, provided it was born alive".

Lord Morton of Shuna in *McWilliams v Lord Advocate* had correctly narrated the background to the passing of the 1976 Act. His opinion, to which full reference was made, was sound in all respects. Reference was made to the opinions both of Potts J and of the judges of the Court of Appeal in *B v Islington Health Authority* and *Burton v Islington Health Authority*; *de Martell v Merton and Sutton Health* I *Authority*.

Turning to the wording and correct construction of s 1 (1) itself, it would be helpful to make it clear what was not in issue. The reclaimer was not seeking to challenge the well established rule that legal personality commenced at birth and not before birth. Secondly, the reclaimer was not seeking to argue that the nasciturus doctrine could be prayed in aid except in the context of giving a right of action to a child J subsequently born alive: relatives could not rely directly on this civil law doctrine. However, in the present case, it was not necessary to do so. The real dispute in this appeal was whether or not the Lord Ordinary had properly understood the expression in the statute, "personal injuries sustained by him". The relative physical injuries were inflicted at a time when the child was in utero and was a foetus. But it was a mistake to look narrowly at individual words or phrases and to suggest, for example, that the words K "by him" coupled with the word "personal" before "injuries" somehow indicated that the relevant injuries could be inflicted only upon a person in life. The whole structure of the section needed to be looked at. There was no warrant for saying that Parliament intended to create a critical requirement by the use of the words "personal injuries sustained by him". The function of the first four lines or so of the section was to direct attention to the liability to pay damages to the now deceased child or conversely to the child's right L to claim damages from the responsible person. Then there followed the critical word "also" which was the key to the structure of the whole section. In essence, therefore, what the section meant was that, provided the deceased child had, before his death, been a person to whom the responsible person had a liability to pay damages, then the responsible person was also liable to pay damages to a qualifying relative. The civil law nasciturus doctrine was not needed either by the child or by the relatives. Even if the Lord Ordinary had been right to regard the words "personal injuries sus-

A tained by him" as embodying a critical requirement, it was submitted that the word "sustained" did not denote a once and only single event occurring at the moment when injuries were inflicted. Reference to the dictionary showed that the word "sustained" was broadly synonymous with such words as endure, bear, and experience. Accordingly it was perfectly appropriate to treat the personal injuries as being sustained from the time they were inflicted until the time when the injured person died. Even if the word "sustained" had to denote a once and for all, single event, that still

B posed no problem for the reclaimer because the relevant tempus inspiciendum has to be at or after birth. Personal injuries could not be sustained except by a person ("by him"). The child at birth was a person who sustained personal injuries. Nothing in the wording of the section directed attention to a foetus. If injury were inflicted to the foetus and the child sustained the immediate sequelae, that was good enough for the reclaimer because the child sustained the sequelae on birth. It might also be said that because

C the foetus became the person it was the child who had sustained the injuries but at an earlier stage. But there was no difficulty with the concept that the child became afflicted by the injuries, because it was the child who later died from them. The expression "personal injuries" included any disease or any impairment of a person's physical condition. This child sustained an impairment of his physical condition when he was born and it was the result of an act or omission by a person for whom the defenders and

D respondents were responsible. The reclaiming motion should be allowed.

Counsel for the respondent conceded that the child could have invoked the civil law nasciturus doctrine in an action raised by the child. There was, however, no room for invoking what had been described as the common law fiction, namely that the child was injured at the date of birth. Any injury took place when the child was a foetus. In relation to the application of the nasciturus doctrine reference was made to the speech

E of Lord Macmillan in *Elliot v Joicey* at p 70. Relatives could not found upon it. In all the quoted Scottish cases which had any bearing upon this matter the deceased was alive at the time when the delictual act happened and injured him. As to the nature of the claim it was not a derivative action but a separate independent action: see *Davidson v Sprengel*, 1909 1 SLT at p 222. *Connachan v SMT*, *Leadbetter v NCB* and *Riddell v Longmuir* all concerned posthumous children. It could be said that the nasciturus doctrine

F lay at the root of these cases; see also *Cohen v Shaw*. *Watson v Fram* was of no value to the reclaimer because it concerned a wholly different statute with different wording and the facts were very different.

The paragraphs founded upon by the reclaimer in the report of the Scottish Law Commission (no 30) were not vouched by any authority. The draft Bill was attached to a different report, report no 31. In these circumstances the principle of construction founded upon and referred to in Maxwell, op cit, had no bearing upon the present dispute. Whatever the

G Scottish Law Commission might have thought, there was no clear and established rule of law to which the principle of statutory construction referred to could apply. What the report did serve to illustrate was that there were different approaches in various different countries with different legal traditions. These different approaches, contained in the appendix to Scot Law Com report no 30, part 2, were referred to in some detail.

As to the statutory construction, the approach of the Lord Ordinary in the present case was correct. If the

H reclaimers' view was correct then many of the words in s 1 (1) were superfluous. In particular, the words "in consequence of personal injuries sustained by him" were unnecessary, and the words "the injured" preceding "person" should be replaced by the word "that". It was a well known rule of statutory construction that each phrase had to be given its appropriate content. It was not to be assumed that Parliament used words and phrases unnecessarily. It was true that a liability to pay damages to the injured

I person was a prerequisite of a claim by a relative but it was not the only prerequisite. It may not have been the express purpose of Parliament to exclude claims by a relative in respect of the death of a child whose death resulted from injuries sustained before birth; but the effect of the section was to exclude any such claim because the whole wording of the phrase which the reclaimers' submission ignored, "in consequence of personal injuries sustained by him", made it plain that the injuries had to be sustained by a person in life.

J It followed that unless it could be said that the injuries were sustained by a person who was in life the statutory condition was not met. On a proper analysis of the word "sustained" it must be accepted that the injuries were sustained at a point in time when they were inflicted. In this case they were not and there could not be personal injuries inflicted upon "him" because when they were inflicted there was no person and no "him". The child did not die of personal injuries which he, the child, had sustained. Lord

K Morton of Shuna's analysis of the background to the 1976 Act was flawed by the fact that the Bill was contained in and the Act was derived directly from the report laid before Parliament in July 1973 (no 31) which contained no mention of ante-natal injuries. If, as indicated in *Pepper v Hart*, it was permissible in certain circumstances (specified in the speech of Lord Browne-Wilkinson) to consider statements in Parliament — though that seemed inappropriate in this case — there was nothing in the ministerial or other state-

L ments to indicate that Parliament had any intention to legislate on the matter of ante-natal injuries at all. Lord Morton of Shuna had been wrong to draw a parallel with the case of *McCluskey v HM Advocate* because that case was concerned with a wholly different statute and the reasoning there was not appropriate to the present case. The recent English cases of *Burton v Islington* and *de Martell* merely showed that different fictions were employed to deal with the difficult case of the posthumous child. But this whole jurisprudence had developed without any reference at all to the interests of third parties such as the present reclaimers. The Lord Ordinary's opinion in the present case was to be preferred. The act of the alleged wrongdoer was completed and the injury was sustained before there was any person. The reclaiming motion should be refused.

In my opinion, the only issue which it is necessary to decide is as to the meaning and application of s 1 (1) of the Damages (Scotland) Act 1976. What that section does is to make a wrongdoer ("the responsible person") liable to pay damages to a "relative" (as defined in the Schedule) of a person who has died. The death of that person must have been in consequence of personal injuries sustained by that person as a result of an act or omission giving rise to liability (in the responsible person) to pay damages to the injured person or his executor. As the act or omission must be one giving rise to liability to pay damages, there can be no liability until both damnum and injuria concur. There can be no liability to pay damages until there is a person in respect of whose loss the claim to damages arises. An unborn person, a foetus, is not a person in the eyes of the law — at least in relation to the law of civil remedies — and there can be no liability to pay damages to a foetus, even although the foetus has sustained injuries resulting from a negligent act or omission constituting a breach of duty owed.

There is no difficulty whatsoever in Scots law in holding that doctors engaged in the delivery of a foetus owe a duty of care to avoid injury to that foetus: that is trite. But once the foetus ceases on birth to be a foetus and becomes a person there is a concurrence of injuria and damnum and the newly born child has a right to sue the person whose breach of duty has resulted in the child's loss. The coming into existence of that right to sue does not depend upon the application of any fiction. It depends upon the neighbourhood doctrine of *Donoghue v Stevenson*. The doctors engaged in the medical work of assisting in the delivery of a child can obviously foresee that a failure to exercise due care and skill by them may result in injuries to the foetus, being injuries which will cause the child to suffer loss: if the loss to the living child is the foreseeable, direct and probable consequence of the failure to exercise due care and skill at an earlier stage, there is a breach of duty owed, in the law of negligence, to the child and that breach occurs when the child is born. If the injuries with which he is born are injuries to his organs or skeleton or tissues then they are properly and sensibly described as "personal injuries" even although when they were inflicted he did not enjoy legal personality; they are injuries to his person although not to his legal persona. They are to him an impairment of his physical condition. To suppose that only one who enjoys legal personality can sustain "personal injuries" is to attach an artificial meaning to the adjective "personal" in s 1 (1). Legal personality is a construct of the law and merely relates to a basket of rights and responsibilities recognised by the law as effeiring to certain specified creatures, including man-made creatures: there are many examples in history of adult, sentient human beings being denied human status and legal personality and of limited liability companies and even of non-human animals being accorded rights and responsibilities normally appropriate only to human beings.

In the circumstances, I see no reason to restrict "personal" in the phrase "personal injuries" so that it means injuries suffered by one on whom the law has conferred legal personality for certain purposes. In my view, it is equally clear that the whole phrase "personal injuries sustained by him" in this context is perfectly apt to include injuries inflicted to the person of a child immediately before his birth and continuing to have their effects on him by impairing his physical condition at and after the time of his birth. Whether or not the phrase would be apt to cover some form of trauma to a foetus in the early days of pregnancy it is not necessary to decide; different legal systems for different purposes have to decide such issues relating to the legal status and rights of a foetus in their context as best they can when they arise: cf *Roe v Wade*. I am not persuaded that the use of the personal pronoun "him" in the phrase "sustained by him" was intended by Parliament to have the bizarre result that there was no one to injure or to sustain injuries in the few days before the child was born. It is perfectly common in ordinary speech to refer to the child in utero as "he", "she", "him" or "her" and I do not feel driven by the use of such ordinary parlance in this section to the view which the Lord Ordinary accepted, that "Parliament envisaged a person sustaining injuries", meaning a person enjoying legal personality. It was this child who sustained injuries to his person and who died in consequence of personal injuries sustained by him. That appears to me to be enough to require me to hold that the responsible person became liable, on the child's birth, to pay damages to him. There being no dispute that the child was a person who died in consequence of the injuries inflicted on him immediately before his birth, it follows, in my opinion, that the responsible person is also liable to pay damages to the pursuers and reclaimers under s 1 (1). It will thus be seen that I prefer the approach of the reclaimer which I have endeavoured to summarise at an earlier stage and that I have simply reformulated the four question test which was promulgated in the reclaimers' submissions.

In relation to the submissions about the background to the passing of the Act I do not find it necessary or helpful to look in any detail at this background. Although the respondents referred us to *Pepper (Inspector of Taxes) v Hart* and to the speeches recorded in the *Official Report* of ministers in the respective Houses of Parliament, speaking in support of the motion for second reading of the relevant Bill, it was not suggested that any real guidance could be obtained from this source. All that was clear was that there was nothing specific said about what cl 1 (1) (later enacted as s 1 (1)) was intended to effect in relation to a child injured before birth and dying from his injuries after birth. Lord Morton of Shuna deals fairly fully with the status of the Scottish Law Commission documents in Parliament prior to the introduction of the 1976 Act. I have no reason to disagree with his narration of this matter but, given that the composition of Parliament was radically changed between 1973 and 1976, and having regard to the fact that the Scottish Law Commission document incorporating the Bill which became the Act was presented to Parliament before the document dealing with liability for ante-natal injury, I doubt if it is realistic and helpful to look to these documents as defining clearly a mischief which s 1 (1) of the Act was designed to remedy in relation to ante-natal injuries.

As to the view expressed by the Scottish Law Commission, to the effect that as at the date of the documents (1973) certain relatives of a child who was injured ante-natally and then died, could at common law have sued for compensation for his death without reliance on the nasciturus fiction, I agree with Lord Caplan and I do not find it necessary to repeat his discussion of *B v Islington Health Authority* and *de Martell v Merton and Sutton Health Authority* and *Watson v Fram*; I agree with it fully.

I noted earlier the respondents' submission that Parliament must not be assumed to have used words and phrases unnecessarily and that the subsection could have been economically worded. It is quite common, however, to find that a provision in an Act of Parliament, once it has been subjected to very close analysis in the light of a particular set of facts, could have been worded differently. Our duty is to look at the provision as a whole and to try to give the words used their ordinary meaning if that is possible. That is, I believe, what I have sought to do. In my opinion the Lord Ordinary has taken too narrow and restricted a view of the meaning and effect of the section and in particular of the one phrase "personal injuries sustained by him".

For these reasons I disagree with the conclusion which the Lord Ordinary has reached. I move your Lordships to sustain the reclaiming motion and to recall the interlocutor of 21 November 1991 sustaining the second plea in law for the defenders and dismissing the action in relation to the first and second conclusions. The appropriate course is to repel that plea in law and to remit the cause to the Lord Ordinary for further procedure.

LORD CAPLAN.—Your Lordship in the chair has fully set out the background to this reclaiming motion and also the respective arguments of the parties so that I need not repeat them.

It is I think accepted that the outcome of this reclaiming motion will depend on the construction to be placed upon s 1 (1) of the Damages (Scotland) Act 1976. For my own part I find it helpful in the first instance when construing the relevant statutory provision to look at it in its entirety and in context rather than place too much emphasis on single words or phrases. The object of the subsection is to secure that when a person dies from injuries caused by delict, and he or his executor would have had a right to claim damages for these injuries, then certain categories of relative should also have a right to claim compensation in respect of the death. Where the subsection applies a right to claim for loss of society is conferred upon close relatives.

A parent who loses a young infant will experience the same sense of loss irrespective of whether the injuries causing death originated shortly before birth or shortly after birth. It is therefore difficult to know what policy objective could have prompted the legislature to confine entitlement to claim compensation to post-natal injuries in a case where the fatality has been caused by the negligence of a third party.

In terms of the subsection the rights of the defined categories of relative only arise where a third party is liable to pay damages to the injured person or his executor. If that liability arises then the person liable to pay damages is also liable to compensate the eligible relatives of the deceased. That consequential liability is quite categorically stated. We must therefore look at the first part of the subsection to discover what particular right of action which would have been available to the injured party or his executor will create a right of action in relatives. The party who originally brought about the fatal injuries to the deceased will only be under liability to pay damages if injuria and damnum co-exist. The first few words of the subsection define the particular damnum which the injured party must suffer before the statutory provision will operate. The critical element of the loss is that the injured party must have died and that death must be in consequence of "personal injuries". Thus the subsection begins by dealing with death and the cause of death so that the emphasis will fall naturally at the time of death and not at some earlier time when injury was first suffered. The respondents argued that the word "personal" in the expression "personal injuries" connotes that the statute is seeking to confine the prerequisite loss to death by injuries inflicted on a living person. It was certainly accepted by the reclaimer that under our law a child in utero does not have the legal status of being a person. It is only upon the event of birth that the foetus becomes a person.

Reading the first few words of the subsection without undue strain, it is not difficult to conclude that if a person dies from injuries (and of course only a living person can die) then the injuries which caused death must essentially be personal injuries. Once the requisite loss is established one looks for the injuria which must underlie the right of action of the deceased or his executor. Thus we come to the phrase "sustained by him as a result of an act or omission of another person". On the face of it the essential question here is "how were the injuries of the deceased caused?", and it would be odd if this question included "at what point of time in the development of his person were they caused?" Thus the link between damnum and injuria is essentially posed by the question: "How were the loss-causing injuries acquired?" In my view "sustained" means little more than "acquired". However because of the damaging and unpleasant quality of injuries, the word "sustained", with its connotation of "injured" or "borne" or "experienced", might be a more apt word than "acquired".

The defenders for their part in support of the view of the Lord Ordinary urged us to read the phrase "sustained by him" as signifying "at the time the harmful injuries were inflicted on a person". "Person" of course in that context would mean a living person. On this construction the legislature were deliberately excluding a right to compensation unless the fatal injuries originated at a point when the deceased was in life. Assuming that it were the intention of the subsection to give effect to such an exclusion and to make a specific provision to exclude rights flowing from harm to an unborn foetus, the matter is expressed in a singularly oblique way. The subsection refers to claims by relatives for death at all ages of injured persons, and a claim arising from the death of a person suffering from ante-natal injuries must be a relatively rare contingency. One may have expected that such a particular proviso would have merited a separate subsection rather than be worked into a general provision. Moreover the 1976 Act was presented to Parliament in consequence of the command paper of the Scottish Law Commission no 31 (*Report on the Law relating to Damages for Injuries causing Death*) and was based on the draft Bill attached to that paper. Insofar as we were referred to the terms of the command paper by the respondents, we were not referred to any proposal to change or restate the law in relation to ante-natal damage.

Senior counsel for the respondents made the point that it is an accepted canon of statutory construction that expressions used must be assumed to have a content. He argued therefore that the phrase "personal injuries sustained by him" can only be given content if it relates to the situation where injuries were sustained by a person in life. It was suggested that if the intention was to include death in consequence of all injuries at whatever stage of development these had been inflicted then the statutory provision could have better read "when a person dies as a result of an act or omission" etc. In any event it was said that the provisions covering ante-natal injury did have a logical basis. The intention was to preserve the pre-existing state of the law since at common law a relative had no claim in respect of a child who had suffered injury before birth. I do not agree that s 1 (1) is merely continuing this view of the common law in relation to ante-natal injuries and I shall develop that point later. However I also do not agree that the reference to "personal injuries sustained by him" has no content unless it is given the meaning urged upon us by the respondents. In relation to direct cause of death, the phrase "dies in consequence of personal injuries" is more specific than "dies as a result of an act or omission by another person".

Senior counsel for the respondents sought to make a distinction between the injuries initially inflicted and their sequelae. The abbreviated formulation suggested by the respondents' senior counsel may well have left a question as to whether the statutory provision only covered the immediate consequences of the delict or also extended to death caused by the sequelae. Looking to the definition of "personal injuries" given in the interpretation section (s 10) of the 1976 Act, we find that "personal injuries" includes any disease or any impairment of a person's physical or mental condition. This definition includes consequences which would often be the sequelae to the original injury to the deceased. "Impairment" is usually measured and assessed after the impact of the initial injury. Equally, in relation say to occupational disease, the body, for example, is assailed by noxious substances and then the disease develops subsequently. Thus in my view the definition in s 10 supports the conclusion that in the present case the child died of "personal injuries", for clearly at the time of its death its physical condition was impaired. On one view of course it is difficult to imagine a person dying of injuries which are not "personal" injuries. The phrase "personal injuries", however, is commonly encountered as relating to a situation where injuries have been suffered by a person. It is often used to differentiate injuries to the person from patrimonial loss. For example the phrase occurs in the Law Reform (Personal Injuries) Act 1948. Section 3 of that Act sets out that the expression "personal injury" includes any disease and any impairment of a person's physical or mental condition, and the expression "injured" shall be construed accordingly. Other examples could be given of the statutory use of the expression "personal injuries" coupled with a definition equivalent to that I have already alluded to. These statutes do not refer to situations where ante-natal injuries could be an issue. However to illustrate in specific terms the point I am making, one need look no further than the very Act we are considering. In s 9 of the 1976 Act the section is declared to apply to "any action for damages in respect of personal injuries sustained by the pursuer". The section thereafter proceeds to deal with matters that have no reference to claims by relatives but instead relate to matters affecting the situation where the injured person has a direct claim. It was accepted by the respondents that an injured foetus who survives birth would have a right of action. Thus in s 9 it is difficult to see what justification there could possibly be for using the phrase "personal injuries sustained by the pursuer" for the purpose of limiting the section to post-natal injuries exclusively.

Given that I have concluded that the meaning of s 1 (1) is unambiguous, there may be no need to proceed further, but we were given a comprehensive argument about the relationship between the subsection and the pre-existing law so that it would be appropriate that I consider this in case my interpretation of the section is otherwise invalid. In effect the reclaimer contended that there is what is effectively a presumption against construing a statute so as to innovate on the preceding common law unless it is perfectly clear from the terms of the statute that change in the pre-existing law is intended. Counsel for the reclaimer argued that at common law claims by relatives, insofar as allowed by the law, would have covered claims in respect of a child who had died from the effects of ante-natal injury. Counsel for the respondents contested this. They argued that under the common law a child who

A had suffered ante-natal injuries could only sue by enlisting the benefit of the civil law fiction to the effect that in matters affecting its interests the unborn child in utero should be deemed to be born. It was contended that this fiction is not available for the benefit of a third party, and I think that in cases where it were necessary to apply the fiction the reclaimer would accept that position. The respondents in these circumstances argued that the legislators adopted the wording of s 1 (1) with a view to taking account of what the respondents perceive to have been the pre-existing law and that it is for this reason that claims by relatives for the death of a child injured ante-natally have been specifically excluded.

B

In this matter I favour the view of the reclaimer. Thus in my opinion before the 1976 Act certain relatives of a child who was injured ante-natally and then died could at common law have sued for compensation for his death, and that without reliance upon the said civil law fiction. As I understand the opinion of the Lord Ordinary, he took the opposite view and this C may have influenced his decision to construe s 1 (1) as he did. More significant however may be the fact that neither the Lord Ordinary's opinion nor indeed the report of his decision in Scots Law Times indicate that the Lord Ordinary was referred to the highly pertinent case of B v Islington Health Authority. In March 1992 the judgment of Potts J in the last mentioned case, and of Phillips J in an equivalent case (de Martell v Merton and Sutton Health Authority), came before the Court of Appeal in England and indeed the majority of that D court went out of their way to indicate that they gave their express approval to these judgments. Of course the Court of Appeal decision was not available when the Lord Ordinary heard the present case. The cases in question are now reported sub nom Burton v Islington Health Authority; de Martell v Merton and Sutton Health Authority. Each of the two judges of first instance and Dillon LJ in the Court of Appeal gave a very extensive analysis of English law in relation to a child who suffers ante-natal injury, and certainly material is set out in these cases which the Lord E Ordinary would have required to consider carefully had the cases been available to him. I may say that for my own part, having given careful consideration to Burton v Islington Health Authority (and the associated case of de Martell), I am in full agreement with most of the views expressed by the judges involved. Nor do I see any reason for supposing that the points made by these judges would not be equally applicable to Scotland. It is probably now trite law that before a right of action to sue for reparation arises in Scotland it is F not necessary that the act of negligence and infliction of harm should be contemporaneous. Indeed Donoghue v Stevenson sets this beyond dispute. Nor is it necessary that the person to whom a duty to take care is owed should be identifiable at the time when such care is neglected, or even for that matter alive at such time. A duty is owed to take care not to cause injury to any member of a class of person who might foreseeably be harmed by an act of negligence. As was said by Gillard J in the Australian case Watt v Rama at p 373: "It would appear from Donoghue v Stevenson and Australian Knitting Mills Ltd v Grant [1936] AC 85, that

it would be immaterial whether at the time of fault the victim was in existence or not, so long as the victim G was a member of a class which might reasonably and probably be affected by the act of carelessness."

Watt v Rama was a decision of the Supreme Court of Victoria and it was followed by the Court of Appeal in Burton. Phillips J quoted the said words of Gillard J with apparent approval and as I have indicated the majority of the Court of Appeal specifically accepted his reasoning. Furthermore in his judgment Dillon LJ (at p 658) quoted with approval from a case at first instance before the High Court of Ontario, namely H Duval v Seguin at p 433. The action arose out of ante-natal injuries in consequence of a motor accident to a child later born and named Ann. Fraser J said: "Ann's mother was plainly one of a class within the area of foreseeable risk and one to whom the defendants therefore owed a duty. Was Ann any the less so? I think not. Procreation is normal and necessary for the preservation of the race. If a driver drives on a highway without due care for other users it is foreseeable that some of the other users of the highway will be preg- I nant women and that a child en ventre sa mère may be injured. Such a child therefore falls well within the area of potential danger which the driver is required to foresee and take reasonable care to avoid."

In my own opinion the validity of these remarks is glaringly obvious. In the present case, given that the deceased infant is alleged to have been damaged in the course of a forceps delivery shortly before birth, it is scarcely contestable that the prospect that a careless use of the forceps could cause serious damage to the J emergent child is an obviously foreseeable danger. Accordingly the doctor in charge of the delivery had a duty to take reasonable care not to do anything which might cause harm to the child about to be born. However the duty is not breached, nor does a right of action arise, at the point when the careless act is committed (assuming there were such an act). The duty which rests upon a person charged with taking care is not the academic responsibility of not being negligent but rather the duty not to cause harm by negligence. K The delict is only committed when the initial negligent act actually causes harm. That is to say the concurrence of injuria and damnum is required. Thus as Lord Reid said in Watson v Fram Reinforced Concrete Co (Scotland) Ltd and Winget Ltd, 1960 SLT at p 327: "The ground of any action based on negligence is a concurrence of breach of duty and damage, and I cannot see how there can be that concurrence unless the duty still exists and is breached when the damage occurs." As Phillips J puts it in de Martell at p 648: "The duty in the law of negligence is not a duty to L exercise reasonable care to avoid risk of causing injury. It is a duty not to cause injury by want of reasonable care."

On the basis of the foregoing reasoning the point when actionable injury is sustained is not the point of time when carelessness is committed, nor even the point in time when that carelessness may have given rise to a physical affront, but rather the point of time when it can first be said that the person affected has suffered (or "sustained" for that matter) material harm because of the preceding negligence. Thus, returning again to *Burton* at p 657, Dillon LJ quotes (again with approval) from the leading judgment of Winneke CJ and Pape J at pp 360-361 of the report in *Watt v Rama*. The said judges stated: "On the facts which for present purposes must be assumed, the child was born with injuries caused by the act or neglect of the defendant in the driving of his car. But as the child could not in the very nature of things acquire rights co-relative to a duty until it became by birth a living person, and as it was not until then that it could sustain injuries as a living person, it was, we think, at that stage that the duty arising out of the relationship was attached to the defendant."

It has to be noticed that what was said was that in a situation where the foetus had suffered ante-natal injuries in a car accident, injuries to a living person were not "sustained" until the point of birth.

In my view the rule of law relating to a child in utero to the effect that it is not a living being (which on one view itself is a fiction) cannot apply in both directions. If the foetus is not a living being then it is mere organic matter — a fuse or conduit which if affected by the negligence of a defender can lead (because it is a feature in the chain of causation) to the emergence of personal injuries when the child is born. In *de Martell* at p 650 Phillips J aptly refers to comments of Holmes J in *Dietrich v Northampton*. Holmes J stated at p 16 of the report: "that, on general principles, an injury transmitted from the actor to a person through his own organic substance, or through his mother, before he became a person, stands on the same footing as an injury transmitted to an existing person through other intervening substances outside him".

The implication of the point I have been making is that even if I am wrong in attributing to "sustained", as the word is used in s 1 (1), a meaning such as "borne" or "experienced", then personal injuries were not "sustained" until the infant was born. Certainly damage was done at an earlier stage to the foetus but it is only at birth that for the first time one could say "here is a living being who has sustained personal injuries". As Phillips J puts it (at p 650 of *de Martell*): "In law and in logic no damage can have been caused to the plaintiff before the plaintiff existed. The damage was suffered by the plaintiff at the moment that, in law, the plaintiff achieved personality and inherited the damaged body for which the health authority (on the assumed facts) was responsible."

The defenders attack the applicability to Scotland of *de Martell* and *Burton*. These cases were both concerned with ante-natal injuries to a child suffered before the passage of the Congenital Disabilities (Civil Liability) Act 1976. Thus the court was concerned with determining the relevant English common law as it existed before the 1976 statute. It appears to me that the reasoning I have set out above, although supported by English and foreign authority, is based on principles which are also applicable to Scots law. The respondents' senior counsel contended that it was not necessary for the court to erect an elaborate argument such as (it is said) happened in *Burton* because in Scot-

land the matter should be determined by the applicability of the civil law fiction. I see no need for fiction at all in relation to the right of a deceased child to raise an action based on what happened to it before birth. The civil law fiction is clearly necessary for the resolution of certain categories of case. I do not think it can be disputed that it is needed to create a right of succession in relation to a posthumous child. It may also be needed in a reparation context in a case such as *Cohen v Shaw* because it is certainly arguable that without the fiction the posthumous child was not a "relative" at the time of the father's death. However in the present case it seems to me that the child would have had a perfectly clear right to sue on the basis of established common law principles. It should be noted that in England the common law recognises a principle equivalent to our civil law fiction. This point is brought out in the judgment of Dillon LJ in *Burton* at pp 655 and 656. His Lordship then states: "For my part, I think it would be open to the English courts to apply the civil law maxim directly to the situations we have in these two appeals, and treat the two plaintiffs as lives in being at the times of the events which injured them as they were later born alive, but it is not necessary to do so".

I would agree with that view in relation to the suggested need to apply the civil law fiction in an equivalent situation in Scotland. I consider that parents who otherwise qualify would have had a right of action for damages prior to 1976 in respect of a child who had died because of ante-natal damage. That is because the child itself would have had a right of action independent of the limiting features of the civil law fiction. That being so, I am confirmed in my view that it was not the intention of the legislature to innovate upon the existing law in respect of the relevant matter. Indeed innovation within the context of the 1976 Act would have been surprising and would have required clear statement.

For the reasons which I have set out I find myself in disagreement with the Lord Ordinary's opinion and I would sustain the reclaiming motion. The consequence would be that the Lord Ordinary's dismissal of the action should be recalled and the case remitted to him for further procedure.

LORD WYLIE. —I have had the opportunity to read the comprehensive opinion of your Lordship in the chair. I agree with it and there is nothing which I feel I could usefully add.

For the reasons fully set out by your Lordship I would accordingly sustain the reclaiming motion and recall the interlocutor of 21 November 1991.

Counsel for Pursuers and Reclaimers, G N H Emslie, QC, A Smith; Solicitors, Balfour & Manson, Nightingale & Bell — Counsel for Defenders and Respondents, A C Hamilton, QC, D I Mackay; Solicitor, J I McCubbin.

D A K

George Thompson Services Ltd v Moore

OUTER HOUSE

LORD WEIR

26 NOVEMBER 1991

Heritable property — Transfer — Disposition — Rectification — Disposition giving effect to missives — Averment of common intention that larger area would be transferred — Relevancy — Law Reform (Miscellaneous Provisions) (Scotland) Act 1985 (c 73), s 8 (1) and (2).

Writ — Rectification — Disposition — Disposition giving effect to missives — Averment of common intention that larger area would be transferred — Relevancy — Law Reform (Miscellaneous Provisions) (Scotland) Act 1985 (c 73), s 8 (1) and (2).

The Law Reform (Miscellaneous Provisions) (Scotland) Act 1985 provides in s 8 for the rectification of the terms of a document which has failed accurately to record the terms of an agreement reached between the parties to the document.

The purchasers of land sought rectification under s 8 of an allegedly defectively expressed conveyance in 1987 of an estate on the Isle of Arran. In terms of the missives, the subjects to be conveyed were said to be Dippin Estate, as described in certain named dispositions, under certain exceptions described by reference to other deeds. The purchasers claimed that it had been the common intention of the parties that a further area of land not mentioned in the missives nor conveyed was also to be transferred to them. The purchasers did not aver that the alleged common intention related to any agreement antecedent to the missives. They founded (1) on a plan which showed the disputed area as part of subjects advertised for sale, and (2) on their occupation of the whole subjects from September 1987. The purchasers contended that it was competent under the statute to look back to a stage before the missives had been concluded in order to ascertain the parties' common intention. There were no averments suggesting that the emergence of the alleged common intention arose in the course of actual negotiations leading up to the agreement. Further, it was not argued that there was any ambiguity in the terms of the missives or subsequent disposition. The purchasers sought a proof of their averments.

Held, that there being no averments either of ambiguity in the missives or of the existence of facts and circumstances demonstrating a verbal agreement between the parties establishing their common intention, the petition was irrelevant as there was no defect in any agreement to correct (pp 636L-637B); and petition *dismissed*.

Shaw v William Grant (Minerals) Ltd, 1989 SLT 121, *referred to.*

Petition for an order under s 8 (1) of the Law Reform (Miscellaneous Provisions) (Scotland) Act 1985

George Thompson Services Ltd presented a petition under s 8 (1) of the Law Reform (Miscellaneous Provisions) (Scotland) Act 1985 seeking rectification of a disposition of an estate on the Isle of Arran. Royston Moore and Mrs Carol Jean Moore, the grantors of the petitioners' title, appeared as respondents.

The petition came on procedure roll before the Lord Ordinary (Weir).

Statutory provisions

The Law Reform (Miscellaneous Provisions) (Scotland) Act 1985 provides:

"*Rectification of defectively expressed documents*

"8.—(1) Subject to section 9 of this Act, where the court is satisfied, on an application made to it, that — (a) a document intended to express or give effect to an agreement fails to express accurately the common intention of the parties to the agreement at the date when it was made; . . . it may order the document to be rectified in any manner that it may specify in order to give effect to that intention.

"(2) For the purposes of subsection (1) above, the court shall be entitled to have regard to all relevant evidence, whether written or oral."

Cases referred to

Anderson v Lambie, 1954 SLT 73; 1954 SC (HL) 43.
Houldsworth v Gordon Cumming, 1909 2 SLT 40; 1910 SC (HL) 49.
Hudson v Hudson's Trustees, 1978 SLT 88; (sub nom *Hudson v St John*) 1977 SC 255.
Shaw v William Grant (Minerals) Ltd, 1989 SLT 121.

On 26 November 1991 his Lordship *dismissed* the petition.

LORD WEIR.—The respondents were formerly owners of the Dippin Estate which is situated in the south eastern corner of the Isle of Arran. The general extent of the estate is shown on a plan, no 16 of process. When the estate was offered for sale it consisted of a house, Dippin Lodge, and a number of farm holdings which are shown as bordered in different colours on the plan. It is unnecessary to go into detail as to the individual components, except to describe a particular area of just under six acres in extent which is the subject of the dispute in these proceedings. This land is bordered in red and lies to the south west of a larger area, also bordered in red, which lies generally to the west or north west of the road (A841) from Whiting Bay to Lagg. The disputed land is known, at least for the purposes of this case, as Dippin Kennels. This piece of land is itself bisected by the road and there is an enclave on the northerly section consisting of a house and ground known as Dippin Kennels House. This property was sold by the respondents in 1982.

The petitioners maintain that when the estate was conveyed to them in 1987 it was the common intention of the parties to the transaction that the land at Dippin Kennels still in the respondents' ownership was to be conveyed along with and as part of the rest of the estate. However the titles of the subjects conveyed do not include Dippin Kennels and this petition has been presented under s 8 (1) (a) of the Law Reform (Miscellaneous Provisions) (Scotland) Act 1985 for rectification of the allegedly defectively expressed conveyance. The respondents submitted that in the circumstances of this case it was not open to the court to order rectification of the Dippin Estate conveyance and in doing so have raised a question as to the scope of the operation of the statutory provision.

The exposure of Dippin Estate for sale was initiated by the publication of particulars of sale prepared by Messrs Strutt & Parker and the plan to which I have referred was annexed to these particulars. The particulars purported to give only a general outline and the introduction states: "The introduction and the particulars are intended to give a fair and substantially correct overall description for the guidance of intending purchasers and do not constitute, nor constitute part of an offer or contract."

Missives of sale were concluded between a Mr and Mrs Thompson and the respondents by letters dated 3, 6, 8 and 9 July 1987 passing between their respective agents. One of the conditions which formed part of the concluded missives was contained in the letter of 6 July by the respondents' solicitors which stated: "26. For the sake of clarification the Schedule of Particulars prepared by Strutt & Parker does not form part of the bargain to follow hereon."

In terms of the missives the subjects to be conveyed were the Dippin Estate as described in certain named dispositions (under exception of five areas of ground which were described by reference to other deeds). The letter of 6 July also stated: "The titles are sent here together with the Quick Copies of the excepted subjects and your clients should be held to have satisfied themselves with regard to the true measurements of the subjects to be conveyed to them." In due course the subjects of sale referred to in the missives were disponed as respects Dippin Lodge to Mr and Mrs Thompson, and as respects the Dippin Estate to the petitioners (a company under the control of the Thompsons). What was not mentioned in the missives nor conveyed was the disputed land, Dippin Kennels, which was held by the respondents on a separate title.

In art 9 of the condescendence, it is averred that Mr and Mrs Thompson and the respondents always intended the Dippin Estate conveyance to transfer and convey to the petitioners the Dippin Kennel subjects and there is an averment in the following terms: "The Dippin Estate conveyance by omitting from its terms the Dippin Kennel subjects . . . failed to reflect accurately the common intention of the said Anthony George William Thompson and Mrs Josette Raymon Giselle Thompson, the petitioners, and respondents in respect of the Dippin Estate conveyance at the date of the said missives."

In other words the petitioners are claiming that the missives and thereafter the disposition failed to express the common intention of the parties. What is important to observe is that the petitioners do not aver that the alleged common intention related to any agreement antecedent to the missives and it is in fact the case that the dispositions to the petitioners conveyed precisely what was specified in the missives.

The petitioners seek proof of certain averments which it is claimed are apt to infer the existence of a prior common intention. They found on the plan which showed the Dippin Kennels as forming part of the subjects advertised for sale. They aver that the petitioners have occupied and farmed these subjects since September 1987. The respondents have left Arran and have made no attempt to exercise rights of ownership over the disputed subjects. It is claimed that the first named respondent showed the Thompsons over the whole estate including these subjects prior to missives being concluded and certain further averments are made which seek to demonstrate actions and statements consistent with the respondents believing that they no longer owned the land.

The central issue in the case is whether statutory rectification can take place not to correct a defect in the written expression of an agreement which had already been reached, but to reflect the alleged common intention of the parties before they had reached any agreement regarding the sale of the land. It is not doubted that if the missives in the transaction had expressly included the Dippin Kennel subjects but the subsequent disposition had not, rectification under the statute would have been in order. The contention of counsel for the petitioners was that it was competent to look back to a stage before the missives were concluded in order to ascertain the common intention of the parties. If that common intention was for the Kennels to be included in any agreement which might later be reached about the sale of the estate, then it would be proper to rectify the defect in the missives (and hence the disposition) because of the failure to express that intention.

It is pertinent to make two further observations before considering the question of law. First, there are no averments to the effect that the emergence of the alleged common intention arose in the course of actual negotiations leading up to an agreement. Secondly, it was not argued that there was any ambiguity in the terms of the missives or the subsequent disposition.

Section 8 of the Law Reform (Miscellaneous Provisions) (Scotland) Act 1985 is preceded by the headnote, and the relevant parts of the section for the purposes of this opinion are in the following terms: [his Lordship quoted the terms of s 8 set out supra and continued:]

Counsel for the petitioners submitted that there must be a document to be rectified. In this instance, the disposition was the document because it echoed precisely the terms of the missives which in turn failed to express the common intention of the parties at the date when the agreement embodied in the missives was made. A common intention meant that the parties

A intended the same thing and it was to this question that inquiry under s 8 (1) had to be directed. Such inquiry was to be directed towards establishing what was the common intention, even although no agreement had been reached when such an intention could be said to have emerged. If after inquiry it transpired that the agreement subsequently entered into defectively expressed that common intention then the court could order rectification of the document. The averments which had been made were sufficient, if proved, to disclose a common intention which was at variance

B with the missives and the disposition.

Counsel for the respondents contended that rectification under s 8 (1) (a) was permissible only where an antecedent agreement was not accurately reflected in the resulting document. He submitted that it was essential for the petitioners to aver the existence of such an agreement, whether written or verbal, before an investigation could be made into what was the common intention of the parties at that time. In the present case the petitioners had been unable to aver

C any antecedent or informal agreement between the parties that the land should be sold and what may have been in minds of the parties at that stage was irrelevant. He submitted that the disposition which the petitioners sought to rectify accurately reflected, as was conceded, the terms of the missives and the missives, being unambiguous, were the unassailable measure of the parties' respective contractual rights and obligations.

D Questions may arise from time to time as to what subjects have actually been conveyed on a feu grant or disposition in implement of a contract of sale of land and where such question arises it has to be decided by consideration of the terms of the contract. This general rule was expressed in this way by Lord Kinnear in *Houldsworth v Gordon Cumming*, 1910 SC (HL) at p 55: "It is manifest, therefore, that if a question arises as to the description to be inserted in a disposition, the first thing to be settled is what is the

E exact subject sold; and that is to be determined not by the existing titles, but by the contract of sale, interpreted, as every document whatsoever must, more or less, be interpreted, by reference to the surrounding circumstances."

An instance of the working of this principle is to be found in the leading case of *Anderson v Lambie*. In that case, the proprietor of an estate which consisted mainly of a farm sold the subjects. The question arose as to the extent of the subjects sold. The disposition,

F as the result of an error by the sellers' solicitors, had the effect of conveying the whole estate. It was claimed by the sellers that their intention was to convey the farm only and this was challenged. The oral evidence established that the parties had entered into an agreement for the sale of the farm alone and as the disposition had failed to give effect to that agreement due to a mistake common to both parties, the disposition fell to be reduced.

It is evident from this case that parole evidence was competent, even before the passing of the Act of 1985,

G in order to ascertain the true intention of the parties when a question arose as to the extent of the subjects conveyed in a deed, but at that time the only remedies which could be utilised in order to rectify an alleged mistake in the deed in reflecting the common intention of the parties was either by an action of declarator or of reduction (see, e g *Hudson v Hudson's Trs*). The purpose of s 8 (1) (a) of the Act is to provide a swifter and more convenient remedy and counsel for both parties were agreed on this point. A useful study of the question is to be found in the report of the Scottish Law Commission (Scot Law Com no 9) on *Rectifica-*

H *tion of Contractual and Other Documents*. So the earlier law is relevant to the consideration of the scope of s 8 (1) (a). Counsel for the petitioners founded in particular on a passage in the speech of Lord Reid in *Anderson v Lambie* at 1954 SLT, p 80: "But when it is sought to reduce a deed it is necessary to go behind the deed and discover the real facts. The fact that the parties had agreed to the missives is important evidence but it is not the only competent evidence. The question is not what the missives mean: if that were

I the question the ordinary rule would apply that the meaning of a document must be found from its terms. The question is whether the real facts are such that the disposition must be reduced and the existence of the missives does not alter the nature of the inquiry."

Counsel for the petitioner submitted that this statement supported his proposition that it was possible to go behind apparently unambiguous missives to find out the "real facts" relating to the common intention. I agree that this passage in the speech of Lord Reid,

J if read in isolation, does lend support to his argument. However, I consider that these observations must be considered in the context of the facts of that case. The most significant fact, as is made clear by Lord Reid at pp 78 and 79 and Lord Keith of Avonholm at p 84, is that the parties to the transaction had already verbally agreed to a sale of the farm lands alone before missives were entered into. It is evident that the terms of the missives were capable of more than one meaning as to the extent of the subjects to be conveyed and accord-

K ingly it was open to the court to consider the oral evidence as to what the parties had agreed. In my opinion, the case of *Anderson v Lambie* is not authority for the wide proposition that a common intention may be determined for the purpose of rectifying a deed even although the existence of an alleged agreement reflecting the parties' common intention is not averred.

In considering s 8 (1) (a) it is important to note that the document which may be subject to rectification is

L one "intended to express or to give effect to an agreement". The question which arises in this case is: what agreement? If it is the missives, there is no problem about them because the disposition expresses exactly the terms of the missives as to the extent of the subjects conveyed. The missives themselves state quite clearly what is the extent of the subjects for sale and need no further interpretation. In my opinion it is implicit in the terms of the subsection that one has to discover the existence of an earlier agreement from which a common intention can be discerned. The word "intention" has a positive character. It is suggestive of something more than a wish or a belief, an indication or even a general understanding. It has a purpose to it and in this context, in my view, it must be related to an agreement. If the petitioners had averred the existence of facts and circumstances demonstrating a verbal agreement between the Thompsons and the respondents that the latter would sell to them (or the petitioners) all the estate, including the Kennels, and in that context that was their common intention, then an inquiry into the facts would have been appropriate. Likewise, if the missives were ambiguous then an inquiry into the surrounding circumstances might have been in order. But in the absence of averments to such effect, it seems to me that there is no defect in any agreement to correct. To give effect to the petitioners' argument would be to innovate on the existing law and I can see nothing in the terms of the subsection which would entitle the court to take such a course. I would venture the opinion that to give effect to the petitioners' submission would result in the introduction of uncertainty into an area where it is important that the law should be, and has hitherto been, plain.

In *Shaw v William Grant (Minerals) Ltd*, Lord McCluskey analysed s 8 of the Act of 1985 and expressed the opinion that "before the court can order rectification it has to be satisfied: (1) that there is a document to be rectified; (2) that that document was intended to express or give effect to an already existing agreement arrived at between two (or more) parties; (3) that there was, when the document was executed, such a pre-existing agreement — whether or not enforceable; (4) that that agreement itself embodied and was an expression of one or more intentions common to (that is to say, shared by) the parties; (5) that the intentions were actual (not deemed) intentions; (6) that the agreement itself must have been reached at a definite point in time (cf 'the date when it was made')" (1989 SLT at p 121). So far as I can discover this is the only case in which s 8 (1) (a) has been examined in detail by the court and it would appear to support the view that I have formed as to the need for there to be an agreement to which a common intention relates.

Since the averments which the petitioners seek to prove do not set out an agreement to which a common intention can be said to relate, I am of opinion that they are irrelevant to the purpose of this petition. The petitioners have failed to plead a case which would entitle the court to consider statutory rectification and it follows therefore that the petition must be dismissed.

For the avoidance of doubt it should be made clear that if the court had been minded to order rectification there was no dispute that such rectification would have been appropriate in the terms set out in the prayer of the petition.

Counsel for Petitioners, Drummond Young, QC, MacIver; Solicitors, Dundas & Wilson, CS — Counsel for Respondents, Sutherland, QC; Solicitors, Drummond Miller, WS.   P A

Hunter v Douglas Reyburn & Co Ltd

OUTER HOUSE

LORD PENROSE

7 FEBRUARY 1992

Process — Commission and diligence — Recovery of documents — Confidentiality — Expert report — Report prepared for purposes of earlier similar litigation — Whether post litem motam — Whether confidential.

A man raised an action of damages against his former employers in respect of personal injuries. He alleged that he had been required to work in areas of their factory in which there had been excessive concentrations of dust in the air. He sought to recover expert reports from the defenders. These reports had been prepared on the instructions of the defenders in the course of preparation of their defence to a previous action based on similar grounds. The previous action had been disposed of. These reports were produced to the court in a sealed envelope since confidentiality was claimed in respect of their contents. The pursuer then moved the court to open up the sealed envelope.

Held, (1) that what was prepared by or on behalf of a litigant or potential litigant post litem motam was confidential (p 638J); and (2) that confidentiality did not cease on completion of the case for which a report had been prepared post litem motam (p 638J-K); and motion *refused.*

Action of damages

James Hunter raised an action of damages against Douglas Reyburn & Co Ltd. He sought damages in respect of personal injuries sustained by him. He alleged that they were caused by fault and negligence on the part of the defenders who were formerly his employers. He alleged that he was required to work in areas of the factory operated by them in which there were excessive concentrations of wool dust in the air.

The pursuer obtained an order for commission and diligence to recover "The report or reports prepared in about 1983 by [two named experts], of dust levels in the areas where the pursuer worked in the defenders' factory." The experts had prepared reports in the course of earlier, similar, actions at the instance of other employees. Documents were produced in answer to the service of the specification of documents, but sealed in an envelope marked "confidential".

The case came before the Lord Ordinary (Penrose) on the motion roll on the pursuer's opposed motion to have the envelope opened up.

Cases referred to

Admiralty v Aberdeen Steam Trawling and Fishing Co Ltd, 1909 1 SLT 2; 1909 SC 335.

Anderson v Ayr and South Ayrshire Local Committee of St Andrew's Ambulance Association, 1942 SLT 278; 1942 SC 555.

Clippens Oil Co Ltd v Edinburgh and District Water Trustees (1906) 13 SLT 985; (1906) 8 F 731.

On 7 February 1992 the Lord Ordinary *refused* the motion.

LORD PENROSE.—On 1 November 1991, commission was granted on the pursuer's motion for the recovery of documents defined in a specification which included a call in the following terms: "2. The report or reports prepared in about 1983 by Mr G E Rushworth and Professor Willey, of dust levels in the areas where the pursuer worked in the defenders' factory."

In due course a sealed envelope was tendered by the haver in obedience to that call. The pursuer has now moved that the sealed envelope be opened up. I was invited by the parties to consider the contents in disposing of the issues raised in the argument before me. In this opinion I refer in particular to Mr Rushworth. Professor Willey was mutatis mutandis, in the same position.

The present action is the third in a series of cases between the defenders and individual employees or former employees. The first case brought to my attention involved an employee Alexander McGaw. It was said on behalf of the pursuer, Mr Hunter, that Mr McGaw's case arose out of circumstances similar to those obtaining in the present case. Mr Hunter claims to have suffered loss, injury and damage as a result of breaches of duty by the defenders in carrying on operations at their mill in Kilmarnock. Fundamental to his case is the allegation that during the time he worked in the premises there were excessive concentrations of wool dust in the air circulating within the areas where he was required to carry out his duties. There were similar allegations in the case at the instance of Mr McGaw. In the course of preparing their defence in Mr McGaw's case, the defenders instructed Mr Rushworth to carry out investigations and to provide them with a report or reports. In due course Mr Rushworth gave evidence at the proof in Mr McGaw's case. Mr McGaw failed to recover damages. A second case then followed at the instance of a Mr Lawrie. Mr Rushworth was, on this occasion, instructed by the pursuer but he did not make use of the data accumulated during the investigations instructed by the defenders in Mr McGaw's case. The pursuer again failed to recover damages. In the present case Mr Rushworth was again instructed by the pursuer. It was, by now, common knowledge among the professional advisers engaged in the litigation that he had carried out certain studies on behalf of the defenders, and it was believed that these included factual investigations and in particular the measurement of dust concentrations within the factory premises of the defenders. The purpose of the call was to recover this material.

There is no doubt whatever that the report in Mr McGaw's case was instructed for the purposes of the defence of his action. That appeared clearly from the submissions of counsel quite apart from anything which might be gleaned from the terms of the contentious documents. Against that background it was argued for the defenders that the documents were not recoverable in the present proceedings for two reasons: (a) they were within the protection of the confidentiality which obtains as between agent and client, since the report had been instructed by the defenders' solicitors; and (b) having been instructed post litem motam they were confidential to the defenders and remained so notwithstanding that the case for which they were instructed had been disposed of. For the pursuer it was argued that the documents were not confidential in any general sense, that there was no justification for extending the confidentiality which applies as between solicitor and client to such a class of document, and that in the absence of any cogent reason for withholding the documents recovery was competent and expedient.

The only authority to which I was referred was *Clippens Oil Co Ltd v Edinburgh and District Water Trs.* That case was not concerned with the basis for the general rule of confidentiality of reports instructed post litem motam, and the circumstances made it irrelevant for present purposes, in my opinion. So far as material, it supported the view that post litem motam reports were confidential in general. This was not in dispute. The question whether confidentiality survives the instant case was never addressed.

I was not referred to the *Admiralty v Aberdeen Steam Trawling and Fishing Co Ltd*, where the opinion of the Lord President at 1909 1 SLT, pp 4-5 might have been of assistance, nor to *Anderson v St Andrew's Ambulance Association*, which might have been of assistance in considering the basis of the general rule.

What is prepared by or on behalf of a litigant or potential litigant post litem motam, is confidential. The opposing party may not recover it by diligence. The disposal of the case removes the interest of the particular opponent, but it makes no change in the relationship between the litigant instructing the report, in a case such as the present, and the witness providing it, or between the instructing party and the havers of the documents containing the report. Unless confidentiality ceases with the disposal of the case for which the report was prepared, it must subsist in favour of the party entitled to protection of the material. If the pursuer's argument were correct, and confidentiality was limited to the instant case for which the report was prepared, it would not avail the party instructing it against another opponent carrying on a parallel case any more than against a later opponent. I am not persuaded that confidentiality flies off on completion of the case for which a report was prepared, post litem motam.

In the circumstances I refuse the motion to open up the sealed envelope. I have reached this decision without reference to the terms of the documents tendered to me. In the circumstances I say nothing about the contents of the envelope.

Counsel for Pursuer, Miller, QC; Solicitors, Drummond Miller, WS (for Shaughnessy, Quigley & McColl, Glasgow) — Counsel for Defenders, P M Macdonald; Solicitors, Balfour & Manson, Nightingale & Bell (for Ross Harper & Murphy, Glasgow).

A J H

Robb v Hillary

A HIGH COURT OF JUSTICIARY

THE LORD JUSTICE CLERK (ROSS),
LORDS CULLEN AND WYLIE

14 MAY 1992

Justiciary — Procedure — Summary procedure — Natural justice — Accused charged with perjury — Sheriff who presided over trial in which accused was alleged to have committed perjury, and who was to be
B *witness in perjury trial, presiding at pleading diet — Defence objecting to sheriff presiding — Sheriff continuing diet without plea overnight but detaining accused in custody — Sheriff thereafter repelling objection — Whether resulting trial involved breach of natural justice — Whether justice seen to be done.*

An accused person was charged with perjury. At the pleading diet the presiding sheriff was the same one as had presided at the trial from which the allegation of perjury arose. The accused objected to the sheriff
C presiding on the basis that he would be a witness in the resulting trial. The sheriff continued the case without plea until the following day and detained the accused overnight. At the continued diet the sheriff repelled the objection, the accused pled not guilty and a trial diet was fixed. At the trial diet the accused renewed the objection and it was stated that justice could not be seen to be done in a case where the principal Crown witness had presided over the first calling of the complaint in court. It was therefore contrary to
D natural justice that the trial should proceed and a motion to desert simpliciter the case against the accused was moved. The sheriff refused the motion. The accused presented a bill of advocation to the High Court.

Held, (1) that although it was unfortunate and objectionable that the pleading diet had been presided over by a sheriff who was going to be a witness in the subsequent trial, the critical question was whether
E what occurred then could have affected what would occur later at the trial (p 640J-K); (2) that what had happened at the pleading diet was purely procedural; arrangements were made for the trial to be presided over by a different sheriff and nothing that happened at the pleading diet would either affect the other sheriff hearing the trial or affect the sheriff who was going to find himself as a witness, and the proceedings could not be said to be in any sense tainted by what had occurred at the pleading diet (p 640K-L); and bill
F *refused.*

Tennant v Houston, 1987 SLT 317, *distinguished.*

Bill of advocation

Karen Jane Robb presented a bill of advocation to the High Court of Justiciary craving that a complaint libelling perjury by her should be deserted simpliciter. Clement Hillary, procurator fiscal, Arbroath, was called in the bill as respondent.

Statement of facts

The bill contained the following statement of facts: G

Stat 1. That the complainer was charged that she had committed perjury at the trial of Scott Petrie on 21 October 1991 at Arbroath Sheriff Court. Sheriff C N R Stein, Esq was the presiding sheriff at the said trial.

Stat 2. The complainer was called on to plead to the said charge at Arbroath sheriff court on 22 October 1991. Sheriff Stein was again the presiding sheriff. The solicitor for the complainer objected that it was not appropriate that Sheriff Stein should conduct the H said pleading diet as he was bound to be an essential Crown witness at the trial. The same objection was stated in respect of the procurator fiscal depute, Miss Ogg.

Stat 3. Sheriff Stein continued the pleading diet, without plea to 23 October 1991. He remanded the complainer in custody.

Stat 4. On 23 October 1991 Sheriff Stein repelled the objection. The complainer pled not guilty and a I diet of trial was fixed for 29 January 1992.

Stat 5. On 29 January 1992 the said objection was renewed before Sheriff Forbes who presided at the trial diet. It was argued by counsel for the complainer that justice could not be seen to be done in a case where the principal Crown witness had presided over the first calling of the complaint in court. It was further argued that the pleading diet could without inconvenience have taken place in the conjoined jurisdiction of the sheriff at Forfar. It was further pointed J out that as a result of the foregoing the said Sheriff Stein had required to consider the complainer's application for bail, and had remanded her in custody overnight. It was submitted that in all the circumstances it was oppressive and contrary to natural justice that the trial should proceed or that any further proceedings should take place. Counsel for the complainer moved Sheriff Forbes to desert the complaint pro loco et tempore.

Stat 6. Sheriff Forbes considered the said submis- K sions and those of the Crown. By interlocutor dated 7 February 1992 Sheriff Forbes refused the said motion. His reasons are set forth in a note of 21 February 1992 which is produced herewith and referred to for its whole terms which are incorporated brevitatis causa.

Stat 7. In the foregoing circumstances the complainer requires to adopt this mode of appeal to your Lordships.

The plea in law for the complainer was in the fol- L lowing terms:

In the circumstances set forth, the proceedings at the pleading diet of 22 October 1991 and at the continuation thereof on 23 October 1991 having been, or appearing to be oppressive and contrary to natural justice the court should desert the said complaint simpliciter.

Case referred to

Tennant v Houston, 1987 SLT 317; 1986 SCCR 556.

The bill was argued before the High Court on 14 May 1992.

Eo die the court *refused* to pass the bill.

The following opinion of the court was delivered by the Lord Justice Clerk (Ross):

OPINION OF THE COURT.—The statement of facts for the complainer shows that she was charged in the sheriff court at Arbroath on a complaint libelling that she had committed perjury at a trial in that sheriff court on 21 October 1991. The presiding sheriff at the trial was Sheriff Stein. The bill goes on to explain that the complainer was called on to plead to the charge of perjury on the following day, 22 October 1991, at Arbroath Sheriff Court. Sheriff Stein was again the presiding sheriff. The solicitor for the complainer objected that it was not appropriate that Sheriff Stein should conduct the pleading diet as he was bound to be an essential Crown witness at the forthcoming trial. Objection was also taken to the fact that the procurator fiscal depute was appearing but today counsel for the complainer has explained that that latter objection is no longer insisted in. What happened on 22 October was that Sheriff Stein continued the pleading diet without plea until the following day, 23 October 1991 and remanded the complainer in custody. On 23 October Sheriff Stein repelled the objection, the complainer pled not guilty, and a diet of trial was fixed for 29 January 1992 and bail was granted.

On 29 January 1992 the case called for trial before Sheriff Forbes. The same objection was stated to him and it was submitted on behalf of the complainer that justice could not be seen to be done in a case where the principal Crown witness had presided over the first calling of the complaint in court. It was submitted that in the circumstances justice could not be seen to be done and it was contrary to natural justice that the trial should proceed, and counsel moved that the diet should be deserted. Sheriff Forbes considered these submissions and refused the motion. The complainer has accordingly presented this bill of advocation. Counsel has drawn attention to what Sheriff Forbes said in his note and she has submitted that he misapprehended the position being adopted by the complainer. She explained that no challenge was being taken to the competency of the proceedings. What was being asserted was that for the trial to proceed would involve a breach of the principles of natural justice. She cited the case of *Tennant v Houston* and maintained that that was a similar case where the court had quashed a sentence upon the view that there had been a breach of natural justice in that the justice hearing the case had been accompanied on the bench by another justice who was a member of the council which had issued the enforcement notice which was the subject matter of the prosecution. We are satisfied, however, that that was a very different case from the present case because the objection in that case was that the other justice had been on the bench with the sentencing justice at the time when sentence was passed. In the course of that opinion it is recorded: "In cir-

cumstances such as I have described here where the councillor was on the bench with the Justice trying the case, we are satisfied that justice was not seen to be done when the Justice proceeded to sentence." It is the fact that this third party was on the bench when the justice proceeded to sentence that supported the allegation of a breach of natural justice. That is, as we say, different on its facts from the present case.

At the end of the day the strongest point which counsel for the complainer made was this. That because the procedure went ahead before Sheriff Stein the result was that on 22 October the complainer was ordered to be detained in custody overnight by order of a person who was going to be a witness at her trial. That she maintained was objectionable and the fact that that had happened meant that the whole proceedings had been tainted. The Solicitor General on the other hand, whilst accepting that it was unfortunate that the pleading diet had been presided over by a sheriff who was going to be a witness in the subsequent trial, maintained that one could not affirm that the whole proceedings had been tainted. The complainer's complaint has to be that she can never receive a fair trial and the question which arises must therefore be whether what occurred on 22 and 23 October must necessarily affect the subsequent trial of the complainer.

We are not persuaded that there is any link between what occurred on 22 and 23 October and the subsequent trial. We agree with the Solicitor General that it was unfortunate to say the least of it that the pleading diet should have been presided over by a sheriff who was himself going to be a witness at the trial of the complainer in the event of the complainer maintaining a plea of not guilty and a trial being necessary. That is something which should not have occurred and was unfortunate and we think objectionable. However the critical question raised in the bill is whether what occurred then can have affected what would occur later at the trial and we are unable to see that what occurred at the pleading diet can have any effect on the subsequent trial. What happened at the pleading diet was purely procedural. The arrangements were made for the trial to be presided over by a different sheriff and we are quite unable to see how what happened at the pleading diet would affect the other sheriff hearing the trial or indeed how it would affect the sheriff who was going to find himself as a witness. We can see no connection between these two matters and we are quite unable to affirm that the proceedings were in any sense tainted by what occurred at the pleading diet. It follows therefore that we must refuse to pass the bill.

Counsel for Complainer, Cowan; Solicitors, Alex Morison & Co, WS (for Herald & Co, Arbroath) — Counsel for Respondent, Solicitor General (Dawson, QC); Solicitor, J D Lowe, Crown Agent.

R F H

McLuckie Brothers Ltd v Newhouse Contracts Ltd

OUTER HOUSE

LORD MILLIGAN

3 JUNE 1992

Company — Winding up — Gratuitous alienation — Transfer of heritable property by insolvent company to third party — Whether made for adequate consideration — Onus on person seeking to uphold transaction — Insolvency Act 1986 (c 45), s 242.

Section 242 of the Insolvency Act 1986 provides that an alienation made to a third party by a company which is thereafter wound up, if made within two years before the date of commencement of the winding up, may be challenged by the liquidator or any creditor of the company, and that upon such challenge the court is to grant decree of reduction or certain other orders unless inter alia any person seeking to uphold the alienation can establish that the alienation was made for adequate consideration.

A company acquired certain lands for development for housing. They commenced building operations and in October 1989 entered into missives for the sale of the partly developed site to a second company for £330,000. The price actually paid was £353,515.31 to include certain works allegedly carried out after the date of the missives. The first company subsequently went into insolvent liquidation and a creditor of that company and the liquidator sought reduction of the disposition in favour of the second company. The second company contended that the sale was for adequate consideration. It led evidence that the price had been arrived at by taking into account the final price to be expected for the houses on the development and the cost of completing the development, allowing for contingencies. No details of such prices and costs were produced. Evidence was also led from an architect who valued the works carried out by 12 July 1989 at £257,650. The site was valued at £106,000. Certain works had been carried out to the buildings between 12 July 1989 and the date of the missives, some of which had been remedial works rendered necessary following the issue of a stop notice by the local authority in August 1989. The liquidator led no evidence and contended first that there was no evidence to show that the figure of £330,000 was adequate consideration, and secondly that what evidence there was pointed to a valuation in excess of £363,000.

Held, that the defenders had failed to establish that the price paid was adequate consideration in that (1) there was no evidence to show what work had been done between the July valuation and the October sale although sufficient work had been done between those dates to have had a material effect on the value of the development, (2) no attempt had been made to market the subjects, and (3) the offer of £330,000 related to the particular circumstances in which the offer had been made (p 644C-I); and decree of reduction *granted.*

Observed, (1) that the absence of evidence from the pursuers could not help the defenders, especially since the pursuers could not be expected to produce even an approximately accurate valuation of the partly developed site when the defenders had not proved in reasonable detail the state of the site at the material time (p 644I-J); and (2) that a defence based on establishing "adequate consideration" would not necessarily fail because, after the event, it appeared that the price actually obtained could have been bettered (p 643H-I).

Dictum in *Short's Tr v Chung,* 1991 SLT 472, *followed.*

Action of reduction

McLuckie Brothers Ltd, as creditors of Havenbel Developments Ltd (formerly Newhouse Construction Ltd), and Alan William O'Boyle, its official liquidator, raised an action against Newhouse Contracts Ltd, seeking reduction of a disposition of heritage by the then Newhouse Construction Ltd to Newhouse Contracts Ltd.

The case came before the Lord Ordinary (Milligan) for proof before answer.

Statutory provisions

The Insolvency Act 1986 provides:

"242.—(1) Where this subsection applies and — (a) the winding up of a company has commenced, an alienation by the company is challengeable by — (i) any creditor who is a creditor by virtue of a debt incurred on or before the date of such commencement, or (ii) the liquidator. . . .

"(4) On a challenge being brought under subsection (1), the court shall grant decree of reduction or for such restoration of property to the company's assets or other redress as may be appropriate; but the court shall not grant such a decree if the person seeking to uphold the alienation establishes — . . . (b) that the alienation was made for adequate consideration."

Case referred to

Short's Tr v Chung, 1991 SLT 472.

On 3 June 1992 the Lord Ordinary *granted* decree of reduction.

LORD MILLIGAN.—This is an action of reduction brought by a company who are admitted to be creditors of Havenbel Developments Ltd, formerly Newhouse Construction Ltd, in which they, and the liquidator of Newhouse Construction Ltd, seek reduction of a disposition by Newhouse Construction Ltd in favour of the defenders. The disposition is dated 24 October 1989 and was recorded in the Land Register on 3 November 1989. The disposition was of subjects consisting of a partly built housing construction site at Kirkhill Road, Wishaw. The second pursuer was appointed provisional liquidator of Newhouse Construction Ltd on 7 March 1990, interim liquidator of

A the company on 9 August 1990 and official liquidator on 28 August 1990. It is accepted that immediately, and all other times, after the alienation concerned in this action the assets of Newhouse Construction Ltd did not exceed its liabilities. The sole point in issue at the proof was whether the defenders established that the alienation was made for adequate consideration. This issue arises from the terms of s 242 of the Insolvency Act 1986 which reads: [his Lordship quoted the terms of s 242 (4) set out supra and continued:] It is accepted that the onus in the matter is upon the

B defenders and the defenders led at the proof.

Evidence was given first by Mr Francis Smith, a director of Newhouse Construction Ltd. He explained that the development concerned was on a greenfield site and comprised phase II of his company's Kirkhill Road development. Phase II involved 12 flatted houses and eight terraced houses. There was also some spare land on the site for possible future development. The phase II development was financed through Hill Samuel Bank and for their purposes periodical valua-

C tions were required as work progressed. He agreed with the bank that such valuations would be provided by Mr McEwan, architect. Mr McEwan provided certificates to the effect that the total value of work done by 12 July 1989 was £257,650. To this figure there fell to be added £100,000 by way of site value. At the time of this valuation, work was ongoing. In about late May and June 1989 difficulty was being experienced with the supply of windows and doors by kit manufac-turers. He said that the roof had to come off several

D times. On 30 August 1989 the local authority placed a stop notice on the site because wrong timbers had been used on the roof of the flatted block. Mr Smith described the cost to his company of the kit problems as horrendous. There had also been difficulties with the supply of wrong materials earlier in the year, in March. His company incurred professional fees in relation to investigation of wrongly designed inter-mediate floors. Mr Smith said that the company was doing what he described as "bits and pieces" between

E the July valuation and the date of the stop notice, when all work on the site had to stop. In due course, Hill Samuel Bank suggested selling off the partly com-pleted site. The bank was threatening to call up its standard security but agreed to give the company time. Mr Smith said that the company advertised by putting a sign up and several local builders were interested. He said that he adjusted a sum with Mr Alex Smith, a director of the defenders, for acquisition by the defenders of the partly completed site. Different solici-

F tors represented the defenders and Newhouse Con-struction Ltd in the negotiation of missives between 12 October 1989 and 16 October 1989.

In cross examination, Mr Smith explained that the land had been purchased in 1988 and work had started in about November or December 1988. No quantity surveyor was involved for economy reasons. Mr McEwan's valuations were based on materials and labour costs incurred together with a percentage for profit, although the main profit would arise at the end of the development work when the houses were com-

G plete. Mr Smith said that following the lifting of the stop notice in September 1989, work was carried out on the roof of the flatted building. Some work was also done on the terraced block. Most of the work done between the valuation in July and the sale in October was remedial work. He thought that the cost of this work during that period was a maximum of £18,000 to £19,000 and may have been only £10,000. After the sale of the site to the defenders he became site agent on behalf of the defenders at the site on a self employed basis. He also signed a guarantee in connec-

H tion with his daughter's involvement as a director of the defenders in acquisition and continuation of the development concerned. With regard to the price paid by the defenders he explained that his brother, Mr Alex Smith, took stock of what the development then comprised on behalf of the defenders and put in his offer of £330,000. The price actually paid into New-house Construction Ltd's account by the defenders was £353,515.32, the difference being a negotiated sum for additional work done not included for in the £330,000 price. Some of this work had been done

I prior to the commencement of negotiation on the mis-sives on 12 October 1989 and some afterwards.

Mr John Clelland, a chartered surveyor, said that on the basis of information supplied by Mr Francis Smith to him as to the number of flats and houses comprised in the development, he provided the valuation of £100,000 for the site which was adopted by Mr McEwan in his valuation of 12 July 1989. He explained in evidence that on the basis of the number

J of units actually created this value would have been £106,000. He would wish to do a check before saying that that sum was an appropriate valuation of the site value as at October 1989 but he would not have expected much increase between July 1989 and October 1989. His valuation had been based upon information about the site and not upon inspection of it.

Mr McEwan, the architect already mentioned, explained that the valuations which he provided for

K the purposes of Hill Samuel Bank might involve an error of 5 per cent or 10 per cent. There was no quan-tity surveyor on the site. He took the actual cost of materials and added Mr Francis Smith's figure for labour which he assumed included builder's profit. For example, Mr Smith might say that the brickwork labour had been £2,000. The figure of £100,000 for site value had been supplied by Mr Smith on the basis of the information obtained from Mr Clelland already mentioned. Work had stopped altogether with the

L service of the stop notice on 30 August 1989. The rectification work could have been measured and valued but he was not asked to do this. The last valua-tion sought from him was that referred to in the cer-tificate of 12 July 1989. In cross examination, Mr McEwan said that there was no interruption in work prior to the stop notice of 30 August 1989. Work had been carrying on normally on site prior to then. During the period between the July valuation and the stop notice he was paying fortnightly visits to the site but he could not remember what work had been done

during this period. It was, moreover, obvious that
A work was going on more on the flatted block than on
the terraced houses. As at the time of the July valuation, tarring of the roof of the flatted block had not
been done. He did not know if flooring work had been
done by then. By the time of the stop notice all of the
roof tiling work would have been done. He remembered advertising boards relating to the houses being
for sale. He did not recollect any board to indicate that
the site was for sale and he was unaware of the sale of
the site to the defenders until some days after it had
B actually occurred.

Mr Alex Smith gave evidence that he had no financial contract with his brother Francis Smith at any
time. He was a self employed building contractor and
property developer. Mr Francis Smith's daughter was
an estate agent and she brought his attention to the
possibility of acquiring the part developed site. He
visited the site over a period of a few weeks. He
arranged for prospective finance from the Bank of
Scotland. He worked out the actual costs of develop-
C ing the site to completion, allowed for contingencies
and profit and decided to offer £330,000 for the site.
He thought that the flatted block was about 60 per
cent complete and the terraced houses about 80 per
cent complete. In addition there was a vacant plot at
the back of the site on which four terraced houses
similar to those being built could be developed. His
price of £330,000 was agreed with Mr Francis Smith.
Thereafter there was a claim for additional work, as
already mentioned, which was compromised for about
D £23,000 additional to the £330,000 price. He said that
this additional sum was all referable to work done after
10 October 1989. His company took possession of the
site on 31 October 1989. He employed his brother Mr
Francis Smith as a site agent. The labour force of
Newhouse Construction Ltd was dismissed. He
wanted to bring on his own labour force, which he did.
Due to financial difficulties arising out of claims made
by the first pursuers in the present action against his
company, which he said were not well founded, the
E Bank of Scotland called up the security on the
development concerned so he was not involved in ultimate completion of the whole development. In cross
examination, Mr Alex Smith said that he kept a low
profile during the period terminating in purchase of
the site. He explained that it was vital to do the deal
and then tell the property world. He did not want the
deal to become public in case somebody else came in
and outbid him. He said that it was common
knowledge in Wishaw that the site was for sale. He
F said that there was a board displayed to that effect.

No evidence was led for the pursuers.

Counsel for the defenders submitted that decree of
reduction should be refused. He accepted that the
onus was upon the defenders to establish as a matter
of fact that the alienation was made for adequate consideration. He said that there were no reported
decisions on the application of s 242 of the Insolvency
Act 1986. There was, however, one reported decision
on the provisions of the Bankruptcy (Scotland) Act

1986, s 34 (4), the terms of which mirror the terms of
s 242. This case was *Short's Tr v Chung*. He founded G
in particular upon an obiter dictum of Lord Weir in
that case when he said (at p 475A-B): "As at present
advised, I am not persuaded that it is necessary for the
person who is seeking to uphold the transaction to
demonstrate that an adequate consideration for the
sale of heritable property necessarily means, with the
benefit of hindsight or otherwise, the best price which
could have been obtained in the open market in a
properly conducted arms length transaction. There
may well be cases where, for particular reasons, the H
consideration has turned out to be less than that but
still be 'adequate' for the purposes of s 34, and it may
be relevant to examine the circumstances in which a
transaction took place." Lord Weir went on to point
out that in the case with which he was dealing such
matters hardly arose as the difference between acceptable valuation and sale price was so wide as to leave
no room for doubt about the matter. I agree with Lord
Weir's observation on this point, and in particular that
a defence based on adequate consideration will not I
necessarily fail because after the event it appears that
the price actually obtained might have been bettered.
Counsel for the defender founded upon the price
agreed between Mr Alex Smith and Mr Francis Smith
as being sound evidence of adequate consideration for
the alienation. Counsel also sought support from Mr
McEwan's valuation of £357,650 in July. He said that
Mr McEwan deducted £8,500 for the value of hired
equipment and his fees, leaving about £349,000. He
estimated the value of remedial work required to J
be about £20,000, leaving £329,000. Thus, Mr
McEwan's valuation supported the price paid as being
adequate consideration.

Counsel for the pursuers submitted that the
defenders had failed to establish that the alienation
was for adequate consideration. He said that there was
no proper evidence at all to suggest that the figure of
£330,000 represented such adequate consideration.
Mr Alex Smith's method of working back from the K
ultimate prospective selling price of the units in the
development to his offer price by calculating the cost
of completion of the development and taking account
of contingency allowances and profit sought, was an
acceptable framework for calculation of the part
developed site as at October 1989. However, Mr Alex
Smith had failed to explain any detail of his purported
calculations and, in any event, the evidence made it
clear that the sum offered by him was not checked
either by or on behalf of Mr Francis Smith. Furthermore, in reaching the figure which he offered, Mr L
Alex Smith was, as he fairly admitted in evidence,
aware that others might offer more. So far as the July
1989 valuation by Mr McEwan was concerned, it was
clear that this was not truly a proper valuation of the
value of the part developed site at that time. This was
so because of the way in which Mr McEwan's valuation figures were reached, as already explained in
reference to his evidence. But even if his July 1989
valuation be taken as a starting point for calculation of
adequate consideration as at October 1989, it was clear

from the evidence that this exercise would show that the part developed site as at October 1989 was worth in excess of £363,000. This was so because the valuation in July 1989 was for £357,000, to which £6,000 required to be added by way of the additional £6,000 spoken to by Mr Clelland as referable to land value in respect of the number of units actually being created. Furthermore, the evidence showed that there would be additional value, perhaps quite substantial additional value, in work done between the July valuation and price agreement in October. For example, it was clear, as shown by the evidence of Mr McEwan, that tiling work had been done on the flatted block between July and October and possibly flooring work also. In addition to this, as indicated by the evidence of Mr Francis Smith, at least some work was done on both the flatted block and the terraced block other than work done to remedy defects present at the time of the July 1989 valuation. Hence the inference that the true site value of the partly developed site as at October 1989 was more than £363,000.

I agree with the submissions made by counsel for the pursuers. In his careful and clear submissions, counsel for the defenders said all that could be said in support of the defenders' case. However, my firm view is that the defenders have failed to establish that the price of £330,000 represented an adequate consideration for the part developed site in terms of s 242 of the Insolvency Act 1986. As to the work being done between the July valuation and the October sale, I found the evidence of Mr McEwan more reliable than that of Mr Francis Smith, from the manner in which their evidence was respectively given. So far as Mr McEwan was able to throw light upon this matter, I found his evidence clear and acceptable. On the other hand, I found the evidence of Mr Francis Smith more hesitant and in many respects rather vague upon this matter. In fairness to Mr Smith, I would add that this may have been wholly, or at least largely, due to the passage of time dimming recollection, especially in the absence of documentation on the matter. In the result, I have no clear detailed picture as to just what work was done between the July valuation and the October sale. What I do find is that the evidence showed that on a balance of probabilities sufficient work of a nature enhancing value was done during that period to have a material effect upon the value of the development between those two dates. While I am satisfied on that point on a balance of probabilities, the evidence does not enable me to quantify the extent of that increase. Upon a correct analysis of the evidence, in my opinion, this results, as counsel for the pursuers submitted, in Mr McEwan's valuation of £357,000, as at July 1989, producing an updated valuation of more than £363,000 in October 1989. I do not find in Mr Alex Smith's evidence any sound reason to hold that the price of £330,000 actually paid was adequate consideration within the meaning of s 242. I was left with the clear impression from Mr Alex Smith's evidence that his offer of £330,000 related to the particular circumstances in which that offer was made. Those particular circumstances included the obvious financial problems of Newhouse Construction Ltd, the knowledge that Mr Francis Smith knew that he would be engaged as site agent by the defenders if the defenders' offer was accepted, the absence of a competing bidder and of meaningful advertising of the sale and the perfectly understandable desire of Mr Alex Smith to achieve as low a price as he could in the rather special circumstances of this particular sale. With regard to advertisement I do not accept Mr Alex Smith's evidence, supported though it was by that of Mr Francis Smith, that the site was advertised for sale, at least that it was so advertised in any meaningful way. If it had been, I cannot envisage that Mr McEwan would have been unaware of that, visiting the site every fortnight as he did. I accept Mr McEwan's evidence that he had no knowledge that the site was being advertised for sale and also his evidence that he, initially at least, had no knowledge of the actual sale. In view of each of the foregoing circumstances, I do not find the offer made by Mr Alex Smith and agreed to by Mr Francis Smith to be of any substantial significance towards ascertaining what was adequate consideration for the alienation concerned.

I record that counsel for the defender founded upon the absence of any evidence from the pursuers. Upon my view of the evidence led for the defenders the absence of any evidence from the pursuers cannot avail the defenders. I would add that I find it difficult to see how the pursuers could have been expected to produce even an approximately accurate valuation of a partly developed site when the defenders cannot prove in reasonable detail the state of the site at the material time, a matter very much for the defenders to establish.

On the whole matter, I hold that the defenders have failed to prove that the alienation was for adequate consideration within the meaning of s 242 of the Insolvency Act 1986 and accordingly I repel the defenders' pleas in law and sustain the plea in law for the pursuers and grant decree of reduction in terms of the first conclusion of the summons.

Counsel for Pursuers, Macnair; Solicitors, Beveridge & Kellas, WS — Counsel for Defenders, J D Campbell; Solicitors, Russel & Aitken, WS.

C N M

Maitland v HM Advocate

HIGH COURT OF JUSTICIARY

THE LORD JUSTICE CLERK (ROSS),
LORDS MORISON AND PENROSE

16 JUNE 1992

Justiciary — Evidence — Appeal — New evidence not heard and not reasonably available at trial — Accused convicted of murder but co-accused acquitted — Evidence at trial that co-accused stabbed deceased — On appeal affidavits lodged showing co-accused before and during trial admitted stabbing deceased — Whether new evidence of materiality justifying hearing it — Whether miscarriage of justice — Criminal Procedure (Scotland) Act 1975 (c 21), ss 228 (2) and 252 (b).

Justiciary — Procedure — Retrial — Appeal on ground of new evidence not heard and not reasonably available at trial — Accused moving for retrial on basis of affidavits containing new evidence — Whether retrial appropriate at that stage — Criminal Procedure (Scotland) Act 1975 (c 21), ss 252 (b), 254 and 255.

Section 252 (b) of the Criminal Procedure (Scotland) Act 1975 provides that the High Court may, for the purposes of an appeal under s 228 (1) of the 1975 Act, hear any additional evidence relevant to any alleged miscarriage of justice or order such evidence to be heard by a judge of the High Court or by such other person as it may appoint for that purpose.

An accused person was charged with, inter alia, murder while acting along with two other persons. The jury convicted the accused but acquitted his two co-accused. There was sufficient evidence that the accused had inflicted the fatal wound but there was also evidence that one of the other accused, Hay, had struck the blow. At trial, the accused gave evidence that he had taken a knife from Hay after the incident. Hay gave evidence to the effect that he suffered from alcoholic amnesia and that he could remember nothing about the incident. The third accused, Smith, gave evidence that after they had left the house where the assault took place, Hay had said to him: "I got him". Another witness said that after the incident Hay passed a knife to the accused. There was also evidence from Smith regarding conversations involving Hay in prison about who had stabbed the deceased. The accused appealed on the ground of the existence and significance of additional evidence not heard at the trial from five witnesses to the effect that either before or during the trial they each had heard Hay admit that he carried out the stabbing though none of the witnesses said that they saw him commit the crime. The accused moved for a retrial to be authorised on the basis of the affidavits of these witnesses.

Held, (1) that the accused's motion for a retrial was premature because before the appeal court could hold that there had been any miscarriage of justice it would be necessary for the court to hear the additional evidence in accordance with s 252 (b) of the 1975 Act (p 648D-E); (2) that the court's task was initially to decide whether the proposed additional evidence could be regarded as evidence which was not available and could not reasonably have been made available at the trial, and whether the evidence was prima facie of materiality (p 648E-F); (3) that the evidence was not of such a nature that the court should hear it since (a) evidence had been led at trial of conversations involving Hay and the proposed new evidence did not add significantly to evidence already given; and (b) no reasonable jury could have regarded the new evidence as reliable evidence of Hay's involvement as actor because none of the witnesses claimed to have seen Hay commit the crime but only that he admitted it, Hay himself in evidence had claimed to have no recollection of the incident and the new evidence would only establish that no reliance could be placed on Hay, whom it was not proposed to call again and who no longer had any interest to deny what was attributed to him (pp 648G-H and 649A-I); and appeal *refused.*

Cameron v HM Advocate, 1988 SLT 169, *applied*; *Temple v HM Advocate*, 1971 SLT 193, and *Morland v HM Advocate*, 1985 SCCR 316, *followed.*

Observed, that if the jury had had available to them the proposed additional evidence it might have inclined them also to convict Hay on an art and part basis since it indicated a greater involvement on his part than he was prepared to admit at his trial (pp 649L-650A).

Indictment

Thomas Maitland was charged along with two others at the instance of the rt hon the Lord Fraser of Carmyllie, Her Majesty's Advocate on an indictment which contained the following charge, inter alia: "(7) [on 10 November 1990 at the house at 64 Drumover Drive, Glasgow] you Alexander Torrie Shand Smith, you Thomas McCreavy Hay and you Thomas Maitland did assault James McGloine then residing there, now deceased, push and pull him about, seize him by the neck, push him against a wall, present knives or similar instruments at him, repeatedly stab him on the body with knives or similar instruments and murder him". The accused pled not guilty and proceeded to trial before Lord Cameron of Lochbroom and a jury in the High Court at Glasgow. After trial the accused was found guilty of this charge but Hay and Smith were acquitted. The accused appealed against conviction by note of appeal to the High Court. The facts of the case appear from the opinion of the court.

Statutory provisions

The Criminal Procedure (Scotland) Act 1975 provides:

"228.—. . . (2) By an appeal under subsection (1) of this section [appeal against conviction on indictment], a person may bring under review of the High Court any alleged miscarriage of justice in the proceedings in which he was convicted, including any alleged miscarriage of justice on the basis of the existence and significance of additional evidence which

A was not heard at the trial and which was not available and could not reasonably have been made available at the trial. . . .

"252. Without prejudice to any existing power of the High Court, that court may for the purposes of an appeal under section 228 (1) of this Act—. . . (b) hear any additional evidence relevant to any alleged miscarriage of justice or order such evidence to be heard by a judge of the High Court or by such other person as it may appoint for that purpose."

B **Cases referred to**
Cameron v HM Advocate, 1988 SLT 169; 1987 SCCR 608.
Morland v HM Advocate, 1985 SCCR 316.
Stillie v HM Advocate, 1992 SLT 279; 1990 SCCR 719.
Temple v HM Advocate, 1971 SLT 193; 1971 JC 1.

Appeal
C The appeal was argued before the High Court on 19 March 1992.

On 16 June 1992 the court *refused* the appeal.

The following opinion of the court was delivered by the Lord Justice Clerk (Ross):

OPINION OF THE COURT.—The appellant is Thomas Maitland who went to trial along with
D Alexander Torrie Shand Smith and Thomas McCreavy Hay at the High Court in Glasgow on an indictment containing a number of charges. Charge 7 libelled that all three accused had murdered James McGloine. The jury found Smith and Hay not guilty of charge 7; by a majority they found the appellant guilty of charge 7. The appellant was also found guilty of charge 4 which was a charge of breach of the peace. Smith was found guilty of charge 4 under certain deletions, and Hay was found guilty as libelled of charges
E 1 and 4 and guilty under deletion of charge 3. These three charges were all charges of breach of the peace. Against his conviction on the charge of murder the appellant has appealed.

In the note of appeal the following was stated to be the ground of appeal: "The appellant states that there was insufficient evidence to convict him of the crime of murder. The appellant also states that the judge erred in his charge to the jury in relation to art and part."

F Subsequently additional grounds of appeal were lodged, and they were in the following terms:

"The nature, quality and state of the evidence led at the trial was such that no reasonable jury would have been entitled to convict the appellant of any part of the indictment.

"Accordingly his conviction was a miscarriage of justice.

"In addition to the above fresh evidence has come to light in respect of admissions made by the co-accused Thomas Hay to fellow prisoners. The said Thomas Hay had admitted committing the murder to G James McLaughlin, Thomas Hendry and Sean Houston. These parties were inmates of HM Prison, Barlinnie while the said Thomas Hay was on remand pending trial. This evidence only came to light following on the conviction of the appellant and was not available to the defence during the trial."

Thereafter the appellant lodged an amended ground of appeal in the following terms:

"The appellant refers to the affidavits of: H

John Clarke
James McLaughlin
Thomas Docherty
Sean Joseph Houston
Thomas Hendry

"In respect of said affidavits he respectfully submits that the said evidence which was not available at trial would, if so available, have at least materially affected the jury's consideration of the charge of murder I against him.

"In these circumstances he submits there has been a miscarriage of justice and the said conviction should be quashed."

On 22 October 1991 the court allowed these additional grounds of appeal to be received, and continued the appeal to enable the trial judge to prepare a supplementary report upon the additional grounds and the relevant affidavits. The continued appeal was heard on J 19 March 1992 when senior counsel who appeared for the appellant submitted that there had been a miscarriage of justice in this case. In his submissions, he made it clear that he was not seeking to support the original grounds of appeal, but that the alleged miscarriage of justice was on the basis of the existence and significance of additional evidence which was not heard at the trial and which was not available and could not reasonably have been made available at the trial in terms of s 228 (2) of the Criminal Procedure K (Scotland) Act 1975.

All three accused had lodged notices of incrimination, and senior counsel for the appellants informed us that the appellant had invited the jury to hold that the murder had in fact been committed by his co-accused Hay and not by himself. Counsel also informed us that evidence had been given to that effect by the appellant, and his evidence was that he had taken a knife from Hay after the incident. Hay also gave evidence and claimed to suffer from alcoholic amnesia, and he L said that he could remember nothing about the incident. Counsel did say that it had to be accepted that there was material available to the jury from a number of sources to the effect that the appellant had been armed with one or two knives at a variety of stages of the incident; there was also evidence to the effect that the appellant had stabbed the deceased.

The material evidence has been summarised by the trial judge in his original report. Under reference to charge 4, which was a charge of breach of the peace, the trial judge tells us that the jury unanimously convicted the appellant of uttering threats of violence to the occupants of the house at 64 Drumover Drive, Glasgow, brandishing knives and forcing their way into the house. He also tells us that there was evidence from witnesses that outside the house the appellant was in possession of two knives. The trial judge's description of the incident giving rise to the murder is as follows: "The incident giving rise to the charge of murder occurred within the house after the appellant had entered. The deceased died from a single stab wound to the chest. In addition at post mortem he was found to have received a wound on the hand and a wound on the buttock, neither of which was life threatening. There was evidence from the witnesses James and Thomas McGloine that the appellant had been in the van when forcing entry to the house. James McGloine, Angela McGloine and Linda Hay gave evidence that within the hallway the appellant had confronted the deceased. James McGloine said that he had attempted to intervene to protect his father but had been seized by the accused Smith. While struggling with Smith, he had seen the appellant lunge forward with a knife in his hand at his father who was then standing with his hands up in the air. The appellant appeared to have struck his father. Angela McGloine, who was standing in the entrance to the house, described seeing the appellant with a hold of her father. The latter was against a wall in the hallway while at the same time the appellant was holding a knife in his hand high in the air. She had screamed and run away, passing Linda Hay in the doorway. Linda Hay described looking in immediately after this and seeing the appellant with a knife close to the deceased. He moved forward and the blade of the knife entered the upper part of the deceased's body."

There was accordingly sufficient evidence, if the jury accepted it, to entitle the jury to conclude that the fatal blow had been struck by the appellant. On the other hand, as the trial judge reminded the jury in his charge, there was also a body of evidence to the effect that the blow had been struck by Hay. Some witnesses spoke to Hay having a knife that night. Morag Smith and the appellant both spoke to the appellant taking a knife away from Hay after the incident in the house. In his evidence the appellant stated that he saw the deceased being stabbed by Hay. The co-accused Smith stated that after they had left the house Hay had stated to him (Smith): "I got him".

The case for the Crown was put upon the basis that the accused were guilty as actors or upon the basis of art and part. In the event the jury acquitted Smith and Hay and convicted the appellant; this must have been upon the basis that they were satisfied that the appellant was guilty as actor and not upon the basis of concert.

The appellant is now maintaining that there was an alleged miscarriage of justice on the basis of additional evidence which he has put forward in the form of affidavits. Affidavits have been produced from the five witnesses named in the amended ground of appeal.

Thomas Hendry has deponed that in January or February 1991 prior to the trial, while he was in custody in Barlinnie prison he heard Hay saying: "It looks as though all the Derry is on Tam Maitland, but I stabbed him." He further explains that "Derry" means "the blame". He also depones that sometime later he heard Hay speaking to two others and saying something to the effect that the appellant Maitland should turn Queen's evidence. He took this to mean that the appellant should simply tell the truth and blame Hay because Hay had committed the crime. He states that after the trial had been completed he told the appellant what he had heard Hay say before the trial.

There is also an affidavit from Sean Joseph Houston. He has deponed that while the trial was taking place, he was seated on a bus beside Hay. They were being taken to court. He states that Hay told him about some of the events on the night in question; he (Hay) had been fighting with Thomas McGloine, and had then gone to his own house in order to obtain two knives and to get the appellant Maitland. He stated that later on he (Hay) had been fighting with McGloine's father, and he said that he had killed McGloine's father by stabbing him. He further deponed that the appellant Maitland had had nothing to do with the stabbing. He also stated that he had told his wife what to say at the trial. He states that after his release from prison at the end of April 1991 he told the appellant's sister what he had heard Hay state.

Thomas Docherty has stated in his affidavit that he was in Barlinnie prison at the time of the trial. On one occasion Hay came to his cell, and someone asked him how the trial was going. Hay replied: "I'm thinking about going in to plead tomorrow." Docherty said: "How's that?" and Hay replied: "My conscience is bothering me." Later he added: "I done it, I stabbed him." He later told the appellant what Hay had said.

James McLaughlin has also given an affidavit. He is serving a sentence for culpable homicide. During the trial of the appellant and his co-accused, Hay came in to Maitland's cell. He said he was going to plead guilty to the murder charge. He said something to the effect: "I'm going to go in and put my hands up to it. I done the stabbing." He also said: "My conscience is bothering me because it looks as though Maitland is going to be the fall guy." Subsequently after the trial had been concluded, he met the appellant and told him what he had heard.

The final affidavit is from John Clarke. Prior to the trial whilst he was being held in custody in Barlinnie prison, he shared a cell with Alexander Torrie Shand Smith. Hay used to come to the cell, and conversations took place. During one of these conversations Hay said to Smith: "I don't want to see you getting done. You and Tam should go into the box and give evidence against me." He said this more than once. According to Clarke, Hay also said that Smith and the appellant had been on the stairs fighting with a young guy when he (Hay) stabbed the man and left the house with the knife. Hay added that at the time he had said:

"I've done that bastard." Some time after the trial had
been concluded, Clarke maintains that he told the
appellant what Hay had said.

The evidence contained in these affidavits is said to
be the basis of the alleged miscarriage of justice. Each
of these five witnesses has deponed that they heard
Hay admitting to having done the stabbing of the
deceased. These alleged admissions appear to have
been made either before the trial of the three accused
began or during the period when the trial was proceeding. At this stage the critical question to determine is
whether the evidence contained in the affidavits is of
such a nature that this court should hear the evidence
in order to determine whether the evidence is of such
a kind and quality that it was likely to have been found
by a reasonable jury and on proper directions to be of
material assistance to them in their consideration of a
critical issue at the trial of these three accused, including the appellant (*Cameron v HM Advocate*). After
hearing the evidence, if it were found to be reliable,
this court would require to be satisfied that its
relevance and significance were such that it was
reasonable to conclude that a verdict reached in ignorance of that evidence must be regarded as a miscarriage of justice.

At this stage what we have to determine is whether
we should allow this additional evidence to be led
before the court and we could only do that if we were
satisfied that if the evidence appeared to us to be credible it was evidence of the nature described above.

At the end of his submissions, senior counsel for the
appellant moved the court to set aside the conviction
of the appellant and to grant authority to the Crown
to bring a new prosecution in accordance with ss 254
and 255 of the Criminal Procedure (Scotland) Act
1975. Such a motion was, in our opinion, clearly
premature. Before the court could hold that there had
been any miscarriage of justice on the basis of the existence and significance of additional evidence which
had not been heard at the trial, it would be necessary
for the court to hear such additional evidence in
accordance with s 252 (b) of the Criminal Procedure
(Scotland) Act 1975. Where precognitions or affidavits
have been lodged to support an appeal based on s 228
(2) of the Act of 1975, and the court is invited to
exercise its power under s 252 (b) to hear additional
evidence, what the court has to decide initially is
whether the proposed additional evidence could be
regarded as evidence which was not available and
could not reasonably have been made available at the
trial, and further whether the alleged additional evidence contained in the affidavits is prima facie of
materiality (*Cameron v HM Advocate*).

According to what the witnesses say in their
affidavits, the admissions which they allege that Hay
made were made either shortly before the trial or
during the trial of the appellant and his co-accused.
Having regard to the circumstances in which these
alleged admissions were made, we are at present prepared to accept that they constitute evidence which
was not available and could not reasonably have been

made available at the trial. Accordingly the critical
question at this stage is to determine whether the
alleged additional evidence is prima facie of materiality, and accordingly whether it is evidence which we
ought to hear under the powers conferred upon us by
s 252 (b) of the Act of 1975.

Having given the matter consideration, we have
come to be of opinion that the evidence is not of such
a nature that we should hear it. In the first place, it is
well established that this court will decline to hear
additional evidence which merely adds to evidence
already given (*Temple v HM Advocate*). We recognise
that if the circumstances are special the court may
allow additional evidence even although its effect will
be merely to add to evidence already given at the trial,
but it is plain that it will not do so unless the circumstances are very special (*Morland v HM Advocate*).

We do not regard the present case as very special in
this sense. At the trial, as we have already observed,
there was evidence supporting the involvement of Hay
in the crime. The appellant stated that he saw the
deceased stabbed by Hay, and the co-accused Smith
said he heard Hay say: "I got him." The appellant also
said that he took a knife away from Hay. Mrs Morag
Smith also said that after the incident Hay passed a
knife to the appellant.

All this evidence was before the jury. So far as Hay
was concerned the trial judge reminded the jury that
there was evidence to the effect that he had delivered
the fatal blow, and that if they were satisfied beyond
doubt that it was he who delivered the fatal blow they
would then require to consider whether that was done
with murderous intent. Alternatively they were
instructed that it would be open to them to consider
whether Hay was guilty on the basis of art and part.

The trial judge also tells us in his supplementary
report that the co-accused Smith in the course of his
evidence in chief spoke of a conversation in Barlinnie
prison shortly after he, the co-accused Hay and the
appellant had been arrested and taken into custody.
According to Smith the appellant suggested that it
must have been Hay who had stabbed the deceased,
and Hay had then gone on to suggest that whoever saw
him stab the deceased should turn Queen's evidence.
When the appellant had said that he had seen Hay
stabbing the deceased Hay had responded to the effect:
"If you seen it, you tell them you seen it." Smith
apparently agreed that Hay had not admitted that he
had stabbed the deceased, but rather had said that he
could not remember what had happened. Smith also
agreed that there had been discussions about the incident a couple of times when the accused were in
Barlinnie. Hay in his evidence stated that there was a
conversation in Barlinnie to the effect that he might
have carried out the stabbing; the appellant's position
was that he never did it and that it must have been
Hay, and that Hay had then said that he himself did
not know that he had done it; he knew nothing
about the incident. He stated that he had had in mind
the possibility that he had carried out the stabbing
until his wife told him later what she had seen. The

A appellant also spoke to conversations to this effect in Barlinnie.

It thus seems plain that at the trial evidence was given regarding conversations involving Hay in Barlinnie prison before the trial. It appeared to be generally agreed by all three accused at that time that Hay's position was that he did not remember what had happened. Evidence was also given at the trial to the effect that Hay had stabbed the deceased. It follows that what the appellant is now seeking to do in inviting the court to hear evidence from the witnesses who

B have sworn affidavits, is merely to add to evidence which has already been given to the effect that it was Hay who stabbed the deceased, that he had admitted the stabbing, and regarding conversations to which Hay was a party in Barlinnie prison. The proposed new evidence does not add significantly to what was already before the jury. This is one reason for concluding that it would not be appropriate to allow this additional evidence to be led.

C There is a further reason for reaching that conclusion. As already observed, the case was presented to the jury upon the basis that they might conclude on the evidence that either the appellant or Hay had delivered the fatal blow. They were also directed upon the doctrine of concert, and, so far as the appellant and Hay were concerned, they were given a direction to the effect that if they were satisfied that the fatal blow had been struck by one or other of the appellant or Hay and that both were throughout acting in concert

D with a common criminal purpose to attack persons in the house with knives, then the jury would be entitled to convict both of them. In the event the jury acquitted both Smith and Hay, and convicted only the appellant of the charge of murder. Accordingly the jury cannot have been satisfied that Smith or Hay was guilty on the basis of concert, and they must have convicted the appellant upon the basis that it was he who had delivered the fatal blow.

E The case against the appellant Maitland depended principally upon the evidence of James McGloine, Angela McGloine and Linda Hay, and that evidence supported the view that the appellant was guilty as actor. The question must be as to what effect if any the proposed new evidence would have had upon the evidence which implicated the appellant as actor. If there had been reliable evidence that Hay had carried out the stabbing, that might have led the jury to reject the evidence which they accepted that the appellant had struck the fatal blow. The evidence led at the trial

F supporting the involvement of Hay in the crime was clearly not accepted by the jury. The proposed new evidence is to the effect that the fatal blow was struck by Hay rather than the appellant, but the source of the evidence is Hay himself, and it is plain that the jury could not have proceeded upon the basis of the evidence given by Hay at the trial, and it is difficult to see how any reasonable jury now could place any reliance upon the evidence of what he had previously said. According to the evidence led at the trial, shortly after his arrest when he was in Barlinnie prison, Hay was

maintaining to the two co-accused that he could not remember what had happened. According to what is G stated in the affidavits, shortly before and during the trial, Hay was telling all and sundry that he had stabbed the deceased. When Hay gave evidence at the trial, he testified that he had no recollection of events in the house where the killing took place. If the proposed new evidence were allowed to be led, it would clearly establish that Hay was not a person on whom any reliance could be placed.

The proposed new witnesses may be telling the truth, but we are satisfied that we could not properly H hold their evidence to be reliable evidence regarding the alleged involvement of Hay in the crime. None of them claims to have seen Hay commit the crime; they merely say that he told them so after the event. Hay gave evidence at the trial, and there is no suggestion that he should be called to give fresh evidence. In any event, since he has been acquitted, he no longer has any interest to deny what is now attributed to him. We are accordingly satisfied that this is a case where we are driven to the conclusion that no reasonable jury I could have regarded the proposed new evidence as reliable evidence of Hay's involvement (*Stillie v HM Advocate*). There is accordingly no reason to think that the proposed new evidence throws any doubt on the evidence on which the jury must have relied in holding that the appellant was guilty as actor.

Senior counsel for the appellant maintained that if the evidence contained in the affidavits had been available to the jury, that evidence (a) might have cast J doubt upon the evidence of Hay; (b) might have cast doubt upon the evidence of Linda Hay; and (c) would have revealed a confession on the part of one of the three accused, namely, Hay.

If the additional evidence would have cast doubt on the evidence of Hay, it is difficult to see how at the same time that evidence should be relied upon as supporting the view that Hay was telling the truth when he is alleged to have confessed to others in Barlinnie prison. Moreover even if the evidence of Linda Hay K were to be left out of account, there was still ample evidence to support the case that the appellant had struck the fatal blow. There was the evidence of James McGloine who spoke to seeing the appellant lunging forward and appearing to stab the deceased. Both Thomas McGloine and Angela McGloine put the deceased and Maitland together, and Angela McGloine stated that the appellant got hold of her father, and that he was holding a knife in his hand high in the air. The jury must have accepted the three L McGloine witnesses as credible and reliable, and even if they had had available to them the evidence contained in the affidavits, there is no reason to think that they would have formed a different view of the evidence of the three McGloines. Of course it is clear that the jury must have rejected the evidence of Hay's confession as spoken to by the co-accused Smith, and the appellant's evidence that it was Hay who stabbed the deceased.

We would only add that if the jury had had available

A to them the proposed additional evidence contained in the affidavits, that might have inclined them to convict Hay on the basis of art and part since it indicates a greater involvement on his part in the attack on the deceased than Hay was prepared to admit at the trial. But there is no reason to think that they would have rejected the clear evidence against the appellant implicating him on the basis of the testimony given by the three McGloines.

B   In all the circumstances senior counsel for the appellant has failed to satisfy us that the proposed additional evidence is of such a nature that it satisfies the test laid down in *Cameron v HM Advocate*; it cannot be regarded as important and reliable evidence which would have been at least likely to have had a material bearing upon, or a material part to play in, the jury's determination of a critical issue in the trial, namely, whether the appellant was guilty of the charge of murder. We are not persuaded that the jury's verdict reached in ignorance of the additional evidence referred to in the affidavits represented any mis-C carriage of justice so far as the appellant is concerned.

For the foregoing reasons the appeal against conviction is refused.

Counsel for Appellant, Findlay, QC, McBride; Solicitors, Beltrami & Co, Glasgow — Counsel for Respondent, McFarlane, QC, AD; Solicitor, J D Lowe, Crown Agent.

D   P W F

(NOTE)

Bain v Grampian Health Board

E
OUTER HOUSE
LORD KIRKWOOD
9 JULY 1992

Damages — Amount — Solatium — Wrist — Fractures of both wrists in elderly woman — Continuing pain and disability.

A 64 year old domestic worker slipped and fell in icy
F conditions, breaking both wrists. The fractures healed with continuing pain and disability in one wrist but only slight twinges in the other.

Opinion, that solatium was properly valued at £6,000.

Agnes McCreadie Bain raised an action of damages against her former employers, Grampian Health Board, following an accident on 11 February 1988. She was then aged 64. She had been employed as a

domestic worker at a hospital. After a proof before the Lord Ordinary (Kirkwood) his Lordship held that the G pursuer had slipped and fallen in icy conditions in the hospital grounds but that she had not established a case of fault against the hospital board. He granted the board absolvitor. In relation to damages his Lordship said:

"Turning to the question of damages, the pursuer gave evidence that after she fell she tried to get up and realised that there was something wrong with her hands. She had difficulty getting up but she managed to walk home and kick the door and her husband then H called a taxi and took her to the accident and emergency department of Aberdeen Royal infirmary. She was in great pain and could not put her hands down. She was x-rayed and told that two bones in her right wrist had been broken and that wrist was placed in plaster. Her left wrist was more painful but at that stage it was just strapped. The next day she returned to hospital and her left wrist was put in an elastic bandage. A week or two later she saw a consultant who told her that her left wrist had been broken as well and I it was put in plaster. She then had both wrists in plaster and they were in plaster for some four to six weeks. During that period her husband had to do everything for her, including washing and dressing her. After the plasters were removed, he had to assist her in the house for a few weeks. She still has continuing pain in her right wrist which is more painful than her left wrist. So far as her left wrist is concerned, she now only gets twinges in the back of the wrist. Her hobby was knitting but she can now only knit about J two rows at a time and she has to knit slowly or there is pain in her right wrist. If she reads a newspaper she at times suffers from cramp in the ring and little fingers of her left hand. She cannot carry such heavy weights as she was able to carry before the accident. For example, she can lift a kettle but not a pressure cooker. She can use a hoover but she cannot lift it. She has not worked since the accident. At the time of the accident she was 64 years of age and she was due to retire from her employment with the defenders in K October 1988. She had intended to obtain another cleaning job after she retired but she will not now be able to do so. She had no loss of wages prior to October 1988. Before the accident she had suffered from a mild degree of arthritis in her fingers but it did not bother her and there had been no disability in either wrist.

"Parties were agreed that the two medical reports in process are the evidence of the authors thereof. The L reports show that on 11 February 1988 an x-ray of the pursuer's right wrist showed an undisplaced fracture of the distal radius and a fragment chipped off the ulnar styloid, and the wrist was immobilised in plaster. The left wrist was initially immobilised using an elastic strapping but repeat x-rays taken on 26 February showed an undisplaced fracture of the radial styloid and that wrist was also placed in plaster. The plasters were removed on 18 March and radiologically both wrists were seen to be healing satisfactorily in good position. An elastic strapping was applied to the right wrist and she was advised to mobilise. On 25 March she had regained a good range of movement and a course of physiotherapy was arranged. By 19 April she had made only slow progress and x-rays showed some osteoporosis. In May 1988 she still had some discomfort in her right wrist but she had regained a good deal of movement and subjectively she was much improved. When she was examined by Mr Graham Page in April 1990 there was no residual tenderness or swelling but movements of the right wrist lacked about 20 degrees in all directions. Movements of the left wrist were virtually full. There was no neurovascular deficit in either limb. There had been pre-existing osteoarthritic changes in both wrists at the time of the accident, the right being worse than the left, and there had been some progress in the changes in the right wrist but the changes in the left wrist had not progressed since she had sustained the fracture. At that time Mr Page anticipated that the discomfort she was experiencing would improve further but considered that it was likely that she would have permanent disability and discomfort in both wrists, the right being worse than the left. He expressed the opinion that, if she does have permanent discomfort in both wrists, then the fractures, superimposed on the pre-existing osteoarthritis, could legitimately be said to have contributed to this longstanding condition. The pursuer was examined by Mr Sharma on 27 March 1992. Clinical examination showed slight swelling on the dorsum of both wrists, the right more so than the left. She also had a slight prominence related to her right ulnar styloid area which was still tender on deep palpation. She had fairly good dorsiflexion. Radial deviation produced some discomfort at 20 degrees on the right side. Ulnar deviation produced some pain on the left wrist. X-rays of both wrists showed no evidence of any acute fractures and no evidence of deformity or abnormality. There had been an avulsion fracture at the tip of the right ulnar styloid process and minimal changes of osteo-arthrosis related to both wrists, the right slightly more obvious than the left. Mr Sharma stated that the pursuer's current symptoms relate to dullness and some low grade pain, especially after doing any heavy work, largely related to her right wrist. Current x-rays suggested minor degenerative changes at the radio-carpal joint but the changes were minimal and in keeping with a lady of her age.

"Parties were agreed (1) that the pursuer suffered no loss of earnings as a result of the accident; (2) that the amount which reflects the extent to which she has suffered a disadvantage on the labour market as a result of the injuries sustained in the accident should be £400; and (3) that the value of the services provided to her by her husband under reference to s 8 of the Administration of Justice Act 1982 is £800. In these circumstances, the only dispute related to the value of the pursuer's claim for solatium.

"Counsel for the pursuer referred to *Hillen v Honeywell Ltd*, 1988 SLT 487 and *Johns v Greater Glasgow Health Board*, 1990 SLT 459 and submitted that an appropriate award of solatium would be in the region

of £8,000-£10,000. Counsel for the defenders, under reference to *Harkin v National Coal Board*, 1981 SLT (Notes) 37 and *McMahon v Sunblest Bakeries (Edinburgh) Ltd*, 1989 SLT 291, submitted that an award of solatiuim should be £3,000. Counsel were agreed that two thirds of the award should be attributed to the past.

"I did not consider that the pursuer attempted in any way to exaggerate her present disabilities and having regard to her evidence, and the terms of the two medical reports, I would have assessed the value of her claim for solatium at £6,000."

Counsel for Pursuer, Mackie; Solicitors, Digby Brown & Co — Counsel for Defenders, Ardrey; Solicitor, R F Macdonald.

C H

(NOTE)

Ahmed's Trustee v Ahmed (No 2)

OUTER HOUSE
LORD ABERNETHY
27 AUGUST 1992

Bankruptcy — Gratuitous alienation — Assignation of lease — Debtor entitled to but not insisting in assignation from uncle — Assignation granted to another relative instead — Uncle ordained to execute assignation to bankrupt's trustee — Assignation to other relative reduced — Bankruptcy (Scotland) Act 1985 (c 66), s 34 (1), (2) and (4).

After an assignation by an uncle to his nephew had been negotiated and, in part, executed, the nephew got into financial difficulty. The assignation was completed in the name of another nephew. On the sequestration of the originally intended assignee, his permanent trustee sought reduction of the executed assignation and an order that an assignation in favour of him as the bankrupt's trustee be executed and delivered.

Held, that the bankrupt's behaviour was a gratuitous alienation in that he had renounced his right to the assignation; and decree for execution and delivery of an assignation, and for reduction of the assignation in favour of the bankrupt's brother, *pronounced.*

Gratuitous alienations by a debtor are struck at by s 34 of the Bankruptcy (Scotland) Act 1985, which provides that an alienation is challengeable by a creditor and others, including a permanent trustee, if any of the debtor's property has been transferred by

A the alienation or any right of the debtor discharged or renounced. On such a challenge the court is empowered by s 34 (4) to "grant decree of reduction or for such restoration of property to the debtor's estate or other redress as may be appropriate".

Colin Anthony Fisher Hastings, permanent trustee on the sequestrated estates of Maqsood Ahmed, raised an action of reduction of a purported assignation of a lease of shop premises by an uncle of the bankrupt to the bankrupt's brother. The permanent trustee also B sought an order ordaining the uncle to execute an assignation of the lease of the premises in favour of the bankrupt and to deliver it to the trustee. Amongst the defenders were (first) the bankrupt, (second) his brother and (third) the grantor of the assignation, an uncle of the first and second defenders. After a proof the Lord Ordinary (Abernethy) held that there had been a verbal agreement between the bankrupt and his uncle for the assignation of the lease to the bankrupt and that that agreement had been rendered enforceable by rei interventus and homologation. His Lord-C ship also held that the assignation by the uncle of the bankrupt to the bankrupt's brother had been executed by all except the brother at a time when it bore to be in favour of the bankrupt and that it had been thereafter altered and completed. In granting decree of reduction of the assignation and an order ordaining the uncle to execute an assignation in favour of the bankrupt's permanent trustee his Lordship said:

"The result of this is that the lease was not the first D defender's property at this time [when the assignation had been executed in favour of the bankrupt but before its alteration and delivery] or indeed at any other time. There can therefore have been no alienation of property in terms of s 34 (2) (a) of the Bankruptcy (Scotland) Act 1985. That, however, is not the end of the matter. Alienation in terms of that subsection may also take place if any claim or right of the debtor has been discharged or renounced. I have already held that the first defender E had a contractual right to an assignation of the lease. At the meeting on 26 February 1988 in [his solicitor's] office he renounced that right. Counsel for the second defender submitted that this was a renunciation back to the third defender rather than a renunciation to the second defender and for that reason was not covered by the section. But in my opinion there is no substance in this point. The section draws no distinction of that kind.

F "The renunciation by the first defender of his right to an assignation of the lease was therefore an alienation within s 34 (2) (a) of the 1985 Act. It took place less than five years before his sequestration. That period is the proper one here because the renunciation was in favour of an associate within the meaning of s 74 (2) and (4). In fact, however, the general period of two years would do in this case (see s 34 (3)). The alienation is therefore challengeable by the pursuer and in terms of s 34 (4) the court 'shall grant decree of reduction or for such restoration of property to the debtor's estate or other redress as may be appropriate',

except in the circumstances thereafter set out in the subsection and subject to the proviso at the end of the G subsection. None of these circumstances applies in this case; neither does the proviso since any interest acquired in the lease by the second defender from the third defender was not for value. The appropriate decree in these circumstances is therefore one in terms of conclusion 2 [an order for execution and delivery of an assignation in favour of the pursuer as the bankrupt's permanent trustee].

"There remains, however, the purported assignation of the lease in favour of the second defender. It H is plain that that document is fatally and incurably flawed as an assignation of the lease to the second defender. None of the signatures on it, with the possible exception of the second defender's, was put on it in relation to a transfer of the lease to the second defender (Smyth v Smyth (1876) 3 R 573). However, it stands as an ex facie valid deed until reduced. Even though it was an alienation not by the first defender, the debtor in the context of s 34 of the 1985 Act, but by the third defender, it is so tied up with and refer- I able only to the alienation by the first defender that it is in my opinion appropriate to reduce it in the exercise of my powers under s 34 (4)."

Counsel for Pursuer, Hodge; Solicitors, Brodies, WS — No appearance for First Defender — Counsel for Second Defender, G M Henderson; Solicitors, Drummond Miller, WS — Counsel for Third Defender, Allardice; Solicitors, Macbeth, Currie & Co, WS. J

C H

(NOTE)

Stark v Lothian and Borders Fire Board K

OUTER HOUSE
TEMPORARY JUDGE J M S HORSBURGH, QC
1 SEPTEMBER 1992

Damages — Amount — Solatium, loss of earnings and loss of earning capacity — Burning injuries and post-traumatic stress disorder — Agreed multiplier of 12 years L applied to loss of future earnings.

Damages — Solatium — Assessment — Whether to be assessed at overall figure or by summation of awards for different consequences.

Damages — Solatium, loss of earnings and loss of earning capacity — Whether separate award should be made for loss of congenial employment.

A 26 year old fire fighter suffered burns to about 24 per cent of his body area while fighting a fire. He

A developed post-traumatic stress disorder with prolonged periods of irritability and depression and had returned to less congenial employment. Separate awards were sought for the burning injuries, the stress disorder and the loss of congenial employment.

Held, that solatium should be assessed as an overall figure and that the appropriate award was £26,000; that future loss of earnings should be calculated using a multiplier of 12 applied to the differential annual wage loss; that £3,000 was the appropriate award for disadvantage on the labour market; but that the award

B for solatium included an element for loss of congenial employment; and decree *pronounced* accordingly.

Christopher Jeffrey Stark sought damages from his employers, the Lothian and Borders Fire Board, in respect of injuries sustained while fighting a fire in a high rise block of flats on 6 February 1990. He was then aged 26. After a proof the temporary judge

C (J M S Horsburgh, QC) held that fault had been established on the ground that the fireman in charge should have appreciated the risk of a "flashover" and taken appropriate steps to avoid injury resulting from flashover. While the pursuer had been in the flat a flashover had occurred with the pursuer only a few feet from the fire. He lost consciousness and suffered burning injuries. In assessing damages, the temporary judge said:

"As a result of the accident Mr Stark suffered burns

D to about 24 per cent of his body area, including his hands, forearms, upper arms and shoulders, both ears, the scalp, the left lumbar region and the left thigh. He underwent grafting operations. He was in considerable pain as a result of his injuries for several months. His left ear is painful when exposed to the sun and now has an irregular shape. The right ear is abnormally shaped. Both are tender to touch. His skin in areas affected by burning causes him discomfort and he requires to apply cream to his hands.

E "At the time of the fire Mr Stark thought he was going to die. Since then he has developed post-traumatic stress disorder and has suffered prolonged periods of irritability and depression. His sleep has been disturbed by recollection of events. For a period he abused alcohol. Professor Bond's evidence in these matters was largely unchallenged. Mr Stark's relationship with his fiancée, to whom he intended to get married in May 1990, was badly affected to the extent that the wedding has been postponed indefinitely.

F "Mr Stark returned to work with the defenders on or about 3 December 1990 in their community education department. He will never be fit to return to fire fighting, and his present post offers no promotion. It is a less secure position than his former one. He finds the work less satisfying than his previous job. He had reasonable prospects of being promoted to leading fireman by about 1991. Although he was keen on his job, Mr Stark was not gifted academically, and his examination record suggested to me that he lacked the application necessary to pass the examinations which

would have improved his chances of advancement. On

G balance therefore I was not satisfied that he would have been likely to have achieved any higher rank. Additionally, Mr Stark claims for the assistance rendered him by his parents and his girlfriend who were responsible for looking after him shortly after he left hospital. They saw to changing his bedding daily, dressing him, cooking his meals, changing bandages, applying medication and driving him about.

Under reference to the cases of *McAleenan, Grant, Murphy and Gibson v National Coal Board*, 1987 SLT

H 106, senior counsel for Mr Stark suggested an award of £12,500 for the physical injuries. In relation to the post-traumatic stress disorder she referred to the relevant Piper Alpha arbitration awards reported in McEwan and Paton at CN 28A-12 et seq and suggested an award of about £12,500. The overall figure of solatium therefore should be £25,000, 70 per cent of which should be attributed to the past. Counsel for the defenders, under reference to the *Calder* and

Clayton cases among the Piper Alpha awards, sug-

I gested an appropriate figure for solatium would be about £20,000.

"Counsel were agreed that in respect of the claim for services provided the appropriate figure was £3,000. To that interest at 7½ per cent to the date of decree falls to be added.

"In relation to past wage loss it was agreed that loss of overtime inclusive of interest to the date of decree be taken at £200.

"As to future loss, senior counsel for Mr Stark

J argued that the weight of the evidence indicated he would have been a candidate for promotion to leading fireman by 1991 and to sub-officer grade by 1993. Under reference to *Watson v City Meat Wholesalers Ltd*, 1981 SLT (Notes) 121, a 12 year multiplier would be appropriate. That was accepted on the defenders' behalf. I am of the view that future wage loss falls to be assessed on the basis of a 12 year multiplier applied to the sum of £750 per annum, which represents the increase on a leading fireman's salary

K above what he presently earns. That gives a figure of £9,000. An award was also sought for the disadvantage Mr Stark will have on the labour market. Under reference to *Clews v B A Chemicals Ltd*, 1988 SLT 29, £5,000 was suggested, but counsel for the defenders argued for £2,500. I have come to the view that a figure of £3,000 would be reasonable.

"Senior counsel for Mr Stark also sought an award for loss of congenial employment distinguishable from

L the award of solatium. She referred to an unreported Queen's Bench case, *Blamey v London Fire and Civil Defence Authority* (16 December 1988). At p 59 of the print the deputy High Court judge referred to a number of cases in which a separate award for loss of job satisfaction had been made and she urged upon me the reasons as set out at p 61 why this should be done in the present case. The first was that loss of job satisfaction is largely unrelated to the severity of the injury. Secondly a separate award would avoid any misleading impression of inflating the solatium element for pain and suffering. Thirdly it was desirable to recognise this real head of damage independently, and fourthly such recognition would avoid the temptation a judge faces to keep his award in conformity with the pain and suffering element. She also referred to *Rieley v Kingslaw Riding School*, 1975 SLT (Notes) 14; 1975 SC 28; *McNee v G R Stein & Co Ltd*, 1981 SLT (Notes) 31 and *Tuttle v University of Edinburgh*, 1984 SLT 172, as cases where the Scottish courts have recognised the distinct nature of an award for loss of job satisfaction, although compensation therefor was included in the solatium award. She suggested £6,000. Counsel for the defenders challenged neither the principle of making this award nor the amount proposed.

"Alternatively, senior counsel for Mr Stark suggested that if I was not satisfied that it was appropriate to make an award for loss of job satisfaction separate from the solatium award, a total solatium award to include this element should be £31,000.

"I do not consider that the English cases referred to assist. The Scots law concept of solatium is wider than a pain and suffering award. I am not satisfied as to the soundness of the reasons advanced in *Blamey* for making a separate award for loss of job satisfaction. I prefer to follow existing Scottish practice and to make a solatium award which comprises an overall figure for pain and suffering, post-traumatic stress disorder and loss of job satisfaction rather than one which represents a total of accumulative elements. £31,000 is over generous in my opinion, and I consider the appropriate figure to be £26,000. Interest should run at 7½ per cent on two thirds of that sum to the date of decree.

"It was agreed that the loss of pension rights to be awarded upon the assumption that Mr Stark would have been promoted to leading fireman is £8,000. I calculate interest on past solatium at £2,500 and interest on the loss of services at £560.

"Accordingly the total award is £52,250 and I grant decree for that sum."

Counsel for Pursuer, Clark, QC, Craddock; Solicitors, Robin Thompson & Partners — Counsel for Defenders, Cheyne; Solicitor, G F G Welsh.

C H

Taylor v Ford

OUTER HOUSE

TEMPORARY JUDGE J M S HORSBURGH, QC

3 SEPTEMBER 1992

Parent and child — Custody — International child abduction — Children removed from Canada to Scotland by parent having Canadian custody award — Effect of subsequent Canadian court orders awarding custody to other parent — Whether removal of children a "wrongful act" — Procedure for resolving issues of Canadian law — Child Abduction and Custody Act 1985 (c 60), s 5 and Sched 1, arts 3, 5, 12 and 13 (b).

The father and mother of two children cohabited in Canada. On 16 July 1991 the father obtained an order from the court in Ontario prohibiting the mother from removing the children from the province. The mother then left the father, taking the children with her. On 19 July 1991 the father obtained an award of custody and delivery of the children from the same court. On 8 August 1991 the father and mother resumed cohabitation in an attempt at reconciliation. On 16 September 1991 however the mother finally left the father, leaving the children with him. The father left Canada with the children on 1 October 1991 and took them to Malta. On 2 October 1991 the mother obtained an order from the Ontario court prohibiting the father from removing the children from the province. On 4 October 1991 she obtained a restraining order and an order for access. On 17 October 1991 the Ontario court rescinded the father's custody and awarded interim custody to the mother.

In 1992 the father arrived in Scotland with the children. The mother presented a petition to the Court of Session under s 5 of the Child Abduction and Custody Act 1985 for an order that the father return the children to Ontario, with interdict and ancillary orders to facilitate the delivery of the children to her. The vacation judge granted interim interdict against the removal of the children from Scotland by the father and ordered him to return the children to the mother. The father then enrolled motions for recall of the interlocutors of the vacation judge and delivery of the children to him. The mother argued (a) that the resumption of cohabitation by the parties had revoked the court order of 19 July 1991; (b) that a letter from the father's lawyer had compromised that order; and (c) that the father was in breach of his and the mother's custody rights, so that the removal was unlawful. The mother further argued that the court should request a decision from the Ontario court on whether the removal was unlawful.

Held, (1) that the removal of the children from Canada by the father was not wrongful within the meaning of art 3 of the Hague Convention as he had obtained a custody order on 19 July 1991, under Canadian law the mother's equal entitlement to custody then ended, and under art 5 of the Convention the father's custody rights included the right to determine the place of residence of the children (p 656G-H); (2) that the mother had not demonstrated that according to Canadian law a resumption of cohabitation terminated a court order for custody (pp 656I-657C); (3) that it was inappropriate to request a decision from the Ontario court as to whether the removal was unlawful in view of (a) an authoritative Canadian precedent which had not been judicially disapproved or not followed, and (b) the need for expedition in deciding applications under the Convention (p 657C-E); (4) that no agreement had been estab-

A lished to revoke the father's custody order, nor did it appear that one or other party could compromise such an order (p 657E-F); and (5) that the mother had had no custodial rights which had been breached by the removal of the children (p 657H-J and K-L); but (6) that standing the interim custody order in favour of the mother, it was inappropriate to order the return of the children to the father (p 658A); and interim interdict *recalled*.

Re H (A Minor) (Abduction) [1990] 2 FLR 439, *distinguished.*

B **Opinion**, that only in the clearest of cases should the court exercise its discretion under art 13 (b) of the Convention, and the third proviso thereto, to refuse to order the return of the children notwithstanding that the removal had been held to be wrongful (p 658B).

Petition under the Child Abduction and Custody Act 1985

C Cheryl Ann Taylor, the mother of two children, presented a petition against Raymond John Ford, the children's father, seeking an order under s 5 of the Child Abduction and Custody Act 1985 for return of the children to Ontario, with an interdict and order for delivery. The children had been taken from Canada to Scotland by their father. On 11 August 1992 the vacation judge granted interim interdict against removal of the children from Scotland by the father. On 12 August 1992 the vacation judge ordered the father to return the children to the mother in Scotland D under the supervision of the social work department. The father enrolled motions for recall of the interlocutors of 11 and 12 August 1992, and for delivery of the children to him.

A hearing took place before the temporary judge (J M S Horsburgh, QC) on 26 and 27 August 1992.

Statutory provisions

The Child Abduction and Custody Act 1985 E provides:

"5. Where an application has been made to a court in the United Kingdom under the Convention, the court may, at any time before the application is determined, give such interim directions as it thinks fit for the purpose of securing the welfare of the child concerned or of preventing changes in the circumstances relevant to the determination of the application."

The Convention on the Civil Aspects of International Child Abduction (The Hague Convention), set F out in Sched 1 to the 1985 Act, provides:

"3. The removal or the retention of a child is to be considered wrongful where — (a) it is in breach of rights of custody attributed to a person, an institution or any other body, either jointly or alone, under the law of the state in which the child was habitually resident immediately before the removal or retention; and (b) at the time of removal or retention those rights were actually exercised, either jointly or alone, or would have been so exercised but for the removal or retention.

"The rights of custody mentioned in sub-paragraph (a) above may arise in particular by operation of law G or by reason of a judicial or administrative decision, or by reason of an agreement having legal effect under the law of that state. . . .

"5. For the purposes of this Convention — (a) 'rights of custody' shall include rights relating to the care of the person of the child and, in particular, the right to determine the child's place of residence; (b) 'rights of access' shall include the right to take a child for a limited period of time to a place other than the child's habitual residence. . . . H

"12. Where a child has been wrongfully removed or retained in terms of Article 3 and, at the date of the commencement of the proceedings before the judicial or administrative authority of the Contracting State where the child is, a period of less than one year has elapsed from the date of the wrongful removal or retention, the authority concerned shall order the return of the child forthwith. . . .

"13. Notwithstanding the provisions of the preced- I ing Article, the judicial or administrative authority of the requested State is not bound to order the return of the child if the person, institution or other body which opposes its return establishes that — . . . (b) there is a grave risk that his or her return would expose the child to physical or psychological harm or otherwise place the child in an intolerable situation."

Cases referred to

C v C (Minor: Abduction: Rights of Custody Abroad) J [1989] 1 WLR 654; [1989] 2 All ER 465.
Dickson v Dickson, 1990 SCLR 692.
Grail v Grail (1990) 27 RFL (3d) 317; 30 RFL (3d) 454.
H (A Minor) (Abduction), Re [1990] 2 FLR 439.
Hatt v Hatt (1976) 17 RFL 58.
MacMillan v MacMillan, 1989 SLT 350; 1989 SCLR 243.
Mongrain v Mongrain (1986) 1 RFL (3d) 330.

K On 3 September 1992 the temporary judge *recalled* the interim interdict.

J M S HORSBURGH, QC.—From the facts admitted in the pleadings, so far as adjusted, in this petition and answers, and from unchallenged information given at the bar, it appears that for about 10 years ending on 16 September 1991 the petitioner and the respondent cohabited in Canada. They both have Canadian nationality, although the respondent is of L Maltese origin. They had two children, now aged 10 and eight. In January and June 1991 the petitioner left the respondent for short periods.

On 16 July 1991, by ex parte application, the respondent obtained an order from an Ontario court prohibiting the petitioner from removing the children from that province. She again left the respondent, taking the children with her. On 19 July 1991 he similarly obtained an award of their custody and an order for their delivery from the same court. On 6 August

1991 he obtained an order for delivery from a court in British Columbia, where the petitioner and the children then were. Numbers 7 (2), 7 (3) and 7 (5) of process are copies of these orders.

On 8 August 1991 the petitioner and the children returned to live with the respondent in Ontario, in an attempted reconciliation. On 16 September 1991 the petitioner again left, leaving the children with the respondent. The petitioner's averments that she left because of abuse and violence by the respondent are denied.

On 1 October 1991 the respondent left Canada with the children and travelled to Malta. On 2 October 1991 the petitioner obtained an order in the Ontario action at the respondent's instance prohibiting his removal of the children from the province. On 4 October 1991 she obtained a similar restraining order and an order for access. On 17 October 1991, on the petitioner's application, the order of 19 July 1991 granting custody to the respondent was rescinded, and she was awarded interim custody of the children. Numbers 7 (6), 7 (7) and 7 (9) of process are copies of these orders.

On 31 March 1992 the children left Malta with the respondent, and travelled to Paisley where he has since lived with a woman.

In this petition the petitioner seeks an order under s 5 of the Child Abduction and Custody Act 1985 that the respondent return the children to Ontario, with associated interdict and orders to facilitate delivery of the children to her. She avers that with the attempted reconciliation between 8 August and 16 September the court order of 19 July in the respondent's favour fell, and her equal entitlement to custody with the respondent under s 20 (1) of the Canadian Children's Law Reform Act 1980 (hereafter referred to as the 1980 Act) revived. She also avers that the children's removal was in breach of her rights of custody to which art 3 of the Hague Convention applied, and which she was actually exercising. She maintains that the removal of the children from Canada was wrongful.

On the other hand the respondent avers that at the time of the children's removal he had an award of custody, while the petitioner had no such right, and in any event, she was not exercising any right she might have at the material time. Thus his removal of the children was not wrongful.

On 11 August 1992 the vacation judge granted interim interdict against the removal of the children from Scotland by the respondent. On 12 August he ordered the respondent to return the children to the petitioner, who had come to Scotland, and directed that her subsequent care of them be subject to social work department supervision. The petitioner recovered care of the children, and they presently live with her.

Motions by the respondent for recall of these interlocutors, and for delivery of the children to him, were argued before me on 26 and 27 August. In essence the arguments presented followed the parties' respective averments, and were directed chiefly to the issue of the effect of the attempted reconciliation on the order of 19 July 1991.

I am of the opinion that the respondent is entitled to recall of the interim interdict pronounced on 11 August.

I have reached that conclusion upon the view that the respondent's removal of the children was not wrongful within the meaning of art 3 of the Hague Convention. On 19 July 1991 he had obtained an order giving him custody of the children. Under s 20 (7) of the 1980 Act the petitioner's equal entitlement to custody then ended, and she had no custodial rights. In terms of art 5 of the Convention the rights the respondent then had included that of determining the place of residence of the children. He was thus entitled to take them out of Canada on 1 October 1991. The respondent's right remained effective till rescinded on 17 October, since which date the petitioner has had an interim order for custody in her favour.

The petitioner's argument was first that resumption of cohabitation by the parties had revoked the court order of 19 July, and secondly that the respondent's lawyer's letter of 1 August 1991, which was no 7 (4) of process, also might have compromised that order. The effect was that the equal custody entitlement given parents by s 20 (1) revived. Thirdly, she argued that in removing the children the respondent was in breach of both his and the petitioner's custody rights, and so the removal was wrongful.

I consider that first argument to be incorrect. As to Canadian law on the matter, I was referred to *Hatt v Hatt.* That case decided that under ss 1 (1) and 2 (1) of the Infants Act, which gave parents equal entitlement to custody unless otherwise ordered by the court, a resumption of cohabitation did not terminate a court order for custody. The Infants Act seems to have been the statutory predecessor of the 1980 Act. In an opinion obtained from Canadian counsel *Hatt* was relied on, and in another opinion reference was also made to a decision of Pat Wallace J in August 1991 to the effect that an interim order for custody and/or support remained effective until changed by the parties. Both opinions supported the view that the attempted reconciliation had not terminated the order of 19 July.

The petitioner's assertion that the reconciliation revived equal custody entitlement relied upon passages in a research memorandum in process. These were to the effect that it was possible that the courts might be persuaded by analogy with *Mongrain v Mongrain* and *Grail v Grail* that the order of 19 July 1991 fell and *Hatt* would be overruled or not followed.

In my opinion that is an inadequate basis for contending that the respondent's removal of the children on 1 October 1991 was wrongful, for two reasons. First, the memorandum merely puts forward the possibility that in the future Canadian courts might not follow *Hatt*. Secondly, the cases of *Mongrain* and *Grail* dealt with a different statute, and related to spouse and child support, not to custody. According to the reports, nos 9 (4), 9 (5) and 9 (6) of process, *Hatt* was not cited or considered. They therefore provide an insufficient basis for the contention that at the time of the removal of the children there were directly conflicting decisions on the issue in the Canadian courts.

The petitioner's argument was also based on an opinion of Canadian counsel which was to the same effect as the memorandum. It does not refer to *Hatt*. It states that Ontario law on the effect of reconciliation on custody orders is unclear, and that judges take different views. I do not consider that variation in practice forms an adequate foundation for finding the respondent's removal of the children to have been wrongful. Even if, as averred by the petitioner, the respondent had been advised by his lawyers that removal of the children would be wrongful, standing the information available to me, that advice cannot be regarded as sound. Accordingly, I do not consider that as a matter of law at least, the respondent's action can be regarded as wrongful.

Counsel for the petitioner also argued that since the question was an open one, I should request a decision from the Ontario court on whether the removal was wrongful. I am not prepared to take that course for two reasons. First, I am not referred to any reported case which disapproved of or did not follow *Hatt*. Secondly the Hague Convention is designed to achieve the speedy return of children wrongfully removed from a jurisdiction, and in the Inner House in *MacMillan v MacMillan* and *Dickson v Dickson* the need for expedition in deciding applications under the Convention has been emphasised. A request to Ontario would cause delay, and I think that course would only be justified if there was a real doubt about the effect of attempted reconciliations on custody orders under Ontario law at the time of the removal. On the information before me such a doubt has not been shown to exist.

I also consider the petitioner's second argument to be unsound. It was maintained that there might be an agreement which revoked the court order of 19 July. I reject the argument because first it is based on speculation. Secondly, I find nothing in s 20 to indicate that one or other party can compromise a court order. Thirdly, on its face no 7 (4) of process does not constitute an agreement between the parties, nor is it a separation agreement such as is referred to in s 20. In any event, its proposals were superseded by the attempted reconciliation.

Lastly, I consider that the respondent's argument receives powerful support from the fact that the petitioner sought and obtained orders for rescission of the order of 19 July on 4 and 17 October respectively. These steps strongly indicate that at the time of the removal of the children the order of 19 July was regarded as being in force. Counsel for the petitioner had no satisfactory explanation for why that was done

if the petitioner's equal right of custody had been revived and the respondent's sole right lost.

I do not consider the petitioner's third contention to be sound.

The argument that the respondent breached his own rights of custody was founded on *Re H (A Minor) (Abduction)*. That case is clearly distinguishable however. In it the award of custody to the mother who removed the child had contained a prohibition against her removing the child from the jurisdiction without the court's leave. The removal was wrongful because she acted in breach of that prohibition. The order of 19 July contains no such prohibition. The respondent, having an order in his favour had the right to determine the residence of the children, and by removing them, he was within his rights. That he did so knowing, as the petitioner avers, that a hearing on custody was imminent, may not be to his credit, but it did not make his actions wrongful in law.

The argument that the respondent acted in breach of the petitioner's own custodial rights was put on the footing that Canadian concepts of custody and access might differ from those of Scots law. I reject that as speculation. It was also contended that the petitioner's right of access was a custodial right. However s 20 of the 1980 Act distinguishes between custody and access. The Ontario court orders produced also make that distinction, as does art 5 of the Convention. It was also suggested that under s 20 (4) and (5) the non-custodial parent had a right to be consulted as to the whereabouts of the children. That reading cannot be supported. It gives no right of consultation or determination in relation to the children's place of residence. No more than a right to inquire and to receive information is given. Accordingly I reject this argument.

It thus becomes unnecessary to decide if the petitioner was actually exercising rights of custody at the time of the children's removal, but I observe that the letter founded on to support that argument, no 7 (4) of process, deals only with access for the respondent.

Reliance was placed by the petitioner on *C v C (Minor: Abduction: Rights of Custody Abroad)* to suggest that custody rights should not be interpreted narrowly. However the basis of that decision was that the mother's removal of the child breached a provision in the order in her favour that neither party would remove the child from the jurisdiction without the other's consent, which had not been obtained. The need for the father's consent was held to be a right to determine the child's place of residence, and hence a custody right. Again the order of 19 July gave the petitioner no such right.

For these reasons I am satisfied that the removal of the children by the respondent was not a wrongful act within the meaning of the Hague Convention. Dismissal of the petition was not sought. Since the respondent was acting within his rights, I consider that he is entitled to recall of the interim interdict, that being designed to protect against his removal of the children from Scotland, he having allegedly wrongfully removed them from Canada.

It does not follow however that an order for the return of the children to him should be made. The petitioner has an interim award of custody in her favour, and that has not been recalled. My decision merely settles that the petitioner's retention of custody cannot depend on the provisions of the Hague Convention. The issue of custody will have to be resolved either in Ontario or in another process in this court, founding on the presence of the children within Scotland.

It should be added that the respondent argued that if his removal of the children was held to be wrongful, I should exercise my discretion under art 13 (b) and the third proviso of that article, and refuse to order the return of the children. In view of my decision it is not necessary to do so. However, I consider that only in the clearest of cases should this means of escaping the mandatory provisions of art 12 of the Convention be entertained by the court. I would not have been prepared to do so on the basis of objections to their return by the children, since I consider that the averments made about this are inadequate. It would only have been with much hesitation that I would have considered that the averments relating to art 13 (b) itself were apt for proof by parole or affidavit evidence.

Counsel for Petitioner, Andrew Smith; Solicitors, Wilson Chalmers & Hendry — Counsel for Respondent, Fitzpatrick; Solicitors, Macbeth, Currie & Co, WS.

P G L H

(NOTE)

Munro v Strathclyde Regional Council

OUTER HOUSE

LORD WEIR

30 OCTOBER 1992

Damages — Amount — Solatium — Nose — Displaced fracture of nose with complete recovery and good alignment.

A 20 year old pedestrian broke her nose in a fall. It required manipulative reduction but there was complete recovery.

Opinion, relying upon awards by the Criminal Injuries Compensation Board, that solatium was reasonably assessed at £1,500.

Mrs Pauline Spalding or Munro raised an action against Strathclyde Regional Council, seeking damages for the consequences of a fall in the street on 7 February 1987. She was then aged 20. The regional council was responsible for the safe condition of the pavement. In the accident the pursuer had fallen about two or three feet into a patio area in front of a shop.

Her main injury was a very serious leg injury caused by a twisting of her knee. After a proof the Lord Ordinary (Weir) held that the leg injury had not been caused by the fall into the patio but by the initial catching of the pursuer's foot in a channel. His Lordship also held that the defenders were not at fault because the accident was unforeseeable. His Lordship assoilzied the defenders. In relation to damages his Lordship said:

"It was agreed that in the event of the pursuer establishing liability on the part of these defenders for *all* of the injuries sustained by her, the amount of damages prior to any deduction in respect of contributory negligence should be £32,500 inclusive of wage loss and of interest to the date of decree. The question of damages does not of course arise but in case it should do there would remain the question of whether the pursuer might be entitled to an award for solatium arising from the injury to her nose. It is arguable that this element of claim is separable upon the view that although the unfenced drop had nothing to do with the initial fall leading to this serious leg injury, the subsequent fall into the patio was the cause of the broken nose. I have already expressed the view that the link between the unfenced drop and the nose injury is not established, but, if I am wrong on that point, I would have assessed damages for the broken nose at £1,500. This was a displaced fracture which required manipulative reduction. It must have been a painful experience but fortunately the pursuer has made a complete recovery with good alignment of the nose and no disfigurement. In making this assessment I have had regard to the level of comparable awards made by the Criminal Injuries Compensation Board and set out in their most recent annual report. No tribunal has more experience in making assessments of injuries of this kind than the board."

Counsel for Pursuer, R W J Anderson; Solicitors, Brown Mair Mackintosh & Co — Counsel for Defenders, Craddock; Solicitors, Simpson & Marwick, WS (for Hennessy, Bowie & Co, Glasgow).

C H

Garvie v Secretary of State for Social Services

FIRST DIVISION

THE LORD PRESIDENT (HOPE),
LORDS SUTHERLAND AND KIRKWOOD

27 NOVEMBER 1992

Social security — Supplementary benefit — Single payments — Discretionary payments to be made in specified circumstances except where claim for "miscellaneous furniture and household equipment needs" — Whether claim for number of specified items constituted separate claims for each item and thereby not a miscellaneous

A claim — Supplementary Benefit (Single Payments) Regulations 1981 (SI 1981/1528), reg 30, as amended.

Process — Authorities — Social security commissioner — Conflicting decisions of tribunals of commissioners — Decision of Court of Appeal in Northern Ireland — Whether commissioner bound to follow latest decision of tribunal of commissioners — Whether commissioner ought to follow decision of Court of Appeal in Northern Ireland.

B Regulation 30 of the Supplementary Benefit (Single Payments) Regulations 1981, as amended, provided for single payments to be made, except where a claim was for miscellaneous furniture and household equipment needs, to meet an exceptional need not otherwise provided for in the regulations if such a payment was the only means by which serious damage or serious risk to the health or safety of the claimant might be prevented. Regulation 9 dealt with claims for furniture and household equipment regarded as essential. By virtue of reg 10A a single payment of a prescribed sum (£75) could be made for miscellaneous furniture C and household equipment needs.

A claimant who was blind applied for a single supplementary benefit payment in respect of expenditure incurred in moving into a house of his own as a first time tenant. A number of items of furniture, fittings and household equipment were claimed. Those items classified as essential were paid for and the prescribed amount of £75 in respect of miscellaneous furniture and household equipment needs was paid in respect of the remainder. It was argued on behalf of the claimant D that he had made a number of separate claims in respect of each individual item and that a discretionary payment should be made for the items claimed since the requirements of reg 30 were met. It was contended that the exclusion in respect of miscellaneous furniture and household equipment needs related to a general claim which would attract only the prescribed amount. The regulation had been interpreted to opposite effects by two tribunals of commissioners, the interpretation by the later of which corresponded with E that of a decision of the Court of Appeal in Northern Ireland. The claimant challenged the commissioner's ruling that he was obliged to follow the decision of the later tribunal.

Held, (1) that although there were separate regulations in Northern Ireland, they were virtually identical to those applicable in the present case and the decision of the Court of Appeal in Northern Ireland should be treated by a commissioner in England or Scotland as persuasive if not binding (p 661C); (2) that it was F reasonable for the commissioner to have followed the decision of the later tribunal of commissioners, which had before it both the decision of the earlier tribunal and that of the Court of Appeal in Northern Ireland (p 661C-D); (3) that if an item of household furniture and equipment was not essential within the terms of reg 9 it fell within reg 10A which dealt with miscellaneous furniture and household equipment needs and was excluded from reg 30 regardless of whether or not a payment in respect of the item would be necessary for the health or safety of the claimant (pp 661I-J and 662A-B); and appeal refused.

Opinion, that the exclusion in reg 30 did not extend to essential furniture and household equipment G needs for which a claim was not otherwise met under the regulations (p 662E-F).

Dictum in Carleton v Department of Health and Social Security, Court of Appeal in Northern Ireland, 29 June 1988, unreported, not followed.

Appeal from the social security commissioner

John Garvie sought a single payment of supplementary benefit in terms of the Supplementary H Benefit (Single Payments) Regulations 1981, as amended, in respect of needs arising from moving into a house of his own for the first time. The adjudication officer allowed claims for essential items of furniture and household equipment and awarded a single payment of £75 for the remaining items. The claimant appealed to the social security appeal tribunal and to the social security commissioner. Both appeals were refused.

The claimant appealed to the Court of Session I under s 14 (1) of the Social Security Act 1980.

Statutory provisions

The Supplementary Benefit (Single Payments) Regulations 1981, as amended, provided:

"10A.—(1) Subject to the further conditions of paragraph (2) a single payment shall be made in respect of miscellaneous furniture and household equipment needs (other than any item to which regulation 9 J [essential items] applies) where the claimant or his partner has within the 28 days immediately preceding the date of claim become the tenant or owner of an unfurnished or partly furnished home. . . .

"30.—(1) Except where a claim is for miscellaneous furniture and household equipment needs, where a claimant is entitled to a pension or allowance and he — (a) claims a single payment for an exceptional need under any of the regulations in Parts II to VII (other than regulation 10A) but fails to satisfy the conditions K for that payment; or (b) claims to have an exceptional need for which no provision for a single payment is made in any regulation in those Parts, a single payment to meet that exceptional need shall be made in his case if, in the opinion of an adjudication officer, such a payment is the only means by which serious damage or serious risk to the health or safety of any member of the assessment unit may be prevented."

Cases referred to

Carleton v Department of Health and Social Security, L Court of Appeal in Northern Ireland, 29 June 1988, unreported.
Decision No R (SB) 10/88.
Decision No R (SB) 1/90.

Appeal

The claimant's grounds of appeal were as follows:

(1) The commissioner misdirected himself in law in holding that reg 30 of the Supplementary Benefit (Single Payments) Regulations 1981 did not apply in

A deciding whether or not the appellant's claim for a single payment should be granted. The appellant's claim was not in respect of miscellaneous furniture and household equipment.

(2) The commissioner misdirected himself in law in holding that he was bound to follow decision R (SB) 1/90 referred to in his said decision.

The appeal was heard by the First Division on 13 November 1992.

B   On 27 November 1992 the court *refused* the appeal.

The following opinion of the court was delivered by Lord Sutherland:

OPINION OF THE COURT.—This is an appeal under s 14 of the Social Security Act 1980 against a decision by the social security commissioner whereby he affirmed a decision of the social security appeal tribunal which in turn had affirmed a decision of the adjudication officer. The claimant, who is blind, had
C moved into a house of his own as a first time tenant. He had no furniture of his own and the claim was accordingly for a large number of items of furniture and household equipment. Some of the items were regarded as essential and were therefore paid for under the appropriate regulation. The remaining items were regarded as miscellaneous furniture and household equipment, and in respect of all of these items taken together, a single payment of £75 was made, this being the figure fixed by the regulations. The claimant
D appealed against this decision on the ground that the items which he claimed should not properly be regarded as being items of miscellaneous furniture and household equipment but should be regarded as items which were necessary to him because he had an exceptional need of them and only a payment for them would be the means by which serious damage or serious risk to his health or safety might be prevented.

It is necessary first to set out the relevant regulations. The Supplementary Benefit (Single Payments)
E Regulations 1981 were amended by the Supplementary Benefit (Miscellaneous Amendments) Regulations 1986 and it is the amended regulations which are relevant in this case. Regulation 9, as amended, reads as follows: "In this Part of the regulations 'essential furniture and household equipment' means the following items". There then follows a list of 11 items including bed, cooker and heater which are regarded as essential items. Some of these items are only to be treated as essential if they satisfy further
F conditions. For example a vacuum cleaner is only regarded as essential if a member of the assessment unit is allergic to house dust. Regulation 10 provides for a single payment for the purchase, repair and installation of an item of essential furniture and household equipment under certain conditions, mainly relating to the circumstances of the claimant. It is not necessary to go into details of these conditions as there is no doubt that the claimant in the present case satisfies the relevant conditions. Regulation 10A is in the following terms: [his Lordship quoted its terms and continued:]

There then follow certain conditions again relating to the circumstances of the claimant. Under para (3) G of reg 10A it is provided that the amount payable in respect of miscellaneous furniture and household equipment needs under this regulation shall be the aggregate of (a) the amount specified in col 2 of Sched 1B for the claimant and (b) the amount specified in col 2 of Sched 1B for each additional member of the assessment unit. The amount specified for a claimant was, at the material time, £75. Regulation 30 deals with discretionary payments and, as amended, provides as follows: [his Lordship quoted the terms of reg H 30 (1) and continued:]

The adjudication officer allowed claims for items on the claimant's list which constituted essential items of furniture and equipment as defined in reg 9. As far as the remaining items were concerned, he held that the claimant satisfied the conditions for a payment under reg 10A and awarded a single payment of £75. The claimant appealed on the ground that the regulations under which the claim had been determined were ultra vires. When the matter came before the social security I appeal tribunal the question of vires was argued and the claimant's argument was rejected. We do not need to say anything further on this aspect of the case, as before this court the claimant did not seek to advance any argument to the effect that the regulations were ultra vires. It was, however, also argued before the tribunal that the items were not included in the term "miscellaneous furniture and household equipment" and accordingly reg 10A did not apply and reg 30 should apply in its place. The tribunal, in considering that argument, accepted that the circumstances of the J claimant were such that he would satisfy the condition under reg 30 that a full payment for each of these items claimed would be the only means by which serious damage or serious risk to the health or safety of the claimant may be prevented, but nevertheless held that because the items claimed fell under reg 10A, any claim under reg 30 was excluded because of the exclusion in that regulation of any claim for miscellaneous furniture and household equipment needs. Before the commissioner the same arguments were K advanced and the commissioner upheld the decision of the tribunal on both aspects of the claim.

In his decision the commissioner referred to two decisions by tribunals of commissioners, namely R (SB) 10/88 and R (SB) 1/90, and a decision of the Court of Appeal in Northern Ireland in the case of *Carleton v DHSS*, 29 June 1988. The commissioner held that he felt obliged to follow the decision in R (SB) 1/90 and accordingly held that the appeal failed. The claimant appeals to this court on the following L grounds: [his Lordship quoted the grounds of appeal and continued:]

It is convenient to deal with the second ground of appeal first. Decision R (SB) 10/88, to which we shall return in more detail later, could be regarded as being favourable to the claimant's argument. The decision by the Court of Appeal in Northern Ireland was to the contrary effect and held that reg 30 could not apply when a number of items of furniture and equipment were being sought, as such a claim was precluded by the terms of the equivalent regulation to reg 10A. The decision in R (SB) 1/90 followed upon these two decisions, and the tribunal of commissioners having considered the matter held that they would follow the decision given by the Court of Appeal in Northern Ireland. It was in that situation that the commissioner in the present case felt that he was obliged to follow R (SB) 1/90. It was argued before us that the Court of Appeal in Northern Ireland had not considered the decision in R (SB) 10/88 and therefore their reasoning was vitiated. Furthermore, a decision by the Court of Appeal in Northern Ireland would not be binding on commissioners in England or Scotland because there were separate regulations for Northern Ireland and therefore any decision could not be binding. For practical purposes therefore there were two conflicting decisions of tribunals of commissioners and the commissioner in the present case should have considered the matter for himself, rather than simply following the later decision of a tribunal of commissioners.

It is perfectly true that a decision by the Court of Appeal in Northern Ireland is not binding on a commissioner in England or Scotland, in that there are separate regulations to be considered. For practical purposes however the regulations are in virtually identical terms as far as the present issue is concerned and therefore any decision of the Court of Appeal in Northern Ireland should be treated as persuasive, if not binding. The important point, however, is that decision R (SB) 1/90 was given by a tribunal of commissioners who considered the previous decision 10/88 and also the Northern Irish decision and having considered these matters came to their own conclusion. It was therefore, in our view, quite reasonable for the commissioner in the present case to take the view that the later decision was the one which he should follow, bearing in mind that the tribunal in that case had before it the decision not only of the earlier tribunal but also of the Court of Appeal in Northern Ireland and fully considered the relevant issues. As far as this court is concerned the issue is an academic one as we are, of course, not bound by any decisions of tribunals of commissioners or indeed of the Court of Appeal in Northern Ireland.

Turning to the principal issue raised in the first ground of appeal, the argument for the appellant as we understood it was that a claim for a number of items should not be treated as a single claim but as a number of separate claims in respect of each individual item. If a claim for a single item was made this could not fall within the terms of reg 10A and, on the assumption that it was not an essential item under reg 9, would necessarily fall to be dealt with under reg 30. The only way in which a claim under reg 30 could be held to be excluded by reason of the exception would be when the claim was in purely general terms for a single payment for miscellaneous furniture and household equipment. If, however, the claim was for a specific item or a number of specific items each claim had to be treated separately and could not be regarded as falling under the head of a generalised claim for miscellaneous equipment. This was the argument which

commended itself to the tribunal of commissioners in R (SB) 10/88 and should be followed.

In our opinion this argument is unsound. Looking at R (SB) 10/88 the claim was made for carpets, curtains, furniture and household goods in general. The tribunal held that it was quite clear that the claim in that case was for what could properly be described as miscellaneous furniture and household equipment needs and that being so, the claim under reg 30 must fail. The tribunal however went on to say: "We should emphasise that nothing that we have written precludes a claim from being made for an individual item under regulation 30 (Part VIII) of the Single Payment Regulations on the ground that without it there is a serious risk to health and safety. Such a claim is not a claim for miscellaneous furniture and household equipment needs. Where more than one item is requested, that is in fact a separate claim in respect of each item. Tentative suggestions were made in argument that one could 'dress up' what is in reality a claim for miscellaneous furniture and household equipment needs in this way. It will be for the adjudicating authority, in each case, to determine the nature of the claim or claims in this connection."

It is in our opinion clear that reg 30 is designed to deal with the situation where a claim is made for items which are necessary for the safety or health of the claimant. Notwithstanding that generality, however, reg 30 makes it abundantly clear at the outset that any claim which is for miscellaneous furniture and household equipment needs is excluded from the purview of reg 30, regardless of whether or not such payment would be necessary for the health or safety of the claimant. What therefore has to be looked at first is whether or not the claim is indeed for miscellaneous furniture and household equipment needs. If that question is answered in the affirmative, then regardless of the safety or health of the claimant reg 30 cannot apply. It is only if the question is answered in the negative that one can go on to consider whether the other conditions set out in reg 30 are applicable.

Turning to regs 9, 10 and 10A the scheme of the regulations appears to be clear. Certain items of furniture and household equipment are regarded as essential and these are dealt with in reg 9. If the conditions set out in reg 9 and the personal conditions relating to the claimant set out in reg 10 are also satisfied a payment will be made for these items. A further payment may be made under reg 10A if the conditions in that regulation are satisfied. Regulation 10A in terms deals with "miscellaneous furniture and household equipment needs (other than any item to which regulation 9 applies)". This in our opinion makes it abundantly clear that furniture and household equipment needs are divided into two parts, namely, essential furniture and equipment and miscellaneous furniture and equipment. Counsel for the appellant argued that there could be a third category midway between these items, and that miscellaneous furniture and equipment should only be treated as dealing with very small and minor items which could not attract any payment under reg 30. In our opinion, however, there is no room in the scheme of these regulations for any third category. We consider it to be quite clear on a proper construction of the regulations that if an item of household furniture and equipment is not essential within the terms of reg 9 then it must fall within the purview of reg 10A, and that the proper construction of reg 10A is to read it as meaning a need for any item of furniture or household equipment which was not covered by reg 9. This may appear somewhat draconian in that items which may be necessary for the safety and health of a claimant are thereby excluded, but we see no escape from that construction of the regulations. This was the view which commended itself to the Court of Appeal in Northern Ireland and to the tribunal of commissioners in R (SB) 1/90 and we agree with those decisions. Any contrary view would involve the invention of a third category not contemplated by the regulations. Furthermore the argument as advanced by the appellant would mean that the effect of the exception set out in reg 30 could be elided by making a claim for a specific item or items rather than a purely general claim and this would mean that for practical purposes the exception would be meaningless. The appeal is accordingly refused.

Having had put before us the full transcript of the decision by the Court of Appeal in Northern Ireland in *Carleton* we consider that there is one matter to which we should draw attention. In giving the decision of the court the Lord Chief Justice said that reg 30 no longer permits a payment to be made under it in respect of furniture or household equipment. The claimant sought leave to appeal to the House of Lords, which was refused. In his judgment refusing leave the Lord Chief Justice added this: "It has been suggested that, when indicating at the end of my judgment the form of answer which I would propose to give to the first question, I may have made a slip by omitting the word 'miscellaneous' before the word 'furniture' in the phrase 'because regulation 30 no longer permits a payment to be made under it in respect of furniture or household equipment'. I think it will be helpful if I say that the omission was not accidental, since my view, in which the other members of the court concurred, is that regulation 30 does not apply to any furniture or household equipment."

We have to say that we are unable to agree with this proposition. If a claim for payment was made under reg 9 but the claim failed to satisfy the conditions relating to specific items in reg 9 or any of the conditions set out in reg 10, there is no reason why a payment should not be made under reg 30. The only exception to reg 30 is in relation to a claim for miscellaneous furniture and household equipment needs and in reg 30 (1) (a) the only exclusion is reg 10A. For our part therefore we would confine our decision to saying that a claim under reg 30 is excluded where the claim is for miscellaneous furniture and household equipment needs, but is not excluded where the claim is for essential furniture and household equipment needs but one or more of the conditions for a claim under regs 9 and 10 is not met.

Counsel for Appellant, Kelly; Solicitors, Erskine, MacAskill & Co — Counsel for Defenders, Davidson; Solicitor, R Brodie, Solicitor in Scotland to the Secretary of State for Social Services.

D K

(NOTE)

McNeil v Clelland

OUTER HOUSE
LORD MILLIGAN
11 DECEMBER 1992

Damages — Amount — Solatium — Hip, leg and arm — Fracture to femur limiting hip movement — Fracture to arm limiting power in arm.

An elderly pedestrian knocked down by a motorcycle suffered fractures of the left femur, right fibula and left ulna leaving him with permanent disabilities.

Held, that solatium was properly valued at £9,000; and decree therefor *pronounced.*

John McNeil raised an action against William Clelland seeking damages for injuries suffered in an accident on 14 December 1989. The pursuer was then aged 68. He had been crossing a road when he was knocked down by a motorcycle which had been driven through traffic lights at red. After a proof the Lord Ordinary (Milligan) held that the defender had been the rider of the motorcycle and that the accident had been the rider's fault. In assessing damages his Lordship said:

"The pursuer claims damages for (i) solatium; (ii) damage to clothing; and (iii) an award under s 8 of the Administration of Justice Act 1982 in respect of assistance provided to him by relatives. It is agreed that the appropriate awards under heads (ii) and (iii) are £100 and £300 respectively. So far as solatium is concerned, the pursuer was rendered unconscious in the accident and was admitted to Hairmyres hospital, where he was found to have sustained fractures of the left femur, left ulna and right fibula and multiple lacerations. He required operative treatment for stabilisation of the left hip. He was detained in hospital for a period of about 10 weeks. He required physiotherapy treatment thereafter. Prior to the accident he was physically fit and capable of walking substantial distances, and of bicycling. He is now unable to do either of these things. The stabilisation of the left hip involved the insertion of a sliding nail plate with six screws and this procedure was uneventful. He made a good recovery from this treatment. The fracture which required this stabilisation was below the hip joint itself, namely a badly shattered fracture of the upper end of the left femur. By March 1992, he was found to be walking well and confidently and his limitations resulting from the injury to the left femur appear to relate to the extent to which he can walk, which is very much less than prior to the accident, to his inability now to go for bicycle runs, and to his inability now to do many gardening jobs which he enjoyed doing previously. The pursuer's displaced fracture of the shaft of the left ulna in the forearm was treated by bracing with a removable brace and physiotherapy. After this the ulna slowly united and by April 1991 appeared stable and painless. As at March 1992, the pursuer noticed occasional creaking or clicking in the area of the forearm. This was not painful and he could perform most activities with the arm apart from heavy lifting, for which he has to use the right hand. This condition is likely to be permanent, involving a loss of 20 per cent of the facility of use of the left arm. The forearm fracture had united with fibrous scar tissue rather than solid bone but did so quite firmly, thereby enabling him to regain 80 per cent of the normal range of movement of elbow, forearm and wrist. His shattered fracture of the mid-shaft of the right fibula in the lower leg, with a secondary fracture of the upper end of the fibula, had healed satisfactorily without deformity or residual swelling by April 1991. The laceration on the top of the scalp healed rapidly without residual symptoms.

"Counsel for the pursuer submitted that the appropriate award for solatium would be within the range of £15,000-£18,000. She described the pursuer as quite a determined individual, a comment which I accept. She founded upon the extent of impairment of his ability to walk and bicycle. She referred to the cases of *Smith v Heeps*, 1990 SLT 871 and *Mackinnon v R & W Scott Ltd*, 1987 SLT 448. In the former case, Lord Cameron of Lochbroom awarded solatium of £19,000 to a 44 year old man who sustained a fracture and dislocation of the hip. The pursuer in that case suffered ongoing pain as the result of osteoarthritic degeneration and would require a hip replacement operation about five years after the accident. Lord Cameron took into account that his surgeons said that there might not be total relief from pain notwithstanding surgical interventions and that there would be substantial restriction of movement of the right hip and thus diminution in the enjoyment of life, which might increase with the years. In the *Mackinnon* case, Lord Cowie awarded solatium of £15,000 to a 70 year old lady who sustained injuries to her left hip and knee and to her right wrist. The main effects of her injuries appear to have been considerable loss of mobility due to the hip injury and associated pain in her left leg. In addition she had continuing pain in her right wrist with marked loss of movement and function. With regard to the pursuer's arm injury, counsel referred to McEwan & Paton on *Damages*, pp 460 and 460/1 and cases there referred to. She submitted that, with ongoing incapacity in the arm, the appropriate award for solatium should include an element of around £3,000-£5,000 for the arm injury. She said that 90 per cent of the award for solatium should be referable to the past so far as interest was concerned.

"Counsel for the defender submitted that an appropriate award for solatium would be about £6,000. He referred to the case of *Clarke v McFadyen*, 1990 SLT 277. In that case Lord Kirkwood awarded solatium of £7,500 to a 19 year old woman injured in an accident in which her sister was killed. She suffered a head injury, a fractured femur and fractures of the pelvic ring. She continued to suffer intermittent pain and discomfort in her leg as well as dizzy spells. She also suffered depression and survivor guilt, a recognised psychiatric illness. Lord Kirkwood found that the pursuer had proved that she was still suffering continuing significant pain and discomfort in her lower back and left leg which interfered with her work and that, while there was likely to be some improvement in her condition in the future, she would never make a full and complete recovery. Prior to the accident she had enjoyed running, hillwalking, badminton and swimming but since the accident she had not been able to participate in any of those activities. Counsel for the defender also referred to the case of *Thomson v British Railways Board*, 1988 SLT 537. In that case Lord Morison awarded £4,200 to a 58 year old fire inspector who fell on an icy surface and sustained a displaced sub-capital fracture of the femur. The fracture had healed leaving a slightly shortened leg, reduced movement of the hip joint and continuing discomfort. Counsel pointed out that in the present case the pursuer had not sustained an actual hip injury as such.

"Taking account of the lay and medical evidence in the present case as to the nature and extent of the pursuer's injuries and the effect of those injuries upon him, and the awards referred to by counsel, with appropriate allowance for differences in circumstances and the dates of the awards concerned, I conclude that the appropriate award for solatium in the present case should be £9,000. In the absence of any objection to the proposal by counsel for the pursuer that 90 per cent of the award for solatium should be referable to the past, I will award interest at the rate of 7½ per cent from the date of the accident on 90 per cent of the award for solatium. So far as the other two heads of award are concerned, I award interest at 15 per cent since the date of the accident on the £100 award for damage to clothing and interest at 15 per cent from 1 April 1990, the approximate mid-point date of the provision of assistance concerned, on the £300 award under s 8 of the 1982 Act."

Counsel for Pursuer, C A G McNeill; Solicitors, J & R A Robertson, WS — Counsel for Defender, L Alonzi; Solicitors, Ketchen & Stevens, WS.

C H

Eclipse Blinds Ltd v Wright

A EXTRA DIVISION

LORDS ALLANBRIDGE, McCLUSKEY AND MORISON

25 OCTOBER 1991

Employment — Unfair dismissal — Employee dismissed on grounds of ill health without prior consultation — Employer seeking to protect employee from full knowledge of illness — Whether duty on employer to consult with
B *employee prior to dismissal — Whether dismissal unfair — Employment Protection (Consolidation) Act 1978 (c 44), s 57 (1) and (3).*

Process — Appeal — Appeal to employment appeal tribunal — Whether employment appeal tribunal entitled to displace decision of industrial tribunal as to weight to attach to particular facts.

A disabled employee with congenital heart disease became too ill to work. Her employers, after ascertain-
C ing from her GP that there was no likelihood of her being fit to resume work in the near future, informed her that it had become necessary to appoint a new employee to fill her position as a telephonist and that her salary would be continued for a few more months. The employers thereafter received a letter from a consultant surgeon stating that the employee was fit to resume work, and offered her suitable clerical work until a telephonist position should become vacant. The employee refused this offer and was accordingly
D dismissed. The employee appealed to an industrial tribunal on the ground that her employers' failure to consult with her prior to dismissing her rendered the dismissal unfair. The industrial tribunal held that the duty to consult depended on the circumstances and that the dismissal had been fair. The employee appealed to the employment appeal tribunal, who held that consultation was necessary, and remitted to the industrial tribunal to assess compensation. The employers appealed to the Court of Session.

E **Held,** (1) that the weight attached to the facts as regards consultation was a matter for the industrial tribunal (p 667C); (2) that in determining whether an employer acted fairly or unfairly the industrial tribunal had to determine as a matter of fact and judgment what consultation if any was necessary or desirable in the known circumstances of the particular case (p 667G); and (3) that the industrial tribunal's decision that the employers' genuine concern to avoid giving the employee information with regard to her
F health of which she did not appear to be aware was not so unreasonable as to render the dismissal unfair, was one which they were entitled to make on the facts, so that it was not open to the employment appeal tribunal to displace that decision (p 667H-J); and appeal *allowed* and decision of industrial tribunal *restored.*

Observed, that what inference was to be drawn from facts was a matter to be determined by the tribunal hearing and deciding the facts, unless there were no facts from which any particular inference could properly be drawn (p 666K-L).

Dictum of Lord Denning MR in *Marriott v Oxford and District Co-operative Society Ltd (No 2)* [1969] G ITR 377, *disapproved.*

Appeal from the employment appeal tribunal

Eclipse Blinds Ltd appealed against the decision of the employment appeal tribunal, reversing an industrial tribunal, that they had unfairly dismissed their employee, Mrs Thomasina C Wright, in that they had failed to consult her prior to dismissing her on grounds of ill health. H

Statutory provisions

The Employment Protection (Consolidation) Act 1978 provides:

"57.— . . . (3) Where the employer has fulfilled the requirements of subsection (1), then, subject to sections 58 to 62, the determination of the question whether the dismissal was fair or unfair, having regard to the reason shown by the employer, shall depend on whether in the circumstances (including the size and I administrative resources of the employer's undertaking) the employer acted reasonably or unreasonably in treating it as a sufficient reason for dismissing the employee; and that question shall be determined in accordance with equity and the substantial merits of the case."

Cases referred to

East Lindsey District Council v Daubney [1977] IRLR 181. J

Hollister v National Farmers' Union [1979] IRLR 238.

Leonard v Fergus & Haynes Civil Engineering Ltd [1979] IRLR 235.

Links (A) & Co Ltd v Rose, 1993 SLT 209.

Marriott v Oxford and District Co-operative Society Ltd (No 2) [1969] ITR 377.

Patterson v Messrs Bracketts [1977] IRLR 137.

Polkey v A E Dayton Services Ltd [1988] AC 344; [1987] 3 WLR 1153; [1987] 3 All ER 974; [1987] IRLR 503. K

Taylorplan Catering (Scotland) Ltd v McInally [1980] IRLR 53.

Watling v William Bird & Son Contractors Ltd (1976) 11 ITR 70.

Williamson v Alcan (UK) Ltd [1977] IRLR 303.

The appeal was heard before an Extra Division on 27 September 1991.

On 25 October 1991 the court *allowed* the appeal L and *restored* the decision of the industrial tribunal.

The following opinion of the court was delivered by Lord Allanbridge:

OPINION OF THE COURT.—This is an appeal from a decision of the employment appeal tribunal under s 136 (4) of the Employment Protection (Consolidation) Act 1978. The judgment of the employment appeal tribunal, dated 1 July 1990, allowed an appeal taken against a decision of an industrial tribunal dated 28 December 1989, which had decided that the respondent (hereinafter referred to as "the applicant") had not been unfairly dismissed by the appellants (hereinafter referred to as "the employers").

The applicant, who was a registered disabled person, had been employed by the employers as a telephonist/receptionist since 1978. Mr McNeil, who was a director of the employers and the only witness for them, said she was an excellent employee despite her disability, but since 1985 her health had deteriorated and her absence due to sickness had increased. She became a part time employee at the end of 1987 following which there was a reduction in the applicant's absences due to sickness. Thereafter there is little dispute on the facts which are summarised in the judgment of the employment appeal tribunal and are as follows:

"In March 1989, the appellant became ill and was off work. She submitted regular medical certificates and was retained as an employee on full pay less her sickness benefit. In May 1989, the appellant visited the personnel officer and handed her a sickness line for 13 weeks. She said she thought that her health was improving. She was asked by the personnel officer for her permission to get in touch with her general practitioner to obtain his views as to her fitness to resume work at the end of the period of 13 weeks. The general practitioner, a Dr MacKay, was accordingly asked for his opinion. On 25 May 1989, Dr MacKay wrote to the personnel officer indicating that the appellant's health was not good, and that he could not see any possibility of her return to work in the near future. He stated that the ultimate prognosis was not good. That letter was passed to Mr McNeil who considered the position for some three weeks. The letter made it clear that, in Dr MacKay's opinion, there was no possibility of the appellant's early return to work.

"The respondents had engaged temporary employees to carry out the appellant's duties while she was off sick, but in view of the length of her absence some difficulties were being encountered. Mr McNeil concluded it would be necessary to engage a permanent replacement for the appellant. The industrial tribunal held that Mr McNeil realised that it would be desirable to speak to the appellant and explain the position to her, but as the appellant had informed the personnel officer that she felt that her health in general was improving, it appeared to Mr McNeil that the appellant did not realise the seriousness of her illness as indicated in Dr MacKay's letter. He, accordingly, decided to write a letter to the appellant, to avoid the risk of being involved in a conversation with her in which it might be difficult to avoid disclosing to her information about her health, of which she was not aware. He accordingly, wrote to the appellant stating that he was sorry that her health was not at its best, and that she was not likely to be able to return to work in the foreseeable future. He then stated: 'Under the circumstances it has been become [sic] necessary for us to appoint a new member of staff to fill your position.' He continued her salary until the end of September and wished her a speedy recovery.

"A few days later, Mr McNeil received a letter from Dr T Fyfe, consultant physician at the Southern General hospital, Glasgow. The letter stated: 'I was disappointed to learn that you intend to terminate Mrs Wright's employment with you. As you know Mrs Wright has congenital heart disease and recently we have had trouble because she has been in cardiac failure. However her problem is now reasonably well controlled on drug therapy and I think that she is now again fit for work as a telephonist. In view of this I wonder if you would consider your decision to dismiss her. Obviously the number of jobs which the patient could do is extremely limited and I would have thought that her job as a telephonist is an ideal one for her.

" 'Now that she is over her recent problems I would be keen that she should return to work. It would be extremely unfortunate to burden her with the problem of unemployment now that she is getting over her health problem.'

"At about that time the appellant telephoned Mr McNeil and he arranged to have a meeting with her. He explained to the appellant that, in view of information which he had received, he had appointed a temporary telephonist who had been employed in a permanent position, and there was no vacancy for a telephonist. He indicated, however, that he would be able to offer her other clerical work to suit her disability, and that as and when a position for a telephonist became vacant, she would be appointed to that post. He said that the appellant's duties would be regulated so that they were consistent with her general ability. At the beginning of September, however, Mr McNeil received a letter from the appellant in which she declined the job which he had offered to her. In these circumstances the appellant's employment terminated at the end of September."

The industrial tribunal came to the conclusion that the employers had not acted unreasonably in dismissing the applicant. They considered the employers were entitled to rely on Dr MacKay's advice. They said that so far as the applicant was concerned the employers had taken a generous view of her disability and that it was only after a long absence and when they received Dr MacKay's opinion to the effect that he could not see any possibility of her return to work in the near future, that the employers felt they had to reconsider the applicant's position. At this stage Mr McNeil decided not to consult with the applicant before writing to her telling her that it had been decided to appoint a new member of staff to fill her position.

It is this failure to consult with the applicant that has occasioned this appeal to this court. The reason given by Mr McNeil was that whilst he realised it would be desirable to speak to the applicant and explain the position to her, the applicant had informed the personnel officer that she thought her health was improving. Mr McNeil said it appeared to him that

A she did not realise the seriousness of her illness as indicated in Dr MacKay's letter. In these circumstances he decided not to consult with the applicant but simply to write a letter to the applicant rather than becoming involved in a conversation with her in which it might be difficult to avoid disclosing to her information about her health of which she was not aware.

The industrial tribunal held that in their opinion Mr McNeil's decision not to consult with the applicant could not be said, in all the circumstances, to be
B so unreasonable as to render the dismissal unfair. The appeal tribunal came to a different conclusion and said that in their view a sensitive consultation could have been carried out and that this was not a case where a failure to consult could be justified. They therefore concluded that the employers ought to have discussed and consulted with the applicant before deciding to dismiss her and accordingly allowed the appeal and remitted back to the industrial tribunal to assess the compensation.
C
Counsel for the appellants drew our attention to the question to be answered by the tribunal which is outlined in s 57 (3) of the 1978 Act, as amended, and which is in the following terms: [his Lordship quoted the terms of s 57 (3) and continued:]

Counsel then submitted that in answering this question the industrial tribunal was answering a question of fact which depended on their view of the whole evidence. All the facts were before that tribunal.
D There was no rule of law that consultation with the applicant before dismissal was absolutely necessary. The necessity for it was a question of fact and degree for the tribunal to decide in all the circumstances of the case. The jurisdiction of the appeal tribunal and this court was limited to determining questions of law in terms of s 136 (1) of the 1978 Act.

Counsel for the appellants referred to three cases decided in 1977 in the employment appeal tribunal in
E England (namely, *East Lindsey District Council v Daubney*; *Patterson v Messrs Bracketts*; and *Williamson v Alcan (UK) Ltd*), which dealt with the question of consultation before dismissal. He drew our attention to what was said by Lord President Emslie about this matter in the Court of Session in 1979 in the case of *Leonard v Fergus & Haynes Civil Engineering Ltd* at p 238. He also drew our attention to the general observations of Lord Denning MR in the Court of Appeal in the case of *Hollister v National Farmers' Union* at p 241. He also referred to what was said by Lord
F Mackay of Clashfern in the House of Lords at [1987] IRLR, p 504 in *Polkey v A E Dayton Services Ltd*. Finally he referred to the recent case of *A Links & Co Ltd v Rose* at p 212K-L where Lord McDonald's observations in the case of *Taylorplan Catering (Scotland) Ltd* are quoted with approval, to the effect that "in the normal case a measure of consultation is expected of an employer before he decides to dismiss an employee for ill health". It was submitted that although these cases recognised that lack of any consultation between an employer and an employee

may normally be regarded as unfair, there was no rule of law to that effect, and no principle that consultation G was always required.

In reply counsel for the respondent submitted that the employment appeal tribunal decided as a matter of law that the industrial tribunal had failed to give sufficient weight to the employers' failure to consult the applicant before dismissing her on the grounds of ill health. He said the appeal tribunal had correctly stated in their judgment that "the cases indicate, however, that not only is consultation almost certainly necessary", but he conceded he could not support the latter H part of that sentence where it goes on to state "but that the true medical position should be ascertained". He accepted that that latter suggestion went too far and would in some circumstances be almost impossible to fulfil. We agree he was right to make that concession. It might well be difficult to ascertain with any certainty what was the true medical position in any given case. An employer is only bound to take reasonable steps to ascertain as best he can in the circumstances the medical condition of the applicant. It is not the I function of an employer to turn himself into some sort of medical appeal tribunal to review the opinions and advice received from their medical advisers (see Phillips J at p 184, para 17 of the *East Lindsey District Council* case).

Counsel for the respondent said that the industrial tribunal were wrong where in their decision they accepted "that in normal circumstances the respondents would have been expected to consult with the J applicant before telling her that she was to be dismissed". The proper test to be applied, as stated in the 1977 cases, was "Unless there are wholly exceptional circumstances, before an employee is dismissed on the ground of ill health it is necessary that he should be consulted" (see Phillips J at p 304, para 8 of *Williamson's* case and p 184, para 18 of *East Lindsey District Council*).

Our attention was also drawn by counsel for the respondent to what was said by Lord Denning MR at K p 380 of *Marriott v Oxford and District Co-operative Society Ltd*, where he stated that the question of what was the proper inference to be drawn from primary facts, was a question of law. That observation may have been apt in the context of that case but, with respect, as a general principle of law we cannot accept it. What inference is to be drawn from facts is a matter to be determined by the tribunal hearing and deciding the facts unless, of course, there are no facts from which any particular inference could properly be L drawn. That is not the situation in the present case.

Counsel then referred us to the three categories of cases that Phillips J had outlined in *Watling v William Bird & Son Contractors Ltd* at pp 71H-72B, into one of which an applicant must put his appeal on a point of law: first, a tribunal must have either misdirected itself in law or misunderstood the law or misapplied the law; secondly, the tribunal must have misunderstood the facts or misapplied the facts; or, thirdly, the decision was "perverse" and there was no evidence to

justify the conclusion that was reached by the
A tribunal. Counsel suggested this appeal fell into the
third category. This case is also interesting because at
p 72E, Phillips J also indicates that the observations of
Lord Denning in *Marriott's* case referred to supra,
require to be read in their context.

In conclusion counsel for the respondent referred to
the three cases decided in 1977, namely, *Patterson,
East Lindsey District Council* and *Williamson* and the
later case of *Polkey.* These are the four cases referred
to in the judgment of the employment appeal tribunal
B in this case. He submitted that the industrial tribunal
had misdirected itself as to the importance of consultation and the appeal tribunal endeavoured to correct
that situation and the appeal should be dismissed.

Having considered the arguments of counsel we do
not think that the industrial tribunal did misdirect
itself in law. The thrust of the applicant's argument to
that effect was based on the submission that that
tribunal gave insufficient weight to the evidence
C regarding the question of consultation by the
employer. In our view such an argument is misconceived. The weight to be attached to any evidence in
any case is a matter for the tribunal determining the
facts. It can never be for an appellate tribunal concerned only with errors in law, to take upon itself the
task of deciding what weight should be attached to
particular facts. However, that is clearly what the
appeal tribunal have done in this case. Throughout
the latter part of their judgment they indicate on
D several occasions what is their "view" of the agreed
facts and in so doing so they fell into the trap of substituting their own views for those of the lower
tribunal so clearly warned against by Lord Denning
MR at the end of para 17 at p 241 of *Hollister's* case.
Moreover in reaching their decision the appeal
tribunal appear to have considered only the conduct of
the employers in failing to consult with the applicant
and to have left out of account the numerous other
circumstances which provided a context in which the
E reasonableness of that conduct had to be assessed.

It is true that Lord McDonald in *Taylorplan Catering (Scotland) Ltd* referred to what is expected in the
"normal case" as regards the necessity for consultation, whereas Phillips J referred to "wholly exceptional circumstances" in several of the English cases in
1977. However, in our opinion these two approaches
to the question of whether or not a consultation should
have been held are not inconsistent with each other.
One is the converse of the other, as if a case is wholly
F exceptional it is not normal. This was the view
reached by this court in the case of *A Links & Co Ltd,*
but it is fair to note that as stated at p 212H, there was
no dispute in that case as to the duty of an employer
who is considering dismissing an employee on the
grounds of ill health, so the alleged inconsistency was
not argued. In that case this court held that it would
require to go to a fresh industrial tribunal to decide
inter alia whether consultation was appropriate in the
circumstances because there had been no consideration given to that matter at the original hearing.

However, in the case of *A Links & Co Ltd* it was
also held by this court, at p 213C, that an industrial G
tribunal in approaching the question as to whether the
employer acted fairly or unfairly must determine, as a
matter of fact and judgment, what consultation, if any,
was necessary or desirable in the known circumstances
of the particular case. We are quite satisfied that that
is the correct approach. We stress that it is a matter of
fact to be determined by the industrial tribunal. This
is also the approach suggested by Lord President
Emslie at p 238, para 14 in *Leonard's* case. Furthermore, the Lord Chancellor in a somewhat different H
case did stress that the matters of consultation or
warning were matters for an industrial tribunal to consider in the light of the circumstances known to the
employer at the time he dismissed the employee (see
Polkey's case at [1987] IRLR, p 504, para 5).

In this case it was quite clear from the agreed facts
that the industrial tribunal did consider all the necessary and relevant facts. This was a case that the industrial tribunal decided was not normal and was
exceptional as regards the question of consulting with I
the applicant. They accepted in terms that in normal
circumstances the employers would have been
expected to consult with the applicant before telling
her she was to be dismissed. However, they decided
that Mr McNeil had a genuine concern to avoid giving
the applicant information with regard to her health of
which she did not appear to be aware and therefore
concluded that his decision could not be said, in all the
circumstances, to be so unreasonable as to render the
dismissal unfair. This was a judgment which the J
industrial tribunal were entitled to make on the facts
and it was therefore not open to the employment
appeal tribunal to displace that judgment on fact by
their own view or judgment. No error in law by the
industrial tribunal had occurred.

In this situation we allow the appeal, reverse the
appeal tribunal and restore the decision of the industrial tribunal.

——————————   K

*Counsel for Appellants, Wright; Solicitors, Bird
Semple Fyfe Ireland, WS — Counsel for Respondent,
Hutchison; Solicitors, Drummond Miller, WS.*

R F H

L

Clark's Trustee, Noter

OUTER HOUSE
LORD OSBORNE
27 FEBRUARY 1992

*Bankruptcy — Sequestration — Trustee — Powers of
interim trustee — Power to sell debtor's assets including
heritage — Bankruptcy (Scotland) Act 1985 (c 66), s 18
(3).*

A *Statute — Construction — Ejusdem generis rule — Whether list in statute comprised a genus — Bankruptcy (Scotland) Act 1985 (c 66), s 18 (3).*

The Bankruptcy (Scotland) Act 1985, s 18 (3), empowers the court to authorise an interim trustee appointed on a debtor's estate before sequestration to do various things concerned with safeguarding the debtor's estate. The final power given to the court is "to make such other order to safeguard the debtor's estate as it thinks appropriate".

B Qualified creditors petitioned for the sequestration of a debtor on the ground that he had become apparently insolvent on his signing a trust deed within four months prior to the presentation of the petition. The debtor's place of business and principal material asset was a licensed public house. The petitioning creditors averred that if this business, which was still operating, ceased, its value would decline materially, hence prejudicing the creditors. Prior to signing the trust deed, the debtor had agreed with the petitioners'
C representatives that he would sign a trust deed in favour of an insolvency practitioner, experienced with regard to licensed premises, and that the public house would be sold to a company who, the petitioners averred, had submitted a very good offer which was materially higher than a recent valuation of the public house. The petitioners were unwilling to fund continued trading by the trustee appointed by the debtor and sought immediate appointment of an interim trustee and the granting to the interim trustee of
D powers to carry on the public house and to borrow money in terms of ss 2 (1) (a) and 18 (3) of the 1985 Act. The Lord Ordinary granted an order for intimation and service and ordained the debtor to appear to show cause why sequestration should not be awarded. The Lord Ordinary further appointed the insolvency practitioner recommended by the petitioners as interim trustee with all the usual powers and duties including powers to borrow money, insofar as necessary for the trustee to safeguard the debtor's estate,
E and to carry on the debtor's business. Subsequently a note was presented by the interim trustee to the court referring to the offer for the public house and the valuation thereof, and seeking power under s 18 (3) of the 1985 Act to sell the public house to safeguard the debtor's estate.

Held, that the wording of s 18 (3) (c) was very wide, that the ejusdem generis rule of construction did not apply to effect a curtailment of the prima facie effect of the words concerned, because no genus could be
F perceived as emerging from the preceding list of powers set out in s 18 (3); and thus that the court had power to grant authority to the noter as interim trustee to sell the public house and business carried on therein (p 670A-C); and prayer of the note *granted*.

Petition for sequestration

Scottish & Newcastle plc, qualified creditors of Thomas Watson Clark, raised a petition for the appointment of an interim trustee with the usual statu-

tory powers. On his appointment Murdoch Lang McKillop, the interim trustee, presented a note G seeking power under s 18 (3) (c) of the 1985 Act to sell a public house owned by the debtor together with the business carried on there.

Statutory provisions

The Bankruptcy (Scotland) Act 1985 provides:

"2.—(1) In every sequestration there shall be appointed under section 13 of this Act an interim trustee whose general functions shall be — (a) to safeguard the debtor's estate pending the appointment of H a permanent trustee under this Act. . . .

"18.— . . . (3) The court, on the application of the interim trustee, may — (a) empower the interim trustee to — (i) carry on any business of the debtor; (ii) borrow money, in so far as it is necessary for the trustee to do so to safeguard the debtor's estate; (b) on cause shown, grant a warrant authorising the interim trustee to enter the house where the debtor resides or his business premises and to search for and take possession of anything mentioned in paragraphs (a) and I (c) of subsection (2) above, if need be by opening shut and lock-fast places; or (c) make such other order to safeguard the debtor's estate as it thinks appropriate."

Case referred to

Crichton Stuart v Ogilvie, 1914 2 SLT 116; 1914 SC 888.

On 27 February 1992 the Lord Ordinary *granted* the prayer of the note.   J

LORD OSBORNE.—In this petition, the petitioners aver that they are "qualified creditors", within the meaning of s 5 (4) of the Bankruptcy (Scotland) Act 1985, of Thomas Watson Clark, who had an established place of business at the Criterion Bar, 54 Guild Street, Aberdeen. As at 30 January 1992, it is said that the debtor's indebtedness to the petitioners amounted to £343,006.77. On 29 January 1992, the debtor signed a trust deed in favour of Michael Reid, K chartered accountant, Aberdeen. Accordingly he became "apparently insolvent" within the meaning of s 7 (1) (c) of the Act of 1985. On 30 January 1992, the petitioners presented the present petition for the sequestration of the debtor upon the ground that he had become "apparently insolvent" within four months before the presentation of the petition concerned, in terms of s 8 (1) (b) of the Act of 1985.

In their petition the petitioners aver: "That the L debtor's place of business and a material asset is a licensed public house ('the public house') which he still operates. If that business ceases, its value would decline materially, causing serious prejudice to the debtor's creditors, such as the petitioners. The debtor cannot properly continue to operate the public house after the making of this application. Reference is made to ss 32 (2), 31 (1) and 12 (4) of the 1985 Act. As set out in stat 2 the debtor has signed a trust deed in favour in his creditors. Before he did so, the debtor had agreed with representatives of the petitioners that

(i) he would sign a trust deed in favour of Murdoch L
McKillop, CA, Edinburgh and Glasgow, who is a
very experienced insolvency practitioner, particularly
in relation to licensed premises, and (ii) that the public
house would be sold to Eagle Taverns Ltd. That
company submitted an offer dated 29 January 1992 of
£575,000 for the public house. The petitioners believe
that that offer is a very good one. It is materially
higher than a valuation dated 29 January 1992 of the
public house, which the petitioners obtained from
Graham & Sibbald, chartered surveyors, Aberdeen.
That valuation gave a value of £450,000 for the public
house. The petitioners believe that if they fund the
continued trading from the public house until the
appointment of Mr McKillop or another person as the
permanent trustee, that offer will remain open. The
petitioners are in the circumstances unwilling to fund
continued trading by the trustee appointed by the
debtor. In these circumstances the petitioners seek (i)
the immediate appointment of an interim trustee in
terms of s 13 of the 1985 Act and (ii) the granting to
the interim trustee of the powers to carry on the public
house and to borrow money in terms of ss 2 (1) (a) and
18 (3) of the 1985 Act. The petitioners suggest that Mr
McKillop is a suitable person to be appointed to that
office. He is qualified and has agreed to act in that
office."

By an interlocutor dated 30 January 1992, the Lord
Ordinary appointed the petition to be intimated in
common form and to be served upon the debtor, who
was appointed, if so advised, to appear within the
Court of Session on 27 February 1992, being a date
not less than six nor more than 14 days after the date
of citation, to show cause why sequestration should
not be awarded. Further, the Lord Ordinary meantime
appointed Murdoch L McKillop, chartered accountant, 199 St Vincent Street, Glasgow, to be interim
trustee on the estates of the said Thomas Watson
Clark, the debtor, with the powers and duties
prescribed by statute and in particular with the powers
to borrow money insofar as it is necessary for the
trustee to do so to safeguard the debtor's estate and to
carry on the business of the debtor.

On 26 February 1992 the interim trustee, Murdoch
Lang McKillop, presented a note to the court. After
narrating the procedure, to which I have already made
reference, he avers: "A major part of the [debtor's]
estates is constituted by a large public house situated
in Guild Street, Aberdeen and known as 'The
Criterion Bar'. The value placed upon that business
by Messrs Graham & Sibbald, chartered surveyors, 38
Carden Place, Aberdeen, retained to value that business, is £450,000. However, an offer to purchase that
public house has been made by Eagle Taverns Ltd,
... wherein that company offers to purchase that
public house for a price of £575,000. . . . The noter
regards that offer as a generous one which, given the
valuation of said public house which is available to
him, he does not expect to be repeated. Said offer is,
however, subject to certain conditions, one of which
stipulates that the purchaser should receive a permanent transfer of the licence relative to said premises

at the meeting of the City of Aberdeen District Licensing Board due to be held on 17 March 1992. The
noter, had he power to accept the said offer and sell
to Eagle Taverns Ltd the said public house, would be
anxious to do so in order to safeguard that part of Mr
Clark's estate which is composed of the premium over
valuation in said offer. Having regard to the earliest
date at which sequestration of Mr Clark's estates may
be awarded by the Court, and the statutory timetable
thereafter which would govern the procedure for the
election and confirmation of a permanent trustee on
said estates with power to sell said public house, the
noter is concerned that the said offer and premium
may be lost to the estates because a permanent trustee
might not be elected and confirmed before 17 March
1992. In any event, even if the said offer were to
remain open until the next meeting of the said Board
in June 1992, a substantial element of said premium
would be lost because the increased overheads and
trading costs which would be incurred by the noter
(and his successor as permanent trustee on said estate)
in running the said public house during the period
March to June 1992 would require to be met from
funds otherwise available for distribution under said
Act . . . the noter accordingly conceives that it is necessary to safeguard that part of the estates of Thomas
Watson Clark which is composed of the premium
element of said offer, that he should be authorised by
the Court to sell the said public house as interim
trustee on the said estates. He therefore seeks to be
authorised as aforesaid by your Lordships pursuant to
the power conferred upon them by s 18 (3) of the said
statute of 1985."

The note by the interim trustee came before me on
27 February 1992, prior to my being asked to grant
the prayer of the petition for sequestration itself. I was
moved to grant the prayer of the note and to authorise
the noter to sell the said public house and the business
carried on therein under s 18 (3) (c) of the Act of 1985.
Counsel for the noter submitted that one of the
general functions of an interim trustee was, in terms
of s 2 (1) (a) of the 1985 Act "to safeguard the debtor's
estate pending the appointment of a permanent trustee
under this Act". In practical terms, it would not be
possible to satisfy condition 3 of the offer made on
behalf of Eagle Taverns Ltd, unless the noter were
authorised to proceed immediately with the sale of the
public house premises and business. If the offer on
behalf of Eagle Taverns Ltd could not be accepted and
the conditions therein satisfied, the estate of the debtor
would suffer serious prejudice, in respect that an offer
£125,000 in excess of the valuation figure given to the
noter by his advisers would be lost. If that happened,
there would have been a failure on the part of the
noter to safeguard that part of the debtor's estate
representing the premium in the offer over the valuation figure.

While there was no specific power enabling the
court to authorise the noter to effect the sale concerned, in response to the offer which he had received,
counsel for the noter submitted that s 18 (3) (c) of the
Act of 1985, which contained general language, had

A the effect of enabling the court to grant such an authorisation. That subsection provided that: "the court on the application of the interim trustee, may . . . (c) make such other order to safeguard the debtor's estate as it thinks appropriate".

I have reached the conclusion that s 18 (3) (c) of the Act of 1985, the terms of which I have quoted above, does, on a proper construction, enable the court to grant to the noter the authority which he seeks to sell the said public house and the business carried on therein. The words of the subsection "such other

B order to safeguard the debtor's estate as it thinks appropriate" are, in my opinion, very wide. I can see nothing in the preceding terms of s 18 (3), or indeed elsewhere in the Act of 1985, which would have the effect of curtailing the very wide scope of those words. In particular, while the words quoted in subpara (c) form part of a list of powers given to the court under s 18 (3), I do not consider that the ejusdem generis rule of construction would apply here to effect a curtailment of the prima facie effect of the words concerned,

C since in my opinion, no genus can be perceived as emerging from the preceding list of powers. In this connection, I refer to the decision in the case of *Crichton Stuart v Ogilvie.*

In all of these circumstances, having regard to the very clear expediency of granting the order sought, in order to safeguard the debtor's estate, I have decided to grant the prayer of the note.

D
Counsel for Petitioner, Howie; Solicitors, Dorman Jeffrey & Co.

P A

E (NOTE)

McFaulds v Reed Corrugated Cases Ltd

OUTER HOUSE
LORD PENROSE
19 MARCH 1992

F *Reparation — Negligence — Breach of statutory duty — Unsafe place of work — Whether seat of forklift truck used in a factory a "place of work" — Factories Act 1961 (9 & 10 Eliz II, c 34), s 29 (1).*

Damages — Amount — Solatium — Minor injury — Leg — Driver trapped by leg for half an hour suffering pain but with no permanent physical consequences.

The Factories Act 1961 provides in s 29 (1) that every place at which any person has to work shall be made and kept safe, so far as reasonably practicable, for any person working there. A 52 year old forklift truck driver was injured while driving a truck inside

a factory. The truck collided with pallets causing the driver's seat and its mounting to be dislodged, thereby G injuring the driver. The collision was held to be the driver's fault. The cases of fault advanced included an allegation of a breach of s 29 (1) of the 1961 Act on the basis that the insecure seat was a place at which the pursuer had to work and that the seat had not been made and kept safe by securing it to the body of the truck. The driver was trapped by the leg for about half an hour after the accident. He suffered a painful injury, but for the most part his pain and discomfort were of short duration.

H
Held, (1) that the forklift truck was not a "place" within the meaning of s 29 (1) of the 1961 Act; and (2) that solatium was properly valued at £1,500.

George McFaulds raised an action against his employers Reed Corrugated Cases Ltd, for damages for injuries sustained in an accident at work on 21 February 1989. He was then aged 52 and employed as I a forklift truck operator. The truck he had been operating was a battery driven Coventry Climax vehicle. In common with other such trucks at the factory, the battery box was located at the rear of the truck. The battery box had a glass fibre lid with a depression on top into which the driver's seat was fitted. The seat was supported on a metal framework attached through the lid to metal strips located on its underside. The lid had a lip, originally continuous, which overlapped the top edge of the battery box on all four sides when in J position. The lid was supported at three places. The two sides of the battery box had raised portions midway along their length. These supported the lid at its outer edges. The main support was provided by the batteries themselves, or, in some cases, by a sheet of material placed over the batteries. There was no form of mechanical fixing of the lid. The lid and seat were maintained in position by friction, essentially by the weight of the driver. Protection against movement of the lid to the rear was provided by the solid back of K the truck which rose above the top of the battery box and by two straps supporting the roof over the operator's cabin. Protection against movement to the sides was provided by the overlap of the lid along the greater parts of the sides to a depth of three quarters of an inch or thereby, but more particularly by the raised portions of the sides of the battery box and the depression accommodating the driver's seat. Protection against movement towards the front was provided by the three quarter inch overlap of the lid along L the rear of the battery box. The leading edge of the battery box was for all practical purposes level with the top of the batteries. There was no seat belt to restrain the operator. The pursuer's injury was caused when, following a collision with pallets stacked on the floor of the premises, the lid and driver's seat were dislodged and pushed forward, trapping his right leg between them and the controls of the truck. The pursuer was the only driver on duty and after the accident he had sat trapped for up to half an hour, during which time he became unconscious due to the

pain he was suffering. He was eventually found,
A released and carried away on a stretcher.

At a proof before the Lord Ordinary (Penrose) the
pursuer contended that the accident had been caused
by an obstruction on the floor. The Lord Ordinary
rejected that suggestion and concluded:

"In summary, then, I consider that the accident
happened because in driving the truck in reverse along
the bottom passage, on or close to the centre line of the
passage, Mr McFaulds, through carelessness, collided
B with the stack of pallets. The point of impact on the
truck was the rear corner of the battery box lid. The
lid was lifted by the impact to such an extent that the
rear portion of the lip came free from the rear side of
the battery box. As the truck continued to reverse, the
lid and seat were forced forward, trapping Mr
McFaulds. The collision was caused by Mr
McFaulds' negligence in driving the truck."

His Lordship then upheld the pursuer's case that it
was obviously necessary for his employers to have
C found a remedy for the lack of fixing of the battery box
lid and continued: "The injuries suffered by Mr
McFaulds were caused by two factors, his own negligence as already discussed, and the fact that at the time
he was operating a truck which was unsafe in the event
of a collision occurring in reverse."

After considering and rejecting cases based on the
alleged negligence of those who had placed the pallets
in position and on breaches of s 28 (1) and s 29 (1) of
the Factories Act 1961 related to duties of keeping the
D passageway free, his Lordship continued:

"In art 6 of the condescendence the pursuer makes
a case in the following terms: 'It was the defenders'
duty so far as reasonably practicable, to make and keep
safe the seat of the said truck, which was a place at
which the pursuer had to work. Reference is made to
s 29 (1) of the Factories Act 1961. The seat was unsafe
in respect that it was secured only to the battery cover
and there was no seat belt to restrain the driver. It
E would have been reasonably practicable for the
defenders to take steps to secure the seat to the body
of the truck, to provide a seat belt to restrain the driver
in his seat.'

"The allegation that the seat of a forklift truck was
a place at which the pursuer had to work was said to
be somewhat novel. But support for the proposition
was sought in a number of cases. *Cox v HCB Angus
Ltd* [1981] ICR 683 was said to support the general
proposition that 'place' was not restricted to the
F premises, but extended to things brought on to the
premises. *Allen v Avon Rubber Co* [1986] ICR 695 was
relied on as a case under s 29 (1) involving a forklift
truck. Reference was made to *Yates v Rockwell
Graphic Systems Ltd* [1988] ICR 8.

"In *Yates*, Steyn J said, at p 14: 'It is, of course,
clear, that "place" within the meaning of s 29 (1) does
not simply mean the floor space within a factory. One
has to have regard to the permanently installed
machinery and the regular activities carried on in the
factory in order to decide whether the place is safe.'

"There is nothing in that case to support the argument that a vehicle such as a forklift truck which G
operates within and outwith buildings would be a
'place' in the sense of the Act. On the contrary, the
identification of permanently installed machinery as
'place' suggests a contrast with mobile plant and
equipment which would be adverse to the pursuer's
case. *Cox* showed that an article brought into a workshop might in certain circumstances properly be
viewed as a 'place' at which a person had to work.
There is no conceptual difficulty with that notion.
Many manufacturing and industrial processes involve H
the creation, adaptation, modification or repair of
articles substantial enough in size to be viewed on a
common sense level as 'place'. It is easy to envisage
situations in which the 'place', the workshop, would
be diminished if the work piece itself did not become
part of the place in substitution for the floor area on
which it rested, and which it covered. It would be odd
if the Act had a more restricted application when work
was in progress than when it was not.

"However, none of these cases supported the pur- I
suer's contention. The lack of safety founded upon in
this case arose from the interaction between place and
plant. The truck was a moveable tool employed within
the place to enable the pursuer to perform his duties
there. The pursuer of course had to sit on the seat to
use the truck and to perform his duties within the
workplace. But in my opinion the truck itself was not
a 'place' within the meaning of s 29 (1) on any view
of its construction. I consider that this case failed for
that reason." J

His Lordship then held that the pursuer, by his
careless driving, and his employers, by their failure to
secure the seat in position, had equally contributed to
the accident and awarded damages modified to one
half for contributory negligence. In assessing total
damages at £1,786 before reduction for contributory
negligence his Lordship said:

"Mr McFaulds' patrimonial loss was agreed at £60
inclusive of interest. There was a dispute as to the K
quantum of solatium. Counsel for the pursuer relied
upon *Gilchrist v D B Marshall (Newbridge)*, 1991 SLT
842 and *Crutchley v Gazzard* [1991] CLY 1480 in
support of his submission that solatium should be
within the band £1,800 to £2,500 and should in fact
be at the upper level of that band, £2,500, which with
interest on two thirds of the principal sum at 7½ per
cent to date amounted to £2,874.99. Counsel for the
defenders relied upon *Crutchley* and also upon
Zdrojewski v British Railways Board, 1986 SLT 642, L
in support of his contention that at most solatium
should be fixed at £1,000. The cases do no more than
provide pointers, but they are valuable for that
purpose. It was proved that the pursuer had suffered
a painful injury, but that for the most part the pain
and discomfort were of short duration. There was no
objective evidence of significant continuing signs and
symptoms attributable to the accident, but a degree of
discomfort and uncertainty affecting the pursuer in
the ordinary course of his work continued. In the

whole circumstances, having regard to the authorities, and the evidence of injury which was agreed, I considered that an appropriate sum for solatium was £1,500. With interest on the basis and at the rate agreed between parties the total sum inclusive of interest to the date of the proof amounts to £1,726. I therefore considered that total damages amounted to £1,786, of which I shall grant decree for one half, £893."

Counsel for Pursuer, Mackinnon; Solicitors, Robin Thompson & Partners — Counsel for Defenders, Andrew Smith; Solicitors, Simpson & Marwick, WS.

C H

Scott v Morrison

HIGH COURT OF JUSTICIARY
THE LORD JUSTICE CLERK (ROSS),
LORDS MORISON AND SUTHERLAND
9 JUNE 1992

Justiciary — Procedure — Summary procedure — Complaint — Amendment — Crown seeking to substitute "cannabis resin" for "cannabis" at close of Crown case — Sheriff refusing leave as unfair to accused — Whether sheriff entitled to refuse leave — Criminal Procedure (Scotland) Act 1975 (c 21), s 335.

Section 335 (1) of the Criminal Procedure (Scotland) Act 1975 provides that it shall be competent at any time prior to the determination of a summary prosecution, unless the court sees just cause to the contrary, to amend the complaint by deletion, alteration or addition so as to cure any error or defect therein or to meet any objection thereto or to cure any discrepancy or variance between the complaint and the evidence.

An accused person was charged on a summary complaint with contraventions of s 5 (2) and (3) of the Misuse of Drugs Act 1971 in respect of his possession of cannabis. After the third of five Crown witnesses had been led, the Crown sought leave to amend the complaint to add "resin" after the word "cannabis". The motion was opposed and was not then insisted in but prior to the close of the Crown case the Crown again sought leave to amend the complaint. The sheriff refused the motion on the ground inter alia that to do so would be unfair to the accused. The sheriff thereafter acquitted the accused in response to a submission, which was not opposed by the Crown, that the accused had no case to answer. The Crown appealed.

Held, that the sheriff was entitled to exercise his discretion so as to refuse leave to amend in the circumstances and in particular the time at which the amendment was sought and after a previous motion had been withdrawn (p 674D-E); and appeal *refused.*

Summary complaint

Allan Thomas Morrison was charged at the instance of George E Scott, procurator fiscal, Falkirk, on a summary complaint which contained the following charges: "You did on 29 November 1990 in the house at 13 Kilbrennan Drive, Tamfourhill, Falkirk, occupied by Mhairi Louise Callaghan (1) have in your possession a controlled drug, namely cannabis, a class B drug, as specified in Sched 2 to the aftermentioned Act, in contravention of s 5 (1) of the said Act: contrary to the Misuse of Drugs Act 1971, s 5 (2); (2) have unlawfully in your possession a controlled drug, namely cannabis, a class B drug, as specified in Sched 2 to the Misuse of Drugs Act 1971, with intent to supply it to another person in contravention of s 4 (1) of the above mentioned Act: contrary to the Misuse of Drugs Act 1971, s 5 (3)."

The accused pled not guilty and proceeded to trial. At the conclusion of the Crown case the sheriff (A V Sheehan) sustained a submission, which was not opposed by the Crown, and acquitted the accused in terms of s 345A of the Criminal Procedure (Scotland) Act 1975. The facts of the case appear from the opinion of the court.

The procurator fiscal appealed by way of stated case to the High Court against the decision of the sheriff.

Statutory provisions

The Criminal Procedure (Scotland) Act 1975 provides:

"335.—(1) It shall be competent at any time prior to the determination of a summary prosecution, unless the court sees just cause to the contrary, to amend the complaint or any notice of penalty or previous conviction relative thereto by deletion, alteration or addition so as to cure any error or defect therein, or to meet any objection thereto, or to cure any discrepancy or variance between the complaint or notice and the evidence.

"(2) Nothing in this section shall authorise an amendment which changes the character of the offence charged, and if the court shall be of the opinion that the accused may in any way be prejudiced in his defence on the merits of the case by any amendment made under this section, the court shall grant such remedy to the accused by adjournment or otherwise as it shall think just."

Cases referred to

Arnott v MacFarlane, 1976 SLT (Notes) 39.
Heywood v Macrae, 1988 SLT 218; 1987 SCCR 627.
MacArthur v MacNeill, 1987 SLT 299; 1986 JC 182; 1986 SCCR 552.
Penman v Crowe, High Court of Justiciary, 25 September 1991, unreported (1991 GWD 36-2186).

The sheriff appended a note to the stated case which was in the following terms, inter alia:

THE SHERIFF (A V SHEEHAN).— . . . With
A regard to the Crown motion to amend the charges by
inserting the word "resin", both parties agreed on 29
November that the Misuse of Drugs Act 1971, Sched
2, Pt II (which refers to class B drugs) contains
separate entries for cannabis and cannabis resin. It was
therefore agreed that they were two quite distinct and
different drugs within the same class. Furthermore, as
held in the case of *Arnott v MacFarlane*, "since the
charge was of possession of cannabis, a finding of
possession of cannabis resin did not establish the con-
B travention".

In the course of his submissions, the appellant's
depute advised me that although the analysts' certificate had not been issued until 16 May 1991, the appellant had intended from the outset to charge the
respondent with possession of cannabis resin, contrary
to s 5 (2) and (3) of the 1971 Act. The omission of the
word "resin" in the complaint was due to a clerical or
typing error. No explanation could be given for the
failure by the appellant to notice this error when the
C complaint was signed, when the complaint was served,
when the complaint called on 25 February 1991, or
when it called for trial on 31 May 1991 and 16
September 1991. The error had not even been noticed
by the appellant's depute at the start of the trial on 19
November 1991 and it had not come to his attention
until after the evidence of the third Crown witness had
been concluded. Even at that stage, while a tentative
motion had been made to amend the complaint, the
motion was withdrawn when it was opposed by the
D respondent's solicitor. Nevertheless, the appellant's
depute submitted that at the conclusion of his evidence I should allow the complaint to be amended
before the determination of his case, in terms of s 335
of the Criminal Procedure (Scotland) Act 1975.

In opposing this motion, the respondent's solicitor
submitted that there was just cause for repelling the
motion since there could be grave prejudice to the
respondent if the amendment were allowed at this late
E stage in the proceedings. Throughout the course of the
trial he had conducted the respondent's defence on the
basis that he was charged with possession of cannabis.
The appellant's depute had not led any evidence relating to cannabis, and while he may have led evidence
about cannabis resin, he (the respondent's solicitor)
had regarded this as irrelevant since there was no
charge to this effect. In addition, the proposed amendment altered the character of the offence. If the
amendment were allowed, even an extreme remedy
F such as allowing all the Crown witnesses to be recalled
for cross examination could not cure the grave
prejudice which would be suffered by the respondent.
The respondent's solicitor did, however, concede that
he could not have argued that there would have been
the same degree of prejudice if the appellant's depute
had moved to amend the complaint at the outset of the
trial before the first witness was called.

In the course of the debate, reference was made to
Heywood v Macrae and *Penman v Crowe*, but I did not
find that either case was particularly relevant to the
exact circumstances of the present case. On the other
hand, it respectfully seemed to me that the issue G
before me was similar to the issue before the court in
MacArthur v MacNeill where it was decided that an
amendment, after all the prosecution evidence had
been led, to delete a reference to breath and substitute
a reference to blood, changed the character of the
offence and was unfair to the defence and should not
have been allowed, albeit that the charge would have
remained one of contravening the same section of the
same statute. To paraphrase the wording in
MacArthur, mutatis mutandis, to allege possession of H
cannabis is one thing but it is an offence of a different
character to allege possession of cannabis resin. Moreover, as in that case, the time at which the amendment
was sought must be one factor to be taken into account
when deciding whether or not the amendment should
be allowed. In the circumstances of the present case,
I decided that it would be unfair and gravely
prejudicial to the respondent if I allowed the amendment and I therefore refused the motion by the appel-
lant's depute.   I

Appeal

The sheriff posed the following question for the
opinion of the High Court:

Did I err in refusing the motion by the appellant's
depute at the close of the Crown case to amend the
complaint by inserting the word "resin" after the
word "cannabis" in line 1 of both charges of the libel?

The appeal was argued before the High Court on 9   J
June 1992.

Eo die the court *answered* the question in the *negative* and *refused* the appeal.

The following opinion of the court was delivered by
the Lord Justice Clerk (Ross):

OPINION OF THE COURT.—This is a Crown
appeal at the instance of the procurator fiscal, Falkirk. K
The respondent is Allan Thomas Morrison. The
respondent went to trial in the sheriff court at Falkirk
on a summary complaint containing two charges. The
first charge was a charge of contravening s 5 (2) of the
Misuse of Drugs Act 1971 and charge 2 was a charge
of contravening s 5 (3) of the same Act. In both
charges it was libelled that he had had, in his possession, a controlled drug, namely cannabis, a class B
drug as specified in Sched 2 to the Misuse of Drugs
Act 1971.   L

The sheriff in the stated case explains that the appellant led evidence from five witnesses, and after the
third witness had completed his evidence the appellant
made a motion to amend the complaint by inserting
the word "resin" after the word "cannabis" where it
occurred in both charges, that is to say that the charge
was now to be a charge libelling possession of cannabis
resin rather than cannabis. The motion to amend was
opposed by the respondent and was then withdrawn
by the appellant. Later, after the last Crown witness

A had been called, the appellant indicated that he intended to close his case but before doing so he again moved to amend the complaint in the manner already described. After hearing both parties the sheriff refused the Crown motion. The appellant then closed his case whereupon the respondent's solicitor made a submission of no case to answer which the sheriff sustained.

The appellant in this case is seeking to appeal against the decision of the sheriff to refuse to allow the complaint to be amended. In the note annexed to the
B case, the sheriff explains why he refused the motion to amend. It was opposed by the respondent upon the ground that the amendment if allowed would have the effect of changing the character of the offence charged and it was also opposed as being unfair. The sheriff, under reference to *MacArthur v MacNeill* held that the proposed amendment would have the effect of changing the character of the offence. He went on to say, moreover, that in the circumstances of the case he concluded that it would be unfair and gravely
C prejudicial to the respondent if he allowed the amendment. Amendment of a complaint is competent in accordance with s 335 of the Criminal Procedure (Scotland) Act 1975. Section 335 (1) provides as follows: [his Lordship quoted the terms of s 335 (1) and then s 335 (2) and continued:]

As we have already observed, the sheriff in the present case appears to have refused the amendment on two separate grounds. The first ground was that it changed the character of the offence; the second was
D that it would be unfair to do so. It is unnecessary in this case to determine whether the amendment which was proposed would have had the effect of changing the character of the offence because we are satisfied that having regard to the fact that the sheriff had a discretion as to whether or not to allow an amendment it cannot be said that in the circumstances of this case he was not entitled to exercise his discretion so as to refuse leave to amend. The sheriff, as we say, makes it plain that in the circumstances of the case as he has
E described them, he concluded that it would be unfair to the respondent if he allowed the amendment.

Having regard to the whole circumstances described by the sheriff and in particular the time at which the amendment was sought at a stage when the Crown had completed leading the whole of its evidence, and after a previous motion to amend had been withdrawn, we are satisfied that the sheriff was entitled to reach the conclusion which he did, namely, that it would be unfair to allow the amendment.

F We shall accordingly answer the one question in the case in the negative and it follows that the appeal in the instance of the Crown is refused.

Counsel for Appellant, Bonomy, AD; Solicitor, J D Lowe, Crown Agent — Counsel for Respondent, McBride; Solicitors, Balfour & Manson, Nightingale & Bell (for Blackadder & McMonagle, Falkirk).

P W F

(NOTE)

Leask v City of Glasgow District Council

G

OUTER HOUSE
TEMPORARY JUDGE J M S HORSBURGH, QC
26 JUNE 1992

Damages — Amount — Solatium — Back — Straining injury causing moderate degree of aggravation of pain from spondylosis for a few months.

H

A 23 year old maintenance engineer injured his back. He suffered from spondylosis of the spine which resulted in a predisposition to back pain and his accident aggravated the condition but only for a period of about four months, after which he had returned to work.

Opinion, that the appropriate award for solatium would have been £1,750.

I

Expenses — Tender — Withdrawal of tender — Whether necessary to be withdrawn by formal minute or whether change of circumstances sufficient.

Process — Action of reparation for personal injuries — Tender — Withdrawal of tender — Whether necessary to be withdrawn by formal minute or whether change of circumstances sufficient.

During the course of a proof the pursuer sought to lodge a minute of acceptance of a tender lodged by the
J defenders and to obtain decree in respect thereof. It was argued that the tender was still capable of acceptance since, although it had been removed from process, no minute of withdrawal of tender had been lodged. The defenders argued that the minute of tender was no longer capable of being accepted because (a) it had been made subject to a time limit which had expired; (b) the solicitors for the pursuer had informed the defenders' solicitors that the tender was inadequate; (c) before the commencement of the
K proof the pursuer's counsel had been informed that no offer was being made; (d) the tender had been withdrawn from process; and (e) evidence had been led the previous day.

Held, that a tender could be withdrawn either by lodging a formal minute of withdrawal or by a material change of circumstances and that the factors founded upon by the defenders, except the leading of evidence, were sufficient to amount to withdrawal; and motion for decree in terms of minute of tender and acceptance L thereof *refused*.

David Leask raised an action against his employers, the City of Glasgow District Council, for damages in respect of personal injuries sustained in an accident at work on 26 October 1987. He was then aged 23 and employed as a maintenance engineer. He had hurt his back while moving a pump from a bench to a barrow. He claimed that he had slipped on oily duckboards.

The temporary judge (J M S Horsburgh, QC) held that the pursuer had not established how or why he had fallen and assoilzied the defenders. In relation to damages the temporary judge said:

"It was common ground that the pursuer suffers from spondylosis of the lumbar sacral junction, which occurs through genetic disposition between the ages of eight and 18 years. Although he denied it, the medical records show the pursuer had a pre-accident history of back trouble. Spondylosis produces a predisposition towards back pain. The accident on 26 October 1987 aggravated that condition to a moderate degree in consequence of which the pursuer suffered pain for a period. I am of the view that the aggravation attributable to the accident had subsided by late February 1988 when the pursuer returned to work. I am satisfied that later referrals for hospital treatment were not related to the occurrence of the accident, and in particular the referral in February 1989 was entirely due to other causative factors.

"Counsel for the pursuer suggested solatium of £4,000 with interest on two thirds of that at 7½ per cent and a loss of employability award of £2,000. Counsel for the defenders stressed that any long term adverse effect on the pursuer was due to spondylosis, not the accident, and its effects had been minimal. He referred to *Gibson v British Coal Corporation*, 1990 SLT 714; *Kane v Norwest Holst Pipework Ltd*, 1988 SLT 28; and *Meek v Burton's Gold Medal Biscuits Ltd*, 1989 SLT 338. He suggested £1,750 to £2,000 as appropriate for solatium. He argued no award should be made for prejudice on the labour market since the pursuer's back trouble was due to spondylosis.

"I agree with the view of counsel for the defenders. I consider that £1,750 is reasonable compensation as solatium. Interest at 7½ per cent on two thirds of that would fall to be added, namely a sum of £415. I was entirely satisfied that any disadvantage in employability which the pursuer might encounter in future because of back trouble would be directly related to the inherited disability, and not in consequence of the accident. Accordingly had I found in favour of the pursuer I would have assessed full liability at £2,165 and made an award, subject to contributory negligence, in his favour of £1,082.50."

In relation to a minute of tender which the pursuer sought to accept in the course of the proof the temporary judge said:

"I should record that at the start of the second day of the proof, counsel for the defenders informed me that on 11 February 1992 a minute of tender had been lodged by the defenders' Edinburgh agents and intimated to the Edinburgh agents for the solicitors now acting for the pursuer. On 18 February the defenders' Edinburgh agents wrote to the pursuer's present solicitors advising that the tender was open for acceptance until 5 pm on Friday, 21 February, and if not accepted it would be withdrawn on 24 February. No indication that the tender was acceptable was received, and it was withdrawn from process, that being marked on the inventory. No formal minute of withdrawal had been lodged. Prior to the start of the proof on 3 March counsel for the defenders had advised counsel for the pursuer that no offer was now being made. Prior thereto the pursuer's present solicitors had telephoned the defenders' Edinburgh agents stating the sum offered by tender was inadequate.

"He contended that the minute of tender was no longer capable of acceptance because of the deadline given, the telephone call which inferred that the tender was unacceptable to the pursuer, the pre-proof discussion between counsel, the withdrawal of the tender from process and the previous day's evidence. Under reference to Maxwell on *Court of Session Practice*, p 246; *Macrae v Edinburgh Street Tramways Co* (1885) 13 R 265; *Bright v Low*, 1940 SLT 171; 1940 SC 280; and *Sommerville v National Coal Board*, 1963 SLT 334; 1963 SC 666 he contended that a formal minute withdrawing a tender was not essential to disable a pursuer from accepting. In the circumstances neither party could be under the misapprehension that an offer to settle was still extant.

"In response counsel for the pursuer contended the present case lacked a change of circumstances of the dramatic and material sort which had occurred in the cases cited, and that accordingly a minute of withdrawal was needed to put acceptance of the tender beyond the pursuer's power. She referred to *McMillan v Meikleham*, 1934 SLT 357. She contended that the letter of 18 February was ambiguous, being capable of meaning that the defenders' agents would arrange for the tender to be withdrawn on 24 February or that they would withdraw it then, and it treated the tender as an extrajudicial offer. She however conceded that discussions between counsel had made it clear that there was now no offer.

"In reply, counsel for the defenders pointed out that there was now no Rule of Court which was equivalent of the Act of Sederunt applied in the *McMillan* case, which was also distinguishable because there had been no intimation of withdrawal given, whereas that had occurred in the present circumstances. Because a tender could not be qualified to contain a deadline, the letter of 18 February had been employed. Its expiry without acceptance was an important change of circumstance. The pursuer's argument relied on the contractual aspect of tender and acceptance, but it was clear that there was no consensus between the parties.

"I reached the view that the contentions of the defenders were correct. In my opinion the minute of tender may be withdrawn effectively either by the lodging of a formal minute to that effect or by a material change in circumstances. In this case the latter was satisfied by the expiry of the deadline for acceptance, the indication on the pursuer's behalf that the tender was unacceptable, the physical withdrawal of the minute of tender from process and the pre-proof discussions between counsel. These factors combined to make plain to the understanding of both sides that there was now no tender capable of acceptance and I so held."

Counsel for Pursuer, Raeburn, QC, Hofford; Solicitors, L & L Lawrence — Counsel for Defenders, Menzies, QC, G M Henderson; Solicitors, Campbell Smith & Co, WS.   C H

Beattie, Petitioner

A HIGH COURT OF JUSTICIARY

THE LORD JUSTICE GENERAL (HOPE),
LORDS ALLANBRIDGE AND MAYFIELD

9 JULY 1992

*Nobile officium — Competency — Appeal court quashing
sentence and imposing different sentence — Accused thereafter petitioning nobile officium to quash appeal court's
sentence — Whether appeal court's sentence subject to*
B *review of nobile officium — Criminal Procedure (Scotland) Act 1975 (c 21), ss 262, 281.*

Sections 262 and 281 of the Criminal Procedure
(Scotland) Act 1975 provide, inter alia, that all interlocutors and sentences pronounced by the High Court
under Pt I of the Act shall be final and conclusive and
not subject to review by any court whatsoever.

An accused person was sentenced in the High Court
to 16 years' imprisonment in respect of a charge under
C s 4 (3) (b) of the Misuse of Drugs Act 1971 which contained 11 subcharges each of which libelled separate
contraventions of the 1971 Act. On appeal the High
Court, considering that the trial judge's sentence was
incompetent as being in excess of the then maximum
sentence of 14 years' imprisonment available under
the 1971 Act, quashed the sentence and imposed both
a sentence of 14 years' imprisonment on the charge
and various periods of imprisonment in respect of each
of the subcharges to run concurrently with the sent-
D ence of 14 years' imprisonment. Thereafter the
accused petitioned the nobile officium to quash the
sentence in its entirety on the basis that it was incompetent. The petition was opposed as incompetent. The
accused argued that the petition was directed not to
the merits of the earlier decision but to the form in
which it was put into effect.

Held, (1) that what the High Court was being asked
to do by the petitioner was to review the appeal court's
earlier decision and substitute its own view of what
E was competent and appropriate for that taken by the
appeal court (p 678D-F); (2) that ss 262 and 281 of the
1975 Act made it abundantly clear that the petitioner
had no such right of further appeal (p 678G); and (3)
that it had not been demonstrated that there was anything extraordinary or unforeseen in the circumstances which would justify the exercise of the nobile
officium in conflict with the intention of the 1975 Act
(p 678G-H); and petition *dismissed* as incompetent.

Dictum in *Perrie, Petr*, 1992 SLT 655, *applied.*

F

Petition to the nobile officium

Brian Andrew Beattie presented a petition to the
nobile officium of the High Court of Justiciary seeking
review of a decision of the High Court, sitting as the
court of criminal appeal, dated 17 October 1986,
whereby the court quashed the sentence imposed on
the petitioner in the High Court at Aberdeen on 18
March 1986 and substituted therefor a lower sentence.
The petitioner maintained that the appeal court's sent-

ence was oppressive and unjust in respect that it was
incompetent. The facts of the case are set forth in the G
opinion of the court.

Statutory provisions

The Criminal Procedure (Scotland) Act 1975
provides:

"262. Subject to the provisions of the next following
section of this Act [prerogative of mercy], all interlocutors and sentences pronounced by the High Court
under this Part of this Act shall be final and conclusive
and not subject to review by any court whatsoever and H
it shall be incompetent to stay or suspend any execution or diligence issuing from the High Court under
this Part of this Act. . . .

"281. All interlocutors and sentences pronounced
by the High Court under the authority of this Part of
this Act shall be final and conclusive, and not subject
to review by any court whatsoever, and it shall be
incompetent to stay or suspend any execution or diligence issuing forth of the High Court under the
authority of the same."   I

Cases referred to

Anderson v HM Advocate, 1974 SLT 239.
MacPherson, Petitioners, 1990 JC 5; 1989 SCCR 518.
Perrie, Petitioner, 1992 SLT 655; 1991 SCCR 475.

The petition was heard before the High Court on 25
June 1992.

On 9 July 1992 the court *dismissed* the petition as J
incompetent.

The following opinion of the court was delivered by
the Lord Justice General (Hope):

OPINION OF THE COURT.—The petitioner
appeared in the High Court at Aberdeen on 18 March
1986 on an indictment in which he was charged with
numerous offences. At the outset of the trial he tendered pleas of guilty which were accepted by the K
Crown. Apart from one breach of the peace which was
libelled in charge 14, the offences to which he pled
guilty were all contained within charge 10 on the
indictment. This charge was one of being concerned
in the supplying of various class A and class B drugs
between 1 January 1980 and 21 December 1985, contrary to s 4 (3) (b) of the Misuse of Drugs Act 1971.
The charge was unusual, in that after an introductory
preamble it contained within it 39 subcharges, each of
which libelled a separate contravention of a provision
of the Act. Each of these subcharges was so worded as L
to be capable of being treated as a separate offence.
But they were all subsumed within the opening narrative of charge 10 as being the respects in which the
principal offence of being concerned in the supplying
of the controlled drugs to others was committed. The
petitioner pled guilty to this charge in respect of the
period between 1 November 1982 and 31 May 1985,
and he also pled guilty to 11 of the subcharges, one of
which was itself subdivided into five further subcharges under s 4 (3) (b) of the Act.

The trial judge decided to sentence the petitioner in
A respect of each of the subcharges rather than in respect
of charge 10 as a whole. Having regard to the manner
in which the pleas were tendered, he was of the
opinion that it was competent to sentence him to
periods of imprisonment up to the statutory maximum
for each offence, and to do so cumulatively if appropriate. He regarded the breach of the peace as an
offence which was totally separate from the statutory
offences and was of the opinion that it merited a
separate consecutive sentence of imprisonment. The
B information which was before him indicated that the
petitioner had, for a number of years, organised and
financed a substantial drug ring in the Aberdeen area,
and he was satisfied that an exemplary and punitive
sentence was appropriate. He imposed various terms
of imprisonment in respect of the subcharges within
charge 10, some to be served concurrently with each
other and others to be served consecutively, resulting
in a total period of 16 years' imprisonment. He also
sentenced the petitioner to one year's imprisonment
C on the charge of breach of the peace, this period to be
served consecutively to the sentences which he had
imposed in respect of charge 10. He also imposed fines
on certain of the subheads of charge 10 amounting in
total to £19,000.

The petitioner then appealed against these sentences
in the exercise of his right of appeal under s 228 (1) of
the Criminal Procedure (Scotland) Act 1975. Among
the various grounds which were advanced in support
of the appeal was the argument that the sentences
D imposed in respect of charge 10 were incompetent
because they amounted in total to more than the
maximum amount which could be imposed on charge
10 itself. At the time when these sentences were pronounced the maximum sentence which could be
imposed for a breach of s 4 (3) (b) of the 1971 Act in
respect of class A or class B drugs was 14 years'
imprisonment or a fine or both. The trial judge had
not imposed any sentence in respect of charge 10
itself, but the effect of the sentences imposed on the
E various subheads was that the petitioner was being
required to serve a total of 16 years' imprisonment for
what had been libelled in that charge as a breach of s 4
(3) (b). On 17 October 1986 the court allowed the petitioner's appeal to the extent that the sentences of
imprisonment imposed by the trial judge in respect of
the various subcharges within charge 10 were all
quashed, and in substitution therefor the petitioner
was sentenced to 14 years' imprisonment on that
charge. The court also sentenced him to various
F periods of imprisonment in respect of each of the subcharges, these all to run concurrently with each other
and concurrently with the sentence which the court
had imposed in respect of charge 10. The appeal was
refused in regard to the various fines which were
imposed in respect of the subcharges within charge 10,
and it was also refused insofar as it was directed
against the sentence imposed on the charge of breach
of the peace.

Section 262 of the 1975 Act provides that all interlocutors and sentences pronounced by the High Court

under that Part of the Act shall be final and conclusive
and not subject to review by any court whatsoever. A
provision in the same terms is to be found also in s 281
of the Act. The petitioner having thus exhausted his
statutory right of appeal, one would have expected
that to have been an end of the matter unless a situation so extraordinary and unforeseen had occurred as
to justify the exercise by the court of its nobile officium. And it is to the nobile officium that the petitioner
has now presented this application, on the ground that
the various concurrent sentences of imprisonment and
the various fines which were imposed in respect of the
subcharges within charge 10 were incompetent. He
has invited us to quash these sentences of imprisonment and fines on this ground. Furthermore, in terms
of an amendment which was lodged by counsel for the
petitioner at the outset of the hearing and which was
not opposed by the learned Solicitor General, we are
being asked to go still further and to quash the sentence in its entirety, or to quash the sentence of 14
years' imprisonment in respect of charge 10 as an
alternative to quashing the various sentences imposed
on the subcharges within that charge.

The basis of this application, as explained in the
averments, is that the sentences which were imposed
by the court on appeal were oppressive and unjust in
respect that they were incompetent. But no attempt
has been made in the averments to face up to the question which must be considered at the outset, which is
whether this application to the nobile officium is itself
competent. It is well settled that the nobile officium
cannot be invoked to bring decisions of the High
Court under review. This is because of the finality
which attaches to its decisions in terms of the statute,
and because the nobile officium may never be invoked
when to do so would conflict with statutory intention,
express or implied. It is sufficient to refer to Lord
Justice General Emslie's statement of this principle in
Anderson v HM Advocate, 1974 SLT at p 240. The
same principle has been applied in several recent
decisions of this court, notably *MacPherson, Petrs* and
Perrie, Petr. In the latter case the principle was
expressed at p 658A-B in these terms: "it is clear that
we cannot exercise the nobile officium on grounds
which would have been the proper subject of an
appeal had a further right of appeal been available
under the statute: see *MacPherson, Petrs* at p 522. The
purpose of the nobile officium is to prevent injustice
or oppression where the circumstances are extraordinary or unforeseen and where no other remedy or
procedure is provided by the law. But the power
cannot be exercised in order to review on the merits
a decision taken by the court under the statutory provisions for appeal".

Counsel for the petitioner recognised this difficulty,
as he submitted that the point which the petitioner
sought to raise was not directed to the merits of the
decision taken in the appeal but to the form in which
its decision was put into effect. That being so, he said,
the application was clearly competent, since it was
open to us now to correct a sentence which could be
shown to have been incompetent and not within the

power of the court to pronounce. The point which he sought to argue was that there had been a duplication of sentences for what was in essence a single offence. Looked at as a whole the sentence was incompetent because its effect was to punish the petitioner twice over for one offence. The proper course would be to excise that part of the sentence which was incompetent. But it was not possible to say whether it was the sentence on charge 10 as a whole or the sentence on the various subcharges within charge 10 which caused the difficulty, since either of these sentences on its own would have been competent. In these circumstances the appropriate course was to regard the whole sentence on both charge 10 and its various subcharges as incompetent and for the sentence as a whole to be quashed.

But it was apparent when counsel sought to develop this argument that the contention that the sentences were incompetent amounted to no more than an assertion on his part for which he was unable to cite any authority. He did not and could not suggest that the sentences imposed by the appeal court were incompetent because they were outwith the powers conferred by the 1971 Act. This is not a case therefore where it can be said that the court has done something in the exercise of its appellate jurisdiction which it was not permitted to do by Parliament. In such a case there may be said to have been a circumstance which was unforeseen, because the statutory provisions for the finality of appeals assume that the appeal court will exercise its appellate jurisdiction in accordance with the statutes. The nobile officium may then be exercised to prevent such injustice or oppression as may result. In the present case however the appeal court upheld the petitioner's appeal against the sentences imposed by the trial judge on the ground that he had exceeded the sentencing powers given to him by the 1971 Act. They then imposed in their place sentences within these sentencing powers which they must be taken to have considered to be competent. The argument that these sentences were incompetent is therefore directed to a point which was for the appeal court itself to decide. It was for the appeal court to say what sentences were competent and appropriate, having regard to the unusual way in which charge 10 was expressed and their view of the criminal conduct disclosed by those parts of it to which the petitioner had pled guilty. It follows that, despite the contention to the contrary, what we are really being asked to do by the petitioner is to review that decision. We are being asked to substitute our own view of what was competent and appropriate for that taken by the appeal court. Moreover, since there is no statutory provision on the point at issue, it would be open to us to take the view that what the appeal court did was competent after all. A further difficulty, which also reveals the true nature of the point at issue in this case, is that there are obvious limitations on our powers, sitting as a court of three judges, to interfere with sentences imposed by the appeal court which were not incompetent in terms of any statute without convening a larger court.

For all these reasons we are in no doubt that this petition must be refused as incompetent. The petitioner's argument is one which would have been the proper subject of an appeal had a further right of appeal been open to him under the statute. But ss 262 and 281 of the 1975 Act make it abundantly clear that he has no such right; and it has not been demonstrated that there is anything extraordinary or unforeseen in the circumstances of this case which would justify the exercise of the nobile officium in conflict with the intention of the Act, which is that decisions of the appeal court are final and not subject to review.

Counsel for Petitioner, Macfadyen, QC; Solicitors, Haig-Scott & Co, WS — Counsel for Respondent, Solicitor General (Dawson, QC); Solicitor, J D Lowe, Crown Agent.

P W F

(NOTE)

Ballantyne v Tesco Stores Ltd

OUTER HOUSE
LORD KIRKWOOD
31 JULY 1992

Damages — Amount — Solatium and necessary services rendered to injured person — Ankle — Fracture of ankle with almost total recovery within a year — Injured person requiring assistance from husband for several weeks.

A 48 year old general assistant fractured her ankle. She was unable to walk on it while it was in plaster and her husband gave up his job temporarily to look after her and the children. The pursuer was off work for three months and had achieved an almost total recovery within a year after the accident.

Held, that solatium was properly valued at £2,250 and that the husband's services claim was properly valued at £250; and decree *pronounced* accordingly.

Mrs Margaret Ballantyne raised an action of damages against her employers, Tesco Stores Ltd, in respect of personal injuries sustained in an accident at work on 15 February 1990. She was then aged 48 and employed as a general assistant in a store operated by the defenders. After a proof before the Lord Ordinary (Kirkwood) it was held that the pursuer had been wheeling a trolley laden with milk in cartons when a stiff wheel on the trolley had come free, causing the trolley to turn, striking her on, and fracturing, her left ankle. Liability was established on the part of the defenders for failing to have a system to cope with defective trolleys. In relation to damages his Lordship said:

A "Turning to the issue of damages, the pursuer gave evidence that her left ankle was stitched and put in plaster. She was sent home but returned to hospital the next day to have another plaster applied. About three weeks later the plaster was removed, the stitches were taken out and another plaster was put on. While her ankle was in plaster she could not walk on it and she had to use crutches and she was unable to do her housework or look after her children properly. Her husband left his job in Wales and returned home to assist her. For about three weeks he made the meals

B and did all the housework, but it was about two months before the pursuer could resume her normal household duties, and she was off work for about three months. After the plaster was removed a double elastic bandage was fitted and the pursuer then became mobile although she limped for a time. The pain in her ankle gradually wore off but she still gets some pain in cold weather. There is a small scar but it does not trouble her. She is now back at work and has no difficulty in carrying out her duties.

C "Parties were agreed that the medical report by Mr Ian Mackay, consultant orthopaedic surgeon, dated 10 November 1990 and the medical report by Mr Thomas Mann, consultant orthopaedic surgeon, dated 4 May 1992 are accurate in all medical particulars and refer to the pursuer. These reports disclose that the pursuer sustained a laceration of the left ankle and an undisplaced fracture of the left lateral malleolus. Three stitches were inserted, a below knee plaster was applied and she was sent home and advised to use

D crutches. The following day the plaster was changed and there was found to be some swelling, bruising and tenderness over the lateral malleolus although ankle movements were full. On 1 March 1990 the wound was seen to be well healed and a new plaster was applied. The plaster was removed on 15 March 1990 when she complained of slight pain at the fracture site, and she was given a supporting bandage. When she was examined by Mr Mackay in September 1990 she was still complaining of intermittent pain. She had no

E obvious limp but she had difficulty fully weight-bearing on the left leg. There was a well healed scar some 3 cm in length and a loss of 20 degrees of dorsiflexion of the left ankle. There was pain at the extremes of plantar flexion. However, Mr Mackay expected that all her problems would settle completely in about six months. When the pursuer was examined by Mr Mann in May 1992 she walked without a trace of a limp and only some very minor deficits remained which did not augur any long term difficulty. In Mr

F Mann's opinion, the pursuer will have no future problems with her ankle.

"Parties were agreed that the pursuer was off work from 15 February 1990 until 5 May 1990 and that during that period her net loss of wages amounted to £657.85 exclusive of interest. There was no claim for future loss of earnings.

"Counsel for the pursuer referred to *Daniels v Greater London Council* (Kemp and Kemp, *Quantum of Damages*, para 13/029) and *Bruce v British Trans-*

port Hotels Ltd, 1981 SLT (Notes) 77, and submitted that an appropriate award of solatium would be G £3,000, all of which should be attributed to the past. With regard to the pursuer's claim in respect of the services rendered to her by her husband, he invited me to make an award of £300. Counsel for the defenders submitted that the value of the pursuer's claim for solatium was £1,700, two thirds of which should be attributed to the past and he referred to *Leck v Hoover Ltd*, 1983 SLT 374; *Ross v National Coal Board*, 1988 SLT 385; *Millar v Fife Regional Council*, 1990 SLT 651; and *Nimmo v British Railways Board*, 1990 SLT H 680. An award of £150 should be made in respect of the services rendered to the pursuer by her husband.

"I was satisfied that the pursuer did not at any stage seek to exaggerate the effects of her injury and on the basis of her evidence, and the terms of the agreed medical reports, I assess the value of her claim for solatium at £2,250 and I would attribute the whole of that sum to the past. With regard to the claim under s 8 of the Administration of Justice (Scotland) Act 1981 I have decided to award the sum of £250." I

Counsel for Pursuer, Dorrian; Solicitors, Robin Thompson & Partners — Counsel for Defenders, Stephenson; Solicitors, Gray Muirhead, WS (for Holmes MacKillop, Glasgow).

C H

J

Hooper v Royal London General Insurance Co Ltd

SECOND DIVISION
THE LORD JUSTICE CLERK (ROSS),
LORDS McCLUSKEY AND KIRKWOOD
29 JANUARY 1993   K

Insurance — Indemnity insurance — Material non-disclosure — Appropriate test of materiality — Non-disclosure of prior conviction — Whether material.

An insured person raised an action in the sheriff court for payment in terms of an insurance contract over house contents. The risks insured against included loss or damage by fire, theft and vandalism. The proposal form requested disclosure of previous convictions and outstanding charges. At the time of completion the pursuer had a conviction for vandalism which was not spent in terms of the Rehabilitation of Offenders Act 1974. He also faced an outstanding charge of theft of which he was later convicted. Neither the conviction nor the charge was disclosed to the insurers. Shortly after the policy took effect there was a fire in the pursuer's home and the contents were destroyed. The defenders refused to meet the claim intimated on the basis of material non-disclosure by the pursuer. After a proof the sheriff dismissed the

action and the pursuer appealed to the Inner House.
A The pursuer contended that the proper test of materiality of non-disclosure was what a reasonable and cautious man proposing insurance would think proper to be disclosed. The defenders contended for the test of what would influence the judgment of a prudent insurer in determining whether to take the risk.

Held, (1) that the appropriate basis for the test of materiality in all types of insurance other than life assurance was that of the prudent or reasonable
B insurer (pp 684D, 688I-J and 691J-K); (2) that the test of materiality was an objective one, that regard had to be had to the terms of the policy, and that the insurance cover sought, the risk, the premium payable, the possible fate of the insured articles and the apparent honesty or dishonesty of the insured were all relevant and significant matters (pp 684H-K, 688L, 689D-E, 692F-G and 692I-K); (3) that the defenders were entitled to hold the contract void as a result of the pursuer's failure to disclose the previous conviction and
C pending charge (pp 685B-C, 689H and 693A); and appeal *refused*.

Life Association of Scotland v Foster (1873) 11 M 351, *distinguished.* Authorities *reviewed*.

Opinion, that even if the test of materiality was on the basis of what an insured considered material, the contract would be void as a reasonable man in the position of the insured would have realised that these matters would influence the insurers' judgment (pp 685A-B, 689A and 692L-693A).

D **Opinion**, further, that where there was sufficient evidence of the general character of the pursuer's loss, but the evidence as to the value of the property destroyed was unsatisfactory, the pursuer would have been entitled to decree for payment of a restricted sum compared to what had been claimed (pp 685G-I, 690D-G and 693B-D).

Appeal from the sheriff court
E Samuel Hooper raised an action in Kirkcaldy sheriff court against Royal London General Insurance Co Ltd seeking payment in respect of a claim under a policy of insurance with the defenders following the loss by fire of the contents of the pursuer's home. The defenders pled material non-disclosure by the pursuer in the proposal form entitling them to void the policy.

The case came to proof before the sheriff.

Statutory provisions
F The Marine Insurance Act 1906 provides:

"18.— . . . (2) Every circumstance is material which would influence the judgment of a prudent insurer in fixing the premium, or determining whether he will take the risk."

The Road Traffic Act 1988 provides:

"151.— . . . (9) . . . (b) 'material' means of such a nature as to influence the judgment of a prudent insurer in determining whether he will take the risk and, if so, at what premium and on what conditions."

Cases referred to
Arif v Excess Insurance Group Ltd, 1982 SLT 183.
Duncan v Gumleys, 1987 SLT 729.
Gifto Fancy Goods Ltd v Ecclesiastical Insurance Office plc and Hannah, OH, 15 November 1990, unreported (1991 GWD 2-117).
Lambert v Co-operative Insurance Society Ltd [1975] 2 Lloyd's Rep 485.
Life Association of Scotland v Foster (1873) 11 M 351.
McCartney v Laverty, 1968 SLT (Notes) 50; 1968 SC 207.
March Cabaret Club & Casino v London Assurance [1975] 1 Lloyd's Rep 169.
Mutual Life Insurance Co of New York v Ontario Metal Products Co Ltd [1925] AC 344.
Reid and Co Ltd v Employers' Accident and Live Stock Insurance Co Ltd (1899) 1 F 1031.
Reynolds and Anderson v Phoenix Assurance Co Ltd [1978] 2 Lloyd's Rep 440.
Zurich General Accident and Liability Insurance Co v Leven, 1940 SLT 350; 1940 SC 406.

Textbook referred to
MacGillivray and Parkington, *Insurance Law* (8th ed), paras 541, 542, 544, 658, 660, 663 and 665.

Terms of proposal form
The insurance proposal form contained the following, inter alia:

"10. Have you, or any member of your family, or any other person permanently residing with you . . . (c) ever been convicted of (or charged but not yet tried with) any offence other than motoring offences? . . .

"IMPORTANT NOTE
"All material facts must be disclosed. Failure to do so could invalidate the policy. A material fact is one which would be likely to influence an insurer in the assessment or acceptance of the risk, e g intended unoccupancy of the property. If in doubt as to whether a fact is material then it should be disclosed to the Company. State any other material fact here."

On 30 November 1990 the sheriff *dismissed* the action.

The pursuer appealed to the Court of Session.

Appeal
The appeal was heard before the Second Division on 24, 25 and 26 November 1992.

On 29 January 1993 the court *refused* the appeal, *recalled* the interlocutor of the sheriff, *sustained* the second and third pleas in law for the defenders and *pronounced* decree of absolvitor in their favour.

THE LORD JUSTICE CLERK (ROSS).—In this action the pursuer is seeking payment from the defenders of sums alleged to be due to him in terms of a contract of insurance. The policy of insurance was entered into by the parties in 1988, and in terms of it the defenders undertook to indemnify the pursuer in respect of damage caused to his house contents by

certain named risks including inter alia damage caused
A by fire. The effective date of the policy was 6 September 1988, and on 29 October 1988 a fire broke out at
the pursuer's property and the whole contents of his
property were destroyed by fire. The pursuer intimated a claim in terms of the policy which the
defenders refused to honour. The defenders maintained that there had been material non-disclosure by
the pursuer in the proposal form upon which the
policy of insurance followed. After sundry procedure
a proof was held before the sheriff at Kirkcaldy, and
B on 30 November 1990 the sheriff pronounced an interlocutor dismissing the action. It is against that interlocutor that the pursuer has appealed to this court.

It was not disputed that the pursuer had signed a
proposal form prior to the policy of insurance being
entered into, and that the proposal form included a
number of questions. Question 10 (c) was in the
following terms: [his Lordship quoted the terms of
question 10 set out supra and continued:] It was not
disputed that that question was answered in the nega-
C tive. By way of explanation the pursuer maintained
that he is semi-literate and that the defenders' agent
Mr Patrick completed the form upon his behalf. The
sheriff states in his note that he is satisfied that the
pursuer is semi-literate and that the proposal form was
read over to him and filled in by Mr Patrick. Subsequently the sheriff states that Mr Patrick did not convince him that he read over all the questions to the
pursuer, and he accordingly found the evidence in a
total state of equilibrium. It was for that reason that
D the sheriff held that the pursuer must fail and he dismissed the action.

It is a matter of regret to have to say that the sheriff's
interlocutor and note appear to me to be woefully
inadequate. Although the sheriff has set out in his
interlocutor findings in fact, he has made no findings
in law, and the findings in fact do not deal adequately
with the evidence which was led before him. He has
appended to his interlocutor a note but the note is
E unsatisfactory as it contains a number of inconsistencies. For example finding 17 is in the following
terms:

"17. The proposal form was read over to the
pursuer by the agent." As already observed, in his
note the sheriff states that he is satisfied that the
proposal form was read over to him and filled in by the
agent, but he also says that the agent did not convince
him that he read over all the questions to the pursuer.
The terms of finding 17 would suggest that the whole
F proposal form was read over to the pursuer by the
agent, and if that was not the case, one would have
expected the sheriff to make an express finding as to
which part or parts of the proposal form were not read
over to the pursuer by Mr Patrick. In the first paragraph of his note the sheriff states in terms that one
of the questions which Mr Patrick asked the pursuer
was the question about previous convictions, and yet
at a later stage of his note the sheriff says that Mr
Patrick did not convince him that he read over all the
questions to the pursuer.

It is, however, accepted that the pursuer signed the
proposal form, and before this court the argument G
proceeded upon the basis that the pursuer was
responsible for what was contained in the completed
proposal form which he signed. It is not therefore
necessary to seek to resolve the conflict in evidence to
which the sheriff referred.

In their pleadings the defenders make it clear that
they are seeking to avoid the contract upon the ground
of material non-disclosure or misrepresentation on the
part of the pursuer. That being so, it is surprising to
discover that the findings in fact are silent upon this H
critical matter. There is no finding in fact to the effect
that there was or was not any non-disclosure or misrepresentation by the pursuer. There is no finding in
fact dealing with the materiality of any non-disclosure
or misrepresentation. Finding in fact 19 is in the following terms: "The policy is entitled to be voided if
there is an effective non-disclosure." That is not a
finding in fact but a finding in law. Moreover all that
it says is that the policy may be voided in the event of
there being an effective non-disclosure, but it is not I
said that there was an effective non-disclosure. In any
event in this branch of the law the test is not whether
any non-disclosure was effective but whether it was
material. The real question in this case was whether
any misrepresentation or non-disclosure on the part of
the pursuer was material. Counsel for the defender
made it clear that he was relying on misrepresentation
or non-disclosure and not on any warranty. The
proposal form included a declaration in the course of
which the pursuer as the insured stated inter alia: "To J
the best of my knowledge and belief all particulars
given on and in connection with this proposal are
correct and complete." This might have supported a
claim that the matter was covered by warranty, but
counsel explained that the defenders as insurers had
never suggested that they were repudiating on the
ground of warranty, and that accordingly counsel was
not now founding on warranty.

As already observed the answer to question 10 (c)
was in the negative. The fact is that the pursuer K
accepted that he had a large number of convictions for
criminal offences prior to 6 September 1988. Most of
these, however, were spent convictions in terms of the
Rehabilitation of Offenders Act 1974. It was not,
however, disputed that as at 6 September 1988 there
was a conviction against the pursuer on 23 February
1987 which was not spent. This was a conviction for
a contravention of s 78 (1) of the Criminal Justice
(Scotland) Act 1980, that is, vandalism. It was also not
disputed that as at 6 September 1988 the pursuer had L
been charged with an offence alleged to have been
committed on 13 August 1988. The charge was of
breach of the peace and theft of a video recorder. On
3 May 1989 he was convicted of these offences.

It was not disputed on behalf of the pursuer that
there had been no disclosure by him to the defenders
of the pending charge on 6 September 1988 nor of the
previous conviction on 23 February 1987. On the pursuer's behalf, however, it was maintained that such
non-disclosure, whether it was regarded as non-

A
disclosure or a misrepresentation, had not been material. In the present case it appears to me that the answer to question 10 (c) on the proposal form constituted both misrepresentation and non-disclosure. A contract of insurance may be voidable on the ground of inter alia misrepresentation and/or non-disclosure (MacGillivray and Parkington on *Insurance Law* (8th ed), para 541). "A misrepresentation may be defined as an inaccurate or untrue statement made by one of the parties to the contract of insurance, or by his agent, prior to the conclusion of the contract" (Mac-

B
Gillivray and Parkington, para 542). It is something directly said in answer to a specific question (*Zurich General Accident and Liability Insurance Co Ltd v Leven* at 1940 SLT, p 354 per the Lord President). The answer to question 10 (c) appears to me to fall within that definition. Because a contract of insurance is a contract uberrima fides, the utmost good faith is required from the parties. There is thus a duty on a party to disclose all relevant facts to enable the other party to make an accurate estimate of what he is under-

C
taking. "In general, non-disclosure means that you have failed to disclose something which was not the subject of a question but which was known to you and which you ought to have considered for yourself would be material" (*Zurich General Accident and Liability Insurance Co v Leven*, p 354).

Non-disclosure of material facts renders a contract of insurance voidable (MacGillivray and Parkington, para 544). Failure to give a true answer to question 10 (c) may therefore also be reviewed as non-disclosure

D
and, of course, such non-disclosure would arise even if question 10 (c) had not been asked. What is critical is to determine whether the misrepresentation or non-disclosure was material.

It was strongly argued on behalf of the pursuer that before it could be held that there had been non-disclosure of, or misrepresentation concerning, material facts justifying avoidance of the contract, three critical matters required to be established: (1)

E
Did the fact founded upon create an additional risk? (2) If the fact had been known to the insurer, would that have influenced his judgment determining whether to take on the risk? (3) Would a reasonable assured in the position of the pursuer have realised both these matters?

In order to determine the validity of the submissions, it is necessary to determine the proper test of materiality which falls to be applied in this context. In this connection counsel for the pursuer referred to

F
MacGillivray and Parkington, paras 658 and 660. Paragraph 658 deals with the test of materiality in English law. It is there pointed out that the test so far as marine insurance is concerned is to be found in s 18 (2) of the Marine Insurance Act 1906 which provides that: "Every circumstance is material which would influence the judgment of a prudent insurer in fixing the premium or determining whether he will take the risk."

It is also pointed out in this paragraph that it has been held that the words of s 18 (2) also represent the

G
law in non-marine insurance. That was so held by the Court of Appeal in *Lambert v Co-operative Insurance Society Ltd*, where it was observed that there was no obvious reason why there should be a rule of disclosure in marine insurance different from the rules in other forms of insurance. That case concerned an "all risk" insurance policy covering jewellery. In reaching their decision the Court of Appeal applied the decision of the Privy Council in *Mutual Life Insurance Co of New York v Ontario Metal Products Co Ltd*, which was a case concerning life insurance. In the course of delivering the judgment of the board Lord Salvesen

H
said: "In their view, it is a question of fact in each case whether, if the matters concealed or misrepresented had been truly disclosed, they would, on a fair consideration of the evidence, have influenced a reasonable insurer to decline the risk or to have stipulated for a higher premium."

It is thus clear that in both marine and non-marine insurance, in England the test is that of the prudent insurer. The court rejected what is sometimes called the "reasonable assured" test which had been

I
expressed in *Mutual Life Assurance Co of New York v Ontario Metal Products Co Ltd* by a Canadian judge as "what any reasonable man would have considered material to tell them when the questions were put to the insured".

Paragraph 660 of MacGillivray and Parkington is headed "Life Assurance and Scots Law". It is there observed that prior to *Lambert v Co-operative Insurance Society Ltd*, there was a line of authority in both

J
England and Scotland to the effect that in life assurance the test of materiality was to ask whether a reasonable man in the position of the assured and with the knowledge of the facts in dispute ought to have realised that they were material to the risk. This is the "reasonable assured" test which was laid down in Scotland in *Life Association of Scotland v Foster*. In para 660 the authors say of that decision: "It is submitted that this decision still represents the law in Scotland, as the Scottish courts are in no way bound

K
to follow the decision of the English Court of Appeal." It is also observed in a footnote that *Life Association of Scotland v Foster* was not cited to the Court of Appeal in *Lambert v Co-operative Insurance Society Ltd*.

Life Association of Scotland v Foster related to a life assurance policy. The proposal form contained a declaration that the insured was "in good health, not being afflicted with any disorder, external or

L
internal". In reply to a question put by the medical officer of the assurance company whether she had a rupture the insured replied in the negative. It was proved that at the date when the assurance was effected the assured had a small swelling on the groin, which was a symptom of rupture, but which she did not know to be so, and which she did not consider of importance and did not disclose. In the course of delivering his opinion in that case Lord President Inglis said (at pp 359-360): "Concealment or non-disclosure of material facts by a person entering into

a contract is, generally speaking, either fraudulent or innocent, and in the case of most contracts where parties are dealing at arm's-length, that which is not fraudulent is innocent. But contracts of insurance are in this, among other particulars, exceptional, that they require on both sides *uberrima fides*. Hence, without any fraudulent intent, and even *in bona fide*, the insured may fail in the duty of disclosure. His duty is carefully and diligently to review all the facts known to himself bearing on the risk proposed to the insurers, and to state every circumstance which any reasonable man might suppose could in any way influence the insurers in considering and deciding whether they will enter into the contract. Any negligence or want of fair consideration for the interests of the insurers on the part of the insured leading to the non-disclosure of material facts, though there be no dishonesty, may therefore constitute a failure in the duty of disclosure which will lead to the voidance of the contract. The fact undisclosed may not have appeared to the insured at the time to be material, and yet if it turned out to be material, and in the opinion of a jury was a fact that a reasonable and cautious man proposing insurance would think material and proper to be disclosed, its non-disclosure will constitute such negligence on the part of the insured as to void the contract."

That decision has stood for over 100 years, and I agree with the authors of MacGillivray and Parkington that it prescribes the test of materiality to be applied in life assurance. Counsel for the pursuer, however, maintained that Lord President Inglis had been speaking of contracts of insurance generally, and they maintained that the same test of materiality fell to be applied in the case of non-life insurance, and in particular that the same test fell to be applied in the case of fire insurance. They recognised that in marine insurance and in motor insurance the test is statutory, but they maintained that for fire insurance the test of the reasonable assured laid down by Lord President Inglis was the correct test.

Counsel for the defenders, on the other hand, maintained that the test laid down in *Life Association of Scotland v Foster* applied only to life assurance. He accepted that the test of materiality was statutory in the case of marine insurance and motor insurance but he contended that there was no justification for applying the reasonable assured test to fire insurance. Counsel for the defenders drew attention to two Outer House cases, although he submitted that they did not in fact give assistance. *Gifto Fancy Goods Ltd v Ecclesiastical Insurance Office plc and Hannah* was a case of fire insurance. Lord Sutherland applied the prudent insurer test, but he did so only because that test of materiality had been agreed between the parties, and he stated that he would have been interested to hear full argument as to whether or not this was in fact the correct test to be applied in Scotland to a non-marine risk. Counsel also referred to *Arif v Excess Insurance Group Ltd* where Lord Wylie also applied the reasonable insurer test. However, he does not appear to have had any full citation of authority, and his decision cannot therefore be regarded as

authoritative. It is certainly clear that neither of these cases is authority for the proposition that the test laid down in *Life Association of Scotland v Foster* applies to all contracts of insurance.

In the course of submissions we were also referred to *Reid and Co Ltd v Employers' Accident and Live Stock Insurance Co Ltd*. That case concerned a policy of insurance against liability for damage caused to third parties by employees. The insurers sought to avoid liability on the ground of material misstatement of fact by the insured. In the course of his opinion Lord Trayner stated (at p 1035): "Now, had the case stood thus, I cannot doubt that upon well-settled principles of law the policy, which was issued on the basis of the truth of the particulars given in the proposal, would be void, and that no claim could be enforced in respect of it. The law is trite, that any misstatement of facts, or non-disclosure of facts, which might reasonably affect the mind of the insurer in undertaking the risk is fatal to the policy. It does not require to that end to be shewn that the misstatements or non-disclosure were intentional or wilfully false." Counsel for the pursuers, however, pointed out that in that case, *Life Association of Scotland v Foster* had not been cited.

The critical question to be determined is whether the test laid down in *Life Association of Scotland v Foster* is to be applied to all contracts of insurance, or whether it is to be applied only to life assurance cases. All contracts of insurance are contracts uberrima fides and Lord President Inglis' comments are expressed quite generally. Nevertheless I have come to be of opinion that life assurance is in a different position to other contracts of insurance, and that there are sound reasons for concluding that a different test of materiality arises in life assurance cases. When a proposal form in relation to life assurance contains questions to be answered by the assured, these questions often relate to personal matters such as the assured's state of health, and whether the assured has had illnesses or has exhibited symptoms of disorder. These matters are all peculiarly within the knowledge of the assured. They are subjective and are not capable of assessment on any objective basis. On the other hand where the contract of insurance is a contract of indemnity the questions addressed to the insured are of a different character to those which feature in life assurance cases. Thus when, as here, the assured is asked whether he has ever been convicted of or charged with any offence, that is no doubt within his own personal knowledge, but whether he has been convicted or charged with an offence is a fact which is known to many persons other than himself. It is quite different to something like the pain or swelling in *Life Association of Scotland v Foster* which could only be known to the assured. Unless the reasonable assured test was adopted in life assurance cases, the result might be that in cases like *Life Association of Scotland v Foster* the insurers would be able to avoid the contract on the ground that a reasonable insurer would not have entered the contract when he was aware that the insured had a swelling in the groin which was a symptom of rupture although the assured did not know that to be so and did not consider the swelling to be of importance. In such cases justice requires the adoption of the reasonable assured test so that the insurers would be liable when it was shown "that the swelling which is proved to have existed at the date of the contract of insurance has not been shewn to be such a fact as a reasonable and cautious person, unskilled in medical science, and with no special knowledge of the law and practice of insurance, would believe to be of any materiality or in any way calculated to influence the insurers in considering and deciding on the risk" (p 360).

In non-life assurance cases, however, I see no justification for adopting the reasonable assured test. It is significant that no authority was cited to us in support of the proposition that the test should be the test of the reasonable assured. In *Reid and Co Ltd v Employers' Accident Insurance Co Ltd* Lord Trayner clearly favoured the "prudent insurer" or "reasonable insurer" test. He stated it to be trite law that any non-disclosure of facts which might reasonably affect the mind of the insurer in undertaking the risk was fatal to the policy. It is true that *Life Association of Scotland v Foster* was not cited to the court, but that may well have been because parties correctly recognised that the latter case was concerned with life assurance only. It is significant that Lord Young was one of the court who decided *Reid and Co Ltd v Employers' Accident Assurance Co Ltd*, and he was also counsel in *Life Association of Scotland v Foster*. If he had thought that *Life Association of Scotland v Foster* had any relevance to a non-life assurance case such as *Reid and Co Ltd v Employers' Accident and Live Stock Insurance Co Ltd*, it is very surprising that he made no mention of that in his opinion in the latter case.

I accordingly conclude that except in life assurance cases, the test of materiality is the same in Scotland as it is in England and that the test to be applied is the test of the prudent or reasonable insurer.

However, even if that is the test, it was strongly argued that in the present case, although there had been non-disclosure, there was insufficient material before the sheriff to establish whether or not the non-disclosure created an additional risk, and, if so, whether that would have influenced the judgment of a prudent or reasonable insurer. Counsel for the pursuer contended that the onus was upon the defenders to establish materiality, and that on the evidence there was insufficient material for them to discharge that onus. Counsel on behalf of the defenders, on the other hand, maintained that if there was an onus upon the defenders in this respect, it had shifted once non-disclosure had been established. Alternatively he submitted that once all the evidence had been led the question of onus did not really arise.

I have reached the conclusion that no question of onus arises here. Applying the reasonable insurer test, I am satisfied that if a prudent insurer had been aware of the pursuer's previous conviction for vandalism and the pending charge for theft, that would have

influenced his judgment on whether to take the risk. In *March Cabaret v London Assurance*, May J (as he then was) observed at p 176 that there is a presumption that matters dealt with in a proposal form are material. It has also been observed that the materiality of a non-disclosed fact may be so obvious that evidence is not necessary to establish the point (MacGillivray and Parkington, para 665). In any event, there was evidence before the sheriff from Mr Tolfts, an assistant claims manager with the defenders, to the effect that if these matters had been disclosed to the defenders they would have rejected the risk. However, he made it clear that he was referring to the practice of his own company, and I accept that a fact is not proved to be material merely because a particular insurer expresses the view that he would regard it to be material (MacGillivray and Parkington, para 663). The test of materiality is an objective one. In determining whether or not non-disclosure was material, I am of opinion that it is important to have regard to the nature of the risk which the insurer was being invited to undertake. The evidence clearly established the nature of the risk. It is clear from the proposal form that the pursuer was applying for a "Home Protection Extra And Home Protection" policy. What was issued to him was a "Home Protection Extra" policy. The policy covered contents, and the contents cover covered inter alia: "loss or damage to the contents in the home by the following causes . . . 3. Riot, civil commotion, strikes, labour and political disturbances, malicious persons or vandals". There was expressly excluded "Malicious damage caused by paying guests, tenants or Insured Persons". The contents cover also covered inter alia "7. Theft or attempted theft". Again there was an express exclusion of "Loss or damage caused by paying guests, tenants or Insured Persons".

Although malicious damage caused by the insured or loss or damage caused by the insured were expressly excluded from the policy cover, I regard it as significant that the policy covered loss or damage due to vandalism or theft. If it had been disclosed to the defenders that the pursuer had recently been convicted of vandalism and that less than four weeks before effecting the insurance he had been charged with theft, I am satisfied that these facts would have influenced them as reasonable insurers in determining whether to adopt the risk of covering the pursuer against inter alia damage due to vandalism or loss due to theft.

In this case a specific question was asked as to whether the pursuer had been charged but not yet tried with any offence. It appears that he was subsequently convicted of the charge, and so had in fact committed the offence. This is an added reason why there had to be disclosure. As Forbes J observed in *Reynolds v Phoenix Assurance Co Ltd* at p 460: "If therefore an allegation of a relevant criminal offence is made, and the allegation is true, the proposer must disclose it not because the allegation has been made but because the offence has in fact been committed; it is not then the allegation which must be disclosed but the underlying fact that a crime has been committed."

I would only add that even if the view were taken that the "reasonable assured" tests fell to be applied, I would still hold that there had been material non-disclosure or misrepresentation. A reasonable man in the position of the pursuer as insured, with the knowledge of the previous conviction for vandalism and the pending charge of theft, would have realised that these facts would have influenced the insurers' judgment. Indeed I agree with counsel for the defenders that it is really inconceivable that a reasonable insured would have considered these matters to be of no relevance to a reasonable insurer. Accordingly, even if the test for which the pursuer contended is applied, the result would be the same, and the defenders would be entitled to avoid the contract on the ground of material non-disclosure or misrepresentation. I am not persuaded that there is inadequate material before the court to enable it to reach a conclusion on this issue.

In these circumstances I am satisfied that the defenders were entitled to hold the contract void by reason of material non-disclosure or misrepresentation on the part of the pursuer. I would accordingly move your Lordships to sustain the second and third pleas in law for the defenders, and to pronounce decree of absolvitor.

I have already referred to the fact that the sheriff's findings do not deal adequately with the evidence. In terms of s 32 (4) of the Court of Session Act 1988, it is necessary for this court, in giving judgment, distinctly to specify in its interlocutor the several facts material to the cause which it finds to be established by the proof. That being so I would move your Lordships to vary the findings in fact in the interlocutor of the sheriff dated 30 November 1990 as follows:

(a) By deleting finding 14 and substituting therefor the following: "The form includes a question as to whether the person seeking insurance has ever been convicted of (or charged but not yet tried with) any offence other than motoring offences."

(b) By deleting finding 15 and substituting therefor the following: "The foregoing question was answered in the negative and no mention was made of any previous convictions or pending charges."

(c) Finding 16 should be altered by inserting at the beginning the words: "The pursuer was convicted of the offence of vandalism (s 78 (1) of the Criminal Justice (Scotland) Act 1980) on 23 February 1987, and that conviction was not spent as at 6 September 1988."

By adding at the end of finding 16 the following: "He had been charged with said offences prior to entering into said policy of insurance, and was aware of that fact."

(d) Finding 19 should be deleted, and should be replaced by a finding in the following terms: "20. The amount of loss sustained by the pursuer in respect of which he would be entitled to payment from the defenders if the policy were not avoided is £6,500."

I would also move your Lordships to add after the findings in fact the following:

"Finds in fact and law that the policy is liable to be avoided if there is a material non-disclosure or misrepresentation, and there was material non-disclosure or misrepresentation in this case."

As already observed, the sheriff did not make any findings in relation to the appellant's loss. This has left the court in a difficult position. I am not, however, persuaded that this court is unable on the evidence to arrive at a just result. The pursuer clearly must have suffered substantial loss, and if he had succeeded in establishing liability against the defenders, I am of opinion that he would have been entitled to the amount claimed by him subject to a discount because of the unsatisfactory nature of the evidence led before the court. Lord McCluskey has dealt with the matter in some detail, and I find myself in agreement with all that he says in this regard. In particular I agree that justice would be done if the figure of £6,500 was placed upon the pursuer's loss. That is the amount to which he would have been entitled if liability had been established against the defenders.

Having regard to my views on the merits, however, I would move your Lordships to refuse this appeal, to recall the interlocutor of the sheriff dated 30 November 1990, to sustain the second and third pleas in law for the defenders, and to pronounce decree of absolvitor in their favour. The interlocutor pronounced by this court will include the findings in fact and the findings in fact and law as amended.

LORD McCLUSKEY.—On 6 September 1988 the pursuer and appellant signed an insurance proposal form of the defenders and respondents whereby he sought insurance cover from them in respect of the contents of the house in which he was then living. Before he signed the proposal form it was completed by the respondents' agent, Peter Patrick; it was he who filled in details of the proposer's name, address, employment and so on; he also ticked in the appropriate "Yes" and "No" boxes in answer to various questions posed in the form. The only writing of the appellant on the form was his signature. The respondents duly accepted the proposal contained in the form and parties entered into a contract of insurance, effective from 6 September 1988, whereby the contents of the house were insured for £12,000, the minimum cover offered by the respondents under the appropriate policy, the "Home Protection Extra" policy. On 29 October 1988 a fire destroyed virtually everything that was in the house. The fire was started deliberately but it is not known who did it; it was not the appellant. The smouldering and fire damaged contents were removed during or shortly after the fire to the district council tip. The appellant duly claimed under the policy. He calculated his loss at over £13,000. However, the claim had to be restricted to a sum no greater than £12,000; and for that and other reasons the claim now advanced is for £10,550.17. The respondents repudiated liability for the claim in its entirety and in this action the appellant seeks

payment from the respondents under the policy to
A indemnify him for what he claims to be his loss.

The circumstance that gave rise to repudiation of
the claim was that, after the fire, the respondents discovered that the appellant had not told them the whole
truth about his brushes with the criminal law. By 6
September 1988 he had acquired a substantial list of
convictions for various breaches of the criminal law.
Although under the Rehabilitation of Offenders Act
1974 he was not obliged to do so, the pursuer volunteered in evidence in chief that he had "quite a few"
B previous convictions, probably as many as 20; he did
not really know. The respondents also learned that on
24 February 1989 he was convicted at Kirkcaldy
sheriff court of several offences committed in
Kirkcaldy on 13 August 1988; these included a breach
of the peace in a house in Kirkcaldy and the theft from
that house of a video recorder; further details are contained in an extract conviction dated 3 May 1989
(which the authors of the pleadings and the sheriff
mistakenly treated as the date of the conviction: see
C finding in fact 16). In the proposal form no mention
was made of any of these convictions or charges,
despite the fact that the signed proposal form itself
contained a specific question in the following terms:
[his Lordship quoted the terms of question 10 set out
supra and continued:] This question was followed by
a blank box to allow "full details" to be given. Underneath that box there was a section inviting disclosure
of other material facts. It read: [his Lordship quoted
the terms of the "Important Note" and continued:]
D There was then a blank box to allow such statement.
The respondents' repudiation of liability was on the
basis which is contained in their second and third
pleas in law which read as follows:

"(2) The contract of insurance between the parties
being voidable by reason of the material non-
disclosure by the pursuer as condescended upon, and
the defenders having held the contract to be void, they
should be assoilzied.

E "(3) The pursuer being in material breach of the
said contract as condescended upon is not entitled to
be indemnified thereunder."

The material non-disclosure there referred to did
not, however, relate to the appellant's whole criminal
record. The material breach upon which the respondents were and are founding was the appellant's
failure to disclose (a) a conviction for vandalism under
s 78 (1) of the Criminal Justice (Scotland) Act 1980 at
F Kirkcaldy sheriff court on 23 February 1987, in
respect of which the appellant was fined £50; and (b)
the fact that on or about 13 August 1988, the appellant
had been charged with the offences of which he was
subsequently convicted on 24 February 1989. There
was some discussion before this court as to whether
the appellant's failure to disclose these matters should
properly be characterised as a "misrepresentation of a
fact" or simply as "non-disclosure", a distinction discussed by the Lord President in *Zurich General
Accident and Liability Insurance Co v Leven* at p 415.
There was undoubtedly no disclosure of these matters

by the appellant; he did not dispute this, his position
being that nobody asked him. Although on the face of G
it he was guilty of a misrepresentation by signing the
proposal form which contained, when he signed it, a
negative response to question 10 (c) and no response
at all to the "Important Note" inviting disclosure of
material facts, the appellant's position was that he was
only semi-literate, that it was Peter Patrick who had
filled in the form for the appellant to sign and that the
questions, and in particular question 10, had not been
brought to his attention in any way; so he had not
consciously made any misrepresentation about the H
matters which the respondents were regarding as
material. Mr Patrick, in evidence, said that the appellant was in fact asked all the questions and gave negative answers, and that the appellant also signed the
proposal form without disclosing that he had any
difficulty whatsoever in reading; indeed the appellant
had signed it after apparently perusing it for a while
without making any suggestion whatsoever that he
was unable to read what it was he was being given the
opportunity to sign.   I

The sheriff regarded this issue of fact as of great
importance because he concluded that the case fell to
be decided on the basis that the pursuer and appellant
had failed to discharge the onus upon him to prove
that he had not been asked to disclose previous convictions, pending charges or any other material matter. In
the course of the appeal debate, however, it became
clear that this was not a decisive issue. What was decisive in the whole case was whether or not the matter
founded upon by the respondents as being "material"   J
fell to be held by the court to be material; for it was
accepted on both sides of the bar that if the
undisclosed matter, namely the appellant's 1987 vandalism conviction and the existence of criminal
charges arising from the events of 13 August 1988, fell
to be treated as "material" for the purposes of this
insurance contract then the appellant had had a duty
to disclose it whether or not he was specifically asked
about it. It was also accepted that if the undisclosed
matter did not fall to be treated as "material" then the K
failure to disclose it, even in answer to a direct and
explicit question or other invitation, would not
amount in the circumstances here to a material breach
of contract entitling the respondents to repudiate
liability under the contract of insurance. In this case
the respondents did not suggest that they had sought
and obtained from the appellant a warranty of the
truth and accuracy of the answers to the questions;
had they done so they might well have been able to
found upon the breach of warranty as a material   L
breach of contract; but no such question arose in this
case. Accordingly, the only issue on the merits in the
appeal was that of materiality. Accepting as I do that
this is the correct view of the case I now turn to consider that issue in the context of this case. The question of the assessment of loss must also be addressed.

On the central issue of materiality, the submission
of the appellant was that, once it was established that
the loss was within the risks covered by the policy, the
respondents could avoid liability only if they could

establish — the onus being on them — that the
A undisclosed matter was material. Three central questions arose: (a) Did the (undisclosed) facts create an
additional risk? (b) Would knowledge of those facts
have influenced the insurers' judgment in the sense in
which Lord Fraser had used that phrase in *McCartney
v Laverty*, 1968 SC at p 213, i e would such
knowledge have affected the result of their consideration as to whether or not to accept the risk or the terms
on which they would have been prepared to accept it?
(c) Would a reasonable assured in the position of the
actual assured have so realised at the time of entering
B into the contract?

This last question was derived in this form principally from the opinion of Lord President Inglis in
Life Association of Scotland v Foster at p 359, where the
Lord President, discussing the proposer's duty to disclose material facts in a contract of insurance, which,
as he said, requires uberrima fides on both sides, said:
"His [scil, the proposer's] duty is carefully and diligently to review all the facts known to himself bearing
C on the risk proposed to the insurers, and to state every
circumstance which any reasonable man might
suppose could in any way influence the insurers in
considering and deciding whether they will enter into
the contract.

The essence of this test, it was submitted, was that
one approached the assessment of materiality from the
viewpoint of the assured rather than from the perspective of the insurer. The perspective of the insurer
appeared to be the correct starting point in England:
D cf *Lambert v Co-operative Insurance Society*. Our attention was also drawn to Lord Trayner's opinion in *Reid
and Co Ltd v Employers' Accident and Live Stock Insurance Co Ltd* at p 1035, which appeared to be more in
line with the *Lambert* approach than with that adopted
in *Foster*. In *Reid and Co Ltd*, concerning an
employer's liability for damage caused to third parties
by his van drivers, Lord Trayner had said: "The law
is trite, that any misstatement of facts, or non-
disclosure of facts, which might reasonably affect the
E mind of the insurer in undertaking the risk is fatal to
the policy." But that, it was pointed out, was obiter.
It was important to note that the *Foster* test involved
looking at the circumstances prevailing at the time
when the proposal was made. In relation to criminal
charges pending at that time it had to be shown that
a proposer, knowing what he knew of the circumstances giving rise to the charges, would reasonably
have concluded that disclosure of the charges and
perhaps those circumstances was necessary because of
their likely relevance to the insurers' judgment on
F whether or not to accept the proposal (or the terms on
which it was to be accepted). In this case, so far as the
matter of the pending charges was concerned, there
was nothing to suggest that they fell to be regarded as
material. The only significant passages in the evidence
relating expressly to them were those in the evidence
of the appellant himself; he had made it plain at the
time when he signed the application form he believed
that the charges connected with the alleged theft of the
video recorder would fail because he had not been
stealing it; he had simply been taking it as security in

respect of an unpaid debt. In these circumstances, it
could not properly be said, in the absence of any evid- G
ence whatsoever to support it, that the pursuer and
appellant as a reasonable man should have appreciated
that this charge, which he regarded as misconceived,
could have any significant influence upon the
insurers' assessment of the risk. The question of
materiality was one of fact and degree; there was no
absolute rule: although there could be cases where the
character and gravity of the charge or conviction could
be enough on its own, the mere fact that a person had
convictions for or faced charges of criminal behaviour H
of the kind founded upon in this appeal by the respondents was not necessarily enough in itself to warrant
any conclusion that the undisclosed matter was
material. More information would be required. The
respondents had never sought any such information
either when they first repudiated liability or at the
proof. The only relevant evidence available for this
court to look at was that of the appellant, evidence
which was, at the very least, extenuating and mitigating. Accordingly, even accepting that the appellant I
was guilty as convicted on 24 February 1989, there
was no sufficient basis for concluding that a reasonable
assured would have had a duty to disclose the outstanding criminal charges as a fact which he should
have appreciated would influence the insurers' judgment. Counsel for the appellant accepted that this
court had to approach the matter of the outstanding
charges on the basis that the appellant was in fact
guilty as convicted and that he must be taken to have
known of the facts establishing his guilt; but, in the J
absence of any evidence on the matter, the appellant
would lose the appeal only if this court concluded that
the reasonable assured would have appreciated that,
by their very nature, the existence, nature and circumstances of the outstanding charges would require to be
disclosed. It all came down to considering degrees of
dishonesty or irresponsibility and moral culpability
and the bearing thereof on the likelihood of there
being any recurrence or repetition of such dishonesty
or the like during the currency of the policy so as to K
create additional risk; without some evidence to
support such a conclusion, the court could not hold
that disclosure was required. The same reasoning
applied to the vandalism conviction which itself had
no obvious bearing on the assessment of the risk.

Counsel for the respondent accepted that in relation
to the test to be applied in deciding the issue of materiality in certain types of case it was possible that there
might be some difference between the law of England
and the law of Scotland and in that regard he accepted L
that para 660 of MacGillivray and Parkington on
Insurance Law (8th ed), founded upon by the appellant, correctly stated the law. He pointed out,
however, that this paragraph related to life assurance.
The court should be careful to draw a distinction
between the type of insurance policy with which this
case was concerned and special cases such as life assurance, marine insurance or motor insurance. The latter
two fell to be considered in the light of the provisions
of the appropriate statutes which defined materiality

A for such types of insurance. But life assurance itself was also a special kind of case; because inevitably a person seeking life assurance might have knowledge of circumstances which could affect the risk, being circumstances of which no one else could have any knowledge. One example, as in *Foster*, would be knowledge by the person in question that he had a pain which he had not yet disclosed to the doctor or anyone else. It might be a harbinger of serious ill health, or it might not. There was no way that such a thing could be found out by any stranger and the

B duty of disclosure simply had to be focused upon the proposer's own assessment, as a reasonable man, of the significance of the information which was known only to him. In that type of case, it was reasonable to apply the test of the reasonable insured person as in *Life Association of Scotland v Foster*, which was just such a case. However, it was perhaps not of very great importance in this particular case which precise formulation of the test was adopted because even if the court were to apply the test formulated by the Lord President in

C *Foster* the result in this case would be the same. It was important in considering the question of materiality to have regard to the subject matter that was covered by the insurance and also to the risks. In this case the contract covered inter alia all the contents of the household. The risk included damage by malicious persons or vandals and loss by theft. Thus the appellant, in applying, sought insurance in respect of these risks. Yet his 1987 conviction was for vandalism. If a reasonable man was seeking insurance cover in respect of loss

D caused by such behaviour and he knew that he had a conviction for that very behaviour he would be bound to consider that he should disclose his record. So far as the pending charge was concerned it was not in dispute that the offence itself was committed on 13 August 1988 and the proposal form was signed by the appellant on 6 September 1988, just over three weeks later. Some of the English cases referred to by the appellant contained observations about very old convictions; for example, in *Reynolds v Phoenix* the con-

E viction was 11 years old; but the conduct in this case was very recent indeed, as was the 1987 conviction. Even if he thought he was innocent or had an extenuating explanation of the circumstances a reasonable man would be bound to disclose the outstanding charges and to offer to disclose the surrounding circumstances. No one had any right to be insured. Any duty of disclosure arose only if a person voluntarily sought insurance. The contract was uberrimae fidei. The insurers were always entitled to accept or refuse

F in terms of the risk. The materiality question also fell to be tested against the amount of the premium, which in this case was £38.40 per annum, and the sum insured which was £12,000. Whatever test was applied the same result was reached, namely that a reasonable man would reveal that he had been charged and no doubt would offer explanations to the effect that he was innocent.

In my opinion, there is no reason in this case to question the submission that the opinion of Lord President Inglis in *Life Association v Foster* correctly

states the law as to the duty of a person applying for life assurance in relation to disclosure of potentially G material facts and circumstances about which he is not expressly asked. No one in this case argued to the contrary. But for myself I can see no good reason why that statement of duty, even if it is thought to state the duty significantly differently in life assurance cases from the way it would be stated in other cases, should be taken to apply in relation to persons seeking insurance in respect of fire and theft. As the submissions made to us acknowledged, materiality is defined by statute in some fields of insurance. The cases to which we H were referred, including *McCartney v Laverty* and *Lambert v Co-operative Insurance Society Ltd*, for example, refer to such statutory definitions. But even in fields of insurance in which there is no applicable statutory definition of materiality it is common to find that the proposal form itself defines materiality for the purposes of the contract. The present case gives an example of that. In the "Important Note" referred to earlier it will be seen that such a definition appears: "A material fact is one which would be likely to I influence an insurer in the assessment or acceptance of the risk." That in itself is effectively the *Lambert* test, without the gloss added by Lord Fraser in *McCartney*. In my view, counsel for the defenders in his submissions demonstrated clearly that none of the cases founded upon by the appellant vouched the application of the *Foster* test outside the field of life assurance; MacGillivray and Parkington (op cit) is always careful in referring to this case to remind the reader that *Foster* was a life assurance case. I find the reasoning J and the discussion of the authorities in *Lambert v Co-operative Insurance Society Ltd* compelling, and like Lawton LJ, I can see no reason why the rule should be different for fire or burglary or all risks insurance from that which has been laid down by statute for marine insurance, namely that what is material is that which would influence the mind of a prudent insurer. In the absence of Scottish authorities requiring me to do so I should be reluctant to hold that the test should be different in Scotland from that applying in K England.

In any event I am not persuaded that the result would be likely to be different in many, if any, cases involving non-disclosure of criminal activities if the *Foster* test were applied rather than the *Lambert* test. The duty as stated by Lord President Inglis is a duty upon the proposer to review all the facts known to himself and then: "to state every circumstance which any reasonable man *might suppose* could *in any way influence* the insurers in considering and deciding L whether they will *enter into the contract*" (my emphasis). This is a statement of the duty resting upon the proposer, but it also recognises that the assessment of materiality is not for the proposer to make subjectively but it is one that falls to be made by standards of the reasonable man. In cases involving recent convictions for, or charges of, relevant criminal activities I find it difficult to conceive of such a circumstance which "would influence the mind of a prudent insurer" (*Lambert*) and would not also be a circumstance which a reasonable man, looking at the matter objectively, might suppose could in *any* way *influence* the particular insurers in considering and deciding whether or not they will enter into the contract. In this I am also in agreement with the approach by counsel for the respondents, which was that in the present case it did not matter precisely which test was applied. In the present case we have a man applying for household insurance in respect of a house to which apparently he had been temporarily "decanted": that is to say he had been temporarily rehoused while his normal house was being refurbished. The contents cover in the policy covered loss of or damage to the contents in that house by a number of causes including "vandals" and "theft or attempted theft". Now it appears to be perfectly obvious that a reasonable man might suppose that knowledge of such circumstances could in some way influence the insurers in deciding whether or not to enter into the contract on the terms on which they did enter into the contract. For the insurers here accepted the risk at a modest annual premium of £38.40 and put themselves at risk for the sum of £12,000. And as the risks included the destruction of the contents by fire or their removal by theft and as this was a "new for old" policy in respect of most items (other than wearing apparel, household linen and pedal cycles) then the honesty of the insured — whose assertions about the precise contents of the house would be virtually uncheckable if those contents were lost or destroyed through theft or fire — would inevitably be of great significance. The outstanding charges would relate to events that were only a few weeks old. They included the charge of theft of a video recorder, a typical article found in any house nowadays. The vandalism conviction itself was only 18 months old. I consider that the court must have regard to the terms of the policy in assessing materiality upon an objective basis and that the cover, the risk, the premium, the possible fate of the insured articles and the apparent honesty or dishonesty of the proposer, and others living with him are all relevant and significant matters. I disagree with any suggestion that the court would need detailed evidence about each and every recent conviction or charge in order to decide upon the issue of materiality. Nor indeed would the insurers need such detail in coming to a decision whether or not to hold the policy void. No doubt there may be cases in which the circumstances undisclosed, including previous convictions, would be such that the court could come to a view that they would have no influence upon the mind of an insurer. Prima facie, however, circumstances of the kind obtaining in the present case would appear highly pertinent to any decision whether or not, and if so on what terms, to grant insurance cover in respect of inter alia theft and vandalism. In my view, if an insurance company is able to put such circumstances before the court in such a case it will have discharged any onus resting upon it in relation to establishing non-disclosure of a material fact.

Although I can conceive of circumstances in which the insured could then place before the court evidence which would so take the sting out of the admitted, undisclosed convictions that the court could hold that nothing material to the assessment of the risk had been left undisclosed, there was nothing of that kind in this case. It is true that the appellant gave evidence in relation to the circumstances allegedly attending the offences committed on 13 August 1988; but it cannot be denied that the explanation he offered in evidence was inconsistent with his guilt; yet he was convicted and punished appropriately. His counsel were accordingly correct to accept that this court must treat that conviction as valid for the purposes of assessing materiality and that the appellant must be deemed to have known on 6 September 1988 that he was guilty of doing the things that led to his later conviction. In my opinion, the respondents have discharged the burden upon them of showing that they were entitled to hold the policy void by reason of material non-disclosure. In these circumstances I would sustain the second and third pleas in law for the defenders and respondents. For reasons which are not disclosed, the sheriff dismissed the action but that was clearly an error.

This court has to determine the findings in fact and I agree with your Lordship in the chair as to what those findings in fact should be, in the light of the submissions made to us and our decisions in relation to them.

It is most unfortunate that the sheriff did not see fit to make findings in relation to the appellant's loss. In making their submissions on this matter counsel for the appellant made reference to all the evidence bearing on the quantification of the loss. It was argued that it was inevitably difficult to give very precise information about what had been lost. What the pursuer and appellant had done was to try to recall and to estimate all the articles, and their number, that had been lost in the fire. The claim, as now modified, excluded any claim for those articles which, under the policy, were subject to depreciation. In relation to the remaining articles, the pursuer had compiled a list of what he estimated these articles to be and had obtained prices for such articles from a current catalogue. This, it was submitted, was a reasonable basis upon which to compute his loss and there was no contrary evidence. The figure of £10,550.17 was that mentioned in the sheriff's note and counsel showed how it was derived from the list of articles and the prices associated therewith. Counsel for the defenders pointed out that in relation to the quantification of damages the court was in a very difficult position indeed. The appellant had not responded to calls contained in the pleadings with the result that the defenders at the proof were unable to check the accuracy of the lists produced. Furthermore the evidence given by the pursuer was inconsistent with the lists in material respects. The catalogue from which the prices were allegedly taken was never produced. No details were given of the goods which were said to be lost, for example, their make or their cost or the like. Although it was true that the respondents had not asked him to vouch the details of his claim at the time

A it was made, that was because the claim had been repudiated in its entirety. Once the claim had been repudiated it was up to the appellant to prove it, if necessary by engaging his own loss adjuster or taking such other steps as were necessary. The court could not simply rubber stamp the list and award the sum sought.

The court has indeed been left in a difficult position both by the sheriff's failure to deal with the matter and by the shortage of evidence laid before the court by the
B pursuer and appellant. Nonetheless the fact that it is difficult to make a precise computation of the loss in respect of which the appellant would have been entitled to be indemnified had his claim been accepted does not necessarily mean that he would not be entitled to receive anything in respect of that loss. There were available to us, as to the sheriff, photographs showing some of the damage to the household contents. There was no real contradiction of much of the evidence given by and on behalf of the appellant
C about the articles which had been damaged. Some very cogent and critical questions were indeed asked in cross examination about certain details and about the computation of the loss; and at the proof no very serious attempt was made by the pursuer to establish the precise character, history, likely current price and so on even of the major articles appearing in the list of contents, such as the three piece suite (£950), the music system (£599), the kitchen white goods, microwave, freezer etc and other such articles. Despite the
D deficiencies in the pursuer's proof, however, this cannot be said to be a case in which the court was asked "to award damages in the absence of evidence upon which to base the award" (per the Lord Justice Clerk in *Duncan v Gumleys* at p 734). There was evidence led before the court in support of the figure of £10,550.17. That figure cannot be described as "a figure plucked from the air", as in *Duncan v Gumleys*. Here we have evidence which is sufficient in law and which is largely uncontradicted as to the general
E character of the loss; the only substantial criticism is of the methods employed both to put a price on the articles missing and, in some instances at least, to assess their number or quality. Even some of the criticisms made at the proof are diminished by the fact that the appellant no longer seeks indemnity in respect of articles of apparel and household linen and the bicycles. Given that there was a substantial loss which was undoubtedly of the broad character of that specified in the list of contents the court, in my opinion,
F must make some assessment based upon the evidence before it. I am not prepared to accept the pursuer's estimates of quantity and the values put upon particular articles at face value but I think nothing entitles the court to ignore the fact that there was a substantial loss of the general kind specified. On a balance of probabilities such a loss is established. In putting a precise figure upon it I am of opinion that the only method that is open to this court is to make a substantial discount from the amount brought out by the list of contents to reflect the unsatisfactory nature of the detailed proof in support of that list. In my view,

G justice would be done if that resulted in our putting the figure of £6,500 upon the pursuer's loss.

In the whole circumstances I agree with your Lordship in the chair as to the disposal of this case.

LORD KIRKWOOD.—I am in full agreement with the opinion of your Lordship in the chair.

In September 1988 the pursuer and defenders entered into a policy of house insurance in terms of which the defenders undertook to indemnify the pursuer in respect of damage caused to the contents of his
H house at 97 Hayfield Road, Kirkcaldy, on the occurrence of certain risks, including fire. The date of the policy was 6 September 1988 and the term of the policy was one year, namely, until 6 September 1989. On or about 29 October 1988 there was a fire at the pursuer's house and considerable damage was caused to the contents of the house. The question which has now arisen is whether or not the defenders are bound to indemnify the pursuer, in terms of the policy, in respect of the damage caused to the contents of the house.
I

On 6 September 1988 the pursuer signed the proposal form which contained inter alia a question in the following terms: [his Lordship quoted the terms of question 10 set out supra and continued:] This question was answered "No".

The proposal form also contained the following statement: [his Lordship quoted the terms of the "Important Note" set out supra and continued:] Below this statement was a box which was left blank.
J

On behalf of the pursuer it was admitted that he failed to disclose: (a) the fact that on 23 February 1987 in Kirkcaldy sheriff court he had been convicted, on a summary complaint, of an offence under s 78 (1) of the Criminal Justice (Scotland) Act 1980 (namely, vandalism); and (b) the fact that as at 6 September 1988 he had been charged with inter alia the theft of a video recorder. It was also admitted that on 24 February 1989 in Kirkcaldy sheriff court he was convicted inter alia of theft of the video recorder and that he was fined
K £50 and ordered to pay compensation of £150. It appeared that the pursuer had a number of other previous convictions for criminal offences prior to 1987. We heard some argument as to whether or not these were spent convictions in terms of the Rehabilitation of Offenders Act 1974 but counsel for the defenders eventually stated that he did not seek to found on these convictions. Counsel for the defenders did not contend that the untrue answer to question 10 had constituted a breach of warranty, in which event
L the issue of materiality would not have arisen, but he did submit that the answer to question 10 amounted to a false misrepresentation and, in any event, that there had been a failure to disclose the 1987 conviction and the pending charge of the theft of the video recorder. As I have said, counsel for the pursuer conceded that there had been non-disclosure. In these circumstances the question which initially arose was whether this was simply a case of non-disclosure or whether there had been both non-disclosure and a misrepresentation. In this connection it seemed to me that

A
there was, in fact, non-disclosure and also a misrepresentation. However, counsel were agreed that in either case the critical question, which was whether the misrepresentation or the failure to disclose had been material, would fall to be answered in the same way. Counsel for the defenders submitted that the facts which were not disclosed, namely, the existence of the 1987 conviction for vandalism and the pending charge of theft, were clearly material and that the defenders were therefore justified in treating the contract as being void. On the other hand, counsel for the
B
pursuer submitted that the facts which were not disclosed were not material and that the pursuer was entitled to be indemnified by the defenders in respect of the loss which he had sustained.

In the foregoing circumstances the first question for consideration is what test is to be applied in determining the issue of materiality. So far as marine insurance is concerned the test of materiality is set out in s 18 (2) of the Marine Insurance Act 1906 which provides as follows: [his Lordship quoted the terms of
C
s 18 (2) set out supra and continued:]

Further, for many years the Road Traffic Acts have contained a definition of "material" in the case of a policy of motor insurance which has been obtained by the non-disclosure of a material fact. Thus, in s 151 of the Road Traffic Act 1988 the test laid down is whether the fact was: "of such a nature as to influence the judgment of a prudent insurer in determining whether he will take the risk and, if so, at what
D
premium and on what conditions".

This test was formerly contained in s 10 (5) of the Road Traffic Act 1934 and in relation thereto Lord Fraser observed in *McCartney v Laverty*, 1968 SC at p 213 that: "facts cannot be said to influence the judgment of a prudent insurer in the relevant sense, if they merely have to be taken into consideration but do not affect the result".

While these statutory provisions adopt the test of
E
the "prudent insurer" they are not, of course, applicable in the case of a contract of fire insurance. In *Life Association of Scotland v Foster*, a case which involved a proposal for life assurance, Lord President Inglis observed (at p 359) that it was the duty of an insured: "to state every circumstance which any reasonable man might suppose could in any way influence the insurers in considering and deciding whether they will enter into the contract".

F
This is what is known as the test of the reasonable assured. In *Reid and Co Ltd v Employers' Accident and Live Stock Insurance Co Ltd* a tradesman had signed a proposal to an insurance company for an insurance against liability for any damage which might be caused by his van drivers to third parties. Lord Trayner observed (at p 1035) that: "the question is whether the difference between the statement made in the proposal and the actual fact as now ascertained was material as likely to affect the mind of the insurer in undertaking the risk". This is the test of the reasonable or prudent insurer.

G
Counsel for the defenders submitted that the test laid down by Lord President Inglis in *Life Association of Scotland v Foster* was not appropriate in a case of fire insurance, but he went on to submit that whichever test was adopted in this case the result would be the same and that the facts which were not disclosed could properly be regarded as being material. Senior counsel for the pursuer submitted that, in considering the issue of materiality, three questions fell to be addressed, namely: (1) Did the fact in question create an additional risk? (2) If it had been known to the
H
insurers would it have influenced their judgment in the sense explained by Lord Fraser in *McCartney v Laverty*? and (3) Would a reasonable insured in the position of the actual insured have realised that it would create an additional risk and influence the judgment of the insurers? Only if all three questions were answered in the affirmative could the fact in question be regarded as material.

There can be no doubt that, in the case of life assurance, the proper test of materiality is that set out by
I
Lord President Inglis in *Life Association of Scotland v Foster*, but I am not persuaded that this is the appropriate test to be applied in other types of insurance, including insurance against fire and theft. In the case of a proposal for life assurance there are likely to be facts relating to the health of the proposer which are known only to him. A proposer may have a symptom which he does not regard as being of any significance and, for that reason, does not disclose to the insurers. However, if the reasonable or prudent
J
insurer test was applied then it would be open to the insurers to contend that had they known of the existence of the symptom, in light of the medical evidence available to them, they would not have accepted the risk and that they were therefore entitled to treat the policy as void. For the reasons given by your Lordship in the chair, I consider that, in cases of life assurance, justice requires the adoption of the reasonable assured test but I can see no justification for importing that test into other forms of insurance. In the case of insurance against fire and theft I am of the opinion that the
K
reasonable assured test does not apply and that the proper test of materiality should be the reasonable or prudent insurer test. As Lord Trayner observed in *Reid and Co Ltd v Employers' Accident and Live Stock Insurance Co Ltd* (at p 1035): "The law is trite, that any misstatement of facts, or non-disclosure of facts, which might reasonably affect the mind of the insurer in undertaking the risk is fatal to the policy."

L
It is, I think, also of significance in this case that the proposal form stated inter alia that "a material fact is one which would be likely to influence an insurer in the assessment or acceptance of the risk", and this appears to be a reference to the test of the reasonable or prudent insurer. Further, the English authorities to which we were referred demonstrate that the test of the reasonable or prudent insurer is also applied in England in cases other than those involving life assurance.

Having determined the test of materiality which

falls to be applied in this case, the next question for
A consideration is whether or not the facts which the
pursuer admittedly failed to disclose were material.
Counsel for the defenders submitted that the 1987
conviction for vandalism and the pending charge of
theft, either separately or taken together, were such as
would be likely to have influenced an insurer in the
assessment or acceptance of the risk and counsel
founded on the evidence given by Mr Tolfts, the
defenders' assistant claims manager. Counsel for the
pursuer submitted that the vandalism conviction was
B not material, particularly as the defenders would not
have been required to indemnify the pursuer if there
had been damage to the contents of his house which
had been caused by vandalism on his part. There was
no absolute rule to the effect that a criminal conviction
fell to be regarded as material. Any conviction must be
looked at in light of its own particular circumstances.
The conviction for vandalism, in respect of which the
pursuer was fined £50, could not be regarded as
material in the circumstances of this case. So far as the
C pending charge was concerned, it had to be borne in
mind that it was a conviction, not a charge, which was
important. However, he accepted that the pursuer had
subsequently been convicted of the theft of the video
recorder and that the court must proceed on the basis,
not only that he was guilty of the theft, but that at the
time he signed the proposal form he knew that he was
guilty. Nevertheless, the materiality or non-materiality
of a criminal charge and conviction must depend on
the nature of the offence and the surrounding circum-
D stances. It may be that, in a case such as the present,
a prior conviction for wilful fire raising, or defrauding
an insurance company, would fall to be regarded as
material. However, the theft of a video recorder, in
respect of which the pursuer was later fined £50 and
had a compensation order for £150 made against him,
did not indicate that there had been the necessary
degree of dishonesty and irresponsibility to satisfy the
test of materiality. The defenders had failed to lead
any evidence relating to the circumstances surround-
E ing the theft in order to indicate that the degree of dishonesty involved was such as to be likely to have
influenced an insurer in the assessment or acceptance
of the risk. Even when the conviction for vandalism
and the pending charge of theft were taken together,
they did not satisfy the test of materiality.

The materiality of an undisclosed fact may be so self
evident that it is not necessary to call any expert evidence to establish the point (MacGillivray and Parkington, *Insurance Law*, para 665). However, evidence
F bearing on the issue of materiality was given by Mr
Tolfts, the defenders' assistant claims manager. He
stated that in his view the fact that an insured had
been charged with theft, an offence of dishonesty,
involved an assessment of moral hazard. The conviction for vandalism also involved a degree of moral
hazard. Mr Tolfts gave evidence that the defenders,
had they known of the facts which had not been disclosed, would not have accepted the risk. However,
the question in this case is not what the defenders
would have done but what attitude would have been

adopted by a reasonable and prudent underwriter
(*Reynolds and Anderson v Phoenix Assurance Co Ltd*, G
per Forbes J at p 458) and in that sense the test is an
objective one. Mr Tolfts went on to state that in
general what he had said went "throughout the
market". When he was asked whether other insurers
might not view a conviction for theft as material, he
replied that there could be some underwriters but he
had never come across one.

When the pursuer gave evidence in relation to the
charge of theft he attempted to put forward an innocent explanation but, having regard to the concession H
that he was, at the time he signed the proposal form,
aware of his guilt, I do not consider that any weight
can be placed on that explanation. The fact of the
matter is that, although the proposal form contained
a question which sought to elicit any previous convictions for offences other than motoring offences, and
any pending charges, the pursuer failed to disclose his
1987 conviction and the pending charge of theft, of
which he knew that he was guilty. The pending charge
was one which involved dishonesty and, taken along I
with the vandalism conviction, it seems to me that
they involved an assessment of what can be described
as moral hazard. In this case the insurance cover
included damage caused by theft and vandalism,
although the insurers would not be under an obligation to indemnify the pursuer against any damage due
to theft or vandalism for which he was responsible.
Nevertheless the character and honesty of the pursuer
must be regarded as being of importance. The conviction for vandalism was only some 18 months old and J
the charge of theft, of which the pursuer was aware
that he was guilty, was pending at the time he signed
the proposal form. In the circumstances, and on the
basis of the admitted facts and the evidence which was
led, I consider that the defenders have succeeded in
establishing that the conviction for vandalism, and the
pending charge of theft, were prima facie material in
the sense that they would be likely to have influenced
an insurer in deciding whether to accept the risk and,
if so, at what premium and on what conditions.   K

It would have been open to the pursuer to seek to
lead evidence of the circumstances surrounding the
offences in question with a view to establishing that
these circumstances mitigated the apparent materiality
of those offences and that, when all the circumstances
were taken into account, the proper conclusion to be
drawn was that the undisclosed facts were not, after
all, material. However, in the circumstances of this
case no acceptable evidence to that effect was led. On L
the whole matter I am satisfied that if it had been disclosed that the pursuer had been convicted of vandalism in 1987 and that the charge of theft was
pending, then these facts would have influenced a
reasonable and prudent insurer in deciding whether to
accept the risk of insuring the pursuer against loss due
to inter alia fire, vandalism and theft and, if the risk
was to be accepted, what terms should be imposed. It
also seems to me that even if the test to be applied in
this case had been the test of the "reasonable assured"
then the non-disclosure and misrepresentation would

still have been material. On the whole matter I consider that there was material non-disclosure and also misrepresentation in this case and that the defenders are therefore not liable to indemnify the pursuer in respect of the damage which was sustained to the contents of the house as a result of the fire.

Turning to the issue of damages, there is no doubt that as a result of the fire the contents of the pursuer's house were seriously damaged and the question in dispute was whether or not the pursuer had led sufficient evidence to establish the extent of his loss. I appreciate that the fact that many of the contents were destroyed meant that the pursuer was faced with certain practical difficulties in attempting to identify, and to establish the value of, the items which had been lost. There were, however, obvious shortcomings in the evidence which the pursuer did lead and it is very unfortunate, in my view, that the sheriff did not see fit to make any findings in relation to the pursuer's loss. In the circumstances of this case the ascertainment of the extent of the pursuer's loss has been rendered difficult but I do not consider that that would justify us in holding that no loss had been established. It is clear, on the evidence, that the pursuer must have sustained substantial loss and I find myself in agreement with Lord McCluskey as to the way in which the assessment of damages should be approached in this case. It seems to me that adopting that approach and placing the figure of £6,500 on the pursuer's loss would have the effect of doing justice between the parties.

However, as the pursuer has failed on the merits, I agree that the appeal should be disposed of as proposed by your Lordship in the chair.

Counsel for Pursuer (Appellant), C M Campbell, QC, Andrew Smith; Solicitors, Simpson & Marwick, WS (for McKenzies, Kirkcaldy) — Counsel for Defenders (Respondents), Hajducki; Solicitors, Lindsays, WS (for Innes Johnston & Co, Kirkcaldy).

R D S

McGillivray v Davidson

OUTER HOUSE

TEMPORARY JUDGE J M S HORSBURGH, QC
30 JULY 1991

Contract — Breach of contract — Joint and several liability — Action laid against defenders jointly and severally — Separate wrongs not causative of whole loss but contributing to same result — Competency.

Contract — Breach of contract — Joint and several liability — Illegal breach of missives by seller and of letter of obligation by seller's solicitors — Whether single wrong suffered by pursuers.

Process — Competency — Action of damages for breach of contract — Joint pursuers — Whether separate conclusions for each pursuer necessary — Competency of single conclusion seeking decree for each pursuer.

Purchasers entered into missives to acquire from the owner subjects which included ground, outbuildings and the business carried on there. The seller gave warranties that no local authority orders or notices adversely affected the subjects. The seller's solicitors granted a letter of obligation undertaking to deliver planning permission, building warrant and completion certificate in respect of alterations to the subjects made by their client, the seller. Soon after the purchasers took entry, they discovered that the local authority had served an enforcement notice on the seller some months earlier for failure to comply with conditions attached to planning permission granted for change of use of the subjects.

The purchasers were left with subjects incapable of business use and sued for loss of business, concluding for payment by both the seller and his solicitors jointly and severally. At a procedure roll debate, the solicitors argued, inter alia, that the action was incompetent in that it had been laid against the seller and the solicitors jointly and severally, whereas the loss caused by the separate breaches of obligation was not identical, since each wrongdoer had not caused the whole of the damage. It was further argued that the purchasers' conclusion seeking decree for each of them was incompetent since they were joint owners of the subjects and joint venturers in business. The conclusion should therefore have been for payment to both pursuers of one sum, or else separate conclusions should have been made for each of them.

Held, (1) that joint and several liability existed when breaches by defenders contributed in different but material ways to a single common result, even where each defender's breach was not a material cause of the whole damage, s 3 of the Law Reform (Miscellaneous Provisions) (Scotland) Act 1940 providing for just and equitable apportionment inter se of liability among those in breach of contract (*Grunwald v Hughes*, 1965 SLT 209 and *Engdiv Ltd v G Percy Trentham Ltd*, 1990 SLT 617, *considered* and *followed*) (pp 695J and 696A-C); (2) that in any event, the breaches of obligation by the defenders were not disconnected but were related to the one transaction, namely the conveyance of the property and the sale of the business; thus both of the separate breaches contributed to the same wrong (p 696C-D); (3) that where pursuers had suffered the same wrong through the defenders' breaches of contract, they might both sue in the same action, provided that claims were separately stated either in separate conclusions or, as here, in the same conclusion (*Harkes v Mowat* (1862) 24 D 701, *applied*) (p 696F-G); and proof before answer allowed.

Action of declarator and damages

Ian Forbes McGillivray and Mrs May Steel McGillivray raised an action of declarator and

damages against (first) David Peter Davidson and
A (second) Messrs MacArthur Stewart & Co. The action
arose out of the sale of heritage by the first defender
to the pursuer. The second defenders had been the
solicitors for the first defender in the transaction and
had given certain undertakings to the pursuers.
Decree in absence was taken against the first defender
on 18 December 1990. The second defenders stated a
plea to the competency, a plea of no title to sue and
a plea to the relevancy of the action. The pursuers
stated a plea to the relevancy of the second defenders'
B defences.

The case came on procedure roll before the temporary judge (J M S Horsburgh, QC).

Statutory provisions

The Law Reform (Miscellaneous Provisions) (Scotland) Act 1940 provides:

"3.—(1) Where in any action of damages in respect
of loss or damage arising from any wrongful acts or
C negligent acts or omissions two or more persons are,
in pursuance of the verdict of a jury or the judgment
of a court found jointly and severally liable in damages
or expenses, they shall be liable *inter se* to contribute
to such damages or expenses in such proportions as
the jury or the court, as the case may be, may deem
just: Provided that nothing in this subsection shall
affect the right of the person to whom such damages
or expenses have been awarded to obtain a joint and
several decree therefor against the persons so found
D liable."

Cases referred to

Engdiv Ltd v G Percy Trentham Ltd, 1990 SLT 617.
Fleming v McGillivray, 1945 SLT 301; 1946 SC 1.
Grunwald v Hughes, 1965 SLT 209.
Harkes v Mowat (1862) 24 D 701.

On 30 July 1991 the temporary judge *repelled* the
second defenders' first plea (to competency), their
E second plea (no title to sue) of consent, *upheld*, of
consent, the pursuers' plea to the extent of excluding
certain averments from probation and quoad ultra
allowed a proof before answer.

J M S HORSBURGH, QC.—In this action which
called before me on procedure roll, the pursuers seek,
first, declarator that the first defender is in breach of
warranty contained in missives entered with the pursuers for the sale to the pursuers of certain subjects at
F Clachan Seil, Argyllshire, secondly, declarator that the
second defenders are in breach of their obligation relative to the missives and the subsequent disposition in
respect of their failure to deliver certain local authority
consents to alterations to the subjects of sale carried
out by the first defender, and thirdly, payment of
£25,000 by the defenders jointly and severally or
severally to each of the pursuers.

The pursuers aver that by missives dated March
1987 they agreed to buy from the first defender subjects known as Strathnaver, Clachan Seil, with the

ground, outbuildings and business of Clachan Seil
Marine Services carried out there. Prior to conclusion G
of the missives the first defender had made substantial
alteration to the subjects and grounds in converting
them to business use, including the building of a car
park with main road access, a workshop, and the
installation of fixed equipment. In terms of the missives the first defender gave certain warranties about
having received no local authority notices or orders
adversely affecting the subjects. On 17 April 1987,
one week after entry, the pursuers were advised that
the local authority had served an enforcement notice H
on the first defender on 28 January 1987 for his non-
compliance with conditions attached to planning permission for change of use of the subjects dated 23 September 1986. That was the only permission relating to
the subjects. The enforcement notice adversely affects
the subjects. The first defender was therefore in
breach of the missives.

The pursuers further aver that on 10 April 1987 the
second defenders, as solicitors for the first defender,
gave a letter of obligation personally undertaking to I
deliver planning permission, building warrant and
completion certificate in respect of the alterations
made by the first defender. The second defenders
cannot do so, as the documents do not exist.

In reply the second defenders aver that the undertaking in the letter of obligation referred only to alterations made by the first defender to the dwellinghouse,
and the undertaking had been satisfied by sending
certain consents to the pursuers' solicitors on 20 May
1987. The pursuers admitted receipt of these. The J
second defenders further aver that only the first
defender was bound by the undertaking, and that any
works effected by him other than to the dwellinghouse
were of a minor nature not requiring local authority
consents.

The pursuers also aver that they suffered loss
through the first defender's breach of missives and the
second defenders' breach of undertaking. They cannot
comply with planning conditions about access and K
parking and must obey the enforcement notice, which
involves expense. They have been left with subjects
capable only of residential use and incapable of
business use, and have and will continue to suffer
inconvenience. With the needed permissions the pursuers would have had an asset worth about £82,000
instead of £50,000, its present value. The business
element was worth about £40,000 with an annual
turnover of nearly £20,000, which the pursuers could
have more than doubled. They had lost the ability to L
earn a substantial net profit.

At debate counsel for the second defenders departed
from their second preliminary plea and invited me to
repel it.

In relation to their first plea it was argued that the
action and the third conclusion were incompetent.
The first and main contention was, under reference to
Grunwald v Hughes, that it was not competent to sue
the defenders jointly and severally. Two defenders
may competently be so sued only where the loss

caused by the separate breaches of obligation is
A identical, i e, each wrongdoer must have caused the
whole of the damage. It is not clear what damage is
said to have been caused by the second defenders'
breach, it is not averred that they caused the whole
damage complained of, nor is it clear that their breach
caused the same damage as the first defender's breach.
The expense of complying with the enforcement
notice which is claimed, is a consequence of the non-
disclosure, not a breach of undertaking by the second
defenders. Likewise, damages claimed for loss of
B business due to the restrictions imposed by the
absence of planning permission, or due to failure by
the first defenders to implement the planning conditions, were matters about which the second
defenders had given no undertakings. The action was
accordingly incompetent.

Secondly, it was contended that in circumstances
where the pursuers were joint owners of the property
and joint venturers in the business the third conclusion which seeks a decree for each pursuer is not
C competent. Either a conclusion for payment to both
pursuers of one sum or separate conclusions for each
with averments to support the claim of each would be
required. Further, the conclusion does not consist
with the interlocutor of 18 December 1990 which
decerned for payment of the sum concluded for "to
the pursuers" by the first defender.

Counsel for the second defenders also argued that
the action was irrelevant for two reasons. [The tem-
D porary judge narrated these arguments, with which
this report is not concerned, and continued:]

Counsel for the pursuers first submitted that since
the second defenders were no longer insisting on their
plea of no title to sue they were departing from their
averred stand of not being bound by the letter of
obligation and their second plea should be repelled,
and the pursuers' eighth plea be partially sustained to
the extent of excluding from probation the passage in
ans 5 for the second defenders from 16D to 17A. This
E was conceded by senior counsel for the second
defenders.

Secondly, he submitted that the second defenders'
first plea, being directed against the competency of the
action, should be repelled since there was no attack on
the second conclusion. In any event, the pursuers
relied on *Grunwald v Hughes* to the effect that joint
and several liability is applicable where two breaches
of contract are not disconnected and contribute to the
same damage. That each defender had caused the
F whole damage was not the test. *Engdiv Ltd v Percy
Trentham Ltd* was to the same effect. Here both
defenders were said to have contributed to the
damage, and the two breaches were not disconnected,
since the contracts were all part of the same conveyancing transaction, and through the absence of planning permission the separate breaches by the
defenders had contributed to the same damage. Condescendence 6 was framed on the basis that the same
damage was said to flow from the two separate
breaches.

With reference to the form of the conclusion counsel
for the pursuers contended that the form of the inter- G
locutor of 18 December 1990 was not ideal, but that
was irrelevant to the debate, and in any event it did not
grant the decree enrolled for. As it stood the conclusion was a convenient way of indicating that each
pursuer was seeking to recover damages. Should its
form be regarded as incompetent, the pursuers should
be given an opportunity to amend, following *Fleming
v McGillivray*. However his submission was that for
the foregoing reasons the action and the third conclusion were competent.   H

[The temporary judge narrated the contentions for
the pursuer in relation to relevancy and continued:]

In support of the pursuers' sixth plea counsel moved
that decree of declarator should be granted in terms of
the second conclusion and a proof on quantum of
damage allowed in relation to the third conclusion,
because it was now accepted that the second defenders
were bound by the letter of obligation. If "subjects"
is not limited in meaning but relates to the subjects of I
sale in general, then since the terms of the enforcement notice were not disputed, and that it was issued
is not disputed, there is no defence on the merits. The
only question left was whether and to what extent the
loss resulted from the second defenders' breach. Proof
therefore should be restricted to quantum and the
second defenders' pleas except for the sixth and
seventh should be repelled.

I deal first with the main competency argument. I
do not agree with the second defenders' reading of J
Grunwald v Hughes to the effect that defenders may
competently be sued jointly and severally only where
their separate breaches of obligation have each caused
the *whole* damage claimed. In my view that case
supports the proposition that joint and several liability
exists when breaches by defenders contribute in different but material ways to a single common result. That
seems clear from the opinion of Lord Justice Clerk
Grant when he said at p 211: "That test is whether the
two defenders have contributed, albeit in different K
ways, to cause a single wrong." I agree with the view
of Lord Prosser in *Engdiv v Percy Trentham Ltd* at
p 620A-B that "wrong" in that context appropriately
describes loss and damage. In *Grunwald* Lord
Strachan said at p 214 that joint and several liability
may follow "where both defenders are in breach of
contract, if both breaches contribute to the one
common result", and Lord Walker at p 214 said that
joint and several liability depends "on the fact that
breach of duty on the part of each is a material cause L
of the . . . damage". I do not consider that these dicta
support the proposition that the breach by each obligant must have caused the whole damage claimed, or
identical damage.

It is true that at p 215 Lord Walker also said: "I can
see no reason in principle why two defenders should
not be jointly and severally liable for their separate
breaches of contract, provided always that each breach
was a material cause of the whole damage." It would
appear that the second defenders' argument depends

A   on that dictum. However, the terms of Lord Walker's proviso do not express the views of the majority of the court, and I respectfully disagree with what his Lordship said. The essence of joint and several liability is that each defender should be liable for the whole damage, but it does not follow from that that each defender's breach must have been a material cause of the whole damage. Again, I agree with Lord Prosser in *Engdiv* at p 620G in referring to a breach of contract "contributing to the loss and damage" as the basis for such a claim, and I consider what he says to

B   be in accord with the ratio of *Grunwald v Hughes*.

For these reasons I disagree with senior counsel for the second defenders who argued that basic principles of justice required that one party should not be held liable if that party's actings had not led to the pursuers' whole loss. In practice the principle of joint and several liability that each defender should be liable for the whole damage is open to modification by the ability of the defenders to seek relief from each other by the application of s 3 of the Law Reform (Miscel-

C   laneous Provisions) (Scotland) Act 1940, as happened in *Engdiv*. By such means a just and equitable split of liability among those in breach of contract can be achieved.

In addition, it appears to me that the second defenders' argument does not properly acknowledge that the breaches of obligation by the defenders are not disconnected, but are related to different aspects of the one transaction, namely the conveyance of the

D   property and the sale of the business. Had the first defender fulfilled his warranty, the second defenders could have satisfied their undertaking in the letter of obligation and service of the enforcement notice would have been unnecessary. Thus both the separate breaches, on the averments, contributed to the same wrong, the loss and damage which the pursuers say they suffered.

Thus applying the ratio of *Grunwald v Hughes* as a test of the pursuers' averments I am of the view that

E   the first sentence of cond 6 makes clear that their case is that both defenders by their respective breaches contributed to the loss suffered. The cost of compliance with the enforcement notice is a loss which appears to me to be but one aspect of the single wrong to the pursuers to which both defenders have contributed through their breaches. The same can be said of the claim for loss of business. These issues may be the subject of relief among the defenders, but in my view the attack on the competency of the action fails. Had

F   I reached the opposite conclusion I would have sustained the second defenders' first plea only to the extent of deleting the third conclusion, since, as was submitted by counsel for the pursuers, the second conclusion was not attacked.

As regards the argument relating to the competency of the form of the third conclusion I have reached the view that the second defenders' contentions are not well founded. Where pursuers have suffered the same wrong by the defenders' breaches as is averred in the present case, they may sue together in the same action,

provided the claims for damages are separately stated. That may be done by a separate conclusion for each G pursuer, but I can see no reason why it cannot also competently be done by one conclusion in which the claim of each pursuer is separately stated, as has happened here. I can see no problems in extracting a decree in favour of each pursuer on the basis of that conclusion. Although I was not referred to it, *Harkes v Mowat* is an example of a case with a conclusion similar to that in the present action, to which the court took no objection. The terms of the interlocutor granting decree against the first defender do not assist the H second defenders' argument about the correct form of the conclusion. For these reasons I reject their contentions that the third conclusion is incompetent.

The next question relates to the specification of the averments of loss. [The temporary judge considered the matter, concluded that proof was required and continued:]

There remains the pursuers' attack upon the relevancy of the second defenders' averments. It follows I from my conclusion that inquiry is needed to determine the proper construction and the effect of breach of undertaking in the letter of obligation that the pursuers' argument cannot be disposed of at this stage. To do so would involve acceptance as fact that the undertaking relates to the transaction as a whole, and/or that there is dispute. Further, the second defenders have tabled a defence based on the proposition that planning consent was not required for certain alterations made by the first defender. This would require to be determined after proof before the issue of quantifica- J tion of damages arises.

Accordingly, on the whole matter, of consent I repel the second defenders' second plea, and have decided to repel their first plea. I reserve their third plea and allow a proof before answer. I sustain the pursuers' eighth plea to the extent of excluding from probation the averments in ans 5 for the second defenders from the words "It was granted" at 16D to the words "and completion certificates" where they occur at 17A. K Beyond that, that plea and the sixth plea are reserved.

Counsel for Pursuers, Sutherland, QC; Solicitors, Drummond Miller, WS — No appearance for First Defender — Counsel for Second Defenders, McEachran, QC, Doherty; Solicitors, Simpson & Marwick, WS.

S J B

L

Davis v British Coal Corporation

OUTER HOUSE

TEMPORARY JUDGE J M S HORSBURGH, QC

10 JANUARY 1992

Expenses — Tender — Acceptance during proof — Finding of expenses in favour of pursuer to date of tender — Remit to auditor to determine reasonable date for acceptance — Defenders' entitlement to expenses thereafter — Competency of motion for expenses after decerniture on the merits — Rules of Court 1965, rules 30 (2) and 348 (1).

Expenses — Tender and acceptance — Acceptance during proof — Date of tender — Whether appropriate for court or auditor to determine effective date of tender.

Process — Interlocutor — Correction — Interlocutor following tender and minute of acceptance — No award of expenses in defenders' favour then made — Subsequent motion for expenses — Whether error in interlocutor — Relevance of misunderstanding of position by defenders' advisers — Rules of Court 1965, rule 30 (2).

Rule of Court 348 (1) provides that the court, when making a finding of entitlement to expenses, should also decern against the party liable in the expenses as they might subsequently be taxed. Rule of Court 30 (2) provides that a judge may on cause shown correct or alter an interlocutor at any time before extract.

The defenders in an action of damages for personal injuries lodged a tender four days prior to the proof. During the second day of the proof the pursuer accepted the tender. The court granted decree for the sum tendered, found the defenders liable in expenses to the date of the tender and, parties having agreed that the auditor should determine a reasonable date for acceptance, remitted the pursuer's account of expenses, when lodged, to the auditor to tax and report. At a later date the defenders moved for the expenses of the second day of the proof and of the subsequent days set down for the proof, arguing that the circumstances justified a departure from the general rule that the auditor should determine the true date of the tender, since the tender had been accepted while the pursuer was being cross examined, and it had become apparent that the pursuer might not succeed in his action against the defenders. The defenders contended that such a motion was competent in view of the current practice of dealing with subsidiary questions of expenses after the making of a finding of expenses; and that because the defenders had been operating on the misunderstanding that the remit to the auditor left the defenders' entitlement to expenses after the date of tender open, it was open to the court under rule 30 (2) to correct the interlocutor.

Held, that the defenders' motion was incompetent in respect that the interlocutor dealing with entitlement to expenses was final and unless expenses were expressly reserved there was no power to award them later, a rule which had not been eroded by recent practice (pp 698L-699C); and motion *refused.*

Opinion, (1) that there was no sufficient reason for departing from the rule that the effective date of the tender should be determined by the auditor (p 699E-F); and (2) that as the interlocutor neither contained an error nor failed to express the court's intention, Rule of Court 30 (2) could not be used to remedy a misunderstanding by the defenders' advisers (p 699F-H).

Action of damages

Robert Davis raised an action of damages for personal injuries against the British Coal Corporation. After proof commenced the pursuer accepted a tender lodged by the defenders some days earlier. The temporary judge granted decree in terms of the minute and acceptance of tender, found the defenders liable in expenses to the date of tender and remitted the pursuer's account of expenses to the auditor of court to tax and to report.

The case then came before the court on the motion roll on the defenders' motion for expenses subsequent to the tender.

Statutory provisions

The Rules of Court 1965 provide:

"30.— . . . (2) The judge who signs an interlocutor may on cause shown correct or alter it at any time before extract. . . .

"348.—(1) Where expenses are found due to a party in any cause and a remit is made to the Auditor of Court for taxation the court shall — (a) pronounce an interlocutor finding that party entitled to expenses; and (b) subject to paragraphs (2) and (3) of Rule 349, and unless satisfied that there is special cause shown for not doing so, decern against the party found liable in expenses as taxed by the Auditor."

Cases referred to

Austin v Austin, 1988 SLT 676.
Baird v GP Inveresk, OH, November 1990, unreported.
Campbell v Campbell, 1934 SLT 45.
Gilbert's Trustee v Gilbert, 1988 SLT 680.
Henderson v Peeblesshire County Council, 1972 SLT (Notes) 35.
Jack v Black, 1911 1 SLT 320; 1911 SC 691.
McLean v Galbraith Stores, 1935 SLT 135; 1935 SC 165.
Smeaton v Dundee Corporation, 1942 SLT 47; 1941 SC 600.
Stewart v Stewart, 1989 SLT 80.
UCB Bank plc v Dundas & Wilson, CS, 1991 SLT 90.

Textbooks referred to

Hastings, *Legal Expenses in Scotland*, p 97.
Maxwell, *Practice of the Court of Session*, pp 246, 609, 621.
Thomson and Middleton, *Court of Session Practice*, p 304.

On 10 January 1992 the temporary judge *refused* the defenders' motion as incompetent.

J M S HORSBURGH, QC.—The leading of evid-
A ence in this reparation action commenced on the afternoon of 22 October 1991. The case was adjourned
owing to the lateness of the hour in the course of the
pursuer's cross examination. At 12.35 pm on 23
October, while the pursuer was still under cross
examination his counsel tendered a minute of acceptance of a tender which had been lodged on 18
December. I allowed that to be lodged, and on the pursuer's motion I granted decree against the defenders
for £45,000, the sum tendered. The pursuer's counsel
B also moved me to find the defenders liable to the
pursuer in the expenses of the cause to the date of the
tender. Counsel on both sides were agreed that a
reasonable date for acceptance of the tender should be
determined by the auditor. I granted that motion, and
remitted the account when lodged to the auditor to tax
and to report. No motion was made on the defenders'
behalf to find the pursuer liable in expenses from the
date of the tender, and there was no reservation of
expenses made.

C   On 30 October the defenders enrolled a motion to
find the pursuer liable to them in the expenses of the
second day of the proof and of the third and fourth
days set down for proof. That called before me on 6
December. In view of the observations of Lord President Dunedin in *Jack v Black* at 1911 1 SLT, p 322
as to the period between which the defenders might be
entitled to expenses, senior counsel for the defenders
amended the motion to exclude the claim for the
expenses of the third and fourth days.
D
    In moving the motion he first argued, under refer-
ence to *Jack v Black* at p 322, *Smeaton v Dundee Corporation*, at 1942 SLT, p 51 and Maxwell, *Court of
Session Practice*, p 246, that since all relevant information was before the court, I, rather than the auditor,
should decide when was a reasonable date for acceptance of the tender. I was also referred to *McLean v
Galbraith Stores* at 1935 SLT, pp 136-137. He maintained that in any event there were exceptional cir-
E cumstances to justify departure from the general rule
that the auditor should determine the "true date" of
the tender, namely that the pursuer had had the whole
morning before the proof started as well as the preceding four days to consider the tender, and that the
tender was accepted when cross examination made
apparent the likelihood that he might lose. On the
basis of the practice referred to in Hastings on
Expenses, p 67, he accepted the pursuer should be
awarded the expenses of the first day of the proof.

F   Secondly he sought an addition to my interlocutor
of 23 October finding the pursuer liable to the
defender in the expenses of the second day of the
proof. He argued this was competent in view of
current practice which demonstrated that courts have
often dealt with subsidiary questions of expenses after
findings of expenses had been made previously.
Examples were to be found in the allowance of additional fees to solicitors and modification of liability
under the legal aid provisions, as in *Austin v Austin*.

    Thirdly and lastly he argued that because of a mis-

understanding at the time of lodging of the minute of
acceptance of tender, it was open to the court under G
Rule of Court 30 (2) to correct the interlocutor of 23
October by making the addition he desired. Although
no motion had been made on the defenders' behalf for
a finding of expenses against the pursuer from the date
of the tender, he had understood that since parties had
agreed reference to the auditor, it would follow that
expenses from the date when it was reasonable for the
tender to have been accepted would be awarded to the
defenders.

    In replying to the defenders' second argument H
counsel for the pursuer contended under reference to
Henderson v Peeblesshire County Council, Thomson
and Middleton, *Court of Session Practice*, p 304 and
Maxwell, p 609 that the motion which sought
expenses after decerniture on the merits came too late
and was incompetent. He also referred to an
unreported decision, *Baird v GP Inveresk*. In that case
the pursuer had apparently accepted a tender and
moved for decree in terms of the minutes of tender and
acceptance and for expenses to the date of the tender. I
That motion was granted on 6 November 1990. On 12
November 1990 the defenders enrolled a motion for
expenses against the pursuer from the date of the
tender. That was refused as incompetent by Lord
Coulsfield since it was made after decerniture on the
merits. Practices relating to the allowance of additional fees and modification of expenses under the
legal aid scheme after findings of expenses had been
made did not support the defenders' argument that a
finding for expenses could be made after decerniture, J
as is demonstrated by *UCB Bank v Dundas & Wilson,
CS* and *Gilbert's Tr v Gilbert*. *McLean v Galbraith
Stores* dealt only with circumstances where the
pursuer had failed in his action, having refused a
tender.

    In dealing with the defenders' third argument
counsel for the pursuer maintained that the motion as
amended sought not merely alteration to the interlocutor of 23 October, but the making of a finding of
expenses in the defenders' favour. The interlocutor K
pronounced had reflected all that the court had been
moved to grant. There was no question of an error on
the part of the court or of the pursuer, and rule 30
could not be resorted to. He further submitted that in
any event there was no reason for treating the case as
an exception to the general rule that it is for the
auditor to determine the date to which the pursuer
should be awarded his expenses.

    In my opinion the defenders' motion must be L
refused as incompetent. Rule of Court 348 requires
the court to make by separate interlocutors a finding
of entitlement to expenses and a decerniture for
expenses. The case of *UCB Bank* makes plain that the
interlocutor dealing with entitlement to expenses,
once pronounced, is final and cannot be recalled in the
Outer House. I am equally satisfied that it is not open
to me to add to it by making a further finding relating
to entitlement to expenses. That would have the effect
of reducing overall the expenses already awarded to
the pursuer.

That case and rule 348 do not affect the general rule set out in Thomson and Middleton, p 304 and founded on in the opinion of Lord Robertson in *Henderson v Peeblesshire County Council* that where there is an interlocutor which exhausts the merits, expenses must be expressly awarded or reserved and where there is no reference made to expenses the court has no power to award them later. In this case the interlocutor of 23 October disposed of the merits but contained no finding of expenses in the defenders' favour after the date of the tender. I am therefore of the view that such a finding cannot now be made.

I am satisfied that the general rule has not been eroded by recent practice. *Baird v GP Inveresk* indicates this. Further, I consider the examples relied on by the defenders do not assist their case. As *UCB Bank* shows, a motion for the late allowance of additional fees does not involve any alteration or addition to the interlocutor containing the decerniture on the merits of the action. Nor does it seek alteration of or addition to the separate interlocutor awarding expenses. If it succeeds, such a motion merely adds a matter for the consideration of the auditor in taxing the account in terms of the finding already made in relation to expenses. By contrast the present motion seeks to alter a final interlocutor containing decerniture on the merits and a finding that the pursuer is entitled to expenses by adding an award of expenses not previously sought. The opinion of the court at p 93L shows this cannot be done.

Likewise the example of modification of legal aid liability is unhelpful to the defenders. *Austin v Austin* does not raise the issue for decision in this case and deals with alteration of the means of assessing expenses from that contained in a decree. It does not deal with entitlement to expenses. By contrast the modification sought in *Gilbert's Tr v Gilbert* was held to be incompetent. That case was followed in *Stewart v Stewart* and approved in *UCB Bank* in the passage to which reference has already been made.

My conclusion that the motion is incompetent makes it unnecessary to deal with the defenders' other arguments. However, I record my opinion in relation to the first argument that the defenders have not demonstrated sufficient reason for departing from the general rule and usual practice referred to in *Jack v Black, Smeaton v Dundee Corporation* and Maxwell, p 246 that it should be left to the auditor to determine the precise date when the tender should reasonably have been accepted and to which the pursuer should be entitled to expenses. The minute of tender and the minute of proceedings are sufficient for the auditor to be seized of the relevant information. I am of the view that the advantage I had of hearing cross examination does not necessarily place me in as good an overall position as the auditor would be to determine the issue. In any event, the defenders did not advance any convincing reason for departing from the agreement of 23 October that the matter be remitted to the auditor for decision.

Lastly I do not consider the defenders' third argument, that reliance can be placed on rule 30 (2), to be sound. The interlocutor was granted on the basis of what I was moved to do; it contains no errors. Nor did it fail to express properly the intentions which I had. It does not require correction or alteration. What the defenders now seek to do is to retrieve the situation from the consequences of their failure to move for a finding of expenses at the proper time. I am afraid it is now too late for them to do so. A misunderstanding on the part of the defenders' advisers does not justify resort to rule 30 (2) in my opinion. The passage in Maxwell, p 621 under reference to *Campbell v Campbell* was not cited to me, but appears to support the view I have reached.

Accordingly I refuse the defenders' motion.

———————————

Counsel for Pursuer, Doherty; Solicitors, Robin Thompson & Partners — Counsel for Defenders, Miller, QC; Solicitors, McClure Naismith Anderson & Gardiner.

C A G M

Devlin v Strathclyde Regional Council

OUTER HOUSE

LORD COULSFIELD

14 FEBRUARY 1992

Reparation — Negligence — Occupiers' liability — Foreseeability — Occupiers aware that children climbed onto roof of building — No knowledge that children would jump onto skylight — Whether accident by falling through skylight reasonably foreseeable.

Reparation — Negligence — Volenti non fit injuria — Injured person's own negligence — Child on roof of school building where he knew he should not be — Jumping onto skylight from above during game of tig.

Damages — Amount — Loss of society — Death of 14 year old son and stepson.

The mother and stepfather of a deceased boy raised an action in respect of his death occasioned by a fall through a skylight at a primary school occupied by and under the control of the defenders. The deceased was 14 years old and a former pupil at the school. With two younger friends he had climbed onto the school roof on a Saturday. The boys were playing tig and the deceased jumped onto a UPVC domed cover which shattered so that he fell through the aperture onto the floor beneath, sustaining fatal injuries. It was not uncommon for children to be on the school roof, and sometimes school staff knew of and supervised their presence there, for instance in the fetching of balls which landed on the roof from the nearby playground. On other occasions, children were advised to

A come down from the roof. The presence of children on the roof was not tolerated but it was well known to the defenders' employees who made no strenuous effort to prevent or deter children from being there. It was well known to the children that they were not supposed to go onto the roof unsupervised. There was no evidence that any accident had ever occurred as a result of children going onto the roof. The pursuers, founding on the Occupiers' Liability (Scotland) Act 1960, con-

B tended that the defenders should have taken reasonable care, first, to prevent children from climbing on to and playing on the roof, and secondly, to instal a skylight that would bear the weight of a child landing on it, and to fence off or strengthen the skylight in question. Expert evidence was led showing that measures could have reasonably been taken to make access to the roof difficult and the skylight covers stronger, both without excessive difficulty or costs. The pursuers sought damages for loss of society. The first pursuer was the deceased's stepfather, who had lived with the boy as his father from a date prior to the

C boy's fourth birthday.

Held, (1) that the deceased's action was so extreme as to be beyond the scope of reasonable foresight on the part of the defenders (p 702H-I); (2) that the duty of an occupier to a particular person was one which depended on all the circumstances of the case, including the age and state of knowledge of the particular person who entered on the premises, and the pursuers had failed to show that the accident to the deceased was caused by any failure in reasonable care on the

D part of the defenders (p 703B-D); and defenders *assoilzied.*

Opinion, (1) that the deceased had been solely to blame for the accident, or had voluntarily accepted the risk of it (p 703E); and (2) that it would not have been appropriate to make any distinction between the pursuers in deciding the amount to be awarded in respect of loss of society, which award would have comprised £5,000 to each pursuer (p 703G).

E

Action of damages

Patrick Devlin and Mrs Ellen Devlin raised an action of damages against Strathclyde Regional Council in respect of the death of their stepson and son Brian Devlin who died on 19 October 1987 as a result of injuries sustained in a fall through a skylight in a school building. He was then aged 14.

F The case came to proof before the Lord Ordinary (Coulsfield).

Cases referred to

Donald v Strathclyde Passenger Transport Executive, 1986 SLT 625.
Gough v National Coal Board [1954] 1 QB 191; [1953] 3 WLR 900; [1953] 2 All ER 1283.
Harvey v Cairns, 1989 SLT 107.
Heap v West Highland Crofters and Farmers, 1985 SLT 191.

McGlone v British Railways Board, 1966 SLT 2; 1966 SC (HL) 1.
G *Titchener v British Railways Board,* 1984 SLT 192; 1984 SC (HL) 34.

On 14 February 1992 his Lordship *sustained* the second and third pleas in law for the defenders and *granted* decree of absolvitor.

LORD COULSFIELD.—The second named pursuer is the mother and the first named pursuer is the stepfather of the late Brian Devlin, who died on 19 H October 1987 as a result of injuries which he sustained on 17 October 1987 by falling through a skylight in New Monkland primary school, Glenmavis, a school occupied by and under the control of the defenders. The deceased was born on 31 May 1973. Some time after the birth of the deceased, the second named pursuer obtained a divorce from his father, and on 5 February 1977 she and the first named pursuer were married. From that time on, the deceased had no contact with his natural father, and was treated by the I first named pursuer as, in all respects, his own child. The pursuers have two other children.

New Monkland primary school is situated in the centre of the village of Glenmavis, and is surrounded by a playground. The playground in front of the school faces a road. At one side of the school there is a church, and at the other side there is the church manse; the school was apparently built on land which formerly belonged to the church. To the rear of the school, the playground is adjacent to a cemetery. J There are walls or railings on all sides of the playground, separating it from the adjacent properties. At the front, these take the form of a wall with railings on top. There are three gates at the front of the school, giving access to the playground. The top of the railings is about 5 ft, or a little more, above ground level, and two of the gates are of a similar height, but one of the gates is only about 4 ft high. The wall at the rear, separating the playground from the cemetery, is about 8 ft high. At the time of the accident, the gates K were kept locked when the premises were not in use. It is, however, clear on the evidence that a normally active child of nine years of age or more could get access to the playground without difficulty by climbing the lowest gate, or possibly the fence, or, in any event, from the cemetery where an adjacent tombstone provided a reasonably convenient access to the top of the wall.

At the material time, the school buildings consisted of three principal elements, namely a two storey block, L a single storey section and a hall with a pitched roof and a projecting tower, the purpose of which was to admit light to a stage which formed part of the hall. The single storey section had a flat roof, which was about 11 or 12 ft above the level of the playground. The hall was situated in the centre of the single storey section, and projected some distance above it. It was possible to walk completely, or almost completely, round the hall on the flat roof. The walls of the hall projected a short distance vertically above the flat roof,

A and above the walls there was a pitched roof which sloped up to a ridge some distance higher still. The slope of the roof was not steep and it would not be difficult for a child of nine years of age to walk on it. The vertical distance from the lowest point of the pitched roof to the flat roof surface was about 5 ft, but at one side of the hall there was a section of flat roof at a slightly higher level, and it would not be particularly difficult for a child of the age mentioned to reach the pitched roof from the flat roof. There were a number of rhone pipes on the exterior of the flat
B roofed section, some of which ran close to windows. The pipes were not boxed in or otherwise prevented from being used as climbing aids, and an active child, perhaps one slightly older, say 11 or 12, would be able to use them to reach the roof with relative ease. There were a number of skylights in the flat roof. These were round apertures which were covered with round domed covers attached to a wooden surround. Some of the covers, which had been in position for some time, were made of glass and held down by two metal strips
C which formed a cross over the dome and were fixed to the surround. In the course of time, some of these glass covers had been replaced with domed covers made of unplasticised polyvinyl chloride (UPVC), bolted to the surround. The aperture of the skylight gave on to a short vertical tunnel, leading down to ceiling level within the building. The precise sizes of the cover, the aperture and the tunnel were not established in evidence. The best estimate was given by the school janitor, Mr Bell, who thought that the cover
D was about 4 ft 6 in in diameter, the aperture about 8 in to 1 ft less and the tunnel about 18 in to 2 ft in diameter. I am inclined to suspect, because of the way the accident happened, that that may be an underestimate, but I do not think that the precise sizes are material for the purposes of the case.

The circumstances of the accident are not really in dispute. On 17 October 1987, which was a Saturday, the deceased, who was then 14 years of age, and was
E no longer a pupil at the school, was in the company of two friends, Stephen Coyle, who was 13, and Thomas Spence, who was almost 12. The three boys met some time about the middle of the day. They had no particular purpose in mind and ended by climbing into the playground from the cemetery. They then, almost immediately, climbed onto the roof of the school, using a rhone pipe and a window ledge beside the side door of the school. On the roof, they played a form of tig, and spent some time sunbathing. In the
F course of running about on the flat part of the roof, they jumped onto one or more of the UPVC skylight covers, in order to bounce off them. It appears that there was enough spring or give in the covers to make this possible. It is not clear how often this was done, but the accounts of Coyle and Spence suggested that each of the boys had done it more than once. Eventually, in the course of a game of tig, the deceased ran up one side of the pitched roof, pursued by the other two, and down the other. When he came to the edge of the pitched roof, he jumped from it directly on to one of the UPVC covers which was situated about 3

ft horizontally from the point from which he jumped and, as I have explained, about 5 ft below it. Both
G Coyle and Spence said that their impression was that the deceased aimed to jump for the cover, in order to bounce off it, although both agreed that they did not know what was in his mind and that he might simply have been trying to escape the pursuit. The deceased did land directly on the cover, which shattered so that he fell through the aperture and onto the floor beneath, sustaining the injuries which led to his death. Spence went to try to obtain help but did not succeed, and came back with a rope which he had found in the
H cemetery, and which was lowered through the aperture in an attempt to reach the deceased. Coyle then went for help, and was successful in finding some persons who came to the scene, one of them entering the premises. About the same time, police officers who had been sent in response to a report that there were youths on the school roof arrived at the scene. The officers arrived at about 2.45 pm, probably half an hour or more after the accident happened.

There was a substantial body of evidence to the
I effect that it was not uncommon for children to be on the roof of the school. Sometimes their presence was known to and supervised by the school staff. Both the headmistress, Mrs Wright, and the janitor, Mr Bell, said that the older boys used to play football in part of the playground and that the ball inevitably went on the roof from time to time. What usually happened then was that the janitor, who was the person who supervised the playground, would assist one of the
J boys to climb onto the roof to fetch it, under his supervision. In addition, however, there was evidence from several witnesses that children were seen from time to time on the roof out of school hours. Mr Ford, the parish minister, said that he would see children on the roof perhaps five or six times in a year, mostly during the summer. Mr Marshall who regularly worked at the church in the evenings and on Saturdays gave a similar estimate. Mrs Logan, the mother of the second pursuer, and Mrs White, both of whom worked as
K cleaners at the school, gave evidence to the effect that there were always children in the playground and that they went onto the roof quite often. All these witnesses said that, when they saw children on the roof, they checked them and told them to come down. Both Coyle and Spence admitted that they had known quite well that they were not supposed to be on the roof and said that the deceased had also been well aware of that. The second pursuer herself had been a pupil at the school and said that she and others had gone on the
L roof of the school, and that if they were seen the janitor or some other adult would shout at them to come down. This chapter of the evidence can, I think, fairly be summarised by saying that, while it would be going too far to say that the presence of children on the roof was tolerated, it was well known to the defenders' employees responsible for the running of the school that children did go on the roof from time to time, and that no strenuous effort was made to prevent or deter them from doing so: while on the other hand, it was well known to the children that they

were not supposed to go onto the roof unsupervised. I should add that there was no averment, and no evidence, that any accident had ever occurred as a result of children going on this roof.

The case against the defenders is pled under the Occupiers' Liability (Scotland) Act 1960, and may be said to fall into three sections: it is averred that the defenders should have taken reasonable care, first, to prevent children from climbing onto and playing on the roof; secondly, to instal a skylight that would bear the weight of a child landing on it, and to fence off or strengthen the skylight in question; and, thirdly, to place a notice beside the skylight warning that it would not take the weight of a person landing on it. The third part of the case did not figure either in the evidence or the submissions.

The evidence principally relied on to support the other two parts of the case came from Mr Cheeseman, a senior lecturer in the department of building engineering and surveying at Heriot-Watt University. Put shortly Mr Cheeseman's evidence was that measures could have been taken, without much difficulty or cost, to make access to the roof difficult, if not impossible for children by putting barbed wire round the tops of the rhone pipes and by boxing in the pipes to prevent them from being used as climbing aids. Objection was taken to this evidence on the ground that there was no specific record for the particular steps which Mr Cheeseman recommended, but, in my opinion, these were just the sort of steps which must obviously be contemplated by an averment that it was the defenders' duty to make access to the roof difficult. As regards the second branch of the case, Mr Cheeseman gave evidence that there were other materials which could have been used to cover the skylight, one of which, polycarbonate, was extremely strong, although he accepted that it was normally used in situations requiring high security such as military establishments; and that it would also have been possible, without excessive difficulty or cost, to fit a metal grille below the skylight to prevent access by it or a person falling through it. Objection was taken to the evidence as to the particular material and to the suggestion that a metal grille should have been installed, on the ground of no record, but, again, it seems to me that the suggestion of fitting a grille is well within an averment that the skylight should have been strengthened, and that in the absence of an averment by the defenders that it was not possible to obtain or use a stronger material for the skylight cover, they were not prejudiced by the evidence naming a specific material as sufficiently strong to bear the impact of a child jumping onto it. In my opinion, there is really little or no difficulty in reaching the conclusion that, if the defenders had appreciated that there was a risk that a child who had climbed onto the roof would jump on the skylight in the way the deceased did, there were reasonable and practicable steps which they could have taken to prevent or materially reduce the risk of injury to such a child. It appears to me, therefore, that the material questions in the case are first, whether conduct of the kind in

which the deceased engaged should have been foreseen and, secondly, whether in the absence of foresight of such conduct, the defenders should have taken any steps beyond those which they did take to discourage access to the roof or to make the roof safer.

As regards the first question, the arguments one way and the other seem to me to fall within a narrow compass. On the one hand, it can be said with force that children may be forgetful, careless and imprudent and that it is precisely for that reason that special care has to be taken to protect them. On the other hand, it can equally well be said that what the deceased did went beyond mere imprudence and carelessness. Balancing the arguments as best I can, I have come to the view that the deceased's action in jumping 5 ft vertically onto a dome which he knew to be a cover over a skylight, made of some form of plastic, was so extreme as to be beyond the scope of reasonable foresight on the part of the defenders. The deceased was 14 years of age and, making all allowances for youth and excitement, I cannot view his action as other than reckless.

Turning to the second question, it is, I think, obvious that, if children obtain access to a roof at all, there must be some danger that they may fall and sustain injury. In this case the flat section of roof was about 10 to 12 ft above ground level and a fall from that height could easily cause serious injury. Nevertheless, if that were the only risk, I do not think that it could be said that the defenders were under a duty to surround the rhones with barbed wire or to box them in, or otherwise seek to make the roof inaccessible. It is, I think, important to bear in mind that the roof had been in much the same state over a long number of years, without any accident, even though children had been in the way of going on the roof from time to time. It is also, I think, obvious that if there are skylights in a roof, there must be some danger that a person walking on the roof may step on one and fall through it. Mr Cheeseman said, indeed, that he would not put his weight on a skylight even if it were made of polycarbonate, a material which is, in itself, as strong as mild steel. There was, however, nothing in the evidence to suggest that the material of which this skylight was made posed a special risk or was materially inferior to the materials of which skylights are commonly made. The alternatives mentioned in Mr Cheeseman's evidence were glass, perspex and wire reinforced PVC, none of which would have offered a significantly better resistance to impact; glass reinforced polyester, which would have been stronger than UPVC, but is still at the lower end of the range of materials in terms of impact resistance, and which is less pleasing in appearance and has poor light transmission properties; and polycarbonate which is, as I have mentioned, usually employed in special situations, and which was, at least until about the end of the 1980s, liable to problems of rapid deterioration, and also might not have been readily available unless specially ordered. It is again relevant to bear in mind that there was no history of accidents at the school, and it is also relevant that the material in fact used was

strong enough to resist the bouncing to which it was
subjected by all three boys for some time before the
accident. I do not, therefore, think that there was anything in the nature or construction of this roof which
should have led the defenders to anticipate any special
danger to children who might be on the roof beyond
those inherent in roofs in general. The defenders did
discourage access to the playground, and to the roof,
and it was made clear to the children that they should
not go on the roof unsupervised. There was no averment or evidence of any general practice in the construction of school roofs, and, in particular, no
evidence of any practice of inserting grilles to prevent
persons falling through skylights.

In considering the question of liability, counsel
referred to the 1960 Act, and to *McGlone v British
Railways Board, Titchener v British Railways Board*
and *Gough v National Coal Board.* I do not think that
it is necessary to quote these cases in detail. It is, in
my opinion, clear that the duty of an occupier is one
which depends on all the circumstances of the case,
including the age and state of knowledge of the particular person who enters on the premises, and that the
duty relates to that person. The defenders had taken
some steps to discourage children from going onto the
roof. In order to go there, it was necessary to surmount
the fence or wall, and to climb up a rhone pipe onto
the roof. The deceased and his companions were well
aware that they should not go on the roof. There was
no special or unusual danger there and the deceased
was of sufficient age to have some understanding of
the risk involved in doing what he knew to be prohibited. In my opinion the pursuers have failed to
show that the accident to the deceased was caused by
any failure in reasonable care on the part of the
defenders.

The defenders also maintained that the accident was
due to the fault of the deceased and further that he had
voluntarily accepted the risk of any injury. As was
indicated by Lord Hailsham LC in *Titchener,* supra, at
1984 SLT, p 193, these different pleas may involve
little more than different ways of formulating the same
result, and I think that that is the case here. I have
already said that the deceased acted recklessly, in my
view, and it follows that, had it been necessary, I
would have been prepared to hold that he was solely
to blame for the accident, or voluntarily accepted the
risk of it.

The deceased was an intelligent boy, who intended
to stay at school until after his highers, and thereafter
apply for entry to the navy. He had lived in family
with his mother and stepfather since 1977, and the
evidence was all to the effect that he treated the first
pursuer as his father, and was very close to him,
although perhaps a little closer to his mother. In the
circumstances of this case, I do not think that it would
have been appropriate to make any distinction
between the pursuers in deciding the amount to be
awarded. I was referred to a number of authorities,
including *Heap v West Highland Crofters, Donald v
Strathclyde Passenger Transport Executive* and *Harvey*

v Cairns. These authorities suggest that the award for
loss of society tends to diminish as the child in question becomes older, and support figures in the region
of £7,500 for a child of six or seven and £3,000 for one
of 17 or 18, at present day values. If I had been in the
pursuers' favour on the merits of the case, I would
have made an award of £5,000 to each of them.

In all the circumstances, however, I shall sustain the
second and third pleas in law for the defenders and
grant decree of absolvitor.

———————

*Counsel for Pursuer, Mure, QC, D M MacNeill; Soli-
citors, Allan McDougall & Co, SSC (for Bell, Russell &
Co, Airdrie) — Counsel for Defenders, Doherty; Solicitors, Balfour & Manson, Nightingale & Bell.*

P A

Westwater v Thomson

HIGH COURT OF JUSTICIARY

THE LORD JUSTICE GENERAL (HOPE),
LORDS ALLANBRIDGE AND COWIE

26 MAY 1992

*Justiciary — Statutory offence — Failing to log location
of fishing catch — Master recording ICES zone but not
more precise statistical rectangle where catch made —
Whether sufficient compliance with requirements —
Fisheries Act 1981 (c 29), s 30 — Sea Fishing (Enforcement of Community Control Measures) Order 1985 (SI
1985/487), art 3 — Commission Regulation (EEC)
2807/83, art 1 (1) and annexes I and IV — Council Regulation (EEC) 2241/87, art 5.1.*

Article 5.1 of EEC Council Regulation 2241/87 provides that the skippers of fishing vessels flying the flag
of, or registered in, a member state and fishing for a
stock or group of stocks subject to total allowable
catches or quotas shall keep a logbook of their operations indicating "as a minimum" the quantities of
each species caught and kept on board, the date and
location of such catches by reference to the smallest
zone for which a total allowable catch or quota has
been fixed and administered and the type of gear used.
Article 14 provides that detailed rules for implementing inter alia art 5 shall be adopted in accordance with
the procedure laid down in art 14 of the EC Regulation 170/83 by virtue of which Commission Regulation 2807/83 was made.

The 1983 Commission Regulation provides in its
preamble that standardised logbooks will ensure Community wide compliance with the conservation measures adopted, should make for more effective
monitoring of current rules, and should facilitate the
scientific analysis of estimates of fish stocks and their
exploitation. Article 1 provides that the logbook shall

be completed in accordance with the instructions set
A out in annexes IV and V. Rule 2.2.1 of annex IV provides inter alia that all the compulsory information
shall be given. Rule 2.4.1 provides that the information required on fishing operations is to be filled in
against the corresponding numbers on the page of the
logbook and provides examples referring to the recording of entries for ICES division and the statistical
rectangle.

An accused person, the master and skipper of a
British registered fishing vessel, the overall length of
B which exceeded 17 m, was charged on a summary
complaint with a contravention of art 3 of the Sea
Fishing (Enforcement of Community Control
Measures) Order 1985, as amended, and s 30 of the
Fisheries Act 1981 in respect that he failed to record
in the vessel's logbook the locations of four catches
made as required by EC Commission Regulation
2807/83, art 1 (1) and annexes I and IV, and EC
Council Regulation 2241/87, art 5. The evidence disclosed that on four occasions the accused entered the
C ICES zone in the logbook but not the statistical rectangle in which the catches were made. A submission that
the accused had no case to answer was upheld by the
sheriff on the ground that the accused had done all
that he was required to do when he recorded the ICES
zone which was the smallest zone for which a total
allowable catch had been fixed. The Crown appealed
on the ground of error in law.

Held, (1) that art 5 of the 1987 Council Regulation
D stated the minimum requirements to be provided for
in the detailed rules and it was open to the Commission, if so advised, to require more information than
the minimum to be given, and that that was, in any
event, the plain effect of the detailed rules in annex IV
to the 1983 Council Regulation when the legislation
was read as a whole (p 709E-F); (2) that on a proper
reading of the detailed rules in annex IV the master
was required to insert in the logbook, in the manner
described by reference to an example, the statistical
E rectangle in which most of the catches were made and
it was not sufficient compliance with the rules for him
to state only the ICES zone in which the catches were
made (p 709J-K); and Crown appeal *allowed.*

Observed, that the accused's submission that the
detailed rules should be construed strictly in his
favour in view of their penal consequences, was inconsistent with Community law which was not penal in
character and had to be applied uniformly throughout
the Community (pp 709L-710A).
F
Observed, further, that the answer to the point at
issue was so obvious as to leave no scope for any
reasonable doubt and that the High Court was under
no obligation to refer the question to the European
Court of Justice for a preliminary ruling under art 177
(p 710F-G and K-L).

*CILFIT Srl and Lanificio di Gavardo SpA v Ministry
of Health* (283/81) [1982] ECR 3415, *applied.*

_____

Summary complaint

John William Campbell Thomson was charged at G
the instance of Henry J Westwater, procurator fiscal,
Dornoch on a summary complaint which contained
the following charge: "that being the master and
skipper of the British fishing boat *St Kilda,* INS 47,
a boat of registered length 22.87 m and overall length
23.99 m, in respect of which there was a failure to
comply with the provisions of Commission Regulation
(EEC) No 2807/83, art 1 (1) and annex I and IV, and
Council Regulation (EEC) No 2241/87, art 5, specified in Column 1 of Part 1 of the Schedule to the H
undermentioned order, in that in relation to four
voyages of said fishing boat departing and landing at
Lochinver, District of Sutherland, on the dates specified in the schedule hereto, the locations of the catches
made were not indicated in the logbook as required by
said regulations, you are guilty of an offence: contrary
to the Sea Fishing (Enforcement of Community
Control Measures) Order 1985, art 3, as amended, and
the Fisheries Act 1981, s 30".

The accused pled not guilty and proceeded to trial. I
After trial the sheriff (J O A Fraser) sustained a sub-
mission in terms of s 345A of the Criminal Procedure
(Scotland) Act 1975 and acquitted the accused.

The procurator fiscal appealed by way of stated case
to the High Court against the decision of the sheriff.

Statutory provisions

EEC Council Regulation 2241/87 provides:

"*Article 5* J

"1. The skippers of fishing vessels flying the flag of,
or registered in, a Member State and fishing for a
stock or group of stocks subject to total allowable
catches (TACs) or quotas shall keep a logbook of their
operations, indicating, as a minimum, the quantities of
each species caught and kept on board, the date and
location of such catches by reference to the smallest
zone for which a TAC or quota has been fixed and
administered and the type of gear used."
K
EEC Commission Regulation 2807/83 provides:

"[Preamble] Having regard to Council Regulation
(EEC) No 170/83 of 25 January 1983 establishing a
Community system for the conservation and manage-
ment of fishery resources,

"Having regard to [Council Regulation (EEC) No
2241/87 of 23 July 1987] establishing certain control
measures for fishing activities by vessels of the
Member States, and in particular [Article 14] thereof, L

"Whereas [Article 5 of Council Regulation (EEC)
No 2241/87] provides that the masters of fishing
vessels flying the flag of, or registered in, a Member
State shall keep a log-book of their fishing operations; Whereas standardized log-books will ensure
Community-wide compliance with the conservation
measures adopted and should make for more effective
monitoring of current rules and facilitate the scientific
analysis of estimates of fish stocks and their exploitation . . .

"Article 1

A   "1. The log-book required under [art 5 of Regulation (EEC) no 2241/87] shall be filled in by the master in accordance with the model shown in Annex I or Annex II, depending on the fishing zone, for all fishing operations relating to species subject to TACs in the respective ICES/NAFO zones as referred to in paragraph 1 of [the said art 5]. The form of log-book shown in Annex I shall be used for all fishing zones except those comprised in NAFO I and ICES Va and XIV, for which the log-book shown in Annex II shall

B   be used. These log-books shall be completed in accordance with the instructions set out in Annexes IV and V respectively . . .

"Annex IV

". . . 2.1.2 *How to complete the log-book* — The log-book shall be completed daily by not later than 2400 hours and at the time of arrival in port. — The log-book shall also be completed at the time of any inspection at sea. — All the compulsory information shall be given. — Rules considered optional at Community

C   level may be made mandatory if a Member State so wishes, in respect of vessels flying its flag or registered therein. In such cases the relevant authorities will issue additional instructions. . . .

"2.4 Information on Fishing Operations

"2.4.1 *Type of information*

"The information required on fishing operations is to be filled in against the corresponding numbers on the page of the log-book, as follows: . . . Reference No

D   in log-book (14): position.

Examples: — 'ICES division or NAFO sub-area': refer to the ICES divisions as shown on the maps inside the cover of the log-book and indicate the code of each division. *e g*: IVa), VIb), VIIg). — 'Statistical rectangle': refer to the ICES statistical rectangle on the charts inside the cover of the log-book. These rectangles are bounded by latitudes and longitudes corresponding to whole figures of degree or whole figures of

E   degree plus 30' for the latitudes and whole figures of degree for the longitudes. Using a combination of figures and a letter indicate the statistical rectangle in which most of the catches were made (e g the area between 56° and 56° 30' latitude North and between 6° and 7° longitude East = ICES code 41/F6). However, optional entries may be made in respect of all the statistical rectangles in which the vessel has fished during the day."

F   The Treaty of Rome provides:

"Article 177

"The Court of Justice shall have jurisdiction to give preliminary rulings concerning: (a) the interpretation of this Treaty; (b) the validity and interpretation of acts of the institutions of the Community; (c) the interpretation of the statutes of bodies established by an act of the Council, where those statutes so provide.

"Where such a question is raised before any court or tribunal of a Member State, that court or tribunal may, if it considers that a decision on the question is

necessary to enable it to give judgment, request the Court of Justice to give a ruling thereon.   G

"Where any such question is raised in a case pending before a court or tribunal of a Member State, against whose decisions there is no judicial remedy under national law, that court or tribunal shall bring that matter before the Court of Justice."

Cases referred to

CILFIT Srl and Lanificio di Gavardo SpA v Ministry of Health (283/81) [1982] ECR 3415.
R v Henn [1981] AC 850.   H

The sheriff in the stated case reported inter alia on the Crown evidence:

(10) The *St Kilda*, whose port of registry is Inverness, and whose port letters and numbers are INS 47, is 23.99 m in overall length, is a fishing vessel registered in the United Kingdom, and is a British fishing boat, date of registration 13 March 1978, current certificate of registry, as at the date of complaint, being 18 May 1989. (11) The respondent was   I at the material time the master and skipper of the *St Kilda*. (12) At the material time the *St Kilda* was fishing for a group of stock subject to total allowable catches, in accordance with a white fish pressure stock licence for the General North Sea and West of Scotland dated 1990. (13) The respondent kept a logbook of the operations of the *St Kilda* including the quantities of each species caught and kept on board, and the dates and locations of such catches for four   J voyages as follows: (a) departure 17 April 1990, landing 19 April 1990; (b) departure 20 April 1990, landing 23 April 1990; (c) departure 24 April 1990, landing 26 April 1990; (d) departure 15 May 1990, landing 16 May 1990. (14) The only zones for which total allowable catches were fixed as at the dates set out in para 13 above, were ICES divisions of the sea, which were therefore by definition the smallest zones. (15) In respect of all four voyages referred to in para 13 above, said logbook disclosed various particulars   K whose legality and accuracy is not challenged and also disclosed in reference (14) of said logbook the ICES division where the fish were caught but not, in any case, the statistical rectangle, where any of said fish were caught.

In his note attached to the stated case the sheriff stated:

THE SHERIFF (J O A FRASER).—The argument between the appellant and the solicitor for the   L respondent in this case was in clear cut and uncomplicated terms although the provisions of the regulations of the Commission and Council of the European Communities were slightly complicated.

The issue between the parties was whether the respondent was obliged in law to complete his logbook for the voyages of the *St Kilda* in respect of the position of the *St Kilda* when the fish were caught by putting in the position in respect of the statistical rectangle as well as the ICES division of the sea. The

argument for the appellant was that he was obliged
A and by the solicitor for the respondent was that he was
not so obliged.

Article 5 of Council Regulation 2241/87 sets out in
general terms the requirement for the skipper of a
vessel, which the respondent was, to keep a logbook,
and in general terms the contents of the logbook.
Commission Regulation 2807/83 sets out by art 1 and
annexes I and IV the form and content of the logbook.

It is not a matter of dispute between the parties and
was indeed manifest that the form of a logbook in
B annex I does contain a section for the completion of
the position with reference to the statistical rectangle
as well as the ICES division.

The argument for the appellant is that given the
form of the logbook, the plain requirement of the provisions of annex IV in relation to the type of information to be recorded in the logbook says that the
position in accordance with reference (14) should be
stated.

C Indeed the appellant reinforced the argument by
pointing to the examples in para 2.4.1 of annex IV in
which examples are given both of ICES division and
of the statistical rectangle showing how these should
be identified and therefore put into the logbook.

His contention was that the Council and Commission regulations were wholly consistent and the Commission regulation particularised the information
generally required by the Council regulation.

D The argument for the respondent was on two
grounds and his weaker ground was that the Commission regulation had to be read with the Council regulation, that the Commission regulation simply stated the
requirement to put in the position and described how
that position would be calculated whether the respondent wished to insert the ICES division or the statistical rectangle, or both. He went on to argue that there
was nothing in the Commission regulation which
derogated from nor was inconsistent with the Council
regulation and the Council regulation at its material
E part required that the logbook should show the location of the catches of fish by reference to the smallest
zone for which a total allowable catch had been fixed
and administered.

It was the evidence of the prosecution, and is, I
understand, not the matter of any dispute, that the
smallest zone for which a total allowable catch has
been fixed as represented by the licence held by the
respondent, is the particular ICES division in which
he is fishing.
F
The argument of the respondent's solicitor therefore, was that that was what the respondent was
required to fill in and nothing more. He had, indis-
putably, done that and had therefore complied with
the provisions of the necessary legislation. He could,
therefore, not be guilty of any offence in accordance
with the Sea Fishing (Enforcement of Community
Control Measures) Order 1985, as amended, and the
Fisheries Act 1981, s 30, those being the United
Kingdom legislation which implemented the Council
and Commission regulations in respect that they

created offences in accordance with the provisions of
the Commission and Council regulations which I have G
already referred to.

The second, and stronger, argument of the respondent's solicitor was that even if there was a doubt
about interpretation it was, at the worst for the respondent, dubious whether it was necessary in law to
include the statistical rectangle in the marking of the
position in the logbook. If that requirement was in any
way dubious then the respondent was facing prosecution for a criminal offence: he had to know, as anyone
has to know, exactly what the law was, and the H
prosecution required to set out beyond dispute that
what they were alleging was an offence was in fact an
offence. On this basis of this argument, the respondent's solicitor contended that it was not clear, on his
second, but stronger, argument that the filling of the
statistical rectangle was necessary in law, and therefore the respondent on the basis of that argument
could not be guilty of an offence on the basis of the
evidence led for the prosecution.

I
In my view the respondent's solicitor was correct on
both accounts. I upheld his submission of no case to
answer on the basis of his first and weaker argument.
It is plain to me that the Commission regulation is a
detailed implementation of the general provision in
the Council regulation. I can see no answer to the
argument presented by the respondent's solicitor, that
the location by reference to the smallest zone for
which a total allowable catch has been fixed was
clearly in his favour and that is an ICES division and
that is what the respondent did fill in. J

It was plain, though not necessary for me to reach,
that the second and stronger argument for the respondent was also a valid one but my decision was made
on the question of interpretation of the first and
weaker argument for the respondent.

The appellant also presented an argument that if I
was not with him on his main contention, I should set
aside the Council regulation and should read the Commission regulation alone. If I did that it was clear that K
the statistical rectangle had to be filled in and the
respondent was therefore guilty of the offence. Of
necessity this argument would have obliged me, if I
had reached this stage at the end of the day, to delete,
in the complaint, the narration of failure to comply
with the provision of the Council regulation and leave
in only the Commission regulation.

This was not an argument which found favour with
me but I do not refer to it further, as, reading the L
matters which the appellant desires to bring under
review, it appears to me that on a proper interpretation of those matters, this argument is not being
advanced by way of appeal and I, therefore, make no
further reference to it.

_____

Appeal
The sheriff posed the following question for the
opinion of the High Court:

Did I err in law in holding that the respondent was
A not obliged to comply with the provisions of the Commission Regulation 2807/83, by entering the locations
of his catches in his logbook by reference to the
statistical rectangles referred to in said regulation?

The appeal was heard in the High Court on 26 May
1992.

Eo die the court *answered* the question in the
affirmative and *remitted* to the sheriff to proceed as
B accords.

The following opinion of the court was delivered by
the Lord Justice General (Hope):

OPINION OF THE COURT.—The respondent,
who is the master and skipper of a British fishing boat
whose overall length exceeds 17 m, was charged on
summary complaint in the sheriff court at Dornoch
with an offence contrary to art 3 of the Sea Fishing
C (Enforcement of Community Control Measures)
Order 1985, as amended, and the Fisheries Act 1981,
s 30. The substance of the charge was that he had
failed to comply with the provisions of Community
regulations in respect of the information to be
recorded in the logbook which the masters of all
fishing vessels more than 17 m in length are required
to keep, irrespective of the duration of the fishing
voyage, in that in relation to four voyages of his
fishing boat the locations of the catches made were not
D indicated in the logbook as required by the regulations. He pled not guilty and went to trial, but at the
end of the Crown case a submission was made on his
behalf that there was no case to answer, which was
upheld by the sheriff and he was found not guilty. The
Crown have now appealed against the sheriff's
decision on the ground that he was wrong to hold that
the entries in the logbook contained all the information as to the location of the catches which was
required by the regulations.

E   There was no dispute about the facts of the case.
The respondent's vessel, *St Kilda*, is a fishing vessel
registered in the United Kingdom. Her port of
registry is Inverness, and her port letters and numbers
are INS 47. Her overall length is 23.99 m. At the
material time she was fishing for a group of stocks
which were subject to total allowable catches, in
accordance with a white fish pressure stock licence for
the General North Sea and West of Scotland dated
1990. The respondent was required by the Com-
F munity regulations to keep a logbook of the operations
of the *St Kilda* and he entered in it the quantities of
each species caught and kept on board, and the dates
and locations of such catches, for four voyages
between 17 April 1990 and 16 May 1990, the dates of
departure and landing of which are set out in the
schedule to the complaint. The point at issue in the
case relates to the entries for the location of these
catches, and in order to understand the argument it is
necessary to say something first about the Community
regulations which contain the requirement.

The charge states that there was a failure to comply
with the provisions of Commission Regulation (EEC) G
no 2807/83, art 1 (1) and annexes I and IV, and
Council Regulation (EEC) no 2241/87, art 5. The
starting point for an examination of these provisions
is the Council regulation, and it is necessary first to
observe that the Regulation no 2241/87 of 23 July
1987 repealed and re-enacted with amendments an
earlier Council Regulation no 2057/82, the purpose of
which, like Regulation 2241/87, was to establish
certain control measures relating to fishing activities.
Article 16.2 of Regulation 2241/87 provides that refer- H
ences to the repealed regulation are to be construed as
referring to that regulation, and it is provided by the
same article that citations and references to the articles
of the repealed Regulation 2057/82 are to be read in
accordance with the correlation table set out in the
annex to Regulation 2241/87. The correlation table, so
far as relevant to the subject matter of the complaint,
provides that art 3 of Regulation 2057/82 is to be
equiparated to art 5 of Regulation 2241/87 and that
art 13 is to be equiparated to art 14. Article 5 of Regu- I
lation 2241/87 is concerned with the monitoring of
catches, and art 14 is concerned with the laying down
of detailed rules for implementing that article among
others which Regulation 2241/87 contains.

Article 5.1 of Regulation 2241/87 is in these terms:
[his Lordship narrated its terms and continued:]
Article 5.2 provides for exemption from the obligations of art 5.1 for vessels of overall length of 10 m or
under and for vessels of over 10 m but not over 17 m
if carrying out a fishing voyage outside the Skagerrak J
or the Kattegat of a maximum of 24 hours measured
from the time of leaving port to the time of re-entering
port. Article 14 of Regulation 2241/87 provides:
"Detailed rules for implementing Articles 3 to 10 of
this Regulation shall be adopted in accordance with
the procedure laid down in Article 14 of Regulation
(EEC) No 170/83".

The detailed rules to which art 14 refers are to be
found in Commission Regulation no 2807/83, references in which to Council Regulation no 2057/82 K
must be read as being references to the equivalent
articles in Council Regulation no 2241/87. Since
much of the discussion relates to the content of these
detailed rules it is appropriate to set out at this stage
those which are relevant to the keeping of the logbook.
In doing so we shall quote the relevant provisions,
substituting for references to Council Regulation no
2057/82 references to the equivalent Council Regulation no 2241/87.

The relevant paragraphs of the preamble to Com- L
mission Regulation no 2807/83, which is binding in its
entirety and directly applicable in all member states,
are as follows: [his Lordship quoted the terms of the
preamble set out supra and continued:]

Article 1 of Commission Regulation no 2807/83,
subject to the same amendment, is in the following
terms: [his Lordship quoted its terms and continued:]

Annex I sets out the form of the logbook, for each

A of the entries in which there is a reference number by which it can be linked to corresponding instructions in annex IV. The entry relative to the position of the vessel bears the reference number (14), and comprises three columns headed "Statistical rectangle", "ICES/NAFO zone" and "Non-member country's fishing zone". The areas of the sea to which these descriptions relate are shown on maps or charts inside the cover of the logbook. The sea is divided up into rectangles by vertical lines of longitude and horizontal lines of latitude as is usual in the case of a map. The reference to

B the statistical rectangle is to the squares formed by the crossing of these lines, each of which can be identified by a number and letter in the manner familiar to anyone who uses plans in common use such as a city guide. The reference to the ICES/NAFO zone is to areas of the sea of variable size, all of which are substantially greater than the statistical rectangle. The North Sea for example is divided into only three such areas. The reference to the non-member country's fishing zone is a reference to those zones which lie

C within the fishing limits of a country which is not a member of the EEC, such as Sweden or Norway. No issue arises in the present case about the entry in the logbook of a non-member country's fishing zone, because the respondent was fishing off the north west of Scotland and landing his catch at Lochinver at the time of the alleged offence. The question is whether it was sufficient for him to enter in his logbook, as he did in respect of all four voyages, the ICES/NAFO zone in which he was fishing or whether it was neces-

D sary for him also to enter the statistical rectangle.

Annex IV of Commission Regulation no 2807/83, which sets out the instructions to masters required to keep a logbook as shown at annex I, contains the following provision so far as relevant to this case: [his Lordship quoted the terms of annex IV set out supra and continued:]

It will be seen that some of the information is described in these provisions as optional, and that rule

E 2.1.2 refers to information which is compulsory. The question is whether it is compulsory for the master of the fishing vessel to fill in the entry relating to the statistical rectangle or whether the only information which is compulsory in regard to the position of the vessel at the time of the catch is the ICES/NAFO zone. It should be noted that the only zones for which total allowable catches were fixed, as at the dates in the schedule to the complaint, were ICES divisions of the sea. The evidence before the sheriff was that these

F divisions were by definition the smallest zones for which a TAC or quota had been fixed: see art 5 of Council Regulation no 2241/87. The sheriff was satisfied — and there can be no dispute about this point — that the Commission regulation is a detailed implementation of the general provision in the Council regulation. Nevertheless he saw no answer to the argument presented by the respondent's solicitor, that the location by reference to the smallest zone for which a total allowable catch had been fixed, which was the ICES zone, was all that was required and that since this was what the respondent had filled in when com-

G pleting his logbook he should be acquitted of the charge.

The sheriff's brief discussion of the matter, in his explanation of his reasons for accepting this argument, seems to ignore the detailed instructions set out in rule 2.4.1 of annex IV. As the Lord Advocate pointed out, he made no attempt to examine or interpret that paragraph. His approach concentrated instead on the provisions of art 5 of the Council regulation, and he appears to have been satisfied that it was sufficient for the respondent to have complied with what that article

H describes as the minimum requirement. Counsel for the respondent renewed that argument in his submissions in reply to the Lord Advocate's contention that the sheriff had erred in law. He also presented an alternative argument in regard to the detailed wording of rule 2.4.1, and he invited us to construe these provisions, if there was any doubt on the matter, strictly in the respondent's favour in view of the penal consequences of these rules if they were breached. We should mention that he indicated also that it was the

I respondent's intention to challenge art 3 of the Sea Fishing (Enforcement of Community Control Measures) Order 1985 on the ground that it had failed to implement the Community legislation according to its terms. But that argument was not presented to the sheriff, and no question about it is raised in the stated case. It is not a matter with which we can deal at this stage in these proceedings, and we make no assumption one way or the other as to its validity.

J The first point to be considered is whether it was sufficient in order to comply with the Community legislation that the respondent entered in his logbook the minimum amount of information in regard to position mentioned in art 5 of Council Regulation no 2241/87. This argument is difficult to reconcile with art 14 which states that detailed rules for implementing the article are to be adopted in accordance with the relative procedure in art 4 in Council Regulation no 170/83, and with the preamble to Commission Regulation no 2807/83. It is plain that the purpose of the

K Commission regulation is to lay down the detailed rules for implementing the requirement stated in art 5 of the Council regulation, and counsel for the respondent did not seek to suggest otherwise. His point was that on a proper reading of the preamble to the Commission regulation its rules must be read subject to art 5 of the Council regulation, and that in so far as the detailed rules might seem to require more than the minimum requirement set out in art 5 they were to be ignored. The Lord Advocate accepted that

L the detailed rules did require more than the minimum stated in art 5. They had "moved on", as he put it, but he maintained that it was open to the Commission to prescribe details which were more stringent and that this was what they had done. Here again the point in dispute was a narrow one, because counsel for the respondent did not contend that it was beyond the competence of the Commission to do this and he did not invite us to consider whether the detailed rules were ultra vires of the Commission. His point came in the end to be that the detailed rules were not to be con-

A strued as innovating on art 5 because there was no indication of an intention to do this in the preamble. He referred in particular to the last paragraph in the quotation from the preamble which we have given above. The provisions of art 5, he said, contained all that was necessary to ensure that there were standardised logbooks, and that being so there was no need to provide any more detailed rule.

But the latter part of the paragraph from the preamble which we have quoted makes reference to "more effective monitoring of current rules" and to

B facilitating "the scientific analysis of estimates of fish stocks and their exploitation". It is not hard to imagine that the Commission, on an examination of what was necessary to achieve these objects, decided that more detailed information than that mentioned in art 5 was required. One only has to look at the map to see that information which is confined only to stating the ICES zone as the location of the catches is imprecise. Zone IVa, in which the respondent was fishing at the relevant time, extends from the northern

C part of the Irish Sea to a point approximately half way between Cape Wrath and the Faeroe Islands. It would not be surprising therefore, given the intention to provide for more effective monitoring and to facilitate scientific analysis, if the detailed rules were to require a more precise location to be given — and the system of giving the location by reference to a statistical rectangle seems much more in keeping with what one would expect. At all events there is no indication whatever in this paragraph of the preamble that in

D case of conflict art 5 of the Council regulation is to prevail over the detailed rules. Moreover an examination of some of the other detailed rules, such as those which require information on the gear used, shows that the respondent's argument, if correct, would cause substantial difficulty. The minimum information about gear which is mentioned in art 5 is the type of gear used, but rule 2.3 of annex IV requires there to be stated also the mesh size in millimetres, with the capacity of the gear in certain other respects to be

E regarded as optional. If counsel for the respondent's argument is carried to its conclusion it would not be compulsory for the master to enter the mesh size in millimetres in his logbook, which would enable him to leave out one of the most important pieces of information required to monitor his fishing activity. It seems to us that the argument involves a misreading of the words "as a minimum" in art 5. The argument was that this was all that required to be stated in the logbook, but the more likely meaning of the article is

F that these are the minimum requirements to be provided for in the detailed rules and that it was open to the Commission, if so advised, to require more information than the minimum to be given. In any event that is the plain effect of the detailed rules, when the relevant legislation is read as a whole.

The second point is whether, on the reading of the detailed rules in annex IV, they require the master to give the location of his catch by reference to the statistical rectangle. As a preliminary to an examination of this argument it should be noted that what we

are concerned with here are rules, and that the stipulation in art 1 of Commission Regulation no 2807/83 is G that the logbooks "shall be completed in accordance with the instructions" set out in annex IV. Rule 2.1.2 of annex IV under the heading "How to complete the log-book" states that "All the compulsory information shall be given". It is also stated that rules considered optional at Community level may be made mandatory if a member state so wishes in respect of vessels flying the flag of that member state or registered there. So the information described as detailed rules falls into two categories — those which are compulsory and H those which are optional. Counsel for the respondent's argument was that the information about the statistical rectangle was optional, but we find that argument impossible to reconcile with the wording of rule 2.4.1. The opening section of that part of the rule which deals with the statistical rectangle is not qualified by any words which suggest that it is optional, whereas the concluding section of it states: "However, optional entries may be made in respect of all the statistical rectangles in which the vessel has fished during the I day". The plain implication of the opening words of this section is that the section which precedes it is compulsory. Counsel for the respondent's argument was in the end directed to the word "Examples" which precedes the detailed instructions about how each column is to be filled in. If these were examples, said counsel for the respondent, they could not be compulsory. But here again his approach seems to involve a misreading of the words used. The purpose of the reference to "Examples" is to give examples of J how to fill in the columns on the form with the information required, not to enable the master to make his own decision as to what is and what is not compulsory. We are in no doubt, that on a proper reading of the detailed rules, the master is required to insert in the logbook, in the manner described by reference to an example, the statistical rectangle in which most of the catches were made. It is not a sufficient compliance with the requirement of the detailed rules for him to state only the ICES zone in which the catches were K made. Counsel for the respondent suggested that it was asking too much of the master to be required to provide detail of this kind while engaged in fishing operations at sea. But we do not have the information which would be needed for us to form a judgment on this point. For all we know it would be relatively easy for the master to do this, given the sophisticated navigation equipment with which the larger fishing vessels to which these rules apply are equipped. In any event this was a matter for the Commission, and we cannot L ignore the plain meaning of the detailed rules by considerations of this kind.

Counsel for the respondent's last point was that we should construe these rules strictly in the respondent's favour in view of their penal consequences. But that submission is inconsistent with Community law which leaves it to the member state to take whatever steps it thinks appropriate, whether penal or otherwise, to give effect to Community legislation. Community legislation as such is not penal in character and it must be applied uniformly throughout the Community. For us to attempt to construe it by reference to domestic rules about the construction of penal legislation would be to apply rules of construction which have no part to play in the construction of regulations issued either by the Council or the Commission. In *R v Henn* [1981] AC at p 904H Lord Diplock issued a warning against the danger of an English court applying English canons of statutory construction to the interpretation of the treaty or for that matter of Community regulations or directives. Furthermore s 3 (1) of the European Communities Act 1972 provides that for the purposes of all legal proceedings any question as to the meaning or effect of any of the treaties, or as to the validity, meaning or effect of any Community instrument, shall be treated as a question of law and, if not referred to the European Court, be for determination as such in accordance with the principles laid down by and any relevant decision of the European Court or any court attached thereto. For these reasons we are quite unable to give effect to this submission, which in any event would only have raised a point of significance if there was reason to think that a strict construction would have led to a different result. In our opinion the wording of rule 2.1.2 is so clear on the point at issue in this case that there is no room for any construction of its provisions other than that the information about the statistical rectangle is to be regarded as compulsory.

Finally we should mention that we have not overlooked our obligation in terms of art 177 of the EEC Treaty, as the court in this country of last resort, to refer to any question as to the interpretation of any Community legislation to the European Court of Justice for a preliminary ruling. Had we been in doubt as to the point of interpretation raised in this case we would have been obliged to make such a reference, even although it was not submitted by either party that we should do so. In our opinion however the proper view of this case is that the point is too plain to raise a question of interpretation appropriate for decision by the European Court of Justice. In *R v Henn* Lord Diplock at p 906C said that English judges should not be too ready to hold that, because the meaning of the English text seemed plain to them, no question of interpretation could be involved. Nevertheless at p 905D he envisaged that there would be cases — the instance which he gave was where there was a series of decisions by the European Court of Justice, amounting to an established body of case law, which applied directly to the case before the court — in which an English court might properly take the view that no real question of interpretation was involved, making a reference under art 177 necessary in order to give judgment. We were informed that there are no decisions of the European Court of Justice as to the proper interpretation of the detailed rules for the keeping of the master's logbook. So it cannot be maintained that in this case there is an established body of case law which determines the point at issue. Nevertheless the answer to the various submissions which have been advanced for the respondent in this case is so plain that in our opinion no real question of interpretation is involved here, and we are in the position to issue our decision without having first obtained a preliminary ruling on the matter from the European Court of Justice.

We find further support for this approach upon a consideration of *Srl CILFIT and Lanificio di Gavardo SpA v Ministry of Health* in which consideration was given by the European Court of Justice to the purpose of art 177 and the scope of the obligation which it imposes on the court of final decision in a member state. It was held that the third paragraph of that article "is to be interpreted as meaning that a court or tribunal against whose decisions there is no judicial remedy under national law is required, where a question of Community law is raised before it, to comply with its obligation to bring the matter before the Court of Justice, unless it has established that the question raised is irrelevant or that the Community provision in question has already been interpreted by the Court or that the correct application of Community law is so obvious as to leave no scope for any reasonable doubt. The existence of such a possibility must be assessed in the light of the specific characteristics of Community law, the particular difficulties to which its interpretation gives rise and the risk of divergences in judicial decisions within the Community".

The judgment in this case tells us that we must bear in mind that Community legislation is drafted in several languages, the different language versions of which are all equally authentic. We must also bear in mind that Community law uses terminology which is peculiar to it and that legal concepts do not necessarily have the same meaning in Community law as in the law of the various member states. Finally we are told that every provision of Community law must be placed in its context and interpreted in the light of the provisions of Community law as a whole. It does not appear to us that the different language versions of the text of the regulations would make any difference to the point which we have been considering in this case, or that any peculiarity of Community terminology or of the legal concepts of the Community is in issue. No difficulty of this kind was drawn to our attention in the course of the argument. We have given full weight to the context in our examination of the text of the regulations and especially to the wording of the preamble to Commission Regulation no 2241/87. It is because we consider, having had regard to all these matters, that the answer to the point at issue in this case is so obvious as to leave no scope for any reasonable doubt that we are of the view that we are under no obligation to refer the question to the European Court.

For these reasons we consider that the sheriff's decision that the respondent was not obliged to enter the locations of his catches in his logbook by reference to the statistical rectangles was erroneous in point of law. We shall answer the question in the case in the affirmative and remit to the sheriff to proceed as accords.

A *Counsel for Appellant, Lord Advocate (Lord Rodger of Earlsferry, QC); Solicitor, J D Lowe, Crown Agent — Counsel for Respondent, Wright; Solicitors, Boyd Jameson, WS (for Mackinnons, Aberdeen).*

P W F

B

Garland v Fairnington

OUTER HOUSE

LORD PENROSE

11 JUNE 1992

Process — Reparation — Personal injuries — Optional procedure — Competency — Whether action cognitionis C *causa tantum competent under optional procedure — Rules of Court 1965, rule 188E.*

A person injured in a road accident raised an action of damages by way of the optional procedure. The driver who was blamed had died since the accident. The action was initially raised against the driver's daughter as "next of kin of the late Bryden Fairnington", concluding for payment of damages. Before defences were lodged, the pursuer lodged a minute of amendment seeking to substitute for the original con-
D clusion new conclusions including a decree for declarator cognitionis causa tantum. The pursuer's motion to have the minute of amendment received was opposed, the defender contending that an action cognitionis causa tantum fell outwith the scope of the optional procedure provided for by Rule of Court 188E.

Held, (1) that the conclusions in an action under the optional procedure were not restricted in scope to a conclusion for payment only, provided that the course
E of action was properly described as within the class of reparation for personal injuries (p 713C-D); and (2) that an action cognitionis causa tantum based upon a claim for damages for personal injuries fell within that class (p 713A-B); and motion *granted.*

Dictum of Lord Guthrie in *Smith v Tasker*, 1955 SLT 347 *commented upon* and *followed.*

F
Action of damages

Edgar Garland raised an action under the optional procedure seeking damages for personal injuries. The action was initially raised against Miss S Fairnington as defender seeking decree as next of kin and representative of the driver of the vehicle which had knocked him down. The pursuer lodged a minute of amendment substituting new conclusions including inter alia a conclusion for declarator cognitionis causa tantum that the sum of damages due was a just and lawful debt of the deceased.

The case called on the motion roll before the Lord Ordinary (Penrose) when counsel for the pursuer G moved the court to allow the minute of amendment to be received and a period of seven days for adjustment. The motion was opposed.

Statutory provisions
The Executors (Scotland) Act 1900, as amended, provides:

"6. When any sole or last surviving trustee or executor has died with any property (whether heritable or H moveable) in Scotland vested in him as trustee or executor, confirmation by his executors (if any) to the proper estate of such trustee or executor, or the probate granted in England and Wales or Northern Ireland to his executors and noting his domicile in England and Wales or in Northern Ireland, as the case may be shall, whether granted before or after the passing of this Act, be valid, and available to such executors for recovering such property, and for assigning and transferring the same to such person or persons as may be legally authorised to continue the I administration thereof, or, where no other act of administration remains to be performed, directly to the beneficiaries entitled thereto, or to any person or persons whom the beneficiaries may appoint to receive and discharge, realise and distribute the same, provided always that a note or statement of such property shall have been appended to any inventory or additional inventory of the personal estate of such deceased trustee or executor given up by his executors in Scotland, and duly confirmed; and provided further J that nothing herein contained shall bind executors of a deceased trustee or executor to make up title to such property, nor prejudice or exclude the right of any other person to complete a title to such property by any proceedings otherwise competent."

The Rules of Court 1965, as amended, provide:

"188E.—(1) The provisions of this section apply to an action of reparation for personal injuries or for the K death of a relative in which election has been made to adopt the procedure in this section.

"(2) Subject to the provisions of this section, the other provisions of the Rules of Court, so far as applicable, apply to the practice and procedure to which this section applies."

Cases referred to
Davidson Pirie & Co v Dihle's Representatives (1900) 7 SLT 384; (1900) 2 F 640. L
Emslie v Tognarelli's Executors, 1967 SLT (Notes) 66.
Mackenzie v Digby Brown & Co, 1992 SLT 891.
Smith v Tasker, 1955 SLT 347.
Stevens v Thomson, 1971 SLT 136.

Textbooks referred to
Bell, *Commentaries*, i, 749.
Erskine, *Institute*, II xii 46 and III ix 35.
Gloag and Henderson, *Introduction to the Law of Scotland* (9th ed), p 755.

A Mackay, *Manual of Court of Session Practice*, p 649.
Maclaren, *Court of Session Practice*, p 805.
Wilson and Duncan, *Trusts, Trustees and Executors*,
    p 463.

On 11 June 1992 the Lord Ordinary *granted* the
motion.

LORD PENROSE.—This is an action by way of
optional procedure at the instance of Edgar Garland
who was injured in a road traffic accident on or about
B 21 January 1989. He was struck and knocked down by
a motor vehicle driven by the late Bryden Fairnington.
Mr Fairnington died on 10 September 1990. At that
time discussions had already been under way for some
time between solicitors representing Mr Garland and
solicitors acting on the instructions of Mr Fairnington's insurers. Mr Garland and his representatives
were unaware of the death. Shortly before the expiry
of the triennium a summons at the instance of Mr
Garland was signeted calling Mr Fairnington as
C defender. Service by messenger at arms failed and it
was discovered that the defender had died. The
summons in the present action was signeted on 28
February 1992. At the motion roll hearing before me
on 29 May 1992 the defender's position on time bar
was expressly reserved and the argument took place on
a strictly limited basis. The action was raised initially
against Miss Fairnington, described in the instance as
"next of kin and representative of the late Bryden
Fairnington". The conclusion was in the following
terms: "For payment by the defender to the pursuer
D of the sum of £50,000 or such greater or smaller sum
as to the court shall seem proper with interest at the
rate of interest in Rule of Court 66 applicable at the
date of decree from the date of decree to follow hereon
until payment".

Before defences had been lodged the pursuer lodged
a minute of amendment to be received and for a period
of seven days for adjustment of its terms.

E   The minute of amendment, so far as material,
sought to substitute for the conclusion quoted above
new conclusions for declarator that the damages
sought by the pursuer were a just and lawful debt due
by the deceased Mr Fairnington; for declarator that
the pursuer was a just and lawful creditor of the
deceased for the same and had an interest in his estate
accordingly; for an order that the defender confirm as
executor and pay the damages or renounce her right;
and in that event for declarator cognitionis causa
F tantum that the sum of damages due was a just and
lawful debt of the deceased. It was anticipated that
failing confirmation by the defender the pursuer
would proceed to seek confirmation qua creditor. New
averments of fact were proposed to reflect the change
of conclusion. I was informed that since the preparation of the minute of amendment the pursuer had
ascertained that following the death of the deceased's
father who had been confirmed as executor dative,
Miss Fairnington had confirmed to the estate of her
late father as his executrix dative and that further
amendment would be required properly to reflect the

whole relevant sequence of events since the death of
Mr Fairnington.   G

I was addressed at length on the nature of the
remedy sought by the pursuer and referred by pursuer's counsel to Wilson and Duncan on *Trusts and
Trustees* at p 463; the Executors (Scotland) Act 1900,
s 6; *Emslie v Tognarelli's Executors*; *Smith v Tasker*;
Davidson Pirie & Co v Dihle's Representatives; *Stevens
v Thomson*, and to the terms of the optional procedure
rules in Rule of Court 188E and following paragraphs.
In response, counsel for Miss Fairnington referred me
to Erskine's *Institute*, Vol I, p 638 and in Vol II at   H
p 1021 at title III ix 35; Bell's *Commentaries*, i, 749;
Mackay's *Manual of Practice*, p 649; Maclaren on
Court of Session Practice at p 805; and *Gloag and
Henderson* (9th ed), p 755. In addition and by way of
analogy, counsel referred me to *Mackenzie v Digby
Brown & Co*.

The point at issue in the end was short. It was
whether an action cognitionis causa tantum was
within the scope of the Rule of Court 188E which   I
made provision for optional procedure in the case of
actions for reparation. The argument for the defender
was that an action cognitionis causa tantum was in a
special category separate from and distinct from
actions for enforcement of the substantive obligations
upon which it rested and that such actions did not
have the character of actions for enforcement of the
primary obligation. The extensive reference to
authority was designed to demonstrate the history of
such procedures and to show that in ancillary matters, J
such as the disposal of expenses, actions cognitionis
causa tantum were dealt with in a way that was
different from and incompatible with actions for
enforcement of the primary obligation. It was submitted that the Rule of Court was drawn in a particularly narrow way and that litigants who chose the
simplified procedure provided for did so at their peril.
The comparison with *Mackenzie v Digby Brown & Co*
was said to be apt. That was an application for interim
damages. Although the pursuer's complaint was   K
founded upon a claim that he had suffered loss and
damages through personal injuries, it was held that
he could not recover interim damages against his
solicitors.

In my opinion the analogy of *Mackenzie v Digby
Brown & Co* did not assist the defenders. On the contrary it pointed to the fundamental error in the
defenders' approach. The cause of action in *Mackenzie*
was the alleged breach of professional duty by the
solicitor to the pursuer. The damages sought to be   L
recovered had to reflect inter alia the reasonable anticipation of the level of award that the pursuer might
have recovered had his action against those responsible to him for breach of a duty of care to avoid injury
not been time barred. However, it was not exclusively
related to that breach and the claim founded on it. In
any event the fundamental difference depended upon
the classification of the cause of action. In the present
case the sole cause of action available to the pursuer
is the alleged breach of duty on the part of the late Mr

A Fairnington in driving his motor vehicle carelessly. Damages, should they be recoverable, will be quantified directly by reference to the loss and damage sustained by the pursuer as a result of any breach of duty by the deceased. The only difference between the present proceedings and proceedings raised directly against the late Mr Fairnington is that decree for payment cannot be enforced directly against the defender, who is called in a representative capacity only and for the purpose of instructing a competent claim against the estate of the deceased, including such

B rights as he had to indemnity under the policy of insurance issued to him during his lifetime. That this is of the nature of an action for reparation is in my opinion amply demonstrated in the opinion of Lord Guthrie in *Smith v Tasker*. It is not lightly to be thought that in describing an action of constitution as one for reparation Lord Guthrie used language in less than an accurate way.

The Rule of Court has as its purpose, in my opinion, the identification of proceedings according to

C cause of action. Counsel for the defender pointed to the appendix to the Rules of Court, and the form of conclusion provided for there, in support of his argument that actions for payment only fell within the scope of the provision. He argued that unless a defender were directly liable to the pursuer, the action could not come within the scope of the rule. In my opinion there is no reason why the form of conclusion cannot be adapted to the requirements of a case such as the present, provided only that the cause of action

D is properly described as within the class of reparation for damages for personal injuries.

Most of the analysis by pursuer's counsel of the historical background to actions cognitionis causa tantum was conceded by defender's counsel. Most of the analysis by defender's counsel was, in my opinion, aimed at establishing the procedural characteristics of such actions and failed to deal with the sole issue of substance, whether on a proper construction of the rule an action cognitionis causa tantum based upon a

E claim for damages for personal injuries fell within its scope. I shall allow the minute of amendment to be received and allow the seven days for adjustment proposed by the pursuer.

As already mentioned, the scope of the argument left untouched the substantial issue between the parties whether the proceedings are in any event competent.

F *Counsel for Pursuer, Clancy; Solicitors, Beveridge & Kellas, WS — Counsel for Defender, Hanretty; Solicitors, Gillam Mackie, SSC.*

P G L H

Stirling Aquatic Technology Ltd v Farmocean AB

G

FIRST DIVISION

THE LORD PRESIDENT (HOPE),
LORDS ALLANBRIDGE AND WEIR

17 JUNE 1992

Process — Commercial action — Motion to appoint action to procedure roll — Discretion of Lord Ordinary — Whether discretion properly exercised — Rules of H *Court 1965, rule 151 (4) (c).*

Rule of Court 151 (4) (c) provides that where in a commercial action the period of adjustment has expired, the court "shall . . . appoint the action to the procedure roll, or allow a proof, or a proof before answer", or make such other order as it thinks fit for the further progress of the action.

At a hearing by order on the commercial roll, the Lord Ordinary refused a motion by the first and I second defenders to appoint the action to the procedure roll and, on the pursuers' motion, allowed the parties a proof before answer. In the action the pursuers sought recovery of losses allegedly sustained when nets supplied by the defenders and used in fish farming, developed a hole with resulting loss of fish. The defenders sought to challenge the relevancy of the averments as to the cause of the hole and of a claim for economic loss. The Lord Ordinary took the view that it was unlikely that there would be sufficient sub- J stance in the defenders' arguments to enable the case to be disposed of without proof. The first and second defenders reclaimed, the second defenders raising the question of whether the Lord Ordinary had had a discretion in the matter.

Held, (1) that one of the principal objects of the procedure on the commercial roll was to enable disputes of a business or commercial nature to be dealt with as quickly as possible under the close supervision K of the court (p 715K); (2) that the word "shall" in rule 151 (4) (c) meant that the Lord Ordinary was required at this stage to choose between one or other of the three options in the rule, or to make such other order as he thought fit, bearing in mind the object of the procedure (p 716A); (3) that accordingly that matter was left to the discretion of the Lord Ordinary (p 716B); and (4) that he had not erred in the exercise of his discretion in this case (p 716G-H and K-L); and reclaiming motion *refused.*

L

Action of damages

Stirling Aquatic Technology Ltd raised a commercial action against (first) Farmocean AB and (second) Cosmos Trawl A/S seeking damages in respect of allegedly defective nets supplied for use on the pursuers' fish farm.

The case came before the Lord Ordinary (Coulsfield) by order on the commercial roll on the

A pursuers' motion for a proof before answer and the defenders' motion for the case to be sent to the procedure roll.

Statutory provisions

The Rules of Court 1965 provide, in relation to commercial actions:

"151.— . . . (4) At the first, or any subsequent hearing by order, the court — (a) may make such further order as it thinks fit for the speedy determination of the question in dispute between the parties;
B (b) may — (i) allow a specified period of adjustment; (ii) allow an amendment; (iii) ordain a party to give further specification of his case in his pleadings; (iv) allow a counter-claim to be lodged; (v) grant warrant for service of a third party notice; (vi) remit to a man of skill; (vii) where it proposes to appoint an action to the procedure roll under sub-paragraph (c) (i), ordain a party to lodge a concise note of his proposed argument within such time as it considers
C appropriate; (c) shall, where adjustment has not been allowed or the period of adjustment has expired — (i) appoint the action to the procedure roll, or allow a proof, or a proof before answer, of the whole or such part of the action as the court shall think fit; or (ii) make such other order as it thinks fit for the further progress of the action."

Case referred to

Muirhead v Industrial Tank Specialities Ltd [1986]
D   QB 507; [1985] 3 WLR 993; [1985] 3 All ER 705.

On 24 January 1992 the Lord Ordinary *allowed* a proof before answer.

LORD COULSFIELD.—This is a commercial cause arising out of a contract between the pursuers and the first defenders for the purchase of certain items including nets for use in commercial fish
E farming. Certain nets were supplied by the first defenders in pursuance of the contract. These nets were manufactured by the second defenders to the order of the first defenders. The ground of action against the first defenders is that the goods were not of merchantable quality, in conformity with s 14 (2) of the Sale of Goods Act 1979. The ground of action against the second defenders is failure to take due care in the manufacture of the nets. The respects in which the nets are said to have been defective are set out in
F art 3 of the condescendence. Briefly, the position is that upper and lower nets required to be attached to one another by lacing them together with thin green twine, a common rope and black twine passed over both the green twine and the common rope. The pursuers aver that in attaching the nets, the second defenders laced the black twine through the nets and the common rope but did not, as would have been reasonably required in the securing of the nets, "stopper off" the black twine by means of secure knots at regular intervals. The pursuers aver that the effect of that failure is that if any part of the twine is

broken, a hole opens up for a considerable distance whereas if the twine was secured at regular intervals G by suitable knots the hole would only develop as far as the next knot. The pursuers aver that on 26 March 1990, a hole about 4 ft square had developed in certain nets which had been used in a fish farm operated by the pursuers, and that as a result there had been a loss of stock. The loss claimed is based on a calculation of the amount of stock lost and the size and anticipated price of the fish comprised in that stock.

The case came before me on 24 January 1992 and H counsel for all parties indicated that no further period for adjustment was sought. Counsel for the pursuers requested that a proof before answer should be allowed and counsel for both the first and second defenders requested that the case be sent to procedure roll. As I understand the position, under Rule of Court 151 (4) (c), the court is entitled, in a commercial cause, to exercise discretion in deciding what the appropriate next step of procedure is. I accordingly asked counsel for the defenders to specify the grounds I on which it was suggested that it would be appropriate to send the case to the procedure roll. Counsel for the first defenders stated that he proposed to argue that in the absence of some explanation from the pursuers of how the hole was alleged to have originated, the case was irrelevant. Counsel for the second defenders indicated that he wished to raise a question of the relevance of a claim for economic loss. It is, it seems to me, obviously impracticable at a hearing of this kind to require the statement of a full argument, but J on the other hand it does appear to be necessary to exercise some judgment as to whether a procedure roll hearing is likely to advance or delay the resolution of the issues in the case. In the present case, it seemed to me unlikely that there would be sufficient substance in the first defenders' argument to enable the case to be disposed of without proof. The pursuers have stated a ground for maintaining that the nets were not of merchantable quality and, as I understand it, their case is to the effect that, given the circumstances in K which the nets were used, any hole that might have developed, however originated, would have been restricted to a limited size if the defenders had performed their obligations. As regards the second defenders' suggestion, it seemed to me that the pursuers' case is, at least primarily, based on a physical loss, namely a loss of stock belonging to them, and accordingly that the matter of the amount and nature of any loss could only be resolved after proof. In these circumstances, I decided that the appropriate course was to allow a L proof before answer.

The defenders reclaimed.

Reclaiming motion

The reclaiming motions were heard before the First Division on 17 June 1992.

Eo die the court *refused* the reclaiming motions.

The following opinion of the court was delivered by
A the Lord President (Hope):

OPINION OF THE COURT.—This is a reclaiming motion against an interlocutor which the Lord Ordinary pronounced on the by order commercial roll refusing a motion by the first and second defenders to appoint the cause to the procedure roll and, on the pursuers' motion, allowing the parties a proof before answer of their respective averments on record.

The Lord Ordinary took the view that, since this is
B a commercial cause and the Rule of Court which regulates the procedure was rule 151 (4) (c), he was entitled to exercise a discretion in deciding what was to be the next step of procedure. He recognised that it was impracticable at a hearing on the by order roll to require the statement of a full argument on the points which the defenders wished to raise. But, in order to enable him to exercise some judgment as to whether a procedure roll hearing was likely to advance or delay the resolution of the issues in the case, he asked
C counsel for the defenders to specify the grounds on which it was suggested that it would be appropriate to send the case to the procedure roll. The information which he was then given did not persuade him that this was the appropriate course. Counsel for the first defenders told him that he proposed to argue that the pursuers' case against them on the merits was irrelevant. But it seemed to the Lord Ordinary unlikely that there would be sufficient substance in their argument to enable the case to be disposed of without proof.
D Counsel for the second defenders indicated that he proposed to raise a question as to the pursuers' claim for damages, on the ground that since this was a claim for economic loss it was irrelevant. But in the view of the Lord Ordinary this also was a matter which could only be resolved after proof, since it seemed to him that the pursuers' case was, at least primarily, based on a physical rather than an economic loss as the claim was for a loss of stock belonging to them. In these circumstances he decided that the appropriate course
E was to allow a proof before answer.

The first question to be considered is whether the Lord Ordinary had a discretion in the matter at all. This point was not discussed in the hearing before him, and his view that he was entitled to exercise a discretion has not been challenged by the first defenders in their grounds of appeal. But the second defenders assert in their fourth ground of appeal that the Lord Ordinary was bound to send the cause to the procedure roll having regard to the motions made by the
F defenders in respect of their preliminary pleas, and that he thus erred in law in failing to do so. This proposition was modified somewhat by counsel for the second defenders at the outset of his argument, since he conceded that there could not be an absolute rule in this matter which obliged a Lord Ordinary to send a case to the procedure roll even where it was obvious that there was no proper basis for the plea. But he maintained that the Lord Ordinary was nevertheless obliged in the circumstances of this case to send the case to the procedure roll. The second defenders had

made it clear that there was a point of relevancy to be argued, and in these circumstances they were entitled G
to insist as of right that it be considered on the procedure roll so that they should not be put to the trouble and expense of a proof.

This argument was directed to the wording of rule 151, which regulates the procedure in commercial causes following the lodging of defences, and in particular to para (4) of that rule which sets out the various orders which the court can make at the first or any subsequent hearing of the case by order. The relevant parts of this paragraph are as follows: "(4) At the H
first, or any subsequent hearing by order, the court — (a) may make such further order as it thinks fit for the speedy determination of the question in dispute between the parties; (b) may — [here follow seven orders of various kinds which may be made, including allowing a specified period of adjustment]; (c) shall, where adjustment has not been allowed or the period of adjustment has expired — (i) appoint the action to the procedure roll, or allow a proof, or a proof before answer, of the whole or such part of the action as the I
court shall think fit; or (ii) make such other order as it thinks fit for the further progress of the action."

The effect of the word "shall" in para (4) (c) was said to be that the court normally had no discretion in the matter. The words "as the court shall think fit" at the end of para (4) (c) (i) ought not to be read as qualifying the whole of that subparagraph, but were to be read as qualifying only the words "such part of the action" at the end of it. Rule 188J (6) (a) (vi) which provides that the Lord Ordinary under the optional J
procedure "may . . . on special cause shown appoint the action to be heard on the procedure roll" had adopted a quite different approach, which was plainly to leave the matter to the discretion of the Lord Ordinary. The wording of the present rule indicated an intention not to innovate on the ordinary practice of the court by which, when parties are heard on the by order (adjustment) roll under Rule of Court 91 (3) (b), there is an opportunity for a party to insist that the case be sent to the procedure roll on a plea to competency or relevancy rather than having the point left K
over for discussion until after a proof.

One of the principal objects of the procedure on the commercial roll is to enable disputes of a business or commercial nature to be dealt with as quickly as possible under the close supervision of the court. The guiding principle is to be seen in para (4) (a). This provides that, at the first or any subsequent hearing by order, the court shall make such further order as it thinks fit for the speedy determination of the question L
in dispute between the parties. The various orders mentioned in para (4) (b) are orders which may or may not be appropriate according to the circumstances. But none of these incidental orders can lead to the determination of the question between the parties. For this to be done a hearing on the procedure roll or a proof or a proof before answer will be required. That is why the court is directed in para (4) (c) that it "shall", where adjustment has not been allowed or the period of adjustment has expired, appoint the action

to the procedure roll or allow a proof or a proof before answer. Now the word "shall" here does not mean that the Lord Ordinary is obliged to appoint the action to the procedure roll simply because a party has asked him to do so. What he is obliged to do at this stage is to choose between one or other of the three alternatives, or to make such other order as he thinks fit for the further progress of the action — see para (4) (c) (ii) — bearing in mind always the guiding principle set out in para (4) (a). The rules relating to the optional procedure are different, but no assistance is to be gained from an examination of these differences in construing the effect of the rules. It is sufficient to say that the wording of para (4) (c) read as a whole, and taken together with para (4) (a), leaves this matter of procedure to the discretion of the Lord Ordinary.

The remainder of the argument was directed to the question whether that discretion was properly exercised in this case. Counsel for the first defenders, while accepting that there were obvious limits to the extent to which the substance of his argument could be examined on the by order roll, submitted that the Lord Ordinary had not fully appreciated the point which he wished to raise. His point, which was directed to the relevancy of the pursuers' case against these defenders under s 14 (2) of the Sale of Goods Act 1979, was not just that there was an absence of explanation as to how the hole in the nets had originated. That had to be seen in the light of the pursuers' averment that the nets had been supplied to them in about August 1988 and had been used thereafter until March 1990 without complaint, and that they had been inspected regularly throughout this period and found to be in a wholly satisfactory condition. In the light of these factors the nets could not be said not to have been of merchantable quality when they were supplied. Accordingly the case was irrelevant and it ought to be disposed of on the procedure roll. He referred also to the expense to the defenders of having to bring witnesses to Scotland from Sweden and Denmark, and submitted that it was entirely consistent with the speedy determination of the question in dispute for the case to be sent for debate on the procedure roll in order to avoid the cost and inconvenience of a proof.

We are not persuaded, however, that the Lord Ordinary erred in the exercise of his discretion in declining to send this argument to the procedure roll. It seems to us that he was right to appreciate, as he explains in his opinion, that the pursuers' case was not related simply to the fact that a hole developed in the nets. He was entitled to take it from the pleadings that the case which was being made against these defenders was that, given the circumstances in which the nets were used, any hole that might have developed would have been restricted, if the defenders had performed their obligations, to such a size that the fish would not have escaped. The assessment that the argument was not of sufficient substance to enable the case to be disposed of without proof was for him to make. It was for him to judge whether the determination of the question between these parties would be advanced or delayed by a discussion of this point on the procedure roll. No doubt it can be said that a proof would be rendered unnecessary if, having heard argument on the procedure roll, the Lord Ordinary were then to sustain the plea to relevancy. On the other hand, time would clearly have been wasted if the only decision which the Lord Ordinary were to feel he could properly take on the procedure roll was to send the case to proof before answer. We can find no indication from what the Lord Ordinary has said in his opinion that he misdirected himself as to the point at issue, or that in any other way his discretion was not properly exercised.

We take the same view about the argument to be advanced by the second defenders. Counsel's point was that the pursuers' claim as averred was one for damages for pure economic loss. He maintained that the Lord Ordinary, to whom it seemed that their case was at least primarily based on the physical loss of their stock of fish, had misdirected himself because he had misunderstood the second defenders' argument. Recent cases such as *Muirhead v Industrial Tank Specialities Ltd* had made it clear that strict limits had been set to the claims which might be made by the ultimate purchaser of goods against their manufacturer, and that pure economic loss was not recoverable. This was an area of law of some complexity in which fine distinctions were often crucial, and there was a point of law of real substance which the Lord Ordinary had prejudged in the reasons which he had given for refusing to allow it to be discussed on the procedure roll.

It seems to us, however, that there may well be force in the Lord Ordinary's observation that the loss claimed by the pursuers in this case is at least primarily a physical loss. The amount of the claim is the net value of the fish which escaped, valued as at the date of the escape, not the loss of profits which may ultimately have resulted from the fact that the fish escaped prematurely from the nets. It was suggested that the only relevant claim would be for the replacement cost of the fish. But it is not obvious from the pleadings that the pursuers could have taken this approach to the quantification of their loss. Furthermore, the Lord Ordinary has not deprived the second defenders of their argument. What he said is that, in his view, the amount and nature of the claim — that is whether the claim is truly one for pure economic loss in the sense indicated in the authorities — could only be resolved after proof. That view was one which he was entitled to take in the circumstances, and we cannot say that he erred in the exercise of his discretion when he decided to reject the second defenders' motion that this point should be discussed first on the procedure roll.

For these reasons we consider that the Lord Ordinary's decision as to the order which he should pronounce was one which he was entitled to take in all the circumstances. Accordingly, we shall refuse these reclaiming motions and adhere to his interlocutor.

A *Counsel for Pursuers and Respondents, Shand; Solicitors, Boyd Jameson, WS — Counsel for First Defenders and Reclaimers, Peoples; Solicitors, Bell & Scott, WS — Counsel for Second Defenders and Reclaimers, Clarke, QC; Solicitors, Bird Semple Fyfe Ireland, WS.*

P A

B (NOTE)

Stark v Nairn Floors Ltd

OUTER HOUSE

LORD OSBORNE

25 JUNE 1992

C *Damages — Amount — Solatium and necessary services rendered to injured person — Hand and fingers — Partial amputation of ring finger.*

A 36 year old factory employee lost part of his right ring finger in an accident at work. He returned to work after about three months.

Opinion, that solatium was properly valued at £3,250, and that the services performed for him by his wife over the course of a few months after the accident were appropriately valued at £500.

D ——————————

Robert Stark raised an action against his employers Nairn Floors Ltd for damages for injuries sustained in an accident at work on 10 September 1986. He was then aged 36. He had trapped the fingers of his right hand between the hooks and the load while working with an overhead transporter in the factory. After a proof the Lord Ordinary (Osborne) held that the pursuer had failed to prove that the accident was the

E fault of his employers and granted absolvitor. In relation to damages, his Lordship continued:

"Despite the conclusion which I have reached on the merits of the action, it is appropriate for me to express my opinion on the matter of the quantification of damages. Two elements of damage were claimed: (1) solatium, and (2) damages under s 8 of the Administration of Justice Act 1982, in respect of services rendered to the pursuer by his wife.

F "Dealing first with the question of solatium, it was agreed that I should proceed upon the basis of the evidence relating to the pursuer's injuries, contained in two medical reports by Mr R A Buxton, a consultant orthopaedic surgeon, dated 3 May 1988 and 16 November 1991. These reports reveal that, following upon the accident, the pursuer was found to have had a traumatic amputation of the ring finger of the right hand immediately distal to the interphalangeal joint and small lacerations to the pulp of the middle and little fingers. He was admitted to the orthopaedic ward of Victoria hospital, Kirkcaldy, and later on the day of

the accident, under general anaesthetic, wound toilet and terminalisation of the right ring finger were per- G formed. It was necessary to do a formal amputation through the neck of the middle phalanx of the right ring finger and the wound was closed. The wounds on the pulps of the little and long fingers were cleaned and repaired using interrupted nylon. Antibiotics were administered against infection. The pursuer was discharged home the next day. The pursuer was subsequently seen in the outpatients department, finally on 23 October 1986, by which time the wounds had almost healed. There was some tingling sensation over H the tip of the amputated finger. The pursuer returned to work in December 1986.

"The position now is that there are very small, well healed scars over the tips of the pulps of the right long and little fingers. There is no related loss of sensation or sweating to these fingers and there is normal flexion and extension. The stump of the middle phalanx of the right ring finger has well healed. There is some diminution of sensation over the tip where there is a one centimetre linear scar which is healed. The subcu- I taneous tissues over the bone are very thin and on tapping it there is a painful sensation. The pursuer has full flexion of the interphalangeal joints of all fingers and although power grip is full on the index, middle and little fingers, it is weak over the right ring finger.

"Mr Buxton's opinion is that the pursuer has been left with some pain on sharp tapping over the tip of the amputation stump and that this will not now improve in the future. There is some consequent J slight loss of power grip due to the amputation. These drawbacks would stay with the pursuer for the rest of his life, but there would be no further untoward consequences of the injury such as osteoarthritis.

"In submitting that £3,500 would be an appropriate figure for solatium, counsel for the pursuer referred me to two decisions. These were *Lind v Lord Advocate*, 1982 SLT 277 and *Boyes v Carnation Foods Ltd*, 1986 SLT 145. Counsel for the defenders referred me in this connection to *McIntosh v Dundee* K *Port Authority*, McEwan and Paton on *Damages in Scotland*, p 480. Having regard to these cases and to the injuries sustained by the pursuer, as described by Mr Buxton, I have reached the conclusion that an appropriate sum for solatium would have been £3,250. It was agreed between the parties that 75 per cent of whatever figure I might award for solatium could properly be seen as attributable to the past. On that proportion of the figure which I have settled for solatium, I would have awarded interest at the rate of L 7½ per cent from the date of the accident to date.

"As regards the claim for damages under s 8 of the Administration of Justice Act 1982, evidence was given by the pursuer and his wife. The pursuer indicated that, after leaving hospital, he was not able to do anything with his right hand for around two months, after which the situation began to improve. As a result the pursuer's wife had to do a number of jobs which he normally did, such as lighting fires and chopping sticks. She also had to perform personal tasks for the pursuer such as helping him put on shoes. He thought that it took his wife up to two hours per day to perform the various tasks which she had to do on account of the consequences of his injury. The pursuer's wife confirmed that she had had to perform a number of additional tasks for the pursuer on account of his inability to do so. These tasks included a range of personal duties such as dressing and undressing the pursuer, washing and drying him, attending to his shoes, and the like. She also had to deal with the consequences of a rewiring operation in the house, which, had he been fit, the pursuer would have dealt with. The pursuer's wife's additional tasks were carried out over a period of about four months after which they tailed off. In connection with this part of the claim, I was referred to the case of *White v University of Dundee*, 1990 SLT 545, where £500 was awarded under this head. It was contended that more was involved in that case than in the present one.

"Doing the best that I can in all the circumstances, the conclusion which I have reached is that a sum of £500 would have been appropriate here as damages under this head."

Counsel for Pursuer, Peebles; Solicitors, Digby, Brown & Co — Counsel for Defenders, Shand; Solicitors, Simpson & Marwick, WS.

C H

Berry v Taylor

OUTER HOUSE

LORD COULSFIELD

17 JULY 1992

Diligence — Arrestment — Effect of subsequent sequestration of common debtor — Whether subjects of arrestment vested in trustee in sequestration — Bankruptcy (Scotland) Act 1985 (c 66), ss 31 (1), 33 (3) and 51.

Section 31 (1) of the Bankruptcy (Scotland) Act 1985 provides that subject to s 33, the whole estate of the debtor shall vest in the permanent trustee for the benefit of the creditors. Section 33 (3) preserves "the right of any secured creditor which is preferable to the rights of the permanent trustee", as does s 51 (6) which deals with priority of distribution of the estate.

A wife suing her husband for divorce effected arrestments on the dependence of the action. She obtained decree and raised an action of furthcoming calling the holder of the arrested funds as first defender. Prior to the raising of said action the husband had been sequestrated. His trustee was called as second defender.

The wife contended that her right was that of a secured creditor in terms of s 33 (3) of the 1985 Act and that the arrested fund did not fall to be included

in the vesting in the trustee by virtue of s 31 (1). She further argued that the lack of provision for payment of a secured creditor in s 51, and the saving provision in s 51 (6), indicated that she was entitled to be paid without going through the machinery of the sequestration.

Held, (1) that the terms of s 31 (1) were effective to vest the arrested fund in the trustee and that the provisions of s 33 (3) were given effect to by requiring the trustee to give effect to the preferences secured by arrestment, these provisions reflecting the earlier bankruptcy legislation (p 720E-F); (2) that while s 51 had no exact parallel it also reflected the pre-existing law whereby the trustee realised subjects, including arrested funds, and ranked the creditors according to their preferences (p 720G-I); and action *dismissed.*

Action of furthcoming

Rebecca Deane or Berry raised an action of furthcoming against (first) Peter Cranbourne Taylor, judicial factor on a business formerly carried on by the pursuer and her former husband Edward Harris Berry, and (second) Graham Ritchie, trustee in sequestration of Edward Harris Berry, in respect of sums arrested on the dependence of the pursuer's action of divorce.

The case came before the Lord Ordinary (Coulsfield) on procedure roll.

Statutory provisions

The Bankruptcy (Scotland) Act 1985 provides:

"31.—(1) Subject to section 33 of this Act, the whole estate of the debtor shall vest as at the date of sequestration in the permanent trustee for the benefit of the creditors; and — (a) the estate shall so vest by virtue of the act and warrant issued on confirmation of the permanent trustee's appointment; and (b) the act and warrant shall, in respect of the heritable estate in Scotland of the debtor, have the same effect as if a decree of adjudication in implement of sale, as well as a decree of adjudication for payment and in security of debt, subject to no legal reversion, had been pronounced in favour of the permanent trustee. . . .

"(4) Any moveable property, in respect of which but for this subsection — (a) delivery or possession; or (b) intimation of its assignation, would be required in order to complete title to it, shall vest in the permanent trustee by virtue of the act and warrant as if at the date of sequestration the permanent trustee had taken delivery or possession of the property or had made intimation of its assignation to him, as the case may be. . . .

"33.—. . . (3) Sections 31 and 32 of this Act are without prejudice to the right of any secured creditor which is preferable to the rights of the permanent trustee. . . .

"51.—. . . (6) Nothing in this section [order of priority in distribution] shall affect — (a) the right of a secured creditor which is preferable to the rights of the permanent trustee".

Case referred to

A *Lindsay v Paterson* (1840) 2 D 1373.

Textbooks referred to

Goudy, *Bankruptcy* (4th ed), pp 254, 330.
Stewart, *Diligence*, p 186.

On 17 July 1992 the Lord Ordinary *sustained* the
second defender's first, second and third pleas in law
and *dismissed* the action.

B **LORD COULSFIELD.**—The pursuer and her
former husband Edward Harris Berry (the common
debtor) at one time carried on business in partnership.
The first defender is the judicial factor on that business: the date of his appointment is not specified but
was earlier than any of the events material for the
present purpose. The pursuer raised proceedings for
divorce against Edward Harris Berry and arrestments
on the dependence of that action were made, in the
C hands of the first defender, on 6 April 1989 and 25
April 1989. The pursuer avers that the arrestments
were for the sums of £200,000 and £825,000 respectively and that a sum of £100,000 was arrested in the
hands of the first defender. Decree in the action
followed on 16 February 1990 and the common debtor
was found liable to pay to the pursuer the sum of
£683,250. The pursuer avers that the sum of
£155,998.78 has been recovered from the common
debtor in respect of that decree. The common debtor
D was thereafter sequestrated, the effective date of the
sequestration being 23 September 1991. The present
action is an action of furthcoming in which the
pursuer seeks decree against the first defender for the
sum arrested in his hands. The first defender admits
that funds have been arrested and avers that the
balance of arrested funds as at 6 November 1991 was
£117,324.09. The first defender's position is that he
cannot pay out the sum arrested in so far as there is
a competition for that sum between the pursuer and
E the second defender and other secured creditors. The
second defender claims that the sum arrested should
be paid over to him so that he can administer it and
give effect to any secured claims which the pursuer
may have. He also makes certain further averments, to
which I shall refer later, but which are not relevant to
the principal issue debated in this case.

The case came before me in the procedure roll on 27
June 1992. Counsel for the second defender submitted
that effect should be given to his principal claim and
F that the sum in question should be paid over to the
second defender under reservation of the rights which
the pursuer had obtained by her arrestment. Counsel
for the pursuer submitted that the arrested funds were
exempted from the general vesting of the bankrupt
estate in the trustee and that the pursuer was entitled
to payment of them.

The relevant statutory provisions are contained in
the Bankruptcy (Scotland) Act 1985. Section 31 (1)
provides: [his Lordship quoted the terms of s 31 (1)
and then s 31 (4) and continued:]

Section 33, by subss (1) and (2), exempts certain
property from the vesting in the permanent trustee
G but those exemptions are not relevant for the present
purpose. Section 33 (3) provides: [his Lordship quoted
the terms of s 33 (3) and continued:]

Section 37 of the Act provides, inter alia, that the
order awarding sequestration shall have the effect, in
relation to diligence done, whether before or after the
date of the sequestration, in respect of any part of the
debtor's estate, of an arrestment in execution and
decree of furthcoming. Section 51 lays down the order
H of priority of distribution of the debtor's estate and
defines certain debts as preferred and certain other
debts as postponed. Section 51 (6) provides: "Nothing
in this section shall affect — (a) the right of a secured
creditor which is preferable to the rights of the permanent trustee".

Section 73 defines the expression "secured creditor"
as "a creditor who holds a security for his debt over
any part of the debtor's estate", and the word
"security" as "any security, heritable or moveable, or
I any right of lien, retention or preference".

Counsel were agreed that the provisions of the 1985
Act with regard to equalisation of diligence did not
affect the arrestment in the present case and that the
pursuer was properly to be regarded as a secured
creditor, for the purposes of the provisions above
quoted. The submission for the second defender was
that the arrested funds were part of the estate of the
bankrupt and were therefore vested in the trustee by
J virtue of s 31 and were not exempted by s 33, the only
effect of which, for the purposes of the present action,
was to preserve the arrestor's priority as a secured
creditor without affecting the vesting of the funds.
Counsel submitted that the position under the law
before the 1985 Act was, very clearly, that the whole
estate vested in the trustee who administered it, and
would give effect to any proper preference established
by an arrestment. That system had been quite
adequate and workable and had ensured that the
K interests of all creditors were satisfied, and there was
nothing in the 1985 Act or in the Scottish Law Commission report no 68, which preceded it, to suggest
that there was any intention to change that system.
Counsel for the pursuer submitted that the cumulative
effect of the statutory provisions was to exempt the
funds in question from vesting in the trustee. The
pursuer was a secured creditor and the question was
how she was to get the benefit of that security,
through the trustee or directly. If, however, the
L benefit was to be obtained through the trustee, that
would largely involve ignoring the terms of the 1985
Act. The provisions of s 31 were clearly subject to
those of s 33 (3). Unlike previous legislation, the 1985
Act set out, in s 51, a specific order of distribution of
the estate and that provision did not include any reference to payment to a secured creditor so that there was
no method by which the trustee could give the pursuer
the preference to which she was entitled. If the only
course which the trustee could take would be to pay
the funds to the creditor who held the security, there

A was no justification for allowing those funds to be included in the vesting and the specific provisions of s 51 (6) themselves indicated that the secured creditor was entitled to be paid without going through the machinery of the sequestration. The provisions in regard to distribution constituted a material departure from the provisions of the earlier legislation and indicated that the system which had operated under that legislation could no longer be given effect to.

The rule of law which was in operation before the 1985 Act is stated in Stewart on *Diligence* as follows:
B "Although the arrestment or poinding has been executed prior to the sixty days before notour bankruptcy, if no decree of furthcoming has been obtained, or sale carried through, at the date of sequestration, the property arrested or poinded vests in the trustee in virtue of his confirmation, and he is entitled to delivery of it; but the arrester or poinder having acquired a preference has this reserved in the ranking" (at p 186).

C A little later it is stated: "If decree of furthcoming has been obtained, or a sale carried through, before the date of sequestration, in virtue of an arrestment or poinding not cut down by the sequestration, the bankrupt having been divested, the subjects arrested or poinded or their proceeds do not pass to the trustee" (cf Goudy, *Bankruptcy* (4th ed), p 254).

The earliest authority cited for these propositions is *Lindsay v Paterson* in which it was held that the effect of the clear words of s 78 of the Bankruptcy Act 1839
D was to transfer the whole estate of the bankrupt to the trustee, who should give effect to any preference obtained by an arrestment. The relevant provisions of s 78 of the 1839 Act were as follows: "that the moveable estate and effects of the bankrupt, wherever situated, so far as attachable for debt, shall, by virtue of the act and warrant of confirmation in favour of the trustee, be transferred to, and vested in him or any succeeding trustee for behoof of the creditors, absolutely and irredeemably, as at the date of the
E sequestration, with all right, title and interest, to the same effect as if actual delivery or possession had been obtained, or intimation made at that date, subject always to such preferable securities as existed at the date of the sequestration, and are not null or reducible".

There is, in my view, no material distinction between the provisions of s 78 of the 1839 Act and those of ss 31 and 33 of the 1985 Act, so far as relevant for the present purpose. In each Act, there is specific
F provision for vesting of the moveable estate in the trustee; and the definition of the effect of that vesting, namely that it is equivalent to delivery or intimation, is in substance the same. Further, the provisions with regard to the preservation of the rights of secured creditors are parallel and no material distinction can be drawn between them. The same can, in my view, be said of the relevant provisions of the Bankruptcy (Scotland) Act 1913, which are found in s 97. Again, there is provision for vesting of the whole estate, for the effect and extent of such vesting and for the preser-

vation of preferable securities which existed at the date of the sequestration. The only difference between the G pre-1985 legislation and the Act of 1985 is that to which counsel for the pursuer drew attention, namely, that s 51 sets out precise provisions directing the trustee how to pay out the bankrupt's estate. It is, so far as I am aware, true that no such precise provisions were found in the 1913 or 1839 statutes. There was, however, provision in s 123 of the 1913 Act for ranking of creditors by which the trustee was required to divide the creditors into three classes, preferable, ordinary and contingent (see Goudy, supra, p 330). H Secured creditors, such as arresters who had not proceeded to a furthcoming, and whose security, therefore, was a mere nexus without possession were included among the preferable creditors, and the trustee would realise the subjects in question and rank the creditors upon them according to their preferences. In my opinion, therefore, all that has been done in s 51 of the 1985 Act is to express precisely the rule of law which was already held to be in operation under the earlier legislation, and there is therefore no I material change brought about by the 1985 Act. It follows, in my view, that the same effect should be given to the clear words of the 1985 Act transferring the whole estate of the bankrupt to the trustee as was given to the clear words of the earlier legislation. The statute provides expressly for vesting of all the estate in the trustee. Subjects which have been arrested are still included in the estate of the bankrupt, even though a nexus has been established over them in favour of the creditor. Since, however, the statute also J expressly saves the rights of secured creditors such as, in this instance, arresters, effect must also be given to that provision and that effect is given by requiring the trustee to work out and give effect to the preferences which have been secured by arrestment.

The facts relevant to the present issue are not in dispute and I shall therefore, as invited by counsel for the second defender, sustain his first three pleas in law and dismiss the action.

I also heard argument as to the relevancy of certain K other averments on record, particularly those of the second defender, relating to the amount of funds arrested and to previous arrestments which are said to have been made and satisfied. I do not think it necessary to discuss these issues, especially as it was, I think, clear that, if the matter were to be taken any further, amendment to make these averments more specific would be necessary.

L

Counsel for Pursuer, Dorrian; Solicitors, Drummond Miller, WS — Counsel for First Defender, Davidson; Solicitors, Shepherd & Wedderburn, WS — Counsel for Second Defender, Ellis; Solicitors, Macbeth, Currie & Co, WS.

S D D N

(NOTE)

Young v Greater Glasgow Health Board

OUTER HOUSE

LORD CAMERON OF LOCHBROOM

27 NOVEMBER 1992

Damages — Amount — Solatium and loss of earnings — Back — Soft tissue injury to back with pre-existing degenerative changes — Contribution of later accident.

A 42 year old nursing auxiliary fell, causing soft tissue injury to her back. She had a history of back injuries and sustained a further injury about one year later. By the time of the proof she was in lighter employment earning about £30 per week less than if she had continued in her pre-accident employment.

Opinion, that solatium was reasonably valued at £2,500 to date and £500 for the future and that an award of future wage loss limited to £2,000 would have been appropriate.

———————

Maureen Young raised an action against her former employers, the Greater Glasgow Health Board, for damages in respect of injuries sustained in an accident at work on 14 August 1988. She was then aged 42. She slipped and fell on a recently washed floor. After a proof before the Lord Ordinary (Lord Cameron of Lochbroom) the case advanced by the pursuer, that the cleaner had not placed in position a warning cone, was disproved and the defenders were assoilzied. In relation to damages his Lordship said:

"On record the pursuer claims that she has suffered from back pain since the time of the accident which had increased with the passage of time and which radiates into her right leg and also causes her to experience paraesthesiae in her right foot. She states that she became increasingly unable to carry out her duties and although she attempted to continue working, was forced to cease working on or about 21 September 1989. She further states that prior to the accident in August 1988 she had no significant episodes of back pain since about 1979 and that any other episodes of back pain were not of significant duration and are not relevant to her present condition.

"In her own evidence the pursuer agreed that she had had trouble with her shoulder as a result of a patient lift in 1978. She described a fall in 1980 when she had a fracture of the coccyx but this had subsequently cleared up. This last episode appears to be that described by Mr McKay, the pursuer's expert medical witness, in his report of 5 June 1992 where he describes a fall down stairs causing the pursuer to hurt the bottom of her back in the midline around the coccyx after which she was off work for some three months. The pursuer however also agreed that she had suffered from backache in September 1979 for a period of two weeks. She had also fallen and strained her back and had an x-ray of her neck in December 1979. In August 1980 she had strained her left shoulder. In July 1981 she had suffered an accident following which she had had pain in her neck and left shoulder. In May 1983 she had a lifting episode following which she had back pain in the thoracic area and in September 1984 she had suffered an episode of muscular back strain. Thereafter until the incident in 1988 she said that she had had no significant trouble except periods of muscular strain from lifting patients. While it would appear from the evidence of Mr Kelly, the defender's expert medical witness, and the terms of the reports from Mr Scott, a surgeon who examined the pursuer twice on instructions from the pursuer's solicitors, that the pursuer was not wholly forthcoming about her medical history prior to 1988, the significance of this extends, in my opinion, only to her credibility and has no immediate relationship to the nature of the accident and the injuries sustained from it in 1988. Of more significance is the fact that in March 1989 an x-ray indicated some minor degenerative changes in the pursuer's lumbar spine indicating the probability that in August 1988 there had been some degenerative changes of the lumbar spine present for some time prior thereto. . . .

"The pursuer gave evidence that on an occasion in June or July 1989 she again slipped on a floor striking her elbow and twisting her back as she went down. She said that she worked on after this accident for some three months or so but eventually stopped work because when lifting patients, she found that the pain in her back was getting worse and worse. The contemporary general practitioner records show that on 21 September 1989, the pursuer was seen and was then complaining of backache following a fall at work. She was at that time certified as unfit for work. Dr Roxby, the pursuer's general practitioner, gave evidence that the complaint of back pain at that time was, she imagined, a product of the fall in August 1988 as she was unaware of a second fall. She also said that the complaints of back pain recorded in the general practitioner records thereafter appeared to be related to the same part of the back as those made prior to September 1989. Reference to a second fall appears in Mr Scott's report after his first examination of the pursuer. He then received an account from the pursuer of the fall as having occurred in July 1989. Subsequently at his second examination in March 1991 Mr Scott reports that the pursuer had told him then that she had 'injured her back' in that fall.

"My clear impression of the whole evidence is that this second incident resulted in an exacerbation of the existing lesion in the pursuer's back. This conclusion is supported by the evidence of each of the three surgeons who examined the pursuer. As Mr Kelly put it, the second fall could have either accelerated or exacerbated the pursuer's previous back condition. He said that if there was continuing pain, the second fall could have contributed to the pursuer's present symptoms even if those symptoms dated from the first fall. Though Mr McKay differed as to the source of the symptoms which followed the first fall, he agreed

that his position was close to the views expressed by
A Mr Kelly and Mr Scott in their reports to the effect
that those symptoms were caused by a combination of
the effects of both falls, though he ascribed more
importance to the first than to the second fall.
However of equal importance is the view that both Mr
Kelly and Mr McKay expressed in evidence that the
pursuer's present condition was also related to her
back history prior to August 1988. This view is also
expressed by Mr Scott in his report dated 27 March
1991, a view from which Mr McKay did not differ.
B This was to the effect that the general practitioner's
records indicated that the pursuer had obviously had
intermittent problems with her neck, back and left
shoulder long before she injured herself in 1988. Mr
Scott's view was that her symptoms in March 1991
then appeared to be worse than they had been previously. He felt that she was then unable to carry out
nursing duties and doubted if she would be able to do
so in the future. He also expressed the view that she
was only moderately restricted but that a job which
C involved repeated lifting, often in awkward situations,
would, he thought, prove impossible for her. His
overall view was that the pursuer had a disability,
which in view of her past history, was partially
attributable to the injury in 1988. This expression of
view was also consistent with that expressed both in
his report and in evidence by Mr Kelly. The pursuer
herself in evidence when speaking to the history of
back trouble prior to August 1988, agreed that she had
been having problems in what she called muscular
D strain when lifting patients. As already noted, the
x-rays taken after August 1988 indicated the presence
of some degenerative changes which, as Mr McKay
put it in his report of 5 June 1992, made any recovery
from a soft tissue injury likely to be more prolonged
than normal and less complete than normal. The
balance of the medical evidence indicates, in my
opinion, that the pursuer was already vulnerable to
further back injury prior to 1988. Even if she had not
suffered an accident in August 1988 it is probable that
E the combination of her prior back condition and a
further injury such as she sustained in July 1989
would have affected her continuing to work as an
auxiliary nurse.

"On the other hand I am satisfied that the continuing complaint of back pain prior to the second fall in
July 1989 suggests that the pursuer was still suffering
from the effects of her accident in August 1988 and
that the probability was that the symptoms would
have persisted for some substantial period of time
F thereafter. The consequence was to make the effects of
the second accident more acute than they would otherwise have been. While there was no specific evidence
which bore on this matter other than Mr McKay's
opinion that the present complaints of back pain are
related to the first rather than to the second accident,
Mr Kelly being unable to reach a clear view as to
which was more important, it is perhaps significant
that Mr McKay in his opinion expressed in his report
of 5 June 1992, at which time he appeared to be
unaware of any problems of back pain prior to August

1988, indicated that the degree and extent of back pain
is frequently related to the type of work in which a G
person is involved and that he was not unduly surprised that the pursuer eventually gave up her rather
heavy work. He observed that back pain in the pursuer's age group was a frequent cause for having to
stop nursing, particularly at the heavier elements of
nursing. He also noted that the current intake of mild
analgesics by the pursuer was relatively modest and he
thought that this was an indication of the level of
trouble that she is now experiencing in much lighter
work. H

"The balance of the evidence points, in my view, to
the probability that even had she not suffered an
accident in August 1988, the pursuer would, having
suffered a fall in July 1989, have been required to consider giving up employment as a nurse within a period
of two or three years thereafter because of continuing
chronic back pain associated with the fall in July 1989.
The chronicity of back pain suffered by her after
August 1988 and prior to July 1989 appeared from her
own evidence and her continuing complaints of pain I
to her general practitioner at that time. In this regard
I also take account of the impression which the
pursuer appeared to give to Mr McKay as a somewhat
anxious person. I consider that while the symptoms of
back pain had eased prior to the second fall, they were
still of a character such as to suggest that they were
persistent and would have taken some time to clear up.

"Counsel for the pursuer suggested that a sum of
£4,500 might be awarded for solatium on the basis J
that the most substantial element in the pursuer's persisting condition is the injury from the first accident.
She referred me to *McGahan v Greater Glasgow Health
Board*, 1988 SLT 270, which with the updating factor
taken from Kemp and Kemp on *Quantum of Damages*
brought out a figure of £4,500. She also made reference to the case of *Thomson v Queensberry House
Hospital*, OH, 18 May 1990, unreported (1990 GWD
21-1194) and *McLachlan v D B Marshall (Newbridge)
Ltd*, 1992 SLT 131. Counsel for the defenders under K
reference to *McGahan* and *McMillan v D B Marshall
(Newbridge) Ltd*, 1991 SLT 229, suggested a figure of
between £2,000 and £2,500. In my opinion, the
pursuer is entitled to solatium for pain and suffering
sustained by her between the date of the accident until
July 1989 together with something for the effects
which that accident continued to have to date in relation to her condition following the second fall. In
broad terms I would assess this at a figure of £2,500
to represent pain and suffering to date. On the medical L
evidence I think it unlikely that the symptoms would
have been fully relieved by the present date but that
any future effect would have been limited. I would
have assessed this at the sum of £500. On the figure
for solatium to date I would have awarded interest at
the rate of 7½ per cent per annum from the date of the
accident to the date of decree.

"Parties are agreed that the past wage loss to date
inclusive of interest is £1,500. So far as future wage
loss is concerned, counsel for the pursuer argued that

A any award should also reflect the pursuer's disability in the earnings market. As a home support worker with Strathclyde Regional Council she is presently working something of the order of 16 hours a week at a maximum as compared with 22 hours a week that she worked as a nursing auxiliary. As a home support worker her hourly rate of pay is £3.8826 per hour. If she had continued in work as a nursing auxiliary her present rate of pay would have been £4.3828 per hour. On a very broad basis she is losing earnings at about £30 per week. Counsel for the pursuer suggested that

B taking a broad approach to future wage loss it should be fixed at a figure of £6,000. On the other hand on the basis that the pursuer would have continued at best to remain in employment as an auxiliary nurse for some uncertain period even from the present but for the accident, counsel for the defender suggested that taking all the imponderables into account a figure of £2,000 should be awarded. I have come to the conclusion that any sum for future loss should be relatively small. The nature of the pursuer's prior back com-

C plaints and the material contribution of the accident in July 1989 to her present state, leads me to take the view that it was likely that even by the present day or at least in the reasonably short term future she would have required to give up employment as an auxiliary nurse. On a broad view I think a figure of £2,000 suggested by counsel for the defenders would have been reasonable."

———

D *Counsel for Pursuer, Caldwell; Solicitors, Robin Thompson & Partners — Counsel for Defenders, R W J Anderson; Solicitor, R F Macdonald.*

C H

E # Quayle Munro Ltd, Petitioners

FIRST DIVISION
THE LORD PRESIDENT (HOPE),
LORDS ALLANBRIDGE AND MAYFIELD
27 SEPTEMBER 1991

Company — Share premium account — Cancellation of account and transfer of credit to special reserve — Application to court for confirmation — Protection of
F *creditors — Undertakings necessary from company — Whether moneys on special reserve distributable profits of company — Whether moneys might be used to redeem redeemable shares — Companies Act 1985 (c 6), ss 160 (1) (a) and 263 (2) and (3).*

A company applied to the court for cancellation of the amount standing to the credit of its share premium account. It undertook that the credit arising in its books would be carried to a special reserve, and that the special reserve would not be treated as realised profit or applied in making any distribution (other

than a capital issue of further shares) by way of divi- G dend, return of capital or otherwise to any of its members so long as there remained outstanding any debt or claim which would have been admissible in proof against the company had it been wound up on the date when the proposed cancellation took effect, except with the prior consent of all persons to whom such debts and claims were due. The latter undertaking was given subject to the proviso that nothing in the undertaking would prevent the company transferring all or part of the special reserve to the profit and loss account from time to time to the extent only H of any accrued losses on that account. The proviso was made subject to a further undertaking that there would be retained within the special reserve a sum sufficient to repay at par the preference shares then in issue until the shares had been redeemed out of the special reserve or from other available sources. The court appointed a reporter, who raised two questions for the court's consideration: first, whether the company was entitled, as envisaged by the proviso, to use the special reserve to write off future losses on its profit and loss I account; and secondly, whether the company was entitled, as envisaged by the further undertaking, to use the special reserve to redeem the redeemable shares.

Held, (1) that there was no objection in principle to the use of the special reserve to write off future losses (p 725C); and (2) that once the statutory requirements for the cancellation of the share premium account had been satisfied, the funds transferable to the special reserve would be available for all purposes to which distributable profits might be applied, subject to the J terms of the undertaking (p 726A-C); and cancellation of the share premium account *confirmed* and registrar of companies *directed* to register the undertaking and the order of the court.

———

Petition for confirmation of reduction of share premium account

Quayle Munro Ltd presented a petition to the Court of Session asking that the court confirm the cancel- K lation of its share premium account effected by special resolution of the company at an extraordinary general meeting on 17 September 1991.

On 27 September 1991 the petition came before the First Division on single bills on the petitioners' motion to grant the prayer of the petition.

Statutory provisions

The Companies Act 1985 provides:

L "160.—(1) Subject to the next subsection and to sections 171 (private companies redeeming or purchasing own shares out of capital) and 178 (4) (terms of redemption or purchase enforceable in a winding up) — (a) redeemable shares may only be redeemed out of distributable profits of the company or out of the proceeds of a fresh issue of shares made for the purposes of the redemption. . . .

"263.— . . . (2) In this Part, 'distribution' means every description of distribution of a company's assets

A to its members, whether in cash or otherwise, except a distribution by way of — (a) an issue of shares as fully or partly paid bonus shares, (b) the redemption or purchase of any of the company's own shares out of capital (including the proceeds of any fresh issue of shares) or out of unrealised profits in accordance with Chapter VII of Part V, (c) the reduction of share capital by extinguishing or reducing the liability of any of the members on any of the company's shares in respect of share capital not paid up, or by paying off paid-up share capital, and (d) a distribution of assets

B to members of the company on its winding up.

"(3) For purposes of this Part, a company's profits available for distribution are its accumulated, realised profits, so far as not previously utilised by distribution or capitalisation, less its accumulated, realised losses, so far as not previously written off in a reduction or reorganisation of capital duly made. This is subject to the provision made by sections 265 and 266 for investment and other companies."

C **Cases referred to**

Drown v Gaumont British Picture Corporation [1937] Ch 402.
Grosvenor Press plc, Re [1985] 1 WLR 980.
Ratners Group plc, Re [1988] BCLC 685.

Terms of undertaking

The petitioners offered the following undertaking:

"We, Quayle Munro Ltd, having our registered
D office at 42 Charlotte Square, Edinburgh EH2 4HQ ('the company') do hereby undertake that, in the event that the cancellation of the company's share premium account effected by the special resolution passed by the shareholders of the company at the extraordinary general meeting held on 17 September 1991 is confirmed by the court, the credit arising in the books of account of the company will be carried to a special reserve ('the special reserve'); we further undertake that so long as there shall remain outstanding any debt
E or claim which would have been admissible in proof against the company had it been wound up on the date when the proposed cancellation shall take effect, the special reserve shall not be treated as realised profit of the company or applied in making any distribution (other than a capital issue of further shares) by way of dividend, return of capital or otherwise to any of the members of the company except with the prior consent of all persons to whom any such debts or claims for the time being outstanding are due and
F owing; provided that notwithstanding the foregoing nothing in this undertaking shall prevent the company transferring all or part of the special reserve to profit and loss account from time to time to the extent only of any accrued losses on profit and loss account but subject always to the further undertaking hereinafter contained; We further undertake that in any event there shall be retained within the special reserve a sum sufficient to repay at par the 210,000 6 per cent preference shares of £1 each and the 300,000 escalating rate redeemable preference shares of £1 each presently in issue until the said shares have been redeemed

whether out of the special reserve or from other available sources." G

Eo die the court *granted* the prayer of the petition, *confirmed* the cancellation of the share premium account and *directed* the registrar of companies to register the undertaking and the order of the court.

The following opinion of the court was delivered by the Lord President (Hope):

OPINION OF THE COURT.—This is an application by a company incorporated under the Companies H
Acts for confirmation of cancellation of the amount standing to the credit of its share premium account. The application came before us today in the single bills on the petitioners' motion to grant the prayer of the petition. We have had the advantage of a full and careful report upon the facts and circumstances and regularity of the proceedings. In the light of that report, the undertaking which has been lodged in process and the submissions which were made to us by counsel we are satisfied that the provisions of s 136 (3) I
to (5) of the Companies Act 1985 need not apply in this case and that the cancellation of the share premium account which has been resolved on by special resolution of the company should be confirmed. But the reporter has raised two points for our consideration in regard to the terms of the undertaking on which we have heard argument, and it is appropriate that we should set out in writing the conclusions which we have reached on these matters.

The petitioners' undertaking is in these terms: [his J
Lordship quoted the terms of the undertaking, and continued:] The practice is now well established for undertakings of this kind to be given to and accepted by the court for the purpose of protecting the interests of creditors. The court requires to be satisfied that creditors of the company are safeguarded so that share capital or money held on share premium account cannot be applied in any way which would be detrimental to their interests: *Re Ratners Group plc*, per K
Harman J at p 687 (c). But as a general rule it is not necessary to do more than safeguard the interests of existing creditors, and the court does not normally require as a condition of any reduction that a reserve be set aside indefinitely to safeguard the interests of future creditors and shareholders. As Nourse J pointed out in *Re Grosvenor Press plc* at p 985, anyone who gives credit to or acquires shares in the company after the reduction takes effect is prima facie adequately protected by the existing statutory safeguards, includ- L
ing the detailed requirements of the Act which provide that a company's accounts shall give a true and fair view of the state of its affairs and of its profits or losses for the financial year. There may be cases where an undertaking to set aside a permanent capital reserve is required. But no such special circumstances are present in this case, so all that is needed here is an undertaking which will secure the interests of existing creditors as at the date when the proposed cancellation of the share premium account takes effect. Sufficient notice of the undertaking will be given to the creditors

of the company by its registration with the registrar of companies together with the order of the court confirming the cancellation. Once this has been done there is no reason to doubt that the undertaking will be effective to ensure that a sufficient amount remains in the hands of the company to meet the debts and claims to which it refers.

The points which have been raised by the reporter for discussion in this case relate to the last two clauses of the undertaking. The first of these is the proviso, which will allow the company to transfer all or part of the special reserve to profit and loss account from time to time to the extent only of any accrued losses on profit and loss account. The effect of this provision, as the reporter has pointed out, is to enable the company to use the special reserve to write off future losses on its profit and loss account as well as those which have already been identified. The writing off of past losses is a common use of such a reserve and is not regarded as objectionable, subject to the giving of an undertaking in terms which are appropriate to protect the creditors of the company. The writing off of future accrued losses is less familiar, but we agree with the reporter that in principle this also is not objectionable. Here again the creditors of the company at the time when cancellation takes effect will be protected by the undertaking to the appropriate extent. The company has undertaken not to make any distribution until the creditors whose claims are outstanding when the proposed cancellation becomes effective have either consented or been paid off. This undertaking applies equally to the use of the special reserve for the writing off of future losses as it does in the case of the deficit on the profit and loss account which has already been identified in respect of past losses.

Although the immediate purpose of this application is to enable the company to write off accrued losses on profit and loss account, the last clause of the undertaking refers to its wish to be able in the longer term to use the special reserve to repay the 210,000 6 per cent preference shares of £1 each and the 300,000 escalating rate preference shares of £1 each presently in issue. So the proposal is that a sufficient amount be kept in the special reserve to provide for the redemption at par of these shares on the appropriate date. This is reflected by the last sentence of the undertaking, which imposes an additional restraint on the company as regards the extent to which the special reserve may be used to write off losses which have accrued on its profit and loss account. This clause is of obvious benefit to the holders of these shares, since it will ensure that their redemption rights will be fully satisfied out of the special reserve should there be no other available sources from which this can be done. Nevertheless the reporter has questioned whether it is legitimate for the special reserve to be used for this purpose. He has suggested that it is for the petitioners to persuade us that the moneys on the special reserve are distributable profits of the company for the purpose of s 160 (1) (a) of the Act.

Approaching this point first as one of statutory construction, we see no reason to doubt that the funds held in the special reserve which it is proposed to create may be treated by the company as profits available for distribution, and thus as distributable profits for the purposes of s 160 (1) (a). Section 263 (3) provides that for the purposes of that Part of the Act, which is concerned with the distribution of profits and assets, a company's profits available for distribution are its accumulated, realised profits so far as not previously utilised by distribution or capitalisation, less its accumulated, realised losses, so far as not previously written off in a reduction or reorganisation of capital duly made. It is not in doubt that the balance on the proposed special reserve, after writing off accrued losses on profit and loss account, will represent a distributable profit from which dividends may be paid. But that is not the only purpose to which a distributable profit may be applied, since s 160 (1) (a) permits redeemable shares to be redeemed out of distributable profits. The expression "distributable profits" is defined for this purpose by s 181 (a) as meaning, in relation to the making of any payment by a company, those profits out of which it could lawfully make a distribution within the meaning given by s 263 (2) equal in value to the payment. Thus, the expression "distributable profits" in s 160 (1) (a) is linked to the provisions of s 263 which defines the profits which are available for distribution by the company in the manner permitted by that Part of the Act. So profits which are available for distribution in that manner are available also as a source from which redeemable shares may be redeemed in terms of s 160 (1) (a).

The point which has troubled the reporter is whether it is appropriate to give this treatment to funds which have been released from the statutory share premium account. He does not doubt that when the funds have been released from the share premium account by virtue of the order of the court they may be treated as realised profits in terms of s 262 (3), by which that expression is taken to refer to such profits of the company as fall to be treated as realised in accordance with principles generally accepted, at the time when the accounts are prepared, with respect to the determination for accounting purposes of realised profits. Nor does he question the position which obtained prior to the coming into operation of s 72 of the Companies Act 1947, which introduced the provisions now to be found in s 130 of the 1985 Act, for the application of share premiums to a share premium account. Before the coming into operation of that legislation, premiums received on the issue of shares were available to be treated as profits and distributed by way of dividend and thus to be treated as profits of the company irrespective of the state of its profit and loss account. His point is that it may not be appropriate to look to the common law position in this matter in view of the detailed provisions which the statute contains, especially in s 171, for a private company to redeem its own shares out of capital.

We do not share the reporter's difficulty on this point. It is to be noted that s 171 applies only where the company wishes to make a payment in respect of

A the redemption or purchase of its own shares otherwise than out of distributable profits or the proceeds
of a fresh issue of shares. A payment so made is
referred to for this purpose as a payment out of capital.
But that description is not apt to a payment made out
of funds which are available for distribution as realised
profits in terms of s 262 (3). The statutory restrictions
which apply to the share premium account prevent
sums held at credit of that account from being distributed as distributable profits of the company. But
once they have been released from the share premium
B account following upon its cancellation, they are available to be distributed, in accordance with the principles described in *Drown v Gaumont British Picture
Corporation,* as profits distributable by way of dividend. So it follows that, in the absence of any statutory
restriction to the contrary, they are available also for
the redemption of redeemable shares of the company
in terms of s 160 (1) (a). In our opinion, therefore,
once the statutory requirements for the cancellation of
share premium account have been satisfied, the funds
C transferred to the special reserve will be available for
all purposes to which distributable profits may be
applied, subject to the terms of the undertaking.

For these reasons we are satisfied that the special
reserve may properly be applied for the purpose indicated by the last clause of the undertaking, and we
approve of its terms. We shall grant an order confirming the cancellation of its share premium account
as sought by the petitioners, and we shall direct the
registrar of companies to register the undertaking
D along with the order of the court.

-----

*Counsel for Petitioners, Philip, QC; Solicitors, Tods
Murray, WS.*

A N

E

Anderson v Gibb

OUTER HOUSE
LORD PENROSE
14 NOVEMBER 1991

*Arbitration — Procedure — Recovery of documents for
F proposed arbitration — Competency — Whether arbitra-
tion "civil proceedings" — Administration of Justice
(Scotland) Act 1972 (c 59), s 1 (1).*

*Statute — Construction — Reference to report of com-
mittee of inquiry — Whether plain meaning of Act to be
restricted by consideration of mischief sought to be
remedied — Contrast with English statutes in pari
materia.*

*Process — Commission and diligence — Recovery of docu-
ments — Before commencement of proceedings — Proposed arbitration — Whether "civil proceedings" —*

*Competency of order — Administration of Justice (Scot-
land) Act 1972 (c 59), s 1 (1).*

G

The Administration of Justice (Scotland) Act 1972,
s 1, empowers the court to order the production and
recovery of documents in connection with "civil
proceedings" already before that court or "likely to be
brought".

The landlords of a farm served a notice on their
tenant requiring him to remedy an alleged breach of
duty under the lease to reside on the farm and to keep
sufficient stock on it, the stock to be his property. The H
landlords then served a notice to quit, alleging failure
to stock the farm and a failure to keep only his own
stock on the farm. The tenant served a counter notice
requiring all questions arising out of the reasons for
the notice to quit to be determined by arbitration
under the Agricultural Holdings (Scotland) Act. The
landlords applied to the court by petition for an order
under s 1 of the 1972 Act for the production, recovery
and retention of documents relating to the ownership
of stock on the farm during the two years prior to the I
date of the application. The purpose of the application
was to recover the documents for use in the arbitration. The tenant challenged the competency of the
application, arguing, inter alia, that "civil proceedings" in s 1 did not include arbitrations and accordingly that the provisions of s 1 could not be relied
upon by the landlords.

The tenant founded on the fact that the mischief
that was sought to be remedied by the statute was
restricted to proposed court actions. J

Held, (1) that a consideration of the terms of the
statute demonstrated, particularly by contrast with the
provisions of earlier statutes, that the mischief
addressed by the statute was wider than that addressed
by the original government report (p 729K); and (2)
that while in its application to proceedings in dependence s 1 (1) related to the powers of the court seized
of the matter, in its application to proceedings which
had not been commenced the expression "civil
proceedings" should receive its general, wide meaning K
and be applied to proceedings of a civil character
irrespective of the court or tribunal before which they
would be raised (p 729E-F and L); and plea to competency *repelled* and petition *continued* for consideration of the terms of the order to be pronounced.

McIntyre v Armitage Shanks Ltd, 1980 SLT 112,
and *Stock v Frank Jones (Tipton) Ltd* [1978] 1 WLR
231, *applied.*

L

**Petition for an order under s 1 (1) of the
Administration of Justice (Scotland) Act 1972**

Graham Frederick Anderson and another, landlords
of South Glassmount farm, Kinghorn, petitioned for
an order under s 1 (1) of the Administration of Justice
(Scotland) Act 1972 for the production, recovery and
retention of documents relating to the ownership of
stock on the farm. They called their tenant, James
Gibb, as respondent.

The petition came before the Lord Ordinary (Penrose) for a hearing on the respondent's objection to the competency of the order sought.

Statutory provisions

The Administration of Justice (Scotland) Act 1972 provides:

"1.—(1) Without prejudice to the existing powers of the Court of Session and of the sheriff court, those courts shall have power, subject to the provisions of subsection (4) of this section, to order the inspection, photographing, preservation, custody and detention of documents and other property (including, where appropriate, land) which appear to the court to be property as to which any question may relevantly arise in any existing civil proceedings before that court or in civil proceedings which are likely to be brought, and to order the production and recovery of any such property, the taking of samples thereof and the carrying out of any experiment thereon or therewith."

Cases referred to

Black-Clawson International Ltd v Papierwerke Waldhof-Aschaffenburg AG [1975] AC 591; [1975] 2 WLR 513; [1975] 1 All ER 810.

McIntyre v Armitage Shanks Ltd, 1980 SLT 112; 1980 SC (HL) 46.

Stock v Frank Jones (Tipton) Ltd [1978] 1 WLR 231; [1978] 1 All ER 948.

Textbooks referred to

Gloag and Henderson, *Introduction to the Law of Scotland* (9th ed), p 6.

Hunter, *Arbitration*, p 274.

Irons and Melville, *Arbitration*, pp 154 and 155.

Maxwell, *Interpretation of Statutes* (12th ed), p 33.

Stair Memorial Encyclopaedia, Vol 2, para 447.

On 14 November 1991 the Lord Ordinary *repelled* the pleas in law for the respondent and *continued* the case for a further hearing on the details of the specification and the form of the order to be pronounced.

LORD PENROSE.—This is an application for an order under s 1 of the Administration of Justice (Scotland) Act 1972 for the production, recovery and retention of documents relating to the ownership of stock on South Glassmount farm, Kinghorn, during the two years prior to the date of the application. The petitioners are the owners of the farm. The respondent is the tenant, by succession, under a lease dated 4 and 5 November 1935. On 14 March 1990 the petitioners' agents served on the respondent a notice requiring him to remedy an alleged breach of the tenants' duty under the lease "constantly to reside on the farm and at all times to keep a sufficient stock thereon which shall be their own bona fide property only". On 8 November 1990 the petitioners served a notice to quit, alleging inter alia (1) failure by the respondent at all times to keep a sufficient stock on the farm; and (2) failure at all times to keep a stock on the farm which was his own property only. A counter notice has been served by the respondent requiring all questions arising out of the reasons for the notice to quit to be determined by arbitration under the Agricultural Holdings (Scotland) Act (now the Act of 1991). The purpose of the present application is to recover documents intended to be used in the arbitration proceedings. No arbiter has been appointed.

At the hearing on 30 October 1991 the respondent challenged the competency of the application. Shortly stated the issue was whether it was competent to proceed by petition under s 1 of the 1972 Act in respect of prospective proceedings which, if raised, would take place before an arbiter. It was agreed that arbitration would be mandatory, in view of the provisions of the agricultural holdings legislation.

Section 1 (1) of the 1972 Act extended the powers of the Court of Session and of the sheriff court to make orders for inspection and other procedures relating to documents and other property "which appear to the court to be property as to which any question may relevantly arise in any existing civil proceedings before that court or in civil proceedings which are likely to be brought".

For the respondent it was argued that it would be anomalous for the second branch of the provision to extend to anticipated arbitration proceedings when the first was restricted to existing court proceedings. The first branch of the provision could not apply to current arbitrations. Recovery of documents in that context depended on the powers of the arbiter, and the court was involved, if at all, only where powers of compulsion were required. Reference was made to Irons and Melville on *Arbitration* at pp 154 and 155. Counsel compared the provisions of s 1 with s 9 of the Civil Evidence (Scotland) Act 1988 where the intention that arbitration proceedings should be within the expression "civil proceedings" was reflected in the definition provision. The lack of a definition provision in the 1972 Act, it was said, demonstrated the intention that its application should be narrower. In view of the anomaly which arose on the interpretation contended for by the petitioners it was both competent and appropriate to consider the mischief the Act was intended to remedy and to construe the provision in the light of that mischief: *Black-Clawson International Ltd v Papierwerke Waldhof-Aschaffenburg AG* and *McIntyre v Armitage Shanks Ltd*. The provisions of s 1 had their origins in proposals contained in the report of the Winn Committee on Personal Injuries Litigation, Cmnd 3691 (1969). In England those proposals received effect, in an extended form, in the Administration of Justice Act 1969, s 21, and in the Administration of Justice Act 1970, ss 31 and 32. Those provisions applied only to proceedings before the ordinary courts of England. The 1972 Act adapted the English proceedings for application in Scotland. Counsel referred to Sheriff Macphail's article in 1972 SLT (News) at p 73. In summary counsel contended that the provisions of s 1 were limited in their scope to civil proceedings in court because (1) otherwise there would be an anomaly as between the two branches of the provisions; (2) the mischief addressed

A was perceived in terms of proceedings in court only; and (3) as the 1988 Act demonstrated, arbitration was provided for specifically where it was intended that the expression "civil proceedings" should extend to cover that form of proceeding.

Counsel for the petitioners argued that the expression "civil proceedings" should receive its ordinary, wide, meaning. Within the subsection there were words of qualification where that was intended. The expression was otherwise plain and unambiguous. Reference was made to the literal rule of construction
B set out in Maxwell on *Interpretation of Statutes* (12th ed), at p 33. The respondent's contentions required that the word "court" be read into the provision as a qualification of the scope of the expression "civil proceedings". That was illegitimate. He argued that there was in any event no anomaly. If an arbiter approved of a specification of such width as the court might approve under the first branch of s 1 (1), subsequent approval by the court would be competent. He referred to Hunter on *Arbitration* at p 274, paras 13.34
C and 13.45 for a statement of the author's understanding of the position. Even if there were an anomaly on the literal and proper interpretation of the provision, that was irrelevant: Gloag and Henderson (9th ed), p 6, and *Stock v Frank Jones (Tipton) Ltd.* If the construction were not clear it was appropriate to have regard to extrinsic material. The article in the *Stair Memorial Encyclopaedia*, Vol 2, para 447, suggested that there might be scope for doubt about construction. However the external circumstances relied
D upon by the respondent were of limited or negligible assistance in the circumstances. It was clear that Parliament had departed from the proposals of the Winn committee report in enacting the English provisions. Those provisions were general in their scope and were not restricted to personal injuries litigation. Further it was apparent that the words of limitation in the 1969 and 1970 Administration of Justice Acts had not been repeated in the Scottish Act. This demonstrated that the intention was that the Scottish provi-
E sion should not be restricted in its scope to civil litigation in the ordinary courts. There was nothing in the Agricultural Holdings (Scotland) Act 1949 or the procedural rules made thereunder to affect the application of s 1 of the 1972 Act in circumstances such as the present. Paragraph 6 of Sched 6 to the Act (now para 6 of Sched 7 to the Act of 1991) envisaged very wide powers in the case of existing arbitrations. Further, the mischief was precisely the same in the case of arbitrations as it was in relation to proceedings
F in court. There was no justification for reading the words "civil proceedings" restrictively. All civil proceedings were covered. The 1988 Civil Evidence (Scotland) Act and s 1 of the 1972 Act dealt with the same field of law, namely the law of evidence, albeit that one was concerned with the recovery of material and the other with admissibility of evidence. One would expect the expression "civil proceedings" to have a similar meaning in each context.

In response respondent's counsel referred to the speech of Lord Simon of Glaisdale in *Stock v Frank*

Jones (Tipton) Ltd in support of his own approach. He
G repeated and reinforced his argument that anomalies would be evident on the approach adopted by the petitioner. He was critical of the passages in Hunter on *Arbitration* relied on by petitioners' counsel. Finally petitioners' counsel stated as his fundamental contention that the provision must have been intended to cover arbitration and that it would be anomalous if such proceedings were excluded.

Since both parties relied upon *Stock v Frank Jones (Tipton) Ltd* I take the statement of the golden rule as
H adapted by Lord Simon of Glaisdale as the starting point for this discussion. As he stated it, the rule of statutory construction was this: you are to apply statutory words and phrases according to their natural and ordinary meaning in their context and according to the appropriate linguistic register without addition or subtraction, unless that meaning produces injustice, absurdity, anomaly or contradiction in which case you may modify the natural and ordinary meaning so as to obviate such injustice, etc, but no further. As a matter
I of textual analysis, s 1 (1) of the 1972 Act confers on the Court of Session and sheriff court extended powers, identical in scope, in two different situations. The first situation is where there is an action in dependence before the court. Then the powers are provided to the court seized of the matter, and are defined by reference to questions which may relevantly arise in the existing litigation. In some respects the language is clumsy. The confusion of the plural and singular in references to the courts is unhelpful. But making allowance for the grammatical infelicity, the meaning
J and purpose of the provision is reasonably plain. The limitation to the court before which the proceedings are in dependence avoids duplication of process. Without such words of limitation it is not inconceivable that an application might have been made in the Court of Session for inspection or other procedure relating to documents or other property in respect of which questions arose in a sheriff court process. The subsection is to be read as identifying the court before which the relevant proceedings are depending as the
K court competent to exercise the extended powers.

It would not have been appropriate to provide for arbitration in this context. Scottish practice is well established. It is for the arbiter to determine the scope of the recovery of documentary and other material, and of any inspection which may be appropriate, according to the powers conferred upon him by the deed of submission or any relevant conditions or regulations applying to the arbitration. After approval of
L the specification, the court is asked to interpone its authority by granting warrant to cite witnesses and havers. In arbitration proceedings under the Agricultural Holdings (Scotland) Act the parties are obliged to comply with requirements of the arbiter inter alia as to the production of samples, books, deeds, papers, accounts, writings and documents within their possession. The scope of an arbiter's powers generally or under such statutory provisions were not matters with which s 1 of the 1972 Act was concerned. It would have been anomalous in a real and substantial sense

had power been conferred on the ordinary courts to order the various procedures provided for in relation to arbitration proceedings already in dependence without a review of the general law and practice relating to evidence and procedure in arbitration.

Similar considerations do not necessarily apply in situations in which proceedings have not been commenced. Prior to the commencement of proceedings there is no duplication of process. There is no arbiter to entertain an application relating to documents of property. Unless it is open to the parties to have resort to the ordinary courts, no one can authorise any step for inspection or preservation of evidence or any of the other procedures envisaged in the Act. I was not persuaded that there was any necessary anomaly in making different provision for what are two patently different situations.

Nevertheless the construction for which the petitioners contend could give rise to anomalies. Section 1 in its second branch defines powers exercisable by the court without reference to any specific provision, whether conventional or regulatory, which might apply to the prospective arbitration. In current practice many arbitrations take place under contracts or regulations which not only stipulate for mandatory arbitration but regulate to a greater or lesser extent the conduct of proceedings. It would be anomalous if a party obliged to arbitrate subject to such provisions were entitled in anticipation of the arbitration to apply to the ordinary courts for an order for procedure which the arbiter subsequently appointed was not empowered himself to authorise. Section 9 (v) of the Civil Evidence Act 1988 recognises this problem by excluding from the scope of that Act cases in which specific provision had been made for the rules of evidence to be applied in the arbitration in question. But exceptions of this kind are not always found. Section 17 of the Law Reform (Miscellaneous Provisions) (Scotland) Act 1968 includes arbitration in the definition of civil proceedings for the purposes of Pt III of that Act without qualification. However construed, s 1 provides a discretionary power. Any inconsistency between the terms of an application and the conventional or regulatory provisions under which arbitration would ensue could be addressed in considering the scope of an order by the court involved. There is no need for conceptual anomalies to be reflected in practical results in this case.

In the whole circumstances I am of opinion that there is no anomaly as between the two branches of the provision attributable to their applying in different contexts and that the primary meaning of the provision must be sought within the framework of the language found in s 1 (1) itself. So approached, I consider that the expression "civil proceedings" should receive its general, wide, meaning, namely that it applies to proceedings of a civil character irrespective of the court or tribunal before which they may be raised.

In any event I consider that there is nothing in the relevant background which would prevent such a view

being taken of the provision. It is clear that in enacting the 1969 and 1972 Administration of Justice Acts Parliament innovated to a considerable extent on the proposals of the Winn committee. The committee had a particular remit. But the problems addressed in the statutes reflect the appreciation that the matters identified by the committee had a more general application. The statutes provided a general remedy, limited to court proceedings. Section 21 of the Administration of Justice Act 1969 provides that the High Court shall have power to make orders, co-extensive with the forms of order provided for in s 1 of the 1972 Act, in relation to property "which appears to the court to be property which may become the subject matter of subsequent proceedings in the court". The 1970 Act extended these provisions to persons who were not parties to the future litigation. Section 31 refers specifically to "subsequent proceedings in that court" in defining the extended powers of the High Court. Section 32 (2) does not contain an express qualification on the other hand. However each of these provisions is further limited in its scope to cases involving personal injury or death, which was the subject matter of the Winn committee report. The words of qualification employed in the more general of the English provisions are omitted in the relevant part of s 1 (1) of the Scottish Act. If any inference arises from the comparison of these provisions it is, in my opinion, that, for whatever reason, Parliament considered it appropriate to extend the scope of the provision in 1972 further than it had proceeded in the English statutes. None of this assists the respondent. The observations of Lord Hailsham LC in *McIntyre* at 1980 SLT, p 117, relating to the use of reports of committees as aids in construction are apt: "Such documents must be used, if at all, with the greatest care because it does not follow either that Parliament, in enacting consequent legislation, has followed minutely all the recommendations of the report, or that, in enacting consequent legislation, Parliament has not seized the opportunity of legislating also on matters altogether outside the recommendations of the report". In this case it is clear that the mischief addressed by the legislation was altogether more extensive than that identified in the Winn committee report. It is appropriate to assume that the variation of expressions found in the 1972 Act, when compared with the earlier statutes, was not casual but reflected a deliberate intention on the part of Parliament to extend the powers provided.

In the whole circumstances I am of opinion that the expression "civil proceedings" is intended in this context to describe the character of the proceedings envisaged in the legislation rather than to circumscribe the operation of the provision by reference to the tribunal or court before which such proceedings arise. There being no basis on which to construe the expression so as to exclude arbitration proceedings I shall repel the first plea in law for the respondent. No argument was advanced in support of the second plea in law and I shall repel it accordingly. Quoad ultra I shall continue the matter. It was agreed between

parties that in the event that the proceedings were held
to be competent a further opportunity would be
required to address the court on the details of the
specification and the precise form of order to be
pronounced.

*Counsel for Petitioners, Mundy; Solicitors, Connell &
Connell, WS — Counsel for Respondent, Hodge; Solicitors, Brodies, WS.*

J P D

Maciocia v Alma Holdings Ltd

OUTER HOUSE

LORD CAPLAN

12 FEBRUARY 1992

*Diligence — Arrestment — Arrestment on dependence —
Recall — Deed for discounting of receivables — Whether
effective trust created affecting funds arrested — Proper
forum for determining effect of trust.*

An employee who had been dismissed raised an
action of damages against his former employers founding on an alleged wrongful termination of the service
agreement between the parties. The summons contained a warrant to arrest on the dependence. An
arrestment was executed against a shop company who,
at the date of the arrestment, apparently owed the
employers a sum in excess of the sum arrested. The
employers sought recall of the arrestment as nimious
and oppressive. They did not offer caution or an alternative security, but argued that the arrestment had not
caught any funds owing to them and founded on the
terms of a deed for the discounting of receivables
entered into between the employers and another
company prior to the raising of the action. The object
of the deed was to effect acquisition by the other
company of book debts at a discount. The employers
argued that this deed effectively created a trust
whereby they held all receivables which had been notified to the other company in trust for that company
and accordingly had no beneficial interest themselves
in the arrested funds. The pursuer argued that the
deed did not create an effective trust and that the
arrestment had effectively attached the arrested funds.

Held, that it was not appropriate in proceedings for
recall of an arrestment to reach a concluded view on
the effect of the deed in question; the respective rights
of those claiming the interest in the arrested funds
should be ascertained in proceedings where the
interested parties had an opportunity to be represented and where the issues between them could be
properly focused by pleadings (p 732A-C); that in the

circumstances recall of the arrestment would be
inappropriate (p 732D); and motion for recall *refused*.

Action of damages

Mario Gustavo Alfredo Maciocia raised an action of
damages for breach of contract against Alma Holdings
Ltd. The summons contained warrant for arrestment
on the dependence. The pursuer effected an arrestment of funds in the hands of Woolworths plc.

The case came before the Lord Ordinary (Caplan)
on the defenders' motion for recall of the arrestment.

Case referred to

Tay Valley Joinery Ltd v C F Financial Services Ltd,
1987 SLT 207.

On 12 February 1992 his Lordship *refused* the
motion in hoc statu.

LORD CAPLAN.—In this action the pursuer sues
the defenders for damages of £200,000 for an alleged
breach of contract. The pursuer had a service agreement with the defenders and claims that this was
wrongfully terminated by them.

The summons in the action contained a warrant to
arrest on the dependence signeted on 25 October 1991
and on 16 November 1991 messengers at arms in
terms of this warrant arrested the sum of £200,000 in
the hands of Woolworths plc, Glasgow. The defenders
are confectionery manufacturers and regularly supply
Woolworths with their products. At the date of the
arrestment Woolworths owed in excess of the sum
arrested in respect of their purchases from the
defenders.

On 17 January 1992 the matter came before me on
the motion roll when the defenders moved to have the
said arrestment recalled. Defenders' counsel
emphasised that the defenders were not offering
caution or alternative security. The argument
advanced was that the arrestment had not caught any
funds owing to the defenders but that its continued
existence was causing commercial embarrassment and
practical difficulty. The defenders founded on the
terms of a deed for the discounting of receivables
entered into on 12 July 1991 between the defenders
and a company called Security Pacific Eurofinance plc
(referred to in the said deed as "the Factor"). The
object of the said deed was to effect acquisition by the
factor of the defenders' book debts at a discount. In
the deed a "receivable" is defined as the amount of
any indebtedness incurred or to be incurred by the
debtor under a supply contract. A "supply contract"
is a contract for the sale of goods by the client (that is
to say the defenders).

Clause 4 of the deed is in the following terms:

"(1) The Client agrees to sell and the Factor to purchase all receivables existing at the commencement
date or arising thereafter during the currency of this
Deed in relation to any Debtor of the class or descrip-

tion specified in paragraph 3 of the Schedule. The ownership of each such receivable shall, as regards receivables existing at the commencement date, vest in the Factor on that date and as regards future receivables, vest in the Factor automatically upon the same coming into existence. If any receivable should fail to vest effectively in the Factor in equity or otherwise the Client shall hold such receivable and any associated rights relating thereto in trust for the Factor.

"(2) Upon any receivable vesting in the Factor under sub-clause (1) there shall also automatically vest in the Factor all the associated rights in relation to such receivable and the Factor shall have the right to require the transfer to it of title to any goods comprised in the relevant supply contract.

"(3) The Client shall at the request of the Factor and at the Client's expense execute a formal written assignment to the Factor of the receivables and associated rights referred to in sub-clause (1) and (2) and deliver to the Factor any instrument of security included therein with any necessary endorsement or other signature."

Clause 8 (2) incorporates the following provisions:

"The Client undertakes in addition to and without limitation to any other undertaking given elsewhere in this Deed, . . . (ii) promptly to notify the Factor in such manner and with such particulars and documents evidencing the receivable as the Factor may from time to time require, of every receivable sold by the Client to the Factor, as soon as the relevant goods have been delivered or, if so required by the Factor, at any other time; . . . (vi) to deliver direct to the Factor (or, if so required by the Factor direct to a bank account specified by the Factor) any remittance received by the Client in payment of or on account of any receivable, and pending such delivery to hold such remittance in trust for the Factor and separate from the Client's own monies; (vii) to co-operate fully with the Factor in the collection of any receivable and enforcement of payment thereof, whether by proceedings or otherwise, and to indemnify the Factor against all legal and other costs and expenses incurred in connection with such enforcement so far as it relates to an unapproved receivable."

Clause 14 of the deed is in the following terms:

"(1) Notwithstanding any provision for notices in accordance with paragraph (v) of Clause 8 (2) and without prejudice to the provisions of paragraph (vi) thereof, the Client shall enforce payment of all receivables at his own expense and, for the purpose of such enforcement is hereby appointed the agent of the Factor. However the Factor may at any time by written notice terminate such agency and following upon such termination until any receivable has become revested in the Client in accordance with Clause 10 the Factor shall have the sole right to collect the receivable and to enforce payment thereof in such manner and to such extent as it shall in its absolute discretion decide, and to institute, defend or compromise in the name of the Factor or the Client and

on such terms as the Factor thinks fit any proceedings brought by or against the Factor in relation to the receivable."

Counsel for the defenders argued that the effect of the deed was to create a trust whereby the defenders held all receivables which had been notified to the factor in trust for the factor. The sums purportedly arrested in the hands of Woolworths were all receivables covered by the deed and documentation was produced to vouch that the creation of such receivables had been intimated to the factor. I do not think that it was contested that the sums which the defenders have arrested are receivables covered by the deed. The defenders relied on the case of *Tay Valley Joinery Ltd v C F Financial Services Ltd* as authority for the view that a deed such as the defenders entered into created an effective trust. The defenders have no beneficial interest in the arrested funds. The existence of the arrestment is causing them commercial embarrassment. They are in breach of their own obligations to the factor. No intimation of the deed required to be made to Woolworths so that company are entitled meanwhile to retain the arrested funds. The pursuer would get no benefit if the arrestment continued. To maintain the arrestment under such circumstances is nimious and oppressive.

Senior counsel for the pursuer opposed the proposed recall of the arrestment. He contended that the arrestment had effectively attached the funds arrested. He did not accept that the said deed had created an effective trust. The case is distinguishable from *Tay Valley Joinery Ltd* where the terms of the deed were different. In *Tay Valley Joinery Ltd* the right of the finance company to receivables vested when the receivable came into existence. However, in the present case in terms of cl 4 the scheme is that "ownership" shall vest. "Ownership" is different from "a right" which could be a right as a beneficiary. It is only in circumstances which are not very clearly stated in the case that a trust arises.

Clause 4 (3) provides that the client shall at the factor's request deliver a formal written assignment to the factor of receivables. This was said to be consistent only with the view that the deed intended absolute ownership of receivables to vest in the factor at their creation. Clause 14 provides that the client is appointed the agent of the factor for the collection of receivables. This is totally inconsistent with the suggestion that the defenders are trustees. If the arguments for the defenders are well founded, then they have no interest in the funds arrested and the party with the interest to contest the validity of the arrestment is the factor who is not represented.

I am not as convinced as senior counsel for the pursuers would have liked me to be that the deed in this case is readily distinguishable from the deed being considered in *Tay Valley Joinery Ltd*. The two deeds have various common features including reference to vesting on the coming into existence of the receivable, assignment being referred to along with trust, and the noting of a legend indicating in the client's books that

A the receivables are held in trust (cl 8 (x)). However, two of the judges in the *Tay Valley Joinery Ltd* case reached their final opinions with a considerable degree of hesitation. Relatively minor differences in the terms of the present deed could have an important bearing on its effect. I do not think that it is appropriate that in proceedings for the recall of an arrestment I should reach a concluded view as to the effect of the deed. If the fund purportedly arrested is effectively attached, then this could provide the pursuer with a critical degree of security should his action succeed. If the B factor has the main beneficial interest in the arrested fund, the principal competition for this fund may prove to be between the factor and the pursuer or even between the factor and the defenders as trustees, but not the defenders in their own right. The attitude of the factor to their rights under the deed is not known. With a large sum such as is involved in the arrestment the respective rights of those claiming an interest in the arrested fund should be ascertained in proceedings where the interested parties have an opportunity to be C represented and where the issues between these parties can be properly focused by pleadings. Questions could arise as to the procedures followed by the parties in the operation of the deed and as to the English law applicable to it. The deed in the present case is governed by English law. *Tay Valley Joinery Ltd* proceeded by way of special case and questions of operating procedures and English law were agreed therein. If the defenders are embarrassed by the continued endurance of the arrestment they can offer D some alternative security. Meanwhile in hoc statu I do not think it would be appropriate to recall the arrestment and the defenders' motion is accordingly refused.

Counsel for Pursuer, Martin, QC; Solicitors, Henderson & Jackson, WS — Counsel for Defenders, Hanretty; Solicitors, Dundas & Wilson, CS.

E   P A

Kamperman v MacIver

OUTER HOUSE

TEMPORARY JUDGE R G McEWAN, QC

F 20 MARCH 1992

Husband and wife — Marriage — Constitution — Irregular marriage — Cohabitation with habit and repute — Relevancy — Circumstances prior to removal of impediment to marriage — Whether period of cohabitation of just over six months after removal of impediment sufficient.

A woman brought an action of declarator that she had been lawfully married by cohabitation with habit and repute to a man who had died on 8 September

1989. She had begun cohabiting with him in May 1984 when they were both married to other persons G and had continued to do so until the date of his death. She was divorced in February 1986 and the deceased in February 1989. The pursuer averred that during the cohabitation the friends and relatives both of her and of the deceased had known her as "Mrs Jackson" and those with whom they dealt had considered them married. The defenders, who were nieces of the deceased, challenged the relevancy of the pursuer's averments at procedure roll on the grounds (1) that the averments did not indicate that the pursuer and the H deceased had formed an intention to marry after February 1989 when the final impediment to marriage had been removed; and (2) that the period of cohabitation of just over six months between February 1989 and the deceased's death was too short.

Held, (1) that only facts and circumstances about cohabitation and repute arising after the parties were free to marry were relevant to infer consent to marriage and that the pursuer's averments relating to the whole period of cohabitation from May 1984 until the I deceased's death, which contained no specific averments related to the period after February 1989, were therefore irrelevant (p 733G-J); (2) that the requirement of habit referred to the length of time of cohabitation which had to be "considerable" and that a period of cohabitation of just over six months could never be categorised as "considerable" for this purpose (p 733J-K); and action *dismissed.*

Lapsley v Grierson (1845) 8 D 34, and *Wallace v Fife J Coal Co*, 1909 1 SLT 509, *followed*; *Shaw v Henderson*, 1982 SLT 211, *not followed.*

Opinion, that while it was not necessary for the pursuer to aver the names and addresses of the persons who dealt with the pursuer and the deceased and from whom she hoped to obtain evidence of repute, specific averments detailing repute ought to have been made (p 734D-E).

K

Action of declarator

Mrs Lillian Marland or Kamperman (known as Jackson) sought declarator that she had been married by cohabitation with habit and repute to James Jackson, deceased. She called as defenders the deceased's two nieces, Miss Fiona MacIver and Miss Isbeth MacIver, who both defended the action, and also the Lord Advocate in the public interest. The Lord Advocate did not enter appearance.   L

The case came before the temporary judge (R G McEwan, QC) on procedure roll.

Cases referred to

Boulting v Elias, 1990 SLT 596.
Lapsley v Grierson (1845) 8 D 34.
Mackenzie v Scott, 1980 SLT (Notes) 9.
Shaw v Henderson, 1982 SLT 211.
Wallace v Fife Coal Co, 1909 1 SLT 509; 1909 SC 682.

Textbooks referred to

A Clive, *Husband and Wife* (2nd ed), pp 59 and 63.
Stair Memorial Encyclopaedia, Vol 10, para. 814.

On 20 March 1992 the temporary judge *dismissed* the action.

R G McEWAN, QC.—This action concerns a dispute over the estate of the late James Jackson who died on 8 September 1989. It is between his two nieces who live in Lewis and the pursuer who claims to have
B been married to him in an irregular marriage. The summons is raised in the pursuer's married name with the words "known as Jackson" added.

The issue argued to me was whether the pursuer has relevantly averred facts and circumstances which, if proved, would support a marriage by cohabitation with habit and repute.

The pursuer avers that she and the deceased cohabited from May 1984 until he died, at two
C different addresses in Ayrshire. To begin with both were already married to other persons. The pursuer was divorced in February 1986 and the deceased in February 1989, i e some six months before he died. It is alleged that during the cohabitation the friends and relatives of both knew the pursuer as "Mrs Jackson" and those with whom they dealt considered them married.

Counsel for the defenders argued that there were no averments indicating that the couple had formed an
D intention to marry after February 1989 when the final impediment was removed. The period of about six months was, in any event, too short. He referred me to *Lapsley v Grierson* at p 61 and *Wallace v Fife Coal Co*, 1909 1 SLT at p 511. The shortest period which had been accepted was 11 months and that was after proof (*Shaw v Henderson* at p 212). Counsel for the defenders maintained that the Lord Ordinary in *Shaw* had misunderstood the decision in *Wallace*. In this case there was nothing to indicate an intention to be
E married when the impediment was gone as opposed to being married in the future (*Mackenzie v Scott* at p 10, col 2). Repute had to be undivided. The pursuer could not be known as Jackson until the divorces were granted. It was not said who were the people with whom they dealt and although the defenders could take steps to find out (Administration of Justice Act 1972, s 1 (1A)), proper pleading demanded that such detail be given on record (*Boulting v Elias* at p 600G).

F Counsel for the pursuer responded that her case was relevantly averred. It was accepted that the period was short but there was no absolute rule as to the length of period. *Wallace* was decided on the facts special to it. There were clear averments as to cohabitation and what was stated in the pleadings was sufficiently specific to establish general repute. There was no need to give names and addresses of potential witnesses. That would simply be to plead evidence. Counsel for the pursuer indicated that her instructing agents undertook to let the defenders' agents know who would be the witnesses in advance of any proof. She

concluded by referring me to passages in Clive on *Husband and Wife* (2nd ed), pp 59 and 63 and to the G *Stair Memorial Encyclopaedia*, Vol 10, para 814.

In my judgment marriage by habit and repute is based upon a presumption. The cohabitation and the repute are evidence from which the necessary consent to enter a marriage is inferred.

In my opinion only facts and circumstances arising after the parties are free to marry can be relevant and circumstances of cohabitation, or anything else prior, while interesting as background can never be relevant H to infer consent. In the present case that would exclude events before 23 February 1989. This is clearly established by the first case cited to me, viz *Lapsley v Grierson*. There are various passages in the opinion of the Lord Justice Clerk (Hope) at p 50 to this effect. There is also a passage to like effect at p 47. The case also is important on proof of habit arising out of the length of time, and I will return to this. In the present case cond 2 makes it clear that the cohabitation began in May 1984. At the outset it was adulterous I and the question arises whether any change in character took place after 23 February 1989 at which could be attributed to the actions of the pursuer and the deceased. Nothing specific is averred in this last period and indeed the last three lines of cond 2 begin with the words "during the said period of cohabitation". That can only refer to the whole period from May 1984 to September 1989 and almost five years of that I hold to be irrelevant for the reasons already given. Nothing is said as to why the cohabitation J ceased to be illicit.

Next comes habit. This refers to the length of time founded upon. In this case it is exactly six and a half months. It is undeniable that this is a very short period. In *Lapsley* Lord Moncrieff stated that the period had to be "considerable" at p 61. In my view, here, as a matter of relevancy, a period of six months and two weeks could never be categorised as considerable in the context of proving a marriage. Proof of marriage is a serious and important matter. K

I now deal with *Wallace* which is binding on me. It concerned compensation following upon the death of a miner. The sheriff substitute sitting as arbitrator had stated a case on his award of compensation. It is clear from his findings that the pursuer, then a 15 year old girl, had left Fife with Wallace in September 1907. They cohabited at various addresses in Lanarkshire and there are findings in fact concerning repute (finding 2). There was also a finding that a ceremony of marriage was postponed (finding 3) and that the L child born on 26 July 1908 was registered as illegitimate (finding 4). Wallace had himself been killed in the defenders' mine on 14 July, i e, two weeks before the birth of the baby.

The Second Division refused to declare a marriage. No specific reasons are given in the opinion of the Lord Justice Clerk except that the facts stated did not support a marriage (1909 1 SLT at p 511). Lord Ardwall, however, made a careful analysis of the facts and in particular the 10½ month period. In my

A opinion his judgment does lay down that 10½ months is too short a period. In *Wallace*, unlike the present case, there was never any issue of an impediment to marriage.

In *Shaw v Henderson* a period of 11 months was accepted after proof. An examination of the case reveals that very little attention was given to the period of habit other than a reference to *Wallace*. In my view the Lord Ordinary misconstrued what was decided in *Wallace*. As I read the case the Lord Justice Clerk left the analysis of the findings to Lord Ardwall.

B Lord Ardwall did not disagree with the Lord Justice Clerk. Lord Lowe simply concurred. What I think is significant about *Shaw* is that *Lapsley v Grierson* was not cited and no argument appears to have been made that the period had to be considerable. For these reasons I do not find *Shaw* of assistance.

Similarly, *Mackenzie v Scott* is only an example on its facts after proof. There the proof was undefended and the period involved was three years. It is perhaps important to observe the careful analysis of repute given by the Lord Ordinary.

C On this aspect of the case I conclude on the authorities that the pursuer has failed relevantly to aver a period which could ever be considerable.

What of repute? I have already indicated that the pursuer has not confined repute to the relevant period. It can also be said that the averments lack detail and give little notice of who the friends are or who dealt with the parties and in what circumstances. This is

D important as the repute has to be general, unvarying and consistent. The problem with allowing such a case to go to proof is that the evidence on these averments is liable to be confusing and unforeseen because the areas of dispute or controversy have not been clearly focused in the pleadings. There is also the risk that the court would hear evidence of lifestyle prior to the relevant period.

I do not think it is incumbent on the pursuer to give names and addresses, but careful preparation ought to

E reveal more information and details of repute which could be the subject of averment and which is plainly lacking here. For this reason also, I criticise the pursuer's case for lack of specification. I have come to the conclusion with some hesitation that the pursuer's case must necessarily fail even if she proves all she avers. In these circumstances I will sustain the first plea in law for the compearing defenders and dismiss the action.

F

Counsel for Pursuer, S Smith; Solicitors, Balfour & Manson, Nightingale & Bell — Counsel for Defenders, Baird; Solicitors, Drummond Miller, WS.

A J H

Mitchell v HAT Contracting Services Ltd (No 2)

OUTER HOUSE

TEMPORARY JUDGE R G McEWAN, QC

20 MARCH 1992

Process — Decree — Summary decree — Whether defences to statutory cases disclosed — Whether appropriate to determine relevancy issue on motion roll — Rules of Court 1965, rule 89B.

A worker raised an action of damages in respect of personal injuries sustained in the course of his employment. He alleged that a defective scaffolding board had broken as he was carrying out some paintwork on an oil installation. He sued his employers and also the concession owners of the oil installation, basing his case on breaches of the Construction (Working Places) Regulations 1966 and the Offshore Installations (Operational Safety, Health and Welfare) Regulations 1976 by the defenders respectively. Having already been awarded interim damages and the record having closed, the pursuer sought summary decree in order to limit proof to quantum of damages. A report by the concession owners, which had been lodged, indicated that the cause of the accident had been a defective scaffolding board. The defenders had not raised the defence of reasonable practicability under the regulations. The employers argued that there was an issue as to whether the 1966 Regulations applied, and that they could not have known about the defect in the scaffolding board.

Held, (1) that the proper test for summary decree was that set out by Lord Cullen in *Robinson v Thomson*, 1987 SLT 120, and that if it unmistakably appeared that there might be an issue of relevancy then the case had to go to procedure roll (p 737B-D); (2) that the applicability to the employers of the 1966 Regulations was such an issue of relevancy (p 737G-H); and (3) that the concession owners' report, taken together with their admissions, amounted to an acceptance of the pursuer's factual case against them and they had no defence to it (p 737I-K); and motion for summary decree *refused* as against the employers but *granted* as against the concession owners; and proof against the second defenders *restricted* to quantum of damages.

Action of damages

Paul Mitchell raised an action of damages in respect of personal injuries sustained as a result of an accident in the course of his employment with the first defenders, HAT Contracting Services Ltd, on an oil installation in respect of which the second defenders, Unocal UK Ltd were the concession owners.

The case came before the temporary judge (R G McEwan, QC) on the pursuer's motion for summary decree in terms of Rule of Court 89B and to restrict any proof to quantum of damages only.

Statutory provisions

A   The Rules of Court 1965 provide:

"89B.—. . . (3) In applying for summary decree the pursuer may move the court — . . . (b) to pronounce an interlocutor sustaining or repelling a plea-in-law; or (c) to dispose of the whole or a part of the subject matter of the action. . . .

"(5) At the hearing of a motion under this Rule the court may — (a) if satisfied that there is no defence to the action or to any part of it to which the motion B   relates, grant the motion for summary decree in whole or in part as the case may be".

The Construction (Working Places) Regulations 1966 provide:

"2.—(1) These regulations apply — . . . (b) to works of engineering construction; undertaken by way of trade or business, or for the purpose of any industrial or commercial undertaking, or by or on behalf of the Crown or any municipal or other public authority, C   and to any line or siding which is used in connection therewith and for the purposes thereof and is not part of a railway or tramway."

The Offshore Installations (Operational Safety, Health and Welfare) Regulations 1976 provide:

"14. At all times all reasonably practicable steps shall be taken to ensure the safety of persons at all places on the installation including the provision of safe means of access to and egress from any such place D   and in particular, but without prejudice to the generality of the foregoing:— (a) all scaffolding on the installation shall be so secured as to prevent accidental displacement; (b) every ladder shall be so fixed that the stiles or sides of the ladder are evenly supported or suspended and so secured as to prevent slipping; (c) every working platform shall be not less than 65 centimetres wide and shall be securely fastened to ledgers, standards or uprights or its movement prevented by other means and any working platform or walkway E   from which a person will be liable to fall a distance of more than two metres or into the sea shall where practicable be provided with a toe board not less than 15 centimetres high and suitable guard rails of adequate strength comprising at least three courses so arranged that the lowest rail is not more than 76 centimetres above the toe board and the highest rail is not less than one metre above the platform or walkway and the openings between the rails are not more than 40 centimetres; (d) where any person is to work at any place F   on the installation from which he will be liable to fall into the sea or a distance of more than two metres and where it is not practicable to comply with paragraph (c) above, safety nets or safety sheets of suitable design and construction shall, if practicable, be so provided in such positions as to prevent, without causing any undue injury to any such person, that person so falling; (e) where any person is to work at any place on the installation from which he will be liable to fall into the sea or a distance of more than two metres and it is not practicable to ensure his safety by the provision

of fencing or safety nets or sheets, there shall be provided for that person, and that person shall use, a G   suitable safety belt which, together with its lines, fittings and anchorages, is so designed and constructed as to prevent serious injury to that person in the event of his falling; and (f) where any person in getting to or from the place at which he is to work will be liable to fall into the sea and it is not practicable to ensure his safety by the provision of the means described in subparagraph (d) or (e) above, there shall be provided for that person and that person shall wear, a suitable lifejacket."   H

Cases referred to

Breslin v Britoil plc, 1992 SLT 414.
Brunswick Bowling and Billiards Corporation v Bedrock Bowl Ltd, 1991 SLT 187.
Curran v William Neill & Son (St Helens) Ltd [1961] 1 WLR 1069; [1961] 3 All ER 108.
Edwards v National Coal Board [1949] 1 KB 704.
Frimokar (UK) Ltd v Mobile Technical Plant (International) Ltd, 1990 SLT 180.   I
Gifto Fancy Goods Ltd v Orion Insurance Co Ltd, OH, 24 July 1991, unreported (1991 GWD 28-1693).
Hamilton v National Coal Board, 1960 SLT 24; 1960 SC (HL) 1.
Mackays Stores Ltd v City Wall (Holdings) Ltd, 1989 SLT 835.
McManus v Speirs Dick and Smith Ltd, 1989 SLT 806.
MacMillan v Wimpey Offshore Engineers and Constructors Ltd, 1991 SLT 515.
Marshall v Gotham Co [1954] AC 360, [1954] 2 WLR   J   812; [1954] 1 All ER 937.
Murray v Rococo Entertainments Ltd, OH, 25 October 1988, unreported (1988 GWD 37-1541).
Nimmo v Alexander Cowan & Sons Ltd, 1967 SLT 277; 1967 SC (HL) 79.
Rankin v Reid, 1987 SLT 352.
Robinson v Thomson, OH, 6 May 1986 (reported on another point, 1987 SLT 120).
Ross v British Coal Corporation, 1990 SLT 854.
Shepherd v Pearson Engineering Services (Dundee) Ltd, K   1981 SLT 197; 1980 SC 268.
Sinclair (P & M) v Bamber Gray Partnership, 1987 SLT 674.
Struthers v British Alcan Rolled Products Ltd, 21 February 1991, unreported (1991 GWD 10-628).
Walker v Imfabco Diving Services Ltd, 1985 SLT 633.
Watson-Towers Ltd v McPhail, 1986 SLT 617.

Textbook referred to

Redgrave, *Health and Safety in Factories* (1990).   L

On 20 March 1992 the temporary judge *refused* the pursuer's motion for summary decree against the first defenders and, quoad the second defenders, *granted* the motion and *restricted* any proof against them to quantum of damages.

R G McEWAN, QC.—This matter appeared before me on a motion for summary decree in terms of Rule of Court 89B.

The pursuer first of all lodged a minute of amendment making a small but important alteration to the specification of his statutory case. There was no opposition to the amendment and neither defender wished to lodge answers.

In the course of the argument I was referred to a large number of authorities which for convenience I list here, viz: [the temporary judge then cited the cases listed above and continued:]

I was also referred in detail to Rules of Court 89A and 89B, and various passages in Redgrave's *Health and Safety* (1990) and *Butterworths Words and Phrases* under the headings "Equipment" and "Parts". I was also invited to consider no 25 of process [a report by the second defenders on the cause of the accident].

It has to be noted that on 3 October 1991 Lord Cameron of Lochbroom made an interim award of damages in favour of the pursuer of £10,000 [1992 SLT 883]. His Lordship expressed himself satisfied that the pursuer was almost certain to succeed against one or other or both defenders on the case relating to a defective scaffolding board and to the security of the scaffold. This decision has not been reclaimed.

The debate was further complicated by the fact that I was told that the cause was to be sent to the procedure roll for an early hearing and that the first defenders were considering an amendment. In my view I have to ignore both of these matters. No date has been fixed. No minute of amendment is before me, not even an indication of what direction it might take. At one stage the various arguments began to assume the character of a full procedure roll discussion and I very much doubt whether rule 89B was meant to allow this (see *Rankin v Reid*, 1987 SLT at p 354A-C). I now summarise the arguments put to me.

The pursuer invited me to sustain his first and fifth pleas in law and to repel each defender's pleas 1, 2 and 3 only so far as they related to breach of statutory duty. That would leave a proof restricted to quantum of damages. Counsel for the pursuer founded on Rule of Court 89B (3) (b) and (c) and (5) (a). He urged me to be satisfied that there was no defence to the action. The pursuer was working from a scaffold at the A2 laydown area on the Heather Alpha oil installation. He was spray painting a lifeboat davit. The first defenders employed him. They had erected the scaffold. The second defenders were the concession owners of the oil installation. On the day in question a scaffolding board broke at a point where there was a knot in the wood. The second defenders' safety officer is said to have been aware of the use of defective boards. The pursuer fell. The first defenders admit they erected the scaffold and that the pursuer had an accident on the relevant date. They do not admit the precise circumstances. Although they go on to aver circumstances relating to inspection and checking, they nowhere raise the issue of what was or was not reasonably practicable. The second defenders admit the breaking of the very scaffolding board and that the pursuer fell. They do not admit any connection. Their production no 25 of process, however, clearly shows that the board was found to be defective and that in consequence the pursuer was injured. The matter is to be given immediate priority to prevent recurrence (see part H). It is dated the day of the accident.

The case against the first defenders was based upon the Construction (Working Places) Regulations 1966, regs 6, 9 and 11. It was argued that these duties were absolute and only limited by a defence of what was not reasonably practicable. No such defence was set out in fact or in law.

The same position applied against the second defenders under the Offshore Installations (Operational Safety, Health and Welfare) Regulations 1976. Regulations 32 (1) and 5 and 14 were absolute except if the defenders raised an issue of reasonable practicability. They had not done so.

Counsel for the pursuer founded particularly on the cases of *Rankin v Reid, Nimmo v Cowan, Edwards v NCB, Marshall v Gotham, Breslin v Britoil, MacMillan v Wimpey*, and in his reply speech *Robinson v Thomson, Frimokar v MTP* and *Struthers v Alcan*.

The argument of counsel who appeared for the first defenders was fourfold.

In the first place he maintained that this case was suitable for procedure roll where full notice of all the appropriate arguments could be given. Here there was a serious issue of law as to whether the regulations applied. (This argument in detail would form his third submission.)

His second point was that the test for summary decree under Rule of Court 89B was more strict than under rule 89A for interim damages. While the degree of satisfaction was the same, with interim damages the merits of the action and the defences were considered. With summary decree, however, when any defence was detected the motion had to be refused. There were safeguards with interim damages, e g insurance, and there were also repayment provisions. With summary decree, however, leave to reclaim was needed.

Thirdly, it was argued that the pursuer had no relevant case under the regulations relied on in art 6. Relevancy was of importance. He referred me to *Murray v Rococo*, although I pause to observe that *Murray* was decided by Lord McCluskey before there was a properly adjusted open record.

The present case had been sent to the procedure roll on 8 January. What was in issue was painting a lifeboat davit. That was not a work of engineering construction in terms of the pursuer's latest amendment. While repainting could be repair, this was expressed to be merely painting. It was not said the oil installation was made of steel or reinforced concrete. Such was not within judicial knowledge. He referred me to *Shepherd v Pearson*.

Finally, he argued that there was a proper defence. He referred to *Ross v British Coal*. The case concerned the supply of scaffolding boards by a third party and these defenders could not be fixed with the knowledge

of the defects. The pursuer's amendment showed that
he was unsure of his own case and the defenders were
entitled to have a trial on the facts where there was a
genuine issue.

Counsel for the second defenders adopted the arguments of counsel for the first defenders on what were
the correct tests for summary decree.

He further argued that the case against his clients in
art 9 was irrelevant. The scaffold was a temporary
structure and was not part of the installation. References to "equipment" in other statutes was unhelpful.
The preamble to reg 14 was not in point. In any event
he was entitled to put the pursuer to proof.

I turn now to my decision.

It respectfully seems to me that the proper test for
summary decree is set out by Lord Cullen in *Robinson
v Thomson* (but not reported on this point). I was
provided with a library copy which states (p 8):
"Before granting a motion for summary decree the
court requires to be 'satisfied that there is no defence
to the action or any part of it to which the motion
relates'. I interpret 'satisfied' in the same way as it has
been interpreted in cases relating to interim damages,
namely as requiring something more than probability
but less than complete certainty. . . . The wording to
which I refer also involves that the court should be
able to identify a part of the case to which it is satisfied
there is no defence".

I am also satisfied that if it unmistakably appears
that there may be an issue of relevancy the matter
must go to procedure roll and summary decree is
inappropriate. (See *Murray v Rococo* and *Rankin v
Reid*.)

In some cases in the Outer House, problems in relation to summary decree have arisen where the action,
as here, is one for reparation. This matter was considered by Lord Prosser in *Ross v British Coal Corporation* at p 856 where his Lordship said this: "I do not
regard the rule as unusable in reparation actions.
There will be many reparation claims where the
defender had direct knowledge of the specific events
founded upon, and will not be entitled to shelter
behind a skeletal defence. Road accidents provide an
obvious example where this might arise, and I think
a comparable situation can be found, even with a corporate defender, if the alleged fault turns upon actions
at the time of the alleged accident, by one who is effectively representing the defender. But in a case where
the alleged fault lies in prior omissions or the like the
defender will at least prima facie be in a position
where he can say that he has no knowledge of the
specific events. That is the position adopted by the
defenders in the present case, and it is one which, in
my view, they are entitled to maintain, notwithstanding that there may be information from others
supporting the pursuer's claim". I refer also in this
context to the opinion of Lord MacLean in *Struthers
v Alcan etc Ltd* where his Lordship carefully analysed
the authorities in the context of reparation.

In this case the record was closed on 6 November

1991 after a three month period on the adjustment
roll. The parties have thus had full opportunity to
adjust the summons and defences.

In my view, here, a clear distinction exists between
the defenders. The first defenders did not supply the
relevant scaffolding board and at this stage I think
they can be heard to say that they have no knowledge
of its defect or how the pursuer came to fall. No 25 of
process is not a document emanating from them, albeit
it is "information from others supporting the pursuer's claim" (Lord Prosser, supra). On the argument
addressed to me I entertain doubts as to whether the
Construction (Working Places) Regulations 1966
apply to what the pursuer says in his pleadings he was
doing at the time. I consider that this matter should be
more fully argued at procedure roll. It cannot be disputed that these defenders have said nothing about the
practicability or otherwise of the measures required to
be taken. If they maintain that attitude they will have
no defence to what may prove to be absolute liability.
However, what they do or do not say matters not at all
if the pursuer has no relevant case.

However, the second defenders are in a different
position. No 25 of process is their report of an investigation made on the date of the accident. It shows that
the board broke, was examined and found to have a
knot. It notes the pursuer's injuries, who were his
employers and explains in some detail the cause of the
"defective scaffolding".

In my view this production taken with the admissions in ans 2 amount to acceptance of the pursuer's
averments of how, why and in what circumstances he
came to be injured.

Various grounds of statutory fault under the 1976
Regulations are made and in particular reg 14 which
provides: "At all times all reasonably practicable steps
shall be taken to ensure the safety of persons at all
places on the installation". That is an absolute duty
(*Breslin v Britoil*). The defenders do not plead an issue
of what was practicable. In my judgment a scaffold
erected at A2 laydown area is "a place". In these
circumstances I am satisfied that the second defenders
have no defence to this part of the case and anything
stated in the defences is merely tactical. I am not concerned with their defence to any other part of the case.

In the result the motion for summary decree against
the first defenders will be refused; but in granting it
against the second defenders I repel their first, second
and third pleas in law. Any proof in respect of these
defenders will accordingly be restricted to quantum of
damages.

---

*Counsel for Pursuer, Sturrock; Solicitors, Balfour &
Manson, Nightingale & Bell — Counsel for First
Defenders, Kinroy; Solicitors, Simpson & Marwick, WS
— Counsel for Second Defenders, Hanretty; Solicitors,
Gillam Mackie, SSC.*

P McC

Rellis v Hart

A   OUTER HOUSE

LORD COULSFIELD

9 JUNE 1992

Parent and child — Custody — Jurisdiction — Habitual residence of child — Child of unmarried parents brought to Scotland by mother with consent of father — No agreement as to duration of visit — Father commencing proceedings in English court when mother refused to return child — Whether Scottish or English court had jurisdiction — Family Law Act 1986 (c 55), ss 9, 10 and 41.

B

The Family Law Act 1986 provides as the principal ground of jurisdiction in relation to custody, where custody is not sought as an ancillary to divorce, the habitual residence of the child. Both in England and Scotland a father has no parental rights in relation to an illegitimate child until he is granted these rights by the court. Section 41 of the 1986 Act provides that a child's habitual residence endures for a year beyond the child's removal or retention outside the particular part of the United Kingdom if that removal or retention is without the consent of all who have the right to determine where the child resides or is in contravention of an order made by a British court.

C

A child of unmarried parents lived with her father after the separation of her parents, occasionally spending a few days with her mother. The father lived in England and the mother in Scotland. In December 1991 the mother collected the child from England, by agreement with the father, and took the child to Scotland for a holiday the duration of which had not been agreed. On 7 January 1992 the mother informed the father that she was not going to return the child. On 8 January the father applied for and obtained an order in the English courts requiring the mother to return the child. He founded jurisdiction on the habitual residence of the child in England. On 10 January a residence order was obtained from the same court. That order included a requirement that the child be returned to the father. The father sought to enforce these orders by registration in the Court of Session. On 23 January the Lord Ordinary refused to make any order and called for a report. On 3 February the English court granted a further order extending the operation of the specific order of 8 January and the residence order of 10 January. That order was also registered in the Court of Session. The father then sought an order for delivery of the child in implement of the registered English order. The mother disputed the father's entitlement to delivery, contending that the child's habitual residence had been in Scotland at all material times since only the mother had parental rights, the child being illegitimate, and the child had accordingly lost its English habitual residence when the mother had removed the child to Scotland.

D

E

F

Held, that the question of habitual residence was one of fact and not of legal right, and that since there had been no agreement that the child should remain permanently or for a long time in Scotland, the child had retained her habitual residence in England until at

least 8 January 1992 (p 741A-D); and order for delivery *pronounced*.

G

Petition for enforcement of custody order

Sean Rellis petitioned for an order for delivery and ancillary orders to enforce a custody order in his favour pronounced in an English court. The child who was the subject of the order was the illegitimate child of the petitioner and Elizabeth Hart. After sundry procedure, including a remit to a reporter to inquire into the circumstances of the child, the petitioner sought an order for delivery of the child.

H

The petition came before the Lord Ordinary (Coulsfield).

Statutory provisions

The Family Law Act 1986 provides:

"8. A court in Scotland may entertain an application for a custody order otherwise than in matrimonial proceedings only if it has jurisdiction under section 9, 10, 12 or 15 (2) of this Act.

I

"9. Subject to section 11 of this Act [concurrent matrimonial proceedings], an application for a custody order otherwise than in matrimonial proceedings may be entertained by — (a) the Court of Session if, on the date of the application, the child concerned is habitually resident in Scotland; . . . .

"10. Subject to section 11 of this Act, an application for a custody order otherwise than in matrimonial proceedings may be entertained by — (a) the Court of Session if, on the date of the application, the child concerned — (i) is present in Scotland; and (ii) is not habitually resident in any part of the United Kingdom. . . .

J

"12. Notwithstanding that any other court, whether within or outside Scotland, has jurisdiction to entertain an application for a custody order, the Court of Session or the sheriff shall have jurisdiction to entertain such an application if — (a) the child concerned is present in Scotland or, as the case may be, in the sheriffdom on the date of the application; and (b) the Court of Session or sheriff considers that, for the protection of the child, it is necessary to make such an order immediately. . . .

K

"25.—(1) Where a custody order made by a court in any part of the United Kingdom is in force with respect to a child who has not attained the age of sixteen, then, subject to subsection (2) below, the order shall be recognised in any other part of the United Kingdom as having the same effect in that other part as if it had been made by the appropriate court in that other part and as if that court had had jurisdiction to make it. . . .

L

"41.—(1) Where a child who — (a) has not attained the age of sixteen, and (b) is habitually resident in a part of the United Kingdom, becomes habitually resident outside that part of the United Kingdom in consequence of circumstances of the kind specified in subsection (2) below, he shall be treated for the purposes of this Part as continuing to be habitually resident in that part of the United Kingdom for the period of one year beginning with the date on which those circumstances arise.

"(2) The circumstances referred to in subsection (1) above exist where the child is removed from or retained outside, or himself leaves or remains outside, the part of the United Kingdom in which he was habitually resident before his change of residence — (a) without the agreement of the person or all the persons having, under the law of that part of the United Kingdom, the right to determine where he is to reside, or (b) in contravention of an order made by a court in any part of the United Kingdom."

Textbooks referred to
Anton, *Private International Law* (2nd ed), p 514.
Cretney and Masson, *Principles of Family Law* (5th ed), p 545.

On 9 June 1992 the Lord Ordinary *granted* the order sought.

LORD COULSFIELD.—The petitioner is the father and the respondent is the mother of Kerri Runa Lee Rellis, who was born on 15 October 1988. The parties lived together for about four years but were never married. The respondent has another child born as a result of a previous association. The petitioner and the respondent met when they were both living in a community in Wales. They initially lived together there and later lived in a truck which was converted to a mobile home. They followed a somewhat nomadic existence until the summer of 1990, when they sold the truck and bought a caravan which was parked on a farm in Wales, where the petitioner obtained casual work. In September 1990, the parties separated for three weeks, during which time the respondent remained in the caravan with Kerri and her other child. They finally separated in November 1990 and at this time the petitioner took Kerri while the other child remained with the respondent. The petitioner and Kerri moved to Bristol, where they lived with a friend, but the petitioner remained in contact with the respondent and when he went on holiday to France early in 1991 the respondent looked after Kerri. At the time of the separation, the respondent became involved with an older man and was quite content that Kerri should live with the petitioner. In June 1991, the respondent discovered that the man with whom she was associating was having an affair with someone else and she became depressed as a result. Later the same month, her father died. As a result of these events she required treatment in a psychiatric hospital, first in England and later in Glasgow. She has now been discharged from the hospital and appears to have fully recovered. By August 1991, the petitioner had met his present girlfriend who was working with Archaos circus. With the circus, the petitioner visited Edinburgh and while there met the respondent and arranged for Kerri to spend one week with her in Glasgow. The petitioner had been given an opportunity to travel with the circus to Canada in Sep-

tember 1991 and it was intended that Kerri should stay with the respondent. However, after having had Kerri for one day, the respondent contacted him and advised that she was unable to cope. As a result, the petitioner took Kerri to Canada with him. After their return, Kerri did spend one week with the respondent in Glasgow. In November 1991, the petitioner obtained a tenancy for a flat in Bristol, where he still resides.

Kerri remained with the petitioner until 28 December 1991 when the respondent went to Bristol and collected her. The parties do not entirely agree as to the basis upon which it was arranged that the respondent should take Kerri to Glasgow. In a report ordered early in 1992, the reporter records the petitioner as stating: "That he was agreeable to the respondent taking Kerri to Scotland for 2/3 weeks but no longer because she was to start back at nursery. The respondent wanted to keep Kerri for a long period but he was not agreeable to this. He was anxious not to disturb Kerri's routine. The parties would appear to have argued over the period of access."

The position of the respondent is recorded as follows: "Ms Hart explained that she found her visit to Bristol in December very difficult. She was living in the same house as the petitioner and his girlfriend and felt uncomfortable. She wanted to spend some time with Kerri in Scotland but the petitioner was being very possessive and dictatorial about the period of access. They were therefore unable to agree on the duration of Kerri's stay in Scotland."

Up to that time, there had evidently been a reasonably flexible arrangement for access and care of Kerri. The respondent was not finally discharged from outpatient attendance at hospital until December 1991. It is also relevant to observe that, according to the report, Kerri had been regularly attending a nursery in Bristol during the period of her residence there with the petitioner.

On 7 January 1992, the petitioner telephoned the respondent to arrange to collect Kerri. The respondent however told him that Kerri was not to be returned to him. On the following day, the petitioner commenced proceedings in England for the return of Kerri. On 8 January 1992 an order was made in Bristol county court requiring the respondent to return Kerri to the petitioner. On 10 January 1992 a further order was made in the same court. This was a residence order and included a requirement that the child be returned to the care of the petitioner. Both of these orders were made on ex parte applications at the instance of the petitioner and without the respondent having been heard. Thereafter, the petitioner commenced the present proceedings in Scotland. On 23 January 1992, the Lord Ordinary refused to make any order in the meantime and remitted to a reporter to report on all the facts and circumstances relating to the care and upbringing of Kerri. The original residence order in the Bristol county court was made for the period to 21 January 1992 but that hearing was

A
adjourned until 3 February and the earlier orders were automatically extended to that date. On 3 February 1992, the county court made an order extending the specific order of 8 January 1992 and the residence order of 10 January 1992 until further order. The respondent was represented at the hearing on 3 February. There may have been some confusion in the minds of those advising the respondent in Scotland as to what the position was at the English hearing on 3 February. Counsel for the respondent informed me that the county court had been told that by that stage

B
the Scottish petition included a claim for custody of Kerri and that the Scottish court was "seized of" the case and accordingly that the county court adjourned the proceedings before it sine die. That understanding, however, is quite at variance with the terms of the order made on 3 February which clearly extends the previous orders, and also gives leave to the respondent to apply to vary or discharge the order within 48 hours. I should observe at this point that it was suggested that the county court had not been given

C
correct information about the respondent's position in that it had been suggested that the respondent had been in hospital for a period of six months, whereas her actual detention had only lasted from June to August 1991. It seems to me, however, that having regard to the fact that the respondent was still under supervision in respect of her psychiatric condition in that she was attending Gartnavel hospital as an outpatient until December 1991 that point is of relatively little significance.

D
On 18 March 1992 there was an application in the Court of Session for access and access was agreed on the understanding that the petitioner's counsel would recommend that the proceedings in Bristol should be dropped. On about 25 March 1992, the report was lodged and following on the report the petitioner declined to accept the recommendation that the Bristol proceedings should be dropped. On 11 May 1992 the order of the Bristol court was registered in the Court of Session.

E
The next stage of the proceedings was a hearing before a Lord Ordinary on 22 May 1992, following the production of the report. The report spoke favourably of both parents and in particularly stated that the petitioner had demonstrated his ability to cope with the problems of looking after a very young child, that the relationship between the father and daughter was very good and that the petitioner's girlfriend is very supportive. It is also stated that the petitioner has provided for Kerri materially and emotionally and

F
attempted to give her some stability. It was also found that the respondent was genuine in her desire to obtain custody of both children and that she had a good relationship with Kerri. The reporter found it difficult to make a recommendation but, on balance, in view of the fact that Kerri was with the respondent, recommended that the status quo should continue.

At the hearing on 22 May 1992 questions about the jurisdiction of the court were, for the first time, raised because it was appreciated that the fact that the child was illegitimate might have some bearing upon the

view which should be taken. It was also suggested in the course of that hearing that it would be logical for G the respondent to attempt to challenge the jurisdiction of the Bristol county court and to consider seeking custody in the Scottish proceedings. Following upon that discussion amendments were made to the petition and the answers and the question came before me on 5 June 1992 on a motion by the petitioner to order delivery of the child Kerri to him.

The issue upon which the grant or refusal of the order turns is that of jurisdiction. Under ss 8 to 13 of the Family Law Act 1986, the factor which determines H whether the Court of Session has jurisdiction, other than jurisdiction in a situation of emergency, in a case which is not a matrimonial proceeding, is the habitual residence of the child. The same rule applies in the English courts. If the county court in Bristol had jurisdiction on 8 January 1992, then in terms of s 41 of the 1986 Act, that jurisdiction will continue for a year because the child will continue to be treated as habitually resident in England. It follows that, if s 41 applies, the Scottish court has no jurisdiction to deal I with the child other than an emergency jurisdiction. As I understood the position, that analysis was not disputed by counsel for the respondent. Counsel for the respondent submitted, however, that the proper course was to sist the cause in order to enable a challenge to be made to the English court order, but as I understood the position, the primary ground on which the challenge would be made would be that the English court did not have jurisdiction to make the original order. J

It was submitted on behalf of the respondent that the English court did not have jurisdiction because, since the child is illegitimate, the only person who has any rights in relation to the child is the respondent; the petitioner does not enjoy any rights as father of the child unless he obtains such rights in virtue of a court order. So far as relevant, the position in regard to the rights of the parents of an illegitimate child is the same in Scotland and in England. It was, accordingly, submitted that there was no question of the petitioner's K consent being required as a matter of law to bring the child to Scotland nor to the respondent's retaining her there. The respondent was the sole person with parental rights. She had every right to retain the child and any question of access or consent or agreement was irrelevant. Since the child had been moved to Scotland and become resident there before any order of the court was made in England and since the father's agreement was not required to that being done, the English court had no jurisdiction. Counsel also questioned whether the English court order was L properly made since in Cretney and Masson, *Principles of Family Law* (5th ed), p 545, it was suggested that a residence order could only be made in favour of the father of an illegitimate child if an order giving parental rights was also made and that did not appear to have been done.

In my view, the respondent's argument places too much emphasis on the question of parental rights at law and too little upon the factual situation. As I understand the position, the question whether

habitual residence has been established is one of fact.
A It is notable that attempts either to define the concept
or to make it dependent upon definitions of legal right,
have been uniformly resisted (cf Anton, *Private International Law* (2nd ed), p 514). Counsel for the respondent accepted that until 30 December 1991, the child
in the present case was habitually resident with her
father in England. It seems to me that to accept, as the
respondent's argument would require, that the
moment the child came to Scotland the effect of the
respondent's parental rights was to terminate her
B habitual residence in England and substitute habitual
residence in Scotland would be to distort the operation
of the rules in the 1986 Act. Habitual residence in one
jurisdiction does not necessarily come to an end
merely because the person concerned leaves the jurisdiction for a short period or for a temporary purpose.
There is some dispute as to whether there was a
precise agreement between the petitioner and the
respondent as to the length of the child's stay in
Glasgow, but from the facts ascertained by the
C reporter it is, I think, clear that there was no agreement that the child should remain permanently or for
a long time in Glasgow. The petitioner clearly
expected the child to return. He had made arrangements for the child's attendance at a nursery and he
took proceedings as soon as the return was delayed. In
these circumstances, it seems to me that on the
admitted facts of this case, the English court did have
jurisdiction on 8 January 1992 when the first order
was made. If so, it follows that the Scottish courts have
D no jurisdiction other than the ancillary jurisdiction or
jurisdiction on the grounds of emergency. The report,
however, makes it clear that there is no question of the
child's welfare being in danger if she is returned to the
care of the petitioner.

At earlier stages in the proceedings in Scotland, it
was suggested that steps might be taken to contest the
English order but, for various reasons, nothing effective has yet been done. Counsel for the respondent
explained some of the reasons for that failure and it
E appears that there may have been some unfortunate
lack of communication between the respondent's
advisers in England and Scotland. I do not, however,
proceed on any ground related to any failure on the
part of the respondent or her advisers to take effective
and timeous steps to contest the English order.

I was also invited, under reference to s 30 of the
1986 Act, to sist the proceedings in order that proceedings might be taken in England. Section 30 appears to
F give a broad discretion, but, in the whole circumstances of this case, I do not think that it would be
appropriate to exercise it to sist these proceedings.
This child has virtually spent her whole life outside
Scotland. Her parents' whole relationship took place
in England or Wales. It is, perhaps, unfortunate that
she has been in Scotland for almost six months while
these proceedings have been in progress but I do not
think that that fact of itself is sufficient to cause one
to depart from the view that the proper court to
regulate questions relating to her welfare is the
English court.

In all these circumstances, I shall grant the order
sought by the petitioner.   G

---

*Counsel for Petitioner (Father), Haddow, QC; Solici-
tors, J & A Hastie, SSC — Counsel for Respondent
(Mother), O'Brien; Solicitors, John G Gray & Co, SSC.*

C H

H

Rehman v Ahmad

OUTER HOUSE
LORD PENROSE
17 JULY 1992

*Writ — Rectification — Document failing to express
accurately the intention of the parties — Requirements
for rectification — Law Reform (Miscellaneous Pro-   I
visions) (Scotland) Act 1985 (c 73), s 8 (1).*

*Evidence — Standard of proof — Rectification of docu-
ment — Whether proof on balance of probabilities or
beyond reasonable doubt — Law Reform (Miscellaneous
Provisions) (Scotland) Act 1985 (c 73), s 8 (1).*

*Statute — Construction — Reference to report of Scottish
Law Commission — Purpose for which reference may be
made.*   J

The petitioner and the respondent carried on business in partnership as restaurateurs. The petitioner
sought rectification of a minute of agreement dissol-
ving the partnership which he averred failed properly
to reflect the terms of dissolution agreed. The issue
between the parties related to the calculation of an
option price at which the petitioner was entitled to
acquire the heritable interest of the respondent in
restaurant premises owned by them. The option as
expressed in the agreement provided for acquisition   K
"at any time . . . at a price equal to one half of the
market value of the said building on a bricks and
mortar basis". The petitioner submitted that it had
been agreed that the price would be equal to one half
of the market value of the premises after deduction of
a second loan, the option being exercisable at any
time. The respondent was to have a cross option postponed to that of the petitioner. The respondent maintained that the parties intended the property to be a
long term investment.   L

In relation to the appropriate standard of proof, the
petitioner submitted that the requirement was for
proof on a balance of probabilities. The respondent
submitted that the standard was akin to proof beyond
reasonable doubt.

Held (after proof), (1) that it was legitimate to have
regard to a memorandum and report of the Scottish
Law Commission in interpreting the statute and that
the appropriate standard of proof was proof on a
balance of probabilities (*Anderson v Lambie*, 1954

SLT 73, *distinguished*) (pp 745F and 746C-E); (2) that in order to succeed the petitioner had to provide proof of an agreement made independently of, and at or prior to the date of, the document or documents intended to give effect to it, coupled with proof that the writing failed to express accurately the common intention of the parties at the point at which the agreement was made, common intention being the intention ascertained objectively in accordance with the normal canons of construction of agreements, and in particular the rules applicable in ascertaining whether consensus in idem had been achieved, and to what effect (pp 751K-752C); and (3) that the petitioner had failed to prove consensus in the sense required to an agreement containing both the points averred (pp 747E, 749F-I, 750J-L and 753D); and prayer of petition *refused*.

Petition under s 8 (1) of the Law Reform (Miscellaneous Provisions) (Scotland) Act 1985

Hafeezur Rehman presented a petition under s 8 (1) of the Law Reform (Miscellaneous Provisions) (Scotland) Act 1985 for rectification of a document purporting to give effect to agreed terms of dissolution of a partnership between them formed to carry on the business of running two restaurants. His former partner, Nazir Ahmad, appeared as respondent.

Terms of agreement

The agreement executed by the parties was in the following terms:

"Whereas the parties have carried on the business of Restaurateurs at Fourteen Princes Street, Falkirk and Twenty/Twenty-four Kirk Wynd, Falkirk sometime as Harris Properties (Glasgow) Limited and thereafter trading under the name as Harris Properties (Glasgow) and it has been agreed to bring the partnership to an end: Therefore it is agreed as follows: First, the date of dissolution of the partnership shall be the date hereof. Second, Books of Accounts shall be prepared by the parties' Accountants to the date of dissolution and the same shall be binding on both parties. Third, The First Party shall take over the restaurant business known as and forming The Sinbad Restaurant, Fourteen Princes Street, Falkirk with immediate effect and the Second Party will take over the restaurant business known as Reflections Restaurant, Twenty/Twenty-four Kirk Wynd, Falkirk also with immediate effect. Fourth, In respect that the parties have purchased the heritable property at Fourteen Princes Street, Falkirk in their joint names no rent or other payment will be made by the First Party in respect of his occupation of the said Restaurant. All mortgage payments in respect of the said building at Fourteen Princes Street, Falkirk and buildings insurance premiums will be borne by the First Party and the buildings insurance premiums will be borne equally by the Parties in equal shares [sic] and each party will retain in effect during the period of the heritable security life insurance in the amount of the loan and will otherwise comply with the terms and condition of the loan. Fifth, The First Party will have the option at any time to purchase the Second Party's interest in the said heritable subjects at Fourteen Princes Street, Falkirk at a price equal to one half of the market value of the said building on a bricks and mortar basis ignoring any value of the Restaurant Business operating therefrom. In the event that the First Party wishes to sell his share in the said building of Fourteen Princes Street, Falkirk he will require to give the first option to purchase his heritable interest to the Second Party again at one half of the market value of the building. In the event of any dispute between the parties as to what constitutes one half of the market value of the said building at Fourteen Princes Street, Falkirk the matter will be referred to a Chartered Surveyor and failing agreement a surveyor appointed by the Dean of the Royal Faculty of Procurators in Glasgow and such surveyor's decision will be final and binding on both parties. Sixth, It is understood that the said Company of Harris Properties (Glasgow) Limited have certain outstanding liabilities and the parties hereby agree and confirm that with regard to the arrears of PAYE, National Insurance Contributions and VAT due by the Company, the First Party shall pay 60 per cent of such arrears and the Second Party shall pay the remaining 40 per cent of such arrears and both parties will be responsible for their own tax liabilities in respect of the said Limited Company and the said partnership up to the date hereof. As regards all other debts due by the said Limited Company the First Party is to have no ongoing liability for any such debts and the Second Party shall be responsible for the same including without prejudice to the foregoing generality all sums due to Tennent Caledonian Breweries Limited, Lombard North Central Finance Company and all other payments due under any leasing agreement or credit sale agreement entered into by the Company. Seventh, Considering that there is a debit balance of approximately seventy thousand pounds £70,000 on the partnership bank account with the Bank of Scotland, Alexandra Parade Branch, Glasgow the First Party undertakes to accept liability for such debit balance to the extent of £43,000 and the Second Party undertakes liability in respect of the said debit balance to the extent of £27,000 and the parties shall be responsible for the interest on the total debit balance with their Bankers to date in the proportion of 60 per cent for the First Party and 40 per cent for the Second Party and each undertakes liability in respect of all interest due or to become due on the proportion of the partnership bank account debit balance for which each hereby accepts responsibility."

Terms of petition

The petitioner sought to have the agreement amended as follows:

"(a) By adding at the end of the first sentence of clause fifth thereof, the following: 'and after first deducting the whole outstanding loan secured over the said heritable subjects';

"(b) at the end of the second sentence of clause fifth thereof, by adding the following: 'calculated as aforesaid and after first deducting the whole of said outstanding loan'; and

"(c) by adding after the second sentence the following: 'in the event of either party exercising his option under this clause, he shall repay the whole of the outstanding loan secured over the said heritable subjects, or, alternatively, assume all obligations under and in terms of the standard security over said heritable subjects'."

In his concluding speech counsel for the petitioner sought leave to amend the prayer of the petition so that para (c) above would read: "in the event of either party wishing to exercise his option under this clause, it shall be a condition of doing so that he shall repay the whole of the outstanding loan secured over the said heritable subjects, or, alternatively, procure the discharge of the other party from all obligations under and in terms of the standard security or undertaken in connection with the said loan over said heritable subjects."

Statutory provisions

The Law Reform (Miscellaneous Provisions) (Scotland) Act 1985 provides:

"8.—(1) Subject to section 9 of this Act, where the court is satisfied, on an application made to it, that — (a) a document intended to express or to give effect to an agreement fails to express accurately the common intention of the parties to the agreement at the date when it was made; or (b) a document intended to create, transfer, vary or renounce a right, not being a document falling within paragraph (a) above, fails to express accurately the intention of the grantor of the document at the date when it was executed, it may order the document to be rectified in any manner that it may specify in order to give effect to that intention.

"(2) For the purposes of subsection (1) above, the court shall be entitled to have regard to all relevant evidence, whether written or oral. . . .

"(4) Subject to section 9 (4) of this Act, a document ordered to be rectified under this section shall have effect as if it had always been so rectified."

Cases referred to

Advocate (Lord) v Ruffle, 1979 SLT 212; 1979 SC 371.
Anderson v Lambie, 1954 SLT 73; 1954 SC (HL) 43.
Angus v Bryden, 1992 SLT 884.
Bank of Scotland v Graham's Trustee, 1993 SLT 252.
Brown v Brown, 1972 SLT 143; 1972 SC 123.
Fowler v Fowler (1859) 4 De G & J 250.
Gribben v Gribben, 1976 SLT 266.
Harris v F, 1991 SLT 242.
Inglis v Buttery & Co (1878) 5 R (HL) 87.
Joscelyne v Nissen [1970] 2 QB 86; [1979] 2 WLR 509; [1970] 1 All ER 1213.
Lennon v Co-operative Insurance Society Ltd, 1986 SLT 98.
MAC Electrical and Heating Engineers Ltd v Calscot Electrical (Distributors) Ltd, 1989 SCLR 498.
McIntyre v Armitage Shanks Ltd, 1980 SLT 112; 1980 SC (HL) 46.
Muirhead & Turnbull v Dickson (1905) 7 F 686.

Oliver v Gaughan, OH, 24 May 1990, unreported (1990 GWD 22-1247).
Sereshky v Sereshky, 1988 SLT 426.
Shaw v William Grant (Minerals) Ltd, 1989 SLT 121.
Thompson (George) Services Ltd v Moore, 1993 SLT 634.
Thomson v James (1855) 18 D 1.
Ward v Chief Constable, Strathclyde Police, 1991 SLT 292.

Textbook referred to

Walker and Walker, *Evidence*, pp 79-80.

On 17 July 1992 the Lord Ordinary *refused* the prayer of the petition.

LORD PENROSE.—The parties carried on business as restaurateurs in Falkirk. In discussions commencing towards the end of 1988 they agreed to dissolve their partnership. They executed a minute of agreement purporting to give effect to the agreed terms of dissolution on 23 February 1989. The petitioner, Hafeezur Rehman, maintained that the minute of agreement failed properly to reflect the terms agreed between them, and sought rectification of its provisions under reference to s 8 of the Law Reform (Miscellaneous Provisions) (Scotland) Act 1985. The respondent, Nazir Ahmad, maintained in his pleadings that the minute of agreement gave effect to the terms agreed between the parties.

The issue between the parties as pled was, superficially, narrow. The order sought related to the calculation of the option price at which the petitioner was entitled to acquire the heritable interest of the respondent in certain restaurant premises owned by them. So far as was disclosed in the evidence and documents the background was of a business conducted with less than strict acknowledgment of the distinct interests of the parties as individuals, as partners, and as members of a limited company. The dissolution negotiations and agreement appeared, on analysis, to have failed to deal with some of the matters one might have expected to find in a properly drafted minute of agreement intended to deal comprehensively with the interests of parties on the break up of their business relationships and the dissolution of partnership. The minute, in which Mr Rehman was the first party, and Mr Ahmad the second party, was in these terms: [his Lordship quoted the terms of the agreement and continued:] The parties consented to registration of this minute for preservation and execution.

The amendments sought were set out in the prayer of the petition as follows: [his Lordship quoted the terms of the petition set out supra and continued:]

I was urged by counsel to deal with the issue raised on the petition narrowly, and to ignore the effect of the agreement as a whole, either as a matter of construction of its provisions, or in the light of material lodged in process which might bear on the structure of the dissolution contract. In particular I was urged to ignore accounts prepared relative to these businesses which might have a bearing upon the com-

mercial reality of what I was invited to do by parties
A in respect of this application.

The parties formed a limited company, latterly
named Harris Properties (Glasgow) Ltd, to carry on
their businesses. The premises at 14 Princes Street
had been let by Central Regional Council to Akhtar
Hussain and Mohammad Arshad in 1984. That lease
was assigned to Harris Properties (Glasgow) Ltd, with
consent, by assignation dated 18 and 26 June and 4
July 1986, for a consideration of £47,000. The lease
contained an option to purchase. Solicitors acting for
B Harris Properties (Glasgow) Ltd concluded missives
for the purchase of the property from the council on
8 August 1988, at a price of £85,000. The price was
funded by a loan of £85,000 obtained from Allied Irish
Finance Co Ltd in November 1988. The terms of
repayment were set out in a letter sent by Allied Irish
to the parties dated 18 November 1988. Instalments,
calculated initially on a 15 year repayment term at an
artificially low rate, were to remain fixed at £1,151.75
per month for the first five years of the loan period,
C after which any deficiency arising from discrepancies
between that rate and the contractual rates applicable
was to be paid and the instalments for the remainder
of the term adjusted. There were stipulations for
additional security, and the offer of finance was
subject to a satisfactory survey report. The parties
instructed Messrs Wilkie & Simpson, chartered surveyors, to provide a bricks and mortar valuation of the
subjects. The surveyors reported on 25 October 1988
that on that basis the subjects had a value of £110,000.
D The disposition of the subjects was executed on 3
February 1989 in favour of "Hafeezur Rehman and
Nazir Ahmad equally between them and . . . their
respective executors, assignees and disponees whomsoever". Business at the Sinbad was carried on latterly
by a partnership using the firm name Harris Properties (Glasgow), of which the parties were the only
partners. Business relationships between the limited
company and the partnership and between the limited
company and the parties as individuals were not
E explored in evidence in a way which would allow one
to make findings in fact with any degree of historical
accuracy. It was the business carried on at the Sinbad
that Hafeezur Rehman agreed to take over on dissolution and in respect of which the option clause in question was to have effect.

The parties were also interested in Reflections, a
restaurant business carried on at 20/24 Kirk Wynd,
Falkirk. It is sufficient to note at this stage that the
F premises there were held on lease, that the history of
the parties' interests was as complex as in the case of
the Sinbad, and that it would be impossible on the
evidence to analyse in any satisfactory way the relationships which arose. Nazir Ahmad agreed to take
over the business of Reflections on dissolution of the
partnership.

The purchase price for the property at 14 Princes
Street was sent by Messrs Clark Boyle & Co, then
acting as solicitors for both parties, to Central
Regional Council under cover of a letter dated 9

February 1989. The first letter in the exchanges of
correspondence constituting the missives was dated 21 G
July 1988. It appeared that early moves in the negotiations for dissolution of the partnership must have
taken place within a few weeks of the conclusion of the
missives, and that those negotiations were concluded
before the transaction to acquire the property was
settled.

There were differences between the parties about
the precise timing of negotiations. But, in evidence,
the petitioner and the respondent agreed in substance
in their description of some factors in the background H
to the dissolution. The businesses had not been
profitable. The petitioner took the initiative and proposed that the parties should go their separate ways.
After discussions, which took place in the ordinary
course of their business meetings towards the end of
1988 and into the beginning of 1989, it was agreed
that the partnership should be dissolved. The respondent was to have the choice of the businesses. He
elected to take over Reflections. It was agreed that the
dissolution would take effect generally on the basis I
that the petitioner should take Sinbad, and become
liable for certain obligations, and the respondent
should take Reflections, and take over certain liabilities. Thereafter a meeting was arranged at the
office of Clark Boyle, the firm's solicitors.

In relation to the critical issues of fact upon which
a remedy under s 8 depended, counsel differed in their
submissions on the standard of proof to be applied. It
is necessary to consider this matter before embarking
on a discussion of the evidence and the matters of fact J
which have to be resolved. Counsel for the petitioner
argued that the appropriate standard was the normal
civil standard of balance of probabilities. There was
nothing in the statute to suggest an alternative standard. There was no reason to adopt the standard of
proof beyond reasonable doubt. This matter had been
canvassed by Lord McCluskey in *Shaw v William
Grant (Minerals) Ltd*. He had said that there were no
special canons of relevancy for this type of case. In
Oliver v Gaughan, Lord MacLean was referred to K
Anderson v Lambie in support of the submissions that
the onus of proof was on the pursuer to overcome the
terms of the deed and that the standard of proof
required was such that would leave no fair and reasonable doubt on the mind. Without expressing any
opinion on the proper test Lord MacLean had been
satisfied to the standard specified. The passages in
Anderson which were relevant were in the speeches of
Lord Reid and Lord Keith. Lord Reid, 1954 SLT at
p 80 said: "There is a heavy onus on a party who seeks L
to reduce a probative deed, but in my opinion, the
appellant has proved his case beyond reasonable
doubt." Lord Keith, at p 83, said: "In the matter of
proof the *onus* is on the appellant. He has to overcome
the terms of the conveyance and the *onus* is not a light
one. It is, in my opinion, rightly expressed by Lord
Chelmsford in *Fowler v Fowler* (1859), 4 De G & J 250,
at p 265, as requiring a standard of proof that will
leave no fair and reasonable doubt upon the mind."

These observations were in a sense irrelevant. It was

A not clear that either of the judges considered any kind of deed other than the particular case before them, which concerned a disposition on a register, a matter of great public significance. There were only two standards of proof in Scotland: Lord Emslie's opinion in *Brown v Brown*, 1972 SLT at p 145. Walker and Walker on *Evidence*, pp 79-80 demonstrated that there were limited classes of cases only in which the higher standard applied unless statute provided otherwise. The Scottish Law Commission memorandum no 43 (1979) dealt with the matter at para 4.3. The standard

B was perceived to be the ordinary civil standard.

Counsel for the respondent argued that the speeches in *Anderson v Lambie* were instructive in indicating the proper approach to the issue. She founded on *Fowler* as demonstrating the attitude of the English court that the power to reformulate a deed was to be used with care, and that it was only in the clearest case that the court should interfere with a document. In response counsel for the petitioner submitted that *Fowler* no longer represented the thinking of the

C English court: see *Joscelyne v Nissen*, where the test of "convincing proof" was applied, and drew attention to the Law Commission's view that in Scotland the ordinary civil test should apply. He also referred to a series of cases indicating the current thinking in Scotland on standard of proof genereally: *Harris v F*; *Ward v Chief Constable of Strathclyde*; *Lennon v Co-operative Insurance Society Ltd*; *Sereshky v Sereshky*; *Lord Advocate v Ruffle* and *Gribben v Gribben*.

D The question is primarily one of interpretation of the terms of the Act. While the context was different, *Harris v F* provides a warning against the indiscriminate use of authority in statutory construction. At p 246D the Lord Justice Clerk dismissed references to authority on the basis that in considering the scope of a statutory jurisdiction the question was wholly one of interpretation. Lord McCluskey and Lord McDonald made similar observations. On the other hand, in *McIntyre v Armitage Shanks Ltd* at pp 117

E and 118, the Lord Chancellor commented on the value, in appropriate cases, of having regard to the mischief sought to be cured by an Act of Parliament and on the use of relevant judicial authority and the reports of commissions and committees charged with proposing technical alterations to the law, emphasising the need for the greatest of care. In the instant case the section enables the provision of a remedy where the court is "satisfied" of certain facts and circumstances. The standard of proof is not specified. In

F these circumstances I consider it legitimate to have regard to relevant authority and to the memorandum and report of the Scottish Law Commission relating to the proposals which led to the enactment of s 8.

I did not find the authorities dealing with proof of criminal conduct in civil litigation or with civil penalty proceedings helpful. The case of *Ruffle* was in the latter category. Lord Jauncey applied the standard of proof beyond reasonable doubt in proceedings under the Taxes Management Act 1970, on the ground that they were quasi-criminal in nature. He

relied in part, by way of analogy, on the comparable rule in actions for breach of interdict: *Gribben v* G *Gribben*. Neither situation is in my opinion a parallel to the present where one is concerned only with proof of disconformity between parties' agreement and the expression of it in writing. *Lennon* involved allegations of wilful fireraising by the pursuer as a defence to a claim under a fire insurance policy. It has a bearing on the present question insofar as it indicates that there is a scale of standards of proof. Lord Kincraig said: "I accept . . . that the standard of proof which the defenders must attain in order to be entitled to judg- H ment is lower than the criminal standard, namely, beyond reasonable doubt, but higher than on a balance of probabilities. . . . I am not able to state in words the extent of that onus, but it is enough that I consider that it is higher than on a balance of probabilities."

Similarly in *Sereshky* Lord Weir had to consider allegations of forgery in proceedings for reduction of a deed. He said (at p 427): "In approaching the question of proof, I am prepared to accept for the purposes of this case that the standard to be met is less than that I required in a criminal case. Nonetheless the pursuer's case must be proved by very clear evidence and to a high degree of probability, having regard to the criminal implications involved."

There are difficulties with an approach which depends on indefinable qualitative distinctions. However in each of these cases the opinions identified a standard of proof intermediate between the civil standard of balance of probabilities and the standard J of proof beyond reasonable doubt where allegations of criminal conduct were made in a civil case not exposing any person to criminal penalties. Whatever the position in such cases, in my opinion, they have no bearing upon the present issue. It is clear that the reason for adopting the intermediate position was in each case the nature of the allegations, and the present case raises no issue of that kind.

In approaching the question of construction, it is, in K my opinion, necessary to distinguish between the definition of the standard of proof required to establish the facts necessary to entitle the applicant to a remedy, and the identification and specification of those facts and relevant circumstances. In *Ward* it was emphasised that the pursuers had to overcome the presumption in favour of police officers that they had acted properly by demonstrating want of probable cause and malice. But proof of those matters was required only on the ordinary civil balance of proba- L bilities. The approach appears to me to provide a helpful analogy in the present case. It is no doubt true that the applicant must overcome the force and effect of a written document. The presumptions of accuracy in a probative deed can be compared with those against lack of probable cause and malice which were dealt with in *Ward*. Proof of the facts and circumstances necessary to overcome the presumption does not require the application of any standard other than balance of probabilities. The status of a written contract is not in doubt. Lord Gifford's observations in

Inglis v Buttery & Co were adopted and repeated in the House of Lords by Lord Blackburn at p 102: "Now, I think it is quite fixed, and no more wholesome or salutory rule relative to written contracts can be devised, that where parties agree to embody, and do actually embody, their contract in a formal written deed, then in determining what the contract really was and really meant, a Court must look to the formal deed, and to that deed alone. . . . The written contract is that which is to be appealed to by both parties, however different it may be from their previous demands or stipulations, whether contained in letters or in verbal conversation. There can be no doubt that this is the general rule."

The presumption that a written document embodied the agreement of the parties is strong. The proponent, if he is to overcome that presumption, requires to prove the series of facts identified in the statute. Given the normal status of the document it will be appropriate to require careful and precise proof of those facts. The presumption in favour of the document must be overcome. To that extent the observations in *Anderson v Lambie* are pertinent and, in my opinion, helpful. But I consider that counsel for the petitioner was correct in distinguishing the case in other respects. It was concerned with a particular class of solemn document. The Act relates to a much wider range of documents. It applies to any agreement reduced to writing. It applies to private documents as it applies to documents on public registers. It applies to probative documents and documents requiring no particular solemnities of execution. Had it related exclusively to documents of the kind dealt with in *Anderson v Lambie*, one might have found in that case both the mischief sought to be remedied, and an indication of the standard of proof envisaged by the House of Lords at that time on analogy with the English remedy. However it is clear that the provision is not so limited in its scope. The Act does not stipulate a standard of proof different from the ordinary civil standard. There is nothing in the terms of the provision which can be read as implying any higher standard. Further the matter was quite clearly canvassed by the Law Commission, and the proposal was for the ordinary civil standard to apply. On the whole I agree with Lord McCluskey in *Shaw v William Grant* that there are no special canons applicable, in this context, under the Act. I did not find the reference to English authority helpful. It seemed to me that counsel for the petitioner was correct in observing that *Joscelyne v Nissen* implied a departure from the approach found in *Fowler*, but the adoption of the test of "convincing proof" in that case undermines its relevance to Scots law, given the views of Lord Emslie in *Brown v Brown*. In any event the English cases had no bearing upon the mischief addressed by the Scottish Act.

In their closing submissions counsel sought to persuade me to treat the petitioner and the respondent respectively as wholly credible and reliable witnesses. I did not find either the petitioner or the respondent to be wholly credible or reliable. Each was an intelligent and experienced businessman who appeared to me to have a keen appreciation of where lay the balance of advantage as he perceived it. The evidence on occasion took on the character of debate as the direction and purpose of counsel's questions were weighed before an answer was given. I was left with a clear impression that in their dealings one with the other manipulation of opportunity for advantage would have been characteristic rather than openness and fairness. In the positions they adopted in evidence, self justification appeared to be a powerful motive in some of the differences between them.

In the circumstances it is necessary to consider credibility and reliability as an aspect of each of the major subdivisions of the dispute in matters of fact rather than in an overall way.

The first chapter of evidence to be considered dealt generally with the background to the parties' business relationships, to their acquisition of the heritable property in Falkirk, and to the early stages in their discussions which led to dissolution of their business relationships. I accepted as altogether more credible and reliable the respondent's evidence as to the common intention of the parties in purchasing the property. The evidence of both parties was that the businesses had not been profitable when conducted by the limited company, nor later when conducted in partnership. The lease of the Sinbad cost £47,000, quite apart from the expenditure on improvements. It was valued at £110,000, ignoring goodwill associated with the restaurant activity, if there were any value in such an asset. It might have made good commercial sense for the parties to purchase the property for £85,000. But it would have made no sense at all for either to undertake the liability for a share of the price, nor to share in the associated expenses of purchase, on a short term basis if the professional valuation were even approximately correct. The petitioner maintained that the valuation was excessive, making a short term investment even less likely in my opinion. Further, the alteration of the arrangements for purchase, involving taking title in the parties' names as individuals on terms which excluded any suggestion of an obligation of trust for the partnership, concluded after they had already agreed to dissolve the firm, points in the direction of an intention separate from their intentions as trading partners. The structure of the funding, with a long initial period of instalments at advantageous rates, and ancillary securities including life assurance on both parties' lives, pointed in the same direction. Mrs Ahmad spoke also of her husband mentioning the investment as having a long term character. I accepted that evidence also. I rejected the evidence of the petitioner so far as it was to a contrary effect as untrue. I also consider it to be clear that in the course of their negotiations the implications of holding the property in the long term were discussed and agreed. Leaving aside the reason he gave for expressing willingness to enter into such a bargain, to which I shall come, the petitioner's evidence of the discussions was that the property of Sinbad restaurant would be kept in joint names, and that he would pay the mortgage instalments. When the property was sold the net profit would be divided after the deduction of the loan which was secured on the subjects. The respondent was consistent in describing the property as a long term investment and he agreed that the petitioner was to pay the mortgage instalments, and have no liability for rent. Arrangements were made for splitting the liability for insurance between them, notwithstanding the confused terms of the minute of agreement in this respect. Accordingly overall it appeared to me to be clear that in entering into the purchase and in structuring it in the way they did the parties had in mind that the equity in the property, likely to grow with time, would be a source of advantage on which both could draw in compensation for the trading debt incurred by them.

On the other hand, I considered that it was equally clear that at least from the time at which negotiations for the dissolution of the partnership began, the petitioner had as a major objective the obtaining of an option which would enable him to appropriate to his own advantage the equity potential in the heritable property. The petitioner explained that the reason he accepted liability for the mortgage instalments was that he would have a first option to buy out the respondent's share, with the respondent having a second option, and that it was his intention to exercise the option after the agreement had been completed. In explaining the reason for the option arrangements he said that the business was his and the property was in joint names and "so I decided that I will have the first option to buy the premises". In cross examination he was more explicit. He discussed his obligation to pay the mortgage instalments in the context of the option. He said "well the discussion of options . . . why I agreed to mortgage payments . . . because I knew after this agreement I would have the first option to buy his share and I will exercise my option so I don't have to pay this instalment not very long, a month or two". I considered it to be inherently probable, in the light of his evidence, and his later conduct, that the petitioner had set out to achieve a situation in which he would be able to exclude the respondent from the benefit of the growth potential of the property.

However, I do not consider it proved that the parties had reached agreement to the effect that the petitioner should have an option of this nature exercisable at any time. The petitioner's own evidence on the point was equivocal. When asked in cross examination whether he told the respondent that he intended to exercise his option within a month or two, he said that the respondent knew very well that he was expecting to exercise his option. But when pressed he said, "No I never told him this one, but I told him a lot of things." He then appeared to contradict himself. In fact he proceeded to exercise the option three days after signing the document. He would not be drawn on whether he had disclosed his intention to the respondent prior to the execution of the document. His final comments on this topic, though relating to the respondent, appeared to reflect the commercial opportunism which characterised his own approach. He dismissed the respondent's position on the matter as "just dreaming in the daylight time". I was firmly of opinion that the petitioner both entertained the ambition to achieve an option right which would enable him to acquire the property and exclude the respondent from the benefit of it and that he failed to disclose his intentions to the respondent while discussing at length the implications of a long term holding of the property. It was clear that the petitioner had initiated the steps towards dissolution. While insisting throughout that the agreement to dissolve the partnership was mutual, when pressed specifically on whose idea it was to dissolve he responded: "Well that is a different question. The idea was mutual, the idea whether it started from me, my idea or his idea, that is a different question." He agreed that it had been his idea. The parties had taken a few weeks to reach agreement. The respondent had not wanted the relationship to be broken up and felt that they should stay together to attempt to work out the difficulties that had already emerged. However the petitioner insisted and the respondent conceded. In the course of these discussions it was clear on the evidence of both that in very general terms at least something approaching cross options was discussed and it was agreed that option provisions should be built in to the dissolution agreement. However had the evidence gone no further than the evidence of the parties in describing their negotiations and discussions at the end of 1988 and the beginning of 1989 I would not have been satisfied that any such option agreement as was set out in the minute of agreement in its original form or either of the proposed amended forms had been agreed.

The impression from the evidence of the parties was of protracted discussions, with certain factors emerging as heads of agreement from time to time, but with a lack of mutual openness and candour preventing the formulation of heads of agreement overall. Nevertheless it was against this background that the petitioner took the initiative again and arranged a meeting with solicitors. The parties attended at the offices of Messrs Clark Boyle & Co, solicitors, on 13 February 1989 with Mr Lawrence Reilly and Miss Sharon Reilly. Mr Reilly was a partner in Clark Boyle & Co and had been the parties' solicitor. Miss Reilly was a partner in Messrs John S Boyle, solicitors. She was Mr Reilly's sister. The circumstances surrounding the arranging of this meeting and the attendance of Miss Reilly require to be considered since they reflect upon the evidence of all parties as to what happened at it. I accepted the evidence of Mr Reilly that when the petitioner contacted him to arrange a meeting he informed him that it was to discuss terms of dissolution of the partnership. Mr Reilly at that stage advised the petitioner that the parties should be separately represented because of the danger of conflict of interest. I accepted the evidence of the petitioner that at that time Mr Reilly proposed that he would arrange for the attendance of his sister who could act as solicitor for the respondent. It was clear that neither the petitioner nor Mr Reilly made any contact with nor communicated any information about this arrangement to the respondent prior to the meeting. What happened was that

A Mr Reilly proceeded about a week before the meeting on 13 February to contact his sister and ask her to attend. She had had no prior dealings with either party and knew nothing about their affairs. She attended the meeting "cold", without information, without instructions, and without making any inquiry of her own as to what might reasonably be required of her as a solicitor attending such a meeting. Mr Reilly for his part could remember no discussion prior to 13 February about the terms of dissolution or any of the surrounding circumstances. When the four participants met on B 13 February Mr Reilly introduced his sister to the respondent and told him that her function was to represent the respondent's interests at the meeting. According to the petitioner he understood that Miss Reilly was there for that purpose. But his evidence was, perhaps not surprisingly, confused. He thought that Mr Reilly was representing both parties but "according to law" he had had to get a solicitor to attend to look after the respondent's interests. Making the best of the evidence, what transpired at the meet-C ing appears to have been that the petitioner maintained his initiative in putting forward proposals which were listened to by Mr Reilly and discussed extensively by him, with Miss Reilly making occasional interventions and discussing matters with the respondent as they arose. Mr Reilly made some notes. Miss Reilly also made some notes as matters progressed.

It is of some significance to note the evidence of the two solicitors as to what they understood was happen-D ing at the meeting. Mr Reilly spoke to fairly detailed discussions on the basis on which the parties were to part company. He could not say whether they or either of them had advised him of any discussions they had had. He could recollect some details of what had taken place. His understanding was that the idea had been that having discussed and agreed terms, the terms would be put in writing by him on behalf of the petitioner. Miss Reilly was almost wholly dependent on her notes. They contained a mixture of notes of discus-E sion and notes of agreement. She could not distinguish within her notes between what was a note of discussion and what was a note of agreement at the meeting. Her impression was that at the end of the meeting there were still some matters which required to be resolved. The picture that emerged from the evidence of the solicitors was of their attendance at a meeting to hear the discussions of the two parties as to a basis for dissolution which was to take place against a background of total ignorance on the part of Sharon Reilly of any relevant fact and on the part of Lawrence Reilly F without his having taken any steps to inform himself of the objectives of the petitioner, whom he selected as his client, nor of his having made any contact whatsoever with the respondent prior to the meeting.

It is perhaps not surprising that the evidence of the two solicitors about what transpired at the meeting was less than satisfactory. It is only necessary to consider the evidence about discussions of option rights for the purposes of the case. The evidence of Mr Reilly was, as already mentioned, that there had been fairly detailed discussions on the basis on which the

parties were to separate. He could recollect some details about the split of the businesses between the G parties, that there was to be an allocation of certain liabilities, and that the interests of the parties in the company were to be dealt with. He remembered that the petitioner was to pay the mortgage of Sinbad because he would not be paying rent for the premises. He was then asked whether any other matter was discussed regarding the heritage and said that the petitioner wished to have the option to acquire the respondent's interest. He thought that that had been discussed. He said that the petitioner had introduced H the question of the option, and he had thought it was at the meeting. It was either at the meeting or subsequently. The price was to be one half of the market value under deduction of the then outstanding loan. He was then asked, without objection: "Did that appear to be the intention of Mr Rehman and Mr Ahmad?" and answered "Sorry?". The question was repeated and he answered "Yes". He described how he saw an option working, on exercise, and was then asked: "We have heard evidence that there was to be I a second option whereby Mr Ahmad might have an option to the property if Mr Rehman was to sell it, does that ring a bell with you?" He answered: "Not really. No." After the meeting he had proceeded to draft a document. In cross examination he was asked about the option. There had clearly been some discussions prior to the meeting, but he thought that the particular point about the option was perhaps something new. He thought that the parties had discussed terms previously but that the terms of the option were J something they had not discussed in great detail. They had agreed certain matters. But they had not agreed about the option or the format of it. The petitioner had brought the matter up. He could not remember how he had arrived at the impression that the price would be one half of market value under deduction of the loan. He explained that his practice in dealing with matters of this kind was to use illustrations, and hypothetical figures, when talking to clients. In response to a question I put, he said that he thought K that there had been discussion on the question of how the option would work. There was some equity on the property. His contemporary note of the agreement was "Rehman option to buy Ahmad's half at market value! Thereafter Rehman gives option to Rehman." He thought that the second sentence had been added later in the discussion. A few days later he had made up a fuller file note containing the item: "In that you have purchased the Sinbad building in joint names Mr Rehman will have the option to buy Mr Ahmad's half L in the building at one half of the market value of the building (ignoring any value the restaurant business has). Mr Ahmad wants a similar option for him in the event that Mr Rehman does not take up his option. This appears to be superfluous."

In dealing with the timing of the option he said that he suspected that it was in the petitioner's mind to exercise his option quickly. That however had not been said at the meeting. He was asked questions about discussions of the mechanics of exercise of the option. His answers in cross examination were less than satisfactory. The matter was taken up again in re-examination. On this occasion the form of questioning was such as to deprive the answers of any value. Because of the form of some of the questioning I asked Mr Reilly what his recollection of the agreement was. He said: "I think the basis of the agreement regarding the option was on a net basis. However, I cannot say specifically how much discussion there was on this point and how this agreement was reached. I don't think it was simply I understood that to be the agreement because that is what one would expect. I think there was discussion of the exact details of the discussion I cannot be absolutely sure of." He did not think that there had been any discussion at all regarding the mechanics of the option. Miss Reilly had taken notes of the discussion.

The critical notes relating to the options were:

"Option to buy Mr A's share or sell.

One half option, one half value of building.

Option to buy equals one half share at market value.

One half share after repay loan. . . .

Operate business 15 years.

If die — business sold — family? . . .

Rehman — first option to buy.

If sell business Ahmad have option to buy — at market value.

After 15 years."

Miss Reilly prepared what purported to be a transcript of her manuscript notes some 10 days prior to the proof. Since she made it clear that she had no recollection independently of her notes, I was not prepared to accept as reliable any addition or emendation produced by her. I refer in particular in this connection to the introduction of the words "at any time" into the description of the petitioner's option right. In cross examination certain obvious inaccuracies in the note were discussed. She would not accept these, which only underlined her lack of any independent recollection, or understanding, of the events and relationships between the parties. In relation to the option price she understood that the price was to be after repayment of the loan. She understood that the price was to be at current market value but after any outstanding loan balance. In re-examination she was again led in discussion of the transcript. But given the general tenor of her evidence I did not accept her views.

The evidence of the professionals in attendance being less than satisfactory, one had the greater difficulty in dealing with the conflict of evidence between the parties themselves. However taking the matter as a whole I was satisfied that there had been discussion of an option right at the meeting and that the respondent had stipulated for a cross option postponed to that of the petitioner. I was satisfied also that the basis of quantification was that the option should be at market value, and that there should be a deduction of the amount of the loan. I was not satisfied that at that meeting there was any agreement as to the timing of exercise of that option and in particular I was not satisfied that there was agreement that the option should be exercisable "at any time". I regarded it as significant that that expression had not appeared in any of the contemporary notes of the meeting. The petitioner's insistence that the language had been used and the respondent's insistence that the long term nature of the investment had been discussed appeared to me on each side to be no more than a reiteration of the objectives of the parties respectively in their negotiations, both before and after 13 February. It did not reflect on either side a statement of agreement between them on the nature of their rights in and options over the property in question. Overall I preferred the evidence of the respondent. I considered it inconceivable that he would have agreed to the package as discussed in the petitioner's evidence had he known of the petitioner's intentions, since he would have been fully aware that the early exercise of the option would have destroyed his prospects of recovering past trading losses from the capital gain on the property. However, his insistence that there had been agreement that the mortgage should be ignored in determining the option price appeared to have been an example of that commercial opportunism that I referred to earlier.

It was not proved that the discussions extended to a consideration of the consequential steps necessary to be resolved upon exercise of the option nor that parties had addressed in a manner likely to give rise to agreement what those steps might be. I have already referred to the evidence of Mr Reilly and Miss Reilly which wholly failed to cover matters of this kind in a satisfactory way. The petitioner said that there was discussion of the terms upon which the options might be exercised. When asked about the particular ways matters might work out, his answer was that that was simple, without complication and well understood. He said that the standard security would be discharged and the person taking over the premises would have the standard security in his name. When asked whether this was a matter of discussion, he said that it automatically followed. He agreed that this was something which he thought to follow naturally from the agreement reached. In cross examination he was pressed on the mechanics of deduction and said that it was mentioned, it was something which was automatic and well understood by every party and secondly, it was mentioned that there was a loan, that that was the condition with the building, that that was the string attached to the building. The respondent's evidence about the meeting of 13 February, so far as relating to the option, was that there had been discussion about the parties having equal options. He denied that there had been an agreement that the petitioner should have a first option. Market value was to be the basis of the price. His evidence amounted to a claim that there had been agreement for cross options. In general he felt that there had been little discussion about options and he could not remember what was

A said. He denied that there was discussion about the petitioner having a first option. In cross examination he said that the parties had gone to Mr Reilly to have their agreement put into legal language. He had not anticipated a sale before the loan had been paid off. It had been left to Mr Reilly to put down in words the agreement for equal options. He was not asked in cross examination about agreement on the mechanics of exercise of option rights.

B After the meeting of 13 February Mr Reilly was again approached by the petitioner. The petitioner pressed him for a further meeting. A second meeting was held on 23 February 1989. At the point at which the petitioner had pressed for this meeting Mr Reilly had not prepared a draft. He proceeded to prepare a draft agreement in some haste. The meeting was attended by the parties and Mr Reilly alone. Mr Reilly, according to his own evidence, had not considered that there was any scope for conflict of interest at this stage, and had therefore not taken steps to arrange for any form of separate representation for the respondent. The petitioner's evidence was that he had thought that Miss Reilly did attend. When they appeared a document prepared by Mr Reilly was produced. There was discussion whether the respondent would sign without ancillary matters being agreed and disposed of. Those matters were dealt with and the petitioner signed a personal bond acknowledging his liability for sums previously borrowed. So far as the minute of agreement was concerned he had not seen the draft before the meeting. It was not discussed at the meeting. The respondent read it and asked for certain amendments. It was then extended and executed. The petitioner maintained that the document reflected generally the agreement of parties, but that the option provision was incorrect. The petitioner maintained that he was not a technical man and just saw the agreement as one of the situations for the reduction of the loan, he having left the technicalities to Mr Reilly. In cross examination he said that he regarded Mr Reilly as acting for both parties at the second meeting. He persisted in his evidence that he had not understood cl fifth because it contained a lot of technical words. He thought that the expression "half of market value" would be after deduction of the loan. The respondent maintained that when he had gone to the second meeting he found the matters that had been discussed worded differently. He had however understood from the document that the petitioner would be able to exercise his option at any time, but he did not think much of that because the intention was that the property be held on a long term basis. If it had been suggested to him that it was not a long term investment he would not have gone ahead. At the second meeting he had looked at the document, he had asked for certain corrections to be made, and he had read and understood cl fifth. He appreciated that it did not reflect the agreement between parties but he decided that he would not pursue the matter. He did not think that the matter would arise because it was a long term investment. Mr Reilly had not gone over the document with parties. The petitioner was anxious to sign the document and he agreed. Mr Reilly had suggested that he could take separate legal advice if he wanted to. But he had decided against that course. In cross examination he maintained that the document did not reflect what had been agreed. It had been up to Mr Reilly how to give them an option that was fair and similar or equal. Mr Reilly in giving evidence about this meeting said that the document was drafted to reflect the agreement between parties. He presented the draft to them on 23 February. He did not think that there would be scope for conflict of interest. But he emphasised to the respondent that he should not sign without the benefit of separate legal advice. Both parties had signed. He had not anticipated that, but had seen the agreement as a working draft drawn up in some haste after the petitioner had asked for a second meeting. He said that both parties had read the dissolution agreement.

The respondent had reported to his wife that the agreement was for an option at market value without deduction of the loan. I accepted her evidence on that matter. Taken along with the respondent's evidence that he had read and understood cl fifth, it appeared to me to be clear that on this occasion the respondent had been fully aware that the expression "at any time" appeared in the document, that that was inconsistent with his understanding, but that he had deliberately decided to accept it because as he understood cl fifth the market price without deduction of the loan represented a material advantage to him. I did not accept the respondent's explanation in evidence that he ignored any difficulty because of his confidence that the parties were in agreement that the investment was of a long term nature. On this matter I considered that the respondent was not giving true evidence. Equally I did not accept the petitioner's evidence that he had been confused that the expression "market value" meant under deduction of loan. Having regard to his general evidence in which he had insisted that the agreement was specific to that effect, it is inconceivable that he would not have picked up the difference had he read the document with care. Rather I think that it is clear that the petitioner considered that Mr Reilly was acting on his behalf alone at this time and could be relied upon to reflect what was in the petitioner's interest in the document. In summary I considered that the petitioner signed the agreement in reliance upon Mr Reilly as his solicitor without himself analysing with care the particular provisions it contained. The respondent on the other hand signed having read the provisions with care in the belief that they represented an advantage to him notwithstanding that they did not reflect what he believed to have been the terms of the agreement between the parties.

After the agreement was signed the petitioner approached Mr Reilly to start the option procedure. The immediate response from the respondent's solicitors was to ask for half of the gross valuation of the premises, exploiting what was seen by the petitioner as a small technical loophole in the document. There was evidence about a meeting in the respondent's solicitors' office, at which the respondent said that he

A understood that there was a small error in the document, and that he was just utilising this error. He understood quite well that a loan had to be taken off before the net share of profit. He understood that the document did not give effect to the agreement. Mr Reilly maintained that the document gave effect to the parties' agreement with the exception of the mistake that it contained. That mistake was the failure to provide that the price was half market value after deduction of the outstanding mortgage. When asked to specify the error he said: "It's not representative of the parties' agreement in that it should say that the price

B should be equal to one half of the market value of the building under deduction or after payment off or on the reduction of the joint outstanding security, the amount of the outstanding secured loan." He then proceeded, in response to leading questions, to give wholly unsatisfactory evidence on the errors in the agreement. I found it impossible to accept his evidence at that stage as a reliable statement of what had occurred at the first meeting, but was not properly

C reflected in the document. He was quite unable to distinguish between what had been agreed and what he thought might be required to deal with the situations being brought to his attention which, clearly, he had never contemplated. That there was any problem at all had only come to his attention when the respondent's solicitors had sought market value without reduction. That had certainly provoked him to a realisation that there had been an error of some kind. He too spoke to the meeting in August or September at the respon-

D dent's solicitors' office. His interpretation of what the respondent had said at that meeting was that if there had not been an acrimonious dispute between him and the petitioner he would have been happy to agree with the petitioner and what he wanted. The respondent's answer to the intimation from his banker that the petitioner was seeking funds to exercise the option was of shock. He had written to Mr Reilly about the matter. He had then taken separate advice. He had consulted an accountant, Mr Bowers. He did not accept that the

E document was in error in specifying the basis of quantification of the price. The stage was set for impasse bringing the parties eventually to court.

Counsel were in agreement, generally, as to the elements requiring to be proved for a remedy. There had to be a document. The document must have been intended to express or give effect to an agreement. There had to have been an agreement reflecting the common intention of the parties at the date it was made. There had to be proof that the document failed

F to express that intention. Reference was made to Lord McCluskey's opinion in *Shaw v William Grant (Minerals) Ltd* for an analysis of those factors in greater depth. Counsel also referred to *George Thompson Services Ltd v Moore*; *Oliver v Gaughan*; *Angus v Bryden*; *MAC Electrical and Heating Engineers Ltd v Calscot Electrical (Distributors) Ltd*; and *Bank of Scotland v Graham*. The case of *MAC* did not provide assistance. Lord Coulsfield in allowing proof before answer in an application for rectification did not make any analysis of the law. In *Thompson* the issue was

expressed by Lord Weir at p 635I as being "whether statutory rectification can take place not to correct a G defect in the written expression of an agreement which had already been reached, but to reflect the alleged common intention of the parties before they had reached any agreement regarding the sale of the land". He held that there must be an agreement to which the common intention could be said to relate and looked to Lord McCluskey's formulation in *Shaw* for support for that view.

In *Bank of Scotland v Graham*, the Lord President, dealing with s 8 (1) (b), said that it would be unwise H to attempt to define all of the circumstances to which the power of rectification could apply. I consider that the same can be said of para (a). If Lord McCluskey's formulation were intended to be an exhaustive statement of the scope of para (a) I would find some difficulty with it. Two aspects of that formulation might call for comment: the emphasis on the requirement for proof of prior agreement at a definite point in time; and the reference in his fifth proposition to "actual (not deemed) intentions". As I understand the I provision it may apply whether the "document" comprises one or more than one element. There is no apparent reason why the normal rule of construction in the Interpretation Act should not apply. If that is so, there must exist circumstances in which agreement is reached through a process of exchange of documents over a period of time. An error of expression of common intention may enter the proceedings at a time prior to the resolution of the last essential of a completed contract, and remain uncorrected when that J final stage is achieved. If the authorities are any guide, one might think typically of an error of description of heritable property in missives overlooked while parties' solicitors negotiated the minutiae of a modern contract for sale of the subjects. The agreement would be made, in many cases, by the delivery of a final letter which might do no more than accept the last counter stipulation and "hold the bargain as completed". The last letter would both complete the agreement and the K exchange of documents intended to express it. I can see no reason to deny a remedy in such a case, if otherwise appropriate, simply because the two events occurred simultaneously. It is clear, in my opinion, that there must be proof of agreement independent of and separate from the completion of the document or documents. *Angus v Bryden* illustrates how difficult it may be to resolve differences between cases where prior understandings and beliefs are superseded in the course of negotiation and cases where agreements L actually made are not accurately expressed in the documents. But one must avoid thinking only of professionally prepared documents in this context. Parties may seek to reduce to writing an agreement instantly made, and err in the expression of it, perhaps because of lack of professional knowledge. What is required, in my opinion, is proof of an agreement made independently of, and at or prior to the date of, the document or documents intended to give effect to it, coupled with proof that the writing failed to express accurately the common intention of the parties at the

point at which the agreement was made. The point,
A which can have been of no significance in *Shaw*,
would be relevant in the present case on one view of
the evidence of the respondent.

Common intention, in the context of making an
agreement, has to be determined objectively: *Thomson
v James*, and *Muirhead & Turnbull v Dickson*. In the
former case, the "actual" intention of Mr James to
enter into any contract at all had been departed from,
but there was held to be a completed bargain, on an
application of the postal rule. In the latter, one finds
B the statement of Lord President Dunedin: "But commercial contracts cannot be arranged by what people
think in their inmost minds. Commercial contracts are
made according to what people say." The description
of intention as "actual" leaves open, perhaps, the
question whether one is concerned with a party's
intention as a matter of subjective perception, or as a
matter of expression, objectively determined. In my
opinion the common intention of parties referred to in
the provision is the common intention ascertained
C objectively in accordance with the normal canons of
construction of agreements, and in particular the rules
applicable in ascertaining whether consensus in idem
has been achieved, and to what effect. It is in that
sense that one must approach the question whether
the petitioner has proved that there was agreement in
which the common intention of the parties was as
expressed in the following terms:

"Fifth. The first party will have the option at any
D time to purchase the second party's interest in the said
heritable subjects at 14 Princes Street, Falkirk, at a
price equal to one half of the market value of the said
building on a bricks and mortar basis ignoring any
value of the restaurant business operating therefrom,
and after first deducting the whole outstanding loan
secured over the said heritable subjects. In the event
that the first party wishes to sell his share in the said
building of 14 Princes Street, Falkirk, he will require
to give the first option to purchase his heritable
E interest to the second party again at one half of the
market value of the building calculated as aforesaid
and after first deducting the whole of said outstanding
loan. In the event of either party wishing to exercise
his option under this clause it shall be a condition of
doing so that he shall repay the whole of the outstanding loan secured over the said heritable subjects, or,
alternatively, procure the discharge of the other party
from all obligations under and in terms of the standard
security", followed by a provision for arbitration.

F I was asked particularly to ignore such questions as
the failure to provide for the life assurance policies,
and the personal bonds, and the other stipulations of
the funding agreement. Having regard to the conclusions I have reached on the facts it is not necessary
to look beyond the terms of cl fifth in this case. But
I would not have been inclined to accept the submissions of counsel which sought to restrict the scope of
the court's powers to have regard to surrounding circumstances. One can give effect to common intention
only in the context of an agreement as a whole. The

structure of a contract, the interrelationships of its
provisions, and its language may be relevant to the G
exercise of the powers conferred by s 8, in my view,
along with all relevant extraneous facts and circumstances.

I did not believe the petitioner's evidence that an
agreement to the effect narrated above had been
arrived at prior to the meeting on 13 February with
Mr and Miss Reilly. As already mentioned I preferred
the evidence of the respondent on this matter. Further
Mr Reilly's impression was that the parties had come
without having discussed the option in great detail. H
They had not agreed about the option and the format
of it. I preferred his evidence when, in response to me,
he said that there had been no discussion at all about
the mechanics of the option. He clearly thought that
his task at the end of the meeting was to prepare a
document on behalf of the petitioner which would be
the subject of further consideration and discussion. In
the end he had prepared a working draft in haste
following pressure from the petitioner for a further
meeting. I accepted the evidence of the respondent I
that at the meeting of 13 February the words "at any
time" were not discussed and agreed. These words did
not appear in the contemporary notes of either solicitor, and I did not find the evidence of Miss Reilly
as to the preparation of her transcript of her manuscript notes to be reliable.

The inclusion of the words "at any time" in the
draft document clearly reflected the intentions of the
petitioner, and the belief on the part of Mr Reilly that
the petitioner intended to exercise the option quickly. J
On 23 February the respondent saw those words in the
draft, appreciated their meaning, and ignored the
danger they represented. I consider that he did so
because he read and accepted the terms of the clause
as a whole which he was soon to attempt to use to his
own advantage. But the only evidence of his acceptance of the terms was in his asking for other matters
to be adjusted and by his executing the extended
agreement in its terms. The evidence of Mrs Ahmad
of his report of the terms of the agreement was K
eloquent of his appreciation of the full significance of
the form in which the agreement had been prepared.
If I were entitled to look into the mind of the respondent, I would have concluded that he appreciated fully
that there had been an error in the drafting of the
agreement involving the omission of the provisions for
the deduction of the loan, and that to achieve the
advantage which he thought that gave him, he was
prepared to accept the reference to time, thinking that
it was in any event irrelevant having regard to the L
intention to keep the property as an investment.
However looking at the matter objectively, his agreement to the form of cl fifth, evidenced by his instructions for the document to be extended, and his
execution of it, related wholly to the form on paper as
it then stood.

If it were of the essence of s 8 that agreement had
to be achieved prior to the execution of the documents
so that the document reflected that which anticipated
it, I would consider that the petitioner must fail in this

case. This follows inevitably from the view that the respondent came to appreciate the significance of the words "at any time" when he saw them, for the first time, in the completed agreement and signed in the light of that appreciation. At the close of the proof, counsel for the petitioner amended the petitioner's pleadings to delete the reference to the meeting on 23 February from line 7 of p 6 of the record, following his adoption of Lord McCluskey's formulation. On the pleadings as so amended, in my opinion, the petitioner must fail. However, as already indicated it seems to me that reflected an over narrow view of s 8 since it fails to have regard to the possibility that parties may in good faith disclose to each other full agreement at the point of execution and yet sign a written document that failed in some material particular to reflect what was agreed between them and can be shown to have been agreed. Accordingly it appears to me that had it been possible to find evidence that the respondent had expressed his acceptance of the terms when confronted by them on 23 February, it would have been proper to hold him bound by the agreement albeit that it was achieved then. The problem however is that his evidence, so far as I accepted it on this matter, related his acceptance of the words "at any time" to his appreciation of the nature of the error of expression of price. Further it is quite clear that he did not express his thoughts at that time, and that they were never communicated to the petitioner or to Mr Reilly. In the whole circumstances I am of opinion that the petitioner has failed to prove consensus in the sense required to an agreement including both the reference to time and the measure of market value for which he contends. He has failed to prove agreement at all as to the mechanics of operation of the option clause. Had the petitioner succeeded in proving agreement on the main terms of the option, a question would have arisen whether one could properly have given effect to the mechanical provisions sought without such proof. Without expressing any view about the competency of inserting purely mechanical provisions intended to give expression to the ordinary consequences of a contractual stipulation, which might in any case be left to professional advisers, I would not have granted this aspect of the prayer. The amendments sought could go to the roots of the option right, and in certain circumstances defeat it if the consent of lenders to the course proposed could not be obtained. To give effect to the application would involve selecting particular solutions from a range of possible approaches open to parties in negotiation, and, in effect, would involve the court in making a contribution to the formulation of the agreement. In my opinion that would exceed the bounds of the powers created by s 8. In these circumstances I shall refuse the prayer of the petition.

Counsel for Petitioner, Sturrock; Solicitors, Brodies, WS — Counsel for Respondent, Illius; Solicitors, Lindsays, WS.

G D M

Kirkcaldy District Council v Burntisland Community Council

OUTER HOUSE
LORD CAPLAN
12 JUNE 1991

Local government — Common good — Alienation and disposal of land forming part of common good — Application to court for authorisation — Exercise of court's discretion where economic benefit to local inhabitants — Local Government (Scotland) Act 1973 (c 65), ss 75 (2) and 222 (2).

Section 75 (2) of the Local Government (Scotland) Act 1973 empowers a local authority wishing to dispose of land forming part of the common good and as to which there is a question as to its alienability, to apply to the court for authority to dispose of the land. The court, in granting authority, may impose conditions.

A district council petitioned the court under s 75 (2) seeking authority to dispose of an area of land forming part of the common good on which they operated a caravan site. They proposed to sell the land to an adjoining industrial proprietor who had made an offer which exceeded the market value of the land. Planning permission had been granted over 40 per cent of the land, but further expansion requiring the use of the whole area of ground was likely to be required within two years. They contended that the local community derived from the land an economic benefit rather than a recreational one, and this would be better served by the proposed disposal. They proposed to credit their common good fund with a sum equal to the district valuer's valuation of the land, and to apply the balance to repay loans incurred in improving the caravan site which had been drawn on their leisure and recreation capital account. The district council had determined that it was not practicable to establish an alternative caravan site in the area.

The local community council and the caravan site owners' association opposed the petition, arguing that the land had been dedicated for the recreational benefit of local inhabitants. They contended that only the portion of land for which planning permission had been granted should be alienated, and that conditions should be imposed requiring the district council to make available alternative land for caravan use and to apply the whole price to the common good fund.

Held, (1) that the economic benefit arising to the local community out of the disposal outweighed any loss resulting from the termination of recreational use of the land (pp 757F, 757L–758A and 758E); (2) that it was impracticable and unnecessary to require alternative land to be made available for caravan use (p 758A–F); but (3) that the whole proceeds of the sale should be held and applied for the benefit of local inhabitants (p 758G–H and K–L); and prayer of the petition *granted*, with a condition that all the sale proceeds be applied to the common good fund.

Opinion, that in proceedings under s 75 (2) of the
A Act the court required to pay attention to the nature
and quality of the rights enjoyed over the land by local
inhabitants, and that those enjoying a specific exercisable right should not be readily disadvantaged
(p 757D).

**Petition under s 75 (2) of the Local Government
(Scotland) Act 1973**

Kirkcaldy District Council presented a petition
B under s 75 (2) of the Local Government (Scotland) Act
1973 seeking authority to sell land held within its
common good fund. The Burntisland Community
Council, Burntisland Caravan Site Owners Association, Robert Connors, and B A Chemicals Ltd lodged
answers. With consent of all parties the court remitted
the cause to a member of the bar to inquire into and
to report on the facts and circumstances. Following
lodging of the report, the cause came before the Lord
Ordinary (Caplan).

C
Statutory provisions

The Local Government (Scotland) Act 1973
provides:

"75.— . . . (2) Where a local authority desire to
dispose of land forming part of the common good with
respect to which land a question arises as to the right
of the authority to alienate, they may apply to the
Court of Session or the sheriff to authorise them to
dispose of the land, and the Court or sheriff may, if
D they think fit, authorise the authority to dispose of the
land subject to such conditions, if any, as they may
impose, and the authority shall be entitled to dispose
of the land accordingly. . . .

"222.— . . . (2) The Secretary of State shall by order
provide that all property held as part of the common
good by an existing local authority on 15th May 1975
shall on 16th May 1975 be transferred to and vest in
such islands or district council as may be specified in
E or determined under the order, and those councils,
other than the district councils of Aberdeen, Dundee,
Edinburgh and Glasgow, shall, in administering that
property, have regard to the interests of the inhabitants of the area to which the common good formerly
related."

Cases referred to

East Lothian District Council v National Coal Board,
1982 SLT 460.
F *Motherwell District Council, Petitioners*, OH, 25 March
1988, unreported (1988 GWD 15-666).
Pearce Brothers v Irons (1869) 7 M 571.

On 12 June 1991 the Lord Ordinary *granted* decree
in terms of the prayer of the petition, with a condition.

LORD CAPLAN.—In this petition Kirkcaldy District Council seek authority under s 75 (2) of the Local
Government (Scotland) Act 1973 to dispose of land
forming part of the common good of Burntisland. The
petition is opposed by the first and second respondents

who are the Burntisland Community Council and the
Burntisland Caravan Site Owners Association respec- G
tively. The third respondent, Robert Connors, did not
appear at the hearing to oppose the grant of the petition. The fourth respondents, B A Chemicals Ltd,
seek to purchase the land which is the subject of the
petition and therefore they appeared to support the
petitioners' application.

The land with which the petition is concerned consists of about six acres of grassland within the town of
Burntisland. The said land was purchased by the
Royal Burgh of Burntisland in 1907. The site is part H
of a neighbourhood known as the Haugh. It was formerly part of Rossend estate. It is adjacent to a factory
complex owned and operated by the fourth respondents. In the disposition of the land recorded on 20
November 1907 from Shepherd's Trustees (the dis-
poners) in favour of the Provost, Magistrates and
Councillors of the Royal Burgh of Burntisland the
subjects were conveyed "to and in favour of the
Provost, Magistrates and Councillors of the Royal
Burgh of Burntisland and to their successors in office I
for behoof of the whole body and community thereof
and to their assignees whomsoever". The council
minutes of 17 July 1907 recorded that the proposal to
buy the land was "to acquire lands in the neighbourhood suitable for recreation grounds and other
municipal purposes". The motion carried by the town
council was "the Town Council on behalf of the
common good resolve to offer for the said Castle and
grounds with a view to their being used as a public
recreation ground and for any other purposes". The J
petitioners acquired the land about 1975 upon the
reorganisation of local government, Burntisland being
within the boundaries of their district.

Following upon its acquisition part of the land with
which the petition is concerned was used for refuse
disposal and this use continued until 1954 when a
different site was made available for the said purpose.
The remainder of the site was originally used as a football pitch and was apparently known as Rossend K
Castle Park. Other small parts of the land were at
different times used for grazing, allotments and other
miscellaneous purposes. However in 1954 all the land
was converted to use as a caravan site and has
remained in that use ever since. The site is operated
by the petitioners' department of leisure and direct
facilities. The land has about 90 caravan pitches. The
caravans are static caravans rather than of the touring
sort and they are left on the site throughout the year.
The site is open from about March to September in
each season. The site has been fully occupied until L
September 1989 when the petitioners' intention to
dispose of the site was intimated to the caravan
owners. There are now about 40 pitches occupied.

The remainder of Rossend estate purchased in 1907,
with which the petition is not concerned, has largely
been used for housing. An area of about 3.9 acres was
conveyed to the fourth respondents with authority of
the sheriff in or about 1975.

In the mid-1980s the petitioners built an amenity

block on the caravan site. This was paid for by borrowings but the money was not drawn on the common good fund but instead was drawn on the leisure and recreation capital account. The said borrowings presently stand at about £110,000. The petitioners lose about £30,000 per annum on the operation of the caravan site and this is principally due to the cost of repaying the said loans incurred for capital expenditure.

It perhaps should also be noted that the common good of the former Royal Burgh of Burntisland also comprises other areas of land and moneys which are kept in a common good account.

The fourth respondents want to construct on the land with which this petition is concerned an extension to their industrial storage facilities and also a lorry parking area. On 14 October 1989 planning permission for the development was granted. These particular developments on the land for which planning permission has been granted comprise about 40 per cent of the said area of six acres. The fourth respondents want to acquire the balance of the site for future development. I was informed by senior counsel for the petitioners that provisional missives have been entered into with the fourth respondents for the sale to them of the said land.

On 21 February 1991 the Lord Ordinary with consent of all parties remitted to Ralph A Smith, advocate, to inquire into and report on the facts and circumstances surrounding (1) the uses to which the land has been put since 1907, (2) whether there are any reasonably practicable alternative uses for the land of beneficial assistance to the local population, and (3) whether there appear to be circumstances justifying the imposition of a condition on disposal that land be supplied in substitution as a caravan site for the land to be disposed of.

The facts I have narrated above are largely taken from Mr Smith's report and I do not think that these particular facts are in any sense disputed. Mr Smith in his report dealt fully with a number of other matters.

With regard to alternative beneficial uses of the land the reporter doubted if the land was eminently suitable for its present use as a caravan site. It is surrounded on two sides by a factory complex. The views from the site are to say the least limited. The factory operates continuously. It emits dust and there is a distinct background noise. The site floods from time to time. However the caravaners who use the site, who come from outside Burntisland and in particular from the west of Scotland, were enthusiastic about continuing to come to the site. This may largely be because the pitch rentals charged are low. The provenance of the caravaners is perhaps supported by the fact that all three representatives of the second respondents who were interviewed by the reporter live in Airdrie.

With regard to the proposed use of the site by the fourth respondents, the reporter seems to have had no hesitation in concluding that the industrial extension which has presently been approved by the planning

authority would be of assistance to the local population. The fourth respondents are the largest single employers in the area and they employ about 550 persons. The majority of these come from Burntisland. Due to the fact that the fourth respondents are a multinational company and also to worldwide economic factors in the aluminium industry, the fourth respondents require to continue to expand and diversify their operations. Should they be unable to do so at Burntisland they would do so elsewhere. Their present premises are congested and the only practical place for expansion is into the caravan site. Land is required for industrial storage. Some storage presently takes place outside Burntisland and this is financially inefficient. The reporter observes: "I was left in no doubt from speaking to the two directors of the fourth respondents that should their expansion not take place at Burntisland it would be likely to occur in other places in England or elsewhere and ultimately the Burntisland operations would become run down." Local jobs would be lost if the expansion does not proceed and safeguarded if it does. The petitioners for their part regard the fourth respondents' operations as very important to the economy of the area and while they recognise that tourism is important to Burntisland's economy they think that this factor is outweighed by the importance to that economy of the fourth respondents' operations.

With regard to the possibility of confining the fourth respondents' acquisition to the 40 per cent of the site for which planning permission has been granted, the petitioners aver in the petition that a caravan site would not be a viable proposition on the remaining 60 per cent of the land. The reporter does not deal specifically with this matter. However it is obvious that a number of the existing caravan pitches would be lost and it is difficult to see how this could be beneficial to a caravan site that is already losing a substantial amount of money. The reporter does observe that having spoken to the fourth respondents' production director, Mr McNeill, the latter's view is that the immediate plans for the site are only an interim solution and that within one or two years further space will be required by the fourth respondents. The reporter states that he was inclined to accept that view and he himself noted that the fourth respondents have little extra space within their existing premises. The petitioners for their part are concerned that the fourth respondents should be able to plan their future development with greater certainty. The reporter concludes that a partial sale of the land to the fourth respondents would only be a short term solution to the latter's problems.

The reporter deals with the possibility of the said land being required for uses other than the present use or that now proposed. He concludes that there is no requirement for such alternative uses.

The reporter accepts that the caravan site will bring a certain amount of money into the local economy particularly to High Street traders during the summer. He accordingly considered the possibility of a condition being attached to any authority to dispose of the

A land to the effect that other land be made available as a caravan site. It should be noted that there are other caravan sites in the area particularly at Kinghorn and Pettycur Bay although not in Burntisland itself. These other caravan sites are said to be more expensive than the Burntisland site. The reporter concludes that there is nowhere in the vicinity of Burntisland which would provide a suitable caravan site without a good deal of difficulty. A site at Lammerlaws was considered but the land is owned by Forth Ports Authority who are not prepared to sell it. In any event there is a serious

B access problem. A new road would be required and this would have to pass through railway sidings. Another site known as Red Mud Pond is thought to be unsuitable because of doubts about the stability of the ground. It is thought that the development of a green site would cost in the region of £500,000. The reporter considered that it was not at all clear whether any new site would be commercially viable. It has to be noted that the second respondents' members who were consulted by the reporter seemed reluctant to use

C a privately owned site and indeed doubted that their rather elderly caravans would be admitted to such a site.

The petitioners appeared before me to move that the petition be granted. Their senior counsel contended that the petition should be granted without conditions. It was conceded that the land under consideration had been dedicated to a common good purpose. However the community receives from the land an economic benefit rather than a recreational benefit and this

D could be better served by the petitioners' proposals. The petitioners are under no obligation to continue the operation of a loss making caravan site and could close it tomorrow. The findings of the reporter that the whole land was required by the fourth respondents and that there was no other land which it would be practicable to offer as a caravan site, should be accepted. With regard to the disposal of the sale proceeds senior counsel told me that the petitioners had negotiated by private bargain a price which would take

E account of their capital expenditure on the land. However the market value of the land was likely to be less than this specially negotiated price. The petitioners would have the land valued by the district valuer and this valuation would take account of the fact that there were certain structures on the land. However, since the district valuer's valuation of the land was likely to be less than the actual price received, the common good fund would be credited with that value and the balance of the price would be

F used to help pay off the loans incurred by the petitioners in respect of the site. With regard to the application of s 75 (2) of the Local Government (Scotland) Act 1973 I was referred to *East Lothian District Council v National Coal Board*.

Counsel for the first and second respondents indicated that he accepted that the land with which the petition was concerned was land in respect of which a question arises as to the rights of the petitioners to alienate it. The land had in effect been dedicated to recreational purposes for the benefit of the inhabitants

of Burntisland. These respondents were not wholly opposed to alienation of some of the land. They recog- G nised the importance of land being available to meet the legitimate needs of the fourth respondents as an important economic unit in the area. However any authority to dispose of the land should be made subject to restrictions or to conditions. In the first place it was said that the petitioners had not established that the whole land was required for their purposes. Accordingly authority should only be granted for the 40 per cent of land for which planning permission had been granted. In any event it should be made H a condition of any authority granted that the whole price realised for the land should be applied to the common good fund. If the whole site was to be disposed of it should be a condition of any authority granted by the court that the petitioners should make available an alternative area of land which could be used as a caravan site. I was referred to s 222 (2) of the Local Government (Scotland) Act 1973 which was to the effect that when common good was transferred to a district under the Act it should be administered I having regard to the interests of the inhabitants of the area to which the common good formerly related. It was also referred to an unreported opinion dated 25 March 1988 of Lord Kirkwood in a petition by Motherwell District Council. It was contended that the petitioners had not satisfactorily proved that at this point of time the fourth respondents require the whole area of land, nor had they proved that it would not be viable to operate the remaining portion of the land as a caravan site. The availability of a caravan site in J Burntisland was important to the community and the reporter's views on alternative sites were not based on sufficiently exhaustive information. If necessary further evidence should be allowed or the facts should once again be remitted to the reporter for amplification.

Counsel for the fourth respondents added his weight to the petitioners' submissions. He suggested that it would be incompetent to allow evidence at this stage or to have a further remit to the reporter. I was K referred to *Pearce Brothers v Irons*. It was argued that the reporter was perfectly entitled to conclude that there were sound reasons for allowing the fourth respondents the whole site.

Section 75 (2) of the Local Government (Scotland) Act 1973, by virtue of which the petitioners present their petition, is in the following terms: [his Lordship narrated its terms and continued:] All the parties represented agreed that a question arises as to the L alienability of the relevant land. I am not at all convinced that the land has been dedicated to any specific public purpose. It seems originally to have been intended primarily as public recreation ground although "other purposes" were mentioned in the motion originally approving of the purchase by Burntisland Town Council. On the other hand despite the terms of the motion it is certainly suggested by the reporter that the securing of a refuse dump may have been the main reason for purchasing the particular site I am concerned with. Certainly for a period of 47 years part of the ground was used as a refuse dump to which presumably the public had access.

On the other hand at least a substantial part of the land has always been used for what may be described as recreational purposes. Originally there was a public football pitch on the land. Since 1954 the land has been used as a caravan site and administered as recreational land. Caravanning is certainly a recreational activity but it is less certain that any of the inhabitants of Burntisland benefit recreationally from the caravan park since the occupiers appear to come exclusively from outside Burntisland. The traders in the town may benefit economically but this is scarcely a recreational use by the inhabitants. Nevertheless, the land since its purchase has been kept available as open space for purposes considered to be beneficial to the inhabitants of the town. The very uncertainty about the status of the land with regard to alienability may be demonstrated by the fact that the parties in the case support the view that at least there is a question about this matter. A portion of what was at the time essentially land held in similar circumstances was the subject of a petition to the court in 1975 and the authority of the sheriff to dispose of the land was granted under s 171 of the Local Government (Scotland) Act 1947. I respectfully agree with Lord Maxwell in *East Lothian District Council* that the power of the court to apply s 75 (2) should not be regarded too narrowly. Clearly the alienability of the land in the present case is at least open to argument and I consider therefore that it would be appropriate to grant authority under s 75 (2) if the circumstances otherwise justified this.

The terms of s 75 (2) invest a wide discretion in the court. Clearly in order to discharge its powers the court requires to pay attention to the nature and quality of the rights which the inhabitants of the locality enjoy over the land under consideration. Any inhabitants who enjoy a specific exercisable right over the land should not be readily disadvantaged. In this regard however it should again be noted that it is not at all certain that any inhabitants of Burntisland have in fact personally used the said land for many years.

The parties do not in fact dispute that some degree of authority to dispose ought to be granted in respect of this land, although the petitioners and fourth respondents differ from the first and second respondents in respect of just what degree of authority should be granted. I have no difficulty in accepting that there could be no question of refusing this petition in its entirety. It is a matter of general agreement that it is important to the economic welfare of the inhabitants of Burntisland that the fourth respondents should be allowed to carry out the specific plans for the expansion of their factory for which they have been granted planning permission. However, that leaves open the question of whether or not I should impose any of the three qualifications suggested by the first and second respondents.

Counsel for the first and second respondents argued that certain facts central to consideration of the disputed issues had not been satisfactorily proved. However this is a case where parties have sensibly, and presumably in order to save an expensive proof, concurred in a remit to a reporter. Thus they were satisfied to have the remitted factual questions decided by the reporter. I do not say that in a petition of this sort there could never be a case where it was appropriate to allow evidence even where there had been a remit of factual questions. However I need not form a concluded view as to that point. Although counsel for the first and second respondents criticised the adequacy of certain of the reporter's findings, neither he nor any other party moved to be allowed to lead evidence. Thus the petitioners rest their case on the findings in the report and I consider that I am entitled to take account of these, bearing in mind of course any criticisms that may have been made of the way in which the reporter reached his conclusions.

In relation to whether or not authority may be granted for the whole area of land the respondents claim that if authority to dispose were limited to the 40 per cent of the land, this may enable the balance to be retained as a caravan site. Certainly the petitioners have not specifically proved that it would not be possible to operate the balance of the land as a caravan site although they do aver that it would not in fact be viable. Alienation of 40 per cent of the land would inevitably reduce the number of caravan pitches and this must reduce the income earned by the site. Even when fully used the site was losing £30,000 per year. There is no obligation on the petitioners to continue to bear this loss nor indeed to continue to operate a caravan park. It is very unlikely that a private operator would take on the site and in any event not in terms which would be acceptable to the present users. Balanced against what is claimed to be a prospect of retaining a caravan facility is the finding of the reporter that the fourth respondents will eventually require more land. The first and second respondents claim that the fourth respondents were possibly seeking merely to acquire what they described as a "land bank". The reporter himself physically observed that the fourth respondents presently would seem to have little extra space. From the other information in the report about prospective use of the land, the industrial use of it by the fourth respondents would seem to be the only likely future use. The suggestions of the first and second respondents are entirely speculative and fly in the face of the reporter's indication that the fourth respondents will in fact require to expand further in one or two years' time. Moreover, in my own view, it is difficult to fault the view of the petitioners that there is merit in the fourth respondents having some additional land so that they can plan their future with greater certainty. If, as seems very possible, the fourth respondents do require the balance of the land in a year or two a further petition to the court would be wasteful and might cause damaging uncertainty to all interested parties. Thus to divide the land at this point of time would offer only at best a conjectural and at worst a highly doubtful prospect that the caravan park would continue to

A operate. Even if it did it is uncertain for how long that situation could continue. On the other hand if the fourth respondents get the whole parcel of land they can solve their immediate problem and would have both assurance and encouragement in respect of any needed future expansion. Thus applying my own discretion to the matter I consider that the petitioners are well justified in their proposal to sell the whole site.

B With regard to the suggestion that I should impose a condition that alternative land be made available for caravan use, I do not regard this as practicable or necessary in the present case. I am prepared to accept the reporter's findings that such land as might be available is likely to be difficult and expensive to develop as a caravan site. It was suggested by counsel for the first and second respondents that the reporter could not appropriately form such a view without more detailed investigations and costings. I think that the kind of in depth investigations which these respondents wanted would have been totally impracticable in this case. Even the present site required capital expen-
C diture to the order of £170,000 to equip it as a caravan site and it is obvious from what the reporter discovered that any alternative site would require considerably more expenditure. Since the petitioners have no legal obligation to continue to operate a caravan site it would be wrong to put them in a position where in order to meet their policy that they should satisfy the fourth respondents' legitimate needs, they would have to assume a greater burden than they have already. Moreover, even if land was merely made available, not
D only is it doubtful whether a private operator would be prepared to develop and operate the site but equally it is doubtful whether a private site developed in such circumstances would be sufficiently economic and flexible in its policy to meet the particular requirements of those who presently use the site at Burntisland. There may be cases where the prospective loss of significant rights enjoyed by the local inhabitants would justify the imposition of a condition that alternative land requires to be provided even if such a con-
E dition put the proposed alienation in material jeopardy. However this is not such a case. There is a clear benefit to the whole community in securing the industrial operations of the fourth respondents. This benefit outweighs any loss to the community as a result of the closure of the caravan park. The petitioners as the local authority charged with certain responsibility regarding the economic welfare of the community are well placed to make that judgment. Accordingly their view is entitled to some respect and
F on the facts it is one with which I have no difficulty in agreeing. If a condition such as is suggested were to be imposed it might well completely prevent the implementation of the disposal. Even if land were to be provided for an alternative site it is far from certain that it would ever operate as a caravan site and that if it did it would operate for any length of time.

The third question I have to address concerns the application of the sale proceeds. Counsel for the petitioners argued that there was a difference between the true market value of the land and the special price that the petitioners might be able to negotiate with the pur-
G chasers. If the common good fund was given the market value of the developed land, the fund would be accorded its full entitlement and any surplus could be used to pay off the loan. This it was argued would be eminently equitable. That may well be so, but such equitable considerations are not applicable to the situation. In terms of s 222 (2) of the Local Government (Scotland) Act 1973 the petitioners in administering the land have to pay regard to the interests of the inhabitants of Burntisland. The land is essentially dedicated to these inhabitants and the petitioners in a
H sense hold the land in trust for them.

The petitioners have applied substantial capital sums to the development of the land. This expenditure was not regarded as a charge on the relevant common good fund so that the position in law appears to be that the petitioners have chosen to amplify the value of the land (and thus the common good fund which it represents) by erecting a building on it. The whole land (including the building and any other fixed structures) is what is held as common good for the
I local inhabitants. If the petitioners translate the fund into money by selling the land the proceeds remain subject to the common good trust. In managing the land for the local inhabitants the petitioners are obliged to get the best possible price for the land for these inhabitants should it be sold. Thus I find it difficult to see the distinction made by their senior counsel between an artificial market price fixed by the district valuer and the price actually realised on sale. What the petitioners propose to do with the proceeds
J seems effectively to be a proposed alienation of part of the common good fund dedicated to local inhabitants. The loans which would be repaid are of course not only a charge on the inhabitants of Burntisland but on the whole Kirkcaldy District. Section 75 (2) of the Act of course only applies to land and the circumstances under which parts of the common good fund other than land may be alienated were not fully explored before me. The first and second respondents argue that the petitioners' proposals are at best highly debat-
K able and would be likely to give rise to further acute controversy. It is certainly true that if I make no condition the law would take its course with regard to the application of the purchase proceeds, but I think I am entitled to take account of the fact that it may be unfair on the inhabitants and generally undesirable that any alienation of the land should create an unsettled situation. The petitioners' proposals certainly threaten that such a situation would arise. I shall therefore make it a condition of the disposal that the whole sale proceeds
L of the land should be applied to the common good account dedicated to the benefit of the inhabitants of Burntisland. In this way the inhabitants will be no worse off after the sale than they were when they had the benefit of the capital asset represented by the land and its buildings. If the petitioners have any enforceable claim on the common good account for moneys which they have expended in developing the land then this could be pursued in the appropriate way.

In the whole circumstances I shall grant the prayer

A of the petition and authorise the disposal of the land in question to the fourth respondents. I shall attach a condition to such disposal to the effect that the whole proceeds of the sale should be applied to the common good account dedicated to the benefit of the inhabitants of Burntisland.

B *Counsel for Petitioners, McNeill; Solicitors, Shepherd & Wedderburn, WS — Counsel for First and Second Respondents, Bovey; Solicitors, Cochran, Sayers & Cook (for James Thomson & Son, Kirkcaldy) — No appearance for Third Respondent — Counsel for Fourth Respondents, Hamilton; Solicitors, Gillespie Macandrew, WS.*

S F M

[The requirement that such petitions be presented in the Inner House, as noted at the end of the report in *East Lothian District Council v National Coal Board*, was altered by the Act of Sederunt (Rules of Court Amendment No 4) 1987 which added such petitions to the list of Outer House petitions con-
C tained in Rule of Court 189.]

The Noble Organisation Ltd v Kilmarnock and Loudoun District Council

D

FIRST DIVISION

THE LORD PRESIDENT (HOPE),
LORDS COWIE AND WYLIE

25 JUNE 1992

Licensing — Licensing committee — Application for public entertainment licence for amusement centre — Objection — Petition signed by objectors — Specification
E *of grounds of objection — Petition stating "Kilmarnock does not need a bigger arcade" — Whether sufficient specification — Civic Government (Scotland) Act 1982 (c 45), Sched 1, para 3 (1).*

Process — Appeal — Grounds of appeal — Late lodging — Adjournment moved at hearing of appeal — No prior intimation of intention to lodge grounds — Whether leave should be granted — Rules of Court 1965, rule 294B (2) (b).

F An application for a public entertainment licence for premises in Kilmarnock was made to the local authority's planning and licensing committee in terms of s 41 of the Civic Government (Scotland) Act 1982. The premises were already being operated by the applicants as a place of public entertainment. The applicants proposed to close an adjacent wine bar and increase the number of electronic machines in the premises from 91 to 170. The committee refused the application on the basis of over provision in the central part of Kilmarnock. At the hearing, an objection was before the committee in the form of a peti-

tion, attached to which were 376 signatures, reading: "Kilmarnock does not need a bigger arcade (Plaza con- G verted into amusements)". The applicants successfully appealed to the sheriff under Sched 1, para 18 to the Act. The sheriff held inter alia that the committee had erred in law, in that the petition failed to specify grounds of objection as required by para 3 (1) (b) of Sched 1 to the Act, and remitted the case to the committee for a rehearing. The licensing authority appealed to the Inner House on the grounds that the sheriff erred in so holding. At the hearing of the appeal the applicants sought an adjournment for the H purpose of lodging late grounds of appeal in order to challenge the sheriff's decision to remit for a rehearing.

Held, (1) that, the applicants having conducted the appeal to the date of hearing on the basis that they accepted the sheriff's decision, insufficient reason had been given by the applicants for seeking to lodge grounds of appeal at such a very late stage (p 761I-J); (2) that while there was a measure of discretion given to the licensing authority about the grounds on which I an application might be refused, para 3 (1) was precise as to what was required of an objection if it was to be a relevant objection for the purposes of Sched 1 and, if an objection did not meet these requirements, the licensing authority were obliged to disregard it (pp 762L-763B); (3) that for a ground of objection to be "specified", enough had to be said to identify the point at issue and give notice to the applicant of the point which he had to meet, and the licensing authority had to be able to determine whether or not J the objection disclosed a relevant ground for refusing the application (p 763C); (4) that that requirement was a strict one, and the licensing authority had to be careful to leave out of account any objection which did not comply with its terms (p 763D); and (5) that the sheriff was entitled to hold that the test of specification was not satisfied as no reason was given for the statement in the petition, and accordingly the committee ought not to have entertained the petition (p 763H-J); and appeal *refused*. K

Observed, (1) that the mere number of objections irrespective of their content could never be a good reason for refusing an application (p 763E); and (2) that an objection was not to be treated more leniently as regards specification simply because it took the form of a petition for public signature (p 763F).

Appeal from the sheriff court L

Kilmarnock and Loudoun District Council appealed to the Court of Session against the decision of the sheriff at Kilmarnock to allow an appeal by The Noble Organisation Ltd against the district council's decision to refuse a public entertainment licence for premises in Kilmarnock, and to remit the case to the council for a rehearing of the application.

Statutory provisions

The Civic Government (Scotland) Act 1982 provides in Sched 1:

"3.—(1) Any objection or representation relating to an application for the grant or renewal of a licence shall, subject to subparagraph (2) below, be entertained by the licensing authority if, but only if, the objection or representation — (a) is in writing; (b) specifies the grounds of the objection or, as the case may be, the nature of the representation; (c) specifies the name and address of the person making it; (d) is signed by him or on his behalf; (e) was made to them within 21 days of whichever is the later or, as the case may be, latest of the following dates — (i) where public notice of the application was given under paragraph 2 (7) above, the date when it was first so given; (ii) where the application relates to a licence for an activity which is wholly or mainly to be carried out in premises and the authority have specified a date under paragraph 2 (6) above, that date; (iii) in any other case, the date when the application was made to them. . . .

"5.—(1) Where an application for the grant or renewal of a licence has been made to a licensing authority they shall, in accordance with this paragraph — (a) grant or renew the licence unconditionally; (b) grant or renew the licence subject to conditions; or (c) refuse to grant or renew the licence. . . .

"(3) A licensing authority shall refuse an application to grant or renew a licence if, in their opinion — (a) the applicant or, where the applicant is not a natural person, any director of it or partner in it or any other person responsible for its management, is either — (i) for the time being disqualified under section 7 (6) of this Act, or (ii) not a fit and proper person to be the holder of the licence; (b) the activity to which it relates would be managed by or carried on for the benefit of a person, other than the applicant, who would be refused the grant or renewal of such a licence if he made the application himself; (c) where the licence applied for relates to an activity consisting of or including the use of premises or a vehicle or vessel, those premises are not or, as the case may be, that vehicle or vessel is not suitable or convenient for the conduct of the activity having regard to — (i) the location, character or condition of the premises or the character or condition of the vehicle or vessel; (ii) the nature and extent of the proposed activity; (iii) the kind of persons likely to be in the premises, vehicle or vessel; (iv) the possibility of undue public nuisance; or (v) public order or public safety; or (d) there is other good reason for refusing the application; and otherwise shall grant the application."

The Rules of Court 1965, as amended, provide:

"294B.— . . . (2) On appearance in the single bills under paragraph (1), in the absence of any opposition, or where any opposition is unsuccessful, the court shall appoint — (a) the reclaimer or appellant; and (b) any respondent wishing to bring any interlocutor under review or challenge the grounds on which the Lord Ordinary or court below has pronounced the interlocutor under review, to lodge grounds of appeal within 28 days."

Case referred to

Noble Organisation v City of Glasgow District Council (No 3), 1991 SLT 213.

The appeal was heard by the First Division on 11 June 1992.

On 25 June 1992 the court *refused* the appeal.

The following opinion of the court was delivered by the Lord President (Hope):

OPINION OF THE COURT.—This is an appeal by the licensing authority for the district of Kilmarnock and Loudoun against an interlocutor of the sheriff allowing an appeal by the applicants against a decision of the authority's planning and licensing committee. The application was for a public entertainment licence for premises situated at Nobles Amusements, Ground Floor, Foregate, Kilmarnock. It was made under s 41 of the Civic Government (Scotland) Act 1982. The premises were already being operated by the applicants as a place of public entertainment together with a snack bar. Adjacent to them were other premises occupied by the applicants which were being operated by them as the Plaza wine bar. The proposal was to close the wine bar with its restaurant and discotheque area and to increase the number of electronic machines in the premises from 91 to 170, thus increasing substantially the area used as a place of public entertainment within the meaning of s 41 (2) of the Act.

The committee refused the application by nine votes to four, for various reasons which were set out in a letter to the respondents' solicitors dated 1 October 1990. They took the view that, having regard to the location of the premises and the nature and extent of the activity, there would be an over provision in the central part of Kilmarnock, that the nature and extent of the activity was not appropriate to the prominent position of the premises and that a large public entertainment facility would be detrimental to the area in which the premises were situated. Although this is not mentioned in the grounds for refusal, it is a matter of agreement that the committee had before them at the hearing an objection which took the form of a petition attached to which were 376 signatures. No one who was named in the petition appeared at the hearing to speak to this objection. The applicants appealed to the sheriff under para 18 of Sched 1 to the Act against the refusal of their application, and their appeal was successful. The sheriff was persuaded that for a number of reasons — one of which was related to the petition — the committee in arriving at their decision erred in law, acted contrary to natural justice and exercised their discretion in an unreasonable manner. These are three of the four grounds on which, in terms of subpara (7) of para 18, the sheriff may uphold an appeal. He was urged to reverse the decision and to grant the application, as he had power to do under subpara (9) of this paragraph. But he decided instead to remit the case to the planning and licensing committee for a rehearing of the application. This was on the view that there had not been a blatant and deliberate contravention of the principles of natural justice, but rather that the matter had been aired in a too disjointed and vague fashion to focus the real issues in the case.

The licensing authority have challenged the sheriff's decision in their grounds of appeal on a number of points. But counsel indicated at the outset of the hearing of the appeal that he proposed to argue only one of them. This was ground 1, which is in these terms: "The learned sheriff erred in holding (record p 55) that the petition signed by objectors was not a competent objection and ought not to have been entertained by the appellants' committee."

He was content to accept the sheriff's decision on all other grounds, from which it follows that the decision to allow the appeal and to remit the case to the committee for a rehearing of the application is no longer objected to by the licensing authority as being erroneous. As counsel explained, however, it would not be open to the committee to look at the petition when the matter came before them again at the rehearing of the application if the sheriff's decision as to its competency was allowed to stand. He submitted that the point remained a live issue in the case, notwithstanding the fact that the licensing authority no longer sought to interfere with the defenders' decision in any other respect. Counsel for the applicants did not resist the request by the licensing authority that we should consider the appeal on this point only. We agree that, on the assumption that the case is to go back to the committee for a rehearing, the point remains a live one and that the licensing authority are entitled to continue with their appeal on this single ground.

Counsel then sought an adjournment of the hearing of the appeal in order to enable the applicants to lodge grounds of appeal challenging the sheriff's decision to remit the case to the committee for a rehearing. He pointed out that a substantial period of time had now elapsed since the sheriff's decision was issued, and he told us that the applicants were anxious to avoid any further delay. They wished to submit that the sheriff had exercised his discretion wrongly in deciding to remit the case to the committee for reconsideration instead of reversing that decision and granting the application. Counsel for the licensing authority told us that he was not in a position to argue this point, since he had received no notice that this was a point on which argument would be required. But he was unable to say that it was important in the public interest that the appeal should be disposed of without delay, and for this reason he did not feel able to oppose the application for an adjournment.

We were not persuaded that a sufficient reason had been made out by counsel for the applicants for seeking to lodge grounds of appeal at this very late stage. Rule of Court 294B (2) (b) as amended, provides inter alia that, on the first appearance of an appeal in the single bills, any respondent wishing to bring any interlocutor under review, or to challenge the grounds on which the court below has pronounced the interlocutor, must lodge grounds of appeal within 28 days. On 12 July 1991 the court pronounced an interlocutor in accordance with this rule, by which the licensing authority and any respondent wishing to bring any interlocutor under review were appointed to lodge their grounds of appeal within 28 days from that date.

The applicants did not lodge any grounds of appeal in terms of that interlocutor, nor did they seek to do so at any date prior to the hearing of this appeal. Nor was it suggested on their behalf when the case came before the court on the by order roll under Rule of Court 294C (7) that it was their intention to challenge the sheriff's decision on this point. On the contrary the parties were agreed when the case came before us on the by order roll that, since the appeal was to be restricted to one point only, the period originally fixed for the hearing of this appeal could be reduced from two days to one day only. It is clear that the applicants had ample opportunity to seek leave to lodge grounds of appeal if they wished to do so, and that up to the date of the hearing of the appeal their case was being conducted on the basis that this would not be necessary because they were content to accept the sheriff's decision and to move that it be affirmed.

Had it not been for the position which was adopted by the applicants at the stage of the by order hearing, we might perhaps have been disposed to consider granting an adjournment and allowing grounds of appeal to be lodged late. But the purpose of the by order hearing is to eliminate, so far as reasonably practicable, disruption to the court's timetable by late adjournments or inaccurate forecasts of the duration of a hearing on the summar roll. That is the stage at which consideration should have been given to the grounds on which the appeal was to be argued, so that the court could be told whether the appeal was to proceed and whether the dates which had been fixed for the hearing were required. Since no good reason was advanced as to why the point which counsel for the applicants sought to take could not have been mentioned at that stage, we were not prepared to grant him the adjournment which would have been necessary to enable this fresh ground of appeal to be argued.

Accordingly the argument to which we listened in this appeal was confined to the single question whether the sheriff was in error in holding that the petition was not a competent objection and that it ought not to have been entertained by the committee. The statutory background to this question is to be found in Sched 1 to the Act, which makes provision for the general system of licensing for activities for which licences are required under Pt II of the Act. It applies in particular to public entertainment licences. The system requires the applicant to make an application in writing to the licensing authority, whereupon various provisions take effect for its intimation to the chief constable and the fire authority and for notice of the application to be given to the public. There is an opportunity for the making of objections or representations and for them to be considered when the application is being disposed of by the licensing authority. Paragraph 3 (1) provides that an objection or representation relating to an application for the grant or renewal of a licence shall be entertained by the licensing authority inter alia "if, but only if, the objection or representation — . . . (b) specifies the grounds of the objection or, as the case may be, the nature of the representation".

A There is also a time limit under para 3 (1) (e) of 21 days for the making of the objection or representation. It is open to the licensing authority under para 3 (2) to entertain an objection or representation which is out of time if they are satisfied that there is a sufficient reason why it was not made within the time required under subpara (1). But no such discretion is given to the licensing authority in regard to an objection or representation which fails to meet the requirement that the grounds of objection or the nature of the representation must be specified.

B Paragraph 5 of Sched 1 provides that where an application for the grant or renewal of a licence has been made to them, the local authority "shall, in accordance with this paragraph — (a) grant or renew the licence unconditionally; (b) grant or renew the licence subject to conditions; or (c) refuse to grant or renew the licence".

The provision which enables the licensing authority to refuse an application is subpara (3) of para 5, which C specifies various grounds of refusal. Grounds (a) and (b) relate to grounds of objection against the applicant himself or the person, other than the applicant, by whom the activity would be managed or for whose benefit it would be carried on. The remaining grounds of objection are in these terms: [his Lordship quoted the terms of subpara (3) (c) and (d) and continued:] The subparagraph concludes by indicating that unless the licensing authority are of opinion that one or more of the specified grounds of refusal has been made out they must grant the application.
D

The petition of objection which was before the planning and licensing committee consisted of a cover sheet and 15 pages on which were set out the names and addresses of the signatories. No reference appears to have been made to the wording of the cover sheet in the argument in the sheriff court. The sheriff does not mention it in his note, and, since no argument was submitted to us about its terms, we need say no more about it. The argument relates only to the meaning E and effect of the words printed in capital letters at the head of each of the following 15 pages, which are as follows: "Kilmarnock does not need a bigger arcade (Plaza converted into amusements)".

The sheriff held that this was not a competent objection, because, as he put it, it would be taking too charitable a view to say that it specified grounds of objection as it was required to do by para 3 (1) (b) of Sched 1. In his view the committee erred in law in regarding it as a competent objection and it ought not F to have been entertained by them.

Counsel for the licensing authority submitted that the sheriff had misdirected himself as to the proper construction of the words used in the document. He contended that they gave a sufficient indication of the ground of objection, which was that if the application were to be granted it would result in an over provision of places of public entertainment in Kilmarnock. He pointed out that the grounds of refusal in para 5 (3) (c) did not include over provision, but he submitted that there could be no doubt that this was another "good

reason" for refusing an application in terms of para 5 (3) (d). If authority was needed on this point it was to G be found in *The Noble Organisation v City of Glasgow District Council (No 3)* where at p 216D the Lord Justice Clerk agreed that over provision of similar facilities in the locality could fall under head (d) of the subparagraph. As for the words in brackets, these indicated that the objection was related to the conversion of the Plaza wine bar into an amusement arcade. So the statement that Kilmarnock did not need a bigger arcade was to be understood as referring not to a shopping or any other kind of arcade but to an amuse- H ment arcade only. Any person with a reasonable amount of local knowledge would understand that what was meant was that the existing amusement arcade was big enough for Kilmarnock — it was implied by the word "bigger" that there was already a smaller one in existence, and a person with local knowledge would know where it was. The signatories were saying simply that enough was enough, and that was sufficient for the committee to be entitled to consider the petition and to take these objections into I account.

It was not disputed by counsel for the applicants that over provision of similar facilities, if established, could be regarded as a good reason for refusing an application for a public entertainment licence. Nor did he dispute the point that it was sufficiently clear, under reference to the passage in parenthesis, that the objection was intended to relate to the pursuers' application to extend the arcade as a place of public entertainment. But he submitted that the words J "Kilmarnock does not need a bigger arcade" failed to meet the requirement in para 3 (1) (b) that the ground of objection should be specified. The sheriff was entitled to find that this requirement was not met by the words used in the petition. No specification was given, since there was nothing more than a bald statement of fact, which might equally be read as an objection on grounds of amenity as one on grounds of over provision. Nothing was said to indicate that objection was being taken on the ground that there were too K many amusement machines, or on any other point of detail to show clearly that the objection was that an over provision would result.

In all these cases about licensing there is a balance to be struck between the legitimate interests of the applicant and those of the public who may be affected by the activity for which the licence is required. The system which the Act lays down is designed to achieve this, and it is important that careful attention is paid L to its various requirements if the balance is not to be disturbed. The open ended list of grounds for refusal which is set out in para 5 (3) gives some flexibility to the system. It may be contrasted with the list of grounds given in s 17 (1) of the Licensing (Scotland) Act 1976, which requires the licensing board to grant the application if none of the particular grounds there listed is made out. Whether there is any other good reason for refusing the application than the reasons which are specifically mentioned in the subparagraph is left to the opinion of the licensing authority. But, while this measure of discretion is given to the licensing authority about the grounds on which an application may be refused, the provisions of para 3 (1) are precise as to what is required of an objection or representation if it is to be a relevant objection or representation for the purposes of the Schedule. An objection or representation which does not meet these requirements is not only one which the licensing authority are not obliged to entertain — it is one which they must also disregard, as the words "but only" in subpara (1) indicate. This is subject only to the discretion given to the licensing authority by subpara (2) in regard to objections or representations which are made to them out of time.

It is important in these circumstances that proper weight should be given to the requirement that the grounds of the objection must be "specified". No doubt some latitude can be given to objectors as to the wording to be used when specifying the grounds. It is not necessary that these should be expressed in the language of para 5 (3) of the Schedule, as the licensing authority is entitled to refuse an application if there is "some other good reason" for doing so than the particular reasons listed there. Nevertheless enough must be said to identify the point at issue. Notice must be given to the applicant of the point which he has to meet, and the licensing authority must be able to determine whether or not the objection discloses a relevant ground for refusing the application. Counsel for the applicants described this as a stringent test, which placed a heavy onus on the objector. We prefer not to describe the requirement in these particular terms. The language of para 3 (1) speaks for itself, as it is only if the objection "specifies" the grounds for the objection that it becomes a relevant objection which must be considered by the licensing authority. It is, however, appropriate to describe the requirement as a strict one, and the licensing authority must be careful to leave out of account any objection which does not comply with its terms.

There is a further point to be made in regard to petitions of objection of the kind which is before us in this case. As the Lord Justice Clerk pointed out in *Noble Organisation v City of Glasgow District Council*, the number of objections on any particular ground cannot of itself be a good reason for refusal. The mere number of objections irrespective of their content can never be a good reason for refusing an application. What matters are the grounds on which the objection is based. This makes it all the more important, when numerous signatures have been obtained to indicate the weight of opinion on the point, for the grounds of the objection to be clearly specified. Unless this is done it cannot be assumed that the signatories are all objecting for the same reason. Lack of precision in the reason given in the petition may indicate that they themselves were not clear in their own minds about the content of the objection with which they wished to be associated. An objection is not to be treated more leniently in this regard simply because it takes the form of a petition for public signature. On the contrary, it is important that the requirement that the grounds of objection must be specified should be applied as strictly in these cases as it must be in the case of an objection by an individual. If this is not done, the licensing authority may be tempted to attach weight to the objection because of the number of persons associated with it regardless of its content, which is something which they are not entitled to do.

The words which have been used in the present case are sufficient to identify the application to which the objection relates. That much is clear from the four words which were placed in parenthesis, and counsel for the applicants was content not to dispute this point. The question is whether the grounds for the objection have been specified in the seven words which remain. Although the point is a narrow one, we have reached the opinion without much difficulty that the sheriff was entitled to hold that this test was not satisfied. It seems to us that these words contain a proposition which simply invites the question, why not? It is in the unspoken answer to that question that the grounds for the objection are concealed, not in the proposition which invites it. And, as counsel pointed out, it is not inconceivable that various answers might be given if the question were to be put to the objectors. Depending on the emphasis given to the word "need" on the one hand, or to the word "bigger" on the other, they might range from over provision of facilities, measured by the number of machines or the places for such facilities in Kilmarnock, to points related to the nature or size of this particular arcade. Too much is left to speculation, and that being so the committee ought not to have entertained this petition of objection.

The sheriff's decision has not, in the end of the day, been challenged on any other point. We shall therefore affirm his interlocutor and refuse the appeal.

Counsel for Pursuers and Respondents (Applicants), Henderson, QC; Solicitors, Bonar Mackenzie, WS — Counsel for Defenders and Appellants (Licensing Authority), Nimmo Smith, QC, Bovey; Solicitors, Cochran, Sayers & Cook.

P A

Stirling v Bartlett

OUTER HOUSE
LORD COULSFIELD
11 AUGUST 1992

Heritable property — Boundary dispute — Boundary marked by medium filum of river — Channel of river destroyed in flood — New channel dug by agreement in different position — Whether boundary marked by medium filum of new channel or old channel.

Property — Heritable property — Boundary dispute —
A *Boundary marked by medium filum of river — Channel*
of river destroyed in flood — New channel dug by agree-
ment in different position — Whether boundary marked
by medium filum of new channel or old channel.

River, loch and sea — River — Boundary dispute —
Boundary marked by medium filum of river — Channel
of river destroyed in flood — New channel dug by agree-
ment in different position — Whether boundary marked
by medium filum of new channel or old channel.

B   A dispute arose between neighbouring landowners
as to part of the boundary between their properties.
According to their titles the boundary was represented
by the medium filum of part of the River Orrin. In
February 1966, debris brought downriver by a flood
caused this part of the river to split into a number of
shallow channels. In 1967 by agreement between the
pursuer and the predecessors in title of the defender,
a clear channel was dug out by bulldozer. The pursuer
argued that the construction of the channel should be
C   taken as fixing the boundary. The defender argued
that the main channel had previously lain to the west
of the new channel and that the boundary did not
move when the channel was built. Evidence led at
proof indicated that the channel of the river had
moved on a number of occasions within the past
century and had at times run where parts of the new
channel had been dug.

Held, that as the proprietors had agreed to restore
a channel which had been effectively destroyed, and as
D   it was not possible on the available evidence to determine where the old channel had been, nor was it a case
of avulsio (a sudden and dramatic change in the course
of the river) or of a wholly new artificial channel being
created, as a matter of common sense the channel dug
in 1967 should be taken to be the channel of the river
for the purpose of determining the boundary for the
time being (p 769C-G); and declarator *granted* in
favour of the pursuer.

E
_____

**Action of declarator, interdict, damages, and
production and reduction**
    Roderick William Kenneth Stirling raised an action
against William Bartlett concluding for declarator
that part of the boundary between their respective
properties was formed by the mid-point of a manmade
channel formed in the River Orrin in 1967 after floods
had destroyed the previous natural channel. He also
sought interdict against encroachment by the
F   defender, damages and production and reduction of a
deed granted in favour of the defenders by his
predecessors in title.

    The case came to proof before the Lord Ordinary
(Coulsfield).

Cases referred to
Att Gen for Southern Nigeria v Holt [1915] AC 559.
Menzies v Marquess of Breadalbane (1901) 4 F 55.
Nebraska v Iowa (1892) US Reports 359.
Tweeddale (Marquis of) v Kerr (1822) 1 S 397.

Textbooks referred to
Justinian, *Institutes,* II i 20.   G
Stair, *Institutions,* II i 35.

    On 11 August 1992 the Lord Ordinary *granted*
decree of declarator and interdict, and quoad ultra
assoilzied the defender.

    LORD COULSFIELD.—The River Orrin rises in
the remote hills of the East Monar forest and pursues
a generally eastward course, passing through a hydro-
electric reservoir, until it makes a sharp turn towards H
the north and, for about the last three kilometres of its
course, flows generally northwards, to join the river
Conon near the ruins of Brahan Castle. Shortly before
its junction with the Conan, the Orrin passes under a
bridge which carries the road from Muir of Ord to
Marybank and Contin. For some distance to the south
of the road bridge, the Orrin constitutes the boundary
between the lands owned by the pursuer, who is the
proprietor of the estate of Fairbairn, and those of the
defender. It is agreed between the parties that, in   I
terms of both their titles, the river constitutes the
boundary between them and it is also agreed that, in
accordance with the normal rule, the boundary is the
medium filum of the river.

    There is, in broad terms, little dispute as to the cir-
cumstances which have led to the present action. The
flow of water in the Orrin varies according to the
season of the year, and the river is capable of rising
very rapidly in spate. When it does so, it carries down
substantial quantities of gravel and stones, as well as, J
on occasion, trees and other debris. In consequence
the precise course of the river is liable to alter. Prior
to 1969, the lands now owned by the defender were
the property of a company, Kings & Co Ltd, who also
owned lands on the east side of the Orrin to the north
of the road bridge. Kings & Co Ltd had carried on
gravel extraction from the lands both north and south
of the bridge for some time and, at least before the
construction of the hydro-electric dam in 1953, had
had the benefit of replacement of the gravel extracted by K
the action of the river. In the course of time, an extensive quantity of gravel was extracted on the east side
of the Orrin to the south of the bridge, that is, on the
land now owned by the defender. By agreement with
the pursuer, extraction also took place on the west side
of the river, on part of his land. According to his evidence, the pursuer received royalties on about 25,000
tons of gravel extracted. These activities had some
effect upon the course of the river, the precise extent
of which will be considered later. The gravel working L
carried out by Kings & Co Ltd came to an end in
about 1966. The area affected by the gravel extraction
extended, on the east side of the river, for about 200
yds to the south of the bridge and then, on both sides
of the river, for a further 300 to 400 yds.

    In February 1966, there was a very large flood,
which brought down substantial quantities of gravel
and trees, tree roots and other rubbish. This material
was deposited, in part, on the area of ground where
the gravel had been worked and caused the river to

become widely spread and divided into a number of channels, most of which were shallow. The road bridge was damaged in the flood. Discussions then took place involving the district fishery board, the Department of Agriculture and Fisheries for Scotland and Highland Regional Council, as the roads authority, as well as the proprietors. The district fishery board were involved because, although the construction of the hydro-electric dam in 1953 had substantially ended salmon fishing in the Orrin, and compensation had been paid on the basis of the full value of the salmon fisheries in the river, nevertheless some netting of salmon was still carried out, at a point upstream of the area in dispute in this action, and, in addition, it was thought that the river was of some value as a nursery area for young salmon. It was decided that a clear channel for the river should be dug out, and this was done by a bulldozer, working from the southern end of the stretch of the river now in dispute, to about the vicinity of the road bridge.

The defender acquired his land from Kings & Co Ltd, and took possession of it, in 1969, although he did not receive a disposition until 1976. By the time he took possession of the land, the new channel had already been excavated. The defender was, however, under the impression, from discussions he had had with a foreman employed by Kings & Co Ltd, that the land which he had purchased extended some way to the west of the new channel. The foreman in question, Mr Macgregor, who has since died, was later involved in the defender's quarrying. After acquiring the property, the defender carried out some quarrying on his side of the river to the north of the bridge; he maintained that he had not carried out any quarrying for profit in the disputed area. His quarrying work came to an end in 1991. In about 1982 the defender established a fish farm on his side of the channel. Water supplies for the farm were at first obtained by pipes from the river, but, some time after 1983, the defender constructed a secondary channel, divided from the main channel by a gravel bank, which took a proportion of the flow of the river towards the fish farm and returned the surplus to the main flow of the river some distance downstream, but still above the road bridge. As a result of these operations, the main channel of the Orrin moved some distance towards the west from the position it occupied after the excavation of the new channel.

In 1984 there was another flood but it does not appear that that flood had serious consequences. In 1989, however, there was another very substantial flood, in the course of which the level of the Orrin rose very rapidly because of an overflow from the hydro-electric dam. The flood passed through the defender's property and caused extensive damage to his fish farm. After the 1989 flood, the defender carried out works for the future protection of his lands and of the fish farm. These works included the construction of a rock armoured bank for a considerable distance along the east side of the river. The defender also instructed work to be carried out on the west side of the channel, as it existed at that date. The operations carried out on the west side of the channel included the excavation of a spur channel in a generally westwards direction; and the clearing of trees and scrub from a substantial area of ground. The area affected by the clearance was variously estimated in the evidence but it is reasonably clear that it included, at least, an area of about 100 yds by 50 yds which lies immediately to the north of the spur channel excavated by the defender. In the course of these operations, the defender caused heaps of gravel to be made on the west side of the existing main channel. He also caused some loads of gravel to be removed from the area of the river bed and used for the works on the east side of the river or stored for future use, and some of the gravel removed was sold. These operations were objected to by the pursuer who obtained interim interdict to prevent their continuance.

In brief, the dispute between the parties is whether the line of their boundary is now represented by the medium filum of the main channel (that is, the channel excavated following the 1966 flood as it now is after taking account of the effects of the later operations in the construction of a secondary channel), or a line further to the west, representing the position of the medium filum of the main course of the river, prior to 1966.

The pursuer's witnesses included Mr Donald Fisher, a chartered geologist and engineer who has qualifications in photography, and has made special studies of aerial photography, and who, in addition, has experience of the area in question through previous employment as a soils engineer and geologist with Inverness County Council and, later, with Highland Regional Council. Mr Fisher had made extremely careful and accurate investigations and presented the results with exemplary clarity. He obtained, from the National Archive of Aerial Photography, such aerial photographs showing the disputed areas as were available and arranged for them to be reduced, by a very accurate process of electronic scanning, to a common scale. Thereafter he interpreted the photographs so as to distinguish areas of standing or running water, on the one hand, and areas of significant ground clearance, revealing sand, gravel or soil, on the other. These interpretations are shown on a series of transparent overlays, on which areas of water are represented in blue and areas of significant soil exposure in red. Mr Fisher made a similar interpretation, so far as possible, of the 1906 Ordnance Survey sheet, which is the map referred to in the titles of the property. He also took several series of aerial photographs of the area as it now is, from different heights. By comparing the various overlays and setting them against either a copy of the Ordnance Survey map or an aerial photograph of the area as it now is, enlarged to the same scale, it is possible to make fairly close comparisons of the position of the river at various dates. The principal deficiency in the evidence is that, unfortunately, no aerial photographs are available for the period immediately preceding the 1966 flood. The nearest photograph in date prior to the flood was taken on 23 May 1963. There is photo-

graphic evidence available for early 1967, shortly after
A the flood, which appears to show the consequences
of it.

It is not easy to express in words what Mr Fisher's
interpretations show, but it is necessary, for the purposes of this opinion, to make some attempt to do so.
The enlarged aerial photograph showing the present
situation is no 32/3 of process. This photograph shows
the disputed stretch of the Orrin to the south of the
road bridge. The bridge itself does not appear in this
photograph. The north end of the stretch of river in
B question is at the right hand side of the photograph
and the river runs approximately across the middle of
the photograph. The channel of the river as it now is,
following the effects of the 1967 excavations and the
later construction of a subsidiary channel, runs in a
reasonably regular shallow curve across the photograph. The apex of the curve is towards the top of the
photograph, i e towards the west. The secondary
channel, now divided into several lagoons, appears
immediately below (that is, to the east of) the main
C channel as it now is, and is, for most of its course,
separated from the main channel by a gravel bank.
Above and to the left of the apex of the shallow curve
is the principal part of the area of ground cleared in
the course of the defender's operations following the
1989 flood. The westward spur, also excavated by the
defender, can be seen to the left of that cleared area.
The defender's fish farm can be seen just below the
secondary channel slightly to the right of the apex of
the curve of the main channel. A comparison of Mr
D Fisher's interpretations of the 1906 Ordnance Survey
sheet, an aerial photograph taken on 9 August 1947,
a further photograph taken on 15 October 1959 and
the photographs taken on 23 May 1963 and 23 April
1967 with no 32/3 shows that, in the stretch towards
the extreme right of no 32/3, the course of the river
has varied little during the whole period. That is not
surprising, since the river must flow into the channel
which passes under the road bridge. For convenience,
I shall refer to the left hand (or southern) end of the
E stretch which has shown little variation as "the
common point". Immediately above the stretch of
river to the right of the common point, a dark curved
line can be seen in no 32/3, among the vegetation on
the west side of the channel; this line probably indicates the line of an earlier channel of the river, but it
is evident that that channel was abandoned by the
river before 1906.

Moving from the common point towards the south,
F in the 1906 interpretation the main river channel runs
slightly above (i e, west) of the present channel to a
point approximately in line with the apex of the bend
in the present channel; it then curves so as to come
approximately to the same point as the apex of the
present bend. From that point, the main 1906 channel
runs considerably to the west of the line of the present
channel until it reaches the left side of no 32/3.
Although, however, the 1906 channel does lie to the
west of the present channel, the west end of the spur
channel recently excavated by the defender projects to
the west of the mid-line of the 1906 channel and some

of the area cleared by the defender also lies to the west
of the mid-line of the 1906 channel. By 1947 the posi- G
tion had altered quite significantly. The main flow of
the river as shown in the 1947 interpretation runs
from the common point, on a line east of the present
channel and then curves sharply westwards so as to
cross the line of the present channel at about the position of the apex of the bend; in consequence there is
a part of the 1947 channel which lies to the east of the
position of the present channel. From the apex, the
1947 channel curves southwards and thereafter runs
on a line similar to, but not identical with, the line H
appearing in the 1906 interpretation. Further south
again, the line of the 1947 channel lies somewhat to
the east of the line of the channel in 1906. The 1959
interpretation shows that the main channel has altered
again. It now runs from the common point a little to
the west of the 1947 line but does not make the sharp
bend towards the west referred to in the description of
the 1947 position. Instead, it crosses the line of the
1947 main channel and runs southwards some
distance to the east of that line. The 1959 line crosses I
the western edge of the cleared area evident in no 32/3
and touches the end of the spur channel excavated by
the defender after 1989; from that point it runs southwards on an irregularly curving line. While the 1959
main channel is, as I have said, somewhat to the east
of the 1947 channel, it is, through all of its length
from the northern part of the cleared area, some distance to the west of the line of the present channel.

The 1963 interpretation shows a somewhat confused picture. It can, I think, be said that there does J
appear to be a channel following approximately the
same line as the 1959 main channel but it is not
entirely clear that that can be regarded as a main
channel. At one section, near the apex of the bend, this
channel does lie some distance to the east of the 1959
channel. It is also evident in the 1963 interpretation
that there are other channels lying to the west of the
channel which may perhaps be the main channel and
that the exposed area of ground has been very substantially extended, particularly on the east side of the K
river. There is a section, admittedly short, to the left
of the common point where the 1963 channel lies
somewhat east of the present channel.

The 1967 photograph shows an even more confused
picture. Towards the left side, there is a channel
which lies to the east of the present channel, but over
much of the stretch in question there is no channel
which can reasonably be said, in my view, to
correspond to the main channel of 1959 or, on the
assumption that the main channel was still the same L
at the later date, 1963. There are possibly five
channels, one of which lies somewhat to the west of
the 1959 main channel and perhaps rather nearer to
the original channel shown in the 1906 map, although
the correspondence is by no means exact: but there are
others, of which one is quite close to the line of the
defender's subsidiary channel, and another lies substantially to the east, crossing the area now occupied
by the fish farm. What is evident from the 1967 photograph, however, is that there are a number of areas of

standing water or subsidiary channels and it is reasonably clear that the 1967 photograph represents the dis-
persed and confused state of the river brought about
by the flood and the heavy deposits of gravel previously mentioned. It is generally true that for much
of its length the channel excavated in 1967, as it now
appears, lies somewhat to the east of any main channel
which can be derived from interpretation of any
photograph prior to 1967 but, as I have mentioned,
there are stretches of the present channel which lie
west of the line of the 1947 and 1963 channels. It can
also, I think, be said that the 1967 photograph shows
water passing through areas which lay to the east of
any previous channel and which appear to be areas in
which gravel working was carried out on the
defender's side of the river.

Both the defender and the pursuer gave evidence as
to the line of the channel from time to time but,
inevitably, with much less accuracy than was possible
for Mr Fisher. The pursuer gave evidence that, as he
recollected the position, the channel dug in 1967 had
been intended to follow the line where, at that time,
the principal flow of water was. I think, however, that
that evidence is not fully supported by the 1967 photograph. As I have mentioned, there was a channel in
1967 which lay near the line of the defender's subsidiary channel, but while it was no doubt the purpose
of the excavation to achieve a satisfactory and clear
line of flow in the river, the photographic record
suggests that the excavation did not follow any principal channel existing at that date. The defender
referred to curved markings in the vegetation, additional to those previously mentioned, lying to the west
of the apex of the bend of the stretch in dispute and
said that the old bed of the river, which he took to be
the boundary of his land, was represented by those
marks and could still be seen upon the ground, at least
at the time of his inspection in 1969. Again, however,
I do not think that that evidence is consistent with the
aerial photographs. The marks to which the defender
referred may perhaps represent part of the course of
the main channel in 1947 and earlier, but it is clear,
in my view, that if there was a main channel in 1963,
it lay further to the east than those marks would
imply. Some evidence was given by other witnesses,
principally in relation to the effects of the 1966 flood,
but their evidence was not accurate enough to add anything of value.

As I have indicated, the crux of the case is whether
the boundary between the parties' lands is now
represented by the medium filum of the channel as it
now exists or by some other line, representing an
earlier position of the channel, some distance to the
west. In summary, the position of the pursuer was that
the construction of the channel in 1967 had been a
lawful operation carried out by agreement of the
various proprietors involved and must be taken as
fixing their boundary. On the other hand, the contention of the defender was, in brief, that if in 1967 a new
channel had been built which moved the Orrin some
distance to the east, in law the boundary did not move
with it. The defender did not undertake, either in his

pleadings or at the proof, to identify a precise line as
the present boundary; in evidence, he said that his
claim was founded on the 1966 position but added that
he thought that the position was the same in 1966 as
it had been in 1948, which cannot, in my view, be
correct. Neither party suggested any other basis for
establishing the boundary. In some cases, although the
position of the main channel or channels may vary it
is possible to identify a relatively defined and stable
alveus, and take the centre line of that as the boundary
(see, e g *Menzies v Marquess of Breadalbane*) but no
attempt was made to apply that approach in the
present case, and the evidence here does not point to
the existence of any such alveus. It follows that the
choice lies between accepting the medium filum of the
1967 channel, as subsequently modified, as representing the boundary of the parties' lands, for the time
being and accepting, on the other hand, that the
boundary lies some distance to the west of that line,
although the precise position of the boundary cannot
be established in these proceedings.

I was given a full citation of authority but both
counsel agreed that there is no previous decision
which precisely covers the point in issue in the present
case. It is, I think, well established that where the
course of a river, which constitutes the boundary
between two properties, changes by the gradual and
imperceptible addition or subtraction of soil on one
bank or the other, the boundary shifts in accordance
with the movement of the river. That is an application
of the principle of alluvio. On the other hand, where
the course of a river changes in a sudden and violent
way, whether by the operation of natural forces or
with human assistance, the boundary does not change.
That is an application of the principle of avulsio. The
principles are stated in the *Institutes* of Justinian (II i
20) as follows: "Praeterea quod per alluvionem agro
tuo flumen adjecit, jure gentium tibi adquiritur. Est
autem alluvio incrementum latens. Per alluvionem
autem id videtur adjici, quod ita paulatim adjicitur, ut
intellegere non possis quantum quoquo momento
temporis adjiciatur. Quodsi vis fluminis partem
aliquam ex tuo praedio detraxerit et vicini praedio
appulerit palam est eam tuam permanere. Plane si
longiore tempore fundo vicini haeserit arboresque
quas secum traxerit in eum fumdum radices egerint ex
eo tempore videntur vicini fundo adquisitae esse".

As Lord Shaw of Dunfermline observed in *Att Gen
for Southern Nigeria v Holt* [1915] AC at p 613, little
has been added to these principles in subsequent
centuries. Some assistance can, however, be obtained
from the case of *Nebraska v Iowa* to which I was
referred. Justice Brewer, giving the opinion of the
court, cites authorities for the application of the principles of alluvio and avulsio in various systems of law,
domestic and international, in which it is pointed out
that the rule is a rule of the jus gentium, based on the
view that the convenience of retaining the river as a
boundary outweighs any gradual detriment which one
party or the other may suffer by the gradual diminution of territory. The River Missouri is a winding
stream, liable to rapid flows of large volumes of water

from melting snows, and it flows through a valley in
A which the underlying substratum is largely quicksand.
In consequence, it is not uncommon for large masses
of soil to be detached from a bank at one time and
carried away, although such large masses are not
swept away to be deposited at one place. On the contrary: "There is, except in such cases of avulsion as
may be noticed hereafter, in all matters of increase of
bank, always a mere gradual and imperceptible
process. There is no heaping up at an instant and
while the eye rests upon the stream of acres or rods on
B the forming side of the river. No engineering skill is
sufficient to say where the earth in the bank washed
away and disintegrating into the river finds its rest and
abiding place. . . . There is, no matter how rapid the
process of subtraction or addition, no detachment of
earth from one side and deposit of the same on the
other. The only thing which distinguishes this river
from other streams, in the matter of accretion, is in the
rapidity of the change caused by the velocity of the
current; and this in itself, in the very nature of things,
C works no change in the principle underlying the rule
of law in respect thereto. Our conclusions are that notwithstanding the rapidity of the changes in the course
of the channel and the washing from the one side and
on to the other, the law of accretion controls on the
Missouri River, as elsewhere."

Justice Brewer went on to say that a case in which
the river suddenly changed course, for example, by
cutting through the neck of a bend, would be treated
as one of avulsio. The significance of this case is that
D it indicates that although the changes which constitute
accretion must be gradual and imperceptible in the
sense that at any given time they cannot be seen to
occur, they need not be gradual in the sense of occurring slowly over a period of years, or even months; it
is sufficient if they occur in such a way that the transfer of soil cannot be seen to happen before the eyes of
the observer (cf Stair, II i 35).

There is some authority in Scotland for treating
E acquiescence as relevant. *Marquis of Tweeddale v Kerr*
was concerned with a change in the course of a river
as a result of which an area of three acres of land came
to be on the side of a proprietor other than the previous owner of them. It was found by the verdict of a
jury that the change had taken place by the imperceptible addition of soil to the bank of the river and the
court held that, in consequence, the three acres had
been added to the property of the proprietor on whose
side of the river they now lay. The court described the
F case as one of alvei mutatio rather than alluvio,
although it seems to have been accepted that, for this
purpose, alvei mutatio must be a gradual process. A
number of judges gave opinions, which vary in detail
and it is not clear what the full reasoning of the judges
was. Several judges do, however, appear to have
accepted that acquiescence was relevant and that a
proprietor who failed to fence or bank his side of the
river so as to prevent the migration of soil must be
held to have acquiesced in any change which took
place. Although the authorities cited in *Nebraska v
Iowa* suggest that the basis of the rule of the jus

gentium is convenience rather than actual or implied
acquiescence, the decision in *Marquis of Tweeddale v* G
Kerr at least opens the door to regarding acquiescence
or consent as a relevant factor.

Counsel for the defender submitted, founding on
Att Gen for Nigeria v Holt, that a change in the course
of a river brought about by artificial means could not
bring about a change in ownership. The full facts of
Holt's case are complex, but, as I understand it, the
case was, in essence, concerned with accretion on the
foreshore resulting from the construction of works
intended to give protection against erosion. It was held H
in the House of Lords that, in view of the facts found
by the lower courts, the accresced land must be treated
as the product of reclamation work on the foreshore
and must therefore belong to the Crown. The case
does, I think, support the conclusion that a change
resulting from accretion brought about by work
carried out by one proprietor alone would not bring
about a change in ownership. Even without specific
authority, there is, I think, no difficulty in reaching
the conclusion that a mere agreement between pro- I
prietors to dig a wholly new channel for a river,
without any agreement to a change in ownership,
would not effect such a change: and, in any event, a
bare agreement, without appropriate formalities,
would not transfer the title to heritage. I do not,
however, think that *Holt's* case goes so far as to
exclude the possibility that a channel created by artificial work carried out with the consent of both proprietors, in a case such as this, may fall to be regarded
as the river channel for the purpose of fixing the J
boundary for the time being.

In the present case, in my opinion, the changes in
the course of the river at least up to 1959 should be
regarded as attributable to alluvio. The changes may
have taken place relatively quickly or relatively slowly,
but there is no evidence to suggest that there was at
any time a sudden or violent change in the course of
the river which might be regarded as a case of avulsio.
By 1963, the position of the main channel of the river K
may have been uncertain, and gravel working carried
out by or with the consent of both proprietors may
have had some effect, but, again, there is no reason to
think that there had been any sudden or violent
change of course, or any new channel artificially
created, and, therefore, there is no reason, in my
opinion, to think that the boundary as at 1963 should
not be the mid-line of the main channel, wherever that
then was. If so, the boundary in 1947 lay along the line
of the main channel then visible: and it follows that
part of the new channel excavated in 1967 lies within L
land which was part of the pursuer's property in 1947.
The same can be said of the position in 1959, although
the length of channel involved is less. Again, parts of
the land on which the defender carried out clearance
work and the excavation of the spur channel after the
1989 flood lay, both in 1906 and 1963, on the
pursuer's side of the main channel and therefore in his
property. It seems to me that, on the evidence available, the sort of changes which occurred prior to the
1966 flood are just the sort of changes which parties

A whose lands are separated by a river like the Orrin have to accept.

What happened between 1963 and 1967 was, however, rather different. The 1967 situation was brought about by the combination of gravel extraction on both sides of the river carried out by both proprietors and the very large flood in 1966. Even then, however, it does not appear that there was a true avulsio, in the sense of a detachment and redeposit of a distinct body of land or a sudden change in the position of a channel. Indeed the effect of the flood was B virtually to leave the river without any main channel. A new channel was then dug on a line agreed between the proprietors, and, although as I have said, for much of its length it lay to the east of any previous channel, it did, in quite significant sections, lie within an area over which the channel had moved, to and fro, in the course of the last century or so. It also lay within the area affected both by the gravel workings which had been carried out on the two sides of the river and by the deposit of material brought down by the flood. It C seems to me that, given the fluctuations to which the Orrin is liable, it is common sense to treat the channel dug out in 1967 as being the channel of the river for the purpose of fixing the boundary for the time being, and subject to any further natural changes, and that there is nothing contrary to any established principle or authority in so holding. On the evidence available, this is not a case where there had been an avulsio, nor is it a case in which a wholly new artificial channel has been created, nor a case in which a change has been D brought about by the actions of one proprietor alone. It is a case in which the proprietors agreed to restore a channel which had been effectively destroyed, and it is in my view entirely consistent with principle to regard the mid-line of that channel as the boundary between them for the time being. There has been some subsequent movement of the channel, and on the principles which I have discussed, and the evidence in this case, the channel as it now is must represent the present boundary.

E A further consideration which supports that approach is, in my view, that if the mid-line of the present channel, subject to future variation, is not to be taken to be the boundary, it is not easy to see where the boundary in fact is. As I have mentioned, the defender did not, and did not require to, adopt a precise position on this point in his pleadings. His position in evidence was that there was a line which could be determined from the course of the river as it was both in 1966 and 1948, but, in the circumstances F which I have attempted to explain, that evidence was incorrect and no such clear line can be ascertained. The difficulty is emphasised by the fact that even if the 1906 line were taken as the boundary, parts of the works carried out by the defender in 1989 would lie on the pursuer's side of that boundary. The fact is, in my opinion, that it is not possible to go back over the history of the river movements and determine a medium filum which was at one time the boundary and which was later departed from in such a way as to leave the boundary unaffected. In all the circumstances, in my view, the only proper solution to the problems in this case is to hold that the main channel of the river as it now is represents the boundary G between the property of the pursuer and that of the defender. It follows that I shall sustain the first plea in law for the pursuer and grant decree of declarator in terms of the first conclusion of the summons.

The second conclusion of the summons is a conclusion for interdict, but, although interim interdict was granted at an earlier stage of these proceedings, I have had some doubt whether it is appropriate to grant a permanent interdict. This is, I think, a bona fide dispute about the position of a boundary; it may well H be that, once the question of the boundary has been settled, the defender is not likely to commit further encroachment. I have however come to the view that I should grant decree in terms of the second conclusion; the interdict can always be recalled if it is unnecessary. There is a conclusion for damages, but no evidence was led which provided any foundation for holding that the operations of the defender had caused material damage to the pursuer or his property. There is also a conclusion for production and reduc- I tion of a deed, described as a corroborative disposition, granted by successors of Kings & Co Ltd in 1990 with a view to fortifying the defender's position in regard to his title. There is, however, no basis in the evidence, in my opinion, for regarding that disposition as null or invalid. It is, of course, ineffective insofar as it purports to convey any property to the west of the appropriate boundary, but that is not, in my view, a sufficient reason for granting decree of reduction. I shall therefore repel the second, third and sixth pleas in law for the pursuer, and assoilzie the defender from J the third and fourth conclusions of the summons.

Counsel for Pursuer, P W Ferguson; Solicitors, Dundas & Wilson, CS — Counsel for Defender, C J MacAulay, QC, Truscott; Solicitors, Morton Fraser Milligan, WS (for Middleton, Ross & Arnot, Dingwall).

P McC

K

(NOTE)

McGunnigal v D B Marshall (Newbridge) Ltd

OUTER HOUSE L

TEMPORARY JUDGE T G COUTTS, QC

18 AUGUST 1992

Process — Reparation — Personal injuries — Optional procedure — Witnesses — Failure by party to provide list of witnesses — Whether to be allowed to lead witnesses — Rules of Court 1965, rule 188L.

Damages — Amount — Solatium and loss of earnings — Minor injury with ensuing neurosis.

A   A 28 year old employee was injured when her arm was drawn into a housing on a conveyer belt. She raised an action under the optional procedure against her employers, who accepted liability subject to a plea of contributory negligence. The employers provided no list of witnesses. At the proof they sought to adduce witnesses to fact, including witnesses who had been on the list intimated by the pursuer but not led on her behalf. The pursuer's injuries were physically minor but gave rise to an anxiety neurosis which would persist until shortly after the proof.

B   **Held,** (1) that the defenders were not entitled to lead any witnesses; and (2) that solatium was properly valued at £4,000 and disadvantage on the labour market also at £4,000; and decree *pronounced* accordingly.

———————————

Rule of Court 188L (1) provides that each party is to intimate to the other party a list of witnesses within 28 days of the allowance of proof. Rule 188L (2) provides that witnesses not on the list may be adduced, where any other party objects, only at the court's discretion.

C

Mrs Helen McGunnigal raised an action under the optional procedure against her former employers, D B Marshall (Newbridge) Ltd, for damages in respect of injuries sustained in an accident at work on 16 August 1990. She was then aged 28. The pursuer's accident happened at the fillet line in the defenders' premises. That line consisted of a series of moving cones on a conveyor belt. Cooked chickens were impaled on these cones and parts of them were removed for further preparation for sale. At the end of the line the belt with the cones entered a steel box, or housing, where it passed over a wheel and returned the cones to the start of the line. Within that box the filleted carcasses were deposited in a bin. Sensors and an emergency stop button were located where the belt entered the box so that the line could be stopped in case of emergency. The pursuer sustained injury when her arm was drawn into the said box causing her to be pulled in up to shoulder level.

D

E

The pursuer had been trapped for about 10 minutes while the box was removed to release her. The pursuer was unable to stop the belt. She screamed and it was stopped promptly by a fellow employee, Jean Reid. The pursuer was treated initially at the works' first aid room, then removed to the accident and emergency department at Hairmyres hospital. She was examined and sent home to the care of her general practitioner.

F

The temporary judge (T G Coutts, QC) held that no contributory negligence had been established. In so doing he said:

"Prior to the proof the defenders lodged a minute admitting liability subject only to their pleas directed to contributory negligence and quantum of damages. By so doing they absolved the pursuer of the necessity of doing other than describing the injury caused while she was working at a machine. The injury was admitted to be due to the defenders' fault to some extent. However, by so framing their minute, the defenders accepted the onus of establishing any contributory negligence on the part of the pursuer. The mere fact that the pursuer's account of the accident is difficult to understand does not mean that it must be inferred that it was due in any part to her own fault.

G

"The defenders were equally unable to establish any contributory negligence. Their difficulty arose principally because they had not intimated in terms of the rules applicable to optional procedure the names of any witnesses. Various preliminary matters occurred prior to the commencement of the proof but even then the defenders did not make any motion about witnesses. It was only after the pursuer's case had been closed that the defenders sought leave to call a witness or witnesses, some of whom had been on the pursuer's list, in order, doubtless, to attempt to establish facts upon which the inference of contributory negligence could be drawn. Counsel for the pursuer objected to any witnesses who had not been properly intimated being called. He stated that his solicitors had drawn the attention of the defenders' solicitors to the omission of a list but that no list had been provided. He referred me to a decision of Lord Osborne in *Alexander Donald McLeod v Kemp Todd Ltd* dated 29 October 1991 (1992 GWD 2-93) in which, in special circumstances, a medical witness who had not previously been intimated was allowed to be nominated as a witness prior to the commencement of the proof. Counsel for the pursuer accepted that medical witnesses may be different and, indeed, had agreed in the present case that the defenders could lead their medical witness, Dr Shenkin, although he had not appeared on a list of witnesses.

H

I

J

"I refused to allow the defenders to lead any witness other than the agreed Dr Shenkin in the absence of proper intimation in terms of the rules. The principal reason for this decision was that the motion to lead the witnesses came far too late, being made, as it was, after the pursuer's case had closed. Whether my attitude would have been different had leave been sought prior to the commencement of the proof, I cannot say, but in my view it is abundantly clear that to attempt to lead unintimated witnesses after the pursuer's case had closed, in the context of optional procedure, is not permissible. The situation was not altered by the fact that two of the witnesses the defenders sought to lead had been on the pursuer's own list. The optional procedure rules must be complied with if that system is to work efficiently. While no doubt there could be circumstances in which witnesses may be allowed to be led albeit that their names do not appear on lists, there was nothing exceptional in the present case to justify that course and certainly nothing to justify that course after the pursuer's own case had been closed, it having been presented on the basis that there were no witnesses who could be led by the defenders. The pursuer is entitled, in my view, to rely upon the rules being complied with and, accordingly, I did not permit the defenders to lead witnesses on a list presented to me after the closing of the pursuer's case."

K

L

In relation to damages the temporary judge
A continued:

"The quantification of damages for the pursuer in
this case has caused considerable difficulty. She was
described by Dr Shenkin as exaggerating her condition. I agree with that and find ample support for such
a view in the evidence of the pursuer and the other
witnesses. Essentially the account of the effects on the
pursuer of her accident depends upon her own evidence. She has given accounts, not only of the accident
and her condition at the time, but also of its alleged
B lasting effects, to various persons whose evidence is
before me. There was evidence from her husband of
her condition and state of mind and of her ability to
undertake household tasks but his evidence did not
demonstrate any serious condition suffered by her. In
particular he was unaware of any nightmares or obtru-
sive recollection of the accident. There was evidence
from Ann Brown and Jane Donnachie of what
happened to her at the accident which indicates a brief
C period of being trapped with no prolonged danger.
There were accounts given to Mr Graham, the
orthopaedic surgeon, in April 1991, and April 1992;
to Dr Shenkin in March 1992; to Mr Hussain in May
1992; to Professor Bond on 2 May 1992. Some of
these witnesses had available to them the GP notes
and although, unfortunately, the general practitioner
was not led as a witness, the general practitioner's
notes were spoken to and commented upon by the
pursuer and others. These notes also contain matters
D which must have appeared there as a result of accounts
given by the pursuer.

"It is notable that the pursuer's account of her
accident and alleged injuries becomes more dramatic
as time passes. So, for example, to Mr Graham on 23
March 1991 she said that she was trapped for 15
minutes; was freed by maintenance engineers; was
taken to the nurses' room where her arm was placed
in a sling and thence to Hairmyres hospital. The right
shoulder was x-rayed and in the absence of any frac-
E ture or dislocation, the arm was rested in a collar and
cuff sling and she was discharged home. After about
two months sensation returned to normal in her hand
and arm, although she never recovered full power in
the right hand. She also told Mr Graham at that time
that she was given analgesic tablets, and required
sleeping tablets to take at night in view of an acute
anxiety condition. To Dr Shenkin on 27 March 1992
she said she was screaming, was frightened and was
helped by colleagues who eventually stopped the
F machinery. She attended her own doctor and was
given sleeping pills and pills for pain. She said she discontinued the sleeping tablets in a short time but took
painkilling tablets until December 1990, ceasing when
she became pregnant. To Professor Bond on 2 May
1992 she said that towards the end of the 15 minutes
she fainted and remembered waking in the nurses'
room. She was told that the muscles and nerves had
been strained. Her GP gave her analgesics and sometime later, when she had difficulty in sleep, had
prescribed tablets, but she ceased to take those tablets.

"In the witness box on 2 June 1992 she said that she
was conscious for most of the time, was hysterical, G
screaming and, significantly, said "I thought I was
going to my death". She said that she had gone to her
general practitioner who had given her painkillers but
nothing to make her sleep or calm her down. Reference to her GP notes would indicate that she had told
her doctor that she had dislocated her right shoulder
and that an analgesic had been prescribed together
with 20 nitrazepam tablets. These were again
prescribed on 25 September 1990 and she then
obtained in November 1990 Inderal tablets. Through- H
out the GP records until he referred her to Mr
Hussain by way of an urgent appointment, it was
assumed that she had dislocated her right shoulder.
When asked about this in the witness box, because in
fact she had not dislocated her shoulder, she explained
the entry by saying that she had been told that by the
nurse at work and not at the hospital, and that she had
told the general practitioner that the nurses thought
she had dislocated her shoulder. There is an elaboration of the injury evident throughout that history of I
events from a straightforward description to Mr
Graham and Dr Shenkin, to fainting described to
Professor Bond and finally in the witness box an
alleged fear of death. I cannot believe that if that last
statement had been uttered to any of the practitioners
who had seen her prior to the proof that they would
not have noted it and in particular that Professor Bond
would not have noted it.

"Further, it is plain from a perusal of the evidence
from the orthopaedic consultants, Mr Graham and Mr J
Hussain, and indeed also from the examinations
carried out by the two psychiatrists, that if indeed
there is any disability in the pursuer's arm it is
minimal and is not such as would prevent her
working, and further that it was not such as would
have prevented her working in December 1990 and
thereafter. She did in fact return to work, against the
advice of her GP, according to her, but in accordance
with the advice given by the orthopaedic department
at Hairmyres hospital. She remained at work until K
August 1991. The stated reason she was signed off
work then by her doctor was pain in the right
shoulder. That was the reason she gave for not
working at the time and to an extent it still is. She
complains, it would seem from the evidence she gave,
of constant pain in her right shoulder all the time
without intermission. There is no physical basis for
such pain. The psychiatrists indicated that an anxiety
state would not cause pain of itself, although it might
prolong a perception of pain held previously. On the L
evidence I hold that there was no physical condition
present in the pursuer which would have prevented
her working at any employment after December 1990.

"Mr Graham in his report of 29 April 1992 might
seem to lend some credence to the possibility of persistent pain to a certain degree even on a permanent
basis. He said however that her condition was somewhat exaggerated by her emotional and psychological
state, although he could detect no impairment in the
sensation in the arm and was unable to assess the

degree of strength in the muscles of the arm since 'she
A did not sustain contraction of any of the muscles
around the elbow or shoulder and tended to give way
when any stress was placed upon them'. He could find
no major abnormality in the shoulder or elbow and no
evidence of any neurological impairment. He thought
she was depressed. When Mr Hussain's views were
put to him in the witness box he indicated that there
was no difference between him and Mr Hussain,
although Mr Hussain has the narration of intermittent
pain in the right arm whereas Mr Graham has the
B narration of pain all the time. I found consistency in
the medical views on the physical aspects of this
injury.

"Mr Graham suggested that there was a psychological component to the pursuer's complaints. In her
GP notes, which were misread by the consultants
examining, it is noted that she was 'very anxious' on
30 November 1990, but the reason given was marital
breakdown. On 21 January 1991 there is a note 'wants
to see psychologist re industrial accident'. She had
C consulted with a solicitor about her industrial accident
prior to that date. Mr Graham saw her in March 1991
and no doubt as a result of his observations the
defenders had the pursuer seen by Dr Shenkin in
March 1992. Dr Graham's evidence as to the pursuer's psychological state is not expert but instead is
proffered to provide an explanation for the pursuer's
complaining of persistent pain without any physical
reason for it. He thought in April 1992 that she was
depressed but neither of the psychologists would
D accept that she suffered from depression. All the
medical witnesses, apart from Dr Shenkin, seem to
have regarded her as giving her account of events
clearly and without exaggeration. I did not so find.
The accounts differed.

"In her evidence she described events after the
accident as being the suffering of constant pain,
anxiety, irritability, nightmares, disturbed sleep and
what she said in evidence were 'flashbacks'. It was
E interesting that she used such a term and she was
asked to explain what she meant. It emerged later that
this was a term mentioned to her by Professor Bond
and used by him in inverted commas in his report. It
is a condition commonly regarded as significant in a
diagnosis of post-traumatic stress disorder. However
what the pursuer described in the witness box was
'reliving the accident' rather than intrusive recollections of it. Counsel for the pursuer did not however in
pleading or submission suggest that the pursuer was
F suffering from post-traumatic stress disorder. This
condition was suggested by Professor Bond in his
report and was described by him as a bundle of
symptoms. That was not regarded as a useful term by
Dr Shenkin, who did not regard a collection of
symptoms arithmetically accumulated as a particularly
useful method of diagnosis. In my view counsel was
correct in his approach. The use of the term post-
traumatic stress disorder may be readily understood in
a disaster such as Piper Alpha or the *Herald of Free
Enterprise,* but the overwhelming nature of such dis-
asters is not here present. Only one person, the

pursuer, was involved. There was not an extended
period of danger; there was not any room for 'survivor G
guilt'. In short, the accident was not out of the run of
ordinary accidents.

"What was apparent not only from the narration of
the events which happened to the pursuer but also
from the evidence of Dr Shenkin and Professor Bond
was that the pursuer did have a very alarming
experience and that thereafter it was to be expected
that to some extent she would suffer from an anxiety
neurosis in the course of which sleep disturbance, distressing recollections of the event and feelings of H
generalised unease, would emerge and persist for some
time. The fact of being involved in a litigation over the
matter in which liability was not admitted until late,
also served to prolong the pursuer's symptoms. I did
not consider this as sinister. Although there could be
argued a case that the persistence of symptoms was
motivated by the prospect of gain, I am prepared to
accept Professor Bond's view that there was not a
deliberately false exaggeration. However, exaggeration
there undoubtedly was.   I

"I consider that the pursuer will have recovered to
an extent which would place her in the position of not
suffering from any psychological injury as desiderated
in *McLoughlin v O'Brian* [1983] AC 410 very shortly
after the conclusion of the proof. She will, however,
in my opinion, always have some fear of working with
certain kinds of machinery and that will limit her
employability in the future. She is pregnant and would
not be working at present. I am not satisfied that there J
has been established, by evidence which I can accept,
any sufficient reason for her ceasing the work she was
doing in August 1991. There was at that time no
physical reason why she should not work and she did
not give up work because of anxiety but because of
alleged pain in her arm.

"I find that the pursuer sustained an alarming but
minor physical injury, that she had recognisable
psychological disturbance as a result of it which
existed at an appreciable level until her return to work K
and to a lessening extent thereafter. It increased
shortly before the proof. Throughout, the account
given of the disturbance and its effects was substantially exaggerated. I consider that an award of
solatium of £4,000, taking into account her alarming
experience and actual injury physical and psychological, is adequate compensation. I consider that the
pursuer will have no significant attributable persisting
psychological disability, and no physical disability
after the date of decree. I therefore attribute the whole L
solatium to the past and award interest thereon at the
rate of 7½ per cent from the date of the accident.

"With regard to loss of earnings it was agreed that
the pursuer, between the date of her accident and her
return to work, had lost £978.80. Interest thereon falls
to be awarded at the rate of 7½ per cent from the date
of the accident until the date of her return to work
which was, according to the GP notes, 14 December
1990 and at the rate of 15 per cent thereafter to the
date of decree. Since I am unable to hold that the

A pursuer was unfit for work thereafter, although in fact she did not work, I make no award in respect of wage loss past or future from that date. On the other hand I recognise that the pursuer has and may well continue to have some difficulty in coping with certain types of machinery involving a particular type of production line. This difficulty is unrelated to her physical condition and it may well prejudice her ability to undertake some kind of employment in the future. I am uncertain whether this fear genuinely played any part in her cessation of work, because the reason given at

B the time was the unsustainable one of arm pain and she is not disturbed by all machinery — she sat and passed her driving test after the accident. I consider however that a 'jury award' of a lump sum of £4,000 reflects her disadvantage on the labour market from 1991 onwards. Accordingly, in the whole circumstances, I repel the defenders' fifth plea in law and grant decree to the pursuer for the sum of £9,847 as follows:

Solatium	£4,000.00
C	Interest to 18 August 1992 at 7½ per cent	600.00
Past loss	978.80
Interest at 7½ per cent from 16 August 1990 to 14 December 1990 at 7½ per cent	24.20
Interest thereafter at 15 per cent from 15 December 1990 to 18 August 1992	244.00
D	Loss of employability	4,000.00
	£9,847.00

Counsel for Pursuer, Bonomy; Solicitors, Robin Thompson & Partners — Counsel for Defenders, Stephenson; Solicitors, Gray Muirhead, WS.

C H

E

Mason v A & R Robertson & Black

OUTER HOUSE

LORD CAMERON OF LOCHBROOM

F 4 NOVEMBER 1992

Heritable property — Sale — Missives — Sellers raising action to enforce missives — Purchasers defending on basis that sellers in material breach and purchasers entitled to rescind — Purchasers counterclaiming for repayment of part payment of price — Decree of dismissal by default of sellers' action and for payment under counterclaim — Whether purchasers thereafter precluded from reconsidering decision to rescind and seeking implement.

Property — Heritable property — Sale — Sellers raising action to enforce missives — Purchasers defending on G *basis that sellers in material breach and purchasers entitled to rescind — Purchasers counterclaiming for repayment of part payment of price — Decree of dismissal by default of sellers' action and for payment under counterclaim — Whether purchasers thereafter precluded from reconsidering decision to rescind and seeking implement.*

Contract — Sale of heritage — Rescission — Sellers raising action to enforce missives — Purchasers defending on basis that sellers in material breach and purchasers H *entitled to rescind — Purchasers counterclaiming for repayment of part payment of price — Decree of dismissal by default of sellers' action and for payment under counterclaim — Whether purchasers thereafter precluded from reconsidering decision to rescind and seeking implement.*

Process — Decree — Decree by default — Pursuers' agents withdrawing from acting — Pursuers failing to obtemper court order that they intimate whether proceeding — Decree of dismissal of principal action and decree under I *counterclaim pronounced on failure to intimate — Whether decree in foro.*

A couple raised an action against their solicitors in respect of alleged professional negligence. In 1981 the pursuers had concluded missives for the purchase of a farm from a limited company. The defenders acted as the pursuers' solicitors during the transaction. The pursuers paid £118,500 of the total purchase price in November 1981 and took possession of the farm. The sellers' agents granted a letter of obligation undertak- J ing to deliver a valid disposition in return for the outstanding balance of the purchase price. In April 1982 the sellers' agents intimated that they were in a position to deliver a valid disposition, but the pursuers refused to settle the transaction as they claimed that the acreage of the farm had been misrepresented. The sellers raised an action against the pursuers for implement of the missives. The pursuers lodged defences, contending that the sellers were in material breach of contract and not entitled to enforce the missives. They K also averred that these breaches amounted to a repudiation of the contract which fell to be rescinded. They lodged a counterclaim seeking repayment of the £118,500 paid. The sellers did not accept the pursuers' rescission. As a result of the sellers' financial circumstances, their solicitors withdrew from acting and the pursuers obtained decree of dismissal in the principal action and decree by default in the counterclaim. The pursuers were unsuccessful in enforcing the decree and petitioned for the sellers' liquidation. The holders of a standard security over the farm L entered into possession and resold the farm.

The alleged negligence was the defenders' failure to advise the pursuers that any decree obtained would be likely to be worthless and also that by obtaining decree the letter of obligation granted by the sellers' agents would fall along with the missives. The defenders challenged the proposition that by taking decree by default in the counterclaim the missives would be rescinded and the letter of obligation rendered unenforceable.

Held, (1) that the letter of obligation was a contract
A collateral to the missives and fell to be read in the
context of the missives (p 778G-H); (2) that both the
decree of dismissal in the principal action and the
decree in the counterclaim were decrees by default and
therefore in foro (pp 778L-779A and 779D-E); (3) that
the decree of dismissal was not res judicata and the
decree in the counterclaim for repayment could be
reclaimed or reduced (p 779E-F and G-H); (4) that the
pursuers' actions in taking decree had not amounted
to an irrevocable election in that as a matter of law the
B missives were not automatically terminated by the
pronouncement of the decrees, and the pursuers' averments that the letter of obligation became ineffective
following the pronouncement of the decrees were
accordingly irrelevant (p 781E-H); and case *put out* by
order for further procedure.

Action of damages

Mr and Mrs Alfred James Mason raised an action of
C damages against their former solicitors, Messrs A & R
Robertson & Black. They sought damages in respect
of alleged negligent advice during a conveyancing
transaction and a subsequent court action. They
averred that the defenders had failed to advise them
that by obtaining decree in an earlier court action the
missives of sale would be rescinded and the letter of
obligation granted by the sellers' solicitors rendered
unenforceable.

D The case came before the Lord Ordinary (Lord
Cameron of Lochbroom) on procedure roll.

Statutory provisions

The Rules of Court 1965 provide:

"84.—(a) It shall be competent for a defender either
in his defences as lodged, or at adjustment, or, subject
to such conditions, if any, as to expenses or otherwise
as the court may think just, by way of amendment at
any later stage of the case at which amendment is com-
E petent, to counterclaim against the pursuer in respect
of any matter forming part of, or arising out of, the
grounds of, the pursuer's action, or the decision of
which is necessary for the determination of the question in controversy between the parties, or which, if
the pursuer had been a person not otherwise subject
to the jurisdiction of the court, might competently
have formed the subject of an action against such
pursuer in which jurisdiction would have arisen *ex
reconventione*; provided that, in any case, the counter-
F claim is such as might have formed matter of a
separate action, and that, if such separate action had
been raised, it would not have been necessary to call
as defender thereto any person other than the
pursuer. . . .

"89.—(a) If in any cause other than a cause in which
it is incompetent to decern without proof a defender
fails to enter appearance in terms of Rule 81, or if,
having duly entered appearance he fails to lodge
defences in terms of paragraph (a) of Rule 83, the
pursuer may enrol for decree in absence; and the cause

will then appear in the printed rolls, in the roll of
undefended causes, on the first available day thereafter G
whether in session or vacation."

Cases referred to

Dryburgh v A & A S Gordon (1896) 4 SLT 113; (1896)
24 R 1.
Forrest v Dunlop (1875) 3 R 15.
Gibson v Hunter Home Designs Ltd (in liquidation),
1976 SLT 94; 1976 SC 23.
Grant and Sillars v Marshall (1863) 1 M 1167.
Johnston v Little, 1960 SLT 129. H
Lawrence v Ritchie (1893) 1 SLT 44.
Panmure (Lord) v Crokat (1854) 17 D 85.
Marjoribanks v Borthwick (1857) 19 D 474.
Wade v Waldon, 1909 1 SLT 215; 1909 SC 571.
Westville Shipping Co v Abram Steamship Co Ltd, 1923
SLT 613; 1923 SC (HL) 68.

Textbooks referred to

Bell, *Principles* (10th ed), para 1938.
Gloag, *Contract* (2nd ed), pp 599-601. I
Greens Encyclopaedia of the Laws of Scotland, Vol 6,
paras 271, 275.
McBryde, *Contract,* p 324, paras 14-69 and 70.
McDonald, *Conveyancing Manual* (4th ed), para 35-49,
p 375.
Mackay, *Manual of Court of Session Practice,* p 310.
Maclaren, *Court of Session Practice,* pp 692, 696,
1094.
Maxwell, *Practice of the Court of Session,* pp 583, 617.
Walker, *Civil Remedies,* pp 174-175.
J

On 4 November 1992 the Lord Ordinary *held* that
the pursuers' averments anent the effect of a decree
upon the missives were irrelevant and *put out* the case
by order for parties to consider further procedure.

LORD CAMERON OF LOCHBROOM.—Proof
before answer in this action was set down for 13
October 1992. On the morning of the proof the
defenders sought to amend their pleadings. This was
initially opposed. After an adjournment, parties K
moved me to allow the closed record to be amended in
terms of the defenders' minute of amendment and the
pursuers' answers, to discharge the diet of proof and
to send the case to the procedure roll in respect of the
defenders' second plea in law. The debate was, of
consent, to be restricted to the issue of the pursuers'
averments relative to the legal effect of the decrees
pronounced in the pursuers' favour on 1 March 1984
in an action raised against the pursuers by Lindsay
Farms Ltd for implement of missives entered into L
between the pursuers and that company and also in a
counterclaim at the pursuers' instance in that action
for repayment of sums paid to that company towards
the purchase price of the subjects of the missives. The
debate was also of consent extended to the pursuers'
fourth plea in law directed to certain averments added
by way of amendment in the defenders' minute of
amendment.

Parties have produced a statement of agreed facts. I
am indebted to them for having done so. From this

statement and from facts admitted in the pleadings I
take the following matters as common ground between
the parties for the purpose of the decision which I am
asked to reach. In 1981 Lindsay Farms Ltd, whom I
refer to hereafter as "the sellers", owned the subjects
known as Carmacoup Farm, Douglas. By letters dated
26 August 1981, 28 August 1981, 28 September 1981,
29 September 1981, and 8 and 9 October 1981 passing
between the parties' solicitors, a concluded agreement
for the purchase by the pursuers of the farm subjects
was effected. The price was agreed at £190,000. Of
that sum 10 per cent was payable within the seven
days from the date of the formal letter concluding the
bargain. It was further provided that the balance of the
purchase price would be paid in full on the date of
entry. This was stated to be 31 October 1981 or such
earlier date as might be mutually agreed. It was
further provided that "at settlement, in exchange for
the purchase price, there would be given a validly
executed disposition of the subjects to the pursuers or
their nominees and there would be delivered or
exhibited a good marketable title including clear
searches in the property and personal registers covering the respective prescriptive periods".

A payment of £19,000 was made by the pursuers to
the sellers on 16 October 1981. On 30 October 1981
the pursuers' solicitors sent a further payment of
£99,500 to account of the balance of the purchase
price under cover of a letter in which it was stated:

"Please hold our payments to account as undelivered pending clear interim reports on the searches,
vacant possession of the subjects of sale being granted
to our clients and in exchange please let us have your
own obligation to deliver on payment in full of the
purchase price, a duly executed disposition in terms of
the draft to be adjusted between us and otherwise to
implement the provisions of the missives which
remain unimplemented."

On or about 3 November 1981 that payment was
received by the sellers' solicitors. On that date they
wrote to the pursuers' agents acknowledging receipt of
the sum of £99,500. The letter enclosed a letter of
obligation addressed to the pursuers' solicitors in the
following terms:

"We acknowledge to have received from you the
sum of One Hundred and Eighteen Thousand and
Five Hundred Pounds (£118,500) to account of the
price of the above subjects, the balance of the price to
lie at interest until paid in terms of the missives.

"We therefore undertake to deliver to you on
payment in full of the purchase price a duly executed
disposition in terms of the draft to be adjusted
between us and otherwise to implement the provisions
of the missives which remain unimplemented."

On or about 3 November 1981 the sellers entered
into occupation of the farm subjects. By letter dated 2
April 1982 the sellers' solicitors advised the defenders
who were the pursuers' solicitors, that they were ready
to settle the transaction. At that date they held a disposition of the subjects executed by the sellers. There-

after the sellers and the pursuers were in dispute about
the extent of the subjects and in particular the total
acreage. In about December 1982 the sellers raised an
action against the pursuers concluding first for implement of the pursuers' obligations under the missives
by making payment of the sum of £71,500 with
interest in exchange for a valid disposition, alternatively, failing implement for a sum of £50,000 in name
of damages. The pursuers lodged defences to the
action. In their defences they contended that the
sellers were in breach of the contract constituted by
the missives or were unable to perform the contract in
a considerable number of respects and were not
entitled to enforce the contract. They further averred
that these respects were each and all matters of materiality which constituted a repudiation of the contract
which fell to be rescinded. As appears from the closed
record in that action, these contentions were denied by
the sellers. The pursuers further lodged a counterclaim concluding for payment of £118,500 with
interest upon averment that the contract for the purchase of the subjects fell to be rescinded. The plea in
law stated that the consideration for which the sum
was paid had failed and the pursuers were entitled to
repayment of it. No answers were lodged by the sellers
to the counterclaim.

The record was closed on 21 September 1983. On
about 9 February 1984 the sellers' legal advisers withdrew from acting. The parties to the present action are
agreed in the belief that the sellers' solicitors withdrew
from acting because the sellers were in financial
difficulties and were not able to make provision for
their agreed fees. On 10 February 1984 an interlocutor
was pronounced upon a motion of the pursuers,
appointing the sellers to intimate to the deputy principal clerk within 14 days after intimation of the interlocutor upon them "whether they intend to insist
upon their action under certificate that if they failed
to do so, the action may be dismissed and a decree in
terms of the counterclaim may be granted against
them". The interlocutor was thereafter intimated to
the sellers. No intimation was received by the deputy
principal clerk within the period stated. Thereafter on
1 March the pursuers moved the court "in respect of
the pursuers' failure to obtemper the terms of the
interlocutor pronounced by Lord Kincraig on 10
February 1984 to dismiss the principal action and to
find the pursuers liable to the defenders in the
expenses thereof and to grant decree in terms of the
conclusion of the counterclaim for the defenders". On
that date decree for dismissal of the principal action
was pronounced in the terms set out in no 23/4 of
process. Decree of payment in the sum of £118,500
was pronounced in the terms set out in no 29/1 of
process. The decree for payment was thereafter
extracted. Letters of inhibition in execution of that
decree were obtained. The letters were personally
served on the sellers on about 14 and 20 March 1984.
Arrestment in execution of the decree was effected
between about 21 and 26 March 1984 in the hands of
the sellers' solicitors. As appears from the letter of 12
April 1984, no 26/271 of process, a sum of £579.43

A was then attached. After 3 November 1981 the pursuers continued in occupation of the farm subjects and were in occupation of them on 1 March 1984. Thereafter in 1984 the sellers went into liquidation upon the petition of the pursuers. The farm subjects were sold by the Clydesdale Bank, the holders of a standard security over the farm subjects, who prior to 6 February 1984 had served a calling up notice in respect of their loan secured over the farm subjects.

B In the present action the pursuers seek damages against their solicitors for professional negligence. The averments of the pursuers which give rise to the debate are to the following effect. First, it is averred in cond 6 that in relation to the decrees pronounced on 1 March 1984, the decree for payment was worthless and furthermore the effect of obtaining that decree on the basis that the missives had been rescinded was to render the letter of obligation worthless. It is also averred that the defenders had given no advice or warning to the pursuers that by taking decree by default in the action, the pursuers would forfeit the protection offered to them by the letter of obligation.

C In cond 7 the pursuers aver inter alia that they were not advised that by defending the action of implement and by taking decree in their counterclaim they would forfeit the protection afforded to them by the letter of obligation and would risk losing the sum of £118,500 already paid to the sellers. The foregoing averments form the basis for certain of the averments of fault in cond 8. In particular it is there averred that the

D defenders knew or ought to have known that if the pursuers took decree in the counterclaim, they would forfeit the protection of the letter of obligation. In addition they form the basis of the averment of duty to warn the pursuers that by moving for decree in the counterclaim in the action raised by the sellers, the pursuers would "thereby rescind the missives and lose the only protection they had (viz said letter of obligation) in respect of said deposits totalling £118,500".

E The parties are at one that it is a question of law whether by the taking of the decree for payment in the counterclaim, the pursuers brought the bargain for the sale of the subjects in the missives to an end and so caused the obligation undertaken by the sellers' solicitors in the letter of obligation to fly off, with the result that thereafter the pursuers forfeited any right to tender payment of the balance of the purchase price and demand delivery of the executed disposition from the sellers' agents.

F Counsel for the defenders submitted in the first place that notwithstanding the pronouncing of the decrees of dismissal and of payment, the missives were not thereby rescinded nor did the decrees have that effect. Consequently the obligation of the sellers' solicitors under the letter of obligation was enforceable thereafter at the pursuers' instance. Counsel further submitted that the decree of dismissal pronounced on 1 March 1984 had no effect upon the merits of the action and that these lay open for determination in the event that the sellers chose thereafter to raise a fresh action seeking implement of the missives. Counsel

G accepted that at the same time it would be necessary to reduce the decree for payment. So far as the decree for payment was concerned, that had, on the pursuers' pleadings, proved worthless notwithstanding that the decree had been extracted and diligence done upon it by way of arrestment and inhibition. No money had been recovered under it. The decree fell to be regarded as a "technicality by the wayside", as counsel put it, while the pursuers attempted to resolve the situation in which they had been placed. The decree having proved worthless, the letter of obligation was still in

H effect and could be applied to by the pursuers. This was because the letter of obligation should be regarded as independent of the missives. It was an obligation which was constituted in a letter between the opposing solicitors for the sellers and purchasers. They were different contracting parties from those in the missives. Reference was made to McDonald's *Conveyancing Manual*, para 35-49 for the purpose of and the extent of the obligation undertaken in a letter of obligation. Counsel also referred to *Johnston v Little* in reference to the nature of the obligation as one

I between solicitors. He also referred to *Gibson v Hunter Home Designs Ltd* as an example of circumstances in which a letter of obligation can be founded upon. Counsel also made reference to *Dryburgh v A & A S Gordon*, but that case did not seem to me to add anything to the foregoing authorities.

The subsidiary argument for the defenders was that on the pleadings it was doubtful if the facts averred by the pursuers were such as to support the proposition

J that they had irrevocably elected to rescind the missives so that they were unable to found upon a continuing obligation in the letter of obligation which was granted not by the sellers but by the sellers' solicitors. It could not be said that on the facts the pursuers had already made their election by the approach adopted by them in their counterclaim. Under reference to *Lord Panmure v Crokat* and in particular to the opinion of Lord President McNeill at p 92, counsel submitted that the present case was not a case in which

K it could be said that in seeking repayment in the counterclaim on the basis of resiling from the missives and thereafter, upon withdrawal of the sellers' solicitors, taking decree in the counterclaim, in the absence of the other party, and doing ineffectual diligence thereon, the pursuers had made an election such as to put it out of their power to abandon that choice and be unable to go back upon the matter to make a different choice and procure a remedy under the letter of obligation. Counsel pointed to the passage in which

L Lord President McNeill had stated that it was a matter of circumstances whether or not the party seeking to take a benefit under one deed was necessarily precluded from abandoning that right and taking himself to an adverse right. In the present case, counsel argued, the right which the pursuers sought to obtain in the counterclaim was a right arising from the missives and arose from their choice to pursue a remedy based on their right to resile from the missives. They had achieved nothing thereby, having taken decree. They were not precluded from abandon-

ing that right to resile, and insisting upon their right
A under the letter of obligation to secure delivery of the
executed disposition upon payment of the balance of
the price, the sellers having already received benefit of
the remainder of the price. Counsel submitted that an
analogous case was to be found in *Lawrence v Ritchie*.
In that case missives had been completed for the sale
of a house. The purchaser had objected to the title
offered to him by the seller. While negotiations were
proceeding between the parties, the seller, after intimation to the purchaser, exposed the subjects for sale
B by public roup. No offers were received. As the purchaser continued to refuse to complete the bargain, the
seller brought an action for implement of the missives.
It was argued for the seller that the purchaser by his
actings had implemented the sale and could not resile.
An argument for the purchaser that the seller was personally barred from insisting in the action having
exposed the subjects for sale by public roup was
rejected and decree was given in terms of the conclusion for implement of the missives.

C   Counsel also referred to *Westville Shipping Co v
Abram Steamship Co* and in particular to the speeches
of Lord Dunedin and of Lord Atkinson for the proposition that, just as with affirmation, so repudiation of
a contract will not be lightly inferred and that clear
and unequivocal acts are required before the court will
so hold. In the present case, said counsel, the mere fact
of taking decree in the absence of the sellers did not
affect the underlying contractual position in relation
to the missives and the letter of obligation. The pur-
D suers could still have insisted upon implementing the
missives. If the sellers or sellers' agents did not thereafter deliver a duly executed disposition, the pursuers
would be entitled to sue the sellers' agents on the letter
of obligation. At worst for the defenders, there was an
issue as to whether or not there had been such clear
and unequivocal expression of repudiation in the
circumstances of the present case, looking to the
actings of the parties, to the missives and to the letter
of obligation both before and after the taking of
E decree, and accordingly proof before answer on the
whole matter should be allowed.

    Counsel for the pursuers, on the other hand, sub-
mitted that the decrees having been pronounced, the
pursuers could not thereafter recover the money paid
to the sellers by means of founding upon the letter of
obligation. That obligation only became enforceable
in the event of the missives being implemented by the
pursuers and did not protect the pursuers against the
F event of their requiring to recover any moneys paid in
the event of material breach entitling the pursuers to
rescind the missives. The critical event was the taking
of decree on the counterclaim and decree of dismissal
in the principal action. The sellers by withdrawing
from the action in the face of the interlocutor of 10
February 1984, had accepted that rescission of the
contract was the consequence of their actings. Thereafter the pursuers were put upon their election. Their
election became irrevocable when decree was taken by
the pursuers. By their withdrawal the sellers had
repudiated the missives by stating in effect that they

did not wish to perform their obligations under the
contract. At that point the pursuers, being the inno- G
cent party, had the choice of rescinding or implementing the contract. The test lay in considering the
pursuers' position after decree had been pronounced.
It was accepted for the defenders that they would have
to reduce the decree for payment. This was because it
was a decree by default which was a decree in foro.
Reponing was not competent in terms of Rule of
Court 89 (f) which applied only to decree in absence.
Reference was also made to Maxwell, *Practice of the
Court of Session*, p 583. There were only limited H
grounds upon which an action of reduction of a decree
pronounced on the merits would be permitted, in any
event. Reference was made to Maclaren, *Court of
Session Practice*, pp 692 and 696. It would be difficult
to imagine grounds of res noviter upon which, for
instance, the pursuers could found to obtain decree of
reduction. Counsel also made reference to McBryde
on *Contract*, p 324 where the author says this:

"On a material breach the 'innocent party' has an
option. . . . The specialty arising from a material I
breach is that the innocent party may decide to end all
future performance of the contract. He may or may
not intimate this decision to the party in breach. If he
does intimate his decision there is 'rescission' of the
contract. But rescission is not always essential."

    In the present case the pronouncing of decrees was
the clearest possible intimation of rescission of the
missives on the part of the pursuers. The decree of
payment took effect from November 1981 in respect J
that interest on the principal sum was awarded from
3 November 1981. As a consequence, the pursuers
were no longer bound to tender performance of any
obligation on their part under the missives. Thereupon the obligation under the letter of obligation fell.
Counsel made reference to *Gibson v Hunter Home
Designs Ltd*. He argued that in that case the missives
had effectively been repudiated upon liquidation of
the defenders, but that the missives only fell if the
repudiation had been accepted by the pursuer. He K
pointed out that both Lord President Emslie and Lord
Cameron referred to that existence of the letter of
obligation, and the possibility of a claim arising from
it. Unlike the present case, nothing more remained to
be done by the purchaser under the missives so that
the obligation under the letter of obligation remained
in existence as against the sellers' solicitors notwithstanding that the court held that the subjects of sale
remained the property of the company and the
company was not, upon commencement of the L
winding up, bound to deliver the disposition which
had already been executed by the company. Repudiation was defined by counsel as material breach or intimation of an intention not to perform the contract.
Intimation of intention not to perform could be
expressly stated or could be implicit from the fact of
the breach itself. But the committing of a manifest
breach of contract did not bring the contract to an end
where there was no judicial determination of the issue.
The sellers' failure to insist in their action in the face
of an interlocutor warning them of the consequences

A of not doing so was in effect to acquiesce in an intimation upon the pursuers on the sellers' part of an intention not to perform their obligations under the missives. At that moment the pursuers were given a choice since the sellers must be held no longer to be challenging the assertion that the sellers had been in material breach of contract. The pursuers thus could treat such intimation as a material breach of contract on the one hand and rescind or could proceed to implement the contract on their part and call upon the sellers to perform their part of the bargain. By taking

B decree the pursuers had effectively terminated the contract in the missives and were no longer in a position to perform their obligation under the missives. Since the missives were terminated by decree pronounced in the counterclaim whereby the sellers were judicially determined to have been in material breach of contract, and since the sellers were no longer in a position to call for performance of the pursuers' obligations, it followed that the sellers' agents, who were underwriting performance of the sellers' obligations under

C the missives, were therefore no longer bound by the letter of obligation. Neither the case of *Lawrence v Ritchie* nor *Lord Panmure v Crokat* was in point. In the present case the pursuers' election was made within the four walls of the missives. The choices were either to obtain decree for payment which was likely to be worthless or to tender the balance of the purchase price and to obtain in exchange a title and thereby reselling the subjects, if necessary, to recover the loss of £118,000. Thus a valuable right was lost

D when decree by default was taken.

Counsel contended that the concept of election or of approbate and reprobate required that a point be reached when the pursuers had a choice to make as to their attitude to the missives to which the notion of approbate and reprobate could be applied. Reference was made to Gloag on *Contract*, pp 599-600, *Green's Encyclopaedia*, Vol 6, paras 271 and 275 and Bell's *Principles*, para 1938. Election required to be the spontaneous, deliberate act of the elector in knowledge of

E his rights. So withdrawal from one position adopted was permissible within a reasonable time if the elector did not know the alternatives between which he was to choose. The pursuers' case was based upon the failure of the defenders to present the alternatives and the legal consequences of them to enable an informed choice to be made while the alternative courses remained available.

In relation to the second submission for the

F defenders, counsel submitted that it must be accepted that since each decree was a decree by default and so a decree in foro, it would be difficult for the sellers to have extracted themselves from the position of having the two decrees against them. Personal bar arguments might then come into play. Reference was made to Walker, *Civil Remedies*, pp 174-175. In the whole circumstances the defenders' challenge to relevancy was without foundation and a proof before answer in all respects should be allowed except in relation to the averments added by amendment. These related to actings of the pursuers after decree had been

G pronounced. These actings could be of no effect standing the finality of the decrees pronounced on 1 March 1984.

I have reached the view that the pursuers' submissions on the matter of law at issue between the parties are misconceived and ill founded. The missives represented a concluded contract between the pursuers and the sellers. I agree with pursuers' counsel that the letter of obligation falls to be read in the context of the missives. It was a contract collateral to and dependent upon the obligations undertaken by the sellers in the missives. It was a unilateral undertaking

H given by the sellers' solicitors whereby they undertook a personal obligation on a certain event to deliver a duly executed disposition in terms of the draft to be adjusted between agents to the pursuers' solicitors. That personal obligation, while standing independent of the obligation on the sellers' part under the missives, became enforceable only upon payment by the defenders as the pursuers' solicitors, or their clients, the pursuers, of the full purchase price or of any balance remaining thereunder. That was the position

I in *Gibson v Hunter Homes Designs Ltd*. In terms of the missives the sellers were entitled, once they considered that they had fulfilled all the obligations undertaken by them in terms of the missives and having duly executed a disposition in terms of the missives, to demand fulfilment by the pursuers of their obligation to tender payment of the balance of the purchase price in exchange for delivery of such duly executed disposition. In April 1982 the sellers considered that they

J were in a position to implement all the obligations lying upon them in terms of the missives and were ready to deliver a duly executed disposition. The pursuers refused to perform their part of the bargain giving reasons therefor. It is plain that the sellers did not accept that those reasons justified the pursuers in withholding performance of their part of the bargain since they then raised the action for implement. This action proceeded upon the basis that the sellers had performed their part of the bargain and were willing to deliver a duly executed disposition for the subjects

K of sale in exchange for the balance of the purchase price. As the pleadings show, they were met by a defence from the pursuers that the missives were no longer binding upon the pursuers by reason of material breach of contract on the sellers' part. Thus the de quo of the action to which the counterclaim was conjoined and upon which the parties had joined issue, was whether or not the missives were binding upon the pursuers. The parties were still maintaining their separate positions in terms of the pleadings at the

L point when the sellers' solicitors withdrew from acting in the action. In the present action the pursuers do not aver that the sellers would have delivered the duly executed disposition if the balance of the purchase price had been tendered to them after 1 March 1984.

I agree with the submissions of counsel for the pursuers that the decrees pronounced on 1 March 1984 were each decrees by default and thus decrees in foro. I did not understand counsel for the defenders to dispute that the decree of dismissal in the principal action fell to be regarded as a decree in foro. It was a decree pronounced after the parties had joined issue in that action. It was pronounced against the sellers as pursuers in the action in respect of their failure to obey an order of the court under certification. It thus fell within the description of a decree by default in Maclaren, *Court of Session Practice*, p 1094. Passages to a similar effect are to be found in Mackay's *Manual of Court of Session Practice*, p 310 and Maxwell, *The Practice of the Court of Session*, p 617. It was, however, argued for the defenders under reference to the provisions of Rule of Court 84 that the counterclaim fell to be regarded as a separate action. The Rule of Court provides that notwithstanding abandonment by a pursuer, the defender in an action may insist in his counterclaim and the proceedings therein shall continue as if the counterclaim were a separate action. Accordingly, argued counsel, when the decree of dismissal was pronounced in the principal action, the counterclaim stood alone without answers, though the sellers as pursuers in the action could have lodged answers to the counterclaim in terms of Rule of Court 84 (k). Accordingly the counterclaim was a separate action in which a decree had been "pronounced against a defender who had . . . after appearance, failed to lodge defences within the statutory time". Counsel made reference to Mackay's *Manual of Court of Session Practice*, p 310 and the cases cited there, namely *Marjoribanks v Borthwick* and *Grant and Sillars v Marshall*. In my opinion, this ingenious argument is misconceived. It takes no account of the provisions of Rule of Court 89. It is plain from that Rule of Court that its provisions are not intended to apply to a counterclaim for the simple reason that a counterclaim cannot exist unless and until there is a principal action in which the defender has lodged defences as provided for by Rule of Court 84 (a). The fact that no answers to the counterclaim were lodged by the sellers is not, in my opinion, decisive. The counterclaim was directly related to the grounds of the sellers' action. It was an extension of that action so that the sellers' case in the principal action was an apt answer to the counterclaim. If the sellers succeeded in that action, the counterclaim was bound to fail. Thus like the decree of dismissal in the principal action pronounced in absence of the sellers as pursuers, the decree of payment was also a decree by default. As such it could only be recalled by the party against whom it was pronounced by way of reclaiming before extract or by reduction. I refer to Maclaren, *Court of Session Practice*, p 1094; Maxwell, *Practice of the Court of Session*, p 617 and Rule of Court 264 (e). On the other hand the decree became enforceable by way of diligence only after it had been extracted.

Counsel for the pursuers also contended that the two decrees having been pronounced by default were res judicata. He supported this by reference to the passages in Maclaren, *Court of Session Practice*, Mackay's *Manual of Court of Session Practice* and Maxwell, *Practice of the Court of Session* to which I have earlier referred. In Maclaren it is stated that a decree by default "is a decree in foro and is res judicata so long as it subsists". This passage is supported by reference to the case of *Forrest v Dunlop*. In that case decree of absolvitor had been pronounced. The rubric correctly states the matter to the effect that a decree of absolvitor is a decree in foro and, so long as it subsists, will exclude a new action upon the same grounds. Such is the effect of a decree of absolvitor pronounced in foro. In the present case, however, the court, upon the pursuers' motion, granted decree of dismissal. That is the form of decree used when it is intended to decide that the particular action should not be allowed to proceed against the defender but which is intended to leave it open to the pursuer to bring another action on the same grounds. At the same time the court, again upon the pursuers' motion, granted decree of payment against the sellers. But that decree was susceptible to recall as I note above and only became enforceable after it had been extracted, so that diligence could be done upon it.

Against that background, I turn to consider the parties' submissions as to the effects upon the missives of the pronouncement of the two decrees on 1 March 1984. At the heart of them is the question whether the missives came to an end and ceased to be enforceable by either party against the other upon the two decrees being pronounced, with the result that the obligation in the letter of obligation could not thereafter be founded upon by the pursuers. Put in another way, the question is whether the pursuers by taking decree put it out of their power thereafter to tender payment of the balance of the purchase price and to demand delivery of the duly executed disposition. It is thus apparent that the pursuers' case must depend upon the proposition that at least up until 1 March 1984 when the decrees were pronounced, the sellers were still bound to implement their part of the bargain if called upon to do so by the pursuers or alternatively, that the sellers had no ground upon which to resist such a demand on the pursuers' part.

There is no doubt, in my opinion, that the obligation under the letter of obligation was co-extensive with the sellers' obligation under the missives to deliver a duly executed disposition. If the sellers would not or could not implement their obligation, the sellers' agents then became personally liable under their obligation to the defenders as the pursuers' solicitors. They were thus in effect undertaking to indemnify the pursuers against loss in the event that the contract could not be implemented by the sellers. I refer to McDonald's *Conveyancing Manual*, p 375. The sellers' agents, however, undertook no obligation to indemnify against the sellers otherwise being in material breach of contract in the respects upon which the pursuers founded in their defence to the sellers' action. Thus before either the sellers' obligation to deliver a duly executed disposition or the correlative obligation upon the sellers' solicitors to do so, arose, it was necessary for the pursuers to tender payment of the balance of the purchase price and so either expressly or by inference depart from any assertion of a right to rescind the bargain and to recover the balance paid over to the sellers' solicitors prior to 3

November 1981. As the pleadings in the sellers' action stood prior to decree, the sellers were maintaining that they were willing to perform their obligation to deliver a duly executed disposition in exchange for the balance of the purchase price. The pursuers on the other hand had from the time when defences were lodged, refused to perform their part of the bargain in the missives. They further took the position that they were holding the bargain as rescinded on the ground of material breach of contract on the sellers' part. The fact of breach and the materiality of any breach were denied by the sellers. The position thus was that the pursuers had intimated a decision on their part that there was rescission of the contract, but this intimation was not accepted by the sellers. So far as the sellers were concerned the bargain contained in the missives for sale of the subjects was still open for completion by both parties. It would have been open to the sellers at that stage to have taken such intimation as repudiation of the missives by the pursuers and brought the bargain to an end. No doubt if they had done so, the issue of whether there had or had not been a material breach of contract would have remained to be decided. But the pursuers would have required to relinquish occupation of the subjects and the sellers to return any part of the purchase price, subject to any claim for damages on the part of either party. On the other hand, as is stated in Gloag on *Contract*, p 600: "If . . . a refusal to perform is not accepted as equivalent to a rescission of the contract, the party who made it is entitled to reconsider it, and to tender performance at the appointed time." Equally, while the sellers were still maintaining that the bargain fell to be implemented and that they were ready on their part to do so, the pursuers could at any stage reconsider their position and tender performance of their part of the bargain, namely payment of the balance of the purchase price, and call upon the sellers to deliver a duly executed disposition. In the pursuers' pleadings there is no suggestion that at the time when the pursuers were advised that the sellers' solicitors were no longer acting for the sellers in the action of implement, the sellers' position had changed and that they then accepted the pursuers' refusal to perform their part of the bargain as equivalent to rescission. The intimation to the sellers of the pursuers' motion calling upon the sellers to state whether they were intending to insist in the action under certification was no more than a continued assertion of the pursuers' refusal to perform their part of the bargain for the reasons stated in their defences and in the counterclaim. Thus so far as the sellers were concerned, the pursuers were maintaining their repudiation of the missives.

It is at this point that, in my opinion, the fallacy in the pursuers' submissions appears. It was said that the sellers' failure to make intimation as to whether they were to insist in the action of implement amounted either to an intimation that they did not intend further to implement the contract so that the pursuers were entitled to take that as repudiation of the contract by the sellers; alternatively the failure to respond to the order of court amounted to acquiescence in the pursuers' assertion that the sellers had been in material breach of contract. In either event, it was submitted, the pursuers had on the one hand a right to rescind the contract or on the other a right to tender payment of the balance of the purchase price and call upon the sellers to deliver the duly executed disposition. That being so, so far as the pursuers were concerned, the bargain in the missives remained available for completion by the parties by payment of the balance of the purchase price by the pursuers with the corresponding obligation upon the sellers then arising to deliver a duly executed disposition. The moving of the motions for decree of dismissal and for payment were unilateral acts of the pursuers. I do not consider that the case of *Gibson v Hunter Homes Designs Ltd* is pertinent to the questions I am asked to answer. There the commencement of the winding up was, in terms of the relevant Companies Act provisions, equivalent to a decree of adjudication of the heritable estate of that company for payment of the whole debts to the company accumulated at that date. For that reason and since the title to the subjects sold remained with the company and thus the subjects remained company property, the company was not bound to deliver the disposition under the personal obligation undertaken by the company in terms of the missives. It was said at one stage by counsel for the pursuers that the taking of the decrees was the clearest possible intimation of rescission of the missives by the pursuers. At another stage, he submitted that in circumstances where there was open to the pursuers the choice of rescinding the missives and taking decree in the counterclaim or effecting performance, the choice once made and communicated was irrevocable and that communication took place when the letters of inhibition were served upon the sellers. But the pursuers were not obliged after the decrees were pronounced in their favour, to extract the decree for payment. As counsel for the pursuers accepted in argument, communication of the choice took place only after the letters of inhibition were served upon the sellers. Neither decree barred the sellers from raising a further action for implement under the missives, though counsel for the defenders accepted that at the same time the decree for payment would have had to be reduced. So far as the sellers were concerned, as counsel for the defenders pointed out, even if their insolvency had occurred at that stage it would not have been equivalent to a refusal to perform their obligation to deliver a duly executed disposition and could not give the pursuers a right to rescind. I refer to Gloag on *Contract*, p 601.

The false premise in the pursuers' submissions is demonstrated by reference to two of the authorities to which reference was made. Thus it is pointed out in Gloag on *Contract*, p 599: "The party who receives intimation that the contract will not be performed is not bound to accept it as final. He may, if he pleases, refuse to rescind the contract, and, when the date of performance arrives, sue for damages calculated on the loss inflicted as at that date." Again in McBryde, p 324, para 14-69, it is stated that "on a material breach the 'innocent party' has an option. He may or may not continue with his performance of the contract". After a reference to the case of *Wade v Waldon*, the author observes (para 14-70) that if the theatre manager had not sent notice of rescission and if Robey had turned up for the first performance, "the decisions on first whether the breach was material, and secondly whether it should be waived or whether further performance should be refused, would still have had to have been taken". The pursuers defended the sellers' action upon the basis that there had been a material breach of contract. But the sellers were maintaining the contract still fell to be performed. Their conclusion for damages was predicated upon a decree ordaining the pursuers to fulfil their part of the bargain having been pronounced but not thereafter implemented. So far as the sellers were concerned the bargain remained to be completed by performance by both parties with the sellers willing still to perform their part. In the present case, however, the pursuers' case proceeds upon the view that notwithstanding the sellers' failure to respond to the court order pronounced on 10 February 1984 and in the face of the sellers' repudiation of the missives, alternatively their acquiescence in the pursuers' assertion of material breach, the missives still fell to be implemented. This means that the pursuers accept that whatever positions the parties had adopted prior to 1 March 1984, each was still entitled to reconsider the position adopted by them and to tender performance or demand performance of the outstanding obligations. This must proceed upon the basis that the time appointed for performance had not yet finally arrived. It may be doubtful that this was the case: the basis of the sellers' action was that the time for performance, and hence completion of the contract, by the pursuers of their obligation had already arisen prior to the raising of the action. Be that as it may, assuming as I must for the purposes of this debate, that the missives remained open for completion after the days had passed for the sellers to obtemper the court order pronounced on 10 February 1984, and in particular that the sellers remained bound by them, the pursuers' action in moving for decree of dismissal in the principal action did not serve to alter the sellers' position. The decree did not constitute a decision on the merits. It was not a decree of absolvitor which would have made the ground of action in the principal action res judicata. The sellers were not thereby cut off from raising a new action on the same grounds. By the same token the decree for payment was ineffective against the sellers at least until it was extracted. In the meantime the sellers could have reclaimed. The pursuers were not bound to extract it. Even thereafter it would have been open to the sellers to reduce it. Accordingly if the sellers had chosen to call upon the pursuers even after the decrees pronounced to perform their obligation to tender payment, the pursuers were not barred by their actings from doing so if they chose. Equally if the pursuers after the decrees had been pronounced, had chosen to tender payment of the balance of the price, the sellers were not barred by the decrees from delivering the duly executed disposition or from giving instructions to their solicitors to do so. That is to say, the decrees only had such legal effect as the pursuers and the sellers chose to give them. The pronouncement of the decrees did not appoint the date for the bargain to be completed as the date of the decrees, namely 1 March 1984. In my opinion the missives were not automatically terminated as a matter of law by the pronouncement of the decrees. They could have been implemented if parties so chose even after the decrees were pronounced. If they had been so, it would not have been some new contract as counsel for the pursuers suggested. Accordingly, the decrees did not have the absolute legal effect which was contended for by the pursuers. Insofar as the pursuers' case is founded upon averments setting out such an absolute legal effect, it is irrelevant.

If I were wrong on this point, parties were agreed that the case should go to proof before answer on the pleadings as they stand with the exception of an argument directed to certain of the averments of actings of parties after 1 March 1984 added by way of minute of amendment. In my opinion these averments may well be relevant to the issue of parties' intentions in relation to the question of whether the missives remained to be implemented and could be implemented by the parties at the dates averred. I would not therefore have sustained at this stage the pursuers' limited plea to the relevancy of the added averments, but left it standing. Otherwise I express no opinion of the arguments addressed to me by counsel since parties' pleas to relevancy will remain standing.

I shall, however, put the case out by order in order that parties may consider their positions in the light of this opinion.

Counsel for Pursuers, Thomson, QC, Abercrombie; Solicitors, Alex Morison & Co, WS — Counsel for Defenders, Galbraith, QC, D I Mackay; Solicitors, Shepherd & Wedderburn, WS.

A R W Y

[When the case came out by order, decree of dismissal was pronounced.]

(NOTE)

Rotary Services Ltd v Honeywell Control Systems Ltd

OUTER HOUSE

LORD MORTON OF SHUNA

26 NOVEMBER 1992

Contract — Breach of contract — Damages — Overheads — Onus of proof that contractor's mark up on subcontract price productive of profit.

Damages — Breach of contract — Overheads — Onus of proof that contractor's mark up on subcontract price productive of profit.

A subcontractor required to make good the main contractor's loss on remedying a defect caused by the breach of contract of one of the subcontractor's sub-subcontractors, and sued the sub-subcontractors to recover their loss. That loss consisted of the cost to the main contractors of the remedial works, being the price quoted to the pursuers by those carrying out the remedial work plus the pursuers' standard mark up of 15 per cent on subcontracts. The defenders disputed the pursuers' entitlement to recover the whole amount on the basis that the mark up would include profit to the pursuers.

Held, that the onus of proving that the mark up included profit rather than overheads was on the defenders and that they had failed to demonstrate that the pursuers had made any profit; and damages as sought by the pursuers *awarded.*

Rotary Services Ltd, nominated subcontractors under a building contract, sought to recover damages from subcontractors to them, Honeywell Control Systems Ltd. The breach of contract by the defenders led to extra work under an extension to the main contract, amounting to £107,014. That sum being recoverable by the employers, Property Services Agency (PSA), from the main contractors, Farrans, and by the main contractors from the pursuers, the pursuers sought to recover it from the defenders. The sum consisted of the charge made to the pursuers by Bellinghee, the company carrying out the remedial works, together with the pursuers' mark up of 15 per cent "as on other subcontract work". The defenders disputed the pursuers' right to recover the whole amount, including the 15 per cent mark up. In allowing recovery in full the Lord Ordinary (Lord Morton of Shuna) said:

"Counsel for the defenders submitted that the damages claimed were irrelevant in that they clearly included profit. The pursuers were only entitled to be put in the same position as they would have been if the breach had not occurred and they had by the defenders' breach been in fact engaged in profitable work. I heard interesting submissions on the vexed question of whether managerial overheads and head office overheads were recoverable.

"I was referred to *Tate & Lyle Food and Distribution Ltd v Greater London Council* [1982] 1 WLR 149; [1981] 3 All ER 716, and by the pursuers' counsel to *Banco de Portugal v Waterlow & Sons Ltd* [1932] AC 452. The figure which the pursuers required to pay was what the eventual customer did pay to get the defect remedied. The evidence does not suggest that if PSA or Farrans had gone to other contractors the cost would have been less. The principle is that the party not in breach is entitled to be restored to what the position would have been if there had been no breach. The party not in breach has a duty to minimise his loss but the *Banco de Portugal* case suggests that the onus of proof of failure to mitigate is on the party in breach and that the court should not judge a pursuer's actings

too strictly, nor fault him for not adopting the best course.

"In the present case there was evidence that the pursuers applied a mark up to the prices quoted to them. A mark up however is not the same thing as a profit, as the mark up is meant to cover a variety of cost items, which I have already mentioned. There is no evidence that the pursuers made any profit from the extra work they and others carried out as a result of the defenders' breach. There was no evidence that the pursuers made a profit on the original contract. On a strict view of the pleadings the defenders' averment that the cost of the remedial work included profit on the part of the pursuers is denied by the pursuers, being covered by their general denial. The defenders have failed to prove that the pursuers made a profit on their work and their argument on this point fails."

Counsel for Pursuers, H H Campbell, QC, Lambert; Solicitors, Murray Beith & Murray, WS — Counsel for Defenders, Moynihan; Solicitors, McClure Naismith Anderson & Gardiner.

C H

McLeod v MacFarlane

HIGH COURT OF JUSTICIARY
THE LORD JUSTICE GENERAL (HOPE),
LORDS ALLANBRIDGE AND COWIE
11 DECEMBER 1992

Justiciary — Statutory offence — Driving while unfit through drink — Specimen of blood or urine — Whether motorist ought to be provided with opportunity to make representations before police decide upon blood or urine — Whether requirement properly made — Road Traffic Act 1988 (c 52), ss 5 (1) (a) and 7 (4).

Section 7 (1) of the Road Traffic Act 1988 provides, inter alia, that in the course of an investigation into whether a person has committed an offence under s 5 a constable may require him to provide a specimen of blood or urine for a laboratory test, and subs (3) (b) provides that where a Camic device or a reliable Camic device is not available a constable may require the driver to provide a specimen of blood or urine at the police station. Subsection (4) provides: "If the provision of a specimen other than a specimen of breath may be required in pursuance of this section the question whether it is to be a specimen of blood or a specimen of urine shall be decided by the constable making the requirement, but if a medical practitioner is of the opinion that for medical reasons a specimen of blood cannot or should not be taken the specimen shall be a specimen of urine."

An accused person was charged on a summary complaint with a contravention of s 5 (1) (a) of the Road

A Traffic Act 1988. The evidence disclosed that the accused was arrested and taken to a police station where there was no Camic device available. The police followed procedures which involved reading out to the accused the following requirement: "You are required to supply a specimen of blood or urine for a laboratory test. The type of specimen shall be decided by me and I will take into account any reason offered by you in response to that decision." The accused was then required to provide a specimen of blood. At the close of the Crown case it was submitted that the accused

B had no case to answer because the evidence of the blood specimen was inadmissible as it had been obtained without the accused being given the opportunity to express his preference as to which type of specimen he would be required to provide. The sheriff upheld the submission and acquitted the accused. The procurator fiscal appealed by stated case.

Held, that since the accused had no right to be given an opportunity to express a preference before the decision was made by the constable as to which speci-

C men he should be required to provide, the requirement that he should provide a specimen of blood for analysis had been properly made (p 786F-G); and appeal *allowed* and case *remitted* to sheriff to proceed as accords.

DPP v Warren [1992] 3 WLR 884, *followed; Carmichael v McKay*, 1991 SCCR 953, *overruled*.

D **Summary complaint**

(Reported 1992 SLT (Sh Ct) 81)

Stanley Barclay MacFarlane was charged at the instance of Iain A McLeod, procurator fiscal, Perth, on a summary complaint which contained the following charge: "On 8 September 1991, on a road or other public place, namely on King Street, Gallowhill and School Wynd, Crieff, Perth and Kinross District, you did drive a motor vehicle, namely a motor van registered number B820 NMS after consuming so

E much alcohol that the proportion of it in your blood was 169 milligrammes of alcohol in 100 millilitres of blood which exceeded the prescribed limit, namely 80 milligrammes of alcohol in 100 millilitres of blood; contrary to the Road Traffic Act 1988, s 5 (1) (a)." The accused pled not guilty and proceeded to trial. At the close of the Crown case the sheriff (J F Wheatley) upheld a submission by the defence in terms of s 345A of the Criminal Procedure (Scotland) Act 1975 and acquitted the accused. (Reported 1992 SLT (Sh Ct)

F 81, where the sheriff's findings in fact and note are set out.)

The procurator fiscal appealed by way of stated case to the High Court against the decision of the sheriff.

Statutory provisions

The Road Traffic Act 1988 provides:

"7.—(1) In the course of an investigation into whether a person has committed an offence under s 4 or 5 of this Act a constable may, subject to the following provisions of this section and section 9 of this Act,

require him — (a) to provide two specimens of breath for analysis by means of a device of a type approved G by the Secretary of State, or (b) to provide a specimen of blood or urine for a laboratory test. . . .

"(4) If the provision of a specimen other than a specimen of breath may be required in pursuance of this section the question whether it is to be a specimen of blood or a specimen of urine shall be decided by the constable making the requirement, but if a medical practitioner is of the opinion that for medical reasons a specimen of blood cannot or should not be taken the specimen shall be a specimen of urine. H

"(5) A specimen of urine shall be provided within one hour of the requirement for its provision being made and after the provision of a previous specimen or urine.

"(6) A person who without reasonable excuse, fails to provide a specimen when required to do so in pursuance of this section is guilty of an offence.

"(7) A constable must, on requiring any person to I provide a specimen in pursuance of this section, warn him that a failure to provide it may render him liable to prosecution. . . .

"8.—. . . (2) If the specimen with the lower proportion of alcohol contains no more than 50 microgrammes of alcohol in 100 millilitres of breath, the person who provided it may claim that it should be replaced by such specimen as may be required under section 7 (4) of this Act and, if he then provides such a specimen, neither specimen of breath shall be used." J

Cases referred to

Carmichael v McKay, 1991 SCCR 953.
DPP v Byrne [1991] RTR 119.
DPP v Warren [1992] 3 WLR 884; [1992] 4 All ER 865.
Hobbs v Clark [1988] RTR 36.
Paterson v DPP [1990] RTR 329.
Pelosi v Jessop, 1991 SLT 155; 1990 JC 273; 1990 SCCR 175. K

Appeal

The sheriff posed the following questions for the opinion of the High Court:

(1) On the evidence led, was I entitled to acquit the respondent?

(2) Was I entitled to reject the evidence of the specimen taken in terms of production 1?

(3) Was I entitled to make finding in fact 4? L

The appeal was argued before the High Court on 1 December 1992.

On 11 December 1992 the court *answered* the questions in the *negative, allowed* the appeal and *remitted* to the sheriff to proceed as accords.

The following opinion of the court was delivered by the Lord Justice General (Hope):

OPINION OF THE COURT.—The respondent

went to trial in the sheriff court at Perth on a charge
of driving with an excess of alcohol in his blood contrary to s 5 (1) (a) of the Road Traffic Act 1988. The
facts were all agreed by way of a joint minute of admissions and the Crown led no further evidence. A
motion was then made on the respondent's behalf
under s 345A of the Criminal Procedure (Scotland)
Act 1975 that there was no case to answer on this
charge. The sheriff upheld that submission and
acquitted the respondent, and it is that decision which
the appellant now seeks to bring under review in this
stated case.

The only question in the case related to the admissibility of the evidence about a specimen of blood which
was obtained from the respondent following a requirement made by a police officer which, on analysis,
showed that there was a proportion of alcohol in it
which was in excess of the prescribed limit. It was
admitted that the respondent was driving his car when
it was stopped late at night by the police, and that the
police were acting in accordance with the statutory
procedures when they took him to the police station in
Crieff for further procedures to be carried out. The
police station there did not have a device of a type
approved by the Secretary of State for subjecting
specimens of breath to analysis, so the police officers
embarked on the statutory procedure where a specimen of blood or urine is required. Section 7 (3) (b)
enables a requirement to provide a specimen of blood
or urine to be made at a police station where, at the
time the requirement is made, a device or a reliable
device of a type approved by the Secretary of State is
not available there, and it is not disputed that the
police officers were entitled to make the requirement.
It is the procedure which they then followed which led
to the argument that the specimen of blood which was
then taken from the respondent by a medical practitioner had been improperly obtained and that evidence
about it was inadmissible.

The objection to the admissibility of this evidence
was directed to the stage at which, having decided to
make the requirement, the police officer read out to
the respondent words printed on a standard form for
use by the police in these circumstances. This was a
form prepared by Tayside police which set out the
procedure to be followed in the police station in cases
where an approved breath specimen device could not
be used, either because no such device was available
there or because it was not reliable or because it was
not practicable to use the device. The words to be read
out to the motorist in these circumstances were as
follows: "You are required to supply a specimen of
blood or urine for a laboratory test. The type of specimen shall be decided by me and I will take into
account any reason offered by you in response to that
decision."

It was agreed in terms of the joint minute that the
police officers followed the procedure laid down in the
standard form, and that this passage was duly read out
to the respondent, who was then required to provide
a specimen of blood for analysis. The decision that the

specimen was to be of blood rather than of urine was
made by the police officers, in accordance with a
standing instruction by the chief constable that, unless
there were compelling reasons to the contrary, the
specimen required under s 7 (4) of the 1988 Act should
be of blood not urine.

Section 7 (4) of the 1988 Act is in these terms: [his
Lordship narrated the terms of s 7 (4) and continued:]

Section 7 (6) provides that a person who, without
reasonable excuse, fails to provide a specimen when
required to do so in pursuance of that section is guilty
of an offence. Section 7 (7) provides that a constable
must, on requiring any person to provide a specimen
in pursuance of that section, warn him that a failure
to provide it may render him liable to prosecution. But
there is no doubt that the decision as to whether the
specimen is to be of blood or urine is left by s 7 (4)
entirely to the constable. There is no indication in the
section that the person who is to provide this specimen
is entitled to be asked for his views on the matter or
has a right to express his preference before the
decision is made by the constable.

The respondent's contention, which was the basis of
the sheriff's decision to acquit him, was that the
wording on the form implied that the constable's
decision had already been taken before the option of
blood or urine was made fully available to the
motorist. It was presented in such a way that the
motorist had no opportunity to express any view he
might have on the question of choice, with the result
that the respondent in this case had no chance to
influence the decision before it was taken by the constable. This submission was based on a line of
decisions by the Court of Appeal in England, notably
Hobbs v Clark in which Roch J said at pp 41-42 that
the constable's decision must be an informed decision,
which it could not be unless the motorist had been
given the opportunity of making representations as to
which of the two types of specimen it should be, and
DPP v Byrne, in which Bingham LJ, as he then was,
said at p 125: "the police officer must convey to the
defendant that the sample to be required may be of
either blood or urine and must give the defendant an
opportunity to consider which sample he would prefer
to give if the choice were his and any reasons he has
for that preference".

The only reported case in Scotland on this point is
Carmichael v McKay, in which Sheriff Simpson,
following the English cases that the decision of the
constable whether to require blood or urine must be
an informed decision, held that the respondent had a
right to make representations to the constable as to his
preference and that there was no proper requirement
for a specimen of blood where the constable, after
reading out words identical to those used in the
present case, had made a requirement for a specimen
of blood without obtaining the appellant's views.

It is hard to reconcile this line of authority with the
statutory language, since s 7 (4) is unequivocal in its
statement that the choice as between the two kinds of
specimen is one to be decided by the constable who

makes the requirement. Nowhere in the procedure
A described in s 7 (3) and 7 (4) is there a choice or option
to be exercised by the motorist. This may be contrasted with s 8 (2) of the Act, which applies to the case
where the requirement by the constable under s 7 (1)
is to provide two specimens of breath for analysis by
means of an approved device. Section 8 (2) is in these
terms: [his Lordship narrated its terms and continued:]

As was pointed out in *Pelosi v Jessop*, 1990 SCCR
at p 177E, it is necessary that the person who is being
B offered the choice to which this subsection refers
should be told precisely what the alternatives are
between which he may choose. The Lord Justice
General went on to say this at p 177E-F: "On the one
hand there is the specimen of breath. On the other
hand there is the specimen of blood or urine. The
choice as between blood or urine is for the police
officer, but the choice as to whether to claim that the
specimen of breath should be replaced is for the
person who has provided that specimen. In order that
C he may be fully informed, he must now be told that
his right is to claim to have the specimen of breath
replaced by a specimen of blood or a specimen of
urine."

For completeness it should be added that he should
also be told that the choice as to whether the replacement is to be by specimen of blood or a specimen of
urine will be made by the police officer. In *Pelosi v
Jessop* the Crown conceded that the proper procedure
had not been carried out by the police. There was,
D however, no choice to be made by the motorist in the
present case because there was no approved device
available in the police station, and the requirement
which was made under s 7 (1) (b) was to provide a
specimen of blood or urine for a laboratory test.

The question whether we ought to follow the line of
authority in England as to what must be said to the
motorist in these circumstances has now been resolved
by the House of Lords in *DPP v Warren*, by which the
E decisions in *Hobbs v Clark* and *DPP v Byrne* were
overruled. It was held that, where a driver was
required to provide a specimen of blood or urine for
one of the reasons set out in s 7 (3) of the 1988 Act,
or claimed the right to provide such a specimen under
s 8 (2), the constable was required by s 7 (4) to inform
him that the specimen was to be of blood or urine and
that it was for the constable to decide which, but that
there was no requirement for him to invite the driver
to express his preference as to which this should be.
F The reasons for the decision were set out in the speech
of Lord Bridge of Harwich, who addressed himself
first to the question what the statute upon its face
value appeared to require. He said this at [1992] 3
WLR, p 890C-D: "It has been said more than once in
the decided cases that section 7 (4) cannot receive
different constructions according to whether resort to
the subsection arises for one of the reasons under
section 7 (3) or because the driver exercises his right
to claim to have his breath specimen replaced under
section 8 (2). This is clearly right. But it does not
follow that there may not be a difference in the pro-

cedures which are appropriate on the one hand in
requiring the driver to provide a specimen of blood or G
urine under section 7 (4) where it is obligatory for him
to do so because one of the circumstances specified in
section 7 (3) has arisen, and on the other hand in
informing the driver of his right under section 8 (2) to
claim that the specimen of breath which he has given
containing the lower proportion of alcohol should be
replaced by a specimen of blood or urine under section
7 (4)."

On the question what a driver who decides to exercise his right under s 8 (2) should be told, he said at H
p 890G: "I can see no ground whatever, on the face
of the statute, why in a section 8 (2) case the driver
should be invited to state whether he prefers to give
blood or urine or to state any reasons for his preference. Indeed, to invite him to do so, it seems to me,
can only be misleading in suggesting that the driver is
entitled to some say in the matter. The statute gives
him no such say. The driver is faced with the prospect
of conviction on the basis of the breath specimen
which he has given containing the lower proportion of I
alcohol. His only chance of escape from that prospect
is by opting to give and then in fact giving a replacement specimen of whichever kind the constable
requires of him, subject only to his right to object to
giving blood on medical grounds, and, if they are
accepted by the doctor, then to give urine instead.
Again, so far as the language of the statute is concerned, I can see no reason in principle why the constable in the course of explaining to the driver his
rights under section 8 (2) should not tell him, if it be J
the case, that he, the constable, will require the
replacement specimen to be of blood."

As to the case where a requirement is made under
s 7 (3), where the driver has no option, he said at
p 891B: "Again, on the face of the statute, I cannot see
any reason why in this case the constable should do
more than tell the driver the reason under section 7 (3)
why breath specimens cannot be taken or used; tell
him that in these circumstances he is required to give
a specimen of blood or urine but that it is for the con- K
stable to decide which; warn him that a failure to
provide the specimen required may render him liable
to prosecution; and then, if the constable decides to
require blood, ask the driver if there are any reasons
why a specimen cannot or should not be taken from
him by a doctor. This will certainly give the driver the
opportunity to raise any objection he may have to
giving blood, either on medical grounds or indeed for
any other reason which might afford a 'reasonable
excuse' under section 7 (6). Here again, provided the L
driver has such an opportunity, I can see nothing in
the language of the statute which would justify a
procedural requirement that the driver be invited to
express his own preference for giving blood or urine,
either before a constable indicates which specimen he
will require or at all."

After a consideration of various cases which had
developed what Bingham LJ referred to in *DPP v
Byrne* as the doctrine of the driver's preference and the
need for an explanation in order that that preference

could be exercised, he said at p 895C that he could find nothing in them which caused him to depart from the view he had reached on the basis of the statutory language. Neither in a case where the requirement is made under s 7 (3) for one of the reasons specified in that subsection nor where the driver's option is exercised under s 8 (2) is there any need for the driver to express his preference for giving blood or urine. This is for the constable to decide, and if he intends to require a specimen of blood to be taken by a medical practitioner the driver should be told that his only right to object to giving blood and to give urine instead will be for medical reasons to be determined by the medical practitioner.

The learned advocate depute invited us to reverse the decision which the sheriff took in this case, and also to overrule the decision in *Carmichael v McKay*, on the view that these decisions were inconsistent with the position as it had now been declared to be for England and Wales by the House of Lords. Counsel for the respondent agreed that he could not properly oppose the advocate depute's motion in the present case. He pointed out however that the wording used by the police in this case, and also in *Carmichael v McKay*, was different from that which had been used by the police in *DPP v Warren* and held to be appropriate. The words set out in the pro forma instruction in *Warren*, quoted at p 887H, were as follows: "The approved evidential breath testing device cannot be used on this occasion because the calibration check has proved unsatisfactory. Accordingly, I require you to provide an alternative specimen, which will be submitted for laboratory analysis. The specimen may be of blood or urine, but it is for me to decide which. If you provide a specimen you will be offered part of it in a suitable container. If you fail to provide a specimen you may be liable to prosecution. Are there any reasons why a specimen of blood cannot or should not be taken by a doctor?"

In the present case the statement "The type of specimen shall be decided by me and I will take into account any reason offered by you in response to that decision" gave rise to difficulty. It was wrong for the driver to be told that any reason offered by him would be taken into account, and in any event it was illogical for him to be told that any such reason should be taken into account "in response" to that decision since this could only be after the decision had been made.

We agree that the words used in the present case are unsatisfactory. No doubt consideration will now be given to this matter, so that revised instructions may be issued as to what should be said by the constable who makes the requirement. But this does not affect the critical issue in the case, which is whether the respondent was entitled to be given an opportunity to express a preference before the decision was made by the constable. On this point we are in no doubt, both on a consideration of the statutory language and of the decision in *DPP v Warren* with which we are, with respect, in full agreement, that the respondent had no such right and that the requirement that he should

provide a specimen of blood for analysis was properly made in this case. We shall therefore allow this appeal, answer all three questions in the negative and remit the case to the sheriff to proceed as accords. It follows that the decision in *Carmichael v McKay* must be overruled. But we should add that the concession in *Pelosi v Jessop* was properly made, since it was consistent with what Lord Bridge said in *DPP v Warren* about the procedure to be followed in those cases where the driver has an option in s 8 (2) of the 1988 Act, with which we also agree.

Counsel for Appellant, Macdonald, QC, AD; Solicitor, J D Lowe, Crown Agent — Counsel for Respondent, Duguid; Solicitors, Garden, Haig, Stirling & Burnet (for Kippen, Campbell & Burt, WS, Perth.

P W F

(NOTE)

Murphy v MRS (Distribution) Ltd

OUTER HOUSE
LORD CLYDE
3 FEBRUARY 1993

Damages — Amount — Solatium — Neck — Whiplash injury — Soft tissue injury with consequences lasting for several years.

A 42 year old van salesman was struck in the side of the head and neck resulting in symptoms, similar to a whiplash injury, rendering him unfit for work for seven weeks, with the pain thereafter lessening but still causing trouble and likely to continue to do so, although on a lessening basis, nearly three years later.

Held, that solatium was properly valued at £3,000; and decree *pronounced* accordingly.

John Murphy raised an action against MRS (Distribution) Ltd for damages for injuries sustained in an accident at work on 12 July 1990. He was then employed as a van salesman and aged 42. A cage containing boxes of fruit and vegetables fell from the tailgate of a lorry while being unloaded and struck the pursuer on the side of the head and neck. Liability was admitted and wage loss agreed at £989.18 inclusive of interest. In assessing solatium at £3,000 the Lord Ordinary (Clyde) said:

"At the time of the accident the pursuer was rendered unconscious for a few minutes. He was taken to the hospital feeling, as he put it, 'a bit groggy' and with a severe pain in his head and neck. No bones were found to have been fractured and he was dis-

A charged home the same day. He was advised to take painkillers and not to drive for 48 hours. The pain in his neck continued so that he could not freely rotate his head to the right nor bend it forward. He was unable to sleep on his left side because of the pain in his neck and, even when sleeping on his right side, was woken two to three times during the night because of pain in the neck.

"Some three days later he consulted his general practitioner Dr Anderson, who advised him to undergo physiotherapy, prescribed both an analgesic
B and an anti-inflammatory drug and signed him off work at fortnightly intervals over July and August for a total of some seven weeks. Dr Anderson described the injury as like a whiplash injury. The pursuer had physiotherapy for some five weeks and wore a surgical collar during the daytime which the physiotherapist provided for him. The pursuer returned to work in the second week of September 1990 and managed to resume his work driving a van and delivering bread satisfactorily. He was able to manage the head move-
C ments required in the operation of driving his van. He later gave up that work in order to return to his trade as a motor mechanic and he has been managing that work satisfactorily dealing with private motor cars. The pain was less by the time he returned to work and had reduced to a dull ache some six months after the accident. He was unable to manage his hobbies of golf and bowls for some eight months after the accident, having attempted to return to them some two months after it only to find his movements restricted by pain
D in the neck. He was able to resume these activities some six months after that. However, as the surgeon, Mr Court-Brown, noted on 19 November 1991, the pursuer's activities at golf and bowls were still affected by his cervical pain, especially his golfing activities. His present general practitioner, Dr McGregor, recalled that in July 1991 the pursuer was still complaining of pain on the left side of the neck. The pain was constantly present as a dull ache but was exacerbated principally by turning his head to the right. He
E was finding it difficult to sleep at night. Mr Court-Brown found a degree of muscle spasm and diagnosed the continuing effects of a soft tissue injury. He considered that the effects would settle in a reasonable time.

"The effects however had not settled when Mr Court-Brown saw the pursuer again on 8 January 1993 and the pursuer himself gave evidence at the proof of their continuance. As he described it, he still had a
F constant dull ache, like a mild toothache, giving rise to some restriction of free movement in turning his head to the right. He still had difficulty in sleeping, particularly on the left side, and takes a painkiller some three or four times a week. He also finds pain developing if he reads for a time with his neck flexed. He considered that his condition was improving but it was only progressing slowly. Mr Court-Brown recorded that on 8 January 1993 the pursuer's symptoms had improved and were continuing to do so. In his opinion, which I accept, the pursuer's condition will probably settle in time, but he will prob-

ably continue to suffer minor discomfort which would not cause him much trouble. I have no hesitation in
G holding the pursuer to be an honest and reliable witness and there was no suggestion that he was exaggerating the discomfort which he has had and he continues to have.

"Counsel for the pursuer submitted that solatium should lie in the range of £3,000 to £4,000. Counsel for the defenders defined the range as between £1,000 and £2,000. Each side referred me to a battery of awards made for the most part in English cases although counsel for the defenders provided some
H Scottish examples. Updated to September 1992 these awards fell broadly within the range of £1,000 to £4,000 covered by the competing submissions. Looking to the particular circumstances of the present case, and obtaining such guidance as I can from the various examples put before me, in the great majority of which the effects of the injury were less longlasting than in the present case, I consider that solatium should be assessed at £3,000. By far the greater proportion of this relates to the past period and while
I counsel for the defenders suggested that only 10 per cent should relate to the future, as opposed to the suggestion of 25 per cent made by counsel for the pursuer, I consider that it should be apportioned as to 80 per cent to the past and 20 per cent to the future. It was agreed that interest should run on the past element at 7½ per cent. The period in question is one of two years and 28 weeks. I calculate the interest on £2,400 at £457. The total award including the agreed sum for the loss of earnings is then £4,446.18. I shall accordingly sustain the first plea in law for the
J pursuer, repel the first to fifth pleas for the defenders and award as damages the sum of £4,446.18."

Counsel for Pursuer, I W F Ferguson; Solicitors, Allan McDougall & Co, SSC — Counsel for Defenders, Paterson; Solicitors, Simpson & Marwick, WS.

C H
K

(NOTE)

Connell v BP Chemicals Ltd

OUTER HOUSE

LORD CAMERON OF LOCHBROOM

18 FEBRUARY 1993
L

Damages — Amount — Solatium — Ankle — Strain to ankle resulting in persisting minor disability.

A 41 year old rigger sustained a strain to his ankle which required to be treated initially with immobilisation in a plaster cast. It healed with no restrictions of function but with minor discomfort on prolonged standing.

Opinion, that solatium was reasonably assessed at £2,200.

A Kenneth Connell raised an action against his employers BP Chemicals Ltd for damages for injuries sustained in an accident at work on 20 December 1989. He was then aged 41. He twisted his ankle while working on a grating walkway. After a proof the Lord Ordinary (Lord Cameron of Lochbroom) held that the pursuer had failed to establish any accident caused by fault on the part of the defenders and granted absolvitor. In relation to damages his Lordship said:

B "The pursuer's claim for damages rests upon a claim for solatium and a claim for wage loss, the latter of which is agreed at a net sum of £797.18. From the medical reports it appears that after the accident the pursuer was removed to Falkirk hospital. He was found to have swelling and tenderness over the lateral side of his ankle and the lateral side of his right foot. It was thought that he had sprained the joints just below his ankle. He was given a below the knee plaster cast which was removed on 24 January 1990. The sprain of the lateral ligament of the right ankle gave rise to pain and swelling. In March 1990 the pursuer C was out walking on uneven ground and sustained further injury. In the report no 15/6 of process it was noted that the tenderness after this episode was on the medial side of the ankle and on the dorsal of the foot, which latter area of pain was more in keeping with a congenital abnormality of the foot which was present prior to the accident. In the opinion of Mr Kerr, the stresses to the foot which arose from the accident had aggravated the pre-existing congenital abnormality. Both surgeons are of opinion that the ankle has now D settled and that the sole complaints of the pursuer are of minor discomfort in the ankle on prolonged standing and that otherwise he has no restrictions of function in the ankle. The ankle is now stable and the continuing consequences of the original injury do not interfere with the pursuer's ability to climb ladders and work at a height. It is agreed that the pursuer was able to resume his employment after the accident on 5 November 1990.

E "Having regard to the terms of the medical reports before me, it cannot be said that this was a trivial injury. There is still some trouble, though minor, arising from it. If I had been in the pursuer's favour on the merits, then, having regard to the nature of the injury, the pain and suffering which followed thereon and the extent of the time during which he was incapacitated from work, I would have awarded £2,200 as solatium. In making this assessment I have had regard to the cases cited to me, namely *Nimmo v British Railways Board*, 1990 SLT 680, *Ross v National Coal Board*, 1988 SLT 385, *Duncan v Glacier* F *Metal Co Ltd*, 1988 SLT 479 and *Millar v Fife Regional Council*, 1990 SLT 651. Parties were agreed that in any award for solatium, three quarters of the award should represent solatium to date and carry interest at the rate of 7½ per cent per annum from the date of the accident. Parties were also agreed that the sum for net wage loss of £797.18 together with the agreed rate of interest of 15 per cent thereon from 5 November 1990 to date would amount to a figure of £1,066.23 in all."

Counsel for Pursuers, J G Thomson; Solicitors, L & L Lawrence — Counsel for Defenders, H K Small; Solicitors, Balfour & Manson, Nightingale & Bell.

C H

McCrum v Ballantyne

FIRST DIVISION
THE LORD PRESIDENT (HOPE),
LORDS WEIR AND KIRKWOOD
18 DECEMBER 1992

Damages — Amount — Solatium and loss of earnings — Multiple injuries — Pelvic, thigh and face injuries — Continuing disability in right thigh — Loss of teeth and facial scarring — Multiplier of 14 applied to wage differential reduced to 11 to take account of possibility of return to pre-accident work and some uncertainty about level of future earnings in pre-accident employment.

Damages — Amount — Solatium and loss of earnings — Multiple injuries — Review by appellate court of award of solatium.

A welder sustained serious, multiple injuries in a road accident when he was aged 21. His injuries included a double fracture of the jaw with loss of teeth and facial scarring, internal injuries to the stomach and liver, and fractures of the pelvis, right thigh and J right ankle with continuing disability. He raised an action of damages against the driver. When the action came before the Lord Ordinary at proof, liability was admitted and the case proceeded on the question of quantum of damages. The Lord Ordinary awarded total damages of £97,920, including solatium of £21,000, £21,272 for loss of earnings to date of decree and £54,648 for future loss of earnings. Future wage loss was calculated by applying a multiplier of 11 to the differential between the pursuer's pre-accident K earnings and those from the employment he had since obtained. The Lord Ordinary had reached a multiplier of 11 by selecting the maximum generally applicable to a man of the pursuer's age and then discounting it to take account of the special factors peculiar to his situation. The defender reclaimed submitting that the award was excessive in each of the three aspects. It was argued (1) that the Lord Ordinary's award for solatium was out of line with awards in similar cases, (2) that he was not entitled to take into account the overtime L figure which he did in calculating the multiplicand for loss of earnings prior to the date of proof, which the employer claimed to know on the basis of personal knowledge, and (3) that the multiplier used for future wage loss was too high.

Held, (1) that the appeal court could only interfere with an award of solatium where it was considered that the Lord Ordinary had awarded a sum which was out of all proportion to the sum which the appeal court considered ought to have been awarded, and on

no view was this such an award (pp 789F-H and
A 790C); (2) that the Lord Ordinary was entitled to
accept the employer's evidence of average overtime
and to include this as part of the multiplicand
(p 790I-K); (3) that to select a multiplier appropriate
in general terms to a pursuer's age and then to discount it to allow for special factors was a legitimate
method of estimating future wage loss and there was
nothing to suggest that the Lord Ordinary had failed
to make sufficient discount (p 791B); and reclaiming
motion *refused*.

B ————————————

Action of damages
(Reported 1992 SLT 620)
Robert McCrum raised an action of damages against
Janice Ballantyne in respect of damages sustained in a
road accident on 22 March 1987. The pursuer was
then aged 21. Liability was not in issue.

The case came to proof on quantum before the Lord
Ordinary (Sutherland).

C
Cases referred to
Barker v Murdoch, 1979 SLT 145.
McColl v Barnes, 1992 SLT 1188.
McGowan v Ayr Products (UK) Ltd, 1991 SLT 591.
Prentice v William Thyne Ltd, 1989 SLT 336.
Purdie v William Allan & Sons, 1950 SLT 29; 1949
    SC 477.
Redman v McRae, 1991 SLT 785.

D On 11 October 1991 the Lord Ordinary *pronounced*
decree for damages of £97,920. (Reported 1992 SLT
620.)

The defender reclaimed.

Reclaiming motion
The reclaiming motion was heard before the First
Division on 8 and 9 December 1992.

E On 18 December 1992 the court *refused* the reclaiming motion.

The following opinion of the court was delivered by
Lord Weir:

OPINION OF THE COURT.—The defender
seeks to challenge the Lord Ordinary's assessment of
damages which he awarded to the pursuer. The total
award was £97,920, and its [principal] constituent
parts were £21,000 for pain and suffering, £21,272 for
F loss of earnings from the date of the accident to the
date of the award and £54,648 for future loss of earnings. It was submitted that the award was excessive in
all three aspects.

In considering whether or not to interfere with an
award for pain and suffering it is well recognised that
this court cannot do so merely by substituting for a
Lord Ordinary's award the figure which it considers
appropriate. An assessment of damages under this
head is essentially a matter of discretion for the Lord
Ordinary, who will have formed a view not least by

seeing and hearing the injured party as well as considering medical and other evidence concerning the G
consequences to a pursuer of the injuries received and
also their effects in the future. The court may interfere
only in limited circumstances and one of these circumstances is where it is considered that a Lord Ordinary
in the exercise of his discretion has awarded a sum
which appears to be out of all proportion to the sum
which an appeal court considers ought to have been
awarded (*Purdie v William Allan & Sons*, per Lord
Justice Clerk Thomson at 1950 SLT, p 30; *Barker v
Murdoch*).   H

The Lord Ordinary summarised the pursuer's
injuries in a manner which was not challenged. He
said: "Basically these consisted of a double fracture of
the jaw, the loss of three upper incisors, internal
injury to the stomach and liver, a fractured pelvis, a
compound comminuted fracture to the right femur
which required major surgery, a fracture of the right
ankle which required screw fixation, a laparotomy
scar, substantially scarring of the outer aspect of the
right thigh and right ankle and three minor scars on   I
the right chin. These injuries were undoubtedly
severe and extensive but fortunately he has made what
is in the circumstances an excellent recovery. There
are certain continuing disabilities, particularly in the
right thigh which cause aching after use, pain when
kneeling and instability. I am satisfied that this is a
genuine and continuing disability."

He also considered that the disability in the right
thigh was permanent, and the other permanent dis- J
abilities were the continuing effects of the loss of three
upper incisors causing some trouble to the pursuer
when biting and chewing, substantial scarring including scarring on the thigh and the laparotomy scar and
also the scarring on the right chin which, although not
very noticeable, obviously caused the pursuer some
embarrassment. The Lord Ordinary concluded as
follows: "Looking at the matter then on a global basis
and taking into account all of the various injuries
which he suffered, the very considerable pain and K
inconvenience which he must have had in the initial
stages, the efforts which he has made to rehabilitate
himself, the necessity of having further operations to
remove the ironmongery and the continuing disabilities which I have already mentioned I am of the
view that the appropriate sum for solatium in this case
is £21,000. Having regard to the pursuer's age and the
fact that therefore the disabilities would exist for a
long period it appears to me to be appropriate to allot
one third of the solatium to the future."   L

We were referred to a number of recent awards to
be found in the reported cases, including *Prentice v
Thyne*; *McColl v Barnes*; *McGowan v Ayr Products
(UK) Ltd*, and *Redman v McRae*. Counsel for the
defender submitted that on a consideration of such
cases it was plain that the Lord Ordinary's award was
very much out of line with the limits of awards for
these types of injury and he contended that it should
not have exceeded £15,000 at most. In our opinion
these decisions, while useful in giving general

guidance as to the level of award to be expected, must
be treated with some caution. First, taken as a whole
they are insufficient by themselves to establish a clear
pattern of award to use as a good point of reference.
Secondly, on analysis there are many points of difference both as to the nature and consequences of the
injuries and the ages of the respective victims which
make these illustrations not particularly reliable as
comparisons. Thirdly, it is to be observed that this is
a case involving multiple injuries of varying degrees of
severity and it is the cumulative effect which has to be
considered in making the assessment. In that connection these cases are of limited assistance.

The Lord Ordinary had the benefit of seeing the
pursuer and was well able with the assistance of the
medical reports to form his own overall impression of
the extent of pain and suffering past, present and
future. We are in no position to know better. It is
possible that if we had been in the same advantageous
position as the Lord Ordinary we might have made an
award approaching the figure contended for by
counsel for the defender but we cannot say that we
would necessarily have done so. It is sufficient for the
disposal of this ground of appeal to say that on no view
can it be said that the award was out of all proportion
to any sum which we might have considered ought to
have been awarded.

The criticism of the Lord Ordinary's award for loss
of earnings from the date of accident to the date of the
proof was concerned with the make up of the multiplicand. The question in dispute before him related to
the amount of overtime which should be taken into
account in assessing the weekly loss of earnings. We
did not understand counsel for the defenders to
contend that overtime should have been left out of
account altogether. The Lord Ordinary was of the
opinion that a figure of 19 hours' overtime per week
was appropriate to take into account but counsel for
the defender contended that the evidence did not
entitle him to reach such a conclusion. He submitted
that a somewhat lower figure should have been
chosen.

The evidence concerning overtime was given by the
pursuer and also, in particular, by his former
employer Robert Miller, a blacksmith and welder. As
the pursuer had only worked for 10 days with Mr
Miller prior to his accident Mr Miller's evidence was
necessarily concerned with the amount of overtime
worked generally by his welders prior and subsequent
to the pursuer's accident in 1987. His evidence was to
the effect that although the pursuer was working a
fortnight's trial period it was intended that he should
be kept on. The business had been active and since the
accident to the pursuer more welders had to be taken
on, at least for a time. Mr Miller confirmed the terms
of a letter in process dated 18 January 1991 which
stated: "Over the last four years an average of 19 hours
overtime per week has been worked. This has been
available to all employees should they wish." He said
that overtime had continued up till a few weeks before
the proof. There was at that time a shortage of work

but he expected it to pick up and for the firm to be
busy as formerly in 1992. Mr Miller stated in evidence
that he could think of no reason why the pursuer
would not have been offered overtime and the pursuer
himself stated that he would have worked overtime if
he had continued in employment.

Mr Miller was asked how the average of 19 hours'
overtime was calculated:

"Q. How did you work out the average? — Basically
from our wages sheets, wages sheets of the people
doing work.

"Q. So are you saying you went through four years'
wages sheets and counted up the hours of overtime? —
It wasn't really necessary, I know just off the top of my
head the wages and how much we have been looking
for people to carry out overtime for us."

Counsel for the defender contended that this was no
more than a guess and that the Lord Ordinary should
not have accepted it as a reliable constituent on which
to calculate the multiplicand. While recognising that
there is some force in that observation, nevertheless it
has to be observed that the answer is capable of more
than one construction. From the answer it can be
inferred that Mr Miller had looked at the wages sheets
as a starting point but then proceeded to reach his conclusion on the basis of personal knowledge. This
seems to us to be a reasonable construction to put on
this answer. Moreover the figure of 19 hours' overtime which was advanced was given as an average
figure. In individual cases it might have been more or
it might have been less. This was a matter for the Lord
Ordinary to resolve. He stated that he accepted the
evidence of Mr Miller and also dealt expressly with
the point. He said: "Mr Miller was criticised in that
he did not closely examine his wages records in order
to arrive at this figure, but in the case of a small business I am satisfied that the owner of the business
knows perfectly well what his employees are doing and
is capable of giving accurate evidence on this matter."

In our opinion the Lord Ordinary was entitled to
accept the figure of an average of 19 hours' overtime
as a reliable basis for calculating the multiplicand, and
there is no substance in this ground of appeal.

Finally it was submitted that the multiplier used for
calculating future loss was too high, although counsel
for the defender did not suggest to us what number
should have been substituted for it. He contended that
the Lord Ordinary had failed to take sufficient account
of the age of the pursuer (who was 26 at the date of
the proof) and of the fact that he had made a good
recovery from his serious injuries and was fit for a
wide range of occupations. Indeed he was fit to do
work as a welder, albeit that he would have to
requalify and would be restricted to welding at a
bench. Although the position was never made quite
clear to us, counsel also appeared to be contending
that it was unrealistic to assume that had he continued
to work with Mr Miller 19 hours' average weekly
overtime would have been available in the future.

The Lord Ordinary's approach was to view a multi-

plier of 14 as being the maximum which would be
A allowed for someone of the pursuer's age. He then proceeded to reduce it to 11 by taking into account the
possibility that he might return to welding, although
he considered that a very remote possibility. Further
in making the reduction he recognised that if the
pursuer had stayed with Mr Miller's firm overtime
might possibly be reduced and he also noted the possibility that the pursuer might in future move to a better
paid job than the particular employment which he was
in at the time of proof.

B   We see no reason to criticise the Lord Ordinary's
approach to the assessment of future loss. To select a
multiplier appropriate in general terms to a pursuer's
age and then to discount it to allow for special factors
is in our view a legitimate method of estimating such
loss and nothing has been said by counsel for the
defender to persuade us that the Lord Ordinary failed
to make sufficient allowance for the factors which he
mentioned in making this discount.

C   For all these reasons the reclaiming motion is
refused.

---

*Counsel for Pursuer and Respondent, Andrew Smith;
Solicitors, Drummond Miller, WS — Counsel for
Defender and Reclaimer, P W Ferguson; Solicitors,
Dundas & Wilson, CS.*

C A G M

D

Rae v Friel

HIGH COURT OF JUSTICIARY

THE LORD JUSTICE CLERK (ROSS),
LORDS MORISON AND SUTHERLAND

E 10 JUNE 1992

*Justiciary — Statutory offence — Careless driving —
Accused driving nearly two miles on motorway at average
speed of 71.24 mph while holding telephone handset in one
hand and overtaking twice — Whether sheriff entitled to
convict — Road Traffic Act 1988 (c 52), s 3.*

An accused person was charged on a summary complaint with careless driving contrary to s 3 of the Road
Traffic Act 1988. The evidence disclosed that for a
F distance of nearly two miles on a motorway with a 70
mph limit the accused drove at an average speed of
71.24 mph whilst holding a telephone handset to his
left ear and embarked on two overtaking manoeuvres
overtaking in total five motor vehicles. The sheriff
found that the accused would have been unable to
react appropriately to any danger or emergency and
convicted him. The accused appealed on the ground
that as he had performed all the proper duties of a
motorist there was no justification for convicting him.

Held, that the sheriff was fully entitled to conclude

that there had been potential danger to which the
accused would not have been able properly to react G
and was therefore entitled to convict (p 793B-D and
G-I); and appeal *refused*.

MacPhail v Haddow, 1990 SLT (Sh Ct) 100,
distinguished.

Summary complaint
    Charles Gordon Rae was charged at the instance of
James Friel, procurator fiscal, Paisley, on a summary
complaint which contained the following charge, after H
amendment: "on 23 October 1990 on the M8 motorway between the M898 and Glasgow airport, Erskine,
District of Renfrew, you, Charles Gordon Rae, did
drive a motor vehicle, namely a motor car registered
number G954 NAG, without due care and attention
and without reasonable consideration for other
persons using the road in respect that you drove said
motor vehicle at a speed in excess of the prevailing
statutory limit and did carry out overtaking
manoeuvres whilst engaged in the use of a hand held I
telephone; contrary to the Road Traffic Act 1988,
s 3". The accused pled not guilty and proceeded to
trial. After trial the sheriff (J Spy) found the accused
guilty.

    The accused appealed by way of stated case to the
High Court against the decision of the sheriff. The
facts of the case are set forth in the opinion of the
court.

Case referred to   J
MacPhail v Haddow, 1990 SLT (Sh Ct) 100; 1990
    SCCR 339.

Appeal
    The sheriff posed the following questions for the
opinion of the High Court, inter alia:

    (2) Was I entitled to make finding in fact no 13?
[Finding 13 stated: "The appellant would have been
unable to react appropriately to any danger or emer- K
gency on the road ahead of him."]

    (3) On the facts stated was I entitled to convict the
appellant of the charge as amended?

    The appeal was argued before the High Court on 10
June 1992.

    Eo die the court *answered* questions 2 and 3 in the
affirmative and *refused* the appeal.
                                                              L
    The following opinion of the court was delivered by
the Lord Justice Clerk (Ross):

    OPINION OF THE COURT.—This is an appeal
at the instance of Charles Gordon Rae. The appellant
went to trial in the sheriff court at Paisley on a complaint libelling a contravention of s 3 of the Road
Traffic Act 1988. The charge libelled that on the M8
motorway, he had driven a motor vehicle, namely a
motor car, without due care and attention, without
reasonable consideration for other persons using the

road in respect that he had driven the motor vehicle and had carried out overtaking manoeuvres whilst engaged in the use of a hand held telephone. During the trial, the Crown sought and obtained leave to amend the complaint by adding the allegation that he had driven the motor vehicle at a speed in excess of the prevailing statutory limit. A submission of no case to answer was made and was repelled. Evidence was then given on behalf of the appellant and after hearing closing submissions, the sheriff found the appellant guilty of the charge as amended.

He has now appealed against conviction by way of stated case. He also appealed against sentence but today on his behalf counsel has explained that he is not proceeding with the appeal against sentence and that he is using the stated case only for the purpose of challenging the conviction. Counsel maintained that the sheriff had not been entitled on the basis of the findings to convict the appellant. He founded strongly upon the fact that in his note the sheriff reports that the procurator fiscal depute advised him that the Crown accepted that apart from the appellant's use of the handset and driving with only one hand on the steering wheel there was nothing wrong in the appellant's driving and overtaking manoeuvres. Counsel submitted that it was not enough to justify a conviction of this charge merely to show that the appellant had been driving with one hand on the steering wheel, but that if he was to be found guilty of contravening s 3, the facts and circumstances would have to justify such an inference. He drew attention to the findings in this case. Putting the matter shortly, it is stated that police officers who were on mobile motorway patrol became aware of the car driven by the appellant. They observed that the appellant was alone in the car and that he was holding the handset of a car telephone to his left ear with his left hand and that only his right hand was on the steering wheel. They accordingly decided to follow him and it took them approximately one mile to catch up with his vehicle. When they caught up with his vehicle, he was still holding the handset in the manner described. On catching up with the vehicle, the police officers proceeded to activate the Vascar device and continued to follow him. It is also stated that the appellant's vehicle moved into the offside lane and he overtook four motor vehicles travelling in the nearside lane. He then returned to the nearside lane. It is also found that during all this manoeuvre, he continued to hold the handset in the manner described and that all appropriate traffic signals for the manoeuvre were given by him. As he approached the St James interchange near Paisley, the appellant overtook one further motor car. Having done so his vehicle returned to the centre lane of the motorway and a description is then given of his continuing along this motorway. The appellant's vehicle was stopped by police officers and it is stated in the findings that the total distance driven by the appellant while holding the handset to his left ear and driving with only his right hand on the steering wheel during the period of the operation of the Vascar device was just short of two miles and that his average speed

during this period was 71.24 miles per hour. There is a finding that apart from his use of the hand held telephone, there was nothing remarkable about his overtaking manoeuvres.

There are three other significant findings to which reference should be made. In finding 10, the sheriff sets forth the terms of rule 54 of the Highway Code. That rule is in the following terms: "Do not use a hand-held microphone or telephone handset while your vehicle is moving, except in an emergency. You should only speak into a fixed neck slung or clipped on microphone when it would not distract your attention from the road. Do not stop on the hard shoulder of a motorway to answer or make a call however urgent."

Finding 13 is in the following terms: "The appellant would have been unable to react appropriately to any danger or emergency on the road ahead of him."

Finding 15 is in the following terms: "The appellant's whole concentration and attention was not on the road ahead and traffic around him."

There is a question in the case challenging finding 13 and asking the question whether the sheriff was entitled to make that finding. Counsel maintained that having regard to the evidence as described by the sheriff in his note and the other findings, the sheriff was not entitled to make finding 13. He recognised that unless he could successfully challenge finding 13, he could not maintain that the sheriff had not been entitled to convict, but he did challenge finding 13 as we say and maintained that the sheriff was not entitled to make it. His submission was that on the findings it was plain that the appellant had performed all the proper duties of a motorist and that there was no justification for concluding that he had been contravening the provisions of s 3. He drew attention to the case of *MacPhail v Haddow*. That was a case where an accused was charged with contravening s 3 in that he had used a portable telephone while driving. There was in that case no evidence of any lack of control over the vehicle or any danger to others and in that case Sheriff Wheatley held that in the absence of any such evidence there was no evidence of a contravention of the section and the accused was acquitted. Counsel founded upon that case which he maintained was not distinguishable from the facts of the present case.

The advocate depute on the other hand maintained that the sheriff had adopted the correct approach in this case and had applied the correct test to the driving of the appellant. He had asked himself whether the driving of the appellant showed that he was exercising the degree of skill, care and attention which the reasonably competent and prudent driver could be reasonably expected to show in the circumstances. The advocate depute then drew attention to what the sheriff said in his note and he maintained that there was adequate material to justify the sheriff in making finding 13 and in finding the appellant guilty.

We have come to the conclusion that the submissions of the Crown are to be preferred. The sheriff in his note explains that in convicting the appellant he took into account the provisions of the Highway Code, rule 54. No doubt the fact that a driver has used a hand held telephone while his vehicle is moving and has been in breach of the provisions of the Highway Code is not conclusive of the question of whether he has contravened s 3, but it is a circumstance to which the sheriff is entitled to have regard. The sheriff goes on to point out that for a distance of nearly two miles, plus the mile in which it took the police officers to catch up with the appellant's vehicle, at an average speed of 71.24 miles per hour the appellant drove his vehicle whilst holding a telephone handset to his left ear. During that period he had only one hand on the steering wheel. Not only that, but during that period of time he embarked upon two overtaking manoeuvres, overtaking a total of five motor vehicles. The sheriff concluded that in so doing the appellant's driving had fallen short of the requisite standard of care to be expected of a reasonably competent and prudent driver. In our opinion, he was entitled to reach such a conclusion in the circumstances. The sheriff explains that he accepted the evidence of the police officers to the effect that during his telephone conversation, the appellant's whole concentration could not have been on the road, and accepted this evidence that during this period with only one hand on the steering wheel he was not in a position to react appropriately to an emergency or danger on the road ahead. In our opinion the sheriff is likewise justified in that conclusion. It is in our view an important feature of the present case that during this period of time the appellant overtook a total of five vehicles. It is obvious that if any one of these vehicles had happened suddenly and unexpectedly to move out into the overtaking lane which the appellant was occupying, an emergency would have been created and in our opinion the sheriff was justified in concluding that if such a danger or emergency had occurred the appellant would not have been able to react appropriately when he had only one hand on the steering wheel.

So far as the case of *MacPhail v Haddow* is concerned, that case appears to us to turn very much upon the special facts which were present in it. Obviously each case must depend upon its facts and we regard the circumstances in the case of *MacPhail* as different to those of the present case and indeed to have been somewhat special. We say that because as Sheriff Wheatley makes plain in his judgment, that the driving in the case of *MacPhail* took place within the centre of the city of Perth and that must have been an area where there was a speed limit of 30 miles per hour. Not only that, but the accused in that case turned into a one way street. The sheriff held that there were no other vehicles in the vicinity of the roads on which the accused was driving at the material time and no pedestrians who might have posed any kind of problem for vehicles engaged in the manoeuvres which he was undertaking. Moreover, Sheriff Wheatley also states in his judgment that there was no indication of potential danger that might have led the accused to be in a position that it could be said that

he would not be able properly to respond. He goes on to say that if such danger had materialised from somewhere in the course of the manoeuvre it was plain from the facts and circumstances and in particular from the absence of any pedestrians and vehicular traffic that the accused would have had ample time to observe such a danger. The facts in the present case are different from the facts in *MacPhail* in a number of important particulars. As has already been observed the appellant at the material time was driving on a motorway where there was a maximum speed limit of 70 miles per hour. He was in fact marginally exceeding that speed limit. Not only that, but far from there being any finding that there were no other vehicles in the vicinity, there are findings which show that during the time that he drove in the manner described in the charge, the appellant at this high speed overtook five other vehicles. In these circumstances we are quite satisfied that in the present case, unlike *MacPhail*, the sheriff was fully entitled to conclude that there was potential danger to which the appellant would not have been able properly to react and respond. For the foregoing reasons we are satisfied that on the facts found in this case the sheriff was entitled to make finding in fact 13 and to convict the appellant. We shall accordingly answer questions 2 and 3 in the affirmative and it follows that the appeal is refused.

Counsel for Appellant, Baird; Solicitors, Bird Semple Fyfe Ireland, WS — Counsel for Respondent, Bonomy, A D; Solicitor, J D Lowe, Crown Agent.

P W F

Farrell v Normand

HIGH COURT OF JUSTICIARY

THE LORD JUSTICE CLERK (ROSS), LORDS GRIEVE AND WYLIE

22 JULY 1992

Justiciary — Crime — Breach of the peace — Accused beckoning young girl over and asking if she wanted a drink — Girl and her two friends alarmed and upset — Whether breach of the peace.

Justiciary — Evidence — Corroboration — Mutual corroboration — Two charges of breach of the peace involving young girls in same area but only one charge involving indecency — Whether mutual corroboration applicable.

An accused person was charged on a summary complaint with two charges of breach of the peace. Charge 1 libelled that on 27 November 1991 in a shopping centre in Cowglen Road, Glasgow, the accused made indecent suggestions to a young girl, E, and placed her in a state of fear and alarm. Charge 2 libelled that on 29 November 1991 in the leisure pool in Cowglen Road the accused placed E and two other young girls

A in a state of fear and alarm. The evidence disclosed in respect of charge 2 that the accused had beckoned E over and asked her if she would like a drink. All three girls were alarmed and upset although only E spoke to what the accused said. On charge 1 only E spoke to the accused offering her money to indulge in a sexual act but the other two girls knew about that earlier incident. The Crown relied on the rule in *Moorov v HM Advocate*, 1930 SLT 596, in respect of that charge. The accused was convicted of both charges and appealed by stated case.

B   **Held**, (1) that as there was such a material difference between the essential features of the charges, because only one charge involved indecency, the rule in *Moorov* could not apply (p 795G-I); (2) that the mere beckoning over of E could not be regarded as conduct which might reasonably be expected to lead to her and others being alarmed or upset and accordingly did not amount to breach of the peace (pp 795L-796B); and appeal *allowed* and convictions *quashed*.

C   *Harvey v HM Advocate* (1975) SCCR Supp 96, *distinguished*.

Summary complaint

Roderick Norman Farrell or Robert Reynolds was charged at the instance of Andrew C Normand, procurator fiscal, Glasgow on a summary complaint which contained the following charges, inter alia: "(1) you did on 27 November 1991 in the Pollok Shopping

D Centre, Cowglen Road, Glasgow, conduct yourself in a disorderly manner, make indecent suggestions to [E], aged 10 years, c/o Pollock Police Office, Glasgow, place her in a state of fear and alarm and did commit a breach of the peace; (2) you did on 29 November 1991 in the Pollok Leisure Pool, 27 Cowglen Road, Glasgow, conduct yourself in a disorderly manner, place said [E], and [A], aged 11 years and [B], aged 10 years, both c/o Pollok Police Office aforesaid, in a state of fear and alarm and did commit a breach of the

E peace." The accused pled not guilty and proceeded to trial. After trial the sheriff (G G Crozier) found the accused guilty.

   The accused appealed by way of stated case to the High Court against the decision of the sheriff.

Findings in fact

   The sheriff found the following facts admitted or proved, inter alia:

F   (1) On 27 November 1991 the complainer, a 10 year old girl [E], was in the Pollok shopping centre in Glasgow. The complainer was unaccompanied and after some time she sat down near a toy machine. (2) The appellant, who was sitting near her, asked her to phone his brother for him. The appellant was a complete stranger to the complainer.... (4) The complainer telephoned as directed. (5) A security guard in the shopping centre asked them to move as the centre was about to close. (6) On leaving the centre the appellant said to the complainer that he would give her £5.00 but he would require to "feel her". (7) The com-

G plainer was frightened on hearing this suggestion and ran away to a nearby house of a . . . close friend of her mother and told her what had happened. (8) On 29 November 1991 the same complainer met some friends at the Pollok leisure pool. (9) She had occasion to go into the toilet and as she came out of the toilet she saw the appellant. (10) The appellant beckoned her over and asked her if she would like a drink.

   (11) The complainer was accompanied by [K], aged 11 years, and [C], aged 10 years, both of whom knew that the appellant had made an indecent suggestion to the complainer two days previously, and they in turn H were afraid and upset by the appellant's beckoning gestures to the complainer. (12) The complainer was alarmed and very upset at being again accosted by the appellant who was a complete stranger to her. (13) The complainer ran from the appellant and told an attendant of the approach which the appellant had made to her and the police were called and arrested the appellant.

Cases referred to   I

Harvey v HM Advocate (1975) SCCR Supp 96.
Moorov v HM Advocate, 1930 SLT 596; 1930 JC 68.
Raffaelli v Heatly, 1949 SLT 284; 1949 JC 101.

Appeal

   The sheriff posed the following questions for the opinion of the High Court, inter alia:

   (1) Was I entitled on the evidence to find that the appellant's behaviour in relation to the second charge amounted to a breach of the peace?   J

   (2) Was I entitled on the evidence to regard the appellant's conduct in both of these charges to be similar enough and in such circumstances as to apply to the *Moorov* doctrine so as to allow the evidence in charge 2 to corroborate the evidence of the complainer in charge 1? . . .

   (4) Was I on the evidence entitled to convict the appellant on either or both charges?   K

   The appeal was heard in the High Court on 22 July 1992.

   Eo die the court *answered* questions 1, 2 and 3 in the *negative, allowed* the appeal and *quashed* the convictions.

   The following opinion of the court was delivered by the Lord Justice Clerk (Ross):

   OPINION OF THE COURT.—The appellant is L Roderick Norman Farrell or Robert Reynolds. He went to trial in the sheriff court at Glasgow on a complaint libelling three charges. He pled not guilty to all three charges and his plea was accepted in respect of charge 3 and the matter proceeded to trial on the first two charges.

   In order to appreciate the point raised in this appeal, it is necessary to set out the terms of these charges. The charges were as follows: [his Lordship quoted the terms of the charges and continued:]

A At the conclusion of the Crown case a submission of no case to answer was made and the sheriff rejected that submission; the appellant then gave evidence and at the end of the day the sheriff convicted the appellant of both charges as libelled. He has now appealed against that conviction.

In presenting the appeal counsel first addressed us on charge 2. He did so because it was plain that the conviction on charge 1 depended upon the so called rule of *Moorov* whereas in the case of charge 2 there was evidence from more than one source. In relation

B to charge 2 counsel pointed out under reference to findings 8, 10, 11 and 12 that on 29 November the complainer was with friends at Pollok leisure pool. When she was coming out of the toilet, the appellant beckoned her over and asked her if she would like a drink. Findings 11 and 12 make it plain that the complainer and her companions were afraid and upset by the appellant's conduct. As will be clear from the terms of charge 2 there were in fact three complainers in that charge, the complainer [E] and her two com-

C panions. The sheriff throughout has referred to [E] as "the complainer" since she was the sole complainer in charge 1 and one of the complainers in charge 2.

Counsel pointed out that the only conduct of the appellant complained of was the beckoning over of the child. Under reference to the note he pointed out also that it appeared it was the complainer [E] alone who spoke to the appellant's having said to her: "Do you want a drink?" He criticised the sheriff's holding that

D the conduct amounted to breach of the peace by pointing out that the sheriff does not say why the conduct was capable of amounting to breach of the peace. His submission was that the findings fell short of what was necessary to point to conduct amounting to breach of the peace. He then turned his attention to charge 1. The question raised was whether there was room for the application of the *Moorov* doctrine. Counsel stressed that the conduct libelled in charge 2 was different from the conduct libelled in charge 1 and he

E maintained that there was no sufficient similarity in circumstances between the two chrges such as would permit the application of the *Moorov* doctrine. In particular he emphasised that in charge 1 the serious part of the libel was that the appellant had made indecent suggestions to the complainer, [E], whereas in charge 2 there was no such suggestion made.

The advocate depute, on the other hand, maintained that so far as charge 1 was concerned the rule of *Moorov* could be relied upon by the Crown. He

F reminded us that in both charges it is stated that an older man has approached or accosted young female children. The advocate depute relied upon *Harvey v HM Advocate*. In that case it was stressed that provided there were sufficient similarities in the circumstances between two charges, in that case, of assault, it did not matter that the particular method of assault was different. No doubt that is so in the case of a charge such as assault but the question here which must be determined is whether there was sufficient similarity in the nature of the charges themselves.

We recognise, as the advocate depute stressed, that the charges were alleged to have taken place within an G interval of only two days. The charges were alleged to have taken place within the same area, and in each case the charge is one of the breach of the peace. These are undoubtedly similarities but we have come to the conclusion that the charges were in essence so different that the role of *Moorov* cannot be relied upon. We say that because it is plain that the principal feature of charge 1 is the making of an indecent suggestion, whereas in charge 2 there is no such allegation made and the terms of charge 2 are simply in standard form H to the effect that the appellant conducted himself in a disorderly manner and placed the three complainers in a state of fear and alarm and thus committed the breach of the peace. It appears to us that there is such a material difference between the essential features of the two charges that this is not a case where one could affirm that the rule of *Moorov* would apply.

That being so we are satisfied that the conviction on charge 1 cannot stand. Although the sheriff does not explain precisely why he found the appellant guilty on I charge 1, it is plain from the second question in the case, which he has stated, that the conviction of the appellant on charge 1 depended upon the *Moorov* doctrine.

The remaining question is whether there was sufficient evidence on charge 2. The advocate depute maintained that there was sufficient evidence. He pointed out that there was no need in this case for the Crown to rely on the *Moorov* doctrine. There were J three complainers who had all given evidence; it was plain from their evidence and from the findings that the appellant had beckoned the complainer, [E], over and it was also plain from the findings that the three complainers were alarmed and upset. It appears that the reason for the alarm and upset was that, so far as [E] was concerned, she had previously come across the appellant in the circumstances which gave rise to charge 1, and she had communicated details of this incident to the two other complainers and it was for K that reason that they were afraid and upset. That is made plain in finding 11. Of course, the circumstances of the first charge were spoken to only by the complainer, [E].

As in all cases where an issue arises as to whether conduct amounted to breach of the peace, one has to bear in mind the well known definition given by Lord Justice Clerk Thomson in *Raffaelli v Heatly*, 1949 SLT at p 285: "where something is done in breach of public order or decorum which might reasonably be L expected to lead to the lieges being alarmed or upset, or tempted to make reprisals at their own hand, the circumstances are such as to amount to a breach of the peace".

The question here is whether the mere beckoning over of the complainer [E] can be regarded as conduct which might reasonably be expected to lead to the girls being alarmed or upset. Although the point is a narrow one, we have come to the conclusion that it cannot be affirmed that mere beckoning over of the

girl in this case can be regarded as conduct which
A might reasonably be expected to lead to her and others
being alarmed or upset. Whether beckoning by an
older person of a child can amount to breach of the
peace must depend upon the circumstances, and all
that we are affirming in the present case is that in the
circumstances as disclosed to us we are not satisfied
that the beckoning over here was such as to be likely
to lead to the girls being alarmed or upset. We can
appreciate that in other circumstances beckoning over
might be such as to lead to some reasonable expecta-
B tion of alarm, for example, if the beckoning had been
persisted in after the girls had exhibited signs of alarm
and upset, then the situation might be different but we
are not prepared to affirm that beckoning over in
itself, as described in the findings here, was conduct
which amounted to breach of the peace.

Accordingly, for the foregoing reasons, we have concluded that the sheriff was not entitled to hold breach
of the peace established in terms of the second charge.
We shall accordingly answer the first question in the
C negative, the second question in the negative and also
the fourth question in the negative and it follows that
the conviction is quashed.

---

*Counsel for Appellant, Baird; Solicitors, Brodies, WS
(for A F Finlayson & Co, Glasgow) — Counsel for Respondent, Macdonald, QC, A D; Solicitor, J D Lowe,
Crown Agent.*

P W F

D

Leisure Inns (UK) Ltd v Perth & Kinross District Licensing Board

SECOND DIVISION
E THE LORD JUSTICE CLERK (ROSS),
LORDS MURRAY AND MORISON
6 MARCH 1991

*Licensing — Licence — Application for provisional grant
of public house licence — Whether premises suitable
"having regard to their location" — Whether confined to
suitability for use as licensed premises or including wider
question of amenity — Whether grant of planning per-
F mission relevant to consideration of effect on amenity —
Licensing (Scotland) Act 1976 (c 66), s 17 (1) (b).*

*Licensing — Licence — Application for provisional grant
of public house licence — Reasons for refusal — Whether
court had power to remit to licensing board to amplify
reasons already given — Act of Sederunt (Appeals under
the Licensing (Scotland) Act 1976) 1977 (SI 1977/1622),
para 5.*

An application was made for the provisional grant of
a public house licence in respect of premises for which
planning permission had been granted for use as a res-

taurant and cafe bar. There were objections from the
four householders situated in dwellinghouses above G
the premises, who suggested that the noise that might
emanate from the premises would seriously affect the
amenity of the houses. The licensing board refused the
application on the ground inter alia of "there being
the strong possibility that the use of the premises as
a public house would have a detrimental effect on the
amenity of the four dwellinghouses". The applicants
appealed to the sheriff, who held that the reasons for
refusal were inadequate and granted the application.
The licensing board appealed to the Court of Session, H
arguing that the reasons given were sufficient to
warrant the refusal and that if it was held that the
board had failed to give adequate reasons the case
should be remitted to the sheriff so that the board
could be given an opportunity of giving fuller reasons
for their decision in terms of the Act of Sederunt
(Appeals under the Licensing (Scotland) Act 1976)
1977, para 5.

Held, (1) that behind every ground for refusal there
had to be adequate reasons and that for those reasons I
there had to be a proper basis in fact (pp 798I and
800A and B-D); (2) that the reasons given by the board
were inadequate in that anyone reading the statement
of reasons would be left in real doubt as to what the
reasons were for refusing the application (pp 798I-K
and 800A and B-D); (3) that there was no adequate
material before the board for holding that the ground
for refusal had been made out and therefore no point
in directing that the case should be remitted to the
board (pp 798L-799B and 800A and D); and appeal J
refused.

Opinion, that when considering "location" under
s 17 (1) (b) loss of amenity would be a relevant consideration, but (per the Lord Justice Clerk (Ross)) that
where planning permission had been granted a licensing board should be slow to hold that any detrimental
effect on amenity was to be apprehended (pp 799D-E
and 800A and B-C).

Doubted, per the Lord Justice Clerk (Ross), K
whether a remit to the licensing board under para 5 of
the Act of Sederunt to give reasons for finding a
ground of refusal established would be competent to
permit the licensing board to amplify their reasons
rather than give reasons where none had previously
been given (p 799J-L).

Opinion reserved, on this point, per Lords
Murray and Morison (p 800B and D-E).

Opinion reserved, per the Lord Justice Clerk
(Ross), whether a strong possibility of damage to L
amenity was sufficient to meet the test of balance of
probabilities (p 799L).

Appeal from the sheriff court
Leisure Inns (UK) Ltd appealed to the sheriff court
against the decision of Perth & Kinross District
Licensing Board to refuse their application for the
provisional grant of a public house licence for
premises in Perth.

Statutory provisions

A   The Licensing (Scotland) Act 1976 provides:

"17.—(1) A licensing board shall refuse an application of the type described in subsection (2) below if it finds that one or more of the following grounds for refusal, being competent grounds, applies to it— . . . (b) that the premises to which an application relates are not suitable or convenient for the sale of alcoholic liquor, having regard to their location, their character and condition, the nature and extent of the proposed use of the premises, and the persons likely to resort to B   the premises; . . . and otherwise shall grant the application."

The Act of Sederunt (Appeals under the Licensing (Scotland) Act 1976) 1977 provides:

"5. Where an appeal is made to the sheriff against a decision of a licensing board and that board has given as reasons for its decision one or more of the statutory grounds of refusal, the sheriff may, at any time prior to pronouncing a final interlocutor request C   the licensing board to give their reasons for finding such ground or grounds of refusal to be established."

Cases referred to

Augustus Barnett Ltd v Bute and Cowal Divisional Licensing Board, 1989 SLT 572.
Hill (William) (Scotland) Ltd v Kyle and Carrick District Licensing Board, 1991 SLT 559.
Wordie Property Co Ltd v Secretary of State for Scotland, 1984 SLT 345.

D

On 26 February 1990 the sheriff (J C McInnes, QC) *sustained* the appeal and *granted* the application.

The licensing board appealed to the Court of Session.

Appeal

The appeal was heard before the Second Division on E   12 and 13 February 1991.

On 6 March 1991 the court *refused* the appeal.

THE LORD JUSTICE CLERK (ROSS).—On 8 November 1989 the appellants who are Perth and Kinross District Licensing Board considered an application by the respondents for the provisional grant of a public house licence for premises at 38 South Street, Perth. The Chief Constable, Tayside Police was F   represented at the meeting of the appellants as were five other parties who had lodged objections to the respondents' application. The chief constable did not lodge any objection to the application. The respondents had already obtained planning permission for a proposed restaurant and cafe bar at the premises. In submitting their application the respondents referred to the proposed layout of the premises and explained that there would be a holding bar area where alcoholic liquor would be served mainly to persons waiting to go in to the attached restaurant or taking bar lunches or suppers; the restaurant would serve a full range of

meals, and a full range of food would be available for service in both areas of the premises throughout their G   opening hours. The proposed bar and restaurant would be small intimate areas. The objectors were principally concerned about the number of licensed premises in the centre of Perth principally providing similar facilities and about disturbance in the area occurring from time to time at present. The objectors occupy houses above the said premises, and on behalf of the objectors, Mr and Mrs A G Cowe, it was stated as one ground of objection, "the noise emanating from the ground floor would be intolerable to our clients". H   Other objectors, Mr and Mrs A C Low claimed that the proposed use of the premises would seriously and substantially affect the amenity of their flat.

The appellants refused the application, and on 10 November 1989 in response to a request for reasons of refusal, they issued a statement of reasons in a letter dated 10 November 1989. It was stated therein: "The Licensing Board decided by eight votes to one that the premises to which the application related were not suitable or convenient for the sale of alcoholic liquor I   as applied for due to their location in a block consisting of the premises and four dwellinghouses above, there being the strong possibility that the use of the premises as a public house would have a detrimental effect on the amenity of the four dwellinghouses."

The respondents appealed to the sheriff against the refusal of their application for the provisional grant of a public house licence, and after hearing parties the sheriff sustained the appeal, holding that the appel- J   lants had acted in an unreasonable manner in deciding to refuse the application by the respondents. He accordingly reversed the appellants' decision and granted the respondents' application. Against that decision of the sheriff the appellants have appealed to this court.

On behalf of the appellants counsel submitted that the sheriff had erred in holding that the appellants had not given sufficient reasons to warrant their refusal of the application, and that he had also erred in basing K   his decision upon the view that the appellants' "reason is at best speculative". He accordingly moved the court to allow the appeal or alternatively to remit the case to the sheriff in order that he might remit the case to the appellants to hear the application de novo in terms of s 39 (6) (a) of the Licensing (Scotland) Act 1976. Alternatively he submitted that this court should remit the case to the sheriff in order that the sheriff might instruct the appellants to give amplified reasons for their decision in terms of para 5 of the Act L   of Sederunt (Appeals under the Licensing (Scotland) Act 1976) 1977.

In presenting the appeal, counsel drew attention to the provisions of s 17 of the Act of 1976, and he accepted that the licensing board required to grant the respondents' application unless one of the grounds for refusal specified in s 17 (1) had been established. In the present case the appellants had refused the application upon a ground for refusal specified in s 17 (1) (b). Counsel explained further that a question of construc-

A tion arose in relation to s 17 (1) (b). The question was whether the words "having regard to their location" were to be given a restricted or a wider interpretation. Counsel submitted also that the learned sheriff had been in error in that he had confused a ground for refusal with the reasons which the appellants had for adopting that ground for refusal. He recognised that the reasons contained in the letter of 10 November 1989 were not very specific, but he submitted that there was just sufficient in the letter to justify the view that the appellants had complied with the obligation
B upon them to give reasons for their decision in terms of s 18 of the Act of 1976. Alternatively, if the court took the view that the appellants had failed to give adequate reasons, then he submitted that the case should be remitted to the sheriff so that the appellants could have an opportunity of giving fuller reasons for their decision.

With reference to the obligation to give reasons for their decision, counsel accepted that the situation was similar to that considered by the court in *Wordie*
C *Property Co Ltd v Secretary of State for Scotland*. That was a case under the town and country planning legislation, but counsel accepted that so far as the giving of reasons was concerned, the approach in the present case should be the same. In that case the Lord President stated at p 348: "So far as para 11 (1) is concerned all that requires to be said is that in order to comply with the statutory duty imposed upon him the Secretary of State must give proper and adequate reasons for his decision which deal with the substantial ques-
D tions in issue in an intelligible way. The decision must, in short, leave the informed reader and the court in no real and substantial doubt as to what the reasons for it were and what were the material considerations which were taken into account in reaching it."

Although no express reference was made to noise in the letter of 10 November 1989, counsel contended that it was clear that the detrimental effect on amenity which was referred to was in fact noise. If, however,
E the court took the view that the reasons were inadequate, then counsel maintained that there should be a remit so that the appellants could amplify their reasons.

On behalf of the respondents, counsel maintained that the appeal should be refused. He submitted that not only were no satisfactory reasons given for the decision of the appellants, but that there was no indication of the basis upon which such reasons could be
F given. He stressed that in the present case planning permission in detail had been obtained for the proposed restaurant and cafe bar, and that conditions had been attached to the planning permission for the express purpose of protecting the amenity of the adjacent residential property. That was something which the sheriff was entitled to have in mind. He examined the material before the sheriff which is contained in the initial writ and the answers, and also in the note annexed to the sheriff's interlocutor. He stressed that it was for the objectors to establish a ground for refusal and he maintained that any such

ground for refusal required to be established upon a balance of probabilities. He further contended that to G say there was a "strong possibility" of damage to amenity was not sufficient to meet the test of a balance of probabilities. In any event, he maintained that there was no material before the sheriff to justify the conclusion arrived at by the appellants. In particular there was no indication in the reasons of what was meant by "a detrimental effect on the amenity of the four dwellinghouses" and there was in fact no material to justify such a conclusion. He further maintained that the words in s 17 (1) (b) "having regard to their loca- H tion" were confined to the location of the premises from the point of view of their suitability for use as licensed premises, and that the words did not cover the wider question of amenity. His principal submission, however, was that there was no material before the appellants to justify them in holding that a ground for refusal under s 17 (1) (b) had been established.

Both counsel referred to a number of other authorities under similar legislation, and in particular under the provisions of the Betting, Gaming and Lotteries I Act 1963 and the Civic Government (Scotland) Act 1982. I do not however find it necessary to consider all these authorities which were laid before the court. I have reached the clear conclusion that counsel for the respondents' principal submission is well founded. I agree with him that behind every ground for refusal there must be adequate reasons, and that for these reasons there must be a proper basis in fact. The reasons given in the letter of 10 November 1989 are not, in my opinion, adequate. Although the appel- J lants' contention was that the detrimental effect on amenity referred to related to noise, it is significant that no express mention of noise is made in the letter. Not only that, but there is no indication as to the circumstances in which it was apprehended that there would be noise detrimental to amenity. How long was the noise to continue? With what frequency was such noise to be experienced? At what time of the day or night was it apprehended that this noise would occur? What degree of noise was anticipated? These are some K of the questions which are not dealt with in the statement of reasons. In my opinion the statement of reasons is unspecific and anyone reading the statement of reasons would be left in real doubt as to what the reasons were for refusing this application.

That the reasons were liable to be regarded as inadequate was recognised by counsel for the appellants, and it was for this reason that he submitted in the alternative that there should be a remit. I accept that L in terms of s 39 (6) the sheriff could have remitted the case to the appellants for reconsideration of their decision, and that this court could competently remit to the sheriff so that he in turn could remit to the appellants for that purpose. I also accept that in a case covered by para 5 of the Act of Sederunt of 1977, the sheriff might remit to the appellants to give reasons, and that in the same way this court could competently remit to the sheriff for him to exercise his power under para 5. However, there would be no point in directing that this case should be remitted to the appellants if there was no material before the appellants to justify their holding that a ground for refusal in terms of s 17 (1) (b) had been established. In the note annexed to his interlocutor, the sheriff explains that it was not suggested during the hearing that he lacked in any way the information which was before the appellants. Although he had not heard the oral submissions as they were made to the appellants, their gist had been put to him, and he had the written objections which had been lodged. There was no question of the appellants having acted on the basis of local knowledge. On the basis of the information contained in the initial writ and answers and in the sheriff's note, I am satisfied that there was no material before the appellants in this case to justify them in concluding that a ground of objection under s 17 (1) (b) had been established.

This was an application for the provisional grant of a new licence, and in terms of s 23 of the Act of 1976 the respondents required to produce a certificate from the planning authority to the effect that they had obtained planning permission. As already indicated, in the present case the respondents had obtained not merely outline planning permission but detailed planning permission. It was plain that the planning authority had had regard to the question of amenity. In my opinion, the question of amenity can properly arise under s 17 (1) (b) where reference is made to "having regard to their location". Under reference to different legislation in *William Hill (Scotland) Ltd v Kyle and Carrick District Licensing Board* I expressed the view that similar words should be given a wider rather than a restricted interpretation, and in particular that when considering "location" loss of amenity to surrounding properties would be a relevant consideration. The submissions made in the present case confirm me in the view which I expressed in that case. Accordingly, contrary to counsel for the respondents' submission, I am satisfied that the appellants were entitled to consider the matter of amenity, although since planning permission had been received for this application for a provisional grant of a licence, the appellants should, in my opinion, have been slow to hold that any detrimental effect on amenity was to be apprehended. In any event, if they were to hold such, they would require to have material before them to justify such a conclusion. Having considered all the material which was before the appellants I am satisfied that they had no sound basis for concluding that there was a strong possibility that the use of the premises would have a detrimental effect on the amenity of the objectors' premises. Other than assertions from the objectors that their amenity would be affected, there appears to be no basis for any such conclusion. It appears from the answers that the objectors made specific mention of other licensed premises in Perth which were similar to the respondents' premises but there is no suggestion anywhere that problems have been encountered there, and in particular no suggestion that these premises have given rise to noise or disturbance. What the appellants state in the letter of 10 November 1989 is that there is a strong possibility that the use of the premises as a public house would have a detrimental effect. There may, however, be some misconception on the part of the appellants because the premises in question are not to be used as a public house in the ordinary sense of that expression. Although the application is for the provisional grant of a public house licence for these premises, it is a condition of the planning permission that there are restrictions on the use of the premises relating to the provision of food. Accordingly there is no question here of the respondents having carte blanche to use the premises as a public house without restrictions; the premises can only be used for the purpose of a restaurant and cafe bar. There is nothing in the material before the appellants to support the view that the use of the premises for such a purpose would have a detrimental effect on the adjoining properties.

Since I am satisfied that there was no adequate material before the appellants to justify their holding that this ground of refusal had been made out, there would be no point in remitting the case to the sheriff so that he could remit the case to them. That being so, it is unnecessary to express any firm conclusions upon arguments which were presented to us regarding the scope of the powers to remit under s 39 (6) and the Act of Sederunt of 1977. It was not disputed that whether or not to remit under either of these provisions was a matter for the discretion of the court, but there could be no question of the court exercising its discretion to remit if the appellants had had no adequate material before them to enable them to hold that the ground for refusal had been established. I would only add that I am not persuaded that a remit under para 5 of the Act of Sederunt of 1977 would be competent in this case since the appellants purported to give reasons for their decision. This was not a case where the only reason offered for the decision was one or more of the statutory grounds of refusal, and accordingly I am inclined to think that it would not be open to the sheriff to make a remit under para 5. It is significant that under para 5 the sheriff may request the licensing board to give their reasons for finding a ground of refusal to be established; it does not entitle him to request the licensing board to amplify their reasons. In *Augustus Barnett Ltd v Bute and Cowal Divisional Licensing Board*, Lord Murray, in his dissenting opinion, expressed the view that a remit might be made under para 5 of the Act of Sederunt of 1977 so that the licensing board might be required to amplify their reasons. With all respect to Lord Murray, I am not persuaded that a remit under para 5 could be used to require a licensing board to amplify reasons; I am inclined to the view that such a remit can only be used where the licensing board have given no reasons and where they are required by the sheriff to give their reasons for finding a ground for refusal to be established. Paragraph 5 empowers the sheriff to request the licensing board "to give their reasons", not "to give or amplify their reasons".

Having regard to my conclusion on counsel for the respondents' principal submission, it is unnecessary to determine whether holding that there was a strong possibility of damage to amenity would meet the test of a balance of probabilities.

A For the foregoing reasons I would move your Lordships to refuse this appeal and to affirm the interlocutor of the sheriff.

LORD MURRAY.—I agree with your Lordship in the chair that this appeal fails for the reasons stated in your opinion. In light of that, as you point out, there is no need for this court to deal with the alternative submission for the appellants that the case should be remitted to the sheriff for him to remit the case to the appellants under the Act of Sederunt of 1977 to
B amplify the reasons which they gave for their decision. I expressed an opinion on this matter in the *Augustus Barnett* case relating to the particular facts of that case. I would reserve judgment, for my part, as to whether para 5 of the Act of Sederunt applies only to a case where a licensing board has given no reasons at all for their decision.

LORD MORISON.—I agree with your Lordship that a detrimental effect of the grant of a licence on the
C amenity of a locality may constitute a ground for refusing the grant, by virtue of the provisions contained in s 17 (1) (b) of the 1976 Act. But the reasons given by the appellants do not disclose in what respects they considered that use of the premises would be likely to have a detrimental effect on the occupation of the dwellinghouses to which they refer, and their general reference to "use of the premises as a public house" appears to ignore the particular character of the premises for which the respondents were applying for
D a provisional grant and in respect of which they had received planning permission. Counsel for the appellants was unable to point to any material which had been the subject of consideration when the application was heard which might provide them with a basis for amplification of the reasons which they gave. There is therefore no point in remitting the case so as to allow the appellants to give further specification of their reasons. Accordingly it is unnecessary to consider what is the extent of the court's power to remit either under s 39 (6) of the Act, or under the Act of Sederunt
E of 1977. I reserve my opinion on that matter, but agree with your Lordship that the appeal should be refused.

Counsel for Pursuers and Respondents (Applicants), Bonomy; Solicitors, Ketchen & Stevens, WS — Counsel for Defenders and Appellants (Licensing Board), Agnew of Lochnaw; Solicitors, W & J Burness, WS.

F   C H A of L

Noble v City of Glasgow District Council

EXTRA DIVISION

LORDS McCLUSKEY, MORISON AND PROSSER

14 FEBRUARY 1992

Licensing — Licensing committee — Application for grant of public entertainment licence — Objection — Purported objections wrongly identifying application — Whether committee entitled to take them into account — Whether committee entitled to have regard to productions accompanying objection not related to subject matter of objection — Necessity for proper specification of objections — Civic Government (Scotland) Act 1982 (c 45), Sched 1, para 3.

The Civic Government (Scotland) Act 1982, Sched 1, para 3, provides that any objection or representation relating to an application for the grant or renewal of a licence shall "be entertained by the licensing authority if, but only if, the objection or represenation — (a) is in writing; (b) specifies the grounds of the objection or, as the case may be, the nature of the representation".

An application was made for the grant of a public entertainment licence. The secretary of a tenants' association wrote objecting to "the renewal of amusement licence". The Lord Provost submitted a letter headed, inter alia, "Amusement with Prizes by means of Membership"; the letter stated, "My constituents, and I agree with them, fear that this would encourage undesirable elements of our community to this venue". A petition objected to "the renewal of a gaming licence". A competent objection was accompanied by a number of productions which bore no relation to the complaint raised in the objection. In the course of the hearing, these productions were referred to by the objector's solicitor, who also represented all the other purported objectors. The committee having refused the application, the applicants appealed to the sheriff and then to the Court of Session on the basis, inter alia, that the committee had erred in law. It was contended that the committee had erred in taking into account the productions attached to the competent objection, and that the other objections were incompetent, the Lord Provost's being also irrelevant.

Held, (1) that it was a matter of construction whether or not any particular document had the character of an objection or representation relating to the application which was before the committee, and having regard to their full terms the committee was entitled in each case to regard the letters as constituting an objection or representation relating to the applicants' application (pp 805G-I, 805K and 806D-F); (2) that a purported objection which was so unspecific as to be plainly irrelevant should not be entertained at all once the irrelevancy was pointed out, and since the Lord Provost's letter fell into this category the correct

A course would have been for the committee to have ruled at the start that the letter did not contain any objection or representation which it might entertain; but having regard to the terms of the committee's decision, the court was not persuaded that the committee had given any weight to the assertions contained in the letter (pp 805L-806D); and (3) that the committee was entitled to have regard to the productions insofar as they lent support to any relevant and competent objection advanced by any of the solicitor's clients, and while some of the documents contained little to

B support objections properly related to the statutory grounds for refusing an application, the court was not persuaded that the committee had founded upon any of the doubtfully relevant material in arriving at its decision (p 806H-I); and appeal *refused* (the court having considered and rejected an argument that the committee had unreasonably exercised its discretion).

Appeal from the sheriff court

C   Michael Noble and another appealed to the sheriff against the refusal by the licensing committee of the City of Glasgow District Council to grant a public entertainment licence in respect of premises at 86 Westmuir Street, Glasgow.

Statutory provisions

The Civic Government (Scotland) Act 1982 provides in Sched 1:

D   "3.—(1) Any objection or representation relating to an application for the grant or renewal of a licence shall . . . be entertained by the licensing authority if, but only if, the objection or representation — (a) is in writing; (b) specifies the grounds of the objection or, as the case may be, the nature of the representation".

Cases referred to

Associated Provincial Picture Houses Ltd v Wednesbury Corporation [1948] 1 KB 223.

E   *Wordie Property Co Ltd v Secretary of State for Scotland*, 1984 SLT 345.

On 29 June 1990 the sheriff *refused* the appeal.

THE SHERIFF (B A LOCKHART).— . . . I deal with the four separate grounds of appeal argued by counsel for the pursuers as follows:

(1) The committee considered objections which were clearly incompetent or lacking in specification and took
F *them into account in reaching their decision.*

As far as the objection by the Beattock and Powfoot Tenants' Association was concerned, I was referred to their letter of objection dated 21 February 1989. This letter stated inter alia: "As secretary of the above Tenants' Association I am writing to you to object to the renewal of Amusement Licence made by Nobles Amusement Centre at 86 Westmuir Street". It was submitted that this letter did not constitute an objection to the application for a public entertainment licence, but purported to be an objection "to the

renewal of Amusement Licence made by Nobles Amusement Centre at 86 Westmuir Street". It was G submitted that a subsequent letter lodged with the subcommittee dated 9 May 1989 correctly stated that the objection was to a public entertainment licence and tacitly accepted that there had been an error in referring to it in the letter of 21 February 1989 as an amusement licence. That letter of 9 May was held by the committee to be incompetent as it had not been lodged within 21 days. It was submitted that the letter of 21 February 1989, which was before the committee, was not an objection to the present application, but purported to be an objection to an application for an H "Amusement Licence". Such an application did not exist. It was submitted that in light of the terms of the letter of 21 February 1989 it could not be considered an objection to the present application and accordingly it had been incompetently considered by the first defenders' subcommittee.

Solicitor for the first defenders stated that the letter of 21 February 1989 stated that the tenants' association was objecting to an "Amusement Licence" and I the place was at "Nobles Amusement Centre". It was submitted that this letter had to be taken in its context and it had to be noted that it was lodged on behalf of members of the public and not a solicitor. There was nothing in the Act to say that the objection required to be headed "public entertainment licence". It was submitted that given the terms of the letter of objection, and the fact that this was the only application made by Nobles, it was difficult to see what else the objection could have referred to. It was submitted that J it was too strict an interpretation of the regulations to insist on the words "entertainment licence" in the letter of objection. It was clear to all that the reference in the letter to an "amusement licence" was sufficient to give proper notice of the intention of the objectors. It was further submitted that the first defenders' subcommittee had clearly understood that letter to be an objection. On 25 July 1989 they sent to the appellant's solicitors a letter which said inter alia "the committee, when considering the application, intend to take into K account . . . (2) letters of objection from:— i. Beattock and Powfoot Tenants' Association". It was this letter to which they referred. It was submitted that the purpose of the Act and the necessity of intimation was to give fair notice to an applicant as to the objection he required to meet. It was submitted that this letter gave that fair notice and the fact that there was a description of the licence as an amusement licence instead of a public entertainment licence was not material.
L
In my opinion the submissions made on behalf of solicitor for the first defenders are well founded. I take the view that the first defenders' subcommittee were entitled to take into account the letter of objection from the Beattock and Powfoot Tenants' Association and the submissions and productions in support thereof during the course of their deliberations.

Counsel for the pursuers then referred to the letter of objection lodged on behalf of the fourth defender, the Lord Provost of the City of Glasgow. This letter was in the following terms: "I refer to your letter of 17 February regarding the above and wish to make a strong recommendation that this application be refused. At my recent surgery I received a deputation of local tenants all objecting to this application. My constituents, and I agree with them, feel that this would encourage undesirable elements of our community to this venue. The entertainment envisaged in these premises would do nothing to improve the community facilities available in the area." The type of entertainment was described in the heading of the letter as "amusement with prizes by means of membership". It was submitted that this objection lacked specification. It purported to be on behalf of unnamed constituents, whose unspecific complaint was being passed to the town clerk by the Lord Provost. The complaint from the unnamed constituents had been made to her, but no complaint by these constituents had been made to the committee. It was submitted that there was also no specification of the grounds of the objection. The section of the letter to which I have referred did not give proper specification of what problems were envisaged. It was further submitted that the whole tenor of the letter envisaged that a new operation was coming into force which had not been operating before. The fact of the matter however was that these facilities had been in existence and the pursuers had been trading since 1985. It was submitted that this application should have been regarded by the committee as incompetent as it lacked specification. The letter appeared to be an objection "to amusement with prizes by means of membership". There was no question of membership of amusement centres. A public entertainment licence does not require members. It was sumitted that this objection should not have been considered by the committee.

Solicitor for the first defenders referred me to the letter from the Lord Provost of 28 February 1989. In the heading of her letter, there is specification of the name of the appellant, the address of the premises, a reference to the Civic Government (Scotland) Act 1982 and an acknowledgment that entertainment is involved. It was argued by solicitor for the defenders that there was no other application to which this letter could refer and that it was reasonable for the first defenders to consider it as an objection to this application. This was the only reasonable inference which could be taken from the letter. It was argued that this was not an objection by the Lord Provost on behalf of her constituents, but a personal objection by the Lord Provost. She says in terms: "I . . . wish to make a strong recommendation that this application be refused". She goes on: "my constituents, *and I agree with them*, fear". This indicated that the objection is at her instance as an individual.

I was referred to para 3 (1) of Sched 1 to the 1982 Act which states that the objection requires to be in writing, to specify the grounds of the objection, the name and the address of the person making it, and to be signed by that person and to be made within 21 days. It was submitted that the ground of objection was clear, namely that the granting of this application would encourage undesirable elements of the community to this venue and that the entertainment envisaged would do nothing to improve the community facilities available in the area. The letter of objection did all that was required in terms of the Act.

Again I accept the submission made by solicitor for the first defenders. It appears to me that this was a competent objection made by the Lord Provost as an individual, the terms of which the committee are entitled to take into account during their deliberations. The Lord Provost chose not to speak to her objection before the committee, or to appoint someone to speak for her. In my opinion the committee are entitled to take the letter into account as it stands and to attach such weight to the terms of it as they think fit.

Counsel for the appellants then referred to the objections lodged on behalf of the fifth to 14th defenders who are signatories to a petition which is production 6/6. This petition states, "We, the undersigned, being tenants at 88 Westmuir Street, Parkhead, Glasgow, do hereby wish to register our objection to the renewal of a gaming licence to Noble Amusements, 86 Westmuir Street, Glasgow, for the following reasons:". It was submitted that this referred to an application for a gaming licence, and not to an application for a public entertainment licence. Michael Noble already had a gaming licence for this establishment. The only application before the committee which had involved a gaming licence had been at the instance of Luxury Leisure Ltd and this had been withdrawn. As these objectors had chosen to lodge an objection to a gaming licence, and not a public entertainment licence, their objection was incompetent and should not be considered by the committee.

Solicitor for the first defenders explained that the only application at the instance of Noble Amusements of Westmuir Street, Glasgow, before the committee was the public entertainment licence. It was pointed out that the objectors used the word "licence", they referred to the applications correctly as "Noble Amusements", and they specified the location to which their objection related. It was submitted that it was clear from that letter, written by lay persons, that what they were objecting to was the licence which has currently been applied for by Noble Amusements. Again it was clear from the letter written by the first defenders' clerk to the appellant's solicitors of 25 July 1989 that that petition was taken as an objection by the clerk.

Again I accept the argument that the only interpretation which could be reasonably placed on this document was that it was an objection to the application at the instance of Noble Amusements relating to a licence of their Westmuir Street premises which was currently before the committee. The letter fairly states the ground of their objection and I am not prepared to regard as material the fact that these lay tenants wrongly refer to a "public entertainment" licence as a "gaming licence".

I accordingly repel the first ground of appeal argued

on behalf of the appellants. In my opinion, for the
reasons I have given, the first defenders were entitled
to take into account in their deliberations the objections lodged by the second and fourth to 14th
defenders.

*(2) The committee entertained an objection from Ian
Monachan Ltd backed up by productions which were in
effect new objections of which due notice had not been
given in terms of the statute.*

The objection dated 21 February 1989 on behalf of
Ian Monachan Ltd had been intimated by the solicitors Holmes Mackillop who stated to the town clerk:
"Our clients have instructed to intimate to you their
objection to this grant and to any extension of their
operators' licence within the premises. Our clients
have become increasingly concerned that their staff
and customers are being exposed to the increased drug
abuse problem in the East end of the city ... our
clients believe that any extension or development of
the amusement business in the East end of the city is
likely to give rise to further opportunity for abuse and
the encouragement of abuse particularly among young
people." It was first suggested that the objection
related only to any extension or development of the
amusement business, and did not apply to the existing
business. Reading the letter as a whole, I do not accept
that interpretation. In my opinion it is clear that the
objection is in respect of the application presently
presented for a public entertainment licence. In
support of his objection at the hearing before the subcommittee, solicitor for the third defenders lodged and
referred to a number of documents which compose the
inventory of productions no 7 of process.

It was submitted that these documents for the most
part were wholly separate from the defenders' objections and represented new objections which were not
timeously lodged. These documents should have been
ruled incompetent. I deal with each document lodged
in turn. 7/1 is an article in the *Evening Times* about a
prosecution for supplying drugs. The youths involved
were said to have been seen "outside Nobles Amusement Arcade in Westmuir Street, Parkhead". There
was no indication that the pursuers' premises were
involved. 7/2 was a letter from the Lord Provost. It
merely advised Messrs Holmes Mackillop that, as
local councillor, she had lodged her own objection to
the grant of the licence. I refer to my previous comments regarding the objection lodged by her. 7/3 is a
letter from David Marshall, MP, the local Member of
Parliament. It is addressed to the solicitors acting for
the objectors and states: "I would also like to make the
point that I am totally opposed to this application
being granted. The local feeling against it is one of the
strongest I have ever come across and it is most
definitely not the sort of facility which is needed in
this area." It was submitted that this was a separate
objection at the instance of David Marshall and should
not have been introduced as a production for the
objectors before the committee. 7/4 was a letter from
the housing department to one of the objectors and 7/5
was a letter from an area manager of the social work

department of Strathclyde Regional Council to the
Parkhead Community Council. Again it was submitted that these two letters represented separate
objections. 7/6 was the petition on Parkhead Community Council notepaper in the following terms:
"We, the undersigned, are opposed to Glasgow District Council granting a gaming licence to Nobles
Amusement Arcade, 86 Westmuir Street. These
premises cause a great deal of disturbance to neighbouring residence and traders. We believe this arcade
is detrimental to the Parkhead area generally." The
petition was signed by 1,000 persons. It was pointed
out that an objection had been lodged by Parkhead
Community Council. It had not been lodged
timeously and was held by the committee to be
incompetent. This petition, lodged on behalf of the
objectors, nevertheless voiced the community
council's concern. It was submitted that the document
produced contained a substantive objection on behalf
of objectors who are not in the proceedings and whose
objections had been ruled as incompetent. These
productions, it was submitted, contained incompetent
material. They were taken into account by the subcommittee in the course of their deliberations. This
was clear from the statement of reasons. In this respect
they had regard to incompetent material and had
thereby erred in law. I was directed to the transcript
of proceedings where solicitor for the pursuers had
submitted to the committee that the documents
produced by solicitor for the objectors appeared to be
fresh objections and that they could not be referred to
at this late stage.

I was asked to hold that these productions were not
properly part of the objections being considered by the
subcommittee. They were separate objections on
behalf of separate parties. They were in effect new
objections of which due notice had not been given in
terms of the statute.

The position of the first defenders was that those
productions were not treated as objections by the committee. They were regarded as documents lodged on
behalf of the objectors as support for their clients'
position. It was submitted that these documents were
to be regarded as in the same position as the precognitions and signed statements lodged by solicitor for the
appellants at the hearing which purported to support
the appellants' position. It was submitted that it was
clear from the statement of reasons that the committee
had only considered objections lodged on behalf of
four objectors, namely Beattock and Powfoot Tenants'
Association, Ian Monachan Ltd, the Lord Provost and
the tenants at 88 Westmuir Street, Glasgow. I was also
referred to the statement of reasons which stated:
"The members also considered and took into account
in reaching their decision a number of productions
submitted on behalf of the applicants and the
objectors."

I take the view that the letters of objection lodged
timeously with the first defenders set out the grounds
of objection which would be canvassed at the hearing.
Notice of these objections, including the grounds, was

A given to the appellants. The productions complained of were lodged by Mr Williamson of Holmes Mackillop who, at the hearing, was representing not only his original clients Ian Monachan Ltd, but also the Beattock and Powfoot Tenants' Association and the tenants of 88 Westmuir Street. These various letters originally lodged by the parties for whom Mr Williamson was acting set out clearly the grounds of their objection. The inventory of productions subsequently lodged by him contains material which purports to lend support to the objectors' position.

B It certainly would have been open to David Marshall, MP, the housing department, the social work department and the Parkhead Community Council to lodge objections on their own behalf. They chose to lend support to existing objectors and to the grounds of objection that these objectors had intimated. Their evidence was put forward by Mr Williamson in support of his clients' objections.

In my view the first defenders were entitled to con-
C sider evidence put forward by the objectors in support of their own stated grounds of objection. The productions in my opinion can properly be said to reinforce the grounds of objection which have already been intimated by the existing objectors. I consider it was a matter within the discretion of the committee as to whether or not they chose to consider these productions. The statement of reasons makes it clear that they have so chosen and in the whole circumstances I do not consider they can be criticised for so doing.

D Accordingly I am not prepared to sustain either of the first two grounds of appeal which had been intimated on behalf of the pursuers. I have to say that, adopting the test set out in the cases of *Associated Provincial Picture Houses Ltd* and *Wordie Property Co Ltd* to which I have already referred, I would have upheld this appeal if I had taken the view that the committee were not entitled to take into account the objections of Beattock and Powfoot Tenants' Association, the Lord Provost, the tenants of 88 Westmuir
E Street and the productions lodged on behalf of all the objectors. I would have then been obliged to conclude that the committee had taken into account material which ought not to have been before them. In my opinion it could properly have been said that the committee had taken into account material irrelevant considerations and the appellants would be entitled to succeed.

[The sheriff then dealt with further grounds with
F which this report is not concerned.]

———————

The applicants appealed to the Court of Session.

Appeal

The applicants' grounds of appeal were as follows:

The sheriff erred in law in holding that the first respondents were entitled to refuse the pursuers' application for a public entertainment licence on the following grounds:

(1) That the objections made on behalf of (a) Beattock
G and Powfoot Tenants' Association, (b) the Lord Provost, and (c) the defenders fifth to 14th named were not incompetent nor lacking in specification and that the first respondents' subcommittee was entitled to take them into account in making its decision.

(2) That the objection made on behalf of Ian Monaghan Ltd which was supported by various productions and a petition was valid and competent and that the first respondents were entitled to take into account in reaching its decision.

H [There were two further grounds with which this report is not concerned.]

The appeal was heard before an Extra Division on 30 January 1992.

On 14 February 1992 the court *refused* the appeal.

The following opinion of the court was delivered by Lord McCluskey:

I **OPINION OF THE COURT.**—This is an appeal to the Court of Session on a point of law against an interlocutor pronounced by Sheriff Lockhart in Glasgow on 29 June 1990 refusing an appeal brought by the pursuers and appellants under para 18 of Sched 1 to the Civic Government (Scotland) Act 1982. The appeal to the sheriff was against a refusal by the first defenders and respondents (the "licensing authority") to grant the appellants a public entertainment licence in respect of premises at 86 Westmuir Street,
J Glasgow. The background to the appellants' application for that licence was that Michael Noble, one of the pursuers and appellants, had been granted a public entertainment licence for those premises on 18 March 1985. That licence was renewed for three years in 1988. However, a change in the management personnel at the premises gave rise to a fresh application for the grant of a new public entertainment licence; it was that application which was heard, determined and refused by the licensing authority's authorised sub-
K committee on 9 November 1989. The fuller history of this matter is given in the note appended by the sheriff to the interlocutor of 29 June 1990. In that the sheriff has also explained comprehensively what took place before the committee on 9 November 1989 before the application was refused. Most of the proceedings are recorded in a transcript from shorthand notes; there was no dispute either before the sheriff or before this court as to what took place; we can therefore content ourselves with referring to the sheriff's note describing
L the course of these proceedings.

The sheriff records in his note the four separate grounds of appeal which he was invited to consider. He then considers each in turn, narrates the submissions for and against each of the four separate grounds and determines all the matters which he was asked to determine. It is unnecessary in this opinion to repeat what the sheriff has recorded but we observe that no criticism was made of his summary of the submissions made to him.

The appeal to this court is presented under para 18 (12) of Sched 1 to the Civic Government (Scotland) Act 1982 which empowers a party to appeal on a point of law from the sheriff's decision to the Court of Session. The sheriff's powers in relation to an appeal before him are set forth in earlier subparas of para 18. For present purposes it is sufficient to note that, in terms of subpara (7), the sheriff cannot uphold an appeal unless he considers that the licensing authority, in arriving at their decision: "(a) erred in law; (b) based their decision on any incorrect material fact; (c) acted contrary to natural justice; or (d) exercised their discretion in an unreasonable manner".

The grounds of appeal to the Court of Session were in the following terms: [his Lordship quoted the grounds of appeal and continued:]

It will be observed that the points raised in grounds of appeal to the Court of Session were essentially the same points as those contained in the four grounds which were presented to the sheriff. The submissions which the sheriff has recorded in his full and helpful note are in substance the same submissions as were made to this court from both sides of the bar in relation to the four grounds of appeal. We refer with gratitude to the sheriff's summary of these matters and need not narrate the submissions again. We can turn at once to our consideration of the four grounds of appeal presented to us.

The first is that the objections specified in ground 1 were incompetent or lacking in specification, or both, and that accordingly the licensing authority were not entitled to take these objections into account; the sheriff's error, it was said, lay in not accepting that ground when it was presented to him. The Beattock and Powfoot Tenants' Association objection is contained in a letter of 21 February 1989 which states inter alia:

"I am writing to you to object to the renewal of Amusement Licence made by Nobles Amusement Centre at 86 Westmuir Street. Sorry if I can not quote the reverence [sic] number as the application is well above eye level and very hard to read what it is about."

The letter goes on to detail why the objection is taken. What was submitted to us was that there was no creature known to law as an "amusement licence". The application to the licensing authority was for a public entertainment licence; this letter was, therefore, not a competent objection to the application before the licensing authority and should not have been considered by the committee. It was pointed out that in a letter of 9 May 1989 the secretary of the association had acknowledged his error and had then sought, when it was too late to do so, to object to "the renewal of the Public Entertainment License [sic]".

Paragraph 3 of Sched 1 to the Act provides that: [his Lordship quoted the terms of para 3 set out supra and continued:] The rest of the paragraph prescribes certain other particulars required of an objection or representation, but none is of any moment in this case. It will be observed that, although certain characteristics of the objection are specifically prescribed and a strict timetable is laid down (subject to para 3 (2)), the opening words of para 3 (1) refer only to an objection or representation "relating to an application for the grant or renewal of a licence". In our opinion, it is clearly a matter of construction whether or not any particular document presented to the authority has the character of an objection or representation relating to the application which is before the authority. It was not in dispute that the application in question, although technically for the grant of a licence, was treated by all concerned as effectively an application for the renewal of a licence, given that there had been a public entertainment licence in respect of the premises for several years and that it was still current. In our opinion the licensing authority were entitled to regard the letter of 21 February 1989 as being an objection or representation relating to the application by the pursuers and, in the light of that, to hold the objection to be competent in terms of para 3 of Sched 1. The letter of 21 February 1989 states that the association are "objecting" and narrates objections, which include: "that drugs addicts are gathering outside these premises and blocking the pavements and obstructing shoppers getting past to use other shops in the vicinity . . ., that mothers are taking children into the premises and they are being allowed to play the machines", and "Some pensioners are afraid to go by this shop because of the drug addicts standing outside".

It is not disputed that these are relevant grounds of objection. They are plainly relevant grounds and the committee were entitled to take that into account in deciding, as they did, that the letter itself was an objection relating to the appellants' application.

In relation to the letter written by Mrs Susan Baird, the Lord Provost, what was submitted was that the letter bore to be a representation about "Amusement with Prizes by means of Membership": this was what the heading on the letter said. We have no difficulty in holding that the committee were entitled to regard this letter as containing an objection or representation relating to the appellants' application before them, even although the heading to the letter contained a mistake. The heading refers not just to "Amusement with Prizes by means of Membership" but also to "Entertainment" and the Civic Government (Scotland) Act 1982: it is clear what it was intended to be. It was further submitted that the body of the letter contained no relevant or sufficiently specific grounds of objection; all that it said was, "my constituents, and I agree with them, fear that this would encourage undesirable elements of our community to this venue". We are disposed to agree with the criticism that this letter does not comply with para 3 (1) (b) of Sched 1, which provides that an objection is to be entertained only if it "specifies the grounds of the objection". It was submitted that the letter did not specify grounds of objection related to any of the statutory grounds upon the basis of which a licensing authority might refuse an application, namely those grounds contained in Sched 1, para 5 (3), sub-subpara

A (c) of which relates to the suitability of the premises having regard inter alia to "the possibility of undue public nuisance" and "public order or public safety". We agree that it is difficult to say which, if any, of those grounds was supported by the vague and unspecific allegations in this letter. A purported objection which is so unspecific as to be plainly irrelevant should not be entertained at all once the irrelevancy is pointed out. In this case, the correct course would have been for the committee to rule at the start that this letter did not contain any objection or representa-

B tion which the licensing authority should entertain. If, when setting forth their reasons for arriving at the decision ultimately taken, they had specified that they accepted that the grant of a licence "would encourage undesirable elements of our community to this venue" then there might well have been a basis for holding that the authority, in arriving at their decision, had acted incompetently by taking into account a consideration which was so vague as to be meaningless and consequently irrelevant. Having regard to the

C reasons given in the decision letter we do not find it possible to say that the committee treated this objection as relevant. It is not in fact discussed in the letter containing the licensing authority's reasons; but there is no need for such a letter to discuss every point raised by would be objectors, particularly points which are apparently irrelevant and are not said to have played any part in the decision. We are not persuaded that the committee gave any weight at all to the assertions contained in this letter.

D The 10 signature petition dated 20 February 1989 from various tenants (the defenders fifth to 14th named) was also said not to be a competent objection. The point taken was one of competency only; it was based solely upon the opening words of the petition which indicated that the objection was "to the renewal of a Gaming Licence to Noble Amusements". Clearly this was not an accurate description of the application or of the proceedings but we have no doubt that the committee were entitled to consider this document in

E its context, to have regard to the detailed reasons given therein in support of the objection relating to matters of safety and nuisance and to conclude that this was intended to be and could properly be treated as an objection or representation relating to the application before the committee. In our opinion, therefore, it cannot be said that the committee was not entitled to take into account any of the objections listed in the first ground of appeal. Accordingly, it was not an error in law to take any of them into account. The sheriff

F was right so to decide and this ground of appeal fails.

It will be observed that the second ground of appeal is really advancing the proposition that the objection on behalf of Ian Monaghan Ltd was expressly confined to one narrow point and that, accordingly, the various productions which are referred to in this ground of appeal could not be looked at as they dealt with matters other than those embraced by the Ian Monaghan Ltd objection. It is correct to say that the Ian Monaghan Ltd objection was specifically related to an alleged drug abuse problem and that the

"various productions" referred to dealt with many other matters. What the appellant's pleadings say on G this point is: "Although that was the sole ground of objection the third defenders' solicitor (i e Mr Williamson, who acted for Ian Monaghan Ltd) was permitted in the course of his submissions to raise extraneous matters not covered by said objection and, in particular, to lodge and refer to a number of documents, including [the documents are then specified]".

This ground of appeal, however, is dependent for its effect upon the first ground of appeal which we have already rejected. Mr Williamson appeared not simply H for Ian Monaghan Ltd, but for the other objectors referred to in ground of appeal 1; their competent objections and representations covered many matters not referred to by the Ian Monaghan Ltd objection. We are satisfied that the committee were entitled to have regard to the productions insofar as they lent support to any relevant and competent objections advanced by any of Mr Williamson's clients. It is not altogether clear what support, if any, could be found in some of the documents for objections properly I related to the grounds for refusal contained in Sched 1, para 5 (3); but we find nothing in the decision letter itself to indicate that the committee founded upon any of the doubtfully relevant material in arriving at their decision. It is also true that very little of what was contained in the documents listed would amount to evidence in a court of law; but a licensing authority exercising its functions under this Schedule to the 1982 Act is not obliged to confine its attention only to material which would be admissible as evidence in a J court of law. Indeed neither party suggested otherwise to this court. Accordingly, the committee were entitled to attach weight to such of this material as was relevant to any of the grounds of refusal which they were statutorily obliged to consider. In our opinion, it has not been shown that the committee fell into error by considering these documents. We should also add that we consider that the sheriff in his fuller treatment of the details of these productions did not fall into error. The second ground of appeal accordingly fails. K

[His Lordship considered, and rejected, the remaining grounds of appeal and concluded:]

In the whole circumstances the present appeal must be refused.

Counsel for Pursuers, Henderson, QC; Solicitors, Cochran, Sayers & Cook (for Gordon & Smyth, Glasgow) — Counsel for First Defenders, Hodge; Soli- L *citors, Simpson & Marwick, WS (for Holmes Mackillop, Johnstone).*

A N

McMonagle v Secretary of State for Scotland

SECOND DIVISION

THE LORD JUSTICE CLERK (ROSS),
LORDS MURRAY AND GRIEVE

5 NOVEMBER 1992

Compulsory powers — Purchase — Power to acquire land for development — Power to acquire land in interests of proper planning — Whether powers mutually exclusive — Town and Country Planning (Scotland) Act 1972 (c 52), s 102 (1).

Compulsory powers — Purchase — Objections to order — Inquiry — Appeal — Other development possible for site but proposal the only one acceptable to local authority to secure proper planning of area — Whether purpose of acquisition "necessary" in interests of proper planning — Town and Country Planning (Scotland) Act 1972 (c 52), s 102 (1).

A local authority may acquire land compulsorily under s 102 (1) (a) of the Town and Country Planning (Scotland) Act 1972 if it is required for development, and under s 102 (1) (b) if it is required for a purpose which it is necessary to achieve in the interests of the proper planning of an area in which the land is situated.

The Secretary of State confirmed a compulsory purchase order which authorised the acquisition of certain subjects by a district council "for the purpose of a commercial and retail development which it is necessary to achieve in the interests of the proper planning of the area in which the land is situated". An inquiry was held before a reporter who concluded that the order had been justified in terms of both s 102 (1) (a) and (b). In an appeal against the Secretary of State's decision, the appellant argued that the order could be made only under one or other of paras (a) and (b) and that it had been promoted and expressed as falling under s 102 (1) (b). The council accordingly required to show that the development was necessary for the area's proper planning, yet the Secretary of State had concluded only that the council's proposal would make good and effective use of the site, which was not the same thing.

Held, (1) that an order could fall under both s 102 (1) (a) and (b), and that it was apparent from the purpose stated in the order, and in particular from the use of the word "development", that it had been made under both paras (a) and (b) (p 808K-L); and (2) that, in any event, while it was true that the reporter, whose conclusion had been adopted by the Secretary of State, had acknowledged that the development was not "necessary" in the sense that there was no possible alternative development of the site, he had found that the council's proposal was necessary to achieve the proper planning of the area because it was the only proposal which was acceptable to the planning authority to achieve that result (p 809F-H); and appeal *refused*.

Appeal from the Secretary of State for Scotland

Edward Joseph McMonagle brought an appeal under para 15 of Sched 1 to the Acquisition of Land (Authorisation Procedure) (Scotland) Act 1947, against the decision of the Secretary of State for Scotland of 5 July 1991, to confirm the Argyle Street / West Campbell Street / Holm Street / Blythswood Street Compulsory Order 1989, which had been made by the City of Glasgow District Council. The Secretary of State and the council were the first and second respondents respectively.

Statutory provisions

The Town and Country Planning (Scotland) Act 1972 (as amended by s 92 (4) of the Local Government, Planning and Land Act 1980) provides:

"102.—(1) A local authority to whom this subsection applies shall, on being authorised to do so by the Secretary of State, have power to acquire compulsorily — (a) any land within their area which is suitable for and is required in order to secure the carrying out of one or more of the following activities, namely, development, redevelopment and improvement; (b) any land which is in their area and which is required for a purpose which it is necessary to achieve in the interests of the proper planning of an area in which the land is situated.

"(1A) A local authority and the Secretary of State in considering for the purposes of subsection (1) (a) above whether land is suitable for development, redevelopment or improvement shall have regard — (a) to the provisions of the development plan, so far as material; (b) to whether planning permission for any development on the land is in force; and (c) to any other consideration which, on an application for planning permission for development on the land, would be material for the purpose of determining that application."

Case referred to

Sharkey v Secretary of State for the Environment (1990) 2 EGLR 191; (1991) 63 P & CR 332.

The appeal was heard before the Second Division on 15 and 16 October 1992.

On 5 November 1992 the court *refused* the appeal.

The following opinion of the court was delivered by the Lord Justice Clerk (Ross):

OPINION OF THE COURT.—This is an appeal at the instance of Edward Joseph McMonagle against a decision of the first respondent dated 5 July 1991 to confirm the Argyle Street / West Campbell Street / Holm Street / Blythswood Street Compulsory Order 1989 (hereinafter referred to as "the order"). In the appeal, the appellant is inviting the court to quash the order upon the view that the first respondent was not empowered to grant authorisation to the order.

In presenting the appeal on behalf of the appellant, counsel drew attention to the terms of the order as confirmed by the first respondent. He emphasised that

the second respondents had purported to make the
order in exercise of the powers conferred on them by
s 102 of the Town and Country Planning Scotland)
Act 1972. He also stressed that the order authorised
the second respondents to purchase the land compulsorily "for the purpose of the erection of a commercial
and retail development which it is necessary to achieve
in the interests of the proper planning of the area in
which the land is situated".

Section 102 (1) of the Town and Country Planning
(Scotland) Act 1972 (as amended by s 92 (4) of the
Local Government, Planning and Land Act 1980)
provides as follows: [his Lordship quoted its terms
and continued:]

Section 92 (4) of the Act of 1980 also introduced a
new s 102 (1A) to the Act of 1972. Section 102 (1A)
is in the following terms: [his Lordship quoted its
terms and continued:]

Counsel for the appellant drew attention to the fact
that in part II of his report, the reporter expressed his
conclusion that the second respondents had been justified in making the order in terms of s 102 (1) (a) and
(b) of the Act of 1972 (para 15.21). Similarly in his
decision letter in para 14, the first respondent stated
inter alia: "In the circumstances the Secretary of State
is satisfied that the Council have justified the making
of the Order in terms of s 102 (1) (a) and (b) of the
1972 Act."

Counsel submitted that the true position was that
the second respondents had promoted the order under
s 102 (1) (b) and not s 102 (1) (a) of the Act of 1972;
and it was not the case that they had made the order
under both these paragraphs. His next submission was
that since the second respondents had promoted the
order under s 102 (1) (b) they had to show that the
mixed commercial and retail development proposed
by the Scottish Development Agency (SDA) referred
to by the reporter was necessary for the proper planning of the area. He contended that the second respondents had failed to establish that.

In support of his submissions counsel stressed that
the appearance in the order of the words "which it is
necessary to achieve in the interests of the proper planning of the area in which the land is situated" made
it clear that the order was being made under s 102 (1)
(b) and not s 102 (1) (a); the language used echoed
s 102 (1) (b). He further maintained that an order
could not be made under both paragraphs. He
accepted that there was an overlap between the two
paragraphs, but he maintained that they were distinctive, and that the second respondents had chosen to go
down one particular road. Section 102 (1) (a) referred
to the carrying out of the activities of development,
redevelopment and improvement, whereas he submitted that s 102 (1) (b) encompassed activities other
than development, redevelopment and improvement
although it could include development. Having regard
to the language used he contended that the activities
referred to in s 102 (1) (a) need not be shown to be for
a purpose which it is necessary to achieve in the
interests of proper planning, whereas if the order was

made under s 102 (1) (b) it must be demonstrated that
the land was required for a purpose which it is necessary to achieve in the interests of proper planning.
This meant that if the order was made under s 102 (1)
(b) it was necessary to consider the whole area within
which the development was taking place. He also
stressed that s 102 (1A) applied only to orders made
under s 102 (1) (a), and this emphasised the difference
between the two paragraphs.

Counsel for the appellant accepted that the second
respondents could have made the order in terms of
s 102 (1) (a) but he maintained that they had not done
so; they had proceeded solely under s 102 (1) (b) and
this meant that the tests contained in s 102 (1) (b)
required to be satisfied.

Counsel on behalf of the first respondent maintained that it was wrong to hold that the order had
been made solely in terms of s 102 (1) (b) and not
under s 102 (1) (a). He submitted that there might be
cases which fell under only s 102 (1) (a) or s 102 (1) (b),
but he also contended that there might be cases which
fell under both paragraphs, and he stated that the
present case was such a one. He emphasised that the
order had been stated to be "for the purpose of the
erection of a commercial and retail development" and
he maintained that the use of the word "development"
showed that it fell under s 102 (1) (a). He also drew
attention to the fact that the second respondents in
making the order purported to be exercising the
powers conferred upon them by s 102, and he drew
attention to p 4 of the reporter's report in para 1.2
where it is recorded that the latest statement of reasons
for making the order dated 18 May 1990 reads as
follows: "This application is submitted in terms of
Section 102 (1) (a) and (b) of the Town and Country
Planning (Scotland) Act 1972".

Counsel for the first respondent also drew attention
to the fact that the inquiry had obviously taken place
upon the basis that both s 102 (1) (a) and s 102 (1) (b)
applied and he accordingly submitted that counsel for
the appellant's first submission was not well founded.

Although counsel for the appellant presented his
submission most persuasively, we have come to be of
opinion that in this respect counsel for the first
respondent's contentions are to be preferred. The
order bears to have been made by the second respondents in exercise of the powers conferred on them by
s 102 of the Act of 1972 and not only under part of
s 102. Although when the purpose of the order is
stated, the language used in s 102 (1) (b) is repeated,
we agree with counsel that the use of the word
"development" in this connection can be taken as
referring to s 102 (1) (a). If it had simply been stated
that the authority to purchase was "for the purpose of
the erection of a commercial and retail development",
there could be little doubt that that would fall to be
construed as a reference to the power contained in
s 102 (1) (a).

We see no reason why an order should not be made
by an authority exercising power under both s 102 (1)
(a) and 102 (1) (b). Both the reporter and the Secretary

of State proceeded upon the basis that the order was
A made in terms of s 102 (1) (a) and s 102 (1) (b) of the
Act of 1972, and in our opinion they were justified in
so concluding.

Counsel for the appellant's second submission was
based upon the assumption that he was well founded
in his contention that the order should be regarded as
having been made under s 102 (1) (b) only. For the
reasons given above we are not satisfied that that
assumption is well founded. However, even if the
order fell to be regarded as having been made solely
B under s 102 (1) (b) we are not persuaded that counsel
is correct in his submission that it had not been established that the land was required for a purpose which
it was necessary to achieve in the interests of proper
planning. Both parties referred to *Sharkey v Secretary
of State for the Environment*. However, that case was
concerned with the meaning of "required" in the
section of the English Act which is equivalent to
s 102. What is put in issue in the present case is not
the meaning of the word "required" but what is meant
C by the word "necessary" in s 102 (1) (b). In submitting
that it has not been demonstrated that the land was
required for a purpose which it was necessary to
achieve in the interests of proper planning, counsel
founded upon a passage in para 14 of the decision
letter. It is therein stated inter alia: "Although accepting the argument that the proposed commercial and
retail development is not necessary in the sense that
there is no known developer for the site, or that an
alternative may equally be acceptable".

D Counsel maintained that that passage showed that it
had not been shown that the land was required for a
purpose which was necessary. He went on to point out
that in para 14, the first respondent goes on to say:
"The Secretary of State agrees with the Reporter that,
in order to achieve the proper planning of the area, the
SDA proposal, which is at present the only acceptable
development, could solve the need to make good and
effective use of a key site from which the wider public
E would benefit in terms of visual amenity, employment
and impact in the City's fast growing, revitalised
character."

Counsel for the appellant maintained that if the
most that could be said was that acquisition of the land
could solve the need to make good and effective use of
the site, that fell short of establishing that the land was
required for a purpose which it was necessary to
achieve in the interests of proper planning.

F We have come to the conclusion that to read these
passages in that way is to read them too narrowly. Part
of the problem appears to be that in para 14 the first
respondent has paraphrased and not accurately
repeated what was stated by the reporter. However, in
para 12 of the decision letter, the first respondent
states that he accepts the reporter's findings of fact and
agrees with his reasoning, views and opinions in his
conclusions and recommendation; he also states that
he adopts them for the purpose of his own decision.
When one looks at the reporter's report in order to
ascertain what his conclusions were, it is clear from

para 15.19 that the reporter did conclude that the
development was necessary within the meaning of G
s 102 (1) (b). What the reporter said in this connection
is: "Although I accept that there is an argument that
the commercial and retail development proposed is
not 'necessary' in the sense that, at present, there is
no known developer, or that some other form of development might be equally acceptable, it is necessary to
achieve the proper planning of the area in that it
relates to the only proposal so far acceptable to the
planning authority to secure that end result — an end
result which would solve a need to make good and H
effective use of a key site from which the wider public
would benefit in terms of visual amenity, employment
and its impact on the City's fast growing, revitalised
character of zest and enhancement."

It thus seems plain that the reporter did conclude
that the land was required for a purpose which it was
necessary to achieve in the interests of proper planning. Accordingly we are satisfied that both the
reporter and the first respondent were entitled to be
satisfied that the second respondents had justified the I
making of the order in terms of both s 102 (1) (a) and
s 102 (1) (b) of the Act of 1972. For the foregoing
reasons the appeal is refused.

---

*Counsel for Appellant, Boyd; Solicitors, Allan
McDougall & Co — Counsel for First Respondent, Fitz-
patrick; Solicitor, R Brodie, Solicitor to the Secretary of
State for Scotland — Counsel for Second Respondents
(Local Authority), Raeburn, QC; Solicitors, Simpson & J
Marwick, WS.*

M G J U

Burns v Wilson

HIGH COURT OF JUSTICIARY   K
THE LORD JUSTICE CLERK (ROSS),
LORDS MURRAY, McCLUSKEY,
MORISON AND PROSSER
12 MARCH 1993

*Justiciary — Procedure — Summary procedure — Sent-
ence — Adjournment before sentence — Accused pleading
guilty and sheriff purporting to defer sentence to obtain
DVLC printout for period exceeding 21 days — Whether
accused convicted prior to date to which diet incom- L
petently adjourned — Whether conviction ought to be
suspended as well as sentence — Criminal Procedure
(Scotland) Act 1975 (c 21), s 380 (1).*

Section 380 (1) of the Criminal Procedure (Scotland)
Act 1975 provides that a court of summary jurisdiction has power, after a person has been convicted or
the court has found that he committed the offence and
before he has been sentenced or otherwise dealt with,
to adjourn the case for the purpose of enabling
inquiries to be made or of determining the most suit-

A able method of dealing with his case, provided that the court shall not adjourn the hearing of the case for a single period exceeding three weeks.

An accused person pled guilty on 2 March 1992 to two charges on a summary complaint libelling contraventions of the Road Traffic Act 1988, and the sheriff, since any driving licence held by the accused was liable to endorsement, purported to defer sentence until 22 April 1992 for the purposes of obtaining a printout from DVLC. On 22 April 1992 the accused submitted that further proceedings were incompetent B as sentence had been deferred for longer than 21 days. The sheriff held the deferment to be competent and sentenced the accused, who sought suspension of the conviction and sentence on the ground that the sheriff ought to have dismissed the complaint. The Crown admitted that the sheriff had no power either under statute or at common law to adjourn the diet for a period exceeding 21 days to allow production of a printout, but contended that no order should be made in respect of the conviction. The accused argued that C he had not been convicted prior to the date to which the diet had been incompetently adjourned.

Held (by a bench of five judges), (1) that where a plea of guilty or a finding of guilty had been recorded in the minutes of procedure and the court had adjourned the hearing of the case for the purpose of enabling inquiries to be made in terms of s 380 (1) or had deferred sentence in terms of s 432 (1) then, unless the minutes made it clear that disposal by absolute dis-D charge or a probation order was still in contemplation, the accused had to be regarded as having been convicted (p 813B); (2) that as there was nothing in the minute to suggest that the accused might still receive an absolute discharge or be placed on probation, he had been convicted on 2 March 1992 of the charges to which he had pled guilty (p 813D); (3) that it was not competent for the sheriff to proceed to sentence but that incompetence did not extend retrospectively to the conviction, which remained in force (p 813F); and E sentence *suspended* but quoad ultra bill *refused*.

Wilson v Donald, 1993 SLT 31, *overruled in part*; *Tennant v Houston*, 1987 SLT 317, *Bassi v Normand*, 1992 SLT 341 and *Geddes v Hamilton*, 1986 SLT 536, *followed*.

Observed, that where the court decided to adjourn under s 380 (1) while disposal by absolute discharge or a probation order was still being contemplated, the entry in the minutes could conveniently read: "The court before proceeding to conviction adjourned under F s 380 (1) of the Criminal Procedure (Scotland) Act 1975 for the purpose of obtaining a printout from DVLC", to put the matter beyond doubt (p 813E).

Bill of suspension

John Burns brought a bill of suspension against A T W Wilson, procurator fiscal, Airdrie, praying the High Court of Justiciary to suspend a pretended conviction and sentence dated 2 March 1992 whereby

sheriff Marcus I Green, in respect of pleas of guilty which were accepted by the Crown, purported to defer G sentence until 22 April 1992 for the purpose of obtaining a printout from DVLC.

Statement of facts and pleas in law

The bill and the answers were in the following terms:

Stat 1. The complainer is John Burns who pleaded guilty on 2 March 1992 in the sheriff court at Airdrie to four charges on a summary complaint, said complaint being produced herewith.   H

Ans 1. Admitted.

Stat 2. On conviction on both said offences any driving licence held or to be held by the complainer was liable to endorsement in terms of s 44 of the Road Traffic Offenders Act 1988. Sentence was deferred for the purposes of obtaining a printout from DVLC until 22 April 1992. On that date the agent who appeared on the complainer's behalf maintained that further proceedings on the said complaint were incompetent. I A hearing for debate was fixed for 23 April 1992 and the complainer was subsequently sentenced on 29 April 1992 to the following sentences namely charge 1 — fine of £10, charge 2 — fine of £80 and nine months' disqualification, charge 3 — fine of £10, charge 4 — fine of £10.

Ans 2. Admitted.

Stat 3. The decision of the said sheriff was erroneous and contrary to law. The learned sheriff had no power J either by means of statute in terms of s 380 of the Criminal Procedure (Scotland) Act 1975 nor by any power at common law to adjourn the diet for such a period as he saw fit to allow the document specified in s 32 of the Road Traffic Offenders Act 1988 to be produced to the court. It is submitted that no further proceedings were competent on said complaint and such complaint ought to have been dismissed.

Ans 3. Admitted that the decision of the said sheriff was erroneous and contrary to law. Admitted that said K sheriff had no power under statute or at common law to adjourn the diet for a period longer than 21 days to allow the production of a printout from the Drivers and Vehicle Licensing Centre. Quoad ultra denied. Averred that although said sheriff had no power to proceed to sentence the complainer he was not entitled in the circumstances to dismiss the complaint.

The plea in law for the complainer was as follows:

The decision of the sheriff on 29 April 1992 holding L that further proceedings on the said complaint were competent being erroneous and contrary to law, should be recalled and the complaint dismissed.

The pleas in law for the respondent were as follows:

(1) The decision of the sheriff on 29 April 1992 holding that further proceedings on said complaint were competent being erroneous and contrary to law, should be recalled and the sentence passed on that date quashed.

(2) Proceedings on said complaint prior to 29 April
1992 not being tainted by said erroneous decision on
that date, no order should be made in respect of the
conviction.

Statutory provisions

The Criminal Procedure (Scotland) Act 1975
provides:

"380.—(1) It is hereby declared that the power of a
court to adjourn the hearing of a case includes power,
after a person has been convicted or the court has
found that he committed the offence and before he has
been sentenced or otherwise dealt with, to adjourn the
case for the purpose of enabling inquiries to be made
or of determining the most suitable method of dealing
with his case and where the court so adjourns the case
it shall remand the accused in custody or on bail or
ordain him to appear at the adjourned diet; Provided
that a court shall not for the purpose aforesaid adjourn
the hearing of a case for a single period exceeding
three weeks. . . .

"432.—(1) It shall be competent for a court to defer
sentence after conviction for a period and on such conditions as the court may determine; and the fact that
the accused has been convicted shall not prevent the
court from making, in due course, a probation order
under section 384 of this Act."

Cases referred to

Advocate (HM) v Clegg, 1991 SLT 192; 1990 JC 318;
1990 SCCR 293.
Bassi v Normand, 1992 SLT 341; 1992 SCCR 413.
Geddes v Hamilton, 1986 SLT 536; 1986 SCCR 165.
MacNeill v MacGregor, 1975 SLT (Notes) 46; 1975 JC
55.
McPherson v Henderson, 1984 SCCR 294.
Normand v Freeman, 1992 SLT 598; 1992 SCCR 417.
Tennant v Houston, 1987 SLT 317; 1986 SCCR 556.
Tudhope v Cullen, 1982 SCCR 276.
Tudhope (P F (Glasgow)) v MacCauley, High Court of
Justiciary, 28 October 1980, reported as an
appendix to *Tudhope v Cullen* at 1982 SCCR 276.
Wilson v Donald, 1993 SLT 31; 1992 SCCR 654.

Textbook referred to

Renton and Brown, *Criminal Procedure* (5th ed), para
15-18.

The bill was heard before a court of five judges on
18 February 1993.

On 12 March 1993 the court *suspended* the sentence
but quoad ultra *refused* to pass the bill.

The following opinion of the court was delivered by
the Lord Justice Clerk (Ross):

OPINION OF THE COURT.—The complainer is
John Burns who was charged in the sheriff court at
Airdrie on a complaint at the instance of the respondent containing four charges, two of which were
stated in the alternative. On 2 March 1992 the complainer pled guilty to charge 1, to the first alternative

of charge 2, to the first alternative of charge 3, and to
charge 4. The charges all libelled contraventions of
various sections of the Road Traffic Act 1988. As any
driving licence held by the complainer was liable to
endorsement in terms of s 44 of the Road Traffic
Offenders Act 1988, the sheriff purported to defer
sentence for the purposes of obtaining a printout from
DVLC until 22 April 1992.

On 22 April 1992, the complainer's agent submitted
that further proceedings on the complaint were
incompetent, and a hearing for debate was fixed for 23
April 1992. On that date, after hearing the solicitor for
the complainer and the respondent on the competency
of deferring sentence for longer than 21 days, the
sheriff held the deferring of sentence to be competent.
He then deferred sentence for personal appearance of
the complainer until 29 April 1992, on which date he
proceeded to sentence the complainer.

The complainer has now presented this bill of suspension in which he seeks to have his conviction and
sentence suspended on the ground that the decision of
the sheriff on 23 April 1992 holding further proceedings to be competent was erroneous and contrary to
law. Both in the statement of facts for the complainer
and in his plea in law it is contended that in the circumstances the complaint should have been dismissed
by the sheriff. In the answers lodged on behalf of the
respondent it is admitted that the decision of the
sheriff on 23 April 1992 was erroneous and contrary
to law, and that the sheriff had no power under statute
or at common law to adjourn the diet for a period
longer than 21 days to allow the production of a printout from the DVLC. It is, however, contended on
behalf of the respondent that although the sheriff had
no power to proceed to sentence the complainer, he
was not entitled to dismiss the complaint. It is clear
from the terms of the pleas in law for the respondent,
that the respondent accepts that the sentence passed
by the sheriff on 29 April 1992 should be quashed, but
that he maintains that no order should be made in
respect of conviction.

Having regard to the terms of the statement of facts
for the complainer and the answers for the respondent,
it is accordingly clear that the sole issue between them
is whether both conviction and sentence should be
quashed and the complaint dismissed or whether it is
only the sentence which should be quashed. In
moving the court to pass the bill, counsel for the complainer reminded us that it was admitted by the
respondent that the sheriff had no power under statute
or at common law to adjourn the diet for a period
longer than 21 days to allow the production of a printout from DVLC. Although the sheriff had purported
on 2 March 1992 to defer sentence for the purpose of
obtaining the printout, the Crown accepted that what
he had in fact done was to adjourn the diet for a period
in excess of 21 days. Having regard to the provisions
of s 380 (1) of the Criminal Procedure (Scotland) Act
1975, this was something which he had no power to
do. Section 380 (1) of the Act of 1975 is in the following terms: [his Lordship quoted the terms of the subsection and continued:]

Having regard to these provisions counsel for the
A complainer maintained that on 23 April the sheriff
ought to have held that the deferring of sentence on 2
March 1992 for longer than 21 days was incompetent.
He further submitted that since the matter could not
have proceeded further, the sheriff ought to have dismissed the complaint.

Counsel submitted that the Crown were ill founded
in claiming that no order should be made in respect of
conviction because there was not in the circumstances
any conviction. The complainer had pled guilty to
B four charges, but the court had not imposed sentence;
there could be no conviction without sentence. In
s 380 (1) reference is made to the stage "after a person
has been convicted or the court has found that he committed the offence". That clearly showed there was a
distinction between being convicted and being found
to have committed the offence.

Counsel maintained that if the court exercised its
power to adjourn for the purpose of enabling inquiries
C to be made in terms of s 380 (1), the result at the end
of the day might be that the accused was placed on
probation or given an absolute discharge without the
court proceeding to conviction (ss 383 and 384 of the
Criminal Procedure (Scotland) Act 1975; Renton &
Brown's *Criminal Procedure* (5th ed), para 15-18). He
submitted that this showed clearly that when the court
exercised its power to adjourn the hearing of a case
under s 380 (1) for the purpose of enabling inquiries
to be made or of determining the most suitable method
D of dealing with the accused, there could be no question
of the accused being convicted so long as there
remained a possibility of his being placed on probation
or given an absolute discharge. Counsel also sought
support for his argument from the provisions of s 46
(3) of the Road Traffic Offenders Act 1988 which provides that where the court has granted an absolute discharge or made a probation order in respect of a
person, he shall be treated as if he had been convicted
of an offence for the purposes of disqualification and
E endorsements under the Road Traffic Acts.

Counsel for the complainer submitted that in determining whether or not a conviction had taken place,
it was relevant to consider whether an accused who
had pled guilty could change his plea. In this connection he referred to *MacNeill v MacGregor* and *P F
(Glasgow) v MacCauley* (28 October 1980), reported in
Tudhope v Cullen. In *MacNeill v MacGregor* the court
held that it was not competent for a sheriff to allow a
plea of guilty to be withdrawn after the sheriff had
F convicted the accused and proceeded to sentence him,
since the sheriff had thereby become functus. In *P F
(Glasgow) v MacCauley* the sheriff did allow a plea of
guilty to be withdrawn on the view that there could
not be a conviction until the court had decided not to
deal with the accused by absolute discharge or probation.

Counsel for the complainer recognised that there
were a number of cases where the court had quashed
sentences on appeal but had left convictions standing.
These cases were adverse to his submission that there

could be no conviction without sentence, but he
sought to distinguish these cases. One such case was G
Tennant v Houston. In that case the complainer had
appealed against conviction and sentence by bill of
suspension, but in the course of the hearing counsel
for the complainer conceded that since the complainer
had pled guilty there could be no question of the court
suspending his conviction. In *Bassi v Normand* the
appellant had appealed against conviction and sentence by stated case, and it could not accordingly be
suggested that he had not been convicted. In *Normand
v Freeman* the sheriff had made an order deferring H
sentence under s 432 (1) of the Criminal Procedure
(Scotland) Act 1975. Such a deferment is competent
only after conviction, and accordingly the case is
different to the present case where it is not disputed
that what the sheriff had been doing was exercising a
power under s 380 (1) of the Act of 1975.

At the end of the day counsel maintained that the
case of *Wilson v Donald* had been correctly decided,
and that the sheriff in the present case ought to have
done what the sheriff had done in *Wilson v Donald*, I
namely, to have held that the provisions of s 380 (1)
had been contravened and should have dismissed the
complaint.

The Lord Advocate in responding to the appeal conceded that it was difficult to reconcile all the relevant
statutory provisions, and that it was not easy to determine precisely when an accused person had been convicted within the meaning of the statute. In the
present case the minutes of procedure showed that J
pleas of guilty had been recorded, but the mere recording of a plea of guilty could not constitute a conviction
since a sheriff in his discretion may allow a plea of
guilty to be withdrawn. Moreover whether there has
been a plea of guilty or a finding of guilty, that cannot
amount to a conviction unless the court has decided
not to deal with the accused by absolute discharge or
probation since for either of these disposals under
summary procedure the court does not proceed to conviction.

K

The Lord Advocate contended that in the present
case the complainer had been convicted. He had tendered pleas of guilty which had been recorded. The
matter did not end there because the minutes of procedure showed that the court had thereafter purported to
defer sentence for the purpose of obtaining a printout
from DVLC. Section 432 (1) of the Criminal Procedure (Scotland) Act 1975 provides: [his Lordship
quoted the terms of s 432 (1) and continued:]

In the present case, however, where purported L
deferral was for the purpose of obtaining a printout,
it was clear that what the sheriff was doing was in fact
exercising his power under s 380 (1) to adjourn the
hearing of the case for the purpose of enabling
inquiries to be made or of determining the most suitable method of dealing with the complainer's case.
Whether under solemn or summary procedure, it was
necessary to distinguish between deferment and
adjournment (*HM Advocate v Clegg*). The Lord
Advocate indicated that it would be difficult to suggest

that the purported deferral here was a competent deferral under s 432, and as we have already observed the answers proceed upon the basis that the sheriff had been proceeding under s 380 (1) and not s 432 (1). However, since the sheriff had purported to defer sentence under s 432, that clearly implied that the sheriff had convicted and was embarking on the sentencing process. For the purpose of appeal against conviction the case was deemed to be finally determined on the date on which sentence was deferred (s 451 (3) of the Act of 1975).

In our opinion where a plea of guilty or a finding of guilty has been recorded in the minutes of procedure, and the court has adjourned the hearing of the case for the purpose of enabling inquiries to be made in terms of s 380 (1) or has deferred sentence in terms of s 432 (1), then unless the minutes make it clear that disposal by absolute discharge or a probation order is still in contemplation, the accused must be regarded as having been convicted.

"A decision not to proceed to conviction is an exceptional step which the court is entitled to take only if it is to make a particular disposal which it has in mind. In practice it is necessary for a sheriff who decides that such a disposal ought to be made to declare that he is not proceeding to conviction and the style of minutes in use in 1964 made special provision for such a situation" (*McPherson v Henderson*, per Lord Justice General at p 298).

In the present case pleas of guilty were recorded and the court purported to defer sentence for the purpose of obtaining a printout. As already pointed out what the court in fact was doing was exercising its power under s 380 (1) to adjourn the hearing of the case for inquiries to be made. All that was being sought was a printout, and there is nothing in the minute to suggest that the complainer might still receive an absolute discharge or be placed on probation. Accordingly in our judgment he had on that date been convicted of the offences to which he had pled guilty.

However, in any similar case in future where the sheriff decides to adjourn under s 380 (1) while disposal by absolute discharge or a probation order is still being contemplated, the entry in the minutes might conveniently read: "The court before proceeding to conviction adjourned under s 380 (1) of the Criminal Procedure (Scotland) Act 1975 for the purpose of obtaining a printout from DVLC". This would put the matter beyond doubt.

Because the court failed to comply with the requirements in the proviso to s 380 (1) the adjournment was incompetent (*Wilson v Donald*). That being so it was not competent for the sheriff to proceed to sentence. Accordingly the sentence which the sheriff did impose now falls to be suspended.

However the incompetence does not extend retrospectively to the conviction which remains in force (*Tennant v Houston*; *Bassi v Normand*; *Geddes v Hamilton*).

In *Wilson v Donald* which was a Crown appeal by way of bill of advocation, the sheriff had dismissed the complaint. The Crown sought to have the case remitted to the sheriff to proceed to sentence but it does not appear to have been contended in the alternative that the sheriff should not have dismissed the complaint but should have left the conviction standing. Insofar as the court in *Wilson v Donald* appears to have accepted that the sheriff was well founded in dismissing the complaint, we are of opinion that *Wilson v Donald* was wrongly decided.

We shall accordingly pass the bill insofar as it seeks suspension of the sentence, and we shall suspend the sentence, but quoad ultra we shall refuse to pass the bill.

Counsel for Complainer, Drummond, QC; Solicitors, John G Gray & Co, SSC (for Robert Carty & Co, Cumbernauld) — Counsel for Respondent, Lord Advocate (Lord Rodger of Earlsferry, QC); Solicitor, J D Lowe, Crown Agent.

P W F

Holburn v Lees

HIGH COURT OF JUSTICIARY

THE LORD JUSTICE CLERK (ROSS), LORDS MURRAY, McCLUSKEY, MORISON AND PROSSER

12 MARCH 1993

Justiciary — Procedure — Summary procedure — Sentence — Adjournment before sentence — Accused found guilty after trial and sheriff purporting to defer sentence to obtain DVLC printout for period exceeding 21 days — Accused legally represented but not objecting to deferment — Whether accused could waive compliance with statutory time limit — Whether accused had waived compliance — Criminal Procedure (Scotland) Act 1975 (c 21), s 380 (1).

Section 380 (1) of the Criminal Procedure (Scotland) Act 1975 provides that a court of summary jurisdiction has power, after a person has been convicted or the court has found that he committed the offence and before he has been sentenced or otherwise dealt with, to adjourn the case for the purpose of enabling inquiries to be made or of determining the most suitable method of dealing with his case, provided that the court shall not for that purpose adjourn the hearing for a single period exceeding three weeks.

An accused person was found guilty after trial on 5 November 1990 of a contravention of s 3 of the Road Traffic Act 1988. The sheriff then purported to defer sentence until 17 December 1990 in order to obtain a DVLC printout. The accused was thereafter fined on 17 December 1990 and sought suspension of both conviction and sentence on the ground that the purported deferment of sentence on 5 November 1990 was incompetent as being in breach of the provisions of s 380 (1). The Crown contended, inter alia, that the accused, who had been legally represented before the sheriff, had waived compliance with s 380 (1) by not objecting to the adjournment on 5 November 1990 and that he was therefore personally barred from insisting in the bill.

Held (by a bench of five judges), (1) that the accused was convicted on 5 November 1990 and the case was thereafter adjourned before sentence under s 380 (1) (*Burns v Wilson*, 1993 SLT 809, *followed*) (p 815C-F); (2) that an accused could waive compliance with the terms of certain statutory provisions but whether or not there had been waiver depended upon the circumstances of the particular case (p 815I); (3) that as there was no suggestion on 5 November 1990 that the court was invoking s 380 (1) there was no basis in fact for waiver as the accused had no reason to take objection (p 815J-K); and sentence *suspended* but quoad ultra bill *refused*.

***

Bill of suspension

Kenneth Holburn brought a bill of suspension against Robert F Lees, procurator fiscal, Edinburgh, praying the High Court of Justiciary to suspend a pretended conviction and sentence dated 17 December 1990 whereby Sheriff C N R Stein found the complainer guilty of a contravention of s 3 of the Road Traffic Act 1988 and fined him. The facts of the case appear from the opinion of the court.

Statutory provisions

The Criminal Procedure (Scotland) Act 1975 provides:

"380.—(1) It is hereby declared that the power of a court to adjourn the hearing of a case includes power, after a person has been convicted or the court has found that he committed the offence and before he has been sentenced or otherwise dealt with, to adjourn the case for the purpose of enabling inquiries to be made or of determining the most suitable method of dealing with his case and where the court so adjourns the case it shall remand the accused in custody or on bail or ordain him to appear at the adjourned diet; Provided that a court shall not for the purpose aforesaid adjourn the hearing of a case for a single period exceeding three weeks."

Cases referred to

Advocate (HM) v McDonald, 1984 SLT 426; 1984 SCCR 229.
Burns v Wilson, 1993 SLT 809; 1993 SCCR 418.
Cordiner v HM Advocate, 1993 SLT 2; 1991 SCCR 652.
Lowson v HM Advocate, 1944 SLT 74; (sub nom *HM Advocate v Lowson*) 1943 JC 141.
Wilson v Donald, 1993 SLT 31; 1992 SCCR 654.

Bill

The bill was heard in the High Court on 18 February 1993.

On 12 March 1993 the court *suspended* the sentence but quoad ultra *refused* to pass the bill.

The following opinion of the court was delivered by the Lord Justice Clerk (Ross):

OPINION OF THE COURT.—The complainer is Kenneth Holburn who went to trial in the sheriff court at Edinburgh on a summary complaint at the instance of the respondent libelling a contravention of s 3 of the Road Traffic Act 1988. At the conclusion of the prosecution case, a submission of no case to answer was made on behalf of the complainer. The sheriff repelled the submission. Thereafter further evidence was led and concluded, and after hearing the respondent and the solicitor for the complainer the sheriff found the complainer guilty as libelled. Neither the complainer's driving licence nor a printout from the DVLC was available for production to the sheriff, and in the statement of facts for the complainer it is stated that the sheriff adjourned the diet until 17 December 1990 for the purpose of obtaining such a printout. On said date the sheriff sentenced the complainer by imposing a fine of £75 and ordering eight penalty points to be endorsed on his driving licence. The complainer appealed against both conviction and sentence by way of stated case, but subsequently abandoned that appeal. In the present proceedings it is contended that the sheriff's actings by way of adjourning the diet for the purposes of obtaining a printout for a period in excess of 21 days were incompetent having regard to the provisions of s 380 (1) of the Criminal Procedure (Scotland) Act 1975.

Section 380 (1) of the Act of 1975 is in the following terms: [his Lordship quoted the terms of s 380 (1) set out supra and continued:]

In the answers to the bill, the respondent avers that the sheriff had in the circumstances both a common law power and a statutory power to defer sentence on the complainer for such period as he saw fit. The respondent also pleads that esto the continuation from 5 November 1990 to 17 December 1990 fell within the terms of s 380 (1), failure to comply with the terms of that subsection did not render further proceedings incompetent. He claims that in the circumstances as the complainer raised no objection to the continuation on 5 November 1990 or on 17 December 1990, the complainer has waived compliance with s 380 (1) and is personally barred from bringing the present bill. He also contends that in any event a conviction was properly recorded against the complainer on 5 November 1990, and that the conviction should not be quashed.

For reasons similar to those expressed in *Burns v Wilson* we are satisfied that although the minutes of procedure show that the sheriff purported to defer sentence in this case on 5 November 1990, he was in fact adjourning the case before sentence. A distinction falls

A to be drawn between adjourning a case before sentence under s 380 (1) and deferring sentence after conviction in terms of s 432 (1) of the Act of 1975.

In the present case the Lord Advocate who appeared on behalf of the respondent explained that he accepted that distinction and that, despite the terms of the answers, he was not suggesting that the sheriff at the time had been exercising a common law power or a statutory power to defer sentence. Since the purported deferral of sentence had been for the purpose of obtaining a printout, the Lord Advocate accepted that B what the sheriff had in fact been doing had been adjourning the case for the purpose of enabling inquiries to be made in terms of s 380 (1).

We understand both counsel for the complainer and the Lord Advocate to accept that the situation was covered by the case of *Wilson v Donald*. Both counsel for the complainer and the Lord Advocate were agreed that *Wilson v Donald* contained a correct statement of the law, the only difference between them being as to C whether the court in *Wilson v Donald* had been correct in holding that it had been appropriate for the sheriff in that case to dismiss the complaint.

For the reasons which we have given in *Burns v Wilson*, we are satisfied that the sentence in the present case falls to be suspended. Counsel for the complainer also submitted that the conviction fell to be suspended whereas the Lord Advocate contended that the conviction should still stand. Counsel's sub-mission was that there had been no conviction in this D case. He recognised that this submission was inconsis-tent with the averment in the statement of facts for the complainer: "Therafter the learned sheriff convicted the complainer of the charge as amended". Counsel submitted that we should regard that averment as meaning no more than that the sheriff had purported to convict the complainer of the charge. This matter was also considered in *Burns v Wilson*, and for the reasons given in that case, we are satisfied that the appellant was convicted on 5 November 1990. E Counsel contended that a conviction only arose where there was a finding of guilt and a sentence imposed therein, but that is clearly not so. That a conviction may take place before sentence is imposed is clear from the terms of s 432 (1) which enables a court to defer sentence after conviction. Faced with that difficulty counsel then submitted that a conviction took place where there had been a finding of guilt and a disposal, but for the reasons given in *Burns v Wilson* we are satisfied that once a finding of guilt has been F recorded in the minutes of procedure, and the court has adjourned the hearing of the case for the purpose of enabling inquiries to be made in terms of s 380 (1) or has deferred sentence in terms of s 432 (1), then unless the minute makes it clear that disposal by abso-lute discharge or a probation order is still in contem-plation, the accused must be regarded as having been convicted. We accordingly conclude that in the present case the conviction should stand.

The Lord Advocate contended that in the circum-stances the complainer had waived compliance with

s 380 (1) of the Act of 1975 and that he was thus per-sonally barred from bringing the present bill. It was G not disputed that on 5 November 1990 when the sheriff purported to defer sentence until 17 December 1990 for the purpose of obtaining a printout, the com-plainer raised no objection to that being done. Nor was any objection taken on 17 December 1990 when the sheriff proceeded to impose sentence. The Lord Advocate referred to *Lowson v HM Advocate* which was authority for the view that the prosecutor could waive his objection to the failure of an accused to comply with the provisions of s 36 of the Criminal H Procedure (Scotland) Act 1887 (now to be found in s 82 (2) of the Act of 1975). He contended that just as the prosecutor could waive an objection of that kind, so an accused could waive compliance with s 380 (1); such waiver could be express or implied. Certain objections can be waived by an accused (*HM Advocate v McDonald*; *Cordiner v HM Advocate*). It was further submitted by the Lord Advocate that the complainer had been personally present when the court purported to defer sentence on 5 November 1990, and that this I court should hold that he had impliedly waived com-pliance with s 380 in that no objection was taken by him or on his behalf when the court purported to defer sentence.

We are satisfied that an accused person may waive compliance with the terms of certain statutory pro-visions, but whether or not there has been waiver in any particular case must depend upon the circum-stances. In the present case we are not satisfied that the complainer can be held to have waived compliance J with the provisions of s 380 (1). The Lord Advocate accepted that if there was waiver in this case it would require to have been given at the diet on 5 November 1990, and that by 17 December 1990 it was too late for any waiver to take place. At the diet of 5 November 1990, it appears from the minutes of procedure that what the court purported to do was to defer sentence until 17 December 1990 for the purpose of obtaining a printout. There was no suggestion made at that time that the court was invoking s 380 (1), and accordingly K there is no basis for contending that the complainer waived compliance with that subsection. He had no notice that the court was exercising its power to adjourn the hearing of the case under s 380 (1), and accordingly had no reason to take objection. There is accordingly no basis in fact for the Lord Advocate's contention that the complainer waived compliance with s 380 (1), and no basis for the submission that he is personally barred from bringing the present bill.

In the circumstances we shall accordingly pass the L bill insofar as it seeks suspension of the sentence, and we shall suspend the sentence, but quoad ultra we shall refuse to pass the bill.

Counsel for Complainer, Murray, QC; Solicitors, Gordon McBain & Co — Counsel for Respondent, Lord Advocate (Lord Rodger of Earlsferry, QC); Solicitor, J D Lowe, Crown Agent.

P W F

Douglas v Jamieson;
A **Douglas v Peddie**

HIGH COURT OF JUSTICIARY

THE LORD JUSTICE GENERAL (HOPE),
LORDS ALLANBRIDGE AND COWIE

21 MAY 1993

Justiciary — Procedure — Summary procedure — Sentence — Accused pleading guilty to some charges, not guilty to others and trial diet fixed — Sheriff adjourning diet in
B *respect of guilty plea for period exceeding three weeks — Whether adjournment competent under statute — Whether adjournment competent at common law — Criminal Procedure (Scotland) Act 1975 (c 21), s 380 (1).*

Section 380 (1) of the Criminal Procedure (Scotland) Act 1975 provides that the power of a court to adjourn the hearing of a case includes the power, after a person has been convicted or the court has found that he committed the offence and before he has been sentenced
C or otherwise dealt with, to adjourn the case for the purpose of enabling inquiries to be made or of determining the most suitable method of dealing with his case, provided that a court shall not for the purpose aforesaid adjourn the hearing of a case for a single period exceeding three weeks.

Two accused persons were charged on separate summary complaints. The first accused was charged along with other persons and in due course pled to a contravention of the Misuse of Drugs Act 1971 while
D another person charged on the same complaint pled not guilty. The sheriff deferred sentence on the first accused until the trial of his co-accused and remanded the accused in custody for a period exceeding three weeks. Thereafter the first accused argued that further proceedings were incompetent as the adjournment had been in breach of s 380 (1). The sheriff sustained the objection and discharged the accused without imposing sentence. The second accused was charged with three offences and pled guilty after amendment to two
E of the charges and not guilty to a third charge. The sheriff deferred sentence on the charges to which the second accused had pled guilty as he had to go to trial on the third charge and adjourned the trial diet until a date more than three weeks later. Thereafter the accused proceeded to trial and was found guilty. The sheriff sustained a submission that further proceedings were incompetent in respect of the two charges to which the second accused had pled guilty because the adjournment was in breach of s 380 (1), and imposed
F no sentence on these charges. The procurator fiscal appealed in respect of each accused by bill of advocation.

Held, (1) that the stage which s 380 (1) contemplated was that where the court was in a position to proceed to sentence but found it appropriate to order an adjournment for the purpose only of obtaining more complete information in that regard (p 821F); (2) that in neither case was the sheriff, when deciding to adjourn, giving any consideration to the question of sentence but was in effect postponing the whole ques-

tion as to the appropriate sentence and as to the inquiries which might be relevant to this matter, to a G later date (p 821G); (3) that matters had therefore not yet reached the stage contemplated by s 380 (1), and the adjournments were not for the purpose which it described and were thus not subject to the time limit (p 821H-I); (4) that the court had power to adjourn at common law at any time when necessary and it was that power which the sheriff was exercising so that the whole question of sentence might be considered at a later stage (p 821J); and bills *passed* and cases *remitted* to the sheriffs to proceed as accords.
H

Bruce v Linton (1860) 23 D 85, *applied.*

Observed, that the court had power, when adjourning a case at common law, either to admit the accused to bail or to detain him in custody, the appropriate method of seeking review of a decision to refuse bail being a petition for interim liberation rather than an appeal under s 380 (2) (pp 821L-822B).

I

Bill of advocation

Ian Douglas, procurator fiscal, Alloa, brought a bill of advocation against Ian Jamieson praying the High Court of Justiciary to recall the decision of Sheriff W M Reid dated 22 March 1993 whereby the respondent was discharged on a complaint without sentence being imposed. The complainer also brought a bill against Henry Peddie praying the court to recall the decision of Sheriff P I McKay dated 5 April 1993 whereby the respondent was discharged on two J charges on a complaint without sentence being imposed. The facts of the cases appear from the opinion of the court.

Statutory provisions

The Criminal Justice (Scotland) Act 1949 provided:

"26. It is hereby declared that the power of a court to adjourn the hearing of a case includes power, after a person has been convicted or the court has found that he committed the offence and before he has been K sentenced or otherwise dealt with, to adjourn the case for the purpose of enabling inquiries to be made or of determining the most suitable method of dealing with his case: Provided that a court shall not for the purpose aforesaid adjourn the hearing of a case for any single period exceeding three weeks."

The Criminal Procedure (Scotland) Act 1975 provides:

"380.—(1) It is hereby declared that the power of a L court to adjourn the hearing of a case includes power, after a person has been convicted or the court has found that he committed the offence and before he has been sentenced or otherwise dealt with, to adjourn the case for the purpose of enabling inquiries to be made or of determining the most suitable method of dealing with his case and where the court so adjourns the case it shall remand the accused in custody or on bail or ordain him to appear at the adjourned diet; Provided that a court shall not for the purpose aforesaid adjourn

A the hearing of a case for a single period exceeding three weeks.''

Cases referred to

Advocate (HM) v Clegg, 1991 SLT 192; 1990 JC 318; 1990 SCCR 293.
Bruce v Linton (1860) 23 D 85.
Burns v Wilson, 1993 SLT 809; 1993 SCCR 418.
Heywood v Thomson, Dundee Sheriff Court, 28 November 1990, unreported.
Lennon v Copland, 1972 SLT (Notes) 68.
B *Long v HM Advocate*, 1984 SCCR 161.
McCulloch v Scott, 1993 SCCR 41.
McKay v Tudhope, 1979 SLT (Notes) 43.
Morrison v Clark, 1962 SLT 113.
Thom v Smith, 1979 SLT (Notes) 25.
Wilson v Donald, 1993 SLT 31; 1992 SCCR 654.

Textbooks referred to

Hume, *Crimes* (3rd ed), i, 463.
Renton and Brown, *Criminal Procedure* (5th ed), para
C   15-14.

The bills were argued before the High Court on 28 April 1993.

On 21 May 1993 the court *passed* the bills, *recalled* the decisions of the sheriffs and *remitted* to the sheriffs to proceed as accords.

The following opinion of the court was delivered by
D the Lord Justice General (Hope):

OPINION OF THE COURT.—The complainer in these bills of advocation is the procurator fiscal at Alloa who seeks the recall of decisions taken by the sheriff in two separate summary complaints by which the respondents, who had pled guilty to various charges on these complaints, were discharged without sentence being imposed. In both cases the sheriff had previously deferred sentence on the respondents for periods which exceeded three weeks, and a submission
E that this was incompetent in terms of s 380 (1) of the Criminal Procedure (Scotland) Act 1975 was upheld. The complainer submits that these adjournments were not for any of the purposes specified in that subsection, and that for this reason the decisions to discharge the respondents without imposing sentence were unjust, erroneous and contrary to law. It is averred that the sheriff had power in these cases both at common law and in terms of s 432 of the Act to defer sentence for such period as he might determine.
F But the learned advocate depute accepted in the course of his argument that it would be difficult to justify what happened here as an exercise of the power to defer sentence after conviction in terms of s 432 (1) of the Act. Accordingly the question at issue is whether these adjournments can be regarded as a competent exercise of the court's power to adjourn at common law.

Ian Jamieson had been charged with three co-accused on a summary complaint which contained various charges under the Misuse of Drugs Act 1971.

One of his co-accused, Scott Jamieson, was charged with having cannabis in his possession at HM Young G Offenders Institution, Glenochil, and with supplying cannabis to the respondent Ian Jamieson who was then an inmate of that institution. The only charge against the respondent on this complaint was that he had cannabis in his possession on the same date and at the same place. There were further charges against Scott Jamieson and two other co-accused of having three different controlled drugs in their possession in a motor car in the public car park of the institution, and there were two charges alleging contraventions of con- H ditions of bail. The respondent and his co-accused all pled not guilty to the various charges against them and they were granted bail. But they all failed to appear at the diet which had been set for trial and warrants were then granted for their apprehension. On 18 January 1993 the respondent and his co-accused Scott Jamieson appeared from custody and tendered various pleas. The respondent pled guilty as libelled to the charge against him, while Scott Jamieson pled guilty to the charge of supplying cannabis to the respondent I and to a contravention of the Bail etc (Scotland) Act. He pled not guilty to the charges of having controlled drugs in his possession in the institution and in the motor car in the public car park. One of Scott Jamieson's pleas of not guilty was accepted by the prosecutor, but his case was adjourned for trial on the other three charges to which he had pled not guilty and sentence was deferred on the two charges to which he had pled guilty. No question arises in the present proceedings about the disposal in the case of Scott J Jamieson. The minute of 18 January 1993 records the following disposal in the case of the respondent: "The court deferred sentence until the trial of co-accused until 15 February 1993 at 11 am and ordered the accused to be detained in custody until such diet, bail having been refused. Reason bail refused: in view of the record of the accused, including three bail contraventions."

An appeal against the refusal of bail was dismissed by the bail judge on 21 January 1993. When the case K called again on 15 February 1993 the trial was further adjourned until 8 April 1993 due to the absence of one of the co-accused. The agent for the respondent took the opportunity to argue that further proceedings against him were incompetent, on the ground that the diet had been adjourned in his case in terms of s 380 (1) of the 1975 Act for more than three weeks. The sheriff decided to defer sentence further on the respondent until 16 February 1993, and there were two further deferments thereafter of periods not exceeding L three weeks. On 22 March 1993 the sheriff upheld the submission that the first adjournment on 18 January 1993 was incompetent and, having regard to the decision in *Burns v Wilson*, he discharged the respondent without imposing sentence.

Henry Peddie had been charged on summary complaint with a breach of the peace, with a contravention of s 78 (1) of the Criminal Justice (Scotland) Act 1980 and with two contraventions of s 41 (1) (a) of the Police (Scotland) Act 1967. All of these offences were

A said to have been committed on the same date outside premises in Mill Street, Alloa. He pled guilty to the charge of breach of the peace and, subject to certain amendments, to one of the charges under s 41 (1) (a) of the 1967 Act, but he pled not guilty to the other two charges. His pleas were accepted except in respect of his plea of not guilty to the charge under s 78 (1) of the 1980 Act. The minute of 21 December 1992 records the following disposal of his case on that date: "The court deferred sentence on charges 1 and 3 as the accused is on trial on another charge. The court

B adjourned the diet for trial quoad charge 2 until 12 February 1993 until 10 am. Bail granted subject to the separate order attached hereto."

On 12 February 1993 the respondent adhered to his plea of not guilty to charge 2 but the diet for trial was adjourned due to lack of court time to 5 April 1993. Sentence on the two charges to which he had pled guilty was again deferred. On 5 April 1993 he was found guilty of charge 2 and a fine was imposed. But having heard submissions to the effect that further

C proceedings against the respondent were incompetent, in respect that they had been adjourned in terms of s 380 of the 1975 Act for more than three weeks, the sheriff discharged the respondent and imposed no sentence on the two charges to which he had pled guilty.

It has not been suggested that there was any error of principle on the part of the sheriff in either of these two cases in deciding not to proceed to sentence

D immediately on the charges to which the respondents had pled guilty. In Ian Jamieson's case, where there were a number of co-accused who were facing other charges on the same complaint to which they had pled not guilty, the sheriff appears to have taken the view that it would be appropriate to postpone consideration of his sentence until the end of the trial against his co-accused. In *Thom v Smith* it was said that it is highly desirable that, where there is more than one accused who has to be sentenced in respect of a particular

E charge, the same sheriff should deal with the disposal of all the accused. The circumstances here were different, because the respondent had pled guilty to a different charge from those which had been brought against his co-accused. But the events regarding all these charges were closely related to each other, and there was plainly much to be said for the view that it was preferable not to proceed to sentence the respondent on a narrative of the facts by the prosecutor when these facts were to be the subject of evidence at the

F trial of the co-accused which was to take place, perhaps before a different sheriff, at a later date. Renton and Brown (5th ed), para 15-14 points out that where a number of accused appear on one complaint and one pleads guilty while the others go to trial it is common practice to postpone sentence on the one who has pleaded guilty until after the trial of the others, and it is clear that this is the practice which the sheriff was seeking to apply in the present case. In Henry Peddie's case, he was the only person charged on the complaint. But his plea of not guilty to one of the charges had not been accepted by the prosecutor, and

the sheriff appears to have taken the view that it would G be desirable not to proceed to sentence him on the charges to which he had pled guilty until the remaining charge had been disposed of. In *Lennon v Copland* it was held to be contrary to ordinary practice and inappropriate for a sheriff to impose sentence on one charge and to defer sentence on another. Again, the circumstances here are different because, while the appellant in that case had been found guilty of both charges, the respondent in the present case had still to go to trial on the charge to which he had pled not guilty. But the charges all appeared to relate to the H same incident, and there were good reasons for thinking that it would be better to await the outcome of the trial before proceeding to sentence the respondent on any of the charges on the complaint. No doubt it was appreciated in this case also that a different sheriff might take the trial and that it was desirable that the whole matter of sentence should be dealt with by the same sheriff.

Accordingly the question is whether these decisions, which we consider to be in accordance with good sen- I tencing practice, are rendered incompetent by the proviso to s 380 (1) of the 1975 Act. That subsection is in these terms: [his Lordship quoted the terms of s 380 (1) and continued:]

The scope of the phrase "for the purpose ... of determining the most suitable method of dealing with his case" is a matter to which we shall return later in this opinion. But it is clear enough that an adjournment of a case after the accused has been convicted or J found to have committed the offence, for the purpose of enabling inquiries to be made before he is sentenced or otherwise dealt with cannot, in terms of the proviso, be for any single period which exceeds three weeks. Thus adjournments for the purpose of obtaining social inquiry and community service reports, or for the obtaining of a printout from the DVLA in a road traffic case, are restricted by the subsection and must be held to be incompetent if they are for a longer period: *HM Advocate v Clegg*; *Wilson v Donald*. It is K also clear that it is not open to the court to resort to the expedient of exercising the power under s 432 to defer sentence after conviction, when the deferment is for the purpose of enabling inquiries to be made or of determining the most suitable method of dealing with the case. It was held in *Clegg* that, where an adjournment is necessary for the obtaining of reports, it is the provisions which deal with the power of the court to adjourn the case before sentence which apply. The substance of what the court is doing, not the choice of L words, is what determines the matter, and there is an important distinction between the two powers available under the statute. The power of the court under s 380 is to adjourn the case before sentence, and it may be exercised at a stage prior to conviction of the accused. In *Burns v Wilson* it was held that the accused must be regarded as having been convicted unless the minutes make it clear that disposal by absolute discharge or a probation order is still in contemplation. But it was recognised in that case that the court has power to adjourn under s 380 (1) while disposal by

A   absolute discharge or a probation order is still being contemplated. The position is different as regards s 432, because a deferment under that section can be made only after conviction. Furthermore a deferment under that section marks the stage of the case at which an accused can no longer withdraw a plea of guilty but can appeal against his conviction by stated case, and it also marks the stage at which the prosecutor can appeal against the accused's acquittal on some other charge in the same complaint: 1975 Act, s 451 (3).

B   The learned advocate depute accepted that he could not in these circumstances support the decisions which were taken in these cases on the ground that the sheriff had deferred sentence under s 432. Although the minutes in each case use the words "deferred sentence", the substance of the matter, according to his argument, was that the sheriffs were postponing consideration of sentence to a later date. He submitted that this was an exercise of a power which was available to the court at common law. And he maintained that that power had not, in the situations with which C   the sheriffs were dealing in these cases, been abrogated or restricted by s 380 (1). It is necessary therefore to examine the nature and scope of the common law power of adjournment, and to look more closely at the wording of s 380 (1) and the context in which it was enacted.

The opening words of s 380 (1) contain an acknowledgment that a court of summary jurisdiction already has a power at common law to adjourn the D   hearing of a case. The purpose of the subsection is therefore in part declaratory of the existing law, but it is also designed to impose a restriction in terms of the proviso. Clear authority to the effect that the court has power to adjourn is to be found in *Bruce v Linton*, which was concerned with a prosecution in the police court at Edinburgh for a licensing offence. The magistrate adjourned the hearing on four occasions before proceeding to a conviction, the last two of which were after he had completed hearing all the evidence. It was E   held that it was within the discretion of the magistrate to adjourn the case for such periods as he might consider necessary. Lord Justice Clerk Inglis explained the reasons for this decision in the following passage at pp 93-94: "The adjournments particularly complained of are the two last, on the ground that, in the circumstances, it was entirely unjustifiable and illegal to adjourn for a period of five weeks after the trial and evidence were completed. If there were any room for saying, that a court of this kind has no power of F   adjournment, except what is given by the statute, I think that would be a very formidable ground of complaint. But, I think, that is altogether untenable; I think that every court must have, inherent in it, the power to adjourn when necessary. The most summary case may turn out to be a very long case, and it may be inconsistent with human strength and patience to finish it in one sitting; and if there were no power of adjournment, the case would fall. And even in such cases as, from their nature, cannot be expected to extend over a day, some accident may occur which may render adjournment necessary; and if there be any

case in which, at common law, from the nature of jurisdiction, a court has power to adjourn, the general   G rule follows of necessity, that a power to adjourn is a power inherent in every court, which must be exercised according to the discretion of the judge. It falls within the maxim, that, with jurisdiction, is given every power that is necessary to the full exercise of the jurisdiction."

In *Wilson v Donald*, 1993 SLT at p 33 Lord Allanbridge pointed out that *Bruce v Linton* was concerned with adjourning a case before conviction. He indicated that the position might be different after conviction, in   H view of the restriction imposed in certain circumstances by s 380 (1). But so far as the power at common law is concerned, as described by Lord Justice Clerk Inglis, it is one which may be exercised at any time when necessary. Furthermore Lord Cowan said at p 95: "The adjournment may very well be made with the view, if the judge shall see cause, of hearing parties upon the proof, or on the defence, or of considering the judgment and sentence."

I   Hume, i, 463 says that the court may, on receiving the verdict, either proceed to sentence forthwith or adjourn at pleasure to some later day. In the light of these authorities there seems to be no good reason for holding that the common law is restricted as to the stage at which the power of adjournment may be exercised. In any event the stage which had been reached in the present cases, where certain charges in the complaint had yet to be dealt with and no evidence had yet been led in respect of them, was one where the   J common law power of adjournment was clearly available unless it was restricted by statute.

The proviso to s 380 (1) applies only where the adjournment of the case is "for the purpose aforesaid". Its application is thus restricted to adjournments which are made for the purpose which the subsection describes. This is "for the purpose of enabling inquiries to be made or of determining the most suitable method of dealing with the case". There appear here to be two purposes, the first of which   K clearly does not apply in the present case, since no reports were called for nor were other inquiries to be made during the period of the adjournment. So the question is whether the adjournments which were ordered here were for the purpose of determining the most suitable method of dealing with the case.

The learned advocate depute invited us to construe these words strictly by looking to the purpose of the adjournment. He submitted that they ought not to be   L read in such a way as to make it practically impossible for the court to await the outcome of the trial against a co-accused on the same complaint, or against the accused on other charges on the same complaint, where good sentencing practice made this desirable. He drew a distinction between a decision to postpone the whole sentencing process, which he said was what had been done in these cases, and a decision taken with a view to the sentence which was appropriate. These were to be seen as different purposes, and the proper inference to draw in the present cases was that the

A sheriff had decided to adjourn the case against each respondent in the exercise of the common law power. He drew our attention to a decision by Sheriff Cox in *Heywood v Thomson*, 28 November 1990, where he held that a decision by a temporary sheriff at the pleading diet to defer sentence on an accused who had pled guilty, to await the outcome of a trial against his co-accused on the same charge on the same complaint, was in the exercise of the common law power to adjourn and was not rendered incompetent by s 380 (1). The sheriff noted that during the interval between B the pleading and trial diet no one would be making inquiries in relation to the accused's sentence and no one would be giving consideration to the most suitable method of dealing with him. The whole question of his sentence was being postponed to another date and to another sheriff, and the purpose in postponing sentence was not one of the purposes mentioned in s 380 (1).

Counsel for the respondent Ian Jamieson submitted that the only reason for the sheriff deferring sentence C on her client when he had pled guilty and remanding him in custody was to determine the most suitable method of dealing with his case. Her information was that, although there was no written record of the reasons for his decision other than that which had been minuted, the sheriff had indicated at the time that this was his reason for deferring sentence on him to a later date. The existence of a common law power to adjourn for this purpose was doubtful, but in any event the matter was now regulated by s 380 (1). She D maintained that, even if there was a common law power to adjourn, there was no power at common law to remand an accused in custody after he had pled guilty and prior to sentence. It was therefore fundamentally wrong for this respondent to be detained in custody for a period in excess of three weeks, since this was in breach of the proviso to the subsection. If he did not have the protection of the proviso, it would be open to the court in summary proceedings to remand an accused in custody indefinitely after he had E been convicted and before sentence, which she submitted would be ludicrous. Counsel for the respondent Peddie, who had not been remanded in custody, confined her submissions to the purpose for which the adjournment had been ordered in his case. She submitted that this was plainly for the purpose of determining the most suitable method of dealing with the respondent. The distinction between this and the postponement of a consideration of the question of sentence was a distinction without a difference, in view of F the wide terminology used in s 380 (1). She submitted that the subsection was so widely expressed as to cover all situations where an adjournment was considered to be necessary before sentencing an accused who had been convicted or found to have committed the offence.

The phrase "for the purpose . . . of determining the most suitable method of dealing with his case" is certainly a very wide one, and we have not found it easy to discover a sound basis for the limited meaning contended for by the advocate depute. This purpose

appears from the terms of the subsection to be a different purpose from that of enabling inquiries to be G made, but we have not found this aspect of the subsection to be of assistance to us in finding a more precise meaning for the phrase which is in issue in this case. Where the purpose is to enable inquiries to be made, it can no doubt be said that it is the intention that these inquiries should be carried out during the period of the adjournment. The intention is that they should be completed and reported on with a view to providing the relevant information to the court at the adjourned diet. But it does not follow that, where the purpose is H to determine the most suitable method of dealing with the case, the intention is that something is to happen during the period of the adjournment. The phrase is appropriate to cover situations where the purpose is to enable evidence to be heard at the adjourned diet so that the court may decide, in the light of that evidence, what sentence would be appropriate. In *McCulloch v Scott* it was held that a continuation of the case for a period of more than three weeks to hear evidence in mitigation fell within the provisions of s 380 (1), and I that, as the proviso in s 380 (1) limiting adjournments to not more than three weeks was mandatory and not directory, the sentence passed at a diet held in contravention of its provisions should be suspended. The Lord Justice Clerk observed at pp 43G-44A that an adjournment of the kind which occurred in that case could properly be regarded as an adjournment for the purpose of enabling inquiries to be made or at least as an adjournment for the purpose of enabling the court to determine the appropriate method of dealing with J the case. For these reasons Sheriff Cox's suggestion in *Heywood v Thomson* that it was sufficient that during the interval between the pleading and the trial diet no one would be making inquiries in relation to the accused's sentence and no one would be giving consideration to the most suitable method of dealing with him does not provide an answer to the problem which we can regard as acceptable.

We have examined the legislative history of this pro- K vision, and the context in which it was enacted, to see if this can provide any assistance. The provision which is to be found in s 380 (1) of the 1975 Act was first enacted in s 26 of the Criminal Justice (Scotland) Act 1949 in these terms: [his Lordship quoted the terms of s 26 and continued:] That Act also contained important new provisions about the treatment of young offenders, including provisions now to be found in s 415 (2) and (4) of the 1975 Act to the effect that no court shall impose imprisonment on a person under 21 years of age unless the court is of opinion L that no other method of dealing with him is appropriate, and that for the purpose of determining whether any other method of dealing with any such person is appropriate the court shall obtain and consider information about his circumstances. Section 21 of the 1949 Act, which made provision for corrective training and preventive detention, provided that before sentencing any offender to this form of training and detention the court was to call for and consider a report on the offender's suitability for such a sentence,

and that the court might require any person concerned
A   in the preparation of the report or with knowledge of
matters dealt with in it to appear with a view to his
examination on oath regarding any of the matters dealt
with in the report. Similar provisions appear in s 20
of the Act with regard to a sentence of borstal training.
These and other provisions in the 1949 Act were
clearly designed to ensure that the court was fully
equipped with the appropriate information before
determining the most suitable method of dealing with
offenders in view of the various methods which were
B   then to be available. In that context it was no doubt
thought appropriate to make it clear that the court had
power to adjourn the case for the purpose which s 26
(1) of the 1949 Act, now s 380 (1) of the 1975 Act,
described and to place a time limit on the period for
which an adjournment for that purpose might be
made. But while that is the context in which the provision was enacted, the purpose as described in it is
wide enough to cover any situation in which the court
considers it appropriate to wait for further information
C   before passing sentence in the case. It is certainly clear
from the other provisions in the 1949 Act that one of
the situations which it contemplated was that where a
continuation was necessary to enable a person concerned in the preparation of the report to be examined
on oath regarding any of the matters dealt with in it.
This provides further support for the view that it is
not essential for the application of s 380 (1) that consideration is to be given during the period of the
adjournment to the most suitable method of dealing
D   with the case, but that it is apt to cover any situation
where the court adjourns the case to enable further
information relevant to sentence to be put before it at
a later date.

On the other hand it appears to us from its context
that the provision was intended to apply only at the
stage when the court was ready to embark on the sentencing process, having reached the stage in the case
when it was appropriate for it to consider the most
suitable method of dealing with the accused. The fact
E   that one of the purposes for which an adjournment
may be made in terms of the subsection is to enable
inquiries to be made is a clear indication that this is
the stage to which this provision was directed. The
other purpose, as we have said, covers a wide range of
possible reasons for adjourning the case to a later date.
But it is significant that it is the second of the two purposes described and is thus not of paramount importance in the subsection, and that the proviso, by using
the phrase "for the purpose aforesaid", indicates that
F   there is such a close relationship between the two that
they ought really to be seen as one and the same. The
stage which it contemplates therefore is that where the
court is in a position to proceed to sentence but finds
it appropriate to order an adjournment for the purpose
only of obtaining more complete information in that
regard. It seems not unreasonable in that situation that
the power to adjourn the hearing of the case at the
stage of sentence should be restricted by the setting of
a short time limit for each adjournment.

That however was not the situation in either of the

two cases with which we are here concerned. The
minutes indicate that in neither case was the sheriff,   G
when deciding to order an adjournment, giving any
consideration to the question of sentence. He was, in
effect, postponing the whole question as to the appropriate sentence, and as to any inquiries which might
be relevant to this matter, to a later date. No reports
were called for and there is no mention in either
minute of any other information relevant to sentence
which the court had decided it wished to have made
available to it at the adjourned diet. The reference in
each minute to the fact that there was to be a trial on   H
other charges in the same complaint shows that the
only reason for the adjournment was that the sheriff
in each case regarded it as premature to deal with sentence until the end of the trial. And, as we mentioned
earlier, it must have been appreciated that the trial
might take place before a different sheriff from the
sheriff who made the adjournment. In our opinion
therefore matters had not yet reached the stage contemplated by s 380 (1), and the adjournments were not
for the purpose which it describes and were thus not   I
subject to the time limit. In *Heywood v Thomson*
Sheriff Cox reached the view, in similar circumstances, that s 380 (1) had no application and that the
adjournment was in the exercise of the common law
power to adjourn. We agree with his decision in that
case, where it was clear from the minutes that no
inquiries were to be made and no thought was to be
given by the court to the proper disposal of the
accused's case until after the trial of his co-accused. In
the present case also it was the common law power to   J
adjourn which was being exercised so that, in accordance with the well established principles which we
mentioned earlier, the whole question of sentence
might be considered at a later date. It would be
unreasonable to restrict the power to adjourn in such
circumstances by the setting of short time limits which
would make it very difficult to give effect to these
principles, and we are satisfied that s 380 (1) does not
have this effect.

We should add that the fact that the respondent Ian   K
Jamieson was remanded in custody, which was much
relied on by counsel, is not in our opinion a point of
critical importance to the decision as to whether the
adjournment in his case was made under s 380 (1) or
at common law. The provision in s 26 of the 1949 Act
made no mention of any power to detain in custody
nor was there any reference in that section to bail. The
requirement that, when making an adjournment for
the purpose now described in s 380 (1) of the 1975
Act, the court must remand the accused in custody or   L
on bail was added by s 5 (a) of the Bail etc (Scotland)
Act 1980 and the further alternative of ordaining the
accused to appear was added by Sched 7 to the Criminal Justice (Scotland) Act 1980. But, as the cases of
Morrison v Clark and *McKay v Tudhope* illustrate, it
was already the practice for offenders to be admitted
to bail or detained in custody, according to the circumstances, when a case was adjourned for the obtaining
of reports. These cases were concerned with the laying
down of the circumstances where it was appropriate to

A admit the accused to bail, and it was not suggested that there was no power to remand him in custody at that stage. There is no doubt that prior to the amendment made by s 5 (a) of the 1980 Act the court's decision to refuse to admit to bail at this stage was subject to review by the High Court. A person who is remanded in custody under s 380 (1) is required now to present his appeal under subs (2) of that section, which was added by s 5 (b) of the 1980 Act: see *Long v HM Advocate*. But that subsection has no application to the case where bail is refused following a decision to

B adjourn the case at common law. The appropriate method of seeking review of a decision to refuse bail in these circumstances is a petition for interim liberation. We do not accept counsel for the first respondent's argument that an accused who is refused bail in such circumstances may be detained in custody indefinitely prior to sentence without the prospect of the refusal of bail being reviewed.

· For these reasons we consider that the adjournments which were ordered in these cases, being adjourn-
C ments which were made in the exercise of the common law power to adjourn, were not incompetent. We shall pass the bills, advocate the proceedings, recall the decisions by which the sheriffs discharged the respondents without imposing sentence and remit to the sheriff in each case to proceed as accords.

———

D *Counsel for Complainer, Macdonald, QC, A D; Solicitor, J D Lowe, Crown Agent — Counsel for Respondent Jamieson, McNeill; Solicitors, Haig-Scott & Co, WS (for K J Douglas & Co, Falkirk) — Counsel for Respondent Peddie, M E Scott; Solicitors, Drummond Miller, WS (for I Allan Grant & Co, Tullibody).*

P W F

E

(NOTE)

Ferguson v McGrandles

OUTER HOUSE
LORD PENROSE
29 MAY 1992

F *Damages — Award — Interim payment — Competency — Driver not insured although insurers of vehicle owner instructing defence and willing to meet award if competent — Rules of Court 1965, rule 89A (1) (d).*

A passenger injured in a road accident sought an award of interim payment of damages against the driver. The defence had been instructed by the insurers of the owners of the vehicle, there not having been in force insurance covering the driving by the defender.

Held, that since the driver was not insured, it was

incompetent to award interim damages; and motion *refused.*   G

———

Rule of Court 89A (1) (d) provides that no order for interim payment of damages shall be made unless the defender is insured in respect of the claim or is a public authority or is a person whose means and resources are such as to enable him to make the interim payment.

David Ferguson raised an action of damages against H
John McGrandles in respect of injuries sustained by the pursuer when a passenger in a vehicle driven by the defender. The pursuer enrolled a motion for interim damages of £50,000. It was opposed. Liability was not admitted, but the pursuer's counsel argued that an award could properly be made in terms of Rule of Court 89A (1) (c) (ii), having regard to the pleadings of the parties at this stage.

The pursuer sustained catastrophic injuries in the accident. He had been a passenger in a hired vehicle I
being driven at the material time by the defender. The pursuer averred that the defender had lost control of the vehicle on a bend, that the vehicle had collided with a tree, that at the time the defender had neither been insured nor licensed to drive and that he was convicted of breaches of a number of provisions of the Road Traffic Act 1988 including s 3, and ss 143 (1) and 97 (3). The defender denied liability. In refusing the motion the Lord Ordinary (Penrose) said:
J

"Counsel for the defender informed me that his instructions emanated from the insurance company, General Accident. General Accident had issued a policy of insurance in favour of the owner of the vehicle covering the risks of the owner, his employees, persons taking the vehicle on hire, and persons nominated as drivers, being over 25 years of age, at the time of the hire. The insurers were not acting as nominees of the Motor Insurers Bureau at this stage, but were instructing the defence on an interim basis while they K
considered whether they should repudiate liability under the policy. If they did repudiate liability under the policy the Bureau would take over, and General Accident might or might not be nominated to conduct any defence in those circumstances. He explained that there were perceived to be difficulties in resolving the insurance position, caused by the terms of s 148 of the Road Traffic Act 1988. In the meantime, General Accident were willing to pay any amount awarded as interim damages, but he maintained that on the pur- L
suer's pleadings, and the terms of the Rule of Court, an award was incompetent. He referred to Rule of Court 89A (1) (d). The defender was not insured as a matter of fact and there was no suggestion that he had the means and resources to enable him to make the interim payment.

"In response counsel for the pursuer stated that the defender's solicitors had hitherto given no indication that such a position was to be adopted. But if the insurers appeared as volunteers and indicated that the funds necessary to meet any award were available, then the defender was a person whose resources were such as to enable him to meet the award.

"It is, at least, surprising that an admitted dominus litis should appear before the court and intimate that the apparent defence to the action had been presented on an interim basis as a holding operation while that body considered whether or not to repudiate liability under an insurance contract to which neither the pursuer nor the defender was party, on any view of the facts. Delay in addressing the pursuer's claim to a remedy for the injuries he admittedly sustained is unfortunate in the circumstances. The terms of the Act, and the facts disclosed by counsel, may indeed suggest the possibility of a dispute between the insurers of the vehicle and the Bureau as to where the cost of meeting any claim the pursuer may have should ultimately lie. The terms of ans 2 for the defender may be intended to draw the pursuer into that controversy. But at this stage it is not a live issue between the parties to the case.

"The defender's argument has an artificial air in all the circumstances. It seeks to avoid a realistic disposal of the question in terms of substantial justice. It is, however, in my view technically correct. The defender is not insured. I understand the rule to relate to a person who has the benefit of a contract of insurance in his favour, or in favour of some other party in terms which cover the risks of the defender. The defender does not have independent means. I understand the rule to refer to a person who can meet the obligation to pay out of funds which are his or are his to dispose of at will. The willingness of General Accident to pay if a competent interlocutor can be pronounced is not what the rule envisages. On neither branch of the rule can the pursuer succeed.

"The result seems to me to be unfortunate. But the terms of the rule are limited to certain prescribed circumstances. Given those terms I have no alternative but to refuse the motion before me."

Counsel for Pursuer, Dorrian; Solicitors, Drummond Miller, WS (for John & W K Gair & Gibson, Falkirk) — Counsel for Defender, D I Mackay; Solicitors, Simpson & Marwick, WS.

C H

(NOTE)

McCreadie v Clairmont Garments (Scotland) Ltd

OUTER HOUSE
LORD SUTHERLAND
2 JULY 1992

Damages — Amount — Solatium — Knee — Contusion of knee joint with discomfort lasting about two years.

An elderly woman machine operator injured her knee when she tripped and fell. There was some contusion in the knee joint, the effect of which had lasted for about two years.

Opinion, that solatium was properly valued at £2,500.

Elizabeth McCreadie raised an action against her former employers, Clairmont Garments (Scotland) Ltd, for damages sustained in an accident on 14 September 1988. She was then aged in her 60s. She claimed that she had tripped and fallen over a raised gate stop. After a proof before the Lord Ordinary (Sutherland) his Lordship held that the pursuer had failed to prove the cause of her fall. He assoilzied the defenders. In relation to damages his Lordship said:

"As far as damages are concerned it was accepted by counsel for the pursuer that the only claim available to the pursuer was for solatium as she had been made redundant about two weeks after the accident and because of her age would have been unlikely to obtain any further employment. There was a dispute on the medical evidence as to the degree of incapacity. Both Mr Mann who gave evidence for the pursuer and Mr Hamilton who gave evidence for the defenders agreed that there would be some contusion in the knee joint. Mr Mann's evidence was that it was of such a nature that the effects would be likely to last for about two years, whereas Mr Hamilton's view was that the maximum period over which the effects would last would be about 12 weeks. Mr Mann examined the pursuer in April 1989 whereas Mr Hamilton's examination was not until September 1991. I accept Mr Mann's evidence that at the time of his examination there were some clinical signs of injury to the knee joint, and if he is correct about that it follows automatically that Mr Hamilton's suggestion that all the ill effects would have gone by the end of 1988 cannot be correct. Mr Mann's evidence was also that he had examined the pursuer again in October 1991 shortly after Mr Hamilton's examination and that at that time the pursuer had made a full recovery. It is therefore perhaps not surprising that Mr Hamilton should not have found any sign of injury when he made his examination. I would therefore have been prepared to hold that the pursuer continued to suffer from discomfort to her knee for a period of about two years after the accident. The extent of the suffering and inconvenience would be difficult to assess because the

A pursuer maintained in the witness box that she is still suffering from considerable disability although both surgeons were quite satisfied that there was no physical justification for these complaints. I was referred to *Leckie v British Railways Board*, 1980 SLT (Notes) 40, where a similar sort of injury attracted an award of £1,000. In that case there was a full recovery in six months. Allowing for inflation this award would now be in the region of £2,000. In my opinion the appropriate award for solatium in the present case would be £2,500."

B

Counsel for Pursuer, I M Scott; Solicitors, L & L Lawrence — Counsel for Defenders, Bolland; Solicitors, Brown, Mair, Mackintosh & Co.

C H

C

Henderson v George Outram and Co Ltd

OUTER HOUSE

LORD ABERNETHY

21 OCTOBER 1992

D *Diligence — Arrestment — Arrestment on dependence — Recall — Caution — Suitable sum for caution — Action of defamation.*

A senior member of the Scottish bar brought an action of damages for defamation against the publishers of a newspaper and against the authors of articles in the newspaper containing material which was allegedly defamatory of him. He sued for £750,000 with interest and expenses. Arrestment on the dependence of the action was effected, arresting two sums totalling £2,400,000 due to the publishers. E The publishers sought recall of these arrestments, conceding that recall should be subject to the provision of suitable security in the form of caution and arguing that suitable caution would be £100,000. The pursuer argued that caution in the sum of £800,000 would be an appropriate sum.

Held, (1) that the pursuer was entitled to use diligence to obtain a proper degree of security for his claim but that it must not be nimious and oppressive (p 825J-K); (2) that as a matter of fairness to the F pursuer balanced by fairness also to the defenders a suitable sum for caution was £400,000 (p 826C-D); and arrestments *recalled* subject to caution in that sum being provided.

Action of damages

Robert Ewart Henderson, QC, raised an action of damages for defamation against (first) George Outram and Co Ltd, publishers of *The Herald* newspaper, and (second, third and fourth) three journalists in respect of material contained in five articles published in the period between 21 September and 2 October 1992. G Sums of £2,400,000 due to the publishers were arrested by virtue of the warrant for arrestment on the dependence contained in the summons.

The case came before the Lord Ordinary (Abernethy) on the defenders' motion for recall of the arrestments.

Cases referred to

Farrell v Willox (1849) 11 D 565. H
Gecas v Scottish Television plc, OH, 17 July 1992, unreported (1992 GWD 30-1786).
Levy v Gardiner, 1964 SLT (Notes) 68.
Manson v Macara (1839) 2 D 208.
Svenska Petroleum AB v HOR Ltd, 1986 SLT 513.
Taylor Woodrow Construction (Scotland) Ltd v Sears Investment Trust Ltd, 1991 SLT 421.

Textbook referred to

Stewart, *Diligence*, pp 198 and 203. I

On 21 October 1992 his Lordship *granted* the defenders' motion and *recalled* the arrestments subject to caution being lodged by the defenders in the sum of £400,000.

LORD ABERNETHY.—In this case the pursuer is a Queen's Counsel who has been in practice as an advocate for many years. He has raised an action for defamation against the defenders in respect of five J articles published between 21 September and 2 October 1992 in *The Herald* newspaper. The first defenders are the publishers of the articles. The second, third and fourth defenders wrote them.

The pursuer seeks damages of £750,000 together with interest on that sum and expenses. As is usual the summons contained a warrant for arrestment on the dependence. In furtherance of the warrant the pursuer has arrested two large sums of money which are due K to the first defenders. These sums total nearly £2,400,000. In a motion before calling, the defenders seek recall of these arrestments.

I was told that the first defenders were a substantial and solvent trading company. They had a substantial asset base. They were substantially in credit with their bank. They were profitable and expected to remain so. Of course, that situation could change and for that reason their senior counsel accepted on the authority of *Taylor Woodrow Construction v Sears Investment* L *Trust*, that any recall of the arrestment would be subject to providing suitable security for the pursuer. He contended that the sum of £100,000 would be sufficient. Senior counsel for the pursuer, for his part, recognised that recall of the arrestments was appropriate if suitable security for his client were provided. He contended, however, for a sum of £800,000.

The issue between the parties is, therefore, what would be a suitable sum as security for the pursuer on the dependence of this action. Senior counsel for the

A defenders pointed first to the averments of loss in the summons. They are contained in art 18 of the summons. There are two heads of loss claimed, namely, solatium and patrimonial loss. With regard to the claim for solatium I was told that the highest award for solatium in an action of defamation in Scotland was £50,000. That was in an action about two years ago in which a female prison officer sought damages for injury to both personal and professional reputation. Even in the recent case of *Gecas v Scottish Television plc*, where the alleged defamation involved the pursuer being branded a war criminal, Lord

B Milligan had assessed damages in the event that he had found for the pursuer (which he did not) at £30,000. Counsel recognised that there were particular reasons in that case why the figure was so apparently low. He submitted, however, that in a general sense awards of solatium in defamation cases in Scotland — and I took it he meant cases of serious defamation — were on present money values in the tens of thousands of pounds rather than anything more.

C With regard to the question of patrimonial loss counsel directed my attention both to the paucity of the averments and to their hypothetical nature. The averments were so unspecific that it was impossible to make any useful estimate of patrimonial loss. As there were no averments even of the pursuer's present income there was no yardstick by which the effect of any patrimonial loss which the pursuer might have suffered could be assessed. In these circumstances, said counsel, the sum sued for was a random sum. In

D that situation he submitted that the court should adopt a conservative approach to the question at issue. In support of his submissions he also referred to *Farrell v Willox*, *Manson v Macara* and *Levy v Gardiner*.

Counsel also submitted that a question of causation arose. Both before and after 21 September 1992 there had been substantial media comment on the facts and circumstances surrounding the events which are the subject of these articles. A similar consideration had served to reduce the assessment of damages in the

E *Gecas* case. It was impossible to reach a conclusion on the effect of this comment at this stage but it was another reason for viewing the pursuer's claims with caution and conservatism.

In reply senior counsel for the pursuer stressed that a pursuer in an action of damages was entitled to use diligence as a remedy against any defender. It was a weapon which was available to him "from the armoury of legal remedies which Scots law provides" (*Svenska Petroleum AB v HOR Ltd*, Lord Cameron at

F p 518J). The use of the remedy, however, was always subject to the control of the court. There was no specialty because this was an action of defamation. Referring to the passage in Graham Stewart on *The Law of Diligence* at p 203, counsel submitted that the sum sued for was not truly a random sum as it was in actions of count, reckoning and payment such as *Farrell v Willox*. On the contrary, the sum sued for here was an estimate of damages and this action was more properly to be compared with other actions of damages where the damages were estimated. It had not

been suggested in the *Taylor Woodrow* case that the remedy of diligence was somehow modified because G the sum claimed was illiquid. So far as the case of *Manson v Macara* was concerned there were particular reasons for modifying caution in that case, which do not apply here. The *Gecas* case was also distinguishable. In that case some of the other damaging publicity had occurred prior to the publication of the defenders' alleged defamation. In the present case the comment in other sections of the media, at least insofar as it identified the pursuer, had occurred after and stemmed from the first article published by the H defenders. In any event, the question of causation was not a matter to be taken into account at this stage.

Counsel submitted that the matter therefore came back to a consideration of the averments. Since these averments were inevitably made shortly after the events giving rise to the action it was impossible to aver precisely the extent of the damage caused to the pursuer. It was clear, however, that both elements of the claim potentially gave rise to very substantial sums I of damages. In their second article the defenders themselves had quoted a description of the allegation involving the pursuer as being "a devastatingly serious allegation". In their third article they had quoted the Dean of Faculty of Advocates as saying that "he could think of no more serious charge against a member of the Bar than that he or she had used professional information for personal advantage". In these circumstances, said counsel, solatium could well reach into six figures.

J So far as patrimonial loss was concerned it was impossible to say at this stage what the damage is. All that can be said is that the pursuer's prospects are damaged. It would take time to clarify matters and if it was appropriate to do so, the defenders could seek a reduction of security at a later stage.

In my opinion the pursuer is entitled to use diligence in order to obtain a proper degree of security on the dependence of his action. There is, indeed, no K dispute between the parties on that point. On the other hand, he is entitled to no more. To have more would be regarded as nimious and oppressive. These are, indeed, two sides of the same coin. In determining what is a proper degree of security it has long been regarded as appropriate to consider the nature of the action (*Farrell v Willox*, Lord Jeffrey at p 568; Graham Stewart on *The Law of Diligence*, p 198, quoted in *Taylor Woodrow Construction v Sears Investment Trust* at p 426). It is also appropriate to consider L the facts and circumstances of the particular case (*Manson v Macara*). This action is one of damages for defamation. It is therefore to be expected that it will be raised shortly after the alleged defamatory statements and at a time when quantification of damage will be necessarily uncertain. So it is not a criticism that the averments of patrimonial loss here are unspecific and hypothetical. But it is nevertheless a fact. On any view patrimonial loss must account for much the greater part of the sum sued for and the sum sought as security. This element may not quite

A amount to a random sum in the sense that that phrase has been used in actions of count, reckoning and payment (*Manson v Macara*) but in my opinion it is in substance closer to that than to the usual case of estimated damages in, say, an action of damages for personal injury. What we are dealing with here is in effect a claim for future loss but there is no information in the averments to enable one to make anything other than the most speculative guess at what the loss might be. In the course of the argument counsel made an attempt at rationalising the calculation by using a sheriff's net salary as a multiplicand B but I regret to say that I found that of no assistance. On the other hand I think it is to be inferred from the averments that until these articles were published the pursuer was practising successfully as a Queen's Counsel principally in criminal defence work. In that situation it is perfectly possible that any patrimonial loss which resulted from the alleged defamation could be very substantial.

C At the end of the day the matter is one of fairness (*Levy v Gardiner; Taylor Woodrow Construction v Sears Investment Trust*). The pursuer's interest must be protected but the sum sought as security must not be disproportionate to his interest. I am prepared to accept that the solatium element in his claim might, if proved, comfortably exceed the highest previous award in Scotland. It might, indeed, reach six figures. As indicated, I am also prepared to accept that his patrimonial loss could be very substantial. But doing the best I can with the information available to me I D do not think that his interest, which also includes, of course, interest on any past loss proved and expenses, can fairly be said to equate to the sum sought by senior counsel for the pursuer as security. In my opinion an appropriate sum as security in this case would be £400,000.

I shall therefore recall the arrestments subject to caution for that sum.

E *Counsel for Pursuer, Hamilton, QC, Reed; Solicitors, Bird Semple Fyfe Ireland, WS — Counsel for Defenders, Martin, QC, Hodge; Solicitors, McGrigor Donald.*

J P D

Kaiser Bautechnik GmbH v GA Group Ltd

OUTER HOUSE

LORD CAMERON OF LOCHBROOM

13 OCTOBER 1992

Expenses — Caution for expenses — Foreign company — Substantial risk of prejudice to defender.

Process — Mandatary — Sist — Foreign company — Whether sufficient basis to require sist of mandatary.

A German company sought payment of a fee for design services undertaken. After defences had been G lodged, which denied that any concluded agreement had been reached, the defenders moved the court to order the pursuers to lodge caution for expenses or alternatively to sist a mandatary. The defenders founded on the pursuer not having a place of business in Scotland and having been at risk of being removed from the German commercial register by reason of the lack of a registered office. The defenders produced documentation relating to an assignation in security granted by the pursuers to a Scottish bank of all sums H due and to become due by the defenders to the pursuers in the subject matter of the claim. The defenders argued that there was a substantial risk that any award of expenses in their favour would not be satisfied. It was accepted by the defenders that any decree in their favour could be registered in the German courts and enforced against the pursuers, but they submitted this would incur additional expense.

Held, (1) that there was no risk of prejudice to the defenders of such a nature or degree as would justify I an order for the pursuers to find caution (p 828C); (2) that the fact that a pursuer was a foreign person was not per se a ground for an order to sist a mandatary, particularly where any decree against the pursuers in favour of the defenders could be registered in the German courts and there enforced (p 828E-F); and motions *refused.*

Action of payment J

Kaiser Bautechnik GmbH raised an action of payment against GA Group Ltd in respect of a fee for work allegedly done in terms of a joint venture agreement. After defences were lodged the defenders enrolled motions to ordain the pursuers to lodge caution for expenses or alternatively to sist a mandatary.

The motions came before the Lord Ordinary (Lord Cameron of Lochbroom). K

Cases referred to

Dean Warwick Ltd v Borthwick, 1981 SLT (Notes) 18.
Dessau v Daish (1897) 5 SLT 74; (1897) 24 R 976.
Overbury v Peek (1863) 1 M 1058.
Renfrew and Brown v Magistrates of Glasgow (1861) 23 D 1003.
Robertson v McCaw, 1911 1 SLT 346; 1911 SC 650.
Walker v Wedderspoon (1843) 2 Bell's App 57.

Textbooks referred to L

Halliday, *Conveyancing Law and Practice*, Vol I, p 231.
Maclaren, *Court of Session Practice*, p 294.
Maclaren, *Expenses*, p 17.
Maxwell, *Practice of the Court of Session*, p 223.

On 13 October 1992 the Lord Ordinary *refused* the motions.

LORD CAMERON OF LOCHBROOM.—This is a commercial action in which the pursuers, a

German company, seek payment of a fee which, it is averred, is due to them from the defenders as provided for in a joint venture agreement entered into in October 1989. The fee is claimed for work done in connection with design work for the building by the defenders of a student residence for the City University in London. It is said that in the case of this building contract, the parties agreed to vary the terms and conditions of the joint venture agreement so that the parties' rights and responsibilities would remain as there provided for notwithstanding there was no joint venture company in existence as stipulated for in the joint venture agreement.

The summons was signeted on 27 March 1992. Defences have been lodged but as yet there has been no adjustment of the parties' pleadings. The defenders at this stage have moved me to appoint the pursuers to find caution for the expenses of the action in the sum of £50,000, or alternatively to ordain the pursuers to sist a mandatary. Each motion proceeds: "In respect (1) that the pursuers' address is wrongly stated in the instance and that it is believed that the pursuers have no place of business in Scotland; (2) that the pursuers are a German company who are at risk of being struck off the German Company Register; (3) that the pursuers have granted an assignation of their claim which is the subject matter of this action to the Bank of Scotland; and (4) in respect of the pursuers' financial position and that they may not be able to make payment of the expenses of the action in the event of its being unsuccessful".

In their defences the defenders deny that any concluded agreement was reached. Counsel for the defenders drew attention to averments to the effect that not only was no agreement concluded but that the conclusion of any agreement had been made conditional upon settlement by the pursuers of a claim for payment by an associated company of the defenders against the pursuers. Further he pointed to averments setting out that the pursuers had in fact received payment for any services rendered by them in the City University development direct from the university itself and that the contract work for the subject had been undertaken not by the defenders but by an associated company in the same group.

In support of his motion for caution counsel for the defenders founded in the first place upon what he termed the "false" address in Scotland which appears in the instance of the summons as the pursuers' place of business there. It is sufficient to say that the pursuers accept that they do not now have any place of business in Scotland, having meantime withdrawn from any contract work in the United Kingdom and their sometime authorised representative, Mr Nawort, referred to in the summons, having ceased to be such. It appears that his is the address in Leslie, Fife, referred to in the summons. I was advised that he was in part responsible for giving instructions for the raising of the present action. From the information tendered to me by counsel for the pursuers as to how it came to be averred that the pursuers had a place of

business at that address, I remain doubtful that in fact that address was ever truly the pursuers' place of business. Be that as it may, the issue falls to be determined upon the basis that the pursuers are a German company who have no place of business in Scotland and whose registered address is in Germany.

Counsel for the defenders next made reference to documents produced which set out that for a period of time in late 1991 there had been some question that the entry of the pursuers in the German commercial register might be deleted by reason of a lack of a registered office. It appears that thereafter service of a change of address had been registered by the pursuers and the matter has not presently been taken further. No material was put before me to suggest that the pursuers are in financial difficulties and would not be able to meet any decree for payment of expenses made against them. I do not consider that any unfavourable inference to that effect can be taken from the facts that they no longer have a place of business in this jurisdiction and that at one stage consideration was being given to their being deleted from the German commercial register.

The next matter upon which the defenders founded was a submission that in the light of the defences the pursuers' ground of action must be regarded as uncertain. I observe that at this stage the pleadings are as yet unadjusted and it is not possible to assert that the pursuers' case on the facts averred by them has no substance or is not relevant. So far as I can judge at this stage there is an issue to try as between the parties. Counsel for the defenders prayed in aid documentary material relating to an assignation dated 24 October 1990 intimated to the defenders by the Bank of Scotland whereby the pursuers bore to assign to the bank all sums due and to become due by the defenders to the pursuers in respect of work to be done with regard to an agreement dated 30 October 1989. No averment appears in the defences concerning this document and there is no plea of no title to sue in them. As counsel for the pursuers rightly observed, an assignation in security such as this appears to be, does not serve to make the bank the true dominus litis: Halliday, *Coneyancing Law and Practice*, Vol I, p 231. Counsel for the defenders referred me to Maclaren on *Expenses*, p 17 and *Walker v Wedderspoon* for the proposition that caution may be required even if the assignation is in security only. But it remains at best a matter for the discretion of the court to determine whether in the whole circumstances it is equitable that the pursuer should find caution.

Counsel for the defenders accepted that the provisions of s 726 (2) of the Companies Act 1985 did not apply to the pursuers as a foreign company. Nevertheless, he submitted, the criterion adopted in cases such as *Dean Warwick Ltd v Borthwick* that the remedy of caution is available where there is a substantial risk that any award of expenses in the defenders' favour will not be satisfied, is apt. Nor is it necessary that there should be impending insolvency (*Robertson v McCaw*). I would accept that in appropriate circumstances in any case the court may require

A caution to be found by a party where the court is satisfied that there is such a substantial risk present and that it would be inequitable that the party, whose circumstances or conduct give rise to that risk, should proceed further in the action without finding caution. In the present case the defenders accept that any decree pronounced in this action awarding expenses in their favour against the pursuers may be registered and become enforceable in the German courts. It was urged that such a step would involve the defenders in further expense. That may be so, but I would assume

B that such additional costs would also be recoverable against the pursuers in like manner as within this jurisdiction. Looking to the factors set out in the defenders' motion, I do not consider that there is any warrant for suggesting that in the instance the pursuers gave a "false" address as that phrase is used in the passage in Maclaren on *Court of Session Practice*, p 294 to which I was referred by counsel for the defenders. In any event, the matter is now clarified. As to the remaining factors, having reviewed the circum-

C stances, I do not consider that there is a risk of prejudice to the defenders of such a nature or degree as would justify an order requiring the pursuers to find caution as a condition precedent to their proceeding further with the present action.

There remains the alternative motion which was pressed before me, namely to require the pursuers to sist a mandatary. Counsel for the defenders referred me to *Renfrew and Brown v Magistrates of Glasgow* and *Overbury v Peek* for the proposition that the sisting of

D a mandatary was necessary for the purpose of having some person within the jurisdiction to be responsible for the proper conduct of the proceedings since the pursuers no longer had a place of business in the jurisdiction. He alluded to the delay and expense that might be occasioned by having to register any award of expenses in the defenders' favour in the German courts. The circumstances of this case are not such as to persuade me that the pursuers should be required to sist a mandatary on the pleadings as they presently

E stand. The fact that a pursuer is a foreign person is not per se ground for granting such a motion, more particularly where mechanism exists for enforcing any decree pronounced in this court against that person in the courts of the country where that person resides. (See Maxwell, *Court of Session Practice*, p 223; *Dessau v Daish*.) The pursuers are subject to the jurisdiction of the German courts. A decree pronounced in this court awarding expenses against them can be registered in the German courts and become enforce-

F able there. There is nothing before me which satisfies me that the pursuers are verging on or moving towards insolvency. In the whole circumstances accordingly I shall refuse both motions.

Counsel for Pursuers, R A Smith; Solicitors, Maclay, Murray & Spens — Counsel for Defenders, G N H Emslie, QC; Solicitors, Lindsay, WS.

I C W

Dominion Technology Ltd v Gardner Cryogenics Ltd (No 1)

OUTER HOUSE
LORD CULLEN
11 NOVEMBER 1992

Process — Commission and diligence — Recovery of documents and other property before commencement of proceedings — Relevancy — Petitioner intending to raise proceedings if appropriate evidence recovered — Whether proceedings likely to be brought — Administration of Justice (Scotland) Act 1972 (c 59), s 1.

The Administration of Justice (Scotland) Act 1972 by s 1 empowers the court to order the inspection and recovery of documents and other property for the purpose of civil proceedings before those proceedings are raised if those proceedings "are likely to be brought".

A company alleged that two other companies had induced a subsidiary of a further company to breach a contract for the supply of diving gas. The first company sought to recover documents and other property in the possession of all four other companies. In their petition for an order for recovery, the petitioners averred that they intended to raise proceedings against the two companies alleged to have induced the breach, if appropriate evidence was available. The respondent companies sought to have the petition dismissed as irrelevant on the grounds that it did not aver the basis on which proceedings were likely to be brought. The petitioners contended that it was sufficient if there was a reasonable prospect of proceedings being brought.

Held, (1) that in an application under s 1 of the Administration of Justice (Scotland) Act 1972 in connection with proceedings not yet raised, it was necessary for the applicant to satisfy the court that proceedings were likely to be brought and that, as a matter of the exercise of the court's discretion, it was appropriate that an order for recovery should be granted (p 832B); (2) that the applicant accordingly required to make adequate averments as to the substance of and basis for the action which he proposed to raise and that the test of "are likely to be brought" required to be applied before any documents or property were recovered (p 832C-D); and petition *dismissed* as irrelevant.

Friel, Petr, 1981 SLT 113, *considered.*

Petition for an order under s 1 of the Administration of Justice (Scotland) Act 1972

Dominion Technology Ltd sought recovery of documents and other property from (first) Gardner Cryogenics Ltd, (second) Air Products plc, (third) Northern Coasters Ltd and (fourth) Stena Holding (UK) Ltd with a view to proceeding against Gardner Cryogenics Ltd and Air Products plc to recover

damages for the loss suffered by the petitioners as a
result of Gardner Cryogenics Ltd and Air Products
plc inducing a subsidiary of Stena Holding (UK) Ltd
to breach a contract for the supply of diving gas. After
hearing counsel for the petitioners, an order was
granted and documents and other property were
recovered and delivered to the Deputy Principal Clerk
of Session. The first and second respondents, supported by the third and fourth respondents, lodged
answers to the petition pleading that the petition
should be dismissed as irrelevant.

The petition came before the Lord Ordinary
(Cullen) on procedure roll on the respondents' plea to
the relevancy of the petition.

Statutory provisions

The Administration of Justice (Scotland) Act 1972
provides:

"1.—(1) Without prejudice to the existing powers of
the Court of Session and of the sheriff court, those
courts shall have power . . . to order the inspection,
photographing, preservation, custody and detention of
documents and other property (including, where
appropriate, land) which appear to the court to be
property as to which any question may relevantly arise
in any existing civil proceedings before that court or
in civil proceedings which are likely to be brought,
and to order the production and recovery of any such
property, the taking of samples thereof and the carrying out of any experiment thereon or therewith. . . .

"(2) Notwithstanding any rule of law or practice to
the contrary, the court may exercise the powers mentioned in subsection (1) or (1A) of this section — . . .
(b) where proceedings have not been commenced, on
the application at any time of a person who appears to
the court to be likely to be a party to or minuter in
proceedings which are likely to be brought."

Cases referred to

*Boyle v Glasgow Royal Infirmary and Associated
    Hospitals*, 1969 SLT 137; 1969 SC 72.
British Motor Trade Association v Gray, 1951 SLT
    247; 1951 SC 586.
Colquhoun, Petitioner, 1990 SLT 43.
*Dunning v United Liverpool Hospitals' Board of Gover-
    nors* [1973] 2 All ER 454; [1973] 1 WLR 586.
Friel, Petitioner, 1981 SLT 113; 1981 SC 1.
Moore v Greater Glasgow Health Board, 1979 SLT 42;
    1978 SC 123.
Shaw v Vauxhall Motors Ltd [1974] 2 All ER 1185;
    [1974] 1 WLR 1035.
Smith, Petitioner, 1985 SLT 461.
Yau v Ogilvie & Co, 1985 SLT 91.

On 11 November 1992 the Lord Ordinary *sustained*
the respondents' plea to the relevancy and *dismissed*
the petition.

LORD CULLEN.—In this petition for an order
under s 1 of the Administration of Justice (Scotland)
Act 1972 the court on 5 February 1991 after hearing
counsel for the petitioners (whom I will refer to as

"Dominion") granted commission and diligence for
the recovery of the documents and property called for
in the second schedule annexed to the petition;
appointed two commissioners and granted warrant
and authorised them to enter Unit 7, Westhill Industrial Estate, Westhill, Aberdeen, and Stena House,
Westhill Industrial Estate, to open lockfast places, and
to take possession of all and any such documents and
magnetic or electronic media as might be found at
their sight at the said premises or any of them and to
deliver the same to the Deputy Principal Clerk of
Session, pending further orders of the court. According to the terms of the petition Unit 7 was the address
of the first and second respondents (referred to here as
"Gardner" and "Air Products"); and Stena House
was the address of the third and fourth respondents
(referred to here as "Stena" and "Stena Holding (UK)
Ltd"). Answers to the petition were lodged by
Gardner and Air Products; and by Stena and Stena
Holding (UK) Ltd.

From the averments of Dominion it can be seen that
Dominion entered into an agreement (referred to here
as "the original agreement") with Stena dated 25
August and 3 September 1988 whereby Stena agreed
to purchase from Dominion, and Dominion agreed to
supply, Stena's total diving gas requirements for a
period of not less than five years from the date of the
original agreement, being 30 November 1988. Stena is
a subsidiary of Stena Holding (UK) Ltd. The purpose
for which Dominion sought the recovery of documents from the respondents was with a view to
proceedings against Gardner and Air Products to
recover damages for the loss suffered by Dominion as
a result of their inducing Stena to breach the original
agreement. Gardner is a subsidiary of Air Products.

On 7, 8 and 12 February 1991 one of the commissioners attended at the offices of Gardner at Westhill
Industrial Estate and there took possession of certain
documents and other property which he considered
fell within the terms of the second schedule to the
petition. However, at a late state of his search he discovered that these offices were not situated at Unit 7,
which was some distance away. He decided to report
the matter to the court, seal up the documents and
other property and deliver them to the Deputy Principal Clerk of Session to await the further orders of the
court. He presented a report to the court on 5 March
1991. On 25 September 1991 Dominion presented a
second petition for an order under s 1 which arose out
of the fact that the documents and other property had
been recovered from premises of Gardner other than
Unit 7. This opinion is not directly concerned with
the second petition. It is sufficient to state that the
documents and other property remain in the hands of
the Deputy Principal Clerk of Session.

On 22 September 1992 the hearing of both petitions
commenced before me. I determined that the hearing
should be directed in the first instance to the preliminary pleas which had been tabled by the respondents
and sought dismissal of both petitions. On 23
September during the course of the discussion I
granted a motion by Dominion for leave to lodge a

A minute of amendment, and allowed the respondents to lodge answers if so advised, within certain periods. At the continued hearing on 16 October 1992 I allowed the record to be amended in terms of Dominion's minute of amendment and the answers lodged on behalf of the respondents, with the exception of paras 3 and 4 of the answers of Stena and Stena Holding (UK) Ltd. Later in this opinion I will give reasons for allowing the pleadings to be amended to this extent.

B Section 1 (1) of the Administration of Justice (Scotland) Act 1972 provides, subject to certain provisions which are of no relevance to the present case, that the Court of Session is to have power "to order the inspection, photographing, preservation, custody and detention of documents and other property (including, where appropriate, land) which appear to the court to be property as to which any question may relevantly arise in any existing civil proceedings before that court or in civil proceedings which are likely to be brought, and to order the production and recovery of any such property, the taking of samples thereof and the carry-C ing out of any experiment thereon or therewith". Subsection (2) of s 1 further provides that the court may exercise the power mentioned in subs (1) where proceedings have not been commenced, "on the application at any time of a person who appears to the court to be likely to be a party to or minuter in proceedings which are likely to be brought".

The submission of counsel for Gardner and Air Products, which was supported by counsel for the D other respondents, was that the diligence which had been granted amounted to a fishing diligence and was one to which Dominion were not entitled since they had not averred the basis of proceedings which were "likely to be brought" within the meaning of s 1 (1). Their averments were accordingly irrelevant and the petition should be dismissed. It followed from the dismissal of the petition that the order which had been granted on 5 February 1991 would be superseded.

The discussion before me fell into two parts. The E first was concerned with the question as to the correct approach for an application under s 1. The second was concerned with the question whether the averments of Dominion satisfied that approach.

In regard to the first question, counsel for the respondents reminded me that in applying s 1 to existing proceedings prior to the making up of an open record, the court had held in *Moore v Greater Glasgow Health Board* that the party seeking recovery of documents required to show that they were necessary to F enable him to make his own averments more specific or to make adequate replies to his opponent's averments. Otherwise the diligence would be regarded as fishing. In regard to prospective proceedings counsel referred me to the opinion of Lord Maxwell in *Friel, Petr.* At 1981 SLT, pp 114-115 his Lordship made certain remarks about the expression "likely to be brought". Having expressed the view that it was probably going too far to say that the applicant required to aver facts which would make an action relevant if averred on a record he said: "There is a real question,

however, as to whether it can be said that proceedings are likely to be brought where, as here, it is clear that G they cannot be brought unless the order is granted. That is to say, where the ascertainment of matters essential to the bringing of proceedings, such as the identity of the prospective defender, is itself the object of the application. I do not consider it necessary or desirable to determine that question in this case."

He then referred to the English case of *Dunning v United Liverpool Hospitals' Board of Governors* which dealt with the similar but not identical wording of s 31 of the Administration of Justice Act 1970 and said: H "My impression from that case is that the judges would have given an affirmative answer to the question in certain circumstances. James LJ, however, said ([1973] 1 WLR at p 593): 'In order to take advantage of the section the applicant for relief must disclose the nature of the claim he intends to make and show not only the intention of making it but also that there is a reasonable basis for making it. Ill-founded, irresponsible and speculative allegations or allegations based merely on hope would not provide a reasonable basis I for an intended claim in subsequent proceedings.' I think that this would equally apply to an application for an order under s 1 of the 1972 Act on the ground that the proceedings 'are likely to be brought'." The case of *Friel* was, however, decided on other grounds.

In *Colquhoun, Petr* Lord Prosser, when refusing a motion for the recovery of documents under s 1, observed at p 44 that the petitioner's averment that he believed that on due investigation the stewardship of certain trustees might be found to have been wanting J did not appear to him to show that at that stage an action of damages against the trustees fell into the category required by s 1 of "civil proceedings which are likely to be brought". He went on to state: "It is to be observed that in the petitioner's pleadings, there is some suggestion that 'due investigation' might lead one to a position where it was likely that proceedings would be brought. In my opinion, the Act requires the court to take the view that such proceedings are likely to be brought at the time of the application. I do not K consider that an order of this type should be granted where such proceedings are merely a possibility, but would be rendered likely on the basis of the documentation recovered." Counsel invited me to adopt a similar approach in the present case.

In response counsel for Dominion submitted that the decisions in regard to existing proceedings were of no assistance in the present case since the courts had adopted the same approach as they had taken before the passing of the Act, as in *Boyle v Glasgow Royal* L *Infirmary and Associated Hospitals*. In his submission the correct test in regard to prospective proceedings was that set out in the opinion of James LJ which Lord Maxwell had quoted in *Friel*. Section 31 of the Administration of Justice Act 1970 posed essentially the same question as did s 1 of the 1972 Act. In *Dunning*, which was concerned with prospective proceedings for medical negligence, the report of a consultant physician and neurologist stated that there was, subject to what might be contained in the hospital notes, no indication of such negligence. There was, however, evidence of a sudden dramatic change in the health of the patient and as to her subsequent medical history. James LJ at [1973] 1 WLR, p 593 said: "Does the opinion of Dr Evans override that evidence so that it no longer provides a reasonable basis for making a claim? I do not think so. It would have done so, in my judgment, had not the report been qualified by Dr Evans' urgent desire to study the clinical notes without which he says the medical assessment was made more difficult. As it stands, it leaves open the possibility that the notes, if available, may add to the existing evidence to support Mrs Dunning's allegations. If the notes do not confirm Dr Evans' professional view, a claim is more than likely. I would construe likely there as meaning a 'reasonable prospect'."

Lord Denning MR went rather further than James LJ. At p 590 he said: "So the likelihood of a claim depends on the outcome of the discovery. It depends on what Dr Evans finds in the medical reports and case notes. How do you apply the section to this situation? It is difficult, but I think that we should construe 'likely to be made' as meaning 'may' or 'may well be made' dependent on the outcome of the discovery. One of the objects of the section is to enable a plaintiff to find out — before he starts proceedings — whether he has a good cause of action or not. This object would be defeated if he had to show — in advance — that he had already got a good cause of action before he saw the documents."

A similar approach had been taken by the Court of Appeal in *Shaw v Vauxhall Motors Ltd.* Counsel went on to submit that in *Colquhoun*, in which *Dunning* had not been cited, Lord Prosser had applied the wrong test by requiring that the "likelihood" should not be dependent upon what was found in the documents recovered. In any event his remarks should be not treated as having general application. In the case of *Yau v Ogilvie* Lord McDonald's approach was consistent with *Dunning* in holding that an application under s 1 should contain "sufficient information to enable the court to know what the action was going to be about and what assistance the documents sought would give in deciding it". However in *Smith, Petr* Lord Wylie was in error in requiring that in a pre-litigation situation "a prima facie case has been made out". Accordingly the correct approach was for Dominion to set out information from which the inference could be drawn that they might well have a case. This would be the "reasonable basis" to which James LJ referred. If the court was satisfied that documents might well exist which would confirm or negate the ground of action there was an appropriate basis for an order under s 1; and the diligence sought would not be a fishing diligence.

In regard to the question whether the averments of Dominion satisfied the correct test, counsel for the respondents pointed out that, after making averments as to actions which they believed Gardner and Air Products had taken, Dominion averred in para 6 of the petition: "In the foregoing circumstances the petitioners intend, if appropriate evidence is available, to raise proceedings against Gardner and Air Products to recover damages for the loss suffered as a result of their inducing the breach of the agreement by Stena. The documentary evidence available to the petitioners in the course of their investigations does not provide sufficient details of such inducement. The petitioners accordingly require access to the business records of Gardner, Air Products, Stena and Stena Holding (UK) Ltd in order to discover whether Gardner or Air Products has been guilty of inducing Stena to terminate the agreement with the petitioners." This plainly showed that Dominion had been seeking the diligence in order to discover whether they had a case or not. It was noted that in *Shaw* Buckley LJ said at [1974] 1 WLR, p 1040: "This power to order discovery before proceedings are commenced is certainly not one which should be used to encourage fishing expeditions to enable a prospective plaintiff to discover whether he has in fact got a case at all." Counsel for the respondents then went on to submit that in any event there were no relevant averments of the breach by Stena of the original agreement. Yet this was essential to an action in respect of the wrong of knowingly and unjustifiably inducing breach of contract, the type of proceedings to which the case of *British Motor Trade Association v Gray* related. Dominion did not state, or at any rate state clearly, that Stena had ever been in breach of contract.

In these circumstances Dominion sought to amend their averments in regard to the breach by Stena of the original agreement. This was opposed by the respondents on the ground that the amendment came too late and implied that the averments had been deficient when the order of 5 February 1991 had been granted. I allowed Dominion to amend their averments since I was satisfied that this did not involve any radical change to their case and that the amendment was necessary in order to determine the true question in issue between the parties. Stena and Stena Holding (UK) Ltd took the opportunity in paras 3 and 4 of their answers to introduce the propositions that Stena could never have been in breach of the original agreement in respect that it was unlawful by virtue of art 85 (2) of the Treaty establishing the European Economic Community; and separatim that it was void in respect that it had not been registered in terms of the Restrictive Trade Practices Act 1976. I considered that this raised separate issues which had no clear bearing on the petition, as opposed to any prospective proceedings against Gardner or Air Products. However, if they were considered to be relevant to the petition they could and should have been raised at an earlier stage.

Following the amendment of the record counsel for the respondents did not pursue further their submission that there were no averments that Stena had ever been in breach. However, they adhered to their submission that in the light of Dominion's averment that they entered into a further agreement ("the termination agreement") with Stena and Stena Holding (UK)

A Ltd dated 10 March 1989, the terms of which were incorporated in their averments, there was no breach of the original agreement which could form part of the essential basis of an action against Gardner and Air Products.

[His Lordship then narrated the submissions on behalf of the petitioners and respondents in relation to the proposition that the petitioners' pleadings demonstrated that there had been no breach, an issue with which this report is not concerned, and continued:]

B   In an application under s 1 of the 1972 Act in connection with prospective proceedings it is, in my view, plainly necessary that the applicant should do more than set out the nature of the proceedings which he is proposing to raise and the relevance to those proceedings of the documents and other property for which he is seeking an order. The court requires to be satisfied that the proceedings "are likely to be brought"; and that as a matter of the exercise of its discretion it is appropriate that the order should be granted. This C entails in my view that the applicant requires to make adequate averments as to the substance of and basis for the case which he proposes to make. To accept less than this would not do justice to the terms of s 1 and would create the risk of an order being granted where the applicant did not know if there was a statable case but hoped to obtain the material for one by means of a fishing expedition.

The assumption which underlies Dominion's averments in the present case, and in particular in para 6, D is that in assessing whether proceedings "are likely to be brought" it is appropriate for the court to rely wholly or partly upon what the recovered documents or other property may show. In my view that approach is not warranted by the terms of s 1. The likelihood of proceedings requires to be shown to exist without reliance on what the recoveries may show.

I have not found the cases of *Dunning* and *Shaw* to be of assistance to me in the present context. Section E 31 of the 1970 Act is concerned with actions in respect of death and personal injuries and is somewhat differently worded from s 1 of the 1972 Act. More importantly, there are notable differences between the approach adopted by members of the Court of Appeal in each of these cases. Further, as was pointed out by counsel for the respondents, it is clear that at least some of their opinions were influenced by considerations related to the use of funds obtained by legal aid and by at least one of the principles governing applications for discovery in England.

F   For these reasons I have reached the view that the basis for recovery set out in para 6 is irrelevant.

However, I have also to consider the other arguments which were addressed to me. While I would agree with Lord Maxwell in *Friel* that an applicant should not require to aver facts which would make an action relevant if averred on a record, it would not be right for a petition to be allowed to proceed if it appeared from the petitioner's averments that there was no way in which a relevant claim in the prospec-

tive proceedings could be made. If this were the case there would be no justification for the view that the G prospective proceedings were "likely to be brought" or for exercising the court's discretion in favour of allowing recovery to proceed. [His Lordship considered the submissions and determined that issue also against the petitioners, and concluded:]

In these circumstances, quite apart from my views as to the correctness of Dominion's general approach in the petition, I consider that their own averments disclose no relevant basis for an application under s 1. H

In these circumstances I will sustain the first plea in law for each of the respondents and dismiss the petition.

―――――――――

Counsel for Petitioners, Philip, QC, Liddle; Solicitors, Brodies, WS — Counsel for First and Second Respondents, Martin, QC, Wolffe; Solicitors, Gray Muirhead, WS — Counsel for Third and Fourth Respondents, Clarke, QC; Solicitors, McGrigor Donald.

I

N W H

[The petitioners enrolled a reclaiming motion which was subsequently abandoned.]

Dominion Technology Ltd v   J
Gardner Cryogenics Ltd
(No 2)

OUTER HOUSE
LORD CULLEN
11 NOVEMBER 1992

Process — Commission and diligence — Recovery of documents and other property — Illegality surrounding posses- K *sion of documents and other property — Warrant pursuant to previous order for recovery exceeded — Administration of Justice (Scotland) Act 1972 (c 59), s 1.*

A company sought, without intimation, and obtained an order under s 1 of the Administration of Justice (Scotland) Act 1972 granting a warrant inter alia authorising commissioners to enter Unit 7 at a particular industrial estate in Aberdeen, to take possession of documents and other property therein and to L deliver the same to the Deputy Principal Clerk of Session, pending further orders from the court. According to the petition, Unit 7 was the address of two of the companies named as respondents. A commissioner searched the offices of one of the companies and took possession of documents and other property from the offices. At a late stage in the search, the commissioner discovered that the offices which he had been searching were not in Unit 7. The commissioner determined to report the matter to the Deputy Principal Clerk of Session and sealed up the documents and other property and delivered them to him. A report was then made. The petitioners later presented a further petition explaining how, in good faith, the petitioners had taken the company's address to be at Unit 7 and seeking to rectify the defects in the procedure whereby the documents and other property had been delivered to the Deputy Principal Clerk of Session. The second petition also sought authority for the commissioner to take possession of the documents and the property by now in the hands of the Deputy Principal Clerk of Session and thereafter redeliver them to the Deputy Principal Clerk of Session. The respondent companies argued that the second petition should be dismissed as incompetent, and that the original recovery had not been warranted by the order of the court and was accordingly unlawful.

Held, that the courts would not order recovery if that meant that advantage was taken of the unlawful use of a previous order of the court, and that accordingly the second petition was incompetent (p 835D-E); and petition *dismissed.*

Observed, that cases on admissibility of unlawfully obtained evidence in criminal and civil proceedings were not relevant to the issue of the competency of an order under s 1 of the Administration of Justice (Scotland) Act 1972 (p 835C-D).

Petition under s 1 of the Administration of Justice (Scotland) Act 1972

Dominion Technology Ltd presented a petition to the Court of Session which sought an order under s 1 of the Administration of Justice (Scotland) Act 1972 to rectify any defects in the procedure whereby documents and other property had been delivered to the Deputy Principal Clerk of Session in purported exercise of an order granted in an earlier petition involving the same parties, and to authorise a commissioner to take possession of documents and other property in the hands of the Deputy Principal Clerk of Session and thereafter to redeliver them to the Deputy Principal Clerk of Session.

The case called on the procedure roll before the Lord Ordinary (Cullen) when counsel for the first and second respondents sought to have the petition dismissed as incompetent.

Statutory provisions

The Administration of Justice (Scotland) Act 1972 provides:

"1.—(1) Without prejudice to the existing powers of the Court of Session and of the sheriff court, those courts shall have power . . . to order the inspection, photographing, preservation, custody and detention of documents and other property (including, where appropriate, land) which appear to the court to be property as to which any question may relevantly arise in any existing civil proceedings before that court or in civil proceedings which are likely to be brought, and to order the production and recovery of any such property, the taking of samples thereof and the carrying of any experiment thereon or therewith."

Cases referred to

Adam v Crowe (1887) 14 R 800.
Advocate (HM) v Turnbull, 1951 SLT 409; 1951 JC 96.
Azcarate v Iturrizaga, 1938 SLT 390; 1938 JC 573.
Lawrie v Muir, 1950 SLT 37; 1950 JC 19.
Leckie v Miln, 1982 SLT 177.
Pringle v Bremner and Stirling (1867) 5 M 55.
Rattray v Rattray (1898) 5 SLT 245; (1897) 25 R 315.

On 11 November 1992 the Lord Ordinary *upheld* the respondents' preliminary plea and *dismissed* the petition.

LORD CULLEN.—This petition for an order under s 1 of the Administration of Justice (Scotland) Act 1972 arises out of what occurred during the execution of a commission and diligence granted on 5 February 1991 in an earlier petition by the petitioners (whom I will refer to as "Dominion").

The interlocutor of 5 February 1991 in that petition granted commission and diligence for the recovery of the documents and property called for in the second schedule annexed to the petition; appointed two commissioners and granted warrant and authorised them to enter Unit 7, Westhill Industrial Estate, Westhill, Aberdeen, and Stena House, Westhill Industrial Estate, to open lockfast places, and to take possession of all and any such documents and magnetic or electronic media as might be found at their sight at the said premises or any of them and to deliver the same to the Deputy Principal Clerk of Session, pending further orders of the court. According to the terms of the petition Unit 7 was the address of the first and second respondents (referred to here as "Gardner" and "Air Products"); and Stena House was the address of the third and fourth respondents (referred to here as "Stena" and "Stena Holding (UK) Ltd").

According to the averments of Dominion the purpose for which they sought the recovery of documents from the respondents was with a view to proceedings against Gardner and Air Products to recover damages for the loss suffered by Dominion as a result of their inducing Stena to breach an agreement. Gardner is a subsidiary of Air Products; and Stena is a subsidiary of Stena Holding (UK) Ltd.

On 7, 8 and 12 February 1991 one of the commissioners attended at the offices of Gardner at Westhill Industrial Estate and there took possession of certain documents and other property which he considered fell within the terms of the second schedule to the petition. However, at a late stage of his search he discovered that these offices were not situated at Unit 7, which was some distance away. He decided to report the matter to the court, seal up the documents and other property and deliver them to the Deputy Principal Clerk of Session to await the further orders of the court. He presented a report to the court on 5 March 1991. On 25 September 1991 Dominion presented the present petition for an order under s 1 of the 1972 Act. In it Dominion averred that having made certain investigations after the disclosure of the commissioner's report they believed it to be true that the premises occupied by Gardner were not Unit 7. They also set out reasons why they had previously supposed that the premises were at that address. They averred that the overall purpose of the petition and the interlocutor of 5 February 1991 had not been departed from; and that they were seeking to rectify any defect in the procedure whereby the documents and property were delivered to the Deputy Principal Clerk of Session; and that to that end they sought an order appointing a commissioner to take possession of the documents and other property in the hands of the Deputy Principal Clerk of Session and thereafter to redeliver them to the Deputy Principal Clerk of Session.

On 27 September 1991 after hearing counsel for Dominion the court granted diligence against havers for the recovery of the documents and property recovered by the original commissioner in terms of the interlocutor of 5 February 1991 and delivered by him to the Deputy Principal Clerk of Session and now in the hands of the Deputy Principal Clerk of Session, and commission to a new commissioner to attend upon the Deputy Principal Clerk of Session and take possession of the said documents and property, authorised the Deputy Principal Clerk of Session to deliver up said documents and property and ordained the commissioner of new to lodge same with the Deputy Principal Clerk of Session. In these circumstances the documents and other property recovered by the first commissioner remain in the hands of the Deputy Principal Clerk of Session. On 22 September 1992 the hearing of both petitions commenced before me. It was agreed that answers which had been lodged on behalf of Air Products and a minute of amendment which had been lodged on behalf of Gardner should be treated as documents lodged on behalf of both Gardner and Air Products. I determined that the hearing should be directed in the first instance to the preliminary pleas which had been tabled by these respondents.

In regard to the first petition I would refer to my separate opinion for the circumstances in which and the reasons for which I have decided to dismiss that petition [1993 SLT 828].

As regards the present petition, counsel for Gardner and Air Products invited me to sustain their plea to the competency of the petition. They also invited me to sustain their plea to the relevancy of Dominion's averments, but presented no separate argument in support of that course of action.

The argument which was presented in support of the submission that the petition should be dismissed was that the recovery of documents and other property from premises other than Unit 7 was not warranted by the interlocutor of 5 February 1991 and accordingly was unlawful. It followed that they were not lawfully delivered into the hands of the Deputy Principal Clerk of Session. It would not have been competent for the court to grant a new order for recovery from Gardner's premises with a view to giving retrospective validity to what had already happened. No order should have been granted which took advantage of what had already been done unlawfully. It followed that the court should not have granted commission to a second commissioner to take possession of the documents and other property from the hands of the Deputy Principal Clerk of Session.

I was referred by counsel for the respondents to a number of criminal cases in which the High Court of Justiciary had required to consider the admissibility of documents which had been recovered without proper warrant (*Lawrie v Muir; HM Advocate v Turnbull;* and *Leckie v Miln*). From these it appeared that whereas the court recognised the unlawfulness of the recovery there was no absolute rule that what had been recovered was not admissible in evidence against the accused. The court applied the test of whether it was unfair to admit it in evidence. In the case of *HM Advocate v Turnbull* Lord Guthrie pointed out at 1951 SLT, p 410 that the initial illegality was not cured by the granting of a later warrant after the contents of the writs had been examined and used to enable the subsequent charges to be brought. He observed that possession and use of the documents had not been obtained under the later warrant. It was not retroactive. It authorised future and not past actions of officers of law.

It was also pointed out by counsel that it was an actionable wrong for police officers to exceed the scope of their warrant (*Pringle v Bremner and Stirling*). In the case of *Rattray v Rattray* the opinion was expressed by Lord Trayner and Lord Moncreiff that a letter written by the defender to the co-defender in a divorce case which the pursuer had stolen from a post office was competent evidence in support of the pursuer's case. At (1897) 24 R, pp 318-319 Lord Trayner said: "The policy of the law in later years (and I think a good policy) has been to admit almost all evidence which will throw light on disputed facts and enable justice to be done." Counsel pointed out that all these cases had been concerned with the admissibility of evidence which had been obtained unlawfully. However, the cases demonstrated that a strict approach was applied in determining what had been obtained unlawfully. Counsel also pointed out that persons who had exceeded the bounds of what was a lawful arrestment had not been permitted to take advantage of what they had achieved thereby (*Azcarate v Iturrizaga;* and *Adam v Crowe*). The averments in the petition did not entitle Dominion to the benefit of a search which had been carried out unlawfully.

In response counsel for Dominion drew my attention to the reasons why Dominion had erroneously but in good faith thought that Unit 7 was the address of Gardner and Air Products. They had not abused any warrant which had been conferred upon them. The present petition proceeded on the basis that it was outwith the authority of the original commissioner to recover the documents and other property from the premises of Gardner. Rather than allow them to be returned to the premises Dominion had sought an order for their recovery from the place where they were. This would give effect to the underlying intention of the court and serve the interests of justice. The difficulty which had arisen was a technicality. No prejudice in the true sense would be suffered by the respondents if the petition was allowed to proceed. Counsel founded in particular on the case of *Rattray* which showed that there was no foundation for the suggestion which had been made by counsel for Gardner and Air Products that in civil proceedings the case for allowing the use of what had been unlawfully recovered was weaker than in criminal proceedings. The court required to weigh against the need for a strict interpretation and application of its orders, the fact that through no fault on the part of Dominion its underlying intention would be frustrated by the dismissal of the petition.

It will be clear from the foregoing that the researches of counsel did not bring to light a previous instance in which the court was asked to grant warrant for the recovery of documents and other property from a person to whom they had been delivered unlawfully as a result of a previous order of the court being exceeded. However, the cases of *Azcarate* and *Adam* are of some assistance in indicating that the courts will not permit a party to take advantage of a situation which has been brought about by an exceeding of the court's warrant. I am not persuaded that the cases which were concerned with the admissibility of evidence in criminal or civil proceedings are of relevance in the context of determining the competency of an order under s 1 of the 1972 Act in the present type of case. In those decisions the court was careful to distinguish between the unlawfulness of the recovery and the question of the admissibility of evidence. The policy which underlies the admission of evidence does not seem to me to assist in the present context which is concerned with the competency of invoking the court's power to order recovery from a person whose possession derives from the unlawful use of a previous order of the court. In my opinion the court should not be asked to order recovery in circumstances in which this would mean that advantage was taken of the unlawful use of the court's previous order. In my view the petition is not competent.

I will accordingly sustain the first plea in law for Gardner and Air Products and dismiss the petition.

Counsel for Petitioners, Philip, QC, Liddle; Solicitors, Brodies, WS — Counsel for First and Second Respondents, Martin, QC, Wolffe; Solicitors, Gray Muirhead, WS — Counsel for Third and Fourth Respondents, Cullen; Solicitors, McGrigor Donald.

N W H

[The petitioners enrolled a reclaiming motion which was subsequently abandoned.]

Mullan v Anderson

COURT OF FIVE JUDGES

THE LORD JUSTICE CLERK (ROSS), LORDS MORISON, PROSSER, PENROSE AND BRAND

17 MARCH 1993

Process — Sheriff court — Remit to Court of Session — Criteria to be considered in assessing "importance or difficulty" of cause — Whether sheriff had discretion not to remit — Allegation of murder in civil action — Sheriff Courts (Scotland) Act 1971 (c 58), s 37 (1) (b).

Evidence — Standard of proof — Criminal allegation in civil action — Allegation of murder.

Section 37 (1) (b) of the Sheriff Courts (Scotland) Act 1971 provides that a sheriff "may . . . if he is of the opinion that the importance or difficulty of the cause makes it appropriate to do so, remit the cause to the Court of Session".

A widow and her children raised an action of damages in the sheriff court against the man who had been acquitted in the High Court of the murder of her husband. The averments made by the family of the deceased amounted to an allegation that the defender had murdered the deceased. This was denied and the defender sought a remit to the Court of Session in terms of s 37 (1) (b) of the Sheriff Courts (Scotland) Act 1971. The sheriff refused the motion and the defender appealed to the Court of Session. As the appeal raised an issue as to the correctness of the decision in *Data Controls (Middlesbrough) Ltd v British Railways Board*, 1991 SLT 426, a bench of five judges was convened. The appellant argued that the sheriff had erred in having regard to considerations which were irrelevant; in adopting an unreasonable approach to the issues of difficulty and importance; and in concluding that the standard of proof required was on a balance of probabilities.

Held, (1) that *Data Controls* was wrongly decided insofar as it held that the only relevant matters were importance and difficulty because (per the Lord Justice Clerk (Ross) and Lord Morison) that while a sheriff might conclude that a prima facie case for remit arose on the grounds of importance or difficulty, he might, in the exercise of his discretion, refrain from remitting because other factors, including practical or procedural advantages, made it inexpedient to take that course (pp 838G-L, 839G-I and 841B-E and J-K); (per Lords Prosser, Penrose and Brand) s 37 (1) (b) required a sheriff to remit a cause to the Court of Session with no further discretion if he was satisfied that its importance or difficulty made remit appropriate, but making that single stage determination should include consideration of the characteristics of the respective fora, and the question of importance included importance to the parties (pp 845E-F and I-J, 845L-846F, 849B-E and H-J and 851H-J); (2) that the sheriff's decision was open to review because (per the Lord Justice Clerk, Lords Morison and Penrose) in considering the importance of the cause the sheriff had erred in leaving out of account various factors such as the importance of the cause to the parties and the public interest involved in a civil court being asked to

reach a conclusion on an allegation of murder (pp
839I-840D, 842J-L and 850H-851B); (per Lords
Prosser and Brand) the sheriff had had regard to these
factors but his decision was one that no reasonable
sheriff could have reached (pp 847D-J and 851H-I); (3)
that the sheriff had correctly considered that the appropriate standard of proof was on a balance of probabilities (pp 840E-F, 842D-E, 846J-K, 851D and 851H-J);
and (4) that considering the matter anew it was appropriate to remit the case having regard to the importance
of the case to the defender and the previous acquittal
in the High Court (pp 840F-G, 842L-843A, 847J-
848A, 851G-H and 851H-I); and appeal *allowed*.

*Data Controls (Middlesbrough) Ltd v British Rail-
ways Board*, 1991 SLT 426, *overruled*.

Observed (per the Lord Justice Clerk, Lords
Morison and Penrose), that it was wrong to suggest
that only cases of unusual or even exceptional importance or difficulty should be remitted (pp 840A-B,
841L and 850D-E).

Dicta in *Shaw v Lanarkshire Health Board*, 1988
SCLR 13, *disapproved*.

Appeal from the sheriff court

Margaret Rush or Mullan and her children raised an
action of damages in Greenock sheriff court against
David William Anderson alleging that he had murdered Raymond Mullan, the husband and father of the
pursuers. The defender denied murder.

After sundry procedure the defender enrolled a
motion to have the cause remitted to the Court of
Session in terms of s 37 (1) (b) of the Sheriff Courts
(Scotland) Act 1971 as amended.

Statutory provisions

The Sheriff Courts (Scotland) Act 1971, as
amended, provides:

"37.—(1) In the case of any ordinary cause brought
in the sheriff court the sheriff (a) shall at any stage, on
the joint motion of the parties to the cause, direct that
the cause be treated as a summary cause, and in that
case the cause shall be treated for all purposes (including appeal) as a summary cause and shall proceed
accordingly; (b) may, subject to section 7 of the Sheriff
Courts (Scotland) Act 1907, on the motion of any of
the parties to the cause, if he is of the opinion that the
importance or difficulty of the cause makes it appropriate to do so, remit the cause to the Court of
Session. . . .

"(3) A decision — (a) to remit, or not to remit, under
subsection (2A), (2B) or (2C) above; or (b) to make, or
not to make, a direction by virtue of paragraph (b) of,
or the proviso to, subsection (2) above, shall not be
subject to review; but from a decision to remit, or not
to remit, under subsection (1) (b) above an appeal shall
lie to the Court of Session."

Cases referred to

Arnott v Burt (1872) 11 M 62.
B v Kennedy, 1987 SLT 765.
Brown v Brown, 1972 SLT 143; 1972 SC 123.
Buick v Jagler, 1973 SLT (Sh Ct) 6.

Butler v Thom, 1982 SLT (Sh Ct) 57.
*Data Controls (Middlesbrough) Ltd v British Railways
Board*, 1991 SLT 426.
Fleming and Ferguson Ltd v Burgh of Paisley, 1948
SLT 457; 1948 SC 547.
G v G [1985] 1 WLR 647.
Guardian Royal Exchange Group v Moffat, 1986 SLT
262.
Halford v Brookes [1991] TLR 427; [1991] 1 WLR
428.
Harris v F, 1991 SLT 242.
Lamb v Lord Advocate, 1976 SLT 151; 1976 SC 110.
Lennon v The Co-operative Insurance Society Ltd, 1986
SLT 98.
McIntosh v British Railways Board (No 1), 1990 SLT
637; 1990 SC 338.
McWilliams v Sir William Arrol & Co Ltd, 1962 SLT
121; 1962 SC (HL) 70.
Paterson v Henry Robb Ltd, 1989 SLT 585.
Pepper (Inspector of Taxes) v Hart [1992] 3 WLR
1032; [1993] 1 All ER 42.
R v Hampshire County Council, ex p Ellerton [1985] 1
WLR 749.
*R v Secretary of State for the Home Department, ex p
Khawaja* [1984] AC 74; [1983] 2 WLR 321;
[1983] 1 All ER 765.
Rehman v Ahmad, 1993 SLT 741.
Shaw v Lanarkshire Health Board, 1988 SCLR 13.
Stevenson v Rogers, 1992 SLT 558.
Thomson v Corporation of Glasgow, 1962 SLT 105;
1962 SC (HL) 36.
Ward v Chief Constable, Strathclyde Police, 1991 SLT
292.

On 20 December 1990 the sheriff *refused* the
motion.

The defender appealed to the Court of Session.

Appeal

The appeal was first heard on 30 April 1992. As an
issue arose as to the correctness of the decision of the
court in a previous case the hearing resumed on 11
February 1993 before a bench of five judges.

On 17 March 1993 the court *allowed* the appeal,
remitted the case to the sheriff and *directed* him to
remit the case to the Court of Session.

THE LORD JUSTICE CLERK (ROSS).—In this
action the pursuers are seeking damages from the
defender as a result of the death of the deceased, who
was the husband of the first named pursuer, and who
died on or about 9 February 1990. The pursuers aver
that the defender was responsible for the death of the
deceased in that he deliberately or recklessly struck the
deceased with a knife whereby the blade penetrated
the deceased's heart and killed him. It is averred by
the pursuers that following upon the death of the
deceased the defender was apprehended and charged
with his murder. The defender went to trial on various
criminal charges, including a charge of murder in the
High Court at Paisley, and on 31 May 1990 the jury
returned a verdict of not proven on this charge with
the result that the defender was acquitted and liberated. In or about June 1990 the pursuers raised the

present action against the defender in the sheriff court
at Greenock. After sundry procedure including some
adjustment of the pleas, the defenders enrolled a
motion to have the cause remitted to the Court of
Session in terms of s 37 of the Sheriff Courts (Scotland) Act 1971, as amended by s 16 of the Law
Reform (Miscellaneous Provisions) (Scotland) Act
1980. On 20 December 1990 the sheriff pronounced
an interlocutor refusing the defender's motion, and
against the interlocutor of the sheriff the defender has
now appealed to this court.

Section 37 of the Sheriff Courts (Scotland) Act 1971
as amended deals with remits. Section 37 (1) is now in
the following terms: [his Lordship quoted its terms
and continued:]

Counsel were agreed that s 37 (1) (b), which in its
present form had been introduced by s 16 of the Law
Reform (Miscellaneous Provisions) (Scotland) Act
1980, had its origins in the *Report of the Grant Committee on the Sheriff Court* (Cmnd 3248, 1967).

As the sheriff makes clear in the note annexed to his
interlocutor of 20 December 1990, the solicitor for the
defender when moving the motion emphasised the
importance of the action not only to the defender as an
individual but also in respect of the legal issues which
it raised; the defender was faced with a repetition of
the allegation in the indictment, namely, murder.
That was an allegation of the utmost gravity. In addition it was maintained that the sum sought in damages
was substantial, namely, £100,000, and there was no
insurance against this type of risk with the result that
an award could affect the defender throughout his lifetime. It was also submitted that the action was important from the point of view of the pursuers themselves.
It was also maintained that the action concerned the
same facts as had been canvassed in the trial in the
High Court, and it was contended that it was not
appropriate for the sheriff court to appear to review
what had been done in the High Court, but that that
should be done by the supreme civil court. It was also
stated that the issues would fall to be determined
perhaps on a different standard of proof.

The pursuers on the other hand maintained before
the sheriff that the motion was premature as the
record had not been closed. They also submitted that
the motion should be refused on its merits. They contended that averments of criminal conduct in actions
of reparation founded upon delict were not unusual,
and that there was nothing difficult about the facts or
the legal duties which were founded upon. The pursuers also maintained that a remit would be financially
prejudicial to the pursuers who were not in receipt of
legal aid.

In determining whether or not to grant the motion,
the sheriff explains that he had regard to what had
been stated in *Butler v Thom, Shaw v Lanarkshire
Health Board* and *Data Controls (Middlesbrough) Ltd v
British Railways Board*. The sheriff concluded that
there did not appear to be any difficulties of fact or law
so special as to make it appropriate to remit the cause.
Although it was stated that the defender had no assets
of significance and that a decree against him would be

a burden upon him for his lifetime, the sheriff observed
that that would be the same whether the cause was
remitted to the Court of Session or remained in the
sheriff court. The sheriff did accept that it was a relevant factor that the pursuers did not have the benefit
of legal aid and that a remit to the Court of Session
could well involve them in significant further expense
over and above that likely to be incurred in the sheriff
court. The sheriff also expressed the view that the
sheriff court would not in any real sense be reviewing
a decision of the High Court. He stated that the
standard of proof in this cause, being a civil claim for
reparation, would be balance of probability, which was
a very different basis from the standard of proof in a
criminal trial. Although accepting that averments in
reparation actions relating to death caused by conduct
amounting to a crime would always be of the utmost
gravity, the sheriff expressed his final conclusion as
follows: "Nonetheless it seems to me unlikely that a
civil action based upon averments which might amount
to serious criminal conduct would be remitted to the
Court of Session merely on the basis of the importance
to the defender as an individual of answering such
allegations. It seems to me with respect that the
defender's solicitor misapprehends the purpose of the
civil action. It is one founded in delict seeking the civil
remedy of damages. It has no criminal connotations.
Indeed in this cause the criminal element in the facts
averred has already been determined in the defender's
favour."

In presenting the appeal counsel for the defender
emphasised that in arriving at his decision the sheriff
had been exercising a discretion. They contended,
however, that the sheriff had erred in exercising that
discretion. Counsel for the defender next dealt with
the proper construction to be placed upon s 37 (1) (b)
of the Act of 1971, and contended that the proper
approach in a case of this kind had been laid down in
*Data Controls (Middlesbrough) Ltd v British Railways
Board*. They maintained, however, that the sheriff in
this case had erred in taking into account irrelevant
factors, namely, the additional cost to the pursuers if
the case were remitted to the Court of Session, and the
financial consequences to the defender. His approach
had been unreasonable so far as the importance and
difficulty of the cause were concerned, and he had also
erred in law in holding that the standard of proof was
the balance of probability. His decision had been one
which no reasonable sheriff could have reached.
Counsel also contended that since the sheriff's
decision was flawed, the matter was at large for this
court and that when all relevant factors were taken
into account, this court should decide that the case
should be remitted to the Court of Session. One factor
favouring the Court of Session as forum, which had
not been considered by the sheriff, was the availability
of jury trial in the Court of Session.

As regards the power of the appellate court to review
the exercise of discretion by a judge in a court below,
the law is clear. In *Thomson v Corporation of Glasgow*,
1962 SLT at p 107, Lord Reid observed that the
House of Lords would not overrule the discretion of
a lower court merely because they might think that
they would have exercised the discretion differently.

He added: "I do not attempt to define the circumstances in which this House might take that course. We might do so if some irrelevant factor had been taken into account or some important relevant factor left out of account or if the decision was unreasonable, and we would no doubt do so if the decision could be said to be unjudicial."

Stevenson v Rogers was a case where the issue to be decided was one of fact and degree where there was room for more than one conclusion. Under reference to *G v G* the court observed that there was room for a wide judicial discretion with which an appellate court would not interfere unless it considered that the judge of first instance had "exceeded the generous ambit within which a reasonable disagreement is possible".

Counsel on both sides of the bar subjected s 37 (1) (b) to a close scrutiny. Counsel for the defender submitted that if the sheriff was of opinion that the importance or difficulty of the cause made it appropriate to remit the action to the Court of Session, he had no discretion not to remit on the basis of other factors. Counsel recognised that that construction of s 37 (1) (b) meant that the word "may" fell to be read as though the word was "shall". Counsel contended that if the sheriff was of opinion that it was appropriate to remit then it followed that it was inappropriate not to remit, and remitting the cause to the Court of Session then became mandatory. Counsel for the defender relied upon the decision in *Data Controls (Middlesbrough) Ltd v British Railways Board*. Counsel pointed out that all three judges in *Data Controls (Middlesbrough) Ltd v British Railways Board* accepted that so far as s 37 (1) (b) was concerned the only criteria to be considered were the importance or difficulty of the case, and that no other factors were relevant. In particular they all expressed the view that additional delay or expense were not matters which a sheriff was entitled to take into account when considering a motion under s 37 (1) (b). Counsel for the pursuers on the other hand maintained that the case of *Data Controls (Middlesbrough) Ltd v British Railways Board* had been wrongly decided. They maintained that exercise of the power contained in s 37 (1) (b) involved two stages. The first stage was for the sheriff to reach an opinion upon whether the importance or difficulty of the cause made it appropriate to remit to the Court of Session. If the sheriff was of the opinion that the importance or difficulty of the cause made it appropriate to remit to the Court of Session, he then required to proceed to the second stage of the exercise and decide whether or not to make the remit. Counsel submitted that if the sheriff had no discretion once he had arrived at the opinion that the importance or difficulty of the cause made it appropriate to remit the cause to the Court of Session, then the subsection would have begun with the word "shall" instead of the word "may". The presence of the word "may" showed that the sheriff had a discretion to remit even if he was of opinion that the importance or difficulty of the cause made it appropriate to remit.

Counsel for the pursuers recognised that in certain circumstances "may" in a statute may mean "shall"

(*Fleming and Ferguson Ltd v Paisley Magistrates*). However they contended that the present case was not one where words which were prima facie permissive fell to be treated as imperative.

In my judgment the reasoning of the Extra Division in *Data Controls (Middlesbrough) Ltd v British Railways Board* falls to be disapproved. Of the three judges who delivered opinions in that case Lord Allanbridge alone expressed any detailed views on the construction to be placed upon s 37 (1) (b). In the course of his opinion he said: "The word 'may' is used because it demonstrates that the sheriff has a discretion in reaching his own opinion on the matter, albeit that that opinion must be directed towards deciding whether the importance or difficulty of the cause makes it appropriate to remit" (p 430F).

I do not consider that that is a satisfactory explanation for the use of the word "may" in s 37 (1) (b). In my judgment counsel for the pursuers are well founded when they contend that if the subsection had the meaning attributed to it by the Extra Division in *Data Controls (Middlesbrough) Ltd v British Railways Board*, the subsection would have commenced with the word "shall" instead of the word "may". I agree with counsel for the pursuers that a sheriff when considering a motion under s 37 (1) (b) must proceed in two stages. The first stage is to form an opinion regarding the importance or difficulty of the cause. If the sheriff is of opinion that the importance or difficulty of the cause makes it appropriate to remit to the Court of Session, he must then proceed to stage 2 and determine having regard to all relevant factors placed before him whether he should remit. It was suggested by counsel for the defender that if the sheriff was of opinion that the importance or difficulty of the cause made it appropriate to remit, it was difficult to envisage any other factors which would cause him to conclude that it was not appropriate to remit. Counsel for the pursuers, on the other hand, maintained that if there was to be additional delay and expense as a result of remitting the cause to the Court of Session, that might make the sheriff decide not to remit. Moreover as counsel for the pursuers submitted s 37 (1) (b) did not contain any time limit as to when a motion for remit might be made, and if the defender was correct in contending that the sheriff had no discretion once he had arrived at the opinion that the importance or difficulty of the cause made it appropriate to remit, the consequence might be that he could be compelled to remit the cause to the Court of Session at a very late stage of the case, for example on the eve of a proof or even after the proof had been completed and the case was at avizandum. I agree with counsel for the pursuers that Parliament can hardly have intended such an unreasonable result, and that this is a further reason for concluding that the sheriff has a discretion even after he has formed the opinion that the importance or difficulty of the cause makes it appropriate to remit.

When considering this issue of statutory construction, counsel on both sides of the bar referred to the Grant committee report (1967). Counsel for the pursuers pointed out that it was now established by the House of Lords that where legislation was ambigu-

ous or obscure or its literal meaning led to an absurdity, it was open to the courts to refer to parliamentary
material as an aid to statutory construction (*Pepper
(Inspector of Taxes) v Hart*).

So far as the Grant committee report is concerned
the Grant committee recommended a power to remit
cases from the sheriff court to the Court of Session
"because of the importance or complexity of the issues
involved". It is clear however that the Grant committee did not intend that importance or complexity of
the issues should be the only matter to be taken into
account because when they also recommended that
civil jury trial in the sheriff court should cease to be
available, they observed, under reference to rights of
remit from the sheriff court to the Court of Session,
that a desire to have the case tried by a jury would be
a factor to be taken into account in deciding whether
a remit should be granted on the motion of either the
defender or the pursuer (para 191).

We were also referred to the proceedings in Parliament relating to the Law Reform (Miscellaneous Provisions) Act 1980 and to the debate which took place
with regard to what became s 16 of that Act which
amended s 37 of the Act of 1971 by introducing s 37
(1) (b) in its present terms. However there is nothing
in that debate which assists in the matter of construction which has now arisen. During the argument
counsel for the defenders drew attention to the terms
of Rule of Court 188J dealing with optional procedure. In Rule 188J (6) (a) (iv) it is provided that at
a hearing on the diet roll the court may "on special
cause shown, or of its own motion, because the difficulty or complexity of the case makes the action
unsuitable for the procedure under this section, order
that the action proceed as an ordinary action and
appoint the cause to the adjustment roll".

This rule was considered in *Paterson v Henry Robb
Ltd*, where the court held that the Lord Ordinary had
erred in taking an irrelevant consideration into
account. Having regard to the difference in the language of the Rule of Court compared to the language
of s 37 (1) (b) I have not found this case of assistance.

Counsel also referred to *McIntosh v British Railways
Board (No 1)*. That was a case concerning remit from
the Court of Session to the sheriff court under the provisions of the Law Reform (Miscellaneous Provisions)
(Scotland) Act 1985. Section 14 of that Act provides
that the Court of Session may remit an action to the
sheriff court where "the nature of the action makes it
appropriate to do so". Again in view of the difference
in language between the Act of 1985 and the Act of
1971, I have not found this case of great assistance.
The case does, however, show that in addition to considering the nature of the action, the court when
invited to make a remit was entitled to consider other
factors such as any practical or procedural advantages
to be found in adopting one forum rather than
another. The court plainly considered that there were
a number of extraneous matters which fell to be taken
into account in addition to the nature of the action.

In the course of the hearing one of your Lordships
suggested that the words "make it appropriate" meant
that the sheriff when forming his opinion about the
importance or difficulty of the case was entitled to
consider other factors as well. I am not impressed by
that suggestion. If the subsection had empowered the
sheriff to remit if he considered it appropriate to do so,
then I accept that he would be entitled to have regard
to any relevant factors bearing on the issue. But that
is not what the subsection empowers the sheriff to do.
It is the importance or difficulty of the cause which
must make it appropriate to remit; and when reaching
his opinion on that matter the sheriff is not entitled to
have regard to extraneous matters. Any other matters
can only be considered at what I have described as the
second stage.

In all the circumstances I am clearly of opinion that
the approach which was adopted by the Extra Division
in *Data Controls (Middlesbrough) Ltd v British Railways Board* was too narrow, and in particular that it
is incorrect to hold that the only relevant matters
under s 37 (1) (b) of the Act of 1971 are importance
and difficulty. In my opinion the decision in *Data
Controls (Middlesbrough) Ltd v British Railways Board*
should be overruled.

The next question to be determined is whether the
sheriff erred in arriving at his decision. In my opinion,
the sheriff did err in a number of respects. The sheriff
stated that the defender's solicitor had misapprehended the purpose of the civil action which was
founded in delict seeking the civil remedy of damages.
He added, "It has no criminal connotations". Counsel
for the pursuer was driven to concede that the civil
action did have criminal connotations, although they
contended that it would be correct to say that it had
no criminal consequences. It clearly has criminal
connotations because the pursuers have chosen to aver
that the defender "either deliberately or recklessly
struck the said Raymond Caraher Mullan with it,
whereby the blade penetrated his heart and killed
him". That plainly means that the pursuers are
seeking to establish that the defender murdered the
deceased, and making such an allegation even in a civil
action plainly has criminal connotations. Admittedly
the criminal courts have already determined this issue,
but I am satisfied that the sheriff was in error in failing
to appreciate that the present action does have criminal connotations.

In the second place the sheriff appears to have
approached the question of the importance of the
cause only from the point of view that it might be said
to be important to the defender as an individual in
answering the allegations made against him. It appears
to me that the sheriff has not had regard to all the submissions made to him on the subject of the importance
of the cause. A cause may be important for a variety
of reasons. It may be a test case or it may be a case
raising a point of principle; it may raise a question
upon which there is a dearth of authority. In my
opinion, such cases should be regarded by a sheriff as
important having regard to the subject matter of the
cause. Of course a case may also be important to the
parties. In this connection it would not be sufficient
merely that one party asserted that the case was important to him or her. But if the case could be regarded

objectively as of importance to the parties, then the sheriff could reasonably form the opinion that it was important. Counsel for the pursuers contended that in s 37 (1) (b) "importance" did not include "importance to the parties"; they submitted that if that had been intended the words "to the parties" would have appeared in the subsection. There is some force in the contention but I have come to the conclusion that the word "importance" should be regarded as having a wide meaning and as including important to the parties. On the other hand, I do not consider that to fall within the ambit of s 37 (1) (b) the cause must be "of unusual, even exceptional difficulty or importance", and I disagree with views to that effect expressed in *Shaw v Lanarkshire Health Board*.

In the present case, I am of opinion that the sheriff has failed to attach proper importance to the fact that an allegation of murder is one of the most serious which can ever be made against any individual, and that the cause is plainly important to the defender since that allegation has been made. Not only that but in my opinion the action is important from the point of view of the public. Whatever the pursuers' motives may be in raising the action, a civil court is being asked to reach a conclusion upon the question of whether the defender murdered the deceased, and in my opinion that gives rise to public interest and concern. Moreover the issue which the civil court will require to determine is not one upon which a sheriff is normally called upon to adjudicate in a civil proof. It is an issue which is normally determined by a jury in the High Court. This appears to me to emphasise that there is both importance and difficulty in this action which would make it appropriate for the action to be heard in the Court of Session as the supreme court rather than in the sheriff court. With all respect to the sheriff it appears to me that he has not given consideration to all the aspects of importance and difficulty which were relied upon by the defender.

Having said that I agree with the sheriff that some of the grounds put forward by the defender were without substance. There is no question of the civil court being asked to review what was done in the High Court; no difficulty should arise so far as standard of proof is concerned because in the civil action the standard of proof will be balance of probability. We were referred to a number of authorities bearing on this issue which I need not rehearse. Having regard to the nature of this action, I do not regard the matter as in doubt (*Lamb v Lord Advocate*, per Lord Justice Clerk, 1976 SLT at p 153; *B v Kennedy*; *Ward v Chief Constable, Strathclyde Police*). I would add that I do not consider that the fact that the sum sought in damages is substantial per se renders the case important. However, for the reasons which I have outlined above, I am of opinion that the sheriff left out of account various relevant factors bearing upon the importance of the case, and that in the circumstances the decision at which he arrived was unreasonable. That being so the issue is at large for this court, and for the reasons which I have already described, I am satisfied that the importance and difficulty of the case make it appropriate that the case should be remitted to the Court of Session, and that these considerations are not outweighed by the fact that a remit may cause additional delay and expense. I am also satisfied that the pursuers' right to choose the sheriff court as the forum is in this case outweighed by the importance and difficulty of the cause. I would add that the availability of jury trial in the Court of Session appears to me to be a further factor favouring remit. In all the circumstances I am satisfied that the present case is one where a case for remit under s 37 (1) (b) has been made out.

In these circumstances I would move your Lordships to uphold the appeal, to remit the case back to the sheriff with a direction that he should remit the cause to the Court of Session in accordance with the motion made to him in terms of s 37 (1) (b) of the Act of 1971.

LORD MORISON.—Your Lordship has set out the circumstances which have given rise to this appeal, and the terms of s 37 (as amended) to the Sheriff Courts (Scotland) Act 1971 under which the defender's motion was made. On behalf of the defender it was submitted inter alia that the sheriff had erred in law in taking into account, as he did, the additional expense which the pursuers would incur if the case were remitted to the Court of Session. It was because of this submission, and in light of the decision which supported it, *Data Controls (Middlesbrough) Ltd v British Railways Board* that the appeal was heard by this court. But it was also submitted that the sheriff had made other errors in his approach to the case, and that his decision was one which could not reasonably have been arrived at, and I deal with these submissions later.

In forming his "opinion" under the section, the sheriff is unambiguously restricted to a consideration only to the effects of any importance or difficulty which the cause may have. The question which he must answer is not, as was canvassed (but not submitted) in the course of the hearing, whether it *is* appropriate to remit the cause, but whether either or both of the features mentioned, and these alone, *make* it appropriate to do so. That being the case, it was submitted that if he has determined that importance or difficulty make it appropriate to remit the case, the sheriff is obliged under the terms of the section to do so; the permissive word "may" should be understood in a mandatory sense, since it would be unreasonable if the sheriff were allowed a discretion to order that the cause should remain in a court which ex hypothesi he has deemed not to be appropriate. Considerations such as the expense or delay which might arise from a remit are therefore irrelevant.

It is true that, as Lord Carmont observed in *Fleming & Ferguson Ltd v Paisley Magistrates*, 1948 SLT at p 462, "statutory permissive language can sometimes be read as imperative", but I agree also with Lord Carmont's further observation that "the burden however is on the person seeking to have an obligation implied from words which are permissive and enabling". That burden is increased where, as in the present case, the section to be construed also contains, in a similar context, words which are clearly imperative. In both subs (1) and in subs (2) of s 37 the word

"may" is used in contrast to the word "shall" in pro-
A visions relating to the sheriff's powers to govern the
procedural future of an action. I would accordingly
only construe the word "may" in subs (1) (b) as
obliging the sheriff to remit (having concluded that
the requirement of importance or difficulty is satisfied) if the context in which the word occurs clearly
indicates that this must have been what the legislature
intended. In my view there is no such indication. No
doubt a prima facie case for a remit arises if it is concluded that it is appropriate to remit on the ground of
importance or difficulty. But I see nothing anomalous
B in a construction of the subsection which, for example,
recognises that the sheriff may conclude that a case is
of such difficulty that it would be appropriate to remit
it, and yet may refrain from doing so because he considers that other factors make it inexpedient to take
that course. Such other factors might include the total
lack of any importance of the case combined with the
fact that its value is incommensurate with the additional expense, whether public or private, which
would be incurred as a result of a remit. In my opinion
C it is unlikely that the legislature intended that this consideration should be ignored, particularly since it is
reasonable that some weight should also be given to a
pursuer's choice of forum which necessarily and
properly takes it into account. It is also unlikely in my
opinion that it was intended that the sheriff must
ignore the possibility that determination of a party's
case might be delayed by a remit to that party's
prejudice, particularly if the motion is made by the
opposing party, as the section allows, at a late stage of
D the sheriff court proceedings. These are matters
which, according to the circumstances of the case,
might justify a refusal to remit even although the
single consideration of importance or that of difficulty
would per se make a remit appropriate. There is in my
view no indication, or at least no sufficient indication,
that it was intended that the word "may" should not
be given its ordinary permissive meaning. In my
opinion therefore the effect of the subsection is to
oblige the sheriff to refuse the motion unless he is of
E opinion that the importance or difficulty of the case
make it appropriate to remit, but otherwise to allow
him to exercise a reasonable discretion whether or not
to grant it, having regard to all the circumstances of
the case.

That view appears to me to be supported by the
decision in *McIntosh v British Railways Board* which
dealt with the provision, contained in s 14 of the Law
Reform (Miscellaneous Provisions) (Scotland) Act
1985, that the Court of Session "may" remit an action
F to the sheriff court, "where in the opinion of the
court, the nature of the action makes it appropriate to
do so". In that case it was held that while the Lord
Ordinary had rightly taken into account the "practical
and procedural advantages" of the Court of Session to
a litigant who wished to take advantage of them, he
had failed to give proper regard to the pursuer's right
to choose the forum in which to pursue his claim, a
right which was apparently regarded as overriding all
other considerations in the case. Although it had
earlier been observed that "the only criterion which
s 14 provides is that 'the nature of the action' makes

it appropriate to remit the action to the sheriff court",
it seems to me to be impossible to describe the prac- G
tical or the procedural advantages to a litigant of
having his case heard in one forum rather than
another, or a litigant's choice of forum, as matters
which have any bearing on "the nature of the action".
If I am correct in this respect, the decision must have
proceeded (although this is not expressly stated) on the
basis that the court is afforded, by the use of the word
"may" in s 14, a general discretion whether or not to
remit, provided that the nature of the action makes it,
in the court's opinion, appropriate to do so. Except
that the words "importance or difficulty of the case" H
are used instead of the expression "nature of the
action", the wording of subs (1) (b) of s 37 is similar,
and the case therefore appears to me to support the
view which I have expressed as to the sheriff's discretion. In any event it clearly supports my view that,
if the legislation permits it, it is reasonable to accord
some weight to the pursuer's choice of forum.

But the case of *Data Controls* is directly contrary to
these views, dealing as it does with the same subsection I
as that with which the present case is concerned.
Although that decision proceeded on a number of
grounds, it was held by all three members of the court
that under the terms of the subsection the sheriff has
to direct his attention only to the importance or difficulty of the case and that no other considerations are
relevant in dealing with the motion. That conclusion
necessarily assumes that the word "may" should be
construed as implying an obligation, although Lord
Allanbridge was the only member of the court who put
forward an explanation why the word was used. The J
explanation given was that its use served to "demonstrate" that the sheriff has a discretion in reaching an
opinion on importance or difficulty. But even if the
forming of an opinion is properly to be regarded as the
exercise of a discretion, I do not regard this as justification for the use of the word where it is intended that
an obligation should arise if the opinion is formed. In
my opinion the case should be overruled. It follows
that I consider that the sheriff committed no error in
law in referring as he did to the additional expense K
which the pursuers would incur if the present action
were remitted, although it should be added that this
consideration might only have had a bearing on the
sheriff's decision if he had validly concluded, which he
did not, that the importance or difficulty of the case
made it appropriate to remit it.

In relation to the sheriff's assessment of that importance and difficulty it was submitted that he had erred
in a number of respects which included an error said L
to have been made in his adoption of an observation
of another sheriff in *Shaw v Lanarkshire Health Board*.
This was to the effect that the provision referred to
cases of "unusual or even exceptional difficulty or
importance". I agree that no such gloss should be put
on the language of the section. The only test is
whether importance or difficulty make it appropriate
to remit, not whether these features are unusual or
exceptional. But in my view it is clear that the adoption of this observation did not have any misleading
effect on the sheriff's conclusions.

It was also submitted that the sheriff erred in holding that "the standard of proof in this case . . . will be balance of probability". It was submitted that it was not clear on the authorities that this was so in a case in which an allegation of murder had been made, and that the uncertainty of the law on the matter raised a question of importance and created a difficulty which the sheriff had ignored. In my opinion there is no such importance or difficulty, since the sheriff was correct in his determination of the appropriate standard of proof. The Scottish authorities cited to us as indicating the contrary were, first, dicta contained in *Arnott v Burt*, particularly Lord Cowan at p 71 and Lord Neaves at p 74. This was a case in which an allegation of forgery was made, but the observations founded on were plainly obiter, were not supported by any authority, and were not made by the Lord Ordinary whose decision was affirmed, nor by the Lord Justice Clerk or Lord Benholme who concurred in it. The appellants also cited a decision of a Lord Ordinary in *Lennon v The Co-operative Insurance Society Ltd* in which he stated in a case involving an allegation of fireraising that the onus was "higher than on a balance of probabilities, somewhere half-way between that and beyond reasonable doubt". It is not stated in the report of this decision that any submission was made on that matter, and in spite of what he had said, the Lord Ordinary appears to have determined the case on the basis that "no facts, apart from the evidence given by the pursuer, point to the fire having been more probably started by an intruder than by the pursuer himself". In my view these authorities are plainly insufficient to displace the well established principle that in civil cases the standard of proof required of a pursuer is that he prove his case on a balance of probabilities, and the suggestion that there exists in Scotland some standard intermediate between a balance of probabilities and beyond reasonable doubt has expressly been rejected in *Brown v Brown*, 1972 SLT at p 145, *Lamb v Lord Advocate*, 1976 SLT at pp 153 and 156, and *B v Kennedy*, 1987 SLT at p 768.

My view that any civil case, including this one, must be determined on a balance of probabilities does not ignore the obvious fact that it is more difficult to prove, according to the required standard, an allegation of murder or serious crime, because it is inherently unlikely that a normal person will commit such a crime. Certain English authorities cited, including the similar case of *Halford v Brookes*, appear to have proceeded on the basis that this difficulty is to be reflected in a variation of the normal standard of proof, but in my view there is no justification in Scotland for that approach, and if it were applied it might well lead to uncertainty in any case where an allegation of serious criminal or immoral conduct was made.

The major respect in which it was submitted that the cause was one of importance arose from the fact that it contains an allegation of murder, and that the defender has been tried and acquitted in the High Court of this charge. It was said that in a civil case the allegation should be determined by the Court of Session, in recognition of the same importance as requires in the criminal field that the charge should be tried in the High Court; that the gravity of the allegation has imposed a great burden on both parties; and that the unique and novel attempt by the pursuers to establish something which the Crown had failed to do in a criminal case raised questions of general importance. It was submitted that in these respects the sheriff had arrived at a conclusion which no sheriff could reasonably have reached, and that in any event he had misdirected himself in his approach to them. It was not submitted that the amount of damages sought rendered the case important, and indeed it is obvious that the primary importance for the pursuers lies not in their wish to obtain compensation but because they seek to rectify what they regard as an injustice of the defender's acquittal.

In my opinion the importance of a cause can only be assessed by reference to its possible effects. I see no reason to exclude from a consideration of these effects the possible effects on the parties to the action as well as those on the public, or on a section of the public. No doubt the court would more readily regard a cause to be important if its result could affect persons other than the parties, but in my view it is clear that its possible effect on either or both of the parties themselves may per se endow a case with the degree of importance which makes it appropriate that it be remitted to the Court of Session. On the other hand the court must look at the question of importance objectively, and although a case may be and often is of crucial importance to one or both of the parties who are involved in it, this is not decisive in the court's assessment of the matter.

It is the opinion of the sheriff which matters, and, although I do not agree with it, I would not have thought it right to interfere with that opinion if his approach to the question had been correct. In my view the decision would not have been unreasonable if the sheriff had taken all relevant matters into account. But I consider it clear that he erroneously approached the question as if there were no consequences of the action other than financial. He emphasises that the purpose of an action founded on delict is the civil remedy of damages, without "criminal connotations". This approach ignores the reality of the matter, which is that the defender is at risk of being branded for the rest of his life as a murderer, and indeed this is the result which the first named pursuer obviously hopes to achieve. Whatever view might be taken of the pursuer's motives, and of the averments which she has chosen to make, it seems to me that the possible consequences of the action to the defender are at least very material to an assessment of its importance, and that the sheriff has not sufficiently, if at all, taken these consequences into account. This court is entitled therefore to look at the matter de novo. In my opinion the case is of importance both because of its possible effect on the defender and also because an allegation of murder made in a civil action, particularly after an acquittal, is a matter of justifiable public concern and interest. These aspects of importance make it appropriate that the case should be remitted to the Court of

A Session, and since there are no other considerations which outweigh them I would allow the appeal and remit to the sheriff to proceed accordingly as proposed by your Lordship.

LORD PROSSER.—This is a reparation action which was raised in the sheriff court at Greenock. The defender moved the sheriff to remit the cause to the Court of Session, in terms of the Sheriff Courts (Scotland) Act 1971, s 37, as amended by s 16 of the Law Reform (Miscellaneous Provisions) (Scotland) Act B 1980. By interlocutor of 20 December 1990, the sheriff refused this motion. The defender appealed to the Court of Session. The appeal was originally heard on 30 April 1992, but in consequence of doubts as to the correctness of the decision in *Data Controls Ltd v British Railways Board* a larger court has been convened.

In terms of s 37 (1) (b) of the 1971 Act, in an ordinary cause in the sheriff court, the sheriff "(b) may, subject to section 7 of the Sheriff Courts (Scot-C land) Act 1907, on the motion of any of the parties to the cause, if he is of the opinion that the importance or difficulty of the cause make it appropriate to do so, remit the cause to the Court of Session". While other parts of the section, and indeed the terms of other statutes, may be of assistance in construing this provision, no other provision is directly in point.

In presenting the appeal, counsel for the appellant intimated certain alterations to the grounds of appeal D which had been lodged. Five grounds remain. The submissions made on behalf of the appellant fall within these five grounds, but were formulated in a different, and I think clearer way. That being so, I do not propose to refer further to the written grounds of appeal.

The criticisms of the sheriff's decision fall into two basic categories. There are specific alleged "errors", where he is said to have misdirected himself as to the law, or to have taken account of factors which were E irrelevant to the performance of his function under s 37 (1) (b). But it was also submitted that the sheriff had acted unreasonably: his approach to certain matters had been one which no reasonable sheriff would have adopted, and in consequence he had come to a conclusion which no reasonable sheriff would have reached. If his decision was flawed in either or both of these ways, this court would require to consider the matter de novo, and on doing so, should conclude that a remit to the Court of Session was F appropriate, and should remit to the sheriff, for him to remit the cause to the Court of Session. On behalf of the pursuers and respondents, it was not disputed that this court could and should reconsider the matter de novo if (but only if) the sheriff had erred or acted unreasonably as contended by the appellant.

As I have said, this is an action of reparation. Reparation is sought for losses, suffering and damage sustained by the pursuers as a result of the defender's delictual actings, and this is expressed in the pursuers' averments and pleas in law in terms of a breach of duties of care. While the pleadings have that very ordinary framework, the matter is more complicated, G even on the pleadings as they stand. The pursuers are the widow and children of Raymond Mullan. Mr Mullan was a taxi driver, and it is a matter of admission that he died on 9 February 1990. Putting the matter shortly, the pursuers aver that on 9 February 1990, in Mr Mullan's taxi, the defender produced a hunting knife, opened it, and "either deliberately or recklessly struck" Mr Mullan with it, whereby the blade penetrated his heart and killed him. It is subsequently averred that the defender "deliberately or H recklessly killed the deceased"; and the pursuers' first plea in law is to the effect that the defender, having breached the duties of care incumbent on him "not to cause the death" of Mr Mullan, in the circumstances condescended upon, "whether deliberately or recklessly", is due to make reparation. On these pleadings, therefore, the pursuers are making, and the defender is faced with, averments that Mr Mullan's death was caused not merely (i) by a breach of duty of care, but (ii) by a deliberate blow which would constitute an assault. Moreover, in relation to breach of duty of I care, the averments are carried (iii) to the level of recklessness, which would entail culpable homicide; and in relation to assault, it appears to me that the averments must be seen (as indeed they have been seen throughout these proceedings) as assertions of murder, either (iv) on the basis that the defender was reckless in relation to Mr Mullan's life, or (v) as an intentional killing.

I am not concerned with niceties of pleading. The pursuers' averments, and in particular those relating J to deliberate or reckless actions, may mean that the pursuers could not succeed by proving simple negligence or simple assault, although either would in principle appear sufficient as a basis for claiming reparation. Correspondingly, although the answers include general denials, I would note that the only specific denial made by the defender is a denial that he "either deliberately or recklessly" struck the deceased with a knife, and that his only plea dealing with liability is to the effect that the pursuers have not K suffered loss, injury and damage "as a result of the deliberate or reckless actings of the defender". I do not question the propriety of the pursuers' making averments of deliberate or reckless actings, up to and including averments which entail murder. It may well be that the facts which they have to prove, in order to succeed in an action of reparation, would inextricably involve these matters, and in any event, if evidence of these matters is available, it might well be important to aver and prove them, in case a more restricted L attempt to prove simple negligence or assault might fail. I am nonetheless perturbed that in invoking deliberate and reckless actings, the case appears to exclude the lesser but sufficient averment of ordinary negligence or assault. While I know nothing of the facts, it might even be that in the course of the action the defender would admit simple negligence. If he were to do so it does not appear to me that any proof on the merits would be required. So far as quantification of damages is concerned it may well be that the quality of the act which caused Mr Mullan's death would still be significant. But it appears that there are at least problems as to the actual recovery of damages, and it seems to me that the pursuers' professional advisers, and indeed the court in which the action proceeds, may have to consider delicate issues if the action is to be held to its proper function, and not to be put to a merely declaratory use, unrelated to the remedy of reparation. A pursuer who seeks that remedy is of course entitled to seek the court's decision on facts which are the necessary basis for that remedy, or for the quantification of damages. But it is not the function of the courts to grant a bare declarator of a fact which a particular pursuer may wish to have stated for other reasons. In particular, in the present case, where it is a matter of admission that the defender has stood trial for the murder of Mr Mullan and has been acquitted, it seems to me that any civil court, and those having recourse to the civil courts, must abide firmly by the principle that civil litigation is for the vindication of civil rights. If that is the true end and purpose of any action, the court will not be inhibited from making the relevant findings in fact, whatever the wider implications of such findings may be. But if that is not the true end and purpose of the action, the court must be careful not to make unnecessary findings, however much, for wider reasons, a party may wish this to be done.

I have thought it useful to make these comments in relation to the action before turning to the criticisms of what the sheriff has done. The question of whether his approach and decision were reasonable is closely related to a scrutiny of the action, its character and its connotation. But before considering these, it is appropriate to consider the more specific errors which the sheriff is said to have made.

It was submitted that the sheriff, in reaching his decision to refuse a remit, had taken account of certain matters which were irrelevant. These were the additional cost to the pursuers of litigating in the Court of Session rather than in the local sheriff court, and the financial consequences for the defender and appellant in the event of the pursuers succeeding. Whether these are irrelevant matters, which the sheriff should properly have ignored, depends essentially on the construction of s 37 (1) (b) of the 1971 Act. On what was called a "narrow" approach, the section would exclude these matters from consideration. On what was called the "broad" interpretation of the section, these would be matters which the sheriff was entitled to consider, although questions might still arise as to the reasonableness of his treatment of these matters.

In terms of s 37 (1) (b), the sheriff "may . . . remit the cause to the Court of Session". If these words were unqualified, they would naturally be described as enabling, or permissive, and would be seen as conferring a discretion, free of any limitation other than the universal requirement to act fairly and reasonably. I do not think that it was suggested that if the sheriff were exercising such an unqualified discretion, he would not be free to take into account the matters which the appellant contends are irrelevant.

But the principal provision of s 37 (1) (b), that the sheriff may remit the cause to the Court of Session, is not unqualified. What is provided is that he may "if he is of the opinion that the importance or difficulty of the cause make it appropriate to do so" remit the cause to the Court of Session. In a perhaps oversimplified form, the "narrow" interpretation of the provision is to the effect that the sheriff has only one task. He is to consider whether the importance or difficulty of the cause makes it appropriate to remit the cause to the Court of Session. Since only two factors are mentioned, importance and difficulty, he is not entitled to have regard to any other factors in carrying out this exercise. And having carried out the exercise, and ex hypothesi being of the opinion that these matters make it appropriate to remit the cause to the Court of Session, he has no remaining discretion. He must remit. The so called "broader" interpretation, again perhaps oversimplified, is to the effect that the conditional clause is a precondition, or the first stage in a two stage process. The sheriff must consider whether the importance or difficulty of the cause make it appropriate to remit. If he thinks not, he has no power to remit. If on the other hand he is of opinion that these factors do indeed make it appropriate to remit, that establishes his power to remit. But he must still consider whether to do so: what is said is that he "may" remit, not that he shall remit, and he is entitled, at this second stage, to have regard to all the possible relevant factors which, as a reasonable man, he sees as relevant to that discretionary decision. In support of this "broader" interpretation, emphasis is laid on the use of the word "may", and its naturally permissive sense, which can be contrasted with the mandatory word "shall" which is indeed used in s 37 (1) (a), where the sheriff has plainly no discretion. In addition, the "broader" interpretation is supported by the argument that the "narrow" interpretation would exclude from consideration factors which justice and common sense suggest should not be excluded. Parliament cannot have intended to exclude them, and since the conditional clause does not allow them in, it must not be read as exhausting the sheriff's function, and the permissive sense of the words "may . . . remit" must be retained, as a second stage exercise. In support of the "narrow" construction, it is submitted that the word "may" has to be interpreted according to its context, and that it frequently has the same effect as the word "shall". When qualified by a conditional provision which effectively exhausts all the possibilities, it must be interpreted as having that effect. That being the position, and the conditional clause having identified two factors, and two only, for consideration, Parliament's intention that other factors must be disregarded is plain.

In my opinion, neither of these interpretations is quite right. I find no real assistance, before looking at the particular context, in the different meanings of "may" and "shall". Even in the absence of qualifying or conditional clauses, an enabling or empowering word such as "may" can have a mandatory import, deriving from the general duties of the person empowered, or from the rights and interests of those who will be affected by the exercise or non-exercise of the power. (See *Fleming and Ferguson v Paisley Magistrates*, Lord Carmont at 1948 SLT, p 463, and the cases there cited.) But where it is provided that something may be

done, and a condition is attached to that provision, it
A appears to me that the import of the word "may" is
heavily dependent upon the terms of the condition. If,
for example, the condition is the simple occurrence of
some extraneous event, then in the absence of other
reasons (such as those I have mentioned) for giving the
word "may" a mandatory meaning, the condition
could naturally be read as merely a precondition for
the exercise of a discretion. At the opposite extreme,
if it is provided that someone may do something if
satisfied that it is essential in the interests of safety, or
B justice or the like, then it appears to me that the
"may" is quite properly and naturally used, since a
power is being conferred; but the terms of the condition are such that once its requirements have been met
the question of whether the power should be exercised
will have been answered. I am not sure that in these
circumstances it is correct to say that the word "may"
is being given a mandatory meaning. The position is
perhaps rather that a power is conferred, and the conditional clause requires a decision which, when taken
C together with general duties, will inevitably entail the
exercise of the power. Between these extremes, there
will be innumerable possible relationships between a
particular power and the conditions to which it is
subjected. It does not appear to me that the may/shall
distinction is of any real significance in such circumstances, and I would indeed regard the word "may" as
more suitable than "shall", in provisons where the
exercise of the power is made conditional upon, but is
implicit in, some decision or conclusion of the person
holding the power.
D

In my opinion, subject to one qualification to which
I shall return, s 37 (1) (b), in the context of a sheriff's
general function and duties, requires to him to remit
a cause to the Court of Session, with no further discretion, in all cases where the requirement of the conditional clause has been met. The natural meaning of
saying that X or Y makes it appropriate to do Z seems
to me to include a conclusion that it is indeed appropriate to do Z. To say that X or Y makes it appropriate
E to do Z is very different from saying that X or Y suggests that it is appropriate to do Z, or that X or Y
points to Z being appropriate, or the like. When a
sheriff has reached the opinion that the importance or
difficulty of the cause makes it appropriate to remit
the cause to this court, he has in my view decided what
is appropriate. That being so, the combination of his
specific power and his general duties appears to me to
give him no alternative: he must do what in his
opinion is appropriate. On that reading of the pro-
F vision, there is no scope for a further, second stage
consideration of what is to be done, or of factors which
have not been taken into account in reaching the
original opinion.

Thus far, therefore, upon the relationship between
the conditional clause and the words "may . . .
remit", the "narrow" interpretation appears to me to
be the natural and correct one, and I cannot myself see
the "broader" interpretation, allowing for a second
stage discretion, as the natural meaning of the words
used. However, this broader interpretation was not

put forward simply as the natural meaning of the
words used. It was said to be justified partly because G
the "narrow" construction entailed excluding from
consideration factors which plainly ought to be considered. That being so, the broader interpretation
should be adopted, even if this involved giving the
words a less natural or more strained meaning. I was
initially inclined to see considerable force in this line
of argument; and if, in accordance with the decision in
Data Controls Ltd, the "single stage" interpretation
excluded from consideration factors which (as it seems
to me) common sense and justice suggest should not H
be excluded, then I would be very sympathetic to the
suggestion that the sheriff's opinion (that the importance or difficulty of the cause made it appropriate to
remit) need not be regarded as a final or exhaustive
decision, but could be regarded as merely an opinion
that a remit would be appropriate if these two factors
alone were taken into account, but might not turn out
to be appropriate when other matters were considered.

In the end, I have come to the view that such an
interpretation of the words would be not merely I
strained, but over strained. Perhaps more importantly,
I do not think that there is a need for the second stage
discretionary consideration of other factors: in my
opinion, all the factors which ought, according to
common sense or the requirements of justice, to be
considered, can be taken into account in the single
stage process, when the sheriff is considering whether
the importance or difficulty of the cause "make it
appropriate" to remit it to the Court of Session.

J
As I have indicated, I think that the narrow interpretation is right in treating an opinion that the importance or difficulty of the cause "make it appropriate"
to remit it to this court as determining the question of
whether to remit. However, I think that the narrow
interpretation underestimates what has to be taken
into account before an opinion can be reached upon
that matter. The sheriff must of course assess the
importance, and the difficulty of the cause. I do not
think that this is merely a matter of degree: difficulty K
can take many forms, and there are many different
reasons for regarding different cases as important. The
sheriff should have the specific characteristics of the
case in mind, when assessing its importance or
difficulty. But having obtained as full a picture as
possible of the importance or difficulty of the cause,
the sheriff has to decide whether these features make
it appropriate to remit the cause from the sheriff court
to this court. In order to assess whether such a remit
is indeed made appropriate by these features of the
cause, I have come to the view that the sheriff must L
form a view of how each court would cope with these
features of the cause, and whether, because of these
features, the Court of Session is where the case more
appropriately belongs. In my opinion, in making this
assessment, the sheriff has a very wide discretion
indeed. In considering what it is about the cause that
might justify a remit, he must take into account only
its importance and its difficulty. But in considering
the appropriateness of the remit, he will be trying to
relate his detailed picture of importance or difficulty

to the characteristics of either court. Some of these characteristics may be matters which he must accept a priori: the greater authority of the Court of Session, for example, and the procedures available in the two courts. There are no doubt many other generally accepted differences, and other differences which might be very much a matter of the individual sheriff's own impressions. Delay and expense may be matters in this last category; but however they are assessed, they might well be seen as areas of significant difference between the Court of Session and the sheriff court, and if they were so, I see no reason why a sheriff should not take them into account, along with other characteristics of either court. He has to decide whether the identified importance or difficulty of the particular cause makes it appropriate to remit it from the sheriff court, with all its characteristics, to the Court of Session, with all its characteristics.

I do not myself believe that this allows the sheriff to go beyond the importance or difficulty of the cause, in considering what might make it appropriate to remit the cause to this court. But in my opinion the question of whether these features make it appropriate to remit must depend in part upon the way in which these features of the cause would be dealt with here or in the sheriff court. The appropriateness of a remit is a practical question, and necessitates a practical assessment not only of the importance and difficulty of the case, but also of how each court can respond to them. To ignore the actual characteristics and procedures of the two courts would in my opinion be unrealistic (and perhaps impossible) even at this first stage; and the conclusion which I reach is that the second stage discretion is not required. I do not however think that there is any difference of effect, between this interpretation of the provision, and the interpretation which leaves a second stage discretion.

In these circumstances, I consider that the decision in *Data Controls Ltd* was sound in its rejection of a second stage discretion, after a sheriff has reached the opinion that the importance or difficulty of the cause make it appropriate to remit the case to this court. But I consider the decision unsound in relation to the other aspect of the "narrow" interpretation: if a sheriff considers that remitting a cause to the Court of Session would give rise to extra delay or expense, that is relevant to his consideration of whether the importance or difficulty of the cause make it appropriate to send it to such a court. So far as the broader interpretation is concerned, the general or purposive arguments in favour of a second stage discretion lose their force, if the sheriff is entitled to take the broader circumstances into account when forming his original opinion.

Analogies were drawn between s 37 (1) (b) and the provisions governing remit from the Court of Session to the sheriff court, and those which allow this court to order that an action which began under optional procedure is to proceed as an ordinary action. Reference was made to *McIntosh v British Railways Board* and *Paterson v Henry Robb Ltd*. I have not however found these cases useful in relation to s 37 (1) (b).

The other matter of interpretation upon which the parties were at issue related to the words "the importance . . . of the cause". It was suggested that in considering the importance of the cause, a sheriff would not be entitled to consider its importance to either of the parties. The matter is of course one for the sheriff, and his opinion, rather than the parties, or their opinions. But if a sheriff is satisfied that the cause is important in some way or to some degree for either of the parties, or both of them, I can see no justification for holding that he must disregard this. Since the court's function, in relation to any action, is to settle an issue inter partes, I should have greater misgivings if the "importance" relied upon by a sheriff was its importance to others, whether other litigants for whom it might provide a test, or for academics or legal theorists. But the word is unqualified, and I see no basis for saying that a sheriff should disregard any form of importance, when considering whether the importance of the cause makes it appropriate to remit. I would add that the same appears to me to be true in relation to difficulty: anything which the sheriff sees as contributing to the difficulty of the cause is a relevant consideration for him.

Having rejected the submission that the "narrow" interpretation is correct, I am satisfied that the sheriff did not take into account any irrelevant matters. He was not therefore in error in that respect. A further error of law was said to have been made by the sheriff in relation to the standard of proof in a civil action, where a crime such as murder had been put in issue. The sheriff proceeded on the view that the standard of proof was the ordinary civil one: the pursuer must prove his case on a balance of probabilities. While counsel for the appellant did not go so far as to submit that this was positively wrong, it was submitted, in effect, that the matter was all very confused and difficult. Reference was made to such cases as *Arnott v Burt* and *Lennon v The Co-operative Insurance Society Ltd*. In my opinion, however, the sheriff was right. The only alternative to proof on a balance of probabilities is proof beyond reasonable doubt (*Brown v Brown*), and I can see nothing in authority or principle which suggests that the higher standard should be adopted in a civil action, simply because that higher standard would be required in proving the same facts in a criminal trial. Whichever standard of proof is being applied, the party upon whom the onus of proof is laid may succeed merely by proving quite bare circumstances. Or he may have to provide a vast wealth of detailed evidence. General assumptions may make the task easy, or they may make it close to impossible, on either standard. Lord Reid's observations in *McWilliams v Sir William Arrol & Co*, 1962 SLT at p 126, appear to me to show with great clarity the way in which general assumptions as to probabilities determine the magnitude or otherwise of a pursuer's task. Having regard to general probabilities, I do not doubt that a pursuer's task is one of some magnitude, if he seeks to prove that a murder has been committed, even on a balance of probabilities. On the other hand, if he can prove detailed facts and circum-

stances, leading to death, he might require little more,
A even to satisfy the higher standard of proof. Whichever standard has to be attained, one may have a long
way to go, or a short way to go, once the basic facts
are proved. I see no justification for departing from
the ordinary civil standard of proof in those cases
where initially, because of the gravity of his allegations, a pursuer apparently has a long way to go. I
would only add that I am not sure that Lord Neaves,
in *Arnott*, at p 74, was really talking about higher
standards of proof. It seems to me that he may merely
B have meant that in certain circumstances, a pursuer
will have a long way to go before he can even establish
his case on a balance of probabilities. I am not persuaded that the sheriff was in any way in error, or
unreasonable, upon this point.

If that is correct, and if the sheriff was not guilty of
taking any irrelevant factors into account, the appeal
can only succeed if as was submitted on behalf of the
defender and appellant, the sheriff was either in error,
or was unreasonable in dealing with the importance of
C the cause. As I have indicated, I would regard the
importance of the cause to an individual party as one
aspect of the importance of the cause. It would therefore be an error to disregard its importance to an individual. The sheriff says that it seems to him "unlikely
that a civil action based upon averments which might
amount to serious criminal conduct would be remitted
to the Court of Session merely on the basis of the
importance to the defender as an individual of answering such allegations". But I do not think he is going
D so far as to say that the importance of a cause to an
individual is an irrelevant consideration, and correspondingly, I do not think that he has committed an
error upon that point. The issue appears to me to
become one of reasonableness rather than specific
error. As I have indicated, I see a sheriff as being
entitled to make a very broad assessment of matters, in
considering whether the importance or difficulty of a
cause makes it appropriate to remit. It will correspondingly be difficult to establish that he has acted in
E that respect as no reasonable sheriff would have acted.
Nonetheless, I have come to the view that that is here
the position.

First, the sheriff mentions certain submissions
which were based upon the fact that the averments
against the defender were "matters of the utmost
gravity". He goes on to say that "averments in reparation actions relating to death or very serious injury
caused by conduct which amounts to a crime will
F always be of the utmost gravity". I do not understand
that comment. The matters to which he refers will be
of varying gravity, and indeed greatly varying gravity.
While the sheriff acknowledges that they might
perhaps "lack the degree of deliberate conduct in an
averment which amounts to one of murder", he
appears to me to play down the extreme gravity of
allegations of murder, and to treat them as if they were
effectively of no more importance to a defender than
other allegations in the category which he identifies. I
do not regard that as a view which could be held by
any reasonable sheriff.

Secondly, the sheriff says that it seems to him that
the defender's solicitor "misapprehends the purpose   G
of the civil action. It is one founded in delict seeking
the civil remedy of damages. It has no criminal connotations". The process is of course a civil one, and not
a criminal one. But to say that it has no criminal
"connotations" appears to me to be quite wrong. The
pursuers seek to prove, in the manner appropriate to
a civil action, that the defender did things which constitute the crime of murder. If they were to succeed,
they would have established that the defender is probably a murderer. While I would agree with the sheriff   H
in rejecting the suggestion that the court would be
"reviewing a decision of the High Court", and while
the functions of the two processes are of course quite
different, the criminal connotations of the civil proof
are in my view very real. Moreover, while one can
properly say that the purpose of a civil action founded
in delict is to obtain the civil remedy of damages, the
obtaining of a remedy depends upon the proof of facts
and liability. That is indeed the primary issue in a civil
action, notwithstanding that the consequential remedy I
of damages will follow. The importance of a civil
action to a party relates not merely to the remedy, but
to the issue on the merits. The sheriff appears to me
to have misdirected himself upon this matter, and to
have failed to consider the importance of the merits.
I would add that this seems particularly strange, when
it appears that in the present case the pursuers'
purpose in bringing the action is perhaps primarily, or
even solely, to obtain a finding in their favour on the
merits, with the remedy (which constitutes the only   J
proper purpose of such an action) mattering little or
not at all. I do not consider that any sheriff acting
reasonably, in endeavouring to reach an opinion of the
kind required under s 37 (1) (b), could have adopted
the approach of this sheriff on these matters.

That being so, it is the duty of this court to consider
the matter de novo. For my part, I consider that averments of murder in a civil action, in any circumstances
which I can envisage, would make the importance of   K
the cause to the defender so great as to make it appropriate to remit the cause to the Court of Session. More
widely, where there has already been an acquittal in
the High Court, I think that it is a matter of public
importance that the issue of whether the crime was
probably committed by the then accused should be
dealt with by the Court of Session, as the civil court
of maximum authority, and the civil court most
closely analogous to the High Court in all its characteristics. It is undesirable in the public interest, as well
as in the defender's interest, that a finding of probable L
murder be made in anything other than a supreme
court. While it was acknowledged on behalf of the
appellant that the mere amount of damages sought was
not of significant importance, the importance of the
issue on the merits, great though it is in itself, must
in my view be regarded as all the greater, considering
that the defender has neither means nor insurance. I
would add this. While one must judge matters on the
basis of the pleadings as they stand, it appears to me
that these pleadings contain within them significant

A elements of difficulty. One difficulty appears to me to be whether the averment of murder should ever go to proof. Both in degree and in kind, that seems to me to be a difficulty in the cause which makes it appropriate to remit to the Court of Session. I would allow the appeal and remit back to the sheriff to remit the cause to this court.

LORD PENROSE.—The pursuers are the widow and children of the late Raymond Caraher Mullan. Mr Mullan was a taxi driver. He was stabbed to death in

B his taxi in the early hours of Friday, 9 February 1990. The pursuers aver that the defender carried out that act "either deliberately or recklessly", striking Mr Mullan with a hunting knife which he had had in his possession. The allegation is of murder. The defender was tried on an indictment for murder at the High Court of Justiciary at Paisley and, on 31 May 1990, was acquitted. The pursuers seek damages from the defender on allegations which are a close parallel to those forming the basis of the criminal indictment.

C The defender has no significant assets and the prospect of recovering any sum upon the award of damages is remote. Both parties now have the benefit of legal aid for these proceedings.

The case was raised in Greenock sheriff court. The defender sought a remit to the Court of Session in terms of s 37 (1) (b) of the Sheriff Courts (Scotland) Act 1971. The sheriff refused the motion. The defender appealed to the Court of Session and the

D appeal was heard first on 30 April 1992. At that hearing it appeared that an issue arose as to the correctness of the decision of the court in *Data Controls Ltd v British Railways Board*. At the resumed hearing of the appeal, it was not disputed that the tests to be applied on appeal against a decision of a sheriff in the exercise of a power involving subjective judgment were as set out in *Thomson v Glasgow Corporation* by Lord Reid at 1962 SLT, p 107; *Stevenson v Rogers* by the Lord Justice Clerk at p 561; and *Guardian Royal Exchange Group v Moffat* by Lord Justice

E Clerk Wheatley at p 266. In presenting the appeal, counsel for the appellants submitted that the sheriff had erred in: (a) having regard to irrelevant considerations, namely the relatively high level of expense of Court of Session proceedings, and the financial consequences of failure for the appellant; (b) in adopting an approach to those issues of difficulty and importance identified in the statutory test which no reasonable sheriff would have adopted, and in arriving at an

F unreasonable result in consequence; and (c) in the view he had formed of the standard of proof required in respect of allegations of criminal conduct in civil proceedings. Their submission was that the court should consider the issue de novo on a proper application of the statutory provision to the facts and circumstances brought to the notice of the court. Counsel for the respondents submitted that the sheriff could not be faulted, either in the construction of the provision which he had applied, or in respect of the factors which he took into account in arriving at his decision. The decision could not be characterised as one which

G no reasonable sheriff, acting in a reasonable way, could have arrived at. If the court did consider it right to deal with the issue de novo, it should arrive at the same conclusion as the sheriff.

In terms of s 37 (1) (b) the sheriff may remit a cause raised in the sheriff court to the Court of Session: "on the motion of any of the parties to the cause, if he is of the opinion that the importance or difficulty of the cause make it appropriate to do so". The power does not apply in cases falling within the privative jurisdiction of the sheriff under s 7 of the Sheriff Courts

H (Scotland) Act 1907.

In *Data Controls* the court adopted a narrow approach to the construction of s 37. Lord Allanbridge, at p 430, expressed the view that only factors of difficulty or of importance could competently be addressed, and that other factors, such as additional delay and additional expense which might be involved in dealing with a cause in the Court of Session, were irrelevant. Lord Wylie adopted a similar view at p 432. Lord McDonald's views at p 433 were less

I positive, and related more particularly to the submissions of counsel. But the result he arrived at reflected a narrow approach. The construction of s 37 (1) (b) is central to the disposal of the present appeal, and it is appropriate to consider that matter at the outset.

In my opinion, a sheriff who is called upon to deal with a motion that a cause should be remitted to the Court of Session must consider, objectively, the factors bearing on the importance or difficulty of the

J cause which are brought to his notice, and then arrive at a decision, as a subjective matter of opinion, whether those factors make it appropriate that the cause should be remitted rather than remain in the court in which it was raised by the pursuer. If he decides that the cause should be remitted, under this provision, he will override the choice of forum initially made by the pursuer, typically in the light of the pursuer's own perception of his interests at that

K stage in having the cause disposed of by the sheriff, against opposition from one or more of the parties to the cause. The issue arises between the parties, to be resolved by the sheriff as any other such issue. Each court is, ex hypothesi, competent to entertain the cause. The central question of construction appears to me to depend on whether in resolving the issue before him, the sheriff is entitled to have regard to factors characteristic of the competing fora. In other words, the question is whether the issue of appropriateness

L depends solely on characteristics of the cause or depends on relating the characteristics of the cause to those of the courts involved. As a matter of ordinary language it appears to me that the test of appropriateness in the solution of any problem of choice is likely to require consideration of factors relating to both elements in the match one attempts to achieve. If one has to decide whether A or B is a more appropriate solution to a problem defined by reference to C, the relevant characteristics of all three components usually have to be identified. In forming an opinion whether

it is appropriate to remit a cause to the Court of
A Session rather than to dispose of it in the sheriff court,
whatever other limiting factors there might be, one
must have in mind at least certain of the characteristics
of the two courts, to provide some context for the
decision. In my opinion there is nothing in the terms
of this provision which would assist one to define
exclusively those characteristics of the two courts
which alone were relevant to the choice. A court, in
general terms, is defined not only by the characteristics of its judicial and other officers, but also, for
B example, by its forms of procedure, the classes of work
it customarily deals with, its location relative to the
residence or place of business of the parties appearing
before it, the qualifications and experience of those
who are entitled to practise before it, the expense
incurred in using the court, and the efficiency of its
programming for the disposal of work. Other factors
might be identified and added to the list. The question
whether it is appropriate for a case of defined importance or difficulty to be remitted from the sheriff courts
C to the Court of Session appears to me necessarily to
require consideration of those factors relevant to the
processing and disposal of the particular cause in the
respective fora which a sheriff acting reasonably, and
being fully conversant with the characteristics of the
two courts, would have in mind.

None of this, in my opinion, requires the resolution
of the provision into two distinct discretionary or
judgmental stages, in the first of which one determines
whether the importance or difficulty of the cause make
D it appropriate to remit it to the Court of Session, and
the second of which requires the application of some
overriding discretion to determine whether a remit
should be made. The initial word "may" seems to me
to be wholly appropriate to define the power conferred
on the sheriff, given the broad judgmental issues
focused in the specification of the power. If the sheriff,
having completed the judgmental process, forms a
view which leaves him no alternative but to remit the
particular cause, if he is to avoid unreasonable
E conduct, then it will be his duty to remit, and one
might properly say that in that case it would be appropriate at that stage to formulate his duty in terms that
he "shall" do so. But the fact that in particular
circumstances the proper exercise of a discretionary
power defines a single course of action to which there
is no alternative is a function of the circumstances in
which the power falls to be exercised rather than of
definition of the power itself.

F In submitting that the subsection required a two
stage approach of this kind, counsel for the respondents contended that the sheriff had to determine in
the first place whether the difficulty or importance of
the cause made it appropriate for the Court of Session,
and then to consider as a matter of discretion whether
to make the remit. I do not agree with that approach.
While it gives full weight to the need for difficulty or
importance to be established before the sheriff can
competently remit the cause, it ignores the language of
the provision, which relates to remit to the Court of
Session and not to the appropriateness of the cause for

the Court of Session, and it superimposes on the
expressed test of importance and difficulty a wholly G
unspecific discretion, constrained only by general
principles of reasonableness, which might be used to
withhold from the Court of Session a cause which the
sheriff had already resolved was appropriate to remit.
Counsel sought support for his approach in *McIntosh
v British Railways Board* in the opinion of the Lord
President at 1990 SLT, p 640, where he agreed with
the Lord Ordinary's views that: "the court is well
entitled to have regard to any practical or procedural
advantages which are to be found in adopting one H
forum rather than another". In my opinion *McIntosh*
supports the views I have formed in the interpretation
of s 37, without resort to the analysis involved in the
respondents' approach.

However, notwithstanding the different approach
which I have adopted to construction from that
involved in the submissions of the respondents'
counsel, the result differs from *Data Controls*. In my
opinion respondents' counsel were correct in submitting that the construction of s 37 (1) (b) supported I
in that decision was wrong. I consider that the view
expressed by Lord Allanbridge, at p 430, fails to take
account of the issues relating to the nature and characteristics of the respective fora which arise in applying
the section and is incorrect. Lord Wylie's view, at
p 432, reflects a construction of the provision which is
incompatible with the views I have set out above, and
is in my opinion incorrect. Lord McDonald's opinion,
at p 433, rejected the submissions of counsel which
were before him, and I am inclined to think that I J
would have taken the same view. But I consider that
he was in error in following the matter through in
other respects. It is not "fairness" as an overriding
consideration qualifying the statutory discretion
which is material, but the sound construction of the
provision itself. In my opinion the ratio of *Data Controls* is not correct. Reference was made to *Paterson v
Henry Robb Ltd* in this context by way of analogy in
construing s 37 (1) (b). The decision in that case
turned on the construction of Rule of Court 188J (6), K
which empowers the court to order that an action commenced under the optional procedure rules should
proceed as an ordinary action on special cause shown,
or of its own motion, because the difficulty or complexity of the case makes the action unsuitable for
optional procedure. There are obvious differences in
language. More fundamentally, however, there is a
difference in the test prescribed. A decision that a case
is unsuitable for one of the forms of procedure
prescribed for a particular court, as against another
form applicable within the same court, is different in L
kind from the decision involving a comparison of two
courts, with all of their respective procedural rules
forming part of the data available in arriving at a conclusion. In any event, counsel agreed that the aspect
of his argument which he sought to support by reference to *Paterson* had not been argued in that case. I
have not found the decision helpful in this case.

The expression "the importance or difficulty of the
clause" requires construction. Counsel disagreed
whether factors personal to the litigants could be con-

sidered in this context at all. The expression is wider
than that used in subs (2B) of the same section. There,
reference is made to "a difficult question of law or a
question of fact of exceptional complexity" in defining
the sheriff's power. Both elements of that expression
appear clearly to be comprised in the head of "difficulty" in subs (1) (b), yet, in cumulo, they cannot
exhaust that head, or, presumably, Parliament would
have employed the same expression in subs (1) (b), at
least after 1988. The "difficulties" envisaged must
include difficulty of law or of fact, but if it has to have
a wider meaning, it must extend to difficulties which
the parties might face of a procedural or evidential
kind unless it is confined to difficulties anticipated by
the sheriff relating to the disposal of the issue in the
sheriff court. "Importance" is importance of the
cause. The cause, as distinct from the issues of fact
and law focused in it, is primarily of importance to the
parties. One would therefore expect that factors of
importance to one or other party would be within the
contemplation of the sheriff under this head. I see no
reason to confine the interpretation of the expression
in any way. If one found that a case of little monetary
value raised an issue of law of the utmost importance
to the public generally, the inconvenience and expense
to which parties were exposed would be a factor in
deciding whether it was appropriate to remit the particular cause to the Court of Session, if I am correct in
the construction of the provision. It is unnecessary to
seek for a construction of "important or difficult"
which might avoid the risk of the cause being remitted
in such circumstances. I would give these words the
widest of interpretations, including factors personal to
the litigants. The sheriff expressed his agreement with
observations in *Shaw v Lanarkshire Health Board* that
"it was not every important or difficult case that came
within the ambit of section 37 (1) (*b*), but only those
that there were so important or so difficult as to merit
the authoritative and persuasive sanction of the Court
of Session, which meant that the cause must be of
unusual or even exceptional difficulty or importance".
In my opinion this rather extensive gloss on the
language of the section is unhelpful and misleading.
The views of Sheriff Macphail in *Butler v Thom* at
p 58 appear to me to reflect much more accurately the
proper approach to this matter.

I have not found it necessary to have regard to the
Grant committee report, nor to the parliamentary
debates on the Bill, in dealing with the construction of
s 37 (1) (b). I do not think that there is any ambiguity
in this case which is incapable of resolution on the
language of the provision. However, and perhaps of
greater significance, I did not find in either source the
clear guidance on the point in issue which would be
required before one could rely on *Pepper v Hart* for
authority to use such sources as aids to construction in
this case.

In the circumstances it is unnecessary to deal with
counsel's submissions on the basis of the construction
of s 37 applied in *Data Controls*. The appellant's
counsel, assuming that a broader approach would be
adopted, first attacked the sheriff's views on the

respective financial positions of the parties. It was said
that the sheriff had less than adequate information
available on financial matters, on the availability of
legal aid to the respondents, and on the nature and
extent of the "fighting fund" available to the respondents to enable him to arrive at the view he did, and
that the remit of the cause to the Court of Session
could well involve the parties in significant further
expense than would be likely to be involved in the
sheriff court. The problems relating to the parties'
means have disappeared on appeal. The respondents
now have legal aid for the case as has the appellant.
However, it appears to me that the risk of additional
expense is a factor which the sheriff would have been
well entitled to have in mind in any case.

Next it was contended that the sheriff had erred in
his approach to considering the importance of the case
to the appellant. In my opinion there is substance in
this criticism. The sheriff, as I understand his opinion,
was inclined to dismiss as unlikely to have weight the
importance to an individual of answering allegations
of murder. The purpose of the civil action was a civil
remedy of damages. The action had no criminal
connotations and, he said, the criminal element in the
facts averred had already been determined in favour of
the appellant. In my opinion, the sheriff in this respect
misconceived the test to be applied, and failed to give
weight to relevant considerations brought to his attention. The importance to the appellant of resisting
allegations of the type on which the respondents'
claims are based is, in my opinion, clear. The allegation against him is of murder. He has already tholed
an assize on an indictment for murder in the High
Court of Justiciary and been acquitted on a verdict of
not proven. The respondents' averments in this case
put that allegation in issue again, in a civil process.
The defender is exposed to the risk of being found, on
the appropriate standard, to have murdered the late
Mr Mullan, that being one of the issues raised by the
respondents in their pleadings. It is important to him
to maintain his innocence of that crime. There is no
more serious allegation that one can make against a
person than that he took the life of another human
being in circumstances properly characterised as
murder. The criminal penalty is imprisonment or
detention for life. The stigma attaching to the convicted murderer is for life also. Proof in civil proceedings that a person committed such a crime must, in
normal circumstances, similarly affect the reputation
of a person for life. Of course there may be a case in
which that would not be so. A person who had committed murder on one or more previous occasions and
been convicted might be less able to maintain that he
was adversely affected by a subsequent allegation in a
civil process. But for the majority of people proof of
the allegation would have devastating consequences,
in a civil as in a criminal court. The fact that there can
be no criminal sanction as a result of the finding in a
civil process that the defender was probably a murderer would be a matter of some significance, but it
would not be of such significance as to deprive the
proceedings of real importance to a defender of normal

A susceptibilities. In my opinion counsel for the appellant were correct in their analysis of the respondents' position in this case. The objective can fairly be said to be proof of the facts constituting the crime of murder, bearing in mind that the defender is legally aided, has no material assets, and has no form of indemnity insurance. There is no prospect of recovering damages. It is not unreasonable to view the action as an attempt to redress the perceived injustice in the acquittal of the appellant in the High Court of Justiciary. If that is so then the proceedings take on

B the importance one would normally associate with a trial for murder in that court.

The sheriff proceeded on the view that the standard of proof to be applied in this case was the ordinary civil standard of balance of probabilities. For the appellant it was argued that that involved an error of law. Counsel referred to *Lennon v Co-operative Insurance Society Ltd*; *Arnott v Burt*; *Halford v Brookes*; *B v Kennedy*; *Harris v F*; *Buick v Jagler*; *Rehman v Ahmad*; and *Shaw v Lanarkshire Health Board.*

C Counsel for the respondents referred, in addition, to *Brown v Brown*; *Lamb v Lord Advocate*; *R v Home Secretary*; *R v Hampshire County Council, ex p Ellerton*; and *Ward v Chief Constable of Strathclyde*. In my opinion the English authorities are not helpful in this context. As a matter of general impression I found Slade LJ's opinion in *Ellerton* at p 761 attractive. However the development of the law in the two jurisdictions has been different, and it is not possible to be confident that the use of similar expressions reflects

D common understanding of the issues involved. The Scottish authorities establish, in my opinion, that there are two standards of proof only in Scotland, proof beyond reasonable doubt and proof on a balance of probabilities: *Brown*, per Lord Emslie at 1972 SLT, p 145; *Lamb*, per Lord Justice Clerk Wheatley at 1976 SLT, p 153 and Lord Kissen at p 156; *B v Kennedy* at p 768. The two standards differ in character, not in degree. Proof to a standard which excludes reasonable doubt on the whole evidence available to the tribunal

E of fact involves a process of analysis and reasoning which differs from that involved in reaching a view whether, among the possibilities which emerge on a consideration of the evidence as a whole, one can be identified which probably reflects the truth. In my opinion it is wholly consistent with such an approach to recognise that certain facts may require evidence of particular weight if they are to be established on either approach. In *Ward* the Lord President adopted precisely that approach, as I understand his comments, at

F p 294, as did Lord Sutherland at p 297 and Lord Clyde at pp 298-299. In *Rehman* I attempted to follow the same approach, in adopting the test of "careful and precise" proof of the facts required to overcome the presumption that a written document embodied the agreement of the parties who subscribed it. In some cases one may have an allegation which, of its very nature is, or appears to be, improbable. It would require evidence of more significant weight to persuade one that a fact of that nature was probably true than it would to persuade one to the same standard

G that a commonplace event had occurred. It is not clear that the observations of Lord Neaves in *Arnott*, at p 74, are inconsistent with this approach. In *Lennon* Lord Kincraig applied the standard of balance of probabilities when he came to decide the case. The opinion of the court in *B v Kennedy* is clearly consistent with the same approach.

In the whole circumstances I am of opinion that the sheriff did err in his decision in this case and it is open to this court to approach the matter de novo. I consider that the importance of the case to the defender and appellant is so great as to override other con-

H siderations that have been brought to the notice of the court and for this reason alone in the circumstances of this case the proper course is that the case should be remitted to the Court of Session. The case should return to the sheriff to be dealt with in that way.

LORD BRAND.—Since formulating my opinion on the questions raised in this appeal I have had the advantage of reading in draft the opinion of Lord Prosser with which I am in complete agreement. I

I agree, in particular, that the sheriff appears to have misdirected himself by failing to consider the importance of the merits of the cause and that averments of murder forming the basis of a civil action would make the importance of the cause to the defender so great as to make it appropriate to remit the cause to the Court of Session.

This appeal was remitted to a bench of five judges for the purpose of reviewing the decision in *Data Controls Ltd v British Railways Board* insofar as it decided

J that the additional expense which might be incurred by the pursuers if a motion under s 37 (1) (b) for a remit to the Court of Session were granted was irrelevant. In my opinion that decision is erroneous. I consider that the extra expense which might be caused by remitting a cause to the Court of Session is relevant to the consideration of whether the importance or difficulty of the cause makes it appropriate to grant or refuse a motion to remit.

K

————————

Counsel for Pursuers and Respondents, Galbraith, QC, Bennett; Solicitors, John G Gray & Co, SSC (for Bradley, Murnin & Campbell, Greenock) — Counsel for Defender and Appellant, C M Campbell, QC, Sturrock; Solicitors, Drummond Miller, WS (for Blair & Bryden, Greenock).

C A G M

L

Grieve v Morrison

A OUTER HOUSE
LORD MORISON
9 APRIL 1986

Heritable property — Common property — Division and sale — Subjects purchased jointly by co-proprietors financed by joint loan and free proceeds of sale of property formerly owned by one co-proprietor contributed in con-
B *templation of marriage — Marriage not undertaken — Condictio causa data causa non secuta — Whether proprietor contributing free proceeds entitled to resist division and sale — Whether proprietor contributing free proceeds entitled to obtain conveyance of other co-proprietor's interest.*

Repetition — Condictio causa data causa non secuta — Heritable property purchased in joint names in anticipation of marriage — Purchase financed by joint loan and free proceeds of sale of property formerly owned by one co-
C *proprietor — Marriage not undertaken — Whether contribution of free proceeds a donation in consideration of marriage — Whether donor entitled to require conveyance of heritable interest of donee — Whether donor entitled to recover part of free proceeds — Necessity of parties' mutual understanding of consideration for donation — Whether discretion in court to refuse to give effect to condictio when applicable.*

A man raised an action of division or sale of a flat to which he held title in joint names with his former
D fiancée. In 1978 the pursuer and the defender decided to live together on the understanding that they would marry when the pursuer was free to do so. The defender purchased a flat as a dwelling for them both, the purchase being financed largely by a loan obtained on advantageous terms from a subsidiary of her employers. This property was sold in 1979 and another property purchased in the defender's name with the proceeds of the sale of the first property and similar loan finance. The defender met all loan repay-
E ments, while the pursuer met the costs of certain renovations and contributed free time to improvement of the property. In August 1983 the parties became engaged to be married and the pursuer, whilst having considerable unexpressed reservations about the proposed marriage, acquiesced in arrangements for the parties' wedding in August 1984.

In October 1983 the parties made a successful joint offer to purchase a further flat. Title was taken in joint names and the purchase was financed by a secured
F loan of approximately £18,000 made jointly to the parties and the free proceeds of the sale of the property purchased in 1979, amounting to approximately £9,000. At the time of the sales and purchases of the properties the pursuer regarded the free proceeds of sale as the proceeds of a joint venture to which he was jointly entitled, notwithstanding that title had previously been taken solely in the name of the defender. While the defender at no time suggested or implied to the pursuer that she was only willing to sell the 1979 property and enter into joint arrangements for the pur-

chase of another flat if their marriage took place, it was established that if the pursuer had informed the G defender that he did not intend to marry her, no question of the purchase of the further flat would have arisen. One month after taking entry to the new property the pursuer told the defender that he was not going to marry her and left the property.

The defender argued that the pursuer was not entitled to insist on a sale of the property or to any part of the free proceeds, and lodged a counterclaim seeking declarator that she was entitled to the pursuer's pro indiviso share of the property and that his H interest should be conveyed to her. The defender's defence and counterclaim rested solely on the condictio causa data causa non secuta, in respect that the pursuer's interest in the property was a gift made by her in consideration of the parties' marriage which did not occur.

Held, (1) that the consideration for which the 1983 property was jointly purchased was receipt of the price from both parties, the major part of that price being I provided by a joint loan, and accordingly the defender had made no gift of heritable property to the pursuer and the condictio had no application to the pursuer's ownership of his pro indiviso share of the property (p 855B-E); (2) that neither the defender's defences nor her counterclaim relevantly related to an entitlement to part of the free proceeds of any sale as distinct from the whole (p 855F-G); (3) that in any event in order that the condictio could apply to any transfer of assets the transfer had to be subject to a mutually agreed understanding, either express or to be implied J from the circumstances, that it was made for the consideration which later failed and on the evidence no such agreement could be implied (p 855 I-J); and declarator *granted* and pursuer *assoilzied* from the conclusions of the counterclaim.

Opinion, (1) that if the defender were entitled to anything by virtue of the condictio she would only be entitled to the amount which she contributed to the pursuer's share of the price (p 855E-F); and (2) that if K the doctrine of the condictio applied the court was not afforded any discretion to refuse to give effect to it (p 855K).

Action of division or sale

George Edward Grieve, a pro indiviso proprietor of a flatted property in Edinburgh, raised an action of division or sale of the property against Alison L Morrison, the remaining pro indiviso proprietor, and Standard Life Assurance Co Ltd, holders of a standard security over the subjects. The first defender contended inter alia that she was entitled to the pursuer's interest in the property upon the principle of the condictio causa data causa non secuta and counterclaimed for conveyance of the pursuer's interest to her or alternatively for the whole proceeds of any sale.

The case came to proof before the Lord Ordinary (Morison).

Cases referred to

A *Cantiere San Rocco SA v Clyde Shipbuilding and Engineering Co Ltd*, 1923 SLT 624; 1923 SC (HL) 105.

Miller (D & S) v Crichton (1893) 1 SLT 262.

On 9 April 1986 the Lord Ordinary *granted* decree of declarator of right of division or sale, subject to reservation of division of the free proceeds until after any sale; *repelled* the first defender's pleas in law and quoad ultra *continued* the cause; and in the counter-
B claim *repelled* the first defender's pleas in law and *assoilzied* the pursuer from the conclusions of the counterclaim.

LORD MORISON.—This is an action for division or sale of a flat in Figgate Street, Portobello, of which the pursuer and the first defender, whom I shall refer to as "the defender", are pro indiviso proprietors. Their title thereto is contained in a disposition in their favour by Teague Homes (Scotland) Ltd, recorded in
C the Register of Sasines on 9 August 1984. It is a matter of agreement that the flat is for practical purposes incapable of division. It is worth about £27,000.

The action is defended by the defender exclusively on the basis that she has a right to the pursuer's interest in the subjects or to the proceeds of sale of that interest upon the principle of condictio causa data causa non secuta. She avers that the flat had been purchased for the sole purpose of providing a matrimonial home for the parties and that she had made a gift to
D the pursuer of his share of the reversionary interest in the property. This gift was made in consideration of their marriage, and must be returned to her since in the event that consideration failed. She has a counter-claim for the pursuer's pro indiviso share or alterna-tively the whole proceeds of sale.

The circumstances in which these claims have arisen are as follows. The parties met in 1977, when the pursuer was and had been for 11 years married to
E another woman. Within a few months they decided to live together, it being then understood according to the defender, whose evidence on the matter I accepted, that they would marry when the pursuer was free to do so. As it transpired, the pursuer was not divorced until 19 November 1982. After deciding to cohabit, the parties looked for a house and in July 1978 the defender purchased for £9,747 a flat which they had found at 4 Hermitage Park, Edinburgh, as a home for both parties. The way in which this purchase was financed is shown in the defender's solicitors' account,
F no 62 of process. Nine thousand pounds was advanced by The Heritable Securities and Mortgage Investment Association Ltd in whose favour the defender granted a standard security over the flat. This company is a subsidiary of the second defenders, by whom the first defender is employed. As a result of that employment the defender was able to obtain very much more advantageous terms for the loan than those which would have been available to the pursuer, and it was therefore an obviously sensible step that the defender rather than the pursuer should obtain the loan and

take the title in her own name. The pursuer, however, obtained a loan of £1,000 which he says was applied G to the expenses of purchase, including a contribution to the price. I accept his evidence to this effect, although the defender said that she was not satisfied that the whole £1,000 was applied to the purchase. The defender also made a small cash contribution to the balance of the price and expenses.

At first the pursuer lived at Hermitage Park by himself, the defender staying with him for two nights a week. The defender later moved in and the parties lived there together as man and wife until they moved H to a more expensive house at 20 Ryehill Avenue in November 1979 where they lived together for a further four years. Title to the house at Ryehill Avenue was again taken in the defender's name. During the parties' cohabitation there were no dis-putes regarding financial matters, and although I heard evidence of domestic expenditure by both parties I do not regard the details as important, the broad picture being clear. Both the pursuer and the defender were employed and bills were paid by I whoever had money available. The pursuer's earnings, which are summarised in a letter from his employers, were about twice those of the defender, and although he had a financial commitment to his wife and child, he probably incurred greater domestic expenditure than did the defender. For example, he usually paid about £20 weekly for food. He met the cost of improvements to the house at Ryehill Avenue, such as the provision of central heating, a new bathroom and rewiring. He also spent a great deal of his spare time J redecorating, thereby increasing the value of the house. The defender, however, also met household expenses, including the whole of the repayments of capital and interest due in respect of the loans obtained from her employers. When the parties moved from Hermitage Park, the loan secured over the flat there was redeemed and the defender obtained a further loan secured over Ryehill Avenue to meet the balance of the price after applying thereto the full pro-ceeds of sale of Hermitage Park. Details of this trans- K action are contained in the solicitors' account no 45 of process. The loan was later increased by about £3,000 to meet the cost of rebuilding an extension. The defender paid about £65 and £16 monthly under the relative loan agreements by way of deductions from her salary. The parties shared the housework. The pursuer usually cooked and prepared the parties' evening meal during the week, since he was on a shift which allowed him to do this.

Whilst they are not directly relevant, these domestic L arrangements have some bearing on parties' intentions in respect of the purchase of the subjects with which the action is concerned. The pursuer regarded the free proceeds of sale of Hermitage Park and, when it came to be sold, those of Ryehill Avenue as the proceeds of a joint venture to which he was jointly entitled, not-withstanding that the title to these houses had been taken in the name of the defender and that she had met the periodical payments due under the loan agree-ments. The defender in her evidence recognised that this had always been his attitude, but she herself, since the titles to both houses were in her name, considered that she was exclusively entitled to the free proceeds on their sale. It was conceded on behalf of the pursuer that in law she was correct in this view, subject to any claim which the pursuer might have arising from contributions which he had made to the capital value of the properties.

So far as the defender was concerned, her intentions in purchasing the property in Figgate Street were also affected by the progress of her relationship with the pursuer. She had always proceeded on the basis that she and the pursuer would be married when he was free to do so. The pursuer, however, became increasingly reluctant to marry the defender, owing to a deterioration in their relationship which occurred whilst they lived at Ryehill Avenue. The evidence led affords no satisfactory basis for a conclusion as to the reasons for this deterioration, but at least part of the trouble was that the defender objected to the pursuer's son, who was 11 years old when the parties moved to Ryehill Avenue and of whom the pursuer was very fond, staying in the house as much as he did, on the view that this interfered with the parties' relationship. Whether for this or other reasons the pursuer on occasions drank too much, and this created further difficulty. However, in August 1983, about eight months after the pursuer was divorced, the parties became engaged to be married. This engagement was undoubtedly entered into on the defender's initiative, but the pursuer said in evidence that because the defender was unable to accept his son he never had any intention of becoming married and only became engaged for the sake of peace and quiet. Although I regarded him as straightforward and honest in all other respects and although he may now believe this to be the case, I do not accept that when he became engaged he had decided not to marry the defender. An engagement ring was purchased either by him or the defender and in autumn 1983 he allowed a date to be fixed with the registrar for their wedding to take place on 3 August 1984; he acquiesced in the defender's father booking a room for the wedding reception, and he himself booked and paid a deposit for a holiday abroad immediately after the reception. I accept that he had very considerable reservations about the proposed marriage but he did not express these either to the defender or to her family until about the time when they separated. I regard his conduct in this respect as most inconsiderate, even making every allowance for his upset at the deterioration in the parties' relationship.

A short time after their engagement the parties became interested in the flat at Figgate Street for which they jointly made an offer to purchase at a price of £26,950 by missive dated 28 October 1983, accepted on 3 November. The property was ultimately disponed to them jointly in April 1984. The purchase was funded by a loan of about £18,000 made jointly to the parties by the second defenders on the security of the property and still on the same favourable terms as previously; and by the free proceeds arising from the sale of Ryehill Avenue which amounted to £9,000. Under this loan agreement parties were and still are jointly and severally liable in respect of the obligations undertaken in the standard security. So far as the pursuer at least was concerned, the fact that the title taken was in the names of the parties jointly had no particular significance; by this time he was divorced and, so long as the same favourable terms could be obtained from the lenders, it was a more natural arrangement that the house where the parties cohabited should be owned jointly rather than exclusively by the defender, and also that they should be jointly liable for repayment of the loan and for interest thereon.

I accept the evidence of both the pursuer and the defender as to their reasons for moving to Figgate Street. The pursuer wanted a more modern house, being apprehensive about the possibility of dry rot which the parties had experienced at Ryehill Avenue. In addition, the flat in Figgate Street had an additional bedroom where his son could stay. So far as the defender was concerned, she was at first unwilling to move, but agreed to do so at least partly because the additional bedroom would provide more accommodation for the family which she was hoping to have after marriage. If the pursuer had told her that he never intended to marry her, the relationship would have ended then and no question of the purchase of another house would have arisen. However, the defender never suggested or implied to the pursuer that she was only willing to move and to enter into the joint arrangement for purchase of another house if their marriage took place; at one stage of her evidence she agreed that although she herself anticipated marriage in taking joint title to the house she did not know what was the pursuer's attitude in that respect.

Parties moved into Figgate Street in January 1984 but at about the end of February after an altercation the pursuer told the defender that he was not going to marry her and he left. The defender suggests in her pleadings that he did so to live with another woman. The evidence demonstrated that this suggestion is untrue, and it was not pursued. The pursuer left against the defender's wishes because, whether as a result of his own conduct or that of the defender, he could no longer tolerate the relationship.

On the basis of the above facts I turn to consider parties' contentions. The pursuer as pro indiviso proprietor of subjects which are unsuitable for division is prima facie entitled to declarator in terms of his alternative declaratory conclusion. The defender pleads that he is not entitled to insist on a sale, or in any event to any part of the free proceeds. Her counterclaim first seeks declarator that she is entitled to the pursuer's pro indiviso share. Originally she sought adjudication of that share in her favour, but during the hearing it was intimated with the pursuer's consent that the latter conclusion would be amended to substitute a claim that she was entitled to have the pursuer's share conveyed to her. As previously indicated, both her defence and her counterclaim rest solely on the principle condictio causa data causa non secuta, in respect that the pursuer's reversionary interest in the property was a gift made by her in consideration of the parties' marriage which did not occur.

The nature of the condictio is set out in the speeches reported in the leading case of *Cantiere San Rocco v Clyde Shipbuilding and Engineering Co*. It rests generally on the liability to make restitution of a thing which has been transferred on a consideration which has failed. A well recognised example of the application of the doctrine is a gift made, for example to a bridegroom, in consideration of marriage. If the marriage does not take place, the gift must be returned.

I am unable to see how the doctrine can have any application to the pursuer's ownership of his pro indiviso share. No doubt the condictio can apply to a gift made by transfer of title to heritable property, equally to one of money or moveable property, so as to require the donee to reconvey the heritage to the donor if the consideration for which the gift has been made fails. In such a case it may well be required that the consideration for which the gift is made must be specified in the deed transferring title or in some other written document so as to qualify in writing the donee's otherwise ex facie absolute right. But it is unnecessary to determine the latter point because in the present case the defender made no gift of heritable property to the pursuer. The consideration for which the property was jointly purchased, as the disposition bears, was receipt of the price from both parties. The major part of that price was provided by a loan for which both parties took equal responsibility. All that the defender did was to provide towards the price a contribution of £9,000 which she had obtained as the free proceeds of the sale of the parties' former home. In respect of the pursuer's pro indiviso share the maximum extent of her generosity was therefore a contribution of £4,500, which having regard to the circumstances in which this sum became available to her is nothing out of the ordinary, and in any event cannot found a claim for the whole of the pursuer's heritable interest. The absurdity of such a claim is illustrated by the fact that if it were upheld the pursuer would remain liable to the security holder in respect of the obligations undertaken in the standard security. This anomaly would not be affected by an undertaking (which was given during the hearing on the defender's behalf) that she would provide an indemnity in respect of these obligations. If the defender were entitled to anything by virtue of the condictio she would only in my view be entitled to the amount which she contributed to the pursuer's share of the price. The defence insofar as it is based on the defender's alleged entitlement to the whole of the pursuer's pro indiviso share therefore fails and the pursuer is entitled to the declarator which he seeks in relation to sale of the subjects.

So far as the proceeds are concerned, although the defender has a plea and a single averment in her defence to the principal action that she is "entitled to the major part of the free proceeds", there is no specification as to what is meant by the "major part". In the counterclaim there is no conclusion, averment or plea relating to a part of the proceeds, as distinct from the whole, notwithstanding that a claim on part of the proceeds would have been open to the defender in the present proceedings, on the authority of the case of *D & S Miller v Crichton*.

I hold in any event that the defender has no case based on the application of the condictio. As I have indicated, the pursuer regarded the free proceeds of the house at Ryehill Avenue as the proceeds of a joint venture. He had no idea that there was an element of donation by the defender in his favour in the arrangement made for the purchase of the subjects at Figgate Street, let alone that any such donation would be returnable by him if the marriage to which he had agreed did not take place. In the ordinary case of transfer of assets made in return for a consideration the terms or circumstances of the transfer would make it clear for what consideration the transfer was made. Thus in the case of a gift made in consideration of marriage the donee would ordinarily understand that this was the intention of the donor. In the present case the defender admitted that she had never suggested to the pursuer that she was only applying the proceeds of the sale of the parties' previous home to the joint purchase of another house on the understanding that the parties would be married. In effect she recognised in her evidence what I hold to be the case, that the pursuer would not have been aware that any obligation towards her connected with the purchase of the new house would arise if the parties did not become married. In my view in order that the condictio should apply, the transfer must be subject to a mutually agreed understanding, either express or to be implied from the circumstances, that it is made for the consideration which later fails. The doctrine is founded on equitable considerations and is inconsistent with a situation in which a person might have undertaken an obligation of which he had no reason to be aware. If it were otherwise it is not difficult to envisage inequitable results. It was suggested by counsel for the defender that such inequitable results could be avoided by the exercise of a discretion vested in the court to refuse to give effect to the doctrine. I know of no principle or authority which supports the view that if the doctrine applies the court is afforded any discretion. In my opinion the obligation to return a thing transferred for a consideration which has failed is, like any other implied condition, one as to which there must be held to be mutual agreement. No such agreement can be implied in the present case.

For these reasons in the action by the pursuer, I sustain his second and third pleas in law and grant decree of declarator that he is entitled to insist in an action of division or sale, and in terms of the alternative declaratory conclusion with the exception of the words "and the free proceeds divided between the pursuer and the first defender". Division of the proceeds should be dealt with after the sale takes place. I

repel all of the first defender's pleas in law. Quoad
ultra I continue the cause. In the counterclaim I repel
both of the first defender's pleas in law, sustain the
pursuer's third and fourth pleas in law and assoilzie
the pursuer from the conclusions of the counterclaim.

---

*Counsel for Pursuer, R K Miller; Solicitors, Beveridge
& Kellas, WS — Counsel for First Defender, J J
Mitchell; Solicitors, Morton Fraser & Milligan, WS —
No appearance for Second Defenders.*

M L B F

[This case has been reported by request.]

(NOTE)

Baird v Sellars

OUTER HOUSE

TEMPORARY JUDGE J M S HORSBURGH, QC

26 JUNE 1992

*Damages — Amount — Solatium and loss of earning
capacity — Neck, shoulder, head and chest — Main
injury to neck resulting in continuing disability.*

A passenger in a taxi was injured in a collision. She
was then aged 37. Her main injury was a neck injury
causing considerable continuing disability and leaving
her unfit for her previous work as a chambermaid.

Held, that solatium was properly valued at £8,000
and that in addition to an award for past wage loss an
award for loss of employability of £5,000 was
appropriate; and decree *pronounced* accordingly.

Eileen Baird raised an action of damages against
Gordon Sellars, the driver of a taxi in which she had
been travelling when it was involved in a collision
with another vehicle. The accident happened on 5
December 1987. The pursuer, a hotel chambermaid,
was then aged 37. The driver of the other vehicle was
also called as a defender. After a proof before the temporary judge (J M S Horsburgh, QC) the taxi driver
was found wholly to blame and the driver of the other
vehicle assoilzied. A plea of contributory negligence
founded on the pursuer not having worn her seatbelt
was rejected as not having been established. The pursuer's injuries included a possible small fracture of the
sternum, a head injury and a neck injury. In relation
to damages the temporary judge said:

"It may be added that both surgeons were agreed
that the major component in the pursuer's injuries was
that to the neck, and wearing a seatbelt would neither
have avoided nor reduced the severity of that parti-

cular injury. The consequences of the head injury
itself, bruising to the face and eyes, a numb sensation
to the left side of the scalp, loss of consciousness for
a short period, a laceration to the tongue and lacerations to the inner and outer aspects of the lower lip on
the left side, were all relatively minor sequelae of the
accident.

"An injury with more long lasting effects was that
to the sternum. Although not serious, it caused the
pursuer discomfort for a period of about 18 months.

"The main injury which the pursuer sustained as a
result of the accident was that to the neck. She was an
inpatient in Inverclyde Royal hospital for six days.
She was given a cervical collar and painkillers. Initially
she was unable to move her head, neck and arm, and
suffered severe pain in these areas and in her chest
and back. Eating and drinking were difficult. By 24
December 1987 she had made some improvement but
she continued to have pain and considerable limitation
in movement of her right shoulder. In early January
1988 she commenced 12 months' physiotherapy. On
21 January 1988 she was found to be suffering from
a subluxation of the right facet joint of C6 on C7,
with a marginal fracture of C7. By April 1988 the pain
had lessened and movement had increased, but until
about May 1988 she was unable to dress or undress,
required help for toilet and experienced difficulty in
travelling and going up and down stairs. She was
unable to do domestic tasks. She continued to make
progress until about August or September 1988 when
she injured her back in attempting to move a wardrobe
at home. Thereafter progress was reduced. This
caused difficulties with everyday tasks and coping
with the injury. Her lack of progress brought about a
state of anxiety. The pursuer is no longer able to
undertake the sort of heavy work involved in her
former employment as a chambermaid.

"The issue between the surgeons is as to the extent
and effect of the neck injury. They were agreed that
subluxation at C6/7 level was diagnosed in January
1988. Mr Hamilton considered that that had rectified
itself by 1990 except for some minimal residual subluxation causing only restriction of rotation to the
right. He accepted that in its early stages the subluxation would cause pain and restriction of movement,
but later only minor discomfort. On the other hand
Mr McGarrity thought the effect of this particular
injury caused considerable disability which extends to
the present.

"I have come to the view that Mr McGarrity's evidence should be preferred to that of Mr Hamilton. [The
temporary judge gave his reasons for preferring Mr
McGarrity's evidence and continued:]

"Mr McGarrity was supported by the evidence of
the pursuer and her husband that she is still troubled
by her neck, and I accept their evidence about this as
truthful.

"Accordingly I am unable to accept Mr Hamilton's
view that the pursuer has made a virtually complete
recovery and his view that she could have returned to

work at a date much earlier than the date of the proof. I prefer the opinion of Mr McGarrity that the restrictions she currently experiences will continue, and will limit the range of employment open to her in the future. I am of the view that the pursuer has not exaggerated her symptoms. That was denied by her, by her husband, and not acceded to by Mr McGarrity who had treated her over a number of years. I regard his observation that the pursuer did not suffer pain or restriction in social movements of the neck and back to be asymptomatic of exaggeration.

"On the matter of quantum, counsel for the pursuer invited me to accept that both the head and neck injuries were serious, but he regarded the neck injury as of the greatest significance. On solatium I was referred to *Johnston v Hardie*, 1990 SLT 744, *McGowan v Air Products (UK)*, 1991 SLT 591, *Hughes v British Railways Board*, 1992 SLT 97 and *Mackenzie v Midland Scottish Omnibuses*, 1992 SLT 752, which cases vouched a range of awards, allowing for inflation, now worth between £6,500 and about £17,000. It was suggested that £12,000 was appropriate in this case for solatium, and that, because progress had been slow, four fifths of that should be attributable to the past with interest at the usual rate.

"On the other hand, counsel for the defenders referred to *McDiarmid v Borders Regional Health Board*, 1985 SLT 79, *Hunter v National Coal Board*, 1988 SLT 241, *Lang v Fife Health Board*, 1990 SLT 626, *Hughes v British Railways Board* and *Smith v Chief Constable, Central Scotland Police*, 1991 SLT 634. These cases suggested that, with an allowance for inflation, the award should be around the range of £5,800 to £6,700. He was of the view that a solatium award of £7,000 with interest on two thirds of that attributable to the past was appropriate.

"In my opinion the pursuer's injuries do not justify as great an award of solatium as was given in those cases which are at the upper end of the range. Indeed I do not regard the pursuer's injuries as disabling as those suffered by the pursuer in *Mackenzie*. I am of the view that an award of £8,000 would be appropriate for solatium. I am also of the opinion that two thirds of that should be attributable to the past with interest thereon at 7½ per cent. That adds a sum of £1,800 to date.

"Next I deal with past wage loss. [The temporary judge assessed it at £11,007 inclusive of interest to the date of decree and continued:]

"Future loss next falls to be considered. Counsel for the pursuer contended that because she was fit for light work but none was available, an award for loss of employability should be made. He referred to *Geddes v British Railways Board*, 1990 SLT 696 and *Murray v British Railways Board*, 1990 SLT 853 where awards of £10,000 and £6,000 respectively were made. He suggested a figure of £5,000 as equivalent to two years' future loss of earnings. The defender's counsel suggested no award be made, but if any was it should not exceed £1,500, having regard to the fact that the pursuer had been in part time employment only and was a low wage earner.

"I am of the view that an award of £5,000 would be appropriate under this head of the claim. I am satisfied that the pursuer's injuries have left a significant risk of future financial loss. Her chances of finding suitable light work in an area of the country where few opportunities for this exist, are very slim in my opinion. I am also of the view that the award to be made under this head should not be restricted by the fact that the pursuer's employment in the past has been on a part time basis. Her evidence was that she had plans to attend to her own life in the future, much of her past having been devoted to looking after the older and younger generations of her family."

Counsel for Pursuer, Batchelor; Solicitors, John G Gray & Co, SSC (for Bradley Murnin & Campbell, Greenock) — Counsel for Defenders, Mackinnon; Solicitors, Bishop & Robertson Chalmers.

C H

(NOTE)

Arbuckle v A H McIntosh & Co Ltd

OUTER HOUSE
LORD ABERNETHY
20 AUGUST 1992

Reparation — Negligence — Breach of statutory duty — Contributory negligence — Failure to adjust guard of circular saw — Whether statutory duty on employee arose when employers failed to supply saw with properly adjusted guard — Woodworking Machines Regulations 1974 (SI 1974/903), reg 14 (1) (a).

An experienced sawyer was injured when using a mechanical circular saw. His employers were held to be in breach of the Woodworking Machines Regulations 1974 in three respects. The employers argued that the pursuer was also in breach of the regulations.

Held, that an employee's duties under the 1974 Regulations only arose when the employers had provided a saw with a properly adjusted guard; and employers' plea of contributory negligence *repelled*.

Alexander Arbuckle raised an action of damages against his employers A H McIntosh & Co Ltd for injuries sustained in an accident that occurred in the defenders' factory. The pursuer was an experienced sawyer. He had been told by his foreman, Wilson, to prepare softwood plinths using a mechanical circular saw. The foreman had demonstrated the job with the blade and guard already set. The pursuer then carried out the job using the saw in the same way as the foreman had and making no adjustments to the blade or guard. He was injured when his hand came in contact with the saw blade. The pursuer founded upon negligence at common law and upon breaches of the Woodworking Machines Regulations 1974. The Lord Ordinary (Abernethy) held negligence established on the ground that, as set, the guard had not provided the protection it should have done, leaving some of the teeth of the saw totally unguarded. Had it been properly set, the pursuer's thumb would have been deflected away from the saw blade by the nose of the guard. In relation to the cases made under the regulations and the defenders' case of contributory negligence, also founded on the regulations, his Lordship said:

"The pursuer pleads three cases of statutory breach of duty. The first alleges a breach of reg 5 (1) of the Woodworking Machines Regulations 1974. It is admitted that these regulations apply in this case. Regulation 5 (1) provides: 'Without prejudice to the other provisions of these Regulations, the cutters of every woodworking machine shall be enclosed by a guard or guards to the greatest extent that is practicable having regard to the work being done thereat, unless the cutters are in such position as to be as safe to every person employed as they would be if so enclosed.'

"It is plain from the findings that I have made that there was a breach of this regulation. The cutters of the saw were not enclosed by a guard to the greatest extent practicable having regard to the work being done and the caveat at the end of the regulation does not apply.

"The pursuer's second statutory case alleges a breach of reg 16 (3) of the same regulations. That regulation provides: 'Without prejudice to the requirements of Regulation 18 (1), that part of the saw blade of every circular sawing machine which is above the machine table shall be guarded with a strong and easily adjustable guard, which shall be capable of being so adjusted and shall be kept so adjusted that it extends from the top of the riving knife to a point above the upper surface of the material being cut which is as close as practicable to the surface or, where squared stock is being fed to the saw blade by hand, to a point which is not more than 12 millimetres above the upper surface of the material being cut.'

"Again it is plain from the findings that I have made that there was a breach of this regulation. While the guard was sufficiently adjustable, it was not kept so adjusted as to meet the requirements of the regulation. Squared stock within the meaning of the regulations was being fed to the saw blade by hand and Mr O'Neill's unchallenged evidence [Mr O'Neill being an engineering expert instructed on behalf of the pursuer] was that the nose of the guard, when it was in the position I have held it was in, was some 2¼ in above the table. That means the gap between the guard and the upper surface of the piece of wood being cut was some 1½ in, well in excess of 12 mm.

"The third statutory case alleges a breach of reg 16 (4) of the same regulations. The relevant part of that regulation provides: 'The guard referred to in the last foregoing paragraph shall have a flange of adequate depth on each side of the saw blade and the said guard shall be kept so adjusted that the said flanges extend beyond the roots of the teeth of the saw blade.'

"In view of the finding I have made as to the setting of the guard at the time of the pursuer's accident, there was a clear breach of that regulation also. These breaches overlap with one another to a certain extent but in my view they all materially contributed to the occurrence of this accident. I therefore hold that each of the statutory cases pled is proved.

"There remains the question of contributory negligence. It was argued by counsel for the defenders in his closing submissions that in terms of reg 14 (1) (a) of the same Woodworking Machines Regulations there was strict liability on the part of the pursuer as an employee to comply with the regulations. The relevant part of that regulation provides: 'Every person employed shall, while he is operating a woodworking machine (a) use and keep in proper adjustment the guards and devices provided in accordance with these Regulations'.

"Accordingly, said counsel, if the regulations were breached, the pursuer must himself accept a degree of contributory negligence. Counsel did not refer to any authority for this proposition. I am unable to accept it. In the first place the defenders have no pleadings to support such an argument. But secondly, and more importantly, the saw with the guard in the setting I have held it was in was handed over to the pursuer like that by Mr Wilson who had himself by way of demonstration cut the first two plinths with the guard in that position. Furthermore, Mr Wilson said that from time to time in the course of his duties as foreman he would have observed the pursuer working at the saw and he said nothing about the position of the guard. In that situation it seems to me impossible to say that the pursuer was contributorily negligent. Counsel for the pursuer referred me to Lay v D & L Studios Ltd [1944] 1 All ER 322. The case was dealing with the Woodworking Machinery Regulations 1922 but that does not matter for present purposes. At p 325 Singleton J explained the interrelation of the duties on the employer and employee in the regulations in this way: 'I think it is the duty of the employers to see that the guard is properly adjusted. . . . Once that guard is properly adjusted, it is the duty of the person employed to use and maintain in proper adjustment the guards provided.' I respectfully agree. The employee's duty in terms of reg 14 (1) (a) only arises when the employers have provided a saw with a guard which is properly adjusted. The saw which the employers provided here did not have such a guard. It follows, therefore, that there is no room for a finding that this accident was caused to any extent by a breach of reg 14 (1) (a) on the part of the pursuer.

"For these reasons I shall sustain the first plea in law for the pursuer, repel the pleas in law for the defenders and grant decree for payment to the pursuer by the defenders of the [agreed] sum of £5,000."

Counsel for Pursuer, Dunlop, QC; Solicitors, Robin Thompson & Partners — Counsel for Defenders, Bennett; Solicitors, Cochran Sayers & Cook.

C H

(NOTE)

McAvoy v City of Glasgow District Council

OUTER HOUSE

TEMPORARY JUDGE T G COUTTS, QC

23 DECEMBER 1992

Evidence — Admissibility — Hearsay — Precognition — Statement made to solicitor — Statement then prepared by solicitor intended to reflect as nearly as possible actual words used by witness — Whether inadmissible as a precognition — Civil Evidence (Scotland) Act 1988 (c 32), ss 2 (1), 3 and 9.

The Civil Evidence (Scotland) Act 1988 permits statements made otherwise than in the course of the proof and which are not precognitions to be admissible in civil proceedings.

A visitor to a council flat sought damages from the council for injuries suffered in a fall at a close doorway, alleging the existence there of a substantial hole. The person visited having died before the proof, the pursuer sought to lead hearsay evidence of what the deceased had told his family and evidence based on statements taken from him by the pursuer's solicitor.

Held, that although what was said by the deceased was competently before the court as hearsay evidence, the statements prepared by the solicitor were inadmissible in evidence since they were precognitions; and objection to their admissibility *sustained.*

Highland Venison Marketing Ltd v Allwild GmbH, 1992 SLT 1127, and *Anderson v Jas B Fraser & Co Ltd,* 1992 SLT 1129, *commented on.*

The Civil Evidence (Scotland) Act 1988 provides by s 2 that: "(1) In any civil proceedings — (a) evidence shall not be excluded solely on the ground that it is hearsay; (b) a statement made by a person otherwise than in the course of the proof shall be admissible as evidence on any matter contained in the statement of which direct oral evidence by that person would be admissible".

Section 3 states: "In any civil proceedings a state-

ment made otherwise than in the course of the proof by a person who at the proof is examined as to the statement shall be admissible as evidence in so far as it tends to reflect favourably or unfavourably on that person's credibility."

Section 9, the interpretation section, provides that " 'statement' includes any representation (however made or expressed) of fact or opinion but does not include a statement in a precognition".

William Joseph McAvoy raised an action against the City of Glasgow District Council for damages for injuries sustained when he was leaving his brother Patrick McAvoy's flat, then owned and factored by the defenders. He averred that he had put his foot in a hole at the entry to the tenement close and had fallen, breaking his ankle. In the course of the proof evidence was adduced under objection as to statements made by Patrick McAvoy. In considering the objection after the proof and sustaining it the Temporary Judge (T G Coutts, QC) said: "The evidence of Mrs Margaret McAvoy, the widow of Patrick, was taken on commission but unfortunately Patrick died prior to his evidence being obtained on a commission which had been granted for that purpose. Patrick McAvoy, had he lived, would have been the principal witness on the merits of the action.

"At the proof the question of the extent to which the court may have regard to hearsay evidence from a deceased witness was sharply raised. The pursuer's own evidence about his accident was vague because of his poor recollection of any events surrounding that accident and would not have served to establish any material fact other than that he had in some manner sustained a fractured ankle when he fell during the evening of 3 January 1988. The pursuer's brother Patrick died on 20 July 1992. His evidence would have been critical. The action was signeted on 21 February 1990 but the record did not close until 7 August 1991 and proof was allowed on 13 March 1992. Had the litigation been pursued more expeditiously, the evidence of Patrick McAvoy could have been given orally and its reliability would have been capable of proper assessment. Instead, evidence was proferred of what he had said both before and after the action was raised to his family and to his brother's solicitor. That the hearsay evidence of what he had said to his family was competently before the court was not disputed. However, evidence was also led in two forms from the pursuer's solicitor, Mr David Whyte. The first was Mr Whyte's recollection of what Patrick McAvoy had said to him; the second was in the form of three typed documents entitled 'statements', nos 20/2, 20/3 and 20/4 of process. These documents were lodged in process and were referred to in evidence but throughout counsel for the defenders maintained his objection to their competence. Mr Whyte described his practice in the taking of these statements. It was elaborate and there is no reason to doubt him on the matter, even if he did begin his evidence by saying that all the statements were taken in the same manner but later said that 20/4 of process as distinct from 20/2 and 20/3 was

a result of a telephone conversation whereas 20/2 and
20/3 were dictated by Mr Whyte in Patrick's presence.
Mr Whyte's evidence was that he had seen Patrick
McAvoy who told him of various matters. He then
said that all the statements were taken in the same
manner, that Patrick McAvoy was interviewed in the
presence of a shorthand typist, that he himself dictated
to the shorthand typist in Patrick McAvoy's presence
the statement which Patrick McAvoy then had the
opportunity to correct. Number 20/2 was taken in
response to questions by him. Patrick McAvoy did not
alter it after dictation. The statement was said to
represent what Patrick McAvoy told Mr Whyte but
not necessarily the precise words which Patrick
McAvoy had used. Mr Whyte's evidence was 'they are
as near as I could keep to the words he used'. Number
20/3 was said to be a distillation of discussion with
Patrick McAvoy dictated by Mr Whyte in Patrick's
presence who agreed with it. Document no 20/4 was
compiled, Mr Whyte thought, as a result of a conversation on the telephone when he was clarifying
matters. It was thus apparent that Patrick McAvoy
could not be present at any dictation or correction of
that statement. Mr Whyte further said that, generally,
he recollected that Patrick McAvoy had never
deviated from his statement from the first time he had
interviewed him. He was incorrect in that recollection
at least so far as detail was concerned.

"While I have no doubt that Mr Whyte was, as he
said, careful to try to keep to an accurate transcription
of what Patrick McAvoy had told him, it is plain from
his evidence that what he had done was to distil and
in many instances translate the words uttered by
Patrick McAvoy into the form of a statement. I do not
regard these statements as being admissible evidence
properly before the court. In so saying I do not criticise the practice of Mr Whyte nor would I underestimate his knowledge, care and experience in such
matters. However, it seemed to me that there is a considerable difference between a witness recounting to
the court the words he recalls a deceased witness uttering and the compilation of a document which, whether
it be called statement or precognition, is admitted to
be an account of what the witness said rather than
what he did in fact say. It seems to me that this distinction is enshrined in and is the purpose of the
exclusion of a 'statement in a precognition' from the
definition of 'statement' in s 9 of the Civil Evidence
(Scotland) Act 1988. [The temporary judge narrated
the terms of the Act set out supra and continued:]

"I was referred to two cases, an opinion of Lord
Cullen in *Highland Venison Marketing Ltd v Allwild
GmbH*, 1992 SLT 1127, and an opinion of Lord
Morton of Shuna in *Anderson v Jas B Fraser & Co
Ltd*, 1992 SLT 1129. In each of these cases evidence
was led from a solicitor in respect of statements made
by a witness. In *Highland Venison* Lord Cullen did not
require to consider the hearsay evidence given by the
solicitor in coming to his decision but did express,
obiter, the view that the evidence was admissible and
that what he had had presented to him was not a precognition within the meaning of s 9 of the Act. In that

case a solicitor interviewed a Mr Epstein and took
notes. She then drafted a precognition which she sent
to Mr Epstein for his revisal. Mr Epstein revised the
precognition, made alterations, had the document
retyped and then signed it. Mr Epstein died prior to
the proof. In *Anderson v Jas B Fraser & Co Ltd*, Lord
Morton of Shuna heard evidence from the defenders'
solicitor of an interview he had with a witness, Rehill,
who was an alleged eye witness of an incident. Lord
Morton's opinion was that a statement in a precognition means what is recorded in a document prepared
by the precognoscer and does not exclude evidence of
what the person said to the precognoscer in interview.
On that basis he said the solicitor's evidence, 'for what
it is worth', was admissible. The evidence was entirely
oral and no attempt was made to lead evidence of any
document to the court. The Act does not define
'precognition', no doubt the draftsman perhaps being
of the view that everyone could recognise a precognition when they saw one. It would appear reasonable
to consider that a precognition is any compilation of
the evidence which it is hoped that a witness will give
derived from statements made by him and reduced to
writing. There may be circumstances in which a
person could adopt such a written document as his
own, which would appear to be the situation envisaged
in *Highland Venison* where not only was the prepared
statement revised by the witness, it was altered,
retyped and signed. That must be a very close approximation indeed to, for example, a letter written by the
witness. The evidence in *Anderson* was that of utterances by a person to another person who, while no
doubt investigating the events of the incident, was not
speaking to a statement she prepared but to the witness's own words. In the present case the statements
were prepared, were not the witness's own words and
even if he stood by and assented to the version
produced by Mr Whyte there can be no doubt in my
judgment that he had not, in the *Highland Venison*
sense, adopted the statements as his own. Accordingly
I disregard and pay no attention to the documents
20/2, 20/3 and 20/4 of process on the ground that they
are precognitions and the statements therein contained
are statements in precognitions and consequently
inadmissible.

"However, Mr Whyte, as indeed did Mrs McAvoy,
Thomas McAvoy and John McAvoy, spoke to utterances of Patrick McAvoy and these were all, subject to
the obvious criticism that they could not be properly
tested in evidence, competently before the court."

The temporary judge continued by considering the
remaining evidence and concluded that the pursuer
had failed to prove that he had sustained injury in any
fall at the door of the tenement, and assoilzied the
defenders.

---

*Counsel for Pursuer, Ellis; Solicitors, Balfour &
Manson, Nightingale & Bell (for Carswell, Kerr,
Mackay & Boyd, Glasgow) — Counsel for Defenders,
Ivey; Solicitors, Campbell, Smith & Co, WS.*

C H

Simpson v McClory

A   HIGH COURT OF JUSTICIARY

THE LORD JUSTICE CLERK (ROSS),
LORDS MURRAY AND MORISON

5 FEBRUARY 1993

Justiciary — Statutory offence — Driving while unfit through drink — Accused in hospital being requested to supply specimen of blood for laboratory test — Accused not told specimen might be blood or urine but that
B   *decision was for police to make — Whether obligation to give such explanation — Road Traffic Act 1988 (c 52), ss 5 (1) (a) and 7 (1) and (4).*

Section 7 (1) of the Road Traffic Act 1988 provides that in the course of an investigation into whether a person has committed an offence under s 4 or 5 a constable may require him to provide inter alia a specimen of blood or urine for a laboratory test. Subsection (4) provides that if the provision of a specimen other than a specimen of breath may be required in pursu-
C   ance of this section, the question whether it is to be a specimen of blood or a specimen of urine shall be decided by the constable making the requirement.

An accused person was tried on a summary complaint with a contravention of inter alia s 5 (1) (a) of the Road Traffic Act 1988. The accused was found by the police in a motor car which had left the road. He was unconscious, slumped over the wheel and apparently injured. He was taken to hospital where a medical practitioner objected to the accused's being
D   required to provide a screening breath test. Thereafter the police informed the accused that it was alleged that he had committed an offence contrary to s 5 of the 1988 Act and that they required him to provide a specimen of blood for a laboratory test. The police warned the accused of the consequences of failure to comply but did not explain to him that the specimen provided might be blood or urine but that it was for them to decide which. At the close of the Crown case it was submitted that there was no case for the accused
E   to answer as the police had not given that explanation to the accused. The sheriff repelled the submission and convicted the accused who appealed by stated case.

Held, that since the accused had no right to make representations before the constable made the decision as between blood and urine, it followed that there was no legal obligation on a constable to tell the accused that he was required to give a specimen of blood or urine but that the decision as to which was for the constable to determine (pp 866L-867A, 867E-F, 868J-K,
F   869C-D, 869K-L and 870H); and appeal *refused.*

McLeod v MacFarlane, 1993 SLT 782 and *DPP v Warren* [1992] 3 WLR 884, *followed.*

Dicta in *DPP v Warren,* on the propriety of making such an explanation, *commented on.*

Summary complaint

Robert John Simpson was charged at the instance of Colin Bruce McClory, procurator fiscal, Lochmaddy,

on a summary complaint which contained the follow-
G   ing charge inter alia: "(2) [on 30 August 1991 on the A865 Lochboisdale to Lochmaddy public road at Ardheisker, Western Isles, you did] drive a motor vehicle, namely motor car registered number PGE 124Y, after consuming so much alcohol that the proportion of it in your blood was 166 milligrammes of alcohol in 100 millilitres of blood which exceeded the prescribed limit, namely, 80 milligrammes of alcohol in 100 millilitres of blood; contrary to the Road Traffic Act 1988, s 5 (1) (a)". The accused pled guilty and proceeded to trial. After trial the sheriff
H   convicted the accused.

The accused appealed by way of stated case to the High Court against the decision of the sheriff.

Findings in fact

The sheriff (J O A Fraser) found the following facts to be admitted or proved:

(1) In the early hours of the morning of 30 August 1991, Angus John MacLellan, driving on the A865
I   Lochboisdale to Lochmaddy public road at Ardheisker, observed on his nearside of the road an Audi 80 car, registered number PGE 124Y, with the appellant slumped over the wheel unconscious, and, apparently, injured. (2) Mr MacLellan summoned help and two police officers attended the scene about 3.40 am on the said date. By that time the appellant was conscious and was assisted out of the car. There was no sign of blood but the appellant complained of injury to his chest. Both police officers observed that the
J   appellant smelled of alcohol, his speech was slurred and he staggered when walking. (3) The appellant was removed by ambulance to Daliburgh hospital where he was attended to and in the care of Dr Afewu. (4) At 4.38 am on said date Dr Afewu was interviewed by said police officers, who informed him that they proposed to subject the appellant to a specific procedure and that he could object to any part of that procedure as being prejudicial to the appellant's proper care and treatment, in which case the requirement contem-
K   plated by the procedure would not be made. (5) This specific procedure proposed and put in terms to Dr Afewu was (a) a screening breath test; (b) a specimen of blood or urine for a laboratory test, the choice to be that of the police officer, with the details of how that specimen would be taken; (c) cautioning or charging the appellant with a criminal offence; (d) examination and possible testing of the appellant by a medical practitioner selected by the police. (6) At 4.42 am on said date Dr Afewu in response informed the said police
L   officers that he objected to the requirement to provide a screening breath test, on the grounds that the injury to the appellant's chest could be worse than was presently apparent, and that he did not object to any of the other proposed requirements. Dr Afewu signed the appropriate form to that effect. (7) At 4.50 am on said date Police Constable Taylor, one of said two officers, spoke to the appellant at Daliburgh hospital, informing him that it was alleged that he had committed an offence contrary to s 5 of the Road Traffic Act 1988. He required the appellant to provide a

A specimen of blood for a laboratory test, warning him of the consequences of failure to comply, and advising him that the specimen would be taken by a medical practitioner selected by the police, divided into two parts, one being supplied to the appellant on request. (8) The appellant agreed to provide the specimen required and said specimen was taken by Dr Afewu at 4.59 am on said date. (9) Said specimen was then divided into two parts and sealed in two phials. The appellant was warned of possible prosecution if analysis showed blood alcohol above the prescribed limit, and was offered one of the two parts, which he selected and accepted, signing the appropriate form to that effect. (10) Thereafter the remaining specimen was sent for analysis, and was analysed by an authorised analyst on 3 September 1991, said analysis disclosing a level of alcohol of 166 milligrammes of alcohol per 100 millilitres of blood.

Statutory provisions

The Road Traffic Act 1988 provides, inter alia:

C "7.—(1) In the course of an investigation into whether a person has committed an offence under section 4 or 5 of this Act a constable may, subject to the following provisions of this section and section 9 of this Act, require him (a) to provide two specimens of breath for analysis by means of a device of a type approved by the Secretary of State, or (b) to provide a specimen of blood or urine for a laboratory test.

"(2) A requirement under this section to provide specimens of breath can only be made at a police station.

"(3) A requirement under this section to provide a specimen of blood or urine can only be made at a police station or at a hospital; and it cannot be made at a police station unless: (a) the constable making the requirement has reasonable cause to believe that for medical reasons a specimen of breath cannot be provided or should not be required, or (b) at the time the requirement is made a device or a reliable device of the type mentioned in subsection (1) (a) above is not available at the police station or it is then for any other reason not practicable to use such a device there, or (c) the suspected offence is one under section 4 of this Act and the constable making the requirement has been advised by a medical practitioner that the condition of the person required to provide the specimen might be due to some drug; but may then be made notwithstanding that the person required to provide the breath specimen has already provided or been required to provide two specimens of breath.

"(4) If the provision of a specimen other than a specimen of breath may be required in pursuance of this section the question whether it is to be a specimen of blood or a specimen of urine shall be decided by the constable making the requirement, but if a medical practitioner is of the opinion that for medical reasons a specimen of blood cannot or should not be taken the specimen shall be a specimen of urine.

"(5) A specimen of urine shall be provided within one hour of the requirement for its provision being made and after the provision of a previous specimen of urine.

"(6) A person who, without reasonable excuse, fails to provide a specimen when required to do so in pursuance of this section is guilty of an offence.

"(7) A constable must, on requiring any person to provide a specimen in pursuance of this section, warn him that a failure to provide it may render him liable to prosecution.

"8.—(1) Subject to subsection (2) below, of any two specimens of breath provided by any person in pursuance of section 7 of this Act that with the lower proportion of alcohol in the breath shall be used and the other shall be disregarded.

"(2) If the specimen with the lower proportion of alcohol contains no more than 50 microgrammes of alcohol in 100 millilitres of breath, the person who provided it may claim that it should be replaced by such specimen as may be required under section 7 (4) of this Act and, if he then provides such a specimen, neither specimen of breath shall be used. . . .

"9.—(1) While a person is at a hospital as a patient he shall not be required to provide a specimen of breath for a breath test or to provide a specimen for a laboratory unless the medical practitioner in immediate charge of his case has been notified of the proposal to make the requirement; and — (a) if the requirement is then made, it shall be for the provision of a specimen at the hospital, but (b) if the medical practitioner objects on the grounds specified in subsection (2) below, the requirement shall not be made.

"(2) The ground on which the medical practitioner may object is that the requirement or the provision of a specimen or, in the case of a specimen of blood or urine, the warning required under s 7 (7) of this Act, would be prejudicial to the proper care and treatment of the patient."

Cases referred to

Carmichael v McKay, 1991 SCCR 953.
DPP v Byrne [1991] RTR 119.
DPP v Gordon [1990] RTR 71.
DPP v Warren [1992] 3 WLR 884; [1992] 4 All ER 865.
Hamilton v Jones, 1989 SCCR 1.
Hobbs v Clark [1988] RTR 36.
McLeod v MacFarlane, 1993 SLT 782; 1993 SCCR 178.
Paterson v DPP [1990] RTR 329.
Pelosi v Jessop, 1991 SLT 155; 1990 SCCR 175.
Pine v Collacott [1985] RTR 282.

In his note appended to the findings in fact the sheriff stated, inter alia:

THE SHERIFF (J O A FRASER).— . . . I considered the arguments for the appellant and respondent very carefully indeed and I also considered all the authorities which were relevant and referred to in the case of Carmichael v McKay including that case. The first question which I had to determine is whether the

line of authority which is challenged by the Crown
A was binding on me and my conclusion in simple terms
is that it is not. With respect I disagree with my
learned brother, Sheriff Simpson. It follows therefore
that I disagree with the English authority which he
interprets absolutely correctly.

The so called right of the appellant in this case is in
my view non-existent. It is similar, and I do not mean
to be flippant in any way, with the type of choice,
where the authorities may select hanging or beheading
as a method of execution, to asking a condemned
B person which one he prefers.

The appellant in this case, and indeed everyone in
the appellant's position, has the right to proffer a
reasonable excuse for a failure to consent to the
requirement to provide blood. That right is not taken
away.

What the appellant does not have is a right to
challenge the police officer's decision as to whether
C urine or blood should be the specimen which is
provided and, in appropriate cases, subsequently
tested. I can see nothing in s 7 (4) which would justify
such an interpretation.

To put the matter another way, subs (4) of s 7
would, in my view, require to provide that the specimen of blood or the specimen of urine would be
decided by the constable making the requirement but
the accused person would have an opportunity to state
his objection to either and the police officer would
D have to have a reasonable regard to that objection in
making his decision. There is no such phrase in the
subsection and to suggest, in effect, that there is,
strains, in my view, the interpretation of the subsection to breaking point.

What the appellant and any accused person required
to do was to provide the sample which the police
officer required unless he had a reasonable excuse in
law not to do so.

E   Although this case is broadly described a "hospital"
case, as I understood the Crown's submission, that is
the type of case which it happens to be. The position
of the respondent was that that interpretation of s 7 (4)
which he advanced, and with which I agree, is the
appropriate interpretation whether it relates to a specimen being taken in hospital, whether it relates to a
specimen of blood or urine where there is no Camic
device or none operating or whether it relates to an
accused person having a choice other than a specimen
F of breath if, say, a blood test discloses a level above the
permitted limit but sufficiently low to give him that
right.

It is not, of course, for me, to rule or comment on
such a wide submission. I must and did confine my
interpretation to the case and type of case with which
I was faced.

For the reasons described above I accepted the argument advanced by the respondent and rejected the
submission of no case to answer.

Appeal

The sheriff posed the following questions for the G
opinion of the High Court:

(1) Did I err in law in repelling the submission made
on behalf of the appellant that he had no case to
answer?

(2) On the facts stated was I entitled to convict the
appellant on charge 2?

The appeal was argued before the High Court on 16
December 1992.   H

On 5 February 1993 the court *answered* question 1
in the *negative*, question 2 in the *affirmative* and
refused the appeal.

THE LORD JUSTICE CLERK (ROSS).—The
appellant is Robert John Simpson who went to trial in
the sheriff court at Lochmaddy on a complaint libelling two charges, namely, a contravention of s 3 of the
Road Traffic Act 1988 and a contravention of s 5 (1)   I
(a) of the same Act. At the conclusion of the Crown
case, a submission of no case to answer was made on
behalf of the appellant. Having heard submissions
from the parties, the sheriff repelled the submission.
The defence elected to lead no evidence, and after
being addressed upon the evidence the sheriff found
the appellant guilty as libelled of both charges.

The appellant has now appealed by way of stated
case. The appeal is taken against the decision of the
sheriff to repel the appellant's submission of no case J
to answer in respect of charge 2 only. In the stated
case the sheriff has set forth the material evidence. In the
early hours of the morning of 30 August 1991 the
appellant was found slumped over the wheel unconscious and apparently injured in a motor car which had
left the A865 road between Lochboisdale and Lochmaddy. The police were called and when they arrived
at the locus they found the appellant conscious. There
was no sign of blood but he complained of injury to
his chest. The appellant smelt of alcohol, his speech   K
was slurred and he staggered when walking. The
appellant was removed to Daliburgh hospital where he
was attended to by Dr Afewu. At the hospital the
police officers informed Dr Afewu that they proposed
to subject the appellant to a specific procedure, and
that he could object to any part of that procedure as
being prejudicial to the appellant's proper care and
treatment, in which event the requirement contemplated by the procedure would not be made. The
police officers informed Dr Afewu that the specific   L
procedure proposed was: (a) a screening breath test; (b)
a specimen of blood or urine for a laboratory test, the
choice to be that of the police officer, with the details
of how that specimen would be taken; (c) cautioning
or charging the appellant with a criminal offence; and
(d) examination and possible testing of the appellant
by a medical practitioner selected by the police.

Dr Afewu informed the police officers that he
objected to the requirement to provide a screening
breath test on the grounds that the injury to the appel-

A lant's chest could be worse than was presently apparent, but that he would not object to any of the other
proposed requirements. He signed the appropriate
form to that effect.

Finding 7 is in the following terms: [his Lordship
quoted the terms of finding 7 and continued:] The
case goes on to record that the appellant agreed to
provide the specimen required, and the specimen was
duly taken by Dr Afewu. The specimen was divided
into two parts and the appellant was offered one of the
two parts which he selected and accepted. The remain-
B ing specimen was sent for analysis, and the analysis
disclosed a level of alcohol of 166 milligrammes of
alcohol per 100 millilitres of blood which was more
than two times the prescribed limit.

Section 9 of the Road Traffic Act 1988 is in the
following terms: [his Lordship quoted the terms of s 9
(1) and (2) and continued:]

In his note the sheriff explains that the appellant's
solicitor accepted that the procedure for the protection
C of hospital patients set out in s 9 had been properly
carried out; the doctor in charge had objected to the
screening breath test, but not to the procedure for
taking a specimen of blood or urine.

The submission of no case to answer in respect of
charge 2 was based upon the construction sought to be
placed upon s 7 (4) of the Act of 1988 and upon authorities in both England and Scotland.

Section 7 of the Act of 1988 is concerned with the
D provision of specimens for analysis. Section 7 is in the
following terms: [his Lordship quoted its terms and
continued:]

The point which is taken in this appeal is that when
the police officers required the appellant to provide a
specimen of blood for a laboratory test they did not
explain to him that the specimen provided might be
blood or urine but that it was for them to decide
which. On behalf of the appellant it was submitted to
the sheriff that he ought to have had the choices
E explained to him so that he could make appropriate
representations to the police officers who could then
make an informed decision as to whether the specimen
required should be blood or urine. In putting forward
this submission the solicitor for the appellant relied
strongly on the case of *Carmichael v McKay* and to the
line of English authority referred to therein. The submission for the respondent was that the case of
Carmichael v McKay had been wrongly decided, and
that the appellant had no right to be told by the police
F officers that the specimen required might be of blood
or urine but that it was for the police to decide which.
The sheriff disagreed with the decision in *Carmichael
v McKay*, and with the English authorities. He concluded that the appellant did not have any right to
challenge the police officers' decision as to whether
urine or blood should be the specimen to be provided.
He accordingly rejected the submission of no case to
answer.

When the appeal first called before this court on 21
October 1992, the court continued the appeal having

been informed that a case raising a similar issue was
under appeal in the House of Lords. When the appeal G
next called on 15 December 1992, the case under
appeal to the House of Lords (*DPP v Warren*) had
been decided and judgment had also been given in a
Scottish case raising a similar issue.

It has to be appreciated that a driver may be
required to provide a specimen in accordance with s 7
(4) of the Act of 1988 in two different situations. The
first situation is where at a police station it has become
impossible or inappropriate to rely on specimens of
breath for one of the reasons set forth in s 7 (3) or H
where (as here) the driver is a patient at a hospital and
the procedure set out in s 9 has been carried out. In
such a situation it is obligatory for the driver under s 7
(1) (b) to provide the specimen of blood or urine which
the police officer decides to require, and such cases
may be described as obligatory cases. The other situation in which a specimen of blood or urine may be
required of a driver under s 7 (4) arises where the
driver has a choice under s 8 of the Act of 1988.
Section 8 provides as follows: [his Lordship quoted I
the terms of s 8 (1) and (2) and continued:] Cases
under these latter provisions may be described as
optional cases.

Hamilton v Jones was an optional case. The sheriff
in that case, following English authority, acquitted the
accused holding that the police officer had a statutory
duty to inform the accused that he could claim to have
the breath specimen replaced by one of blood or urine.
The Crown appealed to the High Court by stated case,
but did not proceed with the appeal.   J

Pelosi v Jessop was another optional case. The appellant had been required to provide breath, and the proportion of alcohol in each specimen was only 42
microgrammes per 100 millilitres of breath. He was
then told that he could claim to give a specimen of
blood but declined to do so. He was subsequently
prosecuted on the basis of the breath specimens. The
conviction was quashed since the Crown conceded
that the proper procedure had not been carried K
through in that the police were obliged to tell the
appellant that he could claim to give either blood or
urine. In delivering the opinion of the court the Lord
Justice General said: "But the advocate-depute has
explained that according to procedures which are now
in force in Scotland it is necessary that the person who
is being offered the choice to which section 8 (2) of the
1988 Act refers be told precisely what the alternatives
are between which he may choose: see *Hamilton v
Jones*. On the one hand there is a specimen of breath.
On the other hand there is the specimen of blood or L
urine. The choice as between blood or urine is for the
police officer, but the choice as to whether to claim
that the specimen of breath should be replaced is for
the person who has provided that specimen. In order
that he may be fully informed, he must now be told
that his right is to claim to have the specimen of breath
replaced by a specimen of blood or a specimen of
urine. There is no finding that that was done, so the
learned advocate-depute feels that he cannot support
this conviction."

A   *Carmichael v McKay* was an obligatory case where the accused was required to provide a specimen of blood because of the absence of a reliable device for analysing breath at the police station. The accused was acquitted by the sheriff upon the view that the accused had a right to make representations to the constable as to his preference for blood or urine, and that the constable had deprived him of that right by deciding to require blood before obtaining the accused's views. In reaching his decision the sheriff relied upon a number of English authorities.

B   In *McLeod v MacFarlane*, which was an obligatory case, the High Court overruled *Carmichael v McKay* and expressed agreement with *DPP v Warren*. In the course of his opinion the Lord Justice General, under reference to s 7 (4), said: "There is no indication in the section that the person who is to provide this specimen is entitled to be asked for his views on the matter or has a right to express his preference before the decision is made by the constable" (1993 SLT at p 784H).

C   Subsequently the Lord Justice General said under reference to *Carmichael v McKay* and the English cases upon which it relied: "It is hard to reconcile this line of authority with the statutory language, since s 7 (4) is unequivocal in its statement that the choice as between the two kinds of specimen is one to be decided by the constable who makes the requirement. Nowhere in the procedure described in s 7 (3) and 7 (4) is there a choice or option to be exercised by the motorist. This may be contrasted with s 8 (2) of the Act, which applies to the case where the requirement by the constable under s 7 (1) is to provide two specimens of breath for analysis by means of an approved device" (p 784L).

D

The Lord Justice General went on to repeat what had been said in *Pelosi v Jessop*.

Subsequently in his opinion the Lord Justice General added: "Neither in a case where the requirement is made under s 7 (3) for one of the reasons specified in that subsection nor where the driver's option is exercised under s 8 (2) is there any need for the driver to express his preference for giving blood or urine. This is for the constable to decide, and if he intends to require a specimen of blood to be taken by a medical practitioner the driver should be told that his only right to object to giving blood and to give urine instead will be for medical reasons to be determined by the medical practitioner."

E

It is very clear from the opinion in this case that the court was satisfied that the accused had no right to be given an opportunity to express a preference between blood and urine before the decision was made by the constable.

F

DPP v Warren was also an obligatory case where the requirement to provide blood was made because of the absence of a reliable device for analysing breath specimens at the police station. The leading speech was delivered by Lord Bridge of Harwich. In the course of his speech, he made it quite clear that where the reason for requiring a specimen of blood or urine arose

under s 7 (3), there was no question of the driver having any option to exercise. Lord Bridge of Harwich G referred to the two situations where a requirement might be made, namely, an obligatory case and an optional case. He also affirmed that there could be no question of s 7 (4) bearing two different constructions according as to whether the requirement was made in an obligatory case or an optional case. Under reference to *DPP v Gordon* and *Paterson v DPP*, he stated: "The essential reasoning in these two cases is that s 7 (4) cannot bear two different constructions. This is an indisputable proposition. But as I have said earlier, I H do not think this necessarily precludes a difference in the procedures which are appropriate on the one hand where it is necessary to explain to the driver his right to claim a replacement specimen taken under s 7 (4) and what the exercise of that right involves and, on the other hand, where the driver is obliged, subject to any rights of objection, to provide the specimen the constable requires" ([1992] 3 WLR at p 894H).

Having regard to the decisions in *McLeod v MacFarlane* and *DPP v Warren* it might be thought I that there could be no doubt that the sheriff in the present case had arrived at the correct conclusion. Indeed the sheriff at Lochmaddy's views are seen to coincide with those of the House of Lords and the High Court of Justiciary. Counsel for the appellant, however, maintained that the appellant had been treated unfairly because he had had no chance to say that he would be prepared to provide urine rather than blood. I am quite satisfied that these two cases make it perfectly clear that an accused has no right to be J given an opportunity of expressing a preference between blood or urine. These two cases have clearly disapproved of the suggestion that a driver has a preference or that a police officer cannot make an informed decision until he has heard representations by an accused.

The advocate depute, however, recognised that a problem arose because of certain passages in the speech of Lord Bridge of Harwich with which the K court in *McLeod v MacFarlane* expressed themselves as being in full agreement. In the course of his speech Lord Bridge of Harwich said (at [1992] 3 WLR, p 891B): "Again, on the face of the statute, I cannot see any reason why in this case the constable should do more than tell the driver the reason under section 7 (3) why breath specimens cannot be taken or used; tell him that in these circumstances he is required to give a specimen of blood or urine but that it is for the constable to decide which; warn him that a failure to L provide the specimen required may render him liable to prosecution; and then, if the constable decides to require blood, ask the driver if there are any reasons why a specimen cannot or should not be taken from him by a doctor. This will certainly give the driver the opportunity to raise any objection he may have to giving blood, either on medical grounds or indeed for any other reason which might afford a 'reasonable excuse' under section 7 (6). Here again, provided the driver has such an opportunity, I can see nothing in the language of the statute which would justify a procedural requirement that the driver be invited to express his own preference for giving blood or urine, either before a constable indicates which specimen he will require or at all."

With all respect to Lord Bridge of Harwich, if there is no question of the driver having any right to express a preference, it is difficult to see why he should be told that in the circumstances he is required to give a specimen of blood or urine but that it is for the constable to decide which. I do not understand why in such circumstances the driver should not simply be required to give a specimen of blood.

Lord Bridge of Harwich returns to this theme later in his speech. Having observed that the effect of *DPP v Gordon* and *Paterson v DPP* was to overrule *Pine v Collacott*, where the divisional court upheld a conviction where a police constable had simply required a driver to provide a specimen of blood, he said: "If *Pine v Collacott* itself had originally been under challenge in your Lordships' House on the ground that in an obligatory section 7 (4) case the simple requirement that the driver provide a specimen of blood without reference to the possible alternative of urine was insufficient, I should have been inclined to reject that challenge. But since the cases of *Gordon* and *Paterson* have now laid down that in obligatory section 7 (4) cases there must be a reference to the possible alternative of giving urine and since this procedural requirement, shorn of the doctrine of driver's preference, appears to present no difficulty to the police, it would now, I think, be inappropriate to reverse those decisions to the extent of abrogating this procedural requirement" (pp 894H–895B).

Again with all respect to Lord Bridge of Harwich, it appears to me to be difficult to reconcile what he says in these two sentences. In the first sentence he appears to be accepting that all that is needed is a simple requirement that the driver provide a specimen of blood without any reference to the alternative of urine, whereas in the second sentence he appears to be giving approval to a practice where the driver is told that he is required to give a specimen of blood or urine, but that it is for the constable to decide which.

In the next paragraph of his speech Lord Bridge of Harwich said: "Restating those views in summary form, in a case where the necessity to require a specimen of blood or urine under s 7 (4) arises for one of the reasons specified in s 7 (3), what is required is no more and no less than the formula used in the instant case or words to the like effect."

The formula used in *DPP v Warren* was the Metropolitan Police proforma which included the words: "The approved evidential breath testing device cannot be used on this occasion because the calibration check has proved unsatisfactory. Accordingly, I require you to provide an alternative specimen, which will be submitted for laboratory analysis. The specimen may be of blood or urine, but it is for me to decide which. If you provide a specimen you will be offered part of it in a suitable container. If you fail to provide a specimen you may be liable to prosecution. Are there any reasons why a specimen of blood cannot or should not be taken by a doctor?" (p 887).

After the driver had replied in the negative to that question he was asked and agreed to provide a specimen of blood. In *McLeod v MacFarlane* the form in use was that prepared by Tayside Police. The words to be read out to the motorist in the circumstances were as follows: "You are required to supply a specimen of blood or urine for a laboratory test. The type of specimen shall be decided by me and I will take into account any reason offered by you in response to that decision."

It will thus be seen that in both *DPP v Warren* and *McLeod v MacFarlane* the form in use made express reference to the requirement to provide a specimen of blood or urine. In the present case the form used was the Northern Constabulary form relative to hospital procedure. Although Dr Afewu was informed that the specimen required of the patient would be either blood or urine, what was stated to the accused was: "It is alleged that you have committed an offence contrary to section 5 of the Road Traffic Act 1988. I require you to provide a specimen of blood for a laboratory test. I must warn you that failure to provide such a specimen without reasonable excuse is an offence and may render you liable to prosecution. The specimen will be taken by a medical practitioner selected by the police. If you provide such a specimen it will be divided into two parts, one of which will be supplied to you on request. Do you agree to provide such a specimen of blood and if not, what is your reason for so refusing?" To that question the appellant gave the answer Yes.

Accordingly unlike *DPP v Warren* and *McLeod v MacFarlane*, the accused was never told that he required to give a specimen of blood or urine but that it was for the constable to decide which. At the end of the day, I understood counsel for the appellant to maintain that the failure to inform the appellant that he was required to supply a specimen of blood or urine was contrary to the procedure approved of in these two cases and was accordingly unfair to him. What was stated in *DPP v Warren* by Lord Bridge of Harwich was said in the context of that particular case and having regard to the Metropolitan Police proforma which had been applied. Likewise the remarks of the Lord Justice General in *McLeod v MacFarlane* were stated in the context of that case and having regard to the form prepared by Tayside Police. As already observed, a different police form was used in the present case. Having regard to the fact that the choice as between the two kinds of specimen is one to be decided by the constable making the requirement, and that it is accepted that the driver has no right to express any preference for giving blood or urine, I am of opinion that there is no legal obligation on a constable to tell the accused that he is required to give a specimen of blood or urine but that the decision as to which is for the constable to determine. In my opinion it is sufficient if the constable simply requires the accused to provide a specimen of blood. Since the driver has no right to express a preference, I see no reason why he should be told that the specimen may be of blood or urine but that it is for the police constable to decide which. I am not persuaded that the courts in Scotland should adopt a particular construction of the Act of 1988 because of the terms of a Metropolitan Police proforma. It is for the courts to construe the statutory provisions, and police proforma should give effect to the construction which the courts have placed upon the statutory provisions.

I respectfully agree with Lord Bridge of Harwich that s 7 (4) cannot bear two different constructions according as to whether the case is an optional one or an obligatory one, and, in my opinion, in both cases when the requirement to provide the specimen is made the constable need do no more than state which type of specimen he requires. In optional cases under s 8 (2), before the actual requirement to provide a specimen is made if the specimen of breath contains no more than 50 microgrammes of alcohol in 100 millilitres of breath, it will be necessary for the person who provided the breath specimen to be informed that he has the right to claim that the specimen of breath should be replaced by a specimen of blood or urine but that it is for the constable to decide which. However, at the stage when the requirement under s 7 (4) is made by the constable, there is no need for mention to be made of the alternatives of blood or urine. As Lord Bridge of Harwich observed in *DPP v Warren*, although s 7 (4) cannot bear two different constructions, "I do not think this necessarily precludes a difference in the procedures which are appropriate on the one hand where it is necessary to explain to the driver his right to claim a replacement specimen taken under section 7 (4) and what the exercise of that right involves and, on the other hand, where the driver is obliged, subject to any rights of objection, to provide the specimen the constable requires".

No doubt this is what the Lord Justice General had in mind when he stated at the end of the opinion of the court: "But we should add that the concession in *Pelosi v Jessop* was properly made, since it was consistent with what Lord Bridge said in *DPP v Warren* about the procedure to be followed in those cases where the driver has an option in s 8 (2) of the 1988 Act, with which we also agree" (1993 SLT at p 786G).

In my opinion, however, when the actual requirement to provide a specimen of blood (or urine) under either s 7 (3) or s 8 (2) is made, there is no necessity for the police constable to tell the driver that he is required to give a specimen of blood or urine but that it is for the constable to decide which. In my opinion the present case can be distinguished from *DPP v Warren* and *McLeod v MacFarlane* in that a different proforma was employed, and the opinions expressed in these two cases must be regarded as applicable to the facts of these cases and in particular the fact that a different proforma was in use. The result may be that different constructions are placed upon the Act of 1988 in Scotland and in England, but this is the result of different police procedures in the two countries.

It follows that in my opinion the sheriff reached the correct decision in this case, and that the reasons which he gave were sound. I would accordingly move your Lordships to answer the first question in the negative and the second question in the affirmative.

LORD MURRAY.—The only issue which requires to be decided in this appeal is whether, as a matter of law, the sheriff was entitled to hold that the appellant had a case to answer for breach of s 5 (1) (a) of the Road Traffic Act 1988, in the light of the procedure which is set out in the findings of fact (which are not in dispute) whereby the appellant was required to provide, and did provide, a sample of blood to determine whether he had driven his motor vehicle with an excess of alcohol in his blood.

Findings in fact 7 and 8 show that the police officer concerned spoke to the appellant in Daliburgh hospital informing him that it was alleged that he had committed an offence under s 5 of the Act. Proceeding on the basis of the Northern Constabulary proforma, which is printed in the stated case, he required the appellant to provide a specimen of blood, warning him of the consequences of failure and advising him that the specimen would be taken by a medical practitioner and divided into two parts, one being available for the appellant. The appellant agreed and the specimen was taken by the hospital doctor who was in charge of the appellant, who had received a chest injury in the course of the road accident in which he had been involved. Because of this chest injury the doctor had objected to a specimen of breath being taken from the appellant.

In urging the sheriff to hold that there was no case to answer, the solicitor for the appellant founded upon the decision of Sheriff Simpson in the case of *Carmichael v McKay*, following a line of English cases relating to the same (or similar) provisions of the Road Traffic Acts. In effect, put shortly, that line of authority requires a police constable to disclose to a suspect that there is a statutory requirement to provide a specimen of blood or urine before proceeding to require the suspect to provide a specimen of blood, subject to the statutory penalty on failure to do so. This is apparently to give the suspect an opportunity to register a preference to the police constable as to which kind of sample he wishes to supply before the constable actually requires him to provide a specimen of a particular kind. In *Carmichael v McKay* and the English cases in question the need for this opportunity had been raised to the level of a formal requirement without which the procedure would be invalidated.

In the present case, contrary to their previous attitude, the Crown had submitted that, on a proper construction of the provisions, there was no statutory basis for this procedural formality and that it was without foundation in law. As there was no other criticism of the procedure which had been adopted the plea of no case to answer should be repelled.

The sheriff after due consideration reached the view that the Crown's submission was sound and fell to be upheld. As he put it at [p 863A-D, supra]:

"The so called right of the appellant in this case is
A in my view non-existent. . . .

"The appellant . . . and indeed everyone in the
appellant's position, has the right to proffer a reasonable excuse for a failure to consent to the requirement
to provide blood. That right is not taken away.

"What the appellant does not have is a right to
challenge the police officer's decision as to whether
urine or blood should be the specimen which is
provided and in appropriate cases subsequently tested.
B I can see nothing in s 7 (4) which would justify such
an interpretation.

"To put the matter another way, subs (4) of s 7
would, in my view, require to provide that the specimen of blood or the specimen of urine would be
decided by the constable making the requirements but
the accused person would have an opportunity to state
his objection to either and the police officer would
have to have a reasonable regard to that objection in
making his decision. There is no such phrase in the
C subsection and to suggest, in effect, that there is,
strains, in my view, the interpretation of the subsection to breaking point."

I find the sheriff's reasoning is cogent and convincing and I would have had no difficulty in affirming his decision that the appellant had a case to answer
had it not been for the subsequent decision of the
House of Lords in the case of *DPP v Warren*, in which
the speeches of their Lordships have been made avail-
D able to us. The reasoning of the House of Lords,
expounded by Lord Bridge of Harwich, vindicates the
sheriff's interpretation of the statutory provisions and
gives it the seal of authority of the House of Lords. A
difficulty arises, however, in that the case of *Warren*
proceeded upon a Metropolitan Police proforma
which, unlike the Northern Constablulary proforma,
mentions both blood and urine, although the facts did
not differ materially otherwise from the present case.
That proforma was in the following terms: "The
E approved evidential breath testing device cannot be
used on this occasion because the calibration check has
proved unsatisfactory. Accordingly, I require you to
provide an alternative specimen, which will be submitted for laboratory analysis. The specimen may be
of blood or urine, but it is for me to decide which. If
you provide a specimen you will be offered part of it
in a suitable container. If you fail to provide a specimen you may be liable to prosecution. Are there any
reasons why a specimen of blood cannot or should not
F be taken by a doctor?"

The House of Lords overruled the case of *DPP v
Byrne* as the source of the driver's preference interpretation which they were rejecting. Reference was
made with favour to the case of *Pine v Collacott* which,
as Lord Bridge of Harwich mentioned in his speech,
had itself been effectively overruled by later cases.

Later cases to which Lord Bridge of Harwich refers
are *Hobbs v Clark* and *DPP v Gordon*. In dealing with
these cases at pp 894G-895B his Lordship said: "The
effect of these cases is to overrule *Pine v Collacott*

[1985] RTR 282. The essential reasoning in these two
cases is that section 7 (4) cannot bear two different G
constructions. This is an indisputable proposition.
But as I have said earlier, I do not think this necessarily precludes a difference in the procedures which
are appropriate on the one hand where it is necessary
to explain to the driver his right to claim a replacement specimen taken under section 7 (4) and what
the exercise of that right involves and, on the other hand,
where the driver is obliged, subject to any rights of
objection, to provide the specimen the constable
requires. If *Pine v Collacott* itself had originally been H
under challenge in your Lordships' House on the
ground that in an obligatory section 7 (4) case the
simple requirement that the driver provide a specimen
of blood without reference to the possible alternative
of urine was insufficient, I should have been inclined
to reject that challenge. But since the *Gordon* and
Paterson cases have now laid down that in obligatory
section 7 (4) cases there must be a reference to the
possible alternative of giving urine and since this procedural requirement, shorn of the doctrine of driver's
preference, appears to present no difficulty to the I
police, it would now, I think, be inappropriate to
reverse those decisions to the extent of abrogating this
procedural requirement."

Later, at p 895C, his Lordship continues: "Restating those views in summary form, in a case where the
necessity to require a specimen of blood or urine
under section 7 (4) arises for one of the reasons specified in section 7 (3), what is required is no more and
no less than the formula used in the instant case or J
words to the like effect."

In saying that what is required is no more and no
less than what is embodied in the Metropolitan Police
proforma Lord Bridge of Harwich has posed a
problem for this court in the present case where a
different police proforma was used, omitting the now
apparently redundant reference to urine. Apart from
that comment I for my part would have had little difficulty in holding that, in light of the interpretation of
the provisions which the House of Lords have K
adopted, the words used in the Northern Constabulary
proforma were of "like effect" to the words used in the
Metropolitan Police proforma.

The observation to which I have just made reference
is, I suppose, strictly obiter. No doubt what the House
of Lords had in mind was to apply their decision with
the minimum of disruption to the decided English
cases. In this court we are free to apply the House of
Lords' reasoning in a jurisdiction where only the case L
of *Carmichael v McKay*, which has been overruled in
the case of *McLeod v MacFarlane*, stood in the way. (I
note that the latter case involved the formula used by
Tayside Police, which differed from both of those
under consideration here.) In the absence of some legal
ground on which the Metropolitan Police formula
may be regarded as preferable to that of the Northern
Constabulary it may be that there is little option but
to accept some divergence between the two jurisdictions on this matter, however undesirable that
may be.

A The question then to be faced is whether there are any reasonable grounds for preferring a police proforma which mentions the alternatives of blood and urine to one which does not. The requirement to provide a specimen of blood, subject to a statutory penalty in the absence of a reasonable excuse, is on the face of it a material inroad upon the liberty of the citizen, even although it is amply justified by the danger to the public of driving while affected by alcohol. At the point of confrontation between the policeman and the citizen which s 7 (4) envisages, one

B may ask, is the range of excuses, and presumably therefore reasonable excuses, likely to be different depending upon whether there is or is not a mention of the possibility of providing a specimen of urine? After some hesitation I have come to the conclusion that it can hardly diminish, and might materially increase, the likelihood of a reasonable excuse being proffered if the possible provision of a specimen of urine is expressly mentioned. Apart from the obvious examples of suspects suffering from haemophilia, leukaemia or some infectious disease of the blood there

C may be others who have a phobia about blood of which they are ashamed, or who suspect that they are HIV positive, who might just be more ready to speak up (which would generally be in the public interest) rather than simply agree or refuse to provide a specimen of blood. On this rather marginal basis I consider that a formula mentioning the possibility of a urine specimen is preferable to one which does not. Despite this preference I cannot conceive that there would be any material miscarriage of justice to a suspect in

D using the Northern Constabulary formula rather than that of the Metropolitan Police.

I agree with your Lordship in the chair that this appeal fails; that the first question in law should be answered in the negative and the second in the affirmative.

LORD MORISON.—This appeal relates to the appellant's conviction on a charge of contravention of

E s 5 (1) (a) of the Road Traffic Act 1988. That section inter alia provides that a person who drives or attempts to drive a motor vehicle after consuming so much alcohol that the proportion of it in his blood exceeds the prescribed limit is guilty of an offence. A sample of blood containing excess alcohol was provided at a hospital to the police by the appellant. In requiring him to provide it, the police were acting or purporting to act in pursuance of s 7 of the 1988 Act.

F Subsection (1) of s 7 provides inter alia that: "In the course of an investigation into whether a person has committed an offence under section . . . 5 . . . a constable may, subject to the following provisions of this section and section 9 of this Act, require him . . . (b) to provide a specimen of blood or urine for a laboratory test."

Subsection (3) restricts the place where such a requirement may be made to a police station or a hospital, and in the former case, but not the latter, only if certain other conditions are fulfilled.

Subsection (4) provides inter alia that: "If the provision of a specimen other than a specimen of breath G may be required in pursuance of this section, the question whether it is to be a specimen of blood or a specimen of urine shall be decided by the constable making the requirement".

Subsection (6) makes it an offence to fail without reasonable excuse to provide a specimen when required.

In this case the constable concerned decided, by virtue of the discretion given to him by subs (4), to H require the appellant to provide a specimen of blood, not of urine. The conditions set out in s 9 of the Act, which apply where, as in the present case, the suspect is at a hospital, were complied with. The constable warned the appellant of the consequences of failure to comply with his requirement, as he was obliged to do by virtue of subs (7) of s 7. The only ground upon which I understand that this appeal is based is that the constable who made the requirement did not inform the appellant that he had the discretion given to him by subs (4) to decide whether the specimen was to be I of blood or of urine: it is maintained that he should have done so, so that the appellant would have the opportunity of making representations on that matter if he wished. The sheriff rejected this argument, which at the time it was presented to him was supported by another sheriff's decision in *Carmichael v McKay*, and by certain English cases, notably *Hobbs v Clark* and *Paterson v DPP*. These cases appear to have proceeded generally upon the view that although there is no express statutory obligation imposed on the J constable to inform the suspect that it is for him to decide whether blood or urine is required, fairness requires that obligation to be implied as part of the statutory procedure, because the constable can only reach a properly informed decision as to the exercise of his discretion in light of any preference or representation which the suspect might wish to express on that matter.

I entirely agree with the sheriff that this argument K strains the interpretation of the statutory provisions to breaking point. If a person who is required to provide a specimen, whether of blood or of urine, has a reasonable excuse for not doing so, his failure to provide that specimen does not, by virtue of the provisions of subs (6) of s 7, constitute an offence. If he has no reasonable excuse for failing to provide the particular specimen which the police officer may choose, I see no reason why he should be thought entitled to make any representation on that matter. If the legislature had intended that, in making his choice, the constable L should have regard to any such representations or to objections which do not amount to a reasonable excuse, there would have been no difficulty in making provision to that effect. In the absence of any such provision it must be assumed that the legislature intended that the police officer's choice should be made without reference to any preference which the suspect might wish to express which falls short of a reasonable excuse. I see nothing at all unreasonable about that result.

This view is now directly supported by the decision in *McLeod v MacFarlane*, issued in December 1992, in which *Carmichael* was overruled. In the opinion of the court delivered by the Lord Justice General it was held that: "There is no indication in the section that the person who is to provide the specimen is entitled to be asked for his views on the matter or has a right to express his preference before the decision is made by the constable."

I would not have considered it necessary to say anything further, were it not for the fact that counsel for the appellant founded on passages contained in a recent judgment of the House of Lords, *DPP v Warren*, which he submitted provided support for his argument. In dealing with the category of case like the present one, which he referred to as "an obligatory section 7 (4) case", Lord Bridge, who delivered the leading speech, said that provided the driver has an opportunity to raise any objection he might have to giving blood, either on medical grounds or indeed for any other reason which might afford a reasonable excuse, he could see "nothing in the language of the statute which would justify a procedural requirement that the driver be invited to express his own preference for giving blood or urine, either before a constable indicates which specimen he will require or at all".

This view of course directly affirms that which I have expressed, and the decision in *McLeod v MacFarlane*. But in a subsequent passage Lord Bridge referred to the cases of *Gordon* and *Paterson* as having in effect overruled *Pine v Collacott*. The latter case was one in which it had been held that a requirement under s 7 (4) to provide a blood specimen might be made without reference to the alternative of urine. In dealing with these cases Lord Bridge said: "If *Pine v Collacott* itself had originally been under challenge in your Lordships' House on the ground that in an obligatory section 7 (4) case the simple requirement that the driver provide a specimen of blood without reference to the possible alternative of urine was insufficient, I should have been inclined to reject that challenge. But since the *Gordon* and *Paterson* cases have now laid down that in obligatory section 7 (4) cases there must be a reference to the possible alternative of giving urine and since this procedural requirement, shorn of the doctrine of driver's preference, appears to present no difficulty to the police, it would now, I think, be inappropriate to reverse those decisions to the extent of abrogating this procedural requirement."

Lord Bridge accordingly concluded that what was required in obligatory s 7 (4) cases was "no more and no less than the formula used in the instant case or words to the like effect". That formula included a reference to the possible alternatives of blood and of urine.

I do not consider that the latter observations can be regarded as indicating a different interpretation of the statutory provisions from that which Lord Bridge had earlier expressed. They appear to be based primarily on the fact that the procedural requirement laid down by the cases of *Gordon* and *Paterson* presents no difficulty to the police. It is to be borne in mind that the principal issue before the House of Lords, and the only certified question which was specifically answered in the judgment, was whether the words contained in the Metropolitan Police proforma sufficiently complied with the requirements of s 7. That issue was not affected by the decision not to reverse *Gordon* and *Paterson*, since the words in the proforma contained reference to the possible alternatives of blood or urine. In my opinion the passages in Lord Bridge's speech which were founded on by the appellant have no application to the present case in which the formula used by the police contained no reference to the two alternatives.

Finally, in view of the observations made both in *Warren* and in *MacFarlane* relating to the procedure to be carried out in relation to provisions contained in s 8 ("driver's option cases"), I would observe that any comparison between that procedure and the procedure which must be adopted where an obligatory requirement is made appears to me to be inappropriate. In the present case the driver's obligation to provide a sample arose not, as it was expressed by Lord Bridge in the case of *Warren*, "for one of the reasons specified in section 7 (3) of the Act" (which subsection appears to me merely to set out conditions which must be met before a requirement to provide a blood or urine sample may be made), but because the requirement was validly made under the provisions of s 7 (1) (b), and because it was an offence not to comply with it without reasonable excuse. However, like the drivers involved in the cases of *Warren* and *MacFarlane*, the appellant in the present case had no option but to comply. The procedure appropriate to such a case appears to me to be far removed from that which is appropriate to the situation described in s 8 (2), in which a driver may claim that a specimen of breath should be replaced by one of blood or urine. In the latter situation the correct procedure is governed, at least in Scotland, by what was said in *Pelosi v Jessop*, 1990 SCCR at p 177E-F, so that the driver may be fully informed as to the exercise of his option. The reference in s 8 (2) to "such specimen as may be required under section 7 (4)" merely describes the nature of the alternative to a breath sample which the driver may choose. That alternative, i e of a blood or urine sample chosen by the constable, is one about which the suspect is not entitled to make any representation, and construction of the provisions contained in s 7 (4) which have that result is in my opinion unaffected by any view of what is required by virtue of s 8 (2).

I agree that the questions in the case should be answered as proposed by your Lordship.

Counsel for Appellant, Veitch; Solicitors, Currie Gilmour & Co (for Anderson MacArthur & Co, Stornoway) — Counsel for Respondent, Macdonald, QC, A D; Solicitors, J D Lowe, Crown Agent.

P W F

A # Narden Services Ltd v Secretary of State for Scotland

SECOND DIVISION

THE LORD JUSTICE CLERK (ROSS),
LORDS MURRAY AND PROSSER

12 FEBRUARY 1993

B *Town and country planning — Planning permission — Competing applications — Inquiries — Procedure — Sufficiency of evidence — Fairness — Town and Country Planning (Scotland) Act 1972 (c 52), s 267 (4).*

A development company (Narden) was one of three parties with competing proposals seeking outline planning permission on separate but adjoining sites. Their proposal for site 1 was for a superstore, filling station and business park. It had the support of the local planning authority which had granted outline planning permission. The application had then been called in by the Secretary of State for Scotland. The proposal for site 2 (by Hermiston) involving a superstore, filling station, business park, retail units and commercial facilities was opposed by the planning authority, as was the proposal for site 3 (by Mackenzie's Trust) for a business, retail and industrial park.

The Secretary of State for Scotland appointed a reporter and a public local inquiry was held looking at the proposals for each of the three sites. At the inquiry Narden and Hermiston led detailed evidence in relation to their respective proposals for sites 1 and 2. Mackenzie's Trust, however, led no witnesses and merely relied upon a written statement, cross examination of certain witnesses for the other parties and a closing submission. Ultimately the reporter recommended that outline planning permission should be granted to Mackenzie's Trust, subject to certain conditions, and that the proposals of Narden and Hermiston for sites 1 and 2 should be rejected. The Secretary of State essentially adopted these recommendations.

Narden appealed to the Court of Session against this decision of the Secretary of State, arguing that the recommendation of the reporter accepted by the Secretary of State was unfair, perverse and open to challenge. The principal arguments were: (first) that it had been unfair to allow Mackenzie's Trust to rely on a written statement, thus depriving the other parties of the opportunity to cross examine witnesses, and that the reporter should have exercised his powers under s 267 (4) of the Town and Country Planning (Scotland) Act 1972 and compelled Mackenzie's Trust to lead evidence; (secondly) that the reporter had not been entitled to come to the conclusion that there was a reasonable prospect that Mackenzie's Trust could reach a satisfactory agreement with the trunk roads authority on roads improvement, given the sparse material before him and the fact that the trust's proposal was the only one to which the authority had maintained opposition at the inquiry; (thirdly) that the reporter's approach to the loss of agricultural land was wrong in that he had noted that while site 3 involved the largest area, the proportion of prime agricultural land was lower than in the other sites; (fourthly) that the trust's proposals were contrary to sound planning principles in that an insufficient area had been allowed for the business park, and in dealing with this head the reporter had commented on a possible low financial return from the business park in relation to Narden only, despite it being equally material to Hermiston and the trust; and (fifthly) that a degree of unfairness sufficient to vitiate the reporter's decision was demonstrated by his view that little weight should be given to the decisions reached by the local planning authority.

Held, (1) that there was no legal requirement that a party was obliged to lead evidence and the question was whether the reporter had material before him to entitle him to decide as he did; the other applicants had had an opportunity to comment on the trust's case and given that no motion had been made at the inquiry for an order under s 267 (4), Narden could not complain that the reporter had failed to make such an order (pp 875C, 876B-D, 877B and E-H, 883G-L, 887A-B and 888H-J and K-L); (2) that given that Mackenzie's Trust had expressed a willingness to negotiate a roads agreement and given the existence of agreements in relation to the other two sites the reporter was entitled to conclude that there was a reasonable prospect of a satisfactory agreement being reached and to attach a suspensive condition concerning such an agreement to the grant of permission (pp 879H-K, 885G, 886L and 891B-E); (3) that although the reporter's approach to proportionality was questionable, he was entitled to consider the longer term position that parts of site 3 were likely to be developed for industrial use in any event and to conclude that this was a factor favouring the Mackenzie's Trust proposal (pp 880E, 884I-J and 891F-G); (4) that as the applications were for outline planning permission the reporter was entitled to conclude that the business park allocation at site 3 could be increased at the expense of other uses; and, while the absence of comment on the rate of return for sites 2 and 3 suggested a lack of evenhandedness, the relative merits of the business park proposals did not appear to feature in his preference for site 3 and his decision could not be regarded as unreasonable or perverse (pp 880I, 881A-C, 884L-885C and 891G); (5) that while there was considerable force in the suggestion that the reporter had exhibited unfairness in the criticisms levelled at the planning authority, his conclusion that little weight should be given to its decision implied that some weight should be given to it, and did not demonstrate such unfairness as to vitiate his decision (pp 881G, 882A-C, 886G-H and 891H-I); and appeal *refused.*

Appeal from the Secretary of State for Scotland

Narden Services Ltd presented an appeal under s 233 of the Town and Country Planning (Scotland) Act 1972 against a decision of the Secretary of State for

Scotland granting outline planning permission to D F Mackenzie's Trust. The decision followed a public inquiry concerning three competing proposals, by the appellants, by D F Mackenzie's Trust and by Hermiston Securities Ltd. In addition to the other two developers and the Secretary of State for Scotland, Highland Regional Council were cited as respondents.

Statutory provisions

The Town and Country Planning (Scotland) Act 1972 provides:

"267.—. . . (4) The person appointed to hold the inquiry may, on the motion of any party thereto or of his own motion, serve a notice in writing on any person requiring him to attend at the time and place set forth in the notice to give evidence or to produce any books or documents in his custody or under his control which relate to any matter in question at the inquiry."

The Town and Country Planning (Inquiries Procedure) (Scotland) Rules 1980 provide:

"10.—(1) Except as otherwise provided in these rules, the procedure at the inquiry shall be such as the reporter shall in his discretion determine.

"(2) The reporter shall state at the commencement of the inquiry the procedure which, subject to consideration of any submission by the parties, he proposes to adopt.

"(3) Unless in any particular case the reporter with the consent of the applicant otherwise determines, the applicant shall be heard first and the other persons entitled or permitted to appear shall be heard in such order as the reporter may determine; and any closing statements shall be made in the same order as that in which the parties were heard, unless the reporter otherwise determines; at the discretion of the reporter the applicant may have the right to reply to the closing statements by the other parties.

"(4) The applicant, the planning authority and the section 26 parties shall be entitled to call evidence and, subject to paragraph (5) of this rule, to cross-examine persons giving evidence and to make closing statements but any other person appearing at the inquiry may do so only to the extent permitted by the reporter.

"(5) Where the reporter considers that further cross-examination of a witness would lead to undue repetition or elaboration, the reporter may disallow further cross-examination of the witness.

"(6) The reporter shall not require or permit the giving or production of any evidence whether written or oral, which would be contrary to the public interest; but save as aforesaid and without prejudice to rule 8 (4) and section 267 (4) and (5) of the Act (evidence at local inquiries) any evidence may be admitted at the discretion of the reporter, who may direct that documents tendered in evidence may be inspected by any person entitled or permitted to appear at the inquiry and that facilities be afforded him to take or obtain copies thereof.

"(7) The reporter may allow the planning authority or the applicant, or both of them, to alter or add to the observations contained in any statement served under rule 6 (2) or (8) or to any list of documents which accompanied such statement, so far as may be necessary for the purpose of determining the questions in controversy between the parties, but shall (if necessary by adjourning the inquiry) give the applicant or the planning authority, as the case may be, and all section 26 parties an adequate opportunity of considering any such fresh observations or document; and the reporter may make in his report a recommendation as to the payment of any additional expenses occasioned by any such adjournment.

"(8) If any person entitled to appear at the inquiry fails to do so, the reporter may proceed with the inquiry at his discretion.

"(9) The reporter shall be entitled (subject to disclosure thereof at the inquiry) to take into account any written representations or statements received by him before the inquiry from any person, but shall circulate such documents in advance where he considers this to be practicable.

"(10) The reporter may from time to time adjourn the inquiry and, if the date, time and place of the adjourned inquiry are announced before the adjournment, no further notice shall be required."

Cases referred to

Anduff Holdings Ltd v Secretary of State for Scotland, 1992 SLT 696.
Ashbridge Investments Ltd v Minister of Housing and Local Government [1965] 1 WLR 1320; [1965] 3 All ER 371.
Att Gen of Hong Kong v Ng Yuen Shiu [1983] 2 AC 629; [1983] 2 WLR 735; [1983] 2 All ER 346.
Bradley (Edwin H) & Sons v Secretary of State for the Environment (1982) 47 P & CR 374.
British Railways Board v Secretary of State for the Environment, CA, 6 October 1992, unreported.
Bushell v Secretary of State for the Environment [1981] AC 75; [1980] 3 WLR 22; [1980] 2 All ER 68.
Council of Civil Service Unions v Minister for the Civil Service [1985] AC 374; [1984] 3 WLR 1174; [1984] 3 All ER 935.
Fairmount Investments Ltd and Southwark London Borough Council v Secretary of State for the Environment [1976] 1 WLR 1255.
French Keir Developments Ltd v Secretary of State for the Environment [1977] 1 All ER 296.
Glasgow District Council (City of) v Secretary of State for Scotland, 1992 SCLR 964.
Grampian Regional Council v City of Aberdeen District Council and Secretary of State for Scotland, 1984 SLT 197; 1984 SC (HL) 58.
Hughes v Hamilton District Council, 1991 SLT 628.
Jones v Secretary of State for Wales [1990] 3 PLR 102.
Ladbroke Racing Ltd v Secretary of State for Scotland, 1990 SCLR 705.
Lakin Ltd v Secretary of State for Scotland, 1988 SLT 780.

Miller (T A) Ltd v Minister of Housing and Local Government [1968] 1 WLR 992; [1968] 2 All ER 633.

Wordie Property Co Ltd v Secretary of State for Scotland, 1984 SLT 345.

Appeal

The appeal was heard by the Second Division on 5, 6, 7 and 8 January 1993.

On 12 February 1993 the court *refused* the appeal.

THE LORD JUSTICE CLERK (ROSS).—This is an appeal at the instance of the appellants under s 233 of the Town and Country Planning (Scotland) Act 1972 against a decision of the Secretary of State dated 30 April 1991. The decision of the Secretary of State was pronounced after an inquiry which concerned three competing development proposals for three separate but adjoining sites fronting onto the south side of the A96 trunk road on the eastern side of Inverness. Site 1 is at West Seafield, site 2 is at East Seafield, and site 3 is at Stratton Farm. The inquiry was into (a) a proposal for a superstore, filling station and business park on site 1 which had the support of the planning authority, Highland Regional Council, and had been called in for determination by the Secretary of State; (b) an appeal and a called in application for site 2, together embracing a superstore, filling station, business park, other retail units and community facilities, both applications being opposed by the planning authority; and (c) an appeal proposal for site 3 for a business, retail, and industrial park, incorporating leisure/retail development, also opposed by the planning authority. The appellants were the applicants in respect of site 1; Hermiston Securities Ltd were the applicants and appellants in respect of site 2; and D F Mackenzie's Trustees were the appellants in respect of site 3.

The inquiry took place over a period of 15 days. Much of the evidence presented at the inquiry was applicable to all three sites, or involved a close comparison of the proposals for each of the sites. It was accepted that there was likely to be a single development opportunity, and that the approval or development of more than one scheme would be likely to lead to serious problems. Accordingly the appraisal of the schemes was to some extent a comparison exercise.

At the end of the day the reporter who held the inquiry recommended that the two applications and appeal at sites 1 and 2 should be rejected, and that the appeal in respect of site 3 should be upheld. He also recommended that outline planning permission should be granted for that development subject to certain conditions.

The Secretary of State accepted the reporter's findings in fact, agreed with his reasoning and recommendations and adopted them except in two respects. He accordingly upheld the appeal by D F Mackenzie's Trust against the planning authority's refusal of planning permission for development at Stratton Farm (site 3); he granted outline planning permission in respect of their application in respect of site 3. He dismissed the appeal by Hermiston Securities Ltd in relation to their application for development at site 2, and he refused to grant outline planning permission for their supplementary application for development at site 2; he also refused to grant outline planning permission to the appellants in respect of their application for development at site 1. The appellants have appealed against this decision of the Secretary of State, and they have moved the court to quash his decision.

In seeking to support the appeal, counsel for the appellants presented a number of submissions. The appellants' appeal contained 19 separate grounds of appeal, but some of these overlapped, and counsel presented the appeal by reference to a number of topics. Their first submission was that having regard to the evidence led and the procedure followed, the reporter's decision had been unfair and perverse. They also contended that the decision of the reporter was open to challenge on a number of other grounds. These grounds related to what the reporter held in respect of road improvements which would be required at site 3, the use of agricultural land, the extent of the proposals for a business park, and criticisms which he made of the approach to the applications of Highland Regional Council. Junior counsel for the appellants also raised an issue in relation to the use of part of the site for housing, but senior counsel intimated that he was not seeking to support this particular ground of appeal.

So far as the first topic is concerned, it relates to both the procedure followed at the inquiry, and the evidence which was available to the reporter. The submission was that there was insufficient evidence before the reporter to entitle him to hold that the case for site 3 had been established; alternatively if there was sufficient evidence, it was submitted that the reporter and the Secretary of State had acted unfairly in the way in which the evidence had been obtained, and the way in which that evidence had been considered.

An unusual feature of this inquiry was that the appellants and Hermiston Securities Ltd led detailed evidence in relation to the proposals in respect of site 1 and site 2 whereas site 3 was in a different situation. At or shortly before the beginning of the inquiry, D F Mackenzie's Trustees intimated that they were unable to present a fully argued case because of the withdrawal of their preferred developers; they intimated that they wished their proposal to be considered alongside the others at the inquiry. The trustees participated in the inquiry to the extent of asking questions of certain witnesses and of making a closing submission, but otherwise they relied upon a written statement (production DFMT1) rather than presenting evidence through witnesses. The reporter records that no exception was taken to this procedure by the other parties to the inquiry for their respective interests, although concern was expressed by them that while the Mackenzie Trustees would have the opportunity to cross examine the witnesses led by

other parties, there would be no opportunity to test
A their case by cross examination. I shall return to this
matter later.

In view of the attitude adopted by the Mackenzie
Trustees, I am satisfied that the reporter was placed in
a difficult position. Having regard to *Lakin v Secretary
of State for Scotland* the reporter clearly felt it essential
to consider the evidence relating to the three competing sites. Even although the Mackenzie Trustees had
decided not to present evidence through witnesses, it
was important that site 3 should be considered at the
B inquiry along with site 1 and site 2. In opening the
appeal, junior counsel for the appellants submitted
that since the Mackenzie Trustees chose to rely only
upon a written statement, this was unfair to the appellants since they were unable to cross examine witnesses about the contents of the written statement.
Counsel contended that except in cases where an
inquiry was a formality in which event a written statement might suffice, it was unfair to allow an applicant
to rely on a written statement and to lead no evidence
C in support of his application. Evidence was adduced
by the appellants and Hermiston Securities Ltd in
relation to sites 1 and 2, and he contended that in that
situation it was unfair for the reporter to allow the
application in respect of site 3 to be considered solely
upon the basis of the written statement. He submitted
that although the written statement (production
DFMT1) was put forward at the inquiry, no evidence
was led in its support nor to explain its terms; no
opportunity was given to the other parties to test what
D was stated in the statement by cross examination. The
Mackenzie Trustees were afforded an opportunity of
cross examining the witnesses led by the appellants
and Hermiston Securities Ltd, but the appellants and
Hermiston Securities Ltd had no corresponding right
to cross examine any witnesses for the Mackenzie
Trustees. No witnesses supported the application of
the Mackenzie Trustees, and the result was that at the
end of the day the reporter had made a recommendation in favour of granting planning permission for site
E 3 despite being faced with evidence which was
opposed to the granting of the application. In these
circumstances it was contended that it was unfair and
perverse for the reporter to decide in favour of the
application in relation to site 3. There were two
aspects to this submission on behalf of the appellants.
In the first place it was contended that it was unfair
for the reporter to decide in favour of site 3 because
there was no evidence entitling him to make such a
recommendation. In the second place it was contended
F that even if there was evidence which favoured site 3,
the reporter had acted unfairly because of the way in
which that evidence had been presented and considered.

Counsel for the Secretary of State, on the other
hand, contended that sufficient material was adduced
before the reporter to entitle him to make the recommendation, and, in any event, that there was no unfairness in the way in which he had dealt with the matter.

Both in the submissions made to this court and in

some of the authorities cited, reference was made to
the question of whether there was evidence to support
G a planning proposal. Indeed junior counsel for the
appellants initially maintained that since there had
been a public local inquiry in this case, before the
reporter could decide in favour of the Mackenzie
Trustees, the trustees would require to have led some
evidence. Counsel recognised that it was not disputed
that there was a need for development in the A96
corridor and in particular development in the form of
business and industrial uses. He also recognised that
some of the evidence led by the appellants and H
Hermiston Securities Ltd would also apply to site 3,
and that the reporter was plainly entitled to rely on
evidence from these sources when considering the
application at the instance of the Mackenzie Trustees.
However, counsel drew attention to the terms of the
Town and Country Planning (Inquiries Procedure)
(Scotland) Rules 1980 (SI 1980/1676). These rules
apply to a situation like the present case where the
decision is to be taken by the Secretary of State
himself; they do not apply to procedure where the
decision is to be based upon written submissions nor I
to the situation where the Secretary of State has delegated the determination of the application to a
reporter. Rule 7 deals with appearances at the inquiry,
and rule 10 deals with procedure. Rule 10 is in the
following terms: [his Lordship quoted its terms and
continued:]

Counsel for the appellants submitted that the 1980
Rules did not contemplate an inquiry, such as the
present inquiry, where a number of applications and J
appeals were conjoined; nor did the rules contemplate
a situation where an applicant sought to rely wholly
upon a written statement. However, he submitted that
there plainly required to be a hearing, and he contended that at any public local inquiry there required
to be an oral statement or a submission which formed
the evidence of the applicant. Subsequently, however,
counsel retreated from this extreme position. In my
opinion he was correct to do so. It is significant that
rule 8 (3) and rule 9 (3) provide that representatives of K
government departments or local authorities "shall
give evidence and be subject to cross-examination to
the same extent as any other witness" but that there
is no similar provision applying to applicants. Rule 10
(4) merely provides that the applicant shall be entitled
to call evidence, but does not place any obligation
upon him to do so.

Counsel for the applicants accordingly conceded
that, speaking generally, an applicant could proceed
without leading evidence but they maintained that the L
principles of openness and fairness, and the principles
of natural justice might preclude an applicant from
proceeding in this way in any particular inquiry. They
maintained that in a minor inquiry which was little
more than a formality, a written statement from an
applicant might suffice, but they maintained that in
any more major inquiry it would be unfair to allow a
principal party to rely on a written statement and to
lead no evidence. They submitted that the reporter
should have insisted on a public exposition of the case

for the Mackenzie Trustees; he should have made it clear to them that he would not consider their written submission without its being spoken to and tested by cross examination. He submitted that unless that were done, there was no level playing field on which all three sites had been examined and assessed.

Counsel for the Secretary of State, on the other hand, maintained that the appellants' submissions were misconceived insofar as they desiderated that there must be evidence before the reporter in relation to all the matters upon which he relied. He contended that the proper question was not whether there was evidence before the reporter but whether there was material before him upon which he could rely. He also submitted that the reporter did not have to have material to justify every conclusion which he reached, but that he was entitled to use his own planning judgment and expertise to supply any deficiencies. He also stressed that even where the reporter or the Secretary of State required to have material to justify a conclusion, there was no requirement that there had to be evidence in the statutory sense. Moreover the weight to be attached to any material was a matter for the reporter and the Secretary of State, and neither the reporter nor the Secretary of State was bound to accept evidence even if it was not contested or challenged. He submitted that there was material before the reporter and the Secretary of State upon which they were entitled to rely in granting planning permission for site 3. That material consisted of the written submission of the Mackenzie Trustees, the documents which had been lodged along with the application, and evidence which had been led at the inquiry by other parties.

So far as this part of the argument is concerned, I feel that the submissions of counsel for the Secretary of State are well founded. As counsel for the appellants themselves ultimately recognised, there is nothing in the 1980 Rules which makes it obligatory upon an applicant to lead evidence. An applicant is entitled to call evidence, and in most cases, particularly where there are competing sites, if he declines to do so, his application may have little prospect of success. Where there are competing sites, if an applicant in relation to one site chooses to lead no evidence, he is no doubt running a grave risk that his application will not succeed. In the present case the reporter came down in favour of the one site in relation to which no evidence had been led. I agree with the appellants that this was a surprising decision, but that is not what is in issue. What is in issue is whether the reporter was entitled to proceed as he did and whether there was any unfairness in his treatment of the appellants.

Since there is no obligation upon an applicant to lead evidence, I agree with counsel for the Secretary of State that the question must always be whether there has been adequate material before the reporter to entitle him to decide as he did. This material may consist of evidence led by other parties or written submissions tendered and documents lodged. In the present case the reporter in para 9.7 states in relation

to site 3: "The summary of evidence below draws upon the pre-inquiry statement, evidence given about the Stratton proposal by other witnesses, and the responses by those witnesses to questions asked by the Trust's representatives." It is unfortunate that the reporter attaches the description "the summary of evidence" to material some of which was not the subject of evidence at all, but it is clear that what the reporter was really doing was summarising the relevant material.

It is well established that a reporter does not require to have material to justify every conclusion that he reaches, that he is not obliged to accept any evidence before him even if it is not contested or challenged, and that he is entitled to use his own expertise and planning judgment. In *Fairmount Ltd v Secretary of State for Environment* at p 1265 Lord Russell of Killowen said: "I entirely accept that such an inspector, in a case such as this, is not merely trying an issue or issues between the local authority and the objector owner, and may from his professional experience supply deficiencies in the case as presented by the local authority. I equally accept that he is not bound to accept as established a contention in evidence for the objector owner simply because it is not, or is not adequately, challenged or contested on the part of the acquiring authority at the hearing. Part of his function lies in his own knowledge of the subject. Nor would I wish to introduce into procedures such as this — which include, prior to report, his inspection of the site — a rigidity more appropriate to a private issue to be decided by a judge; and in that connection I do not believe that a 'view' by a judge is to be equated in any way with such a site inspection by such an inspector, a possibility which (it was said) might have been in the mind of the Court of Appeal in the instant case."

In *Ladbroke Racing Ltd v Secretary of State for Scotland* it was observed that a reporter conducting a public local inquiry was entitled, in reaching his conclusions, to make use of his own planning experience and expertise. Similar views were expressed in *Anduff Holdings Ltd v Secretary of State for Scotland*.

It is also well recognised that the rules of evidence which apply in a court of law are not all applicable at a public local inquiry. In *French Kier Developments Ltd v Secretary of State for the Environment* at p 302 Willis J said: "It hardly needs to be said that legal rules of evidence are not applied at local inquiries, and both oral and documentary evidence is freely admitted in circumstances where even the more relaxed rules of evidence at the present time would not allow of its admission in a court of law."

Whatever material is relied on, it is crucial that the parties must have an opportunity to comment on the material. In *T A Miller Ltd v Minister of Housing and Local Government* the Court of Appeal held that an inspector had been entitled to rely on a letter which had not been proved in evidence. At [1968] 1 WLR, p 995 Lord Denning MR said: "A tribunal of this kind is master of its own procedure, provided that the rules of natural justice are applied. Most of the evidence here was on oath, but that is no reason why hearsay should not be admitted where it can fairly be regarded as reliable. Tribunals are entitled to act on any material which is logically probative, even though it is not evidence in a court of law. . . . Hearsay is clearly admissible before a tribunal. No doubt in admitting it, the tribunal must observe the rules of natural justice, but this does not mean that it must be tested by cross-examination. It only means that the tribunal must give the other side a fair opportunity of commenting on it and of contradicting it."

In *Bushell v Secretary of State for the Environment* Lord Diplock stressed that fairness required that objectors should have an opportunity of communicating to the minister the reasons for their objections and the facts on which they are based. He also held that fairness also required that the objectors should be given sufficient information about the department's reasons to enable them to challenge the accuracy of any facts and the validity of any arguments upon which the department's reasons were based (p 96). But he emphasised that failure to allow cross examination of witnesses is not unfair per se (p 97).

It is not for this court to determine whether they would have arrived at the same result as the reporter and the Secretary of State. What this court has to do is to consider whether there was material before the reporter and the Secretary of State to entitle them to decide the issue as they did. Once it is accepted that there is no obligation upon an applicant to lead evidence, I am satisfied that there was adequate material before the reporter to enable him to determine the issue. He was entitled to attach such weight as he thought was appropriate to the written submission lodged by the Mackenzie Trustees; he was also entitled to attach such weight as he thought appropriate to the various documents before him; and he was entitled to take into account the evidence about site 3 given by other witnesses, including any cross examination of these witnesses by the Mackenzie Trustees' representative. He was also entitled to use his own expertise where that was appropriate. I accept that there was no witness who gave direct evidence supporting site 3, but I am not persuaded that that means that the reporter was not entitled at the end of the day to conclude that site 3 was the best place for the proposed development in the A96 corridor provided that there was no unfairness either in the way in which the material was obtained or in the way in which he considered it. It thus became clear that the critical question was whether there had been unfairness in either or both of these latter respects.

In the passage already quoted from *T A Miller Ltd v Minister of Housing and Local Government,* Lord Denning MR observed that any tribunal, including an inspector holding a local planning inquiry, had to observe the rules of natural justice, and that the inspector had to give the other side a fair opportunity of commenting upon any material upon which he was proposing to rely. The need to act fairly in this way

was also stressed by Lord Diplock in *Bushell v Secretary of State for the Environment.* The importance of affording parties an opportunity of commenting upon a matter relied upon by the reporter on which no evidence had been led was also mentioned in *Anduff Holdings v Secretary of State for Scotland.* In the present case I am satisfied that there is no question of the appellants having been denied a fair opportunity of commenting upon the case which was put forward on behalf of the Mackenzie Trustees and which commended itself at the end of the day to the reporter. It appears that initially, the understanding was that the Mackenzie Trustees would participate in the inquiry in the usual way by leading evidence and cross examining witnesses. It was only on the eve of the inquiry or when the inquiry actually opened that it became clear that they were to participate in the inquiry to a more limited extent. I have already referred to this, and the reporter describes the situation in the letter to the Secretary of State which accompanied his report. In the course of that letter he said: "It should be noted that D. F. Mackenzie's Trust participated in the inquiry to the extent of asking questions of witnesses and making a closing submission but relied on a written statement (Production DFMT1), summarised in chapter 9, rather than presenting evidence through witnesses. The trust was unable to present a fully argued case because of the withdrawal of their preferred developers, but wished its proposal to be considered alongside the others at the public inquiry. No exception was taken by this procedure by the other parties to the inquiry for their respective interests although concern was expressed that while the Mackenzie Trust would have the opportunity to cross-examine the witnesses led by other parties there would be no opportunity to test their case by cross-examination. The findings on the Mackenzie Trust application are based on their written submission, evidence presented at the inquiry by other parties, and the site inspection. The report of the closing submission on behalf of the trustees is, like the others, a summary of what was actually said."

It is plain from a letter from the appellants' solicitors dated 1 November 1990 making comments upon the amendments which the reporter was proposing to make to part I of his report, that in the reporter's letter what is stated regarding the concern expressed by the appellants about the fact that they would not be able to cross examine any witness for the Mackenzie Trust was proposed by the appellants themselves.

As has already been mentioned, the decision of the Mackenzie Trustees not to lead evidence placed the reporter in a position of some difficulty. What the Secretary of State required to do at the inquiry was to consider the merits of competing applications, and that being so each of the applicants whose applications had been called in or were the subject of appeal had the legitimate expectation of a hearing being held into the matter of the alternative sites at which the merits of the alternative sites were considered (*Lakin Ltd v Secretary of State for Scotland*). The fact that the Mackenzie Trustees were not proposing to lead evidence undoubtedly meant that the appellants and Hermiston Securities Ltd would not have any opportunity to test the Mackenzie Trustees' case by cross examination, but what was essential was that they should have an opportunity of commenting upon the Mackenzie Trustees' case. It is plain from the reporter's report that in the course of their evidence various witnesses called by the planning authority (Highland Regional Council), the appellants and Hermiston Securities Ltd did comment in the course of their evidence upon the proposals in relation to site 3. The written submission for the Mackenzie Trustees was in fairly general terms, but the broad outline of what was being proposed was before the reporter and the other parties to the inquiry and could be commented upon by any of the witnesses. Not only that but the Mackenzie Trustees at the end of the day made closing submissions to the reporter and these are summarised by the reporter in part I of his report. Moreover we were informed that the order of proceedings was that the Mackenzie Trustees made their closing submissions and that counsel for the appellants and Hermiston Securities Ltd made their submissions approximately two weeks later. It is clear from the reporter's report that counsel for both the appellants and Hermiston Securities Ltd did make certain comments upon the Mackenzie Trust proposals. Counsel for the appellants appears to have been fairly dismissive of them, but it is certainly clear that he had an opportunity of commenting upon their proposals.

In addition to that the reporter in accordance with normal procedure circulated part I of his report including his findings in fact, and the solicitors for the appellants entered into correspondence with the reporter making certain comments upon various parts of part I of the report including the findings. This too shows that the appellants had an opportunity of commenting upon the findings in fact which the reporter was proposing to make, and which were the basis for his decision. Accordingly, I regard the present case as quite different to *Anduff Holdings v Secretary of State for Scotland* where the appellants had been given no opportunity to comment upon the issues which were the basis of the reporter's decision.

It was at one stage suggested by counsel for the appellants that in fairness to the appellants the reporter ought to have required the Mackenzie Trustees to give evidence by exercising his powers under s 267 (4) of the Town and Country Planning (Scotland) Act 1972. That subsection provides: [his Lordship quoted the terms of s 267 (4) and continued:] It was suggested that in order to be fair to the appellants and Hermiston Securities Ltd the reporter ex proprio motu should have required the principal trustee of Mackenzie Trust to give evidence.

I am not persuaded that this submission is well founded. It is not at all clear that Mr Young as the principal trustee would have been in a position personally to give evidence either as to fact or as an expert witness. However that may be, I am satisfied that the

appellants cannot reasonably complain that the reporter did not require someone from the Mackenzie Trust to give evidence in view of the fact that the appellants at no stage made any motion to the reporter that he should take this course. If the appellants had considered that fairness to themselves made it necessary for some witness to be ordered by the reporter to attend under s 267 (4), then they should have made a motion to that effect. I am not satisfied that they were justified in making no motion, and then in complaining that the reporter should ex proprio motu have required the attendance of a witness. When the appellants discovered that the Mackenzie Trustees were to lead no evidence, it may not have been easy for them to determine whether it was in their interests to let matters continue upon that basis or whether they ought to invoke s 267 (4). That was a matter for their representatives to determine as matter of tactics, and they plainly decided at the time not to invoke s 267 (4). That being so, I am of opinion that they are not entitled now to complain that the reporter failed to exercise his right under s 267 (4) to require a witness from the Mackenzie Trust to give evidence.

On the issue of fairness, counsel for the Secretary of State referred to *CCSU v Minister for Civil Service*, and in particular to what was there said regarding "procedural impropriety" or "procedural irregularity". It was there stressed that there is a duty to act fairly. In *Lakin v Secretary of State for Scotland* at pp 787L-788A I said: "In my opinion, it is clear from these authorities that when the court is being invited to review an administrative decision, it is not for the court to determine whether the decision was fair or unfair. The court is, however, entitled to consider whether the manner in which the decision was taken was fair or unfair. 'Procedural propriety' or 'procedural irregularity' covers that sort of situation; the person making the administrative decision has a duty to act fairly in the manner in which he arrives at his decision. 'Procedural impropriety' or 'procedural irregularity' may arise where there has been a failure to comply with procedural rules; but it may also arise where there has simply been unfairness in the manner in which a decision has been arrived at. This will be so particularly if an individual who has the legitimate expectation of a hearing is denied any hearing before a decision affecting him is taken (*Att. Gen. of Hong Kong v. Ng Yuen Shiu*; *C.C.S.U. v. Minister for Civil Service*)."

In the present case what the court has to determine is whether there was any unfairness in the way in which the reporter arrived at his decision. The suggestion is that there was unfairness in a number of respects. The first matter to be considered relates to road improvements. Initially the trunk road authority had objected to the appellants' proposal because of the effect which the proposal would have upon the road system. That objection was subsequently withdrawn upon the basis of a minute of agreement providing that the appellants would carry out certain agreed improvements to the A96. These improvements included the construction of a new roundabout to form the access

A to the development, and the upgrading of the A96 to a dual carriageway from the Raigmore interchange to that roundabout including bridging the railway at Stoneyfield. A draft s 50 agreement had been exchanged between the planning authority and the appellants.

So far as the Hermiston Securities Ltd proposals were concerned, the trunk road authority had also objected to their application on the grounds that the volume of traffic generated by the proposed development was in excess of the capacity of the existing trunk

B road. That objection had subsequently been withdrawn when Hermiston Securities Ltd proposed to fund the dualling of the A96 from Raigmore to the Smithton junction including a roundabout at the junction up to a value of £2.3 million. The arrangement was to be the subject of a legal agreement.

So far as site 3 is concerned, the situation is entirely different. In his findings in fact the reporter states (D3): "The necessary road works and developer's con-

C tribution for the Mackenzie Trust development have not been identified. The agreements have enabled the Trunk Roads Authority to withdraw its objections to the Narden and Hermiston schemes. Their objection to the Mackenzie Trust proposal is maintained until a satisfactory solution is agreed."

Finding D7 is in the following terms: "D7. In the Mackenzie Trust case, I find that much less is known about the access situation and possible private funding of improvements, as there have been no detailed

D studies of what is required, or discussions as to what the developer would be prepared to pay. However the developer recognises the need to improve both the A96 and the Smithton Distributor; owns the land on both sides of the Distributor and to the north of the A96 to the east of the Smithton Junction; expects to make a financial contribution to the cost of the improvements; and has a much larger potential development area to underwrite the expenditure. Accordingly, I find that there is a reasonable prospect

E that a satisfactory agreement could be reached with the two highway authorities about access and road improvements, as has been the case with the other applicants, as, with suitable safeguards, the developer could not benefit from the main part of the scheme until the necessary improvements had been carried out. As with the other two schemes, improvement of the A96 would involve an enlarged/duplicated bridge over the railway line, and hence authorisation through the Trunk Road Authority."

F Finding H5 is in the following terms: "H5. Findings on traffic and access matters are as set out at D1-D3 and D7 above. In particular, I find that there has been no detailed examination of what road improvements would be necessary to serve the development, nor any specific agreement or financial arrangement with the applicants to secure the funding of such improvements. However, as noted in finding D7 above, I find that there is a recognition on the part of the developer of the need to carry out improvements to both the A96 and the Smithton Distributor,

and to make a financial contribution to the funding of such improvements. Between them, the Trust and the G Highway Authorities own or control the land likely to be needed for improvements in the vicinity of the site. As with the Hermiston Securities scheme, compulsory purchase powers might be required to obtain land to dual the A96, but the Trunk Road Authorities apparently prepared to use such powers as a publicly-funded scheme is intended in any event. This might involve a delay of 18 months but this would still be within the timescale of a planning commission. Accordingly, I find that there is a reasonable prospect that a satisfac- H tory agreement could be reached, as, with suitable safeguards, the developer could not benefit from the scheme until the necessary improvements had been carried out."

In part II of his report dealing with his reasoning and recommendations at para 12.9 the reporter states inter alia: "No detailed discussions have taken place to determine the road improvements required for the development, but the Trustees recognise that improvements comparable to those for the other I schemes would be necessary (H5). They are prepared to contribute to the costs, and I see no reason why a satisfactory solution should not be reached (H5), so that a suspensive condition would be appropriate."

It was not disputed that both the appellants and Hermiston Securities Ltd had led detailed evidence regarding the road improvements which would be required and their willingness to meet certain costs in connection therewith. On the other hand as regards site 3, no investigation had been carried out as to the J precise impact of traffic upon the site nor regarding access into the site. For example it was not plain whether a roundabout would be required or a grade separated junction. In the documents which accompanied their application, the Mackenzie Trustees stated that they would be committed to enter into negotiations with the planning authority on the planning and commitment towards any necessary road improvements with a similar commitment in some part towards the capital costs. In the written submis- K sion, under the heading "Roads" the following is inter alia stated: "The Trustees are entirely confident that satisfactory solutions to the trunk road and distributor road issues can be found without difficulty. The Trustees are also very optimistic that they will be able to reach agreement with both Roads Authorities as to the basis of funding the improvements. The Trustees, however, consider that it would be unrealistic to give a blanket undertaking to cover the costs of the requi- L site road improvements at this stage and indeed until the precise detail of the works required has been determined."

In the course of his closing submissions, Mr Young for the Mackenzie Trustees repeated the view that the trustees were confident that they would have no difficulty in reaching satisfactory agreements with the two roads authorities regarding roads matters. He also stated: "While the Trustees generally favour contributions by developers towards (and even in some cases completely funding) the provision of infrastructure normally provided by the hard pressed Community Charge payer, they would be extremely concerned both individually (as members of the public) and collectively as Trustees and as a party to the inquiry if the promise of such contributions should become an overriding factor in planning considerations. This would be wrong and would establish an extremely dangerous practice with serious implications. The Trustees knew that they had the best site, and wished to see it developed properly. However, they would not offer an empty promise of funding which at a later date they might be unable to fulfil to the letter."

Counsel for the appellants maintained that since there had been no investigation of the impact of traffic upon site no 3 nor as to what road improvements would be required, the trustees' statement that they were optimistic that they would be able to reach agreement with the two roads authorities as to the basis of funding the improvements was meaningless. The trustees did not know the nature of the works required nor the extent of any contribution that would be required of them. In these circumstances counsel contended that the reporter had not been entitled to conclude that there was a reasonable prospect that a satisfactory agreement could be arrived at between the trustees and the two roads authorities. As already observed under reference to para 12.9 the reporter had concluded that a suspensive condition would be appropriate in the circumstances. He had gone on to recommend the granting of planning permission for site 3 and in this connection he stated in para 12.15: "In my view, outline planning permission can be granted for a development provided that the proposal is reasonably clearly specified; is acceptable in principle from a planning point of view; and that there are no major tactical obstacles to development that might prove fatal to the scheme. The test for the latter is whether there is a reasonable prospect of satisfactory arrangements being made, thus allowing a suspensive condition to safeguard the situation. Given the flexible attitude of the Trust towards the precise content and layout of the scheme; the general suitability of the site for the purpose from a planning point of view; and the reasonable practicability of making the necessary infrastructure servicing arrangements, I am satisfied that the three criteria are met and that a satisfactory outline planning permission could be granted."

Counsel for the appellants contended that the reporter was not entitled to conclude that a suspensive condition could be imposed to safeguard the situation. Counsel referred to *Grampian Regional Council v City of Aberdeen District Council and Secretary of State for Scotland*. In that case Lord Keith of Kinkel made it clear that a suspensive condition could properly be imposed provided that it related to something which had a reasonable prospect of being achieved. The critical question here is whether the reporter was entitled to conclude that there was a reasonable prospect of a satisfactory arrangement in relation to road improvements being concluded between the trustees and the two roads authorities.

Counsel for the Secretary of State accepted that before the reporter would be justified in concluding that a suspensive condition was appropriate, he would require to be entitled to conclude that there was a reasonable prospect of a satisfactory agreement being reached. He maintained that the reporter had approached that matter in the correct way. He recognised that there was very little material to allow him to assess the prospects of a satisfactory agreement being made because as the reporter himself had recognised it was very regrettable that the Mackenzie Trustees had been unable to present a detailed case at the inquiry. However, he contended that there was sufficient material before the reporter to reach the conclusion which he did. He accepted that unlike the position in relation to site 1 and site 2, there were certain gaps in respect of matters which were unknown. Thus precisely what improvements would have to be carried out to the Smithton distributor was unknown. It was also unknown as to what land acquisition would be required in this connection. On the other hand as regards the A96 there was no reason to think that the nature of the works required would be any different for site 3 than for site 2.

I have not found this an easy issue to determine because there is obviously considerable force in the submissions put forward on behalf of the appellants. On the other hand I agree with counsel that the reporter did not require to be certain that a satisfactory agreement could be reached between the Mackenzie Trustees and the two roads authorities; it was sufficient if he could conclude that there was a reasonable prospect of a satisfactory agreement being reached. With some hesitation I have come to be of opinion that the reporter was entitled to reach the conclusion which he did. Site 3 was a suitable site from a planning point of view; the owners of the site had expressed willingness to negotiate an agreement with the two roads authorities and were hopeful that it would be possible to do so; it is significant that it has proved possible in relation to site 1 and site 2 for satisfactory agreements to be reached with the two roads authorities. Site 3 is a larger site than sites 1 and 2, and the reporter was entitled to conclude that it ought to be possible for a developer of this site to make a contribution to the costs of the road improvements which would be acceptable to the two roads authorities. The appellants have accordingly failed to satisfy me that the reporter was not entitled to conclude that there was a reasonable prospect of a satisfactory solution being reached and that a suspensive condition was therefore appropriate. In my opinion the present case was different to *Jones v Secretary of State for Wales*.

The next topic raised related to agricultural land. Counsel for the appellants pointed out that there had been three expert witnesses speaking to agricultural matters, and that all three had been opposed to the development proposed for site 3. The Department of Agriculture and Fisheries for Scotland (DAFS) maintained its objection to all three developments, but counsel pointed out that the development which took most agricultural land was site 3. The reporter in his findings in fact recorded that the planning authority and Hermiston Securities (though not the appellants nor the Mackenzie Trustees) envisaged the desirability of further development in the area in due course. He accordingly concluded that the land take resulting from the current proposals might well represent only the first stage of the long term process. Counsel pointed out that there was no specification as to the extent of any future development nor any assurance that future development would take place. In para C4 the reporter found that the proportion of prime land affected at site 3 was lower than at site 1 or site 2. Counsel maintained that this was not a proper approach since it was plain that the objection of DAFS was to the loss of prime agricultural land and not to the proportion of prime land affected by the proposed developments.

Counsel for the first respondent, on the other hand, pointed out under reference to para 2.17 that although the long term strategy (LTS) for Inverness had not been adopted by the planning authority, it still remained their policy that site 3 was the recommended location for industrial development. He also emphasised that DAFS were prepared to consider the loss from agricultural use of the whole of Stratton Farm for an appropriate purpose such as for the re-siting of the Inverness auction mart. He maintained that the national policy on agricultural land was well known, and that all that the reporter required to do was to have regard to that policy. He recognised that there was no particular need to develop good quality agricultural land for residential purposes, but observed that so far as the Mackenzie Trustees' proposals were concerned housing was included as an option rather than a firm proposal.

Counsel for the Secretary of State maintained that the reporter was entitled to consider what proportion of prime land would be affected by the competing sites because if either the appellants' proposals or those of Hermiston Securities Ltd were approved there would still be need for an industrial site, and the prime site for future industrial development was Stratton Farm. This meant that the probability was that further prime land would be lost for industrial development in the future. That being so there was something to be said for the view that favouring site 3 would mean that more efficient use was made of the prime land available on Stratton Farm.

Although I am not wholly persuaded that the reporter's approach to proportionality is a sound one, I have again with some hesitation come to be of opinion that he was entitled to have regard to the fact that it was likely in the longer term that parts of Stratton Farm would be developed for industrial use, and that being so he was entitled to conclude that this was a factor which could be regarded as favouring site 3. I am also of opinion that the reporter was entitled to make the findings which appear in C3 and C5 and that these support the reasoning which he has expressed in 12.9 and 12.10.

The next matter raised related to the proposals for a business park. As already observed the reporter concluded (B4) that a proper high amenity business park would require an area of 20 acres or more. The reporter also recognised that the indicated mix of land uses proposed by the Mackenzie Trustees for site 3 showed a business park with a maximum size of 50,000 sq ft on 4/5 acres. Counsel for the appellants submitted that this showed that the Mackenzie Trustees' proposals were contrary to sound planning principles and requirements. Counsel for the Secretary of State on the other hand drew attention to paras 9.2 and 9.3 and maintained that what was stated in para 9.3 qualified what was stated in 9.2. He accepted that there was an ambiguity between these paragraphs because in para 9.2 the clear impression is that 4/5 acres is the maximum area which is to be allocated to a business park, whereas in para 9.3 reference is made to "a detailed comprehensive development plan to optimise the uses" and he submitted that one construction which could be placed upon these words was that the maximum areas referred to in para 9.2 were open to adjustment, and that the position clearly was that the Mackenzie Trustees were flexible upon this and other matters. He accordingly submitted that the reporter was entitled to conclude that despite the mixed uses described in the Mackenzie Trustees' application, adequate provision could be made for a business park of adequate size on site 3 at the expense of other uses such as residential/leisure or open space (H11).

Having regard to the fact that the competing applications are all for planning permission in outline, I have with some hesitation come to be of opinion that the reporter was entitled to make the findings which he did at H11, and in particular to conclude that the size of site 3 was such that the business park allocation could be increased at the expense of other uses.

The appellants were critical of the reporter's conclusions regarding business parks for another reason. In his finding F4, the reporter refers to the rate of return on the business park on the appellants' site and concludes that unless there is a significant change in economic circumstances, there would be likely to be a slow rate of take-up in the park, and a strong incentive for the developer to seek to increase building densities and widen the range of users permitted to occupy the park in order to make use of the land and to achieve a return on the money spent in preparing the park. Counsel for the appellants pointed out that this criticism was directed at their site only and that it was unfair that the reporter should use this as a criticism of the appellants' site and disregard these matters when considering the other sites and in particular site 3. Counsel contended that the matters referred to in F4 would apply to the other sites as well and that the reasoning of the reporter was defective in respect that in para 12.7 he refers to this matter in relation to the appellants' site, but makes no mention of this consideration in relation to site no 3.

Counsel for the Secretary of State accepted that the reporter had made reference to this matter in order to justify the conclusion at which he had arrived, but he

A maintained that it was not unfair of him to do so. He submitted that the reporter had been entitled to mention this matter in relation to the appellants' site because the business park was a large element in the appellants' proposal, and accordingly the rate of return from it was material. In contrast even an enlarged business park on site 3 would be a less significant part of the whole proposal, and for that reason the rate of return from a business park there was less material. In any event, counsel pointed out under reference to para 12.10 that when the reporter was

B setting forth his reasons for concluding that the Mackenzie Trustees' scheme would offer substantial advantages compared with the other proposals, he did not refer to this matter of the rate of return of the business park.

The fact that the reporter highlighted the rate of return on the business park on the appellants' site, and made no corresponding comment in relation to the other two sites, does appear to me to suggest that his comparison between the sites has not been entirely

C even handed. On the other hand I recognise that when he does give his reasons for preferring the Mackenzie Trustees' scheme to the appellants' scheme he does not appear to suggest that the relative merits of the business park proposals on the two sites have persuaded him to favour site 3, and for that reason, again with some hesitation, I have come to the conclusion that the decision of the reporter in this respect cannot be regarded as unreasonable or perverse.

D The next issue raised was the approach which the reporter adopted to the views of the planning authority. In his reasons (paras 12.1 to 12.5) the reporter explains his attitude to the views of the planning authority. He explains that the most appropriate mechanism for identifying and allocating major land allocations would be the development plan, and that the planning authority were undertaking this in the form of the LTS which was intended to lead to a review of the relevant local plan. That exercise was,

E however, disrupted by the decision of the planning authority to approve the appellants' proposal. He goes on to explain that he shares the views of those who have stated that "it was hasty, premature, and ill considered for the Council to make such a far reaching resolution at that stage". He expresses the view that the obvious thing to have done was to continue the appellants' application to obtain further resolution of access and drainage matters, and at the same time to give fair and comparable consideration to the applica-

F tion by Hermiston Securities Ltd. He is also critical of the council for having prepared the A96 corridor plan. In para 12.5 he says: "I conclude that little weight should be given to the decisions reached by Highland Regional Council on the planning applications considered at the inquiry, or to the A96 Corridor Framework Plan."

Subsequently in para 12.17, when considering whether outline permission should be granted for the development on site 3, he observes that the planning authority has been prepared to bypass the local plan

procedure in favour of a major application which it supports while referring to the local plan as a reason G to reject other proposals, and he says: "I find it difficult to envisage the planning authority making an impartial decision on this part of the local plan review when it has already given such unequivocal support to the West Seafield proposal."

I am bound to say that I think there is considerable force in the suggestion that he has demonstrated unfairness in this respect. Having regard to the findings which he has made, I doubt whether he was justified in the criticisms which he levelled at the H authority. Paragraphs 7.1 to 7.7 describe the way in which the appellants' application was processed. It was plainly a well prepared application, and there is no reason to think that the planning authority did not consider it carefully. The application was supported by an economic appraisal report prepared by consultants, a report on national and local planning policies prepared by planning experts, a civil engineer's report and a series of conceptual artists' impressions and an illustrative layout. These docu- I ments were all before the planning committee when they first considered the application on 26 October. They decided to defer consideration of it to a special meeting of the committee on 17 November 1988. On that date the committee visited the site in the morning and heard some submissions on the site. They then met in the afternoon. The director of planning recommended refusal for a number of reasons. The committee were aware of objections from DAFS which would require the matter to be referred to the Secretary of J State if the council was minded to approve the proposal. The committee resolved to grant outline planning permission for the development subject to appropriate conditions to be decided upon. Subsequently the committee considered a report on suggested conditions and reserved matters and remitted to a subcommittee to deal with these. The subcommittee met on two occasions and determined the details of the conditions and reserved matters which would form the terms of any outline planning K permission.

It thus appears that the planning authority resolved to grant planning permission on a date more than two months after the submission to them of the planning application. Obviously the planning authority might have decided to continue the application in order to resolve questions of access and drainage but an alternative to that was to deal with these matters by way of conditions, and that appears to be what the planning authority decided. There is obviously some force in the reporter's suggestion that the appellants' application should have been continued in order to give fair and comparable consideration to the other application lodged by Hermiston Securities Ltd but the planning authority's decision not to do so does not, in my opinion, justify describing their action as "hasty, premature, and ill considered". In any event, evidence of the views of the planning authority upon the applications was given at the inquiry by Mr J Greaves and Mr M Greaves who were respectively depute director

A of planning and assistant director of planning. Evidence was also given by Councillor Graham, the vice chairman of the regional planning committee. That being so, I am surprised that the reporter should conclude that little weight should be given to the decisions reached by the planning committee on the planning applications, and to the planning authority's decision on the A96 corridor framework plan. The fact of the matter is, as the reporter recognises in para 7.44, that the planning committee decided to set aside certain policies and to grant approval to the appel-

B lants' application. They were quite entitled to do that if they thought that appropriate. The reporter concluded that little weight should be given to their decisions. That statement, however, implies that some weight should be given to them, and accordingly I am not persuaded that the reporter's attitude to the decision of the planning authority is such as to demonstrate a degree of unfairness which would vitiate his decision.

C The reporter expressed the view that it was difficult to envisage the planning authority making an impartial decision on the local plan review if it was left for them to do so prior to determining which of the competing sites should be preferred. The fact that the planning authority have supported the appellants' proposals would not, in my opinion, disable them from making an impartial decision in the event of the decision of the Secretary of State being quashed and the review of the local plan taking place. However, this matter does not appear to have been a significant

D part of the reporter's reasons for his decision.

In all the circumstances, although this is in many ways a marginal case, I have at the end of the day reached the conclusion that the appellants have failed to establish that the reporter's decision was unfair and perverse. The decision was one which he was entitled to make, and the appellants have failed to show that he reached his decision in an unfair manner.

E I would accordingly move your Lordships to refuse the appeal.

LORD MURRAY.—The appellants were one of three parties seeking development of farm sites adjacent to the A96 trunk road between the east side of Inverness and the west side of Culloden/Smithton. The appellants sought outline planning permission to erect inter alia a superstore, conference centre and business park at Seafield Farm West. Hermiston Secu-

F rities Ltd, the second respondents, sought outline planning permission for erection inter alia of shop units, community facilities and a business park at Seafield Farm East. They also appealed against a decision of Highland Regional Council to refuse planning permission for a development comprising a superstore, retail warehousing and filling station on Seafield Farm East. The third respondents, D F Mackenzie's Trust, appealed against the decision of Highland Regional Council to refuse planning permission for a development comprising a business park, retail food/non-food stores, industrial uses, residential

and/or leisure developments at Stratton Farm. The
G Secretary of State called in the applications in respect of Seafield Farm West by Narden Services Ltd (hereinafter referred to as "Narden") and in respect of Seafield Farm East by Hermiston Securities Ltd (hereinafter referred to as "Hermiston"). He decided that the applications should be considered at a public local inquiry and, with the agreement of the parties concerned, also decided that the appeals by Hermiston and by D F Mackenzie's Trust (hereinafter referred to as the "trust") would be heard in conjunction with these applications and would be decided by the Secre-
H tary of State himself. The procedure adopted by the reporter following this conjunction of hearings was the subject of criticism by the appellants (Narden). In due course the reporter made his report and recommendations to the Secretary of State for Scotland. The latter accepted the report and the recommendations with two exceptions. The reporter recommended that the Narden and Hermiston applications should be refused, that the Hermiston appeal should be dismissed and that the trust's appeal should be allowed
I and outline planning permission for development at Stratton Farm granted.

In a preamble to his report to the Secretary of State the reporter narrates that the inquiry commenced on 2 April 1990. A procedure meeting to make arrangements for the inquiry took place earlier on 15 January 1990. After narrating who participated directly in the inquiry and what parties relied on written submissions the reporter proceeds: "It should be noted that D F Mackenzie's Trust participated in the inquiry to the
J extent of asking questions of witnesses and making a closing submission but relied on a written statement (Production DFMT1), summarised in chapter 9, rather than presenting evidence through witnesses. The trust was unable to present a fully argued case because of the withdrawal of their preferred developers, but wished its proposal to be considered alongside the others at the public inquiry. No exception was taken to this procedure by the other parties to the inquiry for their respective interests although
K concern was expressed that while the Mackenzie Trust would have the opportunity to cross-examine the witnesses led by the other parties there would be no opportunity to test their case by cross-examination. The findings on the Mackenzie Trust application are based on their written submission, evidence presented at the inquiry by other parties, and the site inspection. The report of the closing submission on behalf of the trustees is, like the others, a summary of what was actually said." We were informed by counsel that the
L third last sentence of this paragraph was a form of words accepted — and indeed suggested — by the appellants.

Nineteen grounds of appeal are stated by the appellants. Unfortunately, however, these grounds of appeal overlap to a considerable extent and repeat similar points in different contexts. Broadly speaking two interwoven themes pervade the grounds of appeal. The first of these was that the procedure and the arrangements for the presentation of evidence were

such as to be fundamentally unfair to the appellants.
A The second was that certain decisions of the reporter
were ultra vires as being perverse and unreasonable in
light of the material before him.

The substance of the complaint in terms of the first
theme was that, in allowing the trust to participate as
they did on the basis only of written statements, the
reporter had not provided a level playing field for all
the participants, and in particular the appellants had
been materially prejudiced by their inability to cross
examine witnesses for the trust or to probe and test
B their case as they would have been able to do had witnesses been led. In the result they themselves presented a mass of detailed and carefully articulated
evidence to which effect should have been given not
only because it was not contradicted by opposing evidence, but also because, on any fair assessment, the
weight of the evidence decisively favoured the appellants. Counsel for the appellants supported this submission by reference to passages from the speeches of
Lord Diplock (at pp 410C, 411A) and Lord Roskill (at
C pp 414G-415A) in *Council of Civil Service Unions v
Minister for the Civil Service*; *Bushell v Secretary of
State for Environment* (Lord Diplock at p 97B-E, Lord
Edmund Davies at pp 116-117); and to *Lakin v Secre-
tary of State for Scotland* (Lord Justice Clerk Ross at
p 787L). Reference was also made to the cases of
*Ashbridge Investments Ltd v Minister of Housing and
Local Government*; *Bradley v Secretary of State for
Environment* (at pp 387-388); and *Wordie Property Co
v Secretary of State for Scotland* (at p 347).
D

Counsel for the appellants further submitted that
the relevant rules, the Town and Country Planning
(Inquiries Procedure) (Scotland) Rules 1980 (SI
1980/1676), envisaged that participants at inquiries
would lead the evidence of witnesses on oath who
would be subject to cross examination by opponents.
That this was the intention could be seen from s 267
(5) of the 1972 Act and from rule 10 (4). The rules
made no provision for conjoined inquiries, such as
E this, and did not allow for one applicant relying solely
on a written statement while others presented evidence. The reporter had erred in law in adopting this
procedure which was unfair to the appellants.

In reply counsel for the Secretary of State pointed
out that rule 10 (1) gave the reporter an unlimited discretion as to procedure. The appellants had not
challenged his exercise of his discretion at the preliminary meeting on procedure nor at the outset of the
inquiry, though concern had been expressed in a form
F of words which had originated with the appellants.
The appellants had not even challenged the procedure
in their closing submissions. Further s 267 (5) allowed
written statements in lieu of evidence on oath and rule
10 (9) specifically enjoined reporters to take into
account written representations or statements. In any
event the procedure adopted was the same for all participants and each had the same option of leading evidence or relying on written statements. A participant
had no cause for complaint if another made a different
choice. There was no substance in the appellants'

complaint that the reporter had not provided a level
playing field. Reference was made to *Miller v Minister G
of Housing and Local Government* (Lord Denning MR,
at pp 994B, 995G, 996E); *Hughes v Hamilton District
Council* (at p 632B); *French Keir Developments Ltd v
Secretary of State for Environment* (at p 297F); *Fairmount Investments Ltd v Secretary of State for Environment*; and to the unreported case of *British Railways
Board v Secretary of State for Environment*, in which
there was an appeal to the House of Lords in prospect.
Mention was also made of the observations of Lord
Justice Clerk Ross in *Glasgow District Council v Secre- H
tary of State for Scotland* at pp 965G-966B.

I agree with the reasoning of counsel for the Secretary of State and I would make two comments upon
this theme. First, in light of the procedural meeting
which the reporter held and in the absence of any
objection to the course of action which the reporter
narrates in the paragraph which I have quoted, it
appears to me that all the parties had an equal opportunity of presenting their case to the reporter in any I
competent way which they selected. Accepting that,
unlike a court, a reporter can, and indeed must, take
into account written submissions made to him as well
as formal evidence, no valid complaint of unfairness
can be made if a party who voluntarily confines his
case to a written statement, with all the risks which
that entails, is ultimately preferred, for good planning
reasons, over a polished and powerful presentation of
oral testimony and accompanying documents. Unlike
adversarial proceedings in a court of law, onus of proof J
is not a determinative factor nor must one party
succeed if his opponent loses. At first sight it appears
to me that, at least formally, much in the statement of
the grounds of appeal is based upon conceptions of
fairness in evidence and procedure appropriate to
proceedings in a court of law but not in a planning
inquiry. As each party had an equal opportunity of
presenting their case to the reporter the complaint of
procedural unfairness is in my opinion without substance. Secondly if it is accepted that a reporter would K
be entitled to reject uncontradicted and substantial
evidence in support of a party's case if there were
before him good planning reasons for so doing, then
it will not avail that party to complain that the
reporter did not proceed on that evidence or that he
accepted a view which was not expressed as such in
oral testimony. If this is so then many of the grounds
of appeal are, at least formally, inept and the first
theme cannot succeed.

In the course of argument counsel for the appellants L
suggested that the reporter could and should have
invoked s 267 (4) of the 1972 Act to require the trust
to give evidence in support of their application. As
counsel for the Secretary of State pointed out, the
appellants themselves could have moved the reporter
to do this, but did not. In any event, though no doubt
the subsection could be used to that end, I think that
its prime purpose is to ensure the attendance of a
necessary but reluctant witness rather than to compel
an applicant to support his case by oral testimony.

At para 12.5 the reporter states: "In my view, outline planning permission can be granted for a development provided that the proposal is reasonably clearly specified; is acceptable in principle from a planning point of view; and that there are no major practical obstacles to development that might prove fatal to the scheme." I did not understand the appellants to challenge these propositions seriously, but they did maintain that evidence was required, or at the very least a clear sufficiency of material, before any such conclusion could be drawn. This is the subject matter of the second theme taken up in the grounds of appeal.

I must now address the points of substance which remain in the grounds of appeal in terms of the second theme. It was accepted by both counsel that the substantive grounds of appeal could be grouped into six chapters, taking into account that grounds 11 and 15 were not argued by the appellants and that grounds 1, 2 and 19 need not be separately argued.

The first chapter comprised grounds 3, 4, 5, 6, 14 and 18. These dealt with procedure and the material before the reporter. In terms of the second theme ground 3 can be restated that the trust failed to produce evidence or other sufficient material in support of their appeal. That ground falls if it is accepted that their written statement did support their appeal and amounted to a statable and acceptable case. For the rest it depends upon whether the specific complaints embodied in the remaining particular grounds of appeal can be sustained. Ground 4 is based on the trust's failure to lead counter evidence or to rebut evidence for the appellants. This ground falls as such on rejection of the first theme. Ground 5 can be restated as a complaint that the trust produced no material to justify the use of prime agricultural land for their proposed development. Ground 6 can be restated to the effect that there was no material before the reporter to justify him in concluding that the trust were prepared to adjust the size of their proposed business park. Both of these grounds require to be addressed along with grounds 14 and 18 which do not depend upon the first theme.

The fifth ground of appeal is in issue not only under chap 1 but under chap 3 on agricultural land and it is closely related to ground 17 on housing. I propose to consider grounds 5 and 17 together, disregarding ground 4 which falls on rejection of the first theme.

The reporter sets out his reasoning on both of these grounds at paras 12.9 and 12.10 of his reasoning and gives his recommendations in part II of his report. In ground 17 the appellants take the reporter to task on the grounds that he purports to justify the allocation of prime agricultural land for housing in the absence of any evidence or other material which could possibly justify such loss of prime agricultural land. Perusal of para 12.9 reveals that the reporter was aware that there was no material before him to justify the sacrifice of prime agricultural land to housing as a firm proposal. As he puts it in that paragraph: "Housing is included as an option . . . there is no particular need to develop good quality agricultural land for residential purposes, as land of lower quality has already been approved elsewhere . . . however a residential element might better allow integration with the existing houses in Culloden."

It is to my mind quite clear that what the reporter is stating there, on an overall view of the firm proposals which he does make, is that, for reasons of good planning, a minimal sacrifice of good quality agricultural land to provide a residential element might give better integration between the proposed development and the existing houses in Smithton/Culloden. As the appellants I think came to accept, it is difficult to contend that the reporter was not entitled to reach that conclusion if he was otherwise entitled to conclude that the 38 ha of prime agricultural land at Stratton could be taken for the proposed developments as a whole. Turning to ground 5 the appellants maintained that the reporter's justification for preferring the proposal which takes the most prime agricultural land is that proportionally the loss of agricultural land is less than on the competing proposals. If that were the only basis for the reporter's conclusion I would accept at once that it was perverse, being based upon an obvious logical fallacy. Reference to para 12.9 reveals that the reporter's reasoning is based on the circumstances that the absolute difference in the loss of prime agricultural land as between the Narden and the trust proposals is only 8 ha, the DAFS were prepared to consider a total development package in relation to the trust site, and that a wider range of uses was embraced on a larger area of non-prime agricultural land. He also points out that the provision of a business park and industrial site justify the use of some prime agricultural land. To my mind it is clear from his reasoning in this paragraph and in para 12.10 that the reporter's actual reasoning is not invalidated by the proportionality fallacy and that he balances the greater absolute loss of prime agricultural land against the probability of thereby preserving for a longer time in the longer term the remaining prime agricultural land in the A96 corridor. On that basis I conclude that the reporter's approach to this issue was not perverse and unreasonable and that there was material before him to justify his conclusion. For the foregoing reasons I would reject grounds of appeal 5 and 17.

I turn next to consider ground 6 which appears in chap 1 and, along with grounds 7 and 16, in chap 4. Ground 6 is that, in the absence of sufficient material or evidence relating to effects upon the A96 corridor from the trust, there was an inadequate basis for the reporter to make a balanced judgment as between the appellants' and the trust's proposals. In particular, it is said, there was no basis on which the reporter was entitled to conclude that the trust would be flexible as to the size of the proposed business park. This aspect is pursued in ground 7 where it is pointed out that the trust's proposal was for a business park of 4/5 acres with no indication of flexibility beyond that; while the reporter's view was that the minimum size should be 20 acres but preferably it should be twice that size.

Ground 16 complains that at para 12.7 of part II the reporter concluded without any material to justify that conclusion that the rate of return on a business park at West Seafield would be likely to be below what would probably attract private developers. He did not make the same criticism of the trust's proposal for a business park at Stratton. Prima facie these criticisms of the reporter are justified. There was no material before the reporter to indicate any particular flexibility on their part to a proposal, for instance, to quadruple the size of the business park. All that can be said, I think, is that the trust's statement expresses a general intention to be flexible and gives an "indicated mix" only of the proportions of the site to be allocated to particular uses. This, together with other material about business parks in general, may be just enough to provide a very thin basis on which the reporter could attribute willingness on the part of the trust to be flexible as to the size of the business park. As regards his conclusion on the viability of the proposed business park at West Seafield it does appear that there was material in finding in fact F4 and in the evidence recorded at para 3.15 to justify the reporter's conclusion on that matter. Although I think that the reporter's approach to the business park aspect of the Narden and trust proposals is far from satisfactory it cannot be said that there was no material entitling him to draw the inferences which he did. In my view accordingly grounds 6, 7 and 16 fail.

I take up next what is clearly the most difficult issue in this appeal, namely the matter of roads, which is dealt with in chap 2 and touched upon in grounds of appeal 8, 9, 10, 13, 14 and 18. In ground 8, under reference to para 12 of the decision letter, it is contended that the reporter had no basis for concluding that the trust had acknowledged the need for road improvements and would be able and willing to make a financial contribution to them. It is said that that conclusion was indeed contrary to the evidence. Reference is made to para 10.167 of part I quoting the trust's final submission that they would not offer an empty promise of funding which at a later date they might be unable to fulfil to the letter. It is also said that the reporter's finding at D7 that the trust had a larger potential development area from which to underwrite the expenditure was perverse, irrelevant and unreasonable in respect that there was no evidence that a larger area would be developed or that its return would be greater than that of the appellants from the development in their proposals. Beginning with the latter point I read the reporter's conclusion in D7 as saying no more than that the trust has a larger potential development area to underwrite road expenditure, which appears to me to be self evident on the material before the reporter. That may not take the reporter very far but it does appear to me to be an element which he was entitled to take into account when assessing the proposals before him. What the trust actually say on the second page of their applicant's statement is that their proposals would require upgrading of the section of the A96 to the Smithton distributor road turnoff, including upgrading of the

distributor road for which no proposals were committed. They would accept certain road improvement costs as a necessary part of the overall development. They conclude, on the third page, with the words "the applicant would be committed, therefore, to enter into negotiations with the Regional Council on the planning and commitment towards these roads improvements, with a similar commitment in some part towards the capital costs". From that statement taken along with paras 10.165-167 it appears to me that the reporter was entitled to conclude that the trust were willing to make an appropriate contribution to the capital cost of road improvements but could not commit themselves to a definite figure or formula. In these circumstances I conclude that ground of appeal 8 is not made out.

The substance of grounds 9 and 10 is that there was specific evidence for Narden and Hermiston of specific road arrangements and willingness to negotiate a s 50 agreement which led to withdrawal of SDD objections to these applications while, apparently quite unfairly, such considerations were not to be applied to the trust's Stratton development (though by a somewhat tortuous twist of thought their s 50 undertakings were taken as evidence that the trust could also reach such an agreement). This complaint has to be considered along with the reporter's recommendation in para 12.19 (2) that superstore trading should not commence without the necessary road improvements and that this could be achieved by means of a suspensive condition or by a s 50 agreement. The Secretary of State differs from the reporter in rejecting the option of a s 50 agreement and in imposing detailed suspensive conditions at paras 4 and 18 of annex A to the decision letter. Before deciding whether this conclusion is reasonable it has to be borne in mind that both the Narden and the Hermiston proposals plainly involved only limited and specific consequences for the A96 trunk road whereas the trust's proposal really could not be separated in road traffic terms from overall long term proposals for the improvement and upgrading of the A96 and the Smithton distributor. Bearing in mind that much wider planning considerations therefore arose in relation to that matter it could hardly be said to be unreasonable, it may be said, to set more flexible conditions which fit that wider context, particularly when the proposals themselves were put forward in general and relatively flexible terms. But could the reporter and the Secretary of State decide this matter without evidence or at least specific material in relation to roads, including non-trunk roads, and access to the development?

Counsel for the Secretary of State accepted that there was a real gap in this aspect of the case in the sense that neither evidence nor specific material in that regard was before the reporter or the Secretary of State. He submitted, however, that unlike the case of *Anduff Holdings Ltd v Secretary of State for Scotland*, this was a case in which it was appropriate, as in *Ladbroke Racing Ltd v Secretary of State for Scotland*, for the reporter to deal with issues raised on the basis of material before him in light of his own planning experience and expertise. I propose to consider this ground along with the remaining other grounds relating to roads.

It was argued for the appellants under reference to *Grampian Regional Council v City of Aberdeen District Council,* per Lord Keith at 1984 SLT, pp 198-199, and *Jones v Secretary of State for Wales* per Purchas LJ, at p 107, that a "Grampian" condition should not be imposed unless there was evidence that there was at least a reasonable prospect of the action in question being performed. There was no such evidence here nor was there any material before the reporter on the matter. Accordingly the condition that trading should not commence without prior road improvements was not appropriate. In reply counsel for the Secretary of State pointed out that in the passage of the *Grampian* case cited Lord Keith was not dealing with evidential prospects in that case but with the existence of a legal mechanism which was capable of being used to enable the condition to be met. In any event there was just sufficient material before the reporter in the unusual circumstances of this case to enable him to exercise an appropriate judgment on the matter based on his planning experience and expertise.

The appellants' complaint in ground 13 is essentially that it was unreasonable and unfair to attach little weight to the planning authority's decision in favour of the appellants' proposals. They further complain that the reporter was not even handed in being critical of the appellants' proposals for access and drainage but in uncritically accepting the trust's proposals without SDD agreement and without any evidence relating to roads and drainage. Taking the latter point first it is clear from para 12.3 that the reporter was critical of the planning authority for granting the appellants' application when major problems regarding access and drainage from their site remained to be resolved. He sets out what he thinks should have been done and expresses his agreement with those who gave evidence before him and who considered that what the planning authority had done was hasty and ill considered. So far as the trust is concerned, as is pointed out in answer 13 for the Secretary of State, although there was an absence of information regarding access and drainage no issue was raised by other parties regarding that. Furthermore specific conditions 4.9 and 4.10 meeting this requirement had been imposed by the Secretary of State in annexe A to the decision letter.

As regards the first point, giving little weight to the planning authority's decision, the context of the reporter's approach appears to be rather wider than what is said in para 12.3, focusing on access and drainage. In para 12.1 the reporter accepts the need for additional industrial land and a business park in the Inverness area and finds that some high quality agricultural land will be necessary for this purpose. In para 12.2 he points out that the development plan is the most appropriate mechanism for identifying and allocating the necessary land. He observes that the planning authority was undertaking review of the development plan in the form of a long term strategy. In the reporter's view this was inappropriately disrupted by the resolution to approve the appellants' proposal against the recommendation of the director of planning. After referring to the matters in para 12.3 the reporter goes on in 12.4 to point out that the planning authority, having already pre-empted long term planning of the A96 area by approving the appellants' application, ex post facto prepared an "A96 corridor plan" to provide a context for that approval without the benefit of the thorough level of analysis required by the long term strategy. Detailed criticism of this plan is set out in para B.10.

Approaching para 12.5 in the foregoing setting it is apparent that the reporter considered that he had cleared the ground as it were of pre-empting decision making so that each of the applications could be considered equally on their merits as candidates for a single development opportunity on the three criteria which he sets out. I do not consider that it can be plausibly suggested that this reasoning was perverse or without foundation in the material before the reporter.

Although the emphasis of ground 14 is different from that of ground 13 it raises the same issues and can be dealt with in the same way. Ground 18 reverts to the first broad theme of evidence and procedure and repeats the point that in the absence of evidence and of plans which could be considered and tested in the course of a public inquiry there was no justification for granting the trust's application. The comment that the absence of such material was "very regrettable" appears in para 12.14 in the context of a series of paragraphs from 12.10 to 12.18 in which his reasoning is fully set out. So in para 12.12 the reporter says: "I therefore conclude that it is necessary for major development to take place in the A96 corridor and that Stratton Farm is the best place for it among the proposals under consideration at the inquiry." The reporter I think is really saying that, recognising the deficiencies in the presentation of the Stratton Farm proposals, nonetheless its overall planning advantages on the material before him compared with the other applications are clearly demonstrable.

In para 12.18 the reporter narrates that he considers that outline approval of the trust application at this stage would not prejudice the proper local planning of the area and would be much more in line with planning objectives than approval of either of the other proposals. He then observes that if this view is not accepted it would be necessary to refuse the trust application as premature and leave the matter of development of the A96 corridor to be determined by Highland Regional Council by means of the local plan process. The reporter certainly could not have been faulted if he had adopted the latter course. Equally he can only be faulted for adopting the former course not on the basis that another course would be better or had a greater weight of evidence in its support, or had been tested fully in a public inquiry, but on the basis that the material before the reporter was so deficient and the procedure which he adopted so unfair that his recommendations are ultra vires.

As regards the reporter's decision upon the crucial
matter of roads, as raised in grounds 8, 9, 10, 13, 14
and 18, I have come to the conclusion after much hesitation that it cannot be said that the reporter (and in
turn the Secretary of State) did not have material
before him on which he was entitled to reach the conclusion and make the recommendations which he did.

In considering the appeal as a whole I return to the
standard which the reporter set for himself in para
12.15. Despite the deficiencies which have been highlighted by the appellants I conclude that the trust's
scheme for Stratton, though dependent solely upon
written material, was sufficiently clearly specified for
the reporter to consider it along with the schemes supported by detailed and articulated evidence for the
other applicants; that there was just sufficient material
before the reporter overall, from written statements,
oral evidence, site inspection and his own experience
and expertise to enable him reasonably to find it
acceptable from a planning point of view in competition with the alternative schemes which were before
him; and that there were no evident major practical
obstacles to this development which might prove fatal
to it. He was in my opinion accordingly entitled to
reach the decision which he did and the appeal cannot
succeed.

It is easy to understand the concern and disquiet
which the appellants must have had when the reporter
rejected their carefully researched, detailed and
specific evidence for the West Seafield development in
favour of somewhat vague and highly provisional
proposals for Stratton, based on a written presentation
and unsupported by direct evidence. The fact is that
the trust's proposals were, perhaps unnecessarily,
handicapped from the start by the decision not to lead
evidence which might provide further specification
and a legitimate opportunity for testing by opponents.
Despite that the reporter reached a conclusion which
I hold he was entitled to do and decided that the trust's
proposals offered the best planning option which, for
the reasons he gave, the competing proposals could
not match. I do not consider that the appellants have
been able to present any material, or refer to any
matter, suggesting that a different result would be
likely if a further and fuller inquiry were to take place
in consequence of a decision which might have been
made to quash the Secretary of State's action.

I agree with your Lordship in the chair that the
appeal should be refused.

LORD PROSSER.—The appellants seek an order
quashing a decision of the Secretary of State for Scotland dated 30 April 1991. Putting the matter shortly,
that decision disposed of certain planning applications
and appeals relating to three different sites. The effect
of the Secretary of State's decision is that outline planning permission has been refused in respect of sites at
Seafield Farm West and Seafield Farm East, where the
applicants were the present appellants and second
respondents respectively, and has been granted,
subject to conditions, at Stratton Farm, where the

applicants were the present third respondents. It is not
disputed that these are essentially competing applications, only one of which could reasonably be granted.
It is not disputed by the Secretary of State, who is the
only compearing respondent, that if any part of his
decision requires to be quashed, then the whole
decision must be quashed. In the present appeal, the
contentions of the parties related almost entirely to the
grant of planning consent in respect of Stratton Farm,
and the way in which, at the public inquiry and in the
report which followed upon it, the reporter appointed
by the Secretary of State dealt with that particular
application.

As your Lordships have noted, the appeal sets out
a substantial number of separate grounds. While some
attempt was made on each side to relate the actual submissions to these listed grounds, I think that reference
to them tends to obscure rather than clarify the issues
as they actually emerged. The grounds of appeal
which were insisted in may more conveniently be
listed under five simple headings: evidence and procedure, roads, agricultural land, business park and the
reporter's attitude to Highland Regional Council. I
discuss these in that order.

(1) Evidence and procedure
This is a convenient but perhaps inadequate
description of the appellants' fundamental criticism of
the reporter's handling of the Stratton application.
Your Lordships have described the procedure adopted
by the reporter, the events which led up to the adoption of that procedure, and the basis upon which the
reporter, and in due course the Secretary of State
proceeded. I do not rehearse these matters in detail.
Before turning to the criticisms of what the reporter
did, I would mention the fact that at the outset of the
inquiry, no exception was taken to the procedure
adopted by the reporter, although concern was
expressed on the question of cross examination. It is
also to be noted that counsel for the appellants, in his
closing submission, dealt with the Stratton application
by submitting that it failed in various particular
respects and had scarcely been supported at the
inquiry. Despite the order in which closing submissions are set out in the report, we were informed that
the third respondents had made their closing submission some time before counsel for the appellants made
his. Even so, he did not suggest that it was not open
to the reporter to uphold the Stratton appeal; his position was rather the ordinary one, that the reporter
should not do so.

It does not seem to me that the appellants' "failure
to take the point at the time" means that this ground
of appeal is necessarily ill founded. It may be that the
unfairness or unreasonableness of what a reporter has
done can only be appreciated subsequently, once his
report is available. But the course adopted by counsel
for the appellants is worth noting, in my opinion. An
inquiry to dispose of all the applications and appeals
together had been set up. The desirability of dealing
with the Stratton appeal in the same proceedings as
the appellants' application was plain. The fact that the

third respondents were apparently in a weak position, and were not going to be able to mount as full a case as they had intended, may be seen as having put them at a disadvantage. But from the appellants' point of view, that apparent weakness would be an evident advantage, and would make it all the more desirable that the Stratton application should not be left out of the inquiry, for future consideration, but should proceed in its weak state. It was suggested to us on behalf of the appellants that what the reporter had done had denied the appellants (as the current phrase seems to be) "a level playing field". It seems to me that they and their counsel may well have thought that the slope was in their favour; or (to change metaphors) that it was acceptable to play into the wind, given that the opposition were several men short. Similarly, at the close of the inquiry, it would be a perfectly understandable tactical decision to be dismissive of the opposition, rather than dignify their case with meticulous demolition. Even if the appellants were to identify some specific disadvantage to themselves, such as the availability to the reporter of material which was not open to cross examination, the courts should in my view be very slow to move from acceptance that this was a disadvantage, to a finding that the conduct of the inquiry, or the decisions reached thereafter, had involved, because of that one disadvantage, unfairness or unreasonableness, despite perhaps major advantages accruing to the "aggrieved" party in other ways.

The submissions on behalf of the appellants, under this general ground of appeal, took a number of different forms. Not all of these were persisted in. In relation to the Town and Country Planning (Inquiries Procedure) (Scotland) Rules 1980, SI 1980/1676, it was not in the end suggested that the procedure adopted by the reporter was in direct conflict with the rules. I think it is true that these rules do not apparently contemplate conjoined inquiries, dealing with a number of applications or appeals. I am also inclined to accept that the rules do not contemplate a situation where the appellant or applicant at an inquiry seeks to rely wholly on a written statement, without any witness appearing to give evidence, and thus to be subject to cross examination. Nonetheless, the language of the rules does not appear to me to rule out either conjoined inquiries, or the possibility that an applicant will indeed simply submit a written statement. Inquiries can take many forms. The material put forward to them can take many forms. I should regard it as quite wrong to read into references to "appearance" or to being "heard" as carrying any more specific implication; and I do not see, either in the fact that the inquiry is "public", or in any of the procedural requirements, anything which suggests that a principal party, such as an appellant or applicant, "must" give evidence, or loses his right to cross examine witnesses led by others if he himself does not give evidence, or is not allowed to rely simply upon a written statement. In a normal "single" inquiry, reliance merely on a written statement would no doubt normally involve a huge risk, and would probably be

the height of folly. Other parties would be entitled either to be dismissive of it, or to analyse it word by word, and show that it did not merit reliance, either for want of precision, or because its reliability was questioned, and could not be tested in cross examination. But none of this appears to me to be unfair to other parties, in any general sense. The deficiencies of a mere written statement can be exposed by comment, or by leading evidence in rebuttal, if that is thought necessary. Just as the contention that the procedure was in conflict with the rules was in my view unsound, the alternative submission, that principles of openness and fairness, and natural justice, will for the most part preclude a principal party from proceeding by written statement alone appears to me also to be unsound. There may be particular circumstances which render such a procedure unfair or unreasonable, but if that is to be asserted, it is those particular reasons which must be considered.

At one stage, it was submitted on behalf of the appellants that it was contrary to natural justice for the reporter to have considered the written statement, or indeed to look at the supplementary statement which had been attached to the application. However, I think it was in the end accepted that the reporter was right to let the third respondents put forward what they wanted in support of their case, and that a reporter was not obliged to consider merely "evidence" in the strict sense, but could consider material of other (including written) kinds. It was however still submitted that this reporter had been unfair in accepting the written material, contained in the written statement and the previous supplementary statement, "and nothing else". I remain quite unpersuaded by this. In general, it is for the reporter to decide what parties may do, not to lay down what they must do, in support of their case. Still less is it for him to try to force them to adopt a particular course (such as leading witnesses) by refusing to accept what they would normally be entitled to rely upon, such as a written statement. Others can comment or rebut. The sufficiency of what is contained in a written statement, or the weight which it deserves to be given, is another matter. I see nothing unfair in proceeding as the reporter did.

I would add two brief comments on this ground of appeal. First, at a conjoined inquiry, it may well be possible for one of the applicants or appellants to put little or no material before the reporter, if there is a wealth of material from other sources which he thinks will show, or go far to show, that his site is suitable, and indeed the best of the competing sites. That being so, I should be very reluctant to accept that any general proposition can be stated as to what such a party must lead or present in the way of evidence or material. What matters will be the sum total of evidence or material available to the reporter from the inquiry, regardless of who led or presented it, or which application or appeal it was intended to support. Secondly, however, I should not like anything that I have said to be interpreted as an encouragement to applicants or appellants to rely on written statements as a substitute for evidence, or as

an alternative to evidence on particular matters. On
any significant issue, I regard it as normally important
that the position of any party be spoken to in evidence,
not least where matters of opinion, or practicability or
intention are involved. But the reason for regarding
written statements as a very inferior way of presenting
a case is not so much that it is unfair to other parties.
It is rather that if such material is commented on or
rebutted by other parties, in such a way as to show that
it would require testing before it could be relied upon,
the appellant or applicant will himself suffer, and the
reporter may well have insufficient material, or
insufficiently reliable material, to allow him to make
a finding in that party's favour. That more specific
problem arises in relation to certain of the other
grounds of appeal.

(2) Roads

The reporter recommended that outline planning
permission be granted for the Stratton development,
subject to certain conditions set out in an appendix,
and "if necessary, a section 50 agreement covering
phasing and infrastructure services". The conditions
included what seem to be normal requirements in relation to a master plan and reserved matters. They
further contained certain conditions which were to be
fulfilled before use commenced. In particular, condition 16 was to the effect that no part of the development should be brought into use until inter alia the
access roads had been provided, and condition 18 was
to the effect that the retail part of the scheme should
not be brought into use "until improvements to the
A96 and the Smithton Distributor, and the junction of
those two roads, have been carried out, in accordance
with a scheme (or schemes) to be approved by the
respective highway authorities". The conditions
imposed by the Secretary of State — including condition 16, and condition 18 in a somewhat altered
form — state that the improvements in question are to
be carried out not in accordance with a scheme or
schemes, but simply "to the satisfaction of the respective highway authorities". Moreover, in his decision
letter, the Secretary of State differs somewhat from the
reporter in relation to the need for a s 50 agreement.
At para 19.2 of his letter the Secretary of State says
that he does not consider it necessary that the parties
enter into a s 50 agreement with regard to phasing and
the provision of infrastructure services, and does not
accept that the conclusion of a s 50 agreement is a
prerequisite for planning consent. He goes on to say
that he considers that the planning substance of agreements can be appropriately provided for by conditions
attached to the grant of outline planning permission
and by the planning authority's power to enforce such
conditions. The appellants' position is that they themselves, and the second respondents, required s 50
agreements, and that on the very sparse material
before the reporter, he was wrong to conclude that
outline permission could (and correspondingly, the
Secretary of State was wrong to hold that such permission should) be granted without such a prior agreement. Expressing the same point in a different way, it

was contended that on the basis of that sparse
material, the appropriate prerequisites for proceeding
to grant outline permission, subject to a suspensive
condition of the type found in condition 18, were
missing. The requirement of condition 18 was that the
improvements there mentioned must be carried out to
the satisfaction of the respective highway authorities
before the retail part of the scheme could be brought
into use. The question was whether there was a
realistic prospect that this requirement could be met.

At paras 12.10 to 12.12, the reporter states his conclusion that the Stratton scheme would offer substantial advantages compared to the other proposals,
that it is necessary for major development to take place
in the A96 corridor, and that Stratton Farm is the best
place for it among the proposals under consideration
at the inquiry. In paras 12.13 to 12.15, he raises the
question as to whether there is sufficient information
available about the Stratton application to grant an
outline planning permission, and discusses both the
general requirements, if outline planning permission
is to be granted, and particular considerations in the
present case. He states that in his view "outline planning permission can be granted for a development
provided that the proposal is reasonably clearly specified; is acceptable in principle from a planning point
of view; and that there are no practical obstacles to
development that might prove fatal to the scheme".
On this last point, he states that the test is "whether
there is a reasonable prospect of satisfactory arrangements being made, thus allowing a suspensive condition to safeguard the situation". He refers back to
his finding in fact H5, where he finds "that there is
a reasonable prospect that a satisfactory agreement
could be reached, as, with suitable safeguards, the
developer could not benefit from the scheme until the
necessary improvements had been carried out". His
conclusion in paras 12.14 and 12.15 is that a suspensive condition could safeguard the position, that the
three criteria are met and that a satisfactory outline
planning permission could be granted. Standing these
conclusions, and despite his reference to a s 50 agreement in his final recommendation, it does not appear
to me that there is any real departure by the Secretary
of State from the conclusions of the reporter himself.

I did not understand the appellants really to question the three criteria. It appeared to be suggested that
the road proposals themselves required to be "reasonably clearly specified" if the criteria were to be met,
but I do not think that this is correct. What is
required, if outline planning permission is to be
granted, is that the development proposal as a whole
be reasonably clearly specified, and acceptable in principle from a planning point of view. Planning permission is concerned with appropriate land use, and these
are essential requirements if planning permission is to
be granted. If a particular land use is appropriate, and
particularly if the proposed development is regarded
as necessary, and the particular site as the best place
for it, then outline planning permission can be granted
notwithstanding doubt as to whether some essential
requirement can be met.

Such a doubt may be merely a matter of concern to the developer. In such a case, no protective measures are necessary on the part of the planning authority. Failure to meet the essential requirements may simply mean that the development cannot go ahead. But in other situations, it is necessary for the planning authority to have regard to what is likely to happen. It may be necessary to impose phasing conditions, for example, so that the profitable part of the development does not go ahead, leaving unprofitable but highly desirable elements unexecuted. Or the doubtful matter may be one which the developer could ignore, if he were allowed to proceed with his development, leaving that unresolved matter as a problem for others. In such a situation, it may well be necessary simply to postpone the permission, until the unresolved matter has been resolved, for example by a s 50 agreement. But it will not be necessary to postpone the grant of permission pending such an agreement, if there is both (a) a reasonable prospect of satisfactory arrangements being made, and (b) a suspensive condition forbidding the development, or some part of the development until such arrangements have been made.

In my opinion, the stated criteria are of the practical and common sense type which is appropriate, if reasonable progress is to be made with major development proposals. Obviously, the suspensive condition may never be met. If that occurs, a highly desirable development may not proceed. Particularly if there have been other competing proposals, which perhaps could have gone ahead, this may be very unfortunate. But in my opinion it would be unrealistic always to defer the grant of outline permission beyond the point where one can say that there is a reasonable prospect of satisfactory arrangements being made, until a time when something like certainty has been obtained. This appears to me to be consistent with the views expressed in *Grampian Regional Council v City of Aberdeen District Council* and *Jones v Secretary of State for Wales.*

Questions remain, both in a general sense and with reference to this particular case, as to what material would justify the view that there is a reasonable prospect of satisfactory arrangements being made for something like necessary road improvements or alterations. If what is needed is itself something quite simple, then one may hold that there is a reasonable prospect of it coming about, notwithstanding that this is dependent upon positive steps being taken by third parties, perhaps in exercise of a statutory power, but I think also as a simple matter of their discretion. In *Jones,* there had been a refusal of a vital consent. The case illustrates the difference between that position, and the situation where those who had power to consent were not minded to do so at the time of the inquiry, but might well change their mind in future. I would respectfully agree with the view expressed in that case, that one cannot say that there is a reasonable prospect of something coming about, merely because anything can change. Nonetheless, it seems to me that judging whether there is a reasonable prospect of

something coming about is very much a matter of circumstances, and in the absence of a positive indication that there is no reasonable prospect of it coming about, I am disposed to think that one could proceed upon a very broad impression, to the position of saying that there was some prospect of it coming about. Moreover, if there is some prospect of the necessary event coming about, then unless it seems a quite theoretical or fanciful prospect, I think that one can again, upon a very broad assessment of all the facts, conclude without much difficulty that there is a reasonable prospect. Putting it another way, if a person faced with making this assessment has concluded that there is a reasonable prospect, I would find it hard to conclude that that view was an unreasonable or unjustified one, in the absence of positive reasons for substantial doubt.

One reason for saying that there is substantial doubt as to whether the requirement arrangements will ever be made in the present case, is that condition 18 does not in any way identify what the necessary improvements to the roads would be. Even assuming, as one must, that the planning authorities would not unreasonably say that they were not satisfied, and even acknowledging that the s 50 agreements with the other parties throw some light on what would be required on the westmost part of the A96, it is not at all clear what would be required on the Smithton distributor or at the junction between the two. At least at first sight, the less sure one is as to what is required, the less sure one can be as to whether it is attainable. In addition to this uncertainty, counsel for the appellants pointed out that there were ownership problems on the A96, so that compulsory purchase might be necessary; and that there might be both engineering problems and cost problems inherent in whatever turned out to be the necessary traffic solution. Furthermore, and fundamentally, the third parties' willingness to contribute to cost was wholly unspecific, and based on what were really just assertions of optimism. There was effectively no solid material before the reporter on these matters; and having regard to the nature of the issues in question, the absence of material could not be supplied by the reporter's own experience and expertise. This was not a case like *Ladbroke Racing Ltd v Secretary of State for Scotland,* where the reporter was able in this way to supplement what had been presented to him. It was a case comparable with *Anduff Holdings Ltd v Secretary of State for Scotland.* What the reporter had gave him no basis for holding that there was a reasonable prospect of condition 18 being met.

Counsel for the Secretary of State accepted that there were what he called "gaps" in the material available on this matter. But he emphasised that one was not looking for certainty, and contended that even a reporter with no specific professional skill on the matter, could apply his judgment as an experienced reporter, provided that he was not perverse. In *Grampian,* all there had really been was a possibility which was not capable of assessment. There was a problem, but it was one capable of being solved. He accepted that this case was unlike *Grampian* or *Jones*, inasmuch as in those cases the required solution was known. That was one of the gaps, particularly in relation to the Smithton distributor. But no obvious engineering problem had emerged in the material before the reporter, and with a larger development from which to fund any contribution, and a willingness to overcome the problem which he was entitled to regard as sincere, there was enough to justify proceeding by suspensive condition, on the view that there was at least a reasonable prospect of the arrangements being successfully concluded. There was a spectrum of uncertainty: there would be cases like *Jones*, where the prospects were virtually ruled out, and other cases in which there was effectively no doubt that all would be well. Within the spectrum, the court should only interfere if it was satisfied that in giving the appellants the chance to resolve matters, the reporter and the Secretary of State were doing something pointless. The question was not of course one for the court, and its own assessment of what the prospects were. The question was whether no reasonable reporter, in this reporter's position, could have reached the view which he reached.

On this matter, as on certain others, I have some sympathy with the appellants. Having presented a detailed case for their own development, and having gone to the extent of a s 50 agreement, it is no doubt very frustrating for them to find that a proposal presented in much less detail emerges as preferable, and that on this matter deferment for a s 50 agreement has not been seen as necessary. But on the general matter, I do not think it is really helpful to make a comparison between the amount of information on different proposals. For the grant of permission at Stratton, the question is the sufficiency and reliability of the material about Stratton. And once Stratton has emerged as worthy of planning permission, in terms of land use, the general observations which I have already made appear to me to apply. I do not think that any major obstacle had emerged, as it had in *Jones*. I see no positive reason to relate this to the sparseness of the material presented by the third respondents. Other parties might speculatively hope that a more fully presented case would have revealed obstacles, and in particular that such obstacles might have been revealed by cross examination. Nonetheless, this did not happen. The problem is one of upgrading major roads which are already in existence, and not of striking out into the unknown. Counsel for the appellants himself acknowledged that he could not say that there was no prospect of condition 18 being met. There was a prospect, but the reporter was not entitled to hold that it was a reasonable one. It being acknowledged that there was a prospect, I see no basis upon which this court could hold that the reporter or the Secretary of State was not entitled to see that prospect as a reasonable one.

(3) Agricultural land

At para 12.9, the reporter makes the point that the Stratton proposal embraces a much larger area of land than the other proposals. He comments that being larger, the scheme would occupy more prime agricultural land than the other proposals, but observes that this is not pro rata, as almost half the site is not prime land. It is apparently suggested that he has adopted a wrong criterion, since these matters would not justify taking more prime land. It does not appear to me that he is adopting any such criterion. He is I think merely pointing out that despite the much greater size of the site, it does not involve taking a proportionately greater amount of prime land. He goes on to point out that the actual difference is only 8 ha more. On the other issues as to agricultural land, I do not think that there is anything I can usefully add.

(4) Business park

I agree with the opinions of your Lordships, and have nothing to add on this topic.

(5) Attitude to Highland Regional Council

On the general issue, I agree with your Lordships and have nothing to add. I am concerned by the comment in para 12.17, that the reporter finds it difficult to envisage the planning authority making an impartial decision on this part of the local plan review. If they failed to do so, that would be a matter for others. It cannot constitute a reason for removing from the democratic process a matter which belongs there. But I think that the reporter is not making such a suggestion. Any major decision taken in advance of a review of the local plan might be described as pre-empting it. That is not a reason for deferring all major decisions. While I am inclined to see this particular sentence as somewhat ill advised, I think that what the reporter was doing was setting the recommendation which he contemplated making against the broader planning background, and concluding that it would not conflict with other impartial assessments.

On the whole matter, I agree with your Lordships, and would refuse the appeal.

Counsel for Appellants, Bell, QC, Boyd; Solicitors, Paull & Williamsons — Counsel for First Respondent, Moynihan; Solicitor, R Brodie, Solicitor to the Secretary of State for Scotland.

C A G M

Atlas Assurance Co Ltd v Dollar Land Holdings plc

OUTER HOUSE

LORD MURRAY

16 JULY 1992

Contract — Sale of heritage — Missives — Breach — Waiver — Actings of sellers after purchasers failed to pay purchase price — Whether waiver of right to treat failure as material breach of contract.

Heritable property — Sale — Missives — Breach — Waiver — Actings of sellers after purchasers failed to pay purchase price — Whether waiver of right to treat failure as material breach of contract.

Personal bar — Waiver — Actings of sellers after purchasers failed to pay purchase price in terms of missives — Whether waiver of right to treat failure as material breach of contract.

The owners of heritable subjects concluded missives to sell them. The missives provided that if the purchasers failed to pay the full purchase price within 14 days of the stipulated date of entry the sellers would be entitled to serve a notice on the purchasers demanding full payment of the purchase price within a period of not less than 14 days, and that if the period given in the notice expired without such payment this would constitute a material breach of contract on the part of the purchasers entitling the sellers to "resile from" the missives at their option, reserving to them all claims arising from that breach. The date of entry was 11 June 1990. The purchasers did not pay the full purchase price on that date, nor within 14 days thereafter. On 23 July 1990 the sellers served a notice on the purchasers demanding full payment of the purchase price within 21 days of that date. The purchasers did not do so. On 15 October 1990 the sellers wrote to the purchasers indicating that if the purchasers did not pay the full purchase price by 19 October 1990 the sellers would exercise their option to resile from the missives. As at 2 November 1990 the purchasers had still not paid the full purchase price. On that date the sellers served a notice on the purchasers resiling from the missives by reason of the purchasers' material breach of contract in failing to pay the full purchase price. The sellers then raised an action against the purchasers concluding for damages in respect of the purchasers' breach of contract. The purchasers argued that the sellers by continuing to deal with the conveyancing aspects of the transaction between July and November 1990 and by expressly allowing the purchasers further time to settle the transaction, had led the purchasers to believe that the original failure to pay the full purchase price by July 1990 was not viewed by the sellers as a material breach of contract, that in the circumstances the sellers had waived any right they might have had to treat the purchasers' original failure to pay the full purchase price as a material breach of contract and that accordingly the sellers were not entitled to resile in reliance upon their notice of 23 July 1990. The sellers challenged the

relevancy of the purchasers' averments in regard to waiver.

Held, that the purchasers' averments were insufficient to instruct waiver in that (a) they failed to make relevant averments of the facts and circumstances from which abandonment might be inferred, and (b) they failed to state that the purchasers had changed their position in reliance upon any such abandonment (pp 894E-H and I); and defences *repelled* so far as relating to waiver and proof on quantum *allowed*.

Armia Ltd v Daejan Developments Ltd, 1979 SLT 147, and *Lousada & Co Ltd v J E Lesser (Properties) Ltd,* 1990 SLT 823, *followed.*

Action of damages

Atlas Assurance Co Ltd raised an action of damages against Dollar Land Holdings plc in respect of the defenders' alleged breach of missives in failing to pay to the pursuers the full purchase price of the heritable subjects known as Magnet House, Waterloo Street, Glasgow. The defenders contended that the pursuers had not been entitled to resile from the missives because by their actings the pursuers had waived their right to do so. The pursuers challenged the relevancy of the defenders' averments quoad waiver.

The case came before the Lord Ordinary (Murray) on procedure roll on the pursuers' fourth plea in law to the relevancy of the averments quoad waiver.

Cases referred to

Armia Ltd v Daejan Developments Ltd, 1979 SLT 147; 1979 SC (HL) 56.
Lousada & Co Ltd v J E Lesser (Properties) Ltd, 1990 SLT 823.

On 16 July 1992 the Lord Ordinary *sustained* the pursuers' fourth plea in law, *repelled* the defenders' first and fourth pleas in law and *allowed* a proof on the remaining averments related to quantum.

LORD MURRAY.—The parties to this action are companies who agreed by missives dated 12 and 19 April 1990 and 1 May 1990 that the pursuers sell and the defenders purchase heritable subjects known as Magnet House, Waterloo Street, Glasgow. The purchase price was to be £3,850,000 and the date of entry 11 June 1990. By qualified acceptances it was provided inter alia that if the full purchase price was not paid within 14 days of the date of entry the pursuers would be entitled to serve a notice on the defenders or their agents calling for full payment of the price within a period of not less than 14 days. If the period in the notice expired without payment it was provided that this would constitute a material breach of contract on the part of the defenders entitling the pursuers to resile at their option from the missives, reserving to the pursuers all claims against the defenders arising from the said breach, including any capital loss and a continuing payment of interest at the contractual rate from the date of entry until resale proceeds were received by the pursuers. The

foregoing narrative was not in issue between the
parties.

In cond 3 the pursuers aver that on 11 June 1990 the
pursuers were ready and willing to give entry to the
defenders in exchange for the purchase price. The
defenders did not pay the purchase price. The pursuers served a notice on the defenders in terms of the
foregoing condition requiring payment of the purchase price within 21 days. Said notice was served on
23 July 1990. The defenders still failed to make
payment of the purchase price. On 15 October 1990
the pursuers sent a further letter to the defenders
indicating that if the defenders did not settle the price
by 19 October 1990 the pursuers would exercise their
option to resile from the missives. The defenders still
had not paid the purchase price by 2 November 1990.
The pursuers therefore served a notice on the
defenders on 2 November 1990 resiling from the
missives by reason of the defenders' material breach of
contract in not paying the purchase price. It was
further averred that the defenders had in any event
been in breach of contract in not paying the purchase
price since 11 June 1990. In reply in ans 3 the
defenders admitted that on 11 June 1990 the defenders
did not pay the purchase price. They admitted that the
pursuers served a notice on the defenders on 23 July
1990, that on 15 October 1990 the pursuers sent a
further letter to the defenders and that the defenders
had not paid the purchase price by 2 November 1990.
It was further admitted that the pursuers had served
a notice on the defenders on 2 November 1990 purporting to resile from the missives in terms of the foregoing condition. After a general denial the defenders
go on to explain and aver "that after the notice of 23
July 1990 was served on the defenders the pursuers
continued to deal with every aspect of the conveyancing necessary to give effect to the contract between
the parties. They proceeded with the transaction in
the normal manner. There were substantial contacts
between the parties' agents. In addition the pursuers
expressly allowed the defenders further time to settle
the transaction. Throughout their dealings with the
defenders and their agents between July and
November 1990 the pursuers conducted themselves
upon the basis that the contract was to go ahead. By
their actings they led the defenders to believe that
their original failure to settle the transaction by July
1990 was not, so far as the pursuers were concerned,
a material breach of contract. In these circumstances
the pursuers waived any right they may have had to
treat the defenders' original failure to pay the price as
a material breach of contract. Accordingly the pursuers were not entitled to resile in reliance upon their
notice of 23 July 1990".

The pursuers in the action sought payment from the
defenders of two separate sums of over £1,000,000 by
way of damages in respect of the alleged breach of contract by the defenders. Both parties tabled pleas to the
merits and to the quantum of any damages which
might be due.

The case came before me in procedure roll in

respect of the pursuers' fourth plea in law which was
in the following terms: "4. The defences being irrelevant et separatim lacking in specification the defences
should be repelled and decree pronounced de plano."

The defenders' first plea in law was a general plea
to the relevancy. This was not insisted upon and the
defenders were content that it be repelled. Despite the
general terms of the pursuers' fourth plea, their
counsel made it clear in opening that this plea was to
be directed solely to excluding from probation the
defenders' averments in ans 3 in regard to waiver, and
to having the defenders' fourth plea in law on waiver
repelled. It was accepted by both parties that whether
or not waiver was excluded a proof on quantum would
be necessary.

Counsel for the pursuers submitted that the averments of waiver were irrelevant and lacking in specification. Nothing was averred which could justify the
inference that the pursuers had abandoned their claim
for due payment as a material part of the contract.
Further the defenders did not aver that they had done
anything on the basis of any such abandonment. Both
elements were required to constitute waiver: see
Armia Ltd v Daejan Developments Ltd, per Lord
Fraser of Tullybelton at 1979 SLT, p 163; and Lord
Keith of Kinkel at pp 164-165. The defenders' averments were insufficient on both counts to meet the
foregoing requirements of waiver. The case of *Armia*
was considered and applied by the Second Division in
Lousada & Co Ltd v J E Lesser (Properties) Ltd. The
circumstances of that case were similar to the present
one with no express abandonment of the claim in
question and no averment that the parties alleging
waiver had altered their position in reliance on the
alleged conduct of the other parties. At pp 827L-828A
the Lord Justice Clerk said: "Senior counsel for the
pursuers founded upon the fact that the defenders had
taken no action to resile after their right to do so came
into existence on 23 August 1983. . . . I am satisfied
that the actings of the defenders between 23 August
1983 and 6 January 1984 are consistent with their
waiting to see whether negotiations were to have a successful outcome while at the same time holding in
reserve their right to resile. I see no ground for
holding that during this period of just over four
months the defenders gave the pursuers any ground
for concluding that they were departing from their
rights."

In the present case equally there were no averments
whatever that the defenders had altered their position
in reliance on waiver by the pursuers. The pursuers'
fourth plea in law should be sustained and the fourth
plea in law for the defenders repelled.

In reply counsel for the defenders emphasised that
the only matter to be argued was the issue of waiver
which was the subject of both parties' fourth pleas.
The defenders were content that their first plea in law
should be repelled. The defenders' position was that
their averments of waiver were sufficient to justify the
issue going to proof. It had to be borne in mind that
averments would not be excluded from probation

A unless, if proved, they were bound to fail. It was accepted in both *Armia* and *Lousada* that abandonment did not need to be express but could be inferred from actings. The key averment for the defenders was where they averred that the pursuers had expressly allowed the defenders further time to settle the transaction. It could not be said by the pursuers that this averment lacked specification since they themselves had averred in cond 3 that on 15 October 1990 they sent a letter indicating that if the defenders did not settle the price by 19 October 1990 the option to resile would be exercised. They also averred in cond 3 that

B after 13 August 1990 there was correspondence between the parties limited, so far as the pursuers were concerned, to demands for settlement of the price. It was clear that the pursuers had expressly departed from the requirement to pay the price within 21 days on at least two specific subsequent dates. The defenders' point on waiver was limited to the notice which had been served on 23 July 1990. The defenders were averring that the intention to resile by

C reason of that notice was what had been waived by the subsequent actings of the pursuers. If the pursuers had been serious about resiling after expiry of the 21 days they should have served a further notice of intention to resile if they were to avoid the defenders changing their position in reliance on the notice of 23 July 1990 which, as a matter of inference, had plainly been abandoned. In these circumstances the pursuers' fourth plea in law should be repelled and proof allowed leaving the defenders' fourth plea standing.

D The sole contentious issue between the parties, as I understand it, is whether the defenders' averments of waiver in ans 3 are relevant to infer waiver to the standard set by *Armia* and *Lousada*. I note at the outset that the defenders say that the pursuers by their actings "led the defenders to believe that their original failure to settle the transaction by July 1990 was not, so far as the pursuers were concerned, a material breach of contract". This averment appears to go beyond what was argued by the defenders' counsel and

E appears to be inaccurate in that, as the pursuers' pleadings make plain, they are founding upon failure to pay on 11 June 1990 which was the contract date. As the authorities cited demonstrate, there are two requirements for relevant averments of waiver. The first is that, in the absence of express abandonment, there should be facts and circumstances averred from which abandonment may be inferred. I interpret this, on the basis of the passage from the Lord Justice Clerk's opinion which was founded upon, as meaning

F that what is averred must be consistent with abandonment and inconsistent with merely suspending the sanction of resiling by the creditor to give the debtor a further opportunity to fulfil the contract. Taking the defenders' averments in ans 3 at their highest, they appear to me to assert that, on expiry of the notice of 23 July on 13 August 1990, a demand for payment was made by the pursuers rather than intimation that they were resiling. Further on 15 October the pursuers sent a letter requiring the defenders to settle the price by 19 October 1990 otherwise the pursuers would resile

G from the contract. This date again passed without the pursuers exercising any option to resile. As the price had still not been paid by 2 November 1990 the inference to be drawn, it was said, was that the pursuers had abandoned their option to resile. Can it be said, on the basis of the test in *Lousada*, that, from these facts and circumstances, it could reasonably be inferred that the pursuers had abandoned their option to resile? An affirmative answer could be given only if these averments were not also consistent with a desire by the pursuers to enforce the contract even at the expense of further delay in payment of the price which

H was due on 11 June 1990. I have reached the view that the averments on which the defenders found are consistent with that alternative interpretation. I would accept that suspension of the exercise of an option to resile could not be protracted for a long period of time without giving rise to a possible inference of abandonment. In this case the suspension of enforcement was from 13 August to 2 November 1990, a period of less than three months, compared with four months in *Lousada*.

I In my view, accordingly, the defenders have failed to make relevant averments of abandonment. Further, careful scrutiny of ans 3 has not enabled me to discern an averment that the defenders changed their position in reliance upon any such abandonment. The most that could be inferred from what they do aver is that they relied upon getting more time to pay the price. I cannot conceive that that is the kind of reliance which would of itself avail a debtor.

J I shall sustain the fourth plea in law for the pursuers, repel the first and fourth pleas in law for the defenders and allow proof.

Counsel for Pursuers, Peebles; Solicitors, Wright, Johnston & Mackenzie — Counsel for Defenders, Keen; Solicitors, J & R A Robertson, WS.

I H L M

K

Cole, Petitioner

OUTER HOUSE
LORD MAYFIELD
23 JULY 1992   L

Process — Commission and diligence — Inspection of premises — Order sought before commencement of proceedings — Whether proceedings likely to be brought — Whether fishing diligence — Administration of Justice (Scotland) Act 1972 (c 59), s 1.

Section 1 of the Administration of Justice (Scotland) Act 1972 empowers the court, inter alia, to order the inspection of property, including land, prior to the raising of any proceedings, on the application of a

A person who appears to the court to be a party to proceedings which are likely to be brought.

A sales engineer, in the course of his employment, had required to visit factory premises of a customer. While on the premises the sales engineer had followed the company's employee to the shop floor. In doing so he fell on two steps behind a door and was injured. Before raising an action of reparation in respect of these injuries he wished to obtain a report from an independent person about the dimensions and construction of the stairs and their position in relation to the doorway. He averred that they were dangerous, were of different sizes and did not have any warning sign. The company opposed the petition, arguing that any inspection was premature and that no inference of negligence could be drawn from the facts of the accident averred.

Held, that the petitioner was entitled to have an inspection carried out for the purpose of enabling him to make more pointed and specific averments, that he had averred in outline a case of negligence and that he had satisfied the test that proceedings were likely to be brought (pp 896K-897A); and order for inspection *granted*.

Petition for order under the Administration of Justice (Scotland) Act 1972, s 1

David Ian Cole presented a petition under s 1 of the Administration of Justice (Scotland) Act 1972 for an order for inspection of property occupied by Weir Pumps Ltd in respect of injuries which he sustained while visiting the property. The respondents opposed the granting of an order.

The case came before the Lord Ordinary (Mayfield).

Statutory provisions

The Administration of Justice (Scotland) Act 1972, as amended, provides:

"1.—(1) Without prejudice to the existing powers of the Court of Session and of the sheriff court, those courts shall have power, subject to the provisions of subsection (4) of this section, to order the inspection, photographing, preservation, custody and detention of documents and other property (including, where appropriate, land) which appear to the court to be property as to which any question may relevantly arise in any existing civil proceedings before that court or in civil proceedings which are likely to be brought, and to order the production and recovery of any such property, the taking of samples thereof and the carrying out of any experiment thereon or therewith.

"(1A) Without prejudice to the existing powers of the Court of Session and of the sheriff court, those courts shall have power, subject to subsection (4) of this section, to order any person to disclose such information as he has as to the identity of any persons who appear to the court to be persons who — (a) might be witnesses in any existing civil proceedings before that court or in civil proceedings which are likely to be

brought; (b) might be defenders in any civil proceedings which appear to the court to be likely to be brought.

"(2) Notwithstanding any rule of law or practice to the contrary, the court may exercise the powers mentioned in subsection (1) or (1A) of this section — (a) where proceedings have been commenced, on the application at any time after such commencement, of a party to or minuter in the proceedings, or any other person who appears to the court to have an interest to be joined as such party or minuter; (b) where proceedings have not been commenced, on the application at any time of a person who appears to the court to be likely to be a party to or minuter in proceedings which are likely to be brought, unless there is special reason why the application should not be granted."

Cases referred to

Civil Service Building Society v Macdougall, 1988 SLT 687.
Moore v Greater Glasgow Health Board, 1979 SLT 42; 1978 SC 123.
Smith, Petitioner, 1985 SLT 461.
Thorne v Strathclyde Regional Council, 1984 SLT 161.

On 23 July 1992 the Lord Ordinary *granted* the prayer of the petition.

LORD MAYFIELD.—The Administration of Justice (Scotland) Act 1972, as amended, provides: [his Lordship quoted the terms of s 1 of the Act set out supra and continued:]

David Ian Cole, residing at 88 Dryden Road, Low Fell, Gateshead, has presented a petition for an order. He is employed by Mitchell Bearings as a sales engineer. The respondents are Weir Pumps Ltd who have a place of business at Alloa Works, Alloa. The petitioner averred that on 18 April 1991 he was working in the course of his employment. He was required to attend on a Mr J Kennedy employed by the respondents. The petitioner visited Mr Kennedy in his office on the first floor of the office block at Alloa Works, Alloa. They both left and the petitioner followed said Kennedy down a flight of stairs which led to the shop floor. At the foot of said stairs there was a doorway which opened inwards for persons going down the stairs. The petitioner followed said Kennedy through. As he did so he fell on two steps which were behind the doorway and as a result sustained injury.

He has averred that he believes that the accident occurred because the steps behind the door were dangerous. There was no sign or other warning of their existence. He wished to raise an action for reparation in respect of his injuries in order to make his averments more specific and in particular to ascertain the precise mechanism of his fall. He has averred that it is necessary, or in any event advisable, to have a report from an independent person. The said stairs were accordingly property as to which a question may relevantly arise in civil proceedings which are likely to

A be brought. The petitioner's solicitors have requested the respondents to allow facilities for inspection, investigation, tests and photographs. The respondents have refused.

In their answers the respondents admit that the petitioner visited Mr Kennedy, and that he followed Mr Kennedy down a flight of stairs which led to the front door of the office and from there to the shop floor. It was admitted that there was a doorway which opened inwards for persons going down the stairs and that the petitioner followed Mr Kennedy through the

B doorway. The respondents called upon the petitioner to specify or at least to set out his recollection of the way in which he came to fall on the two steps in the manner in which it is alleged the petitioner sustained injuries. It was averred that the petitioner did not lose consciousness. They admit that there was no sign or other warning of the existence of the steps. They called upon the petitioner to specify why he cannot aver the precise mechanism of his fall. He was also

C called upon to specify whether he claimed that the steps themselves were dangerous or merely their presence behind the said door.

In response the petitioner avers that he is not employed at the premises and was not familiar with the steps, nor was he familiar with the flight of stairs where the accident occurred. He does not know the precise position of the steps in relation to the doorway, nor precisely the condition of the steps. He also avers that there is no sign or notice posted to indicate the

D steps were present immediately beyond the doorway. On passing through the doorway, the petitioner missed his footing on the steps. He believes and avers that the first step was not the same size as the second and that he stumbled in consequence. In any event the petitioner did not expect the said steps to be where they were. After the accident the petitioner was in pain and went downstairs and made no inspection of the steps or doorway. He intended to instruct a health and safety consultant to carry out the inspection,

E investigation, test and photographing of said property. The respondents have averred that any inspection is premature and could relevantly and properly be undertaken once any civil proceedings are commenced and when the petitioner had relevantly averred breaches of duty on the part of the respondents. The petitioner is called upon to state why the consultant required to carry out an inspection on the matters described by the petitioner and is called upon to specify what tests and investigation are proposed and

F why those should be carried out by a health and safety consultant. The reply to that averment was that the consultant would be instructed to examine the dimensions and construction of the steps and their position in relation to the doorway. He would be required to consider the petitioner's line of vision; the effectiveness of any warning signs or notices, had they been posted; and the design and condition of the steps.

I was referred to a number of cases. Counsel for the petitioner referred to *Thorne v Strathclyde Regional Council* and *Smith, Petr*. In those cases applications

were made to the court before the commencement of proceedings. *Thorne* was a case relating to inspection G of property. It was submitted that the facts in that case were similar to the circumstances of the present case. In *Thorne* an employee was injured in an accident involving a particular machine. He sought an order under the Act for inspection of the machine, averring that it was necessary and advisable to enable a proper assessment to be made of the particular pieces of the machine. Granting the order sought, Lord Cowie referred to well settled principles governing the grant or refusal of a diligence for the recovery of documents H at the adjustment stage of the pleadings. See Lord Cameron in *Moore v Greater Glasgow Health Board*, 1979 SLT at p 44. I agree with the view expressed by Lord Cowie in *Thorne* that the same principles apply to the inspection, photographing and experimenting on a piece of property in the possession of prospective defenders. Counsel for the petitioner submitted that there were sufficient averments to show that proceedings were likely to be brought and that the petitioner was entitled to have the premises inspected for the I purpose of enabling him to make more pointed or more specific averments in support of the case already outlined (as in *Moore*). He referred to *Civil Service Building Society v Macdougall* where it was held that a diligence be granted to enable the building society to make more pointed or more specific what they had already averred. In reaching that conclusion the court applied *Moore*. Counsel for the respondents submitted that the pleadings did not disclose a prima facie case; they did not support the requirements of s 1 (2) (b) of J the Act. It was also submitted that in effect the application was a fishing diligence and in any event the scope of the petition was too wide. In contrast to *Thorne* he maintained that no inference of negligence could be drawn from the facts of the accident as averred. The inspection was not necessary because the absence of the sign or warning was admitted. The circumstances did not reveal the necessity for an inspection by a health and safety expert. He submitted further that if the second step was different as averred K the incident had obviously happened at that stage. Accordingly the absence of a sign had no relevance.

I have come to the conclusion that I should grant the order. On a proper reading of the petitioner's averments I am satisfied that he was entitled to have an inspection carried out in the manner set out for the purpose of enabling him to make more pointed and more specific the case than already averred.

I reject also the view that the application should be L regarded as a fishing diligence. In *Civil Service Building Society* the Lord Justice Clerk described a fishing diligence as one for which there was no basis in the averments. The basis of the averments in this case is that there was no sign or warning in relation to the steps and the location of the two steps of different dimensions in relation to a door which opened towards the person proceeding down the steps. The petitioner has also stated that he did not work in that particular building and was a visitor there. Further he was injured as a result of the accident. The layout was not

A familiar to him. Accordingly in my view he has averred in outline a case of negligence where a report by an expert might enable the pleadings to be made more specific. I am accordingly satisfied that the petitioner has satisfied the statutory requirements, in particular s 1 (2) (b) of the Act. In these circumstances I shall grant the prayer of the petition.

B *Counsel for Petitioner, Allardice; Solicitors, Robin Thompson & Partners — Counsel for Respondent, R N Thomson; Solicitors, Simpson & Marwick, WS.*

C A G M

McCluskey v HM Advocate

HIGH COURT OF JUSTICIARY

C THE LORD JUSTICE CLERK (ROSS), LORDS SUTHERLAND AND WYLIE

25 SEPTEMBER 1992

Justiciary — Procedure — Prevention of delay — 80 day rule — Indictment served within 80 day period not called but second indictment served outwith period — Accused detained in custody after first indictment fell — Whether proceedings on second indictment fundamentally null —
D *Criminal Procedure (Scotland) Act 1975 (c 21), s 101 (2) (a).*

Section 101 (2) (a) of the Criminal Procedure (Scotland) Act 1975 provides that an accused person who is committed for an offence until liberated in due course of law shall not be detained by virtue of that committal for a total period of more than 80 days unless within that period the indictment is served on him, which failing he shall be liberated forthwith.

E An accused person was committed until liberated in due course of law in custody on 6 November 1991. He was thereafter served with an indictment which called for trial in the High Court on 17 February 1992 when on a co-accused's motion the trial was adjourned to a sitting commencing on 16 March 1992 and the 110 day period was extended to 4 April 1992. The diet was not called on 16 March 1992 but the accused continued to be detained in custody. A second indictment had been served on the accused on 27 February 1992. At the commencement of the trial it was objected that
F the proceedings were fundamentally null because the indictment on which the Crown relied had been served in breach of s 101 (2) (a) of the 1975 Act. The trial judge repelled the objection and the accused proceeded to trial. On the second day of the trial the accused pled guilty and thereafter appealed against conviction on the ground that the trial judge had wrongly repelled his objection.

Held, (1) that s 101 dealt with the prevention of delay in trials and subs (2) (a) with the liberation of accused persons who had been detained for a parti-

cular period of time, and not with the validity of an G indictment, and the trial judge had accordingly reached the right decision (p 898I-K); and appeal *refused.*

HM Advocate v Walker, 1981 SLT (Notes) 111, *followed.*

Indictment

James McCluskey was charged along with another person at the instance of the rt hon the Lord Fraser of H Carmyllie, Her Majesty's Advocate on an indictment with attempted murder and contraventions of ss 1 (1) (a), 4 (4) and 17 (2) and (5) of the Firearms Act 1968 and s 1 (3) (b) of the Bail etc (Scotland) Act 1980. The indictment called for trial before Lord Penrose in the High Court at Glasgow when the accused stated a preliminary objection to the proceedings on the ground that the indictment had been served in breach of s 101 (2) (a) of the Criminal Procedure (Scotland) Act 1975. The trial judge repelled the objection and I on the second day of trial the accused pled guilty.

The accused appealed against conviction by note of appeal. The facts giving rise to the appeal appear from the opinion of the court.

Statutory provisions

The Criminal Procedure (Scotland) Act 1975 provides:

"101.— . . . (2) Subject to subsections (3), (4) and (5) J below, an accused who is committed for any offence until liberated in due course of law shall not be detained by virtue of that committal for a total period of more than — (a) 80 days, unless within that period the indictment is served on him, which failing he shall be liberated forthwith".

Case referred to

Advocate (HM) v Walker, 1981 SLT (Notes) 111; 1981 JC 102; 1981 SCCR 154. K

Appeal

The note of appeal contained the following grounds:

(1) Not brought to trial within 110 days or within any extended period as required by s 101 (2) (a) of the Criminal Procedure (Scotland) Act 1975.

(2) Indictment served outside the 80 day period required by law on remand prisoners. The Crown failed to obtain an extension to the 80 days required L to serve any further indictments whilst I was in custody and on 27 February 1992 served a different indictment with an amended charge 1 and with additional charges. The 80 day period had expired on 24 January 1992 and the second indictment was rendered invalid.

The appeal was argued before the High Court on 25 September 1992.

Eo die the court *refused* the appeal.

The following opinion of the court was delivered by
A the Lord Justice Clerk (Ross):

OPINION OF THE COURT.—The appellant is
James McCluskey. In the course of trial in the High
Court in Glasgow he pled guilty to certain charges on
the indictment. He has now appealed against conviction. The appeal is based upon a submission which
was made before the trial commenced to the effect that
proceedings on the indictment before him were null,
and, putting the matter shortly, the submission was
that there was no valid indictment before the court.
B The trial judge rejected that submission and as we say
the trial proceeded. But it is this issue which it is
sought to raise again in the appeal against conviction.

Counsel for the appellant has drawn attention to the
relative dates which are material and these are indeed
set out clearly by the trial judge in his report. He tells
us that the history of the matter was as follows. The
appellant appeared on petition on 30 October 1991
when he was committed for further examination. He
C was fully committed in custody on 6 November 1991.
The 80 day period for service of an indictment accordingly expired on 25 January 1992. An indictment was
served and called for trial at a sitting of the court commencing on 17 February 1992. On the first day of the
trial at that sitting of the court and on the motion of
the second accused the trial was adjourned to a sitting
commencing on 16 March 1992. The 110 day period
was extended to 4 April 1992. Apparently the case was
not called at the sitting commencing 16 March 1992
D and the instance accordingly fell at the conclusion of
that sitting. The appellant however remained in
custody. On 27 February 1992 a second indictment
was served. As we have noted, at the commencement
of the trial counsel for the appellant raised as a
preliminary matter the question of whether the
proceedings were fundamentally null. The submission
was that there was not a valid indictment, the indictment on which the Crown relied having been served
in breach of s 101 (2) (a) of the Criminal Procedure
E (Scotland) Act 1975. This motion was resisted by the
Crown.

The trial judge informs us that the Crown accepted
as accurate the history of the procedure which we have
just stated, but contended that the provision relied on
by the appellant, namely s 101 (2) (a) of the Act of
1975, was concerned exclusively with the right of the
appellant to liberation and was not concerned with any
question as to the validity of an indictment. The
Crown accordingly contended that if the appellant had
F been unlawfully detained he might have a civil remedy
in damages, but that the Act of 1975 did not provide
him with protection from prosecution upon a further
indictment.

Counsel for the appellant in presenting his submissions sought to rely upon *HM Advocate v Walker*.
That case related to the legality of the continued
detention of an accused in circumstances in which the
only indictment served within the 80 day period had
fallen. A second indictment was served outwith the
time limit and the sheriff had accordingly ordered the

liberation of the accused. That decision was sustained
by the court. But it appears to us from what was stated G
by the court in the court's opinion that it was plain
that the court took the view that it would have been
competent for fresh proceedings on indictment to have
been raised. In the course of that opinion the following
passage appears (1981 SLT (Notes) at p 112): "When
the peremptory diet of 11 May 1981 did not call the
instance fell and that was the end of those proceedings.
The Crown, if so advised, could start fresh proceedings but these would require to begin ab initio and
part of the procedure which had been instituted by the H
original indictment but which had fallen with the
instance could not be imported into and held to be
part of the proceedings under the subsequent
indictment."

In our opinion that passage makes it quite clear that
fresh proceedings could be taken and that if they were
taken the procedure under the earlier indictment
would not be imported into the later proceedings. Yet
that is precisely what counsel for the appellant is
endeavouring to persuade us should be done in the I
present case. Counsel maintained that his client had
been disadvantaged by the actions of the Crown and
that he had been deprived of a remedy under the
criminal law.

If the Act of 1975 does not afford him a remedy then
if he has a remedy at all it must be under the civil law.
When regard is had to the terms of s 101 of the Act
of 1975 it is significant that this is a section dealing
with prevention of delay in trials. When one looks at
s 101 (2) (a) it is plain that the section is concerned J
with liberation of accused persons who have been
detained for a particular period of time and we are not
persuaded that the section is concerned with such
questions as the validity of an indictment. There is
nothing in the language of the section to suggest that
it is concerned with any such question. It follows that
we are satisfied that the trial judge reached the right
decision upon this matter which was raised before him
as a preliminary matter and it follows that counsel has
been unable to persuade us that there is a good ground K
of appeal in this case. There is nothing to cause us to
conclude that there has been a miscarriage of justice
and the appeal against conviction is accordingly
refused.

---

*Counsel for Appellant, McVicar; Solicitors, John G
Gray & Co, SSC (for Anthony Mahon & Co, Glasgow)
— Counsel for Respondent, Macdonald, QC, A D; Soli-* L
citor, J D Lowe, Crown Agent.

P W F

Guthrie v Friel

A HIGH COURT OF JUSTICIARY

THE LORD JUSTICE CLERK (ROSS),
LORDS GRIEVE AND WYLIE

29 SEPTEMBER 1992

*Justiciary — Statutory offence — Attempting to drive
while unfit through drink — Accused unconscious at 2.50
am in driver's seat wearing seatbelt with engine running
and dipped headlights on — Accused in habit of sleeping*
B *overnight in car — Whether sufficient to establish
attempted driving — Road Traffic Act 1988 (c 52), s 5
(1) (a) and (b).*

An accused person was charged on a summary complaint with attempting to drive or alternatively being
in charge of a motor vehicle while unfit through drink
contrary to s 5 (1) (a) or 5 (1) (b) of the Road Traffic
Act 1988. The evidence disclosed that the accused's
car was stationary at about 2.50 am at the kerb of the
street approximately 50 yds from a club where the
C accused had been drinking and approximately 100 yds
from the cemetery where he worked as a gravedigger.
At that period the accused usually slept overnight in
his car, normally within the cemetery grounds. The
accused was in the driving seat with his seatbelt
fastened. All the doors were closed but the driver's
window was open. The engine was running and the
headlights were switched on in a dipped position. The
accused was slumped forward, unconscious, with his
head resting on the steering wheel. The sheriff con-
D victed the accused of attempting to drive. The accused
appealed, contending that the evidence did not justify
such a finding.

Held, that the accused's action might show that he
was preparing to drive but fell short of establishing
that he was attempting to drive (p 901B-C); and appeal
allowed, conviction *quashed* and case *remitted* to the
sheriff to consider the alternative charge.

E **Summary complaint**

Alastair Guthrie was charged at the instance of
James D Friel, procurator fiscal, Paisley, on a
summary complaint which contained the following
charges: "on 9 June 1991 on a road or other public
place, namely West Campbell Street, Paisley, you
Alastair Guthrie did drive a motor vehicle, namely a
motor car registered number A494 RUS, after consuming so much alcohol that the proportion of it in
F your breath was 47 microgrammes of alcohol in 100
millilitres of breath which exceeded the prescribed
limit, namely 35 microgrammes of alcohol in 100
millilitres of breath; contrary to the Road Traffic Act
1988, s 5 (1) (a); *or alternatively*: on 9 June 1991, you
Alastair Guthrie were in charge of a motor vehicle,
namely said motor car registered number A494 RUS,
which was on a road or other public place, namely
West Campbell Street, Paisley, after consuming so
much alcohol that the proportion of it in your breath
was 47 microgrammes of alcohol in 100 millilitres of
breath which exceeded the prescribed limit, namely 35

microgrammes of alcohol in 100 millilitres of breath;
contrary to the Road Traffic Act 1988, s 5 (1) (b)". G

Before evidence was led the Crown were granted
leave to amend the first alternative charge by adding
"or attempt to drive" after the word "drive". After
trial the sheriff (P Ballance) convicted the accused.

The accused appealed by way of stated case to the
High Court against the decision of the sheriff.

Findings in fact

The sheriff found the following facts to be admitted H
or proved, inter alia:

(1) On 9 June 1991 the appellant's car registered
number A494 RUS was stationary in the early hours
of the morning facing west at the south kerb of West
Campbell Street, Paisley. (2) Immediately to the west
the said street bends sharply to the left with a high
wall on the outside of the bend. (3) The said locus is
approximately 50 yds from the St Mirren Club, and
approximately 100 yds from a cemetery where the I
appellant was employed as a gravedigger. (4) The
appellant was at this period usually sleeping overnight
in his said car, normally within the grounds of the said
cemetery. The bothy in the said cemetery is unsuitable
for sleeping in. (5) On the evening of 8 June 1991 the
appellant visited the said St Mirren Club where he
consumed alcohol. (6) At approximately 2.50 am on 9
June 1991, Constables Roy Hadden and James Quinn
were on uniformed mobile patrol in the area, and saw
the said car. (7) The appellant was in the driving seat
with his seat belt fastened. All doors were closed but J
the driver's window was open. (8) The engine was
running, and the headlights were switched on, in the
dipped position. (9) The appellant was slumped
forward unconscious with his head resting on the
steering wheel. (10) At some time before the said
police officers found him, the appellant had attempted
to drive the said car, but had been unable to do so,
having been overcome by sleep.

Statutory provisions   K

The Road Traffic Act 1988 provides:

"5.—(1) If a person — (a) drives or attempts to drive
a motor vehicle on a road or other public place, or (b)
is in charge of a motor vehicle on a road or other
public place, after consuming so much alcohol that the
proportion of it in his breath, blood or urine exceeds
the prescribed limit he is guilty of an offence.

"(2) It is a defence for a person charged with an
offence under subsection (1) (b) above to prove that at L
the time he is alleged to have committed the offence
the circumstances were such that there was no likelihood of his driving the vehicle whilst the proportion
of alcohol in his breath, blood or urine remained likely
to exceed the prescribed limit."

Cases referred to
Ames v MacLeod, 1969 JC 1.
McArthur v Valentine, 1990 SLT 732; 1990 JC 146;
  1989 SCCR 704.

Appeal

A   The sheriff posed the following questions for the opinion of the High Court, inter alia:

(1) On the evidence led by the Crown, was I entitled to repel the appellant's submission that there was no case to answer?

(2) On the basis of the evidence led and accepted, and on the basis of findings 7, 8 and 9, was I entitled to make finding 10?

(5) On the findings, was I entitled to convict the
B   appellant of the first alternative charge?

The appeal was argued before the High Court on 22 July 1992.

On 29 September 1992 the court *answered* the questions in the *negative, allowed* the appeal and *quashed* the conviction but *remitted* to the sheriff to consider the alternative charge.

C   The following opinion of the court was delivered by the Lord Justice Clerk (Ross):

OPINION OF THE COURT.—The appellant is Alastair Guthrie who went to trial in the sheriff court at Paisley on a summary complaint containing two charges expressed as alternatives. The complaint was in the following terms: [his Lordship quoted the terms of the complaint set out supra and continued:]

Before evidence was led the procurator fiscal depute
D   sought and obtained leave to amend the complaint by inserting the words "or attempt to drive" after the word "drive" in the main charge. Evidence was given by two police officers, and at the conclusion of the evidence of the second police officer the procurator fiscal depute sought leave to amend the complaint further by deleting "47" and inserting "46" before the word "microgrammes" in both the main charge and the alternative charge. The motion to amend was opposed by the solicitor for the appellant, but the
E   sheriff allowed the amendment to be made.

At the conclusion of the Crown evidence, the solicitor for the appellant made a submission that there was no case to answer. In relation to the main charge, the submission was that if a person was found asleep in a motor car, that was a classic prima facie case of being in charge, but not of driving, and because he is asleep, not of attempting to drive. He conceded that it might at most illustrate antecedent intent to drive. The solicitor also presented a second submission covering
F   both the main charge and the alternative charge upon the question of whether the Crown had offered sufficient proof that the appellant, in view of the Camic reading being below 50 microgrammes, was properly offered the alternative of providing blood or urine. The submission of no case to answer was rejected by the sheriff.

In his application for a stated case, the appellant intimated three grounds of appeal. The third ground of appeal related to the issue of whether the Crown had proved by corroborated evidence that the appel-
lant had been allowed the opportunity of claiming the right to have the specimens replaced by specimens of   G   blood or urine, but counsel for the appellant informed this court that he did not propose to argue that point. He did however address the court on the other two grounds of appeal which related to the issue of whether the sheriff had been entitled to infer that the appellant was, at the material time, attempting to drive.

The basis for these submissions can be seen in the findings in fact. On the date libelled in the charge the appellant's car was stationary in the early hours of the   H   morning at the south kerb of West Campbell Street, Paisley. The place where the car was situated was approximately 50 yds from the St Mirren Club and approximately 100 yds from a cemetery where the appellant was employed as a gravedigger. Finding 4 is in the following terms: [his Lordship quoted its terms and continued:]

The findings also record that on the previous evening the appellant had visited the St Mirren Club   I   where he had consumed alcohol. At about 2.50 am on the date libelled two police officers saw the car. The appellant was in the driving seat with his seat belt fastened. All doors were closed but the driver's window was opened. The engine was running, and the headlights were switched on, in the dipped position. The appellant was slumped forward unconscious with his head resting on the steering wheel.

Finding 10 is in the following terms: [his Lordship quoted its terms and continued:] There is a question   J   in the case asking whether the sheriff was entitled to make that finding.

Counsel accepted as a general proposition that the court would be entitled to infer that a driver was attempting to drive when he had been found in hours of darkness in the driving seat with his seat belt fastened, with the engine running and with the headlights on. But he maintained that the situation was different here where the appellant was found to be   K   unconscious or asleep. Counsel pointed out that in the course of his note the sheriff expressed his view as follows: "I formed the strong impression that the appellant had been about to drive off when he fell asleep, and it seemed to me that the Crown had established the first alternative charge".

Counsel submitted that the test was not whether the sheriff had formed some particular impression, and he submitted that it was not clear what basis there was for finding 10. At the end of the day his submission was   L   that on the basis of all the evidence as disclosed in the findings, the sheriff was not entitled to infer that the appellant had been attempting to drive.

The advocate depute accepted that whether the appellant had been attempting to drive the car at the time was a nice question. Under reference to *Ames v MacLeod* and *McArthur v Valentine,* he submitted that a person was driving a car where he was in a substantial sense controlling the movement and direction of the car. He accordingly submitted that for a person to be attempting to drive a car he must be attempting to direct the movement and control of the vehicle.

The advocate depute accepted that at the time when the police officers came upon the car, the appellant was not attempting to drive, but he maintained that in view of what the police officers found it was reasonable to conclude that at an earlier stage he had been attempting to drive. In view of the fact that the engine was running, the headlights were on and the safety belt was fastened it was clear that at some time before the police officers had arrived the appellant had been attempting to drive.

Although there is undoubted force in this submission made by the advocate depute, we have come to the conclusion that the sheriff was not entitled to draw the inference that at an earlier stage the appellant had been attempting to drive. Whether or not an individual has reached the stage of attempting to drive must depend upon the particular circumstances. It has often been observed that before a charge of attempting to do something can be established, the individual must have passed from mere preparation to perpetration. We have come to the conclusion that the appellant's action in starting the engine, turning on the headlights and fastening the seat belt, might show that he was preparing to drive, but fell short of what would be necessary to establish that he was attempting to drive. It might have been different if the appellant's actions had gone further and, for example if in addition to starting the engine, switching on the lights and fastening the seat belt, he had put the handbrake off. But that was not the position.

Quite apart from that, in the present case there is the specialty that the appellant usually slept overnight in his car. Admittedly that was normally within the grounds of the cemetery, but the finding that this took place normally within the grounds of the cemetery shows that it did not invariably take place within the cemetery grounds. The locus was only 100 yds away from the cemetery, and the finding, that he usually slept overnight in the car, makes it more difficult to draw the inference that he was attempting to drive on this occasion when he was found in the car asleep.

In the very special circumstances of this case, when all material facts are taken into account, we have come to the conclusion that the sheriff was not entitled to repel the submission of no case to answer in relation to the main charge. After the submission of no case to answer was rejected by the sheriff the appellant gave evidence, and he stated that he did not remember fastening the seat belt. His explanation was that he had the headlights on because they would reflect off a wall some 15 yds ahead and the interior light was faulty; he wanted to roll a cigarette, and he put the engine on to warm himself up and dry his damp clothing. He stated that it was his intention to switch the engine off and to climb into the back seat in order to go to sleep. The sheriff comments that the appellant's assertion that he turned on the engine to warm himself was at variance with the window being opened, and he considered that the fact that he had his seat belt

fastened was hardly consistent with an intention to warm himself up and then climb into the back seat. We appreciate the force of these observations, but we are of opinion that there was insufficient evidence led by the Crown to justify the appellant's conviction of the main charge, and that the submission of no case to answer should have been sustained.

We are accordingly satisfied that the first, second and fifth questions in the case should be answered in the negative.

In the event of our answering that question in the negative, the advocate depute submitted that a question would then arise as to whether the appellant had been guilty of the alternative charge under s 5 (1) (b) of the Act of 1988. He reminded us that in terms of s 452A (1) (c) of the Criminal Procedure (Scotland) Act 1975 it would be open to the court to set aside the verdict of the sheriff and substitute therefor an amended verdict of guilty of the alternative charge. However the advocate depute recognised that s 5 (2) of the Act of 1988 provides a defence to a charge under s 5 (1) (b). That subsection provides: [his Lordship quoted the terms of s 5 (2) and continued:]

It appears that in making his final submissions to the sheriff the solicitor for the appellant drew the sheriff's attention to this defence, but since the sheriff convicted the appellant of the main charge it was unnecessary for him to reach any conclusion upon the issue of whether the defence under s 5 (2) had been established.

Accordingly having answered questions 1, 2 and 5 in the negative, we shall remit the case to the sheriff in order that he can consider the alternative charge and any defence under s 5 (2) of the Road Traffic Act 1988.

Counsel for Appellant, Baird; Solicitors, Drummond Miller, WS (for Cameron, Pinkerton & Co, Renfrew) — Counsel for Respondent, Macdonald, QC, A D; Solicitor, J D Lowe, Crown Agent.

P W F

McCulloch v Scott

HIGH COURT OF JUSTICIARY

THE LORD JUSTICE CLERK (ROSS), LORDS SUTHERLAND AND WYLIE

14 OCTOBER 1992

Justiciary — Procedure — Summary procedure — Adjournment — Accused pleading guilty to speeding and requesting proof in mitigation for totting up provisions under Road Traffic Offenders Act 1988 — Justice adjourning diet for period exceeding three weeks at accused's request — Whether adjournment incompetent — Criminal Procedure (Scotland) Act 1975 (c 21), s 380 (1).

Section 380 (1) of the Criminal Procedure (Scotland) Act 1975 provides that after a person has been convicted or the court has found that he committed the offence and before he has been sentenced or otherwise dealt with, the court may adjourn the case for "the purpose of enabling inquiries to be made or of determining the most suitable method of dealing with his case", provided that a court shall not for that purpose adjourn the hearing of a case for any single period exceeding three weeks.

An accused person was charged in the district court with speeding and pled guilty on 2 July 1992. The justice then adjourned the case for sentence and for a hearing on special reasons until 4 August 1992. When the case called on that date the accused objected to further proceedings on the ground that sentence had been deferred for a period in excess of three weeks and that the proceedings were accordingly incompetent. The justice overruled the objection and proceeded to sentence. The accused sought suspension of the sentence. The Crown opposed the bill on the grounds that the terms of s 380 (1) were not mandatory but merely directory and that, in any event, the deferral was for the purpose of a proof in mitigation in relation to possible disqualification under s 35 of the Road Traffic Offenders Act 1988 and that accordingly s 380 (1) did not apply.

Held, (1) that since the proviso had importance from the point of view of limiting the period within which an accused might be remanded in custody whilst inquiries were made, the language of the proviso was mandatory (p 903H-I); (2) that an adjournment for a proof in mitigation could properly be regarded as an adjournment for the purpose of enabling inquiries to be made or at least for the purpose of enabling the court to determine the appropriate method of dealing with the accused's case, and accordingly the adjournment was in breach of the provisions of s 380 (1) and was incompetent (pp 903K-904A); and bill *passed* and sentence *suspended*.

Wilson v Donald, 1993 SLT 31, *applied*.

Observed, that although the adjournment had been at the request of the accused's solicitor, the Crown did not suggest that the accused could waive or had waived compliance with the provisions of s 380 (1) (p 904A).

Bill of suspension

Richard Stewart McCulloch brought a bill of suspension against George E Scott, procurator fiscal, Falkirk, praying the High Court of Justiciary to suspend a pretended sentence dated 4 August 1992 whereby the justice imposed a fine of £80, ordered endorsation of the complainer's driving licence with three penalty points and disqualified him for a period of six months for a contravention of reg 3 of the Motorways Traffic (Speed Limit) Regulations 1974.

Statement of facts and pleas in law

The bill and the answers were in the following terms:

Stat 1. That the complainer was charged by the respondent that on 19 February 1992, on the M876 Kincardine Bridge/Dennyloanhead motorway, Larbert, near North Broomage sliproad overbridge, he did drive a motor vehicle, namely, motor car, registration G556 KMS at a speed greater than 70 miles per hour, namely, at 92 miles per hour, contrary to the aforementioned regulations and Act. The complainer pled guilty and appeared at Falkirk district court on 2 July 1992. A hearing in mitigation on the complainer's circumstances relating to a disqualification under the "totting up procedure" was fixed for 4 August 1992.

Ans 1. Admitted. The minute of 2 July 1992 states: "The court adjourned the diet for sentence and for hearing on special reasons until 4 August 1992 at 10.00 am." The adjournment was in fact for the purpose of a proof in mitigation under s 35 of the Road Traffic Offenders Act 1988. On 2 July 1992 the complainer took no objection to the competency of the adjournment.

Stat 2. That at the hearing on 4 August, the complainer's agent objected to further proceedings on the basis that sentence had been deferred for a period in excess of three weeks and that the proceedings were, therefore, incompetent. The . . . justices overruled the complainer's agent and the hearing in mitigation continued and as a result the complainer was sentenced, as hereinbefore condescended upon.

Ans 2. Admitted.

The plea in law for the complainer was as follows:

Sentence having been deferred in these proceedings for a period in excess of three weeks, the proceedings on 4 August were incompetent and the proceedings and sentence should be set aside.

The plea in law for the respondent was as follows:

The proceedings on 4 August 1992 being according to law, the prayer of the bill should be refused.

Statutory provisions

The Criminal Procedure (Scotland) Act 1975 provides:

"380.—(1) It is hereby declared that the power of a court to adjourn the hearing of a case includes power, after a person has been convicted or the court has found that he committed the offence and before he has been sentenced or otherwise dealt with, to adjourn the case for the purpose of enabling inquiries to be made or of determining the most suitable method of dealing with his case and where the court so adjourns the case it shall remand the accused in custody or on bail or ordain him to appear at the adjourned diet; Provided that a court shall not for the purpose aforesaid adjourn the hearing of a case for any single period exceeding three weeks."

Cases referred to

Advocate (HM) v Graham, 1985 SLT 498; 1985 SCCR 169.

Wilson v Donald, 1993 SLT 31; 1992 SCCR 654.

The bill was argued before the High Court on 23
A September 1992.

On 14 October 1992 the court *passed* the bill and
suspended the sentence.

The following opinion of the court was delivered by
the Lord Justice Clerk (Ross):

OPINION OF THE COURT.—This is a bill of
suspension in which the complainer is Richard
Stewart McCulloch, and the respondent is the procu-
B rator fiscal, Falkirk. The complainer was charged by
the respondent with a speeding offence. In answer to
the complaint containing the charge, the complainer
pled guilty at Falkirk district court on 2 July 1992. In
the statement of facts for the complainer it is averred
that a hearing in mitigation on the complainer's
circumstances relating to possible disqualification
under the "totting up procedure" was fixed for 4
August 1992. At the hearing on 4 August 1992, the
complainer's solicitor objected to further proceedings
C on the ground that sentence had been deferred on 2
July 1992 for a period in excess of three weeks, and
that accordingly the proceedings were incompetent.
The objection was overruled by the justice, and after
hearing evidence for the complainer, the court proceeded to sentence. The complainer was fined £80,
three penalty points were ordered to be endorsed on
his licence, and under the totting up procedure he was
disqualified from driving for a period of six months.

D   In this bill of suspension, the complainer seeks to
suspend the sentence imposed by the justice. As is
made clear in the plea in law for the complainer, the
ground upon which suspension is sought is that sentence had been deferred for a period in excess of three
weeks, making any further proceedings incompetent.

In moving the court to pass the bill, counsel for the
complainer drew attention to the provisions of s 380
(1) of the Criminal Procedure (Scotland) Act 1975.
That section provides as follows: [his Lordship quoted
E the terms of s 380 (1) and continued:]

Under reference to *Wilson v Donald*, counsel for the
complainer submitted that the language of s 380 (1)
covered an adjournment which was made for the
purpose of hearing mitigation in relation to possible
disqualification under the totting up procedure. He
accordingly submitted that the imposition of a sentence by the justice on 4 August 1992 was incompetent. He explained that there was a tendency in
some courts to adjourn for a period in excess of three
F weeks because of the time which it took to obtain
documentation from the DVLC.

The Solicitor General pointed out that the minutes
of procedure contained the following record of what
had taken place on 2 July 1992: "The accused in
answer to the complaint pled guilty, said plea being
made by said solicitor on behalf of the accused. The
court adjourned the diet for sentence and for hearing
on special reasons until 4 August 1992 at 10 am."

The Solicitor General explained that this showed

that the adjournment was in fact for the purpose of a
proof in mitigation under s 35 of the Road Traffic G
Offenders Act 1988. He stressed that the adjournment
had been at the request of the complainer's solicitor.
At the hearing on 2 July 1992, after it became apparent that an adjournment would be required, the
suggestion was made by the court that the case should
be adjourned until 21 July 1992, but the complainer's
solicitor indicated that this date was not suitable to
him, and for that reason the diet was adjourned until
4 August 1992.

The Solicitor General also submitted that the word   H
"shall" in the proviso to s 380 (1) was directory and
not mandatory. The Solicitor General cited no
authority for his proposition that the word "shall" in
the proviso was directory and not mandatory. The
situation in the present case appears to us to be different to the situation which was considered by the court
in *HM Advocate v Graham*. Although the three week
limitation applies even where an accused is not in
custody, it clearly does apply to custody cases, and in
such cases the proviso has importance from the point   I
of view of limiting the period within which an accused
person may be remanded in custody whilst inquiries
are made and consideration is given to the most suitable means of dealing with the case. In these circumstances we are not persuaded by the Solicitor General
that the language of the proviso is directory rather
than mandatory.

Having regard to the reasons for granting the
adjournment on 2 July 1992, the Solicitor General   J
submitted that the present case did not fall under the
provisions of s 380 (1); he contended that the adjournment in this case had not been for the purpose of
enabling inquiries to be made nor for determining the
most suitable method of dealing with the complainer's
case. He submitted that the case was clearly different
to *Wilson v Donald* where the adjournment was for the
purpose of obtaining a printout from DVLC. In the
present case, it is plain from the terms of the entry in
the minutes of procedure that the adjournment   K
granted on 2 July 1992 was for the purpose of enabling
the court to determine whether there were grounds for
mitigating the normal consequences of the appellant's
conviction and for determining whether he should be
disqualified for less than the minimum period defined
in s 35 or to refrain from disqualification altogether.
In our opinion, an adjournment of that kind can
properly be regarded as an adjournment for the
purpose of enabling inquiries to be made or at least as
an adjournment for the purpose of enabling the court   L
to determine the appropriate method of dealing with
the complainer's case. It was only after evidence had
been heard at the adjourned diet that the justice could
determine whether or not to impose disqualification
on the complainer. Accordingly we are satisfied that
the adjournment on 2 July 1992 did fall within the
provisions of s 380 (1) of the Act of 1975.

For the foregoing reasons we are satisfied that the
adjournment on 2 July 1992 was for a period in excess
of 21 days, and was accordingly in breach of the pro-

visions of s 380 (1) of the Act of 1975. It follows that the adjournment was incompetent. Although the Crown stressed that the adjournment had been made at the request of the complainer's solicitor, the Crown did not suggest that the complainer could waive or had waived compliance with the provisions of s 380 (1) of the Act of 1975.

For the foregoing reasons we shall pass the bill and suspend the sentence imposed by the justice on 4 August 1992.

_____

Counsel for Complainer, Douglas; Solicitors, Drummond Miller, WS (for I Allan Grant & Co, Tullibody) — Counsel for Respondent, Solicitor General (Dawson, QC); Solicitor, J D Lowe, Crown Agent.

P W F

_____

Cumming's Trustee v Glenrinnes Farms Ltd

OUTER HOUSE
LORD WEIR
20 NOVEMBER 1992

Company — Winding up — Petition by contributory — Competency — Petitioner also trustee in sequestration on estate of principal shareholder in company — Petition for winding up proceeding on basis of bankrupt's right as contributory — Whether competent to petition as trustee in sequestration — Whether trustee required to be registered as owner of shares — Bankruptcy (Scotland) Act 1985 (c 66), s 31 — Insolvency Act 1986 (c 45), ss 79, 82 and 124.

Company — Winding up — Whether just and equitable — Principal shareholder sequestrated — Shareholder's affairs substantially intermixed with those of company — Ownership of assets uncertain — Insolvency Act 1986 (c 45), s 122 (1) (g).

Section 122 (1) (g) of the Insolvency Act 1986 provides that a company may be wound up by the court if the court is of opinion that that is just and equitable. Section 124 (2) provides that a contributory is not entitled to present a winding up petition unless the shares in respect of which he is a contributory were held by him and registered in his name for at least six months during the 18 months before the commencement of the winding up. Section 31 (8) (b) of the Bankruptcy (Scotland) Act 1985 gives a trustee the capacity to exercise all such powers in respect of any property as might have been exercised by the debtor for his own benefit as at the date of sequestration.

The trustee on the sequestrated estates of the principal shareholder in a company petitioned for the winding up of the company on the ground that it was

just and equitable. He was appointed provisional liquidator. The company sought recall of that appointment, arguing that as the trustee had not obtained registration of the bankrupt's shares in his own name he had no power to present a petition for a winding up order. The petitioner argued that s 31 (8) (b) of the 1985 Act enabled him to present a petition without first of all securing title to the bankrupt's shares. The company also challenged the relevancy of the averments in support of the winding up order.

Held, (1) that as a member of the company the bankrupt possessed powers including the power to vote and, as a contributory, the power to present a petition for winding up, and in terms of s 31 (8) (b) of the 1985 Act the capacity to exercise such powers had vested in the trustee as at the date of sequestration (p 906F-G); (2) that averments that the affairs of the bankrupt and the company were intermixed to a substantial degree and might be difficult to disentangle, that the company's accounts were hopelessly out of date and that there was doubt as to the ownership of certain assets, were sufficient for proof on the petition (p 906K-L); and motion for recall *refused* and proof before answer *allowed* on the motion for a winding up order.

Opinion, that there was nothing in the provisions of s 31 (1) or (8) of the 1985 Act which had the effect of treating the act and warrant issued on confirmation of the permanent trustee's appointment, as the equivalent of registering in the name of the trustee a bankrupt's shares in a company (p 906E-F).

_____

Petition for winding up

Peter Cranbourne Taylor, trustee on the sequestrated estates of James Mitchell Cumming, petitioned for the winding up of Glenrinnes Farms Ltd on the basis that it was just and equitable that the company should be wound up in terms of s 122 (1) (g) of the Insolvency Act 1986. The petitioner was appointed provisional liquidator.

The petition came before the Lord Ordinary (Weir) on the petitioner's motion to grant the prayer of the petition and on the company's motion to recall the appointment of the petitioner as provisional liquidator of the company.

Statutory provisions

The Bankruptcy (Scotland) Act 1985 provides:

"**31.**—(1) Subject to section 33 of this Act, the whole estate of the debtor shall vest as at the date of sequestration in the permanent trustee for the benefit of creditors; and — (a) the estate shall so vest by virtue of the act and warrant issued on confirmation of the permanent trustee's appointment; and (b) the act and warrant shall, in respect of the heritable estate in Scotland of the debtor, have the same effect as if a decree of adjudication in implement of sale, as well as a decree of adjudication for payment and in security of debt, subject to no legal reversion, had been pronounced in favour of the permanent trustee. . . .

"(8) In subsection (1) above the 'whole estate of the
A debtor' means his whole estate at the date of sequestration, wherever situated, including — (a) any income or
estate vesting in the debtor on that date; and (b) the
capacity to exercise and to take proceedings for exercising, all such powers in, over, or in respect of any
property as might have been exercised by the debtor
for his own benefit as at, or on, the date of sequestration or might be exercised on a relevant date (within
the meaning of section 32 (10) of this Act)."

B The Insolvency Act 1986 provides:

"79.—(1) In this Act and the Companies Act the
expression 'contributory' means every person liable to
contribute to the assets of a company in the event of
its being wound up, and for the purposes of all proceedings for determining, and all proceedings prior to
the final determination of, the persons who are to be
deemed contributories, includes any person alleged to
be a contributory. . . .

"82.—(1) The following applies if a contributory
C becomes bankrupt, either before or after he has been
placed on the list of contributories.

"(2) His trustee in bankruptcy represents him for all
purposes of the winding up, and is a contributory
accordingly. . . .

"122.—(1) A company may be wound up by the
court if — . . . (g) the court is of the opinion that it
is just and equitable that the company should be
wound up. . . .

D "124.—(1) Subject to the provisions of this section,
an application to the court for the winding up of a
company shall be by petition presented either by the
company, or the directors, or by any creditor or creditors (including any contingent or prospective creditor
or creditors), contributory or contributories, or by all
or any of those parties, together or separately.

"(2) Except as mentioned below, a contributory is
not entitled to present a winding-up petition unless
either — (a) the number of members is reduced below
E 2, or (b) the shares in respect of which he is a contributory, or some of them, either were originally
allotted to him, or have been held by him, and registered in his name, for at least 6 months during the 18
months before the commencement of the winding up,
or have devolved on him through the death of a former
holder."

Cases referred to

F *Bolton (H L) Engineering Co Ltd, Re* [1956] Ch 577;
    [1956] 2 WLR 844; [1956] 1 All ER 799.
Morgan v Gray [1953] Ch 83; [1953] 2 WLR 140;
    [1953] 1 All ER 213.

On 20 November 1992 the Lord Ordinary *refused*
the respondents' motion and quoad ultra *allowed* a
proof before answer.

LORD WEIR.—On 2 July 1992 the petitioner was
appointed provisional liquidator of Glenrinnes Farms
Ltd ("the company") and I have before me two

motions for consideration. One is on behalf of the
company for recall of that appointment and the other G
is at the instance of the petitioner in which the court
is asked to grant the prayer of the petition.

The company was incorporated in 1954 with the
objects of carrying on business as farmers, farm
retailers and associated trades and businesses. The
principal shareholder is James Mitchell Cumming.
His wife holds a significant number of shares and one
share is held by Alastair George McOran-Campbell.
The latter individual has lodged answers but was not
represented at the hearing. The petitioner was H
appointed as trustee in sequestration on the estate of
Cumming in June 1992.

The petitioner avers that upon carrying out investigations into the affairs of Mr Cumming he discovered
that assets including Glenrinnes House, the home
farm and other heritable property might not belong, as
he believed, to Mr Cumming as an individual but may
belong to the company. He makes averments to the
general effect that the affairs and business of Mr I
Cumming on the one hand and the company on the
other hand are intermixed. Moreover, in the absence
of up to date accounts, the last available being three
years old, it is impossible to ascertain what are the
assets and liabilities of the company. On the strength
of these averments it was submitted that it was just
and equitable for the company to be wound up.

Section 124 of the Insolvency Act 1986 is in the
following terms: [his Lordship quoted the provisions
of s 124 (1) and (2) and continued:] J

The first submission of counsel for the respondents
in support of the motion for recall was that the petitioner did not come within the categories of those
entitled to present a petition for winding up. On the
face of it, the petitioner bore to be acting as an individual and in no other capacity. I consider this argument is a technicality and can be immediately disposed
of. It is quite plain from the terms of the petition as
a whole that the petitioner was suing in his capacity
as trustee upon the sequestrated estate of Mr K
Cumming, one of the members of the company. The
fact that this is not expressly stated in the instance
seems to me to be of no importance.

The second argument presented by counsel for the
respondents is a substantial one. In this connection it
was not disputed that the petitioner had taken no steps
to register himself as owner of the shares of Mr
Cumming in the company. The question is whether a
trustee of a bankrupt contributory is to be deemed L
himself a contributory so as to entitle him to petition
for the winding up of that company in terms of s 124
of the Act of 1986.

It will be convenient if I refer to further relevant
statutory provisions of the Insolvency Act 1986. [His
Lordship quoted the terms of s 79 (1) and s 82 (1) and
(2) and continued:]

It will be seen that a contributory is not entitled to
present a winding up petition unless either the
number of members is reduced below two (which is

A not the case here), or the shares in respect of which he is a contributory were held for him and registered in his name for at least six months during the 18 months before the commencement of the winding up. It was accepted that Mr Cumming would qualify as a contributory and I understand it to be accepted that the petitioner would stand in his room provided he had taken steps to register himself as a shareholder. If he did so, then in terms of s 82 (2) he would represent the debtor for all purposes of the winding up and be a contributory. As I have said, the question is whether it is

B necessary for the trustee to register as a shareholder in order to be treated as a contributory and as someone entitled to present a winding up petition.

This problem has received some consideration in England in the context of the provisions of the Companies Act 1948 which are for practical purposes to the same effect as the provisions of the Act of 1986 which I have already narrated. It has been held that a bankrupt remains a member of a company and is entitled to vote so long as he remains on the register

C of the company (*Morgan v Gray* [1953] Ch, per Danckwerts J at p 87). It has also been held that the powers of a trustee to represent the debtor for all the purposes of the winding up can only come into effect after a winding up order has been made and that a trustee who had not obtained registration of the bankrupt's shares in his own name has no locus standi as a contributory to present a petition (*Re H L Bolton Engineering Co Ltd* [1956] Ch, per Wynn-Parry J at pp 582-583).

D

Counsel for the respondents founded on these decisions and submitted that applying in particular the ratio of the decision in *Bolton Engineering Co Ltd* it was clear that the petitioner had no power in this case to present a petition for a winding up order. Counsel for the petitioner, recognising that the two judgments which I have referred to have stood unchallenged for many years, accepted that if the law remained as it then was, his client would have no title to seek a

E winding up order. It is, therefore, unnecessary for me to comment on the law as expressed in the English cases. However, he submitted that the position was now different in view of the provisions of s 31 (1) and (8) of the Bankruptcy (Scotland) Act 1985. [His Lordship quoted the terms of s 31 (1) and (8) and continued:]

There is nothing in these provisions, in my view, which has the effect of treating the act and warrant as

F the equivalent of registration. So in a question concerning a trustee's title to the shares of a bankrupt in a company the necessary formality of registration must be undergone before it can be recognised. That has always been the position and remains so. The question as to whether a trustee can present a petition without registering is, however, a different matter and in my opinion s 31 (8) enables him to do so without first of all securing title to the bankrupt's shares. The powers given to a trustee in terms of s 31 (8) (b) are very wide. He is given the capacity to exercise all such powers in respect of any property as might have been exercised

G by the debtor for his own benefit as at the date of sequestration. As a member of the company the debtor in this case had powers including the power to vote and as a contributory the power to present a petition for winding up. In my opinion in terms of s 31 (8) (b) the capacity to exercise such powers vested in his trustee as at the date of sequestration. The position is now different from what it may have been before the coming into force of the Bankruptcy (Scotland) Act 1985.

For these reasons the petitioner is enabled, in my opinion, as from the date of sequestration to assume H the debtor's powers in relation to the company and in particular to petition for the winding up of the company.

Counsel for the respondent finally submitted that the petitioner had failed to make averments to demonstrate that the company was solvent before a winding up order could be made at the instance of a contributory. This argument is demonstrably unsound in view of an admission made by the respondents on record that the company was in fact solvent. I

The motion for recall of the petitioner's appointment as liquidator accordingly fails.

The petitioner's motion was that the court should grant the prayer of the petition. The basis for the winding up order was that the court had to be of opinion that it was just and equitable that the company should be wound up in terms of s 122 (1) (g) of the Insolvency Act 1986. Counsel for the petitioner did not press that motion but moved for a proof before answer. On the other hand counsel for the respondents J contended that the petitioner's averments were insufficient to disclose a case for inquiry. He founded also on the provisions of s 125 (2) of the Act which gives the court the power to refuse to make a winding up order if it is of opinion both that some other remedy is available to the petitioner and that he is acting unreasonably in seeking to have the company wound up instead of pursuing that other remedy.

I have no hesitation in allowing a proof before reaching a decision on this application. It is best that at this K stage I should say as little as possible about the circumstances or about the merits of the submissions advanced by counsel for the petitioner and respondents respectively. However, from the averments of the petitioner and from certain other documentary material presented to me at the bar, the petitioner has demonstrated to my satisfaction the existence of a prima facie case for a winding up. It appears that the affairs of the debtor, Mr Cumming, and the company L are intermixed to a substantial degree and may be difficult to disentangle. The accounts for the company are hopelessly out of date and there is at present considerable uncertainty as to the ownership of the heritage and certain of the moveables and the extent to which, if at all, the heritage or part of it may be subject to an agricultural tenancy or tenancies. A question has been sufficiently raised in my opinion as to the solvency of the company to entitle the court to inquire into the matter.

A Counsel for Petitioner, Menzies, QC, Andrew Smith; Solicitors, John G Gray & Co, SSC — Counsel for Respondents, Macnair; Solicitors, Bennett & Robertson.

GDM

Hopkinson v Williams

B OUTER HOUSE

LORD CAMERON OF LOCHBROOM

18 FEBRUARY 1993

Process — Pleadings — Relevancy and specification — Sale of heritable property — Action of damages for breach of contract — Defence that purchaser's agent and solicitors instructed by agent exceeded their authority — Sufficiency of averments to support reduction ope exceptionis of missives for lack of authority.

C

Process — Pleadings — Relevancy and specification — Sale of heritable property — Action of damages for breach of contract — Defence that purchaser's solicitors acting without authority — Sufficiency of seller's averments — No specific averment that missives entered into with purchaser's authority.

Agent and principal — Sale of heritable property — Whether missives entered into within scope of authority — Whether implication arose from terms of missives — Purchaser's agent and solicitors instructed by agent allegedly exceeding their authority — Whether averments that purchaser not bound by missives relevant and specific.

D

Contract — Sale of heritage — Breach of contract — Purchaser's agent and solicitors instructed by agent alleged by purchaser to have exceeded their authority — Whether seller's averments that purchaser liable and whether purchaser's averments that missives unauthorised sufficiently relevant and specific.

E

The seller under missives of heritable property raised an action of damages against the purported purchaser in respect of the purchaser's failure to pay the purchase price within the stipulated time. The purported purchaser averred that she had not authorised her solicitors to enter into binding missives. She averred that, although she had authorised her sister to negotiate an informal agreement whereby the seller would agree not to sell the subjects before a certain date, her sister had exceeded her authority by instructing solicitors to submit a formal offer to purchase which was conditional upon the defender's sale of her American property, and that the solicitors had exceeded the authorisation given by her sister by entering into unconditional missives. In response the seller averred that the instructions given to the purported purchaser's sister and solicitors were not known and not admitted, but that following the conclusion of missives the purchaser's solicitors had advised that she wished to withdraw from the bargain

F

and had been advised as to the consequences of doing so. No withdrawal had been intimated, and the G defence relating to lack of authority had not been intimated before it had been incorporated in the defences by way of adjustment. On procedure roll the seller argued that the purported purchaser's averments were insufficiently relevant or specific to support her plea that the missives, having been concluded without her authority, should be reduced ope exceptionis. The purported purchaser argued that the seller's pleadings were irrelevant in that they did not include averments that the solicitors had been acting on the purported H purchaser's authority in entering into missives on her behalf.

Held, (1) that the defender had averred a sufficiently relevant and specific defence in that she averred that her sister had had no authority to act on her behalf in entering into, or instructing a solicitor to enter into missives on her behalf (pp 908J-909A); (2) that the terms of the missives gave rise to an inference that the defender's solicitors had specific instructions in relation to the offer to purchase, this inference I being fortified by the averments relating to the conduct of the solicitor after the conclusion of missives (p 909G-J); and proof before answer *allowed*.

Danish Dairy Co v Gillespie, 1922 SLT 487, *distinguished.*

————

Action of damages

Michael Hopkinson raised an action of damages against Jennifer Williams in respect of breach of contract arising out of the defender's failure to implement missives for the sale of heritable property.

J

The case came before the Lord Ordinary (Lord Cameron of Lochbroom) on procedure roll.

Case referred to

Danish Dairy Co v Gillespie, 1922 SLT 487; 1922 SC 656.

K

Textbooks referred to

Begg, *Law Agents*, chap 8, s 14.

Gloag, *Contract* (2nd ed), p 126.

On 18 February 1993 the Lord Ordinary *allowed* a proof before answer.

LORD CAMERON OF LOCHBROOM.—This action came before me on procedure roll for debate on the parties' respective pleas to relevancy and lack of L specification and further the plea of no jurisdiction stated by the defender. [His Lordship dealt with the latter point, which was departed from by the defender, and continued:]

The action is concerned with the purported sale by the pursuer and purchase by the defender of heritable subjects at Thornhill effected by letters passing between solicitors dated 16, 18 and 29 April and 2 May 1991. The pursuer avers that these letters constituted missives whereby the pursuer agreed to sell

A and the defender agreed to purchase the subjects. He goes on to aver that the letter of 18 April 1991 provided that it was an essential condition that the purchase price be paid on the date of entry whether or not entry was then taken by the pursuer and further that the pursuer had an option to rescind the bargain in the event that the purchase price and interest thereon was not paid within 14 days of the date of entry. The pursuer avers that the defender failed to make payment of the price on the agreed date of entry, 28 June 1991, and within 14 days thereafter. Accord-

B ingly, the pursuer being willing and able to execute a valid disposition of the subjects but the defender having failed to implement her part of the bargain, by letter dated 15 August 1991 the pursuer's agents intimated to the opposing solicitors that in terms of the qualification, the pursuer was rescinding the bargain. In reply the defender avers that by about April 1991 she had for some time contemplated the possibility that she might be interested in purchasing the subjects and had held preliminary discussions with the pursuer

C thereanent. She goes on to say that on about 13 April 1991 she learnt from her sister who resides in Thornhill, that the subjects were being put on the market. The defender's answer continues: "The defender thereupon instructed and authorised her sister to enter into negotiations with the pursuer with a view to her agreeing with the pursuer an informal arrangement whereby the pursuer would delay in selling the subjects until 28 June 1991 in order to give the defender an opportunity to sell her house in Los Angeles with

D a view to the defender thereafter, if so advised, to enter into a binding contract for the purchase of the said subjects. The defender's sister had no authority to enter into missives or to instruct a solicitor to enter into missives for the purchase of the subjects. The defender expressly advised her sister that before any formal offer was to be made, her express written authority should be obtained. Notwithstanding the said limited authority the defender's sister instructed Hector MacLeod, solicitor, Stirling, to enter into mis-

E sives to purchase the said subjects which purported missives were, in due course, concluded. Further and in any event, the instructions given by the defender's sister to said solicitor were explicitly that any offer should be made conditional upon the successful sale of the said house in California. The solicitor had no authority to enter into unconditional missives. In these circumstances the said purported contract having been concluded without the authority of the defender, the defender is not bound thereby and the

F said purported missives fall to be reduced ope exceptionis."

In his reply to these averments, the pursuer states inter alia that it is not known and not admitted what instructions the defender gave to her sister or for what purpose any instructions were given and further what instructions were given to Hector MacLeod by the defender's solicitor. The pursuer also avers that following the conclusion of missives Hector MacLeod advised the pursuer's agents that the defender wished to withdraw from the bargain and told them that he

had advised the defender of the consequences of so doing. It is said that no instruction of withdrawal from G the bargain was received by the pursuer's agents. It is further averred that "Prior to the averments thereof being added in the course of adjustment of this action, the defender had not intimated to the pursuer's agents any allegation that said missives had been entered into without her authority".

It is convenient at this point to consider the submissions of counsel for the pursuer to the effect that the defender had no relevant or specific averments sufficient to support the defender's fourth plea in law H to the effect that the pretended missives had been purportedly concluded without the defender's authority and should be reduced ope exceptionis. It was said that ex facie of the letters constituting the missives, the solicitor had authority to enter into the missives and that since missives had been exchanged between solicitors, the pursuer was entitled to assume that the solicitor purporting to act for the defender had authority unless and until advised to the contrary. There was no averment that Hector MacLeod, the I solicitor who purported to act for the defender, should not have relied upon the instructions so far as they came from the defender's sister nor any averment that he was not entitled to do so. The averments were in particular lacking in specification as to how it came to be that the missives were concluded and no explanation was given for the interval of time that passed between the initial offer by letter dated 16 April and the subsequent qualified acceptance on 29 April 1991 at the hand of Hector MacLeod. It was not said that J the missives had been held concluded without instructions.

I have come to the conclusion that it would be going too fast at this stage to hold that the defender's averments are irrelevant and lacking in specification. The crux of the defence is that it was the defender's sister and not the defender who instructed Hector MacLeod to enter into missives for the purchase of the subjects and that the defender's sister had no authority to do K so herself or to instruct a solicitor to do so. The defender also avers that she had given her sister precise instructions that no formal offer was to be made without her express written authority. The defender goes on to aver as an additional case, that insofar as authority was purportedly given to the solicitor by the defender's sister, this did not extend to authorising the solicitor to enter into unconditional missives since the instructions given were explicitly that any offer should be made conditional upon a suc- L cessful sale of the defender's house in California. I am not entirely clear about the precise import of this additional case which might appear at first blush to assume authority had been given to the defender's sister to instruct a solicitor. But I do not consider it appropriate at this stage to exclude these averments from probation since these matters are said to form some part of the circumstances upon which the defender relies in her defence that the purported contract had been concluded without her authority. Certainly the defender's case is founded upon the premise that the

A contract had been concluded without her authority and that her sister had no authority on her behalf to act as she did. For these reasons, I consider that the defender has averred sufficient to entitle her to proof before answer of her averments in support of her fourth plea in law.

I next consider the defender's submission that the action should be dismissed for want of relevant averments that the contract for purchase of the property was entered into on the defender's behalf with the defender's authority. Counsel's argument was short B and succinct. The defender had raised a defence of want of authority on the part of Hector MacLeod. The missives were concluded, not between the parties direct, but between law agents. A law agent had no general authority to conclude a contract for the purchase of heritage. The onus of proving that the solicitor purporting to act for the defender had authority to do so lay upon the pursuer in the circumstances. Reference was made to Gloag on *Contract* (2nd ed), p 126 for the proposition that the question whether an C agent has actual authority to enter into a particular contract is one of fact — the onus of proof resting, generally, on the party who asserts it. Reference was also made to *Danish Dairy Co v Gillespie*. It was therefore incumbent upon the pursuer to aver positively that the contract had been concluded with the defender's authority. There was no such averment. Indeed, at the very highest the defender's averments as to the matter of instructions were said to be not known and not admitted.

D
I am not persuaded that in the present case the pursuer's averments are not sufficient to entitle the court at the end of the day to infer that the defender's solicitors, in concluding missives, were acting with the pursuer's authority. In *Danish Dairy Co v Gillespie*, which was decided after proof, Lord President Clyde at 1922 SLT, p 491 said this: "The next question is as to Mr Marshall's authority from the defender to convert what was an informal and incomplete agreement into E a complete and binding one. It may be that Mr Marshall's first letter of 18 November 1919 implied that his instructions covered authority to arrange for the tenants sitting on for one more year, under the existing lease, at £23. But I cannot read it as being consistent with the view that his instructions covered authority to complete any agreement for a fresh lease for five years. Authority to make a complete and binding agreement on behalf of a client is not to be lightly inferred in the case of a law agent. 'Although F law agents are very frequently employed to conduct negotiations with a view to contracts, especially in conveyancing business, no one is entitled to assume that a law agent professing to act for a client has general powers to conclude a contract on his behalf.' (Begg on Law Agents, cap 8, section 14). Mr Marshall said he had received no such authority; the defender says he had given him none; and the letter of 18th November 1919 certainly does not represent that any had been given. Neither does any of his subsequent letters. Mr Marshall acted as factor on the defender's behalf for certain properties belonging to him, collect-

ing the rents and paying the taxes. But, as it happened, the rents of this particular property were paid by the G tenants to the defender direct. Mr Marshall had nothing to do with the properties otherwise — as regards repairs for example — and his factory, such as it was, did not include power to let."

The circumstances in that case were therefore substantially different from the present. In the present case the pursuer avers that by the missives the pursuer agreed to sell and the defender agreed to purchase the subjects in question. It was agreed between parties that for the purposes of the debate reference could be H made to the specific terms of the missives. The first letter from Hector MacLeod dated 16 April 1991 begins: "On behalf of and as instructed by my client", the defender. This letter constitutes an offer to purchase. The pursuer's solicitors sent a qualified acceptance by letter dated 18 April 1991. On 29 April 1991 Hector MacLeod responded to the letter of 18 April 1991 and stated inter alia: "I am now instructed to accept the terms of that qualified acceptance subject always to the following additional qualification, I namely: (1) entry and vacant possession to the subjects will be given on 28 June 1991 and not as previously stipulated. I look forward to receiving your letter to conclude the bargain in due course." Thereafter the bargain was held to be concluded with the pursuer's solicitor's letter of 2 May 1991. The terms of these letters can give rise to an inference that the writer had specific instructions in relation to the offer to purchase and further instructions in relation to the concluding of a bargain in response to the qualified acceptance of J 18 April 1991. In addition the averments of what happened after the conclusion of the missives in relation to the actings of Hector MacLeod are capable of fortifying an inference that at all times Hector MacLeod was acting with the specific authority of the defender. For these reasons I am not disposed to hold that there are no sufficient and relevant averments from which it could be spelled out that the solicitors who wrote the letters of 16 and 29 April 1991 were acting with the authority of the defender. There is in K my opinion sufficient to go to proof before answer on the matter. [His Lordship concluded by considering questions related to the relevancy and specification of the damages claimed, with which this report is not concerned.]

Counsel for Pursuer, Stuart; Solicitors, Shepherd & Wedderburn, WS (for Hill & Robb, Stirling) — Counsel for Defender, Agnew of Lochnaw; Solicitors, Haig-Scott L *& Co, WS.*

P McC

R, Petitioner

A FIRST DIVISION

THE LORD PRESIDENT (HOPE),
LORDS ALLANBRIDGE AND CULLEN

26 MARCH 1993

Children and young persons — Children's hearing — Application to sheriff for findings whether or not grounds of referral established — Sheriff deciding that grounds established — Additional evidence casting doubt on
B *matter — Whether grounds of referral liable to reconsideration by sheriff.*

Nobile officium — Competency — Children's hearing — Grounds of referral to children's hearing — Challenge to finding that grounds established on basis of additional evidence — Whether grounds of referral liable to reconsideration by sheriff.

Section 50 (1) of the Social Work (Scotland) Act 1968 provides that an appeal shall lie to the Court of
C Session by stated case on a point of law or in respect of any irregularity in the conduct of the case, from any decision of the sheriff under Pt III of the Act, and no other or further appeal shall be competent.

As a result of allegations made by the eldest of three children the reporter referred their cases to a children's hearing. The children's parents did not accept the grounds of referral and an application was made to the sheriff under s 42 (2) (c) of the Social Work (Scotland) Act 1968 for a finding as to whether
D the grounds of referral had been established. After hearing evidence the sheriff was satisfied that the grounds of referral had been established and remitted the cases to the reporter for determination by a children's hearing. The eldest child was taken into the care of the local authority. The remaining children were placed under the supervision of the local authority but were allowed to live with their mother on the condition that their father lived elsewhere.

The eldest child subsequently retracted the allega-
E tions she had made. An application to the children's hearing to review the residency condition of the supervision order in respect of the remaining children was unsuccessful, as was an application to the Secretary of State under s 52 of the 1968 Act seeking to terminate the supervision requirements in respect of all three children. The father of the children then presented a petition to the nobile officium of the Court of Session, seeking an order directing the sheriff to fix a further diet to reconsider whether the grounds of referral were
F established and to exercise of new his powers under s 42 (5) or 42 (6) of the 1968 Act. The reporter opposed the application and challenged its competency. The father argued that the grounds of referral could be reconsidered at any stage as it could not be assumed that the children's hearing could continue to exercise its discretion where there was no need for it to do so.

Held, (1) that while the nobile officium might be exercised in highly special or unforeseen circumstances, it could not be exercised to conflict with or defeat a statutory intention, nor might it be invoked to

extend the provisions of a statute (p 912H-J); (2) that the intention of the 1968 Act was that once the G grounds of referral had been accepted or established the case stood referred to the children's hearing for consideration and determination (p 914G); (3) that the Act did not make provision for any appeal other than under s 50 (1) or for any reconsideration of the grounds of referral, so that the order sought would supplement the statutory provisions and was accordingly incompetent (p 914H-J); and petition *dismissed* as incompetent.

Observed, that as the children's hearing were H empowered to take any change of circumstances into account in deciding whether a child should continue to be subject to a supervision requirement, it would be inappropriate in the present case to exercise the nobile officium, which could affect only the future conduct of the case and could not be invoked as a means of taking past decisions to appeal (pp 915K-916A).

Observed, further, that a petition to the nobile officium might be appropriate in exceptional circumstances, such as where due to mistaken or incomplete I information on a material point, grounds for referral were accepted or held to be established which ought not to have been (p 915F-H).

Petition to the nobile officium

P R, the father of three children referred to a children's hearing, presented a petition to the nobile officium seeking an order that the grounds for the referral of the children be reheard by the sheriff. Frederick J J Kennedy, the reporter to the children's panel for Strathclyde Region, and A R, the mother of the children, appeared as respondents. The reporter challenged the competency of the petition. The facts giving rise to the petition appear from the opinion of the court.

Statutory provisions

The Social Work (Scotland) Act 1968 provides:

"48.—. . . (3) No supervision requirement shall K remain in force without review for a period extending beyond one year, and where a supervision requirement is not reviewed within the period of one year from the making or continuing of the requirement it shall cease to have effect at the expiration of that period. . . .

"49.—(1) A child or his parent or both may, within a period of three weeks beginning with the date of any decision of a children's hearing, appeal to the sheriff in chambers against that decision, and the child or his L parent or both shall be heard by the sheriff as to the reasons for the appeal. . . .

"50.—(1) Subject to the provisions of this section, an appeal shall lie to the Court of Session, by way of stated case on a point of law or in respect of any irregularity in the conduct of the case, at the instance of a child or his parent or both or of a reporter acting on behalf of a children's hearing, from any decision of the sheriff under this Part of this Act, and no other or further appeal shall be competent. . . .

"52. Where, having regard to all the circumstances of a case and the interests of a child, the Secretary of State is satisfied that a supervision requirement in force in respect of the child should be terminated, he may by order terminate the requirement."

Cases referred to

Anderson v HM Advocate, 1974 SLT 239.
Berry, Petitioner, 1985 SCCR 106.
Black, Petitioner, 1991 SCCR 1.
Brodie v HM Advocate, 1993 SCCR 371.
Hobbs (David) v Reporter for Strathclyde Region, 1st Div, 6 December 1989, unreported.
Humphries, Petitioner, 1982 SLT 481; (sub nom *Humphries v X and Y*) 1982 SC 79.
MacPherson, Petitioners, 1990 JC 5; 1989 SCCR 518.
Maitland, Petitioner, 1961 SLT 384; 1961 SC 291.
Mitchell v HM Advocate, 1989 SCCR 502.
O v Rae, 1993 SLT 570.
Sloan, Petitioner, 1991 SLT 527.
Sloan v B, 1991 SLT 530.

The petition was heard before the First Division on 9 March 1993.

On 26 March 1993 the First Division *dismissed* the petition as incompetent.

The following opinion of the court was delivered by the Lord President (Hope):

OPINION OF THE COURT.—This is an application to the nobile officium by the father of three children in respect of whom proceedings were instituted under Pt III of the Social Work (Scotland) Act 1968. The first respondent is the reporter to the children's panel for Strathclyde Region. The second respondent is the petitioner's wife and the mother of the three children.

The grounds for the referral of these cases to the children's hearing were that the eldest child, S, born on 13 January 1977, had been the victim of an offence mentioned in Sched 1 to the Criminal Procedure (Scotland) Act 1975, and that the two younger children, J born on 6 July 1984, and B born on 14 July 1987, were members of the same household as S, all in terms of s 32 (2) (d) of the 1968 Act. The petitioner and his wife did not accept these grounds for referral, and an application was then made to the sheriff under s 42 (2) (c) for a finding as to whether the grounds for the referral were established. The sheriff heard evidence and was satisfied that the grounds for referral had been established in each case. He remitted the cases to the reporter under s 42 (6) (a) to make arrangements for a children's hearing for the consideration and determination of each case. That was duly done, and the children's hearing made supervision requirements in respect of each of the three children. What the petitioner now seeks to do is to have the grounds for the referral reheard by the sheriff, on the ground that additional evidence is now available which casts serious doubt on the credibility of S's evidence that she was the victim of an offence. There is no provision

for a rehearing under Pt III of the 1968 Act, so the petitioner seeks an order to this effect in the exercise of the nobile officium.

The grounds for the referral in each case were based on allegations which S made in November 1990. She alleged that the petitioner had had sexual intercourse with her in the family home on five occasions between April 1989 and August 1990. This allegation, if true, meant that she had been the victim of an offence contrary to the Sexual Offences (Scotland) Act 1976, as amended by the Incest and Related Offences (Scotland) Act 1986, s 2A (1). Such an offence is an offence mentioned in Sched 1 to the Criminal Procedure (Scotland) Act 1975, and one of the conditions mentioned in s 32 (2) in respect of which a child may be in need of compulsory measures of care is that an offence mentioned in that Schedule has been committed in respect of him or in respect of a child who is a member of the same household. In order to decide whether the grounds for the referral were established it was necessary for the sheriff to hear evidence. In the course of the hearing which took place before him between 1 and 4 July 1991 he heard the evidence of a number of witnesses including that of S. He was satisfied that she was telling the truth, and that the petitioner had committed incest with her on three occasions and on two other occasions he had assaulted her with intent to have unlawful sexual intercourse with her. The petitioner then appealed by way of stated case to the Court of Session under s 50 of the 1968 Act. But in October 1991 he abandoned his appeal as it appeared that the material issue before the sheriff was the credibility of the evidence given by S and the sheriff was entitled to accept S's evidence.

The children's hearing then proceeded in terms of s 43 (1) to consider on what course they should decide in the best interests of each of the three children. They decided that they were all in need of compulsory measures of care, and they made supervision requirements in respect of each of them. S, who had already been taken into care, was to remain in care in respect of the requirements which they then made. J and B were required to live with their mother in the family home, subject to various conditions the effect of which was that the petitioner had to reside elsewhere. His contact with the two younger children was restricted to supervised access.

On 18 January 1992 S retracted the allegations which she had made against the petitioner. The petitioner avers that she confessed to social workers that she had fabricated her evidence. She said that she had lied to protect her boyfriend with whom she had been having sexual intercourse. The retraction is said to cast serious doubt on her credibility and on the decision of the sheriff to find the grounds for referral established. There is however a dispute on this point, because the reporter, who admits that S retracted her allegations and has continued to retract them, avers that retraction of allegations by child victims of sexual abuse is common and is part of a recognised pattern of behaviour. So, although both the petitioner and his wife regard the retraction as a clear indication that the

grounds of referral ought not to have been held to be
A established, that is not the view taken by the reporter.

The petitioner then sought a review of the supervision requirements relating to J and B. He appears to
have been content that the supervision requirement
relating to S should remain in force, and we understand that there are other reasons independent of the
allegations which she made against him for thinking
that she may still be in need of compulsory measures
of care. His application in regard to J and B came
before the children's hearing on 1 April 1992. The
B children's hearing decided that the non-residential
supervision requirements relating to these two
children should continue. In their statement of reasons
they noted that S had withdrawn her allegation that
she had been abused by the petitioner. But they also
noted that, as they put it, it had been established in
court that the petitioner was a Sched 1 offender. It is
clear from this comment in their statement of reasons
that they did not see it as being part of their function
to question the sheriff's decision that the grounds for
C referral had been established. But they took note of S's
retraction and of the second respondent's statement
that she now believed that S had not been abused, in
reaching their decision that the supervision requirement should remain unchanged.

The petitioner's solicitors then wrote to the Secretary of State on 27 July 1992 asking him to exercise
his powers under s 52 of the Act by terminating the
supervision requirement in respect of each of the three
children. They submitted that S's retraction cast grave
D doubt on the sheriff's findings, which had all along
been denied by the petitioner. By letter dated 2
October 1992 the Secretary of State intimated that,
having regard to all the circumstances of the case and
the interests of the children, he was not satisfied that
the supervision requirement should be terminated and
that he had decided not to exercise his powers under
s 52 of the Act. He noted that the sheriff was satisfied
in July 1991 that the grounds for referral were established and that an appeal against his decision was
E abandoned. He also noted that a children's hearing
was held under s 48 (3) of the Act subsequent to the
retraction at which it was decided that S should
remain subject to a supervision requirement with a
condition of residence.

It was in these circumstances, having exhausted his
remedies under the Act, that the petitioner made this
application to the court. He seeks an order directing
the sheriff to fix a further diet for the purpose of considering anew whether the original grounds for
F referral were established, to hear such evidence relating to these grounds as the parties may wish to place
before him and to exercise of new the powers conferred upon him by s 42 (5) or s 42 (6) of the Act as
the case may be. The reporter has opposed this application on various grounds including the ground that it
is incompetent, and it was on the preliminary issue as
to its competency that the application came before us
for a hearing on the summar roll.

Before we turn to consider the matter we should
mention, in order to complete the history, that on 26

February 1993 the children's hearing decided to vary
the non-residential supervision requirement relating G
to J and B. They deleted all the conditions in the
original supervision requirement, which was made on
29 November 1991 and had been continued on 1 April
1992 and again on 16 December 1992. They decided
that the time was now right for the petitioner's full
time integration into the family home, although they
considered that continued supervision was still needed
in the best interests of the children to ensure continued protection of them and that the petitioner's
reintegration into the family home was as smooth as H
possible. S remains subject to a supervision requirement with a condition of residence.

There is no dispute between the parties as to the
scope of the power which is available to us in the exercise of the nobile officium. As Lord President Emslie
said in *Humphries, Petr*, at 1982 SLT, p 482, its limits
are well understood and will not be extended. The
power may be exercised in highly special or unforeseen circumstances to prevent injustice and oppression. If the intention of a statute is clear but the I
necessary machinery for carrying out that intention in
special or unforeseen circumstances is lacking, the
power may be invoked to provide that machinery. In
Sloan, Petr for example, where there was no power
either in the 1968 Act or in the Social Work (Sheriff
Court Procedure) Rules 1971 to enable the sheriff to
do what was considered to be appropriate in the exceptional circumstances of that case, a direction was made
in the exercise of the nobile officium to enable the
sheriff to do what was required. But the power cannot J
be exercised in such a way as to conflict with or defeat
a statutory intention, express or implied. Nor may it
be invoked to extend the provisions of an Act of Parliament, such as by supplementing the statutory procedure by what would, in effect, be an amendment of the
statute: *Maitland, Petr*, per Lord President Clyde at
1961 SLT, p 385. There is now ample authority to the
effect that it is incompetent to invoke the nobile officium on a ground which would have been the proper
subject of an appeal where a right of appeal has been K
excluded by Parliament: *Anderson v HM Advocate;
Berry, Petr; MacPherson, Petrs; Black, Petr*. In *Anderson* at pp 240-241 Lord Justice General Emslie
pointed out that the only mode of appeal provided by
Parliament for the review of the merits of a conviction
was by way of stated case, the effect of which was that
in summary proceedings the trial judge was final on all
questions of fact. The petitioner had resorted to and
exhausted that remedy, and it was incompetent for
him then to apply to the nobile officium on a question L
which related to the evaluation of evidence and the
credibility of witnesses. Accordingly, as the Lord
Justice General observed in *MacPherson*, 1990 JC at p
14, it is necessary where the application is made in the
context of a statutory procedure, to examine the limits
which Parliament has set to that procedure by way of
provision for appeal or other methods of review.

The responsibility for the initial investigation of
cases which may require a children's hearing to be
arranged rests with the reporter. If he considers that

the child is in need of compulsory measures of care on

A the ground that any of the conditions mentioned in s 32 (2) applies to him, the reporter is required by s 39 (3) to arrange a children's hearing to whom the case is to be referred for consideration and determination. It is then the duty of the chairman under s 42 (1) to explain to the child and the parent the grounds which have been stated by the reporter for the referral of the case. The child and the parent have the right at this stage to dispute the grounds for referral: see s 35 (5) (b). The significance of these provisions was described

B in *Sloan v B*, 1991 SLT at p 548C-D: "If the grounds are accepted by them then the way is clear for the hearing to proceed to a consideration of the case in terms of s 42 (2) (a) or (b) as the case may be. This may lead to the taking of the various steps mentioned in s 43 and to the making of the supervision requirement in terms of s 44. The protection which exists, both for child and the parent, lies in the right of the child and the parent to dispute the grounds, in which event the matter goes to the sheriff for a finding as to whether

C they have been established."

There is, therefore, a clear separation between the issues of adjudication of the allegations in the grounds for the referral and the consideration of the measures to be applied in a case where the child is considered to be in need of compulsory measures of care. The responsibility for the consideration of the measures to be applied lies with the children's hearing, while disputed questions of fact as to the allegations made are to be resolved by the sheriff sitting in chambers as a

D court of law. The discussion in *Sloan* concludes with this comment at p 548F: "The right to dispute the grounds for the referral is an essential part of the system, and it provides the protection which is needed to ensure that the children's hearing do not proceed to a consideration of the case with a view to the compulsory measures of care which may be required until any such dispute has been resolved."

The Act makes provision in s 49 for an appeal to the

E sheriff against any decision of a children's hearing, and in s 50 for an appeal to the Court of Session from any decision of the sheriff under Pt III of the Act. Thus an appeal may be taken to the sheriff under s 49 against a decision of the children's hearing that the child is in need of compulsory measures of care. An appeal may also be taken to the sheriff against any requirement which a children's hearing may make under s 44 (1) of the Act. There is a right of appeal to the Court of Session under s 50 against the decision

F of the sheriff in such cases, but that is not a matter which is of concern to us in the present case. A decision taken by the sheriff under s 42 (6) that any of the grounds for the referral have been established may be appealed to the Court of Session under s 50 by way of stated case. Subsection (1) of that section is in these terms: [his Lordship quoted its terms and continued:]

The petitioner exercised his right of appeal under that subsection, although he later decided to abandon the appeal. Since an appeal can be made under s 50 on a point of law only or in respect of any irregularity in

the conduct of the case, it is clear that the sheriff is intended by this provision to be final on all questions G of fact, and it is provided expressly that no other or further appeal is to be competent.

The scheme of the Act is that, once the sheriff has held the grounds of referral to be established and any appeal under s 50 has been disposed of, the children's hearing must consider the case. It is open to them to decide under s 43 (2) that no further action is required and they may then discharge the referral. But there is no provision in the Act for the case to be returned to H the sheriff, either at their direction or at the instance of the reporter, for a reconsideration of the grounds for the referral. The Secretary of State has power under s 52, having regard to all the circumstances of the case and the interests of the child, to terminate a supervision requirement. But he has no power to discharge the referral nor does he have power to order the sheriff to reconsider the question whether the grounds for the referral have been established. The structure of these arrangements seems accordingly to be this. Both the child and the parent have the right to dispute the I grounds for the referral. If they do not accept them a finding may then be obtained from the sheriff as to whether or not the grounds are established. The child and the parent both have the right to take the sheriff's decision on this point to appeal under s 50 on a point of law or upon the ground of an irregularity in the case. But they have no other or further right of appeal, nor have they any opportunity under the statute to reopen the question once they have accepted the grounds for the referral or the grounds have been held J by the sheriff to be established. Once the grounds have been accepted or established that is an end of the matter, as far as any disputed questions of fact are concerned. What remain are questions for the children's hearing to consider, once this prerequisite for the exercise of their jurisdiction has been satisfied.

Counsel for the petitioner accepted that he had to satisfy us that what is sought in this application did not conflict with the scheme of the Act. He submitted K that it was the intention of Parliament that children should receive compulsory measures of care only when and so long as they were in need of them. There was therefore a continuing question at every stage of the case whether the child was still in need of such measures. There was an important distinction between the question whether a child was in need of compulsory measures of care and what these measures should be. The children's hearing were not entitled to hold that a child was in need of compulsory measures L of care unless one or more of the conditions mentioned in s 32 (1) of the Act was satisfied. These conditions required to be specified in the grounds for the referral by the reporter under rule 17 (2) of the Children's Hearings (Scotland) Rules 1986. Unless these grounds were accepted or established, the children's hearing had no jurisdiction to consider the case. The question whether they were accepted or established was one which could be reconsidered at any stage, since it was not to be assumed that it was the intention of Parliament that the children's hearing should continue to

A exercise their jurisdiction in circumstances where there was no need for this. What had happened in the present case was that fresh evidence was now available which cast serious doubt on the truth of S's allegations of incest. If these allegations were false the two younger children had been deprived of contact with the petitioner on a basis which was entirely unjustified. This was not in the best interests of these children and it cannot have been intended that their interests should have been prejudiced in this way. The remedy which was now sought was not, however, that

B of an appeal against the sheriff's decision. It was not now being asserted that he was in error on the evidence which was available to him in July 1991. What was being asked for was an order that he should reconsider the grounds in the light of this fresh evidence, since the children's hearing plainly saw it as no part of their function to consider whether or not the grounds for referral ought still to be held to have been established.

C He explained that it had not been thought necessary to ask for our recall of the sheriff's decision that the grounds for the referral were established. The wording of the prayer had been based on the terms of an interlocutor which had been pronounced in *David Hobbs v Reporter for Strathclyde Region*. That was a case where the Secretary of State had been asked to exercise his powers under s 52 of the Act and had not yet done so, although a period of about eight months

D had elapsed since the request was made. No opinions were delivered in the case, which came before the court at short notice on grounds of urgency. The only issue between the parties was whether it was appropriate for the court to intervene while a decision was still being awaited from the Secretary of State. There was a plea that the petition was incompetent in respect that a statutory remedy was available to and had been invoked by the petitioner. The court decided to grant the order sought on the ground that it was not satisfied

E that the particular circumstances which had arisen in that case, which related to fresh medical evidence, were capable of being dealt with expeditiously by the Secretary of State under s 52 of the Act. Counsel for the petitioner did not suggest that the decision which was taken in that case was of assistance to him on the issue of competency, and we agree that the circumstances of that case were so unusual that it is not to be taken as authority on that point.

F But he submitted that, if we were satisfied that the application was competent, it would be appropriate for us to make an order in the same terms, directing the sheriff to hear evidence and to exercise of new the powers conferred on him by s 42 (5) or (6) of the Act as the case may be. We recognise that that approach is consistent with his argument that there is a continuing question at every stage of the case whether the conditions mentioned in s 32 (1) of the Act are satisfied and that the grounds for the referral remain open for reconsideration at every stage.

G In our opinion, however, the plain intention of Pt III of the 1968 Act is that, once the grounds for the referral of a case have been accepted or established, the case stands referred to the children's hearing for its consideration and determination. All decisions as to whether to accept the grounds or as to whether they are established are intended to be final, subject only to an appeal from the sheriff within 28 days of his decision under s 50 where the case has been referred to him for a finding whether the grounds of referral have been established. No provision is made in s 50 for

H the hearing of additional evidence or for any review of the decision taken by the sheriff on questions of fact. The effect of the provision in s 50 (1) that no other or further appeal shall be competent is that the sheriff is final on all matters except on a point of law or in respect of an irregularity in the conduct of the case. Nor is there any provision for the child or the parent to withdraw his acceptance of the grounds of referral, or to consider afresh whether these grounds are accepted in whole or in part, once the children's hearing have proceeded to consider the case. There is

I nothing in the provisions of this Part of the Act to indicate that the grounds for referral are open to reconsideration at any later stage on the ground of a change in circumstances, or that they can be reviewed on the ground that a mistake was made when the grounds were accepted or found to be established. The proposition that the grounds for referral are open for reconsideration at every stage in the case is one which finds no support in the provisions of the Act. We are in no doubt that if we were to grant the order which

J is sought in this case on this ground we would be supplementing the statutory procedure by what would, in effect, be an amendment to the statute. For this reason the application must be held to be incompetent.

Furthermore, we are not persuaded that the absence of a procedure for reconsideration of the grounds for the referral is due to an oversight. Nor do we consider that what has occurred in this case can be described as

K something which is so exceptional and unforeseen that it would be appropriate for us to provide a remedy. The purpose of Pt III is to enable compulsory measures of care to be provided for children who are in need of them. That need may arise in a variety of circumstances, which are set out in the list of conditions in s 32 (2). Section 32 (3) provides that care in this context includes protection, control, guidance and treatment. The first step is to establish that the child may be in need of these measures of care, but once one

L or more of these grounds has been accepted or established the case is one which the children's hearing must consider, since it is for them to decide what should be done in the best interests of the child. The Act recognises that the grounds for the referral may not be accepted by the child or the parent, and it provides them with a right to dispute the grounds. But the right is to dispute the grounds at the outset only, not to continue to dispute them once they have been accepted or held to be established. The fact that neither the children's hearing nor the Secretary of

State, nor indeed the court, is given power to require
the reporter to apply to the sheriff for a reconsideration of the grounds at a later stage is a clear indication
that it was the intention of Parliament to achieve
finality on this matter before the children's hearing
proceed to a consideration of the case. The grounds
for the referral, accepted or established, thus provide
a clear and irrevocable starting point for the making
and review of such supervision requirements as
they may think necessary in the best interests of the
child.

For the reasons which were discussed in *O v Rae*, a
children's hearing is not just a disposing body, and
their powers are not to be seen as confined within the
limits described by the grounds for referral. The
grounds for referral provide a necessary part of the
background to the case, because unless they are
accepted or established the children's hearing cannot
begin to deal with it. But once the grounds are
accepted or established the children's hearing are
entitled to ask for and consider information across a
wide range. They are entitled to obtain the views of
various people including social workers and any
safeguarder as to what would be in the best interests
of the child. They are entitled to take account of any
further information which may be placed before them
during their consideration of the case under rule 19 (2)
of the 1986 Rules. Some of the matters which may
come to their attention in this way may be matters
which could have formed an additional ground of
referral. But the structure of the provisions of Pt III
of the 1986 Act is such that it is unnecessary for the
reporter in that event to go through the procedure of
referring the case to them again for these additional
matters to be accepted or established. This is because
the child is already before the children's hearing as
one who may be in need of compulsory measures of
care. It is not difficult to see that it might cause
difficulty for the children's hearing if it were to be
open to the child or the parent to withdraw his acceptance of the original grounds, or to insist that they be
reconsidered by the sheriff with a view to a finding
that the original grounds were not after all established.
A decision at that stage that the case was no longer
properly before the children's hearing because the
original grounds were no longer accepted or were not
after all established might be quite contrary to the best
interests of the child, since it might be clear for other
reasons that the child was in need of compulsory
measures of care and ought not to be deprived of them
for even the short time that might be needed for the
case to begin again on other grounds. It does not
appear to be consistent with the provisions of this Part
of the Act that the consideration of the case by the
children's hearing should be liable to be interrupted in
this way. The use of the words "accepted" and "established" indicate that, once decisions to that effect have
been taken, the children's hearing are to deal with the
case, secure in the knowledge that it is not liable to be
taken away from them for reconsideration of the
grounds for the referral.

We are conscious of the concern which may arise in

cases where it is apparent that, due to exceptional circumstances, such as mistaken or incomplete information on a point which was material, the grounds for
the referral ought not to have been accepted or held to
be established. It is not the function of the children's
hearing or of the Secretary of State to examine this
question, since they cannot review a decision taken by
the child or the parent to accept the grounds or by the
sheriff to find that the grounds for the referral have
been established. The children's hearing have no
option but to continue to deal with the case on the
assumption that the facts were as stated in the grounds
for the referral, however unreasonable that might
appear on the information now available. A situation
of that kind might be said to be appropriate for the
exercise of the nobile officium, since there is no
machinery in the Act for removing a case from the
children's hearing which ought not to be before them
at all. That however is not the situation in the present
case. There is no suggestion that the sheriff's decision
was arrived at on the basis of mistaken or incomplete
information, and there is a dispute as to whether S's
retraction is a reliable indication that her allegations
were untrue. It is not unusual for witnesses to say that
they wish to retract or to change their evidence after
it has been given and acted upon. Yet it is clear, even
in criminal cases where appeals are allowed on the
ground of additional evidence, that it is not sufficient
that a witness now wishes to give different evidence
from that which he gave at the trial: *Mitchell v HM
Advocate*; *Brodie v HM Advocate*. So the fact that a
witness who gave evidence to the sheriff under s 42 (4)
of the 1968 Act now wishes to withdraw or change his
evidence cannot be regarded as an exceptional or
unforeseen circumstance which justifies the exercise
of the nobile officium.

What the petitioner seeks in this case is a rehearing
of the evidence given by S. But it was on the evidence
which she gave at the original hearing before him that
the sheriff had to decide whether the grounds for the
referral were established. The guiding principle for
the children's hearing in these circumstances is to be
found in s 47 (1) of the 1968 Act, which provides that
no child shall continue to be subject to a supervision
requirement for any time longer than is necessary in
his interest. Any change of circumstances relevant to
the question as to what is in the child's best interests
may be taken into account by the children's hearing in
their examination of this matter. It was therefore
appropriate for the children's hearing to take S's
retraction into account as a factor in their continuing
review of the measures of care which are required.
Their task is to consider what requires to be done now
and in the future, not to attempt to alter what has been
done in the past. That approach can be seen working
itself out in the present case, as the children's hearing
are now satisfied that the time has come for the petitioner to be reintegrated fully into the family home.
We find here a further indication that this is not an
appropriate case for the exercise of the nobile
officium, which could, at best for the petitioner, affect
only the future conduct of this case by the children's

A hearing since it cannot be invoked as a means of taking past decisions to appeal.

For these reasons we must dismiss this petition on the ground that it is incompetent.

Counsel for Petitioner, Dunlop, QC, Murphy; Solicitors, Robson McLean, WS — Counsel for First Respondent (Reporter), M L Clark, QC; Solicitors, Biggart Baillie & Gifford, WS — Counsel for Second Respondent (Mother), G M Henderson; Solicitors, Stuart & Stuart, WS.

B

R D S

Inland Revenue Commissioners v Herd

C HOUSE OF LORDS

THE LORD CHANCELLOR
(LORD MACKAY OF CLASHFERN),
LORD KEITH OF KINKEL,
LORD JAUNCEY OF TULLICHETTLE,
LORD BROWNE-WILKINSON AND
LORD SLYNN OF HADLEY

17 JUNE 1993

D
Revenue — Income tax — Payment of income — Deduction of tax — Gain on shares acquired by company director treated as income liable to income tax — Whether "payment of emoluments" — Whether employers bound to deduct tax from consideration on disposal of shares — Whether collector entitled to require payment of tax by employee — Income and Corporation Taxes Act 1970 (c 10), s 204 — Income Tax (Employments) Regulations 1973 (SI 1973/334), regs 2 (1), 13 and 26 (3).

E Section 204 (1) of the Income and Corporation Taxes Act 1970 provided that "on the making of any payment of, or on account of, any income assessable to income tax under Schedule E", income tax should be deducted by the person making the payment in accordance with regulations made under that section. Regulation 13 of the Income Tax (Employments) Regulations 1973 provides that on the occasion of any payment of emoluments the employer shall ascertain the cumulative emoluments and cumulative tax; reg
F 20 imposes a duty to deduct the tax. Regulation 26 (3), prior to amendment, provided that where the amount deducted was less than that which the employee was liable to pay, the collector on being satisfied inter alia as to the employer's good faith, might direct that the excess be recovered from the employee. "Emoluments" are defined in reg 2 (1) as the full amount of any income to be taken into account in assessing liability under Sched E.

In 1979 a taxpayer was appointed group construction manager to a group of companies. Negotiations

took place between the taxpayer and the group as to G his remuneration for the position, in the course of which the taxpayer proposed that as part of his remuneration he should receive certain shares in one of the group of companies. This proposal was accepted and as a result the taxpayer bought 10,000 shares in a group company for the sum of £1, the then market value. In 1983 the taxpayer sold his shares back to the group for the sum of £380,000. The market value of the shares at that time was £211,300. The Inland Revenue assessed the taxpayer for income tax in respect of the increase in market value under H s 79 of the Finance Act 1972 and in respect of the excess of the price over the market value under s 67 of the Finance Act 1976.

The taxpayer appealed the assessments to the special commissioners, who allowed the appeal while rejecting an argument that if there was a liability to income tax then the payment made by the group for the shares was a payment of emoluments and it was for the group to deduct tax from this payment and account for it, and it was not open to the collector in terms of the I 1973 Regulations to require repayment from the taxpayers. The Inland Revenue appealed to the Court of Session, who held inter alia (by a majority) that the statutory provisions which required income tax to be paid on the gain also defined the gain as income, and the gain was therefore to be treated as emoluments of the employment, and income tax should have been deducted and accounted for by the employer in terms of the 1973 Regulations. The revenue appealed to the House of Lords. J

Held, that in both of the statutory provisions relied upon as creating liability, the liability to tax under Sched E was not attracted by the amount paid but, as in this case, to part only of the amount paid, and that neither the empowering provisions of the Act of 1970 nor the deduction regulations themselves included an obligation on the payer to deduct tax from a payment only part of which was assessable to income tax under Sched E (p 920F-H); and appeal *allowed*. K

Observed, that although there was no finding of fact in this case that any difficulty had been found in arriving at the appropriate market values, it was obvious that the determination of such values could give rise to substantial disputes (p 920K).

Appeal from the special commissioners of income tax
(Reported 1992 SLT 766) L
At a meeting of the Commissioners for the special purposes of the Income Tax Acts Charles Anderson Peden Herd appealed against an additional assessment to income tax for the year 1983-84 in the figure of £379,999, comprising £211,299 under s 79 of the Finance Act 1972 and £168,700 under s 67 of the Finance Act 1976, arising on the disposal by the taxpayer of shares which he had acquired in the Crudens group. The questions for determination were (1) whether the circumstances in which the taxpayer

A acquired the shares were such as were referred to in those provisions, and (2) whether the liability to account for any tax fell on the taxpayer's employer to the exclusion of the taxpayer.

Statutory provisions

The Finance Act 1972 provided:

"79.—(1) Where a person, on or after 6th April 1972, acquires shares or an interest in shares in a body corporate in pursuance of a right conferred on him or opportunity offered to him as a director or employee

B of that or any other body corporate, and not in pursuance of an offer to the public, subsections (4) and (7) of this section shall apply unless their application is excluded by subsections (2) and (3) of this section respectively. . . .

"(4) Where this subsection applies and the market value of the shares at the end of the period mentioned in subsection (6) below exceeds their market value at the time of the acquisition the person making the

C acquisition shall be chargeable to tax under Schedule E for the year of assessment in which that period ends on an amount equal, except as provided by subsection (5) below, to the excess (or, if his interest is less than the full beneficial ownership, such part of that amount as corresponds to his interest); and the amount so chargeable shall be treated as earned income, whether or not it would otherwise fall to be so treated."

The Finance Act 1976 provided:

D "67.—(1) Subsections (2) to (6) of this section apply where after 6th April 1976 — (a) a person employed or about to be employed in director's or higher-paid employment ("the employee"), or a person connected with him, acquires shares in a company (whether the employing company or not); and (b) the shares are acquired at an under-value in pursuance of a right or opportunity available by reason of the employment. . . .

"(7) Where after 6 April 1976 shares are acquired,

E whether or not at an under-value but otherwise as mentioned in subsection (1) above, and — (a) the shares are subsequently disposed of by surrender or otherwise so that neither the employee nor any person connected with him any longer has a beneficial interest in them; and (b) the disposal is for a consideration which exceeds the then market value of the shares, then for the year in which the disposal is effected the amount of the excess is treated as emoluments of the employee's employment and accordingly

F chargeable to income tax under Schedule E."

The Income and Corporation Taxes Act 1970 provided:

"181.—(1) The Schedule referred to as Schedule E is as follows:—

SCHEDULE E

"1. Tax under this Schedule shall be charged in respect of any office or employment on emoluments thereon which fall under one, or more than one, of the following Cases . . .

G "204.—(1) On the making of any payment of, or on account of, any income assessable to income tax under Schedule E, income tax shall, subject to and in accordance with regulations made by the Board under this section, be deducted or repaid by the person making the payment, notwithstanding that when the payment is made no assessment has been made in respect of the income and notwithstanding that the income is in whole or in part income for some year of assessment other than the year during which the payment is made.

H "(2) The Board shall make regulations with respect to the assessment, charge, collection and recovery of income tax in respect of all income assessable thereto under Schedule E, and those regulations may, in particular, include provision — (a) for requiring any person making any payment of, or on account of, any such income, when he makes the payment, to make a deduction or repayment of income tax calculated by reference to tax tables prepared by the Board, and for rendering persons who are required to make any such deduction or repayment accountable to, or, as the case

I may be, entitled to repayment from, the Board, (b) for the production to and inspection by persons authorised by the Board of wages sheets and other documents or records for the purpose of satisfying themselves that income tax has been and is being deducted, repaid and accounted for in accordance with the regulations, (c) for the collection and recovery, whether by deduction from any such income paid in any later year or otherwise, of income tax in respect of any such income which has not been deducted or

J otherwise recovered during the year, (d) for the assessment and charge of income tax by the inspector in respect of income to which this section applies, (e) for appeals with respect to matters arising under the regulations which would not otherwise be the subject of an appeal, and any such regulations shall have effect notwithstanding anything in the Income Tax Acts . . .

"(3) The said tax tables shall be constructed with a

K view to securing that, so far as possible — (a) the total income tax payable in respect of any income assessable under Schedule E for any year of assessment is deducted from such income paid during that year, and (b) the income tax deductible or repayable on the occasion of any payment of, or on account of, any such income is such that the total net income tax deducted since the beginning of the year of assessment bears to the total income tax payable for the year the same proportion that the part of the year which ends with the date of the payment bears to the whole year.

L "In this subsection references to the total income tax payable for the year shall be construed as references to the total income tax estimated to be payable for the year in respect of the income in question, subject to a provisional deduction for allowances and reliefs, and subject also, if necessary, to an adjustment for amounts overpaid or remaining unpaid on account of income tax in respect of income assessable under Schedule E for any previous year.

"For the purpose of estimating the total income tax

A payable as aforesaid, it may be assumed in relation to any payment of, or on account of, income assessable under Schedule E that the income paid in the part of the year for the assessment which ends with the making of the payment will bear to the income for the whole of that year the same proportion as that part of the year bears to the whole year."

The Income Tax (Employments) Regulations 1973, as amended up to 1983, provided:

B "2.—(1) In these regulations, unless the context otherwise requires — . . . 'emoluments' means the full amount of any income to be taken into account in assessing liability under Schedule E after the deduction of allowable superannuation contributions and references to payments of emoluments include references to payments on account of emoluments; . . . 'employee' means any person in receipt of emoluments; 'employer' means any person paying emoluments; . . .

C "6.—(1) Every employer, on making any payment of emoluments during any year to any employee in respect of whom a code authorisation has been issued to him for that year by the Inspector, shall — (a) if he has not already done so, prepare a deductions working sheet for that employee; and (b) deduct or repay tax in accordance with these regulations by reference to the appropriate code, which shall be specified on the code authorisation. . . .

D "26.—. . . (3) If the amount which the employer is liable to pay to the collector under paragraph (1) of this regulation exceeds the amount actually deducted by him from emoluments paid during the relevant income tax month, the collector, on being satisfied by the employer that he took reasonable care to comply with the provisions of these regulations and that the under-deduction was due to an error made in good faith, may direct that the amount of the excess shall be recovered from the employee, and where the collector so directs the employer shall not be liable to pay the amount of the said excess to the collector.

E "(4) If the amount which the employer is liable to pay to the collector under paragraph (1) of this regulation exceeds the amount actually deducted by him from emoluments paid during the relevant income tax month, and the Commissioners of Inland Revenue are of the opinion that an employee has received his emoluments knowing that the employer has wilfully failed to deduct therefrom the amount of tax which he was liable to deduct under these regulations, the said F Commissioners may direct that the amount of the excess shall be recovered from the employee, and where they so direct the employer shall not be liable to pay the amount of the said excess to the collector. . . .

"49.—. . . (2) If the tax payable under the assessment exceeds the total net tax deducted from the employee's emoluments during the year, the Inspector may require the person assessed to pay the excess to the Collector instead of taking it into account in determining the appropriate code for a subsequent year,

and where the Inspector so requires the person assessed shall pay the excess accordingly. G

"(3) For the purpose of determining the amount of any difference or excess as aforesaid, any necessary adjustment shall be made to the aforesaid total net tax in respect of — (a) any tax which the employer was liable to deduct from the employee's emoluments but failed so to deduct, having regard to whether the Commissioners of Inland Revenue or the collector have or have not directed that tax shall be recovered from the employee; (b) any tax overpaid or remaining unpaid for any year; . . . but any such difference resulting H from an adjustment under sub-paragraph (a) of this paragraph shall be disregarded for the purpose of paragraph (1) above and of computing any tax overpaid under sub-paragraph (b) of this paragraph."

Cases referred to

Booth v Mirror Group Newspapers plc [1992] STC 615.
R v Walton General Commissioners, ex p Wilson [1983] STC 464.

The commissioners *answered* question 1 in favour of I the taxpayer and question 2 in favour of the revenue.

The revenue appealed to the Court of Session by stated case on the question whether the commissioners had correctly answered question 1. The taxpayer sought a determination of whether the commissioners had correctly answered question 2.

Appeal
The appeal was heard before an Extra Division on J 17 and 18 December 1991.

On 14 February 1992 the Extra Division *answered* both questions stated by the special commissioners in the *negative*. (Reported 1992 SLT 766.)

The revenue appealed to the House of Lords.

Appeal
The appeal was heard before the Lord Chancellor K (Lord Mackay of Clashfern), Lord Keith of Kinkel, Lord Jauncey of Tullichettle, Lord Browne-Wilkinson and Lord Slynn of Hadley on 15 and 16 February 1993.

On 17 June 1993 the House *allowed* the appeal and *held* that the second question of law posed by the special commissioners should be answered in the *affirmative*.
L

THE LORD CHANCELLOR (LORD MACKAY OF CLASHFERN).—This is an appeal by the Commissioners of Inland Revenue from a decision of an Extra Division of the Court of Session (Lord McCluskey, Lord Coulsfield and Lord Sutherland), which by a majority, Lord Sutherland dissenting, found against the revenue on a question of law stated by the special commissioner in an appeal by the taxpayer against an additional assessment to income tax under Sched E on the taxpayer for the year to April

1984 in respect of the sale of shares. The question is whether on a true construction of s 79 of the Finance Act 1972 and s 67 of the Finance Act 1976, the Income and Corporation Taxes Act 1970 and the Income Tax (Employments) Regulations 1973, the liability to account for any tax payable on the assessment under appeal fell wholly on the taxpayer.

The facts on which this question arises may be summarised as follows, and I am grateful to the parties for their agreement on the statement of facts, which I have largely followed. The taxpayer was appointed an executive director of Cruden Building & Civil Engineering Ltd (hereinafter referred to as "CBCE") on 25 March 1980. At that date, CBCE was a wholly owned subsidiary of Cruden Investments Ltd (hereinafter referred to as "Investments"). Later in 1980 the taxpayer was appointed a director of Investments and he retained that directorship and his directorship of CBCE until 1987. Apart from the taxpayer's shareholding referred to below, CBCE remained a wholly owned subsidiary of Investments at all material times. On 25 March 1980 Investments sold to the taxpayer 10,000 ordinary shares in CBCE which represented 10 per cent of the issued capital of that company. The consideration paid by the taxpayer for those shares was £1.00. That was the market value of the shares as at 25 March 1980. Investments agreed to the sale of the shares solely because of the taxpayer's acceptance of appointment as an executive director of CBCE. The 10,000 ordinary shares in CBCE were acquired by the taxpayer in such circumstances as are set out in s 79 (1) of the Finance Act 1972. The shares were not acquired as an undervalue but otherwise were acquired by the taxpayer in such circumstances as are set out in s 67 (1) of the Finance Act 1976.

On 4 May 1983 the taxpayer sold his 10,000 ordinary shares in CBCE back to Investments for the sum of £380,000. The market value of the shares at that date is agreed to have been £211,300. Investments paid the taxpayer £250,000 at once and the balance on 30 November 1984. In terms of s 79 of the Finance Act 1972 and s 67 of the Finance Act 1976 a charge to income tax under Sched E fell to be made since as a result of the sale of shares on 4 May 1983 the taxpayer ceased to have any beneficial interest in them.

The inspector of taxes made an additional assessment under Sched E on the taxpayer for the year to April 1984 in the figure of £379,999, that is to say £380,000 minus £1.00, in respect of the sale of the shares. The assessment was made under s 79 of the Finance Act 1972 and under s 67 of the Finance Act 1976, as to £211,299 under s 79 of the 1972 Act and as to £168,700 under s 67 of the 1976 Act.

The taxpayer appealed against the additional assessment to the special commissioner who reduced the assessment to nil. The Commissioners of Inland Revenue appealed to the Inner House of the Court of Session. There a number of matters were discussed but the only issue which arises before your Lordships is that which I have stated at the beginning of this speech.

The Income and Corporation Taxes Act 1970, s 181 (1) imposes a charge to tax under Sched E and provides that: "1. Tax under this Schedule shall be charged in respect of any office or employment on emoluments therefrom which fall under one, or more than one, of the following Cases". Section 183 (1) of the Act of 1970 provides that the expression "emoluments" shall include all salaries, fees, wages, perquisites and profits whatsoever.

Section 204 of the Act of 1970 makes provision for the assessment and recovery of income tax under Sched E and provides as follows: [his Lordship quoted the terms of s 204 set out supra and continued:]

The regulations made under that power in force at the material time for the purposes of this appeal are the Income Tax (Employments) Regulations 1973 as amended up to 1983. Regulation 2 (1) of these regulations includes the provision: [his Lordship quoted the terms of reg 2 (1) set out supra and continued:]

The critical regulation is reg 6 (1) which provides: [his Lordship quoted the terms of reg 6 (1) and continued:]

The details of these arrangements are contained in later provisions of the regulations to many of which it is not necessary to refer. Some, however, must be referred to as they have a bearing on the argument addressed to your Lordships on the appeal.

Regulation 26 provides: [his Lordship quoted the terms of reg 26 (3) and (4) and continued:] No direction was made under either of these powers in the present case.

Regulation 48 provides for assessment and appeals. Regulation 49 makes provision with regard to a situation where the amount deducted is less or more than the total due under an assessment under Sched E for the year in question.

Regulation 49 provides: [his Lordship quoted the terms of reg 49 (2) and (3) and continued:]

It follows from the provision I have just quoted that unless the commissioners or the collector have exercised powers which would enable a charge to be made against the employee in respect of sums which the employer should have deducted, the employee cannot be held liable for amounts which the employer ought to have deducted whether or not he has actually done so — in other words, apart from the powers to which I have referred, the Commissioners of Inland Revenue do not have power to claim from the employee tax which the employer was liable to deduct and pay to the commissioners whether or not he has done so.

The scope of the general scheme in respect of Sched E and the regulations to which I have referred is illustrated by the decision of Hobhouse J in *Booth v Mirror Group Newspapers plc* which was cited in argument but has no particular bearing on the problem arising in the present appeal.

It is common ground between the parties to this appeal that wide as the provisions are for deduction of tax from payments, they can apply only in respect of *payments* by the employer to the employee and therefore where benefits in kind not involving payments by an employer are in question they are not directly applicable. On the other hand in considering the coding the Inland Revenue are entitled to take into account benefits in kind which are taxable under Sched E although not the subject of specific deduction of tax under the regulations. See *R v Walton General Commissioners, ex p Wilson.*

It is to be noted, however, at this stage, that the provisions for deduction apply only to a payment of emoluments or a payment on account of emoluments.

I turn now to examine the specific provisions under which tax under Sched E is agreed to be chargeable either on the taxpayer or on Investments in this appeal.

First of all s 79 of the Finance Act 1972, subs (4): [his Lordship quoted the terms of s 79 (4) and continued:]

The period referred to in subs (6) below is a period which may well come to an end without any payment. In this case, however, it came to an end when the taxpayer ceased to have any beneficial interest in the shares in question and following on that payments were made to him by Investments. If these payments were payments of emoluments or a payment on account of emoluments, I would conclude that the requirement to deduct tax applied even if in other situations subs (4) might be triggered where no such payment occurred.

The other provision founded on to create liability under Sched E is s 67 of the Finance Act 1976 which in subs (7) provides: [his Lordship quoted the terms of s 67 (7) and continued:]

It was pointed out by the Commissioners of Inland Revenue that in relation to both of these provisions the taxpayer's argument might involve a person who was an "employer" only for the purposes of the income tax regulations because he made the payment in question, but that he might have no knowledge of the circumstances which gave rise to tax liability. On the other hand counsel for the taxpayer argued strongly that such circumstances were likely to be extremely limited and pointed to the exception to which I have referred for payments in good faith by an employer in the deduction regulations. I am of opinion that your Lordships have not material on which to form a very accurate view of the number of different circumstances in which these provisions apply and in particular the extent to which any third party acquirer of the shares might be ignorant of the circumstances which give rise to liability. I therefore prefer to rest my view on a narrower ground.

In both of the statutory provisions relied upon as creating liability, the liability to tax under Sched E is not attracted by the amount paid but as in this case to part only of the amount paid. The charging mechanism is not one which treats the whole payment made in this case as an emolument and then preserves a right to claim a deduction by way of allowance. Indeed in this case each payment is subject to two different sections which provide the basis for two different charges under Sched E on sums which in total are less than the total of the payments. It is true that the deduction in this case is small but the ascertainment of its amount, involving as it does questions of the market value of shares which are not publicly quoted, could involve considerable calculation and, perhaps even more important, substantial judgments on matters of opinion. Neither the empowering provisions of the Act of 1970 nor the deduction regulations themselves include an obligation on the payer to deduct tax from a payment only part of which is assessable to income tax under Sched E. Indeed, this is emphasised by the provision that the obligation to deduct arises on the making of any payment of, or *on account of,* any income assessable to income tax under Sched E. Where the provision is as detailed as that, if the intention had been to impose an obligation to make a deduction from a payment which was in part to be treated as income under Sched E, I would have expected this to have been expressly provided for and, even more important, some machinery set up for distinguishing in the single payment between the amount to be subject to deduction and the balance.

This does not mean that by making one payment of two separate amounts, each of which can be determined precisely at the time the payment is made, one could avoid the obligation to make a deduction, but I think it is significant, and in support of the view which I have taken, that s 60 of the Finance Act 1976 treats the expenses there in question as emoluments of the employment and accordingly chargeable to income tax under Sched E, preserving in subs (2) a claim for deductions under the appropriate sections of the Taxes Act. So, for example, where remuneration and expenses are paid together the total payment is a payment of emoluments within the provision requiring the payer to make the appropriate deduction of income tax on making the payment.

Although it is true that there is no finding of fact in this case that any difficulty was found in arriving at the appropriate market values, it is obvious that the determination of these values could give rise to substantial disputes.

Although I found the argument for the taxpayer attractive and cogently argued, I have reached the conclusion ultimately that to give effect to it would be to extend the scope of the provisions for deduction of tax under Sched E to situations for which they were not intended and in respect of which there is no machinery for determining in respect of a single payment at the time the payment is made the amount of it which is to be subject to the deduction arrangements.

The taxpayer points to the provisions of reg 26 (3) of the 1973 Regulations. I think it is noteworthy and supportive of the view which I have formed that the regulation speaks about underdeduction due to an error made in good faith and does not appear to me to deal with the situation where the amount of emolu-

A ments paid is in question. There is no provision that I have been able to find which contemplates a question about the amounts of emoluments involved in any particular payment: rather the whole scheme appears to me to proceed on the assumption that all the payments in question are payments of emoluments and that any deductions are in respect of allowances to be made in computing the tax liability consequent upon the payments. I conclude therefore that when the Commissioners of Inland Revenue submit that the decision of the Court of Session should be reversed B "because the consideration paid by Investments for the shares was not a payment of income assessable to income tax under Sched E" they are correct.

The contention advanced by the taxpayer in this case was said by the Commissioners of Inland Revenue to be novel and, in my view, on a proper reading of the statutory provisions in question it falls to be rejected, but it is right that I should emphasise that my view applies only where a particular payment is treated only in part as assessable to income tax C under Sched E. It would not prevent a payer being under an obligation to deduct tax where it was clear that there were two or more payments made together, some of which were emoluments under Sched E while others were not.

The reasons which I have given differ considerably from the reasons given by Lord Sutherland in the Court of Session for reaching the same view and I would not be prepared to affirm his analysis of the D transaction into a capital transaction completed at the time of payment followed by a statutory treatment of certain parts of the payment as income for tax purposes. The reasoning of the majority only takes one the distance of saying that part of the payment was to be treated as emoluments of the taxpayer's employment under Sched E but for the reasons I have given this does not appear to me to be sufficient to sustain the taxpayer's argument and to have obliged the employers to deduct income tax under the 1973 Regu-E lations on making the payment which even on the majority's view was in part only so assessable.

For the reasons I have given I would allow the appeal and hold that the second question of law posed by the special commissioner should be answered in the affirmative.

LORD KEITH OF KINKEL.—I agree that this appeal should be allowed for the reasons set out in the speech of my noble and learned friend the Lord Chan-F cellor.

LORD JAUNCEY OF TULLICHETTLE.—I have had the advantage of reading in draft the speech of my noble and learned friend the Lord Chancellor. For the reasons which he gives I agree that the appeal should be allowed.

LORD BROWNE-WILKINSON.—I have had the advantage of reading in draft the speech of my noble and learned friend the Lord Chancellor. For the

reasons which he gives I agree that the appeal should be allowed.   G

LORD SLYNN OF HADLEY.—I have had the advantage of reading in draft the speech prepared by my noble and learned friend, the Lord Chancellor. For the reasons he gives I too would allow the appeal.

Counsel for Appellants (Revenue), Nimmo Smith, QC, Henderson (English Bar), Keen; Solicitors, T H Scott, Solicitor of Inland Revenue (Scotland), B E Cleave, H *Solicitor of Inland Revenue — Counsel for Respondent (Taxpayer), Drummond Young, QC, Tyre; Solicitors, Shepherd & Wedderburn, WS, Dyson Bell Martin, London.*

M G T

[The relevant provisions of the Finance Act 1972, s 79 now appear in the Income and Corporation Taxes Act 1988, s 138 (1) and (9); those of the Finance Act 1976, s 67 now appear in the 1988 Act, 's 162 (1) and (6); and those of the Income I and Corporation Taxes Act 1970, s 204 (1) now appear in the 1988 Act, s 203 (1).]

Viewpoint Housing Association Ltd v Lothian Regional Council   J

OUTER HOUSE
LORD CAMERON OF LOCHBROOM
30 OCTOBER 1991

Roads and streets — Private road — Public passage toler-ated by owner for less than prescriptive period — Right K *of owner to restrict passage — Roads (Scotland) Act 1984 (c 54), ss 59 and 151.*

Section 59 (3) of the Roads (Scotland) Act 1984, which superseded similar provisions in earlier legislation, empowers a roads authority to require the removal of an unauthorised obstruction on a road. "Road" is defined in s 151 as "any way . . . over which there is a public right of passage".

In about 1973 a housing association acquired a site L for the purpose of erecting sheltered housing. As part of the development they applied to the roads authority for two street orders under and in terms of the Edinburgh Corporation Order Confirmation Act 1967 authorising the construction of a street. The street orders were granted and a street was constructed within the site to the standard necessary for the street to be taken over by the roads authority. From about 1976, when the development was completed, until 1990, members of the public were allowed to use the street without hindrance. On two occasions the

A housing association made application for the roads authority to adopt the street for purposes of maintenance, but the roads authority declined to do so. In 1990 the housing association erected a barrier, in the form of a removable chain and two posts, across the street. The roads authority, founding on s 59 (3) of the 1984 Act, ordered the housing association to remove the barrier. The housing association refused to do so and raised proceedings seeking declarator that they were entitled to erect and maintain the barrier, and interdict against the roads authority, or anyone on their behalf, from removing the barrier. They averred that the street remained private despite the fact that members of the public had been allowed access. The roads authority, whilst accepting that no public right of way existed, argued that a public right of passage, being something less than a public right of way, had been created, and that this entitled them to invoke s 59 (3) of the 1984 Act and require removal of any obstruction.

Held, that the fact that a street had at some time acquired the character of a road for the purposes of s 59 of the 1984 Act did not prevent the owners thereafter from restricting the class of those who would be entitled to use it by erecting a barrier, and that permission by the owner of the street to its use by the public for a period short of the prescriptive period was terminable (pp 925B-D and K-L, 926F-I and 927D-E); and declarator and interdict *granted* in terms of the summons.

Magistrates of Edinburgh v North British Railway Co (1904) 6 F 620, *followed; Cheyne v MacNeill,* 1973 SLT 27, and *Cowie v Strathclyde Regional Council,* 1st Div, 8 July 1986, unreported, *considered.*

Action of declarator and interdict

Viewpoint Housing Association Ltd raised an action against Lothian Regional Council in which the pursuers sought declarator that they were entitled to erect and maintain a barrier across an access road which had been built on land which they owned, and interdict against the defenders, or anyone on their behalf, from removing the barrier.

The case came before the Lord Ordinary (Lord Cameron of Lochbroom) on procedure roll in respect of the pursuers' plea to the relevancy of the defences.

Statutory provisions

The Roads (Scotland) Act 1984 provides:

"59.—(1) Subject to subsection (6) below, nothing shall be placed or deposited in a road so as to cause an obstruction except with the roads authority's consent in writing and in accordance with any reasonable conditions which they think fit to attach to the consent. . . .

"(3) Without prejudice to subsection (2) above, a person who contravenes subsection (1) above may be required by the roads authority or by a constable in uniform to remove the obstruction forthwith, and commits an offence if he fails to do so. . . .

"151.—. . . 'private road' means any road other than

a public road; . . . 'public road' means a road which a roads authority have a duty to maintain; . . . 'road' means . . . any way (other than a waterway) over which there is a public right of passage (by whatever means)".

Cases referred to

Beattie v Scott, 1990 SCCR 435.
Bruce v Glasgow Corporation (1903) 11 SLT 389.
Cheyne v MacNeill, 1973 SLT 27.
Colquhoun v Paton (1859) 21 D 996.
Cowie v Strathclyde Regional Council, 1st Div, 8 July 1986, unreported.
Cumming v Smollet and the Dumbartonshire Road Trustees (1852) 14 D 885.
Dunn v Keane, 1976 JC 39.
Edinburgh (Magistrates of) v North British Railway Co (1904) 6 F 620.
Harrison v Hill, 1931 SLT 598; 1932 JC 13.
Hogg v Nicholson, 1968 SLT 265.
Kinning Park Police Commissioners v Thomson & Co (1877) 4 R 528.
Macpherson v Scottish Rights of Way and Recreation Society Ltd (1888) 15 R (HL) 68.
Mann v Brodie (1885) 12 R (HL) 52.
Paterson v Ogilvy, 1957 SLT 354; 1957 JC 42.
Young v Carmichael, 1993 SLT 167; 1991 SCCR 332.

Textbook referred to

Rankine, *Land-ownership* (4th ed), pp 325-329.

On 30 October 1991 the Lord Ordinary *sustained* the pursuers' preliminary plea, *repelled* the defences and *granted* decree in terms of the conclusions of the summons.

LORD CAMERON OF LOCHBROOM.—In this action the pursuers are a housing association who own subjects at Gillespie Crescent, Edinburgh. They seek declarator that they are entitled to erect and maintain in existence a barrier by means of a removable chain and two posts or some such other means, across the private access to and from the subjects owned by them and comprising 43-47 Gillespie Crescent, Edinburgh. They further seek interdict against the defenders or anyone acting on their behalf from removing the barrier.

From the pleadings it appears that the barrier was erected some time prior to 11 July 1990. On that date the defenders sent a letter to the pursuers which purported to give notice in terms of s 59 (3) of the Roads (Scotland) Act 1984 to remove the barrier forthwith. A similar letter was sent by the defenders to the pursuers on 3 August 1990.

The pursuers maintain that the defenders have no right to remove the barrier which is erected on land owned by the pursuers and which comprises a private access which the defenders have never maintained. The pursuers further aver that the public have no right to use the said private access and in particular have no rights of passage over it and accordingly the pursuers are entitled to erect and maintain in existence the barrier to prevent any such use.

The general background to the dispute is that in about 1973 the pursuers purchased a 2½ acre site adjoining Gillespie Crescent, Edinburgh, for the purpose of developing a sheltered housing complex. As part of the development the pursuers applied to the defenders for two street orders which were subsequently made by the defenders on 13 October 1975 and 1 March 1976. The street orders were made in terms of the Edinburgh Corporation Order Confirmation Act 1967. The street subsequently constructed was constructed wholly within the pursuers' site and made up to the standard required by the defenders, namely the standard necessary for the street to be taken over by the defenders. It is a matter of admission that the street has never been adopted by the defenders for maintenance purposes.

The defenders' case is that the street and some 35 associated parking spaces available at the development have been used by the public without hindrance since completion of the development in about 1976. They further aver that between at least 1979 and 1981, during which time the pursuers made application to the defenders for the defenders to adopt the street, the pursuers intended that the said street should be a road over which the public had unrestricted access, and that such use of the street continued until about 1990. The defenders further aver that any restriction or attempted restriction by the pursuers of such general right of access prior to about June or July 1990 was minimal. The defenders' case is stated in the following averment in ans 4: "Further explained and averred that what the pursuers call a 'private access' is a street within the meaning of said 1967 Order and a road within the meaning of the Roads (Scotland) Act 1984. Reference is also made to s 224 (1) of the said Order of 1967. Once said road has become 'a street' and 'a road' as aforesaid by virtue of the said unrestricted and tolerated use made of it by the public, the pursuers were, and are, unable to deprive it of that statutory character by physically obstructing it."

The pursuers have submitted that the defence to the action which is encapsulated in the above averment is irrelevant and lacking in specification. It is convenient at this juncture to set out the provisions which are referred to in or relevant to the defenders' pleadings. Section 224 (1) of the Edinburgh Corporation Order Confirmation Act 1967 is in the following terms: "(a) A person shall not, without the consent of the Corporation, make, fix or place: (1) any erection, encroachment, obstruction or projection in, on, or over any street".

In s 3 of the Act "street" is defined as meaning "any highway, road, . . . or any part thereof open to be used by the public and whether it is a thoroughfare or not". Furthermore, "private street" is defined as meaning "a street other than a public street", while "public street" is defined as meaning "any street or part thereof which is wholly maintained by the Corporation or of which the Corporation may undertake the maintenance after the commencement of the Order".

In the same Act by s 241 it is provided that: "(1) the

Corporation shall have the charge, control and superintendence of all private streets; (2) all private streets shall be maintained to the satisfaction of the Corporation by the persons responsible for their maintenance".

It is further provided by s 242 that the majority of frontagers may require private streets to be taken over by the corporation.

In terms of the Roads (Scotland) Act 1984, s 59 (1) it is provided inter alia that: "nothing shall be placed or deposited in a road so as to cause an obstruction except with the roads authority's consent in writing and in accordance with any reasonable conditions which they think fit to attach to the consent".

By s 151 of the Act a road "means, subject to subsection (3) below, any way (other than a waterway) over which there is a public right of passage (by whatever means)". Public road is defined as meaning a road which "a roads authority have a duty to maintain" and a private road is defined as "any road other than a public road". By virtue of s 154, where any local enactment provides for any matter which is also provided for by any provision of the 1984 Act, the provision of that Act shall have effect in substitution for the local enactment which shall cease to have effect. Accordingly, since the coming into force of s 59 of the 1984 Act, the provisions of s 224 (1) of the 1967 Confirmation Act have ceased to have effect.

In support of the pursuers' fourth plea in law, counsel submitted that the proper starting place was the Roads (Scotland) Act 1984. It was plain that the street with which this case is concerned was not a public road as defined in s 151 of the 1984 Act, not being a road which the defenders had a duty to maintain. The defenders did not found upon some express grant by the pursuers of a public right of passage over the street. The only other way in which a public right of passage could be acquired was by prescription. The prescriptive period of 20 years for the acquisition of a public right of way to be exempt from challenge had not passed. Reference was made to s 3 (3) of the Prescription and Limitation (Scotland) Act 1973. Even if unrestricted and tolerated use of the street had been made by the public for the period averred, the pursuers were still entitled as owners of the solum of the street to resume exclusive control and discontinue public use. Counsel referred to Rankine, *Landownership in Scotland* (4th ed), p 329 where it is said of a public right of way: "This is the ordinary name given to such a public passage as was not originally created, has not been adopted, and is not maintained or repaired, by any statutory authority. It is scarcely conceivable that a landowner should, by express dedication, throw open to the public irrevocably a passage which neither the public nor any local authority is bound to repair. Accordingly, as a matter of fact, all such rights of way have been acquired through prescription, which ('as a judicial speculation') presumes an informal grant."

Counsel submitted that the fact that a landowner tolerated public use for a period shorter than the

A prescriptive period did not deprive him of the right to withdraw the permission or licence giving rise to such tolerance. He did so under reference to *Magistrates of Edinburgh v North British Railway Co, Kinning Park Police Commissioners v Thomson & Co* and *Bruce v Glasgow Corporation.* While there was some judicial reference in cases to a public right of way being acquired by dedication, that doctrine formed no part of the law of Scotland. Counsel made reference to *Cumming v Smollett and the Dumbartonshire Road Trustees* and in particular the opinion of Lord Ivory at

B p 894, *Colquhoun v Paton* and the unanimous judgment of the court at p 1003, and *Macpherson v Scottish Rights of Way and Recreation Society Ltd* in the speech of Lord Halsbury LC. He submitted that for the constitution of a right of prescriptive user by the public, nothing less than user by the public as a matter of right continuously and without interruption for the full statutory period of 20 years sufficed. Reference was made to the speech of Lord Watson in *Mann v Brodie* at p 57. Accordingly the common law being

C that nothing short of prescription would serve to constitute a public right of way, nothing in the Roads (Scotland) Act 1984 innovated upon the common law. The public right of passage was not defined in the Act. It was however clear from the treatment of highways in Rankine, at pp 325 et seq, that the public right of passage was a concept known to the law of Scotland under the term "highway". At p 329 Rankine distinguished between the term "highway" as the general name for many sorts of public passages which had

D been set up or maintained by public funds and a public right of way as one which was not originally created, had not been adopted and was not maintained or repaired by any statutory authority. The law remained unchanged that the owner of a private road, so long as it was not adopted by the relevant statutory authority, could at any time within the statutory period of 20 years discontinue the hitherto tolerated use of it by the public generally. If he did so the provisions of s 59 (3), which permitted a roads authority to

E require a person who contravened s 59 (1) to remove the obstruction forthwith, gave no power to the defenders to control any barrier erected by the pursuers on the street in question in the exercise of their private right of ownership with the intention of restricting access by means of the barrier to such persons as resided within the development or had legitimate business in the development. The means employed by the pursuers to assert their private right of ownership in the present case were legitimate and

F the fact that the barrier might otherwise prevent members of the public who had previously obtained access to the street or the public generally from obtaining free access in future, was of no relevance.

For the defenders it was submitted that they had set out a sufficiently relevant case as to the nature and extent of the use of the road as to entitle them to a proof before answer. Immediately a road fell within the definition of a road under the 1984 Act, that is to say a road over which there was a public right of passage, s 59 came into play and thereafter the pur-

G suers were powerless to prevent those powers being exercised. The statutory definition did not employ the term "public right of way" although that could have been done. Otherwise there was nothing in the Act to explain the meaning of "public right of passage". Accordingly it was necessary to look at the law prior to 1984 to give content and meaning to the phrase. In counsel's submission the statutory framework applicable to roads prior to the passing of the 1984 Act recognised a right, being something less than a specific public right of way, which was constituted by tolera-

H tion of use by the public generally over ways or streets which were privately owned. If the character of the use was such that it was use by the public and tolerated over a significant period of time, that fact gave rise to a public right of passage which was something less than a public right of way. Counsel referred to the definition of "road" in s 50 of the Roads (Scotland) Act 1970. This provided that "road" included "any highway and any other road to which the public has access". This definition of a road was also that

I employed for the purposes of the Road Traffic Act 1972 by virtue of s 196 (1) of that Act. While accepting that the relevant provisions of the Edinburgh Corporation Order Confirmation Act 1967 had been superseded by the provisions of the 1984 Act, counsel submitted that it was relevant in determining whether in this case a public right of passage had been constituted to have regard to the fact that the application for street orders had been made under ss 247 and 248 of the 1967 Act. Such an order was required for the construction of a new street as that was defined by the

J Act. Therefore the intended street was a private street to be open to be used by the public. Counsel conceded however that this did not constitute dedication and that it was necessary to go further in order to justify the constitution of a public right of passage by establishing subsequent tolerance of public use of the street. That a public right of passage meant something less than a public right of way or express grant was consistent with decisions in road traffic cases since 1930. He referred to *Hogg v Nicholson* and *Dunn v*

K *Keane.* Counsel submitted that once an owner had allowed the public to use a private road for any length of time it became a road within the meaning of the 1984 Act and the owner was thereafter barred from taking any action to place or deposit anything on the road so as to cause an obstruction. The choice open to an owner was either to maintain it as a private road over which the public generally had no access from the start; alternatively, if he chose to allow access to the public generally for a considerable period of time,

L then the road had a public right of passage over it and was thereafter a road for the purposes of the 1984 Act. Counsel made reference to *Young v Carmichael* and *Beattie v Scott.* Counsel also referred to the decision of the Inner House in *Cowie v Strathclyde Regional Council.* In that case Lord President Emslie had said: "Counsel for the respondent was, in our opinion, well founded in saying that the definition of 'road' in the Act of 1984 does not require that there must exist over the 'way' a public right of way. Parliament has not chosen to define 'road' with reference to the well

A understood concept of a public right of way at common law. Under the definition there must at the outset be a 'way' and the pursuer's averments clearly disclose that the lane which he describes is, on any view, a 'way'. All that is required, therefore, in order to establish that the lane is a 'road' within the meaning of the Act of 1984 is to show that there exists over it 'a public right of passage'. It does not, for example, have to be shown that the passage is between one public place and another. Since it is well known that 'roads' within the meaning of the Act include cul-de-

B sacs, and that some exist to provide access and egress to private properties it is evident that the 'right of passage' mentioned in the definition of the word 'road' involves less exacting considerations than those which govern the existence of a public right of way over private land."

The substantial issue in the present case is whether, even if the street in question had at some time or other within the period following its construction acquired the character of a street for the purposes of s 224 (1)

C of the 1967 Act and a road for the purposes of s 59 of the Roads (Scotland) Act 1984 by virtue of the unrestricted and tolerated use made of it for a period by the public, the pursuers were in law deprived thereafter of restricting the class of those who would be entitled to make use of it by means of the erection of a barrier and chain which could only be removed upon permission being granted to selected persons. In my opinion, counsel for the pursuers was well founded in saying that the decision in the *Magistrates of Edinburgh* case

D demonstrated that such was not the effect of the 1967 Act. In that case, the provisions under consideration were those of the Edinburgh Municipal and Police Act 1879. There was no substantial difference between the relevant provisions of that Act and of the 1967 Act. Each provided for a definition of "street" by reference to the phrase "open to be used by the public". Each provided for the local authority to have "sole charge, control and superintendence of all streets including private streets". Each defined private streets by refer-

E ence to maintenance by persons other than the local authority. Each provided that the maintenance of private streets might be undertaken by the local authority in which event they became public streets. At p 638 Lord Kinnear, with whose opinion the remaining members of the court concurred, said this: "But it is said that, so far at least as the railway bridge is concerned, it is covered by the words 'bridges open to be used by the public'. These are words of ordinary

F language, and they do not appear to be very difficult of interpretation. A bridge is not open to the public, if the public is prevented from making use of it by any physical or legal obstruction; and the definition must therefore mean that it is physically accessible, and that the public is either entitled or allowed to enter upon it. But the words of definition describe a condition of fact, without any implication of legal right or liability. So long as that condition of fact continues, the definition applies. If it is lawfully altered, the definition applies no longer. There is nothing in words that are merely descriptive to import a transference of rights of

property from one person to another, or from a private owner to the public."   G

Lord Kinnear then considers an argument that the bridge had vested in the magistrates. After pointing out that the Act vested no right in the magistrates beyond "charge, control and superintendence" and that the criterion of the power to control and regulate was the fact that the street or bridge was open to the public, he continued (at p 639): "If the ground is not already subject to a public right, there is no positive enactment that touches the inherent power of the private owner to exclude the public, and if the public H has been allowed to pass, out of mere goodwill and so long only as their passage is not inconsistent with the use and occupation by the proprietor of his own property, there is nothing in the statute to prevent the proprietor from taking his road or bridge outside the definition by appropriating it to purposes inconsistent with public use. . . But the pursuers' argument is that if they once allow the public to enter upon a road or bridge although not for long enough to found a prescriptive right, and without creating an adverse I right in any other form, the supereminent right of the Magistrates comes in to compel them to keep their property open to the public for all time. This is confiscation of private property for the benefit of the community, without compensation, and without previous notice which is generally exacted before power is given by Parliament even to purchase without the owner's consent. A construction of an Act of Parliament so inconsistent with the ordinary methods of legislation ought not to be adopted if it is J not the plain meaning of clear language, and I find nothing in the Act to support it. The true effect of the clauses founded on seems to me to be that so long as private streets are streets in fact, the owners must submit to the superintendence and control of the Magistrates for the safety and advantage of the community. But I find nothing to interfere with the legal right of private owners to convert their property to other uses, if independently of the police statute it has not become the subject of any public right of way." K

In one part of the opinion of Lord Kinnear he makes reference to a familiar situation that landowners may lay out ground for streets in such a way as "to create an indefeasible right in the public or in a community of feuars". But as I understood the submissions for the defenders, they eschewed any such suggestion in the present case. In my opinion, the reasoning in Lord Kinnear's opinion applies equally to the construction to be applied to the provisions of the 1967 Act to the L effect that there was nothing in that Act which interfered with the pursuers' legal right to restrict or prevent members of the public from entering upon the street. By the same token, while the definition of a road for the purposes of the Roads (Scotland) Act 1970 and the Road Traffic Act 1972 and its precursors was slightly different from the definition of a street in the 1967 Act, I do not think that anything turns upon that fact. In *Cheyne v MacNeill* at p 30 Lord Justice General Emslie considered the definition of road in s 257 (1) of the Road Traffic Act 1960, namely "any

A highway and any other road to which the public has access". He said: "The statute does not in terms require that the access upon which the issue of liability to the statutory provisions depends shall be in respect of any legally enforceable rights of passage. Further, the definition contrasts 'highway' with the words 'road to which the public has access'. Upon a 'highway' the public right of passage is secured by law and its maintenance is the responsibility of a statutory authority. A 'road' within the meaning of the definition would therefore seem to include a way which
B need not possess either of these qualities. From this contrast, it is not difficult to infer that the words 'to which the public has access' are necessarily referable to a situation in which it is found-in-fact that the public has access — access for the purpose of which a road is intended or designed, i.e., passage on foot or in a vehicle. But when the statute refers to access it cannot be assumed that this means access which is obtained unlawfully, e.g., by climbing over or opening gates, or by surmounting walls or fences, designed to
C exclude potential intruders. In our opinion, 'access', as the word is used in the definition, covers access for passage by permission express or implied from, or acquiescence or toleration by, the person or persons with legal right to control the use of the road. The degree or extent of use necessary to bring a particular road within the definition will necessarily be a question of fact in every case. Where there is such permission, acquiescence or tolerance demonstrated by use or otherwise, it can properly be said that there is nothing
D illegal or unlawful in such access as the public is proved to enjoy, and therefore that the public has access lawfully to the road. In using the word 'lawfully' we would attach to it the meaning which was given to the word 'legally' by Lord Justice General Clyde in *Harrison v Hill*, 1932 JC 13 at p 16 where he said: 'There must be, as matter of fact, walking or driving by the public on the road, and such walking or driving must be lawfully performed — that is to say, must be permitted or allowed, either expressly or
E implicitly, by the person or persons to whom the road belongs. I include in permission or allowance the state of matters known in right of way cases as the tolerance of a proprietor.' "

Later in the same opinion the Lord Justice General makes reference to Lord Sands' opinion in *Harrison* where at p 17 Lord Sands said: "In my view, access means, not right of access, but ingress in fact without any physical hindrance and without any wilful intrusion. In one view, it is a technical trespass for any
F person to put a foot upon an owner's land without the owner's permission. But, as is matter of common knowledge, there are many roads upon which members of the public enter without any sense of wilful intrusion. In my view, any road may be regarded as a road to which the public have access upon which members of the public are to be found who have not obtained access either by overcoming a physical obstruction or in defiance of prohibition express or implied."

I find nothing in these cases to suggest that once it

is established that the road is one to which the public
G has access, the owner of the road with legal right to control the use of the road, ceases to be entitled to exercise such legal right. That proposition is, in my opinion, contrary to what can be taken from the case of *Dunn v Keane* and the case of *Paterson v Ogilvy* cited in the opinion of the court. There is nothing in the opinion in *Dunn v Keane* to suggest that, if the subjects to which the private road led had ceased to be of a public character and the person owning the property, including the private road to the hotel, had
H withdrawn any invitation to the public to use the driveway and made it clear that it was only to be used by those residing on the property or having business within it, in such circumstances he would be prevented from doing so by an application of the powers under s 24 of the Roads (Scotland) Act 1970. Accordingly if, as was submitted by counsel for the defenders, the statutory provisions which applied prior to the passage of the 1984 Act can be looked to, there is nothing in them to justify the assertion that once a road had become a street or a road for the pur-
I poses of such prior legislation, the persons having the legal right to control the use of it were unable, by physically restricting the entry to it and thus the persons entering upon it, to deprive the road of that statutory character. It remains only to consider the case of *Cowie v Strathclyde Regional Council*. In my opinion, the passage quoted, upon which counsel for the defenders particularly founded, has to be read in the context of that case. Averments in that case had been added by way of amendment. These suggested
J that vehicular traffic had been using the lane in question as a public access to and from premises in the lane for several decades prior to the pursuer's interference with it, and further that the previous occupier had resided there for some 31 years and had raised no objection to such traffic. In my opinion the point which the Lord President was making was related to the requirement for the constitution of a public user of the nature of a public right of way that it must be of "the whole road, as a means of passage from one ter-
K minus to the other". I refer to the speech of Lord Watson in *Mann v Brodie* at p 57. Nor do I consider that the case of *Beattie v Scott* assists the defenders. In that case the court held that a definable way from a roadway by way of an access into and across a parking area, the surfaces of which had been laid by and the maintenance of which was the responsibility of the local roads authority and over which members of the public requiring access to various premises including a public house drove their cars, was a road for the pur-
L poses of the 1984 Act. That would be wholly consistent with the concept of a highway as defined by Lord Justice General Emslie in *Cheyne v MacNeill*. In *Young v Carmichael* the Crown conceded that on the facts stated there was no public right of passage over the car park in question. It would appear that the Crown emphasised the difference between the definition of "road" in the Roads (Scotland) Act 1984 and that applicable in relation to England and Wales in terms of s 192 (1) of the Road Traffic Act 1988. I am not certain that there is truly any distinction in this differ-

ence. It is true that the definition which now applies in Scotland for the purposes of the Road Traffic Act 1988 is that in the Roads (Scotland) Act 1984, and that the earlier definition which makes reference to "highway and any other road to which the public has access" is no longer applicable. However the new definition makes no reference to the word "highway" which, as noted in *Cheyne v MacNeill,* was a road upon which the public right of passage was secured by law and whose maintenance was the responsibility of a statutory authority. In these circumstances it was not surprising that Parliament employed the phrase "public right of passage" in the substituted definition. If, as counsel for the pursuers contended, the word "right" is to be read as a real legal right, and not something which is obtained by virtue of permission express or implied from, or acquiescence or toleration by, the person or persons with legal right to control the use of the road, the consequences would be startling. It would mean, for instance, that where a road was not a public road but a private road, unless and until a public right of passage had been demonstrated by continuance over the prescriptive period, no such road would fall within the definition and thus a person driving on such a road, albeit the public had access to it, could not be convicted on evidence which would secure his conviction in England and Wales. It is not necessary for me to express a concluded view on this issue since I am content to decide the case on the more limited basis for which counsel for the pursuers contended, namely that the change in the definition of a road in the 1984 Act made no difference to the manner in which a public right of passage could be constituted and that the law remained the same as it had done prior to the passage of the 1984 Act.

In the whole circumstances I am satisfied that there is no relevant legal basis for the averment upon which the defenders' case is founded in ans 4. The defenders only rely upon an unrestricted and tolerated public user prior to the erection of the barrier which is the subject of the declarator. I am satisfied that there is no warrant for the proposition that by virtue of such user, the pursuers were disqualified in law from exercising their proprietorial right to restrict the user of the street to a particular class, if they so chose. It is not suggested that the barrier constitutes an obstruction otherwise than that it prevents those whom the pursuers no longer choose to permit to enter the development from doing so. I am of opinion that in these circumstances the defenders have made no relevant averments to support their assertion that they have a right to remove the barrier and chain by virtue and in terms of s 59 (3) of the Roads (Scotland) Act 1984 because the general public had some legally enforceable right of passage over the street, which the defenders can protect by this means. There is no suggestion in the defenders' pleadings that those who continue to be users of the street under the restricted form of access now available fall into that class of the general public to which Lord Justice General Clyde made reference in *Harrison v Hill* where at p 16 he said: "I think that, when the statute speaks of 'the

public' in this connexion, what is meant is the public generally, and not the special class of members of the public who have occasion for business or social purposes to go to the farmhouse or any part of the farm itself; were it otherwise, the definition might just as well have included all private roads as well as all public highways."

In the result I shall sustain the fourth plea in law for the pursuers and grant decree in terms of the first and second conclusions.

Counsel for Pursuers, M G Clarke, QC; Solicitors, Campbell Smith & Co, WS (for Taits, WS, Kelso) — Counsel for Defenders, Abercrombie; Solicitor, G F G Welsh.

D C R

Fulton v Lees

HIGH COURT OF JUSTICIARY
THE LORD JUSTICE CLERK (ROSS),
LORDS MORISON AND GRIEVE
29 SEPTEMBER 1992

Justiciary — Statutory offence — Byelaws — Offering for hire without permission — Power to make byelaws not covering regulation of vehicular traffic on roads to which road traffic enactments applied — Accused taxi driver picking up fare on road at airport terminal building — Road traffic enactments applying to road — Whether byelaw ultra vires — Airports Act 1986 (c 31), s 63 (2) (d) — Scottish Airports Byelaws 1986, byelaw 5 (14).

Section 63 (1) of the Airports Act 1986 provides that an airport operator may make byelaws for regulating the use and operation of the airport and the conduct of all persons within the airport, and subs (2) (d) provides in particular that any such byelaws may include byelaws for regulating vehicular traffic anywhere within the airport except on roads to which the road traffic enactments apply. Byelaw 5 (14) of the Scottish Airports Byelaws 1986 provides that no person shall sell or distribute anything, offer anything for sale or hire or make any offer of services unless the operator's permission has first been obtained.

An accused person, who was a taxi driver, was charged with a contravention of byelaw 5 (14) by picking up a fare at Edinburgh airport terminal building. He objected to the competency of the charge on the ground that the byelaw was ultra vires s 63 (2) (d) of the 1986 Act as the place where he had picked up the fare was a road to which the road traffic enactments applied. The sheriff repelled the objection after trial and convicted the accused, who appealed and argued further that the road was not part of the airport which was limited to the aerodrome. There was a finding to the effect that the proprietors of the airport also owned the road in question.

Held, (1) that the word "airport" included the landing ground, the terminal building and the curtilage, particularly as the operators of the airport were the proprietors of the land on which the airport was situated including the road (pp 929L-930A); (2) that s 63 (2) (d) did not extend to the use of vehicles for purposes which could not be regarded as being in the context of regulating vehicular traffic and, accordingly, as byelaw 5 (14) was not so concerned, it was apt to cover what the accused did (pp 930J-931B); and appeal *refused*.

Dictum of Lord Denning MR in *Cinnamond v British Airports Authority* [1980] 1 WLR 582 at p 589, *applied*.

Summary complaint

Derek Fulton was charged at the instance of Robert F Lees, procurator fiscal, Edinburgh, on a summary complaint which contained the following charge: "on 30 January 1990 at Edinburgh airport, Jubilee Road, District of Edinburgh, you did offer for hire a taxi without the permission of the British Airports Authority and without other lawful authority or excuse: contrary to the Scottish Airports Byelaws 1986, s 5 (14) and the Airports Act 1986, s 64". The accused objected to the competency of the charge prior to pleading not guilty and proceeding to trial. After trial the sheriff (I A Poole) repelled the plea to competency and convicted the accused.

The accused appealed to the High Court against the decision of the sheriff.

Findings in fact

The sheriff found the following facts to be admitted or proved, inter alia:

(1) The appellant is a taxi driver and holds a licence from Edinburgh District Council as licensing authority to operate a taxi within the District of Edinburgh area. (2) The appellant's taxi is one of the distinctive Edinburgh black hackney "London cab" style taxis. (3) At 9.30 am on 30 January 1990, the appellant drove a customer to Edinburgh airport and discharged him in Jubilee Road outside the terminal buildings. (4) Having paid off his fare, the appellant's taxi's "For Hire" sign was illuminated. (5) Some yards ahead of the appellant were waiting a line of taxis of the saloon type of taxi. (6) The taxi at the head of that queue was driven by a Mr Little and the taxi immediately behind was driven by Mr Niall Brown. (7) Both Mr Little and Mr Brown were licensed by Edinburgh District Council as licensing authority to operate their taxis in and out of Edinburgh airport. (8) Edinburgh District Council has divided the district of Edinburgh for taxi licensing purposes into two areas, namely Edinburgh airport and the rest of Edinburgh District. (9) Mr Little and Mr Brown have permission from Edinburgh Airport Ltd to ply their taxis for hire out of Edinburgh airport and to wait in an airport taxi stance in Jubilee Road outside the terminal buildings there.

(10) For that permission each pays annually £875.00 plus VAT to Edinburgh Airport Ltd. (11) The appellant had no such permission. (12) Edinburgh Airport Ltd are the heritable proprietors of the lands on which Edinburgh airport is situated including Jubilee Road. . . . (14) On 30 January 1990, a Mr Powell, an English businessman, flew up on an Aberdeen Airways flight from East Midlands airport, England. He required to transact business in Kirkcaldy. (15) Mr Powell approached the self drive hire car companies desks at Edinburgh airport in order to hire a car and was quoted hire terms of £93.00 which he considered excessive. (16) Mr Powell then went out of the terminal buildings and approached a taxi driver at the head of the queue who quoted a fare of £52.00 for Kirkcaldy. Mr Powell considered that fare to be excessive. He approached a second driver further down the queue who quoted a fare of £37.00 which Mr Powell considered excessive. (17) Mr Powell then noticed the appellant and his black hackney cab discharging a fare some yards behind the airport taxi rank queue in Jubilee Road. (18) Mr Powell approached the appellant and inquired the fare to Kirkcaldy. (19) The appellant consulted a printed list of charges and stated that it would be £25.00. (20) That fare was similar to the fare which drivers of airport taxis on a metered journey to Kirkcaldy should charge. (21) Mr Powell agreed to that fare and entered the appellant's taxi. . . . (29) On 30 January 1990, the appellant was cautioned and charged that he had offered his taxi for hire without the permission of British Airports Authority and without other lawful authority or excuse contrary to the Scottish Airports Byelaws 1986, s 5 (14) and the Airports Act 1986, s 64. (30) On 30 January 1990 the appellant offered his taxi for hire at Edinburgh airport without the permission of Edinburgh Airport Ltd.

Statutory provisions

The Airports Act 1986 provides:

"63.—(1) Where an airport is either — (a) designated for the purposes of this section by an order made by the Secretary of State, or (b) managed by the Secretary of State, the airport operator (whether the Secretary of State or some other person) may make byelaws for regulating the use and operation of the airport and the conduct of all persons while within the airport.

"(2) Any such byelaws may, in particular, include byelaws — . . . (d) for regulating vehicular traffic anywhere within the airport, except on roads within the airport to which the road traffic enactments apply, and in particular (with that exception) for imposing speed limits on vehicles within the airport and for restricting or regulating the parking of vehicles or their use for any purpose or in any manner specified in the byelaws; . . .

"(3) In paragraph (d) of subsection (2) 'the road traffic enactments' means the enactments (whether passed before or after this Act) relating to road traffic, including the lighting and parking of vehicles, and any order or other instrument having effect by virtue of any such enactment."

The Scottish Airports Byelaws 1986 provide:

A "5. The following acts are prohibited unless the permission of the Authority has first been obtained or unless the act is performed by a person acting with lawful authority or excuse in circumstances in which the obtaining of permission would be likely to hinder that person in so acting: . . . (14) No person shall sell or distribute anything, offer anything for sale or hire or make any offer of services. . . .

"8.—(1) No person shall cause or permit a taxi to ply for hire or load passengers other than at an authorised
B stance provided that it shall not be an offence to load passengers in a public car park or at a distance of more than half a mile from the nearest of such authorised stances or, with the consent of a constable or the Authority, at any distance from such authorised stances. . . .

"(9) Taxi drivers shall not obstruct the road, footpath or buildings or cause annoyance or disturbance to persons in the vicinity."

C
Case referred to

Cinnamond v British Airports Authority [1980] 1 WLR 582; [1980] 2 All ER 368; [1979] RTR 331.

Appeal
The sheriff posed the following question for the opinion of the High Court:

On the foregoing facts admitted or proved was I entitled to find the appellant guilty?
D

The appeal was argued before the High Court on 9 July 1992.

On 29 September 1992 the court *answered* the question in the *affirmative* and *refused* the appeal.

The following opinion of the court was delivered by the Lord Justice Clerk (Ross):

E **OPINION OF THE COURT.**—On 11 April 1991, the appellant appeared in Edinburgh sheriff court in answer to a complaint which libelled a contravention of Scottish Airports Byelaws 1986, s 5 (14) and the Airports Act 1986, s 64. The complaint libelled: [his Lordship quoted the charge set out supra, and continued:]

A challenge to the competency of the complaint was made on behalf of the appellant who adhered to his plea of not guilty. It was agreed by the appellant and
F the respondent that it would be appropriate that evidence should be led first by the respondent, and that thereafter legal argument could be heard. In the event evidence was led for the respondent and further evidence was led for the appellant. The sheriff then heard submissions on behalf of the appellant and the respondent including submissions on the plea to competency. The sheriff reserved judgment until 22 April 1991 when she found the appellant guilty and admonished him. Against his conviction the appellant has now appealed by way of stated case.

At a previous diet, when the appeal called before the court, counsel intimated that he had five principal G submissions to make. It was however conceded by counsel that with one exception his submissions were not covered by the matters sought to be brought under review in the application for the stated case. Counsel was unable to show cause as to why the appellant should be allowed to found any aspect of his appeal on a matter not contained in the application for a stated case, and the court accordingly intimated that it was not prepared to hear argument on the appellant's behalf in respect of four of his five submissions. The H appeal was continued to enable counsel to take instructions.

As a result of that decision of the court the only submission of the appellant which was covered by his application for a stated case was a submission that on a proper construction of the byelaws no offence under the byelaws was shown to have been committed on the facts of the case. Before the sheriff the submission had been that a prosecution in terms of byelaw 8 (1) of the said byelaws would have been incompetent as ultra I vires in respect that the byelaw enacted by that section went beyond the enabling powers in the principal Act of Parliament and was also repugnant to the general law.

At the hearing of the appeal on 9 July 1992, counsel for the appellant drew attention to the relevant findings in fact. The findings revealed that a Mr Powell on 30 January 1990 arrived at Edinburgh airport. He required to transact business in Kirkcaldy and J approached two taxi drivers in a queue of taxis seeking the quotation of a fare for the journey to Kirkcaldy. He regarded the quotations as excessive. He then noticed the appellant in his black hackney cab discharging a fare some yards behind the airport taxi rank queue in Jubilee Road. He approached the appellant and inquired the fare to Kirkcaldy. The appellant stated that the fare would be £25, and Mr Powell agreed to that fare and entered the taxi.

Finding 29 is in the following terms: [his Lordship K quoted its terms and continued:]

Counsel drew attention to the Scottish Airports Byelaws 1986, and pointed out that byelaw 1 dealt with interpretation. It was provided therein inter alia that "the airport" means the "aerodrome known as . . . Edinburgh Airport". Counsel pointed out that in the *Oxford Dictionary* aerodrome is defined as "A course for the use of flying machines; a tract of level ground from which aeroplanes or airships can start". He accordingly submitted that Edinburgh airport did L not include the roadway on which the appellant had been with his taxi at the airport. He submitted that it was clear that the roadway in question was outwith the curtilage of the aerodrome. We are satisfied that that contention is unsound. Section 63 (1) of the Airports Act 1986 empowers the airport operator to make byelaws for regulating the use and operation of the airport and the conduct of all persons while within the airport. "The airport" must, we think, include the landing ground, the terminal building and the cur-

tilage. In any event finding 12 is in the following
A terms: "Edinburgh Airport Ltd are the heritable
proprietors of the lands on which Edinburgh airport
is situated including Jubilee Road".

It is, we think, clear from that finding that Jubilee
Road is part of Edinburgh airport, and that it is incorrect to suggest that the roadway is outwith the curtilage of the airport.

Counsel next referred to byelaw 8 (1). That byelaw
provides as follows: [his Lordship quoted the terms of
B byelaw 8 (1) and continued:]

Counsel stated that although the appellant had not
been charged with any contravention of byelaw 8 (1)
he could have been charged with such an offence. He
also drew attention to the provisions of byelaw 8 (9)
which is in the following terms: [his Lordship quoted
its terms and continued:]

Counsel maintained that byelaws such as 8 (1) and
8 (9) were ultra vires. This was because of the provi-
C sions of s 63 of the Airports Act 1986. Section 63 (1)
empowers the airport operator to make byelaws for
regulating the use and operation of the airport and the
conduct of all persons while within the airport. In s 63
(2) it is provided inter alia as follows: [his Lordship
quoted the terms of s 63 (2) set out supra and then s 63
(3), and continued:]

Counsel submitted that the effect of s 63 (2) (d) was
that the British Airports Authority could not make
byelaws for regulating traffic on roads to which the
D road traffic enactments applied. He submitted that
Jubilee Road was plainly a road to which the road
traffic enactments applied and that accordingly
byelaws such as byelaw 8 (1) and 8 (9) were beyond the
powers of British Airports Authority.

The Crown's answer to this submission was, of
course, that the appellant was not being charged with
contravention of byelaw 8 (1) or 8 (9). What the appellant was being charged with contravening was byelaw
5 (14). Byelaw 5 deals with "acts for which permission
E is required". It provides as follows: [his Lordship
quoted the terms of byelaw 5 set out supra and continued:]

As we understand it, however, counsel's submission
was that on the findings the appellant had offered his
taxi for hire on Jubilee Road and had thereby offered
his services to Mr Powell. That being so the submission appeared to be that the making of byelaw 5 (14)
was struck at by the provisions of s 63 (2) (d) which
F provided in effect that byelaws could not be made for
the purpose of regulating the use of vehicles for any
purpose on roads within the airport to which the road
traffic enactments applied.

The advocate depute contended that the true effect
of s 63 (2) (d) was that on a road within the airport to
which the road traffic enactments applied, the airport
authority could not make byelaws which changed the
road traffic enactments. He stressed however that the
charge in this case libelled a contravention of byelaw
5 (14), and he contended that that byelaw dealt with

the offering for hire of articles, and that the fact that
in this case the article was a vehicle was irrelevant. He G
founded on the findings which made it clear that at the
material time the appellant was offering to hire his taxi
to Mr Powell and was offering his services to Mr
Powell. He submitted under reference to s 63 (2) (d)
that the provisions "restricting or regulating the
parking of vehicles or their use for any purpose" were
confined to restricting or regulating the use of vehicles
in the context of the regulation of vehicular traffic;
these provisions had no application to the use of
vehicles except insofar as such use could be regarded H
as a facet of the regulating of vehicular traffic. So far
as the use of vehicles for any other purpose was concerned, the provisions of s 63 (2) (d) had no application.

We have come to the conclusion that in this respect
the advocate depute's submissions are sound.
Although we agree that the effect of s 63 (2) (d) is that
the airport operator cannot make byelaws for regulating traffic on roads to which the road traffic enactments apply, this does not mean that byelaw 5 (14) is I
in any way ultra vires. The sheriff recognised that
Jubilee Road was a road to which the road traffic
enactments applied, as evidence to that effect had been
given by Inspector Elgin. She realised however that if
the appellant's arguments were sound then as regards
hackney carriages in Jubilee Road, provisions such as
s 63 (2) (e) and (f) would be inapplicable. She concluded that that could not have been the intention of
Parliament. In our opinion, the sheriff was well
founded in accepting that s 63 (2) (d) did not cover the J
use of vehicles for all purposes, but was concerned
solely with the use of vehicles so far as regulating
vehicular traffic was concerned. In the course of her
note the sheriff referred to *Cinnamond v British Airports Authority.* In that case at [1980] 1 WLR, p 589
Lord Denning MR said of byelaws made by the
British Airports Authority: "It seems to me that the
approach nowadays should be different in regard to
modern byelaws. If the byelaw is of such a nature that
something of this kind is necessary or desirable for the K
operation of the airport, then the courts should
endeavour to interpret the byelaw so as to render it
valid rather than invalid. The Latin maxim is Ut res
magis valeat quam pereat — it is better for a thing to
have effect than to be made void. If it is drafted in
words which on a strict interpretation may be said to
be too wide, or too uncertain, or to be unreasonable,
then the court — so long as the words permit it —
should discard the strict interpretation and interpret
them with any reasonable implications or qualifica- L
tions which may be necessary so as to produce a just
and proper result".

We agree that that is the correct approach, and
adopting that approach, we agree with the sheriff that
one should avoid an interpretation which would have
the effect of making a number of safety provisions in
s 63 (2) inapplicable. It is, in our opinion, preferable
and indeed a sound construction to read s 63 (2) (d) as
not extending to the use of vehicles for purposes
which cannot be regarded as being in the context of

A regulating vehicular traffic. Accordingly, so far as roads within the airport to which the road traffic enactments apply are concerned, there is nothing to prevent the airport operator from making byelaws regulating the use of vehicles for any purposes which are not properly concerned with regulating vehicular traffic.

In our opinion byelaw 5 (14) is not concerned with regulating vehicle traffic at all. It is expressed in general terms, and the words are apt to cover the present situation where the findings show that the
B appellant offered his taxi for hire to Mr Powell and offered his services to Mr Powell. The provision in byelaw 5 (14) to the effect that such offers were prohibited unless permission from the British Airports Authority had first been obtained, are not properly to be regarded as provisions regulating vehicular traffic. In other words, we are satisfied that the prohibition upon which the Crown rely in relation to the charge against the appellant has nothing to do with regulating vehicular traffic on Jubilee Road. Byelaw 5 (14) deals
C with selling, distributing, offering for sale or hire, or offering services. The language used is clearly wide enough to cover motor vehicles, but where motor vehicles are concerned the prohibition cannot be regarded as being a provision for regulating vehicular traffic. It is also of significance that the Road Traffic Acts do not deal with the licensing and regulation of taxis, regarding which provisions are to be found in the Civic Government (Scotland) Act 1982.

D For the foregoing reasons we are satisfied that the sheriff arrived at a correct decision in this case. She was well founded in rejecting the plea to competency, and in convicting the appellant of the charge. On a proper construction of the byelaws, an offence under the byelaws was, on the facts found proved, shown to have been committed. We shall accordingly answer the one question in the case in the affirmative, and the appeal is therefore refused.

———————

E
Counsel for Appellant, Bell, QC; Solicitors, Mackay & Norwell, WS — Counsel for Respondent, Macdonald, QC, A D; Solicitor, J D Lowe, Crown Agent.

P W F

F # Beaton v Strathclyde Buses Ltd

OUTER HOUSE

LORD McCLUSKEY

12 NOVEMBER 1992

Limitation of actions — Reparation — Negligence — Time bar — Action raised 18 days outwith triennium — Clear case available against pursuer's solicitors for failing to raise action timeously — Further delay caused

G *by pursuer's solicitors after action raised — Whether equitable to permit action to proceed — Prescription and Limitation (Scotland) Act 1973 (c 52), s 19A.*

Section 19A of the Prescription and Limitation (Scotland) Act 1973 enables the court to allow an action to proceed which would otherwise be time barred under s 17, if it seems to the court equitable to do so.

On 8 March 1988 an individual was injured when a bus crashed into his livingroom. His solicitors inti-
H mated a claim a few months later and in May 1990 requested Edinburgh correspondents to arrange for an action to be raised in the Court of Session. Counsel was instructed to draft a summons in December 1990 but requested further information. Some steps were taken until mid-January 1991, but then no further action was taken before the triennium expired on 8 March 1991. On 25 March 1991 the solicitors discovered the oversight and had a summons drafted, signeted and served the following day, 18 days after the expiry of the triennium. The record closed on 16
I October 1991, but the pursuer's solicitors did not lodge a closed record until 1 August 1992.

At a procedure roll hearing the defenders argued that the action was time barred and should not be allowed to proceed. The defenders founded not only on the delay in raising the action but also on the delay thereafter. The pursuer argued that an action against his solicitors would take longer to complete, and would involve the extra hurdle of showing that the solicitors had been negligent. The pursuer also
J founded on the fact that he had financial assistance from his trade union for the present action but that it was uncertain whether such assistance would be available for an action against his solicitors.

Held, that the defenders would be prejudiced by losing their defence under s 17; that there was a clear case against the pursuer's solicitors who were responsible for the failure to raise the action timeously; that there was no explanation for the delays caused by the
K solicitors; that it was not appropriate to overlook the pursuer's solicitors' conduct before or after the action was raised to the prejudice of the defenders (p 933D-F); and action *dismissed.*

———————

Action of damages

John William Beaton raised an action of damages against Strathclyde Buses Ltd in respect of injuries he
L sustained when a bus driven by one of the defenders' employees crashed into his livingroom on 8 March 1988. The action was raised on 26 March 1991. The record closed on 16 October 1991 and the closed record was not lodged until 1 August 1992.

The action came before the Lord Ordinary (Lord McCluskey) on procedure roll on the defenders' plea of time bar. The pursuer amended his pleadings at the bar to include a plea invoking s 19A of the Prescription and Limitation (Scotland) Act 1973.

Statutory provisions

A   The Prescription and Limitation (Scotland) Act 1973 provides:

"17.— . . . (2) Subject to subsection (3) below and section 19A of this Act, no action to which this section applies shall be brought unless it is commenced within a period of three years after — (a) the date on which the injuries were sustained or, where the act or omission to which the injuries were attributable was a continuing one, that date or the date on which the act or omission ceased, whichever is the later. . . .

B   "19A.—(1) Where a person would be entitled, but for any of the provisions of section 17 or section 18 and 18A of this Act, to bring an action, the court may, if it seems to it equitable to do so, allow him to bring the action notwithstanding that provision."

Cases referred to

Elliot v J & C Finney, 1989 SLT 208.
Forsyth v A F Stoddard & Co Ltd, 1985 SLT 51.
C   *Nicol v British Steel Corporation (General Steels) Ltd*, 1992 SLT 141.

On 12 November 1992 the Lord Ordinary *repelled* the pursuer's plea in law added by amendment, *sustained* the defenders' first plea in law, and *dismissed* the action.

LORD McCLUSKEY.—In this action the pursuer seeks damages of £30,000 from Strathclyde Buses Ltd
D   in respect of an accident which he was said to have sustained on 8 March 1988. According to the pursuer's condescendence he was standing in the livingroom of the ground floor flat at a house in Glasgow when a bus, owned by the defenders and being driven, in the course of his employment, by one of their employees, drove into the livingroom causing the pursuer to sustain severe shock and other consequences which are later condescended upon. There are averments about the manner in which the bus was driven. The
E   defenders do not dispute that the bus driven by their servant did, on the day in question, turn into the street and collide with the brick wall of a house. An explanation is given for the accident, namely that a quantity of mud and water on the roadway caused the bus to skid. At a fairly early stage in 1988, within a few months of the accident, agents acting on behalf of the pursuer intimated a claim to the defenders and that claim was discussed for some time thereafter. In May of 1990 the Glasgow agents for the pursuer wrote to
F   their Edinburgh correspondents to arrange for the preparation and service of a summons. It appears that counsel was instructed in December 1990 for the drafting of such a summons but did not do so and simply wrote a note; and I was informed at the bar that in that note counsel sought further information on the question of loss, injury and damage. Thereafter some consequential steps were taken, until mid-January, but nothing was done thereafter to raise an action before the expiry of the triennium. The triennium expired on 8 March 1991. Some 17 days later it was realised what had happened, and the pursuer's solicitors took

immediate action and had a summons drafted, signeted and served by the following day, namely 26   G March 1991. The record was closed on 16 October 1991 but I was informed that no closed record was lodged until 1 August 1992.

The case appeared before me on procedure roll today in respect of the defenders' first plea in law, to the effect that the pursuer's action was time barred under s 17 of the Prescription and Limitation (Scotland) Act 1973. Pursuer's counsel tendered a minute of amendment at the bar to put on the record a plea   H invoking the terms of s 19A of the 1973 Act. I pause to notice, however, that neither by minute of amendment nor in the original pleadings is there any explanation whatsoever given on behalf of the pursuer for the failure to serve the action within the triennium.

My attention was drawn to a number of cases which relate to the nature of jurisdiction which the court exercises under s 19A. I think the position has now become quite clear and it is comprehensively and fully stated by Lord Sutherland in the case of *Elliot v J &*   I *C Finney* at p 211C-E and also by Lord Coulsfield in the case of *Nicol v British Steel Corporation (General Steels) Ltd*. The court's jurisdiction is an equitable jurisdiction. The exercise of discretion is not specifically fettered but the court must take into account and balance all the factors that bear upon the conduct and interests of the parties.

In inviting me to sustain his plea under s 19A, counsel for the pursuer accepted that this was a case in which, on the face of it, the pursuer could be said   J to have a reasonably strong case against his solicitors in respect of possible loss to him resulting from their failure to raise an action within the triennium. That, however, had to be qualified by the fact that if he pursued such a case it would certainly be likely to take longer than pursuing the present case. In any event, although he had trade union legal aid for the present case, it was uncertain whether he would have such legal aid for a case against the solicitors. Furthermore,   K such a case would involve an extra hurdle for the pursuer to cross, namely, he would have to show both negligence on the part of the solicitors and a material degree of likelihood that he would have recovered damages in the present proceedings had they been raised timeously. Secondly, the pursuer would be prejudiced by the likelihood of delay if he had to pursue a fresh action against the solicitors; it would have to start from the beginning. Thirdly, memories as to the circumstances in which he claimed to have   L received his injuries would inevitably fade with the passing of time, though he acknowledged that that was a double edged consideration, in respect that it might have relevance to the defenders' position as well. He most particularly pointed to the fact that the actual delay here, once the three year period had expired, was only 17 or 18 days and that the pursuer's agents acted with considerable speed once the error had been discovered and had instantly caused the summons to be prepared, signeted and served. Furthermore, this was by no means a stale claim. The position really was that the defenders were seeking to take advantage of what had been described from time to time as the "windfall" defence available to them under s 17. In essence the only prejudice to the defenders was a loss of the protection afforded to them by s 17. He acknowledged, however, that that was a legitimate and proper consideration to be put into the balance of the various interests. I was referred to a number of cases in which judges in the Outer House weighed these various factors, but it appears to me that each case turns upon its own facts and I have not found the particular decisions in the particular cases of great assistance, although I accept the general statement of the court's position in the two cases to which I have referred.

In response, counsel for the defenders pointed out that there were no averments on the record to explain the delays, although certain explanations had been offered at the bar. It was common ground that there appeared to be a strong case for the pursuer against his agents in respect of their failure to raise the action timeously; as the cases showed, that was an important factor. The prejudice to the defenders was real and palpable. They had lost what the Lord Justice Clerk in Forsyth v A F Stoddard & Co Ltd had referred to as a "cast-iron" defence. The lapse of time between the expiry of the triennium in the service of the summons was indeed quite short, but one day was enough and the whole conduct of the solicitors required to be looked at. The court should take account not just of the unexplained delays which had preceded the expiry of the triennium but of the dilatory conduct of the litigation since that time. For example, the record had been lodged some nine months or more late. The particular cases to which reference had been made all turned on their own facts.

In my view, this is a very clear case in which I should not exercise the discretion conferred upon me by s 19A. In the first instance, I consider that there can be no room for argument that the defenders would be prejudiced by the loss of their defence under s 17. In the second place, this appears to be a clear case in which the pursuer should be able to sue his agents who were clearly responsible for the failure to raise an action timeously against the present defenders. It appears to me, though this is of limited importance — except possibly in relation to staleness — that the conduct of the agents, for which the pursuer has to bear responsibility in a question with the present defenders, has been almost as casual since the action was raised as it was before the expiry of the triennium, in respect that no sense of urgency has been shown. There is really no explanation at all before the court as to why any of the several delays had been incurred and I do not consider that it would be a sensible exercise of my discretion to overlook all such conduct, to the prejudice of the defenders. In the circumstances, I consider that there is a clear balance of the relevant considerations in favour of a refusal to exercise the court's discretion under s 19A. I shall, therefore, repel the plea which the pursuer added by minute of amendment; I shall sustain the first plea in law for the defenders and dismiss the action.

Counsel for Pursuer, Hofford; Solicitors, Allan Mac-Dougall & Co, SSC (for B J Lanigan & Co, Glasgow) — Counsel for Defenders, Coutts; Solicitors, Campbell Smith & Co, WS.

P McC

(NOTE)

Ramm v Lothian and Borders Fire Board

OUTER HOUSE

LORD PENROSE

18 NOVEMBER 1992

Expenses — Award — Action of little value — One of grounds of action of importance to defenders as suggesting that widespread practice was negligent — Pursuer failing on that ground but succeeding on another — Whether expenses to be restricted to sheriff court scale — Whether no award to be made.

A fireman injured in an accident sued his employers and was ultimately awarded £688.34 after a three day proof, the fireman having been found two thirds at fault and having failed to prove all but one of his grounds of fault. He sought expenses on the Court of Session scale.

Held, that the defenders had been justified in defending the case insofar as the pursuer sought to establish that the whole system of working was defective, which he had failed to establish, and that otherwise the case was extremely simple and straightforward; and no expenses *found* due to or by either party.

Douglas Ramm raised an action against his employers, the Lothian and Borders Fire Board, for damages for injuries sustained in an accident while fighting a fire. He sued for £15,000. At the proof total damages were agreed at £2,065. The pursuer raised a number of issues. One case was founded on an alleged failure by his employers to provide adequate equipment and to devise a safe system of work. Another case was founded upon the negligence of a colleague who had taken a hose back down a poorly lit and partly smoke filled stairway, instead of coiling it from the branch end, causing a bight in the hose over which the pursuer tripped.

After a proof the Lord Ordinary (Penrose) held that the only case established against the defenders was one that the colleague removing the hose had pulled on it while aware that he had formed a moving bight in it and without being in a position to see or check whether anyone could be affected by his actions in pulling the hose. The Lord Ordinary also found the pursuer two thirds to blame for the accident on the basis that he should have seen the hose and avoided being caught by it. An award of damages of £688.34 was accordingly made. The pursuer then sought expenses on the Court of Session scale. The defenders opposed the award of expenses. In finding no expenses due to or by either party his Lordship said:

"The pursuer's motion for expenses was for expenses on the Court of Session scale. It was argued that when the action was raised on 7 July 1991 the medical evidence available to the pursuer indicated that his condition had not resolved. It was anticipated that it would but there was no certainty about it. Further, it was said that the pursuer had a possible claim for lost wages of about £200 and a claim for services under the 1982 Act. Counsel appearing for the pursuer was unable to give any indication of how the various elements of damages could have justified the sum sued for of £15,000. He argued that the case was one that was appropriate for the Court of Session and in the nature of things that required the employment of counsel. Had the matter been raised in the sheriff court, the nature of the case was such and, in particular, the need for expert evidence was so clear that counsel would have been instructed and sanctioned in the ordinary course. It was therefore contended that if, contrary to counsel's primary submission, I were to award sheriff court expenses it should be on the basis that employment of counsel would have been sanctioned.

"For the defenders the pursuer's motion was opposed. It was contended that any award of expenses should be on a sheriff court scale but that in the circumstances of the case there should be no expenses awarded to or by either party. If expenses were awarded they should be on the sheriff summary scale. The defenders' position was that all along they had conducted the case on the view that the pursuer sought to impugn the methods by which hose reel was withdrawn from tenement buildings and the defenders were entitled to take the view that this was a serious attack upon their general practice and was of considerable public importance. The pursuer, in his pleadings, gave very little indication of the nature of the attack and a motion for further specification had had to be made. Failure in the case would have carried serious repercussions for the defenders. It was for that reason only that the defenders concurred in the view that the Court of Session was an appropriate forum for the case. The case had been set down for proof before Lord Weir in April 1992. The diet was discharged, but, at that stage, his Lordship had expressed dismay at the prospect of hearing a case concerned with the sums involved. The defenders had contended, however, that the general nature of the allegations made the case suitable for hearing in the Court of Session. Apart from that factor the case was not serious and did not involve serious injuries. The defenders would have moved for the case to be remitted to the sheriff court but for their anxiety over the nature of the allegations made.

"On economic grounds, it was said, the defenders would almost certainly have made an offer to settle the case but for the nature of the allegations made. The medical report produced by the pursuer demonstrated that the injury was minor, worth little in terms of damages. The allegation of loss of wages was made but there was never any quantifiable wage loss other than a trivial sum. No specification had ever been tendered of any sum claimed in respect of services and the matter was at the outset and remained at the end of the proceedings purely speculative.

"The proof in this case lasted three days. A substantial amount of that time was taken up in exploring issues raised by the pursuer for which, in the end of the day, the pursuer had no or inadequate evidence. There was evidence about the colour of the hose reel including evidence of continental practice. But, when pressed, the pursuer's expert who clearly had been the originator of this line of inquiry indicated that he could not support a general attack upon the defenders on this basis. The black hose reel used satisfied British Standards requirements and was widely used throughout the United Kingdom. The second main line of attack on the defenders was that they had failed to institute and to maintain and enforce a system of work for the withdrawal of hose reel from tenement buildings. I have dealt in my opinion with the merits of this case and with some of the evidence led. At this stage it is sufficient to say that it occupied a considerable proportion of the court's time and, on final analysis, appeared to have been wholly misconceived. The pursuer led a witness who, among other things, described precisely, as a practice he had followed himself, the method of withdrawal of which the pursuer complained on record though in slightly different circumstances. The pursuer's witness did not support a case of fault against the defenders on the lines indicated, albeit briefly, on record. The pursuer came to court with averments of an accident that happened as he made his way from a second floor flat in the building. I held that the fire had occurred in a first floor flat. The pursuer claimed to have fallen the full length of the stairs from the upper quarter landing to the lower quarter landing at ground floor. I held that he tripped or was pulled off balance at the level of the lower quarter landing. The pursuer succeeded in this case only because I accepted the evidence of Mr Kean and on that evidence held that, given the background described by the pursuer's expert, there was a failure in duty by Mr Kean in the method of withdrawal of the hose which he adopted.

"The evidence in this case demonstrated that the pursuer had initiated and insisted in a case against the defenders themselves for which there was, at best, inadequate evidence and never any evidence of substance. I took the view that balancing the equities involved in this case, it would not have been an appropriate exercise of my discretion to find the defenders liable in expenses in the circumstances of the case. They had been put to very considerable expense in an anxious case in which there was an apparent attack upon fundamental aspects of their approach to the

performance of their public duties as fire authority. In
these matters the pursuer comprehensively failed and
the expense incurred by the defenders was expense
that ought never to have been incurred at all. It
appeared to me that in equity the pursuer should not
be entitled to any award of expenses against the
defenders given the extent to which he had caused
abortive expenditure to be incurred. Had I made an
award of expenses in favour of the pursuer, it would
have been on the sheriff court ordinary scale without
sanction of counsel. Shorn of the complexities introduced by the pursuer without cause, this case was of
an extremely simple and straightforward character.
The issues on which the pursuer largely failed were
issues of fact, as were the issues on which he
succeeded. One must allow a certain latitude over the
limits of the sheriff summary cause jurisdiction and I
would not have restricted the pursuer to summary
cause expenses for that reason. However, nothing in
the case merited the employment of counsel and
accordingly the choice that I faced in a practical way
was between awarding the pursuer expenses on the
sheriff court ordinary scale without sanction of
counsel and reflecting my understanding of the
realities of the situation by making no award of
expenses at all. Having regard to the whole circumstances I considered that the proper disposal was that
there should be no expenses found due to or by either
party.''

Counsel for Pursuer, Ross; Solicitors, Robin Thompson & Partners — Counsel for Defenders, Kinroy; Solicitor, G F G Welsh.

C H

[The pursuer has marked a reclaiming motion against the
finding of no expenses made by the Lord Ordinary.]

Scott v Kelvin Concrete Ltd

OUTER HOUSE
LORD COULSFIELD
25 NOVEMBER 1992

*Reparation — Negligence — Contributory negligence —
Pursuer inadvertently leaving machine switched on,
leading to accident — Machine poorly maintained and
deficient in safety devices — Whether inadvertence
amounted to contributory negligence.*

*Reparation — Negligence — Master and servant —
Breach of statutory duty — Fencing of machinery —
Machine being repaired — Dangerous parts of machine
not protected during repair — Appropriate means of providing protection during repair — Factories Act 1961 (9
& 10 Eliz II, c 34), s 14.*

*Damages — Amount — Solatium, loss of earnings and
earning capacity, loss of services of and necessary services*

*rendered to injured person — Leg — Below knee delayed
amputation of one leg and serious injury to other foot.*

A works manager was injured in an accident at work
on 4 July 1988. He was then aged 35. He had been
involved in attempting to rectify a fault in a hydraulic-
ally and pneumatically operated press for producing
concrete slabs. In the course of his attempts to get the
machine to work properly he had stepped inside it and
had, by accident, caused it to operate, resulting in his
legs being trapped within the machine. He had compound fractures of both bones of both lower legs,
leading eventually to a below the knee amputation of
one leg with continuing disability in the other ankle.
The machine had been designed with various safety
features, including a key control and fencing with
doors connected to safety switches. The key control
had been wired out of the system following the loss of
the key; switches on doors had been taped up to avoid
them operating to switch the machine off; the hopper,
by which the pursuer had entered the machine after
climbing a ladder, could be reached without passing
through any fences; and the feed tray at the bottom of
the hopper was not protected within the hopper. The
pursuer sought damages founding on breaches of his
employers' common law duties of care and also upon
s 14 of the Factories Act 1961 relating to his
employers' alleged failure to take adequate precautions
to make it safe to operate the machine. He also
founded a case upon a fellow employee having
switched the machine on. After proof, the case last
mentioned was held not to be established, the Lord
Ordinary inferring that it was the pursuer himself who
had failed to use the isolator button to switch the
machine off. The employers disputed the case based
upon s 14 of the Factories Act and sought a finding of
contributory negligence against the pursuer.

Held, (1) that the case based upon s 14 of the
Factories Act was established since, if properly fenced
with gates with interlock switches, the machine could
not have been operated while someone was within the
hopper involved in carrying out a repair (p 937F-H);
(2) that the employers were at fault by allowing the
machine to remain in a dangerous state (p 937H-I); (3)
that having regard to the employers' gross failures in
proper care the failure of the pursuer to operate the
isolator button did not amount to contributory negligence (p 937I-K); and (4) that solatium was properly
assessed at £42,500; loss of earnings, resulting from a
less demanding form of employment calculated to date
and applying a 12 year multiplier for the future at
£62,400; disadvantage in the labour market at
£10,000; loss of services rendered by the pursuer at
£2,000; and necessary services supplied to the pursuer
at £2,000 (p 938A-D); and decree *pronounced*
accordingly.

Action of damages

Michael Scott raised an action against his former
employers Kelvin Concrete (Ayrshire) Ltd and against
the liquidators of that company for damages in respect
of injuries sustained in an accident at work on 4 July
1988. He was then aged 35.

The case came to proof before the Lord Ordinary (Coulsfield).

Statutory provisions

The Factories Act 1961 provides:

"14.—(1) Every dangerous part of any machinery, other than prime movers and transmission machinery, shall be securely fenced unless it is in such a position or of such construction as to be as safe to every person employed or working on the premises as it would be if securely fenced.

"(2) In so far as the safety of a dangerous part of any machinery cannot by reason of the nature of the operation be secured by means of a fixed guard, the requirements of subsection (1) of this section shall be deemed to have been complied with if a device is provided which automatically prevents the operator from coming into contact with that part."

Case referred to

Summers (John) & Son Ltd v Frost [1955] AC 740; [1955] 2 WLR 825; [1955] 1 All ER 870.

On 25 November 1992 the Lord Ordinary *sustained* the pursuer's pleas in law, *repelled* the defenders' pleas in law on the merits and in relation to contributory negligence and *awarded* damages totalling £159,189 plus interest.

LORD COULSFIELD.—On 4 July 1988, the pursuer sustained serious injuries while working in the course of his employment as the first defenders' works manager in their factory premises at Auldhall West, Irvine. The first defenders manufactured concrete blocks and slabs and the machinery used for that purpose included a slab press. This was a fairly large machine the components of which included a hopper, the entrance to which was about 10 ft above ground level, into which a concrete mixture was poured, a feed tray positioned at the foot of the hopper, into which the concrete passed and a hydraulic system which transferred the feed tray to a press in which slabs were made. There was also a pneumatic power system which operated the press itself. In the course of the operation of the machine, the feed tray moved backwards and forwards under the lower aperture of the hopper. The hydraulic and pneumatic systems were operated by electric power.

The machine was in a disgraceful state. It had a number of dangerous moving parts and it should have been protected on all sides by a fencing system so arranged that access could not be obtained to any of the moving parts or to the hopper while power was available to move the machine. This could easily have been achieved by a system of gate locks interlocking with the controls of the machine. No such fencing system had been provided. As designed, the machine did have several safety features. There should have been, on a control panel fairly close to the machine, a main switch which could be turned off to isolate the machine from any electrical supply. There was such a switch but it was not operational. Provision was made

in the control panel of the machine for a key control, so designed that removal of the key would immobilise the machine. At the material time, the key was missing and the control panel had been rewired by the defenders, or at least with their knowledge, to bypass the key. There were a number of wire mesh gates and panels giving access to certain parts of the machine. These were fitted, by the manufacturer, with sensors, the object of which was to cut off power if the gates were open, but the sensors had been taped over to prevent them from operating. In consequence, the only controls of the machine remaining operational were, first, a switch situated on a main electrical distribution board about 80 yds away and, secondly, an isolator button and a start button on the control panel. The isolator button was in practice used to stop the machine in the ordinary course of work although its true purpose was as a safety or emergency stop mechanism. Once depressed, the isolator button had to be reset by pulling it out again, before the machine could be restarted by pressing the start button.

In addition to being manifestly very dangerous, the machine did not function efficiently. Problems had been experienced with the manufacture of slabs intermittently for a considerable time prior to 4 July 1988. The principal fault appears to have been that as the slabs left the machine they tended to fall and break. The pursuer had repeatedly drawn the condition of the machine to the attention of the first defenders' production manager who simply refused to provide any expert assistance to repair or service the machine. The pursuer was therefore compelled to do his best to keep the machine running. On the date in question, the machine was again malfunctioning. The pursuer undertook a number of investigations to try to discover what was going wrong. Eventually, he obtained a ladder and climbed up into the hopper in order to check whether there was any fault there. There was no fence which prevented him from getting into the hopper or descending to the foot of it and he did so. While he was there the feed tray moved, trapping his legs and causing him serious injuries.

The only issue, so far as the facts of the case are concerned, is what caused the movement of the tray. The machine could operate either manually or automatically. Inside the hopper there was a contact switch so arranged that automatic operation could continue only while the hopper contained material available to be fed into the tray. At the material time, the hopper was empty and it must be assumed that the immediate cause of the movement of the tray was that the pursuer had contacted the switch inside the hopper. However, unless there was some other fault in the electrical system, in addition to those already mentioned, the tray would not have moved unless the machine had been switched on at the console and it had been in automatic mode. Since attempts had been made to operate the machine earlier in the day it may be assumed that it was set to operate automatically. The pursuer's evidence was that he had depressed the isolator button before entering the hopper. The pursuer was a very experienced engineer and was well aware

of the danger of working on machinery which was not
isolated from its power supply. The pursuer also said
that when the power supply was switched on there was
some noise from a pump which fed, he understood,
the hydraulic system. There was no other machinery
in operation in the factory and the pursuer thought
that the pump noise would have been audible if the
power had been on. There was some evidence from an
expert engineer, Mr McGregor, who said that the
hydraulic system would not produce any noise unless
the pump were actually in operation, and causing
movement of the machinery, but the pneumatic
system might have created some noise, had the
machine been switched on. The pursuer had, however, been attempting to remedy problems with the
machine. In the course of testing the machine, he
would have had to stop and start it, and there must be
a possibility that he had, on this occasion, omitted to
press the isolator button before checking the hopper.
The only other person in the vicinity was the plant
operator, Robert Hunter. Hunter had been operating
the machine earlier that day, but at the material time
he was engaged in clearing up the debris of slabs
which had fallen and broken in the course of earlier
attempts to use the machine. To carry out this work,
he would be positioned at the end of a conveyor belt
which carried finished slabs from the machine, some
distance away from the control panel. Hunter denied
operating the start button. He was aware that the
pursuer was working on or in the vicinity of the
machine but he was not actually aware that he was in
the hopper but and, according to his evidence, his first
knowledge of the accident was when he heard the
pursuer scream. He then pressed the isolator button
but subsequently had to reset it in order to reverse the
machinery and free the pursuer. It is not easy to
resolve the question how the machine came to be on.
I was impressed by the pursuer as a witness; he
seemed to me to be a man who was likely to be careful
and to be well aware of the problems and dangers of
working on the machine with the power on. On the
other hand there was no evidence to indicate a fault in
the machine of a kind which would enable it to start
without the isolator button having been reversed and
there was no reason why Hunter should have reset the
isolator button and restarted the machine. On balance,
I think that the most probable explanation is that the
pursuer having been working on the machine, and
having had to start and then stop it on a number of
occasions, had inadvertently omitted to depress the
isolator button before entering the hopper.

The pursuer's case on record is based in part upon
the allegation that it was Hunter who caused the
machine to operate. The pursuer also has, however,
cases under s 14 of the Factories Act and at common
law based upon the defenders' failure to take adequate
precautions to make it safe to operate the machine. In
my opinion these cases are clearly established. There
was no fencing to protect the pursuer against encoun-
tering the dangerous part of the machinery. There is,
in my opinion, no doubt that it was foreseeable that a
person working at the machine, particularly in view of

its state and condition, might require to enter the
hopper. There was no evidence to indicate that it was
not practicable to fence the dangerous part of
machinery in which the pursuer was trapped. Even if
there were practical difficulties in providing a guard at
the aperture in the hopper which opened into the
feeding tray, a factory inspector's report made after
the accident makes it clear that there was a proper and
practicable way to guard against the dangers posed by
this machine, by surrounding it with fencing so
arranged that an interlock switch at the entrance gate
or gates would prevent the machine from operating
when anyone entered within the fenced area, as would
have been necessary in order to reach the hopper.
Accordingly, in my opinion, the defenders were in
breach of their duties under s 14. The defenders were
also at fault at common law. They had allowed the
machine to be in a dangerous state and had displayed
indifference to the safety of their employees. The
pursuer should, at the very least, have had available to
him two means of ensuring safety in addition to the
use of the isolator button. Both offered more reliable
means of ensuring safety during repair or maintenance
than the isolator button, whose true function was as an
emergency stopping device. It is true that the immediate occasion of the machine being live was the pursuer's inadvertence, and the defenders argued that that
was the cause of the accident and that the pursuer was,
at least to some extent, to blame. This is, perhaps, not
the sort of situation of repetitive work or fatigue in
which inadvertence is most commonly regarded as
something which does not amount to contributory
negligence. Nevertheless, in the particular circumstances of this case, in view of the defenders' gross
failures in proper care and the fact that the pursuer
was required to do his best to make and keep operational a machine which lacked elementary safety
features, it seems to me that, if the pursuer did fail to
operate the isolator button, his failure can properly be
regarded as falling within the principles of cases such
as *John Summers & Son Ltd v Frost* and therefore not
amounting to contributory negligence. In these circumstances, I have no hesitation in holding that the
accident was entirely due to fault and breach of statutory duty on the part of the defenders.

The pursuer sustained very serious injuries. He had
compound fractures of both tibiae and fibulae just
above ankle level. He required a very substantial
operation to stabilise the fracture and further operations for skin grafts and other procedures. By 21
December 1988, the pursuer was weight bearing only
on his left leg. He continued to have pain from an
ulcer which developed in his right foot. A number of
attempts to treat that ulcer failed and eventually, on 21
March 1989, his right leg was amputated below the
knee. He still has substantial defects in his left leg and
problems with his right leg and his ability to walk is
very restricted. He attempted to study at a college but
his attempts had to be discontinued because of the
problems arising from his injuries. He did not obtain
alternative employment until April 1992 and the
employment is of a relatively undemanding kind. It

A was submitted on behalf of the pursuer that the appropriate award of solatium would be in the range of £42,500 to £45,000 and for the defenders that the range should be between £37,000 and £40,000. In my view the bottom end of the pursuer's proposed range is appropriate and I shall award £42,500 as solatium. The pursuer submitted that two thirds of that sum should be held to relate to the past with interest on that part of the sum at 7½ per cent per annum from the date of the accident to the date of proof and I shall accept that submission. The wage loss to date, includ-

B ing interest, is agreed at £40,289. Wage loss is continuing at the rate of £100 per week. The pursuer suggested a multiplier of 12, and the defenders proposed one of 8. The pursuer is 40 years of age and the multiplier proposed on his behalf seems to be reasonable. The award for future wage loss calculated on that basis is £62,400. In addition the pursuer submitted that there should be an award for disadvantage in the labour market, particularly taking account of the fact that his present employment is with employers who

C are working under a limited contract. The sum suggested was £15,000. In my view it is appropriate to make such an award, although the defenders submitted that none should be made. However, the sum proposed on behalf of the pursuer seems to me to be on the high side and I shall award £10,000. The pursuer also sought awards in relation to loss of services and proposed that there should be awards of £5,000 under each of ss 8 and 9 of the 1982 Act. The evidence indicated that Mrs Scott does require to give

D a considerable amount of assistance to the pursuer and also that the pursuer has been considerably restricted in the extent to which he can carry out household tasks and such other tasks such as decorating or other do it yourself work. The sums proposed by the pursuer, however, seem to me too high. The evidence did not disclose any extraordinary circumstances and in my view an award of £2,000 under each head would be adequate. The total award will therefore be £159,189 plus interest at 7½ per cent on £28,330 from the date

E of his accident to the date of proof. I was invited to make further awards to cover the running of interest and loss of wages for the period between the date of proof and the date of judgment, but as I anticipate that the delay will not be great, I think it unnecessary to make any such additional award.

Counsel for Pursuer, Haddow, QC, Davie; Solicitors, Drummond Miller, WS (for Harper Macleod, Glasgow)

F *— Counsel for Defenders, J G Thomson; Solicitors, Wright Johnston & Mackenzie.*

C H

M W Wilson (Lace) Ltd v Eagle Star Insurance Co Ltd

G

SECOND DIVISION
THE LORD JUSTICE CLERK (ROSS),
LORDS McCLUSKEY AND KIRKWOOD
23 DECEMBER 1992

Contract — Insurance contract — Construction — "Bursting or overflowing of water pipes, water apparatus or water tanks" — Damage resulting from steam escap- H *ing after loss of temporary bung in steam heating system — Whether a "water apparatus" — Whether "bursting or overflowing" of apparatus — Whether any ambiguity to be construed contra proferentem.*

Insurance — Indemnity insurance — Construction of contract — "Bursting or overflowing of water pipes, water apparatus or water tanks" — Damage resulting from steam escaping after loss of temporary bung in steam heating system — Whether a "water apparatus" — I *Whether "bursting or overflowing" of apparatus — Whether any ambiguity to be construed contra proferentem.*

A manufacturing company operating factory premises was insured against various risks including destruction of or damage to property caused by bursting or overflowing of water pipes, water apparatus or water tanks. The factory had a steam heating system in which a gas fired boiler converted water into steam, the steam then being forced along pipes at pressure, J thereby heating the premises. As the steam reverted to water it was recycled.

During repairs the system was activated and steam thus created blew a temporary plastic bung out of the end of a cut pipe. The steam escaping from the pipe condensed and damaged the premises and machinery. The insurers maintained that this was not an insured event; that by no ordinary use of language could this incident be described as the bursting of a water apparatus; and that there was no ambiguity in the K policy as common use of language indicated that a water pipe and a steam pipe were different. In granting decree of declarator that the insurers were bound to indemnify in respect of the damage, the temporary judge held that in the absence of any common usage for the words "water apparatus" they required interpretation and the contra proferentes rule applied; that the term was readily capable of being construed so as to comprehend the heating system; and that the loss of integrity of the water apparatus could justifiably be L described as "bursting". The insurers reclaimed.

Held, (1) that there was no ambiguity in the language of the clause which would justify application of the contra proferentes rule (pp 942G-H, 944L-945A, 946F and 947B-D); (2) that the steam pipe which was sealed with the bung could not properly be described as a water pipe nor the steam heating system as "water apparatus" (pp 943C-D, 945H-L, 946A-C and 947F-G and J-K); (3) that what occurred when the bung was blown out could not on any normal meaning of the

A words be regarded as "bursting or overflowing of water pipes, water apparatus or water tanks" (pp 943I-L, 945F-G, 946D-F, 947G-H and 948B-C); and reclaiming motion *allowed* and decree of absolvitor *granted.*

Action of declarator and payment

M W Wilson (Lace) Ltd raised an action of declarator and payment against Eagle Star Insurance Co
B Ltd. The pursuers sought to establish that the terms of an insurance contract covered circumstances in which their premises and machinery had been damaged by an escape and subsequent condensation of steam from the heating system.

The case came before the temporary judge (T G Coutts, QC) for proof before answer.

Cases referred to

Brebner v British Coal Corporation, 1988 SLT 736.
Houghton v Trafalgar Insurance Co Ltd [1954] 1 QB
C   247; [1953] 3 WLR 985; [1953] 2 All ER 1409; [1953] 2 Lloyd's Rep 503.
Life Association of Scotland v Foster (1873) 11 M 351.
London and Lancashire Fire Insurance Co Ltd v Bolands Ltd [1924] AC 836.
Stanley v Western Insurance Co (1868) LR 2 Ex 71.

Textbooks referred to

Gloag, *Contract* (2nd ed), p 400.
MacGillivray and Parkington, *Insurance Law* (8th ed),
D   paras 1071, 1076, 1078, 1082 and 1105.

Terms of contract of insurance

The terms of the insurance contract between the parties included:

"*Additional Perils*

Subject to the special conditions hereinafter contained the insurance by each item of the specification (except where expressly stated to the contrary therein) is extended to include destruction of or damage to the property thereby insured directly caused by such of
E the additional perils detailed below as are stated on page A of this specification to be insured thereunder:— . . .

"*Burst Pipes* 10. Bursting or overflowing of water pipes, water apparatus or water tanks but excluding (a) destruction or damage whilst the building is untenanted; (b) destruction or damage by water discharged or leaking from an installation of automatic sprinklers; (c) the first £100 (or such other sum as is
F stated on Page A of this specification to be the water damage excess) of each and every loss as ascertained after the application of the condition of average."

On 18 December 1991 the temporary judge *granted* decree of declarator.

T G COUTTS, QC.—The pursuers' factory at Greenhead Mills, Newmilns, contained various knitting machines for the manufacture of their products. The factory premises had a steam heating system: ie, a boiler and pipes which were connected to

the boiler. The pipes ran overhead through the
G factory. The system had a gas fired boiler to heat water originating from an open topped tank fed from the mains. The liquid water was converted into steam which thereafter circulated through the system until ultimately it returned as liquid to the open tank (known as a "hot well" tank) and thus was re-used to feed the boiler. The system involved the steam being forced along the pipes at pressure and, as the heat was transferred from the pipes into the atmosphere of the factory, some part of it reverted to water, which was referred to at the proof as "condensate". There were
H devices throughout the system called steam traps at which point condensate collected. Throughout the system as a whole the proportion of condensate did not exceed 0.17 per cent of the content of the pipes, the remainder being steam. It was an essential feature of the system that condensate be removed from the system by re-delivering it to the holding tank.

On 7 August 1988 work was being done on the heating system which involved cutting some of the overhead pipes. About 2 am on 8 August 1988 the
I boiler, for some reason which was not explored at the proof, started to operate and heated the water thus creating steam in the steam heating system. That steam blew a plastic bung out of the cut end of a pipe in building no 5 of the pursuers' premises. The plastic bung had been placed in the cut pipe as a stopper, to seal the system while it was not in operation. The only purpose of such sealing would be to prevent either dust entering the pipes or water escaping therefrom. The breach thus caused meant that the content of the
J pipe escaped and caused damage to the pursuers' premises and machinery. The escape was discovered and the system shut off about 6 am on 8 August 1988. The extent of the damage was not at issue before me, parties having agreed that the proof before answer was to be directed solely to the first, declaratory, conclusion leaving parties to reach agreement on quantum thereafter. The damage was caused by the premises filling with steam which condensed and formed water on the walls, ceiling and machinery in the factory.
K Some condensate must also have escaped from the cut pipe.

The pursuers had entered into a contract of insurance with the defenders in terms of which the pursuers were to be indemnified in the event of any of the contingencies therein mentioned occurring.

The relevant clause in the policy was that concerning additional perils. The short title read: "subject to the special conditions hereinafter contained, the insur-
L ance for each item of the specification (except where expressly stated to the contrary therein) is extended to include destruction of or damage to the property thereby insured directly caused by such of the additional perils detailed below". Paragraph 10 of these additional perils had the side note "Burst Pipes" and read as follows: [the temporary judge quoted the terms of para 10 and continued:] None of these exclusions applied in the present instance.

The proof before me, confined in its scope by the

A sensible agreements of counsel, was concentrated on an attempt to resolve the dispute between the parties about whether the said para 10 applied to the above narrated event. I heard evidence from the persons who were first on the scene; the principal of the pursuing firm (who in the course of his evidence described the pipes in question as "steam pipes"), and from two expert witnesses, one called for each party.

B Dr Gilchrist, a senior lecturer in mechanical engineering and thermodynamics at the University of Strathclyde, described the system as "a gas fired water heater feeding a header system which distributed steam through a system of pipes". Water vapour, he said, fed back to the tank feeding the boiler unit. He stated that it was implicit in the design of the system that water vapour had to be condensed; that there was water vapour in the system; and that the pipes had to be designed so that when steam condensed with the transfer of heat from the pipe to the atmosphere of the room the water could be removed from the system by being led back to the tank. The pipes were set on a C gradual slope for that purpose. Whether steam or liquid it was all water being the chemical substance H_2O. There was a single phase flow and two fluid phases therein, one liquid and one vapour. He described the complete system as a "water apparatus". He agreed that water and steam, although they have the same chemical constituents, have different properties but said they are two physical arrangements of the one substance.

D Kenneth Tanner, who carried on business as a consulting engineer and whose qualifications were described as FIE and MCIBE, stated that he saw a clear distinction between water and steam particularly in the results of the escape of each. Steam will occupy and engulf an entire area whereas water will simply fall. There will always be some condensate if such a system as the pursuers' is breached but the principal constituent would be steam. In cross examination he asserted that it would be illegitimate to describe the E system as a water apparatus. He described some of the pipes in the system as "condensate pipes" and he declined to accept that the feeder tank to the system was a water tank. He called it a "hot well" tank.

For the pursuers it was argued that the system as a whole was a water apparatus in which the proportion of steam and water would vary throughout. It was fundamental to the operation that the pipes could contain water in vapour and in liquid form and therefore the F pipes were pipes to contain water in the ordinary sense. Reference was made to the Shorter Oxford Dictionary under the heading "water" and to Chambers Dictionary. In both dictionaries the word "water" is said to extend to the substance H_2O in solid or gaseous state. In the textbook Words and Phrases Judicially Defined, p 419 under the heading "water", a Canadian case is cited in which it was said: "in view of the fact that it is the defendant's contract of insurance against damage by escaping water, the term water should not be construed as meaning only water in a liquid form but also in a gaseous form". The Canadian

G case there cited had not been traced by counsel further than the reference in "Words and Phrases". Counsel for the pursuers urged upon me that if there was ambiguity the policy should be construed contra proferentem, citing Gloag, Contract (2nd ed), p 400, Life Association of Scotland v Foster and Houghton v Trafalgar Insurance Co Ltd. He also referred me to the Shorter Oxford English Dictionary's definition of "apparatus". He further argued that "bursting or overflowing" was a phrase wide enough to cover the forcing out of a bung, because the apparatus thereby lost its integrity and its contents escaped.

H Counsel for the defenders contended that the basic principle of construction was to use, if possible, the ordinary meaning of the word. He cited MacGillivray and Parkington on Insurance Law (8th ed), para 1071 and argued that the contra proferentem rule did not apply here since there was no essential ambiguity in this case. There was, he said, an essential distinction in properties and indeed in the risk created by water and steam. The common use of language indicated that a water pipe and a steam pipe were different albeit I that steam pipes might contain water in the form of condensate. The two substances were only the same in the sense that they were H_2O but the ordinary use of language did not indicate that the substance within the pursuers' system could be properly described as water. He illustrated that proposition with Stanley v Western Insurance Co. There the use of the word "gas" in a policy of insurance was held not to be apt to cover the gaseous product of a process in a factory but to be applicable only to town gas. That decision was arrived J at no doubt in the context of a very substantial use of town gas for many purposes at that time. In legislation concerned with factories, steam and water were regarded as different substances subject to different regulations. The term "water apparatus" was not apt to describe a gas fired boiler with steam pipes attached. Here it is, as was agreed by the parties in a joint minute, a steam heating apparatus and it would be better described as a steam apparatus. Turning to the mechanism of the incident he contended that the K escape was not an overflow nor could it be said to be the bursting of a water pipe or water apparatus. By no ordinary use of language, he said, could one describe the incident as the bursting of a water apparatus.

I agree with the pursuers' proposition that the system as described can be quite readily and properly described as "water apparatus". The entire arrangement of the heating system within the pursuers' factory depended upon water. Water was introduced L to a boiler fired by gas — a gas boiler — it was converted to steam, which was circulated, and was reconverted to water and reused. I am unable to recognise any common usage for the words "water apparatus". These words are not commonly heard, or used, together. They do not describe anything which is instantly identifiable. They require interpretation. Since they require interpretation, evidence was appropriate and the contra proferentem rule applies. I prefer Dr Gilchrist's approach. In my opinion these words are readily capable of being construed so as to comprehend the pursuers' heating system. While I agree with counsel for the defenders that water pipes and steam pipes are commonly spoken of as different objects and have no doubt that when people talk about water pipes and steam pipes they intend to make a distinction between them, I do not think that assists when construing "water apparatus". I do not think that in this case there was a bursting of a water pipe. A water pipe is readily understood as being something which conveys water to a tap or tank. A steam pipe conveys steam. Both can exist in a "water apparatus".

In my opinion the inclusion of the words "water apparatus" in the contract was intended to provide a convenient general term for all usages of water within a system utilising water in the factory. In this connection the distinction between water and steam becomes of considerably less significance. One is entitled in my view to have regard to the complete system as being the apparatus as opposed to particular bits of it being the apparatus. The general description of the pursuers' system which sits most comfortably is "water apparatus" which was the usage favoured by Dr Gilchrist. I was not impressed by Mr Tanner who declined even to accept that the tank holding water taken from the domestic water supply was a water tank. He described it as a "hot well tank". If, however, one applies the test contended for by the defenders of the ordinary use of language there could be no doubt in my view that the ordinary person would not describe such a tank as other than a water tank. They certainly would not use the words "hot well tank", although it seems some engineers might.

The other difficulty in interpretation which the pursuers must surmount is whether or not the events which happened can be aptly described as "bursting or overflowing". It was strongly submitted for the defenders that a steam escape was not an overflow nor, it was said, could one describe the events as the bursting of a water pipe. However I think one can justifiably describe the said loss of integrity of the water apparatus as bursting. The pipe had been sealed by a bung and that bung burst out with steam pressure. A defective gasket in the system would equally burst. Again what happened was that the contents of the apparatus escaped and flowed from it, and even "overflowing", although perhaps less apt, would not be an inappropriate description of the event.

Accordingly I am of opinion that the pursuers are entitled to the declarator they seek, in terms of their first conclusion. Quoad ultra the cause will be put out "by order" to determine further procedure.

The defenders reclaimed.

Reclaiming motion

The reclaiming motion was heard before the Second Division on 26 and 27 November 1992.

On 23 December 1992 the court *allowed* the reclaiming motion, *recalled* the interlocutor of the temporary judge and *granted* decree of absolvitor.

THE LORD JUSTICE CLERK (ROSS).—In this action the pursuers seek declarator that the defenders are bound to implement their obligations under a contract of insurance between the parties, and that they are bound to indemnify the pursuers in respect of damage which the pursuers sustained in their factory premises at Newmilns on 12 August 1988. They also seek payment from the defenders in respect of the amount of loss which they claim that they are entitled to recover from the defenders in terms of the insurance policy. The defenders repudiated liability in respect of the claim made by the pursuers on the ground that the policy did not cover the damage which arose on this occasion. A proof before answer took place and by agreement of counsel proof was confined to the question of whether the damage which the pursuers had sustained was covered by the terms of the policy. The temporary judge found in favour of the pursuers and pronounced decree in terms of the first conclusion of the summons. Thereafter he allowed parties a proof of their respective averments restricted to quantum only. Against that interlocutor of the temporary judge the defenders have now reclaimed.

In their grounds of appeal, the defenders allege various errors in law on the part of the temporary judge, but parties were agreed that what this court required to do was to place a proper construction on the language used in the contract of insurance. It was not necessary for this court to consider whether the reasoning of the temporary judge was sound; the only question was whether his construction of the language of the policy was correct. What this court had to do was to determine the proper construction to be placed upon the words used.

It is plain from the pleadings and the evidence that the pursuers' factory premises contained a steam heating system comprising a boiler and pipes which were connected to the boiler. The boiler heated water to produce superheated steam. This passed to a header system to which was connected a number of parallel heating pipework units. The steam was fed at reduced pressure into these parallel heating circuits (which were hot pipes). The steam was condensed on the side of the pipes, and heat was transferred from the surface of the pipes to the surrounding environment. There was a slope on the pipes and the condensate ran down the slope and was gathered in a trap at the end from which it entered a condensate pipe which transferred it back to the hot well tank which re-feeds the boiler. The hot well tank on occasions requires to be replenished with water. It was not disputed that the amount of condensate which was produced amounted to 0.17 per cent of the steam volume.

In August 1988 the pursuers were carrying out alterations to their factory premises, and on 11 August 1988 an employee of third party contractors placed a plastic bung on the open end of a pipe in the steam heating system upon which he was working in building no 5 of the pursuers' premises. At about 2 am on the following day, as a result of a defect in a time switch, the boiler started to operate and heated the water creating steam in the steam heating system.

A That steam blew the plastic bung out of the open end of the pipe with the result that steam escaped from the end of the pipe. Damage was caused by this escape of steam; the steam condensed and water dropped on to the machinery in the premises and damaged it.

It is unnecessary to set out in detail the whole terms of the policy of insurance. The policy contains a clause headed "Additional Perils". The short title provides inter alia as follows: [his Lordship quoted the terms of the clause set out supra including para 10 and continued:] None of the exclusions applies in the present case.

B

The critical question is whether what occurred on the occasion in question was "Bursting or overflowing of water pipes, water apparatus or water tanks". The temporary judge took the view that the heating system as described could readily and properly be described as "water apparatus". He also held that the loss of the integrity of the water apparatus which occurred could justifiably be described as "bursting" and that it C would not be inappropriate to describe what occurred as an overflowing of the contents of the apparatus. He accordingly found in favour of the pursuers. Counsel for the defenders maintained that the Lord Ordinary had not applied the correct construction to the words of para 10. They contended that the steam heating system could not reasonably be described as water apparatus, and further that what occurred on the occasion in question could not properly be described as the bursting or overflowing of water pipes or water D apparatus. Counsel for the pursuers on the other hand stressed that it was fundamental that the heating system contained pipes which carried water both in liquid form and in the form of vapour; the pipe which had been opened and stopped with a bung carried steam and water, and could properly be described as a water pipe; and the whole heating system could aptly be described as water apparatus. On the occasion in question the contents of the pipe burst out from their enclosure, and that was accordingly a bursting of a E water pipe or water apparatus. He also contended that water whether in liquid or vapour form could be described as overflowing when it escaped from the pipe.

Both counsel emphasised that the words used in para 10 fell to be given their natural and ordinary meaning, and they referred extensively to dictionary definitions of the words concerned. I agree that the object must be to ascertain the intention of the parties F to the contract of insurance as expressed or implied by the language which they have used. In that connection words which they have used must be given their natural and ordinary meaning. Both parties maintained that a proper application of that rule of construction supported the construction for which they contended. In other words, the primary contention of both parties was that there was no ambiguity in the language used in para 10 and that the court should simply construe the words in accordance with their natural meaning. Counsel for the pursuers had an alternative submission to the effect that the language used was ambiguous and that accordingly the contra proferentes rule fell to be applied.   G

So far as counsel for the pursuers' alternative submission is concerned, I am satisfied that there is no ground for applying the contra proferentes rule in the present case. The present case raises a pure question of construction, and I do not regard it as a case where there is any ambiguity. Although counsel for the pursuers suggested that there was ambiguity, he was unable to satisfy me as to the precise nature of any ambiguity in this case. The difficulty in the present case is not in ascertaining the meaning of the words   H used in para 10, but in determining whether these words apply to the circumstances of the present case.

"It is suggested further that there is some ambiguity about the proviso, and that, under the various well-known authorities, upon the principle of reading words contra proferentes, we ought to construe this proviso, which is in favour of the insurance company, adversely to them. That, however, is a principle which depends upon there being some ambiguity — that is to   I say, some choice of an expression — by those who are responsible for putting forward the clause, which leaves one unable to decide which of two meanings is the right one. In the present case it is a question only of construction. There may be some difficulty, there may be even some difference of opinion, about the construction, but it is a question quite capable of being solved by the ordinary rules of grammar, and it appears to me that there is no ground for saying that there is such an ambiguity as would warrant us in   J reading the clause otherwise than in accordance with its express terms" (*London and Lancashire Fire Insurance Co Ltd v Bolands Ltd,* per Lord Sumner at p 848; MacGillivray and Parkington (8th ed), para 1105).

To some extent the question of the proper construction is one of impression. In my opinion a pipe charged with steam would not normally be described as a "water pipe", and a steam heating system would not normally be described as "water apparatus". Counsel for the pursuers, however, stressed that the   K heating system depended upon water; the boiler heated water in liquid form, it became steam, condensed, and then drained back again as liquid. That being so he maintained that it was appropriate to describe the apparatus as a whole as "water apparatus". As regards the particular pipe which had been sealed with a bung, that pipe carried water in both phases, that is, water as liquid and water as vapour. Counsel for the pursuers pointed out that in the *Shorter Oxford English Dictionary* the first   L meaning of water is: "The liquid of which seas, lakes and rivers are composed, and which falls as rain and issues from springs". The second meaning given is: "The substance of which the liquid 'water' is one form among several; the chemical compound of two volumes of hydrogen and one of oxygen (formula H_2O)".

In *Chambers Dictionary* water is defined as: "In a state of purity, at ordinary temperatures, a clear transparent colourless liquid, perfectly neutral in its reaction, and devoid of taste or smell; extended to the same substance (H_2O) in solid or gaseous state (ice, steam)''.

In the *Shorter Oxford English Dictionary* "steam" is defined as: "A vapour or fume given out by a substance when heated or burned". A subsequent meaning is: "The vapour into which water is converted when heated. In popular language, applied to the visible vapour which floats in the air in the form of a white cloud or mist, and which consists of minute globules or vesicles of liquid water suspended in a mixture of gaseous water and air".

We were also referred to the definition in the *Shorter Oxford English Dictionary* of "apparatus" as including: "Equipments, material, machinery; material appendages or arrangements".

Although steam and ice are water in different states or phases and each of them is the same substance (H_2O), I am of opinion that "water" in its plain and natural meaning refers to water in its liquid state. When water is in a gaseous state, it is commonly referred to not as water but as steam. In the same way when water is in a solid state it is ordinarily referred to as ice and not water. The steam heating system which I have described earlier in this opinion might appropriately be described as "steam apparatus", but in my judgment it would not be appropriate to describe it as "water apparatus". No doubt it is essential to the operation of the steam heating system that water is introduced to it, but the water is converted to steam for the purpose of the heating system, and the pipe which had the bung contained steam and only a small quantity of liquid after condensation had taken place. That being so it is not appropriate to regard it as a "water pipe" or part of a "water apparatus".

I appreciate that water is a chemical substance and that water in liquid form, water in solid form and water in vapour form are all the same chemical substance. But each of them exhibits different physical arrangements of the same substance, and in common parlance, a distinction is drawn between water, ice and steam. As already pointed out, steam and ice are not commonly described as "water".

Counsel referred to *Brebner v British Coal Corporation* where a question arose as to what was meant by "apparatus". In the course of delivering my opinion in that case I said (at p 742E): "In my opinion the word 'apparatus' should be given its natural and ordinary meaning. One of these meanings is 'an assemblage of appliances or materials for a particular use'". What I was doing in that passage was merely repeating the dictionary definition of the word. Counsel for the pursuers maintained that the heating system which I have described above clearly was an assemblage of appliances or materials for a particular use, and I would accept that that was so. The steam heating system may well have been "apparatus" but the critical question is whether it could properly be described as "water apparatus". I do not consider that the mere fact that the apparatus uses water which it converts into steam, means that it is appropriate to describe the apparatus as "water apparatus". As counsel for the defenders pointed out, Stephenson's steam engine would hardly be described as "water apparatus".

In the foregoing circumstances I am not persuaded that the pipe which was sealed with the bung can properly be described as a water pipe nor that the steam heating system as a whole can properly be described as "water apparatus". But the language of para 10 contains further problems for counsel for the pursuers because if para 10 is held to apply, what occurred must have amounted to "bursting or overflowing of water pipes, water apparatus or water tanks". Counsel maintained that what occurred here could properly be regarded as a bursting of water pipes or water apparatus. He referred to the definition in the *Shorter Oxford English Dictionary* of "burst". The first meaning given is: "To break suddenly, snap, crack — To break suddenly when in a state of tension or expansion, to fly asunder or in pieces". He founded however on a subsequent definition which is there given as: "To issue forth suddenly and copiously by breaking an enclosure or the like". He maintained that when the bung was blown out of the open end of the pipe the steam issued forth suddenly, and could properly be described as breaking out of its enclosed position. I am not persuaded that this approach is a sound one. In the first place when the paragraph refers to bursting of water pipes or water apparatus, I regard that as a clear reference to the bursting of water in its liquid state. But quite apart from that I do not consider that what occurred here amounted to a bursting of a water pipe or water apparatus. What happened on the occasion in question was not any breaking or bursting of a pipe or part of the apparatus but the blowing out of a plastic bung. Moreover what issued forth when the bung was blown out was steam and not water in a liquid state.

I am also satisfied that what occurred cannot properly be described as "overflowing of water pipes or water apparatus". I accept that a gas or vapour may be said to flow within a pipe. An obvious example of this would be natural gas which flows in pipes from the North Sea to the mainland of the United Kingdom. But I do not consider that gas or vapour which has escaped from a pipe can properly be described as the "overflowing of a pipe or apparatus". Liquid water which overflows from a container will naturally fall over the edge of the container by means of gravity. But when steam escaped from the open end of this pipe, there was no question of the steam falling down; on the contrary the steam being lighter than air rose and, in my opinion, steam behaving in that way cannot be properly regarded as "overflowing".

I entirely agree that if this had been a conventional heating system which depended upon hot water being conveyed through pipes, the escape of water from the pipes when a bung blew would properly fall within the description of "bursting or overflowing of water pipes or water apparatus". But that was not the type of heating system which the pursuers had. Theirs was a steam heating system, and I am of opinion that the language of para 10 is not apt to describe what occurs when steam within one of the pipes blows a plastic bung and escapes into the atmosphere of the room. I entirely accept, as counsel for the pursuers submitted, that the predominant feature of the steam heating system was to create heat, but it did so by producing steam, and the pipe which was open, which was part of the whole apparatus, was a pipe which carried steam for heating purposes. No doubt condensation took place, but there can be no doubt that the part of the apparatus where the bung blew was designed primarily to contain steam and not water in liquid form.

For the foregoing reasons I am satisfied that the event which gave rise to the damage cannot on any normal meaning of the words be regarded as "bursting or overflowing of water pipes, water apparatus or water tanks". I am accordingly of opinion that the temporary judge reached the wrong conclusion in this case. I would accordingly move your Lordships to sustain this reclaiming motion, recall the temporary judge's interlocutor of 18 December 1991, repel the first plea in law for the pursuers, to sustain the second and third pleas in law for the defenders, and to grant decree of absolvitor.

LORD McCLUSKEY.—The issue which has given rise to this reclaiming motion has been stated in various different ways in the course of the submissions to this court. As I see it, what has to be decided is whether or not the event that occurred at the respondents' Newmilns factory in August 1988 and caused the loss to the respondents was an event falling within the perils described in para 10 of the additional perils listed in the insurance contract which the parties had entered into. In that contract of insurance (commercial combined policy no 72080477 (9)) the reclaimers undertook to indemnify the respondents in the manner therein defined in the event of the happening of any contingency listed therein. The contingencies listed include those described as follows: "*Burst Pipes.* 10. Bursting or overflowing of water pipes, water apparatus or water tanks".

There were certain exclusions but they do not bear upon any point at issue in this case. The temporary judge of the Court of Session concluded that the event fell within the listed perils; the reclaimers submit that he was wrong. The only questions raised are questions as to the correct understanding of the relevant provisions of the policy and their application to the known, agreed circumstances. It is common ground that the temporary judge was not exercising a judicial discretion in deciding the matters he had to decide; and that accordingly the whole matter is at large for this court to determine by arriving at its own conclusions on the matter of construction and application.

The facts, agreed in the pleadings or by joint minute and elucidated by a proof, can be stated shortly. The system of heating the premises was a steam heating system. A gas fired boiler heated water so that it became superheated steam under pressure; that steam was forced into a header system which was connected through valves to several parallel heating pipework circuits. The steam passed through the various circuits, cooling down as it did so, and transferring its heat to the pipework, whence the heat radiated to the interior of the factory. When the steam cooled down sufficiently it started to condense, thus taking a liquid form, as water. The pipes were set so as to have a gradual slope to allow the condensate to drain towards the outlet end of the appropriate heating circuit. There it built up as water till the pressure of the water opened a valve; that water would then drain past the open valve into a collection tank before being returned to the boiler for re-heating and re-use. The collection tank was kept topped up from a mains water supply controlled by a ballcock system. Thus the heating pipework circuit was designed to convey steam, to transfer heat from the steam to the surrounding air space by radiation, to allow condensation inside the pipework and to collect and return the condensate (water) for re-use. On Thursday, 11 August 1988 at about 4.30 pm, while the heating system was switched off for maintenance work, a workman used a plastic bung to seal off the open end of a steam pipe forming part of one of the heating circuits; he had — for the purposes of his work — disconnected the end of the pipe from the adjacent pipe which was designed specifically to carry the condensate back to the collection tank. The purpose of inserting the bung was apparently to stop foreign matter from entering the open pipe or water from dripping out from it. The plastic bung was in no sense a part of the pipe or the system as designed; it was a temporary stopper inserted into a temporary break in the system. Overnight the boiler was accidentally switched on and the resultant steam pressure in the pipe forced the plastic bung to pop out. The steam issued forth for some hours and caused substantial damage. The reclaimers repudiated liability to indemnify in respect of the damage because they considered that the accident which had occurred was not within the listed perils.

Before this court, parties were agreed that in the first instance the words used in this policy were to be given their ordinary meaning, so as to give effect to the intention of the parties to the contract; but that the common intention of the parties was to be gathered from the words used. Words which had an ordinary and popular meaning were to be construed in their ordinary and popular sense, and the court did not need and should neither seek nor use any "expert" guidance as to the meaning of such words. It was not in dispute that, in interpreting a clause in a policy described as a commercial policy, it was correct to bear in mind the commercial object or function of the clause in the context of the whole policy. Reference was made to MacGillivray and Parkington on *Insurance Law* (8th ed), paras 1071, 1076 and 1078. This was not a case where it was being suggested that the ordinary rules of construction were displaced because the words were terms of art or had acquired some special meaning (cf MacGillivray and Parkington, op cit, para 1082). It was also common ground that the contra proferentem rule was to be invoked only if the

meaning of the words to be construed was ambiguous;
A in particular, the rule could not be prayed in aid to
create ambiguity. I am content to proceed upon this
basis which I consider is the correct one.

As your Lordship in the chair has explained, we
were invited to consider various standard definitions
of words appearing in or related derivatively to words
appearing in para 10, notably "water", "burst",
"overflow" and "apparatus". We were also referred to
the dictionary definition of "steam" and to the interpretation of the word "apparatus" as it appeared in
B s 81 of the Mines and Quarries Act 1954: *Brebner v
British Coal Corporation.* With such assistance, and
indeed without it, I am not conscious of having any
great difficulty in understanding the ordinary and
popular meaning of these words. But I am not in quite
the same position in relation to the expression "water
apparatus"; the fact that I understand each of the component words in a phrase where each such word has
a clear meaning does not necessarily mean that I can
confidently claim to understand the expression com-
C posed of two or more such words. Sometimes it is
easy, as in "water tank"; but that is not because the
meaning of each word is clear — though it is — but
because "water tank" is an ordinary everyday expression. But I would say that "water apparatus" is not.
I think that I am entitled to make the judgment that
the term "water apparatus" is not a term in everyday
use. To say that is not necessarily to say that its
meaning is ambiguous or obscure; it is to say no more
than that its meaning is not instantly and crystal clear.
D But instead of trying to tease out the meaning or all
the possible meanings of such an expression it may be
preferable to start at the other end by examining the
thing which is said to be "water apparatus" and to
consider if it readily fits such nomenclature. Part of
that exercise would be to consider whether or not it
would be possible to find ordinary everyday expressions other than "water apparatus" to describe the
thing under scrutiny. In my opinion, that is a legitimate technique in a case such as the present, not least
E because if there existed some other and different,
ordinary, everyday expression which, viewing the
object from the same perspective, described or fitted
much more aptly, then it would not be unreasonable
to conclude that by neglecting to use that other and
more apt expression the authors were referring to
something else. As has often been said, you do not
have to be able to define "elephant" in order to recognise one; similarly you do not have to know that the
creature you are observing is called a rhinoceros in
F order to appreciate that it is not an elephant.

I have, therefore, decided to start by asking whether
on the agreed facts there occurred a "bursting or overflowing of water pipes, water apparatus or water
tanks". Water tanks drop out of consideration at once
because no one suggested that the pipe or apparatus in
question could be described as a water tank. "Overflowing" can be dismissed equally easily. Primarily it
is liquids that flow; and if the volume of liquid comes
to exceed the capacity of the non-closed container in
which it is then the liquid will "overflow". No doubt,

of course, gases can flow or, if heavier than air, can
overflow through any outlet or upper brim in the con-   G
tainer in which they are initially contained. But to
describe as an "overflow" a sudden escape of high
pressure steam from a pipe, owing to the failure of
some sealing device, does such violence to ordinary
language that I can readily conclude that there was
here no "overflowing".

I have next to consider if what happened could
sensibly be described as a "bursting of water pipes" or
of "water apparatus". This involves considering
whether or not the equipment which (to use a neutral   H
term) malfunctioned could properly be described as a
water pipe or as water apparatus (or both); and also
whether or not the event could sensibly and properly
be described as a bursting. But even then, it is important to look at the whole expression and to judge
whether or not there was any bursting of a water pipe
or any bursting of a water apparatus.

I have little difficulty in concluding that the pipe in
question does not fall under the description, "water
pipe". Its function was to act as a heat radiator. It was   I
enabled so to function by acting as a conduit for superheated steam under pressure; it was and would
properly be described as a steam pipe or a steam
heating pipe or a steam heating circuit pipe. Of course
it could and indeed it did indubitably contain water in
normal operation, namely the condensate produced as
the steam cooled. And indeed it was designed to hold
water condensate; that is clearly evidenced by the
presence of the trap valve. But the ordinary man faced
with a choice of description of the pipe, namely,   J
"steam pipe", "steam conduit pipe", "steam heating
pipe", "steam radiator pipe", would surely prefer any
of these to "water pipe" simply because the pipe was
designed to carry away relatively minute quantities of
water produced incidentally as the result of condensation. No doubt the condensate would also contain
minute quantities of calcium or sodium or other such
salts which are commonly found in public water supplies; but it would be nonsensical — just for that
reason — to describe a pipe in which the condensate   K
contained such salts as a calcium pipe or a salt pipe.
The pipe involved in this incident, defined in terms of
its function or role or use, is not a water pipe. In
exactly the same way, a water pipe designed to carry
boiling water could not properly be described as a
"steam pipe" just because boiling water incidentally
produces steam. If the parties had had a common
intention to include in para 10 steam pipes then it
would have been easy to include the words "or steam
pipes" after "water pipes"; their failure to do so   L
points strongly, in my opinion, to the absence of any
intention to embrace this particular pipe in the term
"water pipes".

There can be no doubt that the term "water
apparatus" would be entirely apt to describe some
parts at least of this steam heating system. Thus the
collection tank, the boiler and the pipes in between
them all hold and process water. Counsel on both
sides accepted that "water apparatus" was an acceptable term to use of these parts of the whole system.

Counsel for the pursuers and respondents was able to
argue (though I paraphrase his argument) that the
water went round and round the system sometimes in
one state (liquid) and sometimes in another (steam or
vapour) and that the whole system could, therefore,
properly be described as a water apparatus. In my
opinion, this is not the correct view. It is easy to think
of examples of a complex linear system of devices or
bits of apparatus all linked to achieve one purpose,
some of the constituent elements of which could
properly be described as water apparatus and some of
which could not. Thus, a mill stream could drive a
water mill which in turn would generate mechanical
or electrical power to operate grinders or rollers or the
like. The grinders or rollers would not properly be
said to be water apparatus even though the water mill
which supplied the power might well be described as
water apparatus. A line has to be drawn. I can see no
logical reason for not drawing such a line (or if necessary, more than one) in a system which could be
described as circular rather than as one-way linear. In
my opinion, this apparatus ceased to be water
apparatus once the functional content ceased to be
water and became steam; the incidental presence of
water as condensate inside it did not turn a steam
heated radiator into a water apparatus. If the parties
had shared a common intent to include in the perils a
failure of this pipe then I think they would have recognised that the term "water apparatus" was singularly
inappropriate and would have employed a different
term, using "steam" adjectively.

Finally I consider the concept of "bursting". In
ordinary parlance, when a thing bursts — whether it
be a balloon, a water pipe or an ill fitting garment —
it suffers damage. A burst pipe is a classic example; it
is the pipe that bursts and the contents escape. But if,
for example, the cork shoots out of a bottle of champagne it would be a bizarre use of language to say that
the bottle had "burst". Equally if one blew up a
balloon, then held it by the neck before suddenly
releasing it and allowing a sudden noisy de-inflation,
it would not occur to the ordinary person to say that
it had "burst"; indeed one could show that it had not burst
by repeating the trick many times. To
phrase it more in line with additional perils no 10,
there would have been no "bursting" of the balloon.
Of course, if the contents of a bottle or of a balloon or
of a classroom suddenly issue forth it is usual to speak
of the cork, or of the champagne or of the air or of the
pupils "bursting out"; but that is a metaphor; and in
any event it is not a bursting *of* the bottle, the balloon
or the classroom. In my opinion, even if the equipment could properly be described as water apparatus
or water pipes there was no bursting thereof when the
temporary bung was expelled and the steam began
escaping. In my opinion, the matter is reasonably clear
on a sound application of the tests which we were
invited to apply. The policy did not include cover for
the contingency that happened.

It is no doubt a matter of regret that such accidental
damage and loss are not covered by the policy; but, in
so far as this is relevant at all, it is to be observed that
if the workmen had decided not to put the plastic bung
in, but had left the opening unprotected or simply
wrapped a piece of cloth or paper round it to achieve
the same purpose, it would not have been open to the
respondents to claim that there was any "bursting"; so
the claim would have failed on that simple ground
alone.

In these circumstances I agree with your Lordship
in the chair as to the disposal of this appeal.

LORD KIRKWOOD.—I am in full agreement
with the opinion of your Lordship in the chair.

In this case the relevant facts were not in dispute.
The pursuers' factory premises at Newmilns contained a steam heating system which comprised a
boiler and pipes which were connected to the boiler.
Water was fed into the boiler and turned into steam
and the steam was circulated under pressure through
a network of pipes. As the heat was transferred from
the pipes into the atmosphere of the factory some of
the steam reverted to condensate which was eventually
removed from the system by redelivering it to the
holding tank, known as a hot well tank. Throughout
the pipework system as a whole the proportion of condensate did not exceed 0.17 per cent of the contents
of the pipes, the remainder being steam. The water
which was fed back into the tank was re-used to feed
the boiler. On 11 August 1988 certain work had been
carried out to the heating system and that work had
involved cutting open some of the overhead pipes. In
building no 5 a plastic bung had been placed in the cut
end of a pipe. It was not intended that the heating
system should come back into operation while the
plastic bung was in position and the purpose of the
bung was to prevent dust entering the pipe and condensate dripping therefrom. However, at about 2 am
on 12 August the boiler unexpectedly began to operate
and heated the water thereby creating steam in the
steam heating system. The pressure of the steam
thereby created blew the plastic bung out of the open
end of the cut pipe. As a result steam escaped from the
pipe and caused damage to the pursuers' premises and
machinery. The damage was caused by the premises
filling with steam which condensed and formed water
on the walls, ceilings and machinery.

The pursuers had entered into a contract of insurance with the defenders in terms of which the pursuers
were to be indemnified in the event of any of the contingencies therein mentioned occurring. The insurance cover included destruction of or damage to the
property thereby insured directly caused by such of
the additional perils as were listed in the policy.

Paragraph 10 of the additional perils read as follows:
[his Lordship quoted the terms of para 10 and continued:]

Evidence was led by both parties and that evidence
has been summarised in the opinion of the temporary
judge. Your Lordship in the chair has set out the submissions made on behalf of each of the parties.

The question for determination in this case is

A whether what took place on the morning of 12 August constituted "bursting or overflowing of water pipes, water apparatus or water tanks" and thereby rendered the defenders liable to indemnify the pursuers in respect of the loss and damage directly caused thereby. In my view this issue is to be decided by considering what is the proper construction to be placed on the opening words of para 10, in light of the events which took place, and parties were agreed that this question of construction was at large for this court to deter-

B mine. On behalf of the pursuers it was suggested that there was an ambiguity in the wording of para 10, in the sense that the heating system, viewed as a whole, could be described either as "water apparatus" or "steam apparatus", with the result that the contra proferentes rule fell to be applied, but I agree with your Lordship in the chair that there is, in fact, no ambiguity and accordingly it is not necessary to resort to the expert evidence which was led at the proof in order to assist in determining the proper construction to be placed on the wording of para 10. The temporary

C judge stated that he was unable to recognise any common usage for the words "water apparatus", that these words required interpretation and that, since they required interpretation, evidence was appropriate and the contra proferetens rule applied. I do not agree. Evidence, as a guide to interpretation, is only appropriate where there is an ambiguity but, as I have said, I do not consider that there is any ambiguity in this case and I am of the opinion that the case falls to be determined by considering what is the proper con-

D struction to be placed on the opening words of para 10 and then deciding whether or not what took place on 12 August was one of the perils insured against.

The general rule of construction of a contract is that the words used are to be given their ordinary and natural meaning and, to a certain extent, the construction to be placed on the opening words of para 10 is a matter of impression. On behalf of the defenders it was submitted that there had been an escape of steam, not water. Steam was a substance which would

E normally be regarded as inherently different from water. It looked different, it felt different and its physical properties were different. It was submitted on behalf of the pursuers that steam was simply water which had been heated until it was in vapour form and that, accordingly, steam could be regarded as water for the purpose of construing para 10. In my opinion, however, this is too simplistic an approach. While it is true that H_2O is the chemical composition of both water and steam, I do not consider that superheated

F steam under pressure can properly be described as water. In my opinion, the word "water", in its ordinary and natural meaning, refers to water in its liquid state. In this case there was a network of pipes through which steam was fed under pressure and I do not consider that a pipe which was designed to carry, and did carry, steam under pressure can properly be described as being a water pipe. In my opinion, such a pipe could properly be described as a "steam pipe" rather than a "water pipe". I accept that if there was a pipe which was used to convey water in its liquid

form, and the water in the pipe froze causing the pipe to rupture, then that could properly be regarded as G being the bursting of a water pipe, but this would be because the pipe which was used for the conveyance of water fell within the definition of a "water pipe". In my view the temporary judge was correct when he observed that when people talk about water pipes and steam pipes they intend to make a distinction between them and that the pipe from which steam escaped was not a "water pipe" within the meaning of para 10. I am also of the opinion that the word "overflowing" is quite inappropriate to describe an escape of steam H which is lighter than air and which rises after it has escaped.

Having reached the conclusion that the pipe from which the escape of steam took place could not properly be described as a "water pipe", the next question which arises is whether what took place on 12 August constituted the "bursting of water apparatus". In this connection counsel for the pursuers submitted that the steam heating system, viewed as a whole, could properly be regarded as "water apparatus". An I apparatus is an assemblage of appliances or materials for a particular use and the steam heating system was an apparatus which made use of water in its liquid and vapour form and could therefore properly be described as "water apparatus". Water was fed into the boiler initially and the condensate was eventually delivered back to the hot well tank and was used, once again, to feed the boiler. Counsel for the defenders submitted that, while some part or parts of the heating system might fall within the definition of "water J apparatus", the heating system, taken as a whole, could not be described as "water apparatus". The correct description would be "steam apparatus". While I agree that parts of the heating system could be regarded as "water apparatus" I do not consider that the entire heating system could properly be so described. Parties were agreed that this case concerns a steam heating system and its primary purpose was to create and circulate steam under pressure through a K network of pipes. In the circumstances it does not seem to me that this steam heating system, viewed as a whole, properly falls within the definition of "water apparatus". If the word "apparatus" is to be applied to the system I would have thought that it would properly be described as "steam heating apparatus" or possibly "steam apparatus", as its predominant purpose was the creation and circulation of steam. However, even if the heating system could properly be described as "water apparatus", the further question L arises as to whether what took place amounted to a "bursting" of the apparatus. Counsel for the pursuers conceded that the plastic bung which had been inserted into the open end of the cut pipe had been placed there only temporarily, that it had not been anticipated that the heating system would come into operation while the bung was in position and that the presence of the bung was to keep out dust and prevent condensate dripping out. The bung was not intended to keep steam in. He agreed that if the bung had not been placed in position and steam had escaped from

A the open end of the cut pipe then it could not have been contended that what took place amounted to a bursting of the apparatus or the pipe. However, he submitted that "bursting" implied the breaking out of the contents by force from an enclosure. In this case the plastic bung had been placed in position, albeit temporarily, in order to seal the pipe, which was part of the heating system, and in the circumstances the blowing out of the bung by the steam could properly be described as the bursting of the water pipe or, looking at the system as a whole, the water apparatus.

B The integrity of the sealed system had been breached by the force exerted by the steam. Counsel for the defenders submitted that this was not a case of a water apparatus bursting. The heating system had been partially dismantled and the bung which had been inserted temporarily in the pipe in question was not intended to be part of the system. Bearing in mind (a) the fact that the pipe had been deliberately cut open in the course of the earlier work, (b) the fact that, when the bung was inserted, it was not anticipated
C that the heating system would be turned on while the bung was in position, and (c) the fact that the purpose of the bung was not to keep steam in but that it had been inserted as a temporary measure, to prevent condensate dripping from the open end of the pipe, I cannot regard the blowing out of the bung by the steam, once the heating system was turned on, as constituting the "bursting" either of the pipe in question or of the apparatus viewed as a whole. This was not a case where the integrity of the heating system had
D suddenly and unexpectedly been breached by the failure of a part of the system which was designed to contain the steam passing through it under pressure. On the whole matter I consider that the pursuers have failed to prove that the escape of steam on 12 August was one of the additional perils insured against in terms of para 10 of the policy of insurance. I therefore agree that the reclaiming motion should be disposed of as proposed by your Lordship in the chair.

E

_____

Counsel for Pursuers and Respondents, Hodge; Solicitors, John G Gray & Co, SSC (for Levy & McRae, Glasgow) — Counsel for Defenders and Reclaimers, Jones, QC, Liddell; Solicitors, Simpson & Marwick, WS.

C A G M

F

Love v Wilson

G

HIGH COURT OF JUSTICIARY
THE LORD JUSTICE GENERAL (HOPE),
LORDS COWIE AND MAYFIELD
5 JANUARY 1993

Justiciary — Procedure — Bill of suspension — Competency — Acquiescence — Accused presenting bill of suspension alleging oppressive conduct by sheriff in course of trial approximately 26 months after trial — Sheriff having died and fine having been paid by then — Accused H *explaining that counsel instructed to draft bill 10 days after trial but failing to do so for approximately 25 months despite being reminded — Whether accused acquiescing in judgment — Whether bill incompetent.*

An accused person was convicted of assault after trial on a summary complaint on 10 September 1990. Thereafter counsel was instructed by letter sent on 20 September 1990 to draft a bill of suspension to challenge the conviction. Four reminders were sent to I counsel between 4 October 1990 and 22 July 1991 but the draft bill was not provided by counsel to the accused's solicitors until 4 September 1991. The Crown received the bill on 30 November 1992, warrant for serving a copy of it on the Crown having been granted on 27 November 1992. The sheriff died on 2 April 1991 and the procurator fiscal depute who had conducted the prosecution was, as a result of the passage of time, unable to recollect any details of the evidence or of the procedure adopted by the sheriff. J The bill contained averments complaining that the sheriff had acted oppressively in respect that he had stated that he was unwilling to note certain of the evidence of Crown witnesses in cross examination because he considered the line of evidence to be irrelevant (it being alleged by the accused that the Crown witnesses had conspired to adduce false evidence to secure the dismissal of the accused from his employment as a prison officer) and, in particular, that he was not prepared to note or have any regard to any evidence K adduced from these Crown witnesses as a result of cross examination. The accused had been fined £200 payable at £5 per week but by the time the bill was heard he had paid the fine. The Crown lodged answers maintaining that the accused had acquiesced in the judgment complained of and that the bill should be dismissed as incompetent.

Held, (1) that it required an exceptional state of affairs for the High Court to be able to deal with a bill L of suspension on the complainer's averments alone especially in the absence of concessions by the Crown entitling the court to proceed on the basis that the facts were agreed (p 950A-B); and (2) that in the circumstances and having regard in particular to the length of the delay and the absence of any really convincing explanation for it, the accused had to be taken to have accepted the conviction (p 950C-D); and bill *refused* as incompetent.

_____

Bill of suspension

A   James Alexander Love brought a bill of suspension against Andrew T W Wilson, procurator fiscal, Airdrie, praying the High Court of Justiciary to suspend simpliciter a pretended conviction and sentence dated 10 September 1990 whereby Sheriff J S Boyle found the accused guilty of assault and fined him £200. The Crown lodged answers maintaining that the complainer had acquiesced in the judgment complained of and that the bill should be dismissed. The procedural history of the case appears from the B opinion of the court. The bill was presented to the High Court on 27 November 1992 when a deliverance was pronounced granting warrant to serve a copy of the bill on the respondent.

The bill was argued before the High Court on 5 January 1993.

Eo die the court *refused* the bill as incompetent on the ground of acquiescence.

C   The following opinion of the court was delivered by the Lord Justice General (Hope):

OPINION OF THE COURT.—The complainer is James Alexander Love who was charged in the sheriff court at Airdrie with assault. He pled not guilty and went to trial before Sheriff Boyle and on 10 September 1990 he was convicted of the charge under the deletion of certain words. He was fined the sum of £200 and was allowed to pay that at the rate of £5 per week, the first payment to be made within seven days D from the date of his conviction. No application was made for a stated case, but a bill has now been presented many months after the conviction alleging that there were circumstances at the trial which justify suspension of the conviction and sentence.

The complainer was a prison officer, and two of the principal witnesses for the Crown on the charge of assault were Andrew Stewart and Derek Watson. In the course of their cross examination various questions E were put to them alleging that they had deliberately fabricated their evidence following upon a conspiracy to adduce false evidence with a view to the complainer losing his job as a prison officer.

The sheriff is said to have stated that he was unwilling to note certain of the evidence in cross examination because he considered the line to be irrelevant, and in particular that he was not prepared to note or have any regard to any evidence adduced from either witness as a result of the cross examination. That is F the allegation which is made in the bill. It is then said in the bill that the sheriff, in refusing to accept this evidence as relevant and stating that he was not prepared to have any regard to it, was acting harshly and oppressively and for that reason there was a miscarriage of justice as a result of which the conviction and sentence should be suspended.

The position today is this, that the sheriff is no longer able to provide us with his account of the events of the trial. Unfortunately, on 2 April 1991, some six months after the date of the trial, he died. He last sat in the sheriff court at Airdrie on 24 September 1990, having developed an illness which ultimately led G to his death. The procurator fiscal depute has been asked to comment on the allegations in the bill, but her recollection has been so affected by the lapse of time that it has not been possible for her to recollect any details of the evidence or procedure which was adopted. As a result of this the answers for the respondent have been confined to a statement that the essential facts are not known and not admitted. The plea in law which is stated by the respondent is that, the complainer having acquiesced in the judgment H complained of, the bill is incompetent and should be dismissed.

Counsel who appeared on the complainer's behalf today appreciated that the point which he had to address in his argument at the outset was the question to which the respondent's plea is directed, that is whether the delay in this case has been such that the bill must be dismissed as incompetent. He provided us with a history of the events since 10 September 1990 when the complainer was convicted. We were told that I about 10 days after the conviction counsel was instructed to draft a bill of suspension to challenge the conviction and sentence. The letter was sent to counsel on 20 September 1990, and together with that letter was sent the original file so that he had in his possession all the information which was needed to draft the bill. We are told that various reminders were sent as no draft bill was immediately forthcoming from counsel. There were reminders on 4 and 29 October 1990, again on 5 November 1990 and again, J after a surprisingly long delay, on 22 July 1991, after the sheriff had died, counsel was again reminded that the bill had not yet been produced. It was not until 4 September 1991, some 12 months later, that a draft bill was ultimately provided to the instructing solicitors, according to the information available to counsel. It is right that we should mention that counsel told us also that various correspondence took place with the sheriff clerk at Airdrie to check on the movements of the sheriff. Accordingly, for one reason or K another, preparation of the bill was delayed for nearly a year and well beyond the date of the sheriff's death.

We were told by the learned Solicitor General that it was not until 30 November 1992, some 26½ months after the end of the trial, that the bill was received and instructions were then sought from the procurator fiscal depute about what had occurred. There had been some previous conversation about this between the solicitor and the depute, but the very substantial L delay which occurred before the bill was formally served on the Crown had the effect on recollection to which we have already referred.

The question which is raised in the bill is one which is directed to the actings of the sheriff himself. It raises a very particular question about the steps taken by the sheriff in response to a line of questioning in cross examination. An explanation for the decision which the sheriff took would have been a matter of some importance if justice was to be done in meeting the

A allegation which is made against him in these averments, assuming that they are accurate. The basic difficulty which now arises is that the court does not and cannot now have before it a report from the sheriff, nor does it have any admission from the Crown that the averments which are contained in the bill are correct or any explanation for what occurred.

In this situation it would require an exceptional state of affairs for us to be able to deal with the bill on the averments of the complainer alone, especially in the absence of concessions by the Crown which would

B entitle us to proceed upon the basis that the facts were all agreed. Furthermore we are told that the fine, which was one to be paid over a period of months, has now been paid. And for one reason or another it is plain that the preparation and lodging of the bill were delayed for many months, although it was clearly well known to the complainer's solicitors that the sheriff was ill and there was plainly a risk that his views on what had occurred would be lost forever. Although we are told that several reminders were sent to counsel, no

C steps were taken to complain to others about the delay or to ensure that the bill was prepared within a reasonable time.

In these circumstances and having regard, in particular, to the length of the delay and the absence of any really convincing explanation for it, we are driven to the conclusion that the complainer must be taken to have accepted the conviction which was recorded against him, and that the only conclusion that can

D properly be drawn is that the bill is incompetent on the ground of acquiescence. For these reasons we have decided that the only course we can now take is to refuse the bill.

Counsel for Complainer, McBride; Solicitors, John G Gray & Co, SSC (for Gordon & Smyth, Glasgow) — Counsel for Respondent, Solicitor General (Dawson, QC); Solicitor, J D Lowe, Crown Agent.

E

P W F

Singh v Secretary of State for the Home Department

F OUTER HOUSE
LORD PENROSE
19 MARCH 1992

Immigration — Illegal entry — Detention of entrant — Judicial review — Application for interim liberation pending disposal of application for political asylum — Power of court to review decision to detain — Whether onus on Crown to establish that detention justified — Immigration Act 1971 (c 77), Sched 2, para 16 (2).

Administrative law — Judicial review — Immigration — Detention of illegal entrant — Application for interim G liberation pending disposal of application for political asylum — Power of court to review decision to detain — Whether onus on Crown to establish that detention justified — Immigration Act 1971 (c 77), Sched 2, para 16 (2).

Paragraph 16 (2) of Sched 2 to the Immigration Act 1971 empowers an immigration officer to authorise the detention of persons refused leave to enter the United Kingdom and illegal entrants.

A man was detained as an illegal immigrant. On H being detained, on 11 January 1992, the detainee applied for political asylum in the United Kingdom. He petitioned for judicial review of the decision to detain him on the ground that the decision was one which no reasonable immigration officer could have reached and was unlawful and oppressive. He argued (1) that he should be allowed to remain in the United Kingdom pending disposal of his application, and (2) that he should be released from custody pending disposal of his application. The petitioner sought reduction of the decision of the immigration officer and for I liberation ad interim on such terms and conditions as the court might impose.

On 28 January the Secretary of State intimated by letter that he was minded to refuse the petitioner's application for political asylum. The petitioner was invited to provide any further information which might be relevant to support his application. On 4 February a motion for interim liberation was refused by the Lord Ordinary, counsel for the Secretary of J State having indicated that a final decision on the application would be arrived at and notified to the petitioner within 10 to 14 days. By letter dated 11 February a solicitor acting on behalf of the petitioner requested that the decision be delayed for six to eight weeks to enable documents to be obtained from the Punjab to support the petitioner's application for political asylum. The petitioner renewed his motion for interim liberation. The case was continued for further inquiries to be made. Little additional infor- K mation was available by the date of the continued hearing. The petitioner had given inconsistent accounts of his travel to, arrival in and subsequent residence in the United Kingdom; the Secretary of State considered him a high risk absconder. The petitioner offered caution in implement of any conditions the court might impose; he had obtained a place of residence in Scotland and had found employment. The petitioner argued that it was for the Secretary of State to satisfy the court that detention and continued L detention of a person in the position of the petitioner was justified.

Held, (1) that the decision of an immigration officer on detention was an aspect of the general administrative power conferred upon the Secretary of State by public general legislation (p 953I); (2) that where the indefinite detention of an individual was at stake there was a predisposition in Scots law towards the securing of liberty, but that the power of the court in such cases was no wider than its general power to review administrative acts and there was no independent discretionary power to override the administrative decision (p 953F and I-J); (3) that there was no universal proposition that in all immigration cases there was an onus on the Crown to satisfy the court of substantial grounds for detention, and the petitioner had failed to present any prima facie case which would justify inquiry and his liberty pending such inquiry (p 954B-C and E-F); and petition *dismissed*.

Observed, that any failure to consider new material bearing on the petitioner's position would warrant a fresh application to the court (p 955A).

Observations, on the differences between the two fields of criminal prosecutions and immigration law as respects safeguards against indefinite detention (p 953F-H).

Petition for judicial review

Jaswant Singh applied for judicial review of a decision of the Secretary of State for the Home Department to detain him in custody.

The petition came for a first hearing before the Lord Ordinary (Penrose).

Statutory provisions

The Immigration Act 1971 provides in Sched 2:

"16.—. . . (2) A person in respect of whom directions may be given under any of paragraphs 8 to 14 above may be detained under the authority of an immigration officer pending the giving of directions and pending his removal in pursuance of any directions given."

Cases referred to

Kumar (Vijay) v Home Secretary, OH, reported in *Glasgow Herald*, 17 June 1988.
Singh (Khushal) v Home Secretary, OH, 1 December 1988, unreported.
Sokha v Secretary of State for the Home Department, 1992 SLT 1049.

On 19 March 1992 the Lord Ordinary *dismissed* the petition.

LORD PENROSE.—The petitioner was detained on 11 January 1992. He has been held in custody since then as an illegal immigrant, liable to removal from the United Kingdom in terms of paras 8 to 11 of Sched 2 to the Immigration Act 1971. His detention was ordered by an immigration officer under powers provided by para 16 of that Schedule. The Secretary of State for the Home Department is responsible for the administration and enforcement of the law in this field, and is the respondent in these proceedings.

The petitioner challenges the original decision to detain him, and further, the decision to detain him in HM Prison, Gateside, Greenock, on the ground that the decision was one which no reasonable immigration officer could have reached and, as such, a decision which was unlawful and oppressive. The petitioner

accepts that he is an illegal immigrant. But he has applied for political asylum in the United Kingdom, and, in essence, contends that he should have been allowed to remain, and should now be released and allowed to remain, at liberty pending disposal of his application. He seeks an order for reduction of the decision and for liberation ad interim on such terms and conditions as the court might impose. It is averred on his behalf that friends in this country are able and willing to offer £2,000 or thereby as monetary security for his compliance with conditions imposed by the court. He would live at a specified address, and work at a restaurant in Glasgow. The respondent opposes this application on the ground that the petitioner is a high risk absconder, whose compliance with conditions could not reasonably be secured.

The petitioner's motion for interim liberation was refused by Lord Weir on 4 February 1992. The interlocutor of that date was not reclaimed. The petitioner applied for asylum on 11 January, the day he was detained, by manuscript letter. He was interviewed on 11 January, and on 12 January, when he expanded on his apprehensions and the basis for his application. The circumstances were set out in a letter dated 28 January 1992, intimating that the Secretary of State was minded to refuse the application for asylum. I shall refer to the contents of these documents later. The Secretary of State's letter ended with an invitation to the petitioner to provide any further information which he believed might be relevant to his application.

The petition was drafted and presented on 4 February. At the hearing before Lord Weir counsel for the respondent indicated that there would be no delay in arriving at a decision and that the Secretary of State's decision would be notified to the petitioner within 10 to 14 days. Thereafter the respondent made further inquiries and, I was informed, would have been in a position to implement the undertaking given to the court on 4 February by issuing a decision letter on or about 17 or 18 February but for a fresh initiative taken by the petitioner. By letter dated 11 February, received by the department on 14 February, a solicitor acting on behalf of the petitioner wrote to the department asking that the decision be delayed for a period of six to eight weeks to enable documents to be obtained from the Punjab in support of the petitioner's application for asylum. On 19 February 1992 the petitioner's motion for interim liberation was renewed before me, inter alia on the ground that there would now be a considerable delay in the disposal of his application for asylum. In the course of the discussion on that day it became clear that counsel could not provide answers to certain questions relating to the petitioner's application generally, and, in particular, relating to his arrival in the United Kingdom and his history since that date. I continued the case until 28 February to allow further inquiry to be made.

Little information was contained in the original application presented by the petitioner. The material parts of his letter of 11 January 1992 were: "I wish to claim asylum on the basis that if I return to India as prisoner I shall face long time imprisonment and fear to my life because I am of a Sikh religion and my family support the independent state. Many other allegation has been poured on myself and my family by the authorities which are not true to some extent. I shall provide evidence in due course."

Additional information was provided to immigration officers on 11 and 12 January 1992, as summarised in the departmental letter of 28 January. The information was narrated in the following terms:

"On 11 January 1992 you were interviewed by an immigration officer. You said that you had arrived in the United Kingdom with the help of an agent, who had been paid by the All India Sikh Student Federation (AISSF). You also said that you feared return to India because of the problems there.

"You were interviewed again on 12 January 1992 when you stated that you feared return to India because you Sikhs are being harassed, beaten and even killed by the police. You said that you had joined the AISSF whilst at college in 1986 or 1987. You also said that you held no special post, but had helped to display posters criticising the government. You stated that you were not politically active but, like all young Sikhs, had joined the federation as a protest against the government.

"You said that in March 1986 you had been arrested by the police on suspicion of sheltering members of Att Vadhi. You said that you had been beaten and that you were detained for 12 or 13 days, until your father hired a solicitor to secure your release. You said that following your release the police had visited your house on a weekly basis for some time but that their visits had then become less frequent and more irregular. You explained that you had hidden from the police when these visits occurred. You said that your reason for leaving home in 1990 was that you were afraid the police would arrest you and beat you and you claimed you had heard that your family had been questioned by police a number of times since your departure."

In his petition the petitioner avers that he was a member of the All India Sikh Students' Federation, and gives certain details about that body. He proceeds to make averments about the general conduct alleged to have been carried out by government agents in the Punjab. He narrates certain facts bearing upon the attitudes of the governor of the Punjab and other authorities towards the All India Sikh Students' Federation. He sets out certain allegations about the death of two members of that association. There are references to the Amnesty International report on certain of these allegations. Against this background, which appears in no way to be particular to or related to the petitioner, he proceeds to narrate the events surrounding his arrest in 1986, his interrogation, and his beating. No further information is provided on the period, highlighted by the immigration authorities in this country, between 1986 and the time of his departure from India for the United Kingdom. The position at the first hearing before me remained that certain information was provided about confrontation between the petitioner and the Indian authorities in 1986, but that nothing was said about his subsequent history that had a bearing upon his present claim for asylum.

The respondent's opposition to the application was based inter alia on the view that the petitioner had failed to set out a prima facie case for asylum in correspondence, interview or pleadings and that his dishonesty was warrant for considering him a high risk absconder. No case had been made out for interim liberation in the circumstances.

The circumstances surrounding the petitioner's arrival in this country, as I understand them, are as follows. The petitioner was smuggled aboard a vessel bound for the United Kingdom, somewhere in the Indian subcontinent, by members of the crew of the vessel. They, or other members of the crew, concealed him on board. He was concealed throughout the voyage to the United Kingdom. After the vessel docked, it is said in Manchester, he was smuggled ashore together with another immigrant. He did not know the name of the vessel. He did not know the other immigrant. They were both assisted to evade immigration controls. They reached the public road system and obtained a lift. The petitioner was heading for Glasgow, and they were fortunate enough to attract the attention of a person driving all the way there. The other illegal immigrant was dropped off somewhere on the way north. The petitioner did not know where. On arrival at Glasgow the petitioner sought refuge in the Sikh temple there and inquired after the whereabouts of Amrik Singh whom he knew. Over the weekend following his arrival he found accommodation with Amrik Singh. Arrangements were made through Balvinder Singh, an acquaintance of Amrik Singh, for the petitioner to meet a solicitor. On 27 November 1991 the petitioner had a meeting with Miss Welsh of David W Shaw & Co, solicitors, Ayr. On 28 November 1991 that firm wrote to the petitioner advising him that evidence would be required that he personally had been persecuted or tortured while in India and thus had to leave the country. He was told that such evidence would be membership of the party seeking independence for Khalistan, of arrest, of having taken part in demonstration or even letters from friends advising him to leave the country. He was advised that without such evidence his application would be refused. On 11 January 1992 the petitioner came to the notice of the immigration authorities. He was detained. When interviewed at the Bombay Brasserie, Glasgow, a restaurant where he had worked for a few days by that stage, the petitioner gave a false account. He said he had arrived in the United Kingdom as a visitor some two to four months earlier. He said that he had thereafter applied for political asylum. He claimed that his application had been sent to a solicitor. He gave his address as 3 Kelvinside Gardens, Glasgow. He claimed that his correspondence was in the hands of Malik Singh of that address. An employee at the Bombay Brasserie volunteered to go to Malik Singh and obtain the correspondence. The petitioner was transferred to the police station. There he gave an entirely different account. He said that he had left India in a cargo ship some two to four months earlier, that he did not know the vessel and that on arrival, under cover of darkness, he had slipped ashore evading immigration authorities. He said that he had no passport, having left his in India, that he had managed to get to Glasgow, and that he had initially stayed there in the Sikh temple. He gave the name of the firm of solicitors he had contacted and told of their letter of 28 November 1991. He said that he had replied to that letter but that no application had been made to the Home Office for asylum. He then admitted that he was not residing at the address he had earlier given but was at the address disclosed in the present application.

Counsel for the respondent founded strongly on the dishonesty implicit in the account of the petitioner's travel, his arrival, and his subsequent history in this country. For the petitioner it was contended that such dishonesty was inherent in any attempt to obtain asylum by a man such as the petitioner. The basic proposition was that the barriers in the way of legitimate entry to United Kingdom were insurmountable. Clandestine entry, or entry on false representations as to intention, were the norm. Thus, as I understood the submission, the deception and dishonesty were at least irrelevant, and at best executed by necessity.

Against the general background set out, the application for interim liberation proceeded as follows. It was said that it would take six to eight weeks to obtain the information sought from the Punjab. Then, since the petitioner did not have travel documents, it would be necessary for fresh travel documents to be prepared. This would take three months or thereby. The petitioner could not be removed from the United Kingdom without such documents. In such circumstances the practice of the court was as set out in Lord Prosser's opinion in the application of *Sokha v Secretary of State for the Home Department.* Counsel also relied on his own analysis of the authorities in an article published by him in the *Journal of the Law Society of Scotland* ((1990) 35 JLS 7). He submitted on the basis of the analysis in the article and Lord Prosser's opinion that it was for the respondent to justify to the court the detention and continued detention of a person in the position of the petitioner. The offer of caution for implement of any conditions imposed by the court, his residence and the fact that he had achieved employment, were said to point to his having established a place in the community here.

There is a deep seated abhorrence of indefinite detention of the individual in Scots law. In the criminal field, as was submitted, it is reflected in the statutory requirement that an accused person who is committed in custody must in general be brought to trial not later than the 110th day after being placed on petition. It is reflected also in the decisions of the court on applications in the immigration field, and, in my opinion, rightly so. But it is necessary to recognise the differences between the two fields. In the criminal context the Crown, represented by the Lord Advocate, brings charges of criminal conduct in the public interest and, in order inter alia to ensure that the accused is brought to trial on those charges, seeks the authority of the court for the detention of the accused person. Detention is at all times subject to the control of the court. Expedition in the prosecution of such cases is ensured by the time limits restricting the period of detention pending trial and by the court's powers to control extension of these limits, as well as its powers of control over detention generally. In the field of immigration law, the immigrant may have a statable claim that he or she has a right to enter the United Kingdom. In such a case the policy of the law ensuring freedom so far as possible while that issue is litigated is at its strongest and is, as I understand it, recognised by the respondent in practice. At the other end of the scale the admittedly illegal immigrant has no right to reside in the United Kingdom. Residence depends upon an executive act, an act of administrative authority. The court has power, within recognised limits, to adjudicate on the regularity of procedures adopted and applied in the exercise of administrative powers. But it has no power generally to review the merits of the administrative decision. The decision of an immigration officer on detention is an aspect of the general administrative power conferred upon the respondent by public general legislation. I was informed that the respondent's policy is liberal. But cases do arise in which detention is ordered. In considering such a decision, the court, in my opinion, has no wider power than it has generally to review administrative acts. There is no discretionary power to override the administrative decision and substitute a judicial decision. Accordingly, while the predisposition to secure the liberty of the individual is obvious, and is a powerful factor, it must be seen as an indication of the court's policy in the exercising of its legitimate powers in this field, and not as reflecting an independent and self sufficient discretionary power to secure the liberty of the individual without acknowledging the general constraints on its power to interfere with administrative action.

It was contended by counsel for the petitioner that there was an onus on the respondent to show that detention was justified. This was said to be based firstly on the decision of Lord Weir in the application of *Vijay Kumar,* reported in the *Glasgow Herald* of 17 June 1988, and secondly on the acceptance by Lord Sutherland and counsel for the present respondent of a submission by counsel for the petitioner in the petition of *Khushal Singh* on 1 December 1988. Reference was made to Lord Prosser's opinion in *Sokha v Secretary of State for the Home Department.* No opinion by Lord Sutherland was available, and the circumstances in which counsel's submission was accepted or conceded were not explained.

Lord Weir refused the application in the present petition when first it was made. The basis of his Lordship's opinion and decision in the case of *Vijay Kumar* is clear. He set out the traditional view of Scots law that a man should not be detained indefinitely, with which I fully agree. He stated that counsel for the respondent would have to show very strong reasons why interim liberation should not be granted. He added that had the immigration authorities not lost Mr Kumar's passport he would have been back in India by that very date. In doing so he identified the factor of importance in the view that he took in that particular case. The applicant had come to the United Kingdom with a passport. The passport had been surrendered to the United Kingdom immigration authorities for the purposes of inquiry. Without the passport he could not travel. The immigration authorities had lost the passport and thereby prevented him from leaving the United Kingdom. Their contention was that he should remain in detention until the situation they had created could be resolved. It should cause no surprise to anyone that Lord Weir took the view that detention had to be justified on independent and substantial grounds in these circumstances. The case however has no general relevance and cannot in logic nor in common sense support a universal proposition that in all immigration cases there is an onus on the Crown to satisfy the court of substantial grounds for detention. Wherever there is a prima facie case to try on an immigration issue, undoubtedly one would bend in favour of liberty pending resolution of that issue. The policy of the court has been successful in this respect that there has been no recorded instance of an applicant who has been granted interim liberation absconding. Further, the release of an applicant into the care of a member of a community sharing powerful religious beliefs imposes upon that community as well as the applicant a responsibility to ensure that the confidence of the court is not frustrated by his absconding. The moral authority of such a community is a matter of no small importance. If there were a general discretionary power to override the decision of the immigration authority these are factors, taken along with the provision of monetary security, upon which one would readily rely in ordering liberation. However there may arise cases, and the question is whether this is one, in which the court has no discretion at all because of the total failure of the petitioner to present any basis on which a prima facie case can be identified which would justify inquiry and his liberty pending the resolutions of the issues focused in it.

In this case there is, quite simply, no relevant issue to try on the original detention of the petitioner. The petitioner entered the country by clandestine means which he could not or would not explain. He remained in substantial concealment until his discovery. He lied about his status, his history, and his personal details. When he adopted his current position, it was so lacking in specification and substance as to leave the immigration authority little choice but to decide against him. Further inquiry has failed to resolve the basic question of the substance of his plea for asylum. The time offered by the court for inquiry has not assisted. His present solicitor's letter dated 11 February 1992 did not specify the sources of evidence and the type of evidence which it was hoped would be recovered by the inquiries being made in Punjab. At the resumed hearing of 28 February 1992 counsel was able to provide very little in the way of additional information. Counsel identified the heads of information which it was acknowledged were required as being (a) information dealing with the petitioner's movement to Delhi in about 1986, (b) information to confirm his history of experience in 1986, (c) information about his associates' views about the consequences if he were now to be returned to India, (d) confirmation that his associates did in fact secure his departure, and (e) information about the circumstances and reasons for their doing so, all coupled with information about the general background against which the position of the petitioner ought to be judged. This information was said to be genuinely relevant but to be unavailable. It was explained that the sources of information were the students' federation, the village council, and certain members of the legislative assembly who were involved in obtaining the release from detention of the petitioner. The political activists seeking independence had either been arrested or had gone underground. The students' federation because of a boycott of recent elections had been formally banned by the government. It also had gone underground and no information was likely to be obtained in the near future from it. The village council had not responded to requests for information. The general picture was that while earnest efforts were being made to obtain information to support the allegations of the petitioner, nothing concrete had been obtained nor could it reasonably be forecast when any new information was likely to come to hand. The petitioner himself had not been interviewed. It was explained that in the absence of further legal aid it had not been possible for him to be seen in order to provide additional information himself about the period between 1986 and 1990 which appeared to be material. The general impression created was that the efforts being expended on behalf of the petitioner were designed primarily not to support the case already made but in some way to find material which could be prayed in aid in supplement of that case. As counsel observed, if the information were available, it would be more expeditious to present it to the immigration authorities. Shortly, it appeared from the submissions that the substance of the petitioner's position as presented by counsel was that there was no basis upon which properly to attack the previous decision and that the petitioner and his advisers were not in possession of information to make a more cogent case at this stage. It became a matter of concern that a substantial purpose of the present application was not unconnected with indirect advantages that might accrue to the petitioner in a subsequent application for discretionary treatment permitting him to stay in the United Kingdom if he could establish a record of work and residence in the United Kingdom. On his behalf counsel was prepared to do no more than accept that a prolonged stay and work record could give the petitioner no legal right to residence. This did not deal with the question of the intention underlying his present application.

In substance nothing has changed in this case since Lord Weir's disposal of it.

It would be inappropriate to make a decision against the petitioner which in any way appeared to foreclose further applications should the situation change. I agree with the views expressed by Lord Prosser in *Sokha* that detention is a continuing state requiring review and that any fact which innovates upon the circumstances taken into account requires fresh consideration of the detainee's position. Any failure to consider new material bearing upon the issue would warrant a fresh application to the court. However unless or until the petitioner is able to bring to the attention of the court relevant circumstances instructing a legitimate challenge of the respondent's activities, in my opinion the court has no power to interfere with the administrative decision. In the whole circumstances I shall refuse the petitioner's motion in hoc statu.

Counsel for Petitioner, Bovey; Solicitors, Morton Fraser Milligan, WS — Counsel for Respondent, Reith; Solicitor, R Brodie, Solicitor in Scotland to the Secretary of State for the Home Department.

J P D

Chapman, Petitioners

OUTER HOUSE

LORD PENROSE

17 DECEMBER 1992

Judicial factor — Tutor dative — Whether discretion in court to refuse appointment — Whether appointment appropriate in application principally concerned with management of person's financial affairs — Curators Act 1585 (c 25).

The only children of a person who had become senile and had been admitted to a nursing home, petitioned for the appointment of a tutor dative to their father with powers both to manage his finances and to give directions for the care and custody of his person. The father was incapable of managing his personal finances. There were, however, no decisions required immediately or in the foreseeable future relating to his residential care, medical treatment or any other matter concerned with his person. It was argued for the children that, where an application for a tutor dative was made by those entitled to make it and the court was satisfied that the person was incapax, the court had no discretion but had to appoint the tutor dative.

Held, (1) that a tutor dative would only be appointed where it was necessary for decisions to be taken regarding the physical welfare of a person who was incapable of taking such decisions for himself or participating in them in any meaningful way (p 958E-H); (2) that the present circumstances suggested the need for the appointment of a curator

bonis (p 958K); and (3) that appointment of a tutor dative was a serious matter and ought not to be done as an incidental matter in an application otherwise concerned with the management of the financial affairs of an incapacitated person (p 958H-I); and petition *put out* by order for further procedure.

Observed, that the functions of the tutor and the curator bonis were not mutually exclusive and the court could readily provide for the physical care of a person independently of the proper provision made for the management of that person's estate (p 958I-J).

Dick v Douglas, 1924 SLT 578, *commented on.*

Petition for appointment of tutor dative

Brian Hunter Chapman and another, the only children of Archibald Hunter Chapman, petitioned the court for the appointment of a tutor dative to their father who had become incapacitated by reason of senile dementia. The terms of the prayer, so far as material, were as follows:

"to appoint the said Niall Hugh Robertson Bogie or such other person or persons as to your Lordships shall seem proper, to be tutor dative of the said Archibald Hunter Chapman, and to grant to the tutor dative (first) the power to decide where the said Archibald Hunter Chapman is to live, whether permanently or temporarily; (second) the power to consent to any medical treatment affecting the said Archibald Hunter Chapman; (third) the right to decide in and for the liferent interest of the incapax on the sale of the said heritable property and to confer and agree with the fiars in that regard; (fourth) power to consent to the sale thereof on such terms as the tutor dative may judge appropriate; (fifth) the right to receive the income from the net free proceeds of sale of the said heritage for the benefit of the said Archibald Hunter Chapman all in terms of clause third of the said minute of agreement registered 14 June 1990; and generally all powers of administration and investment of the estate of the incapax to the extent allowed by law; (sixth) any other matters which might appear to the court to appear reasonably to be required to protect the best interests of the said Archibald Hunter Chapman and (seventh) the power generally to provide the said Archibald Hunter Chapman with care, support and guidance".

The case came before the Lord Ordinary (Penrose) on the motion roll when the petitioners sought the appointment of a named solicitor as tutor dative to Mr Chapman.

Statutory provisions

The Curators Act 1585 provides:

"Oure Souerane Lord be aduise of this present parliament statutis and ordanis that the nearest agnettis and kinsmen of naturall foulis Ideottis and furious Salbe seruit ressauit and preferrit according to the dispositioun of the commoun law to thair tutorie and curatorie."

The Exchequer Court (Scotland) Act 1856 provides:

"19. The duties heretofore performed by or incumbent on the Court of Exchequer with regard to the nomination, appointment, or control of tutors dative shall be performed by the Court of Session acting as the Court of Exchequer in Scotland, upon applications for such nomination or appointment to be made to either of the divisions of the said Court by way of summary petition; and the procedure under such petitions may be, as nearly as may be, the same as under other summary petitions to the said Court, but may be regulated and varied from time to time in such way and manner as to the said Court may seem proper."

Cases referred to

AB v CB (1890) 18 R 90; (sub nom *CB v AB*) (1891) 18 R (HL) 40.
Bryce v Grahame (1828) 6 S 425; (1828) 3 W & S 323.
Dick v Douglas, 1924 SLT 578; 1924 SC 787.
Larkin v McGrady (1874) 2 R 170.
Simpson v Simpson (1891) 18 R 1207.

Textbooks referred to

Erskine, *Institute,* I vii 48-50.
Mackenzie, *Observations on the Acts of Parliament,* p 222.
Stair, *Institutions,* I vi 8 and 11.
Walker, *Judicial Factors,* pp 21-22.

On 17 December 1992 the Lord Ordinary *concluded* that no ground had been made out for the appointment of a tutor dative and *put out* the case by order for further procedure.

LORD PENROSE.—The petitioners are the only children of Archibald Hunter Chapman, to whom I shall refer as "Mr Chapman". Mr Chapman suffers from senile dementia, and is incapable of managing, or of giving instructions for the management of, his own affairs. It is unlikely that he will ever be able to resume control of matters of business. When the present application was presented it was anticipated that he would require to be removed to an institution, and that, when that occurred, he would not be expected to return to his home at 1 Dundas Crescent, Dalkeith. During the dependence of the proceedings Mr Chapman was admitted to a nursing home. He is now residing at Cameron Park nursing home, Edinburgh, and it appears that he will never again be capable of sustaining independent life in the community.

Mr Chapman has certain assets. He has some limited deposits with building societies, a reasonably substantial pension, and a heritable liferent interest in the house at 1 Dundas Crescent, Dalkeith.

In 1990 Mr Chapman and his late wife conveyed 1 Dundas Crescent, Dalkeith, to themselves in liferent and to the petitioners in fee. By minute of agreement dated 6 June and registered 14 June 1990 provision was made inter alia for the maintenance of the property during the lifetime of Mr Chapman and his then wife and for the event of the sale of the house. It was provided that upon sale the proceeds might be applied in the purchase of another house or that the proceeds be held by the present petitioners who should pay to Mr Chapman and his wife or the survivor of them the annual income of the proceeds, or on the balance of any proceeds not spent in the purchase of another house.

The petitioners seek the appointment of Mr Niall Hugh Robertson Bogie, solicitor, as tutor dative to Mr Chapman. No issue arises as to Mr Bogie's suitability for such appointment, or for appointment to any alternative office which might be appropriate in the circumstances of the case. The terms of the prayer, so far as material, are as follows: [his Lordship quoted the terms of the prayer set out supra and continued:]

As a practical matter the problem now confronting the petitioners is that with Mr Chapman's care being provided on an institutional basis and it being unlikely that he will ever again be capable of independent life in a home of his own, steps must be taken for the disposal of the house at 1 Dundas Crescent, Dalkeith. It is clearly necessary that the proceeds of sale be held during Mr Chapman's life for his liferent use and enjoyment. Nothing is suggested in the petition and nothing was said in argument before me to indicate that any decisions of any kind require to be taken now or in circumstances that can now be foreseen relating to the residential care or medical treatment of Mr Chapman. As I understood it, it is anticipated that he will remain in Cameron Park nursing home for the foreseeable future. I was not informed of any medical treatment proposed or anticipated which would require the consent of any party for its effective provision. In the circumstances I required counsel to address me on the appropriateness of the appointment of a tutor dative, on the view that the circumstances pointed, prima facie, to the appointment of a curator bonis to Mr Chapman.

Counsel for the petitioners set out to analyse the court's jurisdiction in these matters historically. The appointment of a tutor dative was originally a matter for the royal prerogative, and, in time, fell within the jurisdiction of the Court of Exchequer. Appointment to the office of curator bonis derived from the nobile officium of the Court of Session, and was adopted as a temporary expedient for the management of the affairs of an incapax until some other means emerged. It was trite that a tutor dative had power over the person and property of the ward, whereas a curator bonis was concerned only with the ward's estate. It was important to recognise why that was so, and not simply that it reflected the law. Counsel began with an analysis of the history of the court's jurisdiction to make appointments of tutors. He referred to Stair's *Institutions,* I vi 8 and 11; Erskine's *Institute,* I vii 48-50, the Curators Act 1585 (c 25); Mackenzie's *Observations on the Acts of Parliament,* and the Exchequer Court (Scotland) Act 1856, s 19. Using these sources counsel supported his submission that the court's power to appoint tutors dative belonged in its origins to the royal prerogative, exercised by the late 17th century by the King in Exchequer. The functions of the Court of Exchequer in respect of the

appointment of tutors dative were transferred to the
Court of Session by s 19 of the 1856 Act. So far as was
material, tutors dative to pupils and to persons lacking
capacity in other respects were equiparated.

A definite hierarchy emerged from examining the
early authorities. A tutor nominate was preferred over
a tutor at law or tutor dative. A tutor at law was
preferred over a tutor dative. Originally the King had
an unrestricted power to appoint as tutor dative
whomsoever he wished. The Act of 1585 restricted
that power. The nearest agnates and kinsmen of
"naturall foulis Ideottis and furious" were to be
preferred according to the disposition of the common
law. One therefore had a hierarchy among tutors, with
the prerogative power being available to make an
appointment where there had been no nomination and
the person in right of appointment as tutor at law did
not come forward. Mackenzie's observations had been
to this effect.

The history of the jurisdiction to make appointments to the office of curator bonis was set out by
reference to *Bryce v Grahame,* a case which both
demonstrated the nature of the court's jurisdiction in
that respect and related to the office of curator bonis
to the appointment of tutors. The appointment of a
curator bonis was an exercise in the court's nobile
officium. The appointment of a tutor superseded and
put an end to any subsisting curatory. What emerged
was that the court would act to appoint a curator
where those entitled to purchase and present a brieve
of insanity either failed or delayed to exercise their
rights. The appointment so made was temporary and
liable to be superseded by the appointment of a
regular tutor. Appontment of a curator bonis was
related to the court's concern for the management of
property. The court would not stand by and see
property left without management. Appointments
were made in the frank expectation that they might be
superseded by the appointment of a tutor. The hierar-
chical scheme therefore was carried through from the
structure of tutory appointments into the court's exercise of its nobile officium to make curatory appointments. The same structure appeared from *Larkin v
McGrady* at p 172, a case in which a brieve of insanity
had been purchased by a person who was not the
nearest male agnate.

Counsel moved on to the end of the 19th century.
By that time tutors dative were sought but fitfully. In
1924, when the last reported appointment was made
prior to the revival of the practice recently, appointment was rare. Walker on *Judicial Factors,* pp 21-22,
regarded the matter as of historical importance only.
Dick v Douglas, the last reported appointment, was
unusual in respect that a then existing curatory was
not superseded. For completeness counsel referred me
to *AB v CD* and *Simpson v Simpson.* The recent
revival of the practice recognised that it had never
become incompetent.

The substantial issue raised by counsel was as to the
implications of the revival. Counsel submitted that the
court was impelled by logic now to accept the whole

implications of the appointment of tutors dative.
There was, he accepted, room for development within
the principles which emerged from an examination of
the history. But the court was boxed in by the concept
which it sought to develop. The hierarchy of offices
was inherent in the structure of the two alternative
jurisdictions. If the court were presented with two
competing or alternative applications for the appointment of curator bonis and tutor dative respectively
from the same source or from sources with equivalent
titles, it might exercise a choice. But where there was
a single application for the appointment of a tutor
dative, the court was not in a position to refuse that
appointment. If the proof of incapacity of the ward
were sufficient, the court had to appoint a tutor on the
application of a qualified petitioner. There were no
grounds on which the application could be refused.

I was not persuaded that the different sources of the
jurisdiction of the court were significant for present
purposes. Apart from obvious historical interest,
counsel did not suggest that the court's approach to
the exercise of its jurisdiction differed according to
source, nor that the adaptation of rules and practices
to reflect changing circumstances depended in any
way upon the source of the jurisdiction. In relation to
matters of practice it is, in my opinion, always necessary to bear in mind that the purpose of the court's
procedural rules, however enacted or established, is to
provide a framework for the regular and efficient disposal of the business of the court. Practice, and the
rules themselves, develop and evolve as circumstances
change. *Dick v Douglas* is a particular example of a
modification of practice to meet a particular situation.
In some respects the situation may be or provide in
due course a close parallel to the present. A curator
had been appointed and was in office. The curator had
management of the property of the incapax but circumstances had arisen in which the court was persuaded that care of the person of the incapax should
be committed to a tutor dative. The argument before
the court was that such an appointment was incompetent. It was proposed that the proper course was for
the nearest male agnate to proceed by cognition and
serve as tutor at law. The competency of such a course
was recognised by the court. However the court upon
an analysis of the authorities decided that cognition
was not an obligatory course. The more delicate question was raised by the existence of the curatory. The
service of a tutor at law would supersede the curatory.
What the court had to consider was whether it was
incompetent to appoint a tutor dative to the ward's
person, while allowing the management of his estate
by a curator bonis to continue. It was held that there
was no objection to such a course. The case at once
indicates the willingness and power of the court to
find a practical solution to a defined problem and
demonstrates that counsel's attempt to analyse the
court's jurisdiction according to a strict hierarchy of
offices cannot be correct.

In *AB v CD* Lord McLaren at pp 96 and 97 set out
in a pragmatic way the court's approach to providing
remedies where the management of the affairs of

persons lacking capacity was in issue. As in *Dick v Douglas* there was recognition that one might proceed by cognition but the court defined restrictively the need to use that remedy, noting that the process of cognition had never been within the historical period the only process for determining such questions. It was strictly a proceeding for the appointment of a tutor of law. That was clear in *Larkin v McGrady*. The process of cognition in that case had been completed, but the purchaser of the brieve was held not to be nearest agnate. The process was retoured to chancery so that the nearest agnate might, if he were so inclined, take the office of tutor at law. If he were not so inclined, then application could be made to the court for appointment of a tutor dative or curator bonis. Lord McLaren proceeded to deal with some of the practical factors which by the end of the 19th century had led to a reduction in the number of applications for appointment of tutor dative relative to applications for appointment of curator bonis. He said: "We do not have many applications for the appointments of tutors-dative, — I suppose because it is a gratuitous office, and because it is more convenient that such estates should be managed on the footing of professional responsibility by agents who make it their business, and who are paid for their services."

There is, in my opinion, no doubt that throughout the 20th century the practice has been for professional men to be appointed curators in circumstances in which they can provide, for remuneration, the administration necessary to ensure the proper protection of the estates of persons lacking in capacity and the application of the available resources for the best interests of the ward.

It is now clear that, with changes in the nature of the risks to which individuals are exposed in a high technology society, and the advances made in medical science in dealing with the injured as well as in providing for the physical care of those whose mental capacities diminish, there are emerging situations in which it has been recognised that there is a need to exercise the jurisdiction to appoint persons with powers to take decisions relating to the personal care and custody of individual members of society. However there is equally a recognition in society at large that one should not interfere with the liberty of any individual except to the extent that one is driven by necessity to do so. The position adopted by the petitioners in this case would suggest that the court could do no other than appoint a tutor dative in a case in which a person having the right of election, as it were, chose that course, and established the incapacity of the ward. That I do not accept. It does not emerge from a reading of the authorities. No doubt it is true that where a tutor of law served, or took up office following cognition, his office superseded those of prior tutors dative and curators. Equally, in its origins, the office of tutor dative superseded that of any prior curator who had been appointed. Neither factor bears on the question whether the court should make an appointment in the first instance. That, in my opinion, must depend on proof of the necessity for and of the appropriateness of the appointment in the circumstances of the case. The removal of the administration of the business affairs of an individual into the hands of a third party is no light step to take. It is more serious to make an order which reflects the view that the person has no capacity in relation to his physical care. In my opinion it is appropriate to continue the well established practice of the court and to appoint curators where the identifiable purpose is to ensure the management of the property of a person. That usually involves a professional appointment in an estate of any substance, with proper provision for remuneration of the curator. That is in the interests of the ward. Where it is shown to be necessary for decisions to be taken regarding the welfare of the person, and that the person is incapable of taking those decisions or participating in them in any meaningful way, then appointment of a tutor will, no doubt, be appropriate. However the significance and the seriousness of appointing a tutor with power to give directions for the care and custody of the person of an individual, excluding that person from those decisions on his or her own behalf, must be acknowledged. In my opinion it ought not to be done as an incidental matter in an application otherwise concerned with the management of the financial affairs of the person lacking in capacity. In the light of *Dick v Douglas* it is clear that the functions of tutor and curator are not in any event mutually exclusive and that the court can readily provide for the physical care of an individual independently of the proper provision made for the management of his or her estate.

In this case there are no decisions required as to the care of Mr Chapman on the information presently before me. The time may come when such a need will arise. But for the present his physical care is in the hands of a nursing home. His medical care is in the hands of his ordinary medical advisers. There is no suggestion of present need for decisions which he could not take on his own behalf or which those having charge of his physical and medical care could not take without consent. In the circumstances of this case I consider that it would be appropriate to make an appointment of curator bonis, if asked to do so. However I am not satisfied that any grounds have been made out for the appointment of a tutor dative. I shall instruct the case to be put out by order for further procedure.

Counsel for Petitioners, I G Mitchell, QC; Solicitors, Dickson Smith, WS.

N W H

[When the petition was put out by order, it was continued to enable the application to be amended to a petition for the appointment of a curator bonis.]

Mailley v HM Advocate

A HIGH COURT OF JUSTICIARY

THE LORD JUSTICE GENERAL (HOPE),
LORDS ALLANBRIDGE AND COWIE

4 MARCH 1993

*Justiciary — Procedure — Trial — Charge to jury —
Sheriff wrongly considering that defence case had not been
put to Crown witness — Sheriff directing that jury
entitled to regard defence evidence with some reservation*
B *— Whether misdirection — Whether miscarriage of
justice.*

*Justiciary — Evidence — Cross examination — Whether
defence obliged to put case to Crown witnesses.*

An accused person was tried along with another
person on an indictment charging them with breach of
the peace and assault to severe injury and permanent
disfigurement involving the use of a knife. The complainer spoke to having been punched by the accused
in the kitchen of his house and then having fled
C upstairs pursued by both the accused and his co-
accused (in respect of whom the libel was subsequently withdrawn). He said that the rest of the
assault took place in a bedroom in the course of which
he was struck by the accused with a knife which he
produced from his trouser pocket. There was no
dispute that the accused and his co-accused entered
the complainer's house and that an incident took place
involving the complainer being cut on his leg with a
knife, but the accused's position was that the com-
D plainer sustained the cut while still in the kitchen and
that it was his co-accused who struck the complainer.
The co-accused supported the accused's evidence. The
sheriff, wrongly considering that the accused's position had not been put to the complainer in cross
examination, directed the jury that it should have been
and that accordingly they were entitled to look at the
defence with some reservation. The accused was convicted and appealed on the ground of misdirection.
The Crown moved the court to authorise a retrial if it
were satisfied that a miscarriage of justice had
E occurred.

Held, (1) that there was no obligation for points to
be put to Crown witnesses as a preliminary to the
leading of evidence on these matters for the defence,
and the sheriff erred in accompanying his comments
with an invitation to the jury to treat the defence evidence with reservation (p 962G-H); (2) that the sheriff's
comments were based on an incorrect recollection of
what had occurred during the Crown evidence and
F accordingly there had been a misdirection on a matter
which was crucial to the accused's defence, resulting
in a miscarriage of justice (p 962H); (3) that in the circumstances it was appropriate to authorise a retrial
(p 962I-J); and appeal *allowed,* conviction *set aside* and
retrial *authorised.*

McPherson v Copeland, 1961 SLT 373, *followed.*

Observed, that the Crown would be entitled when
addressing the jury to comment on any failure to put
the defence case to Crown witnesses, and that it would
be open to the presiding judge to direct the jury that

they were entitled to take this into account in considering the evidence (p 962E-F).   G

Indictment

Martin Mailley was charged along with Margaret
Maxwell or Boyle, at the instance of the rt hon the
Lord Fraser of Carmyllie, Her Majesty's Advocate on
an indictment which was in the following terms: "you
did on 21 July 1991 (1) force your way into the house
at 89 Braidwood Place, East Fulton, Linwood,   H
conduct yourselves in a disorderly manner and
commit a breach of the peace; (2) place above libelled
assault Barry Ward, c/o Johnstone police office, punch
him repeatedly on the face and head, pursue him
upstairs, punch him repeatedly on the head, whereby
he fell onto a bed, seize him by the clothing and strike
him on the arm and body with a knife or similar
instrument all to his severe injury and permanent disfigurement". The accused pled not guilty and
proceeded to trial in the sheriff court at Paisley before
Sheriff R G Smith and a jury. After trial the accused   I
was convicted.

The accused appealed to the High Court by way of
note of appeal against conviction. The facts giving rise
to the appeal appear from the opinion of the court.

Case referred to

McPherson v Copeland, 1961 SLT 373; 1961 JC 74.

Appeal

The note of appeal contained the following ground,   J
inter alia:

(1) That the sheriff misdirected the jury in relation
to the following matters, and that the misdirections are
such that there has resulted a miscarriage of justice:

(a) At p 10D to p 11C of his charge, the sheriff
directed the jury that they should, as a matter of law,
regard with reservation evidence led and sought to be
led by the defence that the part of the assault involving
the use of a knife took place not in the bedroom of the   K
house as had been stated by the complainer but in the
kitchen of the house. He further directed that they
should have reservation toward such a line as it was
never put to the complainer (Barry Ward) or to
Matthew Ward (the only other Crown witness at any
time present in the kitchen).

It is respectfully submitted that this amounted to a
fundamental misdirection. In the instant case it was
the defence position that the assault by use of a knife
was committed not by the appellant in the bedroom of   L
the house, but by the appellant's cohabitee (the co-
accused) in the kitchen of the house.

It is respectfully submitted that this was directly put
to the complainer, Barry Ward, in cross examination
for the appellant.

Further, it being the defence position that Crown
witness Matthew Ward (aged 11 years) left the kitchen
prior to any attack taking place, this was put to him
directly and it was thereafter unnecessary to cross

A examine him further in relation to the detail of the subsequent events in the kitchen.

It is respectfully submitted that in these circumstances the direction was such as to prejudice the appellant in relation to the question of who used the knife and at what stage of the incident.

The appeal was argued before the High Court on 4 March 1993.

B Eo die the court *allowed* the appeal, *set aside* the conviction and *authorised* a retrial.

The following opinion of the court was delivered by the Lord Justice General (Hope):

OPINION OF THE COURT.—The appellant went to trial in the sheriff court at Paisley with his cohabitee Margaret Maxwell or Boyle on charges of breach of the peace and assault. They were said to have forced their way into a house in Linwood, con-
C ducted themselves in a disorderly manner and committed a breach of the peace there, and then to have assaulted Barry Ward in the house by punching him, chasing him upstairs, and subjecting him there to various acts of violence including striking him on the arm and body with a knife or similar instrument to his severe injury and permanent disfigurement. In the course of the trial the libel was withdrawn against Mrs Boyle and she was acquitted on both charges. The appellant was found guilty on both of them, and he
D was sentenced to a total of 21 months' imprisonment.

In his note of appeal the appellant has set out three grounds on which he wishes to appeal against his conviction. The first two allege misdirections by the sheriff in his charge to the jury. The third alleges that the sheriff erred in preventing the defence from putting certain questions to Mrs Boyle, who was called as a defence witness and whom the appellant wished to incriminate on the ground that it was she who had obtained the knife and used it to injure the
E complainer. We need say no more about the third ground however because counsel for the appellant informed us that it was clear from the transcript of Mrs Boyle's evidence that this ground was based on a misconception and that he did not insist on it. He also informed us that he did not insist on the second ground, which alleges that the sheriff failed to direct the jury adequately on the question of provocation. What we are left with is the first ground, which is that the sheriff misdirected the jury when he told them that
F they should, as a matter of law, regard with reservation some of the defence evidence about who used the knife and at what stage in the incident it was used.

When the appeal came before us on the previous occasion our attention was drawn to a difference of recollection between the sheriff and the appellant's solicitor about the content of certain passages in the evidence. The advocate depute agreed with the appellant's counsel that, in view of the absence of any discussion of the evidence in the charge and the rather slender information which the sheriff had provided on

this matter in his report, it would be helpful for a transcript of the evidence of four witnesses to be obtained G before there was any further discussion of this ground of appeal. We have now had the advantage of seeing the transcripts of the evidence of the complainer Barry Ward and his younger brother, Matthew Ward, together with that of the appellant and Mrs Boyle. We have been able to examine the relevant passages in the evidence and compare them with what the sheriff said about this evidence in his charge.

The Crown case was that the complainer, who was aged 17, and his brother, who was aged 11, were alone H in the house when the appellant and Mrs Boyle arrived at the door. There had previously been a disturbance in the garden outside the house in the course of which Matthew Ward and Mrs Boyle's son Thomas Boyle had become involved in a fight with each other. Barry Ward intervened to stop the fight and when Thomas Boyle ran off he and his brother went to Mrs Boyle's house where words were exchanged between them and Mrs Boyle. It was shortly after this that Barry Ward, who had returned home, saw the appel- I lant and Mrs Boyle walking up the garden path to the back door of the house. According to his evidence the appellant then forced his way into the house and punched him several times. At that stage Barry Ward was in the kitchen as was his brother Matthew Ward. Barry Ward then fled upstairs pursued by the appellant and Mrs Boyle, and the rest of the assault took place in his bedroom. In the course of it he was struck by the appellant with a knife which the appellant produced from his trouser pocket. The appellant then J proceeded to punch Barry Ward until he managed to push him away and escape from the attack by running downstairs and out of the house. There was no dispute that the appellant and Mrs Boyle entered the complainer's house and that an incident took place there in the course of which Barry Ward was cut on the leg with a knife. But the appellant's position was that Barry Ward sustained this injury while he was still in the kitchen, and that it was Mrs Boyle who inflicted this injury with a knife which she picked up from the K kitchen worktop before he ran upstairs. Mrs Boyle's evidence was that she did this in the course of a struggle between the appellant and Barry Ward which was taking place in the kitchen, and she also said that no weapon was used while the appellant was in the bedroom.

The passage in the sheriff's charge to which the appeal is directed appears at pp 10D–11C and is in these terms: "Before leaving the question of evidence, L ladies and gentlemen, you will have noticed that certain points which the defence wished to bring out were objected to and disallowed. Now, the reason that I was forced to do this is that any points which the defence wishes to raise in their defence, such points must be put to the Crown witnesses beforehand where that Crown witness is directly involved. This is to give the Crown fair notice and also it is to be fair to the main witness, so that the main witness can have a chance to either agree or refute that evidence. So any such evidence which you did hear, which did slip out

contrary to this rule, you are entitled to view with
some reservation. I refer in particular to the evidence,
one, of the kitchen knife being used and, two, that the
knife assault took place not in the boy's bedroom but
in the kitchen before they got to the boy's bedroom.
That was never put to the complainer, Barry Ward,
nor was it put to the young lad Matthew. For that
reason you are entitled to look at that evidence which
did slip out with some reservation, ladies and
gentlemen.''

Counsel for the appellant submitted that these directions were wrong in law and that they were also wrong
in fact. So far as the facts were concerned, the position
was that the point that the knife was used in the
kitchen and not in the bedroom was put in terms to
Barry Ward during his cross examination. The point
was not put specifically to Matthew Ward, but there
was an explanation for this because Matthew Ward
said in his evidence that he left the kitchen and that
he did not see anything which happened there. This
was a crucial point in the appellant's defence, and the
effect of the misdirection, which the sheriff then used
as the basis for telling the jury that they were entitled
to view his evidence on this matter with reservation,
was so prejudicial to him as to amount to a miscarriage
of justice. As to the law on the matter, counsel for the
appellant's argument was that the sheriff went too far
when he told the jury that they were entitled to view
the defence evidence with reservation because points
raised in it had not been put to the Crown witnesses.
He submitted that there was no rule of law that this
had to be done, nor was it correct to say that if points
were not put to the Crown witnesses the defence evidence on these matters was to be viewed with reservation. It might be a matter for comment if a point was
led from the accused or defence witnesses which had
not been put to the witnesses for the Crown, but this
was not a matter on which the trial judge should give
an adverse direction in the course of his charge.

The sheriff tells us in his report that he can find no
direct reference in his notes as to where the assault
with a knife took place. He has no note of any question
suggesting that Mrs Boyle struck the complainer with
the knife in the kitchen before he fled upstairs. It
appears therefore that his notes are consistent with
what he said in his charge. But it is clear from the transcript that the point was put clearly and repeatedly to
Barry Ward in the course of his cross examination. He
was asked at p 44F whether it was possible that he
could have received the cut on his leg when he was
still in the kitchen. At p 51D it was put to him that
he had already been struck with the knife before he got
to his bedroom. At p 54D it was put to him again that
it was possible that the blows with the knife were delivered when he was in the kitchen. At pp 54F-55A it
was put to him that it was Mrs Boyle who had hit him
with the knife when he was in the kitchen while he
was grappling or fighting with the appellant. The
procurator fiscal depute then intervened, asking that
the defence case be clearly put, especially if it was to
be suggested that Mrs Boyle used the knife at some
stage in the bedroom. In the course of the discussion

which then followed the sheriff said this at p 56C: "As
I understand it, he is saying that the knife wounds
were inflicted in the kitchen and not in the bedroom.''

The appellant's solicitor replied that the sheriff had
picked him up correctly, in that he had put to the
witness that the only place where the knife incident
actually took place was in the kitchen and that he had
sustained any injuries caused by the knife by the time
he got to the bedroom. So far as Matthew Ward's evidence is concerned, this witness said at p 9D that he
went into the livingroom and was too scared to go
upstairs. At p 24D he said that he did not think that
he saw everything that happened in the kitchen
because he wasn't looking. He explained that he
became frightened when the appellant, who had
barged in when the door was opened, punched his
brother. He then went into the livingroom when the
others went upstairs. At p 26A it was put to him that
he did not know exactly what Mrs Boyle was doing in
the kitchen, to which he answered "No". In the discussion following the procurator fiscal's objection
during Barry Ward's evidence at p 59 the sheriff said
that his recollection was that Matthew Ward had not
been asked whether the knife was used in the kitchen,
and the appellant's solicitor confirmed that that was
so. But it is clear from Matthew Ward's evidence that
the view could reasonably be taken that he could not
answer specific questions of this kind about what happened during the incident, as he had taken fright and
did not watch what was going on.

The learned advocate depute did not dispute
counsel for the appellant's point that the sheriff was
wrong in his recollection. He accepted that the sheriff
was plainly incorrect when he said to the jury that the
point that the knife assault took place not in the complainer's bedroom but in the kitchen had not been put
to Barry Ward during his evidence. But he took issue
with counsel on the question whether, assuming that
the sheriff had been right about this, he was justified
in drawing attention to the matter on the ground that
there was an obligation on the defence to put the
defence case to the Crown witnesses. He accepted that
the sheriff's words on this point were not well chosen,
and that he had not put the matter correctly when he
referred to the defence evidence as having slipped out
contrary to a rule and told the jury that they were
entitled to view it with reservation. He maintained
however that there was no serious error here, because
the sheriff had not told the jury that they had to view
the evidence with reservation, only that they were
entitled to do so. He submitted that the sheriff was
right to draw attention to the fact that the defence case
ought to be put to the Crown witnesses. This was not
something to be left entirely to the discretion of the
defence, and there was nothing wrong in principle in
the trial judge making a comment on the matter so
long as he used appropriate language to put the point.

In *McPherson v Copeland* the sheriff was held to
have been in error when he stopped the cross examination of a Crown witness about a special method of
identifying stolen goods which had not been put in
cross examination to a previous Crown witness who

had given evidence on the same point. The same error seems to have affected the sheriff's thinking in the present case when he said that he had been forced to disallow certain evidence. It appears from the transcript that, contrary to his recollection, none of the points which the defence wished to bring out was actually disallowed. But his statement that he was forced to disallow these points because they required to be put to the Crown witnesses beforehand shows that this passage in his charge was based on a misconception, as was his reference to this as being a rule. This was the mistake which the sheriff substitute made in *McPherson v Copeland* when he sustained an objection on the ground that the defence must give notice to the Crown, if they wish to put forward any particular line of defence, by cross examining Crown witnesses who give evidence which is contradictory of that defence. As Lord Justice Clerk Thomson pointed out at 1961 SLT, p 375, the principle on which the sheriff substitute sustained the objection may well be of significance in civil proceedings, but there is no such rule in a criminal trial where the burden of proof is on the Crown throughout to establish the case against the accused beyond reasonable doubt. He went on to say this: "It follows that the procurator for the accused may be as selective as he chooses in cross-examination. The worst that can happen to him is that his selection may be criticised and his omissions commented on."

He went on to say that he could not see that there was any obligation to cross examine the first witness as an essential preliminary to his cross examining the second witness on the point at issue. Irrespective of what had been put to the first witness, he was entitled to get what he could out of the second witness on the topic, with a view to raising a reasonable doubt on the evidence as a whole.

That case was not concerned with the question whether points which are material to the defence case must be put to the Crown witnesses as an essential prerequisite to the leading of evidence on these points for the defence. There is, however, no difference in principle between what occurred there and the situation under discussion in the present case. By not cross examining Crown witnesses on points to be taken later from witnesses in the defence case, the accused's procurator will run the risk that this will be a matter of comment, especially when the jury are addressed on the evidence on behalf of the Crown. It will also be open to the presiding judge to remind the jury that points which were made in the course of the defence case were not put to the Crown witnesses, and that they are entitled to take this into account in their consideration of the evidence. It would of course be wholly improper for adverse comments to be made by the defence procurator on the credibility or reliability of the Crown witnesses as compared with those for the defence on points which had not been put to the Crown witnesses while they were giving their evidence. Criticisms of this kind, whether express or implied, can only be made if the witnesses concerned have had a fair opportunity to deal with the matter while they were in the witness box. This rule of professional practice, which relates to what may properly be said to the jury in a closing speech, is however an entirely different matter from the point which the sheriff had in mind about the leading of defence evidence. There is no obligation for points to be put to Crown witnesses as a preliminary to the leading of evidence on these matters for the defence, and the sheriff's error was to accompany his comments with an invitation to the jury to treat the defence evidence with reservation because it had slipped out contrary to a rule. Furthermore his comments were based on an incorrect recollection of what had occurred during the complainer's evidence, and a mistaken view as to what it was appropriate to put to Matthew Ward in view of the limited nature of his evidence.

We are in no doubt that this passage in the sheriff's charge amounted to a misdirection on a matter which was crucial to the appellant's defence, and that there was as a result a miscarriage of justice in this case. The advocate depute invited us, if we were to reach this view, to grant authority to the Crown to bring a new prosecution in accordance with s 255 of the Criminal Procedure (Scotland) Act 1975. He pointed out that no question had been raised about the sufficiency of the evidence. The age of the principal Crown witnesses was not a material factor in this case, of which a very serious view should be taken as it involved an attack on the complainer in his own house by someone who had forced his way into it armed with a knife. We are satisfied that this is an appropriate case for authority to be given for a new prosecution to be brought. It is clear that, but for this one short passage in the sheriff's charge, the appellant would have had no answer to his conviction for what was, on the Crown evidence, plainly a very serious offence. We shall therefore allow the appeal by setting aside his conviction on both charges in this indictment, and we shall grant authority for a new prosecution to be brought in accordance with s 255 of the Act.

Counsel for Appellant, McBride, Solicitors, Drummond Miller, WS (for Cameron, Pinkerton & Co, Renfrew) — Counsel for Respondent, Macdonald, QC, A D; Solicitor, J D Lowe, Crown Agent.

P W F

HM Advocate v Harris

A HIGH COURT OF JUSTICIARY

THE LORD JUSTICE CLERK (ROSS),
LORDS MURRAY, McCLUSKEY, MORISON
AND PROSSER

18 MARCH 1993

Justiciary — Crime — Recklessly causing injury — Relevancy — No allegation that conduct to danger of lieges — Whether crime.

B *Justiciary — Crime — Assault and recklessly causing injury — Relevancy — Accused charged with assault and alternatively recklessly causing injury on same species facti — Whether true alternative charges.*

An accused person was charged on indictment with assault to severe injury and permanent disfigurement by seizing hold of his victim, pushing her on the body and causing her to fall down a flight of stairs and onto the roadway as a result of which she was struck by a motor vehicle. The indictment also libelled an alter-
C native charge to the effect that the accused culpably, wilfully and recklessly seized hold of his victim and did all of the acts libelled in the assault charge to her severe injury and permanent disfigurement. The accused objected to the relevancy of the alternative charge on the ground that it did not disclose a crime known to the law of Scotland. At a preliminary diet the sheriff sustained the objection and dismissed the alternative charge. The Crown appealed contending that reckless conduct resulting in actual injury con-
D stituted a crime and that it was not essential that the conduct be to the danger of the lieges. The accused maintained that the alternative charge was a duplication of the assault charge.

Held (by a bench of five judges), (1) that reckless conduct to the danger of the lieges constituted a crime in Scotland and so too did reckless conduct which caused actual injury (pp 966A-B, 967E-G, 968K-L, 971A-C and K-L and 975D-E); (2) (Lord McCluskey *dissenting*) that the charges were truly alternatives
E since the law drew a distinction between intent and recklessness, and the jury could conclude that the accused had the intent necessary for assault or alternatively that he lacked that intent but had displayed recklessness which caused the victim to fall and sustain injury (pp 966F-I, 967H-J, 971E-G and 973L-974B); and appeal *allowed*.

Quinn v Cunningham, 1956 SLT 55, *overruled*.

Per Lord McCluskey (*dissenting*): The alternative
F charge was irrelevant as there was no crime known to the law of Scotland consisting of wilfully seizing another human being, pushing her on the body and causing her to fall down a flight of stairs except the crime of assault (p 969L).

Indictment

Andrew Harris was charged at the instance of the rt hon the Lord Rodger of Earlsferry, Her Majesty's Advocate on an indictment which was in the following terms: "on 20 March 1991 at Tin Pan Alley, 39
G Mitchell Street, Glasgow, you did assault Jane Breen, c/o Stewart Street police office, Glasgow, seize hold of her, push her on the body and cause her to fall down a flight of stairs and onto the roadway outside the said premises as a result of which she was struck by motor vehicle registered number F594 CHS, then being driven in Mitchell Street, aforesaid by Alexis Jane McLean, c/o Stewart Street police office, Glasgow all to her severe injury and permanent disfigurement; *or alternatively* on 20 March 1991 at Tin Pan Alley, 39 Mitchell Street, Glasgow, you did culpably, wilfully
H and recklessly seize hold of Jane Breen, c/o Stewart Street police office, Glasgow, push her on the body and cause her to fall down a flight of stairs and onto the roadway outside the said premises as a result of which she was struck by motor vehicle registered number F594 CHS, then being driven in Mitchell Street, aforesaid by Alexis Jane McLean, c/o Stewart Street police office, Glasgow all to her severe injury and permanent disfigurement."

The accused objected to the relevancy of the alter-
I native charge on the ground that it did not disclose a crime known to the law of Scotland. At a preliminary diet the sheriff (G H Gordon, QC) sustained the objection and dismissed the alternative charge. The Crown appealed, with leave, to the High Court against the decision of the sheriff.

Statutory provisions

The Criminal Procedure (Scotland) Act 1975
provides:
J
"44. It shall not be necessary in any indictment to specify by any nomen juris the crime which is charged, but it shall be sufficient that the indictment sets forth facts relevant and sufficient to constitute an indictable crime. . . .

"48. It shall not be necessary in any indictment to allege that any act of commission or omission therein charged was done or omitted to be done 'wilfully' or . . . 'culpably and recklessly' . . . or to use any similar words or expressions qualifying any act K charged, but such qualifying allegation shall be implied in every case."

Cases referred to

Advocate (HM) v Latto (1857) 2 Irv 732.
Advocate (HM) v Phipps (1905) 4 Adam 616.
Advocate (HM) v Smith and McNeil (1842) 1 Broun 240.
Advocate (HM) v Young (1839) 2 Swin 376.
Kerr v Hill, 1936 SLT 320; 1936 JC 71.   L
Khaliq v HM Advocate, 1984 SLT 137; 1984 JC 23; 1983 SCCR 483.
McAllister v Abercrombie (1907) 15 SLT 70; 1907 SC (J) 95.
McHaffie (Ezekiel) (1827) Syme (App III) 38.
McLaughlan v Boyd, 1933 SLT 629; 1934 JC 19.
Paton v HM Advocate, 1936 SLT 298; 1936 JC 19.
Quinn v Cunningham, 1956 SLT 55; 1956 JC 22.
Ulhaq v HM Advocate, 1991 SLT 614; 1990 SCCR 593.
W v HM Advocate, 1982 SLT 420; 1982 SCCR 152.

Textbooks referred to

Gordon, *Criminal Law* (2nd ed), paras 29-30, 29-55.
Macdonald, *Criminal Law* (5th ed), pp 115, 141-142.

The sheriff reported to the High Court in the following terms:

THE SHERIFF (G H GORDON, QC).—This case came before me at a preliminary diet in somewhat unusual circumstances, which could perhaps best be described as being in the nature of a shunting exercise. I was informed by counsel for the accused that an indictment in similar, although not quite identical, terms had been the subject of an earlier preliminary diet at which the plea to the relevancy of the alternative charge of culpable and reckless injury had been sustained by the sheriff. That decision had been appealed to the High Court by the Crown. I was informed that after some argument had been heard, which included a reference to the case of *Khaliq v HM Advocate*, the Lord Justice Clerk had expressed a view that the Crown could not succeed in their appeal standing the case of *Quinn v Cunningham*. I was informed further that the home advocate depute had then conceded that *Quinn v Cunningham* governed the case then under appeal, and that the appeal was remitted to a larger court so that *Quinn v Cunningham* could be reconsidered. Thereafter it appears that the Crown inadvertently pulled the wrong lever, as it were, and deserted the indictment. They had then raised the indictment which came before me in an attempt to put the case back on the rails so that it could again come before your Lordships and the question of whether *Quinn v Cunningham* should be overturned could be raised again. The procurator fiscal depute did not challenge counsel's description of the attitude of the Crown when the case was last before your Lordships, but indicated that she had instructions to oppose the preliminary plea. Neither counsel for the accused nor the depute fiscal wished *Quinn v Cunningham* to be distinguished in the context of the present case. They both agreed that the most appropriate way of bringing the matter back before your Lordships would be for me to uphold the accused's plea. In these circumstances, and in light of what happened at the earlier hearing in the High Court, I accepted that the appropriate course was for me to uphold the accused's plea, and to grant the Crown leave to appeal. In these circumstances I do not think that it would be appropriate or necessary for me to express any view as to whether or not *Quinn v Cunningham* was correctly decided, or indeed as to whether or not it can be distinguished from the present case. Nor do I think that it would be appropriate for me to burden your Lordships with any reference to such arguments on the matter as were put before me in a fairly formal manner or any of the more detailed points about the terminology of the indictment which were briefly raised in discussion.

I should perhaps just say that counsel for the accused's position was that while it was an offence to engage in culpable and reckless conduct which endangered the lieges, it was not an offence culpably and recklessly to cause injury to a particular person. He relied for that argument on *Quinn v Cunningham*, and in particular on what was said by the Lord Justice General at 1956 SLT, p 57. He referred also to *McAllister v Abercrombie* and to the case of *Khaliq*. He also made a passing reference to the treatment of the subject in the recent textbook by Jones and Christie.

The procurator fiscal depute argued that *Quinn v Cunningham* was at odds with *Khaliq*, and with the older cases quoted in *Khaliq* which showed that there was a crime of causing reckless injury to particular persons. She referred also to the cases of *Ulhaq v HM Advocate*, which followed *Khaliq*, and *W v HM Advocate* in which a charge of culpably and recklessly injuring a particular person was not challenged, and the only reference to *Quinn v Cunningham* was in relation to its description of the mens rea of such behaviour. Despite that, as I have said, the procurator fiscal depute did not encourage me to distinguish *Quinn v Cunningham*, but was content that I should uphold the appellant's plea as the most convenient way of bringing the matter once again before your Lordships.

Appeal

The appeal was argued before the High Court on 18 February 1993.

On 18 March 1993 the court *allowed* the appeal, *reversed* the decision of the sheriff and *remitted* to him to proceed as accords.

THE LORD JUSTICE CLERK (ROSS).—This is an appeal at the instance of the Crown. The respondent is Andrew Harris. The respondent has been charged in the sheriff court at Glasgow on an indictment containing a charge which is stated in the alternative. The charge is in the following terms: [his Lordship quoted its terms and continued:]

The respondent gave written notice that he intended to raise a matter relating to the relevancy of the alternative charge, and a preliminary diet was held before the sheriff at Glasgow on 23 September 1992. After holding a hearing the sheriff sustained the preliminary plea to the relevancy stated on behalf of the respondent and dismissed the alternative charge as irrelevant. He did so having regard to *Quinn v Cunningham*. The sheriff granted leave to appeal against his decision. The Crown have appealed against the decision of the sheriff in terms of s 76A of the Act of 1975. The ground of the appeal is stated as follows: "The sheriff erred in law in sustaining the plea to the relevancy of the alternative charge on the indictment on the grounds that the libel did not disclose a crime known to the law of Scotland."

When the appeal called before this court on 22 October 1992, the Crown invited the court to remit the appeal to a quorum of five judges on the ground that *Quinn v Cunningham* should be reconsidered. The court acceded to that request, and the hearing before five judges has now taken place.

In opening the appeal, the Lord Advocate explained that the respondent was what is commonly called a bouncer or steward at a discotheque, and as such was expected to exercise control over persons frequenting such an establishment; in particular it had to be recognised that on occasions in the course of his duties a bouncer might find it necessary to seize and take hold of those frequenting the premises with a view to removing them therefrom. The sheriff had upheld the plea to relevancy upon the view that *Quinn v Cunningham* laid down that reckless conduct was not a crime at common law unless it was libelled to be "to the danger of the lieges". That was not libelled in the alternative charge in this indictment, and accordingly on the authority of *Quinn v Cunningham*, the sheriff had sustained the plea to relevancy. The Lord Advocate submitted that it was not necessary in all cases to libel danger to the lieges; reckless conduct would be criminal if it was libelled either as being to the danger of the lieges or as having resulted in actual injury. He referred to a number of cases where charges had been held to be relevant on the basis that the reckless conduct in question had caused actual injury.

In *Ezekiel McHaffie*, a case of careless navigation of a ship was allowed to go to a jury where the accused was charged with "recklessly managing or directing a vessel or steampacket, so as to cause it to run down, sink and destroy another boat or vessel, thereby seriously wounding and injuring the person of a man sailing in such boat or vessel". In *HM Advocate v Latto* a railway signalman pled guilty to a charge of culpable violation of duty in consequence of which an accident happened and several persons were injured. In *HM Advocate v Robert Young*, a plea to relevancy was taken of a charge which libelled "culpable and reckless neglect of duty by a workman in the management or use of machinery or mechanical apparatus whereby lives were lost or bodily injuries suffered or the safety of the lieges put in danger". The plea was taken upon the ground that it was not relevant to libel merely that the safety of the lieges was put in danger, because in order to constitute a crime, there must be a result produced or intended. The court recommended that the words "or the safety of the lieges put in danger" should be struck out of the indictment, and that was done. This case is accordingly clear authority for the view that culpable and reckless conduct which causes actual injury is criminal. In *Smith and McNeil* a charge of wickedly, recklessly and culpably discharging loaded firearms into an inhabited house to the imminent danger of the lives of the persons within the house was held to be a relevant charge. The Lord Justice Clerk observed that to make a relevant charge of reckless conduct it was not necessary to show that there had been actual injury to a person. The Lord Advocate contended that these cases showed that reckless conduct resulting in actual injury would constitute a crime by the law of Scotland. The Lord Advocate also referred to Macdonald, *Criminal Law of Scotland* (5th ed), pp 141-142. The view appears to be accepted that reckless conduct to the danger of the lieges is criminal, and that such offences are "more heinous when injury results to the lieges". The learned editors add: "In other cases, in order to make a relevant charge of danger to the lieges, it may be necessary to specify that injury resulted to some of them."

I agree with the Lord Advocate that these authorities support the proposition that reckless conduct which results in injury constitutes a crime under the law of Scotland. There was no dispute before this court regarding that, and indeed senior counsel for the respondent expressly accepted that reckless conduct causing injury was a crime under our law. That being so, I see no need to embark on any detailed analysis of the theories which may be thought to justify the law being what I have held it to be, particularly when no detailed arguments were presented to us on that matter.

In *Quinn v Cunningham* the accused was charged on a summary complaint with riding a pedal cycle in a reckless manner and causing it to collide with a pedestrian and injure both parties. The court held that as the conduct was not libelled as being "to the danger of the lieges" the complaint was irrelevant. In the course of delivering his opinion the Lord Justice General described the charge as consisting of two separate parts, "firstly riding a pedal cycle in a reckless manner, and secondly causing it to collide with someone whereby slight injury resulted". For myself I would have thought that the proper way to read the charge was that it libelled riding a pedal cycle recklessly so that it collided with a pedestrian and injured him. However that may be, the Lord Justice General went on to say (at 1956 SLT, p 57): "As the law stands therefore this complaint can only be relevant if it libels that degree of recklessness which constitutes the crime at common law, that is to say a recklessness so high as to involve an indifference to the consequences for the public generally."

After citing a passage from the Lord Justice General in *McAllister v Abercrombie*, Lord Justice General Clyde said: "Judged by this standard the present complaint fails to satisfy what is required, for the words 'to the danger of the lieges' as a qualification of the recklessness, are not libelled in this complaint. It charges the appellant therefore with a degree of recklessness which does not constitute a crime."

It is thus clear that Lord Justice General Clyde was holding that in order to make a relevant charge of reckless conduct, it was necessary to libel that the conduct had been "to the danger of the lieges". He went on to say: "Mere recklessness by a pedal cyclist followed by an injury to a foot passenger does not constitute a crime in Scotland, any more than mere recklessness by driving followed by death would constitute culpable homicide." He added: "In the present case the injury to the foot passenger is in no way connected up with the recklessness, and is not libelled as an element of that recklessness."

Lord Sorn had some doubt as to whether the charge did not disclose riding a bicycle recklessly to the danger of the lieges, although the words "to the danger of the lieges" did not appear.

In my opinion, since there is ample authority for the view that reckless conduct causing injury is a crime by the law of Scotland, the case of *Quinn v Cunningham* is an unsatisfactory decision. Insofar as it supports the proposition that it is not enough for the Crown to libel reckless conduct causing actual injury, I am of opinion that it was wrongly decided. Insofar as *Quinn v Cunningham* supports the proposition that it is necessary in all cases to aver reckless conduct "to the danger of the lieges" I am also of opinion that it was wrongly decided. In my judgment there are two ways in which reckless conduct may become criminal. Reckless conduct to the danger of the lieges will constitute a crime in Scotland, and so too will reckless conduct which has caused actual injury. Being satisfied that it was wrongly decided in these respects, I would move your Lordships to overrule *Quinn v Cunningham.*

The relevancy of the charge was challenged upon another ground. Senior counsel for the respondent maintained that the respondent was being charged with the same crime in both the principal charge and the alternative. He appreciated that in the principal charge the respondent is said to have assaulted the complainer and seized hold of her and pushed her on the body and caused her to fall, whereas in the second charge he is libelled to have culpably, wilfully and recklessly seized hold of the complainer, pushed her on the body and caused her to fall. He submitted that both charges libelled assault and that it did not matter that the word "assault" did not appear in the alternative charge because it was not necessary in any indictment to specify by any nomen juris the crime which was charged provided that the indictment set forth facts relevant and sufficient to constitute an indictable crime (s 44 of the Act of 1975). The alternative charge was a charge of assault. There was no need for the Crown to have included the words "wilfully" or "culpably and recklessly" as these words would be implied in a charge of this nature (s 48 of the Act of 1975). In both the principal charge and the alternative charge precisely the same conduct on the part of the respondent was averred. Senior counsel further explained that the defence to both charges would be that the respondent had been carrying out his ordinary duties as a bouncer, and lacked the mens rea necessary for assault.

The Lord Advocate accepted that the words "culpably" and "wilfully" added nothing to the alternative charge and were superfluous. He also accepted that if the respondent had merely been acting carelessly, that would not be sufficient to render his conduct criminal. He did submit however that the Crown were entitled to libel these alternative charges. If the Crown did not succeed in establishing that the appellant had the necessary mens rea for assault, they might still be able to show that he had been guilty of reckless conduct which had caused injury.

I have come to the conclusion that the argument of the Lord Advocate is to be preferred. I appreciate that both the principal charge and the alternative charge libel precisely the same conduct on the part of the respondent, but in my opinion a different mens rea is required for each charge. As Sheriff Gordon points out in his *Criminal Law* (2nd ed), para 29-30: "Assault is a crime of intent and cannot be committed recklessly or negligently."

"Evil intention being of the essence of assault, it differs from culpable homicide in so far as injuries happening from carelessness, however culpable, are not assaults" (Macdonald, *Criminal Law of Scotland* (5th ed), p 115).

The law draws a distinction between intent and recklessness (*HM Advocate v Phipps*). Accordingly, I am satisfied that the charges truly are alternatives. It will be for the jury to determine whether the accused acted in the manner described in the indictment, and if that is established, then although the accused was acting as a bouncer, the jury may conclude that when he seized hold of the complainer and pulled her, he had the intent necessary for assault; alternatively they may conclude that he lacked the intent necessary for assault but had displayed recklessness which caused her to fall and sustain injury. Of course, if the Crown fail to establish that the accused acted in the manner libelled or that he had the mens rea required for either of the alternative charges, they will acquit the accused. I would not anticipate that a sheriff would have any difficulty in giving a jury comprehensible directions in relation to this indictment. In my opinion a jury which has received proper directions should be well able to understand the difference between the alternative charges.

The sheriff sustained the preliminary plea and dismissed the alternative charge on the basis of *Quinn v Cunningham* which was of course binding upon him. As I have already indicated, in my opinion the alternative charge in this indictment is a relevant charge. I would accordingly move your Lordships to sustain this appeal, to reverse the decision of the sheriff dated 23 September 1992 and to remit to the sheriff to proceed as accords.

LORD MURRAY.—The issue raised in this Crown appeal is whether a charge of culpable, wilful and reckless conduct causing severe injury and permanent disfigurement, as an alternative to a charge of assault to severe injury and permanent disfigurement, constitutes a crime known to the law of Scotland. The Crown maintains that the alternative charge does relevantly libel a crime. The accused respondent contends that it does not. His plea to the relevancy of the alternative charge was sustained in the sheriff court. Against that decision the present note of appeal is taken by the Crown. This issue raises the question whether *Quinn v Cunningham* was correctly decided. A full bench was convened in light of the possibility that *Quinn* might require to be overruled.

In presenting the appeal the Lord Advocate referred to substantial authority prior to *Quinn* for the view that reckless conduct causing injury was a crime according to the law of Scotland. This was reflected in textbooks from Hume through Alison to Macdonald, *Criminal Law* (5th ed), at pp 141-142. Illustrative cases included *McHaffie*; *Latto*; *Young*; and *Smith*.

A These cases vouched the proposition that, to constitute a relevant charge of reckless conduct, it was sufficient to aver recklessness causing actual injury. The decision of the court in *Quinn* was a departure from this view. The doubt expressed by Lord Sorn was well founded. It was accepted that in *Quinn* the complaint did not libel recklessness "to the danger of the lieges". Lord Justice General Clyde found this omission fatal because, as he says at 1956 SLT, p 56, he regards the charge as consisting of two separate

B parts: "firstly riding a pedal cycle in a reckless manner, and secondly causing it to collide with someone whereby slight injury resulted". By this approach he does not allow for recklessness to be qualified by the attribute of causing actual injury. On the authorities an inference of danger to the public was to be drawn from actual injury caused. As Lord Sorn put it, "it might be argued that the statement of that fact was equivalent to making use of the *nomen juris*". Section 48 of the Criminal Procedure (Scot-

C land) Act 1975 provided that it was unnecessary to use qualifying words such as "wilfully" or "culpably and recklessly" in indicting for a crime. Section 44 of the Act rendered it unnecessary to specify a charge by any nomen juris, it being enough that the indictment sets forth facts relevant and sufficient to constitute an indictable crime. The case of *Quinn* should be overruled and the previous common law view affirmed.

Counsel for the respondent took his stand upon the position that the alternative charge properly construed

D did not disclose a crime or was simply a charge of assault. It was not necessary to use the actual word "assault" provided that the libel amounted in law to assault. In fact the narratives in the assault charge and in the alternative charge were identical, so that a conviction on the alternative charge would amount as a matter of law to a conviction for assault. Seizing and pushing to severe injury constituted assault, given that there was mens rea. Carelessness, negligence or even recklessness could not provide mens rea without an

E element of danger express or implied.

In my opinion the court in *Quinn* were right to emphasise the high degree of culpability required to be averred and proved before reckless conduct as a crime at common law could be established. Carelessness, negligence or even recklessness in general are not enough. There must, I think, be conduct deliberately done in face of potential danger to another or others in complete disregard of the consequences for him or them. That quality of recklessness can be averred by

F the phrase "to the danger of the lieges" as the case of *Quinn* asserts. But that quality of recklessness may also be inferred from averments that the reckless conduct in fact caused substantial injury to another person. It is to be noted that the case of *Quinn* involved no more than a summary charge and it was averred that only slight injuries resulted. Further the case involved what was in substance a minor road traffic offence. Those considerations incline me to the view that *Quinn* was rightly decided on its facts and the particular terms of the charge. But insofar as the

case asserts that the phrase "to the danger of the lieges" or words to that effect are necessary for a rele- G vant charge of reckless conduct, I beg to differ, on the basis of the line of authority on which the Lord Advocate relies.

I turn now to deal with the respondent's contention that no true alternative is libelled — just the same species facti inferring a crime which is in law assault, whatever it may be called. The words "seize" and "push", it was said, described modes of assault or attack upon the person. If the seizing or the pushing were done with criminal intent it was assault. While H this contention is persuasive it is, I think, fallacious. Not all seizing or pushing is done with intent to injure, which is the mens rea necessary for assault. Persons such as policemen, bus conductors or ambulancemen and others have from time to time to seize and push people, without any criminal intent, in the course of their employment. I do not think that a bouncer is in a different position. He may have to eject people from the premises for which he is responsible by manhandling them with reasonable force. No I criminal intent can be imputed to that. Of course, even lawful handling of another may spill over readily into assault. However if reasonable force is not exceeded, ejection may nonetheless be culpably reckless, I consider, if insisted upon in face of danger to the person being ejected or to that person's actual severe injury. In my view the alternative libel amounts to this, even if it is not too obvious from the wording used in the charge.

For the foregoing reasons I agree with your Lord- J ship in the chair that this appeal succeeds. I also agree that *Quinn v Cunningham* should be overruled in so far as it asserts that an averment of danger to the lieges is required for a relevant charge of culpable recklessness.

LORD McCLUSKEY.—The indictment in this case contains what appear to be two charges, expressed in the alternative. The first, which is a charge of K common law assault, avers against the panel that: [his Lordship quoted the terms of the first alternative charge and continued:]

It is thus in the ordinary form for such a charge: it avers a date, a place, and a series of acts allegedly done by the panel on the occasion specified. It also, by way of notice, alleges that the person on whom the acts were done suffered certain consequences, that is to say, she was caused to fall down stairs and on to the roadway where she was struck by a motor vehicle and L severely injured and disfigured; such consequences constitute aggravations of the charge of assault.

Section 44 of the Criminal Procedure (Scotland) Act 1975 provides: [his Lordship quoted its terms and continued:] Despite that, but in accordance with the usual practice in assault cases on indictment, the charge which I have quoted does specify the nomen juris of the crime charged. But, even if it had not done so, the narrative of the facts there set forth would certainly have been understood as one setting forth facts

relevant and sufficient to constitute an indictable
A crime. Any Scots criminal lawyer would have known
from the narrative itself precisely what the crime was:
it was common law assault (with aggravations). In our
practice, the Crown usually includes in the charge a
nomen juris but sometimes it does not. Thus, in a rape
case, it is now usual to end the charge with the words
"and you did rape her" (the older practice was to say
"and you did ravish her", but "ravish" was simply a
synonym for "rape"). Murder charges invariably
contain the word "murder" —"and you did murder
B him". But a charge of which the nomen juris is "culpable homicide" does not use that precise term. It will
commonly, though not invariably, contain the word
"culpable" or "culpably" and will also use the word
"kill", the associated noun of which is, of course, a
synonym of "homicide". In some cases, the crime
itself is innominate: there is no nomen juris. An
example may be found in *Kerr v Hill*, where the
charge was that the accused falsely represented to the
police that he had seen a road accident between a pedal
C cyclist and an omnibus thus causing the police to
waste their time investigating an accident which had
not occurred and also bringing the lieges under
unjustified suspicion. In that context, Lord Fleming,
at 1936 SLT, p 321, said, reflecting the provision now
contained in s 44: "The *nomen juris* of a charge is,
however, immaterial."

Khaliq v HM Advocate is the best known recent
example of an innominate crime charged without a
nomen juris. In that case the Lord Justice General,
D Lord Emslie, quoted with approval the opinion of
Lord Justice General Clyde in *McLaughlan v Boyd*,
1933 SLT at p 631: "It would be a mistake to imagine
that the criminal common law of Scotland counten-
ances any precise and exact categorisation of the forms
of conduct which amount to crime. It has been pointed
out many times in this Court that such is not the
nature or quality of the criminal law of Scotland. I
need only refer to the well-known passage in the
opening of Baron Hume's institutional work, in which
E the broad definition of crime — a doleful or wilful
offence against society in the matter of 'violence, dishonesty, falsehood, indecency, irreligion' — is laid
down."

Lord Emslie then went on to notice the effect of s 44
(which is a re-enactment of a provision in the 1887
Act). However, for the most part, the modern practice
is to specify a nomen juris in those cases which have
a nomen juris and, I think almost invariably, in assault
F cases on indictment. This practice, however useful
and common, may nonetheless disguise the fact that
what matters is not the nomen juris but the averment
of facts relevant and sufficient to constitute an indictable crime. If such facts *are* averred, the absence of the
word "assault" will not matter, because the indictment will contain an indictable crime. If such facts are
not averred, then the use of the word "assault" will
not make the charge relevant. To put the matter
shortly, therefore, the use of a label, a nomen juris, is
an optional extra; the essential thing is to set forth
facts relevant and sufficient to constitute an indictable

crime. There can, in my opinion, be no doubt that the
averment "you did assault" is not an averment of a G
fact of the kind that is mentioned in the final phrase
in s 44; on the contrary, it is simply a specification of
a nomen juris.

From that discussion of the first charge, I now turn
to the so called alternative charge. What it does is to
set forth *precisely* the same averments of fact without,
however, any specification of a nomen juris. What it
also does, however, is to use a number of familiar
adverbs, namely "culpably, wilfully and recklessly".
As to these adverbs, it may be marked that when this H
case was first indicted the alternative charge did not
contain the word "wilfully". Further, the Lord
Advocate submitted to this court that the words
"culpably" and "wilfully" added nothing at all to the
charge and it would, he submitted, be a relevant
charge if they were simply omitted. He also acknowledged that all these words, whether expressly
included or not, were implied into the charge by virtue
of s 48 which provides, inter alia: "It shall not be
necessary in any indictment to allege that any act of I
commission or omission therein charged was done or
omitted to be done 'wilfully' or . . . 'culpably and
recklessly' . . . or to use any similar words or expressions qualifying any act charged, but such qualifying
allegation shall be implied in every case."

The express inclusion in the alternative charge of
these adverbs seems to me to risk obfuscating and
confusing the issue because, in the context of the averments of fact, the word "wilfully" is quite contradictory of the word "recklessly"; and the role of the J
word "culpably" is wholly obscure because it contradicts "wilfully" and is, in effect, no more than a
milder version of "recklessly". However, the Lord
Advocate submitted that what was really being averred
was that the specified acts were *recklessly* done and
that to do such acts recklessly whether to the danger
of the lieges or to the actual injury of one of them (as
here) was to commit an indictable crime. He gave us
examples of indictable crimes of this character. Senior
counsel for the respondent conceded that certain kinds K
of reckless conduct causing injury or danger to the
lieges would constitute an indictable crime. This concession was, in my opinion, properly given, and like
your Lordships I am content to accept it and need not
here reiterate the examination of the case law on this
matter by your Lordship in the chair and Lord
Prosser. In certain circumstances, reckless conduct
which causes injury or endangers the lieges may well
constitute an indictable crime. For that reason alone,
I have no difficulty in agreeing with your Lordships L
that the reasoning of the Lord Justice General in
Quinn v Cunningham is not supportable in the light of
the full citation of authority which we were privileged
to have.

But, and this I consider to be an essential point,
what is averred in the alternative charge in the present
case is a series of facts that do not constitute the crime
of assault: otherwise the alternative charge would be a
mere duplication of the first charge and the indictment
would then be incompetent. So if it is not assault

which is charged in the alternative, what is it? It is said
A to be — and it would have to be — something *less* than
assault. The Lord Advocate acknowledged that it was
not averred as a crime of negligence; he submitted, as
I understood him, that the libel showed that it was a
crime of *intention*. That being so, it appears to be it
might have been appropriate to use the word "wilfully" and omit the words "culpably" and "recklessly". However, we have to take the charge as we
find it, with the Lord Advocate's acknowledgment
that what was libelled was that the accused acted
B intentionally: the accused, in other words, *intended* to
seize hold of Jane Breen; he *intended* to push her on
the body. I do not see how it could be said that what
is libelled does not involve intention. You cannot
unintentionally "seize hold" of a person and unintentionally "push" her. That must be conduct which
results from, and perhaps evidences, an intention. But
if the accused intended to seize hold of Jane Breen and
intended to push her on the body and did both these
things, in that order, then that must be an assault, if
C the intent is found to have been evil. If it is not an
assault, I do not know what it is. In the course of the
debate the word "manhandle" was used in order to
avoid begging the question at issue; but the charge
does not talk about manhandling that was culpably
excessive. It talks about wilful seizing and pushing.
There is an obvious logical fallacy in using the term
"manhandling" as a synonym for what is actually
averred well in the words actually used in the indictment. A man who wilfully, intentionally seizes hold of
D a woman and pushes her on the body, thereby causing
her to fall down a flight of stairs, is guilty of common
law assault, provided he has the necessary evil intent,
which is an essential ingredient in such a crime. (I
have used the word "thereby" because the Lord
Advocate in his submission said that that word fell to
be implied before the word "cause".) Although evil
intent is a necessary ingredient in the crime of assault,
"evil intent" is not averred when the Crown charges
an accused with assault. No doubt that is because the
E evil intent is treated, for the purposes of proof, not as
a primary fact of which notice has to be given but as
a secondary fact which falls to be proved by inference
from the primary facts (principally the actings of the
accused on the occasion in question).

I would have equal difficulty in understanding how
one can "recklessly" *seize* hold of a person and *push*
her on the body thereby causing her to fall down a
flight of stairs. That just does not seem to me to make
sense. If I were the trial judge and I had to direct the
F jury as to what the alternative crime was, to tell them
how they were to differentiate it from assault, and
what state of mind it was necessary to prove on the
second charge I should not know how to begin. There
was no reported case found in the careful researches of
the Lord Advocate and senior counsel for the respondent in which a person who *intended* to seize another
and manhandle that other by seizing, pushing and
causing that other to fall, and who did these things,
had ever been charged with any crime other than that
of assault. I do not believe there is such a crime. It is

of course not the function of this court nowadays to
invent new crimes, nor indeed were we being G
avowedly invited to do so. This court can acknowledge, and characterise as criminal, conduct which is
really a new way of committing an old crime. But it
cannot be said that wilfully and recklessly seizing hold
of a woman and pushing her on the body causing her
to fall down a flight of stairs is a new way of committing an old crime. It is just an old, and all too common,
way of committing an all too common crime, the crime
of assault. It is always essential to give consideration
before charging a jury as to the directions which are H
appropriate in relation to mens rea. On this indictment it would be necessary to explain to the jury what
constituted mens rea in relation to the first charge
bearing the nomen juris "assault". It would then be
necessary to explain to the jury that, in relation to the
second or alternative charge, they would reach that
charge if, but only if, they had held that they could *not*
infer the mens rea of assault. What then *is* the mens
rea (not being that appropriate to the crime of assault)
which turns the wilful seizing and pushing of the I
victim, thereby causing her to fall, into an innominate
crime? Lord Prosser's discussion of the concepts of
recklessness and danger, intent, gross negligence and
the existence and foreseeability of possible harm to
others — all of which the trial judge would have to
consider explaining to the jury — serves to illustrate
how unnecessarily sophisticated and remote from
reality we are in danger of rendering the law when, in
a matter of this kind, it should be simple and easy for
juries to grasp.   J

I can well understand how in the past the court,
applying the principles which Lord Clyde referred to
in *McLaughlan v Boyd*, discovered various innominate
crimes, the common characteristic of which was that
the conduct was reckless and unconscionable because
it exposed the lieges to unacceptable dangers. Thus, as
noted by Sheriff Gordon in his *Criminal Law* (2nd ed),
at para 29-55, the court had recognised as indictable
crimes such activities as the reckless discharge of fire- K
arms, the negligent driving of horses and railway
engines, the negligent navigation of vessels, the negligent use of explosives and negligence in erecting
buildings. But it appears to me that this series of
extensions of the criminal calendar was necessary only
when there was no known crime which fitted the facts.
Where one has got an averment of wilful seizing of a
person and pushing her on the body thereby causing
her to fall down a flight of stairs there is absolutely no
need to invent any innominate crime. The familiar
crime of assault fits the bill perfectly. I should simply L
be repeating myself if I sought to take the matter any
further. In my opinion, the alternative charge in the
indictment is irrelevant on the ground that it does not
disclose a crime known to the law of Scotland. In my
opinion, there is no crime known to the law of Scotland consisting of wilfully seizing another human
being, pushing her on the body and causing her to fall
down a flight of stairs, except the crime of assault. As
ex hypothesi the alternative charge does not contain a
charge of assault it cannot be relevant.

I appreciate that it is possible for a libel to contain averments of fact, proof of all of which would entitle the jury to convict of one crime or alternatively of another: the obvious example is a murder charge containing a narrative of violent assault. On such a libel the jury can return a verdict of murder or a verdict of culpable homicide, the difference between the two being warranted by the difference between the mens rea required for the respective crimes, or because some circumstance such as provocation warrants a reduction from murder to culpable homicide. But that is, I believe, a special case. Indeed in that type of case there is *never* an alternative charge of culpable homicide set forth in the indictment (and based upon the same species facti). The trial judge nonetheless will direct the jury that, if the necessary mens rea for murder is not established, the alternative verdict of culpable homicide is open to them. I have never known it to be suggested, however, that on an assault charge, particularly one libelling wilful seizing and pushing, the judge should direct the jury that it is open to them to return a verdict not of assault but of wilful, culpable and reckless conduct to the danger of the lieges or to the actual injury of any of them. I can also readily envisage circumstances — quite distinct from those of common assault — in which culpable and reckless conduct involving physical manhandling of others could be charged as a crime. For example, if a person, whether acting out of high spirits or to escape the police or just for bravado, ran the wrong way down an upward moving escalator crowded with people, thus barging into people, he might be guilty of wilful, culpable and reckless conduct. But I doubt very much if that is how such conduct would be charged. It would obviously be charged as a breach of the peace. Similarly, in circumstances not amounting to assault, where a person is accused of manhandling the lieges in such a way as to put them in danger he could certainly be charged with a breach of the peace. Accordingly what the court is being asked to do is to sanction the inclusion in the indictment of a charge which is innominate, has no real precedent, and, if it is a crime, is properly to be described either as an assault or a breach of the peace. I see no reason to lend my support to such a novel and unnecessary step.

We were informed that the accused was employed as a "bouncer" or steward in the premises at which the incident described in the indictment took place. In my view, the character of the accused's employment has no bearing whatsoever upon any matter of law that we have to decide at this stage. There is not one law for bouncers and another law for the rest. The common law in relation to conduct that might be characterised as constituting the crime of assault or of breach of the peace is the same for all persons, even although it is obvious that some, such as policemen, may well find themselves roughly manhandling persons whom they have to restrain in the course of their duty, without themselves being guilty of assault: the legal justification for not regarding as criminal their use of force in such circumstances would be the absence of the mens rea of assault. It may be that others, such as club stewards, might similarly receive the benefit of the doubt from the tribunal of fact if the evidence showed that their genuine and only aim was to preserve the peace and maintain good order at the place where they were employed. The evaluation of mens rea is a jury function to be exercised with common sense. None of this, however, has anything to do with the correct analysis of what this indictment properly means.

LORD MORISON.—The terms of the indictment with which this appeal is concerned are set out in your Lordship's opinion. The first part alleges the crime of assault, and no question as to its competency or relevancy arises. The second part is stated as an alternative to the charge of assault, but the respondent's actings which are libelled as constituting the alternative crime are the same as those which are alleged to have made him guilty of assault. The prosecutor has clearly intended to charge the respondent with having committed the acts libelled either with intention to injure the complainer, which is an assault, or alternatively with having committed the same acts recklessly whereby she was injured, which is not an assault.

The first question which therefore arises is whether the allegation in the alternative charge of reckless conduct causing injury constitutes a crime. This question is of general importance. If the allegation does constitute a crime, the further question arises whether that crime has been relevantly libelled in the present case as an alternative to the charge of assault. This question does not in my view raise any question of general importance. I do not understand any issues to have been raised in this appeal apart from the two questions to which I have referred.

In the sheriff court it was apparently submitted, as it was expressed by the sheriff, that "while it was an offence to engage in culpable and reckless conduct which endangered the lieges, it was not an offence culpably and recklessly to cause injury to a particular person". This submission was primarily based on dicta in *Quinn v Cunningham*, and it was in light of that decision that the case was heard by this court of five judges. But the submission was not advanced to this court, it being conceded on the respondent's behalf that a libel containing an allegation of reckless conduct causing injury might constitute sufficient notice of a crime without specific reference to endangerment of the lieges. In view of this concession the question may be dealt with quite briefly.

I can think of no sensible reason why reckless conduct causing actual injury should to any lesser extent be capable of constituting a crime than the same conduct which merely endangers the lieges, and I do not understand the case of *Quinn* to have decided the contrary. That case determined that a complaint libelling recklessness on the part of a pedal cyclist and that he caused the cycle to collide with someone whereby slight injuries resulted, did not justify the inference that the alleged recklessness reached the high standard of culpability which was required to demonstrate what had been referred to in *Paton v HM Advocate* as

"criminal indifference to consequences". I see no
A reason to doubt the soundness of that decision in light
of the facts of the case, but there are passages in the
opinion of the Lord Justice General which go beyond
it: these are to the effect that the words "to the danger
of the lieges" are "required as an amplification of the
recklessness" before any crime can be held to have
been libelled.

I consider that these passages should be disapproved. The Lord Advocate cited ample authority
to support the view that an allegation of resultant
B injury may be sufficient in itself to demonstrate the
degree of recklessness required to constitute criminal
conduct. It is unnecessary for me to repeat this citation
of authority since its effect was not disputed. Thus I
did not understand the respondent's counsel to submit
that a jury would not be entitled to infer that the
manner in which in the present case the complainer's
injuries were said to have been sustained demonstrated
a sufficient degree of recklessness to constitute
"criminal indifference to consequences". In my
C opinion a jury would be so entitled, and I see no difficulty in directing them on the matter.

Accepting as he did that an allegation of reckless
conduct causing injury could constitute a crime, the
only argument which, according to my understanding,
the respondent's counsel put forward in the present
case was that what was alleged in the alternative
charge was not a true alternative to the first part of the
libel, since both parts involved the same species facti
D on the part of the respondent and the same crime.
This submission as I understood it entirely depended
on the view that the alternative allegation that the
respondent wilfully seized hold of the complainer and
pushed her constituted the same crime, that of assault,
which is contained in the principal charge.

I do not attach any significance to the word "wilfully". That word can imply reckless disregard for
someone's safety as well as intention to injure that
person, and it provides no indication whether or not
E an assault has been alleged.

It was submitted that the deliberate acts of seizing
and pushing the complainer were inconsistent with
the allegation of recklessness. But the word "recklessly" is not used to indicate that these acts were
other than deliberate, but rather to imply that the
respondent performed them with culpable disregard of
their consequences to the complainer. It is quite easy
to envisage circumstances in which deliberate acts of
seizing and pushing someone do not constitute an
F assault, although in the absence of any legitimate
explanation they would be presumed to do so. The
alternative charge assumes, contrary to the allegation
in the principal charge, that such special circumstances existed, no doubt because the respondent was
employed as a "bouncer" at a club, and the legitimate
performance of his duties in that capacity might have,
in certain circumstances, involved him in deliberate
acts of seizing and pushing so as to avoid some danger
which he reasonably apprehended might occur. There
is in my opinion nothing illogical in the allegation that

he performed these acts recklessly, and it is clearly
possible to distinguish between the two alternatives as G
constituting two different crimes. The alternative
charge is in my opinion relevantly libelled and I would
accordingly allow the appeal and remit to the sheriff
to proceed as accords.

LORD PROSSER.—This is an appeal from the
sheriff court in Glasgow. At a preliminary diet, the
sheriff upheld a plea to the relevancy of an alternative
charge contained in the indictment.

The primary charge is to the effect that on 20 March H
1991, at Tin Pan Alley, 39 Mitchell Street, Glasgow,
the now respondent Andrew Harris assaulted one Jane
Breen. What he is said to have done is "seize hold of
her, push her on the body and cause her to fall down
a flight of stairs and onto the roadway outside the
premises as a result of which she was struck by motor
vehicle registered number F594 CHS, then being
driven in Mitchell Street . . . all to her severe injury
and permanent disfigurement". The alternative
charge contains exactly the same factual narrative, but I
in place of the charge of assault, contains a charge that
the respondent "culpably, wilfully and recklessly" did
the same things.

The appeal has an odd procedural background,
which I see no need to discuss. At the preliminary
diet, for reasons which again I see no need to discuss,
the sheriff proceeded upon the basis that standing the
decision in *Quinn v Cunningham* the alternative charge
did not disclose a crime known to the law of Scotland.
The present court has been convened in order that J
Quinn v Cunningham may be reconsidered.

Both the decision in *Quinn*, and the terms of the
present indictment, seem to me to be likely to cause
confusion. I come to these matters later. But this case
has been seen as raising a more general question, and
I deal with that first.

The submission for the Crown, that the alternative
charge does indeed disclose a crime, rests upon this
proposition: that reckless conduct causing injury to K
another is a crime at common law. Before the sheriff,
a contrary contention was apparently advanced, to the
effect that reckless conduct will only be a crime if it
is to the danger of the lieges; and that a libel which
fails to set forth that the allegedly reckless conduct was
to the danger of the lieges will be irrelevant, notwithstanding that it may set forth that the conduct caused
actual injury to another. Before this court, senior
counsel for the respondent accepted, as I understood
him, that reckless conduct causing injury is indeed a L
crime. In my opinion he was plainly right to concede
this, and this court should affirm it.

I can see no basis in principle for holding that reckless conduct which actually causes injury is not a
crime, while reckless conduct causing danger to
others, but no injury, is a crime. It is not suggested
that reckless conduct in itself, in the absence of either
danger or injury to others, might be a crime. At the
other extreme, it is not in doubt that reckless conduct
causing death is a crime. That being so, if the same

conduct has caused injury rather than death, I should expect it in principle to be regarded as a crime. If anything, the doubtful case in principle would be that where no injury has resulted, although the safety of others has been put in danger. Furthermore, the various authorities cited to us by the Lord Advocate in the course of his submissions in my opinion demonstrate, convincingly if not always very clearly, the proposition that in our law, reckless conduct which causes either danger or injury to others is a crime.

The case of *Ezekiel McHaffie*, where one man had died and another had been seriously injured as a result of the same reckless conduct, shows both that such conduct causing such injury is a crime, and that it is this result, rather than any danger, which in these circumstances completes the crime. *HM Advocate v John Latto* is another case of serious injury. The criminality of the conduct causing that injury was treated as analogous to the criminality of culpable homicide in non-assault cases: it was observed that "the criminal neglect was the same whether the persons here were killed or not". But it is also to be noted that the indictment, when dealing with the results which complete the crime, treats injury to the person and danger as alternatives. There is no suggestion in that case, any more than there had been in the earlier case of *HM Advocate v Robert Young*, that where resulting injury is charged, danger must be so also. In *HM Advocate v Smith and McNeil*, the sufficiency of danger as an element which makes reckless conduct criminal, even in the absence of injury, is clearly expressed. That was a case of the reckless discharge of firearms, but it is made clear, by the references to furious driving and reckless steering, that the "reckless conduct" element in the crime is not limited to any particular field of conduct. What is being said relates to reckless conduct of any kind, and the sufficiency of danger, without injury, to complete the crime.

After a reference to this last mentioned case, and the example of reckless steering to the danger of passengers, it is observed in Macdonald, *Criminal Law*, p 142 that "Such offences are, of course, more heinous when injury results to the lieges". The passage continues as follows: "But although acts of rashness such as those above described are punishable even where no accident follows, they are only held to be so because of their manifest wilfulness, and of the general danger caused by such wanton proceedings. In other cases, in order to make a relevant charge of danger to the lieges, it may be necessary to specify that injury resulted to some of them." The first of these sentences seems to me to be a reasonably clear explanation of why, despite the absence of actual injury to anyone, the law nonetheless refuses to see the reckless conduct as a "bare" act with no consequences, and treats it as having "caused" general danger. If danger is thus seen as a result of the conduct, the crime of causing such danger, like the crime of causing injury, falls quite naturally into the category of result crimes. Moreover, while on first reading I did not really understand the second sentence which I have quoted, I have come to the conclusion that it is indeed consistent with the previous sentence, and indeed with the line of authority to which I have referred. I do not think that it is being suggested that where, say, an individual has been injured, that specific injury is to be seen merely as evidence of danger to the lieges, with such danger constituting the essence of the crime. The sentence is I think dealing with a more limited class of cases, where some people have been injured, while others have merely been endangered. In such a situation, the fact that some have actually been injured would go far towards establishing that the conduct which results in their injury constituted a danger to others nearby. And in some such cases, it might be only the occurrence of such injury to some, which would adequately demonstrate that the conduct involved danger to others. If however it is being suggested that taking recklessness as established, there is only a completed crime if it has generally dangerous as well as specifically injurious consequences, then upon the basis of principle, and the other authorities to which I have referred, the sentence should in my opinion be disapproved.

I would add this, in relation to those cases where there has been reckless conduct, but no injury. It is important to make it clear that our common law does not treat as criminal conduct which, even although reckless, is truly to be regarded as having had no consequences. Where danger to others is the consequence which transforms the reckless conduct into a crime, it will be important to libel that, and prove it. What complicates the matter, and has perhaps tended to confuse it, is this. Recklessness and danger are not unrelated concepts. I see no need here to embark upon a definition of recklessness: in relation to reckless conduct causing injury or danger, it has in my opinion the same meaning as it has in relation to culpable homicide, where death has been caused by reckless conduct, and is not a crime of intent, with the death being caused by an assault. Whether one uses the word recklessness, or such descriptions as gross negligence, that is a familiar concept which I think is readily conveyed to, and understood by, juries. But it involves an assessment of duties owed to others, which in turn depend upon the foreseeability of harmful consequences. Analysis probably becomes unreal; but I think that one can say that in deciding that some conduct has been reckless, one will always be at least very close to saying that it involved a failure to pay due regard to foreseeable consequences of that conduct, which were foreseeably likely to cause injury to others, and which could correspondingly reasonably be called dangerous in relation to them. If that is so, then (i) the category of reckless conduct which is not to the danger of others will be empty, or nearly so; (ii) it will make little or no difference whether one considers the recklessness of the conduct before the danger that it causes, or the danger before the recklessness, since the two are in practical terms interdependent; and (iii) even where the libel is to the effect that reckless conduct has caused injury, or indeed death, so that there is no need to libel danger as the result of the conduct, a judgment as to whether the conduct constituted a danger to others will in fact have to be made in this sense, that the existence and foreseeability of possible harm to others will be inherent in deciding whether the conduct can properly be described as reckless. I am not persuaded that there is any real difficulty in all this. But in cases where actual injury has resulted from the allegedly reckless conduct, I think the possibility of danger is relevant not as a result, but as an inherent element in recklessness itself.

I come to the present indictment. If reckless conduct causing injury is a crime, there is no need to libel danger, either to the person allegedly injured, or to others. I did not understand counsel for the respondent to suggest that the alternative charge in the present indictment would be defective on that basis, if it were otherwise a relevant libel of reckless conduct causing injury. Moreover, although the alternative charge asserts that the respondent "culpably, wilfully and recklessly" did what he is alleged to have done, I did not understand counsel for the respondent to submit that the presence of the word "culpably", or the word "wilfully", rendered the alternative charge irrelevant, if in the absence of these words it would be a relevant charge of reckless conduct causing injury. I would however say that I have very considerable doubts as to whether the word "wilfully" should ever be coupled with the word "recklessly" in a libel, where the essence of the crime is reckless conduct causing either danger or injury. The fact that certain of the acts included in the reckless conduct are in themselves conscious or intentional or deliberate acts is adequately expressed by referring to them as acts of the accused, and does not make it necessary to describe the whole course of conduct as being "wilful" as well as "reckless". In my opinion, the word "wilful" should be reserved for crimes of intent. Moreover, in my opinion the word "culpably", although it has a long history in such contexts, is superfluous and confusing in charges of this kind. Despite past usage, I should regard charges of this type as easier to explain and understand if the word "recklessly" were to be used without a run-up of other probably misleading terms. (In this connection, I would add that in my opinion, in those cases where reckless conduct is not said to have caused injury, and where a reference to danger is accordingly appropriate, talk of danger to "the lieges" is unhelpful and undesirable: special legal terminology is often important, but danger to others can be referred to as danger to others, without obsolete terms which need explaining.)

Counsel's criticism of the alternative charge took a rather different form. It was emphasised that the whole factual narrative was identical in the primary charge and in the alternative. The only difference was that in the primary charge, these acts were described as an assault, whereas in the alternative charge (ignoring the words "culpably" and "wilfully") they are described as "recklessly" done. Both charges were really the same. They were indeed not merely the same: the factual narrative was one of an attack on Miss Breen, of the type which would constitute an assault. While the alternative version of the charge

omitted the word "assault", and added the word "recklessly", that extra word would be implied by statute into the primary charge in any event, and the presence of the word "assault" as a nomen juris was not essential. Reference was made to the Criminal Procedure (Scotland) Act 1975, ss 44 and 48.

In my opinion, these criticisms are misconceived. The bare facts set forth in a libel may constitute one crime and no other. Even in such a case, proof of the crime will require not only proof of the essential facts libelled, but proof also of what need not be mentioned in the libel — the mens rea appropriate to that crime. In other cases, the facts set out in the libel may be relevant and sufficient to constitute not one crime only, but any one of two or more crimes, the appropriate verdict depending on the full facts established in evidence, and in particular the nature of any mens rea so established. Such alternative verdicts may be open within a single charge, based on a single narrative of fact. Indeed, in view of the terms of s 48 of the 1975 Act, I think that a verdict of reckless conduct causing injury would at least theoretically have been open to a jury if the present indictment had contained only the primary charge, since the reference to assault could be deleted, and the implied reference to recklessness relied upon. But that possibility is probably theoretical rather than practical, since upon such a charge standing alone in an indictment, the Crown would in most circumstances be regarded as having perilled its case upon proof of assault, and the alternative of recklessness would not need to be put to the jury. In any event, if the Crown, at the time when the indictment is drafted, do not wish to peril their case upon proof of assault, and wish to put before the jury the alternative possibility of reckless conduct causing injury, I am satisfied that the proper and fair course is to include that alternative expressly in the indictment, as has been done here.

If it were thought that there were alternative possibilities in relation to the basic narratives of fact, no doubt that might be reflected in the two alternative libels. That might have happened here, for example, if for the purposes of the assault charge the Crown had felt able to accuse the respondent of assaulting Miss Breen not merely by seizing her and pushing her (with the fall down the stairs as a consequence of the assault) but of an assault which included an intentional push down the stairs. It might be thought that a push of that kind could only be seen as an assault, with no room for regarding it as merely reckless conduct free of the mens rea of assault. In such a situation, if reckless conduct causing injury were to be brought in as an alternative, the factual narrative in the alternative charge would differ, being restricted to an accusation of pushing which caused the fall. But in a case such as the present, I see no significance in the fact that the factual narrative is the same in both charges. The choice for the jury will not be a choice between two different basic accounts of matters. It will be a choice as to which of the two possible crimes, if either, they hold to have been proved, having considered the whole evidence and the differences between recklessness and the mens rea of assault.

I would add that if the alternative charge in this case stood as the only charge in an indictment, I should be very reluctant to hold that the terms of s 44 of the 1975 Act permitted the Crown to seek a conviction of assault. In any event, in a case such as this, where the Crown have explicitly separated the charge of assault from the alternative charge of reckless conduct causing injury, I am satisfied that upon a proper interpretation of the indictment as a whole, each of the alternative charges is to be read as limited to that crime with which it explicitly deals. In my opinion, these are genuine alternatives, properly libelled.

I should mention two perhaps separate aspects of the criticisms made of this indictment. First, I think that it was suggested that once one had allegations of seizing and pushing, of this type, one had inevitably moved into the area of intentional attack amounting to assault, with no room, if the seizing and pushing were proved, for seeing them as simply reckless acts, devoid of the characteristics of an assault. Secondly, and perhaps correspondingly, I think it was suggested that the crime of reckless conduct causing injury could not really be constituted by acts such as seizing and pushing (which would more naturally be seen as the essence of assault) but was a crime which could only occur in circumstances where what was being done belonged to some category of action which generically required great care because of some obvious and general potential for serious damage to life and limb. On this view, reckless conduct causing injury could occur in relation to such things as the handling of explosives or fire, or the control of vessels at sea, or the driving of motor vehicles, but could not arise in relation to such ordinary daily actions as direct physical contact between people.

In my opinion, both of these criticisms are without foundation. Whether seizing and pushing amounts to an assault is a question of circumstances. For one person (and in particular a steward such as the respondent) to seize and push someone else could easily be an entirely innocent action, with such obvious aims as the protection of the person pushed from others who are out of control, making way for medical assistance or the like. Assault is not the only possibility, and in its absence, a want of care, possibly amounting to recklessness, remains on the cards. Nor is it true that one can only be reckless, in the required sense, in the "high risk" situations suggested. In those situations, with their obviously high risks, it may be easier to establish recklessness, because of the high awareness of risk, and high standard of care, to be expected in such circumstances. The nature of the activity will, generally speaking, make a finding of recklessness more likely than a finding of assault. Similarly, the simple and intentional nature of an act like pushing will in general make it easy to infer assault; and in almost all circumstances the very simplicity of the act, and its limited potential for causing significant injury, will make it absurd to suggest that it was reckless in the required sense. But these generalities do not create categories: just as the circumstances may demonstrate that a motor vehicle was driven not merely recklessly, but as a weapon of assault, so also a push, even of relatively light force and with no element of assault in it, may be held to have been reckless, because of the particular circumstances and potential hazards at the particular place and time. The cases in which it will be appropriate to charge reckless conduct causing injury not on its own, but as an alternative to assault, are in my opinion likely to be very few; and the cases in which, after trial, both alternatives require consideration will, I think, be even fewer. But I see no basis in principle for the law laying down a priori areas of human activity from which either of these crimes is deemed to be excluded. Statutory offences are another matter; but I am satisfied that at common law these are ordinary jury issues.

I come to *Quinn v Cunningham*. I am not sure that I can identify the ratio of that decision. The complaint opened with a charge that the accused did, at a time and place specified, "ride a pedal cycle in a reckless manner". If that had been all it said, and even if it had given a factual description of the recklessness, with no indication that this caused either danger or injury, then I satisfied that the complaint would disclose no crime. Even if it is possible to envisage conduct which is reckless in the required sense, without concomitant danger, danger or injury is part of the essence of the crime at common law. Moreover, the decision in *Quinn* is in my opinion plainly sound in identifying the degree of recklessness which is required at common law as being the degree identified in *Paton v HM Advocate*; so that the creation of any offence, on the basis of the lesser or different degree of culpability, would be a matter for Parliament, and not the courts.

But I am left with two concerns. First, it seems to me that the Lord Justice General has interpreted the word "reckless" contained in the complaint as meaning something different from the reckless disregard of consequences, or gross negligence, required by the *Paton* criterion. In my opinion, the word "reckless" should be read as an expression of that criterion, and I do not fully understand why the complaint was read (if it was) as irrelevant in relation to the degree of culpability libelled. Secondly, however, the complaint did not stop after these opening words. It went on with the words "and did cause it to collide with and knock down Francis Conway . . . whereby both sustained slight injuries". The Lord Justice General appears to treat this as a wholly separate matter, and on that basis, points out that this part of the complaint does not constitute a crime. I should have thought it clear that the complaint in that case (like the charges in this case) was concerned with a single matter, with the second part of the complaint specifying the mode of the recklessness, and its consequences.

While the Lord Justice General in *Quinn* did not read the allegation of injury as connected with the recklessness or an element in it, he deals with the submission that it was so connected. On that hypothesis, his concern is still that the appropriate degree of recklessness has not been libelled: "Mere recklessness by a pedal cyclist followed by an injury to a foot passenger does not constitute a crime in Scotland, any

A more than mere recklessness by driving followed by a death would constitute culpable homicide" (1956 SLT at p 57). And where dealing with matters more generally, he treats crimes committed by reckless conduct as belonging in the same category as non-assault culpable homicide: "the standard of culpability must be the same, whether its consequences are death or not". While he emphasises the difference between "a reckless act which in fact happens to result in injury" and "a reckless disregard of the safety of the public which in fact does injure someone", I think

B that the essential distinction which he is there drawing is once more the difference between recklessness of the type required by *Paton*, and "mere" recklessness of a lesser degree.

It is not clear to me why the inclusion of the words "to the danger of the lieges" in a libel should be read as raising the meaning of the word "reckless" from "mere" recklessness to "reckless disregard of consequences" of the type identified in *Paton*. In my opinion, since the common law in this area has no con-

C cern with lower or different degrees of recklessness, the word "reckless" in a libel is to be read as meaning recklessness of the appropriate degree, complete with all its implications as to the appreciation and disregard of consequences. If the meaning of the word "reckless" had been made plain, perhaps in other ways, to his satisfaction, and if he had been persuaded that the causal link between the reckless conduct and injury had also been properly libelled, then I am not at all sure that the Lord Justice General in *Quinn* would

D have seen any need to libel general danger as a result of the recklessness, in addition to the actual resulting injury. I suspect that one comes back to the inherent role of danger in considering whether there has been a reckless disregard of possible consequences, and a confusion between the place of danger in that analysis, and the need for danger to others as a result of the reckless conduct, in those cases where there is no actual resulting injury. In my opinion, the complaint in *Quinn* was relevant, and despite my doubts as to the

E precise ratio of the decision, I am satisfied that it should be overruled.

As regards the present case, I am satisfied that the alternative charge is to be treated as relevant, the only possibly irrelevant element in it being, in my opinion, the use of the word "wilfully", which I think the Lord Advocate accepted should probably not be there, and which was not treated by counsel for the respondent as destructive of the overall relevancy of the charge. I agree that the appeal should be sustained, and the

F decision of the sheriff reversed.

Counsel for Appellant, Lord Advocate (Lord Rodger of Earlsferry, QC); Solicitor, J D Lowe, Crown Agent — Counsel for Respondent, Bell, QC, McVicar; Solicitors, Macbeth, Currie & Co, WS (for Macdonald McCormick & Giusti Martin, Glasgow).

P W F

Zenel v Haddow

G

FIRST DIVISION

LORDS ALLANBRIDGE, MAYFIELD AND MORTON OF SHUNA

20 JULY 1993

Parent and child — Custody — International child abduction — Jurisdiction — Habitual residence of child — Child of unmarried parents taken to Australia in attempted reconciliation of parents — Whether habitual residence of mother established in Australia — Child Abduction and Custody Act 1985 (c 60), Sched 1, arts 3 and 4.

H

Parent and child — Custody — International child abduction — Child removed by mother clandestinely from country of habitual residence — Father having earlier agreed to attempted reconciliation there on understanding that mother could return to Scotland with child if reconciliation not successful — Parties thereafter living together for 15 months — Whether father had consented to removal of child — Child Abduction and Custody Act 1985 (c 60), Sched 1, arts 12 and 13.

I

Evidence — Review — Function of appellate tribunal in reviewing evidence — Weight to be attached to view of judge of first instance — Proof by affidavit evidence — Whether appellate court entitled to review evidence for itself.

The Child Abduction and Custody Act 1985, by incorporation of the Convention on the Civil Aspects of International Child Abduction, provides remedies where a child is wrongfully removed from the country where the child, in terms of art 3, was "habitually resident immediately before the removal". Under art 13 (a) of the Convention, the court of the country from which return of the child is sought is not bound to order return if the person opposing the return establishes that the person whose right to custody was breached by the removal "had consented to or subsequently acquiesced in the removal".

J

A child of unmarried parents was conceived in Australia, born in Scotland and went with her parents to Australia. The mother's return to Australia was averred by her, and accepted by the Lord Ordinary against the father's denial, to have been as part of an attempted reconciliation and subject to the agreement of the father that she and the child would return to Scotland if the attempted reconciliation failed. The father, mother and child lived together in family in Australia for about 15 months in the course of which the parents had had a new kitchen installed in the house they shared and had together contemplated a move to more spacious accommodation. The mother became unhappy in her relationship and clandestinely returned with the child to Scotland, having finally decided to return to Scotland only a few days before she did so. The father petitioned under the 1985 Act for an order for the return of the child to Australia. In the Outer House the mother in resisting such an order argued inter alia (1) that the child had not been habitually resident in Australia immediately before her

K

L

removal to Scotland, (2) that the father had consented to her terms for the attempted reconciliation, and (3) that, since the relationship between the parents had broken down, the father by acceptance of those terms had consented to the removal of the child to Scotland. The Lord Ordinary, after a proof on affidavits, determined that the mother and therefore the child had been habitually resident in Australia immediately before the removal but that the father's acceptance of the terms of the attempted reconciliation amounted to consent to the removal of the child, and dismissed the father's petition. The father reclaimed, arguing (1) that since the proof had been on affidavits, thus depriving the Lord Ordinary of the advantage of assessing credibility from the witnesses' demeanour, it was open to the Inner House to assess credibility and therefore the facts for itself, (2) that the Lord Ordinary had wrongly decided that the terms of the agreement as to reconciliation were still extant at the time of the removal, and (3) that in any event, the terms of the agreement did not amount to consent to the removal in terms of art 13 (a) of the Convention.

Held, that it was for the judge of first instance at the hearing on evidence on the affidavits to assess the weight and effect of that evidence, and his findings would only be displaced on appeal if the court was satisfied that his conclusions were perverse or such as no reasonable Lord Ordinary could have arrived at (pp 981K-L, 985C and 985L); (2) that the Lord Ordinary had been entitled to make the findings in fact that he made, and in particular (a) that the mother and therefore the child had acquired a habitual residence in Australia even although it had also been found that no reconciliation had been effected, and (b) that the terms of the agreement were still extant after 15 months of cohabitation (pp 982G and K-L, 985G-H and K-L and 985L); and (3) (Lord Morton of Shuna *dissenting*) that the agreement to removal did not require to be connected in time to the actual removal (pp 983G-J and 985I-J); and reclaiming motion *refused.*

Per Lord Morton of Shuna (*dissenting*): It was in accordance with the purpose of the Convention that consent to removal should require to be consent to the particular act of removal (p 986C-E).

Observations, per Lords Allanbridge and Morton of Shuna, on the requirement for expedition in dealing with petitions under the 1985 Act (pp 984A-E and 986J-L).

Petition under the Child Abduction and Custody Act 1985

Edji Zenel petitioned the Court of Session for an order under art 12 of the Convention on the Civil Aspects of International Child Abduction for the return of his child Brianne, who had been brought by her mother, Rhona Haddow, to Scotland from Australia. The mother was called as the respondent.

The petition and answers came before the Lord Ordinary (Marnoch) for a proof on affidavits.

Statutory provisions

The Convention on the Civil Aspects of International Child Abduction, set out in Sched 1 to the Child Abduction and Custody Act 1985, provides:

"Article 3

"The removal or the retention of a child is to be considered wrongful where — (a) it is in breach of rights of custody attributed to a person, an institution or any other body, either jointly or alone, under the law of the State in which the child was habitually resident immediately before the removal or retention; and (b) at the time of removal or retention those rights were actually exercised, either jointly or alone, or would have been so exercised but for the removal or retention.

"The rights of custody mentioned in sub-paragraph (a) above may arise in particular by operation of law or by reason of a judicial or administrative decision, or by reason of an agreement having legal effect under the law of that State.

"Article 4

"The Convention shall apply to any child who was habitually resident in a Contracting State immediately before any breach of custody or access rights. The Convention shall cease to apply when the child attains the age of 16 years.

"Article 5

"For the purposes of this Convention — (a) 'rights of custody' shall include rights relating to the care of the person of the child and, in particular, the right to determine the child's place of residence; (b) 'rights of access' shall include the right to take a child for a limited period of time to a place other than the child's habitual residence. . . .

"Article 12

"Where a child has been wrongfully removed or retained in terms of Article 3 and, at the date of the commencement of the proceedings before the judicial or administrative authority of the Contracting State where the child is, a period of less than one year has elapsed from the date of the wrongful removal or retention, the authority concerned shall order the return of the child forthwith. . . .

"Article 13

"Notwithstanding the provisions of the preceding Article, the judicial or administrative authority of the requested State is not bound to order the return of the child if the person, institution or other body which opposes its return establishes that — (a) the person, institution or other body having the care of the person of the child was not actually exercising the custody rights at the time of removal or retention, or had consented to or subsequently acquiesced in the removal or retention".

Cases referred to

A F (A Minor) (Abduction), Re [1992] FCR 269.
Dickson v Dickson, 1990 SCLR 692.
F (A Minor) (Child Abduction), Re [1992] 1 FLR 548.

J (A Minor), Re [1990] 2 AC 562; [1990] 3 WLR 492;
[1990] 2 All ER 961.

R v Barnet London Borough Council, ex p Shah [1983]
2 AC 309; [1983] 2 WLR 16; [1983] 1 All ER
226.

S (A Minor) (Abduction) (Joint Custody), Re [1991] 2
FLR 1.

On 25 March 1993 the Lord Ordinary *dismissed* the
petition.

LORD MARNOCH.—This is an application for
an order for the return of a child said to have been
wrongfully removed from Australia by its mother, the
respondent. The petitioner is the father of the child.
While the parties have at no time been married, it is
accepted by both that, under the relevant Australian
law, they each shared joint custody of the child in
question. As one might expect, the relevant legal provisions are to be found in the Convention on the Civil
Aspects of International Child Abduction as incorporated into UK law by the Child Abduction and
Custody Act 1985.

In her answers to the petition, the respondent
averred that there was a "grave risk" that the return
of the child to Australia would expose her to "physical
or psychological harm or otherwise place the child in
an intolerable situation" within the meaning of art 13
(b) of the Convention. In the course of the hearing,
however, it was accepted that, provided a reasonable
time was allowed to enable the respondent to return to
Australia along with the child, this ground of opposition could no longer be maintained. This was particularly so in view of the petitioner's undertaking that the
respondent and the child would be allowed the free
and exclusive occupancy of the house in which the
parties formerly resided pending the outcome of
custody proceedings in Victoria. In the result, counsel
for the respondent agreed to drop this ground of
opposition, provided extract of any order for return of
the child was superseded for a period of 14 days.

That, however, is by no means an end of the matter,
because the respondent raises as a preliminary issue
the question whether the child was "habitually resident" in Australia immediately prior to its removal
from that country within the meaning of art 3 of the
Convention. Further, even if the child were so resident, it is submitted that in the particular circumstances of the present case the petitioner "consented"
to its removal within the meaning of art 13 (a) of the
Convention. Before dealing with these matters it is
necessary to set out the salient facts against which the
legal issues must be determined.

Happily, most of the facts are not in dispute and can
be summarised as follows.

The respondent is Scottish and went to Australia on
a 12 month working holiday towards the end of 1987.
She met the petitioner in December 1987 and formed
a relationship with him. The petitioner is an
Australian national and the parties lived together for
about two years until separating in November 1990. A

formal separation agreement was then entered into
and has been lodged as no 16/1 of process. In terms of
that agreement the respondent made over to the petitioner her share of the house formerly occupied by
them. Subsequently, when some six months pregnant,
the respondent returned to Scotland in March 1991.
At that stage, however, there was further communication between the parties in the course of which the
respondent wrote the letter of 14 April 1991 (13/7 of
process). In that letter the respondent wrote inter alia
that she could not wait to see the petitioner, that she
hoped they could "get along good" and that she was
"looking forward to getting back to Australia as a
family". The petitioner later came over to Scotland for
the birth of the child, which occurred on 27 June
1991. Following the birth, the petitioner was registered as father of the child and an Australian passport
was obtained for her. The petitioner then returned to
Australia, via America, and some days later he was
joined by the respondent and the child who landed in
Australia on or about 1 September 1991. Thereafter
the parties resided together for a period of some 15
months until, on or about 27 November 1992, the
respondent, having told the petitioner that she was
going to spend the weekend with relatives, instead
boarded an aeroplane and, together with the child,
again returned to Scotland. About a week previously,
however, the petitioner had consulted a solicitor in
Melbourne and had been advised, rightly or wrongly
— but in any event without reference to the Convention — that there was nothing to prevent her taking
the child to Scotland. During the 15 month period of
cohabitation to which I have referred it is not, I think,
disputed that the relationship between the parties was
an uneven one and, in any event, there is clear affidavit evidence to the effect that latterly the respondent
became most unhappy. She herself maintains that the
relationship between the parties was never satisfactory
during that period. Nonetheless, it is the case that,
fairly soon after they returned to Australia, the parties
purchased a new kitchen and that, at a much later
stage, they actively considered selling the house in
which they then resided and moving to more spacious
accommodation. In addition, in March 1992, the
respondent herself obtained temporary employment
and, in June 1992, she took up full time employment
as a personnel assistant. In her affidavit, no 16/4 of
process (para 11), the respondent explains that she had
begun thinking seriously about returning to Scotland
in about July 1992 and that she "finally decided
definitely to do so" a day or two prior to her actual
departure at the end of November 1992.

All that said, there remains one important area of
dispute between the parties and that relates to the
understanding which had been reached between them
prior to the respondent's return to Australia in September 1991. According to his affidavits (nos 13/1 and
18/1 of process) the petitioner "emphatically denies"
that there was any understanding that, if the parties'
relationship did not work out, the respondent would
return to Scotland along with the child. Indeed, in the
later affidavit, he denies that that question was even

A raised and states that the parties' long term plans were simply "not consistent" with any such arrangement. The respondent, on the other hand, maintains that her return to Australia was part of an *attempted* reconciliation and that it was discussed and agreed in terms that, if things did not work out, both she and the child would come back to Scotland. Needless to say, I have not found it at all easy to resolve this factual dispute on the basis, solely, of affidavit evidence. However, that, realistically, is the best evidence which, in fairness to both parties, can be made available in the circumstances. Counsel for the petitioner pointed out

B that the account given of this matter had been embellished in successive affidavits taken from the respondent. This is true enough, but I attach little importance to that fact bearing in mind that, in her first affidavit (no 15/1 of process), the respondent does refer to having had a "talk" with the petitioner when it was agreed that "we would *attempt* a reconciliation" (my italics), and that in her later affidavit (no 16/4 of process) it is explained that the parties had talked

C about this "a great deal" before final agreement was reached. More importantly, however, there is no reference to this matter in either the first affidavit from the respondent's mother (no 16/8 of process) or the letter from the solicitor whom the respondent consulted in Melbourne (no 12/4 of process), or, indeed, in the letter which she wrote to the petitioner at the time of her return to Scotland (no 18/2 of process). Moreover, as counsel for the petitioner again pointed out, according to para 7 of the respondent's own affidavit (no 15/1

D of process), there was apparently no reference to any such arrangement when the respondent first told the petitioner that she was finally leaving him. As against all that, the respondent does, in my opinion, get clear support for her account of events in the affidavits of Fiona Macfarlane and Angela Mellerick (nos 12/1 and 12/3 of process). There are also the circumstantial considerations that the respondent was at no time married to the petitioner and that, having made over her share in the house to the petitioner in accordance with the

E earlier separation agreement, the respondent had no obvious form of long term security in Australia at the time she agreed to return there. Indeed, according to counsel for the petitioner's information, the respondent, on her return, was wholly dependent on social security benefits. It seems to me that in these circumstances it would be very surprising if, in Scotland, there was absolutely no discussion of the possibility that the respondent might again decide to come back and live with her mother. Moreover, I discount as

F being, in my view, unrealistic counsel's submission that any agreement or understanding would most likely have been "formalised" in writing. In the result, and doing the best I can on the evidence available, I find as a fact that when the respondent returned to Australia in September 1991 she did so as part of an attempted reconciliation with the petitioner and on the express understanding that, if the relationship again failed, she and the child would return and live with her mother in Scotland. It may well be that this had been forgotten after 15 months in Australia or that, in the early stages of the trauma of separation,

the respondent still saw for herself a possible future in Australia. In any event, there is no reason to suppose G that she would have regarded the understanding as having any binding quality or legal significance. But, whatever the precise position, I do not think it likely that the respondent would simply have invented this account of events, let alone have arranged for two of her friends to substantiate it.

I should add that, in making these findings, I leave out of account the affidavits lodged on behalf of the respondent on the third day of the hearing (nos 19/1-4 of process), since I agree with counsel for the petitioner that in the circumstances there could be some H doubt as to their spontaneity and reliability. If, however, account were to be taken of these affidavits, then, with one proviso, the argument for the respondent would become that much stronger. The proviso is that, if it be the case that in late November 1992 the matter of the agreement or understanding was foremost in the mind of the respondent, as is deponed to by the respondent's mother, Angela Mellerick and Anna Papadopoulos in their affidavits, nos 19/1, 3 and I 4 of process, it is then difficult to understand why there was no mention of it in the letter written to the petitioner by the respondent at the time of her departure (no 18/2 of process). One possible explanation, however, is that in any communication with the petitioner the respondent regarded mention of the understanding as being somewhat academic in view of his apparent disregard of its validity and/or importance; see in this connection the respondent's affidavits, no 15/1 of process, para 7 and no 16/4 of process, para 9, J and the affidavits, supra, nos 19/1 and 19/3 of process.

In light of the above I now turn to consider, first, the issue of "habitual residence". On that matter there was no real dispute between the parties as to the most relevant authorities. In chronological order these were *Dickson v Dickson, Re J (A Minor), Re S (A Minor)* and *Re A F (A Minor)*. The first of these was a decision of the Inner House and, in the course of delivering the opinion of the court, the Lord President said this (1990 SCLR at p 703B): "It is enough to say that in K our opinion a habitual residence is one which is being enjoyed voluntarily for the time being and with the settled intention that it should continue for some time. The concept is the same for all practical purposes as that of ordinary residence as described by Lord Scarman in *R. v Barnet London Borough Council*, ex parte *Shah* at pp 342 and 343. A person can, we think, have only one habitual residence at any one time and in the case of a child, who can form no intention of his own, it is the residence which is chosen for him by his L parents. If they are living together with him, then they will all have their habitual residence in the same place. Where the parents separate, as they did in this case, the child's habitual residence cannot be changed by one parent only unless the other consents to the change."

Re J (A Minor) was a case which went to the House of Lords and, in a speech concurred in by all the other members of the Judicial Committee, Lord Brandon of Oakbrook had this to say ([1990] 3 WLR at p 504):

A "The first point is that the expression 'habitually resi- dent', as used in article 3 of the Convention, is nowhere defined. It follows, I think, that the expression is not to be treated as a term of art with some special meaning, but is rather to be understood accord- ing to the ordinary and natural meaning of the two words which it contains. The second point is that the question whether a person is or is not habitually resi- dent in a specified country is a question of fact to be decided by reference to all the circumstances of any particular case. The third point is that there is a signi-

B ficant difference between a person ceasing to be habitually resident in country A, and his subsequently becoming habitually resident in country B. A person may cease to be habitually resident in country A in a single day if he or she leaves it with a settled intention not to return to it but to take up long-term residence in country B instead. Such a person cannot, however, become habitually resident in country B in a single day. An appreciable period of time and a settled inten- tion will be necessary to enable him or her to become

C so. During that appreciable period of time the person will have ceased to be habitually resident in country A but not yet have become habitually resident in country B. The fourth point is that, where a child of J.'s age is in the sole lawful custody of the mother, his situa- tion with regard to habitual residence will necessarily be the same as hers."

In the third of the cases cited the facts are fairly complicated but it is to be observed that, in the course of giving the judgment of the Court of Appeal,

D Purchas LJ commented, first, that a period of 12 months was "more than a sufficiently substantial period of time to effect the transfer of habitual resi- dence" and, secondly, that he did not consider as appropriate in the interpretation of the Convention any analogies with the concept of domicile of origin or domicile of choice.

Lastly, in *Re A F (A Minor)* it was held by the Court of Appeal that, with a settled intention to emigrate to

E Australia, three months was sufficient for a child to acquire a "habitual residence" there. Moreover, the comment was made that in such a situation even a month could be an appreciable period of time and that, in general, the court should not strain to find a lack of habitual residence where "on a broad canvas" the child had settled in a particular country.

From the foregoing authorities it is, I think, clear that the intention of a person is an important aspect in deciding his or her "habitual residence" for pur-

F poses of the Convention and, against that background, counsel for the respondent submitted that on his client's account of events, which I have accepted, there never was any "settled intention" that either she or the child should remain in Australia. Accordingly, neither could be said to have become "habitually resi- dent" there. With some hesitation, I have decided to reject that submission. It seems to me that, while intention is undoubtedly a very important considera- tion, there must come a stage when the objective facts point unequivocally to a person's ordinary or habitual

residence being in a particular place. In the present case the parties had lived together in Australia con- G tinuously for 15 months, had installed a new kitchen, and had considered moving house elsewhere in the state of Victoria. In addition, the respondent had herself obtained full time employment some five months prior to her departure from the country. In all these circumstances I do not consider it realistic to regard the "habitual residence" of the respondent, as at November 1992, as being other than in Australia. Happily, the conclusion which I have reached on this matter avoids what might otherwise have been a diffi- H cult, although interesting, question, namely the ascer- tainment of a child's "habitual residence", if any, in a situation where its parents, albeit living together, did not share the same "habitual residence" for purposes of the Convention. In this connection, however, I note that in *R v Barnet London Borough Council, ex p Shah* [1983] 2 AC at pp 343-344 — being in part, at least, the passage cited with approval by the Inner House in *Dickson v Dickson* — Lord Scarman recognises that there can be ordinary or habitual residence for a I period limited by the immediate purpose (e g educa- tion, family or employment) for which it is taken up. If, therefore, that line of reasoning is applied to the present case, it is possible — and this was suggested by counsel for the petitioner — that a trial period of reconciliation might itself be seen as a purpose suffi- cient to found "habitual residence" within the meaning of the Convention.

I turn lastly, then, to the matter of "consent" and, J in so doing, I would accept at the outset that, here again, there must be some limit to how far an agree- ment or understanding of the type in question should remain binding on the parties to it. In short, there must surely come a stage when for all practical pur- poses the parties can be seen as having become wholly reconciled and to have embraced a new life together. The question is whether that stage was reached in the present case. Again, with some hesitation, but doing the best I can with the available evidence, I have K reached the view that that particular question falls to be answered in the negative. In his affidavit (no 11/1 of process), the petitioner himself accepts that the parties had "heated arguments" from time to time and, as I have already remarked, it is clear that latterly the relationship between the parties became a most unhappy one. The picture is accordingly one of a deteriorating, rather than an improving, relationship, and it can accordingly have come as no surprise to the petitioner when the respondent finally announced that she was leaving him. In these circumstances, and in L light of my finding as to the clear understanding reached between the parties in Scotland some 15 months previously, I do not think that the petitioner has any ground for complaint that the respondent and child returned to Scotland when they did. Viewing matters in that light, therefore, I am prepared to hold that the petitioner, both in form and in substance, "consented" to their doing so within the meaning of art 13 (a) of the Convention in question. In this con- nection, it is, I think, nothing to the point that at the

A time of their departure the agreement or understanding had been overlooked, ignored, or even forgotten by either or both of the parties. Once it be accepted that such an agreement or understanding was entered into, and was in the circumstances still extant, then it seems to me that this application must be refused. In all the above circumstances, therefore, I shall sustain the respondent's fourth plea in law (as added by amendment) to that effect.

B   The petitioner reclaimed.

Reclaiming motion

The reclaiming motion was heard before the First Division on 8 and 9 July 1993.

On 20 July 1993 the court *refused* the reclaiming motion.

LORD ALLANBRIDGE.—On 25 March 1993 the
C Lord Ordinary dismissed a petition which had been presented to this court by the reclaimer. The petition was presented under Pt I of the Child Adoption and Custody Act 1985 for return of the child who had been removed from Australia at about the end of November 1992. The petitioner and the respondent had formed a relationship in about December 1987 and there is one female child of the relationship born on 27 June 1991.

D   As is outlined by the Lord Ordinary, most of the facts are not in dispute and are helpfully summarised by him in his opinion of 25 March 1993. The respondent is a Scot and went to Australia on a 12 month working holiday towards the end of 1987. She met the petitioner in December 1987 and formed a relationship with him. The petitioner is an Australian national and the parties lived together for nearly two years until separating in November 1990. A formal separation agreement was then entered into in terms of
E which the respondent made over to the petitioner her share of the house formerly occupied by them and he paid her a certain sum in exchange. Subsequently, when she was about six months pregnant, the respondent returned to Scotland in March 1991.

There were then further communications between the parties in the course of which the respondent wrote a letter, dated 14 April 1991, in which she stated that she had been really missing the petitioner, could not wait to see him, and was "looking forward to
F getting back to Australia as a family". The petitioner came to Scotland for the birth of the child which occurred on 27 June 1991. Following the birth the petitioner was registered as the father of the child and an Australian passport was obtained for the child.

The petitioner then returned to Australia, via America, and some days later he was joined by the respondent and the child who arrived there about 1 September 1991. Thereafter the parties lived together for a period of about 15 months until about 27 November 1992. The respondent, having told the

petitioner that she was going to spend the weekend with relatives, instead boarded an aeroplane and, G together with the child, returned to Scotland. About a week previously, the respondent had consulted a solicitor in Melbourne and had been advised, without any reference being made by the solicitor to the Convention on the Civil Aspects of International Child Abduction (see Sched 1 to the 1985 Act), that she had the option of returning to Scotland and immediately applying for a sole custody order through the Scottish courts (see Melbourne solicitor's letter, dated 5 February 1993).
H
During the parties' 15 month period of cohabitation between September 1991 and November 1992, the Lord Ordinary said he considered that the relationship between them was an uneven one and, in any event, there was clear affidavit evidence to the effect that latterly the respondent had become most unhappy. In her affidavits the respondent maintained that the relationship between the parties was never satisfactory. Nevertheless, the Lord Ordinary accepts that fairly soon after they returned to Australia, the parties I purchased a new kitchen and that, at a much later stage, they actively considered selling the house in which they then resided and moving to more spacious accommodation. In addition, in March 1992, the respondent herself obtained temporary employment and, in June 1992, she took up full time employment as a personnel assistant. In her affidavit (no 16/4 of process) the respondent stated she had begun to think seriously about returning to Scotland in about July 1992 and finally decided definitely to do so a day or J two prior to her departure at the end of November 1992.

At this stage of his opinion the Lord Ordinary then explains there was one important area of dispute between the parties which related to an understanding said by the respondent to have been reached between the parties prior to her return to Australia in September 1991. The petitioner denied that there was any such understanding, and the dispute as to whether it was established in evidence and, if so, what effect, K if any, it had on the proper interpretation of the parties' rights under art 13 of the Convention, lies at the heart of this reclaiming motion. In his opinion, the Lord Ordinary explains that after considering the available evidence he found as a fact (p 978F, supra) that: "when the respondent returned to Australia in September 1991 she did so as part of an attempted reconciliation with the petitioner and on the express understanding that, if the relationship again failed, she and the child would return and live with her mother L in Scotland".

This undertaking, if established in evidence, requires to be considered against the background of the statutory provisions contained in arts 3, 12 and 13 of the Convention. Three matters were originally the subject of dispute between the parties at the hearing before the Lord Ordinary. In the first place it had been averred in the respondent's answers that there was a grave risk that the return of the child to Australia would expose her to physical or psychological harm in terms of art 13 (b), but during the course of the hearing it was accepted by the respondent that this ground of opposition could no longer be maintained after the petitioner had given an undertaking that the respondent and the child would be allowed the free and exclusive occupancy of the house in which the parties formerly resided pending the outcome of custody proceedings in Victoria. In the second place the respondent raised as a preliminary issue the question whether the child was "habitually resident" in Australia prior to her removal from that country within the meaning of art 3. That matter was decided in favour of the petitioner by the Lord Ordinary who held that the respondent, and therefore the child, was so resident in Australia, and the respondent has not reclaimed against that part of his decision.

In the third place the Lord Ordinary said there was a dispute between the parties as to whether the petitioner had consented to the removal of the child in terms of art 13 (a). The Lord Ordinary decided this dispute in favour of the respondent and sustained the respondent's fourth plea in law to the effect that the petitioner having consented to the removal of the child from Australia, the prayer of the petition should be refused. The debate before us was solely concerned with the question of whether the Lord Ordinary had been entitled to sustain the respondent's said fourth plea in law.

The submissions put forward by counsel on behalf of the petitioner fell broadly into two main categories. In the first place she argued that the Lord Ordinary had erred in law in his interpretation of the proper meaning of art 13 (a) as regards the petitioner's alleged consent to the removal of the child from Australia. In the second place she argued that in finding that there had been a prior agreement between the parties on this matter, the Lord Ordinary had erred in holding any agreement in September 1991 established by the evidence and furthermore, even if it was established, he had erred in finding that it was still extant at the time of the actual removal of the child in about November 1992. I think it is convenient to consider first whether the Lord Ordinary erred in arriving at his factual conclusions before deciding whether he erred in law in his interpretation of the provisions of art 13 (a).

At the beginning of her submissions counsel for the petitioner said she founded very strongly on the fact that when the petition and answers came before the Lord Ordinary on the first day of the hearing on 18 March 1993 no question had been raised in the pleadings as to whether or not the petitioner had consented to the removal of the child. In fact the respondent had admitted in her original answers that she had removed the child without the petitioner's consent. The question of consent was raised by the Lord Ordinary himself on the first day of the hearing. After some discussion between him and counsel for the parties, counsel then acting on behalf of the respondent asked for an adjournment to consider his position as regards amending his pleadings regarding the matter of consent. It was not disputed by counsel who appeared for the respondent before us that the Lord Ordinary

had initiated this matter and, having had the opportunity of looking at the minutes of proceedings, I note that on the following day the appropriate minute of amendment for the respondent was allowed subject to the condition that the petitioner, if so advised, could lodge further affidavits by 10 am on Tuesday, 23 March 1993, which was the third day of the four day hearing. On that day counsel for the petitioner lodged a further affidavit from the petitioner, dated 22 March 1993, in which he emphatically denied any suggestion of an agreement between the respondent and himself that she could take the child back to Scotland. Counsel then acting for the respondent lodged four new affidavits. Three of these affidavits were further affidavits from the respondent's mother and two of her friends in Australia, Angela Mellerick and Anna Papadopoulos, which were dated 22 or 23 March 1993 respectively, and an affidavit from a friend of the respondent's family in Scotland, Robert Kenneth Young Sharp, dated 22 March 1993. In his opinion the Lord Ordinary indicates that he took into account in reaching his decision on the facts the most recent affidavit of the petitioner, but left out of account these four affidavits lodged on behalf of the respondent on the third day of the hearing because he agreed with counsel for the petitioner that in the circumstances there could be some doubt as to their spontaneity and reliability (p 978G-H, supra).

Counsel for the petitioner made no attack on, or complaint about, the procedure adopted by the Lord Ordinary in this case and I am satisfied that it was reasonable in the circumstances of such a hearing which proceeded on affidavit evidence alone. However, I have noted her point that the question of consent was initiated by the Lord Ordinary in this case. I have also noted that at the time he did so he had two affidavits of the respondent before him which made reference to a discussion and an agreement between the parties before the respondent's return to Australia (see no 15/1 of process, dated 11 February 1993, and no 12/2 of process, dated 17 February 1993).

Counsel for the petitioner made a detailed and careful analysis of the affidavit evidence in this case in her submissions to us. She stressed that because this court could look at the affidavits and the other documentary evidence in the same way as the Lord Ordinary had done then this court could equally well assess the credibility of the parties and their witnesses. I do not accept that such an approach is open to this court. It is for the judge at the hearing on the affidavit evidence to assess the weight and effect of that evidence and this court can only disturb his findings in fact if it is satisfied that the Lord Ordinary was so plainly wrong that his conclusion on the facts was one at which no reasonable Lord Ordinary could have arrived. Counsel for the petitioner did not dispute that she required to meet such a test but submitted that she could do so in the circumstances of this case.

I do not find it necessary to detail all the submissions that counsel made in her attack on the credibility of the pursuer's witnesses. I can however quote

some examples which she quite properly put before
A the Lord Ordinary and again put before this court. She
pointed out that the Lord Ordinary stated (at p 978D,
supra) that the respondent got clear support for her
account of the events in the affidavits of Fiona
Macfarlane and Angela Mellerick but that the respondent had, in one of her letters, described Angela as a
person who tends to talk "garbage and tell me to say
and do things that I wouldn't think about". Furthermore, counsel for the petitioner said that Fiona
Macfarlane could hardly be said to support the respon-
B dent on the question of the existence of an agreement
because all she said was that when the respondent went
to Australia to attempt a reconciliation "there was no
doubt in my mind that Rhona intended to come home
to Scotland with Brianne if the reconciliation did not
work". Counsel also attacked the credibility of Anna
Papadopoulos because in her first affidavit she said she
first met the respondent in June 1992 whereas in her
second affidavit she referred to what the respondent
had told her in October 1991 when they were visiting
C a food shop together. Counsel then said that the fact
that these witnesses were unreliable, as demonstrated
by the affidavits, reflected on the credibility of the
respondent herself as they were her friends.

I have considered all the criticisms of counsel for the
petitioner regarding the witnesses and her other comments on the evidence, but I consider these were all
matters for the Lord Ordinary to take into account and
I am not persuaded that he failed to do so. A close
D reading of his opinion demonstrates he carefully considered all these matters of credibility, and counsel for
the petitioner very properly accepted that, in view of
the terms of s 1 of the Civil Evidence (Scotland) Act
1988, the Lord Ordinary did not require to find
corroboration of the respondent's evidence before he
could accept her evidence alone as proof of the alleged
agreement.

There were two further main submissions by
counsel for the petitioner on the evidence. She sub-
E mitted that it was inconsistent for the Lord Ordinary
to find the respondent was "habitually resident" in
Australia and at the same time to find that by November 1992 there had not been a reconciliation. The
Lord Ordinary had reviewed the facts having regard to
the relevant case law as to what is required to establish
habitual residence (pp 978J-979G, supra) and reached
the conclusion that in November 1992 the respondent
was habitually resident in Australia as at that date. He
explains that in the present case the parties had lived
F together in Australia continuously for 15 months, had
installed a new kitchen and had considered moving
house elsewhere in the state of Victoria. In addition,
the respondent had herself obtained full time employment some five months prior to her departure from
the country. As explained by Lord President Hope at
p 703B of *Dickson v Dickson*: "It is enough to say that
in our opinion a habitual residence is one which is
being enjoyed voluntarily for the time being and with
the settled intention that it shall continue for some
time."

In the later case of *Re F (A Minor) (Child Abduction)*
[1992] 1 FLR at p 555G, Butler-Sloss LJ considered G
that residence of a period of only a month could be a
sufficient period of time in which to acquire the necessary settled intention. In such a situation I consider
the fact that the court has found the necessary settled
intention established as regards the respondent, does
not preclude her from maintaining that a reconciliation had not then taken place.

However, I find it more difficult to answer the
related but separate question raised in this case as to
whether the particular alleged agreement was still H
extant at the time the respondent left Australia with
the child in November 1992. The Lord Ordinary said
in his opinion (pp 979L-980A, supra) that it did not
matter that at the time of the departure the agreement
or understanding had been overlooked, ignored, or
even forgotten by either or both parties. At first sight
I found this to be a somewhat surprising suggestion
that if at the time she left Australia the respondent was
not doing so in reliance on the agreement, she could
still rely on it when she returned to Scotland. It may I
well be, as suggested by the Lord Ordinary, that both
parties had forgotten of the existence of the agreement
at the time she left Australia. But on reflection I have
come to be of the view that whether the agreement was
extant and in force when the respondent left Australia,
must be a question of fact to be determined by the
judge at the hearing. There is no doubt that he was
well aware of the difficulties arising in this particular
case and the facts relating to it. He states that he
accepted at the outset that there must be some limit as J
to how far an agreement or understanding of the type
in question should remain binding on the parties to it
and that, in short, there must surely come a stage
when for all practical purposes the parties can be seen
as having become wholly reconciled and to have
embraced a new life together (p 979J, supra). That in
my opinion is the correct approach and when he said
the question was whether that stage had been reached
in the present case, he posed the correct question. He
answered that question, with some hesitation but after K
a careful review of the facts, in the negative. Had I
been answering the question myself I might not necessarily have reached the same conclusion, but I am
satisfied it cannot be said in this case that the Lord
Ordinary as the judge of first instance was not entitled
to reach the conclusion that he did. It was a matter of
fact for him to determine and nothing has been said by
counsel for the petitioner that persuades me that the
Lord Ordinary was so plainly wrong that this court is
entitled to interfere with his decision on this matter. L

I am therefore satisfied that the Lord Ordinary was
entitled to find that the agreement, which I have
already quoted earlier in this opinion, was made
between the parties before the respondent returned to
Australia in September 1991 and that it remained in
force until November 1992 when the respondent took
the child away from Australia. Once it is established
that such an agreement was made, then whilst it
remained in existence the respondent was entitled to
remove the child from Australia without seeking the

A permission of the petitioner to do so. He had already given his consent to the happening of that event whenever it might occur, provided always that the agreement had not come to an end by virtue of the fact that a reconciliation had taken place.

The question remains as to whether the Lord Ordinary erred in law in the interpretation of art 13 (a) of the Convention. It is true, as argued by counsel for the respondent, that the only question in the grounds of appeal which deals with an alleged error in law by the judge is the first ground of appeal and it

B failed to raise any question regarding the proper interpretation of art 13 (a) and when read appears to relate to a matter of fact. That ground states that the error in law by the Lord Ordinary was that he had held there existed, at the date of removal of the child, an agreement between the parties anent removal. I accept at once that there is considerable force in what was said on this matter by counsel, but I am prepared to entertain the somewhat different question argued by counsel for the petitioner for a number of reasons. She

C was permitted by this court to present her argument without objection and as this matter was canvassed by her on the first day of the appeal and as counsel for the respondent did not address the court until the following day, he could not and did not argue that he was taken by surprise and thus prejudiced by receiving no proper notice of it. Furthermore, counsel for the petitioner insisted that such an argument was presented to the Lord Ordinary, albeit his opinion is silent on this topic.

D Article 13 (a) must be considered in its context in the Convention. There was no dispute between the parties before us that the removal of the child had been wrongful in terms of art 3 and that, but for the saving provisions of art 13, the court in Scotland would have required to order the return of the child in terms of art 12. Article 13 (a) reads as follows: [his Lordship quoted the terms of art 13 set out supra and continued:]

E The argument of counsel for the petitioner was to the effect that the respondent, who was the person who opposed the return of the child, required to establish that the petitioner, who was the person having the care of the child (by virtue of joint custody according to Australian law) "had consented to *the* removal". The use of the word "the" before the word "removal", according to counsel for the petitioner, meant that consent must have been given by the petitioner to the particular removal in question which pre-

F supposed knowledge on the part of the petitioner of the actual removal at the time so that he could give the necessary consent. Counsel said that this was a clandestine removal by the respondent and she never told the petitioner that she was removing the child in terms of the alleged agreement. Counsel for the petitioner seemed to accept a suggestion made to her from the bench that, if the respondent had wished to exercise such rights in terms of the agreement, she should have gone to the Australian courts which were responsible for matters of custody in Australia, and obtained their agreement to removal of the child, but I consider there

G is nothing in the wording of art 13 (a) which required that to be done.

I have considered closely the terms of art 13 (a) but can find no support for counsel for the petitioner's suggested interpretation of it. The words "at the time of the removal" plainly relate to and qualify the preceding words "not actually exercising the custody rights". The use of the word "the" before the word "removal" must mean the actual removal which took place but it does not follow that the consent must be given instantaneously at the time because consent could clearly be given to a removal which would take

H place at a future and even indefinite date. A person could agree that a child could be removed, for example, when the child came out of hospital and was fit enough to travel. There would be no definite date but consent was being given for a future removal. The use of the past tense in the words "had consented to . . . the removal" demonstrates that at the time of removal the consent had already been given and looks to the past prior to the removal. In other words a person could consent to the removal of a child in the

I future unless some other event occurred, such as the child not being well enough to travel. The present case is analogous to such an example because the agreement found established by the Lord Ordinary was to the effect that the petitioner would consent to the return of the child to Scotland unless the parties had become reconciled. That consent, given in September 1991 by agreement between the parties, remained in force as a matter of fact in November 1992, as found by the Lord Ordinary. In my opinion that situation,

J once accepted, clearly satisfies the requirements of the wording in art 13 (a).

It was finally submitted by counsel for the petitioner that the result of upholding the Lord Ordinary's decision in this case would be to give an opportunity to any person who abducted a child to set up an alleged prior agreement regarding consent and thus defeat the whole purpose of the Convention. That, in my opinion, is not the proper approach. The clear intention of the qualification regarding consent in art

K 13 (a) is to give the person removing the child the opportunity to prove that the removal of the child was with the consent of the "person, institution or other body having the care of the person of the child". If such an opportunity is taken and the relevant consent is established, then the judicial authority of the requested state is not bound to order the return of the child as stated in terms in art 13 of the Convention. The existence of such consent was proved to the satisfaction of the Lord Ordinary in the circumstances of

L this particular case and I can find nothing in the wording of art 13 (a) to prevent him reaching the conclusion that he did. I am therefore satisfied that he did not err in law and that the terms of para (a), properly construed, did not prevent him from finding consent proved and therefore holding that he was "not bound to order the return of the child" and in the circumstances deciding not to do so.

For these reasons I consider that the issues that are decisive in this particular case are issues of fact. The Lord Ordinary was entitled to accept the affidavit

A evidence led on behalf of the respondent and reject that led on behalf of the petitioner where matters relating to consent were in dispute. In my opinion this reclaiming motion therefore fails and I would refuse the appeal and adhere to the Lord Ordinary's interlocutor of 25 March 1993.

I have had the advantage of reading in draft the opinion of Lord Morton of Shuna. At the end of his opinion he expresses the view that the court should act expeditiously in proceedings for the return of children. I agree with that view. As was stated by Lord B President Hope at p 701B of *Dickson v Dickson*: "Article 11 of the Convention provides that the judicial or administrative authorities of the contracting states shall act expeditiously in proceedings for the return of children. The intention is that proceedings should be conducted as quickly as possible in order to secure the return of a child who has been wrongfully removed from his place of habitual residence with the minimum of delay."

C In this particular case the timetable was as follows. On 2 February 1993 the first order for service of the petition was pronounced. On 12 February 1993 a further order was pronounced ordaining both parties to lodge affidavits and on 2 March 1993 a first hearing was fixed for 18 March 1993. The first hearing before the Lord Ordinary lasted for four court days, as stated earlier in this opinion, and was completed on 24 March 1993. The opinion of the Lord Ordinary was issued on 25 March 1993 and on 5 April a reclaiming D motion by the petitioner was marked. Thereafter the grounds of appeal were lodged on 11 May 1993 and on 23 June 1993, after legal aid had been granted to the petitioner, a request for an early diet for the hearing of the appeal was made. The hearing before this court was then arranged and took place on 8 and 9 July 1993. In these circumstances there does not appear to have been any undue delay on the part of the court authorities in this case but this is a matter that will no doubt be kept under constant review in the E future.

LORD MAYFIELD.—On 25 March 1993 the Lord Ordinary dismissed the petition which had been presented to this court by the reclaimer. The petition was presented under Pt I of the Child Abduction and Custody Act 1985 for the return of a child. The respondent is Scottish and went to Australia on a 12 months' working holiday towards the end of 1987. She met the petitioner in December 1987 and formed a F relationship with him. The petitioner is an Australian national and the parties lived together for about two years until separating in November 1990. There was a formal separation agreement. In terms of that agreement the respondent made over to the petitioner her share of the house formerly occupied by them. Subsequently, when some six months pregnant, the respondent returned to Scotland in March 1991. There was further communication between the parties and the respondent wrote to the petitioner on 14 April 1991 in affectionate terms and looking forward to getting back to Australia as a family. The petitioner visited Scot-

land for the birth of the child which occurred on 27 June 1991. The petitioner was registered as father of G the child and an Australian passport was obtained for her. The petitioner then returned to Australia and some days later was joined by the respondent who landed in Australia on about 1 September 1991. Thereafter the parties resided together for a period of some 15 months until on or about 27 November 1992, when the respondent, having told the petitioner that she was going to spend a weekend with relatives, boarded an aeroplane and again returned to Scotland. She had previously consulted a solicitor who had advised that there was nothing to prevent her from H taking the child to Scotland.

In the petition the petitioner seeks an order under the Child Abduction and Custody Act 1985 and the articles of the Hague Convention set out in Sched 1 to the Act. The United Kingdom and Australia are among the contracting states to this Convention, and the effect of the Act is that so far as Scotland is concerned the Court of Session has jurisdiction to entertain applications under the Convention for the return I of a child at the instance of any person who claims that the child has been removed or retained in breach of custody rights, provided that the child was habitually resident in the contracting state immediately before any breach of those rights occurred.

The Lord Ordinary held that while the parties had at no time been married it was accepted that under the relevant Australian law they each shared joint custody of the child in question. The Lord Ordinary held that the relationship between the parties was an uneven J one and observed that there was clear affidavit evidence to the effect that the respondent became very unhappy. In setting out his findings the Lord Ordinary has referred to an important area of dispute. The petitioner in his affidavits emphatically denied there was any understanding that if the parties' relationship did not work out the respondent would return to Scotland along with the child. The respondent on the other hand maintained that her return to Australia was part of an attempted reconciliation and K it was discussed and agreed in terms that if things did not work out both she and the child would come back to Scotland. The Lord Ordinary considered whether or not there was an agreement. He found as a fact that when the respondent returned to Australia in September 1991 she did so as part of an attempted reconciliation with the petitioner and on the express understanding that if the relationship again failed she and the child would return and live with her mother in Scotland. He reached that conclusion after con- L sidering all the facts and circumstances and various affidavits. The Lord Ordinary also found from the facts that the habitual residence of the parties was in Australia. That finding was not disputed before this court, nor was it submitted, as averred in the reclaiming print, that the child would be at grave risk if returned to Australia.

Counsel for the reclaimer submitted that the Lord Ordinary had erred in law in relation to the proper interpretation of art 13 (a) and in reaching the

conclusion that when the respondent returned to
Australia in September 1991 she did so as part of an
attempted reconciliation with the petitioner and on
the express understanding that, if the relationship
again failed, she and the child would return and live
with her mother in Scotland. She submitted that the
Lord Ordinary erred in the conclusions he had
reached on the facts. She maintained that there had
been no agreement between the parties about the
removal of the child. Further, even if there had been
an agreement, the Lord Ordinary erred in holding that
the agreement was still extant at the date of the
removal of the child. Those were the main submissions. It was also submitted and referred to in the
grounds of appeal that the Lord Ordinary erred in
drawing inferences from surrounding circumstances
in order to conclude that the agreement did exist; and
that there was insufficient evidence to find that such
an agreement existed. He also erred in holding that the
affidavit evidence presented by the respondent in
respect of an agreement was credible. In my view,
even in a case such as this which depended on affidavit
evidence, my understanding is that it is for the Lord
Ordinary to assess the evidence and the significance of
the various factors and the weight to be attached to
them. This court cannot interfere in the conclusions
on the facts reached by the Lord Ordinary on the evidence provided, of course, that the findings were not
perverse or that no reasonable Lord Ordinary could
have reached such a conclusion on the facts.

Initially, I was under the impression from the
opening speech of counsel for the reclaimer, as was
counsel who appeared for the respondent, that her
criticisms of the Lord Ordinary's opinion were confined to his conclusions on the facts. However, while
having some sympathy with counsel for the respondent, who submitted that no question of interpretation
of art 13 (a) had been raised in the reclaimer's first
ground of appeal, the court decided that it was appropriate that the matter of interpretation of the relevant
articles be considered. She submitted that the alleged
agreement occurred 15 months before removal and
there was no agreement in relation to the removal of
the child at the date of removal. As stated earlier the
law is such that this court is obliged to accept the Lord
Ordinary's conclusion on the facts. The Lord
Ordinary's conclusion was that the petitioner both in
form and in substance " 'consented' to their doing so
within the meaning of art 13 (a) of the Convention in
question" (p 979L, supra). He accepted that a stage
might arise after an agreement had been entered into
when the parties could be regarded as having become
wholly reconciled and to have embraced a new life
together. The conclusion he reached was that that
stage had not been reached. He explained his reasons
for reaching that conclusion. He then stated that once
it had been accepted that such an agreement or understanding was entered into it was in the circumstances
still extant and the application must be refused.

There are three articles which are relevant to this
case. Article 3 states: [his Lordship narrated the terms
of art 3 and then art 12 set out supra and continued:]

The critical article, however, in my view is contained in art 13, which states: [his Lordship quoted
the terms of art 13 set out supra and continued:]

Counsel for the reclaimer laid considerable emphasis on the finding of the Lord Ordinary that he had
found the habitual residence (referred to in art 3) to be
in Australia. She maintained that there was an inconsistency in the opinion of the Lord Ordinary in that
he had found the habitual residence to be in Australia
but had also reached the conclusion that by November
1992 there had not been a reconciliation. I do not
myself consider that "habitual residence", which can
be established after a short period, is inconsistent with
the Lord Ordinary's finding that reconciliation had
not taken place. Counsel for the reclaimer submitted
that the respondent had to establish that the petitioner
had consented to *the* removal. As I understood her
submission, that meant that the consent by the petitioner must have been given by the petitioner to the
actual removal and at the time of the removal. Consent
applies to the particular removal. She also stated that
the respondent should have gone to the Australian
court in Victoria and obtained their agreement to the
removal of the child.

I am not able to accept counsel for the reclaimer's
contentions.

While the words "the removal" in art 13 (a) refer to
the actual removal which took place it does not in my
view mean that the consent must be given at the time
of removal. The words "had consented to . . . the
removal" are not consistent with that view. In my
view there is nothing in the article which bars consent
to the removal sometime in the future. Nor do I accept
the submission that if the Lord Ordinary was upheld
it would provide an easy opportunity to others to
avoid the provisions of the Convention by merely
claiming that there had been an agreement such as the
one found by the Lord Ordinary in this case.

My understanding of the position is that the object
of the provision in art 13 (a) is to give the party, in this
case the respondent, the opportunity to establish or
satisfy the Lord Ordinary that the removal of the child
was with the consent of the other party. On the facts
of the present case the Lord Ordinary has held as a fact
that there was an agreement and that the agreement
was in force at the time of removal and that the
consent still stood. The Lord Ordinary recognised that
such an agreement and consent did not subsist for all
time. In this case, however, after careful consideration
he found that the agreement remained in force. In that
event he was not bound to order the return of the child
because he was satisfied on the facts that the petitioner
had consented to the removal. In these circumstances
the reclaiming motion should be refused.

LORD MORTON OF SHUNA.—I wholly agree
with your Lordship in the chair on every point except
on the matter of statutory interpretation and in particular on the meaning of the words "had consented
. . . to the removal" in art 13 (a) of the Convention
enacted as Sched 1 to the Child Abduction and
Custody Act 1985.

The Lord Ordinary's finding that the child was habitually resident in the state of Victoria and the acceptance by both parties that by the law of Victoria the petitioner and the respondent had joint custody of the child means that the removal of the child was wrongful under art 3, and under art 12 the court in Scotland is required to order the return of the child unless under art 13 the respondent establishes that: "the person, institution or other body having the care of the person of the child was not actually exercising the custody rights at the time of removal or retention, or had consented to or subsequently acquiesced in the removal or retention".

The Lord Ordinary has held that the agreement entered into when the respondent returned to Australia in September 1991 was to the effect: "that if the relationship again failed she and the child would return and live with her mother in Scotland", and that by entering into that agreement: "the petitioner, both in form and in substance, 'consented' within the meaning of art 13 (a) of the Convention" (pp 978F and 979L, supra).

In my opinion it is quite clear that art 13 (a) is providing only for consent to or acquiescence in a particular act of removal or retention. The first part of art 13 (a), with its reference to a person not actually exercising custody rights at the time of removal or retention, is clearly referring to the particular act of removal or retention in question and in my opinion the phrase "or had consented to or subsequently acquiesced in the removal or retention" clearly is referring also to the particular removal in question. If one deals only with consent to a removal, the wording of art 13 (a) would be "or had consented to the removal". This interpretation appears to me to be the natural meaning of the words in the article and to fit with what I understand to be the purpose of the Convention. It is, I consider, clear that a main purpose of the Convention is that the court of habitual residence should be the court to decide any issue relating to custody of a child, with a discretion given to the court of a state to which the child may have been removed to refuse to order the return if there has been consent to the removal or for any of the other reasons permitted by art 13. To hold that a consent to subsequent removal can be given before habitual residence has begun, and remain in force throughout the period of habitual residence, and, so far as I could understand from the submissions of counsel, could not be withdrawn by the petitioner, seems to me clearly not the type of consent which was contemplated in art 13 (a). The modern concept of the rights and duties involved in custody of children is that the best interests of the child should be paramount. An irrevocable consent to a possible future removal of a child from a situation which might be very different from that contemplated when the consent was given is difficult to fit in with the concept of the best interests of the child being paramount. However if the consent under art 13 is confined to a particular removal contemplated by the other party having custody rights it is more easy to understand that the consent, if given, is given in the best interests of the child, and after consideration of the situation at the time of removal.

In my opinion it is quite clear that when the respondent decided that she could no longer live with the petitioner, the appropriate court to decide any dispute between the parties as to the custody of the child was the appropriate court in the state of Victoria in Australia. The respondent should have gone to that court and sought custody of the child and authority, if that is what she wished, to take the child to Scotland. She could, in that court, have founded on the agreement between herself and the petitioner as an argument in favour of granting permission for that course. The court in Australia, where both parents were living and where the child had lived for most of her life up to the date of the separation of the parents, was clearly in a far better position to reach an informed conclusion on a dispute about custody. The effect of the Lord Ordinary's decision would be that any dispute about custody of the child will require to be decided by a Scottish court on evidence largely from Australia. Instead of going to the court in Australia the respondent clandestinely removed to the opposite side of the world the child when, at that time, both the petitioner and respondent had custody rights to her. That removal appears to me to be precisely the type of action which the Child Abduction and Custody Act 1985 and the Convention sought to prevent or at least discourage. I would have allowed the reclaiming motion and ordered the return of the child to Australia. However as your Lordships have reached a contrary conclusion I must respectfully dissent.

It is, I consider, most unfortunate that this action has taken so long in the Scottish courts. The petition was first in court in February 1993 and the Lord Ordinary issued his opinion on 25 March 1993. The reclaiming motion was heard on 8 and 9 July 1993. Article 11 of the Convention provides that: "The judicial or administrative authority of the contracting States shall act expeditiously in proceedings for the return of children".

The article continues with a paragraph that suggests that a decision should be reached within six weeks. In this case the proceedings have so far taken five months. In England it appears that a decision usually takes much less time, even if appealed. For example in *Re F (A Minor) (Child Abduction)* the summons first came before a judge on 16 July 1991, a hearing took place on 18 July and the judge on 19 July ordered that the child be returned. An appeal was taken to the Court of Appeal and was refused on 31 July 1991. That timetable appears to me to be an exemplary example of expedition. It is very unfortunate that this case, and especially the reclaiming motion, was not treated with the expedition required by the Convention.

Counsel for Petitioner and Reclaimer, Davie; Solicitors, Balfour & Manson, Nightingale & Bell — Counsel for Respondent, Fitzpatrick (Inner House), Dewar (Outer House); Solicitors, Garden, Haig, Stirling & Burnet.

C H

Drury v McGarvie

FIRST DIVISION

THE LORD PRESIDENT (HOPE),
LORDS COWIE AND GRIEVE

5 NOVEMBER 1992

*Heritable property — Servitude — Right of access —
Proprietor of servient tenement erecting swing gates
across access — Dominant proprietors disabled —
Whether gates amounted to an obstruction — Appro-*
B *priate test — Appropriate remedy where gates amounted
to obstruction because of proprietors' disability.*

The title to a cottage situated on farm land some distance from a public road contained an express grant of
a servitude right of vehicular and pedestrian access by
means of an access road, which ran through the farm
fields. The fence along part of the access road was
inadequate to prevent stock straying. The servient
proprietor removed the fencing and erected gates at
the top and bottom end of the access road in order to
C prevent stock straying. The proprietors of the cottage
were disabled and in poor health. They raised an
action in the sheriff court craving interdict of the
defender from obstructing the access and an order for
removal of the gates. They averred that the gates
obstructed their access, rendering them housebound.
They averred that the nature of the obstruction was
such that "it would to a certain extent inconvenience
any able bodied adult". The sheriff held that the
defender was entitled to erect gates across the access
D road; that the averments of disability were irrelevant
and that the averments that the gates amounted to an
obstruction were lacking in specification. He dismissed the action. The pursuers appealed to the Court
of Session, arguing that it was for the defender to
justify the inconvenience caused by the erection of the
gates, that the pursuers had made sufficient averments
that the gates amounted to an obstruction to anyone
who might use the right of access and accordingly
should be taken down, and in any event that because
E of their own physical condition the pursuers were
entitled to have the gates taken down as their use of
the access was obstructed.

Held, (1) that a proprietor of a servient tenement
was entitled to erect swing gates across a public or
private right of way for the purpose of containing
stock provided the gates did not amount to a material
inconvenience (pp 989C and 990C-E); (2) that the
burden of a servitude had to be measured by reference
F to a reasonable but fixed and constant standard and
not to the individual characteristics of the dominant
proprietor from time to time, and the test to be applied
in determining whether gates erected across a servitude amounted to an obstruction was whether a person
of average strength and agility could open the gates
without material inconvenience (p 991L); (3) that the
pursuers' averments were lacking in specification on
that issue or that the gates were of such a nature that
they amounted to an obstruction which could only be
dealt with by taking them down (pp 990K-991A); and
appeal *refused.*

Wood v Robertson, 7 March 1809, FC, and *Sutherland v Thomson* (1876) 3 R 485, *followed*; *Middletweed
Ltd v Murray,* 1989 SLT 11, *approved.*

Observed, that the pursuers had the right to alter
or adapt the gates in some way to suit their convenience at their own expense, and had a right of
access to the defender's land to execute works required
to maintain the servitude (p 992A-B).

_____

Appeal from the sheriff court

George Bush Drury and Mrs Lucy Margaret Drury
raised an action in the sheriff court at Stranraer against
James McGarvie craving declarator of a right of servitude of access, interdict against the defender from
obstructing the access road and an order for the
removal of gates erected across the access road.

After sundry procedure the case came before the
sheriff for debate on the parties' preliminary pleas.

Cases referred to

Donington (Lord) v Mair (1894) 21 R 829.
Middletweed Ltd v Murray, 1989 SLT 11.
Midlothian District Council v McKenzie, 1985 SLT 36.
*Safeway Food Stores Ltd v Wellington Motor Co (Ayr)
    Ltd,* 1976 SLT 53.
Sutherland v Thomson (1876) 3 R 485.
*Wills' Trustees v Cairngorm Canoeing and Sailing
    School Ltd,* 1976 SLT 162; 1976 SC (HL) 30.
Wood v Robertson, 9 March 1809, FC.

Textbooks referred to

Gordon, *Scottish Land Law,* para 24-18.
Green's Encyclopaedia of the Laws of Scotland, Vol 13,
    para 1223.
Rankine, *Land-ownership* (4th ed), pp 417, 420, 421.

On 25 September 1991 the sheriff *sustained* the
defender's plea to the relevancy and *dismissed* the
action.

The pursuers appealed to the Court of Session.

Appeal

The appeal was heard before the First Division on
20 October 1992.

On 5 November 1992 the court *refused* the appeal.

The following opinion of the court was delivered by
the Lord President (Hope):

OPINION OF THE COURT.—The pursuers are
the heritable proprietors of a cottage in Wigtownshire
which is situated on farm land some distance from the
public road. They purchased the cottage in 1975 and
have resided there since that date. Their title to the
property includes, by reference to an express grant in
the original disposition of the subjects by the then
heritable proprietor of the farm, a servitude right of
vehicular and pedestrian access by means of an access
road. This road runs from the direction of the public

A road through the farm land to the perimeter of the subjects on which the cottage is situated. It is bordered on both sides by fields which belong to the proprietor of the farm. A dispute has arisen between the pursuers and the defender, who became the heritable proprietor of the farm when he purchased it in 1980, about the placing of gates across the access road.

The problem has arisen because the defender uses the fields as grazing land. The fencing along the access road was inadequate to stop the defender's stock from straying from the neighbouring land on to the access

B road and from there into the pursuers' garden. The defender decided to remove all the fencing from either side of the access road and to rely instead on two gates. He erected one gate at the lower end of the access road adjacent to his own farmhouse. He erected the other gate at the top end of the access road on the boundary of the pursuers' property. His purpose in erecting the second gate was to stop beasts from straying into the pursuers' property and causing damage there. The purpose of the first gate was to stop beasts from stray-

C ing from the fields into the farmyard and, no doubt, on to the public road. The pursuers object to these gates on the ground that they constitute an obstruction to their right of access. They describe the gates which the defender erected in the first place as makeshift gates which were secured to posts with string. These gates were replaced by the defender after the raising of the action, but the pursuers object to the replacements on the same ground. They described them as heavy, improperly hinged and so placed as to be

D difficult to reach. They say that substantial physical strength and dexterity is required to perform the operation and that, since they are both elderly and suffer from physical disabilities, they have been rendered virtually housebound.

In the action which they raised in the sheriff court at Stranraer they seek declarator that there is a valid and effectual servitude right of way over the access road and that they and their dependants are entitled to

E free ish and entry by it over the defender's land. Thus far there is no dispute between the parties. It is clear that the right of way has been validly constituted by express grant and that the pursuers are vested in that right as the owners of the dominant tenement. They then seek interdict and interim interdict against the defender from interfering with the pursuers or their family in the lawful use and enjoyment of the access road and from obstructing the same, together with an order ordaining the defender to take down the gates.

F On 10 September 1990, the sheriff, on the pursuers' unopposed motion, granted interim interdict. But on 14 September 1990, having heard argument on behalf of both parties, he recalled the interim interdict on the balance of convenience. He pointed out that it was a natural consequence of having a right of way across grazing land that some obstruction of the way would be necessary in the interests of the servient proprietor. The practical consequences of interim interdict would be to compel him to remove the gates and either cease using the fields for grazing or erect new fencing at considerable expense. Alternatively, he could remove the

G gates, leave the stock in the fields and do without fences, in which event the beasts would stray into the pursuers' garden and cause the kind of damage which was the subject of a separate complaint in the initial writ. The sheriff's decision was appealed to the sheriff principal, who refused the appeal and adhered to the sheriff's interlocutor. The defender then lodged defences to the action, which came before the sheriff again on the debate roll for a debate on the preliminary pleas. On 25 September 1991 the sheriff sustained the defender's plea to the relevancy and dismissed the action. It is against his interlocutor of that date that

H the pursuers have now appealed to this court.

The sheriff was satisfied, after considering the authorities, that the proprietor of a servient tenement was entitled to erect gates at either end of an access road for the purpose of containing stock. He rejected the pursuers' argument that it was for the defender to aver that the gates were not obstructions. He held that it was for the pursuers to aver and prove that these gates, which were intended to render the fields stock

I proof, had to be categorised as obstructions and as such had to be removed. Their averments seemed to him not to give fair notice to the defender of the case he had to meet. Their pleadings lacked averments which were both specific and intelligible as to what was wrong with the gates and how the faults could be rectified. He also held that the pursuers' averments about their disabilities were irrelevant, on the view that the proprietor of the servient tenement was not obliged to accommodate the personal characteristics of the dominant proprietor from time to time. With

J regard to the averments about the pursuers' loss and damage, which are not now in issue, he held that they also were lacking in specification and that for this reason as well the action was irrelevant.

Counsel for the pursuers invited us to recall the sheriff's interlocutor and to pronounce decree de plano. He submitted that it was for the defender to justify the inconvenience which he had admittedly caused by putting up the gates. The defender could

K only do this if he was able to show that the gates were not a material obstruction when account was taken of the pursuers' disabilities, that the gates did not interfere with the pursuers' reasonable and constant use of the access way and that the obstruction, such as it was, was necessary for the use of the servient tenement. He contended that the court had a discretion as to whether or not to allow an interference with a right of access, and that it was for the owner of the servient tenement to show that the interference which he had caused

L should be allowed. We were referred in support of this argument to *Lord Donington v Mair*, where at p 832 Lord Justice Clerk Macdonald said this: "In the case of a highway, the right to prevent any erection on the highway is absolute; whereas in the case of a servitude or public right of way it is a question of circumstances whether the right of those who possess the servitude or of the public is to have it removed. But still anything which covers up and prevents the unobstructed use of the ground, subject to the right for its exercise, must be justified by the owner. He may do so by shewing that what he is doing is required for the proper working of his estate, as by dividing fields or the like, and that it is an immaterial interference with the rights of the dominant tenement in the one case or of the public in the other. The case of stiles on a footway is an illustration of this. They are obstructions, but may be put up as not interfering materially with the right, and as being requisite for the reasonable working of the owner's estate."

In *Midlothian District Council v McKenzie,* Lord Allanbridge allowed a proof before answer where the pursuers' case was that the landowner had obstructed a public right of way by erecting a fence which considerably reduced its width. He applied the principles discussed by the Lord Justice Clerk in *Lord Donington's* case, and refused the defender's motion that the action should be dismissed. He pointed out that it was not a sufficient answer for the defender merely to say that what was left unobstructed was sufficient for the use of the right of way by foot passengers.

In our opinion, however, the sheriff was right to reject this argument. There is no doubt that the proprietor of the servient tenement is entitled to put up swing gates across a public or private right of way for the purpose of preventing stock from straying from his land. The case of *Wood v Robertson* has always been regarded as conclusive on this point. It was held that the tenant of the servient tenement was entitled to put up swing gates on a servitude road which ran through his farm. The tenant's wish was to enclose the farm more completely by erecting gates on the road at different places where it crossed his enclosures. The sheriff held that no harm or obstruction could happen to the owner of the dominant tenement by swing gates being put up on the road, provided they were not locked or fastened in any way to prevent foot passengers from opening them at all times. He allowed the gates to be put up. The complainer then presented a bill of advocation in the Court of Session. The Lord Ordinary directed that, as one of the four gates which the tenant wished to put up was not of much importance, only three gates should be put up. A reclaiming motion was refused, on the view that the interference with the exercise of the servitude by the swing gates was not material. It was observed that the liberty of erecting swing gates might be abused, but in that case the court would afford a remedy by removing them. Reference was also made to the fact that the law allowed stiles to be erected across servitude footpaths. The importance of this case for present purposes is that it shows that the owner of the servient tenement is entitled to erect swing gates across a private right of way, provided they can be opened and are not kept locked. Although swing gates which can be opened and are not locked interfere with the use of the way to some extent, this does not necessarily mean that they are an obstruction. The onus is on the dominant proprietor to aver and prove that they are an obstruction if he seeks to have them altered or removed.

In *Sutherland v Thomson,* the decision in *Wood* was applied to a public right of way which ran through land used for grazing purposes. It was held that the owner of the servient tenement was entitled, for grazing purposes, to put swing wicket gates across the footpath, provided the gates were not of an obstructive character. Lord Neaves said at p 489 that the question was whether there was any reasonable ground, in the case of a public footpath, for depriving the proprietor of the privilege of protecting his property from unnecessary injury by putting up gates which, in the case of servitude roads, had been held in *Wood* to be no obstruction. He concluded that since, in the case of servitude roads, a gate which opens is not an obstruction, so also individual members of the public could not complain about the placing of gates which could open across a public right of way. Lord Ormidale said at p 493: "The general right of the owner, or farmer in his place, to erect gates, provided they do not interfere in a fair and reasonable sense of that expression with the public right of passage, is therefore, I take it, beyond dispute." He concluded his opinion with the comment that the only remaining point was whether the gates which were put up were in themselves of an objectionable description. He said that the appellant who, as a member of the public, wished to remove the gates, had failed to show that they were. Here again, we find clear support for the sheriff's view that prima facie the defender was entitled to put up swing gates to prevent stock from straying from his land.

Lord Donington's case, which was the principal foundation for the pursuers' argument, was concerned with the different situation which arises where gates have been erected which are kept locked. In that case there was a public right of way for foot passengers only. The proprietor's problem was that the roadway was wide enough for the use of vehicles, and he sought to protect himself from the use of the way by the public except as foot passengers by erecting gates at the end of it which were kept locked. He also erected at each end of the road a swing gate of appropriate width which was kept unfastened to enable foot passengers to use the road. It was in that context that Lord Justice Clerk Macdonald said at p 832 that it was for the proprietor to justify the putting up of something which prevented the unobstructed use of the way. With regard to the proprietor's contention that what he had done was to protect his property against illegal encroachments while in no material way interfering with the enjoyment of the existing public right, he said that this would be a good answer to the objection to what he had done. But it is his comments at p 833 with regard to the wicket gates which were left open for the use of foot passengers that are more directly relevant to the facts of the present case. Under reference to *Wood,* and to the mention which was made in that case of the accepted practice of placing stiles across footpaths, he said: "It thus, as I hold, is established law, that a right to pass from one place to another over private property is one which does not imply power to prevent the proprietor from beneficial use and protection of his own property, because his mode of obtaining these things may require the right to be exercised at some particular point under some immaterial restriction, which in no true sense injures the enjoyment of the right."

Lord Rutherfurd Clark dissented, but it is significant that on the issue which affects the present case he agreed with the Lord Justice Clerk. He said at p 834 under reference to *Sutherland v Thomson:* "I do not understand the judgment to determine more than that an easily opened swing-gate is not an obstruction to a public footpath. It applied to public footpaths the rule which had been established in the case of *Wood* in regard to a servitude road. Swing gates do not prevent the full use of the footpath. They interpose, no doubt, a certain obstacle to its use, but one which the passenger can easily and at once remove. They are a great benefit to the proprietor, and of no disadvantage to the public, and in view of the benefit the Court thought that the trouble of opening might be thrown out of account."

In his view the proprietor failed because he could not show that the locked gates were not an obstruction. Lord Trayner agreed with the Lord Justice Clerk, on the view that the only effect of the locked gate was to prevent the road being used in a manner in which only the proprietor had a right to use it.

In our opinion there is here a consistent line of authority which supports the view which was taken by the sheriff about the right to put up gates which can be opened without material inconvenience in order to contain stock. The special factor which arose in *Lord Donington's* case does not arise here, because the right of way which exists here is a right for both vehicular and pedestrian access and the defender has put up swing gates which extend right across the full width of the right of way. Nevertheless there are ample averments in the defences to the effect that the purpose for which the gates were put up was to contain stock, that they swing freely and that they are not kept locked. The defender's case is that they do not constitute a substantial or unnecessary obstruction. The pursuers admit that the roadway is used for grazing and they do not suggest that the gates are kept locked. In this situation the sheriff was right to see the true issue in the case as being whether the gates nevertheless constituted an obstruction and to hold that it was for the pursuers to aver and prove that they were.

We turn now to the question whether the sheriff was wrong to dismiss the action, since counsel for the pursuers' alternative argument was that he was wrong to do this and that a proof before answer should have been allowed. This argument was directed to two points which are best examined separately. The first is whether the pursuers have made sufficient averments that the gates are of such a nature that they are an obstruction to anyone who may use the right of access and that they must be taken down. The second is whether, if they are not an obstruction to the use of the way by a normal person, they can nevertheless have them taken down because their own physical condition is such that their use of the way is being obstructed.

On the first point the pursuers' concern is now with the gates which the defender put up after the raising of the action to replace the original makeshift gates. They describe the replacement gates as heavy and improperly hinged. They say that to open them they require to lift them for some height, unloop them from posts and then drag them along the access road. As we understand this averment, one end of the gate remains on its hinges and the other is drawn away from the opposite post to which it was attached until the way is made open. The pursuers then say that the gates must be held open with pieces of wood until access or egress has been effected and then closed by the same process. The argument is that these gates are an obstruction because they are difficult to reach and lift and because substantial physical strength and dexterity is required to perform the operation. But these averments must be understood in the light of the averments which follow about the pursuers' physical disabilities. These averments conclude in art 3 of the condescendence by stating that the extent of the obstruction is such as to cause severe inconvenience and risk of danger to the pursuers. But as regards the point which we propose to consider at this stage in the argument, the critical averment is in these terms: "The nature of the obstruction is such that it would to a certain extent inconvenience any able bodied adult."

There is some force in counsel's argument that the sheriff went too far when he described these averments as failing to say in any specific and intelligible way what is wrong with the gates. The description which the pursuers give is of gates which, although not locked, are in such a condition that it requires some physical effort to open and shut them. But some amount of physical effort is inevitable in the case of gates which have been placed across a farm road which is wide enough for use by vehicles. That some inconvenience is permissible without constituting an obstruction in the sense required for its removal is clear in the case of stiles. A stile must be climbed if the person who uses the way is to get over it. This may be inconvenient, but the authorities show clearly that if the stile can be crossed by a person of normal physique and agility it does not amount to an obstruction of the right of way. So the question is whether the pursuers' averments have taken the matter beyond mere inconvenience to what can properly be described as an obstruction. Furthermore the defender is entitled to require a careful scrutiny of these averments, because the effect of the orders which the pursuers seek will be to require the gates to be taken down. The pursuers would only be entitled to obtain that remedy if they were in a position to prove that the gates were of such a nature that they amounted to an obstruction which could only be dealt with by taking them down. In our opinion their averments fall significantly short of these requirements. At best for them, on this branch of the argument, the gates require some adjustment or repair to minimise the inconvenience in a way that has not been specified. But this is not the remedy which the pursuers seek. While counsel for

A the pursuers suggested that the court had some discretion in the matter, the court can only grant the remedy which the pursuers seek in their crave, and that is the remedy of having the gates removed. In our opinion, unless they are able to rely on their own physical disabilities, their averments must be held to be irrelevant because they are insufficient in law to justify the contention that the gates ought to be removed.

B The question then is whether the pursuers' disabilities are relevant to the question whether the gates constitute an obstruction. Counsel was unable to cite any authority to this effect. He sought to find some support for the proposition in the principle that a servitude right can belong only to the owner of the dominant tenement: see *Safeway Food Stores Ltd v Wellington Motor Co (Ayr) Ltd,* per Lord Maxwell at pp 56-57. He submitted that it followed from this principle that the owner of the servient tenement was obliged to have regard to the circumstances of the dominant proprietor for the time being. The question

C whether the gates were an obstruction fell to be tested by reference to his ability to make use of the right of way. If they were an obstruction to him because his physique or his state of health were such that he could not open or shut the gates with reasonable convenience, the gates should not be permitted. He recognised that an owner's state of health might vary from time to time, and submitted that the matter fell to be tested at the moment when the gates were put up. He demurred to the suggestion that there was a con-

D tinuing obligation on the servient proprietor not to obstruct the right of way and that, if the dominant owner's state of health was relevant, the matter would require to be assessed from day to day. He submitted that it was not unreasonable to have regard to the characteristics of the owner for the time being, since the use of the way was confined to the residents and visitors to the dominant tenement: *Sutherland v Thomson,* per Lord Gifford at p 496.

E But, as counsel for the defender pointed out in his response to this argument, a servitude is praedial in its nature, since it is a real and not a personal right. He submitted that it would be contrary to this essential characteristic that the burden on the servient tenement should alter from time to time according to the personal circumstances of the owner of the dominant tenement. We were referred to Gordon's *Scottish Land Law* (1989), para 24-18, where the author states that, since it passes with the property, a servitude right

F must be for the benefit of the dominant tenement and must not be a mere personal advantage to the owner of that tenement. In its context, however, that is a statement of the principle to be applied in order to decide whether a particular right can or cannot be a servitude. Reference is made in the same paragraph to the discussion of this point in Rankine, *Landownership* (4th ed), pp 420-421 where it is said that there can be no such thing as a servitude of golfing or of strolling or of trout fishing in a loch. We were referred also to the title on servitudes in *Green's Encyclopaedia,* Vol 13, para 1223. But here again the discussion is directed to what is and is not a servitude, rather than the extent of the obligation on the servient G proprietor if one exists.

In *Middletweed Ltd v Murray,* Lord Davidson was concerned with a right of access which was vested in the proprietor of salmon fishings in the River Tweed. The pursuers sought a declarator that they were entitled to take motor vehicles along a track to the fishings, as a number of the fishermen were disabled and required to be transported to the boats. He rejected the pursuers' argument that they were entitled to vehicular access as part of an accessory H right of fishings. At p 14K-L he held that the necessary right of access which attached to property in salmon fishings was restricted to access which was necessary for the beneficial enjoyment of the fishings. He went on: "Since I am satisfied that pedestrian access down the track as well as pedestrian access from the chain bridge are sufficient to enable a person of average strength and agility to fish all the beats in the Lower Pavilion fishings, I conclude that the pursuers are not entitled, in the exercise of their accessory right, I to insist upon vehicular access along the track to the hawthorn tree."

At p 14C-D he said that counsel for the pursuers had been unable to cite any authority in the law of Scotland for the proposition that the extent of a right of access was to be determined by the limitations of a disabled person, and he found support for the contrary view in a passage in the opinion of Lord Fraser of Tullybelton in *Wills' Trs v Cairngorm Canoeing and Sailing School Ltd,* 1976 SLT at p 216.   J

The facts of the present case are different, because we are not concerned here directly with the extent of the right of access, which admittedly includes a right of access by means of vehicles. But questions as to the extent of the right of the dominant proprietor and questions as to the extent of the right of the servient proprietor fall to be decided by reference to the same principles. In our opinion the view expressed by Lord Davidson that the extent of the dominant proprietor's right of access falls to be determined by reference to K a person of average strength and agility provides authority for the view that the question whether a swing gate is an obstruction must be determined by reference to the same criterion. This is consistent with the principle that the servitude is presumed to be as little burdensome to the servient tenement as is consistent with its fair exercise: Rankine, p 417; *Sutherland v Thomson,* per Lord Gifford at p 495. It provides the complete answer to the problem which was inherent in counsel for the pursuers' argument, that a L person who is fit one day may be disabled on another. Since the burden on the servient proprietor is a continuing one, the burden must be measured by reference to a reasonable but fixed and constant standard, and not to the individual characteristics of the dominant proprietor for the time being. Accordingly the test is whether a person of average strength and agility, or to adopt the phrase used in the pursuers' own pleadings, the ordinary able bodied adult, would be able to open the gate without material inconvenience.

A
In our opinion, therefore, the sheriff reached the correct conclusion on this point also, and his decision that the pursuers' action is irrelevant must be affirmed. We would add, however, that the pursuers may not be without a remedy. If the gates, although not unduly inconvenient to the ordinary able bodied adult, are so difficult for them to open because of their particular disabilities, the question to be considered is whether the gates can be altered or adapted in some way to suit their convenience. If they can, the pursuers have a right of access to the defender's land to carry
B
out the necessary work, since the rule is that the owner of the servient tenement must allow the dominant owner access to the servient land to execute works required to maintain his servitude right. But the work will have to be at the pursuers' expense, since all the defender can be obliged to do at his expense is to maintain the gates in such a condition that they can be opened and shut by the ordinary able bodied adult whenever this is required.

C
For these reasons we shall refuse the appeal and affirm the sheriff's interlocutor.

Counsel for Pursuers and Appellants, Allardice; Solicitors, Steedman Ramage, WS (for McAndrew & Co, Stranraer) — Counsel for Defender and Respondent, Agnew of Lochnaw; Solicitors, Lawford Kidd & Co, WS (for Ferguson & Forster, Stranraer).

D
C H A of L

Hamilton v Neizer

HIGH COURT OF JUSTICIARY

THE LORD JUSTICE GENERAL (HOPE),
E LORDS ALLANBRIDGE AND KINCRAIG

3 DECEMBER 1992

Justiciary — Statutory offence — Driving while unfit through drink — Sentence — Accused driving to escape scene of earlier violence when youths again causing disturbance but returning after colliding with road sign — Whether special reasons for reducing period of disqualification — Road Traffic Act 1988 (c 52), s 5 (1) (a) — Road Traffic Offenders Act 1988 (c 53), s 34 (1).

F
An accused person was found guilty of inter alia driving while unfit through drink, contrary to s 5 (1) (a) of the Road Traffic Act 1988. In mitigation the accused sought to establish special reasons for not being disqualified for the minimum mandatory period. The evidence disclosed that the accused and his friend had stopped overnight in Fort William, parked in a lane at the rear of an hotel and had several drinks. As they returned to their car at 1 am they were attacked by about six youths. They suffered injuries and went to hospital, but were discharged and

G
returned to their car. On their way back they saw youths causing a disturbance further along the street near where their car was parked, but they did not become involved in that incident. Shortly after settling down in the car, the accused suddenly said "Let's get out of here" and drove off. Over half a mile later he failed to go round a roundabout and collided with a road sign. He then reversed off the roundabout, drove about 250 yds back in the direction they had come and stopped. When charged by the police the accused replied: "I was in a state of panic following the fight. I thought they were after us again." The sheriff was
H
satisfied that the accused had been frightened and shaken by the attack and that he might have felt compelled to get out of the area, but held that there were no special reasons and disqualified the accused, who appealed.

Held, (1) that necessity was not the test and that a reasonable latitude had to be given to the driver once an explanation amounting to special reasons had been given as to why he started the car (p 995D-E); but (2)
I that the accident on the roundabout interrupted the course of driving so that a fresh explanation was required for the fact that the accused decided to drive the car again, and since the driving from the roundabout could not be attributed to the accused's desire to escape from the lane, there were no special reasons for him not to be disqualified for this part of the journey (p 995E); and appeal *refused.*

J
Summary complaint
Stuart Hamilton was charged at the instance of Agnes Neizer, procurator fiscal, Fort William, on a summary complaint which contained the following charge, inter alia: "That you did on 10 August 1991 . . . (2) [on the bypass road at the west end roundabout] and on the road to the Crannog restaurant, Fort William [District of Lochaber], drive a motor vehicle namely said motor car A194 VGD after consuming so much alcohol that the proportion of it in your breath
K was 69 microgrammes of alcohol in 100 millilitres of breath which exceeded the prescribed limit namely 35 microgrammes of alcohol in 100 millilitres of breath; contrary to the Road Traffic Act 1988, s 5 (1) (a)." The accused pled not guilty and proceeded to trial. After trial the accused was found guilty and disqualified from driving for 12 months.

The accused appealed by way of stated case to the High Court against the decision of the sheriff.

L
Findings in fact
The sheriff (D Noble) found the following facts to be admitted or proved:

(1) The appellant is 23 years old and resides at Houston, Renfrewshire, where he works as a painter and decorator. (2) On Friday, 9 August 1991, the appellant left Houston in his car accompanied by a friend, Alistair McIlvar. Their intention was to drive to Fort William, sleep overnight in the car there and on the following morning drive to Kintail to spend the

weekend fishing with friends there. (3) The appellant
A and Mr McIlvar arrived in Fort William in the early
evening and the appellant parked his car in a lane at
the rear of the Imperial hotel. The High Street in Fort
William runs in approximately a north-south direction, and the Imperial hotel lies about 50 yds west of
the High Street, down a side street near the north end
of the High Street. (4) After parking the car the appellant and Mr McIlvar had several drinks in a public
house and then went on to the discotheque at
MacTavishes Kitchens where they had more drinks.
B MacTavishes Kitchens is on the east side of the High
Street towards its south end. (5) The appellant and Mr
McIlvar left the discotheque when it closed at 1 am
and they were confronted outside by about six 16 year
old youths. The appellant and his companion walked
northwards on High Street and when they saw that the
youths were following them they ran up a lane leading
east from the High Street. They were pursued by the
youths and sought refuge in the garden of a house
where they banged on the door for assistance. The
youths punched and kicked the appellant and Mr
C McIlvar, and eventually left. Shortly afterwards a
police vehicle arrived, apparently in response to a telephone call from the occupants of the house. The
police officers advised the appellant and his companion to go to the casualty department of the Belford
hospital and said that they would make a search for the
youths. (6) The appellant and Mr McIlvar arrived at
the casualty department of the Belford hospital at 1.40
am. Medical reports have been lodged regarding their
injuries which were minor and they were discharged.
D (7) The Belford hospital lies on the east side of the
road leading north out of Fort William. The appellant
and Mr McIlvar had about a half mile walk from the
hospital to where their car was parked at the rear of
the Imperial hotel. Their route required them to cross
the High Street, and as they did so they saw youths
causing some disturbance further along the High
Street. (8) The appellant and his companion arrived at
the car and the appellant got into the driver's seat and
Mr McIlvar into the front passenger seat. They settled
E down with the intention of sleeping overnight in the
car and continuing their journey to Kintail in the
morning. The lane where the car was parked is poorly
lit. (9) Shortly after the appellant and Mr McIlvar had
settled down in the car the appellant suddenly said:
"Let's get out of here". He started the engine,
switched on the lights and drove off. He drove onto
the short bypass which runs parallel to the High Street
and on its west side. At the south end of the bypass
he failed to go round the roundabout and collided with
F a road sign on the roundabout. After the car had come
to a halt on the roundabout the appellant then
reversed the car off the roundabout and drove back
along the bypass in the direction from which he had
come for about 250 yds to the approach road to the
Crannog restaurant where he stopped the car. The
front, front offside wheel and tyre had been damaged
in the accident and the front offside tyre was deflated.
(10) After the Camic machine procedure, when the
appellant was charged he replied: "I was in a state of
panic following the fight. I thought the boys were after
us again."

Cases referred to

MacLeod v MacDougall, 1989 SLT 151; 1988 SCCR
519.
Watson v Hamilton, 1988 SLT 316; 1988 SCCR 13.

Appeal

The sheriff posed the following question for the
opinion of the High Court, inter alia:

(2) Was I entitled to hold that there were no special
reasons for not disqualifying the appellant?

The appeal was argued before the High Court on 5
November 1992.

On 3 December 1992 the court *answered* the question in the *affirmative* and *refused* the appeal.

The following opinion of the court was delivered by
the Lord Justice General (Hope):

OPINION OF THE COURT.—The appellant was
charged in the sheriff court at Fort William on
summary complaint with two offences under the Road
Traffic Act 1988. The first was a breach of s 3 of that
Act, in respect that on the bypass road in Fort
William, at the west end roundabout, he caused the
car which he was driving to collide with a road sign
whereby both the car and the road sign were damaged.
The second was of driving the car with an excess of
alcohol in his breath, contrary to s 5 (1) (a) of the Act.
He pled not guilty, but at the conclusion of the trial
he was found guilty on both charges. The sheriff took
into consideration the fact that he was a first offender
and imposed fines of £75 in respect of each charge. He
disqualified him from driving for a period of 12
months on the second charge.

Two issues arose at the trial which were the subject
of the appellant's application for a stated case. They
both related to the second charge, there being no
dispute that the sheriff was entitled to convict the
appellant on the charge under s 3 of the 1988 Act. The
first issue related to the appellant's defence of necessity, on which he based his submission that he ought
to be acquitted on the second charge. The second
relates to his submission that there were special
reasons why he should not be disqualified. Counsel
intimated at the outset of the appeal that the appellant
no longer insisted on his defence of necessity, and we
shall therefore answer the first question in the case of
consent in the affirmative and refuse the appeal
against conviction. But he contended that the sheriff
was wrong to hold that there were no special reasons
for not disqualifying, having regard to the circumstances of the offence.

There was no dispute that the appellant was driving
the car at the time of the accident and that the alcohol
in his breath was in excess of the prescribed limit. Nor
was it disputed that he had driven the car while he was
in that condition for a distance amounting to more
than half a mile from a lane at the rear of the Imperial
hotel in Fort William, along the bypass road to the
roundabout and from there for a further distance of

about 250 yds back along the bypass road to the entrance to the Crannog restaurant. The explanation which the appellant gave for this in his evidence, which was spoken to also by his friend Alistair McIlvar who was with him in the car, provided the basis both for the defence of necessity and for the argument that the sheriff ought not to disqualify him in this case.

The appellant and his friend, both of whom live in Renfrewshire, set out in the appellant's car to spend the weekend fishing in Kintail. Their intention was to drive to Fort William, sleep there overnight in their car and then drive to Kintail the next morning. They arrived in Fort William in the early evening, and the appellant parked the car in a lane at the rear of the hotel. They had several drinks in a public house and then in a discotheque which they left when it closed at 1 am. At this point they were confronted by about six 16 year old youths who pursued them as they ran up a lane and tried to seek refuge in the garden of a house. The youths caught up with them and punched and kicked them there before they broke off their attack. The police arrived and advised the appellant and his friend to go to the casualty department of the Belford hospital where they were found to have sustained minor injuries and discharged. They then walked the distance of about half a mile from the hospital to the place where the appellant had parked his car in the lane behind the hotel. As they were crossing the High Street they saw youths causing a disturbance further along the street, but they did not become involved in this incident. They got into the car and settled down with the intention of sleeping in it overnight and continuing their journey to Kintail in the morning.

Shortly afterwards the appellant, who was in the driver's seat, suddenly said: "Let's get out of here". He started the engine and then drove off. He drove from the lane through the town onto the bypass. At the south end of it he failed to go round the west end roundabout and collided with a road sign on the roundabout. He then reversed off the roundabout and drove back along the bypass to the approach road to the restaurant, where he stopped the car. When charged by the police he said: "I was in a state of panic following the fight. I thought they were after us again." The sheriff was satisfied that the appellant and his companion had been frightened and shaken by the unprovoked attack upon them by the youths, and that they were in a shaken and nervous state when they returned to their car. He did not believe the appellant's evidence that he had seen and heard a group of youths in the poorly lit lane where the car was parked after he had settled down in the car for the night. But he regarded it as quite possible that the sounds of disturbance in the High Street would have increased tension in the appellant to such an extent that he felt compelled to get out of the area.

The sheriff decided that there were no special reasons in the circumstances of the offence which would entitle him to refrain from imposing the man-datory disqualification under s 34 (1) of the Road Traffic Offenders Act 1988, but he was not referred to any of the cases on this point, and he states in his note that had he had before him one of the two cases to which he referred subsequently he might possibly have decided that special reasons existed for not disqualifying. In the first case, *Watson v Hamilton*, it was held that there were special reasons where the appellant felt impelled to drive his car to deal with a medical emergency after he had taken several steps to try to deal with it by other means. The circumstances of that case were different from those in the present case, although counsel invited us to note from it that special reasons could exist where the car was driven in an unexpected situation caused by a sudden emergency. The sheriff indicates that he would have had more difficulty in distinguishing the other case, *MacLeod v MacDougall*, where the circumstances were not dissimilar, and it was to that case that counsel directed most of his argument.

As in the present case the appellant in *MacLeod v MacDougall* had parked his car with the intention of not driving it again that night. He had booked into an hotel prior to attending a social function in a nearby restaurant. He parked his car in the hotel car park and walked to the restaurant, where he drank a quantity of alcohol before being given a lift back to the hotel. He arrived there between 1 and 2 am, but before he could gain entry he became involved in a heated argument which was provoked by three other men who were the worse for drink. A friend intervened as he was being assaulted, and this ended the argument. As they retreated words were uttered by the other men to the effect: "You had better disappear". The appellant was shaken and frightened by this incident and, as he was still unable to get into the hotel, he and his friend decided that it would be best for him to leave the area in case there was another attack. They felt that it was unwise for him to walk and there was no nearby telephone box. So he and his friend set off in the car, with the appellant driving, to go to his friend's house. He drove for about half a mile, passing a marked police car on the way which followed him. When signalled to stop he drove for a further 400 yds before he eventually did so. His defence of necessity was rejected, but an appeal against his disqualification was allowed on the ground that there were special reasons for not disqualifying. He went on driving for longer than was necessary, as he continued to drive after he had reached the marked police car. But the Lord Justice Clerk said at 1989 SLT, p 152, that it was clear that the appellant would never have begun driving that evening if he had not been assaulted and been frightened and shaken by what had occurred, that he only started to drive in order to escape from his assailants and that for this reason there were special reasons for him not to be disqualified. Counsel said that the circumstances of the present case were very similar, and maintained that the sheriff was wrong to hold that there were no special reasons which would entitle him not to disqualify.

The advocate depute submitted that it was not

enough for the appellant to claim that he had panicked. The sheriff had rejected his evidence that there was an indication of imminent danger in the lane. In any event the appellant had gone on driving for longer than was necessary to remove himself from the lane to a place of safety, since he had driven onto the bypass road and had then continued driving after the accident on the roundabout. There is more to be said for the last part of this submission than for the first. The sheriff was clearly satisfied that the appellant and his companion were genuinely frightened and shaken by the unprovoked attack on them by the six youths. They were still in a shaken and nervous state when they returned to the car, and it is not unreasonable to accept the appellant's explanation that he had intended to remain there but had suddenly felt compelled to drive away from the lane for fear of another attack. If that was the explanation for the entire journey, there would be much to be said for the view that there were special reasons in the circumstances of the case why the appellant should not be disqualified. The difficulty in the case lies in the fact that the appellant went on driving not only onto the bypass to get out of the town but also to remove the car from the place where it had collided with the road sign on the roundabout.

In our opinion the accident on the roundabout gave rise to a new situation which could no longer be explained by the appellant's desire to escape from the lane. It was suggested that he had to remove the car from the roundabout because it would have been a hazard if it had been left there. But the sheriff rejected this, as the roundabout was well lit and there would have been adequate room for the other vehicles to pass. It is not appropriate in these cases where the question of special reasons is in issue to divide up what was really a single piece of driving into separate chapters in order to see at what point the driving ceased to have been necessary. Necessity is not the test, and a reasonable latitude is to be given to the driver once an explanation amounting to special reasons has been given as to why he started to drive the car. But in the present case the accident on the roundabout can properly be seen as interrupting the course of driving, so that a fresh explanation required to be given for the fact that the appellant decided to drive the car again at this stage. In our opinion his course of driving from the roundabout to the entrance to the restaurant cannot be attributed to his desire to escape from the lane, and there were no special reasons in regard to this part of his journey for him not to be disqualified.

We shall therefore answer the second question in the affirmative and refuse the appeal against sentence.

Counsel for Appellant, MacGibbon; Solicitors, Brodies, WS (for McCusker, Mackie & Co, Johnstone) — Counsel for Respondent, Macdonald, QC, A D; Solicitor, J D Lowe, Crown Agent.

P W F

Lord Advocate v Shipbreaking Industries Ltd (No 2)

OUTER HOUSE
LORD COULSFIELD
12 JANUARY 1993

Landlord and tenant — Lease — Construction — Tenant's obligations of maintenance and compensation for damage arising from its operations or negligence — Whether tenant's acceptance of state of subjects at entry in respect of maintenance obligation capable of affecting tenant's obligations under other provisions of lease.

Process — Pleadings — Relevancy — Specification — Alleged liability of tenant for condition of subjects at end of tenancy — Report incorporated in landlord's pleadings — Whether fair notice given of claims for dilapidation.

A tenant under a lease of a port area was bound under cl eighth thereof to accept at entry the subjects of let as being in good tenantable order and repair and to maintain them in a like condition during the currency of the lease. Clause sixteenth of the lease provided that any damage to the subjects arising out of the tenant's operations or due to its negligence should be made good or compensated on the termination of the lease. Entry was taken under the lease in 1972.

Following termination of the lease by the tenant the landlord raised an action against the tenant claiming compensation for deposits of material containing asbestos on the subjects, founding on the tenant's obligations of maintenance in cl eighth and on the tenant's obligation to compensate the landlord for damage through operations or negligence in terms of cl sixteenth. The landlord also claimed for damages under cl eighth in respect of various defects in the subjects specified in a dilapidation report, excluding damage from the deposit of asbestos. The landlord's claim in relation to asbestos damage under cl eighth was repelled as having prescribed, although the landlord's averments concerning that claim remained on record.

The tenant maintained, inter alia, that it was not liable for claims under cl sixteenth for compensation for all asbestos deposits on the subjects as when entry was taken under the lease the site already had substantial quantities of asbestos deposited on it. While denying this, the landlord argued that the tenant was in any event personally barred from maintaining this defence as in terms of cl eighth the tenant had accepted the subjects as being in good tenantable order at entry.

The landlord argued that cl eighth provided the measure of the standard to which the tenant should make the subjects good or pay compensation therefor in terms of cl sixteenth or that, alternatively, the tenant's acceptance of the subjects in terms of cl eighth was relevant in relation to cl sixteenth as evidence in assessing the state of the subjects at entry.

Held, (1) that cll eighth and sixteenth of the lease set out different obligations, that the tenant's accep-

tance of the subjects as in good order and repair for the
A purposes of any obligation under cl eighth had
nothing to do with claims under cl sixteenth, which
could apply only if the landlord demonstrated that the
tenant's operations or negligence had indeed caused
damage, and that there was therefore no substance in
the landlord's case of personal bar (p 998A-B); (2) that
the landlord's claim that the tenant was liable in compensation in relation to the removal of all asbestos was
irreconcilable with the terms of cl sixteenth, which
imposed an obligation specifically limited to damage
B caused by operations or negligence of the tenant, and
was consequently irrelevant (pp 998J-999B); and (3)
that fair notice of the landlord's claims in respect of
the defects in the subjects specified in the dilapidation
report had been given by incorporation of the report
in the landlord's pleadings (p 999B-D); and plea of
personal bar *repelled*, landlord's averments relating to
personal bar and to the costs of removal of asbestos
excluded from probation and quoad ultra proof before
answer *allowed*.

C
_____

Action of damages

The Lord Advocate, acting on behalf of the Secretary of State for Defence as landlord, raised an action
of damages against Shipbreaking Industries Ltd, as
tenant under a lease, in respect of claims relating to
the condition of the subjects of let at removal. After a
hearing on procedure roll one of the landlord's
grounds of claim was repelled as having prescribed
D (see 1991 SLT 838).

The case thereafter came before the Lord Ordinary
(Coulsfield) on procedure roll on the defenders' pleas
to the relevancy of the remainder of the pursuer's
grounds of claim.

Terms of lease

The lease between the parties provided inter alia:

"Eighth. The tenants' obligations of repair to the
E subjects of let shall be as follows: (a) the port area: The
tenant accepts the port area (which expression for the
purposes of this Clause shall mean the whole subjects
of let with exception of the buildings, the approach
line and the fences and bridges hereafter mentioned in
paragraphs (b), (c), and (d) respectively of this Clause)
together with the buildings and other erections,
installations and all roads, paved areas, electric and
water installations, culverts, internal and boundary
walls and fences in and upon the same insofar as
F belonging to the landlord as in good tenantable order
and repair and satisfactory in all respects and save as
hereinafter provided the tenant undertakes to maintain
the same together with any permanent additions
agreed under Clause Seventh hereof in a like condition
during the currency of this Lease . . .

"Sixteenth. The tenant shall at the expiry or earlier
termination of this lease deliver possession of the
subjects of let to the landlord and any damage arising
out of its operations or due to the negligence of the
tenant shall be made good or compensation paid there-

for by the tenant, fair wear and tear excepted,
provided, however, that where buildings, work, plant G
or other erections upon the subjects of let belong to
the tenant, the tenant shall be entitled to and if
required by the landlord to do so shall be bound to
remove them from the site and restore the site to a
level condition clear and redd and also to remove any
obstruction to navigation for which the tenant is
responsible."

On 12 January 1993 the Lord Ordinary *excluded*
from probation the pursuer's averments relating to the
costs of removal of asbestos and quoad ultra *allowed* a H
proof before answer.

LORD COULSFIELD.—The pursuer in this
action is the Lord Advocate acting on behalf of the
Secretary of State for Defence. The defenders are the
lessees under a lease which commenced on 17
December 1972, although it was not actually executed
until 1976. The lease terminated, following a notice
given by the defenders, on 6 October 1981. The subjects of lease were an area of ground known as Faslane I
Port with certain wharves and berths pertaining
thereto and a number of buildings and erections
thereon. The defenders duly entered into possession
under the lease. Clause eighth of the lease provided
inter alia: [his Lordship quoted the terms of cl eighth
set out supra and continued:]

Further provisions of cl eighth defined the subjects
in detail.

Clause sixteenth of the lease provided: [his Lordship J
quoted the terms of the clause and continued:]

On the face of the record, as it presently stands, the
pursuer makes claims against the defenders on three
grounds. First, he alleges that the defenders failed to
maintain the port area and buildings thereon and
claims compensation for defects listed in a dilapidation
report prepared by a firm of consulting engineers.
Secondly, the pursuer makes certain claims against the
defenders arising from the deposit of asbestos material K
on the subjects, which deposit is alleged to have been
due to breach of contract or negligence on the part of
the defenders. Thirdly, the pursuer makes certain
claims against the defenders under cl sixteenth of the
minute of lease in respect of the asbestos material
deposited on the subjects. The defenders pled that the
claims based on negligence or breach of contract had
prescribed. I heard argument on that issue in a procedure roll discussion and, on 23 August 1990, sustained
the defenders' plea of prescription to the extent of L
repelling the pursuer's first plea in law, which was a
plea relating to the breach of contract case [1991 SLT
838]. A reclaiming motion was enrolled but did not
proceed. Notwithstanding the fact that the breach of
contract claim has been held to have prescribed, the
plea and the averments relating to breach of contract
still form part of the record. After the decision not to
proceed with the reclaiming motion, the pleadings
were further amended and the case again came before
me on procedure roll on 27 November 1992. At that
hearing the defenders submitted that the whole case

A was irrelevant and should be dismissed or alternatively that certain parts of the pursuer's case should not be remitted to probation. Before considering the arguments, however, it is necessary to set out some of the pursuer's averments in more detail.

In cond 5, the pursuer avers that the defenders failed to maintain the port area and the relevant buildings in good tenantable order and repair and satisfactory in all respects and further avers that the defenders' failures, with the exception of the failure to remove and dispose of asbestos, are as detailed in the dilapidation report
B which is produced and referred to for its whole terms and incorporated brevitatis causa. In cond 6, the pursuer avers that the defenders have been called upon to make good the dilapidations and return the subjects to the condition in which they should have been at the termination of the lease but refuse or delay to do so. The sum claimed in respect of the dilapidations referred to in this part of the case amounts to £390,950.

C   In cond 7, the pursuer avers: "Further and in any event, the dumping of material including asbestos material on the subjects of let, constituted damage arising out of the defenders' operations or due to the negligence of the defenders. In the course of the defenders' operations carried out on the subjects of let, large quantities of material were removed from ships which were being broken up and said material was dumped on the subjects of let. Much of it contained asbestos material. The presence of this material arose
D directly from the defenders' operations carried out on the subjects of let, viz, the breaking up of ships." The condescendence then proceeds to set out certain averments relating to the case based on breach of contract, which, as I have indicated, has been disposed of and then continues: "Explained and averred that by said minute of lease the defenders accepted said site as in good tenantable order and repair and satisfactory in all respects and undertook to maintain it in a like condition. . . . A site which has substantial quantities of
E asbestos deposited upon it is not in good tenantable order and repair and satisfactory in all respects. The defenders are personally barred by their acceptance of said site as being in good tenantable order and repair and satisfactory in all respects from maintaining in their defence to this action that by 1972 the site already had substantial quantities of asbestos deposited upon it. Furthermore, in 1973 the defenders applied to the Health and Safety Executive for permission to enlarge their asbestos tips on said site and to
F tip further asbestos on the site. This application was granted by the Health and Safety Executive and the defenders proceeded to tip further asbestos on the site thereafter. The Ministry of Defence was never consulted about said application. The Ministry was not aware of said application and did not consent to further tipping of asbestos."

In cond 8 the pursuer makes further reference to the tipping of asbestos, in connection with a case based upon cl eighth of the lease, and there is further reference in that condescendence to the allegation that the

G defenders are personally barred from maintaining that there were substantial quantities of asbestos on the site before 1972. In cond 9 the pursuer avers that the defenders have been called upon to remove asbestos from the site, to return it to the condition in which it should have been and proceeds to make averments as to the areas which were contaminated by asbestos, and to the amount of asbestos which the Ministry of Defence required to remove in order to make the site safe. The amounts of asbestos involved were very large and the sum claimed as the cost of the operation to remove the asbestos is £15,450,000. It is not necessary
H for the present purpose to refer to the defences except to say that the defenders aver that there was a substantial amount of asbestos deposited on the site between 1946 and 1972, arising from the breaking up of warships at the site; that only a small number of warships were broken up after 1972, and that only a small amount of asbestos was deposited after that date. These averments are covered by general denials in the pursuer's pleadings.

I   The first argument advanced on behalf of the defenders was that the pursuer's averments of personal bar were irrelevant. The provision in cl eighth by which the defenders accepted the port area as in good order and repair was one which applied to the obligation of repair; it was not a general deeming provision that the subjects were to be taken to be in good repair and order for all the purposes of the lease and a fiction adopted for one purpose could not be transposed to another contractual obligation. That was highlighted by considering the nature of the obligation under cl
J sixteenth which clearly related to actual damage arising from the tenant's own operations and negligence, not to a deemed liability for other operations or the negligence of others. For the pursuer it was submitted that there were two possible applications of cl eighth, given that the case based on the clause itself was now out of the picture. In the first place, the acceptance of the subjects as in good order and repair might be relevant, in relation to cl sixteenth, as an adminicle of evidence in assessing the state of the
K subjects on entry. On that basis it would at least provide some evidence of their state at that time. Alternatively cl eighth provided the measure, judged by the lease, of the standard to which the tenant should make the subjects good, if he were required to do so. The pursuer's case was entirely that the damage to the subjects had been caused by the tenant. It was further his case that because asbestos was deposited on the site after 1972, the Secretary of State for Defence had required to remove all the asbestos there in order
L to render the site safe. Once the defenders had damaged the site they required to make it good or pay compensation for it. What the defenders had done was to give an assurance as to the whole state of the subjects at the termination of the lease and they were the only persons who had had anything to do on the site or to do with asbestos on it.

This part of the argument raises a short point of construction of the provisions of the lease. Neither party referred to authority, nor was it suggested that any of

A the other provisions of the lease might shed any light upon the two material clauses. In my view, cll eighth and sixteenth set out different obligations. Clause eighth is concerned with the tenant's obligation to maintain the subjects in good tenantable repair. Clause sixteenth sets out an obligation to remedy damage arising from the tenant's operations or caused by his negligence. Whatever may be the effect of the tenant's acceptance of the subjects as in good order and repair for the purposes of any obligation under cl eighth, that acceptance, in my opinion, has nothing to
B do with claims under cl sixteenth, which can only apply if the landlord demonstrates that the tenant's operations or negligence have indeed caused damage. That seems to me to be the plain meaning of the words of the two clauses. There is therefore, in my opinion, no substance in the pursuer's case of personal bar.

As regards the pursuer's alternative justifications for the retention of the averments relating to cl eighth, it seems to me doubtful whether the acceptance in cl eighth can really be founded upon as material in rela-
C tion to the question of fact whether there was any significant amount of asbestos on the site in 1972. However, I do not think that I can exclude the possibility that the averments in relation to cl eighth may be of some significance and therefore I do not think that I can exclude them from probation. The conclusion from this part of the argument is, therefore, that I would sustain the defenders' second plea in law and exclude from probation the averment: "The defenders are personally barred by their acceptance of said site
D as being in good tenantable order and repair and satisfactory in all respects from maintaining in their defence to this action that by 1972 the site already had substantial quantities of asbestos deposited upon it", which appears on p 14 of the closed record as amended in 1992, and the further averment: "As herein before averred, the defenders are personally barred from maintaining in their defence to this action that there were substantial quantities of asbestos material on said site before 1972", which appears on p 16 of the
E record.

The second argument for the defenders related to their general plea to the relevancy of the pursuer's case and was founded principally upon the failure of the pursuer's averments to make any distinction between the situation in regard to the deposit of asbestos prior to 1972 and after 1972. It was submitted that the pursuer's claim was calculated as a claim in respect of the removal of all asbestos material on the subjects at the
F termination of the lease. There was, however, some reason to think, from the pursuer's averments, that there was asbestos deposited prior to the commencement of the lease in 1972. In my view, it is correct to say that it is not easy to appreciate the precise position adopted by the pursuer on his own averments. As I have mentioned, the defenders aver that asbestos was deposited prior to 1972, but these averments are met with a general denial. The pursuer's case is presented as a claim for the cost of the removal of all asbestos which was on the site as at the conclusion of the lease and no attempt is made to distinguish quantities

deposited at an earlier period from any deposited at a later period. The background of the case, however, as G the pursuer's counsel accepted in the course of his submissions, is that these subjects have been used for shipbreaking since at least 1946. As I understood the position, the instructions upon which counsel for the pursuer proceeds are that the Ministry of Defence is unable to say whether or not there was any asbestos on the site prior to 1972, and that the whole basis of the case as presently presented is that it is irrelevant, for the purposes of the claim, to make any distinction between pre-1972 and post-1972 deposits. Counsel for H the defenders submitted that the pursuer's pleadings should be read closely and critically and that there are two averments which suggest that the pursuer does indeed appreciate that asbestos was deposited on the site before 1972. One of these is the averment at the end of cond 8 that the defenders *continued* to dump asbestos material on the foreshore and bed of the sea below high water mark after 1972. The second, and perhaps less significant, reference is found in cond 7 where it is said that in 1973 the defenders applied to the Health and Safety Executive for permission to I enlarge asbestos tips. It seems to me that there is some force in that submission. I do not, however, think that it is necessary to decide whether or not the pursuer should be taken to have admitted that there was asbestos on the site before 1972. It is sufficient to say that, having regard to the doubts which these averments raise, the relevancy of the case should be judged on the basis on which it has been deliberately pled and presented. If so, the only question which arises on these pleadings is whether the pursuer is entitled to J recover the whole cost of removing asbestos from the site, whether or not that asbestos was deposited during the currency of the lease; and, if he is not so entitled, the only case actually made on record, as the averments stand, fails.

Once the question is so stated, it appears to me that the answer, for the purposes of a claim under cl sixteenth of the lease, is obvious. In terms of that clause the tenant is bound to make good or pay com-
K pensation for "any damage arising out of its operations or due to the negligence of the tenant". On no possible view, so far as I can see, can the deposit of asbestos on the subjects prior to the commencement of the tenant's lease be regarded as damage arising out of the operations, or due to the negligence, of the tenant. The argument advanced on behalf of the pursuer was, as I understood it, that since some damage had, according to his averments, been caused to the subjects by the deposit of asbestos after 1972; and since
L it was necessary for all asbestos on the site to be removed, in order to render the site uncontaminated and fit for future occupation, no distinction fell to be made between pre-lease and post-lease deposits, but the tenants were obliged to remove the whole and to return the subjects to a proper state. In my view, that argument confuses the tenant's obligations under cl sixteenth with those under cl eighth; under cl eighth there is a requirement to return the subjects to the condition specified by that clause whereas under cl sixteenth there is no such conventional standard,

express or implied. In any event, the argument is, in my opinion, irreconcilable with the terms of cl sixteenth, which clearly impose an obligation specifically limited to damage caused by the operations or negligence of the tenant. In consequence, in my opinion, the claim in respect of the removal of asbestos as presently advanced is not relevantly pled. It is not necessary to consider at this stage what averments would require to be made to plead a relevant claim in respect of asbestos deposited only after 1972. It is sufficient to say that, on the footing at which the claim is presently advanced, it is irrelevant.

There remains the pursuer's claim in respect of dilapidations. The defenders submitted that this claim also was not relevantly pled because there was no attempt in the pleadings, or in the report referred to, to differentiate between damage caused by the tenant's operations and damage due to their negligence or to say what the negligence was. It was further submitted that in a number of contexts the report refers to vandalism, to demolition and site clearance and to the restoration of parts of the premises to current standards or to conformity with current codes of practice. Counsel for the pursuer, however, pointed out that while the report does make reference to demolition of buildings which have suffered from lack of maintenance or to the restoration of buildings to comply with current standards, the section of the report which sets out the costs claimed against the tenant invariably adopts the cheapest option, as between restoration of the property or demolition and clearance. In my opinion, the report, which is incorporated in the pleadings, does identify the dilapidations which are alleged to have occurred and does give the defenders fair notice of the claims against them. In this respect, therefore, I do not think that the defenders' submission is well founded.

In the whole circumstances in addition to sustaining the second plea in law for the defenders, I shall sustain their third and fourth pleas in law to the extent of excluding from probation the averments in conds 7, 8 and 9 relating to the deposit of asbestos materials upon the subjects of the lease and to the costs of removal of such asbestos. The practical effect of sustaining these pleas is to exclude from probation the whole of arts 7, 8 and 9 of condescendence, so far as not previously excluded from probation in consequence of the interlocutor of 23 August 1990. Quoad ultra, I shall allow a proof before answer.

Counsel for Pursuers, H H Campbell, QC, Menzies, QC; Solicitors, Robson McLean, WS — Counsel for Defenders, Keen; Solicitors, Steedman Ramage, WS.

M L B F

[The pursuer has marked a reclaiming motion.]

Bannon v Bannon

OUTER HOUSE

LORD CAMERON OF LOCHBROOM

29 JANUARY 1993

Husband and wife — Divorce — Financial provision — Valuation of matrimonial property — Pension rights — Method of valuation — Family Law (Scotland) Act 1985 (c 37), s 10 (1) and (5).

The Family Law (Scotland) Act 1985 provides that, on divorce, the net value of matrimonial property should be shared fairly, which s 10 defines as being shared equally or in such other proportions as are justified by special circumstances.

A wife raised an action of divorce against her husband, a serving police officer. The only matrimonial property of any value was the husband's interest in the police pension scheme established under the Police Pensions Act 1976. The husband's interest in the scheme was agreed to constitute matrimonial property to the extent that it was derived from service in the period from marriage until separation. The husband had no present access to any resources from which to meet any award of a capital sum.

The wife submitted that a capital sum should be awarded on the basis that the husband would survive until he had completed 30 years' service, that he would remain in the police service until that date (26 June 1999) and would then receive a lump sum of one and a half times his final annual salary. The husband proposed an alternative valuation by reference to the pension rights which had accrued during the period of marriage up to the date of separation on the assumption that the husband had then withdrawn from the police pension scheme and was to transfer to another scheme. This calculation was based upon the husband's salary at the time of separation and service to that date and the value was proportioned to the period of the marriage. The figure thus calculated was then increased to take account of the fact that, if so withdrawing, the husband could not receive payment until he reached the age of 60 but the deferred pension was index linked from the age of 55. The actuaries who gave evidence for the respective parties agreed that there was no one approved practice which was followed in relation to the valuation of pension rights but that on the whole the more general practice had been to adopt the "continuous service" method contended for on behalf of the wife.

Held, (1) that the "continuous service" method propounded on behalf of the wife was to be preferred and that, using that method, a figure of £46,000 was a fair valuation of the defender's interest in the pension scheme (pp 1003K-1004E and 1004G-K); (2) that a figure of £23,000 (being one half of that value) would represent a fair sharing of the matrimonial property in the circumstances (p 1005D-E); and (3) that since the valuation had been discounted back to the date of separation, whereas the husband would have no resources from which to make payment until 1999, on

A a broad view, the sum awarded should be increased to a figure of £32,000 to be paid on 26 June 1999 with interest thereon from that date until payment (p 1004E-H); and decree *pronounced* accordingly.

Action of divorce

Margaret Reid Cain or Bannon raised an action of divorce against her husband, John Dalgarno Miller Bannon. Decree of divorce and orders for custody of the two children of the parties' marriage in favour of B the wife were not opposed by the husband.

The case came before the Lord Ordinary (Lord Cameron of Lochbroom) for proof principally on the pursuer's conclusion for a capital sum arising from the defender's rights in a police pension scheme.

Statutory provisions

The Family Law (Scotland) Act 1985 provides:

"10.—(1) In applying the principle set out in section C 9 (1) (a) of this Act [fair sharing], the net value of the matrimonial property shall be taken to be shared fairly between the parties to the marriage when it is shared equally or in such other proportions as are justified by special circumstances. . . .

"(4) Subject to subsection (5) below, in this section and in section 11 of this Act 'the matrimonial property' means all the property belonging to the parties or either of them at the relevant date which was acquired by them or him (otherwise than by way of D gift or succession from a third party) — . . . (b) during the marriage but before the relevant date.

"(5) The proportion of any rights or interests of either party under a life policy or occupational pension scheme or similar arrangement referable to the period to which subsection (4) (b) above refers shall be taken to form part of the matrimonial property."

E **Cases referred to**

Bell v Bell, 1988 SCLR 457.
Brooks v Brooks, 1993 SLT 184.
Gulline v Gulline, 1992 SLT (Sh Ct) 71.
Little v Little, 1990 SLT 785 (1st Div); 1989 SCLR 613 (OH).
Muir v Muir, 1989 SLT (Sh Ct) 20; 1989 SCLR 445.
Park v Park, 1988 SCLR 584.

On 29 January 1993 the Lord Ordinary *pronounced* F decree of divorce, ordering that custody of the parties' two children be awarded to the pursuer and that the defender pay to the pursuer aliment of £35 per week in respect of each child and a capital sum of £32,000, payable on 26 June 1999, with interest to run thereafter.

LORD CAMERON OF LOCHBROOM.—The parties were married on 25 September 1971. At that time the defender was, as he still is, a serving police officer. The pursuer was then in employment and remained so until some months before the birth of the

parties' first child, Claire, on 8 January 1978. A second child, Gail, was born on 4 September 1982. G These children reside with the pursuer in accommodation which the pursuer rents from Glenrothes Development Corporation. I am satisfied on the evidence that they are well cared for by the pursuer and that there is satisfactory accommodation for them at their present address.

The pursuer and the defender lived together until about 11 August 1988. On that date the defender left the pursuer to live with another woman, Mrs Griffiths. The parties have not lived together since H said date. I am entirely satisfied on the evidence that the defender had no intention of living together with the pursuer after 11 August 1988 notwithstanding the fact that the pursuer was then willing to become reconciled to him. I am further satisfied that at no time has the defender sought to become reconciled with the pursuer and that there is now no prospect of any reconciliation between the parties. I therefore hold that the parties' marriage has broken down irretrievably. I shall therefore grant decree of divorce and I make the orders for custody of the two children as concluded for.

The only matters in dispute relate to the conclusions for aliment, periodical allowance and payment of a capital sum. After the separation of 11 August 1988 the pursuer continued to live for a period in a police house before obtaining her present accommodation. From the time that she gave up employment prior to the birth of Claire until the separation of the parties, J she was fully engaged in looking after the family and in bringing up the children of the marriage. After the separation she was for a short time employed as a sales assistant over one Christmas period. Otherwise she was unable to find employment which suited the hours which she required to work. More recently on the advice of her local job centre, she has been studying at Glenrothes College with a view to obtaining a certificated qualification in office administration. This course will be completed in about June 1993. She is K at present in receipt of a grant from the Fife Regional Council which meets the course fees of £1,855 and also provides an allowance for maintenance of the pursuer and the children amounting to £5,431 for the year to 31 August 1993. She also is in receipt of interim aliment for herself and for each child by virtue of an order of this court pronounced on 26 March 1992. Under it the defender was ordained to pay interim aliment at the rate of £25 per week to the pursuer, a similar sum per week for the child Claire L and the sum of £20 per week for the child Gail. She is thus receiving by way of grant, benefit and interim aliment a sum of approximately £848 monthly. Her monthly outgoings are set out in no 66/18 of process. These amount to a figure of £487 or thereby. She thus has a weekly sum of about £80 available to meet the cost of items such as clothing, shoes, dental, optical and other medical treatment and any holiday expenses. I accept the pursuer's evidence that she is not able to make any appreciable savings out of her present income and that her ordinary and necessary

outgoings are just met from her present income.
A Furthermore, I accept her evidence that once she has
completed her present course in office administration,
there is no certainty that she will immediately be able
to obtain gainful employment. In such an event she
will require to depend very largely upon payment of
benefit and any aliment which she obtains from the
defender for the continued support of herself and the
two children of the marriage.

On the other hand, the evidence satisfies me that for
the present the defender's circumstances are yet more
B straitened than those of the pursuer. While he earns a
net monthly salary as a police officer of approximately
£860, he is substantially in debt. There is at present
a sum of £318.56 per month which has been arrested
from his earnings towards payment of outstanding
accounts for legal expenses incurred in a sheriff court
action in which he was found liable for his own and
the pursuer's expenses. In addition in 1990 he and
Mrs Griffiths jointly purchased a house. They bought
the house for £73,000. It is presently valued at
C £75,000. They borrowed £72,000 for its purchase.
They have to pay jointly a sum of £715 monthly for
a mortgage. That figure includes a sum to meet outstanding arrears of some £3,000. In addition the
defender is also bound to make payments on overdrawn bank accounts. Mrs Griffiths is presently a
student undertaking an honours degree course in
speech and language pathology and therapy which will
continue for a further two and a half years. It was not
seriously disputed that her present income position is
D no less parlous than that of the defender. In particular
she is dependent on a grant and is not in receipt of any
payment of aliment for her two children by previous
marriages. I am satisfied that there is no real prospect
that she will in the meantime receive any payment
under the outstanding maintenance orders made in her
favour for these children. In the whole circumstances
I am satisfied that the defender's circumstances are at
present such that he could not undertake any further
obligations to pay aliment than he requires to meet by
E virtue of the order pronounced on 26 March 1992.
The defender also spoke to the prospect that if he were
for any reason to be made bankrupt, he might be
required by his chief constable to resign and leave the
service. He pointed out that while he was anxious to
avoid this eventuality, it was not a wholly remote risk
in his present financial state. The evidence also satisfies me that the likelihood of any substantial improvement in the finances of the defender and Mrs Griffiths
in the reasonably foreseeable future is minimal. In
F evidence the pursuer accepted that she did have some
prospects of employment after her present course. She
also expressed a preference that any payments made to
her should in future be directed to alimenting the two
children of the marriage. In these circumstances I am
prepared to make an order for payment of aliment for
each child at the rate of £35 per week and to make no
order for payment to the pursuer herself of a periodical allowance.

I turn now to the matter of the claim for a capital
sum of £70,000. It is common ground between the

parties that the only matrimonial property of any
value is the defender's interest in the police pension G
scheme established under the Police Pensions Act
1976. This provides that all service from the date of
joining a police force, subject to a minimum age
requirement, which does not apply in the defender's
case, shall count as pensionable service. Pensionable
pay is the individual's basic salary. A member of the
scheme may retire on completion of 30 years' service
with full pension, provided he is under the compulsory retirement age which in the defender's case is 55
years of age. He may also elect to retire at 50 provided H
he has completed 25 years' pensionable service by that
date. At retirement after 30 years' service a member is
entitled to a tax free cash sum of at least one and a half
times his final pensionable pay, being the best
pensionable pay in the last three years of pensionable
service. Provision is also made within the scheme for
ill health retirement benefits and for death benefits
where death occurs in the line of duty. A member's
widow is also entitled to restricted pension rights on
the death of a member. Parties are agreed that by I
virtue of s 9 of the 1976 Act these pension rights and
interests cannot be validly assigned nor charged except
for the benefit of a dependant of a pensioner. Parties
are further agreed that the defender's interest in the
police pension scheme constitutes matrimonial
property so far as and to the extent that it is derived
from service, and from pensionable pay earned during
such service, in the period from the date of marriage
until 11 August 1988. Parties are further agreed that
if the defender continues in police service until 26 J
June 1999, when he would be 51½ years of age, he
will complete the required 30 years' service to entitle
him to his full pension. It is further accepted for the
pursuer that in terms of the pension scheme it is
provided that if the defender had left police service at
the date of separation he would have qualified for a
deferred pension payable from the age of 60 years of
age, that the deferred pension would have had its value
fully maintained up to the age of retirement (that is to
say the age of 55) and thereafter would have been K
index linked to the retail price index.

It is accepted for the pursuer that the defender has
at present no access to resources otherwise from which
to meet any award of a capital sum. Nor can he borrow
upon the expectation of his becoming entitled to a
pension nor once he becomes entitled to a pension can
he borrow upon his future pension payment. The only
resource which is therefore likely to be available to the
defender is the capital sum to which he or his estate
would become entitled in any of the various events L
that can give rise to the emergence of pension rights.
In evidence the defender himself made clear his intention, if he can, to complete his full period of 30 years'
service, though there was evidence that he now suffers
from a back complaint which disables him from time
to time and now means that he spends much of his
time in court administration.

Counsel for the pursuer invited me to assess the
award of a capital sum on the basis that the defender
will survive until the age when he completes 30 years'

A service, that he will remain in the police service until that date, that he will then secure a lump sum payment of at least one and a half times his final year's salary and that it is reasonable to anticipate that the payment of that sum will be made within a month of the date upon which the entitlement to a full pension arises. He submitted that the value of the defender's pension rights upon which any award be made, should be calculated by reference to what was called the "continuing service" basis.

B Evidence was led by the pursuer from an actuary, Mr Ritchie, as to the method by which such a valuation was made and the arithmetical calculation whereby he assessed the value of the defender's benefits at the date of separation at £79,000. The evaluation proceeded upon the facts that the defender was born on 29 January 1948 and the pursuer born on 8 February 1941, that the defender entered the police pension scheme on 26 June 1969, that the parties were married on 25 September 1971 and ceased to live C together on 11 August 1988 and that at the time of separation the defender's pensionable remuneration was £15,123. I pause to observe that the defender's actuarial calculations proceeded upon precisely similar information. In reaching a value of £79,000 Mr Ritchie started by estimating what pension would be enjoyed by the defender if he retired upon completion of 30 years' service. Using the base of the defender's pensionable remuneration at the time of separation he assumed an average salary increase of 7 per cent per D annum for each of the 11 years between 1988 and 1999. This percentage was calculated upon an assumption of an average increase over the period in the retail price index of 5½ per cent per annum and an average salary increase over the period of 1½ per cent per annum greater than the increase in the retail price index. Having thereby achieved a figure for the final year's salary, he valued the defender's pension rights which then accrued according to recognised actuarial principles, taking into account the risks of E mortality up to 1999 and thereafter by reference to recognised actuarial tables. Having made that valuation, he had then discounted that figure by 9 per cent per annum to achieve a value for a fund which would be required as at 11 August 1988 to produce the final figure by the date when the defender completed 30 years' service. The figure of £79,000 thus represented the sum which, in August 1988, would have been required for investment in long term index linked gilts as would produce a sufficient fund to underwrite pay-F ment of the defender's pension on retirement after 30 years' service. In cross examination, Mr Ritchie accepted that his calculations had been wrongly based because he had assumed that if the defender were to retire before completing 30 years' service, while his pension payments would be deferred until aged 60, they would be index linked from the date of retirement and not from the age of 55 as provided for in the scheme. He accepted that the effect of this error was to reduce his final valuation by 20 per cent to £63,200. He further agreed that if his assessment of the annual compound rate for salary increase was considered to be

G unreasonably high and were to be related to the annual increase in the retail price index over the period, this would further reduce his final valuation figure by some £13,000 to £50,000. He also accepted that his calculation of the benefits accruing at retirement on full pension had included provision for a widow's pension which would constitute 15 per cent of the final figure. Thus within his adjusted final figure of £63,200 for the value of the defender's interest at the date of separation, the provision for a widow's pension amounted to £11,850.

H Mr Ritchie was shown a contrary valuation of £34,270 prepared for the defender by an actuary, Mr Lee, which was spoken to by him in evidence. This valuation is fully set out in no 68/3 of process. It valued the pension rights which had accrued during the period of marriage up to the date of separation on the assumption that the member had then withdrawn from the police pension scheme and was to transfer to another scheme. These rights were calculated upon the defender's salary at the date of separation and his I service up to that date and were proportioned to the period of marriage, thus leaving out of account service prior to marriage. This figure was then increased to take account of the fact that, if so withdrawing, the defender could not secure payment until he attained the age of 60 but the deferred pension was index linked from the age of 55. The sum produced represented a fund which would, at the time when such deferred pension became payable at the age of 60, be sufficient to allow for the increase of those pension rights in line with an annual increase of 5 per cent in J the retail price index from the age of 55 until the age of 60 and thereafter for an index linked pension when payable. The valuation of those deferred rights was then discounted from the age of 60 to the date of separation at 4 per cent per annum compound. This figure was the equivalent of the figure of 9 per cent per annum gross, being an annual absolute rate 4 per cent greater than the retail price index of 5 per cent. It was said by Mr Lee in evidence that this valuation reflected the true value of the benefits which would be K available to an individual if he had left the force at the date of separation.

In a letter attached to the report, no 68/3 of process, Mr Lee explained that the valuation had been carried out on the basis of gross pension rights and that no allowance had been made for tax which would be paid on the pension upon its payment. It was made clear that it was not possible to estimate the likely levels of taxation that would apply during the defender's retire-L ment, nor could an estimate be made of the defender's overall financial circumstances during retirement. Accordingly the opinion was expressed in that letter that it was not appropriate to incorporate an allowance for tax in the valuation made in the report. In evidence however Mr Lee argued for some reduction to take account of the possibility of the defender's pension being subject to taxation. Mr Ritchie, when asked about this, was critical of such an approach. It was not normally done. He pointed out that money paid in to an approved scheme was not taxed. In any case, as Mr

Lee himself accepted, it was impossible to predict
A what level, if any, of tax would be payable by the
defender. Indeed the effects of taxation could both be
reduced and be increased by the assumed date of
payment at the age of 60. I consider that it is more
equitable to proceed upon the basis that no account be
taken of the incidence of taxation.

In the end of the day neither Mr Ritchie nor Mr Lee
disputed the arithmetic of the other's calculations.
They were agreed that there was no one approved
practice which was followed in relation to the valua-
B tion of pension rights but that on the whole the more
general practice had been to adopt the method which
was followed by Mr Ritchie, namely the continuous
service method. So far as that method was concerned,
Mr Ritchie agreed that by reason of the normal mortality tables, the risk of failing to survive the age of
51½ in a man of the pursuer's age was regarded as
minimal and fell to be discounted. The rationale of the
method adopted by Mr Lee was fully set out in the
appendix to his report and I do not repeat it. The most
C substantial difference between the two methods was
that in the continuous service method provision was
made in calculating the benefits to be valued that the
defender would become entitled to his full pension
rights on 30 years' service and that for that purpose he
would continue to make payments from his salary, the
salary levels being increased annually over the period
from the date of separation until the age of retirement
after 30 years' continuous service. In the alternative
method spoken to by Mr Lee, the assumption was that
D the only pension rights which fell to be valued were
those which had accrued at the date of separation upon
a salary scale which was that received at that date and
which would fall to be paid at the deferred date,
namely the age of 60.

There was no dispute between parties that actuarial
evidence was appropriate for a determination of the
value to be placed upon the prospective pension rights
or interests which had accrued or would accrue to the
E defender as a consequence of payments made by him
to the police pension scheme during his service from
the date of marriage until the date of separation. The
live issue was as to the basis on which a determination
was to be carried out. Reference was made to cases in
which the "leaving service" or "real value" basis had
been accepted: e g *Bell v Bell* and *Park v Park*. On the
other hand in cases such as *Muir v Muir*, *Little v Little*
and *Gulline v Gulline* the "continuing service" basis
was adopted. Reference was also made to an article by
Mr R A Scott, FFA, entitled "Pension Rights on
F Divorce" (1991) 36 JLS 45, in which the author refers
to both approaches and suggests that the "leaving
service" approach is to be preferred. As Mr Scott
properly points out in the article, the first question to
be asked and answered is what it is that is to be valued.
Section 10 (5) of the Family Law (Scotland) Act 1985
provides that amongst other things, matrimonial
property shall include "the proportion of any rights or
interests of either party under a life policy or occupational pension scheme" which is referable to the
period during the marriage up to the date of separa-

tion. In the present case the defender is not yet in right
of a pension. It is therefore the prospective interest of G
the defender under the police pension scheme which
falls to be valued. The matter is complicated by the
fact that unless and until that interest matures, the
defender has no resources from which to meet any
order for a capital payment since he is prevented by the
statutory provisions under which the police
pension scheme operates from assigning or borrowing
upon the security of his prospective interest. That
matter further bears upon a separate though related
issue, namely the extent of the defender's resources. H
Common to both issues however is the assessment of
probability of the occurrence of the events which
would give rise to the defender's interest being
realised. It is clear from the most cursory glance at the
police pension scheme, set out in no 66/14 of process,
that the defender's interest at the relevant date has to
be measured to take account of a number of different
events in which that interest may emerge. It is also
proper to have in mind that the property to be valued
is that proportion of the interests "of either party" I
under the police pension scheme. Because she is
presently the wife of the defender and thus potentially
his widow, the pursuer has an interest in the scheme.
But I agree with Lord Marnoch's view in *Brooks v
Brooks* that since a divorced wife would not be eligible
to claim such rights were they to come into being, they
should not form part of the defender's interest for the
purpose of valuation. Until the parties' divorce, the
pursuer's interest is protected. The claim for a capital
sum only emerges upon divorce, when the pursuer's J
interest flies off. That same interest could only
become available after divorce if the defender remarried. Divorce is the event which gives rise to the
claim for a capital sum. Accordingly thereafter the
widow's interest would reflect the interest of some
party other than that of the pursuer and defender in
this case. Insofar as the pursuer has any "interest"
under the police pension scheme at the relevant date,
it is extinguished upon decree of divorce being pronounced and falls to be disregarded. K

It was argued that since it is only that "proportion"
of the interests of the defender under the police
pension scheme which is referable to the period of
marriage up to the date of separation which falls to be
valued, the pursuer was not entitled to secure any
advantage which the defender might obtain from contributions made by him after the date of separation,
and in particular of any future salary increases. But
the "interests" of the defender which fall to be valued L
depend upon an assessment of his "final salary" since
that will be the basis upon which his actual pension
rights, however they may emerge, are to be determined. I do not consider that this submission should
be acceded to in the present case. The assessment of
the defender's "final salary" requires that an assessment be made of the event to which the final salary is
to be related. In the present case, that event was not
his leaving service at the date of separation. While the
scheme made provision for that event, it was also providing for further and future events as well. I therefore

consider that the "leaving service" basis is flawed
since it assumes as the event giving rise to the assessment of final salary one which is proved not to have
occurred. It also fails to take into account the fact that
the payments already subscribed by the defender
before the date of separation were directed to providing cover for other and future events just as much as
are payments made by the defender after the date of
separation. In these circumstances, I find that the
reasoning of Mr Ritchie in selecting the event upon
which to assess the final salary, namely the defender's
attainment of 30 years' service in June 1999, at which
date the defender will still hold the same rank, is consistent with the evidence. No problems arise as to the
assessment of future promotion. The evidence did not
suggest that the defender was likely to rise above his
present appointment as a police constable. Indeed no
such suggestion was made by the defender himself.
Furthermore, although there was reference made to
present back trouble by the defender which affected
his present working, he himself said that he was
anxious to complete 30 years' service. I can understand that there may in other cases be difficulties in
assessing the extent of the "final salary", but that difficulty does not, in my opinion, arise in the present
case. There was no material risk on the basis of the
mortality tables that the defender would die prior to
that date, at least to the extent of affecting the actuarial
calculations made by Mr Ritchie (and indeed in this
respect I observe that Mr Lee's calculations proceeded
upon the basis that the defender would survive to age
60). Accordingly I am prepared to proceed upon the
basis that it is much more likely than not that the
defender will survive to, and remain in police service
until, the age of 51½ by which time he will have completed a total of 30 years' police service. It follows that
it is reasonable to anticipate that the defender in
accordance with the police pension scheme will then
become entitled to a pension for the remainder of his
life and will at that time be entitled to elect to
commute part of his future pension rights for a tax free
lump sum amounting to one and a half times his final
year's basic salary. I therefore accept as reasonable the
basis for computation of the interest of the defender
which was selected by Mr Ritchie and spoken to in
evidence by him.

In choosing the approach adopted by Mr Ritchie I
have taken account of the fact that in the method
which was proposed by Mr Lee and which is set out
in detail in no 68/3 of process, it is said that that
method "clearly values a member's actual rights at the
relevant date", that is to say the date of separation. I
refer to para 2.3 of that document. This of course is
not the case. No "rights" have emerged at that date
and the member continues to have an interest in the
emergence of benefits upon the occurrence of one of
a number of future events to which both his past and
future contributions are directed. These benefits are
referred to in the same paragraph as "other possible
rights" which "only arise in the happening of certain
future contingencies". It is said that such occurrences
are "only hypothetical at the relevant date", but that
is not to say that no one of them will not, in fact,
occur. It is in that regard that I consider in the present

case the method adopted by Mr Lee is misconceived.
The only difficulty arises in relation to the certainty
which attaches to the event which is selected as the
appropriate one for the purpose of the valuation exercise. As I indicate above, the event selected by Mr
Ritchie, namely the event of the defender leaving
service at the conclusion of 30 years' service and securing his pension then, is a reasonable one in the light
of the whole evidence.

However, I am not prepared to accept the valuation
of £79,000 which Mr Ritchie placed upon it. In the
first place he admittedly proceeded upon a misunderstanding of the police pension scheme. If the defender
was to leave service at the age of 51½, that is to say
before the compulsory retirement age, his pension
would not be index linked until he reached the age of
55. That being so, as Mr Ritchie accepted, his valuation requires to be reduced to a figure of £63,200.
Furthermore, as I indicated above, I consider that the
widow's interest also falls to be deducted. That further
reduces his valuation by a sum of £11,850, to approximately £51,000. Furthermore, there was a disagreement between Mr Ritchie and Mr Lee as to the proper
basis upon which any estimate of salary increase
should be based. In evidence it was accepted that the
salary increase which had been enjoyed by the police
both for the last year and the year before had been of
the order of 6½ per cent. The figure used for the compound rate of increase per annum by Mr Ritchie was
7 per cent between the present date and the date when
the defender would have completed 30 years' service.
This is because he assumed that any salary increase
would be 1½ per cent above the assumed annual rate
of increase in the retail price index of 5½ per cent.
While I consider that it is not unreasonable to anticipate that future salary increases may be slightly above
the assumed rate of increase in the retail price index,
I am not satisfied on the evidence that the figure taken
by Mr Ritchie is consistent with the increases in the
immediate past. It was accepted by Mr Ritchie that if
the salary increase were to be limited to a retail price
index increase of 5½ per cent, a sum of some £13,000
would fall to be deducted. In my opinion an appropriate deduction would not be so great. On a broad
view I would assess it as amounting to under one half
of that sum to bring out a figure of £46,000 as the
value of the defender's interest at the date of separation.

Such a valuation cannot bring out an absolutely
certain figure by reason that the defender's interest is
a prospective entitlement to benefit which must vary
according to the event which gives rise to it. The event
selected is of course not certain. Furthermore, because
of the nature of the police pension scheme that prospective entitlement cannot be realised for cash at any
stage prior to the event which gives rise to the emergence of that entitlement. However, as I have indicated above in my opinion, the method which as a first
step seeks to ascertain the event which will most probably give rise to that entitlement, and thus to the
defender's enjoyment of a pension, is the more appropriate method in this case to secure a proper valuation.
Nevertheless that exercise cannot be absolutely
certain. In other cases, for instance in personal injury

actions, the court has been accustomed to make provision for uncertainty by way of a broad approach to the risks inherent in such an exercise. It is necessary to bear in mind in this case that the valuation figure effectively ignores the risk of death between the present date and 26 June 1999 on the basis of general mortality tables. It also ignores the possibility that even if alive at that latter date the defender will already have retired because of ill health.

Being satisfied therefore that the sum of £46,000 is a reasonable valuation of the defender's interest in the police pension scheme at the date of separation, the next issue that arises is as to what proportion of that sum should be secured to the pursuer and what order be made for its payment. In the first place, it is to be observed that the defender has no resources at present from which to pay any capital sum and it was not suggested that he would be able to do so unless and until he retired and was able to elect for commutation of part of his pension for a tax free lump sum. Accordingly I do not consider that on the evidence the defender will have any sufficient resources from which to make payment of a capital sum until after June 1999 on the reasonable assumptions set out above. As appears from the evidence of Mr Ritchie and Mr Lee, the defender's basic salary for purposes of pension has clearly increased since the date of separation at which time it was £15,123. At present, he receives a basic salary of some £20,000 per annum. It is reasonable to assume that there will be increments in line with the retail price index or a little above until 1999. Even on his present salary scale he would at that time be entitled to a tax free lump sum of at least £30,000. Since the defender has no present resources with which to meet any order for a capital sum, it is clear that any payment has to be deferred. In my opinion, since the value accorded to his interest in the police pension scheme has been discounted back to the date of separation, it is only proper that the pursuer should be recompensed for any deferment of payment from the present date. On the basis of a figure of £46,000 as a fair valuation of the defender's interest and thus of the matrimonial property at the date of settlement, one half would be £23,000. In this case, I would regard such a sum as representing a fair sharing of the matrimonial property in the circumstances. But it represents a value which has been discounted back to the date of separation. Some provision requires, in my opinion, to be made on the one hand for the fact that it must be assumed that the pursuer will be lying out of her share of the matrimonial property until 1999, and, on the other hand, for the possibility that the defender's interest may, because of death or ill health or circumstances such as bankruptcy, forcing him to leave service, emerge sooner and that this may give rise to a lesser sum becoming available to him than would be the case if he were to survive and remain in service until June 1999. On a very broad view I consider that balancing these varying factors there is warrant for making some increase in the capital sum. I do this in preference to making an order for payment of interest thereon from the date of decree since if, notwithstanding the assumption that the defender will survive until June 1999, he had in fact to leave service

at an earlier date for whatever reason that might be, there is no provision under s 12 (4) of the Act for any adjustment of the capital sum itself. It would however be possible for the date on which payment was to be made and the date from which interest was to be paid, to be varied. Accordingly I do not consider it appropriate in the present case that the deferment of payment should be reflected in an order for a payment of a capital sum with interest on it prior to the date of payment. I propose to fix the capital sum at a figure of £32,000 and to order that it be paid on 26 June 1999 with interest thereon at the rate of 15 per cent per annum until payment. I was urged by counsel for the defender that if I took the course which I propose to do, I should fix a date which was not identical to the assumed date of retirement but one month later. I do not propose to do so because in the circumstances the defender may already have made his election and furthermore may then be in a position to borrow money on the security of his interest in his house to meet the order for payment of a capital sum in advance of his receipt of such tax free sum.

Counsel for Pursuer (Wife), J K Mundy; Solicitors, Gray Muirhead, WS (for W J Reid, Dunfermline) — Counsel for Defender (Husband), G M Henderson; Solicitors, Campbell Smith & Co, WS.

G J J

Balfour Beatty Construction (Scotland) Ltd v Scottish Power plc

SECOND DIVISION

THE LORD JUSTICE CLERK (ROSS), LORDS MURRAY AND MORISON

19 MARCH 1993

Contract — Breach of contract — Damages — Remoteness of damage — Reasonable foreseeability of loss — Supply of electricity for construction contract — Interruption of supply leading to requirement to demolish and rebuild partly completed structure — Whether foreseeable.

A construction company engaged in the building of a roadway and associated structures including an aqueduct contracted with the electricity board for the supply of electricity to operate a concrete batching plant. During the course of building the aqueduct, which required a continuous pour operation, the batching plant stopped working. In an action of damages for breach of contract brought by the construction company against the successors of the electricity board, it was established that the electricity supply had been interrupted and that the interruption was a breach of contract by the electricity board. The construction company claimed the cost of demolishing and rebuilding a substantial part of their construction

A works, this having been rendered necessary by the interruption of the electricity supply and the consequent interruption of the required continuous pour.

After proof, the Lord Ordinary found that the defenders had not known of the need for a continuous pour, nor that it would not be possible simply to cut back part of the hardened concrete to a face against which fresh concrete could be poured to form a joint. He therefore concluded that the need to condemn the whole operation had not been within the defenders' reasonable contemplation, and assoilzied them. The

B pursuers reclaimed.

Held, (1) that even if the particular loss in question was not within the defenders' reasonable contemplation, it was sufficient for them to be liable that the loss was of a kind that was within their reasonable contemplation (pp 1010H, 1014D-F and 1015J-L); (2) that it was apparent from the evidence that it was within the defenders' reasonable contemplation that an interruption in the supply of electricity, and thus of concrete, might necessitate remedial work such as cutting back

C the hardened concrete so as to form a joint with fresh concrete (pp 1010A-F, 1014C-D and 1016A-B); and (3) that the distinction between remedial work of that kind, involving removal of part of what had been constructed, and remedial work involving removal of the whole of what had been constructed, was a distinction of degree, and not of kind, and accordingly that the pursuers' loss, while of a greater degree than was within the defenders' reasonable contemplation, was nevertheless of a kind that was within such contem-

D plation (pp 1011A-D, 1014F-G and 1016I-J), and reclaiming motion *allowed*, interlocutor of the Lord Ordinary *recalled*, and decree *granted* against the defenders in the agreed sum.

Hadley v Baxendale (1854) 9 Ex 341, and *H Parsons (Livestock) Ltd v Uttley Ingham & Co Ltd* [1978] 1 QB 791, *applied*.

Per Lord Murray: The defenders having signed a joint minute agreeing that as a result of the pouring operation not being completed the pursuers had no

E reasonable alternative but to demolish and reconstruct the aqueduct at a stated cost, were thereafter barred from challenging the claim on the ground of remoteness (p 1014I-K).

Action of damages
(Reported 1992 SLT 811)

Balfour Beatty Construction (Scotland) Ltd raised an action of damages for breach of contract against the

F South of Scotland Electricity Board. By amendment shortly before the proof Scottish Power plc, who had succeeded to the liabilities of the South of Scotland Electricity Board, were substituted as defenders.

The case came to proof before the Lord Ordinary (Clyde). In the course of the proof the parties lodged a joint minute agreeing that as a result of the events for which the defenders were said to be liable, the pursuers had had no reasonable alternative but to demolish and reconstruct the works then under construction at a total cost of £229,102.53.

Cases referred to

Czarnikow (C) Ltd v Koufos [1969] 1 AC 350; [1967] G 3 WLR 1491; [1967] 3 All ER 686.
Hadley v Baxendale (1854) 9 Ex 341.
Karlshamns Oljefabriker (A/B) v Monarch Steamship Co Ltd, 1949 SLT 51; 1949 SC (HL) 1.
Parsons (H) (Livestock) Ltd v Uttley Ingham & Co Ltd [1978] 1 QB 791; [1977] 3 WLR 990; [1978] 1 All ER 525.
Smith v Johnson (1899) 15 TLR 179.
Transworld Oil Ltd v North Bay Shipping Corporation (The "Rio Claro") [1978] 2 Lloyd's Rep 173. H
Vacwell Engineering Co Ltd v BDH Chemicals Ltd [1971] 1 QB 111; [1969] 3 WLR 927; [1969] 3 All ER 1681.
Victoria Laundry (Windsor) Ltd v Newman Industries, Coulson & Co Ltd [1949] 2 KB 528.

Textbooks referred to
Gloag, *Contract* (2nd ed), p 696.
McGregor, *Damages* (13th ed), pp 131-132.

On 5 February 1991 the Lord Ordinary *assoilzied* I the defenders. (Reported 1992 SLT 811.)

The pursuers reclaimed.

Reclaiming motion
The reclaiming motion was heard before the Second Division on 23 and 24 February 1993.

On 19 March 1993 the court *allowed* the reclaiming motion, *recalled* the interlocutor of the Lord Ordinary, J *sustained* the first plea in law for the pursuers and *granted* decree for payment to the pursuers by the defenders in the agreed sum of £229,102.53 with interest from the date of citation.

THE LORD JUSTICE CLERK (ROSS).—In this action the pursuers are claiming damages from the defenders on the ground of breach of contract. In 1985 the pursuers were engaged in the construction of the Edinburgh city bypass (Sighthill section). This K involved the building of a roadway and associated structures including the Union canal aqueduct across the bypass. The structures including the aqueduct were to be built of concrete, and the pursuers' contract with Lothian Regional Council provided for the pouring of the concrete required to build these structures. A batching plant for the mixing of the concrete had been set up by the pursuers at Hillwood quarry, Edinburgh, and the batching plant was run on a temporary supply of electricity which was being provided by the South of Scotland Electricity Board under a L contract entered into between them and the pursuers. The rights and liabilities of the South of Scotland Electricity Board have now passed to Scottish Power plc who are the defenders in the action, but for convenience I shall follow the course adopted by the Lord Ordinary and refer to the South of Scotland Electricity Board as the defenders.

On 28 October 1985, the pursuers were engaged in pouring the first stage of the aqueduct. After about 12 hours of work when the structure of stage 1 was nearly complete, the batching plant ceased to operate due to a failure of the electricity supply. It was discovered that first one and then the other two of the fuses on the defenders' three phase supply had fractured. The plant was out of action for so long that the construction work was halted, and as the operation required to be achieved in a continuous pour, ultimately the decision was taken to demolish all that had been done and to start the whole of stage 1 again. The pursuers claim that the stoppage was caused by breach of contract on the part of the defenders, and they claim damages in respect of the cost of the remedial work occasioned by that breach.

After sundry procedure a proof before answer took place before the Lord Ordinary. The Lord Ordinary held that the defenders were in breach of their contract with the pursuers. The question then arose as to whether the pursuers had proved that the loss which they had suffered was caused by that breach of contract. The defenders presented various arguments to the effect that the pursuers' loss had not been caused by failure of the electrical supply but was due to other circumstances. Indeed, as the Lord Ordinary observes, the defenders put forward a catalogue of causes for the loss. The Lord Ordinary, however, concluded that the initiating cause, namely the failure of the fuse, materially contributed to the pursuers' loss, and that so far as causation was concerned, the pursuers were well founded in contending that the defenders' breach of contract caused the loss. The Lord Ordinary also held that the defenders had failed to prove that the pursuers themselves were in any way at fault so as to cause or materially contribute to the breakdown of the concrete core. A question, however, arose as to remoteness of damages, and although the Lord Ordinary held that the pursuers had established a liability on the part of the defenders to make reparation to them, he also held that the pursuers had failed to prove the only quantified loss which was before him in the case. He accordingly granted decree of absolvitor in favour of the defenders.

Against that interlocutor of the Lord Ordinary the pursuers have now reclaimed. In the reclaiming motion they have contended that the Lord Ordinary ought to have upheld the pursuers' first plea in law and to have pronounced damages of the amount referred to in the joint minute no 53 of process. [His Lordship then discussed another matter, with which this report is not concerned, and continued:]

Counsel for the pursuers pointed out that the construction of the aqueduct had to be carried out by means of continuous concrete pours in two stages. As already observed stage 1 was very nearly complete when the batching plant ceased to operate due to the failure in supply. In the course of his opinion the Lord Ordinary has explained why what had been done had to be demolished and stage 1 started again. In his opinion he states (1992 SLT at p 812E-H): "After considerable discussion and consultation during the days which followed the stoppage the pursuers decided to demolish all that they had built on 28 October and to reconstruct the length of the aqueduct which they had intended to build. The immediate instruction given by

Mr Jeffs, the pursuers' project manager, on 29 October, was to have the concrete cut back to a face which might form a joint for continuation of the construction. The particular problem here however, was that the concrete required to be watertight, not simply in the sense of keeping water out but as an aqueduct in preventing water leaking through it. While a waterproof lining was to be applied to the structure after the concrete was complete, the contract required the concrete structure to be tested successfully for its ability to hold water before the waterproof lining was applied. Mr Jeffs was not satisfied that a joint against the concrete which had been laid would achieve the desired result. One joint had been intended in the design but the proper method of achieving a watertight joint in such a structure was by the insertion of a waterbar into the structure at the joint and that required to be done when the concrete was laid in place and was still soft at the place where the joint was to be. A waterbar could not be satisfactorily created now that the concrete had hardened. The view was then taken that there was no valid alternative to demolition and reconstruction."

At the start of the proof that view was challenged, but after the evidence of Mr Jeffs had been led in chief, senior counsel for the defenders intimated that the defenders would no longer challenge as unreasonable the decision which had been taken to demolish the work and reconstruct it. A joint minute was accordingly entered into. It states that it has been agreed: "As a result of the stage 1 pour of the Union canal aqueduct not being completed on 28 October 1985 the pursuers had no reasonable alternative but to demolish and reconstruct stage 1 and the costs of doing so and of investigating the breakdown of the power supply as averred in art 5 amounted to £229,102.53 sterling."

Under reference to *Hadley v Baxendale* and subsequent authorities, counsel for the pursuers contended that the damages referred to in the joint minute were recoverable from the defenders as being damages such as might reasonably be supposed to have been in the contemplation of both parties at the time when the contract was made as the probable result of the breach of it. They contended that the defenders had been requested to supply electricity which they were aware was to be used for the operation of a batching plant for the manufacture of concrete; the defenders were also aware that the concrete was to be used in the construction of the Edinburgh city bypass and associated structures including the Union canal aqueduct. It was contended that in these circumstances it was reasonable for the defenders to contemplate that there was to be civil engineering work upon a considerable scale, and that a considerable quantity of concrete would have to be continually manufactured. Moreover as ordinary people without any special knowledge, they should have known that concrete sets within a short period, and that that imposes civil engineering constraints. They should therefore have realised that if there was a breach of contract upon their part and an interruption to the supply of electricity it was foreseeable that some remedial works would be necessary.

What the pursuers were claiming for was the cost of remedial works, and although the scale of these might not have been reasonably foreseeable by the defenders, the remedial works which were carried out were not damage of a different type from those which could reasonably have been foreseen.

The defenders, on the other hand, stressed that remoteness was a question of fact to be determined on a consideration of the facts and circumstances of the particular case, and that this court should be slow to set aside the decision of the Lord Ordinary upon such a question of fact. They emphasised that the defenders should not be regarded as underwriters, and that if the defenders had been aware that loss on this scale might be claimed, they might have decided not to enter into the contract with the pursuers. In Gloag on *Contract* (2nd ed), p 696, the point is made: "that it is unfair to saddle a contracting party, even although he may have broken his contract, with consequences which could not reasonably have been in his contemplation at the time he entered into the contract, and which, if realised, might have led him to elect not to enter into the contract rather than to run the risk".

Counsel for the defenders accepted that the defenders were aware that the electricity supplied by them was for the operation of the concrete batching plant. They were also aware that this plant was to be used for the manufacture of concrete for use on the Edinburgh city bypass and associated structures. However, they contended that the defenders were not aware that a continuous operation was involved and that concrete had to be supplied continuously; they were not aware of the general technique of continuous pouring nor the need nor reason for continuous pouring; neither were they aware of the particular need for continuous pouring so far as the aqueduct was concerned. Counsel for the defenders did, however, ultimately accept that the defenders must have been aware that the concrete which was manufactured at the batching plant was to be poured, and that if there was an interruption to the electricity supply with the result that the batching plant stopped operating, then pouring of concrete, if taking place at the time, would require to stop. In these circumstances, counsel accepted that the defenders might reasonably have had in contemplation that in the event of breach of contract on their part there might be delay caused to the work carried out by the pursuers, but they maintained that the defenders could not reasonably have foreseen that breach of contract on their part would make remedial work necessary. In any event, even if the defenders could reasonably have foreseen that some remedial work was necessary, that would be confined to cutting back part of the concrete which had been poured, which was a different type of loss to what had occurred in the present case involving demolition of almost the whole of stage 1.

The Lord Ordinary held that damages for the costs of the demolition of most of stage 1 and its reconstruction went beyond what the defenders might reasonably have contemplated when the contract was entered into. He accepted that they knew that the supply of electricity was to be made for the operation of a concrete making plant, and that the concrete was required for the making of the bypass and associated structures. He also accepted that the defenders could certainly have contemplated that if the electrical supply failed, the plant would not operate, and that if it was operating at the time, the manufacture of concrete would be interrupted. The Lord Ordinary, however, held that the defenders did not know of the need of preserving a continuous pour for the purposes of this particular operation, and further that they did not know that a construction joint would not be an acceptable solution if the power was prematurely terminated with the result that demolition would be required. Subsequently in his opinion he said (1992 SLT at p 813G-I): "The necessity for a continuous pour and the requirements of the work on which the pursuers were engaged on 28 October 1985 do not seem to me on the evidence to be notorious or obvious or so generally known as to be taken to be within the understanding of the defenders at the time of the contract. It may be that the technique of a continuous pour for certain concrete structures may be a regular part of industrial practice, and it may be that the fact that if concrete is poured into position it will harden is within common knowledge, but the fact that an interruption of the pour could lead to a condemnation of the whole operation seems to me to be beyond the defenders' reasonable contemplation. In my view to allow the pursuers to recover the damages which they claim here would in effect involve a trespass into the realm of the second rule in *Hadley* v. *Baxendale* and that is a course which even the pursuers did not suggest I could take."

Subsequently he says: "But interruption of the work is one thing, the demolition of what has been done is another." Later on he says: "It is that remedial work which, as it seems to me, was beyond the contemplation of the defenders when the contract was made, and yet it is to that work that the claim for damages relates. It was not something in my view which should be regarded as normal or occurring in the usual course of things."

The pursuers criticised the Lord Ordinary's reasoning in a number of respects. They claimed that he was in error when he held that the defenders could not have known that continuous pouring was necessary. They also maintained that the Lord Ordinary was in error in what he said about possible use of a construction joint. The Lord Ordinary appeared to recognise that a construction joint was normally an acceptable solution in circumstances of this kind, and he had erred in concluding that demolition and reinstatement was damage of a different type; demolition and reinstatement was simply one form of remedial work just as cutting back to a construction joint was another form of remedial work and reinstatement. They also stressed that there was no question of the pursuers founding upon the second rule in *Hadley v Baxendale*.

The rule of *Hadley v Baxendale* is well known and applies in Scotland as well as in England (Gloag on *Contract*, p 696). The celebrated passage from the judgment of the court in *Hadley v Baxendale*, delivered by Alderson B, is to the following effect: "Where two parties have made a contract which one of them has broken, the damages which the other party ought to receive in respect of such breach of contract should be such as may fairly and reasonably be considered either arising naturally, i.e., according to the usual course of things, from such breach of contract itself, or such as may reasonably be supposed to have been in the contemplation of both parties, at the time they made the contract, as the probable result of the breach of it. Now, if the special circumstances under which the contract was actually made were communicated by the plaintiffs to the defendants, and thus known to both parties, the damages resulting from the breach of such a contract, which they would reasonably contemplate, would be the amount of injury which would ordinarily follow from a breach of contract under these special circumstances so known and communicated. But, on the other hand, if these circumstances were wholly unknown to the party breaking the contract, he, at the most, could only be supposed to have had in his contemplation the amount of injury which would arise generally, and in the great multitude of cases not affected by any special circumstances, from such a breach of contract. For, had the special circumstances been known, the parties might have specially provided for the breach of contract by special terms as to the damages in that case; and of this advantage it would be very unjust to deprive them."

Since *Hadley v Baxendale* that dictum has been considered and applied in a large number of cases. We were referred to the following cases: *Victoria Laundry (Windsor) Ltd v Newman Industries, Coulson & Co Ltd*; *A/B Karlshamns Oljefabriker v Monarch Steamship Co*; *Czarnikow (C) Ltd v Koufos*; *H Parsons (Livestock) Ltd v Uttley Ingham & Co Ltd*; *Vacwell Engineering Co Ltd v BDH Chemicals Ltd*; *Smith v Johnson*; and *Transworld Oil Ltd v North Bay Shipping Corporation (The "Rio Claro")*.

In some of these cases glosses have been placed upon the law as stated in *Hadley v Baxendale*, and judges have sought to formulate the rules in different language. With all respect to the distinguished judges who have done so, it appears to me that little advantage is gained from altering the language used in *Hadley v Baxendale* and that the law to be applied is as stated by Alderson B in *Hadley v Baxendale*.

However, since counsel relied upon the authorities listed above, it is necessary to say a word about them. In *Monarch Steamship Co*, after referring to a number of authorities, at 1949 SLT, p 58, Lord Wright said: "but the question in a case like the present must always be what reasonable businessmen must be taken to have contemplated as the natural or probable result if the contract was broken. As reasonable businessmen each must be taken to understand the ordinary practices and exigencies of the other's trade or business".

In *Victoria Laundry (Windsor) Ltd v Newman Industries Ltd* at p 539, Asquith LJ said: "In cases of breach of contract the aggrieved party is only entitled to recover such part of the loss actually resulting as was at the time of the contract reasonably foreseeable as liable to result from the breach." Later in his judgment (at p 540), Asquith LJ stressed the objectivity of the test, and spoke of the loss being "a 'serious possibility' or 'a real danger'". He added: "Possibly the colloquialism 'on the cards' indicates the shade of meaning with some approach to accuracy."

In *Czarnikow Ltd v Koufos* some criticism was directed at the observations of Asquith LJ in the previous case. Lord Reid observed that to bring in the test of reasonable foreseeability was confusing the measure of damages in contract with the measure of damages in tort. He also disagreed with the tests of "real danger" or "serious possibility" or "on the cards". None of the other judges appeared to regard the words "on the cards" as being a useful test, and various other expressions were employed. The view was expressed that the defenders should reasonably contemplate that "it was not unlikely" (per Lord Reid), that "the result was liable to be or at least the result was not unlikely to be" (per Lord Morris of Borth-y-Gest); that "the result was liable to be" (per Lord Hodson); and that "there was a serious possibility or real danger" (Lord Pearce and Lord Upjohn).

In *H Parsons (Livestock) Ltd v Uttley Ingham & Co Ltd* Scarman LJ at p 812 appears to favour the test that the damage "was not unlikely" or that "there was a serious possibility" of damage.

For my part I am satisfied that the issue of remoteness of damage falls to be approached along the lines expounded in *Hadley v Baxendale* and that in applying the rule it is appropriate to bear in mind what judges in the House of Lords have said about the meaning of the rule.

In the present case there is no real dispute that the defenders were aware that the electricity which they were supplying was required for the operation of the batching plant which manufactured concrete. They were also aware that the concrete was to be used in the construction of the city bypass and associated structures. I am also satisfied that the defenders must have been aware that the work for which the concrete was required was a civil engineering work on a considerable scale. Although I accept that the defenders were never expressly told by the pursuers that it was their intention to construct the aqueduct by means of continuous concrete pours in two stages, I am satisfied that the defenders must have been aware that the concrete was to be poured, and that at times continuous pouring would be in operation. The pursuers had stipulated for a continuous supply of electricity; the site was floodlit; and since the defenders themselves criticise the pursuers for having no contingency arrangement in operation with another supplier of concrete for the immediate supply of concrete in the event of any interruption in the operation of their own batching plant, it appears to me clear that the defenders must have been aware that on occasions continuous pouring of concrete would be required. In his opinion the Lord Ordinary states (1992 SLT at p 813E): "What they did not know was the necessity

of preserving a continuous pour *for the purposes of the*
A *particular operation*" (my emphasis). That sentence
appears to me to make it clear that what the Lord
Ordinary is saying is that the defenders were not aware
of the necessity of preserving a continuous pour for
the particular work being undertaken at the time, but
it does not follow from that that the defenders were
not aware that continuous pouring would be necessary
on occasions. The Lord Ordinary goes on to say that
the defenders were not told of the practice of having
standby plant for such operations, but the defenders
B themselves raised this matter in their pleadings.

The defenders as ordinary people of common sense
must have known that concrete does set in a short
period, and that that is bound to impose constraints in
civil engineering construction. That being so I am
satisfied that the defenders should have foreseen that
some remedial works would be necessary if there was
an interruption in electricity supply, due to breach of
contract on their part, which brought a halt to any
concrete pouring which was taking place. Indeed, this
C appears to me to be implicit in the Lord Ordinary's
reasoning. He says (at p 813E-F): "Furthermore they
did not know that a construction joint would not be an
acceptable solution if the power was prematurely terminated so that demolition would follow." That sentence appears to me to imply that the defenders must
have been aware that in some situations a construction
joint would be an acceptable solution if there was a
power failure which brought continuous pouring to an
end.
D
I find support for these views from a subsequent
passage in the Lord Ordinary's opinion, at p 813G-H,
where he says: "It may be that the technique of a continuous pour for certain concrete structures may be a
regular part of industrial practice, and it may be that
the fact that if concrete is poured into position it will
harden is within common knowledge, but the fact that
an interruption of the pour could lead to a condemnation of the whole operation seems to me to be beyond
E the defenders' reasonable contemplation."

The first part of the preceding sentence appears to
me to support the view that the defenders should have
been aware that continuous pouring of cement is
necessary for certain concrete structures, and that if
concrete is poured into position it will harden. I agree
that these are matters of common knowledge of which
the defenders must have been aware. Moreover, for
the Lord Ordinary to state that it was beyond the
defenders' reasonable contemplation that an interrup-
F tion of the pour could lead to a condemnation of the
whole operation appears to me to support the view
that it was within their reasonable contemplation that
an interruption of the pour could lead to condemnation of part of the operation.

At the end of the day, what the Lord Ordinary
appears to be accepting is that an interruption of concrete pouring could make remedial work necessary,
but that the defenders could not reasonably have contemplated that cutting back or the creation of a construction joint would prove inadequate, and that

demolition of almost the whole of stage 1 would be
required. That that is what the Lord Ordinary truly G
meant appears clear from a subsequent passage in his
opinion at p 813J where, having referred to the necessity to undo what had been done and to do it all over
again, he says: "It is that remedial work which, as it
seems to me, was beyond the contemplation of the
defenders when the contract was made, and yet it is to
that work that the claim for damages relates."

In my opinion that approach of the Lord Ordinary
to the question of damages is flawed. It is not necessary for the defenders to have been able to foresee the H
precise consequence which flowed from their breach
of contract; it is sufficient if they could reasonably
foresee the type of consequence which occurred.
Provided they could reasonably foresee the type of
consequence which occurred, it does not matter that
the damage of that type which occurred was more
extensive than they could reasonably have contemplated.

In *H Parsons (Livestock) Ltd v Uttley Ingham & Co* I
Ltd [1978] 1 QB at p 813, Scarman LJ agreed with a
statement in McGregor on *Damages* (13th ed), pp
131-132: "in contract as in tort, it should suffice that,
if physical injury or damage is within the contemplation of the parties, recovery is not to be limited
because the degree of physical injury or damage could
not have been anticipated".

Subsequently he stated: "It does not matter, in my
judgment, if they thought that the chance of physical
injury, loss of profit, loss of market, or other loss as J
the case may be, was slight, or that the odds were
against it, provided they contemplated as a serious
possibility the type of consequence, not necessarily the
specific consequence, that ensued upon breach."

In the present case the pursuers submitted that the
loss which had occurred was of a type which the
defenders should reasonably have foreseen, although
the damage was to a greater extent than they could
have foreseen. The defenders on the other hand main- K
tained that what in fact occurred by way of loss and
damage was entirely different from what they could
have contemplated; it was a different type of damage.
The defenders emphasised that following upon the
interruption of the supply of electricity, the pursuers
had attempted other remedial work in the form of
cutting back in order to form a new construction joint.
This showed that demolition was not something in the
contemplation of either parties as a foreseeable consequence of breach of contract. In this connection the
defenders founded upon a passage from the speech of L
Lord Reid in *Czarnikow (C) Ltd v Koufos* [1969] 1 AC
at p 385: "Indeed the decision (*Hadley v Baxendale*)
makes it clear that a type of damage which was plainly
foreseeable as a real possibility but which would only
occur in a small minority of cases cannot be regarded
as arising in the usual course of things or be supposed
to have been in the contemplation of the parties: the
parties are not supposed to contemplate as grounds for
the recovery of damage any type of loss or damage
which on the knowledge available to the defendant

would appear to him as only likely to occur in a small
minority of cases.''

I agree with the pursuers that in his opinion the
Lord Ordinary does not hold that the loss caused by
the need to carry out demolition work was loss of a
different type to loss involved in cutting back to a construction joint. Moreover, in my opinion the Lord
Ordinary is correct when he makes no such finding.
The fact of the matter is that demolishing the work
which had been carried out is one form of remedial
work rendered necessary by the breach of contract. It
is significant that in the joint minute parties are said
to be agreed that the pursuers had no reasonable alternative but to demolish and reconstruct stage 1. That
appears to me to imply that alternative remedial work
was considered but that there was no reasonable alternative in the circumstances but to demolish. This
appears to support the view that what the pursuers are
claiming is not a different type of damage from that
which could reasonably have been contemplated; the
damage is not different in nature although the extent
of the damage may well exceed that which could have
been reasonably contemplated at the time when the
contract was made. In the circumstances it appears to
me to follow that the costs of demolition and reconstruction can properly be regarded as flowing naturally and directly from the defenders' breach of
contract; the defenders should have had in reasonable
contemplation when the contract was made that if
there was an interruption in the electricity supply
pouring of concrete would have to stop in which event
remedial work would be necessary. The costs of demolition and reconstruction are simply the costs of the
remedial work which was necessary as a result of the
defenders' breach of contract.

I would accordingly move your Lordships to grant
the reclaiming motion, to recall the interlocutor of the
Lord Ordinary, to sustain the first plea in law for the
pursuers and to pronounce decree in favour of the pursuers for the agreed sum of £229,102.53 with interest
from the date of citation.

[His Lordship concluded by dealing with a matter
with which this report is not concerned.]

LORD MURRAY.—The pursuers were main contractors for Lothian Regional Council as road
authority in the construction of the Sighthill bypass at
Edinburgh which involved major concrete works. For
this purpose they had a concrete batching plant at
Hillwood quarry, Edinburgh, for which they required
a temporary supply of electricity for the period from
February 1985 to November 1986 in order to power
the plant, which was to provide concrete for use in the
pursuers' contract to construct the Edinburgh city
bypass (Sighthill section) including a canal aqueduct.
By exchange of letters the defenders contracted to
supply electricity for this purpose in accordance with
the pursuers' requirements.

There is no dispute between the parties that in the
course of pouring concrete for stage 1 in the construction of the aqueduct there was an interruption of the
electricity supply which resulted in the concrete
pouring process itself being interrupted. The pursuers
attributed stoppage of the electricity supply to the
defenders' failure to supply fuses at their transformer
which were of sufficient amperage rating. Whether or
not there was fault in this respect was a major issue at
the proof. Before the Inner House it was not disputed
that the defenders were in breach of contract in this
respect. What was disputed in the reclaiming motions
was whether the loss claimed was caused by the breach
and whether the Lord Ordinary had misdirected
himself on the issue of expenses. The Lord Ordinary
held that there had been a material breach of contract
but that the pursuers had failed to prove any resultant
loss. He also found no expenses due to or by either
party. The pursuers reclaim against the whole interlocutor. The defenders reclaim against the finding on
expenses.

The averments as to loss are to be found in cond 5
and ans 5. In cond 5 the pursuers aver: "As a result
of the said loss of electricity supply the pursuers were
unable to complete said stage 1 pour. They were
required by their employers' resident engineer completely to demolish and reconstruct stage 1. This was
required in order to ensure the long term integrity of
the structure of the aqueduct. . . . The requirement to
demolish and reconstruct stage 1 required re-
programming of the remaining works to minimise
delay. Such delay as did occur meant that the said
remaining works had to be carried out during the more
severe conditions of the winter months. The stage 1
pour should have been completed on 28 October 1985.
The demolition of the abortive pour was complete on
or about 6 December 1985 and the reconstruction was
completed by 31 January 1986."

In ans 5 the defenders reply: "The nature and extent
of any loss and damage sustained by the pursuers are
not known and not admitted. Not known and not
admitted that the pursuers were required by the
employers' resident engineer completely to demolish
and to reconstruct stage 1. Quoad ultra denied. . . .
Explained and averred that, esto the defenders were in
breach of contract (which is denied) and esto the pursuers required to demolish stage 1 (which is not known
and not admitted), any loss allegedly sustained as a
result thereof by the pursuers did not arise naturally
from said breach nor was it within the reasonable contemplation of the defenders when they entered into
the contract to supply electricity for the pursuers."

It can be seen from ans 5 that the defenders in their
pleadings put in issue causation of loss and remoteness
of damage. These averments were supported by a
general rather than a specific plea in law as follows:
"(3) The pursuers not having suffered loss and
damage through breach of contract on the part of the
defenders, the defenders should be assoilzied."

In the course of the proof a joint minute was agreed
and lodged. The operative words of the joint minute
were as follows: "as a result of the stage 1 pour of the
Union canal aqueduct not being completed on 28
October 1985 the pursuers had no reasonable alter-

native but to demolish and reconstruct stage 1 and the costs of doing so and of investigating the breakdown of the power supply as averred in art 5 amounted to £229,102.53 sterling''.

Apart from this joint minute no specific evidence of loss was led before the Lord Ordinary and he, quite understandably, proceeded on the basis that the pursuers were claiming the loss specified in the joint minute or nothing at all.

Before the Inner House there was no dispute between the parties as to the law applicable, as encapsulated in the two rules in *Hadley v Baxendale* and applied in subsequent cases in England and Scotland. No exception was taken to the Lord Ordinary's analysis of the legal principles applicable. The pursuers, however, contended that the Lord Ordinary had misapplied the rules in *Hadley v Baxendale* in applying them to the present case. The defenders maintained that he had applied them correctly and was right to conclude that the loss quantified in the joint minute was too remote.

In his opinion, at 1992 SLT, p 813C-F, the Lord Ordinary turns to this issue. He proceeds as follows: "As I have already noticed, the damages claimed are for all practical purposes the costs of the demolition and reconstruction. In my view that goes beyond what the defenders might reasonably have contemplated when the contract was entered into. They knew that the supply of electricity was to be made for the operation of a concrete making plant and that the concrete was required for the making of the bypass and structures associated with that work. At the meeting on 18 December 1985 it seems that little was said in any detail about the purposes for which the concrete was required. . . . The defenders could certainly contemplate that if the supply failed the plant would not operate and that if it was operating at the time the manufacture of concrete would be interrupted. What they did not know was the necessity of preserving a continuous pour for the purposes of the particular operation. They were not told of the practice of having standby plant for such operations nor were they asked to arrange any specially secure supply of electricity. Furthermore they did not know that a construction joint would not be an acceptable solution if the power was prematurely terminated so that demolition would follow. The pursuers do not claim that the defenders had such special knowledge, nor do they found upon the second rule formulated in *Hadley v. Baxendale*.''

I pause to observe that the pursuers confirmed that they were indeed founding only upon the first rule in *Hadley v Baxendale*. Later in his opinion, at p 813G-I, the Lord Ordinary further states: "It may be that the technique of a continuous pour for certain concrete structures may be a regular part of industrial practice, and it may be that the fact that if concrete is poured into position it will harden is within common knowledge, but the fact that an interruption of the pour could lead to a condemnation of the whole operation seems to me to be beyond the defenders' reasonable contemplation. In my view to allow the pursuers to recover the damages which they claim here would

in effect involve a trespass into the realm of the second rule in *Hadley* v. *Baxendale* and that is a course which even the pursuers did not suggest I could take.''

The two rules in *Hadley v Baxendale* are to be found in the report of the case in (1854) 9 Ex 341, in the opinion of the court at p 354 for the first rule and at p 355 for the second rule. The first rule is as follows: "Where two parties have made a contract which one of them has broken, the damages which the other party ought to receive in respect of such breach of contract should be such as may fairly and reasonably be considered either arising naturally, i.e., according to the usual course of things, from such breach of contract itself, or such as may reasonably be supposed to have been in the contemplation of both parties, at the time they made the contract as the probable result of the breach of it.''

The second rule, dealing with the case where special circumstances under which a contract is actually made are or are not communicated by one party to the other, proceeds on the basis that if the special circumstances are communicated they would reasonably be in the contemplation of the parties. It then proceeds: "But, on the other hand, if these special circumstances were wholly unknown to the party breaking the contract, he, at the most, could only be supposed to have had in his contemplation the amount of injury which would arise generally, and in the great multitude of cases not affected by any special circumstances, from such a breach of contract.''

Counsel for the pursuers contended that the Lord Ordinary had selected the right test but had misapplied it to the evidence which he accepted. In the passage at p 813E of his opinion the Lord Ordinary set out what was within the contemplation of the defenders but he had failed to spell out the consequences of that in terms of the first rule in *Hadley v Baxendale*. He ought to have considered what fairly and reasonably would arise naturally, according to the usual course of things, by way of loss arising from this interruption. Instead of that, in a sort of short circuit, the Lord Ordinary proceeded straight to what the defenders did not know and what was not within the contemplation of the defenders. These are then treated as special circumstances which were not communicated by the pursuers to the defenders and so could not be held to have been within their contemplation. After referring to Lord Wright's dictum in the *Monarch Steamship* case, 1949 SLT at p 58, that reasonable businessmen must be taken to understand the ordinary practices and exigencies of each others' trade or business, the Lord Ordinary then observes at p 813G-H that: "The necessity for a continuous pour and the requirements of the work on which the pursuers were engaged on 28 October 1985 do not seem to me on the evidence to be notorious or obvious or so generally known as to be taken to be within the understanding of the defenders at the time of the contract. It may be that the technique of a continuous pour for certain concrete structures may be a regular part of industrial practice, and it may be that the fact that if concrete is poured into position it will harden is

A within common knowledge, but the fact that an interruption of the pour could lead to a condemnation of the whole operation seems to me to be beyond the defenders' reasonable contemplation."

It was submitted for the pursuers that in the last sentence of this passage the Lord Ordinary was accepting that the quick setting character of liquid concrete, and the problems which that generated, were common knowledge; and that the technique of continuous pour for certain concrete structures was a regular part of industrial practice and therefore within the under-
B standing of reasonable businessmen, but the fact that interruption of the pour could lead to total condemnation of the structure was not. This, it was contended, amounted to holding that it was not the type of loss that was beyond the contemplation of the defenders but the scale of that loss. This was erroneous in law for it was the type of loss which mattered, not its scale. Given that the damage was of a type to be expected, which the Lord Ordinary appeared to accept, the joint minute was then conclusive that the pursuers had no
C alternative but to demolish and rebuild at the cost agreed. It was the type not the scale of physical damage which mattered: see Scarman LJ, in the case of *H Parsons (Livestock) Ltd v Uttley Ingham & Co Ltd* [1978] 1 QB at p 806D. There was no basis for the Lord Ordinary's observation at 1992 SLT, p 813H-I that to allow the pursuers to recover damages in respect of demolition and reconstruction "would in effect involve a trespass into the realm of the second rule in *Hadley* v. *Baxendale*". The Lord Ordinary
D appeared to accept that some remedial work required to be done as a result of the interruption but work of the scale involved would not reasonably be in contemplation: "Interruption of the work is one thing, the demolition of what has been done is another" (p 813I). It was not something which should be regarded as normal or occurring in the usual course of things. It was clear from these observations that it was the extent or scale of the remedial work which impressed the Lord Ordinary, not the fact that remedial work was required. The Lord Ordinary had selected the right
E test but had applied it wrongly. The reclaiming motion should be allowed and decree for the sum agreed in the joint minute pronounced. [His Lordship then referred to matters with which this report is not concerned, and continued:]

Counsel for the defenders stressed that the Lord Ordinary had exercised his discretion in reaching a conclusion on the evidence which he accepted. An appeal court should be slow to interfere, and could not
F do so, in the circumstances of this case, unless it could be demonstrated that he had erred in law; only then would it be open to an appeal court to reach its own conclusion on the evidence. However in the present case there was little dispute about the evidence itself. In considering what could be taken as being within the defenders' contemplation at the time of the contract, even assuming that the characteristics of mixed concrete were a matter of common knowledge, regard must be had to certain evidential considerations. First, the defenders had no reason to suppose that the concrete batching plant was to be in continuous operation

to supply mixed concrete continuously. Indeed the evidence was to the contrary. Hence there was no G reason to suppose that a continuous supply of electricity was essential. Secondly, there was no reason to think that the defenders were aware, or should have been aware, of the distinctive concrete mixes needed respectively for roadworks, concrete structures in general or aqueducts in particular. Thirdly, there was no evidence that the defenders were aware, or should have been aware, of the techniques or requirements in relation to continuous pouring. Fourthly, there was no evidence that the defenders knew, or should have H known, about the requirements for concrete for aqueducts, let alone the specific contractual stipulations for this aqueduct: waterproof quality concrete, only two pours which each had to be continuous and only one waterproof construction joint permitted. Further the defenders were not informed that the pursuers were arranging for a standby supply of mixed concrete or that there were grounds for considering a secure electrical supply, such as provided for hospitals, etc. Taking all these considerations together it I was clear that the extent of the damage resulting from interruption of the electricity supply to the pursuers was wholly out of the ordinary and exceptional, and the Lord Ordinary was entitled so to conclude on the evidence. The pursuers had failed to prove that complete demolition of a concrete structure already poured was in the contemplation of the defenders as a consequence of interruption during concrete pouring. Counsel for the pursuers did not even question the defenders' representative, Mr Ormsby, as to what was in his contemplation at the time of the con- J tract. The Lord Ordinary was correct, it was submitted, to find this damage too remote. As to expenses, the Lord Ordinary ought to have followed the normal rule and awarded expenses to the successful party, namely the defenders, in whose favour he pronounced decree of absolvitor. This was particularly so in light of the fact, not mentioned by the Lord Ordinary, that the defenders had tendered a five figure sum which the pursuers had not accepted. The court should adhere to the Lord Ordinary's interlocutor K except as regards expenses which should be awarded to the defenders.

In considering the submissions for the parties it may be convenient to start with the pleadings. In cond 2 the pursuers aver that the defenders were aware that: "The said supply of electricity was required by the pursuers for their concreting batch plant which was to provide concrete for use for the pursuers' contract to construct the Edinburgh city bypass (Sighthill section) and in particular, for the construction of the Union L canal aqueducts."

In reply the defenders admit, in ans 2, that the supply was required for the pursuers' concrete batching plant to provide concrete for use in the Edinburgh city bypass. They later aver as follows: "Not known and not admitted that the pursuers intended to construct the Union canal aqueduct by means of continuous concrete pours in two stages. Quoad ultra denied." They further explained that at no time did the pursuers advise them that they intended to con-

A struct the aqueduct by means of continuous concrete pours in two stages. These averments of the defenders appear to imply that they were, however, aware that the concrete batching plant was to supply concrete for the aqueduct amongst other bypass structures.

The next point to be noted is that the defenders in the Inner House accepted the Lord Ordinary's conclusion that it can be taken on the evidence to be common knowledge that if the electrical supply failed when the concrete batching plant was operating the manufacture of concrete would be interrupted; that continuous B pouring for certain concrete structures is a regular part of industrial practice; and that, if concrete is poured into position next to concrete which has already hardened, a disconformity results which requires remedial work. But the defenders vigorously denied that demolition and reconstruction would have been reasonably within their contemplation on the foregoing basis as they were unaware of the special and peculiar requirements of the pursuers' contract as to pouring and structural requirements for the aqueduct.
C

It seems to me that, from the foregoing propositions, if I am correct in attributing them to the defenders, it follows that they must be taken to have had within their contemplation that, because of the rapid hardening of freshly mixed concrete, interruption of the electricity supply when the plant was operating would be likely to interrupt the manufacture of concrete resulting in delay, hardening of concrete as it waited in the plant and hardening of concrete in situ before further D concrete was available, and that the latter would call for remedial measures of some kind to enable further concrete to be poured to complete the section being poured with proper integrity. All of the foregoing, it appears, the defenders would accept as damage flowing from the interruption of supply according to the usual course of things (in terms of the first rule in *Hadley v Baxendale*). But it does not, they assert, extend to damage arising from a consequence so special and peculiar as remedial work to a partly E poured aqueduct requiring its complete demolition and reconstruction.

This contention has, I think, to be tested against the matters which the defenders now accept and what is not contested in their pleadings. From them two points emerge. First, the defenders must have known that construction of this bypass would require large concrete structures to be poured as well as structures of ordinary size. Secondly, on the view which I have taken of their averments in answer, they knew that an F aqueduct over a roadway was involved. The rapid hardening of poured concrete being a matter of common knowledge, they must therefore in my opinion be taken to have known that any pour, small or large, which is interrupted for a material length of time after concrete has been poured in situ will call for remedial action if the integrity of the structure is to be maintained. If joints are practicable the laid concrete can be cut to form a construction joint. But if such a joint or equivalent remedial work is not practicable, it appears to me that maintenance of the integrity of a structural unit may well require demolition and reconstruction, even in the case of small scale concrete G works such as pouring a garage floor or a piece of pavement. If so, then there is nothing out of the ordinary in demolition and reconstruction of poured concrete on any scale. With the aqueduct the scale was exceptionally large but, it seems to me, the damage was not different in kind, only in extent. This is the error in the Lord Ordinary's reasoning which the pursuers correctly identify at p 813E of his opinion.

Towards the end of his opinion it appears that the Lord Ordinary had reached the view that breach of H contract had been proved and that there was resultant damage, albeit restricted to such consequences as ensued from the delay thereby caused. He accepted then that there must be some quantifiable loss but was evidently frustrated by the absence of any evidence before him on the details of what he conceived to be allowable loss and the failure of the pursuers even to move for an award of nominal damages. It may be that in this situation the Lord Ordinary failed to give full consideration to the wording of the joint minute I agreed during the proof which must, whatever motivated it, have been designed to restrict the leading of further evidence as to quantum. The operative words of the joint minute are: "as a result of the stage 1 pour . . . not being completed on 28 October 1985 the pursuers had no reasonable alternative but to demolish and reconstruct".

I consider that prima facie the effect of those words is that, on proof of breach of contract and on proof that it to a material extent caused the pour to be inter- J rupted, the pursuers had no reasonable alternative but to demolish and reconstruct at the agreed cost. The Lord Ordinary found in fact that both conditions were established on the evidence. Accordingly, on a strict construction of the wording of the joint minute, there was no room thereafter for the defenders' argument on remoteness. It would have been otherwise, no doubt, if the foregoing wording had been prefixed by the word "if" or if the issue of causation had been expressly reserved. In my view it is difficult in the end K to view the wording of the joint minute as other than conclusive against the defenders in the foregoing circumstances.

For the above reasons I am of the view that the Lord Ordinary has been shown to have erred in law and that his interlocutor must be recalled in toto. It is then open to this court to reach its own conclusion on evidence which is not materially disputed. Although the case is indeed very narrow on its facts, I am satisfied L that the pursuers have not only established on a balance of probability breach of contract, but also the damages quantified in the joint minute on the basis of the first rule in *Hadley v Baxendale*. I would allow the reclaiming motion for the pursuers, refuse that for the defenders and pronounce decree for the agreed sum in terms of the first conclusion.

LORD MORISON.—The facts which were held by the Lord Ordinary to have been established and which have given rise to this appeal may be shortly

A stated. The respondents undertook to provide a supply of electricity to the appellants' batching plant, whose function was to mix ingredients so as to provide concrete for the construction by the appellants of the Edinburgh city bypass and associated structures. This construction involved supply of unset concrete from the plant to the nearby site where it was poured to form the structure or that part of the structure upon which the appellants were from time to time engaged. It was held that the respondents, in breach of their contract with the appellants, failed to provide a continuous supply of electricity because of the inadequacy

B of the fuses fitted at their substation. These fuses ruptured and the process of production of concrete at the plant was thereby interrupted. At the time when this occurred the appellants were engaged in pouring concrete for the construction of a length of aqueduct for the Union canal, this operation being referred to as the "stage 1 pour" of the aqueduct. In order to ensure that this structure was watertight the stage 1 pour was intended to be continuous, so as to avoid the need for a joint against concrete which had already

C been laid and which had hardened. The pour was started at about 7 am on 28 October 1985 but was interrupted by the failure of the electricity supply during the evening of the same day.

During the course of the proof parties agreed that as a result of the non-completion of the pour on 28 October the appellants had no reasonable alternative but to demolish and reconstruct the stage of the construction on which they had been engaged, and that the cost of doing so and of investigating the break-

D down of the power supply was £229,102.53. It is this sum which the appellants say should have been awarded to them. They do not claim damages on any basis less than that of the total of the agreed costs. The respondents maintain that expenditure on the work of demolition and reconstruction which largely comprised these costs was expenditure which was not within their reasonable contemplation as a consequence of their breach of contract. This is the single issue involved in the appeal, and in particular it is not

E contended by the respondents that the Lord Ordinary was in error in holding that the work for which the appellants claim reimbursement was incurred as a result of the respondents' failure to comply with their contractual obligations.

In determining the issue of remoteness of damages in favour of the respondents the Lord Ordinary stated that he proceeded on the principle that the recoverable loss was limited to that which the defenders might reasonably have contemplated at the time of the con-

F tract. That principle is derived from what the Lord Ordinary refers to as the "first rule" laid down in *Hadley v Baxendale*. The "second rule" in that case deals with special circumstances under which a contract has been made which are known to both parties. In the present case the appellants did not suggest that there were any special circumstances known to the respondents which brought the loss into the category of what would reasonably have been contemplated by them. They founded on the first rule, maintaining that the loss arose "according to the usual course of things" and that it was of a kind which might reason-

ably be supposed to have been in the respondents' con- G templation as a consequence of their breach of contract. But this submission was obviously not intended to exclude consideration of the respondents' admitted knowledge that the supply of electricity was required for the appellants' batching plant, and that this plant was operated so as to provide concrete for use in the construction of the bypass and associated structures. It was primarily on account of the respondents' knowledge of these facts, combined with the general knowledge that concrete sets quickly after it has been mixed, that the appellants founded their submission that the respondents should have contem- H plated that if the electricity supply was interrupted, remedial work to any structure which was in the course of construction would be required, and that the loss incurred was of that type.

A number of cases were cited to us which contain dicta of high authority apparently intended to explain or improve upon the terminology of the test laid down in *Hadley v Baxendale*. Such dicta are to be found in *Victoria Laundry v Newman*; *A/B Karlshamns Oljefabriker v Monarch Steamship Co*; *Czarnikow v Koufos*; and *H Parsons (Livestock) Ltd v Uttley Ingham* I *& Co Ltd*. These cases provide a bewildering variety of different and sometimes inconsistent expressions which might be used as alternatives for or in supplement of the test that the recoverable loss must be one which was within parties' reasonable contemplation as a consequence of the breach. I have not found any of these alternatives to be of assistance in resolving the question raised by this appeal. In many cases there is little difficulty in determining whether or not a person J is liable for all of the consequences of his breach of contract, but in those cases where any difficulty exists, the issue arises not because of any doubt as to the meaning of the expression "within reasonable contemplation" but in the application of the *Hadley v Baxendale* test to the particular circumstances of the case; it is in the latter respect that there is sometimes room for a divergence of opinion. I proceed only on the basis of what was said in *Hadley v Baxendale*, although it is to be borne in mind that, as was indicated by Lord K Morris in *Czarnikow* [1969] 1 AC at p 399) and by Lord Scarman in *Parsons* [1978] 1 QB at p 807), the test is not what the party in breach did in fact contemplate, but what he would have reasonably contemplated had he applied his mind to the consequences of the breach which occurred. It is also important in the present case to have regard to the principle that liability for a loss is not to be restricted on account of the fact that the degree of that loss is greater than that which could reasonably have been anticipated (per Lord Scarman in *Parsons* at p 813).   L

The respondents' position was based first on their lack of knowledge of the necessity for a "continuous pour" as part of the operations on which the appellants were engaged. In view of this, it was submitted that they could have contemplated no other effect of their breach than that the appellants would be delayed in the construction on which they were engaged, and that the work could be resumed without additional expense thereafter. Secondly it was submitted that even if the respondents had reason to contemplate that

A some remedial work on an existing concrete structure would become necessary as a result of an interruption in the flow of concrete from the plant, the necessity to demolish a structure completely was a consequence causing loss of an exceptional nature and outwith the respondents' reasonable contemplation.

In my opinion it should have been clear to the respondents that interruption of the supply of unset concrete to the site might well have an effect on the civil engineering work which was taking place there, and in particular might well require remedial work to
B a structure or part of a structure which the appellants were in course of constructing when the flow was interrupted. This view is confirmed by evidence of a consultant electrician who had been asked to investigate the failure of the supply, and who in cross examination by the respondents' counsel stated that if a pour was interrupted he assumed that there would be a "civil engineering consequence" due to the setting of the concrete which would become a problem for the remainder of the operation. The respondents
C knew that the batching plant supplied mixed concrete to the site, and in particular, according to the evidence, that it was to be used for construction of structures being built in association with the construction of the road. It is a matter of general knowledge that concrete hardens quickly after its ingredients have been mixed and put in place. Thus during any operation in which pouring was taking place, an interruption of the supply would at least involve the creation of a satisfactory joint between the concrete which had
D already been poured and had hardened and that which would be poured when the operation was resumed. The expedient of a joint was indeed one to which the appellants gave serious consideration in the present case. It would have involved squaring off the existing structure by cutting back the sloping section of the hardened concrete so as to obtain a reasonable vertical line, an operation which according to the appellants' project manager would have taken several days, even although the concrete was still "green" and therefore
E more easily removeable. Some of the hardened concrete was in fact removed while this expedient was still regarded as a possible solution. In my opinion remedial work of this character would clearly have been in the contemplation of the respondents as a consequence of their breach of contract. That conclusion is not affected by the fact that the appellants might have requested, as the Lord Ordinary apparently took into account, a specially secure supply of electricity, nor by the fact that the respondents were not informed
F that it was desirable and in accordance with practice to have standby plant available during the course of a pouring operation. These matters were no doubt relevant in determining whether the respondents were in breach of contract and whether there was any break in the chain of causation leading to the loss. But these questions are not now in issue, and in my view the considerations referred to are not material in determining the inferences to be derived from what the respondents did know or must be held to have known.

The expedient of cutting back to allow a joint to be

G formed was rejected because of the potential weakness of a joint as part of a water retaining structure. As the joint minute relates, there was no reasonable alternative but to demolish and reconstruct stage 1, which it had been intended to complete in a single pour. This particular consequence was one which the respondents had no reason to anticipate, because, as the Lord Ordinary expressed it (1992 SLT at p 813E), "they did not know [of] the necessity of preserving a continuous pour for the purposes of the particular operation", and "they did not know that a construction
H joint would not be an acceptable solution". The Lord Ordinary accordingly held that a "condemnation of the whole operation" was beyond the defenders' reasonable contemplation.

That may be true, but it is not necessary for the appellants to demonstrate that the respondents had knowledge of what was involved in any particular operation nor what particular remedial work would be required in respect of that structure on which they were engaged when the breach of contract occurred. The Lord Ordinary's opinion leaves open the question
I whether the condemnation of the whole of the stage 1 operation was of the same type, although greater in degree, as the type of damage which could have been reasonably contemplated. In my opinion it was. Once it is accepted that the necessity for remedial work to any existing structure, particularly remedial work involving concrete which had hardened, was within the respondents' reasonable contemplation, it seems to me that the distinction between remedial work involving removal of the whole of what had been con-
J structed as part of stage 1 and remedial work (such as the formation of a joint) involving only part of it is a distinction of degree, not of kind. In my opinion therefore the Lord Ordinary was in error in concluding that the amount claimed was not recoverable because it was not within the respondents' reasonable contemplation that the whole operation would be affected rather than part of it only. I would accordingly grant the appellants' reclaiming motion, recall the interlocutor of the Lord Ordinary and grant decree for the agreed sum
K with interest from the date of citation.

[His Lordship concluded by dealing with a matter with which this report is not concerned.]

Counsel for Pursuers and Reclaimers, Galbraith, QC, Brailsford; Solicitors, Alex Morison & Co, WS —
Counsel for Defenders and Respondents, D S Mackay, QC, Sturrock; Solicitors, Shepherd & Wedderburn, WS.
L

M G J U

[An appeal to the House of Lords has been presented.]

Maxwell v Cardle

A HIGH COURT OF JUSTICIARY

THE LORD JUSTICE GENERAL (HOPE),
LORDS ALLANBRIDGE AND COWIE

6 OCTOBER 1992

Justiciary — Procedure — Summary procedure — Verdict — Justice consulting with assessor in open court allegedly suggesting not proven verdict, then saying it did not matter and she would just find accused guilty as accused faced further charges — Justice denying accused's version but not certain what was said — Whether court entitled to proceed on accused's version — Whether proceedings unfair.

B

An accused person was tried for wilful or reckless damage in the district court. After a submission of no case to answer was repelled and, no defence evidence having been led, closing submissions completed, the justice consulted with her assessor in open court. The accused alleged that she then said: "I think I'll return
C that not proven verdict you mentioned", and subsequently: "It doesn't really matter what I do in this case as the accused is coming up for these other matters referred to by the police, I'll just find him guilty." The accused was convicted and appealed, arguing that the justice had convicted on the basis of suppositions unrelated to the evidence and that justice had not been seen to be done. The justice denied using the words attributed to her while stating that she did not recall the conversation clearly.

D **Held,** (1) that the justice's recollection was not to be taken as less reliable than the accused's, and since in the circumstances the only question was whether the prosecution evidence was to be believed, the justice's assurance that she decided the case solely on the evidence was sufficient (p 1018I-K); (2) that since the purpose of the consultation was to enable the justice to receive advice from her assessor, and having regard to the possibility of the conversation having been misheard or misunderstood, the reasonable observer
E would not have concluded that justice was not being done (pp 1018L-1019A); and appeal *refused.*

Summary complaint

John Samuel Maxwell was charged at the instance of James Cardle, procurator fiscal, Dumbarton, on a complaint which libelled an offence under s 78 (1) of the Criminal Justice (Scotland) Act 1980. The accused pled not guilty and proceeded to trial in the district
F court. After trial the accused was found guilty.

The accused appealed against conviction by stated case to the High Court. The facts giving rise to the appeal appear from the opinion of the court.

Appeal

The justice posed the following question for the High Court, inter alia:

(3) Did my conduct during the course of the appellant's trial amount to oppression and result in a miscarriage of justice?

The appeal was heard before the High Court on 6 October 1992.

G

Eo die the court *answered* the third question in the *negative* and *refused* the appeal.

The following opinion of the court was delivered by the Lord Justice General (Hope):

OPINION OF THE COURT.—The appellant is John Samuel Maxwell who went to trial in the district court of Bearsden and Milngavie at Milngavie charged with wilfully or recklessly damaging a motor car by H smashing its rear windscreen, contrary to s 78 (1) of the Criminal Justice (Scotland) Act 1980. A motion that there was no case to answer was made and rejected by the justice. There was no defence evidence, and at the end of the case the justice decided to find the appellant guilty and she imposed a small fine.

An application was made for a stated case indicating that it was desired to bring the conviction under review on two points. The first was related to an I alleged insufficiency in the evidence. But counsel who appeared for the appellant today informed us that he did not propose to argue that point, so, of consent, we shall answer the first question in the case in the negative and the second question in the affirmative.

The other point which it was sought to raise was the subject of submissions by counsel today. This was to the effect that the conduct of the justice during the course of the appellant's trial amounted to oppression and resulted in a miscarriage of justice. The point is J explained in the application in these terms. We are told that it transpired in the course of the evidence that the appellant, when being questioned by the police in connection with the offence with which he had been charged in the district court, was in fact in custody being questioned about other unrelated matters. According to the appellant, after the submission of no case to answer had been repelled, and apparently after it had been intimated that no evidence was to be led for the defence and the completion of the K closing submissions, but prior to the verdict being returned, the justice consulted with her assessor. She is recorded in the application as having stated: "I think I'll return that not proven verdict you mentioned." She went on to say this: "It doesn't really matter what I do in this case as the accused is coming up for these other matters referred to by the police, I'll just find him guilty." It is contended that these statements indicate that the justice was originally considering returning a not proven verdict, but that she L decided instead to convict the appellant not on the basis of the evidence which she had heard but on what are described as unrelated suppositions on her part, the result of which was that the appellant was treated unfairly by the court.

In response to what is narrated in the application, the justice has set out in the stated case her version of what occurred. She states that any comments by her at the stage to which the application refers were made to her assessor and not to the court. It can be said

A immediately that this much is not in dispute. She then goes on to explain that the assessor briefly stated the options which were open to her, of returning a verdict of not guilty, not proven or guilty. Any reference which was made at that point to finding the appellant guilty was made by her to indicate her intention to reject the other two options. She had already been impressed by the argument by the procurator fiscal depute in support of his submission that there was a case to answer, and the police and other prosecution evidence seemed to her to be credible and reliable and
B to have proved beyond reasonable doubt that the appellant was guilty. It was the police evidence which she had in mind when using the term "other matters" in her discussion with the assessor. She concludes her explanation by saying that she does not recall clearly all of her conversation, but that she was thinking ahead of the verdict to the sentence, and wondering whether probation would be appropriate. She cannot imagine that she would have spoken the full sentence which has been attributed to her and she thinks that
C overheard phrases may have been mistakenly conjoined by the appellant's solicitor. She took the opportunity, in her explanation for refusing certain proposed adjustments, of emphasising that the conversation between herself and the assessor was not intended to be part of the court proceedings or to be capable of being overheard. She refutes the suggestion that her verdict at the trial was not based solely on the evidence.

D   In developing his argument, counsel for the appellant submitted that the justice did not appear to deny the words which had been attributed to her in the application. Her position was that she could not recall clearly what she said, and her comments in reply were really based on speculation. We are invited to accept that what had been attributed to her in the application by the appellant's solicitor was an accurate and fair version of what she said. If she did say what was attributed to her in the application, that would be a miscarriage of justice since this indicated that her
E verdict was not based solely on the evidence. Even if that were going too far, justice had to be seen to be done. She should not have given the impression to the contrary by allowing her conversation with the assessor to be overheard. While counsel accepted that those present in court should not be encouraged to listen in to conversations which were intended to be private, he submitted that if the decision was taken to conduct these conversations in the courtroom where they were capable of being overheard, they should not
F be such as to suggest that there was a miscarriage of justice.

For his part the learned Solicitor General informed us that the procurator fiscal depute had not kept a precise note of what had been said. But he confirmed that there had been a murmured discussion between the justice and her assessor, and that it was generally on the lines stated by the appellant.

The first point to be made is that it is perfectly in order for a justice to consult with the assessor in the

courtroom without resorting to an adjournment. The
G legal assessor appointed under s 7 (1) of the District Courts (Scotland) Act 1975 is there to give legal advice whenever it is required and a justice should not feel inhibited from seeking advice at any stage in the case when points of law or procedure arise. It would be unreasonably disruptive to the proceedings to require an adjournment every time so that these conversations may be conducted in private behind closed doors. It is of course necessary that justice should be done and that it should be seen to be done. Discretion must
H therefore be exercised in order that, so far as possible, discussions on sensitive matters are not overheard. Particular care is required at the stage which had apparently been reached in this case, where consideration is being given to the verdict which is to be returned. But even at this stage there is no need for an adjournment if conditions in the courtroom are such that discussions can be conducted without undue risk of their being overheard, or of their being misheard and misconstrued.

I   Now in the present case the justice, having decided to consult him in open court, was unable to prevent part of her conversation with the assessor from being overheard. She claims that words have been attributed to her which she did not use and that phrases which she did utter have been misconstrued. That is precisely what is liable to happen when people listen in to conversations which they are not supposed to hear. We reject the suggestion that the recollection of her conversation by the justice is less reliable than the account which has been given of it by those by whom
J it was overheard. Accordingly we are not prepared to accept that she expressed herself in the terms attributed to her in the application. We accept her assurance that she decided the case solely on the evidence, and that the explanation for some of her remarks was that she was thinking ahead to the sentence which might be appropriate once the verdict had been announced. It would have been better if she had not allowed her thoughts to be diverted to this point until after the appellant had been convicted. But we are not
K persuaded that she based her verdict on what have been described as unrelated suppositions on her part. It is conceded that there was sufficient evidence for a conviction and, in the absence of defence evidence, the only question was whether the prosecution evidence was to be believed.

There remains the point which counsel for the appellant made today that justice was not seen to be done. This is a surprising allegation, given that the
L purpose of the murmured conversation was to enable the justice to receive advice from her assessor. In this situation we do not think that the reasonable observer would be inclined to conclude, from a few overheard remarks, that justice was not being done in this case. Account must be taken of the nature of the conversation, its purpose and the possibility that it was being misheard or misunderstood. We agree with counsel that it would be wrong to encourage listening in to conversations of this kind, and the reasonable observer would make due allowance for all these factors. A

A blatant indiscretion indicating a bias against the accused or some other breach of natural justice is one thing. What occurred in this case is another, and we are not prepared to accept that what the justice was heard to say would have created in the mind of a reasonable man the impression that justice was not being done.

For these reasons we are not persuaded that her conduct amounted to oppression and resulted in a mis-carriage of justice. We shall therefore answer the third question in the case in the negative and refuse the

B appeal.

_____

Counsel for Appellant, McBride; Solicitors, John G Gray & Co, SSC (for Anderton & Co, Milngavie) — Counsel for Respondent, Solicitor General (Dawson, QC); Solicitor, J D Lowe, Crown Agent.

P W F

C

Gilmour v HM Advocate

HIGH COURT OF JUSTICIARY

THE LORD JUSTICE GENERAL (HOPE),
LORDS ALLANBRIDGE AND COWIE

9 OCTOBER 1992

D *Justiciary — Evidence — Corroboration — Rape — Evidence from complainer that appellant ripped her pants and raped her — No independent evidence from which timing of damage to underwear could be inferred — Whether complainer's account corroborated by damaged state of underwear.*

An accused person was charged with rape. The com-plainer gave an account of forcible rape. She also stated that the accused had torn her pants off in the course of the assault. There was no evidence of injury

E to the complainer. When she undressed and handed her clothing to police some time later the pants were torn at the side and the two ends knotted. This was consistent with her account. Forensic evidence was to the effect that the damage would have required con-siderable force but the timing of the damage was not established. A submission of "no case to answer" was rejected at the end of the Crown case and the accused was convicted. He appealed to the High Court on the

F ground that the complainer's evidence was uncor-roborated.

Held, that in the absence of independent evidence from which the time of the damage occurring to the pants could be inferred, their condition could not be attributed to the appellant's actions and there was therefore insufficient evidence to establish the charge, and the submission of no case to answer ought to have been upheld (p 1021A-C); and appeal *allowed* and con-viction *quashed.*

_____

Indictment

John Gilmour was charged at the instance of the G rt hon the Lord Fraser of Carmyllie, Her Majesty's Advocate, on an indictment which contained the following charge: "on 10 or 11 January 1991 in the house at [address], you did assault [X], push her down on a bed, attempt to kiss her, place your hand over her mouth, attempt to pull down her pants, pull up her skirt, lie on top of her and rape her".

The accused pled not guilty and proceeded to trial in the High Court at Ayr on 22 April 1992, before Lord Prosser and a jury. At the end of the Crown case H the trial judge rejected a submission of no case to answer.

The accused was convicted and appealed to the High Court by note of appeal against conviction.

Appeal

The accused lodged grounds of appeal in the follow-ing terms, inter alia:

(2) The learned trial judge erred in rejecting a sub- I mission of no case to answer under s 140A of the Criminal Procedure (Scotland) Act 1975. The only evidence upon which the Crown relied as affording corroboration of the victim's evidence that she had been raped was of the damaged condition of her pants. Further examination of the pants concluded that con-siderable force would have been required to cause the damage to the side waistband. Medical examination of the victim disclosed no injury and in particular no injury opposite the damaged side of the pants. Shortly J prior to the alleged rape the victim had had sexual intercourse with a friend of the panel while the panel had sexual intercourse with a friend of the victim in the same room. Prior to this sexual intercourse the victim had removed her clothing including her pants under the bedcovers. Only the victim gave evidence that she had put her pants back on after this inter-course prior to intercourse with the panel, and only she gave evidence that the pants were undamaged at that time. Forensic examination of the pants con- K cluded that it could not be said when the damage to the pants had occurred and in particular that it could not be said that this was recent damage. The evidence of the pants was therefore not sufficiently independent of the victim to afford corroboration of her evidence that she had been raped. Said error by the learned trial judge amounts to a miscarriage of justice.

The appeal was heard before the High Court on 9 October 1992.

L

Eo die the court *allowed* the appeal and *quashed* the conviction.

THE LORD JUSTICE GENERAL (HOPE).— The appellant was found guilty in the High Court at Ayr on a charge of rape. He has appealed against his conviction on two grounds. The first is that there was a misdirection by the trial judge, in that he failed to direct the jury as to the test they should apply in order to find that the complainer's account was corroborated by evidence of her distress. But it was at no time A suggested by anyone in the course of the trial that the complainer's distress might be regarded as corroborative of her account, and counsel for the appellant informed us that it was now accepted that this ground had been based on a misconception and it was not insisted on. So we are left with the second ground, which is that the trial judge erred in rejecting a submission of no case to answer on the ground that the only evidence relied on by the Crown as corroborative was not capable of corroborating the complainer's B evidence. The point taken, which was rejected by the trial judge, was that there was no sufficient corroboration of the complainer's evidence that the appellant's intercourse with her, which was itself sufficiently established, had been obtained by force.

The complainer had spent the evening with a friend named Fiona Duncan and a number of other young people including the appellant and Walter Hunter. Sometime after 11.30 pm, having been out drinking, they went to the appellant's house and into his C bedroom where there were two beds. The lights were put out and the complainer went to bed with Hunter while her friend went to bed with the appellant. The complainer had sexual intercourse with Hunter and the appellant had or attempted to have sexual intercourse with her friend. Hunter and her friend then departed leaving the complainer in bed. The appellant saw them off and then returned to the bedroom. The complainer's evidence was that she was sitting on the bed when he returned to the room and that he came D and sat beside her. He then pushed her down on her back, held her down and started having sex with her against her will. The trial judge was satisfied that her evidence afforded an ample basis for the jury to regard her account as one of forcible rape.

There was no evidence of any kind of injury in this case and, as I have already mentioned, it was not suggested that corroboration could be found in evidence of distress observed by others after the event. E The only evidence upon which the Crown relied as affording corroboration of the complainer's account that she had been raped was the damaged condition of her pants when she undressed some hours after the incident and handed them over to the police. A forensic scientist gave evidence to the effect that he had examined the pants. The left side was noted to be torn and the two ends were held together with a knot. He expressed the opinion that considerable force would have been required to produce this damage, but F he was unable to say that this damage was recent. There was no direct evidence from any source independent of that of the complainer to show when the damage occurred. Nor was there any independent evidence that the pants were undamaged up to the time of the alleged rape.

The complainer's account was that she had removed her pants when she had intercourse with Hunter. When he left the room she quickly got dressed again and put on her skirt and pants. She was wearing the pants when the appellant returned to the room. When he started having sex with her he lifted up her skirt and ripped her pants. They had not come off com- G pletely and were ripped by being pulled sideways. She said that they had not been like that previously and that she tied them up by knotting them at the side because the appellant ripped them. The forensic evidence was consistent with her explanation that the pants had been ripped. But in order to afford corroboration of her evidence that she was raped by the appellant that damage had to be related to the time of the alleged assault.

Counsel for the appellant accepted that if the H damaged and knotted state of the pants could be related to the time of the alleged assault the requirement for corroboration would be satisfied. But his point was that it was not open to the jury to draw any inference about this from the evidence of the complainer. The trial judge left this to the jury, on the view that it was for them to decide what inference to draw from the existence of the damage as to the time of its occurrence. Yet there was nothing by way of any adminicle in the evidence to enable any such inference I to be drawn. The forensic expert's evidence had been entirely neutral on the point. The only other independent evidence was that of the police officer who saw the condition of the pants when the complainer undressed, but this evidence also was neutral as to the time when they were damaged. In the absence of any adminicle of independent evidence on this point, there was no corroboration of the complainer's evidence that she was raped.

In his reply the learned Solicitor General invited us J to draw a distinction between the sufficiency of the evidence and its quality. He submitted that further evidence as to timing would strengthen the quality of the evidence about the damage to the pants, but it would not affect the issue of sufficiency. The question was whether their damaged condition was consistent with the complainer's account and, if so, whether this was capable of carrying the inference that she was raped. He submitted that both of these questions should be answered in the affirmative. Her account K that the pants had been ripped was supported by the forensic evidence. If the pants were ripped when the appellant was having sex with her this would indicate that his actions were forcible and that this was rape. He did not suggest that there was anything in the evidence to justify any inference about the time of the damage, but he invited us generally to support the view taken by the trial judge.

The crucial point, since there was no other independent evidence to suggest rape, is whether the pants L were ripped during the appellant's intercourse with the complainer. The ripping of the pants would suggest forcible intercourse, but in order to incriminate the appellant the act of ripping the pants had to be attributed to him. The only direct evidence about her dressing again prior to this act of intercourse, and about the condition of the pants until she was seen by the police, came from the complainer. So if the time of the damage was to be related to the alleged assault this could only be by inference. And in

order to support that inference there had to be some
A other evidence independent of that of the complainer
which would enable it to be drawn. The complainer
could not corroborate herself, so all her evidence as to
the timing of the damage had to be left out of account.

I am not persuaded that any inference as to timing
could be drawn merely from the damaged condition of
the pants by being ripped sideways or the fact that the
complainer was wearing them when she was seen by
the police. An inference must be based on something
if it is not to be just speculation. It is only if this
B requirement is satisfied that the matter can be left to
the jury to decide on the quality of the evidence. An
inference that the tearing of the pants occurred when
the appellant was alone with her, if based on some
independent evidence and not merely on speculation
by the jury, would have sufficed to corroborate the
complainer's evidence that it was the appellant who
tore them. But the forensic evidence was neutral on
this point, and there was no other evidence on which
an inference as to the time of the damage could be
C based. In these circumstances the damaged condition
of the pants could not be attributed, by inference from
any independent evidence, to the appellant's actions
when he had intercourse with the complainer.

For these reasons I am satisfied that the evidence
was insufficient in law to justify the appellant being
convicted of the offence with which he was charged.
The submission that there was no case to answer
ought to have been upheld and he should have been
acquitted of the offence. Accordingly I would allow
D the appeal and quash the conviction.

LORD ALLANBRIDGE.—I have read the
opinion of your Lordship in the chair and for the
reasons given therein I agree that this appeal should be
allowed and the conviction quashed.

LORD COWIE.—I concur with the opinion of
your Lordship in the chair.

E *Counsel for Appellant, McBride; Solicitors, Macbeth
Currie & Co, WS — Counsel for Respondent, Solicitor
General (Dawson, QC); Solicitor, J D Lowe, Crown
Agent.*

CAGM

F # R v Lothian Health Board (No 2)

OUTER HOUSE
LORD MACLEAN
27 NOVEMBER 1992

*Mental health — Detention — Patient detained under
emergency powers — Successive periods of detention —
Detention expiring and patient remaining in hospital on
voluntary basis until almost 24 hours later — Further*

*detention then under emergency powers — Whether
"immediately after expiry of the period of detention"* G
*under earlier order — Whether lawful — Mental Health
(Scotland) Act 1984 (c 36), ss 18, 24 and 26.*

*Time — Computation — Detention for 28 day period —
Beginning of period known to the hour — Natural or civil
computation — Mental Health (Scotland) Act 1984
(c 36), s 26.*

The Mental Health (Scotland) Act 1984 provides for
three types of admission to mental hospital: first,
emergency detention, under s 24, for a maximum of H
72 hours; secondly, short term detention, under s 26,
for a maximum of 28 days; and, thirdly, long term
detention, under s 18, for up to six months, for which
application to and approval by the sheriff is required.
Under s 25, an application for admission for emergency detention may be made while a patient is still in
hospital. Section 26 (7) of the Act provides: "A patient
who has been detained under this section shall not be
further detained under this section nor detained under
section 24 of this Act immediately after the expiry of I
the period of detention under this section."

On 3 May 1990 a woman was admitted to hospital
as a voluntary patient. On 10 May she decided to leave
but was made the subject of an emergency order under
s 24 of the 1984 Act, authorising her detention for 72
hours. At 1400 hours on 13 May she was detained
under s 26 for a further period of 28 days from the
expiry of the s 24 period. About two weeks before the
expiry of the s 26 period on 10 June, the patient indicated that she was willing to remain in hospital volun- J
tarily. On 11 June, however, she tried to leave the
hospital, and was detained again, at about 1.45 pm,
under s 24 as a result of an emergency recommendation by a doctor. On 14 June another doctor issued a
report under s 26, thus authorising her detention for
a further 28 days.

The patient brought a petition for judicial review,
seeking declarator that her continued detention was
unlawful, liberation from detention, liberation ad
interim and damages. It was submitted on her behalf K
that her lawful period of detention had expired at midnight on 10 June, since the period of her detention was
to be calculated de die in diem (civilis computatio)
rather than de momento in momentum (naturalis computatio). The respondents argued that in terms of s 26
(3) the first s 26 period had commenced on the expiry
of the first 72 hours' detention under s 24. The period
was thus to be measured by the hour, with the 28 day
period having commenced on the expiry of the 72nd
hour, at 1400 hours on 13 May. The patient further L
argued in that case that the s 24 detention of 11 June
had nevertheless followed "immediately" after the
expiry of the s 26 detention, no material interval of
time having elapsed, and was therefore in contravention of s 26 (7).

Held, (1) that the Act having set its own precise
time limits to the hour and in keeping with the
presumption for freedom, naturalis computatio
applied with the consequence that the petitioner's
period of detention had expired at 1400 hours on 10

A June 1990 (p 1025D-E); and (2) that, although no interpretation of general application could be devised, the circumstances of the petitioner having remained voluntarily for nearly 24 hours after expiry of the first period of detention under s 26, and those who had care of her having had reason to believe that she would so remain, were sufficient to make it impossible to affirm that her further detention had been effected "immediately" after the expiry of the first s 26 period and that there was therefore no contravention of s 26 (7) (pp 1025L and 1026F-G); and prayer of petition B *refused*.

Petition for judicial review

C D R petitioned for judicial review, seeking declarator that her continued detention in the Royal Edinburgh hospital under s 26 of the Mental Health (Scotland) Act 1984 was unlawful, liberation from detention, liberation ad interim and damages.

C On 28 June 1990, on the petitioner's motion for an order for intimation and service and for interim liberation, the Lord Ordinary (Coulsfield) granted interim liberation (reported 1991 SLT 282). A reclaiming motion was enrolled but, of consent, refused.

The petition then came before the Lord Ordinary (MacLean) for a first hearing.

Statutory provisions

The Mental Health (Scotland) Act 1984 provides:

D "18.—(1) A patient may be admitted to a hospital and there detained for the period allowed by this Part of this Act in pursuance of an application in the prescribed form (in this Act referred to as 'an application for admission') approved by the sheriff and made in accordance with this Part of this Act.

"(2) An application for admission shall be founded on and accompanied by 2 medical recommendations which shall be in the prescribed form and each such recommendation shall include the following state-E ments, being statements of opinion, and the grounds on which each statement is based — (a) a statement of the form of mental disorder from which the patient is suffering, being mental illness or mental handicap or both; and (b) a statement as to which of the grounds set out in section 17 (1) of this Act apply in relation to the patient.

"(3) An application for admission shall be of no effect unless the patient is described in each of the medical recommendations as suffering from the same F form of mental disorder, whether or not he is described in either of those recommendations as suffering also from the other form. . . .

"24.—(1) In any case of urgent necessity a recommendation (in this Act referred to as 'an emergency recommendation') may be made by a medical practitioner in respect of a patient stating that by reason of mental disorder it is urgently necessary for his health or safety or for the protection of other persons, that he should be admitted to a hospital, but that compliance with the provisions of this Part of this Act relating to

an application for admission before the admission of the patient to a hospital would involve undesirable G delay. . . .

"(3) An emergency recommendation shall be sufficient authority for the removal of the patient to a hospital at any time within a period of 3 days from the date on which it was made and for his detention therein for a period not exceeding 72 hours from the time of his admission.

"(4) An emergency recommendation shall be made only by a medical practitioner who has personally H examined the patient on the day on which he signed the recommendation. . . .

"25.—(1) An application for admission or an emergency recommendation may be made under this Part of this Act notwithstanding that the patient is already in a hospital; and where the application or recommendation is made in such a case the patient shall be treated for the purposes of this Part of this Act as if he had been admitted to the hospital on the date on which the application was forwarded to the managers I of the hospital, or, as the case may be, the recommendation was made.

"(2) If, in the case of a patient who is already in a hospital receiving treatment for mental disorder and who is not liable to be detained therein under this Part of this Act, it appears to a nurse of the prescribed class — (a) that the patient is suffering from mental disorder to such a degree that it is necessary for his health or safety or for the protection of other persons for him to J be immediately restrained from leaving the hospital; and (b) that it is not practicable to secure the immediate attendance of a medical practitioner for the purpose of making an emergency recommendation, the patient may be detained in the hospital for a period of 2 hours from the time when he was first so detained or until the earlier arrival at the place where the patient is detained of a medical practitioner having power to make an emergency recommendation. . . .

"26.—(1) Where a patient is admitted to a hospital K in pursuance of section 24 of this Act, he may be detained in that hospital after the expiry of the period of 72 hours referred to in subsection (3) of that section if — (a) a report on the condition of the patient has been furnished to the managers of the hospital; and (b) where practicable, consent to the continued detention has been given by the nearest relative of the patient or by a mental health officer.

"(2) The report referred to in subsection (1) (a) of L this section shall — (a) be given by a medical practitioner approved for the purposes of section 20 (1) (b) of this Act who has personally examined the patient and shall include a statement that in the opinion of the medical practitioner — (i) the patient is suffering from mental disorder of a nature or degree which makes it appropriate for him to be detained in a hospital for at least a limited period; and (ii) the patient ought to be so detained in the interests of his own health or safety or with a view to the protection of other persons; (b) include, where consent to the continued detention has

A not been obtained, a statement of the reasons for not obtaining such consent; and (c) contain a statement as to whether the person signing the report is related to the patient and of any pecuniary interest that that person may have in the admission of the patient to hospital.

"(3) Subject to subsection (6) of this section, where a report is duly furnished under subsection (1) of this section the authority for the detention of the patient shall be thereby renewed for a further period of 28 B days from the expiry of the period of 72 hours referred to in the said subsection (1). . . .

"(6) Any patient may, within the period for which the authority for his detention is renewed by virtue of a report furnished in respect of him under this section, appeal to the sheriff to order his discharge and the provisions of section 33 (2) and (4) of this Act shall apply in relation to such an appeal.

"(7) A patient who has been detained in a hospital C under this section shall not be further detained under this section nor detained under section 24 of this Act immediately after the expiry of the period of detention under this section."

Cases referred to
B v F, 1987 SLT 681; (sub nom *B v Forsey*) 1988 SLT 572.
Frew v Morris (1897) 4 SLT 342; (1897) 24 R (J) 50.
Keenan v Carmichael, 1992 SLT 814; 1991 SCCR 681.
D *R v Berkshire Justices* (1879) 4 QBD 469.

Textbook referred to
Stair Memorial Encyclopaedia, Vol 22, para 819.

On 27 November 1992 his Lordship *found* that the averments in the petition disclosed no relevant ground of action and *refused* the prayer of the petition.

E **LORD MACLEAN.**—The petitioner was in June 1990 detained as a patient in the Royal Edinburgh hospital. On 26 June 1990 she brought the present petition for judicial review of an emergency recommendation in terms of s 24 (1) of the Mental Health (Scotland) Act 1984 and a report in terms of s 26 of the same Act, to which I shall refer in this judgment as "the Act", by force of which she was detained in the hospital. The petitioner sought declarator that her continued detention was unlawful, liberation from detention, liberation ad interim and damages. The F petition came before Lord Coulsfield on 27 June 1990 on a motion for an order for intimation and service, and for interim liberation. On 28 June 1990 Lord Coulsfield granted interim liberation to the petitioner, and also, inter alia, granted leave to the respondents to reclaim [1991 SLT 282]. The respondents duly reclaimed. While the cause was awaiting a hearing on the summar roll Mr Stephen Woolman, advocate, was appointed curator ad litem to the petitioner. On 21 November 1991 on the unopposed motion of the respondents and reclaimers the First Division of the

Inner House refused the reclaiming motion and remitted the cause to the Lord Ordinary to proceed as G accords. The petition, to which no answers have yet been lodged, came before me on 21 October for its first hearing.

In his judgment of 28 June 1990 Lord Coulsfield set out the circumstances which gave rise to the petition which do not appear to be in dispute. He said (1991 SLT at p 283 A-D): "The petitioner has a long history of mental disturbance and has been treated since 1981 for a schizophrenic illness. On 3 May 1990, she was H admitted to the Royal Edinburgh hospital as a voluntary patient, after attending an outpatient clinic. On 10 May, after some investigations had been carried out, she decided to leave the hospital and on that date she was made the subject of an emergency recommendation under s 24 (1) of the Mental Health (Scotland) Act 1984. An order under that section authorises detention of the patient for a period of 72 hours. On 13 May, a report was made under s 26 of the Act of 1984 and in consequence, in terms of that section, she I became liable to be detained for a period of 28 days from the expiry of the initial period of 72 hours' detention. She remained in the hospital during the 28 day period. . . . It was understood that the petitioner would remain in the hospital as a voluntary patient. However, on 11 June, the petitioner apparently decided to leave the hospital. As she was doing so, at about 1.45 pm, she met the first respondent who had a discussion with her and thereafter decided to detain her again, purportedly under s 24 of the Act. On 14 J June, the second named respondent issued a further report under s 26 of the Act purporting to authorise the detention of the petitioner for a further period of 28 days".

Having heard counsel, who coincidentally were the same counsel as appeared before me, Lord Coulsfield was of opinion, for the reasons he gave at p 284 A-C, that on behalf of the petitioner there had been made out a reasonably strong prima facie case that, in a case in which the first period of detention expired upon K one day and the second was ordered on the subsequent day, the one followed immediately upon the other; and so he granted the petitioner interim liberation.

Before me, counsel for the petitioner made clear that the averments in art 6 of the petition ("she was stopped . . . back to the said ward") were not well founded. Nor was the averment that the first named respondent on 11 June 1990 had not personally examined the petitioner. For that reason it was not L possible for him to argue what was contained in art 7 (b) of the petition. A similar concession had been made before Lord Coulsfield as appears from p 283 D-E of the report. The only additional material made available to me that was not before Lord Coulsfield was an affidavit dated 4 December 1991 from the first respondent and a further report from Dr Masterton dated 8 September 1992. In the affidavit the first respondent states that when the petitioner was admitted to the hospital she was displaying psychotic symptoms. On 10 May 1990, when the result of an electro-

A encephalogram revealed an abnormality consistent with a diagnosis of epilepsy, the petitioner coincidentally decided to discharge herself from hospital. As, in the opinion of the first respondent, she was still psychotic, he detained her in terms of s 25 of the Act. The petitioner resisted detention and attempted to leave the hospital but was returned from the car park of the hospital to the ward. On 13 May 1990 at 1400 hours she was further detained under s 26 of the Act because the medical staff wished to attempt treatment with anti-psychotic and anti-epileptic medication in

B the light of the findings of the electro-encephalogram. As a result of continuing treatment, progress seemed to have been made, and about two weeks before the expiry of the s 26 period the petitioner indicated that she would be willing to remain in the hospital voluntarily as an informal patient and to receive treatment after the expiry of that period. The view taken then was that a s 18 application for her detention was unnecessary. In the first respondent's view the detention period under the s 26 order expired at 1400 hours

C on 10 June 1990. At that time the petitioner expressed no desire to leave the hospital. (I interject here the report of Dr Masterton, who examined the petitioner on 18 June 1990. He recorded that the petitioner thought, at different times during the interview he had with her, that she had been an informal patient for three days and one and a half days. He thought that indicated her disorder of thought and judgment.) The first respondent at the time believed that the petitioner was aware of the expiry of the 28 day period and of her

D right to leave. When he met her outside the door of his office at 1345 hours on 11 June 1990, she had her coat on, her bags were packed, and she said that she was going to discharge herself from hospital. In his office to which he invited her, she said: "I want to leave. I am not under section. You can't detain me." The first respondent then proceeded to examine her, as he records in his affidavit in para 5. He states: "In view of the fact that [the petitioner] was in the midst of treatment for her psychotic state and we had this new electro-encephalogram abnormality, it was decided by

E myself to detain [the petitioner] once more under s 25 of the Act in full knowledge that s 26 had expired 24 hours previously and that we had not proceeded to s 18 as [the petitioner] had previously agreed to stay in hospital and accept our treatment. At the time I did not feel 24 hours constituted 'immediately after the expiry of the period of detention'".

The question is whether the first respondent was correct in his belief because s 26 (7) of the Act pro-

F vides that a patient who has been detained in hospital under s 26 "shall not be further detained under this section nor detained under section 24 of this Act immediately after the expiry of the period of detention under this section".

For the petitioner counsel submitted, first, that the petitioner's lawful detention ended at midnight on 10 June, notwithstanding the averment in art 6 of the petition to the effect that "the 28 day period expired on 10 June 1990 at or about 2 pm". The petitioner therefore attended voluntarily as an informal patient

G from then, ie midnight on 10 June until about 1.45 pm on 11 June. The period of her detention was to be calculated de die in diem (civilis computatio) rather than de momento in momentum (naturalis computatio). For this purpose the first day of the petitioner's detention (13 May 1990) fell to be excluded entirely.

In support of his submission he referred to the case of *Frew v Morris*. In that case the statutory period under consideration was a period not exceeding 28 days "from the time of the purchase" in a case in which milk was purchased about 9 am on 4 November and the summons relating to that purchase

H was served on the seller respondent about 7.30 pm on 2 December. Lord Justice Clerk Macdonald said at (1897) 24 R (J), p 51: "I think that in the ordinary sense of our criminal law the word 'time' means the day on which the fact or offence occurred, and the rule of law applies, that in computing a period from the time or day of the occurrence of any event, the day of that occurrence is not to be counted. The running of the time is to be counted as from midnight of that day,

I and therefore any proceedings raised before midnight of the day when the statutory period expires are timeously instituted".

The Lord Justice Clerk's observations were considered recently by the Lord Justice General in *Keenan v Carmichael*. In that case the question was at what time an offence had been committed where it was provided that penalty points in respect of an offence committed more than three years before another offence were not to be added in respect of that other

J offence. After pointing out that it was not the practice to record in the endorsement on a driving licence the precise time of day when an offence had been committed, the Lord Justice General went on (at 1992 SLT, p 815 G-H): "In any event naturalis computatio is used only in exceptional circumstances, such as where the statute in question makes it clear that the time is to run from a particular hour in the day to some other similar point of time. The normal rule is that time is computed de die in diem, leaving out of

K account fractions of days and calculating the period in question to the midnight following or preceding the last day of the specified term".

Counsel for the petitioner also referred me to the article on "Time" in Vol 22 of the *Stair Memorial Encyclopaedia of the Laws of Scotland*, and in particular to paras 820 and 823, which were also drawn to the court's attention in *Keenan*. I note that in para 819 the author of the article says generally this: "Except where statute has placed the matter beyond doubt, it

L is essential to look at each time limit independently, and ascertain the computation principles applicable thereto from an examination of the decided cases or by analogy from similar situations".

The correct approach, in my view, is to examine the provisions of the statute with care in the light of practical considerations and basic principles. That, broadly, was the approach urged upon me by counsel for the respondents. In the first place, he said, the key provisions of the Act provide the necessary timetable.

Section 26 (3) of the Act provided for the commencement of the 28 day period from the expiry of the period of 72 hours, being the maximum period for which a patient can be detained under an emergency recommendation under s 24 (3). The starting point, it should be noted, was measured according to the hour, because the patient under such an emergency recommendation could not be detained according to s 24 (3) "for a period exceeding 72 hours from the time of his admission". In the normal case the 28 day period could be expected to begin on the expiry of the 72nd hour. It was possible therefore to calculate to the precise hour when the 28 days in fact expired. In this case the patient was made the subject of an emergency recommendation at 1400 hours on 10 May 1990, and her renewed detention in hospital under s 26 commenced at 1400 hours on 13 May 1990. It followed that it expired, as the petitioner averred, at 1400 hours on 10 June. In any event, as a general principle, that construction was to be favoured which preserved and ensured the liberty of the subject. The presumption was for freedom. If the submission on her behalf was correct the petitioner would be detained for longer than the statute allowed. If, in any case, counsel for the petitioner was well founded in saying, as he did, that the period to midnight on the first day of detention in terms of s 26 was to be ignored, it would follow that the petitioner had been wrongfully detained on that day. There was, said counsel for the respondents, no halfway house. Both the cases of *Frew* and *Keenan* were concerned with the application of penal statutes in which no similar provisions with regard to precise timing were made as in the 1984 Act.

In my opinion, for all the reasons he advanced, counsel for the respondents was well founded. The Act sets its own precise time limits to the hour. This is, therefore, the less common case of the application of *naturalis computatio*. In practical hospital terms exact times of admission and detention are noted. In any event the general presumption is in favour of freedom of the individual and that may quite properly be used as an aid to construction where necessary. No one should be detained for a moment longer than is justified by the warrant to detain and such a warrant should be construed strictly. I therefore hold that the petitioner's period of detention expired at 1400 hours on 10 June 1990. Thereafter, she attended voluntarily as an informal patient for almost 24 hours.

The second submission by counsel for the petitioner was that the detention in terms of s 25 of the Act, at 1345 hours on 10 June 1990, followed immediately after the expiry of the detention in terms of s 26, and so was unlawful. Before a further order for detention could be lawful some material interval of time would have to elapse, and he referred to the obiter observations of the Lord Justice Clerk, Lord Ross, in this connection in *B v F*, 1987 SLT at p 690 L. What was a material interval of time depended on all the circumstances of the particular case. He, for his part, would consider detention two days later to be in contravention of s 26 (7). The circumstances of the case might include the fact whether the patient de facto had left

the hospital at any stage; the reasons the hospital authority had for obtaining the hospital order or orders; the reasons for not invoking the s 18 procedure while the patient was lawfully detained; and the question whether the patient had genuinely been afforded an opportunity to leave after she had, it appeared, remained in the hospital voluntarily on an informal basis. He referred me to the report of Dr Masterton dated 18 June 1990. In that report Dr Masterton had called into question whether those who had charge of the petitioner should properly have relied upon the petitioner's apparent willingness to undergo voluntary drug treatment in the hospital in view of her past history as a patient. He also referred to her disorder of thought and judgment which was reflected in her uncertainty about the period during which she had been an informal patient which varied, according to her recollection, between one and a half and three days. This does however make it clear and confirms the first respondent's statement that the petitioner knew that she was for a period an informal patient at the hospital. It was unsatisfactory, said counsel for the petitioner, for the hospital authorities to say that the second period of detention was lawful merely because the patient herself had assumed the stance of being an informal patient but chose not to leave immediately. If they wished to continue the petitioner's treatment in the hospital, they ought to have invoked the s 18 procedure. That, as it seems to me, is a matter of medical judgment and there may be sound medical reasons why psychiatrists would prefer to treat patients in hospitals without their formal detention there.

Finally, counsel for the petitioner drew my attention to Lord Coulsfield's judgment in which his Lordship expressed the opinion that there was a reasonably strong prima facie case that, in a case in which the first period of detention expired upon one day and the second was ordered on the subsequent day, the one followed immediately upon the other. His Lordship went on (at p 284 A-B): "it seems to me that from a practical and common sense point of view, detention authorised on the day following the day on which the period expires is detention 'immediately after the expiry' of that period, particularly if the patient has not left the hospital. It is true that in this case the patient's legal status altered for a period of about 24 hours, during which she was a voluntary patient, but that does not, in my view, necessarily take away the force of the petitioner's argument".

The question, as I think, is what is comprehended by the adverb "immediately" in s 26 (7). Counsel for the respondents accepted that it was not possible to lay down a construction of the subsection that applied in every case. The phrase "material interval" was not a substitute for the word "immediately" which imported the meaning of "without any delay" or "forthwith". In *R v Justices of Berkshire* (1879) 4 QBD, Cockburn CJ at p 471 said that the word implied "prompt, vigorous action, without any delay, and whether there has been such action is a question of fact, having regard to the circumstances of the parti-

cular case". It was very difficult to say what period of
A time could elapse without breaching this provision.
One had to look at the circumstances of each case, said
counsel for the respondents, and determine whether it
had been breached or not. In point of actual time in
this case, there had been no breach, but that was not
determinative of the question. He figured the case
where the period of detention expired at midnight
when the patient was asleep. A doctor, discovering
this on coming on duty at 9 am, then issued a s 25
detention order. That would breach the terms of s 26
B (7). I agree with that submission.

Some assistance can be obtained from a consideration of the mischief which s 26 (7) was enacted to
remove. That is succinctly set out in the speech of
Lord Keith of Kinkel in *B v Forsey*, 1988 SLT at
pp 576-577 where his Lordship said: "Section 31 of
the Mental Health (Scotland) Act 1960 authorised the
detention in hospital of a mentally disordered person
upon an emergency recommendation made by a
medical practitioner. The authorised period of deten-
C tion was seven days, and a recommendation might be
made in respect of a person who was already a patient
in hospital. There was nothing to prevent successive
emergency recommendations being made each leading
to seven days' detention, and this became a not
uncommon practice. Section 12 of the Mental Health
(Amendment) (Scotland) Act 1983 put a stop to the
practice by introducing into s 31 of the Act of 1960 a
subsection in the terms now found in s 24 (6) of the
Act of 1984. At the same time the period of emergency
D detention was reduced to 72 hours, and provision was
made for short term detention by enacting a new
s 32A. That section is what now appears as s 26 of the
Act of 1984. So it appears that Parliament specifically
set out to outlaw successive periods of emergency
detention, and it also forbade successive periods of
short term detention".

The very difficult professional problem which the
doctors faced in *B v Forsey* has now been resolved with
E the enactment in July 1991 of the Mental Health
(Detention) (Scotland) Act 1991, which makes special
provision where late in a period of detention under
s 26 there is a change in the condition of the patient
that makes it necessary in the interests of his own
health or safety, or with a view to the protection of
other persons, that the patient should continue to be
detained after the expiry of a period of 28 days and it
is not reasonably practicable to submit a s 18 application to the sheriff before the expiry of the 28 day
F period. That, of course, has no application to this case.

It must, I consider, be a matter of impression in each
case whether it can truly be said that the patient has
been further detained immediately after the expiry of
a period of detention under s 26. What impresses me
in this case is that the petitioner knew that the period
had expired; that she knew then that she could leave
but preferred to remain voluntarily as an informal
patient so that her treatment could be continued; that
those who had care of her in the hospital had reason
to believe for some time before the period expired that

they had her co-operation; and that nearly 24 hours
elapsed between the expiry of the 28 day period and G
her further detention. In these circumstances I find it
impossible to affirm that the further detention was
effected immediately after the expiry of the 28 day
period of detention in contravention of s 26 (7) of the
Act. Since no answers have ever been lodged to the
petition, I will simply find that the averments in the
petition disclose no relevant ground of action, and I
will therefore refuse the prayer of the petition.

H

*Counsel for Petitioner, Clancy; Solicitors, Macbeth
Currie & Co, WS — Counsel for Respondents, Keen;
Solicitor, R F Macdonald, WS.*

S J B

McColligan v Normand   I

HIGH COURT OF JUSTICIARY
THE LORD JUSTICE GENERAL (HOPE),
LORDS COWIE AND MAYFIELD
5 JANUARY 1993

*Justiciary — Procedure — Summary procedure —
Verdict — Justice saying "not proven" to assessor in open
court after defence speech — Assessor suggesting that
justice retire — Justice retiring and thereafter convicting* J
*accused — Whether assessor entitled to intervene —
Whether justice entitled to reconsider position — Whether
proceedings unfair.*

An accused person was tried for breach of the peace
in the district court. At the conclusion of the evidence,
and after the speeches for both the prosecution and the
defence, the justice said the words "not proven" to his
assessor in open court. The assessor then suggested
that the justice retire from the bench and both of them
then left the court. On returning to court the justice K
announced a verdict of guilty. The accused sought
suspension of the conviction on the grounds that the
justice had convicted him not solely on a consideration
of the evidence and that he had been denied a fair trial.

Held, that since the stage of actual judgment had
not been reached, as the words "not proven" had been
addressed to the assessor and not the accused, the
assessor was entitled to suggest that the justice retire
and the justice was entitled to alter his position in the
light of the assessor's advice before announcing his L
verdict, and accordingly there was no inherent unfairness in the proceedings (p 1028G-I); and bill *refused*.

Kelly v Rae, 1916 2 SLT 246, *applied*.

Bill of suspension

Terence McColligan brought a bill of suspension
against Andrew C Normand, procurator fiscal,
Glasgow, praying the High Court to suspend a

pretended conviction dated 30 June 1992 whereby the complainer was found guilty of breach of the peace.

Statement of facts and answers

The bill and the answers were in the following terms:

Stat 1. The complainer is Terence McColligan who was convicted in the district court of Glasgow in relation to the charge of breach of the peace as is more fully set out in the summary complaint at the instance of the respondent, a copy of which is appended hereto.

Ans 1. Admitted.

Stat 2. On 30 June 1992, the complainer appeared at the district court in Glasgow in respect of said complaint and the case proceeded to trial. At the conclusion of said trial the complainer was found guilty. The justice of the peace deferred sentence on the complainer for a period of one year for the complainer to be of good behaviour.

Ans 2. Admitted.

Stat 3. At the conclusion of the evidence and the speeches of the prosecution and the solicitor for the complainer, the justice of the peace said to his legal assessor in court the words "not proven". The said legal assessor then moved for the justice of the peace to retire from the bench to reconsider his position. Both then retired from the court.

Ans 3. Admitted that at the conclusion of the evidence and submissions the justice and his assessor retired. Quoad ultra not known and not admitted. The respondent's depute in court was not aware of any exchange between the justice and his assessor before they retired.

Stat 4. The justice of the peace and the said legal assessor returned to the court after an adjournment of a few minutes. The justice of the peace then delivered a verdict of guilty on the complainer.

Ans 4. Admitted.

Stat 5. It is believed and averred that in consequence of the suggestion of an adjournment having been made by the said legal assessor and not solely on consideration of the evidence led and the submissions made to him, the justice of the peace convicted the complainer.

Ans 5. Not known and not admitted.

Stat 6. The said legal assessor acted improperly and illegally in moving the justice of the peace to adjourn to reconsider his position. The justice of the peace had reached a view of the case. The justice of the peace acted improperly in accepting and acting upon the advice of the said legal assessor to have an adjournment to reconsider his position.

Ans 6. Not known and not admitted.

Stat 7. The said adjournment to reconsider in all the circumstances amounted to the complainer being denied the appearance, if not the substance, of a fair trial, as a result of which there was either a miscarriage of justice or the appearance of such.

The pleas in law for the complainer were in the following terms:

(1) The complainer's trial, in respect of all or any of the matters raised above, having been conducted in an improper and illegal manner, the said pretended conviction should be quashed.

(2) The complainer not having been seen to have received a fair trial, in respect of all or any of the matters raised above, the said pretended conviction should be quashed.

Cases referred to

Kelly v Rae, 1916 2 SLT 246; 1917 JC 12.
Maxwell v Cardle, 1993 SLT 1017; 1993 SCCR 15.

The bill was argued before the High Court on 5 January 1993.

Eo die the court *refused* to pass the bill.

The following opinion of the court was delivered by the Lord Justice General (Hope):

OPINION OF THE COURT.—The complainer is Terence McColligan who went to trial in the district court in Glasgow on a charge of breach of the peace. At the conclusion of the trial he was found guilty and the justice of the peace deferred sentence on him for a period of one year to be of good behaviour. The bill is concerned with an irregularity which was said to have taken place at the trial, and what is sought in it is suspension of the conviction and sentence.

The matter which gives rise to this application is described in the statement of facts on these lines. At the conclusion of the evidence and the speeches both for the prosecution and for the complainer the justice said to his legal assessor in open court the words "not proven". The legal assessor then suggested to the justice that he should retire from the bench, and both of them then retired from the court. The legal assessor is said to have moved that the justice should retire from the bench to reconsider his position. But we were told that no actual words were used in the course of this exchange, and that what happened was the legal assessor indicated by a motion of his head that the justice should retire. Having adjourned for a few minutes the justice and his assessor returned to the court, whereupon the justice delivered a verdict of guilty on the charge against the complainer. The proposition on which the bill depends is that in consequence of the suggestion of an adjournment having been made by the legal assessor, and not solely on consideration of the evidence led and the submissions made to him, the justice convicted the complainer. It is said that the legal assessor acted improperly and illegally in moving the justice of the peace to adjourn to reconsider his position, and that in all the circumstances there was a denial to the complainer of a fair trial.

In developing her argument today counsel for the complainer referred us to the provisions of s 18 (4) (a) of the District Courts (Scotland) Act 1975, which state that the function of the assessor is to advise and assist the justice in the performance of his duties. The more accurate reference would have been to s 7 of that Act, since the function which was being performed on this occasion was that of clerk to the district court. Subsection (1) of that section provides that the clerk shall act as legal assessor in that court, and it is part of his function to give advice to the justice whenever this is required: see *Maxwell v Cardle*.

That provision does not take us very far in deciding what the limits are to the extent to which the assessor may interfere with decisions taken by the justice, but some assistance in this matter is to be found in *Kelly v Rae* to which we were also referred by counsel. In that case a person convicted by a magistrate brought a bill of suspension in which he averred that the magistrate stated at the conclusion of the evidence and speeches that he thought that the case had not been proved. The clerk of court thereupon drew his attention to an item in the evidence and suggested that there should be a conviction. It was contended that it was in consequence of this suggestion and not solely on a consideration of the evidence that the magistrate convicted the accused. It was held that the clerk was entitled, at any time prior to actual judgment, to advise the magistrate with regard to any point which had been matter of evidence, and the court refused to suspend the conviction.

The Lord Justice Clerk pointed out at 1916 2 SLT, p 248 that the magistrate had not formally pronounced his judgment as to whether the accused was guilty or not. He had apparently made an observation before pronouncing the judgment, and it was at that point that the clerk intervened. He observed that this intervention may have been wise or unwise and that the advice may have been good or bad, but that this did not matter. He was satisfied that the stage had not yet been reached when a verdict had actually been pronounced. The same point can be found in the opinions delivered by the other judges, and in particular of Lord Dundas who at p 248 said this: "I take it that a magistrate may at any time before actual judgment change his opinion, and I take it also that a clerk of court is entitled, and may be bound, to tender to the magistrate, if he does so timeously, any advice that occurs to him bearing on the decision of the case".

That passage, in our opinion, describes accurately the position which applies today under the District Courts (Scotland) Act 1975 in regard to the functions of the legal assessor when he is performing his duty to advise and assist the justice in the district court.

The particular point which arises in this case to which the argument was directed is whether the intervention was made so late in the day that the actions of the assessor could be described as improper. Counsel's submission was that his intervention came too late, because what the justice had done was not merely to say what he thought might be the verdict but had stated in an unqualified manner what he considered the verdict should be. Furthermore, this exchange took place in open court, and it gave rise to the impression of unfairness that, having expressed himself in these terms, the justice was then persuaded by his assessor to reconsider his position and change the verdict.

In our opinion, however, on a proper reading of the averments in the bill and what we were told about the events by counsel, the stage of actual judgment had not yet been reached in this case. The critical point is that the words "not proven" were addressed to the legal assessor, not to the complainer. It was only after the justice and his assessor returned to court after the adjournment that the justice then delivered what the averments themselves describe as his verdict of guilty on the complainer. This appears to us to be a case which falls on the correct side of what may well be a very narrow dividing line, between the point at which the matter is open to intervention by the assessor and the point when the actual judgment has been pronounced. On the facts of this case we consider that the legal assessor was entitled to suggest to the justice that he should retire to reconsider his position, and that the justice was entitled to alter his opinion in the light of his advice before pronouncing his verdict. That being so, we cannot accept the proposition that the intervention was improper or that there was any inherent unfairness in the proceedings which were adopted in this case.

For these reasons we must refuse to pass this bill.

Counsel for Complainer, M E Scott; Solicitors, Allan McDougall & Co, SSC (for Penman, Currie & Gordon, Glasgow) — Counsel for Respondent, Solicitor General (Dawson, QC); Solicitor, J D Lowe, Crown Agent.

P W F

Kidd v Russell

HIGH COURT OF JUSTICIARY
LORDS COWIE, MILLIGAN AND WYLIE
14 JANUARY 1993

Justiciary — Sentence — Community service order — Sheriff imposing fine and making community service order for single offence — Whether competent to impose fine — Community Service by Offenders (Scotland) Act 1978 (c 49), s 1 (1).

An accused person pled guilty to inter alia a contravention of s 5 (1) (a) of the Road Traffic Act 1988. The sheriff fined the accused and also made a community service order in respect of him for 120 hours. The accused appealed contending that it was incompetent to impose both a fine and a community service order.

Held, that it was incompetent for the sheriff to make a community service order and at the same time

fine the accused (p 1030B); and appeal *allowed* and
A fine *quashed*.

Summary complaint

Andrew David Kidd was charged at the instance of
Edward B Russell, procurator fiscal, Cupar, on a
summary complaint which libelled, inter alia, a contravention of s 143 (1) and (2) of the Road Traffic Act
1988 and a contravention of s 5 (1) (a) of the Act. The
accused pled guilty to these offences and the sheriff (C
B Smith) in respect of the latter offence fined the
accused £250 and made a community service order in
respect of the accused for 120 hours.

The accused appealed to the High Court against the
sentence imposed by the sheriff.

Statutory provisions

The Community Service by Offenders (Scotland)
Act 1978, as amended, provides:

C "1.—(1) Subject to the provisions of this Act, where
a person of or over 16 years of age is convicted of an
offence punishable by imprisonment, other than an
offence the sentence for which is fixed by law, the
court may, instead of imposing on him a sentence of,
or including, imprisonment or any other form of
detention, make an order (in this Act referred to as 'a
community service order') requiring him to perform
unpaid work for such number of hours (being in total
not less than 40 nor more than 240) as may be speci-
D fied in the order."

Cases referred to

R v Carnwell (1978) 68 Cr App R 58.
R v Cruxton (1991) 12 Cr App R (S) 740.

Appeal

The note of appeal contained an amended ground in
the following terms:

That it is incompetent in terms of the Community
E Service by Offenders (Scotland) Act 1978, s 1, to
impose a fine together with a community service
order. Reference is made to s 1 (1) and (7) of the
said Act.

The appeal was argued before the High Court on 14
January 1993.

Eo die the court *allowed* the appeal and *quashed*
the fine.

F

The following opinion of the court was delivered by
Lord Cowie:

OPINION OF THE COURT.—The appellant is
Andrew David Kidd. On 20 August 1992 he pled
guilty at Cupar sheriff court to two charges under the
Road Traffic Act 1988. The first was using a motor
car on a public road without there being in force in
relation to the use of the said motor car a policy of
insurance or such a security in respect of third party
risks, as complied with the requirements of Pt VI of

the Road Traffic Act 1988, contrary to s 143 (1) and
(2) of the said Act.   G

The second charge was driving a motor car on a
public road after consuming so much alcohol that the
proportion of it in his breath was 89 microgrammes of
alcohol in 100 millilitres of breath which exceeded the
prescribed limit, namely 35 microgrammes of alcohol
in 100 millilitres of breath, contrary to s 5 (1) (a) of the
Road Traffic Act 1988.

The sheriff deferred sentence on the appellant until
10 September 1992 for social inquiry and community
service reports and, in the meantime, suspended the   H
appellant's driving licence.

On 10 September 1992 having considered the above
reports the sheriff fined the appellant £100 on the
charge of using the motor car without insurance and
£250 on the charge of driving with an excess of alcohol
in his breath. He allowed the above fines to be
paid by instalments of £10 per week. In addition however, he made a community service order in respect
of the appellant for 120 hours in relation to the   I
latter charge. For the sake of completion the sheriff
ordered endorsement of the appellant's driving licence
on the former charge and disqualified him from
holding or obtaining a driving licence from the date of
sentence on the latter charge and ordered endorsement
of his driving licence on that charge also.

The appellant appealed against that sentence but
only with a view to challenging the competency of
imposing a fine and a community service order in
respect of the charge of driving with an excess of   J
alcohol in his breath.

The original ground of appeal was misconceived and
so the sheriff's attention was not properly directed to
the point on which the appeal was based. When the
appeal came before this court on 30 October 1992
counsel asked leave to be allowed to lodge amended
grounds of appeal and leave was duly granted. The
new ground of appeal is as follows: [his Lordship
quoted the ground of appeal set out supra and continued:]   K

At the commencement of today's hearing the
learned advocate depute on behalf of the Lord
Advocate informed the court that the appeal was not
to be opposed by the Crown, but since we considered
that the point was one of general interest and we were
not referred to any Scottish authority dealing with the
matter we asked the advocate depute to address us
on it.

He explained that community service was intro-   L
duced in Scotland by the Community Service by
Offenders (Scotland) Act 1978. Section 1 (1) of that
Act, as amended by s 61 (3) of the Law Reform (Miscellaneous Provisions) (Scotland) Act 1990, was in the
following terms: [his Lordship quoted the terms of s 1
(1) and continued:]

The advocate depute submitted that it was clear
from the provisions of that section that the court may
make a community service order as an alternative to
imprisonment, but more importantly that it was clear

that it was to be regarded as an alternative to a sentence including imprisonment, for example a sentence of fine and imprisonment. For that reason alone he argued that it was not competent to make a community service order and impose a fine for the same offence. He submitted that the argument was further underlined by the provisions of s 1 (7) of the Act which specified certain orders which could competently be combined with a community service order and the imposition of a fine was not among them. That feature, according to the advocate depute, demonstrated that Parliament had not intended that a fine should be imposed along with a community service order.

We are quite satisfied that the submissions of the advocate depute are well founded and that it was incompetent in the present case for the sheriff to make a community service order and at the same time fine the appellant on the drink driving charge.

We are confirmed in that view by the decisions in two English cases to which we were referred. The first was the case of *Carnwell* and the second was the case of *Cruxton*. The statutory provisions with which those cases were concerned are quite different from the provisions of the 1978 Act as were the facts, but in our view the principle is the same. The point is neatly explained by Lawton LJ in the case of *Carnwell* at p 61 where he says: "In our judgment the reasoning behind both the provision relating to probation and the provision relating to community service orders, is this: if there is a breach of a probation order, the defendant can be brought back and punished for the offence for which he was put on probation; and if, on the making of a probation order, the offender could be fined in addition, there would be complications when there was a breach. There would be the same kind of difficulty with a community service order. A defendant who fails to comply with the terms of the community service order can be brought back to court and punished for the original offence; and just as with a probation order, if he had been fined at the time the community service order was made, there might be complications when he was brought back for breach of the community service order".

In all these circumstances we shall allow the appeal to the extent of quashing the fine of £250 imposed in respect of the charge of driving with an excess of alcohol in the appellant's breath. The fine imposed on the charge of using a motor vehicle without insurance is not affected, (a) because no appeal was taken against it, (b) because it was imposed in respect of a separate statutory offence and (c) because that offence is not one which is punishable by imprisonment and accordingly the making of a community service order would not have been a competent disposal in that case.

Counsel for Appellant, McBride; Solicitors, J & A Hastie, SSC (for Baird & Co, Cupar) — Counsel for Respondent, Boyd, A D; Solicitor, J D Lowe, Crown Agent.

P W F

Barr v Carmichael

HIGH COURT OF JUSTICIARY
THE LORD JUSTICE CLERK (ROSS),
LORDS MURRAY AND MAYFIELD
20 JANUARY 1993

Justiciary — Statutory offence — Driving while uninsured — Accused obtaining insurance cover by falsely declaring that he had no motoring convictions — Accused subsequently agreeing with insurers that insurance policy void — Whether insurance policy void or voidable — Whether accused guilty of driving while uninsured — Road Traffic Act 1988 (c 52), s 143 (1).

An accused person was charged on a summary complaint with four contraventions of s 143 (1) of the Road Traffic Act 1988. The evidence disclosed that the accused had falsely represented to insurance agents that he and two other named drivers had not been convicted of any motoring offences during the past five years when he had been so convicted in 1986. The insurers subsequently issued a certificate of motor insurance covering the accused and the two named individuals in respect of the proposal form containing the false declaration. Thereafter the accused and the two named individuals drove the motor vehicle. Subsequently the insurers wrote to the accused inviting him to sign a statement to the effect that the representation about previous offences was incorrect and that the insurance policy was void. The accused signed the statement after consulting his solicitors who returned it to the insurers with the certificate of insurance. The sheriff convicted the accused on the ground that the insurance policy was void and that, accordingly, when the driving took place there was no policy of motor insurance in force because the accused had accepted so far as the insurers were concerned that the policy was void. The accused appealed, contending that the policy was merely voidable and not void.

Held, that since the policy was agreed by the accused to be void and not voidable, the sheriff was entitled to arrive at the decision which he made (p 1034G-H); and appeal *refused.*

Observed, that a stated case fell to be decided in the light of the findings made and because of the terms of the findings relating to the accused's agreement that the policy was void, the wider question of whether a false declaration rendered a policy void or voidable did not require to be determined (p 1034H).

Summary complaint

Samuel Ferguson Barr was charged at the instance of William George Carmichael, procurator fiscal, Hamilton, on a summary complaint which contained the following charges, inter alia:

"(2) on 22 June 1989 on Muir Street, Motherwell you did cause and permit Matthew Wotherspoon, 32 Orbiston Drive, Bellshill to use a motor vehicle, namely motor car registered no TNS 541W, without

A there being in force in relation to the use of said motor vehicle by said Matthew Wotherspoon such a policy of insurance or such a security in respect of third party risks as complied with the requirements of Pt VI of the Road Traffic Act 1988; contrary to the Road Traffic Act 1988, s 143 (1) and (2);

"(3) on 13 July 1989 on the B996, Kinross to Cowdenbeath Road, you did cause and permit said Matthew Wotherspoon to use a motor vehicle, namely said motor car registered no TNS 541W, without there being in force in relation to the use of said motor

B vehicle by said Matthew Wotherspoon such a policy of insurance or such a security in respect of third pary risks as complied with the requirements of Pt VI of the Road Traffic Act 1988; contrary to the Road Traffic Act 1988, s 143 (1) and (2);

"(4) on 24 July 1989 within Strathclyde Park, Motherwell you did cause and permit said Matthew Wotherspoon to use a motor vehicle, namely said motor car registered no TNS 541W, without there

C being in force in relation to the use of said motor vehicle by said Matthew Wotherspoon such a policy of insurance or such a security in respect of third party risks as complied with the requirements of Pt VI of the Road Traffic Act 1988; contrary to the Road Traffic Act 1988, s 143 (1) and (2);

"(5) on 26 July 1989 on Turquoise Terrace, Bellshill you did cause and permit Alexander Brown, 8 Community Road, Bellshill to use a motor vehicle, namely said motor car registered no TNS 541W,

D without there being in force in relation to the use of said motor vehicle by said Alexander Brown such a policy of insurance or such a security in respect of third party risks as complied with the requirements of Pt VI of the Road Traffic Act 1988; contrary to the Road Traffic Act 1988, s 143 (1) and (2)".

The accused pled not guilty and proceeded to trial. After trial the sheriff (L S Lovat) found the accused guilty.

E The accused appealed by way of stated case to the High Court against the decision of the sheriff.

Cases referred to
Adams v Dunne [1978] Crim LR 365.
Guardian Assurance Co Ltd v Sutherland [1939] 2 All ER 246.
Taylor v Allon [1966] 1 QB 304; [1965] 2 WLR 598; [1965] 1 All ER 557.

F **Textbooks referred to**
Walker, *Principles of Scottish Private Law* (4th ed), Vol 2, pp 525, 867, 868.
Wilkinson, *Road Traffic Offences* (12th ed), para 10-18.

Findings in fact
The sheriff found the following facts admitted or proved:

(1) On 8 May 1989, the appellant, with two witnesses Matthew Wotherspoon and Alexander Brown,

named in the charges, entered the office of G Douglas

G Green & Co, insurance agents, 29 Main Street, Bothwell, and produced a proposal form for motor car insurance addressed to Eagle Star Insurance Co Ltd, 17-19 Blythswood Square, Glasgow. (2) He produced this form, identifying himself, to the witness Miss Angela O'Meara, then a clerkess in said office, and in the nearby presence of the witness, Mrs Elaine Ingleston, then the office manageress. (3) The witness Angela O'Meara, within the hearing of the witness Elaine Ingleston, went over the details of said form

H with the appellant, asking him if the details were correct, which he said they were; and, in particular she asked him if he or the two drivers named on the form had been convicted of any motoring offences (including fixed penalty offences) during the past five years or were any prosecutions pending (question 4a), and he falsely confirmed that the answer was "no", which was written on said form. (4) The appellant paid to the witness Angela O'Meara £54.94 cash in respect of this vehicle insurance, was handed a receipt for this sum and obtained a vehicle insurance cover note. (5) By

I joint minute of admissions lodged in this case, it was confirmed that on 19 February 1986, the appellant had been convicted of contravening ss 99 (b) and 143 (1) of the Road Traffic Act 1972, at Hamilton sheriff court. (6) The proposal form was sent by the insurance agents to Eagle Star Insurance Co Ltd and they issued to the appellant a certificate of motor insurance valid from 8 May 1989 to 8 May 1990 covering any private motor car owned by the appellant, who was the policyholder and the witnesses Matthew Wotherspoon and

J Alexander Brown were also named as entitled to drive. (7) On 22 June 1989, the witness Matthew Wotherspoon, named in charge 2, with permission of the appellant, drove motor car registered number TNS 541W, owned by the appellant, on Muir Street, Motherwell. (8) On 13 July 1989, the witness Matthew Wotherspoon, named again in charge 3, with permission of the appellant, drove said motor car, owned by the appellant, on the B996 road from Kinross to Cowdenbeath. (9) On 24 July 1989, the

K witness Matthew Wotherspoon named again in charge 4, with permission of the appellant, drove said motor car, owned by the appellant, on roads within Strathclyde Park, Motherwell. (10) On 26 July 1989, the witness Alexander Brown, named in charge 5, with permission of the appellant, drove said motor car, owned by the appellant, on Turquoise Terrace, Bellshill.

(11) On the occasions specified in findings in fact 7,

L 8, 9 and 10, the police stopped said motor car driven by said witnesses and issued to the witness Matthew Wotherspoon HO/RT 1 forms and to the witness Alexander Brown HO/RT 1 form. (12) In conformity with these occasions specified in finding in fact 11, the witness Matthew Wotherspoon produced the certificate of motor insurance (a) to the witness Police Constable Gail Miller on 30 June 1989, who completed the HO/RT 2 form annexed to the HO/RT 1 form, (b) to the witness Police Sergeant Peter Chalmers on 2 August 1989, who completed two HO/RT 2 forms

A annexed to the two HO/RT 1 forms; and the witness Alexander Brown produced the certificate of motor insurance (Crown production no 2) to the witness Police Sergeant Peter Chalmers on 2 August 1989, who completed the HO/RT 2 form annexed to the HO/RT 1 form. (13) Subsequently the witness Ronald Peggs, manager of the aforesaid Eagle Star Insurance Co Ltd, who received information from the police concerning the appellant's Road Traffic Act previous convictions, wrote a letter to the appellant dated 13 October 1989, enclosing a photostat copy of the

B proposal form completed by the appellant, drawing his attention to question 4 (a) which the appellant answered in the negative, stating that from information in their possession that answer was incorrect and that they must treat the policy as void from inception and no insurance cover had been in force; and he enclosed a statement which he asked the appellant to read and if he agreed with the contents — the essence of which was that the answer to question 4 (a) was incorrect and acceptance that the policy was void — to

C sign and date the statement and return it together with the current certificate of insurance, in which event, the money paid by the appellant would be returned to him; and he would not have accepted any amendment or alteration by the appellant in the statement, in particular, an alteration of the word "void" to "voidable". (14) The witness Ronald Peggs subsequently received a letter dated 24 October 1989, from Mr Macara, partner in Beltrami & Co, solicitors, Glasgow, stating that he had been consulted by the

D appellant, who agreed with the statement attached to Mr Pegg's letter, which was now returned by Beltrami & Co, signed by the appellant, with the certificate of insurance and a request that £323 would be sent as soon as possible to the appellant. (15) On 6 November 1989, a cheque for £323 was sent by Eagle Star Insurance Co Ltd to the appellant.

The sheriff appended the following note to the findings in fact:

E **THE SHERIFF (L S LOVAT).**—As far as charge 1 [contravention of the Road Traffic Act 1972, s 170 (6)] is concerned, I found the evidence of the witnesses Angela O'Meara and Elaine Ingleston credible, reliable and truthful as distinct from the evidence of the appellant, which was in many respects deplorable. I was able to reach findings in fact 1 to 5. In cross examination in respect of charge 1 he was asked about the relevant previous conviction and answered: "I had

F no doubt about the conviction". He added: "They asked if any previous convictions". He was asked if he accepted that he answered "No" and he replied: "I never answered anything. Mabye I've said breach of the peace". He was asked: "You say she said — any previous convictions?" and he answered "Yes". He was then asked: "What was the reason that you didn't tell her your Road Traffic Act previous convictions?" and he answered "She didn't really ask". He was asked: "Why did you not tell her about the Road Traffic Act previous convictions?" and he answered "I don't know. It's that long ago". He was asked:

"Did you answer 'no'?" and he replied "Maybe I did". He was then asked: "Did you answer 'no'?" and G he replied "I don't accept that". He was eventually asked: "Did you read the form before signing?" and he replied "I never read every word on it but I looked it over". In respect of findings of fact 13 and 14 concerning Crown productions nos 3 and 4, he was asked in cross examination if he signed Crown production no 4, the statement, upon the advice of Mr Macara, and he replied "Yes". Therefore he was logically asked if he accepted that he answered "No" to Angela O'Meara concerning the previous convictions and he H replied "I don't accept that" — and added "Mr Macara told me to sign it — I wasn't going to sign it". These are examples of the lies, gross inconsistencies and contradictions made on oath by the appellant, which were, as I have said, deplorable. I should add that the evidence of the witness Ronald Peggs was sound and reliable. There was no doubt that the appellant was guilty of committing the crime libelled in charge 1.

I pass now to charges 2 to 5 and to cases cited. I I must say that I found it ironical that on behalf of the appellant, Mr Macara contended that the insurance policy was not void but voidable, despite the fact that, as I have confirmed in finding in fact 14, the appellant signed the statement accepting that the policy was void from inception, having consulted Mr Macara, who wrote the letter dated 24 October 1989, returning the signed statement and the certificate of insurance and requesting the return of £323, which was sent as in finding in fact 15. But I must, in justice, deal with J the arguments which were submitted at the conclusion of the evidence in the late afternoon and on a subsequent date.

The procurator fiscal depute commented on the evidence of the witness Ronald Peggs, who was asked in cross examination by Mr Macara that if he had been aware of the appellant's Road Traffic Act convictions, would he have had discretion; and he replied "Not really", because "the type of conviction was serious". K I myself noted that in response to another question, by Mr Macara to Mr Peggs on the same theme with the use of the word "voidable", Mr Peggs replied "We would still have voided his policy". They did so as set out in findings in fact 13 and 14. The procurator fiscal depute referred to *Guardian Assurance Co Ltd v Sutherland,* where it was held that where a policy of motor insurance was obtained by material misrepresentation and non-disclosure of material facts, the insurance company was entitled to void the policy. Since Mr Macara had intimated *Adams v Dunne,* the L procurator fiscal depute made the point that this case did not resolve matters. The charge had been dismissed by the justices as no steps had been taken to void the cover note. There had followed an appeal by the prosecutor and a decision by the Queen's Bench Division that the contract was not void ab initio but merely voidable; so that unless and until the insurers took steps to void the contract, it remained in force, and the cover provided was within the requirements of s 143 (1). They supported the decision by the justices.

In response, Mr Macara contended that the decision in *Adams v Dunne* made by the Queen's Bench Division must supersede the decision in *Guardian Assurance Co Ltd v Sutherland* made by a single judge. He referred briefly to the 12th edition of Wilkinson's *Road Traffic Offences* at para 10-18. He submitted that the *Adams v Dunne* case supported his contention that the insurance in the present case was not void — it was voidable. He added that *Adams v Dunne* was of persuasive authority as there was in that case a "flagrant contravention". The witness Ronald Peggs in the present case had taken steps, when information was brought to his attention, after the dates of driving the vehicle in charges 2 to 5 and the policy was voidable and not void. He also referred to Professor Walker's *Principles of Scottish Private Law,* chap 31, p 525 and chap 46, pp 867 and 868. Mr Macara maintained that the witness Ronald Peggs had discretion. He concluded on this subject by maintaining that "on the face of it" the appellant was entitled to let others drive in light of the insurance policy and that these offences in charges 2 to 5 "could not be committed retroactively".

I agreed with a comment made by the procurator fiscal depute that dealing with English cases is "persuasive not binding"; and I much preferred the reasoning and decision made in *Guardian Assurance Co Ltd v Sutherland.* The witness Ronald Peggs had authority to make the decision, which he made in finding in fact 13, that is, treating the policy as void from inception in light of the gross irresponsible deceit by the appellant disclosed in findings in fact 2 to 5. Thus I found the appellant guilty of charges 2 to 5.

Appeal

The sheriff posed the following questions for the opinion of the High Court:

(1) Was I entitled to hold that the policy of insurance in respect of the motor car was void?

(2) Was I entitled to convict the appellant of charges 2, 3, 4 and 5?

The appeal was heard in the High Court on 20 January 1993.

Eo die the court *answered* the two questions in the *affirmative* and *refused* the appeal.

The following opinion of the court was delivered by the Lord Justice Clerk (Ross):

OPINION OF THE COURT.—The appellant is Samuel Ferguson Barr who went to trial in the sheriff court at Hamilton on a complaint containing a number of charges. The only charges which arise in this appeal are charges 2 to 5 which were all charges of contravening s 143 (1) and (2) of the Road Traffic Act 1988. The appellant was found guilty of inter alia these charges, and it is against his conviction of these charges that he has now appealed by way of stated case.

The facts are set forth by the sheriff in his findings. Putting the matter shortly it was proved that on 8 May 1989 the appellant, along with two witnesses who are the individuals named in the charges, entered the office of insurance agents and produced a proposal form for motor car insurance addressed to the insurers. The clerkess in the office went over the details of the form with the appellant asking him if the details were correct which he said they were. In particular she asked him if he or the two drivers named on the form had been convicted of any motoring offences during the past five years or whether any prosecutions were pending, and he falsely confirmed that the answer was "No" which was written on the form. The appellant paid the clerkess £54.94 in cash in respect of the insurance and obtained a vehicle insurance cover note.

By joint minute of admissions, it was confirmed that on 19 February 1986 the appellant had been convicted of contravening ss 99 (b) and 143 (1) of the Road Traffic Act 1972. The proposal form was sent by the insurance agents to the insurers who issued a certificate of motor insurance valid from 8 May 1989 to 8 May 1990 covering any private car owned by the appellant who was the policy holder and the witnesses Matthew Wotherspoon and Alexander Brown who were also named as entitled to drive. There then follow findings to the effect that on the dates stated in charges 2 to 5, the individuals named in the charges drove the motor car specified in the charge with the permission of the appellant. There are also findings that on the occasions so specified the individuals named in due course produced to the police the certificate of motor insurance which had been issued to the appellant.

Subsequently the insurers' manager, who had received information from the police concerning the appellant's previous convictions, wrote a letter to the appellant dated 13 October 1989 (defence production no 1) enclosing a photostat copy of the proposal form which had been completed by the appellant, drawing his attention to the question regarding previous convictions which had been answered in the negative, and stating that from the information in their possession that answer was incorrect, and that accordingly the insurers must treat the policy as void from its inception and that no insurance cover had been in force. The insurers' manager enclosed a statement which he asked the appellant to read and if he agreed with the contents to sign. The essence of the statement was that the answer to the particular question about previous convictions was incorrect and an acceptance that the policy was void. The insurers' manager subsequently received a letter dated 24 October 1989 from the appellant's solicitor (Crown production no 3) stating that he had been consulted by the appellant who agreed with the statement which had been sent to him and which was now returned to the insurers signed by the appellant along with the certificate of insurance. (The statement is Crown production no 4.) The solicitors also asked that £323 should be sent as soon as possible to the appellant, and on 6 November 1989 a cheque for £323 was sent by the insurers to the appellant.

The issue which is raised in this appeal is whether on the occasions libelled in charges 2 to 5 the policy of insurance was void or voidable. This issue had been raised before the sheriff and two authorities were cited to the sheriff. Before the sheriff the appellant's solicitor relied upon *Adams v Dunne* and the procurator fiscal depute relied upon *Guardian Assurance Co Ltd v Sutherland*. The sheriff held that at the material times the policy of insurance in respect of the car was void, and he accordingly convicted the appellant of the charges.

In presenting the appeal counsel for the appellant submitted that the sheriff had reached the wrong conclusion upon the law. He recognised that the false declaration by the appellant on the proposal form was very serious, and that the insurers had been misled by the appellant. However, he invited the court to follow *Adams v Dunne* and to hold that the action of the appellant did not render the contract void ab initio but merely made it voidable. He emphasised that in *Adams v Dunne* the accused had been charged with contravening s 143 (1) of the Road Traffic Act 1972 which was in very similar terms to s 143 (1) of the Road Traffic Act 1988. He also submitted that *Guardian Assurance Co Ltd v Sutherland* had been decided before *Adams v Dunne* and related to a different statutory provision. Counsel for the appellant accordingly invited the court to answer both questions in the case in the negative.

The advocate depute maintained that on the findings in the present case it was clear that on the dates specified in charges 2 to 5, the policy of insurance in respect of the motor car specified in the charges was void. He submitted that that was clear from findings 13 and 14 and Crown productions nos 3 and 4 and defence production no 1. He contended that in the present case it had been agreed by the appellant and the insurers that the policy was void, and accordingly the sheriff was justified in holding that the policy was void.

The advocate depute went on to submit that if it was necessary to do so the court should decline to follow *Adams v Dunne* and should hold it to have been wrongly decided. He points out that in *Adams v Dunne*, *Guardian Assurance Co Ltd v Sutherland* had not been referred to, nor had *Taylor v Allon*. In that case the defendant had been convicted of contravening the provisions of s 201 of the Road Traffic Act 1960 which is in broadly similar terms to s 143 (1) of the Act of 1972, and it was held that in order to comply with the provisions of s 201 of the Act of 1960, a valid insurance for the purposes of the section had to arise from an enforceable and effective contract. The advocate depute submitted that that decision was consistent with the policy of the legislation since otherwise, despite the fact that the policy was obtained by fraud, the appellant could claim to be insured even though the public would not be protected by the policy.

In view of the findings in the present case, it is not

necessary to determine whether the sheriff was well founded in preferring the reasoning and decision in *Guardian Assurance Co Ltd v Sutherland* to the decision in *Adams v Dunne*. In our opinion the advocate depute was well founded in his first submission. In the present case as is plain from findings 13 and 14 and the three productions already referred to, it is matter of agreement between the insurers and the appellant that the policy on which the appellant sought to rely was void and not merely voidable. Since that policy was agreed by the appellant to be void and not voidable, it follows that the sheriff was entitled to arrive at the decision which he made in this case. A stated case falls to be decided in the light of the findings made, and because of the terms of the findings in the present case the wider question of whether a false declaration renders a policy void or voidable does not require to be determined.

In all the circumstances we shall answer the two questions in the case in the affirmative, and it follows that the appeal is refused.

Counsel for Appellant, McBride; Solicitors, Macbeth Currie & Co, WS (for Beltrami & Co, Glasgow) — Counsel for Respondents, Macdonald, QC, A D; Solicitor, J D Lowe, Crown Agent.

P W F

Scottish Exhibition Centre Ltd v Mirestop Ltd (in administration)

OUTER HOUSE

LORD MORTON OF SHUNA

22 JANUARY 1993

Company — Insolvency — Administration order — Landlord of company in administration seeking leave to commence proceedings against company under irritancy provision in lease — Whether leave should be given — Guidelines to be applied — Insolvency Act 1986 (c 45), s 11 (3) (d).

Section 11 (3) of the Insolvency Act 1986 provides, inter alia, that during the period for which an administration order is in force in relation to a company no proceedings may be commenced or continued against the company except with the consent of the administrator or the leave of the court.

Joint administrators were appointed to a company carrying on business from three leased restaurants. The company's only significant asset was its interest in the lease of the restaurants; its debts to a chargeholder, which exceeded the value of the interest in the lease, were secured by a floating charge and a standard security over the lease. The landlords sought to exercise a right of irritancy in terms of the lease by reason

A of the appointment of the administrators and, the right of irritancy being contested by the administrators and the secured creditor, sought leave to bring an action to determine the right of irritancy and repossession. The landlords argued that the balance in favour of leave being given was established in that their proprietorial rights would be denied if leave were refused and significant loss would result, first, in their being prevented from regaining their property, and secondly, as rent was payable in respect of the restaurants based on gross annual sales, in the tenant's current failure to

B operate one of the restaurants, the functioning of the restaurants being, additionally, important for the landlords' whole enterprise. The administrators argued that the company had fulfilled its obligation to pay rent under the lease, there being no obligation in the lease to keep all three restaurants open, and further time was required to permit the administrators to dispose of the undertaking as a going concern. The administrators also made submissions concerning both the validity of the notice of irritancy and whether the

C landlord was entitled to rely on the irritancy clause.

Held, (1) that it was inappropriate at the stage of considering whether leave should be granted, to express any opinion in relation to an issue in respect of which a party was seeking leave to commence proceedings, unless such an issue raised a short point of law which it was convenient to determine at that stage (p 1036H-I); (2) that the landlords had a seriously arguable case and that, administrators having been appointed for over 18 months without disposal of the

D business and administration being intended to be only an interim and temporary measure, granting a further period before leave to commence proceedings was given would not achieve anything (p 1036I-J); and leave to bring proceedings against the company *granted*.

Re Atlantic Computer Systems plc (No 1) [1992] 2 WLR 367, *applied*.

———

Note in petition for administration order

E Scottish Exhibition Centre Ltd presented a note in the petition for an administration order in relation to Mirestop Ltd, for leave to commence proceedings as landlords against Mirestop Ltd in terms of a provision for irritancy of a lease between the landlords and the company. Answers to the note were lodged by the joint administrators of the company.

The note came before the Lord Ordinary (Lord Morton of Shuna).

F **Statutory provisions**

The Insolvency Act 1986 provides:

"11.— . . . (3) During the period for which an administration order is in force. . . . (d) no other proceedings . . . may be commenced or continued . . . against the company . . . except with the consent of the administrator or the leave of the court".

Case referred to

Re Atlantic Computer Systems plc (No 1) [1992] Ch 505; [1992] 2 WLR 367; [1992] 1 All ER 476.

On 22 January 1993 the Lord Ordinary *granted* the prayer of the note and *granted* leave to bring proceed- G ings against the company.

LORD MORTON OF SHUNA.—Scottish Exhibition Centre Ltd have lodged a note seeking leave to bring proceedings against Mirestop Ltd, a company which is in administration. The respondents are the joint administrators of the company. They were appointed by the court on the petition of the company on the basis that the company was unable to pay its debts and that an administration order should be H made. The company had obtained a valuation of its assets which showed that a valuation on a "going concern" basis was much greater than a valuation on a "for sale" basis. The respondents were appointed joint administrators ad interim on 4 June 1991 and were appointed joint administrators on 16 July 1991.

The noters leased to the company the premises known as "The Pumphouse" at the Scottish Exhibition and Conference Centre in Glasgow. The premises contain three restaurants which are the business the I company carried on. By cl fifth of the lease, it is provided: "if the tenant shall become notour bankrupt or shall make any arrangement with creditors or shall suffer any diligence to be levied on the Subjects, or being a company, shall go into liquidation, whether voluntary or compulsory (otherwise than a voluntary liquidation of a solvent company for the purpose of amalgamation or reconstruction on terms approved by the Landlord in writing), or suffer a receiver or other administrator or manager for creditors to be J appointed, then in any such case it shall be lawful for the landlord at any time thereafter, by notice in writing, to bring this Lease to an end forthwith and to enter the subjects and repossess and enjoy the same". By letters of 18 June 1991 to the respondents and of 19 June 1991 to the company, the noters intimated that they were exercising their right to irritate and terminate the lease. The respondents do not accept that the noters were entitled to irritate the lease and it is said that the holders of a standard security and floating K charge over the company's interests in the lease have intimated an intention to contest any attempt to remove the company from the premises. In these circumstances the noters have presented the note seeking leave to bring an action to resolve the question.

At the hearing before me, counsel for the noters and counsel for the respondents each accepted the guidelines set out in the Court of Appeal judgment in *Re Atlantic Computer Systems plc*. It was agreed that if the noters obtained possession of the property leased to L the company, it would be impossible to sell the undertaking as a going concern, and therefore impossible to achieve the purpose for which the administration order was made. Applying the guidelines suggested by the Court of Appeal, the court then had to carry out a balancing exercise.

For the noters, counsel submitted that various factors tipped the balance in favour of his clients and he accepted that it was for the noters to make out a case for leave to be given. The factors founded on were

A (1) that the lease was the company's only significant asset, and, from the company's petition, it was clear that the secured creditor was owed far more than the value of the lease. The result of this was that the secured creditor was the only creditor with any real interest; (2) if leave were refused, the noters would be denied any opportunity to exercise proprietorial rights; (3) a refusal of leave would result in significant loss to the noters. The primary loss was that they were prevented from regaining their property. A secondary loss occurred because of the parlous financial position

B of the tenants, who were only operating two of the three restaurants in the premises. Under the terms of the lease, the rent payable after 11 November 1992 was based on a percentage of the gross annual sales for each year to the preceding August. As the company was only operating two restaurants, the turnover must be less than if they were operating three, and therefore the rent payable was less. A refusal to grant leave would result in the noters being tied in with a tenant in a poor financial situation, not operating the

C premises, which were part of the exhibition centre, and important for the noters' whole enterprise. Finally, counsel submitted that the respondents had had more than sufficient time to attempt to dispose of the undertaking as a going concern. The respondents had carried out a wide advertising campaign but this had produced no result. A hearing had been fixed to take place in September 1992, but this had been discharged on the motion of the noters because the respondents had entered on the second advertising

D campaign. This was understood to have produced no significant result. In these circumstances leave should be granted. Counsel for the noters founded on the passage in the judgment in *Atlantic Computers* at p 381: "An administration is intended to be only an interim and temporary regime. There is to be a breathing space while the company, under new management in the person of the administrator, seeks to achieve one or more of the purposes set out in section 8 (3). There is a moratorium on the enforcement of debts and

E rights, proprietory and otherwise, against the company, so as to give the administrator time to formulate proposals and lay them before the creditors and then implement any proposals approved by the creditors. In some cases winding up will follow, in others it will not."

For the respondents, counsel accepted that there was a conflict between the rights of the noters as landlords, and the rights of the secured creditor, and

F accepted the guidelines as in *Atlantic Computer Systems*. He submitted that the balance was against leave being granted or, in any event, that the noters had failed to make out a case that it should be granted. The principal obligation under a lease was to pay the rent, and it was not averred that the tenant was unable to pay the rent. There was no obligation in the lease to keep the three restaurants open, and the rent was based on turnover and not on profit. The administrators had not been idle and had endeavoured to dispose of the business as a going concern, and were still endeavouring to do so. Correspondence was produced

G showing that a company had expressed an interest in December 1992 in acquiring the business, but as I understand it, this interest was expressed on the basis of purchasing the premises as well as the business and it would not appear to meet the particular situation. Counsel for the respondents submitted that further time should be allowed for the administrators to try to dispose of the business.

Counsel also made submissions regarding the validity of the notice of irritancy, and both counsel made reference to the averments by the respondents that it

H was not fair and reasonable for the noters to rely on their purported right to irritate the lease under reference to s 5 of the Law Reform (Miscellaneous Provisions) (Scotland) Act 1985. In my opinion, these points would arise for decision only in the subsequent action if leave to raise it were given. It is, in my opinion, inappropriate at this stage to express any opinion on such points in deciding whether leave should be granted. As was said in *Atlantic Computer Systems*: "In some cases there will be a dispute over the existence, validity or nature of the security which

I the applicant is seeking leave to enforce. It is not for the court on the leave application to seek to adjudicate upon that issue unless the issue raises a short point of law which it is convenient to determine without further ado. Otherwise the court needs to be satisfied only that the applicant has a seriously arguable case".

I consider that the noters do have a seriously arguable case, and I do not consider that, as over 18 months

J have already passed, during which time the administrators have endeavoured to dispose of the business, to grant a further period of time would achieve anything, especially as the administration is intended to be only an interim and temporary regime. In these circumstances I consider it appropriate to grant leave to bring proceedings against the company.

Counsel for Noters, Doherty; Solicitors, Dundas & Wilson, CS — Counsel for Respondents, Davidson; Solicitors, Bishop and Robertson Chalmers.

M L B F

G A Estates Ltd v Caviapen Trustees Ltd (No 1)

OUTER HOUSE

LORD COULSFIELD

30 AUGUST 1991

Reparation — Nuisance — Flooding — Construction of culvert on land of upper and lower heritors to alter flow of water in stream — Flooding on land of lower heritor at time of heavy rainfall — Whether nuisance of upper heritor.

Reparation — Negligence — Duty of care — Construction works on behalf of landowner causing loss to adjoining proprietor — Works negligently designed by independent agents of landowner — Reasonably foreseeable that works attended with risk — Whether duty of care owed by landowner to adjoining proprietor in respect of agents' negligence.

River, loch and sea — River — Alteration in flow of water in stream — Opus manufactum — Construction of culvert on land of upper and lower heritors — Flooding of land of lower heritor at time of heavy rainfall — Whether absolute liability of upper heritor for protective measures taken by lower heritor.

Contract — Construction — Contract negotiated between parties — Warranty conceived in favour of one party — Warranty making provision different from term implied in absence of express warranty — Whether construction of warranty contra proferentem.

Contract — Building contract — Construction — Extent of warranties — Warranty of fitness of site — Whether included allegedly inadequate culvert for diversion of burn — Whether contra proferentem rule applicable.

Agent and principal — Negligence of agent — Construction works on land owned by principal causing loss to adjoining proprietor — Works negligently designed by independent agents of principal — Reasonably foreseeable that works attended with risk — Whether duty of care owed by principal to adjoining proprietor in respect of negligence of agent.

The former owners of an area of ground raised an action against the purchasers for payment for development works carried out by the pursuers, after the sale of the ground, in terms of an agreement between the parties. The pursuers had commenced the development of a shopping centre on the ground prior to the sale, employing a design team, including the third parties, who were consulting structural engineers, and contractors. It was decided that in order to construct the centre a stream which flowed across the site should be diverted through a culvert, with entrance and exit ponds at each end. Parts of the rainwater drainage system of the development were designed to discharge into the culvert. The sale took place when much of the development, including the ponds and culvert, was complete. The pursuers retained an area of ground containing inter alia the entrance to the culvert and the entrance pond. The dimensions and design of the culvert and ponds were contained in the development specification and drawings approved in terms of the

development agreement by surveyors acting on behalf of the defenders, while by cl 4 of the agreement the pursuers warranted that "the site is fit for the purpose of carrying out the development thereon". The development was completed on 3 October 1984. On 3 November 1984, after a period of substantial rainfall, the centre became flooded when, the defenders averred, the culvert proved incapable of carrying the whole water flow of the stream and the rainwater drainage from the development system. As a consequence of the flooding the defenders effected preventative works, including laying a new culvert, acquiring the pursuers' retained land including the entrance pond and culvert entrance, and associated landscaping.

The defenders refused to make payment of sums due under the development agreement on the ground of the pursuers' alleged breach of contract and counterclaimed for damages representing the cost of the preventative works on grounds of the pursuers' nuisance, interference by opus manufactum with the course of a stream, and breach of warranty of the development agreement. The defenders averred that the pursuers were responsible for the fault of the third parties in respect of construction works which could be regarded as inherently dangerous. On procedure roll the pursuers challenged the relevancy of the averments of the counterclaim, arguing, first, that there was no causal link between any interference, nuisance or fault of the third parties and the remedial works effected by the defenders; secondly, that averments of works giving rise to interference or nuisance were irrelevant where the works had been effected with the knowledge and for the amenity of the defenders or for the common benefit of both pursuers and defenders; thirdly, in respect of works which could be regarded as inherently dangerous, the pursuers had performed all obligations incumbent upon them to prevent damage to a neighbour by employing competent consultants to design the works; and fourthly, that the warranty was conceived in favour of the defenders and made provision different from any term which would be implied in the absence of any express warranty and should therefore, if ambiguous, be construed in the way least favourable to the defenders' interest, namely not importing a continuing obligation of the pursuers in respect of the site after completion of the development.

Held, (1) that there was no reason in principle why a neighbour who had suffered loss and was at risk of further harm should not be entitled to recover as damages the cost of taking steps to protect himself against repetition of the harm, the expense of protective measures being regarded as arising naturally and directly from the fault or the activity which gave rise to liability and as causally connected with it (p 1041C-D); (2) that in the absence of any express provision that any approval of the design scheme given by the defenders exonerated the pursuers from any responsibility which they would otherwise have had, the question of whether any approval of the scheme given for the purposes of the contract had the

A
effect of barring the defenders' claim depended on the particular facts and circumstances of the case (p 1041J-L); (3) that where a landowner could reasonably foresee that works effected on his land would be attended by risk to a neighbouring proprietor he could not free himself from liability by binding his agent to take effectual precautions and would be liable for such risk if the steps taken to avoid that risk were inadequate because of his agent's negligence (*Dalton v Angus* (1881) 6 App Cas 740 and *Noble's Trs v Economic Forestry (Scotland) Ltd*, 1988 SLT 662,
B
followed) (p 1042G-K); (4) that the warranty was a clause in a mutual contract negotiated between the pursuers and the defenders for their respective interests and no special rule of construction was applicable to it (pp 1043K-1044B) (Gloag, *Contract* (2nd ed), pp 400-401, *approved*; McBryde, *Contract*, para 19-26, *disapproved*); (5) that the clause warranted the suitability of the situation of the development for the purpose of constructing that development and was an obligation capable of continuing after completion
C
of the development (p 1044H-J); and proof before answer *allowed*.

Observed, that there might be difficulty in applying the principle of liability related to the construction of an opus manufactum where part of the opus manufactum was at the time of damage situated on land belonging to the defenders or where the work was for the benefit of the defenders as well as the pursuers (p 1041E-F).

D

Action of payment; counterclaim for damages

G A Estates Ltd raised an action against Caviapen Trustees Ltd, owners of a shopping centre, in which they concluded for payment due under a construction development agreement in respect of the centre. The defenders counterclaimed for damages in respect of the pursuers' alleged breach of a warranty contained in the agreement, nuisance, interference with a stream and fault on the part of Thorburn Associates, con-
E
sulting structural engineers employed by the pursuers in respect of the development, for whose actings, it was alleged, the pursuers were responsible, and who were called by the pursuers as third parties in the counterclaim.

The case came before the Lord Ordinary (Coulsfield) on procedure roll on the pursuers' plea to the relevancy of the counterclaim. The third parties were represented but did not take part in the debate.

F
Cases referred to
Birrell v Dryer (1884) 11 R (HL) 41.
Borders Regional Council v Roxburgh District Council, 1989 SLT 837.
Caledonian Railway Co v Greenock Corporation, 1917 2 SLT 67; 1917 SC (HL) 56.
Canada Steamship Lines Ltd v R [1952] AC 192.
Dalton v Angus (1881) 6 App Cas 740.
Gourock Ropework Co Ltd v Greenock Corporation, 1966 SLT 125.
Kintore (Earl of) v Pirie & Sons (1903) 5 F 818.

Noble's Trustees v Economic Forestry (Scotland) Ltd, 1988 SLT 662.
G
Prosser (A) & Son v Levy [1955] 3 All ER 557; [1955] 1 WLR 1224.
RHM Bakeries (Scotland) Ltd v Strathclyde Regional Council, 1985 SLT 214.
Smith v UMB Chrysler (Scotland) Ltd, 1978 SLT 21; 1978 SC (HL) 1.

Textbooks referred to
Gloag, *Contract* (2nd ed), pp 400-401.
McBryde, *Contract*, para 19-26.
H
Stair Memorial Encyclopaedia, Vol 14, para 2128.
Walker, *Delict* (2nd ed), p 990.

On 30 August 1991 the Lord Ordinary *allowed* proof before answer on the whole case.

LORD COULSFIELD.—The pursuers in this action were formerly proprietors of an area of ground at Lady Road, Edinburgh. In about 1982, they began to build a shopping centre, now known as Cameron Toll shopping centre, on that ground. The pursuers
I
did not themselves carry out the work of construction or, at least so far as is material for the purposes of this action, design, but employed a design team, including architects and the third parties, who are consulting structural engineers, and building contractors. It was decided that, in order to construct the centre, the Braid Burn, which flowed across the site from south west to north east, should be diverted underground, to flow through a culvert. The work carried out to divert the burn included the creation of an entrance pond
J
towards the south west of the pursuers' area of ground, the construction of a culvert which runs from the entrance pond under the southern sector of the ground, and the creation of an exit pond at the downstream end of the culvert.

After a considerable amount of work had been done, including the construction of the ponds and the culvert, which were completed by May 1983, the pursuers, by a disposition recorded on 30 December 1983,
K
conveyed to the defenders a part of the land owned by them, together with the buildings by that time erected thereon. By that time, a part of the centre designed to accommodate a major store had already been let. The area sold to the defenders extended to about 21.7 acres and was the area on which the centre and associated facilities had been built; it included the greater part of the length of the culvert and the exit pond. However, the pursuers retained in their ownership a plot of ground at the south west side of the area sold, and this
L
plot included the entrance pond and the entrance to the culvert itself. By an agreement between the pursuers and defenders dated 28 December 1983 (the "development agreement"), the pursuers undertook, inter alia, to continue to construct and to complete the centre and the defenders undertook to make certain payments to the pursuers. The pursuers did continue with the work. On 3 October 1984, a certificate of practical completion of the work, subject to certain exceptions, was issued by the architects and endorsed by surveyors acting on behalf of the defenders. On the

same date, the centre was opened to the public. On 3 November 1984, after a period of substantial rainfall, the centre became flooded.

In this action the pursuers claim payment of a sum due to them under the development agreement: the defenders do not dispute that a sum is due under the agreement and the amount is also agreed. The defenders, however, refuse to make payment on the ground of alleged breaches of contract on the part of the pursuers, and counterclaim in respect of loss and damage arising, allegedly, from the flood and the conditions which are said to have given rise to it. The grounds of the counterclaim are, in summary, breach of a warranty contained in the development agreement; interference with the course of the Braid Burn; nuisance; and fault on the part of the third parties for whom, it is alleged, the pursuers are responsible. Much the greater part of the loss which the defenders claim to have sustained consists of expenditure on measures to prevent a recurrence of flooding, including the construction of an additional culvert. The pursuers, in turn, maintain that any loss was the result of negligence on the part of the third parties and seek absolvitor from the conclusion of the counterclaim or relief against the third parties, accordingly.

When the action came before me in the procedure roll on 15 and 16 July 1991, the pursuers argued that the counterclaim should be dismissed and that decree de plano should be granted in the action. The defenders submitted that the whole case should be sent to proof before answer. The third parties were represented but did not take any part in the debate. It was agreed between the pursuers and the defenders that the pursuers' claim in the action is a liquid claim under the development agreement, and therefore that the defenders can only withhold payment if they have stated a relevant case of breach of the warranty contained in the development agreement. The pursuers' argument was presented under four heads, namely (1) that there were no relevant averments of a causal connection between any nuisance or interference with the flow of the burn by the pursuers and at least the major part of the loss claimed by the defenders, the expenditure on the new culvert; (2) that there were no relevant averments of any basis on which the defenders could maintain a claim for nuisance or interference with the flow of the burn when the culvert of which they complain was constructed according to plans which they approved and as part of the work which the pursuers were obliged to complete according to the development agreement; (3) that there were no relevant averments of any basis upon which the pursuers could be held liable for fault on the part of the third parties who were independent civil engineers; (4) that there were no relevant averments of any breach of the warranty contained in the development agreement upon which the defenders' case is founded. It was not suggested that the defenders' cases based on interference with the flow of the burn and on nuisance were otherwise irrelevant or that there were no relevant averments of negligence on the part of the third parties.

Before dealing with these arguments in detail, it is necessary to set out more fully some of the defenders' averments. The defenders aver that the diversion of the Braid Burn was an integral and necessary part of the development of the centre; that the pursuers, after considering various possibilities, decided to divert the burn to flow underground; and that there was a metal grille at the entrance to the culvert, designed to prevent persons who might be in the pond from being sucked into the culvert. The third parties aver that the erection of that grille was a requirement of the local drainage authority. With regard to the flood itself, the defenders aver that by about 2 o'clock on 3 November 1984, the surface rainwater drains in the south entrance to the shopping area were not coping with the amount of water and water began to flow into the shopping mall. Despite efforts to control the water, a greater inflow began at about 5 pm, leading to a flood to a depth of several feet and the evacuation of the centre. They then aver: "The cause of the flooding was the inadequacy, particularly having regard to the nature of the site itself, of measures to protect the site from flooding. The pursuers and their agents in the design team . . . were aware, as was obvious, that the site was low lying and sitting in, as it was, a saucer shaped depression. . . . They were aware of the need to take steps to protect the site from flooding, and they did take certain steps to that end, as herein set forth. Said steps, however, were not adequate to protect the site, which was exposed, as at practical completion, to the likelihood of frequent ingress of flood water with which said protective measures were unable to cope."

The defenders aver that it was understood by all parties that the shopping centre was to be built to last for longer than a generation and that, during such a period, inundations, such as happened on 3 November 1984, would probably have happened on a considerable number of occasions. There had been a number of previous incidents of heavy rainfall causing high flow in the burn. The rate of flow on the previous occasions is specified, as is the rate of flow on 3 November 1984, and the defenders proceed to aver that the entry to the culvert and the culvert itself were too small. The dimensions for the framing of the culvert were given in a specification which was part of certain "Approved Plans" defined in the development agreement. The dimensions of the culvert as constructed were greater than those given in the specification, but the culvert was still too small to cope with the rate of flow which could reasonably be anticipated to occur frequently during the existence of the centre. The defenders further aver that, as the pursuers and their agents including the third parties knew or ought to have known, major flooding of the site had only been averted on the previous occasions of high water flow because men had been stationed at the grille to prevent blockage of the entry by debris swept down by the flood. On 3 November 1984, it is stated, the accumulation of debris at the grille contributed to the flooding. Further averments deal with a contribution to the flooding arising from the fact that parts of the local drainage system, which I understand to include

A the drainage from the car park adjacent to the centre, had been led into the burn while flap valves had been inserted to prevent backflooding from the burn into the system; as a result the local drainage system was prevented from discharging into the burn when the level of the burn was high.

In stat 4 of the counterclaim, the defenders plead a case of breach of a warranty contained in the development agreement. In stat 5, they aver that the pursuers interfered with the course of the Braid Burn on their
B property and that the consequence of their said interference was that the burn overflowed and caused damage to the defenders' subjects which were the next subjects downstream. The purpose of that paragraph is, as I understand it, to plead a case of absolute liability founding on the decision in *Caledonian Railway Co v Greenock Corporation* on the view that, in the circumstances of this case, such liability may be enforced without proof of negligence, notwithstanding the decision in *RHM Bakeries (Scotland) Ltd v Strath-*
C *clyde Regional Council*. In stat 6 it is averred that the loss and damage sustained by the defenders were occasioned by nuisance caused by the pursuers who were the owners of the adjacent subjects from which the nuisance came. It is averred that it was the pursuers' duty to take reasonable care in certain respects to minimise the risk of effluxion of water from their property damaging adjacent property and in particular that it was their duty to take reasonable care to ensure that the culvert was adequate to cope with reasonably foreseeable flows of water and that the design of the
D culvert permitted it to accept and cope safely with the inflow from the local storm water drains. Further it is averred that in the event of a grille being placed at the entrance to the culvert, it was the pursuers' duty to take reasonable care to devise and maintain a system for ensuring that it did not become blocked. In stat 7, a case is made on the basis that the loss and damage and nuisance were occasioned by the pursuers and were caused by the fault of the third party for whose
E actings the pursuers are responsible in a question of nuisance between the defenders and the pursuers. Allegations of negligence on the part of the third parties are set out in detail but, since the relevancy of these averments was not challenged, it is not necessary to repeat them. In stat 8, the defenders aver that as a result of the said interference with the stream, et separatim nuisance, et separatim breach of contract, the defenders have sustained loss and damage. They aver that substantial remedial measures have been taken by them in order to avoid further severe flooding
F which would otherwise be likely to recur. The averments continue: "It was considered by the defenders and their professional advisers to be impracticable and uneconomic to enlarge the existing culvert sufficiently to remedy the existing inadequacy. The defenders required to construct an additional culvert below the perimeter of the car park and to build attenuation tanks and carry out related landscaping works. The defenders required to install short term and long term flow warning and flood prevention systems pending the carrying out of the said remedial works. The

G defenders required to purchase a small plot of land adjacent to the entrance to the culvert in order to allow the remedial work to be carried out."

The amounts of the defenders' expenditure under various heads are then specified. The plot of land which the defenders purchased was the plot of land which had remained in the ownership of the pursuers and in which the entrance to the culvert and the entry pond were situated. There is some obscurity in the pleadings as to whether the claim includes any element in respect of damage directly caused by the
H flood and whether, if so, that part of the claim may overlap with another action in court; but I do not think it necessary to pursue that issue at this stage. It seems to be clear that there was in fact some damage directly caused by the flood.

In presenting his argument under the first head, counsel for the pursuers accepted that, if the substantial element of the defenders' claim had been related to damage directly caused by the flood, such as damage to property on the site, it would have been
I appropriate to allow the claim to go to proof, even though it was not accepted that any flood damage, in that sense, was necessarily due to inadequacy of the culvert as opposed to blockage of the entry. However he submitted that any liability of that kind could not extend to include expenditure on the design and construction of a second culvert on land which, by the time the culvert was built, belonged entirely to the defenders. The works which had been carried out were works done by the defenders for their own
J benefit on their own land. The capacity of a culvert was determined by its narrowest point, but where, according to the defenders' averments, it was too narrow throughout, it would have made no difference to the capacity if the small section at the entrance which lay outside the defenders' property at the time of the flood had been double in size or more. If it were necessary to accommodate the size of flow which the defenders averred to be necessary, an increase in the size of the culvert on the defenders' land would be
K required. That however could not be said to be caused by the fact that the entrance section on the pursuers' land was too narrow. The defenders could not say that but for the nuisance, that is the escape of water from the pursuers' land, the major expenditure would not have arisen. A person affected by a nuisance might be entitled to protect himself against repetition but this was not a case where a defence was being provided against a constant nuisance. The complaint here was that the water level would from time to time be too
L high. The same arguments applied to the case based on interference with the flow of water in the burn, and to that based on liability for negligence on the part of the third parties. In reply, counsel for the defenders submitted that what the pursuers had done was to interfere with a water course and that when they did so, they did it in one operation, including the entrance pond, the grille, the culvert and the exit pond. There were adequate averments that the pond and culvert would have surcharged recurrently and if that was correct, what were the defenders to do? If no steps

were taken to protect themselves, on the next occasion on which damage occurred there might be a defence that they had failed to take steps to mitigate their loss. Where the damage was considerable and likely to be repeated it was impossible to say that the defenders were not entitled to protect themselves against it.

As I have indicated, it appears that there was damage to the defenders' land caused by an agency, flood water, which escaped from an artificial work on the pursuers' land. As was explained in *RHM Bakeries (Scotland) Ltd*, in a case of nuisance the liability of the occupier of land from which the agency escapes is based upon fault, and derives from the construction of the opus manufactum. The reasoning is that, in a case in which there is liability, either the work could not be constructed in such a way as to avoid harm to a neighbouring property, in which case there was fault in building it at all, or the work was built negligently. The liability, therefore, does not arise simply from the fact that the agency escapes on an occasion or occasions, but from the action of constructing the opus manufactum. Similarly, in my view, any strict liability arising from interference with the flow of a stream must arise from the action of constructing the work which interferes. That being so, I see no reason in principle why a neighbour who has suffered harm, and is at risk of further harm, should not be entitled to recover as damages the cost of taking steps to protect himself against a repetition of the harm. In many cases, interdict may be a remedy for the proprietor at risk, and may oblige the proprietor of the work to remove it or make it safe: but where that is not practicable or sufficient, the expense of protective measures can, in my view, be regarded as naturally and directly arising from the fault or the activity which gives rise to liability, and as causally connected with it. The protective measures may well be taken entirely on the land of the proprietor at risk of harm, but it does not seem to me that it necessarily follows that they cannot be a natural and direct consequence of the act of building the opus manufactum. The fact that part of the opus manufactum, the culvert, was, at the time of the flood, situated on land belonging to the defenders, may, in my view, give rise to a real difficulty. So far as I am aware, the position in the cases in which liability has been incurred as a result of interference with a water course was that a work constructed on the land of the one proprietor permitted an escape which has damaged property of another proprietor. There is no case in which it might be said, as in the present case, that the work itself was constructed on the land of a single proprietor but subsequently divided so as to come into the ownership of two different proprietors. It seems to me that there may be difficulty in applying the principle of liability for escape of an agency from a work in such circumstances. I am not, however, convinced that the difficulty, if it is a difficulty, is one concerning causation; and, in any event, the problem should, in my view, be considered after evidence has been led. At that stage, it may be possible to have a better appreciation of the role of the entrance, the grille and any temporary obstruction of

it and the culvert itself in bringing about the flood than is possible on the bare averments. In the circumstances, the whole matter should, in my view, go to inquiry.

In presenting the second head of the pursuers' argument, counsel referred to a number of provisions of the development agreement which indicate that the specification for the work, which gave dimensions for the culvert, and certain drawings, had been approved by a surveyor appointed to act on behalf of the defenders, and to other provisions which allow the surveyor to object to, or withhold approval of, the works. Counsel submitted that there was authority that one defence to a case of nuisance or liability for interference with a water course was that the work in question had been done with the knowledge and authority of the complainer, or for the common benefit of both parties, and referred to Walker, *Delict* (2nd ed), p 990, and *A Prosser & Son v Levy* [1955] 3 All ER at p 584. Counsel for the defenders pointed out that the specification which is referred to in the pleadings is very deficient in detail and neither party has made any specific reference, in the pleadings, to any approved drawings: and submitted that for any consent or approval to have any effect on the defenders' right to make a claim, it must be a consent to the harm, under reference to the *Stair Encyclopaedia*, Vol 14, para 2128, and *Earl of Kintore v Pirie & Sons*.

In my view, this argument can be dealt with fairly briefly at this stage. Insofar as the argument depends on the particular provisions of the contract, and any approvals given under them, the pursuers cannot point to any specific provision to the effect that any approval given by or on behalf of the fund exonerates the pursuers from any responsibility which they would otherwise have. Indeed, cl 3.4.8 of the development agreement provides that failure to disapprove the development at any stage shall not constitute a personal bar against a later objection that the development has not been constructed according to the approved plans. That clause may not apply directly to the point in issue in this argument, but it may have some relevance as part of the context in which the effect of any particular approval has, or in terms of the contract has to be considered. In my view, the question whether or not any approval given for the purposes of the contract has any effect in barring the defenders' claim depends on the particular facts and circumstances and can only be determined when they have been fully explored. Insofar as the argument proceeds on the basis that the work was for the benefit of the defenders as well as the pursuers, I can see that it may well have considerable force. It is, in my view, not easy to see that there is much to distinguish the position of the defenders, who acquired part of the work, including part of the culvert, after it was completed, from that of a party who joins in constructing, or authorises, a work which interferes with a water course. That is one reason why, in my view, there may be difficulty in applying the principles of nuisance in the present case. However, the allegations of fault on

A which the case of nuisance is based include allegations of failure to maintain a system for preventing blocking of the grille. Even if the defenders are barred from maintaining a case based on nuisance in relation to the construction of the culvert, they may be able to establish a case based on failure to prevent blocking of the grille. I think therefore that this part of the argument should also be determined after the facts have been established. There is, I think, likely to be even greater difficulty in applying any principle of strict liability in the present case, but it seems to me that if there is to B be a proof, it is better to leave that issue also to be decided after the proof has taken place. The fact that that case remains on record should not add significantly to the length of the proof.

The third head of argument for the pursuers was that it was a general principle, stemming from the decision in *Dalton v Angus*, that a person was under no liability for the fault on the part of an independent contractor, except where the operation being carried out could be regarded as inherently dangerous. *Dalton* C *v Angus* was a case involving negligence, and counsel referred to a number of authorities in order to show that the same principle applied in cases of nuisance, particularly having regard to the decisions in *Gourock Ropework Co Ltd v Greenock Corporation* and *RHM Bakeries (Scotland) Ltd v Strathclyde Regional Council*. It is, however, not necessary to examine these authorities at this stage because counsel for the defenders accepted that, for the present purpose, a nuisance case should be approached in the same way as a case based D on negligence. Counsel for the defenders submitted that he had made sufficient averments of the undertaking of a hazardous operation to bring the case within the exception to the rule laid down in *Dalton v Angus*. In my opinion, that is correct. The defenders aver, as previously noted, that it was obvious that the site was low lying, in a saucer shaped depression in proximity to the Braid Burn and that steps would require to be taken to deal with flooding. Reference was made to *Noble's Trs v Economic Forestry (Scotland)* E *Ltd* in which Lord Jauncey (at p 664) summarised the position as follows: "A landowner will be liable to his neighbour if he carries out operations on his land which will or are likely to cause damage to his neighbour's land however much care is exercised. Similarly will a landowner be liable in respect of carrying out operations, either at his own hand or at the hand of the contractor, if it is necessary to take steps in the carrying out of those operations to prevent damage to a neighbour, and he, the landlord, does not take or F instruct those steps. In the former case the landowner's culpa lies in the actual carrying out of his operations in the knowledge actual or implied of their likely consequences. In the latter case culpa lies in not taking steps to avoid consequences which he should have foreseen would be likely to flow from one method of carrying out the operation."

In that case, Lord Jauncey went on to hold that a landowner was not liable for the consequences of mud having entered a water course because of casual negligence on the part of a contractor carrying out operations for the landowner. Counsel for the pursuers G submitted that the pursuers had employed competent consultants to design the works and had, therefore, performed their obligation to instruct the steps necessary to prevent damage to a neighbour. I do not think, however, that in the passage quoted, Lord Jauncey meant to imply that, in a case in which the landowner can reasonably foresee that the work will be attended by risk, he is not liable if the steps taken to avoid the risk are inadequate because of his contractor's negligence. In *Dalton v Angus* Lord Watson explained the exception from the general rule that there is no H liability for the fault of an independent contractor as follows (p 831): "But in cases where the work is necessarily attended with risk, he cannot free himself from liability by binding the contractor to take effectual precautions. He is bound, as in a question with the party injured, to see that the contract is performed, and is therefore liable, as well as the contractor, to repair any damage which may be done."

The essential feature of the case with which Lord Jauncey was concerned was that there were no aver- I ments that the operations in question were inherently dangerous or likely to be conducted in a dangerous way. Reference was also made to the decision of Lord Dervaird in *Borders Regional Council v Roxburgh District Council*, a case concerned with operations which undermined the foundations of an adjoining building. Lord Dervaird referred (at p 839) to the speech of Lord Watson in *Dalton v Angus* and added: "I take that to mean that the person who instructs the work must know, or at least ought to know that the work J which he is instructing is necessarily attended with risk", and went on to hold that the averments in the particular case did not meet that test. In the present case, the averments are, in my view, sufficient to meet the test, whether it is taken as expressed by Lord Watson or with Lord Dervaird's gloss. It is averred that the pursuers, as well as their agents, were aware of the character of the risk, the presence of the burn and the risk of flooding, and, in my opinion, these averments are sufficient to go to inquiry. K

In order to deal with the last head of the pursuers' argument, it is necessary to refer to the development agreement in more detail. The agreement narrates that the defenders are the heritable proprietors of the centre, that part of the centre has already been leased to a major store and that the developer has constructed the development up to a certain point. In cl 1, a number of expressions are defined. Those which are relevant for the purposes of the present argument are, in the first place, the definition of "the Centre" which L is as follows: "All and Whole that plot of ground at Lady Road, Edinburgh, for identification purposes only delineated within boundaries coloured blue on the plan annexed and executed as relative hereto, together with all buildings from time to time erected thereon and together with all additions, alterations and improvements thereto."

The definition of "the Site" reads: "All and Whole that plot of ground at Lady Road, Edinburgh, together with all buildings from time to time erected thereon and together with all additions, alterations and improvements thereto which plot of ground with the buildings and others thereon consists of the Centre excepting therefrom those parts of the Centre respectively described in and leased to SavaCentre Limited in terms of the SavaCentre lease and described in and leased to the developer in terms of the filling station lease. The site comprises the plot of ground for identification purposes only delineated within boundaries coloured blue as aforesaid excluding the major store (as hereinafter defined) and the subjects described in the filling station lease and which are outlined in red on the said plan."

The area outlined in blue, referred to in both of the above definitions, is the area of land which was conveyed to the defenders by the disposition recorded on 30 December 1983, and the areas outlined in red are smaller areas included within that blue outlined area. The term "the Development" is defined as the erection of certain buildings contemplated by the approved plans upon the site, and the "Approved Plans" are defined as the specification prepared by the architect and the drawings prepared by the architect, listed in a schedule attached to the agreement, which drawings are stated to have been approved by the defenders' surveyor.

Clause 4 of the agreement is headed "Warranties by Developer" and states, inter alia: "The developer hereby warrants that: 4.1 The Site is fit for the purpose of carrying out the development thereon; 4.2 The Approved Plans shall be practicable, accurate and adequate and that the materials and quantities shall be appropriate for the purpose of the erection of soundly designed and constructed buildings on the Site".

In three further subparagraphs, warranties are given in relation to the validity of any relevant permissions, to the use of the pursuers' best endeavours to ensure that all contractors and others involved exercise proper skill and care in the carrying out of work and supply of materials and in relation to the prevention of the use of certain notorious materials in the construction.

The defenders' case of breach of warranty in stat 4 of the counterclaim is founded only on para 4.1 of the agreement. The material averments for the present purpose are as follows: "The 'site' in terms of the said agreement included the said culvert (except insofar as it fell outwith the boundaries of the said plot) which had been completed prior to the execution of the agreement. The site was not fit for the purpose of carrying out the development thereon. The site was unfit for the said purpose because inadequate measures had been taken on the site and on the pond and culvert mouth site immediately adjacent to it to prevent it from flooding."

Before coming to the substantial argument as to the construction of cl 4.1, I should deal with an argument advanced by counsel for the pursuers to the effect that the clause should be construed contra proferentem. Counsel submitted that cl 4.1 was conceived in favour of the defenders and founded upon by them and should therefore be construed, if it was ambiguous, in the manner least favourable to their interest. he referred to Gloag, *Contract* (2nd ed), pp 400-401 and to McBryde, *Contract*, para 19-26. He accepted that the principle of construction contra proferentem was frequently applied where there was a standard form of contract, but submitted that the principle equally applied to onerous clauses affecting liability even where there was no standard form, including, for example, exemption clauses and indemnities. He submitted that an onerous warranty was in a similar position. Reference was also made to *Smith v UMB Chrysler (Scotland) Ltd* and *Birrell v Dryer*. Counsel for the defenders submitted that this was a negotiated contract and there was no reason to regard the clause as conceived in favour of one party rather than the other.

Gloag states (at p 401), that "in order to admit of construction contra proferentem, there must be a proferens" and that, "in ordinary contracts where parties are contracting on an equal footing it may fairly be assumed that the ultimate terms are arrived at by mutual adjustment, and do not represent the language of one party more than the other". That proposition is supported by reference to the decision in *Birrell*. On the other hand, McBryde expresses the view that the correct rule is that where an expression is ambiguous, it will be construed against the party who relies on it, irrespective of which party or parties produced the words: but no specific authority is cited for that proposition. *Birrell* was concerned with the interpretation of a marine insurance policy which contained a provision that cover should not extend to a particular area. In the House of Lords, it was held that there was no ambiguity in the description of the excluded area. However, both Lord Blackburn and Lord Watson observed that the definition of the excluded area was as much a matter of concern and benefit to the shipowner as to the insurers and that this was not a situation in which the contra proferentem rule could be applied. In the light of these observations, in my opinion, McBryde's formulation of the rule must be too wide. The rule may not be confined to standard form contracts, and other cases in which the terms are, in effect, dictated by one party. A similar rule of construction may be applied to clauses which purport to relieve a party of the consequences of his own negligence; and in *Canada Steamship Lines Ltd v R*, Lord Morton of Henryton used the term "the proferens" to describe the party in whose favour such a clause was conceived. The contra proferentem rule, however, is a special rule, and I do not see how such a special rule can be applied as widely as McBryde suggests, given that the fundamental principle of construction is to endeavour to ascertain the true intention of the contracting parties. Standing that principle, it seems to me that the normal rule in commercial contracts between equal parties must be that stated by Gloag, and that there must be some special feature to justify the application of a special rule of construction. Counsel for the pursuers suggested that there was such a feature in the present case in that cl 4.1 contained a warranty, whereas in contracts of sale of heritage no warranties were normally implied. I do not, however, think that the fact that an express term in a contract makes some provision which is different from what would be implied in the absence of any express term can properly be regarded as comparable with a clause which purports to exempt a party from the consequences of his own fault, and as sufficiently special to bring a special rule of construction into play. In my view, cl 4 of the development agreement is a clause in a mutual contract negotiated between both parties for their respective interests, and no special rule of construction is appropriate.

The difficulty in construing cl 4.1 is that the definition of "the Site" in cl 1 clearly includes additions, alterations and improvements, and states "which plot of ground with the buildings and others thereon consists of the Centre", subject to certain exceptions. If this definition of "Site" is applied in cl 4.1, the result appears to be that the warranty applies not only to the ground upon which the development is constructed but also to those parts of the development which had already been constructed by the date of the agreement. Counsel for the pursuers submitted, however, that that could not have been the intention of the parties because the word "Development" included the whole of the work which was to be carried out to create the centre. The word "Development" is used in the preamble to the agreement, in paras (C) and (D), in a way which clearly indicates that it includes the whole of the work to be carried out. Similarly, it is clear that the definition of "the Development" itself, in cl 1, includes the whole of the buildings contained in the approved plans, not merely those parts which remained to be completed after December 1983. Certain other parts of the contract were referred to in support of that construction of the word "Development", but it is not necessary to rehearse them, because counsel for the defenders accepted that the word was not restricted to that part of the works which remained to be carried out after 1983. Counsel for the pursuers submitted that because the word "Development" in cl 4.1 must mean the whole of the contract works, the word "Site" in that clause could not be given its defined meaning. The definition clause itself provides that the definition is to apply unless the context otherwise requires and it was submitted that in the context of cl 4.1 the definition could not appropriately apply. It was further pointed out that the warranty is that the site is fit for the purpose of carrying out the development, not fit for use as a shopping centre. It was therefore submitted that the effect of the warranty in cl 4.1 was merely that the site was suitable for constructing the works; that is, that it was warranted that it would be possible to construct the works on that site, but once the construction had been completed the warranty was spent. There was no warranty, in cl 4.1, as to the fitness or suitability of the culvert. Counsel for the defenders submitted that notwithstanding the meaning which, by his concession, fell to be attributed to the word "Development", the warranty in cl 4.1 applied to the site as it was at December 1983 including the buildings so far erected

upon it. The defenders were not trying to argue that there was a warranty in regard to the fitness of the culvert for its purpose or its suitability. The case was simply that the site was not fit for carrying out the development because it was prone to flooding and continued to be so, so long as the culvert was inadequate.

It is, I think, clear that it is not easy to apply the definitions in cl 1 of the contract in the construction of cl 4. I have come to the view that the construction proposed by counsel for the pursuers for the warranty in cl 4.1 is correct to the extent that the word "Site" in cl 4.1 cannot be taken as including buildings erected on the site before December 1983. The natural meaning of cl 4.1, according to the ordinary sense of the words used, and in the context of the other provisions of cl 4, is, in my opinion, that the pursuers warrant the suitability of the situation in which, and the ground upon which, the development was built for the purpose of building that development. That view is, I think, reinforced by the fact that, as both counsel agreed, the word "Development" must refer to the whole of the works, not those remaining to be constructed after December 1983. On the other hand, it seems to me that even on that view, the warranty is not spent, as counsel for the pursuers argued, when the development is complete. The warranty, in my view, must include matters such as the bearing capacity of the ground; and if, for example, it were found, some time after completion, that the bearing capacity was inadequate so that the buildings collapsed, that would be a situation which would fall within the warranty. Similarly, in my opinion, if the site were liable to repeated flooding, that could amount to a breach of the warranty. It is true that the warranty in cl 4.1 relates to the fitness of the site and not to the adequacy of the buildings and of any protective measures, such as the culvert, required to deal with problems encountered on the site. It is perhaps arguable that the problems which have arisen in this case are as much related to the adequacy of the buildings as to the fitness of the site, and that the appropriate basis for any claim might be found in cl 4.2 rather than in cl 4.1. However, even if some inadequacy of the works did play a part in causing the flood, it may nevertheless be open to the defenders to maintain that unfitness of the site also played some part. I see no reason to think that it is impossible to hold that both factors were at work. I have therefore come to the conclusion that, when the whole facts and circumstances are examined, the defenders may well be able to establish that this loss arose from unfitness of the site, and accordingly that the pursuers' argument cannot be upheld at this stage.

In the circumstances, I shall allow a proof before answer on the whole case.

Counsel for Pursuers, Emslie, QC, J R Campbell; Solicitors, J & F Anderson, WS — Counsel for Defenders, H H Campbell, QC, Doherty; Solicitors, Bird Semple Fyfe Ireland, WS — Counsel for Third Parties, Brailsford; Solicitors, Maclay Murray & Spens.

M L B F

GA Estates Ltd v Caviapen Trustees Ltd (No 2)

OUTER HOUSE

LORD COULSFIELD

10 JULY 1992

Prescription — Negative prescription — Interruption of prescriptive period — Counterclaim averring breaches of various warranties in contract raised prior to expiry of prescriptive period — Deletion of averments in respect of certain warranties — Reintroduction of deleted averments more than five years after lodging of counterclaim but within five years of deletion — Whether obligations extinguished — Prescription and Limitation (Scotland) Act 1973 (c 52), s 6 (1).

Prescription — Negative prescription — Counterclaim averring breaches of various warranties in contract — Deletion and subsequent reinstatement of averments in respect of certain warranties — Whether remaining averments in respect of other warranties constituted "relevant claim" in respect of claim deleted and reinstated — Prescription and Limitation (Scotland) Act 1973 (c 52), s 6 (1).

Contract — Building contract — Construction — Extent of warranties — Warranty of fitness of site — Warranty that plans appropriate for erection of soundly designed and constructed buildings — Whether included allegedly inadequate culvert for diversion of burn.

Contract — Building contract — Construction — Extent of obligations — Obligation to carry out development in good and workmanlike manner — Whether extending to alleged inadequacy in design.

A dispute arose between the developers and owners of a site after flooding occurred in November 1984 owing to a culvert becoming blocked. The developers brought an action of payment; the owners lodged a counterclaim for damages in May 1986 which founded on (a) cl 3.4.1 of the development agreement, which imposed an obligation on the developers "to carry out the Development in a good and workmanlike manner", (b) cl 4.1, by which the developers warranted that "The Site is fit for the purpose of carrying out the Development thereon," and (c) cl 4.2, by which the developers warranted inter alia that "the materials and quantities shall be appropriate for the purpose of the erection of soundly designed and constructed buildings on the Site". In March 1991 the owners lodged a minute of amendment and deleted the averments founding on cll 4.2 and 3.4.1. In January 1992 the owners moved another minute of amendment attempting to introduce further averments relating to these clauses. A debate took place on the developers' plea that any right the owners might have had under cll 4.2 and 3.4.1 had prescribed under s 6 (1) of the 1973 Act. The developers argued on the basis of the pre-existing law and the Scottish Law Commission's report which preceded the 1973 Act, that on the interruption of the prescriptive period by the making of a "relevant claim", a new period began to run from the

date the claim was first made. The owners argued that interruption continued throughout the currency of such a claim. They further argued that a "relevant claim" was constituted by a claim in the appropriate legal class or category and that the claim under cl 4.1, which had always formed part of their counterclaim, was a "relevant claim" in respect of the obligations founded on cll 4.2 and 3.4.1. The developers further argued that the clauses in question did not extend to the blocking of the culvert.

Held, (1) that the 1973 Act was intended to enact a comprehensive new code for prescription and was to be regarded as laying down a positive rule to be interpreted and applied on its own terms (p 1048H-I); (2) that so long as an action seeking to enforce an obligation was in court, a "relevant claim" was being made and accordingly the new prescriptive period, in the instant case, dated from the time the averments concerning cll 4.2 and 3.4.1 were deleted from the pleadings (p 1049G-H); (3) that cll 4.1 and 4.2 were parts of a comprehensive warranty placing the responsibility for the whole site and design on the pursuers; "buildings" in cl 4.2 had to be read as including the whole constructions on the site including the culvert, and the defenders' case under cl 4.2 was relevant (p 1050G-H); but (4) that there was no relevant case under cl 3.4.1 since an obligation of good workmanship did not cover an inadequacy relating to the design of the development (p 1050I-J); and pursuers' plea to prescription *repelled* and their plea to relevancy *sustained* only in relation to the averments concerning cl 3.4.1.

Opinion, (1) that whether or not a claim founded on one clause of a contract could be regarded as a "relevant claim" in respect of obligations under another clause of the same contract, depended on whether or not the clauses should be regarded as separate obligations or different aspects of one obligation (p 1049K-L); (2) that the obligation under cl 3.4.1 was of a different character from those under cll 4.1 and 4.2 (p 1050A); and (3) that cll 4.1 and 4.2 could properly be regarded as setting out not two separate obligations but two aspects of a single obligation (p 1050B).

Action of payment; counterclaim for damages

GA Estates Ltd raised an action against Caviapen Trustees Ltd, owners of a shopping centre, in which they concluded for payment due under a construction development agreement in respect of the centre. The defenders counterclaimed for damages in respect of the pursuers' breach of the agreement, nuisance, interference with a stream and fault on the part of Thorburn Associates, consulting structural engineers employed by the pursuers in respect of the development for whose actings, it was alleged, the pursuers were responsible, and who were called by the pursuers as third parties in the counterclaim.

The case came before the Lord Ordinary (Coulsfield) on procedure roll on the pursuers' plea to the relevancy of the counterclaim.

Statutory provisions

A　　The Prescription and Limitation (Scotland) Act 1973 provides:

"6.—(1) If, after the appropriate date, an obligation to which this section applies has subsisted for a continuous period of five years — (a) without any relevant claim having been made in relation to the obligation, and (b) without the subsistence of the obligation having been relevantly acknowledged, then as from the expiration of that period the obligation shall be extinguished".

B
Cases referred to

British Railways Board v Strathclyde Regional Council, 1982 SLT 55; 1981 SC 90.
Devos Gebroeder (NV) v Sunderland Sportswear Ltd, 1990 SLT 473.
Gobbi v Lazzaroni (1859) 21 D 801.
Grahame v McFarlane, 30 May 1811, FC.
Hood (George A) & Co v Dumbarton District Council, 1983 SLT 238.
C　*Lawrence v J D McIntosh & Hamilton,* 1981 SLT (Sh Ct) 73.
Macleod v Sinclair, 1981 SLT (Notes) 38.

Textbooks referred to

Bell, *Principles,* s 615.
Erskine, *Institute,* III vii 43 and 45.
Gloag and Henderson, *Introduction to the Law of Scotland* (7th ed), p 162.
Maxwell, *Interpretation of Statutes* (12th ed), p 116.
Millar, *A Handbook of Prescription According to the* D　*Law of Scotland,* p 107.
Napier, *Prescription,* p 658.
Walker, *Prescription and Limitation of Actions* (4th ed), p 22.

Terms of development contract

The contract between the pursuers and the defenders provided inter alia:

"4. *Warranties by Developer*

"The Developer hereby warrants that:

E
"4.1 The Site is fit for the purpose of carrying out the Development thereon;

"4.2 The Approved Plans shall be practicable, accurate and adequate and that the materials and quantities shall be appropriate for the purpose of the erection of soundly designed and constructed buildings on the Site;

"4.3 The Relevant Permissions are current and valid and all notifications and publication required by F　the relevant legislation have been validly and timeously effected;

"4.4 It will use its best endeavours to ensure that the Contractors and all other contractors, sub-contractors and suppliers of materials and the professional advisers employed in connection with the Development including the Professional Team shall exercise proper skill and care in the performance of their respective duties or (as the case may be) the supply of materials in accordance with their respective contracts in that behalf;

"4.5 It will not use or permit or cause to be used any high alumina cement, cement containing added G　calcium chloride as a setting agent, asbestos or woodwool slabs in permanent shuttering form or any other substance which is known to be hazardous or not in accordance with good building practice."

On 30 August 1991 the Lord Ordinary *allowed* proof before answer on the whole case. (Reported 1993 SLT 1037.)

The pursuers reclaimed.

H
On 17 March 1992 the Inner House *allowed* the record to be amended in terms of a minute of amendment for the defenders and answers for the pursuers concerning the counterclaim and *remitted* the case to the Outer House for a debate on the question of prescription.

On 10 July 1992 the Lord Ordinary *allowed* proof before answer on the counterclaim under deletion of certain averments.　　　　　　　　　　　　　　　I

LORD COULSFIELD.—On 30 August 1991 I allowed a proof before answer in this case. The nature and circumstances of the action and counterclaim, and the arguments advanced at a procedure roll hearing on 15 and 16 July 1991, are set out in my opinion dated 30 August 1991, to which I refer. The pursuers reclaimed against the interlocutor of that date. On 15 January 1992, the defenders lodged a minute of amendment, in order to introduce averments founding J　on cl 4.2 and cl 3.4.1 of the development agreement. These provisions had been founded on by the defenders at an earlier stage in the development of the pleadings, but were taken out of the case by an amendment on 21 March 1991. The motion to allow the 1992 amendment was heard in the Inner House on 17 March 1992. At that hearing the pursuers submitted that the amendment should not be allowed, first, as a matter of discretion, because it came too late, and, secondly, on the ground that any right which the K　defenders might have had under the contractual provisions in question had prescribed. The Inner House allowed the amendment to be made but remitted the case back to the Outer House to proceed as accords. The purpose of so doing was to allow the question of prescription to be debated; the question whether the amendment should be allowed as a matter of discretion has, as I understand the position, been decided by the Inner House.

Clause 4 is quoted in my previous opinion but it is L　convenient to repeat its terms here. It is headed "Warranties by Developer" and provides: [his Lordship quoted the terms of cl 4 set out supra and continued:]

Clause 3.4 provides that, subject to certain provisions not material for the present purpose, the developer shall "3.4.1 Carry out the Development in a good and workmanlike manner and shall complete the same in accordance with the Approved Plans, the Relevant Permissions and this Agreement and to the reasonable satisfaction of the Fund's surveyor fit for occupation and use as soon as reasonably practicable".

Counsel were agreed that the counterclaim for the defenders, when it was originally lodged in May 1986, contained reference to cl 4.2 and cl 3.4.1, and fell to be regarded as a relevant claim for the purposes of the law of prescription, and that at the date of lodging the counterclaim any claims in respect of breaches of those clauses of the contract had not prescribed. They also agreed that the lodging of the counterclaim interrupted the running of the prescriptive period and that a new prescriptive period of five years would require to elapse after the interruption to extinguish any claim based upon these clauses. The first issue between the parties is whether the new five year period, following the interruption, should date from the making of the relevant claim by the lodging of the counterclaim, or from the date on which the references to cll 4.2 and 3.4.1 were deleted from the counterclaim pleadings. In the former case, the new prescriptive period would have elapsed before the amendment in January 1992; in the latter case the amendment would fall well within the prescriptive period. The second issue between the parties is whether or not the claims now founded on cll 4.2 and 3.4.1 should be regarded as relating to different obligations from the claims founded on cl 4.1, which have all along formed part of the counterclaim. If the claims under cll 4.1, 4.2 and 3.4.1 should all be regarded as relating to one obligation, then, whatever the correct answer on the first issue, the claims introduced by amendment in March 1992 would not have prescribed.

Counsel for the pursuers submitted that it was clear from the wording of s 6 of the Prescription and Limitation (Scotland) Act 1973 that it was intended that the period of interruption should be measured from the time at which a relevant claim is first made. The words of the section were "without any relevant claim having been made". These words directed attention to the point of time at which a claim is made: if something different was meant, wording such as "without a claim being in dependence", might have been used. The words "being made" pointed to a single event. The date on which the interruption occurred was the date on which a claim was made, in that sense, and it was prima facie reasonable to take the same date as the start of the new period. All of the relevant claims listed in s 9 were single events, even including the execution of a diligence. Negatively, there was nothing in the Act to indicate that Parliament had intended to alter the previous common law on the effect of interrupting short negative prescriptions. That was in accordance with a well known principle of statutory construction (Maxwell, *Interpretation of Statutes,* p 116). The previous general law of interruption had been that a new period ran from the date of the initial interruption, not from some later date. That was supported by Erskine, *Institute,* III vii 45, Bell, *Principles,* s 615 and by Napier, *Prescription* (at p 658) and Millar, *Prescription* (at p 107). The same view could be seen in Gloag and Henderson (7th ed at p 162). The same view was reflected in the Scottish Law Commission's 1968

memorandum on *Prescription,* in its discussion of the existing prescriptive periods; the recommendations in the memorandum were to the effect that the period of prescription should commence to run anew as from the date of any interruption. That understanding was also reflected in the Scottish Law Commission report no 15, of 1970, which led to the 1973 Act, and the same recommendation was made there. The pre-existing law as to interruption had not, therefore, been seen as a mischief or defect which required remedy. There was no decided case in which the effect of an abandoned claim on the running of the period had been considered. The only relevant decision was *Gobbi v Lazzaroni* in which it had been held that an action which was raised and abandoned should not count for interruption at all, but that decision was considered to be wrong. There was a distinction between a claim pursued to judgment and one which had been discontinued. If a creditor passed from a claim, it would be unfair to allow him the whole benefit of the abortive period of the dependency of his claim, which would be the effect if the prescriptive period ran anew from the abandonment of the claim. That view was supported by Erskine at III vii 43. The new period in general, therefore, ran from the start of the interrupting claim, but there was an obvious exception when the interrupting claim was pursued to judgment no matter how long that might take. In that case the action would stay alive.

The only relevant decision under the 1973 Act was *Hood v Dumbarton District Council* in which the Lord Ordinary held that the period began anew from the date on which proceedings ceased, but that was wrongly decided. None of the relevant authorities before 1973 had been before the court and the distinction between an action pursued to judgment and one abandoned had not been observed. The effect of the Lord Ordinary's decision was to read words into s 6. In addition the Lord Ordinary had misconstrued the effect of the decision in *British Railways Board v Strathclyde Regional Council.* Although the Lord Justice Clerk in that case had used some words which might be construed as having the effect which the Lord Ordinary had given to them, he had made it clear that he was reaching no settled decision on this particular point and the other two judges had very clearly reserved their opinions upon it.

As regards the second issue, the fact that there had been a continuous claim founded on cl 4.1 could not be regarded as relevant to save a claim based on cl 4.2. In *N V Devos Gebroeder v Sunderland Sportswear Ltd* the correct principles for deciding whether claims were related to the same obligations had been set out. Where a party had abandoned a claim, what remained in his case could hardly be regarded as founded on the same material. In effect the creditor had said that he was not founding on any such obligations. Cases such as *British Railways Board v Strathclyde Regional Council* and *Macleod v Sinclair* were not in point because they were concerned with delictual obligations and in questions of breach of contract there might be different considerations. The question

whether a claim under a contract was relevant to a
A particular obligation did not depend on whether the
claim and the obligation were founded on clauses
appearing in the same piece of paper. It was necessary
to look at the nature and substance of the obligations
to see if there was the requisite identity. A document
might contain indemnities, warranties and many
extraneous matters. Equally it was not sufficient that
the claim arose out of the same facts and circumstances or related to the same loss. Clause 4.1 was distinct and different from cl 4.2. The former referred to
B the site and was a warranty of quality of part of the
subjects of sale. Clause 4.2 related to the adequacy of
plans which were proposed by persons who were
strangers to this particular contract and looked to the
future, not to the present. Clauses 4.4 and 4.5 were
not warranties at all.

Counsel for the defenders submitted that the proposition that interruption continued throughout the
currency of any relevant claim was supported by the
C decision in *Hood* and consistent with the view
expressed, so far as it went, in *British Railways Board
v Strathclyde Regional Council*. It was also supported
by *Grahame v McFarlane*. The underlying principle
on which prescription was founded, in the old law,
was a presumption of abandonment of the claim and
it could scarcely be said that a debt had been abandoned so long as the creditor was actually pursuing it
in court. It followed that time must run from the date
at which abandonment or satisfaction could be pre-
D sumed. Under the old law, where a prescriptive period
was interrupted by the raising of an action, the action
interrupted the running of the period for 40 years.
The view had been expressed by Walker (*Prescription
and Limitation* (4th ed), p 22) that the 40 year interruption rule continued to apply in cases involving
heritage, and there was no reason to think that that
view was not correct. If the 1973 Act did produce an
innovation on that rule, nevertheless the phrasing of
s 6 (1) was not consistent with a once and single inter-
E ruption by the raising of an action. The interruption
by an action must continue so long as the action was
in court. The Scottish Law Commission memorandum of 1968 set out the view which the pursuers
would wish to see established, but that was not in fact
the scheme which had been adopted by the Act. The
memorandum looked for a general rule subject to
certain exceptions, but the position under the Act
simply was that a relevant claim operated an interruption. The construction proposed on behalf of the pur-
F suers required an exception to be written into the Act
for the running of a current action, but such an exception was wholly unexpressed. In any event, even if
there had been no mention in the pleadings prior to
1992 of cll 3.4.1 and 4.2, or if the once and single
interruption point was correct, the amendment was
not precluded by prescription. A relevant claim had
been made about the obligation, whatever clauses
might stand in it. The *British Railways Board* case
showed that a writ could sufficiently interrupt prescription even if it contained no specification at all.
The obligation in question was a legal class or category

of claim, however that claim might be developed.
That was also supported by the case of *Macleod*. G
Lawrence v J D McIntosh & Hamilton was concerned
with two different contracts, and therefore with a
different point. Each of the defenders' claims was of
the same character, namely that the pursuers had
failed to perform their contract and had left the
defenders with a development not of the standard to
which they were entitled, as a result of failures in
respect of the fitness of the site and the soundness of
the design.

It seems to me that it is of little assistance to con- H
sider what the effect of an interruption of the prescriptive period was before 1973. It is evident both from
the terms of the 1973 Act itself, and from the reports
which preceded it, that the Act was intended to enact
a comprehensive new code for prescription (cf *British
Railways Board v Strathclyde Regional Council*, per
Lord Justice Clerk Wheatley at 1982 SLT, p 59).
Arguments based on the proposition that prescription
is founded on a presumption of abandonment of a
claim seem to me much less compelling in relation to I
a prescriptive period of five years than in relation to
periods of 20 or 40 years, and it is, in my opinion,
more appropriate to regard the 1973 Act as laying
down a positive rule, to be interpreted and applied on
its own terms. Equally, it is not, in my opinion, of
much assistance to have regard to the statements in the
memorandum of 1968 because, in material respects,
the proposals in that memorandum were not carried
out in the Act. For example, the memorandum proposed that the right to recover payment on a decree J
should prescribe after five years, whereas in the Act no
such rule is enacted. The terms of the 1970 report do
not assist in the construction of the 1973 Act since,
like the Act itself, they are open to more than one
interpretation. The decision in *Grahame v McFarlane*
turned on a question of interpretation of the Act 1685,
c 14, which provided that all actions proceeding on
certain forms of diligence should prescribe in five
years, if not wakened within that time. It was held that
the period of five years should run from the date of the K
last step in the process, but that is, in my opinion, a
decision specifically related to a form of prescription
which applied to actions and is of no assistance in considering the effect of an action, or other form of interruption, upon a different form of prescription.

The terms of the 1973 Act themselves might be read
in different ways. There is, I think, force in the argument that the words "without any relevant claim
having been *made*" in s 6 do point to a single event.
On the other hand, the words were read in a different L
sense by Lord Kincraig in the case of *Hood*. His Lordship said (at p 239): "In my judgment, the proper way
to construe s 6 is that if an obligation has subsisted for
five years it shall be extinguished unless a relevant
claim has been made on the creditor within that
period. The period of five years relied on must be one
during which no claim was persisted in. If during that
period the debt was being insisted in the section has
no application, the date upon which it was first
insisted in being immaterial. This interpretation

A seems to me to be more in accordance with giving effect to the purpose of the section, which was to extinguish obligations in respect of which nothing had been done for a continuous period of five years.''

That interpretation of the section is clearly also a possible one, although it might be said that it is not clear what basis there is for saying what the purpose of the section is apart from the words of the section themselves. In *British Railways Board v Strathclyde Regional Council*, the Lord Justice Clerk referred to a sheriff court action which had previously been raised
B and said (at 1982 SLT, p 59) that during the currency of that action the relevant claim persisted, so that there was no continuous period of five years running for the purpose of prescription. What the Lord Justice Clerk said does, perhaps, suggest that he read the section in the same way as Lord Kincraig did, but it was made clear that he was not deciding the point. Lord Kissen also used some expressions (at p 61) which might suggest that he was not impressed by the argument that the period of prescription following an interrup-
C tion by raising an action should run from the date on which the action was raised, but both he and Lord Robertson expressly reserved their opinions on the point. The point actually decided in *British Railways Board v Strathclyde Regional Council* was that when the running of a prescriptive period is interrupted by raising an action, the benefit of the interruption is not confined to the particular interrupting action, but is available in respect of a different action or claim. In that case, the second action was raised within five
D years of the first action being commenced, so that the point in the present case did not require to be decided.

If both constructions are possible, on the wording of the section, it can also be said, in my opinion, that neither is entirely free from anomaly. As Lord Kincraig pointed out in *Hood*, the construction which makes the prescriptive period run from the date on which the interrupting claim is first made would have the effect that the obligation might prescribe while an
E action to enforce it was in progress, unless an implied exception, to preserve an obligation which is the subject of a current action, is to be read into the Act. There are, however, no express terms in the Act which have that effect and, in order to reach the appropriate result, it is necessary to imply, in effect, a substantial exception into the terms of the Act. On the other hand, as the pursuers pointed out in the present case, the construction which makes the period of prescription following an interruption run from the last step
F in a process to enforce the obligation has the consequence that the prescriptive period may be prolonged indefinitely by proceedings which may be entirely without substance.

The choice between the possible constructions is, in my view, not an easy one, but, on balance, I have come to the view that the argument of the defenders in the present case should be sustained. The words of s 6 (1), so far as material, are "If, after the appropriate date, an obligation . . . has subsisted for a continuous period of five years — (a) without any relevant claim having

been made in relation to the obligation''. It seems to me that, so long as an action seeking to enforce the G obligation is in court, a relevant claim is being made; and that it cannot be said that a continuous period of five years has elapsed "without a relevant claim having been made" if, at any point during that period, a relevant claim was being made. It is true that, on that reading of the section, there may be cases in which there is uncertainty as to the date on which the new prescriptive period is to start, and that the period may be prolonged, but, like, I think, Lord Kissen in *British Railways Board v Strathclyde Regional Council*, I am H not unduly impressed by these arguments. In the whole circumstances, therefore, I have come to the view that, in the present case, the relevant period did not commence until 21 March 1991, so that the 1992 amendment came well within it.

If that is correct, the second issue does not require to be decided, but I should express a view on it. The issue is whether a claim which founds upon cl 4.1 of the contract can be regarded as a relevant claim in respect of the obligations under cl 4.2 and cl 3.4.1. I That depends, I think, on whether cll 4.1, on the one hand, and 4.2 and 3.4.1 on the other, should be regarded as separate obligations or as different aspects of one obligation. In my opinion, the simple approach adopted by the defenders, in reliance on the decision in *British Railways Board v Strathclyde Regional Council*, is not acceptable in the context of a claim based on breach of contract. In that case, it was held that an initial writ in which damages were claimed for "fault" without any specification whatever, but which J was capable of being made specific by adjustment or amendment, was sufficient to constitute a relevant claim and so interrupt the prescriptive period in relation to a claim subsequently made on the ground of negligence. In that case, however, although the obligation founded on in the "relevant claim" was stated in a quite unspecific form, the nature or character of the obligation, to make reparation for fault, was indicated. The obligation to refrain from causing damage by fault is general and permanent. Obligations which K arise from contracts are quite different: they are particular and may be temporary. In my view, therefore, the approach must be different, and it is necessary to decide whether the obligation sought to be enforced and the obligation on which the "relevant claim" was founded are the same. I do not think that the defenders' approach is compatible with the approach of the Act in general to obligations, particularly bearing in mind the point made by counsel for the pursuers that one contract document may contain L many different obligations of many different characters, nor is it consistent with the decision in *NV Devos Gebroeder v Sunderland Sportswear*. It seems to me, therefore, that it is necessary to consider whether cl 4.1 on the one hand and cll 4.2 and 3.4.1 on the other contain different obligations or are different aspects of one obligation.

In order to do so, it is, in my opinion, necessary to consider the whole context and circumstances of the contractual provisions and the nature and substance of the obligation or obligations in question. On that approach, in my opinion, cl 3.4.1 and cl 4.1 cannot be regarded as forming parts or aspects of a single obligation. Clause 3.4.1, so far as relevant, sets out a simple obligation of good workmanship. That seems to me to be an obligation of a different character from the obligations under cll 4.1 and 4.2. These clauses do not require the pursuer to do anything so much as to accept responsibility for a satisfactory result being achieved. There may be cases in which such obligations are so clearly related that a relevant claim in respect of one would be a relevant claim in respect of the other; but in the present case, I do not think that such a relationship can be said to exist. On the other hand, in my opinion, cll 4.1 and 4.2 can properly be regarded as setting out not two separate obligations but two aspects of a single obligation. It is not, I think, unimportant that these two subclauses occur within one single provision of the contract which is headed "Warranties by the Developer". I think further that the two subclauses have to be read together. I reject the pursuers' argument that there is a difference in the terminology of the clauses which points to them having separate operation or effect. The words "shall be" in cl 4.2 do not, in my opinion, point to some future obligation but are merely a way of expressing the responsibility for the adequacy of the plans which is undertaken by the pursuers. It is, in my view, reasonably obvious that the purpose of cl 4 in general, and cll 4.1 and 4.2 in particular, was to place the responsibility for the site, the plans, the materials and the design upon the pursuers so that the defenders could look to the pursuers for a remedy if they did not obtain soundly designed and constructed buildings on a suitable site. In these circumstances, I have come to the conclusion that a claim made in express reliance on cl 4.1 should nevertheless be regarded as a relevant claim for the purposes of cl 4.2 since cll 4.1 and 4.2 do not express separate obligations.

In addition to the argument on prescription, counsel for the pursuers submitted that the new claims made under cl 4.2 were irrelevant. He submitted that cl 4.2 did not and could not apply to the culvert which was the source of the problem of which the defenders complained, because it was not a warranty of sound design or construction of the development or the works as a whole nor of the flows in the burn in the future. It was a warranty only relating to "buildings". The word "buildings" could not be taken so widely as to cover all manmade constructions and would not therefore include the culvert. He referred to the definition of the "Development" in cl 1 of the contract, which includes the words "buildings and others", and submitted that the development therefore included some items which were classified as buildings and some others which, although constructed, were not. The use of the words "erection, construction and installation" pointed to the same result. He also referred to the contrast between the tenses in cll 4.1 and 4.2 which I have already mentioned. Counsel for the defenders submitted that the word "buildings" must cover all things built and that the requirement of sound design was not met if the buildings stood in a lake because of the inadequacy of the culvert. In my view, the argument for the defenders must be sustained. For the reasons I have already indicated, it seems to me that cll 4.1 and 4.2 are parts of a comprehensive warranty placing the responsibility for the whole site and design upon the pursuers. In the context, the words "soundly designed and constructed buildings on the Site" must, in my view, be read as including the whole constructions on the site and therefore as including the culvert. It follows that the defenders have stated a relevant case in respect of this clause.

It was, however, also submitted that there was no relevant case under cl 3.4.1. That clause, as I have mentioned, requires that the development be carried out in a good and workmanlike manner and completed in accordance with the approved plans, the relevant permissions and the agreement. Counsel for the pursuers submitted that, since it was clear that the sizing of the culvert was included in the plans, the obligation in this clause was an obligation to construct the culvert in the way that it was in fact constructed. He also pointed out that the whole significance of this claim related to the new culvert which the defenders had constructed rather than to any part played by the grille and the cleaning devices which were the subject of averments in the claim. Counsel for the defenders submitted that there were appropriate averments of failure to carry out the work in a workmanlike manner and that the case should go to proof before answer. I have come to the conclusion that, in this instance, the argument for the pursuers is correct. Clause 3.4.1 is, for the reasons I have already given, in my view, a simple obligation of good workmanship and does not entitle the defenders to make any claim based upon the inadequacy of the culvert which, in my view, is a matter relating to the design of the development.

In the whole circumstances I shall repel the first plea in law for the pursuers in the counterclaim but sustain their second plea in law to the extent of excluding from probation the averments in the counterclaim relating to cl 3.4.1 of the contract. The averments in question are those in stat 4 of the counterclaim from the words "in terms" occurring in the fourth line of p 44 of the reclaiming print of the record as amended to the words "by said plans" occurring in the 20th line of the same page.

Counsel for Pursuers, G N H Emslie, QC, J R Campbell; Solicitors, J & F Anderson, WS — Counsel for Defenders, H H Campbell, QC; Solicitors, Bird Semple Fyfe Ireland, WS.

P A A

GA Estates Ltd v Caviapen Trustees Ltd

EXTRA DIVISION

LORDS McCLUSKEY, WEIR AND PENROSE

26 MAY 1993

Contract — Building contract — Construction — Extent of warranties — Warranty of fitness of site — Warranty that plans appropriate for erection of soundly designed and constructed buildings — Whether included allegedly inadequate culvert for diversion of burn — Whether contra proferentem rule applicable.

Prescription — Negative prescription — Interruption of prescriptive period — Counterclaim averring breaches of various warranties in contract raised prior to expiry of prescriptive period — Deletion of averments in respect of certain warranties — Reintroduction of deleted averments more than five years after lodging of counterclaim but within five years of deletion — Whether claim relating to one obligation had any effect on prescription of another obligation in same contract — Whether obligations extinguished — Prescription and Limitation (Scotland) Act 1973 (c 52), s 6 (1).

The developer of a site brought an action for payment of the purchase price. The sale had been concluded when the development was under construction. Before the purchasers had made payment in full, flooding had occurred on the site due to a blocked culvert. The purchasers lodged a counterclaim for inter alia breach of contract and nuisance. The agreement between the developer and the purchaser had included warranties in respect of the fitness of the site for the development and in respect of the adequacy of the plans and the soundness of the buildings. During the course of litigation the purchasers made various alterations to their pleadings insofar as they related to the contractual warranties. After sundry procedure the Lord Ordinary, at procedure roll, repelled the developers' pleas that the purchasers' cases founded on the warranties were irrelevant and, in any event, had prescribed. The developers reclaimed on the relevancy of the cases of breach of warranty and the question of prescription, arguing inter alia that the warranties fell to be construed contra proferentem.

Held, (1) that the warranty provisions could be satisfactorily construed without the application of the contra proferentem rule (pp 1057D-E, 1060D-E and 1064C); (2) (Lord McCluskey *dissenting*), that the warranty related to the fitness of the site for development did not extend to an undertaking that measures would be taken to cope with any problems which might arise at any time and the case based on this clause was irrelevant (pp 1060J-K, 1064B-C and 1064I-1065A); (3) that the case based on the warranty in respect of soundness of buildings was irrelevant in that it did not extend to other works of construction such as the culvert (pp 1059A-C, 1061B-E and 1065F-G); and reclaiming motion *allowed*, decree de plano *granted* in terms· of the first conclusion in the principal action and proof before answer *allowed* on the remaining averments in the counterclaim.

Per Lord McCluskey (*dissenting*): In the warranty of fitness of the site, "the site" went beyond the ground itself and included the works already carried out, such as the culvert, at the date of contract, and the pleadings based on breach of this warranty were relevant for inquiry (p 1058I-K).

Opinion, per Lord McCluskey, that there was no need or room for the contra proferentem rule where equal parties were expertly advised (p 1057C-D).

Opinion, (1) (per Lord McCluskey, provisionally per Lords Weir and Penrose) that prescription did not run while an action was in court, and recommenced on the day that it was dismissed or abandoned (pp 1059F-I, 1060L and 1065I-L); and (2) (per Lord McCluskey, provisionally per Lord Penrose) that the warranties under cl 4.1 and cl 4.2 were separate and independent and a claim under cl 4.1 did not prevent prescription running against a claim under cl 4.2 (pp 1059K-L and 1065I).

George A Hood & Co Ltd v Dumbarton District Council, 1983 SLT 238, *followed.*

Action of payment; counterclaim for damages
(Reported 1993 SLT 1037 and 1045)

GA Estates Ltd raised an action of payment against Caviapen Trustees Ltd in respect of sums allegedly due under a building contract. The defenders lodged a counterclaim for damages, in respect of which the pursuers introduced a third party, Messrs Thorburn Associates.

The case came before the Lord Ordinary (Coulsfield) on the pursuers' plea to the relevancy of the counterclaim.

Statutory provisions

The Prescription and Limitation (Scotland) Act 1973 provides:

"6.—(1) If, after the appropriate date, an obligation to which this section applies has subsisted for a continuous period of five years — (a) without any relevant claim having been made in relation to the obligation, and (b) without the subsistence of the obligation having been relevantly acknowledged, then as from the expiration of that period the obligation shall be extinguished".

Cases referred to

British Railways Board v Strathclyde Regional Council, 1982 SLT 55; 1981 SC 90.
Canada Steamship Lines Ltd v R [1952] AC 192.
Devos Gebroeder (NV) v Sunderland Sportswear Ltd, 1990 SLT 473.
Grahame v McFarlane, 30 May 1811, FC.
Hood (George A) & Co v Dumbarton District Council, 1983 SLT 238.
Lawrence v J D McIntosh & Hamilton, 1981 SLT (Sh Ct) 73.
Macleod v Sinclair, 1981 SLT (Notes) 38.
North of Scotland Hydro Electric Board v D & R Taylor, 1955 SLT 373; 1956 SC 1.

Pillans & Co v Sibbald's Trustees (1897) 5 SLT 186.
Wickman Machine Tool Sales v L Schuler AG [1974]
AC 235; [1973] 2 WLR 683; [1973] 2 All ER 39.

Textbooks referred to
Bell, *Principles*, s 615.
Chitty, *Contracts* (26th ed), paras 809, 815, 836 and 837.
Erskine, *Institute*, III vii 43 and 45.
Gloag, *Contract* (2nd ed), p 400.
Gloag and Henderson, *Introduction to the Law of Scotland* (7th ed), p 162.
McBryde, *Contract*, paras 13-39-13-40.
Maxwell, *Interpretation of Statutes* (12th ed), pp 116-117.
Millar, *A Handbook of Prescription According to the Law of Scotland*, p 107.
Napier, *Prescription*, p 658.
Stair Memorial Encyclopaedia, Vol 12, para 1126.
Walker, *Contracts* (2nd ed), para 24.6.

Terms of development contract
The contract between the pursuers and the defenders contained the following provisions, inter alia:

"4. *Warranties by Developer*

"The developer hereby warrants that:

"4.1 The Site is fit for the purpose of carrying out the Development thereon;

"4.2 The Approved Plans shall be practicable, accurate, and that the materials and quantities shall be appropriate for the purpose of the erection of soundly designed and constructed buildings on the Site".

On 30 August 1991 the Lord Ordinary *allowed* proof before answer on the whole case. (Reported 1993 SLT 1037.)

The pursuers reclaimed.

On 17 March 1992 the Inner House *allowed* the record to be amended in terms of a minute of amendment for the defenders and answers for the pursuers concerning the counterclaim and *remitted* the case to the Outer House for a debate on the question of prescription.

On 10 July 1992 the Lord Ordinary *allowed* proof before answer on the counterclaim under deletion of certain averments. (Reported 1993 SLT 1045.)

The pursuers reclaimed.

Reclaiming motion
The reclaiming motion was heard before an Extra Division on 16, 17 and 18 March 1993.

On 26 May 1993 the court *allowed* the reclaiming motion, *granted* decree de plano in the principal action, *excluded* from probation the defenders' averments in the counterclaim based on alleged breach of

contract and *allowed* proof before answer on the remaining averments in the counterclaim.

LORD McCLUSKEY.—This litigation arises out of the flooding of the Cameron Toll shopping centre on 3 November 1984. The Lord Ordinary has summarised the background to the litigation in his opinion of 30 August 1991. That summary was not criticised by parties to this reclaiming motion and I am content to quote it, so far as relevant to the matters with which we have now to deal. The relevant parts read as follows: [his Lordship quoted the opening part of the opinion at pp 1038H-1039D ("contained in the development agreement") and 1039G-1040A supra and continued:]

The Lord Ordinary then turned in his opinion to consider the submissions made to him and, by interlocutor of 30 August 1991, allowed a proof before answer on the whole case. The pursuers reclaimed against that interlocutor. In the Inner House, the defenders' motion to allow the record to be amended in terms of a minute of amendment, no 48 of process, and the pursuers' answers, no 50 of process, was granted on 17 March 1992. The case was then remitted to the Lord Ordinary "in respect of the matters contained" in the minute and answers. The matters so contained consisted of additional averments by the defenders whereby the defenders sought to found upon alleged breaches of cl 4.2 and cl 3.4.1 of the development agreement, and the pursuers' averments and pleas in response, to the effect that any obligations created by or flowing from cl 4.2 or cl 3.4.1 had prescribed before the date on which the minute no 48 of process had been lodged. The Lord Ordinary's opinion of 10 July 1992 contains his conclusions on these additional matters; the decisions resulting from the Lord Ordinary's conclusions are contained in an interlocutor of that date. In brief, he repelled the pursuers' prescription plea, upheld their plea to the relevancy in respect of the case based on cl 3.4.1 and quoad ultra allowed parties a proof before answer. The pursuers and reclaimers, in presenting this reclaiming motion against both of the Lord Ordinary's interlocutors (of 30 August 1991 and 10 July 1992) invited us to sustain their prescription plea in relation to the defenders' case based on cl 4.2 of the development agreement, to exclude from probation certain averments contained in the counterclaim, to repel the defenders' pleas so far as based on alleged breaches by the pursuers of warranties contained in cl 4 of the development agreement; and, in the main action, to sustain the pursuers' general plea to the relevancy of the defenders' averments (plea 3) and to pronounce decree de plano. Before us there was agreement as to the orders which the court should make in the event of the pursuers' submissions being successful.

Not all the submissions made to the Lord Ordinary were repeated to us. The pursuers and reclaimers were content to accept the Lord Ordinary's decision to allow a proof before answer on all matters other than the relevancy of the defenders' case so far as based on cll 4.1 and 4.2 and the effect on the cl 4.2 case of the Prescription and Limitation (Scotland) Act 1973, s 6. For their part, the defenders and respondents did not

seek to challenge the Lord Ordinary's conclusion that
A the defenders' case based on breach of cl 3.4.1 was
irrelevant.

It is convenient to consider the submissions in the
order in which senior counsel for the pursuers and
reclaimers dealt with them. He considered first the
construction of cl 4.1 and cl 4.2 founded upon by the
defenders and respondents. These, placed in their
context, appear in the development agreement as
follows: [his Lordship quoted the terms of the warranties set out supra and continued:]
B
These, it was submitted, were real warranties, to be
construed in accordance with their terms. But if,
despite all attempts to give meaning to the words used,
the expressed intention of the parties remained in
doubt it would be right to construe them strictly and
against the interests of the defenders and respondents.
In a context such as this where there was real
ambiguity or difficulty in giving literal effect to the
words used, the contra proferentem rule applied, but
C only in the sense that it required a strict reading of
those clauses which, having regard to their nature and
purpose, were seen to be conceived in the interests of
the parties who sought to take the benefit of them by
founding upon them: this was the approach of Lord
Patrick and of Lord McIntosh in *North of Scotland
Hydro Electric Board v D & R Taylor*, 1955 SLT, at
pp 377 and 379 respectively, and of Lord Morton of
Henryton in *Canada Steamship Lines v R* at
p 207. Reference was also made to Trayner's *Latin
Maxims* (4th ed, 1894) at p 45: "An ambiguous
D agreement ought to be interpreted against the person
putting it forward (*i.e.*, maintaining or pleading upon
it)."

Gloag on *Contract* (2nd ed), p 400, put it the same
way, founding upon Stair and Erskine to the same
effect. Reference was also made to McBryde, *The Law
Relating to Contract*, paras 13-39 and 13-40. When one
looked at the nature and purposes of cl 4.1 and cl 4.2
they were plainly designed to create absolute, strict
E liability on the part of the developers and in favour of
the defenders and respondents. Although they were
not indemnity clauses they were very close in
character to indemnity clauses and there was no reason
to apply any different principle of construction to such
a clause if its meaning was otherwise in doubt.

In relation to the construction of cl 4.1, the Lord
Ordinary appeared to have accepted the arguments in
favour of the construction contended for by the pursuers until almost the end of his opinion. It was sub-
F mitted that he had failed then to reach a proper
construction of cl 4.1 in the light of the defenders'
averments on record of breach of that warranty. The
main complaint on record was that quoted by the Lord
Ordinary from stat 4: "The site was not fit for the
purpose of carrying out the development thereon. The
site was unfit for the said purpose because inadequate
measures had been taken on the site and on the pond
and culvert mouth site immediately adjacent to it, to
prevent it from flooding."

What was there being said was that the culvert was

too small. It could be seen that this averment was
entirely circular because the culvert (or at least that G
part constructed within the boundaries of the defined
site) was part of the development as defined. The true
meaning of cl 4.1 was that the site was to be fit for
carrying out the construction of the buildings and
others contemplated, regardless of whether the resulting development was a good or bad one. There could
be no breach of this warranty in respect of something
that was wrong with the completed development
itself, if it was built as designed and planned. But the
defenders were arguing that the site included the
culvert, because "Site" in cl 4.1 had the meaning H
defined for it in the definitions and interpretation
clause, cl 1. The definitions of "the Centre", "the
Site", "the Development" and "the Approved Plans"
were of greatest importance but had to be read along
with heads (C) and (D) of the preamble, namely:

"(C) The Developer has commenced to construct
the Development (as hereinafter defined).

"(D) The Developer has agreed with the Fund to
continue to construct and to complete upon the Site I
(as hereinafter defined) the Development." (It should
be noted that in the Development Agreement the
defenders and respondents are referred to as "the
Fund" and the predecessors of the pursuers and
reclaimers, Gilbert Ash Estates Ltd as "the
Developer".)

It was submitted that if the culvert was part of the
development it could not be part of the site; the
culvert was plainly part of the development and the J
Lord Ordinary had recorded in the penultimate paragraph of the first opinion that both counsel had agreed
that the word "Development" in cl 4.1 must refer to
the whole of the works, not just those remaining to be
constructed after December 1983 when the development agreement was signed. The quoted passages
from the preamble also made it clear that "the
Development" meant the whole works. In these circumstances the word "Site" could not be given in cl
4.1 the defined meaning for "the Site" contained in cl K
1.2. It was clear that "the Site", as defined, excluded
the parts of the centre previously leased to SavaCentre
Ltd in terms of the SavaCentre lease; "Development",
however, included the SavaCentre, having regard to
the definition of "the Approved Plans" and the relative specification and drawings. Clause 4.1 also
referred to "carrying out" the development, not "continuing" or "completing" it. As "Development"
meant the whole development, "Site" in cl 4.1 did not
include partially or previously completed works. The L
concept of "carrying out" the development in cl 4.1
was to be contrasted with the obligation to "complete
the same" in cl 3.4.1. The dispute between the parties
on this matter was not simply a matter of pleading. It
was about the meaning of the warranty itself. In the
circumstances, cl 4.1 was a warranty about the site. It
was not a warranty about the size of the culvert, or
about the design of the development or about the state
or propensities of the Braid Burn. Clause 4.1 said
nothing about these things. The word it used was
"fit". This word pointed perhaps to such considera-

A tions as the bearing capacity of the site for certain purposes and the absence of any likelihood of mining subsidence. It could not be said that the "carrying out" of the development had been hindered or impeded in any way by the site. In these circumstances it was plain that there was no basis for saying that there was a breach of the warranty contained in cl 4.1. Once the development had been completed and the certificate of practical completion had been issued on 3 October 1984 the development was finished, the carrying out was over, and the cl 4.1 warranty was spent.

B   The Lord Ordinary had correctly concluded that the word "Site" in cl 4.1 could not be taken as including buildings erected on the site before December 1983. The error arose when he stated that the natural meaning of cl 4.1 was "that the pursuers warrant the suitability of *the situation in which* and the ground upon which the development was built for the purpose of building that development". Although the Lord Ordinary had recognised that the warranty in cl 4.1

C related to the fitness of the site and not to the adequacy of the buildings and of any protective measures (such as the culvert) required to deal with problems encountered on the site, he had, contrary to the logic of that view, allowed a proof before answer. The view expressed by the Lord Ordinary as to the cl 4.1 warranty did not fit with the defenders' averment already quoted, that "The site was unfit . . . because inadequate measures had been taken on the site and on the pond and culvert mouth site immediately adjacent to it, to prevent it from flooding." Possibly he had been

D misled by the averment in stat 3 that: "It was a term of the contract that the site should be fit for the purpose of, and fit for occupation and use as, a shopping centre with associated car parking facilities."

That, however, was an averment entirely, or at least largely, related to the case based upon cl 3.4.1 — not now insisted upon — and indeed paraphrased some of the wording of that clause. All parties now accepted that cl 3.4.1 related only to the time for completing the

E work, not to the quality of the work. The suggestion now apparently being made by the respondents, that because of the physical character and properties of the site, there was automatically a breach of cl 4.1 from the start, i e at the moment when the development agreement was signed, simply ignored the wording of cl 4.1. A construction to the effect that a party like the developer was entering into a warranty about something that already amounted to a breach of the warranty was one that should be resisted. In this context,

F reference was made to the dictum of Lord Reid in *Wickman Machine Tool Sales Ltd v L Schuler AG* [1974] AC at p 251: "The fact that a particular construction leads to a very unreasonable result must be a relevant consideration. The more unreasonable the result the more unlikely it is that the parties can have intended it, and if they do intend it the more necessary it is that they shall make that intention abundantly clear."

Turning to cl 4.2, again it was a question of looking at the words actually used. The defenders' position

appeared to be that it contained two separate warranties, the first ending with the words "and adequate", and the second beginning with the words G "and that". That was a questionable reading but it made little difference to the reclaimers' position. The adjectives "practicable", "accurate" and "adequate" were really all ejusdem generis. But the fact was that the defenders could not say and did not say that there was anything wrong with "the Approved Plans" in any of the respects specified. The approved plans related to the specification and drawings and there was nothing impracticable, inaccurate or inadequate about H these plans. If, as appeared more probable, the correct reading of cl 4.2 was that the words, "for the purpose of the erection of soundly designed and constructed buildings on the Site" qualified both the reference to the approved plans and the materials and quantities then all that was being warranted related to the erection of "buildings on the Site", which did not include the culvert. In the context of this subclause "buildings" was something less than the development as a whole. That difference indeed appeared by contrasting I the word "buildings" in cl 4.2 with the words "the Development" in cl 4.1. And the definition of "Development" itself included within it "buildings" as well as such items as "sewers, services, access roads and ways, service yards and all works ancillary thereto in accordance with the Approved Plans".

The "buildings" in cl 4.2 were, therefore, something quite distinct from, and did not include, the culvert. Part of the culvert was not on the site at all and nothing in cl 4.2 required the disapplication of the J definition of "the Site". Accordingly in cl 4.2 the culvert was properly part of the site and it had become heritable by accession; so, in construing whatever warranty was created by cl 4.2, the culvert was already part of the site and was excluded from the "buildings" to which the warranty in this subclause related. It should be noted that the developer was warranting that the approved plans "shall be" practicable etc and that the materials "shall be" appropriate etc. This wording, which looked to the future, fell to be contrasted with the word "is" in cl 4.1. If any of these K warranties had been concerned with the design of the culvert or with flood prevention it was extraordinary that such matters were not mentioned. Equally there was no reference in the development agreement to the Braid Burn. It was to be noted that cll 4.4 and 4.5 were not really warranties at all. Everything in cl 4 was to do with the development phase. The Lord Ordinary's view on the relevancy of cl 4.2 seemed to be based upon the view that cll 4.1 and 4.2 were L somehow parts of a comprehensive warranty placing the responsibility for the whole site and design upon the pursuers. There was no justification for this approach. There was no basis for suggesting that the whole was somehow greater than the sum of the parts. In the circumstances the defenders' case based upon cll 4.1 and 4.2 was bound to fail.

The arguments in relation to prescription were substantially those presented to the Lord Ordinary on the second occasion when the matter was before him on

A procedure roll and they are fully recorded by him. In the circumstances I can summarise the submission fairly shortly. It was maintained that it was clear that Parliament's intention had to be sought from the words of the statute; but the simple fact was that the 1973 Act made no provision whatsoever in relation to the point at issue here, namely the date from which the new prescriptive period was to run after the original period was interrupted by the making of a relevant claim in proceedings. One had to look at the words of the statute to see if they gave any guidance.

B It was also legitimate to look at the pre-existing law because there was ample and undisputed authority for the view that Parliament should not be deemed to have changed the existing law unless it did so clearly and expressly: reference was made to Maxwell, *Interpretation of Statutes* (12th ed), pp 116-117 and to the *Stair Encyclopaedia of the Laws of Scotland,* Vol 12, para 1126. It was not disputed that if an action containing a relevant claim was raised timeously, the raising of the action interrupted the short negative prescription

C and indeed would keep the claim alive and unprescribed as long as the action itself containing the relevant claim was being pursued. The issue here was a special one, namely what Parliament had intended if the interrupting claim was formally abandoned. Both the Lord Ordinary in the present case and Lord Kincraig in the case of *Hood v Dumbarton District Council* were wrong in concluding that while the claim was still contained in an action, a new prescriptive period could not start to run against any claims other than the

D one being pursued in that action. There were obiter dicta in the other cases quoted by the Lord Ordinary and they had to be considered, but there was no other relevant decision. It was submitted (first) that the actual terms used, both in s 6, and in the other sections, especially s 4, indicated that the statute was looking at a single event or act to constitute an interruption, not to any continuing state of affairs; the raising of an action was a single act or event and did not fall to be regarded or treated as a continuous

E making and re-making the claim; (second) Parliament's intention was obviously to restrict severely stale claims, yet if the Lord Ordinary's view was correct then the statute was permitting an extremely lax regime which would permit the use of a litigation to keep an obligation alive for a very long period indeed. The pre-existing law was to be found in the passages from Erskine, Bell, Napier, Millar, Gloag and Henderson and the Scottish Law Commission documents referred to by the Lord Ordinary. It was

F legitimate to look at documents of the Scottish Law Commission both to discover what the law was at the time when they were written and, if possible, to discover what the mischief was. Looking at the Scottish Law Commission documents referred to in the opinion of the Lord Ordinary, there was no "mischief" at all which needed to be changed. In these circumstances, given that the statute made no explicit change, one must assume that the legislature deliberately left the law as it had been in relation to this particular point. Reference was made to *Grahame v McFarlane.* The case could not be regarded as

G authority for the proposition that the period of prescription began to run again from the date of the raising of the action (no one was concerned with that date in that action) but it was authority against treating the date of the abandonment of the action as the date when the period began to run. In the highly unusual case of *Pillans & Co v Sibbald's Trs* it was held that the arrestment had prescribed when five years elapsed from the date when the action fell asleep and the personal debt founded upon also suffered prescription by the action having been allowed to go

H to sleep, despite the fact that the action was in court. It could not be submitted that there was any very clear principle established by authority prior to 1973, but the preferable view appeared to be that of the Scottish Law Commission, namely, that it was the single act of making a claim which interrupted the running of a period of prescription and started a new period running. If, by raising an action, a party interrupted the running of a prescription against him, and then abandoned his claim, it would be bizarre if the date of abandonment turned out to be the start of a new

I period of prescription. That was a result which was so absurd that it must be wrong. Finally, it was submitted that the making and continuing of a claim based upon whatever obligation arose from cl 4.1 could not save the right to enforce an obligation arising out of cl 4.2. The test was whether the cl 4.1 claim and the cl 4.2 claim both arose out of the same contractual obligation or not. The fact that they both appeared in the same contract was not conclusive of the matter. The court should deal with the substance

J of the matter, not the form. Reference was made to *Lawrence v J D McIntosh & Hamilton,* approved by the court in *NV Devos Gebroeder v Sunderland Sportswear Ltd.* It was clear that cl 4.1 was concerned with the site, whereas cl 4.2 was concerned with the plans. Breaches of the separate obligations created by these two clauses would be likely to occur in different ways, at different times and with different losses. The nature of the breach would be different in each case. The very fact that the defenders had at one stage abandoned

K their cl 4.2 claim made it difficult for them to say that it gave rise to the same obligation as cl 4.1. In the result, the pleas of the pursuers and reclaimers directed against the case made by the defenders and respondents on the contract should be sustained and decree de plano should be granted.

In response to these submissions, counsel for the defenders and respondents defended the Lord Ordinary's decision to allow a proof before answer. On

L the question of the court's approach to the construction of the warranties it was submitted that the contra proferentem rule could not be invoked to interpret the contract strictly against the defenders. The contra proferentem rule was to be used only as a rule of last resort. But here there was no proferens in the sense in which that term had been traditionally used and understood. In this respect there was no difference between the approaches of the English and Scottish courts. The Lord Ordinary had correctly summarised the argument for the defenders and had reached the right conclusion. The McBryde text referred to stated the rule too widely. Reference was also made to Chitty on *Contracts* (26th ed), paras 809, 815, 836 and 837, and to Walker's *The Law of Contracts and Related Obligations* (2nd ed), para 24.6. If, as was the case here, parties negotiated on an equal basis and drew up a contract not in standard form, the court had to find and apply a construction that gave effect to the parties' intention. The background had to be taken into account: but although there was a measure of agreement between parties as to the background, it was the averments of the defenders and respondents as to that background which had to be treated pro veritate at this stage, and reference was made to the defenders' averments about the topography of the site and the character of the Braid Burn. On this basis, it was plain that the contract might well, after proof, fall to be construed as a contract agreed by parties all of whom knew that the bare site simply would not do for the construction of the proposed centre and, in particular, that major works were required to avoid the flooding risk; and, on that basis, the Lord Ordinary was right to expect, to look for and to find contractual provisions designed to safeguard the position of the funders. This was a commercial document to be construed in a commercial and commonsense way; it fell to be construed so as to make it work, not so as to make it fail.

Turning to the wording of cl 4.1, "Development" clearly included both what had taken place and what was yet to take place: the term looked both forwards and backwards. The site, as defined, was not a single unchanging entity. It consisted of the ground plus all that came to be in it and on it. Thus it was clear that what constituted the development would change over time and what constituted the site would also change over time. Neither definition was of a fixed, unchanging entity. Eventually it was envisaged that the site, as defined, would include the development. The development, so far as constructed, would always be part of the site but the site would always be greater, bigger than the development. In construing cl 4.1 it was not necessary to go beyond the meaning of "Site" as defined in cl 1. The site in that clause consisted of the ground, the solum which the defenders averred to be not fit for the construction of the centre, plus what had already been done to remedy that unfitness. The choice was between construing "Site" in cl 4.1 as meaning the bare site, or as meaning that site together with such works as had been carried out on it when the development agreement was signed. If the view was taken that development was only what was then still to be built it would be seen that, once construction had begun, the site would always have some parts of the development in it. What was warranted was that the site as it existed in December 1983 was fit for the purpose of ensuring that the whole development which was contemplated could be successfully completed on it. Accordingly cl 4.1 really referred to the bare site with the improvements already in and on it at the time when the agreement was signed. On that basis, the warranty in cl 4.1 was perfectly comprehensible. There was no disguising the fact that there was difficulties in giving both the word "Site" and the word "Development" their defined meanings in the context of cl 4.1, but if one of the defined words had to yield some of its meaning it made more sense for "Development" to do so. If "Development" in cl 4.1 was to be treated as meaning the development outstanding as at the date of signing the agreement, the defenders' argument was that the site was not fit for the purpose of carrying out the development when the development agreement was signed and that the pursuers and reclaimers were immediately in breach of warranty.

Turning to cl 4.2, it was submitted there were two warranties contained in this paragraph: reference was made to the repetition of the word "that" within cl 4.2. For the purposes of this case the defenders were founding upon the inadequacy of the approved plans. It was the specification that was inadequate; it should have been adequate to ensure that there would be no flooding on this site. The specification did not achieve this; it was therefore inadequate. The works were badly designed. Furthermore the second part of this warranty should be construed as relating to the design of all the buildings on the site and, in this context, "buildings" included the culvert. Once again it would be expected as a matter of commercial common sense that the fund would look for a warranty of the sound design of all the buildings on the site whether constructed before or after the signature of the development agreement. The test of relevancy was whether or not the case was bound to fail if all the averments of fact were proved. On that basis the defenders' case could not be held to be irrelevant and the Lord Ordinary had reached the right decision in allowing a proof before answer.

On prescription, the respondents submitted that s 6 of the 1973 Act should be looked at from the perspective of one who was trying to determine if there was a valid prescription plea against his claim: he would look back to see if in the five year period a claim had been made. It would be odd if, while a claim was being actively pursued by an action in court, prescription should be running against the right to demand fulfilment of the very obligation which the claimant was then seeking to vindicate in that action. The reclaimers did not dare to go so far, and they had had to concede that prescription did not run against the claim which was in court, while it was in court and as long as it was being pursued in an action. The logic of that concession was that the claim was being made all the time that it was being actively pursued in an action in court. If it ceased to be actively pursued, whether because it was withdrawn or was dismissed then it ceased to be a claim that was "being made", but it ceased to be such only at the moment when it was withdrawn or dismissed. That was the logical starting point for a new five year prescriptive period to commence. The Scottish Law Commission proposals for the reform of the law had not been enacted. The 1973 Act had provided an entirely new statutory scheme and, as prescription was a statutory invention, the observations of the judges in *British Railways Board v Strathclyde Regional Council*, to the effect that the 1973 Act had swept away the old statutory provisions and replaced them with a new code, were entirely correct. The cases of *Grahame v McFarlane* and *Pillans & Co v Sibbald's Trs* were highly unusual cases, decided against their own statutory backgrounds, and they shed no useful light on the present law. Finally, on the question of severability, the present case was a fortiori of *Macleod v Sinclair*. The respondents' position was entirely consistent with the approach of the court in *NV Devos Gebroeder v Sunderland Sportswear Ltd*. The obligation which it was sought to enforce in the present case was one obligation, namely an objection to make good the loss caused by breaches of the contract, i e the breaches of the cl 4 warranties. The nature of the obligation was what was important, not the mere fact that it might derive from more than one contractual source.

In my opinion, when interpreting a contract which has been prepared by professional advisers and entered into by two broadly equal parties to deal with a unique situation in which they both have substantial economic interests, the court's purpose must be to discover what the parties intended; but the search for that intention must be conducted by considering the words that the parties have used to signify their intention. I do not consider that in this type of case there is any need or room for a principle of construction such as the contra proferentem rule. Plainly, the parties were expertly advised as to the terms in which their rights and responsibilities should be spelled out. Neither party was in any superior position. The contract was drafted ad hoc. I do not understand the fairness or the logic of the principles for which counsel for the pursuers contended, namely that each clause fell to be construed strictly against the interests of whichever party sought to rely on it. That approach could in certain circumstances cause the meaning to change according to the posture or claims of the parties. We must simply address ourselves to the words used. These words must, if possible, be given their ordinary meaning, except where they are expressly defined as having a special meaning for the purposes of the contract. In the present case, the contract itself provides that the defined meaning of certain words is to prevail over the ordinary meaning "unless the context otherwise requires": cl 1. It must, of course, be assumed that the parties intended that the provisions in the contract would be meaningful and would "work", that is to say, would regulate in a commercially sensible way the rights and responsibilities of each party when there occurred any circumstances or turn of events, intended or unintended, affecting the subject matter of the contract.

Clause 4.1 contains two defined words, "Site" and "Development". Each word is written with its opening letter as a capital letter, in the same style as occurs in the "*Definitions & Interpretations Clause*", cl 1. So I think it is abundantly plain that the *actual* intention of both parties was that both these words should receive their defined meaning in cl 4.1. The

contractual definitions are lengthy and they include other specially defined words, such as "Centre," "Developer", "SavaCentre", "Filling Station", "Approved Plans", etc. For the purpose of understanding what cl 4.1 is saying I have attempted to rewrite certain of the definitions relatively shortly, without losing their essence, by omitting legalisms, words of style or words that are unduly repetitive or are otherwise irrelevant for any understanding of the clause; I then replace the defined words with the reworded reformulations. I start with "Centre" which is not in cl 4.1. "The Centre", as reformulated, means "the plot of ground at Lady Road delineated on the plan together with all buildings from time to time erected thereon and together with all additions, alterations and improvements thereto". So it is clear that when the contract was entered into, "the Centre" (as defined) then included all the ground plus whatever buildings had been erected on the ground plus any additions, alterations or improvements to the ground. The centre was not defined as a fixed, unchanging entity; the words "from time to time" make that clear. Next, I draw attention to the fact that the preamble (the recital) says, the developer (the appellants) had already, prior to the signing of the agreement, leased part of the centre "*and the buildings and others erected* or to be erected *thereon* to SavaCentre Limited". It is obvious that the definition of "the Centre" itself already included the erected buildings and others; so we see here, in the use of the words underlined, an early example of the unnecessary repetition of certain words; there are many other examples. Another part of the centre had been leased under the "Filling Station Lease". The expression "the Site" was defined in terms that are virtually identical to those used to define "the Centre", but excluding the two parts of the centre previously leased. Accordingly "the Site" is not defined as a fixed unchanging entity; at any given time it must include both the buildings then erected on it and any additions, alterations and improvements that have, at that given time, been made to the ground. In recitals (C) and (D) it is narrated that the developer has already commenced to construct "the Development (as hereinafter defined)" and has agreed both to continue to construct it and to complete it. The "Development" which has been started, and is to be continued and completed, means (again paraphrasing the definition) the erection, construction and installation upon the site of the buildings and others contemplated by the "Approved Plans" (also specifically defined), which "buildings and others" are described as "comprising one hundred and seventy thousand square feet gross or thereby of retail and other space and ancillary storage and other buildings, including a pedestrian mall, and together with car parks . . . sewers, services, access roads and ways, service yards and all works ancillary thereto". The word "contemplated" in the definition might be construed as looking to the future, but "comprising" is clearly looking at the whole contents of the approved plans; so I would read "contemplated by" as synonymous with "described in". The approved plans are defined to include "the Specification". The

"Specification for Shell Construction of The Cameron Toll Centre", which is printed in the appendix, includes, as item (11), "Sub Structure *Ground* Burn diverted by culvert framed in RC sections 3.000 wide × 1.500 high. Banks of burn and pools reformed and reinforced with Enkamat fabric"; the same item also refers to excavations and drainage.

Certain important obligations are noted in the recital. As the development had already been started by the date of the signing of the agreement (as noted in recital (C)), it is plain that recital (D) is recording the developer's agreement to construct the remainder of the development. It will be observed that if one takes the full definition of "Development" and uses it to replace the word "Development" in recital (C), then recital (C) is saying, "The Developer has commenced to construct the erection, construction and installation upon the Site of the buildings". Again we see here an unnecessary repetition (of the notion of construction). The same thing occurs in recital (D). We should be cautioned by such examples against expecting the rest of the document to possess the coherence of a carefully drafted statute; so cautioned we will be less disappointed. But we must also take from such an analysis the need to search for the meaning of the contract benevolently and without being distracted by pedantic, mincing criticisms of style. Thus it is clear enough that the developer agreed to build the remainder of the development upon the ground as it then was, i e including the buildings already on the ground and the works (the additions, alterations and improvements thereto) which were already there at the date of signing. But although the developer's future obligations as recorded in recitals (C), (D) and (E) relate to the remainder of the development, the contractual definition of the development works well enough in recitals (C), (D) and (E) and it is not necessary to replace the defined meaning there with words such as "remainder of the Development".

Reading the paraphrased, shortened definitions both of "Site" and "Development" into cl 4.1, that clause appears to be saying: "Excluding the leased parts, the delineated plot of ground, the buildings now on it and the additions, alterations and improvements already made to the ground constitute an entity which we the Developers warrant is fit for the purpose of carrying out thereon the erection and construction of the buildings and others described in the Approved Plans comprising retail and other space etc."

The development, both in recital (C) and recital (D), means, in my opinion, the whole development. I consider that the signatories to the contract intended it to have the same meaning in cl 4.1, its defined meaning. I recognise that to give it its defined meaning brings awkwardness and some difficulty, but that that is a phenomenon we encounter often in this document and is an inevitable consequence of so defining "Site" and "Development" that if the two terms are used in one sentence there will be a degree of overlap. Perhaps the degree of overlap is not as serious as was sometimes suggested in the debate before us. The site, as defined,

consists of tangible things, namely ground and works of engineering and building construction. The development is defined as a process, a process of erection, construction and installing upon the site the works including retail space described in the plans. It is the words "upon the Site" in the definition of "The Development" that give rise to any difficulty, because while the construction process envisaged appears to be the whole process, the use of the words "upon the Site" (and the terms of the recital) demonstrate that the process had been completed in part; accordingly, the word "Development" in cl 4.1 might appear to mean only the erecting etc that had not yet been done but was still awaiting completion as at the date of the contract.

On the basis of this discussion, I now reformulate cl 4.1. It is intending to say: the delineated ground, including all the works already built or partly built upon it (including the culvert — so far as it has been constructed on the delineated ground) is fit for the purpose of the erection, construction and installation of the building and ancillary works which are to constitute the retail development provided for in the approved plans. Thus the clause appears to me to go beyond a warranty relating merely to the ground itself, for example, that there are no old mine workings or the like that might threaten the foundations of the building. I read the warranty of fitness as being a warranty that the site, being the subjects defined as "the Site" conveyed by the developers to "the Fund" on the same day as the contract was entered into, was fit to build a retail development on. As it is averred that the site was liable to frequent flooding, because of the presence of the Braid Burn and the way in which it had by then been culverted, the site may be said not to have been fit, when the agreement was signed, to build the planned retail development on. Accordingly, if the averments by the defenders and respondents are proved, it appears to me that they are likely to establish that there was a breach of this warranty. In any event, I am not able to conclude at this stage that their case must necessarily fail. That is the test to be applied in determining whether or not pleadings are relevant for inquiry. Accordingly, I conclude that, in relation to the case based upon cl 4.1, it is relevant for inquiry by way of proof before answer. In these circumstances, I consider that in relation to that matter the Lord Ordinary made the correct decision.

In my opinion, cl 4.2 presents no great difficulty. I consider that it does not contain two separate warranties with the last 15 words applying only to the warranty relating to materials and quantity. In my view the last 15 words plainly apply both to the provision about the approved plans and to the provision about materials and quantities. The repetition within the clause of the words "and that" does not appear to me to give any clear indication that the last 15 words of the clause apply only to materials and quantities. What is being said is that the plans shall be "practicable, accurate and adequate" and that the materials and quantities shall be appropriate, *all* for the purpose of the erection of soundly designed and constructed buildings on the site. I agree with counsel for the pursuers that the word "buildings" necessarily has a restricted meaning here having regard to the distinction in the definition of "the Site" between "buildings" and "all additions, alterations and improvements" to the plot of ground; in particular, "buildings" here does not include the culvert. There are other examples to show that "buildings" in cl 4.2 falls to be distinguished from other works of construction. Even if cl 4.2 were to be read as containing two separate parts with the last 15 words qualifying only the warranty relating to materials and quantities, I find no relevant averments to support any breach of the provision that "the Approved Plans shall be practicable, accurate and adequate". Apart from the difficulty of knowing what is meant by "adequate", if that word is divorced from the last 15 words of the clause, it appears to me plain that the obligation here created is an obligation in relation to the plans themselves. It is not, however, the plans that are criticised, at least in relation to the design and construction of buildings or in relation to their practicability, accuracy or adequacy.

Counsel for the pursuers also suggested that the word "shall" indicated that this provision looked to the future. By contrast, it was submitted, cl 4.1 contained the word "is", pointing to the time when the agreement was signed. I do not, however, find this a persuasive consideration. Strictly speaking, the correct word to point to the future is not "shall" but "will"; but, leaving aside that technical point, it appears to me that what is being warranted simply is that the approved plans, whether or not they already exist, will enable buildings (narrowly understood) of sound design and construction to be erected on the site. Obviously, having regard to the definition of "Approved Plans", not all the plans or drawings would be in existence as at the date of the agreement. However, I find nothing in this clause to suggest that it was intended here to enshrine obligations of the kind which at one stage it was submitted were contained in cl 3.4.1. Accordingly, I consider that the case based on cl 4.2 is irrelevant.

As I have indicated, the arguments in relation to prescription on both sides of the bar were substantially the same as those presented to the Lord Ordinary. Given, however, that, in my opinion, the case under cl 4.2 falls to be dismissed as irrelevant, it is not strictly necessary for this court to decide the question of the construction of s 6 of the 1973 Act. However, having regard to the fullness of the argument which was presented to us, I should indicate the view that I would have formed on this matter. In my opinion, the submissions for the respondents are to be preferred. The whole matter turns upon the construction of s 6 (1), para (a), and the words "having been made" therein. They may be compared with the words, "without the subsistence of the obligation *having been relevantly acknowledged*" in s 6 (1) (b). In my opinion the previous law, largely based upon the construction of statutes now repealed, sheds no light upon the interpretation of any of the relevant words in s 6. For

illustration, I consider the words of para (b) first: if in the defences lodged to an action the subsistence of an obligation were to be unequivocally admitted (see s 10 (1) (b)) then no doubt it could be said that the subsistence of the obligation had been relevantly acknowledged when the defences were lodged. But when thereafter the open record was printed and lodged, and when the closed record was lodged with the concurrence of both parties, then if these documents also contained the same admission there would be, on one view, a repetition of the admission. The better view, in my opinion, would be that as long as the pleadings containing the written admission were alive and playing an effective role in the litigation then the obligation was being acknowledged from moment to moment. In the same way, it appears to me that if a person makes a relevant claim in proceedings and then takes any step in the process, such as lodging an open record or a closed record or an amended record or enrolling a motion to cause the case to proceed further, he is of new positively asserting and reasserting his claim. In my view, the only realistic way to look at a litigation in court is to regard it as a continuous making and asserting of the claim which the pursuer seeks to enforce in the proceedings. On that basis, the claim is being made at every moment until the moment when the action ceases to be in court, whether it has been dismissed or abandoned (resulting in dismissal). Accordingly the prescriptive period starts to run from the day when the action is dismissed.

On the question as to whether or not the obligations under cl 4.1 and cl 4.2 are severable, it is not necessary for this court to decide that matter; but I should again briefly indicate my view. What the Lord Ordinary said was: "It is, in my view, reasonably obvious that the purpose of cl 4 in general, and cll 4.1 and 4.2 in particular, was to place the responsibility for the site, the plan, the materials and the design upon the pursuers so that the defenders could look to the pursuers for a remedy if they did not obtain soundly designed and constructed buildings on a suitable site" (at p 1050C-D).

In applying the words of the statute to a particular situation it is necessary to identify the obligation which it is sought to enforce. As it inevitably follows from the view I have taken of the meaning of the two clauses (4.1 and 4.2) that they give rise to different obligations, it also follows that a claim in respect of one is not a claim to enforce the obligation arising from the other. Accordingly, in my opinion, the claim based on breach of the warranty contained in cl 4.1 is not a claim to enforce the same obligation as the respondents seek to enforce by reference to the alleged breach of warranty contained in cl 4.2. I should not, therefore, have regarded the claim based on cl 4.1 as being apt to stop prescription running against a claim based on cl 4.2.

In the whole circumstances, I should be in favour of reserving the first plea in law for the pursuers and allowing a proof before answer on the whole case, other than in relation to the averments in support of

the defenders' case based upon cl 4.2. However, as I
have the misfortune to disagree with your Lordships,
I agree that the course to be followed to give effect to
the majority view is that which your Lordships have
indicated.

LORD WEIR.—I am of opinion that this reclaiming motion should be allowed to the extent and with
the effect of excluding from probation the defenders'
averments in the counterclaim which are based on an
alleged breach of contract. Your Lordship in the chair
has narrated fully the circumstances relating to this
dispute and to the submissions of the parties, and
there is no need for me to rehearse these.

The discussion before us concerned the interpretation of cl 4 and in particular cll 4.1 and 4.2 of the
development agreement between the pursuers and the
defenders. Clause 4 is headed by the title "Warranties
by Developer", and the clauses were described by the
Lord Ordinary as part of a comprehensive warranty.
I do not agree with this view. Clause 4.4 is not
expressed in the manner apt for a warranty and I
doubt if cl 4.5 can be said to have that character either.
The remaining clauses in my view should not be construed as forming part of one obligation but are to be
treated as a list of separate undertakings given by the
pursuers to the defenders at the time the agreement
was entered into. Those contained in cll 4.1 and 4.2
are of an onerous nature and are expressed without
qualification. It was submitted by counsel for the pursuers that they should be construed contra proferentem and we had an interesting debate on the
nature and supposed scope of this rule of construction.
I do not consider that it is either desirable or necessary
to give effect to this contention. To do so would
appear to have the effect of extending the scope of the
rule beyond the clearly defined situations in which
hitherto it has been held to operate. In any case, in my
opinion, the clauses do not contain an ambiguity or a
series of ambiguities which makes it necessary to
invoke this special rule of construction. It is sufficient
to construe these clauses by giving them no more than
the plain meanings expressed therein and, bearing in
mind that these are onerous undertakings, it is necessary to seek to avoid stretching their meaning, whether
by the introduction of supposed implications or otherwise, beyond what they will reasonably bear.

By cl 4.1 the pursuers warranted that the site
was fit for the purpose of carrying out the development thereon. Both the words "Site" and "Development" have defined meanings. "Site" is said to mean
a plot of ground delineated within certain boundaries,
and excluding certain parts therefrom, taken along
with buildings, additions, alterations and improvements. In my view the site means no more than the
land on which the development had taken place or
might take place in the future. In other words it
includes past works as well as future works. This is
made plain by the use of the expression "from time to
time" in the definition of "Site" which is referable to
the buildings erected on the land. In this connection,
I agree with the detailed analysis which is given in the
opinion of Lord Penrose.

What the pursuers warranted was that the ground
should be fit for a specific purpose, namely that of
"carrying out the Development". The development as
defined means the "erection, construction and installation upon the Site" (i e the ground) of buildings and
other works. That is what the ground had to be fit for.
It was conceded, as the Lord Ordinary noted, that the
culvert was part of the development so it was not part
of the site.

So construed, it is necessary to examine the
defenders' averments relating to alleged unfitness.
There is an averment to the effect that the site was low
lying, sitting as it was in a saucer shaped depression,
and senior counsel for the defenders went so far as to
say that the site was unfit on account of the very
existence of a watercourse running through it. No
doubt such an observation could be made with regard
to numerous built up places particularly in conurba-
tions. Such a construction would mean that the warranty in cl 4.1 could never have been properly made
on account of a fundamental unfitness. But that is not
what the defenders' complaint is about as expressed in
their pleadings. Their grievance is concerned with the
alleged inadequacy of measures taken to protect the
site from flooding. They aver that: "The site was unfit
for the said purpose because inadequate measures had
been taken on the site and on the pond and culvert
mouth site adjacent to it to prevent it from flooding."

This is quite different from saying that the "carrying out" of the development was impeded or adversely
affected by the unfitness of the ground. Such a case
might be made, for example, in relation to ground
where there was some inherent geological instability
against which no measures could be taken to ensure its
fitness for development. But that is not what is
averred. There is no room, in my view, for construing
cl 4.1 as implying a warranty that adequate measures
would be taken to cope with any problems which
might be encountered at any time on the site. For
these reasons I consider that the defenders have not
stated a relevant case for inquiry based on an alleged
breach by the pursuers of cl 4.1.

The defenders' other case based on breach of contract refers to cl 4.2. This claim first made its appearance when the counterclaim was lodged in May 1986.
It was removed by an amendment of the defenders'
pleadings in March 1991 but was reintroduced by
leave of the Inner House in March 1992. The pursuers contended both before the Lord Ordinary and
ourselves that this case had by now prescribed and
much of the debate was concerned with this question.
Since I consider that the case sought to be made by the
defenders of a breach of the warranty in cl 4.2 is irrelevant it is unnecessary to decide the prescription
problem. I would only add that I found the problem
and possible solution extremely difficult in relation to
what must be a highly unusual situation, although it
would be right to state that I find the views on this
question expressed by your Lordship in the chair to be
very persuasive.

Clause 4.2 is in the following terms: [his Lordship

narrated its terms and continued:] I do not consider
that the clause can be divided, as was contended by
counsel for the defenders, into two parts by placing,
as it were, a semicolon after the word "adequate".
The main purpose of the clause is a guarantee that there
will be erected on the site soundly designed and constructed buildings. Sound design is to be achieved by
means of practicable, accurate and adequate plans
while sound construction is to result from the use of
appropriate materials and quantities. The Lord
Ordinary was of the view that the words "soundly
designed and constructed buildings on the Site" had
to be read as including the whole constructions on the
site and therefore as including the culvert. On that
basis the averments concerning the inadequacy of the
culvert to cope with the spate of water were held by
him to be relevant.

I am of opinion that the word "buildings" must be
given its plain meaning in a clause of this kind unless
the context requires otherwise. It is not at first sight
obvious that an underground tunnel constructed to
allow for the passage of a river is a building. Moreover
part of the culvert is said to be situated outwith the
site. In terms of the definition of "the Development",
the approved plans contemplated "buildings and
others" to be erected and constructed and installed on
the site. In addition there were also contemplated car
parks, sewers, services, access roads and ways, service
yards and all works ancillary thereto. Although the
culvert is not expressly mentioned in this definition
there seems to me to be a clear distinction between
buildings on the one hand and other features of the
development on the other hand, and in my opinion the
culvert comes plainly into the second category, at the
very least as being ancillary works. It is to be observed
that this agreement was entered into after part of the
development (including the culvert) had been completed and in that context the use of the future tense
in cl 4.2 is quite appropriate as regards buildings
which remained to be constructed on the site. So in
my opinion there is nothing in the context which
would justify the culvert as being given the description of a building. In those circumstances the
defenders' averments concerning the inadequacy of
the plans so far as relating to flood prevention measures are irrelevant.

The contention of the defenders in the last analysis
appeared to be that from a reading of cll 4.1 and 4.2
taken together there can be spelt out a warranty by the
pursuers that all necessary plans had been made and
measures taken to prevent flooding on the site. If that
had been the intention it would have been easy to have
made express provision to that effect, but in the
absence of such a clause so expressed such warranties
as there are must be confined, in my view, to the
meanings which they separately bear and no more.

The consequence is that the interlocutor of the Lord
Ordinary should be recalled. So far as concerns the
counterclaim, the pursuers' second plea in law should
be sustained to the extent and with the effect of
excluding from probation (a) the averment "It was a

term of the contract that the site should be fit for the
purpose of, and fit for occupation and use as, a shopping centre with associated car parking facilities", and
(b) the averments in stat 4 thereof. In addition, the
defenders' fourth plea in law should be repelled and
the fifth plea in law should be repelled insofar as it is
founded on breach of contract. It was agreed by the
parties that in such event, a proof before answer
should be allowed on the remaining averments of the
defenders in the counterclaim, that decree de plano in
terms of the first conclusion of the summons should
be granted in favour of the pursuers in the principal
action and that a proof before answer be allowed on
the averments relating to the second conclusion of the
summons.

LORD PENROSE.—G A Estates Ltd were the
developers of the Cameron Toll shopping centre in
Edinburgh. When they began operations on the site
they owned the land on which the centre was to be
built. Site preparation comprised, inter alia, engineering works which formed an integral and necessary part
of the development project. These works included the
diversion of the Braid Burn. The burn entered the
intended development site on its south west border,
and emerged on its eastern boundary. In its natural
state, the burn ran across parts of the area intended for
development. It was resolved to culvert the burn. The
third parties designed the culvert and associated
works. The operations were approved by the local
authority, and were carried out and completed prior to
May 1983. By disposition dated 28 December 1983,
G A Estates Ltd conveyed to Caviapen an area of
ground extending to some 21.7 acres at Cameron Toll.
The area conveyed comprised the site of the shopping
centre, and included most of the track of the culvert.
It did not include an area of ground at the south west
of the site in which were located a stilling pond to
retain the burn's water prior to entry to the culvert,
the entrance to the culvert itself, and the initial length
of culverting. This area remained in the ownership of
G A Estates Ltd at all material times. The entrance to
the culvert was fitted with a metal grille. The parties
entered into an agreement along with Bovis Ltd relating inter alia to the completion of the shopping centre.

On 3 November 1984 the centre was flooded. In the
early afternoon, according to Caviapen's pleadings, it
was observed that the surface water drains at the south
entrance to the shopping area were not coping, and
surface water began to flow into the mall. At about 5
pm, a more major inflow of water began and parts of
the mall and shopping area were inundated to a depth
of several feet. The cause of the flooding is said to
have been "the inadequacy, particularly having regard
to the nature of the site itself, of measures to protect
the site from flooding". The vulnerability of the site
in its natural state to flooding is narrated, and it is
averred that G A Estates Ltd and their professional
advisers knew of the relevant factors and made an
attempt to deal with the problem. The steps taken
were, however, not adequate to protect the site. It is
then said that the vulnerability of the developed site

A   to flooding was unacceptable, and that: "It was a term of the contract that the site should be fit for the purpose of, and fit for occupation and use as, a shopping centre with associated car parking facilities. Unless and until adequate measures to prevent the site flooding were taken, it was not."

The cross sectional area of the culvert, and its flow capacity, are said to have been less than required for the discharge of anticipated volumes of surface water entering the burn upstream of the culvert. There are averments about the inhibiting effect on the water

B   flow of blockages at the grille, about the lack of facilities for clearing obstructions from the grille, and about the lack of certain monitoring facilities, all by way of detailed complaints about the design of the system.

It was not disputed that Caviapen owed G A Estates Ltd the sum of £708,656.46 first concluded for in the principal action under the agreement. Caviapen contended that they were entitled to set off against that liability a claim for loss and damage arising out of the

C   inadequacy of the flood protection measures incorporated in the design of the centre. It was a matter of agreement that they could resist G A Estates Ltd's motion for decree de plano in terms of the first conclusion if and only if they had a relevant claim founded in contract for the recovery of the amount of their loss. Before the Lord Ordinary, Caviapen advanced a case on the basis of three provisions of the development agreement, cl 3.4.1, cl 4.1 and cl 4.2. The Lord Ordinary sustained the pursuers' plea to the relevancy to the extent of excluding from probation

D   the defenders' averments in support of the case under cl 3.4.1. That decision was not challenged before us. It appeared clear, and it was accepted by counsel for Caviapen, that there should also have been excluded from probation the words: ", and fit for occupation and use as," forming part of the averment already set out. These words were derived from cl 3.4.1, and had no relevance to the remaining contractual cases under cl 4.

E   The contractual provisions which were relied on were in the following terms: [his Lordship quoted the terms of cl 4 set out supra and continued:]

The averments relating to these clauses are set out in stat 4 of the counterclaim. The critical averments relating to cl 4.1 are in these terms: "The 'Site' in terms of the said agreement included the said culvert (except insofar as it fell outwith the boundaries of the said plot), which had been completed prior to the execution of the agreement. The site was not fit for the

F   purpose of carrying out the development thereon. The site was unfit for the said purpose because inadequate measures had been taken on the site and on the pond and culvert mouth site immediately adjacent to it, to prevent it from flooding. Alternatively, esto the 'Site' in terms of the said agreement did not include the said culvert, the said culvert formed part of 'the Development' as defined in the agreement."

In support of the allegations of breach of cl 4.2, it is averred: "Further the pursuers were in breach of the warranty in cl 4.2. In cl 4.2 the pursuers warranted

G   that 'The Approved Plans shall be practicable, accurate and adequate and that the materials and quantities shall be appropriate for the purpose of erection of soundly designed and constructed buildings on the Site.' The Approved Plans were not practicable, and adequate, et separatim were not practicable and adequate for the purpose of erection of soundly designed and constructed buildings on the said site because adequate measures to prevent site flooding had not been taken therein, and in particular the plans did not specify the steps and precautions set out in stat 3."

H   Statement 3 inter alia specified a range of improvements and design characteristics desiderated by Caviapen as standards to be met by a properly designed culverting system for the discharge of surface water in the area. Counsel for Caviapen made clear in their submissions before us that their principal contention on the construction and application of cl 4.1 proceeded on the footing that the term "Site", as used in the clause, comprised all of the development which had taken place prior to the date of execution of the

I   development agreement, and therefore included the culvert so far as it lay within the boundaries of the site. That contention was based on the application of the definition provisions in cl 1.2 of the agreement. The term "Development" was said to comprise the whole works envisaged in the development proposals, whether completed before or after the date of the development agreement.

J   Your Lordship in the chair has set out the detailed submissions of counsel on the construction and application of cl 4.1 to the case on record, and I need not repeat them. The essence of the pursuers' position on record, and in debate, appeared to me to be that, irrespective of the content of the words "Site" and "Development", cl 4.1 was a warranty that related to the physical characteristics of the site, and to its fitness for the operations comprised in the development works. The position of the respondents, on record and

K   in argument, was that to give the clause meaning it was necessary to consider the purpose that the development was to achieve. The clause had to be read as warranting the fitness of the finished product for its purpose as a shopping centre. That is, the development was to produce a centre which was not liable to flood damage.

The terms "Site" and "Development" are both defined in the agreement. Before looking at the language used, it has to be noted that it was agreed by counsel that in the agreement generally, and in cl 4.1

L   in particular, the term "Development" referred to the whole development project, whether completed, in progress or yet to be begun at the date of the agreement.

In my opinion the first question that has to be considered is whether cl 4.1 can be given effect on its terms, applying the conventional definitions provided. The narrative clause of the agreement set out a number of recitals which employed terms defined in the body of the agreement and which had a bearing on the structure of the definition provisions themselves. Recital (B) referred to the "Centre" and to the previous letting of parts of the centre to SavaCentre Ltd and others. It did not use the expression "Development" in any way. Clause 1 defined "Centre" as meaning the plot of ground delineated on the plan appended to the agreement, "together with all buildings from time to time erected thereon and together with all additions, alterations and improvements thereto". The plan area coincided with the land disponed to Caviapen. This was the most comprehensive of the terms relating to the subjects which were defined. It extended to the land and buildings, and appeared to envisage the buildings both in an original form, and with additions, alterations and improvements, without defining a period of time in express terms. Whatever the scope of the provision, it would appear that it must include the structural shell of the shopping centre, and its heritable fittings from time to time, as these were constructed and installed. The expression did not apply exclusively to the state of development achieved on or before the date of the contract, and must have been intended to comprise at least all of the works intended to be carried out in completing the project as defined at the date of the agreement.

The expression "Site" was defined in the same terms initially, with the explanatory words "which plot of ground with the buildings and others thereon consists of the Centre". It then proceeded to except from the description those parts of the Centre which, shortly described, comprised the SavaCentre and filling station subjects which had already been leased out. The term "Site", as defined, therefore comprised the centre less the SavaCentre and filling station parts of the area. The identification of the areas in the plan appended to the agreement coincided with that view.

Recital (C) stated that the developer had commenced to construct "the Development (as hereinafter defined)". Recital (D) was in these terms: "The Developer has agreed with the Fund to continue to construct and to complete upon the Site (as hereinafter defined) the Development."

In each of these recitals one had an explicit reference to the definition later to be set out. It appears to follow that in these provisions the definition provisions had to be employed. If that is correct, the definition of the term "Development" of necessity covered at the date of the agreement at least some elements of the works which had already been carried out, perhaps elements which were currently in construction or development, and certainly elements which were prospective. Whether these were or included integral buildings, or parts of buildings or whatever was not a matter of definition. But it was plain that the definition, to be applicable to the two recitals, had to extend to cover past workings as well as future workings, or the results of such workings.

At the date of the agreement the SavaCentre building had been erected, and certain other works were complete. In particular, the culvert which is central to this case had been completed. It would not necessarily follow that those particular past works were comprised in the definition of "Development". But it is clear from a consideration of the approved plans, which included the specification appended to the agreement, that the diversion of the Braid Burn by culverting was expressly provided for in the specification for the shell construction of Cameron Toll centre appended to the contract. The definition of "the Development" was that the term meant "the erection, construction and installation upon the Site of the buildings and others contemplated by the Approved Plans . . . comprising one hundred and seventy thousand square feet gross or thereby of retail and other space and ancillary storage and other buildings". It was agreed by counsel that the plan area of 170,000 sq ft did not include the Sava-Centre building.

In the definition provision it appeared that the expression "the Site" was intended to relate to the land and its buildings as the project proceeded and to be applicable from time to time as buildings were erected and as additions, alterations and improvements were made thereto, with the exception of the SavaCentre and Filling Station plots and relative buildings. The parties had sought particularly to define the site as a net area, excluding SavaCentre and the filling station, together with the buildings, alterations and others erected, or to be erected upon that net area. The total works comprised in the centre included SavaCentre and the filling station. But it was clearly envisaged that they were not intended to be seen as part of the "Site". But for the agreement among counsel as to the definition of "Development", one might have inclined to adopt a construction of the term "the Development" which similarly excluded the works associated with SavaCentre and the filling station. Counsel's agreement that the specified area of retail and other space, extending to 170,000 sq ft or thereby, excluded SavaCentre might have supported such an approach. It is, at least, difficult to give a wholly satisfactory construction to the definition of "the Development" if it must proceed upon the view that it extends to the erection, construction and installation inter alia of the SavaCentre building and the filling station upon the "Site" which, by definition, excludes the solum of those structures. The problem, it is to be noted, arises on the express terms of the definitions of "the Site" and "the Development" independently of any difficulties that might arise in the construction of cl 4.1.

It is essential for the defenders' case based on cl 4.1 that the expression "the Development" as there used comprised the whole retail centre. It is the completed centre which is said to be unfit for the purpose of a shopping centre. Whether or not it is legitimate in any event to construe the warranty as extending to fitness for the purposes of a shopping centre, no such term could be implied or arise as a matter of construction of the language used if the expression "the Development" meant anything less than the whole works. In my opinion, the interpretation is strained and unnatural. Reading the relevant parts of the definition

A provisions into the warranty, it would appear that for the defenders to be correct the warranty would have to mean that the area of the whole centre, with all buildings and others for the time being erected on it, less the areas let to SavaCentre and for the filling station, was fit for the purpose of carrying on the erection, construction and installation of all of the buildings and others comprised and intended to be comprised in the whole centre. Further it would be necessary for the warranty to extend beyond the completion of the carrying out of those operations and to

B continue in relation to the completed centre. In my opinion, the construction breaks down the spatial relationship between the site and development which is explicit in the reference to carrying out the development on the site. As already indicated I found difficulty in making sense of definition provisions which envisaged development on an area exceeding the defined site. However, as between the positions adopted by counsel, I consider that senior counsel for the pursuers was correct in submitting that the war-

C ranty related to the site, and was not related to the design of the development or any part of it, nor the quality of enjoyment of the development after completion. In my opinion, the contentions of the defenders fall to be rejected.

In my opinion, the warranty provision can be given an adequate and satisfactory construction on the language it employed without the application of any special rule of construction. The expression "the Site"

D has a defined meaning which took account of the fact that by the date of the agreement the SavaCentre and filling station parts had already been completed. It was in relation to that net site that the warranty clause was conceived and, in my view, the words "the Development thereon" fall to be read together as relating to the development that was intended to be completed or carried out on the area of the site. The fitness of the site was warranted for the purpose of carrying out that development. I consider it to be fundamental to a sound construction of the warranty to bear in mind

E that the definition of "the Development" itself was not expressed in terms of buildings achieved by operations, but in terms of the operations of erection, construction and installation of buildings and others, as contemplated by the approved plans. Taking account of that factor, in my opinion, the scope of the warranty is clear. The site was warranted fit for the purpose of the operations envisaged in the approved plans of erection, construction and installation of buildings and others. There is no difficulty in giving such a con-

F struction content and effect. Stability, structural strength, weight bearing characteristics, and the whole range of geological factors normally requiring to be taken into account in anticipation of development works would be comprised. The warranty would satisfy purchasers and acquirers of the site of the suitability of the land for development without relying upon independent structural surveys, site investigations, bore holes, pits and all of the other geological survey work one might expect before commencing major development works. I consider that there is also

something to be said for the view that the clause was and must remain throughout the construction phase G prospective, looking to operations which were yet to be carried out. Such a view would accommodate those elements in the definition of "Site" which themselves were flexible enough to include the progressive carrying out of the works. On such an approach the plan area of the site, as altered and adapted by progressive development, was warranted fit for the carrying on to completion of the residual works at any time requiring to be carried out for the completion of the scheme.

In advancing their contentions, counsel for the pur- H suers argued that "the Site" in cl 4.1, fell to be construed as relating to the virgin site, the whole site for the centre. That construction would have the advantage of relating the site and the whole development spatially. It has the disadvantage, however, of ignoring the conventional definitions in the agreement. It appears to me also to suffer from the deficiency that it relates the term "the Development" to the results of the operations rather than to the operations themselves. I

In my opinion the defenders' case based on cl 4.1 is irrelevant. Not only does it require the strained and artificial construction of the clause to which I have referred, it looks beyond the operations comprised in the definition of "the Development" to the result and requires one to imply in the word "fit", references to the purpose of the completed development. This is inconsistent with the definition of "the Development". It also involves reading into the clause refer- J ences to the completed centre. That approach is inconsistent with the precise distinctions drawn between the definitions of "the Centre" and those of "the Site" and "the Development" in the agreement. Further, it appears to me that the fitness for purpose which is imputed to the language used in cl 4.1, would require a continuing state of fitness whatever might occur. There would be no limit in time to the warranty. The construction for which the defenders contend would appear to make cl 4.1 as compre- K hensive a warranty of fitness of the full development for the purposes of carrying on a shopping centre enterprise as could be conceived. Clause 3.4.1 of the agreement would appear to be unnecessary. Although that clause was not discussed by counsel, given the defenders' acceptance of the Lord Ordinary's decision on it, it remains an important element in the structure of the contract in my view. The provisions of cl 3.8.1 requiring insurance to be provided by the developer down to practical completion give emphasis to it. But they could not be read comfortably with the defenders' L contentions as to the scope of G A Estates Ltd's responsibility under cl 4.1. The list of insured perils in that clause indicates what the parties conceived as possible threats to the site, liable to affect its usefulness as a shopping centre. Flood, explosion, malicious damage, subsidence, earthquake, aircraft impact and so on were all identified. Some at least of these factors are within reasonable contemplation as perils which might affect Cameron Toll. The stipulation for insurance by the developer down to practical completion is typical of the provision one might expect to identify the shift of risk from developer to owner at the achievement of practical completion on a building project of this kind. If the approach of the defenders to cl 4.1 were correct, G A Estates Ltd would have a liability under a warranty provision covering some, at least, of the insured perils both during the construction phase and for an indefinite period after practical completion. The construction appears to me to be wholly at odds with the general structure and intent of the contract.

Clause 4.2 related to the approved plans. The first issue which arose in argument was whether it comprised a single warranty or two separate warranties. In my opinion there is but one warranty comprised in the clause and the attempt to divide it into two failed. The final sections of the clause provide that "materials and quantities shall be appropriate for the purpose of the erection of soundly designed and constructed buildings on the Site". The reference to "soundly designed" buildings would be incongruous if the last part of the clause were to be read as standing alone. If, however, one takes the view that the clause as a whole has to be read as providing a single warranty, the reference to the plans makes perfectly good sense as relating to the sound design of the buildings, whereas the reference to materials and quantities can be read happily with the reference to the sound construction of the buildings. The plans and the specification of materials and quantities together are factors contributing jointly to the single purpose of erecting soundly designed and constructed buildings on the site. In my opinion no sense is made by attempting to disintegrate the clause into two component parts. Further, to read the two sections apart requires one to imply a purpose for the expression "the Approved Plans shall be practicable, accurate and adequate". The word "adequate" is a relative, not an absolute term in its ordinary usage and demands an answer to the question "for what?" when used in the sense for which the defenders contended. The answer might be for the purpose for which plans were drawn. Plans are drawn, one might think, for the instruction of operations such as the erection of buildings. But they may have other purposes not so directly related to the construction phase of operations. They may comprise record drawings, for long term use by the owners or by local and national government agencies, or they may be contractual documents of importance to pricing and the resolution of disputes during and after the construction phase. The purpose, in the absence of definition, is not self evident. In my opinion it would make a nonsense of the clause to ignore the assistance given internally in defining purpose in this case. If one reads the whole together, then again one has a limited scope for the warranty. It related once more to the purpose defined, which would be self limiting in time. In my view, the warranty in cl 4.2 was a warranty that was designed to bind the developers to an undertaking that the plans which were listed as approved plans were capable of being put into effect, were accurate in their terms and were adequate for the purpose of the

erection of buildings of sound design and that the materials and quantities specified in the plans should be appropriate for the construction of such buildings.

In my opinion the defenders' case based on cll 4.1 and 4.2 of the agreement is irrelevant both in the principal action and in the counterclaim. In these circumstances I consider that the reclaiming motion falls to be allowed and the Lord Ordinary's interlocutor recalled. It would follow that decree de plano should be granted in favour of the pursuers so far as the sums involved in the principal action are undisputed. Decree should be granted in terms of the first conclusion of the summons. I agree with Lord Weir's views on parties' pleas in law. The pursuers' entitlement to interest in terms of the second conclusion is disputed and would require proof.

In these circumstances I consider that it is unnecessary to answer the interesting and difficult questions of prescription raised by the reclaimers in the course of the debate. I would have been inclined to favour the defenders' approach to the construction of s 6 of the Prescription and Limitation (Scotland) Act 1973, applied to cl 4.2 as a separate and independent warranty from cl 4.1. The Act identifies the appropriate date from which the prescriptive period initially must run. It identifies those events which operate as interruptions of that period. The Act does not in terms provide definitions or trigger points for the commencement of further prescriptive periods. It is to be implied that prescription after the appropriate date can run from time to time with interruptions. It was not in dispute that litigation commenced and continued to a final disposal operated to prevent argument that the initial or previous prescriptive period continued to run. At any point along the course of that period the imponderables must include, in the nature of things, the possibility of abandonment, the possibility of dismissal, and the possibility of material change in the scope of litigation. If one asked during the currency of the litigation, and before such an event occurred, whether a prescriptive period were running, then in my opinion the proper answer would be in the negative. For the pursuers' case to succeed on this branch of the argument it would be necessary to introduce a qualification that should the action be abandoned or dismissed the period of interruption would be retrospectively cancelled so that prescription was deemed to have begun to run afresh from the original date of the interrupting act. In my opinion, Lord Kincraig's views in *Hood v Dumbarton District Council* were correct. However, it cannot be said that this matter is necessary to the decision of the present action.

Counsel for Pursuers and Reclaimers, Emslie, QC, J R Campbell; Solicitors, Strathern & Blair, WS — Counsel for Defenders and Respondents, H H Campbell, QC, Doherty; Solicitors, Bird Semple Fyfe Ireland, WS.

C A G M

Carmichael v Wilson

A   HIGH COURT OF JUSTICIARY

THE LORD JUSTICE CLERK (ROSS),
LORDS MURRAY AND MORISON

15 DECEMBER 1992

Justiciary — Statutory offence — Driving while unfit through drink — Police first suspecting accused of offence when speaking to him on private property — Accused then required to supply roadside breath test — Accused
B   *arrested following positive test and required to provide further breath specimens at police station — Whether admissibility of evidence of Camic analysis dependent on lawfulness of earlier requirement for roadside breath test — Road Traffic Act 1988 (c 52), ss 6 and 7.*

Section 7 of the Road Traffic Act 1988 provides that "In the course of an investigation into whether a person has committed an offence under section 4 or 5 of this Act", a constable may require that person to
C   provide breath specimens for analysis on an approved device. Section 6 provides that where a constable in uniform has reasonable cause to suspect that a person driving or in charge of a motor vehicle has alcohol in his body he may require that person to give a roadside breath test.

An accused person was charged on a summary complaint with a contravention of s 5 (1) (a) of the 1988 Act. The evidence disclosed that the police had seen the accused driving his motor car on a public road and
D   had decided to stop him for a routine check. The accused's car turned into a driveway leading to a private house before the police could stop him. The police spoke with the accused as he was alighting from his car on the private driveway and then detected a smell of alcohol on his breath. The police required the accused to submit to a breath test which proved positive. The accused was then arrested and taken to a police station where the procedure under s 7 was
E   carried out. The sheriff sustained a submission that there was no case for the accused to answer on the ground that when the police first suspected the accused of having committed an offence they were on a private roadway and had no right to be there; that this was an irregularity for which no excuse was offered; and that accordingly the evidence of the Camic breath analysis was inadmissible. The Crown appealed.

F   **Held,** that the subsequent procedures under s 7 were in no way vitiated by any actions of the police at the earlier stage at the locus (p 1069D-E and H-I); and appeal *allowed.*

Opinion reserved, whether the sheriff was correct to hold that police officers had no right to be in the driveway on private property, and that their being there constituted an irregularity (p 1069B).

Orr v Urquhart, 1993 SLT 406, *followed.*

Summary complaint

G   Thomas Brownlie Wilson was charged at the instance of William G Carmichael, procurator fiscal, Hamilton, on a summary complaint which was in the following terms: "on 2 January 1992 on a road or other public place, namely Silvertonhill Avenue, Hamilton you did drive motor vehicle registered A757 JVU after consuming so much alcohol that the proportion of it in your breath was 88 microgrammes of alcohol in 100 millilitres of breath which exceeded the prescribed limit, namely 35 microgrammes of alcohol in 100 millilitres of breath: contrary to s 5 (1) (a) of the
H   Road Traffic Act 1988". The accused pled not guilty and proceeded to trial. At the close of the Crown case the sheriff (I A MacMillan) sustained a submission in terms of s 345A of the Criminal Procedure (Scotland) Act 1975 and acquitted the accused.

The procurator fiscal appealed by way of stated case to the High Court against the decision of the sheriff.

Statutory provisions

The Road Traffic Act 1988 provides: I

"6.—(1) Where a constable in uniform has reasonable cause to suspect—(a) that a person driving or attempting to drive or in charge of a motor vehicle on a road or other public place has alcohol in his body or has committed a traffic offence whilst the vehicle was in motion, or (b) that a person has been driving or attempting to drive or been in charge of a motor vehicle on a road or other public place with alcohol in his body and that that person still has alcohol in his
J   body, or (c) that a person has been driving or attempting to drive or been in charge of a motor vehicle on a road or other public place and has committed a traffic offence whilst the vehicle was in motion, he may, subject to section 9 of this Act, require him to provide a specimen of breath for a breath test. . . .

"(5) A constable may arrest a person without warrant if—(a) as a result of a breath test he has reasonable cause to suspect that the proportion of alcohol in that person's breath or blood exceeds the prescribed
K   limit, or (b) that person has failed to provide a specimen of breath for a breath test when required to do so in pursuance of this section and the constable has reasonable cause to suspect that he has alcohol in his body, but a person shall not be arrested by virtue of this subsection when he is at a hospital as a patient. . . .

"7.—(1) In the course of an investigation into whether a person has committed an offence under
section 4 or 5 of this Act a constable may, subject to   L
the following provisions of this section . . . require him—(a) to provide two specimens of breath for analysis by means of a device of a type approved by the Secretary of State".

Cases referred to

Cairns v Keane, 1983 SCCR 277.
Fox v Chief Constable of Gwent [1986] AC 281; [1985] 1 WLR 1126; [1985] 3 All ER 392; [1985] RTR 337.

Lawrie v Muir, 1950 SLT 37; 1950 JC 19.

A *Orr v Urquhart*, 1993 SLT 406; 1992 SCCR 295.

Young v Carmichael, 1993 SLT 167; 1991 SCCR 332.

Textbook referred to

Wheatley, *Road Traffic Law in Scotland*, p 66.

The sheriff appended the following note to the stated case:

THE SHERIFF (I A MACMILLAN).—There was a conflict of evidence as between the two police

B officers (the only prosecution witnesses) as to whether the blue flashing light had or had not been operated on the police car just before the respondent turned into the driveway; but it was never claimed on behalf of the appellant that there was any evidence to show that the respondent was aware, or must have been aware that the police were there, or that they wished to stop him, or that his purpose in entering the driveway was other than an innocent one. It was also not in dispute that the police officers had no cause to

C suspect that an offence had been committed until they detected the smell of alcohol, and that they were then on private property.

In the course of the hearing before me it was accepted that the old law as to whether the driver had completed his journey was no longer relevant; and it was also accepted that the preliminary breath test at the locus and subsequent lawful arrest were no longer essential prerequisites of further procedure in prosecutions for offences under s 5. In the end of the day,

D therefore, only two issues were debated before me, and they appeared to be interrelated.

The first was whether the police officers could be said to have been "in the course of an investigation" as to whether the respondent had committed an offence under s 5 when they required him to provide specimens of breath for analysis at the police station, and whether the prosecution was consequently entitled to rely on the evidence of the Camic analysis.

E The second question was whether such evidence must be taken into account, however obtained, in view of the wording of s 15 (2) of the Road Traffic Offenders Act 1988.

The respondent's agent submitted that the police officers were not entitled to enter private property in order to obtain evidence that the accused had been driving on the public road with excessive alcohol. He referred me to *Fox v Chief Constable of Gwent* and sought to distinguish it on the grounds that in that

F case there had been a road accident. He also referred me to Lord Cooper's judgment in *Lawrie v Muir*, 1950 SLT at p 39, and to *Cairns v Keane* as an example of a situation where evidence irregularly obtained was properly admitted.

In the course of the trial there had been no objection to the admission of the evidence of the Camic reading as being irrelevant; but the procurator fiscal depute did not take issue with this, and the respondent's failure to object to evidence led did not play any part in the hearing before me.

The procurator fiscal depute submitted that in terms of s 6 (1) (b) the police officers had been entitled G to require the roadside test because they had reasonable cause to suspect that the accused had been driving on a public road with alcohol in his body, and that he still had alcohol in his body. They were therefore entitled to arrest him in terms of s 6 (5), and having arrested him, they were entitled to carry out the Camic procedure. The fact that the respondent had left the public road and driven on to private property did not invalidate that procedure or render the evidence inadmissible. All that was required in terms of s 7 (1) of H the Road Traffic Act 1988, in order to render the Camic reading admissible, was that it should be shown that the officers were "in the course of an investigation into whether a person had committed an offence under section 4 or 5". It was clear that this was precisely what they were doing when they required the respondent to provide two specimens of breath for analysis at the police station. The procurator fiscal depute pointed out that s 15 (2) of the Road Traffic Offenders Act 1988 provides that evidence of the proportion of I alcohol in a breath specimen "shall, in all cases, be taken into account"; and he referred me to Sheriff Wheatley's comments on this in his recent book on *Road Traffic Law in Scotland* at p 66 where he says that in terms of this section "all such readings, irrespective of how they are obtained, must be considered".

It did not seem to me that the case of *Fox v Chief Constable of Gwent* was of much assistance. In that case it appeared to be taken for granted that the police J were in the course of an investigation, as no doubt they were, as there had been a road accident shortly before they confronted the driver. The case seemed to be mainly concerned with the English rules as to the admissibility of evidence obtained unlawfully, and I noted Lord Fraser's comment that it was a well established rule of English law that any evidence which is relevant is admissible even if it has been obtained illegally — although he excepted evidence obtained oppressively, or by a trick.   K

As to whether the police officers had been "in the course of an investigation" into whether the respondent had committed an offence, the only case to which I was referred was *Young v Carmichael*. In that case your Lordships held that the place where the accused had been driving was not a road or other public place; that the accused therefore could not possibly have committed the offence of driving on a public road with an excessive amount of alcohol; and therefore the L police officers could not have been investigating whether he had committed such an offence. I took it that the effect of that decision must be that officers can only be regarded as being in the course of an investigation where it has been shown that they have something to investigate, and that they must therefore have a legitimate starting point of some kind. It seemed to me that the police cannot simply pluck a motorist off the street without cause, and then seek to justify the Camic evidence subsequently obtained on the basis that they were in the course of an investigation as to

A whether the driver had or had not committed an offence. There had therefore to be some justifiable basis for their investigation. In this case there was no justifiable starting point for any investigation until the officers detected the smell of drink. There had been nothing prior to that to excite their suspicion — no erratic driving; no infringement of traffic regulations; no suggestion even that the respondent had wilfully ignored the officers' attempt to stop him while he was still on the public road. But by the time the officers detected the smell of alcohol from the respondent's

B breath, and thus had occasion for the first time to commence an investigation, they were where they had no right to be. Their being on private property was an irregularity for which no excuse whatsoever was offered. As to the admissibility of the evidence thus irregularly obtained, it seemed to me that the law of Scotland was still as expressed in *Lawrie v Muir*. I concluded that the police officers in this case had no lawful occasion to investigate whether the respondent had committed an offence under s 4 or 5, and that they

C were not entitled to require him to provide specimens of breath for analysis.

As for the submission that s 15 (2) of the Road Traffic Offenders Act necessitates the admission of such evidence "in all cases", it seemed to me that this phrase did not justify the admission of evidence however irregularly obtained, and that Sheriff Wheatley's views as quoted above were too broadly stated.

I therefore sustained the submission under s 345A, and acquitted the respondent.

D

Appeal

The sheriff posed the following questions for the opinion of the High Court:

(1) Did I err in holding that when the police required the respondent to provide specimens of breath for analysis they were not in the course of an investigation in terms of s 7 (1) of the Road Traffic Act

E 1988?

(2) If the police officers were not in the course of such an investigation, did I err in holding that the evidence of the Camic printout was not admissible by reference to s 15 (2) of the Road Traffic Offenders Act 1988?

(3) Did I err in law in holding that in the circumstances the police officers were not entitled to enter private property to speak to the respondent?

F

(4) Was I entitled on the evidence led to sustain the submission that there was no case to answer?

The appeal was argued before the High Court on 15 December 1992.

Eo die the court *answered* question 1 in the *affirmative*, question 4 in the *negative* and *allowed* the appeal.

The following opinion of the court was delivered by the Lord Justice Clerk (Ross):

OPINION OF THE COURT.—This is an appeal at the instance of the procurator fiscal, Hamilton. The G respondent is Thomas Brownlie Wilson. The respondent went to trial in the sheriff court at Hamilton on a complaint libelling a contravention of s 5 (1) (a) of the Road Traffic Act 1988. At the conclusion of the Crown case a submission of no case to answer was made on behalf of the respondent. The sheriff sustained the submission and acquitted the respondent. It is against that decision of the sheriff that the Crown have now appealed.

In presenting the appeal, the advocate depute drew H attention to the narration of the evidence which the sheriff gave in the case. On 2 January 1992 two uniformed police officers saw the respondent driving his car on Silvertonhill Avenue, Hamilton, which is a road or other public place within the meaning of s 5 of the Road Traffic Act 1988. There was nothing in the manner of the respondent's driving to cause the officers to suspect that he had been drinking, or that he might be in contravention of s 5, or of any other section of or regulation made under the Road Traffic I Act 1988. Nevertheless the officers decided to stop the respondent's car for a routine check. He was observed driving on this street for only a short distance of about 50 yds. His car then entered a driveway leading to a private house. The house and driveway belonged to the respondent's passenger, and the respondent had gone there because it was his intention to spend the night there.

The police officers parked their car on the public road at the entrance to the house and proceeded on J foot up the driveway. They arrived at the respondent's car which was parked at the gable wall of the house just as he was in the process of alighting from it. The sheriff goes on to state that the officers were then on private property, and that they had no right to be there. They spoke to the respondent and detected a smell of alcohol from his breath. As a result they suspected that he had been driving his vehicle with alcohol in his body, and they required him to submit to a breath test at the locus. The respondent agreed to K this and the breath test was positive. He was then arrested and conveyed to Blantyre police station where the usual procedure was carried out in terms of s 7 of the Road Traffic Act 1988. The lower of the two readings obtained from the Camic breathalyser analysis of the specimens provided by the respondent was 88 microgrammes, and he was accordingly cautioned and charged as libelled. The sheriff goes on to say that when the police officers required the respondent to provide specimens for analysis, they were not then in L the course of an investigation into whether he had committed an offence under s 4 or s 5. This last mentioned statement was challenged by the Crown.

The advocate depute submitted that the sheriff had been in error when he held that the two police officers had no right to be in the driveway of the house into which the respondent had driven. A great deal of the sheriff's note is concerned with this aspect of the matter and the sheriff makes it plain that it was submitted on behalf of the respondent that the police officers were not entitled to enter private property in order to obtain evidence that the respondent had been driving on the public road with excessive alcohol. In the course of his note the sheriff expressed the view that there was no justifiable starting point for any investigation on the part of the police until the officers had detected a smell of alcohol. There had been nothing prior to that to excite their suspicion. The sheriff went on to express his views as follows:

"But by the time the officers detected the smell of alcohol from the respondent's breath, and thus had occasion for the first time to commence an investigation, they were where they had no right to be. Their being on private property was an irregularity for which no excuse whatsoever was offered."

We do not find it necessary to determine whether the sheriff was well founded in holding that the two police officers had no right to be in the driveway on private property, nor whether their being there constituted an irregularity. In the case there appears to us to be some confusion between the time when the police officers required the respondent to submit to a breath test at the locus, and the subsequent occasion when the procedures were carried out in the police station with the Camic breathalyser. It seems clear that when the police officers required the respondent to provide a breath test at the locus, they were purporting to exercise their powers under s 6 (1) of the Road Traffic Act 1988, whereas when the respondent was required to provide two specimens of breath for analysis at the police station the officers were purporting to act under the provisions of s 7 of the Act of 1988. The sheriff's conclusion that the police officers had no right to be in the driveway and that there was at that stage an irregularity for which no excuse was offered relates to the procedures under s 6. However, in our opinion, any irregularity in the procedures under s 6 had no effect upon the subsequent procedure under s 7. Accordingly even if the sheriff was well founded in concluding that there had been an irregularity at the time when the police officers were purporting to act under s 6, that would not vitiate the procedure laid down under s 7. In the light of the evidence led before the sheriff, there is no doubt that by the time the respondent was required to provide two specimens of breath at the police station, the police officers were in the course of an investigation into whether he had committed an offence under s 4 or s 5 of the Act of 1988. The procedure under s 7 is quite independent of that under s 6. In the opinion of the court delivered in *Orr v Urquhart* it was observed at 1992 SCCR, p 298C-E: "Under the provisions of what is now section 7 of the Act of 1988, the requirement to provide two specimens of breath for analysis can be given in the course of an investigation into whether a person has committed an offence under section 4 or 5 of the Act of 1988. Accordingly it is not necessary for the procedure in section 6 to have been followed at all provided that the procedure laid down in section 7 has been observed. We are also satisfied that there is no reason why any failure to follow the procedural requirements of section 6 should render any subsequent procedure invalid. Indeed, even if the arrest of a person under section 6 (5) should appear to be invalid, that would not, in our opinion, render invalid any procedure properly carried out under section 7. In *Fox v Chief Constable of Gwent*, which was a case under section 6 (1) of the Road Traffic Act 1972, as substituted by section 25 (3) of and Schedule 8 to the Transport Act 1981, the House of Lords held that on a true construction of section 8 (1) of the Act of 1972, a lawful arrest was not an essential prerequisite of a breath test. In his speech, Lord Fraser of Tullybelton observed that following upon the amendments made to the Act of 1972 by the Act of 1981, the Divisional Court had been right 'in treating the fact that the appellant was in the police station because he had been unlawfully arrested merely as a historical fact, with which the court was not concerned'."

In these circumstances even if the sheriff was well founded in concluding that there had been an irregularity when the procedures under s 6 were set in motion, we are satisfied that nothing at that stage can have tainted the subsequent procedures under s 7. Counsel for the respondent maintained that the sheriff had been correct because the police had acted unfairly at the earlier stage at the locus, but, in our opinion, the subsequent procedures under s 7 were in no way vitiated by any actions of the police at the earlier stage at the locus.

The questions posed by the sheriff are properly directed to the procedures which were carried out by the police officers in terms of s 7 of the Act of 1988. For the reasons given above we accordingly answer the first question in the affirmative and the fourth question in the negative. We do not find it necessary to answer questions 2 and 3 in the case.

Counsel for Appellant, Macdonald, QC, A D; Solicitor, J D Lowe, Crown Agent — Counsel for Respondent, Douglas; Solicitors, Macbeth, Currie & Co, WS (for Hughes Dowdall, Glasgow).

P W F

McGlennan v Clark

HIGH COURT OF JUSTICIARY

THE LORD JUSTICE GENERAL (HOPE), LORDS COWIE AND MAYFIELD

5 JANUARY 1993

Justiciary — Statutory offence — Possession of offensive weapon — "Shuriken" (Chinese throwing star) — Non-flexible metal plate with several sharp radiating points found in accused's trouser pocket — Whether offensive weapon per se — Relevance of statutory instrument declaring shuriken an offensive weapon for purposes of another statute — Prevention of Crime Act 1953 (1 & 2 Eliz II, c 14), s 1 (1) — Criminal Justice Act 1988 (Offensive Weapons) Order 1988 (SI 1988/2019), Sched, para 1 (h).

Section 141 of the Criminal Justice Act 1988 provides that any person who manufactures, sells or hires or offers for sale or hire, exposes or has in his possession for the purpose of sale or hire, or lends or gives to any other person, a weapon of a prescribed description shall be guilty of an offence. The Criminal Justice Act 1988 (Offensive Weapons) Order 1988 provides in the Schedule that, inter alia, the weapon sometimes known as a "shuriken", "shaken", or "death star", being a hard non-flexible plate having three or more sharp radiating points and designed to be thrown, shall be a weapon to which s 141 of the 1988 Act shall apply.

An accused person was charged on summary complaint with possessing a Chinese throwing star contrary to s 1 (1) of the Prevention of Crime Act 1953. The accused was searched by police officers who found a shuriken in his trouser pocket. It was a non-flexible metal plate with several sharp radiating points. The accused stated to the police that it was used for throwing. The sheriff sustained a submission that there was no case for the accused to answer on the ground that there was no evidence that the item was a weapon or offensive per se. He refused to take into account the declaration in para 1 (h) of the Schedule to the 1988 Order in determining whether the shuriken was an offensive weapon per se. The Crown appealed.

Held, (1) that the nature of the shuriken was such that the sheriff should have concluded that there was a prima facie case that it was an offensive weapon (p 1072C); (2) that where it was clearly stated in a statutory instrument that an article was to be regarded as an offensive weapon, it could be regarded as an offensive weapon per se for the purposes of the Prevention of Crime Act 1953, and there was accordingly a case to be answered (p 1072E-F); and appeal *allowed* and case *remitted* to sheriff to proceed as accords.

Dictum of Lord Justice Clerk Wheatley in *Tudhope v O'Neill*, 1982 SLT 360, *applied*.

Summary complaint

Stephen Clark was charged at the instance of John G McGlennan, procurator fiscal, Kilmarnock, on a summary complaint which libelled inter alia the following charge: "(2) on [11 October 1991] in a public place, namely [Mayfield Road, Saltcoats], you did, without lawful authority or reasonable excuse, have with you an offensive weapon, namely a Chinese throwing star: contrary to the Prevention of Crime Act 1953, s 1". The accused pled not guilty and proceeded to trial. At the close of the Crown case the sheriff (T M Croan) sustained a submission that there was no case to answer and acquitted him. The facts of the case appear from the opinion of the court.

The procurator fiscal appealed by way of stated case to the High Court against the decision of the sheriff.

Statutory provisions

The Prevention of Crime Act 1953 provides:

"1.—(1) Any person who without lawful authority or reasonable excuse, the proof whereof shall lie on him, has with him in any public place any offensive weapon shall be guilty of an offence. . . .

"(4) In this section . . . 'offensive weapon' means any article made or adapted for use for causing injury to the person, or intended by the person having it with him for such use by him."

The Criminal Justice Act 1988 provides:

"141.—(1) Any person who manufactures, sells or hires or offers for sale or hire, exposes or has in his possession for the purpose of sale or hire, or lends or gives to any other person, a weapon to which this section applies shall be guilty of an offence and liable on summary conviction to imprisonment for a term not exceeding six months or to a fine not exceeding level 5 on the standard scale or both.

"(2) The Secretary of State may by statutory instrument direct that this section shall apply to any description of weapon specified in the order."

The Criminal Justice Act 1988 (Offensive Weapons) Order 1988 provides in the Schedule:

"1. Section 141 of the Criminal Justice Act 1988 (offensive weapons) shall apply to the following descriptions of weapons, other than weapons of those descriptions which are antiques for the purposes of this Schedule: . . . (h) the weapon sometimes known as a 'shuriken', 'shaken', or 'death star', being a hard, non-flexible plate having three or more sharp radiating points and designed to be thrown".

Cases referred to

Tudhope v O'Neill, 1982 SLT 360; 1982 SCCR 45.
R v Williamson (1977) 67 Cr App R 35; [1978] Crim LR 228.
Woods v Heywood, 1988 SLT 849; 1988 SCCR 434.

The sheriff reported in the stated case in the following terms, inter alia:

THE SHERIFF (T M CROAN).— . . . When the Crown case closed the solicitor for the respondent submitted that there was no case to answer. He said that the item was not an offensive weapon per se, i e a weapon made for use for causing personal injury, and there was nothing in the evidence we had heard to indicate that the respondent intended to use it as a weapon. The appellant's depute conceded that there was no evidence of any intention to use the item as a weapon. He maintained that it was an offensive weapon per se. I allowed him an adjournment to produce some authority for that proposition. Thereafter he was unable to produce any case to that effect. He put before me a copy of the Criminal Justice Act 1988 (Offensive Weapons) Order 1988. The Schedule thereto reads: [the sheriff quoted the terms of para 1 of the Schedule set out supra and continued:]

He submitted that in terms of the statutory instrument the item could be held to be an offensive weapon per se. The solicitor for the accused submitted that the statutory instrument did not make the item an offensive weapon per se.

I took the view that there was no case to answer.

A Section 141 of the Criminal Justice Act 1988 strikes at any person who manufactures, sells or hires or offers for sale or hire, exposes or has in his possession for the purpose of sale or hire or lends or gives to any other person a weapon to which that section applies. It does not refer as far as I know to the Prevention of Crime Act 1953 and it was not suggested to me that it did. I have been able to find no case brought under the Prevention of Crime Act in which a "shuriken" has been found to be an offensive weapon per se. The only weapons, apart from those concerning which there is

B no doubt, about which there have been such a finding appear to be rice flails, sword sticks and flick knives. Whether an article is an offensive weapon for the purposes of s 1 of the Prevention of Crime Act 1953 is a question of fact: *R v Williamson*. The first witness simply said that the item was for throwing. Despite being given an opportunity to expand on that answer he merely repeated it. He did not characterise the item as a weapon at all. The second witness only identified the item and said that it was a throwing star. He was

C not asked and gave no opinion on what it was used for. As neither officer gave evidence that the item was a weapon, far less an offensive weapon per se, I upheld the submission and acquitted the respondent. It seemed to me when the appellant's depute referred to the statutory instrument that I was being asked in the absence of evidence to declare that the item mentioned at para 1 (h) therein was an offensive weapon per se which as I apprehend it is beyond my power. I would like to observe that in this court such charges as this

D are regularly brought and in many of them the arresting police officers display the same coyness when asked to state what their evidence is about the items which they find. Deputes who mark and frame such charges do not seem to apply their minds to what they intend to try to prove, which seems to me to be important in view of the generally cautious nature of the evidence given by the police officers in such cases. As I see it, it is not for this court to supplement the actual evidence by declaring what is or is not an offensive

E weapon per se but to deal with the matter in the light of the evidence presented.

Appeal

The sheriff posed the following question for the opinion of the High Court:

On the evidence narrated was I entitled to find no case to answer on the second charge and acquit the respondent?

F

The appeal was argued before the High Court on 5 January 1993.

Eo die the court (of consent of the accused) *answered* the question in the *negative, allowed* the appeal and *remitted* to the sheriff to proceed as accords.

The following opinion of the court was delivered by the Lord Justice General (Hope):

OPINION OF THE COURT.—This is an appeal

by the procurator fiscal at Kilmarnock against Stephen Clark, who was charged in the sheriff court at G Kilmarnock with a breach of the peace and with having with him in a public place, without lawful authority or reasonable excuse, an offensive weapon, namely a Chinese throwing star, contrary to the Prevention of Crime Act 1953, s 1 (1). He pled guilty to the charge of breach of the peace but went to trial on the second charge. A submission was made that there was no case to answer, which the sheriff upheld. Having done so, he acquitted the respondent on the ground that there was insufficient evidence to show H that the throwing star mentioned in the complaint was an offensive weapon.

The evidence for the Crown consisted of that of two police officers. They described a search which they carried out of the respondent who had been placed in a police vehicle after a disturbance. They found an item in his rear right hand trouser pocket which the first police officer said was known as a shuriken, a Chinese throwing star or a death star. When asked what its purpose was he replied it was used for throw- I ing, and the article when examined was described by the police officer as being a non-flexible metal plate with several sharp radiating points. The article itself was produced in court and was identified as label no 1. The second police officer corroborated the first on the finding of this item in the possession of the respondent. He identified it as the throwing star which they found in his possession. It was on that evidence that it was submitted that there was no case to answer.

Section 1 (4) of the Prevention of Crime Act 1953 J contains a definition of the expression "offensive weapon" which is in these terms: "'Offensive weapon' means any article made or adapted for use for causing injury to the person, or intended by the person having it with him for such use by him".

There is no suggestion in this case of any adaptation, and there was no evidence in the Crown case as to its intended use by the respondent. The article was simply found in the rear right hand trouser pocket. K The essential question was whether the nature of the article was such that there was a case to be made against the respondent that it was made for use for causing personal injury.

There are two chapters in the evidence which can be looked at for an answer to this question. Before we do that, however, we should mention that counsel who appeared for the respondent conceded that the nature of the article was such, on the evidence that had been L led for the Crown, that the only purpose which it could be said to have was for causing injury to the person. He accepted that this could be seen readily from the nature of the article itself which has been produced at this trial, and he conceded that this appeal should be allowed and the case remitted to the sheriff to proceed as accords. The learned Solicitor General concurred in that motion, but he also drew our attention to some of the remarks made by the sheriff, particularly about an alleged coyness by arresting police officers as regards items which are said to constitute offensive weapons. He suggested that some comment was necessary to assist the sheriff as to how cases of this kind should be approached.

Turning then to the chapters in the evidence which are of importance, the first is the nature of the article itself. What is plain from the narrative of the evidence, and was no doubt plain from an examination of the article, is that it consisted of a metal plate with several sharp radiating points. It was designed to be thrown. It was designed so that when it reached its target it would be likely to penetrate or at least cut it. Prima facie it was an article made for use as a weapon. This is not one of those cases where it could be suggested that the article had dual purpose, such as, for example, *Woods v Heywood*. There is no hint in the Crown evidence that this was something that could be used as a tool or an implement of some kind, nor is there any suggestion that it had any sporting or innocent recreational use. On the Crown evidence there was no innocent purpose for which a throwing star or death star might be used. Its nature was, therefore, such that the sheriff should have, without hesitation, concluded that there was a prima facie case to be made that this was an offensive weapon on the ground that it was made for use for causing injury to the person.

The second point to be made relates to a provision in the Criminal Justice Act 1988 (Offensive Weapons) Order 1988. The Schedule to that order reads as follows: [his Lordship quoted the terms of the Schedule set out supra and continued:]

One has only to compare the wording of para (h) of the Schedule with the narrative of the evidence to see that the article which is label 1 in the present case falls precisely within the description of an offensive weapon for the purposes of that Schedule. It was submitted to the sheriff that reference could be made to the statutory instrument in order to decide the question whether this was an offensive weapon per se. The sheriff rejected that argument, on the ground that that Schedule did not appear in an instrument made under the Prevention of Crime Act 1953. He considered the question before him to be a question of fact to be determined solely on the evidence. But in *Tudhope v O'Neill*, 1982 SLT at p 361, Lord Justice Clerk Wheatley made the point that assistance can be derived from other statutory provisions, whether they be in primary legislation or in a statutory instrument, which describe what are to be regarded as offensive weapons. Where one finds in a statutory instrument, which must be taken to have been approved by Parliament, that it is clearly stated that an article of the kind produced in the present case is to be regarded as an offensive weapon, with the result that in terms of s 141 of the 1988 Act it is illegal to make, sell, hire or lend or give it to another person, then it seems to follow naturally that it can be regarded for the purposes of the Prevention of Crime Act as an offensive weapon per se which will found the basis for a prosecution under that Act if a person is found in possession of it without lawful authority or reasonable excuse in a public place.

Accordingly this case seems to us to be one where on the Crown evidence there was a case to be answered. We do not accept the criticism the sheriff makes about coyness having been displayed by the police officers, since the article itself spoke so forcibly as to its nature and its use, and the question whether it was an offensive weapon was one for him, not the police officers, to decide. For these reasons we shall, as we were invited to do, answer the question in the case in the negative, and we shall remit to the sheriff with a direction that he should proceed as accords.

Counsel for Appellant, Solicitor General (Dawson, QC); Solicitor, J D Lowe, Crown Agent — Counsel for Respondent, McBride; Solicitors, Macbeth, Currie & Co, WS (for J D Bannatyne & Campbell, Stevenston).

P W F

Poterala v Uniroyal Tyres Ltd

OUTER HOUSE

TEMPORARY JUDGE J M S HORSBURGH, QC

15 JANUARY 1993

Process — Order for disclosure of information — Disclosure of home address of witness — Employers offering interview facilities at witness's place of work — Witness apprehensive about contact with pursuer's solicitors at her home address — Administration of Justice (Scotland) Act 1972 (c 59), s 1 (1A).

Section 1 (1A) of the Administration of Justice (Scotland) Act 1972 empowers the court to "order any person to disclose such information as he has" as to the identity of any persons who appear to the court to be persons who might be witnesses in any existing civil proceedings or who might be defenders in any such proceedings.

A factory nurse was considered by the solicitors acting for an employee pursuing an action of damages in respect of dermatitis allegedly contracted through the fault of the employers, to be a potential witness in the action. The solicitors sought to precognosce the nurse at her home but the employers had not disclosed her home address. They had offered facilities for the nurse to be precognosced at her place of work. The pursuer enrolled a motion for an order under s 1 (1A) of the 1972 Act for the disclosure of the home address of this nurse. It was submitted for the pursuer that his solicitors should be able to contact the witness at her home address to discover her true wishes as to where she should be precognosced, the pursuer's solicitors not being satisfied as to her wishes. The defenders opposed the motion and indicated that the witness was willing to be precognosced by arrangement made

A directly with her at her place of work and that any mail sent to her marked "private and confidential" would be received by her unopened. They also indicated that the witness would be likely to wish a third party to be present during the interview as she had felt "intimidated" and subjected to "undue aggression" on an occasion when previously precognosced by the pursuer's solicitors.

Held, (1) that the concerns of the pursuer's solicitors that interference in communicating with the witness was likely or that undue influence would be B brought to bear on her by her employers were she to be written to at her place of work were speculative and could not support the motion (p 1074B); (2) that given that the solicitors were prepared to interview the witness at her place of work it was difficult to understand the purpose of a letter addressed to her at home (p 1074C); (3) that the defenders had offered an adequate channel of communication to the witness at her place of work, and the solicitors should have accepted the offer (p 1074C-D); and motion *refused*.

C *Mooney v City of Glasgow District Council*, 1989 SLT 863, *followed*.

Opinion, that the prospective witness's apprehension about being in direct contact with the pursuer's solicitors would itself have been a sufficient reason for refusal of the motion (p 1074F).

Action of damages

D Joseph Poterala raised an action against his employers, Uniroyal Tyres Ltd, for damages for dermatitis allegedly caused by his employers' fault.

A motion was enrolled under s 1 (1A) of the Administration of Justice (Scotland) Act 1972 for an order for the disclosure of the home address of a potentially material witness, a factory nurse in the employment of the defenders. The motion was opposed.

The motion was heard by the temporary judge (J M S Horsburgh, QC).

E **Statutory provisions**

The Administration of Justice (Scotland) Act 1972, as amended by s 19 of the Law Reform (Miscellaneous Provisions) (Scotland) Act 1985, provides:

"1.—. . . (1A) Without prejudice to the existing powers of the Court of Session and of the sheriff court, those courts shall have power, subject to subsection (4) of this section, to order any person to disclose such information as he has as to the identity of any persons who appear to the court to be persons who—(a) might F be witnesses in any existing civil proceedings brought before that court or in civil proceedings which are likely to be brought; or (b) might be defenders in any civil proceedings which appear to the court to be likely to be brought."

Cases referred to

Hughes v Asda Stores, OH, Lord Marnoch, unreported.
Mooney v City of Glasgow District Council, 1989 SLT 863.

On 15 January 1993 the temporary judge *refused* the motion.   G

J M S HORSBURGH, QC.—In this action the pursuer seeks damages for dermatitis alleged to have been contracted through the fault of his employers, the defenders. On 14 January counsel for the pursuer moved a motion under s 1 (1A) of the Administration of Justice (Scotland) Act 1972, as amended, to have the defenders' solicitors ordained to disclose the home address of Mrs Margaret Price, who was said to be a material witness in the case, so that they could write H to her there for interview facilities. It is averred that the pursuer and another employee consulted Mrs Price, who was the defenders' factory nurse, about their skin conditions.

I refused the motion, and have been invited to set out my reasons for doing so.

Counsel for the pursuer stated that the defenders had refused to disclose the witness's home address, but had offered facilities to the pursuer's solicitors to precognosce her at her place of work. The pursuer's I solicitors had no objection to interviewing her there in the presence of anyone she chose, provided these were truly her wishes, a matter upon which at present they were not satisfied. To determine her wishes they required to write to her at her home address, when she might indicate her choice to be interviewed at home or at her place of work. Were they required to contact her only at or through her place of work, there could be a risk of prejudice to the pursuer through the witness feeling unduly pressurised.   J

He referred to *Mooney v Glasgow District Council* which related to a pre-litigation petition seeking an order under the same section and in which the Lord Ordinary accepted that the petitioner's solicitors should be entitled to an opportunity to approach witnesses whose home addresses the defenders would not disclose. However, he had refused to make an order since efforts had not been made to contact them at their place of work, a course to which the defenders would assent. Reference was also made to *Hughes v* K *Asda Stores*, in which Lord Marnoch gave a verbal opinion expressing concern about the possibility of undue pressure being brought to bear on defenders' witnesses in the situation of a request for contact at their place of work, with consequent prejudice to the pursuer's side. Apparently he accepted that there might be a residual potential for prejudice where the opportunity for contacting a witness at home is denied.

Counsel for the defenders opposed the motion by L reference to a fax message dated 12 January from the defenders' to the pursuer's solicitors. That indicated the witness was willing to be precognosced by arrangement made directly with her at her place of work, and that any mail addressed to her there as "private and confidential" would be received by her unopened. The fax also indicated that she would be likely to wish a third party, not connected to the case, to be present because of past experience of being precognosced by someone from the pursuer's solicitors. I was informed that opposition to the motion was

A   at the wish of the witness, who had felt "intimidated" and subjected to "undue aggression" on the occasion when previously precognosced. She therefore did not wish to be contacted by them at her home address. An arrangement for precognition made directly and privately with her at her place of work would be adequate to satisfy the interests of the pursuer's solicitors and the witness. A special reason thus existed why the motion should not be granted.

The reasons for my refusing the motion were as follows.

B   First, counsel for the pursuer was unable to make any positive or concrete assertion based on fact that interference in communicating with the witness was likely, or that undue influence would be brought to bear on her by the defenders, were she to be written to at her place of work. The concern expressed was speculative and hypothetical. In my view that was not an adequate foundation for the motion.

C   Secondly, in the absence of any substantial explanation I found it difficult to see how a letter addressed to the witness at home was more likely to enable her to make a free and unfettered choice as to the locus of the interview than one addressed to her at her place of work. Given that the pursuer's solicitors were in fact prepared to interview her there, this point seemed to me to be rather artificial.

Thirdly, I was satisfied that the arrangement offered by the defenders' solicitors gave the pursuer's solicitors an adequate channel of communication with the
D   witness. Where, as here, responsible solicitors have made plain that there would be no interception of mail addressed to the witness, that offer should have been accepted. That means of contact had been rejected, at present at least, without any test of its satisfactoriness having been made. I therefore find myself in agreement with the opinion of Lord Kirkwood in *Mooney v Glasgow District Council* on this matter. I consider that I had insufficient information on the circumstances of and the basis of the decision in *Hughes v*
E   *Asda Stores* available to me for that case to be of assistance to me in deciding this issue. From what I was told that decision would appear to render the number of cases in which the refusal of an order of disclosure would be appropriate very few indeed. From my reading of the statutory provisions that would be a surprising result.

For these reasons it did not appear to me that prima facie it was in the interests of justice that the motion should be granted. Even if I had thought that to be the
F   case, I would have refused the motion, since I was of the opinion that the witness's apprehension about being in direct contact with the pursuer's solicitors constituted special reason why the motion should not be granted. To that extent the information about the witness's attitude differs from the situation in *Mooney* where letters offered no explanation for the witnesses' refusals to have their home addresses disclosed.

I found the defenders entitled to the expenses of the motion.

————————

Counsel for Pursuer, C A L Scott; Solicitors, Robin Thompson & Partners — Counsel for Defenders, Andrew G *Smith; Solicitors, McClure Naismith Anderson & Gardiner.*

J P D

Rea v Parole Board for   H
Scotland

OUTER HOUSE
LORD PENROSE
27 FEBRUARY 1991

Administrative law — Judicial review — Parole Board — Legitimate expectation — Recommendation advising release on licence — Acceptance of recommendation by I *Secretary of State — Subsequent reversal by Parole Board of recommendation — Whether legitimate expectation of hearing on grounds for reversal — Prisons (Scotland) Act 1989 (c 45), ss 18, 22 and 28.*

A prisoner was advised that his release on licence had been recommended by the Parole Board for a date later the same year, and that the Secretary of State had accepted that recommendation. He was transferred to an open prison to train for freedom. Prior to his release he was called before the prison governor in J connection with matters involving suspected irregularities in the use of a visitor pass. Following adjudication, the prisoner was returned to a closed prison. He was invited to make representations against the transfer, and did so. Although further representations on his behalf were made to the Parole Board, the board withdrew its recommendation that he be released on licence. The prisoner sought reduction of the board's decision, suspension of it, and a declarator that he was entitled to (1) written notice K of the grounds on which the decision had been made; (2) a hearing to consider whether those grounds were established, at which he could be represented and lead evidence; and (3) reconsideration by the board of its decision in light of the hearing. The prisoner claimed title and interest on the basis that, upon intimation of a release date, there had emerged a legitimate expectation that the intention to release would be implemented, and that there would be no deviation from that intention because of a change in the board's L recommendation unless the board had satisfied the procedural requirements of which the prisoner sought declarator.

Held, (1) that the Secretary of State could exercise his discretion to release on licence only if that act was supported by a recommendation of the Parole Board at the date it was carried into effect (p 1077E); (2) that there was no basis in the Act for the rights contended for by the prisoner, and the discretion conferred on the board and the Secretary of State should not be

A hampered so as to inhibit the continuous reassessment by the board of its recommendations (pp 1077G and 1077L-1078A); (3) that the petitioner had not established any grounds either by express promise or by implication, for the legitimate expectation of the procedural steps desiderated (pp 1078F-G and 1079C-E); and application *refused*.

Observed, that while it was for the court to enforce the requirement that in carrying out their respective functions in accordance with the scheme, the board and the Secretary of State had to act fairly,
B it was inappropriate to introduce into an administrative scheme rules derived from judicial schemes (p 1078A-C).

———————

Petition for judicial review

James Rea petitioned for judicial review of a decision by the Parole Board for Scotland which had reversed its earlier decision to recommend his release on licence. The board and the Secretary of State for
C Scotland lodged answers. The petitioner sought reduction of the decision, suspension of it, and a declarator that the petitioner was entitled to (1) written notice of the grounds on which the decision was made, (2) a hearing to consider whether the grounds on which the decision was made were established, with an opportunity to the petitioner to be represented and to lead evidence there, and (3) have the board reconsider its decision in light of the hearing.

D The case came before the Lord Ordinary (Penrose) for a first hearing.

Statutory provisions

The Prisons (Scotland) Act 1989 provides:

"18.—. . . (2) It shall be the duty of the [Parole] Board to advise the Secretary of State with respect to — (a) the release on licence under section 22, 25 or 26 of this Act and the recall under section 25, 28, 31 or 32 of this Act of persons whose cases have been
E referred to the Board by the Secretary of State; (b) the conditions of such licences and the variation or cancellation of such conditions; and (c) any other matter so referred which is connected with the recall of persons to whom the said section 31 or 32 applies or the release on licence or recall of persons to whom the said section 22, 25 or 26 applies. . . .

"22.—(1) The Secretary of State may, if recommended to do so by the Parole Board, release on
F licence a person, who is serving a sentence of imprisonment, other than imprisonment for life, or a sentence of detention in a young offender institution imposed in England and Wales, after he has served not less than one-third of his sentence or the specified period, whichever expires the later.

"(2) In subsection (1) above, 'the specified period' means 12 months or such period, not more than 12 months, as the Secretary of State may by order provide. . . .

"28.—(1) Where the Parole Board recommends the

recall of any person who is subject to a licence under
G section 22 or 26 of this Act, the Secretary of State may revoke that person's licence and recall him to prison.

"(2) The Secretary of State may revoke the licence of any such person and recall him as aforesaid without consulting the Board, where it appears to him that it is expedient in the public interest to recall that person before such consultation is practicable.

"(3) A person recalled to prison under the foregoing provisions of this section may make representations in writing with respect to his recall and shall on his
H return to prison be informed of the reasons for his recall and of his right to make such representations."

Cases referred to

Att Gen of Hong Kong v Ng Yuen Shiu [1983] 2 AC 629; [1983] 2 WLR 735; [1983] 2 All ER 346.
Council of Civil Service Unions v Minister for the Civil Service [1985] AC 374; [1984] 3 WLR 1174; [1984] 3 All ER 935.
Findlay, Re [1985] AC 318; [1984] 3 WLR 1159;
I [1984] 3 All ER 801.
Hamilton v Secretary of State for Scotland, OH, 18 December 1990, unreported (1991 GWD 10-624).
Lakin Ltd v Secretary of State for Scotland, 1988 SLT 780.
Payne v Lord Harris of Greenwich [1981] 1 WLR 754.
R v Parole Board, ex p Bradley [1991] 1 WLR 134; [1990] 3 All ER 828.
R v Secretary of State for the Home Department, ex p
J *Gunnell* [1984] Crim LR 170; affd [1985] Crim LR 105.

Textbook referred to

Stair Memorial Encyclopaedia, Vol 1, para 267.

On 27 February 1991 the Lord Ordinary *dismissed* the petition.

LORD PENROSE.—At the first hearing of this
K application for judicial review counsel for the Parole Board for Scotland, and the Secretary of State for Scotland, intimated that the narrative of events set out in the petition was substantially agreed or could at least be accepted for the purposes of the discussion. Both parties lodged documents to which reference was made in the course of the debate. It was further agreed that information available to the court disclosed an issue of law which could properly be dealt with at this stage, accepting the petitioner's averments of fact and
L the representations made by him or on his behalf pro veritate.

The petitioner seeks reduction of the decision of the board taken on 5 June 1990, suspension of that decision, and declarator of his entitlement to (1) written notice of the grounds on which the decision was made; (2) a hearing to consider whether or not the grounds on which the decision was made were established, with an opportunity to the petitioner to be represented and to lead evidence at such hearing; and (3) have the board reconsider its decision in the light of the representations made and evidence led at such a hearing. In addition, the petitioner seeks such further orders as might be thought by the court to be just and reasonable in all of the circumstances of the case. The particular remedy sought was modified in the course of discussion.

The petitioner was sentenced to 12 years' imprisonment in 1983 for offences under the Misuse of Drugs Act 1971. His earliest date of release, with the benefit of full remission, was in May 1991. In accordance with the Secretary of State's general policy, adopted in 1983, of refusing, in all but the most exceptional of cases, to exercise his power to release on licence certain classes of offenders, and in particular drug traffickers, until the final months of their sentences, the earliest date at which the petitioner might have been released on licence would have been in September 1990. The earliest date at which the board would have considered whether to make a recommendation in favour of release on licence would have been in March 1990 accordingly.

The board considered the petitioner's position on 20 March 1990, and recommended that he be released on licence from 11 September 1990. The petitioner was informed. He was further informed that the recommendation had been accepted by the Secretary of State, and that it was intended that he should be released on 11 September. The petitioner was transferred from closed conditions to Penninghame open prison, where there are facilities for training for freedom.

On or about 21 May 1990, the petitioner was called before the acting governor of Penninghame in connection with allegations of irregularities in dealing with visitor passes and allegations of theft of pot plants from the prison grounds. Following the acting governor's adjudication on the report the petitioner was transferred to Shotts prison, and returned to closed conditions. He was invited to make representations against the transfer, and sought legal advice. Subsequently he made representations in writing. In addition solicitors acting on his behalf entered into correspondence with the board and with the Secretary of State. The background to the rather sparse averments in paras 5 and 6 of the petition appears from the correspondence and representations.

The petitioner's solicitors wrote to an officer of the board on 28 May. The letter referred to the invitation to make representations, and stated the writer's inference that that had been done with a view to there taking place some process of review of the decision to release the petitioner on parole. Drawing on both sources, the petitioner's position appears to have been as follows. The petitioner had made arrangements with the authorities at Penninghame for visitor passes for three successive Sundays, namely 6, 13 and 20 May. The visit on 6 May took place as planned. On 13 May there was to be one visitor, his brother, and on 20 May the visitors were to be a Mr Pollock, his wife and children. In the event Mr Pollock arrived on 13 May along with the petitioner's brother. The peti-

tioner was allowed to see him on that occasion. Because Mr Pollock could not come again on 20 May, that day was then free. The petitioner retained the pass issued in respect of the intended visit of Mr Pollock and his family. That was said to be in accordance with the usual arrangements at Penninghame, where prisoners simply presented the passes to the officer on duty at the time of the visit. The sources diverge at this point. The solicitors state that in the course of the week ended 20 May the petitioner was contacted by a friend of his, Mr Bernard Laughlan, who was anxious to visit him, and that the petitioner who now had an extra visit pass for 20 May suggested that Mr Laughlan visit that day, to which Mr Laughlan agreed. The petitioner's statement of representations narrated that in a telephone conversation with his niece she asked if she and her boyfriend, Mr Laughlan, might visit when they were in the area, and 20 May was suggested because it was free. In each case it was stated that the petitioner simply forgot to make the administrative changes required to substitute the new visitors' names despite the fact that that would have been a simple and routine exercise. On 20 May, according to the solicitors' letter, Mr Laughlan arrived at the prison in the company of a Mr Roy, Mrs Roy and a child or children. The visitor pass in the name of Mr Pollock and his family was handed over to the officer on duty by the petitioner and all were admitted. It is said that Mr Laughlan and Mr Roy were both former prisoners, and knew a number of Penninghame prisoners at the time. In the course of the visit, they separated themselves from the petitioner, and went off on their own to speak to other prisoners. After leaving the prison at the end of visiting time, the visitors entered a car, drove a short distance and stopped. Mr Roy left the car and was in the act of uplifting pot plants which had been stolen from the prison when he was apprehended.

At the adjudication on 21 May, it is said, there was no evidence that the petitioner was involved in the theft, but the reporting officer stated that he "had reason to believe" that the petitioner was involved. The petitioner was denied the opportunity to lead evidence. The acting governor indicated that the petitioner had breached his trust, and was being returned to closed conditions. The acting governor did not indicate whether this related to the theft or to the abuse of the passes. The solicitors' letter ended with a plea on behalf of the petitioner that the adjudication should not interfere with his release in September. By letter dated 31 May 1990 the board's deputy secretary acknowledged the solicitors' letter of 28 May, intimated that the incident would be reported to the board in the near future, and gave an assurance that the petitioner's own representations and the letter would be made available to the board at the appropriate time. The board dealt with the matter on 5 June and withdrew its recommendation to the Secretary of State that the petitioner be released on licence. After further correspondence the present application was presented.

The petitioner did not complain of the failure of the Secretary of State to release him on licence. It was accepted that, in terms of s 22 (1) of the Prisons (Scotland) Act 1989, the Secretary of State could release the petitioner only on the recommendation of the board. The petitioner's complaint was with the board. On the intimation of a specific date for release, it was said, there emerged a legitimate expectation that the intention to release would be implemented, and that there would be no deviation from that intention because of a change in the board's recommendation unless the board satisfied certain procedural requirements. The petitioner was entitled to notice of the specific grounds on which the board were to reconsider their recommendation. He was entitled to an opportunity to make representations as to the truth or otherwise of the allegations made against him, and that required specific notice of those allegations. He was entitled to an opportunity to be heard, to be present when his case was considered, and to make oral representations in that connection. He was entitled to be represented, and to lead evidence if he thought fit. All of these rights, or privileges, derived from the legitimate expectation created by the intimation to him of a specific date for release.

Counsel accepted that the board's consideration whether to recommend a prisoner for release on licence was not generally amenable to control by such procedural requirements. Had the Secretary of State refused to release him, the petitioner would have had no complaint even if the board's recommendation had been favourable. The legitimate expectation derived solely from the fact that a release date had been intimated.

The statutory context is found in ss 18, 22 and 28 of the 1989 Act. I was referred by petitioner's counsel to the Local Review Committee (Scotland) Rules 1967, and to the report of the Kincraig committee. Neither party relied on these sources in argument. The rules form an important element in the total system provided for the regulation of the power to release on licence. In the light of the parties' submissions I shall refer in general to the operations of the board only in this opinion. Section 18 prescribes an advisory role for the board relative to the exercise by the Secretary of State of his functions. Section 22 (1) stipulates the conditions which must be satisfied at the date of release. These include a recommendation of the board. It is clear that the Secretary of State may exercise his discretion to release on licence only if that act is supported by a recommendation of the board at the date it is carried into effect. Section 28 provides for the revocation of a licence in certain circumstances. There are two distinct phases in the treatment of the offender, separated by the act of the Secretary of State in releasing a prisoner on licence. The petitioner's contentions in this case would create an intermediate phase; moreover it would appear to be a phase in which the offender had considerably more ample rights than have been provided by Parliament under s 28 (3). Faced with the difficulty created by s 28 (3) counsel for the petitioner accepted that the petitioner could not have more ample rights as a matter of legitimate expectation than s 28 (3) provided for those within the scope of that provision.

The statute does not provide any basis for the requirements desiderated in this case, whether in their more ample form, or in the form of rights within limits derived from a consideration of the terms of s 28 (3). On the contrary, s 28 (3) would either be inconsistent with the existence of such rights or be redundant if they existed. If the equivalent rights applied as a matter of legitimate expectation from an intimation of an intention to release on licence, one would expect no less in respect of an intention to recall. In terms of the statutory scheme, there is no right to notice until after recall. Section 28 (1) envisages that the board may recommend recall and that the Secretary of State may act on that recommendation. The prisoner must be informed of the reasons for his recall, and his right to make representations in writing in respect of that recall. If the prisoner does make representations, the Secretary of State must then refer the matter to the board. There is no provision for a hearing or for the other incidents of inquiry sought in this case. As it happened, in the present case, the petitioner appeared to have been made aware of the reasons for his appearing before the acting governor of Penninghame, and to have been invited to make representations which were considered by the board. Had the Act applied, it may be that he could have demanded no more under its terms. Whether that be so or not, the petition proceeds on the view that such rights existed before the exercise of the Secretary of State's discretion under s 22, at a stage at which Parliament had made no provision of the nature sought.

There has been a consistent refusal to add to the obligations of those responsible for the administration of the Secretary of State's functions in relation to release on licence. No significant distinction exists between the board and the Secretary of State in this connection: *R v Parole Board, ex p Bradley*. In *Payne v Lord Harris of Greenwich*, a prisoner who had applied unsuccessfully for release on licence sought declarations that he was entitled to know the reasons for refusal, so that he could be better prepared for his next application. His application was refused. Lord Denning's observations on p 757 come close to a direct answer to the petitioner in this case: "It seems to me that the statute and the rules together form a comprehensive code. They set out the procedure in such detail that there is nothing more needed to supplement it. They set out the occasions when a man is entitled to make representations; and when he is to be informed of reasons. In particular, it is specifically provided in section 62 (3) of the Act of 1967 that, if he is recalled, he 'shall on his return to prison be informed of the reasons for his recall'. There is no corresponding provision when he is refused a licence. That goes to show that the legislature did not think that reasons were necessary."

Shaw LJ made the same point at pp 762-763, as did Brightman LJ at p 767. The decision in *Payne* was treated as authoritative in *Bradley*. I was referred also to *R v Secretary of State for the Home Department, ex p Gunnell*, where a similar approach was adopted. Counsel for the respondents founded strongly on the

argument that the statutory code was comprehensive
A and self contained, and that the discretion conferred
on the board and the Secretary of State should not be
hampered so as to inhibit the continuous reassessment
of its recommendations by the board. In my opinion
that argument was sound. The statutory scheme distinguished the procedural requirements at its several
stages. It has been recognised that it is for the court
to enforce a requirement that in carrying out their
respective functions in accordance with the scheme
the board and the Secretary of State, and in appro-
B priate cases the local review committee, must act
fairly. However, it does not follow that the court
should, in interpreting and enforcing the duty to act
fairly, in every case elaborate additional procedural
requirements in respect of which the duty to act fairly
would again be enforced incidentally. In particular it
is inappropriate to introduce into the operations of an
administrative scheme rules derived from systems
developed for the resolution of disputes inter partes or
for the trial of crimes and offences. It is necessary to
C avoid substituting a scheme conceived by the court for
that prescribed by the legislature. I refer to the speech
of Lord Scarman in *Re Findlay* [1985] AC at p 339 for
a further illustration of the court's view of the need to
avoid fettering the discretion conferred by this legislation.

The petitioner's contentions reflected a broad
approach to judicial control of administrative actions
and I turn to the submissions which were made. The
language of the petitioner's contentions was derived
D from Professor Bradley's article in Vol 1 of the *Stair
Memorial Encyclopaedia* at para 267, Lord Fraser of
Tullybelton's speech in *CCSU v Minister for the Civil
Service* [1985] AC at p 401 and the opinion of the
Lord Justice Clerk in *Lakin Ltd v Secretary of State for
Scotland*, 1988 SLT at pp 787-788. The petitioner's
counsel indicated that in the light of Lord Milligan's
decision in *Hamilton v Secretary of State for Scotland*,
his whole argument would be based on domestic law.
In *CCSU* Lord Fraser identified the sources of legiti-
E mate expectation as being either an express promise
given on behalf of the public authority or a regular
practice which the claimant could reasonably expect to
continue. *CCSU* was an example of the latter category.
Att Gen of Hong Kong v Ng Yuen Shiu was an example
of the former. These are the authorities cited by the
Lord Justice Clerk in *Lakin* in a passage to which I
will return. It was accepted that there was no practice
of the kind identified by Lord Fraser to support the
contention of the petitioner in this case. Counsel sub-
F mitted that there was implied in the intimation of an
intention to release the petitioner a promise that if he
were not released it would be for some particular
reason, that a decision not to release would not be
arrived at without inquiry, and that he would have the
rights to notice of the reasons, and to make representations and so on for which he contended, so far as was
consistent with the limiting effect of s 28 (3).

It might be sufficient to dismiss the petitioner's contentions on the basis that they fell far short of the
express promise required by Lord Fraser's comments

in *CCSU* as the source of a legitimate expectation. But
in any case it appeared to me to be clear that in the G
absence of an express promise, there was, in substance, no room for implication of the kind of rights
contended for. The general nature of the Parole
Board's functions in respect of release on licence was
examined at length in *Payne*. I would not have found
it easy to accept all of the submissions made on behalf
of the Parole Board in that case. For example, it does
not appear to me to be an attractive or persuasive argument that if there were an obligation to give reasons
for a decision, the decision making body might seek to H
avoid the substance of its obligations by resorting to
short and stereotyped formulations which were less
than full and informative. Again I would hesitate to
accept as a universally valid proposition that the
prisoner would know of the factors adverse to his
release on licence, and therefore would not require
intimation of the reasons of the decision making body.
Such a view gives no weight to the risk of simple error
or to the possibility of misrepresentation, both of
which must exist in any human activity. But the
opinions set out clearly and powerfully the nature of I
the discretion and the context for the actions of the
several bodies involved in its exercise. I refer generally
to the opinion of Shaw LJ, and in particular to his
comments at p 760 where he said: "The Secretary of
State does not, in directing release on licence, accede
to a claim by a prisoner to the benefit of the statute.
As I see it, he is doing an executive act which is considered to be justified in the immediate interests of the
prisoner and, no less importantly, in the general
interests of society when those interests appear to J
coincide. Whether they do so or not, it is the responsibility of the Parole Board to determine and to make
their recommendation to the Secretary of State in
accordance with their determination."

Brightman LJ distinguished the function of investigating charges, and identified a number of factors
which entered into the exercise of the board's functions. There would be a consideration of the prisoner's
file, including all reports which had been made from
time to time by prison staff and reports prepared for K
the purposes of review. The board would require to
assess the prisoner's character and his likely reaction
to a free environment, and also, perhaps more importantly, make an assessment of the public interest.

The emphasis on the particular interests of the petitioner which is implicit in the present application,
ignores the context in which the board must operate
in performing its duties. The petitioner seeks notice of
the reasons for reconsideration of the recommenda- L
tion, and procedures thereafter, which might readily
be compared to the prosecution of a summary offence
of which he was accused. That approach was rejected
by Brightman LJ, in my opinion correctly.

The question of the release of a prisoner on licence
cannot be reduced to one of private right, or even
private privilege, affecting only the prisoner. It is a
matter of general public concern in which the weighing of the respective interests of the individual and the
public must play a significant part. The range of

A factors considered by the board in advising the Secretary of State is potentially wide and, until the date of release on licence, must involve a continuing process in which new facts are additive, extending the total number of relevant considerations, and not necessarily to be dealt with in substitution for material previously available. The weight given to any particular factor must depend on the context provided by the whole information and the body of policy known to and applied by the board. The remedy sought by the petitioner in this case would appear to reduce the issue at

B the stage of reassessment of the recommendation to the particular issue identified in the debate, divorced from the background in all respects.

In *Lakin*, at pp 787-788, the Lord Justice Clerk said: "'Procedural impropriety' or 'procedural irregularity' may arise where there has been a failure to comply with procedural rules; but it may also arise where there has simply been unfairness in the manner in which a decision has been arrived at. This will be so particularly if an individual who has the legitimate

C expectation of a hearing is denied any hearing before a decision affecting him is taken."

The petitioner's counsel founded strongly on that statement, extending it to encompass the whole procedural steps elaborated in the petition. He was unable to identify any source for his propositions other than the implication he sought to derive from the intimation of a release date. Intimation of a release date is not a factor peculiar to the petitioner. Intimation of an intended release date is a common step, taken in the

D interests of the prisoner who would otherwise be released without preparation. The petitioner's contentions are of general importance. It would be unfortunate if the board were inhibited from intimating its recommendations in time to enable the prisoner to prepare for release by apprehension that any reassessment would be encompassed about by a series of precise procedural requirements amenable to judicial control. The probable result of the regime sought by the petitioner would be a reluctance to give any inti-

E mation, with consequent frustration of the training for freedom schemes in relation to potential licensees. That would be highly undesirable. In the general context of the operation of the system of release on licence, I am of opinion that there is no room for the inference on which the petitioner's case relies.

In the circumstances I am of the opinion that the petitioner has not established any grounds for the legitimate expectation of the procedural steps desider-

F ated. I therefore refuse the application.

Counsel for Petitioner, Di Rollo; Solicitors, Drummond & Co, WS — Counsel for Respondents, M G Clarke, QC; Solicitor, R Brodie, Solicitor to the Secretary of State for Scotland.

R N T

HM Advocate v Boyle

G

HIGH COURT OF JUSTICIARY
THE LORD JUSTICE GENERAL (HOPE),
LORDS COWIE AND MAYFIELD

2 OCTOBER 1992

Justiciary — Procedure — Retrial — Accused charged with murder in original proceedings but convicted of culpable homicide "without murderous intent" — Crown authorised to bring new prosecution following appeal against conviction — Crown reindicting for murder — H *Whether proceedings competent — Whether oppressive — Criminal Procedure (Scotland) Act 1975 (c 21), ss 254 (1) (c) and 255 (1).*

Section 254 (1) (c) of the Criminal Procedure (Scotland) Act 1975 provides that the High Court may dispose of an appeal against conviction by setting aside the verdict of the trial court and granting authority to bring a new prosecution in accordance with s 255. Section 255 (1) provides that where such authority is I granted, a new prosecution may be brought charging the accused with the same or any similar offence arising out of the same facts, and the proceedings out of which the appeal arose shall not be a bar to such new prosecution, provided that no sentence may be passed on conviction under the new prosecution which could not have been passed on conviction under the earlier proceedings.

An accused person was tried inter alia for murder but was convicted of culpable homicide, the jury J adding the rider that it was "without murderous intent". He appealed on the ground of misdirection by the trial judge, and the appeal court set aside the conviction and granted authority for the Crown to bring a new prosecution in accordance with s 255. The accused was reindicted for murder and at a preliminary diet argued that it was incompetent, or in any event oppressive, for the Crown to charge him again with murder since the jury's verdict implied his acquittal on the murder charge. The trial judge held that it was competent but oppressive for the accused K to be charged again with murder, and dismissed the charge. The Crown appealed.

Held, (1) that the effect of setting aside a verdict was that the verdict was no longer available to be used for any purpose, verdicts which included deletions from the narrative, verdicts which had riders attached to them and verdicts which reduced the crime libelled to a lesser crime all being in the same position (p 1083I-K); (2) that the power in s 255 (1) related to L the original indictment and the charge or charges in respect of which the accused was convicted and to which he directed his appeal, so that the Crown's bringing a new prosecution for murder was competent (p 1084B-D and F); (3) that as the sole basis for the argument based on oppression was a comparison between the charge in the present indictment and the verdict at the previous trial, and as that verdict had been set aside and ceased to exist, the trial judge had erred in law (p 1084I-J); and appeal *allowed* and case *remitted* to trial judge to proceed as accords.

Observed, that the purpose of the proviso to s 255 (1) was to deal with those cases where the sentence had been regulated by statute and the statutory penalty on conviction for the offence had been increased since the date of the original conviction (p 1084E-F).

Indictment

Daniel Boyle was charged at the instance of the rt hon the Lord Rodger of Earlsferry, Her Majesty's Advocate, on an indictment which libelled, inter alia, the following charge: "(2) on 27 July 1991 in Craigton Road, Glasgow, you did assault William Murray Bennett, formerly residing at 133 Elderpark Street, Glasgow, repeatedly stab him on the body with a knife and did murder him". The accused sought a preliminary diet at which he moved the trial judge (Lord Murray) to dismiss charge 2 as incompetent or in any event oppressive.

Statutory provisions

The Criminal Procedure (Scotland) Act 1975, as amended, provides:

"254.—(1) The High Court may, subject to subsection (4) below, dispose of an appeal against conviction by — (a) affirming the verdict of the trial court; (b) setting aside the verdict of the trial court and either quashing the conviction or substituting therefor an amended verdict of guilty: Provided that an amended verdict of guilty must be one which could have been returned on the indictment before the trial court; or (c) setting aside the verdict of the trial court and granting authority to bring a new prosecution in accordance with section 255 of this Act. . . .

"255.—(1) Where authority is granted under section 254 (1) (c) of this Act, a new prosecution may be brought charging the accused with the same or any similar offence arising out of the same facts; and the proceedings out of which the appeal arose shall not be a bar to such new prosecution: Provided that no sentence may be passed on conviction under the new prosecution which could not have been passed on conviction under the earlier proceedings."

Cases referred to

Advocate (HM) v Stewart, 1980 JC 84.
Stuurman v HM Advocate, 1980 SLT 182; 1980 SLT (Notes) 95; 1980 JC 111.

On 27 August 1992 the trial judge *dismissed* charge 2 as oppressive.

LORD MURRAY.—Counsel for the minuter presented a persuasive argument that the Crown, if given authority by the court to bring a fresh prosecution on appeal, cannot competently libel a more serious offence in the new indictment than that for which the appellant was originally convicted. The relevant charge in this case was murder, but the jury convicted of culpable homicide, explaining in their verdict that they found that the minuter did not have murderous intent. It was pointed out that Parliament had expressly provided for this limitation in corresponding legislation for England and Wales.

The advocate depute, in reply, founded upon the express terms of ss 254 and 255 of the 1975 Act which prima facie entitle the Crown to libel the same or similar charges. Though there is much to be said for the interpretation advanced for the minuter, I am not persuaded, at this point, that it is correct in law.

Accordingly, I am not prepared to hold that it is incompetent for the Crown now to proceed on a charge of murder. Further, I note that in the opinion which allowed the minuter's appeal, the court were asked to impose the restriction on the Crown now sought to be made, but they declined to do so. For all these reasons I am content to assume that the Crown may competently proceed on the present indictment.

A second argument for the minuter is, however, a great deal more difficult to dispose of. It was urged, and not seriously disputed for the Crown, that in Scotland the court retains an inherent power, despite the Lord Advocate's mastery of the instance, to prevent a prosecution if it would be oppressive for it to proceed.

The advocate depute sought to restrict the application of this principle to certain obvious instances. I do not think that oppression can be defined by exhaustive enumeration and I am content to take it as meaning fundamental unfairness, particularly for the accused. The strength of the argument on oppression in this case, it appears to me, is that the jury at the original trial, having heard oral evidence on oath, specifically excluded murderous intent on the part of the minuter. That has to be set against the Crown's firm opinion that the evidence in their possession wholly justifies a charge of murder. To the extent that there are two contrasting reasonable assessments of the available evidence instead of the Crown's alone, which must ordinarily be inviolate, there is plainly room for the court to make its own assessment of the fairness or otherwise of the Crown's proposed course of action.

There is room then for me to make an assessment of that element rather than leave it, as I was invited to do, entirely to the discretion of the Crown. The Crown, however, further pointed out that as the appeal court had set aside the verdict, strictly speaking, nothing remained of it and no regard could any longer be had to the jury's opinion on the minuter's criminal intent. I do not accept that this is necessarily the case, particularly with unusual cases such as the present where the jury have chosen to make an assertion of fact which was not a necessary part of their verdict.

What is important, in my opinion, is whether any assertion made by the jury may be vitiated by the very misdirection which led to their verdict being set aside.

The advocate depute touched upon, but did not develop, a point which has troubled me. The misdirection here was substantially that the jury may have had the impression from the trial judge's charge that self defence, which was the centrepiece of the defence, was not open to them to uphold. There was clearly a risk in the original trial that the jury convicted of the lesser crime of culpable homicide where they might have acquitted completely had they felt free to accept the special defence. Is there a somewhat similar risk that self defence pled in the face of a charge of culpable homicide rather than murder might reduce the impact of the defence?

If the advocate depute is right in his assessment of the evidence, the jury might have the impression that the accused was lucky not to be charged with murder and so pass too easily to a verdict of culpable homicide despite the special defence. This is indeed a material risk, but I have come to the conclusion that it is not one which should deflect me from making an assessment of the fundamental fairness of this prosecution proceeding on the principles which I have already outlined.

In the result, I am prepared to treat the jury's conclusion on criminal intent at the original trial as untainted by misdirection and as standing, as a factual opinion, even although the verdict is set aside in its entirety. Making the best assessment which I can on fundamental fairness I have reached the view that, in the very special — indeed unique — circumstances of this case it would amount to oppression for the present prosecution to proceed on a charge of murder rather than culpable homicide.

The Crown appealed with leave of the trial judge to the High Court.

Appeal

The appeal was argued before the High Court on 23 September 1992.

On 2 October 1992 the court *allowed* the appeal, *reversed* the decision of the trial judge and *remitted* to him to proceed as accords.

The following opinion of the court was delivered by the Lord Justice General (Hope):

OPINION OF THE COURT.—This is an appeal under s 76A of the Criminal Procedure (Scotland) Act 1975 against a decision taken at a preliminary diet by which the principal charge in the indictment was dismissed as oppressive. This was a charge of murder, which had been brought against the respondent under s 255 of the Act following the setting aside of the verdict of the trial court in previous proceedings for the same offence [1993 SLT 577]. Authority was then granted under s 254 (1) (c) for the bringing of a new prosecution in accordance with s 255. The verdict which was set aside was that the respondent, although charged with murder, was guilty of culpable homicide. It was submitted by the respondent at the preliminary diet that it was incompetent and in any event oppressive for him to be charged once again with murder, since the effect of the jury's verdict was to acquit him on that charge. The judge was not prepared to hold that it was incompetent for the Crown to proceed on the present indictment on a charge of murder. But he was satisfied, having regard to the jury's verdict, that it was oppressive for the charge to be one of murder rather than of culpable homicide.

The original indictment contained five charges which were in precisely the same terms as those in the indictment in the present proceedings. Charge 1 was a charge of breach of the peace. It alleged that the respondent conducted himself in a disorderly manner and formed part of a disorderly crowd, which brandished various instruments, shouted, swore, threatened violence to the lieges and threw bottles and other similar objects at them in a road near to a public house. Charge 2 was a charge of murder, in which it was averred that the respondent stabbed the deceased on the body with a knife on the date and at the place libelled in charge 1. Charges 3, 4 and 5 were charges of contravening s 3 (1) (b) of the Bail etc (Scotland) Act 1980 in respect that the respondent committed the offences libelled in charges 1 and 2. Counsel for the respondent conceded at the trial that the respondent was guilty of a breach of the peace as libelled, but in regard to charge 2 there was a special defence of self defence.

The events libelled in charges 1 and 2 were closely associated. In the view of the trial judge they were effectively part of the same event, and, taking them together for this purpose, he imposed a cumulo sentence of 10 years' detention following the respondent's conviction. It was to the directions by the trial judge in regard to the issue of self defence that the respondent's appeal was then directed. For reasons which it is not necessary to discuss in this opinion the court held that these contained misdirections amounting to a miscarriage of justice and that the verdict of the jury had to be set aside. Since the miscarriage of justice came from a misdirection on the part of the trial judge, and in view of the serious nature of charge 2, the Crown were granted authority to bring a new prosecution in terms of ss 254 and 255 of the 1975 Act.

It was suggested in the course of the argument in that appeal that if authority were to be granted for a new prosecution authority should be given only for a fresh prosecution on a charge of culpable homicide, that being the offence of which the respondent had been convicted. But the advocate depute contended that it was not for the court to consider what charge might be brought in the new prosecution, this being a matter for the Crown to decide. In delivering the opinion of the court on this issue the Lord Justice Clerk said: "We agree with the advocate depute. Section 254 (1) (c) enables the court to dispose of an appeal by setting aside the verdict of the trial court and granting authority to bring a new prosecution in accordance with s 255 of the Act of 1975. Section 255 (1) makes it plain that where such authority has been granted, a new prosecution may be brought charging the accused with the same or any similar offence arising out of the same facts. In our opinion, however, it is for the Crown and not the court to determine what charges should be levelled against the accused in the new prosecution. What the court does is to grant authority for the bringing of a new prosecution leaving it to the Crown to decide whether to exercise that right, and if so what charges to bring" (1993 SLT at p 588H-I).

Although the misdirection related only to charge 2 on the indictment, the court held that it was appropriate to set aside the whole verdict of the jury, so that the jury at the new prosecution could hear all the evidence relevant and material to the issues which were the subject of the first indictment. The court's decision that it was appropriate to set aside the verdict of the jury on charges 1, 3, 4 and 5, against which the respondent had not directed any appeal, is the subject of challenge under a separate application to the nobile officium. But the argument on that matter does not affect the issues to which this appeal has been directed, since it is concerned only with the judge's decision at the preliminary diet in regard to the offence libelled in charge 2.

Although the basis for the decision at the preliminary diet was that it was oppressive for the respondent to be charged in these proceedings with murder rather than with culpable homicide, it is necessary first to examine the issue of competency. The two points are closely related to each other, since the learned advocate depute sought to rely on the competency of the charge in his submission that the judge erred in law in holding that it would amount to oppression for the charge to proceed as one of murder. And counsel for the respondent renewed the argument that it was incompetent for the respondent to be charged with murder at this stage as part of his submission that the decision at the preliminary diet should be affirmed.

Section 228 (1) of the 1975 Act provides that any person convicted on indictment may appeal, in accordance with the provisions of that Part of the Act, to the High Court against such conviction. The provisions as to the disposal of an appeal against conviction are set out in s 254 (1) of the Act, as substituted by Sched 2 to the Criminal Justice (Scotland) Act 1980, which is in these terms: [his Lordship quoted the terms of s 254 (1) and continued:]

The powers set out in paras (a) and (b) of this subsection are a re-enactment in substantially the same terms of the powers which were available to the court under ss 254 and 255 of the 1975 Act as originally enacted. But the power to grant authority to bring a new prosecution was introduced for the first time by the 1980 Act, Sched 2 to which substituted a new s 255, subs (1) of which is in these terms: [his Lordship quoted its terms and continued:]

Reference was made in the course of the argument to the power of the Court of Appeal in England in terms of s 7 of the Criminal Appeal Act 1968, as amended by s 43 of the Criminal Justice Act 1988, to order a retrial. This power is available to be exercised where the Court of Appeal has decided to allow an appeal against conviction and it appears to it that the interests of justice so require. There are significant limitations on the order which may then be pronounced. Subsection (2) of s 7 provides that a person shall not under that section be ordered to be retried for any offence other than the offence of which he was convicted at the original trial and in respect of

which his appeal has been allowed by reason of the fresh evidence, or an offence of which he could have been convicted at the original trial on an indictment for that offence, or an offence charged in any alternative count of the indictment in respect of which the jury were disabled from giving a verdict in consequence of convicting him of that offence. It is plain that if a restriction in these terms had been enacted as part of the substituted s 255 (1) of the 1975 Act the Crown would be unable to bring any charge in the new prosecution in this case other than one of culpable homicide. This is because that was the offence of which he was convicted and in respect of which his appeal was allowed. But counsel for the respondent accepted that no advantage was to be gained in seeking to draw a comparison between the Scottish and English legislation on this point, except perhaps to demonstrate that if Parliament had wished to do so it could have enacted a restriction to the same effect in express terms in the Scottish legislation. There are significant differences of approach, since the Court of Appeal in England is empowered by the statute to exercise a much closer control over the process of retrial than has been thought appropriate in Scotland. The Scottish approach is no doubt based on the principle which is fundamental to our system of criminal prosecution that the Crown is at all times the master of the instance, and it has due regard to the discretion which is vested in the public interest in the Lord Advocate.

In the course of the trial in the original indictment the trial judge explained to the jury that it was open to them to convict the respondent on charge 2 either of murder or of culpable homicide. What he said was this: "If you convict him of murder it is quite simple. You simply say in relation to charge 2, the clerk asks you what is your verdict, you reply guilty. And that is guilty of murder. If you return a guilty verdict but not of murder then you would simply say guilty of culpable homicide, and I invite you, although you are not obliged to follow my invitation, if you do return a verdict of culpable homicide to explain whether it is provocation, cruel excess or the absence of murderous intent."

In the event when the jury were asked what their verdict was on charge 2 they found him guilty of culpable homicide, as can be seen from the following exchange between the foreman and the clerk of court:

"*The Clerk*: What is your verdict in respect of the accused Daniel Boyle on charge 2?

"*The Foreman*: Guilty of culpable homicide.

"*The Clerk*: Is that verdict unanimous or by a majority?

"*The Foreman*: By a majority.

"*The Clerk*: Is there anything further you wish to add in respect of charge 2?

"*The Foreman*: It is without murderous intent."

It was to his conviction in consequence of that verdict that the respondent directed his appeal, and in

disposing of the appeal it was that verdict which was
A set aside by the appeal court.

The critical issue, so far as the question of competency is concerned, is whether the authority granted under s 254 (1) (c) to bring a new prosecution is subject to limitation because of the terms of the verdict or whether the verdict, having been set aside, is now to be left entirely out of account so that no such limitation is to be implied. Counsel for the respondent accepted that no such limitation was to be found in the express language either of s 254 (1) (c) or s 255 (1). But
B he contended that the effect of the jury's verdict was, by the clearest implication, to acquit the respondent of murder. His appeal had been directed to the conviction, not the acquittal. And if the verdict was set aside in order to remove the conviction of culpable homicide, that left the implied verdict of acquittal of murder undisturbed. It was contrary to the whole spirit of the Act that the respondent should find himself worse off as a result of a successful appeal against his conviction, as he would be if he were to be
C exposed once more to the charge of murder of which he had been acquitted. It was also illogical that that should be the result of granting authority under s 254 (1) (c) since the statute gave no right to the Crown to appeal against a conviction. The furthest it went, as the result of another amendment introduced by s 37 of the 1980 Act, was to enable the Lord Advocate to refer a question of law to the High Court for their opinion under s 263A. But it was expressly provided by subs (5) of that section that the opinion on the point referred was not to affect the acquittal in the trial.
D

Accepting as he did that no restriction similar to that in the English legislation was expressed in either s 254 (1) (c) or s 255 (1) of the 1975 Act, counsel for the respondent submitted that if there was an ambiguity it should be resolved in favour of the accused. This was, he said, in accordance with the presumption of innocence, and with the general proposition already mentioned that it was unfair for the appellant to be exposed to the risk of being worse off as a result of his
E appeal than he would be if the conviction appealed against were to be allowed to stand and the verdict of the jury was affirmed.

The contrary view which was contended for by the advocate depute is that once the verdict of the jury has been set aside it cannot be founded on for any purpose. Any rider attached to it, as was done in the present case, must also be ignored. This meant that a verdict which had the effect of convicting the accused of a lesser offence than that libelled in the charge was
F in precisely the same position as one by which part of the narrative had been deleted. The scope of the authority granted under s 254 (1) (c) was to be determined by the provisions of s 255 (1), which made no reference to the terms of the verdict. The only restriction on the authority which was granted to the Crown was that expressed in terms of that subsection, by which it was provided that the new prosecution might be brought charging the accused with the same or any similar offence arising out of the same facts. The appropriate point of reference for the purposes of this

restriction was the original indictment, not the verdict of the jury at the trial. It was the facts on the basis of G which the original prosecution had been brought, not the evidence led at the previous trial or the view formed by the jury in the light of that evidence, to which one should have regard.

We agree with counsel for the respondent that by convicting the respondent of culpable homicide the jury at the previous trial were by implication acquitting him of the charge of murder. And it is clear that the respondent's appeal against his conviction on charge 2 was directed against his conviction for culp- H able homicide in terms of the verdict of the jury on that charge. His acquittal on the charge of murder which was implied by that verdict could not have been, and was not, the subject of any appeal. In setting aside the verdict of the trial court in terms of s 254 (1) (c) the appeal court were therefore setting aside the verdict by which the respondent was convicted of culpable homicide, just as they would have been doing if they had set aside the verdict under s 254 (1) (b) as a preliminary to quashing his conviction on that I charge.

But in our opinion the effect of setting aside the verdict is that that verdict is no longer available to be used for any purpose. It must be disregarded entirely, and all its effects and implications have ceased to exist. There is no indication in the statute that, although it ceases to have effect for one purpose, it is to continue to have effect for another. Counsel for the respondent accepted that, if a verdict of guilty which merely deleted part of the narrative of a charge was set aside, J the deletion would fall to be disregarded if a new prosecution were then to be brought charging the accused with the same offence. His point was that a verdict which implied an acquittal of a more serious offence libelled in the same charge was different, because there could be no appeal against the acquittal and only the conviction on that charge was being set aside. We do not accept this distinction. In our view verdicts which include deletions from the narrative, verdicts which have riders attached to them and K verdicts which reduce the crime libelled to a lesser crime are all in the same position. Once the verdict has been set aside under s 254 (1) (c) all exculpatory elements which are expressed in or implied by it are struck out also, as a preliminary to the bringing of a new prosecution.

Much was made of the fact that it was unfair that an accused person who had been convicted of a lesser crime should be put at risk of facing the more serious L charge once again following a successful appeal. But it is necessary to have regard also to the public interest in this matter, since this is an important factor to be taken into account when consideration is given to the question whether authority should be granted for the bringing of a new prosecution. That point was recognised in the present case in the following passage of the opinion delivered by the Lord Justice Clerk: "Since the miscarriage of justice arose from misdirection on the part of the trial judge, and in view of the serious nature of charge 2, we are satisfied that it

A is in the public interest that the Crown should be granted authority to being a new prosecution in terms of ss 254 and 255 of the Criminal Procedure (Scotland) Act 1975" (1993 SLT at p 588D-E).

It is not difficult to envisage cases — a miscarriage of justice due to the existence of significant new evidence which was not available at the trial is one example — where the appropriate course in the public interest would be to wipe the slate clean so that the prosecution may begin again. What Parliament has done is to provide the court with the power to set aside B the verdict in all those cases where it is in the public interest that there should be a fresh prosecution rather than a quashing of the conviction. A single rule that once the verdict is set aside it ceases to have effect for all purposes is consistent with this approach.

The limitations on the new prosecution are to be found therefore in s 255, not in s 254 (1) (c). It is provided here that the new prosecution may be brought charging the accused with the same or any C similar offence arising out of the same facts. The use of the word "similar" shows that a measure of discretion is available to the Crown as to the offence charged, although the facts out of which it arises must be the same. No mention is made at this stage of the verdict, which has been set aside. The point of reference against which to test the sameness or similarity cannot reasonably be the precognition, nor can it be evidence which was led in the proceedings out of which the appeal arose. It must therefore be the terms D of the indictment, and where more than one charge was contained in it, the charge or charges in respect of which the accused was previously convicted and to which he directed his appeal. Taking charge 2 on the original indictment as the point of reference in the present case, we find that in the new prosecution the respondent has been charged with precisely the same offence arising out of precisely the same facts as those set out in the original charge, so this requirement has clearly been satisfied.

E There was a suggestion that to charge the respondent with murder at this stage was inconsistent with the proviso to s 255 (1), by which it is declared that no sentence may be passed on conviction under the new prosecution which could not have been passed on conviction under the earlier proceedings. But we agree with the advocate depute that the purpose of this provision is to deal with those cases where the sentence has been regulated by statute and the statutory penalty on conviction for the offence has been increased since F the date of the original conviction. In the present case the crime libelled in charge 2 in the original indictment was a common law offence, and there has been no change since the original conviction in the sentences available to the court.

For these reasons we are of the opinion that the bringing of the charge of murder on this indictment was competent. The remaining issue is whether for the Crown to charge the respondent with murder at this stage amounted to oppression. Now it is important to notice that it has not been suggested that the

action of the Crown is oppressive in the sense that the respondent would be unable to receive a fair trial. G Accordingly this is not one of those cases, such as *HM Advocate v Stewart* or *Stuurman v HM Advocate*, where the issue was whether there was a risk of prejudice to the accused so grave that no direction by a trial judge could be expected to remove it. The alleged oppression in the present case consists solely in the bringing of the charge as one of murder not one of culpable homicide.

The judge reached the view at the preliminary diet that the circumstances of this case were very special, H and indeed unique, because the jury had decided to assert in the rider to their verdict that the respondent had acted without murderous intent. Comparing this rider with the charge of murder in the present indictment, he concluded that there was a fundamental unfairness in the decision taken by the Crown. Counsel for the respondent sought to support this approach, submitting that there was here a fundamental unfairness in the action of the Crown which could not be cured by any direction from the trial I judge. But this argument, which was submitted as one of principle and thus equally applicable to all cases where the accused had been convicted of a lesser crime on the first occasion, seems to us to be misconceived. The sole basis for the argument is a comparison between the charge in this indictment and the verdict at the previous trial. But, in order to clear the way for the bringing of a new prosecution, that verdict has been set aside. It has ceased to exist, and any attempt to compare the charge on this indictment with the con- J clusion reached by the jury on the evidence led in the earlier proceedings must be rejected as irrelevant.

Furthermore it is clear from their opinion that the appeal court were well aware that the respondent was liable to be tried again for murder if authority were to be given for the bringing of a new prosecution. Yet they held that it was in the public interest that authority to this effect should be granted. In bringing charge 2 against the respondent as one of murder, K therefore, the Crown were acting within the limits of the authority given to them by the court and in accordance with the provisions of the Act. We find it impossible in these circumstances to say that, having decided that this charge should be brought against the respondent as one of murder rather than one of culpable homicide, the Crown were acting oppressively. Furthermore no case was cited to us, and we are not aware of any, in which it has been held that the court is entitled to substitute its own view of what is fair or unfair as regards the charges to be included in an L indictment for that formed by the Lord Advocate.

Accordingly we are of the opinion that the decision taken by the judge at the preliminary diet was unsound in law and must be reversed. We shall accordingly allow this appeal and remit the case to the trial judge to proceed as accords.

Counsel for Appellant, Macdonald, QC, A D; Soli-

citor, *J D Lowe, Crown Agent* — Counsel for Respondent, *Bell, QC*; Solicitors, *Macbeth, Currie & Co, WS (for Beltrami & Co, Glasgow).*

P W F

[The accused also unsuccessfully petitioned the nobile officium of the High Court of Justiciary to review the decision to set aside the verdict on all of the charges and not just the culpable homicide charge: see *Boyle, Petr,* 1993 SLT 1085. At the subsequent trial the accused was acquitted of murder on a verdict of not proven.]

Boyle, Petitioner

HIGH COURT OF JUSTICIARY

THE LORD JUSTICE GENERAL (HOPE), LORDS COWIE AND MAYFIELD

2 OCTOBER 1992

Justiciary — Procedure — Retrial — Accused convicted of five charges but appealing against only one — Appeal court setting aside verdict on all charges and granting authority to bring new prosecution — Whether within powers of appeal court to set aside whole verdict — Criminal Procedure (Scotland) Act 1975 (c 21), ss 254 (1) (c) and 255 (1).

Nobile officium — Competency — Authority to bring new prosecution — Accused convicted of five charges but appealing against only one — Appeal court setting aside verdict on all charges and granting authority to bring new prosecution — Whether within powers of appeal court to set aside whole verdict — Whether for appeal court to determine own jurisdiction — Whether decision subject to review of nobile officium — Criminal Procedure (Scotland) Act 1975 (c 21), ss 254 (1) (c), 255 (1), 262 and 281.

Section 254 (1) (c) of the Criminal Procedure (Scotland) Act 1975 provides that the High Court may dispose of an appeal against conviction by, inter alia, setting aside the verdict of the trial court and granting authority to bring a new prosecution in accordance with s 255. Section 255 (1) provides that where authority is granted, a new prosecution may be brought charging the accused with the same or any similar offence arising out of the same facts and the proceedings out of which the appeal arose shall not be a bar to such new prosecution, provided that no sentence may be passed on conviction under the new prosecution which could not have been passed on conviction under the earlier proceedings. Sections 262 and 281 each provide inter alia that all interlocutors and sentences pronounced by the High Court in solemn proceedings shall be final and conclusive and not subject to review by any court whatsoever.

An accused person was tried for breach of the peace, murder and three contraventions of s 3 (1) (b) of the Bail etc (Scotland) Act 1980. He was found guilty of culpable homicide and the other charges in the indictment and appealed against his conviction of culpable homicide on the ground of misdirection by the trial

judge in relation to self defence. On the day of the hearing the appeal court allowed the appeal, set aside the verdict of the trial court and granted authority to bring a new prosecution. No mention was then made of the extent to which the verdict was being set aside but in an opinion subsequently issued the court made clear that it considered it to be appropriate to set aside the whole verdict and not just the culpable homicide verdict. The determination as recorded by the Deputy Clerk of Justiciary stated that the appeal court "having heard counsel for the appellant and the advocate depute allowed the appeal; set aside the verdict of the High Court sitting at Glasgow on 18 November 1991 and granted authority to bring a new prosecution in accordance with s 255 of the Criminal Procedure (Scotland) Act 1975".

The accused was thereafter served with a new indictment charging him with the same five offences as appeared in the original indictment. He petitioned the nobile officium praying the High Court of Justiciary to review the decision to set aside the verdict on all of the charges and not just the culpable homicide verdict on the grounds that to set aside the whole verdict was incompetent and outwith the appeal court's powers and, in any event, unfair since the accused had not appealed against four of the convictions which were thereby set aside. It was also argued that the notice of determination was an interlocutor which the appeal court had subsequently attempted to alter by issuing their opinion in breach of ss 262 and 281 of the 1975 Act.

Held, (1) that the notice of determination was not an interlocutor and was capable of correction if it appeared later that it was not in accordance with the decision of the court (p 1088K-L); (2) that the determination was consistent with the opinion of the court which was the best evidence of what was decided by the appeal court, and was stated in terms which indicated that the court had acted within the powers conferred by the 1975 Act (pp 1088L-1089B); (3) that to a large extent it was for the High Court in the exercise of its appellate jurisdiction to determine the limits of its own jurisdiction so long as this did not conflict with what Parliament had provided, either expressly or by necessary implication, in any enactment (pp 1090I-J and 1091A-B); (4) that it was an inevitable consequence of this view that the decision which the appeal court took was not open to review in a petition to the nobile officium (p 1091B); and petition *dismissed* as incompetent.

Opinion, that it could not have been held to be unjust or oppressive for the appeal court to act as it did; it was in the public interest that the authority to bring a new prosecution should extend to the ancillary charges, since the jury in the new prosecution ought to be able to hear all the evidence bearing on the principal charge so that they could arrive at a fair verdict (pp 1090F and 1091B-C).

Observed, that it was not the practice of the High Court in appeals under solemn procedure to issue interlocutors signed by the presiding judge (p 1088I-J).

Petition to the nobile officium

A   Daniel Boyle presented a petition to the nobile officium of the High Court of Justiciary praying the court to review the decision of the criminal appeal court dated 10 July 1992 by which the appeal court purported to exercise its powers in terms of ss 254 and 255 of the Criminal Procedure (Scotland) Act 1975 and set aside the whole verdict of the jury and not simply the verdict of the jury on one charge in the indictment.

B   The petition was in the following terms:

Stat 1. That the petitioner is Daniel Boyle who went to trial in the High Court in Glasgow on an indictment containing a number of charges. Charge 1 was a charge of breach of the peace, charge 2 was a charge of murder and charges 3, 4 and 5 were ancillary contraventions of s 3 (1) (b) of the Bail etc (Scotland) Act 1980. The jury by a majority verdict found the petitioner guilty in respect of charge 1 as libelled, by a majority found him guilty of culpable homicide in respect of charge 2 on the basis that he acted "without murderous intent" and unanimously found the petitioner guilty in respect of each of charges 3, 4 and 5 as libelled.

Stat 2. The petitioner was sentenced to a period of 10 years' detention in a young offenders institution in respect of charges 1 and 2 and to three months in respect of charges 3, 4 and 5, these sentences being ordered to run consecutively to each other, but from 30 July 1991.

D   Stat 3. The appellant appealed against his conviction and sentence and at the hearing of the appeal on 10 July 1992 the appeal court set aside the verdict of the jury and allowed the Crown authority for a fresh prosecution in terms of ss 254 and 255 of the Criminal Procedure (Scotland) Act 1975. Reference is made to the interlocutor pronounced in the appeal. Thereafter on 24 August 1992 an opinion was delivered in which the court purported to set aside the verdict on charges 1, 3, 4 and 5 in addition to charge 2.

E   Stat 4. A fresh indictment libelling the original charges which appeared on the original indictment has been served on the petitioner and by means of a preliminary diet the petitioner sought to challenge the decision of the Crown to serve an indictment setting out a charge of murder, it being a more serious crime than the one of which he was originally convicted at the original diet of trial. Lord Murray agreed with that proposition and dismissed the murder charge as being

F   oppressive. The Crown sought leave to appeal against that decision and the appeal was continued until 22 September 1992 in respect of this matter.

Stat 5. During the hearing of the appeal on 10 July 1992, the court was not addressed on the question of the convictions on charges 1, 3, 4 and 5 on the indictment either by counsel for the petitioner or by the learned advocate depute. Furthermore, the court did not invite any submissions on these charges. The grounds of appeal against conviction related to the conviction for the charge of culpable homicide only

and the grounds of appeal do not relate to convictions on charges 1, 3, 4 and 5. Accordingly it is submitted   G that these convictions were not before the appeal court for their consideration.

Stat 6. Section 254 of the Criminal Procedure (Scotland) Act 1975 provides inter alia: "The High Court may . . . dispose of an appeal against conviction by (a) affirming the verdict of the trial court; (b) setting aside the verdict of the trial court and either quashing the conviction or substituting therefor an amended verdict of guilty: . . . (c) setting aside the verdict of the trial court and granting authority to bring a new prosecu-   H tion in accordance with section 255 of this Act." It is respectfully submitted that the power of the appeal court set out in s 254 of the Act of 1975 relates to the verdict of the trial court on the charge which has been appealed against. It would not have been competent for counsel for the appellant to invite the appeal court to set aside the verdict of guilty on the charges 1, 3, 4 and 5, such charges not having been appealed against and not forming any part of the grounds of appeal nor forming any part of submissions.   I

Stat 7. It is accordingly respectfully submitted that the decision of the appeal court dated 10 July 1992 and delivered on 24 August 1992 insofar as it relates to the setting aside of the verdicts of guilty on charges 1, 3, 4 and 5 is unlawful and incompetent. It is respectfully submitted that the decision of the appeal court was ultra vires, they not having power in terms of any Act of Parliament to set aside the verdict of guilty on these charges in these circumstances.   J

Stat 8. Section 281 of the Criminal Procedure (Scotland) Act 1975 provides: "All interlocutors and sentences pronounced by the High Court under the authority of this Part of this Act shall be final and conclusive and not subject to review by any court whatsoever and it shall be incompetent to stay or suspend any execution or diligence issuing forth of the High Court under the authority of the same." It is respectfully submitted that s 281 relates only to a lawful and proper interlocutor pronounced in terms of the power   K of the court set out in the Act of 1975. It is respectfully submitted that the provisions of s 281 do not prevent the petitioner competently seeking to challenge the decision which is said to be unlawful and incompetent, the appeal court not being empowered in terms of any Act of Parliament to pronounce such an interlocutor.

Stat 9. There is no provision in the Criminal Procedure (Scotland) Act 1975 for the petitioner to challenge the decision of the appeal court in these circumstances and accordingly the petitioner is under the   L necessity of applying to the nobile officium of the High Court of Justiciary for an order finding that the interlocutor of the appeal court dated 10 July 1992 relating to the decision to the extent that it purports to set aside the verdicts of guilty on charges 1, 3, 4 and 5 was unlawful, incompetent and ultra vires.

Statutory provisions

The Criminal Procedure (Scotland) Act 1975 provides:

"254.—(1) The High Court may, subject to sub-
A section (4) below, dispose of an appeal against conviction by — (a) affirming the verdict of the trial court;
(b) setting aside the verdict of the trial court and either
quashing the conviction or substituting therefor an
amended verdict of guilty: Provided that an amended
verdict of guilty must be one which could have been
returned on the indictment before the trial court; or (c)
setting aside the verdict of the trial court and granting
authority to bring a new prosecution in accordance
with section 255 of this Act. . . .

B "255.—(1) Where authority is granted under section
254 (1) (c) of the Act, a new prosecution may be
brought charging the accused with the same or any
similar offence arising out of the same facts; and the
proceedings out of which the appeal arose shall not be
a bar to such new prosecution: Provided that no sentence may be passed on conviction under the new
prosecution which could not have been passed on conviction under the earlier proceedings. . . .

C "262. Subject to the provisions of the next following
section of this Act, all interlocutors and sentences
pronounced by the High Court under this Part of this
Act shall be final and conclusive and not subject to
review by any court whatsoever and it shall be
incompetent to stay or suspend any execution or diligence issuing from the High Court under this Part of
this Act. . . .

"281. All interlocutors and sentences pronounced
by the High Court under the authority of this Part of
D this Act shall be final and conclusive, and not subject
to review by any court whatsoever, and it shall be
incompetent to stay or suspend any execution or diligence issuing forth of the High Court under the
authority of the same."

Cases referred to

Beattie, Petitioner, 1993 SLT 676; 1992 SCCR 812.
Morrison v HM Advocate, 1991 SLT 57; 1990 JC 299;
1990 SCCR 235.
E *Perrie, Petitioner*, 1992 SLT 655; 1991 SCCR 475.

The petition was argued before the High Court on
22 September 1992.

On 2 October 1992 the court *dismissed* the petition
as incompetent.

The following opinion of the court was delivered by
the Lord Justice General (Hope):

F **OPINION OF THE COURT.**—This is a petition
to the nobile officium, in which the petitioner seeks
review of a decision of the High Court under s 254 of
the Criminal Procedure (Scotland) Act 1975 when disposing of an appeal at his instance against his conviction.

He had been convicted in the High Court in
Glasgow on an indictment which contained five
charges. Charge 1 was a charge of breach of the peace,
charge 2 was one of murder and charges 3, 4 and 5
were charges of contravening s 3 (1) (b) of the Bail etc

(Scotland) Act 1980. He was found guilty as libelled
on charges 1, 3, 4 and 5, and on charge 2 he was found G
guilty of culpable homicide. He then appealed against
his conviction for culpable homicide on the ground of
misdirection by the trial judge. His grounds of appeal
were all related to the issue of self defence which arose
only in regard to charge 2. There was no suggestion
either in the grounds of appeal or in the course of the
argument that the alleged misdirections affected the
pursuer's conviction on the other four charges, against
which he had not appealed. On 10 July 1992 his
appeal was allowed, and it was disposed of by setting H
aside the verdict of the trial court and granting
authority to bring a new prosecution in accordance
with s 255 of the 1975 Act [see 1993 SLT 577].

No mention was made in the course of the decision
which was intimated on that date of the extent to
which the verdict of the jury was being set aside. But
in an opinion which was subsequently issued on 24
August 1992 it was made clear that the court considered it appropriate to set aside the whole verdict of
the jury, including its verdict on charges 1, 3, 4 and I
5. The petitioner now seeks to challenge that decision
on the ground that his conviction on these charges was
not before the High Court for their consideration in
the appeal, and accordingly that the court had no
power to set aside the verdict of the trial court except
in regard to his conviction of culpable homicide under
charge 2. He claims that this decision was unlawful
and incompetent as being outwith the powers of the
High Court in terms of the 1975 Act. He claims also
that it has resulted in an injustice, because he has now J
been served with an indictment in the new prosecution under s 255 which contains the same five charges
as those which he faced in the original proceedings,
four of which were the subject of convictions against
him which he did not appeal.

It is well settled that the nobile officium of this court
can be invoked only in exceptional circumstances. So
the first question is whether the application is competent, having regard to the finality which attaches to all K
interlocutors and sentences of the High Court in terms
of ss 262 and 281 of the Act. Counsel for the petitioner
submitted that the provisions of these sections did not
preclude a challenge to a decision of the High Court
on the ground that it was unlawful and incompetent,
and that since this was the only point which he sought
to raise we should consider the application and review
the decision to set aside the jury's verdict on these four
charges. The learned advocate depute informed us
that he did not challenge the competency of the appli- L
cation in view of the nature of the argument which
senior counsel wished to present. We were invited to
regard this as a case where, on the petitioner's argument, the High Court had done something in the exercise of its appellate jurisdiction which it was not
permitted to do by Parliament. Reference was made to
Beattie, Petr, in which it was recognised that in such
a case there may be said to have been a circumstance
which was unforeseen because the statutory provisions
for the finality of appeals assume that the High Court
will exercise its jurisdiction in accordance with the

statutes, and that the nobile officium may then be exercised to prevent such injustice or oppression as may result.

But in the present case the issue of competency is incapable of being separated from the merits of the application. This is not one of those cases suggested in argument where, due to a mistake or oversight, the court has acted contrary to the express terms of an enactment, such as by imposing a sentence on a statutory charge other than one provided for by Parliament. The argument here is directed to something which the appeal court did in the belief that what they were doing was competent. It was a decision which was deliberately taken, for reasons which were clearly set out in the following passages in the opinion of the court which was delivered by the Lord Justice Clerk: "Although the misdirection related to charge 2 on the indictment only, it was accepted that charges 1 and 2 were intimately connected and it is clear that charges 3, 4 and 5 were consequential charges. It therefore appears to us to be appropriate to set aside the whole verdict of the jury.

". . . The fact that there is to be a new prosecution emphasises the desirability of setting aside the jury's verdict on all charges, so that the jury at the new prosecution can hear all the evidence which is relevant and material to the issues which were the subject of the first indictment" (1993 SLT at p 588D-F).

Two questions arise in these circumstances. The first is whether it is open to argument that the course taken by the appeal court was one which the High Court was entitled to take in the exercise of its jurisdiction under s 254 (1) of the Act. The second is whether, if the point is open to argument, it is competent for the view which was taken by the appeal court to be reviewed by us in the exercise of the nobile officium, having regard to the final and conclusive nature of all interlocutors and sentences pronounced by the High Court which are declared by statute not to be subject to review. A third question which was raised in the course of argument by counsel for the petitioner is whether it was competent for the appeal court to state in the opinion which was issued on 24 August 1992 that the whole verdict of the jury was to be set aside, since no mention of the setting aside of the verdicts on charges 1, 3, 4 and 5 was made in the decision which was announced on 10 July 1992.

We take first the third question, since it raises a short point on a matter of procedure. Both counsel for the petitioner and the advocate depute were agreed that there was some discussion about the relationship between charges 1 and 2 on the original indictment in the course of the appeal, but they were also agreed that no mention was made of charge 1 or of charges 3, 4 and 5 in the context of the discussion as to what charges might be brought in the new prosecution. As can be seen from the opinion delivered by the Lord Justice Clerk, it was suggested by counsel for the petitioner that the court should only authorise a new prosecution on a charge of culpable homicide, since that was the offence of which the petitioner had been

convicted by the jury on charge 2. The court's decision on that point was that s 254 (1) (c) enabled the court to dispose of an appeal by setting aside the verdict of the trial court and granting authority to bring a new prosecution, leaving it to the Crown to decide whether to exercise that right and if so what charges to bring. Counsel for the petitioner maintained that the impression shared by all those who listened to the court's decision on this point was that it was only the conviction on charge 2 which was being set aside. He then pointed to the determination as recorded by the Depute Clerk of Justiciary, which was in these terms: "The court having heard counsel for the appellant and the advocate depute allowed the appeal; set aside the verdict of the High Court sitting at Glasgow on 18 November 1991 and granted authority to bring a new prosecution in accordance with s 255 of the Criminal Procedure (Scotland) Act 1975." Counsel submitted that this was consistent with what had been discussed and that it was a final interlocutor which was incapable of being altered by the terms of the opinion.

We have no hesitation in rejecting this argument. The suggestion that the appeal court were attempting in the opinion to alter the terms of their own interlocutor was based on a misconception of the function which was being performed by the Depute Clerk of Justiciary. As was pointed out in *Perrie, Petr*, 1992 SLT at p 657, it is not the practice of the High Court in appeals under solemn procedure to issue interlocutors signed by the presiding judge. But s 261 of the 1975 Act provides that on the final determination of any appeal under that part of the Act the Clerk of Justiciary is to give notice of such determination to the appellant or applicant, if he is in custody and was not present at such final determination, to the clerk of the court in which the conviction took place, and to the Secretary of State. The words which we have quoted above were written on a form of notice addressed to the clerk of the trial court, the Director of Prison Services, the governor of HM Prison at Edinburgh and the officer in charge of the Criminal Records Office in Glasgow. They were introduced by these words on the printed form: "This is to Give You Notice, That the Court of Criminal Appeal has finally determined the said Appeal, and on 10-7-92 pronounced the following judgment:—".

It is incorrect to describe the notice of determination given by the Clerk of Justiciary as an interlocutor, or to suggest that its terms are incapable of alteration by the court. The function of the notice is to intimate the determination to those who require to be made aware of its terms. But it is not shown to the presiding judge, and it is always open to him to correct it if it should appear later that it is not in accordance with the decision of the court. In the present case, however, no such correction is required. The notice records the determination of the appeal in terms which reflect precisely the language of s 254 (1) (c) of the 1975 Act. It states that the court allowed the appeal, set aside the verdict of the trial court and granted authority to bring a new prosecution. No express reference is made here

A to any particular charge or charges on the indictment. It is open to the interpretation that the whole verdict of the trial court was being set aside. That interpretation is confirmed by the words which were quoted earlier from the opinion which was subsequently delivered by the Lord Justice Clerk. The opinion is the best evidence of what was decided by the court, and it is consistent with the terms of the notice signed by the Depute Clerk of Justiciary. We can find nothing in this part of counsel for the petitioner's argument which would entitle us to say that the High Court did something here which it was not permitted to do by the 1975 Act.

B

We turn now to the question whether it was within the power of the High Court to set aside the verdict of the trial court on charges which were not the subject of the appeal. This is an issue of some general interest and importance, because the statute contains no express provision for the situation which has arisen in this case. No distinction is made in the statutory framework between cases where the indictment in the original proceedings contained only one charge and C where it contained several. Section 228 (1) provides that any person convicted on indictment may appeal to the High Court against such conviction, and s 254 (1) sets out the powers which the High Court may exercise in disposing of such appeals. In cases where the appeal is to be determined by affirming the verdict of the trial court under s 254 (1) (a) or by setting aside its verdict and quashing the conviction under s 254 (1) (b) there is no difficulty. There is no need in these D cases to look beyond the conviction which was the subject of the appeal. But the position is different when the disposal which has been selected is to set aside the verdict under s 254 (1) (c) and to grant authority for the bringing of a new prosecution under s 255.

It is clear that the powers of the High Court under s 254 (1) are limited to disposing of an appeal against conviction. No mention is made in this subsection of any other steps which may be taken in regard to E verdicts which are not the subject of the appeal. There is no power to set aside the verdict of the trial court on other charges on which the appellant may have been convicted, or to set aside verdicts of acquittal on other charges against which no appeal could competently be taken since no right of appeal is given to the Crown. But the purpose of granting authority for a new prosecution is to enable a new prosecution to be brought for the same or any similar offence arising out of the same facts, and it is expressly provided in s 255 F (1) that the proceedings out of which the appeal arose shall not be a bar to such new prosecution.

The problem, to which no express reference has been made in the statute, arises where the original indictment contains other charges than the charge or charges which were the subject of appeal. These charges could include charges which were in the indictment purely for evidential reasons or as background to the principal charge. Charges of this character would need to be included in the fresh indictment if the new prosecution was to proceed with

any reasonable prospect of success. The principle is that notice must be given in the indictment of the G intention to lead evidence of anything done or omitted to be done by the accused which constitutes a crime. This is so even if the evidence is to be directed only to proof of the principal crime or crimes libelled against him. That principle applies equally to a new prosecution brought under authority granted under s 254 (1) (c) as it does to the original proceedings. For this reason it is not difficult to see that the new prosecution would be at a material disadvantage if the Crown were to be unable to lead evidence relevant to H the principal charge because the events had not been libelled in the indictment. But the petitioner's argument is that that is the effect of ss 254 and 255, since they do not permit the court to interfere with the verdict of the trial court finding the appellant guilty on ancillary charges against which he did not appeal, or with its verdict where, as not infrequently happens for technical reasons, the ancillary charges were disposed of by an acquittal.

In the opinion which we have just delivered in the I Crown's appeal under s 76A of the 1975 Act against a decision taken at a preliminary diet in the new proceedings [*HM Advocate v Boyle*, 1993 SLT 1079], we said that the point of reference to determine whether the accused has been charged under s 255 with the same or any similar offence arising out of the same facts must be the terms of the previous indictment. We also said that, where more than one charge was contained in that indictment, it must be the charge or charges in respect of which the accused was J previously convicted and to which he directed his appeal. But counsel for the petitioner accepted that it would be open to the Crown to expand the narrative in the charge or charges in the indictment in the new prosecution to include what had been libelled separately in the previous indictment in charges to which no appeal had been directed, if this narrative was relevant to the proof of the offence or offences which were now being prosecuted. He made it clear that his objection was to the taking of any step in the K disposal of the appeal which would enable the Crown to libel these facts as separate charges, since it would then be open to the Crown to obtain a fresh conviction in respect of them for offences of which he had already been convicted.

The advocate depute drew our attention to *Morrison v HM Advocate*, 1991 SLT at p 62, where reference was made to what was seen in that case to be an insuperable difficulty. The appellant in that case had L gone to trial on two charges of rape against the same complainer which arose out of what was essentially one incident. He was convicted on the second charge and he appealed against that conviction. But the jury had acquitted him of the first charge, which had been amended to one of attempted rape, and it was accepted that the Crown could not lead evidence in relation to that charge at a retrial of the charge on which the appellant originally had been convicted. In view of the impossible situation which this would create the advocate depute accepted that the court should simply

A   set aside the verdict of the jury in terms of s 254 (1) (b) and quash the conviction. So far as the present case was concerned, however, he submitted that it would be open to the Crown to narrate the events which in the previous indictment had been charged in charge 1 as a breach of the peace, as what he described as a hanging particle to the charge of murder, so that all the events relevant to that charge could be led.

B   Although both counsel for the petitioner and the advocate depute were agreed that the narrative in charge 2 of the original indictment could be expanded to include matters which were previously libelled as a breach of the peace, this course also is not without difficulty. Section 61 (2) of the 1975 Act provides that any part of what is charged in an indictment, constituting in itself an indictable crime, shall be deemed separable to the effect of making it lawful to convict of such a crime. A narrative of the kind suggested would, therefore, leave it open to the jury to convict the petitioner of disorderly conduct amounting to a breach of the peace although they had decided to acquit him of the principal elements of the charge.

C   There seems to us therefore to be no significant distinction for present purposes between narrating this conduct as part of the principal charge and presenting it as a separate charge in the indictment. Either course would leave it open to the Crown to seek a conviction on this narrative for breach of the peace. The only difference is that if the narrative were to be the subject of a separate charge it would be open to the jury to return a separate verdict of guilty of breach of the peace in addition to a verdict of murder or culpable homicide on the principal charge. But the decision of the trial judge in the previous proceedings to take both charges together for the purposes of sentence and to treat them as being effectively part of the same event shows that the practical consequences of either course as regards sentence are likely to be the same.

D

It was suggested by the advocate depute that a statutory basis for the use of the hanging particle was the provision in s 255 (1) that the proceedings out of which the appeal arose are not to be a bar to the new prosecution. He seemed to be reluctant to take that proposition to its logical conclusion, which appears to us to be that nothing which took place in the previous proceedings is to be a bar to a new prosecution for the same or any similar offence arising out of the same facts which were narrated in the charge which gave rise to the appeal. Yet it is at this stage that the real difficulty for the petitioner in this application must be faced. In our opinion there are good reasons for regarding it as appropriate, in those cases where the verdicts not appealed against related to ancillary charges which were intimately connected with the principal charge which gave rise to the appeal, that the authority to bring a new prosecution should extend to these ancillary charges also. This is in the public interest, since the jury in the new prosecution ought to be able to hear all the evidence bearing on the principal charge so that they can arrive at a fair verdict. Furthermore, as the advocate depute pointed out, it is in accordance with the intention of Parliament as indi-

E

F

G   cated by the declaration in s 255 (1) that the previous proceedings are not to be a bar to the new prosecution. And there could not reasonably be said to be any unfairness in this course, since the only purpose of including the ancillary charges in the original indictment would be to enable the Crown to lead all the evidence which was relevant and material to the question whether the accused was guilty of the principal charge. What the appeal court did in this case seems to us therefore to be entirely in accordance with this approach. Unlike the charge of attempted rape in *Morrison,* the appellant's acquittal on which was seen to present an insuperable obstacle to a new prosecution on the other charge, the breach of the peace in the present case was of a minor character in comparison with the offence libelled in charge 2 and would not, taken on its own, have justified the taking of proceedings against the petitioner on indictment.

H

Accordingly the question is whether it was open to argument that the course taken by the appeal court was one which the High Court was entitled to take in the exercise of its jurisdiction under s 254 (1) of the Act. We have put the question in this way because, if it was open to argument, it was clearly a matter for the appeal court to decide and not for us. The High Court, in the exercise of its appellate jurisdiction under the Act, is entitled to do all such things as may be necessary to give effect to that jurisdiction in accordance with the intention of Parliament. Its decisions on these matters are as final and conclusive and beyond the power of review of any court as any other decision or determination in the disposal of an appeal. To a large extent therefore it is for the High Court to determine the limits of its own jurisdiction, so long as this does not conflict with what Parliament has provided, either expressly or by necessary implication, in any enactment.

I

J

So far as the limits of its jurisdiction under s 254 (1) (c) are concerned, the provision that it may dispose of an appeal against conviction "by setting aside the verdict of the trial court" is loosely phrased and open to construction. As against the argument that, in its context, the words "the verdict" must be taken to be the verdict which has been appealed against, there is the point that, in order to give effect to the granting of authority for a new prosecution, s 255 (1) provides that the proceedings out of which the appeal arose shall not be a bar to such new proceedings. Section 254 (1) (c) does not state in terms that only the verdict which has been expressly appealed against can be set aside, and it seems to us at least open to argument that it permits the setting aside of the verdict on all charges which are intimately connected with the charge which was the subject of the appeal. An argument in support of this approach would be that the appellant had, by necessary implication, submitted the verdict on all these charges also to review by the High Court, thus enabling the court, if this was appropriate in the public interest, to set aside the verdict on these other charges so that the jury in the new prosecution could hear all the relevant evidence. The argument has particular force in regard to the charges under the Bail etc

K

L

(Scotland) Act 1980, because it would make no sense
for the convictions under s 3 (1) (b) of that Act, which
were entirely dependent on the petitioner's conviction
for the offences libelled in charges 1 and 2, to remain
standing along with the sentences attached to them
when the verdict of the trial court on the other charges
had been set aside.

For these reasons we are in no doubt that the issue
as to whether this course was competent was one for
the appeal court to decide when disposing of the
appeal. It is an inevitable consequence of this opinion
that the decision which they took is not open to us to
review in these proceedings and that the petition must
therefore be dismissed as incompetent. But we should
add that, even if we had been persuaded that it was a
decision which could be reviewed in the exercise of the
nobile officium, we would have found it impossible to
hold that what occurred in this case had resulted in
such injustice or oppression to the petitioner as would
entitle us to interfere to prevent it. Counsel for the
petitioner confined his argument on this point to the
submission that it was unjust and oppressive for the
court to exercise a power which it did not possess. But,
in the wider context of a decision which was taken for
the express purpose of enabling a new prosecution to
be brought in accordance with s 255 of the Act, that
is not an approach which we can accept. It was not
suggested that the petitioner had been prejudiced by
the decision in any respect which was not necessary to
serve the public interest. By setting aside the verdict
on all charges the appeal court relieved from him the
consequences of his conviction on all of them, leaving
it to the Crown to decide whether or not to bring a
new prosecution. The decision would, in terms of
s 255 (4), have had the effect, for all purposes, of an
acquittal had fresh proceedings not now been brought.
And it has not been suggested that the petitioner is in
any different position as regards the new proceedings
than he was when he went to trial under the previous
indictment. For these reasons also we would have
declined to interfere with the decision of the appeal
court that the whole verdict of the jury should be set
aside.

---

*Counsel for Petitioner, Bell, QC, McBride; Solicitors,
Macbeth, Currie & Co, WS (for Beltrami & Co,
Glasgow) — Counsel for Respondent, Macdonald, QC,
A D; Solicitor, J D Lowe, Crown Agent.*

P W F

(NOTE)
Hunter v Wylie

OUTER HOUSE
LORD ABERNETHY
11 NOVEMBER 1992

*Contract — Breach of contract — Partnership —
Partners withdrawing capital without consent —
Whether material breach disentitling parties from exer-
cising contractual right to dissolve partnership.*

*Partnership — Dissolution — Partners withdrawing
capital without consent in breach of partnership contract
— Whether material breach disentitling partners from
exercising contractual right to dissolve partnership.*

Partners, acting in breach of the terms of the
partnership contract, withdrew capital without the
consent of other partners. They then sought to exercise a contractual right to dissolve the contract.

Held, that there was a prima facie case that the
partners who had withdrawn capital had done so in
material breach of the partnership contract and were
accordingly not entitled to exercise their contractual
right to dissolve the contract; and interdict against
their actings *granted* ad interim.

David Kelso Hunter and others, partners in a firm
of chartered accountants, sought interdict against
James Gordon Wylie and another, the other partners
in the firm, from proceeding with a dissolution of the
firm purportedly under a provision in the partnership
contract. The pursuers argued that the defenders were
not entitled to exercise their contractual power to dissolve the firm since they were in material breach of the
partnership contract in respect of another of its terms.
Each of the defenders had withdrawn £120,000 from
the firm by agreement with each other but not with
the agreement of the other partners. In granting
interim interdict the Lord Ordinary (Abernethy) said:

"Counsel for the pursuers' first submission was that
the defenders were in material breach of cl third of the
contract of copartnership and, that being so, they were
not entitled to exercise their rights to dissolve the
partnership under the contract (*Graham & Co v
United Turkey Red Co*, 1922 SLT 406; 1922 SC 533).
Clause third provides inter alia: 'The Profit Sharing
Partners shall, from time to time, contribute to or
withdraw from the Partnership such amounts as may
be mutually agreed.' The defenders were in material
breach of that clause because they had withdrawn the
amount of capital mentioned without the agreement of
all the profit sharing partners, junior as well as senior.
They were therefore not entitled to issue the notice of
dissolution of 6 November 1992. That notice was
accordingly invalid, as was all that followed it."

His Lordship then summarised and rejected the
defenders' contention that the withdrawals had been
made under another provision of the partnership contract which gave certain powers to the defenders as

"senior profit sharing partners". His Lordship continued: "In these circumstances I am of opinion that these withdrawals could have been made under cl third and, indeed, could only have been made under that clause. But they were not made in accordance with the whole applicable provisions of that clause because they were not made with the agreement of the profit sharing partners. In these circumstances I am of opinion that these withdrawals were made in breach of contract.

"But were they made in material breach of contract? Counsel for the defenders argued that they were not because any breach was easily remediable and in any event on dissolution the sums would automatically be taken into account. In my opinion, however, one must look at the materiality of the breach when it occurs and in its continuing state. I do not think what would otherwise be a material breach can be said to be not material just because it can be easily remedied or taken account of. In my opinion the breach here was material. The sums withdrawn were in the context of this partnership very substantial.

"Since the defenders are in material breach of the contract of copartnership it follows in my opinion that they are not able to invoke their rights to dissolve the contract (*Graham & Co v United Turkey Red Co*). Counsel for the defenders argued that a contract of copartnership was more complex than a sales contract. Accordingly it did not follow that a breach of this contract by them would result in their being unable to enforce any of their rights under the contract. For example they would still be entitled to remuneration. That may be so but I do not think it affects the position with regard to the exercise by the defenders of their power of dissolution.

"This is sufficient to establish a prima facie case for the pursuers for the purposes of interim interdict."

His Lordship then held that the pursuers had averred a prima facie case that the dissolution procedure had in any event been carried out in a manner not authorised by the partnership contract. Having so concluded, his Lordship then determined that the balance of convenience favoured the pursuers and granted interim interdict.

Counsel for Pursuers, Davidson; Solicitors, Bird Semple Fyfe Ireland, WS — Counsel for Defenders, Drummond Young, QC; Solicitors, Dorman Jeffrey & Co.

C H

Saleem v Hamilton District Licensing Board

FIRST DIVISION

THE LORD PRESIDENT (HOPE),
LORDS ALLANBRIDGE AND KIRKWOOD

31 DECEMBER 1992

Process — Sheriff court — Summary application — First calling — Failure by pursuer's agents to be present at first calling — Summary application dismissed — Whether sheriff exercised discretion reasonably in dismissing application — Proper practice for sheriff — Sheriff Courts (Scotland) Act 1907 (7 Edw VII, c 51), ss 3 and 50.

An applicant appealed to the sheriff by way of summary application against a licensing board's refusal of his application for renewal of his off sale licence. At the first calling of the application the applicant's solicitor was not present, having been detained in another court. On the motion of the solicitor for the respondents, the sheriff dismissed the application. The applicant appealed to the Court of Session.

Held, (1) that while the sheriff had a discretion as to how to dispose of the application if the pursuer was not present or represented, he should normally drop the case from the roll and only in exceptional circumstances should he dismiss the application at that stage (p 1095A); (2) that in the present case the sheriff had erred in law in failing to give himself an opportunity to reach a reasoned decision before dismissing the action (p 1095D-E); and appeal *allowed* and application *remitted* to the sheriff to proceed as accords.

Macphail, *Sheriff Court Practice*, para 26-19, *approved*.

Appeal from the sheriff court

Mohammed Saleem appealed to the Court of Session against the dismissal by the sheriff of an appeal by summary application against the decision of the Hamilton District Licensing Board to refuse a renewal of his off sale licence, his solicitor not having been present at the first calling of the application.

Statutory provisions

The Sheriff Courts (Scotland) Act 1907 provides:

"3. In construing this Act (unless where the context is repugnant to such construction)—. . . (p) 'Summary application' means and includes all applications of a summary nature brought under the common law jurisdiction of the sheriff, and all applications, whether by appeal or otherwise, brought under any Act of Parliament which provides, or, according to any practice in the sheriff court, which allows, that the same shall be disposed of in a summary manner, but which does not more particularly define in what form the same shall be heard, tried, and determined. . . .

"50. In summary applications (where a hearing is necessary) the sheriff shall appoint the application to be heard at a diet to be fixed by him, and at that or

A
any subsequent diet (without record of evidence unless the sheriff shall order a record) shall summarily dispose of the matter and give his judgment in writing".

The Act of Sederunt (Appeals under the Licensing (Scotland) Act 1976) 1977 provides:

"2. Any appeal to the sheriff under section 39 of the 1976 Act against a decision of a licensing board shall be made by way of initial writ under the Sheriff Courts (Scotland) Acts 1907 and 1913 and such appeal shall be disposed of as a summary application as
B defined in the said Acts."

Cases referred to

Higgins v Atkinson (1908) 24 Sh Ct Rep 385.
McKay v Banff and Buchan Western Division Licensing Board, 1991 SLT 20.
McKelvie v Scottish Steel Scaffolding Co Ltd, 1938 SLT 159; 1938 SC 278.
Rayment v Jack, 1988 SLT 647.
Simpson v Banff and Buchan District Licensing Board,
C 1991 SLT 18.

Textbooks referred to

Dobie, *Sheriff Court Practice*, p 140.
Macphail, *Sheriff Court Practice*, pp 247, 249 and 880.

The appeal was heard before the First Division on 15 December 1992.

On 31 December 1992 the court *allowed* the appeal
D and *remitted* the case to the sheriff to proceed as accords.

The following opinion of the court was delivered by Lord Allanbridge:

OPINION OF THE COURT.—The appellant is the holder of an off sale licence in respect of premises at 224-226 Silverton Avenue, Hamilton. On 30 April 1992 the respondents refused his application for renewal of that licence after they had been asked to
E reconsider their earlier decision to refuse it by the sheriff at Hamilton.

The appellant then appealed this second decision of the respondents to the sheriff in terms of s 39 of the Licensing (Scotland) Act 1976. The Court of Session was empowered in terms of s 39 (9) to make rules for the conduct of proceedings under this section by Act of Sederunt. The appropriate Act of Sederunt was made on 6 October 1977 (SI 1977/1622) to regulate the appeals procedure under said s 39 and came into
F operation on 29 October 1977. Paragraph 2 thereof is in the following terms: [his Lordship quoted its terms and continued:]

The definition of a "summary application" is to be found in the interpretation section of the Sheriff Courts (Scotland) Act 1907 which is s 3. The relevant definition reads as follows: [his Lordship quoted the terms of s 3 (p) and continued:]

Section 50 of the 1907 Act makes further reference to the disposal of summary applications and the rele-

vant part reads as follows: [his Lordship quoted the terms of s 50 set out supra and continued:]   G

It is to be noted that rules 1, 3, 4, 5 (3), 10 to 12 and 14 to 19 of the ordinary cause rules, which are set out in Sched 1 to the 1907 Act, apply to a summary application insofar as they are not inconsistent with s 50 of the Act of 1907 (see reg 5 of SI 1983/747, as amended by SI 1988/1978).

In the present case the appellant commenced this appeal by initial writ in Hamilton sheriff court and a warrant to cite the defenders in terms of said rule 5 (3) H was obtained in that court on 5 June 1992. Warrant was granted to cite the defenders upon a period of notice of 21 days and it appointed them to answer within the sheriff court house at Hamilton on 8 July 1992 at 10 o'clock forenoon "under certification of being held as confessed".

On 8 July 1992 the case duly called but the appellant's solicitor was not present and the solicitor for the respondents who did appear made a motion to the sheriff to dismiss the cause. The sheriff, by inter- I
locutor dated 8 July 1992, thereupon dismissed the cause and found no expenses due to or by either party. On 10 July 1992 the appellant appealed this interlocutor to this court and requested the sheriff to write a note. The sheriff wrote a note in the following terms:

"The case called in ordinary court on 8 July 1992. The solicitor for the respondents appeared. There was no appearance by or on behalf of the appellant. I acceded to the respondents' solicitor's motion to J
dismiss the action with a finding of no expenses due to or by either party.

"The solicitor for the appellant appeared 10-15 minutes later, having been detained in another court. By that time the solicitor for the respondents had left. Accordingly I was unable to re-call this case as requested by the appellant's solicitor."

Counsel appeared before us for the appellant and argued that, in the context of a summary application K
to the sheriff, the sheriff was wrong to dismiss the cause at the stage he did in respect of the failure of the appellant's solicitor to be present at the first calling of the cause. He explained that the solicitor had been delayed in another court and that the appellant could not raise a fresh application as it was by then time barred in terms of the 1976 Act. He said the proper practice in such a situation was not that an application should be dismissed but that it should be dropped from the roll. Thereafter a pursuer could lodge a L
motion to enrol the cause for further procedure and of new to grant warrant to cite the defender. When that motion was heard, the defender may move for dismissal, while the pursuer may move the sheriff to grant his motion (see Macphail on *Sheriff Court Practice* at p 880). He said he could find no reported case which dealt with this matter, but he sought to draw a comparison with "tabling" in ordinary cause procedure in the sheriff court where a pursuer fails to appear to table the initial writ on the appointed court day. In such a situation the defender's remedy in the

circumstances was not absolvitor but protestation (see
A *Higgins v Atkinson* and Macphail, supra at p 249).
While protestation was not available for a summary
application, counsel for the appellant submitted that
the diet of appearance in a summary cause must necessarily be regarded as tabling (see Dobie on *Sheriff
Court Practice*, p 140).

Counsel for the appellant then submitted a second
argument to the effect that, assuming the sheriff had
a discretion in the matter, he had failed to exercise it
in a proper manner because his note indicated that he
B had not considered whether substantial grounds of
appeal were disclosed in the initial writ. The court
had, for example, indicated in the past that it would
be extremely reluctant that a decree pronounced
against any defender should become final where there
was a substantial defence that had never been heard
(see Lord President Normand at p 160 of *McKelvie v
Scottish Steel Scaffolding Co*, 1938 SLT 159, referred
to by Lord Justice Clerk Ross at pp 649L and 650B-C
of *Rayment v Jack*. It was averred inter alia in the
C present initial writ that the respondents had reached
their decision in private whereas they should have
reached their decision and voted in public (see
Simpson v Banff and Buchan District Licensing Board
and *McKay v Banff and Buchan Western Division
Licensing Board*), and in this situation the court should
have been reluctant to decide that such a statable
ground of appeal should not be heard. Counsel for the
appellant finally asked this court to recall the sheriff's
interlocutor of 8 July 1992 and remit the cause back
D to the sheriff to proceed as accords.

In reply counsel for the respondents stressed that
the present application was a summary application
and not a summary cause, and submitted that it was
not appropriate to compare it with tabling procedure
where, if the pursuer fails to appear, the defender may
crave protestation but if he does not do so the action
is market "Not tabled" and dropped from the roll (see
rules 35 and 36 of the ordinary cause rules and Mac-
E phail, supra at p 247). He said the reference to Dobie,
supra at p 140 was also not appropriate, because the
author was referring to the diet of appearance in a
summary cause which has a different procedure from
that of a summary application.

Counsel for the respondents suggested that, as there
were no rules which applied to the first calling of a
summary application, the sheriff had a discretion to
determine what course to take in the event of non-
appearance by the applicant's solicitor. He could, for
F example, have regard to rule 59 (1) of the ordinary
cause rules which states that in a defended cause "if
one party fails to appear or be represented at a diet, the
sheriff may grant decree as craved or decree of absolvitor, or may dismiss the cause, with expenses". In
these circumstances in the present case the sheriff was
fully entitled in the exercise of his discretion to
dismiss the application and the appeal should be
refused. Counsel for the respondents said he himself
was not aware of any established practice along the
lines suggested in para 26-19 of Macphail, supra at

p 880, and added that it was to be noted that chap 26
was not written by a practising sheriff, as was indi- G
cated on the first page of the textbook which detailed
the authors of certain chapters.

Counsel for the respondents also drew our attention
to the terms of s 39 (8) of the 1976 Act which allowed
an appeal to the Court of Session within 28 days
whereas the time limit in the ordinary cause rules was
stated to be 14 days in rule 91 thereof. However, he
submitted that what was important in the present case
was that the appellant was in effect submitting that the
sheriff had erred in his discretion in dismissing the H
present application and he argued that that error was
not an error "in point of law" as it required to be in
terms of s 39 (8). In this situation this court could
therefore not interfere with the sheriff's decision and
the appeal must be refused.

Having considered the arguments of counsel we
require to decide what a sheriff should do in a situation where an appellant fails to appear or be represented at the first calling of a summary application.   I
There are no rules of court which give the sheriff
guidance as to what he should do in such a situation.
As already outlined in this opinion, there are a very
limited number of the ordinary cause rules which
apply to summary applications (namely, rules 1, 3, 4,
5 (3), 10 to 12 and 14 to 19), and it is apparent that
the procedure is intended to be as simple and expeditious as possible. It is to be noted that the sheriff
retains his dispensing power in rule 1 although, of
course, no breach of any rule is said to have occurred   J
in the present case. Both counsel in their submissions
to us suggested in their respective arguments that
assistance could be gained by looking at a number of
the ordinary cause rules which do not apply to
summary applications. We do not consider it either
advisable or helpful to look at such rules because the
procedure for summary applications is clearly
intended to be different, except in the case of the rules
which have been expressly applied to it, from that for
ordinary or summary causes.   K

There is no authority in case law to which we were
referred which assists us on this matter. It is, however,
specifically dealt with at para 26-19 of Macphail on
Sheriff Court Practice, which was published in 1988.
We are aware that chap 26 was not written by a practising sheriff, and we have not been provided with any
information as to what the practice, if any, is when
such a situation arises in the sheriff court. But as we
understand the purpose of the initial calling of the
case, it is to enable the sheriff to ascertain whether a   L
hearing will be necessary and, if so, to arrange for
further procedure so that a diet of hearing can be fixed
as soon as convenient. The opening words of s 50 of
the 1907 Act read: "50. In summary applications
(where a hearing is necessary) the sheriff shall appoint
the application to be heard at a diet to be fixed by
him".

The warrant in the present case was in the prescribed form (see rule 5 (3) and form B2 in the Appendix to Sched 1 to the 1907 Act), and required the

A defenders to answer within the sheriff court house at Hamilton under certification of being held as confessed. In such a situation, if the defenders were not present or represented on that date, the sheriff would be entitled to grant decree against them as they had clear notice that such a result might follow. However, if the pursuer is not present or represented we are of the opinion that the sheriff should normally drop the case from the roll and that only in exceptional circumstances should he dismiss the application at that stage. We consider that the sheriff has a discretion

B as to how to dispose of the application if such a situation arises, but in our view he should drop the case from the roll unless he has strong reasons for not doing so. We appreciate that the calling of such a case on the roll will usually occur at a time when the sheriff has had neither the time nor the opportunity to examine the initial writ in any detail. He cannot normally be expected to know at that stage whether the appellant or his representative had a reasonable excuse for failing to appear and whether

C the appellant had a statable appeal. In such a situation we consider the procedure outlined in para 26-19 of Macphail on *Sheriff Court Practice* is not only sensible but will normally be appropriate. As is outlined in that paragraph, after the case is dropped from the roll the pursuer may thereafter lodge a motion to enrol the cause for further procedure and of new to grant warrant to cite the defender. When that motion is heard, then the defender may move for dismissal, while the pursuer may move the sheriff to grant his motion for further procedure. At that

D stage the sheriff should be properly appraised of the relevant facts and in a position to reach a reasoned decision as to whether or not to dismiss the application.

In the present case it is quite clear that the sheriff gave himself no opportunity to reach a reasoned decision before he pronounced the interlocutor which dismissed the action. In his brief note he simply acknowledges that he acceded to the respondents'

E solicitor's motion to dismiss the action but gives no reason at all for doing so. In these circumstances we are satisfied that the sheriff erred in law in acting as he did. He should have dismissed the action only if he considered there were good reasons for not dropping it from the roll and giving an opportunity for further procedure to take place. He has not given any such reasons. We will therefore allow this appeal on that ground, which is an appropriate ground in terms of our powers under s 39 (8) of the 1976 Act.

F It only remains to add that we consider it unwise to make any observations as to how the sheriff should exercise his discretion if he is again asked to dismiss the action, as that will be a matter for him on the information then available. On the whole matter we therefore allow this appeal, recall the sheriff's interlocutor of 8 July 1992 and remit the case back to the sheriff to proceed as accords.

———————

Counsel for Appellant, Gale; Solicitors, Drummond Miller, WS — Counsel for Respondents, Truscott; Solicitors, Simpson & Marwick, WS.

C H A of L

(NOTE)

Campbell v Campbell & Isherwood Ltd

OUTER HOUSE
LORD WEIR
29 JANUARY 1993

Damages — Amount — Solatium, loss of personal services of and necessary services rendered to injured person — Chest and lungs — Asbestosis — Elderly man seriously disabled and continuing to deteriorate, and with unrelated medical conditions.

A 73 year old former shipyard worker was held to be suffering from asbestosis, resulting in breathlessness and a serious inability to do anything involving any level of exertion. He had a life expectancy of about five years. His condition was contributed to by chronic bronchitis and a cerebro-vascular "accident", neither being connected with his working conditions.

Held, that solatium was properly valued, after taking into account the unrelated medical factors, at £12,000, that the claim for services of a domestic and nursing character rendered by relatives was reasonably assessed at £4,000 and that no award was appropriate for the loss of the pursuer's services to the household; and decree *pronounced* accordingly.

———————

Hugh Campbell raised an action against his former employers Campbell & Isherwood Ltd. At the date of the proof the pursuer was aged 73 and had been retired for about 10 years. His employment had been as an electrician in shipyards. There he had been exposed to asbestos, causing him to contract asbestosis. After a proof before answer the Lord Ordinary (Weir) found the defenders liable in reparation to the pursuer. In assessing damages his Lordship said:

"The pursuer is aged 73 and has lived with his wife in retirement for about 10 years. He is now in very poor health and doctors do not expect him to live much beyond five years from now. His condition has deteriorated during the last two or three years and this has become more noticeable in recent months. He was unable to come to court and his evidence was taken at home on commission. His main complaint is of breathlessness which greatly affects his ability to move. The two bedrooms of the house in which he and his wife live are on the first floor and he is now largely confined to these rooms. It is only now and

A again that he goes downstairs and that only on a special occasion. He cannot manage the stairs without assistance. He is afraid of falling. The effort of climbing he finds exhausting. His sleep is sometimes interrupted by outbreaks of coughing and breathlessness. On occasions he is incontinent due to his inability to reach the toilet or his urine bottle in time. His wife sleeps in the other bedroom so as to obtain a proper sleep for herself. She has to bathe him regularly and a daughter in law comes in to assist. The pursuer cannot dress or undress without assistance, and all

B meals have to be brought to him. The pursuer used to be taken in the car for a trip but he has not been out of the house for a long time. His devoted wife sums up his way of life as describing it as being confined to shuffling between one bedroom and the other and that 'everything is a terrible bother to him'. His condition will not improve and there is a significant risk of him contracting a respiratory infection such as pneumonia or developing malignant lesions such as lung cancer or mesothelioma. The pursuer is aware of future breath-

C ing problems and is understandably anxious about such possibilities. . . .

"The pursuer's claim for damages comes under three heads. First, there is a claim in respect of pain and suffering. Secondly, there is a claim in respect of services provided by the pursuer's relatives, and thirdly, there is a claim for damages on account of the pursuer's inability himself to provide certain services. There is a conclusion for provisional damages but counsel for the pursuer did not insist upon this claim.

D The departure from this conclusion was, in my opinion, quite appropriate having regard to the circumstances.

"The claim for solatium is complicated by the undoubted existence of the pursuer's chronic bronchitis. Counsel for the defenders submitted that this was the manifest cause of the pursuer's outward problems, the nature of which I have already indicated. Any claim, he said, should be assessed on the

E basis of compensation for "non-problematic" pleural plaques and pleural thickening and that the effect of the fibrosis was "very slight". Dr Fennerty [the defenders' consultant physician] expressed the view that if there was fibrosis it would have a very small effect on the pursuer's respiratory function and assessed it at about 10 per cent. Dr Kerr [the pursuer's consultant physician] described such an assessment as a gross underestimate. His own estimation was that the pursuer's breathlessness was 50 per cent attribut-

F able to asbestos damage to his lungs and the remaining 50 per cent was due to obstructive airways disease taken along with the cerebro-vascular accident. Dr Kerr accepted that such an apportionment was a matter of judgment. The root cause of all the pursuer's disabilities was breathlessness. The fibrosis as revealed in the CT scan was quite extensive and quite dominant in his opinion and it was on this basis that Dr Kerr made his assessment. One of the effects of asbestosis is stiffness of the lung which leads to a greater effort in breathing and hence in part the breathlessness which the pursuer experiences. With-

out the asbestosis element he considered that the pursuer would be more mobile. He would be able to G move about the house more readily although he accepted that difficulty in managing the stairs would exist due to the cerebro-vascular accident. But for the asbestos element he would also be able to be taken out in the car. On the other hand certain other difficulties such as in sleeping, in bathing, in wheezing, and his incontinence problems would have existed in any event on account of his obstructive airways disease.

"I am disposed to assess damages on the basis of Dr Kerr's judgment rather than that of Dr Fennerty since H his expertise and his judgment made him the more reliable witness. I do not consider that it would be a proper approach to arrive at a certain level of award assuming the absence of complicating factors and then discount it by 50 per cent to allow for these. The approach, in my opinion, must be on a broad overall view of the pursuer's condition, making due allowance for the contribution to his condition by medical factors unrelated to his asbestosis. It has to be recognised that an award of solatium would have had to be very much I greater had the pursuer's condition been solely attributable to asbestosis. Indeed the award would have been very substantial indeed in these circumstances, but the effects of the concurrent contributory causes must be regarded as considerable as they are responsible, either in whole or in part, for a number of the pursuer's complaints.

"This is a very sad case. The pursuer suffers from a distressing condition of breathlessness and he is virtually confined to one part of his house. His enjoy- J ment of life is very limited and he has little or nothing to look forward to. He is not unaware of the risk of malignant diseases which are attributable to asbestosis. The risk of lung cancer already exists since the pursuer has been a lifelong smoker [having given up the previous year], but according to Dr Kerr that risk has been greatly heightened in view of the onset of asbestosis. The risk of contracting mesothelioma is also very much greater for the same reason. The pursuer is at risk of contracting pneumonia due to the K general condition of his lungs but due to fibrosis the risk is greater than it would otherwise have been. I infer from the evidence taken on commission that the pursuer is not unaware of these risks. In considering his suffering I have also taken into account the pursuer's realisation that on looking back on his life's work his reward has been to contract this seriously disabling disease.

"Counsel were good enough to supply me with a L number of illustrations from the various digests of awards of damages both in Scotland and in England. These were not of particular assistance since they related to claimants of younger age or to claims uncomplicated by other respiratory diseases or to cases where awards of provisional damages were made. Indeed there is little or no guidance to be derived from these cases. Counsel for the pursuer invited me to make an award of between £15,000 and £20,000 while counsel for the defenders suggested an award of £3,000 inclusive of interest. Whether or not proceeding on the basis of the views of Dr Fennerty, I regard the latter suggestion as derisory. I have to approach the matter broadly and taking into account all the factors as best I can and making full allowance for the unrelated causes I am of opinion that the sum of £12,000 is the proper sum to award by way of solatium. The disease is still in a fairly early stage and its effects seem likely to become more predominant in the future. I would apportion solatium at one third to the past and two thirds to the future.

"The claim by relatives, especially Mrs Campbell, for services to the pursuer must also be treated in a broad way and I understood both counsel to agree that this was the proper approach. The services in question were concerned with the extra work of a domestic and a nursing character undertaken and to be undertaken in the future by the pursuer's wife. That this work was being done and would continue to be done is not in controversy. The extra cost of using the motor car was also claimed and there were specific claims, ultimately departed from, for a shower and mechanical aid for climbing stairs. These costs were scrutinised thoroughly in cross examination by counsel for the defenders and there is some substance in the view that the quantification for nursing help and for fuel in particular is excessive. Counsel for the pursuer did not attempt a precise quantification but he recognised that these services were already being performed and would have had to be performed in a substantial measure even if the asbestosis element had not emerged. It has to be recognised that these services are liable to become more onerous as time goes by. Counsel for the pursuer suggested a figure of £5,000 while counsel for the defenders suggested that it should not exceed £2,000. I am inclined towards the former figure and should award £4,000 under this head, apportioning it for the purposes of interest in the same way as the claim for solatium.

"The loss of the pursuer's services to the household was claimed by counsel for the pursuer at the nominal figure of £100, this being to allow for the fact that he had not greatly contributed in the past in providing these services and recognising the fact that his bronchitis would have prevented him from performing them in any case. I do not consider that any loss is more than de minimis and shall make no award under this head."

Counsel for Pursuer, Bowen, QC, Kelly; Solicitors, Robin Thompson & Partners — Counsel for Defenders, R N Thomson; Solicitors, Cochran Sayers & Cook.

C H

(NOTE)

Falkirk District Council v Falkirk Taverns Ltd

OUTER HOUSE
LORD OSBORNE
29 JANUARY 1993

Landlord and tenant — Lease — Rent review — Waiver — Landlord asserting right to increased rent on review but demanding and accepting original rent — Whether waived right to insist on review.

Personal bar — Waiver — Lease — Rent review — Landlord asserting right to increased rent on review but demanding and accepting original rent — Whether waived right to insist on review.

A landlord was entitled to a review of rent on the occurrence of a specified event but, due to a misunderstanding of its position, the landlord demanded and received the pre-review rent for many years until the mistake was realised and an action raised for recovery of the arrears. All along the landlord had contended in correspondence and oral communications with the tenant that there would be liability to a rent in excess of the rent being claimed and paid.

Held, that the correspondence and communications, if proved, would establish a defence to the plea of waiver; and proof before answer *allowed.*

Banks v Mecca Bookmakers (Scotland) Ltd, 1982 SLT 150; 1982 SC 7, *distinguished.*

Falkirk District Council, the owners of an hotel, raised an action against the tenants, Falkirk Taverns Ltd, for arrears of rent. In terms of the lease entered into in April 1972 the tenants undertook to pay rent at a yearly rate subject to an increase of 15 per cent on any assignation and subject to review to a figure to be fixed by the district valuer on the erection by the tenants of an extension. The extension having been erected in November 1973 the district council, as landlords, sought a reviewed rental figure from the district valuer. The district valuer having given a figure, there was then a dispute between the landlords and the tenants as to the effect of the district valuer's figure, the tenants wrongly contending that there could be negotiations on the district valuer's figure and the landlords believing, wrongly, that the tenants' consent to the reviewed figure was required.

The landlords made elaborate averments concerning the extensive correspondence which took place between them and the tenants over a period of years concerning the matter of rent review. In these averments and in the correspondence to which they related, the landlords continued to adopt the position that the final figure of the increased rent required to be agreed by the tenants. They also averred that, from time to time, the landlords had suggested to the tenants that the latter should make an appropriate

lump sum payment of rent to reflect the increase
A which the landlords assumed would ultimately be
given effect. They averred in addition that they had
invited the tenants to reach a conclusion in their
negotiations with the district valuer. It was only after
many years that the landlords realised their mistake in
believing that the tenants had required to consent to
the rent fixed by the district valuer and raised an
action for the arrears, the landlords having throughout
sought rent at the original rate only. Part of the
defence to the action was that, by demanding and
B accepting rent at the original rate only, the landlords
had waived their right to a rent review. The tenants
sought (a) dismissal at procedure roll on the basis that
there were no relevant averments that a definite
reviewed rent had been provided, and (b) absolvitor at
procedure roll on the basis that the landlords had
waived their right to a review. In relation to the issue
of waiver the Lord Ordinary (Osborne) said:

"Counsel for the defenders went on to submit that,
C having regard to the position taken up in the past prior
to the raising of this action by the pursuers in relation
to the matter of rent review, they were now personally
barred from founding upon the letter [from the district
valuer] of 5 October 1976 as a basis for a contention
that a rent review had occurred. However, counsel for
the defenders quickly departed from that formulation
of his argument, making clear that the defenders' case
in this regard was truly one of waiver rather than personal bar. In connection with this part of his argument
D he referred to *Banks v Mecca Bookmakers (Scotland)
Ltd*, 1982 SLT 150; 1982 SC 7. He drew attention
particularly to the passages in the opinion of Lord
Grieve at 1982 SLT, pp 151-152. In that case it was
apparent that the tenant had tendered and the landlord
had accepted without comment or qualification rental
payments at an existing level for a period of nearly two
years after a point in time at which a rent review might
have been open to the landlord. The court had held
that the only inference which could reasonably be
E drawn from the acceptance of the rents after the time
of review was that the landlord had waived his right
to institute a rent review. Counsel for the defenders
argued that that was what had happened in the present
case. Here, if indeed the district valuer had reviewed
the rent, the pursuers, by their actings in accepting the
old rent without qualification and by the terms of their
correspondence, in which they had accepted that no
review had taken place, must be held to have expressly
or by inference abandoned any right to insist upon the
payment of a new rent allegedly fixed by the district
F valuer, or to argue now that what the district valuer
did was a rent review. Counsel for the defenders recognised that, in a sense, this was a question of fact, but
it was necessary at the stage of a debate on the
relevancy of the pursuers' pleadings to look at the contents of those pleadings. If the pursuers proved everything that they had averred, there was nothing to
gainsay waiver of their right to rely upon a rent review
having taken place. In connection with a case of
waiver, it was, of course, not necessary for the
defenders to aver that they had been prejudiced by the

pursuers' actings. In this connection counsel for the
defenders relied upon the case of *Armia Ltd v Daejan* G
Developments Ltd, 1979 SLT 147; 1979 SC (HL) 56,
particularly per Lord Keith at 1979 SLT, p 165. . . .

"Turning to the matter of waiver, counsel for the
pursuers accepted the statement of the law on the
subject advanced by counsel for the defenders. In
particular he accepted that the element of prejudice
did not require to be established in the making of a
case of waiver. So far as the case of *Banks v Mecca
Bookmakers (Scotland) Ltd* was concerned, it was distinguishable upon its facts from the present case, in H
respect that no attempt had been made to invoke the
rent review clause for a period of nearly two years after
the appropriate time for doing so. In the meantime
rent had been accepted without qualification at an
unreviewed rate. Here, the rent review clause had
been invoked timeously and a review had taken place,
according to the pursuers' argument. Further, in the
present case, unlike the position in *Banks*, the pursuers had written over and over again during a very
prolonged period of time to the effect that they did not I
regard the rent which they were accepting at the old
rate of £450 per annum as the full rent payable for the
premises. They frequently urged the defenders to pay
larger sums on account of a larger rent. In addition, it
was apparent from the decision in *Banks* that parties
had been agreed that no useful purpose would be
served by a proof, no significant facts being in dispute.
However, in the present case there was no such agreement. In particular there was no such agreement in
relation to the facts relevant to the alleged waiver. In J
that connection, it was important to recognise that in
Armia Ltd v Daejan Developments Ltd at p 165 Lord
Keith had said that the question whether or not there
had been waiver of a right was a question of fact, to
be determined objectively upon a consideration of all
the relevant evidence. While there might be cases in
which an issue of waiver could be determined as a
matter of relevancy, this case was not one of them, in
view of the circumstances which were in dispute, or at
least not the subject of admission. K

"Some reliance had been placed by the court in the
decisions cited by the defenders upon the case of
Davies v City of Glasgow Friendly Society, 1935 SC
224. In that case it was held as a matter of relevancy
that the pursuer's contractual claim for remuneration
additional to that paid to him for which he had granted
unqualified receipts was irrelevant and barred upon
the ground of acquiescence. Counsel for the pursuers
pointed out that, in that decision, great weight had L
been attributed to the circumstance that the pursuer
had granted unqualified receipts for salary payments.
The position in the present case was that throughout
the pursuers had protested to the defenders that the
sums being paid by way of rental were insufficient
following upon the rent review. They had committed
those protests to writing. In any event, the present
case was one in which the defenders raised a plea of
waiver. That was not the position in the case of
Davies. Furthermore, it was apparent from the judgment of the Lord Justice Clerk at p 235 that he con-

sidered that special considerations attached to a situation where an employee had granted unqualified receipts for salary. No such situation was involved in the present case. Accordingly *Davies* could be distinguished from the circumstances of the present case.

"In the light of the foregoing arguments I have come to the conclusion that a proof before answer should be allowed. . . .

"On the matter of the rent review, I am satisfied that the pursuers have relevantly averred that a rent review under cl first of the lease has taken place. . . .

"So far as the question of waiver is concerned, in my opinion, the averments of the parties must be sent for proof before answer. There is no doubt that the defenders have averred and pleaded a case of waiver against the pursuers. However, the issue now is whether that case could, at this stage, be sustained in the absence of proof. In my opinion, it could not. Although such a course was taken by Lord Grieve in *Banks v Mecca Bookmakers (Scotland) Ltd*, the situation in that case differed from the present one in respect that both parties agreed that a proof was unnecessary. That is not the position here. Although counsel for the pursuers accepted in the course of the argument that, as a fact, the pursuers had granted unqualified receipts for the rental payments at the old rate of £450 per annum, that does not appear to me to determine the situation in favour of the defenders. Throughout the elaborate and lengthy correspondence which is the subject of averment by the pursuers, but which is not fully admitted by the defenders, it is clear that the pursuers took up the position that, a rent review having occurred, substantial additional rental payments would require to be made by the defenders. Although receipts granted by the pursuers, I was informed, were unqualified, it appears to me that it would be quite wrong for the court to ignore the terms of the correspondence to which I have referred. Furthermore, although I recognise that there may be cases in which an issue of waiver could be determined solely on the basis of the pleadings of the parties, essentially the question raised by such a plea is a question of fact. In this connection I have in mind the observations of Lord Keith in *Armia Ltd v Daejan Developments Ltd* at p 165, which were founded upon by the pursuers. There he stated that whether or not there had been waiver of a right was a question of fact, to be determined objectively upon a consideration of all the relevant evidence. In the light of that observation, it would appear to me to be wrong to follow the course suggested by counsel for the defenders and to deprive the pursuers of an opportunity of establishing the position which they took up in the correspondence which I have mentioned.

"Some reliance was placed by the defenders upon the decision in *Davies v City of Glasgow Friendly Society*. However I note that that case did not involve a plea of waiver. Furthermore, it appears to me that the court was particularly concerned about the implications of any course other than that which it followed in relation to a contract of employment, which was, of course, the kind of contract involved there. Accordingly, for these reasons, it does not appear to me that the decision in that case is of assistance in deciding the present issues.

"In all these circumstances I shall repel pleas in law nos 3 and 4 for the defenders and otherwise allow a proof before answer."

Counsel for Pursuers, Bennett; Solicitors, Gray Muirhead, WS — Counsel for Defenders, Bell, QC; Solicitors, Drummond Miller, WS (for James Turnbull & Co, Stenhousemuir).

C H

Sabre Leasing Ltd v Copeland

FIRST DIVISION

THE LORD PRESIDENT (HOPE), LORDS ALLANBRIDGE AND MACLEAN

18 MARCH 1993

Process — Pleadings — Defences — Specification — Action by finance company based on contract — Defenders having dealt with suppliers, denying dealings with pursuers — Whether open to defenders to argue that no contract existed through pursuers' failure to intimate their acceptance.

Contract — Offer and acceptance — Proof of acceptance — Offer by customer forwarded by supplier to finance company — Whether finance company bound to aver and prove intimation to customer of their acceptance.

A finance company sought payment of a sum claimed by them to be due to them in respect of the hire of a telephone system. The pursuers claimed that the agreement was constituted by the completion and signature on behalf of both parties of a written hire agreement, on a standard printed form. The supplier of the equipment had completed most of the details of the agreement, which was then signed on the defenders' behalf by one of the defenders and was sent by the supplier to the pursuers. Thereafter the pursuers' representative signed the agreement on the pursuers' behalf. In their pleadings the defenders denied that they had had any contact or dealings with the pursuers or that they had entered into any hire agreement with them. At proof the pursuers led no evidence that any steps had been taken to intimate to the defenders that the pursuers had signed the agreement. The defenders submitted that the pursuers had failed as a result to prove that a contract had been entered into. The sheriff refused to hear this argument on the ground that this was not a matter which had been specifically averred. The sheriff principal allowed an appeal by the defenders. The pursuers appealed to the Court of Session, arguing that the defenders had not

A given fair notice in their pleadings of this line of evidence, which was a matter within the defenders' own knowledge. The pursuers would have conducted their case entirely differently if they had had notice that the question of lack of intimation of the acceptance was to be put in issue.

Held, (1) that in the absence of any admission by the defenders on the point, it was for the pursuers to prove their averment by showing not only that there was an offer and an acceptance of it, but also that the offerer had been made aware of the fact that the offer had B been accepted (p 1101H-I); (2) that in the absence of evidence on this point the pursuers had failed to discharge the onus which rested on them since the defenders, by their denials, had given sufficient notice to the pursuers that no admission was being made by them to the effect that an agreement had been entered into between the parties, and the burden of proof resting on the pursuers had accordingly not been discharged (pp 1101L-1102A); and appeal *refused*.

C ———————

Appeal from the sheriff court
Sabre Leasing Ltd raised an action in the sheriff court at Dumfries against Henry C Copeland, Elizabeth G Copeland and John Dalgleish, trading as The Braids Caravan Park, seeking payment of rental arrears in respect of the hire of a telephone system.

The case came to proof before the sheriff.

D **Textbook referred to**
Gloag, *Contract* (2nd ed), p 35.

The sheriff *granted* decree for payment by the defenders to the pursuers of the sum sued for.

The defenders appealed to the sheriff principal, who *sustained* the appeal and *granted* decree of absolvitor.

The pursuers appealed to the Court of Session.

E **Appeal**
The appeal was heard before the First Division on 18 March 1993.

Eo die the court *affirmed* the interlocutor of the sheriff principal and *refused* the appeal.

The following opinion of the court was delivered by the Lord President (Hope):

F **OPINION OF THE COURT.**—This is an action of payment in which the pursuers are a finance company. They seek payment from the defenders, who carry on business in partnership, of a sum of money which they claim to be due and resting owing to them in respect of the hire of a telephone system. The sheriff held that a hire agreement was entered into between the pursuers and the defenders for the hire of the telephone system, and that the defenders were in breach of the agreement in respect of unpaid rentals amounting to the sum sued for. He granted

decree for payment by the defenders to the pursuers of that sum. The defenders then appealed to the G sheriff principal, who held that no binding contract had been entered into between the parties and granted decree of absolvitor. The pursuers have now appealed against his interlocutor to this court.

A number of issues were raised in the course of the appeal to the sheriff principal, but the argument before us was confined to a single point which, as counsel for the pursuers recognised, is fundamental to their case. According to their averments, a hire agreement was entered into between the parties on or about H 29 June 1990 in respect of the hire of a London 8 telephone system. The sum sued for is calculated under reference to the terms of the hire agreement, and the pursuers also found upon a clause in the hire agreement to the effect that they are not liable for any warranties, conditions or guarantees express or implied in respect of the equipment. The defenders, however, lodged answers in which they deny that a hire agreement was entered into between the parties. They also deny that they had any contact or dealings with the I pursuers. They explain that they were approached by a representative acting for a firm known as Copy Consultants Group of Carlisle. The representative solicited an order from them for the hire of a telephone system, and they supplied them with a telephone system after the defenders had explained their requirements. This system proved to be unsuitable and defective and, after an attempt to give it a fair trial, the defenders decided to reject the equipment. They returned all the portable items to Copy Consultants J Group who accepted their return, and they then isolated the fixed equipment so that it could not be used. They deny they are due and resting owing to the pursuers in the sum sued for.

The sheriff before whom the case came for proof was satisfied, after considering the evidence, that the pursuers and the defenders entered into a hire agreement in respect of the telephone system. In his view the agreement was constituted by the completion and K signature on behalf of both parties of a written hire agreement. Most of the details on this agreement, which consisted of a standard printed form, were completed by the supplier of the equipment. It was then signed by the third defender, John Dalgleish, on the defenders' behalf, and it was sent by the supplier to the pursuers for their attention. On 29 June 1990 the pursuers' representative, Miss C A Hammond, signed the agreement on the pursuers' behalf. There was no evidence that any steps were then taken to intimate to L the defenders that the pursuers had signed the agreement. On the contrary there was evidence from the defenders that they received no communication of any kind from the pursuers until they eventually received a letter from them intimating that they were in arrears. Up until that stage all they had was a copy of the hire agreement which had been given to them by the supplier of the equipment on which the only signature was that of Mr Dalgleish. The defenders submitted to the sheriff that the pursuers had failed to prove that a contract was entered into between the parties, because there was no evidence of any intimation to the defenders that the pursuers had signed the agreement. But the sheriff refused to entertain this argument, on the ground that this was not a matter which had been specifically averred by the defenders in their pleadings and it was not therefore open to them to argue the point on which they had given no notice to the pursuers.

The sheriff principal took a different view from the sheriff on this matter. He was satisfied that, when an offer has been made and is accepted outwith the presence of the offerer, the contract is only completed when the offerer is made aware of the fact of the acceptance. It was submitted to him on the pursuers' behalf that the pursuers would only have required to prove intimation of the acceptance if this point had been put in issue by the defenders, and that since this had not been done in the present case there was no need for them to lead evidence on the point. He decided, however, with some hesitation, that the defenders had raised this issue. He noted that the evidence for the defenders that they received no communication from the pursuers was unchallenged, and that one witness for the pursuers said that the suppliers were informed that the offer had been accepted but did not suggest that the defenders had been so informed. He held that in that situation the pursuers had failed to establish that there had been a completed contract between the parties and, having made a finding in fact and law to that effect, he recalled the sheriff's interlocutor and assoilzied the defenders from the crave of the initial writ.

Counsel for the pursuers did not dispute the point that intimation of the fact of the acceptance was necessary to complete the contract. Nor did he suggest that the sheriff principal had formed an incorrect view of the evidence. His point was that the sheriff principal erred in holding that the defenders had given sufficient notice in their pleadings of the argument that there were no concluded contract between the parties because the pursuers had allegedly not intimated their acceptance of the defenders' offer to take the equipment on hire. He submitted that the defenders had not given fair notice in their pleadings of this line of defence. This was, he said, a matter which was within the defenders' own knowledge prior to the proof and they had no good reason for not making any averments about it. They had restricted their defences to what he described as a vague denial that there was a contract, and he submitted that the effect of this was to disable them from developing any specific arguments on the point. He said that the pursuers would have conducted their case entirely differently if they had had notice that the question of lack of intimation of the acceptance was to be put in issue.

The pursuers' pleadings on this matter are confined to a single averment which is in these terms: "On or about 29 June 1990, a hire agreement was entered into between the pursuers and the defenders in respect of the hire of one London 8 telephone system". It will be observed that there is no specification in this averment

of the way in which the alleged agreement was constituted. The date which is mentioned here is the date when the hire agreement was signed by Miss Hammond on the pursuers' behalf, but this point is not explained in the averment. Nevertheless there is no doubt that, by setting out an averment in these terms, the pursuers undertook to prove that a hire agreement was entered into between the parties in respect of the equipment. Gloag on *Contract* (2nd ed), p 35 states: "The onus of proof that acceptance has been posted, or otherwise dispatched, lies on the acceptor. But it is sufficient if he can prove that the offerer were made aware of the fact of acceptance".

It was an essential part of the pursuers' case that the parties entered into a hire agreement in terms of which the sum sued for was to be paid. If the defenders' response to this averment had been to admit that they entered into the hire agreement this would, of course, have relieved the pursuers of the necessity of establishing the point by evidence. But, in the absence of any admission on the point, it was for the pursuers to prove their averment. In order to do this it was necessary for them to show not only that there was an offer and an acceptance of it, but also that the offerer was made aware of the fact that the offer had been accepted. The lack of detail in the pursuers' averments may perhaps have misled them as to what was necessary in order to prove the formation of the contract. But in our opinion the defenders were entitled to put the pursuers to their proof on this point.

Counsel for the pursuers' argument was directed to the lack of notice in the defences. The opening sentences of ans 2 are in these terms: "Denied that a hire agreement was entered into between the pursuers and the defenders. Denied that the defenders had any contact or dealings with the pursuers. Denied they entered into any contract or agreement with them".

In the averments which follow the defenders explain that their dealings in respect of the order for the hire of the telephone system and its rejection were with the suppliers Copy Consultants Group. It is true that they do not aver in terms that the pursuers did not intimate to them that they had accepted the offer. But we agree with the sheriff principal that their denial that they had any contact or dealings with the pursuers, together with their denial that a hire agreement was entered into between the pursuers and the defenders, was sufficient to give notice to the pursuers that the point was in issue. As counsel for the defenders submitted in the course of his argument, it is clear from these denials that the defenders were challenging the existence of a contract between the parties. Accordingly it was for the pursuers in these circumstances to lead sufficient evidence to prove that a contract had been entered into. Since intimation of the acceptance was necessary in order to conclude the contract, there can be no doubt that this was a matter on which the pursuers required to lead evidence in order to prove their averment. In the absence of evidence on this point the pursuers failed to discharge the onus which rested on them, since the defenders, by their denials, gave sufficient notice to the pursuers that no admis-

A sion was being made by them to the effect that an agreement had been entered into between the parties.

The answer to the point raised in this appeal, therefore, is that the pursuers failed to discharge the onus of proof which rested on them. It was an essential part of their case that a hire agreement was entered into between the pursuers and the defenders in respect of the equipment. The defenders not only made no admission on the point but, by their express denials, put the point in issue. They also gave notice of their position that they had no contact or dealings with the
B pursuers at any time but dealt only with the suppliers of the equipment. In this state of the pleadings it was for the pursuers to lead the evidence which would have entitled the sheriff to find as a fact that a hire agreement was entered into between the parties in respect of the equipment. The consequence of their failure to lead this evidence is that the burden of proof which rested on them was not discharged.

For these reasons we shall affirm the interlocutor of
C the sheriff principal and refuse this appeal.

Counsel for Pursuers and Appellants, Kinloch; Solicitors, Anderson Strathern, WS — Counsel for Defenders and Respondents, Ivey; Solicitors, Shepherd & Wedderburn, WS.

P A A

D

McLuskie v City of Glasgow District Council

EXTRA DIVISION

LORDS McCLUSKEY, PROSSER AND WYLIE

26 MARCH 1993

E *Licensing — Licensing committee — Application for renewal of street trader's licence — Application granted for restricted period — Whether application "refused" — Discretion of licensing body in fixing duration — Whether duty to give reasons for restriction of period of licence — Civic Government (Scotland) Act 1982 (c 45), Sched 1, paras 5 (1), 8 (2) and 17.*

Paragraph 5 (1) of Sched 1 to the Civic Government (Scotland) Act 1982 directs a licensing authority, on an application for the grant or renewal of a licence, to
F grant or renew the licence unconditionally or subject to conditions or to refuse to grant or renew the licence. By para 8 (2) a licence shall have effect for three years or such shorter period as the licensing authority may decide. By para 17 (1) a licensing authority shall on being required to do so, give reasons in writing for arriving at any decision inter alia to grant or renew a licence or to refuse to do so.

A Glasgow street trader holding a licence in terms of s 39 of the 1982 Act was granted a three year licence in April 1988 and applied in January 1991 to the

council as the relevant licensing body for a renewal of her licence for a further period of three years. The G licensing committee granted a renewal for a restricted period of two years. The trader's solicitors requested from the licensing body their reasons in writing for granting the licence for a restricted period. The licensing body declined to give reasons for their decision. The trader appealed in terms of para 18 of Sched 1 to the 1982 Act to the sheriff, who refused the appeal, holding that the committee had an absolute discretion as to duration of the licence in terms of para 8 (2) (b) of Sched 1. The trader appealed to the Court of H Session.

The appellant contended that the committee had to be taken as having refused the application and in any event, given the terms of para 17 of Sched 1, that there could be no dispute that the committee were obliged to give reasons in writing for arriving at their decision because they had been requested to do so within the period specified and their decision had to be viewed either as a decision to renew or a decision to refuse to renew. Any decision by the committee on a restriction I of the period was integral with the decision taken to renew. The respondents submitted that there was a renewal of the licence and that at the time when the decision to renew was taken, a separate decision was taken as to the duration of the licence.

Held, (1) that the decision had been to renew the appellant's licence, albeit for a shorter period than that sought (pp 1106F, 1107H and 1108G); (2) that the obligation to give reasons on request under para 17 J had to be read as including a decision to restrict the duration of a licence under para 8 (2) (b) because (per Lords McCluskey and Wylie) whether or not such a decision was integral to the decision to grant or refuse a licence, the matter was of importance to the applicant and the Act should be construed in favour of the liberty of the subject and as providing a remedy for an adverse decision under para 8 (2) (b) (pp 1106G-L, 1107C-D and 1108G); (per Lord Prosser) the question of duration was so closely related to the decision to K grant or renew that it was unrealistic to regard the two matters as separate (p 1108B-E); and (3) that in view of the passage of time since the committee's decision and since the respondents indicated that they did not know what facts might have influenced the committee, the sheriff should now exercise his power under para 18 (9) to modify the decision (pp 1107D-F, 1108F and 1108G); and appeal *allowed* and case *remitted* to the sheriff with an instruction to him to modify the decision of the licensing authority by renewing the L appellant's licence for a period of three years.

Appeal from the sheriff court

Mrs Helen McLuskie applied to the City of Glasgow District Council for a renewal of her street trader's licence in respect of her pitch at the west side of Virginia Street at its junction with Argyle Street, Glasgow. Her application was considered by the council's subcommittee on licensing applications at a

meeting on 13 June 1991, as a result of which her
application was granted but for a restricted period.

Statutory provisions

The Civic Government (Scotland) Act 1982
provides:

"5.—(1) Where an application for the grant or
renewal of a licence has been made to a licensing
authority they shall, in accordance with this paragraph
— (a) grant or renew the licence unconditionally; (b)
grant or renew the licence subject to conditions; or (c)
refuse to grant or renew the licence.

"(2) The conditions referred to in sub-paragraph (1)
(b) above shall be such reasonable conditions as the
licensing authority think fit and, without prejudice to
that generality, may include — (a) conditions restricting the validity of a licence to an area or areas specified
in the licence; and (b) in relation to the grant of a
licence, where that licence is intended to replace an
existing licence, a condition requiring the holder of
the existing licence to surrender it in accordance with
paragraph 13 below. . . .

"8.—(1) Subject to and in accordance with the provisions of this paragraph, a licence shall come into
force on being granted by a licensing authority or on
such later date as they may specify as a condition of
the licence and shall continue in force on being
renewed by them.

"(2) Subject to the provisions of this paragraph, a
licence shall have effect— (a) for a period of three years
from the date when it comes into force; or (b) for such
shorter period as the licensing authority may decide at
the time when they grant or renew the licence. . . .

"17.—(1) A licensing authority shall, within 10 days
of being required to do so under sub-paragraph (2)
below, give reasons in writing for arriving at any
decision of theirs under this Schedule — (a) to grant
or renew a licence or to refuse to do so; (b) to consent
or to refuse to consent to a material change in any
premises, vehicle or vessel; (c) to vary or refuse to vary
the terms of a licence; (d) in relation to paragraph 11
above — (i) to suspend a licence or refuse to do so; (ii)
as to the period of suspension; (iii) ordering immediate
suspension; (e) to suspend a licence under paragraph
12 above or to refuse to do so.

"(2) Reasons for a decision referred to in sub-
paragraph (1) above shall be given by the licensing
authority on a request being made to the authority by
a relevant person within 28 days of the date of the
decision.

"(3) Nothing in this paragraph affects the power of
the sheriff under paragraph 18 below to require a
licensing authority to give reasons for a decision of the
authority — (a) which is being appealed to the sheriff
under that paragraph; and (b) for which reasons have
not been given under this paragraph.

"(4) In this paragraph, 'relevant person' means — (a)
in respect of a decision specified in sub-paragraph (1)
(a) above, the applicant or any person who made a rele-

vant objection or representation (within the meaning
of paragraph 19 below) in relation to the application
to which the decision relates . . .

"18.—(1) Subject to sub-paragraph (2) below, a
person who may, under this Schedule, require a licensing authority to give him reasons for their decision
may appeal to the sheriff against that decision. . . .

"(6) For the purposes of an appeal under this paragraph, the sheriff may, in the case of a decision of a
licensing authority for which reasons have not been
given by the authority under paragraph 17 above,
require the authority to give reasons for that decision,
and the authority shall comply with such a
requirement.

"(7) The sheriff may uphold an appeal under this
paragraph only if he considers that the licensing
authority, in arriving at their decision — (a) erred in
law; (b) based their decision on any incorrect material
fact; (c) acted contrary to natural justice; or (d) exercised their discretion in an unreasonable manner. . . .

"(9) On upholding an appeal under this paragraph,
the sheriff may— (a) remit the case with the reasons for
his decision to the licensing authority for reconsideration of their decision; or (b) reverse or modify the
decision of the authority, and on remitting a case
under sub-sub-paragraph (a) above the sheriff may—
(i) specify a date by which the reconsideration by the
authority must take place; (ii) modify any procedural
steps which otherwise would be required in relation to
the matter by or under any enactment (including this
Act)."

Cases referred to

Baillie v Wilson, 1917 1 SLT 96; 1917 SC 55.
Wolfson v Glasgow District Licensing Board, 1981 SLT
    17; 1980 SC 136.

The applicant appealed to the sheriff in terms of
para 18 of Sched 1 to the 1982 Act.

On 10 March 1992 the sheriff *dismissed* the appeal.

The applicant appealed to the Court of Session.

Appeal

The appeal was heard before an Extra Division on
26 February 1993.

On 26 March 1993 the court *allowed* the appeal and
remitted the case to the sheriff with an instruction to
him to modify the decision of the licensing authority
by renewing the appellant's licence for a period of
three years expiring on the last day of May 1994.

LORD McCLUSKEY.—The appellant is a street
trader with a pitch at the west side of Virginia Street
at its junction with Argyle Street, Glasgow and has
operated there as a street trader for over 30 years.
Since the coming into force of the relevant provisions
in the Civic Government (Scotland) Act 1982 she has
held a street trader's licence of the kind governed by

A s 39 of the 1982 Act. In April 1988 she was granted a three year licence which was due to expire on 31 March 1991. Three years is the maximum period for which such a licence can have effect under para 8 of Sched 1 to the 1982 Act. On 4 January 1991 she applied to the defenders and respondents for a renewal of her licence for a period of three years. She was advised that her application would be considered by the defenders' subcommittee on licensing applications at a meeting to be held on 13 June 1991. She duly attended the meeting accompanied by her solicitor.

B There were no objections to the renewal of the application nor were there any adverse comments from any of the agencies having a possible interest in the matter, including the police, environmental health and building control. There was no discussion at the hearing in the presence of the appellant or her solicitor about the duration of the licence. On 18 June 1991 the solicitor to the respondents wrote a letter to the appellant's solicitors in the following terms:

"Dear Sirs

C *Civic Government (Scotland) Act 1982*
Your Client — Helen McLuskie

"As required by Paragraph 5 (5) of Schedule 1 to the Civic Government (Scotland) Act, 1982, I hereby inform you that the Sub-committee on Licensing Applications at a meeting held on 13 June, 1991 granted your client's application for the renewal of a Street Trader's Licence.

"I would confirm that the Sub-committee also

D granted dispensation from (a) that part of Condition No. 9 relating to the size of the vehicle, kiosk, or moveable stall, and (b) Condition No. 13. It should be noted that this licence, unless otherwise suspended or surrendered, expires on the last day of May 1993. The licence was granted for a restricted period.

"Yours faithfully,

"Solicitor to the Council. (*signature*)"

On 20 June the appellant's solicitors replied to the respondents' solicitor in the following terms:

E "Dear Sir,

Our Client: Helen McLuskie
Civic Government (Scotland) Act, 1982

"We are in receipt of your letter of 18th June and note that the Licence granted is for a restricted period only. We may have misunderstood what was said to us when the decision was communicated. We rather thought that the Committee had granted the Licence for the full period but had restricted the dispensation

F for a period of two years in order to bring it into line with the dispensation granted to Gerard McLuskie as we understood it from Mrs McLuskie. That would have been acceptable. However, we see that the main Licence itself has only been granted for two years and that is not acceptable. Accordingly, we hereby formally on behalf of Mrs McLuskie request reasons in writing for the Committee granting the Licence for a restricted period.

"Yours faithfully,

"Gordon & Smyth"

G It is clear therefore that well within the 10 days specified in para 17 of Sched 1 to the 1982 Act the appellant through her agents was requiring the respondents to give reasons in writing for arriving at the decision which had been intimated in the letter of 18 June quoted above. Nonetheless the respondents declined to give reasons for their decision. Their position all along has been that they were under no obligation to give reasons as their decision to fix the duration of the renewed licence at a period of two years, rather than three years, was a decision lying within their unfettered discretion; as their discretion

H was unfettered they were entitled to decline to give any reason whatsoever to anyone at any time for making the decision as to the duration of the licence. The appellant considered herself aggrieved by the decision of the defenders and also by their failure to give any reasons for deciding the duration of the licence in the way they had done. She accordingly availed herself of the provisions under para 18 of Sched 1 to the 1982 Act and appealed to the sheriff. The respondents lodged answers to her appeal writ.

I Their pleas in law indicate that their position was that they had not acted contrary to natural justice, and had exercised their discretion in a manner that could not be characterised as unreasonable. They also had a general plea to the relevancy and specification of the pursuer and appellant's appeal to the sheriff. They had no plea to the competency. On 10 March 1992 the sheriff, having heard parties' procurators on the application, dismissed the application. The present appeal is taken against that interlocutor. Paragraph 18 (12)

J allows any party to an appeal to the sheriff under para 18 to appeal on a point of law from the sheriff's decision to the Court of Session within 28 days from the date of that decision. The sheriff, at the request of the appellant, wrote a note in respect of the interlocutor of 10 March 1992. It was in the following terms:

"The pursuer appealed on the ground that by renewing her licence for two years instead of three, the defenders had refused her one year's licence and had

K not stated their reasons therefor and that by refusing to do so had acted contrary to natural justice.

"I was of opinion that para 8 (2) (b) of Sched 1 to the Civic Government Act 1982 gave the defenders an absolute discretion as to the time of renewing any licence for reasons quite unconnected with the suitability of an applicant for renewal of licence and that the defenders were not bound to give their reasons therefor, eg planning changes for a locus. The authori-

L ties to whom [sic] the pursuer referred me did not seem to me to derogate from the view I had formed of para 8 (2) (b)".

Counsel for the appellant submitted that what the respondents had done was to refuse the appellant's application. That being so the terms of para 17 obliged the licensing authority to give reasons for the decision to refuse the renewal. But even if what the respondents had done was to grant the renewal the same paragraph still obliged them, if requested timeously, to give reasons in writing for the decision. She drew our attention to the terms of paras 4 (1), 5 (1), (2) and (3), 6, 7, 8 (1) and (2), 10, 17 (1) and (2) and 18. In support of her submission that the respondents had refused her application, she referred us to two liquor licensing cases, *Baillie v Wilson* and *Wolfson v Glasgow District Licensing Board*, but reminded us that different statutory provisions prevailed in relation to such cases. In particular, the position at the time of *Wolfson* was governed by s 30 (3) of the Licensing (Scotland) Act 1976.

It is perhaps convenient to note at least in summary what the quoted paragraphs deal with. Paragraph 4 makes it plain that, except in special circumstances, the licensing authority does not require to have a hearing attended by the applicant. Paragraph 5 empowers the authority to grant or renew the licence unconditionally, to grant or renew it subject to conditions or to refuse to grant or renew the licence. Paragraph 5 (3) requires the licensing authority to refuse an application to grant or renew a licence in certain circumstances, none of which applies in the present case, but it goes on, "and otherwise shall grant the application". Paragraph 7 permits the licensing authority to grant temporary licences for periods not exceeding six weeks. Paragraph 8 includes the following: [his Lordship quoted the terms of para 8 (1) and (2) and continued:]

Paragraph 9 contains provisions about notification by the holder of a licence of any material change of circumstances. Paragraph 10 permits the licensing authority to vary the terms of a licence on any grounds they think fit. Paragraph 11 empowers the licensing authority to suspend a licence in certain specified circumstances. The material parts of para 17 are as follows: [his Lordship quoted the terms of para 17 set out supra and continued:]

Paragraph 18 permits "a person who may, under this Schedule, require a licensing authority to give him reasons for their decision" to appeal to the sheriff against that decision. The sheriff may uphold an appeal in certain circumstances specified in subpara (7). If he upholds an appeal then, under subpara (9), he may "remit the case with reasons for his decision to the licensing authority for reconsideration of their decision; or (b) reverse or modify the decision of the authority". Subparagraph (6) permits the sheriff, in the case of a decision of a licensing authority for which reasons have not been given under para 17, to require the authority to give reasons for that decision.

Counsel for the appellant submitted that, given the terms of para 17, there could be no dispute that the licensing authority were obliged to give reasons in writing for arriving at their decision because they had been requested to do so within the period specified and their decision must be viewed either as a decision to renew or a decision to refuse to renew. She accepted that they were free, under para 8, to decide that the licence should expire within the maximum period of three years; but if they so decided they had to give reasons for doing so. Any such decision was integral

with the decision taken to renew, which was narrated in the letter of 18 June 1991. If the restriction of the period to two years was not to be regarded as a refusal of the application, which was for a licence for three years, then the fixing of the shorter period was integral with the decision to renew and formed part of that decision. In these circumstances, she submitted that the court should remit the case to the sheriff requiring him to exercise his powers under subpara 9. However, having regard to the terms of ans 7 of the writ and answers which were before the sheriff, it was plain that the respondents were not now in a position to give reasons. She referred in particular to the averment there, "Not known and not admitted what facts might have influenced the committee". Having regard to that and the lapse of time the appropriate course would be for the sheriff to reverse the decision of the authority by granting the application for a renewal for a three year period, or to modify the authority's decision by making the licence endure for the three years which had been applied for.

In reply, counsel for the respondents submitted that the critical issue was whether or not the court was satisfied that the respondents were obliged to give a statement of reasons in relation to a decision which had plainly been taken under para 8 (2) (b) as to the duration of the licence. He wished to take no technical pleading point in relation to the appellant's argument, presented on an esto basis, that if the application had not been refused it had been granted but nonetheless attracted the obligation to give reasons in writing. In fact he submitted that there was a renewal of the licence, as intimated in the letter of 18 June, and at the time when the decision to renew was taken a separate decision was taken as to the duration of the licence. The critical matter was that the decision as to duration was not an integral part of the renewal decision. It was a separate decision under a separate provision relating only to the duration of licences. He accepted that para 5 (3) referred to a refusal of an application or a grant or renewal of an application but he drew attention to the fact that para 17 spoke of granting or renewing "a licence", not an application. He submitted that para 17, which required the authority to give reasons in writing if required to do so, did not apply to a decision under para 8 (2). Indeed if one looked at the five separate matters dealt with in para 17 (1), letters (a) to (e) it could be seen that they followed the scheme of the earlier paragraphs: (a) referred to paras 4 and 5; (b) referred to para 9; (c) referred to para 10; (d) referred to para 11; and (e) referred to para 12. None of the five referred to para 8. In his submission para 8 was not referred to in para 17 because Parliament had not intended that the decision as to the duration of a licence, which was undoubtedly left to the absolute discretion of the licensing authority, should be subject to review. Accordingly there was no point in requiring the licensing authority to give reasons in writing for arriving at such a decision. It also followed that the present appeal and the application to the sheriff were both incompetent because para 18 (1) restricted the

A right of appeal to a person who could require the licensing authority to give reasons for the decision. He acknowledged that there was no plea to the competency taken by the respondents but submitted that it was pars judicis to notice the incompetency of the appeal. If an applicant was upset by a decision to restrict the licence to a period less than that applied for the applicant could simply apply again towards the end of the restricted period. The matter at issue was not unimportant; there were many such applicants and they were heard by the licensing authority at fre-

B quent and regular intervals. There was no record of the proceedings and it could be a substantial burden to have to give reasons for decisions made in the exercise of an unfettered discretion. Accordingly it made perfectly good sense for Parliament not to oblige an authority to give a statement of reasons in respect of such a matter lying wholly within their discretion. The cases referred to by counsel for the appellant were clearly distinguishable for the reason which she had acknowledged, namely that they turned upon the

C terms of the statutes which were wholly differently worded. In any event, those cases were concerned with restrictions which affected the manner in which the liquor licence could be operated. In the present instance the licence was granted without any such restriction. It was only the duration that was restricted. The sheriff had reached the right conclusion. If, however, the court concluded that the sheriff had reached the wrong conclusion then the appropriate course would be to remit to the sheriff with an instruc-

D tion to him to exercise his power under para 18 (9) (a) and to remit the case to the licensing authority requiring them to explain their decision.

In my opinion the appellant is entitled to succeed. Paragraph 5 (3) makes it plain that the licensing authority must either refuse an application to renew a licence or grant "the application". This application was for a renewal for a period of three years. Had para 5 stood alone it might be said that they had neither

E granted the application nor refused it; but I accept that under para 8 (2) they had the right to decide that they should renew but for a shorter period. To that extent, para 8 appears to me to modify the terms of para 5 (3). Reading them together therefore the authority is obliged to renew the application or to grant it or to grant it but for a shorter period than that applied for. (Other provisions permit them to adject conditions, but we are not concerned with that.) The real question, therefore, is whether or not the decision they

F took and intimated in the letter of 18 June 1991, which I treat as a decision to renew the licence, falls to be regarded as a decision of the kind specified in para 17 (1) (a) (to grant or renew a licence or to refuse to do so) or really amounts to two decisions, one in relation to renewal and the other in relation to duration. I can see force in the submission by counsel for the respondents as narrated earlier, particularly because the decision as to duration appears to be one lying within the discretion of the licensing authority, and also because the layout of the sub-subparagraphs of 17 (1) reflects the earlier layout of the Schedule and

points to an intention to omit a decision as to duration under 8 (2) (b) from the decisions in respect of which G written reasons can be demanded. But I simply cannot tell, as a matter of law, whether or not the decision in relation to duration of a licence is integral with the decision to renew, even upon the assumption that the decision is to be regarded as a decision to renew a licence. Counsel for the respondents accepted in the course of the debate that, although in this case the period chosen was two years, his argument led to the view that an even shorter period might be decided upon without any reasons given or without any right H of appeal. There is simply no way in which, as a matter of law, one can determine what shorter period would be so short as to vitiate the purported renewal of the licence. The value of the licence to the street trader might or might not be affected by the imposition of a period of less than three years. But one cannot tell that as a matter of law. Nor is it possible, as a matter of law, to determine what the result of the voting by the members of the authority would have been if there had been a division of opinion as to the I appropriate duration of the licence.

I see no reason at all why this court should assume that the decision as to the duration of the licence was necessarily separate from and independent of the decision to renew. Both decisions fall to be taken at the same time in terms of para 8 (2) (b) and I see no reason to assume that the decision on duration might not have influenced the decision in relation to renewal. It may be that it would make sense for Parliament to legislate that a decision on duration should be regarded as a J separate decision which does not need to be explained and cannot be appealed, but I consider that if Parliament had intended so to legislate it could and should have done so expressly. I should be reluctant to imply a denial of a right to a statement of reasons in relation to a matter which might, in the particular circumstances of any individual street trader, be absolutely crucial to the carrying on of his business. All persons in business, including street traders, have to make plans for the future and one could well suppose that K certain street traders would be seriously embarrassed by a decision taken under para 8 (2) (b) to limit the licence for a period materially shorter than that applied for. Yet the respondents' argument is that they had no statutory remedy. Insofar as the matter is in doubt I should construe this Schedule in favour of the liberty of the subject. In doing so I would be following a well established principle of statutory construction. But I should be doing no more than holding that a licensing authority which takes a deliberate decision to L depart from the presumptive period of three years in para 8 (2) (a) and to decide upon a shorter period when renewing the licence should explain why they are doing so.

In any event, the Schedule to the Act is so drawn that the applicant is entitled to demand reasons even for a renewal. Accordingly this appellant was entitled to seek and obtain reasons why her application was granted. But the respondents' position is that while they were obliged to give reasons for renewing (which they did not give), they were not obliged to give reasons for restricting the duration of the renewed licence to a restricted period; nor were they obliged to disclose whether or not the decision to restrict was integral to or separate from the decision to renew. I am not at all impressed by the suggestion that there are a lot of such decisions to be taken and no proper record is kept of the proceedings at which the decisions are made. If the licensing authority chooses to exercise its discretion behind closed doors and does so without having given the applicant the slightest hint that the period for the duration of the licence for which she has applied is unsuitable, and without giving her any opportunity to comment upon the possible effects upon her business of a shorter period, then it places no serious hardship upon the authority to be required, if requested, to give the reason for the restriction at the same time as they gave the reasons for the renewal. Equally it would hardly be surprising if Parliament allowed the applicant a right of appeal in such circumstances. It might well be appropriate in such a case for the appellant to request the sheriff to require the authority to give reasons for their decision under para 18 (6) and, if she persuades the sheriff that there are sound grounds for doing so, to invite the sheriff to remit the case to the licensing authority for reconsideration of their decision. Accordingly, believing as I do that Parliament would not take away the right of appeal conferred in respect of other aspects without some clear and unambiguous provision for doing so, I consider that we should construe para 17 as including a decision of a kind that is included in para 8 (2) (b). I would, therefore, allow the appeal.

In my opinion, it would serve no purpose now to send the case back to the sheriff with instructions to him to remit the case back to the licensing authority. It is now nearly two years since the licensing authority took its decision. The pleadings of the respondents indicate that they do not know what facts might have influenced the committee. It appears to me that having regard to that averment and the passage of time, any reason which was now given for the decision would be likely to be a construction based upon something other than genuine recollection. In any event, para 18 (9) envisages that the sheriff may either remit the case to the licensing authority for "reconsideration" of their decision or that he should reverse or modify the decision of the authority. It does not appear to me that it is appropriate to invite the licensing authority to "reconsider" their decision. That is not and was never the point in relation to this application and appeal. It appears to me that for that reason and because it is now in practical terms too late to require them to give reasons under para 18 (6) the sheriff should exercise his power under para 18 (9). I therefore move that the case be remitted to the sheriff with an instruction to him to modify the decision of the licensing authority by renewing the appellant's licence for a period of three years so that it expires on the last day of May 1994.

LORD PROSSER.—Your Lordship in the chair has described the background to this appeal, and its

statutory context. In contending that the respondents were obliged to give reasons for their decision, the appellant founds upon para 17 (1) (a) of Sched 1 to the Civic Government (Scotland) Act 1982. In terms of that provision, the respondents were obliged to give the appellant reasons for their decision under para 5 of the Schedule, regardless of whether that decision is to be seen as a refusal or a renewal. The appellant required them to give reasons for their decision. They have not done so.

The primary contention advanced on behalf of the appellant was to the effect that the respondents' decision constituted a "refusal" for the purposes of para 17. The sheriff rejected that proposition, and I am entirely satisfied that he was right to do so. The appellant's licence was not refused. It was renewed. The fact that it was renewed for a shorter period than she had applied for does not, in my opinion, justify treating the decision as either a constructive refusal, or a partial refusal, so as to oblige the respondents to give reasons for a "refusal".

The alternative proposition advanced on behalf of the appellant was to the effect that, if the decision was a renewal, the respondents were nonetheless obliged, if required, to give reasons for that decision. In itself, I did not understand that proposition to be disputed by the respondents. It was however emphasised on their behalf that the decision for which reasons had to be given, in terms of para 17, was a decision under para 5; and that reasons for that decision had to be given only if required. It was suggested, I think, that what the appellant had sought, upon a correct construction of her solicitors' letter, had been not their reasons for their decision under para 5, but reasons for their decision under para 8. In any event, even upon the assumption that there had been a valid requirement to give reasons for the decision under para 5, it was submitted that the respondents would only have to provide their reasons for actually renewing the licence, with no obligation (in response to such a requirement or otherwise) to provide reasons for their decision, in terms of para 8, to restrict the duration of the renewed licence to a period of two years.

In my opinion, there is some force in the suggestion that what was being sought by the appellant's solicitors was indeed reasons for the restriction, rather than reasons for the decision. But I have come to the view that this is too stark a contrast, and that what was being sought was the respondents' reasons for their decision, that decision being seen as one which involved both the positive feature of renewal, and the negative feature of a restriction as to time. Whether that was a valid requirement depends upon the substantive question: in giving reasons for their decision, under para 5, to renew the licence, were the respondents obliged to include, within those reasons, their reasons for deciding, in terms of para 8, that the renewal should be for a restricted period rather than the three year period which had been sought, and which, in the absence of a decision to restrict, would be the effective period in terms of para 8?

It is true that the respondents' decision to restrict,
A in terms of para 8, is an unfettered one. That being so,
I do not understand it to be disputed, on behalf of the
appellant, that there would be no implicit need to
express reasons for such a decision; and it is also to be
noted that para 17 imposes no obligation to give
reasons for a decision to restrict, taken under para 8.
There is thus some attraction in the submission made
for the respondents, that there is neither a general nor
a specific reason for holding that the respondents are
ever required to give reasons for a decision to restrict,
B in terms of that paragraph.

I have however come to the view that the treatment
of decisions under para 8 as separate and distinct from
decisions to grant or renew licences, under para 5, is
unsound. Decisions to restrict the period of licences
cannot be taken in the absract, or in general, or as a
matter of policy. Whatever general policy may be, a
specific decision is required at the time of the grant or
renewal of a particular licence. A decision under para
C 5, to grant or renew, rather than refuse, might actually
depend, in particular circumstances, upon the period
for which the licence was to endure. But even in situations where there was no question but that there
would be a grant or renewal, the question of duration
is in my opinion so closely related to the decision to
grant or renew, that it is unrealistic to regard the two
matters as separate. The duration of a licence is in my
opinion properly to be seen as one of its integral
characteristics or terms; and upon that basis, I am
D satisfied that when reasons are given for a decision to
grant or renew, the fact that the grant or renewal is for
a restricted period cannot be ignored in the giving of
reasons, and the reasons must be reasons for the whole
decision, including any restriction. That is what the
respondents were obliged to give, if required; and as
I have indicated, that appears to me to be precisely
what the appellant's solicitors required the respondents to give. I would only add in this connection that
I find the absence of any reference to para 8, in the
E terms of para 17, entirely natural: no separate requirement is needed, since the reasons given for the
decision to grant or renew will include reasons for
choosing any specific duration for that grant or
renewal.

In these circumstances, the respondents have in my
opinion failed to provide the appellant with the
reasons to which she is entitled, including reasons for
the restriction on the duration of her licence.
F Moreover, what is important is not the respondents'
positive reasons for granting a renewal, but their
reasons for restricting it to less than the period that
would otherwise apply. For the reasons given by your
Lordship in the chair, I have come to the conclusion
that in all the circumstances, no purpose would be
served by sending this case back to the licensing
authority. I agree that the case should be remitted to
the sheriff, with an instruction to him to modify the
decision of the licensing authority, by removing the
restriction, and thus making the renewal a normal
renewal for a period of three years.

LORD WYLIE.—I agree with the opinion of your
Lordship in the chair and have nothing useful to add. G

*Counsel for Pursuer and Appellant, Stacey; Solicitors,
Cochran Sayers & Cook (for Gordon & Smyth,
Glasgow) — Counsel for Defenders and Respondents,
Wylie, QC; Solicitors, Simpson & Marwick, WS.*

                                                    P A A

                                                            H

(NOTE)

MacInnes v MacInnes

OUTER HOUSE
LORD MARNOCH   I
21 FEBRUARY 1990

*Husband and wife — Divorce — Financial provision —
Interim aliment — Whether gross or net income to be considered.*

In calculating the interim aliment to be paid for the
wife and children of the marriage, reference was made
to the husband's earnings net of income tax.

Observed, that it remained appropriate to use J
figures without deduction of income tax.

Janette MacInnes raised an action of divorce against
her husband John MacInnes concluding also for
custody of the three children of the marriage and
aliment for them and periodical allowance for herself.
The Income and Corporation Taxes Act 1988, as
amended by the Finance Act 1988, s 36, makes provision for the incidence of income tax in relation to K
maintenance payments. The case came before the
Lord Ordinary (Marnoch) on the motion roll on the
wife's motion for interim aliment. His Lordship
having awarded interim aliment at the rate of £30 a
week for each child and at the rate of £50 a week for
the wife, the husband sought leave to reclaim. In
granting leave to reclaim his Lordship considered the
ground upon which leave was sought (with which this
report is not concerned) and then continued:

"Lest I be wrong in the approach which I have L
taken in this matter I should perhaps record that in
another respect I was perhaps over generous to the
defender. During the motion roll hearing I was
advised by counsel for the defender that his net earnings amounted to £223 per week. When I inquired of
both counsel whether the gross figure might not be
more appropriate, my note is that I was informed that
in this case there was 'not much difference between
the net and gross figures'. My calculations accordingly
proceeded on inter alia the figure of £223 per week.
Today I was informed that there was indeed a material

difference as between the defender's gross and net
A earnings, but it was asserted that since the passing of
s 36 of the Finance Act 1988 it was no longer
appropriate to have regard to gross as opposed to net
figures in assessing awards of aliment. I am not myself
persuaded that this is as self evident as counsel
appeared to think. In the first place, while that section
undoubtedly does effect some changes to the tax treatment of what were formerly 'small maintenance payments', the spouse making what is now termed a
'qualifying maintenance payment' continues to get
relief roughly equivalent to what might loosely be
B termed as the married person's allowance. Secondly,
and as importantly, I do not myself read the dicta in
Gray v Gray, 1968 SLT 254; 1968 SC 185 and
Thomson v Thomson, 1943 SLT 170; 1943 SC 154 as
being confined to and dependent on the tax treatment
of the sums actually paid as aliment. Rather do I think
that the more general sentiment is that it would be
impracticable and undesirable for the court to enter on
an inquiry into the sometimes highly complex tax
treatment of the overall incomes of the respective
C spouses and that instead it should be left to the parties
to work out with the Commissioners of Inland
Revenue their respective liabilities for tax. I might add
for my own part that, to some extent at least, the tax
treatment of alimentary payments must be a matter of
policy for the legislature and, as it seems to me, that
policy in its most recent embodiment is to be found in
s 36 of the Finance Act 1988. Insofar as under that
section the payer is given substantially the same relief
as a cohabiting spouse, the positive indications, as it
D seems to me, are that awards of aliment should continue to be assessed on figures of gross income."

---

*Counsel for Pursuer, MacNair; Solicitors, Brodies,
WS (for Russells, Glasgow) — Counsel for Defender,
O'Brien; Solicitors, Ranken & Reid, SSC (for Murdoch
Jackson, Glasgow).*

C H

E [This case has been reported by request.]

McGlennan v Beatties Bakeries Ltd

F HIGH COURT OF JUSTICIARY
THE LORD JUSTICE GENERAL (HOPE),
LORDS ALLANBRIDGE AND KINCRAIG
8 OCTOBER 1991

*Justiciary — Procedure — Summary procedure — Plea
in bar of trial — Accused a limited company — Written
plea of guilty signed by individual "for and on behalf of"
company — Whether competent — Act of Adjournal
(Consolidation) 1988 (SI 1988/110), rule 88 and Sched,
form 49.*

Rule 88 of the Act of Adjournal (Consolidation)
1988 provides that where an accused is cited on a G
summary complaint the prosecutor shall send him a
reply form for completion and return. That form is
form 49 contained in the Schedule to the Act of
Adjournal which provides for the accused's signature.
No special provision is made in respect of companies
who appear on complaint.

A limited company was charged on a summary complaint with an offence under s 2 (1) of the Food and
Drugs (Scotland) Act 1956. The reply form sent to the
company with the citation was returned to the procu- H
rator fiscal completed in such a way as to indicate that
the company was pleading guilty. The person signing
the form signed his name and alongside his signature
there appeared the words "for and on behalf of" the
company. The sheriff doubted the competency of the
plea, not being satisfied that the form had been written
by the company or with its authority. The case was
continued without plea and in due course a letter was
received from the company, repeating the guilty plea
and signed by another individual after whose name I
was written the word "(Accountant)" and beneath
which were typed the words "for and on behalf of" the
company. The sheriff remained unsatisfied and, the
Crown making no further motion, the sheriff made no
further order. The procurator fiscal brought a bill of
advocation to the High Court.

Held, that as the only formalities required by the
Act of Adjournal were signatures in the appropriate
places to authenticate the pleas which were being submitted in writing in reply to the prosecutor, it was J
sufficient so far as the court was concerned that what
was written on the form indicated that the pleas which
had been tendered were pleas which were made by or
on behalf of the accused; and where, as here, the
accused was a company, a statement by the person
who signed the form that he was signing for and on
behalf of the company was all that was required
(p 1111F-H); and bill *passed.*

Observed, that it might have been different if K
either of the signatories had appeared in court and had
sought to represent the company on a plea of not
guilty (p 1111E-F).

Bill of advocation

John Gregory McGlennan, procurator fiscal,
Kilmarnock, presented a bill of advocation to the High
Court of Justiciary praying for recall of a decision of
Sheriff T F Russell at Kilmarnock sheriff court dated L
28 March 1991, refusing to accept a written plea of
guilty by Beatties Bakeries Ltd to a summary complaint raised at the instance of the complainer.

Statement of facts and plea in law

The statement of facts for the complainer was in the
following terms:

Stat 1. The respondents were charged at the complainer's instance on summary complaint, a copy of
which is annexed hereto and referred to for its terms.

Said complaint first called on 14 February 1991. By reply form Daniel Stevenson, a representative of the respondents, indicated that he wished to plead guilty "For and on behalf of Beatties Bakeries Limited". In addition a letter accompanied said reply form which made a number of points on behalf of the respondent. Said documents are annexed hereto and are referred to for their terms.

Stat 2. On 14 February aforesaid, said Sheriff Russell indicated that said Daniel Stevenson was not a representative of the respondent and indicated that he wished to have a letter from either a solicitor or representative of the respondent. The diet was continued without plea until 7 March 1991 for the respondent to be legally represented.

Stat 3. On 7 March when the case called in court no reply had been received from the respondent and the complainer's depute moved the court to continue the case without plea until 28 March. The complainer's depute wrote to the respondent indicating that the matter had been continued without plea and inviting the representative of the company to clarify the position.

Stat 4. By written intimation dated 14 March from the respondents, John Kelly, an accountant with the respondents, indicated to the complainer that they wished to plead guilty to the charge and said written intimation was signed by John Kelly (Accountant) "For and on behalf of Beatties Bakeries Limited". Said written intimation is referred to for its terms. On 28 March 1991 the complainer's depute tendered said intimation to said sheriff who indicated that he was not satisfied that it was written by the respondent or with the respondent's authority. He indicated that accountants normally dealt with financial matters and there was no evidence that the accountant could bind the respondent by pleading guilty.

Stat 5. The court having heard the complainer's depute on the question of the competency of said written intimation said sheriff stated that he was not prepared to accept it as a plea of guilty, it being incompetent, and that it should be treated as a not guilty plea and the depute should move for a trial diet to be set. The complainer's depute indicated that he did not wish to make any further motion and in the circumstances the sheriff made no order.

The plea in law for the complainer was as follows:

The sheriff's refusal to treat the written intimation as a competent plea of guilty as having been authorised by the accused being unjust, erroneous and contrary to law, said sheriff should be ordained to accept said intimation as a plea of guilty and proceed to hear and dispose of the case in the absence of the accused.

Statutory provisions

The Act of Adjournal (Consolidation) 1988 provides:

"88. The procurator fiscal shall send to the accused person together with the citation — (a) a reply form for completion and return by him stating whether he pleads guilty or not guilty in the form set out in Form 49 of Schedule 1; (b) a means form for completion and return by him and in the form set out in Form 50 of Schedule 1. . . .

"[Sched 1]
"Form 49
"Form of Reply to Complaint
. . .

2. Pleading Guilty

I plead Guilty to the charge(s)

except ....

....

Signed............................. Date............................

Please continue to complete this form

. . .

Name and Address
of Accused

Date of Birth ....
Check that your name, address and date of birth are shown correctly.
Please correct anything that is wrong."

The bill was heard before the High Court on 8 October 1991.

Eo die the court *passed* the bill and *directed* the sheriff to proceed as accords.

The following opinion of the court was delivered by the Lord Justice General (Hope):

OPINION OF THE COURT.—This is a bill of advocation for the procurator fiscal at Kilmarnock. The respondents are Beatties Bakeries Ltd, a company incorporated under the Companies Acts. They were charged at the complainer's instance on summary complaint with an offence under s 2 (1) of the Food and Drugs (Scotland) Act 1956. In accordance with rule 88 of the Act of Adjournal (Consolidation) 1988 the prosecutor sent to the respondents together with the citation a reply form in the form which is set out in form 49 of the Schedule to the Act of Adjournal. That form was returned to the prosecutor completed in such a way as to indicate that the respondents were pleading guilty to the charge. This was done by the completion of s 2 on the reply form which contains the words "I plead guilty to the charge(s)". This was signed by Daniel Stevenson, beside whose signature were written the words "For and on behalf of Beatties Bakeries Limited". There was then, in the section providing for a written explanation if pleading guilty, a reference to a letter which the respondents wished to enter along with the plea. And there was enclosed along with the printed form a letter signed by Mr Stevenson under whose name were written the words "for and on behalf of Beatties Bakeries Limited", setting out some information which he asked to be considered along with the plea of guilty.

The bill tells us that, when the case called on 14
February 1991 and the prosecutor moved for sentence,
the sheriff indicated that he was not satisfied that this
was a competent plea of guilty because he was not
satisfied that the form had been written by the respondents or with their authority. He said that David
Stevenson was not a representative of the respondents
and that he wished a letter from either a solicitor or
a duly appointed representative of the respondents. In
the light of his doubt on this matter the diet was continued without plea and arrangements were made for
a letter to be sent to the respondents to clarify their
position. In due course a letter was received from them
dated 14 March 1991 signed on this occasion by John
Kelly, after whose name was written the word
"(Accountant)" and beneath which were typed the
words "For and on behalf of Beatties Bakeries
Limited". That letter repeated that the respondents
were pleading guilty to the charge and that the previous letter of 24 January 1991 was a statement of the
points which the company wished to be taken into
consideration by the court prior to imposing its
decision. When the case called before him again the
sheriff was still not satisfied that this represented a
competent plea of guilty on the respondents' behalf,
and he indicated that he was not prepared to entertain
this as a plea of guilty and that a trial diet should be
set. The prosecutor's depute then stated that he had
no further motion to make and in the circumstances
the sheriff made no further order. The sheriff has
explained in his report which is before us that he drew
the attention of the procurator fiscal depute to the provisions of s 74 of the Criminal Procedure (Scotland)
Act 1975, and that he also pointed out that the signatory of the first letter of 24 January 1991 was not
designed and that the signatory of the second letter of
14 March 1991 designed himself as an accountant. As
he puts it in his report: "I pointed out that neither
bore to be a person having the management of the
affairs of the body corporate or to have been appointed
by such a person to represent the body corporate in
these proceedings."

In moving us to pass the bill, in the absence of
representation today on behalf of the respondents, the
learned Solicitor General submitted that the formalities required by the Act of Adjournal were satisfied
in this case. He pointed out that s 74 of the 1975 Act
to which the sheriff referred was one which was concerned only with solemn proceedings, and that while
things might have been different if either Mr
Stevenson or Mr Kelly had appeared in court and
sought to represent the company on a plea of not
guilty, the pleas of guilty which were tendered by
them in writing were sufficient to meet the requirements of the rule. We have no difficulty in giving
effect to that submission. The form which was originally tendered is one which is authorised by the Act of
Adjournal. Its purpose is to enable an accused person
who wishes to do so to plead guilty in writing or to
plead not guilty as the case may be. The only formalities which are needed are signatures in the appropriate places to authenticate the pleas which are being

submitted in writing in reply to the prosecutor. So far
as the court is concerned it is sufficient that what is
written on the form indicates that the pleas which
have been tendered are pleas which are made by or on
behalf of the accused. If the accused happens, as in
this case, to be a company, a statement by the person
who signs the form that he is signing for and on behalf
of the company is all that is required. In the present
case there was a statement in writing on the form in
the appropriate place that the signature was given for
and on behalf of the company. That was sufficient to
show for the purposes of the court's disposal of the
case that the person who signed the letter was somebody who had the authority of the company to
represent it in these proceedings. No further formality
was required and the sheriff was in error in referring
to s 74 of the Act, which has no application to
summary proceedings, and requiring some further
authentication to be given to confirm the plea.

For these reasons we are satisfied that the respondents intended to plead guilty and that they did so in
a competent manner by means of the form which was
sent to the prosecutor in reply to service of the
complaint. What we shall do therefore is pass the bill
and direct the sheriff to proceed as accords.

---

*Counsel for Complainer, Solicitor General (Rodger,
QC); Solicitor J D Lowe, Crown Agent — No appearance for Respondents.*

R F H

Darroch v Strathclyde Regional Council

OUTER HOUSE
LORD MACLEAN
5 MARCH 1992

*Administrative law — Judicial review — Competency —
Local authority notifying employee that post politically
restricted — Whether actions of local authority related to
individual contract or raised matter of public law
warranting recourse to supervisory jurisdiction —
Whether determination about status of depute assessor
affecting others as well as petitioner.*

*Local government — Chief officer — Political activity —
Whether assessor a statutory chief officer or a non-
statutory chief officer and thereby disabled from political
activity — Local Government and Housing Act 1989 (c
42), s 2.*

The Local Government and Housing Act 1989 provides in s 2 that certain posts, including non-statutory
chief officers and their deputes, in a local authority
are "politically restricted" and, in s 1, that a person
holding such a post cannot be a member of a local
authority.

An employee of a regional council employed as a depute assessor, depute electoral registration officer and depute community charges registration officer was informed by the council that his post was a politically restricted one in terms of the 1989 Act and that accordingly he was subject to the disqualifications contained in the Act and would in future be subject to further restrictions in respect that regulations made under the Act by the Secretary of State would be incorporated into his contract of employment. The employee sought judicial review of the council's actings and sought (1) a declarator that he was not a depute chief officer in terms of s 2 of the 1989 Act, and (2) an order quashing the council's actings. The council challenged the competency of the petition on the grounds (a) that the petitioner had not been adversely affected by any decision or actings of the council but rather they had only been informing him of the impact of legislation on the occupier of a post such as his, and (b) that the actings of the council related to the petitioner's individual position and were not of general application and accordingly were outwith the supervisory jurisdiction of the court. In relation to the merits of the application the council argued that the assessor was a "non-statutory chief officer" in terms of s 2 (7) of the Act and that the petitioner was accordingly a "deputy chief officer" in terms of s 2 (8), and in any event that he held a politically restricted post by virtue of s 2 (1) (g) in respect that he was a person to whom powers were delegated in terms of s 50G (2) of the Local Government (Scotland) Act 1973 and was specified as such in a list maintained by the council in terms of that Act.

Held, (1) that the council by intimating to the petitioner that they considered him to be a "deputy chief officer" in terms of the Act had plainly considered the matter, exercised their judgment and arrived at a decision or determination of an administrative character which had adverse consequences for the petitioner and which was accordingly properly subject to the supervisory jurisdiction of the court (p 1114F-H); (2) that the council's decision was not one solely between employer and employee since others in the council's employment, such as the assessor and other deputes, could be adversely affected by the respondents' decision, and the restrictions placed on such persons might affect their freedom of speech and association and as such raised a matter of public law which was properly the subject of the supervisory jurisdiction of the court (p 1114I-J); (3) that the duties of the assessor in each of his capacities were laid on him personally by statute, and thus he was not a non-statutory chief officer and his deputies were not deputy chief officers within the definition (pp 1115L-1116A); (4) that it followed that the assessor's post was not properly included in the list maintained by the respondents under s 50G (2) of the 1973 Act (p 1116I-J); and decree of declarator *pronounced*.

Petition for judicial review

Colin Malcolm McEachern Darroch presented a petition for judicial review seeking declarator that he was not a deputy chief officer in terms of s 2 of the Local Government and Housing Act 1989 and an order quashing certain actings by his employers, Strathclyde Regional Council.

The petition came before the Lord Ordinary (MacLean) for a first hearing.

Statutory provisions

The Local Government (Scotland) Act 1973, as amended, provides:

"50G.— . . . (2) A local authority shall maintain a list — (a) specifying those powers of the authority which, for the time being, are exercisable from time to time by officers of the authority in pursuance of arrangements made under this Act or any other enactment for their discharge by those officers; and (b) stating the title of the officer by whom each of the powers so specified is for the time being so exercisable; but this subsection does not require a power to be specified in the list if the arrangements for its discharge by the officer are made for a specified period not exceeding six months. . . .

"116.—. . . (2) Every valuation authority shall appoint, in accordance with the provisions of section 1 of the Valuation and Rating (Scotland) Act 1956, an assessor and such number of depute assessors as the authority may consider necessary for the purposes of the Valuation Acts; and any assessor or depute assessor appointed under the said Acts or under the 1947 Act and holding office immediately before 16th May 1975 (other than an assessor or depute assessor appointed under this section) shall cease to hold office on that date.

"(3) A depute assessor appointed under this section shall have and may exercise all the functions of an assessor so appointed."

The Representation of the People Act 1983 provides:

"8.—(1) For the registration of electors there shall be electoral registration officers (in this Act referred to as 'registration officers'). . . .

"(3) In Scotland, the council of every region and islands area shall appoint an officer of the council for their area or for any adjoining region or islands area, or an officer appointed by any combination of such councils, to be registration officer for any constituency or part of a constituency which is situated within that region or islands area. . . .

"9.—(1) It is every registration officer's duty to prepare and publish in each year — (a) a register of parliamentary electors for each constituency or part of a constituency in the area for which he acts; and (b) a register of local government electors for the local government areas or parts of local government areas included in the area for which he acts."

The Abolition of Domestic Rates Etc (Scotland) Act 1987 provided:

"12.—(1) There shall be a Community Charges Registration Officer (to be known as such but, in this

Act, referred to as 'the registration officer') for every region and islands area.

"(2) The assessor appointed for each region or islands area under section 116 (2) or (5) of the Local Government (Scotland) Act 1973 shall be the registration officer for that area and any depute assessor appointed under the said section 116 (2) or (5) shall be a depute registration officer and shall have all the functions of a registration officer. . . .

"(4) The registration officer shall prepare, maintain and keep up-to-date the register for his registration area."

The Local Government and Housing Act 1989 provides:

"2.—(1) The following persons are to be regarded for the purposes of this Part as holding politically restricted posts under a local authority — . . . (b) the statutory chief officers; (c) a non-statutory chief officer; (d) a deputy chief officer; . . . (g) any person not falling within paragraphs (a) to (f) above whose post is for the time being specified by the authority in a list maintained in accordance with subsection (2) below and any directions under section 3 below or with section 100G (2) of the Local Government Act 1972 or section 50G (2) of the Local Government (Scotland) Act 1973 (list of officers to whom powers are delegated). . . .

"(7) In this section 'non-statutory chief officer' means, subject to the following provisions of this section — (a) a person for whom the head of the authority's paid service is directly responsible; (b) a person who, as respects all or most of the duties of his post, is required to report directly or is directly accountable to the head of the authority's paid service; and (c) any person who, as respects all or most of the duties of his post, is required to report directly or is directly accountable to the local authority themselves or any committee or sub-committee of the authority.

"(8) In this section 'deputy chief officer' means, subject to the following provisions of this section, a person who, as respects all or most of the duties of his post, is required to report directly or is directly accountable to one or more of the statutory or non-statutory chief officers."

Cases referred to

Glasgow (Assessor for) v Finefare Ltd, 1976 SLT 122.
Watt v Strathclyde Regional Council, 1992 SLT 324.

Textbooks referred to

Armour, *Valuation for Rating*, paras 1-15 and 1-17.
Stair Memorial Encyclopaedia, Vol 24, para 408.

On 5 March 1992 the Lord Ordinary *granted* declarator (1) that the petitioner was not a deputy chief officer in terms of s 2 of the Local Government and Housing Act 1989; (2) that the petitioner's post was not comprehended by the respondents' scheme of delegated functions; and (3) that the petitioner did not hold a politically restricted post under the respondents.

LORD MACLEAN.—The petitioner is employed by the respondents as a depute assessor, depute electoral registration officer and depute community charges registration officer. He has been employed in the first two positions since his appointment thereto on 6 January 1986. (See the letter of appointment of 24 December 1985 which is in process.) By letter dated 14 February 1990 the respondents informed the petitioner generally with regard to the provisions of the Local Government and Housing Act 1989 (hereinafter referred to as "the Act") in relation to politically restricted posts. The letter set out nine categories of employee whose posts were subject to disqualifications and political restrictions under the Act. The writer of the letter, the respondents' director of personnel services, drew the petitioner's attention to the fact that in only two of the nine categories were rights of appeal available to holders of these posts. He then informed the petitioner as follows: "On behalf of the Regional Council I hereby notify you formally that your post has been designated a politically restricted post in terms of category 4 referred to above. The disqualifications which I have outlined will therefore apply to you as from 1st March 1990 and the further restrictions on political activities to be the subject of regulations by the Secretary of State will be incorporated into your contract of employment. The details of these restrictions will be notified to you as soon as the regulations are published."

By further letter dated 12 July 1990 the respondents' director of personnel services advised the petitioner that the Secretary of State had promulgated the regulations he had referred to in his letter of 14 February 1990, and there was appended to the letter a copy of the restrictions which, by virtue of the designation in the previous letter, were deemed to be incorporated in the petitioner's contract of employment.

The petitioner maintained that the respondents wrongly designated him as a "Deputy Chief Officer" in their letter of 14 February 1990, which designation he sought to bring under review by the court in terms of Rule of Court 260B. First, however, the respondents submitted in terms of their first plea in law that there were no actings on their part nor any decision of theirs which were properly the subject of judicial review. This submission, which was advanced on two grounds, being a submission in support of a preliminary plea, I shall consider first.

Counsel for the respondents said that the petitioner had misconceived the position that it was a decision of the respondents as local authority that had adversely affected his position. The matter, he said, flowed directly from the statutory provision without any intervention on the part of the local authority. The petitioner maintained that he was not a deputy chief officer. In the petition he proceeded as if something had been done by the respondents requiring to be put right by the court. The persons occupying those posts set out in s 2 (1) (b), (c) and (d) of the Act were identifiable separately and objectively by application of the definition of a "statutory chief officer", and a "non-statutory chief officer", contained in s 2 (6) and (7) of the Act, which any informed observer could do. The

A question with which the petitioner was concerned was one which could be answered by looking at his job and then that of the assessor. In that connection counsel for the respondents referred me to the letter of appointment to which I have already referred and in particular to the paragraph at the foot of p 2 which reads: "The duties applicable to the post will be as prescribed by the Assessor and Electoral Registration Officer or such other person acting on his behalf who will also exercise supervision over your services." The letters of 14 February and 12 July 1990 sent by the

B respondents to the petitioner should be read against the background of the Act. They were merely an intimation by the respondents to their employee of the impact of the Act upon the employee's situation. Whether or not he occupied such a politically affected post was unaffected by any decision of the respondents as his employers. Counsel for the respondents drew my attention to the case of *Watt v Strathclyde Regional Council*, and in particular to the opinion of the Lord President at pp 328 and 329. The supervisory jurisdic-

C tion of the court, which the petitioner had prayed in aid, was concerned essentially with the review of decisions of an administrative or judicial character, as the Lord President had said, and to that counsel for the respondents would add actings of a similar character. In this case there were no such decisions or actings on the part of the respondents to be reviewed.

I consider this submission to be fallacious and I reject it. The question is whether the post which the

D petitioner occupies in his employment with the respondents is one which falls within s 2 (1) (d) of the Act. Is he a "deputy chief officer" in terms of the Act? Section 2 (8) of the Act provides the following definition: "a person who, as respects all or most of the duties of his post, is required to report directly or is directly accountable to one or more of the statutory or non-statutory chief officers". It is accepted that the assessor/electoral registration officer/community charges registration officer is not referred to in terms

E of s 2 (6) of the Act and so is not a "statutory chief officer". But is he a "non-statutory chief officer" in terms of s 2 (7) of the Act? In particular is he "(b) a person who, as respects all or most of the duties of his post, is required to report directly or is directly accountable to the head of the authority's paid service"; or "(c) a person who, as respects all or most of the duties of the post, is required to report directly or is directly accountable to the local authority themselves or any committee or sub-committee of the authority"? The petitioner maintains he was not a

F non-statutory chief officer. The respondents maintained that he was. The point is, however, that the respondents, having considered the matter, reached the view that he was, and that therefore the petitioner, as his depute, was a deputy chief officer in terms of the Act, and they so intimated that view to the petitioner. I have in the previous sentence used the expression "reached the view" to describe the conclusion to which the respondents came, but I could as easily have used the words "decided" or "determined". It was not the case that the respondents simply intimated a

G section of the Act to the petitioner. They exercised their own judgment with regard to the petitioner's position under the Act, a judgment which counsel for the petitioner urges upon me is, in any event, wrong. I am clear that the view which the respondents reached was a decision of an administrative character which has adverse consequences for the petitioner and as such is one that is properly subject to the supervisory jurisdiction of the court in terms of Rule of Court 260B. Indeed, it seems to me disingenuous to suggest otherwise.

H Counsel for the respondents advanced a further subsidiary argument in support of his first plea of competency. He submitted that one did not have here a general decision which could be made the target of judicial review with effect upon a series of individual contracts of employment. In this case the target was the petitioner's individual position. There was no attempt to get at a decision that was above and beyond the individual contract. Thus this application lay outwith the supervisory jurisdiction.

I I do not see this case as involving simply a contractual dispute between employee and employer. It is obvious that the decision made by the respondents, if not challenged, may have consequences for others in their employment, such as the assessor himself and other deputes. The restrictions placed upon the activities of the petitioner do in my opinion raise a matter of public law since they affect his freedom of speech and association as well as that of others. Although the decision appears to relate to one individual contract,

J circumstances do exist to warrant recourse to the supervisory jurisdiction of this court. (See *Watt v Strathclyde Regional Council* cited above, especially per Lord Clyde at pp 331-332.)

I turn now to the question whether the respondents' decision was correct. In view of the relationship between s 2 (7) and (8) of the Act in this case, it is necessary first and fundamentally to consider whether the assessor, as the petitioner's superior and to whom he is required to report or to whom he is accountable,

K is a non-statutory chief officer, because, if he is not, the respondents' decision may be wrong. I say that it "may" be wrong because of the case the respondents advance in the alternative at the end of ans 6 to which I will come in due course. The respondents contend that the assessor qua assessor, electoral registration officer and community charges registration officer in Strathclyde Region is a person who as respects all or most of the duties of his post is required to report

L directly or is directly accountable to the head of the respondents' paid service, i e the chief executive, and they further contend that, in any event, as regards these duties he is required to report directly or is directly accountable to the respondents themselves and their finance committee.

The Assessor of Strathclyde was appointed to the post of assessor and electoral registration officer by letter from the respondents dated 13 April 1982. The letter included the following conditions: "As Assessor and Electoral Registration Officer you will be respon-

sible to the Regional Council through the Finance
Committee and the Chief Executive for the efficient
management of your department and your duties will
include those listed on the attached draft Job Description. Your appointment as Assessor and Electoral
Registration Officer is made in terms of Section 116
(3) of the Local Government (Scotland) Act 1973 and
Section 6 (3) of the Representation of the People Act
1949.''

The job description stated that he would be responsible to Strathclyde Regional Council as valuation
authority. His basic function was to ensure that the
functions of valuation and electoral registration in the
region were effectively and timeously discharged in
accordance with statute. His main duties were as
follows: "To advise the Council, its committees and
the Chief Executive, as required, on the implications
of valuation law and related matters. To ensure that
the statutory requirements imposed on the Region
regarding valuation and electoral registration are fully
and competently discharged. To prepare departmental
policy options and to monitor the departmental
budgetary control. To co-operate with other officials
and to maintain and develop procedures for these
changes of services and information within the
authority. To maintain and review the organisation of
the lands valuation and electoral registration functions
and to manage, direct and control professional, technical, administrative, clerical and other staff employed
within the Assessor's Department.''

One might readily think from the terms of the
assessor's appointment which I have just set out that
he was reasonably to be regarded as an officer of the
local authority as valuation authority employing him.
What, however, I have to consider is whether "as
respects all or most of the duties of his post" he is
required to report directly or is directly accountable to
the local authority's executive or the local authority
themselves or one of their committees. In each of his
three capacities statute provides for his appointment.
(See the Local Government (Scotland) Act 1973, s 116
(2); the Representation of the People Act 1983, s 8 (3);
the Abolition of Domestic Rates Etc (Scotland) Act
1987, s 12 (1).) Statutory duties are laid on the assessor
personally with regard to valuation and the valuation
roll. He has, for example, to submit the arrangements
he has to make with regard to the valuation or revaluation of lands and heritages in his area to the Secretary
of State for approval, and he has to submit to the
advisory council an annual report on the progress of
valuation and revaluation in the area and send a copy
of such a report to the valuation authority for the area.
(See generally the Local Government (Scotland) Act
1975, s 1.) While he is appointed by the valuation
authority they cannot at their own hands dismiss him.

Counsel for the respondents asked me to accept the
following passage in Armour on *Valuation* at para 1-15
as correctly stating the position of the assessor: "An
Assessor holds office during the pleasure of the valuation authority but he can only be removed, or alternatively be required to resign, if the authority has passed
a resolution for his removal or resignation with a

majority of at least two-thirds of the members present
at a meeting for which notice of the matter has been
specifically given and if the Secretary of State consents. Before deciding whether or not to give his
consent the Secretary of State must give the assessor
and the authority an opportunity of being heard by a
person appointed by him. While he is employed by the
local authority the assessor has always been recognised
as having a degree of independence. As Lord Keith
observed in *Assessor for Glasgow v Finefare Limited*,
'Assessors are independent officials, not officers of the
local authorities who appoint them.' Such independence is an essential for the proper performance of his
statutory duties which involve the assessment of valuations in situations where the interests of the local
authority and the ratepayers may well conflict. It is
also important that valuations should be seen to be
free from political influence or interference. The
administration of his department and the overall
expense involved in carrying out his statutory duties
are matters which may be considered and controlled
by the local authority, but the correctness of his valuations or the methods by which he has computed them
are not matters for which he is answerable to the local
authority. Parliament has provided procedures for
challenge by way of appeal and complaint if those
matters are to be questioned or investigated.''

I agree with counsel for the respondents that Lord
Keith's obiter observation cited in the passage in
Armour above may overstate the position with regard
to the assessor not being an officer of the authority,
and for my part I prefer the statement in Vol 24 of the
Stair Memorial Encyclopaedia at para 408 (contributed
by Lord Clyde), namely: "The nature of the assessor's
office and the duties which he has to carry out require
him to possess a degree of independence of the local
authority. Although he is employed by and is an
officer of the valuation authority, it has always been
recognised that in the carrying out of his responsibilities in the field of valuation he is free from any
influence or interference from the authority.''

Similarly, statutory duties are laid on the assessor in
his capacity as electoral registration officer (see ss 9
and 10 of the Representation of the People Act 1983),
and also in his capacity as community charges registration officer (see ss 14, 17, 18A, 20A and 20C of the
Abolition of Domestic Rates Etc (Scotland) Act 1987).
Counsel for the respondents rightly described the
exercise which I must carry out as a difficult balancing
exercise. I have however come to the conclusion that
the assessor's principal duties in all three capacities are
laid upon him personally by statute and are not
primarily owed by him to the employing authority. I
am aware, from earlier judicial experience, of a community charges registration officer for example suing
the local authority for their failure to provide him with
sufficient staff and resources to carry out his statutory
duties. Cases like that emphasise the relative independence of this officer of the local authority. I am unable
to assert that as respects *most* at least of the duties of
his post the assessor is required to report directly or
is directly accountable in terms of s 2 (7) (b) and (c) of

A the Act. The subsections may appear to call for a numerical assessment of these duties, but in my opinion the correct approach is to look at the essential duties of his post and determine whether these fall within the definitions in the subsections. As I have said I do not think they do.

This may seem somewhat surprising in view of the objective in ss 1 to 3 of the Act which is, as I see it, to prohibit those holding certain posts in a local authority's employment from becoming or remaining members of a local authority or from standing for elec-
B tion to Parliament. One might reasonably think that an assessor in Scotland would be so prohibited given the nature of his post and his position as an officer of the local authority. It seems to me odd that he was not included amongst those defined as statutory chief officers in the Act. I am, nonetheless, satisfied that his position is not caught by s 2 (7) (b) and (c). It follows that I am of the opinion that the petitioner is not a deputy chief officer in terms of the Act.

C The matter does not however end there. The respondents go on to aver that, even if he is not, he is a person specified by them in a list of officers to whom powers are delegated, maintained in accordance with s 50G (2) of the Local Government (Scotland) Act 1973. It provides as follows: "A local authority shall maintain a list — (a) specifying those powers of the authority which, for the time being, are exercisable from time to time by officers of the authority in pursuance of arrangements made under this Act or any other enactment for their discharge by those officers;
D and (b) stating the title of the officer by whom each of the powers so specified is for the time being so exercisable." The respondents submit that, in that case, the petitioner falls within s 2 (1) (g) of the Act which (read short) provides that any person not falling within paras (a) to (f) of this section whose post is for the time being specified by the authority in a list maintained in accordance with s 50G (2) of the Local Government (Scotland) Act 1973, is a person who is to be regarded for the purposes of the Act as holding a politically
E restricted post under the local authority.

Counsel for the respondents argued that the local authority had power to appoint staff in terms of s 64 of the Local Government (Scotland) Act 1973 for the proper discharge by the authority of their functions. In the exercise of that power the local authority appointed staff to the assessor's office. The question was whether a depute assessor could be treated as an officer to whom delegation could be made. Even if the assessor was not acting as an officer of the authority
F with regard to certain functions, he might for other purposes be acting as an officer of the authority, as, for example, the head of a department and someone who was maintaining budgetary controls. It would be wrong to go on to say the assessor was never acting as an officer of the local authority. In terms of s 56 (1) of the 1973 Act a local authority was empowered to arrange for the discharge of any of their functions by an officer of the authority. That was what the respondents had done in their scheme of delegated functions promulgated in May 1991, with particular reference to p 21 and (xvii) on p 25. That was what had been done

in relation to the petitioner in this case. Number 18 of process was the list of officers to whom powers were G delegated in terms of s 50G (2) of the 1973 Act, and the assessor as director or head of department was authorised by that list to make appointments of those in the same position as the petitioner. Thus the petitioner was in a politically restricted post.

In reply counsel for the petitioner pointed out that the list was one specifying the powers of the authority which for the time being were exercisable from time to time by officers of the authority. The powers of the assessor were exercisable by him alone: they were not H powers enjoyed by the authority. The scheme in no 18 of process had no reference to depute assessors who in any event, like assessors, were appointed, not under s 64 of the 1973 Act, but under s 116. There was no power in the local authority to delegate the assessor's functions to the depute assessor. No doubt the local authority could appoint staff to the assessor's office in terms of s 64 of the 1973 Act, but that power, as the editors of Armour pointed out at para 1-17, related to discharge of the local authority's functions but the assessor's duties were laid on him directly by s 1 of the I 1975 Act. Thus, the petitioner's job was not included in the list, no 18 of process.

I think that counsel for the petitioner was well founded. I do not consider, looking at the statutory provisions with regard to the assessor's duties in each of his three capacities, that these functions, which are central to his post, are functions of the local authority which are delegable by them. While the list, no 18 of process, may be one falling within the definition of s 2 (1) (g) of the Act, I am of the opinion that the peti- J tioner's post is not properly included within it.

The petitioner seeks two orders. The first is declarator that he is not a deputy chief officer in terms of s 2 of the Act, and the second is an order quashing the respondents' actings. These actings, according to the petitioner's counsel, were to be found in the respondents' letters. He did, however, submit that the declarator would cover, as he put it, the whole matter so that reduction might be thought to be unnecessary. I am K prepared to grant the declarator sought, but it does not, of course, cover the whole matter, since the respondents also contend that the petitioner is on the list to which s 2 (1) (g) refers. I do, however, consider it to be just and reasonable to grant declarator also that the petitioner's post was not comprehended by the respondents' scheme of delegated functions, and accordingly, although the petitioner's plea in law is not expressed thus, I find and declare that he does not hold a politically restricted post under the respondents. L

Counsel for Petitioner, Davidson; Solicitors, McClure Naismith Anderson & Gardiner — Counsel for Respondents, Macfadyen, QC; Solicitors, Simpson & Marwick, WS.

M H O

King v Moore

A OUTER HOUSE
LORD MORTON OF SHUNA
22 OCTOBER 1992

Process — Decree — Summary decree — Sale of heritage — Difference between purchase price and valuation at date purchaser failed to pay under decree for implement — Sufficiency of evidence or averment necessary to resist motion for summary decree.

B   The purchasers of a farm failed to implement the purchase. The vendors sought decree for implement of the missives by the purchasers, failing which damages. Summary decree for implement having been granted in January 1992 and the time limit for payment of the price having expired without payment being made, the vendors sought summary decree for damages. The motion was made shortly before the date set down for the proof in the action. To support the quantum of the damages sought the vendors had
C   lodged valuation reports on the subjects giving the value as at the date the time allowed for implement of the missives had expired. The valuations were substantially less than the price agreed in the missives. The vendors sought summary decree for the difference between the valuation and the price due under the missives with interest from the date for implement. The defenders opposed summary decree but neither produced nor averred any contrary valuation. The time for lodging productions for the proof had
D   elapsed.

Held, that the defenders were not able to advance and establish any defence in the action (pp 1117L and 1118B); and motion for summary decree *granted*.

Rankin v Reid, 1987 SLT 352, *followed*.

Action of specific implement or damages
E   Robert King, Mrs M J King and W T King raised an action of specific implement, which failing damages, against G E Moore and Mrs J M Moore. After obtaining summary decree for implement within 14 days after 8 January 1992, in respect of which the defenders failed to pay the price and implement the bargain, the pursuers enrolled a motion for summary decree for damages.

The case came before the Lord Ordinary (Lord Morton of Shuna) on the motion roll.

F   **Statutory provisions**
The Rules of Court 1965 provide:

"89B.—. . . (2) Subject to paragraphs (3) to (6) of this Rule, in a cause to which this Rule applies, the pursuer may, at any time after a defender has lodged defences, apply by motion to the court for summary decree against that defender on the ground that there is no defence to the action or a part of it disclosed in the defences.

"(3) In applying for summary decree the pursuer

may move the court — (a) to grant decree in terms of all or any of the conclusions of the summons; . . .   G

"(5) At the hearing of a motion under this Rule the court may — (a) if satisfied that there is no defence to the action or to any part of it to which the motion relates, grant the motion for summary decree in whole or in part as the case may be; or (b) order any party, or a partner, director, officer or office-bearer of, any party — (i) to produce any document; or (ii) to lodge an affidavit or affidavits in support of any assertion of fact made in the pleadings or at the bar."

H

Cases referred to
Rankin v Reid, 1987 SLT 352.

On 22 October 1992 the Lord Ordinary *granted* the motion for summary decree.

LORD MORTON OF SHUNA.—The pursuers are the heritable proprietors of Wyseby Hill Farm, Lockerbie. In October 1990 the pursuers entered into   I
missives with the defenders for the sale of the farm for £495,000. The defenders failed to implement the purchase and the present action was raised with conclusions for implement of the missives and, failing implement, for damages of £190,000. On 8 January 1992 Lord Prosser granted summary decree against the defenders for implement in terms of the first conclusion within 14 days from that date. The defenders failed to pay the price and implement the bargain.

On 21 October 1992 the pursuers' motion for   J
summary decree came before me. Counsel for the pursuers restricted his motion to seek £100,000 with interest at 15 per cent per annum from 22 January 1992, being the date by which implement of the first conclusion was ordered by the interlocutor of 8 January 1992. The pursuers had lodged in process valuations from two firms of valuers giving valuations for the farm as at 22 January 1992 at £385,000 and £393,000. In addition to the difference in price between £495,000 and the valuation the pursuers aver   K
in cond 4 that in a resale they will incur additional legal and estate agency fees and will suffer loss and inconvenience. Counsel for the pursuers, in seeking summary decree for £100,000 with interest, stated that if the pursuers obtained decree for that sum the proof fixed for 12 November 1992 would be unnecessary and that the defenders had stated no relevant defence.

Counsel for the defenders opposed summary decree, but did not refer to any contrary valuation and none   L
had been lodged as a production. The defenders make no averment of the value of the farm on the open market and have lodged no valuer's or other report on the value of the farm. The defenders' only positive averment relevant to the motion appeared to be an admission that the pursuer will incur additional legal and estate agency fees. In these circumstances, as the date for lodging of any productions prior to the proof has now passed, it appeared to me that the defenders' scope to challenge the valuation of the pursuers' valuers was very limited.

A I continued the motion until 22 October to allow counsel for the defenders to obtain further instructions and was then informed by him that he had no further instructions or submissions. Counsel for the pursuers sought leave to amend conclusion 2 so that interest ran from 22 January 1992 in the terms of the motion that he had submitted the previous day. As this amendment was designed to prevent the pursuers being awarded interest on interest and was not opposed, I allowed the amendment.

B I was satisfied, following the approach of Lord McCluskey in *Rankin v Reid*, that the defenders are unable to advance and establish any defence in this action. I accordingly granted the pursuers' motion.

C *Counsel for Pursuers, Bonomy; Solicitors, Gillam Mackie, SSC (for John Henderson & Sons, Dumfries) — Counsel for Defenders, S D D Nicoll; Solicitors, Garden, Haig, Stirling & Burnet, WS (for Thomas Purdom & Sons, Hawick).*

C A G M

Chung v Wigtown District Licensing Board

FIRST DIVISION

D THE LORD PRESIDENT (HOPE),
LORDS ALLANBRIDGE AND MAYFIELD

31 DECEMBER 1992

Licensing — Off sale licence — Refusal of licence on ground of over provision — Proper approach of board in considering "the number of licensed premises in the locality" — Whether board bound to take into account application already granted at same meeting — Licensing (Scotland) Act 1976 (c 66), s 17 (1) (d), as amended.

E *Licensing — Licensing board — Application for off sale licence — Refusal on ground of over provision — Proper approach of board in considering "the number of licensed premises in the locality" — Order of consideration of competing applications — Whether reasonable exercise of discretion — Licensing (Scotland) Act 1976 (c 66), ss 17 (1) (d) and 39 (4) (d), as amended.*

The Licensing (Scotland) Act 1976, as amended, provides by s 17 (1) (d) that a licensing board shall
F refuse an application if it finds "that, having regard to — (i) the number of licensed premises in the locality at the time the application is considered; and (ii) the number of premises in respect of which the provisional grant of a new licence is in force, the board is satisfied that the grant of the application would result in the over provision of licensed premises in the locality".

Two applications for off sale licences for the same locality were lodged with the licensing board for consideration at their quarterly meeting in January 1992.

The first application was lodged on 18 December 1991 and the second, that of the appellant, on 20 G December 1991. At the meeting the licensing board dealt with the applications in the order in which they were lodged. They granted the first application and thereafter refused the second application on the ground that, the first application having been granted, there would now be over provision. While they accepted the applicant's intention to provide a dedicated wine shop, they held that they required to consider the number of licensed premises in the locality and the off sale facilities at present available from H these premises, including the subject of the first application. On appeal to the sheriff it was argued that the first application should not have been taken into account when the appellant's application came to be considered. It was also argued that the board erred in taking into account the nature of the off sale provisions proposed by the appellant. The sheriff allowed the appeal. He held that the board should have had regard only to the number of licensed premises in the locality, without having regard to the type of licence. The sheriff also considered that the grant in the first I application should not have been taken into account in considering the appellant's second application, and that the board had exercised its discretion in an unreasonable manner in terms of s 39 (4) (d) of the Act. The board appealed to the Court of Session.

Held, (1) that the proper approach to s 17 (1) (d) as amended was to count the number of premises falling within each of the two categories therein, and then to consider whether the grant of the licence sought by the applicant would result in over provision, the board J being entitled to examine the number of licences of each type listed in Sched 1 to the Act and the facilities which a holder of that type of licence was authorised to provide in the premises, but not now to examine the particular way in which each licence holder was in fact operating the premises for the time being or to consider the particular facilities which the applicant proposed to provide (p 1122G-H); (2) that on that approach there was no error of law either in the board's approach to s 17 (1) (d) or in their reasons for K their decision (p 1122I-K); (3) that a licence to which there was no objection came into force immediately it was granted and accordingly fell to be taken into consideration when any later application was considered at the same board meeting (pp 1122L-1123B); (4) that it was irrelevant under s 17 (1) (d) to consider the facilities which different applicants proposed to provide and the board had exercised its discretion reasonably in taking the applications in the order in which they had been lodged (p 1123F-H); and appeal *allowed*. L

Observed, (1) that a licence granted at a board meeting to which there was an objection, because of the effect of s 30 (1) of the 1976 Act, did not come into force immediately and accordingly fell to be disregarded in considering the number of licensed premises in the locality (p 1123A and H-I).

Opinion, that in view of the limited basis on which the question of over provision might now be considered, there was no fairer way of proceeding than to

consider and dispose of each application in the order
A in which the applications were lodged with the board
(p 1123I).

Appeal from the sheriff court

On Ken Chung applied to the Wigtown District
Licensing Board for an off sale licence. The licensing
board refused the application. The applicant appealed
to the sheriff who allowed the appeal.

The licensing board then appealed to the Court of
B Session.

Statutory provisions

The Licensing (Scotland) Act 1976, as amended,
provides:

"17.—(1) A licensing board shall refuse an application of the type described in subsection (2) below if it
finds that one or more of the following grounds for
refusal, being competent grounds, applies to it — . . .
(d) that, having regard to — (i) the number of licensed
C premises in the locality at the time the application is
considered; and (ii) the number of premises in respect
of which the provisional grant of a new licence is in
force, the board is satisfied that the grant of the application would result in the over provision of licensed
premises in the locality, and otherwise shall grant the
application."

Cases referred to

Augustus Barnett Ltd v Bute & Cowal Divisional
D   *Licensing Board*, 1989 SLT 572.
Collins v Hamilton District Licensing Board, 1984 SLT
    230.
Mohammed v Docherty, 1992 SLT 488.
Pepper v Hart [1992] 3 WLR 1032; [1993] 1 All ER
    42.

Appeal

The appeal was heard before the First Division.

E   On 31 December 1992 the court *allowed* the appeal,
affirmed the decision of the licensing board and
remitted the case to the sheriff to proceed as accords.

The following opinion of the court was delivered by
the Lord President (Hope):

OPINION OF THE COURT.—This is an appeal
under s 39 of the Licensing (Scotland) Act 1976 from
an interlocutor of the sheriff at Stranraer by which he
reversed the decision of the licensing board and
F granted an application for a new off sale licence in
respect of premises at 73/75 Hanover Street,
Stranraer. The licensing board are the appellants in
this appeal and the applicant, whose appeal to the
sheriff was successful, is the respondent.

The application came before the appellants at their
quarterly meeting on 27 January 1992. There were
before them on that date three applications for the
grant or provisional grant of new licences in terms of
s 10 of the 1976 Act. One of these was for an entertainment licence and is not relevant to this appeal. The

other two were applications for the grant of an off sale
licence. The first of these, in order of its appearance   G
on the agenda, was an application by Mrs C Howard
in respect of premises at 39 St John Street, Stranraer.
Her application was lodged with the appellants on 18
December 1991. The second was the respondent's
application, which was lodged on 20 December 1991.
The respective premises were about 100 to 150 yds
apart, and the parties were agreed that they were both
in the same locality for the purposes of s 17 (1) (d) of
the 1976 Act, which sets out one of the grounds on
which an application for a new licence may be refused.   H
No objections were lodged in respect of either application, and the appellants took the view that none of the
grounds of refusal set out in s 17 (1) (a), (b) or (c)
applied in either case. They decided to grant Mrs
Howard's application, which they heard first, and
granted, before they heard submissions on the respondent's application. But the respondent's application
was refused under s 17 (1) (d) on the ground that its
grant would result in the over provision of licensed
premises in the locality of the town centre in
Stranraer. It appears that it was the order in which the   I
respondent's application was heard which made all the
difference, because the appellants had just granted
Mrs Howard's application for the same type of licence
in the same locality.

On 31 December 1991, between the date of the
lodging of these applications and the date of the
meeting at which they were heard, the provisions of Pt
1 of Sched 8 to the Law Reform (Miscellaneous Provisions) (Scotland) Act 1990 were brought into force by
the Law Reform (Miscellaneous Provisions) (Scotland)   J
Act 1990 (Commencement No 9) Order 1991. This
part of the Schedule, read together with s 74 (1) of the
1990 Act, made various amendments to the Licensing
(Scotland) Act 1976. Among these amendments, in
para 6 of the Schedule, was an amendment to para (d)
of subs (1) of s 17 of the 1976 Act, which sets out one
of the grounds for refusal of an application. In its
previous unamended form s 17 (1) (d) was in these
terms: "that, having regard to the facilities of the same   K
or similar kind already available in the locality, or to
facilities of the same or similar kind, in respect of
which the provisional grant of a new licence is in
force, which are to be provided in the locality, the
grant of an application would result in the over-
provision of such facilities".

In its amended form s 17 (1) (d) now provides: "that,
having regard to — (i) the number of licensed premises
in the locality at the time the application is considered;
and (ii) the number of premises in respect of which the   L
provisional grant of a new licence is in force, the board
is satisfied that the grant of the application would
result in the over provision of licensed premises in the
locality".

The appellants were reminded of the terms of s 17
(1) (d) as so amended when they came to consider the
respondent's application. They had before them a plan
showing the location of all licensed premises in
Stranraer, and they also had a list of all the licensed
premises in the locality of the town centre. This list

comprised a total of 26 licensed premises, which were
listed according to the type of licence, as specified in
Sched 1 to the Act, which had been granted in each
case. There were five hotels, seven public houses,
eight off sale premises, three restaurants and three
refreshment premises on this list. There were no
premises on the list for which a provisional grant of a
new licence was in force. In the statement of reasons
which they later gave for their decision under s 18 (2)
of the Act, the appellants acknowledged that, in considering the application, they required to have regard
to the number of licensed premises in the locality notwithstanding the fact that the respondent had made
application for an off sale licence. They then set out
the number of licensed premises in the locality, listing
them by the number of licences granted for each type.
Their reasons then continued in terms of the following
paragraphs:

"10. In considering the application, the Board also
took account of the nature of the off sale facilities proposed to be provided by your client in his premises,
namely a 'dedicated wine shop' and had regard to the
same or similar kind of facility already available in the
locality, with particular regard to off sale facilities
which were provided in the Hotels, Public Houses and
Off Sale premises previously identified by the Board
at 8 (a), (b) & (c) above.

"11. In their deliberations, the Board accepted that,
while it was your client's intention to provide a 'dedicated wine shop' at these premises, they required to
consider the number of licensed premises in the locality and the off sale facilities which were at present
available from these premises.

"12. In considering the number of licensed premises
in the locality, the Board were mindful of the fact that,
earlier in the same meeting, they had granted an application for an Off Sale Licence in respect of the
premises at 39 St John Street, Stranraer.

"13. The Board were also aware that, if they were
to grant the application, it would result in a further
retail outlet for the sale of alcoholic liquor in the
locality."

The reasons concluded with the statement that the
appellants decided to refuse the application given that,
in their view, to grant the application would result in
the over provision of licensed premises in the locality,
as specified in s 17 (1) (d) of the Act.

The respondent appealed to the sheriff against this
decision on the ground that the appellants erred in law
on the question of over provision of facilities, that they
had acted contrary to natural justice and that, in
arriving at their decision, they had exercised their discretion in an unreasonable manner. These are grounds
on which a sheriff may uphold an appeal under s 39
(4) (a), (c) and (d) of the Act. In the discussion before
the sheriff it was submitted that the appellants had
erred in law in taking the grant of Mrs Howard's
application into account, since in terms of s 17 (1) (d)
(i) as amended the "time the application is considered" was the same for Mrs Howard's application

and that of the respondent and accordingly the
number of licensed premises in the locality had to be
taken to be the same in each case. It was also submitted that the appellants erred in law in taking
account of the nature of the off sale facilities proposed
by the respondent and in having regard to other facilities of the same or similar kind. This was because the
requirement in the old s 17 (1) (d) that the board
should have regard to "facilities of the same or similar
kind" had been deleted by the amendment in Sched 8
to the 1990 Act. The whole procedure adopted by the
appellants was also said to be unfair, because of the
order in which they had dealt with the two applications. It was said that it was unreasonable for the
appellants to have heard Mrs Howard's application
first and to have granted it, and then to have refused
the respondent's application on the basis that only
moments before they had granted another licence in
the same locality. The point was made that it could
not be assumed that the respondent or his agent
actually knew about the other application or what
might have been said in relation to it.

The sheriff decided to uphold the respondent's
appeal on two grounds. The first was that the appellants had erred in law, and the second was that they
had exercised their discretion in an unreasonable
manner. He was not persuaded that they had acted
contrary to natural justice.

The first error of law which he saw in the appellants' decision was that they had not confined themselves to a consideration only of the number of
licensed premises in the locality. In his opinion the
effect of the amendment to s 17 (1) (d) by the 1990 Act
was to direct the licensing board to count up the
number of licensed premises in the locality irrespective of the type of licence. To the total of licensed
premises thus produced the licensing board were
required to add the total number of premises in which
a provisional grant was in force. Having done this the
board were required to look to the result of this arithmetic. If they were satisfied that the grant would result
in an over provision they were required to refuse the
application having regard to the arithmetical exercise,
otherwise they were required to grant the application.
He considered that the appellants had misdirected
themselves when they had regard to the type of facilities which were offered by the existing licensed
premises, and then compared with them the facilities
to be provided by the respondent if his application was
granted.

The second error of law was to have regard to the
grant of an off sale licence to Mrs Howard immediately before they turned to consider the respondent's
application. In his opinion s 17 (1) (d) (i) directed
attention to the number of licensed premises physically in the locality at the time when the licensing
board were considering the application. He was not
persuaded that this meant the same thing as the
number of premises in respect of which a licence had
been granted, having regard to the curious results
which this approach would produce in cases where the
applicant decided not to take up the grant of the

licence or where there had been objections and there remained the possibility of a successful appeal. He was also critical of the appellants' reasons, on the ground that they failed to explain why at the stage of Mrs Howard's application there was no over provision and why, having taken this approach at that stage, they then considered that an over provision would result from the grant of the respondent's application. On the question whether the appellants had exercised their discretion in an unreasonable manner, he considered that this was so having regard to the fact that Mrs Howard's application was dealt with first before the respondent or his agent had had a chance to say a word. They had put the respondent in an impossible position when they proceeded to use the decision which they had just made as a basis for refusing his application.

The first question which we have to consider against this background is whether the appellants erred in law, having regard to the provisions of s 17 (1) (d) as amended. The appellants' grounds of appeal challenge the sheriff's decision on this point on two grounds only. The first is that he was wrong to say that the appellants, when looking at the total number of premises in the locality, ought to have had regard only to the licensed premises already operating there at the time the application was being considered. The second is that he had misconstrued the appellants' reasons for their decision in finding that they had taken account of the nature of the facilities to be provided by the respondent, because all the appellants had been doing in this passage of their reasons was to acknowledge the basis upon which his submissions had been made.

The way in which the grounds of appeal had been drafted imply an acceptance of the sheriff's view that the effect of the amendment of s 17 (1) (d) was to confine the licensing board to the simple arithmetical exercise of adding up the number of licensed premises in the locality and then to decide whether or not there was an over provision by looking simply to the result of their arithmetic. Counsel for the appellants submitted that on a proper reading of the reasons for the decision that was all that the appellants had done in this case. As he put it, they had done what Parliament had intended them to do, which was to look simply to the number of licensed premises. He agreed with the sheriff that they were not entitled to have regard to the type of licence or to the nature of the facilities to be provided in the premises. Counsel for the respondent endorsed this approach. He maintained that the plain meaning of the Act was that the licensing board were required to do no more than count up the number of licensed premises and then to assess the effect of the result without making any distinction between the types of licence. But both counsel recognised in the course of the argument that this very restrictive approach to s 17 (1) (d) might create difficulty, and that the paragraph was open to the construction that, while the number of the licensed premises in the locality was something to which the licensing board must have regard in considering whether there was an over provision, they were entitled to take certain other matters into account. The absurdities which the restrictive approach might lead to were noted. For example, it would seem to be unreasonable for the board to be disabled from having regard to the fact that there were in the locality no other premises in respect of which a licence of the type sought by the applicant had been granted. In such a situation it might be desirable for them to grant the application, even although there were already sufficient licences of other types in the locality. It was suggested that this might be a case where, in the light of the recent decision of the House of Lords in *Pepper v Hart*, it might have been helpful, as an aid to construing s 17 (1) (d) in its amended form, to have regard to the ministerial statement when this amendment was being presented to Parliament. But counsel informed us that their researches in *Hansard* had revealed that there was no such statement, perhaps because the amendment with which we are concerned appears in one of several paragraphs in a Schedule containing many amendments to the 1976 Act.

In this situation the best guide to the purpose of the amendment is to examine the effect of the provision for which it was substituted, as it had been interpreted by decisions in this court. The emphasis in the old s 17 (1) (d) was on the word "facilities". The question of over provision had to be approached by having regard to the facilities of the same or similar kind already available in the locality, or to facilities of the same or similar kind which were to be provided in respect of provisional grants in force for a new licence. Thus it was not simply the type of licence which had to be considered, it was the facilities which could be provided as a result of the granting of the licence. Moreover, an examination of any facilities of a specialist nature provided or to be provided in the premises was relevant to the issue, and if this point was raised by the applicant, it was something which the board had to consider in the exercise of its discretion under the Act.

The first point was the subject of a decision in *Collins v Hamilton District Licensing Board*, in which it was held that it was the facilities which had to be the same or similar, not the type of licence. What had to be looked at was the facilities which could be provided as a result of the licence being granted, and the licensing board were held not to have been in error, when considering an application for a public house licence in a locality where there were several public houses and several off sale premises, in taking account of the fact that a public house licence authorises the holder to sell alcohol by retail for consumption on or off the premises. That decision does not seem to have given rise to difficulty, since it was not suggested there that it was necessary to examine the particular facilities to be provided in each of the premises for which licences had been granted. In *Augustus Barnett Ltd v Bute & Cowal Divisional Licensing Board*, however, the point was developed to a stage which might have been thought to be unacceptable. The application was for an off sale licence, and it was refused under s 17 (1) (d) on the ground that there were at that time 38 premises operating an off sales facility in Dunoon.

A The appellants accepted that the board were entitled to take into account those 38 facilities, which it was accepted were of the same or similar kind as those for which a licence had been applied for. But it was contended that the board had failed to consider the range and quality of the facilities which the applicants wished to provide in their premises as compared with the facilities provided in the 38 other premises. It was submitted to the board that only two of these other premises offered a reasonable selection of wines, that

B only one of these was a comparable outlet to that which the applicants sought to provide and they were restricted to one supplier, and that the applicants would offer a superior choice of wine in Dunoon. As the Lord Justice Clerk pointed out in his opinion, the narrow issue raised in the appeal was whether the respondents did take into account the specialist nature of the applicants' premises or whether they failed to do so. As to whether they were bound to take the matter into account he said this, 1989 SLT at

C p 575A-B: "where the issue of the specialist nature of the applicants' proposed premises was raised, I am of opinion that the respondents were obliged to have regard to that aspect also. In *Collins* no issue was raised as to the specialist nature of the pursuers' premises, but there is nothing in the opinion of the court which would suggest that in every case all that a board requires to do is to count up the number of other licensed premises in the locality. Where, as here, it is represented that the proposed off sale premises are

D of a specialist nature different from most of the other off sale premises in the locality, I am of opinion that that is a matter which it is relevant for the board to consider".

In *Mohammed v Docherty*, which was also concerned with a decision taken prior to the amendment, the court agreed with the views expressed by the Lord Justice Clerk. The effect of the old s 17 (1) (d) was therefore to require the board to have regard to the specialist nature of the facility proposed by the appli-

E cants. This may well have been seen as likely to lead to complex and lengthy hearings before licensing boards involving detailed comparisons between the facilities provided in different premises. It may be assumed, therefore, that the purpose of the amendment was to attempt to simplify matters by removing this requirement.

The question is whether the effect of the amendment is to restrict the board's consideration of the question of over provision to an exercise of simple

F arithmetic. On this view the board would be disabled from having regard to the number of licences of different types in the locality and to the facilities which the holder of a licence of each type is authorised to provide. But it is difficult to see how the question of over provision can properly be examined without having some regard to these matters. Moreover, the amendment appears to have been designed to achieve something different, namely to remove from the board's consideration an examination of the particular facilities, including specialist facilities, which are for

the time being provided by the respective licence

G holders and comparing them with the facilities proposed by the applicant. In our opinion the proper approach to the amended s 17 (1) (d) is to count up the number of premises falling within each of the two categories, namely (i) the number of licensed premises in the locality at the time and (ii) the number of premises in respect of which the provisional grant of a new licence is in force. Consideration must then be given to the question whether to grant the licence sought by the applicant would result in an over provision. In its consideration of this question the board

H is entitled to examine the number of licences of each type listed in Sched 1 to the Act and the facilities which, in terms of that Schedule, a holder of that type of licence is authorised to provide in the premises. It is, however, no longer relevant to examine the particular way in which each holder is in fact operating the premises for the time being or to consider the particular facilities which the applicant proposes to provide.

On this approach the reasons given by the appellants

I in this case cannot be faulted. They noted, but disregarded, the respondent's argument that it was his intention to provide a dedicated wine shop. Paragraph 11 of their reasons shows that they confined their consideration of the question of over provision to an examination of the number of licensed premises in the locality and in particular of the off sale facilities which were available in these premises. The sale by retail of alcoholic liquor for consumption off the premises is authorised in the case of public house, off sale and

J hotel licences. In the case of restaurant and refreshment licences, the consumption of alcohol must be in or on the premises. The board clearly thought it appropriate to look at the number of public house, off sale and hotel licences when they came to consider whether a further off sale licence would result in an over provision in the locality, and in our opinion this was something which they were entitled to do. It is hard to see how they could have done otherwise, if they were to arrive at a responsible decision in the

K exercise of their discretion when considering the application. Accordingly there was no error of law either in the appellants' approach to the question of over provision in terms of the amended s 17 (1) (d) or in the reasons which they gave for their decision on this point.

The other ground on which it was held by the sheriff that the appellants erred in law was in their treatment of their previous decision in Mrs Howard's

L application. He held that they were in error in aggregating the grant of her application for a new off sale licence with the number of licensed premises which were already on their list. But we disagree with him on this point also. The amended s 17 (1) (d) is not concerned with what is actually happening in any of the licensed premises or with the particular facilities which are for the time being provided there. The expression used is "licensed premises" which, as defined in s 139 (1) of the Act, means premises in respect of which a licence under the Act is in force.

A Since what is actually being done in the premises is irrelevant, it is of no significance that the premises are closed for the time being or are not yet open for business of the kind which the licence has authorised its holder to provide. A licence which has not yet come into effect because of the provisions of s 30 (1), which gives time for appeals to be disposed of where there were objections, must be disregarded. But in Mrs Howard's case there were no objections. Her licence came into effect as soon as it was granted. The appellants were therefore required by s 17 (1) (d) to take it into account when they came to consider the respondent's application.

B

We turn now to the second question which is whether the appellants exercised their discretion in an unreasonable manner. The sheriff's decision to uphold the respondent's appeal on this ground also was based on the view that there was unfairness in the manner in which the appellants dealt with the two off sale licence applications which were before them that day. He took the view that it was unfair for them to hear C and dispose of Mrs Howard's application first. What they should have done, since the applications were closely linked, was to have heard both of them, then adjourned and considered both at the same time. Counsel for the appellants submitted that there was no authority in the Act for the view that the two applications should have been heard together or that it was unfair to hear and dispose of them separately. His argument on the proper construction of s 17 (1) (d) was that all that required to be done was to count up the D number of licensed premises in the locality, and he pointed out that if the matter was only one of arithmetic the only logical way to proceed was to take the applications one after the other, and that there was no inherent unfairness if this was done. Counsel for the respondent's reply on this point soon developed into an argument that the appellants had acted contrary to natural justice, because the effect of what they did was that the respondent had no notice of the point which he had to meet when the time came for him to present E his argument. Thus he had no opportunity to address the board on the question before the point was effectively decided against him by the granting of Mrs Howard's application. But the sheriff held that the procedure was not so flawed as to amount to a departure from the rules of natural justice, and the respondent has not lodged any ground of appeal directed to this point. We note also that some of the points which counsel sought to raise were not the subject of averment in the appeal in the sheriff court. The only question F tion which we can consider in regard to this matter is whether the sheriff was right to hold that, by dealing with the applications in the order in which they did, the appellants exercised their discretion in an unreasonable manner.

We do not think that the procedure which the appellants adopted in this case is open to that criticism. While we have not accepted counsel's argument that the only question which they had to consider was one of arithmetic, the question whether there was an over provision did in the end depend on the number of licensed premises in the locality for which the licence granted authorised the sale by retail of alcoholic liquor G for consumption off the premises. A comparison between Mrs Howard's application and the respondent's application in this respect, and in particular by reference to the kind of facilities which they each proposed to provide, would have introduced questions which were irrelevant to what they had to consider under s 17 (1) (d). In these circumstances it was a reasonable approach to take the applications in the order in which they had been lodged with the board, and then to reach a decision on each application before H turning to the next. The sheriff has drawn attention to the difficulties which may arise when some applications are the subject of objection and others are not. It was only by chance that Mrs Howard's application was not objected to, with the result that her licence could be taken into account when the respondent's application was considered because it came into force immediately. Where there are objections, the grant of a new licence for other premises on the same day will have to be disregarded, because it cannot be said that the premises in respect of which that licence was I granted are licensed premises within the meaning of the Act. Nevertheless, in view of the limited basis on which the question of over provision may now be considered, the order in which each application is considered is likely to be critical. There can be no fairer way to proceed than to consider and dispose of each application in the order in which the applications were lodged with the board.

For these reasons we consider that the sheriff erred in law and we must sustain this appeal. We shall recall J his interlocutor. This means that the decision of the licensing board dated 27 January 1992 must be affirmed, and the case will be remitted to the sheriff to proceed as accords.

Counsel for Appellant and Respondent (Applicant), Baird; Solicitors, Bishop & Robertson Chalmers — Counsel for Respondents and Appellants (Licensing Board), Bovey; Solicitors, Lawford Kidd & Co, WS. K

C H A of L

(NOTE)

McCormick v City of Aberdeen District Council L

OUTER HOUSE
TEMPORARY JUDGE T G COUTTS, QC
27 NOVEMBER 1992

Damages — Amount — Solatium — Back — Strain to back causing unfitness for work lasting for three months.

A dog warden, then aged 34, hurt her back on two occasions while putting stray dogs into her van. Her

injuries were strains and would have incapacitated her
A from work for about three months.

Opinion, that solatium was appropriately assessed
at £1,750.

Mary McCormick raised an action against her
former employers, the City of Aberdeen District
Council, for damages for injuries sustained in the
course of her employment as a dog warden. She
claimed to have hurt her back first on 22 August 1988
B after which she had returned to work until 27 October
1988 when she again injured her back. She was then
aged 34. In relation to the first accident she said that
she had required to deal with a medium sized mongrel
collie which, while not ferocious, had been unwilling
to go into the van. She said that as she was holding the
lead with both hands and manoeuvring the dog inside
she had felt her back "a bit sore at the bottom". She
had continued with her work. Some three days after
C the incident she had consulted her general practitioner
who had treated her with analgesics. She had returned
to work in September 1988. In relation to the second
accident she said that, while putting a lively dog into
the van, she had felt a twinge in her back. She had
worked on for a while but had then considered herself
to be unfit for work.

After a proof the temporary judge (T G Coutts, QC)
held that the pursuer had failed to prove the circumstances of her accidents and had also failed to establish
D the grounds of fault advanced. He accordingly
assoilzied the defenders. In relation to damages the
temporary judge, who accepted that the pursuer
sustained a low back strain at work in August 1988
and again in October 1988, said:

"So far as quantum of damages were concerned, the
two injuries were not sought to be divided by the
pursuer but obviously the injury which was alleged to
be incapacitating was that of October. According to
E the pursuer she has suffered such backache since that
time that she has been unable to work at all. None of
the medical persons who gave evidence was able to
provide any justification for such a view. They had
anticipated the pursuer resuming work in about three
months after the accident, but this did not happen.
There was no evidence of any attributable injury or
defect in the back which had been caused by the
accident. The view of Mr Chalmers, who gave evidence for the defenders, was that although the pursuer
F did have some pain in her back she was suffering from
the effects of disuse rather than any defect. I accept
that evidence. Mr McLaughlin, for the pursuer,
thought that she had some pre-existing condition of
facet changes in the lumbar spine which might have
been asymptomatic and brought to the fore by the
accident but he expressed that in somewhat tentative
terms in evidence as opposed to the categoric statement in his report of 15 September 1992 which was
produced. He said that in view of the fact that she had
no backache in the past it was fair to assume that it was
an exacerbation of a previously present, asymptomatic

condition. When the suggestion of facet changes was
put to Mr Chalmers, he was inclined to dismiss such G
changes, if any, as having any relevance to the
accidents. The pursuer did not appear to suffer severe
or disabling pain and, when asked about facet hyper-
trophy, he dismissed that as being a minor degenerative change of no significance. I am unable to accept
Mr McLaughlin's assumption of exacerbation. On the
available evidence I consider that the pursuer was able
to resume work so far as the later accident was concerned after about three months and should have done
so. In addition, however, she had a deplorable attend- H
ance history and her job was insecure as a result of that
in any event. On that view there is no wage loss since
she received such payments from the defenders and
has received such national insurance benefits as
wholly to wipe out any past loss. The question of loss
of employability does not arise on the view taken.

"In all the circumstances I would have awarded her
solatium for the effects of her injuries of £1,750; but
the defenders are entitled to absolvitor."

I

*Counsel for Pursuer, Hamilton; Solicitors, Lawford
Kidd & Co, WS — Counsel for Defenders, Mackinnon;
Solicitors, Simpson & Marwick, WS.*

C H

J

Shanks & McEwan (Contractors) Ltd v Mifflin Construction Ltd

OUTER HOUSE
LORD CULLEN
4 DECEMBER 1992

*Administrative law — Judicial review — Arbitration — K
Competency — Alternative statutory remedy — Whether
party can challenge arbiter's decision on procedural
matters — Effect of error of law by arbiter.*

*Arbitration — Judicial review — Competency —
Whether party can challenge arbiter's decision on
procedural matters — Alternative statutory remedy —
Effect of error of law by arbiter.*

The parties to an arbitration challenged the L
relevancy and specification of each other's pleadings.
After a legal debate the arbiter issued proposed findings allowing a proof before answer on the whole averments of each party. Thereafter, the respondent in the
arbitration applied by minute to the arbiter seeking to
have a case stated for the Court of Session on various
questions. The claimant also sought to have a question
stated for the Court of Session. After a further hearing
the arbiter issued an interlocutor postponing consideration of the application for a stated case until the
facts had been ascertained. The respondent in the

A arbitration then presented a note to the Inner House seeking inter alia to have the arbiter ordained to state a case. The claimant lodged answers to the note challenging the competency of the note. A hearing on the note was pending before the Inner House.

Thereafter, the respondent in the arbitration presented a petition for judicial review of the arbiter's interlocutor which had postponed consideration of the application for a stated case. A first hearing took place to consider the competency of the petition. It was argued for the claimant in the arbitration and for the

B arbiter that the petition was incompetent as (1) there was an alternative statutory remedy which was being pursued before the Inner House, and (2) the decision of an arbiter to postpone consideration of an application for a stated case, being a decision on procedural matters, was not subject to judicial review.

Held, (1) that an alternative statutory remedy had to be an effective one and as the proceedings before the Inner House were being challenged by the first respondents as incompetent, those proceedings could

C not found a challenge to the competency of the petition for judicial review (p 1129E-G); (2) that in extreme cases the court would be entitled to interfere with the decision of an arbiter on procedural matters where that decision was unreasonable and therefore the matter was susceptible to judicial review (pp 1129J-L and 1130C-D); and case *put out* by order for further procedure.

Observed, that an error of law by an arbiter was insufficient to found a challenge by judicial review

D unless that error resulted in an excess or abuse of jurisdiction (p 1130D-E).

Dictum of Lord President Hope in *West v Secretary of State for Scotland*, 1992 SLT 636 at p 651, *explained.*

Petition for judicial review

Shanks and McEwan (Contractors) Ltd, respondents in an arbitration, presented a petition seeking

E judicial review of an interlocutor pronounced by the arbiter, Kenneth A McDougall. Answers were lodged by the claimants in the arbitration, Mifflin Construction Ltd (the first respondents) and by the arbiter (the second respondent). Both respondents challenged the competency of the petition.

The petition came before the Lord Ordinary (Cullen) for a first hearing.

F **Cases referred to**

Bennets v Bennet (1903) 10 SLT 609; (1903) 5 F 376.
Biakh v Hyundai [1988] 1 Lloyd's Rep 187.
Brown & Son v Associated Fire Clay Companies Ltd, 1936 SLT 411; 1937 SLT 435; 1936 SC 690; 1937 SC (HL) 42.
Christison's Trustees v Callender-Brodie (1906) 14 SLT 143; (1906) 8 F 928.
Forbes v Underwood (1886) 13 R 465.
Mensah v Secretary of State for the Home Department, 1992 SLT 177.
Mitchell v Cable (1848) 10 D 1297.

Nuttall (Edmund) Ltd v Amec Projects Ltd, 1993 SLT 255.
G
O'Neill v Scottish Joint Negotiating Committee for Teaching Staff, 1987 SLT 648.
Paterson & Sons Ltd v Glasgow Corporation (1901) 3 F (HL) 34.
Strathclyde Buses Ltd, Petitioners, OH, 5 March 1992, unreported.
Tarmac Econowaste Ltd v Assessor for Lothian Region, 1991 SLT 77.
West v Secretary of State for Scotland, 1992 SLT 636.

H **Statutory provisions**

The Administration of Justice (Scotland) Act 1972 provides:

"3.—(1) Subject to express provision to the contrary in an agreement to refer to arbitration, the arbiter or oversman may, on the application of a party to the arbitration, and shall, if the Court of Session on such an application so directs, at any stage in the arbitration state a case for the opinion of that court on any question of law arising in the arbitration."
I

The Rules of Court 1965 provide:

"277. . . . (c) If the application [for a stated case] is presented before the facts have been ascertained by the tribunal, and if the tribunal is of opinion that it is necessary or expedient that the facts should be ascertained before the application is disposed of, it may postpone further consideration of the application until the facts have been ascertained by it. (d) On considera-
J tion of any such application, whether after the facts have been ascertained or at an earlier stage (should the tribunal think it necessary or expedient then to consider it), the tribunal may, if it is of opinion that the proposed question does not arise or that a decision upon it is unnecessary for the purpose of the appeal or is frivolous, refuse to state a case on such question; but in that event it shall intimate its decision to the parties and grant a certificate to the applicant, specifying the reason of refusal and bearing the date of the refusal; and if such refusal is made after the facts have been
K ascertained, such certificate shall be accompanied by a note of the proposed findings in which the facts which have been ascertained, and on which the tribunal proposes to base its decision, shall be set forth, and if such refusal is made before the facts have been ascertained the certificate shall be accompanied by a note of, or sufficient reference to, the averments of the parties in the appeal or their admissions therein on which the refusal is based."

Textbook referred to
L
Bell, *Arbitration,* para 317.

On 4 December 1992 the Lord Ordinary *repelled* the first and second respondents' pleas in law challenging the competency of the petition and *put out* the case by order for further procedure.

LORD CULLEN.—This petition for judicial review relates to an interlocutor issued on 25 September 1991 by the second respondent as arbiter in an arbitration between the first respondent as claimant and the petitioner as respondent in that arbitration. The arbitration relates to a subcontract between the petitioner and the first respondent for the erection by the first respondent of structural steel work as part of contract works undertaken by the petitioner at RAF Leuchars in Fife.

On 5 March 1990 a debate was held in the arbitration at which the petitioner challenged the relevancy and specification of certain of the first respondent's averments; and the first respondent attacked the petitioners' counterclaim. On 21 February 1991 the second respondent issued proposed findings in regard to the debate and in effect allowed a proof before answer. He did not issue a statement of his reasons for doing so. On 10 June 1991 the petitioner applied by minute to the second respondent for a case to be stated for the opinion of the Court of Session under s 3 (1) of the Administration of Justice (Scotland) Act 1972 on eight questions related to the arguments which they have presented. On 28 June 1991 the first respondent applied by a further minute seeking the addition of a question relating to the counterclaim. Following a hearing of the parties on 10 July 1991 the second respondent issued the interlocutor which is under challenge in which he stated, inter alia that "the arbiter is of opinion that it is necessary or expedient that the facts should be ascertained before the applications are disposed of. The arbiter therefore postpones further consideration of the applications until the facts have been ascertained by the arbiter". The second respondent did not state any reasons for coming to that decision.

On 8 October 1991 the petitioner presented a note to the Inner House which was stated to be under s 3 (1) of the 1972 Act, in which it sought to have the first respondent ordained to show cause why a case should not be stated by the second respondent on the eight questions which had been proposed; and thereafter the second respondent ordained to state a case on those questions in the form directed by Rule of Court 279. The first respondent lodged answers to the note in which it pleaded that the application was incompetent. Proceedings in regard to the note are still pending and a hearing has been fixed to take place on 15 December 1992.

In the meantime the petitioner on 30 June 1992 presented the present petition in which it seeks reduction of the interlocutor of 25 September 1991 on the following grounds, as stated in art 4: "(i) that in light of the surrounding circumstances it is unreasonable and irrational, being a decision which is logically excluded; (ii) that it was made through an error of law as to the extent of the second respondent's powers, and in misuse of the powers of fact conferred upon the second respondent under the said submission and rule 277 of the Rules of Court 1965".

In art 7 of the petition the petitioner avers in elaboration of these grounds that: "The issues raised by the questions proposed by the petitioner in its said minute were such as ought not to have been reserved for consideration until after the facts of the submitted dispute had been ascertained. Such reservation in respect of those questions which touched upon the want of essential specification in the first respondent's pleadings is logically excluded by the nature of a plea to the want of essential specification and the result to which it leads in case of success, namely the exclusion of the averments concerned from the proof. To reserve such consideration — and therefore the arguments as to specification themselves — is irrational and prejudicial to the interests of the petitioner insofar as it deprives the petitioner of fair notice of the case it has to meet and extends the ambit of the proof into areas unnecessary to explore and which, though irrelevant, may result in the arbiter's view of other relevant matter being unconsciously coloured. Further, said decision was made through error in law and a misuse of the power afforded the second respondent by rule 277 (c) of the Rules of Court 1965. The questions raised in said minute are not such as may prove, on investigation of the facts of said disputes, to be academic or hypothetical. The said power is intended to permit an arbiter to avoid the necessity to state a case on matters which may prove to be irrelevant to the dispute between the arbitrating parties. The question of the relevancy or otherwise of the first respondent's averments anent prior communings and negotiations will remain an issue for decision after proof has been heard; a proof prejudicial to the petitioner's interest as being likely to increase cost and time incurred in the arbitration to no end, and exposing the petitioner to the said risk of the colouring of other relevant matter in the arbiter's mind. The second respondent's said decision insofar as it affected said question was unreasonable." The petitioner also admits that the note to the Inner House proceeds upon substantially the same factual narrative and substantially the same grounds as the present application.

Section 3 (1) of the 1972 Act provides that: [his Lordship quoted the terms of s 3 (1) and continued:]

Rules of Court 276-280 make provision for procedure in regard to a wide variety of appeals to the Court of Session including all stated cases by an arbiter. Rule 277 (d) provides that the tribunal may refuse to state a case on a proposed question if it is of opinion that it does not arise or that a decision upon it is unnecessary for the purpose of the appeal or is frivolous. In such cases it is to grant a certificate to that effect. This may be after the facts have been ascertained or at an earlier stage. Under rule 278 the applicant may apply by note to the Inner House for an order upon the other party to show cause why a case should not be stated. After intimation to the other parties the note is to be disposed of summarily. On the other hand, Rule of Court 277 (c) provides that if the application for the case is presented before the facts have been ascertained by the tribunal, and if the tribunal is of opinion that it is necessary or expedient that the facts should be ascertained before the application is disposed of, it may postpone further consideration of the application until the facts have been ascertained by it. In the case of such postponement no

A provision is made for the granting of a certificate or for the court ordaining the tribunal to state a case.

In its answers to the petition the first respondent has tabled pleas seeking dismissal of the petition on four grounds, namely that the application is incompetent; lis pendens; that the application is premature; and that the application is irrelevant et separatim lacking in specification. The second respondent has tabled pleas seeking dismissal of the petition on the ground that it is incompetent; and that the petitioner's averments are irrelevant. At the commencement of the first hearing

B before me it was agreed between the parties that the discussion should in the first instance be directed to the respondents' objection to the availability of judicial review of the interlocutor of 25 September 1991 on the grounds set out in the petition. This would leave over for later discussion the question whether the petitioner had made sufficient averments in support of those grounds.

The arguments presented to me were divided into

C two main parts. The first was concerned with the question of the petitioner's alternative remedy under s 3 (1) of the 1972 Act. The second was concerned with the question of the competence of the court's interference with the decision of an arbiter on procedural matters.

In regard to the first part of the arguments, counsel for the first respondent submitted that the fact that the petitioner was pursuing a statutory remedy on substantially the same grounds rendered the present

D application incompetent. It was pointed out that it was well established that the failure to exhaust a statutory remedy as a means of dealing with a petitioner's complaint was a ground for the court dismissing an application for judicial review (see *O'Neill v Scottish Joint Negotiating Committee for Teaching Staff* and *Tarmac Econowaste Ltd v Assessor for Lothian Region*). The same applied a fortiori where the petitioner was simultaneously pursuing the statutory application (see *Strathclyde Buses Ltd, Petrs*). While the first respon-

E dent was admittedly maintaining that the application to the Inner House was also incompetent the important point was that the petitioner was insisting on it. It was undesirable that proceedings should be duplicated, with the consequent risk of conflicting decisions.

In reply counsel for the petitioners submitted that before an alternative remedy could be regarded as a ground for dismissing an application for judicial review it would require to be seen to be an effective

F one. In the present case the recent decision of the First Division in *Edmund Nuttall Ltd v Amec Projects Ltd* had raised doubts as to whether the Inner House would entertain the petitioner's note. In that case an order had been sought under the nobile officium ordaining an arbiter who had decided to postpone an application for a stated case to state one for the opinion of the court. The First Division rejected arguments that rule 277 (c) was outwith the rule making powers of the court and that it did not in any event apply to proceedings before an arbiter. Counsel sub-

G mitted that it was illogical for the first respondent to use the note as a basis for submitting that the present application was incompetent. I was also reminded that in *Mensah v Secretary of State for the Home Department* Lord Coulsfield held that recourse to the court for judicial review was not excluded in the case of ultra vires or similar fundamental invalidity of a decision unless it was specifically excluded by statute.

In regard to the second part of the arguments counsel for both respondents invited me to take the view that the Court of Session in the exercise of its

H supervisory jurisdiction was not entitled to interfere on the grounds set out in the petition with a decision of an arbiter on procedural matters. These arguments could be regarded as going to the competency of the present application or the relevance of the petitioners' averments.

Counsel for the respondents pointed out the restricted extent to which the decisions of an arbiter were challengeable. Leaving aside the special case of challenge under the 25th Act of the Articles of Regula-

I tion 1695, an arbiter's decision was reducible at common law on certain grounds, none of which involved a review of the merits of his decision either in fact or in law. Thus, for example, his decision could be reduced on the grounds that it was ultra fines compromissi or that it was not a true determination or that it was reached in circumstances in which he had failed to observe the rules of natural justice. None of the common law grounds of reduction applied in the present case. As regards the decisions of an arbiter on

J matters of procedure it was well established that he had a wide discretion. Thus it was for him to decide what form, if any, the pleadings were to take (*Christison's Trs v Callender-Brodie*, per Lord President Dunedin at (1906) 8 F, p 931). It was for him to decide what should be the content and standard of the pleadings. It should not be assumed that he required to apply the same standard for relevancy and specification as would be applied in a court of law (Bell, *Arbitration*, para 317). Prima facie it was for him to

K determine questions of procedure (*Paterson & Sons Ltd v Glasgow Corporation*, per Lord Robertson at p 40). It was also pointed out that a refusal by the arbiter to hear evidence which he regarded as irrelevant could not be regarded as infringing the rules of natural justice. See *Brown & Son v Associated Fire Clay Companies*, per Lord Thankerton at 1937 SLT, p 437. In that case in the Court of Session Lord President Normand at 1936 SLT, p 416 said: "If an arbiter declines to entertain the question submitted to him

L and accordingly issues an award which does not dispose of the question, the award is bad. But a *bona fide* decision by an arbiter that averments are irrelevant, even if the decision is wrong and even if it excludes from proof averments which, on a true view of the law, are most material, has no adverse effect on the award." Similarly the arbiter had a wide discretion in deciding whether, despite the arguments presented to him, he should allow a proof before answer. He was entitled to take into consideration that the production of documents might meet a complaint of lack of

specification; that a party who criticised the pleadings
A of his opponent still had the opportunity to maintain
his objection both during and after the proof and seek
an adjournment in order to deal with matters of which
fair notice had not been given. It should not be
assumed that the arbiter would dispose of such matters
by acting outwith his jurisdiction or by acting unfairly
as between the parties to the arbitration. In *Bennets v
Bennet,* in which it was submitted that an arbiter in
allowing a proof despite an argument that certain averments raised matters outwith the reference had
B exceeded his jurisdiction, Lord Kinnear at (1903) 10
SLT, p 612 said: "But he has decided nothing but a
question of procedure. He has held, in effect, that it
is better that the facts should be ascertained before he
decides disputed questions on the merits, or on the
limits of his own jurisdiction. I think that was a question for the arbiter which was within the jurisdiction
of the arbiter to decide, and I do not think this Court
has jurisdiction to review his judgment on it, and to
say that he decided it wrongly." The arbiter was also
C entitled to take into account the consideration that it
was undesirable for the progress of the arbitration to
be delayed by requiring further elaboration of the
pleadings.

Turning to the terms of rule 277 (c) counsel submitted that, far from derogating from the arbiter being
master of his own procedure, they made it clear that
he had a wide discretion as to whether to postpone the
statement of a case. In *Edmund Nuttall Ltd* the Lord
President, after referring to Lord Kinnear's remarks
D in *Bennets,* expressed the view that it was entirely consistent with the existing law and practice of arbitration
in Scotland that an arbiter should be given the discretion which rule 277 (c) extended to all tribunals on the
receipt of an application to state a case. Counsel for
the second respondent emphasised that the terms of
the rule reflected the view of the court as to its non-
intervention with decisions of the arbiter on
procedural matters. It was clearly desirable that the
progress of an arbitration should not be disrupted
E unnecessarily. It was significant that the Rules of
Court made no provision for questioning such a
decision. It followed from the decision in *Edmund
Nuttall Ltd* that a decision of an arbiter to postpone
consideration of the application for a case to be stated
lay beyond judicial review by the Court of Session.
There was no suggestion in the present case that the
arbiter had not acted in bona fide. It was suggested
that if this had been alleged it would be open to the
Inner House to treat his decision as equivalent to a
F refusal despite the absence of a certificate.

While the question of the sufficiency of the petitioners' averments lay beyond what I understood to be
the scope of the present discussion, counsel for the
respondents indicated by way of background to their
submissions that their position was that there was no
relevant foundation for the petitioner's complaint that
the arbiter's decision in the present case was irrational
or unreasonable. If the petitioner was correct the
arbiter would never be entitled to postpone the statement of a case. Even if there were some substance in

the petitioner's criticism of the arbiter's decision it
was no more than a matter of degree on which dif- G
ferent views might well be reached. The basic flaw in
the petitioner's averments was that it assumed that the
arguments which they addressed to the arbiter were
correct, whereas it was for him to decide that matter.

In reply counsel for the petitioner founded strongly
on the decision of the First Division in *West v Secretary of State for Scotland.* Two points were taken from
that case. In the first place the Lord President
provided a clear statement of the ambit of judicial
review in the light of prior decisions including *Forbes* H
v Underwood, in which it was held that the Court of
Session alone had jurisdiction to compel an arbiter to
proceed. The Lord President at p 643A remarked that:
"The importance of this case for present purposes is
that it shows that the principle upon which the supervisory jurisdiction is exercised is not affected by distinctions which may exist for other purposes between
public bodies and those who exercise a jurisdiction
under a private contract." At pp 650-651 he set out
the rules by reference to which the competency of all I
applications to the supervisory jurisdiction was to be
determined. This did not indicate that as regards any
category of case the scope of that jurisdiction was
limited. It was therefore open to the Court of Session
in exercise of that jurisdiction to reduce the decision
of an arbiter, including a decision which determined
a matter of procedure, on the ground that it was
unreasonable. Counsel submitted that the remarks of
the Lord President in *Edmund Nuttall Ltd* should not
be regarded as deciding that the decision of an arbiter J
to postpone consideration of an application for a case
was beyond the scope of judicial review. In support of
this, counsel used an unusual type of authority in the
form of an address given by the Lord President to the
annual general meeting of the Scottish Council for
Arbitration on 18 March 1992, which is reported in
(1992) 37 JLS 223. At p 224, after referring to the
decision in *Edmund Nuttall Ltd* he said: "I should not
like to say that an arbiter whose refusal to state a case
in reliance on that provision was wholly unreasonable K
in the circumstances would not be open to judicial
review — but that is another story." Counsel also
founded on the decision in *Mitchell v Cable* as demonstrating that not all matters of procedure were left in
the unfettered control of the arbiter. In that case the
court set aside the award of an arbiter who had
proceeded on evidence from one side only and had not
given the opposite side the opportunity of bringing
evidence before him. While it was recognised that all
decisions of the arbiter on the merits of the claims of L
the parties were unchallengeable the arbiter in that
case had failed to carry out his duty to do equal justice
between them. Counsel submitted that the arbiter
should not be regarded as being at liberty to proceed
entirely as he thought fit. Thus, for example, he now
required to comply with the terms of the Civil Evidence Act 1988.

In the second place, counsel founded on the statement of the Lord President in *West* at p 651A that:
"An excess or abuse of jurisdiction may involve

stepping outside it, or failing to observe its limits, or departing from the rules of natural justice, or a failure to understand the law, or the taking into account of matters which ought not to have been taken into account." In order to justify an application for judicial review it was sufficient to demonstrate that an arbiter — who fell to be treated as a minor judge — had made an error of law. The terms of rule 277 (c) should be narrowly construed. It was accepted that they could apply to cases where an arbiter in his discretion took the view that the points argued before him were academic or hypothetical or depended on assumptions which might turn out to be ill founded; or turned on questions of mixed fact and law. They should not be construed as justifying the postponement of a case where there were points on relevancy and specification which were "fundamental" to a party's position. The decision of an arbiter on postponement would be final only when his reasons in law were correct.

As regards the averments made by the petitioner in support of the grounds of challenge, counsel for the petitioner indicated that if the dispute on relevancy and specification was not resolved at the present stage the petitioner would suffer prejudice because there would be unnecessary evidence and because there would be unfairness through fundamental lack of specification. In face of the petitioner's arguments it was illogical for the second respondent to say that it was necessary or expedient to ascertain the facts before dealing with the application. No reasonable arbiter properly advised would have reached the view that rule 277 (c) applied. Further, the result of his decision was so unreasonable that he must have misdirected himself in law. There was no adequate basis for the view that it was necessary or expedient that the facts should be ascertained first.

The decisions which were cited to me show that the Court of Session may decline to exercise its supervisory jurisdiction, assuming that it has not been otherwise excluded, if it appears that the petitioner has not exhausted a statutory remedy. There are obviously a number of considerations which could be of significance to the court in deciding whether or not to decline that jurisdiction in the circumstances of the case. It is unnecessary for me to explore those considerations in the present case since the implication which underlies any reference to a statutory remedy is that it is an effective one (cf *Tarmac Econowaste Ltd*, per Lord Clyde at p 79). In the present case the parties did not invite me to come to a view as to whether or not the petitioners' present application in the Inner House is incompetent. However, on any view there appear to be considerable difficulties for the petitioner in pursuing an application under s 3 of the 1972 Act in the light of the terms of the Rules of Court and the decision of the First Division in *Edmund Nuttall Ltd*. It is somewhat singular that the first respondent in the Inner House disputes the competency of the petitioner's application but in the Outer House founds upon it in support of the argument that the present application is incompetent. In my view the proceedings in the Inner House in the present case do not provide a satisfactory basis for sustaining a plea to the competency of the present application or for regarding the present application as premature. Further I do not regard the present situation to be one in which the plea of lis pendens properly applies. While the note is based upon the same narrative and grounds, it seeks to invoke an entirely different procedure with a different legal result.

In approaching the question of the court's interference with the decision of an arbiter on the procedural matters it is important in my opinion to keep in view the nature of the decision which the arbiter required to take. In dealing with the petitioners' application for a stated case he was in effect asked to exercise a discretion in connection with which there were various possible factors to which he could attach whatever weight he considered appropriate. These included, but were not confined to, the view he took of the points of law which had been argued before he decided to allow a proof before answer.

The respondents are correct in submitting that it has been long recognised that matters of procedure are for the arbiter to determine, so long as he observes the rules of natural justice in the way in which he reaches that determination. In passing, I would observe that *Mitchell v Cable* should be regarded as an example of the arbiter's failure to observe them. I do not regard it as deciding that the court is entitled to interfere with the arbiter's judgment on matters of procedure. If matters of procedure are for the arbiter to determine it is but a short step to the conclusion that in dealing with an application for a case to be stated the arbiter has a similar discretion to decide whether it is necessary or expedient that the facts should be ascertained before that application is disposed of.

All these propositions no doubt point to the conclusion that in general the court will not interfere with a decision on procedural matters, and will regard an application for judicial review as incompetent. However, it is one thing to say that such matters of procedure are for the arbiter and not for the court to decide. It is another thing to say that there are no circumstances in which an arbiter's decision on matters of procedure will be interfered with by the court. It is not and could not be disputed that the court would interfere if the decision of an arbiter involved an abuse or an excess of his jurisdiction. Such a decision would be reducible at common law, the basis being that it was contrary to what was implied in the parties' submission to him or, perhaps more accurately, what the law implies when the judicial function is conferred. It is true that no case was cited to me in which it was decided or argued that an arbiter's decision, and in particular a decision which turned on the exercise of a discretion, was invalid in respect that the decision was unreasonable and accordingly involved an excess or abuse of his jurisdiction. It is perhaps not surprising that the point did not arise in cases decided long before the development of the modern law in regard to this ground for judicial review and its adoption in the law of Scotland. I would also observe that the point did not arise for consideration in *Edmund*

A   *Nuttall Ltd.* The reducibility of arbiter's decision on matters of procedure is at least consistent with decision in *West*, although it has to be borne in mind that that decision was essentially concerned with dealing with the suggestion that the scope of judicial review in Scotland was limited to questions of "public law".

Accordingly I have to ask myself — is there any sound reason why the court should not be entitled to reduce the decision of an arbiter on procedural matters on the ground that the decision was unreasonable?

B   Counsel for the respondents maintained that a reason could be found in the fact that the arbiter had been chosen by the parties. However, this does not provide a satisfactory basis for decision since there are many instances, such as cases of statutory arbitration, where the arbiter is not a person chosen by the parties. Another reason was said to be the importance of the point that judicial interference in the arbitral process should be kept to a minimum. In that connection reference was made by counsel for the second respon-

C   dent to the decision of Steyn J in the Commercial Court in *Biakh v Hyundai*. While that case relates to a very different legal regime I accept that this is a formidable consideration. However, it does not, in my view, rule out judicial interference in the extreme situation in which it is contended that a decision was unreasonable. It would be a factor for consideration in the exercise of the court's discretion. Having regard to the nature of the decision to which the present case relates and which involves the exercise of a discretion I am not satisfied that there is a sound reason for

D   excluding the court's entitlement to interfere with such a decision on the ground that it was unreasonable.

As regards the petitioner's submission on error in law I am unable to agree with the contention that the finality of the decision of an arbiter is dependent on whether it is sound in law or that the Lord President in *West* intended to countenance that proposition. As I understand his reference at p 651 to "a failure to

E   understand the law", he meant a failure which was of such a character as to entail an excess or abuse of jurisdiction. When I turn to the terms of para (ii) of art 4 of the petition which I quoted above I find that the reference to an error of law is there qualified, and in my view necessarily qualified, by the words "and in misuse of the powers in fact conferred upon the second respondent". Thus far, the second ground for reduction of the arbiter's interlocutor squares with what according to my understanding would require to

F   be established. However, the petitioner goes on in art 7, as I have indicated above, to aver that: "The questions raised in said minute are not such as may prove, on investigation of the facts of said disputes, to be academic or hypothetical. The said power is intended to permit an arbiter to avoid the necessity to state a case on matters which may prove to be irrelevant to the dispute between the arbitrating parties." This sets unacceptably narrow limits to the scope which the arbiter has for postponing the statement of a case. Further, as I have already stated in my summary of its arguments, the petitioner appears to accept that there

are further grounds upon which the arbiter could elect to postpone consideration of the application, in parti-   G cular where the arguments presented raised questions of mixed fact and law. In these circumstances I do not understand how the present case can be placed in a category which lies beyond the proper province of rule 277 (c). This second ground for the reduction of the arbiter's interlocutor appears to me to pose essentially the same question as the first but in a different form.

In the result I have reached the conclusion that the present application is competent. The next matter which arises for consideration, is whether the peti-   H tioner has made sufficient averments in support of the grounds for reduction to meet the tests of relevancy and specification. As I have already indicated parties have set out their respective positions at least in outline on these matters. I will give them an opportunity to elaborate them if they so wish. In the meantime I refrain from making any comment on what so far has been presented to me.

Accordingly I will repel the first, second and third pleas in law for the first respondent and the first plea   I in law for the second respondent. The case will be put out by order for further procedure.

Counsel for Petitioners, McNeill, QC; Solicitors, MacRoberts — Counsel for First Respondents, Scott, QC, Reid; Solicitors, Maclay, Murray & Spens — Counsel for Second Respondent (Arbiter), Glennie; Solicitors, Campbell Smith & Co, WS.

                                         A R W Y   J

(NOTE)

Moffat v Babcock Thorn Ltd

OUTER HOUSE   K
LORD PROSSER
4 FEBRUARY 1993

Damages — Amount — Solatium — Hearing — Burning injury in ear causing initial pain, deafness for two or three days and tinnitus at significant level for about six months with minor permanent hearing deficit.

A 24 year old welder suffered injury when a drop of molten slag fell into his ear. The initial injury was   L painful and was followed by deafness in that ear for two or three days. He suffered tinnitus at a significant level for about six months, clearing up entirely after about a year. He was left with a minor hearing deficit.

Held, that solatium was properly valued at £1,750; and decree *pronounced* accordingly.

Stuart Moffat raised an action of damages against his employers, Babcock Thorn Ltd, for injuries received in an accident at work on 1 November 1990. He was then aged 24. He was a welder and had been welding in a confined space when a drop of molten slag fell into his ear. The defenders admitted liability. In assessing solatium at £1,750 the Lord Ordinary (Prosser) said:

"The pursuer said that he had realised at once what had happened. There had been a buzzing and hissing, and extreme pain. From the difficult position in which he was at the time, it had taken him about a minute to get clear. He had been screaming, but his workmate only arrived as he himself had almost got out. While trying to get out, he had almost fainted. Thereafter, the pain had been severe for about a day; and for several days after that, there had been a burning sensation. He had only missed three or four days of work, but had been on light duties for a period thereafter.

"In evidence, the pursuer described how initially he had been unable to hear in his left ear. His hearing had come back within about three days. However, within about two days after the burning sensation had gone, he had started suffering from tinnitus. While he had not originally known the term, he described being conscious of a high pitched noise inside his head. He was somewhat imprecise as to how long this had continued, but I am satisfied from his evidence as a whole (and notwithstanding certain possibly conflicting records) that the tinnitus was a significant problem for perhaps six months, and thereafter improved, finally ceasing about a year after the accident. Even during the first six months, the tinnitus was getting better. Quite apart from the tinnitus, when the pursuer's hearing was initially tested, a mild high-frequency depression was revealed on the left side. The hearing in his right ear had been normal throughout.

"When he was seen by Mr A J Smith, a consultant aural surgeon, in February 1991, his hearing was described as "slightly depressed on the left side". Mr Smith in evidence expressed the view that both the tinnitus and this hearing loss were as a result of the accident. By May 1991 (when, as I have indicated, the tinnitus effectively ceased to be a significant problem) the problem with high frequency hearing appears also to have gone. However, when the tympanic membranes of the ears were examined, Mr Smith discovered a small thickened area, posterior on the left side. He attributed this to the healing of the scar caused by the burn, and stated that its principal effect would be to make the tympanic membrane less responsive to incoming sound waves. In particular, it would make the membrane less responsive to low frequency sound waves. Someone having such a thickened membrane would hear low frequency sound less well, and he agreed that this meant that such people were 'slightly deaf'. Conversational assessment had not suggested 'serious loss' of hearing 'within the speech frequencies'. An audiogram had shown that there was low frequency conductive hearing depression on the left side: this related to air conduction, and meant effectively that a person suffering from such a reduction would hear less well, this again being particularly for low frequency sound. When asked to relate this in practical terms to the experience of the person suffering it, Mr Smith said that it had been found that minor differences in hearing ability are 'much, much more perceptible to the sufferer than perhaps audiometric measurement would suggest'. This is likely to be a permanent consequence. Mr Smith acknowledged that people with abnormal mid-ear physiology experience discomfort because of sudden loud sound, but in other respects, he would expect the sufferer to be able to adjust, and use his better ear. The pursuer had been found to suffer from a degree of noise induced deafness, affecting higher frequencies, and Mr Smith gave evidence to the effect that the effect of the two would be additive — because he had the higher frequency difficulty, the lower frequency difficulty would be much more than if he did not have the higher frequency difficulty. So far as Mr Smith was concerned, he said that he would call the hearing loss 'mild', but he emphasised that the important matter was not the simple loss, in terms of decibels, but the fact that the pursuer does not now have symmetrical hearing.

"In relation to hearing difficulties, I have thought it more convenient to deal with the medical evidence before coming to the evidence of the pursuer himself, and the only other lay witness, his girlfriend. I regarded the pursuer as an honest and reliable witness. Referring to the first six months, he said that he felt his hearing had changed. It had been 'definitely down' in comparison with his right ear. There might be a noise on his left side, which he would hear in his right ear. It had been getting better by the time he saw Mr Smith, and was not affecting him greatly by then. He acknowledged that he was not greatly affected now. He would not call it a problem; on the other hand he would not say that it was back to normal. His girlfriend confirmed the general picture, of minor problems in relation to television, doorbells, phones and the like during the first year. She also confirmed the problems relating to tinnitus, and the ringing in the pursuer's ears, and spoke to the element of stress which this had involved.

"In addressing me on damages, counsel for the pursuer treated the question of solatium under three heads. There was the very unpleasant and painful initial accident. Secondly, there was the period of about six months when the pursuer had suffered some initial pain and thereafter both a high frequency hearing problem and the stressful tinnitus. Thirdly, there was the period from May 1991 onwards, and continuing into the future, when one could say that the pursuer had no real problem, but was suffering from a hearing deficit resulting from the accident. While counsel for the defenders accepted that it had been an unpleasant accident, with intense pain, he pointed out that it had to be seen in the context of other and more disastrous accidents. So far as the subsequent position is concerned, he pointed out that any hearing defect was a compounding of a defect which was present in any event, and he naturally relied on the fact that the pursuer had no continuing specific complaint, and indeed no continuing problem.

"The pursuer was born on 5 April 1966, and was

A accordingly aged 24 at the date of the accident. I regard the intense pain which he suffered at the time of the accident, and indeed the whole circumstances of the accident, as serious matters, and I am satisfied that the next six months, and in particular the problem of tinnitus, must have been very unpleasant and worrying. I would furthermore accept that until the tinnitus went completely, there was at least an abiding concern, and as regards the long term position, I regard the low frequency hearing deficit as a material consideration in assessing damages. On the other

B hand, I have not found it possible to draw any close analogy between this long term deficit and cases where permanent hearing loss constitutes a significant problem or disability. Equally, apart from this long term matter, it must be borne in mind that the pursuer's really unpleasant experiences were over within about six months.

"I was referred to a number of cases: *Taylor v Fife Regional Council*, 1991 SLT 80; *Hoey v British Steel Corporation*, 1991 SLT 196; *McLeod v Wiggins Teape*

C *(Stationery) Ltd*, 1991 SLT 406; and *Laidler v Yarrow Shipbuilders Ltd*, 1990 SLT 261. In *Taylor*, where solatium was given for a burn to the hand, I find no real assistance. The other three cases relate to loss of hearing or tinnitus, but their facts all appear to me to be very different, and I have not found them to be of any very direct assistance. I am satisfied that on a comparison with these cases, the pursuer's short term sufferings, and long term minor deficit, cannot justify the level of award sought by his counsel, of some

D £4,000 or more. Equally, I think that counsel for the defenders went too far in suggesting that damages to date could be sufficiently met by an award of £800, with a further £100 for the continuing deficit. In my opinion a fair cumulative figure for solatium would be £1,750, of which I would regard £1,250 as relating to past pain and suffering."

Counsel for Pursuer, Allardice; Solicitors, Robin
E *Thompson & Partners — Counsel for Defenders, R N Thomson; Solicitors, Simpson & Marwick, WS.*

C H

(NOTE)
F # Lothian Regional Council v Lord Advocate

OUTER HOUSE
LORD COULSFIELD
5 FEBRUARY 1993

Process — Fatal accident inquiry — Appeal by way of judicial review — Whether competent — When determination reducible — Extent to which determination

reducible — Fatal Accidents and Sudden Deaths Inquiry (Scotland) Act 1976 (c 14), s 6 (1).   G

Administrative law — Fatal accident inquiry — Appeal by way of judicial review — Whether competent — When determination reducible — Extent to which determination reducible — Fatal Accidents and Sudden Deaths Inquiry (Scotland) Act 1976 (c 14), s 6 (1).

Parties involved in a fatal accident inquiry held under the Fatal Accidents and Sudden Deaths Inquiry (Scotland) Act 1976 sought to bring under review, by a petition for judicial review, the determination by the   H sheriff in the fatal accident inquiry.

Held, (1) (in the absence of argument to the contrary) that judicial review was competent; (2) that where the sheriff had not misdirected himself in law or acted beyond his jurisdiction, his determination could be reduced only if it could be said that the sheriff altogether failed to take into account a matter which he should have taken into account; and (3) that the only part of the determination that could be   I reduced was a part that fell within the specific findings listed in s 6 (1) of the Act.

Section 6 (1) of the Fatal Accidents and Sudden Deaths Inquiry (Scotland) Act 1976 provides:

"At the conclusion of the evidence and any submissions thereon, or as soon as possible thereafter, the sheriff shall make a determination setting out the following circumstances of the death so far as they have   J been established to his satisfaction — (a) where and when the death and any accident resulting in the death took place; (b) the cause or causes of such death and any accident resulting in the death; (c) the reasonable precautions, if any, whereby the death and any accident resulting in the death might have been avoided; (d) the defects, if any, in any system of working which contributed to the death or any accident resulting in the death; and (e) any other facts which are relevant to the circumstances of the death."   K

Lothian Regional Council and four of its employees in its roads department petitioned for judicial review of the determination of the sheriff in a fatal accident inquiry into the death of a car driver who had died on 13 March 1991 in consequence of an accident at the junction of the A71 and A706 roads. The respondent was the Lord Advocate, who appeared in the public interest in order to assist the court. In his determination, the sheriff had held that the employees had   L caused the accident by blocking the westbound lane of the A71, and that they had attempted to conceal the mistake which caused the accident by removing certain road cones. The sheriff had criticised the behaviour of the employees very severely both in respect of the blocking of the road and the removal of the cones and also because, as he had held, they had failed to render assistance to the deceased. In the petition for judicial review, the petitioners sought reduction of part of the determination on the ground that the sheriff had not been entitled to reach the con-

clusions summarised above upon the evidence before
A him and that those conclusions were such as no
reasonable sheriff could have reached upon the evidence. In relation to the competency of the action the
Lord Ordinary (Coulsfield) said:

"In the answers lodged on behalf of the Lord
Advocate, pleas were taken to the competency of the
petition and to the title and interest of the petitioners
to raise it. Those pleas were not, however, insisted in.
It seems to me that the sheriff's comments clearly did
have important consequences for all the petitioners,
B even though the determination of a fatal accident
inquiry cannot be founded upon in any subsequent
legal proceedings. The nature of those consequences is
apparent from some newspaper cuttings produced by
the petitioners in which the sheriff's determination
and his criticisms were fully reported, and in which
criticisms of all the petitioners were strongly
expressed. The Fatal Accidents and Sudden Deaths
Inquiry (Scotland) Act 1976 contains no provision for
appeal against a determination of a sheriff at such an
C inquiry. In the circumstances, in my opinion, I am
entitled to accept, in the absence of any argument to
the contrary, that the present proceedings are competent."

After narrating the background to the accident, his
Lordship continued:

"The sheriff heard evidence from a considerable
number of witnesses including . . . the four individual
petitioners. His determination is set out in the form of
D a reasoned judgment including comments upon the
evidence of particular witnesses. Section 6 of the 1976
Act provides, inter alia [his Lordship quoted the terms
of s 6 (1) set out supra and continued:]

"No statutory form is provided for the sheriff's
determination. As I understand the position, it is at
least a common, if not the normal, practice for sheriffs
to set out specific findings in relation to each of the
five heads specified in s 6 (1), if they are satisfied upon
the evidence that such findings should be made, and
E to set out their reasoning or observations in a note
appended to the findings. In the present case, specific
findings have not been made, and, in consequence, it
is necessary to go through the sheriff's reasoning in
some detail in order to show what he did find. In substance, however, the facts found by the sheriff do
appear to be reasonably clear."

His Lordship then considered the evidence before
the sheriff and the criticisms made of the sheriff's
F determination, one of which was that the sheriff had
ignored, without reason, the evidence of two witnesses, Doyle and McGurk, which criticism his Lordship found justified, and concluded:

"In all the circumstances, if this were an ordinary
appeal, I would have no hesitation in holding that the
sheriff's reasoning was flawed and that it would be
necessary to review the whole evidence in order to see
what conclusions could properly be drawn from it.

"This, however, is not an ordinary appeal but an
application for judicial review. There is no reason to

think that the sheriff misdirected himself in law or
acted beyond his jurisdiction. It was pointed out in G
Black v Scott Lithgow Ltd, 1990 SLT 612 that the
sheriff is not directed to reach any conclusion on a
question of fault, but the statute empowers him, if he
is so satisfied, to make a determination as to the cause
of an accident and as to precautions which might have
been relevant to prevention of it, and I do not think
that the sheriff, in the present case, can be said to have
gone beyond those functions. Further, there was, as I
have attempted to explain, some direct evidence that
the carriageway of the A71 was blocked for westbound H
vehicles, and the sheriff would, no doubt, have been
entitled to weigh that evidence against the evidence of
Mr Doyle and Mr McGurk, and to reject the latter
evidence, if he had reason to do so. It follows, in my
opinion, that the determination can be reduced only if
it can be said that the sheriff altogether failed to take
into account a matter which he should have taken into
account, namely the evidence of Mr Doyle and Mr
McGurk. To justify a reduction of the determination
on this ground, it must, I think, be possible to go I
beyond the inference that the sheriff did not have, or
did not express, adequate reasons for rejecting the
evidence and conclude that he must have overlooked
it entirely or shut it out from his consideration.
Whether such a conclusion can be reached must
depend upon the facts and circumstances of the
individual case. In the present case, the evidence of
Mr Doyle and Mr McGurk was absolutely and
directly relevant to the essential point which had to be
decided. It is wholly contrary to the view which the J
sheriff has taken. There is nothing in the evidence as
recorded to suggest it is intrinsically unreliable or to
give, ex facie, a reason to reject it. The sheriff has
given no reason for rejecting the evidence, but has
wholly ignored it. In the case of Mr Doyle, given that
the sheriff does make reference to part of the evidence
of the witness and place some reliance on that part, it
is difficult to see what reason he could have for passing
over the rest of the evidence without explanation. In
these exceptional circumstances, it seems to me that it K
is legitimate to conclude that the sheriff has excluded
material evidence from his consideration or wholly
overlooked it, and that, therefore, the determination
cannot stand.

"The second material respect in which the sheriff's
determination was criticised was in regard to his comments upon the activities of the four individual petitioners, the workmen present at the time." His
Lordship considered the evidence and concluded:

"No suggestion was made, at any time, to any of the L
employees of the petitioners that their actions had
been improper or unreasonable. In these circumstances, it seems to me that the sheriff's comments
went further than was justified. Of course, if in fact
the employees did occupy themselves with concealing
a blunder rather than giving assistance to the victim of
an accident, that would be conduct which might
reasonably be criticised; but even on that basis, it
would, I think, be better not to express such severe
criticism when the employees had not had an oppor-

A tunity to defend themselves. In the actual circumstances of this case, the decision not to attempt to free the deceased before expert help was available could not be said to be wrong or unreasonable in itself and since, for the reasons already given, the sheriff was not entitled to conclude as he did, that the A71 had been coned off, it follows that there was no sufficient basis for the criticism which he expressed.

"The question which remains is what remedy should be granted. The petitioners seek reduction of the last three sentences of the sheriff's determination
B which, as has been seen, contain the finding that the employees of the first petitioners caused the accident by blocking the westbound lane of the A71 and the adverse comments upon the individual petitioners. It would, I think, be difficult to regard the comments upon the employees, however ill founded, as the proper subject matter of a decree of reduction. These comments really form part of the sheriff's assessment of the evidence rather than of a determination in terms of s 6 of the 1976 Act, a point which would have been
C clearer if the normal practice had been followed in setting out the determination. However, the conclusion that the first petitioners' employees caused the accident by blocking part of the A71 could, I think, be regarded as a determination within para (d) of s 6 (1) of the 1976 Act. It was submitted on behalf of the respondent that it was not possible to separate a part of the sheriff's determination and reduce that part because the sheriff had had evidence before him upon which he was entitled to reach a conclusion, and did
D reach a conclusion, as to the cause of the accident and other relevant matters. It appears to me, however, that s 6 (1) sets out a number of headings under which particular determinations are to be made and that a determination under one heading need not necessarily be so interlinked with a determination upon another as to make it impossible to separate the two. In the circumstances of the present case, it appears to me that insofar as the sheriff has purported to determine that the westbound lane of the A71 was blocked, that part
E of his determination is severable and contains a finding which he was not entitled to make, so that reduction of that part of the determination should be granted. I shall, accordingly, sustain the plea in law for the petitioners, repel the second and fourth pleas in law for the respondent and grant decree of reduction of the determination of the sheriff insofar as it purports to determine, for the purposes of s 6 (1) (d) of the 1976 Act, that the accident was caused by blocking off the westbound carriageway of the A71 road by
F employees of the first petitioners."

Counsel for Petitioners, McGhie, QC, Cowan; Solicitor, G F G Welsh — Counsel for Respondent, Paton, QC; Solicitor, J D Lowe, Crown Agent.

C H

Kennedy v A

G

EXTRA DIVISION

LORDS MURRAY, OSBORNE AND WYLIE

3 MARCH 1993

Children and young persons — Children's hearing — Application to sheriff for findings whether or not grounds of referral established — Whether father assaulted child — Father striking young baby twice with hand on bare bottom — Whether mens rea for assault established.

H

A five month old baby was referred to a children's hearing on the basis that an offence mentioned in Sched 1 to the Criminal Procedure (Scotland) Act 1975 had been committed against her, in that she had been assaulted. The parents did not accept the grounds of referral. The sheriff found that the child's father had had sole care of the child for a limited period of time one day and that "while she was alone in his care Mr A forcibly struck L at least twice on her bare bottom with the palm of his hand". The sheriff
I did not consider this finding to amount to assault, taking the view that it could not be said on a balance of probabilities that at the moment of striking the child the father had the necessary evil intent or wilfulness to justify finding either that he assaulted the child or that he wilfully ill treated the child, and that the grounds of referral had not been established. The reporter appealed.

Held, that the only reasonable inference to be drawn from the findings was that the blows referred J to were struck deliberately, and that if so mens rea was sufficiently established for the blows to constitute assault in the absence of evidence of justification or any other exonerating factor (p 1138B); and case *remitted* to the sheriff to find the grounds of referral established.

Appeal from the sheriff court

Frederick J Kennedy, reporter to the children's K panel for Strathclyde Region, referred a child, L, to a children's hearing, as a child in respect of whom an offence mentioned in Sched 1 to the Criminal Procedure (Scotland) Act 1975 had been committed, in terms of s 32 (2) (d) of the Social Work (Scotland) Act 1968. The child's parents, S A and J A, did not accept the grounds of referral. The children's hearing directed the reporter to apply to the sheriff for a finding as to whether the grounds of referral in question were established. A hearing took place at L Greenock sheriff court before Sheriff Sir S S T Young.

Facts

The following narrative is taken from the opinion of the court:

The sheriff's findings in fact, so far as material, included the following:

"(3) Soon after her birth L began to develop breathing difficulties at night. As a result she was given an apnoea monitor which records her breathing and sets

off an alarm if it stops. She has had to be taken to the
doctor in connection with her breathing difficulties
and she has had several chest infections for which
antibiotics have been prescribed. Otherwise she has
developed normally. . . . (5) At about 8 am on 21 June
1992 (which was a Sunday) Mr A went out to work
leaving Mrs A in the house with L. . . . During the
night L had not slept well and her monitor had gone
off twice. On each occasion it had taken Mrs A
between half an hour and an hour to settle the child.
But in the morning she seemed to Mrs A to be 'fine'.
Mrs A got her up in the usual way, fed, bathed and
changed her. At that stage there was no sign of any
injury on her.''

It is then narrated that Mr and Mrs A went out in
their car with L and another 11 month old child. The
findings then proceed: "(7) After a brief visit to
another part of Greenock . . . Mr and Mrs A returned
to their home . . . with L and Mrs B. By this time it
was about 11.30 am. Mr A and L remained in the
house while Mrs A and Mrs B went out to a nearby
bowling club to do some catering. (8) At this stage L
was asleep in her buggy. She continued to sleep for a
while. When she awoke she appeared to Mr A to be
very tired, hungry and thirsty. He picked her up and
walked around the room with her showing her some
pictures. Then he put her in her baby walker and gave
her some toys to play with including one to chew in
her mouth as she was teething at the time. She was
still, in Mr A's words, 'really tired'. (9) Mr A then
tried feeding L but she was not interested in her food
nor did she want any juice when he offered that to her.
He then tried to play with her but she was still not
happy. She started to cry so he picked her up. She
quietened down and he tried to feed her again but still
she would not eat. She started crying again. (10) Mr
A then decided to telephone Mrs A at her work to see
if she had any idea as to what could be wrong with the
child and as to how he might get her to eat or sleep.
Mrs A suggested that he should put her into her buggy
and walk her over to the bowling club where she was
working in the hope that that might send her to sleep.
By this time it was about 12.50 pm. (11) After
telephoning Mrs A, Mr A proceeded to change L's
nappy. When he had finished doing so he put her in
her buggy where she fell asleep as he took her to the
bowling club. He arrived there about 1.30 pm. (12) At
some stage between 11.30 am and 1.30 pm that day
while she was alone in his care Mr A forcibly struck
L at least twice on her bare bottom with the palm of
his hand. (13) On arrival at the bowling club Mr A
told Mrs A that there was a small bruise on the side
of her left leg. He suggested that this had been caused
by her baby walker. At that point L was asleep so Mrs
A left her undisturbed and carried on working.''

It is then narrated that, because of L's breathing
difficulty, Mr and Mrs A took L to a local health
centre where she saw a doctor between 3 pm and 4
pm. By this time Mrs L had seen the mark to which
Mr A had earlier referred. Between 3 and 4 pm Mrs
A changed L's nappy at home and found that the mark
had grown in extent. She took L back to the health

centre where she was examined by Dr Rutherford who
found an oval mark about three quarters of an inch in
extent of a uniform bluish/black discolouration which
she did not think was a bruise. By about 6.30 pm
markings were visible on the child's body to an even
greater extent. L was taken to the children's ward at
Inverclyde Royal hospital where she was examined by
Dr Sharp. The findings continue:

"(23) . . . she found that the child had blue discolouration resembling fresh bruising on both
buttocks with small petechial areas . . . in the cleft
between the buttocks. The doctor considered the
possibility that L might have a clotting abnormality
but was able to exclude this after a sample of her blood
had been taken . . . the doctor was concerned about
how the markings might have been caused and decided
to seek the opinion of the consultant paediatrician on
call, Dr R C Shepherd. (24) Dr Shepherd . . . found
a confluent extensive bruised area across her buttocks
extending from the hip bones to the buttock fold, i e
at the base of the buttocks. Within this area there were
petechiae which were especially marked at the anal
cleft. The anus itself was unmarked. In addition on
the upper thighs at the back there were two linear
bruises extending from the insides of the thighs round
to the outer sides. (25) The markings on L's bottom
were in Dr Shepherd's opinion of very recent origin.
Judging by the freshness of the bruising and the
presence of the petechiae he thought that they had
probably been caused within the previous 24 hours.
The only way that he could think that they might have
occurred was by L being hit by blunt trauma, almost
certainly the palm of a hand in light of the linear
marks on the thighs. In his view several slaps would
have been required to produce the injuries which he
found. The injuries would have caused L a degree of
distress at the time that they were inflicted but this
would have been only temporary. . . . (27) After Dr
Shepherd had completed his examination of L,
standby social workers were called and in due course
arrangements were made for the child and Mrs A to
spend the night at the hospital. Mr A went home. (28)
The following morning the other consultant paediatrician at Inverclyde Royal hospital, Dr Norman
Coutts . . . found bruises on her buttocks compatible
with her having been slapped, probably twice, once on
each buttock. In his opinion 'a fair degree of force'
would have been required to cause the injuries. He
also considered that the bruising was between 24 and
48 hours old. . . . (30) A place of safety order was
subsequently sought and obtained in respect of L. By
24 June 1992 the markings on her bottom were found
by Dr Shepherd to be fading, and after a short stay in
the hospital she was discharged into the care of foster
parents. She remained in foster care until the discharge of the referral . . . on 21 July 1992. Throughout
that period Mr and Mrs A were fully co-operative with
representatives of the local social work department.
(31) While she was in foster care Mr and Mrs A had
access to L for an hour or two a day between Mondays
and Fridays each week. L appeared to be a bright, alert
and contented baby. She related very well and happily

to Mr and Mrs A. Her face would light up when she
A entered the room and she would throw out her arms
to greet them. She appeared to benefit greatly from the
attention of both parents and would play energetically
with Mr A in particular. Both parents were observed
changing her nappy and both were seen to do so very
carefully."

The findings in fact make it clear that at no point
before L was taken into foster care did the respondents
offer an explanation as to the cause of the markings.

B **Cases referred to**
Advocate's (Lord) Reference No 2 of 1992, 1993 SLT
460; 1992 SCCR 960.
Guest v Annan, 1988 SCCR 275.
R v Senior [1899] 1 QB 83.
Ross v HM Advocate, 1991 SLT 564; 1991 SCCR 823.

Textbooks referred to
Gordon, *Criminal Law* (2nd ed), para 29-30.
Macdonald, *Criminal Law* (5th ed), p 115.
C

The sheriff *found* that the grounds of referral were
not established.

The reporter appealed to the Court of Session.

Appeal
The sheriff stated the following question for the
opinion of the court:

D On the facts found proved or admitted was I entitled
to find that the grounds of referral had not been established?

The appeal was heard before an Extra Division on
3 March 1993.

Eo die the court *answered* the question in the stated
case in the *negative* and *remitted* the case to the sheriff
to find the grounds of referral established and to
E proceed as accords.

The following opinion of the court was delivered by
Lord Murray:

OPINION OF THE COURT.—The appellant in
this stated case is the reporter to the children's panel
for Strathclyde Region. The respondents are the
parents of a child L. On 25 June 1992 she was referred
to a children's hearing on the basis that she was a child
in respect of whom an offence mentioned in Sched 1
F to the Criminal Procedure (Scotland) Act 1975 had
been committed, being ground for referral in terms of
s 32 (2) (d) of the Social Work (Scotland) Act 1968 (as
amended).

In support of the above referral there was a statement of facts to the effect that L was born on 25
January 1992 and normally resided in family with her
mother and father. At all material times the child was
in the custody, charge and care of her parents. On 21
June 1992, within Inverclyde Royal hospital, the child
was examined and the following injuries were noted:

an extensive, confluent bruised area across the buttocks; petechiae within the confluent bruised area in G
particular at the anal cleft; two linear bruises on the
thighs extending from the posterior of the thighs to
the lateral side of the thighs on both sides. The child's
parents were unable to offer an adequate and acceptable explanation for these injuries. The injuries were
consistent with the child being struck a direct blow
with the palm of the hand.

At a children's hearing held on 25 June 1992 the
respondents did not accept the grounds of referral
apart from identification and address. The children's H
hearing were satisfied that the child herself was not
capable of understanding the grounds of referral.
They accordingly directed the appellant in terms of
s 42 (2) (c) and 42 (7) of the Social Work (Scotland) Act
1968 to apply to the sheriff for a finding as to whether
the said grounds were established. On 20 and 21 July
1992 the sheriff heard evidence and submissions for
the parties and decided that the grounds of referral
had not been established. He accordingly dismissed
the application and discharged the referral. I

[His Lordship then narrated the facts as set out
supra and continued:]

In his careful and full note the sheriff explains that
Mr and Mrs A "suggested in the course of their evidence that L might have been injured as a result of
being bounced up and down on her father's knees or
shoulders or while she was in the bath or while she
was moving about in her baby walker. These suggestions were put to the doctors and I was quite satisfied J
that they were right to exclude them as possible
explanations for the markings on L's bottom. I had no
doubt in light of the evidence of Dr Shepherd and Dr
Coutts that the child had been struck forcibly on her
bare bottom with the palm of a hand at least twice. As
Dr Shepherd put it: 'it really has to be a burst of
temper, an aggressive outburst'."

The sheriff makes it clear that he found Mrs A to
be an honest witness but mistaken about how L came
by her injuries. Similarly he accepted that Mr A K
appeared to be giving an honest account of events
except as regards how L came by her injuries, on
which he concluded, for reasons which he sets out
fully, that Mr A was lying. The conclusion which he
drew from the evidence is contained in finding in
fact 12.

The sheriff concludes that the circumstances in
which Mr A did so were that, being in sole charge of
a small child who was ailing and fretful he became
exasperated and desperate, "as in vain he tries every- L
thing he can think of to try and quieten the child. In
such a situation it is possible for the parent's self
control to snap and in a moment of aberration he may
strike or otherwise injure the child in a manner that
is instantly regretted (and most unlikely ever to be
repeated)". He concluded that this was much the most
likely explanation of how L came by her injuries. The
sheriff then proceeds to spell out the reasoning on
which he decided that the grounds of referral had not
been established. This is what the sheriff says:

"In the ordinary course it might have been thought plain that, having struck L as he did, Mr A was thereby guilty of assaulting her at common law or of wilfully ill treating her within the meaning of s 12 of the 1937 Act. But it is axiomatic that evil intent on the part of the perpetrator is an essential element in the crime of assault. Similarly, in the case of wilful ill treatment of a child the reference in s 12 to 'wilfully' means that the act must be done deliberately and intentionally 'not by accident or inadvertence, but so that the mind of the person who does the act goes with it' (R v Senior, Lord Russell CJ at p 291). Every case of this kind must depend upon its own facts and circumstances, and I am very far from saying that in every case in which a child is proving difficult to manage a parent is entitled to strike the child so hard as to cause injuries of the kind described in this case, let alone injuries which may be life threatening. I have already described the circumstances in which I consider Mr A came to strike L on the date in question. Having heard all the evidence I do not believe that he was the type of father who would have deliberately harmed his child in the manner found by the doctors even in the context of a fit of temper. When he had charge of her his overriding purpose would have been to secure her welfare and in my view the last thing that would have entered his mind would have been the possibility of his doing her any harm. In my opinion it would have required momentary total loss of self control such as I have described to have caused him to strike L as he did and in that state of affairs and in the circumstances of this particular case I do not consider that it can be said on a balance of probabilities that, at the moment of striking the child, he had the necessary evil intent or wilfulness to justify a finding either that he assaulted the child or that he wilfully ill treated her within the meaning of s 12 of the 1937 Act. It was for this reason that I decided that the grounds of referral had not been established."

The question for the opinion of the court was: "On the facts found proved or admitted was I entitled to find that the grounds of referral had not been established?"

At the outset of the hearing before the Inner House counsel for the appellant presented an argument that what the sheriff had found in fact amounted in law to an assault upon L and that, without making any concession on the point, he would not present an argument that it also amounted in law to wilful ill treatment in terms of s 12. It was to be noted that the sheriff had made no findings on reasonable chastisement, though it was clear from his note that he had excluded this on the evidence which he had accepted. It was submitted that the sheriff, having correctly made finding in fact 12, erred when he came to consider the issue of mens rea for assault. To establish mens rea in relation to assault it was not necessary in every case to draw an inference of positive intent to harm or injure. In the absence of justification it was sufficient if blows causing injury were struck deliberately, and that was generally a matter of inference from the facts and circumstances proved. The real question was whether blows were struck deliberately rather than carelessly or by inadvertence. That this was the correct approach to mens rea appeared from Lord Advocate's Reference No 2, where an accused charged with assault with intent to rob maintained that there was no mens rea because his admitted actions were carried out as a joke. At 1993 SLT, p 464F-G the Lord Justice Clerk (Ross) said: "In my opinion the accused's assertion that it was a joke means no more than that it was his motive or ulterior intention in acting as he did. It has often been said that evil intention is of the essence of assault (Macdonald's Criminal Law, p 115). But what that means is that assault cannot be committed accidentally or recklessly or negligently (Gordon's Criminal Law (2nd ed), para 29-30). In the present case, it is plain that when the accused entered the shop, presented the handgun at Mrs Daly and uttered the words which he did, he was acting deliberately. That being so, in my opinion, he had the necessary intent for his actions to amount to assault, and his motive for acting as he did was irrelevant."

It was plain from the findings in fact in this case that the sheriff had found that Mr A had inflicted a deliberate blow. That was sufficient to constitute the necessary mens rea. Momentary loss of control or loss of temper was of no relevance, though it might have a bearing on provocation, which was insufficient to exclude mens rea. The necessary test for a defence excluding mens rea had been dealt with in the full bench case of Ross v HM Advocate, Lord Justice General (Hope) at 1991 SLT, p 569C-F, Lord McCluskey at pp 575L-576D.

It was clear that the sheriff had misdirected himself in law on his findings in fact. He had also allowed himself to stray into consideration of what was in the best interests of the child L in the circumstances which he had found. This was properly a matter for the children's hearing. The question for the opinion of the court should be answered in the negative.

Counsel for the respondents accepted that the sheriff's function was confined to determining whether the grounds of referral had been established and, if they were, it was for the children's hearing and not for the sheriff to make a judgment on the future arrangements for the child. The crucial finding in fact 12 in its context of the other findings in fact was neutral as regards mens rea. Although deliberation was in general sufficient to infer mens rea without the need to prove positive intent to harm, there was room in the present circumstances for the sheriff's conclusion that mens rea had not been established. One should not take too rigid an approach and look only at the act. So inadvertence or misjudgment in a chastisement situation should not be excluded, particularly in a parent-child situation where what was involved was no more than slapping on the buttocks, an ordinary mode of parent chastisement. Taking finding in fact 12 along with findings 8 to 10, one had a picture of parental conduct which it would be wrong to stigmatise as criminal. In a parent-child situation it was for the reporter to negative the chastisement

A factor, particularly where, as here, the sheriff had found that Mr A was a devoted and caring father. The case of *Guest v Annan* was analogous to the present case, apart from the age of the child. The court there held that an angry father who lost his temper and hit his daughter repeatedly on the buttocks with his hand to her injury did not have the necessary criminal intent. The sheriff had taken a similar approach and was entitled to hold that the grounds of referral had not been made out.

B Having considered the respective submissions of the parties we are in no doubt that the sheriff's findings in fact provided material from which the only reasonable inference to be drawn was that the blows referred to in finding in fact 12 were struck deliberately. If so, mens rea was sufficiently established for these blows to constitute assault in the absence of evidence of justification or any other exonerating factor. The sheriff, understandably in view of his discriminating assessment of the facts, was reluctant to take the final step of formally attributing assault to a caring father

C who had a moment of aberration when he was driven to distraction by a situation with which he was unable to cope. It may well be that the factors which influenced the sheriff are strongly mitigating and should be given proper consideration by the children's hearing when they come to consider the future arrangements for L in light of all the relevant facts and circumstances, on the footing that the grounds of referral are now held to be established.

D Accordingly we answer the question put to us in the stated case in the negative and remit the case back to the sheriff to find the grounds of referral established and to proceed as accords.

Counsel for Appellant, Macfadyen, QC; Solicitors, Biggart Baillie & Gifford, WS — Counsel for Respondents, Dorrian; Solicitors, Drummond Miller, WS (for Blair & Bryden, Greenock).

E   P A A

Mikhailitchenko v Normand

HIGH COURT OF JUSTICIARY

F THE LORD JUSTICE CLERK (ROSS),
LORDS MURRAY AND MORISON
20 OCTOBER 1992

Justiciary — Procedure — Summary procedure — Interpreter — Accused incapable of understanding English having own interpreter in court — Crown considering their interpreter to be inadequate — Sheriff proceeding to hear Crown motion for adjournment of trial because of absence of essential witness — Whether unfair to hear motion without competent interpreter.

An accused person was charged on a summary complaint. His mother tongue was Russian and he G required the services of an interpreter who was supplied by the Crown to the court. The accused also had an interpreter to facilitate communications between himself and his solicitor; that interpreter was not permitted to take any further part in the proceedings. When the case called over in court the sheriff requested the accused to confirm that he understood the charge and that he was pleading not guilty. The sheriff at one stage asked the interpreter if she was interpreting properly and thereafter, after the Crown H had moved the court to adjourn the diet because of the absence of an essential witness, the sheriff, ex proprio motu, adjourned the diet for one hour to allow the Crown to consider their position in relation to an interpreter. After the adjournment, but before the case was called again, the Crown informed the sheriff that it would be in the interests of justice for another interpreter to be obtained and that one could be provided the next day. The Crown then renewed their motion for an adjournment of the trial diet. The accused's I solicitor opposed the motion but after hearing argument the sheriff granted it and adjourned the trial diet to a date several months later. The accused sought advocation of the sheriff's order on the ground that the absence of a competent interpreter rendered the proceedings unfair.

Held, that since clear prejudice arose to the accused because he was not afforded the opportunity, to which he was entitled, of having an interpreter so that he could understand fully what was taking place before J him, there had been unfairness in the proceedings (p 1140H-I); and bill *passed* and order *recalled*.

Bill of advocation

Alexei Alexandrovich Mikhailitchenko brought a bill of advocation against Andrew C Normand, procurator fiscal, Glasgow, praying the High Court to recall a pretended order dated 20 August 1992 whereby Sheriff C McKay adjourned a trial diet until 14 K January 1993. The facts of the case appear from the opinion of the court.

Cases referred to
Advocate (HM) v Olsson, 1941 SLT 402; 1941 JC 63.
Liszewski v Thomson, 1942 SLT 147; 1942 JC 55.

The bill contained the following plea in law for the complainer:

The said pretended order being incompetent et L separatim wrongous and contrary to law, it should be recalled and the complainer freed and discharged for ever from all question or process relative to the offence presently libelled against him.

The bill contained the following plea in law for the respondent:

The order of the sheriff to adjourn the diet being competent and lawful the prayer of the bill should be refused.

The bill was argued before the High Court on 20 October 1992.

Eo die the court *passed* the bill, *advocated* the proceedings and *recalled* the order of the sheriff.

The following opinion of the court was delivered by the Lord Justice Clerk (Ross):

OPINION OF THE COURT.—This is a bill of advocation in which the complainer is Alexei Alexandrovitch Mikhailitchenko and the respondent is the procurator fiscal, Glasgow. What has given rise to this bill of advocation is that the respondent served on the complainer a complaint which libelled a contravention of s 5 (1) (a) of the Road Traffic Act 1988. The complainer pled not guilty and after sundry procedure was ordained to appear for trial on 20 August 1992.

It is stated in the statement of facts for the complainer that the case called for trial that day. In his answers, the respondent explains that in company with other cases set down for trial that day the case was merely called over to ascertain the accused's plea and to deal, if necessary, with any motions for adjournment. However that may be, the fact of the matter is that included in the minute of proceedings is a minute relating to 20 August 1992 which reveals that the accused was asked to confirm the plea previously tendered of not guilty and that the court then considered a Crown motion to adjourn the diet due to the absence of essential Crown witnesses.

Problems arose because the complainer is Ukrainian and his mother tongue is Russian. He has little or no understanding of the English language. Prior to the calling on 20 August 1992 an interpreter was provided by the Crown and the minute shows that she was a Mrs Nina Petkow and that the oath was duly administered to her. The solicitor for the complainer was granted leave to have present a defence interpreter for the purpose of facilitating confidential communings between himself and his client. The sheriff however made it clear that the defence interpreter was expressly confined to such communings and the defence interpreter was warned by the sheriff to take no other part in the proceedings before the court.

It appears from what is stated in the statement of facts that difficulties arose in relation to the official interpreter and that she, on occasion, sought assistance from the defence interpreter. The statement of facts goes on to explain that the respondent sought an adjournment of the case for the reason that an essential Crown witness was not available. There was some difficulty at that time as to whether the official interpreter was interpreting properly the proceedings in court, and the minute shows that the court ex proprio motu, in respect that the defence intimated that the complainer did not fully understand the proceedings as translated by the interpreter, adjourned the case for one hour to allow the prosecutor to consider his position in relation to the interpreter. It is stated in the statement of facts that after that short adjournment the respondent addressed the court as follows: "During the adjournment, you gave the Crown the opportunity to determine the position in connection with an interpreter. I have spoken directly to the interpreter who was sworn in earlier in regard to her experience and feelings in regard to her duties to be performed. It has been explained to me by way of information she has supplied me with that it would be in the interests of justice to obtain another interpreter, and inquiry has been made in regard to this and the Crown can have a Russian interpreter for tomorrow morning". Counsel for the complainer explained that the official interpreter was apparently Bulgarian and not Russian.

The statement of facts goes on to explain that despite that statement, which was made by the fiscal, the proceedings continued and consideration was given to the motion that had been made for adjournment. The statement of facts contains the statement which we have quoted and which is attributed to the fiscal and it is of importance to observe that the whole of that is admitted by the respondent in his answers. Accordingly the position was that the sheriff was clearly informed that it was the view of the Crown that it was in the interest of justice that another interpreter should be obtained. He was also told that a competent interpreter could be available within 24 hours but despite that the proceedings continued and at the end of the day the sheriff granted the motion to adjourn the trial until 14 January 1993.

It is in these circumstances that this bill of advocation has been presented and the complaint is that the sheriff's order adjourning the case for trial until 14 January 1993 was incompetent, or at least wrong and contrary to law. Counsel has explained that what is complained of is unfairness in the conduct of the proceedings. He stresses that the sheriff was informed that it would be in the interests of justice to obtain another interpreter and that another interpreter would be available the following day, but that instead of adjourning until the following day, so that this fresh interpreter could be available to interpret the proceedings to the complainer, the sheriff entertained a motion to adjourn because of the non-availability of an essential Crown witness and proceeded to grant an adjournment of the proceedings until 14 January 1993. In the statement of facts it is explained that throughout the whole time the matter was before the court, from 10.35 am until approximately 1.35 pm, when the sheriff made the order for adjournment until January of 1993, the complainer was totally confused and did not understand what had transpired.

The sheriff in the note which he has written in connection with this bill explains that many represented accused persons appearing in court, of whatever nationality or education, do not understand all the finer points of procedure and that he leaves that to the pleaders to explain. He also says that he had no doubt that the complainer understood the essence of all that had occurred, although he very frankly states that he may, of course, have been quite wrong in forming that view. Earlier in his note he informs us that he questioned the official interpreter in order to satisfy

A himself that she had interpreted matters for the benefit of the complainer and he expresses the view that she intimated to him that she had indeed translated everything. On the other hand, the sheriff does recognise that in the statement of facts it is averred that when the sheriff asked the official interpreter whether she had interpreted everything she replied: "I do not think so." In his note he tells us that he has no note of the interpreter having used these words but that if the solicitor for the complainer has it so noted, he takes it that that was said.

B   The circumstances under which interpreters should be provided are well known. We need do no more than refer to the case of *Liszewski v Thomson*. The facts of that case are different to the present case but the case is of interest because of what the Lord Justice General said at 1942 SLT, p 48. In that case he expressed the view that what had occurred was inconsistent with the due administration of justice. He said this: "It is clear that the magistrate neglected his judicial duty and failed to take the proper steps to make sure that each C one of these men had the fullest opportunity of understanding the charge that had been made against him and the proceedings which were taking place in Court."

That case makes it quite plain that the purpose of having interpreters is inter alia in order that an accused person may have the fullest opportunity of understanding the proceedings which are taking place in court before him. In the present case, once it is D appreciated that the Crown took the view that it was in the interests of justice to obtain another interpreter because of the failings of the official interpreter, we are quite satisfied that for the proceedings to continue beyond that stage with the same interpreter must mean that the complainer did not have the fullest opportunity of understanding the proceedings which were taking place before him, although he had a right to have that full opportunity.

The advocate depute in the present case emphasised E that throughout the whole proceedings the complainer was represented, and that he had the use of his own private interpreter. That is all very well, but it is an important part of our rules for the administration of justice in this country that an interpreter should be made available to someone such as the complainer who does not understand the language of the court. In *HM Advocate v Olsson*, 1941 SLT at p 403 Lord Jamieson observed: "It is inherent in the proper administration of justice that a person tried on indict-F ment must be present during the proceedings, in order that he may hear the case against him, and it is obvious that the mere physical presence of the accused in this case will not satisfy the requirements of justice, and that provision must be made for having the evidence led communicated to him through an interpreter."

The present proceedings did not proceed upon indictment but under a complaint, but the principle is the same, and as was made plain in the subsequent case of *Liszewski*, to which we have referred, an interpreter should be provided not only in order to inter-

pret the evidence led but also so that the accused person may have the fullest opportunity of under- G standing the proceedings which are taking place before him.

In the present case, we are satisfied that there was a failure to afford the complainer that opportunity to which he was entitled. The advocate depute contended that before the court would be entitled to interfere with what had occurred it would be necessary for it to be demonstrated that there had been some identifiable prejudice.

We are satisfied, however, that the clear prejudice to H the complainer arose because he was not afforded the opportunity to which he was entitled of having an interpreter so that he could understand fully what was taking place before him. It appears from what is stated in the statement of facts that the motion by the Crown to adjourn was opposed by the complainer and that the factual background to that motion was gone into. The complainer being present at the time, he was entitled to be put in the position where facilities were made available to give him the opportunity fully to under- I stand what was taking place when that matter was debated. It appears to us to follow from the fact that the Crown accepted that it was in the interests of justice that another interpreter should be obtained, that the complainer must necessarily have been denied that opportunity.

For these reasons we have come to the conclusion that there was, as counsel for the complainer claims, unfairness in the proceedings and we shall accordingly pass the bill, advocate the proceedings and recall the J order of the sheriff dated 20 August 1992.

Counsel for Complainer, Drummond, QC; Solicitors, J & A Hastie, SSC (for Peacock Johnston, Glasgow) — Counsel for Respondent, Macdonald, QC, A D; Solicitor, J D Lowe, Crown Agent.

P W F

K

Hornall v Scott

HIGH COURT OF JUSTICIARY
THE LORD JUSTICE CLERK (ROSS),
LORDS MURRAY AND MORISON
21 OCTOBER 1992

L
Justiciary — Statutory offence — Failing to report accident as soon as reasonably practicable — Accused involved in accident telephoning for breakdown vehicle to collect car — Accused leaving before breakdown vehicle and police arrived at locus — Police stations near accused's home closed at material time but main police station near accident open — Police visiting accused at home one hour after accused leaving locus and accused reporting accident then — Whether Crown proving accused could have reported accident sooner than he did — Road Traffic Act 1988 (c 52), s 170 (3) and (4).

An accused person was tried on summary complaint
A with failing to report an accident to the police as soon
as reasonably practicable, contrary to s 170 (3) and (4)
of the Road Traffic Act 1988. The accused's motor car
collided with a motorway barrier at about 2 am. His
vehicle was extensively damaged. The accused used
his car telephone immediately to contact one of his
employees to instruct that his car be collected by a
local breakdown service. The accused also telephoned
his wife to collect him and both he and his wife left
the scene of the accident before the breakdown vehicle
B arrived. The police arrived as the motor car was being
removed by the breakdown vehicle. The accused was
visited by the police at his home approximately one
hour after he arrived home, at about 3.15 am. Both
police stations near the accused's home were closed at
the time of the accident but the main police station
near the accident was open. The sheriff, considering
that the accused could have reported the accident by
going to a nearby police station on his way home or
by waiting for the breakdown vehicle and going with
C it via a police station, convicted the accused who
appealed, contending that the sheriff was not entitled
to conclude that the accused could have reported the
accident sooner than he did. The Crown argued before
the appeal court that the accused could have telephoned the police and arranged to call subsequently at
a police station or waited at his home for a police
officer to call on him.

Held, (1) that the onus was on the Crown to establish that there was a failure to report the accident at
D a police station or to a constable as soon as was reasonably practicable, namely sooner than the accused did
(p 1143F-G); (2) that there was nothing in the findings
or evidence to suggest that if the accused had done as
the Crown suggested, he would have been in a
position to report the accident sooner than he did (p
1143F and G); and appeal *allowed* and conviction
quashed.

_____

E **Summary complaint**
    James Hornall was charged at the instance of George
E Scott, procurator fiscal, Falkirk, on a summary complaint which contained the following charge: "On 15
August 1991, on the Dennyloanhead/Kincardine
Bridge Motorway M876, District of Falkirk, being the
driver of a motor vehicle, namely motor car registered
no H896 ATS and an accident having then and there
occurred owing to the presence of said motor vehicle
on said road, as above libelled and not having given
F your name and address to any person having reasonable grounds for requiring same, you did fail to report
said accident at a police station or to a constable as
soon as reasonably practicable, and in any case within
24 hours of the occurrence thereof; contrary to the
Road Traffic Act 1988, s 170 (3) and (4)." The
accused pled not guilty and proceeded to trial. After
trial the sheriff (A J Murphy) convicted the accused.

    The accused appealed by way of stated case to the
High Court of Justiciary against the decision of the
sheriff.

Findings in fact
    The sheriff found the following facts to be admitted G
or proved, inter alia:

    (1) At about 2 am on 15 August 1991 the appellant,
driving a BMW motor car registration no H896 ATS
on the M876 motorway near Falkirk, collided with a
stretch of barrier upon said roadway, damaging the
same and also damaging extensively the said motor
vehicle in which he had been travelling alone. (2)
Immediately after the accident the appellant, by
means of his car telephone, contacted the transport
manager of the company in which he was a director, H
instructing him to arrange for the car to be uplifted by
a local breakdown service. He also telephoned his wife
to come and take him home. The appellant departed
with his wife before the arrival of the breakdown
service. The police arrived at the scene while the
breakdown service vehicle was in the course of removing the appellant's abandoned vehicle from the locus.
(3) At about 3.15 am the police then attended the
appellant's home and found the appellant who
admitted in terms of s 172 of the Road Traffic Act I
1988 that he had been driving the vehicle at the time
of the accident. Both local police stations at Denny
and Bonnybridge were closed around the time of the
accident and at the time the police attended the appellant's home. The nearest police station open around
the time of the accident was the Falkirk police station.
(4) In the course of the accident the appellant had
broken a collar bone. The pain was such that he was
unable to sign the police notebook when they had
attended his home. The appellant had been back home J
for about one hour before the police had arrived. The
appellant had felt no pain at the time of the accident,
but it was only after a period at home that he had
become aware of his injury.

    The sheriff appended a note to the findings in the
following terms, inter alia:

    THE SHERIFF (A J MURPHY).—I considered,
on the facts of the case, that it would have been reason- K
ably practicable for the appellant to report the
accident to the police sooner than he did. The appellant had been unaware of his injured shoulder at the
time of the accident and there would have been
nothing to prevent his having got his wife to take him
to a nearby police station on his way home or for his
having waited until the breakdown service arrived and
gone with it via a police office. Although a telephone
call to a police office would not in itself have fulfilled
the requirements of s 170 of the Act, the appellant had L
a phone available in his car and could have, with relative ease, contacted the police at nearby Falkirk to
attend the scene if they desired. He never contacted
the police himself, nor got his wife nor his transport
manager to get in touch with the police. As it was, he
left the scene completely and returned home.
Although the appellant had sustained, as it transpired,
a broken collar bone, that in itself would not have
prevented his having reported the matter to the police
either at or on the way to a hospital. As it was, he did
not attend the hospital or a police station, but had

proceeded home and remained there when the police arrived an hour after his arrival back home. He made no attempt in the intervening hour or so to bring the accident to the attention of the police. In his evidence the appellant claimed that he intended to contact the police the next day. I considered that, given the number of people the appellant had been in touch with for getting back home, he had ample opportunity to report the matter in terms of the section and that it would have been reasonably practicable in the circumstances for him to have contacted the police before they found him at home more than an hour after the accident.

Appeal

The sheriff posed the following question for the opinion of the High Court, inter alia:

(2) On the facts stated, was I entitled to convict the appellant?

The appeal was argued in the High Court on 21 October 1992.

Eo die the court *answered* question 2 in the *negative*, *allowed* the appeal and *quashed* the conviction.

The following opinion of the court was delivered by the Lord Justice Clerk (Ross):

OPINION OF THE COURT.—This is an appeal at the instance of James Hornall. He went to trial in the sheriff court at Falkirk on a complaint libelling a charge of contravening s 170 (3) and (4) of the Road Traffic Act 1988. The charge libels that being the driver of a motor vehicle on the Dennyloanhead/Kincardine Bridge motorway and an accident having occurred there owing to the presence of that motor vehicle on the road, he, not having given his name and address to any person having reasonable grounds for requiring the same, failed to report the accident at a police station or to a constable as soon as reasonably practicable and in any case within 24 hours of the occurrence. At the end of the Crown case a submission of no case to answer was made and the sheriff rejected that submission. The appellant was subsequently found guilty of the charge and it is against his conviction that he has now appealed.

In presenting his appeal today counsel for the appellant explained that when the stated case had been applied for two grounds had been stated, but he intimated that he was not founding upon the first ground. He did, however, support the second ground which was to the effect that there was not sufficient evidence to justify the sheriff holding that the offence had been committed.

Counsel's first submission was to the effect that there had been a failure on the part of the sheriff in that there was no finding in fact to the effect that it would have been reasonably practicable for the appellant to report the accident to the police sooner than he did. It is true that there is no finding to that effect and

that one might have expected a finding dealing with these matters, but in the note annexed to the stated case the sheriff has indicated what conclusions he drew from the evidence and in the circumstances we are prepared to treat the case upon that basis. Counsel next submitted that the sheriff had failed to take account of all the relevant circumstances of the case and both counsel and the advocate depute were agreed that it was necessary for the sheriff to have regard to the whole circumstances when deciding whether there had been failure to report the accident as soon as reasonably practicable. It was, as the advocate depute put it, a question of fact and degree. The relevant times are clearly set forth in the findings in fact and the whole period with which we are concerned is a relatively short one. The appellant's car, which he was driving, collided with a stretch of barrier on the roadway around 2 am. The barrier was damaged and his vehicle was also extensively damaged. It appears that the appellant's vehicle was fitted with a car telephone and he immediately contacted the transport manager of the company in which he was a director and instructed him to arrange for the car to be uplifted by a local breakdown service. He also telephoned to his wife to come and take him home and it is stated in the findings that the appellant had departed with his wife before the arrival of the breakdown vehicle. The police apparently arrived at the locus while the breakdown vehicle was there and was in the course of removing the appellant's vehicle from the locus. The next material time is that we are told in finding 4 that the appellant had been back home for about one hour before the police arrived. Since the police arrived at about 3.15 am it follows that the appellant must have arrived home around 2.15 am. As we have observed, the police attended at the appellant's home at about 3.15 am and he admitted to them that he had been driving the vehicle. The appellant lives in Bonnybridge and the findings reveal that both local police stations at Denny and Bonnybridge were closed around the time of the accident and when the police attended at the appellant's home. The nearest police station open around the time of the accident was the Falkirk police station and, as finding 1 reveals, the accident took place on the M876 motorway near Falkirk.

In the course of the accident the appellant had broken a collar bone. Apparently he felt no pain at the time of the accident but it was only after a period at home that he became aware of the injury. At the time the police arrived, the pain was such that he was not able to sign the police notebook. The sheriff in his note explains why he reached the conclusion that it would have been reasonably practicable for the appellant to report the accident to the police sooner than he did. He says in his note at [p 1141K, supra] as follows: "The appellant had been unaware of his injured shoulder at the time of the accident and there would have been nothing to prevent his having got his wife to take him to a nearby police station on his way home or for his having waited until the breakdown service arrived and gone with it via a police office." Subsequently, in the final portion of his note, the sheriff says this: "He made no attempt in the intervening hour or so to bring the accident to the attention of the police. In his evidence the appellant claimed that he intended to contact the police the next day. I considered that, given the number of people the appellant had been in touch with for getting back home, he had ample opportunity to report the matter in terms of the section and that it would have been reasonably practicable in the circumstances for him to have contacted the police before they found him at home more than an hour after the accident" [p 1142A-B, supra].

As we say the period with which we are concerned is a relatively short one. It was agreed by both counsel and the advocate depute that the appellant could not have complied with his obligation under the section merely by telephoning the police but that he required to report the accident at a police station or to a constable. The question which we have to determine is whether, on the findings and having regard to what the sheriff says in his note, he was entitled to reach the conclusion that it would have been reasonably practicable for the appellant to report the accident to the police sooner than he did. The sheriff appears to have considered that since the appellant had telephoned the transport manager and his wife he could have contacted the police before they found him at his home. We are not entirely clear what the sheriff means by saying that he could have contacted the police earlier, but as we say, telephoning them would not have been sufficient. As we understood the argument for the advocate depute, the Crown are contending that the appellant could have phoned the police and either arranged to call subsequently at a police station or to have waited at his home for a police constable to come to him so that he could have reported. That is all very well, but the question must arise as to whether the Crown has proved that if he had taken these steps he would have reported the accident any sooner than he did, and we are not persuaded on the findings and from the statement of evidence in the note that that is the result which would have followed if he had taken the steps which the advocate depute suggested he should have taken, namely telephoned the police. It cannot be unreasonable that the appellant, in the circumstances, returned to his home, and it appears that he got there around 2.15 am. If he had taken the steps which the Crown suggested he should have taken and communicated with a police station by telephone, he might well have found that the two local police stations were closed and thereafter have communicated with Falkirk police station. There is nothing in the findings to suggest that if he had done so and had then waited at home for a police officer to come to him, the result would have been that he would have been in a position to report the accident to the police any sooner than he did because, as we have already observed, the police in fact called at his house somewhere around 3.15 am. The onus is on the Crown to establish that there was a failure on the part of the appellant to report the accident at a police station or to a constable as soon as reasonably practic-

able. That must mean, as the sheriff recognised, that it would have been reasonably practicable for the appellant to report the accident to the police sooner than he did. We are not satisfied that the Crown did succeed on the findings and on the evidence in establishing that, and accordingly it follows that we are not satisfied that the sheriff was entitled to draw the inference which he did. We shall accordingly answer the second question in the case in the negative and the appeal therefore succeeds.

Counsel for Appellant, Alonzi; Solicitors, Bennett & Robertson, WS (for McLean & Stewart, Dunblane) — Counsel for Respondent, Macdonald, QC, A D; Solicitor, J D Lowe, Crown Agent.

P W F

Robertson v McNaughtan

HIGH COURT OF JUSTICIARY
THE LORD JUSTICE GENERAL (HOPE),
LORDS ALLANBRIDGE AND COWIE
3 MARCH 1993

Justiciary — Statutory offence — Sentence — Driving while disqualified — Endorsation — Special reasons — Accused driving on two occasions separated by half an hour while unaware that disqualified — Sheriff refraining from disqualifying because of accused's unawareness but ordering endorsation on both offences — Whether two separate offences or one incident — Whether special reasons for not endorsing — Road Traffic Offenders Act 1988 (c 53), ss 28 (4), 35 and 44 (2).

Section 28 (4) of the Road Traffic Offenders Act 1988 provides that where a person is convicted (whether on the same occasion or not) of two or more offences committed on the same occasion and involving obligatory endorsement, the total number of penalty points to be attributed to the offences is the number or highest number that would be attributed on a conviction of one of them. The offence of driving while disqualified contrary to s 103 (1) (b) of the Road Traffic Act 1988 is one for which endorsement is obligatory unless, in terms of s 44 (2) of the Road Traffic Offenders Act 1988, the court for special reasons thinks fit not to order endorsement. Section 35 (1) of the 1988 Act provides that where the number of penalty points on a person's licence reaches 12 he shall be disqualified for a period of six months unless the court is satisfied having regard to all the circumstances that there are grounds for mitigating the normal consequences of the conviction. Section 35 (4) provides inter alia that no account is to be taken under subs (1) of any circumstances that are alleged to make the offence not a serious one or of any hardship other than exceptional hardship.

An accused person pled guilty to two offences of
A driving while disqualified. The first offence was committed at about 11.45 pm on 2 May 1992 and the
second was committed about 30 minutes later on 3
May 1992 on streets which were near each other. At
the material time the accused had appealed against his
conviction on 31 January 1992 which resulted in his
being disqualified but unknown to him his appeal had
been deemed to be abandoned because of his Edinburgh agents' failure to lodge the stated case, and his
disqualification, which had been suspended ad
interim, had been reimposed. The sheriff considered
B that the accused's actual lack of knowledge that the
disqualification had been reimposed amounted to
special reasons for not disqualifying the accused but
that the accused had to be deemed to know the consequences of his failure to proceed with the appeal and
could not avoid responsibility by delegating his obligations to solicitors. The sheriff therefore ordered
endorsement of the accused's licence with six penalty
points for each offence on the ground that they were
separate offences and not part of one incident. The
C accused appealed on the grounds that there were
special reasons for not endorsing and in any event, as
the offences were committed on the same occasion, his
licence should be endorsed with only six penalty
points for both offences in accordance with s 28 (4).

Held, (1) that s 28 (4) was intended to provide for
offences which occurred as part of one incident or at
least as part of a series of incidents which were so
closely related as to be reasonably regarded as one
general incident, and in the present case although the
D times and places were not far apart there was nothing
to suggest that these were anything other than separate
incidents (p 1146H-J); (2) that since the reimposition
of the disqualification was due to a fact of which the
accused was genuinely unaware, namely that the
appeal had been deemed to be abandoned through a
failure by his solicitors, no good reason existed for not
treating his unawareness as a special reason for refraining from ordering endorsation (p 1147K); and appeal
allowed and order for endorsation *quashed.*

E *Carmichael v Shevlin,* 1992 SLT 1113, *commented on.*

Observed, that had the sheriff treated the accused's
unawareness as a special reason for not ordering
endorsation, there would have been no need to go on
and consider whether, in terms of s 35 (1) of the Road
Traffic Offenders Act 1988, there were grounds for
mitigating the normal consequences of the conviction
(p 1147L).

F **Summary complaint**
Neil Robertson was charged at the instance of I S
McNaughtan, procurator fiscal, Peterhead, on a
summary complaint which contained the following
offences, inter alia:

"(2) You being a person disqualified for holding or
obtaining a licence to drive a motor vehicle, did, on 2
May 1992, on Seaforth Street, Fraserburgh, while so
disqualified, drive a motor vehicle, namely a motor
car, contrary to the Road Traffic Act 1988, s 103 (1)
(b). . . .

"(4) You being a person disqualified for holding or
obtaining a licence to drive a motor vehicle, did on 3 G
May 1992, on Saltoun Square and Broad Street, both
Fraserburgh, while so disqualified, drive a motor
vehicle, namely a motor car, contrary to the Road
Traffic Act 1988, s 103 (1) (b)."

The accused pled guilty to these charges and the
sheriff (K A McLernan) ordered the accused's licence
to be endorsed with six penalty points in respect of
each offence.

The accused appealed by note of appeal against
sentence. H

Statutory provisions
The Road Traffic Offenders Act 1988, as amended,
provides:

"28.— . . . (4) Where a person is convicted (whether
on the same occasion or not) of two or more offences
committed on the same occasion and involving obligatory endorsement, the total number of penalty points
to be attributed to them is the number or highest
number that would be attributed on a conviction of I
one of them (so that if the convictions are on different
occasions the number of penalty points to be
attributed to the offences on the later occasion or
occasions shall be restricted accordingly). . . .

"35.—(1) Where — (a) a person is convicted of an
offence to which this subsection applies, and (b) the
penalty points to be taken into account on that
occasion number twelve or more, the court must order
him to be disqualified for not less than the minimum
period unless the court is satisfied, having regard to all J
the circumstances, that there are grounds for mitigating the normal consequences of the conviction and
thinks fit to order him to be disqualified for a shorter
period or not to order him to be disqualified. . . .

"(4) No account is to be taken under subsection (1)
above of any of the following circumstances — (a) any
circumstances that are alleged to make the offence or
any of the offences not a serious one, (b) hardship,
other than exceptional hardship, or (c) any circum- K
stances which, within the three years immediately
preceding the conviction, have been taken into
account under that subsection in ordering the offender
to be disqualified for a shorter period or not ordering
him to be disqualified. . . .

"44.— . . . (2) Where the court does not order the
person convicted to be disqualified, it need not make
an order under subsection (1) above [endorsement] if
for special reasons it thinks fit not to do so."

L
Cases referred to
Brewer v Metropolitan Police Commissioner [1969] 1
WLR 267.
Carmichael v Shevlin, 1992 SLT 1113; 1992 SCCR
247.

Textbook referred to
Wilkinson, *Road Traffic Offences,* para 21.31.

The sheriff reported to the High Court as follows,
inter alia:

THE SHERIFF (K A McLERNAN).— . . . The
A procurator fiscal explained that Mr Robertson had
been found guilty after a trial on 31 January 1992 and
as a result of which he had been disqualified from
driving for a period of six months. He appealed
against conviction on 6 February 1992 and an interim
suspension of the disqualification was granted on 25
February 1992. Thereafter, the appeal was deemed
abandoned on 15 April 1992 and, accordingly, the disqualification period recommenced from that date.
Thereafter, Mr Robertson had been seen to be driving
B on 2 and again on 3 May 1992. I was then advised by
the defence solicitor that the stated case in the appeal
against conviction had been adjusted but the solicitor
concerned had failed to return it to the High Court.
The next the solicitor heard about the matter was
when his Edinburgh correspondent telephoned him
on 28 April 1992 to confirm that the appeal was being
abandoned. At that stage, Mr Robertson was not contacted by the solicitor. The solicitor sent a letter to Mr
Robertson on 5 May 1992 informing him of the end
C of the suspension of disqualification. It was explained
that the police had not stopped Mr Robertson at any
time to warn him and, accordingly, it was argued that
discretionary disqualification should not be imposed
and furthermore, that that explanation was sufficient
to establish special reasons for not ordering endorsement of Mr Robertson's licence. Reference was made
to Wilkinson, *Road Traffic Offences,* para 21.31 and
the insurance cases quoted there. Mr Robertson, it
was argued, had been misled by omission and had
D reasonable cause to believe that he was entitled to
drive. It was further explained that Mr Robertson was
aged 32 years, unemployed and in receipt of state
benefits of £80.00 per fortnight. . . .

I then explained that I did not propose to impose a
discretionary disqualification but I did not consider
there were special reasons which would entitle me not
to endorse and that I therefore required to endorse on
both charges three penalty points. The clerk immedi-
E ately invited me to confirm the pointage and I
observed that I had misread the notice of penalty. It
read two *or* six points. I certiorated myself by consulting the 1988 Act as amended and thereafter confirmed
that I required to endorse with six penalty points and
as I was about to do so, the proceedings were interrupted by Mr Robertson in circumstances which led
to a finding of contempt of court. I thereafter deferred
the whole matter to allow Mr Robertson to be advised
by a solicitor and the matter called again on 7 January
F 1993.

On 7 January 1993 the defence agent asked to be
heard further on the question of endorsation and I
allowed him to be heard. He submitted that the two
offences should be regarded as one because although
the two offences were libelled as occurring on different
days, there was in fact only a time difference between
the two offences of one hour and both offences took
place in the centre of Fraserburgh and therefore the
two offences could be regarded as having occurred on
the same occasion.

As that was the first time that matter had been
raised, I invited the procurator fiscal to comment and G
he confirmed that there was indeed about an hour
between the two separate sightings and that both
offences had occurred in the centre of Fraserburgh.
The defence agent founded upon s 28 (4) as amended
of the Road Traffic Offenders Act 1988.

I took the view that there was no information before
me to justify regarding the two offences as having
occurred "on the same occasion". The mere fact that
they occurred within an hour of each other in streets
very close to each other, does not seem to me to lead H
to a conclusion that the offences occurred on the same
occasion. No argument was advanced as to what
might, and what might not, amount in fact to "same
occasion". I took what I regarded as the ordinary
meaning of that phrase to signify that two offences
must have occurred as part of the one incident or part
of a set of incidents which could be so closely
related as to be reasonably regarded as one general
incident. There was nothing at all to suggest that the
offences were other than two separate incidents, one I
hour apart. In the circumstances, I required to endorse
the six penalty points on each charge. That brought
into operation the provisions of s 35 of the Road
Traffic Offenders Act 1988 (what are loosely referred
to as "the totting up provisions"). It seemed to me that
there were grounds for mitigating the normal consequences of the conviction. Both offences were very
close to each other; both offences occurred as a direct
result of Mr Robertson's lack of knowledge that his
disqualification had been reimposed; the reimposition J
of disqualification had occurred without his knowledge of that fact and he accordingly had no grounds
to suspect he was committing an offence. Accordingly,
I refrained from disqualification. I drew a distinction
between "special reasons" and "exceptional circumstances". In considering the former I considered he
was deemed to know the consequences of his failure to
proceed with the appeal and cannot avoid responsibility or liability by delegating his obligations. In considering the latter I took into account the actual state K
of awareness and the circumstances which brought
that about.

———————

Appeal
The appeal was argued before the High Court on 3
March 1993.

Eo die the court *allowed* the appeal and *quashed* the
order for endorsation.   L

The following opinion of the court was delivered by
the Lord Justice General (Hope):

OPINION OF THE COURT.—The appellant is
Neil Robertson who pled guilty in the sheriff court at
Peterhead to two offences of driving while disqualified. The sheriff accepted that the appellant was not
aware that he was disqualified when he committed
these offences. He rejected a submission that the two

offences should be regarded as one because they were
A committed within a short time of each other. He then
ordered that the appellant's licence was to be endorsed
with six penalty points in respect of each offence, but
refrained from disqualifying him under the totting up
provision. The appellant has now appealed on the
ground that the sheriff ought to have held that there
were special reasons for not ordering his licence to be
endorsed with penalty points, and that in any event he
ought to have held that it should have been endorsed
only with six penalty points in respect that both
B offences were committed on the same occasion.

The offences to which the appellant pled guilty were
committed on 2 and 3 May 1992. On the first occasion
he was seen to be driving a motor car on Seaforth
Street, Fraserburgh. This was at about 11.45 pm that
day. On the second occasion, which occurred about 30
minutes later, at about 15 minutes after midnight on
the following day, he was seen to be driving a motor
car on Saltoun Square and Broad Street, Fraserburgh.
He had been disqualified from holding or obtaining a
C licence to drive a motor vehicle for a period of six
months on 31 January 1992 following his conviction
for certain offences under the Road Traffic Acts. On
6 February 1992 he appealed against his conviction,
and on 25 February 1992 an order was made suspending his disqualification pending the appeal. A draft
stated case was then issued, but the appeal was later
deemed to have been abandoned in terms of s 448 (5)
of the Criminal Procedure (Scotland) Act 1975 due to
his solicitor's failure to lodge the adjusted stated case
D with the Clerk of Justiciary. This was on 15 April
1992, but the appellant was not then aware of what
had occurred since it was not on his instructions that
the appeal had not been proceeded with. His solicitor
also appears not to have appreciated what had
happened until 28 April 1992, when he received a telephone call from his Edinburgh correspondent to
confirm that the appeal was being abandoned. Even
then he did not at that stage inform the appellant that
the appeal was not to proceed and that the suspension
E of his disqualification was at an end. It was not until
5 May 1992 that the solicitor wrote to the appellant
telling him what had happened, by which date the
appellant had committed the two offences libelled in
the complaint. On neither occasion had he previously
been warned by the police that he was disqualified. In
the light of this information the sheriff accepted that
the appellant was still unaware on these dates that his
appeal had been abandoned and that he no longer had
the benefit of the interim suspension of his disqualifi-
F cation.

The sheriff dealt first with the question whether
there were truly two separate offences in this case, and
it is convenient to examine his decision on this point
before turning to discuss the question whether there
were special reasons for ordering that the appellant's
licence should not be endorsed with penalty points.
The argument was that the two offences should be
regarded as one because, although they were libelled
as having been committed on different dates, there was
only a very short time between them and they both

took place in the centre of Fraserburgh. This, it was
said, meant that the two offences could be regarded as G
having occurred on the same occasion for the purposes
of s 28 (4) of the Road Traffic Offenders Act 1988.
That subsection, as substituted by s 27 of the Road
Traffic Act 1991, provides: [his Lordship quoted the
terms of s 28 (4) and continued:]

The sheriff was of the view that the mere fact that
the offences occurred within an hour of each other in
streets very close to each other did not mean that they
occurred on the same occasion. He took the ordinary
meaning of the phrase to signify that the offences must H
have occurred as part of the one incident, or at least
as part of a series of incidents which were so closely
related as to be reasonably regarded as one general
incident. Accordingly he held that he required to
order endorsement of the appellant's licence with six
penalty points on each of the two charges to which he
had pled guilty.

We agree with the sheriff on this point. The typical
example of a case where two or more offences are committed on the same occasion is where a single incident I
has occurred as a result of which the driver is charged
with a number of separate offences involving obligatory endorsement under different provisions of the
Act. This will be the position where the driver is
charged with the offence of careless driving and at the
same time with offences under the Construction and
Use Regulations in circumstances where endorsement
is obligatory. In the present case, however, the appellant pled guilty to driving while disqualified at two
different times and in two different places. The times J
and places were not very far apart, but there was no
information to suggest that these were anything other
than two separate incidents. Had the appellant been
engaged on a single, uninterrupted course of driving
while disqualified, the proper view to take would have
been that he was committing a single offence, albeit it
was being committed in different streets as he
travelled from one place to another in the course of his
journey. In that event, since he would have been
charged with one offence only of driving while dis- K
qualified, the question raised by s 28 (4) would not
have arisen. As it is, the appellant was charged in this
complaint with two separate offences, and the reason
for this was that the offences were being committed on
different occasions and were not all part of a single
incident.

Having disposed of this point the sheriff turned to
the question whether there were grounds for mitigating the normal consequences of the conviction. The
offence of driving while disqualified is one for which L
endorsation is obligatory unless, in terms of s 44 (2) of
the Road Traffic Offenders Act 1988, the court for
special reasons thinks fit not to order the licence to be
endorsed. Furthermore, the effect of endorsing with
six penalty points for each offence was to oblige the
appellant to be disqualified unless, in terms of s 35 (1)
of the Act, the court was satisfied, having regard to all
the circumstances, that there were grounds for
mitigating the normal consequences of the conviction
and for ordering him not to be disqualified. The

sheriff decided that there were no special reasons in this case for not endorsing the appellant's licence with penalty points, but he held that there were grounds for mitigating the normal consequences of the conviction in the light of what he described as "exceptional circumstances". He noted that the two offences were very close to each other and that both of them occurred as a result of the appellant's lack of knowledge that his disqualification had been reimposed. The decision which he took was minuted in these terms: "The court refrained from disqualifying the accused in terms of the totting up procedure as exceptional mitigating factors existed viz that the suspension of his disqualification had been removed without his knowledge of that fact, that he had no grounds to suspect he was committing repeated offences, and the offences were very proximate to each other." He has given these further reasons for his decision in his report: "I drew a distinction between 'special reasons' and 'exceptional circumstances'. In considering the former I considered he was deemed to know the consequences of his failure to proceed with the appeal and cannot avoid responsibility or liability by delegating his obligations. In considering the latter I took into account the actual state of awareness and the circumstances which brought that about."

Counsel for the appellant submitted that the sheriff had erred in the approach which he took to these matters, and his argument was concurred in and elaborated upon by the learned advocate depute. They were agreed that what the sheriff should have done in this case was to hold that there were special reasons for not ordering endorsation on either charge, in view of the fact that the appellant was not aware on the dates when he committed the offences that his disqualification had been reimposed. We are of the same view, but having regard to the unusual circumstances and the way in which the sheriff dealt with the case it is appropriate that we should explain in more detail the reasons why we have decided that we must allow this appeal.

The sheriff rejected the argument that there were special reasons for not ordering endorsement because he considered that the appellant was deemed to know the consequences of his failure to proceed with the appeal. He also said that he could not avoid responsibility or liability by delegating his obligations. As counsel pointed out, however, the appellant's position was not that he was ignorant of the law to be applied in this case following the abandonment of his appeal but that he was ignorant of the facts. The appeal had been abandoned, contrary to his instructions, due to his solicitor's failure to lodge the stated case. He had not been told about this at the time, and he had no reasonable cause to suspect that the appeal had been abandoned and that his disqualification had been reimposed. Nothing had happened prior to his commission of the two offences to put him on his guard on this point or to suggest to him that the interim suspension of his disqualification was at an end.

In our opinion the undisputed facts of this case, which are plainly special to these particular offences,

are capable of amounting to special reasons. We consider that the sheriff was wrong to hold that they did not amount to special reasons for not ordering endorsation of the appellant's licence. The sheriff was satisfied that the appellant was in fact unaware that his disqualification had been reimposed. The basis for his view that the appellant ought to be deemed to have been aware of this was that he must be taken to have known what would be the consequence of what the sheriff described as "his failure" to proceed with the appeal. But the appeal was deemed to have been abandoned due to a failure by the appellant's solicitor, not to anything which the appellant himself did or failed to do. It would have been a different matter if the appellant had given instructions for his appeal to be abandoned. That might well have been said to have been a circumstance which put him on his inquiry, since he could reasonably have been taken to have been aware that the interim suspension of his disqualification would be ended as soon as intimation of the abandonment was made to the court. As it is, there is nothing in the facts of this case to justify fixing him with constructive knowledge of the deemed abandonment of the appeal. The situation is similar to that in *Brewer v Metropolitan Police Commissioner* where a driver had inhaled fumes in the premises of an engineering firm of which he was director which had an alcoholic content, without his being aware that the chemical gave off fumes which could render him unfit to drive. Lord Parker CJ said at p 271F: "Once it is accepted that he in fact did not know that these fumes had any alcohol in them, then the only possibility of holding him, as it were, liable on the basis of constructive knowledge would be if there were circumstances under which he was fixed with the knowledge of the alcohol content. There is nothing whatever of that sort in the regulations or otherwise to give him any warning of the matter, and accordingly in my judgment the general circumstances which were capable of amounting to a special reason did in the circumstances of this case amount to such a special reason."

In the present case the appellant's ignorance of the fact that he was disqualified was capable of amounting to a special reason, and since the reimposition of the disqualification was due to a fact of which he also was genuinely unaware, namely that the appeal had been deemed to be abandoned due to a failure by his solicitor, no good reason existed for not treating his unawareness as a special reason for ordering that there should be no endorsation of his licence with penalty points.

Had the sheriff taken this view of the case that would have been an end of the matter, and there would have been no need for him to go on and consider whether, in terms of s 35 (1) of the Road Traffic Offenders Act 1988, there were grounds for mitigating the normal consequences of the conviction and in particular for ordering the appellant not to be disqualified. As it was, the situation in which he found himself was one of some difficulty, due to the provisions of s 35 (4) which provides: [his Lordship quoted the terms of s 35 (4) and continued:]

The sheriff tells us that he drew a distinction
A between "special reasons" and "exceptional circumstances", and that in finding that there were what he described as "exceptional circumstances" he took into account the appellant's actual state of awareness and the circumstances which brought that about. But there appears to be some confusion in this reasoning, and the sheriff does not seem to have taken proper account of the words used in s 35 (4). The phrase "exceptional circumstances" does not appear anywhere in s 35. There is a reference in s 35 (4) (b) to "exceptional
B hardship", but it was not part of the appellant's argument that he would suffer exceptional hardship if he were to be disqualified. What the sheriff seems to be saying is that there were circumstances relating to the offence which made it an exceptional one, because the appellant was not in fact aware that he was disqualified. But s 35 (4) (a) provides that no account is to be taken of any circumstances which are alleged to make the offence not a serious one. The exceptional circumstances which the sheriff accepted were present in this
C case were indeed exceptional, but what he should have done was to treat them as amounting to special reasons within the meaning of s 44 (2).

The learned advocate depute drew our attention to *Carmichael v Shevlin* which, on one view, might be thought to support what the sheriff did in this case. The sheriff does not mention this decision in his report, and the reasons which he gave for his decision not to disqualify suggest that he had not been referred to it. But the facts were very similar, because in that
D case the respondent had been convicted of driving without insurance when he genuinely believed that he was insured. His licence was ordered to be endorsed with the appropriate number of penalty points, but the sheriff refrained from disqualifying. He noted that in terms of s 35 (4) (a) no account could be taken of any circumstances that were alleged to make the offence not a serious one, and also that there was no question of exceptional hardship. But he felt that the particular circumstances of the case, where the respondent genuinely believed that he was insured, could
E amount to a ground for mitigating the normal consequences of the conviction. This decision was upheld on appeal, on the ground that the mitigating circumstances referred to in s 35 (1) included circumstances relating to the offender as well as to the offence and that his belief that he was insured was a circumstance relating to the offender. The advocate depute submitted that it would have been more correct to view the respondent's belief as a circumstance relating to
F the offence, since this was his explanation as to why he had committed it. He also submitted that Parliament was not to be taken to have intended that what might constitute special reasons for the purposes of s 44 (2), or of s 34 (1) where the offence involves obligatory disqualification, should also amount to mitigating circumstances for the purposes of s 35 (1).

We are bound to say that we see considerable force in these submissions. The situation in *Carmichael v Shevlin* was in some respects unsatisfactory, because there appears to have been no attempt by the respondent in that case to argue that there were special reasons for his licence not to be endorsed with penalty G points. The case proceeded upon the basis that the only way in which the ordinary consequences of the conviction could be mitigated was by finding that there were grounds for doing so in terms of s 35 (1) and for ordering him not to be disqualified. In our view, for the reasons discussed earlier in this opinion, that was the wrong approach. What the sheriff should have been asked to do was to find that the fact that the respondent was not aware that he was uninsured constituted special reasons for ordering his licence not to H be endorsed. That would have been consistent with the principle that the reasons must be special to the particular facts of the case. It would have given due recognition to the fact that it was only because he was not aware that he was uninsured that the respondent had been driving while uninsured at the time of the offence. Had the sheriff taken that course the problem would not have arisen of having to find reasons for mitigating the consequences of the conviction in terms of s 35 (1). That was a difficult task for him, having I regard to the important restrictions which have been imposed by s 35 (4) on the discretion which can be exercised by the court.

The advocate depute made a number of other submissions about *Carmichael v Shevlin*, but we find it unnecessary to consider them because the point which has been taken in the present appeal was not argued in that case. It is sufficient for us to say that, while that decision would have provided support for the sheriff's decision in this case to refrain from disqualifying on J the view that there were grounds for mitigating the normal consequences of the conviction, he ought not to have reached this point at all because what he should have done was to hold that there were special reasons for ordering the appellant's licence not to be endorsed with penalty points. In our opinion that was the proper stage at which to take account of the appellant's genuine lack of awareness that he was disqualified, because this was something which related to the circumstances of the offence and was a reason special K to the particular offence to which he had pled guilty in this case.

For these reasons we shall allow this appeal by quashing the order for endorsement of the appellant's driving licence with six penalty points on each charge. We shall refrain from ordering endorsement on the ground that, as the suspension of the appellant's disqualification had been removed without his knowledge of that fact, special reasons exist for not ordering endorsement in terms of s 44 (2) of the Road Traffic L Offenders Act 1988.

Counsel for Appellant, Armstrong; Solicitors, Balfour & Manson, Nightingale & Bell (for George Mathers & Co, Aberdeen) — Counsel for Respondent, Macdonald, QC, A D; Solicitor, J D Lowe, Crown Agent.

P W F

City of Aberdeen District Council v Secretary of State for Scotland

OUTER HOUSE

LORD CAMERON OF LOCHBROOM

10 MARCH 1993

Town and country planning — Expenses — Appeal to Secretary of State against planning authority's refusal of change of use application — Contrary advice by authority's planning officer — Appeal largely conceded by planning authority — Award of expenses against planning authority — Whether award unreasonable.

Expenses — Town and country planning — Appeal to Secretary of State against planning authority's refusal of change of use application — Contrary advice by authority's planning officer — Appeal largely conceded by planning authority — Award of expenses against planning authority — Whether award unreasonable.

A local planning authority, against the recommendation of its city planning officer, but having received certain objections from third parties, refused an application for change of use of subjects. The applicant appealed to the Secretary of State. The applicant was content that the appeal be dealt with by way of written submissions but the planning authority requested a public inquiry for which a date was then fixed, the decision having been delegated to a reporter. Meantime the planning authority, having received advice from a planning consultant, resolved no longer to resist the appeal if certain conditions were attached by the Secretary of State to the permission. After correspondence between the parties, subject to one or two reservations, agreement was reached between the authority and the applicant on the terms of such conditions. Between the fixing of the date for the inquiry and the date fixed, objections to the application were received by the reporter from two third parties. At the inquiry no third party appeared and the reporter was addressed by the authority and the applicant on the conditions to be attached to the permission. At the close of the inquiry the applicant moved for an award of expenses against the authority. The reporter awarded the applicant the expenses arising directly from the appeal procedure on the grounds that the authority had acted unreasonably by being unduly influenced by the contradictory views of the third parties and by giving insufficient weight to the original advice of the city planning officer. The authority sought partial reduction of the reporter's decision letter insofar as it related to the award of expenses, on the ground that the award was an unreasonable exercise of the reporter's discretion.

Held, that the reporter had been entitled reasonably to take the view that the authority had no reasonable planning grounds upon which to reach their decision to refuse the planning application and that he had accordingly been entitled to make an award of expenses against the authority (p 1154H-J); and petition *dismissed*.

Petition for judicial review

The City of Aberdeen District Council presented a petition for judicial review of a decision by Mr Richard M Hickman, deputy chief reporter, Scottish Office inquiry reporters, the reporter appointed by the Secretary of State to determine an appeal against the refusal by the council of an application by Mr Gordon Bruce for change of use of premises in Aberdeen from public house to class 1 retail use. Mr Hickman was called as first respondent and Mr Bruce as second respondent. The Secretary of State for Scotland lodged answers. The council sought partial reduction of the decision insofar as it awarded against the council the expenses occasioned by a public inquiry after the council had altered its position from opposition to the proposed change of use to insistence on certain conditions being attached to the permission. The council argued that in making this award of expenses the reporter had exercised his discretion in the matter unreasonably.

The petition came before the Lord Ordinary (Lord Cameron of Lochbroom).

Cases referred to

Anduff Holdings Ltd v Secretary of State for Scotland, 1992 SLT 696.

Associated Provincial Picture Houses Ltd v Wednesbury Corporation [1948] 1 KB 223.

Council of Civil Service Unions v Minister for the Civil Service [1985] 1 AC 374; [1984] 3 WLR 1174; [1984] 3 All ER 935.

Pirie v City of Aberdeen District Council, 1993 SLT 1155.

Wordie Property Co Ltd v Secretary of State for Scotland, 1984 SLT 345.

On 10 March 1993 the Lord Ordinary *dismissed* the petition.

LORD CAMERON OF LOCHBROOM.—The petitioners are a local authority who on 1 July 1991 issued a notice of determination refusing an application by the second respondent for change of use of subjects at 28 Great Northern Road, Aberdeen, from public house to class 1 retail use. During the processing of the application it became known to the petitioners that the intended use of the property was for the direction of funerals. When the application came to be considered by the petitioners they had before them a report by the city planning officer recommending approval of the application subject to certain suspensive conditions, and also two letters of objection and a petition signed by 54 neighbouring proprietors in a block containing sheltered accommodation a short distance from the subjects. The objectors all stated that they felt that the location of a funeral directors would be inappropriate and insensitive next to sheltered accommodation. The report from the city planning officer contained an evaluation of the application together with reference to the representations as noted above. It proceeded as follows:

"Whilst the application is only for a change of use from a public house to Class 1 retail, it is understood that the building would be used as a funeral directors.

In the Town & Country Planning (Use Classes) (Scotland) Order 1989, Use Class 1 (Shops) (G) states uses 'for the direction of funerals'. The agent has given assurances that whilst the proposals would include a chapel, rest rooms and arrangement rooms, no embalming or other such processes would take place, nor would any coffin construction or other joinery work. The location of the proposed use may seem insensitive next to a sheltered accommodation for the elderly but as the site fronts onto Great Northern Road, and Clifton Court is located behind the building very few residents would be able to see the activities of the Directors. The application is for a change of Class 1 and it must be determined as such. A change of use from a derelict pub to a different Class 1 use (eg a grocers) would be welcomed by most residents and a change to a Funeral Directors could then take place as a permitted change within Class 1. I therefore feel that, notwithstanding the exact proposed use, this application could not be justifiably refused."

In his recommendation to approve with conditions, the city planning officer included two conditions, the first relating to the servicing, draining, laying out, demarcation and lighting of the proposed car parking area on the subjects and the second to the construction of a screen wall, means of access and gates thereto onto the Great Northern Road frontage of the proposed car parking area, both conditions "in the interests of road safety, the free flow of traffic and visual amenity". A third condition was also proposed in relation to the means of access or egress to the building "in the interests of public safety and in order to preserve the amenity of the neighbourhood".

The notice of determination stated that the reasons for the decision of the council were "on the grounds that the use proposed by the applicants would be incompatible with the residential use of the upper floors of the property and the residential character surrounding the area and consequently detrimental to the amenity and enjoyment both to the upper flats and of the neighbouring sheltered dwellings and detrimental to public safety by reason of problems of egress from the applicants' car park onto a heavily trafficked dual carriageway".

The second respondent appealed against the refusal of planning permission to the Secretary of State on 12 December 1991. Thereafter the Secretary of State sought advice from the petitioners as to their preferred method of determination. As appears from a letter dated 2 March 1992 addressed to the petitioners by the Scottish Office inquiry reporters' unit, the second respondent had previously requested that the appeal be determined by written submissions procedure but by the date of the letter the petitioners had not yet decided upon the procedure to be adopted and were "actively seeking a consultant to advise on the appeal". On 12 March 1992 the petitioners wrote to the inquiry reporters' unit advising that they were insisting on a public inquiry relative to the appeal. In the light of the petitioners' decision the Secretary of State was obliged to comply with the request in terms of s 33 (4) of the Town and Country Planning (Scotland) Act 1972. The second respondent was accordingly so advised by letter dated 23 March 1992.

On 2 April 1992 the petitioners' appeal panel considered a report from the city's solicitor seeking further instructions from the appeals panel following upon an earlier decision authorising him to engage the services of an independent planning consultant in connection with the appeal. As minuted: "the report indicated that the City's Solicitor had approached a number of consultants on the Council's list, none of whom were prepared to support the Council's decision, but that one of the consultants had suggested, as a compromise, the roofing over of the whole or part of the yard area lying to the rear and side of the premises in order to screen the activities from the view of neighbouring upper-floor dwellings; advised that if the appellants were willing to accept that suggestion they would require to lodge a fresh application with the Planning Authority; and recommended that the appeal be not further pursued but that the City's Solicitor be authorised to approach the appellants with a view to gauging their reaction to the compromise solution. The report concluded by intimating that the situation insofar as opposition to the development was concerned was somewhat unclear, in that, in response to an approach by the City's Solicitor to purported objectors, some could not recall having lodged an objection, some were no longer resident in the vicinity of the application site and some did not wish to maintain their objections.

"The panel resolved — (1) to rescind their previous decision to resist the appeal; and (2) to authorise the City's Solicitor to approach the appellants or their agents in order to discuss with them the proposal that the yard area be roofed over in a manner and by means of a structure considered acceptable to the Planning Authority and if they are agreeable to submission by them of a planning application giving effect to that proposal, or, alternatively, in the event of the appellants' refusal to countenance such a proposal, to request the Secretary of State to impose a suitable condition to that effect and other appropriate conditions in his grant of planning permission for the development."

In May 1992 two letters of objection to the proposed change of use were received by the inquiry reporters' unit, one from a local regional councillor and the other from an elected tenants' organisation in the area. This latter objector subsequently intimated to the inquiry reporters' unit that it wished to take part in, and give evidence to, the public local inquiry which had by then been fixed for 4 August 1992.

Subsequent to the decision of the petitioners' appeals panel, discussions took place between the petitioners' planning consultant and the second respondent's agents. In July 1992 the petitioners prepared an amended statement of observations in respect of the appeal in which the Secretary of State was invited to grant planning permission in respect of the subjects and to impose certain conditions as listed in the amended statement for the reasons stated therein. The second respondent's agent having received the amended statement of observations, wrote to the petitioners by letter dated 22 July 1992 intimating that she had written to the Scottish Office inquiry reporters' unit "confirming our agreement to the conditions to be imposed subject to the insertion of a single statement. This is designed to clarify the conditions to be imposed in respect of any Class 1 use, other than category (G) for the direction of funerals".

A copy of the letter sent to the inquiry reporters' unit was enclosed. In this letter the second respondent's agent said this: "It now appears that there is no need for a public enquiry to take place on August 4.

"Although we consider some of these conditions to be superfluous, we have agreed to their imposition: subject to the insertion of one additional statement. This addition is designed to clarify the conditions to be imposed in respect of any Class 1 retail use other than category (G) — 'for the direction of funerals'."

Later on in the same letter the writer continues: "Because of this unusual method of determining an appeal, I have not set out our agreement in more formal terms. To summarise however, the appellant is agreeable to the imposition of the conditions as contained within Aberdeen City Council's amended statement of observations . . . if this will avoid the need for a public enquiry. This agreement is subject to further explanation of the conditions applicable in all categories of Class 1 retail use excluding category (G): in addition, the statement of intent is to be read with the planning consent. We request therefore, that Mr Hickman determines this appeal in the light of agreement between the appellant, Mr Gordon Bruce and Aberdeen City Council, and that he grants conditional planning permission for change of use to Class 1 retail."

On 23 July 1992 the petitioners wrote to the inquiry reporters' unit intimating that following the submission of the petitioners' statement of observations in June 1992, there had been further discussions between the parties and that there was enclosed "An amended statement of observations, setting out conditions which the applicants' planning consultant has indicated would be acceptable. In the circumstances, it would seem to both parties that there are no issues upon which they need to be heard on 4th August 1992 and if the reporter agrees the public local enquiry and site inspection can be cancelled."

On 14 July 1992 the date and the venue of the inquiry were advertised in the *Press and Journal* newspaper. At this stage the first respondent, as the designated inquiry reporter, had before him the two letters of objection by third parties. In their petition, it is stated on behalf of the petitioners that by the time that the letter dated 23 July 1992 was sent by the petitioners' solicitor to the inquiry reporters' unit, "one of the objectors and 21 signatories of the petition had withdrawn their objections". It is proper to note that counsel for the petitioners accepted that this was not strictly accurate. So far as known to the petitioners

and the first respondent the only parties who had advised the first respondent of objections to the appeal were the individual regional councillor and the tenants' association noted previously. The reference to the withdrawal of the objections in the petition relates to the position of those who had originally objected to the application before its determination by the petitioners.

The inquiry was duly held on 4 August 1992. In the event, no third party appeared. The first respondent heard argument on behalf of the petitioners and the second respondent for some half a day relative to the conditions to be attached to any grant of planning permission. At the close of the inquiry a motion for expenses was made on behalf of the second respondent.

On 11 August 1992 the first respondent issued his decision letter addressed to the second respondent's agent. After setting out the facts relating to the subjects and their intended use together with the second respondent's proposal for adaptation of the subjects as funeral directors, the decision letter continues:

"(5) The City Planning Officer recommended approval of the proposal, but the Council decided to reject the application because the particular use proposed was considered to be incompatible with the nearby residential uses, including the sheltered housing, and on traffic grounds.

"(6) After the appeal was lodged, the Council learned that some of the objectors were no longer opposed to the use as a funeral directors, because there was more concern that the previous public house use might be resumed. In addition the Planning Consultant engaged by the Council to fight the appeal advised that it would be difficult to defend the Council's decision, and that the proposal could be approved, subject to specific conditions to regulate the use for funerals. The Council accepted this advice. There were discussions between yourself and the Council's Planning Consultant, resulting in your client's acceptance of the proposed conditions, subject to one or two reservations.

"(7) The inquiry took place as arranged to hear from any remaining objectors, and to discuss the necessity for the various proposed conditions. In the event, no third parties appeared, and their representations remained to be considered as written submissions.

"(8) Both sides accepted that it was in order for the Planning Authority to impose conditions relating to the specific use that was proposed, providing that all conditions met the tests recommended in the Scottish Office Guidance on Planning Conditions (SDD Circular 18/1986)."

Subsequently in his decision letter the first respondent set out certain conclusions including:

"(13) On the basis of the revised attitude of the Planning Authority, the intended conditions that would regulate the development, the existence of the public house use, the absence of objection from the Highway Authority, and the status of a funeral directors as a

Class 1 retail use, I consider that the criticisms of the proposal by the third parties do not justify the withholding of planning permission. However, I accept that it would be very desirable to ensure that the activities at the delivery bay serving the funeral directors are screened from view from the nearby sheltered flats, and that traffic emerging from the site is encouraged to turn left into Great Northern Road. The former objective could probably best be achieved by locating the service bay on the south gable elevation of the building, and by screening it with the canopy."

After dealing with certain other matters the first respondent came to deal with the request for expenses as follows:

"(16) Your request for expenses is based in the contention that the application need never have come to appeal if the District Council had addressed only the question of a Class 1 use, as proposed on the application form, and not the supplementary matter of the particular use as a funeral directors; and that as the Council was eventually prepared to accept the proposal subject to conditions, no appeal would have been necessary if the initial advice of the City Planning Officer had been accepted.

"(17) For the Council, it was submitted that it was for the elected members to reach their own view on planning applications, and that the matter had been processed as quickly as possible once the appeal had been lodged. If an award of expenses was to be made, it should cover only the cost of preparing for the appeal.

"(18) I note that the Council reversed its attitude to this proposal after the advice of the Planning Consultant re-inforced that of the City Planning Officer, and it was learned that there had been a change of view on the part of some or all of the third party objectors. While it is right and proper that the planning authority should give due weight to the views of those making representations, the Council is also obliged to have regard to the provisions of the development plan and other material considerations. Such considerations should have included the status of a funeral directors as a Class 1 use and the amenity and traffic implications of the existing use of the property as a public house. I therefore agree that the Council acted unreasonably in this matter, being unduly influenced by the contradictory views of the third parties, and by giving insufficient weight to the advice of the City Planning Officer, who pointed out that it would be difficult to reject a Class 1 retail use at the site.

"(19) For these reasons, and in exercise of the powers delegated to me, I find that your client's appeal should not have been necessary, and that expenses arising directly from the appeal procedure should be awarded against the District Council in favour of your client."

The petitioners seek partial reduction of the decision letter to the extent that it makes an award of expenses against the petitioners. In the petition the grounds are set out as follows: "Said award of expenses constituted an unreasonable exercise of the first respondent's discretion. Having regard to the conditions which the first respondent imposed and his decision to proceed with the inquiry in order to hear from objectors there was no reasonable basis for the conclusion that the petitioners acted unreasonably by giving insufficient weight to the advice of the city planning officer and being unduly influenced by the contradictory views of third parties. It was for the petitioners to determine what weight to attach to city planning officer's report and relevant representations and objections. Separatim it was wholly unreasonable for the first respondent to award expenses against the petitioners in circumstances where he had determined to proceed with a public inquiry notwithstanding that the petitioners and the second respondent had previously reached agreement as to planning permission being granted for retail use and conditions to be attached thereto such as to render an inquiry unnecessary for their purposes. In the circumstances no reporter acting unreasonably would have made said award of expenses."

Reference was made to the well known passage in the opinion of Lord President Emslie in *Wordie Property Co Ltd v Secretary of State for Scotland* at p 347 as to what constitutes the test of unreasonableness for the purpose of striking down such a decision.

Counsel submitted that it was clear from the terms of the decision letter that the first respondent's determination that the petitioners had acted unreasonably arose from his assessment that the petitioners had been "unduly influenced" by the contradictory views of the third parties and by his assessment that they had given "insufficient weight to the advice of the City Planning Officer who pointed out that it would be difficult to reject a Class 1 retail use at the site".

If a decision was reached by reference to two separate factors each of which was essential to the decision and one of which was shown to be misconceived, then the decision was fatally flawed. He referred to *Pirie v City of Aberdeen District Council* and *Anduff Holdings v Secretary of State for Scotland* and in particular the opinion of the Lord Justice Clerk at p 699. There reference was made to the high test that it was necessary to satisfy to show that a decision was reasonable looking only to the remaining ground in the event that one of the grounds of decision was found to be bad. Counsel submitted that it was not unreasonable per se that the local planning authority should choose not to follow the chief planning officer's advice. There must be something beyond that. He further submitted that the matter of what weight should be attached to any factor in a planning application was for the planning authority to determine. He accepted that if subsequently the weight attached to one factor was shown to be unreasonable then the committee's decision was open to attack, but it was important for the reporter to distinguish between the approach which he was entitled to adopt in relation to the merits of the appeal and in reaching a decision on an award of expenses. As regards the

A former matter, it was accepted for the petitioners that by virtue of s 33 of the 1972 Act, a reporter was entitled to approach the matter of grant or refusal of a planning application on appeal de novo. The first respondent was therefore free to reach a different decision on the merits since it could be based upon different considerations from those which the local authority had had in mind. But insofar as he was concerned with a decision on the matter of expenses, the question for him was whether the planning authority had acted reasonably in the circumstances before

B them. It was thus insufficient for the first respondent simply to say that the petitioners had given insufficient weight to one factor or been unduly influenced by another factor. He was bound to explain why the decision reached by the petitioners was unreasonable. This was a different matter from holding that the local authority had been wrong on the merits after a review of the whole case.

In para 18 of the decision letter the first respondent

C appeared to have taken into account material which had come to the notice of the petitioners after they had determined to refuse the application of the second respondent. In particular, he had made reference to the reinforcement of the city planning officer's advice by that of a planning consultant and the fact that there had been a change of view "on the part of some or all of the third party objectors". In relation to the advice tendered to the petitioners in the city planning officer's report, it was to be noted that it was not there

D suggested that the petitioners were not entitled to have regard to the proposed use as a material consideration in reaching their determination. For instance, different issues as to amenity and traffic hazard might arise depending upon the particular nature of the class 1 retail use proposed. It was not without significance that these were matters which were addressed both by the city planning officer in suggesting conditions and by the first respondent in relation to the conditions which he imposed on the grant of planning permis-

E sion. In the whole circumstances there was no proper basis for finding that the petitioners acted unreasonably and that their determination to refuse the planning application was unwarranted. The decision of the first respondent was one to which no reasonable reporter could come.

Counsel for the petitioners presented a subsidiary submission to the effect that on any view it was wholly unreasonable for the first respondent to have awarded expenses including the expenses of the inquiry itself

F standing the agreement reached between parties in the period prior to the hearing on 4 August 1992. Since the parties are not at one on the facts which would be relevant to this submission, and in particular are not at one on the circumstances which gave rise to the parties making submissions at the hearing to the first respondent, it is agreed that I cannot deal with this argument at this stage. Parties were agreed that if this were the only outstanding issue, it would be necessary to continue these proceedings for evidence either by affidavit or oral, before it could be resolved.

For the first respondent counsel invited me to sustain the second and third pleas in law for this G respondent. He submitted that the petition was misconceived. The proper question for decision was whether there was any factual basis upon which the court could conclude that in reaching his decision to award expenses the first named respondent had reached a decision that was unreasonable in the *Wednesbury* sense. There was no dispute that in terms of s 267 (7) of the 1972 Act and para 5 of Sched 7 to the Act the first respondent had a discretion to award expenses. This discretion fell to be exercised taking account of the terms of a Scottish Office circular H 6/1990. This provided advice on the manner in which the Secretary of State's power to order one party to certain proceedings to meet the expenses of another party was to be exercised in planning appeals such as that which the first respondent was appointed to determine. Paragraph 2 of the circular states: "This circular also explains the conditions which require to be met before an award of expenses will be made. It sets out examples of some of the situations in which an award of expenses may be made either against a I planning authority or against an appellant or other party."

In para 5 it is provided that before an award of expenses is made the following conditions will normally need to have been met: first, that application for an award has been made; secondly, the party against whom the claim is made has acted unreasonably; and thirdly, this unreasonable conduct has caused the party making the application to incur unnecessary expense "either because it should not J have been necessary for the case to come before the Secretary of State for determination or because of the manner in which the party against whom the claim is made had conducted his part of the proceedings".

There then follow illustrations of unreasonable behaviour which may give rise to an award of expenses. In para 7, which contains examples of unreasonable behaviour, it is stated unreasonable behaviour on the part of the planning authority may K include: "Reaching their decision without reasonable planning grounds for doing so".

It was necessary to bear in mind that the question of *Wednesbury* unreasonableness to be applied to the first respondent's decision to award expenses was a high test as was made clear by Lord Diplock in his speech in *CCSU v Minister for the Civil Service*. At [1985] 1 AC, p 410 he said: "By 'irrationality' I mean what can by now be succinctly referred to as '*Wednesbury* unreasonableness'. . . . It applies to a L decision which is so outrageous in its defiance of logic or of accepted moral standards that no sensible person who had applied his mind to the question to be decided could have arrived at it."

In approaching his task the first respondent was not bound to use that same test but rather to ask himself whether there had been shown to have been any good reason for the petitioners having determined the second respondent's planning application as they did. While it was undoubtedly a matter for the petitioners in the first place to make up their minds on the issue, the first named respondent was perfectly entitled in reaching his decision on expenses to take account of the fact that the petitioners had, when the second respondent had appealed, reversed their attitude and thus by their own conduct demonstrated that their original decision was not a justifiable one. Looking to the material which was before the first respondent so far as the merits of the application were concerned, and more particularly his conclusions in para 13 of the decision letter taken along with the matters noted by him in para 18, it could not be said that his view that the petitioners had acted unreasonably in the matter was illogical or absurd. It was plain from the reference there to the petitioners having been unduly influenced by the views of the objectors then before them that that had inclined them to overlook unreasonably the weight of the advice of the city planning officer as set out in his report. This had set out that notwithstanding the exact proposed use of the subjects, the application was one only for change of use from a public house to class 1 retail and could not justifiably be refused. The first respondent's decision fell squarely within one of the stated grounds in the Scottish Office circular, namely that in reaching their decision the local authority had acted without reasonable planning grounds for doing so.

Counsel further dealt with the issue of whether there was sufficient material to support the petitioners' averment that prior to the hearing of the appeal there had been a concluded agreement between the petitioners and the second named respondent on the matter of the conditions to be imposed in the event that a grant of planning permission was to be made by the first respondent. While I think that there may be some force in this contention, if regard is had to the correspondence between parties there appears to have been some degree of concluded view between parties as to the manner in which parties might approach the matter of the appeal. However there is one particular issue concerning the communication of information in a telephone call between the first respondent and the second respondent's agents on 27 July 1992 which may bear on the matter and which is not the subject of an admission. In these circumstances it cannot be determined at this stage as a matter of fact and law what was the agreed position between the petitioners and the second respondent prior to the hearing on 4 August 1992. In any event it is pertinent to observe that unless and until the first respondent had considered the full implications of the proposed conditions and the basis of the objections lodged, on both of which matters the petitioners and the second respondents would have been entitled to address him, there was no basis standing the objections upon which the appeal could then be determined without some form of hearing.

At this stage therefore the only question which can be determined is whether the petitioners have established on the basis of the agreed facts between the parties that the first respondent's decision on the matter of an award of expenses was unreasonable in the *Wednesbury* sense. I have reached the view that on this question the submissions for the first respondent are to be preferred. It is not in dispute that the first respondent was entitled to entertain the second respondent's motion for an award of expenses. Nor did I understand it to be in dispute that his decision was a matter of discretion which could only be struck down if it were shown to have offended against the test of *Wednesbury* unreasonableness. It is said that he failed to take into account that the petitioners were entitled to disagree with the city planning officer and to be influenced by the views expressed by objectors. I do not doubt that as general propositions that is so. The question which the first respondent required to consider was whether in the circumstances placed before him it could be said that the petitioners' decision had been without reasonable planning grounds. The material which he had considered in reaching the view that he did is set out in his decision letter. In particular he had regard to the terms of the advice tendered to the petitioners by the city planning officer as to the proper planning considerations which they should bear in mind. Standing the facts which are not disputed, that the city planning officer had proposed conditions which would have dealt with the issues of amenity and road safety, both of which appeared to be the grounds upon which the petitioners determined to refuse the second respondent's application, and furthermore having in mind that subsequently the city planning officer's advice had been fortified by the views of independent planning consultants, I am of the opinion that the first respondent was entitled reasonably to take the view that the petitioners had no reasonable planning grounds upon which to reach their decision to refuse the planning application. It might well be that a different view might have been reached on the same basis of fact but that is beside the point. The question is whether it has been shown that the discretion exercised by the first respondent has been exercised upon a mistaken basis of fact or in disregard of a material factor, such that his decision could be described as so outrageous in its defiance of logic or of accepted moral standards that no sensible person who had applied his mind to the question to be decided could have arrived at it. Looking to the first respondent's decision and the material before him and the grounds on which it is stated that he reached his decision, I can find no basis for the suggestion that he had proceeded upon either a mistaken basis of fact or had disregarded a material factor. His reference to "undue influence" and to "insufficient weight" in para 18 of the decision letter serves merely to give point to the opinion which he had reached, that the views of the third parties did not give rise to reasonable planning grounds to refuse the application in the light of the advice of the city planning officer that it would be difficult to reject a class 1 retail use at the site, and his suggestion of conditions to be attached to any grant.

In the whole circumstances I shall sustain the second and third pleas in law for the first respondent and dismiss the petition.

A   *Counsel for Petitioners, S L Stuart; Solicitors, Bennett & Robertson, WS — Counsel for Respondent (Secretary of State for Scotland), Moynihan; Solicitor, R Brodie, Solicitor to the Secretary of State for Scotland.*

C H S M

B
Pirie v City of Aberdeen District Council

OUTER HOUSE

LORD CULLEN

3 FEBRUARY 1993

Administrative law — Judicial review — Reasons given by administrative body — Severability — One of two reasons given invalid — Whether reasons severable or
C   *cumulative.*

Housing — Local authority — Decision to refuse admission to housing list — Reliance on ground not within published summary of rules for admission — Whether local authority entitled to rely upon factor not in summary — Housing (Scotland) Act 1987 (c 26), s 21 (1) and (4).

The Housing (Scotland) Act 1987 provides by s 19 (1) (d) that a local authority, in considering whether an
D   applicant for local authority housing is entitled to be admitted to a housing list, is to take no account of any outstanding liability for rent attributable to the tenancy of any house of which the applicant was not the tenant. Section 21 (1) provides that a local authority is to publish and make available in summary form any rules it may have governing admission of applicants to a housing list.

An applicant for a place on a district council's housing waiting list applied by judicial review for
E   reduction of the council's decision to refuse his application. The applicant's wife, with whom the applicant lived, had incurred rent arrears before eviction, she having been the sole tenant of that flat. The applicant's wife had been evicted as a result of conduct amounting to nuisance or annoyance. The refusal by the local authority to admit the applicant to the list was stated to be because of the arrears and because the tenancy had been conducted by the wife in an unsatisfactory manner. The local authority's summary of its
F   rules made no reference, as a reason for refusal, to unsatisfactory behaviour on the part of anyone other than an applicant. In the judicial review proceedings it was accepted by the local authority that reliance on the wife's rent arrears was invalid as a reason for refusal of the applicant's application. The local authority argued that the wife's unsatisfactory conduct of her tenancy was a sufficient reason on its own justifying the local authority's refusal.

Held, that the two matters were stated cumulatively and thus that, even if the second matter on its own

could properly have been relied upon, the fact that the two matters had been considered cumulatively vitiated G the decision (p 1157C-D); and decree of reduction granted.

Malloch v Aberdeen Corporation, 1974 SLT 253, *distinguished.*

Opinion, that the local authority's failure to list in the summary of their rules unsatisfactory behaviour of anyone other than an applicant as a ground for refusing an application, barred the local authority from founding on the behaviour of the applicant's wife H (p 1157 I-K).

Petition for judicial review

Derek Pirie sought judicial review of a decision by the City of Aberdeen District Council, refusing his application to be put on a housing waiting list.

The case came for a first hearing before the Lord Ordinary (Cullen).   I

Statutory provisions

The Housing (Scotland) Act 1987 provides:

"19.—(1) In considering whether an applicant for local authority housing is entitled to be admitted to a housing list, a local authority shall take no account of— . . . (d) any outstanding liability (for payment of rent or otherwise) attributable to the tenancy of any house of which the applicant is not, and was not when the liability accrued, a tenant. . . .   J

"21.—(1) It shall be the duty of every local authority . . . to publish . . . any rules which it may have governing— (a) admission of applicants to any housing list. . . .

"(4) The rules to be published by a body in accordance with subsection (1) or (2) shall be— (a) available for perusal; and (b) on sale at a reasonable price; and (c) available in summary form on request to members of the public, at all reasonable times— (i) in a case K where the body is a local authority or a development corporation, at its principal offices and its housing department offices; and (ii) in any other case, at its principal and other offices."

Cases referred to

Lennon v Hamilton District Council, 1990 SCLR 514.
Malloch v Aberdeen Corporation, 1974 SLT 253; 1973 SC 227.
R v Secretary of State for the Home Department, ex p L *Ruddock* [1987] 1 WLR 1482.

On 3 February 1993 the Lord Ordinary *sustained* the petitioner's pleas in law to the extent of *pronouncing* decree of reduction of the local authority's original and appeal decisions.

LORD CULLEN.—On or about 7 February 1992 the respondents received from the petitioner an application for him to be placed on the waiting list for district council accommodation. In a letter to the petitioner dated 20 March 1992 an official of the respondents' housing division referred to the petitioner's application and stated: "My records indicate that your wife's former tenancy at 9E Richmond Walk which was occupied within the last twelve months has arrears and legal expenses amounting to £1,285.23, and was conducted in an unsatisfactory manner. I would therefore advise you that your application does not qualify for inclusion onto the waiting list at this time."

The petitioner exercised his right to appeal against this decision but his appeal was refused by the respondents' housing (cases) subcommittee on 2 June 1992. The petitioner was notified of this decision by letter dated 8 June 1992.

By way of background to this correspondence it may be noted that the petitioner's wife, whom he married on 24 December 1991, had been the sole tenant of a flat at 9E Richmond Walk, which was owned by the respondents, from 28 October 1988. The petitioner had been living with her at that address from at least 1990. On 3 September 1991 an order was made in the sheriff court at Aberdeen under s 48 (2) (a) of, and para 7 of Sched 3 to, the Housing (Scotland) Act 1987 for the recovery of possession of the flat by the respondents. Paragraph 7 states as one of the grounds for recovery of possession of houses let under secure tenancies that: "The tenant of the house (or any one of joint tenants) or any person residing or lodging with him or any sub-tenant of his has been guilty of conduct in or in the vicinity of the house which is a nuisance or annoyance and it is not reasonable in all the circumstances that the landlord should be required to make other accommodation available to him."

On 12 December 1991 the sheriff principal refused an appeal against this order. The case stated by the sheriff who made the decision on 3 September 1991 contains findings in fact as to the behaviour of the tenant, who in due course became the petitioner's wife, but makes no mention of the conduct of the petitioner himself. The petitioner's application to be placed on the housing list was made after his wife had been evicted from the flat. In his application he referred to himself as having no fixed address.

In this petition for judicial review the petitioner seeks reduction of the decisions which were intimated to him by the letters dated 20 March and 8 June 1992 on the ground that the respondents erred in law.

Before coming to the arguments which were presented at the first hearing of the petition it is convenient to refer to two sections of the 1987 Act. The first of these is s 19, which provides by subs (1) that in considering whether an applicant for local authority housing is entitled to be admitted to a housing list, a local authority is to take no account of, inter alia, "(d) any outstanding liability (for payment of rent or otherwise) attributable to the tenancy of any house of which the applicant is not, and was not when the liability accrued, a tenant".

The second of these sections is s 21 which provides by subs (1) that it is to be the duty of every local authority to publish any rules which it may have

governing, inter alia, admission of applicants to any housing list. It is further provided by subs (4) that the rules to be published are to be "(a) available for perusal; and (b) on sale at a reasonable price; and (c) available in summary form on request to members of the public, at all reasonable times" at the principal offices and the housing department offices of the local authority.

I was referred to a copy of a booklet published by the respondents in January 1992 as a guide to their housing allocations and transfers policies. It was common ground that this represented the summary which was made available to members of the public in accordance with s 21 (4). I should add that there was no suggestion that for present purposes there was any material difference between what was stated in that booklet and the terms of the rules which had been made by the respondents. Under the heading "Who can Apply?" the booklet stated that to be accepted on to the waiting list an applicant must have some degree of housing need as recognised by the scheme. It went on to state various categories of persons whose applications were accepted or who might apply for acceptance. This section of the booklet ended with the following words:

"Applications for the waiting list are NOT normally accepted from

Former tenants of this or any other Housing Authority whose tenancy was conducted unsatisfactorily (subject to the right of appeal to the Housing Committee).

Former tenants of this or any other Housing Authority who owe money in respect of their tenancy unless the City Housing Officer decides otherwise.

Applicants who within the last twelve months have occupied accommodation which reasonably met their needs at the time (in the opinion of the City Housing Officer) and voluntarily gave it up."

At the first hearing it was not in dispute that, having regard to the terms of s 19 (1) (d) of the 1987 Act, the respondents should have taken no account of the arrears in respect of the tenancy of the petitioner's wife at 9E Richmond Walk; and accordingly that this reason for the refusal of the petitioner's application was unsound in law. The issues between the parties accordingly were (i) whether the second reason given in the letter dated 20 March 1992, namely that the tenancy "was conducted in an unsatisfactory manner", represented a severable reason for that decision; and (ii) whether in any event this was a reason which was sound in law.

Counsel for the respondents emphasised that the second reason was distinct in meaning from the first and maintained that by itself it was sufficient to form the basis for the respondents' decision. The respondents were entitled to take into account that the conduct of the petitioner's wife had been totally unacceptable and that they had been successful in recovering possession of the flat. They had a duty to all their tenants to secure the removal of those who were guilty of unsatisfactory conduct. There was no suggestion that the petitioner had been intending to be

A the sole occupier of the accommodation which he was seeking. The respondents would have refused application on the strength of the second ground by itself.

I am not satisfied that the second ground falls to be treated as severable and hence as an independent ground for the refusal of the application. This question turns essentially on the correct interpretation of the respondents' decision. The argument presented by counsel for the respondents appears to me to involve a consideration of what hypothetically would have been their decision if the first reason had been
B excluded. That, however, pursues a wrong line of inquiry. The question for me is as to the effect on the respondents' actual decision of the invalidity of the first reason. Counsel for the respondents accepted that whether an application was to be refused on particular grounds was a matter for the discretion of the respondents. It was not suggested that the respondents were bound to refuse the petitioner's application or that no reasonable authority in the position of the respondents would have failed to do so. Considering therefore the
C way in which the respondents' decision was expressed, I find that the two reasons were presented as the reasons in cumulo for the refusal of the application. They were not presented as alternative reasons or as one arising in default of the other. The language of the decision may be contrasted with the reasons which the education authority adopted in *Malloch v Aberdeen Corporation*, to which I was referred. The second of the two reasons for the dismissal of an unregistered but certificated teacher was introduced by the words
D "and on the additional ground that in any event". Although the first ground was held invalid the second was regarded as providing an independent ground for the dismissal. In these circumstances I am of opinion that the second reason is not severable and that accordingly the respondents' decisions were unsound in law.

In these circumstances it is unnecessary for me to go on to deal with the discussion of the second of the questions which were in issue between the parties.
E However, as the arguments were developed at some length and as the points which were argued may be of general interest, I will briefly outline the argument and my views in relation to it.

Counsel for the petitioner presented a twofold approach. First, he submitted that the implication of the 1987 Act, and in particular s 21, was that the respondents were under a duty to comply with the rules which they were required to publish. If this was not the case the duty to publish would have no
F meaning. He referred to *Lennon v Hamilton District Council* as an example of the enforcement against a local authority of the terms of their current housing allocation policy. In the present case the list of the types of application which were not normally accepted should be regarded as exhaustive in the absence of any contrary indication. Accordingly the respondents were not entitled to refuse the petitioners' application on any other ground. Secondly, the petitioner was in any event entitled to maintain that he had a legitimate expectation that the respondents would conform to the

terms of the rules which they had published. Reference was made to *R v Secretary of State for the Home* G *Department, ex p Ruddock* in which Taylor J held that a legitimate expectation was not confined to cases where the complaint was that of failure to consult or to give the opportunity to make representations before a decision was made.

In response counsel for the respondents maintained that it was not appropriate to interpret the respondents' guide as giving an exhaustive list of those cases in which applications would not normally be accepted. It was not practicable to cover every conceivable H circumstance which might provide a reason for refusing an application. The guide indicated that previous conduct was relevant to whether an application would not be accepted. The respondents were acting in accordance with the intention of the 1987 Act in having regard to the way in which it was likely that a tenancy would be conducted.

The critical question is whether the guide should be understood as giving an exhaustive indication of the I type of cases in which an application for inclusion in the housing list would not normally be accepted. If an application was refused for a reason which was not within the rules indicated in the guide, the respondents would be in breach of their duty under the statute and the resulting decision would be invalid. It would be unnecessary to consider whether the case could be based on the failure to fulfil a legitimate expectation. Counsel for the petitioner was, in my view, correct when he submitted that the rules made J by the local authority and hence those published and summarised in accordance with s 21 are the whole rules by reference to which a particular application is to be decided. I do not regard the terms of the guide as giving any indication that the unsatisfactory conduct of a previous tenancy by any person other than the applicant would entail that the application would not normally be accepted. There is no doubt that it would have been practicable for the respondents to make and publish a rule to this effect if that had been desired. In these circumstances I am of K opinion that the second reason for the refusal of the petitioner's application was invalid in respect that it was not within the rules made and published by the respondents as the rules governing the admission of applicants to their housing list.

Accordingly I will sustain the first and third pleas in law for the petitioner to the extent of pronouncing decree of reduction of the respondents' decisions of 20 March and 8 June 1992. I will repel the second plea L in law for the petitioner which I was not asked to sustain.

Counsel for Petitioner, Bovey; Solicitors, J & R A Robertson, WS (for Lindsay & Kirk, Aberdeen) — Counsel for Respondents, Cowan; Solicitors, Bennett & Robertson, WS.

C H

McCormack v HM Advocate

A   HIGH COURT OF JUSTICIARY

THE LORD JUSTICE GENERAL (HOPE),
LORDS ALLANBRIDGE AND COWIE

19 MARCH 1993

*Justiciary — Crime — Murder — Culpable homicide —
Provocation — Wife telling accused he was not father of
child of marriage — Accused at first not taking her
seriously then having doubts, and strangling wife to*
B   *silence her — Whether sufficient basis for provocation
reducing murder to culpable homicide.*

*Justiciary — Evidence — Appeal — New evidence not
heard and not reasonably available at trial — Accused
suffering amnesia at trial — Accused seeking to lead evidence to substitute for explanation that he could not recall
strangling wife, that he wanted to stop her asserting that
he was not father of child of marriage — Whether evidence not reasonably available at trial — Whether evidence
additional — Criminal Procedure (Scotland) Act 1975*
C   *(c 21), s 228 (2).*

*Justiciary — Procedure — Trial — Charge to jury —
Provocation — Judge directing jury that reasonable or
proportionate relationship must exist between conduct
amounting to provocation and accused's act — Whether
misdirection.*

An accused person was tried for the murder of his
wife. There was no dispute that he had strangled her
in the house to which she had gone to live some
D   months after it had been decided that they should
separate. The accused, who was anxious that there
should be a reconciliation, had arrived at his wife's
house to discuss increased access to the child of the
marriage on the day of her death. There was no animosity between them until the accused's wife became
anxious that the accused would awaken the child. An
argument began and developed into physical violence.
In evidence the accused stated that he and his wife had
struggled, his wife having pulled his hair and sunk her
E   teeth into his forehead. The accused then got on top
of her, kneeled astride her and slapped her face. Then
he next remembered sitting on the edge of a bed
looking down at his apparently lifeless wife on the
floor. There was a bandage in his hand. He could not
recall strangling his wife. In relation to provocation
the trial judge directed the jury, inter alia, that there
had to be a reasonable or proportionate relationship
between the conduct amounting to the provocation
and the accused's act. The accused was convicted of
F   murder and appealed on the ground that the trial
judge had misled the jury into thinking that the
act complained of had to be broadly equal to the
response.

The accused also appealed on the ground of the
existence of evidence which was not heard at the trial
and which was not available and could not reasonably
have been made available at the trial. The accused had
been trying since his conviction to recall more detail
about what happened during the incident and, about
six months after his conviction, he was able to state on

affidavit that in the course of the argument his wife
had repeatedly asserted that the accused was not the   G
child's father and, in order to stop her speaking, he
had tried to stuff a bandage into her mouth and, being
unsuccessful, had put it round her throat and pulled
as he had not wanted to hear that he was not the
child's father. Before the appeal court the Crown
accepted that the accused's amnesia at his trial was
genuine and that the information in his affidavit could
not have been obtained from him at that stage.

Held, (1) that the effect of the direction was simply
to warn the jury that they could not hold that the   H
accused was acting under provocation where there was
an absence of any proper or reasonable relationship
between the provocation offered and the response to
it, and it was sufficient to inform the jury that the
question was one of degree, and there had been no
misdirection (p 1160K-L); (2) that where significant
additional evidence was now available which was not
and could not reasonably have been made available at
the trial, it did not matter that it was the accused who,
having recovered his memory, sought to provide it   I
rather than another witness of whose existence or
identity the accused and his advisers were previously
unaware (p 1163A-B); (3) that the additional details
which the accused now wished to give were not additional evidence but were a different account as he
wished to withdraw his evidence that he could not
recall strangling his wife: it was therefore a more complete account of the accident by the same witness
(p 1163F-H); (4) that in any event, even if it could be
regarded as additional evidence, it was not evidence of   J
such significance that a verdict reached in ignorance
of it had to be regarded as a miscarriage of justice,
since the wife's accusation did not amount to a clear
and unequivocal admission of adultery which was
accepted as such by the accused (p 1163J and L); and
appeal *refused.*

Jones v HM Advocate, 1990 SLT 517, *distinguished;*
McKay v HM Advocate, 1992 SLT 138, *applied.*

               K

Indictment

Hugh Guthrie McCormack was charged at the
instance of the rt hon the Lord Fraser of Carmyllie,
Her Majesty's Advocate, on an indictment which was
in the following terms: "on 19 September 1991 in the
house occupied by Angela Janet McIntyre or
McCormack at 22C Dalry Road, Ardrossan, you did
assault said Angela Janet McIntyre or McCormack,
seize hold of her, struggle with her, repeatedly strike   L
her on the head and body with your hands or feet or
cause her to strike her head and body against solid
objects, place a ligature around her neck and compress
her throat with said ligature and you did murder her".
The accused pled not guilty and proceeded to trial
before Lord MacLean and a jury in the High Court at
Kilmarnock. After trial the accused was found guilty
by a unanimous verdict.

The accused appealed to the High Court by note of
appeal against conviction.

Statutory provisions

A   The Criminal Procedure (Scotland) Act 1975 provides:

"228.—(1) Any person convicted on indictment may appeal in accordance with the provisions of this Part of this Act, to the High Court — (a) against such conviction; (b) against the sentence passed on such conviction; or (c) against both such conviction and such sentence: Provided that there shall be no appeal against any sentence fixed by law.

B   "(2) By an appeal under subsection (1) of this section, a person may bring under review of the High Court any alleged miscarriage of justice in the proceedings in which he was convicted, including any alleged miscarriage of justice on the basis of the existence and significance of additional evidence which was not heard at the trial and which was not available and could not reasonably have been made available at the trial."

C   ## Cases referred to

Advocate (HM) v Hill, 1941 SLT 401; 1941 JC 59.
Brodie v HM Advocate, 1993 SCCR 371.
Jones v HM Advocate, 1990 SLT 517; 1989 SCCR 726.
Low v HM Advocate, 1993 SCCR 493.
McKay v HM Advocate, 1992 SLT 138; 1991 SCCR 364.
Russell v HM Advocate, 1946 SLT 93; 1946 JC 37.
Thomson v HM Advocate, 1986 SLT 281; 1985 SCCR
D   448.

Appeal

The accused, on 8 October 1992, was granted leave by the High Court to lodge an additional ground of appeal and to supplement the original ground which had been lodged. These grounds were in the following terms:

(1) The trial judge erred in that he did not properly and sufficiently direct the jury in respect of provoca-
E   tion. In particular he gave an insufficient direction as to the standard to be applied by the jury in considering whether or not the provocation had been established. The test to be applied is whether a reasonable man would have lost control in the circumstances as narrated in evidence by the accused. The relationship between the conduct causing the loss of control and the response must be conceded [sic] in the context of the control having been lost. The trial judge failed to make this clear and in so doing caused the jury to
F   weigh the conduct causing the loss of control and the response in too fine a balance. The jury were thereby given the impression that the plea of provocation must fail unless the conduct causing the loss of control and the response thereto were broadly speaking equal.

(3) [sic] There has been a miscarriage of justice in that further evidence is now available tending to exculpate the appellant of the crime of murder. Said further evidence was not available and could not reasonably have been made available at the trial diet. Said further evidence is as contained in the affidavit of the appel-

lant which will be produced herewith. Said further
G   evidence was not available at the trial diet because the appellant was unable to remember it. The loss of memory was caused by the medical and mental condition of the accused.

The appeal was again heard in the High Court on 5 March 1993.

On 19 March 1993 the court *refused* the appeal.

The following opinion of the court was delivered by
H   the Lord Justice General (Hope):

OPINION OF THE COURT.—The appellant went to trial in the High Court at Kilmarnock on a charge of murdering his wife in the house to which she had gone to live some months after it had been decided that they should separate. There was no dispute that he was responsible for her death, the cause of which was strangulation with a bandage which the appellant had placed round her neck as a ligature. The only issue at the trial was whether this was murder or culp-
I   able homicide. In the event the jury returned a unanimous verdict that he was guilty of murder and he was sentenced to life imprisonment.

An appeal was taken against his conviction on the ground that the trial judge misdirected the jury on the matter of provocation. It was said that he had given an insufficient direction as to the standard to be applied by the jury in considering whether or not provocation had been established. The appellant was later granted leave to lodge further grounds of appeal, in which the
J   first ground is a restatement of his argument that there was a misdirection in respect of provocation. They included, however, a further ground which is based upon an affidavit by the appellant who claims now to remember things about the circumstances of the offence which he could not remember when he gave evidence at his trial. It is said that there was a miscarriage of justice in that what he can now remember is additional evidence which was not available and could not reasonably have been made available at the
K   trial, which tends to exculpate him of the crime of murder. An opportunity was then given for the appellant to be examined by psychiatrists, and we now have before us three psychiatric reports, two of which were instructed by the appellant and the other by the Crown, in the light of which we have been invited to consider this ground of appeal.

We shall deal first with the argument that there was a misdirection on the matter of provocation. The back-
L   ground to this argument is provided by the account of the incident which the appellant gave in his evidence at the trial. We have been given a full description of his evidence by the trial judge in his report, and it is necessary for us to mention only one or two details at this stage. The marriage had been happy at first, but there were strains between the parties due to financial problems, and they decided to separate. The appellant's wife left the matrimonial home in July 1991 for what he regarded as a trial separation, taking with her the one child of the marriage who was born on 7 May

1990. The appellant appeared to have been anxious that there should be a reconciliation, and the parties were agreed that he should have access to the child for a period each Sunday. He wished, however, to have greater access to her, and it was in order to discuss this matter that he arrived at his wife's house at about 9.15 on the evening of her death. There was no animosity between them until he went to see the child in her bedroom, and his wife then became anxious that his actions would wake the child. An argument began between them, and after a verbal exchange it developed into physical violence. The critical part of the appellant's evidence is summarised by the trial judge in this passage in his report: "They struggled on the bed and, after falling off it, they continued to struggle on the floor. The deceased started to pull his hair. She sunk her teeth into his forehead. He then got on top of her and kneeled astride her. He slapped her face, he recalled. Then the next thing he remembered was sitting on the edge of the bed looking down at his wife who was lying on the floor. She appeared to be lifeless. There was a bandage in his hand. He found that he could not wake his wife up and realised that she was dead. He accepted that he must have strangled her with the bandage, but he could not recall doing so."

It should be noted that there is no suggestion in this account that the appellant was seeking to explain his action on the ground that he was provoked by his wife into doing what he did.

The trial judge decided to direct the jury with regard to provocation, although he was in some doubt as to whether there was sufficient evidence of conduct on the part of the deceased which could reasonably have led to the appellant's loss of control to such a degree that he proceeded to strangle her. He did not think that there was a reasonable proportion between her actions and his actions in applying the ligature with such force and for such a length of time as to cause her death. The appellant's counsel had not taken from him in terms during his evidence that he had been provoked into strangling her, nor did he mention provocation in his speech to the jury. His argument was that the appellant had not intended to do his wife any harm and that he did not therefore have the necessary state of mind for murder. Nevertheless, the advocate depute had mentioned the matter in his speech, and the trial judge, very properly in our opinion, decided to deal with it in his charge. What he said was this: "What would otherwise fall to be regarded as a case of murder is reduced to that of culpable homicide if an accused person killed while acting under provocation. The accused's act in the first place is what he was provoked into doing. He must have reacted or retaliated in the heat of the moment when through fear or agitation he had lost control of his actions. The act or actions must be immediate, that is to say the provocation must be recent. There must be a reasonable or proportionate relationship between the conduct amounting to the provocation and the accused's act. In relation to a death caused by stabbing it was said: 'It takes a tremendous amount of provoca-

tion to palliate the stabbing of a man to death'. So there must be a reasonable or reasonably proportionate relationship between the conduct amounting to provocation and the act or reaction of the accused.''

Counsel for the appellant said that this was a misdirection because the trial judge misled the jury into thinking that the act complained of must be broadly equal to the response. He accepted that there had to be a relationship between that act and the response, but this was not to be weighed in too fine a balance. What was lacking was a more complete description of what could amount to provocation, in order to make it clear that the issue was to be judged broadly. It was wrong to apply a fine balance between the conduct causing the loss of control and the response to it. The impression which was given was that the conduct causing the loss of control and the response to it had more or less to be equal, whereas provocation was commonly recognised to exist where there was an imbalance between that conduct and the response. The advocate depute pointed out that the trial judge had been somewhat generous to the appellant in the direction which he gave, having regard to what the appellant had said in his evidence. He submitted that in any event there was nothing wrong with the direction, as it was in language which was well supported by the authorities.

In our opinion the trial judge said all that needed to be said on this matter in the circumstances of this case. There was, as he explains in his report, very little in the evidence to suggest that there was any basis for saying that the appellant acted as he did under provocation. It appears that the appellant lost control of himself when he acted as he did, but there was no attempt in the evidence to explain his actings on the ground that he was provoked. In this situation the question whether a fine or a broad balance was appropriate in order to determine the matter was not really a live issue in the case. In any event the direction that there must be a reasonable or reasonably proportionate relationship between the conduct amounting to provocation and the act or reaction to it was sufficient to inform the jury that the question was one of degree. There was no indication here that there had to be a precise equivalence between the one and the other or that a fine balance was required. The effect of the direction was simply to warn the jury that they could not hold that the accused was acting under provocation where there was an absence of any proper or reasonable relationship between the provocation offered and the response to it. As the Lord Justice Clerk said in *Low v HM Advocate*, whatever language is used to describe the limitation to the plea of provocation, it must always be a question of circumstances and a question of degree. The language which the trial judge used in this case is very similar to that used by the Lord Justice Clerk and by Lord Hunter in *Thomson v HM Advocate*, 1986 SLT at p 285, and we consider that counsel's criticism of it was not justified. It follows that we must reject this ground of appeal.

We turn now to the question whether there was a

A miscarriage of justice because what the appellant now says in his affidavit amounts to significant additional evidence which was not heard at the trial and which was not available and could not reasonably have been made available at the trial. Counsel for the appellant accepted that an appeal on the ground of additional evidence will not be allowed where a witness merely wishes to change the evidence which he gave at his trial. It is unnecessary therefore for us to go over the ground which was discussed in *Brodie v HM Advocate* in which all the recent authorities on this matter were

B reviewed. His point was that what the appellant was seeking to do here was to give additional evidence, and that there was moreover a sufficient explanation for his wishing to give fresh evidence which took this case out of that general rule.

According to his affidavit the appellant had been trying since his conviction to recall more detail about what happened during the incident which led to his wife's death. It was in about June or July 1992, about six months after his conviction, that he was able to tell

C his solicitor that he remembered the detail. He says that he had held off telling him or anyone else about this in case it affected his position in an action which had been raised for the child's custody. The account which he now gives is that in the course of the argument his wife told him that he was no use. When he asked her what she meant by that she then said that he could not even father his own child, and that he was not her father. He goes on to say this: "I instantly asserted that I was, but she repeated the allegation

D several times and I kept saying that I was the father. My head was in a spin. My heart was telling me that I was [the child's] father, but I began thinking that maybe I was not. I began thinking, did I ever leave my wife alone, were there occasions when someone else could have been with her? Lying under the couch were a couple of trainers and there was a bandage protruding from one of them. I grabbed the bandage. I just wanted my wife to shut up and I tried to stuff the bandage into her mouth. She moved her head about

E and would not accept the bandage into her mouth. There came a time during the struggle when we were lying face to face and in that situation I put the bandage round her throat and pulled. I just wanted not to hear these words anymore, that I was not [the child's] father."

The psychiatrists are agreed that this appears to be a genuine case of retrieval of memory. In her report dated 24 November 1992, Dr M A E Smith, a consul-

F tant psychiatrist at the Douglas Inch Centre, states that emotionally the appellant could be described as over controlled. His ability to remember exactly what had happened was repressed after the incident. His inability to recall was influenced by the horror of the moment and also by his desire that no one else should be aware that his fatherhood had been questioned. His recall was stimulated when he was presented with the information that his daughter's maternal grandparents were applying for her custody and that in that event he could lose contact with his daughter. Dr Smith also says that in her experience, prior to and during trial,

the majority of those accused of murder cannot recall the final words or feelings immediately prior to the act G which caused the death. It is after trial and imprisonment that there is time to think, and the memory of what was actually said and of what actually happened returns. In his report dated 29 December 1992, Dr Norman Clark, a consultant psychiatrist, also of the Douglas Inch Centre, describes the appellant's personality as somewhat over controlled and rigid. He accepts as genuine his statement that his memory blanked out at the time immediately prior to his wife's death, and adds that it is not unknown to find people H convicted of serious offences with such a period of amnesia. The repression of the relevant memories fades as some degree of acceptance of the incident occurs as time passes, and he considers it likely that this is what has happened in this case. He adds that a reaction of intense rage and violence in an otherwise over controlled personality might also serve to cause amnesia due to the strength of the emotions involved, and that such repression of memory could well in his experience lead to a failure of recall over a six to nine I month period as the appellant alleges. Although he points out that he can make no accurate statement as to the veracity or otherwise of his initial amnesia and his present apparent recall, he feels that this is entirely plausible given his experience of such episodes with other prisoners after their conviction.

In his report dated 15 January 1993, Dr J A Baird, a consultant forensic psychiatrist at the State Hospital, Carstairs, says that claims of amnesia are common among those who commit violent crime. While in J some cases the opinion is that the amnesia is not genuine, there are a significant number of cases where it is accepted. The phenomenon is considered to be a psychological process, not related to any mental disorder of any kind. No single theory is universally accepted as being the explanation for it, nor is there any certain method for distinguishing between feigned and genuine amnesia other than resorting to clinical opinion in each case. It is also recognised that as time passes memory can appear to return, and the same K comments apply to the assessment of this event where it occurs. His opinion of the appellant is that he had not even yet been able to give a complete account of his marriage as a whole. He describes his account of it as idealised, simplistic and given from his perspective, but he does not think that there is deliberate dissimulation on his part. He concludes his report with these words: "From all this it would be my opinion that it is consistent with his circumstances and the events in which he has been involved that his account L of these events has changed and developed with time. It is even possible that in the future other details about the relationship with his wife may emerge. I do not consider that this gradual process of increased disclosure is due to deliberate withholding of information or an attempt to deceive on his part".

The learned advocate depute said that he was content to accept that the appellant's amnesia at his trial was genuine and that the information which he now gives in his affidavit could not have been obtained

from him at that stage. Counsel for the appellant's
A position is that he was content to accept the opinion
expressed by Dr Baird, namely that this was a psychological process, and that he did not consider it necessary for the psychiatrists to give evidence because, so
far as he was concerned, there was no material dispute
between them about this case. It was sufficient for the
purposes of his argument that there was agreement
among them all that the sequence of events, leading
from amnesia at the trial to recall at the present time,
was genuine and not due to deliberate withholding of
B information or any attempt to deceive.

From this starting point he submitted that this was
truly additional evidence, which was not available and
could not reasonably have been made available at the
trial. The explanation for this was provided by the
psychiatrists, and it was clear that this was not a case
of someone who was wishing merely to change his
story. There was no element of choice in this case,
because the appellant had been unable to give the
account at his trial which he had now given in his
C affidavit. It was in the interests of justice that he
should be given the opportunity of having the account
which he can now give heard by a jury, since he now
had a genuine recall which provided him with a
defence to the charge of murder. The issue of provocation had been before the jury at his trial, but what he
could now say about the event was significant additional material relevant to that issue which he should
now be allowed to place before a fresh jury in his
D defence.

The advocate depute described this argument as
raising a unique and novel issue. But if the psychiatric
advice is to be accepted the phenomenon of amnesia
followed by recall after conviction is by no means
unique to this case. There is therefore an important
question of principle to be considered, because it is not
difficult to see that, if the appellant's argument in this
case were to be accepted, this could lead to other applications for a conviction to be set aside and a fresh
E prosecution authorised on the ground that the
accused, only after his conviction, has remembered
something which was of material significance to his
defence which he was incapable of recalling at his
trial. Dr Baird tells us that, while in some cases such
amnesia and recall of memory is feigned, there are a
significant number of cases where it is accepted as
genuine. The appellant's argument would seem to
lead to the conclusion that in such cases the verdict
reached at the first trial would have to be regarded as
F provisional only, pending a final resolution of the
matter at a second trial once the accused has recovered
his memory.

As the advocate depute pointed out, it might seem
to be more logical for there to be no trial at all until
the accused has recovered his memory. That would be
more consistent with the principle that a trial should
achieve finality in these matters, subject only to the
power now available to the court to grant authority for
a new prosecution in accordance with s 255 of the
1975 Act where there has been a miscarriage of justice.

But this would not be a solution in those cases where
a conviction is needed to produce the recall. And there G
is another difficulty. In *Russell v HM Advocate* it was
held that the fact that the accused suffered from hysterical amnesia, as a result of which she was unable to
plead to the libel or give instructions for her defence,
afforded no ground for a plea in bar of trial. Lord
Justice Clerk Cooper said at 1946 SLT, p 97: "It is,
I think, plain from the unbroken practice followed
from the earliest dates to which our records extend
that, in dealing with pleas in bar of trial founded on
some abnormal condition in the accused, the Court H
has balanced against each other two major considerations, viz., (1) fairness to the panel, who should not be
tried if and so long as he is not a fit object for trial,
and (2) the public interest which requires that persons
brought before a criminal Court by a public prosecutor should not be permitted to purchase complete
immunity from investigation into the charge by the
simple expedient of proving the existence at the diet
of trial of some mental or physical incapacity or
handicap."
I

He went on to point out that the administration of
criminal justice would be prejudiced if a plea in bar
were to be sustained just because the accused could
not tell his counsel what he was really doing at the
time of the offence. If that were to be so, it would have
to be sustained in cases where the accused had been
under the influence of drink, or had sustained a head
injury at the time of the crime or was a person of
unreliable memory. He concluded his remarks by
saying at p 98 that loss of memory in a person other- J
wise normal and sane plays its full part, if it is
sufficiently proved, in increasing the onus on the
Crown, and in raising doubts to which it may be the
duty of the jury to give effect in a verdict of acquittal
after investigation of the whole case, but that as our
law stands it can have no further or other effect. There
is no doubt therefore that the amnesia from which the
appellant in the present case claims to have been
suffering at the time of his trial would not have
afforded him a ground for a plea in bar of trial. The K
question is whether a conviction can now be set aside
on the ground that the accused has recovered his
memory and is now in a position to give significant
additional evidence which he was unable to give at
the trial.

It seems to us that, in principle, there can be only
one answer to the question which we have just asked
ourselves. If there was a miscarriage of justice, because
the accused is now able to give significant additional
evidence which was not heard at the trial and was not L
available and could not reasonably have been made
available then because of a genuine state of amnesia,
it will be the duty of the court to set aside the conviction and grant authority for the bringing of a new
prosecution. The significance of the amendments
which were made to ss 228 and 254 of the 1975 Act
by the Criminal Justice (Scotland) Act 1980 is that, in
contrast to the situation with which the court was
faced in *Russell*, there are now available to the court
powers which enable a miscarriage of justice to be

corrected by setting aside a conviction on the ground of the existence of additional evidence, leaving it open to the Crown to bring a fresh prosecution based on the whole of the evidence now available. The fresh evidence must of course be additional evidence, and not merely different evidence from that given at the trial. It must also be evidence which was not available and could not reasonably have been made available then, so an accused who is able to give evidence at his trial and chooses not to give evidence is unlikely to satisfy this requirement. But if the case is truly one where significant additional evidence is now available which was not available and could not reasonably have been made available at the trial, it ought not in principle to matter that it is the accused himself who seeks to provide it, having recovered his memory, rather than another witness of whose existence or identity the accused and his advisers were previously unaware.

It is nevertheless important to examine closely counsel's argument that what is now available in this case is truly additional evidence and that it is evidence which is significant. Only if it can properly be so described can it be said that there is a basis for setting aside the verdict on the ground of a miscarriage of justice. Counsel's submission was that this was additional evidence because the appellant was not seeking merely to change the evidence which he gave at his trial but to add to it evidence which, due to a loss of memory, he could not give. The advocate depute's reply was that this was not additional evidence but different evidence. The appellant now wished to change his evidence that he could not recall what had happened and to replace it by giving different evidence. This was different evidence for which there was an explanation, but it was nevertheless merely evidence which was different. He accepted however that, due to the appellant's genuine amnesia, this could not be said to be evidence which could reasonably have been made available at the trial. In this respect the present case differs from *Jones v HM Advocate,* where the appellant sought to be allowed to lead additional evidence about something which he had remembered after the trial. The Lord Justice Clerk said in that case at 1990 SLT, p 523A that since the appellant gave evidence at the trial anything which he could now say about events at or about the time of the stabbing must be evidence which could reasonably have been made available at the trial. That point cannot be made in the present case, in view of the opinions expressed by the psychiatrists and the acceptance by the advocate depute that the appellant's amnesia at his trial was not feigned but genuine. It is therefore on the issue as to whether this is truly additional evidence that the point depends.

The account of the incident which the appellant now wishes to give in terms of his affidavit contains some details which he did not mention at the trial when he gave his evidence. But in our opinion these additional details cannot properly be described as additional evidence. What he is seeking to do is to withdraw that part of his evidence at the trial where he said that the next thing he remembered after slapping his wife's face was sitting on the edge of the bed looking down at her lying on the floor when she appeared to be lifeless. He wishes to substitute, for his evidence that he could not recall strangling her with the bandage, evidence to the effect that he put the bandage around her throat and pulled it because he wanted her to stop saying that he was not the father of the child. It is plain that the appellant was questioned closely during the trial about what occurred in the course of the incident. Accordingly this cannot be said to be a new point about which the jury did not hear his evidence. He gave his account of the incident, as far as he could recall it, at the trial. The account which he now wishes to give is a different account.

Accordingly the fact that this account contains additional elements does not mean that it is additional evidence. What it amounts to is a more complete account by the same witness of the same incident. If he were to give this fresh account at a new trial it would be for the jury to decide whether this account is to be accepted in place of his earlier evidence as more reliable. This would lead inevitably to a comparison between two statements on oath by the same witness about the events of the same incident. This is a clear indication that what we are dealing with in this case is not to be regarded as additional evidence. Additional evidence, within the meaning of s 228 (2) of the Act, is evidence which was not heard at the trial. It is evidence about some new matter which can be looked at afresh, without being drawn into a comparison with a different version given by the same witness on a matter about which he previously gave evidence.

In any event we are not satisfied that, even if this could be regarded as additional evidence, it is evidence of such significance that a verdict which was reached in ignorance of it must be regarded as a miscarriage of justice. The appellant claims that he was provoked into doing what he did by his wife's repeated allegation that he was not the father of the child. The account which he now gives therefore is of provocation by words, not by acts of violence. The traditional view is that, in order to justify a verdict of culpable homicide, the provocation must have been constituted by loss of self control due to acts of violence or perhaps by threats of violence, and not to words or insults however provocative they may be. It has been recognised that a man who finds his wife and paramour in the act of adultery and is so provoked by this that in the heat of the moment he kills them is guilty of culpable homicide. This exception was extended to cases where the husband was provoked by a confession of adultery in the paramour's presence: *HM Advocate v Hill.* In the present case however, the wife's accusation that the appellant was not the father of the child, while carrying with it the implication that she must have committed adultery, did not amount to a clear and unequivocal admission which was accepted as such by the appellant. They were insulting remarks, uttered in the course of a violent quarrel, which at first the appellant did not take seriously and then only raised doubts in his mind. It appears that it was

A because he did not wish to continue to hear these allegations, and not because he actually believed them, that he then tried to silence his wife and ultimately caused her death.

In *McKay v HM Advocate* the appellant killed his wife following a remark made by her that a child conceived during a period of cohabitation between them was not his child. But, as in the present case, no act of infidelity took place in his presence nor was any such act described by her, and it could not be said that she was caught in the act of doing something of that B kind. It was thought to be very doubtful whether an insulting remark of the kind that was made in that case, in the context of a separation and marital breakdown, could provide a sufficient basis for the plea of provocation. The same comments can be made in the present case, and in our opinion it does not fall within the exception which arises where a husband is provoked into causing death by hearing a confession of adultery. The only effect of the additions which the appellant now wishes to make to his evidence would C be to add to the acts of minor violence which he described previously the fact that he was provoked into what he did by his wife's insulting remarks. The unanimous verdict which the jury returned in this case shows that they were satisfied, on the evidence which they heard, that the appellant could not be said to have acted as he did under provocation. In our opinion the additions which the appellant now wishes to make to his account would not, given proper directions on the matter by the trial judge, have made any material D difference to them in their consideration of the appropriate verdict.

For these reasons we are not persuaded that there was a miscarriage of justice in this case. We reject this second ground of appeal because the appellant, having given an account of the incident at the trial, is seeking to do no more than give a different account of it based only on a more complete recollection of what occurred. This is not properly to be regarded as additional evidence, and in any event it is not evid-
E ence which would have been of material assistance to the jury in deciding whether this was a case of murder or of culpable homicide. We must therefore refuse this appeal.

Counsel for Appellant, Jackson, QC; Solicitors, Macbeth, Currie & Co, WS (for McCluskey Browne, Kilmarnock) — Counsel for Respondent, Macdonald, QC, A D; Solicitor, J D Lowe, Crown Agent.

F

P W F

Nordic Oil Services Ltd v Berman

G

OUTER HOUSE
LORD OSBORNE
31 MARCH 1993

Company — Directors — Negligence — Duties of care to creditor of company — Lease of aircraft by owner to company without directors' guarantees — Statutory charges incurred by company in respect of aircraft when H *directors knew that company absolutely insolvent and unable to pay its debts — Lessor paying statutory charges to prevent statutory sale of aircraft — Whether duty of care not to cause aircraft to be operated owed by directors to lessor independently of obligations of company — Insolvency Act 1986 (c 45), ss 212, 213, 214 and 215 (4).*

Reparation — Negligence — Economic loss — Duty of care — Company directors — Duties to owner of aircraft leased to company — Statutory route, navigation and airport charges incurred by company in respect of aircraft I *when directors knew that company absolutely insolvent and unable to pay its debts — Lessor paying statutory charges to prevent statutory sale of aircraft and seeking recovery of sums expended — Whether purely economic loss — Whether duty of care not to cause aircraft to be operated owed by directors to lessor independently of obligations of company — Test to be applied in determining existence and scope of duty of care in circumstances of economic loss.*

In June 1987 a company, trading as an air carrier, J leased an aircraft from its owner. The company's operation of the aircraft gave rise to route, navigation and aircraft charges payable to the Civil Aviation Authority and the British Airports Authority, which authorities held statutory powers of confiscation, detention and sale of the aircraft upon such charges remaining unpaid. The lease between the company and the owner provided inter alia, that the lessee was obliged to pay, and to indemnify the lessor in relation to, these charges and that if such charges remained K unpaid the lessor was at liberty, but not bound, to pay these and to recover from the lessee any sums so expended. On 12 February 1988 a receiver of the property of the company was appointed and on 11 and 15 February 1988 the leased aircraft was statutorily detained by the British Airports Authority and the Civil Aviation Authority respectively by reason of charges arising since October 1987 unpaid to those authorities. The owner, to free the aircraft from detention and to avoid the possibility of further detention and expropriation by a statutory sale, made payment L of these charges to the authorities. On 5 May 1988 the company entered insolvent liquidation.

The owner raised an action of damages against the directors of the company on the ground of their alleged fault, seeking recovery of the sums paid by it to the authorities. The owner averred that from 1 September 1987 the directors had known that the company had been absolutely insolvent and that there had been no reasonable prospect that the company would have been able to make payment of debts

incurred after that date, that the directors had nevertheless continued to cause the aircraft to be operated
and thereby to incur charges payable to the authorities, and that the directors had accordingly breached
duties of care owed by them to the owner, first, to
refrain from doing anything which would expose the
aircraft to the risk of confiscation, detention and
expropriation; secondly, not to cause or permit such
charges to be incurred without reasonable assurance
that the charges would be timeously paid, and thirdly,
in circumstances of the company's absolute insolvency
and inability to pay its debts, not to permit the aircraft
to be operated in and after October 1987.

On the directors' challenge to the relevancy of the
pursuer's case, the pursuer argued, first, that the loss
suffered, being to prevent the sale of the aircraft, which
sale would have been the equivalent of its physical destruction or loss, was the equivalent of or analogous to
physical loss of the aircraft and therefore could not be
characterised as purely economic loss, and the reasonable foreseeability of the loss established the defenders'
duties of care; secondly, that directors of companies
could be liable in delict to third parties, even where
there existed contractual obligations between the
company and the third party and where the director
was not a party to or guarantor of the obligations under
that contract, and that the defenders' reliance on ss 212
to 215 of the Insolvency Act 1986 as delimiting rights
against delinquent directors was misplaced; and
thirdly, that if the pursuer's loss fell to be regarded as
economic loss, the relationship of proximity between
the pursuer and the defenders necessary to constitute
the duties of care contended for was established by the
relationship of the defenders with the company, which
was in direct contractual relationship with the pursuer,
the defenders' causing the aircraft to be used in a situation in which the charges could not be paid by the
company, and the pursuer's proprietary interest in
the aircraft.

Held, (1) that the loss alleged to have been sustained
by the pursuer was not the equivalent of, or analogous
to, physical destruction or loss of the aircraft, and the
pursuer's claim was for economic loss sustained as a
result of the intervention to free the aircraft from
detention (pp 1170K and 1171B); (2) that in determining the existence and scope of a duty of care in a
context in which a claim was made for economic loss
the court had to have particular regard to the traditional categorisation of situations in which duties
might or might not have been recognised in particular
circumstances (dicta in *Leigh and Sillavan Ltd v Aliakmon Shipping Co Ltd* [1983] 1 AC 520 and *Caparo
Industries plc v Dickman* [1990] 2 AC 605, *followed*)
(p 1171J); (3) that directors were not, in the ordinary
course of matters and independently of the tortious or
delictual actings of the company, recognised as liable
in negligence to creditors of the company of which they
were directors unless there existed particular circumstances, by virtue of an agreement or representation or
other special circumstances amounting to proximity
(*Wilson v Lord Bury* (1880) 5 QBD 518; and dicta in
*Kuwait Asia Bank EC v National Mutual Life
Nominees Ltd* [1991] 1 AC 187, *followed*; *Yuille v

B & B Fisheries (Leigh) Ltd [1958] 2 Lloyd's Rep 596,
C Evans & Sons Ltd v Spritebrand Ltd [1985] 1 WLR
317, and *Mancetter Developments Ltd v Garmanson Ltd*
[1986] QB 1212, *distinguished*) (pp 1172A and E-G);
(4) that nothing amounting to particular circumstances
of the relevant kind had been averred by the pursuer,
particularly where the pursuer could have equipped
itself with contractual guarantees by the directors of
the performance by the company of its obligations
under the lease of the aircraft, but omitted to do so, and
the defenders owed no duties of the kind for which the
pursuer contended (p 1172A-C); and action *dismissed*.

Opinion, (1) that had the aircraft been sold by the
statutory authorities, resulting in the pursuer's loss of
its title to the property concerned, such loss would
have constituted purely economic loss (p 1171A-B); (2)
that it was not clear that the provisions of ss 212 to 215
of the 1986 Act were, in substance, inconsistent with
the duties contended for by the pursuer (p 1172H-J).

Observed, that there was no question of the
company having committed a tort or delict (p 1172F).

Action of damages

Nordic Oil Services Ltd raised an action of damages
against (first) Michael John Berman, (second) Stephen
Barham Carter and (third) Sir David Checketts,
KCVO, former directors of South East Air Ltd, in
respect of alleged breaches of duties of care owed by the
directors to the pursuer in relation to the operation of
a contract between South East Air Ltd and the pursuer.

The case came before the Lord Ordinary (Osborne)
on procedure roll on the defenders' plea to the relevancy of the action.

Cases referred to

Anns v Merton London Borough Council [1978] AC 728;
   [1977] 2 WLR 1024; [1977] 2 All ER 492.
Caparo Industries plc v Dickman [1990] 2 AC 605;
   [1990] 2 WLR 358; [1990] 1 All ER 568.
Elkington & Co v Hürter [1892] 2 Ch 452.
Evans (C) & Sons Ltd v Spritebrand Ltd [1985] 1 WLR
   317.
Ferguson v Wilson (1866) 2 Ch App 77.
Hedley Byrne & Co Ltd v Heller & Partners Ltd [1964]
   AC 465; [1963] 3 WLR 101; [1963] 2 All ER 575.
Horsley & Weight Ltd, Re [1982] Ch 442; [1982] 3
   WLR 431; [1982] 3 All ER 1045.
*Kuwait Asia Bank EC v National Mutual Life
   Nominees Ltd* [1991] 1 AC 187; [1990] 3 WLR
   297; [1990] 3 All ER 404.
Leigh and Sillavan Ltd v Aliakmon Shipping Co Ltd
   [1986] AC 785; [1986] 2 WLR 902; [1986] 2 All
   ER 145.
Mancetter Developments Ltd v Garmanson Ltd [1986]
   QB 1212; [1986] 2 WLR 871; [1986] 1 All ER
   449.
Murphy v Brentwood District Council [1991] 1 AC 398;
   [1990] 3 WLR 414; [1990] 2 All ER 908.
*Rainham Chemical Works Ltd v Belvedere Fish Guano
   Co Ltd* [1921] 2 AC 465.
Wilson v Lord Bury (1880) 5 QBD 518.

Wincham Shipbuilding, Boiler and Salt Co, Re (1879) 9
   ChD 322.
Yuille v B & B Fisheries (Leigh) Ltd [1958] 2 Lloyd's
   Rep 596.

Textbook referred to

Palmer, *Company Law* (25th ed), Vol 1, para 8.605.

On 31 March 1993 the Lord Ordinary *dismissed* the
action.

LORD OSBORNE.—In this action the pursuers
seek damages from the defenders of £80,053.16 on the
ground of the defenders' alleged fault. The background
to the matter is as follows. In about 1987, the pursuers
were owners of a Handley Page Dart Herald aircraft,
registered no G-ATIG. At that date, the pursuers
leased their aircraft to a company known as South East
Air Ltd. The business of that company was the carriage
of goods by air using leased and chartered aircraft. The
terms on which the aircraft was leased to that company
can be seen from the lease itself, which terms have been
adopted as part of the defenders' pleadings. The
defenders were, at all material times, directors of South
East Air Ltd. That company ceased to trade on or
about 12 February 1988, on which date a receiver was
appointed. Subsequently, by an extraordinary resolution dated 5 May 1988, that company was wound up
voluntarily. A statement of the affairs of the company
showed a deficit of £905,640.

It is a matter of admission that the operations of
South East Air Ltd, and in particular their use of the
aircraft concerned, gave rise to route and navigation
charges levied by the Civil Aviation Authority and
airport charges levied by the British Airports
Authority. If such charges were not paid timeously, the
result was that the aircraft, the use of which had given
rise to the charges, would have been at risk of confiscation, detention and sale, under the statutory powers
available to both of those bodies to enforce payment of
unpaid charges.

The particular circumstances giving rise to the pursuers' claim are described in the pursuers' averments
in cond 4. There it is averred that South East Air Ltd
had been absolutely insolvent from at least 1 September 1987, as the defenders well knew. The pursuers
aver that the defenders knew that the financial affairs
of that company were such that, after 1 September
1987, there were no reasonable prospects of the
company being able to settle debts incurred to creditors
after 1 September 1987. Notwithstanding their possession of that knowledge, it is averred that the defenders
continued to procure, cause or permit aircraft, including the aircraft G-ATIG, to be operated so as to incur
charges payable to the Civil Aviation Authority and the
British Airports Authority. The aircraft was flown
regularly for the transport of mail between Luton,
Edinburgh and Glasgow and also ad hoc throughout
the United Kingdom, including Scotland and between
the United Kingdom and Europe. The pursuers go on
to aver that, as the defenders knew or ought to have
known, from October 1987, the company failed to pay
the charges incurred in these operations. The opera-

tions continued until 11 February 1988. On that date,
the pursuers' aircraft G-ATIG was detained by the
British Airports Authority at Glasgow, in terms of s 88
of the Civil Aviation Act 1982, in respect of outstanding charges incurred by the company at Glasgow
Airport amounting to £13,988.19 and incurred at other
airports of the British Airports Authority, including
Edinburgh, amounting to £9,441.02. On 15 February
1988, the pursuers' aircraft G-ATIG was detained by
the Civil Aviation Authority at Glasgow Airport, in
terms of reg 10 of the Civil Aviation (Navigation
Services Charges) Regulations 1986, as amended, and
reg 11 of the Civil Aviation (Route Charges for Navigation Services) Regulations 1984, as amended, in
respect of outstanding charges amounting to £9,328.30
and US$43,991.96 respectively. In order to free the
said aircraft from detention and to avoid the risk of
further detention and expropriation by sale under
statutory warrants, the pursuers, as was reasonably
foreseeable by the defenders, made payment of the said
outstanding charges to the British Airports Authority
and the Civil Aviation Authority. It is averred that, as
a result, the pursuers sustained serious loss, injury and
damage. Details of the loss, injury and damage which
the pursuers claim to have sustained are set out in cond
6 and the schedule of costs, which is to be found at the
end of the closed record. It is unnecessary for me to be
concerned with the details of that matter, since no issue
arose in relation to it at the procedure roll debate.
Suffice it to say that the total of the loss and damage
which the pursuers claim is the sum sued for.

The legal basis of the pursuers' claim is to be found
in cond 5. There the pursuers aver that the defenders
owed a duty to the pursuers to take reasonable care not
to do, or to refrain from doing, anything which would
expose the pursuers' aircraft to the risk of confiscation,
detention and expropriation, to the loss, injury and
damage of the pursuers. It is averred to have been the
defenders' duty, in the exercise of due care, not to cause
or permit navigation, route and airport charges to be
incurred without reasonable assurance that the charges
would be timeously paid. It is said to have been their
duty in the circumstances from October 1987 not to
procure, cause or permit the pursuers' aircraft to be
operated. In the performance of these duties it is said
the defenders failed and so caused the pursuers' loss,
injury and damage.

It will be observed that both parties have tabled preliminary pleas. When the case came before me in procedure roll I was informed that the pursuers were
content that a proof before answer should be allowed.
However, the defenders sought dismissal of the action
on the basis of their plea in law no 2.

In support of his motion that the action should be
dismissed, counsel for the defenders pointed out that
the pursuers were seeking to have rendered liable three
of the directors of the company which had leased the
aeroplane, although, of course, the charges in respect
of which the action was brought had been incurred by
the company, of which they were directors. The lease
of the aircraft concerned had been incorporated in the
pleadings by the defenders. Curiously and objection-
ably, the pursuers did not admit the terms of the lease;

nevertheless, for the purposes of the debate they could be considered. The provisions of cl 12 of the lease were of importance in the present circumstances. Under cl 12.1 the lessee was obliged to pay a wide range of outgoings in respect of the use of the aircraft, including charges of the kind which formed the basis of the pursuers' claim in this action. Further, the lessee was to indemnify the lessor in connection with such matters. Under cl 12.2 if any of the outgoings in respect of which the lessor was entitled to an indemnity pursuant to cl 12.1 were not paid, or caused to be paid, by the lessee when due, the lessor was to be at liberty, but not to be bound, to pay the same and the lessee was required on demand forthwith to pay to the lessor any sums so expended. What was notable in the present context was that there were no contractual guarantees in the lease, or associated with it, given by the directors of the lessee, guaranteeing performance of the obligations of the lessee under the lease.

Counsel for the defenders contended that the action was irrelevant in law on two grounds. The first of these was that, in the defenders' submission, a company director was not personally liable for the contractual debts of a company of which he was a director, in respect that the creditor contracted with the company, not the director personally. The director owed duties, not to the creditor, but only to the company. It was a consequence of this state of affairs that no delictual relationship existed between a director and a creditor of the company of which he was a director, in the absence of special circumstances. No such circumstances existed here. It had never been the law that a director was personally liable to a creditor for a company's debts. This was apparent from the decision in *Wilson v Lord Bury*, and in particular the judgments of Brett LJ at pp 520 and 525-526 and Bramwell LJ at p 536. A similar view emerged from *Ferguson v Wilson*, particularly at pp 89-90 in the judgment of Cairns LJ. It followed from these decisions that, merely because directors acted in such a way that might foreseeably cause loss to persons in contract with the company, they were not liable in delict to the third party who had contracted with the company. In this connection, reference was also made to *Elkington & Co v Hürter*, particularly the judgment of Romer J at p 455. The position was that, insofar as directors owed duties in delict, they were owed to the company concerned, not to third parties, in the absence of special circumstances. While it was true that directors might require to consider the interests of the creditors of the company in the proper performance of their duties, that duty was owed to the company itself. In this connection reference was made to *Re Wincham Shipbuilding, Boiler and Salt Co*, particularly to the judgment of Jessel MR at p 328.

Consideration of the more modern law led to similar conclusions. This was apparent from *Re Horsley & Weight Ltd* and the judgment of Buckley LJ at p 453. This position was affirmed in the Privy Council case of *Kuwait Asia Bank EC v National Mutual Life Nominees Ltd* in the advice of the Council at [1991] AC, pp 217-219. In this passage it was recognised that, while directors were not liable as such to the creditors of a company, a director might by agreement or representation assume a special duty to a creditor of the company. A director might accept or assume a duty of care in supplying information to a creditor analogous to the duty described by the House of Lords in *Hedley Byrne & Co Ltd v Heller and Partners Ltd*. In the present pleadings, there were no averments by the pursuers of any special circumstances, such as an agreement or representation by the defenders, which could conceivably have given rise to liability on their part. In the absence of such averments, there was no basis for such a liability. It was not sufficient that the actions of a director might foreseeably involve loss to a creditor. The general law relating to foreseeability and proximity imposing liability did not apply as between directors of companies and creditors of the company. The reason for that was to avoid preference being conferred on one creditor of a company as opposed to the others.

It was instructive to consider the legislation which related to these matters. Under s 212 of the Insolvency Act 1986, a provision existed for a summary remedy against, among others, delinquent directors. Under subs (1) thereof, it was enacted that the section applied if, in the course of the winding up of a company, it appeared that a person who was or had been an officer of the company had been guilty of any misfeasance or breach of any fiduciary or other duty in relation to the company. Under subs (3), the court was empowered, on the application of the official receiver, or the liquidator, or of any creditor or contributory, to examine the conduct of the person referred to in subs (1) and compel him to contribute such sum to the company's assets by way of compensation in respect of the misfeasance or breach of fiduciary or other duty as the court thought just.

Under s 213 (1) of the Act of 1986, it was enacted that, if in the course of the winding up of a company it appeared that any business of the company had been carried on with intent to defraud creditors of the company or creditors of any other person, or for any fraudulent purpose, the provisions of subs (2) of the section were to have effect. Subsection (2) provided that the court, on the application of the liquidator, might declare that any persons who were knowingly parties to the carrying on of business in the manner mentioned in subs (1) were to be liable to make such contribution, if any, to the company's assets as the court might think proper.

Under s 214 of the same Act, provision was made against wrongful trading. Subsection (1) of that section provided that, if in the course of the winding up of a company it appeared that subs (2) of the section applied in relation to a person who was or had been a director of the company, the court, on the application of the liquidator, might declare that that person was to be liable to make such contribution, if any, to the company's assets as the court thought proper. Under subs (2) it was provided that that subsection applied in relation to a person if (a) the company had gone into insolvent liquidation, (b) at some time before the commencement of the winding up of the company, that person knew or ought to have concluded that there was no reasonable prospect that the company would avoid

going into insolvent liquidation, and (c) that person
was a director of the company at that time.

Under s 215 (4) of the Act of 1986, it was provided
that, where the court made a declaration under either
s 213 or 214 in relation to a person who was a creditor
of the company, it could direct that the whole or any
part of any debt owed by the company to that person
and any interest thereon should rank in priority after
all other debts owed by the company and after any
interest on those debts.

These provisions provided what might be called a
statutory code to deal with situations where a director
had been guilty of a breach of duty. What emerged
from these provisions was that Parliament had
intended, in the different circumstances described, that
persons who had behaved wrongfully should make contributions to the assets of the company, not to any third
party who might have suffered loss in consequence of
the objectionable conduct. The defenders submitted
that this statutory scheme could not co-exist with the
duty contended for by the pursuers in this case. That
duty would, if it existed, have the effect of giving a
preference to a particular creditor. That was inconsistent with the object of the statutory scheme.

In advancing his next main submission, counsel for
the defenders proceeded to examine the pursuers'
claim in the light of the general law relating to the
recovery of economic loss. He pointed out that the
claim was one for economic loss, based on the allegedly
negligent performance of duties said to have been
incumbent upon the defenders as directors. The loss
sustained by the pursuers was the amount of money
which they had to pay to certain third parties to secure
the release of the aircraft. Furthermore, it was important to appreciate that this was not a case involving
negligent misstatements or statements leading to
economic loss. Counsel for the defenders began by
referring to certain cases, which were concerned with
economic loss outside the area of negligent misstatement. The first of these was *Leigh and Sillavan Ltd
v Aliakmon Shipping Co Ltd*, particularly the speech of
Lord Brandon at [1986] AC, p 815. There, his Lordship made clear that the well known passage in the
speech of Lord Wilberforce in *Anns v Merton London
Borough Council* at pp 751-752 was not intended to and
did not provide a universally applicable test of the
existence and scope of a duty of care in the law of negligence. Furthermore, Lord Wilberforce had been
dealing in that case with the approach to the questions
of the existence and scope of a duty of care in a novel
type of factual situation which was not analogous to
any factual situation in which the existence of such a
duty had already been held to exist. He had not been
suggesting that the same approach should be adopted
to the existence of a duty of care in a factual situation
in which the existence of such a duty had repeatedly
been denied.

That particular passage was of importance in the
present context, since, from an early stage, courts had
held that directors did not owe duties of the kind contended for here. Counsel for the defenders also relied
upon *Murphy v Brentwood District Council*, a decision
of the House of Lords in which the case of *Anns v*
Merton London Borough Council was departed from.
Great care required to be exercised in extending duties
of care beyond their traditional scope. If the causing of
economic loss was to be categorised as wrongful, it was
necessary to find some factor in the situation beyond
the mere occurrence of the loss and the fact that its
occurrence could be foreseen. In *Caparo Industries plc
v Dickman* the House of Lords declared that, whilst
recognising the importance of the underlying general
principles common to the whole field of negligence, the
law had now moved in the direction of attaching
greater significance to the more traditional categorisation of distinct and recognisable situations as guides to
the existence, the scope and the limits of the varied
duties of care which the law imposed. It had now to be
accepted that there was no simple formula or touch-
stone to which recourse could be had in order to
provide in every case a ready answer to the questions
whether, given certain facts, the law would or would
not impose liability for negligence or, in cases where
such liability could be shown to exist, determine the
extent of that liability. A return to the traditional
categorisation of cases was infinitely preferable to
recourse to somewhat wide generalisations which left
their practical applications matters of difficulty and
uncertainty. Insofar as general concepts could be relied
upon, before a duty could come into being, it was
necessary to identify a relationship involving proximity
as well as foreseeability. Applying this traditional
approach, it was submitted that the existence of a duty
of care between a director and an individual creditor of
the company had been negatived so much in the past
that, in the absence of special circumstances, its existence could not now be affirmed. Further, the implications of a decision in the pursuers' favour would be
serious and absurd. If directors were liable to be sued
by the creditors of companies, the position of so called
"company doctors" would be untenable.

In his third main submission, counsel for the
defenders went on to argue that the pursuers' averments were unspecific and defective. The averment in
cond 4 at p 9D-E of the closed record, as further
amended, was seriously lacking in specification. In
relation to financial affairs of the company after 1
September 1987, there was a bald averment of absolute
insolvency. However, there were no references to
accounts or any specific material. It had to be recognised that these averments were made against the background of the defenders' averment to the effect that the
company continued to pay rental on the aircraft up to
the end of March 1988.

In all these circumstances, the action ought to be dismissed by the sustaining of the defenders' second plea
in law. If that course were not to be followed and a
proof before answer were to be allowed, plea in law no
1 for the defenders had to be reserved.

Counsel for the pursuers submitted that a proof
before answer should be allowed. It was necessary to
examine carefully the nature of the pursuers' claim. As
appeared from the averments at p 10D-E of the closed
record, as further amended, the pursuers were seeking
to recover payments made by them to the British Airports Authority and the Civil Aviation Authority to

A prevent a sale of the aircraft at their instance in respect of the non-payment by the hiring company of the charges imposed by these authorities. There was no dubiety about the fact that these authorities possessed powers under which they could validly sell an aircraft in the event of charges made by them in respect of its operation remaining unpaid. The precise nature of the duty contended for by the pursuers was set out in cond 5. The pursuers' claim flowed from a duty, which it was said the pursuers had, to minimise their loss by preventing the sale of the aircraft. Had the sale of the aircraft taken place, that would have been equivalent to

B its physical destruction. Accordingly, argued counsel for the pursuers, the authorities relied upon by the defenders in relation to duties of care in relation to economic loss were not applicable to the present circumstances. The averments of the pursuers at p 9D-E of the closed record, as further amended, were important. In the knowledge of the company's hopeless financial situation, the defenders had continued the operation of the aircraft and the consequent incurring of charges to the authorities mentioned.

C   Turning to the legal background to the case, counsel for the pursuers submitted that it was quite clear that directors of companies could be liable in tort to third parties. In this connection reference was made to Palmer, *Company Law*, Vol 1, para 8.605 and to the case of *C Evans & Sons Ltd v Spritebrand Ltd*, particularly at pp 323, 324 and 326. In this connection reference was also made to *Yuille v B & B Fisheries (Leigh) Ltd* at pp 597 and 617-619. These cases showed that a director could not escape liability for negligence if he

D was involved in the tort, even as a director. Reliance was also placed upon *Mancetter Developments Ltd v Garmanson Ltd.* In that case the second defendant was held to be liable to a third party because he had directed and procured the commission of the tort of waste by the first defendant to which certain buildings had been leased. The situation was that the second defendant had not been a party to the lease nor a guarantor of the obligations under it. The damage concerned had been of a physical nature. Despite the existence of con-

E tractual obligations between the company involved and the plaintiff, the case demonstrated that a director could be liable for tort.

        Counsel for the pursuers argued that the loss claimed here was not pure economic loss, but was money expended to prevent the occurrence of a valid sale of the aircraft to a third party by the statutory authorities. That was equivalent to physical loss of the aircraft. In this connection it was instructive to note that, in terms of cl 13.1. (i) the seizure of the aircraft by the statutory

F authorities constituted a "termination event", the consequence of which was, in terms of cl 13.2. (1) (b), that the lessee's possession of the aircraft could be terminated at the instance of the lessor.

        If it was recognised that a company director might be liable for negligence to a third party, it was necessary to consider whether, in the particular circumstances of this case, a duty of care existed owed by the defenders to the pursuers. In this connection the appropriate test was to be found in *Caparo Industries plc v Dickman.* As appeared from the speech of Lord Bridge, what

G emerged was that, in addition to the foreseeability of damage, necessary ingredients in any situation giving rise to a duty of care were that there should exist between the party owing the duty and the party to whom it was owed a relationship categorised by the law as one of "proximity" or "neighbourhood" and that the situation should be one in which the court considered it fair, just and reasonable that the law should impose a duty of given scope upon the one party for the benefit of the other. In the end, the matter appeared to be one for the sound exercise of a judicial discretion. In relation to foreseeability, there was no problem for

H the pursuers in the present case, since it was foreseeable that they would step in to prevent a sale of the aircraft. If the seizure of the aircraft could properly be regarded as equivalent to its physical destruction, then the pursuers required nothing beyond reasonable foreseeability to establish the existence of a duty. That was evident from the speech of Lord Oliver in *Murphy v Brentwood District Council.* In that case he said that the infliction of physical injury to the person or property of another universally required to be justified. How-

I ever, on the assumption that the pursuers' loss could not be seen as equivalent to the consequences of physical damage to or destruction of the aircraft, it was necessary to demonstrate a relationship of proximity between the defenders and the pursuers. The circumstances of the present case which were important in demonstrating the existence of proximity were: (1) the defenders were directors of the company which was in a direct contractual relationship with the pursuers; (2) the defenders knowingly caused the aircraft to be used in a situation in which the company was absolutely

J insolvent and to incur charges which could not be paid by the company; and (3) the pursuers had a proprietary interest in the aircraft which was thus misused. These factors did create a relationship of proximity between the defenders and the pursuers sufficient to justify the court holding that a duty was owed by the defenders to the pursuers.

        The case of *Kuwait Asia Bank EC v National Mutual Life Nominees Ltd* dealt with duties owed to creditors. Here the issue was a duty owed to a victim of delict.

K   Reliance had been placed by the defenders on legislation, particularly the provisions of the Insolvency Act 1986. That legislation was not relevant in the circumstances of the present case. If the pursuers' claim was successful, the result would be that the assets of the defenders, the directors of the company, would be diminished. However, the affirmation of a duty to the pursuers on the part of the directors would not affect the assets of the company.

L   Turning to the criticisms made of the specification of the pursuers' averments, it was submitted that the specification of the position set out in cond 4 was as good as the pursuers could make it. The background was that the pursuers had endeavoured to recover documents from the liquidator of the company showing or tending to show the knowledge of the directors of the company's financial position at the material time, as appeared from call 1 (a) and (b) of no 19 of process. The motion for a commission and diligence had been opposed. It was understood by the pursuers

A at that stage that the defenders were not intending to take any point relating to the specification of the pursuers' averments. In these circumstances such criticism should not now be entertained by the court.

In reply, counsel for the defenders argued that the submissions of the pursuers were based upon a misunderstanding of certain of the authorities cited by them. Plainly, if a company committed a delict or tort, a director of the company who had procured or instructed the commission of that delict or tort might be liable along with the company. However, it was a

B precondition of such liability that there should be a delict or tort by the company. There was no such wrong here. At best for the pursuers, there was a breach of contract on the part of the company under the lease of the aircraft. In any event, it was a misconception on the part of the pursuers to suppose that it was the defenders who had used the aircraft in the circumstances described. It was the company which had used the aircraft as lessees of it. There were no averments showing the directors' involvement.

C The case of *Mancetter Developments Ltd v Garmanson Ltd*, relied upon by the pursuers, involved a situation very different from the present case. In *Mancetter*, the court was concerned with responsibility for physical damage to a building. The second defendant was held liable to the plaintiff because he had directed and procured the company, the first defendant, to commit the tort. That was a wholly different situation from the present one. There was no necessary connection between anything done by the company, or

D indeed the defenders, and the pursuers' loss. The pursuers' loss could not be regarded as in any way equivalent to the physical damage with which that case was concerned. In the present case, the pursuers' averments disclosed no tort or delict known to the law. If the pursuers' submissions were correct, it would follow that *Elkington v Hürter* and *Kuwait Asia Bank EC v National Mutual Life Nominees Ltd* were wrongly decided. The cases relied upon by the pursuers were concerned with directors' involvement in the delict of companies. It was perfectly understood that if indi-

E viduals procured the commission of a wrongful act by a company, they would be liable to one who suffered loss as a consequence along with the company. In this connection reference was made to *Rainham Chemical Works Ltd v Belvedere Fish Guano Co Ltd*. The present situation was completely different; the court was considering the position of directors of a company which had breached a contract.

Counsel for the pursuers had attempted to suggest that the lease of the aircraft had been terminated by the

F actions of the company. That was not so, as appeared from cl 13.2. (1) (b) thereof. There was no ipso facto termination of the lease brought about by the detention of the aircraft. In any event, this point, emphasised by the pursuers, did not lead anywhere. The pursuers in the present case were in no better position than the plaintiff in *Wilson v Lord Bury* which had been approved in the case of *Kuwait Asia Bank EC v National Mutual Life Nominees Ltd*.

In reply, counsel for the pursuers recognised that he was not in a position to cite any case which directly

supported the pursuers' propositions. However, it was

G clear that contractual and delictual obligations could co-exist. In certain circumstances, directors could have duties towards third parties. The particular role of the directors in the material facts of this case was a matter for proof.

It was a prominent part of the pursuers' argument in this case that the loss which they claim was the equivalent of, or, at least, analogous to the physical destruction of or loss of the aircraft. This argument was based upon the fact that both the Civil Aviation Authority and the British Airports Authority, whose charges

H were involved, had statutory powers under which they could have sold the aircraft which was the subject of the lease to the company, in the event of their charges remaining unpaid. Such a sale would, of course, have had the effect of permanently depriving the pursuers of their property in the aircraft. The significance attaching to the pursuers' desiderated characterisation of their loss in this way is not hard to appreciate. The cases of *Yuille v B & B Fisheries (Leigh) Ltd* and *Man-*

I *cetter Developments Ltd v Garmanson Ltd* involved personal injuries and physical damage to property respectively. Further, in *Murphy v Brentwood District Council*, Lord Oliver of Aylmerton emphasised the important distinction between the infliction of physical injury to the person or property of another and the causing of economic loss, so far as the matter of the determination of the existence of a duty of care was concerned. At [1991] 1 AC, p 487 he said this: "The infliction of physical injury to the person or property of another universally requires to be justified. The

J causing of economic loss does not. If it is to be characterised as wrongful it is necessary to find some factor beyond the mere occurrence of the loss and the fact that its occurrence could be foreseen. Thus the categorisation of damage as economic serves at least the useful purpose of indicating that something more is required and it is one of the unfortunate features of *Anns* that it resulted initially in this essential distinction being lost sight of."

I have reached the conclusion that, in the circum-

K stances of this case, it would be quite wrong for me to treat the loss alleged to have been sustained by the pursuers as the equivalent of, or analogous to, the physical destruction or loss of the aircraft. The reality disclosed in the pursuers' averments is that there was no question of any physical jeopardy to the aircraft. What occurred was that on 11 February 1988 the pursuers' aircraft was detained by the British Airports Authority at Glasgow in terms of the Civil Aviation Act 1982, s 88, in respect of outstanding charges incurred by the

L company at Glasgow Airport. Further, on 15 February 1988 the aircraft was detained by the Civil Aviation Authority at Glasgow Airport in terms of the Civil Aviation (Navigation Services Charges) Regulations 1986, as amended, reg 10, and the Civil Aviation (Route Charges for Navigation Services) Regulations 1984, as amended, reg 11 in respect of outstanding charges. In order to free the aircraft from detention and to avoid the risk of further detention and expropriation by sale under statutory warrant, the pursuers made payment of the outstanding charges involved. I take it from the pursuers' averments that, as a result of their payment of these charges, they recovered possession of their aeroplane in an intact condition. Further, in my opinion, nothing is said to have happened here which could be regarded as the equivalent of physical destruction or damage. Even if the aircraft had been sold by the statutory authorities under their statutory powers, that would not involve the infliction of physical damage on the pursuers' property. The result would have been the pursuers' loss of their title to the property concerned. In my opinion, that would have constituted economic loss. However, no such sale ever took place, on account of the pursuers' intervention in paying the outstanding charges. In my opinion, the pursuers are claiming economic loss sustained as a result of their intervention in the situation outlined. In these circumstances, in my view, the cases of *Yuille v B & B Fisheries (Leigh) Ltd* and *Mancetter Developments Ltd v Garmanson Ltd* are of no assistance.

What I propose now to do is to examine the authorities cited to me relating to, first, the general law regarding the recovery of economic loss negligently caused, and, secondly, the position of company directors in particular, with a view to determining whether the duty relied upon by the pursuers is one which I can recognise. It is, of course, the case that, in recent years, the scope and nature of duties of care to avoid the causing of economic loss have been extensively discussed at the highest judicial level. It appears to me to be quite inappropriate for me to attempt to trace in detail the history of this debate. I consider that, for my purposes, it is sufficient if I attempt to describe the position as it now stands. In that connection, I recognise that the authority of *Anns* was, in the first instance, substantially limited by what was said in *Leigh and Sillavan Ltd v Aliakmon Ltd*, in particular by Lord Brandon of Oakbrook at [1986] AC, p 815. There he declared, first, that the speech of Lord Wilberforce in *Anns* could not have been intended to provide a universally applicable test of the existence and scope of a duty of care in the law of negligence. Secondly, he considered that Lord Wilberforce had been dealing with "the approach to the questions of the existence and scope of a duty of care in a novel type of factual situation which was not analogous to any factual situation in which the existence of such a duty had already been held to exist. He was not, as I understand the passage, suggesting that the same approach should be adopted to the existence of a duty of care in a factual situation in which the existence of such a duty had repeatedly been held not to exist".

A further milestone in the judicial retreat from an attempt to devise a simple formula, to which recourse could be had in all cases in order to provide a ready answer to the question whether, given certain facts, the law will or will not impose liability for negligence, or in cases where such liability can be shown to exist, determine the extent of that liability, can be found in *Caparo Industries plc v Dickman*. The approach taken by the House of Lords in that case appears to me to be epitomised by the following passage in the speech of Lord Bridge of Harwich at [1990] 2 AC, pp 617-618:

"What emerges is that, in addition to the foreseeability of damage, necessary ingredients in any situation giving rise to a duty of care are that there should exist between the party owing the duty and the party to whom it is owed a relationship characterised by the law as one of 'proximity' or 'neighbourhood' and that the situation should be one in which the court considers it fair, just and reasonable that the law should impose a duty of a given scope upon the one party for the benefit of the other. But it is implicit in the passages referred to that the concepts of proximity and fairness embodied in these additional ingredients are not susceptible to any such precise definition as would be necessary to give them utility as practical tests, but amount in effect to little more than convenient labels to attach to the features of different specific situations which, on a detailed examination of all the circumstances, the law recognises pragmatically as giving rise to a duty of care of a given scope. Whilst recognising, of course, the importance of the underlying general principles common to the whole field of negligence, I think the law has now moved in the direction of attaching greater significance to the more traditional categorisation of distinct and recognisable situations as guides to the existence, the scope and the limits of the varied duties of care which the law imposes."

So far as the argument before me was concerned, the last word was extracted from *Murphy v Brentwood District Council*, in which the House of Lords departed from their previous decision in *Anns v Merton London Borough Council*. In the light of the foregoing cases, it appears to me that, in determining the existence and scope of a duty of care in a context in which a claim is made for economic loss, the court must have particular regard to the traditional categorisation of situations in which duties may or may not have been recognised in particular circumstances. It is to that and, in particular, to the category of previous authorities dealing with the duties of directors of companies to which I now turn.

I was referred to a number of cases concerned in different ways with the issue of duties which might or might not be owed by company directors to third parties. Many of these are conveniently summarised in *Kuwait Asia Bank EC v National Mutual Life Nominees Ltd*, in the advice of the Privy Council, delivered by Lord Lowry at [1991] 1 AC, pp 217-219. Prominent among the cases there reviewed was *Wilson v Lord Bury*, a case which appears to me to be of particular relevance in the present context. In that case, the plaintiff had a contract with a company relating to his investment upon a mortgage. The company had borrowed £1,000 from the plaintiff and covenanted to secure payment by assigning a mortgage to him. The mortgage was paid off and the redemption money paid into the funds of the company, which then became insolvent. The plaintiff sued the directors of the company alleging gross negligence on their part. The claim failed. This decision was quoted with approval by Lord Lowry at pp 218-219. The Privy Council there recognised that directors were not liable as such to creditors of the company of which they were directors. However, a director might, by agreement or

representation, assume a special duty to a creditor of
A his company. It appears to me from Lord Lowry's
review of the authorities and his observations in the
case itself that directors are not, in the ordinary course
of matters, liable to creditors of the company of which
they are directors in negligence. However, in particular
circumstances they may be so, by virtue of an agreement or representation, or other special circumstances
amounting to proximity in the sense mentioned. In my
view, nothing averred by the pursuers here amounts to
special circumstances of the relevant kind. I do not see
B why it should be said that it would be "fair, just and
reasonable" for the court to recognise the duties contended for here, in a situation in which the pursuers
could easily have equipped themselves with contractual guarantees by the defenders of the performance by the company of its obligations under the lease
of the aircraft, but omitted to do so and now seek, by
other means, to obviate the practical consequences of
that omission. Accordingly, having regard to the law
set out in *Wilson v Lord Bury* and *Kuwait Asia Bank*
C *EC v National Mutual Life Nominees Ltd*, and to the
current approach to the recognition of duties of care
where economic loss is involved, which I have already
summarised, all of which, in my opinion, may
properly be regarded as representing the law of Scotland, I reach the conclusion that the defenders in this
case owed no duties of the kind for which the pursuers
contend. I therefore hold that the pursuers' case
against the defenders is irrelevant in law.

D   I have already expressed my view in relation to the
cases of *Yuille v B & B Fisheries (Leigh) Ltd* and
Mancetter Developments Ltd v Garmanson Ltd, relied
upon by the pursuers. It is right that I should also
express my comments in the present context on
C Evans & Sons Ltd v Spritebrand Ltd, relied upon by
the pursuers. In that case, which involved claims
under the Copyright Act 1956, it was held that where
a company director was sought to be made liable for
the tortious acts of his company, the extent of his
E personal involvement in the company's tort had to be
carefully examined; but that where the director had
authorised, directed and procured the acts complained
of it was not an essential precondition of his liability
that he knew that the acts thus authorised were
tortious, or was reckless as to whether or not they were
likely to be tortious, unless the primary tortfeasor's
state of mind or knowledge was an essential ingredient
of the particular tort alleged. In my opinion, that case
does not assist the pursuers in the present circumstances. As I understand it, there was no challenge to
F the legal relevance of the claim made under the copyright legislation against the company. The issue with
which the report is concerned related to the directors'
liability in respect of the tortious acts of the company.
In the present case, there is no question of the
company having committed a tort or delict. The issue
which appears to me to be raised here is whether,
independently of the actings of the company, the
defenders, as directors, owe duties of care to the
pursuers. In my opinion, that is an entirely different
issue from the one with which the case referred to

was concerned. The same comments may be made, in
my opinion, in relation to *Yuille v B & B Fisheries*   G
(Leigh) Ltd and *Mancetter Developments Ltd v Garmanson Ltd*.

As I have narrated, counsel for the defenders
addressed to me arguments based upon the provisions
of the Insolvency Act 1986 and in particular ss 212 to
215 thereof. It is appropriate that I should briefly
express my views in relation to that argument. It was
represented that these sections were part of a statutory
code defining the responsibility of directors and other
company officers towards a company in an insolvency   H
situation. It was further suggested that the provisions
of this statutory scheme were, in substance, inconsistent with the duties contended for by the pursuers.
In my opinion, it is not clear that that is the position.
Section 212 of the Act of 1986 was represented to be
of particular significance in this context. That section
speaks of a director's "breach of any fiduciary or other
duty in relation to the company". The scheme of this
section, in particular, involves the opportunity for the
court to compel directors among others to contribute   I
such sum to the company's assets by way of compensation in respect of a breach of duty as the court thinks
just. If the words "or other duty" were to embrace
duties of the kind contended for by the pursuers here,
I recognise force in the defenders' argument. However, in my opinion, it is far from clear that such is the
position. It appears to me that the words "other duty
in relation to the company" are more likely to be a
reference to duties owed by directors towards the
company itself, rather than to third parties such as   J
persons contracting with the company. Accordingly I
do not find these provisions of particular assistance
and do not rely upon them in reaching a decision in
the present case.

In the whole circumstances and for the reasons
which I have given, I shall sustain plea in law no 2 for
the defenders and dismiss the action.

———————————

Counsel for Pursuer, Burns, QC, P W Ferguson; Soli-   K
citors, Henderson & Jackson, WS — Counsel for
Defenders, Scott, QC; Solicitors, Gillespie Macandrew,
WS.

M L B F

L

Pollock v Secretary of State for Scotland

OUTER HOUSE

LORD CAMERON OF LOCHBROOM

6 AUGUST 1992

Town and country planning — Planning permission — Application for planning permission — No notification to conterminous proprietor — Grant of planning permission by reporter — Expiry of time limit for appeal to court — Competency of application for review of decision — Whether decision void or voidable — Town and Country Planning (Scotland) Act 1972 (c 52), ss 231 and 233.

Administrative law — Judicial review — Competency — Town and country planning — Application for planning permission requiring to be served on conterminous proprietor — Application not so served — Grant of planning permission by reporter — Expiry of time limit for appeal to court — Effect of statutory time limit — Town and Country Planning (Scotland) Act 1972 (c 52), ss 231 and 233.

Section 231 (1) of the Town and Country Planning (Scotland) Act 1972 provides that subject to the following provisions, the validity inter alia of a decision of the Secretary of State on appeal "shall not be questioned in any legal proceedings whatsoever". Section 231 (4) preserves the jurisdiction of the courts in respect of any refusal or failure on the part of the Secretary of State to take certain actions. Section 233 (1) (b) allows an application to the courts within six weeks of an action being taken if the basis of the application is that the action is not within the powers of the Act or that a relevant requirement has not been complied with.

The petitioners were owners of land adjacent to a quarry. An application in respect of planning permission for tipping waste in the quarry was made to the local authority. When the local authority failed to determine the application within the prescribed time the applicants appealed to the Secretary of State for Scotland, who appointed a reporter to inquire into the matter. After an agreement had been reached between the local authority and the owners of the quarry, regulating the management of the waste disposal site, the reporter issued a formal decision sustaining the appeal. The petitioners had a notifiable interest in the application, but they received no notice of the application or the inquiry. There was no suggestion of bad faith on the part of the applicants, but the result was that the petitioners had no opportunity to make objections to the proposals or to challenge judicially the decision of the reporter in terms of the statutory provisions. The petitioners raised proceedings for judicial review, seeking reduction of the reporter's decision.

The petitioners argued that they had a legitimate expectation to have their objections heard; that there was no reason why the existence of a statutory right of appeal should preclude the use of judicial review; that the courts should be slow to exclude a common law remedy where exceptional circumstances excused the failure to use the statutory procedures; that a miscarriage of justice might occur; that in the circumstances of the case the appeal proceedings had been ultra vires; and that no distinction could be made between statutory provisions which ousted the supervisory role of the court absolutely and those which sought to place a time limit on the court's jurisdiction. The respondents argued that the lack of fault on the part of the petitioners was not a legitimate consideration in the construction of the statutory provisions; that the interests of individuals had to be subordinated to the greater public interest; that the court's supervisory jurisdiction could only be exercised within the statutory time limit which the court had no power or discretion to extend; that this power also included actions which were potentially null as a result of a procedural irregularity; and that the effect of a time limited ouster clause would be to exclude the court from exercising its supervisory jurisdiction after the time allowed had expired.

Held, (1) that where the parties concerned had acted in good faith, the decision of the reporter was not void but at best voidable (p 1177G); (2) that the failure to receive notice did not take the petitioners outwith the scheme of the statutory provisions so as to enable them to proceed by way of judicial review at common law (pp 1180A-B and F-I); (3) that the statutory time limit did not oust but only limited the jurisdiction of the court, and the meaning of the provisions was clearly to bar any challenge, from whatever source it might come, after the expiry of the time limit (pp 1181I-J and 1181L-1182A); and petition *dismissed*.

Doubted, (1) whether in the context of administrative law there was a distinction between a void and a voidable order, and (2) whether, if the court retained a discretion as to whether or not to strike down an action, the action complained of could be regarded as void ab initio (p 1182H-I).

Lochore v Moray District Council, 1992 SLT 16; *McCowan v Secretary of State for Scotland,* 1972 SLT 163; *McDaid v Clydebank District Council,* 1984 SLT 162; and *Martin v Bearsden and Milngavie District Council,* 1987 SLT 300, *distinguished.*

Petition for judicial review

John James Pollock and another, the owners of land adjoining Pilmuir landfill site, Newton Mearns, presented a petition for judicial review of a decision by a reporter, appointed by the Secretary of State for Scotland, taken on 9 April 1991 to sustain an appeal by Wimpey Waste Management Ltd which sought alteration of conditions in planning permission relating to the disposal of waste on the site.

A first hearing took place before the Lord Ordinary (Lord Cameron of Lochbroom).

Statutory provisions

The Town and Country Planning (Scotland) Act 1972 provides:

"231.—(1) Except as provided by the following pro-

visions of this Part of this Act, the validity of—. . .
(e) any such action on the part of the Secretary of State
as is mentioned in subsection (3) of this section, shall
not be questioned in any legal proceedings whatsoever. . . .

"(3) The action referred to in subsection (1) (e) of
this section is action on the part of the Secretary of
State of any of the following descriptions, that is to say
— . . . (b) any decision of the Secretary of State on an
appeal under section 33 of this Act. . . .

"(4) Nothing in this section shall affect the exercise
of any jurisdiction of any court in respect of any
refusal or failure on the part of the Secretary of State
to take any such action as is mentioned in subsection
(3) of this section. . . .

"233.—(1) If any person — . . . (b) is aggrieved by
any action on the part of the Secretary of State to
which this section applies and desires to question the
validity of that action, on the grounds that the action
is not within the powers of this Act, or that any of the
relevant requirements have not been complied with in
relation to that action, he may, within six weeks from
the date on which the order is confirmed or the action
is taken, as the case may be, make an application to the
Court of Session under this section. . . .

"(3) This section applies to any such order as is
mentioned in subsection (2) of section 231 of this Act
(other than an order under section 203 (1) (a) of this
Act) and to any such action on the part of the Secretary
of State as is mentioned in subsection (3) of the said
section 231.

"(4) On any application under this section the Court
of Session — (a) may by interim order suspend the
operation of the order or action, the validity whereof
is questioned by the application, until the final determination of the proceedings; (b) if satisfied that the
order or action in question is not within the powers of
this Act, or that the interests of the applicant have
been substantially prejudiced by a failure to comply
with any of the relevant requirements in relation
thereto, may quash that order or action: Provided that
paragraph (a) of this subsection shall not apply to
applications questioning the validity of tree preservation orders. . . .

"(7) In this section 'the relevant requirements', in
relation to any order or action to which this section
applies, means any requirements of this Act or of the
Tribunals and Inquiries Act 1971 (or any enactment
replaced thereby), or of any order, regulations or rules
made under this Act or under that Act (or any such
enactment), which are applicable to that order or
action, and any reference to the authority directly concerned with any order or action to which this section
applies is a reference to the planning authority, and,
in relation to any such decision as is mentioned in
section 231 (3) (i) or (j) of this Act, being a decision
confirming the notice in question subject to the substitution of another local authority or statutory undertakers for the planning authority, shall be construed as
including a reference to that other local authority or
those statutory undertakers."

Cases referred to

Accountant in Bankruptcy v Allans of Gillock Ltd;
Allans of Gillock Ltd v Accountant in Bankruptcy,
1991 SLT 765.
Adair v David Colville & Sons Ltd, 1926 SLT 590;
1926 SC (HL) 51.
Anisminic Ltd v Foreign Compensation Commission
[1969] 2 AC 147; [1969] 2 WLR 163; [1969] 1
All ER 208.
Ashley v Magistrates of Rothesay (1873) 11 M 708; affd
(1874) 1 R (HL) 14.
Bromsgrove District Council v Secretary of State for the
Environment (1991) 62 P & CR 29.
Davy v Spelthorne Borough Council [1984] AC 262;
[1983] 3 WLR 742; [1983] 3 All ER 278.
Griffiths v Secretary of State for the Environment
[1983] 2 AC 51; [1983] 2 WLR 172; [1983] 1 All
ER 439.
Hamilton v Secretary of State for Scotland, 1972 SLT
233; 1972 SC 72.
Holmes & Son v Secretary of State for Scotland, 1965
SLT 41; 1965 SC 1.
Lochore v Moray District Council, 1992 SLT 16.
McCowan v Secretary of State for Scotland, 1972 SLT
163; 1972 SC 93.
McDaid v Clydebank District Council, 1984 SLT 162;
(sub nom *Gill v Clydebank District Council*) 1983
SC 76.
Main v Swansea City Council (1985) 49 P & CR 26;
[1985] JPL 558.
Martin v Bearsden and Milngavie District Council,
1987 SLT 300.
Moss' Empires Ltd v Assessor for Glasgow (sub nom
Moss' Empires Ltd v Walker, 1916 1 SLT 103),
1917 SC (HL) 1.
Philip v Reid, 1927 SLT 168; 1927 SC 224.
R v Cornwall County Council, ex p Huntington [1992]
3 All ER 566.
R v Greenwich London Borough Council, ex p Patel
(1985) 51 P & CR 282; [1985] JPL 851.
R v Secretary of State for the Environment, ex p Kent
[1990] JPL 124.
R v Secretary of State for the Environment, ex p Ostler
[1977] QB 122; [1976] 3 WLR 288; [1976] 3 All
ER 90.
Racal Communications Ltd, Re [1981] AC 374; [1980]
3 WLR 181; [1980] 2 All ER 634.
Routh v Reading Corporation, Bar Library Transcript
No 427, 1970.
Smith v East Elloe Rural District Council [1956] AC
736; [1956] 2 WLR 888; [1956] 1 All ER 855.
Tarmac Econowaste Ltd v Assessor for Lothian Region,
1991 SLT 77.
West v Secretary of State for Scotland, 1992 SLT 636.

Textbooks referred to

Craies, *Statute Law* (7th ed), p 141.
Wade, *Administrative Law* (6th ed), pp 633 and 737.

On 6 August 1992 the Lord Ordinary *dismissed* the
petition.

LORD CAMERON OF LOCHBROOM.—This
petition for judicial review, as presently adjusted, sets
out that the petitioners are owners of land adjoining

A Pilmuir landfill site, Newton Mearns, which I will refer to as Pilmuir quarry. Pilmuir quarry lies within the area of Eastwood District Council. In 1983 the district council granted planning permission, subject to conditions, for the tipping of waste at Pilmuir quarry to Tilcon Ltd.

By application dated 16 December 1987, Wimpey Waste Management Ltd, whom I will call WWM, applied to the district council to amend certain conditions in the existing planning permission, to permit tipping to take place until 31 December 1998 and to B extend the range of wastes permitted to be deposited at Pilmuir quarry. As the district council failed to determine the application within the time prescribed by the Town and Country Planning (Scotland) Act 1972, WWM appealed to the first respondent in terms of s 34 of and Sched 7 to the 1972 Act. The first respondent appointed a reporter to determine the appeal. By letter dated 29 March 1990 the reporter indicated his intention to sustain the appeal subject to the imposition of further conditions and the con-C clusion of an agreement between the district council and Pilmuir Waste Disposal Ltd, the owners of Pilmuir quarry, regulating management of the waste disposal site. On 22 and 25 January 1991 such an agreement was concluded. On 9 April 1991 a formal decision letter sustaining the appeal was issued by the reporter.

The debate before me was, by agreement of parties, limited to the pleas of competency stated by the respondents. For the purpose of the debate parties D were agreed that the debate proceed on the basis of accepting pro veritate the petitioners' averments to the following effect:

(1) Both petitioners had a notifiable interest in neighbouring land to Pilmuir quarry for the purposes of the Town and Country Planning (General Development) (Scotland) Order 1981 as amended. Article 7 of the order provides that it is the duty of an applicant for planning permission to serve on any person with E a notifiable interest a copy of the application together with a notice stating that the plans can be inspected at the local authority office within a prescribed period. No such copy or notice was served on either petitioner.

(2) A planning authority is not entitled to entertain an application for planning permission unless and until there is in its hands a certificate stating that there has been compliance with the said General Development Order as amended. In relation to their applica-F tion WWM signed and lodged a certificate with the district council to the effect that they had complied with the Neighbour Notification Rules. That certificate was materially inaccurate in respect that WWM did not at any time notify the petitioners of their application by post or in any other way.

(3) The Town and Country Planning (Inquiries Procedure) (Scotland) Rules 1980, read with the Town and Country Planning Appeals (Determination by Appointed Person) (Inquiries Procedure) (Scotland) Rules 1980 as amended, provide that the Secretary of

State shall give not less than 28 days' notice in writin of an inquiry into an application, inter alia to "section 26 parties" as therein defined, and that such parties shall be entitled to appear or be represented at such appeal proceedings, if so advised. The petitioners would have been "section 26 parties" had they been properly and lawfully notified of the application by WWM and had they been notified of the appeal as required by the provisions of the rules. Their heritable interests are adversely affected by the grant of planning permission.

H The petitioners allege that by reason of the failure of WWM to notify them of the application for planning permission, separatim by reason of the failure of the Scottish Office Reporters' Unit to advertise the appeal, they have been deprived of their right to state objections to the said application and of their right to submit objections in the said appeal proceedings. The petitioners further allege that the requirements of notice of the application and of the appeal proceedings are mandatory requirements. In the face of failure to I give such notifications, the petitioners say that any subsequent act by a planning authority (including the first respondent as the person in whose name the appeal was determined) is ultra vires and is null and void. The petitioners accordingly seek a declarator that the purported decision of the first respondent dated 9 April 1991 sustaining the appeal of WWM in respect of their application to amend the existing planning permission granted to Tilcon Ltd was ultra vires and further seek decree of reduction of the decision J letter by the reporter dated 9 April 1991.

It is appropriate to record at this juncture that parties were agreed that in the event that I did not sustain the pleas to competency stated by the respondents, the first hearing should be continued to enable the parties to adjust their pleadings further and to enable the pleas to relevancy and lack of specification stated by the respondents to be debated.

The petition itself was lodged on 17 March 1992, that is to say some 11 months after the decision letter K sustaining the appeal of WWM. The petitioners aver that they only learned of the said decision when they were notified in a letter sent by ordinary first class post on 25 October 1991 by McGregor Associates, Edinburgh, of an application for planning permission by said McGregor Associates, whom the petitioners believe to have been acting for either WWM or another company as the proposed operators of Pilmuir quarry, in respect of a facility for handling waste at L Pilmuir quarry. On inquiry at the planning department of the district council, the petitioners were informed for the first time that planning permission had been granted to WWM in respect of the application dated 16 December 1987.

It is proper that I record at this point that counsel for the petitioners specifically accepted that the petitioners did not seek to contend that WWM as applicants, the district council or the first respondent, or rather those through whom on his behalf the appeal procedures had been promoted or the decision reached, had acted other than in good faith. Nor was there any dispute between parties that prima facie the making of the decision issued in the letter of 9 April 1991, being a decision of the first respondent on an appeal under s 33 of the 1972 Act, was, by virtue of subs (3) (b) of s 231 of that Act, an "action" on the part of the Secretary of State in terms of subs (1) of that section. Reading short, s 231 (1) says that "Except as provided by the following provisions of this Part of this Act, the validity of . . . any such action . . . shall not be questioned in any legal proceedings whatsoever".

It remains to notice certain further provisions in that Part of the 1972 Act. Section 231 (4) provides that "Nothing in this section shall affect the exercise of any jurisdiction of any court in respect of any refusal or failure on the part of the Secretary of State to take any such action as is mentioned in subsection (3) of this section". Section 233 provides by subs (1) that "If any person . . . (b) is aggrieved by any action on the part of the Secretary of State to which this section applies and desires to question the validity of that action, on the grounds that the action is not within the powers of this Act, or that any of the relevant requirements have not been complied with in relation to that action, he may, within six weeks from the date on which the order is confirmed or the action is taken, as the case may be, make an application to the Court of Session under this section." Subsection (3) provides that the section applies "to any such action on the part of the Secretary of State as is mentioned in subsection (3) of the said section 231". By subs (7) it is provided that "In this section 'the relevant requirements', in relation to any order or action to which this section applies, means any requirements of this Act or of the Tribunals and Inquiries Act 1971 . . . or of any order, regulations or rules made under this Act . . . which are applicable to that order or action".

In terms of art 12 of the petition from which their ground of action is derived, the petitioners aver that the requirements that they be given notice of the said application, separatim of the said appeal proceedings, are mandatory requirements. The service of such notices as are required under the Act of 1972 is governed by s 269 thereof, which requires service to be by hand, or by registered or recorded delivery post. Neither type of service was effected by WWM upon the petitioners.

For the respondents it was submitted that in the circumstances of the present case the provisions of ss 231 and 233 of the 1972 Act served to exclude any challenge in the courts to the first respondent's decision where, as here, the challenge was not taken by proceedings raised within six weeks after 9 April 1991. The word "action" in s 231 (3) fell to be read as including actions which, as counsel put it, were potentially null, that is to say, liable to be struck down as not valid. The exercise of the court's inherent supervisory jurisdiction was preserved only to the extent provided by s 231 (4). It was therefore only in the limited circumstances contemplated in subs (4) that the supervisory jurisdiction of the court at common

law was exercisable after the time limit imposed by s 233 had passed. Further and in any event, the alleged failure to notify the petitioners did not render the decision null and void but only voidable.

In support of his principal submission, counsel urged me to follow the decision in *Smith v East Elloe Rural District Council.* It had been decided upon provisions very similar, if not identical, to those in the 1972 Act. The decision had been followed in *Hamilton v Secretary of State for Scotland* and *Martin v Bearsden and Milngavie District Council. Smith* fell to be distinguished from the decision in *Anisminic Ltd v Foreign Compensation Commission.* Reference was made to Wade on *Administrative Law* (6th ed), p 633. There was a practical necessity for certainty in this area of administrative law, as was recognised by Lord Bridge in his speech in *Griffiths v Secretary of State for the Environment* when dealing with identical statutory provisions. Failure to notify an interested party by some administrative oversight did not invalidate a decision. Reference was made to *R v Secretary of State for the Environment, ex p Kent.* There was no power or discretion in the court to extend the six week time limit by reference to considerations of fairness, practicality or equity. Reference was made to *Bromsgrove District Council v Secretary of State for the Environment.* While the authorities cited were English, the relevant statutory provisions in relation to planning applications or otherwise were similar if not identical in wording and identical in purpose to the analogous Scottish legislation and the decisions were of persuasive authority. The same model of statutory provision had been considered in *Smith.* The 1972 Act had been passed by Parliament after the decisions in both *Smith* and *Anisminic.* The distinction between what had been called absolute ouster clauses and time limited ouster clauses had been recognised in s 14 of the Tribunals and Inquiries Act 1971. *Anisminic* was concerned with the former and not the latter type of clause.

Under reference to the speeches of Lord Reid ([1969] 2 AC at p 170), Lord Pearce (at pp 199-201) and Lord Wilberforce (at pp 210-212) in *Anisminic* as to the meaning to be given to the word "determination" in the context of the statute in question there, namely a real as opposed to a purported determination or a determination made outwith the limits fixed by Parliament, counsel argued that the phrase "any action" in s 233 (1) of the 1972 Act was not ambiguous and could not be given such a narrow construction. To do so would be to make it impossible to construe the phrase as it occurs in its obvious and appropriate sense. The appeal provision extended to "invalidity" of any action, and that must extend to appeals against not only actions which were nullities in the *Anisminic* sense but also other kinds of nullities arising within the limits fixed by Parliament. The word "any" was wholly unqualified. Counsel therefore invited me to follow the line of authority stemming from *Smith* and followed both in England, for instance in *R v Secretary of State for the Environment, ex p Ostler,* and *R v Cornwall County Council, ex p*

Huntington and also in Scotland in *Hamilton* and
A *Martin.* Insofar as it might be suggested that *McDaid
v Clydebank District Council* was a contrary authority,
the statutory provisions under discussion there were
different and the decision in the case fell to be distinguished for the reasons set out in *Martin.* In
McDaid the statutory provisions considered were concerned with enforcement notices and the code relating
to enforcement of control in Pt V of the Act, in particular that part of the code relating to appeals set out
in ss 84 and 85 of the Act. Counsel made specific refer-
B ence to s 85 (10) which provided that the validity of
an enforcement notice should not, except by way of an
appeal under the section, be questioned in any proceedings whatsoever on any of certain specific grounds
specified in subs (1) of s 85. Thus invalidity was there
a "different beast" as counsel put it, since the reference to grounds of appeal subsumed that the person to
whom a right of appeal was open had had the enforcement notice served upon him in terms of s 84 (5).
Furthermore s 85 (10) was only a partial exclusion
C clause and did not serve to exclude common law
remedies. Reference was made to the speech of Lord
Fraser in *Davy v Spelthorne Borough Council* [1984]
AC at p 272. There Lord Fraser had made observations upon the equivalent provisions in the English
planning legislation and the meaning of validity as
enforceability. Counsel also referred to *R v Greenwich
London Borough Council, ex p Patel* in which the Court
of Appeal in England had declined to follow *McDaid*
while distinguishing it on the facts. Counsel pointed
D out that the common law jurisdiction of the court had
been wholly preserved by s 231 (4) in relation to the
refusal or failure of the Secretary of State to take any
action of the description set out in subs (3) of s 231.
Otherwise the court's jurisdiction was ousted in the
event that no challenge was mounted within the time
limit provided for in s 233 (1). It was significant that
the Rules of Court made specific provision for the
application under the Act just as in similar circumstances they did so in relation to schemes or orders
under the Roads (Scotland) Act 1984.
E

Counsel then turned to his second submission that
on any view the failure of service, even with failure of
advertisement, did not render the decision of the
Secretary of State a nullity in the sense that it was void
ab initio and of no effect. Thus if an appeal to the
court had been made timeously in respect of that
failure, it would have proceeded on the basis of "contrary to requirements" and not as an action outwith
the powers of the Secretary of State. On that ground
F of appeal, if upheld, the court would only quash the
action complained of if satisfied that there was substantial prejudice to the aggrieved person. The provisions themselves postulated a distinction between
void and voidable. Reference was made to *Lochore v
Moray District Council.* Even if *Anisminic* and *McDaid*
were relevant in the context of the present case, it
would have to be on the basis that the Secretary of
State's decision was a nullity in the absolute sense and
that could not be said in the present case.

In passing, I would agree with counsel for the

respondents that where, as here, it is clear that the
defect in the certificate supplied by the applicant to G
the second respondent was not a deliberate or
unauthorised act intended to deceive, that is to say
fraudulent or in mala fide, and further that the local
authority had no reason to suspect that the certificate
was defective so that it did not in fact comply with the
provisions of para 7 (3) of the General Development
Order, any determination upon the application could
not be said to be void but was at best voidable. I agree
with the view expressed on this matter in the opinion
of Lord Cullen in *Lochore* at p 20. The defect here is H
at best one which arises from administrative error on
the part of the respondents. As counsel for the second
respondents in particular pointed out, it is not any
part of the petitioner's case that the failure to comply
was tainted by fraud or bad faith on the part of any
party. It thus does not fall within the kind of case
referred to by Lord Fraser in *Davy* at p 272 in relation
to the issue of an enforcement notice which is
"vitiated by fraud, because one of the appellants'
officers had been bribed to issue it, or had been served I
without the appellants' authority".

Counsel for the petitioners, in inviting me to refuse
the respondents' motion and to allow further procedure, submitted that in this case the approach to be
adopted should be that which found favour in
Anisminic rather than that followed in *Smith* by the
House of Lords. The former was an approach which
accorded with the general principles adopted in this
area of the Court of Session's jurisdiction and in any
event was more consistent with other authorities in J
this area of law.

The Court of Session had a supervisory jurisdiction
independent of statute to regulate the powers by
which administrative decisions were taken. So an
ouster clause did not prevent the court from exercising
its jurisdiction over the process of determination.
Reference was made to *Ashley v Magistrates of
Rothesay.* So the court would exercise such a jurisdiction to see what a statute provided for and whether K
the inferior court kept within the bounds of its jurisdiction. There was no distinction between administrative and judicial bodies in this regard. Accordingly,
any dicta seeking to stress the absolute nature of an
ouster clause were ill founded. In Scots law the court
had jurisdiction to interfere wherever a decision maker
was alleged to have exceeded or abused his powers,
and its competence to do so was not confined to those
areas which English law had accepted as suitable for
judicial review. Reference was made to the opinion of
the court in *West v Secretary of State for Scotland.* L
There was no reason why judicial review should not
exist where there was also a statutory right of appeal.
Nor was there any reason why the existence of such
statutory right should preclude recourse to judicial
review to a petitioner who had remained ignorant of
the appeal process. There was no difference in principle between the situation where the matter which
the petitioner sought to raise as ground of challenge
did not fall within and so could not be dealt with
under the appeal process and that where the petitioner

was at all time ignorant of the existence of the appeal process. In the case of *Griffiths* the House of Lords was concerned with the interests of those who were entitled to and had made representations in the appeal process. If such parties were unaware of the time running against them, the decision to refuse planning permission on appeal became immune to challenge by lapse of time. Both *Hamilton* and *Martin* were cases in which the particular decisions reached could be justified on the particular circumstances of these cases. In *Hamilton* the appellant had already availed himself of his statutory right of appeal. In *Martin* the challenge to the compulsory purchase order was mounted in 1986 against an order made in 1967 and confirmed in 1970 with a subsequent vesting order made in 1972 and recorded in the General Register of Sasines in 1973.

In *Hamilton* Lord Kissen was in error in seeking to distinguish *Smith* from *Anisminic* by reference to the existence or absence of statutory provision for a right of appeal. The real issue must be whether the jurisdiction of the court had been excluded. In *Smith* the argument had been presented on a narrow front related only to the validity of the order in question and was not concerned with questions of whether it was void or voidable or in excess of jurisdiction. The circumstances were different from those in the present case. There was a basis for the exercise of the court's discretion because the supervisory jurisdiction of the court was not excluded by the provisions of the Act in the particular circumstances averred here. The procedural irregularity averred was of a nature such that a common law remedy remained open, notwithstanding the existence of a statutory appeal. Reference was made to *Tarmac Econowaste Ltd v Assessor for Lothian Region.*

No application by way of judicial review had been open to the petitioners prior to the reporter reaching a decision because up till that point the petitioners could have entered the process by lodging objections. A question arose once the decision had been taken since at that stage, not having taken part in the proceedings, there must be doubt as to whether the petitioners would be regarded as aggrieved persons for the purposes of s 233 of the 1972 Act. In any event the court should be slow to exclude any common law remedy where in exceptional circumstances a party could be excused from failing to use the prescribed statutory means of reviewing the decision of the Secretary of State and a miscarriage of justice might occur in the absence of such remedy. Reference was made to *Accountant in Bankruptcy v Allans of Gillock Ltd.* In addition, reference was made to *Main v Swansea City Council.* It was necessary to consider the consequences of a failure to carry through the procedural requirements which could have apprised the petitioners of the existence of the application and hence of their right to object both to the planning authority and to the Secretary of State in the light of the proved facts and the continuing chain of events. The petitioners also relied upon the decisions in *Lochore v Moray District Council, McCowan v Secretary of State for Scotland* and

dicta in the speeches of Lord Reid and Lord Pearce in *Anisminic* at pp 171 and 195 respectively where reference was made to the meaning to be applied to the jurisdiction of a tribunal and to the effect in law of the absence of those formalities or things which were conditions precedent to the tribunal having any jurisdiction to embark on an inquiry. No doubt an appellant had to come into court with clean hands when seeking to invite the court to exercise its discretion in his favour. Furthermore, matters might have changed since the decision had been made, making it appropriate for the court to grant the remedy sought. In the present case, no steps had been taken in pursuance of the grant arising from the Secretary of State's action which were or could be regarded as irrevocable.

Counsel pointed out that all the speeches in *Anisminic* had contained passages expressing reservations about the case of *Smith.* As a consequence of *Anisminic* it was open to a court to go behind the face of the order, so that the concept of jurisdiction in this area of law had been broadened. While no allegation was being made in the present case of bad faith on the part of the decision maker, there was no distinction in principle to be found between the clauses which contained an absolute ouster of the court's jurisdiction and those in which a limited period of time for appealing was given and thereafter there was an ouster clause. If the provision for a limited right of appeal was of no use to an appellant, the courts could intervene to grant a remedy.

It was significant that in the case of *Ostler,* Goff LJ had felt difficulty in attempting a satisfactory distinction between the cases of *Smith* and *Anisminic.* The distinction made in that case by the Court of Appeal proceeded upon a basis which could not be acceptable in Scots law. Counsel submitted that in the law of Scotland the court will exercise its supervisory jurisdiction over inferior tribunals, even if no error on the face of the record appears but there is shown to be an excess of jurisdiction. This applies not only to judicial acts but, having regard to the views of the judges about *Smith,* should apply also to administrative acts. The existence of an appeal procedure should not be a bar to such challenge, although *Smith* was not distinguished on that ground, and, that being so, the existence of an ouster clause should be no bar to subsequent challenge. Reference was made to the case of *Re Racal Communications Ltd* and the speech of Lord Diplock in that case as demonstrating that the Court of Appeal in *Ostler* were in error in their attempts to distinguish the decisions of *Smith* and *Anisminic.*

In any event the provisions of s 14 of the Tribunals and Inquiries Act 1971, being the successor to s 11 of the 1958 Act, did not provide any solution to the issue of competency. Section 11 of the 1958 Act was not dealing with the situation in *Smith* but simply reflected the new system of tribunals which were being established under the 1958 Act. Section 14 (3) was not to be interpreted as exclusive in all circumstances. Reference was made to *Anisminic* and in par-

ticular the speech of Lord Wilberforce in his con-
A sideration of the terms of s 11 (3) of the 1958 Act.

The fundamental question was what was the area
which was entrusted to the jurisdiction of the tribunal.
It should not be limited to the narrow reading of jurisdiction to which Lord Kissen referred in *Hamilton*.
He was wrong in the view that he expressed there as
to the nature of the tribunal's jurisdiction. He had not
been asked to consider an applicant who had had no
opportunity to take advantage of the procedure itself.
The allowance of a right of appeal and non-allowance
B of the right of appeal were to be regarded as different
matters. The petitioners had a legitimate expectation
to a hearing of any objections which they might have,
being directly affected by the matter which was the
subject of the application and the appeal. Theirs was
a notifiable interest of a character which entitled them
to intervene. The cases of *Hamilton* and *Martin* were
in any event different in their circumstances from the
present. There was no suggestion of prejudice to the
second respondents and no irrevocable steps had yet
C been taken. While *McDaid* dealt with different provisions, the approach taken there and in *McCowan*,
and in *Patel* in England, pointed to the common sense
approach which a court would adopt in similar
circumstances.

In his further reply counsel for the first respondents
made reference to the case of *Moss' Empires Ltd v
Assessor for Glasgow* for the proposition that where
there was no ambiguity in the terms of an ouster
clause, the words of the statute were to be given their
D clear meaning. There could be no ambiguity in the
words used in ss 231 and 233. The word "action"
covered actions which were both valid and also potentially null. The fact that the petitioners might come
into court with clean hands was not a legitimate consideration to the construction of statute. While it may
well be that the ouster clause in certain circumstances
could result in injustice to individual parties, their
interest must be subordinated to the greater public
interest.

E At this point it is convenient to deal shortly with the
submissions put forward by the parties in relation to
s 14 (2) and (3) of the Tribunals and Inquiries Act
1971. I agree with counsel for the petitioners that that
section and its provisions do not bear upon the central
issues in this case. Be that as it may, I see no reason
for differing from the opinion expressed by Lord
Kissen in *Hamilton* under reference to the effect of
s 11 (3) of the Tribunals and Inquiries Act 1958, that
F that subsection, which is to all intents and purposes in
terms identical to s 14 (3) of the 1971 Act, was a limitation upon the applicability of s 11 (2) of the 1958 Act,
which again is to all intents and purposes in terms
identical to s 14 (2) of the 1971 Act. At 1972 SLT,
p 237, he put it thus: "Subsection (3) means that
nothing in subs (2) is to apply where there is in the
Act, which is under consideration in subs (2), a provision that a compulsory purchase order shall not be
called into question if that Act makes 'special provision' for an application to the Court of Session
within a time limited in that Act for calling the said

order into question". If the phrase "an action" of the
Secretary of State is substituted for the references to G
a compulsory purchase order, that opinion is exactly
apposite to the present case.

By the same token, I do not find the terms of Rule
of Court 260B bear upon the critical issues in this case
insofar as the Rule of Court is concerned only with
procedural matters and nothing more.

For the purposes of the decision which I am asked
to make, I accept pro veritate the petitioners' averments that the relevant statutory rules required that H
the Secretary of State gave not less than 28 days'
notice of an inquiry into the application for planning
permission upon "section 26 parties" as defined in the
rules, that the petitioners were such parties, that the
petitioners' heritable interests were adversely affected
by the grant of planning permission, that they were
never notified of the application initially nor were they
notified of the appeal and that thereby they had been
deprived of their right to submit objections to the
appeal proceedings. I have concentrated upon the
appeal proceedings by reason that, in the first place, I
the district council made no determination in fact
although for the purposes of the 1972 Act, this failure
to do so was deemed a refusal and, in the second place,
the action of the Secretary of State which is attacked
in this process is the decision of the Secretary of State
dated 9 April 1991 on an appeal under s 33 of the Act.
Such an appeal, as s 33 (3) indicates, is effectively a
new process in which the Secretary of State may have
regard to new material as well as the material before
the local planning authority. In any event, s 233 J
applies only to a such an action and to nothing else.
The preceding failure of the local planning authority
to reach a decision was the mechanism whereby the
appeal came within the purview of the Secretary of
State.

In the course of the debate I asked counsel for the
petitioners whether it would have been open to the
petitioners either while the local authority was deliberating upon the application or while the Secretary of
State was deliberating upon the appeal, the petitioners K
having lodged objections and the determining
authority having refused to accept them for consideration, to raise proceedings for judicial review against
that refusal. I understood counsel to accept that this
would be so under reference to opinions expressed in
each of *Tarmac Econowaste Ltd v Assessor for Lothian
Region* and *Accountant in Bankruptcy v Allans of
Gillock Ltd*. In the latter case Lord Cowie at p 768K-L
went on to say this: "As I understand it the general
principles governing the question whether an action of L
reduction is competent when other means of review
have been available and not exercised, are as follows.
Such an action is not competent as a means of reviewing a decision of an inferior court or of an administrative body where other means are prescribed and not
exercised, unless there are exceptional circumstances
excusing a party from failing to use the prescribed
means. The underlying concept is that the exceptional
circumstances disclose a miscarriage of justice: *Adair
v Colville & Sons Ltd*; and *Philp v Reid* and in particular Lord Anderson at 1927 SLT, p 172."

I refer also to Lord Cullen's opinion in *Lochore* at
A p 20 noted before. But neither passage was dealing
with the effect of an ouster clause and I do not read
the opinions as entrenching upon the authorities
which deal specifically with this effect. The same
observation falls to be made in regard to the decision
in *Main v Swansea City Council*. The concept of an
aggrieved person in terms of s 233 (1) (b) must include
a person who has not had an opportunity to present
his case to the Secretary of State by reason of procedural irregularity before the action was taken by the
B Secretary of State. Subsection (4) provides that on an
application under that section the court may quash the
action if satisfied that the applicant's interests had
been substantially prejudiced by a failure to comply
with any of the relevant requirements as defined by
subs (7) in relation to that action. Plainly, failure to
notify if required by the relevant requirements would
fall within the grounds for such an application. Before
quashing an action complained of, the court would
require to consider what was the purpose and effect of
C the relevant requirements which had not been complied with in relation to the action whose validity is
questioned and to exercise a discretion in deciding
whether or not to quash the action. No doubt in reaching such a decision the court may be influenced by
whether the requirement is mandatory or directory.

Counsel for the petitioners however argued that the
concept of ultra vires extended to cover the kind of
case where the applicant for judicial review was
D deprived, by some mischance of which he was wholly
blameless and ignorant, of the opportunity to intervene at any point in the proceedings following upon
the lodging of an application for planning permission
up until and after the passage of the appeal days
against the Secretary of State's decision upon an
appeal relating to that application. In the petitioners'
pleadings the only ground upon which this application
proceeds is ultra vires actings on the part of the Secretary of State as their first plea in law makes clear,
E although in art 12 of the petition their case depends
upon failure to comply with statutory requirements
for the giving of notice to the petitioners of the
application for planning permission and of the subsequent appeal proceedings. This submission of the
petitioners echoed that which was considered and
rejected by Lord Kissen in *Hamilton* at p 240. I note
in passing that Lord Kissen found support for the
view which he formed, in the opinion of Lord
Wheatley in *Holmes & Son v Secretary of State for
Scotland*, but I was not referred to that case in the
F course of the debate. I find Lord Kissen's reasoning
compelling as to the meaning of and effect to be given
to the first ground of challenge under para 15 of Sched
1 to the Acquisition of Land (Authorisation Procedure) (Scotland) Act 1947 which he was there considering, namely that the authorisation "is not
empowered to be granted under this Act". That
phrase exactly parallels the provision in s 233 (1) of
the 1972 Act, allowing a challenge to the validity of an
order on the ground that "the order is not within the
powers of this Act". I observe that Lord Kissen makes

specific reference to the speech of Lord Reid in *Smith*
at [1956] AC, p 761, where he said, "ultra vires in the G
sense that what was authorised by the order went
beyond what was authorised by the Act under which
it was made". In the present case the Secretary of State
was undoubtedly entitled to enter upon the inquiry
into the appeal. And his determination upon it was
within the powers given to him. In *Martin* at p 303
Lord Clyde, referring to paras 15 and 16 of Sched 1
to the 1947 Act, the latter paragraph having its
parallel in s 231 (1) of the 1972 Act, said: "It cannot
be affirmed that para 16 was not intended to cover an H
order which was open to attack on grounds of nullity.
Nor in the framework of the scheme in Sched 1 can
it be affirmed that para 16 does not exclude a person
on whom the statutory notice has not been served."
That opinion is, in my view, equally applicable to the
scheme in Pt XII of the 1972 Act. As Lord Reid said
in *Smith* in his dissenting judgment, "paragraph 16 is
clearly intended to exclude, and does exclude entirely,
all cases of misuse of power in bona fide". No assertion of mala fides on the part of any party is made in I
the present case. The face that the petitioners had no
notice of the application or the appeal does not, in my
opinion, take them outwith the ambit of the scheme in
Pt XII of the 1972 Act such as to enable them to
proceed by way of judicial review at common law.

I am confirmed in my view by consideration of the
petitioners' argument which depended ultimately
upon the submission that there could be no distinction
in the court's approach to an action in excess or abuse
of jurisdiction in a case where there was provision for J
a limited appeal with an ouster clause operating after
a period, that is to say a time limited ouster clause
such as in *Smith*, and that in a case where there was
the *Anisminic* type of absolute ouster clause. The
availability of judicial review to ensure that the
decision maker does not exceed or abuse his powers or
fail to perform the duty which has been delegated or
entrusted to him is not in doubt. In *West v Secretary
of State for Scotland* the court made clear that it has K
power to intervene to restrain the acts or decisions of
administrative bodies or persons with similar functions as well as those of inferior tribunals where there
has been an excess or abuse of jurisdiction, in the
sense of power to decide, whether it be stepping
outside it, failing to observe its limits, departing from
the rules of natural justice, or taking into account
matter which ought not to have been taken into
account. But in the course of the court's opinion, the
Lord President also made clear that there was no substantive difference between English and Scots law as L
to the grounds on which the process of decision
making may be open to review so that reference may
be made to English cases in order to determine
whether there has been an excess or abuse of the jurisdiction, power or authority or a failure to do what it
requires. The court there did not purport to deal with
the effect of ouster clauses. In parenthesis while I
accept that the ouster clause in the present case is to
be found in Scottish planning legislation, it is not
suggested that its wording is in any different form

from that in equivalent planning legislation applying
A in England and Wales. It seems to me that it is open
to refer to English cases in order to determine the
effect of ouster clauses upon the extent of the court's
power to interfere where similar statutory ouster
clauses are being considered in this court. As I have
already indicated, ss 231 and 233 are in terms parallel
to those to be found in Sched 1 to the Acquisition of
Land (Authorisation Procedure) (Scotland) Act 1947
which were considered in *Hamilton*. In that case, as
Lord Kissen pointed out, those terms of the 1947 Act
B were identical to those in the equivalent English Act
which was considered in *Smith*. I note that *Hamilton*
was decided in January 1972, before the 1972 Act
received royal assent. The 1972 Act, as its long title
bears, was an Act to consolidate certain enactments
relating to town and country planning in Scotland
with amendments to give effect to recommendations of
the Scottish Law Commission. It would seem incongruous to imagine that Parliament enacted the 1972
Act without being aware of the apparent conflict
C between the construction given to absolute ouster
clauses and time limited ouster clauses. I find myself
in agreement with the view expressed by Mann LJ in
R v Cornwall County Council, ex p Huntington when
he said at [1992] 3 All ER, p 575: "The intention of
Parliament when it uses an *Anisminic* clause is that
questions as to validity are not excluded (see [1969] 1
All ER 208 at p 244 per Lord Wilberforce). When
paragraphs such as those considered in *Ex p Ostler* are
used, then the legislative intention is that questions as
D to invalidity may be raised on the specified grounds in
the prescribed manner, but that otherwise the jurisdiction of the court is excluded in the interest of
certainty."

Under reference to the terms of the ouster clause
before the court in that case, which were in effect in
terms similar to those in the 1972 Act, he then
observed that he would have independently formed
the same view, for the legislative intention seemed to
him to be plain from the language employed. As he
E pointed out, "The language does not admit of
differentiations between degrees (if such there be) or
grounds of invalidity, nor does it admit of differing
constructions according as to whether the decision to
make an order is judicial or administrative in
character."

As was pointed out by counsel for the first respondent, if Acts are passed using the forms of words or
clauses in prior Acts which have received judicial construction, unless a contrary intention appears, the
F court will presume that the legislature has adopted the
judicial interpretation, or has used the words in the
sense attributed to them by the courts. See Craies on
Statute Law (7th ed), p 141. In *Griffiths v Secretary of
State for the Environment*, the House of Lords considered the equivalent sections of the English Town
and Country Planning Act in circumstances where the
application for planning permission was refused and
the applicants thereafter appealed. The appeal was
dismissed. The question before the House was
whether time began to run against the appellant from

the date of the decision itself or the date when the
decision was received by the appellant. In his speech G
at [1983] 2 AC, p 67 Lord Bridge, with whom the
majority agreed, considered an argument that the
Secretary of State had never decided the planning
appeal at all and said: "At the outset the appellant
sought to argue that the Secretary of State had never
decided his planning appeal at all. This point is not
open to him on the hearing of the present appeal.
What he sought to question by his notice of motion
was certainly a purported decision of the Secretary of
State on an appeal under section 36 of the Act. The
validity of that purported decision can only be ques- H
tioned if the application was made in due time."

Both *Smith* and *Ostler* were cited in argument to the
House. The House reached their decision that time
ran from the making of the decision, notwithstanding
that it was specifically recognised that it would extend
to circumstances where the aggrieved person might
not be aware of the Secretary of State's action within
the time limit for appeal and thus might lose any right
to challenge it. I refer in particular to the speech of I
Lord Bridge at p 70.

The distinction between the cases of *Smith* and
Anisminic may at first blush be difficult to define with
precision. I am, however, content to adopt the analysis
which is to be found in Wade, *Administrative Law* (6th
ed), at p 737, to the effect that the distinction between
absolute ouster clauses and time limited ouster clauses
is that the latter be regarded not as ousting the jurisdiction, but merely as confining the time within which
it can be invoked. In *R v Cornwall County Council* J
Mann LJ was echoing what had been said by Lord
Kissen in *Hamilton v Secretary of State for Scotland* at
p 239. There Lord Kissen said in relation to the statutory provisions being considered by him, it being
common ground that the scope of the right to make an
application to the court given by them related to a
basis which amounted to a nullity: "The question in
Anisminic was whether the court was precluded from
deciding whether a determination of the said commission was a nullity in the circumstances where the K
statute in question in that case made no provisions of
any kind for applications to the courts for consideration of such nullities. In the statutory provisions
which apply in this case there is a provision for quashing at least some kinds of null orders. I cannot see how
it can be said, on the basis of *Anisminic*, that, as pursuers' counsel maintained, one kind of nullity can be
remedied by the application of said para 15 but all
other kinds can be remedied by ordinary legal proceedings in the courts. If that was the intention of the L
statutory provisions which are under consideration in
this case, it would have been easy to say so. (See
Anisminic, at p 170, per Lord Reid.)"

In the present case the meaning and effect of the
wide words in s 231 (1), "Except as provided by the
following provisions of this Part of this Act, the validity of . . . any such action on the part of the Secretary
of State as is mentioned in subsection (3) of this
section shall not be questioned in any legal proceedings whatsoever", are in my opinion clear in their

meaning and bar any challenge from whatever source
A it may come after the period of six weeks has passed
after the taking of the decision of the Secretary of State
on the appeal. It is not disputed that an appeal was
properly placed before the Secretary of State in this
case. It is not disputed that it lay within his powers to
determine it. Insofar as fraud or bad faith may be
excluded from the ambit of the decision in *Smith*, no
such suggestions are made in the present case.

Counsel for the petitioner sought to support his submissions by reference to *Re Racal Communications Ltd*
B and in particular the speech of Lord Diplock at [1981]
AC, pp 382-383. It is true that in that passage Lord
Diplock refers to *Anisminic* as being concerned only
with decisions of administrative tribunals. Thus he
refers to the presumption that where a decision
making power is conferred on a tribunal or authority
that is not a court of law, Parliament did not intend
to confer upon it power to decide questions of law
without clear words to that effect. At p 383 he said:
"The break-through made by *Anisminic* [1969] 2 AC
C 147 was that, as respects administrative tribunals and
authorities, the old distinction between errors of law
that went to jurisdiction and errors of law that did not,
was for practical purposes abolished. Any error of law
that could be shown to have been made by them in the
course of reaching their decision on matters of fact or
of administrative policy would result in their having
asked themselves the wrong question with the result
that the decision they reached would be a nullity. The
Tribunals and Inquiries Act 1971, which requires
D most administrative tribunals from which there is not
a statutory right of appeal to the Supreme Court on
questions of law, to give written reasons for their
decisions . . . facilitates the detection of errors of law
by those tribunals and by administrative authorities,
generally."

That passage seems to me to support precisely the
distinction made by Goff LJ in *Ex p Ostler* where at
p 139, having considered the difficulties arising in
reconciling *Smith* and *Anisminic* he said: "I think
E there is a real distinction between the case with which
the House was dealing in *Anisminic* and the case of
Smith v East Elloe Rural District Council on that
ground, that in the one case the determination was a
purported determination only, because the tribunal,
however eminent, having misconceived the effect of
the statute, acted outside its jurisdiction, and indeed
without any jurisdiction at all, whereas here one is
dealing with an actual decision made within jurisdiction though sought to be challenged".

F In the result accordingly I am not persuaded by the
submissions for the petitioners that there is any
warrant for Scottish courts ignoring the line of
authority which stems from *Smith* and has been
followed both in England and in Scotland. Counsel for
the petitioner founded upon what he described as a
contrary line of authority, stemming from the case of
McDaid, through *McCowan* and *Lochore*, which he
claimed to be in point and was binding upon me. In
my opinion for the reasons which were outlined in the
case of *Martin*, neither *McDaid* nor *McCowan* is in

point so far as the present case is concerned. They
were concerned with compulsory purchase orders and G
furthermore, as in the case of *Main v Swansea City
Council*, the appellants were the owners of the
property which was affected by the grant and specific
reference was made on the face of the Acts in question
in those cases to the need for notice to be served upon
them. I observe in passing that a similar provision
appears in s 24 of the 1972 Act. The case of *Lochore*
is not in point since in it there was no question of an
appeal to the Secretary of State, nor of the meaning
and effect of ouster clauses. I would also observe that
neither in *McDaid* nor in *McCowan* was any doubt cast H
upon the correctness of the decision in *Hamilton*.

Some argument was addressed to me on the question
of whether, if the action of the Secretary of State was
a nullity, it was void or voidable. It suffices to say that
I doubt whether in the end of the day there is truly a
distinction in the context of administrative law. I am
content to accept what was said by Lord Clyde in
Martin at p 304 on these matters, and the passage
from the opinion of Cairns LJ in *Routh v Reading Cor-*
poration cited there. If *Smith* covers both a void and I
a voidable order, the issue ceases to be one of importance. If, as counsel for the petitioners accepted, the
court retained a discretion whether or not to strike
down the action, for instance, because the remedy was
inappropriate, it is difficult to regard the action complained of as void ab initio.

For all these reasons accordingly I shall sustain the
respondents' pleas to competency and dismiss the
petition. J

---

*Counsel for Petitioners, McNeill, QC; Solicitors,
Russel & Aitken, WS — Counsel for First Respondent,
Moynihan; Solicitor, R Brodie, Solicitor to the Secretary
of State for Scotland — Counsel for Second Respondents
(Local Authority), Nimmo Smith, QC, Liddle; Soli-
citors, Dundas & Wilson, CS.*

R D S
K

Bennett v Houston

HIGH COURT OF JUSTICIARY
THE LORD JUSTICE CLERK (ROSS),
LORDS SUTHERLAND AND WYLIE
23 SEPTEMBER 1992 L

*Justiciary — Crime — Fraud — Relevancy — Charge
libelling that accused pretended to have carried out work
to workmanlike standards and of certain value but not
stating that true value was less — Whether relevant
charge of fraud.*

An accused person was charged on a summary complaint containing nine charges of fraud or attempted
fraud which libelled that the accused had pretended
that he had carried out work in a workmanlike manner

and that the true value of the works including materials was a certain sum of money, the truth being as the accused well knew that he had not carried out the work in a workmanlike manner. There was no specification that the accused knew that the true value of the works was less than the sum represented by him. The accused objected to the relevancy of the charges but the sheriff repelled the objection. The accused appealed.

Held (of consent of the Crown), that it was a fatal defect in each charge that it was not stated that the truth was, as he well knew, that the true value of the work was not the sum which he claimed to be the true value (p 1183J-K); and appeal *allowed*.

Summary complaint

Thomas Bennett was charged at the instance of S R Houston, procurator fiscal, Lanark, on a summary complaint which contained nine charges of fraud or attempted fraud. The accused stated a preliminary objection to the charges on the ground that they did not disclose a relevant crime known to the law of Scotland. The sheriff repelled the objection.

The accused appealed with leave to the High Court against the decision of the sheriff. The facts of the case appear from the opinion of the court.

Case referred to

Tapsell v Prentice, 1910 2 SLT 330; 1911 SC (J) 67; (1910) 6 Adam 354.

Appeal

The appeal was heard in the High Court on 23 September 1992.

Eo die the court (of consent of the Crown) *allowed* the appeal and *remitted* to the sheriff with a direction to him to *dismiss* the complaint as irrelevant.

The following opinion of the court was delivered by the Lord Justice Clerk (Ross):

OPINION OF THE COURT.—This is an appeal at the instance of Thomas Bennett. He was charged in the sheriff court at Lanark on a complaint containing nine charges of fraud or attempted fraud. An objection was taken on his behalf to the relevancy of the complaint and the sheriff duly heard his solicitor in support of the plea and the procurator fiscal in reply. The sheriff rejected the challenge to relevancy and it is against the sheriff's decision on that issue that the appellant has now appealed to this court.

Today, counsel for the appellant has maintained that the complaint discloses no relevant crimes and he maintains that there has been no sufficient specification. He has pointed out that these are what are sometimes called "bogus workmen" cases but that the charges are different to the charges which are normally brought in such circumstances. Under reference to authorities such as *Tapsell v Prentice* he has pointed out that it is an inadequate basis for the criminal offence of fraud merely to aver that an article has been sold in excess of its real value. He has submitted that the charges in the complaint do not state in what respect the work carried out was not workmanlike in manner, and he also has stressed that it is not made clear in the charges what the actual value of the work was. He has maintained that the appellant has been left in the position of not knowing what the allegation is which is made against him.

The Solicitor General on the other hand maintained that the charges were relevant. He pointed out that in each charge a false pretence had been alleged and that in each charge the charge proceeded to libel what the true position was. However, when the Solicitor General proceeded to examine the nature of the false pretences and the nature of the allegation as to what the true position was it became apparent to the court that there was something lacking in each of the charges. This can be demonstrated by reference to charge 1 in the complaint. Reading it shortly it is libelled that the appellant pretended to the complainers that he had carried out work in a workmanlike manner and that the true value of the works including materials was £1,250. It is thus clear that there were two branches of false pretence alleged to have been made by the appellant, first that he had carried out the work in a workmanlike manner and, secondly, that the true value of the work was £1,250. One would then have expected that when one went to the latter portion of the charge and saw what was libelled as being the true position both these false pretences would have been negatived. What in fact is stated in charge 1 is that the truth was as the appellant well knew, that he had not carried out the work to a workmanlike manner. But it is not stated that the truth was as he well knew, that the true value of the work was not £1,250. This appears to us to be a fatal defect in the charge and this defect is repeated in each of the other charges on the complaint.

We understood the Solicitor General ultimately to accept that there was indeed such a fatal defect in each charge in that the false pretence libelled, to the effect that the true value of the works was a certain sum of money, was not dealt with in the latter portion of the charge where the true position is libelled. Because of these defects which occur in each of the charges we have come to the conclusion that the objection to the relevancy taken by the appellant was a sound one and that the sheriff was in error in rejecting the objection on relevancy. We shall accordingly reverse the decision of the sheriff on relevancy and we shall remit the case to him with directions to dismiss the complaint as irrelevant.

Counsel for Appellant, Ogg; Solicitors, J & A Hastie, SSC (for Baird & Co, Kirkcaldy) — Counsel for Respondent, Solicitor General (Dawson, QC); Solicitor, J D Lowe, Crown Agent.

P W F

King v Lees

A HIGH COURT OF JUSTICIARY

THE LORD JUSTICE CLERK (ROSS),
LORDS SUTHERLAND AND WYLIE

9 OCTOBER 1992

Justiciary — Evidence — Corroboration — Burden of proving that statutory assumption is overcome resting on accused — Whether defence evidence need be corroborated.

B *Justiciary — Statutory offence — Driving while unfit through drink — Accused giving evidence of amounts of alcohol consumed before and after driving — Whether accused's evidence need be corroborated — Road Traffic Offenders Act 1988 (c 53), s 15 (2) and (3).*

Section 15 (2) of the Road Traffic Offenders Act 1988 provides that evidence of the proportion of alcohol in a specimen of breath provided by an accused shall in all cases be taken into account and that subject to s 15 (3), it shall be assumed that the C proportion of alcohol in the accused's breath at the time of the alleged offence was not less than in the specimen. Section 15 (3) provides that that assumption shall not be made if the accused proves that he had consumed alcohol after he had ceased to drive and before he provided the specimen and that had he not done so the proportion of alcohol in his breath would not have exceeded the prescribed limit.

An accused person was tried on summary complaint with a contravention of s 5 (1) (a) of the Road Traffic D Act 1988. The accused and his son gave evidence that the accused had consumed alcohol after he had ceased to drive but the accused alone gave evidence as to the amount of alcohol consumed before and after driving. The sheriff accepted that the amount of alcohol which the accused said he had consumed before driving would not have been sufficient to put him above the prescribed limit and that the additional amount which he said he had consumed after ceasing to drive would have been sufficient. The sheriff however held that the E accused required to lead corroborated evidence of the amounts which he had consumed and therefore convicted the accused on the basis that he had failed to discharge the onus imposed on him by s 15 (3). The sheriff also stated that in any event he would not have been persuaded by the accused's evidence that the burden had been discharged. The accused appealed.

Held, (1) that it was in accordance with principle that the evidence led by the accused for the purpose F of s 15 (3) need not be corroborated (p 1187D-E); but (2) that as the sheriff had not found the accused's evidence to be credible and reliable, the accused had failed to prove that the assumption contained in s 15 (2) should not be made (p 1187J); and appeal *refused*.

Summary complaint

George King was charged at the instance of Robert F Lees, procurator fiscal, Edinburgh, on a summary complaint which contained the following charge, inter

alia: "on a road or other public place, namely James Street, Edinburgh, you did drive a motor vehicle, G namely a motor car registered number DSH 640X after consuming so much alcohol that the proportion of it in your breath was 68 microgrammes of alcohol in 100 millilitres of breath which exceeded the prescribed limit, namely 35 microgrammes of alcohol in 100 millilitres of breath: contrary to the Road Traffic Act 1988, s 5 (1) (a)". The accused pled not guilty and proceeded to trial. After trial the temporary sheriff (R Black, QC) found the accused guilty.

The accused appealed by way of stated case to the H High Court against the decision of the sheriff.

Findings in fact

The sheriff found the following facts to be admitted or proved:

(1) At around 1.20 am on 25 May 1991 the appellant drove his motor car, registered number DSH 640X, into James Street, Portobello, and parked the vehicle there, some 50 or 60 yds from his home. (2) At around I 2 am on 25 May 1991 the appellant was interviewed at his home by Police Constables William Slaven and William Harra. From information received and from their own examination of vehicles parked in James Street the police officers had reasonable cause to suspect that the appellant had been driving motor car DSH 640X on James Street and had committed a traffic offence whilst the vehicle was in motion. (3) The appellant was required by Constable Harra to provide a specimen of breath for a breath test by J means of an approved device. This the appellant duly did. The result was positive. He was then arrested and conveyed to Leith police office. (4) On arrival at Leith police office, the appellant, at 2.28 am on 25 May 1991, was required by Constable Harra to provide two specimens of breath for analysis by means of an approved device. He was advised that the specimen with the lower proportion of alcohol would be used and the other disregarded. The appellant provided the specimens of breath as required and was handed a K certified copy of the statement produced by the approved device, which showed that the lower of the two specimens of breath provided by him contained 68 microgrammes of alcohol in 100 millilitres of breath. He was then cautioned and charged. His reply to the charge was "I wasn't driving." (5) After ceasing to drive and before providing his specimens of breath for analysis the appellant consumed alcohol in the form of brandy. (6) The amount of brandy so consumed was not proved by the appellant; nor did he prove the L amount of alcohol that had been consumed by him that night before driving and parking in James Street. (7) If before driving that night the appellant's alcohol consumption had consisted solely of one pint of McEwan's 80/- special beer at around 11.55 pm the proportion of alcohol in his breath would not have exceeded the prescribed limit. If the amount of brandy consumed by the appellant after ceasing to drive and before providing his specimens of breath for analysis had been 8.8 fluid ounces or thereby, the proportion of alcohol in the specimens of breath provided by him

at Leith police office would not have exceeded the
A prescribed limit had it not been for the consumption
of the brandy.

Statutory provisions

The Road Traffic Offenders Act 1988 provides:

"15.— . . . (2) Evidence of the proportion of alcohol
or any drug in a specimen of breath, blood or urine
provided by the accused shall, in all cases, be taken
into account and, subject to subsection (3) below, it
shall be assumed that the proportion of alcohol in the
B accused's breath, blood or urine at the time of the
alleged offence was not less than in the specimen.

"(3) If the proceedings are for an offence under
section 5 of that Act . . . that assumption shall not be
made if the accused proves — (a) that he consumed
alcohol after he had ceased to drive . . . and before he
provided the specimen, and (b) that had he not done
so the proportion of alcohol in his breath, blood or
urine would not have exceeded the prescribed limit".

C ### Cases referred to

Hassan v Scott, 1989 SLT 380; 1989 SCCR 49.
Neish v Stevenson, 1969 SLT 229.

The sheriff appended a note to the findings in fact
in the following terms:

THE SHERIFF (R BLACK, QC).—At the close
of the evidence in this case the sole issue in dispute
between the parties was whether the appellant had
D brought himself within the terms of s 15 (3) of the
Road Traffic Offenders Act 1988.

There was evidence from both the appellant and his
son that the appellant consumed brandy after he had
ceased to drive. I accepted that evidence. However,
the only evidence regarding (a) the amount of brandy
consumed by the appellant after ceasing to drive, and
(b) the amount of alcohol consumed by the appellant
before commencing to drive that night, came from the
E appellant himself. That evidence was to the effect that
before driving he consumed one pint of 80/- beer
(which, on the scientific evidence, I accepted would
not be sufficient to put him above the prescribed
limit); and that after driving he consumed two large
glasses of brandy containing in total 8.8 fluid ounces
(which, on the scientific evidence, I accepted would
have been sufficient to put him above the prescribed
limit at the time when he provided the specimens of
breath for analysis).

F The solicitor for the appellant submitted that if the
evidence of the appellant regarding his pre- and post-
driving alcohol consumption raised a reasonable doubt
in my mind about whether the proportion of alcohol
in the appellant's breath while he was actually driving
was above the prescribed limit, then I should give the
appellant the benefit of that doubt and acquit him,
notwithstanding the result of the breath analysis at
Leith police office.

I did not accept that submission. Section 15 (2) of
the Road Traffic Offenders Act 1988 provides: "Evid-

ence of the proportion of alcohol . . . in a specimen of
breath . . . provided by the accused shall, in all cases, G
be taken into account and, subject to subsection (3)
below, it shall be assumed that the proportion of
alcohol in the accused's breath . . . at the time of the
alleged offence was not less than in the specimen".
Section 15 (3) provides: "If the proceedings are for an
offence under section 5 of [the Road Traffic Act 1988]
. . . that assumption shall not be made if the accused
proves — (a) that he consumed alcohol after he ceased
to drive . . . and before he provided the specimen, and,
(b) that had he not done so the proportion of alcohol H
in his breath . . . would not have exceeded the
prescribed limit".

I took the view that the court *must* make the statutory assumption referred to in s 15 (2) unless the
accused *proves* the two matters specified in s 15 (3);
and that in the absence of such proof the court was
statutorily bound to make the assumption notwithstanding that evidence had been led which, if
accepted, raised a doubt about whether the proportion
of alcohol in the accused's breath while actually I
driving was above the prescribed limit. I concluded
that s 15 (3) placed a persuasive burden of proof upon
the appellant to establish the two matters specified
therein; and that in criminal proceedings when a
persuasive burden is placed upon the accused that
burden can be discharged only by corroborated evidence. I accepted, of course, that the *standard* of proof
required to discharge the burden resting on the
accused was proof on a balance of probabilities: *Neish
v Stevenson.* However, that did not seem to me to J
detract from the principle that in criminal proceedings
where a persuasive burden rests upon a party he can
succeed in discharging it only by leading evidence
which is sufficient in law to do so, i e evidence which
is duly corroborated.

In the present case I formed the view that the persuasive burden resting on the appellant required him
to prove, by corroborated evidence, two essential or
crucial facts: (a) that he consumed alcohol after he had K
ceased to drive, and (b) that had he not done so the
proportion of alcohol in his breath would not have
exceeded the prescribed limit. He succeeded in
proving fact (a) by virtue of his own and his son's evidence. But he adduced insufficient evidence in law to
enable him to prove fact (b) since his own was the only
evidence in the proceedings relating to either (i) how
much alcohol he consumed before driving, or (ii) how
much alcohol he consumed after ceasing to drive. Had
the appellant established by corroborated evidence L
that before driving he consumed only one pint of
McEwan's 80/- beer (which, on the scientific evidence,
I accepted would have placed him under the
prescribed limit), I would have held that he had succeeded in discharging his burden of proof under s 15
(3) although he failed to establish by such evidence
how much alcohol he consumed after ceasing to drive.
Provided always that it is established by legally sufficient evidence that the accused consumed *some* alcohol
after ceasing to drive, it is my view that the burden
resting on the accused under s 15 (3) can be discharged

A by his establishing (by corroborated evidence) *either* (a) that the amount of alcohol consumed by him after driving ceased accounted for his exceeding the prescribed limit at the time of the breath analysis *or* (b) that the amount of alcohol consumed by him before driving was insufficient to place him above the prescribed limit. However, it is my view that the accused must establish, by corroborated evidence, one or the other of the pre-driving or the post-driving alcohol consumption. In the present case the appellant did neither.

B In the course of delivering my decision in this case I indicated that I was holding that there was insufficient evidence in law for me to accept that the accused had proved the fact specified in s 15 (3) (b), but that even if I had felt entitled to proceed on the appellant's own uncorroborated evidence of his pre- and post-driving alcohol consumption I would not have been persuaded by that evidence that the statutory assumption in s 15 (2) had been overcome and that the requirements of s 15 (3) had been established.

C

Appeal

The sheriff posed the following questions for the opinion of the High Court:

(1) Did I err in holding that an accused person seeking to found on s 15 (3) of the Road Traffic Act 1988 requires to prove the facts specified in paras (a) and (b) thereof by corroborated evidence?

D (2) On the facts stated was I entitled to convict the appellant?

The appeal was argued before the High Court on 22 September 1992.

On 9 October 1992 the court *answered* both questions in the *affirmative* and *refused* the appeal.

E The following opinion of the court was delivered by the Lord Justice Clerk (Ross):

OPINION OF THE COURT.—The appellant is George King who appeared for trial in the sheriff court at Edinburgh on a complaint containing four charges. At the conclusion of the Crown case, the prosecutor intimated that she did not seek a conviction against the appellant on charges 1, 2 and 4 on the complaint. The sheriff found the appellant guilty of charge 3, and it is against his conviction on that charge that F he has now appealed by way of stated case.

Charge 3 libelled a contravention of s 5 (1) (a) of the Road Traffic Act 1988. The findings in fact reveal that at 1.20 am on the date libelled the appellant drove his motor car and parked it a short distance from his home. Around 2 am on said date the appellant was interviewed at his home by police officers who had reasonable cause to suspect that he had been driving his motor car and had committed a traffic offence whilst the vehicle was in motion. He was required to provide a specimen of breath for a breath test by means of an approved device. He did so and the result was positive. He was then arrested and taken to a G police station where he provided two specimens of breath for analysis by means of an approved device. The lower of the two specimens of breath provided by him contained an amount of alcohol in excess of the prescribed limit.

What was at issue in the trial was whether the appellant had brought himself within the terms of s 15 (3) of the Road Traffic Offenders Act 1988. Section 15 (2) of that Act provides that evidence of the proportion of alcohol in a specimen of breath provided by an H accused shall in all cases be taken into account, and that subject to s 15 (3) it shall be assumed that the proportion of alcohol in the accused's breath at the time of the alleged offence was not less than in the specimen. Section 15 (3) provides inter alia as follows: [his Lordship quoted the terms of s 15 (3) set out supra and continued:]

Finding 5 is in the following terms: [his Lordship quoted its terms and continued:]   I

In his note the sheriff explains that there was evidence from both the appellant and his son that the appellant consumed brandy after he had ceased to drive. The sheriff states that he accepted that evidence. He goes on to say that the only evidence regarding (a) the amount of brandy consumed by the appellant after ceasing to drive, and (b) the amount of alcohol consumed by the appellant before commencing to drive that night, came from the appellant himself. The appellant's evidence apparently was that J before driving he had consumed one pint of 80/- beer, and that after driving he had consumed two large glasses of brandy containing in total 8.8 fluid ounces. In this connection the sheriff has made a further finding which is finding 7 which is in the following terms: [his Lordship quoted its terms and continued:]

After narrating the provisions of s 15 (2) and (3) the sheriff expresses the following view: "I concluded that s 15 (3) placed a persuasive burden of proof upon the K appellant to establish the two matters specified therein; and that in criminal proceedings when a persuasive burden is placed upon the accused that burden can be discharged only by corroborated evidence. I accepted, of course, that the standard of proof required to discharge the burden resting on the accused was proof on a balance of probabilities: *Neish v Stevenson*. However, that did not seem to me to detract from the principle that in criminal proceedings where a persuasive burden rests upon a party he can L succeed in discharging it only by leading evidence which is sufficient in law to do so, i e evidence which is duly corroborated."

Counsel for the appellant submitted that the sheriff had erred in expressing that view. She maintained that there was no requirement that the evidence of an appellant seeking to rely upon the defence contained in s 15 (3) required to be corroborated. Although she did not cite any authority in support of her submission, she submitted strongly that the sheriff was

wrong in concluding that the appellant's evidence in
A support of the defence under s 15 (3) had to be
corroborated. Counsel did refer to *Hassan v Scott*, and
pointed out that it was plain from the sheriff's note in
that case that there had been no corroboration of the
amount of alcohol which the appellant had drunk after
the accident. Despite that the court held that the
sheriff would have been entitled to acquit the appellant who had been founding upon the provisions of
s 10 (2) of the Road Traffic Act 1972 (as amended by
the Transport Act 1981) which is in similar terms to
B s 15 (2) and (3) of the Road Traffic Offenders Act
1988. Counsel maintained that this showed that the
court was satisfied that the appellant's evidence as to
the amount of alcohol which he had drunk did not
require to be corroborated. She submitted that the
erroneous approach of the sheriff in the present case
vitiated his decision to convict the appellant.

The Solicitor General submitted that although the
sheriff was well founded in stating that the standard of
proof to discharge the burden resting on the appellant
C was proof on a balance of probabilities, the sheriff was
wrong in holding that the appellant required to lead
evidence which was corroborated. He contended that
although the provisions of what is now s 15 (3) of the
Road Traffic Offenders Act 1988 took the case out of
the ordinary position, and required an accused person
to prove something, there was no justification for
holding that evidence led by an accused in support of
his defence required to be corroborated.

D   The learned Solicitor General submitted that there
was no authority which supported the sheriff's conclusion that corroboration was necessary, and he maintained that it was contrary to principle that an accused
should have to lead corroborated evidence in support
of a defence which a statute permitted him to put
forward.

Where, as under the provisions of the Road Traffic
Offenders Act 1988, an assumption falls to be made
unless an accused proves otherwise, it is, we consider,
E in accordance with principle that the evidence led by
the accused for this purpose need not be corroborated;
all that is required is that the court accepts the evidence led by the accused as being credible and reliable.
The law insists upon corroboration where the prosecution require to establish the guilt of an accused beyond
reasonable doubt, but different considerations apply
where the law imposes a burden upon an accused
person to establish a defence; the standard of proof
required of him is on a balance of probabilities, and we
F are not persuaded that there is any requirement for
corroboration.

We are accordingly satisfied that the first question
in the case falls to be answered in the affirmative.
Counsel for the appellant maintained that it followed
that the sheriff had not been entitled to convict. She
recognised, however, that the sheriff had indicated
that even if he had felt able to proceed upon the appellant's uncorroborated evidence as to his consumption
of alcohol both before and after the alleged offence, he
would not have been persuaded that the requirements

of s 15 (3) had been established. In the final paragraph
of his note the sheriff expresses himself as follows: "In G
the course of delivering my decision in this case I indicated that I was holding that there was insufficient
evidence in law for me to accept that the accused had
proved the facts specified in s 15 (3) (b), but that even
if I had felt entitled to proceed on the appellant's own
uncorroborated evidence of his pre- and post-driving
alcohol consumption I would not have been persuaded
by that evidence that the statutory assumption in s 15
(2) had been overcome and that the requirements of
s 15 (3) had been established."   H

It is not entirely clear what the sheriff means by this
passage in his note, but we have come to the conclusion that what it must mean is that the sheriff did
not accept the evidence of the appellant as to his consumption of alcohol before and after the alleged
offence as credible and reliable. It is significant that
the sheriff says in terms in the second paragraph of his
note that he accepted the evidence of the appellant and
his son that the appellant had consumed brandy after
he had ceased to drive. The sheriff then goes on to   I
describe the evidence which the appellant himself
gave regarding his consumption of alcohol before and
after the alleged offence and he does not say that he
found that evidence acceptable. As we have already
indicated, although an accused founding upon this
defence does not require to lead corroborated evidence, before he can be held to have established the
defence he must lead evidence which the sheriff is prepared to accept as credible and reliable. In the present
case the sheriff has stated that he would not have been J
persuaded by the evidence led by the appellant, and
we have come to the conclusion that that can only
mean that the sheriff did not find the evidence of the
appellant as to his pre- and post-driving alcohol consumption to be credible and reliable. That being so it
follows that the appellant failed to prove that the
assumption contained in s 15 (2) should not be made.
The consequence must be that the sheriff was entitled
to convict the appellant. We shall accordingly answer
the second question in the case in the affirmative and K
the appeal against conviction is refused.

Counsel for Appellant, Powrie; Solicitors, McKay &
Norwell, WS — Counsel for Respondent, Solicitor
General (Dawson, QC); Solicitor, J D Lowe, Crown
Agent.

                                              P W F
                                                          L

A v Kennedy

A　SECOND DIVISION

THE LORD JUSTICE CLERK (ROSS),
LORDS MURRAY AND BRAND

20 NOVEMBER 1992

Children and young persons — Children's hearing — Application to sheriff for findings whether or not grounds of referral established — Whether child "member of the same household" as person who had committed an offence
B　*— Factors to be taken into account in determining whether same household — Social Work (Scotland) Act 1968 (c 49), s 32 (2) (d).*

Section 32 (2) (d) of the Social Work (Scotland) Act 1968 provides that a child may be in need of compulsory measures of care if inter alia any of the offences mentioned in Sched 1 to the Criminal Procedure (Scotland) Act 1975 has been committed in respect of him or in respect of a child who is a member of the same household.

C　A reporter referred a child, born on 9 February 1992, to a children's hearing inter alia under s 32 (2) (d). The child's parents had had another child in 1983 who died in infancy having been ill treated. An elder sister, born in 1980, had gone to live with foster parents for a time thereafter but had now been returned to her parents under supervision. After sundry procedure the sheriff held inter alia that that ground had been established. The parents appealed by stated case, arguing that the sheriff had erred in deter-
D　mining that the child was a member of the same household as the deceased child: the "household" was not just the sum total of the persons living in the house, but consideration had to be given to the ages of the members of the household at the relevant times, their gender and their experience.

Held, (1) that it was a question of circumstances, fact and degree whether the household was the same, and that a household might continue to constitute the same household as before even where there were
E　changes in membership of the group which constituted the household; the factors founded on by the parents did not in themselves affect the identity of the household (p 1190K-L); (2) that on the facts of the present case the sheriff was entitled to conclude that as between 1983 and 1992 the household to which the two infants respectively belonged remained the same (pp 1190L-1191A); and appeal *refused* and case *remitted* to the sheriff to proceed as accords.

F　————————————

Appeal from the sheriff court

JA and GA, the parents of a child N, appealed to the Court of Session by way of stated case against the decision of the sheriff at Dumbarton finding that a ground of referral to a children's panel under s 32 (2) (d) of the Social Work (Scotland) Act 1968 was established.

Statutory provisions

The Social Work (Scotland) Act 1968 provides:

"32.—(1) A child may be in need of compulsory measures of care within the meaning of this Part of G this Act if any of the conditions mentioned in the next following subsection is satisfied with respect to him.

"(2) The conditions referred to in subsection (1) of this section are that — . . . (d) any of the offences mentioned in Schedule 1 to the Criminal Procedure (Scotland) Act 1975 has been committed in respect of him or in respect of a child who is a member of the same household".

Cases referred to　　　　　　　　　　　　　　　　　　H
Kennedy v R's Curator ad Litem, 1993 SLT 295.
M v McGregor, 1982 SLT 41.
McGregor v H, 1983 SLT 626.
R v Birmingham Juvenile Court, ex p S [1984] Fam 93; [1984] 3 WLR 387; [1984] 2 All ER 688.

The appeal was heard before the Second Division on 29 and 30 October 1992.

On 20 November 1992 the court *refused* the appeal I and *remitted* the case to the sheriff under s 50 (3) of the Social Work (Scotland) Act 1968 to proceed as accords.

The following opinion of the court was delivered by the Lord Justice Clerk (Ross):

OPINION OF THE COURT.—This is an appeal by way of stated case under s 50 of the Social Work (Scotland) Act 1968. The appeal is against a decision of the sheriff at Dumbarton finding grounds of referral J A and C to have been established, and remitting the case to the reporter to the children's panel, Dumbarton, for disposal in terms of s 42 (6) of the Social Work (Scotland) Act 1968.

The referral related to a child N who was born on 9 February 1992 of whom the appellants are the parents. The reporter had stated three grounds for referral, and they were in the following terms:

"A. That one of the offences mentioned in Sched 1 to the Criminal Procedure (Scotland) Act 1975 namely K wilfully assaulting or ill treating a child in a manner likely to cause unnecessary suffering or injury to health, has been committed against a child, who is a member of the same household, being grounds for referral in terms of s 32 (2) (d) of the Social Work (Scotland) Act 1968, as amended by para 54 (b) of Sched 3 to the Children Act 1975, and/or

"B. That the child is, or is likely to become, a member of the same household as a person who has committed one of the offences mentioned in Sched 1 L to the Criminal Procedure (Scotland) Act 1975, namely wilfully assaulting or ill treating a child in a manner likely to cause unnecessary suffering or injury to health, being grounds for referral in terms of s 32 (2) (dd) of the Social Work (Scotland) Act 1968, as amended by para 54 (c) of Sched 3 to the Children Act 1975, and/or

"C. That lack of parental care is likely to cause the child unnecessary suffering or seriously to impair her health or development, being grounds for referral in terms of s 32 (2) (c) of the Social Work (Scotland) Act 1968, as amended by para 54 (a) of Sched 3 to the Children Act 1975 as specified on the attached statement."

In the statement of facts relied upon it is stated that N would under normal circumstances reside with the appellants, and that an elder sister of the child, namely S, who was born on 14 July 1980, resides in family with the appellants. N also had a brother M who was born on 14 June 1983 and who resided in family with the appellants until his death on 5 August 1983. It is further stated in the statement of facts that between 17 June 1983 and 31 July 1983 at the appellants' then home, M was wilfully assaulted or ill treated whereby he suffered multiple injuries which are specified. Between 30 and 31 July 1983 at the appellants' home M was wilfully assaulted or ill treated whereby he suffered injuries as a result of which he died.

Paragraph 4 of the statement of facts is in the following terms: "4. That at all material times, M was in the custody, charge or care of JA and GA".

Statement of fact 4 was accepted by the appellants. It is further stated in the statement of facts that on 12 October 1983 at Dumbarton sheriff court it was established that a Sched 1 offence had been committed in respect of M and reference was made to detailed statements of fact in relation to him which had been found to be established.

After sundry procedure before the sheriff, and after the respondent had closed his case, a continued hearing took place at which the sheriff held that the respondent had established a prima facie case in respect of grounds of referral A and C, and in respect of all the statements of fact, but that he had failed to establish a prima facie case in respect of ground of referral B. At that stage the representatives of the appellants indicated that they wished to lead evidence, and the hearing was further adjourned. At a subsequent hearing, however, both appellants indicated that it was not their intention to lead any evidence. A safeguarder and curator ad litem had been appointed to N, and the safeguarder and curator ad litem intimated that she was not seeking to present any case. It was in these circumstances that the sheriff arrived at the decision which is now challenged in this stated case. The sheriff explains that both parents applied for a stated case, but that he concluded that since their applications were in identical terms, and their interests appeared to be identical, he had stated one case only rather than two separate cases. At the hearing before this court it was agreed that the sheriff had been entirely correct to state one case only.

In opening the appeal, counsel for the first appellant explained that two issues were to be raised in the appeal. The first was whether the sheriff had erred in determining that the child N was a member of the same household as the deceased child M. The second issue was whether the sheriff had been entitled to hold that the reporter had established a prima facie case in respect of ground of referral C.

So far as the first matter is concerned, the sheriff in his note has dealt with submissions made on behalf of the appellants which laid emphasis on the fact that in s 32 (2) (d) of the Act of 1968 the words are "a child who is a member of the same household" and not "a child who was a member of the same household". Counsel for the first appellant, however, stated that she did not contend that a strict interpretation of "is" was necessary. She recognised that if one construed the language strictly and confined the provision to cases covered by the present tense, this would subvert the intention of the statute. For example, if any of the offences mentioned in Sched 1 to the Act of 1975 had been committed in respect of a child who had been living in a household, and as a result that child was removed from the household, a child subsequently entering the household by birth or otherwise might still require the protection of the statute. Counsel for the first appellant, however, submitted that in the present case the household into which M would go if she was returned to her parents would not be the same household as that to which M belonged. Her submission was that in determining the identity of any particular household, it was necessary to consider the whole family circumstances. She conceded that whether a particular child was a member of the same household as another child was a matter of fact and degree. She conceded that it was not merely a matter of geographical location.

Counsel for the first appellant stressed that M had died on 5 August 1983, and that N had not been born until 9 February 1992. There was thus a considerable lapse of time between the date when M had been a member of the household, and the date when N could have entered the household. She maintained that the "household" was not just the sum total of the persons living in the house but that one had to consider the ages of all members of the household at the relevant time, the sex of the members of the household, and the experiences of the members of the household at the relevant periods. In the latter connection she stressed that the elder sister of N, namely S, had been a member of the household both during the lifetime of M and now, but she emphasised that during the intervening period S had been away from the household living with foster parents although she had now returned to live with the appellants under a supervision requirement. Counsel for the first appellant submitted that the circumstances of the household had developed to such a substantial extent that the sheriff ought to have held that the household into which N would now go was different from the household to which M had belonged during his short life.

Counsel for the respondent on the other hand, submitted that counsel for the first appellant's submissions were not well founded. He agreed with her that it was not appropriate to apply a literal application of the present tense when construing s 32 (2) (d). However, he also submitted that the critical question was whether the household in 1992 into which N would go was the same as the household to which M had belonged in 1983. He submitted that "household"

was a flexible concept, and he agreed with counsel for
A the first appellant that it was a matter of fact and
degree. He maintained that the sheriff was entitled to
reach the conclusion which he did, and that this court
would only be entitled to interfere with his decision if
they were satisfied that the decision was one which no
reasonable sheriff could have reached.

Counsel for the respondent submitted that the
household was the same at the two material times
because the parents were the same, and S provided an
element of continuity since she was a member of the
B household both in 1983 and 1992. In the circumstances it was impossible to point to any relevant
change in the identification of the household.

As counsel on both sides agreed, the starting point
for consideration of this case must be *McGregor v H*.
In that case at p 628, the Lord President (Emslie) said:
"All that is required by s 32 (2) (d) is that the child
shall be 'a member of the same household' as the
victim of a relevant offence. The word 'household' in
C s 32 is plainly intended to connote a family unit or
something akin to a family unit — a group of persons,
held together by a particular kind of tie who normally
live together, even if individual members of the group
may be temporarily separated from it. The language of
s 32 (2) (d) provides no warrant for the geographical
approach of the sheriff."

Similar words to those which occur in s 32 (2) (d)
were considered by the Queen's Bench Division in *R
v Birmingham Juvenile Court, ex p S*. The words in s 1
D of the Children and Young Persons Act 1969 are
"who is or was a member of the household to which
he belongs". In that case in 1978 a care order had been
made in respect of a child A whose home had been
with her mother and father. Subsequently the mother
and father separated and were divorced. The mother
began an association with another man and in 1983 a
child B was born. At that time the mother was cohabiting with B's father. It was held that the magistrates
had been entitled to hold that the child A had been a
E member of the household to which B belonged. In the
course of his judgment Sir John Arnold P stressed that
the question was a matter of fact and degree. He
stated: "But at the heart of the concept it is the
persons who comprise the household which have to be
considered I think and not the place where the household is located as a matter of residence" ([1984] Fam
93, p 98).

He went on to observe that it was entirely reasonable
in that case to think that the mother was a person
F whose presence in the household was of the very first
importance. When B was born the dominant personality in terms of what constituted the household to
which he belonged was the mother. He thus concluded that the magistrates were entitled to hold that
the child A had been a member of the household to
which the child B belonged.

We were also referred to *Kennedy v R's Curator ad
Litem*. In that case a child ER was born on 30 June
1989. She was the half sister of RR who was born on
11 August 1977. On 20 August 1990 grounds for the

referral of the case of RR to a children's hearing under
s 32 (2) (d) were established. On 22 January 1991 the   G
case of ER came before a children's hearing. Shortly
thereafter on 6 February 1991 the child's mother
removed herself from the family home taking ER with
her. The court observed that the fact that persons were
living for the time being in separate houses was not
decisive of the question of whether they were
members of the same household. Lord President Hope
stated (at p 300A): "The important question, since the
issue is whether the child is in need of compulsory
measures of care in terms of s 32 of the Act, is whether H
the ties of affection and regular contact which hold the
parties together as a group of persons still continue."
The court accordingly held that the sheriff had not
been entitled to hold that there was no prima facie case
made out by the reporter's evidence.

As Lord President Emslie observed in *McGregor v H*
the word "household" in s 32 connotes a family unit
or something akin to a family unit. In his opinion he
also observed that "household" was a group of
persons held together by a particular tie who normally I
lived together even if individual members of the group
might be temporarily separated from it. These
remarks were of course made under reference to the
facts of that particular case. In our opinion, a household may continue to constitute the same household as
before even if one or more of the original members
have separated from it permanently. For example, if
parents and a number of children live together in
family, they would clearly constitute a "household".
If in the course of time the eldest child was to leave   J
home to get married and was to set up a home of his
own, in our opinion there would still remain an identifiable household which was the same household as
that which existed when the eldest child was still a
member of the group. In other words, in any household or family unit there will be a certain amount of
coming and going. The group may be expanded by the
addition of new members of the family; likewise the
group may be reduced in size if a member of the group
dies or leaves home and sets up a separate establish- K
ment. Despite such changes, it may be proper to conclude that the household has all along remained the
same household. We are accordingly satisfied that
changes of membership of the group which constitute
the household need not lead to the conclusion that the
household has become different from the household
which previously existed.

We are not persuaded that the factors referred to by
counsel for the first appellant, namely passage of time, L
the gender of the members of the group at any particular time, their experiences, have anything to do
with the identity of the household. As has been
observed it is a question of circumstances whether the
household is the same, and it is a matter of degree. In
the present case, as the sheriff observed, the parents of
M and N were the same, they are still living together,
and they still have a child with them. Moreover, the
elder sister S was a member of the household into
which M was born, and likewise she is a member of
the household into which N was born. In these cir-

cumstances we are quite satisfied that the sheriff was
A entitled to conclude that as between 1983 and 1992
the household to which M and N respectively
belonged remained the same. Indeed, it is difficult to
discover any relevant change in the identification of
the household during the period from 1983 to 1992.
Since the decision on this matter was one which the
sheriff was entitled to make, we can detect no error in
his determination in this regard, and we accordingly
answer the first question in the case in the negative.

B [The court then dealt with another issue, with
which this report is not concerned, and continued:]

Having so answered both questions in the case, we
shall remit the case to the sheriff to proceed as accords.

---

*Counsel for First Appellant (Mother), Cowan; Solici-
tors, Macbeth Currie & Co, WS — Counsel for Second
Appellant (Father), Keane; Solicitors, Macbeth Currie &
Co, WS — Counsel for Respondent (Reporter), Emslie,*
C *QC; Solicitors, Biggart, Baillie & Gifford, WS.*

C H A of L

Moir v HM Advocate

D HIGH COURT OF JUSTICIARY
THE LORD JUSTICE CLERK (ROSS),
LORDS MORISON AND PROSSER
11 DECEMBER 1992

*Justiciary — Crime — Murder — Concert — Several
accused — Whether necessary to prove concert in respect
of all co-accused in order to establish guilt of one.*

Justiciary — Procedure — Trial — Charge to jury —
E *Concert — Conflicting evidence as to participation of
accused in concerted attack — Whether misdirection that
trial judge failed to explain law of concert as applied to
the conflicting evidence.*

*Justiciary — Procedure — Trial — Jury — After retiral
jury requesting repetition of evidence — Whether trial
judge under a duty to give a summary from his notes —
Discretion of presiding judge.*

Three accused were charged inter alia with murder
F and assault to severe injury. The first and second
accused were convicted on both charges; the third
accused was acquitted. During the trial, the evidence
of two of the main witnesses conflicted. The first
witness (M) saw three men attacking a man on the
ground. She saw one man, the deceased, lying on the
pavement and another, the complainer in the assault
charge, pulling himself up against a car. The three
assailants ran off but later returned and resumed the
attack on the man on the ground, and subsequently
left. The other main witness, J, saw two men kicking
a man on the ground and a third attacking another

man who was over the bonnet of a car. The two men
left but then returned and resumed the attack on the G
man on the ground. The third attacker remained.
Thereafter, all three left together.

The trial judge directed the jury, on a concession by
the Crown, that the case against the accused depended
upon the Crown establishing concert as between all
three accused. Having retired, the jury returned and
the foreman stated to the trial judge that the jury
"would like to hear if possible . . . all or part of the
evidence given by [J]". The trial judge refused the
request and told the jury that they must rely upon H
their own recollection of the evidence. The first
accused appealed against conviction on the murder
charge on grounds inter alia of misdirection and that
the trial judge had erred in refusing to allow the jury
to hear his notes of J's evidence.

Held, (1) that the trial judge had misdirected the
jury in respect of concert since it was possible for the
jury to conclude that although there had been three
attackers, the accused was not one of them, but that
such a misdirection was favourable to the accused I
(p 1195E-G); (2) that in respect of the murder charge,
the jury had been told clearly that the case against all
three accused depended upon the Crown establishing
concert, and had been given adequate directions on
what constituted concert; and since on either M's or
J's evidence it was open to the jury to infer that the
appellant was one of the three who had attacked the
deceased, it was unnecessary for the trial judge to
explain in detail how to apply the law of concert in J
respect of the different accounts given by M and J
(p 1196E-F and I-J); (3) that since J could not be
recalled and there was no transcript of his evidence
available, it was open to the trial judge to give a
summary to the jury from his notes of J's evidence,
but it was entirely a matter for him to determine
whether or not to follow that course, and the court was
not in a position to review the discretion of the presiding judge on matters concerning the best way of
conducting the case (p 1197B-E); and appeal *refused.* K

Dictum in *Hamilton v HM Advocate*, 1938 SLT
333, *followed; Docherty v HM Advocate*, 1945 SLT
247, *distinguished.*

Indictment

Scott Moir, Steven Peters and Kevin Alan Finlay
were charged at the instance of the rt hon the Lord
Fraser of Carmyllie, Her Majesty's Advocate, on an L
indictment which contained the following charges,
inter alia: "(1) on 25 or 26 January 1991 in West
Preston Street, Edinburgh, you did assault Stuart
William Bunch, formerly of 78 Kirkbrae, Edinburgh,
now deceased, punch and kick him repeatedly on the
head and body, knock him to the ground and further
kick him repeatedly on the head and thus inflict upon
him injuries from which he died on 19 February 1991
at Edinburgh Royal Infirmary, and you did murder
him; (2) date and place above libelled, you did assault
Fergus Andrew McKinnon, care of Lothian and

A Borders Police, Edinburgh, and repeatedly punch and kick him on the head and body to his severe injury".

The accused pled not guilty and proceeded to trial in the High Court at Edinburgh before Lord Osborne and a jury. After trial the jury by a majority found the first and second accused guilty on charge 1; unanimously found the first accused guilty on charge 2 under certain deletions; by a majority found the second accused guilty on charge 2 under certain deletions; and by a majority found charges 1 and 2 not proven against the third accused.

B The first and second accused appealed to the High Court by note of appeal against conviction on charge 1.

Cases referred to

Docherty v HM Advocate, 1945 SLT 247; 1945 JC 89.
Hamilton v HM Advocate, 1938 SLT 333; 1938 JC 134.
Melvin v HM Advocate, 1984 SLT 365; 1984 SCCR 113.

C

The trial judge gave the following directions to the jury, inter alia:

LORD OSBORNE.— . . . Now, you will see in charges 1 and 2 of the indictment that the accused, the allegation is that all three of the accused were responsible for the criminal acts that are set out there. This situation, where two or more persons are said or alleged to be involved in a crime together, demands
D that I explain to you and direct you in law as to what is called the law of concert or, as it has been called by counsel, the law of art and part. I must emphasise that this is a principle of the greatest importance in the circumstances of this case.

Now, ladies and gentlemen, where two or more persons are alleged to have committed a crime, the ordinary rule is that each person is criminally liable only for the acts proved directly against him. However, the situation is different where it is estab-
E lished that the persons concerned were, at the material time, acting together in pursuance of a common criminal purpose. In that event, and that is referred to as acting in concert, then the evidence affecting one, becomes evidence against the others. If you are satisfied that the crime has been committed, all of those involved are guilty, although only one may have committed the physical act constituting the crime.

You were given an example by counsel quite properly of a bank robbery, where someone goes into
F a bank and threatens the bank teller, to obtain money, a companion stands outside the door keeping a lookout and a third person sits waiting in a motor car to drive away the other two when the crime has been committed — that would be a very clear example of acting in concert. If a robbery at the bank were effected, the result of the application of this principle would be that all of those three people would be guilty of the robbery although only one of them actually went into the bank and forced the bank staff to hand over money.

Now, in this connection two or more persons may join together for a common criminal purpose by arrangement, in advance of the commission of a crime G or alternatively, they may come together for that purpose at or very shortly before the commission of the crime itself. It matters not which. If a common criminal purpose is established and a crime is committed in pursuance of it, all of the participants in that common enterprise are guilty, subject to this important qualification. Members of such a group are not responsible for something done by one, or it may be more, of them, which goes beyond the scope of the group's common criminal purpose in an unforeseeable H manner. For example, if there was a plot between a number of persons to commit a pickpocketing and one of the group, unknown to the others, carried a knife and used that knife upon the victim in the course of committing the pickpocketing, only that person would be guilty of an assault by the use of the weapon, the others would be criminally responsible for the pickpocketing alone, so that is an example of what I meant just now when I mentioned the qualification.

Now ladies and gentlemen, I think I should make it I clear to you that mere presence at the scene of a crime, coupled with a failure to prevent the commission of a crime does not of itself constitute art and part guilt or concert. However, the circumstances of a person's presence at the scene of crime may be such as to enable it to be inferred that that person was involved with the principal actors in the prior conception of a plan for the commission of a crime.

Now ladies and gentlemen, there are a number of ways in which a person may become involved through J the principle of concert or art and part in responsibility for a crime. Perhaps the most common way is the case of an agreement, a plot or if you like a conspiracy, to commit a crime — that is the simplest form of concert and in such a case any of those who are parties to that, if they put that plan into execution, will be implicated in the criminal acts which follow.

Now ladies and gentlemen, it follows from what I have said already regarding the matter of concert that K where concert is charged, as it is here, in relation to charges 1 and 2, the first question which you must consider is whether each person affected by the charge, considered separately, is in the concert or plot or took part in the common criminal purpose. Now, that is a question, and I must emphasise this, which you must consider separately in relation to each accused person.

If an accused person is established to be a participant in the common criminal purpose, the L consequences which I have described will follow. If they are not, then that accused is criminally liable only for his or her own acts proved against them.

Now, and this is important ladies and gentlemen, it is as a result of that, that if you are dealing with a charge involving a number of persons and you hold concert is not proved then, to obtain a conviction, the Crown must show the individual parts played by the accused concerned and if they cannot do that then an acquittal would require to follow.

Now, ladies and gentlemen, that I propose to elaborate in a moment or two in relation to the circumstances of this case, but before I do that I would emphasise that these principles that I mentioned are of the greatest importance in the circumstances here and I would now like to draw your attention to certain features of the Crown's position in this case to which these principles must be applied.

Now, the Crown here accept, and in the circumstances so therefore must you, that in relation to charge 1 their case against the accused must depend upon their establishing concert as between all the three accused, because the Crown accept that they are not in a position to prove, by legally sufficient evidence, the parts actually played individually by those involved. Thus, unless you are satisfied that the Crown have proved such concert, you must acquit the accused on charge 1. In relation to charge 2 the position is a little different and a little more complicated.

Scott Moir, who is the first named accused, has accepted, through his counsel, that he falls to be convicted on charge 2. The background to that is that he accepted in his tape recorded interview, which has been read to you, that he had assaulted Fergus McKinnon for the reason and in the circumstances which he described in the interview. Also, it is not disputed that his palm print was found on the bonnet of the Maestro motor car which was in the street outside Pinocchio's restaurant at the time of the assault as it appears. It is thus understandable that Mr Moir has taken up the position which he did. Incidentally, and you may have appreciated this already, acceptance of guilt of charge 2 by Scott Moir means that it follows that he's accepting guilt of charge 3 since he was on bail at the material time and as I have already said counsel recognised that.

However, all of that still leaves for your consideration the position of the second and third named accused Steven Peters and Kevin Finlay in relation to charge 2. Now, again as I understand it the Crown accept, and so must you, that in relation to charge 2, the Crown case against those accused, nos 2 and 3, must depend upon the Crown establishing concert as between all the three accused. Again, because they are not in a position to prove by legally sufficient evidence the parts actually played individually by those accused. Thus, unless you are satisfied that the Crown have proved concert, you must acquit the accused nos 2 and 3 on charge 2.

For all these reasons ladies and gentlemen you will see the very great importance of this principle to the circumstances of this case. Now, before I part with the matter of concert, I think it right to emphasise a point which counsel for the first accused made in his speech to you yesterday, and that was that his acceptance of Scott Moir's guilt of charge 2 and charge 3 should not be thought by you to involve any concession as to his client's involvement in the concert which the Crown must prove to obtain a conviction on charge 1. . . .

Having been charged, the jury retired but subsequently returned in order to ask a question of the trial judge. The following exchange took place:

Lord Osborne — Now ladies and gentlemen, I gather that you have a question that you wish to ask me and I will just ask whoever is going to speak for you to ask it.

The foreman of the jury — What we would like to hear if possible is all or part of the evidence given by Mr Johnston.

Lord Osborne — Again?

The foreman of the jury — Please.

Lord Osborne — Well, I have to tell you that that is not possible. The statutory procedure under which a trial such as this is held provides for evidence being heard at a certain stage and then for subsequent procedure, and once that procedure has been gone through it has to be followed to its conclusion. We cannot, as it were, go back to an earlier stage of the procedure so I have to answer your question, no. I would say, in addition to that, that in your deliberations, as I have already said, you must rely upon your own recollections of the evidence which you have heard.

Appeal

The grounds of appeal were in the following terms, inter alia:

(2) Standing (a) the concession by the Crown that there was insufficient evidence led to enable the jury to convict the appellant on charge 1, on the basis of his own actings, et separatim (b) the line of defence argued on behalf of the appellant to the effect that the appellant was engaged in a fight with Fergus McKinnon whilst the fatal assault upon the deceased was being carried out by others, et separatim (c) the nature and extent of the evidence against the appellant, the trial judge failed to give the jury adequate directions as to what they would require to hold proved vis à vis the appellant of either murder or culpable homicide on charge 1, on the basis of his art and part involvement with the other two accused.

(3) Contrary to the direction which the jury received from the trial judge to the effect that they required to accept that the Crown case against the appellant on charge 1 depended upon the Crown establishing concert between all three, the appellant and his two co-accused, the jury convicted the appellant and his co-accused Steven Peters on charge 1, and acquitted their co-accused Kevin Alan Finlay of the same charge. . . .

(7) When the foreman of the jury intimated to the trial judge that the jury would like to hear if possible, all or part of the evidence given by the witness William Johnston the trial judge erred in failing to provide the jury with the opportunity of hearing the notes he had made of Mr Johnston's evidence.

The appeal first came before the High Court on 20 February 1992 when it was continued to allow, inter

A alia, the extension of notes of evidence in respect of the witnesses Fiona Elizabeth MacPherson and William Scott Coyne Johnston.

The appeal was further heard before the High Court on 20 November 1992.

On 11 December 1992 the court *refused* the appeal.

The following opinion of the court was delivered by the Lord Justice Clerk (Ross):

B **OPINION OF THE COURT.—**The appellants and a co-accused, Kevin Alan Finlay, went to trial in the High Court at Edinburgh on an indictment containing three charges. The first charge libelled that the appellants and their co-accused had murdered Stuart William Bunch, and the second charge libelled that they had assaulted Fergus Andrew McKinnon to his severe injury. The third charge was directed against the appellant Moir only and libelled a contravention of s 3 (1) (b) of the Bail etc (Scotland) Act 1980.

C At the conclusion of the Crown case, counsel for each accused made a submission of no case to answer in terms of s 140A of the Criminal Procedure (Scotland) Act 1975. Counsel for each of the appellants and their co-accused submitted that there was insufficient evidence to justify conviction on charges 1 and 2. The advocate depute contended that the evidence led supported a concerted attack by the appellants and their co-accused on the two complainers, and moved the court to reject the submissions. The trial judge D rejected the submissions and the trial proceeded. During the advocate depute's address to the jury, he sought and obtained leave of the court to amend charge 2 in the indictment by deletion of the words "and kick" and "severe" where they occurred in charge 2.

The jury by a majority found the two appellants guilty as libelled of murder on charge 1. They unanimously found the appellant Moir guilty of charge 2 as E amended, and they unanimously found him guilty as libelled on charge 3. By a majority they found the appellant Peters guilty of charge 2 as amended. By a majority they found charges 1 and 2 not proven against the co-accused Finlay. Against their conviction on these charges the appellants have now appealed. The evidence disclosed that Stuart William Bunch (hereinafter referred to as "the deceased") and Fergus Andrew McKinnon, the complainer in charge 2, (hereinafter referred to as "the complainer") were F workmates. On Friday 25 January 1991 they both left their place of work about 4.30 pm and went to the Southside snooker centre in Causewayside. They had a couple of drinks and started to play snooker about 5 pm and played for approximately two hours. Thereafter they went to a bar downstairs in the centre for more drinks where they remained until around 11 pm. The complainer admitted to drinking nine or ten pints of beer during this period. While they were in this bar some kind of incident, imperfectly described in evidence, involving the breaking of a glass occurred. On leaving the centre, the deceased and the complainer

made their way to the south side of West Preston Street, a short distance from the centre. In the vicinity G of Pinocchio's restaurant there, they were attacked. As a result of the attack the complainer and the deceased were rendered unconscious and otherwise injured. The deceased sustained injuries from which he died on 19 February 1991 without having recovered consciousness. The complainer regained consciousness soon after the attack, before the police and an ambulance arrived.

As the trial judge makes clear in his report, the precise details of the attack were the subject of H controversy. The complainer was unable to give evidence about it. Evidence regarding the attack was given by Fiona MacPherson, an employee at Pinocchio's restaurant, Rudolpho Ganarin, the proprietor of the restaurant, and Michele Tattolo, the chef there. Evidence was also given by William Johnston, a resident of West Preston Street, who happened to be looking out of a window of his flat at the material time. Of the three witnesses in the restaurant, the most important was Fiona MacPherson. She described seeing a fight I outside the restaurant through a window. Three people appeared to be kicking somebody on the ground and stamping and jumping on him. Later she went outside and saw one man, the deceased, lying on the pavement and another, the complainer, pulling himself up against a car. The three attackers ran off in the direction of South Clerk Street, but they later came back and resumed the attack on the man on the ground, subsequently leaving in the direction of Causewayside. She was unable to identify anyone as J an attacker.

William Johnston described a somewhat different picture. He said he saw a fracas involving some people hitting two others, one of whom was on the pavement and the other of whom was over the bonnet of a car. There were three attackers altogether; he saw two of them kicking the man on the ground and the third attacking the man on the car bonnet. Later the two men started to run in the direction of South Clerk K Street, returned and resumed the attack. The third man did not leave off as did the other two. Thereafter all three walked briskly away in the direction of Causewayside and turned left into it. Johnston could not describe or identify any of the attackers.

As the trial judge observed in his report, one of the principal issues in the case was whether the Crown had proved that the three accused were in fact the three attackers. The Crown relied on a variety of pieces of evidence of which the following were the L most important. [His Lordship described the evidence, referred to the authorising of the extension of notes of evidence and continued:]

From the transcript of the advocate depute's speech, it is clear that the Crown case was that the appellants and their co-accused acting together had attacked the deceased and the complainer. After dealing with the matter of concert, the advocate depute in the course of addressing the jury said: "The Crown's position there is that we have a group of people, three accused on the one hand and two people on the other, that there was a concerted attack by the three upon the two, Mr Bunch and Mr McKinnon." Subsequently, towards the end of his address, he said this: "Look at the various circumstances, the various small pieces of evidence, look at all the evidence together and you may say that it builds up a picture that points in one direction, towards an impression of the three people assisting each other both before and after, in a concerted attack upon the two people mentioned in charges 1 and 2."

In the course of his charge to the jury the trial judge explained to them what was meant by concert, and he then gave them the following direction: "Now, the Crown here accept, and in the circumstances so therefore must you, that in relation to charge 1 their case against the accused must depend upon their establishing concert as between all the three accused, because the Crown accept that they are not in a position to prove, by legally sufficient evidence, the parts actually played individually by those involved. Thus, unless you are satisfied that the Crown have proved such concert, you must acquit the accused on charge 1. In relation to charge 2 the position is a little different and a little more complicated."

Scott Moir

On behalf of the appellant Moir seven grounds of appeal were put forward in the note of appeal. Ground 3 refers to the foregoing direction by the trial judge and makes the point that the jury, contrary to that direction, convicted the two appellants, and acquitted the co-accused of charge 1.

On behalf of the appellant Moir, counsel submitted that the trial judge's direction which we have just quoted was a misdirection, but he recognised that the direction was favourable to the defence, and he did not suggest that it had led to any miscarriage of justice. He confined himself to pointing out that the fact that the jury convicted the two appellants and acquitted their co-accused showed that the jury had found it difficult to arrive at a decision upon the evidence. The advocate depute agreed that what the trial judge had said in this passage of his charge was a misdirection, but he too submitted that no miscarriage of justice had followed from it since the misdirection was favourable to the defence.

We are satisfied that the trial judge was in error when he gave the foregoing direction to the jury. Although the Crown's position was that there were three assailants, and that the appellants and their co-accused had been acting together in attacking the deceased and the complainer, it did not follow that the Crown could only succeed if concert could be established between all three of the accused. It is impossible to know why the jury acquitted the co-accused, but it may simply have been that they were not satisfied that he was identified as one of the three persons taking part in the attack. Having regard to the evidence led before the jury, they may well have concluded that there were three attackers, but not have been satisfied that it had been established beyond reasonable doubt

that the co-accused was one of them. In these circumstances, there was no reason why the jury should not have convicted two only of the three persons accused. There was no need for the trial judge to have given this particular direction, and he was in error in giving it. It was not, however, suggested that the misdirection resulted in a miscarriage of justice.

[His Lordship considered and rejected a submission that there was insufficient evidence to go to the jury, and continued:]

Counsel also sought to support ground 2 of the grounds of appeal to the effect that the trial judge had failed to give the jury adequate directions on the subject of concert and also on what required to be proved against the appellant for either murder or culpable homicide on charge 1. In this connection, counsel founded strongly upon the evidence of William Johnston. Mr Johnston explained that he was interested in astronomy and was using a telescope at the time. He described looking down onto the pavement of West Preston Street and seeing what he described as a fracas. He spoke to seeing two people attacked by three people: "Two people were hitting one person on the pavement. All three were standing at that time and there was one person hitting another person over the front of the bonnet of the car which was in front of the restaurant. There were three apparently attacking two."

Later he stated that the two attacks were not together: "That's where two were attacking one on the pavement and the other instance was one attacking one, roughly where the bonnet of this blue car indicated on photograph F is located." Later he added: "Where one was attacking one it was certainly at the front of the car. Where two were attacking one it was at the centre of the car, but not quite at the rear of the car."

When he first saw the attack, punching was taking place, but shortly afterwards he looked back and saw that the person who was being attacked by the two men was on the ground and was being kicked by two people, while the other victim was now spreadeagled over the front of the bonnet of the car and being punched around the chest and head. He spoke to the person on the ground being kicked repeatedly by two people.

Founding on this evidence counsel maintained that if the jury accepted the evidence of William Johnston, the only reasonable inference was that the appellant Moir had attacked the complainer, and that if he was to be held guilty art and part of the attack upon the deceased, the jury would have required to receive particular directions as to how that could be. In the present case, however, the trial judge had done no more than give the jury general directions on the law of concert, and he had not explained to them how to apply these general directions to the particular circumstances of this case. In particular he had not explained to the jury how to approach the doctrine of concert in the event of their accepting the description given by William Johnston and holding that in the attack, the appellant Moir had been engaged in attacking the complainer while the other two men were apparently attacking the deceased. He submitted that the jury required a clear direction as to the legal basis upon which they could convict the appellant Moir of charge 1 if they took the view that during the fracas he had only been involved in assaulting the complainer in charge 2.

In this connection counsel founded upon *Docherty v HM Advocate.* In that case Lord Moncrieff remarked (1945 SLT at pp 249-250) that if a direction was of critical importance for the defence, the direction must be given quite explicitly and not be left to be derived from the drawing of inference. In our opinion, however, that case was concerned with a different matter which may arise where the Crown are relying upon concert. In *Docherty* the trial judge had failed to direct the jury explicitly that if they failed to find satisfactory proof of concert they were bound to acquit the accused. In the present case the trial judge directed the jury more than once that if the Crown failed to prove concert, they must acquit the accused of charge 1.

It is not disputed that the trial judge gave the jury accurate and sufficient directions on the law of concert generally. The complaint is that he did not explain how the general rules of concert could be applied to the facts of this case. Whether or not it is necessary or desirable to explain to a jury precisely how the law can be applied to the facts of a particular case is very much a matter for the trial judge to determine, and no hard and fast rule can be laid down. In the present case the trial judge might have explained to the jury in detail how to apply the law of concert if they were proceeding upon the description of events given by the witness Fiona MacPherson, and he might then have gone on to explain how the doctrine of concert could be applied to the situation described by William Johnston. However, we are not persuaded that it was essential for the trial judge to go into that amount of detail.

In the present case we are satisfied that the trial judge did give the jury adequate directions on the matter of concert. Under reference to charge 1, the jury were clearly told that the case against all three accused depended on the Crown establishing concert. The jury must have understood that the Crown's case was that the appellant Moir was one of three men who carried out an attack upon the deceased. If the jury accepted the description of events given by the witness Fiona MacPherson, there was evidence from which they could conclude that the appellant Moir was one of three men who attacked the deceased together. Alternatively, if the jury accepted the description of events given by William Johnston, then even if they took the view that the appellant Moir had concentrated his attention upon the complainer, they could nonetheless infer that he was party to the attack on the deceased. The evidence to which we have already referred in connection with the submission of no case to answer was sufficient to entitle the jury to conclude that there had been an attack by three men acting together upon two men; William Johnston's description was of two men being simultaneously attacked by a total of three men at virtually the same locus. Even though William Johnston did not see the assailant of the complainer kicking the deceased on the ground, the jury had been properly directed to the effect that if a common criminal purpose had been established, members of the group were not responsible for something done by one or more of them which went beyond the scope of the group's common criminal purpose in an unforeseeable manner. There was sufficient evidence to entitle the jury to conclude that the appellant Moir was party to the serious attack upon the deceased particularly in view of the fact that the three men had left the centre together, had been engaged together in an attack on two men in West Preston Street, thereafter had returned to the centre together, and that the appellant Moir was present when the appellant Peters described what they had done in the words "We just slapped them on the head round the corner". The trial judge had expressly directed the jury that mere presence at the scene of the crime coupled with a failure to prevent the commission of the crime would not of itself constitute guilt upon the basis of concert.

Moreover, the trial judge also gave the jury adequate directions as to what required to be established before a verdict of guilty of murder could be returned, and he also directed the jury that it would be open to them to return a verdict of culpable homicide if they were not satisfied that the criminal intent necessary for murder had been established. The jury were also clearly directed that they required to consider the case against each of the three accused separately. They obviously understood that because they acquitted the co-accused, Finlay, despite the misdirection of the trial judge to which we have already referred.

In all the circumstances we are satisfied that in this case the jury received adequate directions upon all material matters. We are not persuaded that it is necessary in every case to direct a jury where two or more persons are charged on an art and part basis with murder, that it is open to them to return a verdict of murder against one of the accused and a verdict of culpable homicide against another (*Melvin v HM Advocate*). In the present case, as we say, the jury were directed to consider the case against each accused separately, and they were also directed that if death resulted from an assault, it was culpable homicide unless it was established that there was murderous intent.

So far as the appellant Moir is concerned there remains ground 7 in the note of appeal. After the jury had retired they returned to court and intimated that there was a question which they wished to ask the trial judge. It is recorded in the transcript that the foreman of the jury stated "What we would like to hear if possible is all or part of the evidence given by Mr Johnston." In response to that request, the trial judge indicated that that was not possible and that the jury must rely upon their own recollection of the evidence which they had heard. In this ground of appeal it is stated that the trial judge erred in failing to provide the jury with the opportunity of hearing the notes he had made of Mr Johnston's evidence.

It is not entirely clear what the jury meant by their
A request. In particular it is not clear whether they were
wanting William Johnston recalled as a witness to
repeat his evidence, or whether they were under the
impression that a transcript of his evidence could be
read to them. In his report to us, the trial judge states
that it is his understanding that it is a fundamental
principle of our system of criminal justice that the jury
must proceed on their own recollection of the evidence, not that of judge or counsel.

In the situation which arose, we are satisfied that it
B was for the trial judge to decide whether he could
assist the jury regarding the evidence given by the
witness William Johnston. Plainly there was no question of a transcript of his evidence being available to
be read to them. Equally there was no question of
William Johnston being recalled to repeat his evidence. It would, however, have been open to the trial
judge to give the jury a summary of William
Johnston's evidence based upon his notes, although he
no doubt would have thought it desirable to remind
C the jury that they were not bound to accept what he
said as regards the evidence but that they must
proceed on the basis of their own recollection.
However whether or not he was to follow that course
was entirely a matter for the trial judge to determine.
Although he might have given the jury a summary of
William Johnston's evidence, he may have thought it
undesirable to do so since this might be thought to be
laying undue emphasis upon the evidence of one
witness.

D "But it is a matter very much in his [the trial
judge's] discretion whether he can help the jury by
resuming the evidence on any particular aspect of the
case" (*Hamilton v HM Advocate*, per Lord Justice
General, 1938 SLT at p 337).

In the same case it was observed that a court of
appeal is not in a position to review the discretion of
the presiding judge on matters which concerned the
best way of conducting the case before him.

E In these circumstances counsel has failed to
persuade us that the trial judge was in error in failing
to provide the jury with the opportunity of hearing
any notes which he had made of the evidence of
William Johnston. It follows that the appellant Moir
has failed to persuade us that there was any miscarriage of justice on any of the grounds put forward
in his note of appeal. His appeal against conviction is
accordingly refused.

F [His Lordship then considered and rejected a submission for the appellant Peters concerning the sufficiency of evidence.]

*Counsel for First Appellant (Moir), Mackay, QC,
Powrie; Solicitors, McCourts — Counsel for Second
Appellant (Peters), Henderson, QC; Solicitors, Wilson &
Co — Counsel for Respondent, Macdonald, QC, A D;
Solicitor, J D Lowe, Crown Agent.*

S J B

(NOTE)

Stafford v Renfrew District Council

OUTER HOUSE
LORD OSBORNE
18 DECEMBER 1992

*Damages — Amount — Solatium and loss of earnings —
Arm — Fractures of forearm and wrist with continuing
disability — Multiplier or lump sum award for future loss.*

A 38 year old slater fell from a ladder causing
injuries to an arm which, despite lengthy treatment,
caused permanent disability leaving the pursuer permanently unfit for his pre-accident employment.

Held, that solatium was properly assessed at £9,000,
and that wage loss should be calculated on the basis of
loss of earnings to date together with a lump sum
assessment of £12,000 for the future; and decree
pronounced accordingly.

George Stafford raised an action against his former
employers, Renfrew District Council, for damages for
injuries sustained in an accident at work on 16 January
1987. He was then aged 38. He had been working in
the course of his employment as a slater at a flat
window about 30 ft above ground level when the
ladder he was using moved to the side, causing the
pursuer to fall to the ground. After a proof before the
Lord Ordinary (Osborne) liability was established J
against the defenders for the fault of their foreman and
for breach of the Construction (Working Places) Regulations 1966, subject to a finding of contributory
negligence assessed at 30 per cent. In assessing
damages his Lordship said:

"I turn now to deal with the matter of damages.
Following the occurrence of the accident, the pursuer
was taken to the accident and emergency department
of the Royal Alexandra Hospital, Paisley. On examination there the pursuer was found to have major K
injuries to the left arm, namely posterior dislocation of
the elbow, compounded through a 4 cm antero-medial
wound, and a comminuted fracture-dislocation of the
wrist, compounded through a small anterior puncture
wound, with some impairment of circulation and sensation in the fingers distally. There were contusions
over the low back and both lower limbs, but no other
significant abnormal findings. Thereafter the pursuer
underwent an operative procedure. Reduction of the
dislocated elbow, together with substantial reduction L
of the damaged wrist, procured improvement in distal
circulation, and the wounds at elbow and wrist were
excised, extended and explored, removing all devita-
lised tissue. Following the operation the positions of
elbow and wrist were held in a long arm padded back-
slab. Finger sensory loss gradually improved, allowing
the pursuer to be discharged from hospital on 21
January 1987. Plaster immobilisation of the wrist was
continued until 26 February 1987. Thereafter the
pursuer received physiotherapy, which concentrated
on the restoration of wrist function. Fracture healing

A at the wrist had occurred with shortening and radial and dorsal deformity of the distal radius, with prominence of the distal ulna, which caused discomfort on forearm and wrist movement. Associated weakness persisted despite attention from the therapists. The result was that the pursuer was unable to return to work as a slater.

"Regular outpatient clinic reviews were undertaken in the latter part of 1987 and in the early months of 1988, by which stage no further improvement in strength could be anticipated. A corrective operation B for the radius and ulna was proposed and accepted. Re-admission to hospital for this procedure was arranged for early June and surgery on 10 June 1988 involved shortening of the distal ulna by resection of 1 cm of bone, fixation of the shortened bone by a six hole plate and screws, and use of the resected bone to secure and graft an opening wedge osteotomy of the distal radius, substantially correcting the dorsal and radial angulation deformities. A protective plaster was applied after closure of the wounds and post-operative C recovery was uneventful. The pursuer was discharged from hospital on 13 June 1988. Plaster support was continued until 21 July 1988. Thereafter gentle mobilisation was encouraged during monthly attendances in the clinic until November, when sound healing of the radial osteotomoy was observed, although union of the shortened ulna was less satisfactory. Return to work remained impractical because of persistent weakness and discomfort around the wrist. In any event, the pursuer had been discharged from his employment at or about the first anniversary D of the accident.

"A further operation to revise the ulnar osteotomy was discussed. Arrangements were made for this operative procedure in the early part of 1989. At revision on 31 March 1989, firm tethering of the distal ulna dictated against proper approximation of both fragments at the osteotomy site, and the distal fragment was therefore removed, together with attached plate and screws. Recovery was good and the pursuer was discharged home after 24 hours.

E "As at 28 November 1989, when the pursuer was examined by Mr Ian Cartlidge, a consultant orthopaedic surgeon who had been concerned in his treatment, it was found that the left wrist and hand remained painful and weak, grip being poor and difficulty being experienced on attempts at lifting or holding anything heavy. In the view of Mr Cartlidge, the persisting symptoms of pain and weakness, together with the observed stiffness, were entirely F explicable and reasonable on the basis of the history described. While a minor degree of spontaneous improvement might have been expected until around March 1990 or shortly thereafter, these problems were to be regarded as permanent. Scarring at the wrist and elbow would persist in the long term. It was clear at that stage that the pursuer had no prospect of being able to return to his job as a slater, or to any job requiring strength in the left hand, wrist and forearm.

"Mr Cartlidge gave evidence as to his findings at a further examination of the pursuer on 23 March 1992. There had been some improvement in the discomfort in the left wrist until June 1990, but a degree of pain behind the left elbow resulted in a referral back to the G phsyiotherapist in November 1990 for a short course of treatment. By March 1991, it appeared that the pursuer's symptoms had sufficiently settled to allow a final discharge from the outpatient clinic. Rotation of the forearm remained some five degrees short of the right side in supination, and tenderness persisted over the distal ulna scar. Radial deviation deformity and mobility of the left wrist were unchanged, as were weakness of grip and pinch in the left hand. The practical effects of the pursuer's continuing disabilities H were that he remained unable to contemplate return to his previous employment as a slater, or to do any work involving heavy duties with the left upper limb, in the opinion of Mr Cartlidge. Mr Cartlidge considered that the pursuer's grip in the left hand was between 30 per cent and 50 per cent of the normal grip of the left hand in a right handed person.

"Evidence was led on behalf of the defenders from Mr John G Pollock, a consultant surgeon of Glasgow Royal infirmary. He had examined the pursuer on two I occasions on 8 February 1988 and 9 December 1991. His findings were set forth in two reports in process. As I understand it, there is no significant difference between the evidence of Mr Cartlidge and Mr Pollock as regards the nature of the pursuer's injuries and the treatment which he has received for them. However, Mr Pollock was rather more optimistic than was Mr Cartlidge in relation to the possibilities for the pursuer's future employment. Mr Pollock considered that the wrist function had achieved a good level and that the strength of the wrist and hand could be improved J if the pursuer were to perform exercises to strengthen the muscles. Mr Pollock agreed, however, that it would be impossible for the pursuer safely to return to perform work as a slater. He considered that the pursuer was capable of moderate to 'severe' work at ground level. He thought that the pursuer would be able to do work as a barman or nightwatchman and he saw no reason why he could not drive, if he so desired.

"Counsel for the pursuer submitted that the award of solatium should be in the region of £10,000. In K support of his submission he referred me to three cases, *Jack v City of Glasgow District Council*, 1984 SLT 168; *Lockerbie v National Coal Board*, 1983 SLT 396, and *Laing v Northern Grouting Engineers Ltd*, 1985 SLT 179.

"Counsel for the defenders accepted that there was in fact little serious dispute between the parties in relation to the size of an appropriate solatium award. He referred me to *Laing's* case and to *Campbell v City of Glasgow District Council*, 1991 SLT 616. His submis- L sion was that the award should lie in the region of £8,500 to £9,000.

"While limited assistance in the assessment of solatium can be got from reported decisions in cases where the injuries were different from those in the case under consideration, in my opinion *Laing v Northern Grouting Engineers Ltd* provides the most assistance to me in assessing solatium here. The injuries in that case appear to me to have been broadly similar to those of the pursuer and the subsequent

treatment also bears a similarity to that undergone by
A the pursuer. In that case solatium of £6,000 was
assessed. If allowance is made for inflation, that
represents a figure in present day terms of £8,940. In
all the circumstances, it appears to me that a reasonable award to the pursuer in the present case in respect
of solatium would be £9,000. I shall award interest on
that sum at 7.5 per cent per annum on three quarters
of the amount which I am assessing as solatium, which
I consider to be attributable to the past.

"So far as past wage loss is concerned, having regard
B to the evidence which I heard regarding the pursuer's
injuries and circumstances, I consider it appropriate
that the damages being assessed should include the
whole recoverable wage loss from the time of the
accident until the time of the proof. It was a matter of
agreement that this sum amounted to £21,103, after
deduction of one half of the relevant benefits which
the pursuer had received in the five year period following the accident, this being a case in which such a
deduction is appropriate. Accordingly I assess past
C wage loss at that sum. It is appropriate that interest
should be awarded upon it at the rate of 7.5 per cent
per annum from the date of the accident until the
present time.

"Turning to the matter of future loss, counsel for
the pursuer submitted that this was a case in which it
would be appropriate for the court to award future loss
upon the basis of the multiplier/multiplicand
approach. Having regard to the pursuer's age, 44
years, he suggested a multiplier of 6 being applied to
D an agreed multiplicand of £8,456 per annum. As I
understand it, he faintly submitted that an award
might also be made for loss of prospects in the labour
market. In that connection he referred me to *Hughes
v British Railways Board*, 1992 SLT 97.

"Counsel for the defenders, on the other hand, submitted that this was an appropriate case in which to
award a lump sum for diminished value in the labour
market, having regard to the fact that, on the basis of
the medical evidence and particularly that of Mr
E Pollock, the pursuer was currently fit for a range of
different kinds of employment, although it was
accepted that he could not return to work as a slater.
Reference was made to *Laing v Northern Grouting
Engineers Ltd* as a case where a lump sum was awarded
in this connection. In that case the sum concerned was
£7,500, which translated into modern monetary values
at £11,250. Counsel for the defenders suggested that
a sum in that region or possibly a little more would be
a reasonable award to be made to the pursuer here.

F "In my opinion, having regard particularly to the
medical evidence to which I have referred, which indicates that the pursuer could well follow a number of
different types of employment at the present time, it
appears to me that it is not appropriate to follow the
multiplier/multiplicand approach to the assessment of
future loss. I favour the making of an award of a lump
sum, to represent the pursuer's diminished value in
the labour market. In this connection, there is no
doubt that the pursuer has sustained a serious injury
to the left wrist and arm. The consequences of the
wrist injury are permanent and significant. However,

it has to be recognised that the pursuer is fortunately
a right handed individual. Doing the best that I can in G
all the circumstances, it appears to me that a figure of
£12,000 would be an appropriate assessment of this
element of the pursuer's claim of damages. . . .

"I shall pronounce a decree for damages in the sum
of £29,472, being 70 per cent of the total assessment
of £42,103. Interest at 7.5 per cent per annum is
awarded on a sum of £19,497 from the date of the
accident until the present date. That sum is of course
70 per cent of £27,853, being the sum of the figures
assessed for three quarters of the whole of solatium H
and the whole of past loss."

---

*Counsel for Pursuer, Hofford; Solicitors, Aitken
Nairn, WS (for McVey and Murricane, Glasgow) —
Counsel for Defenders, C D Boyd; Solicitors, Simpson &
Marwick, WS (for Wilson, Chalmers & Hendry,
Glasgow).*

C H

I

Mitchell v HAT Contracting Services Ltd (No 3)

OUTER HOUSE
LORD OSBORNE
11 MARCH 1993   J

*Damages — Award — Interim payment — Repayment
— Pursuer awarded interim payment against two
defenders jointly and severally and subsequently seeking
to abandon against one defender — Whether final decree
— Whether order for repayment then to be made against
other defender — Rules of Court 1965, rule 89A (2).*

Rule of Court 89A (1) provides for interim payment
of damages in certain circumstances while an action of
damages for personal injuries is depending. Rule of K
Court 89A (2) provides for the making of any order as
may be necessary "when final decree is pronounced"
for giving effect to a defender's final liability to the
pursuer.

An injured person who had been awarded an interim
payment of damages paid equally by two defenders
then obtained summary decree against one defender
restricting that defender's defence to quantum, and
sought to abandon the action against the other
defender. The motion for leave to abandon sought an L
order on the remaining defender for repayment to the
defender against whom the pursuer was abandoning of
that defender's share of the interim award. The
remaining defender argued that the motion was
incompetent in that the interlocutor following the
motion to abandon was not a final interlocutor and
that, if it was competent, it was a discretionary matter
and should be refused.

Held, (1) that the motion would result in a final
decree in relation to the defender against whom the

A pursuer was abandoning and that the application for repayment was competent (pp 1201K-1202C); (2) that there being no other person against whom the remaining defender had any claim in the pleadings, there was no good reason for opposition to the motion (p 1202C-D); and pursuer's motion *granted*.

Action of damages

(Reported 1992 SLT 883 and 1993 SLT 734)

B   Paul Mitchell raised an action of damages for injuries sustained in an accident on a North Sea oil installation. He raised the action against (first) HAT Contracting Services Ltd and (second) Unocal UK Ltd. On 3 October 1991 the Lord Ordinary (Lord Cameron of Lochbroom) made an award of interim damages against both defenders jointly and severally. (Reported 1992 SLT 883.) Thereafter the temporary judge (R G McEwan, QC) granted summary decree against the second defenders excluding their defence on the merits. (Reported 1993 SLT 734.) The second

C defenders then commenced amendment procedure to add a case against the first defenders based on an alleged contractual indemnity and to involve another company as third parties. The amendment procedure was incomplete when, following an agreement between the pursuer and the first defenders, the pursuer sought leave to abandon the action against the first defenders and to find the second defenders liable to repay to the first defenders the share of the interim award met by the first defenders.

D   That motion came before the Lord Ordinary (Osborne).

Statutory provisions

The Rules of Court 1965 provide:

"89A (2). Where a defender has made an interim payment under Rule 89A (1), the court may make such order, when final decree is pronounced, with respect to the interim payment as may be necessary for giving effect to the defender's final liability to the pursuer

E and in particular may order — (a) repayment by the pursuer of any sum by which the interim payment exceeds the amount which the defender is liable to pay the pursuer, or (b) payment by any other defender or third party of any part of the interim payment which the defender who made it is entitled to recover from him by way of contribution or indemnity or in respect of any remedy or relief relating to or connected with the pursuer's claim."

F **Case referred to**

Walker v Infabco Diving Services Ltd, 1983 SLT 633.

On 11 March 1993 the Lord Ordinary *granted* the pursuer's motion.

LORD OSBORNE.—In this action, raised in May 1991, the pursuer claims damages from the defenders jointly and severally or severally of £150,000 in respect of personal injuries sustained by him on or about 14 May 1988, while he was working in the course of his employment with the first defenders on

the Heather Alpha oil installation. The pursuer makes cases at common law and under statute against the G first and second defenders. No substantive defence has been stated by either the first or second defenders hitherto, although in plea in law no 4 for the first defenders there is to be found a plea of apportionment under s 3 of the Law Reform (Miscellaneous Provisions) Act 1940, stated on the esto basis that the pursuer has suffered loss, injury and damage due to the fault or breach of statutory duty of the first defenders or their employees. The second defenders have tabled no corresponding plea.
H
On 3 October 1991, the pursuer moved the court for an interim award of damages of £50,000, the action being then still at the adjustment stage. This motion was opposed on behalf of both defenders on the basis that the pursuer was not almost certain to succeed against either defender and that, in any event, the sum sought was excessive. Lord Cameron of Lochbroom formed the view that the pursuer was almost certain to succeed against one, if not both, of the defenders at the very least on his cases of breach of statutory duty I relating to a defective scaffolding board and to the security of the scaffold itself made against the defenders. After a consideration of the quantum of the pursuer's claim, Lord Cameron fixed the award of interim damages at £10,000. He pronounced his interlocutor decerning against the defenders jointly and severally and severally for payment of that sum to the pursuer in name of interim damages. I have been informed that, by arrangement between the insurers of the defenders, a payment of £5,000 was made by each of the defenders to the pursuer.
J
On 8 January 1992, on the motion of the first and second defenders, the action was sent to the procedure roll. However, before any procedure roll hearing took place, on 21 February 1992, Sheriff R G McEwan, sitting as a temporary judge, heard a motion for the pursuer for summary decree. On 20 March 1992, Sheriff McEwan granted summary decree against the second defenders to the extent of repelling their first, second and third pleas in law and refused the motion for summary decree against the first defenders. The K effect of this decision, which was not challenged, was to leave the second defenders facing inevitable liability to the pursuer with a defence on quantum only.

On 8 May 1992 the court allowed a minute of amendment for the second defenders to be received and answered within 14 days. In this minute, as originally framed, the second defenders sought to introduce into their pleadings a case of contractual indemnity against the first defenders. On 10 June L 1992 the court allowed the first defenders' answers to this minute to be received late. Answers for the pursuer were lodged timeously. At some date unknown to me the minute of amendment was adjusted by the addition of a case sought to be made against a concern described as Aberdeen Scaffolding, said to have been the suppliers of the scaffolding board involved in the accident. No amendment has been made to the pleadings in the action in terms of the minute of amendment and the answers thereto.

On 22 January 1993 a motion on behalf of the

second defenders for a warrant to serve a third party notice upon Aberdeen Scaffolding Co Ltd was refused, presumably upon the ground that the requirements of Rule of Court 85 had not been satisfied in respect that the second defenders' pleadings contained no case against the proposed third party. There that matter rests.

On 8 March 1993 the pursuer lodged a minute of abandonment of his action at common law insofar as directed against the first defenders, at the same time enrolling a motion in the following terms: "On behalf of the pursuer, for leave to abandon the action insofar as directed against the first defenders in terms of minute of abandonment no 48; as between the pursuer and the first defenders, to find no expenses due to or by; and under reference to Rule of Court 89A (2) to ordain the second defenders to pay to the first defenders the sum of £5,000 paid by the first defenders to the pursuer as interim damages pursuant upon the interlocutor of the court dated 3 October 1991."

When this motion came before me on 10 March 1993, counsel for the pursuer explained that the pursuer had reached an agreement with the first defenders to abandon his action against them, with a view to breaking what he described as a procedural logjam. He was content that the court should absolve the first defenders from the conclusions of the summons. However, the agreement with the first defenders was conditional upon their being reimbursed in respect of the £5,000 paid by them to the pursuer as interim damages. The pursuer, it was said, was neither able nor willing to make the payment. Hence the pursuer sought an order of the court requiring the second defenders to pay that sum to the first defenders.

Counsel for the second defenders opposed the motion on the grounds (1) that it was incompetent, and (2) that, as a matter of discretion, it should not be granted. He maintained that the terms of Rule of Court 89A (2) did not permit me to accede to that part of the motion relating to the order for reimbursement of the first defenders by the second defenders in respect of the interim damages paid by the former to the pursuer. That Rule of Court is in the following terms: [his Lordship quoted its terms and continued:] In particular he argued that the words "when final decree is pronounced" in the opening part of the rule referred to a stage when all issues in the action were on the point of resolution. In the present action, that stage remained in the future. Further, it could not be said at this present stage that the first defenders were "entitled to recover" their share of the interim payment of damages, the £5,000 in question, within the meaning of para (b) of the rule, having regard to the matters which remained to be determined in the action. In addition, it could not be said that there was any entitlement in the first defenders to recover that sum from the second defenders "by way of contribution or indemnity or in respect of any remedy or relief relating to or connected with the pursuer's claim", within the meaning of para (b) of the rule. In any event, having regard to the procedural position it was inappropriate to grant the motion, so far as brought under Rule of Court 89A (2).

Counsel for the first defenders confirmed the nature of the arrangement between her clients and the pursuer. She maintained that the pursuer's motion was competent. The opening words of Rule of Court 89A (2), "such order . . . as may be necessary for giving effect to the defender's final liability to the pursuer", were so wide as themselves to enable the court to follow the course sought. Paragraphs (a) and (b) were merely examples of what could be done. Accordingly, it was not necessary to bring the case within their terms. Further, she argued that the court was in course of pronouncing a "final decree", so far as the first defenders were concerned, since the only case against them was on the point of being abandoned.

Counsel for the pursuer in reply adopted the submissions of counsel for the first defenders. He argued in addition that, even if the court did not have the wide powers contended for under the opening words of the Rule of Court, the motion could still be granted under para (b). The court could and should now determine that the first defenders were "entitled to recover" the money paid. There was no basis whatever in existence to justify the court concluding that the first defenders had any liability to anyone in the matter. It followed that they must be "entitled to recover" the payment made. The words "in respect of any remedy or relief relating to or connected with the pursuer's claim" were apt to describe the basis of the first defenders' right. The decree for interim damages had been properly pronounced against the first defenders, although they were now seen to have no liability (*Walker v Infabco Diving Services Ltd*). Further, as a matter of discretion, the motion should be granted.

Counsel for the second defenders replied by arguing that the court's powers were not as wide as contended for. Paragraphs (a) and (b) described the only steps the court could take, on a proper view of the rule in the light of the principle of interpretation expressio unius est exclusio alterius.

Dealing first with the matter of the competency of the pursuer's motion, in my opinion, the words "when final decree is pronounced" and "the defender's final liability to the pursuer" may all properly be seen as relating individually to the position of any particular defender in an action, not simply to the position of the last of a number of defenders whose situation is considered by the court at the conclusion of an action. Thus I do not regard these words as constituting a barrier to the consideration of this motion at this time, having regard first to the fact that the pursuer is intending to abandon his action against the first defenders and secondly to the fact that that abandonment would eliminate the first defenders from the action, there being in existence no claim against them other than that of the pursuer. So far as the first defenders are concerned, in my opinion, the point of pronouncing a "final decree" has been reached and their "final liability" to the pursuer can be determined.

A Turning next to the scope of the words "such order . . . as may be necessary", in my judgment, while that expression, read alone, is very wide, it must be read in the context of the remainder of the rule. Having regard to what follows and especially the words "and in particular may order — (a) . . . or (b)", it appears to me that the generality of the initial passage may well be limited to no more than what follows in paras (a) and (b). However, it is unnecessary for me to reach any concluded view upon the point, since I am persuaded that what is proposed by the pursuer here falls clearly within the scope of the terms of para (b). In particular, what is sought in my view, is "payment by any other defender . . . of any part of the interim payment which the defender who made it is entitled to recover from him . . . in respect of any remedy or relief relating to or connected with the pursuer's claim". I consider that it is plain that the first defenders are entitled to recover the sum concerned from the "other defender", the second defenders, since the former are now acknowledged to have no liability to the pursuer, while the second defenders have been found liable in damages to the pursuer. The first defenders, against whom an interim decree was quite properly pronounced, must now be seen as entitled to be relieved by the party determined to be solely liable to the pursuers, by way of "remedy or relief relating to or connected with the pursuer's claim". Thus, I regard the motion as competent.

Turning next to the question of whether what was acknowledged to be a discretionary power should be exercised in the pursuer's favour, I am quite satisfied that the motion should be granted. Indeed I can see no legitimate reason why it should not be granted. It may be that, at some time in the future, the second defenders may seek actually to amend their pleadings in the manner foreshadowed in their minute of amendment. However, I cannot conclude at this stage that the court, in the exercise of its discretion, will necessarily allow the proposed amendment and grant warrant for the associated third party notices. Indeed having regard to the dilatory approach which the second defenders have hitherto adopted towards vindicating their alleged right of indemnity against the first defenders and claim against Aberdeen Scaffolding Co Ltd, and having regard also to the procedural steps which have been taken already in relation to the advancement of the pursuer's claim against the second defenders, although, of course, I express no concluded view on the matter, in my opinion it would be entirely understandable if the court were to decline to allow progress in the pursuer's claim to be further delayed by the working out of such remedies as the second defenders may have against others in this action. If that were to be the course adopted by the court, the second defenders would require to pursue such rights and claims as they may have in other proceedings. In all these circumstances and, in particular, looking to the uncertainty surrounding the manner in which the second defenders may be able to pursue their own rights and claims, in my view it would be quite unreasonable for me now to decline to order the payment by the second defenders to the first defenders

which the pursuer seeks should be made. I therefore grant the motion.

G

Counsel for Pursuer, Sturrock; Solicitors, Balfour & Manson, Nightingale & Bell (for Stephens McDonald & Robson, Newcastle-upon-Tyne) — Counsel for First Defenders, Gibson; Solicitors, Simpson & Marwick, WS — Counsel for Second Defenders, Hanretty; Solicitors, Gillam Mackie, SSC (for Hamilton Burns & Moore, Glasgow).

C H

H

HM Advocate v Ward

HIGH COURT OF JUSTICIARY
LORD McCLUSKEY
25 MARCH 1993

I

Justiciary — Procedure — Trial — Specification of documents — Accused seeking all productions and statements taken by police including statements of Crown witnesses prior to accused's police interview, and precognitions — Police at interview alleging matters purportedly derived from Crown witnesses — Whether all material recoverable — Whether precognitions recoverable.

An accused person was charged on indictment and at a preliminary diet he sought to recover from the Crown J all statements taken by the police from persons whether or not on the Crown list of witnesses, all productions and labels whether or not lodged by the Crown and all precognitions of Crown witnesses and individuals not on the Crown list of witnesses. In particular the accused sought the police statements of three Crown witnesses taken prior to an interview between the accused and the police in which the police made allegations purportedly derived from these witnesses.

K

Held, (1) that there was no authority which entitled the accused to obtain an order from the court in such broad terms (p 1204F); (2) that precognitions were never recoverable because they were confidential documents and could not be put in evidence (p 1204H-I); but (3) that the hearing should be continued in respect of the statements of the three Crown witnesses, without deciding their recoverability, in order to allow the Crown to consider their contents (p 1204J-K); and hearing *continued* as aforesaid and quoad ultra order L *refused.*

Dictum in *Higgins v HM Advocate*, 1990 SCCR 268, *considered.*

Indictment
Francis Ward was charged on indictment with 21 offences. He lodged a minute of notice in terms of s 76 of the Criminal Procedure (Scotland) Act 1975 which was in the following terms:

(1) That the minuter has been indicted at the instance
A of Her Majesty's Advocate for trial in the High Court
of Justiciary sitting at Aberdeen on 29 March 1993.

(2) That the said Francis Ward faces trial on 21
charges of lewd, indecent and libidinous practices and
behaviour; assault to injury; assault; contraventions of
the Sexual Offences (Scotland) Act 1976, s 5; shame-
less indecency and breach of the peace. There are 25
witnesses on the indictment and notice has been served
on the accused in terms of s 81 of the Criminal Procedure (Scotland) Act 1975 adding a further 10 wit-
B nesses. The accused wishes, in order to prepare his
defence properly, to have disclosure made to him of the
following material: (i) all statements taken by the police
from witnesses included in the Crown list of witnesses
prior to 25 October 1991; (ii) all statements taken by
the police prior to 25 October 1991 relevant to this case
from individuals who have not been placed on the list
of witnesses; (iii) all statements taken by the police
from all witnesses included in the Crown list of witnesses since 25 October 1991; (iv) all statements taken
C by the police since 25 October 1991 relevant to the case
from individuals who have not been placed on the list
of witnesses; (v) all material relevant to the case of the
nature of a production or a label which has not been
lodged by the Crown; (vi) all precognitions of witnesses
on the list of witnesses and from individuals who have
not been placed on the list of witnesses but who have
information of relevance to this case minus any comments or observations which were the precognoscers'
notes designed simply to assist Crown counsel or staff.

D
(3) It is submitted that it is in the interests of justice
that an accused person should have disclosure of all of
the above in order that he can properly prepare his
defence. In particular it is necessary to have the detail
of all material available to the police from witnesses
prior to 25 October 1991 in order that proper consideration can be given to a taped interview of the
accused by the police on that date in which various allegations were outlined to him. It is only fair that he
should have access to all other police statements taken
E in order that he can be aware of the full nature of the
allegations made against him and of any points which
were favourable to his defence. Likewise, it is only fair
that he should have sight of all precognitions taken by
the Crown for similar reason to that outlined in respect
of police statements. He has no desire to have access to
material which is not the essence of the precognition
but comprises notes of the precognoscer for the
guidance of the Crown about the witness. He also seeks
access to any unused material relevant to his case and
F in the hands of the Crown. By letter dated 9 March
1993 the accused's solicitors requested the material
sought at 2 (i) and 2 (ii). The Crown responded by
letter dated 11 March 1993. The accused apprehends
in light of the tenor of this letter that the further disclosure sought will not be made.

Cases referred to

Donald v Hart (1844) 6 D 1255.
Dowgray v Gilmour (1907) 14 SLT 906; 1907 SC 715.
Friel, Petitioner, 1981 SLT 113; 1981 JC 1.
Higgins v HM Advocate, 1990 SCCR 268.

A preliminary diet was held in the High Court at
Edinburgh on 25 March 1993 before Lord McCluskey. G

Eo die Lord McCluskey *continued* the diet for the
Crown to consider the statements of three Crown witnesses and quoad ultra *refused* the order sought.

LORD McCLUSKEY.—This matter comes before
me by way of a minute of notice by Francis Ward, who
is charged on indictment with a number of charges
there specified. His trial is set down for 29 March 1993
in Aberdeen. The minute of notice narrates the fact of H
the panel's being indicted and summarises the charges.

Counsel appearing for the panel today invited this
court to make an order to enable the defence to recover
documents specified in para 2 and subparas i, ii, iii, iv,
v and vi.

The submission, which I shall summarise briefly,
was to the effect that as a matter of general principle
it was right and proper that there should be disclosed
by the Crown and, in any event, to the defence here,
all material that might have a bearing upon the conduct I
of the trial. In particular, it was suggested that in
England it was the practice for the prosecuting authorities to make available to the defence all previous statements. In any event, it was plain that if the prosecution
in a Scottish case had access to statements made by a
witness to policemen and, in particular, a statement
made to a policeman who was inquiring into matters
before the panel was in fact accused of any crime, then
the Crown were in the position of being able to
challenge any evidence given by such a witness if it J
proved to be contrary to anything said to the police in
the earlier statement. The defence, having no knowledge of any such statement, were not in a position to
deal with that matter. There was therefore no equality
of arms, as counsel for the accused put it, in relation to
this matter. The Crown, it was also said, had the advantage of being able to pick and choose who appeared on
the Crown list and what productions were included on
the list annexed to the indictment. Furthermore, even
in relation to persons who were not on the Crown list K
of witnesses, it might be that persons were interviewed
by the police but not included on the Crown list, yet
were persons whose evidence might be of value to the
defence. It seemed right and proper that the defence
should have access to, in effect, police inquiries in
order to make their own judgment as to what evidence
might properly be placed before the court.

Separately, it was argued, on a more limited front,
that because the Crown productions included the transcript of a tape and the tape itself related to an inter- L
view conducted by the police with the accused on 25
October 1991, and because it was evident from that
transcript that the police had put to the accused
certain allegations said to be derived from information
obtained from persons named on the Crown list, then
the fairness of that interview, and therefore the
admissibility of evidence derived from it, could not
properly be assessed without knowing whether or not
the police in fact had the information which they
allegedly had when they questioned the accused
person.

There was some discussion on both sides of the bar as to whether or not the necessary information in relation to what preceded the interview on 25 October 1991 could be obtained in the course of the trial or indeed by precognoscing police witnesses and others before the trial. But I am satisfied that it would not necessarily be possible for the defence to obtain, by such ordinary methods of precognoscing policemen and witnesses, all the information which could be obtained by obtaining the statements themselves. Indeed, on any view, whether the statements contained the truth or not, the statements are prima facie the best evidence in relation to this matter.

I was referred to certain authorities and I will simply mention them. Counsel for the accused drew my attention to *Friel, Petr*, and the advocate depute drew my attention to *Donald v Hart, Dowgray v Gilmour*, and to the recent case of *Higgins v HM Advocate*.

From the cases of *Friel, Donald* and *Dowgray* I can take, and indeed this is not in dispute, that the court has power to allow the recovery of documents if the interests of justice require that to be done, even over the objection of the Lord Advocate; that power may be exercised if there is sufficient weighty cause. The Crown did not dispute that and, indeed, the advocate depute expressly conceded that that same power could be exercised by me, sitting at this stage on a s 76 diet in criminal proceedings.

I did raise the question as to whether or not judges considering this matter might have responsibility to assess the documents themselves or other matters, other productions, which were not referred to in the minute, but I am not sure that is a task which the judge can, at this stage, properly undertake. As Lord Maxwell said in *Friel, Petr*, at 1981 JC, p 8: "It is not for me to measure the risk because I do not have the information to do it, but I could not override the Lord Advocate's objection unless I was satisfied that there is another public interest at stake so substantial that the risk to law enforcement must take second place."

I am satisfied that where the possibility of risk does exist, that could be an overriding consideration when a person faces serious charges in the High Court; the possibility of a miscarriage of justice which would not be detectable by the appeal court always exists. That is an important consideration. It must be weighed necessarily against any particular prejudice to which the Crown can point.

I think, however, before I turn to the matter of the interview of 25 October 1991, I should deal with the calls which do not relate to the obtaining of statements from persons on the Crown list who gave statements to the police prior to that date. In my opinion, all the calls other than call (i) are calls which must be refused. No precedent at all was quoted to me, no other authority in favour of the proposition that the defence are entitled to obtain an order from the court in such broad terms. In the field of civil diligence these calls would certainly be described as fishing calls because they are so wide. I know of no authority at all which obliges or entitles me to order the production of so many documents.

The advocate depute, in referring to the case of *Higgins*, drew attention to what was said by the court and, in particular, the opinion which was delivered by Lord Cowie and I quote (p 269B): "there is no obligation on the Crown to disclose any information in their possession which would tend to exculpate the accused".

The advocate depute said the Crown did not wish to be associated with that statement. In these circumstances, I do not consider that I am given any guidance or assistance at all from these observations which were made in the case of *Higgins* which, I observe, were delivered by the court without the benefit of a full argument.

On the view I have taken of the calls which are contained in the minute other than call (i), I shall refuse to make an order for the production of the statements or material or precognitions referred to there. In particular I should say that I do not consider that precognitions are ever recoverable. That is for the additional reason that they are confidential documents and also because they are precognitions which cannot be put in evidence even under the statutory rules that govern the admissibility of statements made on a previous occasion.

However, in relation to call (i), although counsel for the accused maintained that he was entitled to what was asked for there, he did indicate that if I were not prepared to go the length of allowing the recovery of all the statements referred to there, I should order the recovery of the statements which he says were referred to by the police in conducting the interview, namely statements attributable to persons who appeared on the Crown list of witnesses as witnesses nos 1, 2 and 14. The advocate depute's position in relation to that restricted call was that it had not been considered proper to trawl through all the information which was sought in the minute prior to this date and it would be desirable that the Crown should consider what was contained in the statements of these three persons in order to decide whether or not the information contained material which should not be disclosed without proper reason. I think the sensible way of dealing with that matter is to indicate that all the remaining heads of the specification contained in the list are refused and, in relation to (i), I simply continue the matter until tomorrow morning when I will hear parties further in relation to statements attributable to the witnesses 1, 2 and 14, taken prior to noon on 25 October 1991.

At this stage I cannot indicate whether or not, of course, I would grant the motion in respect of these, but I am prepared to entertain it tomorrow morning. So the diet is continued until 26 March 1993 at 10 o'clock in this court.

Counsel for Crown, McFarlane, QC, A D; Solicitor, J D Lowe, Crown Agent — Counsel for Accused, Jackson, QC; Solicitors, Balfour & Manson, Nightingale & Bell (for George Mathers & Co, Aberdeen).

P W F

[The Crown subsequently undertook to lodge the remaining statements in question as productions.]

Chapman v Aberdeen Construction Group plc

SECOND DIVISION

THE LORD JUSTICE CLERK (ROSS),
LORDS McDONALD AND WYLIE

15 MAY 1991

Contract — Unfair contract terms — Contract of employment — Whether "consumer contract" — Unfair Contract Terms Act 1977 (c 50), ss 15 (2), 17 (1) and 25 (1).

Employment — Contract of employment — Construction — Executive share option scheme — Rule of scheme excluding right to damages for loss of rights under scheme on dismissal from employment — Whether employee receiving options entering into contractual relations — Whether rule affecting rights under contract of employment — Unfair Contract Terms Act 1977 (c 50), s 23 (a).

Section 25 (1) of the Unfair Contract Terms Act 1977 defines a "consumer contract" (which by s 15 (2) (b) includes a contract of service) inter alia as a contract in which "one party to the contract deals, and the other party to the contract ('the consumer') does not deal or hold himself out as dealing, in the course of business". Section 23 (a) provides that a contractual term shall be void which excludes or restricts "the exercise, by a party to any other contract, of any right or remedy which arises in respect of that other contract . . . which could not . . . be excluded or restricted by a term of that other contract".

An executive director of a company sought damages for wrongful dismissal. He claimed in respect of loss suffered inter alia that he had been deprived of the right to exercise certain options under an executive share option scheme. The rules of the scheme provided in rule 6 (7) "that in the event of the dismissal of a Participant from employment he shall not become entitled to any damages or compensation or any additional compensation or damages by reason of any alteration of his rights or expectations under the Scheme". The pursuer argued that rule 6 (7) constituted a contractual term affecting the arrangements between himself and the defenders, that his contract of employment was a "consumer contract" within the definition in the 1977 Act and that s 23 (a) struck at rule 6 (7) as affecting his rights under his contract of employment. The Lord Ordinary held that the defenders were, but the pursuer was not, dealing in the course of a business when the parties entered into the contract of employment, which accordingly could fall within the 1977 Act, but that rule 6 (7) had effect only in relation to the pursuer's rights under the option contracts and not his contract of employment, and excluded the relative averments from probation. The pursuer reclaimed.

Held, (1) that the parties entered into contractual relations when the pursuer made an application to the defenders' directors which they decided to grant in return for an obligation to pay a specific sum of money

(pp 1213C-F, 1215L-1216B and 1217D-E); (2) that rule 6 (7) constituted a term of that contract affecting the arrangements between the parties (pp 1213H-I, 1216B-C and 1217D-F); (3) (Lord Wylie *dissenting*) that the pursuer's averments concerning loss of rights under the option scheme were relevant because (per the Lord Justice Clerk (Ross)) rule 6 (7) purported to restrict the defenders' liability to pay damages arising from a breach by the defenders of the pursuer's contract of employment, and that as rule 6 (7) appeared in a secondary contract, it might be struck at by s 23 (a) of the 1977 Act (p 1214A-B and I-J); (per Lord McDonald) rule 6 (7) purported to restrict the defenders' liability to pay damages arising from wrongful dismissal, to which the pursuer would be entitled if he could prove loss arising from his summary dismissal, but rule 6 (7) fell to be regarded as void by virtue of s 23 (p 1216C-E); and reclaiming motion *allowed* in respect of the pursuer's averments relating to this head of damages.

Per Lord Wylie (*dissenting*): As the benefit had been given and acquired in the first instance on the express condition that the loss of that benefit in the event of dismissal would not sound in damages, in accepting the benefit the pursuer did so on the basis of the conditions under which it was granted, and accordingly no right or remedy arose which could be excluded or restricted and no scope arose for s 23 (a) to apply (p 1217J-K).

Action of damages

Alan Chapman raised an action against Aberdeen Construction Group plc seeking damages in respect of his alleged wrongful dismissal by the defenders.

The case came before the Lord Ordinary (Caplan) on procedure roll on the defenders' plea to the relevancy of the pursuer's averments so far as concerning his right to use certain motor cars and rights allegedly lost under an executive share option scheme.

Statutory provisions

The Unfair Contract Terms Act 1977 provides:

"12.—(1) A party to a contract 'deals as consumer' in relation to another party if — (a) he neither makes the contract in the course of a business nor holds himself out as doing so; and (b) the other party does make the contract in the course of a business. . . .

"15.— . . . (2) Subject to subsection (3) below, sections 16 to 18 of this Act apply to any contract only to the extent that the contract — . . . (b) constitutes a contract of service or apprenticeship. . . .

"17.—(1) Any term of a contract which is a consumer contract or a standard form contract shall have no effect for the purpose of enabling a party to the contract — (a) who is in breach of a contractual obligation, to exclude or restrict any liability of his to the consumer or customer in respect of the breach; . . . if it was not fair and reasonable to incorporate the term in the contract.

"(2) In this section 'customer' means a party to a standard form contract who deals on the basis of written standard terms of business of the other party to the contract who himself deals in the course of a business. . . .

"23. Any term of any contract shall be void which purports to exclude or restrict, or has the effect of excluding or restricting — (a) the exercise, by a party to any other contract, of any right or remedy which arises in respect of that other contract in consequence of breach of duty, or of obligation, liability for which could not by virtue of the provisions of this Part of this Act be excluded or restricted by a term of that other contract; (b) the application of the provisions of this Part of this Act in respect of that or any other contract. . . .

"25.—(1) In this Part of this Act — . . . 'business' includes a profession and the activities of any government department or local or public authority; 'consumer' has the meaning assigned to that expression in the definition in this section of 'consumer contract'; 'consumer contract' means a contract (not being a contract of sale by auction or competitive tender) in which — (a) one party to the contract deals, and the other party to the contract ('the consumer') does not deal or hold himself out as dealing, in the course of a business, . . . and for the purposes of this Part of this Act the onus of proving that a contract is not to be regarded as a consumer contract shall lie on the party so contending".

Cases referred to

Abrahams v Reiach (Herbert) Ltd [1922] 1 KB 477.
Ailsa Craig Fishing Co Ltd v Malvern Fishing Co Ltd, 1982 SLT 377; 1982 SC (HL) 14.
Beach v Reed Corrugated Cases Ltd [1956] 1 WLR 807.
Bold v Brough, Nicholson & Hall Ltd [1964] 1 WLR 201; [1963] 3 All ER 849.
Davies v Sumner [1984] 1 WLR 1301; [1984] 3 All ER 831.
Hall Brothers Steamship Co Ltd v Young [1939] 1 KB 748.
Pollock v Macrae, 1922 SLT 510; 1922 SC (HL) 192.
Queen v Postmaster General (1876) 1 QB 648; (1878) 3 QB 428.
R & B Customs Brokers v United Dominions Trust [1988] 1 WLR 321; [1988] 1 All ER 847.
S & U Stores Ltd v Lee [1969] 1 WLR 626; [1969] 2 All ER 417.
S & U Stores Ltd v Wilkes [1974] 3 All ER 401.
Sichi v Biagi, 1946 SN 66.
Stone v MacDonald, 1979 SLT 288; 1979 SC 363.

Textbooks referred to

Gloag, *Contract* (2nd ed), pp 24-25.
Gloag and Henderson, *Introduction to the Law of Scotland* (9th ed), pp 307-308.
Harvey, *Industrial Relations and Employment Law*, Vol II, p 549.
McGregor, *Damages* (15th ed), para 1169.
Walker, *Civil Remedies*, p 590.

On 27 February 1990 the Lord Ordinary *sustained* the defenders' first plea in law to the extent of *excluding* the disputed averments from probation.

LORD CAPLAN.—The pursuer sues the defenders for £150,000 being a claim for damages said to flow from wrongful dismissal.

The pursuer began employment with the defenders in July 1955 and his employment was eventually regulated by a minute of agreement between the parties dated 20 March 1986. In terms of that agreement the pursuer was appointed and subsequently acted as executive director of the defenders. On 8 July 1987 the defenders terminated the pursuer's appointment as executive director. It is claimed by the pursuer that this dismissal was in breach of the said contract. In particular the pursuer claims that he was entitled to six months' notice from the defenders of the termination of his employment which means that his employment should have at least continued until 8 January 1988. The parties are in issue as to the contractual propriety of the defenders' dismissal of the pursuer and it is accepted that this matter can only be resolved after proof before answer. However there are two heads of loss in the pursuer's averments of his damages which the defenders contend are clearly irrelevant and at the procedure roll they asked me to exclude these two items of loss from probation on the basis of their first plea in law which is a general plea to the relevancy of the pursuer's case.

[After considering the first item of loss, with which this report is not concerned, his Lordship continued:]

The second branch of the defenders' attack on the relevancy of the pursuer's averments of loss relates to a case made for the recovery of rights allegedly lost under an executive share option scheme. The defenders at a general meeting on 26 October 1984 adopted rules for such a scheme. In general the scheme provides that options shall be granted to such eligible executives as the directors shall from time to time determine. The options involved were for the option holder having a right to subscribe for shares in accordance with the scheme. Rule 6 of the said rules lays down certain provisions to cover the case where the option holder (therein called a participant) ceases to be in the employment of the company. In particular rule 6 (7) provides: "(7) It shall be a condition of the Scheme that in the event of the dismissal of a Participant from employment he shall not become entitled to any damages or compensation or any additional damages or compensation by reason of any alteration of his rights or expectations under the Scheme."

Rule 9 of the rules in relation to takeover makes the following provisions:

"In the event of another company acquiring a majority of the issued ordinary share capital of the Company as a result of a general offer or offers being made to acquire the whole of the issued ordinary share capital of the Company or such part thereof as is not at the time owned by the offeror or any company con-

trolled by the offeror and/or person acting in concert
A with the offeror:

"(a) A participant will be entitled within six months
of being notified by the Company of that event (but
not later than ten years after the grant of the option or
any earlier date for the lapse of such Option under rule
6) to exercise all or any of the Option which he holds
(irrespective of whether the condition set out in Rule
5 (2) has been satisfied and notwithstanding the provisions of Rule 5 (3)) and subject to performance of the
Company's obligation under (b) below, all the Options
B held by him which he does not so exercise shall automatically lapse upon the expiration of the said six
months; and

"(b) The Company shall use its best endeavours to
procure that if a participant is allotted shares pursuant
to the exercise of Options, then the party by whom the
general offer was made shall offer to acquire from the
participant all those shares upon the same terms as
shares were acquired pursuant to the general offer."

C The pursuer avers that on or about 9 November
1984 he was granted an option in respect of 20,000
shares in the defenders' company at £1.75 per share.
It is further averred that in or about 1985 the pursuer
was granted a second option in respect of 10,000
shares of the defenders at £2.38 per share. It is averred
that if the defenders had given the pursuer the notice
of termination that he was entitled to under the
minute of agreement he would have been in the
defenders' employment in November 1987 when
D the defenders were taken over. If that had been the
position the pursuer would have been able to exercise
his share options as provided for in the said rule 9 of
the scheme. It is averred in art 6 of the condescendence that had the pursuer exercised his options
the cost of doing so would have been £58,800 which
he was ready and willing to pay. It is said that the
shares would have been bought by Raine Industries
plc (the takeover company) for £3.5035 per share.
Allowing for capital gains tax and income tax the
E pursuer, it is said, would have benefited by a net gain
of £32,000 and it is claimed that this gain has been lost
by the defenders' alleged breach of contract.

Senior counsel for the defenders attacked the
relevancy of the pursuer's claim to have suffered
damage through loss of opportunity flowing from the
share option scheme. In this regard he relied particularly on the terms of rule 6 (7), which provides that on
dismissal a participant shall not be entitled to any
damages or compensation by reason of an alteration of
F his rights or expectations under the scheme. "Compensation" is to cover the possibility of compensation
being due in terms of s 68 (2) of the Employment Protection (Consolidation) Act 1978. "Damages" could
only arise in the context of some wrongful act on the
part of the defenders. I was referred to Harvey, *Industrial Relations and Employment Law*, Vol II, p 549,
and *Hall Brothers S S Co Ltd v Young*. The Unfair
Contract Terms Act 1977 did not apply to any of the
contractual provisions relevant to this case.

Senior counsel for the pursuer contended that the

reference to "dismissal" in rule 6 (7) could only be a
dismissal which was in terms of the contract of G
employment and could not relate to a wrongful dismissal. The clause required to be construed strictly. I
was referred to *Pollock v Macrae* per Lord Dunedin at
1922 SLT, p 512, and *Ailsa Craig Fishing Co Ltd v
Malvern Fishing Co Ltd*. There would be cases where
even in the absence of a breach of contract the participant would be entitled to compensation and rule 6
(7) could be read as applying to such cases. Reference
was made to Gloag and Henderson, *Introduction to the
Law of Scotland* (9th ed), pp 307-308. In any event the H
rule only applies to damages or compensation which
arise from alteration of rights or expectations under
the scheme. There was said to be a distinction between
damages resulting from an alteration of rights and
damages flowing from the total loss of rights. The
right under a share option scheme might itself have a
value. In this case there had been a removal of rights
as distinct from an alteration of rights. I was referred
to rule 6 (3) which provides that if after three years
from the grant of an option the participant shall cease I
to be in employment by reason of death, injury or disability or dismissal for redundancy, then he shall for
one year from the cessation of employment be entitled
to exercise the option. Thus (it was argued) dismissal
because of redundancy would result in an alteration of
rights in respect that it shortened the period over
which the option could be exercised to one year from
the date of cessation of employment. Moreover the
contract represented by the options granted to the
pursuer was governed by the Unfair Contract Terms J
Act 1977. I was referred to ss 15 (2) (b), 17 (1) (a), 23
and 25 (1) of the Act. The defenders could not remove
rights which flowed from the contract of employment
by means of a secondary contract such as the option
contracts. I was also referred to *R & B Customs
Brokers v UDT* which was said to be distinguishable.

With regard to the construction of rule 6 (7) I first
have to decide whether the terms of that rule fall to be
construed strictly. Senior counsel for the defenders K
argued that insofar as the rules may represent a contract they do not constitute a mutual contract. In particular I was referred to what Lord Fraser of
Tullybelton said in *Ailsa Craig* (1982 SLT at p 382)
where he indicated in relation to strict standards of
construction: "The reason for imposing such
standards on these clauses is the inherent improb-
ability that the other party to a contract including such
a clause intended to release the proferens from a
liability that would otherwise fall upon him." It was L
argued that since in relation to the enactment of the
rules there was no "other party", the basis for the rule
of strict construction vanished. It is important therefore to determine the status of the rules of the executive option scheme. The scheme was approved by the
defenders to accord with Sched 10 to the Finance Act
1984 and it is not difficult to assume that the main
objective of the scheme was to produce a situation
where share options could be offered to employees in
such a manner as to ensure tax advantage for the
employees. In terms of rule 2 (1) options shall be

granted to eligible executives at the absolute discretion
A of the directors. In terms of rule 2 (2) an eligible executive who is invited by the directors to apply for an
option can do so and then on receipt of the application
the director shall consider whether or not to grant the
option subject to the payment by the option holder of
£1. It has therefore to be noted that the rules themselves confer no concrete rights. All they do is
empower the directors to offer options subject to the
terms of the rules. However in this case the pursuer
claims that he was granted two options under the
B scheme. Thus it is to be assumed that the pursuer was
invited to apply for the options, that he did so apply,
and that his options were thereafter granted to him
upon payment of £1. By granting the pursuer options
which were subject to the rules of the scheme, the
defenders entered into a mutual onerous contract. In
return for the grant of each of the options the
defenders received £1. However, they also may well
have had in mind a more significant consideration. By
granting the options the defenders no doubt hoped to
C secure the commitment of their executives to the
welfare of the company and also to encourage them to
remain in the employment of the company. Insofar as
the rules are incorporated into the grant of the options
and govern them, they are stipulations in a mutual
contract and I consider that since the defenders are
seeking to restrict the pursuer's rights in respect of the
value of the options in the event of his rights thereunder being terminated by dismissal, the principles of
construction set out in *Pollock* and *Ailsa Craig* should
D apply. However in my view that conclusion does not
help the pursuer very much for the rule of strict construction only becomes significant if there is a real
ambiguity. In my opinion the word "damages" can
only mean a sum payable by a party to make up for a
loss caused by him as a result of a wrongful act such
as breach of contract or delict. Thus when rule 6 (7)
speaks of "damages or compensation" the words must
be read disjunctively, and to give each intelligent
meaning it follows that the rule was intended to make
E provision for damages for wrongful dismissal. This
makes perfect sense. The employers were making
what they no doubt considered to be a generous
gesture and it is therefore understandable that they
should not want in doing so to increase any claims
which their employees might have against them in the
event of contracts of employment being terminated for
any reason by dismissal. The ingenious argument
advanced that the provision was only intended to
apply to an alteration of rights following upon dis-
F missal for redundancy is not convincing and in any
event would still leave the word "damages" without
any content. The removal of effective rights under the
scheme is an "alteration of rights" albeit drastic in
effect. In fact in relation to the options granted to the
pursuer by the defenders he retained certain notional
rights under the scheme since he was dismissed before
three years had lapsed after the grant of the options,
which gave him rights under rule 6 (1) to seek the
consent of the directors to a continuation of the
options (although in the circumstances of this case that
was probably a right more theoretical than valuable).

Equally, if the pursuer had been dismissed on only
two weeks' notice, a distinct if nevertheless highly G
reduced right in the scheme would have survived until
the actual cessation of employment. It cannot readily
be supposed that the company wished to protect itself
in respect of claims for damages for dismissal on very
short notice but not to protect itself in a case of no
notice at all. So, in my view, whatever the validity of
rule 6 (7) the intention of the rule is clear.

The claim by senior counsel for the pursuer that the
Unfair Contract Terms Act 1977 applied to the contract raises a difficult and important point. It is signifi- H
cant that in terms of s 15 (2) (b) of the Act contracts
of service are specifically covered by ss 16-18 of the
Act. Thus s 17 (1) of the Act applies to a contract of
service provided that it falls within the definition of a
consumer contract. It is perhaps significant that in
relation to the equivalent provisions in Pt I and Sched
1 (both of which cover English law), contracts of
employment are not exempted from the application of
s 3. Looking to the definition of consumer contracts in
s 25 (1), a service contract would be a consumer con- I
tract if one party to the contract deals and the other
party to the contract (the consumer) does not deal or
hold himself out as dealing in the course of a business.
The first question therefore must be whether in relation to their employment of the pursuer the defenders
were dealing in the course of business. Since "business" is defined as covering the activities of a profession or of a local authority I do not take "deals" to
have any narrow specialist meaning. In my view it
merely means "transacts" (compare s 12 (1) of the J
Act). *R & B Customs Brokers v UDT* concerns a case
where a finance company (who were effectively
trading on behalf of a motor dealer) had sold a motor
car to a company for the business use of one of its
directors. The finance company contended that the
purchasers were not consumers for the purposes of the
Unfair Contract Terms Act because in purchasing the
car they had been acting in the course of their business. Following principles set out in *Davies v Sumner*
it was held by the Court of Appeal that the purchasers K
had not been acting in the course of their business
since the purchase of the car had been incidental
rather than integral to their business activities. In my
view that case is distinguishable from the present case.
The protection which the Act is designed to confer
relates to a situation where the dealer can be expected
to enjoy an advantage over the consumer because the
dealer regularly transacts for profit in transactions of
the type regulated by the Act. Thus *R & B Customs
Brokers* were in no sense dealing in motor cars and L
thus in relation to the purchase of a motor car could
not be expected to stand in a different position to any
other car purchasing consumer. On the other hand I
do not believe that for dealing to be in the course of
business the activity needs to represent the major
trading purpose of the dealer. Thus a distillers' main
business endeavour would be to distil and sell whisky.
However if a distillery buys grain from a local farmer
the purchase, although in a sense incidental to whisky
distilling, must I believe be regarded as an integral

part of the distiller's business activity. It is difficult to suppose that a distillery engaged in the regular activity of grain purchasing could be regarded as a consumer rather than a business dealer. If the regular acquisition of material for a manufacturing purpose would in fact be a course of business dealing on the part of the manufacturer then there is no reason in principle why the regular hiring of labour for the same purpose should not also be regarded as transacting in the course of business. Any type of transaction regularly entered into which is central to the purposes of a business must, in my view, be dealing in the course of business. It is obvious from the very nature of the share option scheme that the defenders regularly employ executives and no doubt this activity is critical to the successful conduct of their business. Thus, in my view, when the defenders employed the pursuer they were dealing in the course of their business. Certainly an employee enters into a contract of employment for gain. The word "business" is notoriously difficult to define precisely, but in my view in its ordinary sense it implies not only activity for gain but a degree of organisation of activity for gain. I do not believe that an employee who hires out his labour can be said to be dealing in the course of a business. Thus the pursuer in this case falls to be regarded as a consumer in relation to his contract of employment with the defenders. It is perhaps odd that an executive director entering into a contract at a substantial salary is to be regarded as a consumer whereas a humble jobbing window cleaner would not receive the protection of the Act, but such anomalies are inevitable. The term "consumer" may not sit comfortably on an employee in relation to his work, but this too may be an inevitable result of an artificial definition imposed by statute.

The pursuer does not attempt to argue that s 17 of the Unfair Contract Terms Act applies directly to the minute of agreement. His argument rather is that the contracts represented by the pursuer's option arrangements with the defenders are secondary contracts which seek to evade the application of the Act to the contract of employment. In terms of s 23 any term of a contract shall be void which purports to exclude or restrict or has the effect of excluding or restricting application of Pt II of the Act in respect of that or any other contract. It is to be noted that the concept of fair and reasonable does not enter into the considerations raised by s 23. The section renders any offending term of a contract void and does not merely render it of no effect (as s 17 provides in respect of terms struck at by that section). I think that must mean that it is necessary to look at the contract at the time it is made to see if the term under scrutiny was valid or void at that time. The pursuer was in the defenders' employment when he was offered his options on 9 November 1984 and in 1985 respectively. The minute of agreement under which he now sues is dated March 1986 so that it has no application to the pursuer's position when he acquired his options. However the pursuer was an eligible executive when he acquired his options and therefore, although the terms of his employment at

that time are not known, there certainly was in existence a contract of employment between himself and the defenders. In the absence of any express averment it cannot be supposed that the pursuer's contract of employment in 1984 or 1985 made any reference to a share option scheme. As an employee the pursuer would have had rights upon wrongful dismissal to be compensated for any loss naturally flowing from the breach of contract or, being reasonably within the contemplation of the parties, as a consequence of dismissal. The pursuer would no doubt have been entitled to remuneration under his contract of employment. If the defenders had sought to introduce into the option contracts, terms restricting or excluding the defenders' liability to compensate the pursuer for any loss of remuneration or other benefit flowing directly from the terms of the contract of employment, then I should have had no hesitation in determining that such a provision was void by virtue of s 23. The defenders also would be due to pay damages to the pursuer (at least in certain circumstances) to cover any loss of rights in a secondary contract which were consequential upon a breach of the contract of employment. Whether or not at the time when the pursuer entered into the relevant contract of employment his rights under the prospective share option scheme could be assumed to have been within the reasonable contemplation of the parties may be a fine point. Certainly the pursuer makes no averment about this. However, even ignoring that particular aspect of the matter, the defenders' liability for such consequential damage would be to recompense the pursuer for such loss of rights under the secondary contract as was occasioned by the dismissal. To ascertain the measure of such rights one would have to look to the secondary contract rather than to the contract of employment. The rights in the secondary contract are not any part of the terms of the contract of employment and any restriction (or for that matter amplification) of these rights would be regulated within the terms of secondary contract alone. Thus in the present case the defenders' radical liability to the pursuer upon wrongful dismissal under his contract of employment was at best for the pursuer to recompense him for such loss of rights as he might have suffered in respect of the option contracts. However the definition of these rights must be found in the option contracts themselves since they do not figure in the contract of employment. Rule 6 (7) has the effect of restricting the defenders' liability under the option contracts but it does not in my view exclude or restrict the defenders' said radical liability under the contract of employment itself. It was not of course contended that the Unfair Contract Terms Act applied to the option contracts, so that the parties were free to define or restrict rights under these contracts as they chose. Thus, rule 6 (7) as incorporated into the option contracts did not seek to affect the application of the 1977 Act to the pursuer's contract of employment and the rule is a perfectly valid contractual term. The pursuer's claim to loss of option benefits is therefore irrelevant.

Accordingly, in the whole circumstances, I shall

sustain the defenders' first plea in law to the effect of excluding from probation the words "and the pursuer's right to use two motor cars belonging to the defenders" and also the sentence beginning with the words "The pursuer reasonably estimates". I shall also exclude from probation the passage from the words "Further explained and averred that the pursuer suffered" to the words "gain as about £32,000" inclusive. Quoad ultra I shall reserve judgment on the said plea in law and allow a proof before answer.

———————

The pursuer reclaimed.

Reclaiming motion
The reclaiming motion was heard before the Second Division on 7 and 8 March 1991.

On 15 May 1991 the court *allowed* the reclaiming motion in part.

THE LORD JUSTICE CLERK (ROSS).—In this action the pursuer is seeking damages from the defenders in respect of alleged breach of contract consisting of the termination without notice and without justification of a contract of employment. After sundry procedure, the case was heard on procedure roll by the Lord Ordinary who sustained the first plea in law for the defenders (a plea to the relevancy and specification) to the effect of excluding from probation three passages from the pursuer's pleadings; quoad ultra the Lord Ordinary allowed a proof before answer. At the hearing before the Lord Ordinary two elements in the claim for damages were attacked, and the Lord Ordinary was invited to exclude from probation certain averments dealing with these two matters. In the event the Lord Ordinary upheld the defenders' submissions and ordered these deletions. Against the interlocutor excluding these three passages from probation the pursuer has now reclaimed.

The first two passages excluded contain averments to the effect that the pursuer's annual remuneration included the right to use two motor cars and further averments relating to the value of that alleged right. Counsel for the pursuer, however, made it plain that the pursuer was no longer challenging that part of the Lord Ordinary's decision. The issue which was raised in the reclaiming motion related to averments regarding loss alleged to have been sustained by the pursuer as a result of his having been deprived of his right to exercise certain share options. In his opinion the Lord Ordinary has described the background to the claim as follows: "The pursuer began employment with the defenders in July 1955 and his employment was eventually regulated by a minute of agreement between the parties dated 20 March 1986. In terms of that agreement the pursuer was appointed and subsequently acted as executive director of the defenders. On 8 July 1987 the defenders terminated the pursuer's appointment as executive director. It is claimed by the pursuer that this dismissal was in breach of the said contract. In particular the pursuer claims that he was

entitled to six months' notice from the defenders of the termination of his employment which means that his employment should have at least continued until 8 January 1988. The parties are in issue as to the contractual propriety of the defenders' dismissal of the pursuer and it is accepted that this matter can only be resolved after proof before answer."

The Lord Ordinary then proceeds to deal with the submission made to him that certain averments should be excluded from probation. In his opinion the Lord Ordinary summarises the background to the pursuer's claim to have been deprived of a right to exercise share options: "The second branch of the defenders' attack on the relevancy of the pursuer's averments of loss relates to a case made for the recovery of rights allegedly lost under an executive share option scheme. The defenders at a general meeting on 26 October 1984 adopted rules for such a scheme. In general the scheme provides that options shall be granted to such eligible executives as the directors shall from time to time determine. The options involved were for the option holder having a right to subscribe for shares in accordance with the scheme. Rule 6 of the said rules lays down certain provisions to cover the case where the option holder (therein called a participant) ceases to be in the employment of the company. In particular rule 6 (7) provides: '(7) It shall be a condition of the Scheme that in the event of the dismissal of a Participant from employment he shall not become entitled to any damages or compensation or any additional damages or compensation by reason of any alteration of his rights or expectations under the Scheme.'"

In art 6 of the condescendence it is averred that on 9 November 1984, the pursuer was granted an option in respect of 20,000 shares of the defenders at £1.75 per share, and that in or about 1985 he was granted a further option in respect of 10,000 shares of the defenders at £2.38 per share. The whole terms of the rules of the executive share option scheme are incorporated into the pleadings and held as repeated therein brevitatis causa. Rule 2 deals with the grant of options, and rule 5 with the exercise of options. In terms of rule 5 (1) an option shall be exercised by the participant giving notice in writing to the company stating that the option is being exercised, and the notice requires to be accompanied by the subscription price. Rule 5 (2) provides: "(2) Subject to the provisions of Rules 6, 9 and 10 no Option may be exercised until the expiration of three years from the date of grant of the Option."

Rule 6 deals with conditions on leaving employment. Rule 6 (1) provides that unless the directors consent to its continuation, an option shall lapse if a participant ceases to be in the employment of the defenders for any reason (other than death) before the expiry of three years from the date of the grant of the option. Rule 6 (2) deals with the situation of a participant who has ceased to be in the employment of the defenders by reason of his death before the expiration of three years from the date of the grant of the option. Rule 6 (3) deals with the situation of a participant who, after the expiration of three years from the grant of the option, ceases to be in the employment of the defenders by reason of his death, injury or disability or dismissal for redundancy. Rule 6 (4) deals with the situation of a participant holding options who after the expiry of three years from the grant of the option ceases to be in the employment of the defenders by reason of retirement. Rule 6 (5) deals with the situation of a participant holding options who ceases to be in the employment of the defenders after the expiry of three years from the date of the grant of the option for any reason other than one of those specified in rule 6 (3) and (4). The terms of rule 6 (7) have already been noted.

Rule 9 deals with takeover. It is in the following terms:

"In the event of another company acquiring a majority of the issued ordinary share capital of the Company as a result of a general offer or offers being made to acquire the whole of the issued ordinary share capital of the Company or such part thereof as is not at the time owned by the offeror or any company controlled by the offeror and/or any person acting in concert with the offeror:

"(a) A participant will be entitled within six months of being notified by the Company of that event (but not later than ten years after the grant of the Option or any earlier date for the lapse of such Option under Rule 6) to exercise all or any of the Option which he holds (irrespective of whether the condition set out in Rule 5 (2) has been satisfied and notwithstanding the provisions of Rule 5 (3)) and subject to performance of the Company's obligation under (b) below, all the Options held by him which he does not so exercise shall automatically lapse upon the expiration of the said six months; and

"(b) The Company shall use its best endeavours to procure that if a participant is allotted shares pursuant to the exercise of Options then the party by whom the general offer was made shall offer to acquire from the participant all those shares upon the same terms as shares were acquired pursuant to the general offer."

In terms of cl eighth of the minute of agreement dated 20 March 1986, it was agreed that in the event of any person or company acquiring one half or more of the issued share capital of the company certain rights would emerge; in particular it was provided that in such circumstances the appellant was entitled to cease to be an executive director and to become a non-executive director and to be paid an annual fee at the rate of two thirds of his annual remuneration as an executive director, and that for a period of three years.

Clause ninth of the said minute of agreement provides: "Either party may terminate this Agreement by giving to the other six months' notice, in writing, except that in the event of such an occurrence as referred to in Clause *Eighth* hereof taking place within six months of the First Party giving such notice the Second Party shall be entitled to exercise his option in terms of Clause *Eighth (b)* hereof notwithstanding the

fact that he has received notice in terms of this Clause."

Before the Lord Ordinary and before this court counsel for the defenders challenged the relevancy of the pursuer's claim to have suffered damage through loss of opportunity flowing from the share option scheme. Counsel relied particularly upon the terms of rule 6 (7) set out above. In response to that challenge counsel for the pursuer maintained inter alia that matters were governed by the terms of the Unfair Contract Terms Act 1977. The opposing contentions of the parties in this regard were fully canvassed before the Lord Ordinary. It is surprising therefore to observe that at no stage in their pleadings do the defenders expressly found upon the provisions of rule 6 (7), and the defenders have not stated any plea in law based upon the provisions of that rule. Likewise there is no reference by either party in the pleadings to the provisions of the Unfair Contract Terms Act 1977, although it is plain from the terms of the Lord Ordinary's opinion that various sections of that Act were founded upon. Pleadings are intended to give parties fair notice of the case being made against them, and it is most unsatisfactory that the foregoing provisions do not feature in the written pleadings. On the other hand, in the debate before the Lord Ordinary and in the submissions made by both parties to this court rule 6 (7) and the Act of 1977 were examined and discussed, and neither party suggested that the court should not consider these matters because they had not been mentioned in the pleadings. Accordingly, although the matter is far from satisfactory, I have reached the conclusion that the court should now entertain and decide upon the submissions made by both parties.

The submission for the pursuer was that the Lord Ordinary had erred in excluding from probation the passage in art 8 of the condescendence dealing with the allegation that the pursuer had suffered loss through being deprived of his right to exercise his share options. The following are the averments in art 8 of the condescendence dealing with this matter: "Further explained and averred that the pursuer suffered loss and damage by reason of being deprived of his right to exercise his share options. The pursuer's loss consisted in his inability to purchase shares in the quantity and at the prices provided for in his options, being 20,000 shares at £1.75 per share and 10,000 shares at £2.35 per share. The cost of acquiring that number of shares at those prices is £58,800. The pursuer was ready, willing and able to pay £58,800 to acquire the said shares. Said shares would have been bought by Raine Industries plc for £3.5035 per share. The pursuer, being prevented aforesaid, therefore lost £47,105. The pursuer would have required to pay capital gains tax and income tax on the exercise of the options. The pursuer reasonably estimates his net gain as about £32,000."

For completeness it should be observed that in ans 8 the defenders aver that the pursuer's net gain upon exercise of his share options would have been £30,543.

In support of the reclaiming motion, counsel for the

pursuer put forward two principal arguments. His first submission was that the Lord Ordinary had erred in construing rule 6 (7) of the scheme as covering a situation of wrongful dismissal in breach of contract. His second submission was that even if rule 6 (7) of the scheme applied to a wrongful dismissal in breach of contract, it was not open to the defenders on the pleadings to seek to take advantage of that rule by reason of certain provisions in the Act of 1977.

Counsel for the pursuer started by summarising the propositions which he had made to the Lord Ordinary. They were to the following effect. The rules of the scheme formed the basis of a contract between those to whom options had been granted and the company; on that hypothesis it was plain that rule 6 (7) purported to restrict any liability of the defenders to pay damages arising from breach by them of a participant's contract of employment; if rule 6 (7) had been a term of the contract of employment itself, such a contract would be a contract to which s 17 of the Act of 1977 applied both by virtue of s 15 (2) (b) of the Act of 1977 which applied the provisions of ss 16 to 18 to inter alia a contract of service, and because a contract of service was a consumer contract within the meaning of s 25 (1) of the Act. Counsel also advanced the proposition that if rule 6 (7) had been part of the contract of employment itself, it would have been of no effect unless it had been fair and reasonable to incorporate the term in the contract of employment; the fact that rule 6 (7) formed part of a contract other than the contract of employment did not avail the defenders because of the provisions of s 23 of the Act of 1977 and in particular the provisions of s 23 (a) and (b). In the foregoing circumstances the pursuer's final proposition was that the defenders could only found upon rule 6 (7) if they could prove that it would have been fair and reasonable to have incorporated such a term in the pursuer's contract of employment; that was something which they were required to aver and prove by virtue of s 24 (4) of the Act of 1977, and they had not done so.

Counsel for the pursuer explained that the Lord Ordinary had accepted some of these propositions, but he maintained that the Lord Ordinary had erred in not accepting that rule 6 (7) purported to restrict any liability of the defenders to pay damages arising from breach of the pursuer's contract of employment, and further that he had erred in concluding that the pursuer could not rely upon s 23 of the Act of 1977.

In dealing first with the argument based upon s 23 of the Act of 1977, counsel drew attention to a passage in the Lord Ordinary's opinion where he stated: "Thus in the present case the defenders' radical liability to the pursuer upon wrongful dismissal under his contract of employment was at best for the pursuer to recompense him for such loss of rights as he might have suffered in respect of the option contracts. However the definition of these rights must be found in the option contracts themselves since they do not figure in the contract of employment. Rule 6 (7) has the effect of restricting the defenders' liability under

the option contracts but it does not in my view exclude or restrict the defenders' said radical liability under the contract of employment itself."

Counsel for the pursuer maintained that the final sentence quoted was wrong since rule 6 (7) did not simply restrict the defenders' liability under the option contract; what rule 6 (7) purported to do was to restrict, in relation to any participant, the damages to which that participant would otherwise be entitled in the event of wrongful dismissal under his contract of employment. That, he maintained, was its plain effect. He further submitted that rule 6 (7) was a rule which tried to avoid or evade the provisions of s 17 of the Act of 1977, and accordingly he maintained that it was struck at by s 23 (a) of the Act of 1977. Section 23 (a) provides as follows: [his Lordship quoted the terms of s 23 to end of para (a) and continued:]

The Lord Ordinary had expressed the view that rule 6 (7) was an integral part of the option rights given to the pursuer, but counsel maintained that that could not affect the proper construction to be placed upon s 23 (a). Whatever the nature of the secondary contract, if it purported to take away rights in another contract which could not be taken away in that other contract, the same result would flow. Counsel also maintained that s 23 could apply even though the other contract had not been in existence at the time when the secondary contract (the options contract) came into being. All that mattered was what ought reasonably to have been known to or in the contemplation of the parties to the contract of employment at the time when it was made (s 24).

Counsel for the defenders, on the other hand, maintained that even if rule 6 (7) could be regarded as falling within the ambit of s 23, the rule, because of its express reference to the scheme, was not an attempt to strike at any provision or remedy flowing from the contract of employment itself (the primary contract) and accordingly was not struck at by s 23. They further maintained that the scheme (and in particular rule 6 (7)) was not "a contractual term", and so fell outwith the ambit of s 23. In the course of his submissions junior counsel for the defenders maintained that the contract of employment was not in terms of the Act a consumer contract. However, senior counsel for the defenders intimated that he was no longer supporting that argument. He accepted that contracts of service fell within s 15, and that the question of whether the contract was a consumer contract depended upon the circumstances. The Lord Ordinary concluded that the pursuer's contract of employment was a consumer contract. Senior counsel maintained that the Lord Ordinary had gone too far in arriving at such a firm conclusion, but he accepted that it could not be stated as matter of relevancy that the contract of employment was not a consumer contract. If the pursuer's case were otherwise relevant this issue would require to be determined after inquiry.

Senior counsel proceeded to expand the submissions made by his junior. He reiterated that on a proper analysis rule 6 (7) did not constitute a term of any relevant contract. He contended that it was plain from s 15 that there must be a contract. The opening words of s 15 were "This Part of this Act applies only to contracts". Senior counsel for the defenders stressed the distinction between a contract on the one hand and a unilateral obligation on the other hand, and he maintained that a term of a contract was distinct from a condition attached to a unilateral obligation. A unilateral obligation was not struck at by s 23. In essence his submission was that this scheme was not a contract. At the time when the pursuer was dismissed he held options which had not been exercised; these options were subject to conditions; the options had come into existence some years before by reason of the terms of the scheme. Even if there had been contracts made in 1984 and 1985 when the options were acquired by the pursuer these contracts had since been discharged. He emphasised that what was important was the nature of the right relied upon by the pursuer and that right was constituted by a unilateral obligation. On a proper analysis rule 6 (7) was a condition of the option and not the term of any contract. It followed that s 23 of the Act of 1977 did not apply.

I have come to the conclusion that senior counsel's submissions in this regard are not well founded. I agree with counsel for the pursuer that rule 6 (7) constitutes a contractual term affecting the arrangements between the pursuer and the defenders. No doubt when the scheme was adopted by the defenders in 1984 it did not constitute a contract; it simply stated the terms upon which options might be offered to eligible executives. When, however, in accordance with the rules contained in the scheme the pursuer made an application to the defenders' directors which they decided to grant in return for an obligation to pay a specific sum of money, then, in my opinion, parties entered into contractual relations with one another in which the defenders offered to give and the pursuer agreed to accept the option subject to the terms of the scheme. In other words the terms of the scheme formed the conditions of the contract between the pursuer and the defenders. In the definition clause of the scheme "Option" means the right of a participant to subscribe for a share at the subscription price in accordance with the scheme. The scheme provides for a payment of a nominal sum of £1 for the grant of an option. Although consideration is not necessary under Scots law, I agree with counsel for the pursuer that the provision in relation to the payment of £1 for the grant of the option underlines the contractual relationship which existed between the parties whereby a payment was made in return for a right being given.

Counsel for the defenders founded upon *Stone v MacDonald* as supporting his contention that the option fell to be regarded as a unilateral obligation. That case concerned the exercise of an option which had already been created. The case did not decide that an option right could only be created by a unilateral promise. In the judgment which I delivered in that case I referred to *Sichi v Biagi* which was a case where the option had been created by the promise, but *Stone v MacDonald* was a case where the option had been

created by contract. In any event, even if the option fell to be regarded as a promise or unilateral obligation on the part of the defenders, that promise was accepted by the payment of £1 by the pursuer and accordingly a contract was thereby constituted (Gloag on *Contract* (2nd ed), pp 24-25).

In my opinion a contract was entered into between the parties when the defenders decided to grant the pursuer the options subject to payment by him of the nominal sum of £1 for each option. That contract contained a number of contractual terms including rule 6 (7). Having regard to the existence of these conditions which were applied to options under the scheme, I cannot regard the contract concluded between the parties as being discharged after the option was conferred. The opening words of rule 6 (7) are: "It shall be a condition of the Scheme". I regard these words as making it clear that rule 6 (7) is a term or stipulation of the contract between the parties. It is significant that it is not therein stated "It shall be a condition of the Option", but "It shall be a condition of the Scheme". By virtue of the contract concluded between the parties when the option was granted, the pursuer acquired a right to subscribe for shares at a subscription price in accordance with the conditions laid down in that contract.

The question then arises as to whether the pursuer has made relevant averments in support of his proposition that rule 6 (7) as a term of the contract is struck at by s 23 of the Act of 1977. For the purposes of s 23 the primary contract is the contract of employment and the contract relating to the options under the scheme is the secondary contract. Senior counsel for the defenders accepted that where there has been wrongful dismissal under a contract of employment, that may give rise to claims under the contract itself and also claims for what may be referred to as "fringe benefits". Whether a claim for loss of fringe benefits can be included in a claim for damages for wrongful dismissal will depend upon the terms upon which the benefits were given. Counsel maintained that if the benefit had been given subject to a condition which would exclude a claim, then loss of these benefits will not be an admissible head of damages. To put it in another way, it would not be a direct and natural consequence of the breach of contract if the benefit had been acquired expressly upon the basis that loss of it would not sound in damages. In the context of s 23 (a) counsel maintained that since in terms of the scheme in the event of dismissal the pursuer could not exercise his option rights, there was no right or remedy under s 23 (a) to be excluded or restricted. Counsel for the pursuer on the other hand maintained that what rule 6 (7) purported to do was to restrict the damages to which the pursuer would otherwise be entitled in the event of his being wrongfully dismissed. If such a clause of restriction had been included in the contract of employment it would have fallen under the provisions of s 17 of the Act of 1977. Since this provision appeared not in the contract of employment but in the secondary contract, namely, the options contract, the provisions of s 23 apply, and it would accordingly be necessary to consider whether it was not fair and reasonable to incorporate such a term in the contract. The defenders stressed that rule 6 (7) was an integral part of the option right granted to the pursuer, but I agree with counsel for the pursuer that that cannot affect the proper construction to be placed upon s 23 (a). To say that rule 6 (7) was an integral part of the option right granted to the pursuer is just another way of saying that the option right was granted to the pursuer subject to conditions. I am not persuaded that the operation of s 23 could be avoided by expressing a particular term of a contract in such a way that it could be regarded as an integral part of a right conferred upon one of the parties. If the true effect of a term of a contract is to exclude or restrict a right or remedy arising in respect of the primary contract in the event of a breach of obligation, then in my opinion s 23 will operate.

Counsel for the defenders maintained that even if rule 6 (7) could be regarded as falling within the ambit of s 23, nonetheless it should not be regarded as an attempt to strike at any provision or remedy flowing from the contract of employment itself (the primary contract). It is true that there is no reference in the contract of employment to the scheme, and that the contract of employment in this case was concluded after the scheme had been adopted by the defenders. It is however agreed that prior to the scheme being adopted by the defenders the pursuer must have had another contract of employment. Rule 6 (7) refers to "any damages or compensation . . . by reason of any alteration of his rights or expectations under the Scheme". The Lord Ordinary expressed the view that the word "damages" could only mean a sum payable by a party to make up for a loss caused to him as a result of a wrongful act such as a breach of contract or delict. It is not easy to determine what the defenders intended the content of this rule to be. Rule 6 (7) is directed to the contingency of a participant being dismissed. Counsel for the defenders maintained that the reference in rule 6 (7) to "damages" implied that the dismissal was wrongful. Accordingly they submitted that in this rule "damages" referred to wrongful dismissal, and "compensation" applied to unfair dismissal in terms of the Employment Protection (Consolidation) Act 1978. Counsel for the pursuer, however, drew attention to the fact that for the purposes of that Act dismissal might arise in a number of different circumstances: (1) if the contract was terminated by the employer with or without notice; (2) where a fixed term contract expired without renewal; and (3) where the employee terminated the contract with or without notice in circumstances such that he is entitled to terminate it without notice by reason of the employer's conduct (ss 54 and 55 of the Act of 1978).

In these circumstances counsel for the pursuer maintained that "damages" in rule 6 (7) was not confined to a monetary payment payable for breach of contract. Both parties referred to *Hall Brothers Steamship Co Ltd v Young*. In that case Sir Wilfrid Greene (as he then was) MR said at p 756: "'damages' to an

English lawyer imports this idea, that the sums payable by way of damages are sums which fall to be paid by reason of some breach of duty or obligation, whether that duty or obligation is imposed by contract, by the general law, or legislation". In the context in which the words "damages or compensation" appear in rule 6 (7) I am of opinion that "compensation" applies to such claims as claims for unfair dismissal in terms of the Employment Protection (Consolidation) Act 1978, and that "damages" are not confined to damages payable for breach of contract but include damages arising from contract, general law or legislation. The present action proceeds upon the basis that the pursuer was wrongfully dismissed. I agree with the Lord Ordinary that as such the pursuer would be entitled to be compensated for any loss naturally flowing from that breach of contract or which was reasonably within the contemplation of the parties as a consequence of the dismissal. I also agree with the Lord Ordinary that if the defenders had sought to introduce into the option contracts terms restricting or excluding the defenders' liability to compensate the pursuer for any loss of remuneration or other benefit flowing from the terms of the contract of employment, such a provision would be void by virtue of s 23. However, I do not agree with the Lord Ordinary that rule 6 (7) does not exclude or restrict what he refers to as the "defenders' radical liability" under the contract of employment. Having regard to the averments made by the pursuer, I am of opinion that rule 6 (7) does purport to restrict any liability of the defenders to pay damages arising from a breach by the defenders of the pursuer's contract of employment, and that since rule 6 (7) appears in a secondary contract, it may be struck at by s 23 (a) of the Act of 1977. In my opinion the averments made are sufficient to necessitate an inquiry into these issues, and that the Lord Ordinary was not well founded in excluding from probation the third passage referred to in his interlocutor of 27 February 1990.

I would only add that in support of his first ground of appeal counsel for the pursuer referred to the cases of *Pollock & Co v Macrae* and *Ailsa Craig Fishing Co Ltd v Malvern Fishing Co Ltd*, and submitted that rule 6 (7) fell to be construed contra proferentes. The Lord Ordinary concluded that the principles of construction set out in these two cases should apply, but he opined that that did not help the pursuer very much since these rules of construction only became significant if there was any real ambiguity. In the present case I am not persuaded that it makes any material difference whether strict rules of construction are applied. As already indicated my opinion is that the word "damages" in rule 6 (7) may well be intended to cover more than damages for wrongful dismissal, but even if the clause should be construed as making provision only for damages for wrongful dismissal, I am of opinion that on the basis of the pleadings a question arises as to whether the restriction sought to be imposed by rule 6 (7) was valid having regard to the terms of s 23 (a) of the Act of 1977.

In these circumstances I am satisfied that the Lord

A Ordinary should not have excluded from probation the third passage specified in his interlocutor of 27 February 1990. These averments should have gone to inquiry along with the remaining averments on record. I would accordingly move your Lordships to grant the reclaiming motion to the extent of recalling that part of the interlocutor of 27 February 1990 in which the Lord Ordinary excluded from probation that third passage. Quoad ultra I would affirm the interlocutor of the Lord Ordinary. A proof before answer has to take place upon the averments which

B have been remitted to probation. If such a proof is to take place in which the defenders propose to rely upon the provisions of rule 6 (7) in order to avoid liability, and in which the pursuer proposes to found upon the provisions of the Act of 1977, then prior to the proof both parties should seek leave to amend their pleadings so as to make it clear that these matters are being raised. Parties were agreed that if the interlocutor of 27 February 1990 was to be recalled even in part, it would be appropriate also to recall the Lord

C Ordinary's second interlocutor of 27 February 1990 dealing with expenses. I would accordingly move your Lordships also to recall that interlocutor of 27 February 1990.

LORD McDONALD.—The pursuer was employed by the defenders from July 1955 until he was summarily dismissed by them on 8 July 1987. At the date of dismissal the terms and conditions of his employment were governed by a minute of agreement

D dated 20 March 1986. In the present action he claims damages from the defenders for wrongful dismissal on the ground that by terminating his employment on 8 July 1987 they were in breach of his contract of employment as contained in the minute of agreement.

The present appeal is confined to the relevancy of one head of damages only. Quoad ultra the parties are content with the proof before answer which the Lord Ordinary has allowed. The matter in dispute is a claim by the pursuer that as a result of his dismissal he has

E been deprived of the right to exercise certain options under an executive share option scheme which was adopted by the defenders in general meeting on 26 October 1984. Thereafter on 9 November 1984 and again in 1985 the pursuer was granted under the scheme options to acquire shares at a certain price at certain times and in certain circumstances in the future. The grant of these options pre-dated his contract of service of 20 March 1986 which was current at the time of his dismissal on 8 July 1987. As at that

F date the pursuer had not exercised these options but avers that, had he been given the period of notice to which he was entitled under his contract of service he could and would have done so.

Rule 6 (7) of the scheme provides that it shall be a condition of the scheme that in the event of the dismissal of a participant (i e the holder of an option) from employment he shall not become entitled to any damages or compensation or any additional damages or compensation by reason of any alteration of his rights or expectations under the scheme. In my

opinion the wording used in this provision, standing by itself, is sufficient to exclude the pursuer's claim G under this head. The use of the word "damages" in rule 6 (7) must mean damages for wrongful dismissal; the word "compensation" on the other hand means a payment to which an employee who is unfairly dismissed may become entitled under the Employment Protection (Consolidation) Act 1978 and other relevant statutes.

It was submitted that this provision should be construed strictly and contra proferentem. I am not persuaded that this is necessarily so. The reason for H imposing such a strict standard of construction is that it is inherently improbable that the other party to a contract which includes such a clause intends to release the proferens from a liability that would otherwise fall upon him (*Ailsa Craig Fishing Co Ltd v Malvern Fishing Co Ltd*, per Lord Fraser of Tullybelton at 1982 SLT, p 381). If the share option scheme does create a contractual relationship between the parties it is one which contains substantial potential benefits to the pursuer and I think it most unlikely I that the presence of rule 6 (7) would prevent the pursuer from accepting the grant of a lucrative option.

Even if the scheme falls to be strictly construed against the defenders, however, I consider that it still effectively excludes the pursuer's claim. It is clearly and unambiguously expressed and in my opinion meets the requirements set out by Lord Dunedin in *Pollock v Macrae*, 1922 SLT at p 512. It is true that rule 6 (1) refers to cessation of employment "for any reason (other than death)" and that rule 6 (9) refers to J the termination of a contract of employment "for whatever reason", but I cannot read these as in any way restricting the clear interpretation of rule 6 (7) that it covers damages for wrongful dismissal.

The pursuer had an alternative argument, however, to the effect that even if rule 6 (7) read by itself excludes his claim, it was void by virtue of s 23 of the Unfair Contract Terms Act 1977. So far as Scotland is concerned the intent of this Act is said to be to K impose limits on the extent to which civil liability can be avoided by means of contract terms. The argument for the pursuer was that the grant and acceptance of an option under the scheme created a contract between him and the defenders; that rule 6 (7) purported to exclude or restrict in part at least his right to damages for wrongful dismissal under his contract of employment; and for that reason rule 6 (7) was void in terms of s 23 of the 1977 Act.

The defenders argued that the share option scheme L was not a contract between them and the pursuer and at no stage became one. The grant of an option was a unilateral act at the discretion of the defenders, and even after an employee had been invited to apply for an option the defenders still had a discretion to refuse to grant it. It was at its highest a unilateral obligation and not a mutual contract which it would require to be if it was to be affected by s 23 of the 1977 Act.

In my opinion once an option had been granted to an employee under the scheme a contractual relationship arose between the employee and the defenders. The employee had an enforceable contractual right to exercise his option at such times and under such circumstances as the scheme provides. He also had to pay a nominal option price of £1. Although the English doctrine of consideration does not apply to Scotland the presence of this provision is a clear indication of the bilateral nature of the relationship. I am therefore prepared to hold that at the material time — the date of dismissal — a contractual relationship existed between the pursuer and the defenders arising out of the scheme and, to that extent, s 23 of the 1977 Act is applicable.

If s 23 is applicable the first question to be decided is whether rule 6 (7) of the scheme is a term of the contract which I have held arises between the pursuer and the defenders once an option had been granted and accepted. In my opinion it is such a term. The actual wording is "it shall be a condition of the Scheme". When the stage is reached where the scheme becomes a contract the word "term" becomes quite appropriate to rule 6 (7).

The next question is whether rule 6 (7) excludes or restricts any right or remedy available to the pursuer arising out of any breach of the defenders' duty to him under his contract of employment. If he was wrongfully dismissed he is entitled to damages to cover the financial loss directly flowing from the defenders' breach of contract. In my opinion the pursuer would be entitled to damages under this heading for any financial loss he could prove to have arisen through his inability to follow up his options as a result of his summary dismissal. The defenders' only defence to such a claim — assuming it can be proved — is rule 6 (7). Rule 6 (7) however falls to be regarded as void by virtue of s 23 of the 1977 Act. The result is that the pursuer's averments relating to this head of damages are, in my opinion, sufficiently relevant to be admitted to proof before answer and I would allow this reclaiming motion to that extent.

LORD WYLIE.—On 26 October 1984 the defenders adopted rules in relation to an executive share option scheme in terms of which options would be granted to such eligible executives as the directors from time to time determined. These options, if granted, conferred on the holders a right to subscribe for shares in accordance with the scheme and amounted in effect to fringe benefits for such eligible executives. Rule 2 deals with the grant of such options at the discretion of the directors, inviting application for a specified maximum number of options at a specified subscription price and a time limit of 21 days within which such application required to be made. The directors would then decide whether or not to grant the option applied for, subject to payment of the sum of £1. Rule 5 relates to the exercise of options by the eligible executive by notice in writing accompanied by the subscription price. In terms of rule 5 (2) no such option could be exercised until three years from the date of the grant had expired, subject to rules 6, 9 and 10. Rule 6 relates to conditions on leaving

employment. In terms of rule 6 (1) should a participant cease to be in the employment "for any reason (other than death)" within the three year period the option lapses unless continued at the directors' discretion. Rule 6 (3) provides that if the holder of such an option ceases to be in the employment "by reason of his death, injury or disability or dismissal for redundancy" after the expiration of three years from the grant the option could be exercised within one year of such cessation. Rule 6 (4) provides that if the employment is terminated by reason of retirement after three years from the date of the grant the holder could exercise the option within a period of 15 months thereafter. Rule 6 (7) is in the terms following: "It shall be a condition of the Scheme that in the event of the dismissal of a Participant from employment he shall not become entitled to any damages or compensation or any additional damages or compensation by reason of any alteration of his rights or expectations under the Scheme." Finally, in terms of rule 9 provision is made in the event of a takeover. It provides that a participant is entitled within six months of notification of such an event to exercise the option, provided that is done within 10 years of the grant at which point the option lapses automatically in terms of rule 5 (5), or any earlier date specified under rule 6.

The pursuer commenced employment with the defenders or their predecessors in July 1955 on conditions of employment latterly determined in terms of a minute of agreement between the parties dated 20 March 1986. In terms of cl ninth it was provided inter alia that "Either party may terminate this Agreement by giving to the other six months' notice in writing". On or about 8 July 1987 the defenders gave notice to the pursuer that his employment with the defenders was terminated as at that date and the pursuer maintains that this constituted a breach of his contract of employment. It is accepted that this is an issue between the parties which can only be resolved after proof before answer. In the meantime, it is averred that on 9 November 1984 the pursuer had been granted an option in respect of 20,000 shares at a price of £1.75 per share and that in or about 1985 he had been granted a further option in respect of 10,000 shares at £2.38 per share. On 12 November 1987 an event of the kind envisaged in rule 9 occurred when Raine Industries plc acquired one half or more of the defenders' share capital. It is the pursuer's contention on averment that if he had been given the six months' notice of termination of his employment to which he was entitled in terms of his contract of employment he would have been able and willing to exercise the share options which he held. The head of damages with which alone the reclaiming motion is concerned relates to the loss allegedly sustained as a consequence of being deprived of his right to exercise these share options.

It was submitted on behalf of the pursuer and reclaimer that the Lord Ordinary had erred in excluding this head of damages from probation. In particular, the Lord Ordinary had fallen into error in holding, as he put it: "Rule 6 (7) has the effect of

restricting the defenders' liability under the option
A contracts but it does not in my view exclude or restrict
the defenders' said radical liability under the contract
of employment itself." On the contrary, it was submitted that rule 6 (7) purported to restrict the damages
to which any option holder would be entitled under
the contract of employment itself in the event of
wrongful dismissal. In these circumstances it was
struck at and rendered void by the provisions of s 23
(a) of the Unfair Contract Terms Act 1977. In the
absence of any averments in relation to the "reason-
B ableness" test the defenders could not rely on a provision in a secondary contract (the option contract)
which could not have been effective, in terms of s 17
(1) of the Act, had it been a provision in the primary
contract (the employment contract).

The primary argument advanced on behalf of the
defenders and respondents was that the option scheme
itself was not a contract and any of its provisions,
including rule 6 (7), did not constitute "Any term of
any contract" to which s 23 (a) of the Act of 1977
C could apply. It was essentially a scheme which gave
powers to the directors to issue invitations to eligible
executives at their entire discretion and, in the event
of an application, to grant an option on payment of a
nominal sum, again at their entire discretion. In terms
of the definition (rule 1) an "'option' means the right
of a participant to subscribe for a share at a Subscription Price in accordance with the scheme".
Counsel drew the distinction between a contractual
term on the one hand and a condition attached to a
D unilateral obligation on the other. Rule 6 (7) accordingly constituted a condition attached to an option
which was not struck at by s 23.

I am satisfied that this submission is not well
founded. When the option scheme was initially
promulgated it could not of course constitute a contract. However, when an application was made by an
eligible executive and in respect of that application an
option was granted in return for payment, in accord-
E ance with the rules of the scheme, I am satisfied that
a contractual relationship was constituted. In normal
circumstances, when the participant came to exercise
the option by notice in writing accompanied by the
subscription price, the company was under an obligation to issue the relevant share and have it registered.
As has been observed, the provision in relation to the
payment of £1 for the grant of the option, although
not a necessary requirement of Scots law, serves to
underline the contractual nature of the relationship
F which had come about.

The pursuer's case turns on the application of s 23
(a) and an alternative argument advanced on the
defenders' behalf, shortly stated, was as follows. Rule
6 (7) attached a condition to the benefit provided
under and in terms of the option scheme. Whether or
not the loss of such a benefit could constitute a head
of damages in a claim arising from breach of the contract of employment would depend on circumstances,
one of which would be the terms on which the benefit
itself had been conferred. In this instance the benefit

had been given and acquired on the basis that the loss
of the benefit would not sound in damages. The G
benefit had been given and accepted on the basis that
in the event of dismissal of a participant from employment, no entitlement to any damages or compensation
in respect of the benefit under the scheme would arise.
It was important, so it was argued, to keep in mind the
essential purpose underlying the section. Its purpose
was essentially to prevent rights conferred in a
primary contract, in this instance the contract of
employment, being cut down or extinguished by a
provision in a secondary contract, in this instance the H
share option contract, when this could not have been
achieved had the provision been incorporated in the
primary contract. It was not intended to outlaw a
qualification which had been annexed to rights conferred in the secondary contract itself. It is perhaps
understandable, when an employer chooses to confer
fringe benefits of this nature on his employees, that he
should wish to cover himself against claims for
damages or compensation in respect of these benefits.
It was submitted that the Lord Ordinary was accord- I
ingly correct in examining, as he did, the provisions of
the share option scheme in reaching a conclusion as to
whether or not s 23 applied. He accepted that any provision in the option contract calculated to restrict or
exclude liability to compensate for any loss flowing
directly from the terms of the contract of employment
would certainly be struck at by the section. In this
instance the rights in the secondary contract formed
no part of the terms of the contract of employment and
any restriction of these rights would be regulated J
within the terms of the secondary contract.

I have not found this an easy issue to resolve but I
have been driven to the view that there is force in this
line of argument and in the reasoning by which the
Lord Ordinary reached the conclusion which he did.
As a consequence of an alleged breach of contract the
pursuer has certainly been unable to exercise the
options which he held and has sustained certain losses
as a consequence. But the benefit had been given and
acquired in the first instance on the express condition K
that the loss of that benefit in the event of dismissal
would not sound in damages. In accepting the benefit
the pursuer did so on the basis of the conditions under
which it was granted, no right or remedy arose which
could be excluded or restricted and accordingly no
scope arose for s 23 (a) to apply.

For these reasons I would refuse the reclaiming
motion and adhere to the interlocutor of the Lord
Ordinary.

L

*Counsel for Pursuer and Reclaimer, D R A Emslie,
QC; Solicitors, Balfour & Manson, Nightingale & Bell
— Counsel for Defenders and Respondents, Hamilton,
QC, Cheyne; Solicitors, W & J Burness, WS.*

P A A

Iqbal v Friel

A HIGH COURT OF JUSTICIARY
THE LORD JUSTICE CLERK (ROSS),
LORDS GRIEVE AND WYLIE
23 JULY 1992

Justiciary — Evidence — Sufficiency — Accused charged with selling alcohol to person under 18 years — Boy identifying accused as having sold him alcohol, stating age and speaking to abbreviated birth certificate —
B *Accused in premises later although two persons serving there — Boy seen leaving shop at time of alleged sale carrying cans of lager and making no attempt to conceal them or run away — Whether sufficient evidence of boy's age — Whether sufficient evidence of sale of alcohol by accused — Registration of Births, Deaths and Marriages (Scotland) Act 1965 (c 49), s 41 (3) — Licensing (Scotland) Act 1976 (c 66), s 68.*

Section 41 (3) of the Registration of Births, Deaths and Marriages (Scotland) Act 1965 provides inter alia
C that every abbreviated certificate of birth duly authenticated under the Act shall be sufficient evidence of the birth.

An accused person was charged on a summary complaint, in the special capacity of the licence holder of licensed shop premises, with selling alcoholic liquor to a boy aged 15 years, contrary to ss 67 and 68 (1) and (7) of the Licensing (Scotland) Act 1976. In the course of the trial the boy identified the accused as the person who had sold him the alcohol, stated his age and spoke
D to an abbreviated certificate of his birth. The evidence also disclosed that the accused was in the shop later when the boy returned with the police although there were two persons serving, and that the boy had been seen leaving the shop at the time of the sale carrying cans of lager but making no attempt to conceal them or run away. At the close of the Crown case it was submitted that there was no case for the accused to answer because there was insufficient evidence of the boy's age, that alcohol had been sold to the boy or that it was
E the accused who had sold him the alcohol. The justice rejected the submission. The accused was convicted and appealed by stated case.

Held, (1) that the abbreviated certificate of birth was sufficient evidence of the birth of the boy on the date stated (p 1219F-G); (2) that since the shop sold lager and the boy openly left it carrying four cans of lager making no attempt to conceal them or run away, there was sufficient evidence, taken along with the boy's evidence, of a sale to the boy (p 1220C); but (3)
F that the boy's identification of the accused was not corroborated by the facts that the accused was the licensee or that he was seen in the shop later (pp 1219K-1220A); and appeal *allowed* and conviction *quashed*.

Paton v Wilson, 1988 SLT 634, and *Lockwood v Walker*, 1909 2 SLT 400, *distinguished*.

Summary complaint
Mohammed Iqbal was charged at the instance of James D Friel, procurator fiscal, Paisley, on a

summary complaint which contained the following charge: "On 9 February 1991 from the shop premises G at 71 Seedhill Road, Paisley, you Mohammed Iqbal, being the licence holder in respect of said premises, did sell alcoholic liquor to a person under the age of 18 years, namely Thomas Andrew Dillon, aged 15 years . . . contrary to the Licensing (Scotland) Act 1976, ss 67 and 68 (1) and (7)." The accused pled not guilty and proceeded to trial. After trial the justice convicted the accused.

The accused appealed by way of stated case to the High Court against the decision of the justice.   H

Findings in fact
The justice found the following facts admitted or proved, inter alia:

(1) Thomas Dillon . . . was 15 years of age on 9 February 1991. (2) On said date the witness, Thomas Dillon, was in the vicinity of 71 Seedhill Road, Paisley, with four friends. They all approached the shop premises there. (3) Mohammed Iqbal, the appellant, is the off sale licence holder of 71 Seedhill Road, I Paisley, granted in terms of s 9 (1) of the Licensing (Scotland) Act 1976. The licence will be effective until March 1992. . . . (5) The witness Thomas Dillon was not carrying anything. He went into the premises at 71 Seedhill Road, aforesaid, on his own. A couple of minutes later he came back out of the premises. He spoke to his friends, he exchanged something with one of them and then re-entered the shop. He was still carrying nothing. (6) In the shop premises there were no other customers. There were two people serving in the shop. The witness Dillon was served by the appel- J lant. The witness Dillon asked the appellant for four cans of Budweiser lager. The appellant gave them to him. The witness Dillon paid for them. The appellant did not make any inquiries as to the age of the witness Dillon. (7) The witness Dillon left the shop carrying four cans of Budweiser lager. He was stopped by the two police officers. . . . (8) On the same evening the police officers and the witness Dillon returned to the entrance of 71 Seedhill Road, aforesaid, where the witness Dillon identified the appellant as the person K who had sold the Budweiser lager to him.

Statutory provisions
The Registration of Births, Deaths and Marriages (Scotland) Act 1965 provides:

"41.— . . . (3) Every extract (but not extracts from parochial registers under section 47 of this Act) and every abbreviated certificate of birth, in either case duly authenticated as aforesaid, shall be sufficient evidence of the birth, death or marriage, as the case L may be."

Cases referred to
Lockwood v Walker, 1909 2 SLT 400; 1910 SC (J) 3; (1910) 6 Adam 124.
Meredith v Lees, 1992 SLT 802; 1992 SCCR 459.
Paton v Wilson, 1988 SLT 634; 1988 SCCR 286.

Appeal
The justice posed the following question for the opinion of the High Court, inter alia:

(7) On the facts stated, was I entitled to convict the
A appellant?

The appeal was heard in the High Court on 23 July
1992.

Eo die the court *answered* question 7 in the *negative,
allowed* the appeal and *quashed* the conviction.

The following opinion of the court was delivered by
the Lord Justice Clerk (Ross):

B   **OPINION OF THE COURT.**—This is a stated
case in which the appellant is Mohammed Iqbal. He
went to trial in the district court of Renfrew on a
charge of contravening ss 67 and 68 (1) and (7) of the
Licensing (Scotland) Act 1976 in that he being the
licence holder in respect of certain specified premises
sold alcoholic liquor to a person under the age of 18,
namely Thomas Andrew Dillon, aged 15. At the conclusion of the Crown case a submission of no case to
answer was made and the justice repelled that submis-
C sion. The justice proceeded at the end of the day to
find the appellant guilty of the charge and it is against
his conviction that he is now appealing by way of
stated case.

In presenting the appeal counsel drew attention to
what the justice says in the case regarding the submissions made to her at the stage of the no case to answer
submission. These were four in number and counsel
intimated that he was not now seeking to support the
submission bearing the number 2. He did however
D address the court on the other submissions. The first
of these was to the effect that there was insufficient
evidence in law with regard to the identification of the
accused. The third was that there was insufficient
evidence in law of the sale of alcohol on the occasion
in question and the fourth was that there was no
corroborated evidence of the age of the complainer. So
far as that latter point is concerned, counsel drew
attention to *Lockwood v Walker* and *Paton v Wilson.*
The situation in the present case appears to be that the
E boy Dillon in his evidence stated his age and thereafter
spoke to an abbreviated birth certificate. Counsel submitted that the boy speaking to his birth certificate
was the same source of evidence as the boy speaking
to his age and that accordingly there was not corroborated evidence of his age. In answer to that point the
learned advocate depute submitted that the present
case could readily be distinguished from *Lockwood v
Walker* and *Paton v Wilson* in that in these cases no
birth certificate had been produced. He pointed out
F that in the present case an abbreviated birth certificate
had been produced and he drew attention to the provisions of s 41 (3) of the Registration of Births, Deaths
and Marriages (Scotland) Act 1965. That subsection
provides: [his Lordship quoted the terms of s 41 (3)
and continued:]

The advocate depute submitted that since the justice
had recorded that the boy Dillon had stated his age
and had thereafter spoken to an abbreviated birth
certificate it followed that that abbreviated birth
certificate was sufficient evidence of the birth of the

boy on the date stated. We are satisfied that that submission of the advocate depute is well founded and   G
that there was accordingly sufficient evidence of the
age of the complainer.

The other two points to some extent merge into one
another but the first submission as we say was that
there was insufficient evidence in law with regard to
the identification of the appellant, that is to say his
identification as the seller of the liquor to the boy. The
advocate depute pointed out that the Crown started off
with the clear evidence from the boy to the effect that   H
it was the appellant who had sold the cans of lager to
him. He gave evidence according to the justice that he
had entered the shop, had purchased alcohol from the
appellant and had then left the shop. The advocate
depute maintained that there were two elements on
which the Crown could rely for corroboration. The
first was that the appellant was charged as being the
licence holder in respect of these particular premises.
By virtue of s 312 (x) of the Criminal Procedure (Scotland) Act 1975, since he had been charged in that   I
special capacity, the fact that he possessed that qualification necessary to the commission of the offence
must be held to have been admitted since it had not
been challenged by a preliminary objection before his
plea was recorded. The second element upon which
the advocate depute relied was what is referred to in
finding 8 which tells us that on the evening upon
which the offence was alleged to have been committed
the police officers along with the boy returned to the
entrance of the shop where the boy identified the   J
appellant as the person who had sold him the lager.
The advocate depute contended that that showed there
was evidence from another source, namely from the
police officers, to the effect that the appellant was in
the shop premises some time after the offence had
been committed. He accepted that there was no direct
corroboration but he maintained that these two factors
were sufficient to identify the appellant as the
individual who had sold the liquor to the boy. He
reminded us of the recent case of *Meredith v Lees.* In   K
that case there was some discussion as to the requirements for corroboration, and under reference to what
was stated by the Lord Justice General in that case, the
advocate depute maintained that the factors upon
which he relied did constitute a sufficient check upon
the evidence which the boy had given and thus were
available as a suitable check of the guilt of the appellant. We are not persuaded that that is so. It is not
merely a question of being able to say that there is
corroboration that the appellant was in the shop (and   L
we recognise that the evidence upon which the
advocate depute was relying might indeed show that,
because there was evidence from the boy that the
appellant was in the shop, and there was evidence
from the police officers that some time later he was
seen to be in the shop, and it was his shop he being
the licence holder), but what is necessary is not evidence that he was in the shop but evidence that he was
the person in the shop who sold the liquor to the
complainer. We are not persuaded that the factors
upon which the Crown rely are sufficient to cor-

A roborate the boy's evidence as to that. It is significant in this case that there is a finding to the effect that there were two people serving in the shop at the material time. We recognise that the situation might well have been different if there had been other evidence to suggest that the only person serving in the shop at the material time was the appellant but that was not the situation. That is sufficient for the disposal of the case.

B We also heard argument on the third point raised which was whether there was sufficient evidence in law of the sale of the alcohol. So far as that is concerned, the advocate depute reminded us that one started off with the boy Dillon speaking to the sale having taken place and he submitted that there was sufficient corroboration from the evidence of a police officer to the effect that the boy had originally gone into the shop, had come out of the shop, spoken to his friends, exchanged something with one of them and had then re-entered the shop and that he had subsequently come out of the shop carrying four cans of

C lager. Having regard to the fact that this was a shop which sold lager and that the boy openly left it carrying four cans of lager, making no attempt to conceal them or to run away, we are of the view that a sale might well be established from that evidence. The difficulty for the Crown however is that the charge libels that it was the appellant personally who had sold the liquor to the boy and as we have already explained we are not satisfied that there is sufficient corroboration of the boy's evidence that it was the appellant who

D had sold the liquor to him. That being so we are satisfied that the justice was not entitled to convict the appellant of the charge and we shall accordingly answer question 7 in the negative and will quash the conviction.

Counsel for Appellant, Baird; Solicitors, J & A Hastie, SSC (for Peacock Johnston, Glasgow) — Counsel for Respondent, Macdonald, QC, A D; Solicitor, J D
E *Lowe, Crown Agent.*

P W F

(NOTE)

Exal Sampling Services Ltd v
F # Massie

OUTER HOUSE
LORD CULLEN
3 DECEMBER 1992

Process — Commission and diligence — Recovery of documents — Whether interlocutor granting commission and diligence capable of being sisted as a partial sist of process.

Commission and diligence for recovery of documents having been granted to pursuers and the pur-

suers then having lodged a minute of amendment raising features which the defenders wished to G challenge, the defenders sought a sist of the order for commission and diligence.

Held, that an order for commission and diligence was final and that it was incompetent to sist it; and motion for sist *refused*.

Exal Sampling Services Ltd, a company providing specialised services to the offshore oil industry, raised H an action against two former employees and a former director, and also against a company set up by those individuals. The action, as raised, was for interdict and an accounting of profits, failing which damages, and was based on averments that information confidential to the pursuers in relation to single phase, pressure compensated sampling systems had been and was being used by the defenders. By interlocutor dated 23 September 1992, when a proof was imminent, the pursuers obtained commission and diligence for the I recovery of records showing details of jobs obtained and work carried out by the defenders using the allegedly confidential system.

Thereafter the pursuers lodged a minute of amendment which disclosed that their whole undertaking had been transferred to another company which it was proposed should be substituted as pursuers. The proof was discharged and the defenders indicated an intention to debate a plea of no title to sue in relation to the proposed new pursuers and that there would be an J argument against the joint and several nature of the remedy sought. The defenders also sought a sist of procedure in relation to the commission and diligence, which had not been executed. In refusing the sist the Lord Ordinary (Cullen) said:

"In support of that motion senior counsel pointed out that the pursuers' minute of amendment had introduced a number of changes. Exal Reservoir Services Ltd, to which the whole business undertaking of the K pursuers had been transferred as at 31 March 1992, were to be substituted as pursuers. This raised a question of law as to how far Exal Reservoir Services Ltd were entitled to protect their own business interests by reference to contracts of employment with the pursuers. Could that company in its own right claim damages in respect of what happened after 31 March 1992? It was counsel's present intention to seek to debate the title to sue of Exal Reservoir Services Ltd. A plea of no title to sue had been taken in the L defenders' answers which had been lodged after he had been consulted in the matter. Counsel also indicated that he intended to challenge the pursuers' attempt to obtain joint and several liability on the part of all four defenders. He pointed out that the second defender was on the one hand an employee of Exal Reservoir Services Ltd and on the other hand a director of the pursuers. He pointed out that according to the pursuers' adjustments to which I have referred above, the case against that defender was to be based on his duty as a director. A plea challenging the

competency of the conclusion for joint and several
A liability of the defenders was also tabled in the
defenders' answers. Counsel also pointed out that in
their adjustments the pursuers had deleted their conclusions for an account of profits, which failing
payment of a sum of money. This left the conclusion
for damages as the only monetary claim which was to
be made. This meant that the defenders' gain was no
longer in issue. He accepted that if a proof was
allowed on amended pleadings the pursuers would be
entitled to recover documents to show what jobs had
B been done by the defenders and where, but as matters
presently stood there was no justification for allowing
recovery to proceed.

"Counsel also pointed out that when I granted the
motion on 23 September 1992 the proof was 'imminent'. This situation no longer existed. Counsel went
on to state that it was his intention in due course to
seek a separation between proof on the merits and
proof on the quantification of the pursuers' claim.
Counsel accepted that confidentiality, which was the
C practical reason for the defenders' motion, did not
provide a complete answer to a claim for recovery of
documents. However, it entailed that the court could
be careful to see that it was respected unless and until
the contrary was required in the interests of justice.
He informed me that information as to the locations
of jobs would enable the identity of his contracting
parties to be ascertained. He informed me that the
market was quite small and that it would be very
damaging for the pursuers, who were the defenders'
D direct competitors, to find out the defenders' pricing
structure and list of customers. This would give them
an unfair commercial advantage.

"On the competency of the motion, counsel claimed
that he was not seeking a recall or variation of the
interlocutor of 23 September. He was seeking the
sisting of the diligence, which was in effect a partial
sist, as opposed to a sist of the whole action. It would
be very strange if where a case underwent radical
E change it was not open to the court to grant a sist. By
way of analogy counsel pointed out that the court
could in the light of a change of pleadings discharge
the allowance of proof. He also pointed to the practice
of the court superseding extract. He also sought
support in the terms of Rule of Court 264 (b) which,
in dealing with reclaiming, refers to an interlocutor
'granting or refusing or recalling a sist of execution or
procedure'.

F "Senior counsel for the pursuers disputed the competency of the motion. The court had no inherent
power to alter its previous interlocutor. He accepted
that if it were an abuse of process for a party to insist
on the recovery of documents there would be a remedy
but he submitted that it would lie in the taking of
separate proceedings, such as for suspension or suspension and interdict. However, in the present case
there was no question of abuse of process. Extract was
superseded in the same interlocutor as that which
granted an extractable decree. The substratum for the
recovery of documents was still present.

"In any event counsel opposed the motion on its
merits. [His Lordship summarised the arguments G
about the merits of the motion and continued:]

"In my view the defenders' motion is incompetent.
I am not persuaded that what is sought amounts to the
partial sist of an action. The interlocutor of 23
September 1992 was not interim in nature but disposed of the application for commission and diligence.
It became final. In these circumstances the defenders'
motion seeks in effect to qualify the operation of the
interlocutor. In my view it is not competent for me to
make such a qualification ex post facto.   H

"I should add that even if I did not take the view
that the motion is incompetent I would refuse it on its
merits. . . . The submissions made by counsel for the
pursuers satisfy me that the diligence which I granted
on 23 September is still relevant and reasonably necessary in order to enable the pursuers to make specific
averments on matters which both sides addressed in
the existing pleadings in connection with the dispute
as to whether or not the pursuers would have obtained
the work which was done by the fourth defenders."   I

*Counsel for Pursuers, Currie, QC, R A Smith; Soli-
citors, W & J Burness, WS — Counsel for Defenders,
Emslie, QC; Solicitors, MacRoberts.*

                                                   C H

[A reclaiming motion was enrolled and, of consent, the
interlocutor allowing commission and diligence, pronounced
on 23 September 1992, was recalled and the reclaiming
motion, so far as relating to the interlocutor of 3 December
1992, was then refused as unnecessary.]   J

C R Smith Glaziers
(Dunfermline) Ltd v Greenan

SECOND DIVISION
THE LORD JUSTICE CLERK (ROSS),
LORDS MURRAY AND MORISON   K

10 DECEMBER 1992

*Contract — Restrictive covenant — Contract of employ-
ment — Disclosure of confidential information — Prohibition on engaging with competitor — Whether latter
restriction necessary for enforcement of former — Balance
of convenience — Factors to be taken into account.*

*Interdict — Interim interdict — Balance of convenience
— Factors to be taken into account — Restrictive
covenant.*   L

A company raised an action against a former
employee seeking to prevent him inter alia from
breaching an undertaking not to engage with any competitor for six months after termination of his employment with the pursuers. The Lord Ordinary refused
the pursuers' motion for interim interdict on the basis
that while both parties had a prima facie case, the
financial consequences would be more serious for the
defender, and that the restraint was far reaching in
geographical terms. The Lord Ordinary also accepted

A the defender's account that he had not signed the restrictive agreement willingly. The pursuers reclaimed.

Held, (1) that the matter was at large for the court since the Lord Ordinary had erred in assessing the balance of convenience in that (i) the loss to the defender was a loss of remuneration which could be readily quantified, whereas the pursuers would be unable to secure adequate protection against loss of trade secrets and would suffer a loss which might be difficult to quantify (p 1223F-G); (ii) the defender
B having signed the agreement had prima facie entered into it voluntarily and the Lord Ordinary was not entitled to hold otherwise solely on the basis of an ex parte statement (p 1223H-I); and (iii) the wide geographical terms of the restraint were not a proper consideration where the pursuers had established a prima facie case (p 1223K-L); (2) that the balance of convenience lay in the pursuers' favour where the restriction had only a short time left to run (p 1224A-B and D-E); and reclaiming motion *allowed* and interim
C interdict *granted*.

Action of interdict

C R Smith Glaziers (Dunfermline) Ltd brought an action against Michael John Greenan, a former employee, concluding after amendment, for interdict against the defender, inter alia (i) disclosing to anyone or using for his own purposes or any purposes except
D those of the pursuers, any confidential information of the pursuers, and (iv) until the expiry of six months from the termination of his employment, directly or indirectly engaging within a defined area in a business supplying products and services substantially similar to those supplied by the pursuers.

The case came before the vacation judge (Lord Milligan) when the pursuers, having already obtained interim interdict in terms of head (i), sought interim interdict in terms of the newly added head (iv).
E

Cases referred to

Bluebell Apparel Ltd v Dickinson, 1980 SLT 157; 1978 SC 16.
Group 4 Total Security Ltd v Ferrier, 1985 SLT 287.
Reed Stenhouse (UK) Ltd v Brodie, 1986 SLT 354.
Smith (C R) Glaziers (Dunfermline) Ltd v McGuire and McKeag, 12 December 1986, unreported (1987 GWD 1-2).

F **Textbook referred to**

Burn-Murdoch, *Interdict,* p 137.

On 23 September 1992 the Lord Ordinary *refused* the pursuers' motion.

The pursuers reclaimed.

Reclaiming motion

The reclaiming motion was heard before the Second Division on 10 December 1992.

Eo die the court *allowed* the reclaiming motion,
G *recalled* the interlocutors of 23 September 1992, *varied* the interlocutor of 21 August 1992 and *granted* interim interdict.

The following opinion of the court was delivered by the Lord Justice Clerk (Ross):

OPINION OF THE COURT.—The pursuers carry on business as suppliers and installers of double glazing. Until 14 July 1992 the defender was employed by the pursuers under and in terms of an agreement dated 5 and 6 March 1992. On 14 July
H 1992 the defender left the employment of the pursuers. Prior to that he had been employed selling the products of the pursuers in the Edinburgh area. The Lord Ordinary was informed that he was employed as a sales accountant until April 1992 when he became an area sales manager. As sales consultant, he was concerned with obtaining contracts for the installation of double glazing, in particular in dwellinghouses. As area sales manager, his role involved the administration of contracts already
I effected by sales consultants although he also accompanied salesmen on calls on occasions. After leaving the employment of the pursuers, the defender became employed by Living Design, a business in competition with the pursuers in the Edinburgh area. Initially he was employed by Living Design as a sales consultant, but since October 1992 he has acted as sales manager. It is stated in the defences that he is now responsible for the training of sales consultants, the administration of contracts secured by sales consul-
J tants and the employing and dismissing from employment of staff of Living Design. It is also stated that from time to time he requires to go on calls to customers when he accompanies sales consultants.

In terms of the agreement between the parties, in return for the sum of £50, and the pursuers continuing to employ him and allowing him to use their confidential information in the course of his duties, the defender gave the pursuers certain undertakings
K which he acknowledged were both fair and necessary to ensure the secrecy of the pursuers' confidential information, and to protect the company against unfair competition; he also acknowledged that damages alone would be an inadequate remedy if he breached any of these undertakings.

The terms of the relevant undertakings have been set forth in art 2 of the condescendence, and it is unnecessary to repeat them here.

In the present action the pursuers seek interdict of L the defender in a number of respects. On 21 August 1992 the vacation judge pronounced interdict against the defender in terms of heads (i), (ii) and (iii) of the first conclusion.

Subsequently it appeared that interim interdict in respect of heads (ii) and (iii) had proceeded upon a misunderstanding of events, and on 23 September 1992, the pursuers invited the Lord Ordinary to recall the interim interdict pronounced under heads (ii) and (iii). At the same time the pursuers sought and obtained

A leave to amend the summons by adding a new head (iv) to the conclusion and adding further averments in support of it. The Lord Ordinary on 23 September 1992 refused a motion by the pursuers to pronounce interim interdict in respect of head (iv) of the conclusion. Against that decision of the Lord Ordinary, the pursuers have now reclaimed.

In presenting the reclaiming motion, counsel for the pursuers submitted that the Lord Ordinary's approach to the matter of interim interdict was flawed. In his opinion the Lord Ordinary states: "I accepted counsel

B for the pursuers' and counsel for the defender's submissions that their respective clients each had a bona fide case to advance on the issue of enforceability of the provision of the agreement concerned".

Counsel submitted that what the Lord Ordinary presumably meant in that passage was that he was satisfied that there was a case to try, and that the parties had each put forward a prima facie case. Counsel for the defender agreed, and we think that the

C Lord Ordinary in the foregoing passage has per incuriam used the expression "bona fide" instead of "prima facie".

The Lord Ordinary then proceeded to deal with the balance of convenience. As we read the Lord Ordinary's opinion, in considering the balance of convenience he had regard to three specific matters — (1) the financial consequences to the parties; (2) the allegation that the defender had entered into the agreement under duress and not willingly; and (3) the fact

D that the restraint imposed upon him was very far reaching in geographical terms.

In considering each of these matters, we are satisfied that the Lord Ordinary's approach was erroneous. "In questions of *interim* interdict, the relative inconvenience resulting to either party from its grant or refusal is the dominating consideration" (Burn-Murdoch on *Interdict*, p 137).

In the present case, if interim interdict is granted,

E the defender will be unable to continue in the employment of the defenders until 15 January 1993. It is claimed that he will lose his present employment, but after 15 January 1993 there will be nothing to prevent him being employed by Living Design or any other firm in this field. Loss of employment will thus involve him in loss of remuneration which can readily be quantified. On the other hand if interim interdict is not granted, the defender will be able to continue in the employment of Living Design, and the pursuers will be unable to secure adequate protection against

F loss of trade secrets. We appreciate that interim interdict still stands in terms of head (i) of the conclusion, but it is well established that a prohibition against disclosing trade secrets is practically worthless unless it is accompanied by a restriction upon the employee possessed of secrets against entering the employment of competitors (*Bluebell Apparel Ltd v Dickinson*, per the Lord President at 1980 SLT, p 160). It accordingly appears to us that if interim interdict is not pronounced in terms of head (iv) the pursuers are likely to sustain loss. The Lord Ordinary concluded

G that any prospective loss to the pursuers was speculative, but we do not agree. It may be difficult to quantify the loss, but we are satisfied that the pursuers would be likely to sustain loss if interim interdict were not pronounced in terms of head (iv). In our opinion the Lord Ordinary failed to give proper weight to this consideration, and in this respect he failed properly to weigh the relative inconvenience to either party from the grant or refusal of the interim interdict.

The Lord Ordinary makes it clear in his opinion that on the information before him he concluded that

H the defender had not entered into the agreement with the pursuers willingly. We are of opinion that there was no justification for the Lord Ordinary so concluding. He had to proceed upon the basis of ex parte statements, and the situation was that the pursuers were maintaining that the agreement had been freely entered into, whereas the defender was maintaining that he had only entered the agreement after threats. The agreement was produced, and it was not disputed that the defender had signed the agreement. That

I being so, in our opinion, prima facie the situation must be that there was an agreement which had been entered into voluntarily. We are not satisfied that on the ex parte statement of the defender alone the Lord Ordinary was entitled to hold that the pursuers' assertion that the agreement had been entered into willingly was shown to be wrong. Moreover the Lord Ordinary explains that he arrived at this conclusion on the weight of the information before him. The position appears to be that the pursuers maintained

J that the agreement had been entered into voluntarily whereas the defender gave a circumstantial account as to the making of threats against him. Before the Lord Ordinary counsel for the pursuers explained that he was not in a position to answer the allegation and he sought and obtained a short adjournment over the lunch interval to obtain further information. In the event he was not able to obtain further information at that time. In granting the adjournment however, the Lord Ordinary indicated that any further information obtained on this particular matter might not be

K material to his decision. In our opinion it was unreasonable for the Lord Ordinary to intimate that further information might not be material to his decision on this matter, and then to decide the issue against the pursuers on the weight of the information before him.

The third matter relied on by the Lord Ordinary was that the restraint which would prohibit the defender working in the field concerned was very far reaching in geographical terms. We are not satisfied

L that this was a proper consideration when weighing the balance of convenience having regard to the fact that the Lord Ordinary must be taken to have held that the pursuers had made out a prima facie case.

In these circumstances we are satisfied that the Lord Ordinary's approach to the balance of convenience was flawed, and that accordingly the matter is now at large for this court.

When we weigh the relative inconvenience to either

party from the grant or refusal of the interim interdict, we are satisfied that the balance of convenience is in favour of granting interim interdict. As we have already observed, in the event of interim interdict being granted the defender would sustain financial loss which can readily be quantified. On the other hand the pursuers will sustain loss if interim interdict is not granted, and although this cannot be quantified, it appears to us that it will likely outweigh any financial loss which the defender will sustain in the period up to 15 January 1993. In considering the balance of convenience we think it is of importance that even if the defender was to lose his employment that would only be for the period up to 15 January 1993. In *C R Smith Glaziers (Dunfermline) Ltd v McGuire and McKeag* this court had occasion to consider different restrictive provisions in a contract of employment. In the course of its opinion reference was made to *Group 4 Total Security Ltd v Ferrier* and *Reed Stenhouse (UK) Ltd v Brodie*. In the former of these cases where the period of restriction had little more than two months to run, the court had held that the equitable course was to recall the interim interdict and to allow the employee to further his employment, leaving it to the employers if so advised to sue for damages for breach of contract. In that connection the court in *C R Smith Glaziers (Dunfermline) Ltd v McGuire and McKeag* stated: "Although there may be cases where that is the appropriate course to take, in our opinion the fact that the particular restrictive covenant only has a relatively short time to run is not a reason for refusing to enforce it. It must be kept in mind that the remedy of damages is not always a practical one owing to the difficulty which an employer may have in establishing breach of the restrictive covenant. Moreover the fact that the restriction has only a short period to run is really double-edged. If it only has a short period to run, any hardship to the employee is necessarily limited too."

In the present case, we are satisfied, particularly because of the short period which the restrictive covenant still has to run, that the balance of convenience favours the pronouncing of interim interdict rather than its refusal. We regard the present case as similar in a number of respects to *C R Smith Glaziers (Dunfermline) Ltd v McGuire and McKeag.*

In seeking to resist the granting of interim interdict, counsel for the defender maintained that there had been some delay on the part of the pursuers in seeking to enforce the restrictive covenant. We are not persuaded that there was any material delay in this case. The defender ceased to be employed by the pursuers on 14 July 1992, and the pursuers obtained interim interdict against him on 21 August 1992. We accept that the issue of interim interdict in terms of head (iv) of the conclusion was not raised until 23 September 1992, but we are not persuaded that any delay in this case supports the view that the pursuers did not regard the matter as involving any great degree of urgency.

In the present case the pursuers have put forward a prima facie case; if interim interdict is not pronounced the pursuers may well sustain loss which it will be difficult to quantify whereas any loss to the defender can be quantified and will probably represent his earnings for a period of approximately five weeks; when one bears in mind that the restriction expires on 15 January 1993 and that the remedy of damages open to the pursuers is not always a practical one because of the difficulty of quantifying loss, we have come to the conclusion that the balance of convenience favours the granting of interim interdict.

We shall accordingly allow the reclaiming motion, recall the Lord Ordinary's interlocutors of 23 September 1992, except insofar as relating to the minute of amendment, we shall vary the interlocutor of 21 August 1992 by substituting the word "authorised" for the word "attended" in that interlocutor, and we shall grant interim interdict in terms of head (iv) of the first conclusion of the summons.

Counsel for Pursuers, Macfadyen, QC; Solicitors, Macbeth, Currie & Co, WS — Counsel for Defender, P W Ferguson; Solicitors, Drummond Miller, WS.

R D S

(NOTE)

Bovis Construction (Scotland) Ltd v Whatlings Construction Ltd

OUTER HOUSE
LORD PROSSER
11 FEBRUARY 1993

Contract — Construction — Prior correspondence — Whether prior correspondence available as aid to construction — Agreement reached by informal correspondence.

Management contractors contracted with a construction company for the construction of part of a building. The management contractors alleged that the construction company was in breach of contract and sought damages. The construction company counterclaimed and also contended that, even if they were in breach, their liability would be restricted to £100,000 by virtue of an agreement contained in letters passing between the parties to that effect. The management contractors disputed that construction of the agreement and sought to refer to prior correspondence between the parties as explanation of the agreement. The construction company argued that it was not proper to refer to the prior correspondence.

Held, that it was almost always necessary, at least with a non-probative contract, to look at prior correspondence for possible assistance in interpretation of a contract, but that in this case no assistance was to be

A found in it in interpreting the terms of the contract documentation; and consideration of the terms of the prior correspondence *excluded* from consideration.

Bovis Construction (Scotland) Ltd raised an action against Whatlings Construction Ltd arising out of a dispute during the construction of a new concert hall in Glasgow for the City of Glasgow District Council. Bovis were the management contractors and Whatlings were subcontracted to construct part of the B building. Disputes arose which were the subject of an action and counterclaim for sums in excess of £1,000,000. The action was sisted for arbitration.

In relation to one part of the Bovis claim, Whatlings contended that any liability on their part was limited to £100,000 by virtue of the terms of certain letters. This contention was disputed by Bovis. The parties wished that particular issue decided by the courts rather than by an arbiter. To achieve this end, the parties entered into a minute of agreement which C preserved the arbitration for all purposes other than resolution of the particular dispute as to limitation, and set out an agreed procedure for resolution of that dispute on the commercial roll. The sist was recalled and it was agreed that, once the limitation dispute had been resolved by the courts, the action would be sisted of new, to await the outcome of the arbitration.

The case then came before the Lord Ordinary (Prosser) for a determination of the limitation question. In deciding that question in favour of Whatlings, D the Lord Ordinary said:

"The limitation dispute, which is the only matter which the parties seek to have resolved at this stage, is essentially a dispute as to the correct interpretation of certain contractual documents. It is agreed that the subcontract was constituted by the offer and qualified acceptance to which I have already referred [an offer from Whatlings of 29 April 1988 (sent in response to certain tender inquiry documentation including a E Bovis 'Form of Agreement between Employer and Sub-contractor') and qualified acceptance dated 15 July 1988] together with (a) three further letters dated 2, 5 and 12 August 1988; (b) the Bovis subcontract terms and conditions, referred to in and insofar as modified by the letters constituting the subcontract; and (c) a group of five letters, relating to the question of limitation, dated 6, 7, 8, 8 (with attached list of contract amendments to date) and 15 July 1988. This last group of letters were expressly included in the subcontract documents in terms of the letter of 15 July F 1988. It will also be necessary to refer to a further six letters which are not themselves part of the subcontract. These six letters are dated 16, 18, 26, 27 and 31 May and 27 June 1988. It is admitted by the pursuers that it was an outcome of this prior correspondence that the parties' subsequent contractual agreement on limitation of the defenders' liability to pay damages was reached. The parties are, however, in dispute as to whether it is appropriate to refer to these six letters, for the purpose of interpreting the actual subcontract documents.

"The pursuers' substantive plea in the present action is to the effect that having suffered loss, injury G and damage as a result of the defenders' breach of contract, they are entitled to reparation. The limitation dispute with which I am concerned is focused in the defenders' fifth plea in law. This is to the effect that the defenders' liability to pay damages to the pursuers in respect of the breach of contract condescended upon being limited to the sum of £100,000 in terms of the parties' contract, decree should not be pronounced as concluded for. At the hearing, it was submitted on behalf of the defenders that I should sustain H this plea, and repel the pursuers' first plea, to the effect that the defenders' averments regarding limitation of liability are irrelevant. The nature of the issue between the parties is in a sense that simple one. It is not disputed that the contract did include a limitation of the defenders' liability. The dispute between the parties is as to the scope and application of that limitation. The contentions advanced on behalf of the pursuers are perhaps the best indication of the real points of difference. Counsel for the pursuers asked me to I make four findings in relation to the parties' agreement about limitation of liability. First, I was asked to hold that the limitation agreement covered damages *for late completion only*. It thus had no application to the facts of the present case. Secondly, I was asked to hold that the limitation agreement had no application in situations where the contract was determined, whatever the nature of the claim might be. Thirdly, I was asked to hold that, at worst for the pursuers, the limitation agreement had no application to any set off J which the pursuers might seek to enforce under cl 11 of the terms and conditions of the subcontract, or indeed to any claim under cl 11 which the arbiter might think competent. Fourthly, and finally, I was asked to hold that the limitation agreement had no application to any claim arising out of defective work, whatever the nature of the losses which that might cause. It is therefore necessary to look at the subcontract documents, in order to discover what it was that the parties agreed in relation to the limitation of the defenders' liability. What was its scope? What K were the situations, or the losses, to which it was intended by the parties to apply?"

His Lordship then considered the terms of the subcontract and the contractual documents dealing with limitation of liability and concluded that Whatlings' liability for the breach of contract condescended on was limited to £100,000. His Lordship then continued:

"That is the conclusion which I would reach if there L were no prior communings. Where one can reach a view as to the intention of the parties from the words which they have used, it is not easy to see why one should look to prior communings, unless the contractual documents themselves indicate that some special meaning for the words used in the contract is to be found in such communings. It is elementary that one is concerned with the intention which the parties have expressed, and not their intentions as they may actually have been: *Inglis v Buttery & Co* (1878) 5 R

A (HL) 87. Since, by definition, the final expression of agreement is to be found in the contract documents, the danger of going back to a period when the parties had not thus agreed, to find out what they did agree, is I think self evident. The limit on its value, where there are divergent suggestions as to what they meant, has been pointed out with great authority: see *Prenn v Simmonds* [1971] 1 WLR 1381, at pp 1383-1385.

"It is nonetheless true that if there is prior correspondence, it will be hard to know, until one has looked at it, whether the terminology of the eventual contract is truly independent of it, or is to be read as having been adopted by the parties precisely because its intended (and perhaps special) meaning had previously been made clear. As was submitted by counsel for the pursuers, it may be that there is greater scope for going back to prior correspondence in cases where the contract itself takes a relatively informal shape. We are not here concerned with probative or formal documents, which might be expected to be self sufficient. One is dealing with the latter end of a continuing correspondence. That being so, the possibility that the later letters depend on what has been said in the earlier ones is probably greater. In any event, I am inclined to think that subject to the basic principle that one is trying to find out the meaning of the intention expressed, rather than a rival intention said to be actual, a court has no real choice but to *look* at background documents, if one of the parties contends that a reading of these will assist in the interpretation of what is said in the contract documents. The justification for at least looking has been expressed in various ways. One may be trying to place oneself in thought in the same position as the parties; one may be trying to find the surrounding circumstances in which they were contracting; one may be looking for the 'factual matrix'. One may invoke 'ambiguity', although in the face of competing interpretations put forward by the parties, I suspect that 'unambiguous meaning' will seldom be simply a reason for refusing to look at prior correspondence. It will rather be a description of a view which one would not expect such correspondence to alter.

"Counsel for the pursuers suggested several reasons for looking at the prior correspondence. He suggested that it was always appropriate, whether the documents were ambiguous or not, to go back to prior correspondence to ascertain the general background which I have mentioned. He further maintained that one should go back if a colloquial phrase with no single precise meaning was employed, and finally he said that one must go back in the present case because the limitation agreement was couched in terms of 'acceptance' or non-acceptance, which constituted a reference back to the prior correspondence. A number of cases were referred to: *Walker v Caledonian Railway Co* (1858) 20 D 1102; *Houldsworth v Gordon Cumming*, 1910 2 SLT 136; 1910 SC (HL) 49; and *Temperance Halls Co-operative Building Society Ltd v Glasgow Pavilion Co Ltd* (1908) 16 SLT 112. I do not however find any specific assistance in these cases. It seems to me that the dangers of misusing past correspondence

are both great and obvious, but that at least in the case of non-probative contract, it is difficult to imagine a situation in which one could decide that past correspondence could not assist in interpretation, without at least looking at it. In the end of the day, in the present case, I did not understand counsel for the defenders to claim that I must shut my eyes to the previous correspondence. The suggestion was rather that I should approach it with great caution, and that I would find nothing useful if I looked at it. That being so, I am satisfied that I ought to look at it. [His Lordship did so and concluded:]

"I think it is fair to say that Whatlings' concern related to the risk of unlimited damages in the event of overrun. On the other hand, they had identified this as a problem arising from the terms of cl 2, and from the absence of any specific limitation or provision for liquidated damages. In putting forward the figure of £100,000 in the letter of 27 June, they related it to 'damages, as proven'. The scope of what they wanted, in saying this, is not clear to me from its context. Over all, I am unable to find, in the pre-contract correspondence, any real clue as to the meaning of the terminology employed in the actual contract. Whatever Whatlings may have been worried about, and whatever they wanted to achieve, I am satisfied that the whole matter is picked up and dealt with on a wider or simpler basis. I do not think I can expand upon this. I simply do not find in the earlier correspondence anything that helps me to determine the meaning of the parties when they subsequently formulated (and indeed re-formulated) their agreement in the documents which constitute the contract itself. It may well be that they were not specifically applying their minds to all types of breach under cl 2. Nonetheless, it appears to me that the simple and wide words that they actually used had that effect.

"One effect of looking at the earlier correspondence is perhaps to alter the nature of the argument on behalf of the pursuers. Looking at the contract documents alone, the argument for the pursuers took the form of contrasting costs with the causes, or breaches of contract, which gave rise to them. It was the former rather than the latter that required to be time related. Looked at in the context of the prior correspondence, the argument for the pursuers can take on a different form. In the prior correspondence, it is plain that the defenders were concentrating upon the possibility of an 'overrun'. As I have already noted, that is a potential cause of costs, and itself a breach of the time requirements. On behalf of the pursuers, it was submitted that there was nonetheless a substantive question as to whether 'time-related costs' were those flowing from every breach of cl 2 (as contended by the defenders) or whether the expression was to be related to one particular type of breach of cl 2, late completion. It was submitted that the expression was indeed limited in this way, that having been the subject matter of the prior correspondence, and losses of that kind being those which the defenders had been seeking to avoid. As I have indicated, the prior correspondence does indeed appear to be concerned with that particular type of breach and its consequences. I am inclined to think that if anything this tends to undermine the contention that the second sentence of the limitation agreement is concerned with consequential costs, without reference to their relationship with the breaches that caused them. I do not however take that into account in interpreting the contractual documents. I am of the view that these must be interpreted upon their own terms, there being no link between these terms and the terms of the prior correspondence which could help for the purposes of interpretation.

"In these circumstances I hold that the defenders' liability to pay damages to the pursuers in respect of the breach of contract condescended upon is limited to the sum of £100,000. It appears that the appropriate course is to repel the pursuers' first plea in law, sustain the defenders' second plea in law in relation to the question of limitation, and sustain the defenders' fifth plea in law to the extent of refusing decree for any sum over the figure of £100,000. Having regard to the somewhat unusual procedural position, and the relationship between this action and the arbitration, I shall however defer pronouncing any interlocutor disposing of pleas meanwhile, and shall put the case out by order for further procedure."

Counsel for Pursuers, G N H Emslie, QC; Solicitors, MacRoberts — Counsel for Defenders, Hamilton, QC, Moynihan; Solicitors, McGrigor Donald.

C H

(NOTE)

Watts v Russell

OUTER HOUSE
LORD MACLEAN
18 FEBRUARY 1993

Damages — Amount — Solatium, loss of earning capacity and necessary services rendered to injured person — Toe — Serious fracture of great toe leading to permanent but limited incapacity.

A 50 year old lady suffered a grossly comminuted fracture of a great toe which left her with persisting disability but minimal persisting discomfort. Her earning capacity was restricted. Her husband had provided her with necessary services, initially intensively and then at a reducing level for a total of about 12 weeks.

Held, that solatium was properly assessed at £4,250 and that her husband's services were properly valued at £750; and damages *awarded* accordingly.

Kathleen Watts raised an action against David Russell for damages for injuries sustained in an accident on 23 July 1989. She was then aged 50. Her left great toe was caught under a heavy radiator that fell. Liability was admitted. In awarding damages assessed at £9,060 including interest to the date of decree the Lord Ordinary (MacLean) said:

"The accident was wholly unexpected and caused immediate shock. She found her whole body shaking almost incessantly for some time afterwards. She was admitted by ambulance to Dundee Royal infirmary where she was found to have a grossly comminuted fracture of the great toe with skin loss. In hospital she was detained for five days and treated by elevation, rest and by regular dressings applied to her fractured toe which was placed in plaster. Drugs were administered to her in order to attempt to control the pain. Her husband came up to Dundee from Gloucester to take her home. The journey was uncomfortable because she had to keep her leg up. Indeed, to accommodate this, the passenger seat had to be taken out, and during the journey she was in considerable discomfort. The day after she returned home her general practitioner, Dr Cookson, visited her at home. Shortly thereafter she saw the orthopaedic surgeon, Mr Tasker, at hospital. She said that at that time she was very frightened because she did not know what was to be done to her toe, it having been totally crushed. Eight days after the accident the plaster was removed. It was noted that there was some exposed bone in the wound. The pursuer described the sight of her foot as: 'Horrible. Just horrendous.' Because of the area of skin loss the dressing had to be changed at hospital twice a day for about four to six weeks. Then her husband did the dressing of the toe until she was discharged in January 1990. During this period she could not wear normal footwear and continued to use a stick. Her husband did the cooking, shopping and housework. He helped her in the shower. He drove her to the hospital, waited for her there for about two and a half hours, and drove her back home again. Latterly in this period she saw the nurse once each week and the surgeon once each month. She herself could not drive, garden or play badminton which she did before the accident about three times per week. Since her discharge, she has been unable to ride a bicycle or wear high heeled shoes, which she wore all the time before the accident. She cannot now climb ladders. She is unable to garden. She has episodes of cramp, and experiences tightness and discomfort in her foot. She can drive for short periods only. She continued to have pins and needles in her foot so that when she stands, she tends to stand on one foot only. Of her husband's contribution she said he was wonderful. She could not have managed without the help he gave her. She was, she said, still affected by the accident. Her left big toe was rigid at its distal end but now causes minimal discomfort.

"At the time of the accident the pursuer was in fact not working. Her employment was seasonal and intermittent, but she always had work when she wanted it. She said: 'I have always had jobs'. She, generally, did promotions, working in Richard Shops where she sold gold jewellery. At the time of the accident her husband's business was floundering. (It closed, in fact, in September 1989.) She and her husband had therefore discussed the need for her to resume employment in the early autumn. On average she earned about £80-£90 net per week before the accident for four to five months in the year and at Christmas. She might have worked longer in order to help her husband financially. He has been employed as a sales manager for White Arrow since February 1990. As it was, she was physically unable to work until April 1990. Then she could not do the type of job she did in a shop. She was employed in an office at the Cheltenham & Gloucester Building Society effectively as a junior between 10 am and 4 pm for about five months. She cannot type, so was restricted to the work of an office junior. In November and December 1990 she was employed by Boots. Finally, from October to December 1991 she was employed by Debenhams. The job agency to whom she had applied found it difficult to place her because jobs did not come which she could do. She could not now work in jobs with longer hours, and part time jobs were not available. She considered that since the accident, even allowing for the relatively intermittent nature of her pre-accident employment, she had lost earnings. At any rate her ability to earn had been adversely affected by the accident, in which opinion her husband concurred.

"I do not think that in her evidence the pursuer minimised her injury and its consequences. Nevertheless, it was a painful injury, causing much inconvenience and discomfort. Of all the cases cited to me as guides to solatium I considered that of *Campbell v D B Marshall (Newbridge) Ltd*, 1991 SLT 837, to be the most apt and comparable. I shall award £4,250 as solatium with interest on 80 per cent thereof at the rate of 7.5 per cent per annum from the accident until decree — that is, approximately 3.5 years. The total thereof is, in round terms, £5,160.

"I am prepared to accept that, but for the accident, the pursuer would have worked longer hours than she had done before in order to help her husband and the household financially. I think that she did lose income in the period until she resumed employment in April 1990. That can be assessed only broadly, as Mr Holroyd submitted. I accept his figure of £1,000 as reasonable. I shall award £1,000 for wage loss until April 1990 with interest thereon at the rate of 15 per cent per annum since then, namely £400. Loss of earnings after that date is more problematical. Her husband, after all, got a job in February 1990, and the pursuer's need then to prop up the family finances was not so clamant. Besides, on the figures in the documentary productions it is not clear to me that she actually lost earnings until at least she left Debenhams. On the other hand, she is now, without doubt, more restricted in the labour market, and something must be allowed for such loss of employability, even at her age. Mr Holroyd suggested the sum of £4,000, but I think that is far too high a figure. In the circumstances I shall award £1,750 under this head.

"I am prepared to accept that for about 12 weeks the pursuer's husband provided her with necessary services within and without the home. For the first half of that period these services were intensive, but they became less so as the pursuer recovered mobility. Taking a broad view and guided by the awards in the cases cited to me, I shall assess the claim for general services provided by her husband in the sum of £750. In the result I shall award the sum of £9,060 with interest thereon at the rate of 15 per cent from the date of decree until payment."

———————

Counsel for Pursuer, Holroyd; Solicitors, L & L Lawrence — Counsel for Defender, Cowan; Solicitors, Maclay Murray & Spens.

C H

MacKenzie v Barr's Trustees

COURT OF FIVE JUDGES

THE LORD PRESIDENT (HOPE),
LORDS ALLANBRIDGE, COWIE,
McCLUSKEY AND WYLIE

21 MAY 1993

Landlord and tenant — Croft — Resumption of croft land — Crofters' share in market value of land resumed — Resumption for purpose of leasing ground to authority possessing compulsory purchase powers for mineral extraction — Whether "acquisition" by authority of land resumed — Market value in which crofters entitled to share — "Croft land" — Crofting Reform (Scotland) Act 1976 (c 21), s 9.

Landlord and tenant — Croft — Resumption of croft land — Crofters' share in market value of land resumed — Resumption for purpose of leasing ground for mineral extraction — Crofters having no rights in minerals — Whether market value of land resumed included its mineral value — Crofters (Scotland) Act 1955 (3 & 4 Eliz II, c 21), s 12 (1) and Sched 2, para 10 — Crofting Reform (Scotland) Act 1976 (c 21), ss 1 (3) and 9.

The Crofting Reform (Scotland) Act 1976, s 9 (1), provides that where the Land Court authorise the resumption of a croft or part thereof, the crofter shall be entitled to receive, in addition to compensation, "a share in the value of the land so resumed the amount whereof shall be one half of the difference between . . . the market value of the land . . . and the crofting value thereof". Section 9 (3) provides that where the purpose for which resumption is authorised "is to be carried out by an authority possessing compulsory purchase powers . . . on the acquisition by them of the land so resumed", the market value shall be a sum equal to the compensation payable in respect of the acquisition. Section 9 (2) provides in other cases for a value by reference to a sale on the open market.

Landlords applied to the Scottish Land Court for an
A order authorising the resumption of an area of
common grazings for the purposes of leasing the area,
as part of a larger area, to Highland Regional Council
for the purposes of gravel extraction. With the consent
of the crofters, the application was granted, but continued for a hearing to determine the amount of compensation that should be paid to the crofters under s 9
of the 1976 Act. The crofters argued that the reasonable purpose for which resumption was being sought
was leasing by the landlord and accordingly compensation fell to be assessed under s 9 (2) of the 1976 Act
B as a building site worth £5,000. The full court found
that no compensation was due because the reasonable
purpose for which the resumption had been granted,
namely mineral extraction, was to be carried out by an
authority possessing compulsory purchase powers.
Compensation therefore required to be calculated in
terms of s 9 (3). The only consideration being paid by
that authority was royalties under a mineral lease in
which (following *Trs of the Tenth Duke of Argyll v
MacCormick*, 1991 SLT 900) the crofters, having no
C mineral rights in the land, were not entitled to share.
The crofters requested the Land Court to state a
special case for the opinion of the Court of Session to
determine whether compensation should have been
determined under s 9 (2) rather than s 9 (3) of the 1976
Act. The Land Court added questions asking whether
Trs of the Tenth Duke of Argyll had been correctly
decided.

Held, (1) that "acquisition" in s 9 (3) of the 1976
Act meant an acquisition by which ownership of the
D land passed from the landlord to the authority possessing compulsory purchase powers, and in the present
case the market value of the land resumed fell to be
determined under s 9 (2) of the 1976 Act because the
reasonable purpose for which the resumption was
authorised was leasing by the landlords for mineral
extraction (pp 1233L-1234C); (2) that the purpose of
the expression "the land so resumed" in s 9 (1) was to
restrict the valuation to what had been resumed by the
landlord, and the crofters were not entitled to share in
E the mineral value of the land because the minerals did
not form part of the land let (pp 1235L-1236C); and
appeal *allowed* in part.

Trustees of the Tenth Duke of Argyll v MacCormick,
1991 SLT 900, *affirmed*.

Opinion, that the definition of "croft land" in s 1
(3) did not apply to the word "land" in s 9 of the 1976
Act, with the result that unapportioned common
grazings were included in the land which had to be
F valued for the purposes of ss 9 and 10 (p 1237A-B).

_____

Appeal from the Scottish Land Court

The Trustees of Miss Sara Neilson Barr applied to
the Land Court for an order authorising the resumption of an area of the Oldshoremore common grazings
for leasing to Highland Regional Council, as part of a
larger area, for gravel extraction. The crofters consented and the resumption was authorised. The Land
Court determined that the compensation payable to

the crofters was to be determined under s 9 (3) of the
Crofting Reform (Scotland) Act 1976. As the only G
compensation being paid by the council was a mineral
royalty the compensation was nil. The crofters,
through their clerk, John Mackenzie, asked the Land
Court to state a special case for the opinion of the
Court of Session.

Statutory provisions

The Crofters (Scotland) Act 1955, as amended,
provides:

"12.—(1) The Land Court may, on the application H
of the landlord and on being satisfied that he desires
to resume the croft, or part thereof, for some reasonable purpose having relation to the good of the croft
or of the estate or to the public interest, authorise the
resumption thereof by the landlord upon such terms
and conditions as they may think fit, and may require
the crofter to surrender his croft, in whole or in part,
to the landlord accordingly, upon the landlord making
adequate compensation to the crofter either by letting
to him other land of equivalent value in the neighbourhood or by compensation in money or by way of an I
adjustment of rent or in such other manner as the
Land Court may determine.

"(2) For the purposes of the foregoing subsection
the expression 'reasonable purpose' shall include the
using, letting or feuing of the land proposed to be
resumed for the building of dwellings. . . .

"(4) The provisions of the Crofters (Scotland) Acts
1955 and 1961 shall cease to apply to any land on its
being resumed in pursuance of an order authorising its J
resumption made under this section by the Land
Court, without prejudice, however, to the subsequent
exercise of any powers conferred by any enactment for
the constitution of new crofts or the enlargement of
existing crofts. . . .

"[Sched 2] 10. The crofter shall permit the landlord
or any person authorised by the landlord in that behalf
to enter upon the croft for the purpose of exercising
(subject always to the payment of such compensation
as in case of dispute the Land Court may find to be K
reasonable in respect of any damage done or occasioned thereby) any of the following rights, and shall
not obstruct the landlord or any person authorised as
aforesaid in the exercise of any of such rights, that is
to say — (a) mining or taking minerals, or digging or
searching for minerals; (b) quarrying or taking stone,
marble, gravel, sand, clay, slate or other workable
mineral".

The Crofting Reform (Scotland) Act 1976 provides: L

"1.— . . . (3) In this Act 'croft land' includes any
land being part of a croft, other than — (a) the site of
the dwelling-house on or pertaining to the croft; (b)
any land, comprising any part of a common grazing,
unless the land has been apportioned under section 27
(4) of the Act of 1955 and is either — (i) adjacent or
contiguous to any other part of the croft, or (ii) arable
machair; (c) any right to mines, metals or minerals or
salmon fishings (not being salmon fishings in Orkney
or Shetland) pertaining to the croft. . . .

"9.—(1) Where the Land Court authorise the resumption of a croft or a part thereof under section 12 of the Act of 1955, the crofter shall be entitled to receive from the landlord, in addition to any compensation payable to him under that section, a share in the value of the land so resumed the amount whereof shall be one half of the difference between, subject to subsection (5) below, the market value of the land (on the date on which resumption thereof is so authorised) as determined by the Land Court in accordance with subsections (2) and (3) below (less any compensation payable as aforesaid) and the crofting value thereof.

"(2) Where the resumption of the land is so authorised for some reasonable purpose which has been or is to be carried out by the landlord or by any person not being an authority possessing compulsory purchase powers, the market value for the purposes of subsection (1) above shall be a sum equal to the amount which the land, if sold in the open market by a willing seller (not being an authority as defined in section 1 (1) (b) of the Community Land Act 1975) might be expected to realise.

"(3) Where the resumption is so authorised for some reasonable purpose which has been or is to be carried out by an authority possessing compulsory purchase powers (not being the landlord) on the acquisition by them of the land so resumed, the market value for the purposes of subsection (1) above shall be a sum equal to the amount of compensation payable by the authority to the landlord in respect of the acquisition: Provided that, where the land so resumed forms part only of the land acquired from the landlord by the authority, the market value shall be a sum equal to such amount as the Land Court may determine to be the proportion of the amount of compensation so payable by the authority which relates to the land so resumed.

"(4) Where the land so resumed forms or forms part of a common grazing, the share of the value of that land payable to the crofters sharing in the common grazing shall be apportioned among such crofters according to the proportion that the right in the common grazing of each crofter bears to the total of such rights; and any sum so apportioned to such a crofter shall be deemed to be the share in the value of such land resumed to which he is entitled under subsection (1) above."

Cases referred to

Argyll (Trustees of the Tenth Duke of) v MacCormick, 1989 SLT (Land Ct) 58; 1991 SLT 900.
Macrae v Secretary of State for Scotland, 1981 SLT (Land Ct) 18.
Ross v Graesser, 1962 SLT 130; 1962 SC 66.
Strathern v MacColl, 1993 SLT 301.

The following questions of law were stated for the crofters in the special case:

(1) Whether on the facts as stated, the court were correct to hold that the purpose of the resumption was for the extraction of minerals?

(2) Whether on the facts as stated, the court were wrong not to hold that the purpose of the resumption was for the purpose of leasing the land, albeit the lease was for the extraction of minerals?

(3) Whether on the facts as stated, the court were correct to construe the words "on acquisition by them of the land so resumed" in s 9 (3) of the Crofting Reform (Scotland) Act 1976 to include the obtaining by Highland Regional Council of a lease of the lands for 10 years with a provision for continuance of the said lease from year to year thereafter until all minerals were exhausted?

(4) Whether on the facts as stated, the court were in error to find that s 9 (2) of the Crofting Reform (Scotland) Act 1976 did not apply to the share in the value payable to the crofters upon the authorisation of this resumption application?

(5) Whether on the facts as stated, the court were correct to hold that s 9 (3) of the Crofting Reform (Scotland) Act 1976 applied to the share in the value payable to the crofters upon the authorisation of this resumption application?

The following questions of law (as amended at the bar) were stated by the Land Court in the special case:

(6) In the event of your Lordships' court finding that s 9 (3) rather than s 9 (2) of the Crofting Reform (Scotland) Act 1976 applies to the said valuation, (a) whether the court were correct in finding that the consequent valuation was nil? or (b) should they have held that despite the decision in *Duke of Argyll's Trs,* the crofters were entitled to share in the value of the land for gravel extraction? or (c) should they have held that they were entitled to share in its value as a potential house site in the absence of mineral working? or (d) in any event, where s 9 (3) of the Crofting Reform (Scotland) Act 1976 applies for the purpose of calculating the crofters' share in the value of the land resumed, whether the decision in *Duke of Argyll's Trs* was correct.

(7) In the event, however, of your Lordships' court finding that s 9 (2) of the Crofting Reform (Scotland) Act 1976 applies for the purpose of calculating the crofters' share in the value of the land resumed, whether the decision of the majority of the Second Division in *Duke of Argyll's Trs* was correct having regard to the provisions of s 12 (4) of the Crofters (Scotland) Act 1955, as amended by para 11 (b) of the First Schedule to the Crofters (Scotland) Act 1961?

The appeal was first heard before the First Division on 15 October 1991 when it was directed that it be heard before a court of five judges.

The appeal was heard before a court of five judges on 4, 5 and 6 May 1993.

On 21 May 1993 the court *allowed* the appeal in part, *found* it unnecessary to answer questions 1, 2, 3 and 6, *answered* questions 4 and 7 in the *affirmative,* question 5 in the *negative* and *remitted* the case to the Land Court to proceed as accords.

The following opinion of the court was delivered by
A the Lord President (Hope):

OPINION OF THE COURT.—This is a special
case under s 25 of the Small Landholders (Scotland)
Act 1911, as applied to matters requiring determination under the legislation relating to crofters by s 34
of the Crofters (Scotland) Act 1955. It has been stated
by the Scottish Land Court at the request of the clerk
to the grazings for and on behalf of the crofters having
rights in the Oldshoremore common grazings with
respect to an application by the trustees of Miss Sara
B Neilson Barr as landlords for an order authorising
resumption of 0.579 ha of the common grazings under
s 12 of the 1955 Act.

The landlords applied for the order authorising the
resumption for the purpose of leasing the area, as part
of a greater area of land, to Highland Regional
Council for the purpose of the extraction of gravel.
The crofters having an interest in the common
grazings consented to the application, and on 16
November 1988 the divisional court found that the
C landlords desired to resume the area for a reasonable
purpose in terms of s 12 of the 1955 Act and
authorised the resumption. The application was continued for the purpose of determining the amount of
compensation payable to the crofters under s 12 of the
1955 Act and the share in the value of the area which
the crofters might be entitled to receive in terms of s 9
of the Crofting Reform (Scotland) Act 1976. On 1
March 1991 the full court found that no compensation
was due to the crofters in terms of s 12 of the 1955
D Act. They also found that the crofters were not
entitled to any share in the value of the land resumed
in terms of s 9 of the 1976 Act. No question now arises
in regard to the question of compensation, but questions of some difficulty and importance have been
raised as regards the crofters' claim that they are
entitled to a share in the value of the land resumed.

When the case first appeared on the summar roll, it
was directed, for the reasons given in the opinion of
E the court dated 15 October 1991, that this case should
be heard by a court of five judges. At that stage there
was no appearance for the landlords, and concern was
expressed at the absence of a contradictor to resist the
arguments which counsel for the crofters wished to
present. At the hearing which then took place before
us both the landlords and the crofters were represented by counsel, and we are indebted to counsel on
both sides for their very full and careful argument
with regard to the various questions on which our
F opinion has been requested.

These questions fall into two distinct chapters, both
of which relate to the proper interpretation of the provisions of s 9 of the Crofting Reform (Scotland) Act
1976. The relevant subsections are in these terms: [his
Lordship quoted the terms of s 9 (1) to (4) and continued:]

Subsection (6) provides that the expression "crofting value", in relation to land resumed, has the same
meaning as it has in s 3 of the Act in relation to croft
land. Section 3 provides that where the crofter is

authorised to acquire the croft land in the exercise of
the right of acquisition conferred upon him by the G
1976 Act, and the crofter and the landlord have failed
to reach agreement about the consideration payable in
respect of the acquisition, the consideration shall be
the crofting value of the croft land as determined by
the Land Court. The expression "croft land" is
defined in s 1 (3) of the 1976 Act as including any land
being part of a croft other than the site of the dwellinghouse on or pertaining to the croft, any land comprising any part of a common grazing unless the land has
been apportioned, and any rights to mines, metals or H
minerals or salmon fishings, not being salmon fishings
in Orkney or Shetland, pertaining to the croft.

It is the fact that the resumption was for the purpose
of leasing the area to Highland Regional Council, and
that this was for the purpose of the extraction of
minerals, that has given rise to questions of some
difficulty. Highland Regional Council are an authority
possessing compulsory purchase powers in terms of
s 71 of the Local Government (Scotland) Act 1973,
although it has not been necessary for their powers of I
compulsory purchase to be exercised in this case. The
landlords agreed to lease the area to them for a period
of 10 years, with a provision that if the minerals are
not exhausted within that period, the parties are to be
bound to renew the lease for a further period of one
year on the same terms and conditions until the
minerals are exhausted. The first chapter of questions
is directed to the issue whether the market value of the
land resumed for the purposes of subs (1) of s 9 of the
1976 Act is to be a sum equal to the open market value J
of the land as defined in subs (2) of that section, or a
sum equal to the amount of the compensation payable
by the authority to the landlord as provided in subs
(3). The full court decided that, as Highland Regional
Council are an authority possessing compulsory purchase powers, subs (2) does not apply in this case and
that the market value of the land resumed was to be
that provided for by subs (3).

The questions relating to this issue which have been K
stated for the crofters are in these terms: [his Lordship
quoted the terms of questions 1-5 and continued:] The
second chapter of questions is directed to the issue
which then arises, as to whether the crofters are
entitled under these provisions to any share in the
market value of the minerals. In *Trs of the Tenth Duke
of Argyll v MacCormick*, it was held by a majority of
the Second Division that the right conferred on a
crofter by s 9 (1) of the 1976 Act was a right to share
in the value of the land resumed by the landlord, and
that this did not include the value of the minerals since L
they never formed any part of the subjects let to the
crofters. A majority of the Land Court had reached a
different conclusion on this point, and the appeal
against their decision was allowed. In the present case,
applying subs (3) in accordance with the decision of
the Second Division in *Duke of Argyll's Trs*, the full
court held that, as the rent payable by Highland
Regional Council under the lease was related only to
the value of the minerals and nothing was included in
it for any other use of the land or even for its bare land

value, the resultant market value of the land as determined under subs (3) was nil and that accordingly no share in the market value of the land resumed was payable to the crofters.

Questions relating to this issue have been inserted into the special case by the Land Court, in order that they may have further directions as to how to make the relevant valuations in cases of this kind. They point out that, while the present case is of small value, it has wide implications because local authorities in the crofting counties normally acquire croft land by resumption through landlords rather than by using their compulsory powers. They say that they have experienced difficulty in applying the statutory provisions because, while the majority of the Second Division in *Duke of Argyll's Trs*, the Lord Justice Clerk and Lord Clyde, held that the words "the land so resumed" in s 9 (1) had the effect of excluding the value of any minerals from the open market value of the land as determined by the Land Court, a different majority of the Second Division, the Lord Justice Clerk and Lord Murray held that the express exclusion of minerals from the definition of "croft land" contained in s 1 (3) (c) of the 1976 Act did not apply to the word "land" where it appears in ss 9 (1) and 10 (1), which deals with the crofters' right to share in the market value of land taken possession of compulsorily. The questions relating to this issue, with the addition of a new question 6 (d) which was added by amendment at the bar, are in these terms: [his Lordship quoted the terms of questions 6 and 7 and continued:]

While we have, in this introduction, set out the two issues separately, it is the cumulative effect of the decisions in each of them which is of particular interest to the parties in this case. If the market value of the land is to be determined under s 9 (2) by reference to its open market value, then, irrespective of the question relating to the minerals, the crofters will be entitled to a share in the value of the land as a site for the erection of a dwellinghouse. The full court held that the evidence had established that, in the absence of quarrying for gravel, planning permission would have been likely to have been granted for a single dwellinghouse and that the site had a value for this purpose of £5,000. If the market value of the land is to be determined under s 9 (3), however, the value of the site of the dwellinghouse must be left out of account, as the "compensation" payable to the landlords by Highland Regional Council under the lease is related only to the value of the minerals. If then the minerals also must be left out of account, in accordance with the decision in *Duke of Argyll's Trs*, the crofters will be left with nothing in respect of the market value of the land resumed. But if that case was wrongly decided, as the crofters contend in this special case, and the market value of the land resumed includes the value of the minerals, the crofters will be entitled to a share of that value as part of the market value of the land resumed. That would involve reconsideration of the question of value by the Land Court, the result of which will depend upon whether the market value is to be determined under s 9 (2) or s 9 (3).

Whether the market value is to be determined under s 9 (2) or under s 9 (3)

We shall deal first with this issue since it is the subject of the first five questions in the case and was dealt with first in the argument. We should mention at the outset, however, that counsel were agreed that, in the circumstances of this case where the land had merely been leased to the authority possessing compulsory purchase powers and had not been purchased by them, the value fell to be determined under s 9 (2). They were agreed that the Land Court had misdirected itself on this point, but it is nevertheless necessary for us to examine the issue and express our own opinion upon it since it has wide implications and is important to a proper understanding of the approach to value in cases of this kind.

Section 9 (2) applies where the resumption of the land is authorised "for some reasonable purpose which has been or is to be carried out by the landlord or by any person not being an authority possessing compulsory purchase powers". These words do not give rise to difficulty if the land has been or is to be resumed for the purpose of its development by the landlord without first leasing or disposing of it to someone else. Nor do they give rise to difficulty if the development is to be carried out by a third party which is not an authority possessing compulsory purchase powers. The case of *Duke of Argyll's Trs* is an example of the latter alternative, because the area of ground in that case was authorised to be resumed for the purpose of leasing it to a firm of quarriers, and it was not disputed that s 9 (2) applied. Section 9 (3) on the other hand applies when the resumption of the land is authorised "for some reasonable purpose which has been or is to be carried out by an authority possessing compulsory purchase powers (not being the landlord)". Here again no difficulty arises if the authority possessing compulsory purchase powers is the landlord, because the effect of the words in parenthesis is to require the valuation to be made under s 9 (2). That was the situation in *Macrae v Secretary of State* in regard to the land authorised to be resumed for road works to be carried out by the Scottish Development Department, since this was to be regarded as a development carried out by the landlord himself. Nor is there any difficulty if ownership of the land is to be acquired by the authority possessing compulsory purchase powers. The references in subs (3) to "an authority possessing compulsory *purchase powers*" and to "the *acquisition* by them of the land" clearly apply to the situation where the ownership of the land is to pass from the landlord to the acquiring authority. The Land Court in *Macrae v Secretary of State* at p 20 summarised the basis of compensation which applies in that situation as follows: "The compensation payable by an authority possessing compulsory purchase powers in our view falls to be assessed as for a compulsory purchase under the compulsory purchase code and with all the statutory assumptions laid down in the Land Compensation (Scotland) Act 1963."

Thus there is a reasonable basis for the assumption in s 9 (3) that the compensation payable will reflect the market value of the land resumed, as the equivalent, in cases falling under this subsection, of the market value of the land if sold in the open market which is the measure of value described in s 9 (2). It is also consistent with the measure of value which applies when the land is taken compulsorily from the landlord by the acquiring authority, and the market value of it has to be assessed under s 10 (2) in order to determine the crofters' share in the value of the land of which possession has been taken.

The present case does not, however, fall into any of these categories. The works of development are to be carried out by Highland Regional Council, since it is they and not the landlords who are to extract the gravel in terms of the lease. But ownership of the land has not been given to Highland Regional Council, so the basis of compensation which applies in the case of an acquisition by agreement which takes the form of a purchase by an authority possessing compulsory purchase powers cannot apply. The "compensation" payable by the authority to the landlord in this case — and this raises at once the question whether "compensation" is the appropriate word to describe it — is the rent payable under the lease which, as the full court have held, was a rent for the extraction of the minerals and not a sum to be paid in respect of the value of the land. This creates an anomaly which will arise in all cases where the land is leased to an authority possessing compulsory purchase powers for the extraction of minerals, and the question is whether it is possible to construe s 9 (2) and (3) in such a way as to prevent this.

The crofters' argument is that the value in this case falls to be determined under s 9 (2) because the resumption of the land has been authorised for a reasonable purpose to be carried out by the landlords. This purpose was to resume the area for the purpose of leasing it for mineral extraction. Counsel for the appellants submitted that it was of no importance who was to be the tenant, and in particular whether or not this was to be an authority possessing compulsory purchase powers. The point was that the landlord's purpose was to be achieved by letting the land for that purpose only, while retaining the ownership of it. Reference was made to the expression "the using, letting or feuing of the land" in s 12 (2) of the 1955 Act, and it was submitted that in all of these cases, whatever the ultimate purpose may be, these are purposes which are to be carried out by the landlord. Then it was argued that the reference to "compulsory purchase powers" in s 9 (3) was an indication that the subsection applied only where the authority had powers of compulsory purchase which would enable them to carry out the development in the manner which was proposed. Reference was made to s 71 of the Local Government (Scotland) Act 1973 which provides that a local authority may be authorised to purchase land compulsorily. It was pointed out that, while a local authority has power to acquire land by agreement under s 70 by means of purchase, feu, lease or excambion, its powers of compulsory acquisition are limited to the purchase of land, to which the

Acquisition of Land (Authorisation Procedure) (Scotland) Act 1947 applies. It was also submitted that the word "acquisition" in s 9 (3), in its context, did not include a transaction not involving the transfer to the authority of ownership of the land. Counsel for the landlord agreed that this case fell under s 9 (2), which he said was apt to include cases where the reasonable purpose was to be effected by the landlord himself or anyone on his behalf or by leasing it so that that purpose could be carried out. It could not be disputed that the Highland Regional Council were an authority possessing compulsory purchase powers, but the question was whether the land had been or was to be acquired by the authority, and since the transaction was that of a lease to extract the minerals they had not acquired the land from the landlord and s 9 (3) did not apply.

In our opinion the market value of the land resumed falls to be determined in this case under s 9 (2). Accordingly it is a sum equal to the amount which the land, if sold on the open market by a willing seller, might be expected to realise. The view which was taken by the Land Court was that s 9 (2) does not apply in this case because the reasonable purpose for which the divisional court authorised resumption was not simply letting the subject but the letting of it for the purpose of extracting gravel. As they point out, the court would never have authorised a resumption for the purpose merely of letting without any precise indication of any other purpose, and the resumption order was clearly to the effect that it was the purpose of leasing the area to Highland Regional Council for the extraction of gravel which was found to be reasonable. We fully understand and agree with this approach to the question of resumption. But in order to decide which of the two subsections applies with regard to the value of the land resumed, it is necessary to examine the language of both subsections in order to ensure that the choice between them is appropriate.

It is, we think, easier to see why s 9 (3) does not apply in this case. The transaction which it contemplates is the acquisition of the land from the landlord by an authority possessing compulsory purchase powers. The market value which applies to that transaction is to be a sum equal to the amount of compensation payable by the authority to the landlord in respect of the acquisition. As the Lord Justice Clerk pointed out in *Duke of Argyll's Trs* at p 904B: "This is an intelligible provision, because if there was not such a provision it might be contended that the amount of compensation payable by the authority in respect of the acquisition was less than the true value of the subjects."

This is because a valuation by the Land Court under s 9 (2), at a sum equal to the amount which the land if sold on the open market by a willing seller might be expected to realise, might result in a different figure from that arrived at by the district valuer. The important point to notice, however, for present purposes is that the transaction which is contemplated by s 9 (2) is that of sale. It must be assumed that this also is the transaction which is contemplated by s 9 (3), other-

A wise an unacceptable distortion between the two levels of value may arise. The phrase "the land acquired from the landlord by the authority" in the proviso to s 9 (3) is a clear indication that what is envisaged by this subsection is an acquisition by which ownership of the land passes from the landlord to the authority. The reference to compulsory *purchase* powers, in contrast to a power to acquire land by agreement, tends to reinforce the impression that a transaction of sale to and purchase by the authority is necessary for s 9 (3) to apply. Since that is not the transaction which was B entered into in this case, the value of the land cannot be determined by reference to this subsection.

This leads inevitably to the conclusion that, despite some imperfection in the language of this subsection, the market value of the land must be determined in this case at its open market value in accordance with s 9 (2). This is not, of course, a case where, if one ignores the landlord for the moment, the reasonable purpose is to be carried out by a person not being an authority possessing compulsory purchase powers. It C is necessary therefore to find an acceptable basis for saying that the reasonable purpose here has been or is to be carried out by the landlord himself. In our opinion a purpose which is to be carried out by leasing the land to a third party for a limited purpose only can reasonably be described as a purpose which is to be carried out by the landlord. The restrictions on the use of the land by the third party which are inherent in the transaction, together with the fact that ownership is to remain throughout with the landlord, seem to us to D support this approach. The alternative situation referred to in the subsection, by which a reasonable purpose is to be carried out by a person not being an authority possessing compulsory purchase powers, will apply where ownership is to be acquired by the third party with a view to carrying out that purpose. Thus, although the wording of this subsection is not as clear on the point as it might be, it can be assumed that s 9 (2) will apply in all cases except those where, because ownership of the land is to pass by agreement E from the landlord to an authority possessing compulsory purchase powers, the case falls clearly under s 9 (3).

For these reasons we shall answer question 4 in the affirmative and question 5 in the negative. We find it unnecessary to answer questions 1, 2 and 3, since they are concerned with the process of reasoning, which has already been described in this opinion, rather than with the particular questions of law which need to be F decided on this issue.

Whether "the land resumed" in terms of s 9 (1) includes minerals

We turn now to the second issue, the difficulty of which is illustrated by the fact that, while the majority of the Land Court in *Trs of the Tenth Duke of Argyll v MacCormick* were in favour of the view that the value of the land resumed included its mineral value, Mr R Macdonald, member of court, expressed the contrary view in his note of dissent which was the view favoured by a majority of the Second Division

when the case came before them on appeal. We have now had the benefit of a full argument on the point G from counsel for both parties and it is fortunate that we are able to express an opinion upon it which is unanimous.

It is clear that the purpose of s 9 (1) was to enable the crofter to receive from the landlord, in addition to the compensation payable to him under s 12 of the 1955 Act, a share in the value of the land resumed by the landlord. This was a new right which the crofter did not previously have upon a resumption, and there can be no doubt that the intention was that the crofter H should be entitled to share with the landlord in the development value of the land which was being resumed. The formula which it sets out to arrive at the crofter's share is quite simple. He is to receive one half of the difference between the market value of the land and its crofting value. This is because the crofting value, as defined by s 9 (6), is the amount of the consideration which would be payable by the crofter under s 3 of the Act for the acquisition of the croft land from the landlord. It is the residue of value I attributable to the landlord's interest in the land as owner, and in particular to the development of the land when freed from the provisions of the Crofters (Scotland) Acts 1955 and 1961 on its being resumed, which is the subject of sharing between the landlord and the crofter.

This analysis still leaves unanswered, however, the question whether the value of any minerals falls to be taken into account. We need mention only briefly the competing views which were expressed on this point J in *Duke of Argyll's Trs*. The majority of the Land Court saw a clear distinction between the compensation payable to the crofter for the loss of his crofting interest and his share in the value of the land resumed. In their view the crofter's right to share in the value of the land resumed was not affected by his preceding tenancy position nor by the fact that, under that tenancy, he was not entitled to extract the minerals. What was to be determined was the open market value of the land at its appropriate valuation date, which was K at the date of the resumption. They noted that the landlord, as owner of the land, owned the minerals and that the crofter was not entitled to extract minerals from the croft. But in their view the minerals nevertheless formed part of the croft holding which was let and their market value fell to be included in the open market value of the land. The approach taken by Mr Macdonald in his note of dissent at pp 64-65 was to look at the rights of the tenant immediately prior to the resumption. In his opinion what was to be valued L was the subjects as tenanted at that point in time, not as they were at a later point when the granting of the resumption had had the effect of uniting into a single subject the different tenements. The words "so resumed" should, in his view, only relate to the land formerly subject to a tenancy.

When the case came before the Second Division, the Lord Justice Clerk referred at p 904L to the majority view of the Land Court that, although the crofter had no right to extract minerals which belonged to the

A landlord, the minerals nevertheless pertained to the croft and formed part of what was let. In his view these propositions were self contradictory. At p 905B he pointed out that, since the minerals had all along been vested in the landlords, all that the landlords had done by applying for resumption was to seek to resume the surface of the land so that they could get at and remove the minerals. Lord Clyde expressed the opinion at p 908A that what is "so resumed" within the meaning of s 9 (1) must be something to which the crofter had right, and that as such possession as the

B crofter had did not include the valuable right of extraction of the minerals, he had no right to the minerals themselves which accordingly did not form part of the land so resumed. He pointed out various anomalies which would arise if the contrary view were correct, but made it clear at p 908E that the primary point on which his opinion was based was that the crofter did not have possession of any minerals in the sense of being able to exploit them. Lord Murray dissented on the ground that the market value contemplated by s 9

C must be something different from the crofting value of the croft land. He pointed out at p 907B that no formula had been provided in the section for assessing the value of the land on any different basis from its open market value. He said that the reference in s 9 (2) to the market value of the land if sold on the open market indicated unambiguously that what was contemplated was land being directly valued for sale. At p 907F he said that this was a novel proprietary right conferred upon crofters which could not reason-

D ably be related to any previous rights, and that it gave a right to the crofters to share in the market value on sale of the land including its minerals. It appears to have been important to his reasoning that there was no express provision in s 9 that the market value of the land had to be arrived at under reservation of the minerals to the landlord.

For the crofters, counsel submitted that the words "the land so resumed" were intended to do more than

E identify the area of land which was to be valued. Once that area had been identified the land had to be valued as a whole, and this led inevitably to the conclusion that the value of the minerals within it, which formed part of the land, had to be taken into account. He pointed out that the expression "croft land" was used elsewhere in the Act to refer to the land tenanted by the crofter. The definition of "croft land" in s 1 (3) did not apply to the word "land" as used in s 9, and here again there was a clear indication that what this

F section was concerned with was something other than the land as tenanted by the crofter. Under reference to the wording in s 10 (1), which deals with the situation where the land is taken possession of compulsorily, and refers to "the land of which possession has been taken", he submitted that the value of the land had to be fixed after possession had been taken from the crofter, and that it was its value to the landlord at that stage which had to be brought into account. He placed particular emphasis on the point that, while the landlord owned the minerals and was entitled under para 10 of the statutory conditions in Sched 2 to the 1955

G Act to enter on the croft for the purpose of exercising his right to take, dig or search for the minerals, he was not, as counsel put it, entitled to derogate from his grant. We were referred on this point to *Strathern v MacColl* where it was said that if the purported exercise of any of the rights mentioned in para 10 would render the crofts incapable of crofting tenure, that would be illegal. Counsel said that was the reason why the landlords had felt it appropriate to seek authorisation for a resumption, since the effect of a resumption in accordance with s 12 (4) of the 1955 Act, as amended by Sched 1 to the Crofters (Scotland) Act

H 1961, was that the provisions of the 1955 and 1961 Acts ceased to apply to any land on its being resumed. The effect of the resumption therefore was to remove this restriction on the landlord's freedom to search for and extract the minerals, and it was appropriate to regard this as something which the landlord had resumed. He submitted that the majority of the Second Division had overlooked this point, and that it was in accordance with the policy of the Act that the development value of the minerals should be shared.

I Reliance was also placed on the crofter's possessory right over minerals which were exposed on the surface, since as the Land Court pointed out at 1989 SLT (Land Ct), p 61E the presence of exposed mineral rock covering large areas of common grazings is not uncommon in the Highlands and Islands. We were also referred to *Ross v Graesser* where it was held that a crofter's interest in common grazings was not a tenancy of land but a right in pasture or grazing land. As we understood counsel's argument on this point,

J he submitted that the effect of the decision of the Second Division was to restrict the value of the land to the value of the crofter's right in the land which, in the case of common grazings, would mean that there would be nothing left to value once the crofting value had been taken into account.

Counsel, in his reply for the landlords, accepted that prior to a resumption the landlord is restricted in the extent to which he can interfere with the surface of the croft to search and extract minerals because of the

K crofter's interest in the land. But it was "the land so resumed" which was to be valued, and the effect of this phrase was to restrict the value to what had passed out of crofting control. It was only the land which was subject to crofting control which could be resumed, and this meant that the valuer was concerned only with the market value of the surface of the land. The right to work and extract the minerals was something which was never in the possession of the crofter, and it should therefore be left out of account. It was recog-

L nised that minerals could in law be the subject of a separate tenement, whether on the surface or subterranean. The timing of the valuation was not important, because whether the value was to be arrived at immediately before or immediately after the resumption it was the land so resumed which was to be valued, which meant by necessary implication that the value of the minerals was to be left out of account.

In our opinion the argument for the landlords is to be preferred on this point, and we find ourselves

A broadly in agreement with the views expressed by Mr Macdonald in his note of dissent and by the majority of the Second Division in *Duke of Argyll's Trs*.

The key to the whole matter is the use, repeatedly throughout the section, of the expression "the land so resumed". It is the value of the land "so resumed" only which is to be shared. Subsection (1) states that the market value is to be determined as at the date on which "resumption thereof" is authorised. And it is recognised in subs (3) that the land so resumed may
B form part only of the land acquired from the landlord by the acquiring authority. This allows in such cases for the compensation, which is to be the measure of the market value in this situation, to be restricted to what has been resumed by the landlord. It was maintained for the crofters that the purpose of the expression was to identify the area which was to be valued, and that once that area had been identified the value of the whole of the land within that area had to be taken into account. But in our opinion the word "extent" rather than "area" is a better one to use to
C describe its function, and its purpose is to restrict the valuation to what has been resumed by the landlord. It would seem to be inconsistent with the use of the phrase to bring into account the value of any part of the land which did not form part of the land let to the crofter. This gives strong prima facie support to the view that, since the crofter had no right to search for and extract the minerals, the value of that part of the land should be left out of account.

D   On this approach it is the extent of the crofter's interest, not the extent of the landlord's ownership, which provides the measure of the extent of the land to be valued. This is because the effect of an order authorising a resumption under s 12 of the 1955 Act is to require the crofter to surrender his croft, in whole or in part, to the landlord with the result that the provisions of the 1955 and 1961 Acts then cease to apply to the land. But we do not think that this is inconsistent with the purpose of s 9, and there are indications
E elsewhere in the legislation that to do otherwise would give rise to anomaly. The purpose of s 9, as we have said earlier, is to enable the crofter to share in the development value of the land which has been resumed by the landlord. The section assumes that he will also be compensated under s 12 in respect of the surrender of his crofting interest, and the crofting value of the land is to be left out of account in arriving at the value which is to be shared. The application of the statutory formula will thus give something additional to the crofter which he did not have before, even
F if the value of the minerals is left out of account. There is no need therefore, in order to confer that additional benefit on the crofter, to go further and give him a right to share in the value of something which he could not enjoy as part of the croft. His right to occupy the surface of the croft, together with any rocky outcrops and exposed minerals, is something which is clearly distinguishable from the valuable right to extract the minerals, which remained all along with the landlord. The fact that the landlord was restricted in his exercise of that right by the principle dis-

cussed in *Strathern v MacColl* at p 303H does not, in
G our opinion, provide a sound argument to the contrary. No doubt the effect of the resumption is to remove the restriction, but the right to the minerals as such was not itself being resumed because possession of that right had never been given to the crofter.

It is significant also, as Lord Clyde pointed out at p 908C, that a construction of the phrase "the land so resumed" which included the right to the minerals could lead to anomalies. The effect would be to give to the crofter a right to share in the value of the
H minerals although he himself never had any right to extract the minerals from the ground while he was in possession of the croft. The rental provisions contained in the lease to Highland Regional Council in the present case show that this would be a strange result, since the value of the minerals is represented by a price per ton for the minerals until they have been exhausted. Furthermore, while the crofter is entitled by s 1 of the 1976 Act to acquire his croft land from the landlord, the definition of "croft land" in s 1 (3)
I excludes the minerals. Accordingly, the crofter is not entitled to acquire the right to work the minerals pertaining to his croft. We agree with Lord Clyde that it would be anomalous in these circumstances that on a resumption he should become entitled to share in the value of that right. There is also the point that the landlord is entitled under para 10 of the statutory conditions in Sched 2 to the 1955 Act to work the minerals, subject to paying compensation for any damage done or occasioned by this activity. As Lord
J Clyde remarked, it would seem to be a very unequal alternative if resumption, which might be a more respectable way of proceeding with the operation, were to involve a payment to the crofter of a share of the mineral rights to which he would not be entitled if the croft were not resumed and the work done in the exercise of the right under para 10.

There was a difference of view in *Duke of Argyll's Trs* as to whether the definition of the expression "croft land" in s 1 (3) of the 1976 Act applied also to
K the word "land" in s 9 (1). The argument was that, if it did so apply, its effect was to exclude expressly the right to the minerals from the crofter's share of the value of the land, as it does from the croft land which he may acquire under s 1 of the Act. We agree with the Lord Justice Clerk and Lord Murray that, as the words "croft land" appear only in s 9 (6), and not in s 9 (1) or elsewhere in that section where the word "land" is used, the implication is that the definition of the expression "croft land" does not apply to the
L word "land" in this section. The direction in s 9 (4) that the share of the value of the land is to be apportioned among the crofters when the land resumed forms or forms part of common grazings seems to be inconsistent with the exclusion of common grazings, unless the land has been apportioned, from "croft land" as defined by s 1 (3). Lord Clyde expressed a different view on this point at p 908B, because he found it hard to disassociate the language of s 9 from the expression "croft land". As a generality there is some force in this observation, because the phrase

"land so resumed" is so closely linked to what is taken
A from and was previously possessed by the crofter. But
on the particular issue as to whether the definition of
the expression "croft land" applies when the word
"land" only is used in s 9, we prefer the contrary view
expressed by the other judges. The point is not in the
end important to our decision that the value of the
minerals must be left out of account. This is because
we have reached that decision for other reasons not
related to the definition of "croft land" in s 1 (3) of the
1976 Act. The view which we have formed on this
B point will however be important in cases where
unapportioned common grazings are involved. The
exclusion of unapportioned common grazings from
"croft land" by the definition in s 1 (3) does not apply
so as to exclude unapportioned common grazings from
the "land" which is to be valued for the purposes of
ss 9 and 10 of the 1976 Act.

Question 6 in the special case is superseded, because
in our opinion it is s 9 (2) rather than s 9 (3) which
applies to the valuation which is to be made in this
C case. For the reasons which we have given we shall
answer question 7 in the affirmative.

_____

Counsel for Applicants and Respondents (Landlords),
Kinroy; Solicitors, Biggart, Baillie & Gifford, WS —
Counsel for Respondents and Appellants (Crofters),
Agnew of Lochnaw; Solicitors, Drummond Miller, WS
(for Macleod & MacCallum, Inverness).

D
C H A of L

Ballantyne's Trustees v Ballantyne

E FIRST DIVISION

THE LORD PRESIDENT (HOPE),
LORDS ALLANBRIDGE AND PROSSER

25 JUNE 1992

Trust — Trust disposition and settlement — Construc-
tion — Forfeiture of entitlement to bequest upon election
for legal rights — Application of provision to issue of
beneficiary — Whether beneficiary's election to claim
F *legal rights resulted in forfeiture of rights of beneficiary's*
issue as conditional institutes.

A truster died in 1937 leaving a trust disposition and
settlement. The deed provided in purpose (lastly) that
on his widow's death the estate should be divided into
nine equal parts, three parts to be paid to his son
Henry, three to be held on behalf of his daughter
Helen and her issue, and three to be held on behalf of
his son Nigel as an alimentary provision. It further
provided that on Nigel's death his share of the residue
or the balance remaining should be "paid over equally

to and amongst his children, the issue of any who may
predecease taking their parent's share". The deed also G
declared that if a beneficiary repudiated the settlement
and claimed legal rights, that beneficiary would forfeit
all interest in the estate and his share would be divided
between the other beneficiaries.

The truster's son Nigel claimed the legitim to which
he was entitled out of the trust estate. In 1950 the
truster's widow died. In 1952 questions arose concerning the distribution of the estate and, in particular,
whether the action of Nigel in electing to claim his
legal rights in the estate resulted in the forfeiture of H
the provisions in favour of his children and their issue
contained in the trust disposition and settlement. A
special case was presented for the opinion and judgment of the Court of Session. The First Division held
inter alia that the claiming of his legal rights by Nigel
had resulted in the forfeiture of the provisions in
favour of his children. In 1990 the daughter Helen
died having married but being without issue. She was
predeceased by both her brothers, both of whom left
issue who survived them. A dispute arose as to I
whether the forfeiture provision had the effect also of
depriving the issue of Nigel of any interest in the share
of the residue of Helen.

Held, that the provision in favour of the conditional
institutes constituted a gift to them which was entirely
separate from any benefit which those issue would
have derived in the event of their parent's death had
his share not been forfeited (pp 1239H, 1242L and
1243B-C); and questions *answered* accordingly.
J

_____

Special case

Sir Charles Annand Fraser, KCVO, WS, and
others, the trustees presently acting under the trust
deed of the late David Ballantyne (the first parties),
together with the issue of the testator's son, Henry
Ballantyne (second parties) and the issue of the
testator's son, Nigel Ballantyne (third party), whose
share of the trust estate was forfeited following his K
election to claim legitim, presented a special case to
the Inner House, concerning the construction of
purpose (lastly) (b) of the trust deed. The special case
was presented following the death of the testator's
daughter Mrs Helen Muriel Ballantyne or Galbraith,
having married but without leaving issue.

Terms of deed

The trust disposition and settlement provided inter
alia:
L

"(Lastly) on the death or remarriage of my said
wife should she survive me, or on my own death in the
event of her predeceasing me, I direct my trustees to
divide the residue of my said means and estate . . . into
nine equal parts or shares and (a) to pay three ninths,
parts or shares to my son Henry Ballantyne, or his
heirs or assignees whomsoever . . . (b) to hold three
ninths, parts or shares for behoof of my daughter
Helen Muriel Ballantyne or Galbraith . . . for payment
of the annual income thereof to my said daughter

A during her life as an alimentary provision, and on her death said share or residue shall be paid equally to and among her children, payable on their respectively attaining twenty one years of age, the issue of any who may predecease taking their parent's share, and in the event of my said daughter dying without leaving lawful children surviving or if such as may survive shall die without issue before attaining majority then such share of residue shall be divided equally between my said son Henry Ballantyne and my son Nigel Keppell Charteris Ballantyne, and the survivor of

B them, . . . declaring that the issue of such of my sons as may have predeceased shall take *per stirpes* the share which would have fallen to such parent had he survived, and (c) with regard to the remaining three ninths parts or shares my Trustees shall retain same in their own hands and pay or apply the annual income or proceeds thereof to or for behoof of my son Nigel Keppell Charteris Ballantyne during his life as an alimentary provision . . . And on the death of the said Nigel Keppell Charteris Ballantyne said share of

C residue, or such balance as may then remain, shall be paid over equally to and amongst his children, the issue of any who may predecease taking their parent's share, payable on their respectively attaining majority: And in the event of the said Nigel Keppell Charteris Ballantyne dying without leaving lawful children surviving, or if such as may survive shall die without issue without attaining majority, then such share of residue so liferented by him, or such balance as may then remain shall be paid equally to and between my

D said son Henry and my daughter the said Helen Muriel Ballantyne or Galbraith and the survivor of them, the issue of such as may have predeceased taking the share their parent would have taken had he, she or they survived . . . And I declare that the foresaid provisions in favour of my said wife and children are and shall be in full of all that she or they could claim by or through my decease in respect of *terce, jus relictae,* and *legitim,* or any other legal claims competent to them respectively, and in the event of any of

E the beneficiaries repudiating this Settlement and claiming their legal rights in place of the foresaid provisions respectively, or if they or any of them shall by any means prevent this settlement from taking effect in whole or in part, then such beneficiary or beneficiaries shall forfeit all right and interest in any share or shares of that part of my estate and effects which I may freely dispose of by law, and they shall have right only to their respective legal rights, and the share or shares of such beneficiary or beneficiaries

F shall in that event accresce and be dealt with in terms of the provisions hereunder in favour of the other beneficiaries who shall abide by this settlement and accept the provisions herein contained".

Cases referred to

Ballantyne's Trustees v Ballantyne, 1952 SLT 425; 1952 SC 458.
Fisher v Dixon (1831) 10 S 55; (1833) 6 W & S 431.
Hurll's Trustees v Hurll, 1964 SC 12.
McCartney's Trustees v McCartney's Executors (Thornton), 1951 SLT 403; 1951 SC 504.

Munro's Trustees, Petitioners, 1971 SLT 313; 1971 SC 280.   G

Textbook referred to

Dykes, *Supplement to McLaren on Wills and Succession,* pp 49-50.

The parties stated the following questions for the opinion of the court:

(1) Has the action of the said Nigel Ballantyne in electing to claim his legal rights in the estate of the testator resulted in the forfeiture of any rights otherwise open to the issue of the said Nigel Ballantyne to share in the residue of the testator's estate under and in terms of purpose (lastly) (b) of said trust disposition and settlement?   H

(2) If the answer to question 1 is in the affirmative, are the first parties bound to distribute the residue remaining in their hands between the second parties?

(3) If the answer to question 1 is in the negative, are the first parties bound to distribute the residue remaining in their hands in equal proportions between first, the second parties, and secondly, the third party?   I

The case was heard before the First Division on 4 and 5 June 1992.

On 25 June 1992 the court *answered* the first question in the special case in the *negative* and the third question in the *affirmative* and *held* that the third party was entitled to succeed to one half of Mrs Helen   J Galbraith's share in the residue of the trust estate. The second question was superseded.

THE LORD PRESIDENT (HOPE).—The question which is before us in this special case was left unanswered in *Ballantyne's Trs v Ballantyne,* on the ground that, as matters stood at the time, it was premature and hypothetical. That is no longer the position, as the events which give rise to it have now occurred. Mrs Helen Muriel Ballantyne or Galbraith   K died on 11 February 1990 without issue. She was predeceased by Nigel Ballantyne, who died on 15 September 1986, survived by his only child. It is now necessary to consider whether, as a consequence of his claiming legitim, Nigel Ballantyne's forfeiture of all right and interest in the testator's estate has the effect that the right of his issue to one half of Mrs Galbraith's share in the residue has also been forfeited.

It is well settled that an express clause of forfeiture   L extending to issue is not indispensable if the will, read as a whole, sufficiently expresses an intention on the part of the testator to this effect. The answer to the question whether such an intention has been demonstrated depends on whether the gift to the issue is separate from and independent of the gift to the parent who has incurred the forfeiture: *Hurll's Trs v Hurll,* per Lord Justice Clerk Grant at 1964 SC, p 18; *Munro's Trs, Petrs,* per Lord Fraser at 1971 SLT, p 315. This is in accordance with the rule in *Fisher v*

Dixon, by which a distinct and separate right given to
the children is not, by implication, where there is no
express provision, to be affected by the parent's forfeiture. Whether there is such a distinct and separate
right amounting to an independent gift to the issue is
to be discovered by looking at the terms of the deed
as a whole. One must examine the terms of the gift as
well as the terms of the clause of forfeiture, in order
to see whether, as Lord President Cooper put it in
Ballantyne's Trs, 1952 SLT at p 429, "there is enough
to exclude the application of that rule".

The provisions of purpose (lastly) which contained
the words of gift which are now in point can be
summarised quite briefly. The testator's bequest of
the residue of the estate begins with a direction to his
trustees to divide it into nine equal parts or shares,
which are then allocated, as to three ninth shares each,
among his three children. All three children survived
the testator, and they also survived his widow who
died on 22 September 1950 having enjoyed a liferent
of his estate. The elder son, Henry Ballantyne, then
became entitled to payment of the capital of his one
third of the residue. In terms of para (a) of purpose
(lastly) this had been bequeathed to him or his heirs
or assignees whomsoever. The daughter, Mrs Helen
Muriel Ballantyne or Galbraith, became entitled to an
alimentary liferent of her one third share in terms of
para (b). She continued to enjoy this liferent until the
date of her death. Since she died without issue and was
predeceased by her two brothers, between whom her
share of the residue would have been divided equally
had they survived, a destination-over in favour of their
issue came into effect. This is contained in a declaration at the end of para (b) which is in these terms:
"declaring that the issue of such of my sons as may
have predeceased shall take *per stirpes* the share which
would have fallen to such parent had he survived".

The phrase "which would have fallen to such
parent" reflects the previous direction in this paragraph that, in the event of Mrs Galbraith dying
without issue, her share of the residue was to be
divided equally between her two brothers and the
survivor of them. It also reflects the use of the expression "falling to" in the direction that, in Henry's case,
the share falling to him was to be paid over to him —
no doubt since he was to be entitled to immediate
payment of his share — whereas in Nigel's case, the
share falling to him was to be added to the share of the
estate which was to be retained by the trustees for him
"and to be dealt with as hereinafter provided with
regard thereto". Had Nigel Ballantyne survived Mrs
Galbraith, and had he not claimed legal rights, he
would have been entitled to an alimentary liferent of
this share in terms of para (c). In terms of that paragraph his own one third share of the residue was
bequeathed to him in alimentary liferent and to his
issue in fee. As it is, since he predeceased her, the
declaration in favour of his issue as conditional institutes in his share of Mrs Galbraith's share of the
residue takes effect.

It was suggested by counsel for the second parties

that the destination-over in terms of this declaration
was not to be regarded as an isolated gift of a share of
residue. The declaration had to be read in the context
of the whole of purpose (lastly) which, it was said, was
a scheme of great complexity. The significance of this
point is that, if the declaration can be shown to be
dependent upon the provisions of para (c) in favour of
Nigel and his issue, it may then be easier to read the
forfeiture clause as applying to it. If, on the other
hand, it contains a separate and distinct gift in favour
of Nigel's issue, in no way conditional on what Nigel
either does or omits to do, one would be the more
inclined to regard the destination as unaffected by the
forfeiture. That is the result of the authorities to
which I have referred. In my opinion, however, the
declaration in para (b) constitutes a gift to Nigel's issue
which is entirely separate from any benefit which
those issue would have derived under para (c) in the
event of Nigel's death had his share not been forfeited.
It seems to me to be unnecessary to refer to any part
of para (c) in order to construe the declaration. The
terms which are used here are entirely consistent with
the provisions of para (b), and the whole matter
appears to me to be contained within this paragraph.

I accept that there is a similar gift to issue in para
(c), where provision is made for the distribution of
Nigel's share of the residue to his children, whom
failing their issue, on his death. But the same cannot
be said of Henry's issue, since they are given no
interest whatever in his share of the residue under para
(a). In their case the declaration is quite clearly a
separate and independent gift, since it cannot be
linked in any way to the provisions of para (a) in
regard to Henry's share. I see no reason for taking a
different view of the declaration when it is applied to
Nigel's issue.

The clause of forfeiture, which applies in the event
of any of the beneficiaries claiming their legal rights,
may be regarded as falling into two parts. The first is
the direction that, in the events contemplated, the
beneficiary is to forfeit "all right and interest in any
share or shares of that part of my estate and effects
which I may freely dispose of by law". Its effect is to
exclude the beneficiary entirely from what may conveniently be described as the dead's part of the
testator's estate. The second part is the declaration
that in that event "the share or shares of such
beneficiary or beneficiaries" shall accresce and be
dealt with in terms of the provisions in favour of the
other beneficiaries who have accepted the settlement.
In *Ballantyne's Trs* it was held that the effect of this
clause was to involve forfeiture of the provisions in
favour of Nigel's issue in Nigel's share, and that his
share as a whole fell to be applied, after making equitable compensation to the widow for the diminution of
her liferent, by paying one half of it to Henry and
adding the other half to the capital of Mrs Galbraith's
share. The contention for the second parties is that the
forfeiture extends also to any interest in the residue of
Mrs Galbraith's share which might otherwise have
gone to Nigel's issue. But on a plain reading of the
clause of forfeiture that does not seem to be its effect.

A The first part of the clause directs the forfeiture in the case only of the beneficiary or beneficiaries who have claimed legal rights. The second part of the clause is concerned only with the destination of the share or shares of such beneficiary or beneficiaries in that event. I can find no indication here of an intention that the forfeiture, if it was to extend to the issue of a beneficiary, was to apply to an interest which the issue are given in some other clause under the settlement.

B But for some of the things said in *Ballantyne's Trs,* I would have reached the opinion without much difficulty that there was here a separate and independent gift to Nigel's issue which was not affected by the clause of forfeiture. The terms of the gift, in a provision relating exclusively to Mrs Galbraith's share of the estate, cannot be said to be dependent in any way upon the provisions which relate to Nigel's share. The conditional institution of his issue depends for its effect solely upon whether or not he has survived Mrs Galbraith. In the event of his failure to survive her, C there is an immediate and direct gift to the issue without reference to anything that might otherwise have happened had he survived. I can find no indication in the clause of forfeiture that it was intended to apply to the interest taken by the issue as conditional institutes in this share of the residue. In the events which have happened, it is a share which was at no time a share of the beneficiary who incurred the forfeiture.

D Counsel for the second parties submitted that the answer to the question was governed precisely by the decision in *Ballantyne's Trs,* to the effect that the forfeiture clause must be held to apply. The effect of the clause was said to be that Nigel's children and their issue had been entirely excluded from all benefit under the will by his decision to claim legal rights. Although the court had declined to answer the question which has now arisen as premature, their decision was nevertheless in general terms, and it was said that there was no good reason at this stage for reaching a E different result. At first sight there was some attraction in this approach. The discussion in that case was introduced by Lord President Cooper's reference at p 429 to the residue clause as consisting of "an elaborate scheme of interlocking provisions with cross destinations-over, so intricate that the possible interests of the parties in all the possible events cannot be briefly summarised". This comment is undoubtedly directed to the residue clause as a whole and not just to that part of it which applies to Nigel's F share. Similarly Lord Carmont's discussion of the matter extends to a consideration of the various provisions which the testator made with regard to the residue. I have come to the view, however, that on a closer analysis, the critical passages in the opinions are directed only to the effect of the forfeiture on Nigel's share, or on interests which Nigel might have taken in other shares had he survived.

Counsel relied especially on Lord President Cooper's comment at p 429 to this effect: "Reading the residue clause as a whole and using it as its own vocabulary, I am forced to the conclusion that the 'share of' each of the three beneficiaries is the one- G third (or three-ninths) of residue set aside on the widow's death for him or her or his or her stirps, and that it is this (and not the limited interest therein which the beneficiary was enjoying when he claimed legal rights) that passes under the destination-over. Each of these three shares is conceived as the subject of a number of interacting directions, some in favour of the parent and others in favour of his or her children or issue — the whole constituting a *unum quid.*"

H But I consider that the last sentence, which is critical, is to be read as a comment on each share of the residue considered separately. It is this which constitutes the unum quid, not the residue clause as a whole. The whole point of the discussion is that the share includes the fiars' interest as well as that of the liferenter. I can find nothing in this passage to suggest that the gift to children or issue of one parent of part of another parent's share as conditional institutes is to be regarded as unum quid with the share given to the I parent.

The passage in Lord Carmont's opinion on which counsel most relied is at p 433, where he examines the point that what is forfeited is the measure of what is directed to accresce to the parties who abide by the provisions of the settlement. Testing the argument that only Nigel's liferent had been forfeited against its effect on the provisions of the will as a whole, which indicated an intention to establish and preserve equality between each of the three children, viewing J each of them as the head of a stirps, he said: "The preservation of this equality is not lessened, in my opinion, by the fact that provision is made, by a destination-over, for the event of either Helen or Nigel or both not leaving issue them surviving. In that state of matters, the family outlook of the settlement comes to the fore and provides for the succession of the surviving brother and sister who are looked to for the possible continuation of the family. But, at such a stage, the possibility of there being any rights to be K preserved for the issue of Nigel would be out of the question."

But the line of thought there seems to be directed only to the question whether the forfeiture extends to the interest of Nigel's issue in Nigel's share. The only significance of the reference to the destinations-over was that they might suggest that the interest in the fee of Nigel's share could be regarded as a separate and independent gift. That argument was rejected for the reason indicated in the last sentence of this paragraph. L This is because, at the stage which it contemplates, Nigel is assumed to have died without leaving issue, so his share had to pass to his brother and sister and their issue to prevent intestacy. This situation was to be seen as equivalent, in its effect, to a forfeiture which extended to the rights of Nigel's issue in Nigel's share. So a forfeiture which extended to their rights in his share was consistent with the family outlook of the settlement, and there was no disharmony as a result.

There was some discussion in the course of

A counsel's argument for the third party as to whether some of the dicta in *Ballantyne's Trs* were too loosely expressed. Reference was made to *McCartney's Trs v McCartney's Exrs,* which appears not to have been cited in *Ballantyne's Trs,* and Lord Fraser's discussion of the issue in *Munro's Trs, Petrs* at pp 315-316. It was said that the comment that there was here an elaborate scheme of interlocking provisions had been overstated, and that too much importance had been attached to the fact that in the case of Nigel's share the trustees had power to advance to Nigel part of the capital of

B the liferented fund. I do not find it necessary to express a view on these arguments, because in my opinion both Lord President Cooper and Lord Carmont were careful in *Ballantyne's Trs* not to say anything which could be taken to affect a decision on the point which has now arisen. The only issue which they were considering in these passages was whether the action of Nigel, in electing to claim his legal rights, had resulted in the forfeiture of the provisions in favour of his children and issue in his own share, with

C the result that that one third share of the residue was to be divided among the other beneficiaries. I think that, carefully read in that context, the passages which I have quoted were directed to that point only, and not to that raised in the sixth question in the case which was whether, in the event of Mrs Galbraith dying without leaving issue, the right of Nigel's issue to one half of her share of residue had been forfeited. They declined to answer that question as premature and hypothetical, and I think that counsel was successful

D in demonstrating that they did not trespass onto that point when expressing their reasons for holding that the forfeiture extended to the provisions in favour of Nigel's children and their issue in Nigel's share.

For these reasons I would answer question 1 in the present case in the negative. Question 2 is superseded, and question 3, which is consequential on our answer to question 1, should be answered in the affirmative.

LORD ALLANBRIDGE.—The main question
E that arises in this special case is whether the action of Nigel Keppel Charteris Ballantyne (hereinafter referred to as "Nigel"), in electing to choose his legal rights in 1946 in the estate of his father (hereinafter referred to as "the testator"), has resulted in the forfeiture of any rights otherwise open to his issue to share in the residue of one third of the testator's estate which was liferented to his sister Mrs Helen Muriel Ballantyne or Galbraith (hereinafter referred to as "Helen"). The testator died in 1937 leaving a widow
F and three children, namely, Henry Ballantyne (hereinafter referred to as "Henry") and Nigel and Helen. The testator's widow enjoyed the liferent of the trust estate until her death in 1950.

Thereafter, in terms of purpose (lastly) of the testator's trust disposition and settlement, the residue was to be divided into three equal shares of three ninths each. One third share was to be paid to Henry who took his share on his mother's death. He died in 1983 leaving three surviving issue who are the second parties. One third share was left to Nigel in liferent

with power to the trustees to advance capital to him and thereafter his share or any balance of it was left to G his issue. The remaining one third share was left in terms of purpose (lastly) (b) to Helen in liferent and her issue in fee and in the event of her dying without issue then her share was to be divided equally between her brothers Henry and Nigel with their issue taking their parent's share, if their parent predeceased Helen. Helen died in 1990 without issue and predeceased by Henry who died in 1983 and by Nigel who died in 1986. Nigel left one child who is the third party.

In a special case in 1952 (*Ballantyne's Trs v* H *Ballantyne*), the First Division held that because Nigel had claimed his legal rights in 1946 this had resulted in the forfeiture of his one third share, which was held to be applied in compensating the trustees of the testator's widow for the loss of income sustained by her as a result of Nigel claiming legitim and thereafter paying one half of the balance to Henry and adding the remaining half to the capital held for Helen in liferent and her issue in fee.

                                                                  I
When the First Division considered the special case in 1952 they did not answer the sixth question put to them because they considered it to be premature. That question was in the following terms: "(6) In the event of said Mrs Helen Muriel Ballantyne or Galbraith dying without leaving lawful children surviving or if such as may survive shall die without issue before attaining majority, has the right of the issue of the fifth party (Nigel) to one half of her share of residue in the testator's estate, been forfeited?"
                                                                  J
The sixth question is in effect the same as the first and main question which arises now in this second special case. Although the First Division had stated that they were not answering the sixth question in the first special case because it was premature, it was submitted on behalf of the second parties in this special case that the opinions of Lord President Cooper and Lord Carmont were so worded that it was clear that they were of the view that Nigel's issue would also forfeit any right they might have had in Helen's share. K At first sight this was an attractive argument but on a close examination of these opinions I do not consider that this is correct. These opinions, in my view, were directed towards an examination of the rights of Nigel's issue in his share only and not their rights in Helen's share.

The problem that arose regarding Nigel's share in the original special case was whether the rule in *Fisher v Dixon* applied. That rule applies where the deed L can be read as conferring distinct and separate rights on the parents and their children. If so then such a disassociation will mean that the children's rights will not be affected by their parents' forfeiture. This disassociation should be looked for both in the actual terms in which the gifts are made and also in the terms of the clause of forfeiture if any. (See Professor Dykes' *Supplement to McLaren on Wills,* pp 49-50, referred to at p 429 of Lord President Cooper's opinion.) In examining this question at p 429, Lord President Cooper referred to the residue clause as consisting of an "elaborate scheme of interlocking provisions with cross destinations-over".

However, Lord President Cooper did not restrict his observations solely to Nigel's share because he went on to say: "Moreover, the third of residue appropriated to Nigel and his stirps might in certain events have been inflated by the addition of one-half of the third share initially appropriated to his sister, Mrs Galbraith. In other words the 'interest' of Nigel's children or issue, viewed prospectively as at the date of the testator's death, might prove to be anything from nothing at all to the capital of half the residue — in this case a very large sum."

This latter sentence was said by counsel for the second parties to support his argument that the "interest" of Nigel's children and issue in Helen's share was forfeited by the fact that Nigel had claimed his legal rights. I do not agree. I consider it is clear that the Lord President was envisaging a situation where Helen died without issue but survived by Nigel. In that event half of her share would be added to "the third of residue appropriated to Nigel and his stirps". If Nigel had predeceased his sister then one half of Helen's share would either have passed to Henry or his heirs or to Nigel's issue in terms of the provisions in the trust deed relating to Helen's share. Furthermore, when in the second last paragraph on p 429 the Lord President refers to a combination of factors satisfying him that Nigel's children or issue are "to be cut out" if Nigel claims his legal rights, he is clearly limiting his remarks to Nigel's share only, as reference to the previous paragraph shows where each of the three shares was said to constitute a unum quid.

Lord Carmont, at p 432, states that: "In the present case, I am of opinion that the children of Nigel (if any come into existence) could have no separate and distinct right from that of Nigel."

However, that is said by Lord Carmont in the context of examining the provisions relating to Nigel's share and the fact that he was given a liferent in it, and I read these words as limited to Nigel's share. At p 432, Lord Carmont does refer to Helen's share being payable in the event of her death without issue, equally between Henry and Nigel. However, he continues by stating that the half so falling to Nigel should be added to his one half share which would be dealt with as provided for in regard to his original share, so that his issue would take no separate right from what they would have taken in regard to Nigel's own share. These observations were also founded on by counsel for the second parties but once again I am satisfied that Lord Carmont was, like Lord President Cooper, not considering the situation which would arise if Nigel predeceased his sister. This view is supported by the fact that both the Lord President and Lord Carmont (at pp 430 and 433 respectively) made it clear that the court was not answering the sixth question which referred in terms to the right of Nigel's issue in Helen's share in the event of her dying without issue, because it was premature and hypothetical.

The way is now clear to consider whether the rule in *Fisher v Dixon* applied to Helen's share in the events which have happened. I first consider the forfeiture clause in the deed. It is to be found in a declaration following on purpose (lastly) of the trust deed and states that in the event of any beneficiary claiming their legal rights then such beneficiary should forfeit their whole right and interest in any share of the trust estate. Thus Nigel could take no interest in the trust estate, but it is important to note that his issue are not mentioned in the forfeiture clause so that their interest must be determined by the actual terms of the deed relating to Helen's share in terms of purpose (lastly) (b) thereof.

It is the declaration at the end of purpose (lastly) (b) that is critical in this case. It is concerned with the disposal of Helen's share in the event of her dying without issue and predeceased by Henry and/or Nigel. It states: "declaring that the issue of such of my sons as may have predeceased shall take *per stirpes* the share which would have fallen to such parent had he survived".

It was submitted by counsel for the third parties that Nigel's issue were conditional institutes who would take a separate and independent right to a one half of Helen's share in the event of her death without issue predeceased by Nigel. He referred to a number of cases in support of this argument including *McCartney's Trs v McCartney's Exrs* and *Hurll's Trs v Hurll.* In the earlier case, Lord Strachan indicated (1951 SLT at p 404) that a series of cases commencing with *Fisher v Dixon* had laid down that if the issue take an interest which is separate and independent, the election of the parent (to take legitim) in no way affects the independent right of the issue. In the later case, the Second Division followed *Fisher v Dixon* and *McCartney's Trs* and held that a gift to a son's issue was separate from and independent of a gift to the son of a liferent in a fund regarding which the trustees had power to advance capital to the son's issue without the consent of the son as liferenter. The Lord Justice Clerk, 1964 SC at pp 18-19, distinguished *Ballantyne's Trs* in 1952 as he said in that case the trustees had power to advance to the repudiating son up to the whole of the capital of which he was given the liferent. We were referred to a number of other cases by counsel for the third parties but I find it unnecessary to detail them because I am quite satisfied that they only serve to reinforce the proper approach in such cases as being determined by whether or not the rights of the issue were distinct and separate from the rights of the parent in the absence of any contrary intention in the forfeiture clause or any other provisions in the deed.

Applying such an approach in the present case I am of the opinion that in the events which have happened, the rights of Nigel's issue as conditional institutes were quite separate from those of Nigel. As was pointed out by Lord Strachan at p 405 of *McCartney's Trs,* in a situation such as applies in the present case, the parent has no control of any kind over the rights of the issue and the respective rights of

the parent and issue were mutually exclusive. In the
present case neither Nigel nor his issue could take a
vested right in Helen's share liferented by her until
her death without issue. If Helen predeceased Nigel
then one half of her share would be added to Nigel's
share and both he and his issue would forfeit all right
to it, as indicated by Lord President Cooper and Lord
Carmont. On the other hand if Nigel predeceased
Helen then he could never take any right in her share
and it was vested on Helen's death without issue in
Nigel's issue as conditional institutes. Thus in the
present case I am quite satisfied that the third party as
Nigel's only issue took a vested right in one half of
Helen's liferented share on her death.

In these circumstances I would answer the first
question in the negative and it follows that question 3
is answered in the affirmative and question 2 is
superseded.

LORD PROSSER.—I agree with your Lordship
in the chair and there is nothing useful I would like
to add.

---

*Counsel for First Parties, MacIver; Solicitors,
Shepherd & Wedderburn, WS — Counsel for Second
Parties, Drummond Young, QC; Solicitors, Tods
Murray, WS — Counsel for Third Party, Hodge;
Solicitors, Balfour & Manson, Nightingale & Bell.*

M C G

Gibson v Strathclyde Regional Council

SECOND DIVISION
THE LORD JUSTICE CLERK (ROSS),
LORDS MURRAY AND WEIR
15 JULY 1992

*Reparation — Negligence — Duty of care — Extent of
duty — Relevancy — Inspection of pavements by roads
authority — Reference to duty of daily inspection of drain
covers without any supporting averments of fact —
Whether court entitled to decide for itself reasonableness
of stated precaution.*

*Process — Pleadings — Relevancy and specification —
Reference to duty of roads authority to inspect drain
covers daily without specifying practice of other similar
defenders or special circumstances existing at locus.*

A woman sustained injury when she stepped into an
uncovered drain inspection hole in a pavement in
central Glasgow. She raised an action of damages
against the defenders as the local authority having
responsibility for the upkeep and maintenance of
public roads and pavements in Glasgow, based on

their failure to take reasonable care to keep the inspection hole covered. The defenders tabled a general plea
to the relevancy and specification of the pursuer's
averments. In the course of a debate the pursuer was
permitted to amend her averments of duty by inserting
the following sentence: "It was reasonable and practicable to inspect daily said drains." The amendment
followed a sentence in which she averred that it was
the defenders' duty to inspect regularly drains such as
the said drain to ensure they were covered. At the
resumed debate the defenders argued that the pursuer's pleadings as amended were irrelevant as there
were no averments of fact which supported the alleged
duty. The sheriff relied upon the decision of the
sheriff principal in *King v Strathclyde Regional Council*
and allowed a proof. The defenders appealed. They
argued that the case of *King* was wrongly decided and
that in the absence of averments of fact establishing a
duty of daily inspection the pursuer's case was irrelevant. The pursuer contended that *King* was correctly
decided and that it was open to the court to draw the
necessary inference from the whole circumstances of
the accident.

Held, that even if the pursuer succeeded in establishing all the facts which she averred, she was bound
to fail, since the court was not entitled to hold that
daily inspection was reasonable or practicable in the
absence of averments to support such a conclusion
(pp 1245K, 1246B, 1247E-F and 1247L); and appeal
allowed and action *dismissed*.

King v Strathclyde Regional Council, Glasgow sheriff
court, 8 January 1991, unreported, *overruled*.

Appeal from the sheriff court
Mrs Mary Gibson raised an action against Strathclyde Regional Council in the sheriff court at Glasgow
seeking damages as a result of certain injuries sustained by her on 17 May 1989 when she stepped into
an uncovered drain inspection hole in a pavement in
central Glasgow. The action was based on a breach of
duty of inspection at common law.

The case called for debate before the sheriff.

Pleadings
The pursuer made the following averments of fault:

"(3) . . . It was the defenders' duty to take reasonable
care to avoid exposing persons using said footpath to
unnecessary risk. It was the duty of the defenders to
inspect regularly drains such as the said drain to
ensure they are covered. It was reasonable and practicable to inspect daily said drains. It was the duty of
the defenders to maintain regularly drains such as the
said drain to ensure they remained covered. It was the
duty of the defenders to take reasonable care to see to
it that the said drain was kept covered. The defenders
knew or ought to have known that persons, such as the
pursuer using the said footpath without adequate
cover on the said drain, were at risk of falling into the
open drain and sustaining injury. They had a duty to
see that if drains were uncovered, they were adequately fenced and there was adequate visible signs

warning of the potential hazard. In all these duties the defenders failed and by their said failure so caused the said accident. But for their said failure in duty, the said accident would not have happened."

The defenders' answer was in the following terms:

"(3) . . . The locus is inspected 12 times per annum. The last inspection of the locus, prior to the date of said accident, was 31 March 1989. No defect was noted on said date. The defenders do not know how long prior to said accident, said Buchan Trap had been uncovered. No complaints had been made to the defenders about the condition of said cover. The defenders could not, by the exercise of a reasonable system of inspection, have ascertained that said cover was missing. It would not be reasonable for the defenders to inspect drains and drain covers daily. No local authorities carry out routine daily inspection of drains and/or drain covers. There is no practice of carrying out such a daily inspection."

Cases referred to

Brown v Rolls Royce Ltd, 1960 SLT 119; 1960 SC (HL) 22.

Buchanan v Glasgow Corporation, 1923 SLT 502; 1923 SC 782.

Jamieson v Jamieson, 1952 SLT 257; 1952 SC (HL) 44.

King (Mary) v Strathclyde Regional Council, Glasgow sheriff court, 8 January 1991, unreported.

Laing v Paull & Williamsons, 1911 2 SLT 437; 1912 SC 196.

McGuffie v Forth Valley Health Board, 1991 SLT 231.

Miller v South of Scotland Electricity Board, 1958 SLT 229; 1958 SC (HL) 20.

Morton v William Dixon Ltd, 1909 1 SLT 346; 1909 SC 807.

Riddell v Reid, 1941 SLT 179; 1941 SC 277.

On 21 February 1992 the sheriff *repelled* the defenders' plea to the relevancy and *allowed* parties a proof.

The defenders appealed to the Court of Session.

Appeal

The appeal was heard by the Second Division on 23 June 1992.

On 15 July 1992 the court *allowed* the appeal and *dismissed* the action.

THE LORD JUSTICE CLERK (ROSS).—In this action the pursuer is seeking damages from the defenders in respect of injuries which she alleges that she received when she sustained an accident while walking on the west footpath of Abercromby Street, Glasgow, on 17 May 1989. The pursuer's case is that as she was moving on the pavement her right leg went down into an uncovered inspection drain situated in the middle of the footpath. The pursuer averred that the drain cover, which was known as a Buchan Trap cover, had been missing from the drain for at least 14

days prior to the accident. The pursuer is suing the defenders as the local authority responsible for the maintenance and upkeep of drains.

In art 3 of the condescence the pursuer sets out her grounds of fault against the defenders. In particular she avers as follows: [his Lordship narrated the terms of cond 3 and then ans 3 set out supra and continued:]

After sundry procedure the case was put out for debate before the sheriff on 13 December 1991. On that date, after hearing parties, the sheriff allowed both parties to make certain amendments to their pleadings and a fresh debate was fixed for 12 February 1992. On 12 February 1992, the sheriff heard parties and made avizandum. On 21 February 1992 the sheriff of consent repelled the pursuer's third plea in law, repelled the defenders' first plea in law and allowed parties a proof of their respective averments. It is against that interlocutor of the sheriff that the defenders have now appealed.

In a note annexed to his interlocutor of 21 February 1992, the sheriff explains that at the first hearing of the debate the solicitor for the defenders attacked the pursuer's averments as irrelevant because of her failure to aver any duty on the defenders to maintain a system of inspection which would have revealed the fault in the drain cover within 14 days of its occurrence, and also because of the absence of any specification as to the meaning of the averment of a duty of regular inspection. He records that in the course of the debate the solicitor for the pursuer conceded that his pleadings were irrelevant as they stood. He then sought and obtained leave to amend by inserting the following averment: "It was reasonable and practicable to inspect daily said drains." At the resumed debate, the question between the parties was whether this amendment made by the pursuer relating to daily inspection made his pleadings relevant. On behalf of the defenders it was maintained that there were only two ways of showing that such a course of conduct was reasonable; one was by showing that it was so obvious that the court could decide on its reasonableness without hearing any evidence on the matter, and the other was by leading evidence of the practice of other similar defenders, or evidence of other special circumstances from which it could be inferred that the requirement was reasonable. The sheriff explains that the solicitor for the pursuer accepted that this was not a case where the court could decide on the reasonableness of what was proposed without hearing any evidence on the matter. For the defenders it was submitted that if the pursuer required to lead evidence of the practice of other local authorities in relation to inspection, averments of such practice would require to be made so as to give the defenders fair notice. If the pursuer failed to make such averments, she would be precluded from leading any evidence on the matter and accordingly her action would be bound to fail. The defenders further contended that if an averment such as that added by the pursuer was sufficient to entitle a pursuer to proof, it would always be open for a pursuer to obtain a proof by making such an averment in a case of this kind simply upon the basis of

the pursuer's instinctive belief that it was well
A founded, without having any objective support for it.

The sheriff explains that he found the submissions
of the defenders highly persuasive but he felt bound
by a decision of the sheriff principal in *King v Strathclyde Regional Council*. In that case the sheriff principal allowed a similar action to go to proof on an
averment that there was a duty of daily inspection.
The sheriff principal's view appeared to be that the
reasonableness of a stated precaution was a question of
fact for the sheriff to decide for himself, and that there
B was no need to make averments of practice to support
the existence of such a precaution. The sheriff accordingly repelled the plea to relevancy taken on behalf of
the defenders and allowed a proof.

Before this court counsel for the defenders submitted that the appeal should be allowed and the
action should be dismissed. He submitted that the
sheriff was well founded in holding that the defenders'
arguments were highly persuasive, and that he had
C arrived at the wrong decision because he had relied
upon the decision of the sheriff principal in *King v
Strathclyde Regional Council* which must be regarded
as having been wrongly decided. He submitted that at
a proof it would not be open to a sheriff to decide
whether daily inspections were reasonable and practicable without having evidence to support such a conclusion; and if there required to be evidence to support
such a conclusion, there also required to be averments
giving notice of the evidence upon which the pursuer
D would rely for this purpose. He submitted that in the
absence of any averments which would entitle the
pursuer to establish that the defenders were negligent
for failing to have daily inspections, the pursuer could
not lead any evidence regarding this, and that accordingly the pursuer's case must fail. That being so he
submitted that the pursuer's case failed to pass the test
of relevancy and that accordingly her action should be
dismissed.

Counsel for the pursuer maintained that the sheriff
E had reached the correct conclusion, and that the case
of *King v Strathclyde Regional Council* had been correctly decided. Although mindful of what had been
said by the Lord President in *Riddell v Reid*, 1941
SLT at p 183 about the need for a pursuer to define
the intervals at which inspection was to take place, he
contended that it was difficult for a pursuer to make
such averments. He maintained that the practice of
other local authorities might not be of any assistance
to the court because there might be special circum-
F stances obtaining with other local authorities. He submitted that once an accident had occurred there was
a presumption of fault on the part of the defenders
(*Laing v Paull & Williamsons*). He also referred to
Buchanan v Glasgow Corporation. He contended that
the court was entitled when considering the relevancy
of the pursuer's case to have regard to what the
defenders had to say upon the matter and he accordingly relied upon the averments in ans 3 which I have
already quoted.

At the end of the day he maintained that all that the

pursuer could be expected to do was to lead evidence
of the accident, and evidence that the cover was G
missing, and then to invite the court to draw the inference that the defenders had been negligent. He submitted that the court would know from the evidence
that the cover had been missing for 14 days, that the
accident had occurred, and that the defenders normally operated a system of monthly inspections. In
these circumstances he contended that the court would
be justified in inferring that there should have been a
daily inspection.

I have come to the conclusion that counsel for the H
defenders' submissions are well founded. I fully
appreciate that the court should not dismiss a reparation action as irrelevant unless the circumstances are
special. As Viscount Simonds said in *Miller v South of
Scotland Electricity Board*, 1958 SLT at p 234: "it is
undesirable, except in a very clear case, to dismiss an
action on the ground that the pursuer's averments are
irrelevant and insufficient in law". In the same case
Lord Keith of Avonholm said: "In claims of damages
for alleged negligence it can only be in rare and excep- I
tional cases that an action can be disposed of on
relevancy." In my opinion, however, the present is
such a case.

The test of relevancy is well known: "The true
proposition is that an action will not be dismissed as
irrelevant unless it must necessarily fail even if all the
pursuer's averments are proved. The onus is on the
defender who moves to have the action dismissed, and
there is no onus on the pursuer to show that if he
proves his averments he is bound to succeed" J
(*Jamieson v Jamieson*, 1952 SLT per Lord Normand
at p 257).

In the same case at p 264 Lord Reid said: "If it can
be shown that, even if the pursuer succeeds in proving
all that he avers, still his case must fail, it appears to
me to be highly advantageous that time and money
should not be spent on fruitless enquiry into the
facts."

K
It appears to me, however, that the present case is
a case where it can properly be said that even if the
pursuer succeeds in establishing all the facts which she
has averred, she will be bound to fail. I say that
because it is not disputed that the pursuer could not
succeed unless it was established that it was reasonable
and practicable to inspect the drains daily. Having
regard to the fact that the defenders maintain that
their system was for monthly inspections and that they
do not in fact appear to have inspected this drain for L
a period of almost seven weeks, the pursuer might
have chosen to make a case based upon failure to carry
out the system of monthly inspections. Alternatively,
having regard to the fact that the pursuer maintains
that the cover was missing from the drain for at least
14 days, she might have made a case for inspections at
weekly or 10 day intervals. The advantage of such a
case from the pursuer's point of view would be that if
such a duty were established, there would be every
prospect of also establishing that if the defenders had
performed that duty the accident would not have

occurred. However that may be, the pursuer has chosen in this case to peril her case upon the assertion that it was reasonable and practicable to inspect the drains daily. There is no doubt that it was necessary for the pursuer to state at what intervals inspections should have been carried out: "It is clear that if you are going to found upon defect of inspection you must define the intervals at which inspection is to take place" (*Riddell v Reid* at p 183).

In this connection I would also refer to *McGuffie v Forth Valley Health Board.* However, I do not accept that where such an averment has been made the court is entitled to hold that daily inspection was reasonable or practicable in the absence of averments to support such a conclusion. If averments had been made to the effect that it was the practice among other local authorities with responsibility for the maintenance and upkeep of drains to carry out daily inspections, that, in my opinion, would have supported the pursuer's case that it was reasonable and practicable to inspect such drains daily. But no such averments have been made. Likewise if the pursuer had been in a position to aver some special circumstances existing at the locus, such averments might have been sufficient to support the assertion that it was reasonable and practicable to inspect the drains daily. For example, if the pursuer had been in a position to say that in the past covers had frequently been removed from drains in this locality, or that the defenders had received numerous complaints regarding the absence of drain covers here, that too might have supported the case for daily inspections. But no such averments have been made, and since there are no such averments, the pursuer could not lead any evidence at the proof to that effect. The result accordingly would be that at the proof the pursuer would be unable to lead any evidence which could form the basis for the sheriff concluding that daily inspections were reasonable and practicable. I am not persuaded that the sheriff would be entitled to conclude that daily inspections were reasonable and practicable without having heard evidence which could form a sound basis for any such conclusion. In the absence of any such evidence the sheriff would not be entitled to conclude that daily inspections were reasonable, far less practicable. If the pursuer did no more than prove that the cover had been missing for 14 days, that the accident occurred, and that the defenders had normally operated a system of monthly inspections, that would not entitle the court to hold that daily inspections were reasonable and practicable. For the foregoing reasons I agree with counsel for the defenders that the pursuer's case is irrelevant. I do not consider that it is any answer for the pursuer to maintain that there is a presumption of fault on the part of the defenders.

In *King v Strathclyde Regional Council* the sheriff principal said: "If one takes the averment that, in respect of this locus, daily inspection was reasonable, and reads it along with the averred condition of the hole, one can fairly conclude that what the pursuer seeks to prove is that the condition of the hole was such that it must have been in existence long enough to have been observed in the course of daily inspection. The circumstances of the locus might warrant a court's holding that daily inspection was reasonable; and the averred condition of the hole might lead a court to hold that the defenders did have sufficient time to apprise themselves of its existence as a danger, and to counter it. I therefore do not think that the pursuer has failed to specify a relevant case."

In my opinion the reasoning of the sheriff principal in the foregoing passage is flawed. I accept that the circumstances of the locus might in an appropriate case warrant a court's holding that daily inspection was reasonable, but the circumstances of the locus would require to be made the subject of averment. There were no averments to that effect in the case of *King,* and likewise there are no such averments in the present case. It follows that the case of *King v Strathclyde Regional Council* was wrongly decided, and I would overrule it. [His Lordship then dealt with another matter with which this report is not concerned and continued:]

For the foregoing reasons, I would move your Lordships to allow the appeal, to recall the interlocutor of the sheriff dated 21 February 1992, to sustain the first plea in law for the defenders, and to dismiss the action.

LORD MURRAY.—According to her averments the pursuer and respondent in this sheriff court action sustained injury when she stepped into an uncovered drain inspection hole in a pavement in central Glasgow in the process of seeking to obtain a taxi. She blames Strathclyde Regional Council, the local authority responsible for upkeep of public roads and pavements in Glasgow, for their failure to take reasonable care to keep the inspection hole covered. The defenders and appellants tabled a general plea to the relevancy of the respondent's averments which was debated before the sheriff. In the course of the debate the respondent was permitted to amend her averments of duty by inserting in cond 3 the following sentence: "It was reasonable and practicable to inspect daily said drains." The amendment immediately follows a sentence in which it is averred that it was the duty of the defenders to inspect regularly drains such as the said drain to ensure that they were covered.

Having heard argument on the matter the sheriff repelled the appellants' plea to the relevancy and allowed a proof. In his note he made it perfectly plain that he did so only because he considered that he was bound by a decision of the Sheriff Principal of Glasgow and Strathkelvin in the case of *King v Strathclyde Regional Council.* It is clear from the brief note appended to the interlocutor of that date that the sheriff was right to consider himself to be bound by that decision which turned on averments clearly not distinguishable from those in the present case. The appellants appeal the sheriff's interlocutor in this case on the basis that the sheriff principal's decision in *King* was wrong and cannot be supported.

The short point taken by counsel for the appellants

was that the averment added by way of amendment
relating to daily inspection was irrelevant. A bald averment that daily inspection was reasonable and practicable did not disclose any evidential basis, such as general practice of roads authorities, upon which it would be open to a court to infer that daily inspection was reasonable and practicable. In the absence of an evidential basis to ground such an inference the case was bound to fail. If there was an intention to lead such evidence fair notice required an indication of what it was to be. If no such evidence was to be led, the inference to be drawn from the complete lack of specification in the amendment was that there would be no factual basis upon which a court could infer that the duty of inspection desiderated was incumbent upon the appellants. This was not a case, as the agents for the respondent had accepted before the sheriff, where particular circumstances were averred from which it could be seen that the duty averred plainly arose. The appeal should be allowed and the case dismissed.

In reply counsel for the respondent submitted that the sheriff principal in *King* had decided correctly and the sheriff had been right to follow that decision. Realistically a pursuer would never be in a position to aver general practice in regard to the inspection and maintenance of roads and pavements by roads authorities. The respondent's averments about the facts of the accident, the locus and the interval of time which had elapsed since the last inspection were a sufficient basis for inference that it was reasonable and practicable to inspect daily and that a duty so to inspect could be inferred. The appeal should be refused.

Both counsel canvassed authorities touching upon this matter in a general sense but I found these citations to be of little assistance in regard to this case and the case of *King*, which turn very much upon the particular averments made.

Approaching the matter from the standpoint of general principle I am not persuaded by the argument for the respondent that the sentence inserted by way of amendment is sufficient to make the respondent's averments of duty relevant. It appears to me that, in the absence of averments of practice or of particular circumstances from which it may reasonably be inferred that daily inspection of city pavements is both reasonable and practicable, what is asserted in the amendment is simply that daily inspection is possible. To make purely formal averments that a possibility is reasonable and practicable adds nothing, in my opinion, to the essential emptiness of the assertion. In the absence of further specification or of an alternative case based upon some wider hypothesis, proof based upon these averments would be bound to fail.

Turning to the sheriff principal's note in *King* it appears to me that the ground of his decision is contained in the third last paragraph. There the sheriff principal says: "In my view one must read the pursuer's averments at this stage, in their best light. If one takes the averment that, in respect of this locus, daily inspection was reasonable, and reads it along with the averred condition of the hole, one can fairly conclude that what the pursuer seeks to prove is that the condition of the hole was such that it must have been in existence long enough to have been observed in the course of daily inspection. The circumstances of the locus might warrant a court's holding that daily inspection was reasonable; and the averred condition of the hole might lead a court to hold that the defenders did have sufficient time to apprise themselves of its existence as a danger, and to counter it. I therefore do not think that the pursuer has failed to specify a relevant case."

In the middle of the next paragraph the sheriff principal says: "It seems to me that the question is not whether, on these grounds, liability may be attached. Rather it is a question whether the court would draw the factual inferences from these circumstances, which the pursuer requires the court to draw."

With all respect to the learned sheriff principal, it appears to me that the foregoing reasoning is incorrect in law. The sheriff principal explicitly deals with the issue as a one dimensional matter of averments of fact rather than a two dimensional matter of fact and law. In the absence of averments of fact from which a duty in law may reasonably be inferred, no duty in law at all is averred. For a relevant case in a situation like the present there require to be averments of fact from which a duty in law can be inferred and further averments of fact from which it can be inferred that there was a failure on the part of the defender to fulfil that duty. If this analysis is correct then the sheriff principal has failed to discriminate between the two kinds of factual averments which are required to state a relevant case in circumstances such as these. Accordingly his reasoning cannot be supported.

I agree with your Lordship in the chair that the appeal succeeds.

LORD WEIR.—I agree that this appeal should be allowed. The sheriff felt unable to distinguish the present case from that of *King v Strathclyde Regional Council* and he considered that he was bound by that decision, being that of the sheriff principal. However, I am of opinion that the decision in *King* cannot be supported. The relevancy of the pursuer's averments in that case, as well as in this case, should be tested by reference to the well known line of authority commencing with *Morton v William Dixon Ltd* and ending with *Brown v Rolls Royce Ltd*. In this case, the pursuer's case is based on a duty on the part of the defenders to carry out a daily inspection of drains in busy city streets such as the one where the pursuer is said to have met with her accident. Their failure to do so is said to have been the cause of her accident. There are no averments that such a system was commonly operated by other local authorities in their city streets. For the pursuer's case to pass the test of relevancy in the absence of averments of practice, in my opinion, there must be averments which make it absolutely clear that the fulfilment of the duty of reasonable care required a system of daily inspection. The sheriff prin-

A cipal in *King* apparently considered that the court could reach its own judgment on this question without evidence and on the basis of a simple averment that such a duty arose. I do not rule out the possibility that in some situations the failure to adopt measures, even in the absence of practice, may give rise to an inference of negligence. But I consider that the circumstances must be special, exceptional and obvious and these are certainly not present in this case. There has to be evidence in the general run of cases to support the reasonableness of a desired precaution and if there

B is to be evidence there have to be supporting averments. The absence of such averments in this case beyond a bald assertion that it was reasonable and practicable to inspect the drains daily, in my view, renders it irrelevant.

Counsel for Pursuer and Respondent, Geary; Solicitors, Henderson & Jackson, WS (for Gibson & McCaffrey, Glasgow) — Counsel for Defenders and
C *Appellants, Keen; Solicitors, Balfour & Manson, Nightingale & Bell (for Hennessy, Bowie & Co, Glasgow).*

M C G

Blake v Lothian Health Board

D OUTER HOUSE

LORD CAPLAN

17 JULY 1992

Limitation of actions — Reparation — Negligence — Time bar — Action raised nearly four years after accident — Pursuer originally thinking he suffered only minor back injury — Back problems resurfacing one year later and progressively worsening — Whether original injuries
E *sufficiently serious to justify his bringing a court action — Prescription and Limitation (Scotland) Act 1973 (c 52), s 17 (2) (b), as amended.*

Limitation of actions — Reparation — Negligence — Time bar — Action raised outwith triennium — Extension of time limit — Action raised nearly four years after accident — Initial effects of accident only marginally serious enough to justify proceedings — More serious effects emerging a year later — Pursuer having difficulty obtaining advice — Whether equitable to allow action to
F *proceed — Prescription and Limitation (Scotland) Act 1973 (c 52), s 19A.*

Section 17 of the Prescription and Limitation (Scotland) Act 1973 provides that any action of damages in respect of personal injuries must be brought within three years of the date when the injuries were sustained, or, if later, the date on which the pursuer became, or it would have been reasonably practicable for him to have become, aware inter alia that the injuries in question were sufficiently serious to justify his bringing an action of damages. Section 19A

enables the court to allow an action to proceed which would otherwise be time barred under s 17, if it seems G equitable to do so.

On 19 September 1986 an employee injured his back in an accident at work. He reported the accident to his employers and visited his general practitioner after work that day. The symptoms apparently cleared up shortly afterwards. A year later pain returned to his back, which progressively worsened and it became necessary for him to take time off work in October 1987. The employee raised an action in respect of the accident on 27 August 1990. At a proof on the H defenders' preliminary plea of time bar the pursuer argued that it was not until October 1987 that he was in a position to be aware that his injuries were sufficiently serious to justify raising an action, and that in any event it was equitable to apply s 19A (1). The defenders argued that the consequences of the accident were known to the pursuer immediately after it had occurred and were themselves sufficient to justify raising an action. Furthermore the pursuer had known in June 1988 that his back trouble could be connected I to the accident in September 1986, and so he had ample time to raise an action before September 1989. His difficulties in obtaining advice from his trade union, due in part to the effects of his injuries, were typical of many claimants in reparation actions.

Held, (1) that the fact that injuries could not be described as minimal or trivial did not necessarily mean that they were sufficiently serious to justify an action; the question was whether a reasonable claimant in all the circumstances would consider that J the facts about the injury which were known or could be ascertained rendered it worthwhile to raise an action (p 1251C-F); (2) that in these circumstances where a claim would have been worth no more than £200 and would have involved irrecoverable expense, worry and loss of wages, a reasonable claimant would have concluded that an action for damages was not worthwhile (p 1251G-I); (3) that in October 1987 the pursuer had a presentable claim for damages and the prerequisites for such an action were present, and the present action was not time barred (p 1251J-K); and K plea in law for defenders *repelled.*

Opinion, that had it been necessary to consider the application of s 19A (1) the equities would have been narrowly in favour of allowing the pursuer to proceed with his action (p 1252F).

Action of damages

James Blake raised an action against Lothian Health L Board for damages in respect of injuries allegedly sustained in an action at work on 19 September 1986. The action was raised on 27 August 1990.

The case came before the Lord Ordinary (Caplan) for preliminary proof before answer on the defenders' plea of time bar.

Statutory provisions

The Prescription and Limitation (Scotland) Act 1973 provides:

"17.— . . . (2) Subject to subsection (3) below and section 19A of this Act, no action to which this section applies shall be brought unless it is commenced within a period of 3 years after — (a) the date on which the injuries were sustained or, where the act or omission to which the injuries were attributable was a continuing one, that date or the date on which the act or omission ceased, whichever is the later; or (b) the date (if later than any date mentioned in paragraph (a) above) on which the pursuer in the action became, or on which, in the opinion of the court, it would have been reasonably practicable for him in all the circumstances to become, aware of all the following facts — (i) that the injuries in question were sufficiently serious to justify his bringing an action of damages on the assumption that the person against whom the action was brought did not dispute liability and was able to satisfy a decree; (ii) that the injuries were attributable in whole or in part to an action or omission; and (iii) that the defender was a person to whose act or omission the injuries were attributable in whole or in part or the employer or principal of such a person. . . .

"19A.—(1) Where a person would be entitled, but for any of the provisions of section 17 or section 18 and 18A of this Act, to bring an action, the court may, if it seems to it equitable to do so, allow him to bring the action notwithstanding that provision."

Cases referred to

Elliot v J & C Finney, 1989 SLT 605.
Mackie v Currie, 1991 SLT 407.
Nicol v British Steel Corporation (General Steels) Limited, 1992 SLT 141.
Pritchard v Tayside Health Board, OH, 23 March 1983, unreported.
Smith v National Coal Board, 1988 SLT 126.

On 17 July 1992 the Lord Ordinary *repelled* the defenders' plea of time bar.

LORD CAPLAN.—The pursuer is 42 years of age and on 19 September 1986 he was employed by the defenders at Gogarburn hospital as a student nurse. On the said date he sustained an accident to his back in the course of lifting a patient. The pursuer concludes for £15,000 being the alleged damages suffered as a result of the accident. The present action was raised on 27 August 1990. The defenders in their first plea in law ask for the action to be dismissed on the basis that it is time barred. The matter has come before me for proof in respect of that preliminary plea.

About 9.45 am on 19 September 1986 the pursuer required in the course of his duties to lift a geriatric patient from a Buxton chair onto a bed. The bed was in a lower position than the pursuer had anticipated and he misjudged the lift. He felt a sharp pain in his lower back. The pain was severe and at the time he doubled up. He thought he had pulled a muscle. He reported the accident to his employers. He continued with his work but the pain persisted and when he had finished work he visited his general practitioner. In the notes the general practitioner made at the time he noted that the pursuer had "acute lumbar back ache". The general practitioner carried out certain mechanical tests to see if there was any indication of disc damage but he found no positive indications of such damage. Accordingly the pursuer was given analgesics and advised to rest. The doctor told the pursuer that he had suffered a muscle strain. The pursuer took a few days off work. About the same time he also had a two week period of leave from work but he thinks that this was probably holiday leave. In any event the rest appears to have benefited him and when he returned to work he suffered nothing other than the occasional nagging pain. The pursuer thought that the back injury had effectively cleared up. He thought the accident had simply been a minor incident and I doubt if the prospect of making a claim even crossed his mind. However after his experience with his back he was more careful when he lifted patients.

The pursuer had no further trouble until the autumn of 1987 when he began to have severe pain in his back. The pain gradually got worse. On 21 October 1987 the pursuer again consulted his general practitioner about his back (he now having changed his general practitioner to a Dr Hay). Between the accident in September 1986 and the visit to the doctor on 21 October 1987 the pursuer had no occasion to consult a doctor about his back. Because of his back the pursuer was off work from 30 September 1987 until 25 October 1987 and his doctor certified that this absence was due to back strain. Following upon the said absence the pursuer's back failed to improve and he required to consult his doctor about the problem from time to time. He was given a course of physiotherapy. From February 1988 he was off work with his back for about two months. When the pursuer consulted his general practitioner on 27 June 1988 the latter noted that the pursuer had a two year history of back pain. Thus by that date at the latest the pursuer and his doctor must in my view have been relating the pursuer's continuing and more severe back pain to the commencement of the back pain at the time of the accident in 1986. By the beginning of 1989 the pursuer's back pain had become chronic. Because of his regular absences from work the defenders referred him to their occupational health schemes and he was seen there by a Dr Briggs. In February 1989 Dr Hay referred the pursuer to Mr Annan, a consultant orthopaedic surgeon at Bangour General hospital. Mr Annan saw the pursuer in about April of that year. He reported that the pursuer was suffering from a typical lumbar disc injury. Both Mr Annan and a Mr Harris, a neurosurgeon, gave evidence before me and I had no difficulty in accepting their unqualified view that the pursuer's subsequent back trouble was due to the injury to his back originally suffered in September 1986. From February 1989 until January 1990 the pursuer was certified as unfit for work and subsequently he has become unfit to work to a degree that has made it necessary for him to give up employment as a staff nurse. He still suffers considerably from his back and requires to use a stick.

By about the end of 1988 the pursuer was concerned

about the effect his illness was having on his employ-
A ment prospects. Accordingly at that time he saw his
shop steward, Staff Nurse Jean Watt. She gave him
advice about a possible claim for benefits and also
advised him to see Mr McLuckie, a more senior union
representative, concerning possible legal action. She
also advised the pursuer that there was a time limit for
making legal claims although details of this limit do
not seem to have been discussed. The pursuer had
difficulty in communicating with Mr McLuckie by
telephone or otherwise and no doubt this difficulty
B was aggravated by the fact that the pursuer was to a
degree bedridden and off work at the time. He wrote
to Mr McLuckie but got no reply. Eventually he went
to see a Mrs Pullin who was a senior official in his
union. He was not quite sure at what date he
approached Mrs Pullin. In any event Mrs Pullin put
him in touch with solicitors and in February 1990, for
the first time, a claim was intimated to the defenders.

The assessment of the evidence at the proof
presented me with no particular difficulty. The
C pursuer gave evidence and there was also evidence
from Mr Harris, Mr Annan and Dr Hay. No evidence
was led on behalf of the defenders. The pursuer was
rather vague about dates but otherwise I had no reason
to disbelieve his evidence on the matters he covered at
this proof.

In addressing me counsel for the pursuer contended
that the case was one where the relevant date for the
commencement of the limitation period ought to be
D determined in terms of s 17 (2) (b) of the Prescription
and Limitation (Scotland) Act 1973 as amended rather
than by s 17 (2) (a). Counsel contended that the injury
sustained in September 1986 did not seem sufficiently
serious at the time to justify contemplation of an
action for damages. It was only in October 1987 that
it would have been reasonably practicable for the
pursuer to have considered inquiring into the possibility of such an action. Thus it was only at the last
mentioned date that the pursuer was in a position to
E be aware that his injuries were sufficiently serious to
justify an action. If the said date was taken as the starting point of the limitation period then the action
which was raised in August 1990 was raised timeously. On the other hand if contrary to this submission
the date of the accident was the appropriate date for
the commencement of the limitation period, then it
would be equitable for the court to override the limitation in terms of s 19A (1) of the 1973 Act. If limitation
applied the pursuer would totally lose what was obvi-
F ously now a valuable claim. The defenders would
suffer no prejudice other than to lose their right to a
good defence. The accident was reported to the
defenders immediately it had occurred and was noted
in their records. They were aware of the development
of the pursuer's subsequent back trouble. Indeed at
the beginning of 1989 they referred the pursuer to
their own occupational health service for a report. The
pursuer had some excuse for his failure to raise his
action in time. He was let down by his union representative. I was referred to *Elliot v J & C Finney* and
Nicol v British Steel Corporation (General Steels) Ltd.

I was also referred to an unreported judgment of Lord
Milligan in *Pritchard v Tayside Health Board*, dated 23 G
March 1983. The test is whether the pursuer knew he
had suffered "a significant injury".

Counsel for the defenders contended that the consequences of the accident which were known to the
pursuer immediately after it had occurred were themselves sufficient to justify his raising an action. I was
referred to *Smith v National Coal Board* and *Mackie
v Currie*. The latter case was founded on strongly. It
was argued that the Lord Ordinary, Lord Kirkwood,
had in effect held that if injuries were not de minimis H
and would sound in damages then they were sufficiently serious to justify bringing an action of
damages. This, it was argued, was the correct
approach and applying it in this case there was no
doubt that the injuries sustained by the pursuer in
1986 would even at the time have justified an action
of damages. It was further submitted for the defenders
that the application of the limitation period in this
case should not be waived by the court as inequitable
in terms of s 19A (1) of the 1973 Act. The pursuer had I
known by June 1988 that his increasing back trouble
could be connected to his experience in September
1986 when his back trouble began. He had ample time
to raise an action before September 1989 and the
excuses he relied upon were in no way extraordinary
but were typical of the difficulties experienced by
many claimants in reparation actions.

There can be little doubt that viewing the matter
with the benefit of hindsight, the accident suffered by J
the pursuer in September 1986 caused a serious injury
which would have justified an action for damages
against the defenders (assuming that they had accepted
liability). Thus Mr Harris said that the accident
produced a significant injury, but that assessment was
based on consideration by him of the sequelae as they
emerged over the years. The first question therefore
must be what did the pursuer know or could he
reasonably have discovered about the seriousness of
his injuries in September 1986? He certainly had no K
reason to suspect then that his injuries were anything
like as serious as they have ultimately proved to be. He
was aware that he had suffered a severe pain at the
time of injury and that some pain had continued until
he saw his doctor later that day. He knew that his
general practitioner had diagnosed a muscular sprain
and that he had required to take two days or so off
work. He also had the benefit of two weeks' leave but
this so far as he can remember was leave he had agreed
to take earlier by way of an exchange arrangement L
with another nurse. There was certainly no evidence
to show that the pursuer would have required to stay
off work for more than two or three days had it been
necessary to go back to work immediately and there
was no evidence that he lost wages over the period
when he was off work. When he returned to work he
suffered twinges of pain but did not claim that this had
disturbed him in any way. The fact is that within a
short period after the accident the pursuer does not
seem to have given the matter any thought. Thus in
terms of the pursuer's actual state of knowledge his

accident had caused him what can only be described
as a minor injury. Nor is there any indication in the
evidence that it would have been reasonably practicable for the pursuer at the time being considered to
discover that his injuries were in fact more severe. The
doctor had not predicted that his injuries might give
rise to any significant trouble. The injuries seemed to
clear up quickly as would any minor sprain. The pursuer's general practitioner did not advise him to seek
further advice and in the circumstances he would have
lacked any effective opportunity or motivation for
doing so.

Thus given the knowledge reasonably available to
the pursuer in September 1986, could it be said that
the limited facts about his injuries which he was aware
of produced knowledge of injuries which in themselves were sufficiently serious to justify his bringing
an action of damages (allowing of course for the statutory assumptions)? In deciding this question I was
asked to pay particular regard to the decision in
Mackie v Currie. I am not at all sure that the injuries
in *Mackie* were comparable to those in the present
case. In *Mackie* the pursuer was knocked down by a
motor car and then removed to hospital. Notwithstanding the fact that it transpired that the pursuer in
Mackie was not seriously injured, the experience of
being knocked down by a motor car may be considerably more traumatic than that of straining one's back
while lifting. Nor am I certain that the Lord Ordinary
was intending to suggest that the facts that an injury
was not de minimis and could sound in damages, were
necessarily equivalent to the injuries being sufficiently
serious to justify an action. In my view the fact that
injuries cannot be described as minimal or trivial, does
not necessarily meet the test that they are sufficiently
serious to justify an action. For almost any injury
which has caused a degree of shock or pain, it would
be possible to establish entitlement to some compensation albeit the amount may be very small. If the statute
wanted to provide that there must be awareness of an
injury other than trivial, it would have been possible
to frame the relevant test taking account of that fact.
However the specific test laid down is that the
claimant must be aware of an injury sufficiently
serious to justify his bringing an action. The word
"his" in the statute may be significant since it may
relate to the personal situation of the claimant (in con-
tradistinction to a phrase such as "the bringing of an
action"). However I need not decide that point
because I did not understand it to be suggested that
there was evidence of any circumstances particularly
distinctive to the pursuer which may have coloured his
view about bringing an action. The proper question in
this case seems to me to be whether a reasonable
claimant would in all the circumstances consider that
the facts about the injury which were known (or could
have been ascertained) rendered it worthwhile to raise
an action (always of course assuming liability was not
in dispute). I am certainly prepared to hold that in
September 1986 the pursuer did not know that his
injuries, as he perceived them then to be, were sufficiently serious to justify his raising an action. Indeed

I doubt if the matter even crossed his mind. However
even if the pursuer had taken all practicable steps to
ascertain his legal position, I doubt if he, or for that
matter any other reasonable claimant, would have considered it worthwhile to litigate. Injuries such as the
pursuer knew he had suffered in September 1986
would scarcely have generated damages amounting to
more than say £200 if that. The appropriate action for
such a claim would have been a small claims action in
the sheriff court. Given the limitation in expenses
awards in such an action the pursuer could have
incurred a degree of irrecoverable expense had he
chosen to litigate. Moreover litigation will involve a
certain expenditure of time, will generate a degree of
worry, and may involve loss of wages. Thus in my
view even with the fullest information about his
rights, the pursuer would in all probability have concluded that an action for damages was not worthwhile
and it could not be said that this would have been
other than a sensible decision. Accordingly he was not
at the relevant time aware of any injuries serious
enough to justify his raising an action of damages. The
object of s 17 is to prevent stale claims for damages for
personal injuries by appointing a limitation period.
However it is appropriate that this period should only
begin to run when the claimant first knew, or ought
to have known, that the essential prerequisites of an
action were all present. If all he knows is that he has
suffered a minor injury which would not give rise to
sufficient prospect of damages to make the prosecution of an action worthwhile, then he cannot be
expected to put in motion at that time any preparations, negotiations or inquiries such as may be
required if the action is to be raised within three years.
The position became quite different in October 1987.
At that stage it would have been quite practicable for
the pursuer to have discovered that his injuries were
producing recurring symptoms affecting his working
capacity and that there was at least a risk, even at that
stage, that these symptoms would continue. In
October 1987 the pursuer had a presentable claim for
damages and the prerequisites for such an action were
all present. Accordingly in terms of s 17 (2) (b) a three
year limitation period would have begun to run in
October 1987, but in that situation the present action
was in fact raised before the expiry of the triennium.

It was contended on behalf of the pursuer that even
if the three year limitation period had begun to run at
the date of the accident, I ought to relieve the pursuer
of the consequences of the limitation in terms of s 19A
(1) of the 1973 Act. In particular it was argued that it
would be inequitable in the circumstances of this case
to allow the limitation to operate. During the three
year limitation period the pursuer's claim on any view
would have emerged as a much more serious matter
than could originally have been envisaged by him. He
has had a long standing chronic back condition and his
work prospects have been seriously affected. The
pursuer thus now has a substantial claim which is very
important to him and if the limitation operates this
will be lost. It was further contended that the
defenders would not in fact suffer any prejudice were

the claim now to proceed. The accident was reported to them immediately after it had occurred and they noted it in their records. They knew that the pursuer had later developed a serious back problem and indeed they themselves referred him to their occupational health unit with the purpose of obtaining a report from that unit.

In my view the mere fact that a pursuer will suffer serious loss by the operation of the limitation period, coupled with the fact that the defenders cannot be shown to be prejudiced were an action to proceed, would not in itself be a situation justifying the intervention by the court in terms of s 19A (1). The operation of a prescribed limitation period in any case is likely to cause a risk of loss to a pursuer and it would be consistent with the purposes of the legislation that defenders should generally receive protection against stale claims even in situations where it cannot be shown that they have suffered specific prejudice. However in the present case there are other special features which, in my view, would justify offering the pursuer relief against the limitation period were that necessary. There seems little doubt that if it could be said that at the time of the accident the pursuer's injuries were sufficiently serious to justify raising an action, then they were only marginally thus serious. The pursuer at the beginning of the triennium would have had little idea of the significance of his claim. It was only as his condition developed after October 1987 that he would have begun to realise that he had sustained a serious injury. Certainly by June 1988 he had every opportunity to discover that his re-emergent back trouble was related to his accident in 1986. However even at that stage he may not have realised how difficult it was going to be to treat his problem effectively. By the end of 1988 he was certainly worried about his employment position and indeed took steps to secure advice from his union. He was not particularly effective at doing this but there may be a degree of excuse in that from about February 1989 until the beginning of 1990 he was unfit for work and indeed seems to have been at least partly bedridden. The balance of equities in this case is not altogether an easy one since there is some force in the contention for the defenders that the pursuer knew by June 1988 that his accident had caused him a serious back problem, that there was ample time between this knowledge and September 1989 to prepare and raise an action and that the difficulties relied upon by the pursuer were such as would confront most claimants suffering from a serious injury. Nevertheless, given the serious nature of the pursuer's claim, the fact that the defenders do not appear to have been prejudiced by delay, coupled with the facts that the pursuer only came to appreciate the gravity of his position relatively well into the triennium and that thereafter he was handicapped to a degree by his ill health and the difficulty he accordingly experienced in communicating with his trade union advisers, then had it been necessary to consider the application of s 19A (1) I should have decided that the equities narrowly favoured allowing the pursuer to proceed with his action.

In the whole circumstances the defenders' first plea in law falls to be repelled.

Counsel for Pursuers, Dorrian; Solicitors, Strathern & Blair, WS — Counsel for Defenders, L A Keane; Solicitor, R F Macdonald.

R D S

Wilson v Pilgrim Systems plc

OUTER HOUSE

LORD CAMERON OF LOCHBROOM

13 NOVEMBER 1992

Expenses — Award — Competency — Decree in favour of pursuer pronounced following upon minutes of tender and acceptance — Expenses after date of tender thereafter sought by defenders.

Defenders, by minute, tendered a sum to a pursuer, together with the taxed expenses of process to date of the tender, in full of the conclusions of a summons. A minute of acceptance was lodged about six months later and an unopposed motion for decree in terms of the minute and acceptance was then granted. Thereafter the defenders enrolled for an award of expenses from the date of the tender. The pursuer argued that the motion was incompetent, the interlocutor following on the tender and acceptance having exhausted the merits of the case and having dealt also with expenses. The defenders argued that the interlocutor was not final as it had not dealt with expenses subsequent to the minute of tender.

Held, that the decree following on the minutes of tender and acceptance, including an award of expenses in favour of the pursuer, having disposed of the whole subject matter of the action, the court had no power to make any further award of expenses (p 1254D-F); and motion *refused*.

Henderson v Peeblesshire County Council, 1972 SLT (Notes) 35, *followed*.

Action of damages

Kenneth Wilson raised an action of damages against Pilgrim Systems plc. The defenders lodged a minute of tender which was subsequently accepted. After decree in terms of the tender and acceptance had been pronounced, the defenders enrolled a motion seeking an award of expenses from the date of the tender.

The motion came before the Lord Ordinary (Lord Cameron of Lochbroom).

Cases referred to

Baird v Barton (1882) 9 R 970.
Caledonian Railway Co v Corporation of Glasgow (1900) 8 SLT 19; (1900) 2 F 871.
Henderson v Peeblesshire County Council, 1972 SLT (Notes) 35.
Ranken v Kirkwood (1855) 18 D 31.
UCB Bank plc v Dundas & Wilson, CS, 1991 SLT 90.

Textbooks referred to

A Maclaren, *Expenses*, p 37.
Thomson and Middleton, *Court of Session Practice*,
p 304.

On 13 November 1992 the Lord Ordinary *refused*
the defenders' motion.

LORD CAMERON OF LOCHBROOM.—The
defenders have moved for the expenses of the action
since the date of a minute of tender dated 13 Sep-
B tember 1991. A minute of acceptance was lodged by
the pursuer on 30 March 1992. Thereafter, on 6 April
1992, a motion was enrolled on the pursuer's behalf to
grant decree in terms of the minutes of tender and
acceptance. The minute of tender bore to tender to the
pursuer the sum of £20,000 sterling, together with the
taxed expenses of process to date of the tender in full
of the conclusions of the summons. This motion had
previously been intimated to the defenders' agents. No
opposition was marked and the motion was accord-
C ingly unopposed. On 8 April 1992 the vacation judge
pronounced the following interlocutor: "The
Vacation Judge in terms of the minutes of tender and
acceptance, nos 9 and 12 of process, decerns against
the defenders for payment to the pursuers of the sum
of twenty thousand pounds sterling in full of the conclusions of the summons; finds the defenders liable to
the pursuer in the expenses of the action to the date
of tender; remits the account thereof when lodged to
the Auditor of Court for taxation."

D   A further interlocutor decerning against the
defenders for payment to the pursuer of expenses as
the same shall be taxed by the auditor of court, was
pronounced on the same date. It remains only to note
that the summons in the action called on 12 June
1991. The record was closed on 30 October 1991.
Thereafter the cause was appointed to the procedure
roll of consent.

On 27 February 1992 the diet of procedure roll was
E discharged and the defenders allowed to lodge a
minute of amendment. The defenders were found
liable to the pursuer in the expenses occasioned by the
discharge. At the same time the court decerned against
the defenders for payment to the pursuer of the
expenses occasioned by the discharge as the same
should be taxed by the auditor of court. Counsel for
the defenders properly accepted that since the interlocutor decerning against the defenders for the
payment of these expenses is final, the decree which
it contains is now not capable of alteration (*UCB Bank
F plc v Dundas & Wilson, CS*). He therefore accepted
that the motion on the defenders' behalf, insofar as its
terms seek to include those expenses already decerned
for against the defenders, could not be granted in those
terms. Counsel for the pursuer accepted that, if the
motion was competent, she could not resist it if it was
restricted to exclude such expenses. She only sought
that any interlocutor granting expenses be pronounced
against the pursuer as an assisted person for the period
from the date of the tender up to 20 February 1992
when his legal aid certificate was terminated.

The principal issue debated before me related to the
competency of the present motion. Counsel for the G
pursuer, in submitting that the motion was incompetent, founded upon the case of *Henderson v Peeblesshire County Council*. The circumstances in that case
were essentially similar to the present, though it
appears that it was explained to the court in *Henderson*
that the failure to mark the pursuer's motion upon
which the interlocutor was pronounced as opposed
and to obtain an agreed finding for expenses for the
defenders for the period subsequent to the date of the
minute of tender, had been due to an oversight. In that H
case Lord Robertson said this: "It was argued on
behalf of the defenders that, although a final interlocutor on the merits could not be reviewed after the
reclaiming days had expired, the court could re-open
the case on the question of expenses if all the expenses
had not been dealt with and if the failure to deal with
the expenses had been due to a mistake. (*Ranken v
Kirkwood* (1855) 18 D 31.) The whole subject matter
of the cause had not been dealt with because the whole
expenses had not been dealt with. (*Caledonian Railway
v Corporation of Glasgow* (1900) 2 F 871, 8 SLT 19.) I

"In my opinion these arguments are unsound. The
general rule is that expenses must be expressly
awarded or reserved. If the interlocutor exhausting the
merits is silent on expenses, the court has no power
thereafter to award them. An interlocutor disposing of
the merits but silent as to expenses exhausts the cause
(see Thomson and Middleton, *Court of Session
Practice*, p 304). In the present case the final interlocutor of 9th February 1971 exhausted the merits and J
dealt with expenses up to a certain date. No reservation of expenses was made. In my view the court
cannot re-open the matter a year later and make a
further finding of expenses for a different period. The
defenders had ample opportunity to make the necessary motion at the proper time and failed to do so. It
may be that their failure to do so was due to a mistake
induced perhaps by reliance upon communings
between the respective solicitors. But such a mistake
could only be rectified de recenti (see *Ranken v Kirkwood*, cit supra). This motion comes too late. I shall K
refuse the motion."

Counsel also referred me to Maclaren on *Expenses*,
p 37, where it is stated: "Expenses must be expressly
awarded, and if the interlocutor exhausting the merits
is silent on the subject, the Court has no power thereafter to make an award. . . . If the failure to make an
award is a mere omission, the interlocutor will
probably be amended if the case is enrolled immediately for that purpose." L

There was no dispute that as a consequence of the
minutes of tender and acceptance and the subsequent
motion to grant decree on their terms, the merits of
the action were exhausted. This is clear from the fact
that the minute of tender bears to be in full of the conclusions of the action. These conclusions include a
conclusion for the expenses of the action. Counsel for
the defenders submitted that the case of *Henderson v
Peeblesshire County Council* was wrongly decided. He
argued that the interlocutor was not final since on the

A face of it, it did not deal with the expenses subsequent to the minute of tender. That being so, it had not dealt with the whole expenses of the cause and thus the whole subject matter of the action. In support of this proposition he referred to the case of *Caledonian Railway v Glasgow Corporation* and to *Baird v Barton*. In the latter action it was held that an interlocutor finding expenses due, pronounced after an interlocutor disposing of the cause otherwise and reserving the question of expenses, was an interlocutor disposing in part of the subject matter of the cause and
B might be reclaimed against at any time within 21 days from its date. Under reference to the Court of Session Act 1868, and in particular the 53rd section of that Act, which reflects the terminology of Rule of Court 264A (1), Lord President Inglis said this: "Now, while that is a positive enactment that the absence of a decree for expenses shall not be held to prevent the whole subject matter of the cause from being disposed of, it also, by very clear implication, provides that until the question of expenses has been disposed of, —
C that is, until one or other of the parties has been found entitled to expenses, or expenses have been found due to neither party, — there has been no final judgment, and the whole subject-matter of the cause, in the language of the Act of 1868, has not been disposed of."

Counsel also referred me to the opinion of Lord Adam in *Caledonian Railway Co* where in a reference to the case of *Baird v Barton*, Lord Adam said that he had since that case been of opinion, "that it was settled that unless the interlocutor dealt with the question of
D expenses, either by awarding or refusing them, the whole subject of the cause, in the sense of the Act of 1868, was not disposed of".

In the present case, it cannot be said that the question of expenses was not dealt with in the interlocutor pronounced on 8 April 1992. It bore to be an interlocutor pronounced in response to the minutes of tender and acceptance. The minute of tender expressly contained an offer of expenses. The offer of the sum
E tendered and expenses was intended to be in full of the conclusions of the summons. In these circumstances I have no hesitation in reaching the view that the interlocutor pronounced on that date was a final interlocutor which disposed of the whole subject matter of the action. It would have been open to the defenders if they thought fit to have opposed the motion and to have sought expenses on their own account from the date of the tender. They did not do so. The interlocutor was silent on that matter. It is now too late to
F seek to raise the matter of expenses, since the court has now no power to make any further award of expenses.

I would add that if counsel for the defenders were correct, it would mean that unless and until the defenders either sought such an award or formally waived their right to do so, the interlocutor pronounced on 8 April 1992 could never be said to be final. Counsel for the defenders, when pressed on this matter, could only reply that any such motion would require to be enrolled within a reasonable time. I can find no authority for such a view. This factor merely

confirms me in the opinion I have already expressed that an attempt at this time to introduce again the G matter of an award of expenses comes too late. I therefore agree with the opinion expressed by Lord Robertson in the case of *Henderson v Peeblesshire County Council*. I will accordingly refuse the motion.

Counsel for Pursuer, L A Keane; Solicitors, Bonar Mackenzie, WS — Counsel for Defenders, Hanretty; Solicitors, Gillam Mackie, SSC (for Clark & Wallace, Advocates, Aberdeen). H

M B

Marr v Heywood

HIGH COURT OF JUSTICIARY I
THE LORD JUSTICE CLERK (ROSS),
LORDS MURRAY AND MAYFIELD
19 JANUARY 1993

Justiciary — Statutory offence — Being found on premises in circumstances inferring intent to commit theft — Person seen climbing complainer's garden fence and accused afterwards found in neighbouring garden shed — Whether accused "found" on complainer's premises — J
Civic Government (Scotland) Act 1982 (c 45), s 57 (1).

The Civic Government (Scotland) Act 1982, s 57 (1), provides that any person who, without lawful authority to be there, "is found in or on a building or other premises", in circumstances in which it might reasonably be inferred that he intended to commit theft, shall be guilty of an offence.

An accused person was charged with contravention of s 57 (1). There was evidence that the complainer, alerted by the back door alarm of his house, had gone K out into his back garden and had seen a figure climbing over the fence. The complainer had followed the figure and found the accused in a neighbour's garden. In response to a subsequent caution and charge, the accused had replied "I didn't get into the house, you can't do me with this." The accused was convicted and appealed, arguing that since the complainer had not identified him on the premises, there was no direct evidence that he had been found there and the sheriff had not been entitled to convict. L

Held, that there was direct evidence from an eyewitness of the presence on the premises of a person who had turned out to be the accused, and since that evidence was corroborated by the accused's reply when cautioned and charged, the sheriff had been entitled to hold that the accused had been "found" on the premises (p 1256E-G); and appeal *refused*.

Maclean v Paterson, 1968 SLT 374, *distinguished*.

Summary complaint

A Gordon John Marr was charged at the instance of Barry Heywood, procurator fiscal, Dundee, on a summary complaint which contained the following charge, inter alia: "(1) on 19 April 1992, without lawful authority to be there, you were found in premises, namely in the garden of the house at 56 St Leonards Road, Dundee, so that from all the circumstances it might reasonably be inferred that you intended to commit theft there: contrary to the Civic Government (Scotland) Act 1982, s 57 (1)". The
B accused pled not guilty and proceeded to trial.

After the Crown case was closed, the defence made a submission of no case to answer in terms of s 345A of the Criminal Procedure (Scotland) Act 1975. The sheriff (G L Cox) repelled the submission and, no defence evidence having been led, convicted the accused.

The accused appealed by way of stated case to the High Court against the decision of the sheriff.

C
Findings in fact

The sheriff found the following facts admitted or proved:

(1) The rear door of the premises of 56 St Leonard Road, Dundee, had an alarm device fixed to it due to attempts to break into the premises. (2) On the evening of 19 April the alarm operated. (3) The householder, Mr Bayne, immediately went to the back door and opened it. (4) The outside light showed a
D figure some 10 yds from the back door climbing over the rear garden fence. (5) Mr Bayne followed the figure, whom he could not identify at that stage. (6) On climbing the fence, Mr Bayne heard noises coming from the vicinity of his neighbour's garden shed some 10 yds from the fence. (7) The appellant was there. (8) Mr Bayne asked the appellant what he was doing there. The appellant replied he had been chased there by a gang. (9) No other sounds or indicators suggested the presence of any other person in either the garden
E of 56 St Leonard Road, Dundee, or in the neighbouring ground, or in the immediate vicinity. (10) When cautioned by police officers the appellant replied "I didn't get into the house, you can't do me with this." (11) The appellant could have been at the back door of the house at 56 St Leonard Road, and in the garden of the said house. He had no authority to be there. (12) The circumstances were such that it could be inferred that he intended to commit theft there.

F ## Statutory provisions

The Civic Government (Scotland) Act 1982 provides:

"57.—(1) Any person who, without lawful authority to be there, is found in or on a building or other premises . . . so that, in all the circumstances, it may reasonably be inferred that he intended to commit theft there shall be guilty of an offence".

Case referred to

Maclean v Paterson, 1968 SLT 374; 1968 JC 67.

Appeal

The sheriff posed the following questions for the G opinion of the High Court:

(1) Was I entitled to reject the submission in terms of s 345A of the Criminal Procedure (Scotland) Act 1975?

(2) Was I entitled to find that the appellant was in the garden of the premises at 56 St Leonard Road, Dundee?

(3) Was I entitled to hold that the appellant was in the premises with the intention of committing theft? H

(4) Was I entitled to convict the appellant?

The appeal was heard before the High Court on 19 January 1993.

Eo die the court *answered* questions 2 and 4 in the *affirmative* and *refused* the appeal.

The following opinion of the court was delivered by I
the Lord Justice Clerk (Ross):

OPINION OF THE COURT.—The appellant is Gordon John Marr who went to trial in the sheriff court at Dundee on a complaint containing two charges. The first charge libelled a contravention of s 57 (1) of the Civic Government (Scotland) Act 1982 and the second charge was a consequential charge of contravening s 3 (1) (b) of the Bail etc (Scotland) Act 1980. He was found guilty of these charges and he has now appealed against conviction by means of a stated J case. In the note, the sheriff explains that at the conclusion of the Crown case a submission of no case to answer was made. The sheriff repelled that submission and no evidence was led on behalf of the appellant.

In presenting the appeal today, counsel for the appellant has drawn attention to the findings in fact which in the circumstances must be based upon the evidence led by the Crown. The premises referred to in the first charge are the garden at the house at 56 St K Leonards Road, Dundee. The findings show that the rear door of the premises at that address had an alarm device fixed to it due to previous attempts to break in. On the evening of the date in question the alarm operated and the householder Mr Bayne immediately went to the back door and opened it. The outside light showed a figure some 10 yds from the back door climbing over the rear garden fence. Mr Bayne followed the figure which he could not identify at that stage. On climbing the fence Mr Bayne heard noises L coming from the vicinity of his neighbour's garden shed some 10 yds from the fence and when he went there he discovered the appellant there. The further finding of significance is to the effect that the police were called and cautioned the appellant who replied "I didn't get into the house, you can't do me with this."

In seeking to persuade the court to allow this appeal, counsel confined his submissions to the issue which is raised in question 2 in the case. Question 2 is in these terms: "Was I entitled to find that the appellant was

A in the garden of the premises at 56 St Leonard Road, Dundee?" He referred to the case of *Maclean v Paterson*. In that case a man had been convicted of having been found in a goods yard in contravention of s 7 of the Prevention of Crimes Act 1871. That statute contained similar language to s 57 (1) in that reference was made to the person accused being found in any premises. There was ample circumstantial evidence that he had been in the yard but no witness had actually seen or heard him there and the court held that in the absence of such direct evidence, he had not been B "found" in the yard. In the course of his opinion in that case the Lord Justice Clerk said: "In my opinion, and I do not propose to deal with borderline cases, the real meaning of the phrase is found physically on the premises at the relevant moment. That would include, for example, being seen there by a witness or being discovered there by somebody who was able to recognise him by his voice. It would not include being proved by circumstantial evidence to *have been* there — though I do not exclude the possibility of a single C contemporaneous witness who saw the accused on the premises being corroborated by circumstantial evidence" (1968 SLT at p 376).

Counsel for the appellant maintained that the present case was similar to *Maclean v Paterson*, in that it depended upon circumstantial evidence, and he submitted that the witness, Mr Bayne, had not identified the appellant on the premises. The sheriff in his note had explained that he distinguished the case of *Maclean v Paterson* but counsel for the appellant main- D tained that he gave no reasons for doing so and that he had not been entitled to distinguish that case. The advocate depute, on the other hand, maintained that *Maclean v Paterson* could properly be distinguished in the present case. He submitted that in the present case, unlike *Maclean v Paterson*, there had been direct evidence of the presence on the premises of a person who turned out to be the appellant, and in these circumstances he maintained that this was a case where there was direct evidence from an eyewitness and E there was undoubtedly adequate corroboration of his evidence from the reply which the appellant had given to the police.

In our opinion this submission of the Crown is correct. This case is different to the case of *Maclean v Paterson* in that there was a witness, namely Mr Bayne, who spoke to having seen on the premises a person who turned out to be the appellant, and who Mr Bayne was able to say was the appellant when F regard was had to what he discovered when he followed this person into the neighbour's garden. That being so, there was in this case direct evidence which was corroborated by the reply which had been given to the police. We also agree with the advocate depute that what is stated in the findings regarding the alarm device is also of significance because there is a finding that the alarm had operated and that Mr Bayne immediately went to the door. When he went to the door he saw a person who was some 10 yds from the door climbing over the rear garden fence. Accordingly, the evidence clearly was that Mr Bayne saw a

G person who was in the premises defined in charge 1 of the complaint. For these reasons we are satisfied that the sheriff was entitled to distinguish *Maclean v Paterson* and that he was entitled to hold that the appellant was shown to have been found in the garden of the house at 56 St Leonards Road, Dundee, at the material time. We shall accordingly answer question 2 in the affirmative and we shall answer question 4 in the affirmative and it follows that the appeal is refused.

Counsel for Appellant, Mackenzie; Solicitors, H *Campbell Smith & Co, WS (for John Macdonald, Dundee) — Counsel for Respondent, MacAulay, QC, A D; Solicitor, J D Lowe, Crown Agent.*

S J B

Gall v Stirling District Council

I

OUTER HOUSE
LORD CULLEN
22 DECEMBER 1992

Employment — Unfair dismissal — Transfer of undertaking — Whether transfer of undertaking prevented termination of employment — Competency of petition for J *interdict of termination of employment and suspension of notices of dismissal — Employment Protection (Consolidation) Act 1978 (c 44), ss 54, 67 and 129 — Transfer of Undertakings (Protection of Employment) Regulations 1981 (SI 1981/1794) — Treaty of Rome, art 189 (3) — Council Directive (EEC) No 77/187.*

Article 4 (1) of the Council Directive 77/187/EEC provides that the transfer of an undertaking, business or part of a business is not to constitute grounds for K dismissal. Regulation 8 (1) of the Transfer of Undertakings (Protection of Employment) Regulations 1981 provides that a person dismissed is to be treated as unfairly dismissed if the transfer was the reason for the dismissal.

A district council invited tenders for grounds maintenance work which until then had been carried out by a number of the council's employees. The council awarded the contract for the work to a tendering L company. The contract was to come into operation on 1 January 1993. In October 1992 the council notified the Department of Employment that 11 of their employees were to be made redundant due to "loss of contract under compulsory competitive tendering legislation". On the same date the council wrote to the employees advising them that as the "in house" bid for the work had been unsuccessful their employment would be terminated with effect from 31 December 1992. The employees presented a petition seeking interdict against termination of their contracts of employment and suspension of the notices of dismissal. They argued that the award of the contract to the company constituted the transfer of an undertaking for the purposes of the Transfer of Undertakings (Protection of Employment) Regulations 1981, enacted to give effect to the Community Directive 77/187/EEC; and that since under the regulations such a transfer could not in itself constitute a ground for dismissal the termination of their employment and the notices of such termination were wrongful. The council argued that the petition was incompetent since, first, it sought interdict against a completed act; secondly, it was in substance directed to enforcing a positive obligation, especially where the obligation was one of employment; and, thirdly, the employees' sole remedy in terms of the legislation was to make a complaint to an industrial tribunal.

Held, that since reg 8 (1) of the 1981 Regulations extended the statutory provisions against unfair dismissal to dismissals based upon a relevant transfer, the employers had failed to establish a prima facie entitlement to invoke the remedies of interdict and suspension even where they had presented their petition for these remedies prior to the date at which the dismissals took effect, the employers already having done all that they needed to do to bring the employees' employment to an end and the issue raising the same matters as could be the subject of a complaint to an industrial tribunal (p 1260A-C); and motion for interim interdict and interim suspension *refused.*

Opinion, that the 1981 Regulations gave full effect to art 4 (1) of the Council Directive 77/187/EEC (p 1260D-E).

Dictum of Lord Templeman in *Litster v Forth Dry Dock & Engineering Co Ltd,* 1989 SLT 540 at p 543L, *followed.*

Petition for suspension and interdict

Kenneth Gall and seven of his fellow employees presented a petition seeking suspension and interdict and interim suspension and interdict, calling as respondents (first) Stirling District Council, their employers, and (second) Brophy plc. The petitioners sought interdict of the respondents from terminating their contracts by way of dismissal and suspension of the notices of dismissal.

The case came before the Lord Ordinary (Cullen) on the motion roll on the petitioners' motion for interim interdict and interim suspension.

Statutory provisions

The Treaty of Rome provides:

"189.—. . . (3) A Directive shall be binding, as to the result to be achieved, upon each Member State to which it is addressed, but shall leave to the national authorities the form and methods."

European Council Directive (77/187/EEC) provides:

"*Article 4*

"1. The transfer of an undertaking, business or part of a business shall not in itself constitute grounds for dismissal by the transferor or the transferee. This provision shall not stand in the way of dismissals that may take place for economic, technical or organizational reasons entailing changes in the workforce.

"Member States may provide that the first subparagraph shall not apply to certain specific categories of employees who are not covered by the laws or practice of the Member States in respect of protection against dismissal.

"2. If the contract of employment or the employment relationship is terminated because the transfer within the meaning of Article 1 (1) involves a substantial change in working conditions to the detriment of the employee, the employer shall be regarded as having been responsible for termination of the contract of employment or of the employment relationship."

The Employment Protection (Consolidation) Act 1978 provides:

"[Pt V] 54.—(1) In every employment to which this section applies every employee shall have the right not to be unfairly dismissed by his employer.

"(2) This section applies to every employment except in so far as its application is excluded by or under any provision of this Part or by section 141 to 149. . . .

"67.—(1) A complaint may be presented to an industrial tribunal against an employer by any person (in this Part referred to as the complainant) that he was unfairly dismissed by the employer. . . .

"129. The remedy of an employee for infringement of any of the rights conferred on him by sections 8 and 53 and Parts II, III, V and VII shall, if provision is made for a complaint or for the reference of a question to an industrial tribunal, be by way of such complaint or reference and not otherwise."

The Transfer of Undertakings (Protection of Employment) Regulations 1981 provide:

"3.—(1) Subject to the provisions of these Regulations, these Regulations apply to a transfer from one person to another of an undertaking situated immediately before the transfer in the United Kingdom or a part of one which is so situated.

"(2) Subject as aforesaid, these Regulations so apply whether the transfer is effected by sale or by some other disposition or by operation of law. . . .

"5.—(1) A relevant transfer shall not operate so as to terminate the contract of employment of any person employed by the transferor in the undertaking or part transferred but any such contract which would otherwise have been terminated by the transfer shall have effect after the transfer as if originally made between the person so employed and the transferee. . . .

"8.—(1) Where either before or after a relevant transfer, any employee of the transferor or transferee is dismissed, that employee shall be treated for the purposes of Part V of the 1978 Act and Articles 20 to 41 of the 1976 Order (unfair dismissal) as unfairly dis-

A missed if the transfer or a reason connected with it is the reason or principal reason for his dismissal."

Cases referred to

Foreningen af Arbejdsledere i Danmark v Daddy's Dance Halls A/S (105/84) [1988] IRLR 315.
Foster v British Gas plc (C-188/89) [1991] 2 AC 306; [1991] 2 WLR 1075; [1991] 2 All ER 705.
Fratelli Costanzo SpA v Comune di Milano (103/88) [1990] 3 CMLR 239.
Grosvenor Developments (Scotland) plc v Argyll Stores Ltd, 1987 SLT 738.

B
Keeney v Strathclyde Regional Council, 1986 SLT 490.
Kincardine and Deeside District Council v Forestry Commission, 1992 SLT 1180.
Litster v Forth Dry Dock & Engineering Co Ltd, 1989 SLT 540 (HL); [1990] 1 AC 546; [1989] 2 WLR 634; [1989] 1 All ER 1134.
McMillan v Free Church (1861) 23 D 1314.
Marleasing SA v La Comercial Internacional de Alimentacion SA [1990] ECR 4135.

C
Murray v Dumbarton County Council, 1935 SLT 239.
R v Secretary of State for Transport, ex p Factortame Ltd (No 2) (C-213/89) [1991] 1 AC 603; [1990] 3 WLR 818; [1991] 1 All ER 70.
Stichting v Bartol (C-29/91) [1992] IRLR 366.

On 22 December 1992 the Lord Ordinary *refused* the petitioners' motion.

D **LORD CULLEN.**—The eight petitioners commenced employment with the first respondents as grounds maintenance workers in their community services department some years before 1992. Between July and August 1992 the first respondents invited tenders for grounds maintenance work which until then had been done by the petitioners in the course of their employment. In due course the first respondents awarded to the second respondents the contract for the work which was to endure for a period of four years from 1 January 1993. On or about 8 October E 1992 the first respondents' head of personnel services notified the Department of Employment that 11 employees of the first respondents were to be made redundant due to "loss of contract under compulsory competitive tendering legislation". By letters to the petitioners on the same date she stated: "As you are probably aware the District Council submitted a tender for the Phase 3 Grounds Maintenance Contract. The In-House bid was unsuccessful and as a result of that I have no option but to dismiss you from F your post in the Community Services Department of Stirling District Council on the grounds of redundancy. Your date of termination will be 31 December 1992 and I am issuing you with twelve weeks notice of your termination. In due course you will receive estimates of your benefits." The petitioners aver that the award of the contract by the first respondents to the second respondents constituted the transfer of an undertaking for the purposes of the Transfer of Undertakings (Protection of Employment) Regulations 1981; and that since such a transfer could not in itself constitute a ground for dismissal the termination

of the petitioners' employment and the notices of such termination were wrongful. They seek (1) interdict of G the first and second respondents or their agents or anyone acting on their behalf from terminating the petitioners' contracts of employment on 31 December 1992 by way of dismissal insofar as the reason for dismissal is the transfer of an undertaking; and (2) suspension of the said notices dated 8 October 1992.

In the vacation court on 22 December 1992 counsel for the petitioners moved me to grant interim interdict and interim suspension in terms of the prayer of the petition. This motion was opposed by counsel for the H first respondents. The second respondents were not represented.

Counsel for the petitioners founded on reg 3 of the 1981 Regulations; and in particular the provisions in reg 3 (1) that the regulations apply to "a transfer from one person to another of an undertaking situated immediately before the transfer in the United Kingdom or a part of one which is so situated"; and in reg 3 (2) that the regulations so applied "whether the transfer is effected by sale or by some other dis- I position or by operation of law". Regulation 5 (1) provides: "A relevant transfer" — which means a transfer to which the regulations apply — "shall not operate so as to terminate the contract of employment of any person employed by the transferor in the undertaking or part transferred but any such contract which would otherwise have been terminated by the transfer shall have effect after the transfer as if originally made between the person so employed and the transferee". Counsel also referred me to the terms of art 4 (1) of J the Council Directive 77/187/EEC which the regulations were intended to implement. It states: "The transfer of an undertaking, business or part of a business shall not in itself constitute grounds for dismissal by the transferor or the transferee. This provision shall not stand in the way of dismissals that may take place for economic, technical or organizational reasons entailing changes in the workforce."

Counsel founded upon the decision of the European Court of Justice in *Stichting v Bartol* in which it was K held that there was a "legal transfer" for the purposes of art 1 (1) of the directive where a public body decided to terminate a subsidy paid to one legal person, as a result of which the activities of that person were terminated; and to transfer it to another legal person with similar aims. So here the first respondents had decided to terminate the performance of grounds maintenance work by the petitioners and to transfer that work to the second respondents. Reference was also made to an earlier decision of the court in L *Foreningen af Arbejdsledere v Daddy's Dance Hall* in which it was held that art 1 (1) applied to a situation where, after the termination of a non-transferable lease, the owner of the undertaking leased to a new lessee who continued to run the business without any interruption with the same staff who had previously been dismissed upon the expiry of the initial lease.

Counsel pointed out that it had also been held by the court in *Fratelli Costanzo SpA v Comune di Milano* that where the provisions of a directive appeared, as

far as their subject matter was concerned, to be unconditional and sufficiently precise these provisions might
be relied upon by an individual against the state where
that state had failed to implement that directive in
national law by the end of a period prescribed or
where it had failed to implement the directive
correctly. Moreover such provisions were binding
upon all the authorities of member states, including
municipalities (cf *Foster v British Gas plc* and
*Kincardine and Deeside District Council v Forestry
Commission*). Thus if there was any doubt as to
whether the petitioners' case was supported by the
terms of the 1981 Regulations, the petitioners could
rely directly on the terms of the directive in a question
with a municipal authority such as the first
respondents.

It was also pointed out that in *Marleasing SA v La
Comercial Internacional de Alimentacion SA* the
European Court of Justice held that national law fell
to be interpreted so far as possible in the light of the
wording and purpose of the relevant directive in order
to achieve the result pursued by the latter and thereby
comply with art 189 (3) of the Treaty which provides:
"A Directive shall be binding, as to the result to be
achieved, upon each Member State to which it is
addressed, but shall leave to the national authorities
the form and methods." In *Lister v Forth Dry Dock
& Engineering Co Ltd* it was held that courts in the
United Kingdom were under a duty to give a purposive construction to the 1981 Regulations in a
manner which would accord with the decisions of the
European Court of Justice on the directive and where
necessary imply words which would achieve that
effect.

In the present case it was clear that the reason for
the dismissals was the transfer of the undertaking. No
account had been taken of the 1981 Regulations. The
second respondents would use the first respondents'
depots, plant and machinery but no employee was
being taken over for the performance of grounds maintenance services on a commercial basis. The dismissal
of an employee on the ground of transfer of the undertaking was prohibited. The petitioners had a clear
interest to keep their jobs. It was no consolation to
them that they would have a remedy for unfair
dismissal.

In response counsel for the first respondents submitted that the petition was incompetent for three
reasons. First, it sought interdict against a completed
act. The first respondents had already given the
notices of dismissal. It was of no avail for the petitioners to attempt to have the notices suspended
without offering to reduce them. There were in any
event no averments which would justify their reduction. Secondly, the petition was in substance directed
to enforcing a positive obligation, which was not a
permissible object of such proceedings. Reference was
made to *Keeney v Strathclyde Regional Council* and
*Grosvenor Developments (Scotland) plc v Argyll Stores
Ltd.* Furthermore it was inappropriate that the court
should compel the continuance of a contract of

employment. See *McMillan v Free Church,* in which at
p 1346 Lord Deas said: "If a master unwarrantedly
dismisses his servant, we give pecuniary redress; but
we do not compel the master to take the servant back
into his service" (cf *Murray v Dumbarton County
Council*). Thirdly, the petitioners' sole remedy was to
make complaint to an industrial tribunal. Regulation
8 (1) of the 1981 Regulations provides that where
either before or after a relevant transfer any employee
of the transferor or transferee is dismissed, that
employee is to be treated for the purposes of Pt V of
the Employment Protection (Consolidation) Act 1978
as unfairly dismissed if the transfer or a reason
connected with it is the reason or principal reason for
his dismissal. Section 129 of the 1978 Act provides
that the remedy of an employee for infringement of
any of the rights conferred on him by, inter alia, Pt V
should, if provision is made for a complaint or for the
reference of a question to an industrial tribunal, be by
way of such complaint or reference and not otherwise.
Section 54, which forms part of Pt V of the Act,
confers a right on every employee to which it applies
not to be unfairly dismissed by his employer. Section
67 provides for the presentation to an industrial
tribunal of complaints of unfair dismissal. In presenting these attacks on the competency of the petition
counsel for the first respondents reserved his position
in regard to the soundness of the submissions which
had been presented by counsel for the petitioners.

Counsel for the petitioners submitted in reply to the
third and last attack on the competency of the petition
that reg 8 of the 1981 Regulations contemplated the
case in which the dismissal had already taken place. In
the present case the petitioners were taking action
prior to that stage. They placed reliance on the terms
of art 4 (1) of the directive. They were entitled to
invoke the support of the courts in ensuring that the
terms and purpose of the directive were carried into
effect. Reference was made to *R v Secretary of State for
Transport, ex p Factortame Ltd (No. 2),* which was
concerned with the granting of interim relief where the
validity of a section of an Act of Parliament was
challenged. At [1990] 3 WLR, p 855 the European
Court of Justice observed in the course of answering
the questions referred to it that "The Court of Justice
has also held that any provision of a national legal
system and any legislative, administrative or judicial
practice which might impair the effectiveness of Community law by withholding from the national court
having jurisdiction to apply such law the power to do
everything necessary at the moment of its application
to set aside national legislative provisions which might
prevent, even temporarily, Community rules from
having full force and effect are incompatible with
those requirements, which are the very essence of
Community law."

In dealing with these submissions in relation to a
motion for interim interdict and interim suspension it
was not for me to determine the competency of the
petition but rather to reach a view as to whether the
petitioners had advanced a sufficiently cogent case in
support of competency. Regulation 8 (1) of the 1981

Regulations, when read with the provisions of the 1978 Act to which I have referred, plainly involved that dismissals based upon a relevant transfer fell to be treated in the same way as unfair dismissals from the point of view of any complaint by the employee who was affected. The right of an employee not to be unfairly dismissed is a creation of statute and the effect of the 1981 Regulations is to extend the same machinery to these other dismissals. I was not persuaded that, despite these provisions, it was open to persons in the position of the petitioners to invoke the remedies of interdict and suspension provided that they presented their petition for these remedies prior to the date as at which the dismissals took effect. In giving notices of the termination of their employment the first respondents had already done all that they needed to do in order to bring their employment to an end at 31 December 1992. The substance of the petitioners' case was that the notices and the consequences of these notices were "wrongful". This appeared to me to raise substantially the same matters as would have been the subject of a complaint to an industrial tribunal. It was not suggested that the notices were reducible. The petitioners' case was that it was wrongful for the first respondents to dismiss the petitioners where the relevant transfer was the reason for the dismissal.

It appeared to be suggested that the 1981 Regulations might have failed to give full effect to art 4 (1) of the directive so far as concerned remedies for non-compliance with that part of the directive. I was unable to agree. Article 4 (1) states what is to be inadmissible as a ground for dismissing an employee. It is true that the 1981 Regulations do not reproduce the declaratory language of art 4 (1). However, they appear to achieve the same effect by the treatment of dismissals for that inadmissible reason in the same way as unfair dismissals. In *Litster* Lord Templeman at 1989 SLT, p 543L observed: "The result of reg 8 (1) is the same as art 4 (1), namely, that if the new owner wishes to dismiss the workers he cannot achieve his purpose either by procuring the old owner to dismiss the workers, prior to the transfer taking place, or by himself dismissing the workers after the date of the transfer."

In these circumstances I took the view that the petitioners had not demonstrated that the petition was at least prima facie competent. Accordingly I refused to grant the petitioners' motion for interim interdict and interim suspension.

Counsel for Petitioners, Bell, QC, L Murphy; Solicitors, Allan McDougall & Co, SSC — Counsel for First Respondents, Mackinnon; Solicitors, Shepherd & Wedderburn, WS — No appearance for Second Respondents.

GDM

Kimmins v Normand

HIGH COURT OF JUSTICIARY
THE LORD JUSTICE GENERAL (HOPE),
LORDS ALLANBRIDGE AND COWIE
3 FEBRUARY 1993

Justiciary — Crime — Culpable and reckless conduct — Relevancy — Accused, detained to be searched, asked if he had needles, syringes or sharp instruments and falsely denying that he had — Constable placing hand in pocket and being injured by hypodermic needle — Whether crime known to Scots law — Whether criminal act libelled — Whether causal connection between denial and end result.

An accused person was charged on summary complaint with culpable and reckless conduct in respect that having been detained under s 23 (2) of the Misuse of Drugs Act 1971 and advised by a constable that he was to be searched, he falsely denied, when asked if he had any needles, syringes or sharp instruments in his possession, being in possession of any such instruments and permitted the constable to place his hand in the accused's pocket, whereupon a needle entered the constable's hand to his injury and exposing him to the risk of infection. The accused objected to the relevancy of the charge but the sheriff repelled the objection. The accused appealed contending that the charge disclosed no crime known to the law of Scotland because no act was performed by the accused and because there was no causal connection between the denial and the injury to the constable.

Held, (1) that by making the denial in the light of the advice he was given as to why he was asked the question, the accused was doing something which could amount to criminal conduct (p 1261F); and (2) that since it must have been clear to the accused why the question was put to him it was a reasonable inference from the denial that his answer would lead to the constable doing what he did (p 1261G-H); and appeal *refused.*

Summary complaint

Edward Kimmins was charged at the instance of Andrew C Normand, procurator fiscal, Glasgow, on a summary complaint which contained the following charge: "The charge against you is that on 25 May 1992 in Dumbarton Road, Glasgow, at Keith Street, having been lawfully detained in terms of the Misuse of Drugs Act 1971, s 23 (2) by Robert Weir, constable, Strathclyde Police, and having been advised by him that you were to be searched in terms of the said section and having been asked if you were in possession of any needles, syringes or any sharp instruments, you well knowing that you were in possession of an unguarded hypodermic needle and syringe in the pocket of your jacket, did culpably and recklessly and with an utter disregard for the safety of the lieges, and in particular said Robert Weir, deny being in possession of any such instruments and you did permit said Robert Weir to place his hand in the pocket of your

jacket and the said hypodermic needle entered said
A Robert Weir's hand to his injury whereby said Robert
Weir was exposed to the risk of infection." The
accused objected to the relevancy of the charge but the
sheriff repelled the objection.

The accused appealed, with leave, to the High
Court against the decision of the sheriff.

Appeal
The appeal was argued before the High Court on 3
February 1993.
B

Eo die the court *affirmed* the decision of the sheriff
and *refused* the appeal.

The following opinion of the court was delivered by
the Lord Justice General (Hope):

OPINION OF THE COURT.—The appellant is
Edward Kimmins who was charged in the sheriff
court at Glasgow with culpable and reckless conduct.
C In answer to the complaint he tendered a plea to the
competency and relevancy of the charge, on the
ground that the charge as libelled did not disclose a
crime known to the law of Scotland. The sheriff
repelled this plea. The appellant then pled not guilty
and he has now appealed.

The charge which was brought against the complainer was in the following terms: [his Lordship
quoted the charge and continued:]

D It can be seen from this carefully framed charge that
it contains within it the following elements. First, that
the complainer was advised that he was to be searched
in terms of the statutory provision; secondly that he
was asked whether he was in possession of any
needles, syringes or any sharp instruments; thirdly,
that he knew very well that he had an unguarded
needle and syringe in the pocket of his jacket and
fourthly, that he denied having any such article in his
possession. These being the four elements, it is then
E said that he permitted the constable to place his hand
in the pocket whereby the constable sustained injury
and was exposed to the risk of infection.

Counsel for the appellant submitted that the sheriff
erred in two respects in the view which he took of this
charge. The first was that there was no crime committed as known to the law of Scotland, in that no act
was performed by the appellant in the sense that he
did not do anything. In our opinion that argument is
not capable of being supported, because the com-
F plainer having been asked the question, in the light of
the advice he was given as to why it was being put to
him, denied being in possession of any such instruments. By making that denial he was undoubtedly
doing something, and we consider that it can properly
be said that there was the commission by him of something which, if the circumstances were appropriate,
could amount to criminal conduct.

The other point which counsel raised was whether
there was a causal connection between the denial and
the end result. On this matter we consider the facts are

perfectly clear in the light of the narrative given in the
charge. The denial must be seen against the back- G
ground of the advice that the appellant was to be
searched. He had no choice but to submit to the search
in terms of the statute. It must have been clear to him
that the reason why the question was being put to him
was that the police officer was about to put his hand
into the pocket of his jacket with a view to conducting
the search. It is a reasonable inference from the denial
in these circumstances that it would lead directly to
the police officer doing what he in fact did, that is
putting his unprotected hand into the appellant's H
pocket with the result that it was injured by the needle
in the pocket. The chain of events follows naturally
from one end of the charge to the other, and we are
satisfied that on these averments in the libel there was
a causal connection between the denial and the end
result.

For these reasons the view taken by the sheriff was,
in our opinion, the correct one and we shall give effect
to his decision by refusing this appeal.
I

---

*Counsel for Appellant, Thorburn; Solicitors, Patrick
Wheatley — Counsel for Respondent, Solicitor General
(Dawson, QC); Solicitors, J D Lowe, Crown Agent.*

P W F

J

Barton Distilling (Scotland) Ltd v Barton Brands Ltd

OUTER HOUSE
LORD OSBORNE
10 MARCH 1993

Contract — Retention — Action of payment for goods K
*supplied — Counterclaim for damages for breach of
earlier contract to supply — Retention of payment by
defenders pending determination of counterclaim —
Exceptions to general rule that illiquid claim cannot be
retained against liquid claim — Whether counterclaim
admitted of instant verification — Whether sufficient
connection between contracts to invoke principle of
mutuality — Whether justice to parties required retention
to be available.*

Whisky suppliers sued for payment for a quantity of L
whisky supplied between June and July 1990 in terms
of a contract entered into in February 1990. The purchasers admitted the supply but counterclaimed for a
sum in excess of the cost of the whisky. The basis of
the counterclaim was that from 1982 until 1990 the
companies had been engaged in a course of dealing;
that in the course of this dealing in about October
1988 the defenders had agreed to purchase from the
suppliers a large quantity of whisky with the intention
of selling the whisky on, and that the suppliers had,

in breach of that contract, failed to supply that whisky, causing the defenders to suffer the loss of profit for which they now counterclaimed. The parties were agreed that the principal action was for a liquid claim and that the counterclaim was illiquid and required proof. The suppliers contended that the defenders were not entitled to retain the sum sued for merely by showing that the various transactions formed part of a course of dealing, arguing that, unless a single contract existed, or a series of transactions which could properly be looked upon as part of a single contract to the extent that there was true mutuality between the parties in respect of all matters arising in that series of transactions, a plea of retention in respect of an illiquid claim could not be upheld against a claim for a liquid debt. The defenders argued that there were four exceptions to the general rule against a plea of retention: (1) where the illiquid claim admitted of instant verification; (2) where both the liquid and the illiquid claim arose out of a mutual contract; (3) where one or other of the parties was bankrupt or vergens ad inopiam; and (4) where, in exceptional circumstances, retention was allowed to meet the justice or convenience of the particular case; and that the defenders could rely on (1), (2) and (4), the claim being capable of instant verification and, in any event, the various supplies being so interconnected as to amount to a mutual contract or at least to render it just that retention be permitted.

Held, (1) that the exception of instant verification could not be invoked, there being a need for (a) proof of a failure to supply the whisky, and (b) proof of the market value of the whisky before the counterclaim could be determined (p 1268I-K); (2) that although the principle of mutuality could be extended to apply to two or more separate contracts where the parties had so agreed, there were insufficient averments on record to establish that the supplies on the different occasions had any agreed quality of mutuality (p 1269B-D); (3) that in the present case involving two commercial entities there was nothing to justify the court exercising its equitable discretion (p 1269G); and decree de plano *granted* in the principal action and proof before answer *allowed* in respect of the counterclaim.

Ross v Ross (1895) 2 SLT 577; (1895) 22 R 461, *distinguished.*

Action of payment

Barton Distilling (Scotland) Ltd raised an action of payment against Barton Brands Ltd for whisky supplied in the sum of £222,740.05. The defenders counterclaimed for payment of the sum of £413,000 on the basis of alleged breach of contract by the pursuers. They pled that they were entitled to retain the sum of £222,470.05 pending determination of the counterclaim, an illiquid claim, which, it was agreed, required a proof.

The case came before the Lord Ordinary (Osborne) on procedure roll.

Cases referred to

Chafer (J W) (Scotland) Ltd v Hope, 1963 SLT (Notes) 11.
Fulton Clyde Ltd v J F McCallum & Co Ltd, 1960 SLT 253; 1960 SC 78.
Grewar v Cross (1904) 12 SLT 84.
Henderson v Turnbull, 1909 1 SLT 78; 1909 SC 510.
Logan v Stephen (1850) 13 D 262.
Lovie v Baird's Trustees (1895) 3 SLT 93; (1895) 23 R 1.
Munro v Macdonald's Executors (1866) 4 M 687.
Niven v Clyde Fasteners Ltd, 1986 SLT 344.
Ross v Ross (1895) 2 SLT 577; (1895) 22 R 461.
Smart v Wilkinson, 1928 SLT 243; 1928 SC 383.
Sutherland v Urquhart (1895) 3 SLT 198; (1895) 23 R 284.

Textbooks referred to

Erskine, *Institute*, III iv 20.
Gloag, *Contract* (2nd ed), p 624.
Gloag and Irvine, *Rights in Security*, pp 304-306 and 319.
Green's Encyclopaedia of the Laws of Scotland, Vol 13, para 15.

On 10 March 1993 the Lord Ordinary *granted* decree for payment by the defenders to the pursuers of the sum of £222,470.05 and *allowed* a proof before answer in respect of the counterclaim.

LORD OSBORNE.—In this action, the pursuers seek payment to them by the defenders of a sum of £222,472.05, with interest thereon as concluded for, upon the basis that the defenders are due and resting owing to the pursuers in the sum concerned. The pursuers' case is based upon a contract between them and the defenders formed in February 1990. The nature of this contract is a matter of averment and admission. In February 1990 the pursuers agreed to arrange for the supply to the defenders of 210,000 regauged litres of alcohol ("RLA") of four year old blended whisky at a price of £4.25 per RLA in tank ex-warehouse. Although there is no admission to this effect in the defenders' pleadings, I was informed when the case came before me in the procedure roll that the defenders accepted that the whisky concerned had been supplied to them. In cond 2, the pursuers aver that the defenders have failed to pay the sum of £222,472.05 due to the pursuers under the said arrangement in terms of invoices CC/D8969, dated 29 June 1990, JTD9018, dated 9 July 1990, and JTD9085, dated 31 July 1990. Again, although this averment is not formally admitted by the defenders, I was informed that the defenders accepted that the averment concerned is correct and that the sum mentioned has not been paid.

The defenders in this action have tabled a counterclaim against the pursuers, in which they seek payment from the pursuers of £413,000, together with interest thereon as concluded for. The counterclaim is one for damages for alleged breach of contract on the part of the pursuers, as appears from the defenders'

pleas in law therein. In para 2 of the statement of facts
A for the defenders in the counterclaim, it is averred on
their behalf that, from at least 1982 until 1990, the
parties were engaged in a course of dealing, in which
the pursuers supplied Scotch whisky to the defenders.
As part of this course of dealing, it is averred that in
about October 1988, the defenders agreed to purchase
from the pursuers 70,000 RLA of a 12 year old Scotch
whisky at a total cost of £392,000. This represents a
price of £5.60 per RLA. The defenders aver that they
intended to sell the said whisky on. The total market
B value thereof was £805,000. They aver that the pursuers failed to supply the said whisky in breach of the
said agreement. Accordingly, the defenders lost the
resale profit which they would have obtained if the
pursuers had fulfilled their said agreement. That lost
resale profit is, of course, the £413,000 for which the
defenders sue, as being loss and damage suffered by
them in consequence of the pursuers' breach of
contract.

C It was made clear by the parties, at an early stage in
the debate before me, that they both recognised that
there would require to be a proof before answer on the
defenders' counterclaim. Furthermore, it was accepted
by the defenders that the only basis upon which they
might be able to resist a decree for payment in the sum
of £222,472.05, being the price for the whisky
supplied to them by the pursuers, which remained
unpaid, was the defenders' contention that they were
entitled to retain that sum, pending the resolution of
the merits of their counterclaim against the pursuers.
D Thus, it was accepted by the defenders that, if the
court were to hold that, in the particular circumstances, the defenders had no such right to retain, a
decree de plano in the pursuers' favour for the sum
sued for by them would be inevitable. That position
is reflected in pleas in law nos 5 and 7 for the
defenders in the principal action.

In order to render comprehensible the account
which I shall give in due course of the arguments of
E the parties, it is necessary for me to make reference to
certain parts of the pleadings of the defenders and to
a lesser extent of the pursuers. The defenders aver that
the agreement, on the basis of which the pursuers sue
in the principal action, was part of an ongoing course
of business between the pursuers and the defenders,
which had subsisted since prior to 1982. In about
October 1982, the defenders acquired the business and
assets of a firm trading under the style of Barton
Brands Ltd. The said assets included the share capital
F of the pursuers. The said share capital was transferred
to the defenders' then parent company, Amalgamated
Distilled Products plc, which, in 1983, merged with
Argyll Foods plc to form Argyll Group plc. In about
March 1987, Barton Incorporated, a Delaware
company, purchased the defenders' business and
assets from Argyll Group plc. Prior to the said acquisition in 1982 and since that date the pursuers had
supplied the defenders with Scotch whisky.

In about October 1988, the defenders agreed to purchase from the pursuers 70,000 RLA of 12 year old

whisky at £5.60 per RLA. This agreement, which
forms the basis of the defenders' counterclaim, is G
averred to have been confirmed by telex messages
dated 12 and 31 October 1988. The defenders aver
that the total cost of this whisky would have been
£392,000. The said 12 year old whisky was not
supplied to the defenders. It was sold and delivered to
a business or company conducted by one Ian Lockwood under the style of Barton International or by
way of a company known as Barton International Ltd.
The said whisky was for onward supply by the
defenders to Allied Distillers. The market value H
thereof was £11.50 per RLA. The total value of the
said 70,000 RLA was accordingly £805,000. The
defenders aver that, as a result of the pursuers' failure
to make the said supply, they sustained a loss of profit
of £413,000. The defenders first learned that there
might be difficulty over the supply of the 12 year old
whisky when Mr Paul Kraus, a consultant employed
by them, received a fax message from Mr Bob Fisher
of Argyll Group plc, the holding company of the pursuers, referring to a request by him to one Cameron, I
who was a director and employee of the pursuers, to
ask United Distillers Group to supply eight tanks of
12 year old and concluding "I will let you know the
position as soon as possible." Said Kraus received a
memorandum from one Murdoch, also a director and
employee of the pursuers, dated 21 July 1989, on the
pursuers' stationery indicating that he was employed
by the pursuers at that date. By fax dated 25 July
1989, the said Fisher advised said Kraus that he had
been advised by said Cameron that Cameron had been J
unable to secure a supply of 12 year old whisky in
1989. The said Kraus confirmed to the said Fisher, by
fax dated 31 July 1989, that the defenders still
required said whisky. Only on receipt of a memorandum from the said Murdoch dated 15 August 1989,
which was copied to the said Fisher and the terms of
which suggested that, as at its date, said Murdoch continued to be employed by or act as the agent of the
pursuers, did the said Kraus learn that the said whisky
was not to be supplied in 1989. In response to the said K
memorandum from said Murdoch, the said Kraus sent
a memorandum, dated 24 August 1989, to the said
Fisher. The said Kraus framed the fourth paragraph
of the said memorandum of 24 August 1989 as a
response to the allegation by Murdoch that it was the
defenders' intention to "dump the tanks on the open
market". In the foregoing circumstances, while dis-
claiming liability to the defenders, the said Fisher, in
a telephone conversation with said Kraus on 19
September 1989, as confirmed by letter dated 20 Sep- L
tember 1989, written on Argyll Group plc notepaper,
offered to supply to the defenders 70,000 RLA of 12
year old Scotch whisky at a price of £7.05 per RLA.
In an attempt to mitigate their damage, consequent
upon the said breach of contract by the pursuers, the
defenders agreed to purchase 70,000 RLA of 12 year
old Scotch whisky at a price of £7.05 per RLA, as confirmed by letter dated 26 September 1989.

By a memorandum dated 30 October 1989, Mr Ellis
Goodman, the chief executive of the defenders,

A requested of the said Fisher that he provide samples of the said 12 year old blend. This was necessary for the purpose of selling on within the United Kingdom. The said Goodman met with the said Fisher about 7 November 1989, on which occasion the proposal to sell on within the United Kingdom was mentioned. Said Fisher made no adverse comment. Only by letter dated 5 December 1989 to Mr Hart of the defenders did the said Fisher state that it was only on the basis that the said whisky be used for the defenders' own bottled brands that the said whisky was offered at

B £7.05 per RLA. The said Goodman replied to the said letter from the said Fisher by a further letter dated 5 December 1989. In said letter it was explained that the defenders had offered the said quantity of 12 year old whisky to Hiram Walker in anticipation of obtaining four year old blended whiskies from them. The letter went on to explain that the defenders would accept 210,000 litres of four year old in place of the 70,000 litres of 12 year old whisky which the pursuers had agreed to supply in September 1989. The said Fisher

C responded by letter addressed to the said Kraus, dated 22 December 1989, offering to supply 210,000 litres of four year old whisky at £4.25 per litre. This is the whisky in respect of which the pursuers sue in the present action. As appears from said letter, it was the position of the said Fisher, on behalf of the pursuers, that a supply of four year old whisky at that price represented a discount from the market value. As aforesaid, the pursuers supplied said whisky as an alternative to the 70,000 RLA of 12 year old at a cost

D of £7.05 per RLA which they had agreed to supply to the defenders in or about September 1989. As aforesaid, the defenders had agreed to take the said 70,000 RLA at £7.05 per RLA in an attempt to mitigate their damage consequent upon the pursuers' breach of contract. The defenders believe and aver that at all relevant dates Fisher was acting on behalf of the pursuers which is a subsidiary of Argyll Group plc and controlled by them. It was only at a meeting at which the said Goodman and said Fisher were present in London

E on or about 7 March 1990 that said Goodman and accordingly the defenders learned of the said supply to Barton International. The defenders aver that, as appears from their counterclaim, the pursuers have refused to pay the damages sustained by the defenders consequent upon the said breach of contract. In the foregoing circumstances, the defenders believe and aver that they are entitled to set off the said loss of £413,000 against the sum sued for and to retain the said sum pending the resolution of the counterclaim,

F the said contracts being consequent upon each other and the subsequent contracts being entered into in an effort to mitigate, in part, the defenders' said loss, injury and damage. In any event, the defenders believe and aver that it would be equitable that decree should not pass in the principal action before a determination is made upon the counterclaim.

In cond 2, in response to the foregoing averments of the defenders, the pursuers make a number of admissions relating to the general background of the matter. In particular they admit that in about October 1988

G the defenders agreed to purchase from the pursuers a quantity of 12 year old whisky at £5.60 per RLA, the amount to be supplied being eight tanks. Two tanks (23,831 RLA) were supplied. Six tanks (71,130 RLA) were diverted. It is also admitted, in particular, that, subject to the explanation given, in about September 1989 the pursuers agreed to supply to the defenders 70,000 RLA of 12 year old Scotch whisky at a cost of £7.05 per RLA. The pursuers aver that Cameron, Murdoch and McFadyen, who was the pursuers' whisky stock controller, left their employment on 30 April 1989, when they joined Barton International.

H The diversion of the said whisky was effected by issuing orders on the pursuers' order forms to United Distillers, requesting delivery to Grangemouth Packing Services instead of Inver House Distillers as was normal and by altering the name of the addressee on the suppliers' invoice from that of the pursuers to Barton International. The first order form, for 42,174 RLA, was issued while Cameron was employed by the pursuers and the issue of the second was written by McFadyen, procured by Cameron, after they had left

I the pursuers' employment. The whisky was delivered to Barton International by United Distillers Stocks and Sales Ltd direct and Barton International paid them directly. From about June 1989, Mr Fisher of Argyll Group plc, acting on behalf of the pursuers, had telephone conversations with Mr Kraus of the defenders in relation to the provision of a supply of 12 year old whisky to replace that which had been diverted. Mr Fisher first became aware that there might be a problem about a supply of whisky when he

J was telephoned by Mr Kraus on or before 12 June 1989. Thereafter, Mr Fisher investigated the position and in early August he suggested to Mr Kraus that he, Fisher, approach other suppliers to see if a supply could be arranged. At that time Mr Fisher requested and Mr Kraus granted an undertaking on behalf of the defenders that they would not use said replacement whisky for bulk trading, but would bottle it themselves. This undertaking was confirmed by a memorandum from Mr Kraus to Mr Fisher, dated 24

K August 1989. Thereafter, by fax message dated 22 September 1989, Mr Fisher asked Mr E M Goodman of the defenders to let him know as soon as possible whether he wished Mr Fisher to commit to the purchase of up to 70,000 RLA at 7.05 per RLA. Shortly thereafter Mr Goodman confirmed to Mr Fisher by telephone that he wished to proceed and indicated that in consideration for the said supply of whisky the defenders would not press any claim against the pursuers in respect of the diversion of the previous order

L of whisky. In these circumstances, the pursuers aver that the defenders have compromised any claim open to them arising out of the failure of the pursuers to supply the whisky ordered in 1988. They also aver that they refrained from delivering the said whisky ordered in 1989 to the defenders because the defenders, contrary to their undertaking, intended to supply the said whisky to Hiram Walker in a swap agreement. Thereafter, the pursuers supplied the defenders with approximately 210,000 litres of four year old at a price of £4.25 per litre, which compared

A with a market price in excess of £5.00 per litre. It is averred by the pursuers that the supply of four year old was not connected with the agreement in relation to the 12 year old.

At the procedure roll hearing, counsel for the pursuers moved me to sustain both pleas in law for the pursuers and grant decree de plano. In elaborating his submissions, he pointed out that there were three contracts or transactions between the parties which had to be considered. These were: (1) the 1988 contract for 70,000 litres of 12 year old at £5.60 per litre; (2) the
B 1989 contract for 70,000 litres of 12 year old at £7.05 per litre; and (3) the 1990 contract for 210,000 litres of four year old at £4.25 per litre. The principal action was concerned with recovering the price of the goods supplied under contract no 3. The counterclaim, on the other hand, was based upon an alleged breach of contract no 1. In their averments, the defenders had attempted to portray all three contracts as being interconnected, being part of a course of dealing. They
C claimed that their entering into contract no 2 was an attempt to mitigate their damage arising from breach of contract no 1. They went on to claim that a problem arose between the parties concerning contract no 2, as appeared from the averments at pp 14C-15A of the record. Finally, the defenders claimed that contract no 3 arose as an alternative to contract no 2, as appeared from the averments at p 15B. Counsel for the pursuers anticipated that the defenders' view of this state of affairs would be that there were sufficient links
D between the three contracts for the defenders' plea of retention to be upheld as an answer to the pursuers' claim based on the third contract, albeit that that plea of retention was based on contract no 1. It was insufficient to justify a plea of retention for the defenders to show merely that the various transactions formed part of a course of dealing. They had to demonstrate that there was a particular degree of connection between the particular contracts involved. The pursuers' submission was that the facts and circumstances
E set out by the defenders did not indicate that there was such a relationship between the parties in relation to these contracts that the plea could be given effect. It was the pursuers' contention that, unless one had a single contract, or a series of transactions which could properly be looked upon as part of a single contract, to the extent that there was true mutuality between the parties in respect of all matters arising in that series of transactions, a plea of retention in respect of an illiquid claim would not be upheld against a claim for
F a liquid debt. It was quite clear from the authorities that a course of dealing, in itself, would not give rise to a right of retention. Accordingly, the defenders in the present action could make nothing of their averments concerning a course of trade. Furthermore, the defenders could make nothing of their alleged effort to mitigate their damage said to have arisen from the breach of contract no 1. The course of action which they had taken was not an agreed one. The defenders' unilateral intentions were irrelevant to the question of a right to retain. It had to be recognised that the defenders did aver that the several contracts were

G "consequent upon each other". The meaning of that averment was obscure. That appeared to be no more than a characterisation of a situation in which it was said that the second and third contracts had been entered into on account of the existence of the first. If that were the position, that did not constitute a sufficient connection between the second and third contracts on the one hand and the first on the other to take the case out of the ordinary course of trading situation. In an ordinary course of dealing, contracts might well be "consequent on" one another. If a trader performed the first contract well, he might find that
H others were placed with him.

In support of his contention regarding the test of mutuality, counsel for the pursuers referred me to a number of authorities. In *J W Chafer (Scotland) Ltd v Hope*, Lord Cameron summarised the law, which was not in dispute, thus: "When a contract is one and indivisible, a counter-claim arising out of one item can be competently pursued in answer to a claim for payment on the whole contract. If there is a series of
I transactions between the parties, and each transaction or group repesents a separate contract, then a counter-claim can only be competently pleaded against claims for payment in respect of that transaction or series of transactions referable to the particular contract in respect of which it is said to arise."

In *Fulton Clyde Ltd v J F McCallum & Co Ltd*, it was held by Lord Migdale that, to justify retention, the liquid and illiquid claims must both arise directly out of the same contract. At 1960 SLT, p 254 he said:
J "I do not think it is enough to justify retention that the defenders placed a succession of orders with the pursuers. If each order is part of a wider contract that might suffice but that is not the case here. To justify retention, I think that the liquid and illiquid claims must both arise directly out of the same contract."

That case showed that, where a "general account" was involved, retention would be open. However, there was no question of a "general account" in the present case. Support for this view of the law could
K also be found in *Smart v Wilkinson*, 1928 SLT at p 246. The case of *Grewar v Cross* was the first reported case in which a plea of retention sought to be based on a course of dealing was rejected. There Lord Pearson said: "The general rule undoubtedly is that a liquid claim is not to be delayed until the constitution of an illiquid counter claim, unless they arise out of counter stipulations in a mutual contract. . . . Nor do I regard the averment as to the two claims having arisen out of the same 'course of dealing', as sufficient
L to take the case out of the rule."

All that the defenders could say in the present case was that they had averred a course of dealing. That was an insufficient basis for retention. There was no other connection between the various contracts concerned. There had been an alleged failure to perform contract no 1; contract no 2 amounted to a unilateral attempt at mitigation of loss, but that had not been implemented. Contract no 3 stood alone. There were no averments to show that the parties had expressly

A agreed to make the obligations arising from these transactions mutually interdependent. In these circumstances the defences were irrelevant and decree de plano should be granted. Pleas nos 5 and 6 for the defenders should be repelled. There was no question in the present case of the amount of the counterclaim being immediately verifiable and accordingly there was no other possible basis of retention. Pleas in law nos 3 and 8 for the defenders, not being supported by relevant averments, ought also to be repelled.

B Counsel for the defenders moved me to allow a proof before answer on the principal action and the counterclaim. He confirmed that there was no dispute between the parties concerning the performance of contract no 3 and the non-payment for the goods supplied thereunder. He agreed that there had been three transactions or contracts between the parties which were relevant to the present issue. His submission was that there was a thread connecting these transactions, showing that they were not just parts of a course of dealing. The defenders submitted that C there was a sufficient connection between the transactions to justify the plea of retention in this case.

Turning to the law of retention, counsel for the defenders emphasised that it related to what was in effect a temporary remedy of retention during a limited period of time during which a claim of damages had to be determined. In this connection he referred to Erskine's *Institute*, III iv 20. Reference was also made to the *Law of Rights in Security*, etc, Gloag D and Irvine, at pp 304-305, where the general rule and the exceptions to it were set forth. Four exceptions were stated by the learned authors. These were: (1) where the illiquid claim admitted of instant verification; (2) where both the liquid and illiquid claim arose out of a mutual contract; (3) where one or other of the parties was bankrupt, or vergens ad inopiam; and (4) where, in exceptional circumstances, retention had been allowed to meet the justice or convenience of the particular case. The defenders proposed to found on E exceptions 1, 2 and 4.

Counsel for the defenders then went on to review the law in relation to these particular exceptions to the general rule. *Logan v Stephen* was a case where observations were made relating to the exception of immediate ascertainment. At p 267 Lord Cuninghame said: "Our ancient Scots Act (1592), sanctions the pursuer's plea, as it only admitted mutual claims which are liquid, to be compensated. . . . No doubt, in practice, we sometimes allow counter claims not yet F constituted, to be held *pro jam liquido*, when they admit almost of immediate ascertainment. But it is always a question of circumstances, and of sound judicial discretion and equity, in what cases that should be allowed."

Henderson v Turnbull was a case which showed that a claim was not necessarily to be regarded as illiquid because it was of the nature of a claim of damages. The quality of immediate ascertainment might entitle retention to be allowed. In the case in question, an arithmetical exercise only was involved. Counsel went

on to refer the case of *Sutherland v Urquhart*, principally, as I understood it, for the explanation which G was contained in the judgment of Lord Kinnear, at (1895) 23 R, p 286, of the decision in *Lovie v Baird's Trs*. He contended that it was there shown that, if an illiquid claim is capable of ascertainment by valuation, it is to be treated as if it were liquid. *Lovie v Baird's Trs* was an example of Gloag and Irvine's exception no 2, where both claim and counterclaim arose out of a mutual contract. In the argument of counsel for the defenders, the present case came within the exception of instant verification. There were admissions by the H pursuers of the contract no 1 and of the failure to perform it. In addition, there were averments by the defenders relating to the price under that contract and the market value of the goods concerned. While the defenders' averment relating to market value was denied, there was in fact no substantive alternative put forward by the pursuers. Looking at the averments thus far, it was apparent that the defenders' counterclaim was instantly verifiable. The situation was, however, complicated by the pursuers' averments of a compromise by the defenders of their claim arising I from contract no 1. These averments were of very doubtful relevance.

Counsel for the pursuers had concentrated his attack on the defenders' position by reference to Gloag and Irvine's exception no 2. It had been said that there was an insufficient connection between contracts nos 1 and 3 to enable the principle of mutuality to be invoked. The defenders' submission was that, in the circumstances narrated, there was a sufficiently close con- J nection between the three arrangements to justify the defenders in their retention posture. There was no dispute between the parties regarding the law. It was its application to the circumstances of the present case that was in issue. The defenders' position was that contract no 3 only came into being because the earlier contractual arrangements had been entered into. The circumstances here amounted to more than a "course of dealing". For exception no 2 to apply, it had to be shown that the arrangements were so intermingled K that to extract one part from the rest would involve unfairness.

Counsel for the defenders went on to rely on exception no 4 enunciated by Gloag and Irvine. It was submitted that retention should be allowed in the present circumstances in order to meet the justice of the case. The law in this connection was in short compass. An account of it was to be found in Gloag and Irvine at p 319 and, from the pen of Professor Gloag, in *Green's* L *Encyclopaedia of the Laws of Scotland*, Vol 13, para 15. There were two modern cases, the first of which was *Munro v Macdonald's Exrs*. Counsel for the defenders acknowledged that this case had the appearance of one involving the instant verification exception, rather than anything else. The other case was *Ross v Ross*. The view of the court there appeared to be that it was not consonant with justice to give the pursuer immediate decree for the sum for which she claimed, having regard to her past conduct. The case also seemed to involve the court making an assessment of the strength of the illiquid claim. Looking at the whole circumstances of the present case, it was contended that the court should exercise a similar power here.

Counsel for the pursuers in reply submitted that the mutuality exception could operate where more than one contract was involved, provided that the parties had expressly provided that the obligations involved in one contract were dependent upon those involved in another. No such agreement was averred here. The three transactions of concern in the present case were, on the face of it, independent of each other. At best for the defenders, the second and third transactions may have come into being because of decisions by the defenders themselves taken in the light of the outcome of transaction no 1. That was an insufficient connection. The case of *Sutherland v Urquhart* relied upon by the defenders was an example of a situation in which there was a close connection between the origins of the different obligations. Nevertheless, the court held that the circumstances were outside the scope of the mutuality exception. The case of *Lovie v Baird's Trs* was of no particular assistance in the circumstances of this case, since the claims there involved on the one side and on the other were mutual claims arising under the obligations of the lease, as appeared from the opinion of Lord Adam at p 2. The fact of the matter was that no case had been cited by the defenders involving two or more contracts or transactions where the exception of mutuality had been allowed.

Turning to the possible relevance of Gloag and Irvine's exception no 4 to the present case, counsel for the pursuers acknowledged that the court did possess an equitable discretion to allow retention. However, what was clear from the cases examined was that that power would be exercised only in very exceptional circumstances. *Munro v Macdonald's Exrs* was not a case of the exercise of this power. It appeared to be a case falling under exception no 1, instant verification. The only case which had been cited where the equitable discretion had been exercised was that of *Ross v Ross*. It was apparent from the judgments in that case that the court had taken a very disapproving view of Lady Ross's conduct. Among the circumstances which were criticised was the fact that she purported to retain capital repesenting the annuity for an instalment of which she was suing. In addition, over a long period of time, during which she had been responsible for the administration of the estate, she had failed to keep proper accounts. Accordingly, she did not approach the court with clean hands. It was in these circumstances that the heir was permitted to retain. Counsel for the pursuers submitted that there were no circumstances existing in the present case which were remotely comparable with those in *Ross v Ross*. In the present case the court was dealing simply with two commercial organisations, where there was absolutely no reason to exercise a discretion in the defenders' favour based on equitable principles. As appeared from *Munro v Macdonald's Exrs*, the court had shown a marked reluctance to depart from the general principle. Turning to the question of instant verification, counsel for the pursuers accepted that, where an illiquid counterclaim was capable of instant verification or almost instant verification, the court would allow retention. He also accepted that where the subject matter of the counterclaim could be referred to the writ or oath of a party, that was to be regarded as a case of instant verification. However, it was necessary to examine how far the principle went beyond cases involving reference to writ or oath. While the instant verification exception was clearly stated in *Logan v Stephen*, neither that case nor Gloag and Irvine contained any detailed analysis of the ambit of the exception. It was said simply to be a question of circumstances, and of sound judicial discretion and equity. Some assistance could be got from the modern case of *Niven v Clyde Fasteners Ltd* where Lord Jauncey said that, for retention to be allowed, the disputed debt must be capable of almost immediate ascertainment as by writ or oath. He later made clear that his view was that, if a proof were necessary, the situation was not one where the counterclaim was capable of instant verification. In that case, there was only one issue which had to go to proof, namely whether the pension contribution arranged by the pursuer for himself had been made with or without the authority of the defenders. The position here was similar to that in *Niven v Clyde Fasteners Ltd*. There was no question of a proof by writ or oath being competent here. There would require to be a proof, in which the defenders would require to show a failure to supply whisky which was in all the circumstances of the case a breach of contract no 1 upon which they could found. The proof would inevitably involve the issue of the possible compromise of the defenders' claim. However, quite apart from that, there were two serious issues which would require determination after proof. These were (1) the question of a breach of contract which could be founded upon by the defenders; and (2) the question of market value of the whisky concerned. While it was recognised by the pursuers that no counter value was pled by them, the pursuers considered that they were entitled to put the defenders to proof on the matter of the market value for which they contended. Whatever might be involved in almost immediate ascertainment, it was quite clear that a proof of the kind necessary in the present case could not be so described.

The defenders here founded upon what was said by Gloag and Irvine at p 306 in the first paragraph. While counsel for the pursuers submitted that that part of that paragraph which referred to verification by writ or oath was unexceptionable, he took issue with the remainder of the paragraph, which in his submission was an unsafe basis for the extension of the principle beyond cases of proof by writ or oath. The case of *Lovie v Baird's Trs* was not authority for Gloag and Irvine's statement. The express basis of the court's decision in *Lovie* was that the principle of mutuality operated. Lord Kinnear's explanation of the case of *Lovie v Baird's Trs* to be found in *Sutherland v Urquhart* was both incomplete and inaccurate.

Counsel for the defenders had relied upon the case of *Henderson v Turnbull*. Counsel for the pursuers con-

A tended that that case was of no assistance in the circumstances here. It was not a case about retention at all. The pursuer's claim was not a liquid one but was an equitable claim for repetition of money paid in error. Further the defenders' claim for dead freight was in its nature illiquid. It was clear from the opinion of Lord Ardwall that he treated the case as one involving the equities of the condictio indebiti. In summary, counsel for the pursuers submitted that the court should be slow to extend the exception of instant verification beyond a situation where proof by writ or
B oath was competent. On any view of the matter the proof which would be required here could not be described as a technical matter. It could not amount to instant verification.

In the arguments before me, reliance was placed by the defenders on three of the four exceptions stated by Gloag and Irvine at p 305 of their work to the general rule that a person who is sued for a debt which he admits to be due and payable, cannot withhold payment on the ground that he has an illiquid claim
C against the creditor who is suing him. I propose to deal with the arguments in the same order as the exceptions are stated in that work. Accordingly I turn first to the exception of instant verification. The nature of this exception, although perhaps not its precise scope, was clearly explained in *Logan v Stephen* by Lord Cuninghame at p 267, where he said: "No doubt, in practice, we sometimes allow counter claims not yet constituted, to be held *pro jam liquido*, where they admit almost of immediate ascertainment. But it is
D always a question of circumstances, and of sound judicial discretion and equity, in what cases that should be allowed."

In that particular case, retention was not permitted to a master, who owed wages to a farm grieve, in respect of his claim against his servant as cautioner for the intromissions of the master's clerk, who had defaulted. In relation to other cases cited by the defenders in this connection, I have to say that I did
E not find either *Lovie v Baird's Trs* or *Sutherland v Urquhart* as of assistance. In the former case, as I read it, the court's ground of decision was that the tenant's liquid claim and the landlord's counterclaim were claims arising from mutual obligations created by the terms of the lease. Indeed, I have great difficulty in understanding why this case was cited by the authors of Gloag and Irvine in the first paragraph on p 306 of their work, which deals with the instant verification exception. In *Sutherland v Urquhart*, the court held
F that the landlord's illiquid counterclaim under the lease was not a relevant basis for retention against the tenant's claim for a sum found due to him as the price of the waygoing crop under a decree arbitral. The court took the view that the tenant's action was founded not on the contract of lease, but on the submission to arbitration. Accordingly the exception of mutuality was not operative. I should say that, once again, I have difficulty in understanding why the authors of Gloag and Irvine and mention this case in the context of their paragraph relating to instant verification on p 306 of their work.

Counsel for the defenders relied upon *Henderson v Turnbull*. In my opinion, that case has no bearing on G the issue with which I am at present concerned. I agree with the submissions of counsel for the pursuers to the effect that the pursuer's claim in that case was an illiquid claim for repetition of money paid in error. The question before the court was whether effect ought to be given to that particular claim in a context in which the ship owners themselves had a claim for dead freight. Properly viewed, in my opinion, this case is not at all concerned with the law of retention.

The case of *Niven v Clyde Fasteners* does however H appear to me to assist in clarifying the limits of the instant verification exception. At p 345, Lord Jauncey plainly had in contemplation proof by writ or oath as an example of almost immediate ascertainment. It is equally plain, however, that he did not regard a proof in relation to the sole issue of whether the pension premium was paid by the pursuer with or without the authority of the defenders as a matter which would involve almost immediate ascertainment.

I
Looking at the circumstances of this case, I have come to the conclusion that the exception of instant verification cannot successfully be invoked. Before the defenders' counterclaim could be determined, there would require to be a proof on two issues. First, the defenders would have to establish a failure to supply whisky which was in all the circumstances a breach of the first contract, upon which they are now entitled to found. Secondly, the issue of the market value of the whisky involved in that contract is one on which the J pursuers put them to proof. While the second issue may not involve any great difficulty at a proof, the same cannot, in my opinion, be said of the first issue. Having regard to the averments made by the pursuers, any proof would involve an inquiry into the quite elaborate negotiations between the parties which are said by the pursuers to have culminated in a compromise by the defenders of their claim arising out of the failure of the pursuers to supply the whisky ordered in 1988. To my mind, such a proof would K necessarily be more complicated than that which Lord Jauncey held in *Niven v Clyde Fasteners* did not involve instant verification. Accordingly I reject the defenders' arguments based upon this exception.

I turn next to the exception of mutuality invoked by the defenders. I did not understand there to be any dispute between the parties in relation to the law applicable to this exception, which is fully stated by Lord Migdale in *Fulton Clyde Ltd v J F McCallum & Co Ltd* at pp 254 and 255. Quoting Gloag on *Contract* L (2nd ed), at p 624 his Lordship said: "'[A] debt which is admittedly due and payable cannot be withheld on the plea of retention in respect of a claim of damages which does not arise directly out of the same contract.'"

At a later stage in his opinion, in relation to an argument based upon a general course of dealing, he said: "I do not think it is enough to justify retention that the defenders placed a succession of orders with the pursuers. If each order is part of a wider contract, that might suffice, but that is not the case here. To justify retention, I think that the liquid and illiquid claims must both arise directly out of the same contract. A 'course of dealing' is not the same thing as a 'general account'."

It is apparent from the judgment of the Lord Justice Clerk in *Smart v Wilkinson*, at 1928 SLT, p 246, that "The exception is based on the familiar principle that a person who is himself in breach of a contract cannot claim implement of that contract as against another person".

Having regard to these and the other authorities cited during the course of the debate, in my opinion, leaving a general account out of the picture, in considering whether this exception can apply or not in any particular circumstances, one must inquire as to whether there exists a mutual contract which gives rise not only to the liquid claim, but also to the illiquid counterclaim. Nevertheless, with counsel for the pursuers, I would be prepared to recognise the possibility in principle of the quality of mutuality attaching to two or more separate contracts, provided that the parties to those contracts had agreed that that would be so. Looking at the defenders' averments in this case, I can find nothing which suggests that the quality of mutuality of stipulations had been conferred by consent of the parties upon the three contracts with which this action is concerned. It appears to me, looking at those averments, that, at best for the defenders, there was a course of dealing between the parties, associated with a purpose on the part of the defenders to gain advantage from later contracts in a situation in which they had been disappointed as regards performance of the first contract. It may be therefore that it is true to say in this case that each contract was a consequence of its predecessor. However, that does not appear to me to assist the defenders in satisfying the criterion for the application of this exception. In all these circumstances, in my judgment, this exception is not applicable to the circumstances here.

I turn finally to the remaining exception to the general rule, which was invoked by the defenders, namely exceptional circumstances where retention must be allowed to meet the justice or convenience of the particular case. I believe that counsel were at one in accepting that the court did have an equitable discretion to allow retention in exceptional cases. Two decisions were discussed in this context, *Munro v Macdonald's Exrs* and *Ross v Ross*. In my opinion, the former case may more properly be seen as a decision relating to the exception of instant verification. However, there is no doubt that *Ross v Ross* is one where the court exercised its equitable discretion in allowing retention on the basis of the heir's illiquid claims. I agree with the submission of counsel for the pursuers that *Ross v Ross* was a wholly exceptional decision. Very strong equitable considerations operated against Lady Ross. In seeking her annuity, she did not come into court with clean hands, having failed to administer the entailed estates out of which the annuity had to be paid in a proper manner. Furthermore, in the accounts which she had prepared,

she had included as a debt on the estate a sum representing the capital value of the annuity for which she sued in the action. In these circumstances, it is easy to understand why the court were prepared to exercise their equitable discretion. In my opinion, no comparable circumstances exist in the present case. The litigants in the present action are two commercial entities, which have experienced certain contractual difficulties in their relationship. I can identify nothing in the circumstances averred here which would justify the court exercising its equitable discretion in this case. On the whole matter therefore, I have reached the conclusion that the submissions of the pursuers are well founded in that none of the recognised exceptions to the general rule exists in this case. It follows that, in my opinion, there is no basis upon which the defenders can retain the sum sued for pending the investigation and determination of their counterclaim for damages. In these circumstances I shall sustain both of the pursuers' pleas in law and grant decree in their favour against the defenders for the sum of £222,472.05 together with interest thereon as concluded for. I shall repel pleas in law nos 2, 3, 5, 6, 7 and 8 for the defenders. On the defenders' counterclaim, I shall allow a proof before answer.

Counsel for Pursuers, McNeill, QC; Solicitors, MacRoberts — Counsel for Defenders, Brodie, QC; Solicitors, Maclay Murray & Spens.

J P D

(NOTE)

Ferguson v McIntyre

OUTER HOUSE
LORD MURRAY
22 JANUARY 1993

Contract — Assignation of heritable right — Missives providing that conditions therein to subsist for limited period after delivery of disposition — Whether competent — Prescription and Limitation (Scotland) Act 1973 (c 52), s 13, as amended.

Prescription — Contract — Assignation of heritable right — Missives providing that conditions therein to subsist for limited period after delivery of disposition — Whether competent — Prescription and Limitation (Scotland) Act 1973 (c 52), s 13, as amended.

Purchasers of a croft had also stipulated in the missives for an assignation of a share in the common grazings to them by the seller. The missives provided that the missives only remained in full force and effect for three months after delivery of the disposition. The purchasers received a disposition but not the assignation. They sued their solicitor for his negligence in failing to obtain the assignation before their right to obtain one under the missives had expired. In defence

A it was argued that it was still possible to compel the seller to deliver the assignation since the three month limit on enforceability was struck at by s 13 of the Prescription and Limitation (Scotland) Act 1973.

Held, that the provisions of the 1973 Act did not operate to limit consensual agreement within the prescriptive period; and proof before answer *allowed*.

Dicta of Lord Kincraig in *McPhail v Cunninghame District Council,* 1985 SLT 149 at p 153, and Lord Wylie in *Pena v Ray,* 1987 SLT 609 at p 611D-E,
B *followed*.

Section 13 of the Prescription and Limitation (Scotland) Act 1973, as amended by the Prescription and Limitation (Scotland) Act 1984, provides:

"Any provision in any agreement purporting to provide in relation to any right or obligation that section 6, 7, 8 or 8A of this Act shall not have effect
C shall be null."

William Ferguson and another raised an action against their former solicitor, G J McIntyre, for damages for professional negligence in respect of instructions given by the pursuers to him to act as solicitor on their behalf in the purchase of a croft on the island of Skye described in a set of particulars which had been provided to the defender. The subjects had included a detached dwellinghouse and approximately 13.6 acres of croft ground. The parti-
D culars had provided that "in addition the croft is entitled to a share in the local common grazing".

Missives had been concluded by the defender for the purchase of the property, including condition 8 in a letter of 3 September 1985 in the following terms: "There is included in the purchase price the assignation of a share in the local common grazings and it is understood that there are no financial obligations incumbent upon the seller with regard to same." They
E also included condition 5 in a letter of 16 September 1985 in the following terms: "With regard to condition 14 of your said offer the missives shall remain in full force and effect for a period of 3 months only after delivery of the disposition in favour of the purchaser."

The pursuers averred that they would not have offered for the croft if the share in the common grazings had not been available and that the price paid had included the price for the assignation of the share in the common grazing. The pursuers had taken entry on
F or about 11 October 1985 but, since a properly executed disposition had not been delivered to the pursuers until about 6 November 1985, the period of time for the missives to be in force in accordance with the said condition 5 had expired about 6 February 1986. No assignation of the right to the share in the grazings had been granted in that time. The pursuers averred that the seller had thereafter refused to grant an assignation.

The defender argued that the provision about delivery within three months was struck at by s 13 of

the 1973 Act. On this issue the pursuers argued, as narrated by the Lord Ordinary (Murray), that "the G
defender's contention that s 13 of the 1973 Act rendered void a three month enforceability period for missives was incorrect in law. Sections 6, 7, 8 and 8A all applied to obligations which had subsisted continuously for the periods therein prescribed, all of which were greatly in excess of three months. The purpose of s 13 (as amended) was to prevent an extension of any such obligation beyond the periods prescribed, but not to put limits upon their subsistence in any way within such periods. The defender's H
construction of s 13 of the 1973 Act was not consistent with the view expressed by Lord Kincraig in *McPhail v Cunninghame District Council,* 1985 SLT 149 at p 153 (1983 SC 246). Lord Kincraig had held that the section assumed a deliberate intention on the part of contracting parties to make an obligation which was not extinguished by lapse of the statutory period. It did not operate, in his view, so as to make illegal a postponement of enforceability. By the same reasoning it would not stop a limitation of enforceability I
within such statutory period. This was also the view of McBryde on *Contract,* para 23-32, p 551. Furthermore the defender's contention was contradicted by the decision of Lord Wylie in *Pena v Ray,* 1987 SLT 609, at p 611D-E, that there was no reason in principle why agreement should not be competently reached as to the timescale within which missives should persist".

In allowing a proof before answer but excluding from probation the defender's averments about s 13 of J
the 1973 Act his Lordship said:

"The second separate issue is what is the proper legal construction of s 13 of the Prescription and Limitation (Scotland) Act 1973. On this point I prefer the argument presented by counsel for the pursuers, fortified as it is by judicial dicta by Lords Kincraig and Wylie and by McBryde on *Contract.* In my view the provisions of ss 6, 7, 8, 8A and 13 of the 1973 Act, considered in their context of the provisions of the Act as a whole including its long title, make it clear K
that there was no intention on the part of the legislature to limit consensual agreement that the enforceability of a contract, or a provision of a contract, could be postponed or limited without restriction within the prescriptive periods. Indeed I understand such limits to be relatively common in missives for the sale of heritage and it would be somewhat surprising, if the argument was well founded, that it had not been advanced successfully in any reported case in the last 20 years."
L

Counsel for Pursuers, Agnew of Lochnaw; Solicitors, W & J Burness, WS — Counsel for Defender, D I Mackay; Solicitors, Simpson & Marwick, WS.

C H

[The defender has enrolled a reclaiming motion.]

Farooq v HM Advocate

A   HIGH COURT OF JUSTICIARY

THE LORD JUSTICE CLERK (ROSS),
LORDS McCLUSKEY AND MORISON

5 JULY 1991

*Justiciary — Procedure — Trial — Charge to jury —
Hearsay evidence admitted at trial as being de recenti
statements — Judge failing to direct jury that only to be
used in assessing credibility and not as evidence of facts
B — Whether misdirection — Whether miscarriage of
justice.*

*Justiciary — Procedure — Retrial — Evidence at original
trial unsatisfactory — Child witnesses — Whether retrial
appropriate — Criminal Procedure (Scotland) Act 1975
(c 21), ss 254 (1) (c) and 255.*

An accused was charged on indictment with various
sexual offences in relation to two children. In the
course of his trial hearsay evidence was admitted
C   without objection as evidence of de recenti statements
bearing on the credibility of witnesses. In his charge
to the jury the trial judge gave no direction of the
limited purpose for which such hearsay evidence
could be used. The accused was convicted and
appealed. In his report to the appeal court the trial
judge stated that he had attempted in his charge to
focus the jury's attention on whether they believed the
complainers and the evidence of the confessions said
to have been made by the accused. He also expressed
D   surprise at the verdict of the jury in view of conflicts
and inconsistencies in the evidence and difficulties
occasioned by the requirement for an interpreter.

Held, (1) (the Crown conceding that there had been
a misdirection) that this was a case where it was essential to explain to the jury the limited purpose for
which evidence of de recenti statements was available,
and that as the jury could have concluded from the
directions given that the hearsay evidence was evid-
E   ence of the facts alleged in the statements, there had
been a miscarriage of justice (pp 1273K-1274A); (2)
that the unsatisfactory nature of the evidence led at
trial and the fact that children would be required to
give evidence again meant that it was not a case where
authority for a fresh prosecution under ss 254 (1) (c)
and 255 of the 1975 Act should be granted (p 1274C-
D); and appeal *allowed* and convictions *quashed.*

F   **Indictment**

Mohammed Farooq was charged at the instance of
the rt hon the Lord Fraser of Carmyllie, Her
Majesty's Advocate, on an indictment which libelled,
inter alia, lewd and libidinous practices and sodomy in
respect of two boys. He pled not guilty and proceeded
to trial in the High Court at Glasgow before Lord
Morton of Shuna and a jury.

The accused was convicted and appealed to the
High Court by note of appeal against conviction.

Cases referred to

Kelly v Docherty, 1991 SLT 419; 1991 SCCR 312.   G
Morton v HM Advocate, 1938 SLT 27; 1938 JC 50.

The trial judge provided a report in the following
terms, inter alia:

LORD MORTON OF SHUNA.—In this case the
appellant was convicted of sexual offences against two
brothers. The offences against the younger boy YA
were alleged to have been committed on one occasion
when it was alleged that YA and the appellant had
shared a bed on a date which the evidence suggested   H
was about October 1987, when YA was near his
seventh birthday. The offences against the elder boy
were said to have been committed on several occasions
between late March 1990 and early May 1990. The
Crown relied for corroboration on confessions said to
have been made by the appellant shortly after the
occasion of the offence against YA and again shortly
after the offence against his brother FA. In the course
of the evidence there was hearsay evidence including
what each boy had said to his mother and in the case   I
of YA to FA. In addition, in the course of the evidence, which was mainly through an interpreter, a
certain amount of hearsay relating to collateral matters
emerged. The ground of appeal is that I failed to give
any direction about hearsay evidence. I gave no such
direction as I took the view, as I tried to make clear
in my charge to the jury, that the only possible
corroboration of the accounts by each boy was the confessions said to have been made by the appellant and
that the jury had to decide whether the confessions   J
had occurred. I attempted to focus the attention of the
jury on the issues of whether they believed each boy
and if so, whether they found the evidence of the confession relating to that boy acceptable.

I was surprised by the verdict of the jury. There
were so many conflicts in the evidence and so many
inconsistencies that these, together with the unavoidable difficulties of comprehension by witnesses who
did not speak English and came from a very different   K
background and the difficulties of assessment of the
reliability of evidence occasioned by the requirement
of an interpreter, made it very difficult to see that a
reasonable jury would have been able to hold that any
crucial fact was established beyond reasonable doubt.
There was no medical or forensic evidence. No medical
examination took place in regard to the younger boy
YA and the medical examination of FA revealed
nothing at all. The police evidence was that when the
appellant was seen and told of the allegations he strenu-   L
ously denied them. The only evidence against the
appellant came from relatives of the complainers. The
mothers of the appellant and of the two complainers
were sisters. There appeared to be difficulties between
the father of the complainers and the appellant and his
father in that the father of the complainers had made
an apparently false accusation of theft against the
appellant and the appellant had written a letter, which
he got his father to sign, to the immigration authorities
accusing the father of the complainers of arranging
illegal immigration from Pakistan.

[His Lordship then dealt at length with the evidence and concluded:]

I have attempted to narrate the evidence at some length to draw attention to the apparent contradictions and inconsistencies in it. If the jury chose to pick and choose fairly carefully, there was evidence which they could accept and other evidence which they could reject so that there would be sufficient evidence for conviction. No motion on the ground of insufficiency of evidence was made by counsel for the appellant. The quality of the evidence was very unsatisfactory. This was possibly affected by the fact that more than half the witnesses required an interpreter and even with this assistance there seemed to be some difficulties in comprehension by the witnesses. There were also the difficulties inherent in what appeared to be a society very different from that normally encountered in Glasgow. In addition to the unsatisfactory quality of the evidence there appeared to be other difficulties in the Crown case. If FA's evidence was correct and the incidents started in early April, it is difficult to have them ending when his mother said that she got his confession about 8-10 days after the end of Ramadan which would be well into May. FA spoke to four occasions each separated by at most two or three days from the previous incident, which would imply that everything happened over a period of about 10 days. It also appeared odd that Mrs A did not tell her husband until some days after he had returned from Pakistan. It was also odd that on the day that [her husband] did return from Pakistan he and his wife were entertained at the appellant's parents' house in the presence of the appellant after Mr and Mrs Mahmood had picked up [the husband] from Glasgow airport. It is also perhaps surprising that when the police investigated the allegations by F in May 1990 nothing was mentioned by anyone to the police about YA. The allegations about YA were only made to the police in October 1990 and according to the appellant this was after he had been informed by his solicitor that the complaints against him regarding F were to be dropped.

It is my impression that a miscarriage of justice has occurred in this case in that the only appropriate verdict for a reasonable jury to arrive at was a verdict of not proven, unless they believed the total and consistent denial by the appellant that anything had happened.

Appeal

The accused lodged a note of appeal in the following terms:

In the course of the trial there was a considerable body of hearsay evidence to the effect that the appellant had committed the crimes libelled. The bulk of this hearsay evidence was admissible as de recenti statements or otherwise bearing on the credibility of witnesses; some hearsay evidence was also allowed to emerge without objection, because of difficulties occasioned by the age and/or language of some of the witnesses.

The trial judge failed to direct the jury that the hearsay evidence could only be used to assist in assessing the credibility of the witnesses and was not evidence of the facts alleged in the hearsay statements and in particular could not provide corroboration of the other evidence that the appellant committed the crimes libelled.

The failure to give said direction amounted to a miscarriage of justice.

A further ground of appeal was subsequently lodged stating:

(1) The nature, quality and state of the evidence led at the trial was such that no reasonable jury would have been entitled to convict the appellant of any part of the indictment. Accordingly, his conviction was a miscarriage of justice. Reference is made to the trial judge's report at p [1272E supra] and previous pages where he sets out "his opinion on the case generally" as required by the Criminal Procedure (Scotland) Act 1975, s 236A.

The appeal was heard before the High Court on 5 July 1991.

Eo die the court *allowed* the appeal and *quashed* the conviction.

The following opinion of the court was delivered by the Lord Justice Clerk (Ross):

OPINION OF THE COURT.—The appellant is Mohammed Farooq. He went to trial in the High Court in Glasgow on an indictment containing four charges. He was found guilty of charge 1, charge 2 and charge 3 (a) and (c). He has now appealed against conviction. The charges of which he was found guilty were charges of lewd, indecent and libidinous practices, attempted sodomy and sodomy in respect of two children who were his cousins. One of the complainers was born on 18 October 1980 and the offences in relation to him were said to have taken place between May 1987 and February 1988. Accordingly he must have been at the most seven years old at the time. The other complainer was born on 12 April 1975 and so far as he was concerned, he must have been approximately 15 years of age at the time of the offences. In the grounds of appeal the point is made that there was a considerable body of hearsay evidence led before the jury. It is said that the bulk of this hearsay was admissible as being de recenti statements, but the ground of appeal emphasises that the trial judge failed to direct the jury that hearsay evidence could only be used to assist in assessing the credibility of the witnesses and was not evidence of the facts alleged in the hearsay statements.

In presenting the appeal today, counsel has drawn attention to what the trial judge said in his report regarding the hearsay evidence. The trial judge tells us in a long and very careful report that in the course of the evidence in relation to the charges against the younger child there was hearsay evidence including

A what each boy had said to his mother and in the case of the younger child what that child had said to his brother who was the other complainer. The trial judge also tells us that as regards the older of the two complainers he testified that the other complainer had told him what had happened the following morning. He also records that evidence was led by the mother of the complainers. She spoke to having questioned the younger complainer about some money which he had in his possession. He was reluctant to say anything to her until she threatened to hit him with a stick and he
B then said to her that the appellant had, in his words, "done a mischief with him" and had given him the £1 note. In a later portion of his report the trial judge also refers to evidence which the mother of the children gave in relation to the elder complainer. There was what appeared to be a lovebite on him and she thought that he had been associating with a girl, but eventually was told by the boy that the mark had been caused by the appellant. She apparently told her husband who had been out of the country and he testified that his
C wife had told him of these allegations two or three days after his return.

In these circumstances counsel maintained that these were three clear instances of hearsay. He reminded us that these statements were not evidence of the facts alleged although he conceded that they were all de recenti and were admissible insofar as they might throw light upon the credibility of the complainers. He drew attention to the well known passage in *Morton v HM Advocate* and in particular to the
D passage from Lord Justice Clerk Aitchison at 1938 SLT, p 28. The Lord Justice Clerk there said: "A statement made by an injured party *de recenti*, unless it can be brought within the rule of *res gestae*, is ordinarily inadmissible as being hearsay only; but an exception is allowed in the case of sexual assaults upon women and children, including sexual offences against young boys. In cases of that kind the Court will allow the evidence of complaints or statements *de recenti* made by the injured party, for the limited purpose of
E shewing that the conduct of the injured party has been consistent and the story is not an afterthought, and, in the case of assaults upon women, to negative consent. A complaint *de recenti* increases the probability that the complaint is true and not concocted, and the absence of complaint where sexual offences are alleged is always a material point for the defence. But it must be clearly affirmed that the evidence is admissible as bearing upon credibility only, and the statements of an injured party, although made *de recenti* of the com-
F mission of a crime, do not in law amount to corroboration."

Counsel for the appellant's complaint was that in the present case the trial judge had given no direction whatsoever on hearsay or as regards the use which might be made of hearsay which is in the form of a de recenti statement. He accordingly maintained that there had been misdirection by the trial judge and that this had produced a miscarriage of justice. He recognised that in his charge the trial judge had presented the case to the jury upon the basis that they would first

of all require to consider the evidence of the complainers and determine whether they were satisfied G
with their evidence. If they did find the evidence of the complainers true and reliable, they were then directed that they would have next to consider whether they were satisfied with the evidence about certain confessions which were alleged to have been made by the appellant. On the other hand, counsel also drew attention to the fact that in his charge the trial judge had reminded the jury that they required to return their verdict according to the evidence and that it is the evidence and only the evidence in the case H
upon which they had to decide the case, and the trial judge added: "It is for you to decide what to make of the evidence; to decide what evidence of any witness you accept as true and reliable, and what evidence you decide to reject as being untrue or unreliable." He also, having directed the jury as to how they should approach the case by considering the evidence of the complainers and the evidence of the confessions, then added a direction as follows: "Now I am not going into the evidence in any way at all. It is not for me. It is I
for you to consider what evidence is significant and what evidence is of little moment. You consider it in the light of the speeches that counsel have made and you retire and consider your verdict." In these circumstances counsel maintained that hearsay evidence had been led before the jury and it had never been explained to them that it was only available for limited purposes. That being so, they may well have considered that they were entitled to attach weight to the hearsay evidence and use it as evidence of the facts J
alleged in the statements.

The advocate depute accepted that the judge had failed to give a direction which he should have given in the circumstances, but he maintained that there had not been a miscarriage of justice. He reminded us of the way in which the trial judge had directed the jury to approach their consideration of the charges and he submitted that, since he had directed them to consider the evidence of the complainers and then to see whether there was corroboration in the confessions, it K
had not been demonstrated that there had been any miscarriage of justice.

We cannot accept the submissions made on behalf of the Crown. This was a case where it was essential for the trial judge to explain to the jury the limited purpose for which the evidence of de recenti statements was available. He gave them no direction on hearsay whatsoever. He gave no direction on the use which may be made of de recenti statements for the L
purpose of assessing the credibility of the complainers and the jury appears to have been left to consider all the evidence, which must of course include the hearsay evidence to which we have already referred. That being so, when the jury were reminded that it was for them to consider what evidence was significant, they may well have concluded that the hearsay evidence was significant and they may erroneously have concluded that such evidence was evidence of the facts alleged in the statement. That being so, we are satisfied that there was a misdirection as the Crown

concede and moreover that there was a miscarriage of justice.

The advocate depute's final submission was that if the court should be of the view that there had been a miscarriage of justice, then instead of quashing the conviction the court should set aside the verdict of the jury and should grant authority to bring a new prosecution in accordance with s 254 (1) (c) and s 255 of the Criminal Procedure (Scotland) Act 1975. He stressed that if there had been any fault in this case it was not fault on the part of the Crown, and since the miscarriage of justice had resulted from a failure on the part of the trial judge, the proper course would be to allow a fresh prosecution to be brought. Counsel for the appellant on the other hand reminded us that this was a case which concerned young children. He pointed out that there had been difficulties at the trial because of the age of the children and because of the fact that much of the evidence had to be taken with the aid of an interpreter. He also reminded us that in his report to us the trial judge has emphasised that the evidence which was led at the trial was unsatisfactory and was full of apparent contradictions and inconsistencies. To such an extent was that so that the trial judge, when giving us his opinion on the case, expresses the view that there had been a miscarriage of justice. When all these matters are taken into account, it appears to us clear that this is not a case where the court should grant authority to bring a fresh prosecution. In *Kelly v Docherty* one of the circumstances which persuaded the court that authority should not be granted for a fresh prosecution was that a child would have to give evidence again and that doing so might well distress the child. That is undoubtedly a factor which we regard as of importance in this case and when we take into account the whole circumstances of this case, including the unsatisfactory nature of the evidence led at the first trial, we have come to the conclusion that this is clearly not a case where authority should be given to bring a fresh prosecution. Accordingly being satisfied that there was a miscarriage of justice in this case, the convictions are now quashed.

Counsel for Appellant, Totten; Solicitors, Macbeth, Currie & Co, WS (for Beltrami & Co, Glasgow) — Counsel for Respondent, Macdonald, QC, A D; Solicitor, J D Lowe, Crown Agent.

S D D N

Stuart Eves Ltd (in liquidation) v Smiths Gore

OUTER HOUSE
LORD COULSFIELD
16 AUGUST 1991

Company — Insolvency — Gratuitous alienation — Cheque drawn on company account in payment of debt due by director of company to third person — Whether alienation by company to third person — Effect of statute on alienation prior to commencement of statutory provisions — Insolvency Act 1986 (c 45), s 242 and Sched 11, paras 4 and 9 — Bankruptcy Act 1621 (c 18).

Process — Pleadings — Relevancy — Challenge to gratuitous alienation — Pursuers founding on statutory provisions — Whether relevant case at common law pled — Insolvency Act 1986 (c 45), s 242.

Section 242 of the Insolvency Act 1986 entitles inter alia a liquidator to challenge an alienation effected by a company whether before or after 1 April 1986. Schedule 11, para 9 (1) to the 1986 Act states: "a . . . transaction entered into before the appointed day shall not be set aside under [s 242] . . . except to the extent that it could have been set aside under the law in force immediately before that day".

During February 1985, the directors of a company became aware that the value of the company's assets was less than the amount of its liabilities. In May 1985 in furtherance of a proposed scheme to refinance the company, the owner of the whole issued share capital of the company and one of its two directors requested the other director to sign six blank cheques drawn on the company's account. The refinancing scheme did not proceed and the first director paid £8,000 to another firm by means of one of these cheques in connection with a shooting syndicate of which the director was a member.

In November 1985 a liquidator was appointed to the company. The liquidator sought declarator that the payment to the firm constituted a challengeable alienation within the meaning of s 242 of the 1986 Act. The firm challenged the relevancy of the pursuers' averments, arguing that the pursuers' claim under s 242 was irrelevant as by virtue of Sched 11 any challenge to an alienation effected prior to the appointed day in terms of the Act had to be made in terms of the statutory law in force prior to the appointed day, namely the Bankruptcy Act 1621. As there was no averment in relation to the requirements of the provisions of the 1621 Act no relevant case was pled. Secondly, there were no relevant averments of an alienation by the company to the firm, but rather any alienation by the company was made to the second defender.

Held, (1) that as the pursuers were entitled to challenge gratuitous alienations at common law, with the liquidator's statutory title to pursue an action for reduction of a gratuitous alienation depending upon s 242 of the 1986 Act, references in the pursuers' pleadings to s 242 were not necessarily inconsistent

with an intention to plead a case at common law
A (p 1277E-G); (2) that, as on the averments the
payment which constituted the alienation was made by
a cheque of the company signed on its behalf by
persons authorised to do so and drawn on the company's bank account, the pursuers had relevantly
averred a gratuitous alienation at common law by the
company to the first defenders (p 1277H-I); and proof
before answer *allowed*.

B **Action of declarator and payment**

Stuart Eves Ltd, a company in voluntary liquidation, and the liquidator thereof raised an action against
(first) Smiths Gore, a partnership carrying on business
in Edinburgh and (second) a former director and
shareholder of the company, for declarator that a
payment of £8,000 made by the company to the first
named defenders constituted a challengeable alienation within the meaning of s 242 of the Insolvency Act
1986 and for payment by the defenders jointly and
severally or severally of the sum of £8,000.
C

The case came before the Lord Ordinary
(Coulsfield) on procedure roll on the first defenders'
plea to the relevancy of the pursuers' averments.

Statutory provisions

The Insolvency Act 1986 provides:

"242.—(1) Where this subsection applies and — (a)
the winding up of a company has commenced, an
alienation by the company is challengeable by — (i)
D any creditor who is a creditor by virtue of a debt
incurred on or before the date of such commencement,
or (ii) the liquidator; (b) an administration order is in
force in relation to a company, an alienation by the
company is challengeable by the administrator.

"(2) Subsection (1) applies where — (a) by the alienation, whether before or after 1st April 1986 (the
coming into force of section 75 of the Bankruptcy
(Scotland) Act 1985), any part of the company's
E property is transferred or any claim or right of the
company is discharged or renounced, and (b) the
alienation takes place on a relevant day. . . .

"(7) A liquidator and an administrator have the same
right as a creditor has under any rule of law to
challenge an alienation of a company made for no consideration or no adequate consideration.

"436. In this Act . . . 'the appointed day' means the
day on which this Act comes into force under section
F 443. . . .

"[Sched 11] 4.—(1) In relation to any winding up
which has commenced, or is treated as having commenced, before the appointed day, the new law does
not apply, and the former law continues to have effect,
subject to the following paragraphs.

"(2) 'The new law' here means any provisions in the
first Group of Parts of this Act which replace sections
66 to 87 and 89 to 105 of the Insolvency Act 1985; and
'the former law' means Parts XX and XXI of the
Companies Act (without the amendments in para-

graphs 23 to 52 of Schedule 6 to the Insolvency Act
1985, or the associated repeals made by that Act). . . . G

"9.—(1) Where a provision in Part VI of this Act
applies in relation to a winding up or in relation to a
case in which an administration order has been made,
a preference given, floating charge created or other
transaction entered into before the appointed day shall
not be set aside under that provision except to the
extent that it could have been set aside under the law
in force immediately before that day, assuming for this
purpose that any relevant administration order had
been a winding up order.   H

"(2) The references above to setting aside a preference, floating charge or other transaction include the
making of an order which varies or reverses any effect
of a preference, floating charge or other transaction."

Case referred to

Bank of Scotland, Petitioners, 1988 SLT 282 (OH);
1988 SLT 690 (1st Div).

Textbooks referred to   I

Palmer, *Company Law* (24th ed), para 90-67.
St Clair and Drummond Young, *Corporate Insolvency*,
para 13-3.

On 16 August 1991 his Lordship *allowed* proof
before answer on the whole case.

LORD COULSFIELD.—The pursuers in this
action are a limited company now in voluntary liquidation and the liquidator thereof. The winding up of J
the company began on 12 November 1985. In this
action the pursuers seek declarator that a payment of
£8,000 made on 15 May 1985 to the first named
defenders, a partnership carrying on business in Edinburgh, constituted a challengeable alienation within
the meaning of s 242 of the Insolvency Act 1986. The
second defender was a director of the company from
1 September 1981 until 24 June 1985 and held the
whole shareholding in the company until 28 June
1985. He was responsible, in the manner hereinafter K
set out, for making the payment which is sought to be
challenged, and by the second conclusion of the
summons, the pursuers seek decree against the
defenders jointly and severally or severally for the sum
of £8,000. The action came before me in procedure
roll on 12 July 1991 and, at the start of the hearing,
counsel for the pursuers intimated that an agreement
had been reached with the second defender, and as a
result the action against him should be dismissed of
consent without any award of expenses. The debate L
proceeded on the first defenders' plea in law, a general
plea to the relevancy, and the first defenders sought
dismissal of the action against them.

The case set out in the pursuers' averments is as
follows: as at 28 February 1985, the current liabilities
of the company, the first named pursuers, exceeded its
total assets by £3,409.98 and in addition there were
sums due to be paid to creditors after more than one
year after 28 February 1985 amounting to £31,630.68.
The profit and loss account of the company for the

year to 28 February 1985 showed a loss in excess of £36,000 after taxation had been taken into account. Accordingly, as at 28 February 1985 the company was absolutely insolvent and it remained so until the appointment of the second named pursuer as liquidator on 12 November 1985. As at 30 June 1985, the liabilities of the first named pursuers exceeded their total assets by £21,806. The second defender was aware of the financial position of the company and in May 1985 he proposed a scheme to the only other director of the company, Stuart G Eves, which would involve the injection of a capital sum by Allied Hambro based upon certain collateral which would be provided by the two directors. In connection with that scheme, the second defender requested Mr Eves to sign six blank cheques, including one number 161537, on the company's account, representing that these would be stage payments to Allied Hambro in pursuance of the scheme. On or about 15 May 1985, the company paid the first named defenders the sum of £8,000 by means of the cheque numbered 161537. That payment was made on the instructions of the second named defender. The pursuers aver that the payment is believed to have been made in connection with a shooting syndicate of which the second named defender was a member, that the first named pursuers received no consideration for the payment and that it became completely effectual less than two years before the date of commencement of the winding up of the first named pursuers. They therefore aver that the payment constitutes a challengeable alienation of the first named pursuers' assets and refer to s 242 of the Insolvency Act 1986 and to paras 4 and 9 of Sched 11 to that Act and in addition to s 615A of the Companies Act 1985. It appears that the scheme did not in fact proceed and that the second defender withdrew a guarantee over the company's account on 7 June 1985, with the consequence that the account was thereafter frozen.

The first defenders challenged the relevancy of the pursuers' averments on two grounds: first, that the averments in support of the pursuers' claim under s 242 of the 1986 Act were irrelevant because there were no averments which would support a claim under the Act 1621, as would be necessary in view of the transitional provisions of the 1986 Act; and, secondly, that there were no relevant averments of an alienation by the company to the first defenders but, on a proper analysis, any alienation by the company was made to the second defender.

Section 242 of the 1986 Act re-enacted certain provisions of the Bankruptcy (Scotland) Act 1985 which amended the Companies Act 1985 by inserting a new s 615A in that Act in terms identical with s 242 as it now stands. The Bankruptcy (Scotland) Act came into effect on 1 April 1986 and the 1986 Act came into effect on 29 December 1986. Section 242 of the 1986 Act, so far as material, provides: [his Lordship quoted the terms of s 242 (1) and (2) and continued:]

Subsection (3) defines the period within which a challenge may be made, and there is no dispute that in the present case the alienation was made within the appropriate period. Subsection (4) provides for the granting of a decree of reduction and for certain defences to an action for reduction the onus of proof being placed on the defender; and subss (5) and (6) make further provision in connection with these matters. Subsection (7) provides: [his Lordship quoted the terms of s 242 (7) and continued:]

Schedule 11 to the Act contains transitional provisions, which are given effect by s 437. Paragraph 4 of Sched 11 provides: [his Lordship quoted the terms of para 4 and then para 9 and continued:]

The significance of the date 1 April 1986 in the provisions of the 1986 Act is that that was the date on which s 615A of the Companies Act 1985, as inserted by the Bankruptcy (Scotland) Act 1985, came into force. The alienation in the present case took place before that date, on 15 May 1985.

Counsel for the first defenders submitted that the only case for the pursuers was one made under statute: there was no alternative common law case. He accepted that, on its terms, s 242 of the 1986 Act does apply to alienations which took place prior to 1 April 1986. He submitted, however, that, in view of the terms of paras 4 and 9 of Sched 11 to the 1986 Act, any challenge made to such an alienation must be based upon the statutory law governing challenges to gratuitous alienations prior to 1 April 1986. The statutory law in force prior to 1 April 1986 was the Act 1621 c 18, which permitted creditors to challenge alienations to conjunct and confident persons and, in the circumstances allowed by the Act, placed the onus of proof of the solvency of the party making the alienation upon the person to whom it was made. In the present case, however, there was no attempt to aver a case which would meet the requirements of the Act 1621 c 18 and in particular no averment that there had been an alienation to a conjunct or confident person, within the meaning of that Act. Counsel accepted that, as was held in *Bank of Scotland, Petrs*, the common law rules allowing challenges of alienations continued in force, so that the alternative of a common law case was open to a liquidator. However, if a liquidator wished to found upon the statute, he required to rely upon the Act 1621 c 18. Counsel submitted that the words "other transaction" in para 9 (1) of Sched 11 to the 1986 Act must include a gratuitous alienation and that the words "the law in force immediately before that day" must refer to the statutory law in force. The whole of the Schedule was dealing with transitional provisions and savings and there was no need for it to deal with the common law, which was not superseded. The statute was dealing, and required to deal, only with law which was being repealed and it was only in relation to repeals that the provisions with regard to the appointed day became relevant. The whole context of the provision was that of a statutory challenge, and the wording "law in force" was more appropriate to express statutory rather than common law, since the implication was that the law would cease to be in force on the appointed day. Counsel also examined the complex provisions in relation to the dates on which the statutory provisions came into effect, and the problems to which those provisions gave rise, under reference to the discussion in Palmer, *Company Law* (24th ed), para 90-67, and St Clair and Drummond Young, *Corporate Insolvency*, para 13-3. However, on the view I take of this case it is not necessary to discuss these problems.

Counsel for the pursuers submitted that the point in the case was the application of s 242 to liquidations commenced before 1 April 1986 and the restriction of that application by the provisions of Sched 11. He agreed that para 9 of Sched 11 extended to, inter alia, gratuitous alienations but suggested that it was not significant to consider precisely what the appointed day meant because, on any view, the alienation in question in the present case preceded both 1 April 1986 and 29 December 1986. He submitted that the expression "the law in force immediately before that day" need not be confined to the statutory law but on its terms related to all the law. There was nothing inconsistent with that in the survival of the common law grounds of challenge of gratuitous alienations after 1 April 1986, since after that date the liquidator had an option whether to rely on the common law or on statute. The effect of the provisions was that, in dealing with an alienation prior to 1 April 1986, the liquidator was entitled to proceed under s 242 but had to take on board the common law onus of proving that the company was insolvent at the time of the liquidation. That had been done in the pursuers' averments and it had also been averred that the company received no consideration for the alienation. He did not seek to take advantage of any benefit in relation to the onus of proof which s 242 might confer in a liquidation commencing after 1 April 1986. The liquidator had no statutory title to challenge any alienation apart from s 242. The whole argument, he submitted, was very technical since there was no doubt that the liquidator could proceed to challenge the alienation in question under the common law.

In my opinion, the issue in this case at this stage resolves into one of pleading. It is not disputed that the pursuers are entitled to challenge a gratuitous alienation at common law, nor that the pursuers' averments contain sufficient material for a relevant case for reduction at common law. The pursuers' averments refer to s 242 of the 1986 Act and to paras 4 and 9 of Sched 11 and there is a plea in law which refers to that section. As I understand the position, prior to the Act of 1985, a liquidator had no express statutory title to pursue an action for reduction of a gratuitous alienation, although such an action could be pursued by the company. The title of a liquidator and, now, an administrator, to pursue such an action depends upon s 242 of the 1986 Act. A reference to s 242 may, therefore, not necessarily be inconsistent with an intention to plead a common law case. Looking to the pleadings as a whole, I am inclined to think that the pleader did have it in mind to found upon the statute, and take advantage of the statutory shift of onus; or at least that he had not clearly excluded that possibility. Nevertheless, in my view, the pursuers' pleadings can properly be treated as setting out a case at common law. The

pursuers offer to prove all the elements necessary to establish such a case, and do not restrict themselves to the relatively limited averments necessary to make a relevant case under s 242. As counsel for the pursuers said, it would be somewhat technical to refuse probation in a case such as this. In my opinion, therefore, the pursuers' case should go to inquiry.

The second argument for the first defenders was that on a proper analysis, the transaction was an alienation by the company to the second defender and was really equivalent to a payment by the company to the second defender used by him to pay off a debt due by him to the first defenders. In my opinion, that argument is unsound. The payment was made by a cheque of the company, signed on its behalf by persons authorised to do so and drawn on the company's bank account. It was paid direct to and received by the first defenders. It is true that funds might have been taken out of the company by a different form of transaction and received by the first defenders in circumstances in which a challenge of this kind could not have been mounted. In my view, however, that is irrelevant. The proper approach is to examine the transaction which did in fact take place. There are ample averments that the payment was made in the way indicated and was received by the first defenders and there is no challenge to the sufficiency of those averments, in other respects, to support a case that there was a gratuitous alienation.

There was some discussion of the pursuers' claim for interest on the sum sought, but it was agreed that that question might be resolved after proof, if proof should take place.

In my opinion, the appropriate course is to allow a proof before answer on the whole case.

Counsel for Pursuers, Philip, QC; Solicitors, Simpson & Marwick, WS — Counsel for First Defender, C M Campbell, QC; Solicitors, Murray, Beith & Murray, WS — Counsel for Second Defender, Cheyne; Solicitors, Campbell Smith & Co, WS.

M L B F

F v Kennedy (No 1)

SECOND DIVISION

THE LORD JUSTICE CLERK (ROSS), LORDS COWIE AND MORISON

18 OCTOBER 1991

Children and young persons — Children's hearing — Application to sheriff for finding whether or not grounds for referral established — Child alleged to be victim of offence — Evidence of child — Hearsay evidence of interviews with social workers — Sheriff not examining child as to whether he knew difference between telling lies and truth, nor admonishing him to tell truth due to child

A *remaining mute throughout proceedings — Whether evidence of what child said to others competent — Civil Evidence (Scotland) Act 1988 (c 32), s 2 (1).*

Evidence — Competency — Hearsay — Proof of grounds for referral to children's hearing — Hearsay evidence of child's interviews with social workers — Sheriff not examining child as to whether he knew difference between telling lies and truth, nor admonishing him to tell truth due to child remaining mute throughout proceedings — Whether evidence of what child said to others competent — Civil Evidence (Scotland) Act 1988 (c 32), s 2 (1).

B
By s 2 (1) (b) of the Civil Evidence (Scotland) Act 1988, provision is made for hearsay evidence to be accepted as evidence of any matter contained in a statement made otherwise than in the course of a proof where direct oral evidence of the person making the statement would be admissible.

Several children were referred to a children's hearing on the ground, inter alia, that they had been subjected to lewd, indecent and libidinous practices.
C The grounds for referral were not accepted by the children's father and an application was made to the sheriff for a finding as to whether or not the grounds for referral had been established. One of the witnesses was one of the children (W) who was aged three at the time of the hearing before the sheriff. When called as a witness W remained silent and refused to answer any questions. The sheriff neither examined the child, to see whether he knew the difference between telling lies and telling the truth, nor admonished him to tell
D the truth. He did, however, allow hearsay evidence of what W had said to social workers and others. In finding that the grounds for referral had been established, the sheriff relied to a certain extent upon that evidence. The father thereafter appealed to the Court of Session by way of stated case and argued, inter alia, that the sheriff had erred in admitting the hearsay evidence as it did not fall within the ambit of s 2 of the 1988 Act.

Held, (1) that before a young child could be
E admitted to give evidence the judge or sheriff had to carry out a preliminary examination of the child to see whether he knew the difference between what was true and what was false and had then to admonish him to tell the truth (p 1280F); (2) that since in the present case it had not been possible for the sheriff to carry out any examination of W to see whether he knew the difference between truth and falsehood or to admonish W to tell the truth because W had remained mute throughout, the provisions of s 2 (1) (b) of the 1988
F Act had not been satisfied with regard to W (p 1280F-G); and (3) that, as the sheriff had admitted to relying upon the hearsay evidence in reaching his findings, the case had to be remitted to him in order for him to make clear the extent to which he had relied upon that evidence (pp 1280L-1281A); and appeal *allowed* and case *remitted* to the sheriff.

Rees v Lowe, 1990 SLT 507 and *Kelly v Docherty,* 1991 SLT 419, *followed; W v Kennedy,* 1988 SLT 583, *distinguished.*

Appeal from the sheriff court

Frederick J Kennedy, reporter to the children's G panel for Strathclyde Region, referred to a children's hearing three children of the same family, namely J, born on 9 January 1985, W, born 18 November 1986, and G, born 15 October 1988. The grounds for referral were the same for each child, the grounds for the child J and the supporting statement of facts being as follows:

"J, born on 9 January 1985, is being referred to a children's hearing for Strathclyde Region on the grounds of the following conditions: That in terms of H s 32 (2) (b) of the Social Work (Scotland) Act 1968 he is falling into bad associations or is exposed to moral danger, and in terms of s 32 (2) (d) of the same Act any of the offences mentioned in Sched 1 to the Criminal Procedure (Scotland) Act 1975 has been committed in respect of him or in respect of a child who is a member of the same household.

"Statement of facts
"In support of the above conditions it is stated that: I

"(1) J was born on 9 January 1985 and is the son of F and Mrs F.

"(2) The child normally resides with his parents and his brothers, W, aged three years, and G, aged one year nine months, at X.

"(3) On several occasions, the exact dates unknown to the reporter, at Y and elsewhere unknown to the reporter, the child has been subjected to lewd, indecent and libidinous practices and behaviour by J adults involving indecent tickling of the child's private parts, and participation in games or acts of an indecent nature when the child and adults were naked or partly clothed.

"(4) On several occasions, the exact dates unknown to the reporter, at Y and elsewhere unknown to the reporter, the child has been encouraged to become actively physically involved in lewd, indecent and libidinous practices and behaviour with adults and K children and that involved in these activities were the child's cousins, M and I, aged eight years and 10 years respectively.

"(5) On 22 June 1990 at Yorkhill hospital, Glasgow, police surgeon, Dr McLay, and paediatrician, Dr Anne Sutton, examined the child's cousins, M and I; that it was the opinion of both doctors that the child's cousins had been sexually abused and, in particular, that M had been the victim of repeated and long term L instances of sexual abuse.

"(6) The child has inappropriate knowledge of full sexual intercourse and sexual behaviour, and displays inappropriate sexual behaviour by attempting to involve adults in sexual activities.

"(7) On several occasions, the exact dates unknown to the reporter, at Y, the child has been inappropriately exposed to body fluids, secretions and excretions in a manner which could be injurious to physical and psychological well being.

"(8) On 20 May 1990 the child's mother was referred to the female and child unit of Ayr police and from there to Seafield hospital, by her general practitioner, Dr Niblock, as she had alleged that her husband had sexually abused the child.

"(9) On Monday, 18 June 1990, being concerned for the safety of the child, the social work department obtained a seven day place of safety warrant signed by a justice of the peace in order to place the child in the care of the local authority."

JF, the father of J, W and G, did not accept the grounds for referral. The reporter made an application to the sheriff court in terms of s 42 (7) of the 1968 Act.

Statutory provisions

The Civil Evidence (Scotland) Act 1988 provides:

"2.—(1) In any civil proceedings — (a) evidence shall not be excluded solely on the ground that it is hearsay; (b) a statement made by a person otherwise than in the course of the proof shall be admissible as evidence of any matter contained in the statement of which direct oral evidence by that person would be admissible; and (c) the court, or as the case may be the jury, if satisfied that any fact has been established by evidence in those proceedings, shall be entitled to find that fact proved by the evidence notwithstanding that the evidence is hearsay."

Cases referred to

K v K [1989] FCR 356.
Kelly v Docherty, 1991 SLT 419; 1991 SCCR 312.
Rees v Lowe, 1990 SLT 507; 1990 JC 96; 1989 SCCR 664.
W v Kennedy, 1988 SLT 583.

Textbook referred to

Walker and Walker, *Evidence*, p 374.

The sheriff *found* the grounds for referral established on the basis, inter alia, of the hearsay evidence of what W had said to social workers, among others.

The father appealed by stated case to the Court of Session.

Appeal

The stated case contained the following question, inter alia:

(6) Was the sheriff entitled to admit the hearsay evidence of witnesses as to what the child W had said on a previous occasion in circumstances in which it had not been established that the child W would have been a competent witness as (a) when the child W was called as a witness he remained silent and would not answer any questions; (b) the child W was aged three at the date of the hearing; (c) the child W could not be examined as to whether he knew the difference between the truth and otherwise; and (d) the child W's statements to the other witnesses were not established to have been in the nature of de recenti statements?

The appeal was heard before the Second Division on 9 and 10 October 1991.

On 18 October 1991 the court *allowed* the appeal and *remitted* the case to the sheriff so that he could make clear to what extent he had relied upon hearsay evidence from W in making his findings.

The following opinion of the court was delivered by the Lord Justice Clerk (Ross):

OPINION OF THE COURT.—This is a stated case under s 50 of the Social Work (Scotland) Act 1968 at the instance of F who is the father of three children, J, born 9 January 1985, W, born 18 November 1986, and G, born 15 October 1988. The respondent is the reporter to Strathclyde Region. The case of the three children had been referred to a children's hearing by the respondent; they had been so referred along with the children of two other families. As the grounds of referral were not accepted by the appellant, an application was made to the sheriff for a finding as to whether the grounds of referral had been established. After hearing evidence the sheriff found the grounds of referral to be established in terms of statements 1 to 6 and 8 and 9, but held that statement 7 was not proved. Having found grounds for referral established, the sheriff remitted the case to the reporter to make arrangements for a children's hearing for consideration and determination of the case. It is against that decision of the sheriff that the appellant has appealed by way of this stated case.

The grounds for referral were the same for each of the three children. In the case of J the grounds for referral were in the following terms: [his Lordship quoted the grounds for referral and statement of facts set out supra and continued:]

The stated case contains 12 questions. A week before the hearing before this court, the appellant sought to have a number of additional questions added to the case, but his motion to have these additional questions added was refused. At the hearing before this court counsel for the appellant began by making certain preliminary points. It is unnecessary to deal with these preliminary points at the present stage, because the court has decided in the first instance that question 6 (as amended) falls to be answered in the negative and the case remitted to the sheriff.

Question 6 is in the following terms: [his Lordship quoted its terms and continued:]

Counsel intimated that para (d) should be deleted from this question, and we allowed the question to be amended to that effect.

What gives rise to this question is that all the children of the appellant, including W, were interviewed on numerous occasions by social workers and evidence was given by the social workers as to what they had said. No notes however had been taken at the interviews and the evidence of what the children had said was based purely upon the recollection of the social workers. It is also made clear in the findings that all the children concerned in these referrals had been interviewed on a number of occasions by social workers, police officers and other concerned persons,

A and that the children were encouraged to speak and "tell" as and when they pleased.

In the note annexed to the interlocutor, the sheriff makes it plain that he has held the hearsay evidence of all the children to be admissible, and that he has taken account of it to some extent in his findings. So far as W was concerned, the sheriff makes it plain that he had been brought into the court room, but he remained mute and had not given evidence. Before the sheriff it was submitted on behalf of the appellant that the hearsay evidence of W was not admissible as he did

B not fall within the terms of s 2 (1) (b) of the Civil Evidence (Scotland) Act 1988. That subsection provides as follows: "(1) In any civil proceedings — . . . (b) a statement made by a person otherwise than in the course of the proof shall be admissible as evidence of any matter contained in the statement of which direct oral evidence by that person would be admissible".

Before this court counsel for the appellant developed the argument in greater detail. He submitted

C that since W had been found unable to give any direct oral evidence, evidence of what he had said to third parties should not be admitted. Section 2 (1) (b) makes it plain that hearsay evidence of a person is only admissible if direct oral evidence by that person would be admissible. Counsel submitted that since W was three years old, he would only be an admissible witness if he appeared able to appreciate the difference between truth and falsehood, and the duty to tell the truth. With a witness of this age the judge or sheriff

D had to determine after examining the child whether the child had this appreciation, and in the present case since the child remained mute the sheriff was not able to arrive at any such determination.

Counsel for the respondent contended that W could not be described as a witness whose evidence would have been inadmissible. He suggested that if W had not been called as a witness at all, then hearsay evidence would have been admissible. He also submitted that even if a child did not know the difference

E between truth and falsehood, what he said to social workers was part of the evidence in the case.

We are satisfied that the submissions of counsel for the appellant upon this matter are well founded. The rules regarding the evidence of young children are clearly stated in Walker and Walker, *Law of Evidence in Scotland*, at p 374: "A child is admissible if he appears to be able to understand what he has seen or heard and to give an account of it and to appreciate the duty to speak the truth. It is for the judge to determine

F whether a child should be examined, after a preliminary interrogation of the child and, if necessary, after hearing other evidence".

The matter has recently been considered in two criminal cases: *Rees v Lowe* and *Kelly v Docherty*. These cases make it plain that before a young child can be admitted to give evidence the judge or sheriff must carry out a preliminary examination of the child to see whether the child knows the difference between what is true and what is false, and must then admonish the child to tell the truth. In the present case it was

not possible for the sheriff to carry out any examination of the child to see whether he knew the difference G
between truth and falsehood, nor was it possible for
him to admonish the child to tell the truth because the
child remained mute throughout. In these circumstances we are satisfied that the provisions of s 2 (1)
(b) of the Act of 1988 were not satisfied with regard
to W. What he may have said to the social workers or
others was not admissible as evidence of any matter
contained in such statement because direct oral evidence by W of any such matter was not admissible since
in the circumstances W himself was not an admissible H
witness. We recognise that W would have been an
admissible witness if he had been examined by the
sheriff as to his ability to distinguish between truth
and falsehood, and if on being satisfied on that matter,
the sheriff had cautioned him to tell the truth, but in
our opinion, the terms of the subsection make it plain
that hearsay is only admissible if it is hearsay of a
person who was in fact an admissible witness.

Counsel for the appellant sought to obtain some
support for his submissions from *K v K*, but although I
s 2 (1) of the Civil Evidence Act 1968 uses language
similar to s 2 (1) (b) of the Civil Evidence (Scotland)
Act 1988, the admissibility of the evidence of young
children appears in England to depend upon different
principles, and accordingly we have not found this
case of assistance.

In his note the sheriff refers to *W v Kennedy*, and in
particular to a passage in the opinion of the court in
that case where it is stated: "Where, however, it is
clear that the purpose and intention of the 1968 Act J
would be thwarted and the interests of the child would
be prejudiced by over rigid application of the rule
against hearsay then further exception to the rule may
be permitted." The sheriff appears to have favoured
giving the words used in s 2 (1) (b) a wide meaning
partly because of the common law. In our opinion,
however, it is important to realise that since *W v
Kennedy* the law regarding hearsay has been made the
subject of legislation. The civil proceedings in which
the provisions of s 2 of the Act of 1988 apply include K
hearings by a sheriff under s 42 of the Social Work
(Scotland) Act 1968 of an application for a finding as
to whether grounds for the referral of a child's case to
a children's hearing are established. Accordingly it is
clear that so far as the present case is concerned the
admissibility of hearsay depends upon the provisions
of the Act of 1988.

For the foregoing reasons we are satisfied that question 6 as amended falls to be answered in the negative. L
As we have already observed, the sheriff has made it
plain that he admitted the hearsay evidence and took
account of it to some extent in his findings. Counsel
for the appellant and for the respondent were agreed
that in the event of question 6 being answered in the
negative it would be necessary for the case to be
remitted to the sheriff so that he could make clear to
what extent he had relied upon hearsay evidence from
W in making his findings. We therefore propose at
this stage to remit the case to the sheriff so that he may
(1) inform this court as to what the hearsay evidence

of W was, (2) report to this court upon the extent to
A which he relied upon the hearsay evidence of W when
making his findings, and (3) make any necessary
alterations to his findings in the light of the fact that
he must exclude from his consideration all hearsay
evidence of W.

---

*Counsel for Appellant, McGhie, QC, N C Stewart;
Solicitors, Dickson Smith & Co, WS — Counsel for
Respondent, Drummond Young, QC, Hajducki;*
B *Solicitors, Biggart Baillie & Gifford, WS.*

R F H

K v Kennedy

C EXTRA DIVISION

LORDS McCLUSKEY, SUTHERLAND AND
GRIEVE

29 NOVEMBER 1991

*Children and young persons — Children's hearing —
Application to sheriff for finding whether or not grounds
for referral established — Child alleged to be victim of
offence — Evidence of child — Hearsay evidence of statement to police — Child retracting statement at children's*
D *hearing and before sheriff — Whether sheriff entitled to
accept original statement as true — Witnesses mentioned
in statement not called to give evidence — Whether
sufficiency of evidence to justify sheriff's findings — Civil
Evidence (Scotland) Act 1988 (c 32), ss 1 and 2.*

*Evidence — Hearsay — Sufficiency — Proof of grounds
for referral to children's hearing — Hearsay evidence of
child — Statement to police — Child retracting statement
at children's hearing and before sheriff — Whether sheriff*
E *entitled to accept original statement as true — Witnesses
mentioned in statement not called to give evidence —
Whether sufficiency of evidence to justify sheriff's findings — Civil Evidence (Scotland) Act 1988 (c 32), ss 1
and 2.*

Section 1 (1) of the Civil Evidence (Scotland) Act
1988 provides that in any civil proceedings the court,
if satisfied that any fact has been established by evidence, shall be entitled to find that fact proved by that
evidence notwithstanding that the evidence is not
F corroborated. Section 2 (1) of the Act provides that in
such proceedings (a) evidence shall not be excluded
solely on the ground that it is hearsay; and (b) a statement made by a person otherwise than in the course
of the proof shall be admissible as evidence of any
matter contained in the statement of which direct oral
evidence by that witness would be admissible.

A reporter referred a child to a children's hearing on
several grounds, one of which being that she had been
subjected to lewd, indecent and libidinous behaviour.
The child had given a statement to the police and was,

at that time, distressed. Before the children's hearing
she retracted her statement. The grounds for referral G
were not accepted by the child's father and an application was made by the reporter to the sheriff for a
finding as to whether or not those grounds had been
established. Before the sheriff the child again retracted
her original statement. The sheriff refused to accept
the retraction and accepted as true the original statement in terms of s 2 of the 1988 Act. In holding that
the grounds for referral had been established, the
sheriff founded on the child's original statement. The
statement had contained references to other witnesses H
who could have given, but had not been called upon
to give, evidence before the sheriff. The sheriff did,
however, take into account, inter alia, evidence from
a friend of the child's family that the child had told
that person that she had been subjected to sexual interference, evidence from a cousin concerning the
father's behaviour on one occasion in the child's
bedroom, and evidence from a police officer that the
child had been distressed at the time she had given her
statement. The father appealed to the Court of I
Session.

Held, (1) that the sheriff had to proceed on the basis
of the evidence that was before him and was not bound
to refrain from relying upon it just because there
might have been other evidence which could have
been of assistance one way or another (p 1283H-I); and
(2) that while there was no doubt that the evidence in
the case was thin, it could not be said that no sheriff
would have been entitled to take the course which the
sheriff had done (p 1283H and K); and appeal *refused*. J

Morrison v J Kelly & Sons Ltd, 1970 SLT 198, *distinguished.*

Observed, that it was unlikely that the evidence
from other witnesses mentioned in the original statement would have added very much as it could be
regarded only as indirect evidence which might at best
be used to test the accuracy of the child's statement on
incidental matters (p 1283J).

K

Appeal from the sheriff court

Frederick J Kennedy, reporter to the children's
panel for Strathclyde Region, referred a child then
aged 13 to the children's panel on three grounds,
namely lack of parental care likely to cause her
unnecessary suffering; that an offence had been committed in respect of her, involving assault, ill treatment or exposure; and that an offence had been
committed in respect of her, namely lewd and L
libidinous behaviour. The child's father, HK, did not
accept the grounds for referral. The reporter made an
application to the sheriff in terms of s 42 (2) of the
Social Work (Scotland) Act 1968.

Statutory provisions

The Law Reform (Miscellaneous Provisions) (Scotland) Act 1968 provided:

"9.—(1) This section applies to any action of
damages where the damages claimed consist of, or

include, damages or solatium in respect of personal injuries (including any disease, and any impairment of physical or mental condition) sustained by the pursuer or any other person.

"(2) Subject to subsection (4) of this section, any rule of law whereby in any proceedings evidence tending to establish any fact, unless it is corroborated by other evidence, is not to be taken as sufficient proof of that fact shall cease to have effect in relation to any action to which this section applies, and accordingly, subject as aforesaid, in any such action the court shall be entitled, if they are satisfied that any fact has been established by evidence which has been given in that action, to find that fact proved by that evidence, notwithstanding that the evidence is not corroborated."

The Civil Evidence (Scotland) Act 1988 provides:

"1.—(1) In any civil proceedings the court or, as the case may be, the jury, if satisfied that any fact has been established by evidence in those proceedings, shall be entitled to find that fact proved by that evidence notwithstanding that the evidence is not corroborated. . . .

"2.—(1) In any civil proceedings — (a) evidence shall not be excluded solely on the ground that it is hearsay; (b) a statement made by a person otherwise than in the course of the proof shall be admissible as evidence of any matter contained in the statement of which direct oral evidence by that person would be admissible; and (c) the court, or as the case may be the jury, if satisfied that any fact has been established by evidence in those proceedings, shall be entitled to find that fact proved by the evidence notwithstanding that the evidence is hearsay."

Cases referred to

Morrison v J Kelly & Sons Ltd, 1970 SLT 198; 1970 SC 65.
W v Kennedy, 1988 SLT 583.

The sheriff *found* the grounds for referral established.

The father appealed to the Court of Session against the finding in respect of the third ground of referral.

Appeal

The appeal was heard before an Extra Division on 5 and 6 November 1991.

On 20 November 1991 the court *refused* the appeal.

The following opinion of the court was delivered by Lord Sutherland:

OPINION OF THE COURT.—The appellant is the father of a girl now aged 14 who was referred to a children's hearing on three grounds, namely, lack of parental care likely to cause her unnecessary suffering; that an offence had been committed in respect of her involving assault, ill treatment or exposure; and that an offence had been committed in respect of her, namely lewd and libidinous behaviour. The grounds of referral were not accepted and accordingly the matter was remitted to the sheriff to consider whether or not the grounds were established. The sheriff found that all three grounds were established. The present appeal is taken by the appellant only in respect of the third ground of referral, namely that an offence of lewd and libidinous behaviour had been committed by him in respect of the girl.

In the stated case the sheriff has made eight findings of fact relating to lewd and libidinous behaviour on the part of the appellant. The peculiarity of this case is that the findings in fact were made largely on the basis of a statement made by the girl to a police officer. This statement was made on 4 December 1990 and at the children's hearing on 7 December it was retracted by the girl. Her retraction was repeated to the police on 9 December, and before the sheriff the girl also maintained that although she had made this statement on 4 December it was not true. The sheriff, for reasons which he explains, did not accept the girl's retraction of the statement and has accepted that the statement admittedly made to the police on 4 December was in fact true. He founded on s 2 of the Civil Evidence (Scotland) Act 1988 to justify this course and in terms of s 1 of that Act it would not be necessary for there to be corroboration.

The sheriff makes it clear that he did not take such a step lightly but only after weighing up all the sources of evidence. The sheriff sets out in his note what the sources of evidence were. In the first place the police officer who took the statement on 4 December gave evidence and spoke not only to the terms of the statement but also to the fact that the girl was distressed while giving it. A friend of the family spoke to the girl telling her on 2 December 1990 about sexual interference from the appellant and it was this friend who arranged for the girl to see social workers and then the police. A cousin of the girl, who had been staying as a lodger for a few months in 1990, also gave evidence. She spoke to one occasion on which she went into the girl's bedroom and found the appellant sitting on the bed "carrying on" with the girl. She said that on most nights the girl would bring bedclothes into her room and ask to sleep beside her but never said why. She also said that although she did not see any direct sexual interference the appellant was always in the girl's bedroom with the door closed but she never really thought much about it. She denied that the girl ever complained to her about sexual interference although in the girl's statement to the police it was suggested that the girl made such a complaint to her. The sheriff, however, found that this witness was not satisfactory in that she appeared more concerned to protect the appellant and in particular he did not accept her denial that the girl had complained to her. The girl herself in evidence admitted that she had made the statement to the police on 4 December but denied that the contents were true. The sheriff formed the view from her demeanour in the witness box that she appeared to be hiding something, was often silent and reluctant to speak, and gave the impression that there was far more behind what she was prepared to

A say. In these circumstances he rejected her retraction of the original statement. The appellant also gave evidence but the sheriff found that his demeanour was shifty, evasive and unreliable and he accordingly rejected his evidence also.

Counsel for the appellant accepted that as a matter of law the sheriff would be entitled in appropriate circumstances to proceed upon the uncorroborated evidence of what was contained in a statement by the girl even though that statement was subsequently retracted. He argued, however, that in the circum-

B stances of the present case no reasonable sheriff could be satisfied that the ground of referral had been made out. This was because the girl herself was admittedly found to be unreliable and there were a number of witnesses who were mentioned in the girl's statement who could have been called to give evidence but were not. Counsel argued that the test to be applied in a case of this nature was the same as was previously applied in cases under s 9 of the Law Reform (Miscellaneous Provisions) (Scotland) Act 1968. He referred

C in particular to *Morrison v Kelly*. In that case the Lord President set out the appropriate test to be applied in cases where it was sought to rely upon a pursuer's evidence alone even though corroborative evidence might have been available. In such circumstances a court would obviously be very slow to proceed upon the pursuer's evidence alone. The test under the subsection is a relatively high one and the court must be "satisfied that the fact is established". The Lord President then asks the rhetorical question, how could it be satisfied if corroborative evidence was available but

D without any explanation not produced? Counsel pointed to the fact that the sheriff in his note said that he did not know the reasons why this possible corroborative evidence was not produced. In these circumstances it was argued that the state of the evidence was so unsatisfactory that no reasonable sheriff could have been satisfied as to the truth of the original statement by the child.

Counsel for the respondent argued that the evidence

E led before the sheriff was sufficient to entitle him to come to the conclusion which he did. In addition to the original statement of the child there was positive evidence that the child had told the family friend about the alleged sexual interference before making the statement to the police and was distressed at the time. The girl did not dispute that she did make such a statement. The cousin, who was referred to in the girl's statement, might not have spoken to all the things that the girl suggested she could have spoken to but nevertheless she did give some evidence which

F would tend to show that the girl's statement was true. The possible witnesses who were not called could only have given similar evidence to that of the family friend rather than direct evidence of sexual interference. In these circumstances there was no need for any further evidence and this court should not interfere with the sheriff's findings, particularly as he had the very considerable advantage of seeing and hearing all the witnesses.

Counsel for the curator ad litem adopted the arguments advanced on behalf of the respondent. He also

argued that s 9 of the Law Reform (Miscellaneous Provisions) (Scotland) Act had nothing whatever to do G with the present case. That section was designed to do away with corroboration in personal injury actions where there were parties to a cause and where the process was adversarial. It is clear from *W v Kennedy* that hearings before a sheriff under the Social Work (Scotland) Act are sui generis and that the purpose of the hearing is to consider what is in the best interests of the child. Strict rules of evidence and procedure which might be appropriate in adversarial cases are not necessarily appropriate in such hearings.

H

In our opinion the sheriff was entitled to come to the conclusion which he did and to make the findings of fact which he did on the basis of the child's original statement. Whatever may be the correct construction of s 9 of the Law Reform (Miscellaneous Provisions) (Scotland) Act we are of opinion that this does not assist in considering what is the appropriate approach to a referral under the Social Work Act. The sheriff has to proceed on the basis of the evidence that is before him and is not bound to refrain from relying I upon it just because there might have been other evidence which could have been of assistance one way or the other. It is clear from his note that the sheriff considered the evidence very carefully in this case and it is also clear that he did not lightly take the step of proceeding on the basis of the original statement by the girl which was subsequently retracted. Support for the girl's original statement came from the evidence of the friend to whom the girl had made similar complaints two days beforehand and there was also some assistance, albeit slight, from the evidence of the J cousin. From what appears in the girl's statement it is unlikely that the evidence from other witnesses mentioned in that statement would have added very much as they could only add indirect evidence which might at best be used to test the accuracy of the girl's statement on incidental matters. Such evidence had already come from the friend of the family and accordingly in our view the sheriff was entitled to be of the opinion that he could properly decide the issues of fact on the basis of the evidence which was adduced. While there K is no doubt that the evidence in this case was thin, we are of opinion that it could not possibly be said that no sheriff was entitled to take the course which the sheriff did in this case.

The questions asked in the stated case are posed in terms of unnecessary detail and we shall substitute for these questions the one question "Was I entitled for the reasons stated in the above note to find the grounds of referral established?", and answer that question in the affirmative.

L

Counsel for Appellant, Coutts, QC, Skinner; Solicitors, Drummond Miller, WS — Counsel for Respondent, Clark, QC; Solicitors, Biggart Baillie & Gifford, WS — Counsel for Curator ad Litem, Hanretty; Solicitors, Aitken Nairn, WS.

R F H

F v Kennedy (No 2)

A SECOND DIVISION

THE LORD JUSTICE CLERK (ROSS),
LORDS COWIE AND MORISON

4 JUNE 1992

*Children and young persons — Children's hearing —
Application to sheriff for findings whether or not grounds
for referral established — Child alleged to be victim of
offence — Whether necessary to name alleged offender —*
B *Evidence of child — Hearsay evidence of interviews with
social workers — Relevance of failure to comply with
guidelines in Cleveland report — Social Work (Scotland)
Act 1968 (c 49), s 32 (2) (d) — Civil Evidence (Scotland)
Act 1988 (c 32), ss 2 (1) (b) and 9.*

*Evidence — Admissibility — Hearsay — Precognition —
Proof of grounds for referral to children's hearing —
Hearsay evidence of children's interviews with social
workers — Whether precognitions — Civil Evidence
(Scotland) Act 1988 (c 32), ss 2 (1) (b) and 9.*
C

*Evidence — Admissibility — Hearsay — Proof of
grounds for referral to children's hearing — Hearsay evidence of child's interviews with social workers — Relevancy of failure to comply with guidelines in Cleveland
report — Child not asked in evidence about statements
made by him on earlier occasion — Witness available not
giving evidence on particular matter — Whether evidence
of statements on earlier occasions competent and admissible — Civil Evidence (Scotland) Act 1988 (c 32), s 2*
D *(1) (b).*

A reporter to the children's panel referred three children, J, W and G, to a children's hearing in respect of
certain allegations that they had been victims of sexual
abuse. The father refused to accept the grounds for
referral. The reporter accordingly applied to the
sheriff for a finding on whether or not the grounds for
referral had been established. The facts spoken to in
evidence included no evidence independent of the
children. The evidence in the case came from, inter
E alios, the children themselves and hearsay evidence
from third parties as to what J and W had said on prior
occasions. When social workers interviewed the
children no notes were taken and the social workers'
hearsay evidence as to what was said was based purely
upon their own recollections. No tape or video recordings were made of the interviews and during some of
them the children told fantasy stories. No psychiatrist
or psychologist was consulted to examine the children
although the children showed some advance signs of
F disturbance. The guidelines laid down in the Cleveland inquiry report were not complied with. The
grounds for referral were found to be established. The
father appealed to the Inner House and contended,
inter alia, (a) that s 2 of the Civil Evidence (Scotland)
Act 1988, which dealt with the admissibility of
hearsay, did not in terms seek to alter the "best evidence rule" so that, as J had given evidence, what he
had said on another occasion to a third party was not
evidence; (b) that although J had not been questioned
in his evidence as to the making of any previous state-

ment of a different nature, he ought to have been
asked in evidence about matters on which other wit- G
nesses subsequently gave hearsay evidence of what he
had said on an earlier occasion; (c) that hearsay evidence of what J and W had said on previous occasions
was in the nature of evidence taken on precognition;
and (d) that because of the way the children had been
interviewed, serious doubt had necessarily to be
thrown upon their reliability and the sheriff had not
been entitled to treat them as reliable witnesses.

Held, (1) that any hearsay evidence of witnesses as
to what J had previously said was not being led in H
order to challenge or support his credibility but as
evidence of matters contained in the statement, so that
there was no need to question J as to any statement
made by him on another occasion and the absence of
questioning did not render incompetent hearsay evidence as to what J had previously said (p 1287A-C); (2)
that s 2 of the 1988 Act, read along with s 9, had the
effect of overriding the best evidence rule, so that the
fact that the maker of the statement had given oral
evidence did not prevent hearsay evidence being given I
of what he had said upon another occasion (p 1287E-
F); (3) that the children's statements were not of the
nature of precognitions, for (a) it was clear that the
purpose of the interviews was not so much to take
precognitions from the children for the purposes of a
litigation but rather to determine whether grounds
existed for concluding that the children were in need
of compulsory measures of care; (b) there was no
reason to think that any document had ever been
prepared by a precognoscer containing what the pre- J
cognoscer thought the child would say in evidence;
and (c) there was no litigation in the normal sense in
existence at the time, the proceedings before the
sheriff being sui generis and not in any proper sense
an adversarial litigation (p 1288H-J); and (4) that
although it was regrettable that many of the guidelines
laid down in the Cleveland inquiry report had not
been followed, credibility and reliability were matters
for the sheriff and he had decided the issue of whether
the grounds for referral had been established in the K
light of the evidence before him, taking into account
all the criticisms which had been made on behalf of
the appellant (p 1289H-I and K-L); and appeal *refused.*

Opinion, that the recommendations in the
Cleveland inquiry report showed what good practice
was in interviewing children, and in the light of
present day views and unless and until other guidelines for Scotland were devised, the recommendations
should in general be followed; but the mere fact that
the guidelines had not been followed did not mean L
that the sheriff was not entitled to accept the evidence
of children as reliable (p 1289F-G).

Appeal from the sheriff court

Frederick J Kennedy, reporter to the children's
panel for Strathclyde Region, referred three children,
J, W and G, of a family to a children's hearing on
grounds of alleged sexual abuse. At the children's
hearing the father did not accept the grounds for

referral. The hearing accordingly directed that the reporter make an application to the sheriff in terms of s 42 of the Social Work (Scotland) Act 1968. The reporter duly presented the application to the court craving that the sheriff find whether or not the grounds for referral were established.

Statutory provisions

The Social Work (Scotland) Act 1968 provides:

"32.—(1) A child may be in need of compulsory measures of care within the meaning of this Part of this Act if any of the conditions mentioned in the next following subsection is satisfied with respect to him.

"(2) The conditions referred to in subsection (1) of this section are that— . . . (d) any of the offences mentioned in Schedule 1 to the Criminal Procedure (Scotland) Act 1975 has been committed in respect of him or in respect of a child who is a member of the same household".

The Civil Evidence (Scotland) Act 1988 provides:

"2.—(1) In any civil proceedings— (a) evidence shall not be excluded solely on the ground that it is hearsay; (b) a statement made by a person otherwise than in the course of the proof shall be admissible as evidence of any matter contained in the statement of which direct oral evidence by that person would be admissible; and (c) the court, or as the case may be the jury, if satisfied that any fact has been established by evidence in those proceedings, shall be entitled to find that fact proved by the evidence notwithstanding that the evidence is hearsay. . . .

"9. In this Act, unless the context otherwise requires — . . . 'statement' includes any representation (however made or expressed) of fact or opinion but does not include a statement in a precognition".

Cases referred to

Anderson v Jas B Fraser & Co Ltd, 1992 SLT 1129.
C and L (Child Abuse: Evidence), Re [1991] FCR 351.
Harris v F, 1991 SLT 242.
Kerr v HM Advocate, 1958 SLT 82; 1958 JC 14.
M v Kennedy, 1993 SLT 431.
McGregor v AB, 1982 SLT 293; 1981 SC 328.
Miller v Jackson, 1972 SLT (Notes) 31.
S v Kennedy, 1987 SLT 667.
Traynor's Executrix v Bairds and Scottish Steel, 1957 SLT 71; 1957 SC 311.
Young v National Coal Board, 1959 SLT (Notes) 77; 1960 SC 6.

Textbook referred to

Walker and Walker, *Law of Evidence in Scotland*.

The sheriff *found* the grounds for referral to have been established.

The father appealed by way of stated case to the Inner House.

Appeal

The appeal was heard before the Second Division on question 6 in the stated case. On 18 October 1991 the

court *refused* that appeal (1993 SLT 1277). The appeal thereafter came before the Second Division when the following questions were argued:

(3) In considering the question of whether or not hearsay evidence should be admitted, did the sheriff give proper consideration to the "best evidence rule"? . . .

(5) Was the sheriff entitled to admit the hearsay evidence of witnesses as to what the child J had previously said in circumstances in which (a) the child J had given evidence in person, (b) the child J had not been questioned as to making any previous statement of a different nature, and (c) the child J was not asked in evidence in chief or otherwise about areas of evidence on which other witnesses subsequently gave hearsay evidence of what the child J had said on earlier occasions? . . .

(7) On the question of whether or not the hearsay evidence of what the children J and W had said on previous occasions was in the nature of evidence taken on precognition, should the sheriff have identified in his note the circumstances in which such statements were made by the said J and W in relation to each fact which was established by hearsay evidence?

(8) Was the sheriff right to consider that the hearsay evidence of what had been said by the children J and W was not in the nature of evidence taken on precognition? Should the sheriff have stated in his note the circumstances surrounding the interviewing of the children J and W which gave rise to the hearsay evidence which was admitted? . . .

(12) [As amended] On the whole evidence in the case, was the sheriff entitled to hold the grounds of referral established?

On 4 June 1992 the court *refused* the appeal.

THE LORD JUSTICE CLERK (ROSS).—I refer to the opinion of the court in this case dated 18 October 1991. That opinion dealt only with question 6 in the stated case, and I now proceed to deal with the other questions. Before doing so, however, it is necessary to take note of certain preliminary points which counsel for the appellant made at the outset of his submissions.

He submitted that it was important that the correct decision should be arrived at in this case because if the children had been abused with the complicity of their parents, they would be removed from the care of their parents; but if they had not been abused at all or if their parents were not parties to any such abuse, serious damage might be done to the children if they were removed from the care of their parents. He reminded us that in the grounds for referral no specific mention was made of the appellant, and there was nothing to indicate what role, if any, the appellant had played in the conduct complained of. Counsel submitted that it would be important for a children's hearing to know whether or not the parents had been involved.

Counsel for the appellant appeared to be anxious that the court should make a finding one way or the other as to whether the appellant had been involved in any abuse of the children. In my opinion, however, counsel's submission in this regard is misconceived. It is now well established that when referring a child to a children's hearing alleging that an offence has been committed in respect of him in terms of s 32 (2) (d) of the Social Work (Scotland) Act 1968, it is not necessary in the grounds for referral to specify the person who is alleged to have committed the offence (*McGregor v AB*). It has been observed that a sheriff should not make unnecessary findings, and that if the name of the alleged abuser has not been specified in the grounds for referral, it would not be appropriate, where the matter goes to the sheriff for proof, for the sheriff to make any finding naming the alleged offender (*S v Kennedy*). I would only add that where it is alleged that a child has been the victim of sexual abuse, it may not be possible to determine who the abuser was. Nonetheless if the child has been the subject of sexual abuse, the sheriff will require to hold that the grounds of referral have been established even though the name of the abuser has not been proved. I would add that the present case is different to *M v Kennedy*, in respect that in the grounds for referral in the present case it is not alleged that the sexual abuse took place within the family home.

Counsel for the appellant's second preliminary point appeared to me to amount to little more than a plea ad misericordiam. Counsel stated that there was another family of children who had not been involved in the original proceedings but had later been made the subject of a place of safety order. The grounds for referral in that case were not accepted and a different sheriff heard evidence from a number of children including two of the children who had given evidence in the present case. It was said that that other sheriff had held the evidence of the children to be incredible, and had accordingly held that the grounds of referral had not been established. In my opinion, however, that is of no moment so far as the present appeal is concerned. The fact that another sheriff may have found the evidence of two children to be incredible, does not mean that the sheriff in the present case was not entitled to hold these children to be credible so far as the matters raised in this appeal are concerned.

Counsel's final preliminary submission was to refer to the Cleveland report on the subject of assessing the evidence of young children alleged to be the victims of sexual abuse. He submitted that the report clearly recognised that young children were susceptible to suggestion, and that great care had to be taken in the way in which they were interviewed. He was critical of the interviewing techniques used in the present case, and at the end of the day submitted that the whole of the evidence of the children was so tainted that it could not be regarded as reliable evidence, and that accordingly the court should not have found the grounds of referral to be established. Counsel intimated that he proposed to develop this argument under reference to question 12 in the case. That question is in the following terms: "On the whole facts of the case found proved, was the sheriff entitled to hold the grounds of referral established?"

Counsel recognised that having regard to the findings which the sheriff had made, it was virtually impossible to suggest that the sheriff was not entitled to hold the grounds of referral established. However, he maintained that what the appellants had all along wished to raise was whether the sheriff was entitled to reach the decision at which he had arrived on the whole evidence in the case, and he sought leave to have question 12 amended so that it read: "On the whole evidence in the case, was the sheriff entitled to hold the grounds of referral established?"

I am satisfied that question 12 is in the proper form. If the appellant wished to contend that the sheriff was not entitled to make certain findings on the evidence, then he ought to have asked the sheriff to include a question directed to that matter. The present case, however, is an unusual one, and I did not understand counsel for the respondent to oppose the amendment to question 12 which had been proposed by counsel. In these circumstances I am prepared to proceed upon the basis that question 12 is in fact in the form proposed by counsel for the appellant.

Counsel for the appellant next drew attention to the fact that certain of the findings related to children in other families. For example, finding 16A refers expressly to J L and his daughter I, and although the games of an indecent nature are said to have involved children, it is not stated that that included J, W and G, with whom the present appeal is concerned. Counsel also drew attention to findings 26 to 34 and submitted that these findings all related to children who were not the subject of the present proceedings and that these findings were accordingly irrelevant. A submission to this effect had been made to the sheriff in the course of adjustment, and he has explained that he felt it necessary to make these findings in order to give the complete overall picture. In my opinion, the sheriff was entitled to make these findings, although at the end of the day the question which he had to determine, so far as J, W and G are concerned, was whether the grounds for referral relating to them had been established.

Counsel then proceeded to consider each of the questions of law in this stated case. He intimated that question 1 need not concern the court, and that he would not address the court on question 2. Neither of these questions accordingly requires to be answered. He then stated that he would take questions 3 and 5 together. Counsel drew attention to the terms of s 2 of the Civil Evidence (Scotland) Act 1988 dealing with the admissibility of hearsay. He submitted, however, that the Act of 1988 did not in terms seek to alter the established rule of evidence relating to "best evidence". He recognised that proceedings of the kind with which we are concerned are proceedings sui generis, but he contended that since J had given evidence, what he had said on another occasion to a third party was not evidence. Under reference to question 5 he frankly stated that he did not attach great importance to (b), i e the fact that J had not been questioned in his evidence as to the making of any previous statement of a different nature, but he submitted that it was important that J had not been asked in evidence about matters on which other witnesses subsequently gave hearsay evidence of what J had said on an earlier occasion.

In my opinion, these submissions are not soundly based. We are not concerned in the present case with the use of a statement made on another occasion to reflect favourably or unfavourably on the witness's credibility. That is provided for in s 3 of the Act of 1988. Any hearsay evidence of witnesses as to what J had previously said was not being led in order to challenge or support his credibility. There was accordingly no need at the proof before the sheriff to question J as to any statement made by him on another occasion. The purpose of leading hearsay evidence here was so that it could be treated as evidence of any matter contained in the statement (s 2 (1) (b) of the Act of 1988). Of course, the fact that J was not asked in his evidence about the statements alleged to have been made by him earlier can no doubt be made a matter of comment, and to that extent it may reflect upon his credibility. In my opinion, however, the fact that J was not asked in his evidence about statements made by him on an earlier occasion did not render incompetent hearsay evidence of witnesses as to what J had previously said.

Counsel for the appellant also submitted that in the present case it was not clear what facts were based on hearsay evidence and what facts on direct evidence; in that situation counsel contended that the whole evidence should be treated with great suspicion and should be subjected to great scrutiny.

In my opinion, it was for the sheriff to determine whether or not he accepted any of the evidence adduced before him and I shall return to this matter later.

Counsel's principal submission was that if a witness is available and has not given evidence upon a particular matter, hearsay evidence of what he has said to others about that matter is not available. In my opinion, counsel for the respondent was well founded in contending that that was not the effect of s 2 (1) (b) of the Act of 1988. In my judgment s 2 (1) (b) does not deal only with the situation where a witness has not given oral evidence. It is significant that "statement" is defined in s 9 of the Act of 1988 as including "any representation (however made or expressed) of fact or opinion". There is no suggestion there that "statement" is limited to a statement by a witness who has not given oral evidence. On the contrary, it is plain from s 9 that the only exception arises where the statement has been made in a precognition. Accordingly, reading s 2 and s 9 together, I am satisfied that the fact that the maker of the statement has given oral evidence does not prevent hearsay evidence being given of what he has said upon another occasion. In this connection the effect of these two sections is that the best evidence rule is overridden.

The provisions of the Act of 1988 apply to civil proceedings as defined in s 9. Included among such civil proceedings are hearings under s 32 of the Social Work (Scotland) Act 1968 of an application for a finding as to whether grounds for referral are established. It is plain that in many such applications the evidence of children will be critical, and there may well be occasions when it will be difficult to take the whole of a child's evidence in court. It may therefore be important for the sheriff to be able to rely to some extent at least on hearsay evidence of what the child has said on other occasions. Having regard to the interpretation which I would place on s 2 and s 9, I am satisfied that this is something which the sheriff can do. Except where an application to a sheriff relates to a ground mentioned in s 32 (2) (g) of the Act of 1968, a sheriff is entitled to hold any fact to be established without there being corroboration, and he is entitled to rely on hearsay evidence (*Harris v F*). I would stress, of course, that it is for the sheriff to determine what weight if any he is to place upon any of the evidence led before him including the hearsay evidence.

For the foregoing reasons I would move your Lordships to answer both questions 3 and 5 in the affirmative.

So far as question 4 is concerned, counsel for the appellant accepted that the issues therein raised had been dealt with by the sheriff in appendix VI. Accordingly it is unnecessary to answer question 4.

The court has already dealt with question 6 in the opinion of the court dated 18 October 1991.

Counsel for the appellant dealt with questions 7 and 8 together. The issue raised in these questions is whether hearsay evidence of what J and W had said on previous occasions was in the nature of evidence taken on precognition. In s 9 of the Act of 1988 "statement" is defined as including "any representation (however made or expressed) of fact or opinion but does not include a statement in a precognition".

Counsel drew attention to the terms of finding 16, where a description was given of the interviewing of J and W. He emphasised that the children, and in particular J, had been interviewed on numerous occasions, and virtually every day between 7 June and 20 July when the hearing began. No records had been kept by the social workers of the dates, times or duration of these interviews, and no notes were taken at the time of what the children said; the hearsay evidence of the social workers was based purely on their own recollections. Moreover at the interviews anatomically correct dolls were regularly given to the children to demonstrate with although none of the interviewers had had any special training in the use of anatomically correct dolls. No tape or video recordings were made of the interviews. Police officers were present at some of the interviews. During the interviews on occasion the children told the social workers fantasy stories. No psychiatrist or psychologist was consulted to examine the children although the children showed advance signs of disturbance. In these circumstances counsel maintained that what each child had said amounted to a statement in a precognition. In this connection he drew attention to various tests which had been laid down in civil cases as to what amounted to a precognition. Section 2 (1) (b) of the Act of 1988 provides for the admissibility of a statement made by a person otherwise than in the course of the proof, and s 9 makes it plain that "statement" does not include a statement in a precognition. In my opinion Parliament must be taken to have used the word "precognition" in the sense in which it has been used in previous case law. As is made clear in Walker and Walker, *Law of Evidence in Scotland*, the word "precognition" is sometimes used as an abstract term to mean the act of taking a statement from a person for the purpose of discovering what his evidence is to be in a cause which has commenced or at least been decided upon, and on other occasions the word "precognition" is used in the concrete sense as referring to a written precognition where a witness's statements are put into consecutive narrative form. In *Traynor's Exrx v Bairds and Scottish Steel*, Lord Guthrie, in holding that a statement made by a deceased person to his solicitor was inadmissible, appears to have based his decision to some extent upon the view that the statement was tainted by self interest. However, in *Young v National Coal Board*, Lord Guthrie held that the statement in question was of the nature of a precognition although the element of self interest was absent. He appears to have been influenced by the fact that the statement in question had not been made in conversation in the ordinary course of the individual's daily life, but had been elicited from him by questions put to him by an investigator. In *Miller v Jackson*, the Lord Ordinary (Lord Emslie) excluded evidence of a statement made by a deceased upon the view that it was "a statement akin to a precognition". The statement in question had been deliberately solicited by a visit to the deceased after the raising of the action by an individual who had a clear interest in the outcome of the action and who was related to one of the parties.

Counsel for the respondent drew attention to what the sheriff said about this matter in his note. The sheriff had been referred to *Kerr v HM Advocate* which was a criminal case. The sheriff stated that he had no difficulty in deciding that the children's statements were not to be regarded as precognitions. He stated: "The evidence related to remarks made by the children from time to time, often in casual conversation, and sometimes in a more 'structured' interview, which I consider gives them considerable spontaneity, and they are very far removed from what is traditionally regarded as a precognition in the sense that a statement taken by the police or the procurator fiscal in a criminal investigation".

Although counsel for the respondent recognised that this case was not concerned with a precognition in the sense of a statement taken by the police or the procurator fiscal in a criminal investigation, he maintained that the sheriff's reasoning was sound and that the sheriff had reached the correct conclusion. He stressed that proceedings under s 42 of the Act of 1968 are not adversarial proceedings. They are proceedings which are undertaken in the interests of the children, and accordingly he submitted that the normal grounds of objection to a precognition were not present. He

pointed out also that in the present case there was no suggestion that there ever had been any written precognition; it could not be said that the statement was in any way tainted by self interest; and he submitted that it was not necessary in every case before a statement could be admitted that it could be regarded as a fair and spontaneous statement.

I have come to the conclusion that the sheriff arrived at the correct decision upon this matter. After the children's mother had alleged that her children had been the subject of abuse, it was plainly the duty of the social workers and the police to investigate the matter with a view to determining whether the children were in need of compulsory measures of care. The sheriff has described in finding 16 how the interviews were conducted. In my opinion, however, it is clear that the purpose of these interviews was not so much to take precognitions from the children for the purposes of a litigation, but rather was to determine whether grounds existed for concluding that these children were in need of compulsory measures of care. There is no reason to think that any document was ever prepared by a precognoscer containing what the precognoscer thought that the child would say in evidence. The present case is therefore different from *Anderson v Jas B Fraser & Co* to which counsel drew attention at the continued hearing. Moreover there was no litigation in the normal sense in existence at the time. There was to be a hearing before the sheriff to determine whether the grounds of referral had been established, but these proceedings are recognised to be sui generis and they are not in any proper sense an adversarial litigation.

In the foregoing circumstances I am satisfied that the sheriff reached the correct conclusion in this case. In finding 16 the sheriff has described the circumstances in which the statements were taken, and I would accordingly move your Lordships to hold that it is unnecessary to answer question 7. So far as question 8 is concerned I would move your Lordships to answer the first part of that question in the affirmative, and to find it unnecessary to answer the second part of the question.

Counsel for the appellant did refer to question 9 but accepted that the point was now academic, and it is accordingly unnecessary to answer question 9.

So far as question 10 is concerned counsel for the respondent conceded that in relation to G there was no evidence available to enable the sheriff to find it established that paras 3, 4, 5 and 6 of the statement of facts were established in relation to him. It follows that question 10 falls to be answered in the negative. This does not, however, mean that the grounds for referral were not established in the case of G. Whether or not the grounds for referral were established in his case depends upon whether grounds of referral have been established in the case of J and W. If grounds for referral are held to have been established in the case of J and W, then counsel for the appellant accepted that grounds for referral would also have been established in the case of G upon the view that offences

A mentioned in Sched 1 to the Criminal Procedure (Scotland) Act 1975 had been committed in respect of a child who was a member of the same household as G.

So far as question 11 is concerned counsel for the appellant again accepted that the issue raised in this question was now academic.

In addressing this court on question 12, counsel maintained that the facts spoken to in evidence included no evidence independent of the children. He stressed that these children had been exposed to a long B series of interviews designed to lead to disclosures by them. Under reference to the Cleveland report he maintained that children are susceptible to suggestions made by adults, that they readily respond to cues and that they say what is expected of them. He further submitted that any statements made by children are reinforced by acceptance and repetition, and that it is difficult for children to know what is truth and what is not. At the end of the day his submission was that the sheriff had not been entitled to proceed upon the C basis of what the children had said. He reminded the court that the solicitor for the appellant had drawn the attention of the sheriff to these criticisms. He had stressed that the social workers had had little or no experience in the use of anatomically correct dolls, that they had not approached the interviews with an open mind, that they had carried out too many interviews, that there had been no proper recordings of interviews, no video recordings had been made of the interviews of J and W and any notes of interviews had D not been produced. He also drew the sheriff's attention to certain of the criticisms made by Dr Furnell, the child psychologist.

Counsel for the appellant maintained that the sheriff had missed the point in holding that the children were truthful and reliable. He accepted that the sheriff was entitled to hold that the children were telling the truth as they saw it, but he maintained that they were not reliable. Counsel referred to a number of English cases, and under reference to these he submitted that E because of the way in which the children had been interviewed in this case, serious doubt must necessarily be thrown upon their reliability, and the sheriff was not entitled to treat them as reliable witnesses.

In my opinion counsel's submission is not a sound one. His approach appears to me to be misconceived. He seeks to elevate the status of the Cleveland report to something approaching gospel. The Cleveland report is an important document and the recommendations which were made in the report no doubt show F what good practice is in interviewing children and in the light of present day views, and unless and until other guidelines for Scotland are devised, the recommendations of the Cleveland report should in general be followed. In any case, however, it is for the judge who hears the evidence to determine what evidence is truthful and reliable. Where criticisms are made of the way in which children have been interviewed, that is something which the sheriff requires to take into account. But the mere fact that the guidelines in the Cleveland report have not been followed, does not

mean that the sheriff is not entitled to accept the evidence of children as reliable. It is significant that in one G of the cases to which counsel for the appellant referred, namely *Re C and L (Child Abuse: Evidence)*, Hollings J appears to have held that care orders should be made in respect of five children although there had been many breaches of the guidelines laid down in the Cleveland report. In that case it was held that there had been serious faults in the way the children had been interviewed, and that in almost every respect the guidelines of the Cleveland report had not been followed. There had been a failure to approach the H interviews with an open mind, leading questions had been asked, there were too many interviews of the children, and there were inadequate video recordings. Despite that Hollings J did hold that care orders should be made in respect of some of the children.

In the present case it is clear that many of the guidelines laid down in the Cleveland report had not been followed. This is regrettable, but the sheriff was well aware that there had been a failure to observe all these guidelines. The sheriff had the assistance of Dr I Furnell who spent a day in the witness box. He criticised the methods used by the social workers, but the sheriff tells us that his evidence did not vitiate the hearsay evidence obtained at the interviews. Dr Furnell made it clear that he made no personal criticism of the social workers themselves; the most he could say was that they were perhaps rather over zealous in their anxieties to protect the interests of the children, and their lack of experience in the rapidly expanding field of research in child sex abuse had left J them somewhat out of their depth. The sheriff tells us that although minor criticisms could be made of the interviewing techniques used in this case and that methods could no doubt be improved and refined in the light of experience, nonetheless he did not consider such criticism sufficient to invalidate any of the hearsay evidence obtained at the various interviews. It may be that the criticisms made were more than "minor" but nonetheless, in my opinion, the sheriff was fully entitled to arrive at the conclusion which he K reached. Credibility and reliability were matters for the sheriff. It was for him to consider the weight of the evidence and to ask himself whether the grounds for referral had been established. It appears to me that the sheriff decided that issue in the light of the evidence before him and taking into account all the criticisms which had been made on behalf of the appellant. The evidence is not before this court and this court cannot substitute its views on the evidence for those of the sheriff.   L

In all these circumstances I am satisfied that the challenge which counsel for the appellant sought to mount against the sheriff's assessment of the witnesses must fail. Having regard to the evidence which was before the sheriff, he was plainly entitled to conclude that the grounds for referral had been established. I would allow the amendment which counsel proposed should be made to question 12, and thereafter I would move your Lordships to answer question 12, as amended, in the affirmative.

LORD COWIE.—I agree with the opinion of your Lordship in the chair and have nothing useful to add.

LORD MORISON.—I agree that the questions in the case should be answered as proposed by your Lordship, for the reasons which your Lordship has given.

Counsel for Appellant, McGhie, QC, N C Stewart; Solicitors, Dickson Smith, WS — Counsel for Respondent, Drummond Young, QC, Hajducki; Solicitors, Biggart Baillie & Gifford, WS.

R F H

Bal v Secretary of State for the Home Department

OUTER HOUSE

LORD COULSFIELD

1 OCTOBER 1992

Immigration — Illegal entry — Detention of entrant — Application for political asylum — Application for interim liberation pending determination of application for political asylum — Applicant having history of absconding but willing to lodge security — Whether interim liberation should be granted.

A citizen of India who had been present, without leave, in the United Kingdom since 1985, applied for political asylum. He had a history of absconding. He was detained in Aberdeen on 23 August 1992. He alleged the detention was unreasonable and sought interim liberation pending the determination of his application for political asylum.

Held, that although there was no known instance of a person who had been granted interim liberation by the Scottish courts absconding before his application for asylum or permission to remain had been disposed of, this was an extreme case and the immigration authorities could not be said to have been wholly unreasonable in regarding the petitioner as a very high risk absconder (p 1290J-L); and interim liberation *refused.*

Petition for judicial review

Bikar Singh Bal petitioned for judicial review of a decision to detain him as an illegal entrant and to keep him in detention, seeking interim liberation pending determination of his application for political asylum. He had been present in the United Kingdom, without leave, since 1985. He was detained in Aberdeen on 23 August 1992. He alleged that the detention was unreasonable.

The petition came before the Lord Ordinary (Coulsfield) on the petitioner's motion for interim liberation.

On 1 October 1992 the Lord Ordinary *refused* the motion.

LORD COULSFIELD.—The petitioner is a citizen of India, having been born in the Punjab on 3 February 1963. He has been present, without leave, in the United Kingdom since 1985 and has applied for political asylum. On 23 August 1992, he was detained in Aberdeen. In this petition, he alleges that the original detention and the continuation of that detention to the present date are unreasonable and seeks interim liberation pending the determination of his application for political asylum. On 29 September 1992, I heard a motion on his behalf for interim liberation. I continued the motion for further information until 1 October 1992 and on that date refused it.

The petitioner first came to the United Kingdom on 18 January 1986, stating that the purpose of his visit was to see relations. He was never granted leave to remain. Since that date he has absconded on three occasions. One of those occasions took place in 1991 in Aberdeen where he was working in a restaurant at the time. The arrest in 1992 also took place in Aberdeen in premises associated with that restaurant. On the petitioner's behalf, I was supplied with information about an alleged address in Slough and it was indicated that security to the value of £4,000 would be provided for the petitioner's subsequent appearance if interim liberation was granted. Unfortunately, however, the information concerning the permanent address in Slough was, in my view, wholly inconsistent with a narrative of the petitioner's movement and history of working given in an interview in connection with his application for political asylum. I should add that the petitioner's arrest in 1992 took place in premises associated with the same restaurant in which he had been working in 1991 and, although on behalf of the petitioner it was explained that he had been merely visiting friends in Aberdeen, the coincidence seemed to me to be striking. In the whole circumstances, it appeared to me that this was an extreme case and that it could not be said that the immigration authorities were taking a wholly unreasonable view in regarding the petitioner as a very high risk absconder. I was informed that it is still the case that there is no known instance of a person who has been granted interim liberation on security by the court in Scotland having absconded before his application for asylum or permission to remain had been disposed of. I entirely accept that interim liberation should be granted wherever possible in cases of this kind and it was only with hesitation and regret that I came to the conclusion that the present case is not one in which interim liberation can be granted.

Counsel for Petitioner, Bovey; Solicitors, Drummond Miller, WS — Counsel for Respondent, O'Brien; Solicitor, R Brodie, Solicitor in Scotland to the Secretary of State for the Home Department.

J P D

Short's Trustee v Keeper of the Registers of Scotland

A

OUTER HOUSE

LORD COULSFIELD

18 DECEMBER 1992

Heritable property — Registration of title — Registrable transactions or events — Decree of reduction of disposition — Whether reduction an event capable of affecting title to a registered interest in land — Whether decree creating inaccuracy in register — Whether Keeper of Registers obliged to register decree of reduction — Conveyancing (Scotland) Act 1924 (14 & 15 Geo V, c 27), s 46 (1) — Land Registration (Scotland) Act 1979 (c 33), ss 2 (1) and (4), 9 (1), (2), (3) and (4) and 12 (1), (2) and (3) (b) — Bankruptcy (Scotland) Act 1985 (c 66), s 34 (4).

B

Administrative law — Judicial review — Competency — Decision by Keeper of Registers — Alternative statutory remedy — Appeal to Lands Tribunal for Scotland possible — Land Registration (Scotland) Act 1979 (c 33), s 25 (1) and (2).

C

The Land Registration (Scotland) Act 1979 provides for the registration of transfers of registered interests in land. In addition s 2 (4) (c) provides that certain other transactions or events which are capable of affecting the title to a registered interest in land shall be registered by the keeper. Section 9 (1) and (3) (a) provides also that the keeper shall, on being ordered by the court, rectify any inaccuracy in the Land Register by inserting, amending or correcting anything therein, such rectification only being exercised against a proprietor in possession where, inter alia, the inaccuracy was caused wholly or substantially by the fraud or carelessness of the proprietor in possession. Section 29 of, and para 11 of Sched 3 to the Act apply to the Land Register s 46 of the Conveyancing (Scotland) Act 1924, which permits an extract of a decree of reduction of a deed to be recorded in the Register of Sasines.

D

E

A trustee in sequestration sought and obtained reduction under s 34 of the Bankruptcy (Scotland) Act 1985 of the dispositions of two properties, as alienations by the debtor for inadequate consideration, and of further gratuitous dispositions by the disponee to his wife.

The dispositions were recorded in the Land Register. The trustee then sought registration in the Land Register of, first, the reduction of the dispositions and, secondly, the debtor's name in the proprietorship section of the respective title sheets in terms of s 2 (4) (c) of the 1979 Act. The keeper did not make any such amendment and the trustee sought judicial review of the keeper's refusal to take the actions sought on the basis of the decree of reduction. The keeper argued that a decree of reduction was of itself not an event capable of affecting the title to a registered interest in land in terms of s 2 (4) (c) of the 1979 Act, but could give rise to an inaccuracy in the register which could be corrected in appropriate circumstances by rectification of the register under s 9

F

of the Act, subject to the restrictions placed on rectification which would prejudice a proprietor in possession in terms of that section; and that the appropriate remedy for the trustee was to seek an order for rectification under s 9 (1) of the Act.

G

Held, (1) that to sustain the trustee's argument for rectification of the register in terms of s 2 (4) (c) would involve significant prejudice to the operation of the system of registration of title; and that, having regard to the Act's recognition in s 12 (3) (b) of rectification of the register in respect of reductions on the ground of bankruptcy, a reduction of a previous writ relating to a property was not an event which was "capable of affecting the title" to a registered interest and therefore was not automatically registrable under s 2 (4) (c) of the Act (p 1297G-I); (2) that the keeper was entitled to refuse to register the trustee's decree of reduction and the proper course was for the trustee to make application to the keeper for rectification of the register (pp 1298L-1299A); and petition *dismissed*.

H

Opinion, that it was difficult to understand how s 46 (1) of the Conveyancing (Scotland) Act 1924 (recording of extract of decree of reduction in the Register of Sasines) was intended to be operated in the context of the system of registration of title (p 1298H-I).

I

Observed, that the question of the competency of the trustee's petition for judicial review, as to which the keeper reserved his position, was not straightforward, as s 25 (2) of the 1979 Act appeared to leave open other remedies which a party might have in addition to the statutory rights of review granted by s 25 (1) (p 1299A-B).

J

Petition for judicial review

George Douglas Laing, as permanent trustee on the sequestrated estates of Alexander Short, presented a petition for judicial review of a decision of the Keeper of the Registers of Scotland refusing to give effect to a decree of reduction in respect of dispositions of properties being registered interests in land by amending the Land Register in respect of the decree. The keeper and the registered proprietor of the properties lodged answers to the petition.

K

The petition came before the Lord Ordinary (Coulsfield) for a first hearing.

Statutory provisions

The Conveyancing (Scotland) Act 1924 provides:

L

"46.—(1) In the case of the reduction of a deed, decree or instrument recorded in the Register of Sasines or forming a midcouple or link of title in a title recorded in the said register there shall be recorded in the said register either an extract of the decree of reduction . . . or a title in which such extract decree forms a midcouple . . . and such decree of reduction shall not be pleadable against a third party who shall in *bona fide* onerously acquire right to the land . . . prior to an extract of such decree of reduction, or a

A title, in which it forms a midcouple or link of title, being recorded in the Register of Sasines."

The Land Registration (Scotland) Act 1979 provides:

"2.—(1) Subject to subsection (2) below, an unregistered interest in land other than an overriding interest shall be registrable — (a) in any of the following circumstances occurring after the commencement of this Act — (i) on a grant of the interest in land in feu, long lease or security by way of contract of ground B annual, but only to the extent that the interest has become that of the feuar, lessee or debtor in the ground annual; (ii) on a transfer of the interest for valuable consideration; (iii) on a transfer of the interest in consideration of marriage; (iv) on a transfer of the interest whereby it is absorbed into a registered interest in land; (v) on any transfer of the interest where it is held under a long lease, udal tenure or a kindly tenancy; (b) in any other circumstances in which an application is made for registration of the C interest by the person or persons having that interest and the Keeper considers it expedient that the interest should be registered. . . .

"(4) There shall also be registrable — (a) any transfer of a registered interest in land including any transfer whereby it is absorbed into another registered interest in land; (b) any absorption by a registered interest in land of another registered interest in land; (c) any other transaction or event which (whether by itself or in conjunction with registration) is capable under any D enactment or rule of law of affecting the title to a registered interest in land but which is not a transaction or event creating or affecting an overriding interest. . . .

"9.—(1) Subject to subsection (3) below, the Keeper may, whether on being so requested or not, and shall, on being so ordered by the court or the Lands Tribunal for Scotland, rectify any inaccuracy in the register by inserting, amending or cancelling anything E therein.

"(2) Subject to subsection (3) (b) below, the powers of the court and of the Lands Tribunal for Scotland to deal with questions of heritable right or title shall include power to make orders for the purposes of subsection (1) above.

"(3) If rectification under subsection (1) above would prejudice a proprietor in possession — (a) the Keeper may exercise his power to rectify only where F — (i) the purpose of the rectification is to note an overriding interest or to correct any information in the register relating to an overriding interest; (ii) all persons whose interests in land are likely to be affected by the rectification have been informed by the Keeper of his intention to rectify and have consented in writing; (iii) the inaccuracy has been caused wholly or substantially by the fraud or carelessness of the proprietor in possession; or (iv) the rectification relates to a matter in respect of which indemnity has been excluded under section 12 (2) of this Act; (b) the court or the Lands Tribunal for Scotland may order the

Keeper to rectify only where sub-paragraph (i), (iii) or (iv) of paragraph (a) above applies. . . .
G

"(4) In this section — (a) 'the court' means any court having jurisdiction in questions of heritable right or title; (b) 'overriding interest' does not include the interest of (i) a lessee under a lease which is not a long lease. . . .

"12.—(1) Subject to the provisions of this section, a person who suffers loss as a result of — (a) a rectification of the register made under section 9 of this Act; (b) the refusal or omission of the Keeper to make such H a rectification; (c) the loss or destruction of any document while lodged with the Keeper; (d) an error or omission in any land or charge certificate or in any information given by the Keeper in writing or in such other manner as may be prescribed by rules made under section 27 of this Act, shall be entitled to be indemnified by the Keeper in respect of that loss.

"(2) Subject to section 14 of this Act, the Keeper may on registration in respect of an interest in land exclude, in whole or in part, any right to indemnity I under this section in respect of anything appearing in, or omitted from, the title sheet of that interest.

"(3) There shall be no entitlement to indemnity under this section in respect of loss where — . . . (b) the loss arises in respect of a title which has been reduced . . . as a gratuitous alienation or fraudulent preference, or has been reduced or varied by an order under section 6 (2) of the Divorce (Scotland) Act 1976 . . . orders relating to settlements and other J dealings. . . .

"29.— . . . (2) Subject to subsection (3) below, any reference, however expressed, in any enactment passed before, or during the same Session as, this Act or in any instrument made before the passing of this Act under any enactment to the Register of Sasines or to the recording of a deed therein shall be construed as a reference to the register or, as the case may be, to registration.
K

"(3) Subsection (2) above does not apply — (a) to the enactments specified in Schedule 3 to this Act".

The Bankruptcy (Scotland) Act 1985 provides:

"34.—(1) Where this subsection applies, an alienation by a debtor shall be challengeable by — (a) any creditor who is a creditor by virtue of a debt incurred on or before the date of sequestration, or before the granting of the trust deed or the debtor's death, as the case may be; or (b) the permanent trustee, the trustee L acting under the trust deed or the judicial factor, as the case may be. . . .

"(4) On a challenge being brought under subsection (1) above, the court shall grant decree of reduction or for such restoration of property to the debtor's estate or other redress as may be appropriate, but the court shall not grant such a decree if the person seeking to uphold the alienation establishes — (a) that immediately, or at any other time, after the alienation the debtor's assets were greater than his liabilities; or (b)

that the alienation was made for adequate considera-
A tion; or (c) that the alienation — (i) was a birthday,
Christmas or other conventional gift; or (ii) was a gift
made, for a charitable purpose, to a person who is not
an associate of the debtor, which having regard to all
the circumstances, it was reasonable for the debtor to
make: Provided that this subsection shall be without
prejudice to any right or interest acquired in good
faith and for value from or through the transferee in
the alienation."

B **Cases referred to**
Jackson v Secretary of State for Scotland, 1992 SLT
572.
Mulhearn v Dunlop, 1929 SLT 59.

Textbooks referred to
Halliday, *Conveyancing Law and Practice,* Vol II, paras
16-62, 21-60, 24-14, 24-22, 24-46; Vol IV, para
52-18.
HMSO, *Registration of Title Practice Book,* paras
B1.15, C.15, C.59, C.62 and H1.02.
C McDonald, *Conveyancing Manual,* paras 36.6 and
36.25.

On 18 December 1992 the Lord Ordinary *dismissed*
the petition.

LORD COULSFIELD.—The petitioner in this
application for judicial review is the permanent trustee
on the sequestrated estates of Alexander Short ("the
debtor"). The estates of the debtor were sequestrated
D on 3 June 1987 and the petitioner was appointed permanent trustee on 4 August 1987. In 1986, the debtor
had bought two flats comprised in a tenement at 62
Great George Street, Glasgow. Towards the end of
1986, he sold the flats to Shek Chung at a price of
£2,500 for each flat. The flats were conveyed to Mr
Chung by dispositions both dated 7 October 1986, one
of which was registered on 1 December 1986, and the
other on 4 December 1986. By two dispositions, both
dated 20 May 1987, and registered on 28 May 1987,
E Mr Chung conveyed the flats to his wife, the second
respondent, "for love, favour and affection". The
dispositions by the debtor to Mr Chung and by Mr
Chung to the second respondent were registered in the
Land Register of Scotland under titles GLA 13339
and GLA 133328. Mr Chung died on 25 January 1988
and the second respondent was confirmed as his sole
personal representative on 8 April 1988. After his
appointment, the petitioner raised an ordinary action
against Mr Chung and the second respondent seeking
F inter alia reduction of the two dispositions in favour
of Mr Chung and the two dispositions in favour of the
second respondent under s 34 of the Bankruptcy (Scotland) Act 1985. Section 34 enables the permanent
trustee or a qualified creditor to challenge alienations
of the property of an insolvent made, according to the
circumstances, within two or five years before a
sequestration; and subs (4) provides: [his Lordship
narrated the terms of s 34 (4) and continued:]

The action was defended, initially by both Mr
Chung and the second respondent and, after Mr
Chung's death, by the second respondent alone. By
interlocutor dated 13 June 1990, the Lord Ordinary, G
after a proof, granted decree of reduction of all four
dispositions. The second respondent reclaimed but on
15 March 1991, the reclaiming motion was refused
[1991 SLT 472]. The Lord Ordinary held that one of
the flats was worth £6,500 and the other £7,000 as at
the date of the dispositions in favour of Mr Chung and
accordingly that the dispositions had not been made
for adequate consideration. The principal contention
on behalf of the second respondent, at least in the
Inner House, was that under s 34 of the 1985 Act the
court had a discretion as to the remedy to be granted H
and that the appropriate remedy was to grant decree
for payment of a sum representing the loss of value to
the debtor's estate rather than decree of reduction.
The argument was complicated by the absence of
pleadings on behalf of the second respondent clearly
directed to the issue of an alternative remedy but it
does appear that the Inner House accepted that reduction remains the primary remedy in a case under s 34.

In giving the judgment of the court, Lord Suther- I
land said: "It is in our opinion clear from a reading of
s 34 (4) that the general purpose is to provide that as
far as possible any property which has been improperly alienated should be restored to the debtor's
estate. In the case of a disposition of heritable property
this can easily be done by reduction of that disposition. We consider that the reference to 'other redress
as may be appropriate' is not intended to give the
court a general discretion to decide a case on equitable
principles but is designed to enable the court to make J
an appropriate order in a case where reduction or
restoration of the property is not a remedy which is
available. As reduction is available in this case, we
consider that it is the proper remedy and for this
reason we would refuse the reclaiming motion" (p
476J-L).

The parties to the present action were agreed that
the argument with which these proceedings are concerned was not before either the Lord Ordinary or the
Inner House in the action of reduction.   K

In this petition, the petitioner avers that notwithstanding the decree of reduction, he does not yet have
a clear title to the properties and that the Land
Register continues to show the dispositions which
have been reduced. He further avers that he has
applied to the first respondent for registration under
and in terms of s 2 (4) (c) of the Land Registration
(Scotland) Act 1979 of the reductions of the dispositions, by entering the name and designation of the L
debtor in the respective title sheets for the registered
titles, in the part of the title sheet showing the name
and designation of the person entitled to the interest
in land as heritable proprietor, or otherwise as might
be in accordance with proper practice to give proper
effect to the decree. In his answers, the first respondent denies that any application has been made under
s 2 (4) (c) of the 1979 Act but nothing turned on that
point in the debate before me. The petitioner proceeds
to aver that the first respondent has refused to register
the reductions of the dispositions or in any way make

new entries on the title sheets on the basis of the decree and that he has contended that in situations such as the present he is not obliged to make any entries on any title sheet unless and until an order for rectification is made under s 9 of the 1979 Act. The first respondent maintains that registration under s 2 (4) (c) would be inappropriate and that the appropriate procedure is for the petitioner to apply to him for rectification of the register under s 9 of the Act. The first respondent also takes a point in relation to competency to which reference will be made later. The second respondent in her answers adopts substantially the same position as the first respondent.

Before turning to the statutory provisions in detail, it is convenient to say something about the history of the introduction of the system of registration of title and the broad characteristics of that system. In 1959, the Secretary of State for Scotland appointed a committee under the chairmanship of Lord Reid to consider the desirability of reform of the system of land titles in Scotland. In 1963, that committee reported, recommending that an expert committee should be immediately appointed to consider proposals for the amendment of the conveyancing statutes and that another expert committee should be appointed to work out details of a scheme for registration of title to land. The first of these committees, which was under the chairmanship of Professor J M Halliday, reported in 1966 and its recommendations were substantially given effect to in the Conveyancing and Feudal Reform (Scotland) Act 1970 and the Land Tenure Reform (Scotland) Act 1974. Some minor recommendations were only given effect by the 1979 Act. The second committee, under the chairmanship of Professor G L F Henry, reported in 1969 and recommended a scheme for the introduction and operation of registration of title to land. A pilot scheme was set up and operated in the Department of the Registers of Scotland and the scheme recommended by the Henry committee was in essentials given effect to by the Land Registration (Scotland) Act 1979. The general effect of the new scheme, as compared with the earlier law, is described by Professor Halliday (*Conveyancing Law and Practice*, Vol II, p 115, para 16-62) as follows: "The Register of Sasines is a register of deeds and the validity of the title conferred by the recorded deed depends upon the sufficiency of the progress of title deeds which precedes it, at least until the operation of positive prescription has rendered the recorded title unchallengeable. Accordingly it is necessary to examine the progress of titles back to the last recorded title prior to the commencement of the relevant period of positive prescription. Under the system of registration of title the Keeper, upon an application for first registration, satisfies himself that the antecedent progress of title is in order and, if so satisfied, issues a land certificate without exclusion of indemnity with the effect of vesting the person named in the certificate in a real right to the registered interest in the land fortified by an indemnity from the Keeper. An uninfeft proprietor of an interest in land which has been regis-

tered does not require to expede and record a notice of title; if the necessary links or midcouples evidencing his right are produced to the Keeper of the title of the proprietor will be registered."

The essential characteristics of the reformed system are further described by Professor Halliday as follows (Vol II, p 471, para 24-14): "(1) A register of interests in land, including any estate, interest, servitude and other heritable right in or over land and any heritable security and long lease subject to such burdens or conditions as are set out on the register. (2) Registration of an interest vests in the registered proprietor a real right therein and to any right, servitude or pertinent forming part of it, subject only to the effect of any matter entered on the title sheet of the interest as adverse to the interest and any overriding interest, and also makes any registered right or obligation relating to a registered interest a real right or obligation. (3) Accurate identification of the land and its boundaries by a plan based on the Ordnance Map. (4) The issue to the registered proprietor of a land certificate which contains a facsimile of the title sheet of the register including the plan identifying the land, which will broadly take the place of prior title deeds and largely avoid the need for their examination. (5) The right of the proprietor of a registered interest is guaranteed by a Government indemnity subject only to certain statutory exclusions from indemnity and any exclusion expressly entered in the title sheet of the interest. (6) The provision of simple forms of deeds relating to registered interests using an identifying title number of the interest. (7) The provision of an official search service which covers entries on the Register of Sasines, the Land Register and the Register of Inhibitions and Adjudications. (8) The preservation of the public character of land registers in Scotland by the express provision to that effect in section 1 (1) of the 1979 Act and the availability on request of office copies of entries in the Land Register."

The title sheet is further described in para 24-22. It is subdivided into four sections, namely the property section, the proprietorship section, the charges section and the burdens section. The principal matters to be inserted in the property section are the title number of the interest, the nature of the interest (for example as proprietor), a description of the subjects and a plan based on the ordnance map. Where the area of land appears to extend to two hectares the area must be inserted but it is excluded from the indemnity. The proprietorship section contains the name or names and designations of the proprietors of the interest, the date of registration, the consideration and the date of entry, with certain other relevant matters. The charges section sets out particulars of heritable securities and other debts affecting the subjects, and the burdens section specifies any subsisting real burden other than one falling to be entered in the charges section and any overriding interests. Servitudes are a leading example of overriding interests.

The provisions of the 1979 Act upon which the present question principally turns are ss 2 and 9. Section 2 (1) provides that, subject to certain exceptions, an unregistered interest in land, other than an overriding interest, shall be registrable on the grant of an interest in land in feu, long lease or security by ground annual; on the transfer of the interest for valuable consideration; on a transfer in consideration of marriage; on a transfer whereby it is absorbed into a registered interest; and on any transfer of an interest held under long lease, udal tenure or kindly tenancy. Subsections (2) and (3) deal with heritable securities, liferents and incorporeal heritable rights. Subsection (4) provides: [his Lordship narrated its terms and continued:]

Section 3 provides that registration shall have the effect of vesting in the person registered as entitled to the registered interest a real right to the interest, subject only to the effect of any matter entered in the title sheet of the interest adverse to the interest or the person's entitlement to it and to any overriding interest whether noted or not. Subsection (2) provides that registration is to supersede recording in the Register of Sasines but, subject to certain exceptions relating to long leases and other special cases, shall be without prejudice to any other means of creating or affecting real rights or obligations under any enactment or rule of law.

Section 9 provides: [his Lordship quoted the terms of s 9 set out supra and continued:]

Section 10 amends the Prescription and Limitation (Scotland) Act 1973 in such a way as to confine the benefit of positive prescription in rendering a title unchallengeable to the one case where such prescription may still be useful under a registration of title system, that is, where the registration has been made subject to an exclusion of indemnity.

Section 12 as originally enacted provided, inter alia: [his Lordship quoted the terms of s 12 set out supra and continued:] Section 12 (3) (b) was amended by, inter alia, the Bankruptcy (Scotland) Act 1985 so as to insert references to ss 34 and 36 of that Act in relation to gratuitous alienations and fraudulent preferences.

Other subheads of subs (3) of s 12 deal with other instances in which there is no entitlement to indemnity. These subheads appear to cover a variety of miscellaneous circumstances and not to be related by a single unifying principle.

The main contentions of the parties can be set out relatively briefly. It is agreed that for the purposes of s 9 (3) of the 1979 Act, the term "proprietor in possession" must mean the person appearing as proprietor on the face of the Land Register, that is, in the present case, the second respondent. It is further agreed that the dispositions in favour of the second respondent have been reduced not on account of any participation by her in any scheme for fraudulent alienation or undue preference but solely because, being gratuitous, they fell upon the reduction of the title in favour of her late husband. For the petitioner, it was submitted that the effect of the position adopted by the first respondent would be that in order to exercise the right to reduction to which he was entitled under s 34 of the

1985 Act, a trustee would now have to overcome an additional hurdle because he would require to show that the register was inaccurate and that the inaccuracy had been caused wholly or substantially by the fraud or carelessness of the proprietor in possession. That was, it was submitted, an unacceptable limitation upon the rights of the trustee and of the creditors of a debtor. The solution was to regard the reduction of a disposition as an event capable of affecting the title to a registered interest in land, therefore registrable in terms of s 2 (4) of the 1979 Act. For the first respondent it was submitted that the whole scheme of the 1979 legislation was designed to render a registered title unchallengeable except in the very limited circumstances envisaged by the Act itself. The petitioner's argument was based on a fundamental misconception of the system of land registration under which the title was distinct from and did not depend upon a disposition, with the result that reduction of a disposition was in itself incapable of affecting the title to the land, which could only be altered by a rectification. A reduction however did give rise to an inaccuracy which could be corrected in appropriate circumstances by rectification of the register under s 9. These broad contentions were supported by a careful analysis of the provisions of the Act and of the various reports and recommendations which lie behind its enactment. It is evident that the question raised by these contentions is one of some importance for the operation of the system of land registration.

The arguments were developed in a number of chapters. First, reference was made to the reports which preceded the 1979 Act and to the legislative history, particularly as disclosing the mischief with which the legislation was designed to deal. Secondly, arguments were addressed with regard to the construction of the wording of the 1979 Act, as compared with that of the 1985 Act, and the presumed intention of Parliament. Thirdly, reference was made to opinions expressed in conveyancing literature. Fourthly, comparisons were attempted with the treatment of certain other situations under the 1979 legislation including adjudication, rectification and compulsory purchase. Fifthly, there was some attempt to compare the position under the 1979 Act with that under the comparable English legislation. In my opinion, the decision really turns on the second group of arguments, with some assistance from the first. It is convenient, however to deal with them in the order set out above.

So far as the Reid committee is concerned it is, I think, sufficient to note that in chap 3 the committee surveyed the existing system of registration in the Register of Sasines and, for example in para 13, laid stress upon the fact that registration of a writ did not guarantee its validity and that there was therefore a need to examine a progress of titles to verify that a good title existed. The committee examined the system of registration of title as it operated in England and went on to point out, in para 60, that the aspects of the then conveyancing system which were open to criticism and had become more important in recent years were, first, that it was unnecessarily expensive and, secondly, that it imposed unnecessary burdens on the legal profession. The Reid committee identified the requirement for examination of a progress of titles as a principal element both in the cost of transactions and in the burden which, as was then understood, was being placed upon a profession undergoing a manpower crisis. In chap 7 the Reid committee set out the main features of a scheme of registration of title for Scotland. They did not attempt to provide the details of such a scheme. In considering the question of the state guarantee of title and the appropriate rules for compensation the Reid committee said, in para 115: "In deciding who is entitled to be compensated, it becomes necessary to decide what weight should be attached to true ownership of the properties. In England we understand that only very exceptionally is the register rectified in the face of possession; whether or not he has a valid title, the person in possession is normally allowed to remain, and compensation is paid to the other claimant. We take the view that the same rules should apply in Scotland."

The Reid committee then went on to compare their proposed scheme of registration of title with a scheme of certification of title and in the course of discussing the relative advantages and disadvantages said, in para 154: "On the other hand, under registration of title, which we advocate, all registered interests become indefeasible except in the rare case in which rectification of the Register is allowed (see paragraph 114 and 115); even in that case the state guarantee will ensure full compensation to the owner, and any other person who suffers loss by reason of any rectification, and any person who suffers loss because the Register is not rectified will also be entitled to compensation."

The Henry report set out a scheme for registration of title in the form, in effect, of a draft Bill, with annotations to the various provisions. Much of the scheme set out in the report found its way into the 1979 Act. Paragraph 23, which, with para 24, became s 3 of the Act, provided that as at the date of registration of a title there should vest in the proprietor a real right in and to the lands, and drew attention to the difference between that consequence and the recording of a deed in the General Register of Sasines which was not in itself sufficient to vest a real right. Rectification was dealt with in para 47 of the scheme; para 47 (4) provided: "Except for the purpose of giving effect to an overriding interest, the Register shall not be rectified unless with the consent of all parties interested, including the Keeper, so as to affect the title of the proprietor who is in possession: (a) unless such proprietor shall be a party or privy or shall have caused or substantially contributed by his act, neglect or default to the fraud, mistake or omission in consequence of which such rectification is sought; or (b) unless the immediate title by which he shall have acquired right is void or has been reduced or the title in favour of any person through whom he shall claim otherwise than for valuable consideration is void or has been reduced; or (c) unless, in any particular case, it shall be unjust not to rectify the Register against

such proprietor — but notwithstanding the foregoing provisions of this sub-paragraph the Register shall not be rectified against any person whose title has been fortified by prescriptive possession."

As the notes to the paragraph make clear, that proposal was closely modelled on the English legislation then in force which was contained in s 82 of the Land Registration Act 1925. However, before the 1979 Act was passed, s 82 was amended, following a Law Commission report which expressed the view that insufficient protection was given by those provisions to a proprietor in possession. Consequently, when the 1979 Act was framed, it appears that the view was taken that the legislation should follow the model of the amended English legislation. As a result, there is no provision in the 1979 Act equivalent to subpara (4) (b) of para 47 above. The English legislation still contains a provision equivalent to para 47 (4) (c) above, but that provision was also omitted from the 1979 legislation. It is not possible to identify, in any report, a specific reason for that omission; as will be seen, it has been suggested that one reason may have been that the wording of subpara (4) (c) was thought too vague.

I do not think that direct conclusions can be drawn from the Reid and Henry reports as to the proper answer to the present problem. The reports do emphasise the importance of achieving a real right by registration in the Land Register and of protecting such a right once registration has been made. It does, however, seem to me that the primary mischief which the reports were addressing was the difficulty and expense of verifying a title by examining recorded writs under the old system, particularly where there might be competing titles. The reports do not directly address the problem of a registered title based upon a writ which turns out to have been invalid. Indeed, so far as it goes, para 47 (4) (b) of the Henry report seems to suggest that the framers of the scheme were prepared to accept that there were circumstances in which a registered title might fall to be rectified simply on the ground that it was derived by or through a deed which had been reduced.

I turn therefore to consider the arguments in relation to the wording of the statutory provisions themselves. On behalf of the petitioner, it was submitted that s 34 (4) of the 1985 Act conferred on the creditors a right to reduction of a deed, subject to the conditions of the section, and also a right to reduction of deeds in relation to property other than heritable and to restoration of such property or other appropriate redress. As had been held in the earlier case, reduction was the primary remedy and refusal of reduction in a case concerning heritage would create an anomaly in the treatment of heritable and moveable assets respectively. It would be astonishing if Parliament had set out to defeat, indirectly, the rights of creditors in relation to heritable estate, by adding the additional requirement found in s 9 (3) (a) (iii) of the 1979 Act, particularly if that had been done without provision for compensation to the creditors. The solution to the dilemma was to be found in the wording of s 2 (4) (c) of the 1979 Act. A reduction was an event which was capable under a rule of law of affecting the title to a registered interest in land and was therefore something which was in itself registrable. It would be inappropriate to regard the reduction of a deed as an inaccuracy for the purposes of s 9. Accordingly a reduction was in itself registrable in the Land Register and the consequence of registering the reduction would be that the bankrupt's estate would appear in the register as proprietor. For the respondents, it was submitted that the view put forward by the petitioner that a reduction was automatically registrable in the register would subvert the whole system of registration of title. It would mean that, instead of the proprietor, and any person dealing with the proprietor, being able to rely on the certificate of title as conferring a real right, it would become necessary for the previous history of the title to the property to be checked, if security were to be available. There was, however, no provision in the 1979 legislation for the preservation or checking of a progress of titles and the law in relation to prescription had been amended so that prescription was excluded in relation to registered title. Prior titles were now wholly irrelevant and the existence of a real right was judged by what appeared on the register. A reduction did not, in any event, fall within s 2 (4) (c) because it was not, under the present law as properly understood, an event capable of affecting the title; a reduction did not affect the title in itself, but only if it was given effect to by way of a rectification. It was perfectly appropriate to regard reduction of a title as a circumstance coming within the power to rectify inaccuracies contained in s 9 of the 1979 Act. The fact that reference had been made in s 12 (3) (b) to reduction of title by reason of a gratuitous alienation or fraudulent preference was an indication that the circumstance had not been overlooked; and, even if the effect of s 12 (3) (b) was that the creditors were not entitled to compensation on a refusal of rectification, that was not a reason for holding that a reduction must automatically be registrable under s 2 (4) (c). As regards s 34 of the 1985 Act, the court was given power to order other appropriate remedies and the position of creditors could be protected by taking advantage of that power.

In assessing these arguments, it seems to me that the first point to be borne in mind is that, in terms of s 34 of the 1985 Act, decree of reduction can only be granted where there is no prejudice to the rights of a third party who has acquired the property in good faith and for value, while rectification is available under the 1979 Act where the inaccuracy is substantially due to fraud or carelessness on the part of the person in possession. Problems of the kind which arise in the present case appear, therefore, to be confined to cases in which the person in possession has not taken the property in good faith and for value, on the one hand, but has not contributed to the inaccuracy by his carelessness or fraud, on the other. That being so, it does not seem to me that to sustain the respondents' argument would be so unreasonable or involve such a limitation on the rights of creditors that it could not

have been intended by Parliament. On the other hand, it does seem to me that to sustain the petitioner's argument would involve significant prejudice to the operation of the system of registration of title. If the petitioner's arguments were accepted, any reduction of a deed by which a registered interest had been transferred would automatically be registrable. The effect of the petitioner's construction of s 2 (4) (c) would not be limited to cases of reduction arising from bankruptcy, but must extend to every reduction, whatever the reason for it. There would be no limit of time after which a reduction of a deed relating to the interest would cease to be registrable, and no way of applying the law of positive prescription to fortify a title derived from a deed which had been reduced. Further, against the background of the scheme as a whole, it is, in my opinion, of great importance that s 12 (3) (b) clearly envisages that reductions on the ground of bankruptcy may be given effect by means of rectification by the first respondent. It may be added that the Henry committee originally envisaged that rectification should be available in the circumstances set out in para 47 (4) (b) and (c) of their scheme, and that tends to support the inference that it was envisaged that the means of giving effect to reduction should, in general, be rectification. In the whole circumstances, in my opinion, the proper conclusion is that a reduction of a previous writ relating to the property is not an event which is "capable of affecting the title" to a registered interest and therefore is not automatically registrable under s 2 (4) (c) of the 1979 Act.

The remaining arguments do not, in my view, really assist in deciding the central question. So far as the opinions of conveyancers are concerned, reference was made to the *Conveyancing Manual* written by Professor A J McDonald. In para 36.6, Professor McDonald stresses the significance of the state guarantee of a registered title and in para 36.25 deals with the power to rectify. I do not, however, think that Professor McDonald's attention was specifically directed to the present problem and I do not find the observations in those paragraphs of particular assistance. Reference was also made to Professor Halliday's *Conveyancing Law and Practice in Scotland* (Vol II, paras 24-14 and 24-46) but in my view the same comment applies. The 1979 Act was published in *Current Law Statutes* with annotations by Professor Halliday. The note on s 2 (4) is of some interest in that it mentions some cases which might fall within that subsection as being events which would affect a registered title. Professor Halliday instances the case of the death of one of the parties to a title taken in the names of A and B and the survivor in which the keeper might, it was suggested, require to bring the title sheet up to date by deleting the interest of the predecessor which would be absorbed into that of the survivor. The only other note which seems to me of particular significance relates to s 12 (3) (b); it is stated that gratuitous alienations or fraudulent preferences are transactions designed wrongfully to defeat the rights of other persons and that when a title has been obtained by a transaction of that character there is no

A right to indemnity when it is reduced by the court. That suggests, so far as it goes, that the limitation of indemnity contained in s 12 (3) (b) is a limitation as against the bankrupt or persons deriving right from him rather than a limitation as against creditors or trustees in the case in which the rectification is refused. If that is correct, of course, that would count against some of the arguments presented in relation to the proper construction of s 2 (4).

B Reference was made to a number of passages in the *Registration of Title Practice Book,* a manual prepared by a joint consultative committee of representatives of the Law Society of Scotland and the Department of the Registers of Scotland designed to assist practitioners in dealing with the new system of registration of title. The *Practice Book* was first published at about the time of the 1979 legislation and was updated in 1983 and 1991. In para C.15, reference is made to consolidation by prescription as a further instance of an event which may be registrable in terms of s 2 (4) (c). Paragraph C.59 stresses the view that the register C should be rectified in the face of possession only very exceptionally and points out that the result of the legislation as ultimately enacted, as compared with the original recommendations of the Henry report, was that the scales were very heavily weighted in favour of the proprietor in good faith in possession as regards his retention of subjects for which he holds a registered title. In para C.62, reference is made to the abandonment of the provision, which stands in the English legislation, regarding rectification in any D particular case in which it would be unjust not to rectify the register against the proprietor in possession; and the comment is made that this provision was dropped, probably, because the word "unjust" was somewhat vague. It is also suggested that the provision related more to concepts of equity as understood in England than to any principle of Scots law. Further instances of events which might affect a registered title are given in para B1.15, and reference is made to the reduced role of prescription in para H1.02, but none E of these references appears to me to add materially to the arguments discussed above.

The first of the arguments based on comparison with the treatment of other problems in the scheme of registration arose from s 46 of the Conveyancing (Scotland) Act 1924. That section provides, so far as material: [his Lordship quoted the terms of the section set out supra and continued:]

Subsection (2) of s 46 made similar provision for F recording a decree of rectification of a document under s 8 of the Law Reform (Miscellaneous Provisions) (Scotland) Act 1985.

Attention was drawn to s 46 initially as part of the background to the 1979 legislation, and as indicating that the 1979 Act must have been intended to deal with the case of reduction of a deed, without reference to the powers of the first respondent. Later, the argument was developed by reference to s 29 of, and para 11 of Sched 3 to the 1979 Act. It was pointed out that the effect of these provisions was that reference to the

Land Register must be substituted for reference to the Register of Sasines in, among other places, s 46 of the G 1924 Act; and it was submitted that it followed that there must exist a possibility of giving effect to the petitioner's decree of reduction despite the alterations to the system of registration. Section 46 of the 1924 Act was construed as giving only limited protection in *Mulhearn v Dunlop.* It seems to be correct that, as counsel for the first respondent pointed out, it has been assumed that s 46 continues to apply to deeds recorded in the General Register of Sasines while s 9 of the 1979 Act governs the position under the Land H Register (see Halliday, supra, para 21-60). It may be added that deeds and instruments are not registered in the Land Register, which will only show the person entitled, not the stages by which that entitlement came about. It is, however, true that para 11 of Sched 3 to the 1979 Act does not exempt s 46 of the 1924 Act from the general provision [in s 29 (2)] that references to the General Register of Sasines are to be read as references to the Land Register. I confess, therefore, to some difficulty in understanding how s 46 of the I 1924 Act is intended to operate in the context of the new registration system. I have however come to the conclusion that any difficulty of that kind does not bear upon the central question of the proper construction of the 1979 Act itself. Whatever the true effect of s 46 now is, it does not, in my view, support any inference as to the true construction of the crucial provisions of the 1979 Act.

Reference was also made to the treatment of compulsory purchase orders and decrees of adjudication J and also to the effect of certain orders under the Civil Aviation Act 1982. The principal point made was that a general vesting declaration was apparently to be registered in the Land Register (see Halliday, Vol IV, para 52-18) even though the terminology of such an order did not fit with that of a transfer under s 2 (4) (a) of the 1979 Act; the declaration must therefore come in under s 2 (4) (c). Similar arguments were addressed to the treatment of adjudication. Counsel for the first respondent however pointed out that there K is a statutory requirement that compulsory purchase proceedings including vesting orders be registered and that such registration could be explained by reference to s 28 (1) (e) or s 6 (1) (g) of the 1979 Act rather than under s 2. That approach seemed to me to be correct; but whether it is or not, I do not think that this argument casts any light on the question in this case. As regards adjudications, given the special nature of the rules applicable to them, it does not appear to me that there is any inconsistency in the treatment of these L events. In any event, the comment made above in relation to s 46 also applies, that is, that the question in the present case is one of the proper construction of the central provisions of the 1979 Act itself.

In all the circumstances, I have come to the view that the argument of the respondents is to be preferred; that, accordingly, the first respondent is entitled to refuse to register the petitioner's decree of reduction; and that the proper course is that application should be made to the first respondent for rectification of the register. It follows that the petition falls to be dismissed.

As I mentioned earlier, there was some discussion of the competency of an application for judicial review of a decision of the first respondent. The question of competency arises because there is provision in s 25 of the 1979 Act for appeal to the Lands Tribunal and the Court of Session against any decision of the first respondent. The matter is not straightforward because s 25 (2) appears to leave open other remedies which any party may have. It is not, however, necessary to consider the arguments in detail. Counsel for the first respondent ultimately adopted the position that, because it was of practical importance to secure a decision on the substantive question as soon as possible, no practical purpose would be served by arguing the plea to competency (see *Jackson v Secretary of State for Scotland*). Counsel made it clear however, that the first respondent does not concede that an application such as the present is competent. In view of the provisions of s 25 (2), I do not think that the point of competency is so obvious that it must be pars judicis to determine it.

_____

Counsel for Petitioner, J W McNeill, QC; Solicitors, MacRoberts — Counsel for First Respondent, Reed; Solicitor, R Brodie, Solicitor to the Secretary of State for Scotland — Counsel for Second Respondent, Andrew Smith; Solicitors, Gillam Mackie, SSC.

M L B F

[On 5 November 1993 the First Division refused a reclaiming motion by the trustee (1993 GWD 38-2506). A report is in preparation.]

(NOTE)

Clark v Chief Constable, Lothian and Borders Police

SECOND DIVISION

THE LORD JUSTICE CLERK (ROSS),
LORDS MORISON AND CAPLAN

19 FEBRUARY 1993

Damages — Amount — Assessment — Loss of earnings and necessary services rendered to injured person — Lack of specific evidence.

Defenders reclaimed against an award which included an assessment of loss of earnings and of necessary services rendered to the injured person where the evidence as to the amount of earnings lost and as to the extent of the necessary services provided was deficient.

Held, that in assessing wage loss the calculation

required to use the lowest figure extracted from the evidence, and that in assessing necessary services, although the absence of precise evidence was not altogether to exclude consideration of the claim, the court should assess the minimum amount which could reasonably be inferred as appropriate on the evidence; and reclaiming motion *allowed* in relation to those two heads of the award.

Dictum in *Forsyth's Curator Bonis v Govan Shipbuilders Ltd*, 1988 SLT 321 at p 327A-B, *approved*.

_____

(Reported 1992 SLT 822)
William Sutherland, the chief constable of Lothian and Borders Police, and Roderick Cooper, a policeman in that police force, the defenders in an action raised by Linda Clark for damages for injuries sustained by her, reclaimed against the interlocutor pronounced by the temporary judge (T G Coutts, QC) awarding the pursuer damages. The accident had happened on 2 April 1987 when the pursuer was aged 35. The temporary judge had awarded damages made up as follows: solatium, £22,500 plus interest on one half thereof from the date of the accident at the rate of 7½ per cent per annum; loss of earnings, £15,000 plus interest at the rate of 7½ per cent per annum from 1 January 1988 in respect of loss of earnings up to the date of the proof and £6,000 for loss of earning capacity thereafter; necessary services provided to the pursuer by her relatives, £4,000 plus interest at 7½ per cent per annum from the date of the accident; and loss of the pursuer's services, £1,000 up to the date of proof and no award thereafter (after taking into account mobility allowance received by the pursuer). The defenders did not contest the award except in relation to (a) loss of earnings to the date of the proof and (b) the award for services provided to the pursuer.

The court allowed the reclaiming motion. In delivering the opinion of the court Lord Morison said:

"The hearing before us related only to the temporary judge's award for past loss of wages, which he assessed at £15,000 to date, with interest at 7½ per cent per annum from 1 January 1988; and his award for a claim made under s 8 of the Administration of Justice Act 1982, assessed at the sum of £8,825, from which was deducted a sum of £4,589 received by way of mobility allowance. A claim under s 9 of the 1982 Act was also made, which was assessed at the sum of £1,000 in respect of the period up to but not beyond the date of proof, and this assessment also was not disputed.

"The temporary judge assessed past loss of wages upon the basis (a) that, if the accident had not occurred, the pursuer who was unemployed at that time would probably have resumed her former employment by the beginning of 1988; (b) that the effects of the accident disabled her from working full time for a period of two years from that date; (c) that for the remaining two years before the proof she would only have worked part time as a result of her back condition which was not proved to be associated with the

A accident; and (d) that the gross amount which she would have earned by working full time would have been £8,000 per annum over the four year period. . . .

"[I]n opening the reclaiming motion counsel for the reclaimers submitted that there was insufficient evidence to justify the making of any award for loss of wages in respect (a) that there was no basis for determining the amount which the pursuer would have earned during the four year period over which her loss was assessed; and (b) that in light of evidence about the B pursuer's back condition given by a consultant surgeon Mr Chalmers, which had been accepted, no date had been established as that upon which the pursuer would have been able to undertake employment if the accident had not occurred. It was further submitted that in any event the assessment of the amount of wages which the pursuer would have earned was excessive, having regard to such evidence as there was on that matter."

C The court found that the temporary judge had been entitled to hold that, but for the accident, the pursuer would have resumed work at the beginning of 1988 and would have worked two years full time and then two years part time. His Lordship continued:

"Although it was submitted that there was no satisfactory evidence upon which the temporary judge was entitled to proceed to allow any calculation of lost earnings to be made, there was some evidence on that matter, notably that of the pursuer herself who said D that she would have hoped to have earned about £6,000-£7,000 gross per annum by resuming her former employment as a medical secretary, and of a consultant surgeon who said that, as far as he knew, the salary of a medical secretary at the date of the proof was approximately £6,800 to about £8,000 or £9,000 per annum, with additional rewards for extra skills. This evidence was plainly deficient, since it did not reveal the net amount which the pursuer personally would have earned from time to time during E the relevant period. Such evidence is usually agreed before a proof, in accordance with proper practice, but in the absence of agreement it is difficult to understand why accurate and complete evidence was not made available. However the figures mentioned were sufficient to afford to the court some basis for assessing the minimum amount of gross earnings which the pursuer must have lost. We agree with counsel for the reclaimers that such a minimum, over the whole of the four year period, should be taken as £6,400 gross per F annum, not the £8,000 per annum figure on which the temporary judge's assessment proceeded. That figure reflects the lowest amount which the pursuer said she hoped to earn on resuming work, and allows for increases which would have occurred thereafter. From the figure of £6,400 there have to be deducted sums which the pursuer would have paid by way of tax, insurance contributions, and other deductions from her gross salary. This was a matter upon which no evidence at all was led. On behalf of the reclaimers it was submitted that in the absence of evidence it would be reasonable to make a deduction of one third from

the gross salary. Submissions were made on behalf of the respondent as to the rates of tax and insurance con- G tributions for which she would have been liable and the effect of personal tax allowances to which she would have been entitled, which it was contended justified a deduction of only 25 per cent. But in the absence of evidence we consider that this court should proceed on the basis suggested by the reclaimers since it represents a deduction which it is unlikely would have been exceeded. It also appears to reflect the submissions which the temporary judge records as having been made on the pursuer's behalf at the proof. H Annual net loss of wages which the pursuer would have earned if she had worked full time is therefore taken as £4,267. If the deduction from gross earnings is excessive, the responsibility lies in the pursuer's failure to lead evidence on the matter.

"It was not disputed, again in the absence of evidence, that the pursuer's part time earnings would have been one half of those which she would have earned full time. Accordingly the net sum which she would have earned over the four years, in two of which she I would have worked part time, is reduced by a quarter. Loss of earnings thus amounts to three times £4,267 which is £12,800. From that sum must be deducted agreed benefits of £2,666, resulting in an award of £10,134 which compares with the temporary judge's assessment of £15,000. Interest on that sum at the rate of 7½ per cent per annum from 1 January 1988 is agreed.

"In relation to the claim made under s 8 of the Administration of Justice Act it was again submitted J with justification that the evidence led as to the services for which remuneration was claimed and what would be a fair rate of remuneration for these services was unsatisfactory. Reference was made to *Forsyth's CB v Govan Shipbuilders*, 1988 SLT 321, in which Lord Clyde at p 327A-B observed that in future cases evidence should be led to enable the court to assess accurately what in all the circumstances a reasonable remuneration would be. Although we agree with this observation, the effect of a failure to lead precise evid- K ence is not altogether to exclude consideration of the claim, but to restrict the court's assessment to an amount, if any, which represents the minimum that can reasonably be inferred as appropriate on the basis of such evidence as there is. This does not seem to have been the approach taken by the temporary judge, who fixed sums of £5,000 for the first year after the accident, £1,500 for each of the two succeeding years, and £825 thereafter until the date of the proof. Further, it appears that the services which he assessed L at these amounts may well have included assistance in caring for the pursuer's children, which is not a claim arising under s 8 (services rendered to an injured person), but under s 9 (services to an injured person's relative). The sum of £1,000 which the temporary judge awarded under s 9 is not disputed.

"Considering de novo the imprecise evidence led in support of the s 8 claim, we regard it as reasonable to suppose, on the basis of what was said by the pursuer and her mother, that at least two hours a day or 14

hours a week would have been devoted to the services
referred to in the section during the first year after the
accident, and that a sum of £3.00 per hour would constitute, as was accepted by counsel for the reclaimers,
the minimum reasonable rate of remuneration for
these services. The appropriate award for the first year
is therefore £2,184 (52 × £42), and for succeeding
years it was agreed that the sum should be reduced pro
rata in the proportions taken by the temporary judge,
i e a total of three fifths for the next two years and
(approximately) one fifth thereafter. The total amount
comes to £3,931, which is less than the sum awarded
to the pursuer by way of mobility allowance for the
period from 1 October 1988 until the date of proof.
Questions were raised before us whether any deduction in respect of this allowance should be made from
the s 8 claim so far as related to the period between the
date of the accident and that on which the allowance
commenced. It was also suggested that to the extent
that the allowance reflected the pursuer's back condition rather than the effects of the accident, no deduction should be made. These matters were not the
subject of any evidence or submission before the
temporary judge, who proceeded, apparently by concession, to apply the decision in *Hodgson v Trapp*
[1989] AC 807, to the effect that the whole sum of
£4,589 was deductible from the amount which would
represent remuneration for the services. Counsel for
the respondent eventually recognised that he was not
in a position to maintain the contrary. The s 8 claim
is therefore extinguished by the deduction.

"In accordance with these findings we grant the
reclaiming motion to the extent of recalling the interlocutor of the temporary judge dated 7 February 1992
and pronouncing decree for the sum of £22,500 in
name of solatium with interest on one half of that sum
at the rate of 7½ per cent per annum from 2 April
1987 until 7 February 1992; decree for the sum of
£1,000 in respect of the s 9 claim with interest on the
said sum at the rate of 7½ per cent per annum from
2 April 1987 until 7 February 1992; decree for
£10,134 in respect of past loss of wages, with interest
on the said sum at the rate of 7½ per cent per annum
from 1 January 1988 until 7 February 1992; and
decree for £6,000 in respect of future loss of wages or
restriction of employment capacity; with interest on
the total of the said sums at the rate of 15 per cent per
annum from 7 February 1992 until payment."

---

*Counsel for Pursuer and Respondent, P M Macdonald;
Solicitors, Gordon Thomson & Co — Counsel for
Defenders and Reclaimers, Liddle; Solicitors, Simpson &
Marwick, WS.*

C H

Barras v Hamilton

OUTER HOUSE

TEMPORARY JUDGE R G McEWAN, QC

11 MARCH 1993

*Landlord and tenant — Lease — Tenant liable for
premiums on building insurance — Damage to subjects let
caused by tenant's negligence — Whether landlord entitled
to recover for damage from tenant.*

*Insurance — Landlord and tenant — Tenant liable for
premiums on building insurance — Damage to subjects let
caused by tenant's negligence — Whether landlord entitled
to recover for damage from tenant.*

A fire broke out on an industrial estate causing considerable damage. The landlord of the estate sued the
tenant of the unit where the fire was said to have
started, one of four units in the same building. The
landlord sought reparation for uninsured damage to
property and averred breach of a number of duties of
care. The landlord had arranged fire insurance for the
whole property and the tenant was liable to pay the
premium for all four units. The policy paid regardless
of who was negligent. The tenant argued that the
effect of the policy of insurance was to relieve him of
liability for the loss: the landlord was entitled solely to
recovery of the proceeds of the insurance, even if the
event causing the loss was the negligence of the tenant
since, by obliging the tenant to pay the premium, the
landlord as a quid pro quo had accepted he had no
claim upon the tenant. It was argued for the landlord
that what was necessary was to identify the tenant's
insurable interest, as he could only be protected to that
extent. Rei interitus applied and the lease ended.
There was thus no remaining insurable interest, as the
tenant had no interest in anything beyond the terms of
the policy such as the landlord's business, loss of
profits or disruption, and therefore the action was
relevant.

Held, that the landlord having arranged the insurance and fixed the amounts to be insured and the
tenant having been bound to pay the premium, the
tenant was discharged from any liability to the landlord in respect of the insured risk (p 1305F-H); and
action *dismissed*.

Mark Rowlands Ltd v Berni Inns Ltd [1985] 1 QB
211, *followed*; *Duke of Hamilton's Trs v Fleming* (1870)
9 M 329, *Clark v Hume* (1903) 10 SLT 509 and
Cantors Properties (Scotland) Ltd v Swears & Wells,
1980 SLT 165, *distinguished*.

Action of damages

Christopher Barras raised an action against William
Hamilton for reparation in respect of damage to
property of which the pursuer was the landlord and of
part of which the defender was the tenant.

The case came before the temporary judge (R G
McEwan, QC) on procedure roll on the defender's
plea to the relevancy of the pursuer's averments.

Cases referred to

A *Cantors Properties (Scotland) Ltd v Swears & Wells Ltd*, 1980 SLT 165; 1978 SC 310.

Clark v Hume (1903) 10 SLT 509; (1902) 5 F 252.

Eaton (T) & Co Ltd v Smith (1977) 92 DLR (3d) 425.

Hamilton's (Duke of) Trustees v Fleming (1870) 9 M 329.

Mumford Hotels v Wheler [1964] Ch 117; [1963] 3 WLR 735; [1963] 3 All ER 250.

Rowlands (Mark) Ltd v Berni Inns Ltd [1986] 1 QB 211; [1985] 3 WLR 964; [1985] 3 All ER 473.

B **Textbook referred to**

MacGillivray and Parkington, *Insurance Law* (8th ed), paras 1240 and 1652.

On 11 March 1993 the temporary judge *sustained* the defender's first plea in law and *dismissed* the action.

R G McEWAN, QC.—On 7 April 1985 a serious C fire broke out in a small industrial estate known as the "Schoolhouse Estate", Addiewell, West Lothian. The fire is said to have occurred because of a spark from a welding torch igniting diesel fuel. Considerable damage resulted.

The pursuer is the heritable proprietor of the industrial estate. The defender was the tenant and occupier of the unit where the fire is said to have started. The pursuer sues the defender in reparation for damage to property, averring breach of a number of duties of D care. The defence to the action is that the matter is covered by a policy of insurance and no claim lies against the defender.

Counsel for the defender opened his argument by inviting me to dismiss the action as irrelevant standing a series of admissions in the pleadings.

The issue, he said, is focused by these admissions which were to this effect. The relationship between the parties was that of landlord and tenant. Four of the units were all part of "The Property" as the policy E appendix described it. These four units were all one "Building" and the defender was the tenant of unit 2. The landlord arranged fire insurance for the whole of the property and the defender was liable to pay the premium for the building consisting of units 1 to 4. The insurers had paid sums in respect of units 1 to 4 and a separate settlement had been made on a separate building housing units 5 and 6.

What the pursuers were trying to do was to recover uninsured losses out of the destruction of units 1 to 4.

F In principle now in insurance law, in such a case the tenant was entitled to say that any loss suffered by the landlord as a result of the subjects covered being destroyed by fire was to be recouped solely from the proceeds of the insurance, even if the event causing the loss was the negligence of the tenant. This had been the subject of express decision by the Court of Appeal in *Mark Rowlands Ltd v Berni Inns Ltd* (hereinafter called *Berni*). On this point the case enjoyed the approval of MacGillivray on *Insurance* (8th ed), paras 1240 and 1652. By obliging the tenant to pay the

premium the landlord as a quid pro quo accepts he has no claim upon him. *Berni* and certain other cases from G common law jurisdictions enunciated principles of the general body of lex mercatoria. These principles should be the same in Scotland as in England, Canada and the United States.

Counsel for the defender then went on to examine at length the case of *Berni*. I intend no disrespect to his careful argument by not repeating his analysis in detail at this point. I shall ingather it later in my judgment.

Counsel then invited attention to the policy which H is incorporated in the pleadings. The exclusions in the policy were similar to those in the one under consideration in *Berni*. It could not be suggested that the policy did not apply to the events here. A global sum of insurance covered the four units which were insured as if they were a unum quid. Where the pleadings referred to "the subjects" that was what was meant. This tenant paid the premium on all the subjects and the policy paid whoever was negligent. Here the risk covered was destruction by fire of the whole I subjects caused by negligence. What was involved was an exoneration for negligence, not a question of assessment for loss.

Whereas in some of the Canadian cases there was no clear obligation on the tenant to pay the premium, that could not be said here. At this point counsel referred me to the Dominion and American authorities.

There were many points of similarity here with *Berni* on the lease, policy, events and payment. Only J the landlord could fix the level of insurance as only he knew what cover was needed.

I was invited to follow *Berni* and to dismiss the action.

In his reply speech counsel for the defender responded to the pursuer's arguments in this way. Although "premises" and "subjects" were used in the pleadings, they were merely descriptive for the purposes of the pleadings and could not override the policy. They were in any event immaterial if *Berni* was K in point. In any case in *Berni* the tenant only insured the basement. Here only one premium was paid for units not differentiated. The insurers covered the whole and the tenant could not possibly know how they might have allocated or divided the premium he paid.

It was fallacious to found on obligations to reinstate as that was not part of the decision in *Berni*.

Also it was incorrect to rely on insurable interest or L how much premium was paid or for what part. These matters were only dealt with in *Berni* out of courtesy to counsel and not for the purposes of the decision. The point was that the tenant was not liable for fire. The Scottish cases dealt with privity and on the policy only the landlord had privity. Only he could go to the insurers and even they did not seem to think they had any claim against the tenant.

For the pursuer counsel stated that the defender's argument was wrong in principle. In this case the "premises" meant the Schoolhouse of which unit 2 was only a part. Where the word "subjects" was used it referred to unit 2. The tenant defender only bore the cost of insurance of that. It was only part of a greater whole. It was agreed that the landlord was not bound to repair or reinstate. The lease did not continue after destruction, but these were immaterial in this case. The esto case was vital. The defender's fifth plea was one to the merits and did not focus the point properly. It should have been a plea of discharge.

Berni should not be followed because the decision was incorrect and was not the law of Scotland. In this case there are no third party risks whereas these were present in *Berni* and vital to its decision. Also there the landlord had been fully indemnified and the case was one of subrogation. That was not present here where the landlord was not claiming for the part his insurers had paid. The case extended the tenant's indemnity far too widely. If it was correct it meant that the tenant and his servants would be indemnified for their own negligence. The landlord could sue a negligent third party for uninsured losses but not his negligent tenant. To make recovery depend upon paying a premium on part of a greater whole could produce absurd results and depend upon luck.

What was necessary was to identify the tenant's insurable interest as he could only be protected to that extent. Here the tenant had no right to demand that the lease continue. Rei interitus applied and the lease ended. There was thus no remaining insurable interest. The tenant had no interest in anything beyond the terms of the policy such as the landlord's business, loss of profits or disruption. In *Berni* by contrast the building was to be reinstated and the lease to continue.

In Scots law the tenant does not have any such insurable interest. *Duke of Hamilton's Trs v Fleming* was in point as were the opinions at pp 338-340. To like effect was *Clark v Hume*. I was referred to the whole of the Lord Ordinary's opinion at (1902) 5 F, p 253. Counsel next referred me to *Cantors Properties v Swears & Wells*, 1980 SLT, at p 171. There the full value was to be covered as well as 12 months' rent. The effect of these authorities was that the pursuer's third plea should be sustained and proof before answer allowed.

The pursuers, however, had a subsidiary position on the basis of their esto case. Upon a proper construction of the policy and these averments the defenders could only escape liability for unit 2, architects' and surveyors' fees for that unit and one year's rent for that unit. The effect of that was to leave quantification of the claim for the other parts.

I turn now to consider the authorities referred to, beginning with the Scottish cases. In *Duke of Hamilton's Trs v Fleming* the pursuers had leased a mill to the defender. The tenant was obliged "to have the whole houses and machinery on the premises constantly insured in some respectable insurance office to the extent of £1,200 sterling, the policy to be taken in name of the proprietor, and he relieving the tenant of one-half of the premium of insurance".

In 1865 the mill and most of the machinery were destroyed by fire. The insurers paid the landlord who did not renew the subjects though asked to do so by the tenant. When the landlord's trustees claimed rent some years later the tenant counterclaimed for an entitlement to moneys paid by the insurers for lost machinery on which he had expended money.

The First Division decided that he was not entitled to any money recovered under the policy. I was directed by counsel for the pursuer to a number of passages but for present purposes it may only be necessary to refer at length to Lord Deas. At p 337 he said this: "in answer to the second question, I think it is plain that the main interest in the machinery during the lease belonged to the tenant, just as the main interest in the buildings during the lease belonged to him, but in neither case was it an interest of property in the subjects. The tenant had an insurable interest undoubtedly, that interest being the profit which he expected to make during the lease. But when we come to the third question, I consider that the insurance was for the benefit of the landlord alone. The whole insurance is on the buildings and machinery, both being the property of the landlord, and the words of the policy shew that it was effected for the sole behoof of the landlord. The tenant pays a proportion of the premium, that is, his rent is increased by that amount, but that does not entitle him to participate in the benefit of this insurance. His insurable interest was not insured by it at all. I therefore think that he is not entitled to any of the insurance money, but that all that money goes to the landlord, along with what remains of the machinery."

Lord Ardmillan (p 338) and Lord Kinloch (p 340) are to like effect on this point, as was Lord President Inglis (p 335) who, however, had dissented on the other point before the court, which is not material for the purposes of this case.

The case was referred to in the next authority cited to me.

Clark v Hume appears to raise again the very point decided in the *Duke of Hamilton's* case. Once again the facts were that a mill and machinery were destroyed by fire. The lease provided that the landlord was to insure for such amount as he thought necessary and the tenant was to pay one half of the annual premium.

The landlord recovered under the policy then told the tenant he was not going to rebuild the mill, leaving the tenant to abandon the lease or remain in possession of other tenanted subjects with the benefit of an abatement of rent.

The tenant sought declarator that the landlord was bound to rebuild. The Lord Ordinary held the landlord was under no such obligation merely because it was expressly provided that he was to insure. The Second Division, delivering short opinions, agreed there was no such obligation.

I am not sure, however, if the court correctly held that the *Duke of Hamilton* case was decisive upon the obligation to rebuild. As I read the four opinions on the insurance point (which were unanimous) they do

A not appear to me to be authority for the proposition that a clause in a lease requiring insurance of this nature means the landlord is not bound to rebuild. Rebuilding was only mentioned by the Lord President (at p 335) and Lord Ardmillan (p 338). My reading of what they said is that rebuilding would have to have been by express agreement. The judgments in *Clark* seem, however, to decide that an insurance clause in these terms in a lease is fatal to any obligation to rebuild.

I shall return later to one further point in the *Duke*
B *of Hamilton*.

In *Cantors Properties* the pursuers owned premises adjoining Trongate and Brunswick Street in Glasgow. They leased them to the defenders who later sublet them back to the pursuers. In the principal lease the tenants were to insure the premises and 12 months' rent against loss or damage by fire. The sublease placed this and other obligations on the subtenant. The main point argued was whether destruction by fire determined the lease and whether the landlord
C could be required to rebuild. The conclusion was for declarator that the lease and the sublease had both been terminated by the fire.

At 1980 SLT, pp 171-172, Lord Cameron, who presided, dealt at length with the clauses of the lease and sublease and pointed up the distinction between the words "replace" and "rebuild". At p 172 he said this under reference to *Clark* about reinstatement: "It is not difficult to see why this should be so and why in the case of a lease for a term of years, if such an obli-
D gation of reinstatement were to be laid on the landlord for whose benefit and unfettered use it might be thought that such insurance monies would accrue, it would require clear and precise stipulation in the contract providing for such an additional burden, which the common law does not provide, being laid on the landlord's shoulders."

In *Mumford Hotels v Wheler* the defendant, who was a widow, was the tenant for life of her late husband's
E mansion house. The property was used as a hotel by the plaintiffs. Mrs Wheler leased it to the plaintiffs covenanting to insure it. The tenant was to pay an insurance rent equal to the premium. When fire destroyed much of the property the landlord refused to reinstate it. Harman LJ, sitting as an additional judge, held that the landlord's obligation to insure, being paid for by the tenant, was intended to benefit both of them. She thus had to reinstate from the insurance if called upon to do so.

F The judge stressed that "the strength of the company's case lies in its obligation to pay the premiums, and its right to see that the policy was adequate. Why these provisions if it is to have no interest in the policy money?" ([1964] Ch, p 126).

The authority which is central to the whole case is *Mark Rowlands Ltd v Berni Inns Ltd*. There the premises in question were a building in Leeds. The plaintiff was the freeholder but did not occupy any part of the building. The defendant company occupied the basement and part of the ground floor

which it used as a restaurant. The remainder of the building was occupied by another tenant who carried G on a furniture business. In January 1980 a fire destroyed the whole building. The cause of the fire was electrical and was due to the defendant's negligence. The loss was valued at over £1 million and the plaintiff fully recovered from its insurers. No additional losses were incurred. The landlord's insurers suing under their right of subrogation sought to recover from the tenant in negligence.

The defendant had a lease with the plaintiff the material terms of which were that the landlord should H insure the whole building against fire, the tenant was to contribute to the cost of the insurance and the landlord would rebuild with the insurance moneys. (The first two conditions are present here.)

It was provided that the premium also insured three years of the highest rent available ("rack rent"), architects', surveyors' and other fees and incidental expenses consequent upon rebuilding. In percentage terms the tenant was paying 25 per cent of the I premium (here also it is said the tenant only paid part of the premium). The policy itself covered the whole building, an agreed sum for loss of rent and fees. The policy made no reference to the defendant nor did it cover consequential loss of any kind. (Again these points are present in this case.)

In the leading opinion by Kerr LJ between pp 224-228 it can be seen that the only question addressed was whether the plaintiff had effected the insurance for the benefit of the defendant. The J opinions of the Court of Appeal on this point were that the insurance was so intended and that the defendant had an insurable interest. That matter, which was decided with reference to *Mumford* and other cases, was not regarded as a material point in the same way as full indemnity was also not a material point in the decision and ratio of the case.

(It has to be said that English law on this issue appears to differ from the Scottish cases already referred to although the detailed terms of the English K leases may be the reason for that.)

Counsel for the defender, passing from his analysis of this, moved me to hold that the real issue was focused by the question posed by Kerr LJ at p 228F where he said: "the real issue . . . is whether the terms of the lease, and the full indemnification of the plaintiff by its receipt of the insurance moneys, preclude it from recovering damages in negligence from the defendant, or whether the plaintiff's right to recover L such damages remains unaffected".

The learned Lord Justice then discussed several Canadian cases where the majority opinions decided that in these circumstances the landlord could not maintain an action for negligence against the tenant. The terms of the leases in the Canadian cases were all different and some were less favourable to the tenant than in *Berni*.

Of importance is what was said by Laskin CJC in *T Eaton & Co Ltd v Smith* (1977) 92 DLR (3d) 425 at p 428. The Chief Justice of Canada said this: "[a tenant] can escape this liability . . . only . . . on the basis that the landlord's covenant to insure is a covenant that runs to the benefit of the tenant, lifting from it the risk of liability for fire arising from its negligence and bringing that risk under insurance coverage. Had the landlord insured without giving a covenant to that effect in the lease, the tenant's risk of liability for fire resulting from negligence would be unquestionable".

Kerr LJ followed the Canadian and American cases and concluded that the landlord had to recover from the insurers and could not sue the tenant. He had made full recovery in the manner envisaged by the lease. Croom-Johnson and Glidewell LJJ delivered concurring opinions.

What then is the effect of the authorities, beginning with the Scottish cases all of which are binding on me?

It is I think important to note that two of the Scottish cases arose out of declaratory conclusions. *Cantors* was a direct declarator and *Clark* was declarator seeking restoration and payment from insurance money. The *Duke's* case was an action for rent with a counterclaim for insurance money.

In none of these cases was there ever any point made about recovery of uninsured losses. It was clearly pointed out in the *Duke's* case that the precise insurance arrangements are a matter entirely within the discretion of the landlord. Lord Kinloch described the position thus ((1870) 9 M at p 340), and I regard what he said as being important in this case: "I consider the whole arrangement of the insurance to have been nothing else than an arrangement by the landlord for his own security. It was in his power to make the security greater or less at his pleasure." After giving an example he continued: "That he did not so arrange the insurance cannot affect the claim of the tenant against him. The landlord only recovered from the insurance company the sum of £200, in consequence of his own limitation of the sum placed on the machinery."

In a sense that is what has happened here. I do not think that anything turns on any pleading distinction between "property" and "subjects". I regard these as merely descriptive, as it was put. What is clear is that the appendix shows insurance values on units 1 to 6, architects' and surveyors' fees and one year's rent on all the units. No other losses are covered and this must be a matter of deliberate choice with the background of insurance against destruction by fire.

I do not think any question arises about the negligence of the tenant. Although it is not specifically mentioned, the terms of the policy are wide enough to include it. It is normal for a policy of fire insurance to cover accident and negligence, and I consider that is what the parties here intended. The lease itself was verbal and so is silent on any question of liability for negligence. The issue I have to address is whether the policy from its terms benefits the tenant by taking away from him the risk of liability for causing a fire by negligence by placing that risk on the insurers.

It respectfully seems to me that this point is not what was decided in the Scottish cases and no obiter remarks were made about it. They were concerned to decide whether the tenant could recover in cash or kind on the policy. I thus find I have to distinguish the three Inner House decisions as not in point.

I have to regard the point as an open question on which there is no Scottish authority. The English and other cases are at best persuasive.

The case before me concerns a verbal lease and it is admitted that the landlord was to arrange the insurance and the tenant to pay. The pursuers moved me to sustain their third plea and the defenders their first. Having regard to the case of *Berni* I am of the view that it is sound in principle and should be followed. There is nothing to be gained by having a proof about this lease. It assumes little detailed significance in the pleadings beyond what has already been mentioned. The policy is admitted and has been looked at.

I accordingly sustain the defender's first plea in law and dismiss the action.

Counsel for Pursuer, Martin, QC, R S Russell; Solicitors, Lindsays, WS — Counsel for Defender, Clarke, QC; Solicitors, Brodies, WS (for Hamilton Burns & Moore, Glasgow).

G D M

Strathclyde Regional Council v M

EXTRA DIVISION

LORDS McCLUSKEY, WEIR AND WYLIE

3 JUNE 1993

Local government — Social work — Care of children in need — Assumption of parental rights — Child subject to supervision order in care of foster parents — Whether "in care" of local authority — Whether authority entitled to pass resolution assuming parental rights — Social Work (Scotland) Act 1968 (c 49), ss 16 (1) and 44 (5).

Section 16 (1) of the Social Work (Scotland) Act 1968 provides that a local authority may resolve that there shall vest in them the parental rights "with respect to any child who is in their care under section 15", if it appears inter alia that throughout the three years preceding the passing of the resolution the child has been in care under s 15. Section 44 (5) provides that a child who is subject to a supervision requirement made by a children's hearing shall for the purposes inter alia of s 16 be in care.

A child was referred to a children's hearing in 1985. After the grounds for referral were held established by the sheriff, the children's hearing made a supervision requirement in terms of s 44 (1) (a) of the 1968 Act requiring him to submit to supervision in accordance with such conditions as they might impose. Since then the child had been continuously subject to compulsory measures of care and had lived with foster parents. In 1990 the regional council resolved under s 16 of the Act that the relevant parental rights and powers should vest in them, on the basis that it appeared to the authority that the child had been in care throughout the three years immediately preceding in terms of s 16 (1) (iv) and also because it appeared to them that there had been a persistent failure without reasonable cause to discharge the obligations of a parent or guardian so as to render the parent or guardian unfit to have care of the child, in terms of s 16 (1) (ii) and (2) (e). The parents served counter notices under s 16 (7). On a summary application by the local authority, the sheriff after proof determined the application in favour of the authority and ordered that the resolution should not lapse. The father of the child appealed, arguing that the local authority could not competently pass the resolution that they purported to pass given the admitted circumstance that the child had never been in their care under s 15 of the Act.

Held, that a child subject to a supervision requirement was deemed by s 44 (5) to be in the care of the local authority for the purposes of s 16; that the purpose of s 16 was to enable the local authority to pass the appropriate vesting resolution; and accordingly that the resolution was competently passed (pp 1308C-D and 1309D); and appeal *refused*.

Strathclyde Regional Council v B, Sheriff Principal J A Dick, QC, 27 March 1985, unreported, *approved*.

Appeal from the sheriff court

NM, the father of a child K, appealed to the Court of Session against an interlocutor of the sheriff following a summary application made by Strathclyde Regional Council under s 16 (8) of the Social Work (Scotland) Act 1968, ordering that a resolution of council that relevant parental rights and powers in respect of K should vest in them, should not lapse.

Statutory provisions

The Social Work (Scotland) Act 1968, as amended, provides:

"15.—(1) Without prejudice to the generality of the foregoing provisions of this Part of this Act, where it appears to a local authority with respect to a child in their area appearing to them to be under the age of 17 — (a) that he has neither parent nor guardian or has been and remains abandoned by his parent or guardian or is lost; or (b) that his parent or guardian is, for the time being or permanently, prevented by reason of illness or mental disorder or bodily disease or infirmity or other incapacity or any other circumstances from providing for his proper accommodation, maintenance and upbringing; and (c) in either case, that the intervention of the local authority under this section is necessary in the interests of the welfare of the child, it shall be the duty of the local authority to receive the child into their care under this section. . . .

"16.—(1) Subject to the provisions of this Part of this Act, a local authority may resolve — (a) that there shall vest in them the relevant parental rights and powers with respect to any child who is in their care under section 15 of this Act; . . . if it appears to the local authority — . . . (iv) that throughout the three years preceding the passing of the resolution the child has been in the care of a local authority under section 15 of this Act. . . .

"(8) Where a counter-notice has been served on a local authority under subsection (7) of this section, the authority may, not later than fourteen days after the receipt by them of the counter-notice, make a summary application in respect thereto to the sheriff having jurisdiction in the area of the authority, and in that event the resolution shall not lapse until the determination of the application; and the sheriff may, on the hearing of the application, order that the resolution shall not lapse by reason of the service of the counter-notice: Provided that the sheriff shall not so order unless satisfied — (a) that it is in the interests of the child to do so; and (b) that the grounds mentioned in subsection (1) of this section on which the local authority purported to pass the resolution were made out; and (c) that at the time of the hearing there continued to be grounds on which a resolution under subsection (1) of this section could be founded. . . .

"44.—(1) Subject to the provisions of this Part of this Act a children's hearing, where, after the consideration of his case, they decide that a child is in need of compulsory measures of care, may make a requirement, in this Act referred to as a supervision requirement, requiring him — (a) to submit to supervision in accordance with such conditions as they may impose . . . and a condition imposed by virtue of head (a) of this subsection may be a condition as to the place where the child is to reside, being a place other than a residential establishment. . . .

"(5) It shall be the duty of the local authority to give effect to a supervision requirement made by a children's hearing for their area, and a child who is subject to such a supervision requirement shall, for the purposes of sections 16 to 18, 20, 20A, 24 to 26, 28 and 29 of this Act and section 18 of the Adoption (Scotland) Act 1978 (which, amongst other things, provides that an application by an adoption agency to dispense with parental agreement to the freeing of a child for adoption is competent only where the child is in the care of the agency), be in their care."

Cases referred to

Beagley v Beagley, 1984 SLT 202.
Central Regional Council v B, 1985 SLT 413.
Lothian Regional Council v Gibbs, Sheriff P G B McNeill at Edinburgh, 10 August 1984, unreported.
Lothian Regional Council v S, 1986 SLT (Sh Ct) 37.
Pepper v Hart [1992] 3 WLR 1032; [1993] 1 All ER 42.
Strathclyde Regional Council v B, Sheriff Principal J A Dick, QC, at Glasgow, 27 March 1985, unreported.

Strathclyde Regional Council v M, 1982 SLT (Sh Ct)
A   106.
Strathclyde Regional Council v R, Sheriff Sir S S T
     Young at Greenock, 16 January 1987,
     unreported.

Textbook referred to
Kearney, *Children's Hearings and the Sheriff Court*,
     pp 143, 144 and 381.

Appeal
B   The ground of appeal for the father was in the
following terms:

One of the grounds upon which the pursuers purported to pass their resolution was that set out in s 16
(1) (a) (iv) [sic] of the Social Work (Scotland) Act 1968,
namely that throughout the three years preceding the
passing of the resolution the child K had been in the
care of the pursuers under s 15 of the Act. The learned
sheriff misdirected himself in his approach to provisos
C   (b) and (c) to s 16 (8) of the Act when he held (i) that
the foregoing ground was made out when the pursuers
purported to pass their resolution, and (ii) that at the
time of the hearing before him that ground was still
apt to found the making of a resolution under s 16 (1).
The foregoing ground was inapplicable at both stages
because the child has never been in the care of the pursuers under s 15 of the Act. The compulsory measures
of care which have been taken in respect of the child
were authorised by ss 37 (2), 42 (2) and 44 (1) (a) of the
D   Act. Section 44 (5) does not have the effect of extending the class of children in respect of whom a s 16 (1)
resolution may be passed beyond those who have been
taken into care under s 15. The case of *Lothian
Regional Council v S* was wrongly decided.

The appeal was heard before an Extra Division on
29 April 1993.

On 3 June 1993 the court *refused* the appeal.

E   The following opinion of the court was delivered by
Lord McCluskey:

OPINION OF THE COURT.—This case concerns a child, K, now aged 12. In the spring of 1985,
while he was in hospital, a place of safety order was
obtained under s 37 (2) of the Social Work (Scotland)
Act 1968 ("the Act") to prevent his removal from
hospital by his parents. Following that, the area
     children's reporter took appropriate action under Pt
F   III for K's case to be brought before a children's
hearing. The grounds of referral were: "that lack of
parental care is likely to cause (K) unnecessary suffering or seriously to impair his health and development
in terms of section 32 (2) (c) of the Social Work (Scotland) Act 1968" and "that an offence mentioned in
Schedule 1 to the Criminal Procedure (Scotland) Act
1975 has been committed in respect of him or in
respect of a child who is a member of the same household in terms of section 32 (2) (d) of the Social Work
(Scotland) Act 1968".

These grounds were not accepted and the children's
hearing directed the reporter to apply to the sheriff   G
under s 42 (2) (c) of the Act. On 1 August 1985, after
a substantial proof, the sheriff held that the grounds
had been established. The children's hearing then
decided that K was in need of compulsory measures of
care and, in terms of s 44 (1), made a supervision
requirement requiring him in terms of para (a) of that
subsection to submit to supervision in accordance with
such conditions as they might impose. Since then the
child has been continuously subject to compulsory
measures of care. On 31 January 1990 the pursuers   H
and respondents resolved, under s 16 of the Act that
the relevant parental rights and powers should vest in
them. That resolution was made under s 16 (1)
because it appeared to the local authority that the case
was one falling under para (iv) of that section and also
because it appeared to them that there existed circumstances specified in s 16 (2) (e), namely that there had
been a persistent failure without reasonable cause to
discharge the obligations of a parent or guardian so as
to render the parent or guardian unfit to have care of   I
the child. As required by s 16, the respondents served
a notice on the parents intimating to them their right
to object to the resolution. Counter notices were
served under s 16 (7) and the respondents then made
a summary application in respect thereto to the sheriff
under s 16 (8). That provision empowers the sheriff to
order that the resolution shall not lapse by reason of
the service of the counter notice: [his Lordship quoted
the terms of the proviso to s 16 (8) and continued:]

After a substantial proof the sheriff determined the   J
summary application made to him under s 16 (8) in
favour of the respondents, who were the applicants in
this summary application, and ordered that the resolution of 31 January 1990 should not lapse. The sheriff's
decision is contained in a full interlocutor and a clear
note dated 4 November 1991. The appeal with which
we are concerned is taken against that interlocutor.

At the hearing before us the second defender in the
summary application, the father of K, was the only   K
appellant. The only ground of appeal advanced was in
the following terms: [his Lordship quoted its terms
and continued:]

None of the findings in fact made by the sheriff in
the interlocutor appealed against was challenged. The
only issue was on a pure question of law, namely
whether or not the local authority could competently
pass the resolution that they purported to pass given
the admitted circumstance that the child had never
been in their care under s 15 of the Act. It is clear that   L
if this argument is sound then the sheriff must have
misdirected himself in holding that he was entitled to
be satisfied as to the requirements contained in the
proviso, paras (b) and (c) contained in s 16 (8).

The relevant parts of s 16 read as follows: [his Lordship quoted the terms of s 16 (1) set out supra and continued:]

Section 15 empowers a local authority with respect
to a child in their area who appears to have been aban-

A doned by his parents or for other reasons to be without parents or guardians to receive the child into their care. Clearly the resolution made by the respondents in respect of K did not relate to a child received into their care under s 15. In fact the child has lived with foster parents since 1985. The sheriff, however, held that it was competent for the local authority to pass the resolution in respect of the child because of the terms of s 44. The relevant parts are in the following terms: [his Lordship quoted the terms of s 44 (1) set out supra and continued:]

B Section 44 (5) provides: "It shall be the duty of a local authority to give effect to a supervision requirement made by a children's hearing for their area, *and a child who is subject to such a supervision requirement shall, for the purposes of sections 16* to 18, 20, 20A, 24 to 26, 28 and 29 of this Act and section 18 of the Adoption (Scotland) Act 1978 (which, amongst other things, provides that an application by an adoption agency to dispense with parental agreement to the freeing of a child for adoption is competent only where C the child is in the care of the agency), *be in their care*" (emphasis added).

The sheriff held that the effect of s 44 (5) was that the child, being subject to a supervision requirement under s 44 (1), was deemed to be in the care of the local authority for the purposes of s 16. As the primary purpose of s 16 is to enable a local authority to pass a resolution vesting in them the relevant parental rights and powers, and as the child was to be D deemed to be in their care for that purpose, the resolution, in the sheriff's view, was competent.

In our opinion it is absolutely clear that the sheriff reached the right conclusion. We are surprised that doubt has ever been cast upon the view that this is the effect of s 44 (5), but it is plain that this reading of it has been questioned. In the course of the hearing of this appeal, counsel for both parties greatly helped the court by referring us to the full discussion of this matter that has taken place in recent years and in E which the arguments in favour of the view that s 44 (5) did not empower the local authority to pass a s 16 (1) resolution in respect of a child who was not actually in their care under s 15 are set forth. We shall refer briefly to the cases and texts to which they drew our attention; and as they contain virtually all the arguments which were presented to us from both sides of the bar, it is unnecessary for us to rehearse fully the submissions which counsel made to us based on and related to the cases and texts referred to.

F It is convenient to refer first to the work by Sheriff Kearney, *Children's Hearings and the Sheriff Court* where, at pp 143, 144 and 381, the author notes that it has been held in more than one sheriff court case that the effect of s 44 (5) is that the local authority can competently make a s 16 (1) resolution under head (iv) in respect of a child who was subject to a supervision requirement under s 44 (1) and who has not been in care under s 15. It is also noted that contrary opinions, albeit obiter, have been expressed in the sheriff court. On p 381 the discussion concluded with the observa-

tion, "the matter requires clarification". In fact the matter was decided in favour of the view that s 44 (5) G empowered a local authority to make such a resolution under s 16 (1) (iv) in respect of a child who was subject to a s 44 (1) requirement in an unreported case, noted by Sheriff Kearney, namely *Strathclyde Regional Council v B*. We have been provided with a copy of the judgment of Sheriff Principal John A Dick, QC, dated 27 March 1985. The only matter which was canvassed in the appeal heard by Sheriff Principal Dick was the question of the proper interpretation and interrelation of ss 16 and 44 of the Social Work (Scotland) Act 1968. Accordingly the decision, although not H authoritative in this court, was directly in point and the ratio of the decision governs the only issue argued in the present appeal. We shall quote the relevant parts of the sheriff principal's reasoning:

"This case raised the difficult question of the proper statutory interpretation of s 44 (5) of the Social Work (Scotland) Act 1968. . . . It is not in dispute that [the children] were removed to a place of safety, pursuant to a warrant under s 37 (2) of the 1968 Act, as substituted by s 83 of the Children Act 1975, on 7 April I 1980, and that on 19 May 1980 a children's hearing made [the children] . . . subject to a residential requirement in terms of s 44 (1) . . . [the children] have since remained continuously subject to a supervision requirement. . . . As I understand it, under s 44 (5) a child is to be in the care of the local authority not 'in respect' of s 16 but for the 'purposes' of ss 16-18 and the other sections narrated, and the primary purpose of s 16, in my view, is to enable a local J authority to assume parental rights and powers in respect of a child in their care on particular and specified grounds. No question arises in this case of the local authority seeking to have any parental rights and powers vested in a voluntary organisation in terms of s 16 (1) (b) and it does not seem to be that any reasonable content is suggested for s 44 (5) by limiting 'purposes' to one incidental feature necessary for the validity of a resolution in respect of a s 16 (1) (b) resolution. If the child is in the care of the local authority K by virtue of s 44 (5), I have difficulty in seeing how any of the purposes of s 16 (1) (b) which concern a child who is 'in the care' of a voluntary organisation have any relevance to the purposes of s 16 now under consideration referred to in s 44 (5). While in *Beagley v Beagley*, 1984 SLT 202 at p 205, Lord Fraser of Tullybelton said, 'The scheme of the 1968 Act laid down by Parliament is that the duty of providing for orphans and neglected children is entrusted to local authorities', which in my humble view, is a clear and L apposite dictum in this context, that case was not concerned with s 15 or with s 44 (5) or with the scheme of the 1968 Act in regard to children in care of a local authority under their duty to give effect to a supervision requirement. While the sheriff accepted, as I do, that in interpreting statutes, rights and, in particular, parental rights are not to be trenched upon unless the statute clearly so provides, I do not accept the argument that the sheriff erred in his approach by considering the best interests of the child, particularly when s 20 is one of the sections referred to in s 44 (5) concerning the duty of the local authority where such a child is in their care to give first consideration to the best interests of the child. Nor do I think that the presumption against trenching on parental rights can stand in the way of a construction of s 44 (5) which gives it what humbly appears to me to be its only effective and reasonable meaning. As matter of construction, and for the reasons given, I think the sheriff arrived at a correct interpretation of s 44 (5) and on that ground I would refuse the appeal. It would appear that a similar interpretation of s 44 (5) was arrived at by Sheriff McNeill in *Lothian Regional Council v Gibbs*, 10 August 1984 (unreported). A similar view was also expressed by Sheriff Presslie in *Central Regional Council v Beagley*, 14 June 1983, p 52 and I find nothing in the judgments in that case in the Inner House (27 December 1984) which suggest that his understanding of s 44 (5) was erroneous."

We should add that the Inner House case there referred to is reported as *Central Regional Council v B*, 1985 SLT 413. We entirely accept the reasoning of Sheriff Principal Dick and it would be idle to attempt to improve upon it. (It was Sheriff Kearney against whose decision his unsuccessful appeal was taken.) We should note that the same conclusion was reached by Sheriff Principal Sir F W F O'Brien, QC, in *Lothian Regional Council v S* in March 1985, 1986 SLT (Sh Ct) 37, being the case referred to in the grounds of appeal. It will be seen that Sheriff Principal O'Brien arrived at his conclusion upon a different basis, namely that if s 44 (5) was to be made to work for the purposes of s 16 it seemed unavoidable that it would also have to apply to s 15, without which, he said, "s. 16 cannot get off the ground". We prefer the approach of Sheriff Principal Dick because it rightly focuses upon the circumstance that s 44 (5) deems the child to be in the care of the local authority "for the purposes of sections 16 to 18" etc. It is the purposes of the sections that matter, and the purpose of s 16 is abundantly plain, namely to enable the local authority to pass the appropriate vesting resolution. It follows that we disagree with those who have expressed the view that there was some error or omission in the drafting of the section; we see no reason to conclude that there was any such error. In his book, Sheriff Kearney correctly notes that the preponderance of shrieval opinion has been in favour of the conclusion arrived at by Sheriff Principal Dick, but he observes that there are shrieval dicta to the contrary and he does so under reference to *Strathclyde Regional Council v M*, 1982 SLT (Sh Ct) 106, a decision of Sheriff Principal R A Bennett, QC, and Sheriff Sir Stephen Young's decision in *Strathclyde Regional Council v R*. We are not persuaded that Sheriff Principal Bennett expressed any view contrary to that arrived at by Sheriff Principal Dick on this matter; the precise point simply did not arise. Sheriff Sir Stephen Young did express a contrary view in the case in 1987 but what he said was: "Fortunately, I do not require to reach a decision on this point. But I am bound to say that I would have considerable difficulty in holding that a child in care under s 44 (5) fell within the scope of s 16 (1) (iv) which is quite explicit in referring to a child 'in the care of a local authority under s 15' of the Act."

Despite the fact that the matter was plainly obiter he went on to express views about the sections and disagreed with the reasoning of Sheriff Principal Dick. Unfortunately his own reasoning is vitiated by the fact that he founds upon an apparent anomaly which is said to rest upon the circumstance that if a child had been received into care under s 15 parental rights could be assumed only if the child was 16 or under. We do not understand where this notion comes from, given the terms of s 15. However, for present purposes, it is sufficient to note that there is no reported case in which any court has reached a decision different from that arrived at by Sheriff Principal Dick and Sheriff Principal O'Brien in the cases referred to.

Agreeing, as we do, with the decision of Sheriff Principal Dick and his reasoning, that is quite sufficient for the decision of the present case. However, we were also favoured by counsel with a very full citation to demonstrate the legislative history of the sections in question which have been amended several times since 1968, though the essential provision has not changed in substance since 1968. Counsel for the appellant before us felt he could, in the light of the terms of the section and the various authorities, go little further than to argue that the matter was in doubt and that the rights of parents should not be removed by interpreting ambiguous provisions against such rights if there was an alternative interpretation which saved those rights. In short, the statutory provisions were ambiguous, obscure and uncertain. That submission had, however, been anticipated by counsel for the respondents who, while arguing that there was no ambiguity, submitted that, if there was, then following the decision of the House of Lords in *Pepper v Hart* the court could look to the parliamentary history for assistance. The relevant history of the enactment of s 44 is contained in the *Official Report* of the proceedings of the House of Lords on 23 April 1968. What is now s 44 was cl 43 of the Bill then considered, on report, by the House. At [Vol 291,] col 533, the minister in charge of the Bill in the House of Lords, Lord Hughes, moved an amendment to insert into cl 43 (now s 44) the material words, namely "and a child who is subject to such a supervision requirement shall for the purposes of sections 15 to 19, 23 to 25, 27 and 28 of this Act, be in their care" (it should be noted that ss 15 to 19, 23 to 25, 27 and 28 there referred to became ss 16 to 18, 20, 24 to 26, 28 and 29 in the 1968 Act by the time it received the Royal Assent). In moving that amendment Lord Hughes said as follows: "My Lords, this Amendment is designed to ensure that the powers which a local authority will be able to exercise on behalf of a child under a supervision requirement (which, under clause 43 (5), has to be administered by the local authority) will be the same as those they can exercise for a child in their care on a voluntary basis. It seems reasonable that a local authority should be able to use these powers which include the assumption of parental rights, the furtherance of the child's best interests, the making of financial and other arrangements for the education and training of children over school age, the aftercare of children who have left the care of the local authority, and related matters. The power to discharge or vary the supervision requirement remains with the children's hearing."

Thus if it be appropriate to look at the parliamentary history of this enactment it is abundantly plain that the intention of the minister (and the amendment was agreed to without challenge) was that the local authority should be able to assume parental rights both in respect of children coming into their care under the generally voluntary scheme in Pt II and in respect of children placed under a supervision requirement under Pt III of the Act (which deals with compulsory measures of care). Because we take the view that both the meaning of s 44 and the way in which it interrelates with s 16 are perfectly clear, it is not necessary for us to found upon that passage from the *Official Report*; but it is comforting to discover that the statute as enacted plainly did what Parliament plainly intended it to do.

Finally, it is worth noting that after several sheriffs, who had to decide this very question, decided it in the way in which we hold it was proper to decide it, and indeed in the way which the minister and Parliament intended that it should be understood (though the sheriffs did not have the benefit of the reference to the House of Lords *Official Report*), Parliament, in October 1985, enacted s 28 of the Law Reform (Miscellaneous Provisions) (Scotland) Act 1985 which further amended s 44 (5) of the 1968 Act. That would have been an excellent opportunity for Parliament to correct the interpretation contained in the line of decisions if Parliament had considered that interpretation to be unsound and contrary to the intentions of Parliament. Parliament did not take that opportunity.

In the whole circumstances we shall refuse the appeal.

Counsel for Applicants and Respondents (Local Authority), Thomson, QC, Maguire; Solicitors, Simpson & Warwick, WS — Counsel for Respondent and Appellant (Father), Fitzpatrick; Solicitors, Lindsays, WS (for Mackintosh & Wylie, Kilmarnock).

P A A

L, Petitioners (No 1)

FIRST DIVISION
THE LORD PRESIDENT (HOPE),
LORDS ALLANBRIDGE AND MAYFIELD
18 JUNE 1993

Children and young persons — Children's hearing — Application to sheriff for finding whether or not grounds for referral established — Sheriff finding grounds for referral established — New evidence only becoming available after sheriff's findings — Application to nobile officium for order remitting case back to sheriff to rehear evidence in case including new evidence — Whether competent for such order to be pronounced under nobile officium — Social Work (Scotland) Act 1968 (c 49), s 50 (1).

Nobile officium — Competency — Children's hearing — New evidence becoming available after sheriff finding grounds for referral established — Application to nobile officium for order remitting case back to sheriff to rehear evidence in case including new evidence — Whether competent for such order to be pronounced under nobile officium — Social Work (Scotland) Act 1968 (c 49), s 50 (1).

Section 50 (1) of the Social Work (Scotland) Act 1968 provides that an appeal shall lie to the Court of Session, by way of stated case on a point of law or in respect of any irregularity in the conduct of the case, from any decision of the sheriff under Pt III of the Act, "and no other or further appeal shall be competent".

Eight children from three families were made the subject of place of safety orders under Pt III of the Social Work (Scotland) Act 1968. The orders were on the grounds that the children had been sexually abused or were members of the same household as children who were sexually abused. The reporter then referred the children to the children's panel. Only one of the parents accepted the grounds for referral, and the matter was referred to the sheriff for a finding as to whether the grounds for referral in each case were established. The cases were conjoined and the sheriff heard 11 days of evidence. The sheriff found the grounds for referral established in each case and remitted the cases to the children's hearing, which decided that all eight children were in need of compulsory care.

The parents then brought an application to the nobile officium of the Court of Session averring that since the hearing before the sheriff they had obtained additional expert evidence which was not available and could not reasonably have been made available at the hearing, and that the additional evidence cast doubt on the sheriff's findings. They also averred that since the sheriff decided the cases the findings of the Orkney inquiry had been published, that following publication of this report there was a greater understanding of the importance of a number of features which were present in the cases of the eight children, and that this understanding would allow the sheriff to look afresh at the evidence in a more critical way. They sought an order that the sheriff should rehear the evidence relating to the children, contending that the circumstances which had arisen were so extraordinary or unforeseen that the court should exercise its nobile officium to prevent injustice. The reporter opposed the order sought as incompetent. He argued that the rehearing of evidence by the sheriff would amount to an appeal, that s 50 (1) of the Act allowed an appeal from the sheriff to the Court of Session on a point of law only and provided that "no other or further appeal" was competent, and that s 50 (1) therefore excluded the order sought. There was therefore no provision in the Act for a rehearing of evidence once the grounds for referral had been found to be established by the sheriff.

Held, (1) that the nobile officium could not be exercised when to do so would conflict with either an express provision of or the necessary implication from an Act of Parliament (p 1315E and H); (2) that the method of review sought by the petitioners did not amount to an appeal, and therefore was not expressly excluded by the Act (p 1316C-F); (3) that Parliament had seen the need, in the interests of the children affected, for a measure of last resort to enable a supervision requirement which was unnecessary to be terminated, but the special problems which had arisen in this case had not been foreseen and the method of review sought by the petitioners was therefore not impliedly excluded by the Act (p 1317C-F and H-L); and respondent's plea to competency *repelled*, and case *continued* for submissions as to whether the petitioners' averments were sufficient to have the cases remitted to the sheriff for a rehearing.

Petition to the nobile officium

JL and others, the parents of eight children who had been committed to compulsory care, brought an application to the nobile officium of the Court of Session seeking an order that the evidence relating to the grounds for referral of the children to the children's hearing should be reheard by the sheriff. Frederick J Kennedy, reporter to the children's panel for Strathclyde Region, was called as respondent and took pleas to the competency and relevancy of the petition.

Statutory provisions

The Social Work (Scotland) Act 1968 provides:

"42.—(1) Subject to the provisions of subsections (7) and (8) of this section, at the commencement of a children's hearing and before proceeding to the consideration of the case, it shall be the duty of the chairman to explain to the child and his parent the grounds stated by the reporter for the referral of the case for the purpose of ascertaining whether these grounds are accepted in whole or in part by the child and his parent.

"(2) Thereafter — . . . (c) in any other case, unless they decide to discharge the referral, the children's hearing shall direct the reporter to make application to the sheriff for a finding as to whether such grounds for the referral, as are not accepted by the child or his parent, are established having regard to the provisions of section 32 of this Act. . . .

"50.—(1) Subject to the provisions of this section, an appeal shall lie to the Court of Session, by way of stated case on a point of law or in respect of any irregularity in the conduct of the case, at the instance of the child or his parent or both or of a reporter acting on behalf of a children's hearing, from any decision of the sheriff under this Part of this Act, and no other or further appeal shall be competent. . . .

"52. Where, having regard to all the circumstances of a case and the interests of a child, the Secretary of State is satisfied that a supervision requirement in force in respect of the child should be terminated, he may by order terminate the requirement."

Cases referred to

Adair v David Colville & Sons Ltd, 1922 SLT 532; 1922 SC 672.
Anderson v HM Advocate, 1974 SLT 239.
E (A Minor) (Child Abuse: Evidence), Re [1991] 1 FLR 420.
F v Kennedy (No 1), 1993 SLT 1277.
F v Kennedy (No 2), 1993 SLT 1284.
Hobbs (David) v Reporter for Strathclyde Region, 1st Div, 6 December 1989, unreported.
Humphries, Petitioner, 1982 SLT 481; (sub nom *Humphries v X and Y*) 1982 SC 79.
Kennedy v H, 1st Div, 22 January 1992, unreported (1992 GWD 7-340).
MacGown v Cramb (1897) 24 R 481.
R, Petitioner, 1993 SLT 910.
Rochdale Borough Council v A [1991] 2 FLR 192.
Sloan v B, 1991 SLT 530.
Wan Ping Nam v Minister of Justice of the German Federal Republic, 1972 SLT 120; 1972 JC 43.

The petition was heard before the First Division on 9 June 1993.

On 18 June 1993 the court *repelled* the respondent's plea to competency and *continued* the case for further submissions.

The following opinion of the court was delivered by the Lord President (Hope):

OPINION OF THE COURT.—This is an application to the nobile officium by the parents of eight children from three separate but closely related families who are the subject of proceedings under Pt III of the Social Work (Scotland) Act 1968. The respondent is the reporter to the children's panel of Strathclyde Region.

The children were made the subject of place of safety orders on 18, 19 and 23 June 1990 and have resided separately from their parents since that date. The orders were made on the grounds that the children had been sexually abused or were members of the same household as children who were sexually abused. The respondent then served upon the petitioners a statement of the grounds on which he had decided that the children were in need of compulsory measures of care. This was done under reference to s 32 (2) of the 1968 Act. The grounds for their referral were not identical in each case, but there was much common ground between them on the facts. In the case of the four children of the first and second petitioners it was alleged that they had fallen into bad associations or were exposed to moral danger in terms of s 32 (2) (b), that offences mentioned in Sched 1 to the Criminal Procedure (Scotland) Act 1975 had been committed in respect of them or in respect of children who were

members of the same household in terms of s 32 (2)
A (d), and that they were, or were likely to become,
members of the same household as a person who had
committed such offences in terms of s 32 (2) (dd) of the
Act. In the case of the child of the third and fourth
petitioners it was alleged, in addition to the grounds
mentioned in s 32 (2) (b), (d) and (dd), that lack of
parental care was likely to cause her unnecessary
suffering or seriously impair her health or development in terms of s 32 (2) (c), while in the case of the
three children of the fifth and sixth petitioners the
grounds of referral were confined to those mentioned
B in s 32 (2) (b) and (d) of the Act. Common to all these
cases were allegations that the children from each of
the three families had been subjected to lewd, indecent
and libidinous practices and behaviour by male and
female adults, that they had been actively physically
involved in such practices and behaviour and that they
had been the victims of sexual abuse over a long period.

The sixth petitioner, who had first drawn the matter
to the attention of the authorities, accepted the
C grounds of referral in respect of her three children.
But the other petitioners did not accept the grounds of
referral, so the children's hearing directed the reporter
in terms of s 42 (2) (c) of the Act to make an application to the sheriff for a finding as to whether the
grounds for the referral in each case were established.
The children continued to be detained in places of
safety in terms of warrants which were issued and
renewed under s 37 (4) and (5) of the Act.

The respondent's applications in respect of all the
D children involved in these cases were conjoined, and
the sheriff heard evidence on Friday 20 July 1990 and
10 further days. There were two further days of hearings on the submissions for the reporter and the first
to fifth petitioners. On 16 August 1990 the sheriff
pronounced interlocutors in which he found the
grounds of referral established in each case and remitted the cases to the children's hearing for disposal in
terms of s 42 (6) of the 1968 Act. Having considered
the grounds of referral and the other information avail-
E able to them the children's hearing decided that all
eight children were in need of compulsory measures of
care. They made a supervision requirement in each
case requiring the children to reside in residential
establishments in terms of s 44 (1) (b) of the Act. We
understand that the children continue to reside in
residential establishments operated by the social work
department of Strathclyde Regional Council, and
there is no suggestion that the children's hearing have
it in mind that they should be returned to live with
F their families.

The first and second petitioners appealed against the
sheriff's interlocutor in respect of their four children.
A draft stated case was prepared, but these petitioners
subsequently abandoned their appeal. The third and
fourth petitioners did not appeal against the sheriff's
decision that the grounds of referral in respect of their
child had been established. The fifth petitioner
appealed against the sheriff's decision in respect of his
three children, but the court held that the sheriff was
entitled to hold that the grounds of referral were estab-

lished in their case. The reasons for this decision are
set out in the opinions of the court of 18 October 1991 G
and 4 June 1992: see *F v Kennedy (No 1)* and *F v
Kennedy (No 2)*. We were informed that there have
been many review hearings under s 48 and that there
have been a number of subsequent appeals to the
sheriff resulting in stated cases to this court. It is clear
that the proceedings have now become very complicated, and the cases in respect of all eight children continue to be strongly contested on both sides.

The point which has now been raised relates not to
these review hearings but to the decision which the H
sheriff took originally in August 1990 when he found
that the grounds of referral had been established. The
petitioners aver that since the hearing before the
sheriff which resulted in these interlocutors they have
obtained additional expert evidence which was not
available and could not reasonably have been made
available at that hearing. They seek an order from this
court in the exercise of the nobile officium that the
evidence relating to the grounds of referral in the case
of all eight children should be reheard by the sheriff, I
or by such other person or persons as we may direct.
Although the prayer of the petition does not ask for
any further order, it is implicit in this application that
the petitioners wish the sheriff to be authorised to
exercise of new the powers conferred on him by s 42
of the Act, and that they are seeking by means of this
application to obtain a review of his original interlocutors in the light of this additional evidence. The
reporter has opposed the application on various
grounds including the ground that the order sought is J
incompetent. When the case came before us for a
hearing on the summar roll we were invited to consider first the issue as to competency, and it is with
that issue only that this opinion is concerned.

It is unnecessary for us to set out in any detail at this
stage the nature and extent of the additional evidence
which the petitioners say is now available to them, but
a brief summary of these averments is appropriate.
The evidence which the sheriff heard at the original K
hearing in July and August 1990 consisted of medical
evidence of examinations of the children by medical
practitioners, evidence from dental practitioners relating to the condition of the teeth of one of the children
of the first and second petitioners, evidence from a
child psychologist relating to a video taped interview
with another child of these petitioners, evidence given
in court by some of the children among whom were
one child from each of the three families, and evidence
from social workers and a woman police constable
relating to certain alleged disclosures previously made L
by some of the children during interviews. All these
interviews were conducted after the children had been
removed from their homes to a place of safety. The
petitioners also gave evidence, in the course of which
they denied any involvement in the abuse alleged in
the statement of facts. The additional evidence, details
of which are set out in the petitioners' averments and
are the subject of various reports and other documents
which are before us as productions in this case, consists
of reports which challenge the validity of the medical

and dental evidence, expert opinion on the interviewing techniques which were adopted by the social workers, reports by a clinical psychologist following his examination of the first and second petitioners, and psychiatric reports on each of the petitioners which have been prepared by a consultant psychiatrist.

Reference is also made in the petitioners' averments to various events since the proof which are said to cast doubt on the admissibility, credibility and reliability of evidence which the sheriff accepted in August 1990. He admitted hearsay evidence given by one of the children of the fifth and sixth petitioners who was only three years old at the date of the proof, and he took account of part of his evidence in his findings. On 18 October 1991 it was held by this court in an appeal by the fifth petitioner that the evidence of this child was · incompetent. The petitioners accept that the sheriff reported to the court on 7 February 1992 that the necessary amendments to his findings in fact did not materially alter his general conclusion that the interlocutors of 16 August 1990 finding the grounds of referral established should stand. The point is nevertheless one which they submit should be taken into account along with other averments when the case is looked at as a whole.

Reference is then made to a decision by another sheriff following a hearing in November 1990 on similar grounds of referral and statements of fact to those in the present case, in which social workers involved in this case also gave evidence. The sheriff is said to have been critical of the evidence of these social workers on various grounds and to have concluded that their evidence was not credible and reliable. Reference is also made to the *Report of the Inquiry into the Removal of Children from Orkney in February 1991* which was submitted to the Secretary of State on 31 July 1992 and ordered by the House of Commons to be printed on 27 October 1992. The petitioners aver that following the publication of that report there is now a greater understanding of the importance of a number of features which were present in this case. They maintain that this report indicates that the social workers were inadequately trained, that much of their evidence consisted of their uninformed interpretations of what they said the children had told them, and that the social workers and police constable involved in this case did not have the appropriate degree of training and experience to recommend acceptance of their interpretations of what they claimed the children had said to them. The argument is that, with the benefit of that report, a sheriff on rehearing the case would be able to look afresh at the evidence in a more critical way and would come to a different view as to its effect.

The petitioners have, therefore, set out in these averments a substantial body of additional material which, they claim, casts serious doubt on the validity of the evidence which was before the sheriff at the proof and on the conclusions which he drew in the light of that evidence. They point also to the fact that the proof was held and concluded within nine weeks of the making of the place of safety orders and in circumstances of some urgency. While the proof was being held the children were still being detained under successive warrants which, in terms of s 37, could not remain in force for more than 12 weeks after the date when the children's hearing first met to consider their case. They also refer to the fact, as part of the general background, that this is one of three important cases of alleged child sexual abuse which have given rise to public concern about the way in which such cases should be handled by the authorities.

The first of these cases occurred in Rochdale, although the judicial proceedings in that case were not held until long after the grounds of referral in the present case had been held to have been established. On 14 June 1990 a number of children were removed by police and social workers of Rochdale Borough Council from their homes in Greater Manchester in the belief that they had been subjected to organised, satanic or ritual abuse. The wardship summonses by the local authority in respect of 17 of these children were consolidated and ordered to be heard together in the Family Division of the High Court. On 7 March 1991, after a hearing lasting 47 days, during which he heard a considerable body of psychiatric and psychological evidence, Douglas Brown J held that the allegations that the children had been victims of satanic or ritual abuse had not been made out. In the course of the opinion which he delivered in that case on 7 March 1991, *Rochdale Borough Council v A*, he was critical of the employees of the local authority, on the ground that the guidelines for the interviewing of children in the *Report into Child Abuse in Cleveland* (Cm 412, 1988) by Butler Sloss LJ and her assessors and in *Re E (A Minor) (Child Abuse: Evidence)* had been largely ignored by the local authority.

Then there was the Orkney case, which followed the removal of nine children from their homes in Orkney to places of safety on the mainland in February 1991 and their return to Orkney in April 1991 in the circumstances described in *Sloan v B*. The hon Lord Clyde was appointed by the Secretary of State for Scotland to conduct an inquiry into the actings of the agencies involved in their removal. The petitioners in the present case rely on various passages in his report and recommendations which were submitted to the Secretary of State on 31 July 1992 following that inquiry. They make the point that the delicacy and importance of the matter in which interviews of children who are suspected of having been abused are now more fully appreciated than they were at the time of the hearing before the sheriff in 1990.

The respondent avers in his answers that all the personnel involved in this case were at the material time at least adequately trained and experienced to deal with cases of child sexual abuse, according to the standards prevailing at the time. We wish to stress therefore that the truth or otherwise of the various allegations which the petitioners have made about the conduct of these interviews still remains to be tested. So we must not be thought to have accepted at this stage that these allegations, or any of them, are true. Nevertheless it is clear that the issues which they have raised are very closely related to those which were considered in so much detail in the Rochdale case and in the Orkney inquiry, against the background of the important recommendations in the Cleveland report.

The speed with which matters were dealt with in this case, as a result of which the hearing before the sheriff was concluded within nine weeks of the making of the place of safety orders, was in itself commendable. As Lord President Emslie said in *Humphries, Petr*, 1982 SLT at p 482, it is possible, on reading ss 37 to 42 of the 1968 Act, to discern the clear intention of Parliament that these matters should be disposed of without any unnecessary delay. But, in the light of what we have said about this background, there appear to us to be at least some grounds for suspecting that the sheriff did not have before him at the proof all the information which was necessary to arrive at a sound decision in the case and that it may well, if examined further, turn out to be one of exceptional difficulty.

It might be thought that there ought, in these circumstances, to be an opportunity for a rehearing of the evidence, since it would plainly not be in the best interests of the children that they should be treated by the children's hearing as in need of compulsory measures of care if there were no grounds for this. But there is no provision in Pt III of the 1968 Act for a rehearing of the evidence once the sheriff has held the grounds for the referral to have been established and the case has been remitted to the children's hearing for determination. The children's hearing have no power to review the sheriff's decision that the grounds for referral have been established. As was said in *R, Petr*, the children's hearing have no option but to continue to deal with the case on the assumption that the facts were as stated in the grounds for the referral, however unreasonable that might appear on the information now available.

The Secretary of State has power under s 52 of the 1968 Act, if satisfied that a supervision requirement in force in respect of a child should be terminated, to terminate the requirement. But in a letter dated 28 July 1992 the Social Work Services Group of the Scottish Office stated that the Secretary of State could not see any justification for exercising the powers contained in s 52 in this case. In a further letter dated 30 April 1993 the Social Work Services Group pointed out that, although the Secretary of State could consider the new evidence as part of the circumstances to which he was to have regard in determining whether or not to exercise his power under s 52, he did not have power under that section to order the new evidence to be examined judicially. We agree that the Secretary of State does not have this power, and it is clear that, if there is to be a judicial examination of this case in the light of this new evidence, the court must assume the responsibility of making an order to this effect in the exercise of its nobile officium.

The respondent submits however that, on a sound view of the authorities and on a proper construction of the provisions of the statute, the court has no power to order a rehearing of the evidence and that the application to the nobile officium is incompetent. Counsel for the respondent made it clear that the respondent was not willing to concede that a rehearing of the evidence would in any event be appropriate. But he invited us to consider the point of competency as one which could be decided as a matter of principle without regard to the circumstances. According to his argument, however exceptional and unforeseen the circumstances might seem to be, the effect of the statutory scheme and in particular of s 50 (1) of the 1968 Act was to exclude any review of the sheriff's decision on any question of fact whatever, including questions as to the effect of additional evidence.

We had occasion in *R, Petr* to consider the scope of the nobile officium in the context of Pt III of the 1968 Act, with particular reference to the provisions of the statute for appeal or other methods of review. In that case the petitioners sought to have the grounds for the referral reheard by the sheriff, on the ground that additional evidence was available which cast serious doubt on the credibility of the evidence of a child that she had been the victim of an offence mentioned in Sched 1 to the Criminal Procedure (Scotland) Act 1975. The additional evidence consisted only of the retraction by the child of the allegations which she had previously made against the petitioner. It was contended in that case that it was the intention of the statute that the grounds of referral should be open to reconsideration at every stage in the case. This was on the view that it was the intention of Parliament that children should receive compulsory measures of care only when and so long as they were in need of them. But the argument was rejected on the grounds that it was the intention of Parliament to achieve finality on this matter before the children's hearing proceeded to a consideration of the case and that, if the court were to grant the order which was sought on this ground, it would be supplementing the statutory procedure by what would, in effect, be an amendment to the statute.

There is, however, an important distinction between that case and the present one, in that it was not contended in *R, Petr* that the circumstances which had arisen there were exceptional or unforeseen. It would not have been possible for the petitioner to maintain that argument, as it is not unusual for a witness who has given evidence against another person to seek to retract that evidence once it has been accepted and acted on by a court. So the petitioner's argument was in effect the same as that which was successful in *Wan Ping Nam v Minister of Justice of the German Federal Republic*, namely that the statutory intention was clear that the relief sought should be available and that the court had power in the exercise of the nobile officium to provide the means to give effect to the intention of the legislature. In the present case, however, the contention is that the circumstances which have arisen are so extraordinary or unforeseen that the court should exercise its nobile officium to prevent injustice or oppression, since no other remedy or procedure is available. It is not part of the petitioners' argument that it was the intention of Parliament that the grounds of referral should be open to review in such circumstances. Their point with regard to the pro-

visions of the statute is put negatively, that is to say,
that it would not conflict with the statutory intention
for us to exercise the nobile officium in the extraordinary circumstances of this case. They rely on the
fact that, towards the end of the opinion in *R, Petr*, the
court said that it might be appropriate in exceptional
circumstances for the nobile officium to be exercised,
since there was no machinery in the Act for removing
a case from the children's hearing which ought not to
be before them at all. Accordingly it is that passage
which forms the starting point for an examination of
the question which has been raised by the petitioners.
It is unnecessary to repeat here the earlier discussion
in *R, Petr* about the scope of the nobile officium and
the scheme of the Act as to which there was, in this
case, no controversy.

The question whether the petitioners have averred
exceptional or unforeseen circumstances which would
justify the exercise of the nobile officium is not in
issue at this stage. But, as counsel for the respondent
made clear in the course of his argument and was not
disputed by counsel for the petitioners, it is not
enough for them to aver exceptional or unforeseen
circumstances. This is because we are dealing here
with the provisions of a statute. So it is necessary for
the petitioners also to satisfy the further requirement
that the exercise of the nobile officium must not conflict with the intention of the statute, express or
implied. And it is the provisions of the statute which
counsel for the respondent submits stand in the way
in the present case. He recognised that if there was a
gap or lacuna in the statute, the nobile officium could
be exercised to cure the omission and prevent an
injustice. But the corollary was that, if Parliament has
prescribed a rule, that rule must be applied. He submitted that the rule which had to be applied in this
case was that set out in s 50 (1) of the 1968 Act, which
is in these terms: [his Lordship quoted the terms of s
50 (1) and continued:]

There is now ample authority to the effect that the
nobile officium cannot be exercised when to do so
would be in conflict with what has been provided for
by Parliament. In the earlier cases it was a conflict
with an express provision by Parliament which was
noted as making it impossible for the nobile officium
to be exercised. In *MacGown v Cramb*, an interlocutor
had become final in terms of s 28 of the Court of
Session Act 1868 and an application for its recall in
the exercise of the nobile officium was refused. Lord
Adam said at p 482 that he had never understood that
the nobile officium could supersede an Act of Parliament. The same point arose in *Adair v Colville &
Sons*, where an appeal was sought to be taken against
an interlocutor of the sheriff applying the verdict in a
jury trial where the parties had agreed to dispense
with a record of the proceedings. Rule 147 of the
Sheriff Courts (Scotland) Act 1907 provided that the
interlocutor applying the verdict was not to be subject
to review in these circumstances. Lord Justice Clerk
Scott Dickson said at 1922 SLT, p 536: "I appreciate
thoroughly the value and province of the *nobile
officium* of the Court, but I agree with what Lord

Adam said in the case that was cited to us —
(*MacGown v Cramb*, 1897, 24 R. 481) — I never heard
of the *nobile officium* being appealed to in order to
override the express provisions of a statute, and I think
it is quite incompetent for the Court to exercise the
nobile officium to do so."

In *Anderson v HM Advocate* at p 240, Lord
President Emslie said under reference to that case that
the nobile officium may never be invoked when to do
so would conflict with statutory intention, express or
clearly implied. This appears to have been the first
time that it was recognised that a conflict with an
implied statutory intention would be sufficient to
defeat the exercise of the nobile officium. But the
statement has been repeated on numerous occasions
subsequently, and it is in accordance with the principle that necessary implication has the same effect as
an express provision when a question is raised as to the
meaning of an Act of Parliament.

So the first question to which we must now turn is
whether s 50 (1) provides expressly that the remedy
which the petitioners seek in this case is not to be
available. If not, the next question is whether it does
so by clear or necessary implication from the words
used in the subsection, when read in the context of Pt
III of the Act as a whole. On this wider question we
have found it helpful to have regard to certain passages
in the Kilbrandon *Report on Children and Young
Persons, Scotland* (Cmnd 2306) of April 1964, since
most of the provisions which are to be found in Pt III
of the 1968 Act were based on the recommendations
of that report.

The critical words in s 50 (1) are those which declare
that "no other or further appeal shall be competent".
The word "further" does not give rise to difficulty
here, because its effect is clearly to prevent a further
appeal being taken from the Court of Session to the
House of Lords. We are not dealing in this case with
an argument that there should be a further appeal
beyond this court. The word "other" may have been
included to make it clear that, although some of the
conditions mentioned in s 32 (2) involve conduct
which might otherwise be treated as criminal, there
was to be no question under Pt III of the Act of an
appeal to the High Court of Justiciary. But as counsel
for the respondent pointed out, the word is apt also to
cover the grounds on which an appeal may be taken.
So it seems likely that the word "other" was intended
also to make it clear that there was to be no appeal
from the sheriff except by way of stated case on a point
of law or in respect of an irregularity in the conduct
of the case, and in particular that the sheriff's decision
on the facts was to be final and not subject to appeal.

In our opinion, however, it does not follow that the
particular remedy which the petitioners seek in this
case has been expressly excluded by the words used in
the subsection. Counsel for the petitioners said that he
was not seeking to appeal against the sheriff's decision
on the facts. He was not asking the Court of Session
to substitute its own view of the facts for that which
the sheriff formed after listening to the evidence.

What he was seeking was a rehearing by the sheriff of the evidence in the light of additional information which was now available, so that the sheriff could consider the whole matter afresh as the sole judge of the facts. He was not, as he put it, seeking to change the forum which the Act had laid down for considering whether the grounds for the referrals had been established. What he was asking us to do in this case ought not therefore to be regarded as an appeal, or at least not an appeal within the meaning of s 50 (1) of the Act. Counsel for the respondent's response to this argument was that it was not possible to regard the application as anything other than an appeal, when regard was had to the effect of the interlocutor which we were being asked to pronounce. Although this application was being presented as one for the rehearing of the evidence, its effect was, if the sheriff were now to reach the view that the grounds of referral were not established, to supersede the orders which he originally made under s 42 (6) by orders under s 42 (5) that the referrals on these grounds were to be discharged. The result would be the same as if the pursuers had appealed against the sheriff's decision on the facts, and it was a misconception to treat this as anything other than an attempt to take his decision on the facts to appeal.

We prefer counsel for the petitioners' argument on this point. It seems to us that, while what the pursuers seek in this case may be described as a means of obtaining a review of the sheriff's decision that the grounds of referral were established, it is not accurate to describe it as an appeal. They are not seeking to have the sheriff's findings on the facts of the case reviewed by this court. They are content that the facts should be heard once again in the sheriff court so that the sheriff may take account of the additional evidence and form his own view of the facts. It is true that, if the sheriff were to reach a different view of the facts from that which was arrived at in the light of the original evidence, it would then be necessary to reverse the decision previously taken. In that respect the result would be the same as if there had been an appeal, since the effect of the sheriff's order will be that the grounds of referral will be discharged. But the route is not that which is ordinarily associated with an appeal, with which there is no direct parallel, and we consider that the method of review which is sought here is not an appeal in the ordinary sense of that word. Furthermore, s 50 (1) does not go so far as to state expressly that the sheriff's decision on the facts is to be final and conclusive and that it is not to be subject to review in any way whatever may be the circumstances. In this respect the subsection lacks an express declaration of finality such as that found in s 262 of the Criminal Procedure (Scotland) Act 1975 or in s 231 (1) of the Town and Country Planning (Scotland) Act 1972. In our opinion the method of review which the pursuers seek in this case has not been expressly excluded by s 50 (1) of the 1968 Act.

The question then is whether the provisions of s 50 (1) have that effect by clear or necessary implication. In our opinion that question must be considered upon an examination of s 50 (1) in the whole context of what Pt III of the 1968 Act seeks to achieve. As Lord President Emslie said in *Humphries, Petr* at p 482, Pt III of the Act is concerned with the welfare of children. It is designed to secure their welfare in the sense that those children who are in need of compulsory measures of care should have the appropriate measures applied in their interests without any unreasonable delay. The court in that case had regard to the best interests of the children and the overriding intention of Parliament in the special and extraordinary circumstances which had arisen. It authorised the children to be detained in a place of safety for their protection pending final disposal of the referral. To do this was not thought to extend the scope of Pt III of the 1968 Act or to defeat the intention of Parliament express or implied. This was despite the fact that s 37 provides that a child may be detained under successive warrants in a place of safety for a total period of only 84 days. There was an obvious conflict between the provisions of the statute which laid down this machinery and the interests of the children, and it was resolved by preferring the interests of the children in order to secure the overriding intention of Parliament. The respondent's argument is that, however extraordinary may be the circumstances, the remedy which the petitioners seek has by implication been excluded by Parliament. So there is the same conflict between what the respondent says is implied by s 50 (1) and the petitioners' argument which is that the interests of the children demand that the grounds of referral should be reviewed.

Counsel for the respondent urged us to regard s 50 (1) as amounting, by the clearest implication, to what he described as a statutory indication of finality. According to his argument, the sheriff's decision under s 42 (6) only opened the door, as he put it, to the main part of the process, which was a consideration and determination of the case by the children's hearing. It was inherent in any decision making process that the decision which was taken might be wrong, but Parliament must be taken to have accepted this possibility when it laid down that the sheriff's decision was to be final on the facts. The interests of children were best served by not exposing them to the risk of having to give evidence again in an inquiry about the facts. It was better to leave it to the children's hearing to consider, in the light of all the circumstances, on what course they should decide in the best interests of the children in terms of ss 43 and 44 of the Act. If a safety valve was needed to deal with exceptional circumstances, it was to be found in s 52 of the Act, by which the Secretary of State is empowered to terminate a supervision requirement when, having regard to all the circumstances of the case and the interests of the child, he is satisfied that a supervision requirement in force in respect of the child should be terminated.

But that argument seems to us to be an inadequate response to the exceptional circumstances which, on the pursuers' averments, have arisen in this case. To say that the sheriff's decision that the grounds of

referral were established only opens the door to a con-
A sideration and determination of the case by the children's hearing overlooks the point which is of crucial
importance to the petitioners, namely that what the
sheriff held to be established must now be assumed for
all purposes to be true. It is no part of the functions
of a children's hearing to question the decision by the
sheriff that the grounds for the referral were established. It was for the sheriff to resolve all questions
about the facts which were in dispute at that stage, and
s 43 (1) of the Act makes it clear that, when the case
B is referred to the children's hearing, they must accept
the grounds as established. It is not difficult to see that
the sheriff's acceptance of the grounds is a stage of
great importance, especially where there are serious
allegations of child abuse over a long period. Any
attempt by the parents to dispute the grounds after the
sheriff has held them to be established must be
rejected by the children's hearing as raising issues
which are not for them to decide. The dilemma for the
parents as to whether or not to accept the sheriff's
C decision is thus a very difficult one. A decision either
way may have adverse consequences for them if it is
assumed that the allegations which the sheriff held to
be established were all true. It seems to us that this
division of function between the sheriff and the
children's hearing, which has many advantages — see
Sloan v B at p 548E — was not designed to deal with
exceptional circumstances such as are said to have
arisen in this case, which may have led to a serious
misunderstanding about the truth of the allegations
which resulted in the children being taken into care.
D

The same difficulty affects the power which has
been given to the Secretary of State by s 52 of the Act.
Counsel for the respondent asked us not to construe
this power too narrowly, but he accepted that it was
not open to the Secretary of State to review the
sheriff's decision that the grounds of referral had been
established. All he can do is to examine all the circumstances including the interests of the child when considering whether or not the supervision requirement
E should be terminated. But here again the fact that the
grounds of referral have been held to be established is
of crucial importance to the exercise of his power. The
Secretary of State must accept, as an important part of
all the circumstances of the case, all the allegations
which the sheriff has held to have been established. It
is not open to him to review the sheriff's decision on
this matter or to order his decision to be reconsidered
either by the sheriff or by this court. There is a clear
indication in s 52 that Parliament saw the need, in the
F interests of children, for a safety valve or measure of
last resort to enable a supervision requirement which
is unnecessary or inappropriate to be terminated. But
the circumstances averred here have revealed the
inadequacy of that provision to deal with a continuing
dispute about the facts of the case, in a situation of
exceptional difficulty and acute controversy which
only a fresh judicial decision can resolve.

This brings us to the question whether such a situation was truly in contemplation when Pt III of the
1968 Act was enacted. Counsel for the respondent

pointed to the fact that the conditions listed in s 32 (2)
are apt to cover the very serious allegations which G
were made in this case. He referred also to para 138
of the Kilbrandon report, in which there is a similar
list of the circumstances where a child might be said
to be in need of special measures of education and
training, including his having been subject to an
unnatural offence or living within the same household
as such a child. It was clear therefore that what was
now referred to as child abuse, or child sexual abuse,
had been expressly contemplated both in the
Kilbrandon report and by Parliament.
H

But the question is, as we see it, one of degree. Of
course, the conditions listed in s 32 (2) are apt to cover
the present case. Had it not been so, the grounds for
the referral would not have been framed as they were.
And we accept counsel for the respondent's point that
the categories of case mentioned in the Kilbrandon
report include what is now known as child abuse. But
we have the clear impression, from our reading of
what is said in para 9 of the report about the class of
children in need of care and protection, and the discussion which follows about the various situations in I
which compulsory measures of education and training
may be required, that the special problems associated
with group activities of the kind said to have arisen in
the present case were not given detailed consideration.
It appears also that some of the more acute problems
about interviewing techniques and the interpretation
of medical evidence were not foreseen. The principal
focus was on the desirability of bringing to an end the
jurisdiction of the juvenile courts in respect of
children who had committed offences, and of bringing J
into a single regime all cases where compulsory
measures involving deprivation of parental rights were
required. On the matter of appeals from a decision of
the sheriff in the hearing of the grounds of referral, or
of appeals from decisions by the panel, the report says
only this, in para 115: "Under our proposals it is, we
consider, desirable that there should be a right of
appeal on questions of law, arising from proceedings
before the Sheriff, to the Court of Session; and we
recommend accordingly."
K

There is no discussion here or anywhere else in the
report of the question whether there should be an
express exclusion of any form of review, however
extraordinary and unforeseen the circumstances
might be.

In our opinion, therefore, s 50 (1) does not have the
effect, when taken in its context, of excluding by
necessary implication the remedy which the pursuers
seek in this case. The interests of the children require
that, if extraordinary circumstances have arisen which L
reveal the machinery in the statute to be inadequate,
it should be open to the court to provide a remedy.
The distinction between what would amount to
extending the scope of Pt III of the Act and what
would not have this effect is no doubt a narrow and
important one. But we are satisfied that what the
petitioners ask us to do in this case would not be
extending the scope of this Part of the Act.

In this connection mention should be made of the
case of *Hobbs v Reporter for Strathclyde Region*, the

circumstances of which were referred to in *R, Petr.*
One of the twin children involved in that case was
admitted to hospital a few months after birth, suffering from injuries which in the doctor's opinion were
not consistent with the parents' explanation. The
grounds for referral of these cases to the children's
hearing under s 32 (2) (c) and (d) were held by the
sheriff to be established. But the parents then obtained
further medical evidence which they said cast serious
doubt on the soundness of that decision. They applied
to the nobile officium of this court for a rehearing of
the question whether the grounds of referral had been
established. The only point of competency which was
taken was that, as a decision on the matter was still
awaited from the Secretary of State under s 52, the
petitioner had not exhausted his statutory remedy.
That argument was rejected, and the court decided to
grant the application in a situation which was agreed
on both sides to be one of urgency, and no opinion was
delivered.

The interlocutor which was pronounced in that case
was in these terms: "The Lords having heard counsel
on the summar roll, in respect that the court is not
satisfied that the particular circumstances which have
arisen in this case are capable of being dealt with
expeditiously by the Secretary of State under and in
terms of s 52 of the Social Work (Scotland) Act 1968,
repel the pleas in law for the respondent, direct the
sheriff (a) to fix a further diet quam primum for the
purpose of considering anew whether the original
grounds of referral in the case of DH and KH are
established; (b) to hear such evidence relating to the
original grounds of referral as the parties may wish to
place before him including any additional evidence
which was not available at the hearing on 25 May and
7 June 1988; (c) to exercise of new the powers conferred on him by s 42 (5) or 42 (6) of the said Act as
the case may be; declare that pending the exercise by
the sheriff of the said powers the existing supervision
requirements in respect of the said children as
reviewed from time to time under s 48 of the said Act
shall remain in force."

That case was subsequently returned to a different
sheriff for a fresh hearing, after which, having considered a substantial amount of medical evidence, the
sheriff held that the grounds for the referral had not
been established. The referrals were discharged and
the children returned to their parents. The sheriff's
decision was appealed by the reporter but the appeal
was later refused by this court: *Kennedy v H.* That
case shows that the remedy which the pursuers seek in
this case is capable of being worked out within the
scope of the system which Pt III of the 1968 Act has
laid down. In our opinion it would not be inconsistent
with these procedures for the present case to be
returned to the sheriff for the purpose of considering
anew whether the original grounds for the referrals are
established.

For these reasons we shall repel the respondent's
plea to the competency of this application. We have
still to consider whether the petitioners' averments are
sufficient to justify an exercise of the nobile officium,

and the hearing will be continued to a later date to
enable us to hear the parties' arguments on this point.

Counsel for Petitioners (Parents), *Jackson, QC,
Caldwell*; Solicitors, *Macbeth, Currie & Co, WS* —
Counsel for Respondent (Reporter), *Macfadyen, QC*;
Solicitors, *Biggart, Baillie & Gifford, WS.*

D A K

Cumbernauld and Kilsyth District Council v Dollar Land (Cumbernauld) Ltd

HOUSE OF LORDS
LORD KEITH OF KINKEL,
LORD BRIDGE OF HARWICH,
LORD JAUNCEY OF TULLICHETTLE,
LORD BROWNE-WILKINSON AND
LORD MUSTILL
22 JULY 1993

*Heritable property — Public right of way — Acquisition
by prescription — Pedestrian walkway through town
centre — Whether use as matter of right rather than tolerance by proprietor — Test of nature of user necessary to
qualify route as public right of way — Prescription and
Limitation (Scotland) Act 1973 (c 52), s 3 (3).*

*Prescription — Positive prescription — Public right of
way — Pedestrian walkway through town centre —
Whether use as matter of right rather than tolerance by
proprietor — Test of nature of user necessary to qualify
route as public right of way — Prescription and Limitation (Scotland) Act 1973 (c 52), s 3 (3).*

Cumbernauld Development Corporation constructed the town centre of Cumbernauld. The Corporation built a walkway through the town centre to
connect the centre to residential areas on either side.
The walkway, known as Tay Walk, was completed
during 1966 and regularly used thereafter by members
of the public both for access to the town centre and as
a means of crossing through the centre. In 1987 a
company acquired title to the town centre properties.
From November 1988 they closed the walkway at
night and at other times to combat vandalism. The
local planning authority, who had a duty under s 46
of the Countryside (Scotland) Act 1967 to assert,
protect and keep open any public right of way within
their area, raised an action of declarator that Tay Walk
was a public right of way and of interdict of the
company from interfering with members of the public
in their lawful use and enjoyment of the public right
of way. After proof before answer, the Lord Ordinary
found not only that Tay Walk had since 1966 been
used to obtain access to the shops and other associated
units in the town centre but that it had also been used

by numerous categories of members of the general
A public for specific purposes. He concluded that all
these uses had the character of general public use of
a town centre pedestrian thoroughfare and he granted
declarator and interdict as concluded for. The
company reclaimed. They did not seek to challenge
the primary facts found by the Lord Ordinary and
accepted that there had been sufficient use of Tay
Walk by the public during the prescriptive period to
satisfy what they described as the preliminary requirements for a public right of way. They argued that
there was no evidence of use which could not reason-
B ably be ascribed to tolerance on the part of the proprietors. The First Division refused the reclaiming
motion, holding that where the user was of such
amount and in such manner as would reasonably be
regarded as being the assertion of a public right, the
owner could not stand by and ask that his inaction be
ascribed to his good nature or to tolerance. If his
position was to be that the user was by his leave and
licence, he had to do something to make the public
aware of that fact so that they would know that the
C route was being used by them only with his permission and not as of right. The company appealed to
the House of Lords. They contended that unless a
public user of a way was adverse to the interests of the
proprietor it had necessarily to be ascribed to tolerance
and that since the user of Tay Walk had been positively encouraged by the development corporation, it
could not amount to user as of right.

Held, that the company's proposition that there had
to be a conflict of interest between the proprietor and
D the users was wholly unsustainable in law and in any
event lacked a basis in fact (p 1321D); and appeal *dismissed*.

Dictum of Lord President Normand in *Marquis of
Bute v McKirdy and McMillan*, 1937 SLT 241 at
pp 251-252, *approved*.

Action of declarator and interdict
E (Reported 1991 SLT 806 and 1992 SLT 1035)
Cumbernauld and Kilsyth District Council, as district planning authority, raised an action of declarator
of a public right of way over Tay Walk, which runs
through the town centre of Cumbernauld, against
Dollar Land (Cumbernauld) Ltd. The district council
also sought interdict of the defenders from interfering
with members of the public in their lawful use and
enjoyment of the public right of way.

The case came to proof before answer before the
F Lord Ordinary (Penrose).

Statutory provisions
The Prescription and Limitation (Scotland) Act
1973 provides:

"3.—. . . (3) If a public right of way over land has
been possessed by the public for a continuous period
of 20 years openly, peaceably and without judicial
interruption, then, as from the expiration of that
period, the existence of the right of way as so
possessed shall be exempt from challenge."

Cases referred to
Bute (Marquis of) v McKirdy and McMillan Ltd, 1937 G
  SLT 241; 1937 SC 93.
Mackintosh v Moir (1871) 9 M 574.
*Macpherson v Scottish Rights of Way and Recreation
  Society Ltd* (1888) 15 R (HL) 68.
Richardson v Cromarty Petroleum Co Ltd, 1982 SLT
  237.

On 22 February 1991 the Lord Ordinary *pronounced*
decree of declarator and interdict. (Reported 1991
SLT 806.)   H

The defenders reclaimed.

Reclaiming motion
The reclaiming motion was heard before the First
Division on 10, 11, 12 and 13 March 1992.

On 8 April 1992 the court *refused* the reclaiming
motion. (Reported 1992 SLT 1035.)
                                                         I
The defenders appealed to the House of Lords.

Appeal
The appeal was heard before Lord Keith of Kinkel,
Lord Bridge of Harwich, Lord Jauncey of Tullichettle, Lord Browne-Wilkinson and Lord Mustill on
30 June 1993.

On 22 July 1993 the House *dismissed* the appeal.

LORD KEITH OF KINKEL.—For the reasons J
given in the speech to be delivered by my noble and
learned friend Lord Jauncey of Tullichettle, which I
have read in draft and with which I agree, I would
dismiss this appeal.

LORD BRIDGE OF HARWICH.—I have had
the advantage of reading in draft the speech of my
noble and learned friend Lord Jauncey of Tullichettle.
I agree with it and, for the reasons he gives, I would K
dismiss the appeal.

LORD JAUNCEY OF TULLICHETTLE.—This
appeal is about a walkway in the town centre of
Cumbernauld which was built by the Cumbernauld
Development Corporation in accordance with their
powers and duties under the New Towns Act 1946
and later the New Towns (Scotland) Act 1968. The
centre was built on a number of levels and part of it
straddled a main road which carried through traffic. It L
was so designed that pedestrian and vehicular traffic
were segregated to a substantial extent. The walkway
in question, known as Tay Walk, ran from north west
to south east over the main road and through the town
centre linking developments known as Seafar and
Carbrain situated respectively at the north west and
south east corners of the town with the town centre
and with each other. It was part of a comprehensive
walkway system related to the segregation of pedestrian and vehicular traffic. That part of Tay Walk
which passed through the town centre was enclosed by

A the surrounding structure which contained shops, banks, public offices and for the first 12 or more years of its life a hotel and a number of residential flats. Tay Walk was completed in 1966 as part of the core works of phase, which was officially opened in 1967. In the late 1970s doors were installed at the north west and south east ends of the enclosed part of Tay Walk and fire doors were also installed within that part.

The town centre structures remained in the owner-ship of the development corporation until June or July 1987 when they were sold to the appellants. While in B the ownership of the development corporation no restriction was placed on the use by the public of Tay Walk and the doors, albeit fitted with locks, were never locked, notwithstanding persistent vandalism which cost the development corporation substantial sums of money. In November 1988 the appellants locked the doors on Tay Walk at night in order to prevent vandalism. Thereafter the respondents, as local planning authority, in pursuance of their duty under s 46 (1) of the Countryside (Scotland) Act 1967 C to protect and keep open any public right of way in their area, raised the present action for declarator that there existed a public right of way over Tay Walk.

The case went to proof before the Lord Ordinary in January 1991 and by interlocutor of 22 February 1991 he granted decree of declarator as concluded for. In a judgment, carefully reasoned both as to fact and law, the Lord Ordinary found that not only was Tay Walk since 1966 used to obtain access to the shops and other associated units in the town centre but that it was also D used inter alia (1) by worshippers going to St Mungo's church at the north west end of the walkway; (2) by persons making their way to and from the railway station; (3) by persons frequenting the town hall; (4) extensively by schoolchildren going to and from school; (5) by residents in Seafar proceeding to facili-ties such as the health centre, swimming pool and technical college on the south eastern side of the town; (6) by persons resorting to entertainment centres in the central development area; (7) by those visiting E banks with cash dispensing machines out of hours; and (8) by mothers with young children in prams crossing the town centre for social purposes. The Lord Ordinary concluded that all these uses had the character of general public use of a town centre pedes-trian thoroughfare. The appellants reclaimed and the First Division refused the reclaiming motion and adhered to the Lord Ordinary's interlocutor.

Before the First Division the appellants did not seek F to challenge the primary facts found by the Lord Ordinary and indeed accepted that there had been sufficient use of Tay Walk by the public during the prescriptive period to satisfy what was described as the preliminary requirements for a public right of way. Their argument was that there was no evidence of use which could not reasonably be ascribed to tolerance on the part of the proprietors. The Lord President con-sidered that the question to be decided was ultimately one of fact. After reviewing the facts he reached the same conclusion as did the Lord Ordinary, namely that the use of Tay Walk "had the character of general

public use of a town centre pedestrian thoroughfare". Lords Cowie and Murray agreed with the Lord G President in reaching this conclusion. However, the Lord President not only considered the facts of the case but, like the Lord Ordinary, carried out a careful analysis of the relevant authorities during which he concluded that the only support for the appellants' argument was to be found in the passage of the judgment of Lord Deas in *Mackintosh v Moir* (1871) 9 M at p 576, which was disapproved by Lord President Normand and Lord Moncrieff in *Marquis of Bute v McKirdy and McMillan*, 1937 SLT at pp 252 H and 257 respectively. The Lord President (Hope) said (1992 SLT at p 1041G): "where the user is of such amount and in such manner as would reasonably be regarded as being the assertion of a public right, the owner cannot stand by and ask that his inaction be ascribed to his good nature or to tolerance. If his position is to be that the user is by his leave and licence, he must do something to make the public aware of that fact so that they know that the route is being used by them only with his permission and not as of right".   I

The proposition was entirely in line with the follow-ing dictum of Lord President Normand in *Marquis of Bute v McKirdy and McMillan*, at pp 251-252: "The question is rather whether, having regard to the sparseness or density of the population, the user over the prescriptive period was in degree and quality such as might have been expected if the road had been an undisputed right of way. If the public user is of that degree and quality, the proprietor, who fails for the J prescriptive period to assert or to put on record his right to exclude the public, must be taken to have remained inactive, not from tolerance, but because the public right could not have been successfully disputed or because he acquiesced in it." I have no doubt that these dicta correctly state the law of Scotland.

Neither in the First Division nor in your Lordships' House did the appellant seek to argue that the position of the original proprietors of Tay Walk as a new town development corporation with wide statutory powers K affected their position as owners of the walkway. The case proceeded on the basis that the development corporation fell to be treated as any other proprietor for the purposes of applying common law principles.

Before this House, counsel for the appellants referred (first) to the following statement of Lord Halsbury LC in *Macpherson v Scottish Rights of Way and Recreation Society Ltd* (1888) 15 R (HL) at p 68, that "if it can be established that for the necessary L period there has in fact been such a use of the way as negatives a mere licence or permission, then, as I understand the law of Scotland, that establishes abso-lutely the right of way in question"; and (secondly) to a statement of Lord Cowie in *Richardson v Cromarty Petroleum Co Ltd*, 1982 SLT at p 238 to the effect that the pursuer in the right of way action before him had to "prove four things: . . . (4) that the use by the public was of such a nature as to show that they were using it as a matter of right as opposed to the tolerance of the proprietor". In reliance on these dicta counsel for

the appellants argued that unless a public user of a
way was adverse to the interests of the proprietor it
must necessarily be ascribed to tolerance and that
since the user of Tay Walk had been positively
encouraged by the development corporation, it could
not amount to user as of right. For a user to be so considered there must, it was argued, be conflict between
the interest of the users and that of the proprietor. For
this somewhat stark proposition counsel could
produce no authority.

There is no principle of law which requires that
there be conflict between the interest of users and that
of a proprietor. As Lord President Normand pointed
out in *Marquis of Bute v McKirdy and McMillan*,
acquiescence on the part of a proprietor in continued
user throughout the prescriptive period without
taking steps to assert or record his right of exclusion
will result in the constitution of a public right of way
against him. If acquiescence in these circumstances
produces such a result, encouragement can even more
readily be said to have the same consequences.
However, not only is there no basis in law for counsel
for the appellants' proposition but it also lacks basis in
fact, having regard to the obvious disadvantage to the
development corporation in having to spend substantial sums repairing vandalised property. As the Lord
President said (1992 SLT at p 1043B): "On the evidence in this case the development corporation were as
liable to be affected in their ownership of the property
by the assertion of a public right of way as any other
proprietor."

My Lords, both the Lord Ordinary and the First
Division have reached a particular view of the facts
which has not been challenged. In drawing inferences
from those facts they have applied long established
principles of law which have also not been challenged.
The appellants' proposition that there must be a conflict of interest between the proprietor and the users
is wholly unsustainable in law and in any event lacks
a basis in fact. It follows that this hopeless appeal, in
which their Lordships did not find it necessary to call
upon the respondents, must be dismissed. Had leave
to appeal been required in this case it would
indubitably have been refused. The appellants will
pay the respondents' costs before this House.

LORD BROWNE-WILKINSON.—I have read in
draft the speech to be delivered by my noble and
learned friend Lord Jauncey of Tullichettle. For the
reasons which he gives I too would dismiss the appeal.

LORD MUSTILL.—I have had the advantage of
reading in draft the speech prepared by my noble and
learned friend Lord Jauncey of Tullichettle, and for
the reasons he gives I, too, would dismiss the appeal.

---

*Counsel for Pursuers and Respondents, McGhie, QC,
Macnair; Solicitors, Allan McDougall & Co, SSC,
Bayer Rosin, London — Counsel for Defenders and
Appellants, Vandore, QC, Clancy; Solicitors, J & R A
Robertson, WS, Nicholson Graham Jones, London.*

M G T

Mejka v HM Advocate

HIGH COURT OF JUSTICIARY
THE LORD JUSTICE CLERK (ROSS),
LORDS KINCRAIG AND BRAND
10 SEPTEMBER 1993

*Justiciary — Procedure — Trial — Commencement of —
Extension of time — Accused indicted for trial with co-
accused on three occasions when diet deserted pro loco et
tempore because of illness or absence of co-accused —
Crown always able to proceed against accused alone —
Crown not investigating co-accused's condition after first
diet deserted — Sheriff granting extension of 12 month
period — Whether cause shown for extension — Criminal
Procedure (Scotland) Act 1975 (c 21), s 101 (1).*

Section 101 (1) of the Criminal Procedure (Scotland)
Act 1975 provides that an accused shall not be tried on
indictment for any offence unless such trial is commenced within a period of 12 months of his first
appearance on petition in respect of that offence,
provided that the sheriff may on cause shown extend
that period.

An accused person appeared on petition on 28 July
1992 on charges of fraud and contraventions of the
Companies Act 1985 and was committed for trial and
released on bail. An indictment was served on him for
trial along with a co-accused on 16 November 1992
but the Crown deserted that diet pro loco et tempore
because the co-accused appeared to be unwell. A
second indictment was served on both accused for trial
on 22 March 1993 but the diet was again deserted pro
loco et tempore for a similar reason. A third indictment was served on the accused to stand trial along
with his co-accused on 26 July 1993 but when the diet
was called the co-accused was absent. On 27 July 1993
a warrant for the co-accused's apprehension was
granted but the warrant was subsequently suspended
by the High Court with the consent of the Crown.
The Crown moved to desert the diet pro loco et
tempore on 27 July 1993. After deserting the diet pro
loco et tempore, the sheriff, on the Crown's motion,
extended the 12 month period on the view that the
Crown had shown cause for such an extension because
(1) it was in the interests of justice that the accused be
tried along with his co-accused, and (2) the Crown had
not been idle since 22 March 1993 as they had considered a neurological report on the co-accused. The
report was not obtained by the Crown but by the co-
accused; the Crown had taken no steps to obtain information on her condition from any other source. It was
also accepted by the Crown that it had not been
impossible to proceed against the accused alone. The
accused appealed against the extension of the period.

Held, that the sheriff had erred in concluding that
cause had been shown for an extension because (1) he
failed to take into account that the right conferred on
an accused person by s 101 (1) was a very important
one of which he ought not to be deprived unless
sufficient reason had been put forward by the Crown
(p 1323G); (2) he gave inadequate weight to the fact
that the Crown could have proceeded against the

accused alone at each of the three trial diets (p 1323H);
(3) his view that the Crown had not been idle was
unwarranted (p 1323K-L); and appeal *allowed*.

Indictment

Raymond Mejka was charged along with a co-
accused at the instance of the rt hon the Lord Rodger
of Earlsferry, Her Majesty's Advocate, on an indictment libelling (as respects the accused Mejka) four
charges of fraud and two contraventions of the Companies Act 1985. After two indictments had been
served and deserted by the Crown pro loco et tempore
because of the illness of the co-accused, the Crown
moved to desert a third indictment pro loco et tempore
and to be granted an extension of the 12 month period
in terms of s 101 (1) (ii) of the Criminal Procedure
(Scotland) Act 1975, when the co-accused failed to
appear. The sheriff (A M Bell) inter alia granted an
extension of three months.

The accused appealed by note of appeal against the
decision of the sheriff. The facts of the case appear
from the opinion of the court.

Statutory provisions

The Criminal Procedure (Scotland) Act 1975
provides:

"101.—(1) An accused shall not be tried on indictment for any offence unless such trial is commenced
within a period of 12 months of the first appearance
of that accused on petition in respect of that offence;
and, failing such commencement within that period,
the accused shall be discharged forthwith and thereafter he shall be forever free from all question of
process for that offence: Provided that — . . . (ii) on
application made for the purpose, the sheriff or, where
an indictment has been served on the accused in
respect of the High Court, a single judge of that court,
may on cause shown extend the said period of 12
months."

Case referred to

Advocate (HM) v Swift, 1985 SLT 26; 1984 JC 83;
1984 SCCR 216.

Appeal

The note of appeal contained the following ground:

That the grant of said extension is unreasonable in
respect that (1) no adequate cause was shown by the
procurator fiscal at the hearing on 27 July 1993 to
justify extension for any period beyond the statutory
limit of 12 months laid down by the terms of s 101 of
the Criminal Procedure (Scotland) Act 1975, and (2)
the sheriff wrongly exercised his discretion in granting
said extension.

The appeal was heard before the High Court on 10
September 1993.

Eo die the court *allowed* the appeal and *reversed* the
decision of the sheriff.

The following opinion of the court was delivered by
the Lord Justice Clerk (Ross):

OPINION OF THE COURT.—This is an appeal
under s 101 (1) and (5) of the Criminal Procedure
(Scotland) Act 1975, as amended by the Criminal
Justice (Scotland) Act 1980. On 28 July 1992 the
appellant appeared on petition at Edinburgh sheriff
court on charges of fraud and contraventions of the
Companies Act 1985. He was committed for trial and
released on bail.

An indictment was served upon him to stand trial
along with a co-accused at Edinburgh sheriff court on
16 November 1992, but that diet was deserted pro loco
et tempore on the basis that the co-accused appeared
to be unwell and the Crown indicated that they would
have her examined. A further indictment was served
upon the appellant to stand trial with his co-accused
on 22 March 1993. On that occasion the diet was again
deserted pro loco et tempore for a similar reason. A
third indictment was then served upon the appellant
to stand trial with his co-accused at Edinburgh sheriff
court on 26 July 1992, that is only two days before the
expiry of the 12 month period under s 101 (1) of the
Criminal Procedure (Scotland) Act 1975.

On 26 July 1993 when the diet was called the co-
accused was absent. When the diet was called the
prosecutor moved for a warrant to apprehend the co-
accused. The sheriff refused the motion and continued
the case until the following day. On the following day,
the sheriff granted the prosecutor's motion for warrant
to apprehend the co-accused. Subsequently a bill of
suspension was presented on behalf of the co-accused
seeking suspension of the warrant. After sundry procedure the Crown consented to the passing of the bill.

On 27 July 1993 the Crown moved the sheriff to
desert the diet pro loco et tempore, and also moved the
sheriff to extend the 12 month period under s 101 (1)
(ii) of the Act of 1975. After hearing parties the sheriff
agreed to hear the motion for desertion first, and after
hearing parties further the sheriff on 27 July 1993
deserted the diet pro loco et tempore.

The sheriff then proceeded to deal with the motion
for extension of the 12 month period. Since the arguments in favour of extension had been put forward by
the Crown when the motion to desert pro loco et
tempore was made, the sheriff heard the appellant's
opposition to the motion for extension first and then
allowed the Crown to reply.

The sheriff granted the Crown's motion and
extended the period of 12 months which would have
expired on 28 July 1993 by three months. It is against
that decision of the sheriff that the present appeal is
taken.

On behalf of the appellant it was contended that the
grant of the extension was unreasonable in that no
adequate cause had been shown to justify an extension, and that the sheriff had wrongly exercised his
discretion in granting the extension.

Before this court counsel for the appellant and the
advocate depute were agreed that in view of the

decision in *HM Advocate v Swift*, the sheriff required
A to consider (1) whether the Crown had shown sufficient reason to justify an extension of the period, and
(2) if the Crown had shown sufficient reason, whether
in the exercise of his discretion the sheriff ought in
fact to extend the period.

In his report the sheriff explains that he adopted
that approach, and that he concluded that the Crown
had shown cause for an extension, and that he ought
to exercise his discretion to grant an extension.

B   Counsel for the appellant submitted that the
sheriff's approach had been flawed. Although he had
correctly identified the two questions which had to be
addressed, he had erred in the material which he had
taken into account. Counsel rehearsed the history of
the matter and this has been dealt with at length in the
sheriff's report and need not now be repeated. Counsel
also dealt at some length with the history of the appellant in relation to a charge of embezzlement which had
resulted in his being fined £32,000 to be paid by 30
C August 1991. That period had been extended, and
although part of the fine had been paid, the alternative
of serving a period of imprisonment for non-payment
of the fine still hung over the appellant.

In his report the sheriff narrates the submissions
made to him. The Crown contended that it was in the
interests of justice that the appellant and his co-
accused should be tried together if reasonably practicable. The Crown had proceeded properly throughout.
The Crown admitted that they were in a position to
D proceed to trial against the appellant alone, and that it
was not impossible to proceed separately against him.
It was said, however, that it would be most inconvenient to do so particularly as the appellant had given
notice of his intention to lead evidence blaming his co-
accused.

In his report the sheriff makes it plain that there
were two factors which weighed with him in concluding that the Crown had shown cause for an extension.
E The first factor was that it would be in the interests
of justice that the trial should proceed against the
appellant and his co-accused together, and the second
factor was that since the diet was deserted on 22
March 1993 "the Crown had not been idle". His
reason for concluding that the Crown had not been
idle was that since March 1993 the Crown had
explored the only avenue then suggested and had considered a neurological examination undergone by the
co-accused.

F   In our opinion these two factors identified by the
sheriff do not justify his conclusion that the Crown
had shown cause for an extension.

As was emphasised in *HM Advocate v Swift*, the
right conferred upon an accused by s 101 (1) is a very
important one and an extension should only be
granted where the Crown show sufficient reason for it,
and the judge is prepared to exercise his discretion in
favour of the Crown. In these circumstances when
consideration is being given to the question of whether
the Crown have shown cause, it is necessary to keep

in mind that Parliament has conferred this very important right upon accused persons. In the present case, G
it appears to us that the sheriff erred in that he reached
his conclusion that cause had been shown for an extension without his having taken into account that the
right conferred upon the appellant by s 101 (1) is a
very important one of which he ought not to be
deprived unless sufficient reason has been put forward
by the Crown. In our opinion the two reasons put
forward by the Crown were not sufficient to justify the
extension. It is clear from the sheriff's report that he
recognised that even if the three month extension were H
now granted the Crown might well have to proceed
against the appellant alone, but he gave inadequate
weight to the consideration that the Crown could have
done this on 16 November 1992, 22 March 1993 or 26
July 1993. In view of the fact that the Crown accepted
that they could have proceeded to trial against the
appellant on any of these three dates, we are not
persuaded that sufficient cause has been made out for
an extension of the 12 month period. No doubt it
would be less convenient if proceedings were taken
against the appellant and his co-accused separately, I
but proceeding to trial against the appellant alone
would not lead to any denial of justice so far as either
he or his co-accused is concerned. The fact that it
would be more convenient if proceedings could be
taken against the appellant and the co-accused
together is not, in our opinion, justification for depriving the appellant of the valuable right conferred upon
him by s 101 (1) of the Act of 1975.

Moreover cause is not shown for extending the 12 J
month period by accepting that the Crown had not
been idle since 22 March 1993. We accept that fault
on the part of the prosecutor is a relevant consideration in considering whether sufficient reason has been
shown for allowing an extension even though there is
no provision similar to s 101 (4) (c) applying to extensions under s 101 (1) (ii), but the absence of fault is not
conclusive.

In any event, the advocate depute was unable to
inform us of any steps taken by the Crown since 22 K
March 1993 to consider whether or not the co-accused
was likely to be able to go to trial on 26 July 1993. The
sheriff states that the Crown within this period had
considered a neurological examination undergone by
the co-accused, but it appeared that this was in fact a
report of a neurological examination obtained by the
co-accused, and there was nothing to suggest that the
Crown had ever taken any steps to obtain information
about her neurological condition from any other source.
On the information available to us it was not clear that L
the Crown had not in fact been idle regarding this
issue since 22 March 1993, and the sheriff's conclusion to that effect does not appear to be warranted.

In all the circumstances we are satisfied that the
sheriff has not stated adequate reasons for concluding
that cause had been shown for an extension. It is not
accordingly necessary to consider whether the sheriff
erred in the exercise of his discretion, but if it had
been necessary to consider this we would have concluded that the sheriff had erred. In the final para-

graph of his report dealing with the exercise of his discretion, there is no reference to the fact that the right conferred upon an accused person by s 101 (1) is a very important one. Nothing which the sheriff says in the final paragraph of his report appears to us to justify his exercising his discretion in favour of the Crown. He expresses the view that he has sympathy for the difficult position in which the Crown found themselves, but having regard to the fact that the Crown could have proceeded against the appellant separately on 16 November 1992, 22 March 1993 and 26 July 1993, this is no justification for exercising discretion in favour of the Crown.

For the foregoing reasons we sustain the appeal at the instance of the appellant and reverse the decision of the sheriff.

Counsel for Appellant, Drummond, QC; Solicitors, John Pryde & Co — Counsel for Respondent, Jarvie, A D; Solicitor, J D Lowe, Crown Agent.

P W F

(NOTE)

Lord Advocate, Petitioner

OUTER HOUSE

LORD CAMERON OF LOCHBROOM

27 MAY 1992

Company — Winding up — Insolvency — Company unable to pay its debts — Leaving of statutory demand at company's registered office — Whether service to be effected by officer of court — Insolvency Act 1986 (c 45), s 123 (1) (a).

A statutory demand seeking payment of money owed was served on a limited company by a person bearing to act for and on behalf of the creditor. The demand not having been met, the creditor petitioned the court for a winding up order.

Held, that it was sufficient service for the demand to have been served by a person duly authorised by the creditor; and first deliverance *granted.*

Lord Advocate v Blairwest Investments Ltd, 1989 SLT (Sh Ct) 97, and *Lord Advocate v Traprain Ltd,* 1989 SLT (Sh Ct) 99, *approved.*

By virtue of s 123 (1) (a) of the Insolvency Act 1986, a company is deemed unable to pay its debts for the purposes of an application for its winding up if a creditor to whom the company is indebted in a sum exceeding £750 then due "has served on the company, by leaving it at the company's registered office, a written demand" for payment and certain circumstances thereafter obtain.

The Lord Advocate, acting on behalf of Her Majesty's Commissioners of Customs and Excise, petitioned for the winding up of Tulloch Castle Ltd. A demand in the statutory form had been served by a person, not an officer of court, acting on behalf of the commissioners. In granting a first deliverance of the petition the Lord Ordinary (Lord Cameron of Lochbroom) said:

"In this petition for an order for winding up I have granted a first deliverance. A question was raised at the outset as to whether, in terms of s 123 (1) (a) of the Insolvency Act 1986, the statutory demand required to be left at the company's registered office by an officer of court. The statutory demand itself is in the form prescribed by para 7.30 of and Sched 5 to the Insolvency (Scotland) Rules 1986 (SI 1986/1915). The statutory form provides that "this demand is served by the creditor". In my opinion, and in agreement with the conclusions and reasoning on this point of the learned sheriffs in *Lord Advocate v Blairwest Investments Ltd,* 1989 SLT (Sh Ct) 97 and *Lord Advocate v Traprain Ltd,* 1989 SLT (Sh Ct) 99, it does not. The opinions in those cases rehearse fully the relevant statutory provisions and I am content to adopt the reasoning and conclusions reached by the learned sheriffs in the matter. No question arises as to the form of the docquet attached to the statutory demand in the present petition, unlike that in *Lord Advocate v Blairwest Investments Ltd.* In the present case the docquet specifically bears that the signatory acted for and on behalf of the Commissioners of Customs and Excise. For service in compliance with the provisions of s 123 (1) (a) of the Act, it is sufficient if such service is effected either by the creditor in person or by some person duly authorised and so acting for and on behalf of the creditor."

Counsel for Petitioning Creditor, Harris; Solicitors, Shepherd & Wedderburn, WS — No appearance for Company.

C H

City of Aberdeen District Council v Secretary of State for Scotland

FIRST DIVISION

LORDS ALLANBRIDGE, COWIE AND WYLIE

28 JUNE 1991

Town and country planning — Planning permission — Change of use to that of hot food retail shop — Loss of amenity — Application refused by district council but allowed by reporter on appeal — Reporter considering matter of litter a matter dealt with by general legislation and not proper reason for withholding planning permission — Whether a matter for reporter to consider in context of residential amenity — Whether reporter erred — Town and Country Planning (Scotland) Act 1972 (c 52), ss 231 and 233 — Town and Country Planning (Use Classes) (Scotland) Order 1973 (SI 1973/1165).

Town and country planning — Planning permission — Change of use — Loss of amenity — Area of mixed commercial and residential use — Proper test of loss of amenity.

A planning authority and local community council appealed to the Court of Session against a decision of a reporter appointed by the Secretary of State for Scotland who had allowed an appeal against a refusal of planning permission for the change of use of certain premises to that of use as a hot food retail shop. The premises were situated in a mixed commercial and residential use area and were restricted to class 1 of the Town and Country Planning (Use Classes) (Scotland) Order 1973, as amended. In his determination the reporter had stated, in relation to the dropping of litter, that although that subject was often raised in connection with hot food shops it was now generally recognised that, as the dropping of litter was dealt with under general legislation, it was not a proper reason for withholding planning permission. The reporter also considered that the test of whether planning permission should be refused in the circumstances of the case was whether use as a hot food retail shop would result in a serious loss of amenity to nearby residents as opposed to loss of amenity of a lesser standard.

Held, that the problem of litter was a matter which the reporter ought to have taken into account notwithstanding the fact that it was dealt with under other legislation and that, having failed to take it into account when the principal issue in the case was whether the proposed use of the premises would result in a serious loss of amenity, such failure constituted an error of law (pp 1326H-J and 1327A); and appeal *allowed*.

Opinion, that as the area was one of mixed commercial and residential use, the test of loss of amenity was a higher one than that for a purely residential area, so that the reporter had not applied too high a test in stating that serious loss of amenity to nearby residents was required (p 1327F-G).

Appeal from the Secretary of State for Scotland

The City of Aberdeen District Council, as planning authority, and Cults, Bieldside and Milltimber Community Council appealed to the Court of Session against a decision of a reporter appointed by the Secretary of State for Scotland granting planning permission to Scotstown Holdings Ltd for the change of use of premises at Unit 7, The Courtyard, 327/329 North Deeside Road, which was restricted to class 1 of the Town and Country Planning (Use Classes) (Scotland) Order 1973, as amended, to use as a hot food retail shop, subject to certain conditions. The Secretary of State for Scotland and Scotstown Holdings Ltd were called as first and second respondents respectively.

Textbook referred to

Young, *Scottish Planning Appeals*, p 175.

The appeal was heard before the First Division on 11 June 1991.

On 28 June 1991 the court *allowed* the appeal and *quashed* the reporter's decision.

The following opinion of the court was delivered by Lord Cowie:

OPINION OF THE COURT.—This is an appeal under the provisions of ss 231 and 233 of the Town and Country Planning (Scotland) Act 1972.

The appellants are the City of Aberdeen District Council as planning authority and Cults, Bieldside and Milltimber Community Council. They are appealing against a decision of the Secretary of State for Scotland who allowed an appeal by Scotstown Holdings Ltd against a refusal of planning permission by the district council for the change of use of premises at Unit 7, The Courtyard, no 327/329 North Deeside Road, Cults, which is restricted to class 1 of the Town and Country Planning (Use Classes) (Scotland) Order 1973 as amended, to use as a hot food retail shop.

The first respondent is the Secretary of State for Scotland and the second is Scotstown Holdings Ltd.

The description of the site and the representations made for and against the application by the parties are fully set out in the reporter's letter of 24 September 1990.

The reporter's conclusion was that having considered all the matters raised in the representations, there were no sound and clear cut reasons for the refusal of planning permission in this instance provided that certain safeguards were provided by way of conditions. He then proceeded to specify certain conditions directed particularly to the question of amenity. These conditions were as follows:

"(1) The development hereby permitted shall be begun before the expiration of five years from the date of this permission.

"(2) The premises shall not open for business

outwith the hours 0800 to 2300 Monday to Saturday, nor at any time on Sunday.

"(3) The change of use hereby permitted shall not begin until provisions for the extraction and filtration of cooking smells have been made in accordance with a scheme to be agreed with the planning authority; any plant installed in accordance with such a scheme shall be maintained to the satisfaction of the planning authority.

"(4) No recorded music shall be played on the premises at a level which would result in a sound level measurement in excess of 55 dB(a) within 10 metres of the premises."

The appellants have appealed against that decision on various grounds which are set out in the case but we were informed by counsel for the appellants that he was only presenting an argument on three of these grounds.

The first was that the reporter had erred in law in considering at para 18 of his decision that, as the dropping of litter in public places was dealt with under other legislation, it was not a proper reason for withholding planning permission.

The second was that there was no evidence before the reporter to allow him to hold at para 17 of his decision that cooking smells can be substantially reduced by the installation of modern filtration equipment, and in any event to attach condition 3 to the grant of planning permission, which assumes that it can be done, was unjustified.

The third was that the reporter had erred in law when he reached the conclusion in para 13 of his decision that the test of whether planning permission should be refused in the circumstances of this case was whether the hot food retail shop would result in a *serious* loss of amenity to nearby residents as opposed to loss of amenity of a lesser standard.

On the first ground it was submitted by counsel for the appellants that it was clear that the reporter had put out of his mind the consideration of litter as a ground for refusing planning permission because, in his view, the control of litter in public places was covered by other legislation. Indeed it was indicated in the answer to this ground of appeal by the first respondent that it would have been improper for him to have refused planning permission by assuming that members of the public would not comply with the law.

In his reply counsel for the first respondent indicated that he did not intend to present an argument in support of that answer and what he submitted was that, on a fair reading of paras 18 and 19 of the reporter's decision, it was clear that the reporter had not put out of his mind the question of litter as being a material consideration in deciding whether planning permission should be refused, but had come to the view on consideration of that matter amongst others that it did not amount to a sound and clear cut reason for the refusal of planning permission.

We are unable to read the reporter's decision in that

way. What he says in para 18 is this: "Turning to other matters raised reference has been made to possible problems of litter. This is often raised in connection with hot food shops but it is now generally recognised that as the dropping of litter is dealt with under general legislation it is not a proper reason for withholding planning permission."

The reporter then goes on to deal with other considerations in the same paragraph.

In our opinion the only proper inference that can be drawn from the words quoted are that having considered the matter of litter, the reporter had decided to put it aside as of no significance because it could be dealt with under other legislation. Nowhere does he say that litter was still a matter which was of relevance in dealing with the question of loss of amenity. In our opinion that would have been very easy for him to say if that had been his view. Furthermore, it would have been consistent with a decision which is referred to in the textbook by Mr Young entitled *Scottish Planning Appeals, Decisions on Law and Procedure* and of which we approve notwithstanding other decisions which appear to be inconsistent with it. In that decision which is reproduced in Section 6 and is numbered 6.22 on p 175 of Mr Young's book, the reporter says this: "While problems of litter and vandalism were primarily matters for the police, they could also affect residential amenity and so they were also matters for consideration by the planning authority."

Likewise, in our opinion, they are matters for the reporter to consider in the context of residential amenity, and to ignore them on the basis that they are dealt with under other legislation is in our opinion an error in law. As was pointed out by counsel for the appellants, in other fields of legislation consideration has to be given to activities which infringe the criminal law and it could not be said that because it is for the police to control these activities they can be ignored. Breach of the peace in licensed premises when considering the renewal of a licence is an example.

It was submitted by counsel for the respondent that although the reporter did not specifically state that he took the question of litter into consideration when looking at the issue of amenity, it was clear from the opening words of para 19 that he had done so because in reaching his conclusion he refers back to para 18 by saying "I have taken account of these and all the other matters raised in the representations".

We do not read these words as referring back to the matter of litter. In our opinion the reporter had already disposed of the matter of litter in para 18 and his reference back to these and all the other matters raised in the representations refers to matters other than litter.

For all these reasons, notwithstanding the valiant attempt by counsel for the first respondent to persuade us that the clear implication to be taken from the reporter's words was that he had taken the matter of litter into consideration when arriving at his conclusion, we are not prepared to accept that submission. Having failed to do so, when, as the reporter himself states, the principal issue in this case was whether the proposed use of the premises would result in a serious loss of amenity, such failure is in our opinion an error in law and accordingly his decision must be quashed.

That is sufficient to dispose of this appeal but it might be helpful if we were to give our views on the other grounds of appeal.

As regards the second ground of appeal we are satisfied that there was sufficient information before the reporter to justify him in deciding that it was not impossible to instal an effective filtration system at the premises and on that account we are satisfied that he was justified in attaching condition 3 to the grant of planning permission requiring the developer to come up with a scheme for dealing with cooking smells. The position might have been different if there had been any suggestion by the appellants that such a system could never be effective because in that situation the condition would have been unjustifiable, but that is not the situation here. All that the reporter has done, on the basis of the information which was before him, was to give the parties the opportunity of reaching agreement on an effective filtration system and we consider that he was entitled to do so on the basis of the representations before him. Accordingly there is no merit in this ground of appeal.

As regards the third ground of appeal the appellants' submission was that the reporter had asked himself the wrong question in respect that he had asked himself, as para 13 of his decision discloses, whether the change of use of the premises to a hot food retail shop would result in a serious loss of amenity.

Counsel's argument was that that was applying too high a test in the circumstances of this case. It was pointed out that these premises were, according to the policy of the district local plan, in an R1 residential area where activities would not be permitted unless the appellants could be satisfied that the use would cause no conflict with or any nuisance to the enjoyment of the existing residential amenity. In these circumstances it was clear that the test of loss of amenity was much lower than that adopted by the reporter.

In any event it was submitted by counsel for the appellants that the reporter had not attached sufficient weight to the difference between the proposed use of this unit as a hot food retail shop and the use of the other units which was restricted to class 1 of the Town and Country Planning (Use Classes) (Scotland) Order 1973 as amended, and argued that the proposed use would have a significant effect on the amenity of the area.

In our opinion, however, the answer to these submissions lies in the undisputed finding that, notwithstanding the fact that this is an R1 residential area and that there is a condition restricting the use of the units, this is an area of mixed commercial and residential use (cf reporter's finding at para 14 of his decision), and

accordingly, that the test of loss of amenity is a higher one than for a purely residential area. For that reason we do not consider that the reporter has applied too high a test and we are of the opinion that this third ground of appeal must also fail.

In view of the fact that the first ground of appeal is in our opinion a sound one we shall allow the appeal and quash the decision of the reporter dated 24 April 1990.

Counsel for Appellants, Boyd; Solicitors, Bennett & Robertson, WS — Counsel for First Respondent, Moynihan; Solicitor, R Brodie, Solicitor to the Secretary of State for Scotland — Counsel for Second Respondents, Kinroy; Solicitors, Bird Semple Fyfe Ireland, WS.

R F H

Salvesen's Trustees, Petitioners

FIRST DIVISION

THE LORD PRESIDENT (HOPE),
LORDS ALLANBRIDGE AND MAYFIELD

28 MAY 1992

Trust — Inter vivos deed of trust — Construction — "Children" — "Issue" — Deed taking effect in 1968 — Children adopted by means of overseas adoptions in 1989 and 1990 — Provisions permitting adopted children to succeed not extending to overseas adoptions in 1968 — Whether adopted children entitled to benefit under deed executed before making of adoption order — Succession (Scotland) Act 1964 (c 41), s 23.

Section 23 (1) of the Succession (Scotland) Act 1964 provides: "For all purposes relating to — (a) the succession to a deceased person (whether testate or intestate), and (b) the disposal of property by virtue of any inter vivos deed, an adopted person shall be treated as the child of the adopter and not of any other person." Section 23 (2) provides: "In any deed . . . executed after the making of an adoption order, unless the contrary intention appears, any reference . . . to the child or children of the adopter shall be construed as, or as including, a reference to the adopted person." Section 23 (5), as amended, gives "adoption order" "the same meaning as in section 38 of the Adoption (Scotland) Act 1978 (whether the order took effect before or after the commencement of this Act)"; by s 38 an adoption order includes an overseas adoption.

In 1947 a truster executed a deed of trust. In 1968 this was varied by interlocutor of the Court of Session pronounced under s 1 of the Trusts (Scotland) Act 1961. Under the new arrangement, the trustees under the deed were directed to pay income and capital from the trust funds to the beneficiaries who were described as the "children" and "issue" of the truster's son. The

A truster's son was married but had no natural children. He adopted two children by means of adoption orders in the USA in 1989 and 1990. These adoption orders were overeseas adoptions within the meaning of the Adoption (Scotland) Act 1978.

The trustees under the trust petitioned for directions as to whether these children were to be considered to be "children" for the purposes of the trust deed, and therefore entitled to benefit under the deed. The curator appointed to the truster's natural grandchildren argued, first, that s 23 (1) of the 1964 Act did

B not extend to overseas adoptions until the coming into force in 1973 of s 4 (2) and (3) of the Adoption Act 1968, and a definition of "children" which was not in force at the time the new arrangement was approved by the court could not apply to the arrangement; and secondly that even if "children" included children adopted overseas, there was an apparent conflict between s 23 (1) and s 23 (2) of the 1964 Act, s 23 (2) having the effect that by inference any reference to children in a deed executed before the making of an

C adoption order did not include adopted children.

Held, (1) that s 23 (5) of the 1964 Act, as amended, had to be read as extending the definition of adopted children to include children adopted by overseas adoptions, whenever the adoption took place (pp 1330L-1331A); (2) that s 23 (2) of the 1964 Act was included for a limited purpose only and had to be read as applying only to cases where a deed had been executed in the knowledge both of the provisions of the Act and

D of an adoption order, in which cases "children" included adopted children unless a contrary intention was expressed in the deed (p 1332D-F); (3) that s 23 (1) applied generally for all purposes relating to both testate and intestate succession and to the disposal of property by virtue of any inter vivos deed, including deeds executed prior to the making of an adoption order, so that in these circumstances the adopted children could be treated as children of the adopter for the purposes of the deed (p 1332B-D and F-G); and

E directions *given* accordingly.

Petition for directions

Trustees acting under an inter vivos deed of trust granted by Iver Ronald Stuart Salvesen presented a petition to the Inner House of the Court of Session under s 6 (vi) of the Court of Session Act 1988. They sought directions from the court as to whether children adopted by means of overseas adoptions after

F the date when the trust deed was executed were to be treated as children of the adopter for the purposes of construing references in the deed to "the beneficiaries", "children" and "issue". Answers were lodged on behalf of the curator to the truster's son's adopted children, and the curator to the natural grandchildren of the truster.

Statutory provisions

The Succession (Scotland) Act 1964, as amended, provides:

"23.—(1) For all purposes relating to — (a) the succession to a deceased person (whether testate or G intestate), and (b) the disposal of property by virtue of any inter vivos deed, an adopted person shall be treated as the child of the adopter and not as the child of any other person. . . .

"(2) In any deed whereby property is conveyed or under which a succession arises, being a deed executed after the making of an adoption order, unless the contrary intention appears, any reference (whether express or implied) — (a) to the child or children of the adopter shall be construed as, or as including, a refer- H ence to the adopted person; . . . Provided that for the purposes of this subsection a deed containing a provision taking effect on the death of any person shall be deemed to have been executed on the date of death of that person. . . .

"(4) Nothing in this section shall affect any deed executed, or the devolution of any property on, or in consequence of, the death of a person who dies, before the commencement of this Act. I

"(5) In this Part of this Act the expression 'adoption order' has the same meaning as in section 38 of the Adoption (Scotland) Act 1978 (whether the order took effect before or after the commencement of this Act); and 'adopted' means adopted in pursuance of an adoption order."

The Adoption (Scotland) Act 1978 provides:

"38.—(1) In this Part 'adoption order' means . . . (d) an overseas adoption within the meaning of section 65 J (2). . . .

"(2) The definition of an adoption order includes, where the context admits, an adoption order which took effect before the commencement of the Children Act 1975."

Cases referred to

Aikman, Petitioner, 1968 SLT 137.
Hay v Duthie's Trustees, 1956 SLT 345; 1956 SC 511.
Pollock-Morris, Petitioners, 1969 SLT (Notes) 60. K
Spencer's Trustees v Ruggles, 1982 SLT 165; 1981 SC 289.
Valentine's Settlement, Re [1965] 1 Ch 831; [1965] 2 WLR 1015; [1965] 2 All ER 226.

The petition was heard before the First Division on 15 May 1992.

On 28 May 1992 the court *answered* the questions posed in the *affirmative*. L

The following opinion of the court was delivered by the Lord President (Hope):

OPINION OF THE COURT.—This is an application presented under s 6 (vi) of the Court of Session Act 1988 by the trustees acting under an inter vivos deed of trust. They seek the directions of the court on certain questions which have arisen as to how the income and capital of the trust fund may be distributed.

The principal point at issue is whether children who were adopted after the date when the trust deed was executed are to be treated as children of the adopter for the purpose of construing references to "the beneficiaries" and to his "children" and "issue" wherever they appear. An additional complication arises because the two children who have been adopted by him were adopted by means of overseas adoptions. The question is whether effect can be given to these adoption orders, in view of the fact that it was not until after the date of execution of the trust deed that s 23 of the Succession (Scotland) Act 1964 was amended so as to apply to persons adopted in pursuance of an overseas adoption.

The petitioners are the trustees of a separately administered share, known as Alastair's issue's share, of funds held in trust under a deed of trust by the late Iver Ronald Stuart Salvesen dated 4 March 1947, as varied by interlocutor of the Court of Session dated 12 March 1968. That interlocutor, which was pronounced under s 1 (1) and (4) of the Trusts (Scotland) Act 1961, approved and authorised an arrangement for variation of the purposes of the original trust deed. Clause 3 (f) of the arrangement provided that on the operative date, following the effecting of certain policies of assurance, the whole purposes of the 1947 deed of trust were to come to an end and be determined, and that the trustees were thereafter to hold various shares of the trust fund, including Alastair's issue's share, for the trust purposes set out in a schedule to the arrangement. It is agreed that the effect of the arrangement was, in the words of Lord President Clyde in *Aikman, Petr* at p 141, fundamentally and almost completely to supersede the original trust provisions and in effect make a new settlement in terms of the schedule. The date of execution of that new settlement, for the purposes of s 23 of the 1964 Act, may be taken to be the date of the interlocutor of 12 March 1968 by which the arrangement was authorised and approved.

The original trust deed predated the Succession (Scotland) Act 1964, since it was executed on 4 March 1947. It took the form of a discretionary trust, and its purpose was to make provision for the children of the truster and their issue. There was no express inclusion of adopted children among the beneficiaries of the trust, and there is no doubt that prior to its variation on 12 March 1968 adopted children were not included among the persons to whom the income and capital of the trust fund might be distributed. In *Pollock-Morris, Petrs*, the court refused to give its approval to an arrangement which sought to introduce an express reference to adopted children as beneficiaries. The application was refused on the ground that to include beneficiaries who were not within the scope of the trust deed as it stood would prejudice the existing and future beneficiaries, with the result that the proposed arrangement was not one to which the court could give its approval. No such objection was taken in the present case. The 1968 arrangement did not contain an express reference to adopted children as being included among the beneficiaries, and no adoption

orders were in existence or in contemplation at that date. In any event it is clear that, since the effect of the arrangement was to supersede the original trust deed by the trust purposes set out in the schedule, it is as effective for this purpose as if it had been entered into by the agreement of all the beneficiaries, being of full age and subject to no other incapacity. The questions which have now arisen must be answered without regard to any prejudice which might arise to the beneficiaries of the original trust. The answer depends upon the proper construction of the schedule to the 1968 arrangement read together with the provisions of s 23 of the Succession (Scotland) Act 1964, as amended.

The relevant provisions of the schedule to the 1968 arrangement concern a share of the trust fund known as Alastair's issue's share. Alastair is the youngest son of the truster Iver Ronald Stuart Salvesen. He is married but has no natural children. He and his wife have two adopted children, Venetia Clare Joanna Salvesen, born on 13 January 1988 and adopted on 15 March 1990 by virtue of a decree of adoption pronounced by a competent court in the United States of America, and George Edward Thomas Salvesen, born on 28 September 1989 and adopted on 20 October 1989 by virtue of a decree pronounced in the same court. Both adoptions are overseas adoptions within the meaning of s 65 (2) of the Adoption (Scotland) Act 1978. They are adoption orders within the meaning of s 23 (5) of the Succession (Scotland) Act 1964, as amended by Sched 3, para 4 to the 1978 Act. This is because s 38 of the 1978 Act included an overseas adoption within the meaning of the expression "adoption order" in Pt IV of that Act. The order which applied these provisions to adoptions effected in the United States of America was the Adoption (Designation of Overseas Adoptions) Order 1973, made under the original provisions relating to overseas adoptions in s 4 (3) of the Adoption Act 1968, which were repealed and re-enacted by the 1978 Act.

In terms of para 4 of the schedule to the 1968 arrangement, read together with para 2 (a) of that schedule, the trustees are directed to pay the income of Alastair's issue's share to such one or more of "the beneficiaries" as they think fit. This provision was subject to a power to accumulate income during the period of 21 years from 12 March 1968, but that period is now at an end and the trustees are now bound to distribute the free income of the fund as it arises to or for the benefit of the beneficiaries. Paragraph 4, read together with para 2 (b) and (c) of the schedule, makes provision for the distribution of the capital of the fund. There is a power to make over capital to Alastair's "issue" at any time, and if on 1 January 2020 any part of Alastair's issue's share remains in their charge, the trustees are directed to hold it absolutely in fee for Alastair's "children" then in life and the issue of predeceasing children. Failing issue of Alastair then in life, the fund is to be held in fee for the grandchildren of the truster then in life and their issue per stirpes.

The effect of these provisions is that the competing interests in this application are those of the two

A adopted children on the one hand, whose contention is that they fall to be included among the beneficiaries as children of Alastair in terms of s 23 of the 1964 Act, and those of the natural children of the truster and their issue on the other hand, who would be entitled to the benefit of Alastair's issue's share in the event of there being no children or remoter issue of Alastair to whom the income and capital can be distributed. Minutes have been lodged on behalf of the curator ad litem to the two adopted children and on behalf of a separate curator ad litem who was appointed to the

B natural grandchildren of the truster who are presently in life. No other beneficiary has entered the process to advance any contention, but we have had the benefit of a full argument from counsel who appeared for the curator ad litem to the adopted children, and from counsel who appeared for the curator ad litem to the natural grandchildren, following an introductory submission by counsel on behalf of the trustees.

The principal difficulty which has arisen in this case relates to the meaning and effect of s 23 (1) when read

C together with s 23 (2) of the Succession (Scotland) Act 1964. But before we discuss this point we should deal with a subsidiary question which was raised by counsel for the curator to the natural grandchildren. This was whether, assuming that the effect of these provisions is that references to children and issue of Alastair in the schedule to the 1968 arrangement are to be taken to include children who were adopted by him by orders made after the date of the arrangement, that result can be applied to the only adoptions which

D have so far taken place in this case which were overseas adoptions made in 1989 and 1990. This issue has not been clearly focused in either of the questions appended to the petition, but since we heard argument on the point it is appropriate that we should express our opinion on it for the guidance of the trustees.

Counsel pointed out that s 23 of the 1964 Act as originally enacted did not extend to overseas adoptions. Its provisions did not have the effect of extend-

E ing to overseas adoptions until 1 February 1973 when s 4 (2) and (3) of the Adoption Act 1968 came into force. The Adoption (Designation of Overseas Adoptions) Order 1973 came into operation on the same date. Counsel submitted that, even it if could be said that the references to Alastair's children and issue in the schedule to the 1968 arrangement were to be construed as including any children adopted by him, that construction could not include any children adopted by means of overseas adoptions since, as matters stood

F in 1968, s 23 did not apply to them. The 1968 Act was enacted on 26 July 1968, after the date of the 1968 arrangement. Accordingly, irrespective of the date of the overseas adoptions or the date of the order by which adoptions effected under the law of that country were specified as overseas adoptions for the purposes of the 1968 Act, it could not have been the intention at the time of the 1968 arrangement that the provisions of s 23 were to apply to adoptions effected overseas. The answer to the question so far as the two overseas adoptions were concerned therefore was to be found in the common law as it stood at the date of the

1968 arrangement. We were referred to *Spencer's Trs*

G *v Ruggles*, where it was held, in regard to a declaration of trust which was executed in 1905, that the words "lawful child" were to be construed in the light of the law as it stood at the date of the creation of the trust, as at which there was no legal machinery for the adoption of a child in the law of Scotland. Lord Cameron pointed out at 1982 SLT, p 168 that, since there was at that time no statutory power of adoption, the truster was not and could not have been concerned with adopted children when setting up the trust. As at the date of the 1968 arrangement the courts of this

H country would only recognise an adoption made in another country if the adopting parents were domiciled there and the child was ordinarily resident there at the time of the adoption: *Re Valentine's Settlement* [1965] 1 Ch, per Lord Denning MR at p 843D. That was not the position in this case, since Alastair Salvesen was not domiciled in the United States of America at the time when the adoptions were effected. Counsel submitted that the common law was of no assistance to the adopted children in this case, and that the extension of s 23 of the 1964 Act to overseas adop-

I tions came too late to be of any relevance for the purposes of the 1968 arrangement.

In our opinion the answer to this point is to be found in the wording of s 23 (5) of the 1964 Act, as amended by para 4 of Sched 3 to the Adoption (Scotland) Act 1978. In consequence of the amendment effected by the 1978 Act that subsection now reads as follows: "In this Part of this Act the expression 'adoption order' has the same meaning as in section 38 of the Adoption (Scotland) Act 1978 (whether the order

J took effect before or after the commencement of this Act); and 'adopted' means adopted in pursuance of an adoption order."

Section 38 (1) (d) of the 1978 Act provides that an overseas adoption within the meaning of s 65 (2) of that Act is to be included within the meaning of the expression "adoption order", and s 38 (2) is in these terms: "The definition of adoption order includes, where the context admits, an adoption order which

K took effect before the commencement of the Children Act 1975."

The date of the effecting of the overseas adoption order is immaterial, since the expression "adoption order" as defined by s 23 (5) of the 1964 Act applies whether the order took effect before or after the commencement of the Act — that is, before or after the commencement of the Succession (Scotland) Act 1964. The provisions of the 1978 Act reflect those of s 4 (2)

L of the 1968 Act by which references to overseas adoptions were first introduced. In the result s 23 of the 1964 Act must be read as extending to overseas adoptions, whether they took effect before or after the commencement of the 1964 Act, as respects anything done or any event occurring after 1 February 1973 when s 4 of the Adoption Act 1968 came into force. As matters now stand, therefore, children who are the children of a person by virtue of an overseas adoption are to be treated in the same way for all the purposes of s 23 of the 1964 Act as children adopted by orders made in

A this country, and no relevant distinction now exists between them for any of the purposes described in this section. They are in exactly the same position so far as the disposal of property in terms of the schedule to the arrangement is concerned as any other adopted children within the meaning of s 23.

We turn now to the principal question on which our directions are sought. The difficulty has arisen due to the fact that the children were adopted after the date of the 1968 arrangement. This is not a point of impor-
B tance so far as the provisions of s 23 (1) of the 1964 Act are concerned, if they are read alone according to their terms. This subsection, so far as relevant, pro-vides: [his Lordship quoted the terms of s 23 (1) set out supra and continued:]

That subsection must be read subject to subs (4), which provides that nothing in that section is to affect any deed executed before the commencement of the Act. But that does not give rise to any difficulty in the present case, because the 1968 arrangement was approved after the commencement of the 1964 Act,
C which was passed on 10 June 1964 and by virtue of s 38 (3) came into operation on 10 September 1964. The significance of the date when the children were adopted is to be seen when one turns to s 23 (2) which, so far as relevant, is in these terms: [his Lordship quoted the terms of s 23 (2) set out supra and con-tinued:]

The 1968 arrangement was executed before the making of either of the adoption orders by which Alastair's adopted children were adopted. Accord-
D ingly, s 23 (2) cannot be invoked by either of them so as to enable the references to children or issue of Alastair in the schedule to the arrangement to be con-strued by virtue of this subsection as including his adopted children.

It is accepted on all hands that there would be no difficulty about the application of s 23 (1) in this case, if its provisions were to be considered alone and without reference to s 23 (2). The only express qualifi-
E cation of its effect is that to be found in s 23 (4), as a result of which it cannot affect any deed executed before 10 September 1964. As events happened in this case, however, it can be applied to the 1968 arrange-ment, and, since the expression "adopted" is now to be taken to include children whose adoption was effected by an overseas adoption whether before or after the commencement of the Act, Alastair's adopted children are, in terms of this subsection, entitled to be treated for all purposes relating to the disposal of
F property by virtue of the schedule to the 1968 arrange-ment as his children. On the other hand, for the reasons mentioned in the previous paragraph, s 23 (2) cannot be applied to the 1968 arrangement, since the arrangement was executed before the making of the adoption orders. The question then is how these two provisions can be reconciled. No words are to be found in either of them which assist as to their rela-tionship, but it must be assumed that it was the inten-tion that both subsections should receive effect. It would not do to place a construction on either of them which would deprive the other of all meaning or

render either of them entirely unnecessary to the scheme of the Act.   G

Counsel for the curator to the adopted children sub-mitted that s 23 (1) provided the complete answer to the problem, since the opening words of the subsec-tion declared that it applied "for all purposes" relating to the disposal of both income and capital under any inter vivos deed. He accepted that s 23 (2) did not sit easily with s 23 (1), but he contended that their rela-tionship was such that the generality of s 23 (1) remained unqualified. Section 23 (1) provided in
H general terms for the entitlement to benefit, whereas s 23 (2) was concerned with the construction of certain particular expressions which might otherwise give rise to difficulty. Subsection (2) was directed to the point decided in *Hay v Duthie's Trs* about the effect of s 15 (2) of the Adoption Act 1950. That subsection provided that the expressions "child", "children" and "issue" in relation to any person were not, unless the contrary intention appeared, to include a person or persons adopted by that person. For the reasons given by Lord President Clyde at 1956 SLT, p 351, it was
I held that it was not admissible to make reference to extrinsic evidence in order to ascertain the intention of the granter of the deed. Section 23 (2) was concerned to make it clear that the presumption was reversed in relation to expressions used in deeds executed after the making of an adoption order. Counsel for the curator to the adopted children accepted that this submission, which was not disputed by counsel for the curator to the natural grandchildren, did not of itself provide a complete answer to the question which had been
J raised about the relationship between the two subsec-tions. He submitted, however, that subs (2) had been included in the section purely to assist, if assistance was needed, in the particular case to which it referred. It was not needed where subs (1) clearly applied to the situation, as it did in the present case. It was enough for him, therefore, that the adopted children could take advantage of subs (1), especially as there was no express restriction or limitation of the provisions of that subsection to be found anywhere in subs (2).   K

Counsel for the curator to the natural grandchildren on the other hand pointed out that subs (2) applies to any deed whereby property is conveyed or under which a succession arises. While s 23 (1) contained a declaration of a general policy, s 23 (2) had to be read as restricting its effect by excluding from the statutory benefit all cases where the deed was prior in date to the making of the adoption order. The intention which underlay the section was to benefit children who had
L already been adopted at the date of the deed and whose existence might therefore reasonably be taken to have been in contemplation when the deed was executed. The opportunity was given in these cases to exclude the adopted child or children from benefit by express-ing clearly an intention to that effect. It was not the purpose of the section to extend the benefit of the deed to adopted children who were not in existence at that date and whose existence had not even been contem-plated. In essence here argument was that, while s 23 (1) was apparently unqualified in its terms, it had

A nevertheless to be read as being subject to s 23 (2) in all cases to which that subsection applied.

The point is in the end purely one of statutory construction. No assistance is to be gained by considering what was in contemplation at the date of the 1968 arrangement, since we are not concerned here with the meaning to be placed upon the words used in the schedule to the 1968 arrangement otherwise than in terms of the Act. The critical question is the relationship between s 23 (2) and s 23 (1). Although the legislation is not as clear on this point as one might have
B expected, we consider that s 23 (2) was included in the section for a limited purpose only, the extent of which is to be found in the wording of that subsection. Section 23 (1) is not qualified in its terms by any express provision elsewhere in the section, and our examination of the section as a whole does not suggest that any qualification to its generality is to be implied.

The section as a whole begins with a declaration in the most general terms in subs (1) that, for all the pur-
C poses to which that subsection refers, an adopted person is to be treated as the child of the adopter and not as the child of any other person. Subject only to the limits about its retrospective effect which subs (4) provides, there is no indication that it is in any way relevant to the effect of the declaration to consider whether the adoption order came before or after the date when the deed was executed. The declaration in this subsection applies generally for all purposes relating to both testate and intestate succession and to the
D disposal of property by virtue of any inter vivos deed. The wording of the subsection, together with the order in which it appears in the section, suggests that it was designed to express the general rule to which all other provisions in the section are to be seen as ancillary or subordinate.

Subsection (2) can, and in our opinion should, be read as dealing with a particular situation only, where a deed has been executed in knowledge both of the
E provisions of the Act and of the existence of an adoption order. It is qualified in the case of provisions with testamentary effect by the proviso that the date of execution is to be taken to be the date of the death of the person on whose death the provision is to take effect. The particular question with which it is designed to deal is whether it was the intention of the person when making the deed, or by leaving an earlier testamentary deed unaltered until his death, knowing of the provisions of the Act and of the existence of the
F adoption order, that references to a natural relationship were to be construed as including relationships arising from the adoption. The effect of the subsection, on a point which it must be assumed was thought to be liable otherwise to create difficulty, is that a contrary intention must be expressed in the deed in these circumstances if it is not to have that result. In our opinion, however, it has no other effect. In particular it cannot be read as restricting the application of subs (1) (a) to only those cases where the inter vivos deed has been executed after the making of an adoption order. There is nothing in the wording of either sub-

G section to indicate that it was the intention that this should be the result. We can think of no good reason why Parliament, having said all that was necessary in subs (4) to prevent the section from having retrospective effect, should have intended that subs (1) was to be further qualified. In our opinion it was intended to have effect, in accordance with its express provision, for all purposes after the commencement of the Act.

For all these reasons we shall give the directions which have been sought by the trustees by answering the two questions in the petition in the affirmative.

H

Counsel for Petitioners, A C Hamilton, QC, Tyre; Solicitors, Murray, Beith & Murray, WS — Counsel for Curator ad Litem to Adopted Children, Nimmo Smith, QC; Solicitors, Tods Murray, WS — Counsel for Curator ad Litem to Natural Grandchildren, Anne Smith; Solicitors, Murray, Beith & Murray, WS.

D A K

I

City of Glasgow District Council v Secretary of State for Scotland

SECOND DIVISION
THE LORD JUSTICE CLERK (ROSS),   J
LORDS ALLANBRIDGE AND WEIR
31 JULY 1992

Town and country planning — Planning permission — Appeal — Determination by reporter — Permission sought for extension to bank contrary to presumption in local plan — "Any other material considerations" — Relevance of private interests of developer — Relevance of previous refusal on appeal of permission for similar development in same area — Town and Country Planning (Scotland) Act 1972 (c 52), s 26 (1).

K

Town and country planning — Planning permission — Appeal — Determination by reporter — Listed building — Planning authority considering development would have prejudicial impact on amenity — Reporter considering dominant use non-residential and granting consent — Whether error by reporter.

Section 26 (1) of the Town and Country Planning (Scotland) Act 1972 provides that in dealing with an   L application for planning permission a planning authority "shall have regard to the provisions of the development plan, so far as material to the application, and to any other material considerations".

A planning authority appealed against decisions by a reporter appointed by the Secretary of State for Scotland to sustain appeals by a bank against the refusal of planning permission and listed building consent for the erection of a rear extension to a bank and frontage alterations at property in Byres Road, Glasgow. The

relevant local plan contained a presumption against
A such development. The authority argued that the
reporter had erred in taking into account circumstances
personal to the applicants, their desire to
provide better conditions for their staff and better
service to their customers, and had paid insufficient
attention to a previous decision by a reporter to refuse
permission to a building society for a similar development
in the same street. The granting of permission
in the present case would create a dangerous precedent.
With regard to the listed building consent, the
B planning authority argued that the reporter had failed
to give sufficient weight to the mix of residential and
commercial use in concluding that the development
would not adversely affect either the amenity of the
area or the character of the listed building.

Held, (1) that the expression "any other material
considerations" should not be construed narrowly,
and that if it was appropriate to have regard to the
private interests of objectors, then it had also to be
relevant to have regard to the private interests of the
C developer (p 1335D and G); (2) that the reporter was
accordingly fully justified in having regard to the fact
that the bank's proposals would permit better operational
efficiency, expanded services, a higher standard
of staff accommodation, and provide a modern bank to
serve the locality in deciding whether the presumption
against such development had been overcome
(p 1335J-K); (3) that the reporter was entitled to determine
that granting planning permission in this case
would not create a dangerous precedent and to conclude
that the circumstances were different from those
D of the 1985 application, which in any event was not to
be regarded as a binding precedent (pp 1335L-1336B);
(4) that having regard to the dominant characteristics
of the immediate area the reporter was fully justified
in concluding that the extension could not adversely
affect either the amenity of the area or the character
of the listed building (p 1336H-J); and appeal *refused.*

Observed, that the court was in no sense a court for
the purpose of reviewing planning decisions on their
E merits; and that as regards planning decisions, the
court could only interfere if the case fell within the
type of situation described by Lord President Emslie
in *Wordie Property Co Ltd v Secretary of State for
Scotland,* 1984 SLT 345 at pp 347-348 (p 1334D-F).

Appeal from the Secretary of State for Scotland
The City of Glasgow District Council appealed to
the Court of Session under s 233 of the Town and
F Country Planning (Scotland) Act 1972 against the
decision of a reporter appointed by the Secretary of
State for Scotland to allow appeals by the Bank of
Scotland against the refusal of planning permission
and listed building consent for the erection of a rear
extension to a bank and frontage alterations at 174
Byres Road, Glasgow, and to grant such permission
and consent.

Statutory provisions
The Town and Country Planning (Scotland) Act
1972, as amended, provides:

"26.—(1) Subject to the provisions of sections 23 to
25 of this Act, and to the following provisions of this G
Act, where an application is made to a planning
authority for planning permission, that authority, in
dealing with the application, shall have regard to the
provisions of the development plan, so far as material
to the application, and to any other material considerations,
and — (a) subject to sections 38, 39 . . . of this
Act, may grant planning permission, either unconditionally
or subject to such conditions as they think
fit; or (b) may refuse planning permission. . . .

"54.— . . . (3) In considering whether to grant plan- H
ning permission for development which affects a listed
building or its setting, and in considering whether to
grant listed building consent for any works, the planning
authority or the Secretary of State, as the case
may be, shall have special regard to the desirability of
preserving the building or its setting or any features of
special architectural or historic interest which it
possesses."

Cases referred to   I
Buxton v Minister of Housing and Local Government
[1961] 1 QB 278; [1960] 3 WLR 866; [1960] 3
All ER 408.
Stringer v Minister of Housing and Local Government
[1970] 1 WLR 1281; [1971] 1 All ER 65.
Westminster City Council v Great Portland Estates plc
[1985] AC 661; [1984] 3 WLR 1035; [1984] 3
All ER 744.
Wordie Property Co Ltd v Secretary of State for Scotland,
1984 SLT 345.   J

The appeal was heard before the Second Division on
18 June 1992.

On 31 July 1992 the court *refused* the appeal.

The following opinion of the court was delivered by
the Lord Justice Clerk (Ross):

OPINION OF THE COURT.—This is an appeal
by the City of Glasgow District Council against K
decisions by a reporter appointed by the Secretary of
State for Scotland to determine appeals by the Bank of
Scotland against the refusal of planning permission
and listed building consent by the appellants for the
erection of rear extension to a bank and frontage
alterations at 174 Byres Road, Glasgow, which
decisions were dated 29 July 1991 and communicated
to the appellants on 30 July 1991. The reporter
sustained the appeals by the Bank of Scotland and
granted planning permission and listed building L
consent for the erection and frontage alterations at 174
Byres Road, Glasgow. Against that decision of the
reporter the appellants have appealed under s 233 of
the Town and Country Planning (Scotland) Act 1972.

In opening the appeals for the appellants, counsel
drew attention to the terms of the decision letter and
in particular the conclusions in the letter. In para 40
the reporter stated that he concluded that the determining
issues in these appeals are whether the
proposal is contrary to the district council's policies

A for extensions into backcourt areas; and if it is, whether there are exceptional circumstances that justify these policies being set aside; and whether the amenity and character of the building is (sic) sufficiently adversely affected for listed building consent to be refused. Counsel submitted that in that passage the reporter had identified properly the issues which fell to be resolved, but he maintained that the reporter's decision was open to challenge. He maintained that the reporter had ignored certain issues, he had taken into account irrelevant matters and had disregarded

B relevant considerations and had thus arrived at an irrational decision.

Planning permission had been refused by the appellants because the proposal would be contrary to policy IC7 of the West End Local Plan which states a presumption against the expansion of industrial or commercial uses in backcourts. In para 41 of the decision letter the reporter stated inter alia: "I consider that the policy is relevant to the area, has contributed to the current amenity and is worthy of

C support in principle." Counsel submitted that the foregoing statement was a sound one but that the reporter had then gone off the rails because he had failed to put forward any proper basis for departing from that policy.

Counsel put forward his submissions with his customary persuasiveness, but we had the clear impression that the appellants' real desire was to have the reporter's decision reviewed on its merits, and that

D the appeal was being dressed up so as to make it appear that the complaint was that the decision was not within the powers of the Act of 1972. It is important to note that this court is in no sense a court for the purpose of reviewing planning decisions on their merits. As regards planning decisions this court may only interfere if the case falls within the type of situation described by Lord President Emslie in *Wordie Property Co Ltd v Secretary of State for Scotland* at pp 347-348: "A decision of the Secretary of State acting

E within his statutory remit is ultra vires if he has improperly exercised the discretion confided to him. In particular it will be ultra vires if it is based upon a material error of law going to the root of the question for determination. It will be ultra vires, too, if the Secretary of State has taken into account irrelevant considerations or has failed to take account of relevant and material considerations which ought to have been taken into account. Similarly it will fall to be quashed on that ground if, where it is one for which a factual basis is required, there is no proper basis in fact to

F support it. It will also fall to be quashed if it, or any condition imposed in relation to a grant of planning permission, is so unreasonable that no reasonable Secretary of State could have reached or imposed it."

This court must always recognise the limited scope of appeals against planning decisions, and must not entertain appeals which are truly outwith the limited jurisdiction which Parliament has conferred upon this court in relation to planning appeals.

No doubt with the dictum of Lord President Emslie

in mind, counsel for the appellants made a number of submissions to the effect that the reporter here had G taken into account irrelevant matters and had failed to take into account relevant considerations in arriving at his decision.

(1) His first submission was that the reporter had had regard to an irrelevant consideration, namely, that all that the Bank of Scotland was endeavouring to do was to provide more convenient conditions of work for its staff and possibly some better service to its customers. He stated that if planning permission were granted, the Bank of Scotland might be able to H compete more effectively with its competitors, but that that was not justification for a planning decision.

(2) Under reference to para 43 of the decision letter, counsel criticised the statement regarding the particular service which the Bank of Scotland provides in the area. He contended that the Bank of Scotland was not unique; there were other banks in the area who also served the needs of the community.

(3) Counsel maintained that the reporter had failed I to pay sufficient attention to one material consideration, namely, the previous planning decision in relation to 290 Byres Road, Glasgow. In that case in 1985 a different reporter had refused an appeal at the instance of a building society against the refusal of permission to erect a rear extension which would extend into the backcourt.

(4) He also submitted that granting planning permission in the present case would create a dangerous precedent. He recognised that the reporter had not J accepted that a dangerous precedent would be created for reasons which he gave in para 47 of his decision letter. His reasons appear to be that other developers did not perform the special role of banks, and that in most other situations other and appropriate expansion solutions could be found. Counsel maintained that there was not a scrap of evidence to support that view.

Counsel for the Secretary of State for Scotland contended that the reporter had committed no error of law. It was clear that in dealing with any application K for planning permission regard had to be had to the provisions of the development plan so far as material to the application "and to any other material considerations" (s 26 (1) of the Town and Country Planning (Scotland) Act 1972). Counsel for the Secretary of State maintained that the operational needs of banks were a relevant planning consideration. He submitted under reference to *Stringer v Minister of Housing and Local Government* that material considerations of a planning nature have a broad ambit. Under reference L to *Westminster City Council v Great Portland Estates plc*, he maintained that the private interests of a developer were material, and that it was also material to consider the wider community interest.

As regards the suggestion that the needs of the community could be served by other banks, counsel maintained that this had never been put in issue before the reporter, and there had been no evidence that other institutions could meet the community needs which the reporter had identified.

In relation to the criticisms of the reporter's reasons for concluding that granting planning permission in this case would not create a dangerous precedent, counsel for the Secretary of State maintained that having regard to the evidence before him the reporter was entitled to conclude that the present case was an exceptional one, and that planning permission might be granted without the risk of creating a dangerous precedent. He also maintained that the reporter was entitled to regard the present case as different to the case determined by another reporter in 1985. In any event, that other decision was in no sense binding upon him.

Counsel for the Bank of Scotland adopted the submissions made by counsel for the Secretary of State. He also maintained further that counsel for the appellants had confused personal circumstances with private interests. Whilst it might be that personal circumstances of an applicant will not be of much relevancy in the consideration of a planning application, he contended that private interests were a material consideration, and that the private interest of an applicant might lead into a public interest. He submitted that that was the situation here and the reporter had recognised that in para 43 when he described the particular role played by the bank in the area and then stated: "This role of the bank conforms with the thrust of the local plan and shopping policy in promoting the long-term viability of the area."

We are clearly of opinion that the arguments for the Secretary of State and the Bank of Scotland are to be preferred. We see no reason why the expression "any other material considerations" should be given a narrow construction. If a consideration is material, it is one to which the reporter was bound to have regard. We entirely agree with what was said by Cooke J in *Stringer v Minister of Housing* at p 1294: "It may be conceded at once that the material considerations to which the Minister is entitled and bound to have regard in deciding the appeal must be considerations of a planning nature. I find it impossible, however, to accept the view that such considerations are limited to matters relating to amenity. So far as I am aware, there is no authority for such a proposition, and it seems to me to be wrong in principle. In principle, it seems to me that any consideration which relates to the use and development of land is capable of being a planning consideration. Whether a particular consideration falling within that broad class is material in any given case will depend on the circumstances."

We also agree with Cooke J when he said at p 1295: "I find it equally difficult to accept that the local planning authority and the Minister on appeal must have regard only to the public interest as opposed to private interests. It is, of course, true, as Salmon J pointed out in the *Buxton* case [1961] 1 QB 278, that the scheme of the legislation is to restrict development for the benefit of the public at large. But it seems to me that it would be impossible for the Minister and local planning authorities to carry out their duties as custodians of the public interest if they were precluded from considering the effect of a proposed development on a particular use of land by a particular occupier in the neighbourhood. The public interest, as I see it, may require that the interests of individual occupiers should be considered."

If it is appropriate to have regard to the private interests of objectors, then in our opinion it must also be relevant to have regard to the private interests of the developer. The matter was put quite clearly by Lord Scarman in *Westminster City Council v Great Portland Estates* at p 670: "Personal circumstances of an occupier, personal hardship, the difficulties of businesses which are of value to the character of a community are not to be ignored in the administration of planning control. It would be inhuman pedantry to exclude from the control of our environment the human factor. The human factor is always present, of course, indirectly as the background to the consideration of the character of land use. It can, however, and sometimes should, be given direct effect as an exceptional or special circumstance. But such circumstances, when they arise, fall to be considered not as a general rule but as exceptions to a general rule to be met in special cases."

There is thus clear authority for the view that it is appropriate in a case of this kind for a reporter to have regard to the personal circumstances of the developer and the operational requirements of his business, when he is considering whether an exceptional case has been made out for departing from the policy of the plan which provides that there is a presumption against development of the type proposed. Accordingly we are quite satisfied that the reporter was fully justified in having regard to the fact that the Bank of Scotland's proposals would permit better operational efficiency, expanded services and a higher standard of staff accommodation, and provide a modern bank to serve the busy shopping street/university/private customers of the bank. It is quite true, as counsel for the appellants said, that the contention of the appellants before the reporter was that the crux of their case was that policy IC7 deserved support. However, that policy did not contain any absolute prohibition of development of the type proposed by the Bank of Scotland; it merely provided that there would be a presumption against the expansion of industrial or commercial uses in backcourts. Such a presumption is capable of being rebutted, and in our opinion the reporter on the material before him and for the reasons given by him was entitled to conclude that the presumption in this case was rebutted.

We are also satisfied that the reporter was entitled to determine that granting planning permission in this case would not create a dangerous precedent. The reporter considered that few, if any, other organisations perform the special role of banks, and that in most other situations other appropriate expansion solutions could be found. These appear to us to be sound reasons for his conclusion that a precedent would not be created by granting planning permission in this case. Similarly we are satisfied that the present case is different to the case decided by the other reporter in 1985. The decision letter relative to 290

A Byres Road, Glasgow, dated 26 November 1985 is relatively short. What is clear, however, is that in the case of 290 Byres Road, Glasgow, no special features were present. There do not appear to have been any special circumstances, and there was no suggestion that the building society would encounter operational difficulties if it required to move to other premises. There is nothing in that decision letter comparable to the evidence narrated in para 20 of the decision letter in the present case. We are accordingly satisfied that the present case can be distinguished from the B previous case in 1985 relative to 290 Byres Road, Glasgow. In any event, we agree with counsel for the Secretary of State and the Bank of Scotland that the earlier decision is not to be regarded as a binding precedent.

In all the circumstances we are satisfied that the attack upon the granting of planning permission by the reporter clearly fails. So far as listed building consent is concerned, counsel for the appellants maintained that the approach of the reporter had been C fundamentally flawed. In dealing with listed building consent, the reporter noted that the appellants were concerned principally with the impact upon the amenity of the backcourt area. In para 49 of the decision letter the reporter stated: "The rear of the appeal building appears to be unique in the locality in that the bank has secured the superiority of the backcourt and has been granted planning permission to create a two metre high walled garden area. To the rear, there are no residential properties on the D opposite side of the access lane and the character is created principally by the adjacent cinema, restaurant, and university buildings. This situation is unusual in the locality and indicates that the dominant use at the rear is not residential."

Counsel for the appellants was criticial of this approach, and maintained that the reporter had erred by concentrating on the situation on the opposite side of the access lane, and in disregarding the situation on the same side of the access lane as the appeal subjects. E We are not persuaded that this criticism is well founded. It appears to us from the decision letter that the reporter was well aware of the situation in the locality. In para 2 of the decision letter, after describing the appeal site, the reporter stated: "The surrounding area is characterized by similar tenemental properties with commercial uses on the ground floor and residential flats above. The nearby properties at the rear are a cinema, a restaurant and university buildings." In para 20 the reporter records: "The F adjoining frontages are in residential and shop use and are not available."

In the circumstances we are satisfied that the reporter was fully justified in taking into account that a two metre high walled garden was to be erected and that there were no residential properties on the opposite side of the access lane.

Counsel for the appellants also drew attention to the provisions of s 54 (3) of the Town and Country Planning (Scotland) Act 1972. He maintained that the

reporter had failed to take into account the setting in which the development was proposed to take place. G Counsel for the Bank of Scotland submitted that there had been no reference to s 54 either in the evidence led before the reporter or in the submissions made to him; at no point during the inquiry had it been suggested that listed building consent should be refused because of the setting in which the development was to take place. There is nothing in the decision letter to suggest that s 54 had been relied on by the appellants in this connection. As we understand it the appellants' submissions in relation to listed building consent were H that what was proposed would have a prejudicial impact upon the amenity of the backcourt area. For reasons which the reporter gives in his decision letter, his conclusion was that the extension would not adversely affect either the amenity of the area or the character of the listed building. He therefore could detect no reason why listed building consent should be withheld. In our opinion the reporter was fully justified in arriving at such a conclusion and we detect no error in his approach to this matter. We see no justifi- I cation for the contention that the reporter had in mind only non-residential building in the area and that he failed to take into account that there were other residential developments nearby. In para 49 he describes the character of the area as being "created principally by the adjacent cinema, restaurant and university buildings". Subsequently he refers to "the dominant use" at the rear as being non-residential. The use of the words "principally" and "dominant" show clearly that the reporter was aware that there J were uses in this area other than non-residential.

For the foregoing reasons we have concluded that counsel for the appellants has failed to establish any error in law on the part of the reporter. He has failed to establish any ground under s 233 of the Act of 1972 which would justify this court in concluding that the reporter's decision was not within the powers of the Act of 1972. It follows that this appeal must be refused.

——————————   K

Counsel for Appellants, Clarke, QC; Solicitors, Gray Muirhead, WS — Counsel for First Respondent, Doherty; Solicitor, R Brodie, Solicitor to the Secretary of State for Scotland — Counsel for Second Respondents (Applicants), Boyd; Solicitors, Brodies, WS.

P A A   L

Robertson v Thom

A HIGH COURT OF JUSTICIARY

THE LORD JUSTICE CLERK (ROSS),
LORDS SUTHERLAND AND WYLIE

23 SEPTEMBER 1992

*Justiciary — Procedure — Summary procedure — Delay
— Accused arrested on petition warrant but not brought
before court in course of first day after being taken into
custody — Accused served with summary complaint and
objecting to competency of proceedings — Whether failure*
B *vitiated subsequent proceedings — Criminal Procedure
(Scotland) Act 1975 (c 21), s 321 (3).*

Section 321 (3) of the Criminal Procedure (Scotland)
Act 1975 provides inter alia that a person apprehended
under a warrant under the section, or by virtue of
powers possessed at common law or conferred by
statute, shall wherever practicable be brought before a
court competent to deal with the case not later than in
the course of the first day after such person shall be
C taken into custody.

An accused person was charged on a summary complaint in the sheriff court at Wick. On 12 July 1991
the sheriff had granted a petition warrant for his
apprehension in relation to the alleged crime and he
was arrested in Glasgow on 24 October 1991. He was
transferred into custody of police officers of the
Northern Constabulary on 25 October 1991 and taken
to Caithness but he was not brought before the court
until 28 October when he was served with the
D summary complaint and trial was fixed. That trial did
not proceed as the Crown deserted the diet pro loco et
tempore and served the accused with a fresh summary
complaint. The accused objected to the competency of
the new proceedings on the ground that there had
occurred a breach of s 321 (3) of the 1975 Act which
vitiated all subsequent proceedings. The procurator
fiscal accepted that the accused could have been
brought before the court on 24 or 25 October 1991.
The sheriff repelled the objection but granted leave to
E appeal. Before the High Court the Crown accepted
that in cases initiated by petition the same considerations applied as under s 321 (3) and the Crown were
obliged to bring an accused person before the court in
the shortest possible period.

Held, that any irregularity because of the failure to
bring the accused before a court timeously did not in
any way vitiate the subsequent proceedings
(pp 1338L-1339A); and appeal *refused.*

F   *HM Advocate v Keith* (1875) 3 Couper 125, and
McVey v HM Advocate, 1911 2 SLT 119, *applied.*

Summary complaint

Alan John Robertson was charged at the instance of
Aileen Thom, procurator fiscal, Wick, on a summary
complaint. He objected to the competency of the
proceedings on the ground that there had been a
breach of s 321 (3) of the Criminal Procedure (Scotland) Act 1975. The sheriff repelled the objection.

The accused appealed with leave to the High Court
against the decision of the sheriff. The facts of the case G
appear from the opinion of the court.

Statutory provisions

The Criminal Procedure (Scotland) Act 1975 provides:

"321.— . . . (3) A person apprehended under any
such warrant as aforesaid [apprehension or search] or
by virtue of the powers possessed at common law, or
conferred by statute, shall wherever practicable be
brought before a court competent to deal with the case H
either by way of trial or by way of remit to another
court not later than in the course of the first day after
such person shall be taken into custody, such day not
being a Saturday, a Sunday or a court holiday
prescribed for that court under section 10 of the Bail
etc. (Scotland) Act 1980: Provided that nothing in this
subsection shall prevent such person being brought
before the court on a Saturday, a Sunday or such a
court holiday where the court is, in pursuance of the
said section 10, sitting on such day for the disposal of I
criminal business."

Cases referred to

Advocate (HM) v Keith (1875) 2 R (J) 27; (1875) 3
    Couper 125.
McVey v HM Advocate, 1911 2 SLT 119; 1911 SC (J)
    94; (1911) 6 Adam 503.

Textbook referred to

Renton and Brown, *Criminal Procedure* (5th ed), para J
    5-29.

Appeal

The appeal was heard before the High Court on 23
September 1992.

Eo die the court *refused* the appeal.

The following opinion of the court was delivered by
the Lord Justice Clerk (Ross):   K

OPINION OF THE COURT.—This is a note of
appeal at the instance of Alan John Robertson, the
appeal being brought under the provisions of s 34 of
the Criminal Procedure (Scotland) Act 1975. The
position is that the appellant was charged on a complaint in Wick sheriff court and objection was taken to
the competency of proceedings. The sheriff heard
parties on this objection and he repelled the objection.
The appellant has now appealed to this court. The
sheriff has provided a very full note dealing with the L
matters which were raised before him. It is unnecessary to go into the matter in very great detail. Suffice
it to say that it appears that on 12 July 1991 the court
granted a petition warrant for the arrest of the appellant and another in relation to the alleged crime. On
24 October 1991 the appellant was arrested in
Glasgow by officers of Strathclyde Police. He was
transferred into the charge of officers of the Northern
Constabulary at about 2 pm on Friday, 25 October.
He was taken to Caithness but was not brought to

court until Monday, 28 October. The explanation
given for the delay was a shortage of police manpower.
It was accepted by the procurator fiscal before the
sheriff that the appellant could have been brought
before a court in Glasgow on 24 or 25 October and it
was conceded that the provisions of s 321 (3) of the Act
of 1975 had been breached.

On 28 October the appellant appeared in Wick
sheriff court from custody, not on the original petition
but on a summary complaint. It is also explained by
the sheriff in his note that trial was fixed for 10
January 1992 but that on that date the cause did not
proceed to trial but the diet was deserted pro loco et
tempore. Subsequently the procurator fiscal raised a
fresh complaint against the appellant and that is the
complaint to which the present appeal relates.

Counsel for the appellant challenged the decision of
the sheriff. In the course of his note the sheriff summarises his conclusions and expresses the view that
the word "shall" in s 321 (3) of the Act of 1975 is
directory and not mandatory. Section 321 (3) provides
as follows: [his Lordship quoted the terms of s 321 (3)
and continued:]

Counsel for the appellant maintained that the sheriff
was in error when he concluded that the word "shall"
was directory and not mandatory and he maintained
that it was indeed mandatory. The Solicitor General
pointed out that strictly speaking we were not concerned in this case with any breach of s 321 (3) of the
Act of 1975 because, as we have already remarked, the
appellant was originally arrested on a petition warrant
and s 321 is of course dealing with summary procedure. However, the Solicitor General accepted that
at common law the same considerations apply and that
the Crown were obliged to bring a person before the
court in the shortest possible period. As we understood it, it was not for the purposes of this case being
disputed that there was a mandatory obligation upon
the Crown to bring a person before a court whether at
common law or under statute in the shortest possible
period, and it was not disputed that there had in this
case been a failure to fulfil that obligation. The submission of counsel for the appellant was that because
of that failure the subsequent proceedings were
vitiated. The sheriff had expressed a contrary view in
his note and had expressed the view that if there had
been an irregularity of this kind the remedy of the
appellant would be a civil claim for damages but that
the irregularity did not vitiate the subsequent proceedings. The Solicitor General supported such a proposition and drew attention first of all to Renton and
Brown's *Criminal Procedure* (5th ed), para 5-29. He
referred to a passage there which was dealing with
arrest but maintained that the same considerations
applied in the case of unlawful detention. It is there
stated inter alia: "The fact that a person was not
originally lawfully arrested does not of itself render his
ultimate trial invalid."

The Solicitor General also pointed out that there
was no provision in any statute suggesting that an
irregularity of this kind would vitiate proceedings

taken in respect of the charges upon which the person
had been arrested nor was there any common law rule
to that effect. He then referred us to a number of
authorities which supported the view for which he was
contending, namely that an irregularity of this kind
does not have an adverse effect upon subsequent
proceedings. He referred first of all to *HM Advocate
v Keith*. In that case Lord Ardmillan dealt with this
matter at (1875) 3 Couper, p 129. He said: "A very
important question is now raised upon the objection
taken in bar of trial, viz whether they can be
prosecuted upon the indictment now before the court,
which contains not only the charge upon which they
have been committed for trial, but in addition several
other charges, in regard to which it is urged no
declaration has been taken from them, and upon
which they have not been separately committed. Upon
that point I think it important to observe, that the
right of the prosecutor to apprehend, and to incar-
cerate, is quite distinct from the right of the Lord
Advocate to prosecute or to indict. Apprehension and
incarceration are steps in securing the custody of an
accused in order to trial. Commitment is a part, and
a most important part, of the procedure for custody."

On p 130 Lord Ardmillan proceeds: "But, on the
other hand, imprisonment for custody is not necessary
to sustain the public prosecutor's right of accusation."

Lord Ardmillan pointed out that accusation was
possible and not illegal without imprisonment. He
added: "But incarceration is not a privilege of the
accused, the absence of which shall shield him from
prosecution, and hush the voice of accusation."

The Solicitor General also referred to the full bench
decision of *McVey v HM Advocate*. At 1911 2 SLT,
p 121 the Lord Justice General said this: "For the
reasons given I should hesitate to say that the commitment was bad, but as this case was sent to a full bench
on the general question, and I have a clear opinion on
that question, I shall assume that this was a bad commitment. This assumption, however, leaves absolutely
untouched the proceedings on the indictment, for the
simple reason that a bad commitment can be no more
in law than a non-commitment, and does not invest
the wrongly-committed person with a charm or amulet
to protect him against all further proceedings."

A similar view was expressed by the Lord Justice
Clerk at p 121 where he said this: "But even assuming, as your Lordship has done, that the commitment
was bad, the further question arises whether such a
blunder can be any obstacle to the Lord Advocate in
serving an indictment and insisting in the prosecution.
I do not think that it can. If such a mistake has been
made, the prisoner has his right of redress against the
person who has made it, but that it should prevent the
Lord Advocate from doing his duty is a proposition to
which I cannot for a moment assent."

We agree with the Solicitor General that these
authorities support the proposition for which he was
contending, namely, that even if there was an irregularity in the present case because of the failure to bring
the appellant before a court timeously, nonetheless

A that did not in any way vitiate the subsequent proceedings. That is sufficient for the determination of this appeal, and for these reasons we are satisfied that the sheriff reached the correct conclusion in this matter and that he was well founded in repelling the objection to the competency of the proceedings. We shall accordingly refuse the appeal.

B *Counsel for Appellant, Douglas; Solicitors, More & Co — Counsel for Respondent, Solicitor General (Dawson, QC); Solicitor, J D Lowe, Crown Agent.*

P W F

Avintair Ltd v Ryder Airline Services Ltd

C

OUTER HOUSE

LORD SUTHERLAND

18 FEBRUARY 1993

Contract — Constitution — Provision of services — Whether agreement as to remuneration essential — Whether implied term possible while negotiations as to remuneration continuing.

D Aviation consultants sought declarator of the existence of a contract between them and an aircraft engineering company whereby the pursuers were entitled to remuneration on commission rates. There was a further conclusion for count, reckoning and payment. The remuneration sought related to the period during which negotiations about the level of commission payments had been continuing. The defenders argued that the pursuers' pleadings did not disclose the existence of a contract. There were no averments of agreement on price, nor of any agreement as to the method by which price could be calculated. The defenders argued that there had been specific negotiations as to the price but that those negotiations had never reached any conclusion; accordingly there had been no concluded contract and they were entitled to decline the pursuers' offer to provide services. The pursuers argued that price was only essential in a contract for sale and that in the present contract price was not an essential element because their work was equivalent to professional employment and there was an implied term that they would be entitled to reasonable remuneration. They contended that, even if the parties had failed to agree as to what constituted reasonable remuneration, they were entitled to rely on an implied term in the contract and to have the court establish what was reasonable remuneration.

Held (1) that since the parties had attempted to negotiate a rate of remuneration but had not agreed one, there was no consensus in idem on what was an essential term of the contract (p 1341E-G); (2) that there could be no implied term where the parties had been attempting to negotiate a contractual term (p 1341H-J); and action *dismissed.*

R & J Dempster Ltd v Motherwell Bridge & Engineering Co Ltd, 1964 SLT 353, and *Neilson v Stewart,* 1991 SLT 523, *distinguished.*

Action of declarator and count, reckoning and payment

Avintair Ltd raised an action against Ryder Airline Services Ltd seeking declarator of the existence of a contract with the defenders and concluding also for count, reckoning and payment.

The case called on procedure roll before the Lord Ordinary (Sutherland) on the defenders' plea to the relevancy of the pursuers' averments.

Cases referred to

Brett (A R) & Co Ltd v Bow's Emporium Ltd, 1928 SC (HL) 19.
Courtney & Fairbairn Ltd v Tolaini Brothers (Hotels) Ltd [1975] 1 WLR 297; [1975] 1 All ER 76.
Dempster (R & J) Ltd v Motherwell Bridge & Engineering Co Ltd, 1964 SLT 353; 1964 SC 308.
Kennedy v Glass (1890) 17 R 1085.
May and Butcher Ltd v The King [1934] 2 KB 17n.
Neilson v Stewart, 1991 SLT 523.
Walker Fraser & Steel v Fraser's Trustees, 1909 2 SLT 453; 1910 SC 222.

Textbooks referred to

Gloag, *Contract* (2nd ed), pp 192, 294.
McBryde, *Contract,* para 6-45.

On 18 February 1993 the Lord Ordinary *dismissed* the action.

LORD SUTHERLAND.—In this action the pursuers seek declarator of the existence of a contract between the parties whereby the pursuers acted for the defenders as aviation consultants in relation to the obtaining for the defenders of contracts for engine overhaul and similar work from Pakistan International Airways, and that the pursuers are entitled to reasonable remuneration for their work assessed at commission rates as set out in the first conclusion. The second conclusion is for count, reckoning and payment and the third conclusion is for payment of £200,000 or such other sum as may be found due as the true balance on said account. Although the third conclusion does not contain the words "failing an accounting" it is clear from the pursuers' third plea in law that this is how the conclusion should be interpreted. The case came on procedure roll on the defenders' motion that the action should be dismissed on the ground that the pursuers' pleadings do not disclose the existence of the contract as contended for, and in any event even if there was a contract between the parties there is no relevant basis averred for ascertainment of the price.

The pursuers aver that on or about 13 February 1990 one of their directors, Mr Husain, spoke to a manager of the defenders in order to discuss assistance that the pursuers could provide for the defenders in the obtaining of contracts with Pakistan International Airways. Thereafter there was contact between Mr Husain and Mr Allan, the marketing manager of the defenders. On 23 May 1990 Mr Husain and Mr Allan had a three hour meeting when the services offered by the pursuers were discussed and the pursuers made clear that payment for their services would be on a commission basis. They proposed certain rates of commission. Mr Allan confirmed that the pursuers were to act for the defenders but it was agreed that the rate of the commission would be a matter of further negotiation. Thereafter it is averred certain lobbying was done by the pursuers on the defenders' behalf and during this period the parties continued negotiations as to the rate of the remuneration to be paid. On 18 June 1990 Mr Allan proposed certain rates of payment which were substantially less than those which had been proposed by the pursuers. On 26 June 1990 the pursuers restated their proposals for commission which did not differ from the proposals originally made on 23 May. Eventually on 16 August 1990 the defenders purported to decline the pursuers' offer of working on their behalf.

Counsel for the defenders argued that the pursuers' pleadings do not disclose the existence of the contract contended for in the first conclusion and that in any event even if there was a contract in existence there was no relevant basis for ascertainment of the price. In either event the action must fail. In support of his first contention counsel argued that in the creation of any contract there must be agreement on the price and the nature of the services. The general principles were set out in the speech of Lord Jauncey in *Neilson v Stewart*. His Lordship there said that it is trite law that an agreement which leaves a part essential to its implementation to be determined by later negotiation does not constitute a concluded and enforceable contract. He referred to the speech of Viscount Dunedin in *May and Butcher Ltd v The King* [1934] 2 KB at p 21 where it was said: "This case arises upon a question of sale, but in my view the principles which we are applying are not confined to sale, but are the general principles of the law of contract. To be a good contract there must be a concluded bargain, and a concluded contract is one which settles everything that is necessary to be settled and leaves nothing to be settled by agreement between the parties. Of course it may leave something which still has to be determined, but then that determination must be a determination which does not depend upon the agreement between the parties. In the system of law in which I was brought up, that was expressed by one of those brocards of which perhaps we have been too fond, but which often expressed very neatly what is wanted: 'certum est quod certum reddi potest.' Therefore, you may very well agree that a certain part of the contract of sale, such as price, may be settled by someone else. As a matter of the general law of contract all the essentials have to be settled. What are the essentials

may vary according to the particular contract under consideration."

His Lordship also referred to a passage in the opinion of Lord Guthrie in *R & J Dempster Ltd v Motherwell Bridge & Engineering Co Ltd*, 1964 SLT at p 367 where it was said: "In the usual case, the price to be paid is one of the essential matters on which agreement is necessary before either party is bound. If they have not agreed upon the actual sum or on a method of deciding that sum, there is not the *consensus in idem* requisite before a contract can be completed. But if they agree that the question of price shall be deferred, and agree on the things to be done to meet the immediate needs of the situation, there is *consensus in idem,* and each can require the other to do what he has undertaken to do before the price is settled. In such circumstances, the matter of price is not 'vital to the arrangement between them'."

On the application of these principles to contracts for services, counsel referred to *Courtney & Fairbairn Ltd v Tolaini Brothers (Hotels) Ltd.* In that case the purported contract included the provision that the parties' quantity surveyors should negotiate fair and reasonable contract sums. It was held that there was no agreement on price or any method by which price could be calculated. It would have been all right if the calculation of the price had been left to third parties or to arbitration but not where it was left to the parties themselves or their representatives to agree. Accordingly counsel argued that in the present case there was nothing to suggest that the parties had agreed the price or had agreed to defer the calculation of the price to a later stage to be determined by anyone other than the parties themselves. While it was accepted that parties to a contract would be entitled to enter into contractual relations without mentioning the price at all and leaving the matter of price to be determined if necessary by the court at a later stage on the basis that the party providing services would be entitled to a reasonable remuneration, such being an implied term of the contract, the position was different where there were specific negotiations as to the price and these negotiations never reached any conclusion.

Counsel for the pursuers argued that while agreement as to price may be an essential in a contract of sale this was not necessarily so in other forms of contract. *Neilson* was a case in which it was held that the term for repayment of a loan was not an essential to the implementation of an agreement to sell shares. In *Dempster*, although the contract was for the sale of steel over a period of three years, the contract was still valid where it was provided "the prices to be mutually settled at a later and appropriate date". *Courtney & Fairbairn* could be distinguished on the basis that that case only involved an agreement to negotiate, and in any event in that case it was said that price in a building contract is of fundamental importance. In the present contract, price was not an essential element because in relation to the pursuers' type of work which was equivalent to professional employment there would be an implied term that they would be entitled to reasonable remuneration. Gloag on *Contract*, p 192

says that brokers and commission agents have a right
to payment without specific agreement. Examples of
this could be found in *Walker Fraser & Steel v Fraser's
Trs, Kennedy v Glass* and *Brett & Co v Bow's
Emporium*. In McBryde, *Contract*, para 6-45 it is said
that where there is a contract for services but no agreement on amount of remuneration the entitlement is to
payment quantum meruit. Therefore it was possible
for a contract for services to be entered into with an
implied term of reasonable remuneration, and the fact
that the parties endeavoured to negotiate for themselves unsuccessfully what that rate of remuneration
should be did not alter the position. If the parties
failed to agree as to what constituted reasonable
remuneration the pursuers were entitled to fall back
on the implied term in the contract and ask the court
to establish what was a reasonable remuneration.

In my opinion in this case the facts do not establish
that there was consensus in idem between the parties
and accordingly there was no concluded contract. It is
true that on 23 May 1990 the pursuers aver that Mr
Allan confirmed that the pursuers were to act for the
defenders and it is also averred that at later stages the
defenders were aware that the pursuers were making
efforts on their behalf and these efforts were actively
encouraged by the defenders. It is however equally
clear that the rate of commission which the pursuers
were to be paid was never a matter of agreement and
indeed the gulf between the parties was a fairly substantial one. The rates of commission proposed by the
pursuers were about 50 per cent above those proposed
by the defenders, and as the pursuers in their third
conclusion estimated the amount of commission due
to be in the region of £200,000, even on the basis of
the defenders' rates of commission it is obvious that a
fairly substantial sum was involved in the negotiations. I entirely accept that in a contract for services
it may not be necessary to discuss price at all and in
that situation there will be an implied term that the
provider of the services will be entitled to reasonable
remuneration. If necessary the amount of that
remuneration can be left to the court to adjust (see
Gloag, p 294). Had there been no discussion in the
present case between the parties about the rate of commission I would have been satisfied that the pursuers
averred enough to show that a concluded contract was
entered into which included a term that the pursuers
would be entitled to a reasonable rate of commission.
As it was, however, there was a dispute between the
parties from the very start as to what the rate of
remuneration would be and, as I have indicated, the
dispute was not about some trivial sum. It is quite
clear that there was no consensus in idem between the
parties on the matter of the rate of remuneration and
it is equally clear in my view that this was a matter of
considerable importance to the implementation of the
alleged contract. This is not a case such as *Neilson*
where the time for repayment of the loan was a collateral issue, nor is it a case like *R & J Dempster* where
parties specifically agreed that the fixing of the price
should be deferred until such time as the steel was
actually delivered during the course of the following

three years, it not being possible to fix the price at any
earlier date. The cases referred to by counsel for the
pursuers were cases in which there was no dispute that
the pursuers were entitled to remuneration and the
only questions were either whether the pursuers'
efforts had led to a sale or as to what constituted
reasonable remuneration in the circumstances. In the
present case the fixing of the rate of remuneration was
clearly a matter in the forefront of the parties' minds
and I regard it in the circumstances of this contract as
being an essential part of any contractual terms.

The pursuers' argument that they are entitled to fall
back on an implied term will, in my opinion, not do.
An implied term means precisely what it says, namely
that the parties are assumed to have included in their
contractual arrangements a term that the provider of
services would be entitled to reasonable remuneration.
The reason why that term is implied in the contract
is because the parties have not, in the course of their
entering into contractual agreements, negotiated any
different term. Where, however, the parties are
actively negotiating as to what constitutes a reasonable
rate of remuneration it cannot be said that they have
entered into a firm contract with an implied term that
the remuneration shall be left to be fixed perhaps by
the court at a later stage. If that had been the position
there would be no need for the proposals and counter
proposals which were in fact made during the whole
course of the negotiations in this case. On the whole
matter I am satisfied that the alleged contract never
got beyond the stage of negotiation on a vital matter,
that accordingly there was no consensus in idem
between the parties and that therefore the pursuers'
claim for declarator must fail.

[His Lordship then dealt with subsidiary arguments
in relation to specification, with which this report is
not concerned, and continued:]

As I have held that an essential term of the contract
was not agreed between the parties I shall sustain the
defenders' first plea in law and dismiss the action as
irrelevant.

---

*Counsel for Pursuers, Ellis; Solicitors, Bird Semple
Fyfe Ireland, WS — Counsel for Defenders, Sturrock;
Solicitors, Maclay Murray & Spens.*

I C W

[A reclaiming motion by the pursuers was due to be heard
on 14 December 1993.]

L, Petitioners (No 2)

A FIRST DIVISION

THE LORD PRESIDENT (HOPE),
LORDS ALLANBRIDGE AND MAYFIELD

15 JULY 1993

Children and young persons — Children's hearing —
Application to sheriff for finding whether or not grounds
for referral established — Sheriff finding grounds for
referral established — New evidence only becoming avail-
B *able after sheriff's findings — Application to nobile*
officium for order remitting case back to sheriff to rehear
evidence in case including new evidence — Relevancy —
Appropriate standard for assessing whether fresh evidence
ought to be heard — Social Work (Scotland) Act 1968
(c 49), Pt III.

Eight children from three families were made the
subjects of place of safety orders under Pt III of the
Social Work (Scotland) Act 1968. The orders were on
the grounds that the children had been sexually
C abused or were members of the same household as
children who had been sexually abused. The reporter
then referred the children to the children's panel. The
parents of five of the children did not accept the
grounds for referral and the matter was referred to the
sheriff for a finding as to whether the grounds for
referral in each case were established. The cases were
conjoined and the sheriff heard 11 days of evidence.
The sheriff found the grounds for referral established
in each case and remitted the cases to the children's
D panel, which decided that all eight children were in
need of compulsory care.

The parents then brought an application to the
nobile officium of the Court of Session averring that
since the hearing before the sheriff they had obtained
additional expert evidence which was not available
and could not reasonably have been made available at
the hearing, and that the additional evidence cast
doubt on the sheriff's findings. They also averred that
E since the sheriff decided the cases the findings of the
Orkney inquiry had been published, and that following publication of that report there was a greater
understanding of the importance of a number of
features which were present in the cases of the eight
children, and this understanding would allow the
sheriff to look afresh at the evidence in a more critical
way. They sought an order that the sheriff should
rehear the evidence relating to the children. The order
was opposed by the reporter. After a hearing the court
F held that the application was competent. At a continued hearing the petitioners argued that, despite
their averments, it was not necessary for them to
satisfy the court that the additional evidence was not
available and could not reasonably have been made
available at the hearing, and that that test only applied
in criminal cases. The reporter argued that the law
had adopted a consistent approach in relation to the
hearing of new evidence, namely, that fresh evidence
was incompetent unless the evidence was not available, or could not reasonably have been made
available, at the time of the hearing, and that it was

inappropriate for that approach to be departed from in
this case.   G

Held, (1) that although the normal rule in civil and
criminal cases was that a party seeking to rely on fresh
evidence had to show that he was not aware of it and
could not with the exercise of reasonable diligence
have been aware of it when evidence in the case was
being heard, in a case of this type, which was sui
generis, it was not necessary that all the fresh evidence
should satisfy this test, but such evidence had to
achieve a high standard of materiality and significance
before it would be appropriate for it to be allowed (pp H
1344K-1345C); (2) that in assessing the materiality
and significance of the fresh evidence it was necessary
for the court to consider whether the sheriff might
have reached a different view on parts or on the whole
of the evidence, and in this case it appeared that the
sheriff did not have all the information before him to
enable him to arrive at a sound decision in the
children's best interests (pp 1345E-F and 1348A-B);
and case *directed* to be reheard before a different
sheriff, with a direction that the sheriff report the case I
to the court before issuing any interlocutor after the
proof.

Petition to the nobile officium
(Reported 1993 SLT 1310)

JL and others, the parents of eight children who had
been committed to compulsory care, brought an
application to the nobile officium of the Court of J
Session seeking an order that the evidence relating to
the grounds for referral of the children to the
children's hearing should be reheard by the sheriff.
Frederick J Kennedy, reporter to the children's panel
for Strathclyde Region, was called as respondent and
took pleas to the competency and relevancy of the
petition.

Cases referred to
Campbell v Campbell (1865) 3 M 501.   K
F v Kennedy (No 1), 1993 SLT 1277.
F v Kennedy (No 2), 1993 SLT 1284.
McCarroll v McKinstery, 1925 SLT 641; 1926 SC
  (HL) 1.
Miller v Mac Fisheries Ltd, 1922 SLT 94; 1922 SC
  157.
Moorov v HM Advocate, 1930 SLT 596; 1930 JC 68.
Rochdale Borough Council v A [1991] 2 FLR 192.
Ross v Ross, 1928 SLT 357; 1928 SC 600.
                                                            L

Textbook referred to
Grant, *New Trials*, p 131.

The petition was heard before the First Division on
9 June 1993 when the respondent's plea to competency was debated.

On 18 June 1993 the court *repelled* the plea to competency and *continued* the case for further submissions. (Reported 1993 SLT 1310.)

The petition was further heard before the First Division on 5, 6, 7 and 8 July 1993.

On 15 July 1993 the court *granted* the petition and *directed* in the exercise of the nobile officium that the case should be reheard.

The following opinion of the court was delivered by the Lord President (Hope):

OPINION OF THE COURT.—The first opinion which we issued in this case was concerned only with the competency of the application to the nobile officium. We have now to deal with the question whether the petitioners' averments are sufficient to justify an exercise of the nobile officium, on which we heard detailed argument from counsel for the petitioners and counsel for the reporter at the continued hearing of this application on the summar roll.

We should make it clear at the outset of what we have to say about this part of the case that we have not heard the evidence of any witnesses. So it is neither practicable nor appropriate for us to form any judgment of our own as to the facts. We have to deal with the case on the basis of what both parties have stated in their pleadings and on our reading of the various documents which have been shown to us. It is not the practice of the court in the exercise of its nobile officium to hear oral evidence from witnesses in order to resolve questions of fact which are disputed. Neither party suggested that we should attempt to do so in this case. Accordingly our task has been to identify and resolve the issues of principle which are raised by this application, and to assess the materiality and significance of the points made by the petitioners in support of their contention that the evidence relating to the grounds of referral in the cases of all these children should now be reheard, assuming that in due course they will be able to substantiate them by evidence.

The nature of the jurisdiction which we are able to exercise in these circumstances affects both the standard which we must apply when carrying out this assessment, and the extent to which it is appropriate for us to comment in detail on the various matters which we have to take into account. As to the first point, the nobile officium may only be exercised where the circumstances are exceptional or unforeseen. This makes it necessary for the petitioners to achieve a high standard of materiality and significance as regards the additional evidence before we can be satisfied that it would be appropriate for the evidence in these cases to be reheard. On the other hand, we do not wish to say anything, in setting out our reasons for deciding that the standard has been satisfied in this case, which might be taken as suggesting that we have formed any view of our own about the quality of the evidence or its effect. These matters will be for the sheriff to decide on the evidence which he hears as to whether the grounds for the referral have been established, and it is important that he should not be diverted from this task by any comments which we may have made about the facts in this opinion.

The first issue of principle with which we must deal relates to the petitioners' averment in stat 11 of the petition that, since the hearing before the sheriff, they have obtained additional evidence which was not available and could not reasonably have been made available then. The hearing before the sheriff began on Friday, 20 July 1990 and it extended over 12 further days. His interlocutors finding the grounds of referral established were pronounced on 16 August 1990. The proposition in this averment relates expressly to the additional expert evidence obtained by the petitioners after that date which is summarised in stats 12 to 15 in the petition. This consists of reports which challenge the validity of the medical and dental evidence, expert evidence on the interviewing techniques which were adopted by the social workers and reports by a clinical psychologist and a consultant psychiatrist. The same point is implicit in the remaining averments which, according to the summary in stat 17, are to the effect that since the proof doubt has been cast upon the admissibility, credibility and reliability of the witnesses whose evidence was accepted by the sheriff. Detailed reference is made in this regard to the Orkney inquiry report, following which it is said there is now a greater understanding of the importance of a number of features which were present in the cases relating to the children of the petitioners.

These averments all seem to imply an acceptance of the test which is relevant to the question whether there has been a miscarriage of justice in a criminal trial, on the basis of the existence and significance of additional evidence. Sections 228 (2) and 442 (2) of the Criminal Procedure (Scotland) Act 1975, as amended by the Criminal Justice (Scotland) Act 1980, enable the High Court of Justiciary, in both solemn and summary cases, to consider additional evidence if it was not heard at the trial and could not reasonably have been made available at the trial. The exacting standard which has been laid down by these provisions has been emphasised in a number of recent decisions in the High Court, and it would not seem unreasonable to regard the present case as appropriate for the exercise of the nobile officium if that standard can be achieved. But counsel for the petitioners submitted that it was not necessary for him to satisfy us that the additional evidence on which the petitioners now seek to rely was not available and could not reasonably have been made available to the sheriff in July or August 1990. He recognised that he could not satisfy this test in respect of all the additional expert evidence, and he also accepted that much of the comment in the Orkney inquiry report on which he relies could be traced back to the Cleveland inquiry report of 1988. He went so far as to submit that it would be wrong to apply the same test as was appropriate in a criminal case to a case involving children. He reminded us that cases under Pt III of the Social Work (Scotland) Act 1968 are conducted under a procedure which is unique to these cases, and that the provisions of this Part of the Act are concerned essentially with the welfare of children. He submitted that, if a mistake had been made at the proof, it should be open to be corrected

A without regard to the question whether evidence was available or could reasonably have been made available at the time to avoid that mistake.

Counsel for the respondent invited us to reject this argument and to apply the criterion which the petitioners had set for themselves in their own pleadings. He submitted that the law had adopted a consistent approach, in a variety of circumstances, to the question of reopening a case on the ground of fresh evidence and that it was inappropriate for that approach to be departed from in this case. He suggested that

B counsel for the petitioners' argument had assumed that the interests of children pointed only in one direction, namely towards the rehearing of the evidence. He pointed out that there were important considerations to the contrary, since any rehearing of the case at this stage would be bound to involve the risk of the loss of evidence due to the passage of time. It should not be assumed that it was in the best interests of the children for the case to be reheard, especially as the sheriff had been satisfied in 1990 that the grounds for

C the referrals had been established. There were very real and delicate problems in balancing the best interests of the children, and there was a substantial doubt as to whether a rehearing more than three years later was a better way of getting at the facts. It was a legitimate approach to ask, since the petitioners were seeking to rely on additional evidence, whether that evidence was available or at least could with reasonable diligence have been made available in 1990. Even if it could not always be satisfied, this was nevertheless

D a useful and appropriate yardstick which we should apply. If the conclusion was that the evidence was available or that it could with reasonable diligence have been made available, the case could not be said to be so extraordinary or unforeseen as to justify the exercise of the nobile officium. He urged us at least to take the view that the material would require to be scrutinised very carefully before the exercise of the nobile officium could be held to be appropriate.

E There is certainly a good deal of authority for the view that a party who seeks to rely on what may conveniently be referred to as fresh evidence must show that he was not aware of it and could not with the exercise of reasonable diligence have been aware of it when evidence in the case was being heard. The principle of res noviter veniens ad notitiam has been applied consistently to this effect, both in motions for a new trial under what is now s 29 (1) (e) of the Court of Session Act 1988 in regard to civil jury trials, and more gener-

F ally in any case where a decree which has been pronounced in a civil cause is sought to be reduced on this ground. In *Campbell v Campbell* (1865) 3 M at p 504, Lord President McNeill said that nothing could be res noviter that was within the power of the party to discover with ordinary care. In *Miller v Mac Fisheries*, 1922 SLT at p 96, Lord President Clyde quoted the following passage from Grant on *New Trials*, published shortly after the Jury Trials (Scotland) Act 1815 was passed: "Where evidence has newly come to the knowledge of the party, where there is, as it is termed in the law of Scotland, *res noviter veniens ad notitiam*,

G with which he neither was nor ought, in reasonable diligence, to have been acquainted at the time of the trial, but which is material to the justice of the case, then undoubtedly justice requires that a new trial should be granted."

In *McCarroll v McKinstery*, 1925 SLT at p 643, Lord Sumner said: "There is abundant authority for saying that, where the pursuer relies on *res noviter*, he must not merely aver that something material has newly come to his knowledge, but he must aver it with such circumstantiality as will shew that he could not

H by the exercise of reasonable diligence have known of it in time to have made use of it in the original action."

In *Ross v Ross*, in which the issue was raised in a motion for an amendment and further proof when the case came before the Division on a reclaiming motion from the Lord Ordinary, at 1928 SLT p 358, Lord President Clyde said: "The ascertainment of the truth and the interests of justice must always go hand in hand; and so long as it appears, as it does from the proposed minute of amendment, that the pursuer could

I not reasonably have been expected to discover the matters to which the minute relates before the conclusion of the proof on the merits, I find it very difficult to hold that our duty is to exclude evidence which may throw . . . light, and possibly important light, upon the true significance of the earlier facts alleged on record as grounds of divorce."

The test which applies in criminal cases, in terms of ss 228 (2) and 442 (2) of the Criminal Procedure (Scotland) Act 1975, namely that the evidence was not

J heard at the trial and could not reasonably have been made available at the trial, is consistent with this approach. The justification for it lies in the principle that there must be finality in litigation, and there is no doubt that it would be inconsistent with that principle for a case to be opened up for a fresh hearing on the same evidence or on evidence which was known and available but which the party chose not to lead. The additional requirement that the evidence could not reasonably have been made available, or could not

K have been discovered with the exercise of reasonable diligence, is a valuable safeguard against resort being made too easily to this remedy, especially where carelessness or inefficiency was the reason for not leading what is now said to be fresh evidence.

In our opinion, however, it is questionable whether a strict adherence to the requirement of reasonable diligence is appropriate in this case. The uniformity of approach which counsel for the respondent found in

L the authorities is explained by the fact that they are all concerned with the application of the principle of res noviter or with the statutory rules of the 1975 Act. There is no statutory rule in the present case, since the 1968 Act makes no provision for appeals on the ground of fresh evidence. Nor is this a case where there can be said to be a complete analogy with the adversarial system under which civil litigation is conducted or which applies in a criminal trial. There is now ample authority for the view that proceedings under s 42 of the 1968 Act are sui generis and are not in a proper sense to be seen as an adversarial litigation. The children were not said to have committed any offence, and while each of the three families was represented at the proof the children themselves have never been separately represented. The court must be especially vigilant in these circumstances to see that the children, whose care and welfare lies at the heart of the case, are not prejudiced one way or the other by the application of strict rules drawn from a different context.

For these reasons we do not consider it necessary, despite the petitioners' pleading on this point, that all the fresh evidence on which they seek to rely in this case should satisfy the test that it could not have been made available at the proof with the exercise of reasonable diligence. On the other hand we consider it entirely appropriate, for the reasons advanced by counsel for the respondent in his careful address on this point, that we should have regard to this test and that we should also look at the evidence with very great care before reaching our decision in this case. We consider that this is consistent with the principle that the nobile officium may only be exercised in exceptional and unforeseen circumstances, and what we have already said about the necessity for the petitioners to achieve a high standard of materiality and significance in regard to the additional evidence.

We turn now to the various chapters of additional evidence on which the petitioners rely. This consists of the various reports and other documents to which they make reference in their averments. The task which we have set ourselves, in evaluating this material, is to place this additional material into the context of the case as summarised by the sheriff in the note which he attached to his interlocutors dated 16 August 1990. As we mentioned in our previous opinion in this case, the sheriff's decision was appealed against by the fifth petitioner. The court held that the sheriff was entitled to hold that the grounds of referral were established in the case of his three children: see *F v Kennedy (No 1)* and *F v Kennedy (No 2)*. The Lord Justice Clerk pointed out in the latter case, at p 1289F, that credibility and reliability were matters for the sheriff and that it was for him to consider the weight of the evidence and to ask himself whether the grounds for referral had been established. It is necessary for us in the present case however, when assessing the materiality and significance of the additional evidence, to consider whether it is apparent from the sheriff's reasoning that he might have reached a different view on parts and indeed the whole of the evidence, had he had before him the additional evidence on which the petitioners now seek to rely.

The first chapter is the medical evidence. The sheriff's findings were based on evidence given at the proof by Dr W D S McLay, chief medical officer, Strathclyde Police, and Dr A M Sutton, consultant paediatrician, Greater Glasgow Health Board. Mr Jackson said that the reports which had been obtained by the petitioners in 1992 from Dr David M Paul, now deceased, and from Dr Raine Roberts cast a real

doubt on these findings. He accepted that the reports by Dr Paul and Dr Roberts were confined to a critical analysis of the written medical reports by Dr McLay and Dr Sutton which were lodged at the proof. He also accepted that this was material which might have been made available at that stage, since there was time between the lodging of these reports and the end of the proof for them to be referred to other doctors for their analysis. But he submitted that account should be taken of the speed at which matters had then to be dealt with, and of the fact that there had been a development of experience over the years since the Cleveland inquiry in 1988. Counsel for the respondent said that no adequate explanation had been given for not taking these matters up with Dr McLay and Dr Sutton at the proof. It was in any event a paper critique which contained very little if any new evidence, and it was unlikely to have made any significant difference to the sheriff's approach.

In our opinion, however, there are a number of reasons for regarding the points made in the 1992 reports as relevant and for treating the critique which they contain as material and significant. The sheriff says in two places in his note that he relied on the medical evidence. At p 8 he says that the evidence of the four children, taken under the application of the *Moorov* doctrine and coupled with the medical evidence, would have satisfied him beyond reasonable doubt, had it been necessary for him to apply this high standard and not that of the balance of probabilities, that the grounds of referral were established. At p 42, after summarising the direct evidence given by these four children, he says that it was corroborated by the medical evidence and refers to the evidence of the two doctors about penetration relating to I and M. But there was no medical evidence to corroborate the boys' evidence about the acts to which they said they had been subjected, and the question whether the medical evidence relating to I and M corroborated their account required a clear and precise understanding of the nature and extent of the findings in these reports. The significance of the critique lies in the greater understanding of the subject which it reveals as compared with the relatively brief details set out in the reports by Dr McLay and Dr Sutton. There is also some new material here, because Dr Roberts relies upon material first published in September 1990 about genital findings in the case of a number of North American girls not thought to have been sexually abused and on a report by a working party of the Royal College of Physicians in April 1991 about physical signs of sexual abuse in children to which Dr Paul gave evidence. It is not for us to attempt to draw any conclusions about the effect of the critique on the evidence given by Dr McLay and Dr Sutton, and we do not accept counsel for the petitioners' submission that the additional medical evidence is sufficient on its own to show that a reconsideration of the grounds of referral is required in this case. But we are satisfied that this is material and significant evidence and that sufficient reasons exist for regarding it as appropriate for us to take it into account.

Then there is the dental evidence relating to an incident when the child D is said to have had his mouth prised open by his aunt who, with the aid of scissors, then removed part of the enamel from the crown of each of the child's second back molar teeth on the upper jaw. The sheriff regarded this as by far the most sinister aspect of the case, suggesting elements of sadism, ritualism and torture. At p 37 of his note he said that he found this part of the case so distressing and terrible that it was almost too extraordinary to believe. But he found adequate corroboration in the medical evidence given by Dr James Reid, a senior lecturer in the Children's Dental Hospital in Glasgow. There was a conflict of opinion on this point, because the families led the evidence of another dentist named Dr Iain Love who attributed the removal of the enamel to natural causes assisted by decay. The sheriff gave reasons at pp 39-40 for preferring Dr Reid's evidence to that of Dr Love, among which were his own view that baby teeth do not normally decay at a uniform rate and that it was unlikely that two baby teeth would lose their caps naturally round about the same time. The petitioners have now obtained a report from a third dentist named Dr G T Craig as well as additional statements from Dr Reid and Dr Love. Counsel for the petitioners accepted that this could not be said to be new or additional evidence, as the petitioners had led evidence on the same matter at the proof through Dr Love. Counsel for the respondent said that all there was here was an additional expert witness who appeared to support a view already given to the sheriff, and that in any event Dr Craig's report was so qualified as to be speculative. In our opinion Dr Craig's evidence on its own would clearly not justify a rehearing of the case, but we do not think that it can be left entirely out of account for two reasons. At the end of his report he states that it is well known that dental decay often affects baby teeth bilaterally and symmetrically, with the same teeth on opposing sides of the upper or lower jaw showing the same extent of decay. This suggests that the sheriff may have misdirected himself on this point, as to which he does not appear to have heard evidence. And it was important, in view of what he himself describes as the extraordinary nature of the evidence, that there should be a sound basis for reconciling the conflicting views of the two witnesses who gave evidence at the proof.

The next chapter consists of reports by Valerie P Mellor, a consultant clinical psychologist, and by Christine Puckering, a lecturer in clinical psychology, on the interviewing techniques adopted by the social workers while interviewing the children. This is a highly sensitive subject, which is closely related to two other matters which are relied on by the petitioners. One is the view formed by the sheriff in another case that the evidence of two of the social workers, who conducted interviews in the present case and also gave evidence, was not credible and reliable. The other is the Orkney inquiry report, from which the petitioners quote several extracts in order to demonstrate that the social workers were inadequately trained and that they approached the interviews with closed minds. They aver that the social workers and the police constable who was also involved in the case did not have the appropriate attitude, degree of training and expertise to recommend acceptance of their interpretations of what they claimed the children said to them. The details of these matters are set out fully and clearly in the petitioners' averments and we do not need to repeat them.

Counsel for the respondent urged us to disregard all this material. He pointed out that the sheriff heard evidence from a child psychologist named Dr James Furnell, who had viewed the videotaped interview of the child M and interviewed the child himself in the presence of a social worker. The sheriff was also referred to the Cleveland inquiry report in the course of the submissions which were made to him at the end of the proof. He heard detailed argument about the interviewing techniques which were used in this case. Accordingly these could not be said to be new points, since they were already available and were developed in the course of their arguments at the proof by the families. Furthermore the techniques described in the Cleveland inquiry report were already well known by the date when the proof took place. What the pursuers were seeking to do was to make the point more forcefully, but there was nothing sufficiently new in the reports which were now available to justify sending the matter back to the sheriff for reconsideration. He accepted that what might appear from these reports to be substantial criticisms had been seen by the sheriff as relatively minor ones. At p 56 the sheriff said that the most that could be said of Dr Furnell's evidence was that the social workers were perhaps rather over zealous in their anxieties to protect the interests of the children, and that their lack of experience in the rapidly expanding fields of research in child sexual abuse had simply left them somewhat out of their depth. But counsel for the respondent pointed out that this was a matter for the sheriff to consider, and he referred to the Lord Justice Clerk's opinion in F v Kennedy (No 2) at p 1289F, where he said that, when criticisms are made of the way in which children have been interviewed, that is something which the sheriff requires to take into account but that the mere fact that the guidelines of the Cleveland report have not been followed does not mean that the sheriff is not entitled to accept the evidence of children as reliable. He resisted counsel for the petitioners' suggestion, which was made under reference to Rochdale Borough Council v A, that these recommendations now had the force of law because they had been accepted and founded upon by the judge in that case.

With reference to the opinion expressed by the sheriff in the other case, counsel for the respondent submitted that the sheriff's comment on the evidence of the social workers was not substantiated by the evidence and that the confusion which had arisen could have been the result of a genuine misunderstanding due to the fact that two sources were involved in the preparation of the document which came under criticism. He also stated that it would be inappropriate to draw any inference from what happened in that case in regard to the evidence of the same social workers in the present case. As to the Orkney inquiry report, he said that it was a misunderstanding of the conclusions in the inquiry to imagine that it had brought the whole subject of interviewing techniques out of darkness into light. All the points in it on which the pursuers relied in this case could be traced back to the Cleveland inquiry report. He suggested that it would be unacceptable to open up for rehearing all cases which had predated the publication of the Orkney inquiry report. On the other hand, if that were to be permitted in this case, it would be that much more difficult to distinguish it from others where the same points were being taken in reliance on that same report.

We are very conscious of counsel's point that there is no evidence that what he described as a step change has occurred since August 1990 in the state of knowledge and understanding of the practice of interviewing. None of the material which has been produced in this case, let alone the Orkney inquiry report, could be said to be evidence to that effect. The Cleveland inquiry report had already been published by August 1990, and all the important points made both in the Rochdale case and in the Orkney inquiry report can be related back to the Cleveland report. But the recognition of these points by specialists on this subject is one thing. It is quite another as to whether their views and recommendations were being followed in practice on the ground. There was no dispute in this case that, at least in some respects, the social workers did not follow the Cleveland guidelines in the course of their interviews. We accept that the significance of these departures from proper practice was the subject of Dr Furnell's evidence and of the submissions for the parties which the sheriff has narrated in his note. To that extent the points now raised by the petitioners are not new. We also reject counsel for the petitioners' submission that the Cleveland guidelines have achieved something approaching the force of law following their acceptance by Douglas Brown J in *Rochdale Borough Council v A*. We agree with the Lord Justice Clerk's observation in *F v Kennedy (No 2)* at p 1289F that the mere fact that the guidelines of the Cleveland report had not been followed did not mean that the sheriff was not entitled to accept the evidence of the children as reliable.

Nevertheless we consider that there is now a greater understanding, following on both the Rochdale and the Orkney cases, of the fundamental importance of these issues to a proper evaluation of the evidence. This is especially so in cases such as the present where children from more than one family are involved and allegations have been made of group sexual abuse involving several adults. In our opinion it is highly unlikely that criticism of social workers for seeking what they thought were the right answers from children in matters of sexual abuse could now be treated as lightly as they appear to have been treated in this case, according to the account which the sheriff gives of Dr Furnell's evidence. The view which the sheriff in the other case formed about the credibility and the reliability of the two social workers cannot in these circumstances be dismissed as irrelevant. There may be a question of fact as to whether the inference which the petitioners seek to draw from this is a legitimate inference. But the close proximity in time and the close relationship between the facts of the two cases is sufficient to persuade us that this matter also cannot be left out of account.

The whole position which is presented by the petitioners' averments is that, despite the efforts of their representatives in the time then available, this chapter was insufficiently explored in evidence at the proof. We are in no doubt that the additional evidence which is now available to them in this matter is material and significant. It is directed to issues of fundamental importance which affect not only the hearsay evidence of the interviews given by the social workers but also the direct evidence of the four children who gave evidence, all of whom had been interviewed by the social workers many times before they gave evidence at the proof. The absence of a detailed discussion of this topic by the sheriff in his evaluation of the evidence of these children, who were aged between three and 10 years when they gave their evidence, is a further indication that, in the light of the reports now available, including especially the report of the Orkney inquiry, there is here a point of substantial importance which, had it been fully before the sheriff in 1990, might well have affected his assessment of their credibility and reliability.

The petitioners have also produced reports by a clinical psychologist, Dr Iain C Murphy, and a consultant psychiatrist, Dr M A E Smith, which tend to suggest that it is unlikely that the petitioners would have indulged in child sexual abuse. The value to be attached to such evidence may be somewhat limited if there is clear evidence that they have participated in such activity. Furthermore counsel accepted that he could not maintain that this evidence could not have been made available with reasonable diligence at the proof. But he said that the importance of the evidence had not been appreciated in 1990, and it seems to us that there is force in the point that it would be unreasonable to blame the petitioners' advisers for this, given the pace at which the case was being handled and the many issues which had to be considered at that stage. We are not inclined, therefore, to disregard this material, and it seems to us that it cannot be dismissed as being of no materiality or significance. Counsel for the respondent criticised the evidence as a pure afterthought, and he said that it was not in the interests of justice for it to be led as new evidence. But the interests of justice seem to us to be an uncertain criterion in a case of this kind, where the whole object of the procedure is to secure the care and welfare of children. And the more factors are introduced which may cast doubt on the case, the more important it becomes for all relevant points to be taken into account.

This was and still is an exceptional and very difficult case. The number of children involved, the nature and number of the allegations, the way in which the case was conducted and the rapid progress from the making of the place of safety orders to the proof created a situation which, as the sheriff remarks at p 4 of his note, no one could have foreseen at the start of the case. In our opinion the additional evidence which the pursuers aver is now available to them suggests strongly that, in the event, the sheriff did not have all the information which was necessary for him to arrive at a sound decision in the children's best interests. Whether his decision would have been different in the end of the day had he heard all this evidence we cannot say, as we cannot examine all the evidence. But we are satisfied that there is more than a sufficient basis, on the information now available, for it to be appropriate for us to issue a direction in the exercise of the nobile officium that the case should be reheard.

A rehearing of the case so long after the original decision that the grounds of referral were established will undoubtedly create new problems. These will relate not only to the conduct of the fresh hearing but also to the consequences of it, should the sheriff find that the grounds for the referral are not established and that they will require to be discharged. In order to do what we can to minimise these difficulties we shall direct that the sheriff who is to be appointed to rehear the case must be a different sheriff from the sheriff who heard the proof in 1990. It would be unreasonable to expect him to re-examine the case with an open mind in view of the strong views which he has expressed about it. For the same reason it would be appropriate that the sheriff who is appointed to rehear the case should be one who has had no previous contact with this case, in view of various appeals which have been heard by the sheriffs under s 49 of the 1968 Act following the many review hearings which have taken place. Clearly the leading of evidence again in this case will require detailed and careful preparation on both sides, and for this reason we shall not attempt to lay down any time limit in the bringing of the matter back to the sheriff for a rehearing. It will be a matter for the sheriff to set such time limits on the preparation of the case as he considers appropriate. In the meantime the existing supervision requirements in respect of the children as reviewed from time to time under s 48 of the Act must remain in force.

As to the future, if the sheriff is of the view that the grounds for the referral are not established, careful attention will then require to be given to the question how the supervision requirements may best be brought to an end and the children returned to their respective families. It would not be satisfactory for these requirements to be instantly terminated, as that might have very undesirable consequences for the children who may not be prepared to face such a sudden change in their circumstances. For this reason we shall direct the sheriff to report the case back to us before issuing any interlocutor after the proof. This will enable us, if his decision is that the grounds for referral should be discharged in terms of s 42 (5) of the 1968 Act, to place such conditions on the disposal of the matter as may then be appropriate in order to ensure that the welfare of the children may be safeguarded.

Counsel for Petitioners, Jackson, QC, Caldwell; Solicitors, Macbeth Currie & Co, WS — Counsel for Respondent, Macfadyen, QC, Kelly; Solicitors, Biggart Baillie & Gifford, WS.

D A K

Wallis v Wallis

HOUSE OF LORDS

LORD KEITH OF KINKEL,
LORD JAUNCEY OF TULLICHETTLE,
LORD LOWRY, LORD SLYNN OF HADLEY
AND LORD WOOLF

22 JULY 1993

Husband and wife — Divorce — Financial provision — Valuation of matrimonial property — House in joint names — Order for transfer of property and payment of capital sum — Application of principle of equal division — Whether competent to take into account change in value of property between relevant date and date of divorce — Family Law (Scotland) Act 1985 (c 37), ss 8, 9 and 10.

A husband raised an action of divorce against his wife. The parties married in March 1986 and separated in March 1987. The only issue between the parties related to their claims for financial provision. The pursuer sought an order ordaining the defender to transfer to him her one half share in the matrimonial home which was held in the joint names of the parties. The sheriff held that an order for transfer of property was justified by the principles set out in s 9 of the Family Law (Scotland) Act 1985 and was reasonable having regard to the resources of the parties, so long as the pursuer made payment to the defender of a capital sum equivalent to one half of the net value of the property. In assessing the amount of the capital sum the sheriff held that it was reasonable to take account of the difference in value of the property between the date of separation (the relevant date) and the date of divorce for the reason that otherwise the pursuer would retain the benefit of the increase in value of his own share for himself but the defender would surrender the benefit of the increase in the value of her share without compensation. The pursuer appealed to the sheriff principal, who refused the appeal, and then to the Court of Session. He argued that it was not competent for the sheriff to take into account the change in value of the property between the relevant date and the date of divorce. The defender contended that if the property was transferred at less than its full value then she was effectively granting a financial provision to the pursuer which was contrary to the principle of equal division. There had to be a balancing act in terms of s 11 (2) of the Act in order to achieve fairness, otherwise the defender would suffer economic disadvantage in terms of s 9 (1) (b). The list of special circumstances in s 10 (6) was not exhaustive and it would be unfair and unfortunate for the defender to be deprived of her share at less than full value. If the sheriff was not entitled to take into account the increase in value subsequent to the relevant date, then the order for transfer of property should not include the defender's share of the matrimonial home. The First Division allowed the appeal and reduced the amount of the capital sum to reflect the value of the matrimonial home at the relevant date. The defender appealed to the House of Lords.

Held, that for the purposes of the division contemplated by s 9 (1) (a) the matrimonial property was to be valued as at the relevant date and in the absence of special circumstances the net value as at that date was to be divided equally between the parties, and there was nothing in the Act capable of justifying a division between the parties of the increase in the net value which had taken place at the time of the proof (pp 1351G and 1352A-C); and appeal *dismissed.*

Observed, that the Act did nothing to address directly the problems which might arise where some item of matrimonial property had increased or fallen in value during the period since the relevant date, especially as the requirements of s 8 (1) (a) and (b) were cumulative, and it was for consideration whether amending legislation was required to enable courts to deal with the problems that such changes in value could create in such a way as to produce fair results (pp 1351G-H and L and 1352H-J).

Doubted, whether changes in value of the matrimonial property could amount to "special circumstances" for the purposes of s 10 (1) (p 1351L).

————————————

Action of divorce
(Reported 1992 SLT 676)
Paul William Mark Wallis raised an action of divorce against his wife Mrs Margaret Jane MacDonald or Wallis in the sheriff court at Falkirk. The merits of the action were not contested.

The case came before the sheriff (A B Wilkinson) for proof on the question of financial provision.

Statutory provisions
The Family Law (Scotland) Act 1985, as originally enacted, provided:

"8.—(1) In an action for divorce, either party to the marriage may apply to the court for one or more of the following orders — (a) an order for the payment of a capital sum or the transfer of property to him by the other party to the marriage; (b) an order for the making of a periodical allowance to him by the other party to the marriage; (c) an incidental order within the meaning of section 14 (2) of this Act.

"(2) Subject to sections 12 to 15 of this Act, where an application has been made under subsection (1) above, the court shall make such order, if any, as is — (a) justified by the principles set out in section 9 of this Act; and (b) reasonable having regard to the resources of the parties.

"(3) An order under subsection (2) above is in this Act referred to as an 'order for financial provision'.

"9.—(1) The principles which the court shall apply in deciding what order for financial provision, if any, to make are that — (a) the net value of the matrimonial property should be shared fairly between the parties to the marriage. . . .

"10.—(1) In applying the principle set out in section 9 (1) (a) of this Act, the net value of the matrimonial property shall be taken to be shared fairly between the parties to the marriage when it is shared equally or in such other proportions as are justified by special circumstances.

"(2) The net value of the matrimonial property shall be the value of the property at the relevant date after deduction of any debts incurred by the parties or either of them — (a) before the marriage so far as they relate to the matrimonial property, and (b) during the marriage, which are outstanding at that date.

"(3) In this section 'the relevant date' means whichever is the earlier of — (a) subject to subsection (7) below, the date on which the parties ceased to cohabit; (b) the date of service of the summons in the action for divorce.

"(4) Subject to subsection (5) below, in this section and in section 11 of this Act 'the matrimonial property' means all the property belonging to the parties or either of them at the relevant date which was acquired by them or him (otherwise than by way of gift or succession from a third party) — (a) before the marriage for use by them as a family home or as furniture or plenishings for such home; or (b) during the marriage but before the relevant date. . . .

"(6) In subsection (1) above 'special circumstances', without prejudice to the generality of the words, may include — (a) the terms of any agreement between the parties on the ownership or division of any of the matrimonial property; (b) the source of the funds or assets used to acquire any of the matrimonial property where those funds or assets were not derived from the income or efforts of the parties during the marriage; (c) any destruction, dissipation or alienation of property by either party; (d) the nature of the matrimonial property, the use made of it (including use for business purposes or as a matrimonial home) and the extent to which it is reasonable to expect it to be realised or divided or used as security; (e) the actual or prospective liability for any expenses of valuation or transfer of property in connection with the divorce."

On 28 September 1990 the sheriff *granted* decree of divorce, *ordered* the defender to transfer to the pursuer the title to her one half pro indiviso share of the former matrimonial home, and *awarded* the defender a capital sum of £31,450.

The pursuer appealed to the sheriff principal (J J Maguire, QC), who *refused* the appeal.

The pursuer appealed to the Court of Session.

Appeal
The appeal was heard before the First Division on 12 and 13 May 1992.

On 27 May 1992 the First Division *allowed* the
A appeal, *recalled* the interlocutor of the sheriff principal
and also that part of the sheriff's interlocutor which
decerned against the pursuer for payment to the
defender of the sum of £31,450, and *substituted* for
that figure the sum of £19,450. (Reported 1992 SLT
676.)

The defender appealed to the House of Lords.

Appeal

The appeal was heard before Lord Keith of Kinkel,
B Lord Jauncey of Tullichettle, Lord Lowry, Lord
Slynn of Hadley and Lord Woolf on 16 June 1993.

On 22 July 1993 the House *dismissed* the appeal.

LORD KEITH OF KINKEL.—The point of issue
in this appeal relates to the proper construction of
certain of the provisions of the Family Law (Scotland)
Act 1985 which deal with the financial consequences
of divorce.

C The pursuer and the defender were married on 4
March 1986 and separated in March 1987. There
were no children of the marriage. The matrimonial
home during the subsistence of the marriage was at 10
Rosebank Avenue, Falkirk, the title to which at the
time of the separation stood in the joint names of the
parties. After the separation the pursuer (the husband)
continued to live in the house and to conduct his business from it. In 1988 the pursuer raised an action of
divorce against the defender in Falkirk sheriff court,
D on the ground [as subsequently amended] of the
irretrievable breakdown of the marriage as established
by the separation of the parties for a period of over two
years. The defender consented to the granting of
decree of divorce and a proof which took place before
Sheriff A B Wilkinson in April 1990 was limited to
the parties' claims for financial provision. On 28
September 1990 the sheriff pronounced an interlocutor granting decree of divorce. He found that the
matrimonial property in March 1987 (the relevant
E date for purposes of s 10 (3) of the Act of 1985) comprised the matrimonial home, the furnishings and
plenishings therein, which were the joint property of
the parties, and a Mercedes motor car which was the
sole property of the pursuer. The matrimonial home
then was worth £44,000 subject to a mortgage
redemption figure of £26,600 (£17,400 net), its
current value being £68,000. The value of the furnishings and plenishings at the same date was £13,500 and
that of the motor car £8,000. The sheriff ordered the
pursuer to pay to the defender the sum of £31,450 and
F the defender to transfer to the pursuer on payment to
her of the said sum her one half share of the former
matrimonial home and of the furnishings and plenishings. The sum of £31,450 represented one half of the
net value of the house at the relevant date (£8,700)
plus one half of the increase in its value since that date
(£12,000) plus one half of the value of the furnishings
and plenishings at the relevant date (£6,750) plus one
half of the value of the motor car at that date (£4,000).

The pursuer appealed to the sheriff principal
contending inter alia that the capital sum payable by

him to the defender should be reduced by the one half
of the increase in the value of the former matrimonial G
home between the relevant date and the date of the
proof. The reduction by £12,000 would result in a
capital sum payable of £19,450. On 21 February 1991
the sheriff principal refused the appeal. However, a
further appeal by the pursuer to the Court of Session
was on 27 May 1992 allowed by the First Division
(Lord President Hope, Lord Allanbridge and Lord
Mayfield) to the effect of substituting £19,450 for
£31,450 as the capital sum payable by the pursuer
(1992 SLT 676). The defender now appeals to your H
Lordships' House. The pursuer was not represented
at the hearing of the appeal and took no part in it.

Section 8 of the Act of 1985 provides: [his Lordship
quoted the terms of s 8, as originally enacted, and continued:]

Nothing in ss 12 to 15 has any relevance for present
purposes. Subsection (2) of s 8 places two limitations
upon the order (or combination of orders) which the
court may make in response to applications made
under subs (1). The first is that the order or combina- I
tion of orders must be justified under one or more of
the principles set out in s 9. The second is that the
order or orders must be reasonable having regard to the
resources of the parties, which must mean their
resources at the date of the hearing. The only one of
the principles set out in s 9 which is suggested as being
relevant in the present case is that in s 9 (1) (a),
namely: "the net value of the matrimonial property
should be shared fairly between the parties to the
marriage". J

This principle is expanded by s 10, which so far as
material provides: [his Lordship quoted the terms of
s 10 (1)-(4) and (6) and continued:]

The effect of s 9 (1) (a) combined with s 10 is that
in the absence of special circumstances the net value
of the matrimonial property at the relevant date, in
this case the date when the parties separated, is to be
shared equally between them. The sheriff found that
there were no special circumstances shown sufficient
to justify departure from the principle of equal K
division, and counsel for the defender did not dispute
that finding. The sheriff went on to express the
opinion that the total net value of the matrimonial
property at the relevant date might be put at £38,900,
giving a sum of £19,450 for each party on an equal
division. However, in arriving at the capital sum to be
paid by the pursuer to the defender as a condition of
the transfer by the defender to the pursuer of her one
half share in the former matrimonial home (a transfer
which he considered appropriate in the circumstances) L
he added to the £19,450 the sum of £12,000, being one
half of the increase in value of the house between the
relevant date and the date of the proof. He observed
that if the property had all been in the pursuer's
ownership effect could have been given to an equal
division of the matrimonial property ascertained at the
relevant date by an order for payment of a capital sum
of £19,450 to the defender, and that the pursuer would
then have taken the benefit of any increase in value
since then. In the sheriff's view, however, the fact that
the house was owned jointly by the pursuer and the

defender and had increased in value since March 1987 led to a different result. He expressed his reasoning as follows: "If the house had been sold or ordered to be sold there would have been no problem. On an equal division each party would have taken an equal share of the proceeds of sale representing, on a strict analysis of the application of the provisions of the Act, a one-half share of the net value at the relevant date to each party, with each party taking the benefit of the increase in value of his own share. In this case, however, the pursuer sought a transfer of the defender's property to him. If the pursuer were to give no more than half of the net value of the house at the relevant date in return for that transfer the equal distribution of the matrimonial property valued as at the relevant date would be disturbed, because the pursuer would receive an asset of considerably greater value than the money he was paying in return. He would retain the benefit of the increase in the value of his own share of the house, but the defender would surrender her share without any compensation for the increase in its value which would instead be transferred to the pursuer. The pursuer would be receiving an asset of £20,700.00 (£8,700.00 net value at the relevant date plus £12,000.00 increase in value) whereas on an equal distribution as at the relevant date he was entitled only to the equivalent of £8,700.00. Accordingly, if the defender's share in the house was to be transferred to the pursuer he must, in my opinion, give value for the difference between its current value and the value in March 1987 in the sum of £12,000.00."

The First Division held that the sheriff's approach was erroneous. Lord President Hope said (1992 SLT at p 679D): "The critical point which the sheriff omitted to observe is that what [was] required to be shared equally between the parties was the net value of the matrimonial property at the relevant date. Various kinds of financial provision may be made to achieve that object, whether by means of an order for payment of a capital sum or an order for the transfer of property or a combination of the two. There is a choice of method by which the financial provision may be made, but whichever method is chosen the only legitimate object is to achieve a fair division of the net value of the matrimonial property at the relevant date. It is irrelevant to this exercise that the value of the matrimonial property, or of any items comprised within it, may have altered between the relevant date and the date of division. The policy of the Act, as declared by s 10 (1) and (2), is to have regard only to its value at the relevant date, namely the date when the parties ceased to cohabit or the date of service of the summons in the action for divorce. The relevance of the date is that it can be taken to mark the date when the marriage for all practical purposes came to an end. For this date, and this date only, to be used to value the property has the merit of providing a logical and convenient reference point. It avoids the expense and complication of repeated revaluations at later dates should there be a delay in obtaining the divorce. At all events it is the only date as at which, for the purposes of the Act, the matrimonial property is to be valued. Accordingly any subsequent changes in value must be left out of account when calculating the value of the matrimonial property and the way in which it is to be divided between the parties."

There can be no doubt that for the purposes of the division contemplated by s 9 (1) (a) the matrimonial property is to be valued as at the relevant date and in the absence of special circumstances the net value as at that date is to be divided equally between the parties. It is clear, moreover, that the Act does nothing to address directly the problems which may arise where some item of matrimonial property has increased or fallen in value during the period since the relevant date, though some of these problems may be capable of being solved by application of s 8 (2) (b). For example, if the matrimonial home, being held in the sole name of one of the parties, were to be destroyed by fire uninsured after the relevant date but before the date of the proof, the party who owned the property might be required to pay the other party half its value at the relevant date if his or her total resources at the date of the proof were sufficient to make it reasonable for such payment to be made, but not if the party in question had no significant resources. Similar considerations could apply where the property in question consisted in a block of shares which had fallen dramatically in value. Further, it would seem to make no difference in principle that the property in question was at the relevant date owned jointly by the parties or indeed by a party who, in contrast to the other, was lacking in resources at the date of the proof. It might well be not only justified by the principle in s 9 (1) (a) but also reasonable under s 8 (2) (b) that the better off party should pay to the worse off one half of the value of the property at the relevant date in exchange for the latter's devalued interest at the date of the proof.

A more intractable problem would arise in the situation where matrimonial property wholly owned by one party had depreciated substantially in value between the relevant date and the date of the proof but at the latter date the party owning it had no other resources. An equal division as at the relevant date involving payment by the party owning the property to the other party of one half of the net value at the relevant date would result in the latter party receiving very much more than the former party would be left with, which might indeed be nothing at all. It does not appear that s 8 (2) (b) could be applied in such a way as to redress the balance in a situation of that kind. The solution might be found in a finding of special circumstances under s 10 (1), though changes in the value of matrimonial property between the relevant date and the date of the proof can hardly, perhaps, be regarded as so unusual as to amount to special circumstances. It is for consideration whether amending legislation is required to enable courts to deal with the kind of problems I have indicated in such a way as to produce fair results.

Given that certain property is matrimonial property the net value of which at the relevant date is to be divided equally, the correct view, in my opinion, is that it is irrelevant for purposes of s 9 (1) (a) which of the parties happened to own it at the relevant date or that it was then owned by them jointly. The sheriff expressed the opinion, rightly in my view, that if the pursuer had happened to be sole owner of the matrimonial home at the relevant date it would have been appropriate for him to keep it on making payment to the defender of one half of its then net value. It makes no difference in principle that the defender then happened to own one half of the house. If circumstances made it appropriate that she should transfer that one half of it to the pursuer then there is nothing in the Act which could warrant her being paid by the pursuer more than one half of its value at the relevant date. As at that date the net value of the asset then notionally left in the hands of the pursuer did not exceed one half of the total net value of the house and the sum of £8,700 payable to the defender also represented one half of that total value. The principles of the Act cannot justify more than that sum being paid to the defender upon an equal division of the net value of the matrimonial home at the relevant date. There is nothing in the Act capable of justifying a division between the parties of the increase in that net value which had taken place at the time of the proof.

In addition to maintaining that the order of the sheriff should be restored, counsel for the appellant argued that the order should be varied to the effect of affirming it in relation to the division of the value of the furnishings and plenishings and the motor car but recalling it insofar as it related to the former matrimonial home, thus leaving the parties in the situation of joint pro indiviso proprietors and enabling the appellant to raise an action of division and sale. I am of opinion, however, that the decision of the First Division, for the reasons I have endeavoured to indicate, correctly gives effect to the principles of the Act of 1985 so far as applicable to the circumstances of this case and accordingly should not be disturbed.

My Lords, I would therefore dismiss the appeal.

LORD JAUNCEY OF TULLICHETTLE.—I have had the advantage of reading in draft the speech of my noble and learned friend, Lord Keith of Kinkel and I entirely agree with the reasons which he gives for dismissing the appeal.

I would, however, like to add a few words to what my noble and learned friend has said about the possible need for amending legislation. In terms of s 8 (2) on an application for an order under s 8 (1) the court "shall make such order, if any, as is (a) justified by the principles set out in s 9 of this Act; and (b) reasonable having regard to the resources of the parties". These requirements are cumulative with the result that unless both are satisfied the court has no power to make an order. Where an application relates to the sharing of the matrimonial property s 9 (1) (a) requires that its net value is shared fairly and s 10 (1) provides that such net value shall be taken to be shared fairly when it is shared equally or in such other proportions as are justified by special circumstances.

Assume a situation in which neither party has any personal capital and the only matrimonial property consists of a house and contents. Assume further that between the relevant date and the date of the hearing the value of the house has diminished by more than one half, for example, as a result of unforeseen subsidence or incompatible adjacent development. In that situation the court could make no order under s 8 because it would be unreasonable having regard to the resources of the spouse in possession for him or her to pay to the other a sum in excess of any available capital. If the title were in joint names the spouse who was not in possession could pursue an action of division and sale, but if it were in the name of the spouse in possession the former could obtain no share even although it might be possible and reasonable for the spouse having the title to raise some money on the house.

The point which I seek to make is simply that there may well be circumstances where an order which satisfies both requirements of s 8 (2) could not be made but where an order sharing the net value of matrimonial property other than on an equal basis would be just and reasonable in all the circumstances and the making of no order would be unjust. There are, as the Lord President has pointed out, considerable advantages in adopting a single date as that upon which matrimonial property has to be valued and in providing a rule of thumb division, as in s 10 (1), but it must be for consideration whether some discretion should not be given to the court in appropriate circumstances to make an order dividing the net value of the matrimonial property other than equally when such an equal division could not satisfy the requirements of s 8 (2) (b). In thus endorsing my noble and learned friend's suggestion of amending legislation I share his doubts as to whether changes in value of the matrimonial property could amount to "special circumstances" for the purposes of s 10 (1).

LORD LOWRY.—I have had the advantage of reading in draft the speech of my noble and learned friend, Lord Keith of Kinkel.

I agree with it and for the reasons which he gives I, too, would dismiss this appeal.

LORD SLYNN OF HADLEY.—For the reasons given by my noble and learned friend, Lord Keith of Kinkel, I too would dismiss this appeal.

LORD WOOLF.—I have had the advantage of reading in draft the speeches of my noble and learned friends, Lord Keith of Kinkel and Lord Jauncey of Tullichettle.

I agree with them and for the reasons which they give I would also dismiss this appeal.

No appearance for Pursuer and Respondent — Counsel for Defender and Appellant, Macfadyen, QC, Macnair; Solicitors, Brodies, WS (for Tilston MacLaurin, Glasgow), Reynolds Porter Chamberlain, London.

M G T

INDEX OF CASES

ACCORDING TO SUBJECT MATTER

L signifies *House of Lords* Decision.

O signifies *Outer House* Decision.

J signifies *Justiciary Court* or *Criminal Appeal Court* Decision.

V signifies *Lands Valuation Appeal Court* and *Valuation Appeal Court* Decision.

★ signifies case reported in note form.

Company — Directors — Negligence — Duties of care to creditor of company — Lease of aircraft by owner to company without directors' guarantees — Statutory charges incurred by company in respect of aircraft when directors knew that company absolutely insolvent and unable to pay its debts — Lessor paying statutory charges to prevent statutory sale of aircraft — Whether duty of care not to cause aircraft to be operated owed by directors to lessor independently of obligations of company — Insolvency Act 1986 (c 45), ss 212, 213, 214 and 215 (4).

Nordic Oil Services Ltd v Berman—O   1164

Company — Insolvency — Administration order — Landlord of company in administration seeking leave to commence proceedings against company under irritancy provision in lease — Whether leave should be given — Guidelines to be applied — Insolvency Act 1986 (c 45), s 11 (3) (d).

Scottish Exhibition Centre Ltd v Mirestop Ltd (in administration)—O   1034

Company — Insolvency — Gratuitous alienation — Cheque drawn on company account in payment of debt due by director of company to third person — Whether alienation by company to third person — Effect of statute on alienation prior to commencement of statutory provisions — Insolvency Act 1986 (c 45), s 242 and Sched 11, paras 4 and 9 — Bankruptcy Act 1621 (c 18).

Stuart Eves Ltd (in liquidation) v Smiths Gore—O   1274

Company — Insolvency — Unfair preference — Reciprocal obligations — Endorsement of cheque from debtor of company in favour of creditor of company in exchange for delivery of supplies — Whether unfair preference — Whether reciprocal obligation involved broad equivalence or strict equivalence — Insolvency Act 1986 (c 45), s 243 (2) (c).

Nicoll v Steelpress (Supplies) Ltd   533

Company — Liquidator — Misfeasance — Procedure — Alleged breach of interdict by liquidator — Leave to raise proceedings against company in liquidation and liquidator — Whether disputed breach of interdict best dealt with in winding up process or interdict process — Insolvency Act 1986 (c 45), s 212 (2) and (3).

Canon (Scotland) Business Machines Ltd v GA Business Systems Ltd (in liquidation)—O   386

Company — Register of members — Transfer of shares — Failure to comply with form provided in articles of association — Petition for rectification of register — Voting rights — Whether transferee should be prevented from exercising voting rights — Transferee having right by contract to control vote of transferor should transferor remain as member — Whether interim interdict appropriate.

Dempsey v Celtic Football and Athletic Co Ltd—O   382

Company — Register of members — Transfer of shares — Failure to comply with form provided in articles of association — Whether proper instrument of transfer — Whether registration of transfer unlawful — Companies Act 1985 (c 6), s 183 (1).

Dempsey v Celtic Football and Athletic Co Ltd—O   382

Company — Share premium account — Cancellation of account and transfer of credit to special reserve — Application to court for confirmation — Protection of creditors — Undertakings necessary from company — Whether moneys on special reserve distributable profits of company — Whether moneys might be used to redeem redeemable shares — Companies Act 1985 (c 6), ss 160 (1) (a) and 263 (2) and (3).

Quayle Munro Ltd, Petitioners   723

Company — Takeover — Agreement by board of offeree company to recommend offer to its members — Whether legally enforceable — Whether implied term not to solicit or co-operate with potential competing offerors — Whether implied term breached.

Dawson International plc v Coats Paton plc—O   80

Company — Winding up — Gratuitous alienation — Transfer of heritable property by insolvent company to third party — Whether made for adequate consideration — Onus on person seeking to uphold transaction — Insolvency Act 1986 (c 45), s 242.

McLuckie Brothers Ltd v Newhouse Contracts Ltd—O   641

★ **Company** — Winding up — Insolvency — Company unable to pay its debts — Leaving of statutory demand at company's registered office — Whether service to be effected by officer of court — Insolvency Act 1986 (c 45), s 123 (1) (a).

Lord Advocate, Petitioner   1324

Company — Winding up — Liquidator — Powers of — Note — Competency of order that winding up of two companies proceed jointly with sequestration of estate of director — Companies Act 1948 (11 & 12 Geo VI, c 38), s 245 (1) (f).

Taylor, Noter   375

Company — Winding up — Petition by contributory — Competency — Petitioner also trustee in sequestration on estate of principal shareholder in company — Petition for winding up proceeding on basis of bankrupts right as contributory — Whether competent to petition as trustee in sequestration — Whether trustee required to be registered as owner of shares — Bankruptcy (Scotland) Act 1985 (c 66), s 31 — Insolvency Act 1986 (c 45), ss 79, 82 and 124.

Cumming's Trustee v Glenrinnes Farms Ltd—O   904

Contract — Sale of heritage — Missives of sale — Breach — Waiver — Actings of sellers after purchasers failed to pay purchase price — Whether waiver of right to treat failure as material breach of contract.

Contract — Sale of heritage — Missives of sale — Collateral obligation to build house in accordance with drawings and specification — Whether obligation limited to works completed after conclusion of missives — Patent defects — Effect of subsequent disposition.

Contract — Sale of heritage — Missives of sale — Construction — Public sector housing — Sale of subjects "as the same shall be determined by the Council" — Whether council entitled to determine area less than that let under existing tenancy — Whether clause a "condition" challengeable before Lands Tribunal — Tenants' Rights, Etc (Scotland) Act 1980 (c 52), ss 2, 4 (1) and 82.

Contract — Sale of heritage — Rescission — Sellers raising action to enforce missives — Purchasers defending on basis that sellers in material breach and purchasers entitled to rescind — Purchasers counterclaiming for repayment of part payment of price — Decree of dismissal by default of sellers' action and for payment under counterclaim — Whether purchasers thereafter precluded from reconsidering decision to rescind and seeking implement.

Contract — Unfair contract terms — Contract of employment — Whether "consumer contract" — Unfair Contract Terms Act 1977 (c 50), ss 15 (2), 17 (1) and 25 (1)

Contract — Unfair contract terms — Disclaimer — Survey report to building society at request of prospective house purchaser — Disclaimer in loan application form signed by prospective purchaser — Whether disclaimer effective — Whether "a term of a contract" — Whether contract "relates to services of whatever kind" — Unfair Contract Terms Act 1977 (c 50), ss 15 (2) (c) and 16 (1).

Crown — Public interest immunity — National Health Service — Records of blood transfusion service — Disclosure of identity of blood donor to person contracting human immune deficiency virus from transfused blood — Whether public interest threatened — Whether information subject to public interest immunity — Whether

petitioner's interest capable of overriding public interest — Considerations for court in assessing claims of Secretary of State and of blood transfusion service — Administration of Justice (Scotland) Act 1972 (c 59), s 1.

★**Damages** — Amount — Assessment — Loss of earnings and necessary services rendered to injured person — Lack of specific evidence.

Damages — Amount — Loss of society — Death of 14 year old son and stepson.

Damages — Amount — Solatium — Ankle — Strain to ankle resulting in persisting minor disability.

★**Damages** — Amount — Solatium — Back — Strain to back causing unfitness for work lasting for three months.

★**Damages** — Amount — Solatium — Back — Straining injury causing moderate degree of aggravation of pain from spondylosis for a few months.

Damages — Amount — Solatium — Breach of contract for sale of heritage — Resultant distress suffered by purchaser.

★**Damages** — Amount — Solatium — Hearing — Burning injury in ear causing initial pain, deafness for two or three days and tinnitus at significant level for about six months with minor permanent hearing deficit.

★**Damages** — Amount — Solatium — Hip, leg and arm — Fracture to femur limiting hip movement — Fracture to arm limiting power in arm.

★**Damages** — Amount — Solatium — Knee — Contusion of knee joint with discomfort lasting about two years.

★**Damages** — Amount — Solatium — Minor injury — Leg — Driver trapped by leg for half an hour suffering pain but with no permanent physical consequences.

Expenses — Town and country planning — Appeal to Secretary of State against planning authority's refusal of change of use application — Contrary advice by authority's planning officer — Appeal largely conceded by planning authority — Award of expenses against planning authority — Whether award unreasonable.

City of Aberdeen District Council v Secretary of State for Scotland—O   1149

Heritable property — Boundary dispute — Boundary marked by medium filum of river— Channel of river destroyed in flood — New channel dug by agreement in different position — Whether boundary marked by medium filum of new channel or old channel.

Stirling v Bartlett—O   763

Heritable property — Common property — Division and sale — Sale by public roup or private bargain — Whether presumption in favour of sale by private bargain — Applicable considerations in exercise by court of equitable jurisdiction.

The Miller Group Ltd v Tasker   207

Heritable property — Common property — Division and sale — Subjects purchased jointly by co-proprietors financed by joint loan and free proceeds of sale of property formerly owned by one co-proprietor contributed in contemplation of marriage — Marriage not undertaken — Condictio causa data causa non secuta — Whether proprietor contributing free proceeds entitled to resist division and sale — Whether proprietor contributing free proceeds entitled to obtain conveyance of other co-proprietor's interest.

Grieve v Morrison—O   852

Heritable property — Disposition — Rectification — Disposition giving effect to missives — Averment of common intention that larger area would be transferred — Relevancy — Law Reform (Miscellaneous Provisions) (Scotland) Act 1985 (c 73), s 8 (1) and (2).

George Thompson Services Ltd v Moore—O.   634

Heritable property — Public right of way — Acquisition by prescription — Pedestrian walkway through town centre — Whether use as matter of right rather than tolerance by proprietor — Text of nature of user necessary to qualify route as public right of way — Prescription and Limitation (Scotland) Act 1973 (c 52), s 3 (3).

Cumbernauld and Kilsyth District Council v Dollar Land (Cumbernauld) Ltd—L . . .   1318

Heritable property — Registration of title — Registrable transactions or events — Decree of reduction of disposition — Whether reduction an event capable of affecting title to a registered interest in land — Whether decree creating

inaccuracy in register — Whether Keeper of Registers obliged to register decree of reduction — Conveyancing (Scotland) Act 1924 (14 & 15 Geo V, c 27), s 46 (1) — Land Registration (Scotland) Act 1979 (c 33), ss 2 (1) and (4), 9 (1), (2), (3) and (4) and 12 (1), (2) and (3) (b) — Bankruptcy (Scotland) Act 1985 (c 66), s 34 (4).

Short's Trustee v Keeper of the Registers of Scotland—O   1291

Heritable property — Sale — Informal agreement followed by homologation — Proof of existence of agreement — Whether writ of defenders referable to agreement.

Stewart's Executors v Stewart—O   440

Heritable property — Sale — Missives — Breach — Waiver — Actings of sellers after purchasers failed to pay purchase price — Whether waiver of right to treat failure as material breach of contract.

Atlas Assurance Co Ltd v Dollar Land Holdings plc—O   892

Heritable property — Sale — Missives — Obligation to build house in accordance with drawings and specification — Whether collateral obligation — Whether obligation limited to works completed after conclusion of missives — Patent defects — Effect of subsequent disposition.

King v Gebbie—O   512

Heritable property — Sale — Missives — Public sector housing — Purchase of dwellinghouse — Secure tenancy — Sale of subjects "as the same shall be determined by the Council" — Whether council entitled to determine area less than that let under existing tenancy — Whether clause a "condition" challengeable before Lands Tribunal — Tenants' Rights, Etc (Scotland) Act 1980 (c 52), ss 2, 4 (1) and 82.

City of Glasgow District Council v Doyle . . .   604

Heritable property — Sale — Missives — Sellers raising action to enforce missives — Purchasers defending on basis that sellers in material breach and purchasers entitled to rescind — Purchasers counterclaiming for repayment of part payment of price — Decree of dismissal by default of sellers' action and for payment under counterclaim — Whether purchasers thereafter precluded from reconsidering decision to rescind and seeking implement.

Mason v A & R Robertson & Black—O . . .   773

Heritable property — Sale — Warrandice — Whether actual or threatened eviction necessary to found claim for breach of warrandice.

Palmer v Beck—O   485

Heritable property — Servitude — Right of access — Proprietor of servient tenement erecting swing gates across access — Dominant proprietors disabled — Whether gates amounted to an obstruction — Appropriate test — Appropriate remedy where gates amounted to obstruction because of proprietors' disability.

Drury v McGarvie 987

Heritable property — Standard security — Defective form — Standard form signed by debtors qua debtors but not qua proprietors — Whether nature of defect such that court empowered to order rectification — Law Reform (Miscellaneous Provisions) (Scotland) Act 1985 (c 73), s 8 (1).

Bank of Scotland v Graham's Trustee 252

Housing — Local authority — Decision to refuse admission to housing list — Reliance on ground not within published summary of rules for admission — Whether local authority entitled to rely upon factor not in summary — Housing (Scotland) Act 1987 (c 26), s 21 (1) and (4).

Pirie v City of Aberdeen District Council—O 1155

Husband and wife — Divorce — Financial provision — Capital sum — Fair sharing of matrimonial property — Interest claimed for period prior to decree — Competency — Circumstances where appropriate — Family Law (Scotland) Act 1985 (c 37), s 14 (1) and (2) (j).

Geddes v Geddes 494

Husband and wife — Divorce — Financial provision — Capital sum — Pension rights — Method of valuation — Whether pension should be valued according to actuarial evidence or by reference to multiplier — Whether income rights or capital value — Family Law (Scotland) Act 1985 (c 37), s 10.

Brooks v Brooks—O 184

Husband and wife — Divorce — Financial provision — Claim for periodical allowance in action raised prior to coming into force of Family Law (Scotland) Act 1985 — Minute of amendment lodged after Act came into force converting claim for periodical allowance into claim for aliment — Whether minute of amendment converted claim into claim under Act — Family Law (Scotland) Act 1985 (c 37), ss 1 (1) (a) and 2 (2) (a).

McColl v McColl 617

Husband and wife — Divorce — Financial provision — Interim aliment — Variation of award of interim aliment — Backdating of variation — Competency — Family Law (Scotland) Act 1985 (c 37), ss 2, 3 (1) (c), 5 and 6.

McColl v McColl 617

★**Husband and wife** — Divorce — Financial provision — Interim aliment — Whether gross or net income to be considered.

MacInnes v MacInnes—O 1108

Husband and wife — Divorce — Financial provision — Joint minute containing agreement on financial provision — Decree in terms thereof pronounced on pursuer's motion — Competency of reclaiming motion by defender — Competency of defender seeking to set aside agreement as not fair and reasonable at time it was entered into — Family Law (Scotland) Act 1985 (c 37), s 16 (1) (b).

Jongejan v Jongejan 595

Husband and wife — Divorce — Financial provision — Periodical allowance — Variation of award made prior to coming into force of Family Law (Scotland) Act 1985 — Competency of varying both level and duration of periodical allowance — Payer alleged to have voluntarily altered his financial position — Divorce (Scotland) Act 1976 (c 39), s 5 (4) — Family Law (Scotland) Act 1985 (c 37), s 28 (3).

Mitchell v Mitchell—O 419

Husband and wife — Divorce — Financial provision — Valuation of matrimonial property — Award of damages made after relevant date in respect of accident occurring between date of marriage and relevant date — Method of valuing right to damages at relevant date — Whether sheriff entitled to take the sum awarded as value of the asset at relevant date — Family Law (Scotland) Act 1985 (c 37), s 10 (4).

Skarpaas v Skarpaas 343

Husband and wife — Divorce — Financial provision — Valuation of matrimonial property — House in joint names — Order for transfer of property and payment of capital sum — Application of principle of equal division — Whether competent to take into account change in value of property between relevant date and date of divorce — Family Law (Scotland) Act 1985 (c 37), ss 8, 9 and 10.

Wallis v Wallis—L 1348

Husband and wife — Divorce — Financial provision — Valuation of matrimonial property — Pension rights — Method of valuation — Family Law (Scotland) Act 1985 (c 37), s 10 (1) and (5).

Bannon v Bannon—O 999

Husband and wife — Divorce — Foreign decree obtained during currency of Scottish action — Recognition by Scottish court — Whether contrary to public policy — Availability of right to financial provision even although party divorced — Matrimonial and Family Proceedings Act 1984 (c 42), s 28 (1) — Family Law Act 1986 (c 55), s 51 (3) (c).

Tahir v Tahir—O 194

Interdict — Breach of interdict — Finding of breach of interdict in respect of an incident not averred in proceedings for breach and not intimated to Lord Advocate for his concurrence — Whether competent to find there had been a breach.

Byrne v Ross 307

Interdict — Breach of interdict — Interdict from "disrupting, impeding or otherwise interfering with" execution of warrant sale — Respondent taking charge of crowd disrupting sale and making inflammatory speech — Whether "impeding" or "interfering" required to be physical act — Whether breach.

McIntyre v Sheridan 412

Interdict — Breach of interdict — Passing off — Proof — Interdict against supplying Scotch whisky for purpose of enabling spirits containing spirits other than Scotch to be passed off as Scotch whisky — Respondents exporting Scotch whisky to Panama under brand name of "King of Scots" which consisted of 20 per cent of Scotch malt and 80 per cent of Panamanian cane spirit — Respondents instructing Panamanian agents to ensure that all labels and materials clearly indicated that product was blend of Scotch whisky and Panamanian spirit — Cartons sold in Panama for use with Scotch whisky and for use with blend to some extent the same — Bottles used to sell Scotch whisky and blend almost identical — Whether calculated to enable passing off to be achieved.

John Walker & Sons Ltd v Douglas Laing & Co Ltd—O 156

Interdict — Breach of interdict — Penalty — Breach of interdict preventing molestation.

Byrne v Ross 307

Interdict — Breach of interdict — Penalty — Interdict against disrupting execution of warrant sale — Public defiance of court orders.

McIntyre v Sheridan 412

★**Interdict** — Breach of interdict — Penalty — Interdict against individual being in particular employment — Interdict recalled a few weeks later but not meantime obtempered — Flagrant and deliberate defiance of court order.

C R Smith Glaziers (Dunfermline) Ltd v Anderson—O 592

Interdict — Breach of interdict — Proof — Whether corroboration required — Civil Evidence (Scotland) Act 1988 (c 32), s 1 (1).

Byrne v Ross 307

Interdict — Interim interdict — Balance of convenience — Defamatory matter in newspaper article about to be published — Article dealing with alleged dispute between parties in the public eye — Public interest.

McMurdo v Ferguson—O 193

Interdict — Interim interdict — Balance of convenience — Factors to be taken into account — Restrictive covenant.

C R Smith Glaziers (Dunfermline) Ltd v Greenan 1221

Interdict — Precision — Interdict from "disrupting, impeding or otherwise interfering with" execution of warrant sale — Whether "impeding" or "interfering" required to be a physical act — Whether interdict expressed too widely to be enforceable.

McIntyre v Sheridan 412

Interest — Partnership — Dissolution — Scheme of division — Assets in hands of one partner — Whether appropriate for judicial factor to allow interest at commercial rather than judicial rate — Whether appropriate to apply compound interest.

Roxburgh Dinardo & Partners' Judicial Factor v Dinardo 16

Interest — Unpaid tax due under assessment — Interest thereon — Prescription — Negative prescription — Interest accruing from day to day — Whether obligation to pay sum of money by way of interest an obligation in respect of a particular period — Taxes Management Act 1970 (c 9), ss 68 (1), 69 and 86 (1) — Prescription and Limitation (Scotland) Act 1973 (c 52), s 6 and Sched 1, para 1 (a).

Lord Advocate v Butt 10

International law — Recognition of foreign decree — Divorce — Whether foreign decree of divorce depriving party of right to claim financial provision — Whether recognition of decree manifestly contrary to public policy where right still available — Family Law Act 1986 (c 55), s 51 (3) (c).

Tahir v Tahir—O 194

International law — Recognition of foreign judgment — Judgment of United States court — Judgment in action resulting from tort — Jurisdiction of court issuing judgment based on locus of tort in territory of court — Whether judgment may only be recognised if defender resident or present in territory of foreign court when action brought there.

Wendel v Moran—O 44

Judicial factor — Factor appointed to solicitor's estates — Factor authorised to divide sum at credit of client account among clients — Solicitor's estates then sequestrated and permanent trustee appointed — Whether funds at credit of client account vested in trustee — Whether accountant of court entitled to order judicial factor to hand over funds to trustee — Solicitors (Scotland) Act 1980 (c 46), s 42 — Bankruptcy (Scotland) Act 1985 (c 66), s 33 (1).

Council of the Law Society of Scotland v McKinnie 238

Justiciary — Evidence — Admissibility — Character of possible associates of accused — Accused charged with being concerned in supplying drugs — Evidence of police officer as to his knowledge of names and nicknames in notebook found in accused's house and that known drug dealers were persons of those names — Whether evidence speculative — Whether prior notice ought to have been given to defence — Whether evidence properly left to jury.

Justiciary — Evidence — Admissibility — Hearsay — Best evidence — Boy witness not available to give evidence — Whether evidence of police officer regarding questions put to boy and his ability to identify anyone at identity parade admissible — Whether miscarriage of justice.

Justiciary — Evidence — Admissibility — Hearsay — Police officers acting on reasonable suspicion — Whether officers entitled to speak to what was said to them by third party.

Justiciary — Evidence — Admissibility — Improperly obtained evidence — Warrant to search house referring to property stolen from furniture store — Items found in wardrobe relating to separate theft of clothing — Sheriff sustaining objection to evidence of one officer who had been searching for items outwith terms of warrant but repelling objection to evidence from second officer who stated that he was searching for furniture — Whether that officer's evidence admissible in light of successful earlier objection.

Justiciary — Evidence — Admissibility — Police having grounds for suspicion that two persons using hired car in possession of drugs — Police stopping car and discovering third occupant — Third occupant being searched — Whether reasonable grounds for suspecting third occupant in possession of controlled drugs — Misuse of Drugs Act 1971 (c 38), s 23 (2).

Justiciary — Evidence — Admissibility — Statement by accused — Statement made to officer in charge of investigation after accused charged.

Justiciary — Evidence — Admissibility — Statement by accused — Whether statement both exculpatory and incriminatory in character — Other evidence pointing to truth of statement — Trial judge directing jury to treat statement as wholly exculpatory — Whether misdirection.

Justiciary — Evidence — Admissibility — Statement by accused — Whether statement partly self exonerating — Whether self exonerating part admissible.

Justiciary — Evidence — Appeal — New evidence not heard and not reasonably available at trial — Accused convicted of murder but co-accused acquitted — Evidence at trial that co-accused stabbed deceased — On appeal affidavits lodged showing co-accused before and during trial admitted stabbing deceased — Whether new evidence of materiality justifying hearing it — Whether miscarriage of justice — Criminal Procedure (Scotland) Act 1975 (c 21), ss 228 (2) and 252 (b).

Justiciary — Evidence — Appeal — New evidence not heard and not reasonably available at trial — Accused suffering amnesia at trial — Accused seeking to lead evidence to substitute for explanation that he could not recall strangling wife, that he wanted to stop her asserting that he was not father of child of marriage — Whether evidence not reasonably available at trial — Whether evidence additional — Criminal Procedure (Scotland) Act 1975 (c 21), s 228 (2).

Justiciary — Evidence — Corroboration — Burden of proving that statutory assumption is overcome resting on accused — Whether defence evidence need be corroborated.

Justiciary — Evidence — Corroboration — Mutual corroboration — Two charges of breach of the peace involving young girls in same area but only one charge involving indecency — Whether mutual corroboration applicable.

Justiciary — Evidence — Corroboration — Rape — Evidence from complainer that appellant ripped her pants and raped her — No independent evidence from which timing of damage to underwear could be inferred — Whether complainer's account corroborated by damaged state of underwear.

Justiciary — Evidence — Corroboration — Rape — Production spoken to only by complainer — Sufficiency of other corroborative evidence where further charge of attempted murder.

Justiciary — Evidence — Credibility — Crown case presented on basis that complainer giving entirely true account — Crown suggesting for first time in address to jury that they could accept part and reject part of complainer's evidence — Whether open to jury to do so.

Justiciary — Procedure — Prevention of delay — 80 day rule — Indictment served within 80 day period not called but second indictment served outwith period — Accused detained in custody after first indictment fell — Whether proceedings on second indictment fundamentally null — Criminal Procedure (Scotland) Act 1975 (c 21), s 101 (2) (a).

McCluskey v HM Advocate—J   897

Justiciary — Procedure — Prevention of delay — 110 day rule — Transfer of serving prisoner within United Kingdom — Accused sentenced in Scotland and transferred to England on Home Secretary's order — Accused absconding in England, committing offences in Scotland and being arrested there — Accused fully committed in custody for offences in Scotland — No formal order re-transferring accused to Scotland — Whether order necessary to prevent running of 110 day period — Criminal Justice Act 1961 (9 & 10 Eliz II, c 39), ss 26 (1) and (4), 28 (1), 29 (1) and 30 (1) and (3) — Criminal Procedure (Scotland) Act 1975 (c 21), s 101 (2) (b).

HM Advocate v Lewis—J   435

Justiciary — Procedure — Retrial — Accused charged with murder but convicted of culpable homicide — Conviction set aside and retrial authorised — Whether court could restrict retrial to culpable homicide charge — Criminal Procedure (Scotland) Act 1975 (c 21), ss 254 (1) (c) and 255 (1).

Boyle v HM Advocate—J   577

Justiciary — Procedure — Retrial — Accused charged with murder in original proceedings but convicted of culpable homicide "without murderous intent" — Crown authorised to bring new prosecution following appeal against conviction — Crown reindicting for murder — Whether proceedings competent — Whether oppressive — Criminal Procedure (Scotland) Act 1975 (c 21), ss 254 (1) (c) and 255 (1).

HM Advocate v Boyle—J   1079

Justiciary — Procedure — Retrial — Accused convicted of five charges but appealing against only one — Appeal court setting aside verdict on all charges and granting authority to bring new prosecution — Whether within powers of appeal court to set aside whole verdict — Criminal Procedure (Scotland) Act 1975 (c 21), ss 254 (1) (c) and 255 (1).

Boyle, Petitioner—J *1085*

Justiciary — Procedure — Retrial — Appeal on ground of new evidence not heard and not reasonably available at trial — Accused moving for retrial on basis of affidavits containing new evidence — Whether retrial appropriate at that stage — Criminal Procedure (Scotland) Act 1975 (c 21), ss 252 (b), 254 and 255.

Maitland v HM Advocate—J   645

Justiciary — Procedure — Retrial — Evidence at original trial unsatisfactory — Child witnesses — Whether retrial appropriate — Criminal Procedure (Scotland) Act 1975 (c 21), ss 254 (1) (c) and 255.

Farooq v H M Advocate—J   1271

Justiciary — Procedure — Search — Police having grounds for suspicion that two persons using hired car in possession of drugs — Police stopping car and discovering third occupant— Third occupant being searched — Whether reasonable grounds for suspecting third occupant in possession of controlled drugs — Misuse of Drugs Act 1971 (c 38), s 23 (2).

Campbell v HM Advocate—J   245

Justiciary — Procedure — Specification of documents — Accused seeking all productions and statements taken by police including statements of Crown witnesses prior to accused's police interview, and precognitions — Police at interview alleging matters purportedly derived from Crown witnesses — Whether all material recoverable — Whether precognitions recoverable.

HM Advocate v Ward—J   1202

Justiciary — Procedure — Summary procedure — 40 day custody rule — Whether 40 day period calculated by including first day — Whether period elapses at first moment of 40th day — Criminal Procedure (Scotland) Act 1975 (c 21), s 331A (1).

Hazlett v McGlennan—J   74

Justiciary — Procedure — Summary procedure — Accused challenging validity of statutory instrument under which prosecuted — Sheriff ordering accused to lead evidence at hearing on competency — No plea being taken but accused appealing to High Court — Criminal Procedure (Scotland) Act 1975 (c 21), s 334 (2A) — Act of Adjournal (Consolidation) 1988 (SI 1988/110), rule 128 (1).

Johnston v McGillivray—J   120

Justiciary — Procedure — Summary procedure — Accused charged with another person, and both appearing at call over at trial diet — Accused subsequently detained on suspicion of interfering with trial witness — Crown moving outwith presence of accused for adjournment of diet to other date — Co-accused present and adhering to not guilty plea — Trial diet adjourned in respect of both accused — Whether adjournment competent — Whether breach of natural justice.

Deigan v Wilson—J   522

Justiciary — Procedure — Summary procedure — Adjournment — Accused pleading guilty to speedng and requesting proof in mitigation for totting up provisions under Road Traffic Offenders Act 1988 — Justice adjourning diet for period exceeding three weeks at accused's request — Whether adjournment incompetent — Crimial Procedure (Scotland) Act 1975 (c 21), s 380 (1).

McCulloch v Scott—J   901

Justiciary — Sentence — Competency — Accused pleading guilty to breach of the peace by threatening violence — Sheriff sentencing accused to six months' imprisonment — Whether an offence inferring personal violence — Criminal Procedure (Scotland) Act 1975 (c 21), s 290 (b).

McMahon v Lees—J................... 593

Justiciary — Sentence — Competency — Child sentenced to be detained without limit of time — Whether sentence available other than in case of murder conviction — Whether requirement to specify period satisfied — Criminal Procedure (Scotland) Act 1975 (c 21), s 206.

K v HM Advocate—J................. 237

Justiciary — Statutory offence — Attempting to drive while unfit through drink — Accused unconscious at 2.50 am in driver's seat wearing seatbelt with engine running and dipped headlights on — Accused in habit of sleeping overnight in car — Whether sufficient to establish attempted driving — Road Traffic Act 1988 (c 52), s 5 (1) (a) and (b).

Guthrie v Friel—J.................... 899

Justiciary — Statutory offence — Being found on premises in circumstances inferring intent to commit theft — Person seen climbing complainer's garden fence and accused afterwards found in neighbouring garden shed — Whether accused "found" on complainer's premises — Civic Government (Scotland) Act 1982 (c 45), s 57 (1).

Marr v Heywood—J................... 1254

Justiciary — Statutory offence — Being in charge of vehicle while unfit through drink — Accused required to provide roadside breath test — No evidence that police officers in uniform — Accused arrested and required to provide specimens for analysis on Camic machine on which prosecution based — Whether necessary for officers to be in uniform — Whether prima facie case — Road Traffic Act 1988 (c 52), s 5 (1) (b).

Orr v Urquhart—J................... 406

Justiciary — Statutory offence — Being in charge of vehicle while unfit through drink — Breath analyser readings 29 microgrammes apart after one minute interval — Machine calibrating properly and not unsatisfactory on previous occasions when used — Whether police entitled to regard machine as reliable — Road Traffic Act 1988 (c 52), ss 5 (1) (b) and 7 (1) (a) and (3) (b).

Carson v Orr—J..................... 362

Justiciary — Statutory offence — Byelaws — Offering for hire without permission — Power to make byelaws not covering regulation of vehicular traffic on roads to which road traffic enactments applied — Accused taxi driver picking up fare on

road at airport terminal building — Road traffic enactments applying to road — Whether byelaw ultra vires — Airports Act 1986 (c 31), s 63 (2) (d) — Scottish Airports Byelaws 1986, byelaw 5 (14).

Fulton v Lees—J..................... 927

Justiciary — Statutory offence — Careless driving — Accused driving nearly two miles on motorway at average speed of 71.24 mph while holding telephone handset in one hand and overtaking twice — Whether sheriff entitled to convict — Road Traffic Act 1988 (c 52), s 3.

Rae v Friel—J...................... 791

Justiciary — Statutory offence — Carrying out gas work without being competent to do it — Failing to carry out gas work in proper and workmanlike manner — Accused installing and thereafter repairing gas central heating boiler — Bad practices employed by accused exposing complainer subsequently to carbon monoxide fumes — Meaning of "competent" — Whether work not done "in a proper and workmanlike manner" — Gas Safety (Installation and Use) Regulations 1984 (SI 1984/1358), regs 3 (1) and 4 (3).

Paterson v Lees—J................... 48

Justiciary — Statutory offence — Construction regulations — Duty of employer to comply with such requirements of regulations "as affect him or any workman employed by him" — Whether supervisor was workman — Whether necessary to prove that workmen actually on scaffold on day libelled — Whether sufficient that scaffold available for use of other workmen — Construction (Lifting Operations) Regulations 1961 (SI 1961/1581), regs 3 (1) (a) and 42 (1) — Construction (Working Places) Regulations 1966 (SI 1966/94), regs 3 (1) (a) and 11.

Wimpey Homes Holdings Ltd v Lees—J.... 564

Justiciary — Statutory offence — Driving while unfit through drink — Accused giving evidence of amounts of alcohol consumed before and after driving — Whether accused's evidence need be corroborated — Road Traffic Offenders Act 1988 (c 53), s 15 (2) and (3).

King v Lees—J...................... 1184

Justiciary — Statutory offence — Driving while unfit through drink — Accused in hospital being requested to supply specimen of blood for laboratory test — Accused not told specimen might be blood or urine but that decision was for police to make — Whether obligation to give such explanation — Road Traffic Act 1988 (c 52), ss 5 (1) (a) and 7 (1) and (4).

Simpson v McClory—J................. 861

Justiciary — Statutory offence — Licensing — Sale of alcohol for consumption other than as ancillary to a meal — Whether both licence holder and employee could be charged and convicted — Licensing (Scotland) Act 1976 (c 66), s 99.

Stainton v McNaughton—J   119

Justiciary — Statutory offence — Possession of offensive weapon — "Shuriken" (Chinese throwing star) — Non-flexible metal plate with several sharp radiating points found in accused's trouser pocket — Whether offensive weapon per se — Relevance of statutory instrument declaring shuriken an offensive weapon for purposes of another statute — Prevention of Crime Act 1953 (1 & 2 Eliz II, c 14), s 1 (1) — Criminal Justice Act 1988 (Offensive Weapons) Order 1988 (SI 1988/2019), Sched, para 1 (h).

McGlennan v Clark—J   1069

Justiciary — Statutory offence — Resisting police in execution of duty — Police restraining accused by placing hand on accused's arm to stop him moving away, in order to warn accused about conduct — Accused "breakdancing" in busy street — Accused struggling, shouting and swearing when police restraining him — Whether restraint lawful — Whether accused entitled to resist — Police (Scotland) Act 1967 (c 77), s 41 (1) (a).

Cardle v Murray—J   525

Justiciary — Statutory offence — Sentence — Driving while disqualified — Endorsation — Special reasons — Accused driving on two occasions separated by half an hour while unaware that disqualified — Sheriff refraining from disqualifying because of accused's unawareness but ordering endorsation on both offences — Whether two separate offences or one incident — Whether special reasons for not endorsing — Road Traffic Offenders Act 1988 (c 53), ss 28 (4), 35 and 44 (2).

Robertson v McNaughtan—J   1143

Landlord and tenant — Croft — Common grazings — Extraction of minerals by landlord — Permanent reduction in extent of grazing available for pasturage — Crofter entitled to compensation for damage to grazing — Whether crofter's security of tenure at risk from landlord's operations — Whether interdict justified where encroachment by landlord not such as to determine crofting tenure — Crofters (Scotland) Act 1955 (3 & 4 Eliz II, c 21), s 3 and Sched 2, para 10.

Strathern v MacColl   301

Landlord and tenant — Croft — Resumption of croft land — Crofters' share in market value of land resumed — Resumption for purpose of leasing ground for mineral extraction — Crofters having no rights in minerals — Whether market value of land resumed included its mineral value — Crofters (Scotland) Act 1955 (3 & 4 Eliz II, c 21),

s 12 (1) and Sched 2, para 10 — Crofting Reform (Scotland) Act 1976 (c 21), ss 1 (3) and 9.

MacKenzie v Barr's Trustees   1228

Landlord and tenant — Croft — Resumption of croft land — Crofters' share in market value of land resumed — Resumption for purpose of leasing ground to authority possessing compulsory purchase powers for mineral extraction — Whether "acquisition" by authority of land resumed — Market value in which crofters entitled to share — "Croft land" — Crofting Reform (Scotland) Act 1976 (c 21), s 9.

MacKenzie v Barr's Trustees   1228

Landlord and tenant — Lease — Construction — Lease of shop unit in shopping centre — Obligation on tenant to keep and use leased premises as retail premises — Whether positive obligation capable of being enforced by decree ad factum praestandum.

Postel Properties Ltd v Miller and Santhouse plc   353

Landlord and tenant — Lease — Construction — Tenant's obligations of maintenance and compensation for damage arising from its operations or negligence — Whether tenant's acceptance of state of subjects at entry in respect of maintenance obligation capable of affecting tenant's obligations under other provisions of lease.

Lord Advocate v Shipbreaking Industries Ltd (No 2)—O   995

Landlord and tenant — Lease — Full repairing and insuring lease — Liability for repairs — Retaining wall — Whether obligations imposed by terms of lease were wide enough to cover both ordinary and extraordinary repairs — Whether tenants under obligation to reimburse landlords for cost of repairs.

House of Fraser plc v Prudential Assurance Co Ltd—O   519

★ **Landlord and tenant** — Lease — Rent review — Waiver — Landlord asserting right to increased rent on review but demanding and accepting original rent — Whether waived right to insist on review.

Falkirk District Council v Falkirk Taverns Ltd—O   1097

Landlord and tenant — Lease — Tenant liable for premiums on building insurance — Damage to subjects let caused by tenant's negligence — Whether landlord entitled to recover for damage from tenant.

Barras v Hamilton—O   1301

Nobile officium — Competency — Children's hearing — New evidence becoming available after sheriff finding grounds for referral established — Application to nobile officium for order remitting case back to sheriff to rehear evidence in case including new evidence — Whether competent for such order to be pronounced under nobile officium — Social Work (Scotland) Act 1968 (c 49), s 50 (1).

L, Petitioners (No 1) 1310

Nobile officium — Competency — Petition to ordain arbiter to state case — Arbiter postponing stating case — Whether provided for by Rules of Court — Whether matter within regulatory powers of court — Whether rule of court ultra vires — Rules of Court 1965, rule 277 (c) — Administration of Justice (Scotland) Act 1972 (c 52), s 3 (1) — Court of Session Act 1988 (c 36), s 5.

Edmund Nuttall Ltd v Amec Projects Ltd .   255

Parent and child — Custody — Best interests of child — Death of mother of young child — Whether child ought to be returned to natural father who maintained contact with her or remain with aunt where she was happy and well settled.

Breingan v Jamieson—O 186

Parent and child— Custody — International child abduction — Child removed by mother clandestinely from country of habitual residence — Father having earlier agreed to attempted reconciliation there on under standing that mother could return to Scotland with child if reconciliation not successful — Parties thereafter living together for 15 months — Whether father had consented to removal of child — Child Abduction and Custody Act 1985 (c 60), Sched 1, arts 12 and 13.

Zenel v Haddow 975

Parent and child — Custody — International child abduction — Children removed from Canada to Scotland by parent having Canadian custody award — Effect of subsequent Canadian court orders awarding custody to other parent — Whether removal of children a "wrongful act" — Procedure for resolving issues of Canadian law — Child Abduction and Custody Act 1985 (c 60), s 5 and Sched 1, arts 3, 5, 12 and 13 (b).

Taylor v Ford—O 654

Parent and child — Custody — International child abduction — Jurisdiction — Habitual residence of child — Child of unmarried parents taken to Australia in attempted reconciliation of parents — Whether habitual residence of mother established in Australia — Child Abduction and Custody Act 1985 (c 60), Sched 1, arts 3 and 4.

Zenel v Haddow 975

Parent and child — Custody — Jurisdiction — Habitual residence of child — Child of unmarried parents brought to Scotland by mother with consent of father — No agreement as to duration of visit — Father commencing proceedings in English court when mother refused to return child — Whether Scottish or English court had jurisdiction — Family Law Act 1986 (c 55), ss 9, 10 and 41.

Rellis v Hart—O 738

★**Partnership** — Dissolution — Partners withdrawing capital without consent in breach of partnership contract — Whether material breach disentitling partners from exercising contractual right to dissolve partnership.

Hunter v Wylie—O 1091

Partnership — Dissolution — Scheme of division — Assets in hands of one partner — Whether appropriate for judicial factor to allow interest at commercial rather than judicial rate — Whether appropriate to apply compound interest.

Roxburgh Dinardo & Partners' Judicial Factor v Dinardo 16

Personal bar — Waiver — Actings of sellers after purchasers failed to pay purchase price in terms of missives — Whether waiver of right to treat failure as material breach of contract.

Atlas Assurance Co Ltd v Dollar Land Holdings plc—O 892

★**Personal bar** — Waiver — Lease — Rent review — Landlord asserting right to increased rent on review but demanding and accepting original rent — Whether waived right to insist on review.

Falkirk District Council v Falkirk Taverns Ltd—O 1097

★**Prescription** — Contract — Assignation of heritable right — Missives providing that conditions therein to subsist for limited period after delivery of disposition — Whether competent — Prescription and Limitation (Scotland) Act 1973 (c 52), s 13, as amended.

Ferguson v McIntyre—O 1269

Prescription — Negative prescription — Claim for unpaid taxes assessed — Interest thereon — Interest accruing from day to day — Whether "sum of money due . . . by way of interest" — Whether due "in respect of a particular period" — Taxes Management Act 1970 (c 9), ss 68 (1), 69 and 86 (1) — Prescription and Limitation (Scotland) Act 1973 (c 52), s 6 and Sched 1, para 1 (a).

Lord Advocate v Butt 10

Process — Decree — Decree ad factum praestandum — Whether competent against limited company — Law Reform (Miscellaneous Provisions) (Scotland) Act 1940 (3 & 4 Geo VI, c 42), s 1.

Postel Properties Ltd v Miller and Santhouse plc—O 353

Process — Decree — Decree by default — Pursuers' agents withdrawing from acting — Pursuers failing to obtemper court order that they intimate whether proceeding — Decree of dismissal of principal action and decree under counterclaim pronounced on failure to intimate — Whether decree in foro.

Mason v A & R Robertson & Black—O . . . 773

Process — Decree — Decree in foreign currency — Patrimonial loss suffered and to be suffered by Swiss resident — Competency of awarding such loss in foreign currency.

Fullemann v McInnes's Executors—O 259

Process — Decree — Summary decree — Sale of heritage — Difference between purchase price and valuation at date purchaser failed to pay under decree for implement — Sufficiency of evidence or averment necessary to resist motion for summary decree.

King v Moore—O 1117

Process — Decree — Summary decree — Whether defences to statutory cases disclosed — Whether appropriate to determine relevancy issue on motion roll — Rules of Court 1965, rule 89B.

Mitchell v HAT Contracting Services Ltd (No 2)—O 734

Process — Division or sale — Remit to person of skill — Objections to report — Relevancy of objections — Whether competent to object that reporter had not dealt with certain issues when not required by terms of remit to do so — Whether party entitled to require remit to reporter for reconsideration in light of objections to report — Whether reporter entitled to entertain arguments for division based on sentimental interests of one party where pecuniary interests of other party would be prejudiced — Whether appropriate on remit for reconsideration to expand on terms of original remit.

Williams v Cleveland and Highland Holdings Ltd—O 398

Process — Divorce — Joint minute containing agreement on financial provision — Decree in terms thereof pronounced on pursuer's motion — Competency of reclaiming motion by defender — Competency of defender seeking to set aside agreement as not fair and reasonable at time it was entered into — Family Law (Scotland) Act 1985 (c 37), s 16 (1) (b).

Jongejan v Jongejan 595

★ **Process** — Fatal accident inquiry — Appeal by way of judicial review — Whether competent — When determination reducible — Extent to which determination reducible — Fatal Accidents and Sudden Deaths Inquiry (Scotland) Act 1976 (c 14), s 6 (1).

Lothian Regional Council v Lord Advocate—O 1132

Process — Form of action — Alleged failure to pay benefit due under contract of employment — Action of damages for breach of contract rather than of payment under contract — Whether relevant.

Rutherford v Radio Rentals Ltd 221

Process — Interlocutor — Correction — Interlocutor following tender and minute of acceptance — No award of expenses in defenders' favour then made — Subsequent motion for expenses — Whether error in interlocutor — Relevance of misunderstanding of position by defenders' advisers — Rules of Court 1965, rule 30 (2).

Davis v British Coal Corporation—O 697

Process — Mandatary — Sist — Foreign company — Whether sufficient basis to require sist of mandatory.

Kaiser Bautechnik GmbH v G A Group Ltd—O 826

Process — Mode of inquiry — Proof or jury trial — Defamation — Complex issues of fact — Difficult and complex issues of mixed fact and law — Television broadcast in which conduct in business of pursuer and another stated to be fraudulent or inept — Pursuer having involvement in various different capacities in a multiplicity of limited companies — Companies entering into a series of complex inter-company transactions and schemes — Separate defences of veritas and fair comment — Nine separate innuendos set out — Whether "special cause" for withholding case from jury trial — Court of Session Act 1988 (c 36), s 9.

Shanks v British Broadcasting Corporation—O 326

Process — Mode of inquiry — Proof or jury trial — Medical negligence — Whether complexity of likely proof outweighed simplicity of parties' pleadings.

Miller v Lanarkshire Health Board—O 453

Process — Order for disclosure of information — Disclosure of home address of witness — Employers offering interview facilities at witness's place of work — Witness apprehensive about contact with pursuer's solicitors at her home address — Administration of Justice (Scotland) Act 1972 (c 59), s 1 (1A).

Poterala v Uniroyal Tyres Ltd—O 1072

Process — Order for disclosure of information — Petitioner contracting human immune deficiency virus through transfusion of infected blood — Petitioner seeking information as to person donating blood for transfusion — Public interest — Secretary of State claiming risk to supply of blood for transfusion — Whether petitioner's right to sue donor should prevail over public interest — Administration of Justice (Scotland) Act 1972 (c 59), s1.

AB v Glasgow amd West of Scotland Blood Transfusion Service—O   36

Process — Pleadings — Defences — Specification — Action by finance company based on contract — Defenders having dealt with suppliers, denying dealings with pursuers — Whether open to defenders to argue that no contract existed through pursuers' failure to intimate their acceptance.

Sabre Leasing Ltd v Copeland   1099

Process — Pleadings — Relevancy — Challenge to gratuitous alienation — Pursuers founding on statutory provisions — Whether relevant case at common law pled — Insolvency Act 1986 (c 45), s 242.

Stuart Eves Ltd (in liquidation) v Smiths Gore—O   1274

Process — Pleadings — Relevancy — Novus actus interveniens — Causation — Whether determinable without proof.

Davidson v City of Glasgow District Council—O   479

Process — Pleadings — Relevancy and specification — Alleged liability of tenant for condition of subjects at end of tenancy — Report incorporated in landlord's pleadings — Whether fair notice given of claims for dilapidation.

Lord Advocate v Shipbreaking Industries Ltd (No 2)—O   995

Process — Pleadings — Relevancy and specification — Reference to duty of roads authority to inspect drain covers daily without specifying practice of other similar defenders or special circumstances existing at locus.

Gibson v Strathclyde Regional Council   1243

Process — Pleadings — Relevancy and specification — Sale of heritable property — Action of damages for breach of contract — Defence that purchaser's agent and solicitors instructed by agent exceeded their authority — Sufficiency of averments to support reduction ope exceptionis of missives for lack of authority.

Hopkinson v Williams—O   907

Process — Pleadings — Relevancy and specification — Sale of heritable property — Action of damages for breach of contract — Defence that purchaser's solicitors acting without authority — Sufficiency of seller's averments — No specific averment that missives entered into with purchaser's authority.

Hopkinson v Williams—O   907

★ **Process** — Proof — Reopening of proof — Action of damages for personal injuries — Second defenders' proof proceeding and closing before first defenders' proof — Pursuer abandoning against first defenders before first defenders' proof opened — Whether second defenders to be allowed to reopen proof to lead evidence of medical witness who was to have been witness for first defenders.

Wilson v Imrie Engineering Services Ltd—O   235

Process — Reclaiming motion — Competency — Defender reclaiming against interlocutor pronounced on pursuer's motion but in terms of joint minute.

Jongejan v Jongejan   595

★ **Process** — Remit to sheriff court — Action of divorce defended on financial conclusions only — Action raised in Court of Session to avoid local publicity — Extra expense to defender in defending in Court of Session — Whether remit appropriate — Law Reform (Miscellaneous Provisions) (Scotland) Act 1985 (c 73), s 14.

Gribb v Gribb—O   178

Process — Reparation — Personal injuries — Optional procedure — Competency — Whether action cognitionis causa tantum competent under optional procedure — Rules of Court 1965, rule 188E.

Garland v Fairnington—O   711

★ **Process** — Reparation — Personal injuries — Optional procedure — Witnesses — Failure by party to provide list of witnesses — Whether to be allowed to lead witnesses — Rules of Court 1965, rule 188L.

McGunnigal v D B Marshall (Newbridge) Ltd—O   769

Process — Review — Reduction as mode of review — Whether decree may be reduced even though other means of review were available but not used — Whether reduction competent where failure to seek review by other means was result of advice from solicitors — Whether decree may be reduced where statutory remedy still available to pursuer with no consequent miscarriage of justice.

Spence v Davie—O   217

Reparation — Negligence — Occupiers' liability — Foreseeability — Occupiers aware that children climbed onto roof of building — No knowledge that children would jump onto skylight — Whether accident by falling through skylight reasonably foreseeable.

Devlin v Strathclyde Regional Council—O . .   699

★ **Reparation** — Negligence — Road accident— Allocation of blame — Car driver negligently losing control of car on motorway slip road — Lorry driver negligently failing to observe crashed car and driving into collision with it — Liability to be apportioned to each driver.

BOC Ltd v Groves—O   360

★ **Reparation** — Negligence — Road accident — Allocation of blame — Pedestrian crossing road without keeping proper lookout — Driver also not keeping proper lookout.

Malcolm v Fair—O   342

Reparation — Negligence — Vicarious liability — Independent contractor — Test to be applied in determining whether person an independent contractor or a casual employee.

United Wholesale Grocers Ltd v Sher—O   284

Reparation — Negligence — Volenti non fit injuria — Injured person's own negligence — Child on roof of school building where he knew he should not be — Jumping onto skylight from above during game of tig.

Devlin v Strathclyde Regional Council—O . .   699

Reparation — Nuisance — Flooding — Construction of culvert on land of upper and lower heritors to alter flow of water in stream — Flooding on land of lower heritor at time of heavy rainfall — Whether nuisance of upper heritor.

G A Estates Ltd v Caviapen Trustees Ltd (No 1)—O   1037

Repetition — Condictio causa data causa non secuta — Heritable property purchased in joint names in anticipation of marriage — Purchase financed by joint loan and free proceeds of sale of property formerly owned by one co-proprietor — Marriage not undertaken — Whether contribution of free proceeds a donation in consideration of marriage — Whether donor entitled to require conveyance of heritable interest of donee — Whether donor entitled to recover part of free proceeds — Necessity of parties' mutual understanding of consideration for donation — Whether discretion in court to refuse to give effect to condictio when applicable.

Grieve v Morrison—O   852

Revenue — Capital transfer tax — Valuation of shares in private company — Whether previous agreements as to value of sums paid in transfers between relatives relevant to valuation — Finance Act 1975 (c 7), s 38.

Inland Revenue Commissioners v Stenhouse's Trustees—O   248

Revenue — Income tax — Necessary expenses — Journalists required to purchase newspapers for background reading — Whether condition of employment — Whether expenses incurred "necessarily in the performance of" their duties — Income and Corporation Taxes Act 1970 (c 10), s 189 (1).

Fitzpatrick v Inland Revenue Commissioners   54

Revenue — Income tax — Payment of income — Deduction of tax — Gain on shares acquired by company director treated as income liable to income tax — Whether "payment of emoluments" — Whether employers bound to deduct tax from consideration on disposal of shares — Whether collector entitled to require payment of tax by employee — Income and Corporation Taxes Act 1970 (c 10), s 204 — Income Tax (Employments) Regulations 1973 (SI 1973/334), regs 2 (1), 13 and 26 (3).

Inland Revenue Commissioners v Herd—L . .   916

Revenue — Income tax — Prescription — Negative prescription — Unpaid tax due under assessment — Interest thereon — Interest accruing from day to day — Whether "sum of money due . . . by way of interest" — Whether due "in respect of a particular period" — Taxes Management Act 1970 (c 9), ss 68 (1), 69 and 86 (1) — Prescription and Limitation (Scotland) Act 1973 (c 52), s 6 and Sched 1, para 1 (a).

Lord Advocate v Butt   10

River, loch and sea — River — Alteration in flow of water in stream — Opus manufactum — Construction of culvert on land of upper and lower heritors — Flooding of land of lower heritor at time of heavy rainfall — Whether absolute liability of upper heritor for protective measures taken by lower heritor.

G A Estates Ltd v Caviapen Trustees Ltd (No 1)—O   1037

River, loch and sea — River — Boundary dispute — Boundary marked by medium filum of river — Channel of river destroyed in flood — New channel dug by agreement in different position — Whether boundary marked by medium filum of new channel or old channel.

Stirling v Bartlett—O   763

Roads and streets — Private road — Public passage tolerated by owner for less than prescriptive period — Right of owner to restrict passage — Roads (Scotland) Act 1984 (c 54), ss 59 and 151.

Viewpoint Housing Association Ltd v Lothian Regional Council—O   921

Social security — Supplementary benefit — Single payments — Discretionary payments to be made in specified circumstances except where claim for "miscellaneous furniture and household equipment needs" — Whether claim for number of specified items constituted separate claims for each item and thereby not a miscellaneous claim — Supplementary Benefit (Single Payments) Regulations 1981 (SI 1981/1528), reg 30, as amended.

Garvie v Secretary of State for Social Services   658

Solicitor — Judicial factor appointed to solicitor's estates — Factor authorised to divide sum at credit of client account among clients — Solicitor's estates then sequestrated and permanent trustee appointed — Whether funds at credit of client account vested in trustee — Whether accountant of court entitled to order judicial factor to hand over funds to trustee — Solicitors (Scotland) Act 1980 (c 46), s 42 — Bankruptcy (Scotland) Act 1985 (c 66), s 33 (1).

Council of the Law Society of Scotland v McKinnie   238

Statute — Construction — Ejusdem generis rule — Whether list in statute comprised a genus — Bankruptcy (Scotland) Act 1985 (c 66), s 18 (3).

Clark's Trustee, Noter—O   667

Statute — Construction — Reference to report of committee of inquiry — Whether plain meaning of Act to be restricted by consideration of mischief sought to be remedied — Contrast with English statutes in pari materia.

Anderson v Gibb—O   726

Statute — Construction — Reference to report of Scottish Law Commission — Purpose for which reference may be made.

Rehman v Ahmad—O   741

Statute — Construction — Reference to report of Scottish Law Commission — Purpose for which reference may be made — Statute not ambiguous.

Archer Car Sales (Airdrie) Ltd v Gregory's Trustee—O   223

Statutes and orders—
Act of Adjournal (Consolidation) 1988.
                                    120, 1109
Act of Adjournal (Consolidation Amendment No 2) (Evidence of Children) 1991   395
Act of Sederunt (Appeals under the Licensing (Scotland) Act 1976) 1977.
                                    109, 796
Act of Sederunt (Ordinary Cause Rules, Sheriff Court) 1983   109
Administration of Justice (Scotland) Act 1972 ....36, 255, 409, 726, 828, 832,
                                    894, 1072
Airports Act 1986   927

Bankruptcy Act 1621   1274
Bankruptcy (Scotland) Act 1913   375
Bankruptcy (Scotland) Act 1985 .....223, 238,
                        651, 667, 718, 904, 1291
Burial Grounds (Scotland) Act 1855 ...   505
Child Abduction and Custody Act 1985
                                    654, 975
Civic Government (Scotland) Act 1982   759,
                        800, 1102, 1254
Civil Evidence (Scotland) Act 1988 ..307, 859,
                        1277, 1281, 1284
Civil Jurisdiction and Judgments Act 1982   409
Civil Legal Aid (Scotland) Regulations 1987   147
Community Drivers' Hours and Recording Equipment (Exemptions and Supplementary Provisions) Regulations 1986   279
Community Service by Offenders (Scotland) Act 1978   1028
Companies Act 1948   375
Companies Act 1985 ....170, 383, 723
Construction (Lifting Operations) Regulations 1961   564
Construction (Working Places) Regulations 1966   564
Conveyancing (Scotland) Act 1924   1291
Court of Session Act 1988 .....255, 326, 551
Criminal Justice Act 1961   435
Criminal Justice Act 1988 (Offensive Weapons) Order 1988   1069
Criminal Procedure (Scotland) Act 1975   2, 31,
        33, 74, 77, 120, 237, 290, 358, 435, 455,
        471, 541, 564, 593, 599, 645, 672, 676,
        809, 813, 816, 897, 901, 1079, 1085,
                        1158, 1271, 1321, 1337
Crofters (Scotland) Act 1955 ....301, 1228
Crofters (Scotland) Act 1961   301
Crofting Reform (Scotland) Act 1976 ..   1228
Curators Act 1585   955
Damages (Scotland) Act 1976   624
Divorce (Scotland) Act 1976   419
Domicile and Matrimonial Proceedings Act 1973   123
EEC Directive 77/187   1256
EEC Regulation 2807/83   703
EEC Regulation 3820/85   279
EEC Regulation 3821/85   279
EEC Regulation 2241/87   703
Employment Protection (Consolidation) Act 1978 ....209, 664, 1256
Estate Agents Act 1979   23
Factories Act 1961 ....670, 935
Family Law Act 1986 ....194, 738
Family Law (Scotland) Act 1985 ....184, 343,
                419, 494, 595, 617, 999, 1348
Fatal Accidents and Sudden Deaths Inquiry (Scotland) Act 1976   1132
Finance Act 1975   248
Fisheries Act 1981   703
Gaming Act 1968   537
Gas Safety (Installation and Use) Regulations 1984   48

Succession — Testate — Trust disposition and settlement — Construction — "Issue" — "Great-grandchildren" — Scottish deeds executed in 1917 and 1925 — Succession to residue liferented by granddaughter domiciled in England and dying in 1989 — Children of granddaughter legitimated by operation of Legitimacy Act 1959 — Whether children entitled to take share of residue — Legitimacy Act 1959 (7 & 8 Eliz II, c 73), s 1 (1).

Wright's Trustees v Callender—L.........   556

Time — Computation — Detention for 28 day period — Beginning of period known to the hour — Natural or civil computation — Mental Health (Scotland) Act 1984 (c 36), s 26.

R v Lothian Health Board (No 2)—O.....   1021

Town and country planning — Expenses — Appeal to Secretary of State against planning authority's refusal of change of use application — Contrary advice by authority's planning officer — Appeal largely conceded by planning authority — Award of expenses against planning authority — Whether award unreasonable.

City of Aberdeen District Council v Secretary of State for Scotland—O...........   1149

Town and country planning — Planning permission — Appeal — Determination by reporter — Listed building — Planning authority considering development would have prejudicial impact on amenity — Reporter considering dominant use non-residential and granting consent — Whether error by reporter.

City of Glasgow District Council v Secretary of State for Scotland   1332

Town and country planning — Planning permission — Appeal — Determination by reporter — Permission sought for extension to bank contrary to presumption in local plan — "Any other material considerations" — Relevance of private interests of developer — Relevance of previous refusal on appeal of permission for similar development in same area — Town and Country Planning (Scotland) Act 1972 (c 52), s 26 (1).

Town and country planning — Planning permission — Appeal — Determination by Secretary of State — Departure from recommendations of reporter — Whether sufficient reasons given for decision.

Town and country planning — Planning permission — Appeal — "Person aggrieved" — Local resident not objecting to application — Application inadequately described — Resident becoming aware of nature of application prior to appeal by applicants but not appearing in appeal — Whether "person aggrieved" — Whether entitled to appeal against grant of planning permission — Town and Country Planning (Scotland) Act 1972 (c 52), s 233 (1).

Town and country planning — Planning permission — Appeal — Secretary of State directing that he would himself determine an appeal which would, by regulations, normally be determined by reporter — Secretary of State involved in promoting subject of planning application — Whether contrary to natural justice for Secretary of State to hear appeal.

Town and country planning — Planning permission — Application for outline permission — Full details of application not given in application itself or in advertisement in local newspaper — Whether application and advertisement required to give full details of application — Whether grant of application ultra vires — Town and Country Planning (General Development (Scotland) Order 1981 (SI 1981/830), arts 7 (5) (c) and 8, as amended.

Town and country planning — Planning permission — Application for planning permission — No notification to conterminous proprietor — Grant of planning permission by reporter — Expiry of time limit for appeal to court — Competency of application for review of decision — Whether decision void or voidable — Town and Country Planning (Scotland) Act 1972 (c 52), ss 231 and 233.

Town and country planning — Planning permission — Change of use — Loss of amenity — Area of mixed commercial and residential use — Proper test of loss of amenity.

Town and country planning — Planning permission — Change of use to that of hot food retail shop — Loss of amenity — Application refused by district council but allowed by reporter on appeal — Reporter considering matter of litter a matter dealt with by general legislation and not proper reason for withholding planning permission — Whether a matter for reporter to consider in context of residential amenity — Whether reporter erred — Town and Country Planning (Scotland) Act 1972 (c 52), ss 231 and 233 — Town and County Planning (Use Classes) (Scotland) Order 1973 (SI 1973/1165).

Town and country planning — Planning permission — Competing applications — Inquiries — Procedure — Sufficiency of evidence — Fairness — Town and Country Planning (Scotland) Act 1972 (c 52), s 267 (4).

Town and country planning — Planning permission — Enterprise zone — Scheme originally authorising residential development without permission amended to require permission — Building warrant in respect of proposed residential development applied for prior to amendment of scheme but issued after amendment — Development commenced prior to amendment of scheme and prior to issue of warrant — Enforcement notice — Whether development lawfully commenced — Whether developers entitled to found on works prior to issue of building warrant as specified operations determining date of commencement of development — Extent of development commenced by works undertaken — Town and Country Planning (Scotland) Act 1972 (c 52), s 40 (1) and (2) — Local Government, Planning and Land Act 1980 (c 65), Sched 32, para 21.

Trade marks and names — Passing off — Interdict — Breach — Interdict against supplying Scotch whisky for purpose of enabling spirits containing spirits other than Scotch to be passed off as Scotch whisky — Respondents exporting Scotch whisky to Panama under brand name of "King of Scots" which consisted of 20 per cent of Scotch malt and 80 per cent of Panamanian cane spirit — Respondents instructing Panamanian agents to ensure that all labels and materials clearly indicated that product was blend of Scotch whisky and Panamanian spirit — Cartons sold in

Panama for use with Scotch whisky and for use with blend to some extent the same — Bottles used to sell Scotch whisky and blend almost identical — Whether calculated to enable passing off to be achieved.

Trust — Inter vivos deed of trust — Construction — "Children" — "Issue" — Deed taking effect in 1968 — Children adopted by means of overseas adoptions in 1989 and 1990 — Provisions permitting adopted children to succeed not extending to overseas adoptions in 1968 — Whether adopted children entitled to benefit under deed executed before making of adoption order — Succession (Scotland) Act 1964 (c 41), s 23.

Trust — Trust disposition and settlement — Construction — Forfeiture of entitlement to bequest upon election for legal rights — Application of provision to issue of beneficiary — Whether beneficiary's election to claim legal rights resulted in forfeiture of rights of beneficiary's issue as conditional institutes.

Trust — Trust disposition and settlement — Construction — "Issue" — "Great-grandchildren" — Scottish deeds executed in 1917 and 1925 — Succession to residue liferented by granddaughter domiciled in England and dying in 1989 — Children of granddaughter legitimated by operation of Legitimacy Act 1959 — Whether children entitled to take share of residue — Legitimacy Act 1959 (7 & 8 Eliz II, c 73), s 1 (1).

Writ — Rectification — Disposition — Disposition giving effect to missives — Averment of common intention that larger area would be transferred — Relevancy — Law Reform (Miscellaneous Provisions) (Scotland) Act 1985 (c 73), s 8 (1) and (2).

Writ — Rectification — Document failing to express accurately the intention of the parties — Requirements for rectification — Law Reform (Miscellaneous Provisions) (Scotland) Act 1985 (c 73), s 8 (1).

Writ — Rectification — Standard security — Proforma personal bond and standard security only completed quoad personal bond — Whether competent to rectify quoad standard security — Law Reform (Miscellaneous Provisions) (Scotland) Act 1985 (c 73), s 8 (1) (b).